THE NORTON ANTHOLOGY OF

AMERICAN

LITERATURE

SHORTER NINTH EDITION

VOLUME II: 1865 TO THE PRESENT

VOLUME 1

American Literature, Beginnings to 1820 · GUSTAFSON
American Literature 1820–1865 · LEVINE

VOLUME 2

American Literature 1865–1914 · ELLIOTT
American Literature 1914–1945 · LOEFFELHOLZ
American Literature since 1945 · HUNGERFORD

Michael A. Elliott
ASA GRIGGS CANDLER PROFESSOR OF ENGLISH AND AMERICAN STUDIES
EMORY UNIVERSITY

Sandra M. Gustafson
PROFESSOR OF ENGLISH AND AMERICAN STUDIES
UNIVERSITY OF NOTRE DAME

Amy Hungerford
BIRD WHITE HOUSUM PROFESSOR OF ENGLISH AND AMERICAN STUDIES
AND DIRECTOR OF THE DIVISION OF THE HUMANITIES
YALE UNIVERSITY

Mary Loeffelholz
PROFESSOR OF ENGLISH
NORTHEASTERN UNIVERSITY

THE NORTON ANTHOLOGY OF

AMERICAN

LITERATURE

SHORTER NINTH EDITION

Robert S. Levine, *General Editor*

PROFESSOR OF ENGLISH AND
DISTINGUISHED UNIVERSITY PROFESSOR AND
DISTINGUISHED SCHOLAR–TEACHER
University of Maryland, College Park

VOLUME II: 1865 TO THE PRESENT

W · W · NORTON & COMPANY
NEW YORK · LONDON

W. W. Norton & Company has been independent since its founding in 1923, when William Warder Norton and Mary D. Herter Norton first published lectures delivered at the People's Institute, the adult education division of New York City's Cooper Union. The firm soon expanded its program beyond the Institute, publishing books by celebrated academics from America and abroad. By midcentury, the two major pillars of Norton's publishing program—trade books and college texts—were firmly established. In the 1950s, the Norton family transferred control of the company to its employees, and today—with a staff of four hundred and a comparable number of trade, college, and professional titles published each year—W. W. Norton & Company stands as the largest and oldest publishing house owned wholly by its employees.

Editor: Julia Reidhead
Managing Editor, College: Marian Johnson
Manuscript Editors: Kurt Wildermuth, Harry Haskell, Michael Fleming, Tenyia Lee
Assistant Editor: Rachel Taylor
Media Editor: Carly Fraser Doria
Assistant Media Editor: Ava Bramson
Managing Editor, College Digital Media: Kim Yi
Media Project Editor: Kristin Sheerin
Marketing Manager, Literature: Kimberly Bowers
Production Manager: Sean Mintus
Art Director: Debra Morton Hoyt
Cover Design: Tiani Kennedy
Photo Editor: Cat Abelman
Permissions Manager: Megan Jackson Schindel
Permissions Clearing: Margaret Gorenstein
Composition: Westchester Book Group

The Library of Congress has cataloged an earlier edition as follows:
Library of Congress Cataloging-in-Publication Data

Names: Levine, Robert S. (Robert Steven), 1953- editor.
Title: The Norton anthology of American literature / Robert S. Levine,
general editor ; Michael A. Elliott, Sandra M. Gustafson, Amy Hungerford,
Mary Loeffelholz.
Description: Ninth edition. | New York : W. W. Norton & Company, 2017. |
Includes bibliographical references and index.
Identifiers: LCCN 2016043347| ISBN 9780393935714 (pbk., v. a : alk. paper) |
ISBN 9780393264470 (pbk., v. b : alk. paper) | ISBN 9780393264487 (pbk., v. c :
alk. paper) | ISBN 9780393264494 (pbk., v. d : alk. paper) | ISBN 9780393264500
(pbk., v. e : alk. paper)
Subjects: LCSH: American literature. | United States—Literary collections.
Classification: LCC PS507 .N65 2016 | DDC 810.8—dc23 LC record available
at https://lccn.loc.gov/2016043347

This edition: ISBN 978-0-393-26453-1

W. W. Norton & Company, Inc., 500 Fifth Avenue, New York, NY 10110
www.wwnorton.com

W. W. Norton & Company Ltd., 15 Carlisle Street, London W1D 3BS

6 7 8 9 0

Contents

PREFACE xxi

ACKNOWLEDGMENTS xxxiii

American Literature 1865–1914

INTRODUCTION 1

TIMELINE 18

WALT WHITMAN (1819–1892)   21
Song of Myself (1881) 25
Crossing Brooklyn Ferry 69
The Wound-Dresser 74
When Lilacs Last in the Dooryard Bloom'd 76

EMILY DICKINSON (1830–1886)   82
122 [These are the days when Birds come back -] 86
202 ["Faith" is a fine invention] 87
207 [I taste a liquor never brewed -] 87
236 [Some keep the Sabbath going to Church -] 87
260 [I'm Nobody! Who are you?] 88
269 [Wild Nights - Wild Nights!] 88
320 [There's a certain Slant of light] 90
339 [I like a look of Agony] 90
340 [I felt a Funeral, in my Brain] 90
353 [I'm ceded—I've stopped being Their's] 91
359 [A Bird, came down the Walk -] 92
365 [I know that He exists] 92
409 [The Soul selects her own Society -] 93
411 [Mine - by the Right of the White Election!] 93
446 [This was a Poet -] 94
479 [Because I could not stop for Death -] 94
518 [When I was small, a Woman died -] 95
519 [This is my letter to the World] 96
591 [I heard a Fly buzz - when I died -] 96

620 [Much Madness is divinest Sense -] 96
656 [I started Early - Took my Dog -] 97
706 [I cannot live with You -] 97
788 [Publication - is the Auction] 99
1096 [A narrow Fellow in the Grass] 1694 99
1263 [Tell all the Truth but tell it slant -] 100
1577 [The Bible is an antique Volume -] 100

MARK TWAIN (SAMUEL L. CLEMENS) (1835–1910) 101
The Notorious Jumping Frog of Calaveras County 104
Adventures of Huckleberry Finn 108
  CRITICAL CONTROVERSY: RACE AND THE ENDING OF
    ADVENTURES OF HUCKLEBERRY FINN 291
  LEO MARX: From Mr. Eliot, Mr. Trilling, and Huckleberry Finn 292
  JULIUS LESTER: From Morality and Adventures of Huckleberry
    Finn 295
  DAVID L. SMITH: From Huck, Jim, and American Racial
    Discourse 296
  JANE SMILEY: From Say It Ain't So, Huck: Second Thoughts on
    Mark Twain's "Masterpiece" 299
  TONI MORRISON: From Introduction to Adventures of Huckleberry
    Finn 300
  ALAN GRIBBEN: From Introduction to the NewSouth Edition 302
  MICHIKO KAKUTANI: Light Out, Huck, They Still Want to Sivilize
    You 304

BRET HARTE (1836–1902) 306
The Luck of Roaring Camp 307

WILLIAM DEAN HOWELLS (1837–1920) 314
Editha 316

AMBROSE BIERCE (1842–C. 1914) 326
An Occurrence at Owl Creek Bridge 327
Chickamauga 333

HENRY JAMES (1843–1916) 338
Daisy Miller: A Study 342
The Real Thing 382
The Beast in the Jungle 399

EMMA LAZARUS (1849–1887) 429
In the Jewish Synagogue at Newport 430
1492 431
The New Colossus 432

SARAH ORNE JEWETT (1849–1909) 432
A White Heron 434

Kate Chopin (1850–1904)   441
Désirée's Baby   442
The Story of an Hour   446
At the 'Cadian Ball   448
The Storm   455

Mary E. Wilkins Freeman (1852–1930)   459
A New England Nun   460

Booker T. Washington (1856–1915)   469
Up from Slavery   471
    Chapter XIV. The Atlanta Exposition Address   471

Charles W. Chesnutt (1858–1932)   479
The Goophered Grapevine   481
The Wife of His Youth   488

Pauline Elizabeth Hopkins (1859–1930)   497
Talma Gordon   498

Charlotte Perkins Gilman (1860–1935)   509
The Yellow Wall-paper   511
Why I Wrote "The Yellow Wallpaper"?   523

Edith Wharton (1862–1937)   524
The Other Two   526
Roman Fever   540

Sui Sin Far (Edith Maud Eaton) (1865–1914)   549
Mrs. Spring Fragrance   550

W. E. B. Du Bois (1868–1963)   559
The Souls of Black Folk   561
    I. Of Our Spiritual Strivings   562
    III. Of Mr. Booker T. Washington and Others   568

REALISM AND NATURALISM   578
WILLIAM DEAN HOWELLS: *From* Editor's Study   579
HENRY JAMES: *From* The Art of Fiction   584
FRANK NORRIS: A Plea for Romantic Fiction   586
JACK LONDON: *From* What Life Means to Me   590
CHARLOTTE PERKINS GILMAN: *From* Masculine Literature   593

THEODORE DREISER (1871–1945)   595
Sister Carrie   597
     Chapter I   597
     Chapter III   603

STEPHEN CRANE (1871–1900)   611
The Open Boat   614
From War Is Kind   631

PAUL LAURENCE DUNBAR (1872–1906)   633
An Ante-Bellum Sermon   634
We Wear the Mask   636
Sympathy   636
Harriet Beecher Stowe   637
Frederick Douglass   638

JACK LONDON (1876–1916)   639
To Build a Fire   641

ZITKALA-ŠA (GERTRUDE SIMMONS BONNIN) (1876–1938)   652
Impressions of an Indian Childhood   655
     I. My Mother   655
     II. The Legends   656
     VII. The Big Red Apples   658
The Soft-Hearted Sioux   660

American Literature 1914–1945

INTRODUCTION   667

TIMELINE   686

EDWIN ARLINGTON ROBINSON (1869–1935)   688
Richard Cory   689
Miniver Cheevy   689
Eros Turannos   690

WILLA CATHER (1873–1947)   691
Neighbour Rosicky   694
The Sculptor's Funeral   714

AMY LOWELL (1874–1925)   724
The Captured Goddess   726
Venus Transiens   727
Madonna of the Evening Flowers   727
September, 1918   728

GERTRUDE STEIN (1874–1946)   729
The Making of Americans 731
    [Introduction] 731

ROBERT FROST (1874–1963)   735
The Pasture 736
Mowing 736
Mending Wall 737
The Death of the Hired Man 738
After Apple-Picking 742
The Wood-Pile 743
The Road Not Taken 744
Birches 744
"Out, Out—" 746
Fire and Ice 746
Nothing Gold Can Stay 747
Stopping by Woods on a Snowy Evening 747
Desert Places 747
Design 748
Neither Out Far Nor In Deep 748
Directive 749

SUSAN GLASPELL (1876–1948)   750
Trifles 751

SHERWOOD ANDERSON (1876–1941)   761
Winesburg, Ohio 763
    Hands 763
    Mother 767

CARL SANDBURG (1878–1967)   772
Chicago 773
Fog 774
Grass 774

WALLACE STEVENS (1879–1955)   775
The Snow Man 777
A High-Toned Old Christian Woman 777
The Emperor of Ice-Cream 778
Disillusionment of Ten O'Clock 778
Sunday Morning 779
Anecdote of the Jar 782
Thirteen Ways of Looking at a Blackbird 782
The Idea of Order at Key West 784
Of Modern Poetry 785

WILLIAM CARLOS WILLIAMS (1883–1963) 786

The Young Housewife 788
Portrait of a Lady 789
Queen-Anne's-Lace 789
The Widow's Lament in Springtime 790
Spring and All 790
To Elsie 791
The Red Wheelbarrow 793
This Is Just to Say 793
A Sort of a Song 794
The Dance ("In Brueghel's great picture, The Kermess") 794
Landscape with the Fall of Icarus 795

EZRA POUND (1885–1972) 795

To Whistler, American 797
Portrait d'une Femme 798
A Pact 799
In a Station of the Metro 799
The River-Merchant's Wife: A Letter 799
The Cantos 800
      I ("And then went down to the ship") 800

MODERNIST MANIFESTOS 803

F. T. MARINETTI: *From* Manifesto of Futurism 804
MINA LOY: Feminist Manifesto 806
EZRA POUND: *From* A Retrospect 809
WILLA CATHER: *From* The Novel Démeublé 812
WILLIAM CARLOS WILLIAMS: *From* Spring and All 814
LANGSTON HUGHES: *From* The Negro Artist and the Racial
   Mountain 816

H.D. (HILDA DOOLITTLE) (1886–1961) 818

Mid-day 820
Oread 820
Leda 821
Helen 822

MARIANNE MOORE (1887–1972) 822

Poetry 824
To a Snail 825
The Paper Nautilus 825
The Mind Is an Enchanting Thing 826

T. S. ELIOT (1888–1965)   827
    The Love Song of J. Alfred Prufrock 830
    The Waste Land 834
    The Hollow Men 847
    Four Quartets 850
            Burnt Norton 850

EUGENE O'NEILL (1888–1953)   854
    Long Day's Journey into Night 857

CLAUDE McKAY (1889–1948)   934
    The Harlem Dancer 936
    Harlem Shadows 936
    The Lynching 937
    If We Must Die 937
    Africa 937
    America 938

KATHERINE ANNE PORTER (1890–1980)   938
    Flowering Judas 940

ZORA NEALE HURSTON (1891–1960)   948
    Sweat 950
    How It Feels to Be Colored Me 958

E. E. CUMMINGS (1894–1962)   961
    in Just- 962
    O sweet spontaneous 963
    Buffalo Bill 's 964
    "next to of course god america i 964
    i sing of Olaf glad and big 965
    somewhere i have never travelled,gladly beyond 966
    anyone lived in a pretty how town 966

JEAN TOOMER (1894–1967)   967
    Cane 968
            Georgia Dusk 968
            Fern 969
            Portrait in Georgia 972
            Seventh Street 972

F. SCOTT FITZGERALD (1896–1940)   973
    Winter Dreams 975
    Babylon Revisited 991

WILLIAM FAULKNER (1897–1962)   1005
    A Rose for Emily 1009
    Barn Burning 1015

HART CRANE (1899–1932)   1028
Chaplinesque 1028
At Melville's Tomb 1029

ERNEST HEMINGWAY (1899–1961)   1030
Hills Like White Elephants 1032

LANGSTON HUGHES (1902–1967)   1036
The Negro Speaks of Rivers 1037
Mother to Son 1037
I, Too 1038
The Weary Blues 1039
Mulatto 1039
Song for a Dark Girl 1041
Visitors to the Black Belt 1041
Note on Commercial Theatre 1042
Democracy 1042
Theme for English B 1043

JOHN STEINBECK (1902–1968)   1044
The Chrysanthemums 1045

COUNTEE CULLEN (1903–1946)   1053
Yet Do I Marvel 1054
Incident 1054
Heritage 1054

RICHARD WRIGHT (1908–1960)   1058
The Man Who Was Almost a Man 1059

American Literature since 1945

INTRODUCTION 1069

TIMELINE 1087

THEODORE ROETHKE (1908–1963)   1091
Cuttings 1092
Cuttings (later) 1092
My Papa's Waltz 1093
Dolor 1093
The Waking 1093
Elegy for Jane 1094
I Knew a Woman 1095

EUDORA WELTY (1909–2001)   1096
Petrified Man 1097

ELIZABETH BISHOP (1911–1979)   1106
  The Fish 1108
  At the Fishhouses 1109
  The Armadillo 1111
  Sestina 1112
  In the Waiting Room 1113
  One Art 1115

TENNESSEE WILLIAMS (1911–1983)   1116
  A Streetcar Named Desire 1119

JOHN CHEEVER (1912–1982)   1182
  The Swimmer 1183

ROBERT HAYDEN (1913–1980)   1191
  Middle Passage 1193
  Homage to the Empress of the Blues 1197
  Those Winter Sundays 1198

RANDALL JARRELL (1914–1965)   1199
  The Death of the Ball Turret Gunner 1201
  Second Air Force 1201
  Thinking of the Lost World 1202

JOHN BERRYMAN (1914–1972)   1205
  The Dream Songs 1206
       1 ("Huffy Henry hid   the day") 1206
       14 ("Life, friends, is boring. We must not say so") 1207
       29 ("There sat down, once, a thing on Henry's heart") 1207
       384 ("The marker slants, flowerless, day's almost done") 1208

RALPH ELLISON (1914–1994)   1209
  Invisible Man 1210
       Chapter I [Battle Royal] 1210

ARTHUR MILLER (1915–2005)   1221
  Death of a Salesman 1223

ROBERT LOWELL (1917–1977)   1289
  The Quaker Graveyard in Nantucket 1291
  Mr. Edwards and the Spider 1295
  Skunk Hour 1296
  For the Union Dead 1298

GWENDOLYN BROOKS (1917–2000) 1300
  A Street in Bronzeville 1301
        kitchenette building 1301
        the mother 1301
        the white troops had their orders but the Negroes looked like men 1302
  We Real Cool 1303
  The Last Quatrain of the Ballad of Emmett Till 1303
  To the Diaspora 1304

PATRICIA HIGHSMITH (1921–1995) 1304
  The Quest for *Blank Claveringi* 1306

JACK KEROUAC (1922–1969) 1316
  On the Road 1318
        Part One, Chapter 1 1318
        Part Five 1323

DENISE LEVERTOV (1923–1997) 1327
  To the Snake 1328
  The Jacob's Ladder 1329
  In Mind 1329

JAMES BALDWIN (1924–1987) 1330
  Going to Meet the Man 1331
  Sonny's Blues 1343

FLANNERY O'CONNOR (1925–1964) 1366
  Good Country People 1367
  A Good Man Is Hard to Find 1381

ALLEN GINSBERG (1926–1997) 1392
  Howl 1394
  Footnote to Howl 1402
  A Supermarket in California 1402

JOHN ASHBERY (1927–2017) 1403
  Illustration 1405
  Soonest Mended 1406
  Myrtle 1408

ANNE SEXTON (1928–1974) 1408
  The Starry Night 1409
  Sylvia's Death 1410
  Little Girl, My String Bean, My Lovely Woman 1412

ADRIENNE RICH (1929–2012) 1414
  Snapshots of a Daughter-in-Law 1416
  A Valediction Forbidding Mourning 1420

    Diving into the Wreck 1421
    Transcendental Etude 1423

TONI MORRISON (1931–2019)   1427
    Recitatif 1429

SYLVIA PLATH (1932–1963)   1442
    Morning Song 1444
    Lady Lazarus 1444
    Daddy 1447
    Blackberrying 1449
    Child 1450

JOHN UPDIKE (1932–2009)   1450
    Separating 1452

PHILIP ROTH (1933–2018)   1460
    Defender of the Faith 1462

AMIRI BARAKA (LEROI JONES) (1934–2014)   1483
    An Agony. As Now. 1484
    A Poem for Willie Best 1485

AUDRE LORDE (1934–1992)   1490
    Coal 1491
    The Woman Thing 1492
    Black Mother Woman 1493

LUCILLE CLIFTON (1936–2010)   1494
    miss rosie 1495
    the lost baby poem 1496
    homage to my hips 1496
    wild blessings 1497
    wishes for sons 1497
    the mississippi river empties into the gulf 1498
    [oh antic God] 1498

DON DELILLO (b. 1936)   1499
    White Noise 1501
        Part II: Airborne Toxic Event 1501

THOMAS PYNCHON (b. 1937)   1519
    Entropy 1520

RAYMOND CARVER (1938–1988)   1531
    Cathedral 1532

MAXINE HONG KINGSTON (b. 1940)   1543
    The Woman Warrior 1544
        No Name Woman 1544

BILLY COLLINS (b. 1941)   1553
    Forgetfulness 1554
    I Chop Some Parsley While Listening to Art Blakey's
        Version of "Three Blind Mice" 1555
    The Night House 1556

GLORIA ANZALDÚA (1942–2004)   1557
    How to Tame a Wild Tongue 1558

ALICE WALKER (b. 1944)   1567
    Everyday Use 1568

YUSEF KOMUNYAKAA (b. 1947)   1574
    Facing It 1576
    My Father's Love Letters 1577
    Slam, Dunk, & Hook 1578
    When Dusk Weighs Daybreak 1579

LESLIE MARMON SILKO (b. 1948)   1579
    Lullaby 1580

ART SPIEGELMAN (b. 1948)   1587
    From Maus 1588

JOY HARJO (b. 1951)   1605
    Call It Fear 1606
    White Bear 1607

RITA DOVE (b. 1952)   1608
    Adolescence—I 1610
    Adolescence—II 1610
    Parsley 1611
    Rosa 1613

SANDRA CISNEROS (b. 1954)   1613
    Woman Hollering Creek 1614

LOUISE ERDRICH (b. 1954)   1622
    Dear John Wayne 1624
    I Was Sleeping Where the Black Oaks Move 1625
    Grief 1626
    Fleur 1626

LI-YOUNG LEE (b. 1957)   1635
   Persimmons 1636
   Eating Alone 1638
   Eating Together 1638
   This Room and Everything in It 1639

CREATIVE NONFICTION   1641
EDWARD ABBEY: Havasu   1642
BARRY LOPEZ: The Raven   1647
JAMAICA KINCAID: Girl   1649
HUNTER S. THOMPSON: *From* Fear and Loathing in Las Vegas   1651
JOAN DIDION: *From* Slouching Towards Bethlehem   1653
DAVID FOSTER WALLACE: *From* Consider the Lobster   1656
EDWIDGE DANTICAT: *From* Brother, I'm Dying   1661

GEORGE SAUNDERS (b. 1958)   1664
   CivilWarLand in Bad Decline 1665

SHERMAN ALEXIE (b. 1966)   1677
   At Navajo Monument Valley Tribal School 1678
   Pawn Shop 1679
   Crow Testament 1680

NATASHA TRETHEWEY (b. 1966)   1681
   Vignette 1683
   Graveyard Blues 1684
   Photograph: Ice Storm, 1971 1685
   Native Guard 1685
   Miracle of the Black Leg 1689

JHUMPA LAHIRI (b. 1967)   1691
   Sexy 1692

JUNOT DÍAZ (b. 1968)   1708
   Drown 1709

SELECTED BIBLIOGRAPHIES A1

PERMISSIONS ACKNOWLEDGMENTS A50

INDEX A57

Preface to the Shorter Ninth Edition

The Ninth Edition of *The Norton Anthology of American Literature* is the first for me as General Editor; for the Eighth Edition, I served as Associate General Editor under longstanding General Editor Nina Baym. On the occasion of a new general editorship, we have undertaken one of the most extensive revisions in our long publishing history. Three new section editors have joined the team: Sandra M. Gustafson, Professor of English and Concurrent Professor of American Studies at the University of Notre Dame, who succeeds Wayne Franklin and Philip Gura as editor of "American Literature, Beginnings to 1820"; Michael A. Elliott, Professor of English at Emory University, who succeeds Nina Baym, Robert S. Levine, and Jeanne Campbell Reesman as editor of "American Literature, 1865–1914"; and Amy Hungerford, Professor of English and American Studies at Yale University, who succeeds Jerome Klinkowitz and Patricia B. Wallace as editor of "American Literature since 1945." These editors join Robert S. Levine, editor of "American Literature, 1820–1865," and Mary Loeffelholz, editor of "American Literature, 1914–1945." Each editor, new or continuing, is a well-known expert in the relevant field or period and has ultimate responsibility for his or her section of the anthology, but we have worked closely from first to last to rethink all aspects of this new edition. Period introductions, author headnotes, thematic clusters, annotations, illustrations, and bibliographies have all been updated and revised. We have also added a number of new authors, selections, and thematic clusters. We are excited about the outcome of our collaboration and anticipate that, like the previous eight editions, this edition of *The Norton Anthology of American Literature* will continue to lead the field.

From the anthology's inception in 1979, the editors have had three main aims: first, to present a rich and substantial enough variety of works to enable teachers to build courses according to their own vision of American literary history (thus, teachers are offered more authors and more selections than they will probably use in any one course); second, to make the anthology self-sufficient by featuring many works in their entirety along with extensive selections for individual authors; third, to balance traditional interests with developing critical concerns in a way that allows for the complex, rigorous, and capacious study of American literary traditions. As early as 1979, we anthologized work by Anne Bradstreet, Mary Rowlandson, Sarah Kemble Knight, Phillis Wheatley, Margaret Fuller, Harriet Beecher Stowe, Frederick Douglass, Sarah Orne Jewett, Kate Chopin, Mary E. Wilkins Freeman, Booker T. Washington, Charles W. Chesnutt, Edith Wharton, W. E. B. Du

Bois, and other writers who were not yet part of a standard canon. Yet we never shortchanged writers—such as Franklin, Emerson, Whitman, Hawthorne, Melville, Dickinson, Hemingway, Fitzgerald, and Faulkner—whose work many students expected to read in their American literature courses, and whom most teachers then and now would not think of doing without.

The so-called canon wars of the 1980s and 1990s usefully initiated a review of our understanding of American literature, a review that has enlarged the number and diversity of authors now recognized as contributors to the totality of American literature. The traditional writers look different in this expanded context, and they also appear different according to which of their works are selected. Teachers and students remain committed to the idea of the literary—that writers strive to produce artifacts that are both intellectually serious and formally skillful—but believe more than ever that writers should be understood in relation to their cultural and historical situations. We address the complex interrelationships between literature and history in the period introductions, author headnotes, chronologies, and some of the footnotes. As in previous editions, we have worked with detailed suggestions from many teachers on how best to present the authors and selections. We have gained insights as well from the students who use the anthology. Thanks to questionnaires, face-to-face and phone discussions, letters, and email, we have been able to listen to those for whom this book is intended. For the Shorter Ninth Edition, we have drawn on the careful commentary of over 130 reviewers and reworked aspects of the anthology accordingly.

Our new materials continue the work of broadening the canon by representing new writers in depth, without sacrificing widely assigned writers, many of whose selections have been reconsidered, reselected, and expanded. Our aim is always to provide extensive enough selections to do the writers justice, including complete works wherever possible. Our Shorter Ninth Edition offers sixteen complete longer works, including such newly added works as Charles Brockden Brown's *Memoirs of Carwin the Biloquist* and James Baldwin's "Sonny's Blues." Two complete works—Eugene O'Neill's *Long Day's Journey into Night* and Tennessee Williams's *A Streetcar Named Desire*—are exclusive to *The Norton Anthology of American Literature*. Charles Brockden Brown, Louisa May Alcott, and Junot Díaz are among the writers added to the prior edition, and to this edition we have introduced George Saunders and Natasha Tretheway, among others. We have also expanded and in some cases reconfigured such central figures as Franklin, Hawthorne, Dickinson, Twain, and Hemingway, offering new approaches in the headnotes, along with some new selections. In fact, the headnotes and, in many cases, selections for such frequently assigned authors as William Bradford, Washington Irving, James Fenimore Cooper, William Cullen Bryant, Henry Wadsworth Longfellow, Ralph Waldo Emerson, Harriet Beecher Stowe, Mark Twain, William Dean Howells, Henry James, Kate Chopin, W. E. B. Du Bois, Edith Wharton, Willa Cather, and William Faulkner have been revised, updated, and in some cases entirely rewritten in light of recent scholarship. The Shorter Ninth Edition further expands its selections of women writers and writers from diverse ethnic, racial, and regional backgrounds—always with attention to the critical acclaim that recognizes their contributions to the American literary record. New and recently added writers such as Samson Occom, along with the figures represented in the new cluster "Native American Oral Literature," enable teachers to bring early Native American writing and oratory into their syllabi, or, should they prefer, to focus on these selections as a freestanding unit leading toward the moment after 1945 when Native writers fully entered the mainstream of literary activity.

We are pleased to continue our popular innovation of topical gatherings of short texts that illuminate the cultural, historical, intellectual, and literary concerns of their respective periods. Designed to be taught in a class period or two, or used as background, each of the nine clusters consists of brief, carefully excerpted primary and (in one case) secondary texts, about six to ten per cluster, and an introduction. Diverse voices—many new to the anthology—highlight a range of views current when writers of a particular time period were active, and thus allow students better to understand some of the large issues that were being debated at particular historical moments. For example, in "Slavery, Race, and the Making of American Literature," texts by David Walker, William Lloyd Garrison, Angelina Grimké, Sojourner Truth, James M. Whitfield, and Martin R. Delany speak to the great paradox of pre–Civil War America: the contradictory rupture between the realities of slavery and the nation's ideals of freedom.

The Shorter Ninth Edition strengthens this feature with seven new and revised clusters attuned to the requests of teachers. To help students address the controversy over race and aesthetics in *Adventures of Huckleberry Finn*, we have revised a cluster that shows what some of the leading critics of the past few decades thought was at stake in reading and interpreting slavery and race in Twain's canonical novel. The 1865–1914 section also features "Realism and Naturalism," and we continue to include the useful "Modernist Manifestos" in the section covering 1914–1945. We have added to the popular "Creative Nonfiction" in the post-1945 section new selections by David Foster Wallace, Hunter S. Thompson, and Joan Didion, which join texts by such writers as Jamaica Kincaid and Edwidge Danticat.

The Shorter Ninth Edition features an expanded illustration program, both of the black-and-white images, 107 of which are placed throughout the volumes, and of the color plates so popular in the last two editions. In selecting color plates—from Elizabeth Graham's embroidered map of Washington, D.C., at the start of the nineteenth century to Jeff Wall's "After 'Invisible Man'" at the beginning of the twenty-first—the editors aim to provide images relevant to literary works in the anthology while depicting arts and artifacts representative of each era. In addition, graphic works— segments from Art Spiegelman's canonical graphic novel, *Maus*, and a facsimile page of Emily Dickinson manuscript, along with the many new illustrations—open possibilities for teaching visual texts.

Period-by-Period Revisions

American Literature, Beginnings to 1820. Sandra M. Gustafson, the new editor for this period, has substantially revised this section. Prior editions broke this period into two historical sections, with two introductions and a dividing line at the year 1700; Gustafson has dropped that artificial divide to tell a more coherent and fluid story (in her new introduction) about the variety of American literatures during this long period. The section continues to feature narratives by early European explorers of the North American continent as they encountered and attempted to make sense of the diverse cultures they met, and as they sought to justify their aim of claiming the territory for Europeans. In addition to the standing material by John Smith and William Bradford, we include new material by Roger Williams and Charles Brockden Brown's *Memoirs of Carwin the Biloquist* (the complete "prequel" to his first novel, *Wieland*). We continue to offer substantial selections from Rowlandson's enormously influential *A Narrative of the Captivity and Restoration of Mrs. Mary Rowlandson* and Benjamin Franklin's *Autobiography* (which remains one of the most compelling works on the emergence of an "American" self). New and revised thematic clusters of texts highlight themes central to this long historical period. . "Native American Oral Literature" features creation stories, trickster tales, oratory, and poetry from a spectrum of traditions, while "Native American Eloquence" collects speeches and accounts by Canassatego and Native American women (both new to the volume), Pontiac, Chief Logan (as cited by Thomas Jefferson), and Tecumseh, which, as a group, illustrate the centuries-long pattern of initial peaceful contact between Native Americans and whites mutating into bitter and violent conflict. The Native American presence in the volume is further expanded with increased representation of Samson Occom, which includes an excerpt from his sermon at the execution of Moses Paul. The new cluster "Ethnographic and Naturalist Writings" includes writings by Sarah Kemble Knight, William Bartram, and Hendrick Aupaumut. With this cluster, and a number of new selections and revisions in the other historical sections, the Ninth Edition pays greater attention to the impact of science on American literary traditions.

American Literature, 1820–1865. Under the editorship of Robert S. Levine, this section over the past several editions has become more diverse. Included here are the complete texts of Emerson's *Nature*, Douglass's *Narrative*, Whitman's *Song of Myself*, Melville's *Benito Cereno*, and Rebecca Harding Davis's *Life in the Iron Mills*. At the same time, aware of the important role of African American writers in the period, and the omnipresence of race and slavery as literary and political themes, we have recently added the major African American writer Frances E. W. Harper. A generous selection from Stowe's *Uncle Tom's Cabin*, and the cluster "Slavery, Race, and the Making of American Literature," also help remind students of how central slavery was to the literary and political life of the nation during this period. "Native Americans: Resistance and Removal" gathers oratory and writings—by Native Americans such as Black Hawk and whites such as Ralph Waldo Emerson—protesting Andrew Jackson's ruthless national policy of Indian removal. Political themes, far from diluting the literary imagination of American authors, served to inspire some of the most memorable writing of the pre–Civil War period.

Recently added prose fiction includes a chapter from Cooper's *The Last of the Mohicans*. Poetry by Emily Dickinson is now presented in the texts established by R. W. Franklin and includes a facsimile page from Fascicle 10. For this edition we have added several poems by Dickinson that were inspired by the Civil War. Other selections added to this edition include Poe's popular short story "The Cask of Amontillado."

American Literature, 1865–1914. Newly edited by Michael A. Elliott, this section includes expanded selections of key works, as well as new ones that illustrate how many of the struggles of this period prefigure our own. Complete longer works include Twain's *Adventures of Huckleberry Finn* and James's *Daisy Miller*. In the Eighth Edition, we introduced a section on the critical controversy surrounding race and the conclusion of *Adventures of Huckleberry Finn*. That section remains as important as ever, and new additions incorporate a recent debate about the value of an expurgated edition of the novel.

We have substantially revised clusters designed to give students a sense of the cultural context of the period. New selections in "Realism and Naturalism" demonstrate what was at stake in the debate over realism, among them a feminist response from Charlotte Perkins Gilman. We have also added fiction by African American authors, including Pauline Hopkins's "Talma Gordon." The 1865–1914 period saw a rise in immigration that helped to make the country what it is today. A newly added selection of poems by Emma Lazurus brings this theme into focus.

American Literature 1914–1945. Edited by Mary Loeffelholz, "American Literature 1914–1945" offers a number of complete longer works, including Eugene O'Neill's *Long Day's Journey into Night* (exclusive to the Norton Anthology). New selections by Zora Neale Hurston ("Sweat") and John Steinbeck ("The Chrysanthemums") further contribute to the volume's exploration of issues connected with racial and social geographies. Selections by Ezra Pound, T. S. Eliot, Marianne Moore, Hart Crane, and Langston Hughes encourage students and teachers to contemplate the interrelation of modernist aesthetics with ethnic, regional, and popular writing. In "Modernist Manifestos," F. T. Marinetti, Mina Loy, Ezra Pound, Willa Cather, William Carlos Williams, and Langston Hughes show how the manifesto as a form exerted a powerful influence on international modernism in all the arts. Other recent and new additions to this section include Faulkner's popular "A Rose for Emily," Gertrude Stein's introduction to *The Making of Americans*, Hemingway's "Hills Like White Elephants," and poems by Edwin Arlington Robinson.

American Literature since 1945. Amy Hungerford, the new editor of "American Literature since 1945," has revised the section to present a wider range of writing in poetry, prose, drama, and nonfiction. As before, the section offers the complete texts of Tennessee Williams's *A Streetcar Named Desire* (exclusive to this anthology), Arthur Miller's *Death of a Salesman*, and Allen Ginsberg's *Howl*. New to this edition is Don DeLillo. The selection from *White Noise*, one of DeLillo's most celebrated novels, tells what feels like a contemporary story about a nontraditional family navigating an environmental disaster in a climate saturated by mass media. Two newly added stories—Patricia Highsmith's "The Quest for *Blank Claveringi*" and George Saunders's "CivilWarLand in Bad Decline"—reveal the impact of science fiction, fantasy, horror, and (especially in the case of Saunders) mass media on literary fiction. Recognized literary figures in all genres, ranging from Elizabeth Bishop to Leslie Marmon Silko and Toni Morrison, continue to be richly represented. In response to instructors' requests, we now include Flannery O'Connor's "A Good Man Is Hard to Find" and James Baldwin's "Sonny's Blues."

One of the most distinctive features of twentieth- and twenty-first-century American literature is a rich vein of African American poetry. This edition adds a contemporary poet from this living tradition: Natasha Trethewey, whose selections include personal and historical elegies. Trethewey joins African American poets whose work has long helped define the anthology—Rita Dove, Gwendolyn Brooks, Robert Hayden, Audre Lorde, and others.

This edition gives even greater exposure to literary and social experimentation during the 1960s, 1970s, and beyond. To our popular cluster "Creative Nonfiction" we have added a new selection by Joan Didion, from "Slouching Towards Bethlehem," which showcases her revolutionary style of journalism as she comments on experiments with public performance and communal living during the 1960s. A new selection from David Foster Wallace in the same cluster pushes reportage on the Maine Lobster Festival into philosophical inquiry: how can we fairly assess the pain of other creatures? Standing authors in the anthology, notably John Ashbery and Amiri Baraka, fill out the section's survey of radical change in the forms, and social uses, of literary art.

We are delighted to offer this revised Shorter Ninth Edition to teachers and students, and we welcome your comments.

Additional Resources from the Publisher

We are also pleased to offer the Ninth Edition in an ebook format. The Digital Anthologies include all the content of the print volumes, with print-corresponding page and line numbers for seamless integration into the print-digital mixed classroom. Annotations are accessible with a click or a tap, encouraging students to use them with minimal interruption to their reading of the text. The e-reading platform facilitates active reading with a powerful annotation tool and allows students to do a full-text search of the anthology and read online or off. The Digital Editions can be accessed from any computer or device with an Internet browser and are available to students at a fraction of the print price at digital.wwnorton.com/americanlit9shorter. For exam copy access to the Digital Editions and for information on making the Digital Editions available through the campus bookstore or packaging the Digital Editions with the print anthology, instructors should contact their Norton representative.

To give instructors even more flexibility, Norton is making available the full list of 254 Norton Critical Editions. A Norton Critical Edition can be included with any volume at a discounted price (see your Norton representative for details). Each Norton Critical Edition gives students an authoritative, carefully annotated text accompanied by rich contextual and critical materials prepared by an expert in the subject. The publisher also offers the much-praised guide *Writing about American Literature*, by Karen Gocsik (University of California–San Diego) and Coleman Hutchison (University of Texas–Austin), free with either volume.

In addition to the Digital Editions, for students using *The Norton Anthology of American Literature*, the publisher provides a wealth of free resources at digital.wwnorton.com/americanlit9shorter. There students will find more than fifty reading-comprehension quizzes on the period introductions and widely taught works with extensive feedback that points them back to the text. Ideal for self-study or homework assignments, Norton's sophisticated quizzing engine allows instructors to track student results and improvement. For over twenty-five works in the anthology, the sites also offer Close Reading Workshops that walk students step-by-step through analysis of a literary work. Each workshop prompts students to read, reread, consider contexts, and answer questions along the way, making these perfect assignments to build close-reading skills.

The publisher also provides extensive instructor-support materials. New to the Ninth Edition is an online Interactive Instructor's Guide at iig.wwnorton.com/americanlit9/full. Invaluable for course preparation, this resource provides hundreds of teaching notes, discussion questions, and suggested resources from the much-praised *Teaching with* The Norton Anthology of American Literature: *A Guide for Instructors* by Edward Whitley (Lehigh University). Also at this searchable and sortable site are quizzes, images, and lecture PowerPoints for each introduction, topic cluster, and twenty-five widely taught works. A PDF of *Teaching with NAAL* is available for download at wwnorton.com/instructors.

Finally, Norton Coursepacks bring high-quality digital media into a new or existing online course. The coursepack includes all the reading comprehension quizzes (customizable within the coursepack), the Writing about Literature video series, a bank of essay and exam questions, bulleted summaries of the period introductions, and "Making Connections" discussion or essay prompts to encourage students to draw connections across the anthology's authors and works. Coursepacks are available in a variety of formats, including Blackboard, Canvas, Desire2Learn, and Moodle, at no cost to instructors or students.

Editorial Procedures

As in past editions, editorial features—period introductions, headnotes, annotations, and bibliographies—are designed to be concise yet full and to give students necessary information without imposing a single interpretation. The editors have updated all apparatus in response to new scholarship: period introductions have been entirely or substantially rewritten, as have many headnotes. All selected bibliographies and each period's general-resources bibliographies, categorized by Reference Works, Histories, and Literary Criticism, have been thoroughly updated. The Ninth Edition retains two editorial features that help students place their reading in historical and cultural context—a Texts/Contexts timeline following each period introduction and a map on the front endpaper of each volume.

Whenever possible, our policy has been to reprint texts as they appeared in their historical moment. There is one exception: we have modernized most spellings and (very sparingly) the punctuation in Volume 1 on the principle that archaic spellings and typography pose unnecessary problems for beginning students. We have used square brackets to indicate titles supplied by the editors for the convenience of students. Whenever a portion of a text has been omitted, we have indicated that omission with three asterisks. If the omitted portion is important for following the plot or argument, we give a brief summary within the text or in a footnote. After each work, we cite the date of first publication on the right; in some instances, the latter is followed by the date of a revised edition for which the author was responsible. When the date of composition is known and differs from the date of publication, we cite it on the left.

The editors have benefited from commentary offered by hundreds of teachers throughout the country. Those teachers who prepared detailed critiques, or who offered special help in preparing texts, are listed under Acknowledgments, on a separate page. We also thank the many people at Norton who contributed to the Ninth Edition: Julia Reidhead, who supervised the Ninth Edition; Marian Johnson, managing editor, college; Carly Fraser Doria, media editor; manuscript editors Kurt Wildermuth, Michael Fleming, Harry Haskell, Candace Levy, and Tenyia Lee; Rachel Taylor and Ava Bramson, assistant editors; Sean Mintus, production manager; Cat Abelman, photo editor; Julie Tesser, photo researcher; Debra Morton Hoyt, art director; Tiani Kennedy, cover designer; Megan Jackson Schindel, permissions manager; and Margaret Gorenstein, who cleared permissions. We also wish to acknowledge our debt to the late George P. Brockway, former president and chairman at Norton, who invented this anthology, and to the late M. H. Abrams, Norton's advisor on English texts. All have helped us create an anthology that, more than ever, testifies to the continuing richness of American literary traditions.

ROBERT S. LEVINE, General Editor

Acknowledgments

Among our many critics, advisors, and friends, the following were of especial help toward the preparation of the Shorter Ninth Edition, either with advice or by providing critiques of particular periods of the anthology: Rolena Adorno (Yale University); M. Lee Alexander (William and Mary); John Allen (Milwaukee Area Technical College); Kathaleen Amende (Alabama State University); Dr. Andrew S. Andermatt (Paul Smith's College); Brian Anderson (Central Piedmont Community College); David L. Anderson (Butler County Community College); Peter Antelyes (Vassar College); Christopher Apap (Oakland University); Susanna Ashton (Clemson University); John Baffa (Morton College); Amy Bagwell (Central Piedmont Community College); Heidi Bauer (Lower Columbia College); Jenny Beaver (Rowan-Cabarrus Community College); Rebecca Belcher-Rankin (Olivet Nazarene University); Roger A. Berger (Everett Community College); Kyle Bishop (Southern Utah University); Susanne Bloomfield (University of Nebraska–Kearney); Anne Boyd Rioux (University of New Orleans); Alan Brown (University of West Alabama); Martin Brückner (University of Delaware); John Bruni (Grand Valley State University); Joanna Brooks (San Diego State University); Dr. Eugenia Bryan (Georgia Southwestern State University); Lisa Carl (North Carolina Central University); Allison Carpenter (Northampton Community College); Thomas Cassidy (South Carolina State University); Patrick Cesarini (University of South Alabama); Kathleen Chescattie (Harrisburg Area Community College); Lauren Coats (Louisiana State University); Tiffany Collins (Ogeechee Technical College); Josh Cohen (Emory University); Matt Cohen (University of Texas at Austin); James H. Cox (The University of Texas at Austin); Laura Dassow Walls (University of Notre Dame); Matthew Davis (University of Wisconsin–Stevens Point); Mike Davis (Beaufort Community College); Christopher G. Diller (Berry College); James J. Donahue (SUNY Potsdam); Philip J. Egan (Western Michigan University); Patrick Erben (University of West Georgia); Duncan Faherty (The City University of New York); Daniel Fineman (Occidental College); Edward Gallagher (Danville Area Community College); Armida Gilbert (Georgia Perimeter College); Paul Gilmore (Rutgers University); Cory R. Goehring (Waynesburg University); Mary Goodwin (National Taiwan Normal University); Jurgen E. Grandt (University of North Georgia–Gainesville Campus); James N. Green (Library Company of Philadelphia); Kathy Griffith Fish (University of the Cumberlands); Annemarie Hamlin (Central Oregon Community College); Matthew Hartman (Ball State University); Terry Heller (Coe College); Alexander Hollenberg (Sheridan College); Greg Horn (Southwest Virginia Community

College); Coleman Hutchison (University of Texas, Austin); S. Selina Jamil (Prince George's Community College); Joel J. Janicki (Soochow University); Gwendolyn Jones Harold (Clayton State University); Michael Joslin (Lees-McRae College); Cheung Kai Chong (Shih Shin University); Mark Kamrath (University of Central Florida); Kristi Key (Oklahoma Baptist University); Mabel Khawaja (Hampton University, Virginia); James Kirkpatrick (Central Piedmont Community College); Dawn Knopf (Clark College); Kristie Knotts; Jonathan Malcolm Lampley (Dalton State College); Andrew Lanham (Yale University); Marianne Layer (New River Community and Technical College); Richard Leith; Alfred J. López (Purdue University); Bridget Marshall (University of Massachusetts, Lowell); David McCracken (Coker College); John McGreevy (University of Notre Dame); Nancy McKinney (Illinois State University); Fiona McWilliam (University of Texas, San Antonio); Jim McWilliams (Dickinson State University); Christine Mihelich (Marywood University); Joshua Miller (University of Akron); Jesus Montano (Hope College); Laura Morgan Green (Northeastern University); David J. Nackley (Mohawk Valley Community College); Bernard G. Neff (Mount Aloysius College); David Neimeyer (Washington Adventist University); Lee Ogletree (Wiregrass Georgia Technical College); Dawn Oshiro (Kapiolani Community College); Jason Palmer; Martha H. Patterson (McKendree University); Jay Peterson (Atlantic Cape Community College); Christopher Phillips (Lafayette College); Roxanna Pisiak (Morrisville State College); Ben Railton (Fitchburg State University); Palmer Rampell (Yale University); Joseph Rezek (Boston University); Danielle Roach (Miami University); Marc Robinson (Yale University); J. B. Rollins (National Chung Cheng University); Shelbey Rosengarten (St. Petersburg College); Debby Rosenthal (John Carroll University); Phillip Round (University of Iowa); Karin Russell (Keiser University); Melissa Ryan (Alfred University); Claire Satlof (Valley Forge Military College); Gordon Sayre (University of Oregon); Judith Scheffler (West Chester University); William Scott Hanna (West Liberty University); Susan Scott Parrish (University of Michigan); Gabriela Serrano (Angelo State University); Marvin Jerome Severson (Kennesaw State University); Anna Shectman (Yale University); Lincoln Shlensky (University of Victoria); Kim Smith (Baker College); John Springer (University of Central Oklahoma); Kelsey Squire (Ohio Dominican University); Julia Stern (Northwestern University); Dorothy Stringer (Temple University); Kyle Taylor (West Georgia Technical College); Dorothy Terry (Tougaloo College); Jade Tsui-yu Lee (National Kaohsiung Normal University); Barbara Urban (Central Piedmont Community College); Kim Vanderlaan (California University of Pennsylvania); Joanne van der Woude (University of Groningen); Abram van Engen (Washington University); Susan VanZanten (Seattle Pacific University); Jeremy Voigt (Whatcom Community College); Bryan Waterman (New York University); Belinda Wheeler (Claflin University); Elizabeth Wiet (Yale University); Keith Wilhite (Siena College); Andrea N. Williams (The Ohio State University); K. Jamie Woodlief (West Chester University); Curtis A. Yehnert (Western Oregon University); Aiping Zhang (California State University, Chico).

American Literature 1865–1914

THE GILDED AGE

In 1873, Mark Twain and Charles Dudley Warner published *The Gilded Age: A Tale of To-day*. The novel, Twain's first, portrays the United States as a nation consumed by greed and corruption, a land of get-rich-quick schemes, rampant speculation, and bribery. Twain and Warner filled their pages with Americans—from country villagers to big-city dwellers—who were caught up in the fantasy of making an easy fortune, willing to sacrifice their scruples for the sake of material success. The book revealed an age that too easily mistook gilding for gold.

Commercially and critically, *The Gilded Age* enjoyed only modest success. Some readers were put off by the "pungent" satire; others thought the book was "confused and inartistic." One reviewer compared the novel to "a salad dressing badly mixed." But Twain and Warner's contemporaries agreed that *The Gilded Age* had accurately captured something important, if unsettling, about the time in which they lived, and the book shaped the way that we think about this period of American life. Even today, many historians follow Twain and Warner in referring to the late nineteenth century in America as "the Gilded Age."

Just as important, Twain and Warner's novel reveals significant trends that were emerging in the literature of the United States in the decades following the Civil War. Rather than being concerned with introspection or the perfection of literary forms, American literature in the late nineteenth century privileged the description and documentation of a rapidly changing society—a nation undergoing tremendous changes in terms of the composition of its population, the struc-

Children Sleeping in Mulberry Street, 1890, Jacob Riis. For more information about this image, see the color insert in this volume.

ture of its economy, and the customs of its people. American writers scrutinized the world around them, and their observations on the page were frequently accompanied by social commentary and sometimes, as in the case of Twain, comic wit. Instead of the romantic idealism of antebellum authors like Ralph Waldo Emerson and Harriet Beecher Stowe, Gilded Age America fostered a more measured and pragmatic way of looking at the world. The role of literature, in the words of Twain's contemporary Ambrose Bierce, was to "cultivate a taste for the distasteful," to "endeavor to see things as they are, not as they ought to be."

Labels for literary and cultural periods offer a convenient shorthand for characterizing the complicated reality of any cultural moment. We use them, usually with the benefit of hindsight, to reduce the chaos of the past to some kind of narrative order. For most of the twentieth century, literary histories of the Gilded Age celebrated American authors for their willingness to present a series of increasingly distasteful truths, particularly through novels depicting the excesses and foibles of the urban environments where new fortunes were being won and lost. Mark Twain, Henry James, Stephen Crane, Edith Wharton, and Theodore Dreiser—all authors included in this volume—were recognized as writers who advanced an aesthetic of "realism." The editor and author William Dean Howells was identified as the leading proponent of this movement, and literary historians carefully analyzed his advocacy in the pages of magazines like the *Atlantic Monthly* and *Harper's*.

During the last three decades, scholars of American literature have been concerned that this period in American literature has been too narrowly defined. They have noted that how one defines what is "real" depends on where one sits in society—and that the authors named above were largely located in the nation's urban centers, where they focused primarily on the lives of native-born whites. Scholars have also observed that editors like Howells were in fact interested in cultivating a wider variety of perspectives, including authors from regions across the United States, immigrant writers, and African American authors. If one of the roles of literature is to "see things as they are," then our definition of literature could also expand beyond fiction and poetry to include other forms of writing—such as autobiography, sketches, and folk tales—that proliferated during this period.

Literature, though, does not merely show how things are. It amuses, provokes, cajoles, and inspires. Twain was one of the fiercest critics of his time, but he was also one of its finest entertainers. His writing not only reflected the world that surrounded him, but it also played a significant role in shaping how his readers (including us) understand that world. The realism that flourished between the Civil War and World War I raises as many questions about the purpose of literature as it answers. How should literature respond to the social problems of its time? How can language capture what is real? Who gets to decide what counts as realism and what counts as fantasy? How can literature help us to understand competing perspectives on reality?

These questions remain as pertinent in our time as they were in Twain's. Many of the changes sweeping through Twain's world seem to foreshadow the struggles of our own time. The period encompassing the end of the nineteenth century and the beginning of the twentieth witnessed an influx of immigrants to America, questions about racial equality and racial violence, anxiety about shifting gender roles, and concerns about the accumulation and concentration of wealth. The distance between the late nineteenth century and the present is substantial and the differences between that period and ours are significant, but there are good reasons that some have called the early twenty-first century a "second Gilded Age."

RECONSTRUCTING AMERICA

The Civil War transformed the lives of the four million African Americans who obtained their freedom from slavery, but its costs were staggering. The combined death toll from the Union and Confederate armies equaled more than 620,000 soldiers—or about 2 percent of the total U.S. population. Historians have offered a conservative estimate of an additional 50,000 civilian casualties, mostly in areas that declared secession from the Union. Of those who survived battle, hundreds of thousands sustained injuries, and the fighting obliterated fields, factories, and homes in the war's path. In the face of so much destruction and suffering, the rebuilding of the United States required more than simply repairing railroads and clearing away the debris of war. The reconstruction of America also required a reimagination of what it meant to be an American.

In their quest to rebuild the United States, Americans in the post–Civil War era looked in a variety of directions for the resources needed for renewal: abroad, for immigrant populations that would provide the labor necessary for economic growth; to the west, where land, minerals, and other natural resources seemed to be abundant; and to the south, where the destruction left by the war created opportunities for entrepreneurial investors. Finally, by the turn of the twentieth century, Americans were looking to foreign lands in a new way, as the United States sought to claim its place on the world stage as an imperial power. What united these disparate energies was a drive for material prosperity—an unquestioned belief in economic progress. Signs of this creed were visible in the New York mansions constructed on Fifth Avenue; in the thrumming activity of the stockyards and market exchanges of Chicago; and in the new forms of leisure activities—amusement parks, dance halls, nickleodeons—that catered to working-class people who found they had some extra time and money to spend on pleasure.

But that prosperity came at a price. Though wages for blue- and white-collar workers rose during the late nineteenth century, the gains for laborers were far smaller than the fortunes being made and lost by the industrial capitalists who seemed to control a larger and larger share of the American economy every year. The laissez-faire capitalism that generated such spectacular opportunities was also fraught with risk—and the nation endured the consequences of a series of financial panics and market crashes. Though the Homestead Act of 1862 promised free or cheap acreage to every individual or family who would settle and "improve" land according to a set formula, much of the available land was donated to railroads to encourage their growth. The expansion of the railroad network was critical to the larger economic development of the United States, yet it meant that farmers found themselves at the mercy of the large corporations that transported their goods—an economic order that the writer Frank Norris characterized as a giant "octopus" that wielded its power across the land. In the end, large-scale farming took over from the

Golden Spike Ceremony. Joining the tracks for the first transcontinental railroad, Promontory, Utah Territory, 1869.

family farm, increasing agricultural yields but forcing many farmers to join the swelling populations of American cities.

The rapid urbanization of the United States in the late nineteenth century permanently changed the cultural landscape of the nation. Between 1865 and the turn of the twentieth century, New York grew from a population of 500,000 to nearly 3.5 million. Chicago, with a population of only 29,000 in 1850, had more than 2 million inhabitants by 1910. Yet Upton Sinclair titled his great novel of Chicago life *The Jungle* (1906) for good reason. Urban workers often faced brutal, even dangerous, conditions, and the late nineteenth century witnessed the rise of industrial labor movements. Americans were shocked when strikes turned violent in cities such as Pittsburgh and Chicago, though ultimately neither blue-collar laborers nor small farmers were fully successful in opposing the forces of capital. Until the regulations of the early twentieth century, legislators and other elected officials believed that the welfare of the nation required that the forces of capitalism remain unchecked. Kickbacks, bribes, and other forms of corruption further ensured that corporate and industrial interests were well-represented by politicians.

The growth of industry and the urbanization of the United States were fueled by unprecedented levels of immigration. In 1870, the U.S. population was 38.5 million; by 1910, 92 million; by 1920, 123 million. A large percentage of this increase came from the arrival of immigrants from southern and eastern Europe: Russia, Poland, Italy, and the Balkan nations. As much as these new Americans were crucial to the prosperity of the nation, they were also a source of anxiety who provoked recurring questions about what it means to acquire an American identity. Throughout this period, native-born Americans, particularly whites, worried that the surge of immigrants would

Ellis Island. Staff interviewing new immigrants, c. 1910. From 1892 to 1954, New York's Ellis Island was the gateway for millions of immigrants to the United States.

change the racial and religious character of the nation. From a very different perspective, immigrant writers like Abraham Cahan—a Jew fleeing the oppression of his native Belarus—told stories about newcomers to America grappling with the demands of a new language and new customs, including in his novel *Yekl: A Tale of the New York Ghetto* (1896). After the turn of the twentieth century, Americans found a new metaphor to describe the experience of immigrants. The hero of Israel Zangwill's play *The Melting-Pot*—first staged in the United States in 1909—proclaims: "America is God's Crucible, the great Melting-Pot where all the races of Europe are melting and reforming!"

Not everyone, of course, wanted to melt or reform. For American Indians living in the western half of the continent, the expansion of the United States threatened their political and cultural autonomy. From the time of the earliest treaties with the United States, Native nations had agreed to cede large tracts of land with some territory specifically "reserved" for themselves. What we currently think of as Indian reservations came about as a result of President Ulysses S. Grant's policies of the late 1860s, which sought—and mostly forced—the agreement of various Native nations to limit themselves to lands designated by the federal government. In the 1880s, an organization of eastern philanthropists calling itself "Friends of the Indian" began to implement an agenda for assimilating Native Americans into the white mainstream. This organization meant well, but its methods inevitably devalued Native ways of life in favor of white schooling, white patterns of town settlement and agriculture, and above all white religion. Native writers such as Zitkala-Ša (Yankton Sioux), Francis LaFlesche (Omaha), and John Milton Oskison (Cherokee) wrote about the effects of such efforts on their people. At the same time that government and missionary boarding schools were attempting to strip American Indians of their tribal cultures, the government was working to separate them from their land. In 1887, the U.S. Congress approved the Dawes Severalty Act, which set in motion a process for dissolving the communal land holdings of tribal reservations and assigning smaller parcels of land to individual Indians. The Dawes Act fragmented the collectively held tribal lands and reduced the total Native land base by some ninety million acres before the policy was abandoned in 1934.

For most white Americans, the melting pot also excluded African Americans. Of all the social conflicts that animate the literature of the late nineteenth and early twentieth centuries, none matches the force or complexity of the continued subjugation of black Americans during this period. After the surrender of the Confederacy, U.S. federal troops occupied its former states and attempted to make good on the promise of equality. Twelve years later, in 1877, that promise was abandoned as members of Congress worked out a deal that would break a deadlocked presidential election. In exchange for sending Rutherford B. Hayes, a Republican, to the White House, members of his party agreed that the federal government would withdraw soldiers from the South and appropriate funds for railroads and other infrastructure needs there. In the years that followed, this political compromise would give way to a broader cultural consensus among white Americans. Reconciliation between North and South became of paramount importance, and white Americans would avoid reopening sectional wounds by ignoring the growing political and economic disempowerment of African Americans in the former states of the Confederacy. In spite of the genuine progress that had occurred since the Civil War, African Americans often found themselves returning to the questions that had underlain that terrible conflict. Speaking on "The Race Problem in America" at the World's Columbian Exposition in 1893, the famed abolitionist Frederick Douglass faced down a crowd of hecklers. "Men talk of the Negro problem," he declaimed. "There is no Negro problem. The problem is whether the American people have honesty enough, loyalty enough, honor enough, patriotism enough to live up to their own Constitution."

THE LITERARY MARKETPLACE

Douglass's words remind us that for all that was new about post–Civil War America, there were also substantial continuities with what had come before. Writers like Ralph Waldo Emerson, Harriet Beecher Stowe, and Walt Whitman remained active and influential figures into the 1880s and the 1890s. Emily Dickinson's most productive years as a poet occurred during the Civil War, but she would not become widely known as a poet until the 1890s, when her verses were published in heavily edited versions. Herman Melville published three books of poetry in the 1870s and 1880s, and then composed the masterful novella *Billy Budd*, which remained unpublished until long after his death in 1891.

In spite of the influence of such writers in the years following the Civil War, many American writers of this era began to understand themselves as belonging to a distinct generation. Indeed, the late nineteenth century was when scholars and critics began dividing the literature of the United States into distinct historical periods, seeking to create a coherent history of

American writing. The turn of the twentieth century witnessed the publication of several influential anthologies of American literature—and even the first college courses on the subject. By that time, the realm of literature— of literary writing and reading—had undergone substantial changes. The post–Civil War decades saw the United States create and import many features of the literary marketplace that we now take for granted: the standardization and proliferation of book reviewing; the circulation of best-seller lists; the growth, simultaneously, of several classes of readers, including well-educated white-collar readers, middle-class readers who attended book clubs, and increasingly literate working classes who might encounter literature through newspapers or dime novels. The commercial realm governing both author and text changed in significant ways, most crucially with the ratification of the International Copyright Act of 1891, a law supported by literary figures such as Mark Twain and William Dean Howells. The act extended copyright protection to foreign writers in the United States and enabled American authors to receive the same protection abroad.

During this period, the center of the growing publishing industry migrated from New England to New York, and commercial publishing became a more professional and specialized enterprise. As the American reading public grew, publishing houses increasingly focused on different segments of the literary marketplace and devised new methods to excite publicity and increase sales. The turn of the twentieth century fostered the rise of literary celebrity in the United States, most obviously epitomized by Mark Twain. Like later authors such as Jack London, Ernest Hemingway, and Gertrude Stein, Twain became a public figure whose actions and words were reported regularly in newspapers and in the press, and he was arguably the most recognizable American in the world for several decades.

The development of the railroads and the growth of urban markets both contributed to the development of mass cultural expression in the post–Civil War United States. Readers of literature could purchase new works by subscribing to them, as one might subscribe to a magazine, or find them in the increasing number of lending libraries—or they might encounter poems, short stories, and serialized novels in periodicals. Middle- and professional-class readers were the target audience of magazines such as the *Atlantic*, *Century*, and *Harper's*—where they could find writers such as Henry James, Constance Fenimore Woolson, and Sarah Orne Jewett. In San Francisco, the *Overland Monthly* emerged as the leading western literary periodical with a regional focus; it published Bret Harte, Ambrose Bierce, Sui Sin Far, and Mark Twain, among others. Abraham Cahan founded the Yiddish newspaper the *Jewish Daily Forward* in 1897, and Pauline E. Hopkins serialized her sensational novels in the *Colored American Magazine*, founded in 1900. As these examples suggest, new forms of cultural expression did not translate into a single, unified reading public. For white nativists—who were worried about the increasing number of immigrants from eastern and southern Europe, as well as the influence of African Americans and Asian Americans—the visible diversity of American literature exacerbated their fears about the future of their country.

FORMS OF REALISM

Nowhere was the anxiety about the state of American literature and its relationship to the American populace more on display than in the debates about literary realism that transpired in the last two decades of the nineteenth century. *Realism* was (and is) a slippery term, one that could be applied to a variety of literary projects; most commonly, it was used to refer to literary fiction that was rooted in the observation and documentation of the details of everyday life. American realists saw themselves as being influenced by the development of realist fiction in Britain and continental Europe; they looked to writers as diverse as George Eliot (England), Ivan Turgenev (Russia), and Henrik Ibsen (Norway). However, the author and editor William Dean Howells contended that literary realism had a particular function in the democratic society of the United States. Howells held that by documenting the speech and manners of a wide variety of people—representing a diversity of social classes—literary realism could foster a shared democratic culture. "Democracy in literature . . . wishes to know and to tell the truth," he wrote. At a time when American society seemed on the verge of fracturing into divisions of class, race, and ethnicity, literature could help cultivate empathetic bonds that would hold it together. Howells continued, "Men are more alike than unlike one another: let us make them know one another better, that they may be all humbled and strengthened with a sense of their fraternity."

A cluster in this section presents several key arguments about realism and how it might be defined, including an example of the substantial criticism that Howells's vision faced. Some critics believed that realism abandoned the moral purpose of art in favor of the vulgar and commonplace; others believed that realist fiction relied too much on dull observation instead of dramatic storytelling. In spite of this opposition, Howells's ideas set the agenda for the American literary establishment in his time. Indeed, this volume is filled with writers that Howells encouraged, published, or reviewed favorably during his career. He was an early champion of his contemporaries Henry James and Mark Twain—maintaining close ties with both writers for decades—and later promoted younger writers such as Stephen Crane, Paul Laurence Dunbar, and Charles Chesnutt. These writers, he believed, would usher in an age in which the United States could stand on the world stage as an equal to other nations as a contributor to world letters.

The interest in forms of literary realism was especially welcoming of regional writing from throughout the United States. On a practical level, regional writing flourished with the proliferation of mass magazines, for which short stories and sketches were ideal, and which catered to urban audiences with an interest in learning about distant peoples and their cultures. By the end of the nineteenth century, virtually every region of the country had one or more "local colorists" dedicated to capturing its natural, social, and linguistic features. These works, such as Joel Chandler Harris's plantation tales, could be suffused with nostalgia. In other cases, such as in the writing of Constance Fenimore Woolson and Charles Chesnutt about the South, or the Maine fiction of Sarah Orne Jewett, regional writers portrayed the stresses and complexities of particular locales under the pressure of tremendous change. Hamlin Garland, a visible advocate of regional writing, depicted midwestern farmers coming to terms with harsh economic truths, and Mary Wilkins Freeman explored the effects of tradition on the lives of New England women. The appetite for regional writing played a large role in launching the careers of writers from the American West. First published in 1865, Mark Twain's tall tale from the California frontier, "The Notorious Jumping Frog of Calaveras County," remained his best known work for many years, and Bret Harte became a national figure in 1868 with "The Luck of Roaring Camp," a story that explores and exploits colorful myths of the West.

Literary realism and regionalism also influenced the way that writers portrayed the lives of racial and ethnic "others"—nonwhites seen as different from the majority of American readers. Both white and African American writers, for instance, depicted black characters as speaking in a vernacular that was distinct from the speech of their white characters, and they often took advantage of white interest in African American folk beliefs. Joel Chandler Harris's "Wonderful Tar Baby Story" (1881), told by Uncle Remus, was immensely popular, and the superstitions voiced by Jim in Mark Twain's *Adventures of Huckleberry Finn* (1884) contributed to its success. Charles Chesnutt's conjure tales offered a new take on the practice of presenting African American traditions to white readers, one that allows the reader to see an African American storyteller as much less naïve in his engagement with white audiences. The interest in vernacular speech extended to poetry as well, as Paul Laurence Dunbar manipulated the rhythms of African American speech into some of the best-known verse of his time.

In their representations of African Americans, these authors sought to depict ways of speaking that were notably different in vocabulary and pronunciation from the English spoken by their readers. To capture that difference, they represented African American voices in the form of a *dialect*—a variation of a language that is particular to a group or region. For writers, putting dialect on the page involved changing the spelling and punctuation of characters' dialogue so that it purported to match the spoken patterns of a particular race, class, or ethnicity. This practice of writing dialogue in the form of a dialect became common in the late nineteenth century, and it extended to the representation of all those thought to be outside the mainstream society of middle- to upper-class Anglo-America. African Americans, recent immigrants, and the urban poor were all presented in literature as speaking a non-standard English. This vogue for dialect literature, which extended from newspaper sketches to literary novels, can make the writing of this period challenging for the twenty-first-century reader. But the difficulty serves a purpose. For writers like Mark Twain, Charles Chesnutt, and Stephen Crane, transcribing dialogue as nonstandard dialect was a means of representing the social distances that existed among their characters— distances that could have results that were comic, tragic, or both—as well as the distance these writers presumed between their characters and their middle-class readers. Indeed, it could, in fact, be part of the purpose of a work of literature that readers must struggle to understand speakers from racial or ethnic backgrounds different from their own.

By the turn of the twentieth century, the literary interest in the traditions of "the folk" was visible everywhere in American literature. When Kate

A Feast Day at Acoma, Edward S. Curtis, 1904. In 1892 Curtis (1868–1952) opened a studio in Washington Territory and began to photograph local Indians. Curtis traveled widely, portraying Native people and scenes in an elegiac manner, attempting to document what he understood to be the last days of the "vanishing Indian." Whatever his intentions, *A Feast Day at Acoma* shows a bustling scene of Pueblo people in the Southwest.

Chopin sought an audience for her tales of rural Louisiana, she titled her volume *Bayou Folk* (1894). When W. E. B. Du Bois published his ground-breaking collection of essays about race and racism in the United States, he called the book *The Souls of Black Folk* (1903). During the final decades of the nineteenth century, the publication of dialect literature, folktales, and local-color sketches coincided with the rise and professionalization of social sciences that were oriented toward the same materials. For Native Americans, the development of anthropology in the United States had particular significance. Even as American Indians were a target of assimilation campaigns to erase their languages, cultures, and religions, anthropologists were traveling the continent attempting to document those very things. Sponsored both by the federal government and by universities, the anthropologists transcribed songs, stories, and ceremonials—collecting them on the page just as they collected physical artifacts for natural history museums. Native American authors such as Zitkala-Ša could find their way into print by producing their own versions of tribal stories, a practice that continues to this day. Just as important, she and other Native writers reminded Americans that Indians would continue to persist *outside* of museums.

In expanding the diversity of American writing, realism did not cure any of the social ills of the Gilded Age. However, the interest in realism allowed for a more socially engaged literature, one in which the boundaries between fiction and nonfiction could become blurred. Looking back to the Civil War, Ambrose Bierce's dark, violent tales of the conflict and Twain's comic "Private History of a Campaign That Failed" (1885) were both published alongside the more serious accounts of battles and generals; Constance Fenimore Woolson and Charles W. Chesnutt both wrote searing stories of Reconstruction at a time when the economic future of the South was a frequent topic of national discussion; and Booker T. Washington's *Up from Slavery*, published in 1901, offered a blueprint for African American uplift and was instantly recognized as a masterpiece of autobiography, only to meet with a sharp rejoinder two years later by W. E. B. Du Bois in *The Souls of Black Folk*—a mix of memoir, polemic, social science, and fiction. The turn of the twentieth century was a time of lively, even heated, argument about the future of the nation, and literary realism was an invitation for authors to dive into those debates rather than to turn away.

THE "WOMAN QUESTION"

One such debate was about how the role of women in American life would be defined—or even whether it should be defined at all. In the post–Civil War era, females raised in middle- and professional-class homes had increasing access to secondary and even higher education. They had access to new forms of mass entertainment, and urbanization offered new forms of cultural and political activity. The consumer culture of the late nineteenth century allowed women increasing opportunity to assert their own wants and desires, and the decreasing price of magazines was coupled by an increase in the number of periodicals that sought a female readership.

During the last two decades of the nineteenth century, women increasingly participated in social clubs of all kinds, a movement that facilitated the discussion among women of the cultural and political issues of the moment. Women's clubs might invite speakers or select books for discussion, and the "clubwoman" could exert significant influence in a community. While women's clubs were often identified, in the popular press, with liberal attitudes about gender roles, they could also act as conservative forces—organized around traditional lines of class, religion, and race. Indeed, in the 1890s women formed separate national organizations for white and African American women's clubs. For immigrant and working-class communities, women's clubs were an opportunity to discuss the challenges of urban environments. For African American women, clubs allowed members to share in an agenda of racial advancement and to achieve the middle-class respectability often denied them in their daily lives.

The "Woman Question," to use a common phrase from this period, was actually more than a single question; it was a host of issues related to education, participation in the workforce, and the social influence of women on issues such as temperance. Although marriage and matrimony defined, in the popular imagination, the conventional roles for women of all classes, changes in the divorce laws during the 1890s fueled debates about female autonomy and the institution of marriage. The chief political issue identified with women during this period was suffrage. Proponents of female suffrage were bitterly disappointed by the 1870 ratification of the Fifteenth Amendment to the Constitution, which extended—at least in theory—the voting franchise to African American men but not to women of any race. Membership in the National Woman Suffrage Association, founded in 1869, grew dramatically in the late nineteenth century. However, the question of voting rights also fostered racial and ethnic division throughout the period, as white, native-born women often raised their claims to the ballot by deriding the fact that others they deemed less worthy, including new immigrant and African American men, could vote. Black suffragists were often excluded from national events, and many formed their own suffrage organizations.

The quest for female suffrage would not be complete until the ratification of the Nineteenth Amendment in 1920, but throughout the decades between the Civil War and World War I, Americans had a sense that women were claiming new forms of autonomy. At such a time, even something as ordinary as a bicycle, increasingly popular in the late nineteenth century, could become a symbol of female emancipation. ("It gives women a feeling of freedom and self-reliance," Susan B. Anthony famously said.) The questions and anxieties about the changing place of women in American culture reverberate throughout the literature of this period. By portraying an "American girl" attempting to navigate the world of leisure and desire, Henry James struck a nerve with the publication of *Daisy Miller* in 1879, and he returned to these themes throughout his long career as a novelist. In a different vein, Charlotte Perkins Gilman's "The Yellow Wall-paper"—a story that was quickly recognized as a classic when it was first published in 1892—depicts how the medical regime of the late nineteenth century attempted to contain the creative energies of American women. Two important novels published within a year of one another, Kate Chopin's *The Awakening* (1899) and Theodore Dreiser's *Sister Carrie* (1900), both feature protagonists who attempt to achieve autonomy and fulfill their desires—with very different outcomes. Edith Wharton's short stories, including those that appear in this volume, find comedy and pathos in an upper-class world in which divorce is increasingly common.

Female writers of color wrote about many of these same issues, but they also addressed the ways in which racism created a social landscape even more challenging than that faced by their white counterparts. Ida B. Wells-Barnett's accounts of lynching and other forms of anti-black violence revealed the cruelties that threatened the safety and well-being of all African Americans, male and female; in her autobiographical essays, Zitkala-Ša wrote about the pressures of assimilation brought to bear on Native Americans who sought an education; and Pauline Hopkins published sensational tales, like "Talma Gordon" (1900), that called into question the social fictions that upheld racial inequality. Taken together, these works reveal that categories like "race" and "gender" could mean quite distinct things to writers at the turn of the twentieth century. What all of these authors share, though, is a sense that writing had a vital function to play in helping Americans to understand the complex problems of their time.

UNSEEN FORCES

As the century neared its close, Americans increasingly felt that their society was being shaped by unseen forces beyond their control. The industrialization of the United States created large corporations that seemed to obey their own laws; engineers were harnessing the power of electricity, bringing energy to cities that were growing faster than anything Americans had previously seen; in 1895, scientists discovered how to harness X-rays to penetrate the secrets of the body; and a communications network that included telephones and telegraphs spread across the nation and the globe, delivering news at unprecedented speed. By the end of the first decade of the twentieth century, an American could drive an automobile, see the flickering image of a moving picture, and hear voices recorded on a phonograph—all wonders of a new age. Surrounded by the machinery and scientific advances on display at the Great Exposition in Paris in 1900, Henry Adams described himself as having "his historical neck broken by the sudden irruption of forces totally new." For the sixty-two-year-old historian, the grandson and great-grandson of U.S. presidents, the turn of the twentieth century was a time of promise and peril, unleashing "occult, supersensual, irrational" forces that exerted the same power in the modern world that the Christian cross had wielded in the Middle Ages.

One force that changed how many Americans understood the physical and social world was the emerging theory of evolution. In *The Origin of Species* (1859) and *The Descent of Man* (1871), Charles Darwin theorized that human beings had developed over the ages from nonhuman forms of life, successfully adapting to changing environmental conditions. Darwin, a naturalist, was not interested in the competition that took place among human societies, but in the 1860s the English philosopher Herbert Spencer began using the theory of natural selection as a lens for understanding competition among people. Spencer coined the phrase "survival of the fittest" to describe this process, and Darwin even included it in later editions of *The Origin of Species*. Though relatively few Americans read Spencer himself—and even fewer actually read Darwin—ideas about evolution, natural selection, and competition would shape American thought over the next half century. As it was most often invoked, evolution could describe a social world in which progress was achieved only through ruthless competition. Given the collateral damage caused by the dramatic booms and busts of the business cycle during the late nineteenth century, it is small wonder that some of the leading American businessmen happily adopted this rhetoric to describe the value of capitalism. Andrew Carnegie, for example, argued that unrestrained competition was the equivalent of a law of nature designed to eliminate those unfit for the new economic order.

Darwinism could justify other forms of violence as well. Fear that the racial character of the United States would be contaminated by Asian blood—and therefore rendered "unfit"—was one rationale offered for the Chinese Exclusion Act of 1882, which prohibited immigration from China. White Americans believed that the forces of evolution destined American Indians to the margins of history, and this belief drove both the final nineteenth-century campaigns to eradicate Native military resistance to the United States and the

Americanization efforts of self-described "Friends of the Indian." In the South, the language of social evolution and racial competition contributed to the violent suppression of African Americans, particularly African American men. White supremacists claimed that they were protecting the purity of white women and ensuring the future of the white race as they terrorized their black neighbors through the spectacle of lynching. In this distortion of Darwinian evolution, it was all too easy to understand any form of group violence as nothing more than the expression of natural law.

In the realm of literature, American authors at the end of the nineteenth century began to grapple more explicitly with the meaning of evolution and other social forces in the development of literary *naturalism* in the United States. Naturalism grew from, and overlapped with, literary realism, but there were key differences. Like Howells and his fellow realists, literary naturalists felt that they had an obligation to bring social conflict to the page, but they found Howells and his followers too mild and too focused on the manners of the professional and upper classes. Naturalists thought that realism had left literature bloodless by failing to depict the genuine violence that they saw everywhere in the ruthless, modern world; they sought to explore how biology, environment, and other material forces shaped lives—particularly the lives of lower-class people, who had less control over their lives than those who were better off. Naturalism introduces characters from the fringes and depths of society, far from the middle class, whose lives really do spin out of control; their fates are seen to be the outcome of degenerate heredity, a sordid environment, and the bad luck that can often seem to control the lives of people without money or influence. The protagonist of Stephen Crane's *Maggie: A Girl of the Streets* (1893) cannot escape the seamy violence of Manhattan's Lower East Side; Upton Sinclair's *The Jungle* (1906) compares the working-class immigrants of Chicago's meatpacking district to the pigs that they slaughter.

Literary naturalists emphasized plot to a greater degree than did the realists of previous decades. Their works engaged more deliberately with romance and myth, even when the result was to deflate conventional notions of heroism, as in Crane's Civil War novel *The Red Badge of Courage* (1895). In the twentieth century, Jack London would take this romantic turn further with his adventure novels and stories—works that often returned to the theme of the bestial instincts that lay beneath civilization. In London's highly popular *The Call of the Wild* (1903), the canine protagonist Buck is stolen from a California ranch and transported to Alaska, where he awakens to his primal memories of wild life and becomes transformed into the "Ghost Dog" of the wilderness. London later wrote *White Fang* (1906), a novel that reverses this movement by bringing a dog of the "savage, frozen-hearted Northland Wild" into the civilization and domesticity of the south. In both cases, the drama turns on a clash between the power of social environment and the primal force of instinct.

With their emphasis on men of action—whether in the gold fields of Alaska or the stock exchanges of Chicago—the naturalist fictions of London, Frank Norris, Theodore Dreiser, and Upton Sinclair portrayed a world of masculine violence. (Even Jack London's canine protagonists are male.) For decades, some commentators in the United States had expressed concerns that "overcivilization," thanks to the growth of professional and

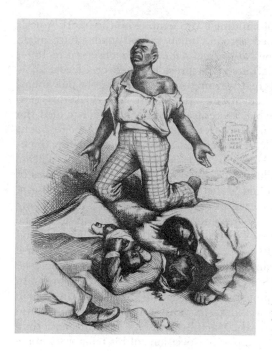

Race and Reconstruction. This 1876 cartoon by Thomas Nast (1840–1902) comments on the failure of the federal government to protect African Americans in the South. The caption reads, "Is this a republican form of government? Is this protecting life, liberty, or property? Is this equal protection of the laws?" *Harper's Weekly,* September 2, 1876.

white-collar occupations, was leading to a kind of softness among American men. This anxiety was shaped by the growing material prosperity of the upper and professional classes, who increasingly worked in occupations that did not require physical strength, and it was also a response to the efforts by women to increase their cultural, economic, and political power. Throughout this period, cultural commentators spent considerable time and effort wringing their hands about what the fluctuating roles of men and women would mean for the future of American civilization.

THE NEW AMERICAN EMPIRE

The increasing assertiveness of American women—or the "New Woman," to use a phrase made popular in the 1890s—made it all the more imperative to shape American manhood properly. One late-nineteenth-century movement, "muscular Christianity," attempted to merge physical and moral development through institutions like the Young Men's Christian Association. Indeed, a central premise of the age was that white men could best prepare themselves for the Darwinian struggle by becoming both mentally *and* physically fit. Theodore Roosevelt urged men to engage in the "strenuous life," and he looked back on *The Winning of the West* (1889–96)—the title of his four-volume history of American expansion—as a grand drama of heroism and sacrifice. However, in the eyes of most white Americans, the West had already been "won" by the 1890s. The historian Frederick Jackson Turner declared in 1893 that the western frontier, which he regarded as crucial to the formation of America's democratic character, no longer existed.

Having completed the work of building a U.S. empire on the North American continent, Americans looked abroad. "Idleness and luxury have made men flabby," a contributor to the *North American Review* observed in 1894, "and the man at the head of affairs [U.S. president Grover Cleveland] is beginning to ask seriously if a great war might not help them to pull themselves together." When the United States went to war with Spain in 1898, Americans quickly embraced what Secretary of State John Hay called the "splendid little war" in Cuba, and Roosevelt organized a volunteer regiment of "rough riders" that he could lead into combat. For those advocating imperial expansion, the Spanish–American War addressed several problems simultaneously. It gave U.S. industry access to new markets, easing fears of "overproduction"; it gave the United States the chance to establish itself as a legitimate rival to European imperial powers; and it created a new proving ground for American men. At the resolution of the conflict in 1898, the nation had acquired new territories in Puerto Rico and the Philippines, and it would acquire the territory of Hawaii that same year. One ostensible cause of the conflict was the American desire to secure Cuban independence, yet after Spain's defeat the United States did not hurry to withdraw its troops. In effect, Cuba remained a U.S. protectorate for decades. In 1892, the Cuban patriot José Martí had written a manifesto, "Our America," warning Latin America of the "giant" to their north. Martí lived in New York for more than a decade, and he understood the imperial aspirations of his temporary home all too well.

In 1899, the Filipino independence movement began to revolt against the U.S. military forces occupying the islands, and the armed conflict lasted for three years. Increasingly vocal critics founded the American Anti-Imperialist league. The anti-imperialists included figures as diverse as the industrialist Andrew Carnegie, the social worker Jane Addams, and the philosopher William James (Henry's brother). As in any movement, participants' motives varied. For some, the prospect of empire seemed in conflict with the principle of self-determination that they believed to be a core American value; others were, less nobly, anxious about any territorial grab that could increase the number of nonwhites living under the American flag. William Dean Howells and Mark Twain were members of the Anti-Imperialist League, and both distrusted the exercise of military power and the rhetoric of patriotism that accompanied it. In his story "Editha" (1905), Howells depicts a young woman so captivated by the romance of war that she sends her fiancé off to die in it—and suffers no regret, even after she encounters the scornful mother of the deceased. Twain, whose celebrity made his views especially newsworthy, penned several works opposing military ventures abroad, including "The War Prayer," a story so dark in its outlook that, after a magazine rejected it for publication in 1905, he left it unpublished in his own lifetime. Twain explained his decision in a letter to a friend: "None but the dead are permitted to tell the truth."

With Twain's passing in 1910, the generation of men and women who had lived through the American Civil War was passing too. By the early 1900s, the first stirrings of modernism were visible: Henry James's deep explorations of consciousness in his late novels anticipated the prose experiments of Virginia Woolf and James Joyce; in 1912 James Weldon Johnson would publish his *Autobiography of an Ex-Colored Man*, a novel that presages the fiction of the Harlem Renaissance in its fascination with alienation and the boundaries of racial identity; and for many readers, the tight, elliptical verses of Emily Dickinson, first published in the 1890s, seem now to have more in common with the twentieth-century verse of poets like Hilda Doolittle or William Carlos Williams than with anything written in her own time. Indeed, many of the authors considered today to be significant influences on American modernism—such as Robert Frost, Ezra Pound, and Gertrude Stein— were already writing and publishing by the year of Twain's death. Realism and naturalism, in other words, overlapped considerably with the artistic movements that would dominate the decades following World War I. When the United States entered the Great War in 1917, its transformation into a global power became complete; as Europe imploded, the United States exerted political and cultural power far beyond what anyone might have imagined a half century earlier, when America was coming to terms with the aftermath of its own terrible war.

AMERICAN LITERATURE 1865–1914

TEXTS	CONTEXTS
1855 Walt Whitman, *Leaves of Grass*	
1860–65 Emily Dickinson writes several hundred **poems**	**1860** Short-lived Pony Express runs from Missouri to California
	1861 South Carolina batteries fire on Fort Sumter, initiating the Civil War • Southern states secede from the Union and found the Confederate States of America
1865 Walt Whitman, *Drum-Taps*	**1865** Civil War ends • Reconstruction begins • Lincoln assassinated • Thirteenth Amendment ratified, prohibiting slavery
1867 Mark Twain, *The Notorious Jumping Frog of Calaveras County and Other Sketches* • Horatio Alger, *Ragged Dick*	**1867** United States purchases Alaska from Russia • Jesse Chisholm maps out the Chisholm Trail, connecting Texas cattle ranches to railheads in Kansas City, Cheyenne, Dodge City, and Abilene
1868 Louisa May Alcott, *Little Women*	**1868** Fourteenth Amendment passed, guaranteeing citizenship to all peoples born in the United States (exclusive of Native peoples) • Congress institutes eight-hour workday for federal employees • sweatshops, using mostly immigrant labor, begin to proliferate in cities
	1869 First transcontinental railroad completed by construction crews composed largely of Chinese laborers • Susan B. Anthony elected president of American Equal Rights Association; Elizabeth Cady Stanton elected president of National Woman Suffrage Association
1870 Bret Harte, *The Luck of Roaring Camp and Other Sketches*	**1870** Fifteenth Amendment, giving African American men the right to vote, ratified
	1871 Indian Appropriation Act ends the practice of negotiating treaties with the tribes as sovereign nations
1872 Mark Twain, *Roughing It*	**1872** Yellowstone, first U.S. national park, established
	1873 Economic panic; financial depression lasts until 1879
	1874 Women's Christian Temperance Union founded in Cleveland • invention of barbed wire effectively ends the open range
1876 Charlot, "[He has filled graves with our bones]"	**1876** Custer's regiment defeated by the Sioux and Cheyenne at Little Big Horn River, Montana • Alexander Graham Bell invents the telephone
	1877 Reconstruction ends • segregationist Jim Crow laws begin
1878 Henry James, *Daisy Miller*	

Boldface titles indicate works in the anthology.

TEXTS	CONTEXTS
1879 Chief Joseph, "An Indian's Views of Indian Affairs"	1879 Thomas Edison invents the electric lightbulb • female lawyers permitted to argue before Supreme Court
1880 Joel Chandler Harris, *Uncle Remus: His Songs and Sayings* • Constance Fenimore Woolson, *Rodman the Keeper: Southern Sketches*	1880–1910 Massive immigration from Europe
	1881 Tuskegee Institute founded
	1882 J. D. Rockefeller organizes Standard Oil Trust • Chinese Exclusion Act instituted
1883 Emma Lazarus, "**The New Colossus**"	
1884 Twain, *Adventures of Huckleberry Finn*	1884 Tailors' strike in New York City brings national attention to sweatshops
	1886 Statue of Liberty dedicated • Haymarket Square labor riot leaves eleven dead • American Federation of Labor organized
	1887 General Allotment Act or Dawes Act permits the president to divide tribally owned lands into individual allotments to be held in trust for twenty-five years, with "surplus" lands to be sold to non-Indians. This led the Indians to lose some 90 million acres of land by the time Dawes was repealed in 1934.
1889 Theodore Roosevelt, *The Winning of the West* • Hamlin Garland, "Under the Lion's Paw" • Andrew Carnegie, "The Gospel of Wealth"	
1890 Ambrose Bierce, "**An Occurrence at Owl Creek Bridge**" • Emily Dickinson, *Poems*	1890 U.S. Bureau of the Census declares the "frontier" "to be closed." There is no more "free" or "unoccupied" land • Sitting Bull killed. Massacre of Big Foot's Minneconjou band by federal troops at Wounded Knee Creek ends the Ghost Dance among the Sioux • Ellis Island Immigration Station opens
1891 José Martí, "Our America" • Mary E. Wilkins Freeman, "**A New England Nun**"	
1892 Anna Julia Cooper, *A Voice from the South* • Charlotte Perkins Gilman, "The Yellow Wall-paper"	
1893 Stephen Crane, *Maggie: A Girl of the Streets* • Frederick Jackson Turner, *The Significance of the Frontier*	1893 World's Columbian Exposition held in Chicago • economic panic and depression, set off by the collapse of the Philadelphia and Reading Railroads
1895 Crane, *Black Riders* and *The Red Badge of Courage*	
1896 Paul Laurence Dunbar, *Lyrics of a Lowly Life* • James Mooney publishes *Ghost Dance Songs* • Abraham Cahan, *Yekl: A Tale of the New York Ghetto* • Sarah Orne Jewett, *The Country of the Pointed Firs*	1896 *Plessy v. Ferguson* upholds segregated transportation
1897 Crane, *The Open Boat and Other Tales of Adventure*	1897–98 Klondike Gold Rush

TEXTS	CONTEXTS
	1898 United States annexes Hawaii
	1898–99 Spanish–American War
1899 Charles Chesnutt, *The Conjure Woman* and *The Wife of His Youth and Other Stories of the Color Line* • Kate Chopin, *The Awakening* • Frank Norris, *McTeague*	
1900 Theodore Dreiser, **Sister Carrie** • Ida B. Wells-Barnett, *Mob-Rule in New Orleans* • Pauline Hopkins, *Contending Forces* • Francis LaFlesche, *The Middle Five*	1900 U.S. population exceeds seventy-five million
1901 Zitkala-Ša, **Impressions of an Indian Childhood and The School Days of an Indian Girl** • Norris, *The Octopus* • Jack London, "The Law of Life" • Booker T. Washington, **Up from Slavery**	1901 J. P. Morgan founds U.S. Steel Corporation • first transatlantic radio • oil discovered in Spindletop, Texas
1903 W. E. B. Du Bois, **The Souls of Black Folk** • London, *The Call of the Wild*	1903 Henry Ford founds Ford Motor Co. • Wright brothers make the first successful airplane flight • *The Great Train Robbery* is first U.S. cinematic narrative
1904 Edith Wharton, **"The Other Two"**	1904 National Child Labor Committee formed
1905 William Dean Howells, **"Editha"**	1905 Industrial Workers of the World (the Wobblies) founded
1906 Upton Sinclair, *The Jungle*	1906 April 18: San Francisco earthquake and fire • dozens of African Americans killed in Atlanta race riots
1907 Henry Adams, *The Education of Henry Adams*, privately printed	
	1908 Israel Zangwill's "The Melting Pot" first performed
	1909 National Association for the Advancement of Colored People (NAACP) founded
1910 Jane Addams, *Twenty Years at Hull-House* • Sui Sin Far, **"Mrs. Spring Fragrance"**	1910 Mexican Revolution
1912 James Weldon Johnson, *The Autobiography of an Ex-Colored Man*	
	1914 U.S. Marines invade and occupy Vera Cruz, Mexico • Panama Canal opens

WALT WHITMAN
1819–1892

Walt Whitman revolutionized American poetry. Responding to Emerson's call in "The Poet" (1842) for an American bard who would address all "the facts of the animal economy, sex, nutriment, gestation, birth," Whitman put the living, breathing, sexual body at the center of much of his poetry, challenging conventions of the day. Responding to Emerson's call for a "metre-making argument," he rejected traditions of poetic scansion and elevated diction, improvising the form that has come to be known as free verse, while adopting a wide-ranging vocabulary opening new possibilities for poetic expression. A poet of democracy, Whitman celebrated the mystical, divine potential of the individual; a poet of the urban, he wrote about the sights, sounds, and energy of the modern metropolis. In his 1855 preface to *Leaves of Grass*, he declared that "the proof of a poet is that his country absorbs him as affectionately as he has absorbed it." On the evidence of his enormous influence on later poets—Hart Crane, Langston Hughes, Robert Lowell, Allen Ginsberg, Adrienne Rich, Cherríe Moraga, and countless others, including Spain's Federico García Lorca and Chile's Pablo Neruda—Whitman not only was affectionately absorbed by his own country but remains a persistent presence in poetry throughout the world.

Whitman was born on May 31, 1819, in West Hills, Long Island (New York), the second of eight surviving children of the Quakers Louisa Van Velsor and Walter Whitman. In 1823, Whitman's father, a farmer turned carpenter, sought to take advantage of a building boom by moving the family to Brooklyn—then a town at the western and most urbanized part of Long Island. Whitman left school when he was eleven, and was soon employed in the printing office of a newspaper; when his family moved east on Long Island in 1833, he remained in Brooklyn on his own. He began contributing to newspapers in his midteens and spent five years teaching at country and small-town schools on Long Island, interrupting his teaching to start a newspaper of his own in 1838 and to work briefly on another Long Island paper. By early 1840 he had started the series "Sun-Down Papers from the Desk of a School-Master" for the Jamaica, New York, *Democrat* and was writing poems and fiction. One of his stories prophetically culminated with the dream of writing "a wonderful and ponderous book."

Just before he turned twenty-one Whitman stopped teaching, moved to Manhattan, began work at the literary weekly *New World*, and soon became editor of a Manhattan daily, the *Aurora*. He also began a political career by speaking at Democratic rallies and writing for the *Democratic Review*, the foremost magazine of the Democratic Party. He exulted in the extremes of the city, where street-gang violence was countered by the lectures of Emerson and where even a young editor could get to know the poet William Cullen Bryant, editor of the *Evening Post*. Fired from the *Aurora*, which publicly charged him with laziness, he wrote a temperance novel, *Franklin Evans, or the Inebriate*, for a one-issue extra of the *New World* late in 1842. After three years of various literary and political jobs, he returned to Brooklyn in 1845, becoming a special contributor to the *Long Island Star*, assigned to Manhattan events, including theatrical and musical performances. All through the 1840s he attended operas on his journalist's passes and he would later say that without the "emotions, raptures, uplifts" of opera he could never have written *Leaves of Grass*. Just before he was twenty-seven he took over the editorship of the *Brooklyn Eagle*, writing most of the literary reviews, which included books by Carlyle, Emerson, Melville, Fuller, and Goethe, among

Leaves of Grass. Frontispiece and title page of the first edition (1855).

others. Like most Democrats, he was able to justify the Mexican War (1846–48) by hailing the great American mission of "peopling the New World with a noble race." Yet at the beginning of 1848 he was fired from the *Eagle* because, like Bryant, he had become a Free-Soiler, opposed to the acquisition of more territory for slavery. Whitman served as a delegate to the Buffalo Free-Soil convention and helped to found the Free-Soil newspaper the *Brooklyn Freeman*. Around this time he began writing poetry in a serious way, experimenting with form and prosody; he published several topical poems in 1850, including "Europe," which would later appear in *Leaves of Grass*.

Whitman's notebook fragments suggest that he began to invent the overall shape of his first volume of poetry during the period 1853–54. On May 15, 1855, he took out a copyright for *Leaves of Grass*, and he spent the spring and early summer seeing his book through the press, probably setting some of the type himself. Published in Brooklyn, New York, during the first week of July, the volume, bound in dark green cloth with a sprig of grass in gilt on the cover, contained twelve untitled poems (including the initial version of "Song of Myself"), along with an exuberant preface declaring his ambition to be the American bard. In the image of Whitman on the book's frontispiece, which was based on an 1854 daguerreotype, the bearded Whitman—rejecting the conventional suit jacket, buttoned-up shirt, and high collar of the formal studio portrait—stands with one arm akimbo, one hand in a pocket, workingman's hat on slightly cocked head, shirt unbuttoned at the collar, looking directly at the reader. (See the reproduction above.) The image, like the poetry itself, defied convention by aligning the poet with working people. The poems, with their absence of standard verse and stanza patterns (although strongly rhythmic and controlled by numerous poetic devices of repetition and variation), also introduced his use of "catalogs"—journalistic and encyclopedic listings—that were to become a hallmark of his style. Whitman sent out numerous presentation and review copies of his book, receiving an immediate response from Emerson, who greeted him "at the beginning of a great career," but otherwise attracting little notice. As weeks passed, Whitman chose to publish a few anonymous reviews himself, praising *Leaves of Grass* in the *American Phrenological Journal*, for instance, as one of "the most glorious triumphs, in the known history of literature." In October he let Horace Greeley's *New York Tribune* print Emerson's private letter of praise, and he put clippings of the letter in presentation copies to Longfellow, among others. Emerson termed Whitman's appropriation of the letter "a strange, rude thing," but he remained interested in meeting the poet. While Whitman was angling for reviews in England and working on expanding his book, Emerson visited him in December of 1855. Thoreau, who admired *Leaves of Grass* but found several of its poems "simply sensual," visited him later in 1856. That year also saw the appearance of the second edition of *Leaves of Grass*, now with thirty-three poems, including "Crossing Brooklyn Ferry" under its initial title, "Sundown Poem."

Returning to miscellaneous journalism, Whitman edited the *Brooklyn Times* from 1857 to 1859 and published several pieces in the *Times* affirming his Free-Soiler hopes for a continued national expansion into the western territories that would not entail the expansion of slavery. In the third (1860) edition of *Leaves of Grass*, Whitman began to group his poems thematically. For a section called "Enfans d'Adam," later retitled "Children of Adam," he wrote fifteen poems focused on what he termed the "amative" love of man for woman, in contrast to the "adhesive" love of man for man. Adhesive love figured in forty-five poems in a section titled "Calamus." These two sections in the 1860 edition differ from the sections in the final 1891–92 edition, for in the intervening editions (1867, 1871, 1881) Whitman revised and regrouped some of the poems, as he would with numerous other poems in the expanded editions he would go on to publish.

With the outbreak of the Civil War, Whitman began to visit the wounded and eventually offered his services as a nurse. He started at New-York Hospital, but in early 1863, after visiting with his wounded brother George in an army camp in Virginia, he moved to Washington, D.C., and began to work at the huge open-air military hospitals there. Nursing gave Whitman a profound sense of vocation. As he wrote a friend in 1863: "I am very happy . . . I was never so beloved. I am running over with health, fat, red & sunburnt in face. I tell thee I am just the one to go to our sick boys." But ministering to tens of thousands of maimed and dying young men took its toll. He succinctly voiced his anguish in a notebook entry of 1864: "the dead, the dead, the dead, our dead." During this time he worked on a series of poems that conveyed his evolving view of the war from heroic celebration to despair at the horrifying carnage. He later wrote a chapter in his prose work *Specimen Days* (1882) titled "The Real War Will Never Get in the Books," but to incorporate the "real war" into a book of poetry became one of the dominant impulses of the *Drum-Taps* collection, which he published in 1865. After Lincoln's assassination, Whitman reissued the volume with a sequel including "O Captain! My Captain!" and "When Lilacs Last in the Dooryard Bloom'd," his famous elegy for the murdered president.

As he prepared *Drum-Taps and Sequel* for publication in late 1865, Whitman was also revising *Leaves of Grass* at his desk in the Department of the Interior, where he had obtained a position as clerk. The new secretary of the interior, James Harlan, read the annotated copy and fired Whitman for writing an obscene book, objecting to Whitman's frankness about bodily functions and heterosexual love. Whitman's friend William O'Connor, a poet, found him another clerical position in the attorney general's office; and in his rage at the firing, O'Connor wrote *The Good Gray Poet* (1866), identifying Whitman with Jesus and Harlan with the forces of evil. Whitman continued to rework *Leaves of Grass*, incorporating *Drum-Taps* into it in 1867, and with his friends' help continued to propagandize for its recognition as a landmark in the history of poetry. He also published essays in the 1867 and 1868 numbers of the New York periodical *Galaxy*, which he expanded into *Democratic*

Vistas (1870), a book conveying his sometimes sharply condemnatory appraisal of postwar democratic culture.

The Washington years came to an abrupt end in 1873 when Whitman suffered a paralytic stroke. His mother died a few months later, and Whitman joined his brother George's household in Camden, New Jersey, to recuperate. During the second year of his illness, the government ceased to hold his clerk job open for him, and he became dependent for a living on occasional publication in newspapers and magazines. The 1867 edition of *Leaves of Grass* had involved much reworking and rearrangement, and the fifth edition (1871) continued that process, adding a new section titled "Passage to India." In 1876 Whitman privately published a prose work, *Memoranda during the War*, and six years later he brought out *Specimen Days*, which has affinities with his early editorial accounts of strolls through the city but is even more intensely personal, the record of representative days in the life of a poet who had lived in the midst of great national events.

During the 1870s and early 1880s, Whitman was increasingly noticed by the leading writers of the time, especially in England. The English poet Algernon Swinburne sent him a poem, the poet laureate Alfred Lord Tennyson sent him an admiring letter, and both Longfellow and Oscar Wilde visited him in Camden. In the United States, writers of a younger generation than Whitman's began to recognize his importance as a poetic voice and organized events to support him. Despite his frail health, Whitman lectured on Thomas Paine in Philadelphia in 1877 and on Abraham Lincoln in New York in 1879 (he would continue to deliver public lectures on Lincoln until 1890). Opposition to his poetry because of its supposed immorality began to dissipate, and readers, having become accustomed over time to Whitman's poetic devices, began to recognize the poet as an artist. Still, in 1881, when the reputable Boston firm of James R. Osgood & Company printed the sixth edition of *Leaves of Grass*, the Boston district attorney threatened to prosecute on the grounds of obscenity. Ironically, when the Philadelphia firm of Rees Welsh and Company reprinted this edition in 1882, the publicity contributed to Whitman's greatest sales in his lifetime: he earned nearly $1,500 in royalties from that edition (around $25,000 in today's value), compared to the $25 he had earned from the Osgood edition before the publisher withdrew it.

In 1884, the still infirm Whitman moved to a cottage at 328 Mickle Street in Camden, which he purchased for $1,750. A year later friends and admirers, including Mark Twain and John Greenleaf Whittier, presented him with a horse and buggy for local travel. He had another stroke in 1888 and in 1890 made preparations for his death by signing a $4,000 contract for the construction in Camden's Harleigh Cemetery of a granite mausoleum, or what he termed a "burial house," suitable for a national bard. In 1891 he did the final editing of *Complete Prose Works* (1892) and oversaw the preparations of the "deathbed" edition of the now more than three hundred poems in *Leaves of Grass* (1891–92), which was in fact a reissue of the 1881 edition with the addition of two later groups of poems, "Sands at Seventy" and "Good-bye My Fancy." Whitman died in Camden on March 26, 1892, and was buried in Harleigh Cemetery in the mausoleum he had helped design.

All the Whitman poems reprinted here, regardless of when they were first composed and printed, are given in their final form: that of the 1891–92 edition of *Leaves of Grass*.

Song of Myself[1]

1

I celebrate myself, and sing myself,
And what I assume you shall assume,
For every atom belonging to me as good belongs to you.

I loafe and invite my soul,
I lean and loafe at my ease observing a spear of summer grass.   5

My tongue, every atom of my blood, form'd from this soil, this air,
Born here of parents born here from parents the same, and their parents
    the same,
I, now thirty-seven years old in perfect health begin,
Hoping to cease not till death.

Creeds and schools in abeyance,   10
Retiring back a while sufficed at what they are, but never forgotten,
I harbor for good or bad, I permit to speak at every hazard,
Nature without check with original energy.

2

Houses and rooms are full of perfumes, the shelves are crowded with
    perfumes,
I breathe the fragrance myself and know it and like it,   15
The distillation would intoxicate me also, but I shall not let it.

The atmosphere is not a perfume, it has no taste of the distillation, it is
    odorless,
It is for my mouth forever, I am in love with it,
I will go to the bank by the wood and become undisguised and naked,
I am mad for it to be in contact with me.   20

The smoke of my own breath,
Echoes, ripples, buzz'd whispers, love-root, silk-thread, crotch and vine,
My respiration and inspiration, the beating of my heart, the passing of
    blood and air through my lungs,
The sniff of green leaves and dry leaves, and of the shore and dark-color'd
    sea-rocks, and of hay in the barn,
The sound of the belch'd words of my voice loos'd to the eddies of the
    wind,   25
A few light kisses, a few embraces, a reaching around of arms,
The play of shine and shade on the trees as the supple boughs wag,

---

1. In the 1855 first edition of *Leaves of Grass*, the poem later called "Song of Myself" appeared without a title and without numbered sections or stanzas. For the 1856 edition, Whitman titled it "Poem of Walt Whitman, an American," and in the 1860 edition he titled it "Walt Whitman"; it retained that title in the 1867 and 1871 editions, and in the 1881 edition was named "Song of Myself." Whitman made numerous other changes to the poem from the first 1855 printing to the 1881 final version.

The delight alone or in the rush of the streets, or along the fields and hill-
    sides,
The feeling of health, the full-noon trill, the song of me rising from bed
    and meeting the sun.

Have you reckon'd a thousand acres much? have you reckon'd the earth
    much?   30
Have you practis'd so long to learn to read?
Have you felt so proud to get at the meaning of poems?

Stop this day and night with me and you shall possess the origin of all
    poems,
You shall possess the good of the earth and sun, (there are millions of
    suns left,)
You shall no longer take things at second or third hand, nor look through
    the eyes of the dead, nor feed on the spectres in books,   35
You shall not look through my eyes either, nor take things from me,
You shall listen to all sides and filter them from your self.

3

I have heard what the talkers were talking, the talk of the beginning and
    the end,
But I do not talk of the beginning or the end.

There was never any more inception than there is now,   40
Nor any more youth or age than there is now,
And will never be any more perfection than there is now,
Nor any more heaven or hell than there is now.

Urge and urge and urge,
Always the procreant urge of the world.   45

Out of the dimness opposite equals advance, always substance and
    increase, always sex,
Always a knit of identity, always distinction, always a breed of life.

To elaborate is no avail, learn'd and unlearn'd feel that it is so.

Sure as the most certain sure, plumb in the uprights, well entretied,[2]
    braced in the beams,
Stout as a horse, affectionate, haughty, electrical,   50
I and this mystery here we stand.

Clear and sweet is my soul, and clear and sweet is all that is not my soul.

Lack one lacks both, and the unseen is proved by the seen,
Till that becomes unseen and receives proof in its turn.

2. Cross-braced; reinforced.

Showing the best and dividing it from the worst age vexes age,   55
Knowing the perfect fitness and equanimity of things, while they discuss
     I am silent, and go bathe and admire myself.

Welcome is every organ and attribute of me, and of any man hearty and
     clean,
Not an inch nor a particle of an inch is vile, and none shall be less familiar
     than the rest.

I am satisfied—I see, dance, laugh, sing;
As the hugging and loving bed-fellow sleeps at my side through the night,
     and withdraws at the peep of the day with stealthy tread,   60
Leaving me baskets cover'd with white towels swelling the house with
     their plenty,
Shall I postpone my acceptation and realization and scream at my eyes,
That they turn from gazing after and down the road,
And forthwith cipher³ and show me to a cent,
Exactly the value of one and exactly the value of two, and which is
     ahead?
                                                                            65

4

Trippers and askers surround me,
People I meet, the effect upon me of my early life or the ward and city I
     live in, or the nation,
The latest dates, discoveries, inventions, societies, authors old and new,
My dinner, dress, associates, looks, compliments, dues,
The real or fancied indifference of some man or woman I love,   70
The sickness of one of my folks or of myself, or ill-doing or loss or lack
     of money, or depressions or exaltations,
Battles, the horrors of fratricidal war, the fever of doubtful news, the fitful
     events;
These come to me days and nights and go from me again,
But they are not the Me myself.

Apart from the pulling and hauling stands what I am,   75
Stands amused, complacent, compassionating, idle, unitary,
Looks down, is erect, or bends an arm on an impalpable certain rest,
Looking with side-curved head curious what will come next,
Both in and out of the game and watching and wondering at it.

Backward I see in my own days where I sweated through fog with
     linguists and contenders,
                                                                            80
I have no mockings or arguments, I witness and wait.

5

I believe in you my soul, the other I am must not abase itself to you,
And you must not be abased to the other.

_____
3. Calculate.

Loafe with me on the grass, loose the stop from your throat,
Not words, not music or rhyme I want, not custom or lecture, not even
    the best,   85
Only the lull I like, the hum of your valvèd voice.

I mind how once we lay such a transparent summer morning,
How you settled your head athwart my hips and gently turn'd over upon
    me,
And parted the shirt from my bosom-bone, and plunged your tongue to
    my bare-stript heart,
And reach'd till you felt my beard, and reach'd till you held my feet.   90

Swiftly arose and spread around me the peace and knowledge that pass
    all the argument of the earth,
And I know that the hand of God is the promise of my own,
And I know that the spirit of God is the brother of my own,
And that all the men ever born are also my brothers, and the women my
    sisters and lovers,
And that a kelson[4] of the creation is love,   95
And limitless are leaves stiff or drooping in the fields,
And brown ants in the little wells beneath them,
And mossy scabs of the worm fence,[5] heap'd stones, elder, mullein and
    poke-weed.

6

A child said *What is the grass?* fetching it to me with full hands;
How could I answer the child? I do not know what it is any more than
    he.   100

I guess it must be the flag of my disposition, out of hopeful green stuff woven.

Or I guess it is the handkerchief of the Lord,
A scented gift and remembrancer designedly dropt,
Bearing the owner's name someway in the corners, that we may see and
    remark, and say *Whose?*

Or I guess the grass is itself a child, the produced babe of the vegetation.   105

Or I guess it is a uniform hieroglyphic,
And it means, Sprouting alike in broad zones and narrow zones,
Growing among black folks as among white,
Kanuck, Tuckahoe, Congressman, Cuff,[6] I give them the same, I receive
    them the same.

And now it seems to me the beautiful uncut hair of graves.   110

---

4. A basic structural unit; a reinforcing timber bolted to the keel (backbone) of a ship.
5. Fence built of interlocking rails in a zigzag pattern.
6. From the African word *cuffee* (name for black male born on a Friday). "Kanuck": French Canadian (now sometimes considered pejorative). "Tuckahoe": Virginian, from eaters of the American Indian food plant tuckahoe.

Tenderly will I use you curling grass,
It may be you transpire from the breasts of young men,
It may be if I had known them I would have loved them,
It may be you are from old people, or from offspring taken soon out of
    their mothers' laps,
And here you are the mothers' laps.   115

This grass is very dark to be from the white heads of old mothers,
Darker than the colorless beards of old men,
Dark to come from under the faint red roofs of mouths.

O I perceive after all so many uttering tongues,
And I perceive they do not come from the roofs of mouths for
    nothing.   120

I wish I could translate the hints about the dead young men and women,
And the hints about old men and mothers, and the offspring taken soon
    out of their laps.

What do you think has become of the young and old men?
And what do you think has become of the women and children?

They are alive and well somewhere,   125
The smallest sprout shows there is really no death,
And if ever there was it led forward life, and does not wait at the end to
    arrest it,
And ceas'd the moment life appear'd.

All goes onward and outward, nothing collapses,
And to die is different from what any one supposed, and luckier.   130

                                    7

Has any one supposed it lucky to be born?
I hasten to inform him or her it is just as lucky to die, and I know it.

I pass death with the dying and birth with the new-wash'd babe, and
    am not contain'd between my hat and boots,
And peruse manifold objects, no two alike and every one good,
The earth good and the stars good, and their adjuncts all good.   135

I am not an earth nor an adjunct of an earth,
I am the mate and companion of people, all just as immortal and
    fathomless as myself,
(They do not know how immortal, but I know.)

Every kind for itself and its own, for me mine male and female,
For me those that have been boys and that love women,   140
For me the man that is proud and feels how it stings to be slighted,
For me the sweet-heart and the old maid, for me mothers and the mothers
    of mothers,

For me lips that have smiled, eyes that have shed tears,
For me children and the begetters of children.

Undrape! you are not guilty to me, nor stale nor discarded,   145
I see through the broadcloth and gingham whether or no,
And am around, tenacious, acquisitive, tireless, and cannot be shaken
    away.

8

The little one sleeps in its cradle,
I lift the gauze and look a long time, and silently brush away flies with
    my hand.

The youngster and the red-faced girl turn aside up the bushy hill,   150
I peeringly view them from the top.

The suicide sprawls on the bloody floor of the bedroom,
I witness the corpse with its dabbled hair, I note where the pistol has
    fallen.

The blab of the pave, tires of carts, sluff of boot-soles, talk of the
    promenaders,
The heavy omnibus, the driver with his interrogating thumb, the clank
    of the shod horses on the granite floor,   155
The snow-sleighs, clinking, shouted jokes, pelts of snow-balls,
The hurrahs for popular favorites, the fury of rous'd mobs,
The flap of the curtain'd litter, a sick man inside borne to the hospital,
The meeting of enemies, the sudden oath, the blows and fall,
The excited crowd, the policeman with his star quickly working his
    passage to the centre of the crowd,   160
The impassive stones that receive and return so many echoes,
What groans of over-fed or half-starv'd who fall sunstruck or in fits,
What exclamations of women taken suddenly who hurry home and
    give birth to babes,
What living and buried speech is always vibrating here, what howls
    restrain'd by decorum,
Arrests of criminals, slights, adulterous offers made, acceptances,
    rejections with convex lips,   165
I mind them or the show or resonance of them—I come and I depart.

9

The big doors of the country barn stand open and ready,
The dried grass of the harvest-time loads the slow-drawn wagon,
The clear light plays on the brown gray and green intertinged,
The armfuls are pack'd to the sagging mow.   170

I am there, I help, I came stretch'd atop of the load,
I felt its soft jolts, one leg reclined on the other,
I jump from the cross-beams and sieze the clover and timothy,
And roll head over heels and tangle my hair full of wisps.

10

Alone far in the wilds and mountains I hunt,   175
Wandering amazed at my own lightness and glee,
In the late afternoon choosing a safe spot to pass the night,
Kindling a fire and broiling the fresh-kill'd game,
Falling asleep on the gather'd leaves with my dog and gun by my side.

The Yankee clipper is under her sky-sails, she cuts the sparkle and scud, 180
My eyes settle the land, I bend at her prow or shout joyously from the deck.

The boatmen and clam-diggers arose early and stopt for me,
I tuck'd my trowser-ends in my boots and went and had a good time;
You should have been with us that day round the chowder-kettle.

I saw the marriage of the trapper in the open air in the far west, the bride
     was a red girl,   185
Her father and his friends sat near cross-legged and dumbly smoking,
     they had moccasins to their feet and large thick blankets hanging from
     their shoulders,
On a bank lounged the trapper, he was drest mostly in skins, his luxuriant
     beard and curls protected his neck, he held his bride by the hand,
She had long eyelashes, her head was bare, her coarse straight locks
     descended upon her voluptuous limbs and reach'd to her feet.

The runaway slave came to my house and stopt outside,
I heard his motions crackling the twigs of the woodpile,   190
Through the swung half-door of the kitchen I saw him limpsy[7] and weak,
And went where he sat on a log and led him in and assured him,
And brought water and fill'd a tub for his sweated body and bruis'd feet,
And gave him a room that enter'd from my own, and gave him some coarse
     clean clothes,
And remember perfectly well his revolving eyes and his awkwardness,   195
And remember putting plasters on the galls of his neck and ankles;
He staid with me a week before he was recuperated and pass'd north,
I had him sit next me at table, my fire-lock lean'd in the corner.

11

Twenty-eight young men bathe by the shore,
Twenty-eight young men and all so friendly;   200
Twenty-eight years of womanly life and all so lonesome.

She owns the fine house by the rise of the bank,
She hides handsome and richly drest aft the blinds of the window.

Which of the young men does she like the best?
Ah the homeliest of them is beautiful to her.   205

7. Limping or swaying.

Where are you off to, lady? for I see you,
You splash in the water there, yet stay stock still in your room.

Dancing and laughing along the beach came the twenty-ninth bather,
The rest did not see her, but she saw them and loved them.

The beards of the young men glisten'd with wet, it ran from their long
    hair,   210
Little streams pass'd over their bodies.

An unseen hand also pass'd over their bodies,
It descended tremblingly from their temples and ribs.

The young men float on their backs, their white bellies bulge to the sun,
    they do not ask who seizes fast to them,
They do not know who puffs and declines with pendant and bending
    arch,   215
They do not think whom they souse with spray.

12

The butcher-boy puts off his killing-clothes, or sharpens his knife
    at the stall in the market,
I loiter enjoying his repartee and his shuffle and break-down.[8]

Blacksmiths with grimed and hairy chests environ the anvil,
Each has his main-sledge, they are all out, there is a great heat in the
    fire.   220

From the cinder-strew'd threshold I follow their movements,
The lithe sheer of their waists plays even with their massive arms,
Overhand the hammers swing, overhand so slow, overhand so sure,
They do not hasten, each man hits in his place.

13

The negro holds firmly the reins of his four horses, the block swags
    underneath on its tied-over chain,   225
The negro that drives the long dray of the stone-yard, steady and tall he
    stands pois'd on one leg on the string-piece,[9]
His blue shirt exposes his ample neck and breast and loosens over his hip-
    band,
His glance is calm and commanding, he tosses the slouch of his hat away
    from his forehead,
The sun falls on his crispy hair and mustache, falls on the black of his
    polish'd and perfect limbs.

I behold the picturesque giant and love him, and I do not stop there,   230
I go with the team also.

---

8. Dances familiar in popular entertainment and minstrelsy. The "shuffle" involves the sliding of feet across the floor, and the "break-down" is faster and noisier.
9. Long, heavy timber used to keep a load in place.

In me the caresser of life wherever moving, backward as well as forward
    sluing,[1]
To niches aside and junior[2] bending, not a person or object missing,
Absorbing all to myself and for this song.

Oxen that rattle the yoke and chain or halt in the leafy shade, what is
    that you express in your eyes?   235
It seems to me more than all the print I have read in my life.

My tread scares the wood-drake and wood-duck on my distant and
    day-long ramble.
They rise together, they slowly circle around.

I believe in those wing'd purposes,
And acknowledge red, yellow, white, playing within me,   240
And consider green and violet and the tufted crown intentional,
And do not call the tortoise unworthy because she is not something else,
And the jay in the woods never studied the gamut,[3] yet trills pretty well
    to me,
And the look of the bay mare shames silliness out of me.

14

The wild gander leads his flock through the cool night,   245
Ya-honk he says, and sounds it down to me like an invitation,
The pert may suppose it meaningless, but I listening close,
Find its purpose and place up there toward the wintry sky.

The sharp-hoof'd moose of the north, the cat on the house-sill, the
    chickadee, the prairie-dog,
The litter of the grunting sow as they tug at her teats,   250
The brood of the turkey-hen and she with her half-spread wings,
I see in them and myself the same old law.

The press of my foot to the earth springs a hundred affections,
They scorn the best I can do to relate them.

I am enamour'd of growing out-doors,   255
Of men that live among cattle or taste of the ocean or woods,
Of the builders and steerers of ships and the wielders of axes and mauls,
    and the drivers of horses,
I can eat and sleep with them week in and week out.

What is commonest, cheapest, nearest, easiest, is Me,
Me going in for my chances, spending for vast returns,   260
Adorning myself to bestow myself on the first that will take me,
Not asking the sky to come down to my good will,
Scattering it freely forever.

1. Twisting.
2. Smaller.
3. Notes of the musical scale.

15

The pure contralto sings in the organ loft,
The carpenter dresses his plank, the tongue of his foreplane whistles
    its wild ascending lisp,   265
The married and unmarried children ride home to their Thanksgiving
    dinner,
The pilot seizes the king-pin,[4] he heaves down with a strong arm,
The mate stands braced in the whale-boat, lance and harpoon are ready,
The duck-shooter walks by silent and cautious stretches,
The deacons are ordain'd with cross'd hands at the altar,   270
The spinning-girl retreats and advances to the hum of the big wheel,
The farmer stops by the bars as he walks on a First-day[5] loafe and looks
    at the oats and rye,
The lunatic is carried at last to the asylum a confirm'd case,
(He will never sleep any more as he did in the cot in his mother's
    bed-room;)
The jour printer[6] with gray head and gaunt jaws works at his case,   275
He turns his quid of tobacco while his eyes blurr with the manuscript;
The malform'd limbs are tied to the surgeon's table,
What is removed drops horribly in a pail;
The quadroon[7] girl is sold at the auction-stand, the drunkard nods by the
    bar-room stove,
The machinist rolls up his sleeves, the policeman travels his beat, the
    gate-keeper marks who pass,   280
The young fellow drives the express-wagon, (I love him, though I do not
    know him;)
The half-breed straps on his light boots to compete in the race,
The western turkey-shooting draws old and young, some lean on their
    rifles, some sit on logs,
Out from the crowd steps the marksman, takes his position, levels his
    piece;
The groups of newly-come immigrants cover the wharf or levee,   285
As the woolly-pates[8] hoe in the sugar-field, the overseer views them
    from his saddle,
The bugle calls in the ball-room, the gentlemen run for their partners,
    the dancers bow to each other,
The youth lies awake in the cedar-roof'd garret and harks to the musical
    rain,
The Wolverine[9] sets traps on the creek that helps fill the Huron,
The squaw wrapt in her yellow-hemm'd cloth is offering moccasins and
    bead-bags for sale,   290
The connoisseur peers along the exhibition-gallery with half-shut eyes
    bent sideways,
As the deck-hands make fast the steamboat the plank is thrown for the
    shore-going passengers,

---

4. The extended spoke of the pilot wheel, used to maintain leverage during storms.
5. Sunday. Whitman frequently uses the numerical Quaker designations for the names of days and months. "Bars": i.e., of a rail fence.
6. I.e., a journeyman printer, or one who has passed an apprenticeship and is fully qualified for all professional work.
7. Term used at the time (often in reference to slaves) to refer to light-complected people thought to be one-fourth black.
8. Black slaves (with stereotypical emphasis on "woolly" hair).
9. Inhabitant of Michigan.

The young sister holds out the skein while the elder sister winds it off
    in a ball, and stops now and then for the knots,
The one-year wife is recovering and happy having a week ago borne her
    first child,
The clean-hair'd Yankee girl works with her sewing-machine or in the
    factory or mill,   295
The paving-man[1] leans on his two-handed rammer, the reporter's lead
    flies swiftly over the note-book, the sign-painter is lettering with blue
    and gold,
The canal boy trots on the tow-path, the book-keeper counts at his desk,
    the shoemaker waxes his thread,
The conductor beats time for the band and all the performers follow him,
The child is baptized, the convert is making his first professions,
The regatta is spread on the bay, the race is begun, (how the white sails
    sparkle!)   300
The drover watching his drove sings out to them that would stray,
The pedler sweats with his pack on his back, (the purchaser higgling
    about the odd cent;)
The bride unrumples her white dress, the minute-hand of the clock
    moves slowly,
The opium-eater reclines with rigid head and just-open'd lips,
The prostitute draggles her shawl, her bonnet bobs on her tipsy and
    pimpled neck,   305
The crowd laugh at her blackguard oaths, the men jeer and wink to each
    other,
(Miserable! I do not laugh at your oaths nor jeer you;)
The President holding a cabinet council is surrounded by the great
    Secretaries,
On the piazza walk three matrons stately and friendly with twined arms,
The crew of the fish-smack pack repeated layers of halibut in the hold,   310
The Missourian crosses the plains toting his wares and his cattle,
As the fare-collector goes through the train he gives notice by the jingling
    of loose change,
The floor-men are laying the floor, the tinners are tinning the roof, the
    masons are calling for mortar,
In single file each shouldering his hod pass onward the laborers;
Seasons pursuing each other the indescribable crowd is gather'd, it is the
    fourth of Seventh-month,[2] (what salutes of cannon and small arms!) 315
Seasons pursuing each other the plougher ploughs, the mower mows,
    and the winter-grain falls in the ground;
Off on the lakes the pike-fisher watches and waits by the hole in the
    frozen surface,
The stumps stand thick round the clearing, the squatter strikes deep
    with his axe,
Flatboatmen make fast towards dusk near the cotton-wood or pecan-trees,
Coon-seekers go through the regions of the Red river or through those
    drain'd by the Tennessee, or through those of the Arkansas,   320
Torches shine in the dark that hangs on the Chattahooch or Altamahaw,[3]

---

1. Man building or repairing streets.   3. Georgia rivers.
2. I.e., the Fourth of July.

Patriarchs sit at supper with sons and grandsons and great-grandsons
    around them,
In walls of adobie, in canvas tents, rest hunters and trappers after their
    day's sport,
The city sleeps and the country sleeps,
The living sleep for their time, the dead sleep for their time,   325
The old husband sleeps by his wife and the young husband sleeps by his
    wife;
And these tend inward to me, and I tend outward to them,
And such as it is to be of these more or less I am,
And of these one and all I weave the song of myself.

16

I am of old and young, of the foolish as much as the wise,   330
Regardless of others, ever regardful of others,
Maternal as well as paternal, a child as well as a man,
Stuff'd with the stuff that is coarse and stuff'd with the stuff that is fine,
One of the Nation of many nations, the smallest the same and the largest
    the same,
A Southerner soon as a Northerner, a planter nonchalant and hospitable
    down by the Oconee[4] I live,   335
A Yankee bound my own way ready for trade, my joints the limberest joints
    on earth and the sternest joints on earth,
A Kentuckian walking the vale of the Elkhorn[5] in my deer-skin leggings, a
    Louisianian or Georgian,
A boatman over lakes or bays or along coasts, a Hoosier, Badger, Buckeye;[6]
At home on Kanadian[7] snow-shoes or up in the bush, or with fishermen
    off Newfoundland,
At home in the fleet of ice-boats, sailing with the rest and tacking,   340
At home on the hills of Vermont or in the woods of Maine, or the Texan
    ranch,
Comrade of Californians, comrade of free North-Westerners, (loving their
    big proportions,)
Comrade of raftsmen and coalmen, comrade of all who shake hands and
    welcome to drink and meat,
A learner with the simplest, a teacher of the thoughtfullest,
A novice beginning yet experient of myriads of seasons,   345
Of every hue and caste am I, of every rank and religion,
A farmer, mechanic, artist, gentleman, sailor, quaker,
Prisoner, fancy-man, rowdy, lawyer, physician, priest.

I resist any thing better than my own diversity,
Breathe the air but leave plenty after me,   350
And am not stuck up, and am in my place.

(The moth and the fish-eggs are in their place,
The bright suns I see and the dark suns I cannot see are in their place,
The palpable is in its place and the impalpable is in its place.)

4. River in central Georgia.
5. River in Nebraska.
6. Inhabitants of Indiana, Wisconsin, and Ohio, respectively.
7. Canadian.

17

These are really the thoughts of all men in all ages and lands, they are
  not original with me,   355
If they are not yours as much as mine they are nothing, or next to
  nothing,
If they are not the riddle and the untying of the riddle they are nothing,
If they are not just as close as they are distant they are nothing.

This is the grass that grows wherever the land is and the water is,
This the common air that bathes the globe.   360

18

With music strong I come, with my cornets and my drums,
I play not marches for accepted victors only, I play marches for conquer'd
  and slain persons.

Have you heard that it was good to gain the day?
I also say it is good to fall, battles are lost in the same spirit in which they
  are won.

I beat and pound for the dead,   365
I blow through my embouchures[8] my loudest and gayest for them.

Vivas to those who have fail'd!
And to those whose war-vessels sank in the sea!
And to those themselves who sank in the sea!
And to all generals that lost engagements, and all overcome heroes!   370
And the numberless unknown heroes equal to the greatest heroes
  known!

19

This is the meal equally set, this the meat for natural hunger,
It is for the wicked just the same as the righteous, I make appointments
  with all,
I will not have a single person slighted or left away,
The kept-woman, sponger, thief, are hereby invited,   375
The heavy-lipp'd slave is invited, the venerealee[9] is invited;
There shall be no difference between them and the rest.

This is the press of a bashful hand, this the float and odor of hair,
This is the touch of my lips to yours, this the murmur of yearning,
This the far-off depth and height reflecting my own face,   380
This the thoughtful merge of myself, and the outlet again.

Do you guess I have some intricate purpose?
Well I have, for the Fourth-month showers have, and the mica on the
  side of a rock has.

8. Mouthpieces of musical instruments such as
the cornet.

9. Someone afflicted with a venereal (sexually
transmitted) disease.

Do you take it I would astonish?
Does the daylight astonish? does the early redstart twittering through
    the woods?   385
Do I astonish more than they?

This hour I tell things in confidence,
I might not tell everybody, but I will tell you.

20

Who goes there? hankering, gross, mystical, nude;
How is it I extract strength from the beef I eat?   390

What is a man anyhow? what am I? what are you?

All I mark as my own you shall offset it with your own,
Else it were time lost listening to me.

I do not snivel that snivel the world over,
That months are vacuums and the ground but wallow and filth.   395

Whimpering and truckling fold with powders for invalids, conformity
    goes to the fourth-remov'd,[1]
I wear my hat as I please indoors or out.

Why should I pray? why should I venerate and be ceremonious?

Having pried through the strata, analyzed to a hair, counsel'd with
    doctors and calculated close,
I find no sweeter fat than sticks to my bones.   400

In all people I see myself, none more and not one a barley-corn[2] less,
And the good or bad I say of myself I say of them.

I know I am solid and sound,
To me the converging objects of the universe perpetually flow,
All are written to me, and I must get what the writing means.   405

I know I am deathless,
I know this orbit of mine cannot be swept by a carpenter's compass,
I know I shall not pass like a child's carlacue[3] cut with a burnt stick at
    night.

I know I am august,
I do not trouble my spirit to vindicate itself or be understood,   410
I see that the elementary laws never apologize,
(I reckon I behave no prouder than the level I plant my house by, after all.)

---

1. Those remote in relationship, such as "third cousin, fourth removed." "Fold with powders": a reference to the custom of wrapping a dose of medicine in a piece of paper.
2. The seed or grain of barley, but also a unit of measure equal to about one-third of an inch.
3. Or *curlicue*, a fancy flourish made with a writing implement, here made in the dark with a lighted stick.

I exist as I am, that is enough,
If no other in the world be aware I sit content,
And if each and all be aware I sit content.   415

One world is aware and by far the largest to me, and that is myself,
And whether I come to my own to-day or in ten thousand or ten million
      years,
I can cheerfully take it now, or with equal cheerfulness I can wait.

My foothold is tenon'd and mortis'd⁴ in granite,
I laugh at what you call dissolution,   420
And I know the amplitude of time.

                                    21

I am the poet of the Body and I am the poet of the Soul,
The pleasures of heaven are with me and the pains of hell are with me,
The first I graft and increase upon myself, the latter I translate into a
      new tongue.

I am the poet of the woman the same as the man,   425
And I say it is as great to be a woman as to be a man,
And I say there is nothing greater than the mother of men.

I chant the chant of dilation or pride,
We have had ducking and deprecating about enough,
I show that size is only development.   430

Have you outstript the rest? are you the President?
It is a trifle, they will more than arrive there every one, and still pass on.

I am he that walks with the tender and growing night,
I call to the earth and sea half-held by the night.

Press close bare-bosom'd night—press close magnetic nourishing night!   435
Night of south winds—night of the large few stars!
Still nodding night—mad naked summer night.

Smile O voluptuous cool-breath'd earth!
Earth of the slumbering and liquid trees!
Earth of departed sunset—earth of the mountains misty-topt!   440
Earth of the vitreous pour of the full moon just tinged with blue!
Earth of shine and dark mottling the tide of the river!
Earth of the limpid gray of clouds brighter and clearer for my sake!
Far-swooping elbow'd earth—rich apple-blossom'd earth!
Smile, for your lover comes.   445

Prodigal, you have given me love—therefore I to you give love!
O unspeakable passionate love.

---

4. Here, mason's terms for a particular way of joining two stones together. A mortise is a cavity in a stone
into which is placed the projection (tenon) from another stone.

22

You sea! I resign myself to you also—I guess what you mean,
I behold from the beach your crooked inviting fingers,
I believe you refuse to go back without feeling of me,   450
We must have a turn together, I undress, hurry me out of sight of the land,
Cushion me soft, rock me in billowy drowse,
Dash me with amorous wet, I can repay you.

Sea of stretch'd ground-swells,
Sea breathing broad and convulsive breaths,   455
Sea of the brine of life and of unshovell'd yet always-ready graves,
Howler and scooper of storms, capricious and dainty sea,
I am integral with you, I too am of one phase and of all phases.

Partaker of influx and efflux I, extoller of hate and conciliation,
Extoller of amies[5] and those that sleep in each others' arms.   460

I am he attesting sympathy,
(Shall I make my list of things in the house and skip the house that
    supports them?)

I am not the poet of goodness only, I do not decline to be the poet of
    wickedness also.

What blurt is this about virtue and about vice?
Evil propels me and reform of evil propels me, I stand indifferent,   465
My gait is no fault-finder's or rejecter's gait,
I moisten the roots of all that has grown.

Did you fear some scrofula[6] out of the unflagging pregnancy?
Did you guess the celestial laws are yet to be work'd over and rectified?

I find one side a balance and the antipodal side a balance,   470
Soft doctrine as steady help as stable doctrine,
Thoughts and deeds of the present our rouse and early start.

This minute that comes to me over the past decillions,[7]
There is no better than it and now.

What behaved well in the past or behaves well to-day is not such a
    wonder,   475
The wonder is always and always how there can be a mean man or an
    infidel.

23

Endless unfolding of words of ages!
And mine a word of the modern, the word En-Masse.

5. Friends (French).
6. Form of tuberculosis characterized by swelling of the lymph glands.
7. The number one followed by thirty-three zeroes.

A word of the faith that never balks,
Here or henceforward it is all the same to me, I accept Time absolutely. 480

It alone is without flaw, it alone rounds and completes all,
That mystic baffling wonder alone completes all.

I accept Reality and dare not question it.
Materialism first and last imbuing.

Hurrah for positive science! long live exact demonstration! 485
Fetch stonecrop mixt with cedar and branches of lilac,
This is the lexicographer, this the chemist, this made a grammar of the
    old cartouches,[8]
These mariners put the ship through dangerous unknown seas,
This is the geologist, this works with the scalpel, and this is a
    mathematician.

Gentlemen, to you the first honors always! 490
Your facts are useful, and yet they are not my dwelling,
I but enter by them to an area of my dwelling.

Less the reminders of properties told my words,
And more the reminders they of life untold, and of freedom and extrication,
And make short account of neuters and geldings, and favor men and
    women fully equipt, 495
And beat the gong of revolt, and stop with fugitives and them that plot and
    conspire.

24

Walt Whitman, a kosmos, of Manhattan the son,
Turbulent, fleshy, sensual, eating, drinking and breeding,
No sentimentalist, no stander above men and women or apart from
    them,
No more modest than immodest. 500

Unscrew the locks from the doors!
Unscrew the doors themselves from their jambs!

Whoever degrades another degrades me,
And whatever is done or said returns at last to me.

Through me the afflatus[9] surging and surging, through me the current
    and index. 505

I speak the pass-word primeval, I give the sign of democracy,
By God! I will accept nothing which all cannot have their counterpart of
    on the same terms.

---

8. On tablets of Egyptian hieroglyphics, the orna-   "Stonecrop": a fleshy-leafed plant.
mental area noting the name of a ruler or deity.   9. Divine wind or spirit.

Through me many long dumb voices,
Voices of the interminable generations of prisoners and slaves,
Voices of the diseas'd and despairing and of thieves and dwarfs,   510
Voices of cycles of preparation and accretion,
And of the threads that connect the stars, and of wombs and of the
    fatherstuff,
And of the rights of them the others are down upon,
Of the deform'd, trivial, flat, foolish, despised,
Fog in the air, beetles rolling balls of dung.   515

Through me forbidden voices,
Voices of sexes and lusts, voices veil'd and I remove the veil,
Voices indecent by me clarified and transfigur'd.

I do not press my fingers across my mouth,
I keep as delicate around the bowels as around the head and heart,   520
Copulation is no more rank to me than death is.

I believe in the flesh and the appetites,
Seeing, hearing, feeling, are miracles, and each part and tag of me is a
    miracle.

Divine am I inside and out, and I make holy whatever I touch or am
    touch'd from,
The scent of these arm-pits aroma finer than prayer,   525
This head more than churches, bibles, and all the creeds.

If I worship one thing more than another it shall be the spread of my own
    body, or any part of it,
Translucent mould of me it shall be you!
Shaded ledges and rests it shall be you!
Firm masculine colter¹ it shall be you!   530
Whatever goes to the tilth² of me it shall be you!
You my rich blood! your milky stream pale strippings of my life!
Breast that presses against other breasts it shall be you!
My brain it shall be your occult convolutions!
Root of wash'd sweet-flag! timorous pond-snipe! nest of guarded duplicate
    eggs! it shall be you!   535
Mix'd tussled hay of head, beard, brawn, it shall be you!
Trickling sap of maple, fibre of manly wheat, it shall be you!
Sun so generous it shall be you!
Vapors lighting and shading my face it shall be you!
You sweaty brooks and dews it shall be you!   540
Winds whose soft-tickling genitals rub against me it shall be you!
Broad muscular fields, branches of live oak, loving lounger in my winding
    paths, it shall be you!
Hands I have taken, face I have kiss'd, mortal I have ever touch'd, it shall
    be you.

---

1. The blade at the front of a plow.   2. Cultivation or tillage of the soil.

I dote on myself, there is that lot of me and all so luscious,
Each moment and whatever happens thrills me with joy,   545
I cannot tell how my ankles bend, nor whence the cause of my faintest
  wish,
Nor the cause of the friendship I emit, nor the cause of the friendship I
  take again.

That I walk up my stoop, I pause to consider if it really be,
A morning-glory at my window satisfies me more than the metaphysics of
  books.

To behold the day-break!   550
The little light fades the immense and diaphanous shadows,
The air tastes good to my palate.

Hefts³ of the moving world at innocent gambols silently rising freshly
  exuding,
Scooting obliquely high and low.

Something I cannot see puts upward libidinous prongs,   555
Seas of bright juice suffuse heaven.

The earth by the sky staid with, the daily close of their junction,
The heav'd challenge from the east that moment over my head,
The mocking taunt, See then whether you shall be master!

25

Dazzling and tremendous how quick the sun-rise would kill me,   560
If I could not now and always send sun-rise out of me.

We also ascend dazzling and tremendous as the sun,
We found our own O my soul in the calm and cool of the day-break.

My voice goes after what my eyes cannot reach,
With the twirl of my tongue I encompass worlds and volumes of worlds. 565

Speech is the twin of my vision, it is unequal to measure itself,
It provokes me forever, it says sarcastically,
Walt you contain enough, why don't you let it out then?

Come now I will not be tantalized, you conceive too much of articulation,
Do you not know O speech how the buds beneath you are folded?   570
Waiting in gloom, protected by frost,
The dirt receding before my prophetical screams,
I underlying causes to balance them at last,
My knowledge my live parts, it keeping tally with the meaning of all things,
Happiness, (which whoever hears me let him or her set out in search of
  this day.)   575

---

3. Something being heaved or raised upward.

My final merit I refuse you, I refuse putting from me what I really am,
Encompass worlds, but never try to encompass me.
I crowd your sleekest and best by simply looking toward you.

Writing and talk do not prove me,
I carry the plenum[4] of proof and every thing else in my face,   580
With the hush of my lips I wholly confound the skeptic.

26

Now I will do nothing but listen,
To accrue what I hear into this song, to let sounds contribute toward it.

I hear bravuras of birds, bustle of growing wheat, gossip of flames, clack
    of sticks cooking my meals,
I hear the sound I love, the sound of the human voice,   585
I hear all sounds running together, combined, fused or following,
Sounds of the city and sounds out of the city, sounds of the day and night,
Talkative young ones to those that like them, the loud laugh of work-people
    at their meals,
The angry base of disjointed friendship, the faint tones of the sick,
The judge with hands tight to the desk, his pallid lips pronouncing a
    death-sentence,   590
The heave'e'yo of stevedores unlading ships by the wharves, the refrain
    of the anchor-lifters,
The ring of alarm-bells, the cry of fire, the whirr of swift-streaking engines
    and hose-carts with premonitory tinkles and color'd lights,
The steam-whistle, the solid roll of the train of approaching cars,
The slow march play'd at the head of the association marching two and
    two,
(They go to guard some corpse, the flag-tops are draped with black
    muslin.)   595

I hear the violoncello ('tis the young man's heart's complaint,)
I hear the key'd cornet, it glides quickly in through my ears,
It shakes mad-sweet pangs through my belly and breast.

I hear the chorus, it is a grand opera,
Ah this indeed is music—this suits me.   600

A tenor large and fresh as the creation fills me,
The orbic flex of his mouth is pouring and filling me full.

I hear the train'd soprano (what work with hers is this?)
The orchestra whirls me wider than Uranus[5] flies,
It wrenches such ardors from me I did not know I possess'd them,   605
It sails me, I dab with bare feet, they are lick'd by the indolent waves,
I am cut by bitter and angry hail, I lose my breath,

4. Fullness.
5. Seventh planet from the sun, thought at the time to be the outermost limit of the solar system.

Steep'd amid honey'd morphine, my windpipe throttled in fakes[6] of death,
At length let up again to feel the puzzle of puzzles,
And that we call Being.   610

27

To be in any form, what is that?
(Round and round we go, all of us, and ever come back thither,)
If nothing lay more develop'd the quahaug[7] in its callous shell were
      enough.

Mine is no callous shell,
I have instant conductors all over me whether I pass or stop,   615
They seize every object and lead it harmlessly through me.

I merely stir, press, feel with my fingers, and am happy,
To touch my person to some one else's is about as much as I can stand.

28

Is this then a touch? quivering me to a new identity,
Flames and ether making a rush for my veins,   620
Treacherous tip of me reaching and crowding to help them,
My flesh and blood playing out lightning to strike what is hardly different
      from myself,
On all sides prurient provokers stiffening my limbs,
Straining the udder of my heart for its withheld drip,
Behaving licentious toward me, taking no denial,   625
Depriving me of my best as for a purpose,
Unbuttoning my clothes, holding me by the bare waist,
Deluding my confusion with the calm of the sunlight and pasture-fields,
Immodestly sliding the fellow-senses away,
They bribed to swap off with touch and go and graze at the edges of me,   630
No consideration, no regard for my draining strength or my anger,
Fetching the rest of the herd around to enjoy them a while,
Then all uniting to stand on a headland and worry me.

The sentries desert every other part of me,
They have left me helpless to a red marauder,   635
They all come to the headland to witness and assist against me.

I am given up by traitors,
I talk wildly, I have lost my wits, I and nobody else am the greatest traitor,
I went myself first to the headland, my own hands carried me there.

You villain touch! what are you doing? my breath is tight in its throat,   640
Unclench your floodgates, you are too much for me.

---

6. Coils of rope.   7. Edible clam of the Atlantic coast.

29

Blind loving wrestling touch, sheath'd hooded sharp-tooth'd touch!
Did it make you ache so, leaving me?

Parting track'd by arriving, perpetual payment of perpetual loan,
Rich showering rain, and recompense richer afterward.   645

Sprouts take and accumulate, stand by the curb prolific and vital,
Landscapes projected masculine, full-sized and golden.

30

All truths wait in all things,
They neither hasten their own delivery nor resist it,
They do not need the obstetric forceps of the surgeon,   650
The insignificant is as big to me as any,
(What is less or more than a touch?)

Logic and sermons never convince,
The damp of the night drives deeper into my soul.

(Only what proves itself to every man and woman is so,   655
Only what nobody denies is so.)

A minute and a drop of me settle my brain,
I believe the soggy clods shall become lovers and lamps,
And a compend[8] of compends is the meat of a man or woman,
And a summit and flower there is the feeling they have for each other,   660
And they are to branch boundlessly out of that lesson until it becomes
      omnific,[9]
And until one and all shall delight us, and we them.

31

I believe a leaf of grass is no less than the journey-work of the stars,
And the pismire[1] is equally perfect, and a grain of sand, and the egg of
      the wren,
And the tree-toad is a chief-d'œuvre for the highest,   665
And the running blackberry would adorn the parlors of heaven,
And the narrowest hinge in my hand puts to scorn all machinery,
And the cow crunching with depress'd head surpasses any statue,
And a mouse is miracle enough to stagger sextillions of infidels.

I find I incorporate gneiss,[2] coal, long-threaded moss, fruits, grains,
      esculent roots,   670
And am stucco'd with quadrupeds and birds all over,

8. I.e., a compendium, where something is
reduced to a short, essential summary.
9. All-encompassing.

1. Ant.
2. Metamorphic rock in which minerals are
arranged in layers.

And have distanced what is behind me for good reasons,
But call any thing back again when I desire it.

In vain the speeding or shyness,
In vain the plutonic rocks[3] send their old heat against my approach,   675
In vain the mastodon retreats beneath its own powder'd bones,
In vain objects stand leagues off and assume manifold shapes,
In vain the ocean settling in hollows and the great monsters lying low,
In vain the buzzard houses herself with the sky,
In vain the snake slides through the creepers and logs,   680
In vain the elk takes to the inner passes of the woods,
In vain the razor-bill'd auk sails far north to Labrador,
I follow quickly, I ascend to the nest in the fissure of the cliff.

32

I think I could turn and live with animals, they are so placid and
      self-contain'd,
I stand and look at them long and long.   685

They do not sweat and whine about their condition,
They do not lie awake in the dark and weep for their sins,
They do not make me sick discussing their duty to God,
Not one is dissatisfied, not one is demented with the mania of owning
      things,
Not one kneels to another, nor to his kind that lived thousands of
      years ago,   690
Not one is respectable or unhappy over the whole earth.

So they show their relations to me and I accept them,
They bring me tokens of myself, they evince them plainly in their possession.

I wonder where they get those tokens,
Did I pass that way huge times ago and negligently drop them?   695

Myself moving forward then and now and forever,
Gathering and showing more always and with velocity,
Infinite and omnigenous,[4] and the like of these among them,
Not too exclusive toward the reachers of my remembrancers,
Picking out here one that I love, and now go with him on brotherly
      terms.   700

A gigantic beauty of a stallion, fresh and responsive to my caresses,
Head high in the forehead, wide between the ears,
Limbs glossy and supple, tail dusting the ground,
Eyes full of sparkling wickedness, ears finely cut, flexibly moving.

His nostrils dilate as my heels embrace him,   705
His well-built limbs tremble with pleasure as we race around and return.

3. Rock of igneous (fire-created) or magmatic (mol-   4. Belonging to every form of life.
ten) origin; from Pluto, ruler of infernal regions.

I but use you a minute, then I resign you, stallion,
Why do I need your paces when I myself out-gallop them?
Even as I stand or sit passing faster than you.

33

Space and Time! now I see it is true, what I guess'd at,   710
What I guess'd when I loaf'd on the grass,
What I guess'd while I lay alone in my bed,
And again as I walk'd the beach under the paling stars of the morning.

My ties and ballasts leave me, my elbows rest in sea-gaps,[5]
I skirt sierras, my palms cover continents,   715
I am afoot with my vision.

By the city's quadrangular houses—in log huts, camping with lumbermen,
Along the ruts of the turnpike, along the dry gulch and rivulet bed,
Weeding my onion-patch or hoeing rows of carrots and parsnips, crossing
     savannas,[6] trailing in forests,
Prospecting, gold-digging, girdling the trees of a new purchase,   720
Scorch'd ankle-deep by the hot sand, hauling my boat down the shallow
     river,
Where the panther walks to and fro on a limb overhead, where the buck
     turns furiously at the hunter,
Where the rattlesnake suns his flabby length on a rock, where the otter is
     feeding on fish,
Where the alligator in his tough pimples sleeps by the bayou,
Where the black bear is searching for roots or honey, where the beaver
     pats the mud with his paddle-shaped tail;   725
Over the growing sugar, over the yellow-flower'd cotton plant, over the rice
     in its low moist field,
Over the sharp-peak'd farm house, with its scallop'd scum and slender
     shoots from the gutters,[7]
Over the western persimmon, over the long-leav'd corn, over the delicate
     blue-flower flax,
Over the white and brown buckwheat, a hummer and buzzer there with
     the rest,
Over the dusky green of the rye as it ripples and shades in the breeze;   730
Scaling mountains, pulling myself cautiously up, holding on by low
     scragged limbs,
Walking the path worn in the grass and beat through the leaves of the
     brush,
Where the quail is whistling betwixt the woods and the wheat-lot,
Where the bat flies in the Seventh-month eve, where the great gold-bug[8]
     drops through the dark,
Where the brook puts out of the roots of the old tree and flows to the
     meadow,   735

---

5. Estuaries or bays.
6. Grasslands.
7. I.e., plants growing from soil lodged in house gutters and drain pipes. "Scallop'd scum": rain-washed and sometimes weedy sediment on the roofs of old farmhouses.
8. Beetle.

Where cattle stand and shake away flies with the tremulous shuddering
    of their hides,
Where the cheese-cloth hangs in the kitchen, where andirons straddle the
    hearth-slab, where cobwebs fall in festoons from the rafters;
Where trip-hammers crash, where the press is whirling its cylinders,
Wherever the human heart beats with terrible throes under its ribs,
Where the pear-shaped balloon is floating aloft, (floating in it myself and
    looking composedly down,)   740
Where the life-car[9] is drawn on the slip-noose, where the heat hatches
    pale-green eggs in the dented sand,
Where the she-whale swims with her calf and never forsakes it,
Where the steam-ship trails hind-ways its long pennant of smoke,
Where the fin of the shark cuts like a black chip out of the water,
Where the half-burn'd brig is riding on unknown currents,   745
Where shells grow to her slimy deck, where the dead are corrupting below;
Where the dense-star'd flag is borne at the head of the regiments,
Approaching Manhattan up by the long-stretching island,
Under Niagara, the cataract falling like a veil over my countenance,
Upon a door-step, upon the horse-block of hard wood outside,   750
Upon the race-course, or enjoying picnics or jigs or a good game of
    baseball,
At he-festivals, with blackguard gibes, ironical license, bull-dances,[1]
    drinking, laughter,
At the cider-mill tasting the sweets of the brown mash, sucking the juice
    through a straw,
At apple-peelings wanting kisses for all the red fruit I find,
At musters, beach-parties, friendly bees,[2] huskings, house-raisings;   755
Where the mocking-bird sounds his delicious gurgles, cackles, screams,
    weeps,
Where the hay-rick[3] stands in the barn-yard, where the dry-stalks are
    scatter'd, where the brood-cow waits in the hovel,
Where the bull advances to do his masculine work, where the stud to the
    mare, where the cock is treading the hen,
Where the heifers browse, where geese nip their food with short jerks,
Where sun-down shadows lengthen over the limitless and lonesome
    prairie,   760
Where herds of buffalo make a crawling spread of the square miles far
    and near,
Where the humming-bird shimmers, where the neck of the long-lived
    swan is curving and winding,
Where the laughing-gull scoots by the shore, where she laughs her
    near-human laugh,
Where bee-hives range on a gray bench in the garden half hid by the high
    weeds,
Where band-neck'd partridges roost in a ring on the ground with their
    heads out,   765
Where burial coaches enter the arch'd gates of a cemetery,

9. Watertight compartment for lowering passengers from a ship when emergency evacuation is
required.
1. Rowdy backwoods dances for which men took
male partners.

2. Gatherings where people work while socializing
with their neighbors. "Musters": assemblages of
people, particularly gatherings of military troops
for drill.
3. Hayrack, from which livestock eat hay.

Where winter wolves bark amid wastes of snow and icicled trees,
Where the yellow-crown'd heron comes to the edge of the marsh at night
    and feeds upon small crabs,
Where the splash of swimmers and divers cools the warm noon,
Where the katy-did works her chromatic[4] reed on the walnut-tree over
    the well,   770
Through patches of citrons[5] and cucumbers with silver-wired leaves,
Through the salt-lick or orange glade, or under conical firs,
Through the gymnasium, through the curtain'd saloon, through the office
    or public hall;
Pleas'd with the native and pleas'd with the foreign, pleas'd with the new
    and old,
Pleas'd with the homely woman as well as the handsome,   775
Pleas'd with the quakeress as she puts off her bonnet and talks
    melodiously,
Pleas'd with the tune of the choir of the whitewash'd church,
Pleas'd with the earnest words of the sweating Methodist preacher,
    impress'd seriously at the camp-meeting;
Looking in at the shop-windows of Broadway the whole forenoon, flatting
    the flesh of my nose on the thick plate glass,
Wandering the same afternoon with my face turn'd up to the clouds, or
    down a lane or along the beach,   780
My right and left arms round the sides of two friends, and I in the
    middle;
Coming home with the silent and dark-cheek'd bush-boy, (behind me he
    rides at the drape of the day,)
Far from the settlements studying the print of animals' feet, or the
    moccasin print,
By the cot in the hospital reaching lemonade to a feverish patient,
Nigh the coffin'd corpse when all is still, examining with a candle;   785
Voyaging to every port to dicker and adventure,
Hurrying with the modern crowd as eager and fickle as any,
Hot toward one I hate, ready in my madness to knife him,
Solitary at midnight in my back yard, my thoughts gone from me a long
    while,
Walking the old hills of Judæa with the beautiful gentle God by my side,   790
Speeding through space, speeding through heaven and the stars,
Speeding amid the seven satellites[6] and the broad ring, and the diameter
    of eighty thousand miles,
Speeding with tail'd meteors, throwing fire-balls like the rest,
Carrying the crescent child that carries its own full mother in its belly,[7]
Storming, enjoying, planning, loving, cautioning,   795
Backing and filling, appearing and disappearing,
I tread day and night such roads.

I visit the orchards of spheres and look at the product,
And look at quintillions ripen'd and look at quintillions green.

---

4. In music, encompassing a full tonal range.
5. Here, small, hard-skinned watermelons.
6. The then known moons of Saturn.

7. I.e., a crescent moon, with the full moon also
palely visible.

I fly those flights of a fluid and swallowing soul,   800
My course runs below the soundings of plummets.

I help myself to material and immaterial,
No guard can shut me off, no law prevent me.

I anchor my ship for a little while only,
My messengers continually cruise away or bring their returns to me.   805

I go hunting polar furs and the seal, leaping chasms with a pike-pointed
    staff, clinging to topples of brittle and blue.[8]

I ascend to the foretruck,[9]
I take my place late at night in the crow's-nest,
We sail the arctic sea, it is plenty light enough,
Through the clear atmosphere I stretch around on the wonderful
    beauty,   810
The enormous masses of ice pass me and I pass them, the scenery is
    plain in all directions,
The white-topt mountains show in the distance, I fling out my fancies
    toward them,
We are approaching some great battle-field in which we are soon to be
    engaged,
We pass the colossal outposts of the encampment, we pass with still feet
    and caution,
Or we are entering by the suburbs some vast and ruin'd city,   815
The blocks and fallen architecture more than all the living cities of the globe.

I am a free companion, I bivouac by invading watchfires,
I turn the bridegroom out of bed and stay with the bride myself,
I tighten her all night to my thighs and lips.

My voice is the wife's voice, the screech by the rail of the stairs,   820
They fetch my man's body up dripping and drown'd.

I understand the large hearts of heroes,
The courage of present times and all times,
How the skipper saw the crowded and rudderless wreck of the steam-ship,
    and Death chasing it up and down the storm,
How he knuckled tight and gave not back an inch, and was faithful of days
    and faithful of nights,   825
And chalk'd in large letters on a board, *Be of good cheer, we will not desert you;*
How he follow'd with them and tack'd with them three days and would not
    give it up,
How he saved the drifting company at last,
How the lank loose-gown'd women look'd when boated from the side of
    their prepared graves,
How the silent old-faced infants and the lifted sick, and the sharp-lipp'd
    unshaved men;   830

8. Toppled pieces of ice.   9. Highest platform of a foremast.

All this I swallow, it tastes good, I like it well, it becomes mine,
I am the man, I suffer'd, I was there.[1]

The disdain and calmness of martyrs,
The mother of old, condemn'd for a witch, burnt with dry wood, her
    children gazing on,
The hounded slave that flags in the race, leans by the fence, blowing,
    cover'd with sweat,   835
The twinges that sting like needles his legs and neck, the murderous
    buckshot and the bullets,
All these I feel or am.

I am the hounded slave, I wince at the bite of the dogs,
Hell and despair are upon me, crack and again crack the marksmen,
I clutch the rails of the fence, my gore dribs, thinn'd with the ooze of
    my skin,[2]   840
I fall on the weeds and stones,
The riders spur their unwilling horses, haul close,
Taunt my dizzy ears and beat me violently over the head with whip-stocks.

Agonies are one of my changes of garments,
I do not ask the wounded person how he feels, I myself become the
    wounded person,   845
My hurts turn livid upon me as I lean on a cane and observe.

I am the mash'd fireman with breast-bone broken,
Tumbling walls buried me in their debris,
Heat and smoke I inspired, I heard the yelling shouts of my comrades,
I heard the distant click of their picks and shovels,   850
They have clear'd the beams away, they tenderly lift me forth.

I lie in the night air in my red shirt, the pervading hush is for my sake,
Painless after all I lie exhausted but not so unhappy,
White and beautiful are the faces around me, the heads are bared of
    their fire-caps,
The kneeling crowd fades with the light of the torches.   855

Distant and dead resuscitate,
They show as the dial or move as the hands of me, I am the clock myself.

I am an old artillerist, I tell of my fort's bombardment,
I am there again.

Again the long roll of the drummers,   860
Again the attacking cannon, mortars,
Again to my listening ears the cannon responsive.

1. Whitman describes the wreck of the *San Francisco*, which sailed from New York on December 22, 1853, bound for South America, and was caught in a storm a day later. The ship drifted helplessly until early January. Over 150 died in the disaster, which was reported widely in the New York papers.
2. Dribbles down, diluted with sweat.

I take part, I see and hear the whole,
The cries, curses, roar, the plaudits of well-aim'd shots,
The ambulanza slowly passing trailing its red drip,   865
Workmen searching after damages, making indispensable repairs,
The fall of grenades through the rent roof, the fan-shaped explosion,
The whizz of limbs, heads, stone, wood, iron, high in the air.

Again gurgles the mouth of my dying general, he furiously waves with
    his hand,
He gasps through the clot *Mind not me—mind—the entrenchments.*   870

34

Now I tell what I knew in Texas in my early youth,
(I tell not the fall of Alamo,[3]
Not one escaped to tell the fall of Alamo,
The hundred and fifty are dumb yet at Alamo,)
'Tis the tale of the murder in cold blood of four hundred and twelve
    young men.   875

Retreating they had form'd in a hollow square with their baggage for
    breastworks,
Nine hundred lives out of the surrounding enemy's, nine times their
    number, was the price they took in advance,
Their colonel was wounded and their ammunition gone,
They treated for an honorable capitulation, receiv'd writing and seal,
    gave up their arms and march'd back prisoners of war.

They were the glory of the race of rangers,   880
Matchless with horse, rifle, song, supper, courtship,
Large, turbulent, generous, handsome, proud, and affectionate,
Bearded, sunburnt, drest in the free costume of hunters,
Not a single one over thirty years of age.

The second First-day morning they were brought out in squads and
    massacred, it was beautiful early summer,   885
The work commenced about five o'clock and was over by eight.

None obey'd the command to kneel,
Some made a mad and helpless rush, some stood stark and straight,
A few fell at once, shot in the temple or heart, the living and dead lay
    together,
The maim'd and mangled dug in the dirt, the new-comers saw them
    there,   890
Some half-kill'd attempted to crawl away,

3. During the Texas Revolution of 1835–36, emigrants from the United States to Texas—at the
time part of Mexico—attempted to make Texas
into an independent republic. Among the battles
fought in what is now the state of Texas were the
battle of the Alamo (a Spanish mission church
compound in San Antonio)—the Alamo fell on
March 6, 1836, after a siege by Mexican forces
beginning on February 23, when around two hundred men were killed—and the battle of Goliad,
when some four hundred secessionist troops were
killed after surrendering to the Mexicans on
March 19 of the same year.

These were despatch'd with bayonets or batter'd with the blunts of muskets,
A youth not seventeen years old seiz'd his assassin till two more came to
    release him,
The three were all torn and cover'd with the boy's blood.

At eleven o'clock began the burning of the bodies;   895
That is the tale of the murder of the four hundred and twelve young men.

35

Would you hear of an old-time sea-fight?[4]
Would you learn who won by the light of the moon and stars?
List to the yarn, as my grandmother's father the sailor told it to me.

Our foe was no skulk in his ship I tell you, (said he,)   900
His was the surly English pluck, and there is no tougher or truer, and
    never was, and never will be;
Along the lower'd eve he came horribly raking us.

We closed with him, the yards entangled, the cannon touch'd,
My captain lash'd fast with his own hands.

We had receiv'd some eighteen pound shots under the water,   905
On our lower-gun-deck two large pieces had burst at the first fire, killing
    all around and blowing up overhead.

Fighting at sun-down, fighting at dark,
Ten o'clock at night, the full moon well up, our leaks on the gain, and five
    feet of water reported,
The master-at-arms loosing the prisoners confined in the after-hold to give
    them a chance for themselves.

The transit to and from the magazine[5] is now stopt by the sentinels,   910
They see so many strange faces they do not know whom to trust.

Our frigate takes fire,
The other asks if we demand quarter?
If our colors are struck and the fighting done?

Now I laugh content, for I hear the voice of my little captain,   915
We have not struck, he composedly cries, *we have just begun our part of
    the fighting.*

Only three guns are in use,
One is directed by the captain himself against the enemy's mainmast,

4. This passage alludes to the famous Revolutionary War sea battle on September 23, 1779, between the American *Bon-Homme Richard*, commanded by John Paul Jones (1747–1792), and the British *Serapis* off the coast of northern England. When Jones was asked to surrender, he famously declared, "I have not yet begun to fight." The American ship eventually defeated the *Serapis*.
5. Storeroom for ammunition.

Two well serv'd with grape and canister[6] silence his musketry and clear
    his decks.

The tops[7] alone second the fire of this little battery, especially the
    main-top,   920
They hold out bravely during the whole of the action.

Not a moment's cease,
The leaks gain fast on the pumps, the fire eats toward the powder-
    magazine.

One of the pumps has been shot away, it is generally thought we are
    sinking.

Serene stands the little captain,   925
He is not hurried, his voice is neither high nor low,
His eyes give more light to us than our battle-lanterns.

Toward twelve there in the beams of the moon they surrender to us.

36

Stretch'd and still lies the midnight,
Two great hulls motionless on the breast of the darkness,   930
Our vessel riddled and slowly sinking, preparations to pass to the one
    we have conquer'd,
The captain on the quarter-deck coldly giving his orders through a
    countenance white as a sheet,
Near by the corpse of the child that serv'd in the cabin,
The dead face of an old salt with long white hair and carefully curl'd
    whiskers,
The flames spite of all that can be done flickering aloft and below,   935
The husky voices of the two or three officers yet fit for duty,
Formless stacks of bodies and bodies by themselves, dabs of flesh upon
    the masts and spars,
Cut of cordage, dangle of rigging, slight shock of the soothe of waves,
Black and impassive guns, litter of powder-parcels, strong scent,
A few large stars overhead, silent and mournful shining,   940
Delicate sniffs of sea-breeze, smells of sedgy grass and fields by the shore,
    death-messages given in charge to survivors,
The hiss of the surgeon's knife, the gnawing teeth of his saw,
Wheeze, cluck, swash of falling blood, short wild scream, and long, dull,
    tapering groan,
These so, these irretrievable.

---

6. Grapeshot ("grape"), clusters of small iron balls, was packed inside a metal cylinder ("canister") and fired from a cannon.

7. I.e., the sailors manning the tops—platforms enclosing the heads of each mast.

37

You laggards there on guard! look to your arms! 945
In at the conquer'd doors they crowd! I am possess'd!
Embody all presences outlaw'd or suffering,
See myself in prison shaped like another man,
And feel the dull unintermitted pain.

For me the keepers of convicts shoulder their carbines and keep
watch, 950
It is I let out in the morning and barr'd at night.

Not a mutineer walks handcuff'd to jail but I am handcuff'd to him and
walk by his side,
(I am less the jolly one there, and more the silent one with sweat on my
twitching lips.)

Not a youngster is taken for larceny but I go up too, and am tried and
sentenced.

Not a cholera patient lies at the last gasp but I also lie at the last
gasp, 955
My face is ash-color'd, my sinews gnarl, away from me people retreat.

Askers embody themselves in me and I am embodied in them,
I project my hat, sit shame-faced, and beg.

38

Enough! enough! enough!
Somehow I have been stunn'd. Stand back! 960
Give me a little time beyond my cuff'd head, slumbers, dreams, gaping,
I discover myself on the verge of a usual mistake.

That I could forget the mockers and insults!
That I could forget the trickling tears and the blows of the bludgeons
and hammers!
That I could look with a separate look on my own crucifixion and bloody
crowning. 965

I remember now,
I resume the overstaid fraction,
The grave of rock multiplies what has been confided to it, or to any
graves,
Corpses rise, gashes heal, fastenings roll from me.

I troop forth replenish'd with supreme power, one of an average unending
procession, 970
Inland and sea-coast we go, and pass all boundary lines,
Our swift ordinances on their way over the whole earth,
The blossoms we wear in our hats the growth of thousands of years.

Eleves,[8] I salute you! come forward!
Continue your annotations, continue your questionings.   975

39

The friendly and flowing savage, who is he?
Is he waiting for civilization, or past it and mastering it?

Is he some Southwesterner rais'd out-doors? is he Kanadian?
Is he from the Mississippi country? Iowa, Oregon, California?
The mountains? prairie-life, bush-life? or sailor from the sea?   980

Wherever he goes men and women accept and desire him,
They desire he should like them, touch them, speak to them, stay with
    them.

Behavior lawless as snow-flakes, words simple as grass, uncomb'd head,
    laughter, and naiveté,
Slow-stepping feet, common features, common modes and emanations,
They descend in new forms from the tips of his fingers,   985
They are wafted with the odor of his body or breath, they fly out of the
    glance of his eyes.

40

Flaunt of the sunshine I need not your bask—lie over!
You light surfaces only, I force surfaces and depths also.

Earth! you seem to look for something at my hands,
Say, old top-knot,[9] what do you want?   990

Man or woman, I might tell how I like you, but cannot,
And might tell what it is in me and what it is in you, but cannot,
And might tell that pining I have, that pulse of my nights and days.

Behold, I do not give lectures or a little charity,
When I give I give myself.   995

You there, impotent, loose in the knees,
Open your scarf'd chops till I blow grit[1] within you,
Spread your palms and lift the flaps of your pockets,
I am not to be denied, I compel, I have stores plenty and to spare,
And any thing I have I bestow.   1000

I do not ask who you are, that is not important to me,
You can do nothing and be nothing but what I will infold you.

---

8. Students (French).
9. An epithet common in frontier humor, deriving from the fact that some Native Americans gathered their hair into tufts at the top of the head. The poet seems to be addressing an older Indian, perhaps picking up on the reference to "the friendly and flowing savage" of the previous stanza.
1. Courage. "Scarf'd chops": lined, worn-down jaw or face.

To cotton-field drudge or cleaner of privies I lean,
On his right cheek I put the family kiss,
And in my soul I swear I never will deny him.   1005

On women fit for conception I start bigger and nimbler babes,
(This day I am jetting the stuff of far more arrogant republics.)

To any one dying, thither I speed and twist the knob of the door,
Turn the bed-clothes toward the foot of the bed,
Let the physician and the priest go home.   1010

I seize the descending man and raise him with resistless will,
O despairer, here is my neck,
By God, you shall not go down! hang your whole weight upon me.

I dilate you with tremendous breath, I buoy you up,
Every room of the house do I fill with an arm'd force,   1015
Lovers of me, bafflers of graves.

Sleep—I and they keep guard all night,
Not doubt, not decease shall dare to lay finger upon you,
I have embraced you, and henceforth possess you to myself,
And when you rise in the morning you will find what I tell you is so.   1020

41

I am he bringing help for the sick as they pant on their backs,
And for strong upright men I bring yet more needed help.

I heard what was said of the universe,
Heard it and heard it of several thousand years;
It is middling well as far as it goes—but is that all?   1025

Magnifying and applying come I,
Outbidding at the start the old cautious hucksters,
Taking myself the exact dimensions of Jehovah,[2]
Lithographing Kronos, Zeus his son, and Hercules[3] his grandson,
Buying drafts of Osiris, Isis, Belus, Brahma, Buddha,[4]   1030
In my portfolio placing Manito loose, Allah[5] on a leaf, the crucifix
    engraved,
With Odin and the hideous-faced Mexitli[6] and every idol and image,
Taking them all for what they are worth and not a cent more,
Admitting they were alive and did the work of their days,

2. God of the Jews and Christians.
3. Son of Zeus and the mortal Alcmene, won immortality by performing twelve supposedly impossible feats. Kronos (or Cronus), in Greek mythology, was the Titan who ruled the universe until dethroned by Zeus, his son, the chief of the Olympian gods.
4. The Indian sage Siddhartha Gautama (known as the "Buddha"), founder of Buddhism. Osiris was the Egyptian god who annually died and was reborn, symbolizing the fertility of nature. Isis was the Egyptian goddess of fertility and the sister and wife of Osiris. Belus was a legendary god-king of Assyria. Brahma, in Hinduism, is the divine reality in the role of the creator god.
5. Arabic word for God, the supreme being in Islam. Manito was the nature god of the Algonquian Indians.
6. An Aztec war god. Odin was the chief Norse god.

(They bore mites as for unfledg'd birds who have now to rise and fly and
    sing for themselves,)   1035
Accepting the rough deific sketches to fill out better in myself, bestowing
    them freely on each man and woman I see,
Discovering as much or more in a framer framing a house,
Putting higher claims for him there with his roll'd-up sleeves driving the
    mallet and chisel,
Not objecting to special revelations, considering a curl of smoke or a hair
    on the back of my hand just as curious as any revelation,
Lads ahold of fire-engines and hook-and-ladder ropes no less to me than
    the gods of the antique wars,   1040
Minding their voices peal through the crash of destruction,
Their brawny limbs passing safe over charr'd laths, their white foreheads
    whole and unhurt out of the flames;
By the mechanic's wife with her babe at her nipple interceding for every
    person born,
Three scythes at harvest whizzing in a row from three lusty angels with
    shirts bagg'd out at their waists,
The snag-tooth'd hostler with red hair redeeming sins past and to
    come,   1045
Selling all he possesses, traveling on foot to fee lawyers for his brother
    and sit by him while he is tried for forgery;
What was strewn in the amplest strewing the square rod about me, and
    not filling the square rod then,
The bull and the bug never worshipp'd half enough,[7]
Dung and dirt more admirable than was dream'd,
The supernatural of no account, myself waiting my time to be one of the
    supremes,   1050
The day getting ready for me when I shall do as much good as the best,
    and be as prodigious;
By my life-lumps![8] becoming already a creator,
Putting myself here and now to the ambush'd womb of the shadows.

42

A call in the midst of the crowd,
My own voice, orotund sweeping and final.   1055

Come my children,
Come my boys and girls, my women, household and intimates,
Now the performer launches his nerve, he has pass'd his prelude on the
    reeds within.

Easily written loose-finger'd chords—I feel the thrum of your climax
    and close.

My head slues round on my neck,   1060
Music rolls, but not from the organ,
Folks are around me, but they are no household of mine.

---

7. As Whitman implies, the bull and the bug had been worshiped in earlier religions, the bull in several,
the scarab beetle as an Egyptian symbol of the soul.
8. Testicles.

Ever the hard unsunk ground,
Ever the eaters and drinkers, ever the upward and downward sun, ever
    the air and the ceaseless tides,
Ever myself and my neighbors, refreshing, wicked, real,   1065
Ever the old inexplicable query, ever that thorn'd thumb, that breath of
    itches and thirsts,
Ever the vexer's *hoot! hoot!* till we find where the sly one hides and bring
    him forth,
Ever love, ever the sobbing liquid of life,
Ever the bandage under the chin, ever the trestles[9] of death.

Here and there with dimes on the eyes[1] walking,   1070
To feed the greed of the belly the brains liberally spooning,
Tickets buying, taking, selling, but in to the feast never once going,
Many sweating, ploughing, thrashing, and then the chaff for payment
    receiving,
A few idly owning, and they the wheat continually claiming.

This is the city and I am one of the citizens,   1075
Whatever interests the rest interests me, politics, wars, markets,
    newspapers, schools,
The mayor and councils, banks, tariffs, steamships, factories, stocks,
    stores, real estate and personal estate.

The little plentiful manikins skipping around in collars and tail'd coats,
I am aware who they are, (they are positively not worms or fleas,)
I acknowledge the duplicates of myself, the weakest and shallowest is
    deathless with me,   1080
What I do and say the same waits for them,
Every thought that flounders in me the same flounders in them.

I know perfectly well my own egotism,
Know my omnivorous lines and must not write any less,
And would fetch you whoever you are flush with myself.   1085

Not words of routine this song of mine,
But abruptly to question, to leap beyond yet nearer bring;
This printed and bound book—but the printer and the printing-office boy?
The well-taken photographs—but your wife or friend close and solid in
    your arms?
The black ship mail'd with iron, her mighty guns in her turrets—but the
    pluck of the captain and engineers?   1090
In the houses the dishes and fare and furniture—but the host and
    hostess, and the look out of their eyes?
The sky up there—yet here or next door, or across the way?
The saints and sages in history—but you yourself?
Sermons, creeds, theology—but the fathomless human brain,
And what is reason? and what is love? and what is life?   1095

9. I.e., sawhorses or similar supports holding up a coffin.

1. Coins were placed on eyelids of corpses to hold them closed until burial.

43

I do not despise you priests, all time, the world over,
My faith is the greatest of faiths and the least of faiths,
Enclosing worship ancient and modern and all between ancient and
    modern,
Believing I shall come again upon the earth after five thousand years,
Waiting responses from oracles, honoring the gods, saluting the sun,   1100
Making a fetich of the first rock or stump, powowing with sticks in the
    circle of obis.[2]
Helping the llama or brahmin[3] as he trims the lamps of the idols,
Dancing yet through the streets in a phallic procession, rapt and austere
    in the woods a gymnosophist,[4]
Drinking mead from the skull-cup, to Shastas and Vedas admirant,
    minding the Koran,[5]
Walking the teokallis,[6] spotted with gore from the stone and knife,
    beating the serpent-skin drum,   1105
Accepting the Gospels,[7] accepting him that was crucified, knowing
    assuredly that he is divine,
To the mass kneeling or the puritan's prayer rising, or sitting patiently
    in a pew,
Ranting and frothing in my insane crisis, or waiting dead-like till my spirit
    arouses me,
Looking forth on pavement and land, or outside of pavement and land,
Belonging to the winders of the circuit of circuits.   1110

One of that centripetal and centrifugal gang I turn and talk like a man
    leaving charges before a journey.

Down-hearted doubters dull and excluded,
Frivolous, sullen, moping, angry, affected, dishearten'd, atheistical,
I know every one of you, I know the sea of torment, doubt, despair and
    unbelief.

How the flukes[8] splash!   1115
How they contort rapid as lightning, with spasms and spouts of blood!

Be at peace bloody flukes of doubters and sullen mopers,
I take my place among you as much as among any,
The past is the push of you, me, all, precisely the same,
And what is yet untried and afterward is for you, me, all, precisely the
    same.   1120

---

2. Magical charms, such as shells, used in African and West Indian religious practices. "Fetich": i.e., fetish; object of worship.
3. Here, also a Buddhist priest. "Llama": i.e., lama; a Buddhist monk of Tibet or Mongolia.
4. Member of an ancient Hindu ascetic sect.
5. The other worshipers include ancient warriors drinking mead (an alcoholic beverage made of fermented honey) from the skulls of defeated enemies; admiring or wondering readers of the sastras (or shastras or shasters, books of Hindu law) or of the Vedas (the oldest sacred writings of Hinduism); and those attentive to the Koran (the sacred book of Islam, containing Allah's revelations to Muhammad).
6. An ancient Central American temple built on a pyramidal mound.
7. Of the New Testament of the Bible.
8. The flat parts on either side of a whale's tail; here used figuratively.

I do not know what is untried and afterward,
But I know it will in its turn prove sufficient, and cannot fail.

Each who passes is consider'd, each who stops is consider'd, not a single
    one can it fail.

It cannot fail the young man who died and was buried,
Nor the young woman who died and was put by his side,   1125
Nor the little child that peep'd in at the door, and then drew back and
    was never seen again,
Nor the old man who has lived without purpose, and feels it with
    bitterness worse than gall,
Nor him in the poor house tubercled by rum and the bad disorder,[9]
Nor the numberless slaughter'd and wreck'd, nor the brutish koboo[1]
    call'd the ordure of humanity,
Nor the sacs merely floating with open mouths for food to slip in,   1130
Nor any thing in the earth, or down in the oldest graves of the earth,
Nor any thing in the myriads of spheres, nor the myriads of myriads
    that inhabit them,
Nor the present, nor the least wisp that is known.

44

It is time to explain myself—let us stand up.

What is known I strip away,   1135
I launch all men and women forward with me into the Unknown.

The clock indicates the moment—but what does eternity indicate?

We have thus far exhausted trillions of winters and summers,
There are trillions ahead, and trillions ahead of them.

Births have brought us richness and variety,   1140
And other births will bring us richness and variety.

I do not call one greater and one smaller,
That which fills its period and place is equal to any.

Were mankind murderous or jealous upon you, my brother, my sister?
I am sorry for you, they are not murderous or jealous upon me,   1145
All has been gentle with me, I keep no account with lamentation,
(What have I to do with lamentation?)

I am an acme of things accomplish'd, and I an encloser of things to be.

My feet strike an apex of the apices[2] of the stairs,
On every step bunches of ages, and larger bunches between the steps,   1150
All below duly travel'd, and still I mount and mount.

9. I.e., syphilis.   2. The highest points (variant plural of *apex*).
1. Native of Sumatra.

Rise after rise bow the phantoms behind me,
Afar down I see the huge first Nothing, I know I was even there,
I waited unseen and always, and slept through the lethargic mist,
And took my time, and took no hurt from the fetid carbon.[3]   1155

Long I was hugg'd close—long and long.

Immense have been the preparations for me,
Faithful and friendly the arms that have help'd me.

Cycles[4] ferried my cradle, rowing and rowing like cheerful boatmen,
For room to me stars kept aside in their own rings,   1160
They sent influences to look after what was to hold me.

Before I was born out of my mother generations guided me,
My embryo has never been torpid, nothing could overlay it.

For it the nebula cohered to an orb,
The long slow strata piled to rest it on,   1165
Vast vegetables gave it sustenance,
Monstrous sauroids[5] transported it in their mouths and deposited it with
    care.

All forces have been steadily employ'd to complete and delight me,
Now on this spot I stand with my robust soul.

45

O span of youth! ever-push'd elasticity!   1170
O manhood, balanced, florid and full.

My lovers suffocate me,
Crowding my lips, thick in the pores of my skin,
Jostling me through streets and public halls, coming naked to me at
    night,
Crying by day Ahoy! from the rocks of the river, swinging and chirping
    over my head,   1175
Calling my name from flower-beds, vines, tangled underbrush,
Lighting on every moment of my life,
Bussing[6] my body with soft balsamic busses,
Noiselessly passing handfuls out of their hearts and giving them to be mine.

Old age superbly rising! O welcome, ineffable grace of dying days!   1180

Every condition promulges[7] not only itself, it promulges what grows after
    and out of itself,
And the dark hush promulges as much as any.

---

3. The "lethargic mist" (line 1154) and "fetid carbon" suggest a time before the appearance of
human beings on earth.
4. Centuries.

5. Prehistoric large reptiles or dinosaurs, thought
to have carried their eggs in their mouths.
6. Kissing.
7. Promulgates, officially announces.

I open my scuttle[8] at night and see the far-sprinkled systems,
And all I see multiplied as high as I can cipher edge but the rim of the
    farther systems.

Wider and wider they spread, expanding, always expanding,   1185
Outward and outward and forever outward.

My sun has his sun and round him obediently wheels,
He joins with his partners a group of superior circuit,
And greater sets follow, making specks of the greatest inside them.

There is no stoppage and never can be stoppage,   1190
If I, you, and the worlds, and all beneath or upon their surfaces, were
    this moment reduced back to a pallid float,[9] it would not avail in the
    long run,
We should surely bring up again where we now stand,
And surely go as much farther, and then farther and farther.

A few quadrillions of eras, a few octillions of cubic leagues, do not hazard[1]
    the span or make it impatient,
They are but parts, any thing is but a part.   1195

See ever so far, there is limitless space outside of that,
Count ever so much, there is limitless time around that.

My rendezvous is appointed, it is certain,
The Lord will be there and wait till I come on perfect terms,
The great Camerado, the lover true for whom I pine will be there.   1200

46

I know I have the best of time and space, and was never measured and
    never will be measured.

I tramp a perpetual journey, (come listen all!)
My signs are a rain-proof coat, good shoes, and a staff cut from the
    woods,
No friend of mine takes his ease in my chair,
I have no chair, no church, no philosophy,   1205
I lead no man to a dinner-table, library, exchange,[2]
But each man and each woman of you I lead upon a knoll,
My left hand hooking you round the waist,
My right hand pointing to landscapes of continents and the public road.

Not I, not any one else can travel that road for you,   1210
You must travel it for yourself.

8. Roof hatch (as on a ship).
9. I.e., returned to the era before the formation of
the solar system.

1. Imperil, make hazardous.
2. Stock exchange, bank.

It is not far, it is within reach,
Perhaps you have been on it since you were born and did not know,
Perhaps it is everywhere on water and on land.

Shoulder your duds dear son, and I will mine, and let us hasten forth,   1215
Wonderful cities and free nations we shall fetch as we go.

If you tire, give me both burdens, and rest the chuff[3] of your hand on
    my hip,
And in due time you shall repay the same service to me,
For after we start we never lie by again.

This day before dawn I ascended a hill and look'd at the crowded
    heaven,   1220
And I said to my spirit *When we become the enfolders of those orbs, and
the pleasure and knowledge of every thing in them, shall we be fill'd
and satisfied then?*
And my spirit said *No, we but level that lift to pass and continue beyond.*

You are also asking me questions and I hear you,
I answer that I cannot answer, you must find out for yourself.

Sit a while dear son,   1225
Here are biscuits to eat and here is milk to drink,
But as soon as you sleep and renew yourself in sweet clothes, I kiss you
    with a good-by kiss and open the gate for your egress hence.

Long enough have you dream'd contemptible dreams,
Now I wash the gum from your eyes,
You must habit yourself to the dazzle of the light and of every moment
    of your life.   1230

Long have you timidly waded holding a plank by the shore,
Now I will you to be a bold swimmer,
To jump off in the midst of the sea, rise again, nod to me, shout, and
    laughingly dash with your hair.

47

I am the teacher of athletes,
He that by me spreads a wider breast than my own proves the width of
    my own,   1235
He most honors my style who learns under it to destroy the teacher.

The boy I love, the same becomes a man not through derived power, but
    in his own right,
Wicked rather than virtuous out of conformity or fear,
Fond of his sweetheart, relishing well his steak,
Unrequited love or a slight cutting him worse than sharp steel cuts,   1240

---

3. The fleshy part of the palm.

First-rate to ride, to fight, to hit the bull's eye, to sail a skiff, to sing a
    song or play on the banjo,
Preferring scars and the beard and faces pitted with small-pox over all
    latherers,
And those well-tann'd to those that keep out of the sun.

I teach straying from me, yet who can stray from me?
I follow you whoever you are from the present hour,   1245
My words itch at your ears till you understand them.

I do not say these things for a dollar or to fill up the time while I wait for
    a boat,
(It is you talking just as much as myself, I act as the tongue of you,
Tied in your mouth, in mine it begins to be loosen'd.)

I swear I will never again mention love or death inside a house,   1250
And I swear I will never translate myself at all, only to him or her who
    privately stays with me in the open air.

If you would understand me go to the heights or water-shore,
The nearest gnat is an explanation, and a drop or motion of waves a key,
The maul, the oar, the hand-saw, second my words.

No shutter'd room or school can commune with me,   1255
But roughs and little children better than they.

The young mechanic is closest to me, he knows me well,
The woodman that takes his axe and jug with him shall take me with him
    all day,
The farm-boy ploughing in the field feels good at the sound of my voice,
In vessels that sail my words sail, I go with fishermen and seamen and
    love them.   1260

The soldier camp'd or upon the march is mine,
On the night ere the pending battle many seek me, and I do not fail
    them,
On that solemn night (it may be their last) those that know me seek me.

My face rubs to the hunter's face when he lies down alone in his blanket,
The driver thinking of me does not mind the jolt of his wagon,   1265
The young mother and old mother comprehend me,
The girl and the wife rest the needle a moment and forget where they
    are,
They and all would resume what I have told them.

48

I have said that the soul is not more than the body,
And I have said that the body is not more than the soul,   1270
And nothing, not God, is greater to one than one's self is,
And whoever walks a furlong without sympathy walks to his own funeral
    drest in his shroud,

And I or you pocketless of a dime may purchase the pick of the earth,
And to glance with an eye or show a bean in its pod confounds the
    learning of all times,
And there is no trade or employment but the young man following it
    may become a hero,   1275
And there is no object so soft but it makes a hub for the wheel'd
    universe,
And I say to any man or woman, Let your soul stand cool and composed
    before a million universes.

And I say to mankind, Be not curious about God,
For I who am curious about each am not curious about God,
(No array of terms can say how much I am at peace about God and
    about death.)   1280

I hear and behold God in every object, yet understand God not in the
    least,
Nor do I understand who there can be more wonderful than myself.

Why should I wish to see God better than this day?
I see something of God each hour of the twenty-four, and each moment then,
In the faces of men and women I see God, and in my own face in the
    glass,   1285
I find letters from God dropt in the street, and every one is sign'd by
    God's name,
And I leave them where they are, for I know that wheresoe'er I go,
Others will punctually come for ever and ever.

49

And as to you Death, and you bitter hug of mortality, it is idle to try to
    alarm me.

To his work without flinching the accoucheur[4] comes,   1290
I see the elder-hand pressing receiving supporting,
I recline by the sills of the exquisite flexible doors,
And mark the outlet, and mark the relief and escape.

And as to you Corpse I think you are good manure, but that does not
    offend me,
I smell the white roses sweet-scented and growing,   1295
I reach to the leafy lips, I reach to the polish'd breasts of melons.

And as to you Life I reckon you are the leavings of many deaths,
(No doubt I have died myself ten thousand times before.)

I hear you whispering there O stars of heaven,
O suns—O grass of graves—O perpetual transfers and promotions,   1300
If you do not say any thing how can I say any thing?

4. Midwife (French).

Of the turbid pool that lies in the autumn forest,
Of the moon that descends the steeps of the soughing twilight,
Toss, sparkles of day and dusk—toss on the black stems that decay in
    the muck,
Toss to the moaning gibberish of the dry limbs.   1305

I ascend from the moon, I ascend from the night,
I perceive that the ghastly glimmer is noonday sunbeams reflected,
And debouch[5] to the steady and central from the offspring great or small.

50

There is that in me—I do not know what it is—but I know it is in me.

Wrench'd and sweaty—calm and cool then my body becomes,   1310
I sleep—I sleep long.

I do not know it—it is without name—it is a word unsaid,
It is not in any dictionary, utterance, symbol.

Something it swings on more than the earth I swing on,
To it the creation is the friend whose embracing awakes me.   1315

Perhaps I might tell more. Outlines! I plead for my brothers and
    sisters.

Do you see O my brothers and sisters?
It is not chaos or death—it is form, union, plan—it is eternal life—it is
    Happiness.

51

The past and present wilt—I have fill'd them, emptied them,
And proceed to fill my next fold of the future.   1320

Listener up there! what have you to confide to me?
Look in my face while I snuff the sidle[6] of evening,
(Talk honestly, no one else hears you, and I stay only a minute longer.)

Do I contradict myself?
Very well then I contradict myself,   1325
(I am large, I contain multitudes.)

I concentrate toward them that are nigh, I wait on the door-slab.

Who has done his day's work? who will soonest be through with his supper?
Who wishes to walk with me?

Will you speak before I am gone? will you prove already too late?   1330

---

5. Pour forth.   6. I.e., extinguish the last glimmers of evening.

52

The spotted hawk swoops by and accuses me, he complains of my gab
and my loitering.

I too am not a bit tamed, I too am untranslatable.
I sound my barbaric yawp over the roofs of the world.

The last scud of day[7] holds back for me,
It flings my likeness after the rest and true as any on the shadow'd
wilds,
It coaxes me to the vapor and the dusk. 1335

I depart as air, I shake my white locks at the runaway sun,
I effuse my flesh in eddies,[8] and drift it in lacy jags.

I bequeath myself to the dirt to grow from the grass I love,
If you want me again look for me under your boot-soles. 1340

You will hardly know who I am or what I mean,
But I shall be good health to you nevertheless,
And filter and fibre your blood.

Failing to fetch me at first keep encouraged,
Missing me one place search another, 1345
I stop somewhere waiting for you.

1855, 1881

Crossing Brooklyn Ferry[1]

1

Flood-tide below me! I see you face to face!
Clouds of the west—sun there half an hour high—I see you also face to
face.

Crowds of men and women attired in the usual costumes, how curious
you are to me!
On the ferry-boats the hundreds and hundreds that cross, returning home,
are more curious to me than you suppose,
And you that shall cross from shore to shore years hence are more to me,
and more in my meditations, than you might suppose. 5

2

The impalpable sustenance of me from all things at all hours of the day,
The simple, compact, well-join'd scheme, myself disintegrated, every one
disintegrated yet part of the scheme,
The similitudes of the past and those of the future,

---

7. Wind-driven clouds, or the last rays of the sun.
8. Air currents. "Effuse": pour forth.
1. First published as "Sun-Down Poem" in the 2nd
edition of *Leaves of Grass* (1856). "Crossing Brooklyn Ferry" was given its final title in 1860.

The glories strung like beads on my smallest sights and hearings, on the
    walk in the street and the passage over the river,
The current rushing so swiftly and swimming with me far away,   10
The others that are to follow me, the ties between me and them,
The certainty of others, the life, love, sight, hearing of others.

Others will enter the gates of the ferry and cross from shore to shore,
Others will watch the run of the flood-tide,
Others will see the shipping of Manhattan north and west, and the
    heights of Brooklyn to the south and east,   15
Others will see the islands large and small;
Fifty years hence, others will see them as they cross, the sun half an hour
    high,
A hundred years hence, or ever so many hundred years hence, others will
    see them,
Will enjoy the sunset, the pouring-in of the flood-tide, the falling-back to
    the sea of the ebb-tide.

3

It avails not, time nor place—distance avails not,   20
I am with you, you men and women of a generation, or ever so many
    generations hence,
Just as you feel when you look on the river and sky, so I felt,
Just as any of you is one of a living crowd, I was one of a crowd,
Just as you are refresh'd by the gladness of the river and the bright flow, I
    was refresh'd,
Just as you stand and lean on the rail, yet hurry with the swift current, I
    stood yet was hurried,   25
Just as you look on the numberless masts of ships and the thick-stemm'd
    pipes of steamboats, I look'd.

I too many and many a time cross'd the river of old,
Watched the Twelfth-month[2] sea-gulls, saw them high in the air floating
    with motionless wings, oscillating their bodies,
Saw how the glistening yellow lit up parts of their bodies and left the rest
    in strong shadow,
Saw the slow-wheeling circles and the gradual edging toward the south, 30
Saw the reflection of the summer sky in the water,
Had my eyes dazzled by the shimmering track of beams,
Look'd at the fine centrifugal spokes of light round the shape of my head
    in the sunlit water,
Look'd on the haze on the hills southward and south-westward,
Look'd on the vapor as it flew in fleeces tinged with violet,   35
Look'd toward the lower bay to notice the vessels arriving,
Saw their approach, saw aboard those that were near me,
Saw the white sails of schooners and sloops, saw the ships at anchor,
The sailors at work in the rigging or out astride the spars,
The round masts, the swinging motion of the hulls, the slender
    serpentine pennants,   40

2. December.

The large and small steamers in motion, the pilots in their pilot-houses,
The white wake left by the passage, the quick tremulous whirl of the
    wheels,
The flags of all nations, the falling of them at sunset.
The scallop-edged waves in the twilight, the ladled cups, the frolicsome
    crests and glistening,
The stretch afar growing dimmer and dimmer, the gray walls of the
    granite storehouses by the docks,   45
On the river the shadowy group, the big steam-tug closely flank'd on
    each side by the barges, the hay-boat, the belated lighter,[3]
On the neighboring shore the fires from the foundry chimneys burning
    high and glaringly into the night,
Casting their flicker of black contrasted with wild red and yellow light
    over the tops of houses, and down into the clefts of streets.

4

These and all else were to me the same as they are to you,
I loved well those cities, loved well the stately and rapid river,   50
The men and women I saw were all near to me,
Others the same—others who looked back on me because I look'd
    forward to them,
(The time will come, though I stop here to-day and to-night.)

5

What is it then between us?
What is the count of the scores or hundreds of years between us?   55

Whatever it is, it avails not—distance avails not, and place avails not,
I too lived, Brooklyn of ample hills was mine,
I too walk'd the streets of Manhattan island, and bathed in the waters
    around it,
I too felt the curious abrupt questionings stir within me,
In the day among crowds of people sometimes they came upon me,   60
In my walks home late at night or as I lay in my bed they came upon me,
I too had been struck from the float forever held in solution,
I too had receiv'd identity by my body,
That I was I knew was of my body, and what I should be I knew I should
    be of my body.

6

It is not upon you alone the dark patches fall,   65
The dark threw its patches down upon me also,
The best I had done seem'd to me blank and suspicious,
My great thoughts as I supposed them, were they not in reality meagre?
Nor is it you alone who know what it is to be evil,

---

3. Barge used to load or unload a cargo ship.

I am he who knew what it was to be evil, 70
I too knitted the old knot of contrariety,
Blabb'd, blush'd, resented, lied, stole, grudg'd,
Had guile, anger, lust, hot wishes I dared not speak,
Was wayward, vain, greedy, shallow, sly, cowardly, malignant,
The wolf, the snake, the hog, not wanting in me, 75
The cheating look, the frivolous word, the adulterous wish, not wanting,
Refusals, hates, postponements, meanness, laziness, none of these
    wanting,
Was one with the rest, the days and haps of the rest,
Was call'd by my nighest name by clear loud voices of young men as they
    saw me approaching or passing,
Felt their arms on my neck as I stood, or the negligent leaning of their
    flesh against me as I sat, 80
Saw many I loved in the street or ferry-boat or public assembly, yet never
    told them a word,
Lived the same life with the rest, the same old laughing, gnawing, sleeping,
Play'd the part that still looks back on the actor or actress,
The same old role, the role that is what we make it, as great as we like,
Or as small as we like, or both great and small. 85

7

Closer yet I approach you,
What thought you have of me now, I had as much of you—I laid in my
    stores in advance,
I consider'd long and seriously of you before you were born.

Who was to know what should come home to me?
Who knows but I am enjoying this? 90
Who knows, for all the distance, but I am as good as looking at you now,
    for all you cannot see me?

8

Ah, what can ever be more stately and admirable to me than mast-hemm'd
    Manhattan?
River and sunset and scallop-edg'd waves of flood-tide?
The sea-gulls oscillating their bodies, the hay-boat in the twilight, and
    the belated lighter?
What gods can exceed these that clasp me by the hand, and with voices I
    love call me promptly and loudly by my nighest name as I approach? 95
What is more subtle than this which ties me to the woman or man that
    looks in my face?
Which fuses me into you now, and pours my meaning into you?

We understand then do we not?
What I promis'd without mentioning it, have you not accepted?
What the study could not teach—what the preaching could not
    accomplish is accomplish'd, is it not? 100

9

Flow on, river! flow with the flood-tide, and ebb with the ebb-tide!
Frolic on, crested and scallop-edg'd waves!
Gorgeous clouds of the sunset! drench with your splendor me, or the
    men and women generations after me!
Cross from shore to shore, countless crowds of passengers!
Stand up, tall masts of Mannahatta![4] stand up, beautiful hills of
    Brooklyn!   105
Throb, baffled and curious brain! throw out questions and answers!
Suspend here and everywhere, eternal float of solution!
Gaze, loving and thirsting eyes, in the house or street or public assembly!
Sound out, voices of young men! loudly and musically call me by my
    nighest name!
Live, old life! play the part that looks back on the actor or actress!   110
Play the old role, the role that is great or small according as one makes it!
Consider, you who peruse me, whether I may not in unknown ways be
    looking upon you;
Be firm, rail over the river, to support those who lean idly, yet haste with
    the hasting current;
Fly on, sea-birds! fly sideways, or wheel in large circles high in the air;
Receive the summer sky, you water, and faithfully hold it till all downcast
    eyes have time to take it from you!   115
Diverge, fine spokes of light, from the shape of my head, or any one's
    head, in the sunlit water!
Come on, ships from the lower bay! pass up or down, white-sail'd
    schooners, sloops, lighters!
Flaunt away, flags of all nations! be duly lower'd at sunset!
Burn high your fires, foundry chimneys! cast black shadows at nightfall!
    cast red and yellow light over the tops of the houses!
Appearances, now or henceforth, indicate what you are,   120
You necessary film, continue to envelop the soul,
About my body for me, and your body for you, be hung our divinest aromas,
Thrive, cities—bring your freight, bring your shows, ample and sufficient
    rivers,
Expand, being than which none else is perhaps more spiritual,
Keep your places, objects than which none else is more lasting.   125

You have waited, you always wait, you dumb, beautiful ministers,
We receive you with free sense at last, and are insatiate henceforward,
Not you any more shall be able to foil us, or withhold yourselves from us,
We use you, and do not cast you aside—we plant you permanently within
    us,
We fathom you not—we love you—there is perfection in you also,   130
You furnish your parts toward eternity,
Great or small, you furnish your parts toward the soul.

                    1856, 1881

---

4. Variant of Manhattan.

The Wound-Dresser[1]

1

An old man bending I come among new faces,
Years looking backward resuming in answer to children,
Come tell us old man, as from young men and maidens that love me,
(Arous'd and angry, I'd thought to beat the alarum, and urge relentless war,
But soon my fingers fail'd me, my face droop'd and I resign'd myself,   5
To sit by the wounded and soothe them, or silently watch the dead;)
Years hence of these scenes, of these furious passions, these chances,
Of unsurpass'd heroes, (was one side so brave? the other was equally
    brave;)
Now be witness again, paint the mightiest armies of earth,
Of those armies so rapid so wondrous what saw you to tell us?   10
What stays with you latest and deepest? of curious panics,
Of hard-fought engagements or sieges tremendous what deepest remains?

2

O maidens and young men I love and that love me,
What you ask of my days those the strangest and sudden your talking
    recalls,
Soldier alert I arrive after a long march cover'd with sweat and dust,   15
In the nick of time I come, plunge in the fight, loudly shout in the rush
    of successful charge,
Enter the captur'd works[2]—yet lo, like a swift-running river they fade,
Pass and are gone they fade—I dwell not on soldiers' perils or soldiers' joys,
(Both I remember well—many the hardships, few the joys, yet I was
    content.)

But in silence in dreams' projections,   20
While the world of gain and appearance and mirth goes on,
So soon what is over forgotten, and waves wash the imprints off the sand,
With hinged knees returning I enter the doors, (while for you up there,
Whoever you are, follow without noise and be of strong heart.)

Bearing the bandages, water and sponge,   25
Straight and swift to my wounded I go,
Where they lie on the ground after the battle brought in,
Where their priceless blood reddens the grass the ground,
Or to the rows of the hospital tent, or under the roof'd hospital,
To the long rows of cots up and down each side I return,   30
To each and all one after another I draw near, not one do I miss,
An attendant follows holding a tray, he carries a refuse pail,
Soon to be fill'd with clotted rags and blood, emptied, and fill'd again.

I onward go, I stop,
With hinged knees and steady hand to dress wounds,   35

1. From *Drum-Taps*.
2. Fortified earthworks.

I am firm with each, the pangs are sharp yet unavoidable,
One turns to me his appealing eyes—poor boy! I never knew you,
Yet I think I could not refuse this moment to die for you, if that would
   save you.

3

On, on I go, (open doors of time! open hospital doors!)
The crush'd head I dress, (poor crazed hand tear not the bandage away,)   40
The neck of the cavalry-man with the bullet through and through I
   examine,
Hard the breathing rattles, quite glazed already the eye, yet life struggles
   hard,
(Come sweet death! be persuaded O beautiful death!
In mercy come quickly.)

From the stump of the arm, the amputated hand,   45
I undo the clotted lint, remove the slough, wash off the matter and blood,
Back on his pillow the soldier bends with curv'd neck and side-falling head,
His eyes are closed, his face is pale, he dares not look on the bloody stump,
And has not yet look'd on it.

I dress a wound in the side, deep, deep,   50
But a day or two more, for see the frame all wasted and sinking,
And the yellow-blue countenance see.

I dress the perforated shoulder, the foot with the bullet-wound,
Cleanse the one with a gnawing and putrid gangrene, so sickening, so
   offensive,
While the attendant stands behind aside me holding the tray and pail.   55

I am faithful, I do not give out,
The fractur'd thigh, the knee, the wound in the abdomen,
These and more I dress with impassive hand, (yet deep in my breast a fire,
   a burning flame.)

4

Thus in silence in dreams' projections,
Returning, resuming, I thread my way through the hospitals,   60
The hurt and wounded I pacify with soothing hand,
I sit by the restless all the dark night, some are so young,
Some suffer so much, I recall the experience sweet and sad,
(Many a soldier's loving arms about this neck have cross'd and rested,
Many a soldier's kiss dwells on these bearded lips.)   65

1865, 1881

When Lilacs Last in the Dooryard Bloom'd[1]

1

When lilacs last in the dooryard bloom'd,
And the great star[2] early droop'd in the western sky in the night,
I mourn'd, and yet shall mourn with ever-returning spring.

Ever-returning spring, trinity sure to me you bring,
Lilac blooming perennial and drooping star in the west,   5
And thought of him I love.

2

O powerful western fallen star!
O shades of night—O moody, tearful night!
O great star disappear'd—O the black murk that hides the star!
O cruel hands that hold me powerless—O helpless soul of me!   10
O harsh surrounding cloud that will not free my soul.

3

In the dooryard fronting an old farm-house near the white-wash'd palings,
Stands the lilac-bush tall-growing with heart-shaped leaves of rich green,
With many a pointed blossom rising delicate, with the perfume strong I love,
With every leaf a miracle—and from this bush in the dooryard,   15
With delicate-color'd blossoms and heart-shaped leaves of rich green,
A sprig with its flower I break.

4

In the swamp in secluded recesses,
A shy and hidden bird is warbling a song.

Solitary the thrush,   20
The hermit withdrawn to himself, avoiding the settlements,
Sings by himself a song.

Song of the bleeding throat,
Death's outlet song of life, (for well dear brother I know,
If thou wast not granted to sing thou would'st surely die.)   25

5

Over the breast of the spring, the land, amid cities,
Amid lanes and through old woods, where lately the violets peep'd from
     the ground, spotting the gray debris,
Amid the grass in the fields each side of the lanes, passing the endless
     grass,

1. Composed in the months following Lincoln's assassination on April 14, 1865, this elegy was printed in the fall of that year as an appendix to the recently published *Drum-Taps* volume. In the 1881 edition of *Leaves of Grass*, it and three shorter poems were joined to make up the section *Memories of President Lincoln*.
2. Literally Venus, although it becomes associated with Lincoln himself.

Passing the yellow-spear'd wheat, every grain from its shroud in the dark-
    brown fields uprisen,
Passing the apple-tree blows[3] of white and pink in the orchards,   30
Carrying a corpse to where it shall rest in the grave,
Night and day journeys a coffin.[4]

6

Coffin that passes through lanes and streets,
Through day and night with the great cloud darkening the land,
With the pomp of the inloop'd flags with the cities draped in black,   35
With the show of the States themselves as of crape-veil'd women standing,
With processions long and winding and the flambeaus[5] of the night,
With the countless torches lit, with the silent sea of faces and the
    unbared heads,
With the waiting depot, the arriving coffin, and the sombre faces,
With dirges through the night, with the thousand voices rising strong
    and solemn,
                                          40
With all the mournful voices of the dirges pour'd around the coffin,
The dim-lit churches and the shuddering organs—where amid these you
    journey,
With the tolling tolling bells' perpetual clang,
Here, coffin that slowly passes,
I give you my sprig of lilac.   45

7

(Nor for you, for one alone,
Blossoms and branches green to coffins all I bring,
For fresh as the morning, thus would I chant a song for you O sane and
    sacred death.

All over bouquets of roses,
O death, I cover you over with roses and early lilies,   50
But mostly and now the lilac that blooms the first,
Copious I break, I break the sprigs from the bushes,
With loaded arms I come, pouring for you,
For you and the coffins all of you O death.)

8

O western orb sailing the heaven,   55
Now I know what you must have meant as a month since I walk'd,
As I walk'd in silence the transparent shadowy night,
As I saw you had something to tell as you bent to me night after night,
As you droop'd from the sky low down as if to my side, (while the other
    stars all look'd on,)
As we wander'd together the solemn night, (for something I know not
    what kept me from sleep,)   60

---

3. Blossoms.
4. The train carrying Lincoln's body traveled from
Washington, D.C., to Springfield, Illinois.
5. Torches.

As the night advanced, and I saw on the rim of the west how full you
    were of woe,
As I stood on the rising ground in the breeze in the cool transparent
    night,
As I watch'd where you pass'd and was lost in the netherward black of the
    night,
As my soul in its trouble dissatisfied sank, as where you sad orb,
Concluded, dropt in the night, and was gone.   65

9

Sing on there in the swamp,
O singer bashful and tender, I hear your notes, I hear your call,
I hear, I come presently, I understand you,
But a moment I linger, for the lustrous star has detain'd me,
The star my departing comrade holds and detains me.   70

10

O how shall I warble myself for the dead one there I loved?
And how shall I deck my song for the large sweet soul that has gone?
And what shall my perfume be for the grave of him I love?

Sea-winds blown from east and west,
Blown from the Eastern sea and blown from the Western sea, till there
    on the prairies meeting,   75
These and with these and the breath of my chant,
I'll perfume the grave of him I love.

11

O what shall I hang on the chamber walls?
And what shall the pictures be that I hang on the walls,
To adorn the burial-house of him I love?   80

Pictures of growing spring and farms and homes,
With the Fourth-month[6] eve at sundown, and the gray smoke lucid and
    bright,
With floods of the yellow gold of the gorgeous, indolent, sinking sun,
    burning, expanding the air,
With the fresh sweet herbage under foot, and the pale green leaves of the
    trees prolific,
In the distance the flowing glaze, the breast of the river, with a
    wind-dapple here and there,   85
With ranging hills on the banks, with many a line against the sky, and
    shadows,
And the city at hand with dwellings so dense, and stacks of chimneys,

6. April.

And all the scenes of life and the workshops, and the workmen homeward
    returning.

12

Lo, body and soul—this land,
My own Manhattan with spires, and the sparkling and hurrying tides,
    and the ships,   90
The varied and ample land, the South and the North in the light, Ohio's
    shores and flashing Missouri,
And ever the far-spreading prairies cover'd with grass and corn.

Lo, the most excellent sun so calm and haughty,
The violet and purple morn with just-felt breezes,
The gentle soft-born measureless light,   95
The miracle spreading bathing all, the fulfill'd noon,
The coming eve delicious, the welcome night and the stars,
Over my cities shining all, enveloping man and land.

13

Sing on, sing on you gray-brown bird,
Sing from the swamps, the recesses, pour your chant from the bushes,   100
Limitless out of the dusk, out of the cedars and pines.

Sing on dearest brother, warble your reedy song,
Loud human song, with voice of uttermost woe.

O liquid and free and tender!
O wild and loose to my soul!—O wondrous singer!   105
You only I hear—yet the star holds me, (but will soon depart,)
Yet the lilac with mastering odor holds me.

14

Now while I sat in the day and look'd forth,
In the close of the day with its light and the fields of spring, and the
    farmers preparing their crops,
In the large unconscious scenery of my land with its lakes and forests,   110
In the heavenly aerial beauty, (after the perturb'd winds and the storms,)
Under the arching heavens of the afternoon swift passing, and the voices
    of children and women,
The many-moving sea-tides, and I saw the ships how they sail'd,
And the summer approaching with richness, and the fields all busy with
    labor,
And the infinite separate houses, how they all went on, each with its
    meals and minutia of daily usages,   115
And the streets how their throbbings throbb'd, and the cities pent—lo,
    then and there,
Falling upon them all and among them all, enveloping me with the rest,

Appear'd the cloud, appear'd the long black trail,
And I knew death, its thought, and the sacred knowledge of death.

Then with the knowledge of death as walking one side of me,   120
And the thought of death close-walking the other side of me,
And I in the middle as with companions, and as holding the hands of
    companions,
I fled forth to the hiding receiving night that talks not,
Down to the shores of the water, the path by the swamp in the dimness,
To the solemn shadowy cedars and ghostly pines so still.   125

And the singer so shy to the rest receiv'd me,
The gray-brown bird I know receiv'd us comrades three,
And he sang the carol of death, and a verse for him I love.

From deep secluded recesses,
From the fragrant cedars and the ghostly pines so still,   130
Came the carol of the bird.

And the charm of the carol rapt me,
As I held as if by their hands my comrades in the night,
And the voice of my spirit tallied the song of the bird.

Come lovely and soothing death,   135
Undulate round the world, serenely arriving, arriving,
In the day, in the night, to all, to each,
Sooner or later delicate death.

Prais'd be the fathomless universe,
For life and joy, and for objects and knowledge curious,   140
And for love, sweet love—but praise! praise! praise!
For the sure-enwinding arms of cool-enfolding death.

Dark mother always gliding near with soft feet,
Have none chanted for thee a chant of fullest welcome?
Then I chant it for thee, I glorify thee above all,   145
I bring thee a song that when thou must indeed come, come unfalteringly.

Approach strong deliveress,
When it is so, when thou hast taken them I joyously sing the dead,
Lost in the loving floating ocean of thee,
Laved in the flood of thy bliss O death.   150

From me to thee glad serenades,
Dances for thee I propose saluting thee, adornments and feastings for thee,
And the sights of the open landscape and the high-spread sky are fitting,
And life and the fields, and the huge and thoughtful night.

The night in silence under many a star,   155
The ocean shore and the husky whispering wave whose voice I know,
And the soul turning to thee O vast and well-veil'd death,
And the body gratefully nestling close to thee.

Over the tree-tops I float thee a song,
Over the rising and sinking waves, over the myriad fields and the prairies
    wide,   160
Over the dense-pack'd cities all and the teeming wharves and ways,
I float this carol with joy, with joy to thee O death.

15

To the tally of my soul,
Loud and strong kept up the gray-brown bird,
With pure deliberate notes spreading filling the night.   165

Loud in the pines and cedars dim,
Clear in the freshness moist and the swamp-perfume,
And I with my comrades there in the night.

While my sight that was bound in my eyes unclosed,
As to long panoramas of visions.   170

And I saw askant[7] the armies,
I saw as in noiseless dreams hundreds of battle-flags,
Borne through the smoke of the battles and pierc'd with missiles I saw them,
And carried hither and yon through the smoke, and torn and bloody,
And at last but a few shreds left on the staffs, (and all in silence,)   175
And the staffs all splinter'd and broken.

I saw battle-corpses, myriads of them,
And the white skeletons of young men, I saw them,
I saw the debris and debris of all the slain soldiers of the war,
But I saw they were not as was thought,   180
They themselves were fully at rest, they suffer'd not,
The living remain'd and suffer'd, the mother suffer'd,
And the wife and the child and the musing comrade suffer'd,
And the armies that remain'd suffer'd.

16

Passing the visions, passing the night,   185
Passing, unloosing the hold of my comrades' hands,
Passing the song of the hermit bird and the tallying song of my soul,
Victorious song, death's outlet song, yet varying ever-altering song,
As low and wailing, yet clear the notes, rising and falling, flooding the
    night,
Sadly sinking and fainting, as warning and warning, and yet again
    bursting with joy,   190
Covering the earth and filling the spread of the heaven,
As that powerful psalm in the night I heard from recesses,
Passing, I leave thee lilac with heart-shaped leaves,
I leave thee there in the door-yard, blooming, returning with spring.

---

7. Sideways, aslant.

I cease from my song for thee,   195
From my gaze on thee in the west, fronting the west, communing with
    thee,
O comrade lustrous with silver face in the night.

Yet each to keep and all, retrievements out of the night,
The song, the wondrous chant of the gray-brown bird,
And the tallying chant, the echo arous'd in my soul,   200
With the lustrous and drooping star with the countenance full of woe,
With the holders holding my hand nearing the call of the bird,
Comrades mine and I in the midst, and their memory ever to keep, for
    the dead I loved so well,
For the sweetest, wisest soul of all my days and lands—and this for his
    dear sake,
Lilac and star and bird twined with the chant of my soul,   205
There in the fragrant pines and the cedars dusk and dim.

1865–66, 1881

EMILY DICKINSON
1830–1886

Emily Dickinson is recognized as one of the greatest American poets, a poet who continues to exert an enormous influence on the way writers think about the possibilities of poetic craft and vocation. Little known in her own lifetime, she was first publicized in almost mythic terms as a reclusive, eccentric, death-obsessed spinster who wrote in fits and starts as the spirit moved her—the image of the woman poet at her oddest. As with all myths, this one has some truth to it, but the reality is more interesting and complicated. Though she lived in her parents' homes for all but a year of her life, she was acutely aware of current events and drew on them for some of her poetry. Her dazzlingly complex poems—compressed statements abounding in startling imagery and marked by an extraordinary vocabulary— explore a wide range of subjects: psychic pain and joy, the relationship of self to nature, the intensely spiritual, and the intensely ordinary. Her poems about death confront its grim reality with honesty, humor, curiosity, and above all a refusal to be comforted. In her poems about religion, she expressed piety and hostility, and she was fully capable of moving within the same poem from religious consolation to a rejection of doctrinal piety and a querying of God's plans for the universe. Her many love poems seem to have emerged in part from close relationships with at least one woman and several men. It is sometimes possible to extract autobiography from her poems, but she was not a confessional poet; rather, she used personae— first-person speakers—to dramatize the various situations, moods, and perspectives she explored in her lyrics. Though each of her poems is individually short, when collected in one volume her nearly eighteen hundred surviving poems (she probably wrote hundreds more that were lost) have the feel of an epic produced by a person who devoted much of her life to her art.

Emily Elizabeth Dickinson was born on December 10, 1830, in Amherst, Massachusetts, the second child of Emily Norcross Dickinson and Edward Dickinson. Economically, politically, and intellectually, the Dickinsons were among Amherst's most prominent families. Edward Dickinson, a lawyer, served as a state representative and a state senator. He helped found Amherst College as a Calvinist alternative to the more liberal Harvard and Yale, and was its treasurer for thirty-six years. During his term in the U.S. House of Representatives (1853–54), Emily visited him in Washington, D.C., and stayed briefly in Philadelphia on her way home, but travel of any kind was unusual for her. She lived most of her life in the spacious Dickinson family house in Amherst called the Homestead. Among her closest friends and lifelong allies were her brother, Austin, a year and a half older than she, and her younger sister, Lavinia. In 1856, when her brother married Emily's close friend Susan Gilbert, the couple moved into what was called the Evergreens, a house next door to the Homestead, built for the newlyweds by Edward Dickinson. Neither Emily nor Lavinia married. The two women stayed with their parents, as was typical of unmarried middle- and upper-class women of the time. New England in this period had many more women than men in these groups, owing to the exodus of the male population during the California gold rush years (1849 and after) and the carnage of the Civil War. For Dickinson, home was a place of "Infinite power."

Dickinson attended Amherst Academy from 1840 through 1846, and then boarded at the Mount Holyoke Female Seminary—located in South Hadley, some ten miles from Amherst—for less than a year, never completing the three-year course of study. The school, presided over by the devoutly Calvinist Mary Lyon, was especially interested in the students' religious development, and hoped that those needing to support themselves or their families would become missionaries. Students were regularly queried as to whether they "professed faith," had "hope," or were resigned to "no hope"; Dickinson remained adamantly among the small group of "no hopes." Arguably, her assertion of no hope was a matter of defiance, a refusal to capitulate to the demands of orthodoxy. A year after leaving Mount Holyoke, Dickinson, in a letter to a friend, described her failure to convert with darkly comic glee: "*I am one of the lingering bad ones*," she said. But she went on to assert that it was her very "failure" to conform to the conventional expectations of her evangelical culture that helped liberate her to think on her own—to "pause," as she put it, "and ponder, and ponder."

Once back at home, Dickinson embarked on a lifelong course of reading. Her deepest literary debts were to the Bible and classic English authors, such as Shakespeare and Milton. Through the national magazines the family subscribed to and books ordered from Boston, she encountered the full range of the English and American literature of her time, including among Americans Longfellow, Holmes, Lowell, Hawthorne, and Emerson. She read the novels of Charles Dickens as they appeared and knew the poems of Robert Browning and the British poet laureate Tennyson. But the English contemporaries who mattered most to her were the Brontë sisters, George Eliot, and above all, as an example of a successful contemporary woman poet, Elizabeth Barrett Browning.

No one has persuasively traced the precise stages of Dickinson's artistic growth from this supposedly "somber Girl" to the young woman who, within a few years of her return from Mount Holyoke, began writing a new kind of poetry, with its distinctive voice, style, and transformation of traditional form. She found a paradoxical poetic freedom within the confines of the meter of the "fourteener"—seven-beat lines usually broken into stanzas alternating four and three beats—familiar to her from earliest childhood. This is the form of nursery rhymes, ballads, church hymns, and some classic English poetry—strongly rhythmical, easy to memorize and recite.

But Dickinson veered sharply from this form's expectations. If Walt Whitman at this time was heeding Emerson's call for a "metre-making argument" by turning to an open form—as though rules did not exist—Dickinson made use of this and other familiar forms only to break their rules. She used dashes and syntactical fragments to convey her pursuit of a truth that could best be communicated indirectly; these fragments dispensed with prosy verbiage and went directly to the core. Her use of enjambment (the syntactical technique of running past the conventional stopping place of a line or a stanza break) forced her reader to learn where to pause to collect the sense before reading on, often creating dizzying ambiguities. She multiplied aural possibilities by making use of what later critics termed "off" or "slant" rhymes that, as with her metrical and syntactical experimentations, contributed to the expressive power of her poetry. Poetic forms thought to be simple, predictable, and safe were altered irrevocably by Dickinson's language experiments.

Dickinson wrote approximately half of her extant poems during the Civil War. Unsurprisingly, there has been increasing critical interest in Dickinson as a Civil War poet whose work can be read in relation to the Civil War poetry of Melville and Whitman. There are risks to interpreting any Dickinson poem as only referring to particular events in her life or the world beyond her home, but there are also risks in overemphasizing Dickinson's isolation from current events and popular culture. In her poetry, which at times can appear to be hauntingly private, Dickinson regularly responded to her nineteenth-century world, which she engaged through her reading, conversations, and friendships, epistolary and otherwise.

Writing about religion, science, music, nature, books, and contemporary events both national and local, Dickinson often presented her poetic ideas as terse, striking definitions or propositions, or dramatic narrative scenes, in a highly abstracted moment or setting, often at the boundaries between life and death. The result was a poetry that focused on the speaker's response to a situation rather than the details of the situation itself. Her "nature" poems offer precise observations that are often as much about psychological and spiritual matters as about the specifics of nature. The sight of a familiar bird—the robin—in the poem beginning "A Bird, came down the Walk" leads to a statement about nature's strangeness rather than the expected statement about friendly animals. Whitman generally seems intoxicated by his ability to appropriate nature for his own purposes; Dickinson's nature is much more resistant to human schemes, and the poet's experiences of nature range from a sense of its hostility to an ability to become an "Inebriate of Air" and "Debauchee of Dew." Openly expressive of sexual and romantic longings, her personae reject conventional gender roles. In one of her most famous poems, for instance, she imagines herself as a "Loaded Gun" with "the power to kill."

Dickinson's private letters, in particular three drafts of letters to an unidentified "Master," and dozens of love poems have convinced biographers that she fell in love a number of times; candidates include Benjamin Newton, a law clerk in her father's office; one or more married men; and Susan Gilbert Dickinson, the friend who became her sister-in-law. The exact nature of any of these relationships is hard to determine, in part because Dickinson's letters and poems could just as easily be taken as poetic meditations on desire as writings directed to specific people. On the evidence of the approximately five hundred letters that Dickinson wrote to Susan, many of which contained drafts or copies of her latest poems, that relationship melded love, friendship, intellectual exchange, and art. One of the men she was involved with was Samuel Bowles, editor of the *Springfield Republican*, whom Dickinson described (in a letter to Bowles himself) as having "the most triumphant face out of paradise"; another was the Reverend Charles Wadsworth, whom she met in Philadelphia in 1855 and who visited her in Amherst in 1860. Evidence suggests that she was upset by his decision to move to San Francisco in 1862, but none of her letters to Wadsworth survive.

Knowing her powers as a poet, Dickinson wanted to be published, but only around a dozen poems appeared during her lifetime. She sent many poems to Bowles, perhaps hoping he would publish them in the *Republican*. Although he did publish a few, he also edited them into more conventional shape. She also sent poems to editor Josiah Holland at *Scribner's*, who chose not to publish her. She sent four poems to Thomas Wentworth Higginson, a contributing editor at the *Atlantic Monthly*, after he printed "Letter to a Young Contributor" in the April 1862 issue. Her cover letter of April 15, 1862, asked him, "Are you too deeply occupied to say if my Verse is alive?" Higginson, like other editors, saw her formal innovations as imperfections. But he remained intrigued by Dickinson and in 1869 invited her to visit him in Boston. When she refused, he visited her in 1870. He would eventually become one of the editors of her posthumously published poetry.

But if Dickinson sought publication, she also regarded it as "the Auction / Of the Mind of Man," as she put it in poem 788; at the very least, she was unwilling to submit to the changes, which she called "surgery," imposed on her poems by editors. Some critics have argued that Dickinson's letters constituted a form of publication, for Dickinson included poems in many of her letters. Even more intriguing, beginning around 1858 Dickinson began to record her poems on white, unlined paper, in some cases marking moments of textual revision, and then folded and stacked the sheets and sewed groups of them together in what are called fascicles. She created thirty such fascicles, ranging in length from sixteen to twenty-four pages; and there is evidence that she worked at the groupings, thinking about chronology, subject matter, and specific thematic orderings within each. These fascicles were left for others to discover after her death, neatly stacked in a drawer. It can be speculated that Dickinson, realizing that her unconventional poetry would not be published in her own lifetime as written, became a sort of self-publisher. Critics remain uncertain, however, about just how self-conscious her arrangements were and argue over what is lost and gained by considering individual poems in the context of their fascicle placement. There is also debate about whether the posthumous publication of Dickinson's manuscript poetry violates the visual look of the poems—their inconsistent dashes and even some of the designs that Dickinson added to particular poems. The selections printed here include a photographic reproduction of poem 269, which can be compared to the now-standard printed version, also included here.

Dickinson's final decades were marked by health problems and a succession of losses. Beginning in the early 1860s she suffered from eye pain. She consulted with an ophthalmologist in Boston in 1864 and remained concerned about losing her vision. In 1874 her father died in a Boston hotel room after taking an injection of morphine for his pain, and one year later her mother had a stroke and would remain bedridden until her death in 1882. Her beloved eight-year-old nephew, Gilbert, died of typhoid fever in 1883, next door at the Evergreens; and in 1885, her close friend from childhood, Helen Hunt Jackson, who had asked to be Dickinson's literary executor, died suddenly in San Francisco. Dickinson's seclusion late in life may have been a response to her grief at these losses or a concern for her own health, but ultimately a focus on the supposed eccentricity of her desire for privacy draws attention away from the huge number of poems she wrote—she may well have secluded herself so that she could follow her vocation. She died on May 15, 1886, perhaps from a kidney disorder called "Bright's Disease," the official diagnosis, but just as likely from hypertension.

In 1881 the astronomer David Todd, with his young wife, Mabel Loomis Todd, arrived in Amherst to direct the Amherst College Observatory. The next year, Austin Dickinson and Mabel Todd began an affair that lasted until Austin's death in 1895. Despite this turn of events, Mabel Todd and Emily Dickinson established a friendship without actually meeting (Todd saw Dickinson once, in her coffin), and Todd decided that the poet was "in many respects a genius." Soon after Dickinson's death,

Mabel Todd (at Emily's sister Lavinia's invitation) painstakingly transcribed many of her poems. The subsequent preservation and publication of her poetry and letters was initiated and carried forth by Todd. She persuaded Higginson to help her see a posthumous collection of poems into print in 1890 and a second volume of poems in 1891; she went on to publish a collection of Dickinson's letters in 1894 and a third volume of poems in 1896. Though Dickinson's poetry perplexed some critics, it impressed many others; the three volumes were popular, going through more than ten printings and selling over ten thousand copies. To make Dickinson's violation of the laws of meter more palatable, Todd and Higginson edited some of the poems heavily. During the 1890s, Susan Dickinson and her daughter, Martha Dickinson Bianchi, also published a few of Dickinson's poems in journals such as the *Century*.

By 1900 or so, Dickinson's work had fallen out of favor, and had Martha Dickinson Bianchi not resumed publication of her aunt's poetry in 1914 (she published eight volumes of Dickinson's work between 1914 and 1937), Dickinson's writings might never have achieved the audience they have today. Taken together, the editorial labors of Todd, Higginson, Susan Dickinson, and Bianchi set in motion the critical and textual work that would help establish Dickinson as one of the great American poets. They also made her poetry available to the American modernists, poets such as Hart Crane and Marianne Moore; Dickinson and Whitman are the nineteenth-century poets who exerted the greatest influence on American poetry to come.

The texts of the poems, and the numbering, are from R. W. Franklin's one-volume edition, *The Poems of Emily Dickinson: Reading Edition* (1999), which draws on his three-volume variorum, *The Poems of Emily Dickinson* (1998). The dating of Dickinson's poetry remains uncertain. The date following each poem corresponds to Franklin's estimate of Dickinson's first finished draft; if the poem was published in Dickinson's lifetime, that date is supplied as well.

122[1]

These are the days when Birds come back -
A very few - a Bird or two -
To take a backward look.

These are the days when skies resume
The old - old sophistries[2] of June -   5
A blue and gold mistake.

Oh fraud that cannot cheat the Bee.
Almost thy plausibility
Induces my belief,

Till ranks of seeds their witness bear -   10
And softly thro' the altered air
Hurries a timid leaf.

Oh sacrament of summer days,
Oh Last Communion[3] in the Haze -
Permit a child to join -   15

1. Dickinson published a version of this poem in the *Drum Beat*, March 11, 1864.
2. Deceptively subtle reasonings.

3. The end of summer is compared to the death of Christ commemorated by the Christian sacrament of Communion.

Thy sacred emblems to partake -
Thy consecrated bread to take
And thine immortal wine!

1859, 1864

202

"Faith" is a fine invention
For Gentlemen who *see*!
But Microscopes are prudent
In an Emergency!

1861

207

I taste a liquor never brewed -
From Tankards scooped in Pearl -
Not all the Frankfort Berries
Yield such an Alcohol!

Inebriate of air - am I -   5
And Debauchee of Dew -
Reeling - thro' endless summer days -
From inns of molten Blue -

When "Landlords" turn the drunken Bee
Out of the Foxglove's door -   10
When Butterflies - renounce their "drams" -
I shall but drink the more!

Till Seraphs[1] swing their snowy Hats -
And Saints - to windows run -
To see the little Tippler   15
Leaning against the - Sun!

1861

236

Some keep the Sabbath going to Church -
I keep it, staying at Home -
With a Bobolink for a Chorister -
And an Orchard, for a Dome -

1. Angels.

Some keep the Sabbath in Surplice[1]
I, just wear my Wings -
And instead of tolling the Bell, for Church,
Our little Sexton[2] - sings.   5

God preaches, a noted Clergyman -
And the sermon is never long,   10
So instead of getting to Heaven, at last -
I'm going, all along.

                                                        1861

260

I'm Nobody! Who are you?
Are you - Nobody - too?
Then there's a pair of us!
Dont tell! they'd advertise - you know!

How dreary - to be - Somebody!   5
How public - like a Frog -
To tell one's name - the livelong June -
To an admiring Bog!

                                                        1861

269[1]

Wild nights - Wild nights!
Were I with thee
Wild nights should be
Our luxury!

Futile - the winds -   5
To a Heart in port -
Done with the Compass -
Done with the Chart!

Rowing in Eden -
Ah - the Sea!   10
Might I but moor - tonight -
In thee!

                                                        1861

1. Open-sleeved ceremonial robe worn by
clergymen.
2. Church custodian.

1. See the opposite page for a reproduction of the
manuscript of this poem.

Poem 269 of Fascicle 11, from vol. 1 of *The Manuscript Books of Emily Dickinson* (1981), ed. R. W. Franklin, reproduced with the permission of Harvard University Press. Dickinson's handwriting, which changed over the years, can be dated by comparison with her letters.

320

There's a certain Slant of light,
Winter Afternoons -
That oppresses, like the Heft
Of Cathedral Tunes -

Heavenly Hurt, it gives us -   5
We can find no scar,
But internal difference -
Where the Meanings, are -

None may teach it - Any -
'Tis the Seal Despair -   10
An imperial affliction
Sent us of the Air -

When it comes, the Landscape listens -
Shadows - hold their breath -
When it goes, 'tis like the Distance   15
On the look of Death -

1862

339

I like a look of Agony,
Because I know it's true -
Men do not sham Convulsion,
Nor simulate, a Throe -

The eyes glaze once - and that is Death -   5
Impossible to feign
The Beads opon the Forehead
By homely Anguish strung.

1862

340

I felt a Funeral, in my Brain,
And Mourners to and fro
Kept treading - treading - till it seemed
That Sense was breaking through -

And when they all were seated,   5
A Service, like a Drum -
Kept beating - beating - till I thought
My mind was going numb -

And then I heard them lift a Box
And creak across my Soul   10
With those same Boots of Lead, again,
Then Space - began to toll,

As all the Heavens were a Bell,
And Being, but an Ear,
And I, and Silence, some strange Race   15
Wrecked, solitary, here -

And then a Plank in Reason, broke,
And I dropped down, and down -
And hit a World, at every plunge,
And Finished knowing - then -   20

1862

353

I'm ceded - I've stopped being Their's -
The name They dropped opon[1] my face
With water, in the country church
Is finished using, now,
And They can put it with my Dolls,   5
My childhood, and the string of spools,
I've finished threading - too -

Baptized, before, without the choice,
But this time, consciously, Of Grace -
Unto supremest name -   10
Called to my Full - The Crescent dropped -
Existence's whole Arc, filled up,
With one - small Diadem -

My second Rank - too small the first -
Crowned - Crowing - on my Father's breast -   15
A half unconscious Queen -
But this time - Adequate - Erect,
With Will to choose,
Or to reject,
And I choose, just a Crown -   20

1862

1. Upon.

359

A Bird, came down the Walk -
He did not know I saw -
He bit an Angle Worm in halves
And ate the fellow, raw,

And then, he drank a Dew   5
From a convenient Grass -
And then hopped sidewise to the Wall
To let a Beetle pass -

He glanced with rapid eyes,
That hurried all abroad -   10
They looked like frightened Beads, I thought,
He stirred his Velvet Head. -

Like one in danger, Cautious,
I offered him a Crumb,
And he unrolled his feathers,   15
And rowed him softer Home -

Than Oars divide the Ocean,
Too silver for a seam,
Or Butterflies, off Banks of Noon,
Leap, plashless[1] as they swim.   20

1862

365

I know that He exists.
Somewhere - in silence -
He has hid his rare life
From our gross eyes.

'Tis an instant's play-   5
'Tis a fond Ambush -
Just to make Bliss
Earn her own surprise!

But - should the play
Prove piercing earnest -   10
Should the glee - glaze -
In Death's - stiff - stare -

1. Splashless.

Would not the fun
Look too expensive!
Would not the jest -   15
Have crawled too far!

1862

409

The Soul selects her own Society -
Then - shuts the Door -
To her divine Majority -
Present no more -

Unmoved - she notes the Chariots - pausing -   5
At her low Gate -
Unmoved - an Emperor be kneeling
Opon her Mat -

I've known her - from an ample nation -
Choose One -   10
Then - close the Valves of her attention -
Like Stone -

1862

411

Mine - by the Right of the White Election!
Mine - by the Royal Seal!
Mine - by the sign in the Scarlet prison -
Bars - cannot conceal!

Mine - here - in Vision - and in Veto!   5
Mine - by the Grave's Repeal -
Titled - Confirmed -
Delirious Charter!
Mine - long as Ages steal!

1862

446

This was a Poet -
It is That
Distills amazing sense
From Ordinary Meanings -
And Attar[1] so immense   5

From the familiar species
That perished by the Door -
We wonder it was not Ourselves
Arrested it - before -

Of Pictures, the Discloser -   10
The Poet - it is He -
Entitles Us - by Contrast -
To ceaseless Poverty -

Of Portion - so unconscious -
The Robbing - could not harm -   15
Himself - to Him - a Fortune -
Exterior - to Time -

                                                    1862

479

Because I could not stop for Death -
He kindly stopped for me -
The Carriage held but just Ourselves -
And Immortality.

We slowly drove - He knew no haste   5
And I had put away
My labor and my leisure too,
For His Civility -

We passed the School, where Children strove
At Recess - in the Ring -   10
We passed the Fields of Gazing Grain -
We passed the Setting Sun -

Or rather - He passed Us -
The Dews drew quivering and Chill -
For only Gossamer,[1] my Gown -   15
My Tippet - only Tulle[2] -

---

1. Fragrance.
1. Delicate, light fabric.

2. Thin silk. "Tippet": scarf for covering neck and shoulders.

We paused before a House that seemed
A Swelling of the Ground -
The Roof was scarcely visible -
The Cornice[3] - in the Ground -   20

Since then - 'tis Centuries - and yet
Feels shorter than the Day
I first surmised the Horses' Heads
Were toward Eternity -

1862

518

When I was small, a Woman died -
Today - her Only Boy
Went up from the Potomac[1]-
His face all Victory

To look at her - How slowly   5
The Seasons must have turned
Till Bullets clipt an Angle
And He passed quickly round -

If pride shall be in Paradise -
Ourself cannot decide -   10
Of their imperial conduct -
No person testified -

But, proud in Apparition -
That Woman and her Boy
Pass back and forth, before my Brain   15
As even in the sky -

I'm confident, that Bravoes -
Perpetual break abroad
For Braveries, remote as this
In Yonder Maryland[2] -   20

1863

3. Decorative molding beneath a roof.
1. River along the mid-Atlantic coast, flowing from Maryland, through Washington, D.C., and into the Virginias.
2. This reference may have been intended to evoke a specific battle, such as the battle of Antietam near Sharpsburg, Maryland, where over twenty thousand soldiers were killed and injured on a single day (September 17, 1862). Despite the reference to Maryland, some critics believe the poem was inspired by the death of Frazar Stearns (1840–1862), the son of Amherst College's president, who died in March 1862 at the battle of New Bern in North Carolina. Dickinson lamented the death in a letter to her cousins Louise and Frances Norcross, referring to "brave Frazar."

519

This is my letter to the World
That never wrote to Me -
The simple News that Nature told -
With tender Majesty

Her Message is committed   5
To Hands I cannot see -
For love of Her - Sweet - countrymen -
Judge tenderly - of Me

1863

591

I heard a Fly buzz - when I died -
The Stillness in the Room
Was like the Stillness in the Air -
Between the Heaves of Storm -

The Eyes around - had wrung them dry -   5
And Breaths were gathering firm
For that last Onset - when the King
Be witnessed - in the Room -

I willed my Keepsakes - Signed away
What portion of me be   10
Assignable - and then it was
There interposed a Fly -

With Blue - uncertain - stumbling Buzz -
Between the light - and me -
And then the Windows failed - and then   15
I could not see to see -

1863

620

Much Madness is divinest Sense -
To a discerning Eye -
Much Sense - the starkest Madness -
'Tis the Majority
In this, as all, prevail -   5
Assent - and you are sane -
Demur - you're straightway dangerous -
And handled with a Chain -

1863

656

I started Early - Took my Dog -
And visited the Sea -
The Mermaids in the Basement
Came out to look at me -

And Frigates - in the Upper Floor   5
Extended Hempen Hands -
Presuming Me to be a Mouse -
Aground - opon the Sands -

But no Man moved Me - till the Tide
Went past my simple Shoe -   10
And past my Apron - and my Belt
And past my Boddice - too -

And made as He would eat me up -
As wholly as a Dew
Opon a Dandelion's Sleeve -   15
And then - I started - too -

And He - He followed - close behind -
I felt His Silver Heel
Opon my Ancle[1] - Then My Shoes
Would overflow with Pearl -   20

Until We met the Solid Town -
No One He seemed to know -
And bowing - with a Mighty look -
At me - The Sea withdrew -

1863

706

I cannot live with You -
It would be Life -
And Life is over there -
Behind the Shelf

The Sexton keeps the key to -   5
Putting up
Our Life - His Porcelain -
Like a Cup -

Discarded of the Housewife -
Quaint - or Broke -   10

---

1. Upon my ankle.

A newer Sevres[1] pleases -
Old Ones crack -

I could not die - with You -
For One must wait
To shut the Other's Gaze down -   15
You - could not -

And I - Could I stand by
And see You - freeze -
Without my Right of Frost -
Death's privilege?   20

Nor could I rise - with You -
Because Your Face
Would put out Jesus' -
That New Grace

Glow plain - and foreign   25
On my homesick eye -
Except that You than He
Shone closer by -

They'd judge Us - How -
For You - served Heaven - You know,   30
Or sought to -
I could not -

Because You saturated sight -
And I had no more eyes
For sordid excellence   35
As Paradise

And were You lost, I would be -
Though my name
Rang loudest
On the Heavenly fame -   40

And were You - saved -
And I - condemned to be
Where You were not
That self - were Hell to me -

So we must meet apart -   45
You there - I - here -
With just the Door ajar
That Oceans are - and Prayer -
And that White Sustenance -
Despair -   50

1863

---

1. Porcelain china (French), usually elaborately decorated.

788

Publication - is the Auction
Of the Mind of Man -
Poverty - be justifying
For so foul a thing

Possibly - but We - would rather   5
From Our Garret go
White - unto the White Creator -
Than invest - Our Snow -

Thought belong to Him who gave it -
Then - to Him Who bear   10
It's Corporeal illustration - sell
The Royal Air -

In the Parcel - Be the Merchant
Of the Heavenly Grace -
But reduce no Human Spirit
To Disgrace of Price -

1863

1096[1]

A narrow Fellow in the Grass
Occasionally rides -
You may have met him? Did you not
His notice instant is -

The Grass divides as with a Comb -   5
A spotted Shaft is seen,
And then it closes at your Feet
And opens further on -

He likes a Boggy Acre -
A Floor too cool for Corn -   10
But when a Boy and Barefoot
I more than once at Noon

Have passed I thought a Whip Lash
Unbraiding in the Sun
When stooping to secure it   15
It wrinkled And was gone -

Several of Nature's People
I know and they know me

1. Dickinson published a version of this poem in the *Springfield Daily Republican*, February 14, 1866.

I feel for them a transport
Of Cordiality   20

But never met this Fellow
Attended or alone
Without a tighter Breathing
And Zero at the Bone.

                                                      1865, 1866

1263

Tell all the truth but tell it slant -
Success in Circuit lies
Too bright for our infirm Delight
The Truth's superb surprise
As Lightning to the Children eased   5
With explanation kind
The Truth must dazzle gradually
Or every man be blind -

                                                            1872

1577

The Bible is an antique Volume -
Written by faded Men
At the suggestion of Holy Spectres -
Subjects - Bethlehem -
Eden - the ancient Homestead -   5
Satan - the Brigadier -
Judas - the Great Defaulter -
David - the Troubadour -
Sin - a distinguished Precipice
Others must resist -   10
Boys that "believe" are very lonesome -
Other Boys are "lost" -
Had but the Tale a warbling Teller -
All the Boys would come -
Orpheus' Sermon[1] captivated -   15
It did not condemn -

                                                            1882

---

1. In Greek mythology, Orpheus played music that would transfix wild beasts and still rivers.

MARK TWAIN (SAMUEL L. CLEMENS)
1835–1910

Samuel Langhorne Clemens, the third of five children, was born on November 30, 1835, in the village of Florida, Missouri, and grew up in the somewhat larger Mississippi River town of Hannibal, Missouri—a place that he reimagined in his writing as St. Petersburg, the most famous boyscape in American literature. Twain's father, a justice of the peace who had unsuccessfully tried to become a storekeeper, died when Twain was twelve, and from that time on Twain worked to support himself and the rest of the family. He was apprenticed to a printer, and in 1851, when his brother Orion became a publisher in Hannibal, Twain went to work for him. But Twain soon escaped from his brother's print shop, as he was being paid virtually nothing for his work, often running the entire operation by himself. In 1853 he began three years of travel, stopping in St. Louis, New York, Philadelphia, Keokuk (Iowa), and Cincinnati, in each place working as an itinerant journeyman printer. In 1856 he left Cincinnati for New Orleans by steamboat, intending to go to the Amazon. He changed his plans, however, and instead apprenticed himself to Horace Bixby, a Mississippi riverboat pilot. After training for eighteen months, virtually committing the river to memory, Twain became a pilot himself. He practiced this lucrative and prestigious trade until 1861, when the Civil War virtually ended commercial river traffic.

Slavery was legal in Missouri, though the state did not join the Confederacy, and Twain may have seen brief service in a woefully unorganized Confederate militia, an experience that he later fictionalized in "The Private History of a Campaign That Failed" (1885). In 1861, as the Mississippi was being closed by Union blockades, Twain went west with his brother Orion, who had been appointed secretary of the Nevada territorial government. This move started him on the path toward his life as a humorist, lecturer, journalist, and author. In the West, Twain began writing for newspapers, first the *Territorial Enterprise* in Virginia City and then, after 1864, the *Californian* in San Francisco. The fashion of the time called for a pen name, and so from a columnist for the New Orleans *Times-Picayune*, he borrowed "Mark Twain," riverboat jargon for "two fathoms deep," or "safe water." His early writing was modeled on the humorous journalism of the day, especially that practiced by his friend and roommate in Nevada, who wrote under the pen name Dan De Quille. Also important to his development during these years were friendships with the western writer Bret Harte, the famous professional lecturer and comic Artemus Ward, and the obscure amateur raconteur Jim Gillis. Harte was particularly important to launching Twain's career. He was Twain's editor at the *Californian*, and was considered the leading writer of the city. The fastidious Harte and the slovenly Twain made an unlikely pair, but they became friends. During this time, Twain made his reputation as a lecturer and landed his first major success as a writer by skillfully retelling a well-known tall tale, "The Notorious Jumping Frog of Calaveras County," first published in 1865. Widely reprinted across the United States, the sketch did more than introduce Twain to a national audience; it inaugurated a new chapter in the literature of the American West.

In this same year Twain signed with the *Sacramento Union* to write a series of letters covering the newly opened steamboat passenger service between San Francisco and Honolulu. In these letters he used a fictitious character, Mr. Brown, to present inelegant ideas and unorthodox views, attitudes, and information, often in impolite language. This device allowed him to say just about anything he wanted, provided he could convincingly claim he was simply reporting what others said and did. As he refined it, this deadpan technique became a staple of his lectures. Twain's first book of this period, and still one of his most popular, was *Innocents Abroad* (1869), consisting, in revised form, of the letters he wrote for the *Alta California* and *New York Tribune* during his 1867 excursion on the *Quaker City* to the Mediterranean and Holy Land. With his fare paid for by the *Alta California*, Twain, through letters to that San Francisco newspaper, provided a running account of the first great modern American tourist raid on the Old World. Twain wrote hilarious satires of his fellow passengers as well as the pretentious, decadent, and undemocratic Old World as viewed by a citizen of a young country on the rise. A characteristically impertinent note was sounded in a remark he made upon disembarking in New York: When Twain was asked for his impressions of the Holy Land, he said he knew for a fact there would be no Second Coming, for if Jesus had been there once he certainly wouldn't go back. Such scoffing drew angry editorials and speeches, publicity that helped make *Innocents Abroad* even more successful.

In *Roughing It* (1872), Twain returned to the West; he fictionally elaborated the Clemens brothers' stagecoach adventures on the way to Carson City and recounted his unsuccessful schemes for making money (including mining the Comstock lode in Virginia City) once he got there. Throughout *Roughing It*, which also covers his stint in San Francisco as a reporter and his half-hearted gold mining in the Sierra Nevada mountains, Twain debunked the idea of the West as a place where fortunes could be easily made and showed its disappointing and even brutal side. In this respect, Twain joined the group of writers who were trying to tell Eastern readers what the West was really like, while exalting in the freedom and outright craziness of western startup towns and encampments, operating far from Eastern laws, orthodoxies, and even common sense.

Twain's publishers sold *Innocents Abroad*, *Roughing It*, and most of his other books mainly by subscription, with door-to-door salespeople offering sometimes gaudy, always lavishly illustrated volumes of his books as diversion and entertainment. Though the trade was regarded as low, and though many books sold by subscription were not reviewed by the established literary and general interest magazines of the time, subscription houses accounted for nearly two-thirds of American bookselling in the 1870s. Twain's shrewd understanding of the dynamics of the publishing industry, including the importance of lining up first-rate illustrators, helped to establish him as a popular author during this time.

Twain's many travels, including later lecture tours around the globe, did not obscure the rich material of his Missouri boyhood, which ran deep in his memory and imagination. He tentatively probed this material as early as 1870 in an early version of *The Adventures of Tom Sawyer* called *A Boy's Manuscript*. In 1875 he wrote *Old Times on the Mississippi* in seven installments for the *Atlantic Monthly*—edited by his friend William Dean Howells, who tirelessly promoted Twain's career. The sometimes idyllic, sometimes dangerous river towns of the antebellum border states proved to be the creative landscape that would make Twain famous. He would later incorporate his magazine writing on this region into *Life on the Mississippi* (1883), completed after Twain took a monthlong steamboat trip on the Mississippi, stopping along the way to visit Hannibal. The resulting book—part history, part memoir, part travelogue—offers, among other things, a critique of the southern romanticism Twain believed had made the Civil War inevitable, a theme that would reappear in his masterpiece, *Adventures of Huckleberry Finn* (1884).

Twain had married Olivia Langdon, daughter of a wealthy coal dealer from Buffalo, New York, in 1870. This entry into a higher stratum of society than he had previously known, along with his increasing fascination with wealth, created a constant struggle in his work between the conventional and the disruptive—a tension that fuels much of his best humor. In the perennially popular *The Adventures of Tom Saw-*

yer (1876), the struggle emerges in the contrast between the entrepreneurial but entirely respectable Tom and his disreputable friend Huck. In this narrative, Twain also mingles childhood pleasures with childhood fears of the violence, terror, and death lurking at the edges of the village. This book has long been recognized as an adult classic as well as a children's book, and its publication further consolidated Twain's status as a writer of popular fiction.

Twain began *Adventures of Huckleberry Finn* in 1876 as a sequel to *Tom Sawyer*, but he put the manuscript aside for several years and finished it in 1884, when his thinking about Huck and his story had changed and matured considerably. In recent years the racial (and racist) implications of *Huck Finn* have been the subjects of critical debate, as have questions about the racial beliefs of the author. (For more on the critical controversy, see the selections in "Race and the Ending of *Adventures of Huckleberry Finn*" immediately following the novel.) Similar questions have been raised about gender and sexuality in Twain's life and work. In Twain's own day *Huck Finn* was banned in many libraries and schools around the country and denounced in pulpits—not for its racial content but for its supposedly encouraging boys to swear, smoke, and run away. Nevertheless, *Huck Finn* has enjoyed extraordinary popularity since its publication. It broke literary ground as a novel written in the vernacular and established the vernacular's capacity to yield high art. Its unpretentious, colloquial, yet poetic style, its wide-ranging humor, its embodiment of the enduring and widely shared dream of innocence and freedom, and its recording of a vanished way of life in the pre–Civil War Mississippi Valley have made the book popular from the moment of its publication: *Huck Finn* sold 51,000 copies in its first fourteen months, compared to *Tom Sawyer*'s 25,000 in the same period. Ernest Hemingway once called it the source of "all modern American literature."

Twain's next novel was also successful, but *A Connecticut Yankee in King Arthur's Court* (1889) is marked by an even sharper satiric bite. The novel describes sixth-century Arthurian England as seen through the eyes of a crafty "Yankee," Hank Morgan, who is transported back thirteen centuries and tries to "introduce," in Twain's words, the "great and beneficent civilization of the nineteenth century" into the chivalric and decidedly undemocratic world of Camelot. But Hank's "Gilded Age" schemes end in their own destruction and the massacre of thousands of knights. *The Tragedy of Pudd'nhead Wilson* (1894) similarly offers a dark and troubling view of nineteenth-century American values. Set in a Mississippi River town of the 1830s, the novel follows the tragic consequences of switching two babies at birth—one free, one slave, and both children of the same white, slave-owning father. The novel provides an intense, sometimes chaotic meditation on the absurdities of defining individuals in relation to race; on the impact on personality and fate of labels like "white" and "black"; and on biological, legal, and social descriptions of human identity.

In the time following the completion of *Pudd'nhead Wilson*, Twain experienced a series of calamities. His spectacularly poor judgment as an investor—combined with the panic of 1893—led to his bankruptcy. His health turned bad; his youngest daughter, Jean, was diagnosed as epileptic; his oldest daughter, Susy, died of meningitis while he was away; and his wife, Livy, began to decline into permanent invalidism. For several years writing was both agonized labor and necessary therapy. The results of these circumstances were a travel book, *Following the Equator* (1897), which records the round-the-world lecture tour that Twain undertook to pay off debts; a sardonically brilliant short story that interrogates middle-class American morality, "The Man That Corrupted Hadleyburg" (1900); an embittered treatise on humanity's foibles, follies, and venality, *What Is Man?* (1906); and the bleakly despairing novel *The Mysterious Stranger*, first published in an inaccurate and unauthorized version by Albert Bigelow Paine, Twain's first biographer, in 1916. Scholars continue to study the large bulk of Twain's unfinished or (until recently) unpublished writings and have called for reevaluation of his work from the decade after 1895. His late writings, most of which Twain declined to see published while he lived, reveal a darkening worldview and an upwelling of anger against orthodoxies of every sort, including organized religious belief and international capitalism and colonialism.

In his later years, Twain, by now an international celebrity, found himself consulted by the press on every subject of general interest. He became an outspoken opponent of U.S. and European imperialism, a stance he shared with Howells. Though Twain's views on political, military, and social subjects were often acerbic, it was only to his best friends that he confessed the depth of his disillusionment. Much of this bitterness informs such published works as "To a Person Sitting in Darkness" (1901), "The United States of Lyncherdom" (1901), and "King Leopold's Soliloquy" (1905), as well as other writings unpublished in his lifetime, such as "The War Prayer," an acid commentary on the practice of praying for military victory.

In 1906, Twain embarked on a scheme to dictate his autobiography. He would allow himself to wander freely through his reminiscences—often speaking from bed—to produce a kind of "diary and history combined." An important part of Twain's project was that the full product would not be available until 100 years after his death, so that he could speak freely of his subjects without fear of hurting their feelings or reputation. Though he published excerpts while still alive, he stuck to this broader plan. The first volume of *The Autobiography of Mark Twain* appeared in 2010 and immediately became a bestseller. Twain's appeal endures because of his deep understanding of the culture that produced him; he remains America's most celebrated humorist and its most caustic critic. As his friend Howells observed, Twain was unlike any of his contemporaries in American letters: "Emerson, Longfellow, Lowell, Holmes—I knew them all and all the rest of our sages, poets, seers, critics, humorists; they were like one another and like other literary men; but Clemens was sole, incomparable, the Lincoln of our literature."

The Notorious Jumping Frog of Calaveras County[1]

In compliance with the request of a friend of mine, who wrote me from the East, I called on good-natured, garrulous old Simon Wheeler, and inquired after my friend's friend, Leonidas W. Smiley, as requested to do, and I hereunto append the result. I have a lurking suspicion that *Leonidas W.* Smiley is a myth; that my friend never knew such a personage; and that he only conjectured that if I asked old Wheeler about him, it would remind him of his infamous *Jim* Smiley, and he would go to work and bore me to death with some exasperating reminiscence of him as long and as tedious as it should be useless to me. If that was the design, it succeeded.

I found Simon Wheeler dozing comfortably by the barroom stove of the dilapidated tavern in the decayed mining camp of Angel's, and I noticed that he was fat and bald-headed, and had an expression of winning gentleness and simplicity upon his tranquil countenance. He roused up, and gave me good-day. I told him a friend of mine had commissioned me to make some inquiries about a cherished companion of his boyhood named *Leonidas W.* Smiley—*Rev. Leonidas W.* Smiley, a young minister of the Gospel, who he had heard was at one time a resident of Angel's Camp. I added that if Mr. Wheeler could tell me anything about this Rev. Leonidas W. Smiley, I would feel under many obligations to him.

1. The story first appeared in the *New York Saturday Press* of November 18, 1865, and was subsequently revised several times. The source of the text is the version published in *Mark Twain's* *Sketches, New and Old* (1875). In a note, Twain instructs his readers that "Calaveras" is pronounced *Cal-e-VA-ras.*

Simon Wheeler backed me into a corner and blockaded me there with his chair, and then sat down and reeled off the monotonous narrative which follows this paragraph. He never smiled, he never frowned, he never changed his voice from the gentle-flowing key to which he tuned his initial sentence, he never betrayed the slightest suspicion of enthusiasm; but all through the interminable narrative there ran a vein of impressive earnestness and sincerity, which showed me plainly that, so far from his imagining that there was anything ridiculous or funny about his story, he regarded it as a really important matter, and admired its two heroes as men of transcendent genius in *finesse*. I let him go on in his own way, and never interrupted him once.

Rev. Leonidas W. H'm, Reverend Le—well, there was a feller here once by the name of *Jim* Smiley, in the winter of '49—or may be it was the spring of '50—I don't recollect exactly, somehow, though what makes me think it was one or the other is because I remember the big flume[2] warn't finished when he first come to the camp; but any way, he was the curiosest man about always betting on anything that turned up you ever see, if he could get anybody to bet on the other side; and if he couldn't he'd change sides. Any way that suited the other man would suit *him*—any way just so's he got a bet, *he* was satisfied. But still he was lucky, uncommon lucky; he most always come out winner. He was always ready and laying for a chance; there couldn't be no solit'ry thing mentioned but that feller'd offer to bet on it, and take ary side you please, as I was just telling you. If there was a horse-race, you'd find him flush or you'd find him busted at the end of it; if there was a dog-fight, he'd bet on it; if there was a cat-fight, he'd bet on it; if there was a chicken-fight, he'd bet on it; why, if there was two birds setting on a fence, he would bet you which one would fly first; or if there was a camp-meeting, he would be there reg'lar to bet on Parson Walker, which he judged to be the best exhorter about here, and so he was too, and a good man. If he even see a straddle-bug start to go anywheres, he would bet you how long it would take him to get to—to wherever he was going to, and if you took him up, he would foller that straddle-bug to Mexico but what he would find out where he was bound for and how long he was on the road. Lots of the boys here has seen that Smiley, and can tell you about him. Why, it never made no difference to *him*—he'd bet on *any* thing—the dangdest feller. Parson Walker's wife laid very sick once, for a good while, and it seemed as if they warn't going to save her; but one morning he come in, and Smiley up and asked him how she was, and he said she was considable better—thank the Lord for his inf'nite mercy—and coming on so smart that with the blessing of Prov'dence she'd get well yet; and Smiley, before he thought says, "Well, I'll resk two-and-a-half she don't anyway."

Thish-yer Smiley had a mare—the boys called her the fifteen-minute nag, but that was only in fun, you know, because of course she was faster than that—and he used to win money on that horse, for all she was so slow and always had the asthma, or the distemper, or the consumption, or something of that kind. They used to give her two or three hundred yards start, and then pass her under way; but always at the fag end of the race she'd get excited and desperate-like, and come cavorting and straddling up, and scattering her legs around limber, sometimes in the air, and sometimes out to one side among the fences, and kicking up m-o-r-e dust and raising m-o-r-e racket with her cough-

2. A narrow channel filled with water, used for conveying logs or timber.

ing and sneezing and blowing her nose—and *always* fetch up at the stand just about a neck ahead, as near as you could cipher it down.

And he had a little small bull-pup, that to look at him you'd think he warn't worth a cent but to set around and look ornery and lay for a chance to steal something. But as soon as money was up on him he was a different dog; his under-jaw'd begin to stick out like the fo'castle[3] of a steamboat, and his teeth would uncover and shine like the furnaces. And a dog might tackle him and bully-rag him, and bite him, and throw him over his shoulder two or three times, and Andrew Jackson—which was the name of the pup—Andrew Jackson would never let on but what *he* was satisfied, and hadn't expected nothing else—and the bets being doubled and doubled on the other side all the time, till the money was all up; and then all of a sudden he would grab that other dog jest by the j'int of his hind leg and freeze to it—not chaw, you understand, but only just grip and hang on till they throwed up the sponge, if it was a year. Smiley always come out winner on that pup, till he harnessed a dog once that didn't have no hind legs, because they'd been sawed off in a circular saw, and when the thing had gone along far enough, and the money was all up, and he come to make a snatch for his pet holt, he see in a minute how he's been imposed on, and how the other dog had him in the door, so to speak, and he 'peared surprised, and then he looked sorter discouraged-like, and didn't try no more to win the fight, and so he got shucked out bad. He give Smiley a look, as much as to say his heart was broke, and it was *his* fault, for putting up a dog that hadn't no hind legs for him to take holt of, which was his main dependence in a fight, and then he limped off a piece and laid down and died. It was a good pup, was that Andrew Jackson, and would have made a name for hisself if he'd lived, for the stuff was in him and he had genius—I know it, because he hadn't no opportunities to speak of, and it don't stand to reason that a dog could make such a fight as he could under them circumstances if he hadn't no talent. It always makes me feel sorry when I think of that last fight of his'n, and the way it turned out.

Well, thish-yer Smiley had rat-tarriers, and chicken cocks, and tomcats and all them kind of things, till you couldn't rest, and you couldn't fetch nothing for him to bet on but he'd match you. He ketched a frog one day, and took him home, and said he cal'lated to educate him; and so he never done nothing for three months but set in his back yard and learn that frog to jump. And you bet you he *did* learn him, too. He'd give him a little punch behind, and the next minute you'd see that frog whirling in the air like a doughnut— see him turn one summerset, or may be a couple, if he got a good start, and come down flat-footed and all right, like a cat. He got him up so in the matter of ketching flies, and kep' him in practice so constant, that he'd nail a fly every time as fur as he could see him. Smiley said all a frog wanted was education, and he could do 'most anything—and I believe him. Why, I've seen him set Dan'l Webster[4] down here on this floor—Dan'l Webster was the name of the frog—and sing out, "Flies, Dan'l, flies!" and quicker'n you could wink he'd spring straight up and snake a fly off'n the counter there, and flop down on the floor ag'in as solid as a gob of mud, and fall to scratching the side of his head with his hind foot as indifferent as if he hadn't no idea he'd

---

3. The forecastle is the forward part of a ship's upper deck.

4. The name of a noted American senator, states- man, and orator (1782–1852).

been doin' any more'n any frog might do. You never see a frog so modest and straightfor'ard as he was, for all he was so gifted. And when it come to fair and square jumping on a dead level, he could get over more ground at one straddle than any animal of his breed you ever see. Jumping on a dead level was his strong suit, you understand; and when it come to that, Smiley would ante up money on him as long as he had a red. Smiley was monstrous proud of his frog, and well he might be, for fellers that had traveled and been everywheres all said he laid over any frog that ever *they* see.

Well, Smiley kep' the beast in a little lattice box, and he used to fetch him down town sometimes and lay for a bet. One day a feller—a stranger in the camp, he was—come acrost him with his box, and says:

"What might it be that you've got in the box?"

And Smiley says, sorter indifferent-like, "It might be a parrot, or it might be a canary, maybe, but it ain't—it's only just a frog."

And the feller took it, and looked at it careful, and turned it round this way and that, and says, "H'm—so 'tis. Well, what's *he* good for?"

"Well," Smiley says, easy and careless, "he's good enough for *one* thing, I should judge—he can outjump any frog in Calaveras county."

The feller took the box again, and took another long, particular look, and give it back to Smiley, and says, very deliberate, "Well," he says, "I don't see no p'ints about that frog that's any better'n any other frog."

"Maybe you don't," Smiley says. "Maybe you understand frogs and maybe you don't understand 'em; maybe you've had experience, and maybe you ain't only an amature, as it were. Anyways, I've got *my* opinion and I'll resk forty dollars that he can outjump any frog in Calaveras county."

And the feller studied a minute, and then says, kinder sad like, "Well, I'm only a stranger here, and I ain't got no frog; but if I had a frog, I'd bet you."

And then Smiley says, "That's all right—that's all right—if you'll hold my box a minute, I'll go and get you a frog." And so the feller took the box, and put up his forty dollars along with Smiley's, and set down to wait.

So he set there a good while thinking and thinking to hisself, and then he got the frog out and prized his mouth open and took a teaspoon and filled him full of quail shot—filled him pretty near up to his chin—and set him on the floor. Smiley he went to the swamp and slopped around in the mud for a long time, and finally he ketched a frog, and fetched him in, and give him to this feller, and says:

"Now, if you're ready, set him alongside of Dan'l, with his forepaws just even with Dan'l's, and I'll give the word." Then he says, "One—two—three-*git!*" and him and the feller touched up the frogs from behind, and the new frog hopped off lively, but Dan'l give a heave, and hysted up his shoulders—so—like a Frenchman, but it warn't no use—he couldn't budge; he was planted as solid as a church, and he couldn't no more stir than if he was anchored out. Smiley was a good deal surprised, and he was disgusted too, but he didn't have no idea what the matter was, of course.

The feller took the money and started away; and when he was going out at the door, he sorter jerked his thumb over his shoulder—so—at Dan'l, and says again, very deliberate, "Well," he says, "*I* don't see no p'ints about that frog that's any better'n any other frog."

Smiley he stood scratching his head and looking down at Dan'l a long time, and at last he says, "I do wonder what in the nation that frog throw'd off for—I wonder if there ain't something the matter with him—he 'pears to look mighty baggy, somehow." And he ketched Dan'l by the nap of the neck, and hefted him, and says, "Why blame my cats if he don't weigh five pound!" and turned him upside down and he belched out a double handful of shot. And then he see how it was, and he was the maddest man—he set the frog down and took out after that feller, but he never ketched him. And——"

[Here Simon Wheeler heard his name called from the front yard, and got up to see what was wanted.] And turning to me as he moved away, he said: "Just set where you are, stranger, and rest easy—I ain't going to be gone a second."

But, by your leave, I did not think that a continuation of the history of the enterprising vagabond *Jim* Smiley would be likely to afford me much information concerning the *Rev. Leonidas W.* Smiley, and so I started away.

At the door I met the sociable Wheeler returning, and he button-holed me and recommenced:

"Well, thish-yer Smiley had a yaller one-eyed cow that didn't have no tail, only jest a short stump like a bannanner, and——"

However, lacking both time and inclination, I did not wait to hear about the afflicted cow, but took my leave.

1865, 1867

Adventures of Huckleberry Finn[1]

(Tom Sawyer's Comrade)

Scene: The Mississippi Valley

Time: Forty to Fifty Years Ago[2]

NOTICE
Persons attempting to find a motive in this narrative will be prosecuted; persons attempting to find a moral in it will be banished; persons attempting to find a plot in it will be shot.

BY ORDER OF THE AUTHOR
PER G. G., CHIEF OF ORDNANCE.

Explanatory

In this book a number of dialects are used, to wit: the Missouri negro dialect; the extremest form of the backwoods South-Western dialect; the ordi-

---

1. *Adventures of Huckleberry Finn* was first published in England in December 1884. The text printed here is a corrected version of the first American edition of 1885.
2. I.e., between 1835 and 1845—well before the Civil War.

Huck. E. W. Kemble's illustration of Huckleberry
Finn on the frontispiece of the first edition (1884).

nary "Pike-County"[3] dialect; and four modified varieties of this last. The
shadings have not been done in a hap-hazard fashion, or by guess-work; but
pains-takingly, and with the trustworthy guidance and support of personal
familiarity with these several forms of speech.

I make this explanation for the reason that without it many readers would
suppose that all these characters were trying to talk alike and not succeeding.

THE AUTHOR

Chapter I

You don't know about me, without you have read a book by the name of "The
Adventures of Tom Sawyer,"[4] but that ain't no matter. That book was made
by Mr. Mark Twain, and he told the truth, mainly. There was things which
he stretched, but mainly he told the truth. That is nothing. I never seen anybody but lied, one time or another, without it was Aunt Polly, or the widow,
or maybe Mary. Aunt Polly—Tom's Aunt Polly, she is—and Mary, and the
Widow Douglas, is all told about in that book—which is mostly a true book;
with some stretchers, as I said before.

---

3. Pike County, Missouri.   4. Published in 1876.

Now the way that the book winds up, is this: Tom and me found the money that the robbers hid in the cave, and it made us rich. We got six thousand dollars apiece—all gold. It was an awful sight of money when it was piled up. Well, Judge Thatcher, he took it and put it out at interest, and it fetched us a dollar a day apiece, all the year round—more than a body could tell what to do with. The Widow Douglas, she took me for her son, and allowed she would sivilize me; but it was rough living in the house all the time, considering how dismal regular and decent the widow was in all her ways; and so when I couldn't stand it no longer, I lit out. I got into my old rags, and my sugar-hogshead[5] again, and was free and satisfied. But Tom Sawyer, he hunted me up and said he was going to start a band of robbers, and I might join if I would go back to the widow and be respectable. So I went back.

The widow she cried over me, and called me a poor lost lamb, and she called me a lot of other names, too, but she never meant no harm by it. She put me in them new clothes again, and I couldn't do nothing but sweat and sweat, and feel all cramped up. Well, then, the old thing commenced again. The widow rung a bell for supper, and you had to come to time. When you got to the table you couldn't go right to eating, but you had to wait for the widow to tuck down her head and grumble a little over the victuals, though there warn't really anything the matter with them. That is, nothing only everything was cooked by itself. In a barrel of odds and ends it is different; things get mixed up, and the juice kind of swaps around, and the things go better.

After supper she got out her book and learned me about Moses and the Bulrushers;[6] and I was in a sweat to find out all about him; but by-and-by she let it out that Moses had been dead a considerable long time; so then I didn't care no more about him; because I don't take no stock in dead people.

Pretty soon I wanted to smoke, and asked the widow to let me. But she wouldn't. She said it was a mean practice and wasn't clean, and I must try to not do it any more. That is just the way with some people. They get down on a thing when they don't know nothing about it. Here she was a bothering about Moses, which was no kin to her, and no use to anybody, being gone, you see, yet finding a power of fault with me for doing a thing that had some good in it. And she took snuff too; of course that was all right, because she done it herself.

Her sister, Miss Watson, a tolerable slim old maid, with goggles on, had just come to live with her, and took a set at me now, with a spelling-book. She worked me middling hard for about an hour, and then the widow made her ease up. I couldn't stood it much longer. Then for an hour it was deadly dull, and I was fidgety. Miss Watson would say, "Don't put your feet up there, Huckleberry"; and "don't scrunch up like that, Huckleberry—set up straight"; and pretty soon she would say, "Don't gap and stretch like that, Huckleberry—why don't you try to behave?" Then she told me all about the bad place, and I said I wished I was there. She got mad, then, but I didn't mean no harm. All I wanted was to go somewheres; all I wanted was a change, I warn't particular. She said it was wicked to say what I said; said she wouldn't say it for the whole world; *she* was going to live so as to go to

---

5. A large barrel.
6. Pharaoh's daughter discovered the infant Moses floating in the Nile in a basket woven from bul-rushes (Exodus 2). She adopted him into the royal family just as the widow has adopted Huck.

the good place. Well, I couldn't see no advantage in going where she was going, so I made up my mind I wouldn't try for it. But I never said so, because it would only make trouble, and wouldn't do no good.

Now she had got a start, and she went on and told me all about the good place. She said all a body would have to do there was to go around all day long with a harp and sing, forever and ever.[7] So I didn't think much of it. But I never said so. I asked her if she reckoned Tom Sawyer would go there, and, she said, not by a considerable sight. I was glad about that, because I wanted him and me to be together.

Miss Watson she kept pecking at me, and it got tiresome and lonesome. By-and-by they fetched the niggers[8] in and had prayers, and then everybody was off to bed. I went up to my room with a piece of candle and put it on the table. Then I set down in a chair by the window and tried to think of something cheerful, but it warn't no use. I felt so lonesome I most wished I was dead. The stars was shining, and the leaves rustled in the woods ever so mournful; and I heard an owl, away off, who-whooing about somebody that was dead, and a whippowill and a dog crying about somebody that was going to die; and the wind was trying to whisper something to me and I couldn't make out what it was, and so it made the cold shivers run over me. Then away out in the woods I heard that kind of a sound that a ghost makes when it wants to tell about something that's on its mind and can't make itself understood, and so can't rest easy in its grave and has to go about that way every night grieving. I got so down-hearted and scared, I did wish I had some company. Pretty soon a spider went crawling up my shoulder, and I flipped it off and it lit in the candle; and before I could budge it was all shriveled up. I didn't need anybody to tell me that that was an awful bad sign and would fetch me some bad luck, so I was scared and most shook the clothes off of me. I got up and turned around in my tracks three times and crossed my breast every time; and then I tied up a little lock of my hair with a thread to keep witches away. But I hadn't no confidence. You do that when you've lost a horse-shoe that you've found, instead of nailing it up over the door, but I hadn't ever heard anybody say it was any way to keep off bad luck when you'd killed a spider.

I set down again, a shaking all over, and got out my pipe for a smoke; for the house was all as still as death, now, and so the widow wouldn't know. Well, after a long time I heard the clock away off in the town go boom— boom—boom—twelve licks—and all still again—stiller than ever. Pretty soon I heard a twig snap, down in the dark amongst the trees— something was a stirring. I set still and listened. Directly I could just barely hear a *"me-yow! me-yow!"* down there. That was good! Says I, *"me-yow! me-yow!"* as soft as I could, and then I put out the light and scrambled out of the window onto the shed. Then I slipped down to the ground and crawled in amongst the trees, and sure enough there was Tom Sawyer waiting for me.

7. Conventional conceptions of the Christian heaven were satirized early and late in Twain's writings.
8. This word is now unacceptable, but at the time of this novel's setting (before the Civil War) it was a common, though vulgar, term among whites without the powerfully negative connotations it has since acquired. For debate on the racial politics of *Huckleberry Finn*, see the selections in "Critical Controversy: Race and the Ending of *Adventures of Huckleberry Finn*," pp. 291–306.

Chapter II

We went tip-toeing along a path amongst the trees back towards the end of the widow's garden, stooping down so as the branches wouldn't scrape our heads. When we was passing by the kitchen I fell over a root and made a noise. We scrouched down and laid still. Miss Watson's big nigger, named Jim, was setting in the kitchen door; we could see him pretty clear, because there was a light behind him. He got up and stretched his neck out about a minute, listening. Then he says,

"Who dah?"

He listened some more; then he come tip-toeing down and stood right between us; we could a touched him, nearly. Well, likely it was minutes and minutes that there warn't a sound, and we all there so close together. There was a place on my ankle that got to itching; but I dasn't scratch it; and then my ear begun to itch; and next my back, right between my shoulders. Seemed like I'd die if I couldn't scratch. Well, I've noticed that thing plenty of times since. If you are with the quality, or at a funeral, or trying to go to sleep when you ain't sleepy—if you are anywheres where it won't do for you to scratch, why you will itch all over in upwards of a thousand places. Pretty soon Jim says:

"Say—who is you? Whar is you? Dog my cats ef I didn' hear sumf'n. Well, I knows what I's gwyne to do. I's gwyne to set down here and listen tell I hears it agin."

So he set down on the ground betwixt me and Tom. He leaned his back up against a tree, and stretched his legs out till one of them most touched one of mine. My nose begun to itch. It itched till the tears come into my eyes. But I dasn't scratch. Then it begun to itch on the inside. Next I got to itching underneath. I didn't know how I was going to set still. This miserableness went on as much as six or seven minutes; but it seemed a sight longer than that. I was itching in eleven different places now. I reckoned I couldn't stand it more'n a minute longer, but I set my teeth hard and got ready to try. Just then Jim begun to breathe heavy; next he begun to snore—and then I was pretty soon comfortable again.

Tom he made a sign to me—kind of a little noise with his mouth—and we went creeping away on our hands and knees. When we was ten foot off, Tom whispered to me and wanted to tie Jim to the tree for fun; but I said no; he might wake and make a disturbance, and then they'd find out I warn't in. Then Tom said he hadn't got candles enough, and he would slip in the kitchen and get some more. I didn't want him to try. I said Jim might wake up and come. But Tom wanted to resk it; so we slid in there and got three candles, and Tom laid five cents on the table for pay. Then we got out, and I was in a sweat to get away; but nothing would do Tom but he must crawl to where Jim was, on his hands and knees, and play something on him. I waited, and it seemed a good while, everything was so still and lonesome.

As soon as Tom was back, we cut along the path, around the garden fence, and by-and-by fetched up on the steep top of the hill the other side of the house. Tom said he slipped Jim's hat off of his head and hung it on a limb right over him, and Jim stirred a little, but he didn't wake. Afterwards Jim said the witches bewitched him and put him in a trance, and rode him all over the State, and then set him under the trees again and hung his hat on a limb to show who done it. And next time Jim told it he said they rode him down to New Orleans; and after that, every time he told it he spread it more and more, till by-and-by he said they rode him all over the world, and tired him most to death, and his back was all over saddle-boils. Jim was monstrous proud about it, and he got so he wouldn't hardly notice the other niggers. Niggers would come miles to hear Jim tell about it, and he was more looked up to than any nigger in that country. Strange niggers[9] would stand with their mouths open and look him all over, same as if he was a wonder. Niggers is always talking about witches in the dark by the kitchen fire; but whenever one was talking and letting on to know all about such things, Jim would happen in and say, "Hm! What you know 'bout witches?" and that nigger was corked up and had to take a back seat. Jim always kept that five-center piece around his neck with a string and said it was a charm the devil give to him with his own hands and told him he could cure anybody with it and fetch witches whenever he wanted to, just by saying something to it; but he never told what it was he said to it. Niggers would come from all around there and give Jim anything they had, just for a sight of the five-center piece; but they wouldn't touch it, because the devil had had his hands on it. Jim was most ruined, for a servant, because he got so stuck up on account of having seen the devil and been rode by witches.

Well, when Tom and me got to the edge of the hill-top, we looked away down into the village[1] and could see three or four lights twinkling, where there was sick folks, may be; and the stars over us was sparkling ever so fine; and down by the village was the river, a whole mile broad, and awful still and grand. We went down the hill and found Jo Harper, and Ben Rogers, and two or three more of the boys, hid in the old tanyard. So we unhitched a skiff and pulled down the river two mile and a half, to the big scar on the hill-side, and went ashore.

We went to a clump of bushes, and Tom made everybody swear to keep the secret, and then showed them a hole in the hill, right in the thickest part of the bushes. Then we lit the candles and crawled in on our hands and knees. We went about two hundred yards, and then the cave opened up. Tom poked about amongst the passages and pretty soon ducked under a wall where you wouldn't a noticed that there was a hole. We went along a narrow place and got into a kind of room, all damp and sweaty and cold, and there we stopped. Tom says:

"Now we'll start this band of robbers and call it Tom Sawyer's Gang. Everybody that wants to join has got to take an oath, and write his name in blood."

Everybody was willing. So Tom got out a sheet of paper that he had wrote the oath on, and read it. It swore every boy to stick to the band, and never tell any of the secrets; and if anybody done anything to any boy in the band, whichever boy was ordered to kill that person and his family must do it, and he mustn't eat and he mustn't sleep till he had killed them and hacked a cross in their breasts, which was the sign of the band. And nobody that didn't belong to the band could use that mark, and if he did he must be sued; and if he done it again he must be killed. And if anybody that belonged to the

9. Those who did not live in the immediate area.
1. The village, called St. Petersburg here and in *Tom Sawyer*, is modeled on Hannibal, Missouri.

band told the secrets, he must have his throat cut, and then have his carcass burnt up and the ashes scattered all around, and his name blotted off
of the list with blood and never mentioned again by the gang, but have a
curse put on it and be forgot, forever.

Everybody said it was a real beautiful oath, and asked Tom if he got it out
of his own head. He said, some of it, but the rest was out of pirate books,
and robber books, and every gang that was high-toned had it.

Some thought it would be good to kill the *families* of boys that told the
secrets. Tom said it was a good idea, so he took a pencil and wrote it in. Then
Ben Rogers says:

"Here's Huck Finn, he hain't got no family—what you going to do 'bout
him?"

"Well, hain't he got a father?" says Tom Sawyer.

"Yes, he's got a father, but you can't never find him, these days. He used
to lay drunk with the hogs in the tanyard, but he hain't been seen in these
parts for a year or more."

They talked it over, and they was going to rule me out, because they said
every boy must have a family or somebody to kill, or else it wouldn't be fair
and square for the others. Well, nobody could think of anything to do—
everybody was stumped, and set still. I was most ready to cry; but all at once
I thought of a way, and so I offered them Miss Watson—they could kill her.
Everybody said:

"Oh, she'll do, she'll do. That's all right. Huck can come in."

Then they all stuck a pin in their fingers to get blood to sign with, and I
made my mark on the paper.

"Now," says Ben Rogers, "what's the line of business of this Gang?"

"Nothing only robbery and murder," Tom said.

"But who are we going to rob? houses—or cattle—or—"

"Stuff! stealing cattle and such things ain't robbery, it's burglary," says Tom
Sawyer. "We ain't burglars. That ain't no sort of style. We are highwaymen.
We stop stages and carriages on the road, with masks on, and kill the people
and take their watches and money."

"Must we always kill the people?"

"Oh, certainly. It's best. Some authorities think different, but mostly it's
considered best to kill them. Except some that you bring to the cave here
and keep them till they're ransomed."

"Ransomed? What's that?"

"I don't know. But that's what they do. I've seen it in books; and so of
course that's what we've got to do."

"But how can we do it if we don't know what it is?"

"Why blame it all, we've *got* to do it. Don't I tell you it's in the books? Do
you want to go to doing different from what's in the books, and get things
all muddled up?"

"Oh, that's all very fine to *say,* Tom Sawyer, but how in the nation[2] are
these fellows going to be ransomed if we don't know how to do it to them?
that's the thing I want to get at. Now what do you *reckon* it is?"

"Well I don't know. But per'aps if we keep them till they're ransomed, it
means that we keep them till they're dead."

---

2. Damnation.

"Now, that's something *like*. That'll answer. Why couldn't you said that before? We'll keep them till they're ransomed to death—and a bothersome lot they'll be, too, eating up everything and always trying to get loose."

"How you talk, Ben Rogers. How can they get loose when there's a guard over them, ready to shoot them down if they move a peg?"

"A guard. Well, that *is* good. So somebody's got to set up all night and never get any sleep, just so as to watch them. I think that's foolishness. Why can't a body take a club and ransom them as soon as they get here?"

"Because it ain't in the books so—that's why. Now Ben Rogers, do you want to do things regular, or don't you?—that's the idea. Don't you reckon that the people that made the books knows what's the correct thing to do? Do you reckon *you* can learn 'em anything? Not by a good deal. No, sir, we'll just go on and ransom them in the regular way."

"All right. I don't mind; but I say it's a fool way, anyhow. Say—do we kill the women, too?"

"Well, Ben Rogers, if I was as ignorant as you I wouldn't let on. Kill the women? No—nobody ever saw anything in the books like that. You fetch them to the cave, and you're always as polite as pie to them; and by-and-by they fall in love with you and never want to go home any more."

"Well, if that's the way, I'm agreed, but I don't take no stock in it. Mighty soon we'll have the cave so cluttered up with women, and fellows waiting to be ransomed, that there won't be no place for the robbers. But go ahead, I ain't got nothing to say."

Little Tommy Barnes was asleep, now, and when they waked him up he was scared, and cried, and said he wanted to go home to his ma, and didn't want to be a robber any more.

So they all made fun of him, and called him cry-baby, and that made him mad, and he said he would go straight and tell all the secrets. But Tom give him five cents to keep quiet, and said we would all go home and meet next week and rob somebody and kill some people.

Ben Rogers said he couldn't get out much, only Sundays, and so he wanted to begin next Sunday; but all the boys said it would be wicked to do it on Sunday, and that settled the thing. They agreed to get together and fix a day as soon as they could, and then we elected Tom Sawyer first captain and Jo Harper second captain of the Gang, and so started home.

I clumb up the shed and crept into my window just before day was breaking. My new clothes was all greased up and clayey, and I was dog-tired.

Chapter III

Well, I got a good going-over in the morning, from old Miss Watson, on account of my clothes; but the widow she didn't scold, but only cleaned off the grease and clay and looked so sorry that I thought I would behave a while if I could. Then Miss Watson she took me in the closet[3] and prayed, but nothing come of it. She told me to pray every day, and whatever I asked for I would get it. But it warn't so. I tried it. Once I got a fish-line, but no hooks. It warn't any good to me without hooks. I tried for the hooks three or four

---

3. "But thou, when thou prayest, enter into thy closet" (Matthew 6.6) is apparently the admonition Miss Watson has in mind.

times, but somehow I couldn't make it work. By-and-by, one day, I asked Miss Watson to try for me, but she said I was a fool. She never told me why, and I couldn't make it out no way.

I set down, one time, back in the woods, and had a long think about it. I says to myself, if a body can get anything they pray for, why don't Deacon Winn get back the money he lost on pork? Why can't the widow get back her silver snuff-box that was stole? Why can't Miss Watson fat up? No, says I to myself, there ain't nothing in it. I went and told the widow about it, and she said the thing a body could get by praying for it was "spiritual gifts." This was too many for me, but she told me what she meant—I must help other people, and do everything I could for other people, and look out for them all the time, and never think about myself. This was including Miss Watson, as I took it. I went out in the woods and turned it over in my mind a long time, but I couldn't see no advantage about it—except for the other people—so at last I reckoned I wouldn't worry about it any more, but just let it go. Sometimes the widow would take me one side and talk about Providence in a way to make a boy's mouth water; but maybe next day Miss Watson would take hold and knock it all down again. I judged I could see that there was two Providences, and a poor chap would stand considerable show with the widow's Providence, but if Miss Watson's got him there warn't no help for him any more. I thought it all out, and reckoned I would belong to the widow's, if he wanted me, though I couldn't make out how he was agoing to be any better off then than what he was before, seeing I was so ignorant and so kind of low-down and ornery.

Pap he hadn't been seen for more than a year, and that was comfortable for me; I didn't want to see him no more. He used to always whale me when he was sober and could get his hands on me; though I used to take to the woods most of the time when he was around. Well, about this time he was found in the river drowned, about twelve mile above town, so people said. They judged it was him, anyway; said this drowned man was just his size, and was ragged, and had uncommon long hair—which was all like pap—but they couldn't make nothing out of the face, because it had been in the water so long it warn't much like a face at all. They said he was floating on his back in the water. They took him and buried him on the bank. But I warn't comfortable long, because I happened to think of something. I knowed mighty well that a drownded man don't float on his back, but on his face. So I knowed, then, that this warn't pap, but a woman dressed up in a man's clothes. So I was uncomfortable again. I judged the old man would turn up again by-and-by, though I wished he wouldn't.

We played robber now and then about a month, and then I resigned. All the boys did. We hadn't robbed nobody, we hadn't killed any people, but only just pretended. We used to hop out of the woods and go charging down on hog-drovers and women in carts taking garden stuff to market, but we never hived[4] any of them. Tom Sawyer called the hogs "ingots," and he called the turnips and stuff "julery" and we would go to the cave and pow-wow over what we had done and how many people we had killed and marked. But I couldn't see no profit in it. One time Tom sent a boy to run about town with a blazing stick, which he called a slogan (which was the sign for the Gang

4. Captured, secured.

to get together), and then he said he had got secret news by his spies that next day a whole parcel of Spanish merchants and rich A-rabs was going to camp in Cave Hollow with two hundred elephants, and six hundred camels, and over a thousand "sumter" mules,[5] all loaded with di'monds, and they didn't have only a guard of four hundred soldiers, and so we would lay in ambuscade, as he called it, and kill the lot and scoop the things. He said we must slick up our swords and guns, and get ready. He never could go after even a turnip-cart but he must have the swords and guns all scoured up for it; though they was only lath and broom-sticks, and you might scour at them till you rotted and then they warn't worth a mouthful of ashes more than what they was before. I didn't believe we could lick such a crowd of Spaniards and A-rabs, but I wanted to see the camels and elephants, so I was on hand next day, Saturday, in the ambuscade; and when we got the word, we rushed out of the woods and down the hill. But there warn't no Spaniards and A-rabs, and there warn't no camels nor no elephants. It warn't anything but a Sunday-school picnic, and only a primer-class at that. We busted it up, and chased the children up the hollow; but we never got anything but some doughnuts and jam, though Ben Rogers got a rag doll, and Jo Harper got a hymn-book and a tract; and then the teacher charged in and made us drop everything and cut. I didn't see no di'monds, and I told Tom Sawyer so. He said there was loads of them there, anyway; and he said there was A-rabs there, too, and elephants and things. I said, why couldn't we see them, then? He said if I warn't so ignorant, but had read a book called "Don Quixote,"[6] I would know without asking. He said it was all done by enchantment. He said there was hundreds of soldiers there, and elephants and treasure, and so on, but we had enemies which he called magicians, and they had turned the whole thing into an infant Sunday school, just out of spite. I said, all right, then the thing for us to do was to go for the magicians. Tom Sawyer said I was a numskull.

"Why," says he, "a magician could call up a lot of genies, and they would hash you up like nothing before you could say Jack Robinson. They are as tall as a tree and as big around as a church."

"Well," I says, "s'pose we got some genies to help *us*—can't we lick the other crowd then?"

"How you going to get them?"

"I don't know. How do *they* get them?"

"Why they rub an old tin lamp or an iron ring, and then the genies come tearing in, with the thunder and lightning a-ripping around and the smoke a-rolling, and everything they're told to do they up and do it. They don't think nothing of pulling a shot tower[7] up by the roots, and belting a Sunday-school superintendent over the head with it—or any other man."

"Who makes them tear around so?"

"Why, whoever rubs the lamp or the ring. They belong to whoever rubs the lamp or the ring, and they've got to do whatever he says. If he tells them to build a palace forty miles long, out of di'monds, and fill it full of chewing gum, or whatever you want, and fetch an emperor's daughter from China

---

5. Pack mules.
6. Tom is here alluding to stories in *The Arabian Nights Entertainments* (1838–41) and to the hero

in Cervantes' *Don Quixote* (1605).
7. A device in which gunshot was formed by dripping molten lead into water.

for you to marry, they've got to do it—and they've got to do it before sun-up next morning, too. And more—they've got to waltz that palace around over the country whenever you want it, you understand."

"Well," says I, "I think they are a pack of flatheads for not keeping the palace themselves 'stead of fooling them away like that. And what's more— if I was one of them I would see a man in Jericho before I would drop my business and come to him for the rubbing of an old tin lamp."

"How you talk, Huck Finn. Why, you'd *have* to come when he rubbed it, whether you wanted to or not."

"What, and I as high as a tree and as big as a church? All right, then; I *would* come; but I lay I'd make that man climb the highest tree there was in the country."

"Shucks, it ain't no use to talk to you, Huck Finn. You don't seem to know anything, somehow—perfect sap-head."

I thought all this over for two or three days, and then I reckoned I would see if there was anything in it. I got an old tin lamp and an iron ring and went out in the woods and rubbed and rubbed till I sweat like an Injun,[8] calculating to build a palace and sell it; but it warn't no use, none of the genies come. So then I judged that all that stuff was only just one of Tom Sawyer's lies. I reckoned he believed in the A-rabs and the elephants, but as for me I think different. It had all the marks of a Sunday school.

Chapter IV

Well, three or four months run along, and it was well into the winter, now. I had been to school most all the time, and could spell, and read, and write just a little, and could say the multiplication table up to six times seven is thirty-five, and I don't reckon I could ever get any further than that if I was to live forever. I don't take no stock in mathematics, anyway.

At first I hated the school, but by-and-by I got so I could stand it. When- ever I got uncommon tired I played hookey, and the hiding I got next day done me good and cheered me up. So the longer I went to school the easier it got to be. I was getting sort of used to the widow's ways, too, and they warn't so raspy on me. Living in a house, and sleeping in a bed, pulled on me pretty tight, mostly, but before the cold weather I used to slide out and sleep in the woods, sometimes, and so that was a rest to me. I liked the old ways best, but I was getting so I liked the new ones, too, a little bit. The widow said I was coming along slow but sure, and doing very satisfactory. She said she warn't ashamed of me.

One morning I happened to turn over the salt-cellar at breakfast. I reached for some of it as quick as I could, to throw over my left shoulder and keep off the bad luck, but Miss Watson was in ahead of me, and crossed me off. She says, "Take your hands away, Huckleberry—what a mess you are always making." The widow put in a good word for me, but that warn't going to keep off the bad luck, I knowed that well enough. I started out, after breakfast, feeling worried and shaky, and wondering where it was going to fall on me, and what it was going to be. There is ways to keep off some kinds of bad

---

8. Common, vulgar term for "Indian," used frequently in Huck's time.

luck, but this wasn't one of them kind; so I never tried to do anything, but just poked along low-spirited and on the watch-out.

I went down the front garden and clumb over the stile,[9] where you go through the high board fence. There was an inch of new snow on the ground, and I seen somebody's tracks. They had come up from the quarry and stood around the stile a while, and then went on around the garden fence. It was funny they hadn't come in, after standing around so. I couldn't make it out. It was very curious, somehow. I was going to follow around, but I stooped down to look at the tracks first. I didn't notice anything at first, but next I did. There was a cross in the left boot-heel made with big nails, to keep off the devil.

I was up in a second and shinning down the hill. I looked over my shoulder every now and then, but I didn't see nobody. I was at Judge Thatcher's as quick as I could get there. He said:

"Why, my boy, you are all out of breath. Did you come for your interest?"

"No sir," I says; "is there some for me?"

"Oh, yes, a half-yearly is in, last night. Over a hundred and fifty dollars. Quite a fortune for you. You better let me invest it along with your six thousand, because if you take it you'll spend it."

"No sir," I says, "I don't want to spend it. I don't want it at all—nor the six thousand, nuther. I want you to take it; I want to give it to you—the six thousand and all."

He looked surprised. He couldn't seem to make it out. He says:

"Why, what can you mean, my boy?"

I says, "Don't you ask me no questions about it, please. You'll take it—won't you?"

He says:

"Well I'm puzzled. Is something the matter?"

"Please take it," says I, "and don't ask me nothing—then I won't have to tell no lies."

He studied a while, and then he says:

"Oho-o. I think I see. You want to *sell* all your property to me—not give it. That's the correct idea."

Then he wrote something on a paper and read it over, and says:

"There—you see it says 'for a consideration.' That means I have bought it of you and paid you for it. Here's a dollar for you. Now, you sign it."

So I signed it, and left.

Miss Watson's nigger, Jim, had a hair-ball[1] as big as your fist, which had been took out of the fourth stomach of an ox, and he used to do magic with it. He said there was a spirit inside of it, and it knowed everything. So I went to him that night and told him pap was here again, for I found his tracks in the snow. What I wanted to know, was, what he was going to do, and was he going to stay? Jim got out his hair-ball, and said something over it, and then he held it up and dropped it on the floor. It fell pretty solid, and only rolled about an inch. Jim tried it again, and then another time, and it acted just the same. Jim got down on his knees and put his ear against it and listened. But it warn't no use; he said it wouldn't talk. He said sometimes it wouldn't talk without money. I told him I had an old slick counterfeit quarter that

---

9. Steps that flank and straddle a fence.
1. Clump of hair found in an animal's stomach; believed by Jim and Huck to have magical powers.

warn't no good because the brass showed through the silver a little, and it wouldn't pass nohow, even if the brass didn't show, because it was so slick it felt greasy, and so that would tell on it every time. (I reckoned I wouldn't say nothing about the dollar I got from the judge.) I said it was pretty bad money, but maybe the hair-ball would take it, because maybe it wouldn't know the difference. Jim smelt it, and bit it, and rubbed it, and said he would manage so the hair-ball would think it was good. He said he would split open a raw Irish potato and stick the quarter in between and keep it there all night, and next morning you couldn't see no brass, and it wouldn't feel greasy no more, and so anybody in town would take it in a minute, let alone a hair-ball. Well, I knowed a potato would do that, before, but I had forgot it.

Jim put the quarter under the hair-ball and got down and listened again. This time he said the hair-ball was all right. He said it would tell my whole fortune if I wanted it to. I says, go on. So the hair-ball talked to Jim, and Jim told it to me. He says:

"Yo' ole father doan' know, yit, what he's a-gwyne to do. Sometimes he spec he'll go 'way, en den agin he spec he'll stay. De bes' way is to res' easy en let de ole man take his own way. Dey's two angels hoverin' roun' 'bout him. One uv 'em is white en shiny, en 'tother one is black. De white one gits him to go right, a little while, den de black one sail in en bust it all up. A body can't tell, yit, which one gwyne to fetch him at de las'. But you is all right. You gwyne to have considable trouble in yo' life, en considable joy. Sometimes you gwyne to git hurt, en sometimes you gwyne to git sick; but every time you's gwyne to git well agin. Dey's two gals flyin' 'bout you in yo' life. One uv 'em's light en 'tother one is dark. One is rich en 'tother is po'. You's gwyne to marry de po' one fust en de rich one by-en-by. You wants to keep 'way fum de water as much as you kin, en don't run no resk, 'kase it's down in de bills[2] dat you's gwyne to git hung."

When I lit my candle and went up to my room that night, there set pap, his own self!

Chapter V

I had shut the door to. Then I turned around, and there he was. I used to be scared of him all the time, he tanned me so much. I reckoned I was scared now, too; but in a minute I see I was mistaken. That is, after the first jolt, as you may say, when my breath sort of hitched—he being so unexpected; but right away after, I see I warn't scared of him worth bothering about.

He was most fifty, and he looked it. His hair was long and tangled and greasy, and hung down, and you could see his eyes shining through like he was behind vines. It was all black, no gray; so was his long, mixed-up whiskers. There warn't no color in his face, where his face showed; it was white; not like another man's white, but a white to make a body sick, a white to make a body's flesh crawl—a tree-toad white, a fish-belly white. As for his clothes—just rags, that was all. He had one ankle resting on 'tother knee; the boot on that foot was busted, and two of his toes stuck through, and he worked them now and then. His hat was laying on the floor; an old black slouch with the top caved in, like a lid.

2. Predestined.

I stood a-looking at him; he set there a-looking at me, with his chair tilted back a little. I set the candle down. I noticed the window was up; so he had clumb in by the shed. He kept a-looking me all over. By-and-by he says:

"Starchy clothes—very. You think you're a good deal of a big-bug, *don't* you?"

"Maybe I am, maybe I ain't," I says.

"Don't you give me none o' your lip," says he. "You've put on considerble many frills since I been away. I'll take you down a peg before I get done with you. You're educated, too, they say; can read and write. You think you're better'n your father, now, don't you, because he can't? *I'll* take it out of you. Who told you you might meddle with such hifalut'n foolishness, hey?—who told you you could?"

"The widow. She told me."

"The widow, hey?—and who told the widow she could put in her shovel about a thing that ain't none of her business?"

"Nobody never told her."

"Well, I'll learn her how to meddle. And looky here—you drop that school, you hear? I'll learn people to bring up a boy to put on airs over his own father and let on to be better'n what *he* is. You lemme catch you fooling around that school again, you hear? Your mother couldn't read, and she couldn't write, nuther, before she died. None of the family couldn't, before *they* died. *I* can't; and here you're a-swelling yourself up like this. I ain't the man to stand it—you hear? Say—lemme hear you read."

I took up a book and begun something about General Washington and the wars. When I'd read about a half a minute, he fetched the book a whack with his hand and knocked it across the house. He says:

"It's so. You can do it. I had my doubts when you told me. Now looky here; you stop that putting on frills. I won't have it. I'll lay for you, my smarty; and if I catch you about that school I'll tan you good. First you know you'll get religion, too. I never see such a son."

He took up a little blue and yaller picture of some cows and a boy, and says:

"What's this?"

"It's something they give me for learning my lessons good."

He tore it up, and says—

"I'll give you something better—I'll give you a cowhide."[3]

He set there a-mumbling and a-growling a minute, and then he says—

"*Ain't* you a sweet-scented dandy, though? A bed; and bedclothes; and a look'n-glass; and a piece of carpet on the floor—and your own father got to sleep with the hogs in the tanyard. I never see such a son. I bet I'll take some o' these frills out o' you before I'm done with you. Why there ain't no end to your airs—they say you're rich. Hey?—how's that?"

"They lie—that's how."

"Looky here—mind how you talk to me; I'm a-standing about all I can stand, now—so don't gimme no sass. I've been in town two days, and I hain't heard nothing but about you bein' rich. I heard about it away down the river, too. That's why I come. You git me that money to-morrow—I want it."

3. A beating with a cowhide whip.

"I hain't got no money."

"It's a lie. Judge Thatcher's got it. You git it. I want it."

"I hain't got no money, I tell you. You ask Judge Thatcher; he'll tell you the same."

"All right. I'll ask him; and I'll make him pungle,[4] too, or I'll know the reason why. Say—how much you got in your pocket? I want it."

"I hain't got only a dollar, and I want that to—"

"It don't make no difference what you want it for—you just shell it out."

He took it and bit it to see if it was good, and then he said he was going down town to get some whiskey; said he hadn't had a drink all day. When he had got out on the shed, he put his head in again, and cussed me for putting on frills and trying to be better than him; and when I reckoned he was gone, he come back and put his head in again, and told me to mind about that school, because he was going to lay for me and lick me if I didn't drop that.

Next day he was drunk, and he went to Judge Thatcher's and bullyragged him and tried to make him give up the money, but he couldn't, and then he swore he'd make the law force him.

The judge and the widow went to law to get the court to take me away from him and let one of them be my guardian; but it was a new judge that had just come, and he didn't know the old man; so he said courts mustn't interfere and separate families if they could help it; said he'd druther not take a child away from its father. So Judge Thatcher and the widow had to quit on the business.

That pleased the old man till he couldn't rest. He said he'd cowhide me till I was black and blue if I didn't raise some money for him. I borrowed three dollars from Judge Thatcher, and pap took it and got drunk and went a-blowing around and cussing and whooping and carrying on; and he kept it up all over town, with a tin pan, till most midnight; then they jailed him, and next day they had him before court, and jailed him again for a week. But he said *he* was satisfied; said he was boss of his son, and he'd make it warm for *him*.

When he got out the new judge said he was agoing to make a man of him. So he took him to his own house, and dressed him up clean and nice, and had him to breakfast and dinner and supper with the family, and was just old pie to him, so to speak. And after supper he talked to him about temperance and such things till the old man cried, and said he'd been a fool, and fooled away his life; but now he was agoing to turn over a new leaf and be a man nobody wouldn't be ashamed of, and he hoped the judge would help him and not look down on him. The judge said he could hug him for them words; so *he* cried, and his wife she cried again; pap said he'd been a man that had always been misunderstood before, and the judge said he believed it. The old man said that what a man wanted that was down, was sympathy; and the judge said it was so; so they cried again. And when it was bedtime, the old man rose up and held out his hand, and says:

"Look at it gentlemen, and ladies all; take ahold of it; shake it. There's a hand that was the hand of a hog; but it ain't so no more; it's the hand of a man that's started in on a new life, and 'll die before he'll go back. You mark them words—don't forget I said them. It's a clean hand now; shake it—don't be afeard."

---

4. Pay.

So they shook it, one after the other, all around, and cried. The judge's wife she kissed it. Then the old man he signed a pledge—made his mark. The judge said it was the holiest time on record, or something like that. Then they tucked the old man into a beautiful room, which was the spare room, and in the night sometime he got powerful thirsty and clumb out onto the porch-roof and slid down a stanchion and traded his new coat for a jug of forty-rod,[5] and clumb back again and had a good old time; and towards day-light he crawled out again, drunk as a fiddler, and rolled off the porch and broke his left arm in two places and was almost froze to death when some-body found him after sun-up. And when they come to look at that spare room, they had to take soundings before they could navigate it.

The judge he felt kind of sore. He said he reckoned a body could reform the ole man with a shot-gun, maybe, but he didn't know no other way.

Chapter VI

Well, pretty soon the old man was up and around again, and then he went for Judge Thatcher in the courts to make him give up that money, and he went for me, too, for not stopping school. He catched me a couple of times and thrashed me, but I went to school just the same, and dodged him or out-run him most of the time. I didn't want to go to school much, before, but I reckoned I'd go now to spite pap. That law trial was a slow business; appeared like they warn't ever going to get started on it; so every now and then I'd borrow two or three dollars off of the judge for him, to keep from getting a cowhiding. Every time he got money he got drunk; and every time he got drunk he raised Cain around town; and every time he raised Cain he got jailed. He was just suited—this kind of thing was right in his line.

He got to hanging around the widow's too much, and so she told him at last, that if he didn't quit using[6] around there she would make trouble for him. Well, *wasn't* he mad? He said he would show who was Huck Finn's boss. So he watched out for me one day in the spring, and catched me, and took me up the river about three mile, in a skiff, and crossed over to the Illinois shore where it was woody and there warn't no houses but an old log hut in a place where the timber was so thick you couldn't find it if you didn't know where it was.

He kept me with him all the time, and I never got a chance to run off. We lived in that old cabin, and he always locked the door and put the key under his head, nights. He had a gun which he had stole, I reckon, and we fished and hunted, and that was what we lived on. Every little while he locked me in and went down to the store, three miles, to the ferry, and traded fish and game for whiskey and fetched it home and got drunk and had a good time, and licked me. The widow she found out where I was, by-and-by, and she sent a man over to try to get hold of me, but pap drove him off with the gun, and it warn't long after that till I was used to being where I was, and liked it, all but the cowhide part.

It was kind of lazy and jolly, laying off comfortable all day, smoking and fishing, and no books nor study. Two months or more run along, and my

5. Home-distilled whiskey strong enough to knock   6. Loitering.
a person forty rods, or 220 yards.

clothes got to be all rags and dirt, and I didn't see how I'd ever got to like it so well at the widow's, where you had to wash, and eat on a plate, and comb up, and go to bed and get up regular, and be forever bothering over a book and have old Miss Watson pecking at you all the time. I didn't want to go back no more. I had stopped cussing, because the widow didn't like it; but now I took to it again because pap hadn't no objections. It was pretty good times up in the woods there, take it all around.

But by-and-by pap got too handy with his hick'ry, and I couldn't stand it. I was all over welts. He got to going away so much, too, and locking me in. Once he locked me in and was gone three days. It was dreadful lonesome. I judged he had got drowned and I wasn't ever going to get out any more. I was scared. I made up my mind I would fix up some way to leave there. I had tried to get out of that cabin many a time, but I couldn't find no way. There warn't a window to it big enough for a dog to get through. I couldn't get up the chimbly, it was too narrow. The door was thick solid oak slabs. Pap was pretty careful not to leave a knife or anything in the cabin when he was away; I reckon I had hunted the place over as much as a hundred times; well, I was 'most all the time at it, because it was about the only way to put in the time. But this time I found something at last; I found an old rusty wood-saw without any handle; it was laid in between a rafter and the clap-boards of the roof. I greased it up and went to work. There was an old horse-blanket nailed against the logs at the far end of the cabin behind the table, to keep the wind from blowing through the chinks and putting the candle out. I got under the table and raised the blanket and went to work to saw a section of the big bottom log out, big enough to let me through. Well, it was a good long job, but I was getting towards the end of it when I heard pap's gun in the woods. I got rid of the signs of my work, and dropped the blanket and hid my saw, and pretty soon pap come in.

Pap warn't in a good humor—so he was his natural self. He said he was down to town, and everything was going wrong. His lawyer said he reck-oned he would win his lawsuit and get the money, if they ever got started on the trial; but then there was ways to put it off a long time, and Judge Thatcher knowed how to do it. And he said people allowed there'd be another trial to get me away from him and give me to the widow for my guardian, and they guessed it would win, this time. This shook me up considerable, because I didn't want to go back to the widow's any more and be so cramped up and sivilized, as they called it. Then the old man got to cussing, and cussed everything and everybody he could think of, and then cussed them all over again to make sure he hadn't skipped any, and after that he polished off with a kind of general cuss all round, including a considerable parcel of people which he didn't know the names of, and so called them what's-his-name, when he got to them, and went right along with his cussing.

He said he would like to see the widow get me. He said he would watch out, and if they tried to come any such game on him he knowed of a place six or seven mile off, to stow me in, where they might hunt till they dropped and they couldn't find me. That made me pretty uneasy again, but only for a minute; I reckoned I wouldn't stay on hand till he got that chance.

The old man made me go to the skiff and fetch the things he had got. There was a fifty-pound sack of corn meal, and a side of bacon, ammunition, and a four-gallon jug of whiskey, and an old book and two newspapers for wadding, besides some tow.[7] I toted up a load, and went back and set down on the bow of the skiff to rest. I thought it all over, and I reckoned I would walk off with the gun and some lines, and take to the woods when I run away. I guessed I wouldn't stay in one place, but just tramp right across the country, mostly night times, and hunt and fish to keep alive, and so get so far away that the old man nor the widow couldn't ever find me any more. I judged I would saw out and leave that night if pap got drunk enough, and I reckoned he would. I got so full of it I didn't notice how long I was staying, till the old man hollered and asked me whether I was asleep or drownded.

I got the things all up to the cabin, and then it was about dark. While I was cooking supper the old man took a swig or two and got sort of warmed up, and went to ripping again. He had been drunk over in town, and laid in the gutter all night, and he was a sight to look at. A body would a thought he was Adam, he was just all mud.[8] Whenever his liquor begun to work, he most always went for the govment. This time he says:

"Call this a govment! why, just look at it and see what it's like. Here's the law a-standing ready to take a man's son away from him—a man's own son, which he has had all the trouble and all the anxiety and all the expense of raising. Yes, just as that man has got that son raised at last, and ready to go to work and begin to do suthin' for *him* and give him a rest, the law up and goes for him. And they call *that* govment! That ain't all, nuther. The law backs that old Judge Thatcher up and helps him to keep me out o' my property. Here's what the law does. The law takes a man worth six thousand dollars and upards, and jams him into an old trap of a cabin like this, and lets him go round in clothes that ain't fitten for a hog. They call that govment! A man can't get his rights in a govment like this. Sometimes I've a mighty notion to just leave the country for good and all. Yes, and I *told* 'em so: I told old Thatcher so to his face. Lots of 'em heard me, and can tell what I said. Says I, for two cents I'd leave the blamed country and never come anear it agin. Them's the very words. I says, look at my hat—if you call it a hat—but the lid raises up and the rest of it goes down till it's below my chin, and then it ain't rightly a hat at all, but more like my head was shoved up through a jint o' stove-pipe. Look at it, says I—such a hat for me to wear—one of the wealthiest men in this town, if I could git my rights.

"Oh, yes, this is a wonderful govment, wonderful. Why, looky here. There was a free nigger there, from Ohio; a mulatter,[9] most as white as a white man. He had the whitest shirt on you ever see, too, and the shiniest hat; and there ain't a man in that town that's got as fine clothes as what he had; and he had a gold watch and chain and a silver-headed cane—the awfulest old gray-headed nabob[1] in the State. And what do you think? they said he was a p'fessor in a college, and could talk all kinds of languages, and knowed every thing. And that ain't the wust. They said he could *vote*, when he was at home. Well, that let me out. Thinks I, what is the country a-coming to? It was 'lection day, and I was just about to go and vote, myself, if I warn't too drunk to get there; but when they told me there was a State in this country where they'd let that nigger vote, I drawed out. I says I'll never vote agin. Them's the very

---

7. Cheap rope. "Wadding": material (here paper) used to pack the gunpowder in a rifle.
8. God created Adam from earth in Genesis 2.7.

9. Mulatto, of mixed white and black ancestry. Ohio was a free state.
1. Someone of conspicuous wealth.

words I said; they all heard me; and the country may rot for all me—I'll never vote agin as long as I live. And to see the cool way of that nigger—why, he wouldn't a give me the road if I hadn't shoved him out o' the way. I says to the people, why ain't this nigger put up at auction and sold?—that's what I want to know. And what do you reckon they said? Why, they said he couldn't be sold till he'd been in the State six months, and he hadn't been there that long yet. There, now—that's a specimen. They call that a govment that can't sell a free nigger till he's been in the State six months. Here's a govment that calls itself a govment, and lets on to be a govment, and thinks it is a govment, and yet's got to set stock-still for six whole months before it can take ahold of a prowling, thieving, infernal, white-shirted free nigger, and[2]—"

Pap was agoing on so, he never noticed where his old limber legs was taking him to, so he went head over heels over the tub of salt pork, and barked both shins, and the rest of his speech was all the hottest kind of language— mostly hove at the nigger and the govment, though he give the tub some, too, all along, here and there. He hopped around the cabin considerble, first on one leg and then on the other, holding first one shin and then the other one, and at last he let out with his left foot all of a sudden and fetched the tub a rattling kick. But it warn't good judgment, because that was the boot that had a couple of his toes leaking out of the front end of it; so now he raised a howl that fairly made a body's hair raise, and down he went in the dirt, and rolled there, and held his toes; and the cussing he done then laid over anything he had ever done previous. He said so his own self, afterwards. He had heard old Sowberry Hagan in his best days, and he said it laid over him, too; but I reckon that was sort of piling it on, maybe.

After supper pap took the jug, and said he had enough whiskey there for two drunks and one delirium tremens. That was always his word. I judged he would be blind drunk in about an hour, an then I would steal the key, or saw myself out, one or 'tother. He drank, and drank, and tumbled down on his blankets, by-and-by; but luck didn't run my way. He didn't go sound asleep, but was uneasy. He groaned, and moaned, and thrashed around this way and that, for a long time. At last I got so sleepy I couldn't keep my eyes open, all I could do, and so before I knowed what I was about I was sound asleep, and the candle burning.

I don't know how long I was asleep, but all of a sudden there was an awful scream and I was up. There was pap, looking wild and skipping around every which way and yelling about snakes. He said they was crawling up his legs; and then he would give a jump and scream, and say one had bit him on the cheek—but I couldn't see no snakes. He started to run round and round the cabin, hollering "take him off! take him off! he's biting me on the neck!" I never see a man look so wild in the eyes. Pretty soon he was all fagged[3] out, and fell down panting; then he rolled over and over, wonderful fast, kicking things every which way, and striking and grabbing at the air with his hands, and screaming, and saying there was devils ahold of him. He wore out, by-and-by, and laid still a while, moaning. Then he laid stiller, and didn't make

---

2. Missouri's original constitution prohibited the entrance of freed slaves and mulattoes into the state, but the second Missouri Compromise of 1820 deleted the provision. In the 1830s and 1840s, however, increasingly strict antiblack laws were passed, and by 1850 a black person without freedom papers could be sold downriver with a mere sworn statement of ownership from a white man.

3. Tired.

a sound. I could hear the owls and the wolves, away off in the woods, and it seemed terrible still. He was laying over by the corner. By-and-by he raised up, part way, and listened, with his head to one side. He says very low:

"Tramp—tramp—tramp; that's the dead; tramp—tramp—tramp; they're coming after me; but I won't go—Oh, they're here! don't touch me—don't! hands off—they're cold; let go—Oh, let a poor devil alone!"

Then he went down on all fours and crawled off begging them to let him alone, and he rolled himself up in his blanket and wallowed in under the old pine table, still a-begging; and then he went to crying. I could hear him through the blanket.

By-and-by he rolled out and jumped up on his feet looking wild, and he see me and went for me. He chased me round and round the place, with a clasp-knife, calling me the Angel of Death and saying he would kill me and then I couldn't come for him no more. I begged, and told him I was only Huck, but he laughed *such* a screechy laugh, and roared and cussed, and kept on chasing me up. Once when I turned short and dodged under his arm he made a grab and got me by the jacket between my shoulders, and I thought I was gone; but I skid out of the jacket quick as lightning, and saved myself. Pretty soon he was all tired out, and dropped down with his back against the door, and said he would rest a minute and then kill me. He put his knife under him, and said he would sleep and get strong, and then he would see who was who.

So he dozed off, pretty soon. By-and-by I got the old split bottom[4] chair and clumb up, as easy as I could, not to make any noise, and got down the gun. I slipped the ramrod down it to make sure it was loaded, and then I laid it across the turnip barrel, pointing towards pap, and set down behind it to wait for him to stir. And how slow and still the time did drag along.

Chapter VII

"Git up! what you 'bout!"

I opened my eyes and looked around, trying to make out where I was. It was after sun-up, and I had been sound asleep. Pap was standing over me, looking sour—and sick, too. He says—

"What you doin' with this gun?"

I judged he didn't know nothing about what he had been doing, so I says:

"Somebody tried to get in, so I was laying for him."

"Why didn't you roust me out?"

"Well I tried to, but I couldn't; I couldn't budge you."

"Well, all right. Don't stand there palavering all day, but out with you and see if there's a fish on the lines for breakfast. I'll be along in a minute."

He unlocked the door and I cleared out, up the river bank. I noticed some pieces of limbs and such things floating down, and a sprinkling of bark; so I knowed the river had begun to rise. I reckoned I would have great times, now, if I was over at the town. The June rise used to be always luck for me; because as soon as that rise begins, here comes cord-wood floating down, and pieces of log rafts—sometimes a dozen logs together; so all you have to do is to catch them and sell them to the wood yards and the sawmill.

---

4. I.e., splint-bottom, made by interweaving thin strips of wood.

I went along up the bank with one eye out for pap and 'tother one out for what the rise might fetch along. Well, all at once, here comes a canoe; just a beauty, too, about thirteen or fourteen foot long, riding high like a duck. I shot head first off of the bank, like a frog, clothes and all on, and struck out for the canoe. I just expected there'd be somebody laying down in it, because people often done that to fool folks, and when a chap had pulled a skiff out most to it they'd raise up and laugh at him. But it warn't so this time. It was a drift-canoe, sure enough, and I clumb in and paddled her ashore. Thinks I, the old man will be glad when he sees this—she's worth ten dollars. But when I got to shore pap wasn't in sight yet, and as I was running her into a little creek like a gully, all hung over with vines and willows, I struck another idea; I judged I'd hide her good, and then, stead of taking to the woods when I run off, I'd go down the river about fifty mile and camp in one place for good, and not have such a rough time tramping on foot.

It was pretty close to the shanty, and I thought I heard the old man coming, all the time; but I got her hid; and then I out and looked around a bunch of willows, and there was the old man down the path apiece just drawing a bead on a bird with his gun. So he hadn't seen anything.

When he got along, I was hard at it taking up a "trot" line.[5] He abused me a little for being so slow, but I told him I fell in the river and that was what made me so long. I knowed he would see I was wet, and then he would be asking questions. We got five catfish off of the lines and went home.

While we laid off, after breakfast, to sleep up, both of us being about wore out, I got to thinking that if I could fix up some way to keep pap and the widow from trying to follow me, it would be a certainer thing than trusting to luck to get far enough off before they missed me; you see, all kinds of things might happen. Well, I didn't see no way for a while, but by-and-by pap raised up a minute, to drink another barrel of water, and he says:

"Another time a man comes a-prowling round here, you roust me out, you hear? That man warn't here for no good. I'd a shot him. Next time, you roust me out, you hear?"

Then he dropped down and went to sleep again—but what he had been saying give me the very idea I wanted. I says to myself, I can fix it now so nobody won't think of following me.

About twelve o'clock we turned out and went along up the bank. The river was coming up pretty fast, and lots of drift-wood going by on the rise. By-and-by, along comes part of a log raft—nine logs fast together. We went out with the skiff and towed it ashore. Then we had dinner. Anybody but pap would a waited and seen the day through, so as to catch more stuff; but that warn't pap's style. Nine logs was enough for one time; he must shove right over to town and sell. So he locked me in and took the skiff and started off towing the raft about half-past three. I judged he wouldn't come back that night. I waited till I reckoned he had got a good start, then I out with my saw and went to work on that log again. Before he was 'tother side of the river I was out of the hole; him and his raft was just a speck on the water away off yonder.

I took the sack of corn meal and took it to where the canoe was hid, and shoved the vines and branches apart and put it in; then I done the same with

---

5. A long fishing line fastened across a stream; to this line several shorter baited lines are attached.

the side of bacon; then the whiskey jug; I took all the coffee and sugar there was, and all the ammunition; I took the wadding; I took the bucket and gourd, I took a dipper and a tin cup, and my old saw and two blankets, and the skillet and the coffee-pot. I took fish-lines and matches and other things—everything that was worth a cent. I cleaned out the place. I wanted an axe, but there wasn't any, only the one out at the wood pile, and I knowed why I was going to leave that. I fetched out the gun, and now I was done.

I had wore the ground a good deal, crawling out of the hole and dragging out so many things. So I fixed that as good as I could from the outside by scattering dust on the place, which covered up the smoothness and the saw-dust. Then I fixed the piece of log back into its place, and put two rocks under it and one against it to hold it there,—for it was bent up at the place, and didn't quite touch ground. If you stood four or five foot away and didn't know it was sawed, you wouldn't ever notice it; and besides, this was the back of the cabin and it warn't likely anybody would go fooling around there.

It was all grass clear to the canoe; so I hadn't left a track. I followed around to see. I stood on the bank and looked out over the river. All safe. So I took the gun and went up a piece into the woods and was hunting around for some birds, when I see a wild pig; hogs soon went wild in them bottoms after they had got away from the prairie farms. I shot this fellow and took him into camp.

I took the axe and smashed in the door—I beat it and hacked it consider-able, a-doing it. I fetched the pig in and took him back nearly to the table and hacked into his throat with the ax, and laid him down on the ground to bleed—I say ground, because it *was* ground—hard packed, and no boards. Well, next I took an old sack and put a lot of big rocks in it,—all I could drag—and I started it from the pig and dragged it to the door and through the woods down to the river and dumped it in, and down it sunk, out of sight. You could easy see that something had been dragged over the ground. I did wish Tom Sawyer was there, I knowed he would take an interest in this kind of business, and throw in the fancy touches. Nobody could spread himself like Tom Sawyer in such a thing as that.

Well, last I pulled out some of my hair, and bloodied the ax good, and stuck it on the back side, and slung the ax in the corner. Then I took up the pig and held him to my breast with my jacket (so he couldn't drip) till I got a good piece below the house and then dumped him into the river. Now I thought of something else. So I went and got the bag of meal and my old saw out of the canoe and fetched them to the house. I took the bag to where it used to stand, and ripped a hole in the bottom of it with the saw, for there warn't no knives and forks on the place—pap done everything with his clasp-knife, about the cooking. Then I carried the sack about a hundred yards across the grass and through the willows east of the house, to a shallow lake that was five mile wide and full of rushes—and ducks too, you might say, in the season. There was a slough or a creek leading out of it on the other side, that went miles away, I don't know where, but it didn't go to the river. The meal sifted out and made a little track all the way to the lake. I dropped pap's whetstone there too, so as to look like it had been done by accident. Then I tied up the rip in the meal sack with a string, so it wouldn't leak no more, and took it and my saw to the canoe again.

It was about dark, now; so I dropped the canoe down the river under some willows that hung over the bank, and waited for the moon to rise. I made fast to a willow; then I took a bite to eat, and by-and-by laid down in the canoe to smoke a pipe and lay out a plan. I says to myself, they'll follow the track of that sackful of rocks to the shore and then drag the river for me. And they'll follow that meal track to the lake and go browsing down the creek that leads out of it to find the robbers that killed me and took the things. They won't ever hunt the river for anything but my dead carcass. They'll soon get tired of that, and won't bother no more about me. All right; I can stop anywhere I want to. Jackson's Island[6] is good enough for me; I know that island pretty well, and nobody ever comes there. And then I can paddle over to town, nights, and slink around and pick up things I want. Jackson's Island's the place.

I was pretty tired, and the first thing I knowed, I was asleep. When I woke up I didn't know where I was, for a minute. I set up and looked around, a little scared. Then I remembered. The river looked miles and miles across. The moon was so bright I could a counted the drift logs that went a slipping along, black and still, hundreds of yards out from shore. Everything was dead quiet, and it looked late, and *smelt* late. You know what I mean—I don't know the words to put it in.

I took a good gap and a stretch, and was just going to unhitch and start, when I heard a sound away over the water. I listened. Pretty soon I made it out. It was that dull kind of a regular sound that comes from oars working in rowlocks when it's a still night. I peeped out through the willow branches, and there it was—a skiff, away across the water. I couldn't tell how many was in it. It kept a-coming, and when it was abreast of me I see there warn't but one man in it. Thinks I, maybe it's pap, though I warn't expecting him. He dropped below me, with the current, and by-and-by he come a-swinging up shore in the easy water, and he went by so close I could a reached out the gun and touched him. Well, it *was* pap, sure enough—and sober, too, by the way he laid to his oars.

I didn't lose no time. The next minute I was a-spinning down stream soft but quick in the shade of the bank. I made two mile and a half, and then struck out a quarter of a mile or more towards the middle of the river, because pretty soon I would be passing the ferry landing and people might see me and hail me. I got out amongst the drift-wood and then laid down in the bottom of the canoe and let her float. I laid there and had a good rest and a smoke out of my pipe, looking away into the sky, not a cloud in it. The sky looks ever so deep when you lay down on your back in the moonshine; I never knowed it before. And how far a body can hear on the water such nights! I heard people talking at the ferry landing. I heard what they said, too, every word of it. One man said it was getting towards the long days and the short nights, now. 'Tother one said *this* warn't one of the short ones, he reckoned—and then they laughed, and he said it over again and they laughed again; then they waked up another fellow and told him, and laughed, but he didn't laugh; he ripped out something brisk and said let him alone. The first fellow said he 'lowed to tell it to his old woman—she would think it was pretty good; but he said that warn't nothing to some things he had said in his time. I heard one man say it was nearly three o'clock, and he hoped daylight wouldn't wait more than about a week longer.

---

6. The same island that serves for an adventure in *Tom Sawyer* (ch. 13).

After that, the talk got further and further away, and I couldn't make out the words any more, but I could hear the mumble; and now and then a laugh, too, but it seemed a long ways off.

I was away below the ferry now. I rose up and there was Jackson's Island, about two mile and a half down stream, heavy-timbered and standing up out of the middle of the river, big and dark and solid, like a steamboat without any lights. There warn't any signs of the bar at the head—it was all under water, now.

It didn't take me long to get there. I shot past the head at a ripping rate, the current was so swift, and then I got into the dead water and landed on the side towards the Illinois shore. I run the canoe into a deep dent in the bank that I knowed about; I had to part the willow branches to get in; and when I made fast nobody could a seen the canoe from the outside.

I went up and set down on a log at the head of the island and looked out on the big river and the black driftwood, and away over to the town, three mile away, where there was three or four lights twinkling. A monstrous big lumber raft was about a mile up stream, coming along down, with a lantern in the middle of it. I watched it come creeping down, and when it was most abreast of where I stood I heard a man say, "Stern oars, there! heave her head to stabboard!"[7] I heard that just as plain as if the man was by my side.

There was a little gray in the sky, now; so I stepped into the woods and laid down for a nap before breakfast.

Chapter VIII

The sun was up so high when I waked, that I judged it was after eight o'clock. I laid there in the grass and the cool shade, thinking about things and feeling rested and ruther comfortable and satisfied. I could see the sun out at one or two holes, but mostly it was big trees all about, and gloomy in there amongst them. There was freckled places on the ground where the light sifted down through the leaves, and the freckled places swapped about a little, showing there was a little breeze up there. A couple of squirrels set on a limb and jabbered at me very friendly.

I was powerful lazy and comfortable—didn't want to get up and cook breakfast. Well, I was dozing off again, when I thinks I hears a deep sound of "boom!" away up the river. I rouses up and rests on my elbow and listens; pretty soon I hears it again. I hopped up and went and looked out at a hole in the leaves, and I see a bunch of smoke laying on the water a long ways up—about abreast the ferry. And there was the ferry-boat full of people, floating along down. I knowed what was the matter, now. "Boom!" I see the white smoke squirt out of the ferry-boat's side. You see, they was firing cannon over the water, trying to make my carcass come to the top.

I was pretty hungry, but it warn't going to do for me to start a fire, because they might see the smoke. So I set there and watched the cannon-smoke and listened to the boom. The river was a mile wide, there, and it always looks pretty on a summer morning—so I was having a good enough time seeing them hunt for my remainders, if I only had a bite to eat. Well, then I

---

7. Starboard, the right-hand side of a boat, facing forward.

happened to think how they always put quicksilver[8] in loaves of bread and float them off because they always go right to the drownded carcass and stop there. So says I, I'll keep a lookout, and if any of them's floating around after me, I'll give them a show. I changed to the Illinois edge of the island to see what luck I could have, and I warn't disappointed. A big double loaf come along, and I most got it, with a long stick, but my foot slipped and she floated out further. Of course I was where the current set in the closest to the shore—I knowed enough for that. But by-and-by along comes another one, and this time I won. I took out the plug and shook out the little dab of quicksilver, and set my teeth in. It was "baker's bread"—what the quality eat—none of your low-down corn-pone.[9]

I got a good place amongst the leaves, and set there on a log, munching the bread and watching the ferry-boat, and very well satisfied. And then something struck me. I says, now I reckon the widow or the parson or somebody prayed that this bread would find me, and here it has gone and done it. So there ain't no doubt but there is something in that thing. That is, there's something in it when a body like the widow or the parson prays, but it don't work for me, and I reckon it don't work for only just the right kind.

I lit a pipe and had a good long smoke and went on watching. The ferry-boat was floating with the current, and I allowed I'd have a chance to see who was aboard when she come along, because she would come in close, where the bread did. When she'd got pretty well along down towards me, I put out my pipe and went to where I fished out the bread, and laid down behind a log on the bank in a little open place. Where the log forked I could peep through.

By-and-by she came along, and she drifted in so close that they could a run out a plank and walked ashore. Most everybody was on the boat. Pap, and Judge Thatcher, and Bessie Thatcher, and Jo Harper, and Tom Sawyer, and his old Aunt Polly, and Sid and Mary, and plenty more. Everybody was talking about the murder, but the captain broke in and says:

"Look sharp, now; the current sets in the closest here, and maybe he's washed ashore and got tangled amongst the brush at the water's edge. I hope so, anyway."

I didn't hope so. They all crowded up and leaned over the rails, nearly in my face, and kept still, watching with all their might. I could see them first-rate, but they couldn't see me. Then the captain sung out:

"Stand away!" and the cannon let off such a blast right before me that it made me deef with the noise and pretty near blind with the smoke, and I judged I was gone. If they'd a had some bullets in, I reckon they'd a got the corpse they was after. Well, I see I warn't hurt, thanks to goodness. The boat floated on and went out of sight around the shoulder of the island. I could hear the booming, now and then, further and further off, and by-and-by after an hour, I didn't hear it no more. The island was three mile long. I judged they had got to the foot, and was giving it up. But they didn't yet a while. They turned around the foot of the island and started up the channel on the Missouri side, under steam, and booming once in a while as they went.

8. Mercury.　　　　　　　9. Cornbread.

I crossed over to that side and watched them. When they got abreast the head of the island they quit shooting and dropped over to the Missouri shore and went home to the town.

I knowed I was all right now. Nobody else would come a-hunting after me. I got my traps out of the canoe and made me a nice camp in the thick woods. I made a kind of a tent out of my blankets to put my things under so the rain couldn't get at them. I catched a cat fish and haggled him open with my saw, and towards sundown I started my camp fire and had supper. Then I set out a line to catch some fish for breakfast.

When it was dark I set by my camp fire smoking, and feeling pretty satisfied; but by-and-by it got sort of lonesome, and so I went and set on the bank and listened to the currents washing along, and counted the stars and drift-logs and rafts that come down, and then went to bed; there ain't no better way to put in time when you are lonesome; you can't stay so, you soon get over it.

And so for three days and nights. No difference—just the same thing. But the next day I went exploring around down through the island. I was boss of it; it all belonged to me, so to say, and I wanted to know all about it; but mainly I wanted to put in the time. I found plenty strawberries, ripe and prime; and green summer-grapes, and green razberries; and the green blackberries was just beginning to show. They would all come handy by-and-by, I judged.

Well, I went fooling along in the deep woods till I judged I warn't far from the foot of the island. I had my gun along, but I hadn't shot nothing; it was for protection; thought I would kill some game nigh home. About this time I mighty near stepped on a good sized snake, and it went sliding off through the grass and flowers, and I after it, trying to get a shot at it. I clipped along, and all of sudden I bounded right on to the ashes of a camp fire that was still smoking.

My heart jumped up amongst my lungs. I never waited for to look further, but uncocked my gun and went sneaking back on my tip-toes as fast as ever I could. Every now and then I stopped a second, amongst the thick leaves, and listened; but my breath come so hard I couldn't hear nothing else. I slunk along another piece further, then listened again; and so on, and so on; if I see a stump, I took it for a man; if I trod on a stick and broke it, it made me feel like a person had cut one of my breaths in two and I only got half, and the short half, too.

When I got to camp I warn't feeling very brash, there warn't much sand in my craw;[1] but I says, this ain't no time to be fooling around. So I got all my traps into my canoe again so as to have them out of sight, and I put out the fire and scattered the ashes around to look like an old last year's camp, and then clumb a tree.

I reckon I was up in the tree two hours; but I didn't see nothing, I didn't hear nothing—I only *thought* I heard and seen as much as a thousand things. Well, I couldn't stay up there forever; so at last I got down, but I kept in the thick woods and on the lookout all the time. All I could get to eat was berries and what was left over from breakfast.

By the time it was night I was pretty hungry. So when it was good and dark, I slid out from shore before moonrise and paddled over to the Illinois

---

1. Slang for not feeling very brave.

bank—about a quarter of a mile. I went out in the woods and cooked a supper, and I had about made up my mind I would stay there all night, when I hear a *plunkety-plunk, plunkety-plunk,* and says to myself, horses coming; and next I hear people's voices. I got everything into the canoe as quick as I could, and then went creeping through the woods to see what I could find out. I hadn't got far when I hear a man say:

"We'd better camp here, if we can find a good place; the horses is about beat out. Let's look around."[2]

I didn't wait, but shoved out and paddled away easy. I tied up in the old place, and reckoned I would sleep in the canoe.

I didn't sleep much. I couldn't, somehow, for thinking. And every time I waked up I thought somebody had me by the neck. So the sleep didn't do me no good. By-and-by I says to myself, I can't live this way; I'm agoing to find out who it is that's here on the island with me; I'll find it out or bust. Well, I felt better, right off.

So I took my paddle and slid out from shore just a step or two, and then let the canoe drop along down amongst the shadows. The moon was shining, and outside of the shadows it made it most as light as day. I poked along well onto an hour, everything still as rocks and sound asleep. Well by this time I was most down to the foot of the island. A little ripply, cool breeze begun to blow, and that was as good as saying the night was about done. I give her a turn with the paddle and brung her nose to shore; then I got my gun and slipped out and into the edge of the woods. I set down there on a log and looked out through the leaves. I see the moon go off watch and the darkness begin to blanket the river. But in a little while I see a pale streak over the tree-tops, and knowed the day was coming. So I took my gun and slipped off towards where I had run across that camp fire, stopping every minute or two to listen. But I hadn't no luck, somehow; I couldn't seem to find the place. But by-and-by, sure enough, I catched a glimpse of fire, away through the trees. I went for it, cautious and slow. By-and-by I was close enough to have a look, and there laid a man on the ground. It most give me the fan-tods.[3] He had a blanket around his head, and his head was nearly in the fire. I set there behind a clump of bushes, in about six foot of him, and kept my eyes on him steady. It was getting gray daylight, now. Pretty soon he gapped, and stretched himself, and hove off the blanket, and it was Miss Watson's Jim! I bet I was glad to see him. I says:

"Hello, Jim!" and skipped out.

He bounced up and stared at me wild. Then he drops down on his knees, and puts his hands together and says:

"Doan' hurt me—don't! I hain't ever done no harm to a ghos'. I awluz liked dead people, en done all I could for 'em. You go en git in de river agin, whah you b'longs, en doan' do nuffn to Ole Jim, 'at 'uz awluz yo' fren'."

Well, I warn't long making him understand I warn't dead. I was ever so glad to see Jim. I warn't lonesome, now. I told him I warn't afraid of *him* telling the people where I was. I talked along, but he only set there and looked at me; never said nothing. Then I says:

---

2. Apparently this episode is a vestige of an early conception of the novel involving Pap in a murder plot and court trial.

3. A state of tension, uneasiness, or nervousness—what we might now call "the willies."

"It's good daylight. Let's get breakfast. Make up your camp fire good."

"What's de use er makin' up de camp fire to cook strawbries en sich truck? But you got a gun, hain't you? Den we kin git sumfn better den strawbries."

"Strawberries and such truck," I says. "Is that what you live on?"

"I couldn' git nuffn else," he says.

"Why, how long you been on the island, Jim?"

"I come heah de night arter you's killed."

"What, all that time?"

"Yes-indeedy."

"And ain't you had nothing but that kind of rubbage to eat?"

"No, sah—nuffn else."

"Well, you must be most starved, ain't you?"

"I reck'n I could eat a hoss. I think I could. How long you ben on de islan'?"

"Since the night I got killed."

"No! W'y, what has you lived on? But you got a gun. Oh, yes, you got a gun. Dat's good. Now you kill sumfn en I'll make up de fire."

So we went over to where the canoe was, and while he built a fire in a grassy open place amongst the trees, I fetched meal and bacon and coffee, and coffee-pot and frying-pan, and sugar and tin cups, and the nigger was set back considerable, because he reckoned it was all done with witchcraft. I catched a good big cat-fish, too, and Jim cleaned him with his knife, and fried him.

When breakfast was ready, we lolled on the grass and eat it smoking hot. Jim laid it in with all his might, for he was most about starved. Then when we had got pretty well stuffed, we laid off and lazied.

By-and-by Jim says:

"But looky here, Huck, who wuz it dat 'uz killed in dat shanty, ef it warn't you?"

Then I told him the whole thing, and he said it was smart. He said Tom Sawyer couldn't get up no better plan than what I had. Then I says:

"How do you come to be here, Jim, and how'd you get here?"

He looked pretty uneasy, and didn't say nothing for a minute. Then he says:

"Maybe I better not tell."

"Why, Jim?"

"Well, dey's reasons. But you wouldn' tell on me ef I 'uz to tell you, would you, Huck?"

"Blamed if I would, Jim."

"Well, I b'lieve you, Huck. I—I *run off*."

"Jim!"

"But mind, you said you wouldn't tell—you know you said you wouldn't tell, Huck."

"Well, I did. I said I wouldn't, and I'll stick to it. Honest *injun* I will. People would call me a low down Ablitionist and despise me for keeping mum—but that don't make no difference. I ain't agoing to tell, and I ain't agoing back there anyways. So now, le's know all about it."

"Well, you see, it 'uz dis way. Ole Missus—dat's Miss Watson—she pecks on me all de time, en treats me pooty rough, but she awluz said she wouldn' sell me down to Orleans. But I noticed dey wuz a nigger trader roun' de place considable, lately, en I begin to git oneasy. Well, one night I creeps to de do', pooty late, en de do' warn't quite shet, en I hear ole missus tell de widder she gwyne to sell me down to Orleans, but she didn' want to, but she could git eight hund'd dollars for me, en it 'uz sich a big stack o' money she couldn' resis'. De widder she try to git her to say she wouldn' do it, but I never waited to hear de res'. I lit out mighty quick, I tell you.

"I tuck out en shin down de hill en 'spec to steal a skift 'long de sho' som'ers 'bove de town, but dey wuz people a-stirrin' yit, so I hid in de ole tumble-down cooper shop on de bank to wait for everybody to go 'way. Well, I wuz dah all night. Dey wuz somebody roun' all de time. 'Long 'bout six in de mawnin', skifts begin to go by, en 'bout eight or nine every skift dat went 'long wuz talkin' 'bout how yo' pap come over to de town en say you's killed. Dese las' skifts wuz full o' ladies en genlmen agoin' over for to see de place. Sometimes dey'd pull up at de sho' en take a res' b'fo' dey started acrost, so by de talk I got to know all 'bout de killin'. I 'uz powerful sorry you's killed, Huck, but I ain't no mo', now.

"I laid dah under de shavins all day. I 'uz hungry, but I warn't afeared; bekase I knowed ole missus en de widder wuz goin' to start to de camp-meetn' right arter breakfas' en be gone all day, en dey knows I goes off wid de cattle 'bout daylight, so dey wouldn' 'spec to see me roun' de place, en so dey wouldn' miss me tell arter dark in de evenin'. De yuther servants wouldn' miss me, kase dey'd shin out en take holiday, soon as de ole folks 'uz out'n de way.

"Well, when it come dark I tuck out up de river road, en went 'bout two mile er more to whah dey warn't no houses. I'd made up my mind 'bout what I's agwyne to do. You see ef I kep' on tryin' to git away afoot, de dogs 'ud track me; ef I stole a skift to cross over, dey'd miss dat skift, you see, en dey'd know 'bout whah I'd lan' on de yuther side en whah to pick up my track. So I says, a raff is what I's arter; it doan' *make* no track.

"I see a light a-comin' roun' de p'int, bymeby, so I wade' in en shove' a log ahead o' me, en swum more'n half-way acrost de river, en got in 'mongst de drift-wood, en kep' my head down low, en kinder swum agin de current tell de raff come along. Den I swum to de stern uv it, en tuck aholt. It clouded up en 'uz pooty dark for a little while. So I clumb up en laid down on de planks. De men 'uz all 'way yonder in de middle, whah de lantern wuz. De river wuz arisin' en dey wuz a good current; so I reck'n'd 'at by fo' in de mawnin' I'd be twenty-five mile down de river, en den I'd slip in, jis' b'fo' daylight, en swim asho' en take to de woods on de Illinoi side.[4]

"But I didn' have no luck. When we 'uz mos' down to de head er de islan', a man begin to come aft wid de lantern. I see it warn't no use fer to wait, so I slid overboad, en struck out fer de islan'. Well, I had a notion I could lan' mos' anywhers, but I couldn'—bank too bluff. I 'uz mos' to de foot er de islan' b'fo' I foun' a good place. I went into de woods en jedged I wouldn' fool wid raffs no mo', long as dey move de lantern roun' so. I had my pipe en a plug er dog-leg,[5] en some matches in my cap, en dey warn't wet, so I 'uz all right."

"And so you ain't had no meat nor bread to eat all this time? Why didn't you get mud-turkles?"

4. Though Illinois was not a slave state, by state law any black person without freedom papers could be arrested and subjected to forced labor. Jim's chances for escape would be improved if he went down the Mississippi and then up the Ohio.

5. Cheap tobacco.

"How you gwyne to git'm? You can't slip up on um en grab um; en how's a body gwyne to hit um wid a rock? How could a body do it in de night? en I warn't gwyne to show myself on de bank in de daytime."

"Well, that's so. You've had to keep in the woods all the time, of course. Did you hear 'em shooting the cannon?"

"Oh, yes. I knowed dey was arter you. I see um go by heah; watched um thoo de bushes."

Some young birds come along, flying a yard or two at a time and lighting. Jim said it was a sign it was going to rain. He said it was a sign when young chickens flew that way, and so he reckoned it was the same way when young birds done it. I was going to catch some of them, but Jim wouldn't let me. He said it was death. He said his father laid mighty sick once, and some of them catched a bird, and his old granny said his father would die, and he did.

And Jim said you mustn't count the things you are going to cook for dinner, because that would bring bad luck. The same if you shook the table-cloth after sundown. And he said if a man owned a bee-hive, and that man died, the bees must be told about it before sun-up next morning, or else the bees would all weaken down and quit work and die. Jim said bees wouldn't sting idiots; but I didn't believe that, because I had tried them lots of times myself, and they wouldn't sting me.

I had heard about some of these things before, but not all of them. Jim knowed all kinds of signs. He said he knowed most everything. I said it looked to me like all the signs was about bad luck, and so I asked him if there warn't any good-luck signs. He says:

"Mighty few—an' *dey* ain' no use to a body. What you want to know when good luck's a-comin' for? want to keep it off?" And he said: "Ef you's got hairy arms en a hairy breas', it's a sign dat you's agwyne to be rich. Well, dey's some use in a sign like dat, 'kase it's so fur ahead. You see, maybe you's got to be po' a long time fust, en so you might git discourage' en kill yo'sef 'f you didn' know by de sign dat you gwyne to be rich bymeby."

"Have you got hairy arms and a hairy breast, Jim?"

"What's de use to ax dat question? don' you see I has?"

"Well, are you rich?"

"No, but I ben rich wunst, and gwyne to be rich agin. Wunst I had foteen dollars, but I tuck to specalat'n', en got busted out."

"What did you speculate in, Jim?"

"Well, fust I tackled stock."

"What kind of stock?"

"Why, live stock. Cattle, you know. I put ten dollars in a cow. But I ain't gwyne to resk no mo' money in stock. De cow up 'n' died on my han's."

"So you lost the ten dollars."

"No, I didn' lose it all. I on'y los' 'bout nine of it. I sole de hide en taller for a dollar en ten cents."

"You had five dollars and ten cents left. Did you speculate any more?"

"Yes. You know dat one-laigged nigger dat b'longs to old Misto Bradish? well, he sot up a bank, en say anybody dat put in a dollar would git fo' dollars mo' at de en' er de year. Well, all de niggers went in, but dey didn' have much. I wuz de on'y one dat had much. So I stuck out for mo' dan fo' dollars, en I said 'f I didn' git it I'd start a bank myself. Well o' course dat nigger want' to keep me out er de business, bekase he say dey warn't business 'nough for two banks, so he say I could put in my five dollars en he pay me thirty-five at de en' er de year.

"So I done it. Den I reck'n'd I'd inves' de thirty-five dollars right off en keep things a-movin'. Dey wuz a nigger name' Bob, dat had ketched a wood-flat,[6] en his marster didn' know it; en I bought it off'n him en told him to take de thirty-five dollars when de en' er de year come; but somebody stole de wood-flat dat night, en nex' day de one-laigged nigger say de bank 's busted. So dey didn' none uv us git no money."

"What did you do with the ten cents, Jim?"

"Well, I 'uz gwyne to spen' it, but I had a dream, en de dream tole me to give it to a nigger name' Balum—Balum's Ass[7] dey call him for short, he's one er dem chuckle-heads, you know. But he's lucky, dey say, en I see I warn't lucky. De dream say let Balum inves' de ten cents en he'd make a raise for me. Well, Balum he tuck de money, en when he wuz in church he hear de preacher say dat whoever give to de po' len' to de Lord, en boun' to git his money back a hund'd times. So Balum he tuck en give de ten cents to de po', en laid low to see what wuz gwyne to come of it."

"Well, what did come of it, Jim?"

"Nuffn never come of it. I couldn' manage to k'leck dat money no way; en Balum he couldn'. I ain' gwyne to len' no mo' money 'dout I see de security. Boun' to git yo' money back a hund'd times, de preacher says! Ef I could git de ten cents back, I'd call it squah, en be glad er de chanst."

"Well, it's all right anyway, Jim, long as you're going to be rich again some time or other."

"Yes—en I's rich now, come to look at it. I owns mysef, en I's wuth eight hund'd dollars. I wisht I had de money, I wouldn' want no mo'."

Chapter IX

I wanted to go and look at a place right about the middle of the island, that I'd found when I was exploring; so we started, and soon got to it, because the island was only three miles long and a quarter of a mile wide.

This place was a tolerable long steep hill or ridge, about forty foot high. We had a rough time getting to the top, the sides was so steep and the bushes so thick. We tramped and clumb around all over it, and by-and-by found a good big cavern in the rock, most up to the top on the side towards Illinois. The cavern was as big as two or three rooms bunched together, and Jim could stand up straight in it. It was cool in there. Jim was for putting our traps in there, right away, but I said we didn't want to be climbing up and down there all the time.

Jim said if we had the canoe hid in a good place, and had all the traps in the cavern, we could rush there if anybody was to come to the island, and they would never find us without dogs. And besides, he said them little birds had said it was going to rain, and did I want the things to get wet?

So we went back and got the canoe and paddled up abreast the cavern, and lugged all the traps up there. Then we hunted up a place close by to hide

---

6. A flat-bottomed boat used to transport timber.
7. In the Old Testament, God's avenging angel interrupts the journey of Balaam, a prophet, to curse the Israelites by standing in his path. Balaam is blind to the angel's presence, but his donkey sees the angel clearly and swerves off the road. The donkey receives the power to speak and complains to Balaam of its treatment (Numbers 22).

the canoe in, amongst the thick willows. We took some fish off of the lines and set them again, and begun to get ready for dinner.

The door of the cavern was big enough to roll a hogshead in, and on one side of the door the floor stuck out a little bit and was flat and a good place to build a fire on. So we built it there and cooked dinner.

We spread the blankets inside for a carpet, and eat our dinner in there. We put all the other things handy at the back of the cavern. Pretty soon it darkened up and begun to thunder and lighten; so the birds was right about it. Directly it begun to rain, and it rained like all fury, too, and I never see the wind blow so. It was one of these regular summer storms. It would get so dark that it looked all blue-black outside, and lovely; and the rain would thrash along by so thick that the trees off a little ways looked dim and spider-webby; and here would come a blast of wind that would bend the trees down and turn up the pale underside of the leaves; and then a perfect rip-per of a gust would follow along and set the branches to tossing their arms as if they was just wild; and next, when it was just about the bluest and blackest—*fst!* it was as bright as glory and you'd have a little glimpse of tree-tops a-plunging about, away off yonder in the storm, hundreds of yards further than you could see before; dark as sin again in a second, and now you'd hear the thunder let go with an awful crash and then go rumbling, grumbling, tumbling down the sky towards the under side of the world, like rolling empty barrels down stairs, where it's long stairs and they bounce a good deal, you know.

"Jim, this is nice," I says. "I wouldn't want to be nowhere else but here. Pass me along another hunk of fish and some hot cornbread."

"Well, you wouldn' a ben here, 'f it hadn' a ben for Jim. You'd a ben down dah in de woods widout any dinner, en gittn' mos' drownded, too, dat you would, honey. Chickens knows when its gwyne to rain, en so do de birds, chile."

The river went on raising and raising for ten or twelve days, till at last it was over the banks. The water was three or four foot deep on the island in the low places and on the Illinois bottom. On that side it was a good many miles wide; but on the Missouri side it was the same old distance across—a half a mile—because the Missouri shore was just a wall of high bluffs.

Daytimes we paddled all over the island in the canoe. It was mighty cool and shady in the deep woods even if the sun was blazing outside. We went winding in and out amongst the trees; and sometimes the vines hung so thick we had to back away and go some other way. Well, on every old broken-down tree, you could see rabbits, and snakes, and such things; and when the island had been overflowed a day or two, they got so tame, on account of being hungry, that you could paddle right up and put your hand on them if you wanted to; but not the snakes and turtles—they would slide off in the water. The ridge our cavern was in, was full of them. We could a had pets enough if we'd wanted them.

One night we catched a little section of a lumber raft—nice pine planks. It was twelve foot wide and about fifteen or sixteen foot long, and the top stood above water six or seven inches, a solid level floor. We could see saw-logs go by in the daylight, sometimes, but we let them go; we didn't show ourselves in daylight.

Another night, when we was up at the head of the island, just before day-light, here comes a frame house down, on the west side. She was a two-story, and tilted over, considerable. We paddled out and got aboard—clumb in at an up-stairs window. But it was too dark to see yet, so we made the canoe fast and set in her to wait for daylight.

The light begun to come before we got to the foot of the island. Then we looked in at the window. We could make out a bed, and a table, and two old chairs, and lots of things around about on the floor; and there was clothes hanging against the wall. There was something laying on the floor in the far corner that looked like a man. So Jim says.

"Hello, you!"

But it didn't budge. So I hollered again, and then Jim says:

"De man ain' asleep—he's dead. You hold still—I'll go en see."

He went and bent down and looked, and says:

"It's a dead man. Yes, indeedy; naked, too. He's ben shot in de back. I reck'n he's ben dead two er three days. Come in, Huck, but doan' look at his face—it's too gashly."

I didn't look at him at all. Jim throwed some old rags over him, but he needn't done it; I didn't want to see him. There was heaps of old greasy cards scattered around over the floor, and old whiskey bottles, and a couple of masks made out of black cloth; and all over the walls was the ignorantest kind of words and pictures, made with charcoal. There was two old dirty calico dresses, and a sun-bonnet, and some women's under-clothes, hanging against the wall, and some men's clothing, too. We put the lot into the canoe; it might come good. There was a boy's old speckled straw hat on the floor; I took that too. And there was a bottle that had had milk in it; and it had a rag stopper for a baby to suck. We would a took the bottle, but it was broke. There was a seedy old chest, and an old hair trunk with the hinges broke. They stood open, but there warn't nothing left in them that was any account. The way things was scattered about, we reckoned the people left in a hurry and warn't fixed so as to carry off most of their stuff.

We got an old tin lantern, and a butcher-knife without any handle, and a bran-new Barlow knife[8] worth two bits in any store, and a lot of tallow candles, and a tin candlestick, and a gourd, and a tin cup, and a ratty old bedquilt off the bed, and a reticule with needles and pins and beeswax and buttons and thread and all such truck in it, and a hatchet and some nails, and a fish-line as thick as my little finger, with some monstrous hooks on it, and a roll of buckskin, and a leather dog-collar, and a horse-shoe, and some vials of medicine that didn't have no label on them; and just as we was leaving I found a tolerable good curry-comb, and Jim he found a ratty old fiddlebow, and a wooden leg. The straps was broke off of it, but barring that, it was a good enough leg, though it was too long for me and not long enough for Jim, and we couldn't find the other one, though we hunted all around.

And so, take it all around, we made a good haul. When we was ready to shove off, we was a quarter of a mile below the island, and it was pretty broad day; so I made Jim lay down in the canoe and cover up with the quilt, because if he set up, people could tell he was a nigger a good ways off. I paddled over to the Illinois shore, and drifted down most a half a mile doing it. I crept up the dead water under the bank, and hadn't no accidents and didn't see nobody. We got home all safe.

---

8. Pocketknife with one blade, named for the inventor.

Chapter X

After breakfast I wanted to talk about the dead man and guess out how he come to be killed, but Jim didn't want to. He said it would fetch bad luck; and besides, he said, he might come and ha'nt us; he said a man that warn't buried was more likely to go a-ha'nting around than one that was planted and comfortable. That sounded pretty reasonable, so I didn't say no more; but I couldn't keep from studying over it and wishing I knowed who shot the man, and what they done it for.

We rummaged the clothes we'd got, and found eight dollars in silver sewed up in the lining of an old blanket overcoat. Jim said he reckoned the people in that house stole the coat, because if they'd a knowed the money was there they wouldn't a left it. I said I reckoned they killed him, too; but Jim didn't want to talk about that. I says:

"Now, you think it's bad luck; but what did you say when I fetched in the snake-skin that I found on the top of the ridge day before yesterday? You said it was the worst bad luck in the world to touch a snake-skin with my hands. Well, here's your bad luck! We've raked in all this truck and eight dollars besides. I wish we could have some bad luck like this every day, Jim."

"Never you mind, honey, never you mind. Don't you git too peart.[9] It's a-comin'. Mind I tell you, it's a-comin'."

It did come, too. It was Tuesday that we had that talk. Well, after dinner Friday, we was laying around in the grass at the upper end of the ridge, and got out of tobacco. I went to the cavern to get some, and found a rattlesnake in there. I killed him, and curled him up on the foot of Jim's blanket, ever so natural, thinking there'd be some fun when Jim found him there. Well, by night I forgot all about the snake, and when Jim flung himself down on the blanket while I struck a light, the snake's mate was there, and bit him.

He jumped up yelling, and the first thing the light showed was the varmint curled up and ready for another spring. I laid him out in a second with a stick, and Jim grabbed pap's whiskey jug and began to pour it down.

He was barefooted, and the snake bit him right on the heel. That all comes of my being such a fool as to not remember that whenever you leave a dead snake its mate always comes there and curls around it. Jim told me to chop off the snake's head and throw it away, and then skin the body and roast a piece of it. I done it, and he eat it and said it would help cure him. He made me take off the rattles and tie them around his wrist, too. He said that that would help. Then I slid out quiet and throwed the snakes clear away amongst the bushes; for I warn't going to let Jim find out it was all my fault, not if I could help it.

Jim sucked and sucked at the jug, and now and then he got out of his head and pitched around and yelled; but every time he come to himself he went to sucking at the jug again. His foot swelled up pretty big, and so did his leg; but by-and-by the drunk begun to come, and so I judged he was all right; but I'd druther been bit with a snake than pap's whiskey.

Jim was laid up for four days and nights. Then the swelling was all gone and he was around again. I made up my mind I wouldn't ever take aholt of a snake-skin again with my hands, now that I see what had come of it. Jim said he reckoned I would believe him next time. And he said that handling

9. Impertinent.

a snake-skin was such awful bad luck that maybe we hadn't got to the end of it yet. He said he druther see the new moon over his left shoulder as much as a thousand times than take up a snake-skin in his hand. Well, I was getting to feel that way myself, though I've always reckoned that looking at the new moon over your left shoulder is one of the carelessest and foolishest things a body can do. Old Hank Bunker done it once, and bragged about it; and in less than two years he got drunk and fell off of the shot tower and spread himself out so that he was just a kind of layer, as you may say; and they slid him edgeways between two barn doors for a coffin, and buried him so, so they say, but I didn't see it. Pap told me. But anyway, it all come of looking at the moon that way, like a fool.

Well, the days went along, and the river went down between its banks again; and about the first thing we done was to bait one of the big hooks with a skinned rabbit and set it and catch a cat-fish that was as big as a man, being six foot two inches long, and weighed over two hundred pounds. We couldn't handle him, of course; he would a flung us into Illinois. We just set there and watched him rip and tear around till he drowned. We found a brass button in his stomach, and a round ball, and lots of rubbage. We split the ball open with the hatchet, and there was a spool in it. Jim said he'd had it there a long time, to coat it over so and make a ball of it. It was as big a fish as was ever catched in the Mississippi, I reckon. Jim said he hadn't ever seen a bigger one. He would a been worth a good deal over at the village. They peddle out such a fish as that by the pound in the market house there; everybody buys some of him; his meat's as white as snow and makes a good fry.

Next morning I said it was getting slow and dull, and I wanted to get a stirring up, some way. I said I reckoned I would slip over the river and find out what was going on. Jim liked that notion; but he said I must go in the dark and look sharp. Then he studied it over and said, couldn't I put on some of them old things and dress up like a girl? That was a good notion, too. So we shortened up one of the calico gowns and I turned up my trowser-legs to my knees and got into it. Jim hitched it behind with the hooks, and it was a fair fit. I put on the sun-bonnet and tied it under my chin, and then for a body to look in and see my face was like looking down a joint of stove-pipe. Jim said nobody would know me, even in the daytime, hardly. I practiced around all day to get the hang of the things, and by-and-by I could do pretty well in them, only Jim said I didn't walk like a girl; and he said I must quit pulling up my gown to get at my britches pocket. I took notice, and done better.

I started up the Illinois shore in the canoe just after dark.

I started across to the town from a little below the ferry landing, and the drift of the current fetched me in at the bottom of the town. I tied up and started along the bank. There was a light burning in a little shanty that hadn't been lived in for a long time, and I wondered who had took up quarters there. I slipped up and peeped in at the window. There was a woman about forty year old in there, knitting by a candle that was on a pine table. I didn't know her face; she was a stranger, for you couldn't start a face in that town that I didn't know. Now this was lucky, because I was weakening; I was getting afraid I had come; people might know my voice and find me out. But if this woman had been in such a little town two days she could tell me all I wanted to know; so I knocked at the door, and made up my mind I wouldn't forget I was a girl.

Chapter XI

"Come in," says the woman, and I did. She says:

"Take a cheer."

I done it. She looked me all over with her little shiny eyes, and says:

"What might your name be?"

"Sarah Williams."

"Where 'bouts do you live? In this neighborhood?"

"No'm. In Hookerville, seven mile below. I've walked all the way and I'm all tired out."

"Hungry, too, I reckon. I'll find you something."

"No'm, I ain't hungry. I was so hungry I had to stop two mile below here at a farm; so I ain't hungry no more. It's what makes me so late. My mother's down sick, and out of money and everything, and I come to tell my uncle Abner Moore. He lives at the upper end of the town, she says. I hain't ever been here before. Do you know him?"

"No; but I don't know everybody yet. I haven't lived here quite two weeks. It's a considerable ways to the upper end of the town. You better stay here all night. Take off your bonnet."

"No," I says, "I'll rest a while, I reckon, and go on. I ain't afeard of the dark."

She said she wouldn't let me go by myself, but her husband would be in by-and-by, maybe in a hour and a half, and she'd send him along with me. Then she got to talking about her husband, and about her relations up the river, and her relations down the river, and how much better off they used to was, and how they didn't know but they'd made a mistake coming to our town, instead of letting well alone—and so on and so on, till I was afeard I had made a mistake coming to her to find out what was going on in the town; but by-and-by she dropped onto pap and the murder, and then I was pretty willing to let her clatter right along. She told about me and Tom Sawyer finding the six thousand dollars (only she got it ten) and all about pap and what a hard lot he was, and what a hard lot I was, and at last she got down to where I was murdered. I says:

"Who done it? We've heard considerable about these goings on, down in Hookerville, but we don't know who 'twas that killed Huck Finn."

"Well, I reckon there's a right smart chance of people *here* that'd like to know who killed him. Some thinks old Finn done it himself."

"No—is that so?"

"Most everybody thought it at first. He'll never know how nigh he come to getting lynched. But before night they changed around and judged it was done by a runaway nigger named Jim."

"Why *he*—"

I stopped. I reckoned I better keep still. She run on, and never noticed I had put in at all.

"The nigger run off the very night Huck Finn was killed. So there's a reward out for him—three hundred dollars. And there's a reward out for old Finn too—two hundred dollars. You see, he come to town the morning after the murder, and told about it, and was out with 'em on the ferry-boat hunt, and right away after he up and left. Before night they wanted to lynch him, but he was gone, you see. Well, next day they found out the nigger was gone; they found out he hadn't ben seen sence ten o'clock the night the murder was done. So then they put it on him, you see, and while they was full of it, next day back comes old Finn and went boohooing to Judge Thatcher to get money to hunt for the nigger all over Illinois with. The judge give him some, and that evening he got drunk and was around till after midnight with a couple of mighty hard looking strangers, and then went off with them. Well, he hain't come back sence, and they ain't looking for him back till this thing blows over a little, for people thinks now that he killed his boy and fixed things so folks would think robbers done it, and then he'd get Huck's money without having to bother a long time with a lawsuit. People do say he warn't any too good to do it. Oh, he's sly, I reckon. If he don't come back for a year, he'll be all right. You can't prove anything on him, you know; everything will be quieted down then, and he'll walk into Huck's money as easy as nothing."

"Yes, I reckon so, 'm. I don't see nothing in the way of it. Has everybody quit thinking the nigger done it?"

"Oh no, not everybody. A good many thinks he done it. But they'll get the nigger pretty soon, now, and maybe they can scare it out of him."

"Why, are they after him yet?"

"Well, you're innocent, ain't you! Does three hundred dollars lay round every day for people to pick up? Some folks thinks the nigger ain't far from here. I'm one of them—but I hain't talked it around. A few days ago I was talking with an old couple that lives next door in the log shanty, and they happened to say hardly anybody ever goes to that island over yonder that they call Jackson's Island. Don't anybody live there? says I. No, nobody, says they. I didn't say any more, but I done some thinking. I was pretty near certain I'd seen smoke over there, about the head of the island, a day or two before that, so I says to myself, like as not that nigger's hiding over there; anyway, says I, it's worth the trouble to give the place a hunt. I hain't seen any smoke sence, so I reckon maybe he's gone, if it was him; but husband's going over to see—him and another man. He was gone up the river; but he got back to-day and I told him as soon as he got here two hours ago."

I had got so uneasy I couldn't set still. I had to do something with my hands; so I took up a needle off of the table and went to threading it. My hands shook and I was making a bad job of it. When the woman stopped talking, I looked up, and she was looking at me pretty curious, and smiling a little. I put down the needle and thread and let on to be interested—and I was, too—and says:

"Three hundred dollars is a power of money. I wish my mother could get it. Is your husband going over there to-night?"

"Oh, yes. He went up town with the man I was telling you of, to get a boat and see if they could borrow another gun. They'll go over after midnight."

"Couldn't they see better if they was to wait till daytime?"

"Yes. And couldn't the nigger see better too? After midnight he'll likely be asleep, and they can slip around through the woods and hunt up his camp fire all the better for the dark, if he's got one."

"I didn't think of that."

The woman kept looking at me pretty curious, and I didn't feel a bit comfortable. Pretty soon she says:

"What did you say your name was, honey?"

"M—Mary Williams."

Somehow it didn't seem to me that I said it was Mary before, so I didn't look up; seemed to me I said it was Sarah; so I felt sort of cornered, and was afeared maybe I was looking it, too. I wished the woman would say something more; the longer she set still, the uneasier I was. But now she says:

"Honey, I thought you said it was Sarah when you first come in?"

"Oh, yes'm, I did. Sarah Mary Williams. Sarah's my first name. Some calls me Sarah, some calls me Mary."

"Oh, that's the way of it?"

"Yes'm."

I was feeling better, then, but I wished I was out of there, anyway. I couldn't look up yet.

Well, the woman fell to talking about how hard times was, and how poor they had to live, and how the rats was as free as if they owned the place, and so forth, and so on, and then I got easy again. She was right about the rats. You'd see one stick his nose out of a hole in the corner every little while. She said she had to have things handy to throw at them when she was alone, or they wouldn't give her no peace. She showed me a bar of lead, twisted up into a knot, and she said she was a good shot with it generly, but she'd wrenched her arm a day or two ago, and didn't know whether she could throw true, now. But she watched for a chance, and directly she banged away at a rat, but she missed him wide, and said "Ouch!" it hurt her arm so. Then she told me to try for the next one. I wanted to be getting away before the old man got back, but of course I didn't let on. I got the thing, and the first rat that showed his nose I let drive, and if he'd a stayed where he was he'd a been a tolerable sick rat. She said that that was first-rate, and she reckoned I would hive[1] the next one. She went and got the lump of lead and fetched it back and brought along a hank of yarn, which she wanted me to help her with. I held up my two hands and she put the hank over them and went on talking about her and her husband's matters. But she broke off to say:

"Keep your eye on the rats. You better have the lead in your lap, handy."

So she dropped the lump into my lap, just at that moment, and I clapped my legs together on it and she went on talking. But only about a minute. Then she took off the hank and looked me straight in the face, but very pleasant, and says:

"Come, now—what's your real name?"

"Wh-what, mum?"

"What's your real name? Is it Bill, or Tom, or Bob?—or what is it?"

I reckon I shook like a leaf, and I didn't know hardly what to do. But I says:

"Please to don't poke fun at a poor girl like me, mum. If I'm in the way, here I'll—"

"No, you won't. Set down and stay where you are. I ain't going to hurt you, and I ain't going to tell on you, nuther. You just tell me your secret, and trust me. I'll keep it; and what's more, I'll help you. So'll my old man, if you want him to. You see, you're a run-away 'prentice—that's all. It ain't anything. There ain't any harm in it. You've been treated bad, and you made up your mind to cut. Bless you, child, I wouldn't tell on you. Tell me all about it, now—that's a good boy."

1. Get.

So I said it wouldn't be no use to try to play it any longer, and I would just make a clean breast and tell her everything, but she mustn't go back on her promise. Then I told her my father and mother was dead, and the law had bound me out to a mean old farmer in the country thirty mile back from the river, and he treated me so bad I couldn't stand it no longer; he went away to be gone a couple of days, and so I took my chance and stole some of his daughter's old clothes, and cleared out, and I had been three nights coming the thirty miles; I traveled nights, and hid daytimes and slept, and the bag of bread and meat I carried from home lasted me all the way and I had a plenty. I said I believed my uncle Abner Moore would take care of me, and so that was why I struck out for this town of Goshen.

"Goshen, child? This ain't Goshen. This is St. Petersburg. Goshen's ten mile further up the river. Who told you this was Goshen?"

"Why, a man I met at day-break this morning, just as I was going to turn into the woods for my regular sleep. He told me when the roads forked I must take the right hand, and five mile would fetch me to Goshen."

"He was drunk I reckon. He told you just exactly wrong."

"Well, he did act like he was drunk, but it ain't no matter now. I got to be moving along. I'll fetch Goshen before day-light."

"Hold on a minute. I'll put you up a snack to eat. You might want it."

So she put me up a snack, and says:

"Say—when a cow's laying down, which end of her gets up first? Answer up prompt, now—don't stop to study over it. Which end gets up first?"

"The hind end, mum."

"Well, then, a horse?"

"The for'rard end, mum."

"Which side of a tree does the most moss grow on?"

"North side."

"If fifteen cows is browsing on a hillside, how many of them eats with their heads pointed the same direction?"

"The whole fifteen, mum."

"Well, I reckon you *have* lived in the country. I thought maybe you was trying to hocus me again. What's your real name, now?"

"George Peters, mum."

"Well, try to remember it, George. Don't forget and tell me it's Elexander before you go, and then get out by saying it's George Elexander when I catch you. And don't go about women in that old calico. You do a girl tolerable poor, but you might fool men, maybe. Bless you, child, when you set out to thread a needle, don't hold the thread still and fetch the needle up to it; hold the needle still and poke the thread at it—that's the way a woman most always does; but a man always does 'tother way. And when you throw at a rat or anything, hitch yourself up a tip-toe, and fetch your hand up over your head as awkard as you can, and miss your rat about six or seven foot. Throw stiff-armed from the shoulder, like there was a pivot there for it to turn on—like a girl; not from the wrist and elbow, with your arm out to one side, like a boy. And mind you, when a girl tries to catch anything in her lap, she throws her knees apart; she don't clap them together, the way you did when you catched the lump of lead. Why, I spotted you for a boy when you was threading the needle; and I contrived the other things just to make certain. Now trot along to your uncle, Sarah Mary Williams George Elexander Peters, and if you get into trouble you send word to Mrs. Judith Loftus, which is me, and I'll do what I can to get you out of it. Keep the river road, all the way, and next time you tramp, take shoes and socks with you. The river road's a rocky one, and your feet 'll be in a condition when you get to Goshen, I reckon."

I went up the bank about fifty yards, and then I doubled on my tracks and slipped back to where my canoe was, a good piece below the house. I jumped in and was off in a hurry. I went up stream far enough to make the head of the island, and then started across. I took off the sun-bonnet, for I didn't want no blinders on, then. When I was about the middle, I hear the clock begin to strike; so I stops and listens; the sound come faint over the water, but clear—eleven. When I struck the head of the island I never waited to blow, though I was most winded, but I shoved right into the timber where my old camp used to be, and started a good fire there on a high-and-dry spot.

Then I jumped in the canoe and dug out for our place a mile and a half below, as hard as I could go. I landed, and slopped through the timber and up the ridge and into the cavern. There Jim laid, sound asleep on the ground. I roused him out and says:

"Git up and hump yourself, Jim! There ain't a minute to lose. They're after us!"

Jim never asked no questions, he never said a word; but the way he worked for the next half an hour showed about how he was scared. By that time everything we had in the world was on our raft and she was ready to be shoved out from the willow cove where she was hid. We put out the camp fire at the cavern the first thing, and didn't show a candle outside after that.

I took the canoe out from shore a little piece and took a look, but if there was a boat around I couldn't see it, for stars and shadows ain't good to see by. Then we got out the raft and slipped along down in the shade, past the foot of the island dead still, never saying a word.

Chapter XII

It must a been close onto one o'clock when we got below the island at last, and the raft did seem to go mighty slow. If a boat was to come along, we was going to take to the canoe and break for the Illinois shore; and it was well a boat didn't come, for we hadn't ever thought to put the gun into the canoe, or a fishing-line or anything to eat. We was in ruther too much of a sweat to think of so many things. It warn't good judgment to put *everything* on the raft.

If the men went to the island, I just expect they found the camp fire I built, and watched it all night for Jim to come. Anyways, they stayed away from us, and if my building the fire never fooled them it warn't no fault of mine. I played it as low-down on them as I could.

When the first streak of day begun to show, we tied up to a tow-head in a big bend on the Illinois side, and hacked off cotton-wood branches with the hatchet and covered up the raft with them so she looked like there had been a cave-in in the bank there. A tow-head is a sand-bar that has cotton-woods on it as thick as harrow-teeth.

We had mountains on the Missouri shore and heavy timber on the Illinois side, and the channel was down the Missouri shore at that place, so we warn't afraid of anybody running across us. We laid there all day and watched the rafts and steamboats spin down the Missouri shore, and up-bound steamboats fight the big river in the middle. I told Jim all about the time I had jabbering with that woman; and Jim said she was a smart one, and if she was to start after us herself *she* wouldn't set down and watch a camp fire—no, sir, she'd fetch a dog. Well, then, I said, why couldn't she tell her husband to fetch a dog? Jim said he bet she did think of it by the time the men was ready to start, and he believed they must a gone up town to get a dog and so they lost all that time, or else we wouldn't be here on a tow-head sixteen or seventeen mile below the village—no, indeedy, we would be in that same old town again. So I said I didn't care what was the reason they didn't get us, as long as they didn't.

When it was beginning to come on dark, we poked our heads out of the cottonwood thicket and looked up, and down, and across; nothing in sight; so Jim took up some of the top planks of the raft and built a snug wigwam to get under in blazing weather and rainy, and to keep the things dry. Jim made a floor for the wigwam, and raised it a foot or more above the level of the raft, so now the blankets and all the traps was out of the reach of steamboat waves. Right in the middle of the wigwam we made a layer of dirt about five or six inches deep with a frame around it for to hold it to its place; this was to build a fire on in sloppy weather or chilly; the wigwam would keep it from being seen. We made an extra steering oar, too, because one of the others might get broke, on a snag or something. We fixed up a short forked stick to hang the old lantern on; because we must always light the lantern whenever we see a steamboat coming down stream, to keep from getting run over; but we wouldn't have to light it up for upstream boats unless we see we was in what they call "crossing;" for the river was pretty high yet, very low banks being still a little under water; so up-bound boats didn't always run the channel, but hunted easy water.

This second night we run between seven and eight hours, with a current that was making over four mile an hour. We catched fish, and talked, and we took a swim now and then to keep off sleepiness. It was kind of solemn, drifting down the big still river, laying on our backs looking up at the stars, and we didn't ever feel like talking loud, and it warn't often that we laughed, only a little kind of a low chuckle. We had mighty good weather, as a general thing, and nothing ever happened to us at all, that night, nor the next, nor the next.

Every night we passed towns, some of them away up on black hillsides, nothing but just a shiny bed of lights, not a house could you see. The fifth night we passed St. Louis, and it was like the whole world lit up. In St. Petersburg they used to say there was twenty or thirty thousand people in St. Louis,[2] but I never believed it till I see that wonderful spread of lights at two o'clock that still night. There warn't a sound there; everybody was asleep.

Every night now, I used to slip ashore, towards ten o'clock, at some little village, and buy ten or fifteen cents' worth of meal or bacon or other stuff to eat; and sometimes I lifted a chicken that warn't roosting comfortable, and

2. St. Louis is 170 miles down the Mississippi from Hannibal.

took him along. Pap always said, take a chicken when you get a chance, because if you don't want him yourself you can easy find somebody that does, and a good deed ain't ever forgot. I never see pap when he didn't want the chicken himself, but that is what he used to say, anyway.

Mornings, before daylight, I slipped into corn fields and borrowed a watermelon, or a mushmelon, or a punkin, or some new corn, or things of that kind. Pap always said it warn't no harm to borrow things, if you was meaning to pay them back, sometime; but the widow said it warn't anything but a soft name for stealing, and no decent body would do it. Jim said he reckoned the widow was partly right and pap was partly right; so the best way would be for us to pick out two or three things from the list and say we wouldn't borrow them any more—then he reckoned it wouldn't be no harm to borrow the others. So we talked it over all one night, drifting along down the river, trying to make up our minds whether to drop the watermelons, or the cantelopes, or the mushmelons, or what. But towards daylight we got it all settled satisfactory, and concluded to drop crabapples and p'simmons. We warn't feeling just right, before that, but it was all comfortable now. I was glad the way it come out, too, because crabapples ain't ever good, and the p'simmons wouldn't be ripe for two or three months yet.

We shot a water-fowl, now and then, that got up too early in the morning or didn't go to bed early enough in the evening. Take it all around, we lived pretty high.

The fifth night below St. Louis we had a big storm after midnight, with a power of thunder and lightning, and the rain poured down in a solid sheet. We stayed in the wigwam and let the raft take care of itself. When the lightning glared out we could see a big straight river ahead, and high rocky bluffs on both sides. By-and-by says I, "Hel-*lo* Jim, looky yonder!" It was a steamboat that had killed herself on a rock. We was drifting straight down for her. The lightning showed her very distinct. She was leaning over, with part of her upper deck above water, and you could see every little chimbly-guy[3] clean and clear, and a chair by the big bell, with an old slouch hat hanging on the back of it when the flashes come.

Well, it being away in the night, and stormy, and all so mysterious-like, I felt just the way any other boy would a felt when I see that wreck laying there so mournful and lonesome in the middle of the river. I wanted to get aboard of her and slink around a little, and see what there was there. So I says:

"Le's land on her, Jim."

But Jim was dead against it, at first. He says:

"I doan' want to go fool'n 'long er no wrack. We's doin' blame' well, en we better let blame' well alone, as de good book says. Like as not dey's a watchman on dat wrack."

"Watchman your grandmother," I says; "there ain't nothing to watch but the texas[4] and the pilot-house; and do you reckon anybody's going to resk his life for a texas and a pilot-house such a night as this, when it's likely to break up and wash off down the river any minute?" Jim couldn't say nothing to that, so he didn't try. "And besides," I says, "we might borrow something worth having, out of the captain's stateroom. Seegars, *I* bet you—and cost

---

3. Wire used to steady the chimney stacks.
4. The large cabin on the top deck located just behind or beneath the pilothouse; it serves as officers' quarters.

five cents apiece, solid cash. Steamboat captains is always rich, and get sixty dollars a month, and *they* don't care a cent what a thing costs, you know, long as they want it. Stick a candle in your pocket; I can't rest, Jim, till we give her a rummaging. Do you reckon Tom Sawyer would ever go by this thing? Not for pie, he wouldn't. He'd call it an adventure—that's what he'd call it; and he'd land on that wreck if it was his last act. And wouldn't he throw style into it?—wouldn't he spread himself, nor nothing? Why, you'd think it was Christopher C'lumbus discovering Kingdom-Come. I wish Tom Sawyer *was* here."

Jim he grumbled a little, but give in. He said we mustn't talk any more than we could help, and then talk mighty low. The lightning showed us the wreck again, just in time, and we fetched the starboard derrick,[5] and made fast there.

The deck was high out, here. We went sneaking down the slope of it to lab-board, in the dark, towards the texas, feeling our way slow with our feet, and spreading our hands out to fend off the guys, for it was so dark we couldn't see no sign of them. Pretty soon we struck the forward end of the skylight, and clumb onto it; and the next step fetched us in front of the captain's door, which was open, and by Jimminy, away down through the texas-hall we see a light! and all in the same second we seem to hear low voices in yonder!

Jim whispered and said he was feeling powerful sick, and told me to come along. I says, all right; and was going to start for the raft; but just then I heard a voice wail out and say:

"Oh, please don't, boys; I swear I won't ever tell!"

Another voice said, pretty loud:

"It's a lie, Jim Turner. You've acted this way before. You always want more'n your share of the truck and you've always got it, too, because you've swore 't if you didn't you'd tell. But this time you've said it jest one time too many. You're the meanest, treacherousest hound in this country."

By this time Jim was gone for the raft. I was just a-biling with curiosity; and I says to myself, Tom Sawyer wouldn't back out now, and so I won't either; I'm agoing to see what's going on here. So I dropped on my hands and knees, in the little passage, and crept aft in the dark, till there warn't but about one stateroom betwixt me and the cross-hall of the texas. Then, in there I see a man stretched on the floor and tied hand and foot, and two men standing over him, and one of them had a dim lantern in his hand, and the other one had a pistol. This one kept pointing the pistol at the man's head on the floor and saying—

"I'd *like* to! And I orter, too, a mean skunk!"

The man on the floor would shrivel up, and say: "Oh, please don't, Bill—I hain't ever goin' to tell."

And every time he said that, the man with the lantern would laugh and say:

" 'Deed you *ain't*! You never said no truer thing 'n that, you bet you." And once he said, "Hear him beg! and yit if we hadn't got the best of him and tied him, he'd a killed us both. And what *for*? Jist for noth'n. Jist because we stood on our *rights*—that's what for. But I lay you ain't agoin' to threaten nobody any more, Jim Turner. Put *up* that pistol, Bill."

5. Boom for lifting cargo.

Bill says:

"I don't want to, Jake Packard. I'm for killin' him—and didn't he kill old Hatfield jist the same way—and don't he deserve it?"

"But I don't *want* him killed, and I've got my reasons for it."

"Bless yo' heart for them words, Jake Packard! I'll never forget you, long's I live!" says the man on the floor, sort of blubbering.

Packard didn't take no notice of that, but hung up his lantern on a nail, and started towards where I was, there in the dark, and motioned Bill to come. I crawfished[6] as fast as I could, about two yards, but the boat slanted so that I couldn't make very good time; so to keep from getting run over and catched I crawled into a stateroom on the upper side. The man come a-pawing along in the dark, and when Packard got to my stateroom, he says:

"Here—come in here."

And in he come, and Bill after him. But before they got in, I was up in the upper berth, cornered, and sorry I come. Then they stood there, with their hands on the ledge of the berth, and talked. I couldn't see them, but I could tell where they was, by the whiskey they'd been having. I was glad I didn't drink whiskey; but it wouldn't made much difference, anyway, because most of the time they couldn't a treed me because I didn't breathe. I was too scared. And besides, a body *couldn't* breathe, and hear such talk. They talked low and earnest. Bill wanted to kill Turner. He says:

"He's said he'll tell, and he will. If we was to give both our shares to him *now*, it wouldn't make no difference after the row, and the way we've served him. Shore's you're born, he'll turn State's evidence; now you hear *me*. I'm for putting him out of his troubles."

"So'm I," says Packard, very quiet.

"Blame it, I'd sorter begun to think you wasn't. Well, then, that's all right. Les' go and do it."

"Hold on a minute; I hain't had my say yit. You listen to me. Shooting's good, but there's quieter ways if the thing's *got* to be done. But what I say, is this; it ain't good sense to go court'n around after a halter,[7] if you can git at what you're up to in some way that's jist as good and at the same time don't bring you into no resks. Ain't that so?"

"You bet it is. But how you goin' to manage it this time?"

"Well, my idea is this: we'll rustle around and gether up whatever pickins we've overlooked in the staterooms, and shove for shore and hide the truck. Then we'll wait. Now I say it ain't agoin' to be more 'n two hours befo' this wrack breaks up and washes off down the river. See? He'll be drownded, and won't have nobody to blame for it but his own self. I reckon that's a considerble sight better'n killin' of him. I'm unfavorable to killin' a man as long as you can git around it; it ain't good sense, it ain't good morals. Ain't I right?"

"Yes—I reck'n you are. But s'pose she *don't* break up and wash off?"

"Well, we can wait the two hours, anyway, and see, can't we?"

"All right, then; come along."

So they started, and I lit out, all in a cold sweat, and scrambled forward. It was dark as pitch there; but I said in a kind of a coarse whisper, "Jim!" and he answered up, right at my elbow, with a sort of a moan, and I says:

---

6. Crept backward on all fours.   7. Hangman's noose.

"Quick, Jim, it ain't no time for fooling around and moaning; there's a gang of murderers in yonder, and if we don't hunt up their boat and set her drifting down the river so these fellows can't get away from the wreck, there's one of 'em going to be in a bad fix. But if we find their boat we can put *all* of 'em in a bad fix—for the Sheriff 'll get 'em. Quick—hurry! I'll hunt the labboard side, you hunt the stabboard. You start at the raft, and—"

"Oh, my lordy, lordy! *Raf'?* Dey ain' no raf' no mo', she done broke loose en gone!—'en here we is!"

Chapter XIII

Well, I catched my breath and most fainted. Shut up on a wreck with such a gang as that! But it warn't no time to be sentimentering. We'd *got* to find that boat, now—had to have it for ourselves. So we went a-quaking and down the stabboard side, and slow work it was, too—seemed a week before we got to the stern. No sign of a boat. Jim said he didn't believe he could go any further—so scared he hadn't hardly any strength left, he said. But I said come on, if we get left on this wreck, we are in a fix, sure. So on we prowled, again. We struck for the stern of the texas, and found it, and then scrabbled along forwards on the skylight, hanging on from shutter to shutter, for the edge of the skylight was in the water. When we got pretty close to the cross-hall door there was the skiff, sure enough! I could just barely see her. I felt ever so thankful. In another second I would a been aboard of her; but just then the door opened. One of the men stuck his head out, only about a couple of foot from me, and I thought I was gone; but he jerked it in again, and says:

"Heave that blame lantern out o' sight, Bill!"

He flung a bag of something into the boat, and then got in himself, and set down. It was Packard. Then Bill *he* come out and got in. Packard says, in a low voice:

"All ready—shove off!"

I couldn't hardly hang onto the shutters, I was so weak. But Bill says:

"Hold on—'d you go through him?"

"No. Didn't you?"

"No. So he's got his share o' the cash, yet."

"Well, then, come along—no use to take truck and leave money."

"Say—won't he suspicion what we're up to?"

"Maybe he won't. But we got to have it anyway. Come along." So they got out and went in.

The door slammed to, because it was on the careened side; and in a half second I was in the boat, and Jim come a tumbling after me. I out with my knife and cut the rope, and away we went!

We didn't touch an oar, and we didn't speak nor whisper, nor hardly even breathe. We went gliding swift along, dead silent, past the tip of the paddle-box, and past the stern; then in a second or two more we was a hundred yards below the wreck, and the darkness soaked her up, every last sign of her, and we was safe, and knowed it.

When we was three or four hundred yards down stream, we see the lantern show like a little spark at the texas door, for a second, and we knowed by that that the rascals had missed their boat, and was beginning to understand that they was in just as much trouble, now, as Jim Turner was.

Then Jim manned the oars, and we took out after our raft. Now was the first time that I begun to worry about the men—I reckon I hadn't had time to before. I begun to think how dreadful it was, even for murderers, to be in such a fix. I says to myself, there ain't no telling but I might come to be a murderer myself, yet, and then how would I like it? So says I to Jim:

"The first light we see, we'll land a hundred yards below it or above it, in a place where it's a good hiding-place for you and the skiff, and then I'll go and fix up some kind of a yarn, and get somebody to go for that gang and get them out of their scrape, so they can be hung when their time comes."

But that idea was a failure; for pretty soon it begun to storm again, and this time worse than ever. The rain poured down, and never a light showed; everybody in bed, I reckon. We boomed along down the river, watching for lights and watching for our raft. After a long time the rain let up, but the clouds staid, and the lightning kept whimpering, and by-and-by a flash showed us a black thing ahead, floating, and we made for it.

It was the raft, and mighty glad was we to get aboard of it again. We seen a light, now, away down to the right, on shore. So I said I would go for it. The skiff was half full of plunder which that gang had stole, there on the wreck. We hustled it onto the raft in a pile, and I told Jim to float along down, and show a light when he judged he had gone about two mile, and keep it burning till I come; then I manned my oars and shoved for the light. As I got down towards it, three or four more showed—up on a hillside. It was a village. I closed in above the shore-light, and laid on my oars and floated. As I went by, I see it was a lantern hanging on the jackstaff of a double-hull ferry-boat. I skimmed around for the watchman, a-wondering whereabouts he slept; and by-and-by I found him roosting on the bitts,[8] forward, with his head down between his knees. I give his shoulder two or three little shoves, and begun to cry.

He stirred up, in a kind of startlish way; but when he see it was only me, he took a good gap and stretch, and then he says:

"Hello, what's up? Don't cry, bub. What's the trouble?"

I says:

"Pap, and mam, and sis, and—"

Then I broke down. He says:

"Oh, dang it, now, *don't* take on so, we all has to have our troubles and this'n 'll come out all right. What's the matter with 'em?"

"They're—they're—are you the watchman of the boat?"

"Yes," he says, kind of pretty-well-satisfied like. "I'm the captain and the owner, and the mate, and the pilot, and watchman, and head deck-hand; and sometimes I'm the freight and passengers. I ain't as rich as old Jim Hornback, and I can't be so blame' generous and good to Tom, Dick and Harry as what he is, and slam around money the way he does; but I've told him a many a time 't I wouldn't trade places with him; for, says I, a sailor's life's the life for me, and I'm derned if I'd live two mile out o' town, where there ain't nothing ever goin' on, not for all his spondulicks[9] and as much more on top of it. Says I—"

I broke in and says:

"They're in an awful peck of trouble, and—"

<hr>

8. Vertical wooden posts to which cables can be secured.
9. Money (slang).

"*Who* is?"

"Why, pap, and mam, and sis, and Miss Hooker; and if you'd take your ferry-boat and go up there—"

"Up where? Where are they?"

"On the wreck."

"What wreck?"

"Why, there ain't but one."

"What, you don't mean the *Walter Scott*?"[1]

"Yes."

"Good land! what are they doin' *there*, for gracious sakes?"

"Well, they didn't go there a-purpose."

"I bet they didn't! Why, great goodness, there ain't no chance for 'em if they don't git off mighty quick! Why, how in the nation did they ever git into such a scrape?"

"Easy enough. Miss Hooker was a-visiting, up there to the town—"

"Yes, Booth's Landing—go on."

"She was a-visiting, there at Booth's Landing, and just in the edge of the evening she started over with her nigger woman in the horse-ferry, to stay all night at her friend's house, Miss What-you-may-call her, I disremember her name, and they lost their steering-oar, and swung around and went a-floating down, stern-first, about two mile, and saddle-baggsed[2] on the wreck, and the ferry man and the nigger woman and the horses was all lost, but Miss Hooker she made a grab and got aboard the wreck. Well, about an hour after dark, we come along down in our trading-scow, and it was so dark we didn't notice the wreck till we was right on it; and so *we* saddle-baggsed; but all of us was saved but Bill Whipple—and oh, he *was* the best cretur!—I most wish't it had been me, I do."

"My George! It's the beatenest thing I ever struck. And *then* what did you all do?"

"Well, we hollered and took on, but it's so wide there, we couldn't make nobody hear. So pap said somebody got to get ashore and get help somehow. I was the only one that could swim, so I made a dash for it, and Miss Hooker she said if I didn't strike help sooner, come here and hunt up her uncle, and he'd fix the thing. I made the land about a mile below, and been fooling along ever since, trying to get people to do something, but they said, 'What, in such a night and such a current? there ain't no sense in it; go for the steam-ferry.' Now if you'll go, and—"

"By Jackson, I'd *like* to, and blame it I don't know but I will; but who in the dingnation's agoin' to *pay* for it? Do you reckon your pap—"

"Why *that's* all right. Miss Hooker she told me, *particular*, that her uncle Hornback—"

"Great guns! is *he* her uncle? Look here, you break for that light over yonder-way, and turn out west when you git there, and about a quarter of a mile out you'll come to the tavern; tell 'em to dart you out to Jim Hornback's and he'll foot the bill. And don't you fool around any, because he'll want to

---

1. Twain blamed the feudalistic fantasies of the pre–Civil War South on the romantic novels of Sir Walter Scott (1771–1832). He expressed himself most vividly on this subject in *Life on the Mississippi* (ch. 46), where he observes: "Sir Walter had so large a hand in making Southern character, as it existed before the war, that he is in great measure responsible for the war."

2. Broken and doubled around the wreck.

"We turned in and slept." E. W. Kemble illustration from the first edition (1884).

know the news. Tell him I'll have his niece all safe before he can get to town. Hump yourself, now; I'm agoing up around the corner here, to roust out my engineer."

I struck for the light, but as soon as he turned the corner I went back and got into my skiff and bailed her out and then pulled up shore in the easy water about six hundred yards, and tucked myself in among some woodboats; for I couldn't rest easy till I could see the ferry-boat start. But take it all around, I was feeling ruther comfortable on accounts of taking all this trouble for that gang, for not many would a done it. I wished the widow knowed about it. I judged she would be proud of me for helping these rapscallions, because rapscallions and dead beats is the kind the widow and good people takes the most interest in.

Well, before long, here comes the wreck, dim and dusky, sliding along down! A kind of cold shiver went through me, and then I struck out for her. She was very deep, and I see in a minute there warn't much chance for anybody being alive in her. I pulled all around her and hollered a little, but there wasn't any answer; all dead still. I felt a little bit heavy-hearted about the gang, but not much, for I reckoned if they could stand it, I could.

Then here comes the ferry-boat; so I shoved for the middle of the river on a long down-stream slant; and when I judged I was out of eye-reach, I laid on my oars, and looked back and see her go and smell around the wreck for Miss Hooker's remainders, because the captain would know her uncle Hornback would want them; and then pretty soon the ferry-boat give it up and went for shore, and I laid into my work and went a-booming down the river.

It did seem a powerful long time before Jim's light showed up; and when it did show, it looked like it was a thousand mile off. By the time I got there the sky was beginning to get a little gray in the east; so we struck for an island, and hid the raft, and sunk the skiff, and turned in and slept like dead people.

Chapter XIV

By-and-by, when we got up, we turned over the truck the gang had stole off of the wreck, and found boots, and blankets, and clothes, and all sorts of other things, and a lot of books, and a spyglass, and three boxes of seegars. We hadn't ever been this rich before, in neither of our lives. The seegars was prime. We laid off all the afternoon in the woods talking, and me reading the books, and having a general good time. I told Jim all about what happened inside the wreck, and at the ferry-boat; and I said these kinds of things was adventures; but he said he didn't want no more adventures. He said that when I went in the texas and he crawled back to get on the raft and found her gone, he nearly died; because he judged it was all up with *him*, anyway it could be fixed; for if he didn't get saved he would get drownded; and if he did get saved, whoever saved him would send him back home so as to get the reward, and then Miss Watson would sell him South, sure. Well, he was right; he was most always right; he had an uncommon level head, for a nigger.

I read considerable to Jim about kings, and dukes, and earls, and such, and how gaudy they dressed, and how much style they put on, and called each other your majesty, and your grace, and your lordship, and so on, 'stead of mister; and Jim's eyes bugged out, and he was interested. He says:

"I didn't know dey was so many un um. I hain't hearn 'bout none un um, skasely, but ole King Sollermun, onless you counts dem kings dat's in a pack er k'yards. How much do a king git?"

"Get?" I says; "why, they get a thousand dollars a month if they want it; they can have just as much as they want; everything belongs to them."

"*Ain'* dat gay? En what dey got to do, Huck?"

"*They* don't do nothing! Why how you talk. They just set around."

"No—is dat so?"

"Of course it is. They just set around. Except maybe when there 's a war; then they go to the war. But other times they just lazy around; or go hawking—just hawking and sp—Sh!—d' you hear a noise?"

We skipped out and looked; but it warn't nothing but the flutter of a steamboat's wheel, away down coming around the point; so we come back.

"Yes," says I, "and other times, when things is dull, they fuss with the parlyment; and if everybody don't go just so he whacks their heads off. But mostly they hang round the harem."

"Roun' de which?"

"Harem."

"What's de harem?"

"The place where he keep his wives. Don't you know about the harem? Solomon had one; he had about a million wives."

"Why, yes, dat's so; I—I'd done forgot it. A harem's a bo'd'n-house, I reck'n. Mos' likely dey has rackety times in de nussery. En I reck'n de wives quarrels considable; en dat 'crease de racket. Yit dey say Sollermun de wises' man dat ever live.' I doan' take no stock in dat. Bekase why: would a wise man want to live in de mids' er sich a blimblammin' all de time? No—'deed he wouldn't. A wise man 'ud take en buil' a biler-factry; en den he could shet *down* de biler-factry when he want to res'."

"Well, but he *was* the wisest man, anyway; because the widow she told me so, her own self."

"I doan k'yer what de widder say, he *warn'* no wise man, nuther. He had some er de dad-fetchedes' ways I ever see. Does you know 'bout dat chile dat he 'uz gwyne to chop in two?"[3]

"Yes, the widow told me all about it."

"*Well*, den! Warn' dat de beatenes' notion in de worl'? You jes' take en look at it a minute. Dah's de stump, dah—dat's one er de women; heah's you—dat's de yuther one; I's Sollermun; en dish-yer dollar bill's de chile. Bofe un you claims it. What does I do? Does I shin aroun' mongs' de neighbors en fine out which un you de bill do b'long to, en han' it over to de right one, all safe en soun', de way dat anybody dat had any gumption would? No—I take en whack de bill in *two*, en give half un it to you, en de yuther half to de yuther woman. Dat's de way Sollermun was gwyne to do wid de chile. Now I want to ask you: what's de use er dat half a bill?—can't buy noth'n wid it. En what use is a half a chile? I wouldn' give a dern for a million un um."

"But hang it, Jim, you've clean missed the point—blame it, you've missed it a thousand mile."

"Who? Me? Go 'long. Doan' talk to *me* 'bout yo' pints. I reck'n I knows sense when I sees it; en dey ain' no sense in sich doin's as dat. De 'spute warn't 'bout a half a chile, de 'spute was 'bout a whole chile; en de man dat think he kin settle a 'spute 'bout a whole chile wid a half a chile, doan' know enough to come in out'n de rain. Doan' talk to me 'bout Sollermun, Huck, I knows him by de back."

"But I tell you you don't get the point."

"Blame de pint! I reck'n I knows what I knows. En mine you, de *real* pint is down furder—it's down deeper. It lays in de way Sollermun was raised. You take a man dat's got on'y one er two children; is dat man gwyne to be waseful o' chillen? No, he ain't; he can't 'ford it. *He* know how to value 'em. But you take a man dat's got 'bout five million chillen runnin' roun' de house, en it's diffunt. *He* as soon chop a chile in two as a cat. Dey's plenty mo'. A chile er two, mo' er less, warn't no consekens to Sollermun, dad fetch him!"

I never see such a nigger. If he got a notion in his head once, there warn't no getting it out again. He was the most down on Solomon of any nigger I ever see. So I went to talking about other kings, and let Solomon slide. I told about Louis Sixteenth that got his head cut off in France long time ago; and about his little boy the dolphin,[4] that would a been a king, but they took and shut him up in jail, and some say he died there.

"Po' little chap."

"But some says he got out and got away, and come to America."

3. In 1 Kings 3.16–28. When two women appeared before him claiming to be the mother of the same infant, Solomon ordered the child cut in two, expecting the real mother to object. The real mother pleaded with him to save the baby and to give it to the other woman, who had maliciously agreed to Solomon's original plan.

4. The Dauphin, Louis Charles, next in line of the succession to the throne, was eight years old when his father, Louis XVI, was beheaded (1793). Though the boy died in prison, probably in 1795, legends of his escape to America (and elsewhere) persisted, and Twain owned a book on the subject by Horace W. Fuller: *Imposters and Adventurers, Noted French Trials* (1882).

"Dat's good! But he'll be pooty lonesome—dey ain' no kings here, is dey, Huck?"

"No."

"Den he cain't git no situation. What he gwyne to do?"

"Well, I don't know. Some of them gets on the police, and some of them learns people how to talk French."

"Why, Huck, doan' de French people talk de same way we does?"

"No, Jim; you couldn't understand a word they said—not a single word."

"Well now, I be ding-busted! How do dat come?"

"I don't know; but it's so. I got some of their jabber out of a book. Spose a man was to come to you and say *Polly-voo-franzy*—what would you think?"

"I wouldn' think nuff'n; I'd take en bust him over de head. Dat is, if he warn't white. I wouldn't 'low no nigger to call me dat."

"Shucks, it ain't calling you anything. It's only saying do you know how to talk French?"

"Well, den, why couldn't he *say* it?"

"Why, he *is* a-saying it. That's a Frenchman's *way* of saying it."

"Well, it's a blame' ridicklous way, en I doan' want to hear no mo' 'bout it. Dey ain' no sense in it."

"Looky here, Jim; does a cat talk like we do?"

"No, a cat don't."

"Well, does a cow?"

"No, a cow don't, nuther."

"Does a cat talk like a cow, or a cow talk like a cat?"

"No, dey don't."

"It's natural and right for 'em to talk different from each other, ain't it?"

" 'Course."

"And ain't it natural and right for a cat and a cow to talk different from *us*?"

"Why, mos' sholy it is."

"Well, then, why ain't it natural and right for a *Frenchman* to talk different from us? You answer me that."

"Is a cat a man, Huck?"

"No."

"Well, den, dey ain' no sense in a cat talkin' like a man. Is a cow a man?—er is a cow a cat?"

"No, she ain't either of them."

"Well, den, she ain' got no business to talk like either one er the yuther of 'em. Is a Frenchman a man?"

"Yes."

"*Well,* den! Dad blame it, why doan' he *talk* like a man? You answer me *dat!*"

I see it warn't no use wasting words—you can't learn a nigger to argue. So I quit.

Chapter XV

We judged that three nights more would fetch us to Cairo,[5] at the bottom of Illinois, where the Ohio River comes in, and that was what we was after.

---

5. Pronounced *CAY-ro*, the town is 364 miles from Hannibal, 194 miles from St. Louis.

We would sell the raft and get on a steamboat and go way up the Ohio amongst the free States, and then be out of trouble.[6]

Well, the second night a fog begun to come on, and we made for a tow-head to tie to, for it wouldn't do to try to run in fog; but when I paddled ahead in the canoe, with the line, to make fast, there warn't anything but little saplings to tie to. I passed the line around one of them right on the edge of the cut bank, but there was a stiff current, and the raft come booming down so lively she tore it out by the roots and away she went. I see the fog closing down, and it made me so sick and scared I couldn't budge for most a half a minute it seemed to me—and then there warn't no raft in sight; you couldn't see twenty yards. I jumped into the canoe and run back to the stern and grabbed the paddle and set her back a stroke. But she didn't come. I was in such a hurry I hadn't untied her. I got up and tried to untie her, but I was so excited my hands shook so I couldn't hardly do anything with them.

As soon as I got started I took out after the raft, hot and heavy, right down the tow-head. That was all right as far as it went, but the tow-head warn't sixty yards long, and the minute I flew by the foot of it I shot out into the solid white fog, and hadn't no more idea which way I was going than a dead man.

Thinks I, it won't do to paddle; first I know I'll run into the bank or a tow-head or something; I got to set still and float, and yet it's mighty fidgety business to have to hold your hands still at such a time. I whooped and listened. Away down there, somewheres, I hears a small whoop, and up comes my spirits. I went tearing after it, listening sharp to hear it again. The next time it come, I see I warn't heading for it but heading away to the right of it. And the next time, I was heading away to the left of it—and not gaining on it much, either, for I was flying around, this way and that and 'tother, but it was going straight ahead all the time.

I did wish the fool would think to beat a tin pan, and beat it all the time, but he never did, and it was the still places between the whoops that was making the trouble for me. Well, I fought along, and directly I hears the whoops *behind* me. I was tangled good, now. That was somebody's else's whoop, or else I was turned around.

I throwed the paddle down. I heard the whoop again; it was behind me yet, but in a different place; it kept coming, and kept changing its place, and I kept answering, till by-and-by it was in front of me again and I knowed the current had swung the canoe's head down stream and I was all right, if that was Jim and not some other raftsman hollering. I couldn't tell nothing about voices in a fog, for nothing don't look natural nor sound natural in a fog.

The whooping went on, and in about a minute I come a booming down on a cut bank[7] with smoky ghosts of big trees on it, and the current throwed me off to the left and shot by, amongst a lot of snags that fairly roared, the current was tearing by them so swift.

In another second or two it was solid white and still again. I set perfectly still, then, listening to my heart thump, and I reckon I didn't draw a breath while it thumped a hundred.

---

6. Southern Illinois was proslavery in sentiment. The state, moreover, had a system of indentured labor, not unlike slavery, to which a black person without proof of free status might be subjected. Although even in the "free" states there were sim- ilar dangers for Jim, the chances of his making his way to freedom and safety in Canada from Ohio or Pennsylvania would be much greater.
7. Steep bank carved out by the force of the current.

I just give up, then. I knowed what the matter was. That cut bank was an island, and Jim had gone down 'tother side of it. It warn't no tow-head, that you could float by in ten minutes. It had the big timber of a regular island; it might be five or six mile long and more than a half a mile wide.

I kept quiet, with my ears cocked, about fifteen minutes, I reckon. I was floating along, of course, four or five mile an hour; but you don't ever think of that. No, you *feel* like you are laying dead still on the water; and if a little glimpse of a snag slips by, you don't think to yourself how fast *you're* going, but you catch your breath and think, my! how that snag's tearing along. If you think it ain't dismal and lonesome out in a fog that way, by yourself, in the night, you try it once—you'll see.

Next, for about a half an hour, I whoops now and then; at last I hears the answer a long ways off, and tries to follow it, but I couldn't do it, and directly I judged I'd got into a nest of tow-heads, for I had little dim glimpses of them on both sides of me, sometimes just a narrow channel between; and some that I couldn't see, I knowed was there, because I'd hear the wash of the current against the old dead brush and trash that hung over the banks. Well, I warn't long losing the whoops, down amongst the tow-heads; and I only tried to chase them a little while, anyway, because it was worse than chasing a Jack-o-lantern. You never knowed a sound dodge around so, and swap places so quick and so much.

I had to claw away from the bank pretty lively, four or five times, to keep from knocking the islands out of the river; and so I judged the raft must be butting into the bank every now and then, or else it would get further ahead and clear out of hearing—it was floating a little faster than what I was.

Well, I seemed to be in the open river again, by-and-by, but I couldn't hear no sign of a whoop nowheres. I reckoned Jim had fetched up on a snag, maybe, and it was all up with him. I was good and tired, so I laid down in the canoe and said I wouldn't bother no more. I didn't want to go to sleep, of course; but I was so sleepy I couldn't help it; so I thought I would take just one little cat-nap.

But I reckon it was more than a cat-nap, for when I waked up the stars was shining bright, the fog was all gone, and I was spinning down a big bend stern first. First I didn't know where I was; I thought I was dreaming; and when things begun to come back to me, they seemed to come up dim out of last week.

It was a monstrous big river here, with the tallest and the thickest kind of timber on both banks; just a solid wall, as well as I could see, by the stars. I looked away down stream, and seen a black speck on the water. I took out after it; but when I got to it it warn't nothing but a couple of saw-logs made fast together. Then I see another speck, and chased that; then another, and this time I was right. It was the raft.

When I got to it Jim was setting there with his head down between his knees, asleep, with his right arm hanging over the steering oar. The other oar was smashed off, and the raft was littered up with leaves and branches and dirt. So she'd had a rough time.

I made fast and laid down under Jim's nose on the raft, and begun to gap, and stretch my fists out against Jim, and says:

"Hello, Jim, have I been asleep? Why didn't you stir me up?"

"Goodness gracious, is dat you, Huck? En you ain' dead—you ain' drownded—you's back agin? It's too good for true, honey, it's too good for true. Lemme look at you, chile, lemme feel o' you. No, you ain' dead? you's back agin, 'live en soun', jis de same ole Huck—de same ole Huck, thanks to goodness!"

"What's the matter with you, Jim? You been a drinking?"

"Drinkin'? Has I ben a drinkin'? Has I had a chance to be a drinkin'?"

"Well, then, what makes you talk so wild?"

"How does I talk wild?"

"*How?* why, haint you been talking about my coming back, and all that stuff, as if I'd been gone away?"

"Huck—Huck Finn, you look me in de eye; look me in de eye. *Hain't* you ben gone away?"

"Gone away? Why, what in the nation do you mean? *I* hain't been gone anywhere. Where would I go to?"

"Well, looky here, boss, dey's sumf'n wrong, dey is. Is I *me*, or who *is* I? Is I heah, or whah *is* I? Now dat's what I wants to know?"

"Well, I think you're here, plain enough, but I think you're a tangle-headed old fool, Jim."

"I is, is I? Well you answer me dis. Didn't you tote out de line in de canoe, fer to make fas' to de tow-head?"

"No, I didn't. What tow-head? I hain't seen no tow-head."

"You hain't seen no tow-head? Looky here—didn't de line pull loose en de raf' go a hummin' down de river, en leave you en de canoe behine in de fog?"

"What fog?"

"Why *de* fog. De fog dat's ben aroun' all night. En didn't you whoop, en didn't I whoop, tell we got mix' up in de islands en one un us got 'los' en 'tother one was jis' as good as los', 'kase he didn' know whah he wuz? En didn't I bust up agin a lot er dem islands en have a turrible time en mos' git drownded? Now ain' dat so, boss—ain't it so? You answer me dat."

"Well, this is too many for me, Jim. I hain't seen no fog, nor no islands, nor no troubles, nor nothing. I been setting here talking with you all night till you went to sleep about ten minutes ago, and I reckon I done the same. You couldn't a got drunk in that time, so of course you've been dreaming."

"Dad fetch it, how is I gwyne to dream all dat in ten minutes?"

"Well, hang it all, you did dream it, because there didn't any of it happen."

"But Huck, it's all jis' as plain to me as—"

"It don't make no difference how plain it is, there ain't nothing in it. I know, because I've been here all the time."

Jim didn't say nothing for about five minutes, but set there studying over it. Then he says:

"Well, den, I reck'n I did dream it, Huck; but dog my cats ef it ain't de powerfullest dream I ever see. En I hain't ever had no dream b'fo' dat's tired me like dis one."

"Oh, well, that's all right, because a dream does tire a body like everything, sometimes. But this one was a staving[8] dream—tell me all about it, Jim."

So Jim went to work and told me the whole thing right through, just as it happened, only he painted it up considerable. Then he said he must start in and " 'terpret" it, because it was sent for a warning. He said the first tow-

8. Vivid, compelling.

head stood for a man that would try to do us some good, but the current was another man that would get us away from him. The whoops was warnings that would come to us every now and then, and if we didn't try hard to make out to understand them they'd just take us into bad luck, 'stead of keeping us out of it. The lot of tow-heads was troubles we was going to get into with quarrelsome people and all kinds of mean folks, but if we minded our business and didn't talk back and aggravate them, we would pull through and get out of the fog and into the big clear river, which was the free States, and wouldn't have no more trouble.

It had clouded up pretty dark just after I got onto the raft, but it was clearing up again, now.

"Oh, well, that's all interpreted well enough, as far as it goes, Jim," I says; "but what does *these* things stand for?"

It was the leaves and rubbish on the raft, and the smashed oar. You could see them first rate, now.

Jim looked at the trash, and then looked at me, and back at the trash again. He had got the dream fixed so strong in his head that he couldn't seem to shake it loose and get the facts back into its place again, right away. But when he did get the thing straightened around, he looked at me steady, without ever smiling, and says:

"What do dey stan' for? I's gwyne to tell you. When I got all wore out wid work, en wid de callin' for you, en went to sleep, my heart wuz mos' broke bekase you wuz los', en I didn' k'yer no mo' what become er me en de raf'. En when I wake up en fine you back agin', all safe en soun', de tears come en I could a got down on my knees en kiss' yo' foot I's so thankful. En all you wuz thinkin' 'bout wuz how you could make a fool uv ole Jim wid a lie. Dat truck dah is *trash*; en trash is what people is dat puts dirt on de head er dey fren's en makes 'em ashamed."

Then he got up slow, and walked to the wigwam, and went in there, without saying anything but that. But that was enough. It made me feel so mean I could almost kissed *his* foot to get him to take it back.

It was fifteen minutes before I could work myself up to go and humble myself to a nigger—but I done it, and I warn't ever sorry for it afterwards, neither. I didn't do him no more mean tricks, and I wouldn't done that one if I'd a knowed it would make him feel that way.

Chapter XVI

We slept most all day, and started out at night, a little ways behind a monstrous long raft that was as long going by as a procession. She had four long sweeps[9] at each end, so we judged she carried as many as thirty men, likely. She had five big wigwams aboard, wide apart, and an open camp fire in the middle, and a tall flagpole at each end. There was a power of style about her. It *amounted* to something being a raftsman on such a craft as that.

We went drifting down into a big bend, and the night clouded up and got hot. The river was very wide, and was walled with solid timber on both sides; you couldn't see a break in it hardly ever, or a light. We talked about Cairo,

---

9. Long oars used chiefly for steering.

and wondered whether we would know it when we got to it. I said likely we wouldn't, because I had heard say there warn't but about a dozen houses there, and if they didn't happen to have them lit up, how was we going to know we was passing a town? Jim said if the two big rivers joined together there, that would show. But I said maybe we might think we was passing the foot of an island and coming into the same old river again. That disturbed Jim—and me too. So the question was, what to do? I said, paddle ashore the first time a light showed, and tell them pap was behind, coming along with a trading-scow, and was a green hand at the business, and wanted to know how far it was to Cairo. Jim thought it was a good idea, so we took a smoke on it and waited.

There warn't nothing to do, now, but to look out sharp for the town, and not pass it without seeing it. He said he'd be mighty sure to see it, because he'd be a free man the minute he seen it, but if he missed it he'd be in the slave country again and no more show for freedom. Every little while he jumps up and says:

"Dah she is!"

But it warn't. It was Jack-o-lanterns, or lightning-bugs; so he set down again, and went to watching, same as before. Jim said it made him all over trembly and feverish to be so close to freedom. Well, I can tell you it made me all over trembly and feverish, too, to hear him, because I begun to get it through my head that he *was* most free—and who was to blame for it? Why, *me*. I couldn't get that out of my conscience, no how nor no way. It got to troubling me so I couldn't rest; I couldn't stay still in one place. It hadn't ever come home to me before, what this thing was that I was doing. But now it did; and it staid with me, and scorched me more and more. I tried to make out to myself that *I* warn't to blame, because I didn't run Jim off from his rightful owner; but it warn't no use, conscience up and says, every time, "But you knowed he was running for his freedom, and you could a paddled ashore and told somebody." That was so—I couldn't get around that, noway. That was where it pinched. Conscience says to me, "What had poor Miss Watson done to you, that you could see her nigger go off right under your eyes and never say one single word? What did that poor old woman do to you, that you could treat her so mean? Why, she tried to learn you your book, she tried to learn you your manners, she tried to be good to you every way she knowed how. *That's* what she done."

I got to feeling so mean and so miserable I most wished I was dead. I fidgeted up and down the raft, abusing myself to myself, and Jim was fidgeting up and down past me. We neither of us could keep still. Every time he danced around and says, "Dah's Cairo!" it went through me like a shot, and I thought if it *was* Cairo I reckoned I would die of miserableness.

Jim talked out loud all the time while I was talking to myself. He was saying how the first thing he would do when he got to a free State he would go to saving up money and never spend a single cent, and when he got enough he would buy his wife, which was owned on a farm close to where Miss Watson lived; and then they would both work to buy the two children, and if their master wouldn't sell them, they'd get an Ab'litionist to go and steal them.

It most froze me to hear such talk. He wouldn't ever dared to talk such talk in his life before. Just see what a difference it made in him the minute he judged he was about free. It was according to the old saying, "give a nigger an inch and he'll take an ell." Thinks I, this is what comes of my not thinking.

Here was this nigger which I had as good as helped to run away, coming right out flat-footed and saying he would steal his children—children that belonged to a man I didn't even know; a man that hadn't ever done me no harm.

I was sorry to hear Jim say that, it was such a lowering of him. My conscience got to stirring me up hotter than ever, until at last I says to it, "Let up on me—it ain't too late, yet—I'll paddle ashore at the first light, and tell." I felt easy, and happy, and light as a feather, right off. All my troubles was gone. I went to looking out sharp for a light, and sort of singing to myself. By-and-by one showed. Jim sings out:

"We's safe, Huck, we's safe! Jump up and crack yo' heels, dat's de good ole Cairo at las', I jis knows it!"

I says:

"I'll take the canoe and go see, Jim. It mightn't be, you know."

He jumped and got the canoe ready, and put his old coat in the bottom for me to set on, and give me the paddle; and as I shoved off, he says:

"Pooty soon I'll be a-shout'n for joy, en I'll say, it's all on accounts o' Huck; I's a free man, en I couldn't ever ben free ef it hadn' ben for Huck; Huck done it. Jim won't ever forgit you, Huck; you's de bes' fren' Jim's ever had; en you's de *only* fren' ole Jim's got now."

I was paddling off, all in a sweat to tell on him; but when he says this, it seemed to kind of take the tuck all out of me. I went along slow then, and I warn't right down certain whether I was glad I started or whether I warn't. When I was fifty yards off, Jim says:

"Dah you goes, de ole true Huck; de on'y white genlman dat ever kep' his promise to ole Jim."

Well, I just felt sick. But I says, I *got* to do it—I can't get *out* of it. Right then, along comes a skiff with two men in it, with guns, and they stopped and I stopped. One of them says:

"What's that, yonder?"

"A piece of raft," I says.

"Do you belong on it?"

"Yes, sir."

"Any men on it?"

"Only one, sir."

"Well, there's five niggers run off to-night, up yonder above the head of the bend. Is your man white or black?"

I didn't answer up prompt. I tried to, but the words wouldn't come. I tried, for a second or two, to brace up and out with it, but I warn't man enough—hadn't the spunk of a rabbit. I see I was weakening; so I just give up trying, and up and says—

"He's white."

"I reckon we'll go and see for ourselves."

"I wish you would," says I, "because it's pap that's there, and maybe you'd help me tow the raft ashore where the light is. He's sick—and so is mam and Mary Ann."

"Oh, the devil! we're in a hurry, boy. But I s'pose we've got to. Come—buckle to your paddle, and let's get along."

I buckled to my paddle and they laid to their oars. When we had made a stroke or two, I says:

"Pap'll be mighty much obleeged to you, I can tell you. Everybody goes away when I want them to help me tow the raft ashore, and I can't do it myself."

"Well, that's infernal mean. Odd, too. Say, boy, what's the matter with your father?"

"It's the—a—the—well, it ain't anything, much."

They stopped pulling. It warn't but a mighty little ways to the raft, now. One says:

"Boy, that's a lie. What *is* the matter with your pap? Answer up square, now, and it'll be the better for you."

"I will, sir, I will, honest—but don't leave us, please. It's the—the—gentlemen, if you'll only pull ahead, and let me heave you the head-line you won't have to come a-near the raft—please do."

"Set her back, John, set her back!" says one. They backed water. "Keep away, boy—keep to looard.[1] Confound it, I just expect the wind has blowed it to us. Your pap's got the small-pox,[2] and you know it precious well. Why didn't you come out and say so? Do you want to spread it all over?"

"Well," says I, a-blubbering, "I've told everybody before, and then they just went away and left us."

"Poor devil, there's something in that. We are right down sorry for you, but we—well, hang it, we don't want the small-pox, you see. Look here, I'll tell you what to do. Don't you try to land by yourself, or you'll smash everything to pieces. You float along down about twenty miles and you'll come to a town on the left-hand side of the river. It will be long after sun-up, then, and when you ask for help, you tell them your folks are all down with chills and fever. Don't be a fool again, and let people guess what is the matter. Now we're trying to do you a kindness; so you just put twenty miles between us, that's a good boy. It wouldn't do any good to land yonder where the light is—it's only a wood-yard. Say—I reckon your father's poor, and I'm bound to say he's in pretty hard luck. Here—I'll put a twenty dollar gold piece on this board, and you get it when it floats by. I feel mighty mean to leave you, but my kingdom! it won't do to fool with small-pox, don't you see?"

"Hold on, Parker," says the other man, "here's a twenty to put on the board for me. Good-bye boy, you do as Mr. Parker told you, and you'll be all right."

"That's so, my boy—good-bye, good-bye. If you see any runaway niggers, you get help and nab them, and you can make some money by it."

"Good-bye, sir," says I, "I won't let no runaway niggers get by me if I can help it."

They went off, and I got aboard the raft, feeling bad and low, because I knowed very well I had done wrong, and I see it warn't no use for me to try to learn to do right; a body that don't get *started* right when he's little, ain't got no show—when the pinch comes there ain't nothing to back him up and keep him to his work, and so he gets beat. Then I thought a minute, and says to myself, hold on,—s'pose you'd a done right and give Jim up; would you felt better than what you do now? No, says I, I'd feel bad—I'd feel just the same way I do now. Well, then, says I, what's the use you learning to do right, when it's troublesome to do right and ain't no trouble to do wrong, and the wages is just the same? I was stuck. I couldn't answer that.

---

1. I.e., leeward, or downwind.   2. A highly infectious, often fatal disease.

So I reckoned I wouldn't bother no more about it, but after this always do whichever come handiest at the time.

I went into the wigwam; Jim warn't there. I looked all around; he warn't anywhere. I says:

"Jim!"

"Here I is, Huck. Is dey out o' sight yit? Don't talk loud."

He was in the river, under the stern oar, with just his nose out. I told him they was out of sight, so he come aboard. He says:

"I was a-listenin' to all de talk, en I slips into de river en was gwyne to shove for sho' if dey come aboard. Den I was gwyne to swim to de raf' agin when dey was gone. But lawsy, how you did fool 'em, Huck! Dat *wuz* de smartes' dodge! I tell you, chile, I 'speck it save' ole Jim—ole Jim ain' gwyne to forgit you for dat, honey."

Then we talked about the money. It was a pretty good raise, twenty dollars apiece. Jim said we could take deck passage on a steamboat now, and the money would last us as far as we wanted to go in the free States. He said twenty mile more warn't far for the raft to go, but he wished we was already there.

Towards daybreak we tied up, and Jim was mighty particular about hiding the raft good. Then he worked all day fixing things in bundles, and getting all ready to quit rafting.

That night about ten we hove in sight of the lights of a town away down in a left-hand bend.

I went off in the canoe, to ask about it. Pretty soon I found a man out in the river with a skiff, setting a trot-line. I ranged up and says:

"Mister, is that town Cairo?"

"Cairo? no. You must be a blame' fool."

"What town is it, mister?"

"If you want to know, go and find out. If you stay here botherin' around me for about a half a minute longer, you'll get something you won't want."

I paddled to the raft. Jim was awful disappointed, but I said never mind, Cairo would be the next place, I reckoned.

We passed another town before daylight, and I was going out again; but it was high ground, so I didn't go. No high ground about Cairo, Jim said. I had forgot it. We laid up for the day, on a tow-head tolerable close to the left-hand bank. I begun to suspicion something. So did Jim. I says:

"Maybe we went by Cairo in the fog that night."

He says:

"Doan' less' talk about it, Huck. Po' niggers can't have no luck. I awluz 'spected dat rattle-snake skin warn't done wid it's work."

"I wish I'd never seen that snake-skin, Jim—I do wish I'd never laid eyes on it."

"It ain't yo' fault, Huck; you didn't know. Don't you blame yo'sef 'bout it."

When it was daylight, here was the clear Ohio water in shore, sure enough, and outside was the old regular Muddy! So it was all up with Cairo.[3]

---

3. The "Muddy" here refers to the sediment carried by the Mississippi River. Cairo is located at the confluence of the Ohio and Mississippi rivers. Therefore, this combination of clear (Ohio) and muddy (Mississippi) water tells Huck and Jim that they have passed Cairo and lost the opportunity to sell the raft and travel up the Ohio by steamboat to freedom.

We talked it all over. It wouldn't do to take to the shore; we couldn't take the raft up the stream, of course. There warn't no way but to wait for dark, and start back in the canoe and take the chances. So we slept all day amongst the cotton-wood thicket, so as to be fresh for the work, and when we went back to the raft about dark the canoe was gone!

We didn't say a word for a good while. There warn't anything to say. We both knowed well enough it was some more work of the rattle-snake skin; so what was the use to talk about it? It would only look like we was finding fault, and that would be bound to fetch more bad luck—and keep on fetching it, too, till we knowed enough to keep still.

By-and-by we talked about what we better do, and found there warn't no way but just to go along down with the raft till we got a chance to buy a canoe to go back in. We warn't going to borrow it when there warn't anybody around, the way pap would do, for that might set people after us.

So we shoved out, after dark, on the raft.[4]

Anybody that don't believe yet, that it's foolishness to handle a snake-skin, after all that that snake-skin done for us, will believe it now, if they read on and see what more it done for us.

The place to buy canoes is off of rafts laying up at shore. But we didn't see no rafts laying up; so we went along during three hours and more. Well, the night got gray, and ruther thick, which is the next meanest thing to fog. You can't tell the shape of the river, and you can't see no distance. It got to be very late and still, and then along comes a steamboat up the river. We lit the lantern, and judged she would see it. Up-stream boats didn't generly come close to us; they go out and follow the bars and hunt for easy water under the reefs; but nights like this they bull right up the channel against the whole river.

We could hear her pounding along, but we didn't see her good till she was close. She aimed right for us. Often they do that and try to see how close they can come without touching; sometimes the wheel bites off a sweep, and then the pilot sticks his head out and laughs, and thinks he's mighty smart. Well, here she comes, and we said she was going to try to shave us; but she didn't seem to be sheering off a bit. She was a big one, and she was coming in a hurry, too, looking like a black cloud with rows of glow-worms around it; but all of a sudden she bulged out, big and scary, with a long row of wide-open furnace doors shining like red-hot teeth, and her monstrous bows and guards hanging right over us. There was a yell at us, and a jingling of bells to stop the engines, a pow-wow of cussing, and whistling of steam—and as Jim went overboard on one side and I on the other, she come smashing straight through the raft.

I dived—and I aimed to find the bottom, too, for a thirty-foot wheel had got to go over me, and I wanted it to have plenty of room. I could always stay under water a minute; this time I reckon I staid under water a minute and a half. Then I bounced for the top in a hurry, for I was nearly busting. I popped out to my arm-pits and blowed the water out of my nose, and puffed a bit.

4. Twain was "stuck" at this point in the writing of the novel and put the 400-page manuscript aside for approximately three years. In the winter of 1879–80 he added the two chapters dealing with the feud (XVII and XVIII) and then the three chapters (XIX–XXI) in which the king and duke enter the story and for a time dominate the action. The novel was not completed until 1883, when Twain wrote the last half of it in a few months of concentrated work. As late as 1882, he was not confident he would ever complete the book.

Of course there was a booming current; and of course that boat started her engines again ten seconds after she stopped them, for they never cared much for raftsmen; so now she was churning along up the river, out of sight in the thick weather, though I could hear her.

I sung out for Jim about a dozen times, but I didn't get any answer; so I grabbed a plank that touched me while I was "treading water," and struck out for shore, shoving it ahead of me. But I made out to see that the drift of the current was towards the left-hand shore,[5] which meant that I was in a crossing; so I changed off and went that way.

It was one of these long, slanting, two-mile crossings; so I was a good long time in getting over. I made a safe landing, and clum up the bank. I couldn't see but a little ways, but I went poking along over rough ground for a quarter of a mile or more, and then I run across a big old-fashioned double log house before I noticed it. I was going to rush by and get away, but a lot of dogs jumped out and went to howling and barking at me, and I knowed better than to move another peg.

Chapter XVII

In about half a minute somebody spoke out of a window, without putting his head out, and says:

"Be done, boys! Who's there?"

I says:

"It's me."

"Who's me?"

"George Jackson, sir."

"What do you want?"

"I don't want nothing, sir. I only want to go along by, but the dogs won't let me."

"What are you prowling around here this time of night, for—hey?"

"I warn't prowling around, sir; I fell overboard off of the steamboat."

"Oh, you did, did you? Strike a light there, somebody. What did you say your name was?"

"George Jackson, sir. I'm only a boy."

"Look here; if you're telling the truth, you needn't be afraid—nobody'll hurt you. But don't try to budge; stand right where you are. Rouse our Bob and Tom, some of you, and fetch the guns. George Jackson, is there anybody with you?"

"No, sir, nobody."

I heard the people stirring around in the house, now, and see a light. The man sung out:

"Snatch that light away, Betsy, you old fool—ain't you got any sense? Put it on the floor behind the front door. Bob, if you and Tom are ready, take your places."

"All ready."

"Now, George Jackson, do you know the Shepherdsons?"

"No, sir—I never heard of them."

5. Kentucky, where the feud in chapters XVII and XVIII is set.

"Well, that may be so, and it mayn't. Now, all ready. Step forward, George Jackson. And mind, don't you hurry—come mighty slow. If there's anybody with you, let him keep back—if he shows himself he'll be shot. Come along, now. Come slow; push the door open, yourself—just enough to squeeze in, d' you hear?"

I didn't hurry, I couldn't if I'd a wanted to. I took one slow step at a time, and there warn't a sound, only I thought I could hear my heart. The dogs were as still as the humans, but they followed a little behind me. When I got to the three log door-steps, I heard them unlocking and unbarring and unbolting. I put my hand on the door and pushed it a little and a little more, till somebody said, "There, that's enough—put your head in." I done it, but I judged they would take it off.

The candle was on the floor, and there they all was, looking at me, and me at them, for about a quarter of a minute. Three big men with guns pointed at me, which made me wince, I tell you; the oldest, gray and about sixty, the other two thirty or more—all of them fine and handsome—and the sweetest old gray-headed lady, and back of her two young women which I couldn't see right well. The old gentleman says:

"There—I reckon it's all right. Come in."

As soon as I was in, the old gentleman he locked the door and barred it and bolted it, and told the young men to come in with their guns, and they all went in a big parlor that had a new rag carpet on the floor, and got together in a corner that was out of range of the front windows—there warn't none on the side. They held the candle, and took a good look at me, and all said, "Why *he* ain't a Shepherdson—no, there ain't any Shepherdson about him." Then the old man said he hoped I wouldn't mind being searched for arms, because he didn't mean no harm by it—it was only to make sure. So he didn't pry into my pockets, but only felt outside with his hands, and said it was all right. He told me to make myself easy and at home, and tell all about myself; but the old lady says:

"Why bless you, Saul, the poor thing's as wet as he can be; and don't you reckon it may be he's hungry?"

"True for you, Rachel—I forgot."

So the old lady says:

"Betsy" (this was a nigger woman), "you fly around and get him something to eat, as quick as you can, poor thing; and one of you girls go and wake up Buck and tell him—Oh, here he is himself. Buck, take this little stranger and get the wet clothes off from him and dress him up in some of yours that's dry."

Buck looked about as old as me—thirteen or fourteen[6] or along there, though he was a little bigger than me. He hadn't on anything but a shirt, and he was very frowsy-headed. He come in gaping and digging one fist into his eyes, and he was dragging a gun along with the other one. He says:

"Ain't they no Shepherdsons around?"

They said, no, 'twas a false alarm.

"Well," he says, "if they'd a ben some, I reckon I'd a got one."

They all laughed, and Bob says:

6. In a notebook entry, Twain identifies Huck as "a boy of 14."

"Why, Buck, they might have scalped us all, you've been so slow in coming."

"Well, nobody come after me, and it ain't right. I'm always kep' down; I don't get no show."

"Never mind, Buck, my boy," says the old man, "you'll have show enough, all in good time, don't you fret about that. Go 'long with you now, and do as your mother told you."

When we got up stairs to his room, he got me a coarse shirt and a round-about[7] and pants of his, and I put them on. While I was at it he asked me what my name was, but before I could tell him, he started to telling me about a blue jay and a young rabbit he had catched in the woods day before yesterday, and he asked me where Moses was when the candle went out. I said I didn't know; I hadn't heard about it before, no way.

"Well, guess," he says.

"How'm I going to guess," says I, "when I never heard tell about it before?"

"But you can guess, can't you? It's just as easy."

"*Which* candle?" I says.

"Why, any candle," he says.

"I don't know where he was," says I; "where was he?"

"Why he was in the *dark*! That's where he was!"

"Well, if you knowed where he was, what did you ask me for?"

"Why, blame it, it's a riddle, don't you see? Say, how long are you going to stay here? You got to stay always. We can just have booming times—they don't have no school now. Do you own a dog? I've got a dog—and he'll go in the river and bring out chips that you throw in. Do you like to comb up, Sundays, and all that kind of foolishness? You bet I don't, but ma she makes me. Confound these ole britches, I reckon I'd better put 'em on, but I'd ruther not, it's so warm. Are you all ready? All right—come along, old hoss."

Cold corn-pone, cold corn-beef, butter and butter-milk—that is what they had for me down there, and there ain't nothing better that ever I've come across yet. Buck and his ma and all of them smoked cob pipes, except the nigger woman, which was gone, and the two young women. They all smoked and talked, and I eat and talked. The young women had quilts around them, and their hair down their backs. They all asked me questions, and I told them how pap and me and all the family was living on a little farm down at the bottom of Arkansaw, and my sister Mary Ann run off and got married and never was heard of no more, and Bill went to hunt them and he warn't heard of no more, and Tom and Mort died, and then there warn't nobody but just me and pap left, and he was just trimmed down to nothing, on account of his troubles; so when he died I took what there was left, because the farm didn't belong to us, and started up the river, deck passage, and fell overboard; and that was how I come to be here. So they said I could have a home there as long as I wanted it. Then it was most daylight, and everybody went to bed, and I went to bed with Buck, and when I waked up in the morning, drat it all, I had forgot what my name was. So I laid there about an hour trying to think and when Buck waked up, I says:

"Can you spell, Buck?"

"Yes," he says.

"I bet you can't spell my name," says I.

7. Short, close-fitting jacket.

"I bet you what you dare I can," says he.

"All right," says I, "go ahead."

"G-o-r-g-e J-a-x-o-n—there now," he says.

"Well," says I, "you done it, but I didn't think you could. It ain't no slouch of a name to spell—right off without studying."

I set it down, private, because somebody might want *me* to spell it, next, and so I wanted to be handy with it and rattle it off like I was used to it.

It was a mighty nice family, and a mighty nice house, too. I hadn't seen no house out in the country before that was so nice and had so much style. It didn't have an iron latch on the front door, nor a wooden one with a buckskin string, but a brass knob to turn, the same as houses in a town. There warn't no bed in the parlor, not a sign of a bed; but heaps of parlors in towns has beds in them. There was a big fireplace that was bricked on the bottom, and the bricks was kept clean and red by pouring water on them and scrubbing them with another brick; sometimes they washed them over with red water-paint that they call Spanish-brown, same as they do in town. They had big brass dog-irons that could hold up a saw-log.[8] There was a clock on the middle of the mantel-piece, with a picture of a town painted on the bottom half of the glass front, and a round place in the middle of it for the sun, and you could see the pendulum swing behind it. It was beautiful to hear that clock tick; and sometimes when one of these peddlers had been along and scoured her up and got her in good shape, she would start in and strike a hundred and fifty before she got tuckered out. They wouldn't took any money for her.

Well, there was a big outlandish parrot on each side of the clock, made out of something like chalk, and painted up gaudy. By one of the parrots was a cat made of crockery, and a crockery dog by the other; and when you pressed down on them they squeaked, but didn't open their mouths nor look different nor interested. They squeaked through underneath. There was a couple of big wild-turkey-wing fans spread out behind those things. On a table in the middle of the room was a kind of a lovely crockery basket that had apples and oranges and peaches and grapes piled up in it which was much redder and yellower and prettier than real ones is, but they warn't real because you could see where pieces had got chipped off and showed the white chalk or whatever it was, underneath.

This table had a cover made out of beautiful oil-cloth, with a red and blue spread-eagle painted on it, and a painted border all around. It come all the way from Philadelphia, they said. There was some books too, piled up perfectly exact, on each corner of the table. One was a big family Bible, full of pictures. One was "Pilgrim's Progress," about a man that left his family it didn't say why. I read considerable in it now and then. The statements was interesting, but tough. Another was "Friendship's Offering," full of beautiful stuff and poetry; but I didn't read the poetry. Another was Henry Clay's Speeches, and another was Dr. Gunn's Family Medicine, which told you all about what to do if a body was sick or dead. There was a Hymn Book, and a lot of other books.[9] And there was nice split-bottom

8. A log large enough to be sawed into planks.

9. The neatly stacked, unread books are meant to define the values and tastes of the time and place. The Bible, John Bunyan's *Pilgrim's Progress* (1678), and the hymn book establish Calvinistic piety; the speeches of the Kentucky politician Henry Clay (1777–1852) convey political orthodoxy; Gunn's *Domestic Medicine* (1830) suggests popular notions of science and medical practice. *Friendship's Offering* was a popular gift book.

chairs, and perfectly sound, too—not bagged down in the middle and busted, like an old basket.

They had pictures hung on the walls—mainly Washingtons and Lafayettes, and battles, and Highland Marys, and one called "Signing the Declaration."[1] There was some that they called crayons, which one of the daughters which was dead made her own self when she was only fifteen years old. They was different from any pictures I ever see before; blacker, mostly, than is common. One was a woman in a slim black dress, belted small under the armpits, with bulges like a cabbage in the middle of the sleeves, and a large black scoop-shovel bonnet with a black veil, and white slim ankles crossed about with black tape, and very wee black slippers, like a chisel, and she was leaning pensive on a tombstone on her right elbow, under a weeping willow, and her other hand hanging down her side holding a white handkerchief and a reticule, and underneath the picture it said "Shall I Never See Thee More Alas." Another one was a young lady with her hair all combed up straight to the top of her head, and knotted there in front of a comb like a chair-back, and she was crying into a handkerchief and had a dead bird laying on its back in her other hand with its heels up, and underneath the picture it said "I Shall Never Hear Thy Sweet Chirrup More Alas." There was one where a young lady was at a window looking up at the moon, and tears running down her cheeks; and she had an open letter in one hand with black sealing-wax showing on one edge of it, and she was mashing a locket with a chain to it against her mouth, and underneath the picture it said "And Art Thou Gone Yes Thou Art Gone Alas." These was all nice pictures, I reckon, but I didn't somehow seem to take to them, because if ever I was down a little, they always give me the fan-tods. Everybody was sorry she died, because she had laid out a lot more of these pictures to do, and a body could see by what she had done what they had lost. But I reckoned, that with her disposition, she was having a better time in the graveyard. She was at work on what they said was her greatest picture when she took sick, and every day and every night it was her prayer to be allowed to live till she got it done, but she never got the chance. It was a picture of a young woman in a long white gown, standing on the rail of a bridge all ready to jump off, with her hair all down her back, and looking up to the moon, with the tears running down her face, and she had two arms folded across her breast, and two arms stretched out in front, and two more reaching up towards the moon—and the idea was, to see which pair would look best and then scratch out all the other arms; but, as I was saying, she died before she got her mind made up, and now they kept this picture over the head of the bed in her room, and every time her birthday come they hung flowers on it. Other times it was hid with a little curtain. The young woman in the picture had a kind of a nice sweet face, but there was so many arms it made her look too spidery, seemed to me.

---

1. Painting in the U.S. Capitol Rotunda by John Trumbull (1756–1843), completed in 1819 and widely reproduced during the antebellum period. "Highland Mary" depicts the Scottish poet Robert Burns's first love, who died a few months after they met. He memorialized her in several poems, especially "To Mary in Heaven" (1792).

This young girl kept a scrap-book when she was alive, and used to paste obituaries and accidents and cases of patient suffering in it out of the *Presbyterian Observer*, and write poetry after them out of her own head. It was very good poetry.[2] This is what she wrote about a boy by the name of Stephen Dowling Bots that fell down a well and was drownded:

ODE TO STEPHEN DOWLING BOTS, DEC'D

And did young Stephen sicken,
    And did young Stephen die?
And did the sad hearts thicken,
    And did the mourners cry?

No; such was not the fate of
    Young Stephen Dowling Bots;
Though sad hearts round him thickened,
    'Twas not from sickness' shots.

No whooping-cough did rack his frame,
    Nor measles drear, with spots;
Not these impaired the sacred name
    Of Stephen Dowling Bots.

Despised love struck not with woe
    That head of curly knots,
Nor stomach troubles laid him low,
    Young Stephen Dowling Bots.

O no. Then list with tearful eye,
    Whilst I his fate do tell.
His soul did from this cold world fly,
    By falling down a well.

They got him out and emptied him;
    Alas it was too late;
His spirit was gone for to sport aloft
    In the realms of the good and great.

If Emmeline Grangerford could make poetry like that before she was fourteen, there ain't no telling what she could a done by-and-by. Buck said she could rattle off poetry like nothing. She didn't ever have to stop to think. He said she would slap down a line, and if she couldn't find anything to rhyme with it she would just scratch it out and slap down another one, and go ahead. She warn't particular, she could write about anything you choose to give her to write about, just so it was sadful. Every time a man died, or a woman died, or a child died, she would be on hand with her "tribute" before he was cold. She

2. This parody derives in particular from two poems by "The Sweet Singer of Michigan," Julia A. Moore (1847–1920), whose sentimental poetry was popular at the time Twain was writing *Huck Finn*. In one of the two poems, "Little Libbie," the heroine "was choken on a piece of beef." The graveyard and obituary (or "sadful") schools of popular poetry are much older and more widespread.

called them tributes. The neighbors said it was the doctor first, then Emmeline, then the undertaker—the undertaker never got in ahead of Emmeline but once, and then she hung fire[3] on a rhyme for the dead person's name, which was Whistler. She warn't ever the same, after that; she never complained, but she kind of pined away and did not live long. Poor thing, many's the time I made myself go up to the little room that used to be hers and get out her poor old scrapbook and read in it when her pictures had been aggravating me and I had soured on her a little. I liked all the family, dead ones and all, and warn't going to let anything come between us. Poor Emmeline made poetry about all the dead people when she was alive, and it didn't seem right that there warn't nobody to make some about her, now she was gone; so I tried to sweat out a verse or two myself, but I couldn't seem to make it go, somehow. They kept Emmeline's room trim and nice and all the things fixed in it just the way she liked to have them when she was alive, and nobody ever slept there. The old lady took care of the room herself, though there was plenty of niggers, and she sewed there a good deal and read her Bible there, mostly.

Well, as I was saying about the parlor, there was beautiful curtains on the windows: white, with pictures painted on them, of castles with vines all down the walls, and cattle coming down to drink. There was a little old piano, too, that had tin pans in it, I reckon, and nothing was ever so lovely as to hear the young ladies sing, "The Last Link is Broken" and play "The Battle of Prague"[4] on it. The walls of all the rooms was plastered, and most had carpets on the floors, and the whole house was whitewashed on the outside.

It was a double house, and the big open place betwixt them was roofed and floored, and sometimes the table was set there in the middle of the day, and it was a cool, comfortable place. Nothing couldn't be better. And warn't the cooking good, and just bushels of it too!

Chapter XVIII

Col. Grangerford was a gentleman, you see. He was a gentleman all over; and so was his family. He was well born, as the saying is, and that's worth as much in a man as it is in a horse, so the Widow Douglas said, and nobody ever denied that she was of the first aristocracy in our town; and pap he always said it, too, though he warn't no more quality than a mudcat,[5] himself. Col. Grangerford was very tall and very slim, and had a darkish-paly complexion, not a sign of red in it anywheres; he was clean-shaved every morning, all over his thin face, and he had the thinnest kind of lips, and the thinnest kind of nostrils, and a high nose, and heavy eyebrows, and the blackest kind of eyes, sunk so deep back that they seemed like they was looking out of caverns at you, as you may say. His forehead was high, and his hair was black and straight, and hung to his shoulders. His hands was long and thin, and every day of his life he put on a clean shirt and a full suit from head to foot made out of linen so white it hurt your eyes to look at it; and on

---

3. Was delayed by, or "hung up." The term comes from an unexpected delay between the trigger of a firearm and its firing—a more common problem in older firearms.
4. A bloody story told in clichéd style, written by the Czech composer Franz Kotswara (1750–

1791) in about 1788; Twain first heard it in 1878. William Clifton's *The Last Link Is Broken* was published about 1840.
5. General term for a number of species of catfish; in this context the lowliest and least esteemed.

Sundays he wore a blue tail-coat with brass buttons on it. He carried a mahogany cane with a silver head to it. There warn't no frivolishness about him, not a bit, and he warn't ever loud. He was as kind as he could be—you could feel that, you know, and so you had confidence. Sometimes he smiled, and it was good to see; but when he straightened himself up like a liberty-pole,[6] and the lightning begun to flicker out from under his eyebrows you wanted to climb a tree first, and find out what the matter was afterwards. He didn't ever have to tell anybody to mind their manners—everybody was always good mannered where he was. Everybody loved to have him around, too; he was sunshine most always—I mean he made it seem like good weather. When he turned into a cloud-bank it was awful dark for a half a minute and that was enough; there wouldn't nothing go wrong again for a week.

When him and the old lady come down in the morning, all the family got up out of their chairs and give them good-day, and didn't set down again till they had set down. Then Tom and Bob went to the sideboard where the decanters was, and mixed a glass of bitters and handed it to him, and he held it in his hand and waited till Tom's and Bob's was mixed, and then they bowed and said "Our duty to you, sir, and madam;" and *they* bowed the least bit in the world and said thank you, and so they drank, all three, and Bob and Tom poured a spoonful of water on the sugar and the mite of whiskey or apple brandy in the bottom of their tumblers, and give it to me and Buck, and we drank to the old people too.

Bob was the oldest, and Tom next. Tall, beautiful men with very broad shoulders and brown faces, and long black hair and black eyes. They dressed in white linen from head to foot, like the old gentleman, and wore broad Panama hats.[7]

Then there was Miss Charlotte, she was twenty-five, and tall and proud and grand, but as good as she could be, when she warn't stirred up; but when she was, she had a look that would make you wilt in your tracks, like her father. She was beautiful.

So was her sister, Miss Sophia, but it was a different kind. She was gentle and sweet, like a dove, and she was only twenty.

Each person had their own nigger to wait on them—Buck, too. My nigger had a monstrous easy time, because I warn't used to having anybody do anything for me, but Buck's was on the jump most of the time.

This was all there was of the family, now; but there used to be more—three sons; they got killed; and Emmeline that died.

The old gentleman owned a lot of farms, and over a hundred niggers. Sometimes a stack of people would come there, horseback, from ten or fifteen miles around, and stay five or six days, and have such junketings round about and on the river, and dances and picnics in the woods, day-times, and balls at the house, nights. These people was mostly kin-folks of the family. The men brought their guns with them. It was a handsome lot of quality, I tell you.

There was another clan of aristocracy around there—five or six families—mostly of the name of Shepherdson. They was as high-toned, and well born,

6. A tall pole, like a flagpole, on which an ensign or "liberty cap" might be raised as a signal.

7. A brimmed straw hat, originally made in Ecuador and shipped through the Panama isthmus.

and rich and grand, as the tribe of Grangerfords. The Shepherdsons and the Grangerfords used the same steamboat landing, which was about two mile above our house; so sometimes when I went up there with a lot of our folks I used to see a lot of Shepherdsons there, on their fine horses.

One day Buck and me was away out in the woods, hunting, and heard a horse coming. We was crossing the road. Buck says:

"Quick! Jump for the woods!"

We done it, and then peeped down the woods through the leaves. Pretty soon a splendid young man come galloping down the road, setting his horse easy and looking like a soldier. He had his gun across his pommel. I had seen him before. It was young Harney Shepherdson. I heard Buck's gun go off at my ear, and Harney's hat tumbled off from his head. He grabbed his gun and rode straight to the place where we was hid. But we didn't wait. We started through the woods on a run. The woods warn't thick, so I looked over my shoulder, to dodge the bullet, and twice I seen Harney cover Buck with his gun; and then he rode away the way he come—to get his hat, I reckon, but I couldn't see. We never stopped running till we got home. The old gentleman's eyes blazed a minute—'twas pleasure, mainly, I judged—then his face sort of smoothed down, and he says, kind of gentle:

"I don't like that shooting from behind a bush. Why didn't you step into the road, my boy?"

"The Shepherdsons don't, father. They always take advantage."

Miss Charlotte she held her head up like a queen while Buck was telling his tale, and her nostrils spread and her eyes snapped. The two young men looked dark, but never said nothing. Miss Sophia she turned pale, but the color come back when she found the man warn't hurt.

Soon as I could get Buck down by the corn-cribs under the trees by ourselves, I says:

"Did you want to kill him, Buck?"

"Well, I bet I did."

"What did he do to you?"

"Him? He never done nothing to me."

"Well, then, what did you want to kill him for?"

"Why nothing—only it's on account of the feud."

"What's a feud?"

"Why, where was you raised? Don't you know what a feud is?"

"Never heard of it before—tell me about it."

"Well," says Buck, "a feud is this way. A man has a quarrel with another man, and kills him; then that other man's brother kills *him*; then the other brothers, on both sides, goes for one another; then the *cousins* chip in—and by-and-by everybody's killed off, and there ain't no more feud. But it's kind of slow, and takes a long time."

"Has this one been going on long, Buck?"

"Well I should *reckon*! it started thirty year ago, or som'ers along there. There was trouble 'bout something and then a lawsuit to settle it; and the suit went agin one of the men, and so he up and shot the man that won the suit—which he would naturally do, of course. Anybody would."

"What was the trouble about, Buck?—land?"

"I reckon maybe—I don't know."

"Well, who done the shooting?—was it a Grangerford or a Shepherdson?"

"Laws, how do *I* know? it was so long ago."

"Don't anybody know?"

"Oh, yes, pa knows, I reckon, and some of the other old folks; but they don't know, now, what the row was about in the first place."

"Has there been many killed, Buck?"

"Yes—right smart chance of funerals. But they don't always kill. Pa's got a few buck-shot in him; but he don't mind it 'cuz he don't weigh much anyway. Bob's been carved up some with a bowie, and Tom's been hurt once or twice."

"Has anybody been killed this year, Buck?"

"Yes, we got one and they got one. 'Bout three months ago, my cousin Bud, fourteen year old, was riding through the woods, on t'other side of the river, and didn't have no weapon with him, which was blame' foolishness, and in a lonesome place he hears a horse a-coming behind him, and sees old Baldy Shepherdson a-linkin' after him with his gun in his hand and his white hair a-flying in the wind; and 'stead of jumping off and taking to the brush, Bud 'lowed he could outrun him; so they had it, nip and tuck, for five mile or more, the old man a-gaining all the time; so at last Bud seen it warn't any use, so he stopped and faced around so as to have the bullet holes in front, you know, and the old man he rode up and shot him down. But he didn't git much chance to enjoy his luck, for inside of a week our folks laid *him* out."

"I reckon that old man was a coward, Buck."

"I reckon he *warn't* a coward. Not by a blame' sight. There ain't a coward amongst them Shepherdsons—not a one. And there ain't no cowards amongst the Grangerfords, either. Why, that old man kep' up his end in a fight one day, for a half an hour, against three Grangerfords, and come out winner. They was all a-horseback; he lit off of his horse and got behind a little wood-pile, and kep' his horse before him to stop the bullets; but the Grangerfords staid on their horses and capered around the old man, and peppered away at him, and he peppered away at them. Him and his horse both went home pretty leaky and crippled, but the Grangerfords had to be *fetched* home—and one of 'em was dead, and another died the next day. No, sir, if a body's out hunting for cowards, he don't want to fool away any time amongst them Shepherdsons, becuz they don't breed any of that *kind*."

Next Sunday we all went to church, about three mile, everybody a-horseback. The men took their guns along, so did Buck, and kept them between their knees or stood them handy against the wall. The Shepherdsons done the same. It was pretty ornery preaching—all about brotherly love, and such-like tiresomeness; but everybody said it was a good sermon, and they all talked it over going home, and had such a powerful lot to say about faith, and good works, and free grace, and preforeordestination,[8] and I don't know what all, that it did seem to me to be one of the roughest Sundays I had run across yet.

About an hour after dinner everybody was dozing around, some in their chairs and some in their rooms, and it got to be pretty dull. Buck and a dog was stretched out on the grass in the sun, sound asleep. I went up to our room, and judged I would take a nap myself. I found that sweet Miss Sophia standing in her door, which was next to ours, and she took me in her room and shut the door very soft, and asked me if I liked her, and I said I did; and

---

8. Huck combines the closely related Presbyterian terms *predestination* and *foreordination*.

she asked me if I would do something for her and not tell anybody, and I said I would. Then she said she'd forgot her Testament, and left it in the seat at church, between two other books and would I slip out quiet and go there and fetch it to her, and not say nothing to nobody. I said I would. So I slid out and slipped off up the road, and there warn't anybody at the church, except maybe a hog or two, for there warn't any lock on the door, and hogs like a puncheon floor[9] in summer-time because it's cool. If you notice, most folks don't go to church only when they've got to; but a hog is different.

Says I to myself something's up—it ain't natural for a girl to be in such a sweat about a Testament; so I give it a shake, and out drops a little piece of paper with *"Half-past two"* wrote on it with a pencil. I ransacked it, but couldn't find anything else. I couldn't make anything out of that, so I put the paper in the book again, and when I got home and up stairs, there was Miss Sophia in her door waiting for me. She pulled me in and shut the door; then she looked in the Testament till she found the paper, and as soon as she read it she looked glad; and before a body could think, she grabbed me and give me a squeeze, and said I was the best boy in the world, and not to tell anybody. She was mighty red in the face, for a minute, and her eyes lighted up and it made her powerful pretty. I was a good deal astonished, but when I got my breath I asked her what the paper was about, and she asked me if I had read it, and I said no, and she asked me if I could read writing, and I told her "no, only coarse-hand,"[1] and then she said the paper warn't anything but a book-mark to keep her place, and I might go and play now.

I went off down to the river, studying over this thing, and pretty soon I noticed that my nigger was following along behind. When we was out of sight of the house, he looked back and around a second, and then comes a-running, and says:

"Mars Jawge, if you'll come down into de swamp, I'll show you a whole stack o' water-moccasins."

Thinks I, that's mighty curious; he said that yesterday. He oughter know a body don't love water-moccasins enough to go around hunting for them. What is he up to anyway? So I says—

"All right, trot ahead."

I followed a half a mile, then he struck out over the swamp and waded ankle deep as much as another half mile. We come to a little flat piece of land which was dry and very thick with trees and bushes and vines, and he says—

"You shove right in dah, jist a few steps, Mars Jawge, dah's whah dey is. I's seed 'm befo', I don't k'yer to see 'em no mo'."

Then he slopped right along and went away, and pretty soon the trees hid him. I poked into the place a-ways, and come to a little open patch as big as a bedroom, all hung around with vines, and found a man laying there asleep—and by jings it was my old Jim!

I waked him up, and I reckoned it was going to be a grand surprise to him to see me again, but it warn't. He nearly cried, he was so glad, but he warn't surprised. Said he swum along behind me, that night, and heard me yell

9. A crude floor made from log slabs in which set in the dirt.
the flat side is turned up and the rounded side is 1. Block printing.

every time, but dasn't answer, because he didn't want nobody to pick *him* up, and take him into slavery again. Says he—

"I got hurt a little, en couldn't swim fas', so I wuz a considable ways behine you, towards de las'; when you landed I reck'ned I could ketch up wid you on de lan' 'dout havin' to shout at you, but when I see dat house I begin to go slow. I 'uz off too fur to hear what dey say to you—I wuz 'fraid o' de dogs—but when it 'uz all quiet again, I knowed you's in de house, so I struck out for de woods to wait for day. Early in de mawnin' some er de niggers come along, gwyne to de fields, en dey tuck me en showed me dis place, whah de dogs can't track me on accounts o' de water, en dey brings me truck to eat every night, en tells me how you's a gitt'n along."

"Why didn't you tell my Jack to fetch me here sooner, Jim?"

"Well, 'twarn't no use to 'sturb you, Huck, tell we could do sumfn—but we's all right, now. I ben a-buyin' pots en pans en vittles, as I got a chanst, en a patchin' up de raf', nights, when—"

"*What* raft, Jim?"

"Our ole raf'."

"You mean to say our old raft warn't smashed all to flinders?"

"No, she warn't. She was tore up a good deal—one en' of her was—but dey warn't no great harm done, on'y our traps was mos' all los'. Ef we hadn' dive' so deep en swum so fur under water, en de night hadn' ben so dark, en we warn't so sk'yerd, en ben sich punkin-heads, as de sayin' is, we'd a seed de raf'. But it's jis' as well we didn't, 'kase now she's all fixed up agin mos' as good as new, en we's got a new lot o' stuff, too, in de place o' what 'uz los'."

"Why, how did you get hold of the raft again, Jim—did you catch her?"

"How I gwyne to ketch her, en I out in de woods? No, some er de niggers foun' her ketched on a snag, along heah in de ben', en dey hid her in a crick, 'mongst de willows, en dey wuz so much jawin' 'bout which un 'um she b'long to de mos', dat I come to heah 'bout it pooty soon, so I ups en settles de trouble by tellin' um she don't b'long to none uv um, but to you en me; en I ast 'm if dey gwyne to grab a young white genlman's propaty, en git a hid'n for it? Den I gin 'm ten cents apiece, en dey 'uz mighty well satisfied, en wisht some mo' raf's 'ud come along en make 'm rich agin. Dey's mighty good to me, dese niggers is, en whatever I wants 'm to do fur me, I doan' have to ast 'm twice, honey. Dat Jack's a good nigger, en pooty smart."

"Yes, he is. He ain't ever told me you was here; told me to come, and he'd show me a lot of water-moccasins. If anything happens, *he* ain't mixed up in it. He can say he never seen us together, and it'll be the truth."

I don't want to talk much about the next day. I reckon I'll cut it pretty short. I waked up about dawn, and was agoing to turn over and go to sleep again, when I noticed how still it was—didn't seem to be anybody stirring. That warn't usual. Next I noticed that Buck was up and gone. Well, I gets up, a-wondering, and goes down stairs—nobody around; everything as still as a mouse. Just the same outside; thinks I, what does it mean? Down by the wood-pile I comes across my Jack, and says:

"What's it all about?"

Says he:

"Don't you know, Mars Jawge?"

"No," says I, "I don't."

"Well, den, Miss Sophia's run off! 'deed she has. She run off in de night, sometime—nobody don't know jis' when—run off to git married to dat young Harney Shepherdson, you know—leastways, so dey 'spec. De fambly foun' it out, 'bout half an hour ago—maybe a little mo'—en' I *tell* you dey warn't no time los'. Sich another hurryin' up guns en hosses *you* never see! De women folks has gone for to stir up de relations, en ole Mars Saul en de boys tuck dey guns en rode up de river road for to try to ketch dat young man en kill him 'fo' he kin git acrost de river wid Miss Sophia. I reck'n dey's gwyne to be mighty rough times."

"Buck went off 'thout waking me up."

"Well I reck'n he *did*! Dey warn't gwyne to mix you up in it. Mars Buck he loaded up his gun en 'lowed he's gwyne to fetch home a Shepherdson or bust. Well, dey'll be plenty un 'm dah, I reck'n, en you bet you he'll fetch one ef he gits a chanst."

I took up the river road as hard as I could put. By-and-by I begin to hear guns a good ways off. When I come in sight of the log store and the wood-pile where the steamboats land, I worked along under the trees and brush till I got to a good place, and then I clumb up into the forks of a cotton-wood that was out of reach, and watched. There was a wood-rank four foot high,[2] a little ways in front of the tree, and first I was going to hide behind that; but maybe it was luckier I didn't.

There was four or five men cavorting around on their horses in the open place before the log store, cussing and yelling, and trying to get at a couple of young chaps that was behind the wood-rank alongside of the steamboat landing—but they couldn't come it. Every time one of them showed himself on the river side of the wood-pile he got shot at. The two boys was squatting back to back behind the pile, so they could watch both ways.

By-and-by the men stopped cavorting around and yelling. They started riding towards the store; then up gets one of the boys, draws a steady bead over the wood-rank, and drops one of them out of his saddle. All the men jumped off of their horses and grabbed the hurt one and started to carry him to the store; and that minute the two boys started on the run. They got half-way to the tree I was in before the men noticed. Then the men see them, and jumped on their horses and took out after them. They gained on the boys, but it didn't do no good, the boys had too good a start; they got to the wood-pile that was in front of my tree, and slipped in behind it, and so they had the bulge[3] on the men again. One of the boys was Buck, and the other was a slim young chap about nineteen years old.

The men ripped around awhile, and then rode away. As soon as they was out of sight, I sung out to Buck and told him. He didn't know what to make of my voice coming out of the tree, at first. He was awful surprised. He told me to watch out sharp and let him know when the men come in sight again; said they was up to some devilment or other—wouldn't be gone long. I wished I was out of that tree, but I dasn't come down. Buck began to cry and rip, and 'lowed that him and his cousin Joe (that was the other young chap) would make up for this day, yet. He said his father and his two brothers was killed, and two or three of the enemy. Said the Shepherdsons laid for them, in

2. Half a cord of stacked firewood.   3. Upper hand.

ambush. Buck said his father and brothers ought to waited for their relations—the Shepherdsons was too strong for them. I asked him what was become of young Harney and Miss Sophia. He said they'd got across the river and was safe. I was glad of that; but the way Buck did take on because he didn't manage to kill Harney that day he shot at him—I hain't ever heard anything like it.

All of a sudden, bang! bang! bang! goes three or four guns—the men had slipped around through the woods and come in from behind without their horses! The boys jumped for the river—both of them hurt—and as they swum down the current the men run along the bank shooting at them and singing out, "Kill them, kill them!" It made me so sick I most fell out of the tree. I ain't agoing to tell *all* that happened!—it would make me sick again if I was to do that. I wished I hadn't ever come ashore that night, to see such things. I ain't ever going to get shut of them—lots of times I dream about them.

I staid in the tree till it begun to get dark, afraid to come down. Sometimes I heard guns away off in the woods; and twice I seen little gangs of men gallop past the log store with guns; so I reckoned the trouble was still agoing on. I was mighty downhearted; so I made up my mind I wouldn't ever go anear that house again, because I reckoned I was to blame, somehow. I judged that that piece of paper meant that Miss Sophia was to meet Harney somewheres at half-past two and run off; and I judged I ought to told her father about that paper and the curious way she acted, and then maybe he would a locked her up and this awful mess wouldn't ever happened.

When I got down out of the tree, I crept along down the river bank a piece, and found the two bodies laying in the edge of the water, and tugged at them till I got them ashore; then I covered up their faces, and got away as quick as I could. I cried a little when I was covering up Buck's face, for he was mighty good to me.

It was just dark, now. I never went near the house, but struck through the woods and made for the swamp. Jim warn't on his island, so I tramped off in a hurry for the crick, and crowded through the willows, red-hot to jump aboard and get out of that awful country—the raft was gone! My souls, but I was scared! I couldn't get my breath for most a minute. Then I raised a yell. A voice not twenty-five foot from me, says—

"Good lan'! is dat you, honey? Doan' make no noise."

It was Jim's voice—nothing ever sounded so good before. I run along the bank a piece and got aboard, and Jim he grabbed me and hugged me, he was so glad to see me. He says—

"Laws bless you, chile, I 'uz right down sho' you's dead agin. Jack's been heah, he say he reck'n you's ben shot, kase you didn' come home no mo'; so I's jes' dis minute a startin' de raf' down towards de mouf er de crick, so's to be all ready for to shove out en leave soon as Jack comes agin en tells me for certain you *is* dead. Lawsy, I's mighty glad to git you back agin, honey."

I says—

"All right—that's mighty good; they won't find me, and they'll think I've been killed, and floated down the river—there's something up there that'll help them to think so—so don't you lose no time, Jim, but just shove off for the big water as fast as ever you can."

I never felt easy till the raft was two mile below there and out in the middle of the Mississippi. Then we hung up our signal lantern, and judged that we was free and safe once more. I hadn't had a bite to eat since yesterday; so Jim he got out some corn-dodgers[4] and buttermilk, and pork and cabbage, and greens—there ain't nothing in the world so good, when it's cooked right—and whilst I eat my supper we talked, and had a good time. I was powerful glad to get away from the feuds, and so was Jim to get away from the swamp. We said there warn't no home like a raft, after all. Other places do seem so cramped up and smothery, but a raft don't. You feel mighty free and easy and comfortable on a raft.

Chapter XIX

Two or three days and nights went by; I reckon I might say they swum by, they slid along so quiet and smooth and lovely. Here is the way we put in the time. It was a monstrous big river down there—sometimes a mile and a half wide; we run nights, and laid up and hid day-times; soon as night was most gone, we stopped navigating and tied up—nearly always in the dead water under a tow-head; and then cut young cottonwoods and willows and hid the raft with them. Then we set out the lines. Next we slid into the river and had a swim, so as to freshen up and cool off; then we set down on the sandy bottom where the water was about knee deep, and watched the daylight come. Not a sound, anywheres—perfectly still—just like the whole world was asleep, only sometimes the bull-frogs a-cluttering, maybe. The first thing to see, looking away over the water, was a kind of dull line—that was the woods on t'other side—you couldn't make nothing else out; then a pale place in the sky; then more paleness, spreading around; then the river softened up, away off, and warn't black any more, but gray; you could see little dark spots drifting along, ever so far away—trading scows, and such things; and long black streaks—rafts; sometimes you could hear a sweep screaking; or jumbled up voices, it was so still, and sounds come so far; and by-and-by you could see a streak on the water which you know by the look of the streak that there's a snag there in a swift current which breaks on it and makes that streak look that way; and you see the mist curl up off of the water, and the east reddens up, and the river, and you make out a log cabin in the edge of the woods, away on the bank on t'other side of the river, being a wood-yard, likely, and piled by them cheats so you can throw a dog through it anywheres;[5] then the nice breeze springs up, and comes fanning you from over there, so cool and fresh, and sweet to smell, on account of the woods and the flowers; but sometimes not that way, because they've left dead fish laying around, gars, and such, and they do get pretty rank; and next you've got the full day, and everything smiling in the sun, and the song-birds just going it!

A little smoke couldn't be noticed, now, so we would take some fish off of the lines, and cook up a hot breakfast. And afterwards we would watch the lonesomeness of the river, and kind of lazy along, and by-and-by lazy off to sleep. Wake up, by-and-by, and look to see what done it, and maybe see a steamboat coughing along up stream, so far off towards the other side you couldn't tell nothing about her only whether she was stern-wheel or side-wheel; then for about an hour there wouldn't be nothing to hear nor noth-

4. Hard cornmeal rolls or cakes.
5. Stacks of wood in this yard were sold by their volume, gaps and holes included.

ing to see—just solid lonesomeness. Next you'd see a raft sliding by, away off yonder, and maybe a galoot[6] on it chopping, because they're almost always doing it on a raft; you'd see the ax flash, and come down—you don't hear nothing; you see that ax go up again, and by the time it's above the man's head, then you hear the *k'chunk!*—it had took all that time to come over the water. So we would put in the day, lazying around, listening to the stillness. Once there was a thick fog, and the rafts and things that went by was beating tin pans so the steamboats wouldn't run over them. A scow or a raft went by so close we could hear them talking and cussing and laughing—heard them plain; but we couldn't see no sign of them; it made you feel crawly, it was like spirits carrying on that way in the air. Jim said he believed it was spirits; but I says:

"No, spirits wouldn't say, 'dern the dern fog.'"

Soon as it was night, out we shoved; when we got her out to about the middle, we let her alone, and let her float wherever the current wanted her to; then we lit the pipes, and dangled our legs in the water and talked about all kinds of things—we was always naked, day and night, whenever the mosquitoes would let us—the new clothes Buck's folks made for me was too good to be comfortable, and besides I didn't go much on clothes, nohow.

Sometimes we'd have that whole river all to ourselves for the longest time. Yonder was the banks and the islands, across the water; and maybe a spark—which was a candle in a cabin window—and sometimes on the water you could see a spark or two—on a raft or a scow, you know; and maybe you could hear a fiddle or a song coming over from one of them crafts. It's lovely to live on a raft. We had the sky, up there, all speckled with stars, and we used to lay on our backs and look up at them, and discuss about whether they was made, or only just happened—Jim he allowed they was made, but I allowed they happened; I judged it would have took too long to *make* so many. Jim said the moon could a *laid* them; well, that looked kind of reasonable, so I didn't say nothing against it, because I've seen a frog lay most as many, so of course it could be done. We used to watch the stars that fell, too, and see them streak down. Jim allowed they'd got spoiled and was hove out of the nest.

Once or twice of a night we would see a steamboat slipping along in the dark, and now and then she would belch a whole world of sparks up out of her chimbleys, and they would rain down in the river and look awful pretty; then she would turn a corner and her lights would wink out and her powwow shut off and leave the river still again; and by-and-by her waves would get to us, a long time after she was gone, and joggle the raft a bit, and after that you wouldn't hear nothing for you couldn't tell how long, except maybe frogs or something.

After midnight the people on shore went to bed, and then for two or three hours the shores was black—no more sparks in the cabin windows. These sparks was our clock—the first one that showed again meant morning was coming, so we hunted a place to hide and tie up, right away.

One morning about day-break, I found a canoe and crossed over a chute[7] to the main shore—it was only two hundred yards—and paddled about a mile up a crick amongst the cypress woods, to see if I couldn't get some berries. Just as

---

6. Awkward, ungainly person (slang).   7. A narrow channel with swift-flowing water.

I was passing a place where a kind of a cow-path crossed the crick, here comes a couple of men tearing up the path as tight as they could foot it. I thought I was a goner, for whenever anybody was after anybody I judged it was *me*—or maybe Jim. I was about to dig out from there in a hurry, but they was pretty close to me then, and sung out and begged me to save their lives—said they hadn't been doing nothing, and was being chased for it—said there was men and dogs a-coming. They wanted to jump right in, but I says—

"Don't you do it. I don't hear the dogs and horses yet; you've got time to crowd through the brush and get up the crick a little ways; then you take to the water and wade down to me and get in—that'll throw the dogs off the scent."

They done it, and soon as they was aboard I lit out for our tow-head, and in about five or ten minutes we heard the dogs and the men away off, shouting. We heard them come along towards the crick, but couldn't see them; they seemed to stop and fool around a while; then, as we got further and further away all the time, we couldn't hardly hear them at all; by the time we had left a mile of woods behind us and struck the river, everything was quiet, and we paddled over to the tow-head and hid in the cotton-woods and was safe.

One of these fellows was about seventy, or upwards, and had a bald head and very gray whiskers. He had an old battered-up slouch hat on, and a greasy blue woolen shirt, and ragged old blue jeans britches stuffed into his boot tops, and home-knit galluses[8]—no, he only had one. He had an old long-tailed blue jeans coat with slick brass buttons, flung over his arm, and both of them had big fat ratty-looking carpet-bags.

The other fellow was about thirty and dressed about as ornery. After breakfast we all laid off and talked, and the first thing that come out was that these chaps didn't know one another.

"What got you into trouble?" says the baldhead to t'other chap.

"Well, I'd been selling an article to take the tartar off the teeth—and it does take it off, too, and generly the enamel along with it—but I staid about one night longer than I ought to, and was just in the act of sliding out when I ran across you on the trail this side of town, and you told me they were coming, and begged me to help you to get off. So I told you I was expecting trouble myself and would scatter out *with* you. That's the whole yarn—what's yourn?"

"Well, I'd ben a-runnin' a little temperance revival[9] thar, 'bout a week, and was the pet of the women-folks, big and little, for I was makin' it mighty warm for the rummies, I *tell* you, and takin' as much as five or six dollars a night—ten cents a head, children and niggers free—and business a growin' all the time; when somehow or another a little report got around, last night, that I had a way of puttin' in my time with a private jug, on the sly. A nigger rousted me out this mornin', and told me the people was getherin' on the quiet, with their dogs and horses, and they'd be along pretty soon and give me 'bout half an hour's start, and then run me down, if they could; and if they got me they'd tar and feather me and ride me on a rail, sure. I didn't wait for no breakfast—I warn't hungry."

8. Suspenders.
9. A religious gathering aimed at producing commitment to a life without alcoholic beverages.

"Old man," says the young one, "I reckon we might double-team it together; what do you think?"

"I ain't undisposed. What's your line—mainly?"

"Jour printer,[1] by trade; do a little in patent medicines; theatre-actor—tragedy, you know; take a turn at mesmerism and phrenology,[2] when there's a chance; teach singing-geography[3] school for a change; sling a lecture, sometimes—oh, I do lots of things—most anything that comes handy, so it ain't work. What's your lay?"[4]

"I've done considerable in the doctoring way in my time. Layin' on o' hands[5] is my best holt—for cancer, and paralysis, and sich things; and I k'n tell a fortune pretty good, when I've got somebody along to find out the facts for me. Preachin's my line, too; and workin' camp-meetin's; and missionaryin' around."

Nobody never said anything for a while; then the young man hove a sigh and says—

"Alas!"

"What 're you alassin' about?" says the baldhead.

"To think I should have lived to be leading such a life, and be degraded down into such company." And he begun to wipe the corner of his eye with a rag.

"Dern your skin, ain't the company good enough for you?" says the baldhead, pretty pert and uppish.

"Yes, it *is* good enough for me; it's as good as I deserve; for who fetched me so low, when I was so high? *I* did myself. I don't blame *you*, gentlemen—far from it; I don't blame anybody. I deserve it all. Let the cold world do its worst; one thing I know—there's a grave somewhere for me. The world may go on just as its always done, and take everything from me—loved ones, property, everything—but it can't take that. Some day I'll lie down in it and forget it all, and my poor broken heart will be at rest." He went on a-wiping.

"Drot your pore broken heart," says the baldhead; "what are you heaving your pore broken heart at *us* f'r? *We* hain't done nothing."

"No, I know you haven't. I ain't blaming you, gentlemen. I brought myself down—yes, I did it myself. It's right I should suffer—perfectly right—I don't make any moan."

"Brought you down from whar? Whar was you brought down from?"

"Ah, you would not believe me; the world never believes—let it pass—'tis no matter. The secret of my birth—"

"The secret of your birth? Do you mean to say—"

"Gentlemen," says the young man, very solemn, "I will reveal it to you, for I feel I may have confidence in you. By rights I am a duke!"

Jim's eyes bugged out when he heard that; and I reckon mine did, too. Then the baldhead says: "No! you can't mean it?"

"Yes. My great-grandfather, eldest son of the Duke of Bridgewater, fled to this country about the end of the last century, to breathe the pure air of freedom; married here, and died, leaving a son, his own father dying about the same time. The second son of the late duke seized the title and estates—the

1. A journeyman printer (not yet a salaried master-printer), who worked by the day.
2. The study of the shape of the skull as an indicator of intelligence and character. "Mesmerism": a form of hypnotism.
3. Chants or rhymes that allowed the singers to memorize geographic facts such as rivers, capitals, mountains, etc.
4. Work, in the sense here of hustle or scheme.
5. Faith healing.

infant real duke was ignored. I am the lineal descendant of that infant—
I am the rightful Duke of Bridgewater; and here am I, forlorn, torn from my
high estate, hunted of men, despised by the cold world, ragged, worn, heart-
broken, and degraded to the companionship of felons on a raft!"

Jim pitied him ever so much, and so did I. We tried to comfort him, but he
said it warn't much use, he couldn't be much comforted; said if we was a mind
to acknowledge him, that would do him more good than most anything else;
so we said we would, if he would tell us how. He said we ought to bow, when
we spoke to him, and say "Your Grace," or "My Lord," or "Your Lordship"—
and he wouldn't mind it if we called him plain "Bridgewater," which he said
was a title, anyway, and not a name; and one of us ought to wait on him at
dinner, and do any little thing for him he wanted done.

Well, that was all easy, so we done it. All through dinner Jim stood around
and waited on him, and says, "Will yo' Grace have some o' dis, or some o'
dat?" and so on, and a body could see it was mighty pleasing to him.

But the old man got pretty silent, by-and-by—didn't have much to say, and
didn't look pretty comfortable over all that petting that was going on around
that duke. He seemed to have something on his mind. So, along in the afternoon, he says:

"Looky here, Bilgewater,"[6] he says, "I'm nation sorry for you, but you ain't
the only person that's had troubles like that."

"No?"

"No, you ain't. You ain't the only person that's ben snaked down wrongfully out'n a high place."

"Alas!"

"No, you ain't the only person that's had a secret of his birth." And by jings,
he begins to cry.

"Hold! What do you mean?"

"Bilgewater, kin I trust you?" says the old man, still sort of sobbing.

"To the bitter death!" He took the old man by the hand and squeezed it,
and says, "The secret of your being: speak!"

"Bilgewater, I am the late Dauphin!"[7]

You bet you Jim and me stared, this time. Then the duke says:

"You are what?"

"Yes, my friend, it is too true—your eyes is lookin' at this very moment on
the pore disappeared Dauphin, Looy the Seventeen, son of Looy the Sixteen
and Marry Antonette."

"You! At your age! No! You mean you're the late Charlemagne;[8] you must
be six or seven hundred years old, at the very least."

"Trouble has done it, Bilgewater, trouble has done it; trouble has brung
these gray hairs and this premature balditude. Yes, gentlemen, you see before
you, in blue jeans and misery, the wanderin', exiled, trampled-on and sufferin' rightful King of France."

Well, he cried and took on so, that me and Jim didn't know hardly what
to do, we was so sorry—and so glad and proud we'd got him with us, too. So
we set in, like we done before with the duke, and tried to comfort *him*. But

---

6. This corruption of "Bridgewater" refers to the
water that collects at the bottom of a boat, the bilge.
7. The Dauphin, born in 1785, would have been
in his mid-fifties or sixties had he survived.
8. Charlemagne (742–814), emperor of the West
(800–814).

he said it warn't no use, nothing but to be dead and done with it all could do him any good; though he said it often made him feel easier and better for a while if people treated him according to his rights, and got down on one knee to speak to him, and always called him "Your Majesty," and waited on him first at meals, and didn't set down in his presence till he asked them. So Jim and me set to majestying him, and doing this and that and t'other for him, and standing up till he told us we might set down. This done him heaps of good, and so he got cheerful and comfortable. But the duke kind of soured on him, and didn't look a bit satisfied with the way things was going; still, the king acted real friendly towards him, and said the duke's great-grandfather and all the other Dukes of Bilgewater was a good deal thought of by *his* father and was allowed to come to the palace considerable; but the duke staid huffy a good while, till by-and-by the king says:

"Like as not we got to be together a blamed long time, on this h-yer raft, Bilgewater, and so what's the use o' your bein' sour? It'll only make things oncomfortable. It ain't my fault I warn't born a duke, it ain't your fault you warn't born a king—so what's the use to worry? Make the best o' things the way you find 'em, says I—that's my motto. This ain't no bad thing that we've struck here—plenty grub and an easy life—come, give us your hand, Duke, and less all be friends."

The duke done it, and Jim and me was pretty glad to see it. It took away all the uncomfortableness, and we felt mighty good over it, because it would a been a miserable business to have any unfriendliness on the raft; for what you want, above all things, on a raft, is for everybody to be satisfied, and feel right and kind towards the others.

It didn't take me long to make up my mind that these liars warn't no kings nor dukes, at all, but just low-down humbugs and frauds. But I never said nothing, never let on; kept it to myself; it's the best way; then you don't have no quarrels, and don't get into no trouble. If they wanted us to call them kings and dukes, I hadn't no objections, 'long as it would keep peace in the family; and it warn't no use to tell Jim, so I didn't tell him. If I never learnt nothing else out of pap, I learnt that the best way to get along with his kind of people is to let them have their own way.

Chapter XX

They asked us considerable many questions; wanted to know what we covered up the raft that way for, and laid by in the daytime instead of running—was Jim a runaway nigger? Says I—

"Goodness sakes, would a runaway nigger run *south?*"

No, they allowed he wouldn't. I had to account for things some way, so I says:

"My folks was living in Pike County, in Missouri, where I was born, and they all died off but me and pa and my brother Ike. Pa, he 'lowed he'd break up and go down and live with Uncle Ben, who's got a little one-horse place on the river, forty-four mile below Orleans. Pa was pretty poor, and had some debts; so when he'd squared up there warn't nothing left but sixteen dollars and our nigger, Jim. That warn't enough to take us fourteen hundred mile, deck passage nor no other way. Well, when the river rose, pa had a streak of luck one day; he ketched this piece of a raft; so we reckoned we'd go down to Orleans on it. Pa's luck didn't hold out; a steamboat run over the forrard corner of the raft, one night, and we all went overboard and dove under the wheel; Jim and me come up, all right, but pa was drunk, and Ike was only four years old, so they never come up no more. Well, for the next day or two we had considerable trouble, because people was always coming out in skiffs and trying to take Jim away from me, saying they believed he was a runaway nigger. We don't run day-times no more, now; nights they don't bother us."

The duke says—

"Leave me alone to cipher out a way so we can run in the daytime if we want to. I'll think the thing over—I'll invent a plan that'll fix it. We'll let it alone for to-day, because of course we don't want to go by that town yonder in daylight—it mightn't be healthy."

Towards night it begun to darken up and look like rain; the heat lightning was squirting around, low down in the sky, and the leaves was beginning to shiver—it was going to be pretty ugly, it was easy to see that. So the duke and the king went to overhauling our wigwam, to see what the beds was like. My bed was a straw tick[9]—better than Jim's, which was a corn-shuck tick; there's always cobs around about in a shuck tick, and they poke into you and hurt; and when you roll over, the dry shucks sound like you was rolling over in a pile of dead leaves; it makes such a rustling that you wake up. Well, the duke allowed he would take my bed; but the king allowed he wouldn't. He says—

"I should a reckoned the difference in rank would a sejested to you that a corn-shuck bed warn't just fitten for me to sleep on. Your Grace'll take the shuck bed yourself."

Jim and me was in a sweat again, for a minute, being afraid there was going to be some more trouble amongst them; so we was pretty glad when the duke says—

" 'Tis my fate to be always ground into the mire under the iron heel of oppression. Misfortune has broken my once haughty spirit; I yield, I submit; 'tis my fate. I am alone in the world—let me suffer; I can bear it."

We got away as soon as it was good and dark. The king told us to stand well out towards the middle of the river, and not show a light till we got a long ways below the town. We come in sight of the little bunch of lights by-and-by—that was the town, you know—and slid by, about a half a mile out, all right. When we was three-quarters of a mile below, we hoisted up our signal lantern; and about ten o'clock it come on to rain and blow and thunder and lighten like everything; so the king told us to both stay on watch till the weather got better; then him and the duke crawled into the wigwam and turned in for the night. It was my watch below, till twelve, but I wouldn't a turned in, anyway, if I'd had a bed; because a body don't see such a storm as that every day in the week, not by a long sight. My souls, how the wind did scream along! And every second or two there'd come a glare that lit up the white-caps for a half a mile around, and you'd see the islands looking dusty through the rain, and the trees thrashing around in the wind; then comes a *h-wack!*—bum! bum! bumble-umble-um-bum-bum-bum-bum—and the thunder would go rumbling and grumbling away, and quit—and then *rip* comes another flash and another sock-dolager.[1] The

9. Mattress.
1. Something exceptionally strong or climactic (slang).

waves most washed me off the raft, sometimes, but I hadn't any clothes on, and didn't mind. We didn't have no trouble about snags; the lightning was glaring and flittering around so constant that we could see them plenty soon enough to throw her head this way or that and miss them.

I had the middle watch, you know, but I was pretty sleepy by that time, so Jim he said he would stand the first half of it for me; he was always mighty good, that way, Jim was. I crawled into the wigwam, but the king and the duke had their legs sprawled around so there warn't no show for me; so I laid outside—I didn't mind the rain, because it was warm, and the waves warn't running so high, now. About two they come up again, though, and Jim was going to call me, but he changed his mind because he reckoned they warn't high enough yet to do any harm; but he was mistaken about that, for pretty soon all of a sudden along comes a regular ripper, and washed me overboard. It most killed Jim a-laughing. He was the easiest nigger to laugh that ever was, anyway.

I took the watch, and Jim he laid down and snored away; and by-and-by the storm let up for good and all; and the first cabin-light that showed, I rousted him out and we slid the raft into hiding-quarters for the day.

The king got out an old ratty deck of cards, after breakfast, and him and the duke played seven-up a while, five cents a game. Then they got tired of it, and allowed they would "lay out a campaign," as they called it. The duke went down into his carpet-bag and fetched up a lot of little printed bills, and read them out loud. One bill said "The celebrated Dr. Armand de Montalban of Paris," would "lecture on the Science of Phrenology" at such and such a place, on the blank day of blank, at ten cents admission, and "furnish charts of character at twenty-five cents apiece." The duke said that was *him*. In another bill he was the "world renowned Shaksperean tragedian, Garrick the Younger,[2] of Drury Lane, London." In other bills he had a lot of other names and done other wonderful things, like finding water and gold with a "divining rod," "dissipating witch-spells," and so on. By-and-by he says—

"But the histrionic muse is the darling. Have you ever trod the boards, Royalty?"

"No," says the king.

"You shall, then, before you're three days older, Fallen Grandeur," says the duke. "The first good town we come to, we'll hire a hall and do the sword-fight in Richard III. and the balcony scene in Romeo and Juliet. How does that strike you?"

"I'm in, up to the hub, for anything that will pay, Bilgewater, but you see I don't know nothing about play-actn', and hain't ever seen much of it. I was too small when pap used to have 'em at the palace. Do you reckon you can learn me?"

"Easy!"

"All right. I'm jist a-freezn' for something fresh, anyway. Less commence, right away."

So the duke he told him all about who Romeo was, and who Juliet was, and said he was used to being Romeo, so the king could be Juliet.

"But if Juliet's such a young gal, Duke, my peeled head and my white whiskers is goin' to look oncommon odd on her, maybe."

2. David Garrick (1717–1779) was a famous tragedian at the Theatre Royal in Drury Lane, London.

"No, don't you worry—these country jakes won't ever think of that. Besides, you know, you'll be in costume, and that makes all the difference in the world; Juliet's in a balcony, enjoying the moonlight before she goes to bed, and she's got on her night-gown and her ruffled night-cap. Here are the costumes for the parts."

He got out two or three curtain-calico suits, which he said was meedyevil armor for Richard III. and t'other chap, and a long white cotton night-shirt and a ruffled night-cap to match. The king was satisfied; so the duke got out his book and read the parts over in the most splendid spread-eagle way, prancing around and acting at the same time, to show how it had got to be done; then he give the book to the king and told him to get his part by heart.

There was a little one-horse town about three mile down the bend, and after dinner the duke said he had ciphered out his idea about how to run in daylight without it being dangersome for Jim; so he allowed he would go down to the town and fix that thing. The king allowed he would go too, and see if he couldn't strike something. We was out of coffee, so Jim said I better go along with them in the canoe and get some.

When we got there, there warn't nobody stirring; streets empty, and perfectly dead and still, like Sunday. We found a sick nigger sunning himself in a back yard, and he said everybody that warn't too young or too sick or too old, was gone to camp-meeting, about two mile back in the woods. The king got the directions, and allowed he'd go and work that camp-meeting for all it was worth, and I might go, too.[3]

The duke said what he was after was a printing office. We found it; a little bit of a concern, up over a carpenter shop—carpenters and printers all gone to the meeting, and no doors locked. It was a dirty, littered-up place, and had ink marks, and handbills with pictures of horses and runaway niggers on them, all over the walls. The duke shed his coat and said he was all right, now. So me and the king lit out for the camp-meeting.

We got there in about a half an hour, fairly dripping, for it was a most awful hot day. There was as much as a thousand people there, from twenty mile around. The woods was full of teams and wagons, hitched everywheres, feeding out of the wagon troughs and stomping to keep off the flies. There was sheds made out of poles and roofed over with branches, where they had lemonade and gingerbread to sell, and piles of watermelons and green corn and such-like truck.

The preaching was going on under the same kinds of sheds, only they was bigger and held crowds of people. The benches was made out of outside slabs of logs, with holes bored in the round side to drive sticks into for legs. They didn't have no backs. The preachers had high platforms to stand on, at one end of the sheds. The women had on sunbonnets; and some had linsey-woolsey frocks, some gingham ones, and a few of the young ones had on calico. Some of the young men was barefooted, and some of the children didn't have on any clothes but just a tow-linen[4] shirt. Some of the old women was knitting, and some of the young folks was courting on the sly.

3. Notoriously easy pickings for confidence men, camp meetings are extended outdoor evangelical meetings.
4. Coarse linen cloth. "Linsey-woolsey": cheap, often homespun, unpatterned cloth composed of wool and flax. "Gingham" and "calico" are inexpensive, store-bought printed cotton.

The first shed we come to, the preacher was lining out a hymn. He lined out two lines, everybody sung it, and it was kind of grand to hear it, there was so many of them and they done it in such a rousing way; then he lined out two more for them to sing—and so on. The people woke up more and more, and sung louder and louder; and towards the end, some begun to groan, and some begun to shout. Then the preacher begun to preach; and begun in earnest, too; and went weaving first to one side of the platform and then the other, and then a leaning down over the front of it, with his arms and his body going all the time, and shouting his words out with all his might; and every now and then he would hold up his Bible and spread it open, and kind of pass it around this way and that, shouting, "It's the brazen serpent in the wilderness! Look upon it and live!" And people would shout out, "Glory!—A-a-men!" And so he went on, and the people groaning and crying and saying amen:

"Oh, come to the mourners' bench![5] come, black with sin! (amen!) come, sick and sore! (amen!) come, lame and halt, and blind! (amen!) come, pore and needy, sunk in shame! (a-a-men!) come all that's worn, and soiled, and suffering!—come with a broken spirit! come with a contrite heart! come in your rags and sin and dirt! the waters that cleanse is free, the door of heaven stands open—oh, enter in and be at rest!" (a-a-men! glory, glory hallelujah!)

And so on. You couldn't make out what the preacher said, any more, on account of the shouting and crying. Folks got up, everywheres in the crowd, and worked their way, just by main strength, to the mourners' bench, with the tears running down their faces; and when all the mourners had got up there to the front benches in a crowd, they sung, and shouted, and flung themselves down on the straw, just crazy and wild.

Well, the first I knowed, the king got agoing; and you could hear him over everybody; and next he went a-charging up on to the platform and the preacher he begged him to speak to the people, and he done it. He told them he was a pirate—been a pirate for thirty years, out in the Indian Ocean, and his crew was thinned out considerable, last spring, in a fight, and he was home now, to take out some fresh men, and thanks to goodness he'd been robbed last night, and put ashore off of a steamboat without a cent, and he was glad of it, it was the blessedest thing that ever happened to him, because he was a changed man now, and happy for the first time in his life; and poor as he was, he was going to start right off and work his way back to the Indian Ocean and put in the rest of his life trying to turn the pirates into the true path; for he could do it better than anybody else, being acquainted with all the pirate crews in that ocean; and though it would take him a long time to get there, without money, he would get there anyway, and every time he convinced a pirate he would say to him, "Don't you thank me, don't you give me no credit, it all belongs to them dear people in Pokeville camp-meeting, natural brothers and benefactors of the race—and that dear preacher there, the truest friend a pirate ever had!"

And then he busted into tears, and so did everybody. Then somebody sings out, "Take up a collection for him, take up a collection!" Well, a half a dozen made a jump to do it, but somebody sings out, "Let *him* pass the hat around!" Then everybody said it, the preacher too.

So the king went all through the crowd with his hat, swabbing his eyes, and blessing the people and praising them and thanking them for being so

5. Front-row pews filled by penitents.

good to the poor pirates away off there; and every little while the prettiest kind of girls, with the tears running down their cheeks, would up and ask him would he let them kiss him, for to remember him by; and he always done it; and some of them he hugged and kissed as many as five or six times—and he was invited to stay a week; and everybody wanted him to live in their houses, and said they'd think it was an honor; but he said as this was the last day of the camp-meeting he couldn't do no good, and besides he was in a sweat to get to the Indian Ocean right off and go to work on the pirates.

When we got back to the raft and he come to count up, he found he had collected eighty-seven dollars and seventy-five cents. And then he had fetched away a three-gallon jug of whiskey, too, that he found under a wagon when we was starting home through the woods. The king said, take it all around, it laid over any day he'd ever put in in the missionarying line. He said it warn't no use talking, heathens don't amount to shucks, alongside of pirates, to work a camp-meeting with.

The duke was thinking *he'd* been doing pretty well, till the king come to show up, but after that he didn't think so so much. He had set up and printed off two little jobs for farmers, in that printing office—horse bills—and took the money, four dollars. And he had got in ten dollars worth of advertisements for the paper, which he said he would put in for four dollars if they would pay in advance—so they done it. The price of the paper was two dollars a year, but he took in three subscriptions for half a dollar apiece on condition of them paying him in advance; they were going to pay in cordwood and onions, as usual, but he said he had just bought the concern and knocked down the price as low as he could afford it, and was going to run it for cash. He set up a little piece of poetry, which he made, himself, out of his own head—three verses—kind of sweet and saddish—the name of it was, "Yes, crush, cold world, this breaking heart"—and he left that all set up and ready to print in the paper and didn't charge nothing for it. Well, he took in nine dollars and a half, and said he'd done a pretty square day's work for it.

Then he showed us another little job he'd printed and hadn't charged for, because it was for us. It had a picture of a runaway nigger, with a bundle on a stick, over his shoulder, and "$200 reward" under it. The reading was all about Jim, and just described him to a dot. It said he run away from St. Jacques' plantation, forty mile below New Orleans, last winter, and likely went north, and whoever would catch him and send him back, he could have the reward and expenses.

"Now," says the duke, "after to-night we can run in the daytime if we want to. Whenever we see anybody coming, we can tie Jim hand and foot with a rope, and lay him in the wigwam and show this handbill and say we captured him up the river, and were too poor to travel on a steamboat, so we got this little raft on credit from our friends and are going down to get the reward. Handcuffs and chains would look still better on Jim, but it wouldn't go well with the story of us being so poor. Too much like jewelry. Ropes are the correct thing—we must preserve the unities,[6] as we say on the boards."

6. Of time, place, and action in classical drama; here the duke is using the term to mean "consistent with the rest of our story."

We all said the duke was pretty smart, and there couldn't be no trouble about running daytimes. We judged we could make miles enough that night to get out of the reach of the pow-wow we reckoned the duke's work in the printing office was going to make in that little town—then we could boom right along, if we wanted to.

We laid low and kept still, and never shoved out till nearly ten o'clock; then we slid by, pretty wide away from the town, and didn't hoist our lantern till we was clear out of sight of it.

When Jim called me to take the watch at four in the morning, he says—

"Huck, does you reck'n we gwyne to run acrost any mo' kings on dis trip?"

"No," I says, "I reckon not."

"Well," says he, "dat's all right, den. I doan' mine one er two kings, but dat's enough. Dis one's powerful drunk, en de duke ain' much better."

I found Jim had been trying to get him to talk French, so he could hear what it was like; but he said he had been in this country so long, and had so much trouble, he'd forgot it.

Chapter XXI

It was after sun-up, now, but we went right on, and didn't tie up. The king and the duke turned out, by-and-by, looking pretty rusty; but after they'd jumped overboard and took a swim, it chippered them up a good deal. After breakfast the king he took a seat on a corner of the raft, and pulled off his boots and rolled up his britches, and let his legs dangle in the water, so as to be comfortable, and lit his pipe, and went to getting his Romeo and Juliet by heart. When he had got it pretty good, him and the duke begun to practice it together. The duke had to learn him over and over again, how to say every speech; and he made him sigh, and put his hand on his heart, and after while he said he done it pretty well; "only," he says, "you mustn't bellow out *Romeo!* that way, like a bull—you must say it soft, and sick, and languishy, so—R-o-o-meo! that is the idea; for Juliet's a dear sweet mere child of a girl, you know, and she don't bray like a jackass."

Well, next they got out a couple of long swords that the duke made out of oak laths, and begun to practice the sword-fight—the duke called himself Richard III.; and the way they laid on, and pranced around the raft was grand to see. But by-and-by the king tripped and fell overboard, and after that they took a rest, and had a talk about all kinds of adventures they'd had in other times along the river.

After dinner, the duke says:

"Well, Capet,[7] we'll want to make this a first-class show, you know, so I guess we'll add a little more to it. We want a little something to answer encores with, anyway."

"What's onkores, Bilgewater?"

The duke told him, and then says:

"I'll answer by doing the Highland fling or the sailor's hornpipe; and you— well, let me see—oh, I've got it—you can do Hamlet's soliloquy."

"Hamlet's which?"

---

7. The family name of Louis XVI, who was guillotined in 1793.

"Hamlet's soliloquy, you know; the most celebrated thing in Shakespeare. Ah, it's sublime, sublime! Always fetches the house. I haven't got it in the book—I've only got one volume—but I reckon I can piece it out from memory. I'll just walk up and down a minute, and see if I can call it back from recollection's vaults."

So he went to marching up and down, thinking, and frowning horrible every now and then; then he would hoist up his eyebrows; next he would squeeze his hand on his forehead and stagger back and kind of moan; next he would sigh, and next he'd let on to drop a tear. It was beautiful to see him. By-and-by he got it. He told us to give attention. Then he strikes a most noble attitude, with one leg shoved forwards, and his arms stretched away up, and his head tilted back, looking up at the sky; and then he begins to rip and rave and grit his teeth; and after that, all through his speech he howled, and spread around, and swelled up his chest, and just knocked the spots out of any acting ever *I* see before. This is the speech—I learned it, easy enough, while he was learning it to the king:[8]

To be, or not to be; that is the bare bodkin
That makes calamity of so long life;
For who would fardels bear, till Birnam Wood do come to Dunsinane,
But that the fear of something after death
Murders the innocent sleep,
Great nature's second course,
And makes us rather sling the arrows of outrageous fortune
Than fly to others that we know not of.
There's the respect must give us pause:
Wake Duncan with thy knocking! I would thou couldst;
For who would bear the whips and scorns of time,
The oppressor's wrong, the proud man's contumely,
The law's delay, and the quietus which his pangs might take,
In the dead waste and middle of the night, when churchyards yawn
In customary suits of solemn black,
But that the undiscovered country from whose bourne no traveler returns,
Breathes forth contagion on the world,
And thus the native hue of resolution, like the poor cat i' the adage,
Is sicklied o'er with care,
And all the clouds that lowered o'er our housetops,
With this regard their currents turn awry,
And lose the name of action.
'Tis a consummation devoutly to be wished. But soft you, the fair Ophelia:
Ope not thy ponderous and marble jaws,
But get thee to a nunnery—go!

Well, the old man he liked that speech, and he mighty soon got it so he could do it first rate. It seemed like he was just born for it; and when he had his hand in and was excited, it was perfectly lovely the way he would rip and tear and rair up behind when he was getting it off.

8. The comical garbling of Shakespeare was another stock-in-trade of the southwestern humorists in whose tradition Twain follows. The soliloquy is composed chiefly of phrases from *Hamlet* and *Macbeth*, but Twain also draws on several other plays.

The first chance we got, the duke he had some show bills printed; and after that, for two or three days as we floated along, the raft was a most uncommon lively place, for there warn't nothing but sword-fighting and rehearsing—as the duke called it—going on all the time. One morning, when we was pretty well down the State of Arkansaw, we come in sight of a little one-horse town in a big bend; so we tied up about three-quarters of a mile above it, in the mouth of a crick which was shut in like a tunnel by the cypress trees, and all of us but Jim took the canoe and went down there to see if there was any chance in that place for our show.

We struck it mighty lucky; there was going to be a circus there that afternoon, and the country people was already beginning to come in, in all kinds of old shackly wagons, and on horses. The circus would leave before night, so our show would have a pretty good chance. The duke he hired the court house, and we went around and stuck up our bills. They read like this:

Shaksperean Revival!!!
Wonderful Attraction!
For One Night Only!
The world renowned tragedians,
David Garrick the younger, of Drury Lane Theatre, London,
and
Edmund Kean the elder,[9] of the Royal Haymarket Theatre, White-
chapel, Pudding Lane, Piccadilly, London, and the
Royal Continental Theatres, in their sublime
Shaksperean Spectacle entitled
The Balcony Scene
in
Romeo and Juliet!!!

Romeo . . . . Mr. Garrick.
Juliet . . . . Mr. Kean.
Assisted by the whole strength of the company!
New costumes, new scenery, new appointments!
Also:
The thrilling, masterly, and blood-curdling
Broad-sword conflict
In Richard III.!!!

Richard III . . . . Mr. Garrick.
Richmond . . . . Mr. Kean.
also:
(by special request,)
Hamlet's Immortal Soliloquy!!
By the Illustrious Kean!
Done by him 300 consecutive nights in Paris!
For One Night Only,
On account of imperative European engagements!
Admission 25 cents; children and servants, 10 cents.

---

9. Here, as elsewhere, the duke garbles the facts. Garrick, Edmund Kean (1787–1833), and Charles John Kean (1811–1868) were all famous tragedians at the Theatre Royal in Drury Lane, London.

Then we went loafing around the town. The stores and houses was most all old shackly dried-up frame concerns that hadn't ever been painted; they was set up three or four foot above ground on stilts, so as to be out of reach of the water when the river was overflowed. The houses had little gardens around them, but they didn't seem to raise hardly anything in them but jimpson weeds, and sunflowers, and ash-piles, and old curled-up boots and shoes, and pieces of bottles, and rags, and played-out tin-ware. The fences was made of different kinds of boards, nailed on at different times; and they leaned every which-way, and had gates that didn't generly have but one hinge—a leather one. Some of the fences had been whitewashed, some time or another, but the duke said it was in Clumbus's time, like enough. There was generly hogs in the garden, and people driving them out.

All the stores was along one street. They had white-domestic awnings[1] in front, and the country people hitched their horses to the awning-posts. There was empty dry-goods boxes under the awnings, and loafers roosting on them all day long, whittling them with their Barlow knives; and chawing tobacco, and gaping and yawning and stretching—a mighty ornery lot. They generly had on yellow straw hats most as wide as an umbrella, but didn't wear no coats nor waistcoats; they called one another Bill, and Buck, and Hank, and Joe, and Andy, and talked lazy and drawly, and used considerable many cuss-words. There was as many as one loafer leaning up against every awning-post, and he most always had his hands in his britches pockets, except when he fetched them out to lend a chaw of tobacco or scratch. What a body was hearing amongst them, all the time was—

"Gimme a chaw 'v tobacker, Hank."

"Cain't—I hain't got but one chaw left. Ask Bill."

Maybe Bill he gives him a chaw; maybe he lies and says he ain't got none. Some of them kinds of loafers never has a cent in the world, nor a chaw of tobacco of their own. They get all their chawing by borrowing—they say to a fellow, "I wisht you'd len' me a chaw, Jack, I jist this minute give Ben Thompson the last chaw I had"—which is a lie, pretty much every time; it don't fool anybody but a stranger; but Jack ain't no stranger, so he says—

"*You* give him a chaw, did you? so did your sister's cat's grandmother. You pay me back the chaws you've awready borry'd off'n me, Lafe Buckner, then I'll loan you one or two ton of it, and won't charge you no back intrust, nuther."

"Well, I *did* pay you back some of it wunst."

"Yes, you did—'bout six chaws. You borry'd store tobacker and paid back nigger-head."[2]

Store tobacco is flat black plug, but these fellows mostly chaws the natural leaf twisted. When they borrow a chaw, they don't generly cut it off with a knife, but they set the plug in between their teeth, and gnaw with their teeth and tug at the plug with their hands till they get it in two—then sometimes the one that owns the tobacco looks mournful at it when it's handed back, and says, sarcastic—

"Here, gimme the *chaw*, and you take the *plug*."

All the streets and lanes was just mud, they warn't nothing else *but* mud—as black as tar, and nigh about a foot deep in some places; and two or three

1. Awnings made from canvas.
2. This racist term describes an inferior form of tobacco.

inches deep in *all* the places. The hogs loafed and grunted around, every-wheres. You'd see a muddy sow and a litter of pigs come lazying along the street and whollop herself right down in the way, where folks had to walk around her, and she'd stretch out, and shut her eyes, and wave her ears, whilst the pigs was milking her, and look as happy as if she was on salary. And pretty soon you'd hear a loafer sing out, "Hi! *so* boy! sick him, Tige!" and away the sow would go, squealing most horrible, with a dog or two swinging to each ear, and three or four dozen more a-coming; and then you would see all the loafers get up and watch the thing out of sight, and laugh at the fun and look grateful for the noise. Then they'd settle back again till there was a dog-fight. There couldn't anything wake them up all over, and make them happy all over, like a dog-fight—unless it might be putting turpentine on a stray dog and setting fire to him, or tying a tin pan to his tail and see him run himself to death.

On the river front some of the houses was sticking out over the bank, and they was bowed and bent, and about ready to tumble in. The people had moved out of them. The bank was caved away under one corner of some others, and that corner was hanging over. People lived in them yet, but it was dangersome, because sometimes a strip of land as wide as a house caves in at a time. Sometimes a belt of land a quarter of a mile deep will start in and cave along and cave along till it all caves into the river in one summer. Such a town as that has to be always moving back, and back, and back, because the river's always gnawing at it.

The nearer it got to noon that day, the thicker and thicker was the wag-ons and horses in the streets, and more coming all the time. Families fetched their dinners with them, from the country, and eat them in the wagons. There was considerable whiskey drinking going on, and I seen three fights. By-and-by somebody sings out—

"Here comes old Boggs!—in from the country for his little old monthly drunk—here he comes, boys!"

All the loafers looked glad—I reckoned they was used to having fun out of Boggs. One of them says—

"Wonder who he's a gwyne to chaw up this time. If he'd a chawed up all the men he's ben a gwyne to chaw up in the last twenty year, he'd have con-siderable ruputation, now."

Another one says, "I wisht old Boggs'd threaten me, 'cuz then I'd know I warn't gwyne to die for a thousan' year."

Boggs comes a-tearing along on his horse, whooping and yelling like an Injun, and singing out—

"Cler the track, thar. I'm on the war-path, and the price uv coffins is a gwyne to raise."

He was drunk, and weaving about in his saddle; he was over fifty year old, and had a very red face. Everybody yelled at him, and laughed at him, and sassed him, and he sassed back, and said he'd attend to them and lay them out in their regular turns, but he couldn't wait now, because he'd come to town to kill old Colonel Sherburn, and his motto was, "meat first, and spoon vittles to top off on."

He see me, and rode up and says—

"Whar'd you come f'm, boy? You prepared to die?"

Then he rode on. I was scared; but a man says—

"He don't mean nothing; he's always a carryin' on like that, when he's drunk. He's the best-naturedest old fool in Arkansaw—never hurt nobody, drunk nor sober."

Boggs rode up before the biggest store in town and bent his head down so he could see under the curtain of the awning, and yells—

"Come out here, Sherburn! Come out and meet the man you've swindled. You're the houn' I'm after, and I'm a gwyne to have you, too!"

And so he went on, calling Sherburn everything he could lay his tongue to, and the whole street packed with people listening and laughing and going on. By-and-by a proud-looking man about fifty-five—and he was a heap the best dressed man in that town, too—steps out of the store, and the crowd drops back on each side to let him come. He says to Boggs, mighty ca'm and slow—he says:

"I'm tired of this; but I'll endure it till one o'clock. Till one o'clock, mind—no longer. If you open your mouth against me only once, after that time, you can't travel so far but I will find you."

Then he turns and goes in. The crowd looked mighty sober; nobody stirred, and there warn't no more laughing. Boggs rode off blackguarding Sherburn as loud as he could yell, all down the street; and pretty soon back he comes and stops before the store, still keeping it up. Some men crowded around him and tried to get him to shut up, but he wouldn't; they told him it would be one o'clock in about fifteen minutes, and so he *must* go home—he must go right away. But it didn't do no good. He cussed away, with all his might, and throwed his hat down in the mud and rode over it, and pretty soon away he went a-raging down the street again, with his gray hair a-flying. Everybody that could get a chance at him tried their best to coax him off of his horse so they could lock him up and get him sober; but it warn't no use—up the street he would tear again, and give Sherburn another cussing. By-and-by somebody says—

"Go for his daughter!—quick, go for his daughter; sometimes he'll listen to her. If anybody can persuade him, she can."

So somebody started on a run. I walked down street a ways, and stopped. In about five or ten minutes, here comes Boggs again—but not on his horse. He was a-reeling across the street towards me, bareheaded, with a friend on both sides of him aholt of his arms and hurrying him along. He was quiet, and looked uneasy; and he warn't hanging back any, but was doing some of the hurrying himself. Somebody sings out—

"Boggs!"

I looked over there to see who said it, and it was that Colonel Sherburn. He was standing perfectly still, in the street, and had a pistol raised in his right hand—not aiming it, but holding it out with the barrel tilted up towards the sky. The same second I see a young girl coming on the run, and two men with her. Boggs and the men turned round, to see who called him, and when they see the pistol the men jumped to one side, and the pistol barrel come down slow and steady to a level—both barrels cocked. Boggs throws up both of his hands, and says, "O Lord, don't shoot!" Bang! goes the first shot, and he staggers back clawing at the air—bang! goes the second one, and he tumbles backwards onto the ground, heavy and solid, with his arms spread out. That young girl screamed out, and comes rushing, and down she throws herself on her father, crying, and saying, "Oh, he's killed him, he's killed him!"

The crowd closed up around them, and shouldered and jammed one another, with their necks stretched, trying to see, and people on the inside trying to shove them back, and shouting, "Back, back! give him air, give him air!"

Colonel Sherburn he tossed his pistol onto the ground, and turned around on his heels and walked off.

They took Boggs to a little drug store, the crowd pressing around, just the same, and the whole town following, and I rushed and got a good place at the window, where I was close to him and could see in. They laid him on the floor, and put one large Bible under his head, and opened another one and spread it on his breast—but they tore open his shirt first, and I seen where one of the bullets went in. He made about a dozen long gasps, his breast lifting the Bible up when he drawed in his breath, and letting it down again when he breathed it out—and after that he laid still; he was dead.[3] Then they pulled his daughter away from him, screaming and crying, and took her off. She was about sixteen, and very sweet and gentle-looking, but awful pale and scared.

Well, pretty soon the whole town was there, squirming and scrouging and pushing and shoving to get at the window and have a look, but people that had the places wouldn't give them up, and folks behind them was saying all the time, "Say, now, you've looked enough, you fellows; 'taint right and 'taint fair, for you to stay thar all the time, and never give nobody a chance; other folks has their rights as well as you."

There was considerable jawing back, so I slid out, thinking maybe there was going to be trouble. The streets was full, and everybody was excited. Everybody that seen the shooting was telling how it happened, and there was a big crowd packed around each one of these fellows, stretching their necks and listening. One long lanky man, with long hair and a big white fur stove-pipe hat on the back of his head, and a crooked-handled cane, marked out the places on the ground where Boggs stood, and where Sherburn stood, and the people following him around from one place to t'other and watching everything he done, and bobbing their heads to show they understood, and stooping a little and resting their hands on their thighs to watch him mark the places on the ground with his cane; and then he stood up straight and stiff where Sherburn had stood, frowning and having his hat-brim down over his eyes, and sung out, "Boggs!" and then fetched his cane down slow to a level, and says "Bang!" staggered backwards, says "Bang!" again, and fell down flat on his back. The people that had seen the thing said he done it perfect; said it was just exactly the way it all happened. Then as much as a dozen people got out their bottles and treated him.

Well, by-and-by somebody said Sherburn ought to be lynched. In about a minute everybody was saying it; so away they went, mad and yelling, and snatching down every clothes-line they come to, to do the hanging with.

Chapter XXII

They swarmed up the street towards Sherburn's house, a-whooping and yelling and raging like Injuns, and everything had to clear the way or get run over and tromped to mush, and it was awful to see. Children was heeling it

---

3. Twain had witnessed a shooting very much like this one when he was ten years old. His father was the presiding judge at the trial, which ended in acquittal.

ahead of the mob, screaming and trying to get out of the way; and every window along the road was full of women's heads, and there was nigger boys in every tree, and bucks and wenches looking over every fence; and as soon as the mob would get nearly to them they would break and skaddle back out of reach. Lots of the women and girls was crying and taking on, scared most to death.

They swarmed up in front of Sherburn's palings as thick as they could jam together, and you couldn't hear yourself think for the noise. It was a little twenty-foot yard. Some sung out "Tear down the fence! tear down the fence!" Then there was a racket of ripping and tearing and smashing, and down she goes, and the front wall of the crowd begins to roll in like a wave.

Just then Sherburn steps out on to the roof of his little front porch, with a double-barrel gun in his hand, and takes his stand, perfectly ca'm and deliberate, not saying a word. The racket stopped, and the wave sucked back.

Sherburn never said a word—just stood there, looking down. The stillness was awful creepy and uncomfortable. Sherburn run his eye slow along the crowd; and wherever it struck, the people tried a little to outgaze him, but they couldn't; they dropped their eyes and looked sneaky. Then pretty soon Sherburn sort of laughed; not the pleasant kind, but the kind that makes you feel like when you are eating bread that's got sand in it.

Then he says, slow and scornful:

"The idea of *you* lynching anybody! It's amusing. The idea of you thinking you had pluck enough to lynch a *man*! Because you're brave enough to tar and feather poor friendless cast-out women that come along here, did that make you think you had grit enough to lay your hands on a *man*? Why, a *man's* safe in the hands of ten thousand of your kind—as long as it's daytime and you're not behind him.

"Do I know you? I know you clear through. I was born and raised in the South, and I've lived in the North; so I know the average all around. The average man's a coward. In the North he lets anybody walk over him that wants to, and goes home and prays for a humble spirit to bear it. In the South one man, all by himself, has stopped a stage full of men, in the day-time, and robbed the lot. Your newspapers call you a brave people so much that you think you *are* braver than any other people—whereas you're just *as* brave, and no braver. Why don't your juries hang murderers? Because they're afraid the man's friends will shoot them in the back, in the dark—and it's just what they *would* do.

"So they always acquit; and then a *man* goes in the night, with a hundred masked cowards at his back, and lynches the rascal. Your mistake is, that you didn't bring a man with you; that's one mistake, and the other is that you didn't come in the dark, and fetch your masks. You brought *part* of a man—Buck Harkness, there—and if you hadn't had him to start you, you'd a taken it out in blowing.

"You didn't want to come. The average man don't like trouble and danger. *You* don't like trouble and danger. But if only *half* a man—like Buck Harkness, there—shouts 'Lynch him, lynch him!' you're afraid to back down—afraid you'll be found out to be what you are—*cowards*—and so you raise a yell, and hang yourselves onto that half-a-man's coat tail, and come raging up here, swearing what big things you're going to do. The pitifulest thing out is a mob; that's what an army is—a mob; they don't fight with courage that's born in them, but with courage that's borrowed from their mass, and from their officers. But a mob without any *man* at the head of it, is *beneath* pitifulness. Now the thing for *you* to do, is to droop your tails and go home and crawl in a hole. If any real lynching's going to be done, it will be done in the dark, Southern fashion; and when they come they'll bring their masks, and fetch a *man* along. Now *leave*—and take your half-a-man with you"— tossing his gun up across his left arm and cocking it, when he says this.

The crowd washed back sudden, and then broke all apart and went tearing off every which way, and Buck Harkness he heeled it after them, looking tolerable cheap. I could a staid, if I'd a wanted to, but I didn't want to.

I went to the circus, and loafed around the back side till the watchman went by, and then dived in under the tent. I had my twenty-dollar gold piece and some other money, but I reckoned I better save it, because there ain't no telling how soon you are going to need it, away from home and amongst strangers, that way. You can't be too careful. I ain't opposed to spending money on circuses, when there ain't no other way, but there ain't no use in *wasting* it on them.

It was a real bully circus. It was the splendidest sight that ever was, when they all come riding in, two and two, a gentleman and lady, side by side, the men just in their drawers and under-shirts, and no shoes nor stirrups, and resting their hands on their thighs, easy and comfortable—there must a' been twenty of them—and every lady with a lovely complexion, and perfectly beautiful, and looking just like a gang of real sure-enough queens, and dressed in clothes that cost millions of dollars, and just littered with diamonds. It was a powerful fine sight; I never see anything so lovely. And then one by one they got up and stood, and went a-weaving around the ring so gentle and wavy and graceful, the men looking ever so tall and airy and straight, with their heads bobbing and skimming along, away up there under the tent-roof, and every lady's rose-leafy dress flapping soft and silky around her hips, and she looking like the most loveliest parasol.

And then faster and faster they went, all of them dancing, first one foot stuck out in the air and then the other, the horses leaning more and more, and the ring-master going round and round the centre-pole, cracking his whip and shouting "hi!—hi!" and the clown cracking jokes behind him; and by-and-by all hands dropped the reins, and every lady put her knuckles on her hips and every gentlemen folded his arms, and then how the horses did lean over and hump themselves! And so, one after the other they all skipped off into the ring, and made the sweetest bow I ever see, and then scampered out, and everybody clapped their hands and went just about wild.

Well, all through the circus they done the most astonishing things; and all the time that clown carried on so it most killed the people. The ring-master couldn't ever say a word to him but he was back at him quick as a wink with the funniest things a body ever said; and how he ever *could* think of so many of them, and so sudden and so pat, was what I couldn't noway understand. Why, I couldn't a thought of them in a year. And by-and-by a drunk man tried to get into the ring—said he wanted to ride; said he could ride as well as anybody that ever was. They argued and tried to keep him out, but he wouldn't listen, and the whole show come to a standstill. Then the people begun to holler at him and make fun of him, and that made him mad, and he begun to rip and tear; so that stirred up the people, and a lot of men began to pile down off of the benches and swarm towards the ring, saying "Knock him down! throw him out!" and one or two women begun to scream. So, then, the ring-master he made a little speech, and said he hoped there wouldn't be no disturbance, and if the man would promise he wouldn't make no more trouble, he would let him ride, if he thought he could stay on the horse. So everybody laughed and said all right, and the man got on. The minute he was on, the horse begun to rip and tear and jump and cavort around, with two circus men hanging onto his bridle trying to hold him, and the drunk man hanging onto his neck, and his heels flying in the air every jump, and the whole crowd of people standing up shouting and laughing till the tears rolled down. And at last, sure enough, all the circus men could do, the horse broke loose, and away he went like the very nation, round and round the ring, with that sot laying down on him and hanging to his neck, with first one leg hanging most to the ground on one side, and then t'other one on t'other side, and the people just crazy. It warn't funny to me, though; I was all of a tremble to see his danger. But pretty soon he struggled up astraddle and grabbed the bridle, a-reeling this way and that; and the next minute he sprung up and dropped the bridle and stood! and the horse ago-ing like a house afire too. He just stood up there, a-sailing around as easy and comfortable as if he warn't ever drunk in his life—and then he begun to pull off his clothes and sling them. He shed them so thick they kind of clogged up the air, and altogether he shed seventeen suits. And then, there he was, slim and handsome, and dressed the gaudiest and prettiest you ever saw, and he lit into that horse with his whip and made him fairly hum—and finally skipped off, and made his bow and danced off to the dressing-room, and everybody just a-howling with pleasure and astonishment.

Then the ring-master he see how he had been fooled, and he *was* the sick-est ring-master you ever see, I reckon. Why, it was one of his own men! He had got up that joke all out of his own head, and never let on to nobody. Well, I felt sheepish enough, to be took in so, but I wouldn't a been in that ring-master's place, not for a thousand dollars. I don't know; there may be bullier circuses than what that one was, but I never struck them yet. Any-ways it was plenty good enough for *me*; and wherever I run across it, it can have all of *my* custom, everytime.

Well, that night we had *our* show; but there warn't only about twelve people there; just enough to pay expenses. And they laughed all the time, and that made the duke mad; and everybody left, anyway, before the show was over, but one boy which was asleep. So the duke said these Arkansaw lunkheads couldn't come up to Shakspeare; what they wanted was low comedy—and may be something ruther worse than low comedy, he reckoned. He said he could size their style. So next morning he got some big sheets of wrapping-paper and some black paint, and drawed off some handbills and stuck them up all over the village. The bills said:

AT THE COURT HOUSE!

FOR 3 NIGHTS ONLY!
The World-Renowned Tragedians
DAVID GARRICK THE YOUNGER
AND
EDMUND KEAN THE ELDER!

Of the London and Continental
Theatres,
In their Thrilling Tragedy of
THE KING'S CAMELOPARD[4]
OR
THE ROYAL NONESUCH!!!
Admission 50 cents.

Then at the bottom was the biggest line of all—which said:

LADIES AND CHILDREN NOT ADMITTED.

"There," says he, "if that line don't fetch them, I don't know Arkansaw!"

Chapter XXIII

Well, all day him and the king was hard at it, rigging up a stage, and a cur-tain, and a row of candles for footlights; and that night the house was jam full of men in no time. When the place couldn't hold no more, the duke he quit tending door and went around the back way and come onto the stage and stood up before the curtain, and made a little speech, and praised up this tragedy, and said it was the most thrillingest one that ever was; and so he went on a-bragging about the tragedy and about Edmund Kean the Elder, which was to play the main principal part in it; and at last when he'd got everybody's expectations up high enough, he rolled up the curtain, and the next minute the king come a-prancing out on all fours, naked; and he was painted all over, ring-streaked-and-striped, all sorts of colors, as splendid as a rainbow. And—but never mind the rest of his outfit, it was just wild, but it was awful funny. The people most killed themselves laughing; and when the king got done capering, and capered off behind the scenes, they roared and clapped and stormed and haw-hawed till he come back and done it over again; and after that, they made him do it another time. Well, it would a made a cow laugh to see the shines that old idiot cut.

Then the duke he lets the curtain down, and bows to the people, and says the great tragedy will be performed only two nights more, on accounts of pressing London engagements, where the seats is all sold aready for it in Drury Lane; and then he makes them another bow, and says if he has suc-ceeded in pleasing them and instructing them, he will be deeply obleeged if they will mention it to their friends and get them to come and see it.

Twenty people sings out:

"What, is it over? Is that *all?*"

The duke says yes. Then there was a fine time. Everybody sings out "sold,"[5] and rose up mad, and was agoing for that stage and them tragedians. But a big fine-looking man jumps up on a bench, and shouts:

"Hold on! Just a word, gentlemen." They stopped to listen. "We are sold—mighty badly sold. But we don't want to be the laughing-stock of this whole town, I reckon, and never hear the last of this thing as long as we live. *No.* What we want, is to go out of here quiet, and talk this show up, and sell the *rest* of

4. An archaic name for a giraffe, but also describes a legendary spotted beast the size of a camel.
5. Cheated.

the town! Then we'll all be in the same boat. Ain't that sensible?" ("You bet it is!—the jedge is right!" everybody sings out.) "All right, then—not a word about any sell. Go along home, and advise everybody to come and see the tragedy."

Next day you couldn't hear nothing around that town but how splendid that show was. House was jammed again, that night, and we sold this crowd the same way. When me and the king and the duke got home to the raft, we all had a supper; and by-and-by, about midnight, they made Jim and me back her out and float her down the middle of the river and fetch her in and hide her about two mile below town.

The third night the house was crammed again—and they warn't new-comers, this time, but people that was at the show the other two nights. I stood by the duke at the door, and I see that every man that went in had his pockets bulging, or something muffled up under his coat—and I see it warn't no perfumery neither, not by a long sight. I smelt sickly eggs by the barrel, and rotten cabbages, and such things; and if I know the signs of a dead cat being around, and I bet I do, there was sixty-four of them went in. I shoved in there for a minute, but it was too various for me, I couldn't stand it. Well, when the place couldn't hold no more people, the duke he give a fellow a quarter and told him to tend door for him a minute, and then he started around for the stage door, I after him; but the minute we turned the corner and was in the dark, he says:

"Walk fast, now, till you get away from the houses, and then shin for the raft like the dickens was after you!"

I done it, and he done the same. We struck the raft at the same time, and in less than two seconds we was gliding down stream, all dark and still, and edging towards the middle of the river, nobody saying a word. I reckoned the poor king was in for a gaudy time of it with the audience; but nothing of the sort; pretty soon he crawls out from under the wigwam, and says:

"Well, how'd the old thing pan out this time, Duke?"

He hadn't been up town at all.

We never showed a light till we was about ten mile below that village. Then we lit up and had a supper, and the king and the duke fairly laughed their bones loose over the way they'd served them people. The duke says:

"Greenhorns, flatheads! *I* knew the first house would keep mum and let the rest of the town get roped in; and I knew they'd lay for us the third night, and consider it was *their* turn now. Well, it *is* their turn, and I'd give something to know how much they'd take for it. I *would* just like to know how they're putting in their opportunity. They can turn it into a picnic, if they want to—they brought plenty provisions."

Them rapscallions took in four hundred and sixty-five dollars in that three nights. I never see money hauled in by the wagon-load like that, before.

By-and-by, when they was asleep and snoring, Jim says:

"Don't it 'sprise you, de way dem kings carries on, Huck?"

"No," I says, "it don't."

"Why don't it, Huck?"

"Well, it don't, because it's in the breed. I reckon they're all alike."

"But, Huck, dese kings o' ourn is reglar rapscallions; dat's jist what dey is; dey's reglar rapscallions."

"Well, that's what I'm a-saying; all kings is mostly rapscallions, as fur as I can make out."

"Is dat so?"

"You read about them once—you'll see. Look at Henry the Eight; this'n 's a Sunday-School Superintendent to *him*. And look at Charles Second, and Louis Fourteen, and Louis Fifteen, and James Second, and Edward Second, and Richard Third, and forty more; besides all them Saxon heptarchies that used to rip around so in old times and raise Cain. My, you ought to seen old Henry the Eight when he was in bloom. He *was* a blossom. He used to marry a new wife every day, and chop off her head next morning. And he would do it just as indifferent as if he was ordering up eggs. 'Fetch up Nell Gwynn,' he says. They fetch her up. Next morning, 'Chop off her head!' And they chop it off. 'Fetch up Jane Shore,' he says; and up she comes. Next morning 'Chop off her head'—and they chop it off. 'Ring up Fair Rosamun.' Fair Rosamun answers the bell. Next morning, 'Chop off her head.' And he made every one of them tell him a tale every night; and he kept that up till he had hogged a thousand and one tales that way, and then he put them all in a book, and called it Domesday Book—which was a good name and stated the case. You don't know kings, Jim, but I know them; and this old rip of ourn is one of the cleanest I've struck in history. Well, Henry he takes a notion he wants to get up some trouble with this country. How does he go at it— give notice?—give the country a show? No. All of sudden he heaves all the tea in Boston Harbor overboard, and whacks out a declaration of independence, and dares them to come on. That was *his* style—he never give anybody a chance. He had suspicions of his father, the Duke of Wellington. Well, what did he do?—ask him to show up? No—drownded him in a butt of mamsey, like a cat. Spose people left money laying around where he was— what did he do? He collared it. Spose he contracted to do a thing; and you paid him, and didn't set down there and see that he done it—what did he do? He always done the other thing. Spose he opened his mouth—what then? If he didn't shut it up powerful quick, he'd lose a lie, every time. That's the kind of a bug Henry was; and if we'd a had him along 'stead of our kings, he'd a fooled that town a heap worse than ourn done. I don't say that ourn is lambs, because they ain't, when you come right down to the cold facts; but they ain't nothing to *that* old ram, anyway. All I say is, kings is kings, and you got to make allowances. Take them all around, they're a mighty ornery lot. It's the way they're raised."[6]

"But dis one do *smell* so like de nation, Huck."

"Well, they all do, Jim. *We* can't help the way a king smells; history don't tell no way."

"Now de duke, he's a tolerable likely man, in some ways."

"Yes, a duke's different. But not very different. This one's a middling hard lot, for a duke. When he's drunk, there ain't no near-sighted man could tell him from a king."

"Well, anyways, I doan' hanker for no mo' un um, Huck. Dese is all I kin stan'."

"It's the way I feel, too, Jim. But we've got them on our hands, and we got to remember what they are, and make allowances. Sometimes I wish we could hear of a country that's out of kings."

---

6. Huck's "history" of kingly behavior is a hodgepodge of fact and fiction, drawn from English and American history.

What was the use to tell Jim these warn't real kings and dukes? It wouldn't a done no good; and besides, it was just as I said; you couldn't tell them from the real kind.

I went to sleep, and Jim didn't call me when it was my turn. He often done that. When I waked up, just at day-break, he was setting there with his head down betwixt his knees, moaning and mourning to himself. I didn't take notice, nor let on. I knowed what it was about. He was thinking about his wife and his children, away up yonder, and he was low and homesick; because he hadn't ever been away from home before in his life; and I do believe he cared just as much for his people as white folks does for their'n. It don't seem natural, but I reckon it's so. He was often moaning and mourning that way, nights, when he judged I was asleep, and saying "Po' little 'Lizabeth! po' little Johnny! its mighty hard; I spec' I ain't ever gwyne to see you no mo', no mo'!" He was a mighty good nigger, Jim was.

But this time I somehow got to talking to him about his wife and young ones; and by-and-by he says:

"What makes me feel so bad dis time, 'uz bekase I hear sumpn over yonder on de bank like a whack, er a slam, while ago, en it mine me er de time I treat my little 'Lizabeth so ornery. She warn't on'y 'bout fo' year ole, en she tuck de sk'yarlet-fever, en had a powful rough spell; but she got well, en one day she was a-stannin' aroun', en I says to her, I says:

"'Shet de do'.'

"She never done it; jis' stood dar, kiner smilin' up at me. It make me mad; en I says agin, mighty loud, I says:

"'Doan' you hear me?—shet de do'!'

"She jis' stood de same way, kiner smilin' up. I was a-bilin'! I says:

"'I lay I *make* you mine!'

"En wid dat I fetch' her a slap side de head dat sont her a-sprawlin'. Den I went into de yuther room, en 'uz gone 'bout ten minutes; en when I come back, dah was dat do' a-stannin' open *yit*, en dat chile stannin' mos' right in it, a-lookin' down and mournin', en de tears runnin' down. My, but I *wuz* mad, I was agwyne for de chile, but jis' den—it was a do' dat open innerds— jis' den, 'long come de wind en slam it to, behine de chile, *ker-blam!*—en my lan', de chile never move'! My breff mos' hop outer me; en I feel so— so—I doan' know *how* I feel. I crope out, all a-tremblin', en crope aroun' en open de do' easy en slow, en poke my head in behine de chile, sof' en still, en all uv a sudden, I says *pow!* jis' as loud as I could yell. *She never budge!* Oh, Huck, I bust out a-cryin' en grab her up in my arms, en say, 'Oh, de po' little thing! de Lord God Amighty fogive po' ole Jim, kaze he never gwyne to fogive hisself as long's he live!' Oh, she was plumb deef en dumb, Huck, plumb deef en dumb—en I'd ben a'treat'n her so!"

Chapter XXIV

Next day, towards night, we laid up under a little willow tow-head out in the middle, where there was a village on each side of the river, and the duke and the king begun to lay out a plan for working them towns. Jim he spoke to the duke, and said he hoped it wouldn't take but a few hours, because it got mighty heavy and tiresome to him when he had to lay all day in the wigwam tied with the rope. You see, when we left him all alone we had to tie him, because if anybody happened on him all by himself and not tied, it wouldn't look much like he was a runaway nigger, you know. So the duke said it *was* kind of hard to have to lay roped all day, and he'd cipher out some way to get around it.

He was uncommon bright, the duke was, and he soon struck it. He dressed Jim up in King Lear's outfit—it was a long curtain-calico gown, and a white horse-hair wig and whiskers; and then he took his theatre-paint and painted Jim's face and hands and ears and neck all over a dead bull solid blue, like a man that's been drownded nine days. Blamed if he warn't the horriblest looking outrage I ever see. Then the duke took and wrote out a sign on a shingle so—

Sick Arab—but harmless when not out of his head.

And he nailed that shingle to a lath, and stood the lath up four or five foot in front of the wigwam. Jim was satisfied. He said it was a sight better than laying tied a couple of years every day and trembling all over every time there was a sound. The duke told him to make himself free and easy, and if anybody ever come meddling around, he must hop out of the wigwam, and carry on a little, and fetch a howl or two like a wild beast, and he reckoned they would light out and leave him alone. Which was sound enough judgment; but you take the average man, and he wouldn't wait for him to howl. Why, he didn't only look like he was dead, he looked considerable more than that.

These rapscallions wanted to try the Nonesuch again, because there was so much money in it, but they judged it wouldn't be safe, because maybe the news might a worked along down by this time. They couldn't hit no project that suited, exactly; so at last the duke said he reckoned he'd lay off and work his brains an hour or two and see if he couldn't put up something on the Arkansaw village; and the king he allowed he would drop over to t'other village, without any plan, but just trust in Providence to lead him the profitable way—meaning the devil, I reckon. We had all bought store clothes where we stopped last; and now the king put his'n on, and he told me to put mine on. I done it, of course. The king's duds was all black, and he did look real swell and starchy. I never knowed how clothes could change a body before. Why, before, he looked like the orneriest old rip that ever was; but now, when he'd take off his new white beaver[7] and make a bow and do a smile, he looked that grand and good and pious that you'd say he had walked right out of the ark, and maybe was old Leviticus[8] himself. Jim cleaned up the canoe, and I got my paddle ready. There was a big steamboat laying at the shore away up under the point, about three mile above town—been there a couple of hours, taking on freight. Says the king:

"Seein' how I'm dressed, I reckon maybe I better arrive down from St. Louis or Cincinnati, or some other big place. Go for the steamboat, Huckleberry; we'll come down to the village on her."

I didn't have to be ordered twice, to go and take a steamboat ride. I fetched the shore a half a mile above the village, and then went scooting along the bluff bank in the easy water. Pretty soon we come to a nice innocent-looking young country jake setting on a log swabbing the sweat

---

7. Hat.
8. The third book of the Old Testament is here confused with Noah.

off of his face, for it was powerful warm weather; and he had a couple of big carpet-bags by him.

"Run her nose in shore," says the king. I done it. "Wher' you bound for, young man?"

"For the steamboat; going to Orleans."

"Git aboard," says the king. "Hold on a minute, my servant 'll he'p you with them bags. Jump out and he'p the gentleman, Adolphus"—meaning me, I see.

I done so, and then we all three started on again. The young chap was mighty thankful; said it was tough work toting his baggage such weather. He asked the king where he was going, and the king told him he'd come down the river and landed at the other village this morning, and now he was going up a few mile to see an old friend on a farm up there. The young fellow says:

"When I first see you, I says to myself, 'It's Mr. Wilks, sure, and he come mighty near getting here in time.' But then I says again, 'No, I reckon it ain't him, or else he wouldn't be paddling up the river.' You *ain't* him, are you?"

"No, my name's Blodgett—Elexander Blodgett—*Reverend* Elexander Blodgett, I spose I must say, as I'm one o' the Lord's poor servants. But still I'm jist as able to be sorry for Mr. Wilks for not arriving in time, all the same, if he's missed anything by it—which I hope he hasn't."

"Well, he don't miss any property by it, because he'll get that all right; but he's missed seeing his brother Peter die—which he mayn't mind, nobody can tell as to that—but his brother would a give anything in this world to see *him* before he died; never talked about nothing else all these three weeks; hadn't seen him since they was boys together—and hadn't ever seen his brother William at all—that's the deef and dumb one—William ain't more than thirty or thirty-five. Peter and George was the only ones that come out here; George was the married brother; him and his wife both died last year. Harvey and William's the only ones that's left now; and, as I was saying, they haven't got here in time."

"Did anybody send 'em word?"

"Oh, yes; a month or two ago, when Peter was first took; because Peter said then that he sorter felt like he warn't going to get well this time. You see, he was pretty old, and George's g'yirls was too young to be much company for him, except Mary Jane the red-headed one; and so he was kinder lonesome after George and his wife died, and didn't seem to care much to live. He most desperately wanted to see Harvey—and William too, for that matter—because he was one of them kind that can't bear to make a will. He left a letter behind for Harvey, and said he'd told in it where his money was hid, and how he wanted the rest of the property divided up so George's g'yirls would be all right—for George didn't leave nothing. And that letter was all they could get him to put a pen to."

"Why do you reckon Harvey don't come? Wher' does he live?"

"Oh, he lives in England—Sheffield—preaches there—hasn't ever been in this country. He hasn't had any too much time—and besides he mightn't a got the letter at all, you know."

"Too bad, too bad he couldn't a lived to see his brothers, poor soul. You going to Orleans, you say?"

"Yes, but that ain't only a part of it. I'm going in a ship, next Wednesday, for Ryo Janeero,[9] where my uncle lives."

"It's a pretty long journey. But it'll be lovely; I wisht I was agoing. Is Mary Jane the oldest? How old is the others?"

"Mary Jane's nineteen, Susan's fifteen, and Joanna's about fourteen—that's the one that gives herself to good works and has a hare-lip."[1]

"Poor things! to be left alone in the cold world so."

"Well, they could be worse off. Old Peter had friends, and they ain't going to let them come to no harm. There's Hobson, the Babtis' preacher; and Deacon Lot Hovey, and Ben Rucker, and Abner Shackleford, and Levi Bell, the lawyer; and Dr. Robinson, and their wives, and the widow Bartley, and—well, there's a lot of them; but these are the ones that Peter was thickest with, and used to write about sometimes, when he wrote home; so Harvey'll know where to look for friends when he gets here."

Well, the old man he went on asking questions till he just fairly emptied that young fellow. Blamed if he didn't inquire about everybody and everything in that blessed town, and all about all the Wilkses; and about Peter's business—which was a tanner; and about George's—which was a carpenter; and about Harvey's—which was a dissentering[2] minister, and so on, and so on. Then he says:

"What did you want to walk all the way up to the steamboat for?"

"Because she's a big Orleans boat, and I was afeard she mightn't stop there. When they're deep they won't stop for a hail. A Cincinnati boat will, but this is a St. Louis one."

"Was Peter Wilks well off?"

"Oh, yes, pretty well off. He had houses and land, and it's reckoned he left three or four thousand in cash hid up som'ers."

"When did you say he died?"

"I didn't say, but it was last night."

"Funeral to-morrow, likely?"

"Yes, 'bout the middle of the day."

"Well, it's all terrible sad; but we've all got to go, one time or another. So what we want to do is to be prepared; then we're all right."

"Yes, sir, it's the best way. Ma used to always say that."

When we struck the boat, she was about done loading, and pretty soon she got off. The king never said nothing about going aboard, so I lost my ride, after all. When the boat was gone, the king made me paddle up another mile to a lonesome place, and then he got ashore, and says:

"Now hustle back, right off, and fetch the duke up here, and the new carpet-bags. And if he's gone over to t'other side, go over there and git him. And tell him to git himself up regardless. Shove along, now."

I see what *he* was up to; but I never said nothing, of course. When I got back with the duke, we hid the canoe and then they set down on a log, and the king told him everything, just like the young fellow had said it—every last word of it. And all the time he was a doing it, he tried to talk like an Englishman; and he done it pretty well too, for a slouch. I can't

9. Rio de Janeiro, Brazil.
1. An outdated term for a cleft palate.
2. Dissenting ministers belonged to Christian denominations that had separated from the Church of England.

imitate him, and so I ain't agoing to try to; but he really done it pretty good. Then he says:

"How are you on the deef and dumb, Bilgewater?"

The duke said, leave him alone for that; said he had played a deef and dumb person on the histrionic boards. So then they waited for a steamboat.

About the middle of the afternoon a couple of little boats come along, but they didn't come from high enough up the river; but at last there was a big one, and they hailed her. She sent out her yawl, and we went aboard, and she was from Cincinnati; and when they found we only wanted to go four or five mile, they was booming mad, and give us a cussing, and said they wouldn't land us. But the king was ca'm. He says:

"If gentlemen kin afford to pay a dollar a mile apiece, to be took on and put off in a yawl, a steamboat kin afford to carry 'em, can't it?"

So they softened down and said it was all right; and when we got to the village, they yawled us ashore. About two dozen men flocked down, when they see the yawl a coming; and when the king says—

"Kin any of you gentlemen tell me wher' Mr. Peter Wilks lives?" they give a glance at one another, and nodded their heads, as much as to say, "What d' I tell you?" Then one of them says, kind of soft and gentle:

"I'm sorry, sir, but the best we can do is to tell you where he *did* live yesterday evening."

Sudden as winking, the ornery old cretur went all to smash, and fell up against the man, and put his chin on his shoulder, and cried down his back, and says:

"Alas, alas, our poor brother—gone, and we never got to see him; oh, it's too, *too* hard!"

Then he turns around, blubbering, and makes a lot of idiotic signs to the duke on his hands, and blamed if *he* didn't drop a carpet-bag and bust out a-crying. If they warn't the beatenest lot, them two frauds, that ever I struck.

Well, the men gethered around, and sympathized with them, and said all sorts of kind things to them, and carried their carpet-bags up the hill for them, and let them lean on them and cry, and told the king all about his brother's last moments, and the king he told it all over again on his hands to the duke, and both of them took on about that dead tanner like they'd lost the twelve disciples. Well, if ever I struck anything like it, I'm a nigger. It was enough to make a body ashamed of the human race.

Chapter XXV

The news was all over town in two minutes, and you could see the people tearing down on the run, from every which way, some of them putting on their coats as they come. Pretty soon we was in the middle of a crowd, and the noise of the tramping was like a soldier-march. The windows and dooryards was full; and every minute somebody would say, over a fence:

"Is it *them*!"

And somebody trotting along with the gang would answer back and say:

"You bet it is."

When we got to the house, the street in front of it was packed, and the three girls was standing in the door. Mary Jane *was* red-headed, and that don't make no difference, she was most awful beautiful, and her face and her eyes was all lit up like glory, she was so glad her uncles was come. The king he spread his arms, and Mary Jane she jumped for them, and the hare-lip jumped for the duke, and there they *had* it! Everybody most, leastways women, cried for joy to see them meet again at last and have such good times.

Then the king he hunched the duke, private—I see him do it—and then he looked around and see the coffin, over in the corner on two chairs; so then, him and the duke, with a hand across each other's shoulder, and t'other hand to their eyes, walked slow and solemn over there, everybody dropping back to give them room, and all the talk and noise stopping, people saying "Sh!" and all the men taking their hats off and drooping their heads, so you could a heard a pin fall. And when they got there, they bent over and looked in the coffin, and took one sight, and then they bust out a crying so you could a heard them to Orleans, most; and then they put their arms around each other's necks, and hung their chins over each other's shoulders; and then for three minutes, or maybe four, I never see two men leak the way they done. And mind you, everybody was doing the same; and the place was that damp I never see anything like it. Then one of them got on one side of the coffin, and t'other on t'other side, and they kneeled down and rested their foreheads on the coffin, and let on to pray all to theirselves. Well, when it come to that, it worked the crowd like you never see anything like it, and so everybody broke down and went to sobbing right out loud—the poor girls, too; and every woman, nearly, went up to the girls, without saying a word, and kissed them, solemn, on the forehead, and then put their hand on their head, and looked up towards the sky, with the tears running down, and then busted out and went off sobbing and swabbing, and give the next woman a show. I never see anything so disgusting.

Well, by-and-by the king he gets up and comes forward a little, and works himself up and slobbers out a speech, all full of tears and flapdoodle about its being a sore trial for him and his poor brother to lose the diseased, and to miss seeing diseased alive, after the long journey of four thousand mile, but it's a trial that's sweetened and sanctified to us by this dear sympathy and these holy tears, and so he thanks them out of his heart and out of his brother's heart, because out of their mouths they can't, words being too weak and cold, and all that kind of rot and slush, till it was just sickening; and then he blubbers out a pious goody-goody Amen, and turns himself loose and goes to crying fit to bust.

And the minute the words was out of his mouth somebody over in the crowd struck up the doxolojer,[3] and everybody joined in with all their might, and it just warmed you up and made you feel as good as church letting out. Music *is* a good thing; and after all that soul-butter and hogwash, I never see it freshen up things so, and sound so honest and bully.

Then the king begins to work his jaw again, and says how him and his nieces would be glad if a few of the main principal friends of the family would take supper here with them this evening, and help set up with the ashes of the diseased; and says if his poor brother laying yonder could speak, he knows who he would name, for they was names that was very dear to him, and mentioned often in his letters; and so he will name the same, to-wit, as

3. I.e., doxology, or hymn of praise to God. The particular doxology referred to here begins "Praise God, from whom all blessings flow."

follows, vizz:—Rev. Mr. Hobson, and Deacon Lot Hovey, and Mr. Ben Rucker, and Abner Shackleford, and Levi Bell, and Dr. Robinson, and their wives, and the widow Bartley.

Rev. Hobson and Dr. Robinson was down to the end of the town, a-hunting together; that is, I mean the doctor was shipping a sick man to t'other world, and the preacher was pinting him right. Lawyer Bell was away up to Louisville on some business. But the rest was on hand, and so they all come and shook hands with the king and thanked him and talked to him; and then they shook hands with the duke, and didn't say nothing but just kept a-smiling and bobbing their heads like a passel of sapheads whilst he made all sorts of signs with his hands and said "Goo-goo—goo-goo-goo," all the time, like a baby that can't talk.

So the king he blatted along, and managed to inquire about pretty much everybody and dog in town, by his name, and mentioned all sorts of little things that happened one time or another in the town, or to George's family, or to Peter; and he always let on that Peter wrote him the things, but that was a lie, he got every blessed one of them out of that young flathead that we canoed up to the steamboat.

Then Mary Jane she fetched the letter her father left behind, and the king he read it out loud and cried over it. It give the dwelling-house and three thousand dollars, gold, to the girls; and it give the tanyard (which was doing a good business), along with some other houses and land (worth about seven thousand), and three thousand dollars in gold to Harvey and William, and told where the six thousand cash was hid, down cellar. So these two frauds said they'd go and fetch it up, and have everything square and above-board; and told me to come with a candle. We shut the cellar door behind us, and when they found the bag they spilt it out on the floor, and it was a lovely sight, all them yallerboys.[4] My, the way the king's eyes did shine! He slaps the duke on the shoulder, and says:

"Oh, *this* ain't bully, nor noth'n! Oh, no, I reckon not! Why, Biljy, it beats the Nonesuch, *don't* it!"

The duke allowed it did. They pawed the yaller-boys, and sifted them through their fingers and let them jingle down on the floor; and the king says:

"It ain't no use talkin'; bein' brothers to a rich dead man, and representatives of furrin heirs that's got left, is the line for you and me, Bilge. Thishyer comes of trust'n to Providence. It's the best way, in the long run. I've tried 'em all, and ther' ain't no better way."

Most everybody would a been satisfied with the pile, and took it on trust; but no, they must count it. So they counts it, and it comes out four hundred and fifteen dollars short. Says the king:

"Dern him, I wonder what he done with that four hundred and fifteen dollars?"

They worried over that a while, and ransacked all around for it. Then the duke says:

"Well, he was a pretty sick man, and likely he made a mistake—I reckon that's the way of it. The best way's to let it go, and keep still about it. We can spare it."

---

4. Gold coins.

"Oh, shucks, yes, we can *spare* it. I don't k'yer noth'n 'bout that—it's the *count* I'm thinkin' about. We want to be awful square and open and above-board, here, you know. We want to lug this h'yer money up stairs and count it before everybody—then ther' ain't noth'n suspicious. But when the dead man says ther's six thous'n dollars, you know, we don't want to—"

"Hold on," says the duke. "Less make up the deffisit"—and he begun to haul out yallerboys out of his pocket.

"It's a most amaz'n good idea, duke—you *have* got a rattlin' clever head on you," says the king. "Blest if the old Nonesuch ain't a heppin' us out agin"—and *he* begun to haul out yallerjackets and stack them up.

It most busted them, but they made up the six thousand clean and clear.

"Say," says the duke, "I got another idea. Le's go up stairs and count this money, and then take and *give it to the girls.*"

"Good land, duke, lemme hug you! It's the most dazzling idea 'at ever a man struck. You have cert'nly got the most astonishin' head I ever see. Oh, this is the boss dodge,[5] ther' ain't no mistake 'bout it. Let 'em fetch along their suspicions now, if they want to—this'll lay 'em out."

When we got up stairs, everybody gathered around the table, and the king he counted it and stacked it up, three hundred dollars in a pile—twenty elegant little piles. Everybody looked hungry at it, and licked their chops. Then they raked it into the bag again, and I see the king begin to swell himself up for another speech. He says:

"Friends all, my poor brother that lays yonder, has done generous by them that's left behind in the vale of sorrers. He has done generous by these-yer poor little lambs that he loved and sheltered, and that's left fatherless and motherless. Yes, and we that knowed him, knows that he would a done *more* generous by 'em if he hadn't been afeard o' woundin' his dear William and me. Now, *wouldn't* he? Ther' ain't no question 'bout it, in *my* mind. Well, then—what kind o' brothers would it be, that 'd stand in his way at sech a time? And what kind o' uncles would it be that 'd rob—yes, *rob*—sech poor sweet lambs as these 'at he loved so, at sech a time? If I know William—and I *think* I do—he—well, I'll jest ask him." He turns around and begins to make a lot of signs to the duke with his hands; and the duke he looks at him stupid and leather-headed a while, then all of sudden he seems to catch his meaning, and jumps for the king, goo-gooing with all his might for joy, and hugs him about fifteen times before he lets up. Then the king says, "I knowed it; I reckon *that* 'll convince anybody the way *he* feels about it. Here, Mary Jane, Susan, Joanner, take the money—take it *all*. It's the gift of him that lays yonder, cold but joyful."

Mary Jane she went for him, Susan and the hare-lip went for the duke, and then such another hugging and kissing I never see yet. And everybody crowded up with the tears in their eyes, and most shook the hands off of them frauds, saying all the time:

"You *dear* good souls!—how *lovely!*—how *could* you!"

Well, then, pretty soon all hands got to talking about the diseased again, and how good he was, and what a loss he was, and all that; and before long a big iron-jawed man worked himself in there from outside, and stood a

5. Best confidence trick.

listening and looking, and not saying anything; and nobody saying anything to him either, because the king was talking and they was all busy listening. The king was saying—in the middle of something he'd started in on—

"—they bein' partickler friends o' the diseased. That's why they're invited here this evenin'; but to-morrow we want *all* to come—everybody; for he respected everybody, he liked everybody, and so it's fitten that his funeral orgies sh'd be public."

And so he went a-mooning on and on, liking to hear himself talk, and every little while he fetched in his funeral orgies again, till the duke he couldn't stand it no more; so he writes on a little scrap of paper, "*obsequies*, you old fool," and folds it up and goes to goo-gooing and reaching it over people's heads to him. The king he reads it, and puts it in his pocket, and says:

"Poor William, afflicted as he is, his *heart's* aluz right. Asks me to invite everybody to come to the funeral—wants me to make 'em all welcome. But he needn't a worried—it was jest what I was at."

Then he weaves along again, perfectly ca'm, and goes to dropping in his funeral orgies again every now and then, just like he done before. And when he done it the third time, he says:

"I say orgies, not because it's the common term, because it ain't—obsequies bein' the common term—but because orgies is the right term. Obsequies ain't used in England no more, now—it's gone out. We say orgies now, in England. Orgies is better, because it means the thing you're after, more exact. It's a word that's made up out'n the Greek *orgo*, outside, open, abroad; and the Hebrew *jeesum*, to plant, cover up; hence in*ter*. So, you see, funeral orgies is an open er public funeral."[6]

He was the *worst* I ever struck. Well, the iron-jawed man he laughed right in his face. Everybody was shocked. Everybody says, "Why *doctor!*" and Abner Shackleford says:

"Why, Robinson, hain't you heard the news? This is Harvey Wilks."

The king he smiled eager, and shoved out his flapper, and says:

"*Is* it my poor brother's dear good friend and physician? I—"

"Keep your hands off of me!" says the doctor. "*You* talk like an Englishman—*don't* you? It's the worse imitation I ever heard. *You* Peter Wilks's brother. You're a fraud, that's what you are!"

Well, how they all took on! They crowded around the doctor, and tried to quiet him down, and tried to explain to him, and tell him how Harvey'd showed in forty ways that he *was* Harvey, and knowed everybody by name, and the names of the very dogs, and begged and *begged* him not to hurt Harvey's feelings and the poor girls' feelings, and all that; but it warn't no use, he stormed right along, and said any man that pretended to be an Englishman and couldn't imitate the lingo no better than what he did, was a fraud and a liar. The poor girls was hanging to the king and crying; and all of a sudden the doctor ups and turns on *them*. He says:

"I was your father's friend, and I'm your friend; and I warn you *as* a friend, and an honest one, that wants to protect you and keep you out of harm and trouble, to turn your backs on that scoundrel, and have nothing to do with him, the ignorant tramp, with his idiotic Greek and Hebrew as he calls it.

6. The comic etymology was a stock-in-trade of the southwestern humorists and is still popular in comedy routines.

He is the thinnest kind of an impostor—has come here with a lot of empty names and facts which he has picked up somewheres, and you take them for *proofs*, and are helped to fool yourselves by these foolish friends here, who ought to know better. Mary Jane Wilks, you know me for your friend, and for your unselfish friend, too. Now listen to me; turn this pitiful rascal out—I *beg* you to do it. Will you?"

Mary Jane straightened herself up, and my, but she was handsome! She says:

"*Here* is my answer." She hove up the bag of money and put it in the king's hands, and says, "Take this six thousand dollars, and invest it for me and my sisters any way you want to, and don't give us no receipt for it."

Then she put her arm around the king on one side, and Susan and the hare-lip done the same on the other. Everybody clapped their hands and stomped on the floor like a perfect storm, whilst the king held up his head and smiled proud. The doctor says:

"All right, I wash *my* hands of the matter. But I warn you all that a time's coming when you're going to feel sick whenever you think of this day"—and away he went.

"All right, doctor," says the king, kinder mocking him, "we'll try and get 'em to send for you"—which made them all laugh, and they said it was a prime good hit.

Chapter XXVI

Well, when they was all gone, the king he asks Mary Jane how they was off for spare rooms, and she said she had one spare room, which would do for Uncle William, and she'd give her own room to Uncle Harvey, which was a little bigger, and she would turn into the room with her sisters and sleep on a cot; and up garret was a little cubby, with a pallet in it. The king said the cubby would do for his valley—meaning me.

So Mary Jane took us up, and she showed them their rooms, which was plain but nice. She said she'd have her frocks and a lot of other traps took out of her room if they was in Uncle Harvey's way, but he said they warn't. The frocks was hung along the wall, and before them was a curtain made out of calico that hung down to the floor. There was an old hair trunk in one corner, and a guitar box in another, and all sorts of little knickknacks and jimcracks around, like girls brisken up a room with. The king said it was all the more homely and more pleasanter for these fixings, and so don't disturb them. The duke's room was pretty small, but plenty good enough, and so was my cubby.

That night they had a big supper, and all them men and women was there, and I stood behind the king and the duke's chairs and waited on them, and the niggers waited on the rest. Mary Jane she set at the head of the table, with Susan along side of her, and said how bad the biscuits was, and how mean the preserves was, and how ornery and tough the fried chickens was— and all that kind of rot, the way women always do for to force out compliments; and the people all knowed everything was tip-top, and said so—said "How *do* you get biscuits to brown so nice?" and "Where, for the land's sake *did* you get these amaz'n pickles?" and all that kind of humbug talky-talk, just the way people always does at a supper, you know.

And when it was all done, me and the hare-lip had supper in the kitchen off of the leavings, whilst the others was helping the niggers clean up the things. The hare-lip she got to pumping me about England, and blest if I didn't think the ice was getting mighty thin, sometimes. She says:

"Did you ever see the king?"

"Who? William Fourth?[7] Well, I bet I have—he goes to our church." I knowed he was dead years ago, but I never let on. So when I says he goes to our church, she says:

"What—regular?"

"Yes—regular. His pew's right over opposite ourn—on 'tother side the pulpit."

"I thought he lived in London?"

"Well, he does. Where *would* he live?"

"But I thought *you* lived in Sheffield?"[8]

I see I was up a stump. I had to let on to get choked with a chicken bone, so as to get time to think how to get down again. Then I says:

"I mean he goes to our church regular when he's in Sheffield. That's only in the summer-time, when he comes there to take the sea baths."

"Why, how you talk—Sheffield ain't on the sea."

"Well, who said it was?"

"Why, you did."

"I *didn't*, nuther."

"You did!"

"I didn't."

"You did."

"I never said nothing of the kind."

"Well, what *did* you say, then?"

"Said he come to take the sea *baths*—that's what I said."

"Well, then! how's he going to take the sea baths if it ain't on the sea?"

"Looky here," I says, "did you ever see any Congress water?"[9]

"Yes."

"Well, did you have to go to Congress to get it?"

"Why, no."

"Well, neither does William Fourth have to go to the sea to get a sea bath."

"How does he get it, then?"

"Gets it the way people down here gets Congress water—in barrels. There in the palace at Sheffield they've got furnaces, and he wants his water hot. They can't bile that amount of water away off there at the sea. They haven't got no conveniences for it."

"Oh, I see, now. You might a said that in the first place and saved time."

When she said that, I see I was out of the woods again, and so I was comfortable and glad. Next, she says:

"Do you go to church, too?"

"Yes—regular."

"Where do you set?"

"Why, in our pew."

"*Whose* pew?"

"Why, *ourn*—your Uncle Harvey's."

"His'n? What does *he* want with a pew?"

"Wants it to set in. What did you *reckon* he wanted with it?"

"Why, I thought he'd be in the pulpit."

Rot him, I forgot he was a preacher. I see I was up a stump again, so I played another chicken bone and got another think. Then I says:

"Blame it, do you suppose there ain't but one preacher to a church?"

"Why, what do they want with more?"

"What!—to preach before a king? I never see such a girl as you. They don't have no less than seventeen."

"Seventeen! My land! Why, I wouldn't set out such a string as that, not if I *never* got to glory. It must take 'em a week."

"Shucks, they don't *all* of 'em preach the same day—only *one* of 'em."

"Well, then, what does the rest of 'em do?"

"Oh, nothing much. Loll around, pass the plate—and one thing or another. But mainly they don't do nothing."

"Well, then, what are they *for?*"

"Why, they're for *style*. Don't you know nothing?"

"Well, I don't *want* to know no such foolishness as that. How is servants treated in England? Do they treat 'em better 'n we treat our niggers?"

"*No!* A servant ain't nobody there. They treat them worse than dogs."

"Don't they give 'em holidays, the way we do, Christmas and New Year's week, and Fourth of July?"

"Oh, just listen! A body could tell *you* hain't ever been to England, by that. Why, Hare-l—why, Joanna, they never see a holiday from year's end to year's end; never go to the circus, nor theatre, nor nigger shows[1] nor nowheres."

"Nor church?"

"Nor church."

"But *you* always went to church."

Well, I was gone up again. I forgot I was the old man's servant. But next minute I whirled in on a kind of an explanation how a valley was different from a common servant, and *had* to go to church whether he wanted to or not, and set with the family, on account of it's being the law. But I didn't do it pretty good, and when I got done I see she warn't satisfied. She says:

"Honest injun, now, hain't you been telling me a lot of lies?"

"Honest injun," says I.

"None of it at all?"

"None of it at all. Not a lie in it," says I.

"Lay your hand on this book and say it."

I see it warn't nothing but a dictionary, so I laid my hand on it and said it. So then she looked a little better satisfied, and says:

"Well, then, I'll believe some of it; but I hope to gracious if I'll believe the rest."

"What is it you won't believe, Joe?" says Mary Jane, stepping in with Susan behind her. "It ain't right nor kind for you to talk so to him, and him a stranger and so far from his people. How would you like to be treated so?"

---

1. Minstrel shows.

"That's always your way, Maim—always sailing in to help somebody before they're hurt. I hain't done nothing to him. He's told some stretchers, I reckon; and I said I wouldn't swallow it all; and that's every bit and grain I *did* say. I reckon he can stand a little thing like that, can't he?"

"I don't care whether 'twas little or whether 'twas big, he's here in our house and a stranger, and it wasn't good of you to say it. If you was in his place, it would make you feel ashamed; and so you ought'nt to say a thing to another person that will make *them* feel ashamed."

"Why, Maim, he said—"

"It don't make no difference what he *said*—that ain't the thing. The thing is for you to treat him *kind*, and not be saying things to make him remember he ain't in his own country and amongst his own folks."

I says to myself, *this* is a girl that I'm letting that old reptile rob her of her money!

Then Susan *she* waltzed in; and if you'll believe me, she did give Hare-lip hark from the tomb![2]

Says I to myself, And this is *another* one that I'm letting him rob her of her money!

Then Mary Jane she took another inning, and went in sweet and lovely again—which was her way—but when she got done there warn't hardly anything left o' poor Hare-lip. So she hollered.

"All right, then," says the other girls, "you just ask his pardon."

She done it, too. And she done it beautiful. She done it so beautiful it was good to hear; and I wished I could tell her a thousand lies, so she could do it again.

I says to myself, this is *another* one that I'm letting him rob her of her money. And when she got through, they all jest laid theirselves out to make me feel at home and know I was amongst friends. I felt so ornery and low down and mean, that I says to myself, My mind's made up; I'll hive that money for them or bust.

So then I lit out—for bed, I said, meaning some time or another. When I got by myself, I went to thinking the thing over. I says to myself, shall I go to that doctor, private, and blow on these frauds? No—that won't do. He might tell who told him; then the king and the duke would make it warm for me. Shall I go, private, and tell Mary Jane? No—I dasn't do it. Her face would give them a hint, sure; they've got the money, and they'd slide right out and get away with it. If she was to fetch in help, I'd get mixed up in the business, before it was done with, I judge. No, there ain't no good way but one. I got to steal that money, somehow; and I got to steal it some way that they won't suspicion that I done it. They've got a good thing, here; and they ain't agoing to leave till they've played this family and this town for all they're worth, so I'll find a chance time enough. I'll steal it, and hide it; and by-and-by, when I'm away down the river, I'll write a letter and tell Mary Jane where it's hid. But I better hive it to-night, if I can, because the doctor maybe hasn't let up as much as he lets on he has; he might scare them out of here, yet.

---

2. A scolding. The phrase refers to a hymn, "Hark! From the Tomb a Doleful Sound," by Isaac Watts (1674–1748).

So, thinks I, I'll go and search them rooms. Up stairs the hall was dark, but I found the duke's room, and started to paw around it with my hands; but I recollected it wouldn't be much like the king to let anybody else take care of that money but his own self; so then I went to his room and begun to paw around there. But I see I couldn't do nothing without a candle, and I dasn't light one, of course. So I judged I'd got to do the other thing—lay for them, and eavesdrop. About that time, I hears their footsteps coming, and was going to skip under the bed; I reached for it, but it wasn't where I thought it would be; but I touched the curtain that hid Mary Jane's frocks, so I jumped in behind that and snuggled in amongst the gowns, and stood there perfectly still.

They come in and shut the door; and the first thing the duke done was to get down and look under the bed. Then I was glad I hadn't found the bed when I wanted it. And yet, you know, it's kind of natural to hide under the bed when you are up to anything private. They sets down, then, and the king says:

"Well, what is it? and cut it middlin' short, because it's better for us to be down there a whoopin'-up the mournin', than up here givin' 'em a chance to talk us over."

"Well, this is it, Capet. I ain't easy; I ain't comfortable. That doctor lays on my mind. I wanted to know your plans. I've got a notion, and I think it's a sound one."

"What is it, duke?"

"That we better glide out of this, before three in the morning, and clip it down the river with what we've got. Specially, seeing we got it so easy—*given* back to us, flung at our heads, as you may say, when of course we allowed to have to steal it back. I'm for knocking off and lighting out."

That made me feel pretty bad. About an hour or two ago, it would a been a little different, but now it made me feel bad and disappointed. The king rips out and says:

"What! And not sell out the rest o' the property? March off like a passel o' fools and leave eight or nine thous'n dollars' worth o' property layin' around jest sufferin' to be scooped in?—and all good salable stuff, too."

The duke he grumbled; said the bag of gold was enough, and he didn't want to go no deeper—didn't want to rob a lot of orphans of *everything* they had.

"Why, how you talk!" says the king. "We shan't rob 'em of nothing at all but jest this money. The people that *buys* the property is the suff'rers; because as soon's it's found out 'at we didn't own it—which won't be long after we've slid—the sale won't be valid, and it'll all go back to the estate. These-yer orphans 'll git their house back agin, and that's enough for *them*; they're young and spry, and k'n easy earn a livin'. *They* ain't agoing to suffer. Why, jest think—there's thous'n's and thous'n's that ain't nigh so well off. Bless you, *they* ain't got noth'n to complain of."

Well, the king he talked him blind; so at last he give in, and said all right, but said he believed it was blame foolishness to stay, and that doctor hanging over them. But the king says:

"Cuss the doctor! What do we k'yer for *him*? Hain't we got all the fools in town on our side? and ain't that a big enough majority in any town?"

So they got ready to go down stairs again. The duke says:

"I don't think we put that money in a good place."

That cheered me up. I'd begun to think I warn't going to get a hint of no kind to help me. The king says:

"Why?"

"Because Mary Jane 'll be in mourning from this out; and first you know the nigger that does up the rooms will get an order to box these duds up and put 'em away; and do you reckon a nigger can run across money and not borrow some of it?"

"Your head's level, agin, duke," says the king; and he come a fumbling under the curtain two or three foot from where I was. I stuck tight to the wall, and kept mighty still, though quivery; and I wondered what them fellows would say to me if they catched me; and I tried to think what I'd better do if they did catch me. But the king he got the bag before I could think more than about a half a thought, and he never suspicioned I was around. They took and shoved the bag through a rip in the straw tick that was under the feather bed, and crammed it in a foot or two amongst the straw and said it was all right, now, because a nigger only makes up the feather bed, and don't turn over the straw tick only about twice a year, and so it warn't in no danger of getting stole, now.

But I knowed better. I had it out of there before they was halfway down stairs. I groped along up to my cubby, and hid it there till I could get a chance to do better. I judged I better hide it outside of the house somewheres, because if they missed it they would give the house a good ransacking. I knowed that very well. Then I turned in, with my clothes all on; but I couldn't a gone to sleep, if I'd a wanted to, I was in such a sweat to get through with the business. By-and-by I heard the king and the duke come up; so I rolled off of my pallet and laid with my chin at the top of my ladder and waited to see if anything was going to happen. But nothing did.

So I held on till all the late sounds had quit and the early ones hadn't begun, yet; and then I slipped down the ladder.

Chapter XXVII

I crept to their doors and listened; they was snoring, so I tip-toed along, and got down stairs all right. There warn't a sound anywheres. I peeped through a crack of the dining-room door, and see the men that was watching the corpse all sound asleep on their chairs. The door was open into the parlor, where the corpse was laying, and there was a candle in both rooms, I passed along, and the parlor door was open; but I see there warn't nobody in there but the remainders of Peter; so I shoved on by; but the front door was locked, and the key wasn't there. Just then I heard somebody coming down the stairs, back behind me. I run in the parlor, and took a swift look around, and the only place I see to hide the bag was in the coffin. The lid was shoved along about a foot, showing the dead man's face down in there, with a wet cloth over it, and his shroud on. I tucked the money-bag in under the lid, just down beyond where his hands was crossed, which made me creep, they was so cold, and then I run back across the room and in behind the door.

The person coming was Mary Jane. She went to the coffin, very soft, and kneeled down and looked in; then she put up her handkerchief and I see she begun to cry, though I couldn't hear her, and her back was to me. I slid out, and as I passed the dining-room I thought I'd make sure them watchers hadn't seen me; so I looked through the crack and everything was all right. They hadn't stirred.

I slipped up to bed, feeling ruther blue, on accounts of the thing playing out that way after I had took so much trouble and run so much resk about it. Says I, if it could stay where it is, all right; because when we get down the river a hundred mile or two, I could write back to Mary Jane, and she could dig him up again and get it; but that ain't the thing that's going to happen; the thing that's going to happen is, the money 'll be found when they come to screw on the lid. Then the king 'll get it again, and it 'll be a long day before he gives anybody another chance to smouch it from him. Of course I *wanted* to slide down and get it out of there, but I dasn't try it. Every minute it was getting earlier, now, and pretty soon some of them watchers would begin to stir, and I might get catched—catched with six thousand dollars in my hands that nobody hadn't hired me to take care of. I don't wish to be mixed up in no such business as that, I says to myself.

When I got down stairs in the morning, the parlor was shut up, and the watchers was gone. There warn't nobody around but the family and the widow Bartley and our tribe. I watched their faces to see if anything had been happening, but I couldn't tell.

Towards the middle of the day the undertaker come, with his man, and they set the coffin in the middle of the room on a couple of chairs, and then set all our chairs in rows, and borrowed more from the neighbors till the hall and the parlor and the dining-room was full. I see the coffin lid was the way it was before, but I dasn't go to look in under it, with folks around.

Then the people begun to flock in, and the beats and the girls took seats in the front row at the head of the coffin, and for a half an hour the people filed around slow, in single rank, and looked down at the dead man's face a minute, and some dropped in a tear, and it was all very still and solemn, only the girls and the beats holding handkerchiefs to their eyes and keeping their heads bent, and sobbing a little. There warn't no other sound but the scraping of the feet on the floor, and blowing noses—because people always blows them more at a funeral than they do at other places except church.

When the place was packed full, the undertaker he slid around in his black gloves with his softy soothering ways, putting on the last touches, and getting people and things all shipshape and comfortable, and making no more sound than a cat. He never spoke; he moved people around, he squeezed in late ones, he opened up passage-ways, and done it all with nods, and signs with his hands. Then he took his place over against the wall. He was the softest, glidingest, stealthiest man I ever see; and there warn't no more smile to him than there is to a ham.

They had borrowed a melodeum[3]—a sick one; and when everything was ready, a young woman set down and worked it, and it was pretty skreeky and colicky, and everybody joined in and sung, and Peter was the only one that had a good thing, according to my notion. Then the Reverend Hobson opened up, slow and solemn, and begun to talk; and straight off the most outrageous

3. A melodeon, small keyboard organ.

row busted out in the cellar a body ever heard; it was only one dog, but he made a most powerful racket, and he kept it up, right along; the parson he had to stand there, over the coffin, and wait—you couldn't hear yourself think. It was right down awkward, and nobody didn't seem to know what to do. But pretty soon they see that long-legged undertaker make a sign to the preacher as much as to say, "Don't you worry—just depend on me." Then he stooped down and begun to glide along the wall, just his shoulders showing over the people's heads. So he glided along, and the pow-wow and racket getting more and more outrageous all the time; and at last, when he had gone around two sides of the room, he disappears down cellar. Then, in about two seconds we heard a whack, and the dog he finished up with a most amazing howl or two, and then everything was dead still, and the parson begun his solemn talk where he left off. In a minute or two here comes this undertaker's back and shoulders gliding along the wall again; and so he glided, and glided, around three sides of the room, and then rose up, and shaded his mouth with his hands, and stretched his neck out towards the preacher, over the people's heads, and says, in a kind of a coarse whisper, *"He had a rat!"* Then he drooped down and glided along the wall again to his place. You could see it was a great satisfaction to the people, because naturally they wanted to know. A little thing like that don't cost nothing, and it's just the little things that makes a man to be looked up to and liked. There warn't no more popular man in town than what that undertaker was.

Well, the funeral sermon was very good, but pison long and tiresome; and then the king he shoved in and got off some of his usual rubbage, and at last the job was through, and the undertaker begun to sneak up on the coffin with his screw-driver. I was in a sweat then, and watched him pretty keen. But he never meddled at all; just slid the lid along, as soft as mush, and screwed it down tight and fast. So there I was! I didn't know whether the money was in there, or not. So, says I, spose somebody has hogged that bag on the sly?—now how do *I* know whether to write to Mary Jane or not? 'Spose she dug him up and didn't find nothing—what would she think of me? Blame it, I says, I might get hunted up and jailed; I'd better lay low and keep dark, and not write at all; the thing's awful mixed, now; trying to better it, I've worsened it a hundred times, and I wish to goodness I'd just let it alone, dad fetch the whole business!

They buried him, and we come back home, and I went to watching faces again—I couldn't help it, and I couldn't rest easy. But nothing come of it; the faces didn't tell me nothing.

The king he visited around, in the evening, and sweetened every body up, and made himself ever so friendly; and he give out the idea that his congregation over in England would be in a sweat about him, so he must hurry and settle up the estate right away, and leave for home. He was very sorry he was so pushed, and so was everybody; they wished he could stay longer, but they said they could see it couldn't be done. And he said of course him and William would take the girls home with them; and that pleased everybody too, because then the girls would be well fixed, and amongst their own relations; and it pleased the girls, too—tickled them so they clean forgot they ever had a trouble in the world; and told him to sell out as quick as he wanted to, they would be ready. Them poor things was that glad and happy it made my heart ache to see them getting fooled and lied to so, but I didn't see no safe way for me to chip in and change the general tune.

Well, blamed if the king didn't bill the house and the niggers and all the property for auction straight off—sale two days after the funeral; but anybody could buy private beforehand if they wanted to.

So the next day after the funeral, along about noontime, the girls' joy got the first jolt; a couple of nigger traders come along, and the king sold them the niggers reasonable, for three-day drafts[4] as they called it, and away they went, the two sons up the river to Memphis, and their mother down the river to Orleans. I thought them poor girls and them niggers would break their hearts for grief; they cried around each other, and took on so it most made me down sick to see it. The girls said they hadn't ever dreamed of seeing the family separated or sold away from the town. I can't ever get it out of my memory, the sight of them poor miserable girls and niggers hanging around each other's necks and crying; and I reckon I couldn't a stood it all but would a had to bust out and tell on our gang if I hadn't knowed the sale warn't no account and the niggers would be back home in a week or two.

The thing made a big stir in the town, too, and a good many come out flatfooted and said it was scandalous to separate the mother and the children that way. It injured the frauds some; but the old fool he bulled right along, spite of all the duke could say or do, and I tell you the duke was powerful uneasy.

Next day was auction day. About broad-day in the morning, the king and the duke come up in the garret and woke me up, and I see by their look that there was trouble. The king says:

"Was you in my room night before last?"

"No, your majesty"—which was the way I always called him when nobody but our gang warn't around.

"Was you in there yisterday er last night?"

"No, your majesty."

"Honor bright, now—no lies."

"Honor bright, your majesty, I'm telling you the truth. I hain't been anear your room since Miss Mary Jane took you and the duke and showed it to you."

The duke says:

"Have you seen anybody else go in there?"

"No, your grace, not as I remember, I believe."

"Stop and think."

I studied a while, and see my chance, then I says:

"Well, I see the niggers go in there several times."

Both of them give a little jump; and looked like they hadn't ever expected it, and then like they *had*. Then the duke says:

"What, *all* of them?"

"No—leastways not all at once. That is, I don't think I ever see them all come *out* at once but just one time."

---

4. Bank drafts or checks payable three days later.

"Hello—when was that?"

"It was the day we had the funeral. In the morning. It warn't early, because I overslept. I was just starting down the ladder, and I see them."

"Well, go on, go on—what did they do? How'd they act?"

"They didn't do nothing. And they didn't act anyway, much, as fur as I see. They tip-toed away; so I seen, easy enough, that they'd shoved in there to do up your majesty's room, or something, sposing you was up; and found you warn't up, and so they was hoping to slide out of the way of trouble without waking you up, if they hadn't already waked you up."

"Great guns, this is a go!" says the king; and both of them looked pretty sick, and tolerable silly. They stood there a thinking and scratching their heads, a minute, and then the duke he bust into a kind of a little raspy chuckle, and says:

"It does beat all, how neat the niggers played their hand. They let on to be sorry they was going out of this region! and I believed they was sorry. And so did you, and so did everybody. Don't ever tell me any more that a nigger ain't got any histrionic talent. Why, the way they played that thing, it would fool anybody. In my opinion there's a fortune in 'em. If I had capital and a theatre, I wouldn't want a better lay out than that—and here we've gone and sold 'em for a song. Yes, and ain't privileged to sing the song, yet. Say, where is that song?—that draft."

"In the bank for to be collected. Where would it be?"

"Well, that's all right then, thank goodness."

Says I, kind of timid-like:

"Is something gone wrong?"

The king whirls on me and rips out:

"None o' your business! You keep your head shet, and mind y'r own affairs—if you got any. Long as you're in this town, don't you forgit that, you hear?" Then he says to the duke, "We got to jest swaller it, and say noth'n: mum's the word for us."

As they was starting down the ladder, the duke he chuckles again, and says:

"Quick sales and small profits! It's a good business—yes."

The king snarls around on him and says,

"I was trying to do for the best, in sellin' 'm out so quick. If the profits has turned out to be none, lackin' considable, and none to carry, is it my fault any more'n it's yourn?"

"Well, they'd be in this house yet, and we wouldn't if I could a got my advice listened to."

The king sassed back, as much as was safe for him, and then swapped around and lit into me again. He give me down the banks[5] for not coming and telling him I see the niggers come out of his room acting that way—said any fool would a knowed something was up. And then waltzed in and cussed himself a while; and said it all come of him not laying late and taking his natural rest that morning, and he'd be blamed if he'd ever do it again. So they went off a jawing; and I felt dreadful glad I'd worked it all off onto the niggers and yet hadn't done the niggers no harm by it.

5. To scream insults or criticism (slang).

Chapter XXVIII

By-and-by it was getting-up time; so I come down the ladder and started for down stairs, but as I come to the girls' room, the door was open, and I see Mary Jane setting by her old hair trunk, which was open and she'd been packing things in it—getting ready to go to England. But she had stopped now, with a folded gown in her lap, and had her face in her hands, crying. I felt awful bad to see it; of course anybody would. I went in there, and says:

"Miss Mary Jane, you can't abear to see people in trouble, and *I* can't—most always. Tell me about it."

So she done it. And it was the niggers—I just expected it. She said the beautiful trip to England was most about spoiled for her; she didn't know *how* she was ever going to be happy there, knowing the mother and the children warn't ever going to see each other no more—and then busted out bitterer than ever, and flung up her hands, and says:

"Oh, dear, dear, to think they ain't *ever* going to see each other any more!"

"But they *will*—and inside of two weeks—and I *know* it!" says I.

Laws it was out before I could think!—and before I could budge, she throws her arms around my neck, and told me to say it *again*, say it *again*, say it *again*!

I see I had spoke too sudden, and said too much, and was in a close place. I asked her to let me think a minute; and she set there, very impatient and excited, and handsome, but looking kind of happy and eased-up, like a person that's had a tooth pulled out. So I went to studying it out. I says to myself, I reckon a body that ups and tells the truth when he is in a tight place, is taking considerable many resks, though I ain't had no experience, and can't say for certain; but it looks so to me, anyway; and yet here's a case where I'm blest if it don't look to me like the truth is better, and actuly *safer*, than a lie. I must lay it by in my mind, and think it over some time or other, it's so kind of strange and unregular. I never see nothing like it. Well, I says to myself at last, I'm agoing to chance it; I'll up and tell the truth this time, though it does seem most like setting down on a kag of powder and touching it off just to see where you'll go to. Then I says:

"Miss Mary Jane, is there any place out of town a little ways, where you could go and stay three or four days?"

"Yes—Mr. Lothrop's. Why?"

"Never mind why, yet. If I'll tell you how I know the niggers will see each other again—inside of two weeks—here in this house—and *prove* how I know it—will you go to Mr. Lothrop's and stay four days?"

"Four days!" she says; "I'll stay a year!"

"All right," I says, "I don't want nothing more out of *you* than just your word—I druther have it than another man's kiss-the-Bible." She smiled, and reddened up very sweet, and I says, "If you don't mind it, I'll shut the door—and bolt it."

Then I come back and set down again, and says:

"Don't you holler. Just set still, and take it like a man. I got to tell the truth, and you want to brace up, Miss Mary, because it's a bad kind, and going to be hard to take, but there ain't no help for it. These uncles of yourn ain't no uncles at all—they're a couple of frauds—regular dead-beats. There, now we're over the worst of it—you can stand the rest middling easy."

It jolted her up like everything, of course; but I was over the shoal water now, so I went right along, her eyes a blazing higher and higher all the time, and told her every blame thing, from where we first struck that young fool going up to the steamboat, clear through to where she flung herself onto the king's breast at the front door and he kissed her sixteen or seventeen times—and then up she jumps, with her face afire like sunset, and says:

"The brute! Come—don't waste a minute—not a *second*—we'll have them tarred and feathered, and flung in the river!"[6]

Says I;

"Cert'nly. But do you mean, *before* you go to Mr. Lothrop's, or—"

"Oh," she says, "what am I *thinking* about!" she says, and set right down again. "Don't mind what I said—please don't—you *won't*, now, *will* you?" Laying her silky hand on mine in that kind of a way that I said I would die first. "I never thought, I was so stirred up," she says; "now go on, and I won't do so any more. You tell me what to do, and whatever you say, I'll do it."

"Well," I says, "it's a rough gang, them two frauds, and I'm fixed so I got to travel with them a while longer, whether I want to or not—I druther not tell you why—and if you was to blow on them this town would get me out of their claws, and *I'd* be all right, but there'd be another person that you don't know about who'd be in big trouble. Well, we got to save *him*, hain't we? Of course. Well, then, we won't blow on them."

Saying them words put a good idea in my head. I see how maybe I could get me and Jim rid of the frauds; get them jailed here, and then leave. But I didn't want to run the raft in day-time, without anybody aboard to answer questions but me; so I didn't want the plan to begin working till pretty late to-night. I says:

"Miss Mary Jane, I'll tell you what we'll do—and you won't have to stay at Mr. Lothrop's so long, nuther. How fur is it?"

"A little short of four miles—right out in the country, back here."

"Well, that'll answer. Now you go along out there, and lay low till nine or half-past, to-night, and then get them to fetch you home again—tell them you've thought of something. If you get here before eleven, put a candle in this window, and if I don't turn up, wait *till* eleven, and *then* if I don't turn up it means I'm gone, and out of the way, and safe. Then you come out and spread the news around, and get these beats jailed."

"Good," she says, "I'll do it."

"And if it just happens so that I don't get away, but get took up along with them, you must up and say I told you the whole thing beforehand, and you must stand by me all you can."

"Stand by you, indeed I will. They sha'n't touch a hair of your head!" she says, and I see her nostrils spread and her eyes snap when she said it, too.

"If I get away, I sha'n't be here," I says, "to prove these rapscallions ain't your uncles, and I couldn't do it if I *was* here. I could swear they was beats and bummers, that's all; though that's worth something. Well, there's others can do that better than what I can—and they're people that ain't going to be doubted as quick as I'd be. I'll tell you how to find them. Gimme a pencil and a piece of paper. There—'*Royal Nonesuch, Bricksville.*' Put it away, and

6. The victim of this fairly commonplace mob punishment was tied to a rail, smeared with hot tar, and covered with feathers. Then the victim would be ridden out of town on the rail to the jeers of the mob.

don't lose it. When the court wants to find out something about these two, let them send up to Bricksville and say they've got the men that played the Royal Nonesuch, and ask for some witnesses—why, you'll have that entire town down here before you can hardly wink, Miss Mary. And they'll come a-biling, too."

I judged we had got everything fixed about right, now. So I says:

"Just let the auction go right along, and don't worry. Nobody don't have to pay for the things they buy till a whole day after the auction, on accounts of the short notice, and they ain't going out of this till they get that money—and the way we've fixed it the sale ain't going to count, and they ain't going to *get* no money. It's just like the way it was with the niggers—it warn't no sale, and the niggers will be back before long. Why, they can't collect the money for the *niggers*, yet—they're in the worst kind of a fix, Miss Mary."

"Well," she says, "I'll run down to breakfast now, and then I'll start straight for Mr. Lothrop's."

" 'Deed, *that* ain't the ticket, Miss Mary Jane," I says, "by no manner of means; go *before* breakfast."

"Why?"

"What did you reckon I wanted you to go at all for, Miss Mary?"

"Well, I never thought—and come to think, I don't know. What was it?"

"Why, it's because you ain't one of these leather-face people. I don't want no better book than what your face is. A body can set down and read it off like coarse paint. Do you reckon you can go and face your uncles, when they come to kiss you good-morning, and never—"

"There, there, don't! Yes, I'll go before breakfast—I'll be glad to. And leave my sisters with them?"

"Yes—never mind about them. They've got to stand it yet a while. They might suspicion something if all of you was to go. I don't want you to see them, nor your sisters, nor nobody in this town—if a neighbor was to ask how is your uncles this morning, your face would tell something. No, you go right along, Miss Mary Jane, and I'll fix it with all of them. I'll tell Miss Susan to give your love to your uncles and say you've went away for a few hours for to get a little rest and change, or to see a friend, and you'll be back to-night or early in the morning."

"Gone to see a friend is all right, but I won't have my love given to them."

"Well, then, it sha'n't be." It was well enough to tell *her* so—no harm in it. It was only a little thing to do, and no trouble; and it's the little things that smoothes people's roads the most, down here below; it would make Mary Jane comfortable, and it wouldn't cost nothing. Then I says: "There's one more thing—that bag of money."

"Well, they've got that; and it makes me feel pretty silly to think *how* they got it."

"No, you're out, there. They hain't got it."

"Why, who's got it?"

"I wish I knowed, but I don't. I *had* it, because I stole it from them: and I stole it to give to you; and I know where I hid it, but I'm afraid it ain't there no more. I'm awful sorry, Miss Mary Jane, I'm just as sorry as I can be; but I done the best I could; I did, honest. I come nigh getting caught, and I had to shove it into the first place I come to, and run—and it warn't a good place."

"Oh, stop blaming yourself—it's too bad to do it, and I won't allow it— you couldn't help it; it wasn't your fault. Where did you hide it?"

I didn't want to set her to thinking about her troubles again; and I couldn't seem to get my mouth to tell her what would make her see that corpse laying in the coffin with that bag of money on his stomach. So for a minute I didn't say nothing—then I says:

"I'd rather not *tell* you where I put it, Miss Mary Jane, if you don't mind letting me off; but I'll write it for you on a piece of paper, and you can read it along the road to Mr. Lothrop's; if you want to. Do you reckon that'll do?"

"Oh, yes."

So I wrote: "I put it in the coffin. It was in there when you was crying there, away in the night. I was behind the door, and I was mighty sorry for you, Miss Mary Jane."

It made my eyes water a little, to remember her crying there all by her-self in the night, and them devils laying there right under her own roof, shaming her and robbing her; and when I folded it up and give it to her, I see the water come into her eyes, too; and she shook me by the hand, hard, and says:

"*Good*-bye—I'm going to do everything just as you've told me; and if I don't ever see you again, I sha'n't ever forget you, and I'll think of you a many and a many a time, and I'll *pray* for you, too!"—and she was gone.

Pray for me! I reckoned if she knowed me she'd take a job that was more nearer her size. But I bet she done it, just the same—she was just that kind. She had the grit to pray for Judus if she took the notion—there warn't no backdown to her, I judge. You may say what you want to, but in my opinion she had more sand in her than any girl I ever see; in my opinion she was just full of sand.[7] It sounds like flattery, but it ain't no flattery. And when it comes to beauty—and goodness too—she lays over them all. I hain't ever seen her since that time that I see her go out of that door; no, I hain't ever seen her since, but I reckon I've thought of her a many and a many a mil-lion times, and of her saying she would pray for me; and if ever I'd a thought it would do any good for me to pray for *her*, blamed if I wouldn't a done it or bust.

Well, Mary Jane she lit out the back way, I reckon; because nobody see her go. When I struck Susan and the hare-lip, I says:

"What's the name of them people over on t'other side of the river that you all goes to see sometimes?"

They says:

"There's several; but it's the Proctors, mainly."

"That's the name," I says; "I most forgot it. Well, Miss Mary Jane she told me to tell you she's gone over there in a dreadful hurry—one of them's sick."

"Which one?"

"I don't know; leastways I kinder forget; but I think it's—"

"Sakes alive, I hope it ain't *Hanner*?"

"I'm sorry to say it," I says, "but Hanner's the very one."

7. Courage.

"My goodness—and she so well only last week! Is she took bad?"

"It ain't no name for it. They set up with her all night, Miss Mary Jane said, and they don't think she'll last many hours."

"Only think of that, now! What's the matter with her!"

I couldn't think of anything reasonable, right off that way, so I says: "Mumps."

"Mumps your granny! They don't set up with people that's got the mumps."

"They don't, don't they? You better bet they do with *these* mumps. These mumps is different. It's a new kind, Miss Mary Jane said."

"How's it a new kind?"

"Because it's mixed up with other things."

"What other things?"

"Well, measles, and whooping-cough, and erysiplas, and consumption, and yaller janders, and brain fever, and I don't know what all."

"My land! And they call it the *mumps*?"

"That's what Miss Mary Jane said."

"Well, what in the nation do they call it the *mumps* for?"

"Why, because it *is* the mumps. That's what it starts with."

"Well, ther' ain't no sense in it. A body might stump his toe, and take pison, and fall down the well, and break his neck, and bust his brains out, and somebody come along and ask what killed him, and some numskull up and say, 'Why, he stumped his *toe*.' Would ther' be any sense in that? *No*. And ther' ain't no sense in *this*, nuther. Is it ketching?"

"Is it *ketching*? Why, how you talk. Is a *harrow* catching?—in the dark? If you don't hitch onto one tooth, you're bound to on another, ain't you? And you can't get away with that tooth without fetching the whole harrow along, can you? Well, these kind of mumps is a kind of a harrow, as you may say— and it ain't no slouch of a harrow, nuther, you come to get it hitched on good."

"Well, it's awful, *I* think," says the hare-lip. "I'll go to Uncle Harvey and—"

"Oh, yes," I says, "I *would*. Of *course* I would. I wouldn't lose no time."

"Well, why wouldn't you?"

"Just look at it a minute, and maybe you can see. Hain't your uncles obleeged to get along home to England as fast as they can? And do you reckon they'd be mean enough to go off and leave you to go all that journey by your- selves? *You* know they'll wait for you. So fur, so good. Your uncle Harvey's a preacher, ain't he? Very well, then; is a *preacher* going to deceive a steam- boat clerk? is he going to deceive a *ship clerk*?—so as to get them to let Miss Mary Jane go aboard? Now *you* know he ain't. What *will* he do, then? Why, he'll say, 'It's a great pity, but my church matters has got to get along the best way they can; for my niece has been exposed to the dreadful pluribus- unum[8] mumps, and so it's my bounden duty to set down here and wait the three months it takes to show on her if she's got it.' But never mind, if you think it's best to tell your uncle Harvey—"

"Shucks, and stay fooling around here when we could all be having good times in England whilst we was waiting to find out whether Mary Jane's got it or not? Why, you talk like a muggins."[9]

---

8. Huck reaches for the handiest Latin phrase he could be expected to know; meaning "out of many, one" (the motto of the United States).

9. A fool.

"Well, anyway, maybe you better tell some of the neighbors."

"Listen at that, now. You do beat all, for natural stupidness. Can't you *see* that *they'd* go and tell? Ther' ain't no way but just to not tell anybody at *all.*"

"Well, maybe you're right—yes, I judge you *are* right."

"But I reckon we ought to tell Uncle Harvey she's gone out a while, anyway, so he wont be uneasy about her?"

"Yes, Miss Mary Jane she wanted you to do that. She says, 'Tell them to give Uncle Harvey and William my love and a kiss, and say I've run over the river to see Mr.—Mr.—what *is* the name of that rich family your uncle Peter used to think so much of?—I mean the one that—"

"Why, you must mean the Apthorps, ain't it?"

"Of course; bother them kind of names, a body can't ever seem to remember them, half the time, somehow. Yes, she said, say she has run over for to ask the Apthorps to be sure and come to the auction and buy this house, because she allowed her uncle Peter would ruther they had it than anybody else; and she's going to stick to them till they say they'll come, and then, if she ain't too tired, she's coming home; and if she is, she'll be home in the morning anyway. She said, don't say nothing about the Proctors, but only about the Apthorps—which'll be perfectly true, because she *is* going there to speak about their buying the house; I know it, because she told me so, herself."

"All right," they said, and cleared out to lay for their uncles, and give them the love and the kisses, and tell them the message.

Everything was all right now. The girls wouldn't say nothing because they wanted to go to England; and the king and the duke would ruther Mary Jane was off working for the auction than around in reach of Doctor Robinson. I felt very good; I judged I had done it pretty neat—I reckoned Tom Sawyer couldn't a done it no neater himself. Of course he would a throwed more style into it, but I can't do that very handy, not being brung up to it.

Well, they held the auction in the public square, along towards the end of the afternoon, and it strung along, and strung along, and the old man he was on hand and looking his level piousest, up there longside of the auctioneer, and chipping in a little Scripture, now and then, or a little goody-goody saying, of some kind, and the duke he was around goo-gooing for sympathy all he knowed how, and just spreading himself generly.

But by-and-by the thing dragged through, and everything was sold. Everything but a little old trifling lot in the graveyard. So they'd got to work *that* off—I never see such a girafft[1] as the king was for wanting to swallow *everything*. Well, whilst they was at it, a steamboat landed, and in about two minutes up comes a crowd a whooping and yelling and laughing and carrying on, and singing out:

"*Here's* your opposition line! here's your two sets o' heirs to old Peter Wilks—and you pays your money and you takes your choice!"

---

1. Giraffe.

Chapter XXIX

They was fetching a very nice looking old gentleman along, and a nice look-ing younger one, with his right arm in a sling. And my souls, how the people yelled, and laughed, and kept it up. But I didn't see no joke about it, and I judged it would strain the duke and the king some to see any. I reckoned they'd turn pale. But no, nary a pale did *they* turn. The duke he never let on he suspicioned what was up, but just went a goo-gooing around, happy and satisfied, like a jug that's googling out buttermilk; and as for the king, he just gazed and gazed down sorrowful on them newcomers like it give him the stomach-ache in his very heart to think there could be such frauds and rascals in the world. Oh, he done it admirable. Lots of the principal people gethered around the king, to let him see they was on his side. That old gentle-man that had just come looked all puzzled to death. Pretty soon he begun to speak, and I see, straight off, he pronounced *like* an Englishman, not the king's way, though the king's *was* pretty good, for an imitation. I can't give the old gent's words, nor I can't imitate him; but he turned around to the crowd, and says, about like this:

"This is a surprise to me which I wasn't looking for; and I'll acknowledge, candid and frank, I ain't very well fixed to meet it and answer it; for my brother and me has had misfortunes, he's broke his arm, and our baggage got put off at a town above here, last night in the night by a mistake. I am Peter Wilks's brother Harvey, and this is his brother William, which can't hear nor speak—and can't even make signs to amount to much, now 't he's only got one hand to work them with. We are who we say we are; and in a day or two, when I get the baggage, I can prove it. But, up till then, I won't say nothing more, but go to the hotel and wait."

So him and the new dummy[2] started off; and the king he laughs, and blethers out:

"Broke his arm—*very* likely *ain't* it?—and very convenient, too, for a fraud that's got to make signs, and hain't learnt how. Lost their baggage! That's *mighty* good!—and mighty ingenious—under the *circumstances!*"

So he laughed again; and so did everybody else, except three or four, or maybe half a dozen. One of these was that doctor; another one was a sharp looking gentleman, with a carpet-bag of the old-fashioned kind made out of carpet-stuff, that had just come off of the steamboat and was talking to him in a low voice, and glancing towards the king now and then and nodding their heads—it was Levi Bell, the lawyer that was gone up to Louisville; and another one was a big rough husky that come along and listened to all the old gentleman said, and was listening to the king now. And when the king got done, this husky up and says:

"Say, looky here; if you are Harvey Wilks, when'd you come to this town?"

"The day before the funeral, friend," says the king.

"But what time o' day?"

"In the evenin'—'bout an hour er two before sundown."

"*How'd* you come?"

"I come down on the *Susan Powell*, from Cincinnati."

2. A person who can't hear or speak.

"Well, then, how'd you come to be up at the Pint in the *mornin'*—in a canoe?"

"I warn't up at the Pint in the mornin'."

"It's a lie."

Several of them jumped for him and begged him not to talk that way to an old man and a preacher.

"Preacher be hanged, he's a fraud and a lair. He was up at the Pint that mornin'. I live up there, don't I? Well, I was up there, and he was up there. I *see* him there. He come in a canoe, along with Tim Collins and a boy."

The doctor he up and says:

"Would you know the boy again if you was to see him, Hines?"

"I reckon I would, but I don't know. Why, yonder he is, now. I know him perfectly easy."

It was me he pointed at. The doctor says:

"Neighbors. I don't know whether the new couple is frauds or not; but if *these* two ain't frauds, I am an idiot, that's all. I think it's our duty to see that they don't get away from here till we've looked into this thing. Come along, Hines; come along, the rest of you. We'll take these fellows to the tavern and affront them with t'other couple, and I reckon we'll find out *something* before we get through."

It was nuts for the crowd, though maybe not for the king's friends; so we all started. It was about sundown. The doctor he led me along by the hand, and was plenty kind enough, but he never let *go* my hand.

We all got in a big room in the hotel, and lit up some candles, and fetched in the new couple. First, the doctor says:

"I don't wish to be too hard on these two men, but *I* think they're frauds, and they may have complices that we don't know nothing about. If they have, won't the complices get away with that bag of gold Peter Wilks left? It ain't unlikely. If these men ain't frauds, they won't object to sending for that money and letting us keep it till they prove they're all right—ain't that so?"

Everybody agreed to that. So I judged they had our gang in a pretty tight place, right at the outstart. But the king he only looked sorrowful, and says:

"Gentlemen, I wish the money was there, for I ain't got no disposition to throw anything in the way of a fair, open, out-and-out investigation o' this misable business; but alas, the money ain't there; you k'n send and see, if you want to."

"Where is it, then?"

"Well, when my niece give it to me to keep for her, I took and hid it inside o' the straw tick o' my bed, not wishin' to bank it for the few days we'd be here, and considerin' the bed a safe place, we not bein' used to niggers, and suppos'n' 'em honest, like servants in England. The niggers stole it the very next mornin' after I had went down stairs; and when I sold 'em, I hadn't missed the money yit, so they got clean away with it. My servant here k'n tell you 'bout it gentlemen."

The doctor and several said "Shucks!" and I see nobody didn't altogether believe him. One man asked me if I see the niggers steal it. I said no, but I see them sneaking out of the room and hustling away, and I never thought nothing, only I reckoned they was afraid they had waked up my master and was trying to get away before he made trouble with them. That was all they asked me. Then the doctor whirls on me and says:

"Are *you* English too?"

I says yes; and him and some others laughed, and said, "Stuff!"

Well, then they sailed in on the general investigation, and there we had it, up and down, hour in, hour out, and nobody never said a word about supper, nor ever seemed to think about it—and so they kept it up, and kept it up; and it *was* the worst mixed-up thing you ever see. They made the king tell his yarn, and they made the old gentleman tell his'n; and anybody but a lot of prejudiced chuckleheads would a *seen* that the old gentleman was spinning truth and t'other one lies. And by-and-by they had me up to tell what I knowed. The king he give me a left-handed look out of the corner of his eye, and so I knowed enough to talk on the right side. I begun to tell about Sheffield, and how we lived there, and all about the English Wilkses, and so on; but I didn't get pretty fur till the doctor begun to laugh; and Levi Bell, the lawyer says:

"Set down, my boy, I wouldn't strain myself, if I was you. I reckon you ain't used to lying, it don't seem to come handy; what you want is practice. You do it pretty awkward."

I didn't care nothing for the compliment, but I was glad to be let off, anyway.

The doctor he started to say something, and turns and says:

"If you'd been in town at first, Levi Bell—"

The king broke in and reached out his hand, and says:

"Why, is this my poor dead brother's old friend that he's wrote so often about?"

The lawyer and him shook hands, and the lawyer smiled and looked pleased, and they talked right along a while, and then got to one side and talked low; and at last the lawyer speaks up and says:

"That'll fix it. I'll take the order and send it, along with your brother's, and then they'll know it's all right."

So they got some paper and a pen, and the king he set down and twisted his head to one side, and chawed his tongue, and scrawled off something; and then they give the pen to the duke—and then for the first time, the duke looked sick. But he took the pen and wrote. So then the lawyer turns to the new old gentleman and says:

"You and your brother please write a line or two and sign your names."

The old gentleman wrote, but nobody couldn't read it. The lawyer looked powerful astonished, and says:

"Well, it beats *me*"—and snaked a lot of old letters out of his pocket, and examined them, and then examined the old man's writing, and then *them* again; and then says: "These old letters is from Harvey Wilks; and here's *these* two's handwritings, and anybody can see *they* didn't write them" (the king and the duke looked sold and foolish, I tell you, to see how the lawyer had took them in), "and here's *this* old gentleman's handwriting, and anybody can tell, easy enough, *he* didn't write them—fact is, the scratches he makes ain't properly *writing*, at all. Now here's some letters from—"

The new old gentleman says:

"If you please, let me explain. Nobody can read my hand but my brother there—so he copies for me. It's *his* hand you've got there, not mine."

"*Well!*" says the lawyer, "this *is* a state of things. I've got some of William's letters too; so if you'll get him to write a line or so we can com—"

"He *can't* write with his left hand," says the old gentleman. "If he could use his right hand, you would see that he wrote his own letters and mine too. Look at both, please—they're by the same hand."

The lawyer done it, and says:

"I believe it's so—and if it ain't so, there's a heap stronger resemblance than I'd noticed before, anyway. Well, well, well! I thought we was right on the track of a slution, but it's gone to grass, partly. But anyway, *one* thing is proved—*these* two ain't either of 'em Wilkses"—and he wagged his head towards the king and the duke.

Well, what do you think?—that muleheaded old fool wouldn't give in *then*! Indeed he wouldn't. Said it warn't no fair test. Said his brother William was the cussedest joker in the world, and hadn't *tried* to write—*he* see William was going to play one of his jokes the minute he put the pen to paper. And so he warmed up and went warbling and warbling right along, till he was actuly beginning to believe what he was saying, *himself*—but pretty soon the new old gentleman broke in, and says:

"I've thought of something. Is there anybody here that helped to lay out my br—helped to lay out the late Peter Wilks for burying?"

"Yes," says somebody, "me and Ab Turner done it. We're both here."

Then the old man turns towards the king, and says:

"Peraps this gentleman can tell me what was tatooed on his breast?"

Blamed if the king didn't have to brace up mighty quick, or he'd a squshed down like a bluff bank that the river has cut under, it took him so sudden—and mind you, it was a thing that was calculated to make most *anybody* sqush to get fetched such a solid one as that without any notice—because how was *he* going to know what was tatooed on the man? He whitened a little; he couldn't help it; and it was mighty still in there, and everybody bending a little forwards and gazing at him. Says I to myself, *Now* he'll throw up the sponge—there ain't no more use. Well, did he? A body can't hardly believe it, but he didn't. I reckon he thought he'd keep the thing up till he tired them people out, so they'd thin out, and him and the duke could break loose and get away. Anyway, he set there, and pretty soon he begun to smile, and says:

"Mf! It's a *very* tough question, *ain't* it! Yes, sir, I k'n tell you what's tatooed on his breast. It's jest a small, thin, blue arrow—that's what it is; and if you don't look clost, you can't see it. *Now* what do you say—hey?"

Well, *I* never see anything like that old blister for clean out-and-out cheek.

The new old gentleman turns brisk towards Ab Turner and his pard, and his eye lights up like he judged he'd got the king *this* time, and says:

"There—you've heard what he said! Was there any such mark on Peter Wilks's breast?"

Both of them spoke up and says:

"We didn't see no such mark."

"Good!" says the old gentleman. "Now, what you *did* see on his breast was a small dim P, and a B (which is an initial he dropped when he was young), and a W, with dashes between them, so: P—B—W"—and he marked them that way on a piece of paper. "Come—ain't that what you saw?"

Both of them spoke up again, and says:

"No, we *didn't*. We never seen any marks at all."

Well, everybody *was* in a state of mind, now; and they sings out:

"The whole *bilin'* of 'm 's frauds! Le's duck 'em! le's drown 'em! le's ride 'em on a rail!" and everybody was whooping at once, and there was a rattling pow-wow. But the lawyer he jumps on the table and yells, and says:

"Gentlemen—gentle*men*! Hear me just a word—just a *single* word—if you PLEASE! There's one way yet—let's go and dig up the corpse and look."

That took them.

"Hooray!" they all shouted, and was starting right off; but the lawyer and the doctor sung out:

"Hold on, hold on! Collar all these four men and the boy, and fetch *them* along, too!"

"We'll do it!" they all shouted: "and if we don't find them marks we'll lynch the whole gang!"

I *was* scared, now, I tell you. But there warn't no getting away, you know. They gripped us all, and marched us right along, straight for the graveyard, which was a mile and a half down the river, and the whole town at our heels, for we made noise enough, and it was only nine in the evening.

As we went by our house I wished I hadn't sent Mary Jane out of town; because now if I could tip her the wink, she'd light out and save me, and blow on our dead-beats.

Well, we swarmed along down the river road, just carrying on like wild-cats; and to make it more scary, the sky was darking up, and the lightning beginning to wink and flitter, and the wind to shiver amongst the leaves. This was the most awful trouble and most dangersome I ever was in; and I was kinder stunned; everything was going so different from what I had allowed for; stead of being fixed so I could take my own time, if I wanted to, and see all the fun, and have Mary Jane at my back to save me and set me free when the close-fit come, here was nothing in the world betwixt me and sudden death but just them tatoo-marks. If they didn't find them—

I couldn't bear to think about it; and yet, somehow, I couldn't think about nothing else. It got darker and darker, and it was a beautiful time to give the crowd the slip; but that big husky had me by the wrist—Hines—and a body might as well try to give Goliar[3] the slip. He dragged me right along, he was so excited; and I had to run to keep up.

When they got there they swarmed into the graveyard and washed over it like an overflow. And when they got to the grave, they found they had about a hundred times as many shovels as they wanted, but nobody hadn't thought to fetch a lantern. But they sailed into digging, anyway, by the flicker of the lightning, and sent a man to the nearest house a half a mile off, to borrow one.

So they dug and dug, like everything; and it got awful dark, and the rain started, and the wind swished and swushed along, and the lightning come brisker and brisker, and the thunder boomed; but them people never took no notice of it, they was so full of this business; and one minute you could see everything and every face in that big crowd, and the shovelfuls of dirt sailing up out of the grave, and the next second the dark wiped it all out, and you couldn't see nothing at all.

---

3. Goliath, a Philistine giant who challenged the Israelites. In 1 Samuel, David, a young shepherd, accepts his challenge and kills him with a stone thrown from a sling.

At last they got out the coffin, and begun to unscrew the lid, and then such another crowding, and shouldering, and shoving as there was, to scrouge in and get a sight, you never see; and in the dark, that way, it was awful. Hines he hurt my wrist dreadful, pulling and tugging so, and I reckon he clean forgot I was in the world, he was so excited and panting.

All of a sudden the lightning let go a perfect sluice of white glare, and somebody sings out:

"By the living jingo, here's the bag of gold on his breast!"

Hines let out a whoop, like everybody else, and dropped my wrist and give a big surge to bust his way in and get a look, and the way I lit out and shinned for the road in the dark, there ain't nobody can tell.

I had the road all to myself, and I fairly flew—leastways I had it all to myself except the solid dark, and the now-and-then glares, and the buzzing of the rain, and the thrashing of the wind, and the splitting of the thunder; and sure as you are born I did clip it along!

When I struck the town, I see there warn't nobody out in the storm, so I never hunted for no back streets, but humped it straight through the main one; and when I begun to get towards our house I aimed my eye and set it. No light there; the house all dark—which made me feel sorry and disappointed, I didn't know why. But at last, just as I was sailing by, *flash* comes the light in Mary Jane's window! and my heart swelled up sudden, like to bust; and the same second the house and all was behind me in the dark, and wasn't ever going to be before me no more in this world. She *was* the best girl I ever see, and had the most sand.

The minute I was far enough above the town to see I could make the tow-head, I begun to look sharp for a boat to borrow; and the first time the lightning showed me one that wasn't chained, I snatched it and shoved. It was a canoe, and warn't fastened with nothing but a rope. The tow-head was a rattling big distance off, away out there in the middle of the river, but I didn't lose no time; and when I struck the raft at last, I was so fagged I would a just laid down to blow and gasp if I could afforded it. But I didn't. As I sprung aboard I sung out:

"Out with you Jim, and set her loose! Glory be to goodness, we're shut of them!"

Jim lit out, and was a coming for me with both arms spread, he was so full of joy; but when I glimpsed him in the lightning, my heart shot up in my mouth, and I went overboard backwards; for I forgot he was old King Lear and a drownded A-rab all in one, and it most scared the livers and lights out of me. But Jim fished me out, and was going to hug me and bless me, and so on, he was so glad I was back and we was shut of the king and the duke, but I says:

"Not now—have it for breakfast, have it for breakfast! Cut loose and let her slide!"

So, in two seconds, away we went, a sliding down the river, and it *did* seem so good to be free again and all by ourselves on the big river and nobody to bother us. I had to skip around a bit, and jump up and crack my heels a few times, I couldn't help it; but about the third crack, I noticed a sound that I knowed mighty well—and held my breath and listened and waited—and sure enough, when the next flash busted out over the water, here they come!—

and just a laying to their oars and making their skiff hum! It was the king and the duke.

So I wilted right down onto the planks, then, and give up; and it was all I could do to keep from crying.

Chapter XXX

When they got aboard, the king went for me, and shook me by the collar, and says:

"Tryin' to give us the slip, was ye, you pup! Tired of our company—hey!"
I says:

"No, your majesty, we warn't—*please* don't, your majesty!"

"Quick, then, and tell us what *was* your idea, or I'll shake the insides out o' you!"

"Honest, I'll tell you everything, just as it happened, your majesty. The man that had aholt of me was very good to me, and kept saying he had a boy about as big as me that died last year, and he was sorry to see a boy in such a dangerous fix; and when they was all took by surprise by finding the gold, and made a rush for the coffin, he lets go of me and whispers, 'Heel it, now, or they'll hang ye, sure!' and I lit out. It didn't seem no good for *me* to stay—I couldn't do nothing, and I didn't want to be hung if I could get away. So I never stopped running till I found the canoe; and when I got here I told Jim to hurry, or they'd catch me and hang me yet, and said I was afeard you and the duke wasn't alive, now, and I was awful sorry, and so was Jim, and was awful glad when we see you coming, you may ask Jim if I didn't."

Jim said it was so; and the king told him to shut up, and said, "Oh, yes, it's *mighty* likely!" and shook me up again, and said he reckoned he'd drownded me. But the duke says:

"Leggo the boy, you old idiot! Would *you* a done any different? Did you inquire around for *him*, when you got loose? *I* don't remember it."

So the king let go of me, and begun to cuss that town and everybody in it. But the duke says:

"You better a blame sight give *yourself* a good cussing, for you're the one that's entitled to it most. You hain't done a thing, from the start, that had any sense in it, except coming out so cool and cheeky with that imaginary blue-arrow mark. That *was* bright—it was right down bully; and it was the thing that saved us. For if it hadn't been for that, they'd a jailed us till them Englishmen's baggage come—and then—the penitentiary, you bet! But that trick took 'em to the graveyard, and the gold done us a still bigger kindness; for if the excited fools hadn't let go all holts and made that rush to get a look, we'd a slept in our cravats[4] to-night—cravats warranted to *wear*, too—longer than *we'd* need 'em."

They was still a minute—thinking—then the king says, kind of absent-minded like:

"Mf! And we reckoned the *niggers* stole it!"

That made me squirm!

4. Nooses from a hanging.

"Yes," says the duke, kinder slow, and deliberate, and sarcastic, "*We* did."

After about a half a minute, the king drawls out:

"Leastways—*I* did."

The duke says, the same way:

"On the contrary—*I* did."

The king kind of ruffles up, and says:

"Looky here, Bilgewater, what'r you referrin' to?"

The duke says, pretty brisk:

"When it comes to that, maybe you'll let me ask, what was *you* referring to?"

"Shucks!" says the king, very sarcastic; "but *I* don't know—maybe you was asleep, and didn't know what you was about."

The duke bristles right up, now, and says:

"Oh, let *up* on this cussed nonsense—do you take me for a blame' fool? Don't you reckon *I* know who hid that money in that coffin?"

"*Yes,* sir! I know you *do* know—because you done it yourself!"

"It's a lie!"—and the duke went for him. The king sings out:

"Take y'r hands off!—leggo my throat!—I take it all back!"

The duke says:

"Well, you just own up, first, that you *did* hide that money there, intending to give me the slip one of these days, and come back and dig it up, and have it all to yourself."

"Wait jest a minute, duke—answer me this one question, honest and fair; if you didn't put the money there, say it, and I'll b'lieve you, and take back everything I said."

"You old scoundrel, I didn't, and you know I didn't. There, now!"

"Well, then, I b'lieve you. But answer me only jest this one more—now *don't* git mad; didn't you have it in your *mind* to hook the money and hide it?"

The duke never said nothing for a little bit; then he says:

"Well—I don't care if I *did*, I didn't *do* it, anyway. But you not only had it in mind to do it, but you *done* it."

"I wisht I may never die if I done it, duke, and that's honest. I won't say I warn't *goin'* to do it, because I *was*; but you—I mean somebody—got in ahead o' me."

"It's a lie! You done it, and you got to *say* you done it, or—"

The king begun to gurgle, and then he gasps out:

" 'Nough!—I *own up*!"

I was very glad to hear him say that, it made me feel much more easier than what I was feeling before. So the duke took his hands off, and says:

"If you ever deny it again, I'll drown you. It's *well* for you to set there and blubber like a baby—it's fitten for you, after the way you've acted. I never see such an old ostrich for wanting to gobble everything—and I a trusting you all the time, like you was my own father. You ought to be ashamed of yourself to stand by and hear it saddled onto a lot of poor niggers and you never say a word for 'em. It makes me feel ridiculous to think I was soft enough to *believe* that rubbage. Cuss you, I can see, now, why you was so anxious to make up the deffesit—you wanted to get what money I'd got out of the Nonesuch and one thing or another, and scoop it *all*!"

The king says, timid, and still a snuffling:

"Why, duke, it was you that said make up the deffersit, it warn't me."

"Dry up! I don't want to hear no more *out* of you!" says the duke. "And *now* you see what you *got* by it. They've got all their own money back, and all of *ourn* but a shekel[5] or two, *besides*. G'long to bed—and don't you deffersit *me* no more deffersits, long 's *you* live!"

So the king sneaked into the wigwam, and took to his bottle for comfort; and before long the duke tackled *his* bottle; and so in about a half an hour they was as thick as thieves again, and the tighter they got, the lovinger they got; and went off a snoring in each other's arms. They both got powerful mellow, but I noticed the king didn't get mellow enough to forget to remember to not deny about hiding the money-bag again. That made me feel easy and satisfied. Of course when they got to snoring, we had a long gabble, and I told Jim everything.

Chapter XXXI

We dasn't stop again at any town, for days and days; kept right along down the river. We was down south in the warm weather, now, and a mighty long ways from home. We begun to come to trees with Spanish moss on them, hanging down from the limbs like long gray beards. It was the first I ever see it growing, and it made the woods look solemn and dismal. So now the frauds reckoned they was out of danger, and they begun to work the villages again.

First they done a lecture on temperance; but they didn't make enough for them both to get drunk on. Then in another village they started a dancing school; but they didn't know no more how to dance than a kangaroo does; so the first prance they made, the general public jumped in and pranced them out of town. Another time they tried a go at yellocution; but they didn't yellocute long till the audience got up and give them a solid good cussing and made them skip out. They tackled missionarying, and mesmerizering, and doctoring, and telling fortunes, and a little of everything; but they couldn't seem to have no luck. So at last they got just about dead broke, and laid around the raft, as she floated along, thinking, and thinking, and never saying nothing, by the half a day at a time, and dreadful blue and desperate.

And at last they took a change, and begun to lay their heads together in the wigwam and talk low and confidential two or three hours at a time. Jim and me got uneasy. We didn't like the look of it. We judged they was studying up some kind of worse deviltry than ever. We turned it over and over, and at last we made up our minds they was going to break into somebody's house or store, or was going into the counterfeit-money business, or something. So then we was pretty scared, and made up an agreement that we wouldn't have nothing in the world to do with such actions, and if we ever got the least show we would give them the cold shake, and clear out and leave them behind. Well, early one morning we hid the raft in a good safe place about two mile below a little bit of a shabby village, named Pikesville, and the king he went ashore, and told us all to stay hid whilst he went up to town and smelt around to see if anybody had got any wind of the Royal Nonesuch there yet. ("House to rob, you *mean*," says I to myself; "and when you get through robbing it you'll come back here and wonder what's become of

---

5. Coin of ancient Israel used here colloquially to suggest a coin of low value.

me and Jim and the raft—and you'll have to take it out in wondering.") And he said if he warn't back by midday, the duke and me would know it was all right, and we was to come along.

So we staid where we was. The duke he fretted and sweated around, and was in a mighty sour way. He scolded us for everything, and we couldn't seem to do nothing right; he found fault with every little thing. Something was a-brewing, sure. I was good and glad when midday come and no king; we could have a change, anyway—and maybe a chance for *the* change, on top of it. So me and the duke went up to the village, and hunted around there for the king, and by-and-by we found him in the back room of a little low doggery,[6] very tight, and a lot of loafers bullyragging him for sport, and he a cussing and threatening with all his might, and so tight he couldn't walk, and couldn't do nothing to them. The duke he begun to abuse him for an old fool, and the king begun to sass back; and the minute they was fairly at it, I lit out, and shook the reefs out of my hind legs, and spun down the river road like a deer—for I see our chance; and I made up my mind that it would be a long day before they ever see me and Jim again. I got down there all out of breath but loaded up with joy, and sung out—

"Set her loose, Jim, we're all right, now!"

But there warn't no answer, and nobody come out of the wigwam. Jim was gone! I set up a shout—and then another—and then another one; and run this way and that in the woods, whooping and screeching; but it warn't no use—old Jim was gone. Then I set down and cried; I couldn't help it. But I couldn't set still long. Pretty soon I went out on the road, trying to think what I better do, and I run across a boy walking, and asked him if he'd seen a strange nigger, dressed so and so, and he says:

"Yes."

"Whereabouts?" says I.

"Down to Silas Phelps's place, two mile below here. He's a runaway nigger, and they've got him. Was you looking for him?"

"You bet I ain't! I run across him in the woods about an hour or two ago, and he said if I hollered he'd cut my livers out—and told me to lay down and stay where I was; and I done it. Been there ever since; afeard to come out."

"Well," he says, "you needn't be afraid no more, becuz they've got him. He run off f'm down South, som'ers."

"It's a good job they got him."

"Well, I *reckon*! There's two hundred dollars reward on him. It's like picking up money out'n the road."

"Yes, it is—and *I* could a had it if I'd been big enough; I see him *first*. Who nailed him?"

"It was an old fellow—a stranger—and he sold out his chance in him for forty dollars, becuz he's got to go up the river and can't wait. Think o' that, now! You bet *I'd* wait, if it was seven year."

"That's me, every time," says I. "But maybe his chance ain't worth no more than that, if he'll sell it so cheap. Maybe there's something ain't straight about it."

"But it *is*, though—straight as a string. I see the handbill myself. It tells all about him, to a dot—paints him like a picture, and tells the plantation

6. Cheap barroom.

he's frum, below New*rleans*. No-siree-*bob*, they ain't no trouble 'bout *that* speculation, you bet you. Say, gimme a chaw tobacker, won't ye?"

I didn't have none, so he left. I went to the raft, and set down in the wig-wam to think. But I couldn't come to nothing. I thought till I wore my head sore, but I couldn't see no way out of the trouble. After all this long journey, and after all we'd done for them scoundrels, here was it all come to noth-ing, everything all busted up and ruined, because they could have the heart to serve Jim such a trick as that, and make him a slave again all his life, and amongst strangers, too, for forty dirty dollars.

Once I said to myself it would be a thousand times better for Jim to be a slave at home where his family was, as long as he'd *got* to be a slave, and so I'd better write a letter to Tom Sawyer and tell him to tell Miss Watson where he was. But I soon give up that notion, for two things: she'd be mad and disgusted at his rascality and ungratefulness for leaving her, and so she'd sell him straight down the river again; and if she didn't, everybody naturally despises an ungrateful nigger, and they'd make Jim feel it all the time, and so he'd feel ornery and disgraced. And then think of *me*! It would get all around, that Huck Finn helped a nigger to get his freedom; and if I was to ever see anybody from that town again, I'd be ready to get down and lick his boots for shame. That's just the way: a person does a low-down thing, and then he don't want to take no consequences of it. Thinks as long as he can hide it, it ain't no disgrace. That was my fix exactly. The more I studied about this, the more my conscience went to grinding me, and the more wicked and low-down and ornery I got to feeling. And at last, when it hit me all of a sudden that here was the plain hand of Providence slapping me in the face and letting me know my wickedness was being watched all the time from up there in heaven, whilst I was stealing a poor old woman's nigger that hadn't ever done me no harm, and now was showing me there's One that's always on the lookout, and ain't agoing to allow no such miserable doings to go only just so fur and no further, I most dropped in my tracks I was so scared. Well, I tried the best I could to kinder soften it up somehow for myself, by saying I was brung up wicked, and so I warn't so much to blame; but something inside of me kept saying, "There was the Sunday school, you could a gone to it; and if you'd a done it they'd a learnt you, there, that people that acts as I'd been acting about the nigger goes to everlasting fire."

It made me shiver. And I about made up my mind to pray; and see if I couldn't try to quit being the kind of a boy I was, and be better. So I kneeled down. But the words wouldn't come. Why wouldn't they? It warn't no use to try and hide it from Him. Nor from *me*, neither. I knowed very well why they wouldn't come. It was because my heart warn't right; it was because I warn't square; it was because I was playing double. I was letting *on* to give up sin, but away inside of me I was holding on to the biggest one of all. I was trying to make my mouth *say* I would do the right thing and the clean thing, and go and write to that nigger's owner and tell where he was; but deep down in me I knowed it was a lie—and He knowed it. You can't pray a lie—I found that out.

So I was full of trouble, full as I could be; and didn't know what to do. At last I had an idea; and I says, I'll go and write the letter—and *then* see if I can pray. Why, it was astonishing, the way I felt as light as a feather, right straight off, and my troubles all gone. So I got a piece of paper and a pencil, all glad and excited, and set down and wrote:

Miss Watson your runaway nigger Jim is down here two mile below Pikesville and Mr. Phelps has got him and he will give him up for the reward if you send.

Huck Finn.

I felt good and all washed clean of sin for the first time I had ever felt so in my life, and I knowed I could pray now. But I didn't do it straight off, but laid the paper down and set there thinking—thinking how good it was all this happened so, and how near I come to being lost and going to hell. And went on thinking. And got to thinking over our trip down the river; and I see Jim before me, all the time, in the day, and in the night-time, sometimes moonlight, sometimes storms, and we a floating along, talking, and singing, and laughing. But somehow I couldn't seem to strike no places to harden me against him, but only the other kind. I'd see him standing my watch on top of his'n, stead of calling me, so I could go on sleeping; and see him how glad he was when I come back out of the fog; and when I come to him again in the swamp, up there where the feud was; and such-like times; and would always call me honey, and pet me, and do everything he could think of for me, and how good he always was; and at last I struck the time I saved him by telling the men we had small-pox aboard, and he was so grateful, and said I was the best friend old Jim ever had in the world, and the *only* one he's got now; and then I happened to look around, and see that paper.

It was a close place. I took it up, and held it in my hand. I was a trembling, because I'd got to decide, forever, betwixt two things, and I knowed it. I studied a minute, sort of holding my breath, and then says to myself:

"All right, then, I'll *go* to hell"—and tore it up.

It was awful thoughts, and awful words, but they was said. And I let them stay said; and never thought no more about reforming. I shoved the whole thing out of my head; and said I would take up wickedness again, which was in my line, being brung up to it, and the other warn't. And for a starter, I would go to work and steal Jim out of slavery again; and if I could think up anything worse, I would do that, too; because as long as I was in, and in for good, I might as well go the whole hog.

Then I set to thinking over how to get at it, and turned over considerable many ways in my mind; and at last fixed up a plan that suited me. So then I took the bearings of a woody island that was down the river a piece, and as soon as it was fairly dark I crept out with my raft and went for it, and hid it there, and then turned in. I slept the night through, and got up before it was light, and had my breakfast, and put on my store clothes, and tied up some others and one thing or another in a bundle, and took the canoe and cleared for shore. I landed below where I judged was Phelps's place, and hid my bundle in the woods, and then filled up the canoe with water, and loaded rocks into her and sunk her where I could find her again when I wanted her, about a quarter of a mile below a little steam sawmill that was on the bank.

Then I struck up the road, and when I passed the mill I see a sign on it, "Phelps's Sawmill," and when I come to the farmhouses, two or three hundred yards further along, I kept my eyes peeled, but didn't see nobody around, though it was good daylight, now. But I didn't mind, because I didn't want to see nobody just yet—I only wanted to get the lay of the land. According to my plan, I was going to turn up there from the village, not from below.

So I just took a look, and shoved along, straight for town. Well, the very first man I see, when I got there, was the duke. He was sticking up a bill for the Royal Nonesuch—three-night performance—like that other time. *They* had the cheek, them frauds! I was right on him, before I could shirk. He looked astonished, and says:

"Hel-*lo*! Where'd *you* come from?" Then he says, kind of glad and eager, "Where's the raft?—got her in a good place?"

I says:

"Why, that's just what I was agoing to ask your grace."

Then he didn't look so joyful—and says:

"What was your idea for asking *me*?" he says.

"Well," I says, "when I see the king in that doggery yesterday, I says to myself, we can't get him home for hours, till he's soberer; so I went a loafing around town to put in the time, and wait. A man up and offered me ten cents to help him pull a skiff over the river and back to fetch a sheep, and so I went along; but when we was dragging him to the boat, and the man left me aholt of the rope and went behind him to shove him along, he was too strong for me, and jerked loose and run, and we after him. We didn't have no dog, and so we had to chase him all over the country till we tired him out. We never got him till dark, then we fetched him over, and I started down for the raft. When I got there and see it was gone, I says to myself, 'they've got into trouble and had to leave; and they've took my nigger, which is the only nigger I've got in the world, and now I'm in a strange country, and ain't got no property no more, nor nothing, and no way to make my living'; so I set down and cried. I slept in the woods all night. But what *did* become of the raft then?—and Jim, poor Jim!"

"Blamed if *I* know—that is, what's become of the raft. That old fool had made a trade and got forty dollars, and when we found him in the doggery the loafers had matched half dollars with him and got every cent but what he'd spent for whiskey; and when I got him home late last night and found the raft gone, we said, 'That little rascal has stole our raft and shook us, and run off down the river.'"

"I wouldn't shake my *nigger*, would I?—the only nigger I had in the world, and the only property."

"We never thought of that. Fact is, I reckon we'd come to consider him *our* nigger; yes, we did consider him so—goodness knows we had trouble enough for him. So when we see the raft was gone, and we flat broke, there warn't anything for it but to try the Royal Nonesuch another shake. And I've pegged along ever since, dry as a powderhorn. Where's that ten cents? Give it here."

I had considerable money, so I give him ten cents, but begged him to spend it for something to eat, and give me some, because it was all the money I had, and I hadn't had nothing to eat since yesterday. He never said nothing. The next minute he whirls on me and says:

"Do you reckon that nigger would blow on us? We'd skin him if he done that!"

"How can he blow? Hain't he run off?"

"No! That old fool sold him, and never divided with me, and the money's gone."

"*Sold* him?" I says, and begun to cry; "why, he was *my* nigger, and that was my money. Where is he?—I want my nigger."

"Well, you can't *get* your nigger, that's all—so dry up your blubbering. Looky here—do you think *you'd* venture to blow on us? Blamed if I think I'd trust you. Why, if you *was* to blow on us—"

He stopped, but I never see the duke look so ugly out of his eyes before. I went on a-whimpering, and says:

"I don't want to blow on nobody; and I ain't got no time to blow, nohow. I got to turn out and find my nigger."

He looked kinder bothered, and stood there with his bills fluttering on his arm, thinking, and wrinkling up his forehead. At last he says:

"I'll tell you something. We got to be here three days. If you'll promise you won't blow, and won't let the nigger blow, I'll tell you where to find him."

So I promised, and he says:

"A farmer by the name of Silas Ph—" and then he stopped. You see he started to tell me the truth; but when he stopped, that way, and begun to study and think again, I reckoned he was changing his mind. And so he was. He wouldn't trust me; he wanted to make sure of having me out of the way the whole three days. So pretty soon he says: "The man that bought him is named Abram Foster—Abram G. Foster—and he lives forty mile back here in the country, on the road to Lafayette."

"All right," I says, "I can walk it in three days. And I'll start this very afternoon."

"No you won't, you'll start *now*; and don't you lose any time about it, neither, nor do any gabbling by the way. Just keep a tight tongue in your head and move right along, and then you won't get into trouble with *us*, d'ye hear?"

That was the order I wanted, and that was the one I played for. I wanted to be left free to work my plans.

"So clear out," he says; "and you can tell Mr. Foster whatever you want to. Maybe you can get him to believe that Jim *is* your nigger—some idiots don't require documents—leastways I've heard there's such down South here. And when you tell him the handbill and the reward's bogus, maybe he'll believe you when you explain to him what the idea was for getting 'em out. Go 'long, now, and tell him anything you want to; but mind you don't work your jaw any *between* here and there."

So I left, and struck for the back country. I didn't look around, but I kinder felt like he was watching me. But I knowed I could tire him out at that. I went straight out in the country as much as a mile, before I stopped; then I doubled back through the woods towards Phelps's. I reckoned I better start in on my plan straight off, without fooling around, because I wanted to stop Jim's mouth till these fellows could get away. I didn't want no trouble with their kind. I'd seen all I wanted to of them, and wanted to get entirely shut of them.

Chapter XXXII

When I got there it was all still and Sunday-like, and hot and sunshiny— the hands was gone to the fields; and there was them kind of faint dronings of bugs and flies in the air that makes it seem so lonesome and like everybody's dead and gone; and if a breeze fans along and quivers the leaves, it makes you feel mournful, because you feel like it's spirits whispering— spirits that's been dead ever so many years—and you always think they're talking about *you*. As a general thing it makes a body wish *he* was dead, too, and done with it all.

Phelps's was one of these little one-horse cotton plantations; and they all look alike. A rail fence round a two-acre yard; a stile, made out of logs sawed off and up-ended, in steps, like barrels of a different length, to climb over the fence with, and for the women to stand on when they are going to jump onto a horse; some sickly grass-patches in the big yard, but mostly it was bare and smooth, like an old hat with the nap rubbed off; big double log house for the white folks—hewed logs, with the chinks stopped up with mud or mortar, and these mud-stripes been whitewashed some time or another; round-log kitchen, with a big broad, open but roofed passage joining it to the house; log smoke-house back of the kitchen; three little log nigger-cabins in a row t'other side the smokehouse; one little hut all by itself away down against the back fence, and some outbuildings down a piece the other side; ash-hopper,[7] and big kettle to bile soap in, by the little hut; bench by the kitchen door, with bucket of water and a gourd; hound asleep there, in the sun; more hounds asleep, round about; about three shade-trees away off in a corner; some currant bushes and gooseberry bushes in one place by the fence; outside of the fence a garden and a water-melon patch; then the cotton fields begins; and after the fields, the woods.

I went around and clumb over the back stile by the ash-hopper, and started for the kitchen. When I got a little ways, I heard the dim hum of a spinning-wheel wailing along up and sinking along down again; and then I knowed for certain I wished I was dead—for that *is* the lonesomest sound in the whole world.

I went right along, not fixing up any particular plan, but just trusting to Providence to put the right words in my mouth when the time come; for I'd noticed that Providence always did put the right words in my mouth, if I left it alone.

When I got half-way, first one hound and then another got up and went for me, and of course I stopped and faced them, and kept still. And such another pow-wow as they made! In a quarter of a minute I was a kind of a hub of a wheel, as you may say—spokes made out of dogs—circle of fifteen of them packed together around me, with their necks and noses stretched up towards me, a barking and howling; and more a coming; you could see them sailing over fences and around corners from everywheres.

A nigger woman come tearing out of the kitchen with a rolling-pin in her hand, singing out, "Begone! *you* Tige! you Spot! begone, sah!" and she fetched first one and then another of them a clip and sent him howling, and then the rest followed; and the next second, half of them come back, wagging their tails around me and making friends with me. There ain't no harm in a hound, nohow.

And behind the woman comes a little nigger girl and two little nigger boys, without anything on but tow-linen shirts, and they hung onto their mother's gown, and peeped out from behind her at me, bashful, the way they always do. And here comes the white woman running from the house, about forty-five or fifty year old, bare-headed, and her spinning-stick in her hand; and behind her comes her little white children, acting the same way the little

7. A container for lye used in making soap.

niggers was doing. She was smiling all over so she could hardly stand—and says:

"It's *you*, at last!—*ain't* it?"

I out with a "Yes'm," before I thought.

She grabbed me and hugged me tight; and then gripped me by both hands and shook and shook; and the tears come in her eyes, and run down over; and she couldn't seem to hug and shake enough, and kept saying, "You don't look as much like your mother as I reckoned you would, but law sakes, I don't care for that, I'm *so* glad to see you! Dear, dear, it does seem like I could eat you up! Children, it's your cousin Tom!—tell him howdy."

But they ducked their heads, and put their fingers in their mouths, and hid behind her. So she run on:

"Lize, hurry up and get him a hot breakfast, right away—or did you get your breakfast on the boat?"

I said I had got it on the boat. So then she started for the house, leading me by the hand, and the children tagging after. When we got there, she set me down in a split-bottomed chair, and set herself down on a little low stool in front of me, holding both of my hands, and says:

"Now I can have a *good* look at you; and laws-a-me, I've been hungry for it a many and a many a time, all these long years, and it's come at last! We been expecting you a couple of days and more. What's kep' you?—boat get aground?"

"Yes'm—she—"

"Don't say yes'm—say Aunt Sally. Where'd she get aground?"

I didn't rightly know what to say, because I didn't know whether the boat would be coming up the river or down. But I go a good deal on instinct; and my instinct said she would be coming up—from down toward Orleans. That didn't help me much, though; for I didn't know the names of bars down that way. I see I'd got to invent a bar, or forget the name of the one we got aground on—or—Now I struck an idea, and fetched it out:

"It warn't the grounding—that didn't keep us back but a little. We blowed out a cylinder-head."

"Good gracious! anybody hurt?"

"No'm. Killed a nigger."

"Well, it's lucky; because sometimes people do get hurt. Two years ago last Christmas, your uncle Silas was coming up from Newrleans on the old *Lally Rook*,[8] and she blowed out a cylinder-head and crippled a man. And I think he died afterwards. He was a Babtist. Your uncle Silas knowed a family in Baton Rouge that knowed his people very well. Yes, I remember, now he *did* die. Mortification[9] set in, and they had to amputate him. But it didn't save him. Yes, it was mortification—that was it. He turned blue all over, and died in the hope of a glorious resurrection. They say he was a sight to look at. Your uncle's been up to the town every day to fetch you. And he's gone again, not more'n an hour ago; he'll be back any minute, now. You must a met him on the road, didn't you?—oldish man, with a—"

"No, I didn't see nobody, Aunt Sally. The boat landed just at daylight, and I left my baggage on the wharf-boat and went looking around the town

8. "Lalla Rookh" (1817), a popular Romantic poem by the Irish poet Thomas Moore (1779–1852).   9. Gangrene.

and out a piece in the country, to put in the time and not get here too soon; and so I come down the back way."

"Who'd you give the baggage to?"

"Nobody."

"Why, child, it'll be stole!"

"Not where *I* hid it I reckon it won't," I says.

"How'd you get your breakfast so early on the boat?"

It was kinder thin ice, but I says:

"The captain see me standing around, and told me I better have something to eat before I went ashore; so he took me in the texas to the officers' lunch, and give me all I wanted."

I was getting so uneasy I couldn't listen good. I had my mind on the children all the time; I wanted to get them out to one side, and pump them a little, and find out who I was. But I couldn't get no show, Mrs. Phelps kept it up and run on so. Pretty soon she made the cold chills streak all down my back, because she says:

"But here we're a running on this way, and you hain't told me a word about Sis, nor any of them. Now I'll rest my works a little, and you start up yourn; just tell me *everything*—tell me all about 'm all—every one of 'm; and how they are, and what they're doing, and what they told you to tell me; and every last thing you can think of."

Well, I see I was up a stump—and up it good. Providence had stood by me this fur, all right, but I was hard and tight aground, now. I see it warn't a bit of use to try to go ahead—I'd *got* to throw up my hand. So I says to myself, here's another place where I got to resk the truth. I opened my mouth to begin; but she grabbed me and hustled me in behind the bed, and says:

"Here he comes! stick your head down lower—there, that'll do; you can't be seen, now. Don't you let on you're here. I'll play a joke on him. Children, don't you say a word."

I see I was in a fix, now. But it warn't no use to worry; there warn't nothing to do but just hold still, and try to be ready to stand from under when the lightning struck.

I had just one little glimpse of the old gentleman when he come in, then the bed hid him. Mrs. Phelps she jumps for him and says:

"Has he come?"

"No," says her husband.

"Good-*ness* gracious!" she says, "what in the world *can* have become of him?"

"I can't imagine," says the old gentleman; "and I must say, it makes me dreadful uneasy."

"Uneasy!" she says, "I'm ready to go distracted! He *must* a come; and you've missed him along the road. I *know* it's so—something *tells* me so."

"Why Sally, I *couldn't* miss him along the road—*you* know that."

"But oh, dear, dear, what *will* Sis say! He must a come! You must a missed him. He—"

"Oh, don't distress me any more'n I'm already distressed. I don't know what in the world to make of it. I'm at my wit's end, and I don't mind acknowledging 't I'm right down scared. But there's no hope that he's come; for he *couldn't* come and me miss him. Sally, it's terrible—just terrible—something's happened to the boat, sure!"

"Why, Silas! Look yonder!—up the road!—ain't that somebody coming?"

He sprung to the window at the head of the bed, and that give Mrs. Phelps the chance she wanted. She stooped down quick, at the foot of the bed, and give me a pull, and out I come; and when he turned back from the window, there she stood, a-beaming and a-smiling like a house afire, and I standing pretty meek and sweaty alongside. The old gentleman stared, and says:

"Why, who's that?"

"Who do you reckon 't is?"

"I hain't no idea. Who *is* it?"

"It's *Tom Sawyer!*"

By jings, I most slumped through the floor. But there warn't no time to swap knives;[1] the old man grabbed me by the hand and shook, and kept on shaking; and all the time, how the woman did dance around and laugh and cry; and then how they both did fire off questions about Sid, and Mary, and the rest of the tribe.

But if they was joyful, it warn't nothing to what I was; for it was like being born again, I was so glad to find out who I was. Well, they froze to me for two hours; and at last when my chin was so tired it couldn't hardly go, any more, I had told them more about my family—I mean the Sawyer family—than ever happened to any six Sawyer families. And I explained all about how we blowed out a cylinder-head at the mouth of the White River[2] and it took us three days to fix it. Which was all right, and worked first rate; because *they* didn't know but what it would take three days to fix it. If I'd a called it a bolt-head it would a done just as well.

Now I was feeling pretty comfortable all down one side, and pretty uncomfortable all up the other. Being Tom Sawyer was easy and comfortable; and it stayed easy and comfortable till by-and-by I hear a steamboat coughing along down the river—then I says to myself, spose Tom Sawyer come down on that boat?—and spose he steps in here, any minute, and sings out my name before I can throw him a wink to keep quiet? Well, I couldn't *have* it that way—it wouldn't do at all. I must go up the road and waylay him. So I told the folks I reckoned I would go up to the town and fetch down my baggage. The old gentleman was for going along with me, but I said no, I could drive the horse myself, and I druther he wouldn't take no trouble about me.

Chapter XXXIII

So I started for town, in the wagon, and when I was half-way I see a wagon coming, and sure enough it was Tom Sawyer, and I stopped and waited till he come along. I says "Hold on!" and it stopped alongside, and his mouth opened up like a trunk, and staid so; and he swallowed two or three times like a person that's got a dry throat, and then says:

"I hain't ever done you no harm. You know that. So then, what you want to come back and ha'nt *me* for?"

I says:

"I hain't come back—I hain't been *gone*."

When he heard my voice, it righted him up some, but he warn't quite satisfied yet. He says:

---

1. I.e., change plans.
2. The White River meets the Mississippi in Desha County, Arkansas.

"Don't you play nothing on me, because I wouldn't on you. Honest injun, now, you ain't a ghost?"

"Honest injun, I ain't," I says.

"Well—I—I—well, that ought to settle it, of course; but I can't somehow seem to understand it, no way. Looky here, warn't you ever murdered *at all?*"

"No. I warn't ever murdered at all—I played it on them. You come in here and feel of me if you don't believe me."

So he done it; and it satisfied him; and he was that glad to see me again, he didn't know what to do. And he wanted to know all about it right off; because it was a grand adventure, and mysterious, and so it hit him where he lived. But I said, leave it along till by-and-by; and told his driver to wait, and we drove off a little piece, and I told him the kind of a fix I was in, and what did he reckon we better do? He said, let him alone a minute, and don't disturb him. So he thought and thought, and pretty soon he says:

"It's all right, I've got it. Take my trunk in your wagon, and let on it's your'n; and you turn back and fool along slow, so as to get to the house about the time you ought to; and I'll go towards town a piece, and take a fresh start, and get there a quarter or a half an hour after you; and you needn't let on to know me, at first."

I says:

"All right; but wait a minute. There's one more thing—a thing that *nobody* don't know but me. And that is, there's a nigger here that I'm trying to steal out of slavery—and his name is *Jim*—old Miss Watson's Jim."

He says:

"What! Why Jim is—"

He stopped and went to studying. I says:

"*I* know what you'll say. You'll say it's dirty low-down business; but what if it is?—*I'm* low down; and I'm agoing to steal him, and I want you to keep mum and not let on. Will you?"

His eye lit up, and he says:

"I'll *help* you steal him!"

Well, I let go all holts then, like I was shot. It was the most astonishing speech I ever heard—and I'm bound to say Tom Sawyer fell, considerable, in my estimation. Only I couldn't believe it. Tom Sawyer a *nigger stealer!*

"Oh, shucks," I says, "you're joking."

"I ain't joking, either."

"Well, then," I says, "joking or no joking, if you hear anything said about a runaway nigger, don't forget to remember that *you* don't know nothing about him, and *I* don't know nothing about him."

Then we took the trunk and put it in my wagon, and he drove off his way, and I drove mine. But of course I forgot all about driving slow, on accounts of being glad and full of thinking; so I got home a heap too quick for that length of trip. The old gentleman was at the door, and he says:

"Why, this is wonderful. Who ever would a thought it was in that mare to do it. I wish we'd a timed her. And she hain't sweated a hair—not a hair. It's wonderful. Why, I wouldn't take a hundred dollars for that horse now; I wouldn't, honest; and yet I'd a sold her for fifteen before, and thought 'twas all she was worth."

That's all he said. He was the innocentest, best old soul I ever see. But it warn't surprising; because he warn't only just a farmer, he was a preacher, too, and had a little one-horse log church down back of the plantation, which he built it himself at his own expense, for a church and school-house, and never charged nothing for his preaching, and it was worth it, too. There was plenty other farmer-preachers like that, and done the same way, down South.

In about half an hour Tom's wagon drove up to the front stile, and Aunt Sally she see it through the window because it was only about fifty yards, and says:

"Why, there's somebody come! I wonder who 'tis? Why, I do believe it's a stranger. Jimmy" (that's one of the children), "run and tell Lize to put on another plate for dinner."

Everybody made a rush for the front door, because, of course, a stranger don't come *every* year, and so he lays over the yaller fever, for interest, when he does come. Tom was over the stile and starting for the house; the wagon was spinning up the road for the village, and we was all bunched in the front door. Tom had his store clothes on, and an audience—and that was always nuts for Tom Sawyer. In them circumstances it warn't no trouble to him to throw in an amount of style that was suitable. He warn't a boy to meeky along up that yard like a sheep; no, he come ca'm and important, like the ram. When he got afront of us, he lifts his hat ever so gracious and dainty, like it was the lid of a box that had butterflies asleep in it and he didn't want to disturb them, and says:

"Mr. Archibald Nichols, I presume?"

"No, my boy," says the old gentleman, "I'm sorry to say 't your driver has deceived you; Nichols's place is down a matter of three mile more. Come in, come in."

Tom he took a look back over his shoulder, and says, "Too late—he's out of sight."

"Yes, he's gone, my son, and you must come in and eat your dinner with us; and then we'll hitch up and take you down to Nichols's."

"Oh, I *can't* make you so much trouble; I couldn't think of it. I'll walk—I don't mind the distance."

"But we won't *let* you walk—it wouldn't be Southern hospitality to do it. Come right in."

"Oh, *do*," says Aunt Sally; "it ain't a bit of trouble to us, not a bit in the world. You *must* stay. It's a long, dusty three mile, and we *can't* let you walk. And besides, I've already told 'em to put on another plate, when I see you coming; so you mustn't disappoint us. Come right in, and make yourself at home."

So Tom he thanked them very hearty and handsome, and let himself be persuaded, and come in; and when he was in, he said he was a stranger from Hicksville, Ohio, and his name was William Thompson—and he made another bow.

Well, he run on, and on, and on, making up stuff about Hicksville and everybody in it he could invent, and I getting a little nervous, and wondering how this was going to help me out of my scrape; and at last, still talking along, he reached over and kissed Aunt Sally right on the mouth, and then settled back again in his chair, comfortable, and was going on talking; but she jumped up and wiped it off with the back of her hand, and says:

"You owdacious puppy!"

He looked kind of hurt, and says:

"I'm surprised at you, m'am."

"You're s'rp—Why, what do you reckon *I* am? I've a good notion to take and—say, what do you mean by kissing me?"

He looked kind of humble, and says:

"I didn't mean nothing, m'am. I didn't mean no harm. I—I—thought you'd like it."

"Why, you born fool!" She took up the spinning-stick, and it looked like it was all she could do to keep from giving him a crack with it. "What made you think I'd like it?"

"Well, I don't know. Only, they—they—told me you would."

"*They* told you I would. Whoever told you's *another* lunatic. I never heard the beat of it. Who's *they*?"

"Why—everybody. They all said so, m'am."

It was all she could do to hold in; and her eyes snapped, and her fingers worked like she wanted to scratch him; and she says:

"Who's everybody? Out with their names—or ther'll be an idiot short."

He got up and looked distressed, and fumbled his hat, and says:

"I'm sorry, and I warn't expecting it. They told me to. They all told me to. They all said kiss her; and said she'll like it. They all said it—every one of them. But I'm sorry, m'am, and I won't do it no more—I won't, honest."

"You won't, won't you? Well, I sh'd *reckon* you won't!"

"No'm, I'm honest about it; I won't ever do it again. Till you ask me."

"Till *I* ask you! Well, I never see the beat of it in my born days! I lay you'll be the Methusalem-numskull[3] of creation before ever *I* ask you—or the likes of you."

"Well," he says, "it does surprise me so. I can't make it out, somehow. They said you would, and I thought you would. But—" He stopped and looked around slow, like he wished he could run across a friendly eye, somewhere's; and fetched up on the old gentleman's, and says, "Didn't *you* think she'd like me to kiss her, sir?"

"Why, no, I—I—well, no, I b'lieve I didn't."

Then he looks on around, the same way, to me—and says:

"Tom, didn't *you* think Aunt Sally 'd open out her arms and say, 'Sid Sawyer—'"

"My land!" she says, breaking in and jumping for him, "you impudent young rascal, to fool a body so—" and was going to hug him, but he fended her off, and says:

"No, not till you've asked me, first."

So she didn't lose no time, but asked him; and hugged him and kissed him, over and over again, and then turned him over to the old man, and he took what was left. And after they got a little quiet again, she says:

"Why, dear me, I never see such a surprise. We warn't looking for *you*, at all, but only Tom. Sis never wrote to me about anybody coming but him."

"It's because it warn't *intended* for any of us to come but Tom," he says; "but I begged and begged, and at the last minute she let me come, too; so, coming down the river, me and Tom thought it would be a first-rate surprise for him to come here to the house first, and for me to by-and-by tag along

---

3. Methuselah was a biblical patriarch said to have lived 969 years.

and drop in and let on to be a stranger. But it was a mistake, Aunt Sally. This ain't no healthy place for a stranger to come."

"No—not impudent whelps, Sid. You ought to had your jaws boxed; I hain't been so put out since I don't know when. But I don't care, I don't mind the terms—I'd be willing to stand a thousand such jokes to have you here. Well, to think of that performance! I don't deny it, I was most putrified[4] with astonishment when you give me that smack."

We had dinner out in that broad open passage betwixt the house and the kitchen; and there was things enough on that table for seven families—and all hot, too; none of your flabby tough meat that's laid in a cupboard in a damp cellar all night and tastes like a hunk of old cold cannibal in the morning. Uncle Silas he asked a pretty long blessing over it, but it was worth it; and it didn't cool it a bit, neither, the way I've seen them kind of interruptions do, lots of times.

There was a considerable good deal of talk, all the afternoon, and me and Tom was on the lookout all the time, but it warn't no use, they didn't happen to say nothing about any runaway nigger, and we was afraid to try to work up to it. But at supper, at night, one of the little boys says:

"Pa, mayn't Tom and Sid and me go to the show?"

"No," says the old man, "I reckon there ain't going to be any; and you couldn't go if there was; because the runaway nigger told Burton and me all about that scandalous show, and Burton said he would tell the people; so I reckon they've drove the owdacious loafers out of town before this time."

So there it was!—but I couldn't help it. Tom and me was to sleep in the same room and bed; so, being tired, we bid good-night and went up to bed, right after supper, and clumb out of the window and down the lightning-rod, and shoved for the town; for I didn't believe anybody was going to give the king and the duke a hint, and so, if I didn't hurry up and give them one they'd get into trouble sure.

On the road Tom he told me all about how it was reckoned I was murdered, and how pap disappeared, pretty soon, and didn't come back no more, and what a stir there was when Jim run away; and I told Tom all about our Royal Nonesuch rapscallions, and as much of the raft-voyage as I had time to; and as we struck into the town and up through the middle of it—it was as much as half-after eight, then—here comes a raging rush of people, with torches, and an awful whooping and yelling, and banging tin pans and blowing horns; and we jumped to one side to let them go by; and as they went by, I see they had the king and the duke astraddle of a rail—that is, I knowed it *was* the king and the duke, though they was all over tar and feathers, and didn't look like nothing in the world that was human—just looked like a couple of monstrous big soldier-plumes. Well, it made me sick to see it; and I was sorry for them poor pitiful rascals, it seemed like I couldn't ever feel any hardness against them any more in the world. It was a dreadful thing to see. Human beings *can* be awful cruel to one another.

We see we was too late—couldn't do no good. We asked some stragglers about it, and they said everybody went to the show looking very innocent; and laid low and kept dark till the poor old king was in the middle of his

---

4. Petrified or stunned.

cavortings on the stage; then somebody give a signal, and the house rose up and went for them.

So we poked along back home, and I warn't feeling so brash as I was before, but kind of ornery, and humble, and to blame, somehow—though I hadn't done anything. But that's always the way; it don't make no difference whether you do right or wrong, a person's conscience ain't got no sense, and just goes for him *anyway*. If I had a yaller dog that didn't know no more than a person's conscience does, I would pison him. It takes up more room than all the rest of a person's insides, and yet ain't no good, nohow. Tom Sawyer he says the same.

Chapter XXXIV

We stopped talking, and got to thinking. By-and-by Tom says:

"Looky here, Huck, what fools we are, to not think of it before! I bet I know where Jim is."

"No! Where?"

"In that hut down by the ash-hopper. Why, looky here. When we was at dinner, didn't you see a nigger man go in there with some vittles?"

"Yes."

"What did you think the vittles was for?"

"For a dog."

"So'd I. Well, it wasn't for a dog."

"Why?"

"Because part of it was watermelon."

"So it was—I noticed it. Well, it does beat all, that I never thought about a dog not eating watermelon. It shows how a body can see and don't see at the same time."

"Well, the nigger unlocked the padlock when he went in, and he locked it again when he come out. He fetched uncle a key, about the time we got up from table—same key, I bet. Watermelon shows man, lock shows prisoner; and it ain't likely there's two prisoners on such a little plantation, and where the people's all so kind and good. Jim's the prisoner. All right—I'm glad we found it out detective fashion; I wouldn't give shucks for any other way. Now you work your mind and study out a plan to steal Jim, and I will study out one, too; and we'll take the one we like the best."

What a head for just a boy to have! If I had Tom Sawyer's head, I wouldn't trade it off to be a duke, nor mate of a steamboat, nor clown in a circus, nor nothing I can think of. I went to thinking out a plan, but only just to be doing something; I knowed very well where the right plan was going to come from. Pretty soon, Tom says:

"Ready?"

"Yes," I says.

"All right—bring it out."

"My plan is this," I says. "We can easy find out if it's Jim in there. Then get up my canoe to-morrow night, and fetch my raft over from the island. Then the first dark night that comes, steal the key out of the old man's britches, after he goes to bed, and shove off down the river on the raft, with Jim, hiding daytimes and running nights, the way me and Jim used to do before. Wouldn't that plan work?"

"*Work?* Why cert'nly, it would work, like rats a fighting. But it's too blame' simple; there ain't nothing *to* it. What's the good of a plan that ain't no more trouble than that? It's as mild as goose-milk. Why, Huck, it wouldn't make no more talk than breaking into a soap factory."

I never said nothing, because I warn't expecting nothing different; but I knowed mighty well that whenever he got *his* plan ready it wouldn't have none of them objections to it.

And it didn't. He told me what it was, and I see in a minute it was worth fifteen of mine, for style, and would make Jim just as free a man as mine would, and maybe get us all killed besides. So I was satisfied, and said we would waltz in on it. I needn't tell what it was, here, because I knowed it wouldn't stay the way it was. I knowed he would be changing it around, every which way, as we went along, and heaving in new bullinesses wherever he got a chance. And that is what he done.

Well, one thing was dead sure; and that was, that Tom Sawyer was in earnest and was actuly going to help steal that nigger out of slavery. That was the thing that was too many for me. Here was a boy that was respectable, and well brung up; and had a character to lose; and folks at home that had characters; and he was bright and not leather-headed; and knowing and not ignorant; and not mean, but kind; and yet here he was, without any more pride, or rightness, or feeling, than to stoop to this business, and make himself a shame, and his family a shame, before everybody. I *couldn't* understand it, no way at all. It was outrageous, and I knowed I ought to just up and tell him so; and so be his true friend, and let him quit the thing right where he was, and save himself. And I *did* start to tell him; but he shut me up, and says:

"Don't you reckon I know what I'm about? Don't I generly know what I'm about?"

"Yes."

"Didn't I *say* I was going to help steal the nigger?"

"Yes."

"*Well* then."

That's all he said, and that's all I said. It warn't no use to say any more; because when he said he'd do a thing, he always done it. But *I* couldn't make out how he was willing to go into this thing; so I just let it go, and never bothered no more about it. If he was bound to have it so, I couldn't help it.

When we got home, the house was all dark and still; so we went on down to the hut by the ash-hopper, for to examine it. We went through the yard, so as to see what the hounds would do. They knowed us, and didn't make no more noise than country dogs is always doing when anything comes by in the night. When we got to the cabin, we took a look at the front and the two sides; and on the side I warn't acquainted with—which was the north side—we found a square window-hole, up tolerable high, with just one stout board nailed across it. I says:

"Here's the ticket. This hole's big enough for Jim to get through, if we wrench off the board."

Tom says:

"It's as simple as tit-tat-toe, three-in-a-row, and as easy as playing hooky. I should *hope* we can find a way that's a little more complicated than *that*, Huck Finn."

"Well, then," I says, "how'll it do to saw him out, the way I done before I was murdered, that time?"

"That's more *like*," he says, "It's real mysterious, and troublesome, and good," he says; "but I bet we can find a way that's twice as long. There ain't no hurry; le's keep on looking around."

Betwixt the hut and the fence, on the back side, was a lean-to, that joined the hut at the eaves, and was made out of plank. It was as long as the hut, but narrow—only about six foot wide. The door to it was at the south end, and was padlocked. Tom he went to the soap kettle, and searched around and fetched back the iron thing they lift the lid with; so he took it and prized out one of the staples. The chain fell down, and we opened the door and went in, and shut it, and struck a match, and see the shed was only built against the cabin and hadn't no connection with it; and there warn't no floor to the shed, nor nothing in it but some old rusty played-out hoes, and spades, and picks, and a crippled plow. The match went out, and so did we, and shoved in the staple again, and the door was locked as good as ever. Tom was joyful. He says:

"Now we're all right. We'll *dig* him out. It'll take about a week!"

Then we started for the house, and I went in the back door—you only have to pull a buckskin latch-string, they don't fasten the doors—but that warn't romantical enough for Tom Sawyer: no way would do him but he must climb up the lightning-rod. But after he got up half-way about three times, and missed fire and fell every time, and the last time most busted his brains out, he thought he'd got to give it up; but after he rested, he allowed he would give her one more turn for luck, and this time he made the trip.

In the morning we was up at break of day, and down to the nigger cabins to pet the dogs and make friends with the nigger that fed Jim—if it *was* Jim that was being fed. The niggers was just getting through breakfast and starting for the fields; and Jim's nigger was piling up a tin pan with bread and meat and things; and whilst the other was leaving, the key come from the house.

This nigger had a good-natured, chuckle-headed face, and his wool was all tied up in little bunches with thread. That was to keep witches off. He said the witches was pestering him awful, these nights, and making him see all kinds of strange things, and hear all kinds of strange words and noises, and he didn't believe he was ever witched so long, before, in his life. He got so worked up, and got to running on so about his troubles, he forgot all about what he'd been agoing to do. So Tom says:

"What's the vittles for? Going to feed the dogs?"

The nigger kind of smiled around graduly over his face, like when you heave a brickbat in a mud puddle, and he says:

"Yes, Mars Sid, *a* dog. Cur'us dog too. Does you want to go en look at 'im?"

"Yes."

I hunched Tom, and whispers:

"You going, right here in the day-break? *That* warn't the plan."

"No, it warn't—but it's the plan *now*."

So, drat him, we went along, but I didn't like it much. When we got in, we couldn't hardly see anything, it was so dark; but Jim was there, sure enough, and could see us; and he sings out:

"Why, *Huck*! En good *lan*'! ain' dat Misto Tom?"

I just knowed how it would be; I just expected it. *I* didn't know nothing to do; and if I had, I couldn't done it; because that nigger busted in and says:

"Why, de gracious sakes! do he know you genlmen?"

We could see pretty well, now. Tom he looked at the nigger, steady and kind of wondering, and says:

"Does *who* know us?"

"Why, dish-yer runaway nigger."

"I don't reckon he does; but what put that into your head?"

"What *put* it dar? Didn' he jis' dis minute sing out like he knowed you?"

Tom says, in a puzzled-up kind of way:

"Well, that's mighty curious. *Who* sung out? *When* did he sing out? *What* did he sing out?" And turns to me, perfectly ca'm, and says, "Did *you* hear anybody sing out?"

Of course there warn't nothing to be said but the one thing; so I says:

"No; *I* ain't heard nobody say nothing."

Then he turns to Jim, and looks him over like he never see him before; and says:

"Did you sing out?"

"No, sah," says Jim; "*I* hain't said nothing, sah."

"Not a word?"

"No, sah, I hain't said a word."

"Did you ever see us before?"

"No, sah; not as *I* knows on."

So Tom turns to the nigger, which was looking wild and distressed, and says, kind of severe:

"What do you reckon's the matter with you, anyway? What made you think somebody sung out?"

"Oh, it's de dad-blame' witches, sah, en I wisht I was dead, I do. Dey's awluz at it, sah, en dey do mos' kill me, dey sk'yers me so. Please to don't tell nobody 'bout it sah, er old Mars Silas he'll scole me; 'kase he say dey *ain't* no witches. I jis' wish to goodness he was heah now—*den* what would he say! I jis' bet he couldn' fine no way to git aroun' it *dis* time. But it's awluz jis' so; people dat's *sot*, stays sot; dey won't look into nothn' en fine it out f'r deyselves, en when *you* fine it out en tell um 'bout it, dey doan' b'lieve you."

Tom give him a dime, and said we wouldn't tell nobody; and told him to buy some more thread to tie up his wool with; and then looks at Jim, and says:

"I wonder if Uncle Silas is going to hang this nigger. If I was to catch a nigger that was ungrateful enough to run away, *I* wouldn't give him up, I'd hang him." And whilst the nigger stepped to the door to look at the dime and bite it to see if it was good, he whispers to Jim and says:

"Don't ever let on to know us. And if you hear any digging going on nights, it's us: we're going to set you free."

Jim only had time to grab us by the hand and squeeze it, then the nigger come back, and we said we'd come again some time if the nigger wanted us to; and he said he would, more particular if it was dark, because the witches went for him mostly in the dark, and it was good to have folks around then.

Chapter XXXV

It would be most an hour, yet, till breakfast, so we left, and struck down into the woods; because Tom said we got to have *some* light to see how to dig by, and a lantern makes too much, and might get us into trouble; what we must have was a lot of them rotten chunks that's called fox-fire[5] and just makes a soft kind of a glow when you lay them in a dark place. We fetched an armful and hid it in the weeds, and set down to rest, and Tom says, kind of dissatisfied:

"Blame it, this whole thing is just as easy and awkard as it can be. And so it makes it so rotten difficult to get up a difficult plan. There ain't no watchman to be drugged—now there *ought* to be a watchman. There ain't even a dog to give a sleeping-mixture to. And there's Jim chained by one leg, with a ten-foot chain, to the leg of his bed; why, all you got to do is to lift up the bedstead and slip off the chain. And Uncle Silas he trusts everybody; sends the key to the punkin-headed nigger, and don't send nobody to watch the nigger. Jim could a got out of that window hole before this, only there wouldn't be no use trying to travel with a ten-foot chain on his leg. Why, drat it, Huck, it's the stupidest arrangement I ever see. You got to invent *all* the difficulties. Well, we can't help it, we got to do the best we can with the materials we've got. Anyhow, there's one thing—there's more honor in getting him out through a lot of difficulties and dangers, where there warn't one of them furnished to you by the people who it was their duty to furnish them, and you had to contrive them all out of your own head. Now look at just that one thing of the lantern. When you come down to the cold facts, we simply got to *let on* that a lantern's resky. Why, we could work with a torchlight procession if we wanted to, *I* believe. Now, whilst I think of it, we got to hunt up something to make a saw out of, the first chance we get."

"What do we want of a saw?"

"What do we *want* of it? Hain't we got to saw the leg of Jim's bed off, so as to get the chain loose?"

"Why, you just said a body could lift up the bedstead and slip the chain off."

"Well, if that ain't just like you, Huck Finn. You *can* get up the infant-schooliest ways of going at a thing. Why, hain't you ever read any books at all?—Baron Trenck, nor Casanova, nor Benvenuto Chelleeny, nor Henri IV.[6] nor none of them heroes? Whoever heard of getting a prisoner loose in such an old-maidy way as that? No; the way all the best authorities does, is to saw the bedleg in two, and leave it just so, and swallow the sawdust, so it can't be found, and put some dirt and grease around the sawed place so the very keenest seneskal[7] can't see no sign of it's being sawed, and thinks the bedleg is perfectly sound. Then, the night you're ready, fetch the leg a kick, down she goes; slip off your chain, and there you are. Nothing to do but hitch your rope-ladder to the battlements, shin down it, break your leg in the moat—because a rope-ladder is nineteen foot too short, you know—and there's your

---

5. Phosphorescent glow of fungus on rotting wood.
6. Baron Friedrich von der Trenck (1726–1794), an Austrian soldier, and Henry IV of France (1553–1610), military heroes. Benvenuto Cellini (1500–1571), an artist, and Giovanni Jacopo

Casanova (1725–1798) were both famous lovers. All four were involved in daring escape attempts.
7. Seneschal, powerful official in the service of medieval nobles.

horses and your trusty vassles, and they scoop you up and fling you across a saddle and away you go, to your native Langudoc, or Navarre,[8] or wherever it is. It's gaudy, Huck. I wish there was a moat to this cabin. If we get time, the night of the escape, we'll dig one."

I says:

"What do we want of a moat, when we're going to snake him out from under the cabin?"

But he never heard me. He had forgot me and everything else. He had his chin in his hand, thinking. Pretty soon, he sighs, and shakes his head; then sighs again, and says:

"No, it wouldn't do—there ain't necessity enough for it."

"For what?" I says.

"Why, to saw Jim's leg off," he says.

"Good land!" I says, "why, there ain't *no* necessity for it. And what would you want to saw his leg off for, anyway?"

"Well, some of the best authorities has done it. They couldn't get the chain off, so they just cut their hand off, and shoved. And a leg would be better still. But we got to let that go. There ain't necessity enough in this case; and besides, Jim's a nigger and wouldn't understand the reasons for it, and how it's the custom in Europe, so we'll let it go. But there's one thing—he can have a rope-ladder; we can tear up our sheets and make him a rope-ladder easy enough. And we can send it to him in a pie; it's mostly done that way. And I've et worse pies."

"Why, Tom Sawyer, how you talk," I says; "Jim ain't got no use for a rope-ladder."

"He *has* got use for it. How *you* talk, you better say; you don't know nothing about it. He's *got* to have a rope ladder; they all do."

"What in the nation can he *do* with it?"

"*Do* with it? He can hide it in his bed, can't he? That's what they all do; and he's got to, too. Huck, you don't ever seem to want to do anything that's regular; you want to be starting something fresh all the time. Spose he *don't* do nothing with it? ain't it there in his bed, for a clew, after he's gone? and don't you reckon they'll want clews? Of course they will. And you wouldn't leave them any? That would be a *pretty* howdy-do *wouldn't* it! I never heard of such a thing."

"Well," I says, "if it's in the regulations, and he's got to have it, all right, let him have it; because I don't wish to go back on no regulations; but there's one thing, Tom Sawyer—if we go tearing up our sheets to make Jim a rope-ladder, we're going to get into trouble with Aunt Sally, just as sure as you're born. Now, the way I look at it, a hickry-bark ladder don't cost nothing, and don't waste nothing, and is just as good to load up a pie with, and hide in a straw tick, as any rag ladder you can start; and as for Jim, he hain't had no experience, and so *he* don't care what kind of a—"

"Oh, shucks, Huck Finn, if I was as ignorant as you, I'd keep still—that's what *I'd* do. Who ever heard of a state prisoner escaping by a hickry-bark ladder? Why, it's perfectly ridiculous."

"Well, all right, Tom, fix it your own way; but if you'll take my advice, you'll let me borrow a sheet off of the clothes-line."

---

8. Provinces in France and Spain, respectively.

He said that would do. And that give him another idea, and he says:

"Borrow a shirt, too."

"What do we want of a shirt, Tom?"

"Want it for Jim to keep a journal on."

"Journal your granny—*Jim* can't write."

"Spose he *can't* write—he can make marks on the shirt, can't he, if we make him a pen out of an old pewter spoon or a piece of an old iron barrel-hoop?"

"Why, Tom, we can pull a feather out of a goose and make him a better one; and quicker, too."

"*Prisoners* don't have geese running around the donjon-keep to pull pens out of, you muggins. They *always* make their pens out of the hardest, toughest, troublesomest piece of old brass candlestick or something like that they can get their hands on; and it takes them weeks and weeks, and months and months to file it out, too, because they've got to do it by rubbing it on the wall. *They* wouldn't use a goose-quill if they had it. It ain't regular."

"Well, then, what'll we make him the ink out of?"

"Many makes it out of iron-rust and tears; but that's the common sort and women; the best authorities uses their own blood. Jim can do that; and when he wants to send any little common ordinary mysterious message to let the world know where he's captivated, he can write it on the bottom of a tin plate with a fork and throw it out of the window. The Iron Mask[9] always done that, and it's a blame' good way, too."

"Jim ain't got no tin plates. They feed him in a pan."

"That ain't anything; we can get him some."

"Can't nobody *read* his plates."

"That ain't got nothing to *do* with it, Huck Finn. All *he's* got to do is to write on the plate and throw it out. You don't *have* to be able to read it. Why, half the time you can't read anything a prisoner writes on a tin plate, or anywhere else."

"Well, then, what's the sense in wasting the plates?"

"Why, blame it all, it ain't the *prisoner's* plates."

"But it's *somebody's* plates, ain't it?"

"Well, spos'n it is? What does the *prisoner* care whose—"

He broke off there, because we heard the breakfast-horn blowing. So we cleared out for the house.

Along during that morning I borrowed a sheet and a white shirt off of the clothes-line; and I found an old sack and put them in it, and we went down and got the fox-fire, and put that in too. I called it borrowing, because that was what pap always called it; but Tom said it warn't borrowing, it was stealing. He said we was representing prisoners; and prisoners don't care how they get a thing so they get it, and nobody don't blame them for it, either. It ain't no crime in a prisoner to steal the thing he needs to get away with, Tom said; it's his right; and so, as long as we was representing a prisoner, we had a perfect right to steal anything on this place we had the least use for, to get ourselves out of prison with. He said if we warn't prisoners it would be a very different thing, and nobody but a mean ornery person would steal when he warn't a prisoner. So we allowed we would steal everything there

---

9. The chief character in Alexandre Dumas's novel *Le Vicomte de Bragelonne* (1848–50), part of which was translated into English as *The Man in the Iron Mask.*

was that come handy. And yet he made a mighty fuss, one day, after that, when I stole a watermelon out of the nigger patch and eat it; and he made me go and give the niggers a dime, without telling them what it was for. Tom said that what he meant was, we could steal anything we *needed*. Well, I says, I needed the watermelon. But he said I didn't need it to get out of prison with, there's where the difference was. He said if I'd a wanted it to hide a knife in, and smuggle it to Jim to kill the seneskal with, it would a been all right. So I let it go at that, though I couldn't see no advantage in my representing a prisoner, if I got to set down and chaw over a lot of gold-leaf distinctions like that, every time I see a chance to hog a watermelon.

Well, as I was saying, we waited that morning till everybody was settled down to business, and nobody in sight around the yard; then Tom he carried the sack into the lean-to whilst I stood off a piece to keep watch. Byand-by he come out, and we went and set down on the wood-pile, to talk. He says:

"Everything's all right, now, except tools; and that's easy fixed."

"Tools?" I says.

"Yes."

"Tools for what?"

"Why, to dig with. We ain't agoing to *gnaw* him out, are we?"

"Ain't them old crippled picks and things in there good enough to dig a nigger out with?" I says.

He turns on me looking pitying enough to make a body cry, and says:

"Huck Finn, did you *ever* hear of a prisoner having picks and shovels, and all the modern conveniences in his wardrobe to dig himself out with? Now I want to ask you—if you got any reasonableness in you at all—what kind of a show would *that* give him to be a hero? Why, they might as well lend him the key, and done with it. Picks and shovels—why they wouldn't furnish 'em to a king."

"Well, then," I says, "if we don't want the picks and shovels, what do we want?"

"A couple of case-knives."[1]

"To dig the foundations out from under that cabin with?"

"Yes."

"Confound it, it's foolish, Tom."

"It don't make no difference how foolish it is, it's the *right* way—and it's the regular way. And there ain't no *other* way, that ever *I* heard of, and I've read all the books that gives any information about these things. They always dig out with a case-knife—and not through dirt, mind you; generly it's through solid rock. And it takes them weeks and weeks and weeks, and for ever and ever. Why, look at one of them prisoners in the bottom dungeon of the Castle Deef,[2] in the harbor of Marseilles, that dug himself out that way; how long was *he* at it, you reckon?"

"I don't know."

"Well, guess."

"I don't know. A month and a half?"

---

1. Ordinary kitchen knives.
2. The hero of Alexandre Dumas's popular Romantic novel *The Count of Monte Cristo* (1844) was held prisoner at the Château d'If, a castle built by Francis I in 1524 on a small island in Marseilles harbor and used for many years as a state prison.

"*Thirty-seven year*—and he come out in China. *That's* the kind. I wish the bottom of *this* fortress was solid rock."

"*Jim* don't know nobody in China."

"What's *that* got to do with it? Neither did that other fellow. But you're always a-wandering off on a side issue. Why can't you stick to the main point?"

"All right—*I* don't care where he comes out, so he *comes* out; and Jim don't, either, I reckon. But there's one thing, anyway—Jim's too old to be dug out with a case-knife. He won't last."

"Yes he will *last*, too. You don't reckon it's going to take thirty-seven years to dig out through a *dirt* foundation, do you?"

"How long will it take, Tom?"

"Well, we can't resk being as long as we ought to, because it mayn't take very long for Uncle Silas to hear from down there by New Orleans. He'll hear Jim ain't from there. Then his next move will be to advertise Jim, or something like that. So we can't resk being as long digging him out as we ought to. By rights I reckon we ought to be a couple of years; but we can't. Things being so uncertain, what I recommend is this: that we really dig right in, as quick as we can; and after that, we can *let on*, to ourselves, that we was at it thirty-seven years. Then we can snatch him out and rush him away the first time there's an alarm. Yes, I reckon that'll be the best way."

"Now, there's *sense* in that," I says. "Letting on don't cost nothing; letting on ain't no trouble; and if it's any object, I don't mind letting on we was at it a hundred and fifty year. It wouldn't strain me none, after I got my hand in. So I'll mosey along now, and smouch a couple of case-knives."

"Smouch three," he says; "we want one to make a saw out of."

"Tom, if it ain't unregular and irreligious to sejest it," I says, "there's an old rusty saw-blade around yonder sticking under the weatherboarding behind the smoke-house."

He looked kind of weary and discouraged-like, and says:

"It ain't no use to try to learn you nothing, Huck. Run along and smouch the knives—three of them." So I done it.

Chapter XXXVI

As soon as we reckoned everybody was asleep, that night, we went down the lightning-rod, and shut ourselves up in the lean-to, and got out our pile of fox-fire, and went to work. We cleared everything out of the way, about four or five foot along the middle of the bottom log. Tom said he was right behind Jim's bed now, and we'd dig in under it, and when we got through there couldn't nobody in the cabin ever know there was any hole there, because Jim's counterpin[3] hung down most to the ground, and you'd have to raise it up and look under to see the hole. So we dug and dug, with case-knives, till most midnight; and then we was dog-tired, and our hands was blistered, and yet you couldn't see we'd done anything, hardly. At last I says:

"This ain't no thirty-seven year job, this is a thirty-eight year job, Tom Sawyer."

---

3. Counterpane or bedspread.

He never said nothing. But he sighed, and pretty soon he stopped digging, and then for a good little while I knowed he was thinking. Then he says:

"It ain't no use, Huck, it ain't agoing to work. If we was prisoners it would, because then we'd have as many years as we wanted, and no hurry; and we wouldn't get but a few minutes to dig, every day, while they was changing watches, and so our hands wouldn't get blistered, and we could keep it up right along, year in and year out, and do it right, and the way it ought to be done. But *we* can't fool along, we got to rush; we ain't got no time to spare. If we was to put in another night this way, we'd have to knock off for a week to let our hands get well—couldn't touch a case-knife with them sooner."

"Well, then, what we going to do, Tom?"

"I'll tell you. It ain't right, and it ain't moral, and I wouldn't like it to get out—but there ain't only just the one way; we got to dig him out with the picks, and *let on* it's case-knives."

"*Now* you're *talking!*" I says; "your head gets leveler and leveler all the time, Tom Sawyer," I says. "Picks is the thing, moral or no moral; and as for me, I don't care shucks for the morality of it, nohow. When I start in to steal a nigger, or a watermelon, or a Sunday-school book, I ain't no ways particular how it's done so it's done. What I want is my nigger; or what I want is my watermelon; or what I want is my Sunday-school book; and if a pick's the handiest thing, that's the thing I'm agoing to dig that nigger or that water-melon or that Sunday-school book out with; and I don't give a dead rat what the authorities thinks about it nuther."

"Well," he says, "there's excuse for picks and letting-on in a case like this; if it warn't so, I wouldn't approve of it, nor I wouldn't stand by and see the rules broke—because right is right, and wrong is wrong, and a body ain't got no business doing wrong when he ain't ignorant and knows better. It might answer for *you* to dig Jim out with a pick, *without* any letting-on, because you don't know no better; but it wouldn't for me, because I do know better. Gimme a case-knife."

He had his own by him, but I handed him mine. He flung it down, and says:

"Gimme a *case-knife*."

I didn't know just what to do—but then I thought. I scratched around amongst the old tools, and got a pick-ax and give it to him, and he took it and went to work, and never said a word.

He was always just that particular. Full of principle.

So then I got a shovel, and then we picked and shoveled, turn about, and made the fur fly. We stuck to it about a half an hour, which was as long as we could stand up; but we had a good deal of a hole to show for it. When I got up stairs, I looked out at the window and see Tom doing his level best with the lightning-rod, but he couldn't come it, his hands was so sore. At last he says:

"It ain't no use, it can't be done. What you reckon I better do? Can't you think up no way?"

"Yes," I says, "but I reckon it ain't regular. Come up the stairs, and let on it's a lightning-rod."

So he done it.

Next day Tom stole a pewter spoon and a brass candlestick in the house, for to make some pens for Jim out of, and six tallow candles; and I hung around the nigger cabins, and laid for a chance, and stole three tin plates. Tom said it wasn't enough; but I said nobody wouldn't ever see the plates that Jim throwed out, because they'd fall in the dog-fennel and jimpson weeds under the window-hole—then we could tote them back and he could use them over again. So Tom was satisfied. Then he says:

"Now, the thing to study out is, how to get the things to Jim."

"Take them in through the hole," I says, "when we get it done."

He only just looked scornful, and said something about nobody ever heard of such an idiotic idea, and then he went to studying. By-and-by he said he had ciphered out two or three ways, but there warn't no need to decide on any of them yet. Said we'd got to post Jim first.

That night we went down the lightning-rod a little after ten, and took one of the candles along, and listened under the window-hole, and heard Jim snoring; so we pitched it in, and it didn't wake him. Then we whirled in with the pick and shovel, and in about two hours and a half the job was done. We crept in under Jim's bed and into the cabin, and pawed around and found the candle and lit it, and stood over Jim a while, and found him looking hearty and healthy, and then we woke him up gentle and gradual. He was so glad to see us he most cried; and called us honey, and all the pet names he could think of; and was for having us hunt up a cold chisel to cut the chain off of his leg with, right away, and clearing out without losing any time. But Tom he showed him how unregular it would be, and set down and told him all about our plans, and how we could alter them in a minute any time there was an alarm; and not to be the least afraid, because we would see he got away, *sure*. So Jim he said it was all right, and we set there and talked over old times a while, and then Tom asked a lot of questions, and when Jim told him Uncle Silas come in every day or two to pray with him, and Aunt Sally come in to see if he was comfortable and had plenty to eat, and both of them was kind as they could be, Tom says:

"*Now* I know how to fix it. We'll send you some things by them."

I said, "Don't do nothing of the kind; it's one of the most jackass ideas I ever struck;" but he never paid no attention to me; went right on. It was his way when he'd got his plans set.

So he told Jim how we'd have to smuggle in the rope-ladder pie, and other large things, by Nat, the nigger that fed him, and he must be on the look-out, and not be surprised, and not let Nat see him open them; and we would put small things in uncle's coat pockets and he must steal them out; and we would tie things to aunt's apron strings or put them in her apron pocket, if we got a chance; and told him what they would be and what they was for. And told him how to keep a journal on the shirt with his blood, and all that. He told him everything. Jim he couldn't see no sense in the most of it, but he allowed we was white folks and knowed better than him; so he was satisfied, and said he would do it all just as Tom said.

Jim had plenty corn-cob pipes and tobacco; so we had a right down good sociable time; then we crawled out through the hole, and so home to bed, with hands that looked like they'd been chawed. Tom was in high spirits. He said it was the best fun he ever had in his life, and the most intellectural; and said if he only could see his way to it we would keep it up all the rest of our lives and leave Jim to our children to get out; for he believed Jim would come to like it better and better the more he got used to it. He said that in that way it could be strung out to as much as eighty year, and would be the best time on record. And he said it would make us all celebrated that had a hand in it.

In the morning we went out to the wood-pile and chopped up the brass candlestick into handy sizes, and Tom put them and the pewter spoon in his pocket. Then we went to the nigger cabins, and while I got Nat's notice off, Tom shoved a piece of candlestick into the middle of a corn-pone that was in Jim's pan, and we went along with Nat to see how it would work, and it just worked noble; when Jim bit into it it most mashed all his teeth out; and there warn't ever anything could a worked better. Tom said so himself. Jim he never let on but what it was only just a piece of rock or something like that that's always getting into bread, you know; but after that he never bit into nothing but what he jabbed his fork into it in three or four places, first.

And whilst we was a standing there in the dimmish light, here comes a couple of the hounds bulging in, from under Jim's bed; and they kept on piling in till there was eleven of them, and there warn't hardly room in there to get your breath. By jings, we forgot to fasten that lean-to door. The nigger Nat he only just hollered "witches!" once, and kneeled over onto the floor amongst the dogs, and begun to groan like he was dying. Tom jerked the door open and flung out a slab of Jim's meat, and the dogs went for it, and in two seconds he was out himself and back again and shut the door, and I knowed he'd fixed the other door too. Then he went to work on the nigger, coaxing him and petting him, and asking him if he'd been imagining he saw something again. He raised up, and blinked his eyes around, and says:

"Mars Sid, you'll say I's a fool, but if I didn't b'lieve I see most a million dogs, er devils, er some'n, I wisht I may die right heah in dese tracks. I did, mos' sholy. Mars Sid, I *felt* um—I *felt* um, sah; dey was all over me. Dad fetch it, I jis' wisht I could git my han's on one er dem witches jis' wunst—on'y jis' wunst—it's all I'd ast. But mos'ly I wisht dey'd lemme 'lone, I does."

Tom says:

"Well, I tell you what I think. What makes them come here just at this runaway nigger's breakfast-time? It's because they're hungry; that's the reason. You make them a witch pie; that's the thing for *you* to do."

"But my lan', Mars Sid, how's I gwyne to make 'm a witch pie? I doan' know how to make it. I hain't ever hearn er sich a thing b'fo.'"

"Well, then, I'll have to make it myself."

"Will you do it, honey?—will you? I'll wusshup de groun' und' yo' foot, I will!"

"All right, I'll do it, seeing it's you, and you've been good to us and showed us the runaway nigger. But you got to be mighty careful. When we come around, you turn your back; and then whatever we've put in the pan, don't you let on you see it at all. And don't you look, when Jim unloads the pan—something might happen, I don't know what. And above all, don't you *handle* the witch-things."

"*Hannel* 'm Mars Sid? What *is* you a talkin' 'bout? I wouldn' lay de weight er my finger on um, not f'r ten hund'd thous'n' billion dollars, I wouldn't."

Chapter XXXVII

That was all fixed. So then we went away and went to the rubbage-pile in the back yard where they keep the old boots, and rags, and pieces of bottles, and wore-out tin things, and all such truck, and scratched around and found an old tin washpan and stopped up the holes as well as we could, to bake the pie in, and took it down cellar and stole it full of flour, and started for breakfast and found a couple of shingle-nails that Tom said would be handy for a prisoner to scrabble his name and sorrows on the dungeon walls with, and dropped one of them in Aunt Sally's apron pocket which was hanging on a chair, and t'other we stuck in the band of Uncle Silas's hat, which was on the bureau, because we heard the children say their pa and ma was going to the runaway nigger's house this morning, and then went to breakfast, and Tom dropped the pewter spoon in Uncle Silas's coat pocket, and Aunt Sally wasn't come yet, so we had to wait a little while.

And when she come she was hot, and red, and cross, and couldn't hardly wait for the blessing; and then she went to sluicing out coffee with one hand and cracking the handiest child's head with her thimble with the other, and says:

"I've hunted high, and I've hunted low, and it does beat all, what *has* become of your other shirt."

My heart fell down amongst my lungs and livers and things, and a hard piece of corn-crust started down my throat after it and got met on the road with a cough and was shot across the table and took one of the children in the eye and curled him up like a fishing-worm, and let a cry out of him the size of a war-whoop, and Tom he turned kinder blue around the gills, and it all amounted to a considerable state of things for about a quarter of a minute or as much as that, and I would a sold out for half price if there was a bidder. But after that we was all right again—it was the sudden surprise of it that knocked us so kind of cold. Uncle Silas he says:

"It's most uncommon curious, I can't understand it. I know perfectly well I took it *off*, because——"

"Because you hain't got but one on. Just *listen* at the man! *I* know you took it off, and know it by a better way than your wool-gethering memory, too, because it was on the clo'es-line yesterday—I see it there myself. But it's gone—that's the long and the short of it, and you'll just have to change to a red flann'l one till I can get time to make a new one. And it'll be the third I've made in two years; it just keeps a body on the jump to keep you in shirts; and whatever you do manage to *do* with 'm all, is more'n *I* can make out. A body'd think you *would* learn to take some sort of care of 'em, at your time of life."

"I know it, Sally, and I do try all I can. But it oughtn't to be altogether my fault, because you know I don't see them nor have nothing to do with them except when they're on me; and I don't believe I've ever lost one of them *off* of me."

"Well, it ain't *your* fault if you haven't, Silas—you'd a done it if you could, I reckon. And the shirt ain't all that's gone, nuther. Ther's a spoon gone; and *that* ain't all. There was ten, and now ther's only nine. The calf got the shirt I reckon, but the calf never took the spoon, *that's* certain."

"Why, what else is gone, Sally?"

"Ther's six *candles* gone—that's what. The rats could a got the candles, and I reckon they did; I wonder they don't walk off with the whole place, the way you're always going to stop their holes and don't do it; and if they warn't fools they'd sleep in your hair, Silas—*you'd* never find it out; but you can't lay the *spoon* on the rats, and that I *know*."

"Well, Sally, I'm in fault, and I acknowledge it; I've been remiss; but I won't let to-morrow go by without stopping up them holes."

"Oh, I wouldn't hurry, next year'll do. Matilda Angelina Araminta *Phelps!*"

Whack comes the thimble, and the child snatches her claws out of the sugar-bowl without fooling around any. Just then, the nigger woman steps onto the passage, and says:

"Missus, dey's a sheet gone."

"A *sheet* gone! Well, for land's sake!"

"I'll stop up them holes *to-day*," says Uncle Silas, looking sorrowful.

"Oh, *do* shet up!—spose the rats took the *sheet? Where's* it gone, Lize?"

"Clah to goodness I hain't no notion, Miss Sally. She wuz on de clo's-line yistiddy, but she done gone; she ain' dah no mo', now."

"I reckon the world *is* coming to an end. I *never* see the beat of it, in all my born days. A shirt, and a sheet, and a spoon, and six can—"

"Missus," comes a young yaller wench, "dey's a brass candlestick miss'n."

"Cler out from here, you hussy, er I'll take a skillet to ye!"

Well, she was just a biling. I begun to lay for a chance; I reckoned I would sneak out and go for the woods till the weather moderated. She kept a raging right along, running her insurrection all by herself, and everybody else mighty meek and quiet; and at last Uncle Silas, looking kind of foolish, fishes up that spoon out of his pocket. She stopped, with her mouth open and her hands up, and as for me, I wished I was in Jeruslem or somewheres. But not long; because she says:

"It's *just* as I expected. So you had it in your pocket all the time; and like as not you've got the other things there, too. How'd it get there?"

"I reely don't know, Sally," he says, kind of apologizing, "or you know I would tell. I was a-studying over my text in Acts Seventeen,[4] before breakfast, and I reckon I put it in there, not noticing, meaning to put my Testament in, and it must be so, because my Testament ain't in, but I'll go and see, and if the Testament is where I had it, I'll know I didn't put it in, and that will show that I laid the Testament down and took up the spoon, and——"

"Oh, for the land's sake! Give a body a rest! Go 'long now, the whole kit and biling of ye; and don't come nigh me again till I've got back my peace of mind."

I'd a heard her, if she'd a said it to herself, let alone speaking it out; and I'd a got up and obeyed her, if I'd a been dead. As we was passing through the setting-room, the old man he took up his hat, and the shingle-nail fell out on the floor, and he just merely picked it up and laid it on the mantel-shelf, and never said nothing, and went out. Tom see him do it, and remembered about the spoon, and says:

"Well, it ain't no use to send things by *him* no more, he ain't reliable." Then he says: "But he done us a good turn with the spoon, anyway, without knowing it, and so we'll go and do him one without *him* knowing it—stop up his rat-holes."

There was a noble good lot of them, down cellar, and it took us a whole hour, but we done the job tight and good, and ship-shape. Then we heard steps on the stairs, and blowed out our light, and hid; and here comes the old man, with a candle in one hand and a bundle of stuff in t'other, looking as absent-minded as year before last. He went a mooning around, first to one rat-hole and then another, till he'd been to them all. Then he stood about

---

4. In Acts 17, Paul's preaching to the Athenians berates both their false gods and snobbery; verse 29 declares that "we are all God's offspring."

five minutes, picking tallow-drip off of his candle and thinking. Then he turns off slow and dreamy towards the stairs, saying:

"Well, for the life of me I can't remember when I done it. I could show her now that I warn't to blame on account of the rats. But never mind—let it go. I reckon it wouldn't do no good."

And so he went on a mumbling up stairs, and then we left. He was a mighty nice old man. And always is.

Tom was a good deal bothered about what to do for a spoon, but he said we'd got to have it; so he took a think. When he had ciphered it out, he told me how we was to do; then we went and waited around the spoon-basket till we see Aunt Sally coming, and then Tom went to counting the spoons and laying them out to one side, and I slip one of them up my sleeve, and Tom says:

"Why, Aunt Sally, there ain't but nine spoons, *yet*."

She says:

"Go 'long to your play, and don't bother me. I know better, I counted 'm myself."

"Well, I've counted them twice, Aunty, and *I* can't make but nine."

She looked out of all patience, but of course she come to count—anybody would.

"I declare to gracious ther' *ain't* but nine!" she says. "Why, what in the world—plague *take* the things, I'll count 'm again."

So I slipped back the one I had, and when she got done counting, she says:

"Hang the troublesome rubbage, ther's *ten* now!" and she looked huffy and bothered both. But Tom says:

"Why, Aunty *I* don't think there's ten."

"You numskull, didn't you see me *count* 'm?"

"I know, but—"

"Well, I'll count 'm *again*."

So I smouched one, and they come out nine same as the other time. Well, she *was* in a tearing way—just a trembling all over, she was so mad. But she counted and counted, till she got that addled she'd start to count-in the *basket* for a spoon, sometimes; and so, three times they come out right, and three times they come out wrong. Then she grabbed up the basket and slammed it across the house and knocked the cat galley-west;[5] and she said cle'r out and let her have some peace, and if we come bothering around her again betwixt that and dinner, she'd skin us. So we had the odd spoon; and dropped it in her apron pocket whilst she was giving us our sailing-orders, and Jim got it all right, along with her shingle-nail, before noon. We was very well satisfied with the business, and Tom allowed it was worth twice the trouble it took, because he said *now* she couldn't ever count them spoons twice alike again to save her life; and wouldn't believe she'd counted them right, if she *did*; and said that after she'd about counted her head off, for the last three days, he judged she'd give it up and offer to kill anybody that wanted her to ever count them any more.

So we put the sheet back on the line, that night, and stole one out of her closet; and kept on putting it back and stealing it again, for a couple of days, till she didn't know how many sheets she had, any more, and said she didn't

---

5. Into confusion.

care, and warn't agoing to bullyrag[6] the rest of her soul out about it, and wouldn't count them again not to save her life, she druther die first.

So we was all right now, as to the shirt and the sheet and the spoon and the candles, by the help of the calf and the rats and the mixed-up counting; and as to the candlestick, it warn't no consequence, it would blow over by-and-by.

But that pie was a job; we had no end of trouble with that pie. We fixed it up away down in the woods, and cooked it there; and we got it done at last, and very satisfactory, too; but not all in one day; and we had to use up three washpans full of flour, before we got through, and we got burnt pretty much all over, in places, and eyes put out with the smoke; because, you see, we didn't want nothing but a crust, and we couldn't prop it up right, and she would always cave in. But of course we thought of the right way at last; which was to cook the ladder, too, in the pie. So then we laid in with Jim, the second night, and tore up the sheet all in little strings, and twisted them together, and long before daylight we had a lovely rope, that you could a hung a person with. We let on it took nine months to make it.

And in the forenoon we took it down to the woods, but it wouldn't go in the pie. Being made of a whole sheet, that way, there was rope enough for forty pies, if we'd a wanted them, and plenty left over for soup, or sausage, or anything you choose. We could a had a whole dinner.

But we didn't need it. All we needed was just enough for the pie, and so we throwed the rest away. We didn't cook none of the pies in the washpan, afraid the solder would melt; but Uncle Silas he had a noble brass warming-pan which he thought considerable of, because it belonged to one of his ancestors with a long wooden handle that come over from England with William the Conqueror in the *Mayflower*[7] or one of them early ships and was hid away up garret with a lot of other old pots and things that was valuable, not on account of being any account because they warn't, but on account of them being relicts, you know, and we snaked her out, private, and took her down there, but she failed on the first pies, because we didn't know how, but she come up smiling on the last one. We took and lined her with dough, and set her in the coals, and loaded her up with rag-rope, and put on a dough roof, and shut down the lid, and put hot embers on top, and stood off five foot, with the long handle, cool and comfortable, and in fifteen minutes she turned out a pie that was a satisfaction to look at. But the person that et it would want to fetch a couple of kags of toothpicks along, for if that rope-ladder wouldn't cramp him down to business, I don't know nothing what I'm talking about, and lay him in enough stomach-ache to last him till next time, too.

Nat didn't look, when we put the witch-pie in Jim's pan; and we put the three tin plates in the bottom of the pan under the vittles; and so Jim got everything all right, and as soon as he was by himself he busted into the pie and hid the rope-ladder inside of his straw tick, and scratched some marks on a tin plate and throwed it out of the window-hole.

6. To nag mercilessly.
7. William the Conqueror lived in the 11th century. The *Mayflower* made its crossing in 1620.

Chapter XXXVIII

Making them pens was a distressid-tough job, and so was the saw; and Jim allowed the inscription was going to be the toughest of all. That's the one which the prisoner has to scrabble on the wall. But we had to have it; Tom said we'd *got* to; there warn't no case of a state prisoner not scrabbling his inscription to leave behind, and his coat of arms.

"Look at Lady Jane Grey," he says; "look at Gilford Dudley; look at old Northumberland![8] Why, Huck, spose it *is* considerable trouble?—what you going to do?—how you going to get around it? Jim's *got* to do his inscription and coat of arms. They all do."

Jim says:

"Why, Mars Tom, I hain't got no coat o' arms; I hain't got nuffn but dishyer old shirt, en you knows I got to keep de journal on dat."

"Oh, you don't understand, Jim; a coat of arms is very different."

"Well," I says, "Jim's right, anyway, when he says he hain't got no coat of arms, because he hain't."

"I reckon *I* knowed that," Tom says, "but you bet he'll have one before he goes out of this—because he's going out *right*, and there ain't going to be no flaws in his record."

So whilst me and Jim filed away at the pens on a brickbat[9] apiece, Jim a making his'n out of the brass and I making mine out of the spoon, Tom set to work to think out the coat of arms. By-and-by he said he'd struck so many good ones he didn't hardly know which to take, but there was one which he reckoned he'd decide on. He says:

"On the scutcheon[1] we'll have a bend *or* in the dexter base, a saltire *murrey* in the fess, with a dog, couchant, for common charge, and under his foot a chain embattled, for slavery, with a chevron *vert* in a chief engrailed, and three invected lines on a field *azure*, with the nombril points rampant on a dancette indented; crest, a runaway nigger, *sable*, with his bundle over his shoulder on a bar sinister: and a couple of gules for supporters, which is you and me; motto, *Maggiore fretta, minore atto.* Got it out of a book—means, the more haste, the less speed."

"Geewhillikins," I says, "but what does the rest of it mean?"

"We ain't got no time to bother over that," he says, "we got to dig in like all git-out."

"Well, anyway," I says, "what's *some* of it? What's a fess?"

"A fess—a fess is—*you* don't need to know what a fess is. I'll show him how to make it when he gets to it."

"Shucks, Tom," I says, "I think you might tell a person. What's a bar sinister?"

"Oh, *I* don't know. But he's got to have it. All the nobility does."

That was just his way. If it didn't suit him to explain a thing to you, he wouldn't do it. You might pump at him a week, it wouldn't make no difference.

---

8. The story of Lady Jane Grey (1537–1554), her husband, Guildford Dudley, and his father, the duke of Northumberland, was told in W. H. Ainsworth's romance *The Tower of London* (1840). The duke was at work carving a poem on the wall of his cell when the executioners came for him.

9. A fragment of brick.
1. An escutcheon is the shield-shaped surface on which a coat of arms is inscribed. The details are expressed in the technical terminology of heraldry.

He'd got all that coat of arms business fixed, so now he started in to finish up the rest of that part of the work, which was to plan out a mournful
inscription—said Jim got to have one, like they all done. He made up a lot,
and wrote them out on a paper, and read them off, so:

1. *Here a captive heart busted.*
2. *Here a poor prisoner, forsook by the world and friends, fretted out his
sorrowful life.*
3. *Here a lonely heart broke, and a worn spirit went to its rest, after thirty-
seven years of solitary captivity.*
4. *Here, homeless and friendless, after thirty-seven years of bitter captivity,
perished a noble stranger, natural son of Louis XIV.*

Tom's voice trembled, whilst he was reading them, and he most broke
down. When he got done, he couldn't no way make up his mind which one
for Jim to scrabble onto the wall, they was all so good; but at last he allowed
he would let him scrabble them all on. Jim said it would take him a year to
scrabble such a lot of truck onto the logs with a nail, and he didn't know
how to make letters, besides; but Tom said he would block them out for
him, and then he wouldn't have nothing to do but just follow the lines. Then
pretty soon he says:
"Come to think, the logs ain't agoing to do; they don't have log walls in a
dungeon: we got to dig the inscriptions into a rock. We'll fetch a rock."
Jim said the rock was worse than the logs; he said it would take him such
a pison long time to dig them into a rock, he wouldn't ever get out. But Tom
said he would let me help him do it. Then he took a look to see how me and
Jim was getting along with the pens. It was most pesky tedious hard work
and slow, and didn't give my hands no show to get well of the sores, and we
didn't seem to make no headway, hardly. So Tom says:
"I know how to fix it. We got to have a rock for the coat of arms and
mournful inscriptions, and we can kill two birds with that same rock. There's
a gaudy big grindstone down at the mill, and we'll smouch it, and carve the
things on it, and file out the pens and the saw on it, too."
It warn't no slouch of an idea; and it warn't no slouch of a grindstone
nuther; but we allowed we'd tackle it. It warn't quite midnight, yet, so we
cleared out for the mill, leaving Jim at work. We smouched the grindstone,
and set out to roll her home, but it was a most nation tough job. Sometimes, do what we could, we couldn't keep her from falling over, and she
come mighty near mashing us, every time. Tom said she was going to get
one of us, sure, before we got through. We got her half way; and then we
was plumb played out, and most drownded with sweat. We see it warn't no
use, we got to go and fetch Jim. So he raised up his bed and slid the chain
off of the bed-leg, and wrapt it round and round his neck, and we crawled
out through our hole and down there, and Jim and me laid into that
grindstone and walked her along like nothing; and Tom superintended.
He could out-superintend any boy I ever see. He knowed how to do everything.
Our hole was pretty big, but it warn't big enough to get the grindstone
through; but Jim he took the pick and soon made it big enough. Then Tom
marked out them things on it with the nail, and set Jim to work on them,

with the nail for a chisel and an iron bolt from the rubbage in the lean-to for a hammer, and told him to work till the rest of his candle quit on him, and then he could go to bed, and hide the grindstone under his straw tick and sleep on it. Then we helped him fix his chain back on the bed-leg, and was ready for bed ourselves. But Tom thought of something, and says:

"You got any spiders in here, Jim?"

"No, sah, thanks to goodness I hain't, Mars Tom."

"All right, we'll get you some."

"But bless you, honey, I doan' *want* none. I's afeard un um. I jis' 's soon have rattlesnakes aroun'."

Tom thought a minute or two, and says:

"It's a good idea. And I reckon it's been done. It *must* a been done; it stands to reason. Yes, it's a prime good idea. Where could you keep it?"

"Keep what, Mars Tom?"

"Why, a rattlesnake."

"De goodness gracious alive, Mars Tom! Why, if dey was a rattlesnake to come in heah, I'd take en bust right out thoo dat log wall, I would, wid my head."

"Why, Jim, you wouldn't be afraid of it, after a little. You could tame it."

"*Tame* it!"

"Yes—easy enough. Every animal is grateful for kindness and petting, and they wouldn't *think* of hurting a person that pets them. Any book will tell you that. You try—that's all I ask; just try for two or three days. Why, you can get him so, in a little while, that he'll love you; and sleep with you; and won't stay away from you a minute; and will let you wrap him round your neck and put his head in your mouth."

"*Please*, Mars Tom—*doan'* talk so! I can't *stan'* it! He'd *let* me shove his head in my mouf—fer a favor, hain't it? I lay he'd wait a pow'ful long time 'fo' I *ast* him. En mo' en dat, I doan' *want* him to sleep wid me."

"Jim, don't act so foolish. A prisoner's *got* to have some kind of a dumb pet, and if a rattlesnake hain't ever been tried, why, there's more glory to be gained in your being the first to ever try it than any other way you could ever think of to save your life."

"Why, Mars Tom, I doan' *want* no sich glory. Snake take 'n bite Jim's chin off, den *whah* is de glory? No, sah, I doan' want no sich doin's."

"Blame it, can't you *try*? I only *want* you to try—you needn't keep it up if it don't work."

"But de trouble all *done*, ef de snake bite me while I's a tryin' him. Mars Tom, I's willin' to tackle mos' anything 'at ain't onreasonable, but ef you en Huck fetches a rattlesnake in heah for me to tame, I's gwyne to *leave*, dat's *shore*."

"Well, then, let it go, let it go, if you're so bullheaded about it. We can get you some garter-snakes and you can tie some buttons on their tails, and let on they're rattlesnakes, and I reckon that'll have to do."

"I k'n stan' *dem*, Mars Tom, but blame' 'f I couldn't get along widout um, I tell you dat. I never knowed b'fo', 't was so much bother and trouble to be a prisoner."

"Well, it *always* is, when it's done right. You got any rats around here?"

"No, sah, I hain't seed none."

"Well, we'll get you some rats."

"Why, Mars Tom, I doan' *want* no rats. Dey's de dad-blamedest creturs to sturb a body, en rustle roun' over 'im, en bite his feet, when he's tryin' to sleep, I ever see. So, sah, gimme g'yarter-snakes, 'f I's got to have 'm, but doan' gimme no rats. I ain' got not use f'r um, skasely."

"But Jim, you *got* to have 'em—they all do. So don't make no more fuss about it. Prisoners ain't ever without rats. There ain't no instance of it. And they train them, and pet them, and learn them tricks, and they get to be as sociable as flies. But you got to play music to them. You got anything to play music on?"

"I ain't got nuffn but a coase comb en a piece o' paper, en a juice-harp; but I reck'n dey wouldn't take no stock in a juice-harp."

"Yes, they would. *They* don't care what kind of music 'tis. A jews-harp's[2] plenty good enough for a rat. All animals likes music—in a prison they dote on it. Specially, painful music; and you can't get no other kind out of a jews-harp. It always interests them; they come out to see what's the matter with you. Yes, you're all right; you're fixed very well. You want to set on your bed, nights, before you go to sleep, and early in the mornings, and play your jews-harp; play The Last Link is Broken[3]—that's the thing that'll scoop a rat, quicker'n anything else: and when you've played about two minutes, you'll see all the rats, and the snakes, and spiders, and things begin to feel worried about you, and come. And they'll just fairly swarm over you, and have a noble good time."

"Yes, *dey* will, I reck'n, Mars Tom, but what kine er time is *Jim* havin'? Blest if I kin see de pint. But I'll do it ef I got to. I reck'n I better keep de animals satisfied, en not have no trouble in de house."

Tom waited to think over, and see if there wasn't nothing else; and pretty soon he says:

"Oh—there's one thing I forgot. Could you raise a flower here, do you reckon?"

"I doan' know but maybe I could, Mars Tom; but it's tolable dark in heah, en I ain' got no use f'r no flower, nohow, en she'd be a pow'ful sight o' trouble."

"Well, you try it, anyway. Some other prisoners has done it."

"One er dem big cat-tail-lookin' mullen-stalks would grow in heah, Mars Tom, I reck'n, but she wouldn' be wuth half de trouble she'd coss."

"Don't you believe it. We'll fetch you a little one, and you plant it in the corner, over there, and raise it. And don't call it mullen, call it Pitchiola— that's its right name, when it's in a prison.[4] And you want to water it with your tears."

"Why, I got plenty spring water, Mars Tom."

"You don't *want* spring water; you want to water it with your tears. It's the way they always do."

"Why, Mars Tom, I lay I kin raise one er dem mullen-stalks twyste wid spring water whiles another man's a *start'n* one wid tears."

"That ain't the idea. You *got* to do it with tears."

"She'll die on my han's, Mars Tom, she sholy will; kase I doan' skasely ever cry."

---

2. Also known as a mouth harp and by other names, a small instrument that the player holds between his or her teeth and produces notes by striking a metal tongue. Despite this name, it has no particular connection to Judaism or the Jewish people; rather, the name is a corruption of *jaw's harp*.
3. A popular love song of this time.
4. *Picciola* (1836) was a popular romantic novel by Xavier Saintine (pseudonym for Joseph Xavier Boniface, 1798–1865), in which a plant helps a prisoner survive.

So Tom was stumped. But he studied it over, and then said Jim would have to worry along the best he could with an onion. He promised he would go to the nigger cabins and drop one, private, in Jim's coffee-pot, in the morning. Jim said he would "jis' 's soon have tobacker in his coffee;" and found so much fault with it, and with the work and bother of raising the mullen, and jews-harping the rats, and petting and flattering up the snakes and spiders and things, on top of all the other work he had to do on pens, and inscriptions, and journals, and things, which made it more trouble and worry and responsibility to be a prisoner than anything he ever undertook, that Tom most lost all patience with him; and said he was just loadened down with more gaudier chances than a prisoner ever had in the world to make a name for himself, and yet he didn't know enough to appreciate them, and they was just about wasted on him. So Jim he was sorry, and said he wouldn't behave so no more, and then me and Tom shoved for bed.

Chapter XXXIX

In the morning we went up to the village and bought a wire rat trap and fetched it down, and unstopped the best rat hole, and in about an hour we had fifteen of the bulliest kind of ones; and then we took it and put it in a safe place under Aunt Sally's bed. But while we was gone for spiders, little Thomas Franklin Benjamin Jefferson Elexander Phelps found it there, and opened the door of it to see if the rats would come out, and they did; and Aunt Sally she come in, and when we got back she was standing on top of the bed raising Cain, and the rats was doing what they could to keep off the dull times for her. So she took and dusted us both with the hickry, and we was as much as two hours catching another fifteen or sixteen, drat that meddlesome cub, and they warn't the likeliest, nuther, because the first haul was the pick of the flock. I never see a likelier lot of rats than what that first haul was.

We got a splendid stock of sorted spiders, and bugs, and frogs, and caterpillars, and one thing or another; and we like-to got a hornet's nest, but we didn't. The family was at home. We didn't give it right up, but staid with them as long as we could; because we allowed we'd tire them out or they'd got to tire us out, and they done it. Then we got allycumpain⁵ and rubbed on the places, and was pretty near all right again, but couldn't set down convenient. And so we went for the snakes, and grabbed a couple of dozen garters and house-snakes, and put them in a bag, and put it in our room, and by that time it was supper time, and a rattling good honest day's work; and hungry?—oh, no I reckon not! And there warn't a blessed snake up there, when we went back—we didn't half tie the sack, and they worked out, somehow, and left. But it didn't matter much, because they was still on the premises somewheres. So we judged we could get some of them again. No, there warn't no real scarcity of snakes about the house for a considerble spell. You'd see them dripping from the rafters and places, every now and then; and they generly landed in your plate, or down the back of your neck, and most of the time where you didn't want them. Well, they was handsome, and striped, and there warn't no harm in a million of them; but that never

5. Elecampane is an herb that Tom and Huck are using to relieve the pain of the hornet stings.

made no difference to Aunt Sally, she despised snakes, be the breed what
they might, and she couldn't stand them no way you could fix it; and every
time one of them flopped down on her, it didn't make no difference what she
was doing, she would just lay that work down and light out. I never see such
a woman. And you could hear her whoop to Jericho. You couldn't get her to
take aholt of one of them with the tongs. And if she turned over and found
one in bed, she would scramble out and lift a howl that you would think the
house was afire. She disturbed the old man so, that he said he could most
wish there hadn't ever been no snakes created. Why, after every last snake
had been gone clear out of the house for as much as a week, Aunt Sally
warn't over it yet; she warn't near over it; when she was setting thinking
about something, you could touch her on the back of her neck with a feather
and she would jump right out of her stockings. It was very curious. But Tom
said all women was just so. He said they was made that way; for some reason or other.

We got a licking every time one of our snakes come in her way; and she
allowed these lickings warn't nothing to what she would do if we ever loaded
up the place again with them. I didn't mind the lickings, because they didn't
amount to nothing; but I minded the trouble we had, to lay in another lot.
But we got them laid in, and all the other things; and you never see a cabin
as blithesome as Jim's was when they'd all swarm out for music and go for
him. Jim didn't like the spiders, and the spiders didn't like Jim; and so they'd
lay for him and make it mighty warm for him. And he said that between the
rats, and the snakes, and the grindstone, there warn't no room in bed for
him, skasely; and when there was, a body couldn't sleep, it was so lively, and
it was always lively, he said, because *they* never all slept at one time, but took
turn about, so when the snakes was asleep the rats was on deck, and when
the rats turned in the snakes come on watch, so he always had one gang
under him, in his way, and t'other gang having a circus over him, and if he
got up to hunt a new place, the spiders would take a chance at him as he
crossed over. He said if he ever got out, this time, he wouldn't ever be a prisoner again, not for a salary.

Well, by the end of three weeks, everything was in pretty good shape. The
shirt was sent in early, in a pie, and every time a rat bit Jim he would get up
and write a little in his journal whilst the ink was fresh; the pens was made,
the inscriptions and so on was all carved on the grindstone; the bed-leg was
sawed in two, and we had et up the sawdust, and it give us a most amazing
stomach-ache. We reckoned we was all going to die, but didn't. It was the
most undigestible sawdust I ever see; and Tom said the same. But as I was
saying, we'd got all the work done, now, at last; and we was all pretty much
fagged out, too, but mainly Jim. The old man had wrote a couple of times to
the plantation below Orleans to come and get their runaway nigger, but
hadn't got no answer, because there warn't no such plantation; so he allowed
he would advertise Jim in the St. Louis and New Orleans papers; and when
he mentioned the St. Louis ones, it give me the cold shivers, and I see we
hadn't no time to lose. So Tom said, now for the nonnamous letters.

"What's them?" I says.

"Warnings to the people that something is up. Sometimes it's done one
way, sometimes another. But there's always somebody spying around, that
gives notice to the governor of the castle. When Louis XVI was going to light

out of the Tooleries,[6] a servant girl done it. It's a very good way, and so is the nonnamous letters. We'll use them both. And it's usual for the prisoner's mother to change clothes with him, and she stays in, and he slides out in her clothes. We'll do that too."

"But looky here, Tom, what do we want to *warn* anybody for, that something's up? Let them find it out for themselves—it's their lookout."

"Yes, I know; but you can't depend on them. It's the way they've acted from the very start—left us to do *everything*. They're so confiding and mullet-headed they don't take notice of nothing at all. So if we don't *give* them notice, there won't be nobody nor nothing to interfere with us, and so after all our hard work and trouble this escape 'll go off perfectly flat: won't amount to nothing—won't be nothing *to* it."

"Well, as for me, Tom, that's the way I'd like."

"Shucks," he says, and looked disgusted. So I says:

"But I ain't going to make no complaint. Anyway that suits you suits me. What you going to do about the servant-girl?"

"You'll be her. You slide in, in the middle of the night, and hook that yaller girl's frock."

"Why, Tom, that'll make trouble next morning; because of course she prob'bly hain't got any but that one."

"I know; but you don't want it but fifteen minutes, to carry the nonnamous letter and shove it under the front door."

"All right, then, I'll do it; but I could carry it just as handy in my own togs."

"You wouldn't look like a servant-girl *then*, would you?"

"No, but there won't be nobody to see what I look like, *anyway*."

"That ain't got nothing to do with it. The thing for us to do, is just to do our *duty*, and not worry about whether anybody *sees* us do it or not. Hain't you got no principle at all?"

"All right, I ain't saying nothing; I'm the servant-girl. Who's Jim's mother?"

"I'm his mother. I'll hook a gown from Aunt Sally."

"Well, then, you'll have to stay in the cabin when me and Jim leaves."

"Not much. I'll stuff Jim's clothes full of straw and lay it on his bed to represent his mother in disguise: and Jim 'll take Aunt Sally's gown off of me and wear it, and we'll all evade together. When a prisoner of style escapes, it's called an evasion. It's always called so when a king escapes, f'rinstance. And the same with a king's son; it don't make no difference whether he's a natural one or an unnatural one."

So Tom he wrote the nonnamous letter, and I smouched the yaller wench's frock, that night, and put it on, and shoved it under the front door, the way Tom told me to. It said:

> Beware, Trouble is brewing. Keep a sharp lookout.
> UNKNOWN FRIEND.

Next night we stuck a picture which Tom drawed in blood, of a skull and crossbones, on the front door; and next night another one of a coffin, on the back door. I never see a family in such a sweat. They couldn't a been worse scared if the place had a been full of ghosts laying for them behind

---

6. Twain probably read this episode of the Tuileries, a palace in Paris, in Thomas Carlyle's *French Revolution* (1837).

everything and under the beds and shivering through the air. If a door banged, Aunt Sally she jumped, and said "ouch!" if anything fell, she jumped and said "ouch!" if you happened to touch her, when she warn't noticing, she done the same; she couldn't face noway and be satisfied, because she allowed there was something behind her every time—so she was always a whirling around, sudden, and saying "ouch," and before she'd get two-thirds around, she'd whirl back again, and say it again; and she was afraid to go to bed, but she dasn't set up. So the thing was working very well, Tom said; he said he never see a thing work more satisfactory. He said it showed it was done right.

So he said, now for the grand bulge! So the very next morning at the streak of dawn we got another letter ready, and was wondering what we better do with it, because we heard them say at supper they was going to have a nigger on watch at both doors all night. Tom he went down the lightning-rod to spy around; and the nigger at the back door was asleep, and he stuck it in the back of his neck and come back. This letter said:

> Don't betray me, I wish to be your friend. There is a desprate gang of cut-throats from over in the Ingean Territory[7] going to steal your runaway nigger to-night, and they have been trying to scare you so as you will stay in the house and not bother them. I am one of the gang, but have got relliggion and wish to quit it and lead a honest life again, and will betray the helish design. They will sneak down from northards, along the fence, at midnight exact, with a false key, and go in the nigger's cabin to get him. I am to be off a piece and blow a tin horn if I see any danger; but stead of that, I will BA like a sheep soon as they get in and not blow at all; then whilst they are getting his chains loose, you slip there and lock them in, and can kill them at your leasure. Don't do anything but just the way I am telling you, if you do they will suspicion something and raise whoopjamboreehoo. I do not wish any reward but to know I have done the right thing.
>
> UNKNOWN FRIEND.

Chapter XL

We was feeling pretty good, after breakfast, and took my canoe and went over the river a fishing, with a lunch, and had a good time, and took a look at the raft and found her all right, and got home late to supper, and found them in such a sweat and worry they didn't know which end they was standing on, and made us go right off to bed the minute we was done supper, and wouldn't tell us what the trouble was, and never let on a word about the new letter, but didn't need to, because we knowed as much about it as anybody did, and as soon as we was half up stairs and her back was turned, we slid for the cellar cupboard and loaded up a good lunch and took it up to our room and went to bed, and got up about half-past eleven, and Tom put on Aunt Sally's dress that he stole and was going to start with the lunch, but says:

"Where's the butter?"

"I laid out a hunk of it," I says, "on a piece of a corn-pone."

"Well, you *left* it laid out, then—it ain't here."

---

7. Indian country; part of Oklahoma reserved for Native Americans beginning in the 1830s. Because federal law did not apply there, outlaws used it as a base of operations throughout the 19th century.

"We can get along without it," I says.

"We can get along *with* it, too," he says; "just you slide down cellar and fetch it. And then mosey right down the lightning-rod and come along. I'll go and stuff the straw into Jim's clothes to represent his mother in disguise, and be ready to *ba* like a sheep and shove soon as you get there."

So out he went, and down cellar went I. The hunk of butter, big as a person's fist, was where I had left it, so I took up the slab of corn-pone with it on, and blowed out my light, and started up stairs, very stealthy, and got up to the main floor all right, but here comes Aunt Sally with a candle, and I clapped the truck in my hat, and clapped my hat on my head, and the next second she see me; and she says:

"You been down cellar?"

"Yes'm."

"What you been doing down there?"

"Noth'n."

"*Noth'n!*"

"No'm."

"Well, then, what possessed you to go down there, this time of night?"

"I don't know'm."

"You don't *know?* Don't answer me that way, Tom, I want to know what you been *doing* down there?"

"I hain't been doing a single thing, Aunt Sally, I hope to gracious if I have."

I reckoned she'd let me go, now, and as a generl thing she would; but I spose there was so many strange things going on she was just in a sweat about every little thing that warn't yard-stick straight; so she says, very decided:

"You just march into that setting-room and stay there till I come. You been up to something you no business to, and I lay I'll find out what it is before *I'm* done with you."

So she went away as I opened the door and walked into the setting-room. My, but there was a crowd there! Fifteen farmers, and every one of them had a gun. I was most powerful sick, and slunk to a chair and set down. They was setting around, some of them talking a little, in a low voice, and all of them fidgety and uneasy, but trying to look like they warn't; but I knowed they was, because they was always taking off their hats, and putting them on, and scratching their heads, and changing their seats, and fumbling with their buttons. I warn't easy myself, but I didn't take my hat off, all the same.

I did wish Aunt Sally would come, and get done with me, and lick me, if she wanted to, and let me get away and tell Tom how we'd overdone this thing, and what a thundering hornet's nest we'd got ourselves into, so we could stop fooling around, straight off, and clear out with Jim before these rips got out of patience and come for us.

At last she come, and begun to ask me questions, but I *couldn't* answer them straight, I didn't know which end of me was up; because these men was in such a fidget now, that some was wanting to start right *now* and lay for them desperadoes, and saying it warn't but a few minutes to midnight; and others was trying to get them to hold on and wait for the sheep-signal; and here was aunty pegging away at the questions, and me a shaking all over and ready to sink down in my tracks I was that scared; and the place getting hotter and hotter, and the butter beginning to melt and run down my neck and behind my ears: and pretty soon, when one of them says, "*I'm* for going and getting in the cabin *first*, and right *now*, and catching them when they come," I most dropped; and a streak of butter came a trickling down my forehead, and Aunt Sally she see it, and turns white as a sheet, and says:

"For the land's sake what *is* the matter with the child!—he's got the brain fever[8] as shore as you're born, and they're oozing out!"

And everybody runs to see, and she snatches off my hat, and out comes the bread, and what was left of the butter, and she grabbed me, and hugged me, and says:

"Oh, what a turn you did give me! and how glad and grateful I am it ain't no worse; for luck's against us, and it never rains but it pours, and when I see that truck I thought we'd lost you, for I knowed by the color and all, it was just like your brains would be if—Dear, dear, whyd'nt you *tell* me that was what you'd been down there for, *I* wouldn't a cared. Now cler out to bed, and don't lemme see no more of you till morning!"

I was up stairs in a second, and down the lightning-rod in another one, and shinning through the dark for the lean-to. I couldn't hardly get my words out, I was so anxious; but I told Tom as quick as I could, we must jump for it, now, and not a minute to lose—the house full of men, yonder, with guns!

His eyes just blazed; and he says:

"No!—is that so? *Ain't* it bully! Why, Huck, if it was to do over again, I bet I could fetch two hundred! If we could put it off till—"

"Hurry! *Hurry!*" I says. "Where's Jim?"

"Right at your elbow; if you reach out your arm you can touch him. He's dressed, and everything's ready. Now we'll slide out and give the sheep-signal."

But then we heard the tramp of men, coming to the door, and heard them begin to fumble with the padlock; and heard a man say:

"I *told* you we'd be too soon; they haven't come—the door is locked. Here, I'll lock some of you into the cabin and you lay for 'em in the dark and kill 'em when they come; and the rest scatter around a piece, and listen if you can hear 'em coming."

So in they come, but couldn't see us in the dark, and most trod on us whilst we was hustling to get under the bed. But we got under all right, and out through the hole, swift but soft—Jim first, me next, and Tom last, which was according to Tom's orders. Now we was in the lean-to, and heard trampings close by outside. So we crept to the door, and Tom stopped us there and put his eye to the crack, but couldn't make out nothing, it was so dark; and whispered and said he would listen for the steps to get further, and when he nudged us Jim must glide out first, and him last. So he set his ear to the crack and listened, and listened, and listened, and the steps a scraping around, out there, all the time; and at last he nudged us, and we slid out, and stooped down, not breathing, and not making the least noise, and slipped stealthy towards the fence, in Injun file, and got to it, all right, and me and Jim over it; but Tom's britches catched fast on a splinter on the top rail, and then he hear the steps coming, so he had to pull loose, which snapped the splinter and made a noise; and as he dropped in our tracks and started, somebody sings out:

"Who's that? Answer, or I'll shoot!"

---

8. A common term for diseases related to inflammation of the brain.

But we didn't answer; we just unfurled our heels and shoved. Then there was a rush, and a *bang, bang, bang*! and the bullets fairly whizzed around us! We heard them sing out:

"Here they are! They've broke for the river! after 'em, boys! And turn loose the dogs!"

So here they come, full tilt. We could hear them, because they wore boots, and yelled, but we didn't wear no boots, and didn't yell. We was in the path to the mill; and when they got pretty close onto us, we dodged into the bush and let them go by, and then dropped in behind them. They'd had all the dogs shut up, so they wouldn't scare off the robbers; but by this time somebody had let them loose, and here they come, making pow-wow enough for a million; but they was our dogs; so we stopped in our tracks till they catched up; and when they see it warn't nobody but us, and no excitement to offer them, they only just said howdy, and tore right ahead towards the shouting and clattering; and then we up steam again and whizzed along after them till we was nearly to the mill, and then struck up through the bush to where my canoe was tied, and hopped in and pulled for dear life towards the middle of the river, but didn't make no more noise than we was obleeged to. Then we struck out, easy and comfortable, for the island where my raft was; and we could hear them yelling and barking at each other all up and down the bank, till we was so far away the sounds got dim and died out. And when we stepped onto the raft, I says:

"*Now*, old Jim, you're a free man *again*, and I bet you won't ever be a slave no more."

"En a mighty good job it wuz, too, Huck. It 'uz planned beautiful, en it 'uz *done* beautiful; en dey aint' *nobody* kin git up a plan dat's mo' mixed-up en splendid den what dat one wuz."

We was all as glad as we could be, but Tom was the gladdest of all, because he had a bullet in the calf of his leg.

When me and Jim heard that, we didn't feel so brash as what we did before. It was hurting him considerble, and bleeding; so we laid him in the wigwam and tore up one of the duke's shirts for to bandage him, but he says:

"Gimme the rags, I can do it myself. Don't stop, now; don't fool around here, and the evasion booming along so handsome; man the sweeps, and set her loose! Boys, we done it elegant!—'deed we did. I wish *we'd* a had the handling of Louis XVI, there wouldn't a been no 'Son of Saint Louis, ascend to heaven!'[9] wrote down in *his* biography: no, sir, we'd a whooped him over the *border*—that's what we'd a done with *him*—and done it just as slick as nothing at all, too. Man the sweeps—man the sweeps!"

But me and Jim was consulting—and thinking. And after we'd thought a minute, I says:

"Say it, Jim."

So he says:

"Well, den, dis is de way it look to me, Huck. Ef it wuz *him* dat 'uz bein' sot free, en one er de boys wuz to git shot, would he say, 'Go on en save me, nemmine 'bout a doctor f'r to save dis one?' Is dat like Mars Tom Sawyer? Would he say dat? You *bet* he wouldn't! *Well*, den, is *Jim* gwyne to say it?

---

9. Taken from the Scottish historian Thomas Carlyle's rendering of the king's execution in *The French Revolution* (1837).

No, sah—I doan' budge a step out'n dis place, 'dout a *doctor*; not if its forty year!"

I knowed he was white inside, and I reckoned he'd say what he did say— so it was all right, now, and I told Tom I was agoing for a doctor. He raised considerble row about it, but me and Jim stuck to it and wouldn't budge; so he was for crawling out and setting the raft loose himself; but we wouldn't let him. Then he give us a piece of his mind—but it didn't do no good.

So when he see me getting the canoe ready, he says:

"Well, then, if you're bound to go, I'll tell you the way to do, when you get to the village. Shut the door, and blindfold the doctor tight and fast, and make him swear to be silent as the grave, and put a purse full of gold in his hand, and then take and lead him all around the back alleys and everywheres, in the dark, and then fetch him here in the canoe, in a roundabout way amongst the islands, and search him and take his chalk away from him, and don't give it back to him till you get him back to the village, or else he will chalk this raft so he can find it again. It's the way they all do."

So I said I would, and left, and Jim was to hide in the woods when he see the doctor coming, till he was gone again.

Chapter XLI

The doctor was an old man; a very nice, kind-looking old man, when I got him up. I told him me and my brother was over on Spanish Island hunting, yesterday afternoon, and camped on a piece of a raft we found, and about midnight he must a kicked his gun in his dreams, for it went off and shot him in the leg, and we wanted him to go over there and fix it and not say nothing about it, nor let anybody know, because we wanted to come home this evening, and surprise the folks.

"Who is your folks?" he says.

"The Phelpses, down yonder."

"Oh," he says. And after a minute, he says: "How'd you say he got shot?"

"He had a dream," I says, "and it shot him."

"Singular dream," he says.

So he lit up his lantern, and got his saddle-bags, and we started. But when he see the canoe, he didn't like the look of her—said she was big enough for one, but didn't look pretty safe for two. I says:

"Oh, you needn't be afeard, sir, she carried the three of us, easy enough."

"What three?"

"Why, me and Sid, and—and—and *the guns*; that's what I mean."

"Oh," he says.

But he put his foot on the gunnel, and rocked her; and shook his head, and said he reckoned he'd look around for a bigger one. But they was all locked and chained; so he took my canoe, and said for me to wait till he come back, or I could hunt around further, or maybe I better go down home and get them ready for the surprise, if I wanted to. But I said I didn't; so I told him just how to find the raft, and then he started.

I struck an idea, pretty soon. I says to myself, spos'n he can't fix that leg just in three shakes of a sheep's tail, as the saying is? spos'n it takes him three or four days? What are we going to do?—lay around there till he lets the cat out of the bag? No, sir, I know what *I'll* do. I'll wait, and when he comes back, if he says he's got to go any more, I'll get him down there, too, if I swim; and we'll take and tie him, and keep him, and shove out down the river; and when Tom's done with him, we'll give him what it's worth, or all we got, and then let him get shore.

So then I crept into a lumber pile to get some sleep; and next time I waked up the sun was away up over my head! I shot out and went for the doctor's house, but they told me he'd gone away in the night, some time or other, and warn't back yet. Well, thinks I, that looks powerful bad for *Tom*, and I'll dig out for the island, right off. So away I shoved, and turned the corner, and nearly rammed my head into Uncle Silas's stomach! He says:

"Why, Tom! Where you been, all this time, you rascal?"

"*I* hain't been nowheres," I says, "only just hunting for the runaway nigger—me and Sid."

"Why, where ever did you go?" he says. "Your aunt's been mighty uneasy."

"She needn't," I says, "because we was all right. We followed the men and the dogs, but they out-run us, and we lost them; but we thought we heard them on the water, so we got a canoe and took out after them, and crossed over but couldn't find nothing of them; so we cruised along up-shore till we got kind of tired and beat out; and tied up the canoe and went to sleep, and never waked up till about an hour ago, then we paddled over here to hear the news, and Sid's at the post-office to see what he can hear, and I'm a branching out to get something to eat for us, and then we're going home."

So then we went to the post-office to get "Sid"; but just as I suspicioned, he warn't there; so the old man he got a letter out of the office, and we waited a while longer but Sid didn't come; so the old man said come along, let Sid foot it home, or canoe-it, when he got done fooling around—but we would ride. I couldn't get him to let me stay and wait for Sid; and he said there warn't no use in it, and I must come along, and let Aunt Sally see we was all right.

When we got home, Aunt Sally was that glad to see me she laughed and cried both, and hugged me, and give me one of them lickings of hern that don't amount to shucks, and said she'd serve Sid the same when he come.

And the place was plumb full of farmers and farmers' wives, to dinner; and such another clack a body never heard. Old Mrs. Hotchkiss was the worst; her tongue was agoing all the time. She says:

"Well, Sister Phelps, I've ransacked that-air cabin over an' I b'lieve the nigger was crazy. I says so to Sister Damrell—didn't I, Sister Damrell?—s'I, he's crazy, s'I—them's the very words I said. You all hearn me: he's crazy, s'I; everything shows it, s'I. Look at that-air grindstone, s'I; want to tell *me*'t any cretur 'ts in his right mind 's agoin' to scrabble all them crazy things onto a grindstone, s'I? Here sich 'n' sich a person busted his heart; 'n' here so 'n' so pegged along for thirty-seven year, 'n' all that—natcherl son o' Louis some-body, 'n' sich everlast'n rubbage. He's plumb crazy, s'I; it's what I says in the fust place, it's what I says in the middle, 'n' it's what I says last 'n' all the time—the nigger's crazy—crazy's Nebookoodneezer,[1] s'I."

"An' look at that-air ladder made out'n rags, Sister Hotchkiss," says old Mrs. Damrell, "what in the name o'goodness *could* he ever want of—"

---

1. Nebuchadnezzar (605–562 B.C.E.), king of Babylon, is described in Daniel 4.33 as going mad and eating grass.

"The very words I was a-sayin' no longer ago th'n this minute to Sister Utterback, 'n' she'll tell you so herself. Sh-she, look at that-air rag ladder, sh-she; 'n' s'I, yes, *look* at it, s'I—what *could* he a wanted of it, s'I. Sh-she, Sister Hotchkiss, sh-she—"

"But how in the nation'd they ever *git* that grindstone *in* there, *anyway*? 'n' who dug that-air *hole*? 'n' who—"

"My very *words*, Brer Penrod! I was a-sayin'—pass that-air sasser o' m'lasses, won't ye?—I was a-sayin' to Sister Dunlap, jist this minute, how *did* they git that grindstone in there, s'I. Without *help*, mind you—'thout *help*! *Thar's* wher' 'tis. Don't tell *me*, s'I; there *wuz* help, s'I; 'n' ther' wuz a *plenty* help, too, s'I; ther's ben a *dozen* a-helpin' that nigger, 'n' I lay I'd skin every last nigger on this place, but *I'd* find out who done it, s'I; 'n' moreover, s'I—"

"A *dozen* says you!—*forty* couldn't a done everything that's been done. Look at them case-knife saws and things, how tedious they've been made; look at that bed-leg sawed off with 'em, a week's work for six men; look at that nigger made out'n straw on the bed; and look at—"

"You may *well* say it, Brer Hightower! It's jist as I was a-sayin' to Brer Phelps, his own self. S'e, what do *you* think of it, Sister Hotchkiss, s'e? think o' what, Brer Phelps, s'I? think o' that bed-leg sawed off that a way, s'e? *think* of it, s'I? I lay it never sawed *itself* off, s'I—somebody sawed it, s'I; that's my opinion, take it or leave it, it mayn't be no 'count, s'I, but sich as 't is, it's my opinion, s'I, 'n' if anybody k'n start a better one, s'I, let him *do* it, s'I, that's all. I says to Sister Dunlap, s'I—"

"Why, dog my cats, they must a ben a house-full o' niggers in there every night for four weeks, to a done all that work, Sister Phelps. Look at that shirt—every last inch of it kivered over with secret African writ'n done with blood! Must a ben a raft uv 'm at it right along, all the time, amost. Why, I'd give two dollars to have it read to me; 'n' as for the niggers that wrote it, I 'low I'd take 'n' lash 'm t'll—"

"People to *help* him, Brother Marples! Well, I reckon you'd *think* so, if you'd a been in this house for a while back. Why, they've stole everything they could lay their hands on—and we a watching, all the time, mind you. They stole that shirt right off o' the line! and as for that sheet they made the rag ladder out of ther' ain't no telling how many times they *didn't* steal that; and flour, and candles, and candlesticks, and spoons, and the old-warming-pan, and most a thousand things that I disremember, now, and my new calico dress; and me, and Silas, and my Sid and Tom on the constant watch day *and* night, as I was a telling you, and not a one of us could catch hide nor hair, nor sight nor sound of them; and here at the last minute, lo and behold you, they slides right in under our noses, and fools us, and not only fools *us* but the Injun Territory robbers too, and actuly gets *away* with that nigger, safe and sound, and that with sixteen men and twenty-two dogs right on their very heels at that very time! I tell you, it just bangs anything I ever *heard* of. Why, *spirits* couldn't a done better, and been no smarter. And I reckon they must a *been* spirits—because, *you* know our dogs, and ther' ain't no better; well, them dogs never even got on the *track* of 'm, once! You explain *that* to me, if you can!—*any* of you!"

"Well, it does beat—"

"Laws alive, I never—"

"So help me, I wouldn't a be—"

"*House* thieves as well as—"

"Goodnessgracioussakes, I'd a ben afeard to *live* in sich a—"

" 'Fraid to *live*!—why, I was that scared I dasn't hardly go to bed, or get up, or lay down, or *set* down, Sister Ridgeway. Why, they'd steal the very— why, goodness sakes, you can guess what kind of a fluster *I* was in by the time midnight come, last night. I hope to gracious if I warn't afraid they'd steal some o' the family! I was just to that pass, I didn't have no reasoning faculties no more. It looks foolish enough, *now*, in the day-time; but I says to myself, there's my two poor boys asleep, 'way up stairs in that lonesome room, and I declare to goodness I was that uneasy 't I crep' up there and locked 'em in! I *did*. And anybody would. Because, you know, when you get scared, that way, and it keeps running on, and getting worse and worse, all the time, and your wits gets to addling, and you get to doing all sorts o' wild things, and by-and-by you think to yourself, spos'n *I* was a boy, and was away up there, and the door ain't locked, and you—" She stopped, looking kind of wondering, and then she turned her head around slow, and when her eye lit on me—I got up and took a walk.

Says I to myself, I can explain better how we come to not be in that room this morning, if I go out to one side and study over it a little. So I done it. But I dasn't go fur, or she'd a sent for me. And when it was late in the day, the people all went, and then I come in and told her the noise and shooting waked up me and "Sid," and the door was locked, and we wanted to see the fun, so we went down the lightning-rod, and both of us got hurt a little, and we didn't never want to try *that* no more. And then I went on and told her all what I told Uncle Silas before; and then she said she'd forgive us, and maybe it was all right enough anyway, and about what a body might expect of boys, for all boys was a pretty harum-scarum lot, as fur as she could see; and so, as long as no harm hadn't come of it, she judged she better put in her time being grateful we was alive and well and she had us still, stead of fretting over what was past and done. So then she kissed me, and patted me on the head, and dropped into a kind of a brown study; and pretty soon jumps up, and says:

"Why, lawsamercy, it's most night, and Sid not come yet! What *has* become of that boy?"

I see my chance; so I skips up and says:

"I'll run right up to town and get him," I says.

"No, you won't," she says. "You'll stay right wher' you are; *one's* enough to be lost at a time. If he ain't here to supper, your uncle 'll go."

Well, he warn't there to supper; so right after supper uncle went.

He come back about ten, a little bit uneasy; hadn't run across Tom's track. Aunt Sally was a good *deal* uneasy; but Uncle Silas he said there warn't no occasion to be—boys will be boys, he said, and you'll see this one turn up in the morning, all sound and right. So she had to be satisfied. But she said she'd set up for him a while, anyway, and keep a light burning, so he could see it.

And then when I went up to bed she come up with me and fetched her candle, and tucked me in, and mothered me so good I felt mean, and like I couldn't look her in the face; and she set down on the bed and talked with me a long time, and said what a splendid boy Sid was, and didn't seem to want to ever stop talking about him; and kept asking me every now and then, if I reckoned he could a got lost, or hurt, or maybe drownded, and might be laying at this minute, somewhere, suffering or dead, and she not by him to help him, and so the tears would drip down, silent, and I would tell her that Sid was all right, and would be home in the morning, sure; and she would squeeze my hand, or maybe kiss me, and tell me to say it again, and keep on saying it, because it done her good, and she was in so much trouble. And when she was going away, she looked down in my eyes, so steady and gentle, and says:

"The door ain't going to be locked, Tom; and there's the window and the rod; but you'll be good, *won't* you? And you won't go? For *my* sake."

Laws knows I *wanted* to go, bad enough, to see about Tom, and was all intending to go; but after that, I wouldn't a went, not for kingdoms.

But she was on my mind, and Tom was on my mind; so I slept very restless. And twice I went down the rod, away in the night, and slipped around front, and see her setting there by her candle in the window with her eyes towards the road and the tears in them; and I wished I could do something for her, but I couldn't, only to swear that I wouldn't never do nothing to grieve her any more. And the third time, I waked up at dawn, and slid down, and she was there yet, and her candle was most out, and her old gray head was resting on her hand, and she was asleep.

Chapter XLII

The old man was up town again, before breakfast, but couldn't get no track of Tom; and both of them set at the table, thinking, and not saying nothing, and looking mournful, and their coffee getting cold, and not eating anything. And by-and-by the old man says:

"Did I give you the letter?"

"What letter?"

"The one I got yesterday out of the post-office."

"No, you didn't give me no letter."

"Well, I must a forgot it."

So he rummaged his pockets, and then went off somewheres where he had laid it down, and fetched it, and give it to her. She says:

"Why, it's from St. Petersburg—it's from Sis."

I allowed another walk would do me good; but I couldn't stir. But before she could break it open, she dropped it and run—for she see something. And so did I. It was Tom Sawyer on a mattress; and that old doctor; and Jim, in *her* calico dress, with his hands tied behind him; and a lot of people. I hid the letter behind the first thing that come handy, and rushed. She flung herself at Tom, crying, and says:

"Oh, he's dead, he's dead, I know he's dead!"

And Tom he turned his head a little, and muttered something or other, which showed he warn't in his right mind; then she flung up her hands and says:

"He's alive, thank God! And that's enough!" and she snatched a kiss of him, and flew for the house to get the bed ready, and scattering orders right and left at the niggers and everybody else, as fast as her tongue could go, every jump of the way.

I followed the men to see what they was going to do with Jim; and the old doctor and Uncle Silas followed after Tom into the house. The men was very huffy, and some of them wanted to hang Jim, for an example to all the other niggers around there, so they wouldn't be trying to run away, like Jim done, and making such a raft of trouble, and keeping a whole family scared most to death for days and nights. But the others said, don't do it, it wouldn't answer at all, he ain't our nigger, and his owner would turn up and make us pay for him, sure. So that cooled them down a little, because the people that's always the most anxious for to hang a nigger that hain't done just right, is always the very ones that ain't the most anxious to pay for him when they've got their satisfaction out of him.

They cussed Jim considerble, though, and give him a cuff or two, side the head, once in a while, but Jim never said nothing, and he never let on to know me, and they took him to the same cabin, and put his own clothes on him, and chained him again, and not to no bed-leg, this time, but to a big staple drove into the bottom log, and chained his hands, too, and both legs, and said he warn't to have nothing but bread and water to eat, after this, till his owner come or he was sold at auction, because he didn't come in a certain length of time, and filled up our hole, and said a couple of farmers with guns must stand watch around about the cabin every night, and a bull-dog tied to the door in the day time; and about this time they was through with the job and was tapering off with a kind of generl good-bye cussing, and then the old doctor comes and takes a look and says:

"Don't be no rougher on him than you're obleeged to, because he ain't a bad nigger. When I got to where I found the boy, I see I couldn't cut the bullet out without some help, and he warn't in no condition for me to leave, to go and get help; and he got a little worse and a little worse, and after a long time he went out of his head, and wouldn't let me come anigh him, any more, and said if I chalked his raft he'd kill me, and no end of wild foolishness like that, and I see I couldn't do anything at all with him; so I says, I got to have *help*, somehow; and the minute I says it, out crawls this nigger from somewheres, and says he'll help, and he done it, too, and done it very well. Of course I judged he must be a runaway nigger, and there I *was*! and there I had to stick, right straight along all the rest of the day, and all night. It was a fix, I tell you! I had a couple of patients with the chills, and of course I'd of liked to run up to town and see them, but I dasn't, because the nigger might get away, and then I'd be to blame; and yet never a skiff come close enough for me to hail. So there I had to stick, plumb till daylight this morning; and I never see a nigger that was a better nuss or faithfuller, and yet he was resking his freedom to do it, and was all tired out, too, and I see plain enough he'd been worked main hard, lately. I liked the nigger for that; I tell you, gentlemen, a nigger like that is worth a thousand dollars—and kind treatment, too. I had everything I needed, and the boy was doing as well there as he would a done at home—better, maybe, because it was so quiet; but there I *was*, with both of 'm on my hands; and there I had to stick, till about dawn this morning; then some men in a skiff come by, and as good luck would have it, the nigger was setting by the pallet with his head propped on his knees, sound asleep; so I motioned them in, quiet, and they slipped up on him and grabbed him and tied him before he knowed what he was about, and we never had no trouble. And the boy being in a kind of a flighty sleep, too, we muffled the oars and hitched the raft on, and towed her over very nice and quiet, and the nigger never made the least row nor said a word, from the start. He ain't no bad nigger, gentlemen; that's what I think about him."

Somebody says:

"Well, it sounds very good, doctor, I'm obleeged to say."

Then the others softened up a little, too, and I was mighty thankful to that old doctor for doing Jim that good turn; and I was glad it was according to my judgment of him, too; because I thought he had a good heart in him and was a good man, the first time I see him. Then they all agreed that Jim had acted very well, and was deserving to have some notice took of it, and reward. So every one of them promised, right out and hearty, that they wouldn't cuss him no more.

Then they come out and locked him up. I hoped they was going to say he could have one or two of the chains took off, because they was rotten heavy, or could have meat and greens with his bread and water, but they didn't think of it, and I reckoned it warn't best for me to mix in, but I judged I'd get the doctor's yarn to Aunt Sally, somehow or other, as soon as I'd got through the breakers that was laying just ahead of me. Explanations, I mean, of how I forgot to mention about Sid being shot, when I was telling how him and me put in that dratted night paddling around hunting the runaway nigger.

But I had plenty time. Aunt Sally she stuck to the sick-room all day and all night; and every time I see Uncle Silas mooning around, I dodged him.

Next morning I heard Tom was a good deal better, and they said Aunt Sally was gone to get a nap. So I slips to the sick-room, and if I found him awake I reckoned we could put up a yarn for the family that would wash. But he was sleeping, and sleeping very peaceful, too; and pale, not fire-faced the way he was when he come. So I set down and laid for him to wake. In about a half an hour, Aunt Sally comes gliding in, and there I was, up a stump again! She motioned me to be still, and set down by me, and begun to whisper, and said we could all be joyful now, because all the symptoms was first rate, and he'd been sleeping like that for ever so long, and looking better and peacefuller all the time, and ten to one he'd wake up in his right mind.

So we set there watching, and by-and-by he stirs a bit, and opened his eyes very natural, and takes a look, and says:

"Hello, why I'm at *home*! How's that? Where's the raft?"

"It's all right," I says.

"And *Jim*?"

"The same," I says, but couldn't say it pretty brash. But he never noticed, but says:

"Good! Splendid! *Now* we're all right and safe! Did you tell Aunty?"

I was about to say yes; but she chipped in and says:

"About what, Sid?"

"Why, about the way the whole thing was done."

"What whole thing?"

"Why, *the* whole thing. There ain't but one; how we set the runaway nigger free—me and Tom."

"Good land! Set the run—What *is* the child talking about! Dear, dear, out of his head again!"

"*No*, I ain't out of my HEAD; I know all what I'm talking about. We *did* set him free—me and Tom. We laid out to do it, and we *done* it. And we done it elegant, too." He'd got a start, and she never checked him up, just set and stared and stared, and let him clip along, and I see it warn't no use for *me* to put in. "Why, Aunty, it cost us a power of work—weeks of it—hours and hours, every night, whilst you was all asleep. And we had to steal candles, and the sheet, and the shirt, and your dress, and spoons, and tin plates, and case-knives, and the warming-pan, and the grindstone, and flour, and just no end of things, and you can't think what work it was to make the saws, and pens, and inscriptions, and one thing or another, and you can't think *half* the fun it was. And we had to make up the pictures of coffins and things, and nonnamous letters from the robbers, and get up and down the lightning-rod, and dig the hole into the cabin, and make the rope-ladder and send it in cooked up in a pie, and send in spoons and things to work with, in your apron pocket"—

"Mercy sakes!"

—"and load up the cabin with rats and snakes and so on, for company for Jim; and then you kept Tom here so long with the butter in his hat that you come near spiling the whole business, because the men come before we was out of the cabin, and we had to rush, and they heard us and let drive at us, and I got my share, and we dodged out of the path and let them go by, and when the dogs come they warn't interested in us, but went for the most noise, and we got our canoe, and made for the raft, and was all safe, and Jim was a free man, and we done it all by ourselves, and *wasn't* it bully, Aunty!"

"Well, I never heard the likes of it in all my born days! So it was *you,* you little rapscallions, that's been making all this trouble, and turn everybody's wits clean inside out and scared us all most to death. I've as good a notion as ever I had in my life, to take it out o' you this very minute. To think, here I've been, night after night, a—*you* just get well once, you young scamp, and I lay I'll tan the Old Harry[2] out o' both o' ye!"

But Tom, he *was* so proud and joyful, he just *couldn't* hold in, and his tongue just *went* it—she a-chipping in, and spitting fire all along, and both of them going it at once, like a cat-convention; and she says:

"*Well,* you get all the enjoyment you can out of it *now,* for mind I tell you if I catch you meddling with him again—"

"Meddling with *who?*" Tom says, dropping his smile and looking surprised.

"With *who?* Why, the runaway nigger, of course. Who'd you reckon?"

Tom looks at me very grave, and says:

"Tom, didn't you just tell me he was all right? Hasn't he got away?"

"*Him?*" says Aunt Sally; "the runaway nigger? 'Deed he hasn't. They've got him back, safe and sound, and he's in that cabin again, on bread and water, and loaded down with chains, till he's claimed or sold!"

Tom rose square up in bed, with his eye hot, and his nostrils opening and shutting like gills, and sings out to me:

"They hain't no *right* to shut him up! *Shove!*—and don't you lose a minute. Turn him loose! he ain't no slave; he's as free as any cretur that walks this earth!"

"What *does* the child mean?"

"I mean every word I *say,* Aunt Sally, and if somebody don't go, *I'll* go. I've knowed him all his life, and so has Tom, there. Old Miss Watson died two months ago, and she was ashamed she ever was going to sell him down the river, and *said* so; and she set him free in her will."

2. The devil.

"Then what on earth did *you* want to set him free for, seeing he was already free?"

"Well, that *is* a question, I must say; and *just* like women! Why, I wanted the *adventure* of it; and I'd a waded neck-deep in blood to—goodness alive, AUNT POLLY!"[3]

If she warn't standing right there, just inside the door, looking as sweet and contented as an angel half-full of pie, I wish I may never!

Aunt Sally jumped for her, and most hugged the head off of her, and cried over her, and I found a good enough place for me under the bed, for it was getting pretty sultry for *us*, seemed to me. And I peeped out, and in a little while Tom's Aunt Polly shook herself loose and stood there looking across at Tom over her spectacles—kind of grinding him into the earth, you know. And then she says:

"Yes, you *better* turn y'r head away—I would if I was you, Tom."

"Oh, deary me!" says Aunt Sally; "*is* he changed so? Why, that ain't *Tom* it's Sid; Tom's—Tom's—why, where is Tom? He was here a minute ago."

"You mean where's Huck *Finn*—that's what you mean! I reckon I hain't raised such a scamp as my Tom all these years, not to know him when I *see* him. That *would* be a pretty howdy-do. Come out from under the bed, Huck Finn."

So I done it. But not feeling brash.

Aunt Sally she was one of the mixed-upest looking persons I ever see; except one, and that was Uncle Silas, when he come in, and they told it all to him. It kind of made him drunk, as you may say, and he didn't know nothing at all the rest of the day, and preached a prayer-meeting sermon that night that give him a rattling ruputation, because the oldest man in the world couldn't a understood it. So Tom's Aunt Polly, she told all about who I was, and what; and I had to up and tell how I was in such a tight place that when Mrs. Phelps took me for Tom Sawyer—she chipped in and says, "Oh, go on and call me Aunt Sally, I'm used to it, now, and 'tain't no need to change"— that when Aunt Sally took me for Tom Sawyer, I had to stand it—that warn't no other way, and I knowed he wouldn't mind, because it would be nuts for him, being a mystery, and he'd make an adventure out of it and be perfectly satisfied. And so it turned out, and he let on to be Sid, and made things as soft as he could for me.

And his Aunt Polly she said Tom was right about old Miss Watson setting Jim free in her will; and so, sure enough, Tom Sawyer had gone and took all that trouble and bother to set a free nigger free! and I couldn't ever understand, before, until that minute and that talk, how he *could* help a body set a nigger free, with his bringing-up.

Well, Aunt Polly she said that when Aunt Sally wrote to her that Tom and *Sid* had come, all right and safe, she says to herself:

"Look at that, now! I might have expected it, letting him go off that way without anybody to watch him. So now I got to go and trapse all the way down the river, eleven hundred mile, and find out what that creetur's up to, *this* time; as long as I couldn't seem to get any answer out of you about it."

---

3. Tom Sawyer's aunt and guardian, who appears in *The Adventures of Tom Sawyer*.

"Why, I never heard nothing from you," says Aunt Sally.

"Well, I wonder! Why, I wrote to you twice, to ask you what you could mean by Sid being here."

"Well, I never got 'em, Sis."

Aunt Polly, she turns around slow and severe, and says:

"You, Tom!"

"Well—*what?*" he says, kind of pettish.

"Don't you what *me*, you impudent thing—hand out them letters."

"What letters?"

"*Them* letters. I be bound, if I have to take aholt of you I'll—"

"They're in the trunk. There, now. And they're just the same as they was when I got them out of the office. I hain't looked into them, I hain't touched them. But I knowed they'd make trouble, and I thought if you warn't in no hurry, I'd—"

"Well, you *do* need skinning, there ain't no mistake about it. And I wrote another one to tell you I was coming; and I spose he—"

"No, it come yesterday; I hain't read it yet, but *it's* all right, I've got that one."

I wanted to offer to bet two dollars she hadn't, but I reckoned maybe it was just as safe to not to. So I never said nothing.

Chapter the Last

The first time I catched Tom, private, I asked him what was his idea, time of the evasion?—what it was he'd planned to do if the evasion worked all right and he managed to set a nigger free that was already free before? And he said, what he had planned in his head, from the start, if we got Jim out all safe, was for us to run him down the river, on the raft, and have adventures plumb to the mouth of the river, and then tell him about his being free, and take him back up home on a steamboat, in style, and pay him for his lost time, and write word ahead and get out all the niggers around, and have them waltz him into town with a torchlight procession and a brass band, and then he would be a hero, and so would we. But I reckoned it was about as well the way it was.

We had Jim out of the chains in no time, and when Aunt Polly and Uncle Silas and Aunt Sally found out how good he helped the doctor nurse Tom, they made a heap of fuss over him, and fixed him up prime, and give him all he wanted to eat, and a good time, and nothing to do. And we had him up to the sickroom; and had a high talk; and Tom give Jim forty dollars for being prisoner for us so patient, and doing it up so good, and Jim was pleased most to death, and busted out, and says:

"*Dah*, now, Huck, what I tell you?—what I tell you up dah on Jackson islan'? I *tole* you I got a hairy breas', en what's de sign un it; en I *tole* you I ben rich wunst, en gwineter to be rich *agin*; en it's come true; en heah she *is! Dah*, now! doan' talk to *me*—signs is *signs*, mine I tell you; en I knowed jis' 's well 'at I 'uz gwineter be rich agin as I's a stannin' heah dis minute!"

And then Tom he talked along, and talked along, and says, le's all three slide out of here, one of these nights, and get an outfit, and go for howling adventures amongst the Injuns, over in the Territory, for a couple of weeks or two; and I says, all right, that suits me, but I ain't got no money for to buy the outfit, and I reckon I couldn't get none from home, because it's likely pap's been back before now, and got it all away from Judge Thatcher and drunk it up.

"No he hain't," Tom says; "it's all there, yet—six thousand dollars and more; and your pap hain't ever been back since. Hadn't when I come away, anyhow."

Jim says, kind of solemn:

"He ain't a comin' back no mo', Huck."

I says:

"Why, Jim?"

"Nemmine why, Huck—but he ain't comin' back no mo'."

But I kept at him; so at last he says:

"Doan' you 'member de house dat was float'n down de river, en dey wuz a man in dah, kivered up, en I went in en unkivered him and didn' let you come in? Well, den, you k'n git yo' money when you wants it; kase dat wuz him."

Tom's most well, now, and got his bullet around his neck on a watch-guard for a watch, and is always seeing what time it is, and so there ain't nothing more to write about, and I am rotten glad of it, because if I'd a knowed what a trouble it was to make a book I wouldn't a tackled it and ain't agoing to no more. But I reckon I got to light out for the Territory ahead of the rest, because Aunt Sally she's going to adopt me and sivilize me and I can't stand it. I been there before.

THE END. YOURS TRULY, HUCK FINN.

1876–83   1884

Critical Controversy:
Race and the Ending of
Adventures of Huckleberry Finn

Celebrated by Ernest Hemingway as the source of all modern American literature, and regarded by many as a great American novel, *Adventures of Huckleberry Finn* has always been controversial. In Twain's day it was criticized for taking as its hero a boy who smoked, loafed, and preferred the company of a runaway slave to Sunday School. Banned in some school districts and denounced by some scholars and teachers as racist, it has been defended by others as a powerful attack on racism. Its lengthy and ambiguous final section, when the plot to free Jim gives way to an account of Tom Sawyer's pranks, has also provoked controversy. This short selection of critical writings provides a sampling of modern debate on the novel.

Below are the conflicting voices of literary critics and novelists on Jim as a character, on Huck's relationship with Jim, on the use of the "n-word," on race in general, and on the problematic ending. Some of the writers here are sharply critical of the book for what they see as its failure to follow through on its initial premise, that Jim is an admirable character whose drive for freedom expresses a basic human need. Others argue that there is no such failure, that the book maintains its attack on those who deny Jim's status as a human being. The controversy is possible because Twain's ironic humor makes his own position difficult to identify. Leo Marx thinks Jim's drive for freedom is trivialized by an ending in which Huck becomes Tom Sawyer's yes-man. Julius Lester criticizes the book's depiction of Jim along the same lines, arguing that Jim becomes more of a minstrel-show figure than the admirable person he had earlier been. Jane Smiley, also disturbed by Twain's depiction of this black character, proposes Harriet Beecher Stowe's *Uncle Tom's Cabin* (1852) as a better model for American literature. In contrast, David L. Smith argues that the novel undercuts racist discourse with a trenchant critique of nineteenth-century conceptions of "the Negro." Toni Morrison offers insights into her own experience of reading the novel a number of times over many years, concluding that *Huckleberry Finn* is a classic in part because of the powerful way that it raises but does not answer questions about race, culture, character, and nation. Finally, Alan Gribben explains his decision to create a new edition of the novel, published in 2011, that replaces its most infamous racial epithet with the word "slave"; Michiko Kakutani, writing in the *New York Times*, argues that Gribben's substitution whitewashes the "harsh historical realities" that Twain's novel portrays.

LEO MARX

From Mr. Eliot, Mr. Trilling, and *Huckleberry Finn*[1]

* * *

I believe that the ending of *Huckleberry Finn* makes so many readers uneasy because they rightly sense that it jeopardizes the significance of the entire novel. To take seriously what happens at the Phelps farm is to take lightly the entire downstream journey. What is the meaning of the journey? With this question all discussion of *Huckleberry Finn* must begin. It is true that the voyage down the river has many aspects of a boy's idyl. We owe much of its hold upon our imagination to the enchanting image of the raft's unhurried drift with the current. The leisure, the absence of constraint, the beauty of the river—all these things delight us. "It's lovely to live on a raft." And the multitudinous life of the great valley we see through Huck's eyes has a fascination of its own. Then, of course, there is humor—laughter so spontaneous, so free of the bitterness present almost everywhere in American humor that readers often forget how grim a spectacle of human existence Huck contemplates. Humor in this novel flows from a bright joy of life as remote from our world as living on a raft.

Yet along with the idyllic and the epical and the funny in *Huckleberry Finn*, there is a coil of meaning which does for the disparate elements of the novel what a spring does for a watch. The meaning is not in the least obscure. It is made explicit again and again. The very words with which Clemens launches Huck and Jim upon their voyage indicate that theirs is not a boy's lark but a quest for freedom. From the electrifying moment when Huck comes back to Jackson's Island and rouses Jim with the news that a search party is on the way, we are meant to believe that Huck is enlisted in the cause of freedom. "Git up and hump yourself, Jim!" he cries. "There ain't a minute to lose. They're after us!" What particularly counts here is the *us*. No one is after Huck; no one but Jim knows he is alive. In that small word Clemens compresses the exhilarating power of Huck's instinctive humanity. His unpremeditated identification with Jim's flight from slavery is an unforgettable moment in American experience, and it may be said at once that any culmination of the journey which detracts from the urgency and dignity with which it begins will necessarily be unsatisfactory. Huck realizes this himself, and says so when, much later, he comes back to the raft after discovering that the Duke and the King have sold Jim:

> After all this long journey . . . here it was all come to nothing, every-
> thing all busted up and ruined, because they could have the heart to
> serve Jim such a trick as that, and make him a slave again all his life,
> and amongst strangers, too, for forty dirty dollars.

1. From *American Scholar* 22 (1953): 423–40. A pioneering scholar in the field of American studies, Leo Marx (b. 1919) is best known as the author of *The Machine in the Garden: Technology and the Pastoral Ideal in America* (1964). The title of this essay refers to admiring introductions to *Huckleberry Finn* (1948 and 1950, respectively) written by the critic Lionel Trilling (1905–1975) and the poet T. S. Eliot (1888–1965).

OUT OF BONDAGE.

Out of bondage. E. W. Kemble's illustration for the final chapter of the
first edition (1884).

Huck knows that the journey will have been a failure unless it takes Jim to
freedom. It is true that we do discover, in the end, that Jim is free, but we
also find out that the journey was not the means by which he finally reached
freedom.

The most obvious thing wrong with the ending, then, is the flimsy contrivance by which Clemens frees Jim. In the end we not only discover that
Jim has been a free man for two months, but that his freedom has been
granted by old Miss Watson. If this were only a mechanical device for terminating the action, it might not call for much comment. But it is more than
that: it is a significant clue to the import of the last ten chapters. Remember
who Miss Watson is. She is the Widow's sister whom Huck introduces in
the first pages of the novel. It is she who keeps "pecking" at Huck, who tries
to teach him to spell and to pray and to keep his feet off the furniture. She
is an ardent proselytizer for piety and good manners, and her greed provides
the occasion for the journey in the first place. She is Jim's owner, and he
decides to flee only when he realizes that she is about to break her word (she
cannot resist a slave trader's offer of eight hundred dollars) and sell him down
the river away from his family.

Miss Watson, in short, is the Enemy. If we except a predilection for physical violence, she exhibits all the outstanding traits of the valley society. She pronounces the polite lies of civilization that suffocate Huck's spirit. The freedom which Jim seeks, and which Huck and Jim temporarily enjoy aboard the raft, is accordingly freedom *from* everything for which Miss Watson stands. Indeed, the very intensity of the novel derives from the discordance between the aspirations of the fugitives and the respectable code for which she is a spokesman. Therefore her regeneration, of which the deathbed freeing of Jim is the unconvincing sign, hints a resolution of the novel's essential conflict. Perhaps because this device most transparently reveals that shift in point of view which he could not avoid, and which is less easily discerned elsewhere in the concluding chapters, Clemens plays it down. He makes little attempt to account for Miss Watson's change of heart, a change particularly surprising in view of Jim's brazen escape.

* * *

Huckleberry Finn is a masterpiece because it brings Western humor to perfection and yet transcends the narrow limits of its conventions. But the ending does not. During the final extravaganza we are forced to put aside many of the mature emotions evoked earlier by the vivid rendering of Jim's fear of capture, the tenderness of Huck's and Jim's regard for each other, and Huck's excruciating moments of wavering between honesty and respectability. None of these emotions are called forth by the anticlimactic final sequence. I do not mean to suggest that the inclusion of low comedy per se is a flaw in *Huckleberry Finn*. One does not object to the shenanigans of the rogues; there is ample precedent for the place of extravagant humor even in works of high seriousness. But here the case differs from most which come to mind: the major characters themselves are forced to play low comedy roles. Moreover, the most serious motive in the novel, Jim's yearning for freedom, is made the object of nonsense. The conclusion, in short, is farce, but the rest of the novel is not.

* * *

Tom reappears. Soon Huck has fallen almost completely under his sway once more, and we are asked to believe that the boy who felt pity for the rogues is now capable of making Jim's capture the occasion for a game. He becomes Tom's helpless accomplice, submissive and gullible. No wonder that Clemens has Huck remark, when Huck first realizes Aunt Sally has mistaken him for Tom, that "it was like being born again." Exactly. In the end, Huck regresses to the subordinate role in which he had first appeared in *The Adventures of Tom Sawyer*. Most of those traits which made him so appealing a hero now disappear. He had never, for example, found pain or misfortune amusing.

* * *

What I have been saying is that the flimsy devices of plot, the discordant farcical tone, and the disintegration of the major characters all betray the failure of the ending.

* * *

JULIUS LESTER

From Morality and *Adventures of Huckleberry Finn*[1]

* * *

The novel plays with black reality from the moment Jim runs away and does not immediately seek his freedom. It defies logic that Jim did not know Illinois was a free state. Yet, Twain wants us not only to believe he didn't, but to accept as credible that a runaway slave would sail *south* down the Mississippi River, the only route to freedom he knew being at Cairo, Illinois, where the Ohio River meets the Mississippi. If Jim knew that the Ohio met the Mississippi at Cairo, how could he not have known of the closer proximity of freedom to the east in Illinois or north in Iowa? If the reader must suspend intelligence to accept this, intelligence has to be dispensed with altogether to believe that Jim, having unknowingly passed the confluence of the Ohio and Mississippi Rivers, would continue down the river and go deeper and deeper into the heart of slave country. A century of white readers have accepted this as credible, a grim reminder of the abysmal feelings of superiority with which whites are burdened.

The least we expect of a novel is that it be credible, if not wholly in fact then in emotion, for it is emotions that are the true subject matter of fiction. As Jim floats down the river further and further into slave country without anxiety about his fate, without making the least effort to reverse matters, we leave the realm of factual and emotional credibility and enter the all too familiar one of white fantasy in which blacks have all the humanity of Cabbage Patch dolls.

* * *

The depth of Twain's contempt for blacks is not revealed fully until Tom Sawyer clears up something that had confused Huck. When Huck first proposed freeing Jim, he was surprised that Tom agreed readily. The reason Tom did so is because he knew all the while that Miss Watson had freed Jim when she died two months before.

Once again credibility is slain. Early in the novel Jim's disappearance from the town coincides with Huck's. Huck, having manufactured "evidence" of his "murder" to cover his escape, learns that the townspeople believe that Jim killed him. Yet, we are now to believe that an old white lady would free a black slave suspected of murdering a white child. White people might want to believe such fairy tales about themselves, but blacks know better.

But this is not the nadir of Twain's contempt, because when Aunt Sally asks Tom why he wanted to free Jim, knowing he was already free, Tom replies: "Well, that *is* a question, I must say; and *just* like women! Why, I wanted the *adventure* of it . . ." (Ch. 42). Now Huck understands why Tom was so eager to help Jim "escape."

---

1. From the *Mark Twain Journal* 22 (1984): 43–46. A professor at the University of Massachusetts for over thirty years, Julius Lester (b. 1939) is an award-winning author of books for children and adults.

Tom goes on to explain that his plan was "for us to run him down the river on the raft, and have adventures plumb to the mouth of the river." Then he and Huck would tell Jim he was free and take him "back up home on a steamboat, in style, and pay him for his lost time." They would tell everyone they were coming and "get out all the niggers around, and have them waltz him into town with a torchlight procession and a brass-band, and then he would be a hero, and so would we" ("Chapter the Last").

There is no honor here: * * * Jim is a plaything, an excuse for "the *adventure* of it," to be used as it suits the fancies of the white folk, whether that fancy be a journey on a raft down the river or a torch-light parade. What Jim clearly is not is a human being, and this is emphasized by the fact that Miss Watson's will frees Jim but makes no mention of his wife and children.

Twain doesn't care about the lives the slaves actually lived. Because he doesn't care, he devalues the world.

DAVID L. SMITH

From Huck, Jim, and American Racial Discourse[1]

In July 1876, exactly one century after the American Declaration of Independence, Mark Twain began writing *Adventures of Huckleberry Finn*, a novel that illustrates trenchantly the social limitations that American "civilization" imposes on individual freedom. The book takes special note of ways in which racism impinges upon the lives of Afro-Americans, even when they are legally "free." It is therefore ironic that *Huckleberry Finn* has often been attacked and even censored as a racist work. I would argue, on the contrary, that except for Melville's work, *Huckleberry Finn* is without peer among major Euro-American novels for its explicitly antiracist stance. Those who brand the book racist generally do so without having considered the specific form of racial discourse to which the novel responds. Furthermore, *Huckleberry Finn* offers much more than the typical liberal defenses of "human dignity" and protests against cruelty. Though it contains some such elements, it is more fundamentally a critique of those socially constituted fictions— most notably romanticism, religion, and the concept of "the Negro"—which serve to justify and disguise selfish, cruel, and exploitative behavior.

When I speak of "racial discourse," I mean more than simply attitudes about race or conventions of talking about race. Most importantly, I mean that race itself is a discursive formation which delimits social relations on the basis of alleged physical differences. "Race" is a strategy for relegating a segment of the population to a permanent inferior status. It functions by insisting that each "race" has specific, definitive, inherent behavioral tendencies and capacities which distinguish it from other races. Though scientifically specious, race has

---

1. From *Satire or Evasion? Black Perspectives on Huckleberry Finn*, ed. James S. Leonard, Thomas A. Tenney, and Thadious M. Davis (1992), 103–20. David L. Smith is a professor at Williams College.

been powerfully effective as an ideology and as a form of social definition that serves the interests of Euro-American hegemony. In America, race has been deployed against numerous groups, including Native Americans, Jews, Asians, and even—for brief periods—an assortment of European immigrants.

For obvious reasons, however, the primary emphasis historically has been on defining "the Negro" as a deviant from Euro-American norms. "Race" in America means white supremacy and black inferiority, and "the Negro," a socially constituted fiction, is a generalized, one-dimensional surrogate for the historical reality of Afro-American people. It is this reified fiction that Twain attacks in *Huckleberry Finn*.

Twain adopts a strategy of subversion in his attack on race. That is, he focuses on a number of commonplaces associated with "the Negro" and then systematically dramatizes their inadequacy. He uses the term "nigger," and he shows Jim engaging in superstitious behavior. Yet he portrays Jim as a compassionate, shrewd, thoughtful, self-sacrificing, and even wise man. Indeed, his portrayal of Jim contradicts every claim presented in Jefferson's description of "the Negro."[2] Jim is cautious, he gives excellent advice, he suffers persistent anguish over separation from his wife and children, and he even sacrifices his own sleep so that Huck may rest. Jim, in short, exhibits all the qualities that "the Negro" supposedly lacks. Twain's conclusions do more than merely subvert the justifications of slavery, which was already long since abolished. Twain began his book during the final disintegration of Reconstruction, and his satire on antebellum southern bigotry is also an implicit response to the Negrophobic climate of the post-Reconstruction era. It is troubling, therefore, that so many readers have completely misunderstood Twain's subtle attack on racism.

Twain's use of the term "nigger" has provoked some readers to reject the novel. As one of the most offensive words in our vocabulary, "nigger" remains heavily shrouded in taboo. A careful assessment of this term within the context of American racial discourse, however, will allow us to understand the particular way in which the author uses it. If we attend closely to Twain's use of the word, we may find in it not just a trigger to outrage but, more important, a means of understanding the precise nature of American racism and Mark Twain's attack on it.

Most obviously, Twain uses "nigger" throughout the book as a synonym for "slave." There is ample evidence from other sources that this corresponds to one usage common during the antebellum period. We first encounter it in reference to "Miss Watson's big nigger, named Jim" (chap. 2). This usage, like the term "nigger stealer," clearly designates the "nigger" as an item of property: a commodity, a slave. This passage also provides the only apparent textual justification for the common critical practice of labeling Jim "Nigger Jim," as if "nigger" were a part of his proper name. This loathsome habit goes back at least as far as Albert Bigelow Paine's biography of Twain (1912). In any case, "nigger" in this sense connotes an inferior, even subhuman, creature who is properly owned by and subservient to Euro-Americans.

2. A reference to Thomas Jefferson's *Notes on the State of Virginia* (1787), Query XIV.

Both Huck and Jim use the word in this sense. For example, when Huck fabricates his tale about the riverboat accident, the following exchange occurs between him and Aunt Sally:

> "Good gracious! anybody hurt?"
> "No'm. Killed a nigger."
> "Well, it's lucky; because sometimes people do get hurt." (Chap. 32)

Huck has never met Aunt Sally prior to this scene, and in spinning a lie which this stranger will find unobjectionable, he correctly assumes that the common notion of Negro subhumanity will be appropriate. Huck's offhand remark is intended to exploit Aunt Sally's attitudes, not to express Huck's own. A nigger, Aunt Sally confirms, is not a person. Yet this exchange is hilarious precisely because we know that Huck is playing on her glib and conventional bigotry. We know that Huck's relationship to Jim has already invalidated for him such obtuse racial notions. The conception of the "nigger" is a socially constituted and sanctioned fiction, and it is just as false and absurd as Huck's explicit fabrication, which Aunt Sally also swallows whole.

In fact, the exchange between Huck and Aunt Sally reveals a great deal about how racial discourse operates. Its function is to promulgate a conception of "the Negro" as a subhuman and expendable creature who is by definition feeble-minded, immoral, lazy, and superstitious. One crucial purpose of this social fiction is to justify the abuse and exploitation of Afro-American people by substituting the essentialist fiction of "Negroism" for the actual character of individual Afro-Americans. Hence, in racial discourse every Afro-American becomes just another instance of "the Negro"—just another "nigger." Twain recognizes this invidious tendency of race thinking, however, and he takes every opportunity to expose the mismatch between racial abstractions and real human beings.

* * *

As a serious critic of American society, Twain recognized that racial discourse depends upon the deployment of a system of stereotypes which constitute "the Negro" as fundamentally different from and inferior to Euro-Americans. As with his handling of "nigger," Twain's strategy with racial stereotypes is to elaborate them in order to undermine them. To be sure, those critics are correct who have argued that Twain uses this narrative to reveal Jim's humanity. Jim, however, is just one individual. Twain uses the narrative to expose the cruelty and hollowness of that racial discourse which exists only to obscure the humanity of *all* Afro-American people.

JANE SMILEY

From Say It Ain't So, Huck: Second Thoughts on Mark Twain's "Masterpiece"[1]

* * *

As with all bad endings, the problem really lies at the beginning, and at the beginning of *The Adventures of Huckleberry Finn* neither Huck nor Twain takes Jim's desire for freedom at all seriously; that is, they do not accord it the respect that a man's passion deserves. The sign of this is that not only do the two never cross the Mississippi to Illinois, a free state, but they hardly even consider it. In both *Tom Sawyer* and *Huckleberry Finn*, the Jackson's Island scenes show that such a crossing, even in secret, is both possible and routine, and even though it would present legal difficulties for an escaped slave, these would certainly pose no more hardship than locating the mouth of the Ohio and then finding passage up it. It is true that there could have been slave catchers in pursuit (though the novel ostensibly takes place in the 1840s and the Fugitive Slave Act was not passed until 1850), but Twain's moral failure, once Huck and Jim link up, is never even to account for their choice to go down the river rather than across it. What this reveals is that for all his lip service to real attachment between white boy and black man, Twain really saw Jim as no more than Huck's sidekick, homoerotic or otherwise. All the claims that are routinely made for the book's humanitarian power are, in the end, simply absurd. Jim is never autonomous, never has a vote, always finds his purposes subordinate to Huck's, and, like every good sidekick, he never minds. He grows ever more passive and also more affectionate as Huck and the Duke and the Dauphin and Tom (and Twain) make ever more use of him for their own purposes. But this use they make of him is not supplementary; it is integral to Twain's whole conception of the novel. Twain thinks that Huck's affection is a good enough reward for Jim.

The sort of meretricious critical reasoning that has raised Huck's paltry good intentions to a "strategy of subversion" (David L. Smith) and a "convincing indictment of slavery" (Eliot)[2] precisely mirrors the same sort of meretricious reasoning that white people use to convince themselves that they are not "racist." If Huck *feels* positive toward Jim, and *loves* him, and *thinks* of him as a man, then that's enough. He doesn't actually have to act in accordance with his feelings. White Americans always think racism is a feeling, and they reject it or they embrace it. To most Americans, it seems more honorable and nicer to reject it, so they do, but they almost invariably fail to understand that how they *feel* means very little to black Americans, who understand racism a way of structuring American culture, American politics, and the American economy. To invest *The Adventures of Huckleberry*

---

1. From *Harper's Magazine* (January 1996): 61–67. Jane Smiley (b. 1949) won the Pulitzer Prize for her novel *A Thousand Acres* (1991).

2. See T. S. Eliot's "The Boy and the River: Without Beginning or End," his introduction to a 1950 edition of *Huckleberry Finn*.

Finn with "greatness" is to underwrite a very simplistic and evasive theory of what racism is and to promulgate it, philosophically, in schools and the media as well as in academic journals. Surely the discomfort of many readers, black and white, and the censorship battles that have dogged *Huck Finn* in the last twenty years are understandable in this context. No matter how often the critics "place in context" Huck's use of the word "nigger," they can never excuse or fully hide the deeper racism of the novel—the way Twain and Huck use Jim because they really don't care enough about his desire for freedom to let that desire change their plans. And to give credit to Huck suggests that the only racial insight Americans of the nineteenth or twentieth century are capable of is a recognition of the obvious—that blacks, slave and free, are human.

Ernest Hemingway, thinking of himself, as always, once said that all American literature grew out of *Huck Finn*. It undoubtedly would have been better for American literature, and American culture, if our literature had grown out of one of the best-selling novels of all time, another American work of the nineteenth century, *Uncle Tom's Cabin*, which for its portrayal of an array of thoughtful, autonomous, and passionate black characters leaves *Huck Finn* far behind. *Uncle Tom's Cabin* was published in 1852, when Twain was seventeen, still living in Hannibal and contributing to his brother's newspapers.

* * *

I would rather my children read *Uncle Tom's Cabin*, even though it is far more vivid in its depiction of cruelty than *Huck Finn*, and this is because Stowe's novel is clearly and unmistakably a tragedy. No whitewash, no secrets, but evil, suffering, imagination, endurance, and redemption—just like life. Like little Eva, who eagerly but fearfully listens to the stories of the slaves that her family tries to keep from her, our children want to know what is going on, what has gone on, and what we intend to do about it. If "great" literature has any purpose, it is to help us face up to our responsibilities instead of enabling us to avoid them once again by lighting out for the territory.

TONI MORRISON

From Introduction to *Adventures of Huckleberry Finn*[1]

* * *

In the early eighties I read *Huckleberry Finn* again, provoked, I believe, by demands to remove the novel from the libraries and required reading lists of public schools. These efforts were based, it seemed to me, on a narrow notion of how to handle the offense Mark Twain's use of the term "nigger" would occasion for black students and the corrosive effect it would have on

1. From "Introduction," *Adventures of Huckleberry Finn* (New York: Oxford University Press, 1996), xxxi–xli. Toni Morrison (b. 1931) is the author of *Beloved* (1987) and other novels; in 1993 she was awarded the Nobel Prize for Literature.

white ones. It struck me as a purist yet elementary kind of censorship designed to appease adults rather than educate children. Amputate the problem, band-aid the solution. A serious comprehensive discussion of the term by an intelligent teacher certainly would have benefited my eighth-grade class and would have spared all of us (a few blacks, many whites—mostly second-generation immigrant children) some grief. Name calling is a plague of childhood and a learned activity ripe for discussion as soon as it surfaces. Embarrassing as it had been to hear the dread word spoken, and therefore sanctioned, in class, my experience of Jim's epithet had little to do with my initial nervousness the book had caused. Reading "nigger" hundreds of times embarrassed, bored, annoyed—but did not faze me. In this latest reading I was curious about the source of my alarm—my sense that danger lingered after the story ended. I was powerfully attracted to the combination of delight and fearful agitation lying entwined like crossed fingers in the pages. And it was significant that this novel which had given so much pleasure to young readers was also complicated territory for sophisticated scholars.

Usually the divide is substantial: if a story that pleased us as novice readers does not disintegrate as we grow older, it maintains its value only in its retelling for other novices or to summon uncapturable pleasure as playback. Also, the books that academic critics find consistently rewarding are works only partially available to the minds of young readers. *Adventures of Huckleberry Finn* manages to close that divide, and one of the reasons it requires no leap is that in addition to the reverence the novel stimulates is its ability to transform its contradictions into fruitful complexities and to seem to be deliberately cooperating in the controversy it has excited. The brilliance of *Huckleberry Finn* is that it *is* the argument it raises.

My 1980s reading, therefore, was an effort to track the unease, nail it down, and learn in so doing the nature of my troubled relationship to this classic American work. * * *

If the emotional environment into which Twain places his protagonist is dangerous, then the leading question the novel poses for me is, What does Huck need to live without terror, melancholy and suicidal thoughts? The answer, of course, is Jim. When Huck is among society—whether respectable or deviant, rich or poor—he is alert to and consumed by its deception, its illogic, its scariness. Yet he is depressed by himself and sees nature more often as fearful. But when he and Jim become the only "we," the anxiety is outside, not within. ". . . we would watch the lonesomeness of the river . . . for about an hour . . . just solid lonesomeness." Unmanageable terror gives way to a pastoral, idyllic, intimate timelessness minus the hierarchy of age, status or adult control. It has never seemed to me that, in contrast to the entrapment and menace of the shore, the river itself provides this solace. The consolation, the healing properties Huck longs for, is made possible by Jim's active, highly vocal affection. It is in Jim's company that the dread of contemplated nature disappears, that even storms are beautiful and sublime, that real talk—comic, pointed, sad—takes place. Talk so free of lies it produces an aura of restfulness and peace unavailable anywhere else in the novel.* * *

So there will be no "adventures" without Jim. The risk is too great. To Huck and to the novel. When the end does come, when Jim is finally, tortuously, unnecessarily freed, able now to be a father to his own children, Huck runs. Not back to the town—even if it is safe now—but a further run, for the "territory." And if there are complications out there in the world, Huck, we are to assume, is certainly ready for them. He has had a first-rate education in social and individual responsibility, and it is interesting to note that the lessons of his growing but secret activism begin to be punctuated by speech, not silence, by moves toward truth, rather than quick lies.

* * *

The source of my unease reading this amazing, troubling book now seems clear: an imperfect coming to terms with three matters Twain addresses— Huck Finn's estrangement, soleness and morbidity as an outcast child; the disproportionate sadness at the center of Jim's and his relationship; and the secrecy in which Huck's engagement with (rather than escape from) a racist society is necessarily conducted. It is also clear that the rewards of my effort to come to terms have been abundant. My alarm, aroused by Twain's precise rendering of childhood's fear of death and abandonment, remains—as it should. It has been extremely worthwhile slogging through Jim's shame and humiliation to recognize the sadness, the tragic implications at the center of his relationship with Huck. My fury at the maze of deceit, the risk of personal harm that a white child is forced to negotiate in a race-inflected society, is dissipated by the exquisite uses to which Twain puts that maze, that risk.

Yet the larger question, the danger that sifts from the novel's last page, is whether Huck, minus Jim, will be able to stay those three monsters as he enters the "territory." Will that undefined space, so falsely imagined as "open," be free of social chaos, personal morbidity, and further moral complications embedded in adulthood and citizenship? Will it be free not only of nightmare fathers but of dream fathers too? Twain did not write Huck there. He imagined instead a reunion—Huck, Jim and Tom, soaring in a balloon over Egypt.

For a hundred years, the argument that this novel *is* has been identified, reidentified, examined, waged and advanced. What it cannot be is dismissed. It is classic literature, which is to say it heaves, manifests and lasts.

ALAN GRIBBEN

From Introduction to the NewSouth Edition[1]

* * *

The n-word possessed, then as now, demeaning implications more vile than almost any insult that can be applied to other racial groups. There is no equivalent slur in the English language. As a result, with every passing decade this affront appears to gain rather than lose its impact. Even at the level of college and graduate school, students are capable of resenting textual encounters with this racial appellative. In the 1870s and 1880s, of

---

1. From the Introduction to the NewSouth edition of *The Adventures of Tom Sawyer and Huckleberry Finn,* published in 2011. Alan Gribben, a professor of English at Auburn University in Montgomery, Alabama, produced an edition of Twain's most famous novels that replaced racial slurs with language that is more acceptable by twenty-first-century standards. For instance, he substituted "slave" for "nigger" and "Indian" for "Injun." Gribben's edition was deeply controversial and widely criticized for its alteration of Twain's language.

course, Twain scarcely had to concern himself about the feelings of African American or Native American readers. These population groups were too occupied with trying, in the one case, to recover from the degradation of slavery and the institution of Jim Crow segregation policies, and, in the other case, to survive the onslaught of settlers and buffalo-hunters who had decimated their ways of life, than to bother about objectionable vocabulary choices in two popular books.

*　*　*

Through a succession of firsthand experiences, this editor gradually concluded that an epithet-free edition of Twain's books is necessary today. For nearly forty years I have led college classes, bookstore forums, and library reading groups in detailed discussions of *Tom Sawyer* and *Huckleberry Finn* in California, Texas, New York, and Alabama, and I always refrained from uttering the racial slurs spoken by numerous characters, including Tom and Huck. I invariably substituted the word "slave" for Twain's ubiquitous n-word whenever I read any passages aloud. Students and audience members seemed to prefer this expedient, and I could detect a visible sense of relief each time, as though a nagging problem with the text had been addressed. Indeed, numerous communities currently ban *Huckleberry Finn* as required reading in public schools owing to its offensive racial language and have quietly moved the title to voluntary reading lists. The American Library Association lists the novel as one of the most frequently challenged books across the nation.

*　*　*

During the 1980s, educator John H. Wallace unleashed a fierce and protracted dispute by denouncing *Huckleberry Finn* as "the most grotesque example of racist trash ever written." In 1984 I had to walk past a picket line of African American parents outside a scholarly conference in Pennsylvania that was commemorating, among other achievements in American humor, the upcoming centenary anniversary of Twain's *Adventures of Huckleberry Finn*. James S. Leonard, then the editor of the newsletter for the Mark Twain Circle of America, conceded in 2001 that the racist language and unflattering stereotypes of slaves in *Huckleberry Finn* can constitute "real problems" in certain classroom settings. Another scholar, Jonathan Arac, has urged that students be prompted to read other, more unequivocally abolitionist works rather than this one novel that has been consecrated as the mandatory literary statement about American slavery. The once-incontestable belief that the reading of this book at multiple levels of schooling ought to be essential for every American citizen's education is cracking around the edges.

My personal turning point on the journey toward this present NewSouth Edition was a lecture tour I undertook in Alabama in 2009. I had written the introduction for an edition of *The Adventures of Tom Sawyer* designed to interest younger readers in older American literature. The volume was published by NewSouth Books for a consortium of Alabama libraries in connection with the "Big Read," an initiative sponsored by the National Endowment for the Arts. As I traveled around the state and spoke about the novel to reading groups of adults and teenagers in small towns like Valley, Dadeville, Prattville, Eufaula, Wetumpka, and Talladega, and in larger cities like Montgomery and Birmingham, I followed my customary habit of substituting the word "slave" when reading the characters' dialogue aloud. In several towns I was taken aside after my talk by earnest middle and high school teachers who lamented the fact that they no longer felt justified in assigning either of Twain's boy books because of the hurtful n-word. Here was further proof that this single debasing label is overwhelming every other consideration about *Tom Sawyer* and *Huckleberry Finn*, whereas what these novels have to offer readers hardly depends upon that one indefensible slur.

MICHIKO KAKUTANI

Light Out, Huck, They Still Want to Sivilize You[1]

"All modern American literature," Ernest Hemingway once wrote, "comes from one book by Mark Twain called *Huckleberry Finn.*"

Being an iconic classic, however, hasn't protected *Adventures of Huckleberry Finn* from being banned, bowdlerized, and bleeped. It hasn't protected the novel from being cleaned up, updated, and "improved."

A new effort to sanitize *Huckleberry Finn* comes from Alan Gribben, a professor of English at Auburn University, at Montgomery, Alabama, who has produced a new edition of Twain's novel that replaces the word "nigger" with "slave." *Nigger,* which appears in the book more than 200 times, was a common racial epithet in the antebellum South, used by Twain as part of his characters' vernacular speech and as a reflection of mid-nineteenth-century social attitudes along the Mississippi River.

Mr. Gribben has said he worried that the N-word had resulted in the novel falling off reading lists, and that he thought his edition would be welcomed by schoolteachers and university instructors who wanted to spare "the reader from a racial slur that never seems to lose its vitriol." Never mind that today *nigger* is used by many rappers, who have reclaimed the word from its ugly past. Never mind that attaching the epithet *slave* to the character Jim—who has run away in a bid for freedom—effectively labels him as property, as the very thing he is trying to escape.

Controversies over *Huckleberry Finn* occur with predictable regularity. In 2009, just before Barack Obama's inauguration, a high school teacher named John Foley wrote a guest column in the *Seattle Post-Intelligencer* in which he asserted that *Huckleberry Finn, To Kill a Mockingbird* and *Of Mice and Men* don't belong on the curriculum anymore. "The time has arrived to update the literature we use in high school classrooms," he wrote. "Barack Obama is president-elect of the United States, and novels that use the 'N-word' repeatedly need to go."

Haven't we learned by now that removing books from the curriculum just deprives children of exposure to classic works of literature? Worse, it relieves teachers of the fundamental responsibility of putting such books in context—of helping students understand that *Huckleberry Finn* actually

---

1. Michiko Kakutani is a Pulitzer Prize–winning book critic for the *New York Times*, where this article appeared in 2011.

stands as a powerful indictment of slavery (with Nigger Jim its most noble character), of using its contested language as an opportunity to explore the painful complexities of race relations in this country. To censor or redact books on school reading lists is a form of denial: shutting the door on harsh historical realities—whitewashing them or pretending they do not exist.

Mr. Gribben's effort to update *Huckleberry Finn* (published in an edition with *The Adventures of Tom Sawyer* by NewSouth Books), like Mr. Foley's assertion that it's an old book and "we're ready for new," ratifies the narcissistic contemporary belief that art should be inoffensive and accessible; that books, plays, and poetry from other times and places should somehow be made to conform to today's democratic ideals. It's like the politically correct efforts in the eighties to exile great authors like Conrad and Melville from the canon because their work does not feature enough women or projects colonialist attitudes.

Authors' original texts should be sacrosanct intellectual property, whether a book is a classic or not. Tampering with a writer's words underscores both editors' extraordinary hubris and a cavalier attitude embraced by more and more people in this day of mash-ups, sampling, and digital books—the attitude that all texts are fungible, that readers are entitled to alter as they please, that the very idea of authorship is old-fashioned.

Efforts to sanitize classic literature have a long, undistinguished history. Everything from Chaucer's *Canterbury Tales* to Roald Dahl's *Charlie and the Chocolate Factory* have been challenged or have suffered at the hands of uptight editors. There have even been purified versions of the Bible (all that sex and violence!). Sometimes the urge to expurgate (if not outright ban) comes from the right, evangelicals and conservatives, worried about blasphemy, profane language, and sexual innuendo. Fundamentalist groups, for instance, have tried to have dictionaries banned because of definitions offered for words like *hot, tail, ball,* and *nuts.*

In other cases the drive to sanitize comes from the left, eager to impose its own multicultural, feminist worldviews and worried about offending religious or ethnic groups. Michael Radford's 2004 film version of *The Merchant of Venice* (starring Al Pacino) revised the play to elide potentially offensive material, serving up a nicer, more sympathetic Shylock and blunting tough questions about anti-Semitism. More absurdly, a British theater company in 2002 changed the title of its production of *The Hunchback of Notre Dame* to *The Bellringer of Notre Dame.*

Whether it comes from conservatives or liberals, there is a patronizing Big Brother aspect to these literary fumigations. We, the censors, need to protect you, the naïve, delicate reader. We, the editors, need to police writers (even those from other eras), who might have penned something that might be offensive to someone sometime.

* * *

Although it's hard to imagine a theater company today using one of Shakespeare adaptations—say, changing "Out, damned spot! Out, I say!" in *Macbeth* to "out, crimson spot!"—the language police are staging a comeback. Not just with an expurgated *Huckleberry Finn* but with political efforts to clamp down on objectionable language. Last year the *Boston Globe* reported that California lawmakers first voted for, then tabled a resolution declaring a No Cuss Week, that South Carolina had debated a sweeping anti-profanity bill, and that conservative groups like the Parents Television Council have complained about vulgarities creeping into family-hour shows on network television.

But while James V. O'Connor, author of the book *Cuss Control*, argues that people can and should find word substitutions, even his own Web site grants Rhett Butler a "poetic license" exemption in *Gone With the Wind*. "Frankly, my dear, I don't give a hoot"?[2] Now that's damnable.

2. The original line of dialogue from *Gone With the Wind* (1936)—made famous by Clark Gable in the 1939 film adaptation—is "Frankly, my dear, I don't give a damn."

BRET HARTE
1836–1902

Francis Bret[t] Harte was born August 25, 1836, in Albany, New York, of English, Dutch, and Jewish descent. His father, Henry, a schoolteacher, died in 1845, and nine years later, Harte followed his mother, Elizabeth Rebecca, and his elder sister and brother to Oakland, California. When he turned twenty-one, he left to seek employment farther north in California, where he worked for a time for a stagecoach express company (he claimed that he "rode shotgun") and also as a miner, teacher, tutor, pharmacist's clerk, and printer. From 1858 to 1860 he set type and served as an editorial assistant on the staff of the Uniontown *Northern Californian*. In late February 1860, while the editor-in-chief was out of town, Harte wrote an editorial expressing outrage over the massacre in nearby Eureka of sixty Native Americans, mostly women and children, by a small gang of white vigilantes. After the appearance of the editorial, his life was apparently threatened, and within a month he left for San Francisco.

Harte quickly found a job setting type for *The Golden Era*, a monthly magazine, and soon began contributing poems, stories, and sketches, many under the pseudonym "The Bohemian." Harte's career as a writer was confirmed in 1868 when he became the first editor of the newly established *Overland Monthly*, a publication that quickly became influential throughout the United States as the representative journal of the burgeoning, often unruly culture of the Pacific coast. In the second issue, Harte published "The Luck of Roaring Camp," which made him a national celebrity. In this story, as elsewhere, Harte's success rested on his ability to portray distinctive characters whom he connected to the western settings.

Harte's popularity and influence could be felt throughout the late-nineteenth-century boom in regional or local color writing, fiction that situates its characters in carefully drawn local environments. Writing primarily for readers who were generally distant from its terrain or people, Harte helped to create a compelling vision of the West through a combination of romantic adventure and gritty realism. Perhaps what most distinguished him from other writers who exploited the myths of the Wild West is an ironic perspective that often went undetected by readers unfamiliar with California. His writing frequently challenged the dime-novel treatment of the West, with its chivalrous heroes and black-hearted villains, by focusing on characters—stagedrivers, miners, schoolmarms—who never quite made their fortune in the California gold rush. In 1870, Harte published a collection called "*The Luck of Roaring Camp" and Other Sketches*, which included works from *The Golden Era* and *Overland Monthly*. This popular book established many ideas about the West that were later circulated in various forms by other western writers, including Mark Twain, Joaquin Miller, Ambrose Bierce, and, later, Jack London.

Harte, who had married Anna Griswold in 1862, left San Francisco early in 1871 at the height of his fame in hopes that his literary reputation would grow even more in the East. After a cross-country journey that was covered by the daily press, the publisher James T. Fields offered Harte the unheard-of sum of ten thousand dollars to write twelve or more poems and sketches to be published in the *Atlantic Monthly* and *Every Saturday* magazines during the course of the year. Unfortunately, Harte did not produce much writing in the twelve months following, and his contract was not renewed. At the same time, his drinking was harming his lecturing career, which was already shaky due to performances that some saw as "dandified" and not at all those of a rugged western character. Whenever Harte departed from his standard western stories, he was castigated by critics, and so remained trapped in formula and self-parody. Within a few years after his lucrative contract ended, Harte was desperate and nearly penniless.

The last three decades of Harte's life constitute a decline in his personal and literary fortunes. His novel *Gabriel Conroy* (1876) sold well but was slammed by the critics, and though his two plays, *Two Men of Sandy Bar* (1876) and (with Mark Twain) *Ah Sin* (1877), were produced, neither was successful. In 1878 Harte moved to Europe when he was appointed consul to Krefeld, Prussia; in 1880 he took up the consulship in Glasgow, Scotland. But when Grover Cleveland became president in 1885, Harte lost his post. Though his American audience waned, Harte's English readers continued to receive his work favorably until his death in May 1902. Today he is still regarded as one of the progenitors of the literature of the American West—a figure who challenged the supremacy of eastern publishers, expanded the literary terrain of the nation, and set the stage for a more capacious view of American literature.

The Luck of Roaring Camp[1]

There was commotion in Roaring Camp. It could not have been a fight, for in 1850 that was not novel enough to have called together the entire settlement. The ditches and claims were not only deserted, but "Tuttle's grocery" had contributed its gamblers, who, it will be remembered, calmly continued their game the day that French Pete and Kanaka Joe[2] shot each other to death over the bar in the front room. The whole camp was collected before a rude cabin on the outer edge of the clearing. Conversation was carried on in a low tone, but the name of a woman was frequently repeated. It was a name familiar enough in the camp,—"Cherokee Sal."

Perhaps the less said of her the better. She was a coarse and, it is to be feared, a very sinful woman. But at that time she was the only woman in Roaring Camp, and was just then lying in sore extremity, when she most needed the ministration of her own sex. Dissolute, abandoned, and irreclaimable, she was yet suffering a martyrdom hard enough to bear even when veiled by sympathizing womanhood, but now terrible in her loneliness. The

1. First appearing in 1868 in *Overland Monthly*, the tale was reprinted by Osgood of Boston in 1870 in "*The Luck of Roaring Camp" and Other Sketches* and by Houghton Mifflin in 1878 in "*The Luck of Roaring Camp" and Other Tales*; the present text is taken from the 1878 revision.
2. Hawaiian word for adult man, used (nonpejoratively) by both Hawaiians and Americans at the time.

primal curse had come to her in that original isolation which must have made the punishment of the first transgression so dreadful. It was, perhaps, part of the expiation of her sin that, at a moment when she most lacked her sex's intuitive tenderness and care, she met only the half-contemptuous faces of her masculine associates. Yet a few of the spectators were, I think, touched by her sufferings. Sandy Tipton thought it was "rough on Sal," and, in the contemplation of her condition, for a moment rose superior to the fact that he had an ace and two bowers[3] in his sleeve.

It will be seen also that the situation was novel. Deaths were by no means uncommon in Roaring Camp, but a birth was a new thing. People had been dismissed the camp effectively, finally, and with no possibility of return; but this was the first time that anybody had been introduced *ab initio*.[4] Hence the excitement.

"You go in there, Stumpy," said a prominent citizen known as "Kentuck," addressing one of the loungers. "Go in there, and see what you kin do. You've had experience in them things."

Perhaps there was a fitness in the selection. Stumpy, in other climes, had been the putative head of two families; in fact, it was owing to some legal informality in these proceedings that Roaring Camp—a city of refuge—was indebted to his company. The crowd approved the choice, and Stumpy was wise enough to bow to the majority. The door closed on the extempore surgeon and midwife, and Roaring Camp sat down outside, smoked its pipe, and awaited the issue.

The assemblage numbered about a hundred men. One or two of these were actual fugitives from justice, some were criminal, and all were reckless. Physically they exhibited no indication of their past lives and character. The greatest scamp had a Raphael[5] face, with a profusion of blonde hair; Oakhurst, a gambler, had the melancholy air and intellectual abstraction of a Hamlet; the coolest and most courageous man was scarcely over five feet in height, with a soft voice and an embarrassed, timid manner. The term "roughs" applied to them was a distinction rather than a definition. Perhaps in the minor details of fingers, toes, ears, etc., the camp may have been deficient, but these slight omissions did not detract from their aggregate force. The strongest man had but three fingers on his right hand; the best shot had but one eye.

Such was the physical aspect of the men that were dispersed around the cabin. The camp lay in a triangular valley between two hills and a river. The only outlet was a steep trail over the summit of a hill that faced the cabin, now illuminated by the rising moon. The suffering woman might have seen it from the rude bunk whereon she lay,—seen it winding like a silver thread until it was lost in the stars above.

A fire of withered pine boughs added sociability to the gathering. By degrees the natural levity of Roaring Camp returned. Bets were freely offered and taken regarding the result. Three to five that "Sal would get through with it;" even that the child would survive; side bets as to the sex and complexion of the coming stranger. In the midst of an excited discussion an exclamation came from those nearest the door, and the camp stopped to listen. Above the swaying and moaning of the pines, the swift rush of the river, and the crack-

---

3. In the card game euchre, jacks of the trump suit or the other suit of the same color.
4. From the beginning (Latin).

5. Raffaello Sanzio (1483–1520), painter and architect of the Italian High Renaissance, best known for his Madonnas.

ling of the fire rose a sharp, querulous cry,—a cry unlike anything heard before in the camp. The pines stopped moaning, the river ceased to rush, and the fire to crackle. It seemed as if Nature had stopped to listen too.

The camp rose to its feet as one man! It was proposed to explode a barrel of gunpowder; but in consideration of the situation of the mother, better counsels prevailed, and only a few revolvers were discharged; for whether owing to the rude surgery of the camp, or some other reason, Cherokee Sal was sinking fast. Within an hour she had climbed, as it were, that rugged road that led to the stars, and so passed out of Roaring Camp, its sin and shame, forever. I do not think that the announcement disturbed them much, except in speculation as to the fate of the child. "Can he live now?" was asked of Stumpy. The answer was doubtful. The only other being of Cherokee Sal's sex and maternal condition in the settlement was an ass. There was some conjecture as to fitness, but the experiment was tried. It was less problematical than the ancient treatment of Romulus and Remus,[6] and apparently as successful.

When these details were completed, which exhausted another hour, the door was opened, and the anxious crowd of men, who had already formed themselves into a queue, entered in single file. Beside the low bunk or shelf, on which the figure of the mother was starkly outlined below the blankets, stood a pine table. On this a candle-box was placed, and within it, swathed in staring red flannel, lay the last arrival at Roaring Camp. Beside the candle-box was placed a hat. Its use was soon indicated. "Gentlemen," said Stumpy, with a singular mixture of authority and *ex officio*[7] complacency,—"gentlemen will please pass in at the front door, round the table, and out at the back door. Them as wishes to contribute anything toward the orphan will find a hat handy." The first man entered with his hat on; he uncovered, however, as he looked about him, and so unconsciously set an example to the next. In such communities good and bad actions are catching. As the procession filed in comments were audible,—criticisms addressed perhaps rather to Stumpy in the character of showman: "Is that him?" "Mighty small specimen;" "Hasn't more'n got the color;" "Ain't bigger nor a derringer." The contributions were as characteristic: A silver tobacco box; a doubloon; a navy revolver, silver mounted; a gold specimen; a very beautifully embroidered lady's handkerchief (from Oakhurst the gambler); a diamond breastpin; a diamond ring (suggested by the pin, with the remark from the giver that he "saw that pin and went two diamonds better"); a slung-shot; a Bible (contributor not detected); a golden spur; a silver teaspoon (the initials: I regret to a say, were not the giver's); a pair of surgeon's shears; a lancet;[8] Bank of England note for £5; and about $200 in loose gold and silver coin. During these proceedings Stumpy maintained a silence as impassive as the dead on his left, a gravity as inscrutable as that of the newly born on his right. Only one incident occurred to break the monotony of the curious procession. As Kentuck bent over the candle-box half curiously, the child turned, and, in a spasm of pain, caught at his groping finger, and held it fast for a moment. Kentuck looked foolish and embarrassed. Some-

---

6. Twin brothers Romulus and Remus, traditionally honored as founders of Rome, were sons of Mars and Rhea, daughter of King Numitor of Alba Longa. When Numitor's brother Amulius deposed him, he made Rhea a Vestal Virgin (and thus forbidden to marry). But when Mars fell in love with her and she bore him the twins, Amulius, fearing they would grow up to overthrow him, left them by the banks of the River Tiber to fend for themselves; they were found by a she-wolf who took pity on them and fed them with her milk.

7. By virtue of one's office, or position (Latin).

8. A small surgical knife.

thing like a blush tried to assert itself in his weather-beaten cheek. "The d—d little cuss!" he said, as he extricated his finger, with perhaps more tenderness and care than he might have been deemed capable of showing. He held that finger a little apart from its fellows as he went out, and examined it curiously. The examination provoked the same original remark in regard to the child. In fact, he seemed to enjoy repeating it. "He rastled with my finger," he remarked to Tipton, holding up the member, "the d—d little cuss!"

It was four o'clock before the camp sought repose. A light burnt in the cabin where the watchers sat, for Stumpy did not go to bed that night. Nor did Kentuck. He drank quite freely, and related with great gusto his experience, invariably ending with his characteristic condemnation of the newcomer. It seemed to relieve him of any unjust implication of sentiment, and Kentuck had the weaknesses of the nobler sex. When everybody else had gone to bed, he walked down to the river and whistled reflectingly. Then he walked up the gulch past the cabin, still whistling with demonstrative unconcern. At a large redwood-tree he paused and retraced his steps, and again passed the cabin. Halfway down to the river's bank he again paused, and then returned and knocked at the door. It was opened by Stumpy. "How goes it?" said Kentuck, looking past Stumpy toward the candle-box. "All serene!" replied Stumpy. "Anything up?" "Nothing." There was a pause—an embarrassing one—Stumpy still holding the door. Then Kentuck had recourse to his finger, which he held up to Stumpy. "Rastled with it,—the d—d little cuss," he said, and retired.

The next day Cherokee Sal had such rude sepulture as Roaring Camp afforded. After her body had been committed to the hillside, there was a formal meeting of the camp to discuss what should be done with her infant. A resolution to adopt it was unanimous and enthusiastic. But an animated discussion in regard to the manner and feasibility of providing for its wants at once sprang up. It was remarkable that the argument partook of none of those fierce personalities with which discussions were usually conducted at Roaring Camp. Tipton proposed that they should send the child to Red Dog,—a distance of forty miles,—where female attention could be procured. But the unlucky suggestion met with fierce and unanimous opposition. It was evident that no plan which entailed parting from their new acquisition would for a moment be entertained. "Besides," said Tom Ryder, "them fellows at Red Dog would swap it, and ring in somebody else on us."[9] A disbelief in the honesty of other camps prevailed at Roaring Camp, as in other places.

The introduction of a female nurse in the camp also met with objection. It was argued that no decent woman could be prevailed to accept Roaring Camp as her home, and the speaker urged that "they did n't want any more of the other kind." This unkind allusion to the defunct mother, harsh as it may seem, was the first spasm of propriety,—the first symptom of the camp's regeneration. Stumpy advanced nothing. Perhaps he felt a certain delicacy in interfering with the selection of a possible successor in office. But when questioned, he averred stoutly that he and "Jinny"—the mammal before alluded to—could manage to rear the child. There was something original, independent, and heroic about the plan that pleased the camp. Stumpy was retained. Certain articles were sent for to Sacramento. "Mind," said the treasurer, as he

9. That is, Tom fears that the men of Red Dog might substitute another baby for theirs.

pressed a bag of gold-dust into the expressman's hand, "the best that can be got,—lace, you know, and filigree-work and frills,—d—n the cost!"

Strange to say, the child thrived. Perhaps the invigorating climate of the mountain camp was compensation for material deficiencies. Nature took the foundling to her broader breast. In that rare atmosphere of the Sierra foothills,—that air pungent with balsamic odor, that ethereal cordial at once bracing and exhilarating,—he may have found food and nourishment, or a subtle chemistry that transmuted ass's milk to lime and phosphorus.[1] Stumpy inclined to the belief that it was the latter and good nursing. "Me and that ass," he would say, "has been father and mother to him! Don't you," he would add, apostrophizing the helpless bundle before him, "never go back on us."

By the time he was a month old the necessity of giving him a name became apparent. He had generally been known as "The Kid," "Stumpy's Boy," "The Coyote" (an allusion to his vocal powers), and even by Kentuck's endearing diminutive of "The d—d little cuss." But these were felt to be vague and unsatisfactory, and were at last dismissed under another influence. Gamblers and adventurers are generally superstitious, and Oakhurst one day declared that the baby had brought "the luck" to Roaring Camp. It was certain that of late they had been successful. "Luck" was the name agreed upon, with the prefix of Tommy for greater convenience. No allusion was made to the mother, and the father was unknown. "It's better," said the philosophical Oakhurst, "to take a fresh deal all round. Call him Luck, and start him fair." A day was accordingly set apart for the christening. What was meant by this ceremony the reader may imagine who has already gathered some idea of the reckless irreverence of Roaring Camp. The master of ceremonies was one "Boston," a noted wag, and the occasion seemed to promise the greatest facetiousness. This ingenious satirist had spent two days in preparing a burlesque of the Church service, with pointed local allusions. The choir was properly trained, and Sandy Tipton was to stand godfather. But after the procession had marched to the grove with music and banners, and the child had been deposited before a mock altar, Stumpy stepped before the expectant crowd. "It ain't my style to spoil fun, boys," said the little man, stoutly eyeing the faces around him, "but it strikes me that this thing ain't exactly on the squar. It's playing it pretty low down on this yer baby to ring in fun on him that he ain't goin' to understand. And ef there's goin' to be any godfathers round, I'd like to see who's got any better rights than me." A silence followed Stumpy's speech. To the credit of all humorists be it said that the first man to acknowledge its justice was the satirist thus stopped of his fun. "But," said Stumpy, quickly following up his advantage, "we're here for a christening, and we'll have it. I proclaim you Thomas Luck, according to the laws of the United States and the State of California, so help me God." It was the first time that the name of the Deity had been otherwise uttered than profanely in the camp. The form of christening was perhaps even more ludicrous than the satirist had conceived; but strangely enough, nobody saw it and nobody laughed. "Tommy" was christened as seriously as he would have been under a Christian roof, and cried and was comforted in as orthodox fashion.

---

1. Both lime and phosphorus are used as fertilizer, and both are generally white; the suggestion is that the ass's milk would help the child's bones grow strong.

And so the work of regeneration began in Roaring Camp. Almost impercep-
tibly a change came over the settlement. The cabin assigned to "Tommy
Luck"—or "The Luck," as he was more frequently called—first showed signs
of improvement. It was kept scrupulously clean and whitewashed. Then it was
boarded, clothed, and papered. The rosewood cradle, packed eighty miles by
mule, had, in Stumpy's way of putting it, "sorter killed the rest of the furniture." So the rehabilitation of the cabin became a necessity. The men who were
in the habit of lounging in at Stumpy's to see "how 'The Luck' got on" seemed
to appreciate the change, and in self-defense the rival establishment of "Tuttle's
grocery" bestirred itself and imported a carpet and mirrors. The reflections of
the latter on the appearance of Roaring Camp tended to produce stricter habits
of personal cleanliness. Again Stumpy imposed a kind of quarantine upon
those who aspired to the honor and privilege of holding The Luck. It was a
cruel mortification to Kentuck—who, in the carelessness of a large nature and
the habits of frontier life, had begun to regard all garments as a second cuticle,
which, like a snake's, only sloughed off through decay—to be debarred this
privilege from certain prudential reasons. Yet such was the subtle influence of
innovation that he thereafter appeared regularly every afternoon in a clean
shirt and face still shining from his ablutions. Nor were moral and social sanitary laws neglected. "Tommy," who was supposed to spend his whole existence
in a persistent attempt to repose, must not be disturbed by noise. The shouting
and yelling, which had gained the camp its infelicitous title, were not permitted
within hearing distance of Stumpy's. The men conversed in whispers or smoked
with Indian gravity. Profanity was tacitly given up in these sacred precincts,
and throughout the camp a popular form of expletive, known as "D—n the
luck!" and "Curse the luck!" was abandoned, as having a new personal bearing.
Vocal music was not interdicted, being supposed to have a soothing, tranquilizing quality; and one song, sung by "Man-o'-War Jack," an English sailor from
her Majesty's Australian colonies, was quite popular as a lullaby. It was a lugu-
brious recital of the exploits of "the Arethusa,[2] Seventy-four," in a muffled
minor, ending with a prolonged dying fall at the burden of each verse, "On
b-oo-o-ard of the Arethusa." It was a fine sight to see Jack holding The Luck,
rocking from side to side as if with the motion of a ship, and crooning forth this
naval ditty. Either through the peculiar rocking of Jack or the length of his
song,—it contained ninety stanzas, and was continued with conscientious
deliberation to the bitter end,—the lullaby generally had the desired effect. At
such times the men would lie at full length under the trees in the soft summer
twilight, smoking their pipes and drinking in the melodious utterances. An
indistinct idea that this was pastoral happiness pervaded the camp. "This 'ere
kind o' think," said the Cockney Simmons, meditatively reclining on his elbow,
"is 'evingly." It reminded him of Greenwich.[3]

On the long summer days The Luck was usually carried to the gulch from
whence the golden store of Roaring Camp was taken. There, on a blanket
spread over pine boughs, he would lie while the men were working in the
ditches below. Latterly there was a rude attempt to decorate this bower with
flowers and sweet-smelling shrubs, and generally some one would bring him

2. In Greek mythology, a nymph who was transformed into a fountain; the name is a popular
one for ships, as in the song described here.
3. A town on the Thames River in England,
birthplace of Henry VIII and site of the Royal
Naval College, venerated by seafarers for its
keeping of official, or Greenwich Mean, time.

a cluster of wild honeysuckles, azaleas, or the painted blossoms of Las Mariposas. The men had suddenly awakened to the fact that there were beauty and significance in these trifles, which they had so long trodden carelessly beneath their feet. A flake of glittering mica, a fragment of variegated quartz, a bright pebble from the bed of the creek, became beautiful to eyes thus cleared and strengthened, and were invariably put aside for The Luck. It was wonderful how many treasures the woods and hillsides yielded that "would do for Tommy." Surrounded by playthings such as never child out of fairyland had before, it is to be hoped that Tommy was content. He appeared to be serenely happy, albeit there was an infantine gravity about him, a contemplative light in his round gray eyes, that sometimes worried Stumpy. He was always tractable and quiet, and it is recorded that once, having crept beyond his "corral,"—a hedge of tessellated pine boughs, which surrounded his bed,—he dropped over the bank on his head in the soft earth, and remained with his mottled legs in the air in that position for at least five minutes with unflinching gravity. He was extricated without a murmur. I hesitate to record the many other instances of his sagacity, which rest, unfortunately, upon the statements of prejudiced friends. Some of them were not without a tinge of superstition. "I crep' up the bank just now," said Kentuck one day, in a breathless state of excitement, "and dern my skin if he wasn't a-talking to a jaybird as was a-sittin' on his lap. There they was, just as free and sociable as anything you please, a-jawin' at each other just like two cherrybums." Howbeit, whether creeping over the pine boughs or lying lazily on his back blinking at the leaves above him, to him the birds sang, the squirrels chattered, and the flowers bloomed. Nature was his nurse and playfellow. For him she would let slip between the leaves golden shafts of sunlight that fell just within his grasp; she would send wandering breezes to visit him with the balm of bay and resinous gum; to him the tall redwoods nodded familiarly and sleepily, the bumblebees buzzed, and the rooks cawed a slumbrous accompaniment.

Such was the golden summer of Roaring Camp. They were "flush times," and the luck was with them. The claims had yielded enormously. The camp was jealous of its privileges and looked suspiciously on strangers. No encouragement was given to immigration, and, to make their seclusion more perfect, the land on either side of the mountain wall that surrounded the camp they duly preëmpted. This, and a reputation for singular proficiency with the revolver, kept the reserve of Roaring Camp inviolate. The expressman— their only connecting link with the surrounding world—sometimes told wonderful stories of the camp. He would say, "They've a street up there in 'Roaring' that would lay over any street in Red Dog. They've got vines and flowers round their houses, and they wash themselves twice a day. But they're mighty rough on strangers, and they worship an Ingin baby."

With the prosperity of the camp came a desire for further improvement. It was proposed to build a hotel in the following spring, and to invite one or two decent families to reside there for the sake of The Luck, who might perhaps profit by female companionship. The sacrifice that this concession to the sex cost these men, who were fiercely skeptical in regard to its general virtue and usefulness, can only be accounted for by their affection for Tommy. A few still held out. But the resolve could not be carried into effect for three months, and the minority meekly yielded in the hope that something might turn up to prevent it. And it did.

The winter of 1851 will long be remembered in the foothills. The snow lay deep on the Sierras, and every mountain creek became a river, and every river a lake. Each gorge and gulch was transformed into a tumultuous watercourse that descended the hillsides, tearing down giant trees and scattering its drift and débris along the plain. Red Dog had been twice under water, and Roaring Camp had been forewarned. "Water put the gold into them gulches," said Stumpy. "It's been here once and will be here again!" And that night the North Fork suddenly leaped over its banks and swept up the triangular valley of Roaring Camp.

In the confusion of rushing water, crashing trees, and crackling timber, and the darkness which seemed to flow with the water and blot out the fair valley, but little could be done to collect the scattered camp. When the morning broke, the cabin of Stumpy, nearest the river-bank, was gone. Higher up the gulch they found the body of its unlucky owner; but the pride, the hope, the joy, The Luck, of Roaring Camp had disappeared. They were returning with sad hearts when a shout from the bank recalled them.

It was a relief-boat from down the river. They had picked up, they said, a man and an infant, nearly exhausted, about two miles below. Did anybody know them, and did they belong here?

It needed but a glance to show them Kentuck lying there, cruelly crushed and bruised, but still holding The Luck of Roaring Camp in his arms. As they bent over the strangely assorted pair, they saw that the child was cold and pulseless. "He is dead," said one. Kentuck opened his eyes. "Dead?" he repeated feebly. "Yes, my man, and you are dying too." A smile lit the eyes of the expiring Kentuck. "Dying!" he repeated; "he's a-taking me with him. Tell the boys I've got The Luck with me now;" and the strong man, clinging to the frail babe as a drowning man is said to cling to a straw, drifted away into the shadowy river that flows forever to the unknown sea.

1868   1870, 1878

WILLIAM DEAN HOWELLS
1837–1920

As a novelist, playwright, critic, essayist, reviewer, poet, and editor, William Dean Howells was always in the public eye, and his influence during the 1880s and 1890s on a growing middle-class readership was incalculable. Known at the height of his career as "the Dean of American Letters," Howells carefully balanced the traditional and the innovative through his promotion of a new American realism. In the "Editor's Study" essays he wrote for *Harper's New Monthly Magazine* starting in 1886, Howells attacked sentimentality of thought and feeling, which he believed presented readers with a false representation of the moral and ethical choices that they would face in their own lives. He believed that realism "was nothing more or less than the truthful treatment of material," especially the motives and actions of *ordinary* men and women. A selection from these influential essays appears in the "Realism and Naturalism" section on pages 579–83 in this volume.

Howells was born in Martinsville, Ohio, on March 1, 1837, and had little formal schooling, assisting his father—a newspaper publisher and printer—from a very early age. As a teenager he was writing for newspapers in Columbus and Cincinnati, becoming city editor of the *Ohio State Journal* in 1858. During 1859–60, Howells's essays, poems, and reviews appeared in such national publications as the *Atlantic Monthly* and the *Saturday Press*. His increasingly national visibility as an author and active supporter of the Republican Party in Columbus helped him to land the job of writing Abraham Lincoln's campaign biography, which appeared in 1860. In that year, with the money he earned from the biography, he made a literary pilgrimage to New England—the center of American literary culture at that time—where he was welcomed by such figures as James Russell Lowell, Oliver Wendell Holmes, Ralph Waldo Emerson, and Nathaniel Hawthorne. When Lincoln became president in 1861, he appointed Howells as U.S. consul to Venice. There Howells wrote a series of travel letters, eventually published as *Venetian Life* (1866). In December 1862, he married Elinor Mead, with whom he would have three children. Returning to America after the Civil War, he worked briefly for the *Nation* in New York City until James T. Fields offered him the assistant editorship of Boston's *Atlantic Monthly*. In effect, Howells assumed control of the magazine from the very beginning, and he succeeded officially to the editorship in 1871, a position he held until 1881.

Howells had been finding his way as a novelist during his ten years as editor, publishing seven novels during that timespan, beginning with *Their Wedding Journey* (1871). These early novels are short, uncomplicated linear narratives that deliberately avoid the exaggerated characterizations and plots of romantic fiction in favor of a more ordinary realism. Howells came into his own as a novelist in the 1880s, after he left the *Atlantic Monthly*. *A Modern Instance* (1882) examines psychic, familial, and social disintegration under the pressure of the secularization and urbanization of post–Civil War America, which would become one of Howells's central subjects for the rest of his career. In 1885 Howells published his most famous novel, *The Rise of Silas Lapham*, which traces the economic collapse (and moral journey) of Silas Lapham, a typical American entrepreneur who has built a paint manufacturing company out of a combination of hard work, sheer luck, and shady business dealings. Within a year of its publication, Howells was profoundly affected by Russian novelist Leo Tolstoy's ideas of nonviolence, Spartan living, and economic equality and, at great risk to his reputation, publicly defended the "Haymarket Anarchists," a group of Chicago workers, several of whom were executed without clear proof of their participation in a bombing at a public demonstration in May 1886.

In 1891 Howells moved from Boston to New York to assume the editorship of the *Cosmopolitan*, which he hoped to make into a forum for his increasingly radical political views; he resigned in 1893 when he failed to gain support for his political agenda from the magazine's wealthy owner. As a fiction writer, he had begun to offer more direct political explorations of social and economic injustice in novels such as the sprawling *A Hazard of New Fortunes* (1890), which depicts class and ethnic conflict in New York City from the perspective of an editor who has moved from Boston to New York and appreciates the city as an outsider; the tighter, more psychologically focused *An*

William Dean Howells, c. 1871, when he became editor of the *Atlantic Monthly*.

Imperative Duty (1892), which depicts racial passing; and the utopian romance *A Traveller from Altruria* (1894). Howells publicly opposed the Spanish–American War (1898), which was presented by its supporters as an unselfish effort to liberate Cuba from Spain, but which Howells feared was actually about U.S. expansionists' designs on Cuba, Puerto Rico, the Philippines, and other Spanish colonial possessions. In "Editha" (1905), Howells characteristically explores the moral failure of individuals who have been corrupted by their culture's worst values. Though the Spanish–American War is not specifically mentioned in the story, its satire of romantic conceptions of battlefield glory and the rush to war responded to the political moment.

In the course of his lifelong career as a literary authority, Howells was international in outlook and promoted such European contemporaries as Ivan Turgenev, Benito Perez Caldós, Leo Tolstoy, Henrik Ibsen, Émile Zola, George Eliot, and Thomas Hardy. In the constant stream of reviews he wrote over five decades, he also supported many younger American writers and early on recognized and publicized the work of talented African American and women writers, including Paul Dunbar, Charles Chesnutt, Sarah Orne Jewett, Mary E. Wilkins Freeman, Edith Wharton, and Emily Dickinson. He actively promoted the careers of such emerging realists and naturalists as Stephen Crane, Hamlin Garland, and Frank Norris, and from the 1860s on was the friend and literary champion of both Henry James and Mark Twain. Given the astonishing roster of writers whom Howells knew and promoted, it is easy to forget that his advocacy of literary realism and his belief in the social value of fiction were often the target of ridicule from his contemporaries in the late nineteenth century.

By the time Howells died of pneumonia in 1920, he had served for thirteen years as the first president of the American Academy of Arts and Letters and was himself a national institution. For rebels and iconoclasts of the 1930s, Howellsian realism stood for literary conservatism. Frank Norris set the tone for this criticism when he called Howells's novels "teacup tragedies." Indeed, Howells' fiction often seems tame in its focus on the white middle-class, but he strongly believed that fiction could make its greatest contribution by telling stories of everyday life. An outspoken cultural critic and novelistic innovator, Howells focused his passions and intellect on a wide array of contemporary issues in politics and art, regularly revealing his fascination with the lives of Americans of all backgrounds.

Editha[1]

The air was thick with the war feeling,[2] like the electricity of a storm which has not yet burst. Editha sat looking out into the hot spring afternoon, with her lips parted, and panting with the intensity of the question whether she could let him go. She had decided that she could not let him stay, when she saw him at the end of the still leafless avenue, making slowly up towards the house, with his head down and his figure relaxed. She ran impatiently out on the veranda, to the edge of the steps, and imperatively demanded greater haste of him with her will before she called aloud to him: "George!"

He had quickened his pace in mystical response to her mystical urgence, before he could have heard her; now he looked up and answered, "Well?"

"Oh, how united we are!" she exulted, and then she swooped down the steps to him. "What is it?" she cried.

"It's war," he said, and he pulled her up to him and kissed her.

1. First printed in the January 1905 issue of *Harper's Monthly*, the source of the present text. 2. Presumably the "war fever" preceding the Spanish–American War (1898), which Howells opposed.

She kissed him back intensely, but irrelevantly, as to their passion, and uttered from deep in her throat. "How glorious!"

"It's war," he repeated, without consenting to her sense of it; and she did not know just what to think at first. She never knew what to think of him; that made his mystery, his charm. All through their courtship, which was contemporaneous with the growth of the war feeling, she had been puzzled by his want of seriousness about it. He seemed to despise it even more than he abhorred it. She could have understood his abhorring any sort of bloodshed; that would have been a survival of his old life when he thought he would be a minister, and before he changed and took up the law. But making light of a cause so high and noble seemed to show a want of earnestness at the core of his being. Not but that she felt herself able to cope with a congenital defect of that sort, and make his love for her save him from himself. Now perhaps the miracle was already wrought in him. In the presence of the tremendous fact that he announced, all triviality seemed to have gone out of him; she began to feel that. He sank down on the top step, and wiped his forehead with his handkerchief, while she poured out upon him her question of the origin and authenticity of his news.

All the while, in her duplex emotioning, she was aware that now at the very beginning she must put a guard upon herself against urging him, by any word or act, to take the part that her whole soul willed him to take, for the completion of her ideal of him. He was very nearly perfect as he was, and he must be allowed to perfect himself. But he was peculiar, and he might very well be reasoned out of his peculiarity. Before her reasoning went her emotioning: her nature pulling upon his nature, her womanhood upon his manhood, without her knowing the means she was using to the end she was willing. She had always supposed that the man who won her would have done something to win her; she did not know what, but something. George Gearson had simply asked her for her love, on the way home from a concert, and she gave her love to him, without, as it were, thinking. But now, it flashed upon her, if he could do something worthy to *have* won her—be a hero, *her* hero—it would be even better than if he had done it before asking her; it would be grander. Besides, she had believed in the war from the beginning.

"But don't you see, dearest," she said, "that it wouldn't have come to this, if it hadn't been in the order of Providence? And I call any war glorious that is for the liberation of people who have been struggling for years against the cruelest oppression. Don't you think so, too?"

"I suppose so," he returned, languidly. "But war! Is it glorious to break the peace of the world?"

"That ignoble peace! It was no peace at all, with that crime and shame at our very gates." She was conscious of parroting the current phrases of the newspapers, but it was no time to pick and choose her words. She must sacrifice anything to the high ideal she had for him, and after a good deal of rapid argument she ended with the climax: "But now it doesn't matter about the how or why. Since the war has come, all that is gone. There are no two sides, any more. There is nothing now but our country."

He sat with his eyes closed and his head leant back against the veranda, and he said with a vague smile, as if musing aloud, "Our country—right or wrong."[3]

---

3. Part of a toast given by American naval officer Stephen Decatur (1779–1820): "Our country! In her intercourse with foreign nations may she always be in the right; but our country right or wrong."

"Yes, right or wrong!" she returned, fervidly. "I'll go and get you some lemonade." She rose rustling, and whisked away; when she came back with two tall glasses of clouded liquid, on a tray, and the ice clucking in them, he still sat as she had left him, and she said as if there had been no interruption: "But there is no question of wrong in this case. I call it a sacred war. A war for liberty, and humanity, if ever there was one. And I know you will see it just as I do, yet."

He took half the lemonade at a gulp, and he answered as he set the glass down: "I know you always have the highest ideal. When I differ from you, I ought to doubt myself."

A generous sob rose in Editha's throat for the humility of a man, so very nearly perfect, who was willing to put himself below her.

Besides, she felt, more subliminally, that he was never so near slipping through her fingers as when he took that meek way.

"You shall not say that! Only, for once I happen to be right." She seized his hand in her two hands, and poured her soul from her eyes into his. "Don't you think so?" she entreated him.

He released his hand and drank the rest of his lemonade, and she added, "Have mine, too," but he shook his head in answering, "I've no business to think so, unless I act so, too."

Her heart stopped a beat before it pulsed on with leaps that she felt in her neck. She had noticed that strange thing in men: they seemed to feel bound to do what they believed, and not think a thing was finished when they said it, as girls did. She knew what was in his mind, but she pretended not, and she said, "Oh, I am not sure," and then faltered.

He went on as if to himself without apparently heeding her. "There's only one way of proving one's faith in a thing like this."

She could not say that she understood, but she did understand.

He went on again. "If I believed—if I felt as you do about this war—Do you wish me to feel as you do?"

Now she was really not sure; so she said, "George, I don't know what you mean."

He seemed to muse away from her as before. "There is a sort of fascination in it. I suppose that at the bottom of his heart every man would like at times to have his courage tested, to see how he would act."

"How can you talk in that ghastly way?"

"It *is* rather morbid. Still, that's what it comes to, unless you're swept away by ambition, or driven by conviction. I haven't the conviction or the ambition, and the other thing is what it comes to with me. I ought to have been a preacher, after all; then I couldn't have asked it of myself, as I must, now I'm a lawyer. And you believe it's a holy war, Editha?" he suddenly addressed her. "Oh, I know you do! But you wish me to believe so, too?"

She hardly knew whether he was mocking or not, in the ironical way he always had with her plainer mind. But the only thing was to be outspoken with him.

"George, I wish you to believe whatever you think is true, at any and every cost. If I've tried to talk you into anything, I take it all back."

"Oh, I know that, Editha. I know how sincere you are, and how—I wish I had your undoubting spirit! I'll think it over; I'd like to believe as you do.

But I don't, now; I don't, indeed. It isn't this war alone; though this seems peculiarly wanton and needless; but it's every war—so stupid; it makes me sick. Why shouldn't this thing have been settled reasonably?"

"Because," she said, very throatily again, "God meant it to be war."

"You think it was God? Yes, I suppose that is what people will say."

"Do you suppose it would have been war if God hadn't meant it?"

"I don't know. Sometimes it seems as if God had put this world into men's keeping to work it as they pleased."

"Now, George, that is blasphemy."

"Well, I won't blaspheme. I'll try to believe in your pocket Providence," he said, and then he rose to go.

"Why don't you stay to dinner?" Dinner at Balcom's Works was at one o'clock.

"I'll come back to supper, if you'll let me. Perhaps I shall bring you a convert."

"Well, you may come back, on that condition."

"All right. If I don't come, you'll understand."

He went away without kissing her, and she felt it a suspension of their engagement. It all interested her intensely; she was undergoing a tremendous experience, and she was being equal to it. While she stood looking after him, her mother came out through one of the long windows, on to the veranda, with a catlike softness and vagueness.

"Why didn't he stay to dinner?"

"Because—because—war has been declared," Editha pronounced, without turning.

Her mother said, "Oh, my!" and then said nothing more until she had sat down in one of the large Shaker chairs[4] and rocked herself for some time. Then she closed whatever tacit passage of thought there had been in her mind with the spoken words: "Well, I hope *he* won't go."

"And *I* hope he *will*," the girl said, and confronted her mother with a stormy exaltation that would have frightened any creature less unimpressionable than a cat.

Her mother rocked herself again for an interval of cogitation. What she arrived at in speech was: "Well, I guess you've done a wicked thing, Editha Balcom."

The girl said, as she passed indoors through the same window her mother had come out by: "I haven't done anything—yet."

In her room, she put together all her letters and gifts from Gearson, down to the withered petals of the first flower he had offered, with that timidity of his veiled in that irony of his. In the heart of the packet she enshrined her engagement ring which she had restored to the pretty box he had brought it her in. Then she sat down, if not calmly yet strongly, and wrote:

> "GEORGE:—I understood—when you left me. But I think we had better emphasize your meaning that if we cannot be one in everything we had better be one in nothing. So I am sending these things for your keeping till you have made up your mind.

---

4. Sturdy unadorned chairs made by the Shaker sect.

"I shall always love you, and therefore I shall never marry any one else. But the man I marry must love his country first of all, and be able to say to me,

> "'I could not love thee, dear, so much,
> Loved I not honor more.'[5]

"There is no honor above America with me. In this great hour there is no other honor.

"Your heart will make my words clear to you. I had never expected to say so much, but it has come upon me that I must say the utmost.

EDITHA"

She thought she had worded her letter well, worded it in a way that could not be bettered; all had been implied and nothing expressed.

She had it ready to send with the packet she had tied with red, white, and blue ribbon, when it occurred to her that she was not just to him, that she was not giving him a fair chance. He had said he would go and think it over, and she was not waiting. She was pushing, threatening, compelling. That was not a woman's part. She must leave him free, free, free. She could not accept for her country or herself a forced sacrifice.

In writing her letter she had satisfied the impulse from which it sprang; she could well afford to wait till he had thought it over. She put the packet and the letter by, and rested serene in the consciousness of having done what was laid upon her by her love itself to do, and yet used patience, mercy, justice.

She had her reward. Gearson did not come to tea, but she had given him till morning, when, late at night there came up from the village the sound of a fife and drum with a tumult of voices, in shouting, singing, and laughing. The noise drew nearer and nearer; it reached the street end of the avenue; there it silenced itself, and one voice, the voice she knew best, rose over the silence. It fell; the air was filled with cheers; the fife and drum struck up, with the shouting, singing, and laughing again, but now retreating; and a single figure came hurrying up the avenue.

She ran down to meet her lover and clung to him. He was very gay, and he put his arm round her with a boisterous laugh. "Well, you must call me Captain, now; or Cap, if you prefer; that's what the boys call me. Yes, we've had a meeting at the town hall, and everybody has volunteered; and they selected me for captain, and I'm going to the war, the big war, the glorious war, the holy war ordained by the pocket Providence that blesses butchery. Come along; let's tell the whole family about it. Call them from their downy beds, father, mother, Aunt Hitty, and all the folks!"

But when they mounted the veranda steps he did not wait for a larger audience; he poured the story out upon Editha alone.

"There was a lot of speaking, and then some of the fools set up a shout for me. It was all going one way, and I thought it would be a good joke to sprinkle a little cold water on them. But you can't do that with a crowd that adores you. The first thing I knew I was sprinkling hell-fire on them. 'Cry havoc, and let slip the dogs of war.'[6] That was the style. Now that it had come

---

5. From "Lucasta, Going to the Wars," by the English poet Richard Lovelace (1618–1658).

6. From Antony's soliloquy after the murder of Caesar, in Shakespeare's *Julius Caesar* (3.1.274).

to the fight, there were no two parties; there was one country, and the thing was to fight the fight to a finish as quick as possible. I suggested volunteering then and there, and I wrote my name first of all on the roster. Then they elected me—that's all. I wish I had some ice-water!"

She left him walking up and down the veranda, while she ran for the ice-pitcher and a goblet, and when she came back he was still walking up and down, shouting the story he had told her to her father and mother, who had come out more sketchily dressed than they commonly were by day. He drank goblet after goblet of the ice-water without noticing who was giving it, and kept on talking, and laughing through his talk wildly. "It's astonishing," he said, "how well the worse reason looks when you try to make it appear the better. Why, I believe I was the first convert to the war in that crowd tonight! I never thought I should like to kill a man; but now, I shouldn't care; and the smokeless powder lets you see the man drop that you kill. It's all for the country! What a thing it is to have a country that *can't* be wrong, but if it is, is right, anyway!"

Editha had a great, vital thought, an inspiration. She set down the ice-pitcher on the veranda floor, and ran up-stairs and got the letter she had written him. When at last he noisily bade her father and mother, "Well, good night. I forgot I woke you up; I sha'n't want any sleep myself," she followed him down the avenue to the gate. There, after the whirling words that seemed to fly away from her thoughts and refuse to serve them, she made a last effort to solemnize the moment that seemed so crazy, and pressed the letter she had written upon him.

"What's this?" he said. "Want me to mail it?"

"No, no. It's for you. I wrote it after you went this morning. Keep it—keep it—and read it sometime—" She thought, and then her inspiration came: "Read it if ever you doubt what you've done, or fear that I regret your having done it. Read it after you've started."

They strained each other in embraces that seemed as ineffective as their words, and he kissed her face with quick, hot breaths that were so unlike him, that made her feel as if she had lost her old lover and found a stranger in his place. The stranger said: "What a gorgeous flower you are, with your red hair, and your blue eyes that look black now, and your face with the color painted out by the white moonshine! Let me hold you under my chin, to see whether I love blood, you tiger-lily!" Then he laughed Gearson's laugh, and released her, scared and giddy. Within her willfulness she had been frightened by a sense of subtler force in him, and mystically mastered as she had never been before.

She ran all the way back to the house, and mounted the steps panting. Her mother and father were talking of the great affair. Her mother said: "Wa'n't Mr. Gearson in rather of an excited state of mind? Didn't you think he acted curious?"

"Well, not for a man who'd just been elected captain and had to set 'em up for the whole of Company A," her father chuckled back.

"What in the world do you mean, Mr. Balcom? Oh! There's Editha!" She offered to follow the girl indoors.

"Don't come, mother!" Editha called, vanishing.

Mrs. Balcom remained to reproach her husband. "I don't see much of anything to laugh at."

"Well, it's catching. Caught it from Gearson. I guess it won't be much of a war, and I guess Gearson don't think so, either. The other fellows will back down as soon as they see we mean it. I wouldn't lose any sleep over it. I'm going back to bed, myself."

Gearson came again next afternoon, looking pale, and rather sick, but quite himself, even to his languid irony. "I guess I'd better tell you, Editha, that I consecrated myself to your god of battles last night by pouring too many libations to him down my own throat. But I'm all right now. One has to carry off the excitement, somehow."

"Promise me," she commanded, "that you'll never touch it again!"

"What! Not let the cannikin clink? Not let the soldier drink?[7] Well, I promise."

"You don't belong to yourself now; you don't even belong to *me*. You belong to your country, and you have a sacred charge to keep yourself strong and well for your country's sake. I have been thinking, thinking all night and all day long."

"You look as if you had been crying a little, too," he said with his queer smile.

"That's all past. I've been thinking, and worshipping *you*. Don't you suppose I know all that you've been through, to come to this? I've followed you every step from your old theories and opinions."

"Well, you've had a long row to hoe."

"And I know you've done this from the highest motives—"

"'Oh, there won't be much pettifogging to do till this cruel war is—'"

"And you haven't simply done it for my sake. I couldn't respect you if you had."

"Well, then we'll say I haven't. A man that hasn't got his own respect intact wants the respect of all the other people he can corner. But we won't go into that. I'm in for the thing now, and we've got to face our future. My idea is that this isn't going to be a very protracted struggle; we shall just scare the enemy to death before it comes to a fight at all. But we must provide for contingencies, Editha. If anything happens to me—"

"Oh, George!" She clung to him sobbing.

"I don't want you to feel foolishly bound to my memory. I should hate that, wherever I happened to be."

"I am yours, for time and eternity—time and eternity." She liked the words; they satisfied her famine for phrases.

"Well, say eternity; that's all right; but time's another thing; and I'm talking about time. But there is something! My mother! If anything happens—"

She winced, and he laughed. "You're not the bold soldier-girl of yesterday!" Then he sobered. "If anything happens, I want you to help my mother out. She won't like my doing this thing. She brought me up to think war a fool thing as well as a bad thing. My father was in the civil war, all through it; lost his arm in it." She thrilled with the sense of the arm round her; what if that should be lost? He laughed as if divining her: "Oh, it doesn't run in the family, as far as I know!" Then he added, gravely: "He came home with misgivings about war, and they grew on him. I guess he and mother agreed

<hr>

7. Allusion to Shakespeare's *Othello* (2.3.64–68), in which Iago sings a soldier's drinking song.

between them that I was to be brought up in his final mind about it; but that was before my time. I only knew him from my mother's report of him and his opinions; I don't know whether they were hers first; but they were hers last. This will be a blow to her. I shall have to write and tell her—"

He stopped, and she asked: "Would you like me to write too, George?"

"I don't believe that would do. No, I'll do the writing. She'll understand a little if I say that I thought the way to minimize it was to make war on the largest possible scale at once—that I felt I must have been helping on the war somehow if I hadn't helped keep it from coming, and I knew I hadn't; when it came, I had no right to stay out of it."

Whether his sophistries satisfied him or not, they satisfied her. She clung to his breast, and whispered, with closed eyes and quivering lips: "Yes, yes, yes!"

"But if anything should happen, you might go to her, and see what you could do for her. You know? It's rather far off; she can't leave her chair—"

"Oh, I'll go, if it's the ends of the earth! But nothing will happen! Nothing *can*! I—"

She felt herself lifted with his rising, and Gearson was saying, with his arm still round her, to her father: "Well, we're off at once, Mr. Balcom. We're to be formally accepted at the capital, and then bunched up with the rest somehow, and sent into camp somewhere, and got to the front as soon as possible. We all want to be in the van,[8] of course; we're the first company to report to the Governor. I came to tell Editha, but I hadn't got round to it."

She saw him again for a moment at the capital, in the station, just before the train started southward with his regiment. He looked well, in his uniform, and very soldierly, but somehow girlish, too, with his clean-shaven face and slim figure. The manly eyes and the strong voice satisfied her, and his preoccupation with some unexpected details of duty flattered her. Other girls were weeping and bemoaning themselves, but she felt a sort of noble distinction in the abstraction, the almost unconsciousness, with which they parted. Only at the last moment he said: "Don't forget my mother. It mayn't be such a walk-over as I supposed," and he laughed at the notion.

He waved his hand to her as the train moved off—she knew it among a score of hands that were waved to other girls from the platform of the car, for it held a letter which she knew was hers. Then he went inside the car to read it, doubtless, and she did not see him again. But she felt safe for him through the strength of what she called her love. What she called her God, always speaking the name in a deep voice and with the implication of a mutual understanding, would watch over him and keep him and bring him back to her. If with an empty sleeve, then he should have three arms instead of two, for both of hers should be his for life. She did not see, though, why she should always be thinking of the arm his father had lost.

There were not many letters from him, but they were such as she could have wished, and she put her whole strength into making hers such as she imagined he could have wished, glorifying and supporting him. She wrote to his mother glorifying him as their hero, but the brief answer she got was

---

8. Short for vanguard, the foremost division of an army.

merely to the effect that Mrs. Gearson was not well enough to write herself, and thanking her for her letter by the hand of someone who called herself "Yrs truly, Mrs. W. J. Andrews."

Editha determined not to be hurt, but to write again quite as if the answer had been all she expected. But before it seemed as if she could have written, there came news of the first skirmish, and in the list of the killed, which was telegraphed as a trifling loss on our side, was Gearson's name. There was a frantic time of trying to make out that it might be, must be, some other Gearson; but the name and the company and the regiment, and the State were too definitely given.

Then there was a lapse into depths out of which it seemed as if she never could rise again; then a lift into clouds far above all grief, black clouds, that blotted out the sun, but where she soared with him, with George, George! She had the fever that she expected of herself, but she did not die in it; she was not even delirious, and it did not last long. When she was well enough to leave her bed, her one thought was of George's mother, of his strangely worded wish that she should go to her and see what she could do for her. In the exaltation of the duty laid upon her—it buoyed her up instead of burdening her—she rapidly recovered.

Her father went with her on the long railroad journey from northern New York to western Iowa; he had business out at Davenport, and he said he could just as well go then as any other time; and he went with her to the little country town where George's mother lived in a little house on the edge of illimitable corn-fields, under trees pushed to a top of the rolling prairie. George's father had settled there after the civil war, as so many other old soldiers had done; but they were Eastern people, and Editha fancied touches of the East in the June rose overhanging the front door, and the garden with early summer flowers stretching from the gate of the paling fence.

It was very low inside the house, and so dim, with the closed blinds, that they could scarcely see one another: Editha tall and black in her crapes which filled the air with the smell of their dyes; her father standing decorously apart with his hat on his forearm, as at funerals; a woman rested in a deep armchair, and the woman who had let the strangers in stood behind the chair.

The seated woman turned her head round and up, and asked the woman behind her chair: "*Who* did you say?"

Editha, if she had done what she expected of herself, would have gone down on her knees at the feet of the seated figure and said, "I am George's Editha," for answer.

But instead of her own voice she heard that other woman's voice, saying: "Well, I don't know as I *did* get the name just right. I guess I'll have to make a little more light in here," and she went and pushed two of the shutters ajar.

Then Editha's father said, in his public will-now-address-a-few-remarks tone: "My name is Balcom, ma'am—Junius H. Balcom, of Balcom's Works, New York; my daughter—"

"Oh!" the seated woman broke in, with a powerful voice, the voice that always surprised Editha from Gearson's slender frame. "Let me see you! Stand round where the light can strike on your face," and Editha dumbly obeyed. "So, you're Editha Balcom," she sighed.

"Yes," Editha said, more like a culprit than a comforter.

"What did you come for?" Mrs. Gearson asked.

Editha's face quivered and her knees shook. "I came—because—because George—" She could go no further.

"Yes," the mother said, "he told me he had asked you to come if he got killed. You didn't expect that, I suppose, when you sent him."

"I would rather have died myself than done it!" Editha said with more truth in her deep voice than she ordinarily found in it. "I tried to leave him free—"

"Yes, that letter of yours, that came back with his other things, left him free."

Editha saw now where George's irony came from.

"It was not to be read before—unless—until—I told him so," she faltered.

"Of course, he wouldn't read a letter of yours, under the circumstances, till he thought you wanted him to. Been sick?" the woman abruptly demanded.

"Very sick." Editha said, with self-pity.

"Daughter's life," her father interposed, "was almost despaired of, at one time."

Mrs. Gearson gave him no heed. "I suppose you would have been glad to die, such a brave person as you! I don't believe *he* was glad to die. He was always a timid boy, that way; he was afraid of a good many things; but if he was afraid he did what he made up his mind to. I suppose he made up his mind to go, but I knew what it cost him, by what it cost me when I heard of it. I had been through *one* war before. When you sent him you didn't expect he would get killed."

The voice seemed to compassionate Editha, and it was time. "No," she huskily murmured.

"No, girls don't; women don't, when they give their men up to their country. They think they'll come marching back, somehow, just as gay as they went, or if it's an empty sleeve, or even an empty pantaloon, it's all the more glory, and they're so much the prouder of them, poor things!"

The tears began to run down Editha's face; she had not wept till then; but it was now such a relief to be understood that the tears came.

"No, you didn't expect him to get killed," Mrs. Gearson repeated in a voice which was startlingly like George's again. "You just expected him to kill some one else, some of those foreigners, that weren't there because they had any say about it, but because they had to be there, poor wretches—conscripts, or whatever they call 'em. You thought it would be all right for my George, *your* George, to kill the sons of those miserable mothers and the husbands of those girls that you would never see the faces of." The woman lifted her powerful voice in a psalmlike note. "I thank my God he didn't live to do it! I thank my God they killed him first, and that he ain't livin' with their blood on his hands!" She dropped her eyes, which she had raised with her voice, and glared at Editha. "What you got that black on for?" She lifted herself by her powerful arms so high that her helpless body seemed to hang limp its full length. "Take it off, take it off, before I tear it from your back!"

The lady who was passing the summer near Balcom's Works was sketching Editha's beauty, which lent itself wonderfully to the effects of a colorist. It had come to that confidence which is rather apt to grow between artist and sitter, and Editha told her everything.

"To think of your having such a tragedy in your life!" the lady said. She added: "I suppose there are people who feel that way about war. But when you consider the good this war has done—how much it has done for the country! I can't understand such people, for my part. And when you had come all the way out there to console her—got up out of a sick-bed! Well!"

"I think," Editha said, magnanimously, "she wasn't quite in her right mind; and so did papa."

"Yes," the lady said, looking at Editha's lips in nature and then at her lips in art, and giving an empirical touch to them in the picture. "But how dreadful of her! How perfectly—excuse me—how *vulgar!*"

A light broke upon Editha in the darkness which she felt had been without a gleam of brightness for weeks and months. The mystery that had bewildered her was solved by the word; and from that moment she rose from grovelling in shame and self-pity, and began to live again in the ideal.

1905

AMBROSE BIERCE
1842–c. 1914

Ambrose Gwinnett Bierce was born on June 24, 1842, in Meigs County, Ohio, the tenth of thirteen children. After the family moved to Indiana, he attended school and then struck out on his own at age fifteen. He worked as a printer's apprentice for a newspaper in Indiana, spent a term at a military school in Kentucky, and enlisted in the Union Army during the Civil War. Bierce saw action in some of the bloodiest battles of the war, including Shiloh, Chickamauga, and the Atlanta campaign. In 1864, at Kennesaw Mountain, he was struck in the temple by a bullet that miraculously lodged beneath the skin without penetrating the skull. In his *Devil's Dictionary*, Bierce would later define war as a "by-product of the arts of peace" and peace as "a period of cheating between two periods of fighting"—an unsentimental attitude that carried over to his fiction about the war including the bitter war narrative "Chickamauga" (1889) and the suspenseful "An Occurrence at Owl Creek Bridge" (1890).

When the war ended, Bierce moved to San Francisco to begin the journalistic career he followed for the rest of his life. San Francisco in the late 1860s and 1870s was becoming home to a journalism-based literary culture, as writers worked to make the West better known to eastern readers and to counter the image of the "wild West," so popular in dime-novel fiction, by showing San Francisco as the center of a cultivated society. Bierce married in 1872 and he went with his wife to England for four years, where he continued to hone his literary skills. Returning to San Francisco in 1875, he made a reputation through his newspaper columns as a satirist of elegance and bite. From 1886 to 1906, he was employed by William Randolph Hearst's *San Francisco Examiner*, and many of his best-known stories and essays appeared first in the *Examiner*. He published the story collections *Tales of Soldiers and Civilians* (1891) and *Can Such Things Be?* (1893), and then, while working as a correspondent in Washington, D.C., began collecting his witticisms from newspaper columns dating back to the 1880s into book form. This volume was first published in 1906 as *The Cynic's Word Book*. Between 1909 and 1912 his collected works came out in twelve volumes, and the *Word Book* appeared under Bierce's preferred title, *The Devil's Dictionary*.

Bierce and his wife separated in 1888 and divorced five years later. They had three children; one of his two sons seems to have been shot to death in 1889 in a brawl over a woman, and the other died from alcoholism-related pneumonia in 1913. In that year, Bierce went to Mexico and disappeared. It is supposed that he planned to take part in the Mexican Revolution on the side of pro-democracy rebels led by the general Pancho Villa, a cause endorsed by some politically engaged Americans of the era (but not by the U.S. government).

Among writers active after the Civil War, Bierce was known as the most consistently pessimistic; he was called "Bitter Bierce" by many. His stories merged the hallucinatory and the paranormal with everyday events, attempting to catch the intensity of extreme human experience. Rejecting the national preference for optimism and happy endings, he strove to produce essays, fiction, and commentaries that would remain in his readers' minds as much for the tight pungency of his prose style as for the ideas that motivated them. In both of the stories included here, Bierce turns to extraordinary observers—a condemned man preparing to die and a child who has stumbled into the horrors of combat—to tell stories of the Civil War stripped of their usual patina of glory and nobility.

An Occurrence at Owl Creek Bridge[1]

I

A man stood upon a railroad bridge in Northern Alabama, looking down into the swift waters twenty feet below. The man's hands were behind his back, the wrists bound with a cord. A rope closely encircled his neck. It was attached to a stout cross-timber above his head, and the slack fell to the level of his knees. Some loose boards laid upon the sleepers[2] supporting the metals of the railway supplied a footing for him, and his executioners—two private soldiers of the Federal army, directed by a sergeant, who in civil life may have been a deputy sheriff. At a short remove upon the same temporary platform was an officer in the uniform of his rank, armed. He was a captain. A sentinel at each end of the bridge stood with his rifle in the position known as "support," that is to say, vertical in front of the left shoulder, the hammer resting on the forearm thrown straight across the chest—a formal and unnatural position, enforcing an erect carriage of the body. It did not appear to be the duty of these two men to know what was occurring at the centre of the bridge; they merely blockaded the two ends of the foot planking that traversed it.

Beyond one of the sentinels nobody was in sight; the railroad ran straight away into a forest for a hundred yards, then, curving, was lost to view. Doubtless there was an outpost farther along. The other bank of the stream was open ground—a gentle acclivity crowned with a stockade of vertical tree trunks, loopholed for rifles, with a single embrasure through which protruded the muzzle of a brass cannon commanding the bridge. Midway of the slope between bridge and fort were the spectators—a single company of infantry in line, at "parade rest," the butts of the rifles on the ground, the barrels inclining slightly backward against the right shoulder, the hands crossed upon the

---

1. First published in the *San Francisco Examiner* on July 13, 1890, this story was subsequently reprinted as part of the collection *Tales of Soldiers and Civilians* (1891), the source of the text printed here.

2. The wooden cross-braces supporting railroad tracks.

stock. A lieutenant stood at the right of the line, the point of his sword upon the ground, his left hand resting upon his right. Excepting the group of four at the center of the bridge not a man moved. The company faced the bridge, staring stonily, motionless. The sentinels, facing the banks of the stream, might have been statues to adorn the bridge. The captain stood with folded arms, silent, observing the work of his subordinates but making no sign. Death is a dignitary who, when he comes announced, is to be received with formal manifestations of respect, even by those most familiar with him. In the code of military etiquette silence and fixity are forms of deference.

The man who was engaged in being hanged was apparently about thirty-five years of age. He was a civilian, if one might judge from his dress, which was that of a planter. His features were good—a straight nose, firm mouth, broad forehead, from which his long, dark hair was combed straight back, falling behind his ears to the collar of his well-fitting frock coat. He wore a mustache and pointed beard but no whiskers; his eyes were large and dark gray and had a kindly expression which one would hardly have expected in one whose neck was in the hemp. Evidently this was no vulgar assassin. The liberal military code makes provision for hanging many kinds of people, and gentlemen are not excluded.

The preparations being complete, the two private soldiers stepped aside and each drew away the plank upon which he had been standing. The sergeant turned to the captain, saluted and placed himself immediately behind that officer, who in turn moved apart one pace. These movements left the condemned man and the sergeant standing on the two ends of the same plank, which spanned three of the cross-ties of the bridge. The end upon which the civilian stood almost, but not quite, reached a fourth. This plank had been held in place by the weight of the captain; it was now held by that of the sergeant. At a signal from the former, the latter would step aside, the plank would tilt and the condemned man go down between two ties. The arrangement commended itself to his judgment as simple and effective. His face had not been covered nor his eyes bandaged. He looked a moment at his "unsteadfast footing," then let his gaze wander to the swirling water of the stream racing madly beneath his feet. A piece of dancing driftwood caught his attention and his eyes followed it down the current. How slowly it appeared to move! What a sluggish stream!

He closed his eyes in order to fix his last thoughts upon his wife and children. The water, touched to gold by the early sun, the brooding mists under the banks at some distance down the stream, the fort, the soldiers, the piece of drift—all had distracted him. And now he became conscious of a new disturbance. Striking through the thought of his dear ones was a sound which he could neither ignore nor understand, a sharp, distinct, metallic percussion like the stroke of a blacksmith's hammer upon the anvil; it had the same ringing quality. He wondered what it was, and whether immeasurably distant or near by—it seemed both. Its recurrence was regular, but as slow as the tolling of a death knell. He awaited each stroke with impatience and—he knew not why—apprehension. The intervals of silence grew progressively longer; the delays became maddening. With their greater infrequency the sounds increased in strength and sharpness. They hurt his ear like the thrust of a knife; he feared he would shriek. What he heard was the ticking of his watch.

He unclosed his eyes and saw again the water below him. "If I could free my hands," he thought, "I might throw off the noose and spring into the stream. By diving I could evade the bullets and, swimming vigorously, reach the bank, take to the woods, and get away home. My home, thank God, is as yet outside their lines; my wife and little ones are still beyond the invader's farthest advance."

As these thoughts, which have here to be set down in words, were flashed into the doomed man's brain rather than evolved from it, the captain nodded to the sergeant. The sergeant stepped aside.

II

Peyton Farquhar was a well-to-do planter, of an old and highly respected Alabama family. Being a slave owner, and, like other slave owners, a politician he was naturally an original secessionist and ardently devoted to the Southern cause. Circumstances of an imperious nature which it is unnecessary to relate here, had prevented him from taking service with the gallant army that had fought the disastrous campaigns ending with the fall of Corinth,[3] and he chafed under the inglorious restraint, longing for the release of his energies, the larger life of the soldier, the opportunity for distinction. That opportunity, he felt, would come, as it comes to all in war time. Meanwhile he did what he could. No service was too humble for him to perform in aid of the South, no adventure too perilous for him to undertake if consistent with the character of a civilian who was at heart a soldier, and who in good faith and without too much qualification assented to at least a part of the frankly villainous dictum that all is fair in love and war.

One evening while Farquhar and his wife were sitting on a rustic bench near the entrance to his grounds, a gray-clad soldier rode up to the gate and asked for a drink of water. Mrs. Farquhar was only too happy to serve him with her own white hands. While she was gone to fetch the water her husband approached the dusty horseman and inquired eagerly for news from the front.

"The Yanks are repairing the railroads," said the man, "and are getting ready for another advance. They have reached the Owl Creek bridge, put it in order, and built a stockade on the other bank. The commandant has issued an order, which is posted everywhere, declaring that any civilian caught interfering with the railroad, its bridges, tunnels, or trains will be summarily hanged. I saw the order."

"How far is it to the Owl Creek bridge?" Farquhar asked.

"About thirty miles?"

"Is there no force on this side the creek?"

"Only a picket post[4] half a mile out, on the railroad, and a single sentinel at this end of the bridge."

"Suppose a man—a civilian and student of hanging—should elude the picket post and perhaps get the better of the sentinel," said Farquhar, smiling, "what could he accomplish?"

3. Corinth, Mississippi, fell to the Union forces under General Ulysses S. Grant following the Battle of Shiloh on April 6 and 7, 1862.
4. Guard post.

The soldier reflected. "I was there a month ago," he replied. "I observed that the flood of last winter had lodged a great quantity of driftwood against the wooden pier at this end of the bridge. It is now dry and would burn like tow."

The lady had now brought the water, which the soldier drank. He thanked her ceremoniously, bowed to her husband, and rode away. An hour later, after nightfall, he repassed the plantation, going northward in the direction from which he had come. He was a Federal scout.

III

As Peyton Farquhar fell straight downward through the bridge, he lost consciousness and was as one already dead. From this state he was awakened—ages later, it seemed to him—by the pain of a sharp pressure upon his throat, followed by a sense of suffocation. Keen, poignant agonies seemed to shoot from his neck downward through every fiber of his body and limbs. These pains appeared to flash along well-defined lines of ramification and to beat with an inconceivably rapid periodicity. They seemed like streams of pulsating fire heating him to an intolerable temperature. As to his head, he was conscious of nothing but a feeling of fullness—of congestion. These sensations were unaccompanied by thought. The intellectual part of his nature was already effaced; he had power only to feel, and feeling was torment. He was conscious of motion. Encompassed in a luminous cloud, of which he was now merely the fiery heart, without material substance, he swung through unthinkable arcs of oscillation, like a vast pendulum. Then all at once, with terrible suddenness, the light about him shot upward with the noise of a loud plash; a frightful roaring was in his ears, and all was cold and dark. The power of thought was restored; he knew that the rope had broken and he had fallen into the stream. There was no additional strangulation; the noose about his neck was already suffocating him and kept the water from his lungs. To die of hanging at the bottom of a river!—the idea seemed to him ludicrous. He opened his eyes in the blackness and saw above him a gleam of light, but how distant, how inaccessible! He was still sinking, for the light became fainter and fainter until it was a mere glimmer. Then it began to grow and brighten, and he knew that he was rising toward the surface—knew it with reluctance, for he was now very comfortable. "To be hanged and drowned," he thought, "that is not so bad; but I do not wish to be shot. No; I will not be shot; that is not fair."

He was not conscious of an effort, but a sharp pain in his wrist apprised him that he was trying to free his hands. He gave the struggle his attention, as an idler might observe the feat of a juggler, without interest in the outcome. What splendid effort!—what magnificent, what superhuman strength! Ah, that was a fine endeavor! Bravo! The cord fell away; his arms parted and floated upward, the hands dimly seen on each side in the growing light. He watched them with a new interest as first one and then the other pounced upon the noose at his neck. They tore it away and thrust it fiercely aside, its undulations resembling those of a water snake. "Put it back, put it back!" He thought he shouted these words to his hands, for the undoing of the noose had been succeeded by the direst pang that he had yet experienced. His neck ached horribly; his brain was on fire; his heart, which had been fluttering faintly, gave a great leap, trying to force itself out at his mouth. His whole body was racked and wrenched with an insupportable anguish! But his disobedient hands gave no heed to the command. They beat the water vigorously with quick, downward strokes, forcing him to the surface. He felt his head emerge; his eyes were blinded by the sunlight; his chest expanded convulsively, and with a supreme and crowning agony his lungs engulfed a great draught of air, which instantly he expelled in a shriek!

He was now in full possession of his physical senses. They were, indeed, preternaturally keen and alert. Something in the awful disturbance of his organic system had so exalted and refined them that they made record of things never before perceived. He felt the ripples upon his face and heard their separate sounds as they struck. He looked at the forest on the bank of the stream, saw the individual trees, the leaves and the veining of each leaf—saw the very insects upon them: the locusts, the brilliant-bodied flies, the gray spiders stretching their webs from twig to twig. He noted the prismatic colors in all the dewdrops upon a million blades of grass. The humming of the gnats that danced above the eddies of the stream, the beating of the dragon flies' wings, the strokes of the water spiders' legs, like oars which had lifted their boat—all these made audible music. A fish slid along beneath his eyes and he heard the rush of its body parting the water.

He had come to the surface facing down the stream; in a moment the visible world seemed to wheel slowly round, himself the pivotal point, and he saw the bridge, the fort, the soldiers upon the bridge, the captain, the sergeant, the two privates, his executioners. They were in silhouette against the blue sky. They shouted and gesticulated, pointing at him; the captain had drawn his pistol, but did not fire; the others were unarmed. Their movements were grotesque and horrible, their forms gigantic.

Suddenly he heard a sharp report and something struck the water smartly within a few inches of his head, spattering his face with spray. He heard a second report, and saw one of the sentinels with his rifle at his shoulder, a light cloud of blue smoke rising from the muzzle. The man in the water saw the eye of the man on the bridge gazing into his own through the sights of the rifle. He observed that it was a gray eye, and remembered having read that gray eyes were keenest and that all famous marksmen had them. Nevertheless, this one had missed.

A counter swirl had caught Farquhar and turned him half round; he was again looking into the forest on the bank opposite the fort. The sound of a clear, high voice in a monotonous singsong now rang out behind him and came across the water with a distinctness that pierced and subdued all other sounds, even the beating of the ripples in his ears. Although no soldier, he had frequented camps enough to know the dread significance of that deliberate, drawling, aspirated chant; the lieutenant on shore was taking a part in the morning's work. How coldly and pitilessly—with what an even, calm intonation, presaging and enforcing tranquillity in the men—with what accurately-measured intervals fell those cruel words:

"Attention, company. . . . Shoulder arms. . . . Ready. . . . Aim. . . . Fire."

Farquhar dived—dived as deeply as he could. The water roared in his ears like the voice of Niagara, yet he heard the dulled thunder of the volley, and, rising again toward the surface, met shining bits of metal, singularly flattened, oscillating slowly downward. Some of them touched him on the face and hands, then fell away, continuing their descent. One lodged between his collar and neck; it was uncomfortably warm, and he snatched it out.

As he rose to the surface, gasping for breath, he saw that he had been a long time under water; he was perceptibly farther down stream—nearer to safety. The soldiers had almost finished reloading; the metal ramrods flashed all at once in the sunshine as they were drawn from the barrels, turned in the air, and thrust into their sockets. The two sentinels fired again, independently and ineffectually.

The hunted man saw all this over his shoulder; he was now swimming vigorously with the current. His brain was as energetic as his arms and legs; he thought with the rapidity of lightning.

"The officer," he reasoned, "will not make that martinet's error a second time. It is as easy to dodge a volley as a single shot. He has probably already given the command to fire at will. God help me, I cannot dodge them all!"

An appalling plash within two yards of him, followed by a loud, rushing sound, *diminuendo*,[5] which seemed to travel back through the air to the fort and died in an explosion which stirred the very river to its deeps! A rising sheet of water, which curved over him, fell down upon him, blinded him, strangled him! The cannon had taken a hand in the game. As he shook his head free from the commotion of the smitten water, he heard the deflected shot humming through the air ahead, and in an instant it was cracking and smashing the branches in the forest beyond.

"They will not do that again," he thought; "the next time they will use a charge of grape.[6] I must keep my eye upon the gun; the smoke will apprise me—the report arrives too late; it lags behind the missile. It is a good gun."

Suddenly he felt himself whirled round and round—spinning like a top. The water, the banks, the forests, the now distant bridge, fort and men—all were commingled and blurred. Objects were represented by their colors only; circular horizontal streaks of color—that was all he saw. He had been caught in a vortex and was being whirled on with a velocity of advance and gyration which made him giddy and sick. In a few moments he was flung upon the gravel at the foot of the left bank of the stream—the southern bank— and behind a projecting point which concealed him from his enemies. The sudden arrest of his motion, the abrasion of one of his hands on the gravel, restored him and he wept with delight. He dug his fingers into the sand, threw it over himself in handfuls and audibly blessed it. It looked like gold, like diamonds, rubies, emeralds; he could think of nothing beautiful which it did not resemble. The trees upon the bank were giant garden plants; he noted a definite order in their arrangement, inhaled the fragrance of their blooms. A strange, roseate light shone through the spaces among their trunks and the wind made in their branches the music of aeolian harps.[7] He had no wish to perfect his escape, was content to remain in that enchanting spot until retaken.

A whizz and rattle of grapeshot among the branches high above his head roused him from his dream. The baffled cannoneer had fired him a random farewell. He sprang to his feet, rushed up the sloping bank, and plunged into the forest.

---

5. In music, diminishing (Italian).
6. Grapeshot, a cluster of small iron balls used as a cannon charge.

7. Stringed instruments activated by the wind (Aeolus was the keeper of the winds in classical mythology).

All that day he traveled, laying his course by the rounding sun. The forest seemed interminable; nowhere did he discover a break in it, not even a wood-man's road. He had not known that he lived in so wild a region. There was something uncanny in the revelation.

By nightfall he was fatigued, footsore, famishing. The thought of his wife and children urged him on. At last he found a road which led him in what he knew to be the right direction. It was as wide and straight as a city street, yet it seemed untraveled. No fields bordered it, no dwelling anywhere. Not so much as the barking of a dog suggested human habitation. The black bodies of the great trees formed a straight wall on both sides, terminating on the horizon in a point, like a diagram in a lesson in perspective. Overhead, as he looked up through this rift in the wood, shone great golden stars looking unfamiliar and grouped in strange constellations. He was sure they were arranged in some order which had a secret and malign significance. The wood on either side was full of singular noises, among which—once, twice, and again—he distinctly heard whispers in an unknown tongue.

His neck was in pain, and, lifting his hand to it, he found it horribly swol-len. He knew that it had a circle of black where the rope had bruised it. His eyes felt congested; he could no longer close them. His tongue was swollen with thirst; he relieved its fever by thrusting it forward from between his teeth into the cold air. How softly the turf had carpeted the untraveled ave-nue! He could no longer feel the roadway beneath his feet!

Doubtless, despite his suffering, he fell asleep while walking, for now he sees another scene—perhaps he has merely recovered from a delirium. He stands at the gate of his own home. All is as he left it, and all bright and beautiful in the morning sunshine. He must have traveled the entire night. As he pushes open the gate and passes up the wide white walk, he sees a flutter of female garments; his wife, looking fresh and cool and sweet, steps down from the veranda to meet him. At the bottom of the steps she stands waiting, with a smile of ineffable joy, an attitude of matchless grace and dig-nity. Ah, how beautiful she is! He springs forward with extended arms. As he is about to clasp her, he feels a stunning blow upon the back of the neck; a blinding white light blazes all about him, with a sound like the shock of a cannon—then all is darkness and silence!

Peyton Farquhar was dead; his body, with a broken neck, swung gently from side to side beneath the timbers of the Owl Creek bridge.

1890, 1891

Chickamauga[1]

One sunny autumn afternoon a child strayed away from its rude home in a small field and entered a forest unobserved. It was happy in a new sense of freedom from control—happy in the opportunity of exploration and

1. First published on January 20, 1889, in the *San Francisco Examiner*, the story was reprinted in the collection *Tales of Soldiers and Civilians* (1891), the source of the text printed here. Chick-amauga was one of the bloodiest single-day battles of the Civil War, a costly Union defeat along a creek south of Chattanooga, Tennessee, on Sep-tember 19, 1863.

Chickamauga. "The Battle of Chickamauga; Thomas's Men Repulsing the Charge of the Rebels." *Harper's Weekly*, October 21, 1863.

adventure; for this child's spirit, in bodies of its ancestors, had for many thousands of years been trained to memorable feats of discovery and conquest—victories in battles whose critical moments were centuries, whose victors' camps were cities of hewn stone. From the cradle of its race it had conquered its way through two continents, and, passing a great sea, had penetrated a third, there to be born to war and dominion as a heritage.

The child was a boy, aged about six years, the son of a poor planter. In his younger manhood the father had been a soldier, had fought against naked savages, and followed the flag of his country into the capital of a civilized race to the far South. In the peaceful life of a planter the warrior-fire survived; once kindled it is never extinguished. The man loved military books and pictures, and the boy had understood enough to make himself a wooden sword, though even the eye of his father would hardly have known it for what it was. This weapon he now bore bravely, as became the son of an heroic race, and, pausing now and again in the sunny space of the forest, assumed with some exaggeration, the postures of aggression and defense that he had been taught by the engraver's art. Made reckless by the ease with which he overcame invisible foes attempting to stay his advance, he committed the common enough military error of pushing the pursuit to a dangerous extreme, until he found himself upon the margin of a wide but shallow brook, whose rapid waters barred his direct advance against the flying foe that had crossed with illogical ease. But the intrepid victor was not to be baffled; the spirit of the race which had passed the great sea burned unconquerable in that small breast and would not be denied. Finding a place where some bowlders in the bed of the stream lay but a step or a leap apart, he made his way across and fell again upon the rear guard of his imaginary foe, putting all to the sword.

Now that the battle had been won, prudence required that he withdraw to his base of operations. Alas! like many a mightier conqueror, and like one, the mightiest, he could not

curb the lust for war,
Nor learn that tempted Fate will leave the loftiest star.[2]

Advancing from the bank of the creek, he suddenly found himself confronted with a new and more formidable enemy; in the path that he was following, bolt upright, with ears erect and paws suspended before it, sat a rabbit. With a startled cry the child turned and fled, he knew not in what direction, calling with inarticulate cries for his mother, weeping, stumbling, his tender skin cruelly torn by brambles, his little heart beating hard with terror—breathless, blind with tears—lost in the forest! Then, for more than an hour, he wandered with erring feet through the tangled undergrowth, till at last, overcome by fatigue, he lay down in a narrow space between two rocks, within a few yards of the stream, and, still grasping his toy sword, no longer a weapon but a companion, sobbed himself to sleep. The wood birds sang merrily above his head; the squirrels, whisking their bravery of tail, ran barking from tree to tree, unconscious of the pity of it, and somewhere far away was a strange, muffled thunder, as if the partridges were drumming in celebration of nature's victory over the son of her immemorial enslavers. And back at the little plantation, where white men and black were hastily searching the fields and hedges in alarm, a mother's heart was breaking for her missing child.

Hours passed, and then the little sleeper rose to his feet. The chill of the evening was in his limbs, the fear of the gloom in his heart. But he had rested, and he no longer wept. With some blind instinct which impelled to action he struggled through the undergrowth about him and came to a more open ground—on his right the brook, to the left a gentle acclivity studded with infrequent trees; over all the gathering gloom of twilight. A thin, ghostly mist rose along the water. It frightened and repelled him; instead of recrossing, in the direction whence he had come, he turned his back upon it, and went forward toward the dark inclosing wood. Suddenly he saw before him a strange moving object which he took to be some large animal—a dog, a pig—he could not name it; perhaps it was a bear. He had seen pictures of bears, but knew of nothing to their discredit, and had vaguely wished to meet one. But something in form or movement of this object—something in the awkwardness of its approach—told him that it was not a bear, and curiosity was stayed by fear. He stood still, and as it came slowly on, gained courage every moment, for he saw that at least it had not the long, menacing ears of the rabbit. Possibly his impressionable mind was half conscious of something familiar in its shambling, awkward gait. Before it had approached near enough to resolve his doubts, he saw that it was followed by another and another. To right and to left were many more; the whole open space about him was alive with them—all moving toward the brook.

They were men. They crept upon their hands and knees. They used their hands only, dragging their legs. They used their knees only, their arms hang-

2. From Canto 3 of Byron's poem *Childe Harold's Pilgrimage* (1812–18), these lines refer to Napoleon at the Battle of Waterloo.

ing useless at their sides. They strove to rise to their feet, but fell prone in the attempt. They did nothing naturally, and nothing alike, save only to advance foot by foot in the same direction. Singly, in pairs, and in little groups, they came on through the gloom, some halting now and again while others crept slowly past them, then resuming their movement. They came by dozens and by hundreds; as far on either hand as one could see in the deepening gloom they extended and the black wood behind them appeared to be inexhaustible. The very ground seemed in motion toward the creek. Occasionally one who had paused did not again go on, but lay motionless. He was dead. Some, pausing, made strange gestures with their hands, erected their arms and lowered them again, clasped their heads; spread their palms upward, as men are sometimes seen to do in public prayer.

Not all of this did the child note; it is what would have been noted by an older observer; he saw little but that these were men, yet crept like babes. Being men, they were not terrible, though some of them were unfamiliarly clad. He moved among them freely, going from one to another and peering into their faces with childish curiosity. All their faces were singularly white and many were streaked and gouted with red. Something in this—something too, perhaps, in their grotesque attitudes and movements—reminded him of the painted clown whom he had seen last summer in the circus, and he laughed as he watched them. But on and ever on they crept, these maimed and bleeding men, as heedless as he of the dramatic contrast between his laughter and their own ghastly gravity. To him it was a merry spectacle. He had seen his father's negroes creep upon their hands and knees for his amusement—had ridden them so, "making believe" they were his horses. He now approached one of these crawling figures from behind and with an agile movement mounted it astride. The man sank upon his breast, recovered, flung the small boy fiercely to the ground as an unbroken colt might have done, then turned upon him a face that lacked a lower jaw—from the upper teeth to the throat was a great red gap fringed with hanging shreds of flesh and splinters of bone. The unnatural prominence of nose, the absence of chin, the fierce eyes, gave this man the appearance of a great bird of prey crimsoned in throat and breast by the blood of its quarry. The man rose to his knees, the child to his feet. The man shook his fist at the child; the child, terrified at last, ran to a tree near by, got upon the farther side of it, and took a more serious view of the situation. And so the uncanny multitude dragged itself slowly and painfully along in hideous pantomime—moved forward down the slope like a swarm of great black beetles, with never a sound of going—in silence profound, absolute.

Instead of darkening, the haunted landscape began to brighten. Through the belt of trees beyond the brook shone a strange red light, the trunks and branches of the trees making a black lacework against it. It struck the creeping figures and gave them monstrous shadows, which caricatured their movements on the lit grass. It fell upon their faces, touching their whiteness with a ruddy tinge, accentuating the stains with which so many of them were freaked and maculated.[3] It sparkled on buttons and bits of metal in their clothing. Instinctively the child turned toward the growing splendor

3. Spotted, blemished. "Freaked": streaked or flecked.

and moved down the slope with his horrible companions; in a few moments had passed the foremost of the throng—not much of a feat, considering his advantages. He placed himself in the lead, his wooden sword still in hand, and solemnly directed the march, conforming his pace to theirs and occasionally turning as if to see that his forces did not straggle. Surely such a leader never before had such a following.

Scattered about upon the ground now slowly narrowing by the encroachment of this awful march to water, were certain articles to which, in the leader's mind, were coupled no significant associations; an occasional blanket, tightly rolled lengthwise, doubled and the ends bound together with a string; a heavy knapsack here, and there a broken musket—such things, in short, as are found in the rear of retreating troops, the "spoor"[4] of men flying from their hunters. Everywhere near the creek, which here had a margin of lowland, the earth was trodden into mud by the feet of men and horses. An observer of better experience in the use of his eyes would have noticed that these footprints pointed in both directions; the ground had been twice passed over—in advance and in retreat. A few hours before, these desperate, stricken men, with their more fortunate and now distant comrades, had penetrated the forest in thousands. Their successive battalions, breaking into swarms and reforming in lines, had passed the child on every side—had almost trodden on him as he slept. The rustle and murmur of their march had not awakened him. Almost within a stone's throw of where he lay they had fought a battle; but all unheard by him were the roar of the musketry, the shock of the cannon, "the thunder of the captains and the shouting."[5] He had slept through it all, grasping his little wooden sword with perhaps a tighter clutch in unconscious sympathy with his martial environment, but as heedless of the grandeur of the struggle as the dead who had died to make the glory.

The fire beyond the belt of woods on the farther side of the creek, reflected to earth from the canopy of its own smoke, was now suffusing the whole landscape. It transformed the sinuous line of mist to the vapor of gold. The water gleamed with dashes of red, and red, too, were many of the stones protruding above the surface. But that was blood; the less desperately wounded had stained them in crossing. On them, too, the child now crossed with eager steps; he was going to the fire. As he stood upon the farther bank, he turned about to look at the companions of his march. The advance was arriving at the creek. The stronger had already drawn themselves to the brink and plunged their faces in the flood. Three or four who lay without motion appeared to have no heads. At this the child's eyes expanded with wonder; even his hospitable understanding could not accept a phenomenon implying such vitality as that. After slaking their thirst these men had not the strength to back away from the water, nor to keep their heads above it. They were drowned. In rear of these the open spaces of the forest showed the leader as many formless figures of his grim command as at first; but not nearly so many were in motion. He waved his cap for their encouragement and smilingly pointed with his weapon in the direction of the guiding light—a pillar of fire to this strange exodus.

4. The track, trail, or droppings of a wild animal.   5. Job 39.25.

Confident of the fidelity of his forces, he now entered the belt of woods, passed through it easily in the red illumination, climbed a fence, ran across a field, turning now and again to coquette with his responsive shadow, and so approached the blazing ruin of a dwelling. Desolation everywhere. In all the wide glare not a living thing was visible. He cared nothing for that; the spectacle pleased, and he danced with glee in imitation of the wavering flames. He ran about collecting fuel, but every object that he found was too heavy for him to cast in from the distance to which the heat limited his approach. In despair he flung in his sword—a surrender to the superior forces of nature. His military career was at an end.

Shifting his position, his eyes fell upon some outbuildings which had an oddly familiar appearance, as if he had dreamed of them. He stood considering them with wonder, when suddenly the entire plantation, with its inclosing forest, seemed to turn as if upon a pivot. His little world swung half around; the points of the compass were reversed. He recognized the blazing building as his own home!

For a moment he stood stupefied by the power of the revelation, then ran with stumbling feet, making a half circuit of the ruin. There, conspicuous in the light of the conflagration, lay the dead body of a woman—the white face turned upward, the hands thrown out and clutched full of grass, the clothing deranged, the long dark hair in tangles and full of clotted blood. The greater part of the forehead was torn away, and from the jagged hole the brain protruded, overflowing the temple, a frothy mass of gray, crowned with clusters of crimson bubbles—the work of a shell!

The child moved his little hands, making wild, uncertain gestures. He uttered a series of inarticulate and indescribable cries—something between the chattering of an ape and the gobbling of a turkey—a startling, soulless, unholy sound, the language of a devil. The child was a deaf mute.

Then he stood motionless, with quivering lips, looking down upon the wreck.

1889, 1891

HENRY JAMES
1843–1916

As a young man Henry James set out to be a "literary master" in the European sense. His writings, the product of more than half a century as a publishing author, include tales, novellas, novels, plays, autobiographies, criticism, travel pieces, letters, reviews, and biographies—altogether perhaps as many as one hundred volumes, a prodigious output even by late-nineteenth-century standards. The recognition of his importance as well as his wide influence as novelist and critic increased in the years between the world wars, when James's fiction was recognized as a forerunner of transatlantic literary modernism. Since that time James has been firmly established as one of America's greatest novelists and critics, a subtle psychological realist, and an unsurpassed literary stylist.

Henry James was born in New York City on April 15, 1843. His father was a religious philosopher who had inherited enough wealth for his family to live comfortably and travel without his needing to earn an income; his mother, Mary Robertson Walsh James, like many women of her day, stayed home and was the family mainstay. James's older brother, William, would become America's first notable psychologist and one of its most influential philosophers. The family also included two younger brothers and a sister, Alice, herself a perceptive observer and diarist. First taken to Europe as an infant, James spent his boyhood in a then almost bucolic Washington Square in New York City until, when he was twelve, the family once again left for the Continent. His father wanted the children to have a rich, "sensuous education," and

Henry James in the early 1890s.

during the next four years, with stays in England, Switzerland, and France, he brought them to galleries, libraries, museums, and (of special interest to James) theaters. James's formal schooling was unsystematic, but he mastered French well enough to begin a lifelong study of its literature, and from childhood on he was fascinated by the literary and historical traditions in Europe that, as he later lamented in *Hawthorne* (1879), he believed were mostly absent in the United States.

James early developed what he described in *A Small Boy and Others* (1913) as the "practice of wondering and dawdling and gaping." This memoir also tells about a "horrid even if obscure hurt" that he suffered while fighting a stable fire in his late teens. The exact nature of this injury and its consequences have been the subject of intense speculation by biographers and critics, and it probably prevented James from serving in the Civil War. By this time, James's interest in literature and in writing had intensified; before he reached the age of twenty-one he was publishing reviews and stories in some of the leading American journals—the *Atlantic Monthly*, the *North American Review*, the *Galaxy*, and the *Nation*. He attended Harvard Law School briefly in 1862 but then decided that literature was his calling. He settled permanently in England in 1876 (after moving back and forth between America and Europe and after trial residences in France and Italy). James never married, and in recent decades the portrayal of sexual desire in his fiction and the question of his own sexual orientation have engaged his critics and biographers. He maintained close ties with his family, including William's children. He kept up a large correspondence, was extremely sociable, and knew most of his contemporaries in the arts. His prodigious creative energy was invested for more than fifty years in what he called the "sacred rage" of his art.

Leon Edel's influential, multi-volume biography of James, published from 1953 to 1972, divides James's mature literary career into three phases. In the first, which culminated with *The Portrait of a Lady* (1881), James felt his way toward and appropriated the so-called international theme—the drama, comic and tragic, of Americans in Europe and occasionally of Europeans in America. In the second period, he experimented with diverse themes and forms—initially in novels dealing explicitly with the social and political currents of the 1870s and 1880s, such as *The Princess Casamassima* (1886), then in writing for the theater, and finally in shorter fictions exploring the relationship of artists to society and the troubled psyches of oppressed children, as in *What Maisie Knew* (1897). In his last period, the so-called major phase, which culminated with *The Golden Bowl* (1904), he returned to international and cosmopolitan subjects in elaborately complex narratives of great epistemological and moral challenge to readers.

Three of his earliest books, *A Passionate Pilgrim* (stories), *Transatlantic Sketches* (travel pieces), and *Roderick Hudson* (a novel), were published in 1875. *The American* (1877) was James's first successful extended treatment of the naïve young American in conflict with the traditions, customs, and values of the Old World. *Daisy Miller* (1878), with its portrayal of the "new" American girl, brought him widespread popularity, so much so that the name of the title character became used frequently in contemporary debates about the role of women in the United States. In this fictional "study," as it was originally subtitled, a stubbornly naïve American girl willfully resists European (and American) social mores. These works show James as neither a national patriot nor a resentful émigré but a true cosmopolitan concerned with exploring American national character as it is tested by cultural displacement. In *Daisy Miller* in particular, James's skillful use of the limited point of view depicts a young American man who is himself limited by self-absorption and class position—and who is thus unable to see Daisy for who she is. In *Daisy Miller* and other works written during the 1870s, James was already developing the hallmarks of his later works. The drama of his fiction became increasingly concerned with the question of knowledge, whether characters' knowledge of each other or readers' struggles with deliberately limited information.

Despite their appeal, the relatively simple characters of Christopher Newman (*The American*) and Daisy Miller evoke romance, melodrama, and pathos more than psychological complexity and genuine tragedy, which required for James a broader canvas. In the character and career of Isabel Archer he found the focus for one of his most influential works on the international theme, *The Portrait of a Lady*. Here, the complex inner lives of his American characters are rendered with greater depth and stylistic innovation. The last third of *Portrait* depicts the heroine's awakened understanding and her attempts to escape her miserable marriage without sacrificing her principles or harming other people she cares about. James's tendency to have his main characters sacrifice their own happiness for the sake of principle has been criticized by some for its rejection of self-expression. But in *Portrait* and other of his works, James elucidates his belief that renunciation *is* a form of self-expression. During this same period, James formulated his own views on "The Art of Fiction" (1884) in a polemical essay that is reprinted in the "Realism and Naturalism" section of this volume.

From 1885 to 1890 James was largely occupied by writing *The Bostonians* (1886), *The Princess Casamassima* (1886), and *The Tragic Muse* (1889). These novels of reformers, radicals, and revolutionaries are better appreciated, perhaps, in our time than they were in his. Out of a sense of artistic challenge as well as financial need, James attempted to regain the popularity of *Daisy Miller* and earn money by turning dramatist. Between 1890 and 1895 he wrote seven plays; two were produced, and both were painful public failures for their author, leading him into a period of intense self-doubt. Between 1895 and 1900 he returned to fiction, especially to experimental works with three dominant subjects that he often combined: misunderstood or troubled writers and artists; ghosts and apparitions; and doomed or threatened children and adolescents. (The latter two themes conjoin to powerful effect in *The Turn of the Screw* [1898].) "The Beast in the Jungle" (1903, 1909) depicts the life of an egocentric man whose obsessive concern over the vague prospect of personal disaster destroys his chances for love and life in the present. Some of James's biographers have linked the guilt in this tale to the suicide of the writer Constance Fenimore Woolson in 1894, which she may have resorted to partly out of unrequited (and entirely unrecognized) love for James. More recently, Eve Kosofsky Sedgwick and other critics have linked the character's lack of interest in women to repressed homosexuality. However it is interpreted, "The Beast in the Jungle" remains a chilling tale of a failed life.

In his last three great novels—*The Wings of the Dove* (1902), *The Ambassadors* (1903), and *The Golden Bowl* (1904)—James experimented further with representing the complexity and uncertainty of human consciousness. All three of these books return to the international theme, but with a new and remorseless insight into how people make their own realities through their perceptions, impressions, and inner motivations. American innocence, at this point, becomes only a willful refusal to see, while awareness of one's own character as well as others' provides the wisdom to escape the designs that lead to disaster—though disaster is rarely thwarted in time, and we are usually left both with insight and with the knowledge that it has come "too late." James's remedy for unhappiness is sometimes more unhappiness, but more importantly the willingness to entertain diverse points of view on moral struggles. His treatment of such an extraordinarily complex theme allows him an unparalleled richness of syntax, sentence structure, metaphoric webs, symbols, characterization, point of view, and organizing rhythms. The world of these late novels is the one James defined in "The Art of Fiction" (1884) as representing "the very atmosphere of the mind." Though they found only a limited readership in James's own time, these dramas of perception are widely considered to be James's most influential contribution to the craft of fiction. He became, in the words of Joseph Conrad, "the historian of fine consciences."

When James was not writing fiction, he often wrote about it—either his own or others'. He was, as he noted in a letter, "a critical, a *non-naif*, a questioning, worrying reader." His inquiries into the achievement of other writers—preserved in such volumes as *French Poets and Novelists* (1878), *Partial Portraits* (1888), and *Notes on Novelists* (1914)—are remarkable for their breadth, balance, and acuteness. More broadly theoretical than his reviews or essays on individual writers, "The Art of Fiction" (an excerpt from which appears later in this volume) encapsulates James's central aesthetic conceptions. Calling attention to the unparalleled opportunities open to the artist of fiction and the beauty of the novel form, James also insists that "the deepest quality of a work of art will always be the quality of the mind of the producer" and that "no good novel will ever proceed from a superficial mind." James left no better record than this essay of his always twinned concerns over the moral and formal qualities of fiction, of the relationship between aesthetic and moral perception.

James was an extremely self-conscious writer, and his *Complete Notebooks*, edited and published in 1987, reveal a subtle, intense mind in the act of discovering subjects, methods, and principles. The prefaces he wrote for Scribner's lavish twenty-four-volume New York Edition (1907–9) of his extensively revised novels and tales contain James's final analyses of the works he considered to best represent his achievement—not to mention the extensive revisions themselves. As the culmination of a lifetime of reflection on the art of fiction, they provide extraordinary accounts of the origins and growth of his major writings and exquisite analyses of the fictional problems each work posed.

During his 1904–5 visit to the United States, his first after nearly twenty years, James traveled extensively and lectured in his native land and in Canada. The chief result of this visit was *The American Scene* (1907). This "absolutely personal" book explores the profound changes that occurred in America between the Civil War and World War I, the period James characterized as the "Age of the Mistake." The same richness of personal rumination is found in three other autobiographical reminiscences he wrote later in life: *A Small Boy and Others* (1913), *Notes of a Son and Brother* (1914), and the fragmentary and posthumously published *The Middle Years* (1917).

Henry James became a naturalized British subject out of impatience with America's reluctance to enter World War I. Starting in 1915, he involved himself in war-relief work. He was awarded the British Order of Merit in 1916. Despite their considerable difficulty, most of James's novels and tales have remained in print. The rich depth of his work—especially his incisive psychological renderings of *why* people do the things they do, or *don't* do the things they might or even ought to do—has continued to attract readers and scholars. As a writer who was born an American citizen and died British, and as an author whose writing has been celebrated both as the pinnacle of literary realism and an early example of modernist fiction, James eludes easy categorization. The social world that he describes may seem distant from our own, but his fiction still commands attention, both because of his stylistic prowess and because of the complexity of his insights. The short works included in this volume all show, in different ways, James's ability to create a landscape of ambiguity and doubt, where easy moral judgments become unsettled.

Daisy Miller: A Study[1]

I

At the little town of Vevey, in Switzerland, there is a particularly comfortable hotel. There are, indeed, many hotels; for the entertainment of tourists is the business of the place, which, as many travelers will remember, is seated upon the edge of a remarkably blue lake[2]—a lake that it behoves every tourist to visit. The shore of the lake presents an unbroken array of establishments of this order, of every category, from the "grand hotel" of the newest fashion, with a chalk-white front, a hundred balconies, and a dozen flags flying from its roof, to the little Swiss *pension*[3] of an elder day, with its name inscribed in German-looking lettering upon a pink or yellow wall, and an awkward summer-house in the angle of the garden. One of the hotels at Vevey, however, is famous, even classical, being distinguished from many of its upstart neighbors by an air both of luxury and of maturity. In this region, in the month of June, American travelers are extremely numerous; it may be said, indeed, that Vevey assumes at this period some of the characteristics of an American watering-place. There are sights and sounds which evoke a vision, an echo, of Newport and Saratoga.[4] There is a flitting hither and thither of "stylish" young girls, a rustling of muslin flounces, a rattle of dance-music in the morning hours, a sound of high-pitched voices at all times. You receive an impression of these things at the excellent inn of the "Trois Couronnes,"[5] and are transported in fancy to the Ocean House or to Congress Hall. But at the "Trois Couronnes," it must be added, there are other features that are much at variance with these suggestions: neat German waiters, who look like secretaries of legation; Russian princesses sitting in the garden; little Polish boys walking about, held by the hand, with their governors; a

---

1. First published in the *Cornhill Magazine* 37 (June–July 1878). The text reprinted here follows the first British book edition, published by Macmillan in 1879.
2. Lac Léman, or Lake Geneva.
3. Boardinghouse.
4. Newport, Rhode Island, and Saratoga, New York, resort areas for the rich, where the Ocean House and Congress Hall hotels are located.
5. Three Crowns (French).

Daisy Miller. This illustration by Harry McVickar appeared as the frontispiece to the 1892 edition of *Daisy Miller*, which was published by Harper and Brothers.

view of the snowy crest of the Dent du Midi and the picturesque towers of the Castle of Chillon.[6]

I hardly know whether it was the analogies or the differences that were uppermost in the mind of a young American, who, two or three years ago, sat in the garden of the "Trois Couronnes," looking about him, rather idly, at some of the graceful objects I have mentioned. It was a beautiful summer morning, and in whatever fashion the young American looked at things, they

---

6. Medieval castle on an island in Lake Geneva, famous as the setting for Byron's poem "The Prisoner of Chillon" (1816). "Dent du Midi": the highest peak in a mountain group in the Swiss Alps.

must have seemed to him charming. He had come from Geneva the day before, by the little steamer, to see his aunt, who was staying at the hotel—Geneva having been for a long time his place of residence. But his aunt had a headache—his aunt had almost always a headache—and now she was shut up in her room, smelling camphor,[7] so that he was at liberty to wander about. He was some seven-and-twenty years of age; when his friends spoke of him, they usually said that he was at Geneva, "studying." When his enemies spoke of him they said—but, after all, he had no enemies; he was an extremely amiable fellow, and universally liked. What I should say is, simply, that when certain persons spoke of him they affirmed that the reason of his spending so much time at Geneva was that he was extremely devoted to a lady who lived there—a foreign lady—a person older than himself. Very few Americans—indeed I think none—had ever seen this lady, about whom there were some singular stories. But Winterbourne had an old attachment for the little metropolis of Calvinism;[8] he had been put to school there as a boy, and he had afterwards gone to college there—circumstances which had led to his forming a great many youthful friendships. Many of these he had kept, and they were a source of great satisfaction to him.

After knocking at his aunt's door and learning that she was indisposed, he had taken a walk about the town, and then he had come in to his breakfast. He had now finished his breakfast, but he was drinking a small cup of coffee, which had been served to him on a little table in the garden by one of the waiters who looked like an *attaché*.[9] At last he finished his coffee and lit a cigarette. Presently a small boy came walking along the path—an urchin of nine or ten. The child, who was diminutive for his years, had an aged expression of countenance, a pale complexion, and sharp little features. He was dressed in knickerbockers, with red stockings, which displayed his poor little spindleshanks;[1] he also wore a brilliant red cravat. He carried in his hand a long alpenstock,[2] the sharp point of which he thrust into everything that he approached—the flower-beds, the garden-benches, the trains of the ladies' dresses. In front of Winterbourne he paused, looking at him with a pair of bright, penetrating little eyes.

"Will you give me a lump of sugar?" he asked, in a sharp, hard little voice—a voice immature, and yet, somehow, not young.

Winterbourne glanced at the small table near him, on which his coffee-service rested, and saw that several morsels of sugar remained. "Yes, you may take one," he answered; "but I don't think sugar is good for little boys."

This little boy stepped forward and carefully selected three of the coveted fragments, two of which he buried in the pocket to his knickerbockers, depositing the other as promptly in another place. He poked his alpenstock, lance-fashion, into Winterbourne's bench, and tried to crack the lump of sugar with his teeth.

"Oh, blazes; it's har-r-d!" he exclaimed, pronouncing the adjective in a peculiar manner.

7. An aromatic substance made from bark and wood, used at the time for the relief of minor pain.
8. I.e., Geneva, where the French Protestant reformer John Calvin (1509–1564) attempted to establish a community based on his theological beliefs.
9. I.e., like a member of the diplomatic corps.
1. Legs.
2. Walking stick.

Winterbourne had immediately perceived that he might have the honor of claiming him as a fellow-countryman. "Take care you don't hurt your teeth," he said, paternally.

"I haven't got any teeth to hurt. They have all come out. I have only got seven teeth. My mother counted them last night, and one came out right afterwards. She said she'd slap me if any more came out. I can't help it. It's this old Europe. It's the climate that makes them come out. In America they didn't come out. It's these hotels."

Winterbourne was much amused. "If you eat three lumps of sugar, your mother will certainly slap you," he said.

"She's got to give me some candy, then," rejoined his young interlocutor. "I can't get any candy here—any American candy. American candy's the best candy."

"And are American little boys the best little boys?" asked Winterbourne.

"I don't know. I'm an American boy," said the child.

"I see you are one of the best!" laughed Winterbourne.

"Are you an American man?" pursued this vivacious infant. And then, on Winterbourne's affirmative reply—"American men are the best," he declared.

His companion thanked him for the compliment; and the child, who had now got astride of his alpenstock, stood looking about him, while he attacked a second lump of sugar. Winterbourne wondered if he himself had been like this in his infancy, for he had been brought to Europe at about this age.

"Here comes my sister!" cried the child, in a moment. "She's an American girl."

Winterbourne looked along the path and saw a beautiful young lady advancing. "American girls are the best girls," he said, cheerfully, to his young companion.

"My sister ain't the best!" the child declared. "She's always blowing[3] at me."

"I imagine that is your fault, not hers," said Winterbourne. The young lady meanwhile had drawn near. She was dressed in white muslin, with a hundred frills and flounces, and knots of pale-colored ribbon. She was bareheaded; but she balanced in her hand a large parasol, with a deep border of embroidery; and she was strikingly, admirably pretty. "How pretty they are!" thought Winterbourne, straightening himself in his seat, as if he were prepared to rise.

The young lady paused in front of his bench, near the parapet of the garden, which overlooked the lake. The little boy had now converted his alpenstock into a vaulting-pole, by the aid of which he was springing about in the gravel, and kicking it up not a little.

"Randolph," said the young lady, "what *are* you doing?"

"I'm going up the Alps," replied Randolph. "This is the way!" And he gave another little jump, scattering the pebbles about Winterbourne's ears.

"That's the way they come down," said Winterbourne.

"He's an American man!" cried Randolph, in his little hard voice.

The young lady gave no heed to this announcement, but looked straight at her brother. "Well, I guess you had better be quiet," she simply observed.

It seemed to Winterbourne that he had been in a manner presented. He got up and stepped slowly towards the young girl, throwing away his ciga-

3. Nagging.

rette. "This little boy and I have made acquaintance," he said, with great civility. In Geneva, as he had been perfectly aware, a young man was not at liberty to speak to a young unmarried lady except under certain rarely-occurring conditions; but here at Vevey, what conditions could be better than these?—a pretty American girl coming and standing in front of you in a garden. This pretty American girl, however, on hearing Winterbourne's observation, simply glanced at him; she then turned her head and looked over the parapet, at the lake and the opposite mountains. He wondered whether he had gone too far; but he decided that he must advance farther, rather than retreat. While he was thinking of something else to say, the young lady turned to the little boy again.

"I should like to know where you got that pole," she said.

"I bought it!" responded Randolph.

"You don't mean to say you're going to take it to Italy!"

"Yes, I am going to take it to Italy!" the child declared.

The young girl glanced over the front of her dress, and smoothed out a knot or two of ribbon. Then she rested her eyes upon the prospect again. "Well, I guess you had better leave it somewhere," she said, after a moment.

"Are you going to Italy?" Winterbourne inquired, in a tone of great respect.

The young lady glanced at him again.

"Yes, sir," she replied. And she said nothing more.

"Are you—a—going over the Simplon?"[4] Winterbourne pursued, a little embarrassed.

"I don't know," she said, "I suppose it's some mountain. Randolph, what mountain are we going over?"

"Going where?" the child demanded.

"To Italy," Winterbourne explained.

"I don't know," said Randolph. "I don't want to go to Italy. I want to go to America."

"Oh, Italy is a beautiful place!" rejoined the young man.

"Can you get candy there?" Randolph loudly inquired.

"I hope not," said his sister. "I guess you have had enough candy, and mother thinks so too."

"I haven't had any for ever so long—for a hundred weeks!" cried the boy, still jumping about.

The young lady inspected her flounces and smoothed her ribbons again; and Winterbourne presently risked an observation upon the beauty of the view. He was ceasing to be embarrassed, for he had begun to perceive that she was not in the least embarrassed herself. There had not been the slightest alteration in her charming complexion; she was evidently neither offended nor fluttered. If she looked another way when he spoke to her, and seemed not particularly to hear him, this was simply her habit, her manner. Yet, as he talked a little more, and pointed out some of the objects of interest in the view, with which she appeared quite unacquainted, she gradually gave him more of the benefit of her glance; and then he saw that this glance was perfectly direct and unshrinking. It was not, however, what would have been called an immodest glance, for the young girl's eyes were singularly honest and fresh. They were wonderfully pretty eyes; and, indeed, Winterbourne

4. A mountain pass in the Alps between Switzerland and Italy.

had not seen for a long time anything prettier than his fair countrywoman's various features—her complexion, her nose, her ears, her teeth. He had a great relish for feminine beauty; he was addicted to observing and analyzing it; and as regards this young lady's face he made several observations. It was not at all insipid, but it was not exactly expressive; and though it was eminently delicate, Winterbourne mentally accused it—very forgivingly— of a want of finish. He thought it very possible that Master Randolph's sister was a coquette; he was sure she had a spirit of her own; but in her bright, sweet, superficial little visage there was no mockery, no irony. Before long it became obvious that she was much disposed towards conversation. She told him that they were going to Rome for the winter—she and her mother and Randolph. She asked him if he was a "real American"; she wouldn't have taken him for one; he seemed more like a German—this was said after a little hesitation, especially when he spoke. Winterbourne, laughing, answered that he had met Germans who spoke like Americans; but that he had not, so far as he remembered, met an American who spoke like a German. Then he asked her if she would not be more comfortable in sitting upon the bench which he had just quitted. She answered that she liked standing up and walking about; but she presently sat down. She told him she was from New York State—"if you know where that is." Winterbourne learned more about her by catching hold of her small, slippery brother and making him stand a few minutes by his side.

"Tell me your name, my boy," he said.

"Randolph C. Miller," said the boy, sharply. "And I'll tell you her name"; and he leveled his alpenstock at his sister.

"You had better wait till you are asked!" said this young lady, calmly.

"I should like very much to know your name," said Winterbourne.

"Her name is Daisy Miller!" cried the child. "But that isn't her real name; that isn't her name on her cards."

"It's a pity you haven't got one of my cards!" said Miss Miller.

"Her real name is Annie P. Miller," the boy went on.

"Ask him *his* name," said his sister, indicating Winterbourne.

But on this point Randolph seemed perfectly indifferent; he continued to supply information with regard to his own family. "My father's name is Ezra B. Miller," he announced. "My father ain't in Europe; my father's in a better place than Europe."

Winterbourne imagined for a moment that this was the manner in which the child had been taught to intimate that Mr. Miller had been removed to the sphere of celestial rewards. But Randolph immediately added, "My father's in Schenectady. He's got a big business. My father's rich, you bet."

"Well!" ejaculated Miss Miller, lowering her parasol and looking at the embroidered border. Winterbourne presently released the child, who departed, dragging his alpenstock along the path. "He doesn't like Europe," said the young girl. "He wants to go back."

"To Schenectady, you mean?"

"Yes; he wants to go right home. He hasn't got any boys here. There is one boy here, but he always goes round with a teacher; they won't let him play."

"And your brother hasn't any teacher?" Winterbourne inquired.

"Mother thought of getting him one, to travel round with us. There was a lady told her of a very good teacher; an American lady—perhaps you know her—Mrs. Sanders. I think she came from Boston. She told her of this teacher, and we thought of getting him to travel round with us. But Randolph said he didn't want a teacher traveling round with us. He said he wouldn't have lessons when he was in the cars.[5] And we *are* in the cars about half the time. There was an English lady we met in the cars—I think her name was Miss Featherstone; perhaps you know her. She wanted to know why I didn't give Randolph lessons—give him 'instruction,' she called it. I guess he could give me more instruction than I could give him. He's very smart."

"Yes," said Winterbourne; "he seems very smart."

"Mother's going to get a teacher for him as soon as we get to Italy. Can you get good teachers in Italy?"

"Very good, I should think," said Winterbourne.

"Or else she's going to find some school. He ought to learn some more. He's only nine. He's going to college." And in this way Miss Miller continued to converse upon the affairs of her family, and upon other topics. She sat there with her extremely pretty hands, ornamented with very brilliant rings, folded in her lap, and with her pretty eyes now resting upon those of Winterbourne, now wandering over the garden, the people who passed by, and the beautiful view. She talked to Winterbourne as if she had known him a long time. He found it very pleasant. It was many years since he heard a young girl talk so much. It might have been said of this unknown young lady, who had come and sat down beside him upon a bench, that she chattered. She was very quiet, she sat in a charming tranquil attitude; but her lips and her eyes were constantly moving. She had a soft, slender, agreeable voice, and her tone was decidedly sociable. She gave Winterbourne a history of her movements and intentions, and those of her mother and brother, in Europe, and enumerated, in particular, the various hotels at which they had stopped. "That English lady in the cars," she said—"Miss Featherstone—asked me if we didn't all live in hotels in America. I told her I had never been in so many hotels in my life as since I came to Europe. I have never seen so many—it's nothing but hotels." But Miss Miller did not make this remark with a querulous accent; she appeared to be in the best humor with everything. She declared that the hotels were very good, when once you got used to their ways, and that Europe was perfectly sweet. She was not disappointed—not a bit. Perhaps it was because she had heard so much about it before. She had ever so many intimate friends that had been there ever so many times. And then she had had ever so many dresses and things from Paris. Whenever she put on a Paris dress she felt as if she were in Europe.

"It was a kind of wishing-cap," said Winterbourne.

"Yes," said Miss Miller, without examining this analogy; "it always made me wish I was here. But I needn't have done that for dresses. I am sure they send all the pretty ones to America; you see the most frightful things here. The only thing I don't like," she proceeded, "is the society. There isn't any society; or, if there is, I don't know where it keeps itself. Do you? I suppose there is some society somewhere, but I haven't seen anything of it. I'm very fond of society, and I have always had a great deal of it. I don't mean only in Schenectady, but in New York. I used to go to New York every winter. In New York I had lots of society. Last winter I had seventeen dinners given

5. Railway cars.

me; and three of them were by gentlemen," added Daisy Miller. "I have more friends in New York than in Schenectady—more gentlemen friends; and more young lady friends too," she resumed in a moment. She paused again for an instant; she was looking at Winterbourne with all her prettiness in her lively eyes and in her light, slightly monotonous smile. "I have always had," she said, "a great deal of gentlemen's society."

Poor Winterbourne was amused, perplexed, and decidedly charmed. He had never yet heard a young girl express herself in just this fashion; never, at least, save in cases where to say such things seemed a kind of demonstrative evidence of a certain laxity of deportment. And yet was he to accuse Miss Daisy Miller of actual or potential *inconduite*,[6] as they said at Geneva? He felt that he had lived at Geneva so long that he had lost a good deal; he had become dishabituated to the American tone. Never, indeed, since he had grown old enough to appreciate things, had he encountered a young American girl of so pronounced a type as this. Certainly she was very charming; but how deucedly sociable! Was she simply a pretty girl from New York State—were they all like that, the pretty girls who had a good deal of gentlemen's society? Or was she also a designing, an audacious, an unscrupulous young person? Winterbourne had lost his instinct in this matter, and his reason could not help him. Miss Daisy Miller looked extremely innocent. Some people had told him that, after all, American girls were exceedingly innocent; and others had told him that, after all, they were not. He was inclined to think Miss Daisy Miller was a flirt—a pretty American flirt. He had never, as yet, had any relations with young ladies of this category. He had known, here in Europe, two or three women—persons older than Miss Daisy Miller, and provided, for respectability's sake, with husbands— who were great coquettes—dangerous, terrible women, with whom one's relations were liable to take a serious turn. But this young girl was not a coquette in that sense; she was very unsophisticated; she was only a pretty American flirt. Winterbourne was almost grateful for having found the formula that applied to Miss Daisy Miller. He leaned back in his seat; he remarked to himself that she had the most charming nose he had ever seen; he wondered what were the regular conditions and limitations of one's intercourse with a pretty American flirt. It presently became apparent that he was on the way to learn.

"Have you been to that old castle?" asked the young girl, pointing with her parasol to the far-gleaming walls of the Château de Chillon.

"Yes, formerly, more than once," said Winterbourne. "You too, I suppose, have seen it?"

"No; we haven't been there. I want to go there dreadfully. Of course I mean to go there. I wouldn't go away from here without having seen that old castle."

"It's a very pretty excursion," said Winterbourne, "and very easy to make. You can drive, you know, or you can go by the little steamer."

"You can go in the cars," said Miss Miller.

"Yes; you can go in the cars," Winterbourne assented.

"Our courier[7] says they take you right up to the castle," the young girl continued. "We were going last week; but my mother gave out. She suffers dreadfully from dyspepsia. She said she couldn't go. Randolph wouldn't go

---

6. Misconduct (French).   7. Social guide.

either; he says he doesn't think much of old castles. But I guess we'll go this week, if we can get Randolph."

"Your brother is not interested in ancient monuments?" Winterbourne inquired, smiling.

"He says he don't care much about old castles. He's only nine. He wants to stay at the hotel. Mother's afraid to leave him alone, and the courier won't stay with him; so we haven't been to many places. But it will be too bad if we don't go up there." And Miss Miller pointed again at the Château de Chillon.

"I should think it might be arranged," said Winterbourne. "Couldn't you get some one to stay—for the afternoon—with Randolph?"

Miss Miller looked at him a moment; and then, very placidly—"I wish *you* would stay with him!" she said.

Winterbourne hesitated a moment. "I would much rather go to Chillon with you."

"With me?" asked the young girl, with the same placidity.

She didn't rise, blushing, as a young girl at Geneva would have done; and yet Winterbourne, conscious that he had been very bold, thought it possible she was offended. "With your mother," he answered very respectfully.

But it seemed that both his audacity and his respect were lost upon Miss Daisy Miller. "I guess my mother won't go, after all," she said. "She don't like to ride round in the afternoon. But did you really mean what you said just now; that you would like to go up there?"

"Most earnestly," Winterbourne declared.

"Then we may arrange it. If mother will stay with Randolph, I guess Eugenio will."

"Eugenio?" the young man inquired.

"Eugenio's our courier. He doesn't like to stay with Randolph; he's the most fastidious man I ever saw. But he's a splendid courier. I guess he'll stay at home with Randolph if mother does, and then we can go to the castle."

Winterbourne reflected for an instant as lucidly as possible—"we" could only mean Miss Daisy Miller and himself. This programme seemed almost too agreeable for credence; he felt as if he ought to kiss the young lady's hand. Possibly he would have done so—and quite spoiled the project; but at this moment another person—presumably Eugenio—appeared. A tall, handsome man, with superb whiskers, wearing a velvet morning-coat and a brilliant watch-chain, approached Miss Miller, looking sharply at her companion. "Oh, Eugenio!" said Miss Miller, with the friendliest accent.

Eugenio had looked at Winterbourne from head to foot; he now bowed gravely to the young lady. "I have the honor to inform mademoiselle that luncheon is upon the table."

Miss Miller slowly rose. "See here, Eugenio," she said. "I'm going to that old castle, any way."

"To the Château de Chillon, mademoiselle?" the courier inquired. "Mademoiselle had made arrangements?" he added, in a tone which struck Winterbourne as very impertinent.

Eugenio's tone apparently threw, even to Miss Miller's own apprehension, a slightly ironical light upon the young girl's situation. She turned to Winterbourne, blushing a little—a very little. "You won't back out?" she said.

"I shall not be happy till we go!" he protested.

"And you are staying in this hotel?" she went on. "And you are really an American?"

The courier stood looking at Winterbourne, offensively. The young man, at least, thought his manner of looking an offence to Miss Miller; it conveyed an imputation that she "picked up" acquaintances. "I shall have the honor of presenting to you a person who will tell you all about me," he said smiling, and referring to his aunt.

"Oh well, we'll go some day," said Miss Miller. And she gave him a smile and turned away. She put up her parasol and walked back to the inn beside Eugenio. Winterbourne stood looking after her; and as she moved away, drawing her muslin furbelows over the gravel, said to himself that she had the *tournure*[8] of a princess.

II

He had, however, engaged to do more than proved feasible, in promising to present his aunt, Mrs. Costello, to Miss Daisy Miller. As soon as the former lady had got better of her headache he waited upon her in her apartment; and, after the proper inquiries in regard to her health, he asked her if she had observed, in the hotel, an American family—a mamma, a daughter, and a little boy.

"And a courier?" said Mrs. Costello. "Oh, yes, I have observed them. Seen them—heard them—and kept out of their way." Mrs. Costello was a widow with a fortune; a person of much distinction, who frequently intimated that, if she were not so dreadfully liable to sick-headaches, she would probably have left a deeper impress upon her time. She had a long pale face, a high nose, and a great deal of very striking white hair, which she wore in large puffs and *rouleaux*[9] over the top of her head. She had two sons married in New York, and another who was now in Europe. This young man was amusing himself at Homburg,[1] and, though he was on his travels, was rarely perceived to visit any particular city at the moment selected by his mother for her own appearance there. Her nephew, who had come up to Vevey expressly to see her, was therefore more attentive than those who, as she said, were nearer to her. He had imbibed at Geneva the idea that one must always be attentive to one's aunt. Mrs. Costello had not seen him for many years, and she was greatly pleased with him, manifesting her approbation by initiating him into many of the secrets of that social sway which, as she gave him to understand, she exerted in the American capital. She admitted that she was very exclusive; but, if he were acquainted with New York, he would see that one had to be. And her picture of the minutely hierarchical constitution of the society of that city, which she presented to him in many different lights, was, to Winterbourne's imagination, almost oppressively striking.

He immediately perceived, from her tone, that Miss Daisy Miller's place in the social scale was low. "I am afraid you don't approve of them," he said.

"They are very common," Mrs. Costello declared. "They are the sort of Americans that one does one's duty by not—not accepting."

8. Grace, poise (French).
9. Rolls, coils (French).

1. A resort in Germany.

"Ah, you don't accept them?" said the young man.

"I can't, my dear Frederick. I would if I could, but I can't."

"The young girl is very pretty," said Winterbourne, in a moment.

"Of course she's pretty. But she is very common."

"I see what you mean, of course," said Winterbourne, after another pause.

"She has that charming look that they all have," his aunt resumed. "I can't think where they pick it up; and she dresses in perfection—no, you don't know how well she dresses. I can't think where they get their taste."

"But, my dear aunt, she is not, after all, a Comanche savage."

"She is a young lady," said Mrs. Costello, "who has an intimacy with her mamma's courier?"

"An intimacy with the courier?" the young man demanded.

"Oh, the mother is just as bad! They treat the courier like a familiar friend—like a gentleman. I shouldn't wonder if he dines with them. Very likely they have never seen a man with such good manners, such fine clothes, so like a gentleman. He probably corresponds to the young lady's idea of a Count. He sits with them in the garden, in the evening. I think he smokes."

Winterbourne listened with interest to these disclosures; they helped him to make up his mind about Miss Daisy. Evidently she was rather wild. "Well," he said, "I am not a courier, and yet she was very charming to me."

"You had better have said at first," said Mrs. Costello with dignity, "that you had made her acquaintance."

"We simply met in the garden, and we talked a bit."

"*Tout bonnement!*[2] And pray what did you say?"

"I said I should take the liberty of introducing her to my admirable aunt."

"I am much obliged to you."

"It was to guarantee my respectability," said Winterbourne.

"And pray who is to guarantee hers?"

"Ah, you are cruel!" said the young man. "She's a very nice girl."

"You don't say that as if you believed it," Mrs. Costello observed.

"She is completely uncultivated," Winterbourne went on. "But she is wonderfully pretty, and, in short, she is very nice. To prove that I believe it, I am going to take her to the Château de Chillon."

"You two are going off there together? I should say it proved just the contrary. How long had you known her, may I ask, when this interesting project was formed. You haven't been twenty-four hours in the house."

"I had known her half-an-hour!" said Winterbourne, smiling.

"Dear me!" cried Mrs. Costello. "What a dreadful girl!"

Her nephew was silent for some moments.

"You really think, then," he began earnestly, and with a desire for trustworthy information—"you really think that—" But he paused again.

"Think what, sir," said his aunt.

"That she is the sort of young lady who expects a man—sooner or later—to carry her off?"

"I haven't the least idea what such young ladies expect a man to do. But I really think that you had better not meddle with little American girls that are uncultivated, as you call them. You have lived too long out

2. Quite simply! (French).

of the country. You will be sure to make some great mistake. You are too innocent."

"My dear aunt, I am not so innocent," said Winterbourne, smiling and curling his moustache.

"You are too guilty, then?"

Winterbourne continued to curl his moustache, meditatively. "You won't let the poor girl know you then?" he asked at last.

"Is it literally true that she is going to the Château de Chillon with you?"

"I think that she fully intends it."

"Then, my dear Frederick," said Mrs. Costello, "I must decline the honor of her acquaintance. I am an old woman, but I am not too old—thank Heaven—to be shocked!"

"But don't they all do these things—the young girls in America?" Winterbourne inquired.

Mrs. Costello stared a moment. "I should like to see my granddaughters do them!" she declared, grimly.

This seemed to throw some light upon the matter, for Winterbourne remembered to have heard that his pretty cousins in New York were "tremendous flirts." If, therefore, Miss Daisy Miller exceeded the liberal license allowed to these young ladies, it was probable that anything might be expected of her. Winterbourne was impatient to see her again, and he was vexed with himself that, by instinct, he should not appreciate her justly.

Though he was impatient to see her, he hardly knew what he should say to her about his aunt's refusal to become acquainted with her; but he discovered, promptly enough, that with Miss Daisy Miller there was no great need of walking on tiptoe. He found her that evening in the garden, wandering about in the warm starlight, like an indolent sylph, and swinging to and fro the largest fan he had ever beheld. It was ten o'clock. He had dined with his aunt, had been sitting with her since dinner, and had just taken leave of her till the morrow. Miss Daisy Miller seemed very glad to see him; she declared it was the longest evening she had ever passed.

"Have you been all alone?" he asked.

"I have been walking round with mother. But mother gets tired walking round," she answered.

"Has she gone to bed?"

"No; she doesn't like to go to bed," said the young girl. "She doesn't sleep—not three hours. She says she doesn't know how she lives. She's dreadfully nervous. I guess she sleeps more than she thinks. She's gone somewhere after Randolph; she wants to try to get him to go to bed. He doesn't like to go to bed."

"Let us hope she will persuade him," observed Winterbourne.

"She will talk to him all she can; but he doesn't like her to talk to him," said Miss Daisy, opening her fan. "She's going to try to get Eugenio to talk to him. But he isn't afraid of Eugenio. Eugenio's a splendid courier, but he can't make much impression on Randolph! I don't believe he'll go to bed before eleven." It appeared that Randolph's vigil was in fact triumphantly prolonged, for Winterbourne strolled about with the young girl for some time without meeting her mother. "I have been looking round for that lady you want to introduce me to," his companion resumed. "She's your aunt." Then, on Winterbourne's admitting the fact, and expressing some curiosity as to how she had learned it, she said she had heard all about Mrs. Costello from the chambermaid. She was very quiet and very *comme il faut*; she wore white puffs; she spoke to no one, and she never dined at the *table d'hôte*.[3] Every two days she had a headache. "I think that's a lovely description, headache and all!" said Miss Daisy, chattering along in her thin, gay voice. "I want to know her ever so much. I know just what *your* aunt would be; I know I should like her. She would be very exclusive. I like a lady to be exclusive; I'm dying to be exclusive myself. Well, we *are* exclusive, mother and I. We don't speak to every one—or they don't speak to us. I suppose it's about the same thing. Any way, I shall be ever so glad to know your aunt."

Winterbourne was embarrassed. "She would be most happy," he said, "but I am afraid those headaches will interfere."

The young girl looked at him through the dusk. "But I suppose she doesn't have a headache every day," she said, sympathetically.

Winterbourne was silent a moment. "She tells me she does," he answered at last—not knowing what to say.

Miss Daisy Miller stopped and stood looking at him. Her prettiness was still visible in the darkness; she was opening and closing her enormous fan. "She doesn't want to know me!" she said suddenly. "Why don't you say so? You needn't be afraid. I'm not afraid!" And she gave a little laugh.

Winterbourne fancied there was a tremor in her voice; he was touched, shocked, mortified by it. "My dear young lady," he protested, "she knows no one. It's her wretched health."

The young girl walked on a few steps, laughing still. "You needn't be afraid," she repeated. "Why should she want to know me?" Then she paused again; she was close to the parapet of the garden, and in front of her was the starlit lake. There was a vague sheen upon its surface, and in the distance were dimly-seen mountain forms. Daisy Miller looked out upon the mysterious prospect, and then she gave another little laugh. "Gracious! she *is* exclusive!" she said. Winterbourne wondered whether she was seriously wounded, and for a moment almost wished that her sense of injury might be such as to make it becoming in him to attempt to reassure and comfort her. He had a pleasant sense that she would be very approachable for consolatory purposes. He felt then, for the instant, quite ready to sacrifice his aunt, conversationally; to admit that she was a proud, rude woman, and to declare that they needn't mind her. But before he had time to commit himself to this perilous mixture of gallantry and impiety, the young lady, resuming her walk, gave an exclamation in quite another tone. "Well; here's mother! I guess she hasn't got Randolph to go to bed." The figure of a lady appeared, at a distance, very indistinct in the darkness, and advancing with a slow and wavering movement. Suddenly it seemed to pause.

"Are you sure it is your mother? Can you distinguish her in this thick dusk?" Winterbourne asked.

"Well!" cried Miss Daisy Miller, with a laugh, "I guess I know my own mother. And when she has got on my shawl, too! She is always wearing my things."

The lady in question, ceasing to advance, hovered vaguely about the spot at which she had checked her steps.

---

3. A common table for guests in a restaurant or hotel (French). "*Comme il faut*": well mannered (French).

"I am afraid your mother doesn't see you," said Winterbourne. "Or per-haps," he added—thinking, with Miss Miller, the joke permissible—"perhaps she feels guilty about your shawl."

"Oh, it's a fearful old thing!" the young girl replied, serenely. "I told her she could wear it. She won't come here, because she sees you."

"Ah, then," said Winterbourne, "I had better leave you."

"Oh, no; come on!" urged Miss Daisy Miller.

"I'm afraid your mother doesn't approve of my walking with you."

Miss Miller gave him a serious glance. "It isn't for me; it's for you—that is, it's for *her*. Well; I don't know who it's for! But mother doesn't like any of my gentlemen friends. She's right down timid. She always makes a fuss if I introduce a gentleman. But I *do* introduce them—almost always. If I didn't introduce my gentlemen friends to mother," the young girl added, in her little soft, flat monotone, "I shouldn't think I was natural."

"To introduce me," said Winterbourne, "you must know my name." And he proceeded to pronounce it.

"Oh, dear; I can't say all that!" said his companion, with a laugh. But by this time they had come up to Mrs. Miller, who, as they drew near, walked to the parapet of the garden and leaned upon it, looking intently at the lake and turning her back upon them. "Mother!" said the young girl, in a tone of deci-sion. Upon this the elderly lady turned round. "Mr. Winterbourne," said Miss Daisy Miller, introducing the young man very frankly and prettily. "Common" she was, as Mrs. Costello had pronounced her; yet it was a wonder to Winter-bourne that, with her commonness, she had a singularly delicate grace.

Her mother was a small, spare, light person, with a wandering eye, a very exiguous nose, and a large forehead, decorated with a certain amount of thin, much-frizzled hair. Like her daughter, Mrs. Miller was dressed with extreme elegance; she had enormous diamonds in her ears. So far as Winterbourne could observe, she gave him no greeting—she certainly was not looking at him. Daisy was near her, pulling her shawl straight. "What are you doing, poking round here?" this young lady inquired; but by no means with that harshness of accent which her choice of words may imply.

"I don't know," said her mother, turning towards the lake again.

"I shouldn't think you'd want that shawl!" Daisy exclaimed.

"Well—I do!" her mother answered, with a little laugh.

"Did you get Randolph to go to bed?" asked the young girl.

"No; I couldn't induce him," said Mrs. Miller, very gently. "He wants to talk to the waiter. He likes to talk to that waiter."

"I was telling Mr. Winterbourne," the young girl went on; and to the young man's ear her tone might have indicated that she had been uttering his name all her life.

"Oh, yes!" said Winterbourne; "I have the pleasure of knowing your son."

Randolph's mamma was silent; she turned her attention to the lake. But at last she spoke. "Well, I don't see how he lives!"

"Anyhow, it isn't so bad as it was at Dover,"[4] said Daisy Miller.

"And what occurred at Dover?" Winterbourne asked.

"He wouldn't go to bed at all. I guess he sat up all night—in the public parlour. He wasn't in bed at twelve o'clock: I know that."

---

4. English coastal town, across from France.

"It was half-past twelve," declared Mrs. Miller, with mild emphasis.

"Does he sleep much during the day?" Winterbourne demanded.

"I guess he doesn't sleep much," Daisy rejoined.

"I wish he would!" said her mother. "It seems as if he couldn't."

"I think he's real tiresome," Daisy pursued.

Then, for some moments, there was silence. "Well, Daisy Miller," said the elder lady, presently, "I shouldn't think you'd want to talk against your own brother!"

"Well, he *is* tiresome, mother," said Daisy, quite without the asperity of a retort.

"He's only nine," urged Mrs. Miller.

"Well, he wouldn't go to that castle," said the young girl. "I'm going there with Mr. Winterbourne."

To this announcement, very placidly made, Daisy's mamma offered no response. Winterbourne took for granted that she deeply disapproved of the projected excursion; but he said to himself that she was a simple, easily managed person, and that a few deferential protestations would take the edge from her displeasure. "Yes," he began; "your daughter has kindly allowed me the honor of being her guide."

Mrs. Miller's wandering eyes attached themselves, with a sort of appealing air, to Daisy, who, however, strolled a few steps farther, gently humming to herself. "I presume you will go in the cars," said her mother.

"Yes; or in the boat," said Winterbourne.

"Well, of course, I don't know," Mrs. Miller rejoined. "I have never been to that castle."

"It is a pity you shouldn't go," said Winterbourne, beginning to feel reassured as to her opposition. And yet he was quite prepared to find that, as a matter of course, she meant to accompany her daughter.

"We've been thinking ever so much about going," she pursued; "but it seems as if we couldn't. Of course Daisy—she wants to go round. But there's a lady here—I don't know her name—she says she shouldn't think we'd want to go to see castles *here*; she should think we'd want to wait till we got to Italy. It seems as if there would be so many there," continued Mrs. Miller, with an air of increasing confidence. "Of course, we only want to see the principal ones. We visited several in England," she presently added.

"Ah, yes! in England there are beautiful castles," said Winterbourne. "But Chillon, here, is very well worth seeing."

"Well, if Daisy feels up to it—," said Mrs. Miller, in a tone impregnated with a sense of the magnitude of the enterprise. "It seems as if there was nothing she wouldn't undertake."

"Oh, I think she'll enjoy it!" Winterbourne declared. And he desired more and more to make it a certainty that he was to have the privilege of a *tête-à-tête*[5] with the young lady, who was still strolling along in front of them, softly vocalizing. "You are not disposed, madam," he inquired, "to undertake it yourself?"

Daisy's mother looked at him, an instant, askance, and then walked forward in silence. Then—"I guess she had better go alone," she said, simply.

Winterbourne observed to himself that this was a very different type of maternity from that of the vigilant matrons who massed themselves in

5. Private talk (French).

the forefront of social intercourse in the dark old city at the other end of the lake. But his meditations were interrupted by hearing his name very distinctly pronounced by Mrs. Miller's unprotected daughter.

"Mr. Winterbourne!" murmured Daisy.

"Mademoiselle!" said the young man.

"Don't you want to take me out in a boat?"

"At present?" he asked.

"Of course!" said Daisy.

"Well, Annie Miller!" exclaimed her mother.

"I beg you, madam, to let her go," said Winterbourne, ardently; for he had never yet enjoyed the sensation of guiding through the summer starlight a skiff freighted with a fresh and beautiful young girl.

"I shouldn't think she'd want to," said her mother. "I should think she'd rather go indoors."

"I'm sure Mr. Winterbourne wants to take me," Daisy declared. "He's so awfully devoted!"

"I will row you over to Chillon, in the starlight."

"I don't believe it!" said Daisy.

"Well!" ejaculated the elderly lady again.

"You haven't spoken to me for half-an-hour," her daughter went on.

"I have been having some very pleasant conversation with your mother," said Winterbourne.

"Well; I want you to take me out in a boat!" Daisy repeated. They had all stopped, and she had turned round and was looking at Winterbourne. Her face wore a charming smile, her pretty eyes were gleaming, she was swinging her great fan about. No; it's impossible to be prettier than that, thought Winterbourne.

"There are half-a-dozen boats moored at that landing-place," he said, pointing to certain steps which descended from the garden to the lake. "If you will do me the honor to accept my arm, we will go and select one of them."

Daisy stood there smiling; she threw back her head and gave a little light laugh. "I like a gentleman to be formal!" she declared.

"I assure you it's a formal offer."

"I was bound I would make you say something," Daisy went on.

"You see it's not very difficult," said Winterbourne. "But I am afraid you are chaffing me."

"I think not, sir," remarked Mrs. Miller, very gently.

"Do, then, let me give you a row," he said to the young girl.

"It's quite lovely, the way you say that!" said Daisy.

"It will be still more lovely to do it."

"Yes, it would be lovely!" said Daisy. But she made no movement to accompany him; she only stood there laughing.

"I should think you had better find out what time it is," interposed her mother.

"It is eleven o'clock, madam," said a voice, with a foreign accent, out of the neighboring darkness; and Winterbourne, turning, perceived the florid personage who was in attendance upon the two ladies. He had apparently just approached.

"Oh, Eugenio," said Daisy, "I am going out in a boat!"

Eugenio bowed. "At eleven o'clock, mademoiselle?"

"I am going with Mr. Winterbourne. This very minute."

"Do tell her she can't," said Mrs. Miller to the courier.

"I think you had better not go out in a boat, mademoiselle," Eugenio declared.

Winterbourne wished to Heaven this pretty girl were not so familiar with her courier; but he said nothing.

"I suppose you don't think it's proper!" Daisy exclaimed, "Eugenio doesn't think anything's proper."

"I am at your service," said Winterbourne.

"Does mademoiselle propose to go alone?" asked Eugenio of Mrs. Miller.

"Oh, no; with this gentleman!" answered Daisy's mamma.

The courier looked for a moment at Winterbourne—the latter thought he was smiling—and then, solemnly, with a bow, "As mademoiselle pleases!" he said.

"Oh, I hoped you would make a fuss!" said Daisy. "I don't care to go now."

"I myself shall make a fuss if you don't go," said Winterbourne.

"That's all I want—a little fuss!" And the young girl began to laugh again.

"Mr. Randolph has gone to bed!" the courier announced, frigidly.

"Oh, Daisy; now we can go!" said Mrs. Miller.

Daisy turned away from Winterbourne, looking at him, smiling and fanning herself. "Good night," she said; "I hope you are disappointed, or disgusted, or something!"

He looked at her, taking the hand she offered him. "I am puzzled," he answered.

"Well; I hope it won't keep you awake!" she said, very smartly; and, under the escort of the privileged Eugenio, the two ladies passed towards the house.

Winterbourne stood looking after them; he was indeed puzzled. He lingered beside the lake for a quarter of an hour, turning over the mystery of the young girl's sudden familiarities and caprices. But the only very definite conclusion he came to was that he should enjoy deucedly "going off" with her somewhere.

Two days afterwards he went off with her to the Castle of Chillon. He waited for her in the large hall of the hotel, where the couriers, the servants, the foreign tourists were lounging about and staring. It was not the place he would have chosen, but she had appointed it. She came tripping downstairs, buttoning her long gloves, squeezing her folded parasol against her pretty figure, dressed in the perfection of a soberly elegant travelling-costume. Winterbourne was a man of imagination and, as our ancestors used to say, of sensibility; as he looked at her dress and, on the great staircase, her little rapid, confiding step, he felt as if there were something romantic going forward. He could have believed he was going to elope with her. He passed out with her among all the idle people that were assembled there; they were all looking at her very hard; she had begun to chatter as soon as she joined him. Winterbourne's preference had been that they should be conveyed to Chillon in a carriage; but she expressed a lively wish to go in the little steamer; she declared that she had a passion for steamboats. There was always such a lovely breeze upon the water, and you saw such lots of people. The sail was not long, but Winterbourne's companion found time to say a great many things. To the young man himself their little excursion was so much of an escapade—an adventure—that, even allowing for her habitual sense of freedom, he had some expectation of seeing her regard it in the same way. But it must be confessed that, in this particular, he was disappointed. Daisy

Miller was extremely animated, she was in charming spirits; but she was apparently not at all excited; she was not fluttered; she avoided neither his eyes nor those of any one else; she blushed neither when she looked at him nor when she saw that people were looking at her. People continued to look at her a great deal, and Winterbourne took much satisfaction in his pretty companion's distinguished air. He had been a little afraid that she would talk loud, laugh overmuch, and even, perhaps, desire to move about the boat a good deal. But he quite forgot his fears; he sat smiling, with his eyes upon her face, while, without moving from her place, she delivered herself of a great number of original reflections. It was the most charming garrulity he had ever heard. He had assented to the idea that she was "common"; but was she so, after all, or was he simply getting used to her commonness? Her conversation was chiefly of what metaphysicans term the objective cast; but every now and then it took a subjective turn.

"What on *earth* are you so grave about?" she suddenly demanded, fixing her agreeable eyes upon Winterbourne's.

"Am I grave?" he asked. "I had an idea I was grinning from ear to ear."

"You look as if you were taking me to a funeral. If that's a grin, your ears are very near together."

"Should you like me to dance a hornpipe[6] on the deck?"

"Pray do, and I'll carry round your hat. It will pay the expenses of our journey."

"I never was better pleased in my life," murmured Winterbourne.

She looked at him a moment, and then burst into a little laugh. "I like to make you say those things! You're a queer mixture!"

In the castle, after they had landed, the subjective element decidedly prevailed. Daisy tripped about the vaulted chambers, rustled her skirts in the corkscrew staircases, flirted back with a pretty little cry and a shudder from the edge of the *oubliettes*,[7] and turned a singularly well-shaped ear to everything that Winterbourne told her about the place. But he saw that she cared very little for feudal antiquities, and that the dusky traditions of Chillon made but a slight impression upon her. They had the good fortune to have been able to walk about without other companionship than that of the custodian; and Winterbourne arranged with this functionary that they should not be hurried—that they should linger and pause wherever they chose. The custodian interpreted the bargain generously—Winterbourne, on his side, had been generous—and ended by leaving them quite to themselves. Miss Miller's observations were not remarkable for logical consistency; for anything she wanted to say she was sure to find a pretext. She found a great many pretexts in the rugged embrasures of Chillon for asking Winterbourne sudden questions about himself—his family, his previous history, his tastes, his habits, his intentions—and for supplying information upon corresponding points in her own personality. Of her own tastes, habits, and intentions Miss Miller was prepared to give the most definite, and indeed the most favourable, account.

"Well; I hope you know enough!" she said to her companion, after he had told her the history of the unhappy Bonivard.[8] "I never saw a man that knew

6. An English dance similar to the jig.
7. Secret pitlike dungeons with an opening only at the top; places where one is forgotten (French).
8. Hero of Byron's poem "The Prisoner of Chil-

lon"; François de Bonivard (1496–1570), Swiss patriot and martyr, was confined for seven years in the Castle of Chillon.

so much!" The history of Bonivard had evidently, as they say, gone into one ear and out of the other. But Daisy went on to say that she wished Winterbourne would travel with them and "go round" with them; they might know something, in that case. "Don't you want to come and teach Randolph?" she asked. Winterbourne said that nothing could possibly please him so much; but that he had unfortunately other occupations. "Other occupations? I don't believe it!" said Miss Daisy. "What do you mean? You are not in business." The young man admitted that he was not in business; but he had engagements which, even within a day or two, would force him to go back to Geneva. "Oh, bother!" she said. "I don't believe it!" and she began to talk about something else. But a few moments later, when he was pointing out to her the pretty design of an antique fireplace, she broke out irrelevantly, "You don't mean to say you are going back to Geneva?"

"It is a melancholy fact that I shall have to return to Geneva to-morrow."

"Well, Mr. Winterbourne," said Daisy; "I think you're horrid!"

"Oh, don't say such dreadful things!" said Winterbourne—"just at the last."

"The last!" cried the young girl; "I call it the first. I have half a mind to leave you here and go straight back to the hotel alone." And for the next ten minutes she did nothing but call him horrid. Poor Winterbourne was fairly bewildered; no young lady had as yet done him the honor to be so agitated by the announcement of his movements. His companion, after this, ceased to pay any attention to the curiosities of Chillon or the beauties of the lake; she opened fire upon the mysterious charmer in Geneva, whom she appeared to have instantly taken it for granted that he was hurrying back to see. How did Miss Daisy Miller know that there was a charmer in Geneva? Winterbourne, who denied the existence of such a person, was quite unable to discover; and he was divided between amazement at the rapidity of her induction and amusement at the frankness of her *persiflage*.[9] She seemed to him, in all this, an extraordinary mixture of innocence and crudity. "Does she never allow you more than three days at a time?" asked Daisy, ironically. "Doesn't she give you a vacation in summer? There's no one so hard worked but they can get leave to go off somewhere at this season. I suppose, if you stay another day, she'll come after you in the boat. Do wait over till Friday, and I will go down to the landing to see her arrive!" Winterbourne began to think he had been wrong to feel disappointed in the temper in which the young lady had embarked. If he had missed the personal accent, the personal accent was now making its appearance. It sounded very distinctly, at last, in her telling him she would stop "teasing" him if he would promise her solemnly to come down to Rome in the winter.

"That's not a difficult promise to make," said Winterbourne. "My aunt has taken an apartment in Rome for the winter, and has already asked me to come and see her."

"I don't want you to come for your aunt," said Daisy; "I want you to come for me." And this was the only allusion that the young man was ever to hear her make to his invidious kinswoman. He declared that, at any rate, he would certainly come. After this Daisy stopped teasing. Winterbourne took a carriage, and they drove back to Vevey in the dusk; the young girl was very quiet.

9. Frivolous, bantering talk (French).

In the evening Winterbourne mentioned to Mrs. Costello that he had spent the afternoon at Chillon, with Miss Daisy Miller.

"The Americans—of the courier?" asked this lady.

"Ah, happily," said Winterbourne, "the courier stayed at home."

"She went with you all alone?"

"All alone."

Mrs. Costello sniffed a little at her smelling-bottle. "And that," she exclaimed, "is the young person you wanted me to know!"

III

Winterbourne, who had returned to Geneva the day after his excursion to Chillon, went to Rome towards the end of January. His aunt had been established there for several weeks, and he had received a couple of letters from her. "Those people you were so devoted to last summer at Vevey have turned up here, courier and all," she wrote. "They seem to have made several acquaintances, but the courier continues to be the most *intime*. The young lady, however, is also very intimate with some third-rate Italians, with whom she rackets about in a way that makes much talk. Bring me that pretty novel of Cherbuliez's[1]—'Paule Méré'—and don't come later than the 23rd."

In the natural course of events, Winterbourne, on arriving in Rome, would presently have ascertained Mrs. Miller's address at the American banker's and have gone to pay his compliments to Miss Daisy. "After what happened at Vevey I certainly think I may call upon them," he said to Mrs. Costello.

"If, after what happens—at Vevey and everywhere—you desire to keep up the acquaintance, you are very welcome. Of course a man may know every one. Men are welcome to the privilege!"

"Pray what is it that happens—here, for instance?" Winterbourne demanded.

"The girl goes about alone with her foreigners. As to what happens farther, you must apply elsewhere for information. She has picked up half-a-dozen of the regular Roman fortune-hunters, and she takes them about to people's houses. When she comes to a party she brings with her a gentleman with a good deal of manner and a wonderful moustache."

"And where is the mother?"

"I haven't the least idea. They are very dreadful people."

Winterbourne meditated a moment. "They are very ignorant—very innocent only. Depend upon it they are not bad."

"They are hopelessly vulgar," said Mrs. Costello. "Whether or no being hopelessly vulgar is being 'bad' is a question for the metaphysicians. They are bad enough to dislike, at any rate; and for this short life that is quite enough."

The news that Daisy Miller was surrounded by half-a-dozen wonderful moustaches checked Winterbourne's impulse to go straightway to see her. He had perhaps not definitely flattered himself that he had made an ineffaceable impression upon her heart, but he was annoyed at hearing of a state of affairs so little in harmony with an image that had lately flitted in and out

---

1. Victor Cherbuliez (1829–1899), which James spelled "Cherbuliex," a popular French novelist of Swiss origin. His 1865 novel *Paule Méré* focused on a young woman who violates Geneva's social conventions.

of his own meditations; the image of a very pretty girl looking out of an old Roman window and asking herself urgently when Mr. Winterbourne would arrive. If, however, he determined to wait a little before reminding Miss Miller of his claims to her consideration, he went very soon to call upon two or three other friends. One of these friends was an American lady who had spent several winters at Geneva, when she had placed her children at school. She was a very accomplished woman and she lived in the Via Gregoriana.[2] Winterbourne found her in a little crimson drawing-room, on a third floor; the room was filled with southern sunshine. He had not been there ten minutes when the servant came in, announcing "Madame Mila!" This announcement was presently followed by the entrance of little Randolph Miller, who stopped in the middle of the room and stood staring at Winterbourne. An instant later his pretty sister crossed the threshold; and then, after a considerable interval, Mrs. Miller slowly advanced.

"I know you!" said Randolph.

"I'm sure you know a great many things," exclaimed Winterbourne, taking him by the hand. "How is your education coming on?"

Daisy was exchanging greetings very prettily with her hostess; but when she heard Winterbourne's voice she quickly turned her head. "Well, I declare!" she said.

"I told you I should come, you know," Winterbourne rejoined smiling.

"Well—I didn't believe it," said Miss Daisy.

"I am much obliged to you," laughed the young man.

"You might have come to see me!" said Daisy.

"I arrived only yesterday."

"I don't believe that!" the young girl declared.

Winterbourne turned with a protesting smile to her mother; but this lady evaded his glance, and seating herself, fixed her eyes upon her son. "We've got a bigger place than this," said Randolph. "It's all gold on the walls."

Mrs. Miller turned uneasily in her chair. "I told you if I were to bring you, you would say something!" she murmured.

"I told *you!*" Randolph exclaimed. "I tell *you,* sir!" he added jocosely, giving Winterbourne a thump on the knee. "It *is* bigger, too!"

Daisy had entered upon a lively conversation with her hostess; Winterbourne judged it becoming to address a few words to her mother. "I hope you have been well since we parted at Vevey," he said.

Mrs. Miller now certainly looked at him—at his chin. "Not very well, sir," she answered.

"She's got the dyspepsia," said Randolph. "I've got it too. Father's got it. I've got it worst!"

This announcement, instead of embarrassing Mrs. Miller, seemed to relieve her. "I suffer from the liver," she said. "I think it's the climate; it's less bracing than Schenectady, especially in the winter season. I don't know whether you know we reside at Schenectady. I was saying to Daisy that I certainly hadn't found any one like Dr. Davis, and I didn't believe I should. Oh, at Schenectady, he stands first; they think everything of him. He has so much to do, and yet there was nothing he wouldn't do for me. He said he never saw anything like my dyspepsia, but he was bound to cure it. I'm sure

2. A fashionable street in Rome.

there was nothing he wouldn't try. He was just going to try something new when we came off. Mr. Miller wanted Daisy to see Europe for herself. But I wrote to Mr. Miller that it seems as if I couldn't get on without Dr. Davis. At Schenectady he stands at the very top; and there's a great deal of sickness there, too. It affects my sleep."

Winterbourne had a good deal of pathological gossip with Dr. Davis's patient, during which Daisy chattered unremittingly to her own companion. The young man asked Mrs. Miller how she was pleased with Rome. "Well, I must say I am disappointed," she answered. "We had heard so much about it; I suppose we had heard too much. But we couldn't help that. We had been led to expect something different."

"Ah, wait a little, and you will become very fond of it," said Winterbourne.

"I hate it worse and worse every day!" cried Randolph.

"You are like the infant Hannibal,"[3] said Winterbourne.

"No, I ain't!" Randolph declared, at a venture.

"You are not much like an infant," said his mother. "But we have seen places," she resumed, "that I should put a long way before Rome." And in reply to Winterbourne's interrogation, "There's Zurich," she observed; "I think Zurich is lovely; and we hadn't heard half so much about it."

"The best place we've seen is the City of Richmond!" said Randolph.

"He means the ship," his mother explained. "We crossed in that ship. Randolph had a good time on the City of Richmond."

"It's the best place I've seen," the child repeated. "Only it was turned the wrong way."

"Well, we've got to turn the right way some time," said Mrs. Miller, with a little laugh. Winterbourne expressed the hope that her daughter at least found some gratification in Rome, and she declared that Daisy was quite carried away. "It's on account of the society—the society's splendid. She goes round everywhere; she has made a great number of acquaintances. Of course she goes round more than I do. I must say they have been very sociable; they have taken her right in. And then she knows a great many gentlemen. Oh, she thinks there's nothing like Rome. Of course, it's a great deal pleasanter for a young lady if she knows plenty of gentlemen."

By this time Daisy had turned her attention again to Winterbourne. "I've been telling Mrs. Walker how mean you were!" the young girl announced.

"And what is the evidence you have offered?" asked Winterbourne, rather annoyed at Miss Miller's want of appreciation of the zeal of an admirer who on his way down to Rome had stopped neither at Bologna nor at Florence, simply because of a certain sentimental impatience. He remembered that a cynical compatriot had once told him that American women—the pretty ones, and this gave a largeness to the axiom—were at once the most exacting in the world and the least endowed with a sense of indebtedness.

"Why, you were awfully mean at Vevey," said Daisy. "You wouldn't do anything. You wouldn't stay there when I asked you."

"My dearest young lady," cried Winterbourne, with eloquence, "have I come all the way to Rome to encounter your reproaches?"

"Just hear him say that!" said Daisy to her hostess, giving a twist to a bow on this lady's dress. "Did you ever hear anything so quaint?"

3. The Carthaginian general (247–183 B.C.E.), from his infancy, had a lifelong hatred of Rome.

"So quaint, my dear?" murmured Mrs. Walker, in the tone of a partisan of Winterbourne.

"Well, I don't know," said Daisy, fingering Mrs. Walker's ribbons. "Mrs. Walker, I want to tell you something."

"Mother-r," interposed Randolph, with his rough ends to his words, "I tell you you've got to go. Eugenio'll raise something!"

"I'm not afraid of Eugenio," said Daisy, with a toss of her head. "Look here, Mrs. Walker," she went on, "you know I'm coming to your party."

"I am delighted to hear it."

"I've got a lovely dress."

"I am very sure of that."

"But I want to ask a favor—permission to bring a friend."

"I shall be happy to see any of your friends," said Mrs. Walker, turning with a smile to Mrs. Miller.

"Oh, they are not my friends," answered Daisy's mamma, smiling shyly, in her own fashion. "I never spoke to them!"

"It's an intimate friend of mine—Mr. Giovanelli," said Daisy, without a tremor in her clear little voice or a shadow on her brilliant little face.

Mrs. Walker was silent a moment, she gave a rapid glance at Winterbourne. "I shall be glad to see Mr. Giovanelli," she then said.

"He's an Italian," Daisy pursued, with the prettiest serenity. "He's a great friend of mine—he's the handsomest man in the world—except Mr. Winterbourne! He knows plenty of Italians, but he wants to know some Americans. He thinks ever so much of Americans. He's tremendously clever. He's perfectly lovely!"

It was settled that this brilliant personage should be brought to Mrs. Walker's party, and then Mrs. Miller prepared to take her leave. "I guess we'll go back to the hotel," she said.

"You may go back to the hotel, mother, but I'm going to take a walk," said Daisy.

"She's going to walk with Mr. Giovanelli," Randolph proclaimed.

"I am going to the Pincio,"[4] said Daisy, smiling.

"Alone, my dear at this hour?" Mrs. Walker asked. The afternoon was drawing to a close—it was the hour for the throng of carriages and of contemplative pedestrians. "I don't think it's safe, my dear," said Mrs. Walker.

"Neither do I," subjoined Mrs. Miller. "You'll get the fever[5] as sure as you live. Remember what Dr. Davis told you!"

"Give her some medicine before she goes," said Randolph.

The company had risen to its feet; Daisy, still showing her pretty teeth, bent over and kissed her hostess. "Mrs. Walker, you are too perfect," she said. "I'm not going alone; I am going to meet a friend."

"Your friend won't keep you from getting the fever," Mrs. Miller observed.

"Is it Mr. Giovanelli?" asked the hostess.

Winterbourne was watching the girl; at this question his attention quickened. She stood there smiling and smoothing her bonnet-ribbons; she glanced at Winterbourne. Then, while she glanced and smiled, she answered without a shade of hesitation, "Mr. Giovanelli—the beautiful Giovanelli."

4. The Pincian Hill, offering a fine view of Rome.
5. Malaria, whose means of transmission (the mosquito) was unknown in James's day, but which was associated with damp, dark places.

"My dear young friend," said Mrs. Walker, taking her hand, pleadingly, "don't walk off to the Pincio at this hour to meet a beautiful Italian."

"Well, he speaks English," said Mrs. Miller.

"Gracious me!" Daisy exclaimed, "I don't want to do anything improper. There's an easy way to settle it." She continued to glance at Winterbourne. "The Pincio is only a hundred yards distant, and if Mr. Winterbourne were as polite as he pretends he would offer to walk with me!"

Winterbourne's politeness hastened to affirm itself, and the young girl gave him gracious leave to accompany her. They passed downstairs before her mother, and at the door Winterbourne perceived Mrs. Miller's carriage drawn up, with the ornamental courier whose acquaintance he had made at Vevey seated within. "Good-bye, Eugenio!" cried Daisy, "I'm going to take a walk." The distance from the Via Gregoriana to the beautiful garden at the other end of the Pincian Hill is, in fact, rapidly traversed. As the day was splendid, however, and the concourse of vehicles, walkers, and loungers numerous, the young Americans found their progress much delayed. This fact was highly agreeable to Winterbourne, in spite of his consciousness of his singular situation. The slow-moving, idly-gazing Roman crowd bestowed much attention upon the extremely pretty young foreign lady who was passing through it upon his arm; and he wondered what on earth had been in Daisy's mind when she proposed to expose herself, unattended, to its appreciation. His own mission, to her sense, apparently, was to consign her to the hands of Mr. Giovanelli; but Winterbourne, at once annoyed and gratified, resolved that he would do no such thing.

"Why haven't you been to see me?" asked Daisy. "You can't get out of that."

"I have had the honor of telling you that I have only just stepped out of the train."

"You must have stayed in the train a good while after it stopped!" cried the young girl, with her little laugh. "I suppose you were asleep. You have had time to go to see Mrs. Walker."

"I knew Mrs. Walker—" Winterbourne began to explain.

"I knew where you knew her. You knew her at Geneva. She told me so. Well, you knew me at Vevey. That's just as good. So you ought to have come." She asked him no other question than this; she began to prattle about her own affairs. "We've got splendid rooms at the hotel; Eugenio says they're the best rooms in Rome. We are going to stay all winter—if we don't die of the fever; and I guess we'll stay then. It's a great deal nicer than I thought; I thought it would be fearfully quiet; I was sure it would be awfully poky. I was sure we should be going round all the time with one of those dreadful old men that explain about the pictures and things. But we only had about a week of that, and now I'm enjoying myself. I know ever so many people, and they are all so charming. The society's extremely select. There are all kinds— English, and Germans, and Italians. I think I like the English best. I like their style of conversation. But there are some lovely Americans. I never saw anything so hospitable. There's something or other every day. There's not much dancing; but I must say I never thought dancing was everything. I was always fond of conversation. I guess I shall have plenty at Mrs. Walker's—her rooms are so small." When they had passed the gate of the Pincian Gardens, Miss Miller began to wonder where Mr. Giovanelli might be. "We had better go straight to that place in front," she said, "where you look at the view."

"I certainly shall not help you to find him," Winterbourne declared.

"Then I shall find him without you," said Miss Daisy.

"You certainly won't leave me!" cried Winterbourne.

She burst into her little laugh. "Are you afraid you'll get lost—or run over? But there's Giovanelli, leaning against that tree. He's staring at the women in the carriages: did you ever see anything so cool?"

Winterbourne perceived at some distance a little man standing with folded arms, nursing his cane. He had a handsome face, an artfully poised hat, a glass in one eye, and a nosegay in his button-hole. Winterbourne looked at him a moment and then said, "Do you mean to speak to that man?"

"Do I mean to speak to him? Why, you don't suppose I mean to communicate by signs?"

"Pray understand, then," said Winterbourne, "that I intend to remain with you."

Daisy stopped and looked at him, without a sign of troubled consciousness in her face; with nothing but the presence of her charming eyes and her happy dimples. "Well, she's a cool one!" thought the young man.

"I don't like the way you say that," said Daisy. "It's too imperious."

"I beg your pardon if I say it wrong. The main point is to give you an idea of my meaning."

The young girl looked at him more gravely, but with eyes that were prettier than ever. "I have never allowed a gentleman to dictate to me, or to interfere with anything I do."

"I think you have made a mistake," said Winterbourne. "You should sometimes listen to a gentleman—the right one?"

Daisy began to laugh again, "I do nothing but listen to gentlemen!" she exclaimed. "Tell me if Mr. Giovanelli is the right one?"

The gentleman with the nosegay in his bosom had now perceived our two friends, and was approaching the young girl with obsequious rapidity. He bowed to Winterbourne as well as to the latter's companion; he had a brilliant smile, an intelligent eye; Winterbourne thought him not a bad-looking fellow. But he nevertheless said to Daisy—"No, he's not the right one."

Daisy evidently had a natural talent for performing introductions; she mentioned the name of each of her companions to the other. She strolled along with one of them on each side of her; Mr. Giovanelli, who spoke English very cleverly—Winterbourne afterwards learned that he had practiced the idiom upon a great many American heiresses—addressed her a great deal of very polite nonsense; he was extremely urbane, and the young American, who said nothing, reflected upon that profundity of Italian cleverness which enables people to appear more gracious in proportion as they are more acutely disappointed. Giovanelli, of course, had counted upon something more intimate; he had not bargained for a party of three. But he kept his temper in a manner which suggested far-stretching intentions. Winterbourne flattered himself that he had taken his measure. "He is not a gentleman," said the young American; "he is only a clever imitation of one. He is a music-master, or a penny-a-liner,[6] or a third-rate artist. Damn his good looks!" Mr. Giovanelli had certainly a very pretty face; but Winterbourne felt a superior indignation at his own lovely fellow-countrywoman's

6. Hack writer.

not knowing the difference between a spurious gentleman and a real one. Giovanelli chattered and jested and made himself wonderfully agreeable. It was true that if he was an imitation the imitation was very skillful. "Nevertheless," Winterbourne said to himself, "a nice girl ought to know!" And then he came back to the question whether this was in fact a nice girl. Would a nice girl—even allowing for her being a little American flirt—make a rendezvous with a presumably low-lived foreigner? The rendezvous in this case, indeed, had been in broad daylight, and in the most crowded corner of Rome; but was it not impossible to regard the choice of these circumstances as a proof of extreme cynicism? Singular though it may seem, Winterbourne was vexed that the young girl, in joining her *amoroso*,[7] should not appear more impatient of his own company, and he was vexed because of his inclination. It was impossible to regard her as a perfectly well-conducted young lady; she was wanting in a certain indispensable delicacy. It would therefore simplify matters greatly to be able to treat her as the object of one of those sentiments which are called by romancers "lawless passions." That she should seem to wish to get rid of him would help him to think more lightly of her, and to be able to think more lightly of her would make her much less perplexing. But Daisy, on this occasion, continued to present herself as an inscrutable combination of audacity and innocence.

She had been walking some quarter of an hour, attended by her two cavaliers, and responding in a tone of very childish gaiety, as it seemed to Winterbourne, to the pretty speeches of Mr. Giovanelli, when a carriage that had detached itself from the revolving train drew up beside the path. At the same moment Winterbourne perceived that his friend Mrs. Walker—the lady whose house he had lately left—was seated in the vehicle and was beckoning to him. Leaving Miss Miller's side, he hastened to obey her summons. Mrs. Walker was flushed; she wore an excited air. "It is really too dreadful," she said. "That girl must not do this sort of thing. She must not walk here with you two men. Fifty people have noticed her."

Winterbourne raised his eyebrows. "I think it's a pity to make too much fuss about it."

"It's a pity to let the girl ruin herself!"

"She is very innocent," said Winterbourne.

"She's very crazy!" cried Mrs. Walker. "Did you ever see anything so imbecile as her mother? After you had all left me, just now, I could not sit still for thinking of it. It seemed too pitiful, not even to attempt to save her. I ordered the carriage and put on my bonnet, and came here as quickly as possible. Thank heaven I have found you!"

"What do you propose to do with us?" asked Winterbourne, smiling.

"To ask her to get in, to drive her about here for half-an-hour, so that the world may see she is not running absolutely wild, and then to take her safely home."

"I don't think it's a very happy thought," said Winterbourne; "but you can try."

Mrs. Walker tried. The young man went in pursuit of Miss Miller, who had simply nodded and smiled at his interlocutrix in the carriage and had gone her way with her own companion. Daisy, on learning that Mrs. Walker

7. Lover (Italian).

wished to speak to her, retraced her steps with a perfect good grace and with Mr. Giovanelli at her side. She declared that she was delighted to have a chance to present this gentleman to Mrs. Walker. She immediately achieved the introduction, and declared that she had never in her life seen anything so lovely as Mrs. Walker's carriage-rug.

"I am glad you admire it," said this lady, smiling sweetly. "Will you get in and let me put it over you?"

"Oh, no, thank you," said Daisy. "I shall admire it much more as I see you driving round with it."

"Do get in and drive with me," said Mrs. Walker.

"That would be charming, but it's so enchanting just as I am!" and Daisy gave a brilliant glance at the gentlemen on either side of her.

"It may be enchanting, dear child, but it is not the custom here," urged Mrs. Walker, leaning forward in her victoria[8] with her hands devoutly clasped.

"Well, it ought to be, then!" said Daisy. "If I didn't walk I should expire."

"You should walk with your mother, dear," cried the lady from Geneva, losing patience.

"With my mother dear!" exclaimed the young girl. Winterbourne saw that she scented interference. "My mother never walked ten steps in her life. And then, you know," she added with a laugh, "I am more than five years old."

"You are old enough to be more reasonable. You are old enough, dear Miss Miller, to be talked about."

Daisy looked at Mrs. Walker, smiling intensely. "Talked about? What do you mean?"

"Come into my carriage and I will tell you."

Daisy turned her quickened glance again from one of the gentlemen beside her to the other. Mr. Giovanelli was bowing to and fro, rubbing down his gloves and laughing very agreeably; Winterbourne thought it a most unpleasant scene. "I don't think I want to know what you mean," said Daisy presently. "I don't think I should like it."

Winterbourne wished that Mrs. Walker would tuck in her carriage-rug and drive away; but this lady did not enjoy being defied, as she afterwards told him. "Should you prefer being thought a very reckless girl?" she demanded.

"Gracious me!" exclaimed Daisy. She looked again at Mr. Giovanelli, then she turned to Winterbourne. There was a little pink flush in her check; she was tremendously pretty. "Does Mr. Winterbourne think," she asked slowly, smiling, throwing back her head and glancing at him from head to foot, "that—to save my reputation—I ought to get into the carriage?"

Winterbourne colored; for an instant he hesitated greatly. It seemed so strange to hear her speak that way of her "reputation." But he himself, in fact, must speak in accordance with gallantry. The finest gallantry, here, was simply to tell her the truth; and the truth, for Winterbourne, as the few indications I have been able to give have made him known to the reader, was that Daisy Miller should take Mrs. Walker's advice. He looked at her exquisite prettiness; and then he said very gently, "I think you should get into the carriage."

8. A horse-drawn carriage for two with a raised seat in front for the driver.

Daisy gave a violent laugh. "I never heard anything so stiff! If this is improper, Mrs. Walker," she pursued, "then I am all improper, and you must give me up. Good-bye; I hope you'll have a lovely ride!" and, with Mr. Giovanelli, who made a triumphantly obsequious salute, she turned away.

Mrs. Walker sat looking after her, and there were tears in Mrs. Walker's eyes. "Get in here, sir," she said to Winterbourne, indicating the place beside her. The young man answered that he felt bound to accompany Miss Miller; whereupon Mrs. Walker declared that if he refused her this favor she would never speak to him again. She was evidently in earnest. Winterbourne overtook Daisy and her companion and, offering the young girl his hand, told her that Mrs. Walker had made an imperious claim upon his society. He expected that in answer she would say something rather free, something to commit herself still farther to that "recklessness" from which Mrs. Walker had so charitably endeavored to dissuade her. But she only shook his hand, hardly looking at him, while Mr. Giovanelli bade him farewell with a too emphatic flourish of the hat.

Winterbourne was not in the best possible humor as he took his seat in Mrs. Walker's victoria. "That was not clever of you," he said candidly, while the vehicle mingled again with the throng of carriages.

"In such a case," his companion answered, "I don't wish to be clever, I wish to be *earnest!*"

"Well, your earnestness has only offended her and put her off."

"It has happened very well," said Mrs. Walker. "If she is so perfectly determined to compromise herself, the sooner one knows it the better; one can act accordingly."

"I suspect she meant no harm," Winterbourne rejoined.

"So I thought a month ago. But she has been going too far."

"What has she been doing?"

"Everything that is not done here. Flirting with any man she could pick up; sitting in corners with mysterious Italians; dancing all the evening with the same partners; receiving visits at eleven o'clock at night. Her mother goes away when visitors come."

"But her brother," said Winterbourne, laughing, "sits up till midnight."

"He must be edified by what he sees. I'm told that at their hotel every one is talking about her, and that a smile goes round among the servants when a gentleman comes and asks for Miss Miller."

"The servants be hanged!" said Winterbourne angrily. "The poor girl's only fault," he presently added, "is that she is very uncultivated."

"She is naturally indelicate," Mrs. Walker declared. "Take that example this morning. How long had you known her at Vevey?"

"A couple of days."

"Fancy, then, her making it a personal matter that you should have left the place!"

Winterbourne was silent for some moments; then he said, "I suspect, Mrs. Walker, that you and I have lived too long at Geneva!" And he added a request that she should inform him with what particular design she had made him enter her carriage.

"I wished to beg you to cease your relations with Miss Miller—not to flirt with her—to give her no farther opportunity to expose herself—to let her alone, in short."

"I'm afraid I can't do that," said Winterbourne. "I like her extremely."

"All the more reason that you shouldn't help her to make a scandal."

"There shall be nothing scandalous in my attentions to her."

"There certainly will be in the way she takes them. But I have said what I had on my conscience," Mrs. Walker pursued. "If you wish to rejoin the young lady I will put you down. Here, by-the-way, you have a chance."

The carriage was traversing that part of the Pincian Garden which overhangs the wall of Rome and overlooks the beautiful Villa Borghese.[9] It is bordered by a large parapet, near which there are several seats. One of the seats, at a distance, was occupied by a gentleman and a lady, towards whom Mrs. Walker gave a toss of her head. At the same moment these persons rose and walked towards the parapet. Winterbourne had asked the coachman to stop; he now descended from the carriage. His companion looked at him a moment in silence; then, while he raised his hat, she drove majestically away. Winterbourne stood there; he had turned his eyes towards Daisy and her cavalier. They evidently saw no one; they were too deeply occupied with each other. When they reached the low garden-wall they stood a moment looking off at the great flat-topped pine-clusters of the Villa Borghese; then Giovanelli seated himself familiarly upon the broad ledge of the wall. The western sun in the opposite sky sent out a brilliant shaft through a couple of cloud-bars; whereupon Daisy's companion took her parasol out of her hands and opened it. She came a little nearer and he held the parasol over her; then, still holding it, he let it rest upon her shoulder, so that both of their heads were hidden from Winterbourne. This young man lingered a moment, then he began to walk. But he walked—not towards the couple with the parasol; towards the residence of his aunt, Mrs. Costello.

IV

He flattered himself on the following day that there was no smiling among the servants when he, at least, asked for Mrs. Miller at her hotel. This lady and her daughter, however, were not at home; and on the next day, after repeating his visit, Winterbourne again had the misfortune not to find them. Mrs. Walker's party took place on the evening of the third day, and in spite of the frigidity of his last interview with the hostess, Winterbourne was among the guests. Mrs. Walker was one of those American ladies who, while residing abroad, make a point, in their own phrase, of studying European society; and she had on this occasion collected several specimens of her diversely-born fellow-mortals to serve, as it were, as text-books. When Winterbourne arrived Daisy Miller was not there; but in a few moments he saw her mother come in alone, very shyly and ruefully. Mrs. Miller's hair, above her exposed-looking temples, was more frizzled than ever. As she approached Mrs. Walker, Winterbourne also drew near.

"You see I've come all alone," said poor Mrs. Miller. "I'm so frightened; I don't know what to do; it's the first time I've ever been to a party alone—especially in this country. I wanted to bring Randolph or Eugenio, or someone, but Daisy just pushed me off by myself. I ain't used to going round alone."

9. Seventeenth-century palace.

"And does not your daughter intend to favor us with her society?" demanded Mrs. Walker, impressively.

"Well, Daisy's all dressed," said Mrs. Miller, with that accent of the dispassionate, if not of the philosophic, historian with which she always recorded the current incidents of her daughter's career. "She's got dressed on purpose before dinner. But she's got a friend of hers there; that gentleman—the Italian—that she wanted to bring. They've got going at the piano; it seems as if they couldn't leave off. Mr. Giovanelli sings splendidly. But I guess they'll come before very long," concluded Mrs. Miller hopefully.

"I'm sorry she should come—in that way," said Mrs. Walker.

"Well, I told her that there was no use in her getting dressed before dinner if she was going to wait three hours," responded Daisy's mamma. "I didn't see the use of her putting on such a dress as that to sit round with Mr. Giovanelli."

"This is most horrible!" said Mrs. Walker, turning away and addressing herself to Winterbourne. "*Elle s'affiche.*[1] It's her revenge for my having ventured to remonstrate with her. When she comes I shall not speak to her."

Daisy came after eleven o'clock, but she was not, on such an occasion, a young lady to wait to be spoken to. She rustled forward in radiant loveliness, smiling and chattering, carrying a large bouquet and attended by Mr. Giovanelli. Every one stopped talking, and turned and looked at her. She came straight to Mrs. Walker. "I'm afraid you thought I never was coming, so I sent mother off to tell you. I wanted to make Mr. Giovanelli practice some things before he came; you know he sings beautifully, and I want you to ask him to sing. This is Mr. Giovanelli; you know I introduced him to you; he's got the most lovely voice and he knows the most charming set of songs. I made him go over them this evening, on purpose; we had the greatest time at the hotel." Of all this Daisy delivered herself with the sweetest, brightest audibleness, looking now at her hostess and now round the room, while she gave a series of little pats, round her shoulders, to the edges of her dress. "Is there anyone I know?" she asked.

"I think every one knows you!" said Mrs. Walker pregnantly, and she gave a very cursory greeting to Mr. Giovanelli. This gentleman bore himself gallantly. He smiled and bowed and showed his white teeth, he curled his moustaches and rolled his eyes, and performed all the proper functions of a handsome Italian at an evening party. He sang, very prettily, half-a-dozen songs, though Mrs. Walker afterwards declared that she had been quite unable to find out who asked him. It was apparently not Daisy who had given him his orders. Daisy sat at a distance from the piano, and though she had publicly, as it were, professed a high admiration for his singing, talked, not inaudibly, while it was going on.

"It's a pity these rooms are so small; we can't dance," she said to Winterbourne, as if she had seen him five minutes before.

"I am not sorry we can't dance," Winterbourne answered; "I don't dance."

"Of course you don't dance; you're too stiff," said Miss Daisy. "I hope you enjoyed your drive with Mrs. Walker."

"No, I didn't enjoy it; I preferred walking with you."

"We paired off, that was much better," said Daisy. "But did you ever hear anything so cool as Mrs. Walker's wanting me to get into her carriage and

1. She's making a spectacle of herself (French).

drop poor Mr. Giovanelli; and under the pretext that it was proper? People have different ideas! It would have been most unkind; he had been talking about that walk for ten days."

"He should not have talked about it at all," said Winterbourne; "he would never have proposed to a young lady of this country to walk about the streets with him."

"About the streets?" cried Daisy, with her pretty stare. "Where then would he have proposed to her to walk? The Pincio is not the streets, either; and I, thank goodness, am not a young lady of this country. The young ladies of this country have a dreadfully pokey time of it, so far as I can learn; I don't see why I should change my habits for *them*."

"I am afraid your habits are those of a flirt," said Winterbourne gravely.

"Of course they are," she cried, giving him her little smiling stare again. "I'm a fearful, frightful flirt! Did you ever hear of a nice girl that was not? But I suppose you will tell me now that I am not a nice girl."

"You're a very nice girl, but I wish you would flirt with me, and me only," said Winterbourne.

"Ah! thank you, thank you very much; you are the last man I should think of flirting with. As I have had the pleasure of informing you, you are too stiff."

"You say that too often," said Winterbourne.

Daisy gave a delighted laugh. "If I could have the sweet hope of making you angry, I would say it again."

"Don't do that; when I am angry I'm stiffer than ever. But if you won't flirt with me, do cease at least to flirt with your friend at the piano; they don't understand that sort of thing here."

"I thought they understood nothing else!" exclaimed Daisy.

"Not in young unmarried women."

"It seems to me much more proper in young unmarried women than in old married ones," Daisy declared.

"Well," said Winterbourne, "when you deal with natives you must go by the custom of the place. Flirting is a purely American custom; it doesn't exist here. So when you show yourself in public with Mr. Giovanelli and without your mother—"

"Gracious! Poor mother!" interposed Daisy.

"Though you may be flirting, Mr. Giovanelli is not; he means something else."

"He isn't preaching, at any rate," said Daisy with vivacity. "And if you want very much to know, we are neither of us flirting; we are too good friends for that; we are very intimate friends."

"Ah," rejoined Winterbourne, "if you are in love with each other it is another affair."

She had allowed him up to this point to talk so frankly that he had no expectation of shocking her by this ejaculation; but she immediately got up, blushing visibly, and leaving him to exclaim mentally that little American flirts were the queerest creatures in the world. "Mr. Giovanelli, at least," she said, giving her interlocutor a single glance, "never says such very disagreeable things to me."

Winterbourne was bewildered; he stood staring. Mr. Giovanelli had finished singing; he left the piano and came over to Daisy. "Won't you come into the other room and have some tea?" he asked, bending before her with his decorative smile.

Daisy turned to Winterbourne, beginning to smile again. He was still more perplexed, for this inconsequent smile made nothing clear, though it seemed to prove, indeed, that she had a sweetness and softness that reverted instinctively to the pardon of offences. "It has never occurred to Mr. Winterbourne to offer me any tea," she said, with her little tormenting manner.

"I have offered you advice," Winterbourne rejoined.

"I prefer weak tea!" cried Daisy, and she went off with the brilliant Giovanelli. She sat with him in the adjoining room, in the embrasure of the window, for the rest of the evening. There was an interesting performance at the piano, but neither of these young people gave heed to it. When Daisy came to take leave of Mrs. Walker, this lady conscientiously repaired the weakness of which she had been guilty at the moment of the young girl's arrival. She turned her back straight upon Miss Miller and left her to depart with what grace she might. Winterbourne was standing near the door; he saw it all. Daisy turned very pale and looked at her mother, but Mrs. Miller was humbly unconscious of any violation of the usual social forms. She appeared, indeed, to have felt an incongruous impulse to draw attention to her own striking observance of them. "Good night, Mrs. Walker," she said; "we've had a beautiful evening. You see if I let Daisy come to parties without me, I don't want her to go away without me." Daisy turned away, looking with a pale, grave face at the circle near the door; Winterbourne saw that, for the first moment, she was too much shocked and puzzled even for indignation. He on his side was greatly touched.

"That was very cruel," he said to Mrs. Walker.

"She never enters my drawing-room again," replied his hostess.

Since Winterbourne was not to meet her in Mrs. Walker's drawing-room, he went as often as possible to Mrs. Miller's hotel. The ladies were rarely at home, but when he found them the devoted Giovanelli was always present. Very often the polished little Roman was in the drawing-room with Daisy alone, Mrs. Miller being apparently constantly of the opinion that discretion is the better part of surveillance. Winterbourne noted, at first with surprise, that Daisy on these occasions was never embarrassed or annoyed by his own entrance; but he very presently began to feel that she had no more surprises for him; the unexpected in her behavior was the only thing to expect. She showed no displeasure at her tête-à-tête with Giovanelli being interrupted; she could chatter as freshly and freely with two gentlemen as with one; there was always, in her conversation, the same odd mixture of audacity and puerility. Winterbourne remarked to himself that if she was seriously interested in Giovanelli it was very singular that she should not take more trouble to preserve the sanctity of their interviews, and he liked her the more for her innocent-looking indifference and her apparently inexhaustible good humor. He could hardly have said why, but she seemed to him a girl who would never be jealous. At the risk of exciting a somewhat derisive smile on the reader's part, I may affirm that with regard to the women who had hitherto interested him it very often seemed to Winterbourne among the possibilities that, given certain contingencies, he should be afraid— literally afraid—of these ladies. He had a pleasant sense that he should never be afraid of Daisy Miller. It must be added that this sentiment was not altogether flattering to Daisy; it was part of his conviction, or rather of his apprehension, that she would prove a very light young person.

But she was evidently very much interested in Giovanelli. She looked at him whenever he spoke; she was perpetually telling him to do this and to do that; she was constantly "chaffing" and abusing him. She appeared completely to have forgotten that Winterbourne had said anything to displease her at Mrs. Walker's little party. One Sunday afternoon, having gone to St. Peter's[2] with his aunt, Winterbourne perceived Daisy strolling about the great church in company with the inevitable Giovanelli. Presently he pointed out the young girl and her cavalier to Mrs. Costello. This lady looked at them a moment through her eyeglasses, and then she said:

"That's what makes you so pensive in these days, eh?"

"I had not the least idea I was pensive," said the young man.

"You are very much preoccupied, you are thinking of something."

"And what is it," he asked, "that you accuse me of thinking of?"

"Of that young lady's, Miss Baker's, Miss Chandler's—what's her name?—Miss Miller's intrigue with that little barber's block."[3]

"Do you call it an intrigue," Winterbourne asked—"an affair that goes on with such peculiar publicity?"

"That's their folly," said Mrs. Costello, "it's not their merit."

"No," rejoined Winterbourne, with something of that pensiveness to which his aunt had alluded. "I don't believe that there is anything to be called an intrigue."

"I have heard a dozen people speak of it; they say she is quite carried away by him."

"They are certainly very intimate," said Winterbourne.

Mrs. Costello inspected the young couple again with her optical instrument. "He is very handsome. One easily sees how it is. She thinks him the most elegant man in the world, the finest gentleman. She has never seen anything like him; he is better even than the courier. It was the courier probably who introduced him, and if he succeeds in marrying the young lady, the courier will come in for a magnificent commission."

"I don't believe she thinks of marrying him," said Winterbourne, "and I don't believe he hopes to marry her."

"You may be very sure she thinks of nothing. She goes on from day to day, from hour to hour, as they did in the Golden Age. I can imagine nothing more vulgar. And at the same time," added Mrs. Costello, "depend upon it that she may tell you any moment that she is 'engaged.'"

"I think that is more than Giovanelli expects," said Winterbourne.

"Who is Giovanelli?"

"The little Italian. I have asked questions about him and learned something. He is apparently a perfectly respectable little man. I believe he is in a small way a *cavaliere avvocato*.[4] But he doesn't move in what are called the first circles. I think it is really not absolutely impossible that the courier introduced him. He is evidently immensely charmed with Miss Miller. If she

---

2. Ornate Renaissance church in Vatican City, and the worldwide center of Catholic observances.

3. A dandy.

4. Lawyer (Italian). *"Cavaliere"*: a term of respect.

thinks him the finest gentleman in the world, he, on his side, has never found himself in personal contact with such splendor, such opulence, such expensiveness, as this young lady's. And then she must seem to him wonderfully pretty and interesting. I rather doubt whether he dreams of marrying her. That must appear to him too impossible a piece of luck. He has nothing but his handsome face to offer, and there is a substantial Mr. Miller in that mysterious land of dollars. Giovanelli knows that he hasn't a title to offer. If he were only a count or a *marchese*![5] He must wonder at his luck at the way they have taken him up."

"He accounts for it by his handsome face, and thinks Miss Miller a young lady *qui se passe ses fantaisies*!"[6] said Mrs. Costello.

"It is very true," Winterbourne pursued, "that Daisy and her mamma have not yet risen to that stage of—what shall I call it?—of culture, at which the idea of catching a count or a *marchese* begins. I believe that they are intellectually incapable of that conception."

"Ah! but the *cavalier* can't believe it," said Mrs. Costello.

Of the observation excited by Daisy's "intrigue," Winterbourne gathered that day at St. Peter's sufficient evidence. A dozen of the American colonists in Rome came to talk with Mrs. Costello, who sat on a little portable stool at the base of one of the great pilasters. The vesper-service was going forward in splendid chants and organ-tones in the adjacent choir, and meanwhile, between Mrs. Costello and her friends, there was a great deal said about poor little Miss Miller's going really "too far." Winterbourne was not pleased with what he heard; but when, coming out upon the great steps of the church, he saw Daisy, who had emerged before him, get into an open cab with her accomplice and roll away through the cynical streets of Rome, he could not deny to himself that she was going very far indeed. He felt very sorry for her—not exactly that he believed that she had completely lost her head, but because it was painful to hear so much that was pretty and undefended and natural assigned to a vulgar place among the categories of disorder. He made an attempt after this to give a hint to Mrs. Miller. He met one day in the Corso[7] a friend—a tourist like himself—who had just come out of the Doria Palace, where he had been walking through the beautiful gallery. His friend talked for a moment about the superb portrait of Innocent X. by Velasquez,[8] which hangs in one of the cabinets of the palace, and then said, "And in the same cabinet, by-the-way, I had the pleasure of contemplating a picture of a different kind—that pretty American girl whom you pointed out to me last week." In answer to Winterbourne's inquiries, his friend narrated that the pretty American girl—prettier than ever—was seated with a companion in the secluded nook in which the great papal portrait is enshrined.

"Who was her companion?" asked Winterbourne.

"A little Italian with a bouquet in his button-hole. The girl is delightfully pretty, but I thought I understood from you the other day that she was a young lady *du meilleur monde*."[9]

---

5. Marquis (Italian).
6. Who is indulging her whims (French).
7. Via del Corso: main street in Central Rome.
8. Diego Rodríguez de Silva y Velásquez (1599–

1660), Spanish painter. Velásquez's painting of Pope Innocent X is exhibited in a small gallery of the Doria Palace.
9. Of the better society (French).

"So she is!" answered Winterbourne; and having assured himself that his informant had seen Daisy and her companion but five minutes before, he jumped into a cab and went to call on Mrs. Miller. She was at home; but she apologized to him for receiving him in Daisy's absence.

"She's gone out somewhere with Mr. Giovanelli," said Mrs. Miller. "She's always going round with Mr. Giovanelli."

"I have noticed that they are very intimate," Winterbourne observed.

"Oh! it seems as if they couldn't live without each other!" said Mrs. Miller. "Well, he's a real gentleman, anyhow. I keep telling Daisy she's engaged!"

"And what does Daisy say?"

"Oh, she says she isn't engaged. But she might as well be!" this impartial parent resumed. "She goes on as if she was. But I've made Mr. Giovanelli promise to tell me, if *she* doesn't. I should want to write to Mr. Miller about it—shouldn't you?"

Winterbourne replied that he certainly should; and the state of mind of Daisy's mamma struck him as so unprecedented in the annals of parental vigilance that he gave up as utterly irrelevant the attempt to place her upon her guard.

After this Daisy was never at home, and Winterbourne ceased to meet her at the houses of their common acquaintances, because, as he perceived, these shrewd people had quite made up their minds that she was going too far. They ceased to invite her, and they intimated that they desired to express to observant Europeans the great truth that, though Miss Daisy Miller was a young American lady, her behavior was not representative—was regarded by her compatriots as abnormal. Winterbourne wondered how she felt about all the cold shoulders that were turned towards her, and sometimes it annoyed him to suspect that she did not feel at all. He said to himself that she was too light and childish, too uncultivated and unreasoning, too provincial, to have reflected upon her ostracism or even to have perceived it. Then at other moments he believed that she carried about in her elegant and irresponsible little organism a defiant, passionate, perfectly observant consciousness of the impression she produced. He asked himself whether Daisy's defiance came from the consciousness of innocence or from her being, essentially, a young person of the reckless class. It must be admitted that holding oneself to a belief in Daisy's "innocence" came to seem to Winterbourne more and more a matter of fine-spun gallantry. As I have already had occasion to relate, he was angry at finding himself reduced to chopping logic about this young lady; he was vexed at his want of instinctive certitude as to how far her eccentricities were generic, national, and how far they were personal. From either view of them he had somehow missed her, and now it was too late. She was "carried away" by Mr. Giovanelli.

A few days after his brief interview with her mother, he encountered her in that beautiful abode of flowering desolation known as the Palace of the Cæsars. The early Roman spring had filled the air with bloom and perfume, and the rugged surface of the Palatine[1] was muffled with tender verdure. Daisy was strolling along the top of one of those great mounds of ruin that are embanked with mossy marble and paved with monumental inscriptions. It seemed to him that Rome had never been so lovely as just then. He stood looking off at the enchanting harmony of line and color that remotely encir-

1. A park on a hill in the center of Rome, with palatial ruins and historical monuments.

cles the city, inhaling the softly humid odors and feeling the freshness of the year and the antiquity of the place reaffirm themselves in mysterious interfusion. It seemed to him also that Daisy had never looked so pretty; but this had been an observation of his whenever he met her. Giovanelli was at her side, and Giovanelli, too, wore an aspect of even unwonted brilliancy.

"Well," said Daisy, "I should think you would be lonesome!"

"Lonesome?" asked Winterbourne.

"You are always going round by yourself. Can't you get any one to walk with you?"

"I am not so fortunate," said Winterbourne, "as your companion."

Giovanelli, from the first, had treated Winterbourne with distinguished politeness; he listened with a deferential air to his remarks; he laughed, punctiliously, at his pleasantries; he seemed disposed to testify to his belief that Winterbourne was a superior young man. He carried himself in no degree like a jealous wooer; he had obviously a great deal of tact; he had no objection to your expecting a little humility of him. It even seemed to Winterbourne at times that Giovanelli would find a certain mental relief in being able to have a private understanding with him—to say to him, as an intelligent man, that, bless you, *he* knew how extraordinary was this young lady, and didn't flatter himself with delusive—or at least *too* delusive—hopes of matrimony and dollars. On this occasion he strolled away from his companion to pluck a sprig of almond blossom, which he carefully arranged in his button-hole.

"I know why you say that," said Daisy, watching Giovanelli. "Because you think I go round too much with *him*!" And she nodded at her attendant.

"Everyone thinks so—if you care to know," said Winterbourne.

"Of course I care to know!" Daisy exclaimed seriously. "But I don't believe it. They are only pretending to be shocked. They don't really care a straw what I do. Besides, I don't go round so much."

"I think you will find they do care. They will show it—disagreeably."

Daisy looked at him a moment. "How—disagreeably?"

"Haven't you noticed anything?" Winterbourne asked.

"I have noticed you. But I noticed you were as stiff as an umbrella the first time I saw you."

"You will find I am not so stiff as several others," said Winterbourne, smiling.

"How shall I find it?"

"By going to see the others."

"What will they do to me?"

"They will give you the cold shoulder. Do you know what that means?"

Daisy was looking at him intently; she began to color. "Do you mean as Mrs. Walker did the other night?"

"Exactly!" said Winterbourne.

She looked away at Giovanelli, who was decorating himself with his almond-blossom. Then looking back at Winterbourne—"I shouldn't think you would let people be so unkind!" she said.

"How can I help it?" he asked.

"I should think you would say something."

"I do say something"; and he paused a moment. "I say that your mother tells me that she believes you are engaged."

"Well, she does," said Daisy very simply.

Winterbourne began to laugh. "And does Randolph believe it?" he asked.

"I guess Randolph doesn't believe anything," said Daisy. Randolph's scepticism excited Winterbourne to farther hilarity, and he observed that Giovanelli was coming back to them. Daisy, observing it too, addressed herself again to her countryman. "Since you have mentioned it," she said, "I *am* engaged." . . . Winterbourne looked at her; he had stopped laughing. "You don't believe it!" she added.

He was silent a moment; and then, "Yes, I believe it!" he said.

"Oh, no, you don't," she answered. "Well, then—I am not!"

The young girl and her cicerone[2] were on their way to the gate of the enclosure, so that Winterbourne, who had but lately entered, presently took leave of them. A week afterwards he went to dine at a beautiful villa on the Cælian Hill,[3] and, on arriving, dismissed his hired vehicle. The evening was charming, and he promised himself the satisfaction of walking home beneath the Arch of Constantine and past the vaguely-lighted monuments of the Forum.[4] There was a waning moon in the sky, and her radiance was not brilliant, but she was veiled in a thin cloud-curtain which seemed to diffuse and equalize it. When, on his return from the villa (it was eleven o'clock), Winterbourne approached the dusky circle of the Colosseum,[5] it occurred to him, as a lover of the picturesque, that the interior, in the pale moonshine, would be well worth a glance. He turned aside and walked to one of the empty arches, near which, as he observed, an open carriage—one of the little Roman street-cabs—was stationed. Then he passed in among the cavernous shadows of the great structure, and emerged upon the clear and silent arena. The place had never seemed to him more impressive. One-half of the gigantic circus was in deep shade; the other was sleeping in the luminous dusk. As he stood there he began to murmur Byron's famous lines, out of "Manfred";[6] but before he had finished his quotation he remembered that if nocturnal meditations in the Colosseum are recommended by the poets, they are deprecated by the doctors. The historic atmosphere was there, certainly; but the historic atmosphere, scientifically considered, was not better than a villainous miasma. Winterbourne walked to the middle of the arena, to take a more general glance, intending thereafter to make a hasty retreat. The great cross in the center was covered with shadow; it was only as he drew near it that he made it out distinctly. Then he saw that two persons were stationed upon the low steps which formed its base. One of these was a woman, seated; her companion was standing in front of her.

Presently the sound of the woman's voice came to him distinctly in the warm night air. "Well, he looks at us as one of the old lions or tigers may have looked at the Christian martyrs!" These were the words he heard, in the familiar accent of Miss Daisy Miller.

2. Guide (Italian).
3. One of the seven hills upon which ancient Rome had been built.
4. Ruins of the governmental and religious center of ancient Rome. "Arch of Constantine": built in the fourth century to celebrate a key military victory of Rome's first Christian emperor.
5. Ancient Roman amphitheater, known for its battles between gladiators and public executions of Christians.
6. Byron's 1817 dramatic poem contains the following lines: ". . . the night / Hath been to me a more familiar face / Than that of man; and in her starry shade / Of dim and solitary loveliness, / I learn'd the language of another world. / I do remember me, that in my youth, / When I was wandering,—upon such a night / I stood within the Colosseum's wall, / 'Midst the chief relics of almighty Rome; / The trees which grew along the broken arches / Waved dark in the blue midnight, and the stars / Shone through the rents of ruin. . . ."

"Let us hope he is not very hungry," responded the ingenious Giovanelli. "He will have to take me first; you will serve for dessert!"

Winterbourne stopped, with a sort of horror; and, it must be added, with a sort of relief. It was as if a sudden illumination had been flashed upon the ambiguity of Daisy's behavior and the riddle had become easy to read. She was a young lady whom a gentleman need no longer be at pains to respect. He stood there looking at her—looking at her companion, and not reflecting that though he saw them vaguely, he himself must have been more brightly visible. He felt angry with himself that he had bothered so much about the right way of regarding Miss Daisy Miller. Then, as he was going to advance again, he checked himself; not from the fear that he was doing her injustice, but from a sense of the danger of appearing unbecomingly exhilarated by this sudden revulsion from cautious criticism. He turned away towards the entrance of the place; but as he did so he heard Daisy speak again.

"Why, it was Mr. Winterbourne! He saw me—and he cuts me!"

What a clever little reprobate she was, and how smartly she played an injured innocence! But he wouldn't cut her. Winterbourne came forward again, and went towards the great cross. Daisy had got up; Giovanelli lifted his hat. Winterbourne had now begun to think simply of the craziness, from a sanitary point of view, of a delicate young girl lounging away the evening in this nest of malaria. What if she *were* a clever little reprobate? that was no reason for her dying of the *perniciosa*.[7] "How long have you been there?" he asked, almost brutally.

Daisy, lovely in the flattering moonlight, looked at him a moment. Then— "All the evening," she answered gently. . . . "I never saw anything so pretty."

"I am afraid," said Winterbourne, "that you will not think Roman fever very pretty. This is the way people catch it. I wonder," he added, turning to Giovanelli, "that you, a native Roman, should countenance such a terrible indiscretion."

"Ah," said the handsome native, "for myself, I am not afraid."

"Neither am I—for you! I am speaking for this young lady."

Giovanelli lifted his well-shaped eyebrows and showed his brilliant teeth. But he took Winterbourne's rebuke with docility. "I told the Signorina it was a grave indiscretion; but when was the Signorina ever prudent?"

"I never was sick, and I don't mean to be!" the Signorina declared. "I don't look like much, but I'm healthy! I was bound to see the Colosseum by moonlight; I shouldn't have wanted to go home without that; and we have had the most beautiful time, haven't we, Mr. Giovanelli! If there has been any danger, Eugenio can give me some pills. He has got some splendid pills."

"I should advise you," said Winterbourne, "to drive home as fast as possible and take one!"

"What you say is very wise," Giovanelli rejoined. "I will go and make sure the carriage is at hand." And he went forward rapidly.

Daisy followed with Winterbourne. He kept looking at her; she seemed not in the least embarrassed. Winterbourne said nothing; Daisy chattered about the beauty of the place. "Well, I *have* seen the Colosseum by moonlight!" she exclaimed. "That's one good thing." Then, noticing Winterbourne's silence, she asked him why he didn't speak. He made no answer; he only

7. Malaria (Italian).

began to laugh. They passed under one of the dark archways; Giovanelli was in front with the carriage. Here Daisy stopped a moment, looking at the young American. "*Did* you believe I was engaged the other day?" she asked.

"It doesn't matter what I believed the other day," said Winterbourne, still laughing.

"Well, what do you believe now?"

"I believe that it makes very little difference whether you are engaged or not!"

He felt the young girl's pretty eyes fixed upon him through the thick gloom of the archway; she was apparently going to answer. But Giovanelli hurried her forward. "Quick, quick," he said; "if we get in by midnight we are quite safe."

Daisy took her seat in the carriage, and the fortunate Italian placed himself beside her. "Don't forget Eugenio's pills!" said Winterbourne, as he lifted his hat.

"I don't care," said Daisy, in a little strange tone, "whether I have Roman fever or not!" Upon this the cab-driver cracked his whip, and they rolled away over the desultory patches of the antique pavement.

Winterbourne—to do him justice, as it were—mentioned to no one that he had encountered Miss Miller, at midnight, in the Colosseum with a gentleman; but nevertheless, a couple of days later, the fact of her having been there under these circumstances was known to every member of the little American circle, and commented accordingly. Winterbourne reflected that they had of course known it at the hotel, and that, after Daisy's return, there had been an exchange of jokes between the porter and the cab-driver. But the young man was conscious at the same moment that it had ceased to be a matter of serious regret to him that the little American flirt should be "talked about" by low-minded menials. These people, a day or two later, had serious information to give: the little American flirt was alarmingly ill. Winterbourne, when the rumor came to him, immediately went to the hotel for more news. He found that two or three charitable friends had preceded him, and that they were being entertained in Mrs. Miller's salon by Randolph.

"It's going round at night," said Randolph—"that's what made her sick. She's always going round at midnight. I shouldn't think she'd want to—it's so plaguey dark. You can't see anything here at night, except when there's a moon. In America there's always a moon!" Mrs. Miller was invisible; she was now, at least, giving her daughter the advantage of her society. It was evident that Daisy was dangerously ill.

Winterbourne went often to ask for news of her, and once he saw Mrs. Miller, who, though deeply alarmed, was—rather to his surprise—perfectly composed, and, as it appeared, a most efficient and judicious nurse. She talked a good deal about Dr. Davis, but Winterbourne paid her the compliment of saying to himself that she was not, after all, such a monstrous goose. "Daisy spoke of you the other day," she said to him. "Half the time she doesn't know what she's saying, but that time I think she did. She gave me a message: she told me to tell you. She told me to tell you that she never was engaged to that handsome Italian. I am sure I am very glad; Mr. Giovanelli hasn't been near us since she was taken ill. I thought he was so much of a gentleman; but I don't call that very polite! A lady told me that he was afraid I was angry with him for taking Daisy round at night. Well, so

I am; but I suppose he knows I'm a lady. I would scorn to scold him. Any way, she says she's not engaged. I don't know why she wanted you to know; but she said to me three times—'Mind you tell Mr. Winterbourne.' And then she told me to ask if you remembered the time you went to that castle, in Switzerland. But I said I wouldn't give any such messages as that. Only, if she is not engaged, I'm sure I'm glad to know it."

But, as Winterbourne had said, it mattered very little. A week after this the poor girl died; it had been a terrible case of the fever. Daisy's grave was in the little Protestant cemetery, in an angle of the wall of imperial Rome, beneath the cypresses and the thick spring-flowers. Winterbourne stood there beside it, with a number of other mourners; a number larger than the scandal excited by the young lady's career would have led you to expect. Near him stood Giovanelli, who came nearer still before Winterbourne turned away. Giovanelli was very pale; on this occasion he had no flower in his button-hole; he seemed to wish to say something. At last he said, "She was the most beautiful young lady I ever saw, and the most amiable." And then he added in a moment, "And she was the most innocent."

Winterbourne looked at him, and presently repeated his words, "And the most innocent?"

"The most innocent!"

Winterbourne felt sore and angry. "Why the devil," he asked, "did you take her to that fatal place?"

Mr. Giovanelli's urbanity was apparently imperturbable. He looked on the ground a moment, and then he said, "For myself, I had no fear; and she wanted to go."

"That was no reason!" Winterbourne declared.

The subtle Roman again dropped his eyes. "If she had lived, I should have got nothing. She would never have married me, I am sure."

"She would never have married you?"

"For a moment I hoped so. But no, I am sure."

Winterbourne listened to him; he stood staring at the raw protuberance among the April daisies. When he turned away again Mr. Giovanelli, with his light slow step, had retired.

Winterbourne almost immediately left Rome; but the following summer he again met his aunt, Mrs. Costello, at Vevey. Mrs. Costello was fond of Vevey. In the interval Winterbourne had often thought of Daisy Miller and her mystifying manners. One day he spoke of her to his aunt—said it was on his conscience that he had done her injustice.

"I am sure I don't know," said Mrs. Costello. "How did your injustice affect her?"

"She sent me a message before her death which I didn't understand at the time. But I have understood it since. She would have appreciated one's esteem."

"Is that a modest way," asked Mrs. Costello, "of saying that she would have reciprocated one's affection?"

Winterbourne offered no answer to this question; but he presently said, "You were right in that remark that you made last summer. I was booked to make a mistake. I have lived too long in foreign parts."

Nevertheless, he went back to live at Geneva, whence there continue to come the most contradictory accounts of his motives of sojourn: a report that he is "studying" hard—an intimation that he is much interested in a very clever foreign lady.

1878, 1879

The Real Thing[1]

I

When the porter's wife, who used to answer the house-bell, announced "A gentleman and a lady, sir" I had, as I often had in those days—the wish being father to the thought—an immediate vision of sitters. Sitters my visitors in this case proved to be; but not in the sense I should have preferred. There was nothing at first however to indicate that they mightn't have come for a portrait. The gentleman, a man of fifty, very high and very straight, with a moustache slightly grizzled and a dark grey walking-coat admirably fitted, both of which I noted professionally—I don't mean as a barber or yet as a tailor—would have struck me as a celebrity if celebrities often were striking. It was a truth of which I had for some time been conscious that a figure with a good deal of frontage was, as one might say, almost never a public institution. A glance at the lady helped to remind me of this paradoxical law: she also looked too distinguished to be a "personality." Moreover one would scarcely come across two variations together.

Neither of the pair immediately spoke—they only prolonged the preliminary gaze suggesting that each wished to give the other a chance. They were visibly shy; they stood there letting me take them in—which, as I afterwards perceived, was the most practical thing they could have done. In this way their embarrassment served their cause. I had seen people painfully reluctant to mention that they desired anything so gross as to be represented on canvas; but the scruples of my new friends appeared almost insurmountable. Yet the gentleman might have said "I should like a portrait of my wife," and the lady might have said "I should like a portrait of my husband." Perhaps they weren't husband and wife—this naturally would make the matter more delicate. Perhaps they wished to be done together—in which case they ought to have brought a third person to break the news.

"We come from Mr. Rivet," the lady finally said with a dim smile that had the effect of a moist sponge passed over a "sunk"[2] piece of painting, as well as of a vague allusion to vanished beauty. She was as tall and straight, in her degree, as her companion, and with ten years less to carry. She looked as sad as a woman could look whose face was not charged with expression; that is her tinted oval mask showed waste as an exposed surface shows friction. The hand of time had played over her freely, but to an effect of elimination. She was slim and stiff, and so well-dressed, in dark blue cloth, with lappets[3] and pockets and buttons, that it was clear she employed the same tailor as her husband. The couple had an indefinable air of prosperous

---

1. This "little gem of bright, quick vivid form," as James called it, first appeared in the April 16, 1892, issue of *Black and White*; then in "*The Real Thing*" and Other Tales (1893); and finally in Vol. 18 (1909) of the New York edition, the source of the text printed here.
2. When colors lose their brilliance after they have dried on the canvas, they are said to have "sunk in."
3. Decorative flaps or folds.

thrift—they evidently got a good deal of luxury for their money. If I was to be one of their luxuries it would behove me to consider my terms.

"Ah Claude Rivet recommended me?" I echoed; and I added that it was very kind of him, though I could reflect that, as he only painted landscape, this wasn't a sacrifice.

The lady looked very hard at the gentleman, and the gentleman looked round the room. Then staring at the floor a moment and stroking his moustache, he rested his pleasant eyes on me with the remark: "He said you were the right one."

"I try to be, when people want to sit."

"Yes, we should like to," said the lady anxiously.

"Do you mean together?"

My visitors exchanged a glance. "If you could do anything with *me* I suppose it would be double," the gentleman stammered.

"Oh yes, there's naturally a higher charge for two figures than for one."

"We should like to make it pay," the husband confessed.

"That's very good of you," I returned, appreciating so unwonted a sympathy—for I supposed he meant pay the artist.

A sense of strangeness seemed to draw on the lady.

"We mean for the illustrations—Mr. Rivet said you might put one in."

"Put in—an illustration?" I was equally confused.

"Sketch her off, you know," said the gentleman, colouring.

It was only then that I understood the service Claude Rivet had rendered me; he had told them how I worked in black-and-white, for magazines, for storybooks, for sketches of contemporary life, and consequently had copious employment for models. These things were true, but it was not less true—I may confess it now; whether because the aspiration was to lead to everything or to nothing I leave the reader to guess—that I couldn't get the honours, to say nothing of the emoluments, of a great painter of portraits out of my head. My "illustrations" were my pot-boilers; I looked to a different branch of art—far and away the most interesting it had always seemed to me—to perpetuate my fame. There was no shame in looking to it also to make my fortune; but that fortune was by so much further from being made from the moment my visitors wished to be "done" for nothing. I was disappointed; for in the pictorial sense I had immediately *seen* them. I had seized their type—I had already settled what I would do with it. Something that wouldn't absolutely have pleased them, I afterwards reflected.

"Ah you're—you're—a—?" I began as soon as I had mastered my surprise. I couldn't bring out the dingy word "models": it seemed so little to fit the case.

"We haven't had much practice," said the lady.

"We've got to *do* something, and we've thought that an artist in your line might perhaps make something of us," her husband threw off. He further mentioned that they didn't know many artists and that they had gone first, on the off-chance—he painted views of course, but sometimes put in figures; perhaps I remembered—to Mr. Rivet, whom they had met a few years before at a place in Norfolk where he was sketching.

"We used to sketch a little ourselves," the lady hinted.

"It's very awkward, but we absolutely *must* do something," her husband went on.

"Of course we're not so *very* young," she admitted with a wan smile.

With the remark that I might as well know something more about them the husband had handed me a card extracted from a neat new pocket-book—their appurtenances were all of the freshest—and inscribed with the words "Major Monarch." Impressive as these words were they didn't carry my knowledge much further; but my visitor presently added: "I've left the army and we've had the misfortune to lose our money. In fact our means are dreadfully small."

"It's awfully trying—a regular strain," said Mrs. Monarch.

They evidently wished to be discreet—to take care not to swagger because they were gentlefolk. I felt them willing to recognise this as something of a drawback, at the same time that I guessed at an underlying sense—their consolation in adversity—that they *had* their points. They certainly had; but these advantages struck me as preponderantly social; such for instance as would help to make a drawing-room look well. However, a drawing-room was always, or ought to be, a picture.

In consequence of his wife's allusion to their age Major Monarch observed: "Naturally it's more for the figure that we thought of going in. We can still hold ourselves up." On the instant I saw that the figure was indeed their strong point. His "naturally" didn't sound vain, but it lighted up the question. "*She* has the best one," he continued, nodding at his wife with a pleasant after-dinner absence of circumlocution. I could only reply, as if we were in fact sitting over our wine, that this didn't prevent his own from being very good; which led him in turn to make answer: "We thought that if you ever have to do people like us we might be something like it. *She* particularly—for a lady in a book, you know."

I was so amused by them that, to get more of it, I did my best to take their point of view; and though it was an embarrassment to find myself appraising physically, as if they were animals on hire or useful blacks, a pair whom I should have expected to meet only in one of the relations in which criticism is tacit, I looked at Mrs. Monarch judicially enough to be able to exclaim after a moment with conviction: "Oh yes, a lady in a book!" She was singularly like a bad illustration.

"We'll stand up, if you like," said the Major; and he raised himself before me with a really grand air.

I could take his measure at a glance—he was six feet two and a perfect gentleman. It would have paid any club in process of formation and in want of a stamp to engage him at a salary to stand in the principal window. What struck me at once was that in coming to me they had rather missed their vocation; they could surely have been turned to better account for advertising purposes. I couldn't of course see the thing in detail, but I could see them make somebody's fortune—I don't mean their own. There was something in them for a waistcoat-maker, an hotel-keeper or a soap-vendor. I could imagine "We always use it" pinned on their bosoms with the greatest effect; I had a vision of the brilliancy with which they would launch a table d'hôte.[4]

Mrs. Monarch sat still, not from pride but from shyness, and presently her husband said to her; "Get up, my dear, and show how smart you are." She obeyed, but she had no need to get up to show it. She walked to the end

---

4. Host's table (French); a common dining table for guests at a hotel.

of the studio and then came back blushing, her fluttered eyes on the partner of her appeal. I was reminded of an incident I had accidentally had a glimpse of in Paris—being with a friend there, a dramatist about to produce a play, when an actress came to him to ask to be entrusted with a part. She went through her paces before him, walked up and down as Mrs. Monarch was doing. Mrs. Monarch did it quite as well, but I abstained from applauding. It was very odd to see such people apply for such poor pay. She looked as if she had ten thousand a year. Her husband had used the word that described her: she was in the London current jargon essentially and typically "smart." Her figure was, in the same order of ideas, conspicuously and irreproachably "good." For a woman of her age her waist was surprisingly small; her elbow moreover had the orthodox crook. She held her head at the conventional angle, but why did she come to *me*? She ought to have tried on jackets at a big shop. I feared my visitors were not only destitute but "artistic"—which would be a great complication. When she sat down again I thanked her, observing that what a draughtsman most valued in his model was the faculty of keeping quiet.

"Oh *she* can keep quiet," said Major Monarch. Then he added jocosely: "I've always kept her quiet."

"I'm not a nasty fidget, am I?" It was going to wring tears from me, I felt, the way she hid her head, ostrich-like, in the other broad bosom.

The owner of this expanse addressed his answer to me. "Perhaps it isn't out of place to mention—because we ought to be quite business-like, oughtn't we?—that when I married her she was known as the Beautiful Statue."

"Oh dear!" said Mrs. Monarch ruefully.

"Of course I should want a certain amount of expression," I rejoined.

"Of *course*!"—and I had never heard such unanimity.

"And then I suppose you know that you'll get awfully tired."

"Oh we *never* get tired!" they eagerly cried.

"Have you had any kind of practice?"

They hesitated—they looked at each other. "We've been photographed—*immensely*," said Mrs. Monarch.

"She means the fellows have asked us themselves," added the Major.

"I see—because you're so good-looking."

"I don't know what they thought, but they were always after us."

"We always got our photographs for nothing," smiled Mrs. Monarch.

"We might have brought some, my dear," her husband remarked.

"I'm not sure we have any left. We've given quantities away," she explained to me.

"With our autographs and that sort of thing," said the Major.

"Are they to be got in the shops?" I enquired as a harmless pleasantry.

"Oh yes, *hers*—they used to be."

"Not now," said Mrs. Monarch with her eyes on the floor.

II

I could fancy the "sort of thing" they put on the presentation copies of their photographs, and I was sure they wrote a beautiful hand. It was odd how quickly I was sure of everything that concerned them. If they were now so poor as to have to earn shillings and pence they could never have had much of a margin. Their good looks had been their capital, and they had good-humouredly made the most of the career that this resource marked out for them. It was in their faces, the blankness, the deep intellectual repose of the twenty years of country-house visiting that had given them pleasant into-nations. I could see the sunny drawing-rooms, sprinkled with periodicals she didn't read, in which Mrs. Monarch had continuously sat; I could see the wet shrubberies in which she had walked, equipped to admiration for either exercise. I could see the rich covers[5] the Major had helped to shoot and the wonderful garments in which, late at night, he repaired to the smoking-room to talk about them. I could imagine their leggings and waterproofs, their knowing tweeds and rugs, their rolls of sticks and cases of tackle and neat umbrellas; and I could evoke the exact appearance of their servants and the compact variety of their luggage on the platforms of country stations.

They gave small tips, but they were liked; they didn't do anything them-selves, but they were welcome. They looked so well everywhere; they grati-fied the general relish for stature, complexion and "form." They knew it without fatuity or vulgarity, and they respected themselves in consequence. They weren't superficial; they were thorough and kept themselves up—it had been their line. People with such a taste for activity had to have some line. I could feel how even in a dull house they could have been counted on for the joy of life. At present something had happened—it didn't matter what, their little income had grown less, it had grown least—and they had to do something for pocket-money. Their friends could like them, I made out, with-out liking to support them. There was something about them that repre-sented credit—their clothes, their manners, their type; but if credit is a large empty pocket in which an occasional chink reverberates, the chink at least must be audible. What they wanted of me was to help to make it so. Fortu-nately they had no children—I soon divined that. They would also perhaps wish our relations to be kept secret: this was why it was "for the figure"—the reproduction of the face would betray them.

I liked them—I felt, quite as their friends must have done—they were so simple; and I had no objection to them if they would suit. But somehow with all their perfections I didn't easily believe in them. After all they were ama-teurs, and the ruling passion of my life was the detestation of the amateur. Combined with this was another perversity—an innate preference for the represented subject over the real one: the defect of the real one was so apt to be a lack of representation. I liked things that appeared; then one was sure. Whether they *were* or not was a subordinate and almost always a prof-itless question. There were other considerations, the first of which was that I already had two or three recruits in use, notably a young person with big feet, in alpaca, from Kilburn, who for a couple of years had come to me regu-larly for my illustrations and with whom I was still—perhaps ignobly—satisfied. I frankly explained to my visitors how the case stood, but they had taken more precautions than I supposed. They had reasoned out their oppor-tunity, for Claude Rivet had told them of the projected *édition de luxe* of one of the writers of our day—the rarest of the novelists—who, long neglected by the multitudinous vulgar and dearly prized by the attentive (need I men-

5. Game birds.

tion Philip Vincent?) had had the happy fortune of seeing, late in life, the dawn and then the full light of a higher criticism; an estimate in which on the part of the public there was something really of expiation. The edition preparing, planned by a publisher of taste, was practically an act of high reparation; the wood-cuts with which it was to be enriched were the homage of English art to one of the most independent representatives of English letters. Major and Mrs. Monarch confessed to me they had hoped I might be able to work *them* into my branch of the enterprise. They knew I was to do the first of the books, "Rutland Ramsay," but I had to make clear to them that my participation in the rest of the affair—this first book was to be a test—must depend on the satisfaction I should give. If this should be limited my employers would drop me with scarce common forms. It was therefore a crisis for me, and naturally I was making special preparations, looking about for new people, should they be necessary, and securing the best types. I admitted however that I should like to settle down to two or three good models who would do for everything.

"Should we have often to—a—put on special clothes?" Mrs. Monarch timidly demanded.

"Dear yes—that's half the business."

"And should we be expected to supply our own costumes?"

"Oh no; I've got a lot of things. A painter's models put on—or put off—anything he likes."

"And you mean—a—the same?"

"The same?"

Mrs. Monarch looked at her husband again.

"Oh she was just wondering," he explained, "if the costumes are in *general* use." I had to confess that they were, and I mentioned further that some of them—I had a lot of genuine greasy last-century things—had served their time, a hundred years ago, on living world-stained men and women; on figures not perhaps so far removed, in that vanished world, from *their* type, the Monarchs', *quoi!*[6] of a breeched and bewigged age. "We'll put on anything that *fits*," said the Major.

"Oh I arrange that—they fit in the pictures."

"I'm afraid I should do better for the modern books. I'd come as you like," said Mrs. Monarch.

"She has got a lot of clothes at home: they might do for contemporary life," her husband continued.

"Oh I can fancy scenes in which you'd be quite natural." And indeed I could see the slipshod rearrangements of stale properties—the stories I tried to produce pictures for without the exasperation of reading them—whose sandy tracts the good lady might help to people. But I had to return to the fact that for this sort of work—the daily mechanical grind—I was already equipped: the people I was working with were fully adequate.

"We only thought we might be more like *some* characters," said Mrs. Monarch mildly, getting up.

Her husband also rose; he stood looking at me with a dim wistfulness that was touching in so fine a man. "Wouldn't it be rather a pull sometimes to

6. What! (French).

have—a—to have—?" He hung fire;[7] he wanted me to help him by phrasing what he meant. But I couldn't—I didn't know. So he brought it out awkwardly: "The *real* thing; a gentleman, you know, or a lady." I was quite ready to give a general assent—I admitted that there was a great deal in that. This encouraged Major Monarch to say, following up his appeal with an unacted gulp: "It's awfully hard—we've tried everything." The gulp was communicative; it proved too much for his wife. Before I knew it Mrs. Monarch had dropped again upon a divan and burst into tears. Her husband sat down beside her, holding one of her hands; whereupon she quickly dried her eyes with the other, while I felt embarrassed as she looked up at me. "There isn't a confounded job I haven't applied for—waited for—prayed for. You can fancy we'd be pretty bad first. Secretaryships and that sort of thing? You might as well ask for a peerage. I'd be *anything*—I'm strong; a messenger or a coal- heaver. I'd put on a gold-laced cap and open carriage-doors in front of the haberdasher's; I'd hang about a station to carry portmanteaux;[8] I'd be a postman. But they won't *look* at you; there are thousands as good as yourself already on the ground. *Gentlemen*, poor beggars, who've drunk their wine, who've kept their hunters!"

I was as reassuring as I knew how to be, and my visitors were presently on their feet again while, for the experiment, we agreed on an hour. We were discussing it when the door opened and Miss Churm came in with a wet umbrella. Miss Churm had to take the omnibus to Maida Vale[9] and then walk half a mile. She looked a trifle blowsy and slightly splashed. I scarcely ever saw her come in without thinking afresh how odd it was that, being so little in herself, she should yet be so much in others. She was a meagre little Miss Churm, but was such an ample heroine of romance. She was only a freckled cockney,[1] but she could represent everything, from a fine lady to a shepherdess; she had the faculty as she might have had a fine voice or long hair. She couldn't spell and she loved beer, but she had two or three "points," and practice, and a knack, and mother-wit, and a whimsical sensibility, and a love of the theatre, and seven sisters, and not an ounce of respect, especially for the *h*. The first thing my visitors saw was that her umbrella was wet, and in their spotless perfection they visibly winced at it. The rain had come on since their arrival.

"I'm all in a soak; there *was* a mess of people in the 'bus. I wish you lived near a stytion," said Miss Churm. I requested her to get ready as quickly as possible, and she passed into the room in which she always changed her dress. But before going out she asked me what she was to get into this time.

"It's the Russian princess, don't you know?" I answered; "the one with the 'golden eyes,' in black velvet, for the long thing in the *Cheapside*."[2]

"Golden eyes? I *say*!" cried Miss Churm, while my companions watched her with intensity as she withdrew. She always arranged herself, when she was late, before I could turn around; and I kept my visitors a little on purpose, so that they might get an idea, from seeing her, what would be expected

---

7. Delayed. The term comes from an unexpected delay between the triggering of a firearm and its firing—a common problem in older firearms.
8. Large suitcases.
9. Residential district in West London.

1. Native of London, especially the East End. The cockney dialect is known for dropping *h*'s; e.g., *hair* would be pronounced *air*.
2. Imaginary magazine named after a main business street in London.

of themselves. I mentioned that she was quite my notion of an excellent model—she was really very clever.

"Do you think she looks like a Russian princess?" Major Monarch asked with lurking alarm.

"When I make her, yes."

"Oh if you have to *make* her—!" he reasoned, not without point.

"That's the most you can ask. There are so many who are not makeable."

"Well now, *here's* a lady"—and with a persuasive smile he passed his arm into his wife's—"who's already made!"

"Oh I'm not a Russian princess," Mrs. Monarch protested a little coldly. I could see she had known some and didn't like them. There at once was a complication of a kind I never had to fear with Miss Churm.

This young lady came back in black velvet—the gown was rather rusty and very low on her lean shoulders—and with a Japanese fan in her red hands. I reminded her that in the scene I was doing she had to look over some one's head. "I forget whose it is; but it doesn't matter. Just look over a head."

"I'd rather look over a stove," said Miss Churm; and she took her station near the fire. She fell into position, settled herself into a tall attitude, gave a certain backward inclination to her head and a certain forward droop to her fan, and looked, at least to my prejudiced sense, distinguished and charming, foreign and dangerous. We left her looking so while I went downstairs with Major and Mrs. Monarch.

"I believe I could come about as near it as that," said Mrs. Monarch.

"Oh, you think she's shabby, but you must allow for the alchemy of art."

However, they went off with an evident increase of comfort founded on their demonstrable advantage in being the real thing. I could fancy them shuddering over Miss Churm. She was very droll about them when I went back, for I told her what they wanted.

"Well, if *she* can sit I'll tyke to bookkeeping," said my model.

"She's very ladylike," I replied as an innocent form of aggravation.

"So much the worse for *you*. That means she can't turn round."

"She'll do for the fashionable novels."

"Oh yes, she'll *do* for them!" my model humorously declared. "Ain't they bad enough without her?" I had often sociably denounced them to Miss Churm.

III

It was for the elucidation of a mystery in one of these works that I first tried Mrs. Monarch. Her husband came with her, to be useful if necessary—it was sufficiently clear that as a general thing he would prefer to come with her. At first I wondered if this were for "propriety's" sake—if he were going to be jealous and meddling. The idea was too tiresome, and if it had been confirmed it would speedily have brought our acquaintance to a close. But I soon saw there was nothing in it and that if he accompanied Mrs. Monarch it was—in addition to the chance of being wanted—simply because he had nothing else to do. When they were separate his occupation was gone and they never *had* been separate. I judged rightly that in their awkward situation their close union was their main comfort and that this union had no weak spot. It was a real marriage, an encouragement to the hesitating, a nut for pessimists to crack. Their address was humble—I remember afterwards thinking it had been the only thing about them that was really professional—and I could fancy the lamentable lodgings in which the Major would have been left alone. He could sit there more or less grimly with his wife—he couldn't sit there anyhow without her.

He had too much tact to try and make himself agreeable when he couldn't be useful; so when I was too absorbed in my work to talk he simply sat and waited. But I liked to hear him talk—it made my work, when not interrupting it, less mechanical, less special. To listen to him was to combine the excitement of going out with the economy of staying at home. There was only one hindrance—that I seemed not to know any of the people this brilliant couple had known. I think he wondered extremely, during the term of our intercourse, whom the deuce I *did* know. He hadn't a stray sixpence of an idea to fumble for, so we didn't spin it very fine; we confined ourselves to questions of leather and even of liquor—saddlers and breeches-makers and how to get excellent claret cheap—and matters like "good trains" and the habits of small game. His lore on these last subjects was astonishing—he managed to interweave the station-master with the ornithologist. When he couldn't talk about greater things he could talk cheerfully about smaller, and since I couldn't accompany him into reminiscences of the fashionable world he could lower the conversation without a visible effort to my level.

So earnest a desire to please was touching in a man who could so easily have knocked one down. He looked after the fire and had an opinion on the draught of the stove without my asking him, and I could see that he thought many of my arrangements not half knowing. I remember telling him that if I were only rich I'd offer him a salary to come and teach me how to live. Sometimes he gave a random sigh of which the essence might have been: "Give me even such a bare old barrack as *this*, and I'd do something with it!" When I wanted to use him he came alone; which was an illustration of the superior courage of women. His wife could bear her solitary second floor, and she was in general more discreet; showing by various small reserves that she was alive to the propriety of keeping our relations markedly professional—not letting them slide into sociability. She wished it to remain clear that she and the Major were employed, not cultivated, and if she approved of me as a superior, who could be kept in his place, she never thought me quite good enough for an equal.

She sat with great intensity, giving the whole of her mind to it, and was capable of remaining for an hour almost as motionless as before a photographer's lens. I could see she had been photographed often, but somehow the very habit that made her good for that purpose unfitted her for mine. At first I was extremely pleased with her ladylike air, and it was a satisfaction, on coming to follow her lines, to see how good they were and how far they could lead the pencil. But after a little skirmishing I began to find her too insurmountably stiff; do what I would with it my drawing looked like a photograph or a copy of a photograph. Her figure had no variety of expression—she herself had no sense of variety. You may say that this was my business and was only a question of placing her. Yet I placed her in every conceivable position and she managed to obliterate their differences. She was always a lady certainly, and into the bargain was always the same lady. She was the real thing, but always the same thing. There were moments when I rather writhed under the serenity of her confidence that she *was* the real thing. All her dealings with me and all her husband's were an implication that this was lucky for *me*. Meanwhile I found myself trying to invent types that approached her own, instead of making her own transform itself—in the clever way that was not impossible for instance to poor Miss Churm. Arrange as I would and take the precautions I would, she always came out, in my pictures, too tall—landing me in the dilemma of having represented a fascinating woman as seven feet high, which (out of respect perhaps to my own very much scantier inches) was far from my idea of such a personage.

The case was worse with the Major—nothing I could do would keep *him* down, so that he became useful only for representation of brawny giants. I adored variety and range, I cherished human accidents, the illustrative note; I wanted to characterise closely, and the thing in the world I most hated was the danger of being ridden by a type. I had quarrelled with some of my friends about it; I had parted company with them for maintaining that one *had* to be, and that if the type was beautiful—witness Raphael and Leonardo[3]— the servitude was only a gain. I was neither Leonardo nor Raphael—I might only be a presumptuous young modern searcher; but I held that everything was to be sacrificed sooner than character. When they claimed that the obsessional form could easily *be* character I retorted, perhaps superficially, "Whose?" It couldn't be everybody's—it might end in being nobody's.

After I had drawn Mrs. Monarch a dozen times I felt surer even than before that the value of such a model as Miss Churm resided precisely in the fact that she had no positive stamp, combined of course with the other fact that what she did have was a curious and inexplicable talent for imitation. Her usual appearance was like a curtain which she could draw up at request for a capital performance. This performance was simply suggestive; but it was a word to the wise—it was vivid and pretty. Sometimes even I thought it, though she was plain herself, too insipidly pretty; I made it a reproach to her that the figures drawn from her were monotonously (*bête-ment*,[4] as we used to say) graceful. Nothing made her more angry: it was so much her pride to feel she could sit for characters that had nothing in common with each other. She would accuse me at such moments of taking away her "reputytion."

It suffered a certain shrinkage, this queer quantity, from the repeated visits of my new friends. Miss Churm was greatly in demand, never in want of employment, so I had no scruple in putting her off occasionally, to try them more at my ease. It was certainly amusing at first to do the real thing—it was amusing to do Major Monarch's trousers. There *were* the real thing, even if he did come out colossal. It was amusing to do his wife's back hair—it was so mathematically neat—and the particular "smart" tension of her tight stays. She lent herself especially to positions in which the face was somewhat averted or blurred; she abounded in ladylike back views and *profils perdus*.[5] When she stood erect she took naturally one of the attitudes in which

---

3. Leonardo da Vinci (1452–1519), Florentine painter, sculptor, architect, and engineer. Raffaello Santi or Sanzio (1483–1520), Italian painter.

4. Unthinkingly (French).
5. Lost profiles (French); poses in which the subject turns away.

court-painters represent queens and princesses; so that I found myself wondering whether, to draw out this accomplishment, I couldn't get the editor
of the *Cheapside* to publish a really royal romance, "A Tale of Buckingham
Palace." Sometimes however the real thing and the make-believe came into
contact; by which I mean that Miss Churm, keeping an appointment or coming to make one on days when I had much work in hand, encountered her
invidious rivals. The encounter was not on their part, for they noticed her
no more than if she had been the housemaid; not from intentional loftiness,
but simply because as yet, professionally, they didn't know how to fraternise,
as I could imagine they would have liked—or at least that the Major would.
They couldn't talk about the omnibus—they always walked; and they didn't
know what else to try—she wasn't interested in good trains or cheap claret.
Besides, they must have felt—in the air—that she was amused at them,
secretly derisive of their ever knowing how. She wasn't a person to conceal
the limits of her faith if she had had a chance to show them. On the other
hand Mrs. Monarch didn't think her tidy; for why else did she take pains to
say to me—it was going out of the way, for Mrs. Monarch—that she didn't
like dirty women?

One day when my young lady happened to be present with my other
sitters—she even dropped in, when it was convenient, for a chat—I asked
her to be so good as to lend a hand in getting tea, a service with which she
was familiar and which was one of a class that, living as I did in a small
way, with slender domestic resources, I often appealed to my models to render. They liked to lay hands on my property, to break the sitting, and sometimes the china—it made them feel Bohemian. The next time I saw Miss
Churm after this incident she surprised me greatly by making a scene about
it—she accused me of having wished to humiliate her. She hadn't resented
the outrage at the time, but had seemed obliging and amused, enjoying
the comedy of asking Mrs. Monarch, who sat vague and silent, whether she
would have cream and sugar, and putting an exaggerated simper into
the question. She had tried intonations—as if she too wished to pass for
the real thing—till I was afraid my other visitors would take offence.

Oh they were determined not to do this, and their touching patience was
the measure of their great need. They would sit by the hour, uncomplain-
ing, till I was ready to use them; they would come back on the chance of
being wanted and would walk away cheerfully if it failed. I used to go to the
door with them to see in what magnificent order they retreated. I tried to
find other employment for them—I introduced them to several artists. But
they didn't "take," for reasons I could appreciate, and I became rather anxiously aware that after such disappointments they fell back upon me with a
heavier weight. They did me the honour to think me most *their* form. They
weren't romantic enough for the painters, and in those days there were few
serious workers in black-and-white. Besides, they had an eye to the great job
I had mentioned to them—they had secretly set their hearts on supplying
the right essence for my pictorial vindication of our fine novelist. They knew
that for this undertaking I should want no costume-effects, none of the frip-
pery of past ages—that it was a case in which everything would be contemporary and satirical and presumably genteel. If I could work them into
it their future would be assured, for the labour would of course be long and
the occupation steady.

One day Mrs. Monarch came without her husband—she explained his absence by his having had to go to the City.[6] While she sat there in her usual relaxed majesty there came at the door a knock which I immediately recognised as the subdued appeal of a model out of work. It was followed by the entrance of a young man whom I at once saw to be a foreigner and who proved in fact an Italian acquainted with no English word but my name, which he uttered in a way that made it seem to include all others. I hadn't then visited his country, nor was I proficient in his tongue; but as he was not so meanly constituted—what Italian is?—as to depend only on that member for expression he conveyed to me, in familiar but graceful mimicry, that he was in search of exactly the employment in which the lady before me was engaged. I was not struck with him at first, and while I continued to draw I dropped few signs of interest or encouragement. He stood his ground however—not importunately, but with a dumb dog-like fidelity in his eyes that amounted to innocent impudence, the manner of a devoted servant—he might have been in the house for years—unjustly suspected. Suddenly it struck me that this very attitude and expression made a picture; whereupon I told him to sit down and wait till I should be free. There was another picture in the way he obeyed me, and I observed as I worked that there were others still in the way he looked wonderingly, with his head thrown back, about the high studio. He might have been crossing himself in Saint Peter's. Before I finished I said to myself "The fellow's a bankrupt orange-monger, but a treasure."

When Mrs. Monarch withdrew he passed across the room like a flash to open the door for her, standing there with the rapt pure gaze of the young Dante spellbound by the young Beatrice.[7] As I never insisted, in such situations, on the blankness of the British domestic, I reflected that he had the making of a servant—and I needed one, but couldn't pay him to be only that—as well as of a model; in short I resolved to adopt my bright adventurer if he would agree to officiate in the double capacity. He jumped at my offer, and in the event my rashness—for I had really known nothing about him—wasn't brought home to me. He proved a sympathetic though a desultory ministrant, and had in a wonderful degree the *sentiment de la pose*.[8] It was uncultivated, instinctive, a part of the happy instinct that had guided him to my door and helped him to spell out my name on the card nailed to it. He had had no other introduction to me than a guess, from the shape of my high north window, seen outside, that my place was a studio and that as a studio it would contain an artist. He had wandered to England in search of fortune, like other itinerants, and had embarked, with a partner and a small green hand-cart, on the sale of penny ices. The ices had melted away and the partner had dissolved in their train. My young man wore tight yellow trousers with reddish stripes and his name was Oronte. He was sallow but fair, and when I put him into some old clothes of my own he looked like an Englishman. He was as good as Miss Churm, who could look, when requested, like an Italian.

IV

I thought Mrs. Monarch's face slightly convulsed when, on her coming back with her husband, she found Oronte installed. It was strange to have to recognise in a scrap of a lazzarone[9] a competitor to her magnificent Major. It was she who scented danger first, for the Major was anecdotically unconscious. But Oronte gave us tea, with a hundred eager confusions—he had never been concerned in so queer a process—and I think she thought better of me for having at last an "establishment." They saw a couple of drawings that I had made of the establishment, and Mrs. Monarch hinted that it never would have struck her he had sat for them. "Now the drawings you make from *us*, they look exactly like us," she reminded me, smiling in triumph; and I recognised that this was indeed just their defect. When I drew the Monarchs I couldn't anyhow get away from them—get into the character I wanted to represent; and I hadn't the least desire my model should be discoverable in my picture. Miss Churm never was, and Mrs. Monarch thought I hid her, very properly, because she was vulgar; whereas if she was lost it was only as the dead who go to heaven are lost—in the gain of an angel the more.

By this time I had got a certain start with "Rutland Ramsay," the first novel in the great projected series; that is I had produced a dozen drawings, several with the help of the Major and his wife, and I had sent them in for approval. My understanding with the publishers, as I have already hinted, had been that I was to be left to do my work, in this particular case, as I liked, with the whole book committed to me; but my connexion with the rest of the series was only contingent. There were moments when, frankly, it *was* a comfort to have the real thing under one's hand; for there were characters in "Rutland Ramsay" that were very much like it. There were people presumably as erect as the Major and women of as good a fashion as Mrs. Monarch. There was a great deal of country-house life—treated, it is true, in a fine fanciful ironical generalised way—and there was a considerable implication of knickerbockers and kilts.[1] There were certain things I had to settle at the outset; such things for instance as the exact appearance of the hero and the particular bloom and figure of the heroine. The author of course gave me a lead, but there was a margin for interpretation. I took the Monarchs into my confidence, I told them frankly what I was about, I mentioned my embarrassments and alternatives. "Oh take *him*!" Mrs. Monarch murmured sweetly, looking at her husband; and "What could you want better than my wife?" the Major enquired with the comfortable candour that now prevailed between us.

I wasn't obliged to answer these remarks—I was only obliged to place my sitters. I wasn't easy in mind, and I postponed a little timidly perhaps the solving of my question. The book was a large canvas, the other figures were numerous, and I worked off at first some of the episodes in which the hero and the heroine were not concerned. When once I had set *them* up I should have to stick to them—I couldn't make my young man seven feet high in one place and five feet nine in another. I inclined on the whole to the latter measurement, though the Major more than once reminded me that *he* looked

9. Beggar (Italian).
1. Knickerbockers (close-fitting short pants gathered at the knee) and kilts (knee-length pleated skirts, usually of tartan, worn by Scottish men) suggest a rural, outdoor attire.

about as young as any one. It was indeed quite possible to arrange him, for the figure, so that it would have been difficult to detect his age. After the spontaneous Oronte had been with me a month, and after I had given him to understand several times over that his native exuberance would presently constitute an insurmountable barrier to our further intercourse, I waked to a sense of his heroic capacity. He was only five feet seven, but the remaining inches were latent. I tried him almost secretly at first, for I was really rather afraid of the judgment my other models would pass on such a choice. If they regarded Miss Churm as little better than a snare what would they think of the representation by a person so little the real thing as an Italian street-vendor of a protagonist formed by a public school?

If I went a little in fear of them it wasn't because they bullied me, because they had got an oppressive foothold, but because in their really pathetic decorum and mysteriously permanent newness they counted on me so intensely. I was therefore very glad when Jack Hawley came home: he was always of such good counsel. He painted badly himself, but there was no one like him for putting his finger on the place. He had been absent from England for a year; he had been somewhere—I don't remember where—to get a fresh eye. I was in a good deal of dread of any such organ, but we were old friends; he had been away for months and a sense of emptiness was creeping into my life. I hadn't dodged a missile for a year.

He came back with a fresh eye, but with the same old black velvet blouse, and the first evening he spent in my studio we smoked cigarettes till the small hours. He had done no work himself, he had only got the eye; so the field was clear for the production of my little things. He wanted to see what I had produced for the *Cheapside*, but he was disappointed in the exhibition. That at least seemed the meaning of two or three comprehensive groans which, as he lounged on my big divan, his leg folded under him, looking at my latest drawings, issued from his lips with the smoke of the cigarette.

"What's the matter with you?" I asked.

"What's the matter with *you?*"

"Nothing save that I'm mystified."

"You are indeed. You're quite off the hinge. What's the meaning of this new fad?" And he tossed me, with visible irreverence, a drawing in which I happened to have depicted both my elegant models. I asked if he didn't think it good, and he replied that it struck him as execrable, given the sort of thing I had always represented myself to him as wishing to arrive at; but I let that pass—I was so anxious to see exactly what he meant. The two figures in the picture looked colossal, but I supposed this was *not* what he meant, inasmuch as, for aught he knew the contrary, I might have been trying for some such effect. I maintained that I was working exactly in the same way as when he last had done me the honour to tell me I might do something some day. "Well, there's a screw loose somewhere," he answered; "wait a bit and I'll discover it." I depended upon him to do so: where else was the fresh eye? But he produced at last nothing more luminous than "I don't know—I don't like your types." This was lame for a critic who had never consented to discuss with me anything but the question of execution, the direction of strokes and the mystery of values.

"In the drawings you've been looking at I think my types are very handsome."

"Oh they won't do!"

"I've been working with new models."

"I see you have. *They* won't do."

"Are you very sure of that?"

"Absolutely—they're stupid."

"You mean *I* am—for I ought to get round that."

"You *can't*—with such people. Who are they?"

I told him, so far as was necessary, and he concluded heartlessly: "*Ce sont des gens qu'il faut mettre à la porte.*"[2]

"You've never seen them; they're awfully good"—I flew to their defence.

"Not seen them? Why all this recent work of yours drops to pieces with them. It's all I want to see of them."

"No one else has said anything against it—the *Cheapside* people are pleased."

"Everyone else is an ass, and the *Cheapside* people the biggest asses of all. Come, don't pretend at this time of day to have pretty illusions about the public, especially about publishers and editors. It's not for *such* animals you work—it's for those who know, *coloro che sanno*;[3] so keep straight for *me* if you can't keep straight for yourself. There was a certain sort of thing you used to try for—and a very good thing it was. But this twaddle isn't *in* it." When I talked with Hawley later about "Rutland Ramsay" and its possible successors he declared that I must get back into my boat again or I should go to the bottom. His voice in short was the voice of warning.

I noted the warning, but I didn't turn my friends out of doors. They bored me a good deal; but the very fact that they bored me admonished me not to sacrifice them—if there was anything to be done with them—simply to irritation. As I look back at this phase they seem to me to have pervaded my life not a little. I have a vision of them as most of the time in my studio, seated against the wall on an old velvet bench to be out of the way, and resembling the while a pair of patient courtiers in a royal ante-chamber. I'm convinced that during the coldest weeks of the winter they held their ground because it saved them fire. Their newness was losing its gloss, and it was impossible not to feel them objects of charity. Whenever Miss Churm arrived they went away, and after I was fairly launched in "Rutland Ramsay" Miss Churm arrived pretty often. They managed to express to me tacitly that they supposed I wanted her for the low life of the book, and I let them suppose it, since they had attempted to study the work—it was lying about the studio—without discovering that it dealt only with the highest circles. They had dipped into the most brilliant of our novelists without deciphering many passages. I still took an hour from them, now and again, in spite of Jack Hawley's warning: it would be time enough to dismiss them, if dismissal should be necessary, when the rigour of the season was over. Hawley had made their acquaintance—he had met them at my fireside—and thought them a ridiculous pair. Learning that he was a painter they tried to approach him, to show him too that they were the real thing; but he looked at them, across the big room, as if they were miles away: they were a compendium of everything he most objected to in the social system of his country. Such people

2. Such people should be shown the door (French).
3. A misquotation of a phrase Dante applied to Aristotle in *The Divine Comedy*, "Inferno," 4.131, which reads, *"el maestro di color che sanno,"* literally, "the master of those who know."

as that, all convention and patent-leather, with ejaculations that stopped conversation, had no business in a studio. A studio was a place to learn to see,
and how could you see through a pair of feather-beds?

The main inconvenience I suffered at their hands was that at first I was
shy of letting it break upon them that my artful little servant had begun to
sit to me for "Rutland Ramsay." They knew I had been odd enough—they
were prepared by this time to allow oddity to artists—to pick a foreign vagabond out of the streets when I might have had a person with whiskers and
credentials, but it was some time before they learned how high I rated his
accomplishments. They found him in an attitude more than once, but they
never doubted I was doing him as an organ-grinder. There were several things
they never guessed, and one of them was that for a striking scene in the
novel, in which a footman briefly figured, it occurred to me to make use of
Major Monarch as the menial. I kept putting this off, I didn't like to ask him
to don the livery—besides the difficulty of finding a livery to fit him. At last,
one day late in the winter, when I was at work on the despised Oronte, who
caught one's idea on the wing, and was in the glow of feeling myself go very
straight, they came in, the Major and his wife, with their society laugh about
nothing (there was less and less to laugh at); came in like country-callers—
they always reminded me of that—who have walked across the park after
church and are presently persuaded to stay to luncheon. Luncheon was over,
but they could stay to tea—I knew they wanted it. The fit was on me, however, and I couldn't let my ardour cool and my work wait, with the fading
daylight, while my model prepared it. So I asked Mrs. Monarch if she would
mind laying it out—a request which for an instant brought all the blood to
her face. Her eyes were on her husband's for a second, and some mute teleg-
raphy passed between them. Their folly was over the next instant; his cheerful shrewdness put an end to it. So far from pitying their wounded pride, I
must add, I was moved to give it as complete a lesson as I could. They bus-
tled about together and got out the cups and saucers and made the kettle
boil. I know they felt as if they were waiting on my servant, and when the
tea was prepared I said: "He'll have a cup, please—he's tired." Mrs. Monarch brought him one where he stood, and he took it from her as if he had
been a gentleman at a party squeezing a crush-hat with an elbow.

Then it came over me that she had made a great effort for me—made it
with a kind of nobleness—and that I owed her a compensation. Each time
I saw her after this I wondered what the compensation could be. I couldn't
go on doing the wrong thing to oblige them. Oh it *was* the wrong thing, the
stamp of the work for which they sat—Hawley was not the only person to
say it now. I sent in a large number of the drawings I had made for "Rutland
Ramsay," and I received a warning that was more to the point than Hawley's. The artistic adviser of the house for which I was working was of opinion that many of my illustrations were not what had been looked for. Most
of these illustrations were the subjects in which the Monarchs had figured.
Without going into the question of what *had* been looked for, I had to face
the fact that at this rate I shouldn't get the other books to do. I hurled myself
in despair on Miss Churm—I put her through all her paces. I not only
adopted Oronte publicly as my hero, but one morning when the Major looked
in to see if I didn't require him to finish a *Cheapside* figure for which he had
begun to sit the week before, I told him I had changed my mind—I'd do the

drawing from my man. At this my visitor turned pale and stood looking at me. "Is *he* your idea of an English gentleman?" he asked.

I was disappointed, I was nervous, I wanted to get on with my work; so I replied with irritation: "Oh my dear Major—I can't be ruined for *you!*"

It was a horrid speech, but he stood another moment—after which, without a word, he quitted the studio. I drew a long breath, for I said to myself that I shouldn't see him again. I hadn't told him definitely that I was in danger of having my work rejected, but I was vexed at his not having felt the catastrophe in the air, read with me the moral of our fruitless collaboration, the lesson that in the deceptive atmosphere of art even the highest respectability may fail of being plastic.

I didn't owe my friends money, but I did see them again. They reappeared together three days later, and, given all the other facts, there was something tragic in that one. It was a clear proof they could find nothing else in life to do. They had threshed the matter out in a dismal conference—they had digested the bad news that they were not in for the series. If they weren't useful to me even for the *Cheapside* their function seemed difficult to determine, and I could only judge at first that they had come, forgivingly, decorously, to take a last leave. This made me rejoice in secret that I had little leisure for a scene; for I had placed both my other models in position together and I was pegging away at a drawing from which I hoped to derive glory. It had been suggested by the passage in which Rutland Ramsay, drawing up a chair to Artemisia's piano-stool, says extraordinary things to her while she ostensibly fingers out a difficult piece of music. I had done Miss Churm at the piano before—it was an attitude in which she knew how to take on an absolutely poetic grace. I wished the two figures to "compose" together with intensity, and my little Italian had entered perfectly into my conception. The pair were vividly before me, the piano had been pulled out; it was a charming show of blended youth and murmured love, which I had only to catch and keep. My visitors stood and looked at it, and I was friendly to them over my shoulder.

They made no response, but I was used to silent company and went on with my work, only a little disconcerted—even though exhilarated by the sense that *this* was at least the ideal thing—at not having got rid of them after all. Presently I heard Mrs. Monarch's sweet voice beside or rather above me: "I wish her hair were a little better done." I looked up and she was staring with a strange fixedness at Miss Churm, whose back was turned to her. "Do you mind my just touching it?" she went on—a question which made me spring up for an instant as with the instinctive fear that she might do the young lady a harm. But she quieted me with a glance I shall never forget—I confess I should like to have been able to paint *that*—and went for a moment to my model. She spoke to her softly, laying a hand on her shoulder and bending over her; and as the girl, understanding, gratefully assented, she disposed her rough curls, with a few quick passes, in such a way as to make Miss Churm's head twice as charming. It was one of the most heroic personal services I've ever seen rendered. Then Mrs. Monarch turned away with a low sigh and, looking about her as if for something to do, stooped to the floor with a noble humility and picked up a dirty rag that had dropped out of my paint-box.

The Major meanwhile had also been looking for something to do, and, wandering to the other end of the studio, saw before him my breakfast-things neglected, unremoved. "I say, can't I be useful *here?*" he called out to me with an irrepressible quaver. I assented with a laugh that I fear was awkward, and for the next ten minutes, while I worked, I heard the light clatter of china and the tinkle of spoons and glass. Mrs. Monarch assisted her husband—they washed up my crockery, they put it away. They wandered off into my little scullery, and I afterwards found that they had cleaned my knives and that my slender stock of plate had an unprecedented surface. When it came over me, the latent eloquence of what they were doing, I confess that my drawing was blurred for a moment—the picture swam. They had accepted their failure, but they couldn't accept their fate. They had bowed their heads in bewilderment to the perverse and cruel law in virtue of which the real thing could be so much less precious than the unreal; but they didn't want to starve. If my servants were my models, then my models might be my servants. They would reverse the parts—the others would sit for the ladies and gentlemen and *they* would do the work. They would still be in the studio—it was an intense dumb appeal to me not to turn them out. "Take us on," they wanted to say—"we'll do *anything*."

My pencil dropped from my hand; my sitting was spoiled and I got rid of my sitters, who were also evidently rather mystified and awestruck. Then, alone with the Major and his wife I had a most uncomfortable moment. He put their prayer into a single sentence: "I say, you know—just let *us* do for you, can't you?" I couldn't—it was dreadful to see them emptying my slops; but I pretended I could, to oblige them, for about a week. Then I gave them a sum of money to go away, and I never saw them again. I obtained the remaining books, but my friend Hawley repeats that Major and Mrs. Monarch did me a permanent harm, got me into false ways. If it be true I'm content to have paid the price—for the memory.

1892, 1909

The Beast in the Jungle[1]

I

What determined the speech that startled him in the course of their encounter scarcely matters, being probably but some words spoken by himself quite without intention—spoken as they lingered and slowly moved together after their renewal of acquaintance. He had been conveyed by friends an hour or two before to the house at which she was staying; the party of visitors at the other house, of whom he was one, and thanks to whom it was his theory, as always, that he was lost in the crowd, had been invited over to luncheon. There had been after luncheon much dispersal, all in the interest of the original motive, a view of Weatherend itself and the fine things, intrinsic features, pictures, heirlooms, treasures of all the arts, that made the place almost famous; and the great rooms were so numerous that guests could wander at their will, hang back from the principal group and in cases

---

1. James initially recorded the idea for this story in 1895, but it first appeared in the collection *The Better Sort* (1903). It was reprinted, with minor revisions, in the *Altar of the Dead* volume of the New York edition, Vol. 17 (1909), the source of the text printed here.

where they took such matters with the last seriousness give themselves up to mysterious appreciations and measurements. There were persons to be observed, singly or in couples, bending toward objects in out-of-the-way corners with their hands on their knees and their heads nodding quite as with the emphasis of an excited sense of smell. When they were two they either mingled their sounds of ecstasy or melted into silences of even deeper import, so that there were aspects of the occasion that gave it for Marcher much the air of the "look round," previous to a sale highly advertised, that excites or quenches, as may be, the dream of acquisition. The dream of acquisition at Weatherend would have had to be wild indeed, and John Marcher found himself, among such suggestions, disconcerted almost equally by the presence of those who knew too much and by that of those who knew nothing. The great rooms caused so much poetry and history to press upon him that he needed some straying apart to feel in a proper relation with them, though this impulse was not, as happened, like the gloating of some of his companions, to be compared to the movements of a dog sniffing a cupboard. It had an issue promptly enough in a direction that was not to have been calculated.

It led, briefly, in the course of the October afternoon, to his closer meeting with May Bartram, whose face, a reminder, yet not quite a remembrance, as they sat much separated at a very long table, had begun merely by troubling him rather pleasantly. It affected him as the sequel of something of which he had lost the beginning. He knew it, and for the time quite welcomed it, as a continuation, but didn't know what it continued, which was an interest or an amusement the greater as he was also somehow aware— yet without a direct sign from her—that the young woman herself hadn't lost the thread. She hadn't lost it, but she wouldn't give it back to him, he saw, without some putting forth of his hand for it; and he not only saw that, but saw several things more, things odd enough in the light of the fact that at the moment some accident of grouping brought them face to face he was still merely fumbling with the idea that any contact between them in the past would have had no importance. If it had had no importance he scarcely knew why his actual impression of her should so seem to have so much; the answer to which, however, was that in such a life as they all appeared to be leading for the moment one could but take things as they came. He was satisfied, without in the least being able to say why, that this young lady might roughly have ranked in the house as a poor relation; satisfied also that she was not there on a brief visit, but was more or less a part of the establishment— almost a working, a remunerated part. Didn't she enjoy at periods a protection that she paid for by helping, among other services, to show the place and explain it, deal with the tiresome people, answer questions about the dates of the building, the styles of the furniture, the authorship of the pictures, the favourite haunts of the ghost? It wasn't that she looked as if you could have given her shillings—it was impossible to look less so. Yet when she finally drifted toward him, distinctly handsome, though ever so much older—older than when he had seen her before—it might have been as an effect of her guessing that he had, within the couple of hours, devoted more imagination to her than to all the others put together, and had thereby penetrated to a kind of truth that the others were too stupid for. She *was* there on harder terms than any one; she was there as a consequence of things suffered, one way and another, in the interval of years; and she remembered him very much as she was remembered—only a good deal better.

By the time they at last thus came to speech they were alone in one of the rooms—remarkable for a fine portrait over the chimney-place—out of which their friends had passed, and the charm of it was that even before they had spoken they had practically arranged with each other to stay behind for talk. The charm, happily, was in other things too—partly in there being scarce a spot at Weatherend without something to stay behind for. It was in the way the autumn day looked into the high windows as it waned; the way the red light, breaking at the close from under a low sombre sky, reached out in a long shaft and played over old wainscots, old tapestry, old gold, old colour. It was most of all perhaps in the way she came to him as if, since she had been turned on to deal with the simpler sort, he might, should he choose to keep the whole thing down, just take her mild attention for a part of her general business. As soon as he heard her voice, however, the gap was filled up and the missing link supplied; the slight irony he divined in her attitude lost its advantage. He almost jumped at it to get there before her. "I met you years and years ago in Rome. I remember all about it." She confessed to disappointment— she had been so sure he didn't; and to prove how well he did he began to pour forth the particular recollections that popped up as he called for them. Her face and her voice, all at his service now, worked the miracle—the impression operating like the torch of a lamplighter who touches into flame, one by one, a long row of gas-jets. Marcher flattered himself the illumination was brilliant, yet he was really still more pleased on her showing him, with amusement, that in his haste to make everything right he had got most things rather wrong. It hadn't been at Rome—it had been at Naples; and it hadn't been eight years before—it had been more nearly ten. She hadn't been, either, with her uncle and aunt, but with her mother and her brother; in addition to which it was not with the Pembles *he* had been, but with the Boyers, coming down in their company from Rome—a point on which she insisted, a little to his confusion, and as to which she had her evidence in hand. The Boyers she had known, but didn't know the Pembles, though she had heard of them, and it was the people he was with who had made them acquainted. The incident of the thunderstorm that had raged round them with such violence as to drive them for refuge into an excavation—this incident had not occurred at the Palace of the Cæsars, but at Pompeii,[2] on an occasion when they had been present there at an important find.

He accepted her amendments, he enjoyed her corrections, though the moral of them was, she pointed out, that he *really* didn't remember the least thing about her; and he only felt it as a drawback that when all was made strictly historic there didn't appear much of anything left. They lingered together still, she neglecting her office—for from the moment he was so clever she had no proper right to him—and both neglecting the house, just waiting as to see if a memory or two more wouldn't again breathe on them. It hadn't taken them many minutes, after all, to put down on the table, like the cards of a pack, those that constituted their respective hands; only what came out was that the pack was unfortunately not perfect—that the past, invoked, invited, encouraged, could give them, naturally, no more than it

2. Pompeii is near Naples, not Rome.

had. It had made them anciently meet—her at twenty, him at twenty-five; but nothing was so strange, they seemed to say to each other, as that, while so occupied, it hadn't done a little more for them. They looked at each other as with the feeling of an occasion missed; the present would have been so much better if the other, in the far distance, in the foreign land, hadn't been so stupidly meagre. There weren't apparently, all counted, more than a dozen little old things that had succeeded in coming to pass between them; trivialities of youth, simplicities of freshness, stupidities of ignorance, small possible germs, but too deeply buried—too deeply (didn't it seem?) to sprout after so many years. Marcher could only feel he ought to have rendered her some service—saved her from a capsized boat in the Bay or at least recovered her dressing-bag, filched from her cab in the streets of Naples by a lazzarone[3] with a stiletto. Or it would have been nice if he could have been taken with fever all alone at his hotel, and she could have come to look after him, to write to his people, to drive him out in convalescence. *Then* they would be in possession of the something or other that their actual show seemed to lack. It yet somehow presented itself, this show, as too good to be spoiled; so that they were reduced for a few minutes more to wondering a little helplessly why—since they seemed to know a certain number of the same people—their reunion had been so long averted. They didn't use that name for it, but their delay from minute to minute to join the others was a kind of confession that they didn't quite want it to be a failure. Their attempted supposition of reasons for their not having met but showed how little they knew of each other. There came in fact a moment when Marcher felt a positive pang. It was vain to pretend she was an old friend, for all the communities were wanting, in spite of which it was as an old friend that he saw she would have suited him. He had new ones enough—was surrounded with them for instance on the stage of the other house; as a new one he probably wouldn't have so much as noticed her. He would have liked to invent something, get her to make-believe with him that some passage of a romantic or critical kind *had* originally occurred. He was really almost reaching out in imagination—as against time—for something that would do, and saying to himself that if it didn't come this sketch of a fresh start would show for quite awkwardly bungled. They would separate, and now for no second or no third chance. They would have tried and not succeeded. Then it was, just at the turn, as he afterwards made it out to himself, that, everything else failing, she herself decided to take up the case and, as it were, save the situation. He felt as soon as she spoke that she had been consciously keeping back what she said and hoping to get on without it; a scruple in her that immensely touched him when, by the end of three or four minutes more, he was able to measure it. What she brought out, at any rate, quite cleared the air and supplied the link—the link it was so odd he should frivolously have managed to lose.

"You know you told me something I've never forgotten and that again and again has made me think of you since; it was that tremendously hot day when we went to Sorrento,[4] across the bay, for the breeze. What I allude to was what you said to me, on the way back, as we sat under the awning of the boat enjoying the cool. Have you forgotten?"

3. Beggar (Italian).   4. Resort town across the bay from Naples.

He had forgotten and was even more surprised than ashamed. But the great thing was that he saw in this no vulgar reminder of any "sweet" speech. The vanity of women had long memories, but she was making no claim on him of a compliment or a mistake. With another woman, a totally different one, he might have feared the recall possibly of even some imbecile "offer." So, in having to say that he had indeed forgotten, he was conscious rather of a loss than of a gain; he already saw an interest in the matter of her mention. "I try to think—but I give it up. Yet I remember the Sorrento day."

"I'm not very sure you do," May Bartram after a moment said; "and I'm not very sure I ought to want you to. It's dreadful to bring a person back at any time to what he was ten years before. If you've lived away from it," she smiled, "so much the better."

"Ah if *you* haven't why should I?" he asked.

"Lived away, you mean, from what I myself was?"

"From what *I* was. I was of course an ass," Marcher went on; "but I would rather know from you just the sort of ass I was than—from the moment you have something in your mind—not know anything."

Still, however, she hesitated. "But if you've completely ceased to be that sort—?"

"Why I can then all the more bear to know. Besides, perhaps I haven't."

"Perhaps. Yet if you haven't," she added. "I should suppose you'd remember. Not indeed that *I* in the least connect with my impression the invidious name you use. If I had only thought you foolish," she explained, "the thing I speak of wouldn't so have remained with me. It was about yourself." She waited as if it might come to him; but as, only meeting her eyes in wonder, he gave no sign, she burnt her ships.[5] "Has it ever happened?"

Then it was that, while he continued to stare, a light broke for him and the blood slowly came to his face, which began to burn with recognition. "Do you mean I told you—?" But he faltered, lest what came to him shouldn't be right, lest he should only give himself away.

"It was something about yourself that it was natural one shouldn't forget—that is if one remembered you at all. That's why I ask you," she smiled, "if the thing you then spoke of has ever come to pass?"

Oh then he saw, but he was lost in wonder and found himself embarrassed. This, he also saw, made her sorry for him, as if her allusion had been a mistake. It took him but a moment, however, to feel it hadn't been, much as it had been a surprise. After the first little shock of it her knowledge on the contrary began, even if rather strangely, to taste sweet to him. She was the only other person in the world then who would have it, and she had had it all these years, while the fact of his having so breathed his secret had unaccountably faded from him. No wonder they couldn't have met as if nothing had happened. "I judge," he finally said, "that I know what you mean. Only I had strangely enough lost any sense of having taken you so far into my confidence."

"Is it because you've taken so many others as well?"

"I've taken nobody. Not a creature since then."

"So that I'm the only person who knows?"

"The only person in the world."

5. I.e., proceeded boldly; "burned her bridges."

"Well," she quickly replied, "I myself have never spoken. I've never, never repeated of you what you told me." She looked at him so that he perfectly believed her. Their eyes met over it in such a way that he was without a doubt. "And I never will."

She spoke with an earnestness that, as if almost excessive, put him at ease about her possible derision. Somehow the whole question was a new luxury to him—that is from the moment she was in possession. If she didn't take the sarcastic view she clearly took the sympathetic, and that was what he had had, in all the long time, from no one whomsoever. What he felt was that he couldn't at present have begun to tell her, and yet could profit perhaps exquisitely by the accident of having done so of old. "Please don't then. We're just right as it is."

"Oh I am," she laughed, "if you are!" To which she added: "Then you do still feel in the same way?"

It was impossible he shouldn't take to himself that she was really interested, though it all kept coming as perfect surprise. He had thought of himself so long as abominably alone, and lo he wasn't alone a bit. He hadn't been, it appeared, for an hour—since those moments on the Sorrento boat. It was *she* who had been, he seemed to see as he looked at her—she who had been made so by the graceless fact of his lapse of fidelity. To tell her what he had told her—what had it been but to ask something of her? something that she had given, in her charity, without his having, by a remembrance, by a return of the spirit, failing another encounter, so much as thanked her. What he had asked of her had been simply at first not to laugh at him. She had beautifully not done so for ten years, and she was not doing so now. So he had endless gratitude to make up. Only for that he must see just how he had figured to her. "What, exactly, was the account I gave—?"

"Of the way you did feel? Well, it was very simple. You said you had had from your earliest time, as the deepest thing within you, the sense of being kept for something rare and strange, possibly prodigious and terrible, that was sooner or later to happen to you, that you had in your bones the foreboding and the conviction of, and that would perhaps overwhelm you."

"Do you call that very simple?" John Marcher asked.

She thought a moment. "It was perhaps because I seemed, as you spoke, to understand it."

"You do understand it?" he eagerly asked.

Again she kept her kind eyes on him. "You still have the belief?"

"Oh!" he exclaimed helplessly. There was too much to say.

"Whatever it's to be," she clearly made out, "it hasn't yet come."

He shook his head in complete surrender now. "It hasn't yet come. Only, you know, it isn't anything I'm to *do*, to achieve in the world, to be distinguished or admired for. I'm not such an ass as *that*. It would be much better, no doubt, if I were."

"It's to be something you're merely to suffer?"

"Well, say to wait for—to have to meet, to face, to see suddenly break out in my life; possibly destroying all further consciousness, possibly annihilating me; possibly, on the other hand, only altering everything, striking at the root of all my world and leaving me to the consequences, however they shape themselves."

She took this in, but the light in her eyes continued for him not to be that of mockery. "Isn't what you describe perhaps but the expectation—or at any rate the sense of danger, familiar to so many people—of falling in love?"

John Marcher wondered. "Did you ask me that before?"

"No—I wasn't so free-and-easy then. But it's what strikes me now."

"Of course," he said after a moment, "it strikes you. Of course it strikes *me*. Of course what's in store for me may be no more than that. The only thing is," he went on, "that I think if it had been that I should by this time know."

"Do you mean because you've *been* in love?" And then as he but looked at her in silence: "You've been in love, and it hasn't meant such a cataclysm, hasn't proved the great affair?"

"Here I am, you see. It hasn't been overwhelming."

"Then it hasn't been love," said May Bartram.

"Well, I at least thought it was. I took it for that—I've taken it till now. It was agreeable, it was delightful, it was miserable," he explained. "But it wasn't strange. It wasn't what *my* affair's to be."

"You want something all to yourself—something that nobody else knows or *has* known?"

"It isn't a question of what I 'want'—God knows I don't want anything. It's only a question of the apprehension that haunts me—that I live with day by day."

He said this so lucidly and consistently that he could see it further impose itself. If she hadn't been interested before she'd have been interested now. "Is it a sense of coming violence?"

Evidently now too again he liked to talk of it. "I don't think of it as—when it does come—necessarily violent. I only think of it as natural and as of course above all unmistakeable. I think of it simply as *the* thing. *The* thing will of itself appear natural."

"Then how will it appear strange?"

Marcher bethought himself. "It won't—to *me*."

"To whom then?"

"Well," he replied, smiling at last, "say to you."

"Oh then I'm to be present?"

"Why you *are* present—since you know."

"I see." She turned it over. "But I mean at the catastrophe."[6]

At this, for a minute, their lightness gave way to their gravity; it was as if the long look they exchanged held them together. "It will only depend on yourself—if you'll watch with me."

"Are you afraid?" she asked.

"Don't leave me *now*," he went on.

"Are you afraid?" she repeated.

"Do you think me simply out of my mind?" he pursued instead of answering. "Do I merely strike you as a harmless lunatic?"

"No," said May Bartram. "I understand you. I believe you."

"You mean you feel how my obsession—poor old thing!—may correspond to some possible reality?"

"To some possible reality."

---

6. Final event, usually of a play, and not necessarily catastrophic.

"Then you *will* watch with me?"

She hesitated, then for the third time put her question. "Are you afraid?"

"Did I tell you I was—at Naples?"

"No, you said nothing about it."

"Then I don't know. And I should *like* to know," said John Marcher. "You'll tell me yourself whether you think so. If you'll watch with me you'll see."

"Very good then." They had been moving by this time across the room, and at the door, before passing out, they paused as for the full wind-up of their understanding. "I'll watch with you," said May Bartram.

II

The fact that she "knew"—knew and yet neither chaffed him nor betrayed him—had in a short time begun to constitute between them a goodly bond, which became more marked when, within the year that followed their afternoon at Weatherend, the opportunities for meeting multiplied. The event that thus promoted these occasions was the death of the ancient lady her great-aunt, under whose wing, since losing her mother, she had to such an extent found shelter, and who, though but the widowed mother of the new successor to the property, had succeeded—thanks to a high tone and a high temper—in not forfeiting the supreme position at the great house. The deposition of this personage arrived but with her death, which, followed by many changes, made in particular a difference for the young woman in whom Marcher's expert attention had recognised from the first a dependent with a pride that might ache though it didn't bristle. Nothing for a long time had made him easier than the thought that the aching must have been much soothed by Miss Bartram's now finding herself able to set up a small home in London. She had acquired property, to an amount that made that luxury just possible, under her aunt's extremely complicated will, and when the whole matter began to be straightened out, which indeed took time, she let him know that the happy issue was at last in view. He had seen her again before that day, both because she had more than once accompanied the ancient lady to town and because he had paid another visit to the friends who so conveniently made of Weatherend one of the charms of their own hospitality. These friends had taken him back there; he had achieved there again with Miss Bartram some quiet detachment; and he had in London succeeded in persuading her to more than one brief absence from her aunt. They went together, on these latter occasions, to the National Gallery and the South Kensington Museum,[7] where, among vivid reminders, they talked of Italy at large—not now attempting to recover, as at first, the taste of their youth and their ignorance. That recovery, the first day at Weatherend, had served its purpose well, had given them quite enough; so that they were, to Marcher's sense, no longer hovering about the headwaters of their stream, but had felt their boat pushed sharply off and down the current.

They were literally afloat together; for our gentleman this was marked, quite as marked as that the fortunate cause of it was just the buried treasure of her knowledge. He had with his own hands dug up this little hoard, brought

7. Art museums in London; the South Kensington Museum is now called the Victoria and Albert Museum.

to light—that is to within reach of the dim day constituted by their discretions and privacies—the object of value the hiding-place of which he had, after putting it into the ground himself, so strangely, so long forgotten. The rare luck of his having again just stumbled on the spot made him indifferent to any other question; he would doubtless have devoted more time to the odd accident of his lapse of memory if he hadn't been moved to devote so much to the sweetness, the comfort, as he felt, for the future, that this accident itself had helped to keep fresh. It had never entered into his plan that any one should "know," and mainly for the reason that it wasn't in him to tell any one. That would have been impossible, for nothing but the amusement of a cold world would have waited on it. Since, however, a mysterious fate had opened his mouth betimes, in spite of him, he would count that a compensation and profit by it to the utmost. That the right person *should* know tempered the asperity of his secret more even than his shyness had permitted him to imagine; and May Bartram was clearly right, because—well, because there she was. Her knowledge simply settled it; he would have been sure enough by this time had she been wrong. There was that in his situation, no doubt, that disposed him too much to see her as a mere confidant, taking all her light for him from the fact—the fact only—of her interest in his predicament; from her mercy, sympathy, seriousness, her consent not to regard him as the funniest of the funny. Aware, in fine, that her price for him was just in her giving him this constant sense of his being admirably spared, he was careful to remember that she had also a life of her own, with things that might happen to *her,* things that in friendship one should likewise take account of. Something fairly remarkable came to pass with him, for that matter, in this connexion—something represented by a certain passage of his consciousness, in the suddenest way, from one extreme to the other.

He had thought himself, so long as nobody knew, the most disinterested person in the world, carrying his concentrated burden, his perpetual suspense, ever so quietly, holding his tongue about it, giving others no glimpse of it nor of its effect upon his life, asking of them no allowance and only making on his side all those that were asked. He hadn't disturbed people with the queerness of their having to know a haunted man, though he had had moments of rather special temptation on hearing them say they were forsooth "unsettled." If they were as unsettled as he was—he who had never been settled for an hour in his life—they would know what it meant. Yet it wasn't, all the same, for him to make them, and he listened to them civilly enough. This was why he had such good—though possibly such rather colourless—manners; this was why, above all, he could regard himself, in a greedy world, as decently—as in fact perhaps even a little sublimely—unselfish. Our point is accordingly that he valued this character quite sufficiently to measure his present danger of letting it lapse, against which he promised himself to be much on his guard. He was quite ready, none the less, to be selfish just a little, since surely no more charming occasion for it had come to him. "Just a little," in a word, was just as much as Miss Bartram, taking one day with another, would let him. He never would be in the least coercive, and would keep well before him the lines on which consideration for her—the very highest—ought to proceed. He would thoroughly establish the heads under which her affairs, her requirements, her peculiarities—he went so far as to give them the latitude of that name—would come into their intercourse. All this naturally was a sign of how much he took the intercourse itself for granted. There was nothing more to be done about *that*. It simply existed; had sprung into being with her first penetrating question to him in the autumn light there at Weatherend. The real form it should have taken on the basis that stood out large was the form of their marrying. But the devil in this was that the very basis itself put marrying out of the question. His conviction, his apprehension, his obsession, in short, wasn't a privilege he could invite a woman to share; and that consequence of it was precisely what was the matter with him. Something or other lay in wait for him, amid the twists and the turns of the months and the years, like a crouching beast in the jungle. It signified little whether the crouching beast were destined to slay him or to be slain. The definite point was the inevitable spring of the creature; and the definite lesson from that was that a man of feeling didn't cause himself to be accompanied by a lady on a tiger-hunt. Such was the image under which he had ended by figuring his life.

They had at first, none the less, in the scattered hours spent together, made no allusion to that view of it; which was a sign he was handsomely alert to give that he didn't expect, that he in fact didn't care, always to be talking about it. Such a feature in one's outlook was really like a hump on one's back. The difference it made every minute of the day existed quite independently of discussion. One discussed of course *like* a hunchback, for there was always, if nothing else, the hunchback face. That remained, and she was watching him; but people watched best, as a general thing, in silence, so that such would be predominantly the manner of their vigil. Yet he didn't want, at the same time, to be tense and solemn; tense and solemn was what he imagined he too much showed for with other people. The thing to be, with the one person who knew, was easy and natural—to make the reference rather than be seeming to avoid it, to avoid it rather than be seeming to make it, and to keep it, in any case, familiar, facetious even, rather than pedantic and portentous. Some such consideration as the latter was doubtless in his mind for instance when he wrote pleasantly to Miss Bartram that perhaps the great thing he had so long felt as in the lap of the gods was no more than this circumstance, which touched him so nearly, of her acquiring a house in London. It was the first allusion they had yet again made, needing any other hitherto so little; but when she replied, after having given him the news, that she was by no means satisfied with such a trifle as the climax to so special a suspense, she almost set him wondering if she hadn't even a larger conception of singularity for him than he had for himself. He was at all events destined to become aware little by little, as time went by, that she was all the while looking at his life, judging it, measuring it, in the light of the thing she knew, which grew to be at last, with the consecration of the years, never mentioned between them save as "the real truth" about him. That had always been his own form of reference to it, but she adopted the form so quietly that, looking back at the end of a period, he knew there was no moment at which it was traceable that she had, as he might say, got inside his idea, or exchanged the attitude of beautifully indulging for that of still more beautifully believing him.

It was always open to him to accuse her of seeing him but as the most harmless of maniacs, and this, in the long run—since it covered so much ground—was his easiest description of their friendship. He had a screw loose for her, but she liked him in spite of it and was practically, against the rest of the world, his kind wise keeper, unremunerated but fairly amused and, in the absence of other near ties, not disreputably occupied. The rest of the world of course thought him queer, but she, she only, knew how, and above all why, queer; which was precisely what enabled her to dispose the concealing veil in the right folds. She took his gaiety from him—since it had to pass with them for gaiety—as she took everything else; but she certainly so far justified by her unerring touch his finer sense of the degree to which he had ended by convincing her. *She* at least never spoke of the secret of his life except as "the real truth about you," and she had in fact a wonderful way of making it seem, as such, the secret of her own life too. That was in fine how he so constantly felt her as allowing for him; he couldn't on the whole call it anything else. He allowed for himself, but she, exactly, allowed still more; partly because, better placed for a sight of the matter, she traced his unhappy perversion through reaches of its course into which he could scarce follow it. He knew how he felt, but, besides knowing that, she knew how he *looked* as well; he knew each of the things of importance he was insidiously kept from doing, but she could add up the amount they made, understand how much, with a lighter weight on his spirit, he might have done, and thereby establish how, clever as he was, he fell short. Above all she was in the secret of the difference between the forms he went through—those of his little office under Government,[8] those of caring for his modest patrimony, for his library, for his garden in the country, for the people in London whose invitations he accepted and repaid—and the detachment that reigned beneath them and that made of all behaviour, all that could in the least be called behaviour, a long act of dissimulation. What it had come to was that he wore a mask painted with the social simper, out of the eyeholes of which there looked eyes of an expression not in the least matching the other features. This the stupid world, even after years, had never more than half-discovered. It was only May Bartram who had, and she achieved, by an art indescribable, the feat of at once—or perhaps it was only alternately—meeting the eyes from in front and mingling her own vision, as from over his shoulder, with their peep through the apertures.

So while they grew older together she did watch with him, and so she let this association give shape and colour to her own existence. Beneath *her* forms as well detachment had learned to sit, and behaviour had become for her, in the social sense, a false account of herself. There was but one account of her that would have been true all the while and that she could give straight to nobody, least of all to John Marcher. Her whole attitude was a virtual statement, but the perception of that only seemed called to take its place for him as one of the many things necessarily crowded out of his consciousness. If she had moreover, like himself, to make sacrifices to their real truth, it was to be granted that her compensation might have affected her as more prompt and more natural. They had long periods, in this London time, during which, when they were together, a stranger might have listened to them without in the least pricking up his ears; on the other hand the real truth was equally liable at any moment to rise to the surface, and the auditor would then have wondered indeed what they were talking about. They had from

8. I.e., his position as a minor government official.

an early hour made up their mind that society was, luckily, unintelligent, and the margin allowed them by this had fairly become one of their commonplaces. Yet there were still moments when the situation turned almost fresh—usually under the effect of some expression drawn from herself. Her expressions doubtless repeated themselves, but her intervals were generous. "What saves us, you know, is that we answer so completely to so usual an appearance: that of the man and woman whose friendship has become such a daily habit—or almost—as to be at last indispensable." That for instance was a remark she had frequently enough had occasion to make, though she had given it at different times different developments. What we are especially concerned with is the turn it happened to take from her one afternoon when he had come to see her in honour of her birthday. This anniversary had fallen on a Sunday, at a season of thick fog and general outward gloom; but he had brought her his customary offering, having known her now long enough to have established a hundred small traditions. It was one of his proofs to himself, the present he made her on her birthday, that he hadn't sunk into real selfishness. It was mostly nothing more than a small trinket, but it was always fine of its kind, and he was regularly careful to pay for it more than he thought he could afford. "Our habit saves you at least, don't you see? because it makes you, after all, for the vulgar, indistinguishable from other men. What's the most inveterate mark of men in general? Why the capacity to spend endless time with dull women—to spend it I won't say without being bored, but without minding that they are, without being driven off at a tangent by it; which comes to the same thing. I'm your dull woman, a part of the daily bread for which you pray at church. That covers your tracks more than anything."

"And what covers yours?" asked Marcher, whom his dull woman could mostly to this extent amuse. "I see of course what you mean by your saving me, in this way and that, so far as other people are concerned—I've seen it all along. Only what is it that saves *you*? I often think, you know, of that."

She looked as if she sometimes thought of that too, but rather in a different way. "Where other people, you mean, are concerned?"

"Well, you're really so in with me, you know—as a sort of result of my being so in with yourself. I mean of my having such an immense regard for you, being so tremendously mindful of all you've done for me. I sometimes ask myself if it's quite fair. Fair I mean to have so involved and—since one may say it—interested you. I almost feel as if you hadn't really had time to do anything else."

"Anything else but be interested?" she asked. "Ah what else does one ever want to be? If I've been 'watching' with you, as we long ago agreed I was to do, watching's always in itself an absorption."

"Oh certainly," John Marcher said, "if you hadn't had your curiosity—! Only doesn't it sometimes come to you as time goes on that your curiosity isn't being particularly repaid?"

May Bartram had a pause. "Do you ask that, by any chance, because you feel at all that yours isn't? I mean because you have to wait so long."

Oh he understood what she meant! "For the thing to happen that never does happen? For the beast to jump out? No, I'm just where I was about it. It isn't a matter as to which I can *choose*, I can decide for a change. It isn't one as to which there *can* be a change. It's in the lap of the gods. One's in the hands of one's law—there one is. As to the form the law will take, the way it will operate, that's its own affair."

"Yes," Miss Bartram replied; "of course one's fate's coming, of course it *has* come in its own form and its own way, all the while. Only, you know, the form and the way in your case were to have been—well, something so exceptional and, as one may say, so particularly *your* own."

Something in this made him look at her with suspicion. "You say 'were to *have* been,' as if in your heart you had begun to doubt."

"Oh!" she vaguely protested.

"As if you believed," he went on, "that nothing will now take place."

She shook her head slowly but rather inscrutably. "You're far from my thought."

He continued to look at her. "What then is the matter with you?"

"Well," she said after another wait, "the matter with me is simply that I'm more sure than ever my curiosity, as you call it, will be but too well repaid."

They were frankly grave now; he had got up from his seat, had turned once more about the little drawing-room to which, year after year, he brought his inevitable topic; in which he had, as he might have said, tasted their intimate community with every sauce, where every object was as familiar to him as the things of his own house and the very carpets were worn with his fitful walk very much as the desks in old counting-houses are worn by the elbows of generations of clerks. The generations of his nervous moods had been at work there, and the place was the written history of his whole middle life. Under the impression of what his friend had just said he knew himself, for some reason, more aware of these things; which made him, after a moment, stop again before her. "Is it possibly that you've grown afraid?"

"Afraid?" He thought, as she repeated the word, that his question had made her, a little, change colour; so that, lest he should have touched on a truth, he explained very kindly: "You remember that that was what you asked *me* long ago—that first day at Weatherend."

"Oh yes, and you told me you didn't know—that I was to see for myself. We've said little about it since, even in so long a time."

"Precisely," Marcher interposed—"quite as if it were too delicate a matter for us to make free with. Quite as if we might find, on pressure, that I *am* afraid. For then," he said, "we shouldn't, should we? quite know what to do."

She had for the time no answer to his question. "There have been days when I thought you were. Only, of course," she added, "there have been days when we have thought almost anything."

"Everything. Oh!" Marcher softly groaned as with a gasp, half-spent, at the face, more uncovered just then than it had been for a long while, of the imagination always with them. It had always had its incalculable moments of glaring out, quite as with the very eyes of the very Beast, and, used as he was to them, they could still draw from him the tribute of a sigh that rose from the depths of his being. All they had thought, first and last, rolled over him; the past seemed to have been reduced to mere barren speculation. This in fact was what the place had just struck him as so full of—the simplification of everything but the state of suspense. That remained only by seeming to hang in the void surrounding it. Even his original fear, if fear it had been, had lost itself in the desert. "I judge, however," he continued, "that you see I'm not afraid now."

"What I see, as I make it out, is that you've achieved something almost unprecedented in the way of getting used to danger. Living with it so long and so closely you've lost your sense of it; you know it's there, but you're indifferent, and you cease even, as of old, to have to whistle in the dark. Considering what the danger is," May Bartram wound up, "I'm bound to say I don't think your attitude could well be surpassed."

John Marcher faintly smiled. "It's heroic?"

"Certainly—call it that."

It was what he would have liked indeed to call it. "I *am* then a man of courage?"

"That's what you were to show me."

He still, however, wondered. "But doesn't the man of courage know what he's afraid of—or *not* afraid of? I don't know *that*, you see. I don't focus it. I can't name it. I only know I'm exposed."

"Yes, but exposed—how shall I say?—so directly. So intimately. That's surely enough."

"Enough to make you feel then—as what we may call the end and the upshot of our watch—that I'm not afraid?"

"You're not afraid. But it isn't," she said, "the end of our watch. That is it isn't the end of yours. You've everything still to see."

"Then why haven't *you?*" he asked. He had had, all along, to-day, the sense of her keeping something back, and he still had it. As this was his first impression of that it quite made a date. The case was the more marked as she didn't at first answer; which in turn made him go on. "You know something I don't." Then his voice, for that of a man of courage, trembled a little. "You know what's to happen." Her silence, with the face she showed, was almost a confession—it made him sure. "You know, and you're afraid to tell me. It's so bad that you're afraid I'll find out."

All this might be true, for she did look as if, unexpectedly to her, he had crossed some mystic line that she had secretly drawn round her. Yet she might, after all, not have worried; and the real climax was that he himself, at all events, needn't. "You'll never find out."

III

It was all to have made, none the less, as I have said, a date; which came out in the fact that again and again, even after long intervals, other things that passed between them wore in relation to this hour but the character of recalls and results. Its immediate effect had been indeed rather to lighten insistence—almost to provoke a reaction; as if their topic had dropped by its own weight and as if moreover, for that matter, Marcher had been visited by one of his occasional warnings against egotism. He had kept up, he felt, and very decently on the whole, his consciousness of the importance of not being selfish, and it was true that he had never sinned in that direction without promptly enough trying to press the scales the other way. He often repaired his fault, the season permitting, by inviting his friend to accompany him to the opera; and it not infrequently thus happened that, to show he didn't wish her to have but one sort of food for her mind, he was the cause of her appearing there with him a dozen nights in the month. It even happened that, seeing her home at such times, he occasionally went in with her to finish, as he called it, the evening, and, the better to make his point, sat down to the frugal but always careful little supper that awaited his pleasure. His point was made, he thought, by his not eternally insisting with her on himself; made for instance, at such hours, when it befell that, her piano at hand and each of them familiar with it, they went over passages of the opera together. It chanced to be on one of these occasions, however, that he reminded her of her not having answered a certain question he had put to her during the talk that had taken place between them on her last birthday. "What is it that saves *you?*"—saved her, he meant, from that appearance of variation from the usual human type. If he had practically escaped remark, as she pretended, by doing, in the most important particular, what most men do—find the answer to life in patching up an alliance of a sort with a woman no better than himself—how had she escaped it, and how could the alliance, such as it was, since they must suppose it had been more or less noticed, have failed to make her rather positively talked about?

"I never said," May Bartram replied, "that it hadn't made me a good deal talked about."

"Ah well then you're not 'saved.'"

"It hasn't been a question for me. If you've had your woman I've had," she said, "my man."

"And you mean that makes you all right?"

Oh it was always as if there were so much to say! "I don't know why it shouldn't make me—humanly, which is what we're speaking of—as right as it makes you."

"I see," Marcher returned. "'Humanly,' no doubt, as showing that you're living for something. Not, that is, just for me and my secret."

May Bartram smiled. "I don't pretend it exactly shows that I'm not living for you. It's my intimacy with you that's in question."

He laughed as he saw what she meant. "Yes, but since, as you say, I'm only, so far as people make out, ordinary, you're—aren't you?—no more than ordinary either. You help me to pass for a man like another. So if I *am*, as I understand you, you're not compromised. Is that it?"

She had another of her waits, but she spoke clearly enough. "That's it. It's all that concerns me—to help you to pass for a man like another."

He was careful to acknowledge the remark handsomely. "How kind, how beautiful, you are to me! How shall I ever repay you?"

She had her last grave pause, as if there might be a choice of ways. But she chose. "By going on as you are."

It was into this going on as he was that they relapsed, and really for so long a time that the day inevitably came for a further sounding of their depths. These depths, constantly bridged over by a structure firm enough in spite of its lightness and of its occasional oscillation in the somewhat vertiginous air, invited on occasion, in the interest of their nerves, a dropping of the plummet and a measurement of the abyss. A difference had been made moreover, once for all, by the fact that she had all the while not appeared to feel the need of rebutting his charge of an idea within her that she didn't dare to express—a charge uttered just before one of the fullest of their later discussions ended. It had come up for him then that she "knew" something and that what she knew was bad—too bad to tell him. When he had spoken of it as visibly so bad that she was afraid he might find it out, her reply had left the matter too equivocal to be let alone and yet, for Marcher's special sensibility, almost too formidable again to touch. He circled about it at a distance that alternately narrowed and widened and that still wasn't much affected by the consciousness in him that there was nothing she could "know," after all, any better than he did. She had no source of knowledge he hadn't equally—except of course that she might have finer nerves. That was what women had where they were interested; they made out things, where people were concerned, that the people often couldn't have made out for themselves. Their nerves, their sensibility, their imagination, were conductors and revealers, and the beauty of May Bartram was in particular that she had given herself so to his case. He felt in these days what, oddly enough, he had never felt before, the growth of a dread of losing her by some catastrophe—some catastrophe that yet wouldn't at all be *the* catastrophe: partly because she had almost of a sudden begun to strike him as more useful to him than ever yet, and partly by reason of an appearance of uncertainty in her health, coincident and equally new. It was characteristic of the inner detachment he had hitherto so successfully cultivated and to which our whole account of him is a reference, it was characteristic that his complications, such as they were, had never yet seemed so as at this crisis to thicken about him, even to the point of making him ask himself if he were, by any chance, of a truth, within sight or sound, within touch or reach, within the immediate jurisdiction, of the thing that waited.

When the day came, as come it had to, that his friend confessed to him her fear of a deep disorder in her blood, he felt somehow the shadow of a change and the chill of a shock. He immediately began to imagine aggravations and disasters, and above all to think of her peril as the direct menace for himself of personal privation. This indeed gave him one of those partial recoveries of equanimity that were agreeable to him—it showed him that what was still first in his mind was the loss she herself might suffer. "What if she should have to die before knowing, before seeing—?" It would have been brutal, in the early stages of her trouble, to put that question to her; but it had immediately sounded for him to his own concern, and the possibility was what most made him sorry for her. If she did "know," moreover, in the sense of her having had some—what should he think?—mystical irresistible light, this would make the matter not better, but worse, inasmuch as her original adoption of his own curiosity had quite become the basis of her life. She had been living to see what would *be* to be seen, and it would quite lacerate her to have to give up before the accomplishment of the vision. These reflexions, as I say, quickened his generosity; yet, make them as he might, he saw himself, with the lapse of the period, more and more disconcerted. It lapsed for him with a strange steady sweep, and the oddest oddity was that it gave him, independently of the threat of much inconvenience, almost the only positive surprise his career, if career it could be called, had yet offered him. She kept the house as she had never done; he had to go to her to see her—she could meet him nowhere now, though there was scarce a corner of their loved old London in which she hadn't in the past, at one time or another, done so; and he found her always seated by her fire in the deep old-fashioned chair she was less and less able to leave. He had been struck one day, after an absence exceeding his usual measure, with her suddenly looking much older to him than he had ever thought of her being; then he recognised that the suddenness was all on his side—he had just simply and suddenly noticed. She looked older because inevitably, after so many years, she *was* old, or almost; which was of course true in still greater measure of her companion. If she was old, or almost, John Marcher assuredly was, and yet it was her showing of the lesson, not his own, that brought the truth home to him. His surprises began here; when once they had begun they multiplied; they came rather with a rush: it was as if, in the oddest way in the world, they had all been kept back, sown in a thick cluster, for the late afternoon of life, the time at which for people in general the unexpected has died out.

One of them was that he should have caught himself—for he *had* so done—*really* wondering if the great accident would take form now as nothing more than his being condemned to see this charming woman, this admirable friend, pass away from him. He had never so unreservedly qualified her as while confronted in thought with such a possibility; in spite of which there was small doubt for him that as an answer to his long riddle the mere effacement of even so fine a feature of his situation would be an abject anticlimax. It would represent, as connected with his past attitude, a drop of dignity under the shadow of which his existence could only become the most grotesque of failures. He had been far from holding it a failure—long as he had waited for the appearance that was to make it a success. He had waited for quite another thing, not for such a thing as that. The breath of his good faith came short, however, as he recognised how long he had waited, or how long at least his companion had. That she, at all events, might be recorded as having waited in vain—this affected him sharply, and all the more because of his at first having done little more than amuse himself with the idea. It grew more grave as the gravity of her condition grew, and the state of mind it produced in him, which he himself ended by watching as if it had been some definite disfigurement of his outer person, may pass for another of his surprises. This conjoined itself still with another, the really stupefying consciousness of a question that he would have allowed to shape itself had he dared. What did everything mean—what, that is, did *she* mean, she and her vain waiting and her probable death and the soundless admonition of it all—unless that, at this time of day, it was simply, it was overwhelmingly too late? He had never at any stage of his queer consciousness admitted the whisper of such a correction; he had never till within these last few months been so false to his conviction as not to hold that what was to come to him had time, whether *he* struck himself as having it or not. That at last, at last, he certainly hadn't it, to speak of, or had it but in the scantiest measure— such, soon enough, as things went with him, became the inference with which his old obsession had to reckon: and this it was not helped to do by the more and more confirmed appearance that the great vagueness casting the long shadow in which he had lived had, to attest itself, almost no margin left. Since it was in Time that he was to have met his fate, so it was in Time that his fate was to have acted; and as he waked up to the sense of no longer being young, which was exactly the sense of being stale, just as that, in turn, was the sense of being weak, he waked up to another matter beside. It all hung together; they were subject, he and the great vagueness, to an equal and indivisible law. When the possibilities themselves had accordingly turned stale, when the secret of the gods had grown faint, had perhaps even quite evaporated, that, and that only, was failure. It wouldn't have been failure to be bankrupt, dishonoured, pilloried, hanged; it was failure not to be anything. And so, in the dark valley into which his path had taken its unlooked-for twist, he wondered not a little as he groped. He didn't care what awful crash might overtake him, with what ignominy or what monstrosity he might yet be associated—since he wasn't after all too utterly old to suffer—if it would only be decently proportionate to the posture he had kept, all his life, in the threatened presence of it. He had but one desire left—that he shouldn't have been "sold."

IV

Then it was that, one afternoon, while the spring of the year was young and new she met all in her own way his frankest betrayal of these alarms. He had gone in late to see her, but evening hadn't settled and she was presented to him in that long fresh light of waning April days which affects us often with a sadness sharper than the greyest hours of autumn. The week had been warm, the spring was supposed to have begun early, and May Bartram sat, for the first time in the year, without a fire; a fact that, to Marcher's sense, gave the scene of which she formed part a smooth and ultimate look, an air of knowing, in its immaculate order and cold meaningless cheer, that it would never see a fire again. Her own aspect—he could scarce have said why—intensified this note. Almost as white as wax, with the marks and signs in her face as numerous and as fine as if they had been etched by a needle, with soft white draperies relieved by a faded green scarf on the delicate tone of which the years had further refined, she was the picture of a serene and exquisite but impenetrable sphinx, whose head, or indeed all whose person, might have been powdered with silver. She was a sphinx, yet with her white petals and green fronds she might have been a lily too—only an artificial lily, wonderfully imitated and constantly kept, without dust or stain, though not exempt from a slight droop and a complexity of faint creases, under some clear glass bell. The perfection of household care, of high polish and finish, always reigned in her rooms, but they now looked most as if everything had been wound up, tucked in, put away, so that she might sit with folded hands and with nothing more to do. She was "out of it," to Marcher's vision; her work was over; she communicated with him as across some gulf or from some island of rest that she had already reached, and it made him feel strangely abandoned. Was it—or rather wasn't it—that if for so long she had been watching with him the answer to their question must have swum into her ken and taken on its name, so that her occupation was verily gone? He had as much as charged her with this in saying to her, many months before, that she even then knew something she was keeping from him. It was a point he had never since ventured to press, vaguely fearing as he did that it might become a difference, perhaps a disagreement, between them. He had in this later time turned nervous, which was what he in all the other years had never been; and the oddity was that his nervousness should have waited till he had begun to doubt, should have held off so long as he was sure. There was something, it seemed to him, that the wrong word would bring down on his head, something that would so at least ease off his tension. But he wanted not to speak the wrong word; that would make everything ugly. He wanted the knowledge he lacked to drop on him, if drop it could, by its own august weight. If she was to forsake him it was surely for her to take leave. This was why he didn't directly ask her again what she knew; but it was also why, approaching the matter from another side, he said to her in the course of his visit: "What do you regard as the very worst that at this time of day *can* happen to me?"

He had asked her that in the past often enough; they had, with the odd irregular rhythm of their intensities and avoidances, exchanged ideas about it and then had seen the ideas washed away by cool intervals, washed like figures traced in sea-sand. It had ever been the mark of their talk that the oldest allusions in it required but a little dismissal and reaction to come out again, sounding for the hour as new. She could thus at present meet his enquiry quite freshly and patiently. "Oh yes, I've repeatedly thought, only it always seemed to me of old that I couldn't quite make up my mind. I thought of dreadful things, between which it was difficult to choose; and so must you have done."

"Rather! I feel now as if I had scarce done anything else. I appear to myself to have spent my life in thinking of nothing *but* dreadful things. A great many of them I've at different times named to you, but there were others I couldn't name."

"They were too, too dreadful?"

"Too, too dreadful—some of them."

She looked at him a minute, and there came to him as he met it an inconsequent sense that her eyes, when one got their full clearness, were still as beautiful as they had been in youth, only beautiful with a strange cold light—a light that somehow was a part of the effect, if it wasn't rather a part of the cause, of the pale hard sweetness of the season and the hour. "And yet," she said at last, "there are horrors we've mentioned."

It deepened the strangeness to see her, as such a figure in such a picture, talk of "horrors," but she was to do in a few minutes something stranger yet—though even of this he was to take the full measure but afterwards—and the note of it already trembled. It was, for the matter of that, one of the signs that her eyes were having again the high flicker of their prime. He had to admit, however, what she said. "Oh yes, there were times when we did go far." He caught himself in the act of speaking as if it all were over. Well, he wished it were; and the consummation depended for him clearly more and more on his friend.

But she had now a soft smile. "Oh far—!"

It was oddly ironic. "Do you mean you're prepared to go further?"

She was frail and ancient and charming as she continued to look at him, yet it was rather as if she had lost the thread. "Do you consider that we went far?"

"Why I thought it the point you were just making—that we *had* looked most things in the face."

"Including each other?" She still smiled. "But you're quite right. We've had together great imaginations, often great fears; but some of them have been unspoken."

"Then the worst—we haven't faced that. I *could* face it, I believe, if I knew what you think it. I feel," he explained, "as if I had lost my power to conceive such things." And he wondered if he looked as blank as he sounded. "It's spent."

"Then why do you assume," she asked, "that mine isn't?"

"Because you've given me signs to the contrary. It isn't a question for you of conceiving, imagining, comparing. It isn't a question now of choosing." At last he came out with it. "You know something I don't. You've shown me that before."

These last words had affected her, he made out in a moment, exceedingly, and she spoke with firmness. "I've shown you, my dear, nothing."

He shook his head. "You can't hide it."

"Oh, oh!" May Bartram sounded over what she couldn't hide. It was almost a smothered groan.

"You admitted it months ago, when I spoke of it to you as of something you were afraid I should find out. Your answer was that I couldn't, that I wouldn't, and I don't pretend I have. But you had something therefore in mind, and I now see how it must have been, how it still is, the possibility that, of all possibilities, has settled itself for you as the worst. This," he went on, "is why I appeal to you. I'm only afraid of ignorance to-day—I'm not afraid of knowledge." And then as for a while she said nothing: "What makes me sure is that I see in your face and feel here, in this air and amid these appearances, that you're out of it. You've done. You've had your experience. You leave me to my fate."

Well, she listened, motionless and white in her chair, as on a decision to be made, so that her manner was fairly an avowal, though still, with a small fine inner stiffness, an imperfect surrender. "It *would* be the worst," she finally let herself say. "I mean the thing I've never said."

It hushed him a moment. "More monstrous than all the monstrosities we've named?"

"More monstrous. Isn't that what you sufficiently express," she asked, "in calling it the worst?"

Marcher thought. "Assuredly—if you mean, as I do, something that includes all the loss and all the shame that are thinkable."

"It would if it *should* happen," said May Bartram. "What we're speaking of, remember, is only my idea."

"It's your belief," Marcher returned. "That's enough for me. I feel your beliefs are right. Therefore if, having this one, you give me no more light on it, you abandon me."

"No, no!" she repeated. "I'm with you—don't you see?—still." And as to make it more vivid to him she rose from her chair—a movement she seldom risked in these days—and showed herself, all draped and all soft, in her fairness and slimness. "I haven't forsaken you."

It was really, in its effort against weakness, a generous assurance, and had the success of the impulse not, happily, been great, it would have touched him to pain more than to pleasure. But the cold charm in her eyes had spread, as she hovered before him, to all the rest of her person, so that it was for the minute almost a recovery of youth. He couldn't pity her for that; he could only take her as she showed—as capable even yet of helping him. It was as if, at the same time, her light might at any instant go out; wherefore he must make the most of it. There passed before him with intensity the three or four things he wanted most to know; but the question that came of itself to his lips really covered the others. "Then tell me if I shall consciously suffer."

She promptly shook her head. "Never!"

It confirmed the authority he imputed to her, and it produced on him an extraordinary effect. "Well, what's better than that? Do you call that the worst?"

"You think nothing is better?" she asked.

She seemed to mean something so special that he again sharply wondered, though still with the dawn of a prospect of relief. "Why not, if one doesn't *know?*" After which, as their eyes, over his question, met in a silence, the dawn deepened and something to his purpose came prodigiously out of her very face. His own, as he took it in, suddenly flushed to the forehead, and he gasped with the force of a perception to which, on the instant, everything fitted. The sound of his gasp filled the air; then he became articulate. "I see—if I don't suffer!"

In her own look, however, was doubt. "You see what?"

"Why what you mean—what you've always meant."

She again shook her head. "What I mean isn't what I've always meant. It's different."

"It's something new?"

She hung back from it a little. "Something new. It's not what you think. I see what you think."

His divination drew breath then; only her correction might be wrong. "It isn't that I *am* a blockhead?" he asked between faintness and grimness. "It isn't that it's all a mistake."

"A mistake?" she pityingly echoed. *That* possibility, for her, he saw, would be monstrous; and if she guaranteed him the immunity from pain it would accordingly not be what she had in mind. "Oh no," she declared; "it's nothing of that sort. You've been right."

Yet he couldn't help asking himself if she weren't, thus pressed, speaking but to save him. It seemed to him he should be most in a hole if his history should prove all a platitude. "Are you telling me the truth, so that I shan't have been a bigger idiot than I can bear to know? I *haven't* lived with a vain imagination, in the most besotted illusion? I haven't waited but to see the door shut in my face?"

She shook her head again. "However the case stands *that* isn't the truth. Whatever the reality, it *is* a reality. The door isn't shut. The door's open," said May Bartram.

"Then something's to come?"

She waited once again, always with her cold sweet eyes on him. "It's never too late." She had, with her gliding step, diminished the distance between them, and she stood nearer to him, close to him, a minute, as if still charged with the unspoken. Her movement might have been for some finer emphasis of what she was at once hesitating and deciding to say. He had been standing by the chimney-piece, fireless and sparely adorned, a small perfect old French clock and two morsels of rosy Dresden[9] constituting all its furniture; and her hand grasped the shelf while she kept him waiting, grasped it a little as for support and encouragement. She only kept him waiting, however; that is he only waited. It had become suddenly, from her movement and attitude, beautiful and vivid to him that she had something more to give him; her wasted face delicately shone with it—it glittered almost as with the white lustre of silver in her expression. She was right, incontestably, for what he saw in her

9. Fine German porcelain.

face was the truth, and strangely, without consequence, while their talk of it as dreadful was still in the air, she appeared to present it as inordinately soft. This, prompting bewilderment, made him but gape the more gratefully for her revelation, so that they continued for some minutes silent, her face shining at him, her contact imponderably pressing, and his stare all kind but all expectant. The end, none the less, was that what he had expected failed to come to him. Something else took place instead, which seemed to consist at first in the mere closing of her eyes. She gave way at the same instant to a slow fine shudder, and though he remained staring—though he stared in fact but the harder—turned off and regained her chair. It was the end of what she had been intending, but it left him thinking only of that.

"Well, you don't say—?"

She had touched in her passage a bell near the chimney and had sunk back strangely pale. "I'm afraid I'm too ill."

"Too ill to tell me?" It sprang up sharp to him, and almost to his lips, the fear she might die without giving him light. He checked himself in time from so expressing his question, but she answered as if she had heard the words.

"Don't you know—now?"

"'Now'—?" She had spoken as if some difference had been made within the moment. But her maid, quickly obedient to her bell, was already with them. "I know nothing." And he was afterwards to say to himself that he must have spoken with odious impatience, such an impatience as to show that, supremely disconcerted, he washed his hands of the whole question.

"Oh!" said May Bartram.

"Are you in pain?" he asked as the woman went to her.

"No," said May Bartram.

Her maid, who had put an arm round her as if to take her to her room, fixed on him eyes that appealingly contradicted her; in spite of which, however, he showed once more his mystification. "What then has happened?"

She was once more, with her companion's help, on her feet, and, feeling withdrawal imposed on him, he had blankly found his hat and gloves and had reached the door. Yet he waited for her answer. "What *was* to," she said.

V

He came back the next day, but she was then unable to see him, and as it was literally the first time this had occurred in the long stretch of their acquaintance he turned away, defeated and sore, almost angry—or feeling at least that such a break in their custom was really the beginning of the end—and wandered alone with his thoughts, especially with the one he was least able to keep down. She was dying and he would lose her; she was dying and his life would end. He stopped in the Park, into which he had passed, and stared before him at his recurrent doubt. Away from her the doubt pressed again; in her presence he had believed her, but as he felt his forlornness he threw himself into the explanation that, nearest at hand, had most of a miserable warmth for him and least of a cold torment. She had deceived him to save him—to put him off with something in which he should be able to rest. What could the thing that was to happen to him be, after all, but just this thing that had begun to happen? Her dying, her death, his consequent solitude—*that* was what he had figured as the Beast in the

Jungle, that was what had been in the lap of the gods. He had had her word for it as he left her—what else on earth could she have meant? It wasn't a thing of a monstrous order; not a fate rare and distinguished; not a stroke of fortune that overwhelmed and immortalised; it had only the stamp of the common doom. But poor Marcher at this hour judged the common doom sufficient. It would serve his turn, and even as the consummation of infinite waiting he would bend his pride to accept it. He sat down on a bench in the twilight. He hadn't been a fool. Something had *been*, as she had said, to come. Before he rose indeed it had quite struck him that the final fact really matched with the long avenue through which he had had to reach it. As sharing his suspense and as giving herself all, giving her life, to bring it to an end, she had come with him every step of the way. He had lived by her aid, and to leave her behind would be cruelly, damnably to miss her. What could be more overwhelming than that?

Well, he was to know within the week, for though she kept him a while at bay, left him restless and wretched during a series of days on each of which he asked about her only again to have to turn away, she ended his trial by receiving him where she had always received him. Yet she had been brought out at some hazard into the presence of so many of the things that were, consciously, vainly, half their past, and there was scant service left in the gentleness of her mere desire, all too visible, to check his obsession and wind up his long trouble. That was clearly what she wanted, the one thing more for her own peace while she could still put out her hand. He was so affected by her state that, once seated by her chair, he was moved to let everything go; it was she herself therefore who brought him back, took up again, before she dismissed him, her last word of the other time. She showed how she wished to leave their business in order. "I'm not sure you understood. You've nothing to wait for more. It *has* come."

Oh how he looked at her! "Really?"

"Really."

"The thing that, as you said, *was* to?"

"The thing that we began in our youth to watch for."

Face to face with her once more he believed her; it was a claim to which he had so abjectly little to oppose. "You mean that it has come as a positive definite occurrence, with a name and a date?"

"Positive. Definite. I don't know about the 'name,' but oh with a date!"

He found himself again too helplessly at sea. "But come in the night—come and passed me by?"

May Bartram had her strange faint smile. "Oh no, it hasn't passed you by!"

"But if I haven't been aware of it and it hasn't touched me—?"

"Ah your not being aware of it"—and she seemed to hesitate an instant to deal with this—"your not being aware of it is the strangeness *in* the strangeness. It's the wonder *of* the wonder." She spoke as with the softness almost of a sick child, yet now at last, at the end of all, with the perfect straightness of a sibyl. She visibly knew that she knew, and the effect on him was of something co-ordinate, in its high character, with the law that had ruled him. It was the true voice of the law; so on her lips would the law itself have sounded. "It *has* touched you," she went on. "It has done its office. It has made you all its own."

"So utterly without my knowing it?"

"So utterly without your knowing it." His hand, as he leaned to her, was on the arm of her chair, and, dimly smiling always now, she placed her own on it. "It's enough if *I* know it."

"Oh!" he confusedly breathed, as she herself of late so often had done.

"What I long ago said is true. You'll never know now, and I think you ought to be content. You've *had* it," said May Bartram.

"But had what?"

"Why what was to have marked you out. The proof of your law. It has acted. I'm too glad," she then bravely added, "to have been able to see what it's *not*."

He continued to attach his eyes to her, and with the sense that it was all beyond him, and that *she* was too, he would still have sharply challenged her hadn't he so felt it an abuse of her weakness to do more than take devoutly what she gave him, take it hushed as to a revelation. If he did speak, it was out of the foreknowledge of his loneliness to come. "If you're glad of what it's 'not' it might then have been worse?"

She turned her eyes away, she looked straight before her; with which after a moment: "Well, you know our fears."

He wondered. "It's something then we never feared?"

On this slowly she turned to him. "Did we ever dream, with all our dreams, that we should sit and talk of it thus?"

He tried for a little to make out that they had; but it was as if their dreams, numberless enough, were in solution in some thick cold mist through which thought lost itself. "It might have been that we couldn't talk?"

"Well"—she did her best for him—"not from this side. This, you see," she said, "is the *other* side."

"I think," poor Marcher returned, "that all sides are the same to me." Then, however, as she gently shook her head in correction: "We mightn't, as it were, have got across—?"

"To where we are—no. We're *here*"—she made her weak emphasis.

"And much good does it do us!" was her friend's frank comment.

"It does us the good it can. It does us the good that *it* isn't here. It's past. It's behind," said May Bartram. "Before—" but her voice dropped.

He had got up, not to tire her, but it was hard to combat his yearning. She after all told him nothing but that his light had failed—which he knew well enough without her. "Before—?" he blankly echoed.

"Before, you see, it was always to *come*. That kept it present."

"Oh I don't care what comes now! Besides," Marcher added, "it seems to me I liked it better present, as you say, than I can like it absent with *your* absence."

"Oh mine!"—and her pale hands made light of it.

"With the absence of everything." He had a dreadful sense of standing there before her for—so far as anything but this proved, this bottomless drop was concerned—the last time of their life. It rested on him with a weight he felt he could scarce bear, and this weight it apparently was that still pressed out what remained in him of speakable protest. "I believe you; but I can't begin to pretend I understand. *Nothing*, for me, is past; nothing *will* pass till I pass myself, which I pray my stars may be as soon as possible. Say, however," he added, "that I've eaten my cake, as you contend, to the last crumb—how can the thing I've never felt at all be the thing I was marked out to feel?"

She met him perhaps less directly, but she met him unperturbed. "You take your 'feelings' for granted. You were to suffer your fate. That was not necessarily to know it."

"How in the world—when what is such knowledge but suffering?"

She looked up at him a while in silence. "No—you don't understand."

"I suffer," said John Marcher.

"Don't, don't!"

"How can I help at least *that?*"

"*Don't!*" May Bartram repeated.

She spoke it in a tone so special, in spite of her weakness, that he stared an instant—stared as if some light, hitherto hidden, had shimmered across his vision. Darkness again closed over it, but the gleam had already become for him an idea. "Because I haven't the right—?"

"Don't *know*—when you needn't," she mercifully urged. "You needn't—for we shouldn't."

"Shouldn't?" If he could but know what she meant!

"No—it's too much."

"Too much?" he still asked but, with a mystification that was the next moment of a sudden to give way. Her words, if they meant something, affected him in this light—the light also of her wasted face—as meaning *all*, and the sense of what knowledge had been for herself came over him with a rush which broke through into a question. "Is it of that then you're dying?"

She but watched him, gravely at first, as to see, with this, where he was, and she might have seen something or feared something that moved her sympathy. "I would live for you still—if I could." Her eyes closed for a little, as if, withdrawn into herself, she were for a last time trying. "But I can't!" she said as she raised them again to take leave of him.

She couldn't indeed, as but too promptly and sharply appeared, and he had no vision of her after this that was anything, but darkness and doom. They had parted for ever in that strange talk; access to her chamber of pain, rigidly guarded, was almost wholly forbidden him; he was feeling now moreover, in the face of doctors, nurses, the two or three relatives attracted doubtless by the presumption of what she had to "leave," how few were the rights, as they were called in such cases, that he had to put forward, and how odd it might even seem that their intimacy shouldn't have given him more of them. The stupidest fourth cousin had more, even though she had been nothing in such a person's life. She had been a feature of features in *his*, for what else was it to have been so indispensable? Strange beyond saying were the ways of existence, baffling for him the anomaly of his lack, as he felt it to be, of producible claim. A woman might have been, as it were, everything to him, and it might yet present him in no connexion that any one seemed held to recognise. If this was the case in these closing weeks it was the case more sharply on the occasion of the last offices rendered, in the great grey London cemetery, to what had been mortal, to what had been precious, in his friend. The concourse at her grave was not numerous, but he saw himself treated as scarce more nearly concerned with it than if there had been a thousand others. He was in short from this moment face to face with the fact that he was to profit extraordinarily little by the interest May Bartram had taken in him. He couldn't quite have said what he expected, but he hadn't surely expected this approach to a double privation. Not only had her interest failed him, but he seemed to feel himself unattended—and for a reason he couldn't seize—by the distinction, the dignity, the propriety, if nothing else, of the man markedly bereaved. It was as if in the view of society he had not *been* markedly bereaved, as if there still failed some sign or proof of it, and as if none the less his character could never be affirmed nor the deficiency ever made up. There were moments as the weeks went by when he would have liked, by some almost aggressive act, to take his stand on the intimacy of his loss, in order that it *might* be questioned and his retort, to the relief of his spirit, so recorded; but the moments of an irritation more helpless followed fast on these, the moments during which, turning things over with a good conscience but with a bare horizon, he found himself wondering if he oughtn't to have begun, so to speak, further back.

He found himself wondering at many things, and this last speculation had others to keep it company. What could he have done, after all, in her lifetime, without giving them both, as it were, away? He couldn't have made known she was watching him, for that would have published the superstition of the Beast. This was what closed his mouth now—now that the Jungle had been threshed to vacancy and that the Beast had stolen away. It sounded too foolish and too flat; the difference for him in this particular, the extinction in his life of the element of suspense, was such as in fact to surprise him. He could scarce have said what the effect resembled; the abrupt cessation, the positive prohibition, of music perhaps, more than anything else, in some place all adjusted and all accustomed to sonority and to attention. If he could at any rate have conceived lifting the veil from his image at some moment of the past (what had he done, after all, if not lift it to *her*?) so to do this today, to talk to people at large of the Jungle cleared and confide to them that he now felt it as safe, would have been not only to see them listen as to a goodwife's tale, but really to hear himself tell one. What it presently came to in truth was that poor Marcher waded through his beaten grass, where no life stirred, where no breath sounded, where no evil eye seemed to gleam from a possible lair, very much as if vaguely looking for the Beast, and still more as if acutely missing it. He walked about in an existence that had grown strangely more spacious, and, stopping fitfully in places where the undergrowth of life struck him as closer, asked himself yearningly, wondered secretly and sorely, if it would have lurked here or there. It would have at all events *sprung*; what was at least complete was his belief in the truth of the assurance given him. The change from his old sense to his new was absolute and final: what was to happen *had* so absolutely and finally happened that he was as little able to know a fear for his future as to know a hope; so absent in short was any question of anything still to come. He was to live entirely with the other question, that of his unidentified past, that of his having to see his fortune impenetrably muffled and masked.

The torment of this vision became then his occupation; he couldn't perhaps have consented to live but for the possibility of guessing. She had told him, his friend, not to guess; she had forbidden him, so far as he might, to know, and she had even in a sort denied the power in him to learn: which were so many things, precisely, to deprive him of rest. It wasn't that he wanted, he argued for fairness, that anything past and done should repeat itself; it was only that he shouldn't, as an anticlimax, have been taken sleeping so sound as not to be able to win back by an effort of thought the lost stuff of consciousness. He declared to himself at moments that he would either win it back or have done with consciousness for ever; he made this idea his one motive in fine, made it so much his passion that none other, to compare with it, seemed ever to have touched him. The lost stuff of consciousness became thus for him as a strayed or stolen child to an unappeasable father; he hunted it up and down very much as if he were knocking at doors and enquiring of the police. This was the spirit in which, inevitably, he set himself to travel; he started on a journey that was to be as long as he could make it; it danced before him that, as the other side of the globe couldn't possibly have less to say to him, it might, by a possibility of suggestion, have more. Before he quitted London, however, he made a pilgrimage to May Bartram's grave, took his way to it through the endless avenues of the grim suburban metropolis, sought it out in the wilderness of tombs, and, though he had come but for the renewal of the act of farewell, found himself, when he had at last stood by it, beguiled into long intensities. He stood for an hour, powerless to turn away and yet powerless to penetrate the darkness of death; fixing with his eyes her inscribed name and date, beating his forehead against the fact of the secret they kept, drawing his breath, while he waited, as if some sense would in pity of him rise from the stones. He kneeled on the stones, however, in vain; they kept what they concealed; and if the face of the tomb did become a face for him it was because her two names became a pair of eyes that didn't know him. He gave them a last long look, but no palest light broke.

VI

He stayed away, after this, for a year; he visited the depths of Asia, spending himself on scenes of romantic interest, of superlative sanctity; but what was present to him everywhere was that for a man who had known what *he* had known the world was vulgar and vain. The state of mind in which he had lived for so many years shone out to him, in reflexion, as a light that coloured and refined, a light beside which the glow of the East was garish cheap and thin. The terrible truth was that he had lost—with everything else—a distinction as well; the things he saw couldn't help being common when he had become common to look at them. He was simply now one of them himself— he was in the dust, without a peg for the sense of difference; and there were hours when, before the temples of gods and the sepulchres of kings, his spirit turned for nobleness of association to the barely discriminated slab in the London suburb. That had become for him, and more intensely with time and distance, his one witness of a past glory. It was all that was left to him for proof or pride, yet the past glories of Pharaohs were nothing to him as he thought of it. Small wonder then that he came back to it on the morrow of his return. He was drawn there this time as irresistibly as the other, yet with a confidence, almost, that was doubtless the effect of the many months that had elapsed. He had lived, in spite of himself, into his change of feeling, and in wandering over the earth had wandered, as might be said, from the circumference to the centre of his desert. He had settled to his safety and accepted perforce his extinction; figuring to himself, with some colour, in the likeness of certain little old men he remembered to have seen, of whom, all meagre and wizened as they might look, it was related that they had in their time fought twenty duels or been loved by ten princesses. They indeed had been wondrous for others while he was but wondrous for himself; which, however, was exactly the cause of his haste to renew the wonder by getting back, as he might put it, into his own presence. That had quickened his steps and checked his delay. If his visit was prompt it was because he had been separated so long from the part of himself that alone he now valued.

It's accordingly not false to say that he reached his goal with a certain elation and stood there again with a certain assurance. The creature beneath the sod *knew* of his rare experience, so that, strangely now, the place had lost for him its mere blankness of expression. It met him in mildness—not, as before, in mockery; it wore for him the air of conscious greeting that we find, after absence, in things that have closely belonged to us and which seem to confess of themselves to the connexion. The plot of ground, the graven tablet, the tended flowers affected him so as belonging to him that he resembled for the hour a contented landlord reviewing a piece of property. Whatever had happened—well, had happened. He had not come back this time with the vanity of that question, his former worrying "What, *what?*" now practically so spent. Yet he would none the less never again so cut himself off from the spot; he would come back to it every month, for if he did nothing else by its aid he at least held up his head. It thus grew for him, in the oddest way, a positive resource; he carried out his idea of periodical returns, which took their place at last among the most inveterate of his habits. What it all amounted to, oddly enough, was that in his finally so simplified world this garden of death gave him the few square feet of earth on which he could still most live. It was as if, being nothing anywhere else for any one, nothing even for himself, he were just everything here, and if not for a crowd of witnesses or indeed for any witness but John Marcher, then by clear right of the register that he could scan like an open page. The open page was the tomb of his friend, and *there* were the facts of the past, there the truth of his life, there the backward reaches in which he could lose himself. He did this from time to time with such effect that he seemed to wander through the old years with his hand in the arm of a companion who was, in the most extraordinary manner, his other, his younger self; and to wander, which was more extraordinary yet, round and round a third presence—not wandering she, but stationary, still, whose eyes, turning with his revolution, never ceased to follow him, and whose seat was his point, so to speak, of orientation. Thus in short he settled to live—feeding all on the sense that he once *had* lived, and dependent on it not alone for a support but for an identity.

It sufficed him in its way for months and the year elapsed; it would doubtless even have carried him further but for an accident, superficially slight, which moved him, quite in another direction, with a force beyond any of his impressions of Egypt or of India. It was a thing of the merest chance—the turn, as he afterwards felt, of a hair, though he was indeed to live to believe that if light hadn't come to him in this particular fashion it would still have come in another. He was to live to believe this, I say, though he was not to live, I may not less definitely mention, to do much else. We allow him at any rate the benefit of the conviction, struggling up for him at the end, that, whatever might have happened or not happened, he would have come round of himself to the light. The incident of an autumn day had put the match to the train laid from of old by his misery. With the light before him he knew that even of late his ache had only been smothered. It was strangely drugged, but it throbbed;

at the touch it began to bleed. And the touch, in the event, was the face of a fellow mortal. This face, one grey afternoon when the leaves were thick in the alleys, looked into Marcher's own, at the cemetery, with an expression like the cut of a blade. He felt it, that is, so deep down that he winced at the steady thrust. The person who so mutely assaulted him was a figure he had noticed, on reaching his own goal, absorbed by a grave a short distance away, a grave apparently fresh, so that the emotion of the visitor would probably match it for frankness. This face alone forbade further attention, though during the time he stayed he remained vaguely conscious of his neighbour, a middle-aged man apparently, in mourning, whose bowed back, among the clustered monuments and mortuary yews, was constantly presented. Marcher's theory that these were elements in contact with which he himself revived, had suffered, on this occasion, it may be granted, a marked, an excessive check. The autumn day was dire for him as none had recently been, and he rested with a heaviness he had not yet known on the low stone table that bore May Bartram's name. He rested without power to move, as if some spring in him, some spell vouchsafed, had suddenly been broken for ever. If he could have done that moment as he wanted he would simply have stretched himself on the slab that was ready to take him, treating it as a place prepared to receive his last sleep. What in all the wide world had he now to keep awake for? He stared before him with the question, and it was then that, as one of the cemetery walks passed near him, he caught the shock of the face.

His neighbour at the other grave had withdrawn, as he himself, with force enough in him, would have done by now, and was advancing along the path on his way to one of the gates. This brought him close, and his pace was slow, so that—and all the more as there was a kind of hunger in his look— the two men were for a minute directly confronted. Marcher knew him at once for one of the deeply stricken—a perception so sharp that nothing else in the picture comparatively lived, neither his dress, his age, nor his presumable character and class; nothing lived but the deep ravage of the features he showed. He *showed* them—that was the point; he was moved, as he passed, by some impulse that was either a signal for sympathy or, more possibly, a challenge to an opposed sorrow. He might already have been aware of our friend, might at some previous hour have noticed in him the smooth habit of the scene, with which the state of his own senses so scantly consorted, and might thereby have been stirred as by an overt discord. What Marcher was at all events conscious of was in the first place that the image of scarred passion presented to him was conscious too—of something that profaned the air; and in the second that, roused, startled, shocked, he was yet the next moment looking after it, as it went, with envy. The most extraordinary thing that had happened to him—though he had given that name to other matters as well—took place, after his immediate vague stare, as a consequence of this impression. The stranger passed, but the raw glare of his grief remained, making our friend wonder in pity what wrong, what wound it expressed, what injury not to be healed. What had the man *had*, to make him by the loss of it so bleed and yet live?

Something—and this reached him with a pang—that *he*, John Marcher, hadn't; the proof of which was precisely John Marcher's arid end. No passion had ever touched him, for this was what passion meant; he had survived and maundered and pined, but where had been *his* deep ravage? The extraordinary thing we speak of was the sudden rush of the result of this question. The sight that had just met his eyes named to him, as in letters of quick flame, something he had utterly, insanely missed, and what he had missed made these things a train of fire, made them mark themselves in an anguish of inward throbs. He had seen *outside* of his life, not learned it within, the way a woman was mourned when she had been loved for herself: such was the force of his conviction of the meaning of the stranger's face, which still flared for him as a smoky torch. It hadn't come to him, the knowledge, on the wings of experience; it had brushed him, jostled him, upset him, with the disrespect of chance, the insolence of accident. Now that the illumination had begun, however, it blazed to the zenith, and what he presently stood there gazing at was the sounded void of his life. He gazed, he drew breath, in pain; he turned in his dismay, and, turning, he had before him in sharper incision than ever the open page of his story. The name on the table smote him as the passage of his neighbour had done, and what it said to him, full in the face, was that *she* was what he had missed. This was the awful thought, the answer to all the past, the vision at the dread clearness of which he grew as cold as the stone beneath him. Everything fell together, confessed, explained, overwhelmed; leaving him most of all stupefied at the blindness he had cherished. The fate he had been marked for he had met with a vengeance—he had emptied the cup to the lees; he had been the man of his time, *the* man, to whom nothing on earth was to have happened. That was the rare stroke—that was his visitation. So he saw it, as we say, in pale horror, while the pieces fitted and fitted. So *she* had seen it while he didn't, and so she served at this hour to drive the truth home. It was the truth, vivid and monstrous, that all the while he had waited the wait was itself his portion. This the companion of his vigil had at a given moment made out, and she had then offered him the chance to baffle his doom. One's doom, however, was never baffled, and on the day she told him his own had come down she had seen him but stupidly stare at the escape she offered him.

The escape would have been to love her; then, *then* he would have lived. *She* had lived—who could say now with what passion?—since she had loved him for himself; whereas he had never thought of her (ah, how it hugely glared at him!) but in the chill of his egotism and the light of her use. Her spoken words came back to him—the chain stretched and stretched. The Beast had lurked indeed, and the Beast, at its hour, had sprung; it had sprung in that twilight of the cold April when, pale, ill, wasted, but all beautiful, and perhaps even then recoverable, she had risen from her chair to stand before him and let him imaginably guess. It had sprung as he didn't guess; it had sprung as she hopelessly turned from him, and the mark, by the time he left her, had fallen where it *was* to fall. He had justified his fear and achieved his fate; he had failed, with the last exactitude, of all he was to fail of; and a moan now rose to his lips as he remembered she had prayed he mightn't know. This horror of waking—*this* was knowledge, knowledge under the breath of which the very tears in his eyes seemed to freeze. Through them, none the less, he tried to fix it and hold it; he kept it there before him so that he might feel the pain. That at least, belated and bitter, had something of the taste of life. But the bitterness suddenly sickened him, and it was as if, horribly, he saw, in the truth, in the cruelty of his image, what had been appointed and done. He saw the Jungle of his life and saw the lurking Beast; then, while he looked, perceived it, as by a stir of the air, rise, huge and hideous, for the leap that was to settle him.

His eyes darkened—it was close; and, instinctively turning, in his hallucination, to avoid it, he flung himself, face down, on the tomb.

1901   1903, 1909

EMMA LAZARUS
1849–1887

S ince 1903, Emma Lazarus's sonnet "The New Colossus" has been on public
view inside the base of the Statue of Liberty; its last several lines, especially "huddled masses yearning to breathe free," have become part of the national vocabulary through which Americans describe the ideals of their nation.

Lazarus was born in New York City on July 22, 1849, to Moses Lazarus, a wealthy sugar refiner, and Esther Nathan Lazarus, both from families long resident in New York. Her father's family were Sephardic Jews from Portugal who had settled in New York while it was New Amsterdam. She grew up in luxury in Manhattan and summered in fashionable Newport, Rhode Island. Educated by tutors in three modern languages and literatures besides English, Lazarus was precocious, and when her father paid for the publication of *Poems and Translations . . . Written between the Ages of Fourteen and Sixteen* in 1866, she sent copies to several well-known poets, among them Ralph Waldo Emerson, who politely offered to be her "professor" in stylistic matters. In addition to Emerson, Lazarus came to know many American writers of the time, and her enthusiasm for Whitman, Thoreau, and other American writers culminated in her short manifesto "American Literature" (1881).

Early in her literary life, Lazarus identified with the German-Jewish poet Heinrich Heine, who had felt both at home in and estranged from a Christian society and non-Hebraic literature. Though Lazarus had written such poems as "In the Jewish Synagogue at Newport," her intellectual efforts into the early 1880s focused on the continuities and distinctions between American and English literature. But in 1882, horrified that newspapers were minimizing Russian atrocities against Jews, Lazarus fashioned herself into a Jewish spokeswoman on international themes as they affected American national policy on immigration. Her essay "Russian Christianity *versus* Modern Judaism," published in the *Century* in 1882, describes the reign of "murder, rape, arson" during which tens of thousands of Jewish families in Eastern Europe had been reduced "to homeless beggary." That November, playing on Paul's New Testament letter, she began serial publication in the *American Hebrew* of "An Epistle to the Hebrew." There she urged American Jews to become more, not less, "tribal," and to recognize that their freedom depended upon the freedom of Jews in Russia and elsewhere. The following year, in "The Jewish Problem," Lazarus spoke out as an early Zionist, echoing the fervent determination of George Eliot's title character in *Daniel Deronda* to make the Jews "a nation again." And she began visiting the "undesirable" new immigrants detained on Ward's Island in the East River, those deemed too destitute or too infirm to be allowed into American society. In 1883 she founded the Society for the Improvement and Colonization of Eastern European Jews.

Lazarus's poetry combines free-flowing, often powerful imagery with a careful attention to poetic form. Those qualities are on display in "The New Colossus," which Lazarus composed in 1883 as part of a fundraising effort to support the building of the pedestal for the Statue of Liberty. The statue, a gift from France to the United States, had been conceived as a memorial to France's aid of the colonies during the American Revolution. In hailing the female figure as the "Mother of Exiles," Lazarus redefined the "mighty woman with a torch" into the national welcomer of "huddled masses" seeking refuge. Building on her own knowledge of immigrants arriving in New York Harbor, she redefined the significance of the statue away from the past and toward the future.

Lazarus traveled to Europe in 1883 and 1885, meeting several famous poets, including Robert Browning. Her death, from cancer, in 1887 cut short a remarkable career, and her reputation was solidified the following year, when her sisters posthumously published *The Poems of Emma Lazarus*.

In the Jewish Synagogue at Newport[1]

Here, where the noises of the busy town,
    The ocean's plunge and roar can enter not,
We stand and gaze around with tearful awe,
    And muse upon the consecrated spot.

No signs of life are here: the very prayers   5
    Inscribed around are in a language dead;[2]
The light of the "perpetual lamp"[3] is spent
    That an undying radiance was to shed.

What prayers were in this temple offered up,
    Wrung from sad hearts that knew no joy on earth,   10
By these lone exiles of a thousand years,
    From the fair sunrise land that gave them birth!

Now as we gaze, in this new world of light,[4]
    Upon this relic of the days of old,
The present vanishes, and tropic bloom   15
    And Eastern towns and temples we behold.

Again we see the patriarch[5] with his flocks,
    The purple seas, the hot blue sky o'erhead,
The slaves of Egypt,—omens, mysteries,—
    Dark fleeing hosts by flaming angels led,[6]   20

A wondrous light upon a sky-kissed mount,[7]
    A man who reads Jehovah's written law,

1. The text is from *Admetus and Other Poems* (1871), where it is dated "July 1867." It is a companion piece to Henry Wadsworth Longfellow's similarly meditative "The Jewish Cemetery at Newport," about the cemetery attached to the Touro Synagogue, the oldest in the United States, dating from 1763. The synagogue was closed during the years that Lazarus summered in Newport at her family's country house.
2. "Dead" because at that time Hebrew was not used in everyday life.
3. In a synagogue, the light above the ark which holds the Torah (the first five books of the Hebrew scriptures—Genesis, Exodus, Leviticus, Numbers, Deuteronomy).
4. The United States.
5. Abraham (Genesis 24.35), his son Isaac, or Isaac's sons. Lazarus is not striving for specificity but evoking images of Jewish history.
6. The enslavement of Jews in Egypt is described in Exodus 1. After the Hebrews crossed the Red Sea, a pillar of cloud by day and a pillar of fire by night led them through the desert (Exodus 13.21–22).
7. Mount Sinai, where God gave Moses the Ten Commandments (Exodus 34).

'Midst blinding glory and effulgence rare,
    Unto a people prone with reverent awe.

The pride of luxury's barbaric pomp,   25
    In the rich court of royal Solomon—[8]
Alas! we wake: one scene alone remains—
    The exiles by the streams of Babylon.[9]

Our softened voices send us back again
    But mournful echoes through the empty hall;   30
Our footsteps have a strange unnatural sound,
    And with unwonted gentleness they fall.

The weary ones, the sad, the suffering,
    All found their comfort in the holy place,
And children's gladness and men's gratitude   35
    Took voice and mingled in the chant of praise.

The funeral and the marriage, now, alas!
    We know not which is sadder to recall;
For youth and happiness have followed age,
    And green grass lieth gently over all.   40

Nathless[1] the sacred shrine is holy yet,
    With its lone floors where reverent feet once trod.
Take off your shoes as by the burning bush,
    Before the mystery of death and God.

1867   1871

1492[1]

Thou two-faced year, Mother of Change and Fate,
Didst weep when Spain cast forth with flaming sword,
The children of the prophets of the Lord,
Prince, priest, and people, spurned by zealot hate.
Hounded from sea to sea, from state to state,   5
The West[2] refused them, and the East abhorred.
No anchorage the known world could afford,
Close-locked was every port, barred every gate.[3]
Then smiling, thou unveil'dst, O two-faced year,

8. Solomon's magnificence is described in 1
Kings 4; the building of the First Temple (in
Jerusalem) is described in 1 Kings 5–8.
9. The First Temple was destroyed around 588–
586 B.C.E. and the Jews exiled to Babylon, the site
of the modern Hilla, in Iraq, south of Baghdad.
1. Nevertheless (poetic archaism).
1. This poem, reprinted from *Poems* (1888),
acknowledges two events in Spain in 1492. Early
in the year King Ferdinand and Queen Isabella
drove from Spain all Jews who would not convert
to Catholicism. A few months later they invested
in Christopher Columbus's voyage into the
Atlantic in the hope of establishing a new trade
route to the East Indies.
2. Northern Europe, as opposed to the eastern
Mediterranean.
3. The Jews expelled from Spain spread out over
the Mediterranean region, many being robbed,
many dying of the plague, some being enslaved,
some murdered.

A virgin world where doors of sunset part,   10
Saying, "Ho, all who weary, enter here!
There falls each ancient barrier that the art
Of race or creed or rank devised, to rear
Grim bulwarked hatred between heart and heart!"

1883   1888

The New Colossus[1]

Not like the brazen giant of Greek fame,[2]
With conquering limbs astride from land to land;
Here at our sea-washed, sunset gates shall stand
A mighty woman with a torch, whose flame
Is the imprisoned lightning, and her name   5
Mother of Exiles. From her beacon-hand
Glows world-wide welcome; her mild eyes command
The air-bridged harbor that twin cities[3] frame.
"Keep, ancient lands, your storied pomp!" cries she
With silent lips. "Give me your tired, your poor,   10
Your huddled masses yearning to breathe free,
The wretched refuse of your teeming shore.
Send these, the homeless, tempest-tost to me,
I lift my lamp beside the golden door!"

1883   1888

1. The footnote to the 1888 *Poems of Emma Lazarus*, the source of the present text, reads "Written in aid of Bartholdi Pedestal Fund, 1883." The sculpture was by Frédéric-Auguste Bartholdi (1834–1904).
2. The gigantic statue of the sun god, Helios, created by the sculptor Chares of Lindos, loomed over the harbor of the Greek island of Rhodes for several decades before being destroyed in an earthquake in 225 B.C.E. Later reports exaggerated the size, saying that the legs of the statue straddled the harbor.
3. New York City and Jersey City, New Jersey.

SARAH ORNE JEWETT
1849–1909

When Sarah Orne Jewett was born in South Berwick, Maine, in 1849, the town and region she would memorialize in her fiction were already changing rapidly. Her grandfather had been a sea captain, shipowner, and merchant, and as a child she was exposed to the bustle of this small inland port. By the end of the Civil War, however, textile mills and a cannery had largely replaced agriculture, shipbuilding, and logging as the economic base of the community, and the arrival of French Canadian and Irish immigrants brought greater ethnic diversity to the area. The stable, secure, and remote small town Jewett knew and loved as a child was experiencing the economic, technological, and demographic pressures that transformed much of America in her lifetime.

Jewett and her two sisters led happy and generally carefree childhoods. Their father was a kindly, hardworking obstetrician who encouraged Jewett's reading. As a small child she accompanied him on his horse-and-buggy rounds, meeting the rural people who would later populate her fiction. Jewett loved her father deeply, and some of her strong feelings for him are invested in *A Country Doctor* (1884), a novel that also celebrates the independence of its female protagonist. Jewett's relationship with her mother was less intense; it was not until her mother became an invalid in the 1880s that mother and daughter became close. As Jewett confessed in a letter to editor and friend Thomas Bailey Aldrich: "I never felt so near to my mother . . . as I have since she died."

In part inspired by Harriet Beecher Stowe's novel about Maine seacoast life, *The Pearl of Orr's Island* (1862), Jewett began to write and publish verse and stories in her teens. One of her first efforts was accepted for publication in 1869 by William Dean Howells—then assistant editor for the prestigious *Atlantic Monthly*. In her early twenties, encouraged by Howells, she wrote a group of stories and sketches about a fictional coastal town in Maine to which she gave the name Deephaven; she published her first collection of short pieces in 1877 under that title. With the publication of this book, she entered the company of the many post–Civil War regional writers who were depicting the topographies, people, speech patterns, and modes of life of the nation's distinctive regions as they came under pressure from modernizing forces.

From the late 1870s on, Jewett was part of a circle of prominent writers, artists, and editors who lived in or near Boston. The relationship between Jewett and Annie Adams Fields, the wife of the highly influential editor and publisher James T. Fields, was the most important of her many friendships with men and women. Though they had known each other since the late 1870s, it was not until Annie Fields's husband died in 1881 that they established a bond that was to sustain both women until Jewett's death in 1909. During the winter months, Jewett lived at Fields's house in Boston and in the spring and summer was often to be found at Fields's oceanside home a few miles north of Boston in Manchester-by-the-Sea. Jewett maintained her residence in South Berwick, and she and Fields would spend time together there as well. Their relationship, common at the turn of the century among single women who lived and traveled together, was often called a "Boston marriage." Scholars interested in the nineteenth-century history of same-sex desire have frequently turned both to Jewett's biography and to her fiction, where deep, emotionally complicated attachments between women figure prominently.

Jewett reached artistic maturity with the publication of *A White Heron and Other Stories* in 1886; later collections of sketches and stories include *The King of Folly Island* (1888), *A Native of Winby* (1893), and *The Life of Nancy* (1895). In these works the local landscape, people, and dialect are recorded with understanding and sympathy. In "A White Heron," reprinted here, a young girl's conflicted loyalties to her conception of herself in nature and to the world of men she will soon encounter are memorably and sensitively drawn. Long-time residents of these small Maine communities make up the bulk of Jewett's fiction, including her most enduring work, *The Country of the Pointed Firs* (1896). This book is comprised of a series of linked sketches filtered through the consciousness of a summer visitor, much like the person Jewett had become. In this work, bits and pieces of the lives of a small group of men and women are quilted into a unified impression of life in a once-prosperous shipping village. The strong older women who survive in the region form a female community that, for many critics, is a hallmark of New England regionalism. The chapters of the book reproduced here introduce the summer visitor and the community of Dunnet Landing—as well as its history of maritime activity through the figure of Captain Littlepage. The book was well received, and Jewett would go on to publish four additional stories set in Dunnet Landing. Before her death in 1909, Jewett met the admiring Willa Cather, who would celebrate and edit Jewett's work in the decades to come. For Cather, *The Country of the Pointed Firs* ranked with *The Scarlet Letter* and *Adventures of Huckleberry Finn* as a landmark of American literature.

A White Heron[1]

I

The woods were already filled with shadows one June evening, just before eight o'clock, though a bright sunset still glimmered faintly among the trunks of the trees. A little girl was driving home her cow, a plodding, dilatory, provoking creature in her behavior, but a valued companion for all that. They were going away from whatever light there was, and striking deep into the woods, but their feet were familiar with the path, and it was no matter whether their eyes could see it or not.

There was hardly a night the summer through when the old cow could be found waiting at the pasture bars; on the contrary, it was her greatest pleasure to hide herself away among the high huckleberry bushes, and though she wore a loud bell she had made the discovery that if one stood perfectly still it would not ring. So Sylvia had to hunt for her until she found her, and call Co'! Co'! with never an answering Moo, until her childish patience was quite spent. If the creature had not given good milk and plenty of it, the case would have seemed very different to her owners. Besides, Sylvia had all the time there was, and very little use to make of it. Sometimes in pleasant weather it was a consolation to look upon the cow's pranks as an intelligent attempt to play hide and seek, and as the child had no playmates she lent herself to this amusement with a good deal of zest. Though this chase had been so long that the wary animal herself had given an unusual signal of her whereabouts, Sylvia had only laughed when she came upon Mistress Moolly at the swamp-side, and urged her affectionately homeward with a twig of birch leaves. The old cow was not inclined to wander farther, she even turned in the right direction for once as they left the pasture, and stepped along the road at a good pace. She was quite ready to be milked now, and seldom stopped to browse. Sylvia wondered what her grandmother would say because they were so late. It was a great while since she had left home at half past five o'clock, but everybody knew the difficulty of making this errand a short one. Mrs. Tilley had chased the hornéd torment too many summer evenings herself to blame any one else for lingering, and was only thankful as she waited that she had Sylvia, nowadays, to give such valuable assistance. The good woman suspected that Sylvia loitered occasionally on her own account; there never was such a child for straying about out-of-doors since the world was made! Everybody said that it was a good change for a little maid who had tried to grow for eight years in a crowded manufacturing town, but, as for Sylvia herself, it seemed as if she never had been alive

---

1. First published in book form in *A White Heron and Other Stories* (1886), the source of the text printed here.

at all before she came to live at the farm. She thought often with wistful compassion of a wretched geranium that belonged to a town neighbor.

"'Afraid of folks,'" old Mrs. Tilley said to herself, with a smile, after she had made the unlikely choice of Sylvia from her daughter's houseful of children, and was returning to the farm. "'Afraid of folks,' they said! I guess she won't be troubled no great with 'em up to the old place!" When they reached the door of the lonely house and stopped to unlock it, and the cat came to purr loudly, and rub against them, a deserted pussy, indeed, but fat with young robins, Sylvia whispered that this was a beautiful place to live in, and she never should wish to go home.

The companions followed the shady woodroad, the cow taking slow steps, and the child very fast ones. The cow stopped long at the brook to drink, as if the pasture were not half a swamp, and Sylvia stood still and waited, letting her bare feet cool themselves in the shoal water, while the great twilight moths struck softly against her. She waded on through the brook as the cow moved away, and listened to the thrushes with a heart that beat fast with pleasure. There was a stirring in the great boughs overhead. They were full of little birds and beasts that seemed to be wide awake, and going about their world, or else saying good-night to each other in sleepy twitters. Sylvia herself felt sleepy as she walked along. However, it was not much farther to the house, and the air was soft and sweet. She was not often in the woods so late as this, and it made her feel as if she were a part of the gray shadows and the moving leaves. She was just thinking how long it seemed since she first came to the farm a year ago, and wondering if everything went on in the noisy town just the same as when she was there; the thought of the great red-faced boy who used to chase and frighten her made her hurry along the path to escape from the shadow of the trees.

Suddenly this little woods-girl is horror-stricken to hear a clear whistle not very far away. Not a bird's whistle, which would have a sort of friendliness, but a boy's whistle, determined, and somewhat aggressive. Sylvia left the cow to whatever sad fate might await her, and stepped discreetly aside into the bushes, but she was just too late. The enemy had discovered her, and called out in a very cheerful and persuasive tone, "Halloa, little girl, how far is it to the road?" and trembling Sylvia answered almost inaudibly, "A good ways."

She did not dare to look boldly at the tall young man, who carried a gun over his shoulder, but she came out of her bush and again followed the cow, while he walked alongside.

"I have been hunting for some birds," the stranger said kindly, "and I have lost my way, and need a friend very much. Don't be afraid," he added gallantly. "Speak up and tell me what your name is, and whether you think I can spend the night at your house, and go out gunning early in the morning."

Sylvia was more alarmed than before. Would not her grandmother consider her much to blame? But who could have foreseen such an accident as this? It did not seem to be her fault, and she hung her head as if the stem of it were broken, but managed to answer "Sylvy," with much effort when her companion again asked her name.

Mrs. Tilley was standing in the doorway when the trio came into view. The cow gave a loud moo by way of explanation.

"Yes, you'd better speak up for yourself, you old trial! Where'd she tucked herself away this time, Sylvy?" But Sylvia kept an awed silence; she knew by instinct that her grandmother did not comprehend the gravity of the situation. She must be mistaking the stranger for one of the farmer-lads of the region.

The young man stood his gun beside the door, and dropped a lumpy game-bag beside it; then he bade Mrs. Tilley good-evening, and repeated his wayfarer's story, and asked if he could have a night's lodging.

"Put me anywhere you like," he said. "I must be off early in the morning, before day; but I am very hungry, indeed. You can give me some milk at any rate, that's plain."

"Dear sakes, yes," responded the hostess, whose long slumbering hospitality seemed to be easily awakened. "You might fare better if you went out to the main road a mile or so, but you're welcome to what we've got. I'll milk right off, and you make yourself at home. You can sleep on husks or feathers," she proffered graciously. "I raised them all myself. There's good pasturing for geese just below here towards the ma'sh. Now step round and set a plate for the gentleman, Sylvy!" And Sylvia promptly stepped. She was glad to have something to do, and she was hungry herself.

It was a surprise to find so clean and comfortable a little dwelling in this New England wilderness. The young man had known the horrors of its most primitive housekeeping, and the dreary squalor of that level of society which does not rebel at the companionship of hens. This was the best thrift of an old-fashioned farmstead, though on such a small scale that it seemed like a hermitage. He listened eagerly to the old woman's quaint talk, he watched Sylvia's pale face and shining gray eyes with ever growing enthusiasm, and insisted that this was the best supper he had eaten for a month, and afterward the new-made friends sat down in the door-way together while the moon came up.

Soon it would be berry-time, and Sylvia was a great help at picking. The cow was a good milker, though a plaguy thing to keep track of, the hostess gossiped frankly, adding presently that she had buried four children, so Sylvia's mother, and a son (who might be dead) in California were all the children she had left. "Dan, my boy, was a great hand to go gunning," she explained sadly. "I never wanted for pa'tridges or gray squer'ls while he was to home. He's been a great wand'rer, I expect, and he's no hand to write letters. There, I don't blame him, I'd ha' seen the world myself if it had been so I could.

"Sylvia takes after him," the grandmother continued affectionately, after a minute's pause. "There ain't a foot o' ground she don't know her way over, and the wild creaturs counts her one o' themselves. Squer'ls she'll tame to come an' feed right out o' her hands, and all sorts o' birds. Last winter she got the jay-birds to bangeing[2] here, and I believe she'd 'a' scanted herself of her own meals to have plenty to throw out amongst 'em, if I hadn't kep' watch. Anything but crows, I tell her, I'm willin' to help support—though Dan he had a tamed one o' them that did seem to have reason same as folks. It was round here a good spell after he went away. Dan an' his father they didn't hitch,—but he never held up his head ag'in after Dan had dared him an' gone off."

2. Hanging around.

The guest did not notice this hint of family sorrows in his eager interest in something else.

"So Sylvy knows all about birds, does she?" he exclaimed, as he looked round at the little girl who sat, very demure but increasingly sleepy, in the moonlight. "I am making a collection of birds myself. I have been at it ever since I was a boy." (Mrs. Tilley smiled.) "There are two or three very rare ones I have been hunting for these five years. I mean to get them on my own ground if they can be found."

"Do you cage 'em up?" asked Mrs. Tilley doubtfully, in response to this enthusiastic announcement.

"Oh, no, they're stuffed and preserved, dozens and dozens of them," said the ornithologist, "and I have shot or snared every one myself. I caught a glimpse of a white heron three miles from here on Saturday, and I have followed it in this direction. They have never been found in this district at all.[3] The little white heron, it is," and he turned again to look at Sylvia with the hope of discovering that the rare bird was one of her acquaintances.

But Sylvia was watching a hop-toad in the narrow footpath.

"You would know the heron if you saw it," the stranger continued eagerly. "A queer tall white bird with soft feathers and long thin legs. And it would have a nest perhaps in the top of a high tree, made of sticks, something like a hawk's nest."

Sylvia's heart gave a wild beat; she knew that strange white bird, and had once stolen softly near where it stood in some bright green swamp grass, away over at the other side of the woods. There was an open place where the sunshine always seemed strangely yellow and hot, where tall, nodding rushes grew, and her grandmother had warned her that she might sink in the soft black mud underneath and never be heard of more. Not far beyond were the salt marshes just this side the sea itself, which Sylvia wondered and dreamed about, but never had seen, whose great voice could sometimes be heard above the noise of the woods on stormy nights.

"I can't think of anything I should like so much as to find that heron's nest," the handsome stranger was saying. "I would give ten dollars to anybody who could show it to me," he added desperately, "and I mean to spend my whole vacation hunting for it if need be. Perhaps it was only migrating, or had been chased out of its own region by some bird of prey."

Mrs. Tilley gave amazed attention to all this, but Sylvia still watched the toad, not divining, as she might have done at some calmer time, that the creature wished to get to its hole under the door-step, and was much hindered by the unusual spectators at that hour of the evening. No amount of thought, that night, could decide how many wished-for treasures the ten dollars, so lightly spoken of, would buy.

The next day the young sportsman hovered about the woods, and Sylvia kept him company, having lost her first fear of the friendly lad, who proved to be most kind and sympathetic. He told her many things about the birds and what they knew and where they lived and what they did with themselves. And he gave her a jack-knife, which she thought as great a treasure as if she

---

3. Several species of herons were endangered during Jewett's time because hat-makers sought their dramatic wing feathers.

were a desert-islander. All day long he did not once make her troubled or afraid except when he brought down some unsuspecting singing creature from its bough. Sylvia would have liked him vastly better without his gun; she could not understand why he killed the very birds he seemed to like so much. But as the day waned, Sylvia still watched the young man with loving admiration. She had never seen anybody so charming and delightful; the woman's heart, asleep in the child, was vaguely thrilled by a dream of love. Some premonition of that great power stirred and swayed these young creatures who traversed the solemn woodlands with soft-footed silent care. They stopped to listed to a bird's song; they pressed forward again eagerly, parting the branches,—speaking to each other rarely and in whispers; the young man going first and Sylvia following, fascinated, a few steps behind, with her gray eyes dark with excitement.

She grieved because the longed-for white heron was elusive, but she did not lead the guest, she only followed, and there was no such thing as speaking first. The sound of her own unquestioned voice would have terrified her,—it was hard enough to answer yes or no when there was need of that. At last evening began to fall, and they drove the cow home together, and Sylvia smiled with pleasure when they came to the place where she heard the whistle and was afraid only the night before.

II

Half a mile from home, at the farther edge of the woods, where the land was highest, a great pine-tree stood, the last of its generation. Whether it was left for a boundary mark, or for what reason, no one could say; the wood-choppers who had felled its mates were dead and gone long ago, and a whole forest of sturdy trees, pines and oaks and maples, had grown again. But the stately head of this old pine towered above them all and made a landmark for sea and shore miles and miles away. Sylvia knew it well. She had always believed that whoever climbed to the top of it could see the ocean; and the little girl had often laid her hand on the great rough trunk and looked up wistfully at those dark boughs that the wind always stirred, no matter how hot and still the air might be below. Now she thought of the tree with a new excitement, for why, if one climbed it at break of day, could not one see all the world, and easily discover from whence the white heron flew, and mark the place, and find the hidden nest?

What a spirit of adventure, what wild ambition! What fancied triumph and delight and glory for the later morning when she could make known the secret! It was almost too real and too great for the childish heart to bear.

All night the door of the little house stood open and the whippoorwills came and sang upon the very step. The young sportsman and his old hostess were sound asleep, but Sylvia's great design kept her broad awake and watching. She forgot to think of sleep. The short summer night seemed as long as the winter darkness, and at last when the whippoorwills ceased, and she was afraid the morning would after all come too soon, she stole out of the house and followed the pasture path through the woods, hastening toward the open ground beyond, listening with a sense of comfort and companionship to the drowsy twitter of a half-awakened bird, whose perch she had jarred in passing. Alas, if the great wave of human interest which flooded for the first time this dull little life should sweep away the satisfactions of an existence heart to heart with nature and the dumb life of the forest!

There was the huge tree asleep yet in the paling moonlight, and small and silly Sylvia began with utmost bravery to mount to the top of it, with tingling, eager blood coursing the channels of her whole frame, with her bare feet and fingers, that pinched and held like bird's claws to the monstrous ladder reaching up, up, almost to the sky itself. First she must mount the white oak tree that grew alongside, where she was almost lost among the dark branches and the green leaves heavy and wet with dew; a bird fluttered off its nest, and a red squirrel ran to and fro and scolded pettishly at the harmless housebreaker. Sylvia felt her way easily. She had often climbed there, and knew that higher still one of the oak's upper branches chafed against the pine trunk, just where its lower boughs were set close together. There, when she made the dangerous pass from one tree to the other, the great enterprise would really begin.

She crept out along the swaying oak limb at last, and took the daring step across into the old pine-tree. The way was harder than she thought; she must reach far and hold fast, the sharp dry twigs caught and held her and scratched her like angry talons, the pitch made her thin little fingers clumsy and stiff as she went round and round the tree's great stem, higher and higher upward. The sparrows and robins in the woods below were beginning to wake and twitter to the dawn, yet it seemed much lighter there aloft in the pine-tree, and the child knew that she must hurry if her project were to be of any use.

The tree seemed to lengthen itself out as she went up, and to reach farther and farther upward. It was like a great main-mast to the voyaging earth; it must truly have been amazed that morning through all its ponderous frame as it felt this determined spark of human spirit winding its way from higher branch to branch. Who knows how steadily the least twigs held themselves to advantage this light, weak creature on her way! The old pine must have loved his new dependent. More than all the hawks, and bats, and moths, and even the sweet voiced thrushes, was the brave, beating heart of the solitary gray-eyed child. And the tree stood still and frowned away the winds that June morning while the dawn grew bright in the east.

Sylvia's face was like a pale star, if one had seen it from the ground, when the last thorny bough was past, and she stood trembling and tired but wholly triumphant, high in the tree-top. Yes, there was the sea with the dawning sun making a golden dazzle over it, and toward that glorious east flew two hawks with slow-moving pinions. How low they looked in the air from that height when one had only seen them before far up, and dark against the blue sky. Their gray feathers were as soft as moths; they seemed only a little way from the tree, and Sylvia felt as if she too could go flying away among the clouds. Westward, the woodlands and farms reached miles and miles into the distance; here and there were church steeples, and white villages; truly it was a vast and awesome world!

The birds sang louder and louder. At last the sun came up bewilderingly bright. Sylvia could see the white sails of ships out at sea, and the clouds that were purple and rose-colored and yellow at first began to fade away. Where was the white heron's nest in the sea of green branches, and was this wonderful sight and pageant of the world the only reward for having climbed to such a giddy height? Now look down again, Sylvia, where the green marsh is set among the shining birches and dark hemlocks; there where you saw the white heron once you will see him again; look, look! a white spot of him like a single floating feather comes up from the dead hemlock and grows larger, and rises, and comes close at last, and goes by the landmark pine with steady sweep of wing and outstretched slender neck and crested head. And wait! wait! do not move a foot or a finger, little girl, do not send an arrow of light and consciousness from your two eager eyes, for the heron has perched on a pine bough not far beyond yours, and cries back to his mate on the nest, and plumes his feathers for the new day!

The child gives a long sigh a minute later when a company of shouting cat-birds comes also to the tree, and vexed by their fluttering and lawlessness the solemn heron goes away. She knows his secret now, the wild, light, slender bird that floats and wavers, and goes back like an arrow presently to his home in the green world beneath. Then Sylvia, well satisfied, makes her perilous way down again, not daring to look far below the branch she stands on, ready to cry sometimes because her fingers ache and her lamed feet slip. Wondering over and over again what the stranger would say to her, and what he would think when she told him how to find his way straight to the heron's nest.

"Sylvy, Sylvy!" called the busy old grandmother again and again, but nobody answered, and the small husk bed was empty and Sylvia had disappeared.

The guest waked from a dream, and remembering his day's pleasure hurried to dress himself that might it sooner begin. He was sure from the way the shy little girl looked once or twice yesterday that she had at least seen the white heron, and now she must really be made to tell. Here she comes now, paler than ever, and her worn old frock is torn and tattered, and smeared with pine pitch. The grandmother and the sportsman stand in the door together and question her, and the splendid moment has come to speak of the dead hemlock-tree by the green marsh.

But Sylvia does not speak after all, though the old grandmother fretfully rebukes her, and the young man's kind, appealing eyes are looking straight in her own. He can make them rich with money; he has promised it, and they are poor now. He is so well worth making happy, and he waits to hear the story she can tell.

No, she must keep silence! What is it that suddenly forbids her and makes her dumb? Has she been nine years growing and now, when the great world for the first time puts out a hand to her, must she thrust it aside for a bird's sake? The murmur of the pine's green branches is in her ears, she remembers how the white heron came flying through the golden air and how they watched the sea and the morning together, and Sylvia cannot speak; she cannot tell the heron's secret and give its life away.

Dear loyalty, that suffered a sharp pang as the guest went away disappointed later in the day, that could have served and followed him and loved him as a dog loves! Many a night Sylvia heard the echo of his whistle haunting the pasture path as she came home with the loitering cow. She forgot even her sorrow at the sharp report of his gun and the sight of thrushes and sparrows dropping silent to the ground, their songs hushed and their pretty feathers stained and wet with blood. Were the birds better friends than their hunter might have been,—who can tell? Whatever treasures were lost to her, woodlands and summer-time, remember! Bring your gifts and graces and tell your secrets to this lonely country child!

1886

KATE CHOPIN
1850–1904

The Irish immigrant father of Katherine O'Flaherty, known to us now as the author Kate Chopin, was a successful businessman who died in a train wreck when his daughter was five years old. The family enjoyed a high place in St. Louis society; and her mother, grandmother, and great-grandmother were active, pious Catholics of French heritage. Chopin grew up in the company of loving, intelligent, independent women—all of whom had been widowed at a young age and none of whom had remarried. Chopin's strong-willed great-grandmother, moreover, was a compelling and tireless storyteller who may have influenced Chopin's later development as a writer of short fiction and novels.

Chopin was nine years old when she entered St. Louis Academy of the Sacred Heart, but she was already well read in English and French authors. By the time she graduated from the academy in 1868, the nuns of the Academy had instructed her further in literature, history, and science. But it was French writers who most strongly influenced Chopin. She read and admired French classical authors as well as more contemporary figures such as Gustave Flaubert, Madame de Staël, Émile Zola, and Guy de Maupassant. What she said of Maupassant as a writer she might have said of herself: "Here was a man who had escaped from tradition and authority, who had entered into himself and looked out upon life through his own being and with his own eyes; and who in a direct and simple way, told us what he saw." Whether focusing on St. Louis, New Orleans, or the Louisiana countryside, she described the tension between individual erotic inclination and the constraints placed on desire—especially on women's sexual desire—by traditional social mores. She described directly and without moral judgment the challenge of women in the male-dominated culture that limited all aspects of women's lives—even the lives of comfortably situated women—and tried to control their psyches as well. Her new, modern perspectives, especially on female sexuality, paralleled those of Edith Wharton and Theodore Dreiser.

At the age of nineteen she married Oscar Chopin and spent the next decade in New Orleans, where her husband first prospered, then failed, as a cotton broker. They lived for a few years in Cloutierville, a village in northwest Louisiana near Natchitoches, where her husband opened a general store and managed a family cotton plantation. He died in 1883 from swamp fever (probably malaria), and a year later she returned to St. Louis permanently. Then her mother died, in 1885, and at the age of thirty-five Chopin was left essentially alone to raise her six young children. Having recognized the marketplace for "local color," or regional, fiction, Chopin decided to fashion a literary career out of her experiences with the cultural diversity of Louisiana. She depicted Cajuns, descendants of French immigrants who arrived in Louisiana after being deported from Canada in the eighteenth century, as well as French Creoles, elite members of Louisiana society whose ancestry included the French and Spanish colonists of the region. Both groups distinguished themselves from the more recently arrived Americans.

Chopin claimed that she wrote on impulse, that she was "completely at the mercy of unconscious selection" of subject, and that "the polishing up process . . . always proved disastrous." In the relatively few years of her writing career—scarcely more than a decade—she completed three novels, more than 150 stories and sketches, and a substantial body of poetry, reviews, and criticism. (She also translated the stories of Maupassant, but did little to publish them.) A first novel, *At Fault*, was self-published in 1890, but it was her stories of Louisiana rural life, especially in the collection *Bayou Folk* (1894), that won her national recognition. A second collection of stories, *A Night in Acadie*, was published three years later and increased her reputation as a local colorist. Chopin, who wrote about her own time, did not concern herself with the prewar South, but stories such as "Désirée's Baby" reveal the pernicious residues of an outdated social ideology. At the same time, the influence of French fiction on her work showed in stories that were much more erotic—and guilt-free—than the American norm. Her awareness of a disconnect between her work and American culture may explain why she did not submit "The Storm" for publication; it was not published until 1969 as part of Per Seyersted's edition of *The Complete Works of Kate Chopin*.

Chopin's major work, *The Awakening*, was published in 1899. The novel, which traces the sensual and sexual coming to consciousness of a young woman, predictably aroused hostility among contemporary reviewers. Edna Pontellier is not a "new woman" demanding social, economic, and political equality; instead she can appear to be an unrepentant (if ultimately psychologically confused) sensualist, leading some critics to charge that the book was "essentially vulgar" and "unhealthily introspective and morbid in feeling." (Even Willa Cather, in her review of *The Awakening*, wondered why Chopin "devoted so exquisite and sensitive, well-governed a style to so trite and sordid a theme.") But the readers who objected to Edna's behavior missed Chopin's portrayal of Edna's psychological turmoil. Though some commentators found much to praise in *The Awakening*, Chopin's only published response to reviews of the novel was to claim, "I never dreamed of Mrs. Pontellier making such a mess of things and working out her own damnation as she did. If I had had the slightest intimation of such a thing I would have excluded her from the company." In the years following publication of the novel, Chopin's health deteriorated, and she wrote little. After her death, Chopin fell into obscurity for over a half a century, and it was not until the 1970s that *The Awakening* and a number of her stories came to be recognized as among the major achievements of turn-of-the-century American literary culture.

Désirée's Baby[1]

As the day was pleasant, Madame Valmondé drove over to L'Abri to see Désirée and the baby.

It made her laugh to think of Désirée with a baby. Why, it seemed but yesterday that Désirée was little more than a baby herself; when Monsieur in riding through the gateway of Valmondé had found her lying asleep in the shadow of the big stone pillar.

1. The story was first published in the January 4, 1893, *Vogue* as "The Father of Désirée's Baby— The Lover of Mentine," and then included in *Bayou Folk* (1894) with its present title. The text is taken from Per Seyersted's edition of *The Complete Works of Kate Chopin* (1969).

The little one awoke in his arms and began to cry for "Dada." That was as much as she could do or say. Some people thought she might have strayed there of her own accord, for she was of the toddling age. The prevailing belief was that she had been purposely left by a party of Texans, whose canvas-covered wagon, late in the day, had crossed the ferry that Coton Maïs kept, just below the plantation. In time Madame Valmondé abandoned every speculation but the one that Désirée had been sent to her by a beneficent Providence to be the child of her affection, seeing that she was without child of the flesh. For the girl grew to be beautiful and gentle, affectionate and sincere,—the idol of Valmondé.

It was no wonder, when she stood one day against the stone pillar in whose shadow she had lain asleep, eighteen years before, that Armand Aubigny riding by and seeing her there, had fallen in love with her. That was the way all the Aubignys fell in love, as if struck by a pistol shot. The wonder was that he had not loved her before; for he had known her since his father brought him home from Paris, a boy of eight, after his mother died there. The passion that awoke in him that day, when he saw her at the gate, swept along like an avalanche, or like a prairie fire, or like anything that drives headlong over all obstacles.

Monsieur Valmondé grew practical and wanted things well considered: that is, the girl's obscure origin. Armand looked into her eyes and did not care. He was reminded that she was nameless. What did it matter about a name when he could give her one of the oldest and proudest in Louisiana? He ordered the *corbeille*[2] from Paris, and contained himself with what patience he could until it arrived; then they were married.

Madame Valmondé had not seen Désirée and the baby for four weeks. When she reached L'Abri she shuddered at the first sight of it, as she always did. It was a sad looking place, which for many years had not known the gentle presence of a mistress, old Monsieur Aubigny having married and buried his wife in France, and she having loved her own land too well ever to leave it. The roof came down steep and black like a cowl, reaching out beyond the wide galleries that encircled the yellow stuccoed house. Big, solemn oaks grew close to it, and their thick-leaved, far-reaching branches shadowed it like a pall. Young Aubigny's rule was a strict one, too, and under it his negroes had forgotten how to be gay, as they had been during the old master's easy-going and indulgent lifetime.

The young mother was recovering slowly, and lay full length, in her soft white muslins and laces, upon a couch. The baby was beside her, upon her arm, where he had fallen asleep, at her breast. The yellow[3] nurse woman sat beside a window fanning herself.

Madame Valmondé bent her portly figure over Désirée and kissed her, holding her an instant tenderly in her arms. Then she turned to the child.

"This is not the baby!" she exclaimed, in startled tones. French was the language spoken at Valmondé in those days.

"I knew you would be astonished," laughed Désirée, "at the way he has grown. The little *cochon de lait*![4] Look at his legs, mamma, and his hands

2. Basket (French), short for *corbeille de mar-riage*: lavish wedding gifts from bridegroom to bride, traditionally presented in a wicker basket.
3. Anachronistic, generally pejorative term for a

lightly complected African American.
4. Literally, a "pig in milk" (French); the term applies to a Cajun method of roasting pork.

and fingernails,—real finger-nails. Zandrine had to cut them this morning. Isn't it true, Zandrine?"

The woman bowed her turbaned head majestically, "Mais si,[5] Madame."

"And the way he cries," went on Désirée, "is deafening. Armand heard him the other day as far away as La Blanche's cabin."

Madame Valmondé had never removed her eyes from the child. She lifted it and walked with it over to the window that was lightest. She scanned the baby narrowly, then looked as searchingly at Zandrine, whose face was turned to gaze across the fields.

"Yes, the child has grown, has changed," said Madame Valmondé, slowly, as she replaced it beside its mother. "What does Armand say?"

Désirée's face became suffused with a glow that was happiness itself.

"Oh, Armand is the proudest father in the parish, I believe, chiefly because it is a boy, to bear his name; though he says not,—that he would have loved a girl as well. But I know it is n't true. I know he says that to please me. And mamma," she added, drawing Madame Valmondé's head down to her, and speaking in a whisper, "he has n't punished one of them—not one of them—since baby is born. Even Négrillon, who pretended to have burnt his leg that he might rest from work—he only laughed, and said Négrillon was a great scamp. Oh, mamma, I 'm so happy; it frightens me."

What Désirée said was true. Marriage, and later the birth of his son had softened Armand Aubigny's imperious and exacting nature greatly. This was what made the gentle Désirée so happy, for she loved him desperately. When he frowned she trembled, but loved him. When he smiled, she asked no greater blessing of God. But Armand's dark, handsome face had not often been disfigured by frowns since the day he fell in love with her.

When the baby was about three months old, Désirée awoke one day to the conviction that there was something in the air menacing her peace. It was at first too subtle to grasp. It had only been a disquieting suggestion; an air of mystery among the blacks; unexpected visits from far-off neighbors who could hardly account for their coming. Then a strange, an awful change in her husband's manner, which she dared not ask him to explain. When he spoke to her, it was with averted eyes, from which the old love-light seemed to have gone out. He absented himself from home; and when there, avoided her presence and that of her child, without excuse. And the very spirit of Satan seemed suddenly to take hold of him in his dealings with the slaves. Désirée was miserable enough to die.

She sat in her room, one hot afternoon, in her *peignoir*,[6] listlessly drawing through her fingers the strands of her long, silky brown hair that hung about her shoulders. The baby, half naked, lay asleep upon her own great mahogany bed, that was like a sumptuous throne, with its satin-lined half-canopy. One of La Blanche's little quadroon[7] boys—half naked too—stood fanning the child slowly with a fan of peacock feathers. Désirée's eyes had been fixed absently and sadly upon the baby, while she was striving to penetrate the threatening mist that she felt closing about her. She looked from her child to the boy who stood beside him, and back again; over and over.

---

5. Absolutely, yes (French).
6. Woman's dressing gown (French).
7. Term used in the 19th century (less often in the 20th century) for people thought to be one-

fourth black; more generally, "quadroon," like "mulatto," was used for light-skinned people of mixed racial ancestry.

"Ah!" It was a cry that she could not help; which she was not conscious of having uttered. The blood turned like ice in her veins, and a clammy moisture gathered upon her face.

She tried to speak to the little quadroon boy; but no sound would come, at first. When he heard his name uttered, he looked up, and his mistress was pointing to the door. He laid aside the great, soft fan, and obediently stole away, over the polished floor, on his bare tiptoes.

She stayed motionless, with gaze riveted upon her child, and her face the picture of fright.

Presently her husband entered the room, and without noticing her, went to a table and began to search among some papers which covered it.

"Armand," she called to him, in a voice which must have stabbed him, if he was human. But he did not notice. "Armand," she said again. Then she rose and tottered towards him. "Armand," she panted once more, clutching his arm, "look at our child. What does it mean? tell me."

He coldly but gently loosened her fingers from about his arm and thrust the hand away from him. "Tell what it means!" she cried despairingly.

"It means," he answered lightly, "that the child is not white; it means that you are not white."

A quick conception of all that this accusation meant for her nerved her with unwonted courage to deny it. "It is a lie; it is not true, I am white! Look at my hair, it is brown; and my eyes are gray, Armand, you know they are gray. And my skin is fair," seizing his wrist. "Look at my hand; whiter than yours, Armand," she laughed hysterically.

"As white as La Blanche's," he returned cruelly; and went away leaving her alone with their child.

When she could hold a pen in her hand, she sent a despairing letter to Madame Valmondé.

"My mother, they tell me I am not white. Armand has told me I am not white. For God's sake tell them it is not true. You must know it is not true. I shall die. I must die. I cannot be so unhappy, and live."

The answer that came was as brief:

"My own Désirée: Come home to Valmondé; back to your mother who loves you. Come with your child."

When the letter reached Désirée she went with it to her husband's study, and laid it open upon the desk before which he sat. She was like a stone image: silent, white, motionless after she placed it there.

In silence he ran his cold eyes over the written words. He said nothing. "Shall I go, Armand?" she asked in tones sharp with agonized suspense.

"Yes, go."

"Do you want me to go?"

"Yes, I want you to go."

He thought Almighty God had dealt cruelly and unjustly with him; and felt, somehow, that he was paying Him back in kind when he stabbed thus into his wife's soul. Moreover he no longer loved her, because of the unconscious injury she had brought upon his home and his name.

She turned away like one stunned by a blow, and walked slowly towards the door, hoping he would call her back.

"Good-by, Armand," she moaned.

He did not answer her. That was his last blow at fate.

Désirée went in search of her child. Zandrine was pacing the somber gallery with it. She took the little one from the nurse's arms with no word of explanation, and descending the steps, walked away, under the live-oak branches.

It was an October afternoon; the sun was just sinking. Out in the still fields the negroes were picking cotton.

Désirée had not changed the thin white garment nor the slippers which she wore. Her hair was uncovered and the sun's rays brought a golden gleam from its brown meshes. She did not take the broad, beaten road which led to the far-off plantation of Valmondé. She walked across a deserted field, where the stubble bruised her tender feet, so delicately shod, and tore her thin gown to shreds.

She disappeared among the reeds and willows that grew thick along the banks of the deep, sluggish bayou; and she did not come back again.

Some weeks later there was a curious scene enacted at L'Abri. In the centre of the smoothly swept back yard was a great bonfire. Armand Aubigny sat in the wide hallway that commanded a view of the spectacle; and it was he who dealt out to a half dozen negroes the material which kept this fire ablaze.

A graceful cradle of willow, with all its dainty furbishings, was laid upon the pyre, which had already been fed with the richness of a priceless *layette*.[8] Then there were silk gowns, and velvet and satin ones added to these; laces, too, and embroideries; bonnets and gloves; for the *corbeille* had been of rare quality.

The last thing to go was a tiny bundle of letters; innocent little scribblings that Désirée had sent to him during the days of their espousal. There was the remnant of one back in the drawer from which he took them. But it was not Désirée's; it was part of an old letter from his mother to his father. He read it. She was thanking God for the blessing of her husband's love:—

"But, above all," she wrote, "night and day, I thank the good God for having so arranged our lives that our dear Armand will never know that his mother, who adores him, belongs to the race that is cursed with the brand of slavery."

1893   1894

The Story of an Hour[1]

Knowing that Mrs. Mallard was afflicted with a heart trouble, great care was taken to break to her as gently as possible the news of her husband's death.

It was her sister Josephine who told her, in broken sentences; veiled hints that revealed in half concealing. Her husband's friend Richards was there,

---

8. A set of clothes for a newborn child (French).
1. The story was first published in the April 19, 1894, *Vogue* as "The Dream of an Hour," and then reprinted in the January 5, 1895, *St. Louis*

Life with its present title. The text is taken from Per Seyersted's edition of *The Complete Works of Kate Chopin* (1969).

too, near her. It was he who had been in the newspaper office when intelligence of the railroad disaster was received, with Brently Mallard's name leading the list of "killed." He had only taken the time to assure himself of its truth by a second telegram, and had hastened to forestall any less careful, less tender friend in bearing the sad message.

She did not hear the story as many women have heard the same, with a paralyzed inability to accept its significance. She wept at once, with sudden, wild abandonment, in her sister's arms. When the storm of grief had spent itself she went away to her room alone. She would have no one follow her.

There stood, facing the open window, a comfortable, roomy armchair. Into this she sank, pressed down by a physical exhaustion that haunted her body and seemed to reach into her soul.

She could see in the open square before her house the tops of trees that were all aquiver with the new spring life. The delicious breath of rain was in the air. In the street below a peddler was crying his wares. The notes of a distant song which some one was singing reached her faintly, and countless sparrows were twittering in the eaves.

There were patches of blue sky showing here and there through the clouds that had met and piled one above the other in the west facing her window.

She sat with her head thrown back upon the cushion of the chair, quite motionless, except when a sob came up into her throat and shook her, as a child who has cried itself to sleep continues to sob in its dreams.

She was young, with a fair, calm face, whose lines bespoke repression and even a certain strength. But now there was a dull stare in her eyes, whose gaze was fixed away off yonder on one of those patches of blue sky. It was not a glance of reflection, but rather indicated a suspension of intelligent thought.

There was something coming to her and she was waiting for it, fearfully. What was it? She did not know; it was too subtle and elusive to name. But she felt it, creeping out of the sky, reaching toward her through the sounds, the scents, the color that filled the air.

Now her bosom rose and fell tumultuously. She was beginning to recognize this thing that was approaching to possess her, and she was striving to beat it back with her will—as powerless as her two white slender hands would have been.

When she abandoned herself a little whispered word escaped her slightly parted lips. She said it over and over under her breath: "free, free, free!" The vacant stare and the look of terror that had followed it went from her eyes. They stayed keen and bright. Her pulses beat fast, and the coursing blood warmed and relaxed every inch of her body.

She did not stop to ask if it were or were not a monstrous joy that held her. A clear and exalted perception enabled her to dismiss the suggestion as trivial.

She knew that she would weep again when she saw the kind, tender hands folded in death; the face that had never looked save with love upon her, fixed and gray and dead. But she saw beyond that bitter moment a long procession of years to come that would belong to her absolutely. And she opened and spread her arms out to them in welcome.

There would be no one to live for her during those coming years; she would live for herself. There would be no powerful will bending hers in that blind persistence with which men and women believe they have a right to impose a private will upon a fellow-creature. A kind intention or a cruel intention made the act seem no less a crime as she looked upon it in that brief moment of illumination.

And yet she had loved him—sometimes. Often she had not. What did it matter! What could love, the unsolved mystery, count for in face of this possession of self-assertion which she suddenly recognized as the strongest impulse of her being!

"Free! Body and soul free!" she kept whispering.

Josephine was kneeling before the closed door with her lips to the keyhole, imploring for admission. "Louise, open the door! I beg; open the door—you will make yourself ill. What are you doing, Louise? For heaven's sake open the door."

"Go away. I am not making myself ill." No; she was drinking in a very elixir of life through that open window.

Her fancy was running riot along those days ahead of her. Spring days, and summer days, and all sorts of days that would be her own. She breathed a quick prayer that life might be long. It was only yesterday she had thought with a shudder that life might be long.

She arose at length and opened the door to her sister's importunities. There was a feverish triumph in her eyes, and she carried herself unwittingly like a goddess of Victory. She clasped her sister's waist, and together they descended the stairs. Richards stood waiting for them at the bottom.

Some one was opening the front door with a latchkey. It was Brently Mallard who entered, a little travel-stained, composedly carrying his grip-sack and umbrella. He had been far from the scene of accident, and did not even know there had been one. He stood amazed at Josephine's piercing cry; at Richards' quick motion to screen him from the view of his wife.

But Richards was too late.

When the doctors came they said she had died of heart disease—of joy that kills.

1894   1895

At the 'Cadian Ball[1]

Bobinôt, that big, brown, good-natured Bobinôt, had no intention of going to the ball, even though he knew Calixta would be there. For what came of those balls but heartache, and a sickening disinclination for work the whole week through, till Saturday night came again and his tortures began afresh? Why could he not love Ozéina, who would marry him tomorrow; or Fronie, or any one of a dozen others, rather than that little Spanish vixen? Calixta's slender foot had never touched Cuban soil; but her mother's had, and the Spanish was in her blood all the same. For that reason the prairie people forgave her much that they would not have overlooked in their own daughters or sisters.

---

1. First published in *Two Tales* (October 1892); first published in book form in *Bayou Folk* (1894), the source of the text printed here.

Her eyes,—Bobinôt thought of her eyes, and weakened,—the bluest, the drowsiest, most tantalizing that ever looked into a man's; he thought of her flaxen hair that kinked worse than a mulatto's close to her head; that broad, smiling mouth and tiptilted nose, that full figure; that voice like a rich contralto song, with cadences in it that must have been taught by Satan, for there was no one else to teach her tricks on that 'Cadian prairie. Bobinôt thought of them all as he plowed his rows of cane.

There had even been a breath of scandal whispered about her a year ago, when she went to Assumption,[2]—but why talk of it? No one did now. "C'est Espagnol, ça,"[3] most of them said with lenient shoulder-shrugs. "Bon chien tient de race,"[4] the old men mumbled over their pipes, stirred by recollections. Nothing was made of it, except that Fronie threw it up to Calixta when the two quarreled and fought on the church steps after mass one Sunday, about a lover. Calixta swore roundly in fine 'Cadian French and with true Spanish spirit, and slapped Fronie's face. Fronie had slapped her back; "Tiens, cocotte, va!"[5] "Espèce de lionèse; prends ça, et ça!"[6] till the curé himself was obliged to hasten and make peace between them. Bobinôt thought of it all, and would not go to the ball.

But in the afternoon, over at Friedheimer's store, where he was buying a trace-chain,[7] he heard some one say that Alcée Laballière would be there. Then wild horses could not have kept him away. He knew how it would be—or rather he did not know how it would be—if the handsome young planter came over to the ball as he sometimes did. If Alcée happened to be in a serious mood, he might only go to the card-room and play a round or two; or he might stand out on the galleries talking crops and politics with the old people. But there was no telling. A drink or two could put the devil in his head,—that was what Bobinôt said to himself, as he wiped the sweat from his brow with his red bandanna; a gleam from Calixta's eyes, a flash of her ankle, a twirl of her skirts could do the same. Yes, Bobinôt would go to the ball.

That was the year Alcée Laballière put nine hundred acres in rice. It was putting a good deal of money into the ground, but the returns promised to be glorious. Old Madame Laballière, sailing about the spacious galleries in her white *volante*,[8] figured it all out in her head. Clarisse, her goddaughter, helped her a little, and together they built more air-castles than enough. Alcée worked like a mule that time; and if he did not kill himself, it was because his constitution was an iron one. It was an every-day affair for him to come in from the field well-nigh exhausted, and wet to the waist. He did not mind if there were visitors; he left them to his mother and Clarisse. There were often guests: young men and women who came up from the city, which was but a few hours away, to visit his beautiful kinswoman. She was worth going a good deal farther than that to see. Dainty as a lily; hardy as a sunflower; slim, tall, graceful, like one of the reeds that grew in the marsh. Cold and kind and cruel by turn, and everything that was aggravating to Alcée.

He would have liked to sweep the place of those visitors, often. Of the men, above all, with their ways and their manners; their swaying of fans like

2. I.e., Assumption Parish, Louisiana.
3. That's a Spaniard for you (French).
4. Just like her mother (French).
5. Listen, you flirt, get out of here! (French).

6. You bitch; take that and that! (French).
7. Equipment used to harness horses.
8. A flowing garment.

women, and dandling about hammocks. He could have pitched them over the levee into the river, if it hadn't meant murder. That was Alcée. But he must have been crazy the day he came in from the rice-field, and, toil-stained as he was, clasped Clarisse by the arms and panted a volley of hot, blistering love-words into her face. No man had ever spoken love to her like that.

"Monsieur!" she exclaimed, looking him full in the eyes, without a quiver. Alcée's hands dropped and his glance wavered before the chill of her calm, clear her eyes.

"*Par exemple!*"[9] she muttered disdainfully, as she turned from him, deftly adjusting the careful toilet that he had so brutally disarranged.

That happened a day or two before the cyclone came that cut into the rice like fine steel. It was an awful thing, coming so swiftly, without a moment's warning in which to light a holy candle or set a piece of blessed palm burning. Old Madame wept openly and said her beads, just as her son Didier, the New Orleans one, would have done. If such a thing had happened to Alphonse, the Laballière planting cotton up in Natchitoches,[1] he would have raved and stormed like a second cyclone, and made his surroundings unbearable for a day or two. But Alcée took the misfortune differently. He looked ill and gray after it, and said nothing. His speechlessness was frightful. Clarisse's heart melted with tenderness; but when she offered her soft, purring words of condolence, he accepted them with mute indifference. Then she and her nénaine[2] wept afresh in each other's arms.

A night or two later, when Clarisse went to her window to kneel there in the moonlight and say her prayers before retiring, she saw that Bruce, Alcée's negro servant, had led his master's saddle-horse noiselessly along the edge of the sward that bordered the gravel-path, and stood holding him near by. Presently, she heard Alcée quit his room, which was beneath her own, and traverse the lower portico. As he emerged from the shadow and crossed the strip of moonlight, she perceived that he carried a pair of well-filled saddle-bags which he at once flung across the animal's back. He then lost no time in mounting, and after a brief exchange of words with Bruce, went cantering away, taking no precaution to avoid the noisy gravel as the negro had done.

Clarisse had never suspected that it might be Alcée's custom to sally forth from the plantation secretly, and at such an hour; for it was nearly midnight. And had it not been for the telltale saddle-bags, she would only have crept to bed, to wonder, to fret and dream unpleasant dreams. But her impatience and anxiety would not be held in check. Hastily unbolting the shutters of her door that opened upon the gallery, she stepped outside and called softly to the old negro.

"Gre't Peter! Miss Clarisse. I was n' sho it was a ghos' o' w'at, stan'in' up dah, plumb in de night, dataway."

He mounted halfway up the long, broad flight of stairs. She was standing at the top.

"Bruce, w'ere has Monsieur Alcée gone?" she asked.

"W'y, he gone 'bout he business, I reckin," replied Bruce, striving to be non-committal at the outset.

9. For example (French, literal trans.); here, "Get ahold of yourself!"

1. Parish in northwest Louisiana.
2. Female attendant, in this case his mother.

"W'ere has Monsieour Alcée gone?" she reiterated, stamping her bare foot. "I won't stan' any nonsense or any lies; mine, Bruce."

"I don' ric'lic ez I eva tole you lie yit, Miss Clarisse. Mista Alcée, he all broke up, sho."

"Were—has—he gone? Ah, Sainte Vierge! faut de la patience! butor, va!"[3]

"W'en I was in he room, a-breshin' off he clo'es to-day," the darkey began, settling himself against the stair-rail, "he look dat speechless an' down, I say, 'you 'pear to me like some pussun w'at gwine have a spell o' sickness, Mista Alcée.' He say, 'You reckin?' 'I dat he git up, go look hisse'f stiddy in de glass. Den he go to de chimbly an' jerk up de quinine bottle an' po' a gre't hoss-dose on to he han'. An' he swalla dat mess in a wink, an' wash hit down wid a big dram o' w'iskey w'at he keep in he room, against he come all soppin' wet outen de fiel'.

"He 'lows, 'No, I ain' gwine be sick, Bruce.' Den he square off. He say, 'I kin mak out to stan' up an' gi' an' take wid any man I knows, lessen hit's John L. Sulvun.[4] But w'en God A'mighty an' a 'oman jines fo'ces agin me, dat's one too many fur me.' I tell 'im, 'Jis so,' whils' I 'se makin' out to bresh a spot off w'at ain' dah, on he coat colla. I tell 'im, 'You wants li'le res', suh.' He say, 'No, I wants li'le fling; dat w'at I wants; an' I gwine git it. Pitch me a fis'ful o' clo'es in dem 'ar saddle-bags.' Dat w'at he say. Don't you bodda, missy. He jis' gone a-caperin' yonda to de Cajun ball. Uh—uh—de skeeters is fair' a-swarmin' like bees roun' yo' foots!"

The mosquitoes were indeed attacking Clarisse's white feet savagely. She had unconsciously been alternately rubbing one foot over the other during the darkey's recital.

"The 'Cadian ball," she repeated contemptuously. "Humph! *Par exemple!*[5] Nice conduc' for a Laballière. An' he needs a saddle-bag, fill' with clothes, to go to the 'Cadian ball!"

"Oh, Miss Clarisse; you go on to bed, chile; git yo' soun' sleep. He 'low he come back in couple weeks o' so. I kiarn be repeatin' lot o' truck w'at young mans say, out heah face o' young gal."

Clarisse said no more, but turned and abruptly reëntered the house.

"You done talk too much wid yo' mouf a'ready, you ole fool nigga, you," muttered Bruce to himself as he walked away.

Alcée reached the ball very late, of course—too late for the chicken gumbo which had been served at midnight.

The big, low-ceiled room—they called it a hall—was packed with men and women dancing to the music of three fiddles. There were broad galleries all around it. There was a room at one side where sober-faced men were playing cards. Another, in which babies were sleeping, was called *le parc aux petits.*[6] Any one who is white may go to a 'Cadian ball, but he must pay for his lemonade, his coffee and chicken gumbo. And he must behave himself like a 'Cadian. Grosbœuf was giving this ball. He had been giving them since he was a young man, and he was a middle-aged one, now. In that time he could recall but one disturbance, and that was caused by American rail-

3. Ah, Blessed Virgin! Give me patience! Lout, get out of here! (French).
4. American heavyweight boxing champion

(1855–1918).
5. Here, "Quite an example!"
6. Playroom (French).

roaders, who were not in touch with their surroundings and had no business there. "Ces maudits gens du raiderode,"[7] Grosbœuf called them.

Alcée Laballière's presence at the ball caused a flutter even among the men, who could not but admire his "nerve" after such misfortune befalling him. To be sure, they knew the Laballières were rich—that there were resources East, and more again in the city. But they felt it took a *brave homme*[8] to stand a blow like that philosophically. One old gentleman, who was in the habit of reading a Paris newspaper and knew things, chuckled gleefully to everybody that Alcée's conduct was altogether *chic, mais chic.* That he had more *panache*[9] than Boulanger. Well, perhaps he had.

But what he did not show outwardly was that he was in a mood for ugly things to-night. Poor Bobinôt alone felt it vaguely. He discerned a gleam of it in Alcée's handsome eyes, as the young planter stood in the doorway, looking with rather feverish glance upon the assembly, while he laughed and talked with a 'Cadian farmer who was beside him.

Bobinôt himself was dull-looking and clumsy. Most of the men were. But the young women were very beautiful. The eyes that glanced into Alcée's as they passed him were big, dark, soft as those of the young heifers standing out in the cool prairie grass.

But the belle was Calixta. Her white dress was not nearly so handsome or well made as Fronie's (she and Fronie had quite forgotten the battle on the church steps, and were friends again), nor were her slippers so stylish as those of Ozéina; and she fanned herself with a handkerchief, since she had broken her red fan at the last ball, and her aunts and uncles were not willing to give her another. But all the men agreed she was at her best to-night. Such animation! and abandon! such flashes of wit!

"Hé, Bobinôt! Mais w'at's the matta? W'at you standin' *planté là*[1] like ole Ma'ame Tina's cow in the bog, you!"

That was good. That was an excellent thrust at Bobinôt, who had forgotten the figure[2] of the dance with his mind bent on other things, and it started a clamor of laughter at his expense. He joined good-naturedly. It was better to receive even such notice as that from Calixta than none at all. But Madame Suzonne, sitting in a corner, whispered to her neighbor that if Ozéina were to conduct herself in a like manner, she should immediately be taken out to the mule-cart and driven home. The women did not always approve of Calixta.

Now and then were short lulls in the dance, when couples flocked out upon the galleries for a brief respite and fresh air. The moon had gone down pale in the west, and in the east was yet no promise of day. After such an interval, when the dancers again assembled to resume the interrupted quadrille, Calixta was not among them.

She was sitting upon a bench out in the shadow, with Alcée beside her. They were acting like fools. He had attempted to take a little gold ring from her finger; just for the fun of it, for there was nothing he could have done with the ring but replace it again. But she clinched her hand tight. He pretended that it was a very difficult matter to open it. Then he kept the hand

7. Those cursed railroad people (French).
8. Sturdy fellow (French).
9. Style.

1. Rooted there (French).
2. The pattern of steps.

in his. They seemed to forget about it. He played with her earring, a thin crescent of gold hanging from her small brown ear. He caught a wisp of the kinky hair that had escaped its fastening, and rubbed the ends of it against his shaven cheek.

"You know, last year in Assumption, Calixta?" They belonged to the younger generation, so preferred to speak English.

"Don't come say Assumption to me, M'sieur Alcée. I done yeard Assumption till I'm plumb sick."

"Yes, I know. The idiots! Because you were in Assumption, and I happened to go to Assumption, they must have it that we went together. But it was nice—*hein*,[3] Calixta?—in Assumption?"

They saw Bobinôt emerge from the hall and stand a moment outside the lighted doorway, peering uneasily and searchingly into the darkness. He did not see them, and went slowly back.

"There is Bobinôt looking for you. You are going to set poor Bobinôt crazy. You'll marry him some day; *hein*, Calxita?"

"I don't say no, me," she replied, striving to withdraw her hand, which he held more firmly for the attempt.

"But come, Calixta; you know you said you would go back to Assumption, just to spite them."

"No, I neva said that, me. You mus' dreamt that."

"Oh, I thought you did. You know I'm going down to the city."

"W'en?"

"To-night."

"Betta make has'e, then; it's mos' day."

"Well, to-morrow'll do."

"W'at you goin' do, yonda?"

"I don't know. Drown myself in the lake, maybe; unless you go down there to visit your uncle."

Calixta's senses were reeling; and they well-nigh left her when she felt Alicée's lips brush her ear like the touch of a rose.

"Mista Alcée! Is dat Mista Alcée?" the thick voice of a negro was asking; he stood on the ground, holding to the banister-rails near which the couple sat.

"W'at do you want now?" cried Alcée impatiently. "Can't I have a moment of peace?"

"I ben huntin' you high an' low, suh," answered the man. "Dey—dey some one in de road, onda de mulbare-tree, want see you a minute."

"I wouldn't go out to the road to see the Angel Gabriel. And if you come back here with any more talk, I'll have to break your neck." The negro turned mumbling away.

Alcée and Calixta laughed softly about it. Her boisterousness was all gone. They talked low, and laughed softly, as lovers do.

"Alcée! Alcée Laballière!"

It was not the negro's voice this time; but one that went through Alcée's body like an electric shock, bringing him to his feet.

Clarisse was standing there in her riding-habit, where the negro had stood. For an instant confusion reigned in Alcée's thoughts, as with one

3. Huh.

who awakes suddenly from a dream. But he felt that something of serious import had brought his cousin to the ball in the dead of night.

"W'at does this mean, Clarisse?" he asked.

"It means something has happen' at home. You mus' come."

"Happened to maman?" he questioned, in alarm.

"No: nénaine is well, and asleep. It is something else. Not to frighten you. But you mus' come. Come with me, Alcée."

There was no need for the imploring note. He would have followed the voice anywhere.

She had now recognized the girl sitting back on the bench.

"Ah, c'est vous, Calixta? Comment ça va, mon enfant?"[4]

"Tcha va b'en; et vous, mam'zélle?"[5]

Alcée swung himself over the low rail and started to follow Clarisse, without a word, without a glance back at the girl. He had forgotten he was leaving her there. But Clarisse whispered something to him, and he turned back to say "Good-night, Calixta," and offer his hand to press through the railing. She pretended not to see it.

"How come that? You settin' yere by yo'se'f, Calixta?" It was Bobinôt who had found her there alone. The dancers had not yet come out. She looked ghastly in the faint, gray light struggling out of the east.

"Yes, that's me. Go yonda in the *parc aux petits* an' ask Aunt Olisse fu' my hat. She knows w'ere 't is. I want to go home, me."

"How you came?"

"I come afoot, with the Cateaus. But I'm goin' now. I ent goin' wait fu' 'em. I'm plumb wo' out, me."

"Kin I go with you, Calixta?"

"I don' care."

They went together across the open prairie and along the edge of the fields, stumbling in the uncertain light. He told her to lift her dress that was getting wet and bedraggled; for she was pulling at the weeds and grasses with her hands.

"I don't care; it's got to go in the tub, anyway. You been sayin' all along you want to marry me, Bobinôt. Well, if you want, yet, I don' care, me."

The glow of a sudden and overwhelming happiness shone out in the brown, rugged face of the young Acadian. He could not speak, for very joy. It choked him.

"Oh well, if you don' want," snapped Calixta, flippantly, pretending to be piqued at his silence.

"*Bon Dieu!*[6] You know that makes me crazy, w'at you sayin'. You mean that, Calixta? You ent goin' turn roun' agin?"

"I neva tole you that much *yet*, Bobinôt. I mean that. *Tiens*,"[7] and she held out her hand in the business-like manner of a man who clinches a bargain with a hand-clasp. Bobinôt grew bold with happiness and asked Calixta to kiss him. She turned her face, that was almost ugly after the night's dissipation, and looked steadily into his.

4. Ah, is it you, Calixta? How's it going my little one? (French).
5. Everything's fine; and with you, Miss? (French).
6. Good God! (French).
7. Well (French).

"I don' want to kiss you, Bobinôt," she said, turning away again, "not to-day. Some other time. *Bonté divine!*[8] ent you satisfy, *yet!*"

"Oh, I'm satisfy, Calixta," he said.

Riding through a patch of wood, Clarisse's saddle became ungirted, and she and Alcée dismounted to readjust it.

For the twentieth time he asked her what had happened at home.

"But, Clarisse, w'at is it? Is it a misfortune?"

"Ah Dieu sait!"[9] It's only something that happen' to me."

"To you!"

"I saw you go away las' night, Alcée, with those saddle-bags," she said, haltingly, striving to arrange something about the saddle, "an' I made Bruce tell me. He said you had gone to the ball, an' wouldn' be home for weeks an' weeks. I thought, Alcée—maybe you were going to—to Assumption. I got wild. An' then I knew if you didn't come back, *now*, tonight, I couldn't stan' it,—again."

She had her face hidden in her arm that she was resting against the saddle when she said that.

He began to wonder if this meant love. But she had to tell him so, before he believed it. And when she told him, he thought the face of the Universe was changed—just like Bobinôt. Was it last week the cyclone had well-nigh ruined him? The cyclone seemed a huge joke, now. It was he, then, who, an hour ago was kissing little Calixta's ear and whispering nonsense into it. Calixta was like a myth, now. The one, only, great reality in the world was Clarisse standing before him, telling him that she loved him.

In the distance they heard the rapid discharge of pistol-shots; but it did not disturb them. They knew it was only the negro musicians who had gone into the yard to fire their pistols into the air, as the custom is, and to announce *"le bal est fini."*[1]

1892, 1894

The Storm

A *Sequel to "The 'Cadian Ball"*[1]

I

The leaves were so still that even Bibi thought it was going to rain. Bobinôt, who was accustomed to converse on terms of perfect equality with his little son, called the child's attention to certain sombre clouds that were rolling with sinister intention from the west, accompanied by a sullen, threatening roar. They were at Friedheimer's store and decided to remain there till the storm had passed. They sat within the door on two empty kegs. Bibi was four years old and looked very wise.

---

8. Goodness gracious! (French).
9. God knows! (French).
1. The Ball is over (French).
1. Chopin's notebooks show that this story was written on July 18, 1898, just six months after she had submitted *The Awakening* to a publisher. As its subtitle indicates, it was intended as a

sequel to her tale "At the 'Cadian Ball" (1892). "The Storm" was apparently never submitted for publication and did not see print until the publication of Per Seyersted's edition of *The Complete Works of Kate Chopin* in 1969, the basis for the text printed here.

"Mama'll be 'fraid, yes," he suggested with blinking eyes.

"She'll shut the house. Maybe she got Sylvie helpin' her this evenin'," Bobinôt responded reassuringly.

"No; she ent got Sylvie. Sylvie was helpin' her yistiday," piped Bibi.

Bobinôt arose and going across to the counter purchased a can of shrimps, of which Calixta was very fond. Then he returned to his perch on the keg and sat stolidly holding the can of shrimps while the storm burst. It shook the wooden store and seemed to be ripping furrows in the distant field. Bibi laid his little hand on his father's knee and was not afraid.

II

Calixta, at home, felt no uneasiness for their safety. She sat at a side window sewing furiously on a sewing machine. She was greatly occupied and did not notice the approaching storm. But she felt very warm and often stopped to mop her face on which the perspiration gathered in beads. She unfastened her white sacque[2] at the throat. It began to grow dark, and suddenly realizing the situation she got up hurriedly and went about closing windows and doors.

Out on the small front gallery she had hung Bobinôt's Sunday clothes to dry and she hastened out to gather them before the rain fell. As she stepped outside, Alcée Laballière rode in at the gate. She had not seen him very often since her marriage, and never alone. She stood there with Bobinôt's coat in her hands, and the big rain drops began to fall. Alcée rode his horse under the shelter of a side projection where the chickens had huddled and there were plows and a harrow piled up in the corner.

"May I come and wait on your gallery till the storm is over, Calixta?" he asked.

"Come 'long in, M'sieur Alcée."

His voice and her own startled her as if from a trance, and she seized Bobinôt's vest. Alcée, mounting to the porch, grabbed the trousers and snatched Bibi's braided jacket that was about to be carried away by a sudden gust of wind. He expressed an intention to remain outside, but it was soon apparent that he might as well have been out in the open: the water beat in upon the boards in driving sheets, and he went inside, closing the door after him. It was even necessary to put something beneath the door to keep the water out.

"My! what a rain! It's good two years since it rain' like that," exclaimed Calixta as she rolled up a piece of bagging and Alcée helped her to thrust it beneath the crack.

She was a little fuller of figure than five years before when she married; but she had lost nothing of her vivacity. Her blue eyes still retained their melting quality; and her yellow hair, disheveled by the wind and rain, kinked more stubbornly than ever about her ears and temples.

The rain beat upon the low, shingled roof with a force and clatter that threatened to break an entrance and deluge them there. They were in the dining room—the sitting room—the general utility room. Adjoining was her bed room, with Bibi's couch along side her own. The door stood open, and the room with its white, monumental bed, its closed shutters, looked dim and mysterious.

Alcée flung himself into a rocker and Calixta nervously began to gather up from the floor the lengths of a cotton sheet which she had been sewing.

2. Loose-fitting dress.

"If this keeps up, *Dieu sait* if the levees[3] goin' to stan' it!" she exclaimed.

"What have you got to do with the levees?"

"I got enough to do! An' there's Bobinôt with Bibi out in that storm—if he only didn' left Friedheimer's!"

"Let us hope, Calixta, that Bobinôt's got sense enough to come in out of a cyclone."

She went and stood at the window with a greatly disturbed look on her face. She wiped the frame that was clouded with moisture. It was stiflingly hot. Alcée got up and joined her at the window, looking over her shoulder. The rain was coming down in sheets obscuring the view of far-off cabins and enveloping the distant wood in a gray mist. The playing of the lightning was incessant. A bolt struck a tall chinaberry tree at the edge of the field. It filled all visible space with a blinding glare and the crash seemed to invade the very boards they stood upon.

Calixta put her hands to her eyes, and with a cry, staggered backward. Alcée's arm encircled her, and for an instant he drew her close and spasmodically to him.

"*Bonté!*"[4] she cried, releasing herself from his encircling arm and retreating from the window, "the house'll go next! If I only knew w'ere Bibi was!" She would not compose herself; she would not be seated. Alcée clasped her shoulders and looked into her face. The contact of her warm, palpitating body when he had unthinkingly drawn her into his arms, had aroused all the old-time infatuation and desire for her flesh.

"Calixta," he said, "don't be frightened. Nothing can happen. The house is too low to be struck, with so many tall trees standing about. There! aren't you going to be quiet? say, aren't you?" He pushed her hair back from her face that was warm and steaming. Her lips were as red and moist as pomegranate seed. Her white neck and a glimpse of her full, firm bosom disturbed him powerfully. As she glanced up at him the fear in her liquid blue eyes had given place to a drowsy gleam that unconsciously betrayed a sensuous desire. He looked down into her eyes and there was nothing for him to do but to gather her lips in a kiss. It reminded him of Assumption.[5]

"Do you remember—in Assumption, Calixta?" he asked in a low voice broken by passion. Oh! she remembered; for in Assumption he had kissed her and kissed and kissed her; until his senses would well nigh fail, and to save her he would resort to a desperate flight. If she was not an immaculate dove in those days, she was still inviolate; a passionate creature whose very defenselessness had made her defense, against which his honor forbade him to prevail. Now—well, now—her lips seemed in a manner free to be tasted, as well as her round, white throat and her whiter breasts.

They did not heed the crashing torrents, and the roar of the elements made her laugh as she lay in his arms. She was a revelation in that dim, mysterious chamber; as white as the couch she lay upon. Her firm, elastic flesh that was knowing for the first time its birthright, was like a creamy lily that the sun invites to contribute its breath and perfume to the undying life of the world.

---

3. Built-up earthen banks designed to keep the river from flooding the surrounding land. "*Dieu sait*": God knows (French).

4. Goodness! (French).

5. I.e., Assumption Parish, Louisiana, the setting for "At the 'Cadian Ball."

The generous abundance of her passion, without guile or trickery, was like a white flame which penetrated and found response in depths of his own sensuous nature that had never yet been reached.

When he touched her breasts they gave themselves up in quivering ecstasy, inviting his lips. Her mouth was a fountain of delight. And when he possessed her, they seemed to swoon together at the very borderland of life's mystery.

He stayed cushioned upon her, breathless, dazed, enervated, with his heart beating like a hammer upon her. With one hand she clasped his head, her lips lightly touching his forehead. The other hand stroked with a soothing rhythm his muscular shoulders.

The growl of the thunder was distant and passing away. The rain beat softly upon the shingles, inviting them to drowsiness and sleep. But they dared not yield.

III

The rain was over; and the sun was turning the glistening green world into a palace of gems. Calixta, on the gallery, watched Alcée ride away. He turned and smiled at her with a beaming face; and she lifted her pretty chin in the air and laughed aloud.

Bobinôt and Bibi, trudging home, stopped without at the cistern to make themselves presentable.

"My! Bibi, w'at will yo' mama say! You ought to be ashame'. You oughta' put on those good pants. Look at 'em! An' that mud on yo' collar! How you got that mud on yo' collar, Bibi? I never saw such a boy!" Bibi was the picture of pathetic resignation. Bobinôt was the embodiment of serious solicitude as he strove to remove from his own person and his son's the signs of their tramp over heavy roads and through wet fields. He scraped the mud off Bibi's bare legs and feet with a stick and carefully removed all traces from his heavy brogans. Then, prepared for the worst—the meeting with an over-scrupulous housewife, they entered cautiously at the back door.

Calixta was preparing supper. She had set the table and was dripping coffee at the hearth. She sprang up as they came in.

"Oh, Bobinôt! You back! My! but I was uneasy. W'ere you been during the rain? An' Bibi? he ain't wet? he ain't hurt?" She had clasped Bibi and was kissing him effusively. Bobinôt's explanations and apologies which he had been composing all along the way, died on his lips as Calixta felt him to see if he were dry, and seemed to express nothing but satisfaction at their safe return.

"I brought you some shrimps, Calixta," offered Bobinôt, hauling the can from his ample side pocket and laying it on the table.

"Shrimps! Oh, Bobinôt! you too good fo' anything!" and she gave him a smacking kiss on the cheek that resounded, "*J'vous réponds,*[6] we'll have a feas' to night! umph-umph!"

Bobinôt and Bibi began to relax and enjoy themselves, and when the three seated themselves at table they laughed much and so loud that anyone might have heard them as far away as Laballière's.

---

6. I promise you (French).

IV

Alcée Laballière wrote to his wife, Clarisse, that night. It was a loving letter, full of tender solicitude. He told her not to hurry back, but if she and the babies liked it at Biloxi, to stay a month longer. He was getting on nicely; and though he missed them, he was willing to bear the separation a while longer—realizing that their health and pleasure were the first things to be considered.

V

As for Clarisse, she was charmed upon receiving her husband's letter. She and the babies were doing well. The society was agreeable; many of her old friends and acquaintances were at the bay. And the first free breath since her marriage seemed to restore the pleasant liberty of her maiden days. Devoted as she was to her husband, their intimate conjugal life was something which she was more than willing to forego for a while.

So the storm passed and every one was happy.

1898   1969

MARY E. WILKINS FREEMAN
1852–1930

M ary E. Wilkins Freeman, who won literary acclaim for her depiction of New England village life, was born on October 31, 1852, in Randolph, Massachusetts, a small town twenty miles south of Boston. She was frequently ill in a household that knew sickness all too well: two other Wilkins children died before they reached three years of age; her sister Anne only lived to be seventeen. Freeman's parents were pious Christians and orthodox in following the prescriptions of the Congregationalist denomination; she was thus subject to a strict code of behavior. When she became a writer, Freeman would frequently dramatize the constraints of religious belief, the legacy of confining traditions, and especially the impact of orthodoxy on the inner lives of women.

In 1867, Freeman's father became part owner of a dry-goods store in Brattleboro, Vermont, where she graduated from high school. In 1870 she entered Mount Holyoke Female Seminary, which Emily Dickinson had attended two decades earlier. Like Dickinson, Freeman left after a year in which she resisted the school's pressure on all students to offer public testimony as to their Christian commitment. She finished her formal education with a year at West Brattleboro Seminary, though the reading and discussions with her friend Evelyn Sawyer about the novels and poetry of Europe and America were probably more important than her schoolwork in developing her literary taste.

After the failure of her father's business in 1876, Freeman's family moved into the Brattleboro home of the Reverend Thomas Pickman Tyler, where her mother became housekeeper. Poverty was hard for the Wilkinses to bear, especially because their Puritan heritage led them to believe that it was a punishment for sin. Freeman's mother died in 1880, her father three years later, leaving Freeman alone at the age of twenty-eight, with a legacy of less than one thousand dollars.

Fortunately, she had begun to sell poems and stories to such leading magazines as *Harper's Bazaar*, and by the mid-1880s Freeman had a ready market for her work. As soon as she achieved a measure of economic independence, she returned to Randolph, where she lived with her childhood friend Mary Wales. Her early stories, especially those gathered and published in *A Humble Romance* (1887), are set in the Vermont countryside. She wrote in a preface to one edition of these stories that the characters are generalized "studies of the descendants of the Massachusetts Bay colonists, in whom can still be seen traces of those features of will and conscience, so strong as to be almost exaggerations and deformities, which characterized their ancestors." More specifically, the title story dramatizes a theme Freeman was to return to frequently: the potential for unpredictable revolt in outwardly meek and downtrodden natures, such as that of the central character in "The Revolt of 'Mother.'"

"A New England Nun" and Other Stories, which appeared in 1891, contains several of her best stories, most notably the title story, which illustrates Freeman's deep interest in the social restrictions placed on women and the resulting rebelliousness. In addition to providing a vivid sense of place, local dialect, and personality types, Freeman also offers in her best work insight into the individual psychology and interior life that results when confining, inherited codes of tradition are subject to the pressure of a rapidly changing secular and urban world. Freeman's interest in how women, individually and collectively, assert their power to overturn an exhausted Puritan patriarchy resonated with readers throughout the United States, where the role of women was being hotly debated during the turn of the twentieth century.

Freeman continued to write for another three decades. Although she is best known today for her New England short stories, she also wrote plays and a number of successful novels—including *Pembroke* (1894) and *The Shoulders of Atlas* (1908). She was both prolific and wide-ranging: her work includes historical fiction, stories of the occult, novels depicting labor unrest, and even a book of animal tales. She married Dr. Charles Freeman in 1902, when she was forty-nine, and moved to Metuchen, New Jersey; after a few happy years, her husband's drinking developed into destructive alcoholism, and he had to be institutionalized in 1920. In 1926, Freeman was awarded the W. D. Howells medal for fiction by the American Academy of Arts and Letters and she was elected to the National Institute of Arts and Letters, honors rarely bestowed on women writers or regionalists at that time.

A New England Nun[1]

It was late in the afternoon, and the light was waning. There was a difference in the look of the tree shadows out in the yard. Somewhere in the distance cows were lowing and a little bell was tinkling; now and then a farm-wagon tilted by, and the dust flew; some blue-shirted laborers with shovels over their shoulders plodded past; little swarms of flies were dancing up and down before the peoples' faces in the soft air. There seemed to be a gentle stir arising over everything for the mere sake of subsidence—a very premonition of rest and hush and night.

This soft diurnal commotion was over Louisa Ellis also. She had been peacefully sewing at her sitting-room window all the afternoon. Now she quilted her needle carefully into her work, which she folded precisely, and laid in a basket with her thimble and thread and scissors. Louisa Ellis could

---

1. From *"A New England Nun" and Other Stories* (1891), the source of the text printed here.

not remember that ever in her life she had mislaid one of these little feminine appurtenances, which had become, from long use and constant association, a very part of her personality.

Louisa tied a green apron round her waist, and got out a flat straw hat with a green ribbon. Then she went into the garden with a little blue crockery bowl, to pick some currants for her tea. After the currants were picked she sat on the back door-step and stemmed them, collecting the stems carefully in her apron, and afterwards throwing them into the hen-coop. She looked sharply at the grass beside the step to see if any had fallen there.

Louisa was slow and still in her movements; it took her a long time to prepare her tea; but when ready it was set forth with as much grace as if she had been a veritable guest to her own self. The little square table stood exactly in the centre of the kitchen, and was covered with a starched linen cloth whose border pattern of flowers glistened. Louisa had a damask napkin on her tea-tray, where were arranged a cut-glass tumbler full of teaspoons, a silver cream-pitcher, a china sugar-bowl, and one pink china cup and saucer. Louisa used china every day—something which none of her neighbors did. They whispered about it among themselves. Their daily tables were laid with common crockery, their sets of best china stayed in the parlor closet, and Louisa Ellis was no richer nor better bred than they. Still she would use the china. She had for her supper a glass dish full of sugared currants, a plate of little cakes, and one of light white biscuits. Also a leaf or two of lettuce, which she cut up daintily. Louisa was very fond of lettuce, which she raised to perfection in her little garden. She ate quite heartily, though in a delicate, pecking way; it seemed almost surprising that any considerable bulk of the food should vanish.

After tea she filled a plate with nicely baked thin corn-cakes, and carried them out into the back-yard.

"Cæsar!" she called. "Cæsar! Cæsar!"

There was a little rush, and the clank of a chain, and a large yellow-and-white dog appeared at the door of his tiny hut, which was half hidden among the tall grasses and flowers. Louisa patted him and gave him the corn-cakes. Then she returned to the house and washed the tea-things, polishing the china carefully. The twilight had deepened; the chorus of the frogs floated in at the open window wonderfully loud and shrill, and once in a while a long sharp drone from a tree-toad pierced it. Louisa took off her green gingham apron, disclosing a shorter one of pink and white print. She lighted her lamp, and sat down again with her sewing.

In about half an hour Joe Dagget came. She heard his heavy step on the walk, and rose and took off her pink-and-white apron. Under that was still another—white linen with a little cambric edging on the bottom; that was Louisa's company apron. She never wore it without her calico sewing apron over it unless she had a guest. She had barely folded the pink and white one with methodical haste and laid it in a table-drawer when the door opened and Joe Dagget entered.

He seemed to fill up the whole room. A little yellow canary that had been asleep in his green cage at the south window woke up and fluttered wildly, beating his little yellow wings against the wires. He always did so when Joe Dagget came into the room.

"Good-evening," said Louisa. She extended her hand with a kind of solemn cordiality.

"Good-evening, Louisa," returned the man, in a loud voice.

She placed a chair for him, and they sat facing each other, with the table between them. He sat bolt-upright, toeing out his heavy feet squarely, glancing with a good-humored uneasiness around the room. She sat gently erect, folding her slender hands in her white-linen lap.

"Been a pleasant day," remarked Dagget.

"Real pleasant," Louisa assented, softly. "Have you been haying?" she asked, after a little while.

"Yes, I've been haying all day, down in the ten-acre lot. Pretty hot work."

"It must be."

"Yes, it's pretty hot work in the sun."

"Is your mother well to-day?"

"Yes, mother's pretty well."

"I suppose Lily Dyer's with her now?"

Dagget colored. "Yes, she's with her," he answered, slowly.

He was not very young, but there was a boyish look about his large face. Louisa was not quite as old as he, her face was fairer and smoother, but she gave people the impression of being older.

"I suppose she's a good deal of help to your mother," she said, further.

"I guess she is; I don't know how mother'd get along without her," said Dagget, with a sort of embarrassed warmth.

"She looks like a real capable girl. She's pretty-looking too," remarked Louisa.

"Yes, she is pretty fair looking."

Presently Dagget began fingering the books on the table. There was a square red autograph album, and a Young Lady's Gift-Book[2] which had belonged to Louisa's mother. He took them up one after the other and opened them; then laid them down again, the album on the Gift-Book.

Louisa kept eying them with mild uneasiness. Finally she rose and changed the position of the books, putting the album underneath. That was the way they had been arranged in the first place.

Dagget gave an awkward little laugh. "Now what difference did it make which book was on top?" said he.

Louisa looked at him with a deprecating smile. "I always keep them that way," murmured she.

"You do beat everything," said Dagget, trying to laugh again. His large face was flushed.

He remained about an hour longer, then rose to take leave. Going out, he stumbled over a rug, and trying to recover himself, hit Louisa's work-basket on the table, and knocked it on the floor.

He looked at Louisa, then at the rolling spools; he ducked himself awkwardly toward them, but she stopped him. "Never mind," said she; "I'll pick them up after you're gone."

She spoke with a mild stiffness. Either she was a little disturbed, or his nervousness affected her, and made her seem constrained in her effort to reassure him.

---

2. Popular annual miscellanies, containing stories, essays, and poems, usually with a polite or moral tone. They were lavishly printed and decorated for use as Christmas or New Year's gifts.

When Joe Dagget was outside he drew in the sweet evening air with a sigh, and felt much as an innocent and perfectly well-intentioned bear might after his exit from a china shop.

Louisa, on her part, felt much as the kind-hearted, long-suffering owner of the china shop might have done after the exit of the bear.

She tied on the pink, then the green apron, picked up all the scattered treasures and replaced them in her work-basket, and straightened the rug. Then she set the lamp on the floor, and began sharply examining the carpet. She even rubbed her fingers over it, and looked at them.

"He's tracked in a good deal of dust," she murmured. "I thought he must have."

Louisa got a dust-pan and brush, and swept Joe Dagget's track carefully.

If he could have known it, it would have increased his perplexity and uneasiness, although it would not have disturbed his loyalty in the least. He came twice a week to see Louisa Ellis, and every time, sitting there in her delicately sweet room, he felt as if surrounded by a hedge of lace. He was afraid to stir lest he should put a clumsy foot or hand through the fairy web, and he had always the consciousness that Louisa was watching fearfully lest he should.

Still the lace and Louisa commanded perforce his perfect respect and patience and loyalty. They were to be married in a month, after a singular courtship which had lasted for a matter of fifteen years. For fourteen out of the fifteen years the two had not once seen each other, and they had seldom exchanged letters. Joe had been all those years in Australia, where he had gone to make his fortune, and where he had stayed until he made it. He would have stayed fifty years if it had taken so long, and come home feeble and tottering, or never come home at all, to marry Louisa.

But the fortune had been made in the fourteen years, and he had come home now to marry the woman who had been patiently and unquestioningly waiting for him all that time.

Shortly after they were engaged he had announced to Louisa his determination to strike out into new fields, and secure a competency[3] before they should be married. She had listened and assented with the sweet serenity which never failed her, not even when her lover set forth on that long and uncertain journey. Joe, buoyed up as he was by his sturdy determination, broke down a little at the last, but Louisa kissed him with a mild blush, and said good-by.

"It won't be for long," poor Joe had said, huskily; but it was for fourteen years.

In that length of time much had happened. Louisa's mother and brother had died, and she was all alone in the world. But greatest happening of all—a subtle happening which both were too simple to understand—Louisa's feet had turned into a path, smooth maybe under a calm, serene sky, but so straight and unswerving that it could only meet a check at her grave, and so narrow that there was no room for any one at her side.

Louisa's first emotion when Joe Dagget came home (he had not apprised her of his coming) was consternation, although she would not admit it to herself, and he never dreamed of it. Fifteen years ago she had been in love

3. Income or savings sufficient to support a certain standard of living.

with him—at least she considered herself to be. Just at that time, gently acquiescing with and falling into the natural drift of girlhood, she had seen marriage ahead as a reasonable feature and a probable desirability of life. She had listened with calm docility to her mother's views upon the subject. Her mother was remarkable for her cool sense and sweet, even temperament. She talked wisely to her daughter when Joe Dagget presented himself, and Louisa accepted him with no hesitation. He was the first lover she had ever had.

She had been faithful to him all these years. She had never dreamed of the possibility of marrying any one else. Her life, especially for the last seven years, had been full of a pleasant peace, she had never felt discontented nor impatient over her lover's absence; still she had always looked forward to his return and their marriage as the inevitable conclusion of things. However, she had fallen into a way of placing it so far in the future that it was almost equal to placing it over the boundaries of another life.

When Joe came she had been expecting him, and expecting to be married for fourteen years, but she was as much surprised and taken aback as if she had never thought of it.

Joe's consternation came later. He eyed Louisa with an instant confirmation of his old admiration. She had changed but little. She still kept her pretty manner and soft grace, and was, he considered, every whit as attractive as ever. As for himself, his stent[4] was done; he had turned his face away from fortune-seeking, and the old winds of romance whistled as loud and sweet as ever through his ears. All the song which he had been wont to hear in them was Louisa; he had for a long time a loyal belief that he heard it still, but finally it seemed to him that although the winds sang always that one song, it had another name. But for Louisa the wind had never more than murmured; now it had gone down, and everything was still. She listened for a little while with half-wistful attention; then she turned quietly away and went to work on her wedding clothes.

Joe had made some extensive and quite magnificent alterations in his house. It was the old homestead; the newly-married couple would live there, for Joe could not desert his mother, who refused to leave her old home. So Louisa must leave hers. Every morning, rising and going about among her neat maidenly possessions, she felt as one looking her last upon the faces of dear friends. It was true that in a measure she could take them with her, but, robbed of their old environments, they would appear in such new guises that they would almost cease to be themselves. Then there were some peculiar features of her happy solitary life which she would probably be obliged to relinquish altogether. Sterner tasks than these graceful but half-needless ones would probably devolve upon her. There would be a large house to care for; there would be company to entertain; there would be Joe's rigours and feeble old mother to wait upon; and it would be contrary to all thrifty village traditions for her to keep more than one servant. Louisa had a little still, and she used to occupy herself pleasantly in summer weather with distilling the sweet and aromatic essences from roses and peppermint and spearmint. By-and-by her still must be laid away. Her store of essences was already considerable, and there would be no time for her to distil for the mere pleasure of it. Then Joe's mother would think it foolishness; she had already hinted her opinion in the

4. I.e., "stint," task.

matter. Louisa dearly loved to sew a linen seam, not always for use, but for the simple, mild pleasure which she took in it. She would have been loath to confess how more than once she had ripped a seam for the mere delight of sewing it together again. Sitting at her window during long sweet afternoons, drawing her needle gently through the dainty fabric, she was peace itself. But there was small chance of such foolish comfort in the future. Joe's mother, domineering, shrewd old matron that she was even in her old age, and very likely even Joe himself, with his honest masculine rudeness, would laugh and frown down all these pretty but senseless old maiden ways.

Louisa had almost the enthusiasm of an artist over the mere order and cleanliness of her solitary home. She had throbs of genuine triumph at the sight of the window-panes which she had polished until they shone like jewels. She gloated gently over her orderly bureau-drawers, with their exquisitely folded contents redolent with lavender and sweet clover and very purity. Could she be sure of the endurance of even this? She had visions, so startling that she half repudiated them as indelicate, of coarse masculine belongings strewn about in endless litter; of dust and disorder arising necessarily from a coarse masculine presence in the midst of all this delicate harmony.

Among her forebodings of disturbance, not the least was with regard to Cæsar. Cæsar was a veritable hermit of a dog. For the greater part of his life he had dwelt in his secluded hut, shut out from the society of his kind and all innocent canine joys. Never had Cæsar since his early youth watched at a woodchuck's hole; never had he known the delights of a stray bone at a neighbor's kitchen door. And it was all on account of a sin committed when hardly out of his puppyhood. No one knew the possible depth of remorse of which this mild-visaged, altogether innocent-looking old dog might be capable; but whether or not he had encountered remorse, he had encountered a full measure of righteous retribution. Old Cæsar seldom lifted up his voice in a growl or a bark; he was fat and sleepy; there were yellow rings which looked like spectacles around his dim old eyes; but there was a neighbor who bore on his hand the imprint of several of Cæsar's sharp white youthful teeth, and for that he had lived at the end of a chain, all alone in a little hut, for fourteen years. The neighbor, who was choleric and smarting with the pain of his wound, had demanded either Cæsar's death or complete ostracism. So Louisa's brother, to whom the dog had belonged, had built him his little kennel and tied him up. It was now fourteen years since, in a flood of youthful spirits, he had inflicted that memorable bite, and with the exception of short excursions, always at the end of the chain, under the strict guardianship of his master or Louisa, the old dog had remained a close prisoner. It is doubtful if, with his limited ambition, he took much pride in the fact, but it is certain that he was possessed of considerable cheap fame. He was regarded by all the children in the village and by many adults as a very monster of ferocity. St. George's dragon[5] could hardly have surpassed in evil repute Louisa Ellis's old yellow dog. Mothers charged their children with solemn emphasis not to go too near him, and the children listened and believed greedily, with a fascinated appetite for terror, and ran by Louisa's house stealthily, with many sidelong and backward glances at the terrible dog. If perchance

5. The story of St. George (patron saint of England) and the dragon is an allegorical expression of the triumph of the Christian hero over evil.

he sounded a hoarse bark, there was a panic. Wayfarers chancing into Louisa's yard eyed him with respect, and inquired if the chain were stout. Cæsar at large might have seemed a very ordinary dog, and excited no comment whatever; chained, his reputation overshadowed him, so that he lost his own proper outlines and looked darkly vague and enormous. Joe Dagget, however, with his good-humored sense and shrewdness, saw him as he was. He strode valiantly up to him and patted him on the head, in spite of Louisa's soft clamor of warning, and even attempted to set him loose. Louisa grew so alarmed that he desisted, but kept announcing his opinion in the matter quite forcibly at intervals. "There ain't a better-natured dog in town," he would say, "and it's downright cruel to keep him tied up there. Some day I'm going to take him out."

Louisa had very little hope that he would not, one of these days, when their interests and possessions should be more completely fused in one. She pictured to herself Cæsar on the rampage through the quiet and unguarded village. She saw innocent children bleeding in his path. She was herself very fond of the old dog, because he had belonged to her dead brother, and he was always very gentle with her; still she had great faith in his ferocity. She always warned people not to go too near him. She fed him on ascetic fare of corn-mush and cakes, and never fired his dangerous temper with heating and sanguinary diet of flesh and bones. Louisa looked at the old dog munching his simple fare, and thought of her approaching marriage and trembled. Still no anticipation of disorder and confusion in lieu of sweet peace and harmony, no forebodings of Cæsar on the rampage, no wild fluttering of her little yellow canary, were sufficient to turn her a hair's-breadth. Joe Dagget had been fond of her and working for her all these years. It was not for her, whatever came to pass, to prove untrue and break his heart. She put the exquisite little stitches into her wedding-garments, and the time went on until it was only a week before her wedding-day. It was a Tuesday evening, and the wedding was to be a week from Wednesday.

There was a full moon that night. About nine o'clock Louisa strolled down the road a little way. There were harvest-fields on either hand, bordered by low stone walls. Luxuriant clumps of bushes grew beside the wall, and trees—wild cherry and old apple-trees—at intervals. Presently Louisa sat down on the wall and looked about her with mildly sorrowful reflectiveness. Tall shrubs of blueberry and meadow-sweet, all woven together and tangled with blackberry vines and horsebriers, shut her in on either side. She had a little clear space between. Opposite her, on the other side of the road, was a spreading tree; the moon shone between its boughs, and the leaves twinkled like silver. The road was bespread with a beautiful shifting dapple of silver and shadow; the air was full of a mysterious sweetness. "I wonder if it's wild grapes?" murmured Louisa. She sat there some time. She was just thinking of rising, when she heard footsteps and low voices, and remained quiet. It was a lonely place, and she felt a little timid. She thought she would keep still in the shadow and let the persons, whoever they might be, pass her.

But just before they reached her the voices ceased, and the footsteps. She understood that their owners had also found seats upon the stone wall. She was wondering if she could not steal away unobserved, when the voice broke the stillness. It was Joe Dagget's. She sat still and listened.

The voice was announced by a loud sigh, which was as familiar as itself. "Well," said Dagget, "you've made up your mind, then, I suppose?"

"Yes," returned another voice; "I'm going day after to-morrow."

"That's Lily Dyer," thought Louisa to herself. The voice embodied itself in her mind. She saw a girl tall and full-figured, with a firm, fair face, looking fairer and firmer in the moonlight, her strong yellow hair braided in a close knot. A girl full of a calm rustic strength and bloom, with a masterful way which might have beseemed a princess. Lily Dyer was a favorite with the village folk; she had just the qualities to arouse the admiration. She was good and handsome and smart. Louisa had often heard her praises sounded.

"Well," said Joe Dagget, "I ain't got a word to say."

"I don't know what you could say," returned Lily Dyer.

"Not a word to say," repeated Joe, drawing out the words heavily. Then there was silence. "I ain't sorry," he began at last, "that that happened yesterday—that we kind of let on how we felt to each other. I guess it's just as well we knew. Of course I can't do anything any different. I'm going right on an' get married next week. I ain't going back on a woman that's waited for me fourteen years, an' break her heart."

"If you should jilt her to-morrow, I wouldn't have you," spoke up the girl, with sudden vehemence.

"Well, I ain't going to give you the chance," said he; "but I don't believe you would, either."

"You'd see I wouldn't. Honor's honor, an' right's right. An' I'd never think anything of any man that went against 'em for me or any other girl; you'd find that out, Joe Dagget."

"Well, you'll find out fast enough that I ain't going against 'em for you or any other girl," returned he. Their voices sounded almost as if they were angry with each other. Louisa was listening eagerly.

"I'm sorry you feel as if you must go away," said Joe, "but I don't know but it's best."

"Of course it's best. I hope you and I have got common-sense."

"Well, I suppose you're right." Suddenly Joe's voice got an undertone of tenderness. "Say, Lily," said he, "I'll get along well enough myself, but I can't bear to think—You don't suppose you're going to fret much over it?"

"I guess you'll find out I sha'n't fret much over a married man."

"Well, I hope you won't—I hope you won't, Lily. God knows I do. And—I hope—one of these days—you'll—come across somebody else—"

"I don't see any reason why I shouldn't." Suddenly her tone changed. She spoke in a sweet, clear voice, so loud that she could have been heard across the street. "No, Joe Dagget," said she, "I'll never marry any other man as long as I live. I've got good sense, an' I ain't going to break my heart nor make a fool of myself; but I'm never going to be married, you can be sure of that. I ain't that sort of a girl to feel this way twice."

Louisa heard an exclamation and a soft commotion behind the bushes; then Lily spoke again—the voice sounded as if she had risen. "This must be put a stop to," said she. "We've stayed here long enough. I'm going home."

Louisa sat there in a daze, listening to their retreating steps. After a while she got up and slunk softly home herself. The next day she did her housework methodically; that was as much a matter of course as breathing; but she did not sew on her wedding-clothes. She sat at her window and meditated. In the evening Joe came. Louisa Ellis had never known that she had any diplomacy in her, but when she came to look for it that night she found it, although meek of its kind, among her little feminine weapons. Even now she could hardly believe that she had heard aright, and that she would not do Joe a terrible injury should she break her troth-plight. She wanted to sound him without betraying too soon her own inclinations in the matter. She did it successfully, and they finally came to an understanding; but it was a difficult thing, for he was as afraid of betraying himself as she.

She never mentioned Lily Dyer. She simply said that while she had no cause of complaint against him, she had lived so long in one way that she shrank from making a change.

"Well, I never shrank, Louisa," said Dagget. "I'm going to be honest enough to say that I think maybe it's better this way; but if you'd wanted to keep on, I'd have stuck to you till my dying day. I hope you know that."

"Yes, I do," said she.

That night she and Joe parted more tenderly than they had done for a long time. Standing in the door, holding each other's hands, a last great wave of regretful memory swept over them.

"Well, this ain't the way we've thought it was all going to end, is it, Louisa?" said Joe.

She shook her head. There was a little quiver on her placid face.

"You let me know if there's ever anything I can do for you," said he. "I ain't ever going to forget you, Louisa." Then he kissed her, and went down the path.

Louisa, all alone by herself that night, wept a little, she hardly knew why; but the next morning, on waking, she felt like a queen who, after fearing lest her domain be wrested away from her, sees it firmly insured in her possession.

Now the tall weeds and grasses might cluster around Cæsar's little hermit hut, the snow might fall on its roof year in and year out, but he never would go on a rampage through the unguarded village. Now the little canary might turn itself into a peaceful yellow ball night after night, and have no need to wake and flutter with wild terror against its bars. Louisa could sew linen seams, and distil roses, and dust and polish and fold away in lavender, as long as she listed. That afternoon she sat with her needle-work at the window, and felt fairly steeped in peace. Lily Dyer, tall and erect and blooming, went past; but she felt no qualm. If Louisa Ellis had sold her birthright she did not know it, the taste of the pottage[6] was so delicious, and had been her sole satisfaction for so long. Serenity and placid narrowness had become to her as the birthright itself. She gazed ahead through a long reach of future days strung together like pearls in a rosary, every one like the others, and all smooth and flawless and innocent, and her heart went up in thankfulness. Outside was the fervid summer afternoon; the air was filled with the sounds of the busy harvest of men and birds and bees; there were halloos, metallic clatterings, sweet calls, and long hummings. Louisa sat, prayerfully numbering her days, like an uncloistered nun.

1891

6. In Genesis 25, Esau sells his birthright as oldest son of Isaac and Rebekah to his younger brother Jacob for a bowl of pottage (lentil stew).

BOOKER T. WASHINGTON
1856–1915

Between the last decade of the nineteenth century and the beginning of World War I, no one influenced the public discourse about race relations in the United States more than Booker Taliaferro Washington, arguably the most visible African American leader in the United States during this time. Washington advocated for the economic uplift of African Americans through an educational program of vocational training and for their peaceful incorporation into the American credo of hard work and upward mobility. His works have been contrasted with the dynamic and often sharply critical efforts of Frederick Douglass (whose mantle of leadership Washington sought to assume) and the intellectual and professional initiatives of the fiercely independent W. E. B. Du Bois.

Washington's birth date is uncertain; as an adult he selected April 5, 1856. His mother was born a slave in Hale's Ford, Virginia (now West Virginia); his father was a white man whose identity is unknown. As a boy, he had, like most slaves, only a first name, and it was not until he entered school that he adopted the surname Washington, which was the first name of Washington Ferguson, a slave whom his mother had married. Washington's account of his early life describes his deprivation and struggle in moving detail. At the end of the Civil War, when he was nine years old, he accompanied his mother to Malden, West Virginia, to join his stepfather, who had found work there in a salt furnace. From 1865 to 1872, Washington worked as a salt packer, coal miner, and house servant while attending school in the off-hours and thus beginning to satisfy his "intense longing" to learn to read and write. In 1872, he set out on a five hundred–mile, month-long journey by rail, cart, and foot to reach Hampton, Virginia, where he would attend the Hampton Normal and Agricultural Institute, a school established by the American Missionary Association to train African Americans as teachers. There Washington paid his way by working as a janitor. In the quasi-military atmosphere of the school, he was drilled in the values of cleanliness, thrift, and diligent labor that became central to his life and educational philosophy.

After graduating from Hampton in 1875 with honors and a certificate to teach in a trade school, Washington returned to Malden and found work with a local school. He studied for a while at Wayland Seminary and in 1878 was hired by Samuel Armstrong, the principal of Hampton, to teach in a program for Native Americans. Then, in 1881, he became the first principal of what was to become the Tuskegee Institute, a school established by the Alabama legislature to train African American men and women in agricultural and mechanical trades and teaching. Tuskegee began with thirty students, and Washington, the staff, and the students constructed the school buildings from bricks they made themselves. But through his considerable powers as a conciliator and fund-raiser, and aided by publicity that highlighted his goals of instilling Christian virtues and encouraging simple, disciplined living among the students, Washington soon developed Tuskegee into a thriving institution.

Washington emerged as a national figure in 1895 as the result of a short speech, included below as part of his autobiography, to a crowd of two thousand at the Atlanta Exposition of 1895. In the speech, popularly known as the "Atlanta Compromise," Washington argued that African Americans should defer the quest for immediate, full equality in return for basic economic opportunities. "In all things that are purely social," he declared, "we can be as separate as the fingers, yet one as the hand in all

Booker T. Washington. Washington in his office at Tuskegee
Institute, c. 1905.

things essential to mutual progress." This formulation suggested that economic uplift
could coexist with segregation, an approach that appealed to many whites and even
some blacks across the nation. The immense popularity of Washington's rhetoric
reveals much about the context of the years between 1885 and 1910, when some
thirty-five hundred African Americans were lynched and when, following the end of
Reconstruction, most southern states effectively disenfranchised African Americans.
Even such militant African American leaders as Du Bois and T. Thomas Fortune
initially praised the speech and supported the philosophy of conciliation that was its
pragmatic basis. Their opposition to Washington did not develop until several years
later, when they felt it was again time to insist on civil, social, and political equality
for all African Americans.

Washington believed in rewarding deserving individuals rather than in policies
treating African Americans as a group. His writings argue that success should be
measured not so much by the position a person has reached as by the obstacles overcome while trying to succeed. In his work he instructs African Americans to emulate
the proverbial ship captain who urged his crew to "cast down your buckets where you
are" even though they were still at sea, and who thus found fresh water at the mouth
of a river. Washington argued that by seeking improvement African Americans would
inevitably rise as individuals. Yet he also urged whites not to judge African American children against white children until they had had a chance to catch up in school.
In short, Washington proposed a middle ground wherein African Americans would
raise themselves by individual effort and white Americans would appreciate the efforts
being made and judge accordingly.

In the years following the Atlanta speech, Washington was sometimes referred to
as the "Moses of his race," and he worked to consolidate that position. Nothing did
more to enhance this mythic stature than his autobiography, *Up from Slavery* (1901),
a masterpiece of the genre that was widely praised in the United States and read in
translation around the world. The early chapters included here reveal the physical
and psychological realities of Washington's origins, realities that were shared by
many of the slaves set "free" at the conclusion of the Civil War. Later chapters
show Washington at the peak of his success as an African American spokesperson,

particularly as a master of rhetoric that allowed him to appear both as sincerely humble and as a force to be reckoned with—a man of selfless industry and one of considerable political know-how. *Up from Slavery* is important as a literary production and as a record of a time, place, and person. The autobiography carefully constructs the public figure of Washington, who presents himself as a plainspoken truth-teller rather than a shrewd master of rhetoric, metaphor, and narrative. Even those who have criticized Washington's assimilationist political message have admired the power of his craft—and no critic denies that his message played a substantial role in the shape of African American education in the twentieth century. Washington was awarded an honorary degree by Harvard University, invited to dine by President Theodore Roosevelt, and widely consulted on policy questions by white political and business leaders. On November 5, 1915, Washington was taken ill and entered St. Luke's Hospital in New York City; diagnosed with arteriosclerosis, he was told that he did not have long to live. He traveled to Tuskegee, where he died on November 14. Over eight thousand people attended his funeral, which was held in the Tuskegee Institute Chapel.

From Up from Slavery[1]

Chapter XIV. *The Atlanta Exposition Address*

The Atlanta Exposition,[2] at which I had been asked to make an address as a representative of the Negro race, as stated in the last chapter, was opened with a short address from Governor Bullock.[3] After other interesting exercises, including an invocation from Bishop Nelson, of Georgia, a dedicatory ode by Albert Howell, Jr., and addresses by the President of the Exposition and Mrs. Joseph Thompson, the President of the Woman's Board, Governor Bullock introduced me with the words, "We have with us to-day a representative of Negro enterprise and Negro civilization."

When I arose to speak, there was considerable cheering, especially from the coloured people. As I remember it now, the thing that was uppermost in my mind was the desire to say something that would cement the friendship of the races and bring about hearty coöperation between them. So far as my outward surroundings were concerned, the only thing that I recall distinctly now is that when I got up, I saw thousands of eyes looking intently into my face. The following is the address which I delivered:—

Mr. President and Gentlemen of the Board of Directors and Citizens:

One-third of the population of the South is of the Negro race. No enterprise seeking the material, civil, or moral welfare of this section can disregard this element of our population and reach the highest success. I but convey to you, Mr. President and Directors, the sentiment of the masses of my race when I say that in no way have the value and manhood

1. Published serially in *Outlook* from November 3, 1900, to February 23, 1901, *Up from Slavery* was first published in book form by Doubleday, Page and Company (1901), the source of the text printed here.

2. Opening on September 18, 1895, the Cotton States and International Exposition was a major southern trade fair.

3. Rufus Bullock (1834–1907) served as Georgia governor from 1868 to 1871. A northern-born businessman, he was widely reviled as a carpetbagger and targeted by white supremacists because of his support for African American political equality. Bullock was accused of corruption and fled the state upon resigning his office. He returned to Atlanta in 1876, stood trial, and after being acquitted of all charges he went on to become one of Atlanta's most prominent businessmen.

of the American Negro been more fittingly and generously recognized than by the managers of this magnificent Exposition at every stage of its progress. It is a recognition that will do more to cement the friendship of the two races than any occurrence since the dawn of our freedom.

Not only this, but the opportunity here afforded will awaken among us a new era of industrial progress. Ignorant and inexperienced, it is not strange that in the first years of our new life we began at the top instead of at the bottom; that a seat in Congress or the state legislature was more sought than real estate or industrial skill; that the political convention or stump speaking had more attractions than starting a dairy farm or truck garden.

A ship lost at sea for many days suddenly sighted a friendly vessel. From the mast of the unfortunate vessel was seen a signal, "Water, water; we die of thirst!" The answer from the friendly vessel at once came back, "Cast down your bucket where you are." A second time the signal, "Water, water; send us water!" ran up from the distressed vessel, and was answered, "Cast down your bucket where you are." And a third and fourth signal for water was answered, "Cast down your bucket where you are." The captain of the distressed vessel, at last heeding the injunction, cast down his bucket, and it came up full of fresh, sparkling water from the mouth of the Amazon River. To those of my race who depend on bettering their condition in a foreign land or who underestimate the importance of cultivating friendly relations with the Southern white man, who is their next-door neighbour, I would say: "Cast down your bucket where you are"—cast it down in making friends in every manly way of the people of all races by whom we are surrounded.

Cast it down in agriculture, mechanics, in commerce, in domestic service, and in the professions. And in this connection it is well to bear in mind that whatever other sins the South may be called to bear, when it comes to business, pure and simple, it is in the South that the Negro is given a man's chance in the commercial world, and in nothing is this Exposition more eloquent than in emphasizing this chance. Our greatest danger is that in the great leap from slavery to freedom we may overlook the fact that the masses of us are to live by the productions of our hands, and fail to keep in mind that we shall prosper in proportion as we learn to dignify and glorify common labour and put brains and skill into the common occupations of life; shall prosper in proportion as we learn to draw the line between the superficial and the substantial, the ornamental gewgaws of life and the useful. No race can prosper till it learns that there is as much dignity in tilling a field as in writing a poem. It is at the bottom of life we must begin, and not at the top. Nor should we permit our grievances to overshadow our opportunities.

To those of the white race who look to the incoming of those of foreign birth and strange tongue and habits for the prosperity of the South, were I permitted I would repeat what I say to my own race, "Cast down your bucket where you are." Cast it down among the eight millions of Negroes whose habits you know, whose fidelity and love you have tested in days when to have proved treacherous meant the ruin of your firesides. Cast down your bucket among these people who have, without strikes and labour wars, tilled your fields, cleared your forests, builded your railroads and cities, and brought forth treasures from the bowels of the earth, and helped make possible this magnificent representation of the progress of the South. Casting down your bucket among my people, helping and encouraging them as you are doing on these grounds, and to education of head, hand, and heart, and you will find that they will buy your surplus land, make blossom the waste places in your fields, and run your factories. While doing this, you can be sure in the future, as in the past, that you and your families will be surrounded by the most patient, faithful, law-abiding, and unresentful people that the world has seen. As we have proved our loyalty to you in the past, in nursing your children, watching by the sick-bed of your mothers and fathers, and often following them with tear-dimmed eyes to their graves, so in the future, in our humble way, we shall stand by you with a devotion that no foreigner can approach, ready to lay down our lives, if need be, in defence of yours, interlacing our industrial, commercial, civil, and religious life with yours in a way that shall make the interests of both races one. In all things that are purely social we can be as separate as the fingers, yet one as the hand in all things essential to mutual progress.

There is no defence or security for any of us except in the highest intelligence and development of all. If anywhere there are efforts tending to curtail the fullest growth of the Negro, let these efforts be turned into stimulating, encouraging, and making him the most useful and intelligent citizen. Effort or means so invested will pay a thousand per cent interest. These efforts will be twice blessed—"blessing him that gives and him that takes."[4]

There is no escape through law of man or God from the inevitable:—

> "The laws of changeless justice bind
>   Oppressor with oppressed;
> And close as sin and suffering joined
>   We march to fate abreast."[5]

Nearly sixteen millions of hands will aid you in pulling the load upward, or they will pull against you the load downward. We shall constitute one-third and more of the ignorance and crime of the South, or one-third its intelligence and progress; we shall contribute one-third to the business and industrial prosperity of the South, or we shall prove a veritable body of death, stagnating, depressing, retarding every effort to advance the body politic.

Gentlemen of the Exposition, as we present to you our humble effort at an exhibition of our progress, you must not expect overmuch. Starting thirty years ago with ownership here and there in a few quilts and pumpkins and chickens (gathered from miscellaneous sources), remember the path that has led from these to the inventions and production of agricultural implements, buggies, steam-engines, newspapers, books, statuary, carving, paintings, the management of drug-stores and banks, has not been trodden without contact with thorns and thistles. While we take pride in what we exhibit as a result of our independent efforts,

4. "It blesseth him that gives and him that takes" (Shakespeare, *The Merchant of Venice* 3.1.167).
5. From "Song of the Negro Boatman" (1861), by the Massachusetts poet and abolitionist John Greenleaf Whittier (1807–1892).

we do not for a moment forget that our part in this exhibition would fall far short of your expectations but for the constant help that has come to our educational life, not only from the Southern states, but especially from Northern philanthropists, who have made their gifts a constant stream of blessing and encouragement.

The wisest among my race understand that the agitation of questions of social equality is the extremest folly, and that progress in the enjoyment of all the privileges that will come to us must be the result of severe and constant struggle rather than of artificial forcing. No race that has anything to contribute to the markets of the world is long in any degree ostracized. It is important and right that all privileges of the law be ours, but it is vastly more important that we be prepared for the exercises of these privileges. The opportunity to earn a dollar in a factory just now is worth infinitely more than the opportunity to spend a dollar in an opera-house.

In conclusion, may I repeat that nothing in thirty years has given us more hope and encouragement, and drawn us so near to you of the white race, as this opportunity offered by the Exposition; and here bending, as it were, over the altar that represents the results of the struggles of your race and mine, both starting practically empty-handed three decades ago, I pledge that in your effort to work out the great and intricate problem which God has laid at the doors of the South, you shall have at all times the patient, sympathetic help of my race; only let this be constantly in mind, that, while from representations in these buildings of the product of field, of forest, of mine, of factory, letters, and art, much good will come, yet far above and beyond material benefits will be that higher good, that, let us pray God, will come, in a blotting out of sectional differences and racial animosities and suspicions, in a determination to administer absolute justice, in a willing obedience among all classes to the mandates of law. This, this, coupled with our material prosperity, will bring into our beloved South a new heaven and a new earth.

The first thing that I remember, after I had finished speaking, was that Governor Bullock rushed across the platform and took me by the hand, and that others did the same. I received so many and such hearty congratulations that I found it difficult to get out of the building. I did not appreciate to any degree, however, the impression which my address seemed to have made, until the next morning, when I went into the business part of the city. As soon as I was recognized, I was surprised to find myself pointed out and surrounded by a crowd of men who wished to shake hands with me. This was kept up on every street on to which I went, to an extent which embarrassed me so much that I went back to my boarding-place. The next morning I returned to Tuskegee. At the station in Atlanta, and at almost all of the stations at which the train stopped between the city and Tuskegee, I found a crowd of people anxious to shake hands with me.

The papers in all the parts of the United States published the address in full, and for months afterward there were complimentary editorial references to it. Mr. Clark Howell, the editor of the Atlanta *Constitution*, telegraphed to a New York paper, among other words, the following, "I do not exaggerate when I say that Professor Booker T. Washington's address yesterday was one of the most notable speeches, both as to character and as to the warmth of its reception, ever delivered to a Southern audience. The address was a revelation. The whole speech is a platform upon which blacks and whites can stand with full justice to each other."

The Boston *Transcript* said editorially: "The speech of Booker T. Washington at the Atlanta Exposition, this week, seems to have dwarfed all the other proceedings and the Exposition itself. The sensation that it has caused in the press has never been equalled."

I very soon began receiving all kinds of propositions from lecture bureaus, and editors of magazines and papers, to take the lecture platform, and to write articles. One lecture bureau offered me fifty thousand dollars, or two hundred dollars a night and expenses, if I would place my services at its disposal for a given period. To all these communications I replied that my life-work was at Tuskegee; and that whenever I spoke it must be in the interests of the Tuskegee school and my race, and that I would enter into no arrangements that seemed to place a mere commercial value upon my services.

Some days after its delivery I sent a copy of my address to the President of the United States, the Hon. Grover Cleveland.[6] I received from him the following autograph reply:—

Gray Gables
Buzzard's Bay, Mass., October 6, 1895

Booker T. Washington, Esq.:

My Dear Sir: I thank you for sending me a copy of your address delivered at the Atlanta Exposition.

I thank you with much enthusiasm for making the address. I have read it with intense interest, and I think the Exposition would be fully justified if it did not do more than furnish the opportunity for its delivery. Your words cannot fail to delight and encourage all who wish well for your race; and if our coloured fellow-citizens do not from your utterances father new hope and form new determinations to gain every valuable advantage offered them by their citizenship, it will be strange indeed. Yours very truly,

Grover Cleveland

Later I met Mr. Cleveland, for the first time, when, as President, he visited the Atlanta Exposition. At the request of myself and others he consented to spend an hour in the Negro Building, for the purpose of inspecting the Negro exhibit and of giving the coloured people in attendance an opportunity to shake hands with him. As soon as I met Mr. Cleveland I became impressed with his simplicity, greatness, and rugged honesty. I have met him many times since then, both at public functions and at his private residence in Princeton, and the more I see of him the more I admire him. When he visited the Negro Building in Atlanta he seemed to give himself up wholly, for that hour, to the coloured people. He seemed to be as careful to shake hands with some old coloured "auntie" clad partially in rags, and to take as

6. American politician (1837–1908), twenty-second (1885–89) and twenty-fourth (1893–97) president of the United States.

much pleasure in doing so, as if he were greeting some millionaire. Many of the coloured people took advantage of the occasion to get him to write his name in a book or on a slip of paper. He was as careful and patient in doing this as if he were putting his signature to some great state document.

Mr. Cleveland has not only shown his friendship for me in many personal ways, but has always consented to do anything I have asked of him for our school. This he has done, whether it was to make a personal donation or to use his influence in securing the donations of others. Judging from my personal acquaintance with Mr. Cleveland, I do not believe that he is conscious of possessing any colour prejudice. He is too great for that. In my contact with people I find that, as a rule, it is only the little, narrow people who live for themselves, who never read good books, who do not travel, who never open up their souls in a way to permit them to come into contact with other souls—with the great outside world. No man whose vision is bounded by colour can come into contact with what is highest and best in the world. In meeting men, in many places, I have found that the happiest people are those who do the most for others; the most miserable are those who do the least. I have also found that few things, if any, are capable of making one so blind and narrow as race prejudice. I often say to our students, in the course of my talks to them on Sunday evenings in the chapel, that the longer I live and the more experience I have of the world, the more I am convinced that, after all, the one thing that is most worth living for—and dying for, if need be—is the opportunity of making some one else more happy and more useful.

The coloured people and the coloured newspapers at first seemed to be greatly pleased with the character of my Atlanta address, as well as with its reception. But after the first burst of enthusiasm began to die away, and the coloured people began reading the speech in cold type, some of them seemed to feel that they had been hypnotized. They seemed to feel that I had been too liberal in my remarks toward the Southern whites, and that I had not spoken out strongly enough for what they termed the "rights" of the race. For a while there was a reaction, so far as a certain element of my own race was concerned, but later these reactionary ones seemed to have been won over to my way of believing and acting.

While speaking of changes in public sentiment, I recall that about ten years after the school at Tuskegee was established, I had an experience that I shall never forget. Dr. Lyman Abbott, then the pastor of Plymouth Church, and also editor of the *Outlook*[7] (then the *Christian Union*), asked me to write a letter for his paper giving my opinion of the exact condition, mental and moral of the coloured ministers in the South, as based upon my observations. I wrote the letter, giving the exact facts as I conceived them to be. The picture painted was a rather black one—or, since I am black, shall I say "white"? It could not be otherwise with a race but a few years out of slavery, a race which had not had time or opportunity to produce a competent ministry.

What I said soon reached every Negro minister in the country, I think, and the letters of condemnation which I received from them were not few. I think that for a year after the publication of this article every association and every conference or religious body of any kind, of my race, that met, did not fail before adjourning to pass a resolution condemning me, or calling

---

7. The weekly magazine that first published *Up from Slavery* in serial form.

upon me to retract or modify what I had said. Many of these organizations went so far in their resolutions as to advise parents to cease sending their children to Tuskegee. One association even appointed a "missionary" whose duty it was to warn the people against sending their children to Tuskegee. This missionary had a son in the school, and I noticed that, whatever the "missionary" might have said or done with regard to others, he was careful not to take his son away from the institution. Many of the coloured papers, especially those that were the organs of religious bodies, joined in the general chorus of condemnation or demands for retraction.

During the whole time of the excitement, and through all the criticism, I did not utter a word of explanation or retraction. I knew that I was right, and that time and the sober second thought of the people would vindicate me. It was not long before the bishops and other church leaders began to make a careful investigation of the conditions of the ministry, and they found out that I was right. In fact, the oldest and most influential bishop in one branch of the Methodist Church said that my words were far too mild. Very soon public sentiment began making itself felt, in demanding a purifying of the ministry. While this is not yet complete by any means, I think I may say, without egotism, and I have been told by many of our most influential ministers, that my words had much to do with starting a demand for the placing of a higher type of men in the pulpit. I have had the satisfaction of having many who once condemned me thank me heartily for my frank words.

The change of the attitude of the Negro ministry, so far as regards myself, is so complete that at the present time I have no warmer friends among any class than I have among the clergymen. The improvement in the character and life of the Negro ministers is one of the most gratifying evidences of the progress of the race. My experience with them, as well as other events in my life, convince me that the thing to do, when one feels sure that he has said or done the right thing, and is condemned, is to stand still and keep quiet. If he is right, time will show it.

In the midst of the discussion which was going on concerning my Atlanta speech, I received a letter which I give below, from Dr. Gilman, the President of Johns Hopkins University,[8] who had been made chairman of the judges of award in connection with the Atlanta Exposition:—

> Johns Hopkins University, Baltimore
> President's Office, September 30, 1895
>
> Dear Mr. Washington: Would it be agreeable to you to be one of the Judges of Award in the Department of Education at Atlanta? If so, I shall be glad to place your name upon the list. A line by telegraph will be welcomed. Yours very truly,
>
> D. C. Gilman

I think I was even more surprised to receive this invitation than I had been to receive the invitation to speak at the opening of the Exposition. It was to be a part of my duty, as one of the jurors, to pass not only upon the exhibits of the coloured schools, but also upon those of the white schools. I accepted

---

8. As President of Johns Hopkins from 1875 to 1901, Daniel Coit Gilman (1831–1908) exerted tremendous influence on American higher education.

the position, and spent a month in Atlanta in performance of the duties which it entailed. The board of jurors was a large one, consisting in all of sixty members. It was about equally divided between Southern white people and Northern white people. Among them were college presidents, leading scientists and men of letters, and specialists in many subjects. When the group of jurors to which I was assigned met for organization, Mr. Thomas Nelson Page,[9] who was one of the number, moved that I be made secretary of that division, and the motion was unanimously adopted. Nearly half of our division were Southern people. In performing my duties in the inspection of the exhibits of white schools I was in every case treated with respect, and at the close of our labours I parted from my associates with regret.

I am often asked to express myself more freely than I do upon the political condition and the political future of my race. These recollections of my experience in Atlanta give me the opportunity to do so briefly. My own belief is, although I have never before said so in so many words, that the time will come when the Negro in the South will be accorded all the political rights which his ability, character, and material possessions entitle him to. I think, though, that the opportunity to freely exercise such political rights will not come in any large degree through outside or artificial forcing, but will be accorded to the Negro by the Southern white people themselves, and that they will protect him in the exercise of those rights. Just as soon as the South gets over the old feeling that it is being forced by "foreigners," or "aliens," to do something which it does not want to do, I believe that the change in the direction that I have indicated is going to begin. In fact, there are indications that it is already beginning in a slight degree.

Let me illustrate my meaning. Suppose that some months before the opening of the Atlanta Exposition there had been a general demand from the press and public platform outside the South that a Negro be given a place on the opening programme, and that a Negro be placed upon the board of jurors of award. Would any such recognition of the race have taken place? I do not think so. The Atlanta officials went as far as they did because they felt it to be a pleasure, as well as a duty, to reward what they considered merit in the Negro race. Say what we will, there is something in human nature which we cannot blot out, which makes one man, in the end, recognize and reward merit in another, regardless of colour or race.

I believe it is the duty of the Negro—as the greater part of the race is already doing—to deport himself modestly in regard to political claims, depending upon the slow but sure influences that proceed from the possession of property, intelligence, and high character for the full recognition of his political rights. I think that the according of the full exercise of political rights is going to be a matter of natural, slow growth, not an over-night, gourd-vine affair. I do not believe that the Negro should cease voting, for a man cannot learn the exercise of self-government by ceasing to vote, any more than a boy can learn to swim by keeping out of the water, but I do believe that in his voting he should more and more be influenced by those of intelligence and character who are his next-door neighbours.

I know coloured men who, through the encouragement, help, and advice of Southern white people, have accumulated thousands of dollars' worth of

9. Popular Virginia diplomat and author (1853–1922), best known for *In Ole Virginia* (1887).

property, but who, at the same time, would never think of going to those same persons for advice concerning the casting of their ballots. This, it seems to me, is unwise and unreasonable, and should cease. In saying this I do not mean that the Negro should truckle, or not vote from principle, for the instant he ceases to vote from principle he loses the confidence and respect of the Southern white man even.

I do not believe that any state should make a law that permits an ignorant and poverty-stricken white man to vote, and prevents a black man in the same condition from voting. Such a law is not only unjust, but it will react, as all unjust laws do, in time; for the effect of such a law is to encourage the Negro to secure education and property, and at the same time it encourages the white man to remain in ignorance and poverty. I believe that in time, through the operation of intelligence and friendly race relations, all cheating at the ballot-box in the South will cease. It will become apparent that the white man who begins by cheating a Negro out of his ballot soon learns to cheat a white man out of his, and that the man who does this ends his career of dishonesty by the theft of property or by some equally serious crime. In my opinion, the time will come when the South will encourage all of its citizens to vote. It will see that it pays better, from every standpoint, to have healthy, vigorous life than to have that political stagnation which always results when one-half of the population has no share and no interest in the Government.

As a rule, I believe in universal, free suffrage, but I believe that in the South we are confronted with peculiar conditions that justify the protection of the ballot in many of the states, for a while at least, either by an educational test, a property test, or by both combined; but whatever tests are required, they should be made to apply with equal and exact justice to both races.

1901

CHARLES W. CHESNUTT
1858–1932

I n his short fiction and novels, Charles W. Chesnutt created a provocative, engaging body of writing that challenged some of the most entrenched social conventions of his time. With humor and wit, Chesnutt consistently confronted the logic of racial identification and hierarchy in the United States. His career is also instructive for what it reveals about both the opportunities available to African American writers at the turn of the twentieth century and the obstacles that they faced in finding an audience for their work.

Charles Waddell Chesnutt was born on June 20, 1858, in Cleveland, Ohio. His parents were free-born blacks from North Carolina; his father served in the Union Army and after the Civil War moved his family back to Fayetteville, North Carolina. Chesnutt went to a school established by the Freedman's Bureau during

Reconstruction and worked as a teacher, school principal, newspaper reporter, and accountant. He married Susan Perry, a Fayetteville schoolteacher, in 1878; they had four children. During the late 1870s, Chesnutt declared in his journal his intention to move to the North and "strike for an entering wedge in the literary world." In 1883 he returned to Cleveland and began work as a legal stenographer, passing the Ohio bar exam in 1887. That same year the *Atlantic Monthly* published "The Goophered Grapevine," the first of a group of stories in the regional-dialect folktale tradition earlier made nationally popular by Joel Chandler Harris. Chesnutt's contemporaries would have recognized the trappings of the story—including the figure of a storytelling former slave and the emphasis on authenticity in language, customs, and setting. Perceptive readers then and now, though, also find in "The Goophered Grapevine" a sophisticated, often ironic, reworking of the plantation tale tradition that emphasizes the cruelty of slavery, the power of its legacy, and the slipperiness of power relations between the races. In both "The Goophered Gravpevine" and "Po' Sandy," published the following year, the new owners of a former plantation must contend with the complex history of human bondage that has shaped the land and its people. In the former slave Julius McAdoo, Chesnutt portrays a master storyteller who cannily deploys his art for white auditors struggling to understand the human landscape of the South during Reconstruction.

With age and fame Chesnutt became more direct in his exploration of the psychological and historical implications of racial thinking in the United States. Chesnutt was himself light-skinned but had never tried to hide his racial identity; it was not until 1899, however, the year he began to write full-time, that he revealed himself to his readers as a black man. In that year, his dialect stories set in rural North Carolina were gathered and published as *The Conjure Woman*. Conjure (or hoodoo) is the name given to a set of folk beliefs that combine Caribbean and West African healing and spiritual practices with elements of Christian belief. Practitioners of conjure are thought to know how to get in touch with and direct the powers of nature to make something happen—or to keep something from happening. Two other books by Chesnutt appeared in 1899: a collection of mostly non-dialect and urban stories titled *The Wife of His Youth and Other Stories of the Color Line* and a biography of Frederick Douglass. A number of Chesnutt's stories written in the 1890s dealt with the psychological and social tensions of light-skinned blacks attempting to pass as whites. "The Wife of His Youth," included here, affirms the importance of upwardly mobile, light-complected blacks remembering and honoring their collective past. A second story from that collection, "The Passing of Grandison," shows the limits of whites' understanding of the African American desire for freedom.

Chesnutt's first novel, *The House behind the Cedars* (1900), focuses on interracial relationships between men and women in the South, a subject that recurs throughout his fiction and essays. Though Chesnutt argued that the laws prohibiting interracial marriage were both illogical and absurd, he also understood the powerful, violent response that interracial unions provoked among many white Southerners. These themes are central to *The Marrow of Tradition* (1901), his most ambitious novel, which culminates in a massacre of blacks based on the Wilmington (North Carolina) Riot of 1898. Chesnutt's third novel on the problem of race relations in the post–Civil War South, *The Colonel's Dream* (1905), depicts the failed efforts of the reform-minded Colonel Henry French to institute modernizing economic practices and to challenge white supremacy in a small southern town. Despite the overwhelming pessimism of the novel, Chesnutt dedicated it to "the great number of those who are seeking, in whatever manner or degree, from near at hand or far away, to bring the forces of enlightenment to bear upon the vexed problems which harass the South." The novel received few reviews and sold poorly.

Early in his career, in 1880, Chesnutt had recorded in his journal his youthful ambitions as a writer:

> The object of my writings would be not so much the elevation of the colored people as the elevation of the whites—for I consider the unjust spirit of caste which is so insidious as to pervade a whole nation, and so powerful as to subject a whole race and all connected with it to scorn and social ostracism—I consider this a barrier to the moral progress of the American people; and I would be one of the first to head a determined, organized crusade against it.

With his shrewd depictions of racial thinking in the South, and particularly of the fluidity of the color line, Chesnutt emerged as the first great short-story writer in the African American tradition, and as the first African American fiction writer to be taken seriously in the white press. However, by the time he began composing *The Colonel's Dream*, Chesnutt realized that the reading public did not embrace his work in numbers sufficient for him to support his family. Chesnutt continued to write, but publishers became uninterested in his work; recent years have seen the posthumous first publications of four Chesnutt novels that he left in manuscript form at his death. In his own time, Chesnutt remained esteemed among black writers and readers as a pioneering author committed to representing racial issues in all their historical and social complexity. In 1928 the National Association for the Advancement of Colored People awarded him the Spingarn Medal for his groundbreaking contribution "as a literary artist depicting the life and struggles of Americans of Negro descent." Chesnutt has since come to be widely recognized as one of the most powerful literary artists of the color line.

The Goophered Grapevine[1]

About ten years ago my wife was in poor health, and our family doctor, in whose skill and honesty I had implicit confidence, advised a change of climate. I was engaged in grape-culture in northern Ohio, and decided to look for a location suitable for carrying on the same business in some Southern State. I wrote to a cousin who had gone into the turpentine business in central North Carolina, and he assured me that no better place could be found in the South than the State and neighborhood in which he lived: climate and soil were all that could be asked for, and land could be bought for a mere song. A cordial invitation to visit him while I looked into the matter was accepted. We found the weather delightful at that season, the end of the summer, and were most hospitably entertained. Our host placed a horse and buggy at our disposal, and himself acted as guide until I got somewhat familiar with the country.

I went several times to look at a place which I thought might suit me. It had been at one time a thriving plantation, but shiftless cultivation had wellnigh exhausted the soil. There had been a vineyard of some extent on the place, but it had not been attended to since the war, and had fallen into utter neglect. The vines—here partly supported by decayed and broken-down arbors, there twining themselves among the branches of the slender saplings

1. First published in the August 1887 issue of the *Atlantic Monthly*, the source of the text reprinted here. A revised version of the story later appeared in the collection *The Conjure Woman* (1899). "Goophered": bewitched, hexed (as in voodoo).

which had sprung up among them—grew in wild and unpruned luxuriance, and the few scanty grapes which they bore were the undisputed prey of the first comer. The site was admirably adapted to grape-raising; the soil, with a little attention, could not have been better; and with the native grape, the luscious scuppernong, mainly to rely upon, I felt sure that I could introduce and cultivate successfully a number of other varieties.

One day I went over with my wife, to show her the place. We drove between the decayed gate-posts—the gate itself had long since disappeared—and up the straight, sandy lane to the open space where a dwelling-house had once stood. But the house had fallen a victim to the fortunes of war, and nothing remained of it except the brick pillars upon which the sills had rested. We alighted, and walked about the place for a while; but on Annie's complaining of weariness I led the way back to the yard, where a pine log, lying under a spreading elm, formed a shady though somewhat hard seat. One end of the log was already occupied by a venerable-looking colored man. He held on his knees a hat full of grapes, over which he was smacking his lips with great gusto, and a pile of grape-skins near him indicated that the performance was no new thing. He respectfully rose as we approached, and was moving away, when I begged him to keep his seat.

"Don't let us disturb you," I said. "There's plenty of room for us all."

He resumed his seat with somewhat of embarrassment.

"Do you live around here?" I asked, anxious to put him at his ease.

"Yas, suh. I lives des ober yander, behine de nex' san'-hill, on de Lumberton plank-road."

"Do you know anything about the time when this vineyard was cultivated?"

"Lawd bless yer, suh, I knows all about it. Dey ain' na'er a man in dis settlement w'at won' tell yer ole Julius McAdoo 'uz bawn an' raise' on dis yer same plantation. Is you de Norv'n gemman w'at's gwine ter buy de ole vimya'd?"

"I am looking at it," I replied; "but I don't know that I shall care to buy unless I can be reasonably sure of making something out of it."

"Well, suh, you is a stranger ter me, en I is a stranger ter you, en we is bofe strangers ter one anudder, but 'f I 'uz in yo' place, I wouldn' buy dis vimya'd."

"Why not?" I asked.

"Well, I dunner whe'r you b'lieves in cunj'in er not,—some er de w'ite folks don't, er says dey don't,—but de truf er de matter is dat dis yer old vimya'd is goophered."

"Is what?" I asked, not grasping the meaning of this unfamiliar word.

"Is goophered, cunju'd, bewitch'."

He imparted this information with such solemn earnestness, and with such an air of confidential mystery, that I felt somewhat interested, while Annie was evidently much impressed, and drew closer to me.

"How do you know it is bewitched?" I asked.

"I wouldn' spec' fer you ter b'lieve me 'less you know all 'bout de fac's. But ef you en young miss dere doan' min' lis'n'in' ter a ole nigger run on a minute er two while you er restin', I kin 'splain to yer how it all happen'."

We assured him that we would be glad to hear how it all happened, and he began to tell us. At first the current of his memory—or imagination—seemed somewhat sluggish; but as his embarrassment wore off, his language flowed more freely, and the story acquired perspective and coherence. As he became more and more absorbed in the narrative, his eyes assumed a dreamy expression, and he seemed to lose sight of his auditors, and to be living over again in monologue his life on the old plantation.

"Ole Mars Dugal' McAdoo bought dis place long many years befo' de wah, en I 'member well w'en he sot out all dis yer part er de plantation in scuppernon's. De vimes growed monst'us fas', en Mars Dugal' made a thousan' gallon er scuppernon' wine eve'y year.

"Now, ef dey's an'thing a nigger lub, nex' ter 'possum, en chick'n, en water-millyums, it's scuppernon's. Dey ain' niffin dat kin stan' up side'n de scuppernon' fer sweetness; sugar ain't a suckumstance ter scuppernon'. W'en de season is nigh 'bout ober, en de grapes begin ter swivel up des a little wid de wrinkles er ole age,—w'en de skin git sof' en brown,—den de scuppernon' make you smack yo' lip en roll yo' eye en wush fer mo'; so I reckon it ain' very 'stonishin' dat niggers lub scuppernon'.

"Dey wuz a sight er niggers in de naberhood er de vimya'd. Dere wuz ole Mars Henry Brayboy's niggers, en ole Mars Dunkin McLean's niggers, en Mars Dugal's own niggers; den dey wuz a settlement er free niggers en po' buckrahs[2] down by de Wim'l'ton Road, en Mars Dugal' had de only vimya'd in de naberhood. I reckon it ain' so much so nowadays, but befo' de wah, in slab'ry times, er nigger didn' mine goin' fi' er ten mile in a night, w'en dey wuz sump'n good ter eat at de yuther een.

"So atter a w'ile Mars Dugal' begin ter miss his scuppernon's. Co'se he 'cuse' de niggers er it, but dey all 'nied it ter de las'. Mars Dugal' sot spring guns en steel traps, en he en de oberseah sot up nights once't er twice't, tel one night Mars Dugal'—he 'uz a monst'us keerless man—got his leg shot full er cow-peas.[3] But somehow er nudder dey couldn' nebber ketch none er de niggers. I dunner how it happen, but it happen des like I tell yer, en de grapes kep' on a-goin des de same.

"But bimeby ole Mars Dugal' fix' up a plan ter stop it. Dey 'uz a cunjuh 'ooman livin' down mongs' de free niggers on de Wim'l'ton Road, en all de darkies fum Rockfish ter Beaver Crick wuz feared uv her. She could wuk de mos' powerfulles' kind er goopher,—could make people hab fits er rheuma-tiz, er make 'em des dwinel away en die; en dey say she went out ridin' de niggers at night, for she wuz a witch 'sides bein' a cunjuh 'ooman. Mars Dugal' hearn 'bout Aun' Peggy's doin's, en begun ter 'flect whe'r er no he couldn' git her ter he'p him keep de niggers off'n de grapevimes. One day in de spring er de year, ole miss pack' up a basket er chick'n en poun'-cake, en a bottle er scuppernon' wine, en Mars Dugal' tuk it in his buggy en driv ober ter Aun' Peggy's cabin. He tuk de basket in, en had a long talk wid Aun' Peggy. De nex' day Aun' Peggy come up ter de vimya'd. De niggers seed her slippin' 'roun', en dey soon foun' out what she 'uz doin' dere. Mars Dugal' had hi'ed her ter goopher de grapevimes. She sa'ntered 'roun' mongs' de vimes, en tuk a leaf fum dis one, en a grape-hull fum dat one, en a grape-seed fum anudder one; en den a little twig fum here, en a little pinch er dirt fum dere,—en put it all in a big black bottle, wid a snake's toof en a speckle' hen's gall en some ha'rs fum a black cat's tail, en den fill' de bottle wid scuppernon' wine. W'en she got de goopher all ready en fix', she tuk 'n went out in de woods en buried it under de root uv a red oak tree, en den come back en tole one er de niggers she done goopher de grapevimes, en a'er a nigger w'at eat dem grapes 'ud be sho ter die inside'n twel' mont's.

"Atter dat de niggers let de scuppernons' lone, en Mars Dugal' didn' hab no 'casion ter fine no mo' fault; en de season wuz mos' gone, w'en a strange gemman stop at de plantation one night ter see Mars Dugal' on some business; en his coachman, seein' de scuppernon's growin' so nice en sweet, slip 'roun behine de smoke-house, en et all de scuppernon's he could hole. Nobody didn' notice it at de time, but dat night, on de way home, de gemman's hoss runned away en kill' de coachman. W'en we hearn de noos, Aun' Lucy, de cook, she up 'n say she seed de strange nigger eat'n er de scuppernon's behind de smoke-house; en den we knowed de goopher had b'en er wukkin. Den one er de nigger chilluns runned away fum de quarters one day, en got in de scuppernon's, en died de nex' week. W'ite folks say he die' er de fevuh, but de niggers knowed it wuz de goopher. So you k'n be sho de darkies didn' hab much ter do wid dem scuppernon' vimes.

"W'en de scuppernon' season 'uz ober fer dat year, Mars Dugal' foun' he had made fifteen hund'ed gallon er wine; en one er de niggers hearn him laffin' wid de oberseah fit ter kill, en sayin' dem fifteen hund'ed gallon er wine wuz monst'us good intrus' on de ten dollars he laid out on de vimya'd. So I 'low ez he paid Aun' Peggy ten dollars fer to goopher de grapevimes.

"De goopher didn' wuk no mo' tel de nex' summer, w'en 'long to'ds de middle er de season one er de fiel' han's died; en ez dat lef' Mars Dugal' sho't er han's, he went off ter town fer ter buy anudder. He fotch de noo nigger home wid 'im. He wuz er ole nigger, er de color er a gingy-cake, en ball ez a hoss-apple on de top er his head. He wuz a peart ole nigger, do', en could do a big day's wuk.

"Now it happen dat one er de niggers on de nex' plantation, one er ole Mars Henry Brayboy's niggers, had runned away de day befo', en tuk ter de swamp, en ole Mars Dugal' en some er de yuther nabor w'ite folks had gone out wid dere guns en dere dogs fer ter he'p 'em hunt fer de nigger; en de han's on our own plantation wuz all so flusterated dat we fuhgot ter tell de noo han' 'bout de goopher on de scuppernon' vimes. Co'se he smell de grapes en see de vimes, an atter dahk de fus' thing he done wuz ter slip off ter de grapevimes 'dout sayin' nuffin ter nobody. Nex' mawnin' he tole some er de niggers 'bout de fine bait er scuppernon' he et de night befo'.

"W'en dey tole 'im 'bout de goopher on de grapevimes, he 'uz dat tarrified dat he turn pale, en look des like he gwine ter die right in his tracks. De oberseah come up en axed w'at 'uz de matter; en w'en dey tol 'im Henry be'n eatin' er de scuppernon's, en got de goopher on 'im, he gin Henry a big drink er w'iskey, en 'low dat de nex' rainy day he take 'im ober ter Aun' Peggy's, en see ef she wouldn' take de goopher off'n him, seein' ez he didn't know nuffin erbout it tel he done et de grapes.

"Sho nuff, it rain de nex' day, en de oberseah went ober ter Aun' Peggy's wid Henry. En Aun' Peggy say dat bein' ez Henry didn' know 'bout de goopher, en et de grapes in ign'ance er de quinseconces, she reckon she mought be able fer ter take de goopher off'n him. So she fotch out er bottle wid some cunjuh medicine in it, en po'd some out in a go'd fer Henry ter drink. He manage ter git it down; he say it tas'e like whiskey wid sump'n bitter in it. She 'lowed dat 'ud keep de goopher off'n him tel de spring; but w'en de sap begin ter rise in de grapevimes he ha ter come en see her agin, en she tell him w'at e's ter do.

"Nex' spring, w'en de sap commence' ter rise in de scuppernon' vime, Henry tuk a ham one night. Whar'd he git de ham? *I* doan know; dey wa'nt no hams on de plantation 'cep'n w'at 'uz in de smoke-house, but *I* never see Henry 'bout de smoke-house. But ez I wuz a-sayin', he tuk de ham ober ter Aun' Peggy's; en Aun' Peggy tole 'im dat w'en Mars Dugal' begin ter prume de grapevimes, he mus' go en take 'n scrape off de sap whar it ooze out'n de cut een's er de vimes, en 'n'int his ball head wid it; en ef he do dat once't a year de goopher wouldn' wuk agin 'im long ez he done it. En bein 'ez he fotch her de ham, she fix' it so he kin eat all de scuppernon' he want.

"So Henry 'n'int his head wid de sap out'n de big grapevime des ha'f way 'twix' de quarters en de big house, en de goopher nebber wuk agin him dat summer. But de beatenes' thing you eber see happen ter Henry. Up ter dat time he wuz ez ball ez a sweeten' 'tater, but des ez soon ez de young leaves begun ter come out on de grapevimes de ha'r begun ter grow out on Henry's head, en by de middle er de summer he had de bigges' head er ha'r on de plantation. Befo' dat, Henry had tol'able good ha'r 'roun' de aidges, but soon ez de young grapes begun ter come Henry's ha'r begun ter quirl all up in little balls, des like dis yer reg'lar grapy ha'r, en by de time de grapes got ripe his head look des like a bunch er grapes. Combin' it didn' do no good; he wuk at it ha'f de night wid er Jim Crow,[4] en think he git it straighten' out, but in de mawnin' de grapes 'ud be dere des de same. So he gin it up, en tried ter keep de grapes down by havin' his ha'r cut sho't.

"But dat wa'nt de quares' thing 'bout de goopher. When Henry come ter de plantation, he wuz gittin' a little ole an stiff in de j'ints. But dat summer he got des ez spray en libely ez any young nigger on de plantation; fac' he got so biggity dat Mars Jackson, de oberseah, ha' ter th'eaten ter whip 'im, ef he didn' stop cuttin' up his didos[5] en behave hisse'f. But de mos' cur'ouses' thing happen' in de fall, when sap begin ter go down in de grapevimes. Fus', when de grapes 'uz gethered, de knots begun ter straighten out'n Henry's h'ar; en w'en de leaves begin ter fall, Henry's ha'r begin ter drap out; en w'en de vimes 'uz b'ar, Henry's head wuz baller'n it wuz in de spring, en he begin ter git ole en stiff in de j'ints ag'in, en paid no mo' tention ter de gals dyoin' er de whole winter. En nex' spring, w'en he rub de sap on ag'in, he got young ag'in, en so soopl en libely dat none er de young niggers on de plantation could n' jump, ner dance, ner hoe ez much cotton ez Henry. But in de fall er de year his grapes begun ter straighten out, en his j'ints ter git stiff, en his ha'r drap off, en de rheumatiz begin ter wrastle wid 'im.

"Now, ef you'd a knowed ole Mars Dugal' McAdoo, you'd a knowed dat it ha' ter be a mighty rainy day when he could n' fine sump'n fer his niggers ter do, en it ha' ter be a mightly little hole he couldn' crawl thoo, en ha' ter be a monst'us cloudy night w'en a dollar git by him in de dahkness; en w'en he see how Henry git young in de spring en ole in de fall, he 'lowered ter hisse'f ez how he could make mo' money outen Henry dan by wukkin' him in de cotton fiel'. 'Long de nex' spring, atter de sap commence' ter rise, en Henry 'n'int 'is head en commence fer ter git young en soopl, Mars Dugal' up'n tuk

---

4. A small card, resembling a curry-comb in construction, and used by negroes in the rural districts instead of a comb [Chesnutt's note].
5. Behaving in a silly or mischievous way.

Henry ter town, en sole 'im fer fifteen hunder' dollars. Co'se de man w'at bought Henry didn' know nuffin 'bout de goopher, en Mars Dugal' didn' see no 'casion fer ter tell 'im. Long to'ds de fall, w'en de sap went down, Henry begin ter git ole again same ez yuzhal, en his noo marster begin ter git skeered les'n he gwine ter lose his fifteen-hunder'-dollar nigger. He sent fer a mighty fine doctor, but de med'cine didn' 'pear ter do no good; de goopher had a good holt. Henry tole de doctor 'bout de goopher, but de doctor des laff at 'im.

"One day in de winter Mars Dugal' went ter town, en wuz santerin' 'long de Main Street, when who should he meet but Henry's noo marster. Dey said 'Hoddy,' en Mars Dugal' ax 'im ter hab a seegyar; en atter dey run on awhile 'about de craps en de weather, Mars Dugal' ax 'im, sorter keerless, like ez ef he des thought of it,—

"'How you like de nigger I sole you las' spring?'

"Henry's marster shuck his head en knock de ashes off'n his seegyar.

"'Spec' I made a bad bahgin when I bought dat nigger. Henry done good wuk all de summer, but sence de fall set in he 'pears ter be sorter pinin' away. Dey ain' nuffin pertickler de matter wid 'im—leastways de doctor say so— 'cep'n' a tech er de rheumatiz; but his ha'r is all fell out, en ef he don't pick up his strenk mighty soon, I spec' I'm gwine ter lose 'im.'

"Dey smoked on awhile, en bimeby ole mars say, 'Well, a bahgin's a bahgin, but you en me is good fren's, en I doan wan' ter see you lose all de money you paid fer dat digger; en ef w'at you say is so, en I ain't 'sputin' it, he ain't wuf much now. I spec's you wukked him too ha'd dis summer, er e'se de swamps down here don't agree wid de san'-hill nigger. So you des lemme know, en ef he gits any wusser I'll be willin' ter gib yer five hund'ed dollars fer 'im, en take my chances on his livin'.'

"Sho nuff, when Henry begun ter draw up wid de rheumatiz en it look like he gwine ter die fer sho, his noo marster sen' fer Mars Dugal', en Mars Dugal' gin him what he promus, en brung Henry home ag'in. He tuk good keer uv 'im dyoin' er de winter,—give 'im w'iskey ter rub his rheumatiz, en terbacker ter smoke, en all he want ter eat,—'caze a nigger w'at he could make a thousan' dollars a year off'n didn' grow on eve'y huckleberry bush.

"Nex' spring, w'en de sap ris en Henry's ha'r commence' ter sprout, Mars Dugal' sole 'im ag'in, down in Robeson County dis time; en he kep' dat sellin' business up fer five year er mo'. Henry nebber say nuffin 'bout de goopher ter his noo marsters, 'caze he knew he gwine ter be tuk good keer uv de nex' winter, w'en Mars Dugal' buy him back. En Mars Dugal' made 'nuff money off'n Henry ter buy anudder plantation ober on Beaver Crick.

"But long 'bout de een' er dat five year dey come a stranger ter stop at de plantation. De fus' day he 'us dere he went out wid Mars Dugal' en spent all de mawnin' lookin' ober de vimya'd, en atter dinner dey spent all de evenin' playin' kya'ds. De niggers soon 'skiver' dat he wuz a Yankee, en dat he come down ter Norf C'lina fer ter learn de w'ite folks how to raise grapes en make wine. He promus Mars Dugal' he cud make de grapevimes ba'r twice't ez many grapes, en dat de noo wine-press he wuz a-sellin' would make mo' d'n twice't ez many gallons er wine. En ole Mars Dugal' des drunk it all in, des 'peared ter be bewitched wid dat Yankee. W'en de darkies see dat Yankee runnin' 'roun de vimya'd en diggin' under de grapevimes, dey shuk dere heads, en 'lowed dat dey feared Mars Dugal' losin' his min'. Mars Dugal' had all de dirt dug away fum under de roots er all de scuppernon' vimes, an' let 'em stan' dat away fer a week er mo'. Den dat Yankee made de niggers fix up a mixtry er lime en ashes en manyo,[6] en po' it roun' de roots er de grape-vimes. Den he 'vise' Mars Dugal' fer ter trim de vimes close't, en Mars Dugal' tuck 'n done eve'ything de Yankee tole him ter do. Dyoin' all er dis time, mind yer, 'e wuz libbin' off'n de fat er de lan', at de big house, en playin' kyards wid Mars Dugal' eve'y night; en dey say Mars Dugal' los' mo'n a thousan' dollars dyoin' er de week dat Yankee wuz a runnin' de grapevimes.

"W'en de sap ris nex' spring, old Henry 'n'inted his head ez yuzhal, en his ha'r commence' ter grow des de same ez it done eve'y year. De scuppernon' vimes growed monst's fas', en de leaves wuz greener en thicker dan dey eber be'n dyowin my rememb'ance; en Henry's ha'r growed out thicker dan eber, en he 'peared ter git younger 'n younger, en soopler 'n soopler; en seein' ez he wuz sho't er han's dat spring, havin' tuk in consid'able noo groun', Mars Dugal' 'cluded he would n' sell Henry 'tel he git de crap in en de cotton chop'. So he kep' Henry on de plantation.

"But 'long 'bout time fer de grapes ter come on de scuppernon' vimes, dey 'peared ter come a change ober dem; de leaves wivered en swivel' up, en de young grapes turn' yaller, en bimeby eve'ybody on de plantation could see dat de whole vimya'd wuz dyin'. Mars Dugal' tuck'n water de vimes en done all he could, but 't wan' no use: dat Yankee done bus' de watermillyum. One time de vimes picked up a bit, en Mars Dugal' thought dey wuz gwine ter come out ag'in; but dat Yankee done dug too close unde' de roots, en prune de branches too close ter de vime, en all dat lime en ashes done burn' de life outen de vimes, en dey des kep' a with'in' en a swivelin'.

"All dis time de goopher wuz a-wukkin'. W'en de vimes commence' ter wither, Henry commence' ter complain er his rheumatiz, en when de leaves begin ter dry up his ha'r commence' ter drap out. When de vimes fresh up a bit Henry 'ud git peart agin, en when de vimes wither agin Henry 'ud git ole agin, en des kep' gittin' mo' en mo' fitten fer nuffin; he des pined away, en fine'ly tuk ter his cabin; en when de big vime whar he got de sap ter 'n'int his head withered en turned yaller en died, Henry died too,—des went out sorter like a cannel. Dey didn't 'pear ter be nuffin de matter wid 'im, cep'n' de rheumatiz, but his strenk des dwinel' away, 'tel he didn' hab ernuff lef' ter draw his bref. De goopher had got de under holt, en th'owed Henry fer good en all dat time.

"Mars Dugal' tuk on might'ly 'bout losin' his vimes en his nigger in de same year; en he swo' dat ef he could git holt er dat Yankee he'd wear 'im ter a frazzle, en den chaw up de frazzle; en he'd done it, too, for Mars Dugal' 'uz a monst'us brash man w'en he once git started. He sot de vimya'd out ober agin, but it wuz th'ee er fo' year befo' de vimes got ter b'arin' any scup-pernon's.

"W'en de wah broke out, Mars Dugal' raise' a comp'ny, en went off ter fight de Yankees. He say he wuz mighty glad dat wah come, en he des want ter kill a Yankee fer eve'y dollar he los' 'long er dat grape-raisin' Yankee. En I 'spec' he would a done it, too, ef de Yankees hadn' s'picioned sump'n, en killed him fus'. Atter de s'render ole miss move' ter town, de niggers all scat-tered 'way fum de plantation, en de vimya'd ain' be'n cultervated sence."

6. Manure.

"Is that story true?" asked Annie, doubtfully, but seriously, as the old man concluded his narrative.

"It's des ez true ez I'm a-settin' here, miss. Dey's a easy way ter prove it: I kin lead de way right ter Henry's grave ober yander in de plantation buryin'-groun'. En I tell yer w'at, marster, I wouldn' 'vise yer to buy dis yer ole vimya'd, 'caze de goopher's on it yit, en dey ain' no tellin' w'en it's gwine ter crap out."

"But I thought you said all the old vines died."

"Dey did 'pear ter die, but a few ov 'em come out ag'in, en is mixed in mongs' de yuthers. I ain' skeered ter eat de grapes, 'caze I knows de old vimes fum de noo ones; but wid strangers dey ain' no tellin' w'at might happen. I wouldn' 'vise yer ter buy dis vimya'd."

I bought the vineyard, nevertheless, and it has been for a long time in a thriving condition, and is referred to by the local press as a striking illustration of the opportunities open to Northern capital in the development of Southern industries. The luscious scuppernong holds first rank among our grapes, though we cultivate a great many other varieties, and our income from grapes packed and shipped to the Northern markets is quite considerable. I have not noticed any developments of the goopher in the vineyard, although I have a mild suspicion that our colored assistants do not suffer from want of grapes during the season.

I found, when I bought the vineyard, that Uncle Julius had occupied a cabin on the place for many years, and derived a respectable revenue from the neglected grapevines. This, doubtless, accounted for his advice to me not to buy the vineyard, though whether it inspired the goopher story I am unable to state. I believe, however, that the wages I pay him for his services are more than an equivalent for anything he lost by the sale of the vineyard.

1887

The Wife of His Youth[1]

I

Mr. Ryder was going to give a ball. There were several reasons why this was an opportune time for such an event.

Mr. Ryder might aptly be called the dean of the Blue Veins. The original Blue Veins were a little society of colored persons organized in a certain Northern city shortly after the war. Its purpose was to establish and maintain correct social standards among a people whose social condition presented almost unlimited room for improvement. By accident, combined perhaps with some natural affinity, the society consisted of individuals who were, generally speaking, more white than black. Some envious outsider made the suggestion that no one was eligible for membership who was not white enough to show blue veins. The suggestion was readily adopted by those who were not of the favored few, and since that time the society, though possessing a longer and more pretentious name, had been known far and wide as the "Blue Vein Society," and its members as the "Blue Veins."

1. First published in the July 1898 issue of the *Atlantic* and reprinted in the collection *"The Wife of His Youth" and Other Stories of the Color Line* (1899), the source of the text printed here.

The Blue Veins did not allow that any such requirement existed for admission to their circle, but, on the contrary, declared that character and culture were the only things considered; and that if most of their members were light-colored, it was because such persons, as a rule, had had better opportunities to qualify themselves for membership. Opinions differed, too, as to the usefulness of the society. There were those who had been known to assail it violently as a glaring example of the very prejudice from which the colored race had suffered most; and later, when such critics had succeeded in getting on the inside, they had been heard to maintain with zeal and earnestness that the society was a life-boat, an anchor, a bulwark and a shield,—a pillar of cloud by day and of fire by night, to guide their people through the social wilderness. Another alleged prerequisite for Blue Vein membership was that of free birth; and while there was really no such requirement, it is doubtless true that very few of the members would have been unable to meet it if there had been. If there were one or two of the older members who had come up from the South and from slavery, their history presented enough romantic circumstances to rob their servile origin of its grosser aspects.

While there were no such tests of eligibility, it is true that the Blue Veins had their notions on these subjects, and that not all of them were equally liberal in regard to the things they collectively disclaimed. Mr. Ryder was one of the most conservative. Though he had not been among the founders of the society, but had come in some years later, his genius for social leadership was such that he had speedily become its recognized adviser and head, the custodian of its standards, and the preserver of its traditions. He shaped its social policy, was active in providing for its entertainment, and when the interest fell off, as it sometimes did, he fanned the embers until they burst again into a cheerful flame.

There were still other reasons for his popularity. While he was not as white as some of the Blue Veins, his appearance was such as to confer distinction upon them. His features were of a refined type, his hair was almost straight; he was always neatly dressed; his manners were irreproachable, and his morals above suspicion. He had come to Groveland a young man, and obtaining employment in the office of a railroad company as messenger had in time worked himself up to the position of stationery clerk, having charge of the distribution of the office supplies for the whole company. Although the lack of early training had hindered the orderly development of a naturally fine mind, it had not prevented him from doing a great deal of reading or from forming decidedly literary tastes. Poetry was his passion. He could repeat whole pages of the great English poets; and if his pronunciation was sometimes faulty, his eye, his voice, his gestures, would respond to the changing sentiment with a precision that revealed a poetic soul and disarmed criticism. He was economical, and had saved money; he owned and occupied a very comfortable house on a respectable street. His residence was handsomely furnished, containing among other things a good library, especially rich in poetry, a piano, and some choice engravings. He generally shared his house with some young couple, who looked after his wants and were company for him; for Mr. Ryder was a single man. In the early days of his connection with the Blue Veins he had been regarded as quite a catch, and young ladies and their mothers had manœuvred with much ingenuity to capture him. Not, however, until Mrs. Molly Dixon visited Groveland had any woman ever made him wish to change his condition to that of a married man.

Mrs. Dixon had come to Groveland from Washington in the spring, and before the summer was over she had won Mr. Ryder's heart. She possessed many attractive qualities. She was much younger than he; in fact, he was old enough to have been her father, though no one knew exactly how old he was. She was whiter than he, and better educated. She had moved in the best colored society of the country, at Washington, and had taught in the schools of that city. Such a superior person had been eagerly welcomed to the Blue Vein Society, and had taken a leading part in its activities. Mr. Ryder had at first been attracted by her charms of person, for she was very good looking and not over twenty-five; then by her refined manners and the vivacity of her wit. Her husband had been a government clerk, and at his death had left a considerable life insurance. She was visiting friends in Groveland, and, finding the town and the people to her liking, had prolonged her stay indefinitely. She had not seemed displeased at Mr. Ryder's attentions, but on the contrary had given him every proper encouragement; indeed, a younger and less cautious man would long since have spoken. But he had made up his mind, and had only to determine the time when he would ask her to be his wife. He decided to give a ball in her honor, and at some time during the evening of the ball to offer her his heart and hand. He had no special fears about the outcome, but, with a little touch of romance, he wanted the surroundings to be in harmony with his own feelings when he should have received the answer he expected.

Mr. Ryder resolved that this ball should mark an epoch in the social history of Groveland. He knew, of course,—no one could know better,—the entertainments that had taken place in past years, and what must be done to surpass them. His ball must be worthy of the lady in whose honor it was to be given, and must, by the quality of its guests, set an example for the future. He had observed of late a growing liberality, almost a laxity, in social matters, even among members of his own set, and had several times been forced to meet in a social way persons whose complexions and callings in life were hardly up to the standard which he considered proper for the society to maintain. He had a theory of his own.

"I have no race prejudice," he would say, "but we people of mixed blood are ground between the upper and the nether millstone. Our fate lies between absorption by the white race and extinction in the black. The one doesn't want us yet, but may take us in time. The other would welcome us, but it would be for us a backward step. 'With malice towards none, with charity for all,'[2] we must do the best we can for ourselves and those who are to follow us. Self-preservation is the first law of nature."

His ball would serve by its exclusiveness to counteract leveling tendencies, and his marriage with Mrs. Dixon would help to further the upward process of absorption he had been wishing and waiting for.

II

The ball was to take place on Friday night. The house had been put in order, the carpets covered with canvas, the halls and stairs decorated with palms

2. From Abraham Lincoln's second inaugural address (1865).

and potted plants; and in the afternoon Mr. Ryder sat on his front porch, which the shade of a vine running up over a wire netting made a cool and pleasant lounging place. He expected to respond to the toast "The Ladies" at the supper, and from a volume of Tennyson—his favorite poet—was fortifying himself with apt quotations. The volume was open at "A Dream of Fair Women."[3] His eyes fell on these lines, and he read them aloud to judge better of their effect:—

> "At length I saw a lady within call,
>   Stiller than chisell'd marble, standing there;
> A daughter of the gods, divinely tall,
>   And most divinely fair."

He marked the verse, and turning the page read the stanza beginning,—

> "O sweet pale Margaret,
>   O rare pale Margaret."[4]

He weighed the passage a moment, and decided that it would not do. Mrs. Dixon was the palest lady he expected at the ball, and she was of a rather ruddy complexion, and of lively disposition and buxom build. So he ran over the leaves until his eye rested on the description of Queen Guinevere:[5]—

> "She seem'd a part of joyous Spring:
> A gown of grass-green silk she wore,
> Buckled with golden clasps before;
> A light-green tuft of plumes she bore
> Closed in a golden ring.
>
> •　•　•　•　•
>
> "She look'd so lovely, as she sway'd
> The rein with dainty finger-tips,
> A man had given all other bliss,
> And all his worldly worth for this,
> To waste his whole heart in one kiss
> Upon her perfect lips."

As Mr. Ryder murmured these words audibly, with an appreciative thrill, he heard the latch of his gate click, and a light foot-fall sounding on the steps. He turned his head, and saw a woman standing before his door.

She was a little woman, not five feet tall, and proportioned to her height. Although she stood erect, and looked around her with very bright and restless eyes, she seemed quite old; for her face was crossed and recrossed with a hundred wrinkles, and around the edges of her bonnet could be seen protruding here and there a tuft of short gray wool. She wore a blue calico gown of ancient cut, a little red shawl fastened around her shoulders with an old-fashioned brass brooch, and a large bonnet profusely ornamented with faded red and yellow artificial flowers. And she was very black,—so black that her toothless gums, revealed when she opened her mouth to speak, were not red, but blue. She looked like a bit of the old plantation life, sum-

---

3. Poem by the English writer Alfred, Lord Tennyson (1809–1892), published in 1832.
4. From Tennyson's "Margaret" (1832).

5. Wife of the legendary King Arthur, described in the stanzas that follow from Tennyson's "Sir Launcelot and Queen Guinevere" (1842).

moned up from the past by the wave of a magician's wand, as the poet's fancy had called into being the gracious shapes of which Mr. Ryder had just been reading.

He rose from his chair and came over to where she stood.

"Good-afternoon, madam," he said.

"Good-evenin', suh," she answered, ducking suddenly with a quaint curtsy. Her voice was shrill and piping, but softened somewhat by age. "Is dis yere whar Mistuh Ryduh lib, suh?" she asked, looking around her doubtfully, and glancing into the open windows, through which some of the preparations for the evening were visible.

"Yes," he replied, with an air of kindly patronage, unconsciously flattered by her manner, "I am Mr. Ryder. Did you want to see me?"

"Yas, suh, ef I ain't 'sturbin' of you too much."

"Not at all. Have a seat over here behind the vine, where it is cool. What can I do for you?"

" 'Scuse me, suh," she continued, when she had sat down on the edge of a chair, " 'scuse me, suh, I's lookin' for my husban'. I heerd you wuz a big man an' had libbed heah a long time, an' I 'lowed you wouldn't min' ef I'd come roun' an' ax you ef you'd ever heerd of a merlatter[6] man by de name er Sam Taylor 'quirin' roun' in de chu'ches ermongs' de people fer his wife 'Liza Jane?"

Mr. Ryder seemed to think for a moment.

"There used to be many such cases right after the war," he said, "but it has been so long that I have forgotten them. There are very few now. But tell me your story, and it may refresh my memory."

She sat back farther in her chair so as to be more comfortable, and folded her withered hands in her lap.

"My name's 'Liza," she began, " 'Liza Jane. W'en I wuz young I us'ter b'long ter Marse Bob Smif, down in ole Missoura. I wuz bawn down dere. W'en I wuz a gal I wuz married ter a man named Jim. But Jim died, an' after dat I married a merlatter man named Sam Taylor. Sam wuz free-bawn, but his mammy and daddy died, an' de w'ite folks 'prenticed him ter my marster fer ter work fer 'im 'tel he wuz growed up. Sam worked in de fiel', an' I wuz de cook. One day Ma'y Ann, ole miss's maid, came rushin' out ter de kitchen, an' says she, ' 'Liza Jane, ole marse gwine sell yo' Sam down de ribber.'

" 'Go way f'm yere,' says I; 'my husban' 's free!'

" 'Don' make no diff'ence. I heerd ole marse tell ole miss he wuz gwine take yo' Sam 'way wid 'im ter-morrow, fer he needed money, an' he knowed whar he could git a t'ousan' dollars fer Sam an' no questions axed.'

"W'en Sam come home f'm de fiel' dat night, I tole him 'bout ole marse gwine steal 'im, an' Sam run erway. His time wuz mos' up, an' he swo' dat w'en he wuz twenty-one he would come back an' he'p me run erway, er else save up de money ter buy my freedom. An' I know he'd 'a' done it, fer he thought a heap er me, Sam did. But w'en he come back he didn' fin' me, fer I wuzn' dere. Ole marse had heerd dat I warned Sam, so he had me whip' an' sol' down de ribber.

6. Mulatto.

"Den de wah broke out, an' w'en it wuz ober de cullud folks wuz scattered. I went back ter de ole home; but Sam wuzn' dere, an' I couldn' l'arn nuffin' 'bout 'im. But I knowed he'd be'n dere to look for me an' hadn' foun' me, an' had gone erway ter hunt fer me.

"I's be'n lookin' fer 'im eber sence," she added simply, as though twenty-five years were but a couple of weeks, "an' I knows he's be'n lookin' fer me. Fer he sot a heap er sto' by me, Sam did, an' I know he's be'n huntin' fer me all dese years,—'less'n he's be'n sick er sump'n, so he couldn' work, er out'n his head, so he couldn' 'member his promise. I went back down de ribber, fer I 'lowed he'd gone down dere lookin' fer me. I's be'n ter Noo Orleens, an' Atlanty, an' Charleston, an' Richmon'; an' w'en I'd be'n all ober de Souf I come ter de Norf. Fer I knows I'll fin' 'im some er dese days," she added softly, "er he'll fin' me, an' den we'll bofe be as happy in freedom as we wuz in de ole days befo' de wah." A smile stole over her withered countenance as she paused a moment, and her bright eyes softened into a far-away look.

This was the substance of the old woman's story. She had wandered a little here and there. Mr. Ryder was looking at her curiously when she finished.

"How have you lived all these years?" he asked.

"Cookin', suh. I's a good cook. Does you know anybody w'at needs a good cook, suh? I's stoppin' wid a cullud fam'ly round' de corner yonder 'tel I kin git a place."

"Do you really expect to find your husband? He may be dead long ago."

She shook her head emphatically. "Oh no, he ain' dead. De signs an' de tokens tells me. I dremp three nights runnin' on'y dis las' week dat I foun' him."

"He may have married another woman. Your slave marriage would not have prevented him, for you never lived with him after the war, and without that your marriage doesn't count."[7]

"Wouldn' make no diff'ence wid Sam. He wouldn' marry no yuther 'ooman 'tel he foun' out 'bout me. I knows it," she added. "Sump'n's be'n tellin' me all dese years dat I's gwine fin' Sam 'fo' I dies."

"Perhaps he's outgrown you, and climbed up in the world where he wouldn't care to have you find him."

"No, indeed, suh," she replied, "Sam ain' dat kin' er man. He wuz good ter me, Sam wuz, but he wuzn' much good ter nobody e'se, fer he wuz one er de triflin'es' han's on de plantation. I 'spec's ter haf ter suppo't 'im w'en I fin' 'im, fer he nebber would work 'less'n he had ter. But den he wuz free, an' he didn' git no pay fer his work, an' I don' blame 'im much. Mebbe he's done better sence he run erway, but I ain' 'spectin' much."

"You may have passed him on the street a hundred times during the twenty-five years, and not have known him; time works great changes."

She smiled incredulously. "I'd know 'im 'mongs' a hund'ed men. Fer dey wuz n' no yuther merlatter man like my man Sam, an' I couldn' be mistook. I's toted his picture roun' wid me twenty-five years."

"May I see it?" asked Mr. Ryder. "It might help me to remember whether I have seen the original."

As she drew a small parcel from her bosom he saw that it was fastened to a string that went around her neck. Removing several wrappers, she brought to light an old-fashioned daguerreotype in a black case. He looked long and

7. Slave marriages had no legal standing in the pre–Civil War South.

intently at the portrait. It was faded with time, but the features were still distinct, and it was easy to see what manner of man it had represented.

He closed the case, and with a slow movement handed it back to her.

"I don't know of any man in town who goes by that name," he said, "nor have I heard of any one making such inquiries. But if you will leave me your address, I will give the matter some attention, and if I find out anything I will let you know."

She gave him the number of a house in the neighborhood, and went away, after thanking him warmly.

He wrote the address on the fly-leaf of the volume of Tennyson, and, when she had gone, rose to his feet and stood looking after her curiously. As she walked down the street with mincing step, he saw several persons whom she passed turn and look back at her with a smile of kindly amusement. When she had turned the corner, he went upstairs to his bedroom, and stood for a long time before the mirror of his dressing-case, gazing thoughtfully at the reflection of his own face.

III

At eight o'clock the ballroom was a blaze of light and the guests had begun to assemble; for there was a literary programme and some routine business of the society to be gone through with before the dancing. A black servant in evening dress waited at the door and directed the guests to the dressing-rooms.

The occasion was long memorable among the colored people of the city; not alone for the dress and display, but for the high average of intelligence and culture that distinguished the gathering as a whole. There were a number of school-teachers, several young doctors, three or four lawyers, some professional singers, an editor, a lieutenant in the United States army spending his furlough in the city, and others in various polite callings; these were colored, though most of them would not have attracted even a casual glance because of any marked difference from white people. Most of the ladies were in evening costume, and dress coats and dancing pumps were the rule among the men. A band of string music, stationed in an alcove behind a row of palms, played popular airs while the guests were gathering.

The dancing began at half past nine. At eleven o'clock supper was served. Mr. Ryder had left the ballroom some little time before the intermission, but reappeared at the supper-table. The spread was worthy of the occasion, and the guests did full justice to it. When the coffee had been served, the toast-master, Mr. Solomon Sadler, rapped for order. He made a brief introductory speech, complimenting host and guests, and then presented in their order the toasts of the evening. They were responded to with a very fair display of after-dinner wit.

"The last toast," said the toast-master, when he reached the end of the list, "is one which must appeal to us all. There is no one of us of the sterner sex who is not at some time dependent upon woman,—in infancy for protection, in manhood for companionship, in old age for care and comforting. Our good host has been trying to live alone, but the fair faces I see around me to-night prove that he too is largely dependent upon the gentler sex for most that makes life worth living,—the society and love of friends,—and rumor is at fault if he does not soon yield entire subjection to one of them. Mr. Ryder will now respond to the toast,—The Ladies."

There was a pensive look in Mr. Ryder's eyes as he took the floor and adjusted his eye-glasses. He began by speaking of woman as the gift of Heaven to man, and after some general observations on the relations of the sexes he said: "But perhaps the quality which most distinguishes woman is her fidelity and devotion to those she loves. History is full of examples, but has recorded none more striking than one which only to-day came under my notice."

He then related, simply but effectively, the story told by his visitor of the afternoon. He gave it in the same soft dialect, which came readily to his lips, while the company listened attentively and sympathetically. For the story had awakened a responsive thrill in many hearts. There were some present who had seen, and others who had heard their fathers and grandfathers tell, the wrongs and sufferings of this past generation, and all of them still felt, in their darker moments, the shadow hanging over them. Mr. Ryder went on:—

"Such devotion and confidence are rare even among women. There are many who would have searched a year, some who would have waited five years, a few who might have hoped ten years; but for twenty-five years this woman has retained her affection for and her faith in a man she has not seen or heard of in all that time.

"She came to me to-day in the hope that I might be able to help her find this long-lost husband. And when she was gone I gave my fancy rein, and imagined a case I will put to you.

"Suppose that this husband, soon after his escape, had learned that his wife had been sold away, and that such inquiries as he could make brought no information of her whereabouts. Suppose that he was young, and she much older than he; that he was light, and she was black; that their marriage was a slave marriage, and legally binding only if they chose to make it so after the war. Suppose, too, that he made his way to the North, as some of us have done, and there, where he had larger opportunities, had improved them, and had in the course of all these years grown to be as different from the ignorant boy who ran away from fear of slavery as the day is from the night. Suppose, even, that he had qualified himself, by industry, by thrift, and by study, to win the friendship and be considered worthy the society of such people as these I see around me to-night, gracing my board and filling my heart with gladness; for I am old enough to remember the day when such a gathering would not have been possible in this land. Suppose, too, that, as the years went by, this man's memory of the past grew more and more indistinct, until at last it was rarely, except in his dreams, that any image of this bygone period rose before his mind. And then suppose that accident should bring to his knowledge the fact that the wife of his youth, the wife he had left behind him,—not one who had walked by his side and kept pace with him in his upward struggle, but one upon whom advancing years and a laborious life had set their mark,—was alive and seeking him, but that he was absolutely safe from recognition or discovery, unless he chose to reveal himself. My friends, what would the man do? I will presume that he was one who loved honor, and tried to deal justly with all men. I will even carry the case further, and suppose that perhaps he had set his heart upon another, whom he had hoped to call his own. What would he do, or rather what ought he to do, in such a crisis of a lifetime?

"It seemed to me that he might hesitate, and I imagined that I was an old friend, a near friend, and that he had come to me for advice; and I argued the case with him. I tried to discuss it impartially. After we had looked upon the matter from every point of view, I said to him, in words that we all know:—

> "This above all: to thine own self be true,
> And it must follow, as the night the day,
> Thou canst not then be false to any man."[8]

Then, finally, I put the question to him, 'Shall you acknowledge her?'

"And now, ladies and gentlemen, friends and companions, I ask you, what should he have done?"

There was something in Mr. Ryder's voice that stirred the hearts of those who sat around him. It suggested more than mere sympathy with an imaginary situation; it seemed rather in the nature of a personal appeal. It was observed, too, that his look rested more especially upon Mrs. Dixon, with a mingled expression of renunciation and inquiry.

"This is the woman, and I am the man."
Clyde O. DeLand's illustration for the first book publication (1899) of "The Wife of His Youth."

She had listened, with parted lips and streaming eyes. She was the first to speak: "He should have acknowledged her."

"Yes," they all echoed, "he should have acknowledged her."

"My friends and companions," responded Mr. Ryder, "I thank you, one and all. It is the answer I expected, for I knew your hearts."

He turned and walked toward the closed door of an adjoining room, while every eye followed him in wondering curiosity. He came back in a moment, leading by the hand his visitor of the afternoon, who stood startled and trembling at the sudden plunge into this scene of brilliant gayety. She was neatly dressed in gray, and wore the white cap of an elderly woman.

"Ladies and gentlemen," he said, "this is the woman, and I am the man, whose story I have told you. Permit me to introduce to you the wife of my youth."

1899

8. Shakespeare, *Hamlet* 1.3.

PAULINE ELIZABETH HOPKINS
1859–1930

As an author and editor, Pauline E. Hopkins played a significant role in the development of African American literature in the United States. Though she was also an outspoken journalist, she is best known to us today as a gifted storyteller whose fiction mingles suspenseful, even sensational story lines with forceful analysis of turn-of-the-century debates on race. Unlike Booker T. Washington, Hopkins was suspicious of political accommodation with whites as long as blacks were subjected to Jim Crow segregationist practices and remained vulnerable to lynching and other acts of racist violence. She believed that fiction in particular could play a crucial role in encouraging African Americans to continue their struggle for civil rights in the United States, while taking pride in their larger diasporic connections to blacks of the southern Americas and Africa. Hopkins wrote in the introduction to one of her novels, "Fiction is of great value to any people as a preserver of manners and customs—religious, political, and social. It is a record of growth and development from generation to generation. No one will do this for us; we must ourselves develop the men and women who will faithfully portray the inmost thoughts and feelings of the Negro with all the fire and romance which lies dormant in our history, and, as yet, unrecognized by writers of the Anglo-Saxon race."

Hopkins was born in Portland, Maine, the only child of Sarah A. Allen and Benjamin Northrup, members of prominent African American families based in Exeter, New Hampshire, and Providence, Rhode Island, respectively. Her forebears included the Reverends Nathaniel and Thomas Paul, founders of the first Baptist church in Boston for blacks, their activist sister Susan Paul, and the poet James M. Whitfield. The family moved to Boston when Hopkins was ready for school, and she was encouraged to become involved with the intellectual and cultural life of black Boston. As a teen, she was recognized for her writing in an essay contest, and she received the prize from no less a figure than William Wells Brown, the formerly enslaved author and abolitionist. Hopkins also performed with her family, which had established the Hopkins Colored Troubadours, as an actress, singer, and musician. Several years after graduating from the Girls' High School, an integrated public school in Boston, her play *The Slaves' Escape; or, the Underground Railroad* was performed in Boston in 1880 by her family's theatrical company. Inspired by the group of African American women whom W. E. B. Du Bois would call "the New Women of Color" of the "Black Brahmin" class of Boston, Hopkins during the 1880s and 1890s participated in various literary and reading societies, gave lectures on black history, and joined the National Association of Colored Women when it was founded in 1896. To support herself, she took a job as a stenographer for the Massachusetts Bureau of Statistics of Labor, work she continued until 1900, when she helped to found the *Colored American Magazine*, a journal aiming to make literature relevant to African Americans' political and intellectual advancement.

The turn of the twentieth century was a period of unprecedented literary activity by African American artists such as Charles W. Chesnutt and Paul Laurence Dunbar. At this time, Hopkins began writing in earnest as well, producing a large corpus of writing in prose that included short fiction, history, and biographical sketches. In 1900 she published her first and best-known novel, *Contending Forces: A Romance Illustrative of Negro Life North and South* (1900). While working at the

Colored American Magazine, initially as editor of the Women's Department and then as literary editor, Hopkins published in the journal a number of essays and short stories as well as three serialized novels: *Hagar's Daughter: A Story of Southern Caste Prejudice* (1901); *Winona: A Tale of Negro Life in the South and Southwest* (1902); and *Of One Blood; or, the Hidden Self* (1902). Hopkins's four novels focus on African American female protagonists and are often melodramatic, with surprising twists and an interest in the supernatural and occult. Her fiction borrows from the traditions of sentiment and sensation, with plots that, as in "Talma Gordon," frequently turn on secret family histories and mysterious, unsolved crimes. Like her contemporary Chesnutt, she uses these narrative devices to stir readers into rethinking the assumptions that supported racial inequality and even the concept of race itself—a provocation that continues to bring new readers to her fiction.

Hopkins's association with the *Colored American Magazine* ended in 1904 when Booker T. Washington gained control of the journal and had her fired because of her resistance to his accommodationist approach to race relations. Hopkins complained in a letter to a friend about "the revengeful tactics of Mr. Washington's men." The loss of her job at the *Colored American Magazine* made Hopkins considerably less visible as a literary presence. But she continued to work in journalism, and in 1905 she cofounded her own publishing company, P. E. Hopkins and Co.; its only book, published the same year, was her *Primer of Facts Pertaining to the Early Greatness of the African Race and the Possibility of Restoration by Its Descendents—With an Epilogue.* She cofounded and became an editor at the *New Era Magazine* in 1916, but the journal failed. She worked as a stenographer at the Massachusetts Institute of Technology for many years, with her achievements as an editor, publisher, and writer going virtually unrecognized in her lifetime. In the late 1980s, Oxford University Press republished Hopkins's novels as part of the Schomburg Library of Nineteenth-Century Black Women Writers, an event that generated a new audience for her fiction among contemporary readers.

Talma Gordon[1]

The Canterbury Club of Boston was holding its regular monthly meeting at the palatial Beacon-street residence of Dr. William Thornton, expert medical practitioner and specialist. All the members were present, because some rare opinions were to be aired by men of profound thought on a question of vital importance to the life of the Republic, and because the club celebrated its anniversary in a home usually closed to society. The Doctor's winters, since his marriage, were passed at his summer home near his celebrated sanatorium. This winter found him in town with his wife and two boys. We had heard much of the beauty of the former, who was entirely unknown to social life, and about whose life and marriage we felt sure a romantic interest attached. The Doctor himself was too bright a luminary of the professional world to remain long hidden without creating comment. We had accepted the invitation to dine with alacrity, knowing that we should be welcomed to a banquet that would feast both eye and palate; but we had not

---

1. Originally published in the October 1900 issue of the *Colored American Magazine*, from which the present text is taken.

been favored by even a glimpse of the hostess. The subject for discussion was: "Expansion: Its Effect upon the Future Development of the Anglo-Saxon throughout the World."

Dinner was over, but we still sat about the social board discussing the question of the hour. The Hon. Herbert Clapp, eminent jurist and politician, had painted in glowing colors the advantages to be gained by the increase of wealth and the exalted position which expansion would give the United States in the councils of the great governments of the world. In smoothly flowing sentences marshalled in rhetorical order, with compact ideas, and incisive argument, he drew an effective picture with all the persuasive eloquence of the trained orator.

Joseph Whitman, the theologian of world-wide fame, accepted the arguments of Mr. Clapp, but subordinated all to the great opportunity which expansion would give to the religious enthusiast. None could doubt the sincerity of this man, who looked once into the idealized face on which heaven had set the seal of consecration.

Various opinions were advanced by the twenty-five men present, but the host said nothing; he glanced from one to another with a look of amusement in his shrewd gray-blue eyes. "Wonderful eyes," said his patients who came under their magic spell. "A wonderful man and a wonderful mind," agreed his contemporaries, as they heard in amazement of some great cure of chronic or malignant disease which approached the supernatural.

"What do you think of this question, Doctor?" finally asked the president, turning to the silent host.

"Your arguments are good; they would convince almost anyone."

"But not Doctor Thornton," laughed the theologian.

"I acquiesce which ever way the result turns. Still, I like to view both sides of a question. We have considered but one tonight. Did you ever think that in spite of our prejudices against amalgamation,[2] some of our descendants, indeed many of them, will inevitably intermarry among those far-off tribes of dark-skinned peoples, if they become a part of this great Union?"

"Among the lower classes that may occur, but not to any great extent," remarked a college president.

"My experience teaches me that it will occur among all classes, and to an appalling extent," replied the Doctor.

"You don't believe in intermarriage with other races?"

"Yes, most emphatically, when they possess decent moral development and physical perfection, for then we develop a superior being in the progeny born of the intermarriage. But if we are not ready to receive and assimilate the new material which will be brought to mingle with our pure Anglo-Saxon stream, we should call a halt in our expansion policy."

"I must confess, Doctor, that in the idea of amalgamation you present a new thought to my mind. Will you not favor us with a few of your main points?" asked the president of the club, breaking the silence which followed the Doctor's remarks.

---

2. Intermarriage and reproduction between members of different racial or ethnic groups.

"Yes, Doctor, give us your theories on the subject. We may not agree with you, but we are all open to conviction."

The Doctor removed the half-consumed cigar from his lips, drank what remained in his glass of the choice Burgundy, and leaning back in his chair contemplated the earnest faces before him.

"We may make laws, but laws are but straws in the hands of Omnipotence.

> 'There's a divinity that shapes our ends,
> Rough-hew them how we will.'[3]

And no man may combat fate. Given a man, propinquity, opportunity, fascinating femininity, and there you are. Black, white, green, yellow—nothing will prevent intermarriage. Position, wealth, family, friends—all sink into insignificance before the God-implanted instinct that made Adam, awakening from a deep sleep and finding the woman beside him, accept Eve as bone of his bone; he cared not nor questioned whence she came. So it is with the sons of Adam ever since, through the law of heredity which makes us all one common family. And so it will be with us in our re-formation of this old Republic. Perhaps I can make my meaning clearer by illustration, and with your permission I will tell you a story which came under my observation as a practitioner.

"Doubtless all of you heard of the terrible tragedy which occurred at Gordonville, Mass., some years ago, when Capt. Jonathan Gordon, his wife, and little son were murdered. I suppose that I am the only man on this side the Atlantic, outside of the police, who can tell you the true story of that crime.

"I knew Captain Gordon well; it was through his persuasions that I bought a place in Gordonville and settled down to spending my summers in that charming rural neighborhood. I had rendered the Captain what he was pleased to call valuable medical help, and I became his family physician. Captain Gordon was a retired sea captain, formerly engaged in the East India trade. All his ancestors had been such; but when the bottom fell out of that business he established the Gordonville Mills with his first wife's money, and settled down as a money-making manufacturer of cotton cloth. The Gordons were old New England Puritans who had come over in the *Mayflower*; they had owned Gordon Hall for more than a hundred years. It was a baronial-like pile of granite with towers, standing on a hill which commanded a superb view of Massachusetts Bay and the surrounding country. I imagine the Gordon star was under a cloud about the time Captain Jonathan married his first wife, Miss Isabel Franklin of Boston, who brought to him the money which mended the broken fortunes of the Gordon house, and restored this old Puritan stock to its rightful position. In the person of Captain Gordon the austerity of manner and indomitable will-power that he had inherited were combined with a temper that brooked no contradiction.

"The first wife died at the birth of her third child, leaving him two daughters, Jeannette and Talma. Very soon after her death the Captain married again. I have heard it rumored that the Gordon girls did not get on very well with their stepmother. She was a woman with no fortune of her own, and envied the large portion left by the first Mrs. Gordon to her daughters.

3. Shakespeare, *Hamlet* 5.2.

"Jeannette was tall, dark, and stern like her father; Talma was like her dead mother, and possessed of great talent, so great that her father sent her to the American Academy at Rome, to develop the gift. It was the hottest of July days when her friends were bidden to an afternoon party on the lawn and a dance in the evening, to welcome Talma Gordon among them again. I watched her as she moved about among her guests, a fairylike blonde in floating white draperies, her face a study in delicate changing tints, like the heart of a flower, sparkling in smiles about the mouth to end in merry laughter in the clear blue eyes. There were all the subtle allurements of birth, wealth and culture about the exquisite creature:

'Smiling, frowning evermore,
Thou art perfect in love-lore,
Ever varying Madeline,'[4]

quoted a celebrated writer as he stood apart with me, gazing upon the scene before us. He sighed as he looked at the girl.

"'Doctor, there is genius and passion in her face. Sometime our little friend will do wonderful things. But is it desirable to be singled out for special blessings by the gods? Genius always carries with it intense capacity for suffering: "Whom the gods love die young."'

"'Ah,' I replied, 'do not name death and Talma Gordon together. Cease your dismal croakings; such talk is rank heresy.'

"The dazzling daylight dropped slowly into summer twilight. The merriment continued; more guests arrived; the great dancing pagoda built for the occasion was lighted by myriads of Japanese lanterns. The strains from the band grew sweeter and sweeter, and 'all went merry as a marriage bell.'[5] It was a rare treat to have this party at Gordon Hall, for Captain Jonathan was not given to hospitality. We broke up shortly before midnight, with expressions of delight from all the guests.

"I was a bachelor then, without ties. Captain Gordon insisted upon my having a bed at the Hall. I did not fall asleep readily; there seemed to be something in the air that forbade it. I was still awake when a distant clock struck the second hour of the morning. Suddenly the heavens were lighted by a sheet of ghastly light; a terrific midsummer thunderstorm was breaking over the sleeping town. A lurid flash lit up all the landscape, painting the trees in grotesque shapes against the murky sky, and defining clearly the sullen blackness of the waters of the bay breaking in grandeur against the rocky coast. I had arisen and put back the draperies from the windows, to have an unobstructed view of the grand scene. A low muttering coming nearer and nearer, a terrific roar, and then a tremendous downpour. The storm had burst.

"Now the uncanny howling of a dog mingled with the rattling volleys of thunder. I heard the opening and closing of doors; the servants were about looking after things. It was impossible to sleep. The lightning was more vivid. There was a blinding flash of a greenish-white tinge mingled with the crash of falling timbers. Then before my startled gaze arose columns of red flames reflected against the sky. 'Heaven help us!' I cried; 'it is the left tower; it has been struck and is on fire!'

4. From "Madeline," by English poet Alfred, Lord Tennyson (1809–1892).

5. From "Eve of Waterloo," by English poet Lord Byron (1788–1824).

"I hurried on my clothes and stepped into the corridor; the girls were there before me. Jeannette came up to me instantly with anxious face. 'Oh, Doctor Thornton, what shall we do? Papa and Mamma and little Johnny are in the old left tower. It is on fire. I have knocked and knocked, but get no answer.'

"'Don't be alarmed,' said I soothingly. 'Jenkins, ring the alarm bell,' I continued, turning to the butler who was standing near; 'the rest follow me. We will force the entrance to the Captain's room.'

"Instantly, it seemed to me, the bell boomed out upon the now silent air, for the storm had died down as quickly as it arose: and as our little procession paused before the entrance to the old left tower, we could distinguish the sound of the fire engines already on their way from the village.

"The door resisted all our efforts; there seemed to be a barrier against it which nothing could move. The flames were gaining headway. Still the same deathly silence within the rooms.

"'Oh, will they never get here?' cried Talma, ringing her hands in terror. Jeannette said nothing, but her face was ashen. The servants were huddled together in a panic-stricken group. I can never tell you what a relief it was when we heard the first sound of the firemen's voices, saw their quick movements, and heard the ringing of the axes with which they cut away every obstacle to our entrance to the rooms. The neighbors who had just enjoyed the hospitality of the house were now gathered around offering all the assistance in their power. In less than fifteen minutes the fire was out, and the men began to bear the unconscious inmates from the ruins. They carried them to the pagoda so lately the scene of mirth and pleasure, and I took up my station there, ready to assume my professional duties. The Captain was nearest me; and as I stooped to make the necessary examination I reeled away from the ghastly sight which confronted me—*gentlemen, across the Captain's throat was a deep gash that severed the jugular vein!*"

The Doctor paused, and the hand with which he refilled his glass trembled violently.

"'What is it, Doctor?' cried the men gathering about me.

"'Take the women away; this is murder!'

"'Murder!' cried Jeannette, as she fell against the side of the pagoda.

"'Murder!' screamed Talma, staring at me as if unable to grasp my meaning.

"I continued my examination of the bodies, and found that the same thing had happened to Mrs. Gordon and to little Johnny.

"The police were notified; and when the sun rose over the dripping town he found them in charge of Gordon Hall, the servants standing in excited knots talking over the crime, the friends of the family confounded, and the two girls trying to comfort each other and realize the terrible misfortune that had overtaken them.

"Nothing in the rooms of the left tower seemed to have been disturbed. The door of communication between the rooms of the husband and wife was open, as they had arranged it for the night. Little Johnny's crib was placed beside his mother's bed. In it he was found as though never awakened by the storm. It was quite evident that the assassin was no common ruffian. The chief gave strict orders for a watch to be kept on all strangers or suspicious characters who were seen in the neighborhood. He made inquiries among the servants, seeing each one separately, but there was nothing gained from them. No one had heard anything suspicious; all had been awakened by the storm. The chief was puzzled. Here was a triple crime for which no motive could be assigned.

"'What do you think of it?' I asked him, as we stood together on the lawn.

"'It is my opinion that the deed was committed by one of the higher classes, which makes the mystery more difficult to solve. I tell you, Doctor, there are mysteries that never come to light, and this, I think, is one of them.'

"While we were talking Jenkins, the butler, an old and trusted servant, came up to the chief and saluted respectfully. 'Want to speak with me, Jenkins?' he asked. The man nodded, and they walked away together.

"The story of the inquest was short, but appalling. It was shown that Talma had been allowed to go abroad to study because she and Mrs. Gordon did not get on well together. From the testimony of Jenkins it seemed that Talma and her father had quarrelled bitterly about her lover, a young artist whom she had met at Rome, who was unknown to fame, and very poor. There had been terrible things said by each, and threats even had passed, all of which now rose up in judgment against the unhappy girl. The examination of the family solicitor revealed the fact that Captain Gordon intended to leave his daughters only a small annuity, the bulk of the fortune going to his son Jonathan, junior. This was a monstrous injustice, as everyone felt. In vain Talma protested her innocence. Someone must have done it. No one would be benefited so much by these deaths as she and her sister. Moreover, the will, together with other papers, was nowhere to be found. Not the slightest clue bearing upon the disturbing elements in this family, if any there were, was to be found. As the only surviving relatives, Jeannette and Talma became joint heirs to an immense fortune, which only for the bloody tragedy just enacted would, in all probability, have passed them by. Here was the motive. The case was very black against Talma. The foreman stood up. The silence was intense: 'We find that Capt. Jonathan Gordon, Mary E. Gordon, and Jonathan Gordon, junior, all deceased, came to their deaths by means of a knife or other sharp instrument in the hands of Talma Gordon.' The girl was like one stricken with death. The flower-like mouth was drawn and pinched; the great sapphire-blue eyes were black with passionate anguish, terror, and despair. She was placed in jail to await her trial at the fall session of the criminal court. The excitement in the hitherto quiet town rose to fever heat. Many points in the evidence seemed incomplete to thinking men. The weapon could not be found, nor could it be divined what had become of it. No reason could be given for the murder except the quarrel between Talma and her father and the ill will which existed between the girl and her stepmother.

"When the trial was called Jeannette sat beside Talma in the prisoner's dock; both were arrayed in deepest mourning. Talma was pale and careworn, but seemed uplifted, spiritualized, as it were. Upon Jeannette the full realization of her sister's peril seemed to weigh heavily. She had changed much too: hollow cheeks, tottering steps, eyes blazing with fever, all suggestive of rapid and premature decay. From far-off Italy Edward Turner, growing famous in the art world, came to stand beside his girl-love in this hour of anguish.

"The trial was a memorable one. No additional evidence had been collected to strengthen the prosecution; when the attorney-general rose to open the case against Talma he knew, as everyone else did, that he could not convict solely on the evidence adduced. What was given did not always bear upon the case, and brought out strange stories of Captain Jonathan's methods. Tales were told of sailors who had sworn to take his life, in revenge for injuries inflicted upon them by his hand. One or two clues were followed, but without avail. The judge summed up the evidence impartially, giving the prisoner the benefit of the doubt. The points in hand furnished valuable collateral evidence, but were not direct proof. Although the moral presumption was against the prisoner, legal evidence was lacking to actually convict. The jury found the prisoner 'Not Guilty,' owing to the fact that the evidence was entirely circumstantial. The verdict was received in painful silence; then a murmur of discontent ran through the great crowd.

"'She must have done it,' said one; 'who else has been benefited by the horrible deed?'

"'A poor woman would not have fared so well at the hands of the jury, nor a homely one either, for that matter,' said another.

"The great Gordon trial was ended; innocent or guilty, Talma Gordon could not be tried again. She was free; but her liberty, with blasted prospects and fair fame gone forever, was valueless to her. She seemed to have but one object in her mind: to find the murderer or murderers of her parents and half-brother. By her direction the shrewdest of detectives were employed and money flowed like water, but to no purpose; the Gordon tragedy remained a mystery. I had consented to act as one of the trustees of the immense Gordon estates and business interests, and by my advice the Misses Gordon went abroad. A year later I received a letter from Edward Turner, saying that Jeannette Gordon had died suddenly at Rome, and that Talma, after refusing all his entreaties for an early marriage, had disappeared, leaving no clue as to her whereabouts. I could give the poor fellow no comfort, although I had been duly notified of the death of Jeannette by Talma, in a letter telling me where to forward her remittances, and at the same time requesting me to keep her present residence secret, especially from Edward.

"I had established a sanitarium for the cure of chronic diseases at Gordonville, and absorbed in the cares of my profession I gave little thought to the Gordons. I seemed fated to be involved in mysteries.

"A man claiming to be an Englishman, and fresh from the California gold fields, engaged board and professional service at my retreat. I found him suffering in the grasp of the tubercle[6] fiend—the last stages. He called himself Simon Cameron. Seldom have I seen so fascinating and wicked a face. The lines of the mouth were cruel, the eyes cold and sharp, the smile mocking and evil. He had money in plenty but seemed to have no friends, for he had received no letters and had had no visitors in the time he had been with us. He was an enigma to me; and his nationality puzzled me, for of course I did not believe his story of being English. The peaceful influence of the house seemed to sooth him in a measure, and make his last steps to the mysterious valley[7] as easy as possible. For a time he improved, and would sit or walk about the grounds and sing sweet songs for the pleasure of the other inmates. Strange to say, his malady only affected his voice at times. He sang quaint

6. Tuberculosis. 7. Alludes to the "valley of death" (Psalm 23).

songs in a silvery tenor of great purity and sweetness that was delicious to the
listening ear:

> 'A wet sheet and a flowing sea,
> A wind that follows fast,
> And fills the white and rustling sail
> And bends the gallant mast;
> And bends the gallant mast, my Boys;
> While like the eagle free,
> Away the good ship flies, and leaves
> Old England on the lea.'[8]

"There are few singers on the lyric stage who could surpass Simon
Cameron.

"One night, a few weeks after Cameron's arrival, I sat in my office making up my accounts when the door opened and closed; I glanced up, expecting to see a servant. A lady advanced toward me. She threw back her veil,
and then I saw that Talma Gordon, or her ghost, stood before me. After the
first excitement of our meeting was over, she told me she had come direct
from Paris, to place herself in my care. I had studied her attentively during
the first moments of our meeting, and I felt that was right; unless something unforeseen happened to arouse her from the stupor into which she
seemed to have fallen, the last Gordon was doomed to an early death. The
next day I told her I had cabled Edward Turner to come to her.

"'It will do no good; I cannot marry him,' was her only comment.

"'Have you no feeling of pity for that faithful fellow?' I asked her sternly,
provoked by her seeming indifference. I shall never forget the varied emotions depicted on her speaking face. Fully revealed to my gaze was the sight
of a human soul tortured beyond the point of endurance; suffering all things,
enduring all things, in the silent agony of despair.

"In a few days Edward arrived and Talma consented to see him and explain
her refusal to keep her promise to him. 'You must be present, Doctor; it is
due your long, tried friendship to know that I have not been fickle, but have
acted from the best and strongest motives.'

"I shall never forget that day. It was directly after lunch that we met in
the library. I was greatly excited, expecting I knew not what. Edward was
agitated, too. Talma was the only calm one. She handed me what seemed
to be a letter, with the request that I would read it. Even now I think I can
repeat every word of the document, so indelibly are the words engraved upon
my mind:

> MY DARLING SISTER TALMA: When you read these lines I shall be no
> more, for I shall not live to see your life blasted by the same knowledge
> that has blighted mine.
>
> One evening, about a year before your expected return from Rome,
> I climbed into a hammock in one corner of the veranda outside the
> breakfast-room windows, intending to spend the twilight hours in lazy
> comfort, for it was very hot, enervating August weather. I fell asleep. I
> was awakened by voices. Because of the heat the rooms had been left in
> semi-darkness. As I lay there, lazily enjoying the beauty of the perfect

---

8. From "Sea Song," by Scottish poet Allan Cunningham (1784–1842).

summer night, my wandering thoughts were arrested by words spoken by our father to Mrs. Gordon, for they were the occupants of the breakfast-room.

"Never fear, Mary; Johnny shall have it all—money, houses, land and business."

"But if you do go first, Jonathan, what will happen if the girls contest the will? People will think that they ought to have the money as it appears to be theirs by law. I never could survive the terrible disgrace of the story."

"Don't borrow trouble; all you would need to do would be to show them papers I have drawn up, and they would be glad to take their annuity and say nothing. After all, I do not think it is so bad. Jeannette can teach; Talma can paint; six hundred dollars a year is quite enough for them."

I had been somewhat mystified by the conversation until now. This last remark solved the riddle. What could he mean? teach, paint, six hundred a year! With my usual impetuosity I sprang from my resting-place, and in a moment stood in the room confronting my father, and asking what he meant. I could see plainly that both were disconcerted by my unexpected appearance.

"Ah, wretched girl! you have been listening. But what could I expect of your mother's daughter?"

At these words I felt the indignant blood rush to my head in a torrent. So it had been all my life. Before you could remember, Talma, I had felt my little heart swell with anger at the disparaging hints and slurs concerning our mother. Now was my time. I determined that tonight I would know why she was looked upon as an outcast, and her children subjected to every humiliation. So I replied to my father in bitter anger:

"I was not listening; I fell asleep in the hammock. What do you mean by a paltry six hundred a year each to Talma and to me? 'My mother's daughter' demands an explanation from you, sir, of the meaning of the monstrous injustice that you have always practised toward my sister and me."

"Speak more respectfully to your father, Jeannette," broke in Mrs. Gordon.

"How is it, madam, that you look for respect from one whom you have delighted to torment ever since you came into this most unhappy family?"

"Hush, both of you," said Captain Gordon, who seemed to have recovered from the dismay into which my sudden appearance and passionate words had plunged him. "I think I may as well tell you as to wait. Since you know so much you may as well know the whole miserable story." He motioned me to a seat. I could see that he was deeply agitated. I seated myself in a chair he pointed out, in wonder and expectation,— expectation of I knew not what. I trembled. This was a supreme moment in my life; I felt it. The air was heavy with the intense stillness that had settled over us as the common sounds of day gave place to the early quiet of the rural evening. I could see Mrs. Gordon's face as she sat within the radius of the lighted hallway. There was a smile of triumph upon it. I clinched my hands and bit my lips until the blood came, in the effort to keep from screaming. What was I about to hear? At last he spoke:

"I was disappointed at your birth, and also at the birth of Talma. I wanted a male heir. When I knew that I should again be a father I was torn by hope and fear, but I comforted myself with the thought that luck would be with me in the birth of the third child. When the doctor brought me word that a son was born to the house of Gordon, I was wild with delight, and did not notice his disturbed countenance. In the midst of my joy he said to me:

'Captain Gordon, there is something strange about this birth. I want you to see this child.'

Quelling my exultation I followed him to the nursery, and there, lying in the cradle, I saw a child dark as a mulatto, with the characteristic features of the Negro! I was stunned. Gradually it dawned upon me that there was something radically wrong. I turned to the doctor for an explanation.

'There is but one explanation, Captain Gordon; there is Negro blood in the child.'

'There is no Negro blood in my veins,' I said proudly. Then I paused— *the mother!*—I glanced at the doctor. He was watching me intently. The same thought was in his mind. I must have lived a thousand years in that cursed five seconds that I stood there confronting the physician and trying to think. 'Come,' said I to him, 'let us end this suspense.' Without thinking of consequences, I hurried away to your mother and accused her of infidelity to her marriage vows. I raved like a madman. Your mother fell into convulsions; her life was despaired of. I sent for Mr. and Mrs. Franklin, and then I learned the truth. They were childless. One year while on a Southern tour, they befriended an octoroon[9] girl who had been abandoned by her white lover. Her child was a beautiful girl baby. They, being Northern born, thought little of caste distinction because the child showed no trace of Negro blood. They determined to adopt it. They went abroad, secretly sending back word to their friends at a proper time, of the birth of a little daughter. No one doubted the truth of the statement. They made Isabel their heiress, and all went well until the birth of your brother. Your mother and the unfortunate babe died. This is the story which, if known, would bring dire disgrace upon the Gordon family.

To appease my righteous wrath, Mr. Franklin left a codicil to his will by which all the property is left at my disposal save a small annuity to you and your sister."

I sat there after he had finished his story, stunned by what I had heard. I understood, now, Mrs. Gordon's half contemptuous toleration and lack of consideration for us both. As I rose from my seat to leave the room, I said to Captain Gordon:

"Still, in spite of all, sir, I am a Gordon, legally born. I will not tamely give up my birthright."

I left that room a broken-hearted girl, filled with a desire for revenge upon this man, my father, who, by his manner disowned us without regret. Not once in that remarkable interview did he speak of our mother as his wife. He quietly repudiated her and us with all the cold

---

9. Term for a person of one-eighth African or African American ancestry.

cruelty of relentless caste prejudice. I heard the treatment of your lover's proposal; I knew why Captain Gordon's consent to your marriage was withheld.

The night of the reception and dance was the chance for which I had waited, planned and watched. I crept from my window into the ivy-vines, and down, down, until I stood upon the window-sill of Captain Gordon's room in the old left tower. How did I do it, you ask? I do not know. The house was silent after the revel; the darkness of the gathering storm favored me, too. The lawyer was there that day. The will was signed and put safely away among my father's papers. I was determined to have the will and the other documents bearing upon the case, and I would have revenge, too, for the cruelties we had suffered. With the old East Indian dagger firmly grasped I entered the room and found—that my revenge had been forestalled! The horror of the discovery I made that night restored me to reason and a realization of the crime I meditated. Scarce knowing what I did, I sought and found the papers, and crept back to my room as I had come. Do you wonder that my disease is past medical aid?"

"I looked at Edward as I finished. He sat, his face covered with his hands. Finally he looked up with a glance of haggard despair: 'God! Doctor, but this is too much. I could stand the stigma of murder, but add to that the pollution of Negro blood! No man is brave enough to face such a situation.'

"'It is as I thought it would be,' said Talma sadly, while the tears poured over her white face. 'I do not blame you, Edward.'

"He rose from his chair, wrung my hand in a convulsive clasp, turned to Talma and bowed profoundly, with his eyes fixed upon the floor, hesitated, turned, paused, bowed again, and abruptly left the room. So those two who had been lovers, parted. I turned to Talma, expecting her to give way. She smiled a pitiful smile, and said: 'You see, Doctor, I knew best.'

"From that on she failed rapidly. I was restless. If only I could rouse her to an interest in life, she might live to old age. So rich, so young, so beautiful, so talented, so pure; I grew savage thinking of the injustice of the world. I had not reckoned on the power that never sleeps. Something was about to happen.

"On visiting Cameron next morning I found him approaching the end. He had been sinking for a week very rapidly. As I sat by the bedside holding his emaciated hand, he fixed his bright, wicked eyes on me, and asked: 'How long have I got to live?'

"'Candidly, but a few hours.'

"'Thank you; well, I want death; I am not afraid to die. Doctor, Cameron is not my name.'

"'I never supposed it was.'

"'No? You are sharper than I thought. I heard all your talk yesterday with Talma Gordon. Curse the whole race!'

"He clasped his bony fingers around my arm and gasped: '*I murdered the Gordons!*'

"Had I the pen of a Dumas[1] I could not paint Cameron as he told his story. It is a question with me whether this wheeling planet, home of the suffer-

---

1. Alexandre Dumas was the name of a popular French playwright and novelist (1802–1870), as well as the name of his son (1824–1895). Notably, the genealogy of the Dumas family included an enslaved African woman.

ing, doubting, dying, may not hold worse agonies on its smiling surface than those of the conventional hell. I sent for Talma and a lawyer. We gave him stimulants, and then with broken intervals of coughing and prostration we got the story of the Gordon murder. I give it to you in a few words:

"'I am an East Indian, but my name does not matter, Cameron is as good as any. There is many a soul crying in heaven and hell for vengeance on Jonathan Gordon. Gold was his idol; and many a good man walked the plank, and many a gallant ship was stripped of her treasure, to satisfy his lust for gold. His blackest crime was the murder of my father, who was his friend, and had sailed with him for many a year as mate. One night these two went ashore together to bury their treasure. My father never returned from that expedition. His body was afterward found with a bullet through the heart on the shore where the vessel stopped that night. It was the custom then among pirates for the captain to kill the men who helped bury their treasure. Captain Gordon was no better than a pirate. An East Indian never forgets, and I swore by my mother's deathbed to hunt Captain Gordon down until I had avenged my father's murder. I had the plans of the Gordon estate, and fixed on the night of the reception in honor of Talma as the time for my vengeance. There is a secret entrance from the shore to the chambers where Captain Gordon slept; no one knew of it save the Captain and trusted members of his crew. My mother gave me the plans, and entrance and escape were easy.'"

"So the great mystery was solved. In a few hours Cameron was no more. We placed the confession in the hands of the police, and there the matter ended."

"But what became of Talma Gordon?" questioned the president. "Did she die?"

"Gentlemen," said the Doctor, rising to his feet and sweeping the faces of the company with his eagle gaze, "gentlemen, if you will follow me to the drawing-room, I shall have much pleasure in introducing you to my wife— *nee* Talma Gordon."

1900

CHARLOTTE PERKINS GILMAN
1860–1935

Charlotte Perkins Gilman lived much of her life on the margins of a society whose economic assumptions about and social definitions of women she vigorously repudiated. Out of her resistance to conventional values that she described as "masculinist," Gilman produced the large body of polemical writing and self-consciously feminist fiction that made her a leading theoretician, speaker, and writer on women's issues of her time.

Charlotte Anna Perkins was born in Hartford, Connecticut, on July 3, 1860. Her father, Frederic Beecher Perkins, belonged to the famous New England Beecher family, which included theologian Lyman Beecher, minister Henry Ward Beecher, and the novelist Harriet Beecher Stowe. Her mother was Mary A. Fitch, whose family had lived in Rhode Island since the middle of the seventeenth century. When Gilman's father deserted his family and left for San Francisco shortly after her birth, her mother returned to Providence, Rhode Island, where she supported herself and her two children with great difficulty. She apparently withheld from them all physical expressions of love, hoping to prevent their later disillusionment over broken relationships. Given these circumstances, it is easy to understand why in her autobiography Gilman described her childhood as painful and lonely.

Between 1880 and her marriage in May 1884 to Charles Stetson, a promising Providence artist, Gilman supported herself in Providence as a governess, art teacher, and designer of greeting cards. During those years she had increasingly become aware of the injustices inflicted on women, and she had begun to write poems—one in defense of prostitutes—in which she developed her own views on women's rights. She entered into the marriage reluctantly, anticipating the difficulties of reconciling her ambition to be a writer with the demands of being a wife, mother, and housekeeper. Within eleven months, their only child, Katharine, was born; following the birth, Gilman became increasingly despondent, and marital tensions increased. Believing that Gilman needed rest and willpower to overcome her depression, her husband and mother persuaded her to go to Philadelphia for treatment by Dr. S. Weir Mitchell, the most famous American neurologist of the day. A specialist in women's "nervous" disorders, Mitchell usually prescribed a "rest cure" consisting of total bedrest for several weeks and limited intellectual activity thereafter. As Gilman put it in "Why I Wrote 'The Yellow Wallpaper'?" (1913), this treatment led her to "the edge of madness" before she drew back by returning to her life as a writer and frequent contributor to the Boston *Woman's Journal*. A few years later Gilman wrote her most famous story. Writing, however, did not keep Gilman from suffering all her life from extended periods of depression.

In 1888, convinced that her marriage threatened her sanity, Gilman moved with her daughter to Pasadena, California, and in 1894 she was granted a divorce. Her former husband promptly married her best friend, the writer Grace Ellery Channing, and not long thereafter Gilman sent her daughter east to live with them. Such actions generated much publicity and hostile criticism in the press, but nothing kept Gilman from pursuing her double career as a writer and lecturer on women, labor, and social organization. In these years she was particularly influenced by the sociologist Lester Ward and the utopian novelist Edward Bellamy.

In 1898 Gilman published *Women and Economics*, the book that earned her immediate celebrity and is still considered her most important nonfiction work. This powerful feminist manifesto argues that women's economic dependency on men has stunted the growth of the entire human species. For instance, she contended that because of the dependency of women on men for food and shelter, the sexual and maternal aspects of their personalities had been developed excessively and to the detriment of their other productive capacities. To free women to develop in a more balanced and socially constructive way, Gilman urged such reforms as centralized nurseries (in *Concerning Children*, 1900) and professionally staffed collective kitchens (in *The Home*, 1904). Later, in *The Man-Made World* (1911)—reprinted partly in the "Realism and Naturalism" cluster of this section—Gilman contrasted the competitiveness and aggressiveness of men with the cooperativeness and nurturance of women; she posited that until women played a larger part in national and international life, social injustice and war would continue to characterize industrialized societies. Similarly, in *His Religion and Hers* (1923) Gilman predicted that only when women influenced theology would the fear of death and punishment cease to be central to religious institutions and practices.

Gilman's poetry and fiction, primarily written when she was well past forty, extended her feminist inquiry into the role of gender in social organization. Her stories and her utopian novels—such as *Moving the Mountain* (1911), *Herland* (1915), and *With Her in Ourland* (1916)—offer vivid dramatizations of the social ills (and

their potential remedies) that result from a competitive economic system in which
women are subordinate to men and accept their subordination. In *Herland*, for
instance, Gilman offers a vision of an all-female society in which caring women
collectively raise children (reproduced by parthenogenesis) in a world that is both
prosperous and ecologically sound.

Gilman committed suicide in 1935 after being diagnosed with inoperable cancer.
Her vast corpus of writing influenced feminism for generations, and her works offer
intellectual historians a remarkable window into questions of gender and sexuality
in the late nineteenth and early twentieth centuries. "The Yellow Wall-Paper" remains
Gilman's most widely read and discussed literary work, immediately regarded as a masterpiece by her contemporaries and, more recently, rediscovered by new generations of
readers.

The Yellow Wall-paper[1]

It is very seldom that mere ordinary people like John and myself secure
ancestral halls for the summer.

A colonial mansion, a hereditary estate, I would say a haunted house, and
reach the height of romantic felicity—but that would be asking too much of
fate!

Still I will proudly declare that there is something queer about it.

Else, why should it be let so cheaply? And why have stood so long unten-
anted?

John laughs at me, of course, but one expects that in marriage.

John is practical in the extreme. He has no patience with faith, an intense
horror of superstition, and he scoffs openly at any talk of things not to be
felt and seen and put down in figures.

John is a physician, and *perhaps*—(I would not say it to a living soul, of
course, but this is dead paper and a great relief to my mind)—*perhaps* that is
one reason I do not get well faster.

You see he does not believe I am sick!

And what can one do?

If a physician of high standing, and one's own husband, assures friends
and relatives that there is really nothing the matter with one but temporary
nervous depression—a slight hysterical tendency[2]—what is one to do?

My brother is also a physician, and also of high standing, and he says the
same thing.

So I take phosphates or phosphites—whichever it is—and tonics, and journeys, and air, and exercise, and am absolutely forbidden to "work" until I
am well again.

Personally, I disagree with their ideas.

---

1. The complete and complex textual history of
the extant fair copy manuscript and seven editions of the story during Gilman's lifetime is
available in Julie Bates Dock's *Charlotte Perkins
Gilman's "The Yellow Wall-paper" and the History of Its Publication and Reception: A Critical
Edition and Documentary Casebook* (Pennsylvania State University Press, 1998). Dock's volume
also contains a detailed textual apparatus and
notes, a variety of background material, early

reviews, and other commentary. Professor Dock
and Pennsylvania State University Press have
kindly granted permission to use her eclectic
critical edition of this story.

2. *Hysteria* was a term used to describe a wide
variety of symptoms, thought to be particularly
prevalent among women, that indicated emotional
disturbance or dysfunction. Depression, anxiety,
excitability, and vague somatic complaints were
among the conditions treated as "hysteria."

Personally, I believe that congenial work, with excitement and change, would do me good.

But what is one to do?

I did write for a while in spite of them; but it *does* exhaust me a good deal—having to be so sly about it, or else meet with heavy opposition.

I sometimes fancy that in my condition if I had less opposition and more society and stimulus—but John says the very worst thing I can do is to think about my condition, and I confess it always makes me feel bad.

So I will let it alone and talk about the house.

The most beautiful place! It is quite alone, standing well back from the road, quite three miles from the village. It makes me think of English places that you read about, for there are hedges and walls and gates that lock, and lots of separate little houses for the gardeners and people.

There is a *delicious* garden! I never saw such a garden—large and shady, full of box-bordered paths, and lined with long grape-covered arbors with seats under them.

There were greenhouses, too, but they are all broken now.

There was some legal trouble, I believe, something about the heirs and co-heirs; anyhow, the place has been empty for years.

That spoils my ghostliness, I am afraid, but I don't care—there is something strange about the house—I can feel it.

I even said so to John one moonlight evening, but he said what I felt was a *draught*, and shut the window.

I get unreasonably angry with John sometimes. I'm sure I never used to be so sensitive. I think it is due to this nervous condition.

But John says if I feel so, I shall neglect proper self-control; so I take pains to control myself—before him, at least, and that makes me very tired.

I don't like our room a bit. I wanted one downstairs that opened on the piazza and had roses all over the window, and such pretty old-fashioned chintz hangings! But John would not hear of it.

He said there was only one window and not room for two beds, and no near room for him if he took another.

He is very careful and loving, and hardly lets me stir without special direction.

I have a schedule prescription for each hour in the day; he takes all care from me, and so I feel basely ungrateful not to value it more.

He said we came here solely on my account, that I was to have perfect rest and all the air I could get. "Your exercise depends on your strength, my dear," said he, "and your food somewhat on your appetite; but air you can absorb all the time." So we took the nursery at the top of the house.

It is a big, airy room, the whole floor nearly, with windows that look all ways, and air and sunshine galore. It was nursery first and then playroom and gymnasium, I should judge; for the windows are barred for little children, and there are rings and things in the walls.

The paint and paper look as if a boys' school had used it. It is stripped off—the paper—in great patches all around the head of my bed, about as far as I can reach, and in a great place on the other side of the room low down. I never saw a worse paper in my life.

One of those sprawling flamboyant patterns committing every artistic sin.

It is dull enough to confuse the eye in following, pronounced enough to constantly irritate and provoke study, and when you follow the lame uncertain curves for a little distance they suddenly commit suicide—plunge off at outrageous angles, destroy themselves in unheard of contradictions.

The color is repellent, almost revolting; a smouldering unclean yellow, strangely faded by the slow-turning sunlight.

It is a dull yet lurid orange in some places, a sickly sulphur tint in others.

No wonder the children hated it! I should hate it myself if I had to live in this room long.

There comes John, and I must put this away—he hates to have me write a word.

• • • • • •

We have been here two weeks, and I haven't felt like writing before, since that first day.

I am sitting by the window now, up in this atrocious nursery, and there is nothing to hinder my writing as much as I please, save lack of strength.

John is away all day, and even some nights when his cases are serious.

I am glad my case is not serious!

But these nervous troubles are dreadfully depressing.

John does not know how much I really suffer. He knows there is no *reason* to suffer, and that satisfies him.

Of course it is only nervousness. It does weigh on me so not to do my duty in any way!

I meant to be such a help to John, such a real rest and comfort, and here I am a comparative burden already!

Nobody would believe what an effort it is to do what little I am able—to dress and entertain, and order things.

It is fortunate Mary is so good with the baby. Such a dear baby!

And yet I *cannot* be with him, it makes me so nervous.

I suppose John never was nervous in his life. He laughs at me so about this wall-paper!

At first he meant to repaper the room, but afterwards he said that I was letting it get the better of me, and that nothing was worse for a nervous patient than to give way to such fancies.

He said that after the wall-paper was changed it would be the heavy bedstead, and then the barred windows, and then that gate at the head of the stairs, and so on.

"You know the place is doing you good," he said, "and really, dear, I don't care to renovate the house just for a three months' rental."

"Then do let us go downstairs," I said, "there are such pretty rooms there."

Then he took me in his arms and called me a blessed little goose, and said he would go down cellar, if I wished, and have it whitewashed into the bargain.

But he is right enough about the beds and windows and things.

It is as airy and comfortable a room as any one need wish, and, of course, I would not be so silly as to make him uncomfortable just for a whim.

I'm really getting quite fond of the big room, all but that horrid paper.

Out of one window I can see the garden, those mysterious deep-shaded arbors, the riotous old-fashioned flowers, and bushes and gnarly trees.

Out of another I get a lovely view of the bay and a little private wharf belonging to the estate. There is a beautiful shaded lane that runs down there from the house. I always fancy I see people walking in these numerous paths and arbors, but John has cautioned me not to give way to fancy in the least. He says that with my imaginative power and habit of story-making, a nervous weakness like mine is sure to lead to all manner of excited fancies, and that I ought to use my will and good sense to check the tendency. So I try.

I think sometimes that if I were only well enough to write a little it would relieve the press of ideas and rest me.

But I find I get pretty tired when I try.

It is so discouraging not to have any advice and companionship about my work. When I get really well, John says we will ask Cousin Henry and Julia down for a long visit; but he says he would as soon put fireworks in my pillow-case as to let me have those stimulating people about now.

I wish I could get well faster.

But I must not think about that. This paper looks to me as if it *knew* what a vicious influence it had!

There is a recurrent spot where the pattern lolls like a broken neck and two bulbous eyes stare at you upside down.

I get positively angry with the impertinence of it and the everlastingness. Up and down and sideways they crawl, and those absurd, unblinking eyes are everywhere. There is one place where two breadths didn't match, and the eyes go all up and down the line, one a little higher than the other.

I never saw so much expression in an inanimate thing before, and we all know how much expression they have! I used to lie awake as a child and get more entertainment and terror out of blank walls and plain furniture than most children could find in a toy-store.

I remember what a kindly wink the knobs of our big, old bureau used to have, and there was one chair that always seemed like a strong friend.

I used to feel that if any of the other things looked too fierce I could always hop into that chair and be safe.

The furniture in this room is no worse than inharmonious, however, for we had to bring it all from downstairs. I suppose when this was used as a play-room they had to take the nursery things out, and no wonder! I never saw such ravages as the children have made here.

The wall-paper, as I said before, is torn off in spots, and it sticketh closer than a brother[3]—they must have had perseverance as well as hatred.

Then the floor is scratched and gouged and splintered, the plaster itself is dug out here and there, and this great heavy bed, which is all we found in the room, looks as if it had been through the wars.

But I don't mind it a bit—only the paper.

There comes John's sister. Such a dear girl as she is, and so careful of me! I must not let her find me writing.

She is a perfect and enthusiastic housekeeper, and hopes for no better profession. I verily believe she thinks it is the writing which made me sick!

---

3. Proverbs 18.24: "There is a friend that sticketh closer than a brother."

But I can write when she is out, and see her a long way off from these windows.

There is one that commands the road, a lovely shaded winding road, and one that just looks off over the country. A lovely country, too, full of great elms and velvet meadows.

This wall-paper has a kind of sub-pattern in a different shade, a particularly irritating one, for you can only see it in certain lights, and not clearly then.

But in the places where it isn't faded and where the sun is just so—I can see a strange, provoking, formless sort of figure, that seems to skulk about behind that silly and conspicuous front design.

There's sister on the stairs!

• • • • • •

Well, the Fourth of July is over! The people are all gone and I am tired out. John thought it might do me good to see a little company, so we just had mother and Nellie and the children down for a week.

Of course I didn't do a thing. Jennie sees to everything now.

But it tired me all the same.

John says if I don't pick up faster he shall send me to Weir Mitchell[4] in the fall.

But I don't want to go there at all. I had a friend who was in his hands once, and she says he is just like John and my brother, only more so!

Besides, it is such an undertaking to go so far.

I don't feel as if it was worth while to turn my hand over for anything, and I'm getting dreadfully fretful and querulous.

I cry at nothing, and cry most of the time.

Of course I don't when John is here, or anybody else, but when I am alone.

And I am alone a good deal just now. John is kept in town very often by serious cases, and Jennie is good and lets me alone when I want her to.

So I walk a little in the garden or down that lovely lane, sit on the porch under the roses, and lie down up here a good deal.

I'm getting really fond of the room in spite of the wall-paper. Perhaps *because* of the wall-paper.

It dwells in my mind so!

I lie here on this great immovable bed—it is nailed down, I believe—and follow that pattern about by the hour. It is as good as gymnastics, I assure you. I start, we'll say, at the bottom, down in the corner over there where it has not been touched, and I determine for the thousandth time that I *will* follow that pointless pattern to some sort of a conclusion.

I know a little of the principle of design, and I know this thing was not arranged on any laws of radiation, or alternation, or repetition, or symmetry, or anything else that I ever heard of.

It is repeated, of course, by the breadths, but not otherwise.

4. Silas Weir Mitchell (1829–1914), American physician, novelist, and specialist in nerve disorders, popularized the "rest cure" in the management of hysteria, nervous breakdowns, and related disorders. A friend of W. D. Howells, he was the model for the nerve specialist in Howells's novel *The Shadow of a Dream* (1890).

Looked at in one way each breadth stands alone, the bloated curves and flourishes—a kind of "debased Romanesque" with *delirium tremens*[5]—go waddling up and down in isolated columns of fatuity.

But, on the other hand, they connect diagonally, and the sprawling outlines run off in great slanting waves of optic horror, like a lot of wallowing seaweeds in full chase.

The whole thing goes horizontally, too, at least it seems so, and I exhaust myself in trying to distinguish the order of its going in that direction.

They have used a horizontal breadth for a frieze,[6] and that adds wonderfully to the confusion.

There is one end of the room where it is almost intact, and there, when the crosslights fade and low sun shines directly upon it, I can almost fancy radiation after all—the interminable grotesques seem to form around a common centre and rush off in headlong plunges of equal distraction.

It makes me tired to follow it. I will take a nap I guess.

• • • • • •

I don't know why I should write this.

I don't want to.

I don't feel able.

And I know John would think it absurd. But I *must* say what I feel and think in some way—it is such a relief!

But the effort is getting to be greater than the relief.

Half the time now I am awfully lazy, and lie down ever so much.

John says I mustn't lose my strength, and has me take cod liver oil and lots of tonics and things, to say nothing of ale and wine and rare meat.

Dear John! He loves me very dearly, and hates to have me sick. I tried to have a real earnest reasonable talk with him the other day, and tell him how I wish he would let me go and make a visit to Cousin Henry and Julia.

But he said I wasn't able to go, nor able to stand it after I got there; and I did not make out a very good case for myself, for I was crying before I had finished.

It is getting to be a great effort for me to think straight. Just this nervous weakness I suppose.

And dear John gathered me up in his arms, and just carried me upstairs and laid me on the bed, and sat by me and read to me till it tired my head.

He said I was his darling and his comfort and all he had, and that I must take care of myself for his sake, and keep well.

He says no one but myself can help me out of it, that I must use my will and self-control and not let any silly fancies run away with me.

There's one comfort, the baby is well and happy, and does not have to occupy this nursery with the horrid wall-paper.

If we had not used it, that blessed child would have! What a fortunate escape! Why, I wouldn't have a child of mine, an impressionable little thing, live in such a room for worlds.

I never thought of it before, but it is lucky that John kept me here after all, I can stand it so much easier than a baby, you see.

---

5. Latin for "shaking frenzy," a condition caused by alcohol withdrawal in chronic alcoholics. "Debased Romanesque": degraded version of a medieval decorative style characterized by orna-mental complexity and repeated motifs and figures.

6. An ornamental border at the top of the wall.

Of course I never mention it to them any more—I am too wise—but I keep watch of it all the same.

There are things in that paper that nobody knows but me, or ever will.

Behind that outside pattern the dim shapes get clearer every day.

It is always the same shape, only very numerous.

And it is like a woman stooping down and creeping about behind that pattern. I don't like it a bit. I wonder—I begin to think—I wish John would take me away from here!

• • • • • •

It is so hard to talk with John about my case, because he is so wise, and because he loves me so.

But I tried it last night.

It was moonlight. The moon shines in all around just as the sun does.

I hate to see it sometimes, it creeps so slowly, and always comes in by one window or another.

John was asleep and I hated to waken him, so I kept still and watched the moonlight on that undulating wall-paper till I felt creepy.

The faint figure behind seemed to shake the pattern, just as if she wanted to get out.

I got up softly and went to feel and see if the paper *did* move, and when I came back John was awake.

"What is it, little girl?" he said. "Don't go walking about like that—you'll get cold."

I thought it was a good time to talk, so I told him that I really was not gaining here, and that I wished he would take me away.

"Why, darling!" said he, "our lease will be up in three weeks, and I can't see how to leave before.

"The repairs are not done at home, and I cannot possibly leave town just now. Of course if you were in any danger, I could and would, but you really are better, dear, whether you can see it or not. I am a doctor, dear, and I know. You are gaining flesh and color, your appetite is better, I feel really much easier about you."

"I don't weigh a bit more," said I, "nor as much; and my appetite may be better in the evening when you are here, but it is worse in the morning when you are away!"

"Bless her little heart!" said he with a big hug, "she shall be as sick as she pleases! But now let's improve the shining hours[7] by going to sleep, and talk about it in the morning!"

"And you won't go away?" I asked gloomily.

"Why, how can I, dear? It is only three weeks more and then we will take a nice little trip of a few days while Jennie is getting the house ready. Really, dear, you are better!"

---

7. In his poem "Against Idleness and Mischief," Isaac Watts (1674–1748) writes:

> How doth the little busy bee
> Improve each shining hour,
> And gather honey all the day
> From every opening flower!

"Better in body perhaps—" I began, and stopped short, for he sat up straight and looked at me with such a stern, reproachful look that I could not say another word.

"My darling," said he, "I beg of you, for my sake and for our child's sake, as well as for your own, that you will never for one instant let that idea enter your mind! There is nothing so dangerous, so fascinating, to a temperament like yours. It is a false and foolish fancy. Can you not trust me as a physician when I tell you so?"

So of course I said no more on that score, and we went to sleep before long. He thought I was asleep first, but I wasn't, and lay there for hours trying to decide whether that front pattern and the back pattern really did move together or separately.

• • • • • •

On a pattern like this, by daylight, there is a lack of sequence, a defiance of law, that is a constant irritant to a normal mind.

The color is hideous enough, and unreliable enough, and infuriating enough, but the pattern is torturing.

You think you have mastered it, but just as you get well underway in following, it turns a back-somersault and there you are. It slaps you in the face, knocks you down, and tramples upon you. It is like a bad dream.

The outside pattern is a florid arabesque, reminding one of a fungus. If you can imagine a toadstool in joints, an interminable string of toadstools, budding and sprouting in endless convolutions—why, that is something like it.

That is, sometimes!

There is one marked peculiarity about this paper, a thing nobody seems to notice but myself, and that is that it changes as the light changes.

When the sun shoots in through the east window—I always watch for that first long, straight ray—it changes so quickly that I never can quite believe it.

That is why I watch it always.

By moonlight—the moon shines in all night when there is a moon—I wouldn't know it was the same paper.

At night in any kind of light, in twilight, candlelight, lamplight, and worst of all by moonlight, it becomes bars! The outside pattern, I mean, and the woman behind it is as plain as can be.

I didn't realize for a long time what the thing was that showed behind, that dim sub-pattern, but now I am quite sure it is a woman.

By daylight she is subdued, quiet. I fancy it is the pattern that keeps her so still. It is so puzzling. It keeps me quiet by the hour.

I lie down ever so much now. John says it is good for me, and to sleep all I can.

Indeed he started the habit by making me lie down for an hour after each meal.

It is a very bad habit, I am convinced, for you see I don't sleep.

And that cultivates deceit, for I don't tell them I'm awake—O no!

The fact is I am getting a little afraid of John.

He seems very queer sometimes, and even Jennie has an inexplicable look.

It strikes me occasionally, just as a scientific hypothesis, that perhaps it is the paper!

I have watched John when he did not know I was looking, and come into the room suddenly on the most innocent excuses, and I've caught him several times *looking at the paper!* And Jennie too. I caught Jennie with her hand on it once.

She didn't know I was in the room, and when I asked her in a quiet, a very quiet voice, with the most restrained manner possible, what she was doing with the paper—she turned around as if she had been caught stealing, and looked quite angry—asked me why I should frighten her so!

Then she said that the paper stained everything it touched, that she had found yellow smooches on all my clothes and John's, and she wished we would be more careful!

Did not that sound innocent? But I know she was studying that pattern, and I am determined that nobody shall find it out but myself!

• • • • • •

Life is very much more exciting now than it used to be. You see I have something more to expect, to look forward to, to watch. I really do eat better, and am more quiet than I was.

John is so pleased to see me improve! He laughed a little the other day, and said I seemed to be flourishing in spite of my wall-paper.

I turned it off with a laugh. I had no intention of telling him it was *because* of the wall-paper—he would make fun of me. He might even want to take me away.

I don't want to leave now until I have found it out. There is a week more, and I think that will be enough.

• • • • • •

I'm feeling ever so much better! I don't sleep much at night, for it is so interesting to watch developments; but I sleep a good deal in the daytime.

In the daytime it is tiresome and perplexing.

There are always new shoots on the fungus, and new shades of yellow all over it. I cannot keep count of them, though I have tried conscientiously.

It is the strangest yellow, that wall-paper! It makes me think of all the yellow things I ever saw—not beautiful ones like buttercups, but old foul, bad yellow things.

But there is something else about that paper—the smell! I noticed it the moment we came into the room, but with so much air and sun it was not bad. Now we have had a week of fog and rain, and whether the windows are open or not, the smell is here.

It creeps all over the house.

I find it hovering in the dining-room, skulking in the parlor, hiding in the hall, lying in wait for me on the stairs.

It gets into my hair.

Even when I go to ride, if I turn my head suddenly and surprise it—there is that smell!

Such a peculiar odor, too! I have spent hours in trying to analyze it, to find what it smelled like.

It is not bad—at first—and very gentle, but quite the subtlest, most enduring odor I ever met.

In this damp weather it is awful, I wake up in the night and find it hanging over me.

It used to disturb me at first. I thought seriously of burning the house—to reach the smell.

But now I am used to it. The only thing I can think of that it is like is the *color* of the paper! A yellow smell.

There is a very funny mark on this wall, low down, near the mopboard. A streak that runs round the room. It goes behind every piece of furniture, except the bed, a long, straight, even *smooch*, as if it had been rubbed over and over.

I wonder how it was done and who did it, and what they did it for. Round and round and round—round and round and round—it makes me dizzy!

• • • • • •

I really have discovered something at last.

Through watching so much at night, when it changes so, I have finally found out.

The front pattern *does* move—and no wonder! The woman behind shakes it!

Sometimes I think there are a great many women behind, and sometimes only one, and she crawls around fast, and her crawling shakes it all over.

Then in the very bright spots she keeps still, and in the very shady spots she just takes hold of the bars and shakes them hard.

And she is all the time trying to climb through. But nobody could climb through that pattern—it strangles so; I think that is why it has so many heads.

They get through, and then the pattern strangles them off and turns them upside down, and makes their eyes white!

If those heads were covered or taken off it would not be half so bad.

• • • • • •

I think that woman gets out in the daytime!

And I'll tell you why—privately—I've seen her!

I can see her out of every one of my windows!

It is the same woman, I know, for she is always creeping, and most women do not creep by daylight.

I see her in that long shaded lane, creeping up and down. I see her in those dark grape arbors, creeping all around the garden.

I see her on that long road under the trees, creeping along, and when a carriage comes she hides under the blackberry vines.

I don't blame her a bit. It must be very humiliating to be caught creeping by daylight!

I always lock the door when I creep by daylight. I can't do it at night, for I know John would suspect something at once.

And John is so queer now, that I don't want to irritate him. I wish he would take another room! Besides, I don't want anybody to get that woman out at night but myself.

I often wonder if I could see her out of all the windows at once.

But, turn as fast as I can, I can only see out of one at one time.

And though I always see her, she *may* be able to creep faster than I can turn!

I have watched her sometimes away off in the open country, creeping as fast as a cloud shadow in a high wind.

· · · · · ·

If only that top pattern could be gotten off from the under one! I mean to try it, little by little.

I have found out another funny thing, but I shan't tell it this time! It does not do to trust people too much.

There are only two more days to get this paper off, and I believe John is beginning to notice. I don't like the look in his eyes.

And I heard him ask Jennie a lot of professional questions about me. She had a very good report to give.

She said I slept a good deal in the daytime.

John knows I don't sleep very well at night, for all I'm so quiet!

He asked me all sorts of questions, too, and pretended to be very loving and kind.

As if I couldn't see through him!

Still, I don't wonder he acts so, sleeping under this paper for three months.

It only interests me, but I feel sure John and Jennie are secretly affected by it.

· · · · ·

Hurrah! This is the last day, but it is enough. John had to stay in town over night, and won't be out until this evening.

Jennie wanted to sleep with me—the sly thing!—but I told her I should undoubtedly rest better for a night all alone.

That was clever, for really I wasn't alone a bit! As soon as it was moonlight and that poor thing began to crawl and shake the pattern, I got up and ran to help her.

I pulled and she shook, I shook and she pulled, and before morning we had peeled off yards of that paper.

A strip about as high as my head and half around the room.

And then when the sun came and that awful pattern began to laugh at me, I declared I would finish it to-day!

We go away to-morrow, and they are moving all my furniture down again to leave things as they were before.

Jennie looked at the wall in amazement, but I told her merrily that I did it out of pure spite at the vicious thing.

She laughed and said she wouldn't mind doing it herself, but I must not get tired.

How she betrayed herself that time!

But I am here, and no person touches this paper but me—not *alive*!

She tried to get me out of the room—it was too patent! But I said it was so quiet and empty and clean now that I believed I would lie down again and sleep all I could; and not to wake me even for dinner—I would call when I woke.

So now she is gone, and the servants are gone, and the things are gone, and there is nothing left but that great bedstead nailed down, with the canvas mattress we found on it.

We shall sleep downstairs to-night, and take the boat home to-morrow.

I quite enjoy the room, now it is bare again.

How those children did tear about here!

This bedstead is fairly gnawed!

But I must get to work.

I have locked the door and thrown the key down into the front path.

I don't want to go out, and I don't want to have anybody come in, till John comes.

I want to astonish him.

I've got a rope up here that even Jennie did not find. If that woman does get out, and tries to get away, I can tie her!

But I forgot I could not reach far without anything to stand on!

This bed will *not* move!

I tried to lift and push it until I was lame, and then I got so angry I bit off a little piece at one corner—but it hurt my teeth.

Then I peeled off all the paper I could reach standing on the floor. It sticks horribly and the pattern just enjoys it! All those strangled heads and bulbous eyes and waddling fungus growths just shriek with derision!

I am getting angry enough to do something desperate. To jump out of the window would be admirable exercise, but the bars are too strong even to try.

Besides, I wouldn't do it. Of course not. I know well enough that a step like that is improper and might be misconstrued.

I don't like to *look* out of the windows even—there are so many of those creeping women, and they creep so fast.

I wonder if they all come out of that wall-paper as I did?

But I am securely fastened now by my well-hidden rope—you don't get *me* out in the road there!

I suppose I shall have to get back behind the pattern when it comes night, and that is hard!

It is so pleasant to be out in this great room and creep around as I please!

I don't want to go outside. I won't, even if Jennie asks me to.

For outside you have to creep on the ground, and everything is green instead of yellow.

But here I can creep smoothly on the floor, and my shoulder just fits in that long smooch around the wall, so I cannot lose my way.

Why, there's John at the door!

It is no use, young man, you can't open it!

How he does call and pound!

Now he's crying for an axe.

It would be a shame to break down that beautiful door!

"John, dear!" said I in the gentlest voice, "the key is down by the front steps, under a plantain leaf!"

That silenced him for a few moments.

Then he said—very quietly indeed—"Open the door, my darling!"

"I can't," said I. "The key is down by the front door under a plantain leaf!"

"Now why should that man have fainted?" Joseph Henry
Hatfield's illustration from the original magazine publication of
"The Yellow Wall-paper," *New England Magazine*, January 1892.

And then I said it again, several times, very gently and slowly, and said it
so often that he had to go and see, and he got it of course, and came in. He
stopped short by the door.

"What is the matter?" he cried. "For God's sake, what are you doing!"

I kept on creeping just the same, but I looked at him over my shoulder.

"I've got out at last," said I, "in spite of you and Jane! And I've pulled off
most of the paper, so you can't put me back!"

Now why should that man have fainted? But he did, and right across my
path by the wall, so that I had to creep over him every time!

1892

Why I Wrote "The Yellow Wallpaper"?[1]

Many and many a reader has asked that. When the story first came out, in
the *New England Magazine* about 1891,[2] a Boston physician made protest
in *The Transcript*. Such a story ought not to be written, he said; it was enough
to drive anyone mad to read it.

Another physician, in Kansas I think, wrote to say that it was the best
description of incipient insanity he had ever seen, and—begging my pardon—
had I been there?

Now the story of the story is this:

For many years I suffered from a severe and continuous nervous breakdown tending to melancholia—and beyond. During about the third year of
this trouble I went, in devout faith and some faint stir of hope, to a noted
specialist[3] in nervous diseases, the best known in the country. This wise man
put me to bed and applied the rest cure, to which a still good physique
responded so promptly that he concluded there was nothing much the matter

1. First published in the *Forerunner* (October   2. The correct date is January 1892.
1913), the source of the text printed here.   3. Silas Weir Mitchell; see n. 4, p. 515.

with me, and sent me home with solemn advice to "live as domestic a life as far as possible," to "have but two hours' intellectual life a day," and "never to touch pen, brush or pencil again as long as I lived." This was in 1887.

I went home and obeyed those directions for some three months, and came so near the border line of utter mental ruin that I could see over.

Then, using the remnants of intelligence that remained, and helped by a wise friend,[4] I cast the noted specialist's advice to the winds and went to work again—work, the normal life of every human being; work, in which is joy and growth and service, without which one is a pauper and a parasite; ultimately recovering some measure of power.

Being naturally moved to rejoicing by this narrow escape, I wrote "The Yellow Wallpaper," with its embellishments and additions to carry out the ideal (I never had hallucinations or objections to my mural decorations) and sent a copy to the physician who so nearly drove me mad. He never acknowledged it.

The little book is valued by alienists[5] and as a good specimen of one kind of literature. It has to my knowledge saved one woman from a similar fate—so terrifying her family that they let her out into normal activity and she recovered.

But the best result is this. Many years later I was told that the great specialist had admitted to friends of his that he had altered his treatment of neurasthenia[6] since reading "The Yellow Wallpaper."

It was not intended to drive people crazy, but to save people from being driven crazy, and it worked.

1913

4. This is almost certainly the writer Grace Channing (1862–1937). Channing and Gilman had been friends since they were teenagers; in 1894, after Gilman and Charles Stetson were divorced, Channing and Stetson married.
5. Those who treat diseases of the mind.
6. A medical condition believed to be caused by the exhaustion of the nervous system.

EDITH WHARTON
1862–1937

Few novelists in American literary history have enjoyed the combination of commercial success and critical acclaim that Edith Wharton earned during her lifetime. As someone raised in the nineteenth century who became a major writer in the twentieth, Wharton cultivated a sensibility poised on the cusp between the traditions of the past and the shock of the modern. She is well-known for her portrayal of the moneyed classes of old New York, epitomized by the Pulitzer Prize–winning novel *Age of Innocence* (1920); other works, like *Ethan Frome* (1911), depict village life in New England that seems relatively untouched by modernity. However, in Wharton's fiction conventions rarely withstand careful scrutiny; fortunes fail, marriages crumble, traditions once thought comforting become painfully confining. Wharton's recent biographer, Hermione Lee, calls Wharton's mode of fiction "compassionate realism"—a style of sympathetic observation of her characters that leaves room for satiric commentary on the world in which they live.

Edith Newbold Jones was born in New York City on January 24, 1862, into a patriarchial, moneyed, and rather rigid family that, like others in its small circle, disdained and feared the drastic changes in American society brought on by the rapid pace of industrialization and increasing immigration after the Civil War. She spent much of her youth in Europe with her family, and later remarked that she felt like an exile in America after the age of ten. In 1885 she married the Bostonian Edward Wharton, a social equal thirteen years her senior who never provided her with intellectual companionship. Though they lived together (in New York; Newport,

Edith Wharton, 1905.

Rhode Island; Lenox, Massachusetts; and Paris) for twenty-eight years, the marriage was not a happy one. Her success as a writer provided her with both the financial resources to maintain her standard of living despite her husband's poor business judgment and the means to cultivate the relationships with other intellectuals that would sustain her. Wharton engaged in an affair with Morton Fullerton, an expatriate journalist, from 1906 to 1909; she and her husband divorced in 1913, after he began to show signs of mental illness.

Wharton had begun to write as a teenager. By the age of fifteen, she had written (in secret) a thirty-thousand-word novella titled *Fast and Loose*. She had also composed a substantial amount of lyric poetry, and her practice of writing both fiction and verse would continue throughout her writing life. In 1889, she successfully submitted poems to *Scribner's*, *Harper's*, and the *Century*—her first foray into a commercial magazine market that would be crucial to her future success. However, it was not until Wharton was in her late thirties—in the late 1890s—that she fully embraced authorship as a career. She wrote in a variety of genres, publishing short stories, travel literature, works on design and architecture, and historical fiction. The 1905 publication of *The House of Mirth* brought her to the attention of a wide and appreciative public, establishing her place in the literary landscape. The novel was highly successful in its serial publication in *Scribner's Magazine* as well as in book form, and *The House of Mirth* forever linked Wharton to its setting and themes: the old aristocracy of New York, the struggle of characters trapped by social forces, and especially the challenges that faced women attempting to secure financial and social security amidst a shifting terrain of regulation. The novel tells the story of the beautiful Lily Bart, trained to be a decorative upper-class wife but ultimately unwilling to sell herself as merchandise. In *The Custom of the Country* (1913), which Wharton considered her masterpiece, a ruthless midwesterner, Undine Spragg, makes her way up the social ladder, stepping on Americans and Europeans alike in her pursuit of money and the power that goes with it.

With her interest in the lives of leisured elite and her portrayal of Americans abroad, Wharton was frequently compared by reviewers and critics to Henry James—a pairing that continued to shape critical studies of her work after her death. James was Wharton's senior by more than twenty years, and the two enjoyed an intellectual and social relationship that was important to both. It was James, in fact, who suggested that Wharton focus on "the American subject" just as she was preparing to compose *House of Mirth*. However, Wharton also found the repeated comparison of her fiction to James's—which began with her first volume of short stories—to be deeply annoying. (In one letter from 1904, she complained that the "continued cry that I am an echo of Mr. James" left her feeling "rather hopeless.") Like James, Wharton was interested in the manners and motives of upperclass Americans, but the differences are significant. Wharton was less interested than James in the kind of narrative impressionism that he employed in his final novels to explore consciousness; and by comparison with James's, Wharton's fiction is generally more driven by plot and action, including the rising and falling fortunes of her characters. Moreover, Wharton enjoyed a popularity that James never reached. Indeed, in 1912 Wharton even directed her publisher, Charles Scribner, to divert secretly some of her own royalties into a large advance for her aging friend.

By this time, Wharton had taken up permanent residence in France, where she spent the rest of her life. During World War I, Wharton organized relief efforts for the refugees and orphans displaced by the advance of the German army and was active in many other committees and organizations dealing with the devastation wrought by the war. She was relentless in her fundraising, and even edited *The Book of the Homeless* (1916), a collection of literary works and art by international artists, to generate further financial support for French charities. Wharton also wrote extensively about her visits to the front line; she published a collection of these dispatches and would later write two war novels: *The Marne* (1918) and *A Son at the Front* (1923). Wharton's literary output was truly prolific: she produced more than eighty short stories, twenty-two novellas and novels, and three volumes of poetry. Though the Pulitzer Prize–winning *Age of Innocence* is the last of her best-known novels, she published consistently until the time of her death, continuing to enjoy a wide readership. She published an autobiography, *A Backward Glance*, in 1934.

Wharton's achievements as a novelist have overshadowed her mastery of the shortstory form, where she often achieves in a handful of pages a depth of characterization and incident more often realized in much longer novels. Included here are works that represent themes to which she repeatedly returned; "The Other Two" (1904) explores the new age of divorce, while "Roman Fever" (1934) concerns a lifelong rivalry between two leisure-class women, a long-buried secret of illicit love, and the tensions between the old world and new. Considered together, they reveal the shrewdness of Wharton's social chronicles and her ability to deliver penetrating insight into a world that was rapidly changing around her.

The Other Two[1]

I

Waythorn, on the drawing-room hearth, waited for his wife to come down to dinner.

It was their first night under his own roof, and he was surprised at his thrill of boyish agitation. He was not so old, to be sure—his glass gave him little more than the five-and-thirty years to which his wife confessed—but he had fancied himself already in the temperate zone; yet here he was listening for her step with a tender sense of all it symbolized, with some old trail of verse about the garlanded nuptial doorposts floating through his enjoyment of the pleasant room and the good dinner just beyond it.

---

1. First appeared in *Collier's Weekly* (February 1904).

They had been hastily recalled from their honeymoon by the illness of Lily Haskett, the child of Mrs. Waythorn's first marriage. The little girl, at Waythorn's desire, had been transferred to his house on the day of her mother's wedding, and the doctor, on their arrival, broke the news that she was ill with typhoid, but declared that all the symptoms were favorable. Lily could show twelve years of unblemished health, and the case promised to be a light one. The nurse spoke as reassuringly, and after a moment of alarm Mrs. Waythorn had adjusted herself to the situation. She was very fond of Lily—her affection for the child had perhaps been her decisive charm in Waythorn's eyes—but she had the perfectly balanced nerves which her little girl had inherited, and no woman ever wasted less tissue in unproductive worry. Waythorn was therefore quite prepared to see her come in presently, a little late because of a last look at Lily, but as serene and well-appointed as if her goodnight kiss had been laid on the brow of health. Her composure was restful to him; it acted as ballast to his somewhat unstable sensibilities. As he pictured her bending over the child's bed he thought how soothing her presence must be in illness: her very step would prognosticate recovery.

His own life had been a gray one, from temperament rather than circumstance, and he had been drawn to her by the unperturbed gaiety which kept her fresh and elastic at an age when most women's activities are growing either slack or febrile. He knew what was said about her; for, popular as she was, there had always been a faint undercurrent of detraction. When she had appeared in New York, nine or ten years earlier, as the pretty Mrs. Haskett whom Gus Varick had unearthed somewhere—was it in Pittsburgh or Utica?—society, while promptly accepting her, had reserved the right to cast a doubt on its own indiscrimination. Inquiry, however, established her undoubted connection with a socially reigning family, and explained her recent divorce as the natural result of a runaway match at seventeen; and as nothing was known of Mr. Haskett it was easy to believe the worst of him.

Alice Haskett's remarriage with Gus Varick was a passport to the set whose recognition she coveted, and for a few years the Varicks were the most popular couple in town. Unfortunately the alliance was brief and stormy, and this time the husband had his champions. Still, even Varick's stanchest supporters admitted that he was not meant for matrimony, and Mrs. Varick's grievances were of a nature to bear the inspection of the New York courts. A New York divorce is in itself a diploma of virtue, and in the semiwidowhood of this second separation Mrs. Varick took on an air of sanctity, and was allowed to confide her wrongs to some of the most scrupulous ears in town. But when it was known that she was to marry Waythorn there was a momentary reaction. Her best friends would have preferred to see her remain in the role of the injured wife, which was as becoming to her as crepe to a rosy complexion. True, a decent time had elapsed, and it was not even suggested that Waythorn had supplanted his predecessor. People shook their heads over him, however, and one grudging friend, to whom he affirmed that he took the step with his eyes open, replied oracularly: "Yes—and with your ears shut."

Waythorn could afford to smile at these innuendoes. In the Wall Street phrase, he had "discounted" them. He knew that society has not yet adapted itself to the consequences of divorce, and that till the adaptation takes place every woman who uses the freedom the law accords her must be her own social justification. Waythorn had an amused confidence in his wife's ability to justify herself. His expectations were fulfilled, and before the wedding took place Alice Varick's group had rallied openly to her support. She took it all imperturbably: she had a way of surmounting obstacles without seeming to be aware of them, and Waythorn looked back with wonder at the trivialities over which he had worn his nerves thin. He had the sense of having found refuge in a richer, warmer nature than his own, and his satisfaction, at the moment, was humorously summed up in the thought that his wife, when she had done all she could for Lily, would not be ashamed to come down and enjoy a good dinner.

The anticipation of such enjoyment was not, however, the sentiment expressed by Mrs. Waythorn's charming face when she presently joined him. Though she had put on her most engaging tea gown she had neglected to assume the smile that went with it, and Waythorn thought he had never seen her look so nearly worried.

"What is it?" he asked. "Is anything wrong with Lily?"

"No; I've just been in and she's still sleeping." Mrs. Waythorn hesitated. "But something tiresome has happened."

He had taken her two hands, and now perceived that he was crushing a paper between them.

"This letter?"

"Yes—Mr. Haskett has written—I mean his lawyer has written."

Waythorn felt himself flush uncomfortably. He dropped his wife's hands.

"What about?"

"About seeing Lily. You know the courts—"

"Yes, yes," he interrupted nervously.

Nothing was known about Haskett in New York. He was vaguely supposed to have remained in the outer darkness from which his wife had been rescued, and Waythorn was one of the few who were aware that he had given up his business in Utica and followed her to New York in order to be near his little girl. In the days of his wooing, Waythorn had often met Lily on the doorstep, rosy and smiling, on her way "to see papa."

"I am so sorry," Mrs. Waythorn murmured.

He roused himself. "What does he want?"

"He wants to see her. You know she goes to him once a week."

"Well—he doesn't expect her to go to him now, does he?"

"No—he has heard of her illness; but he expects to come here."

"Here?"

Mrs. Waythorn reddened under his gaze. They looked away from each other.

"I'm afraid he has the right. . . . You'll see. . . ." She made a proffer of the letter.

Waythorn moved away with a gesture of refusal. He stood staring about the softly-lighted room, which a moment before had seemed so full of bridal intimacy.

"I'm so sorry," she repeated. "If Lily could have been moved—"

"That's out of the question," he returned impatiently.

"I suppose so."

Her lip was beginning to tremble, and he felt himself a brute.

"He must come, of course," he said. "When is—his day?"

"I'm afraid—tomorrow."

"Very well. Send a note in the morning."

The butler entered to announce dinner.

Waythorn turned to his wife. "Come—you must be tired. It's beastly, but try to forget about it," he said, drawing her hand through his arm.

"You're so good, dear. I'll try," she whispered back.

Her face cleared at once, and as she looked at him across the flowers, between the rosy candleshades, he saw her lips waver back into a smile.

"How pretty everything is!" she sighed luxuriously.

He turned to the butler. "The champagne at once, please. Mrs. Waythorn is tired."

In a moment or two their eyes met above the sparkling glasses. Her own were quite clear and untroubled: he saw that she had obeyed his injunction and forgotten.

II

Waythorn, the next morning, went downtown earlier than usual. Haskett was not likely to come till the afternoon, but the instinct of flight drove him forth. He meant to stay away all day—he had thoughts of dining at his club. As his door closed behind him he reflected that before he opened it again it would have admitted another man who had as much right to enter it as himself, and the thought filled him with a physical repugnance.

He caught the elevated at the employees' hour, and found himself crushed between two layers of pendulous humanity. At Eighth Street the man facing him wriggled out, and another took his place. Waythorn glanced up and saw that it was Gus Varick. The men were so close together that it was impossible to ignore the smile of recognition on Varick's handsome overblown face. And after all—why not? They had always been on good terms, and Varick had been divorced before Waythorn's attentions to his wife began. The two exchanged a word on the perennial grievance of the congested trains, and when a seat at their side was miraculously left empty the instinct of self-preservation made Waythorn slip into it after Varick.

The latter drew the stout man's breath of relief. "Lord—I was beginning to feel like a pressed flower." He leaned back, looking unconcernedly at Waythorn. "Sorry to hear that Sellers is knocked out again."

"Sellers?" echoed Waythorn, starting at his partner's name.

Varick looked surprised. "You didn't know he was laid up with the gout?"

"No. I've been away—I only got back last night." Waythorn felt himself reddening in anticipation of the other's smile.

"Ah—yes; to be sure. And Sellers' attack came on two days ago. I'm afraid he's pretty bad. Very awkward for me, as it happens, because he was just putting through a rather important thing for me."

"Ah?" Waythorn wondered vaguely since when Varick had been dealing in "important things." Hitherto he had dabbled only in the shallow pools of speculation, with which Waythorn's office did not usually concern itself.

It occurred to him that Varick might be talking at random, to relieve the strain of their propinquity. That strain was becoming momentarily more apparent to Waythorn, and when, at Cortlandt Street, he caught sight of an acquaintance and had a sudden vision of the picture he and Varick must present to an initiated eye, he jumped up with a muttered excuse.

"I hope you'll find Sellers better," said Varick civilly, and he stammered back: "If I can be of any use to you—" and let the departing crowd sweep him to the platform.

At his office he heard that Sellers was in fact ill with the gout, and would probably not be able to leave the house for some weeks.

"I'm sorry it should have happened so, Mr. Waythorn," the senior clerk said with affable significance. "Mr. Sellers was very much upset at the idea of giving you such a lot of extra work just now."

"Oh, that's no matter," said Waythorn hastily. He secretly welcomed the pressure of additional business, and was glad to think that, when the day's work was over, he would have to call at his partner's on the way home.

He was late for luncheon, and turned in at the nearest restaurant instead of going to his club. The place was full, and the waiter hurried him to the back of the room to capture the only vacant table. In the cloud of cigar smoke Waythorn did not at once distinguish his neighbors: but presently, looking about him, he saw Varick seated a few feet off. This time, luckily, they were too far apart for conversation, and Varick, who faced another way, had probably not even seen him; but there was an irony in their renewed nearness.

Varick was said to be fond of good living, and as Waythorn sat dispatching his hurried luncheon he looked across half enviously at the other's leisurely degustation of his meal. When Waythorn first saw him he had been helping himself with critical deliberation to a bit of Camembert at the ideal point of liquefaction, and now, the cheese removed, he was just pouring his *café double* from its little two-storied earthen pot. He poured slowly, his ruddy profile bent over the task, and one beringed white hand steadying the lid of the coffeepot; then he stretched his other hand to the decanter of cognac at his elbow, filled a liqueur glass, took a tentative sip, and poured the brandy into his coffee cup.

Waythorn watched him in a kind of fascination. What was he thinking of—only of the flavor of the coffee and the liqueur? Had the morning's meeting left no more trace in his thoughts than on his face? Had his wife so completely passed out of his life that even this odd encounter with her present husband, within a week after her remarriage, was no more than an incident in his day? And as Waythorn mused, another idea struck him: had Haskett ever met Varick as Varick and he had just met? The recollection of Haskett perturbed him, and he rose and left the restaurant, taking a circuitous way out to escape the placid irony of Varick's nod.

It was after seven when Waythorn reached home. He thought the footman who opened the door looked at him oddly.

"How is Miss Lily?" he asked in haste.

"Doing very well, sir. A gentleman—"

"Tell Barlow to put off dinner for half an hour," Waythorn cut him off, hurrying upstairs.

He went straight to his room and dressed without seeing his wife. When he reached the drawing room she was there, fresh and radiant. Lily's day had been good; the doctor was not coming back that evening.

At dinner Waythorn told her of Sellers' illness and of the resulting complications. She listened sympathetically, adjuring him not to let himself be overworked, and asking vague feminine questions about the routine of the office. Then she gave him the chronicle of Lily's day; quoted the nurse and doctor, and told him who had called to inquire. He had never seen her more serene and unruffled. It struck him, with a curious pang, that she was very happy in being with him, so happy that she found a childish pleasure in rehearsing the trivial incidents of her day.

After dinner they went to the library, and the servant put the coffee and liqueurs on a low table before her and left the room. She looked singularly soft and girlish in her rosy-pale dress, against the dark leather of one of his bachelor armchairs. A day earlier the contrast would have charmed him.

He turned away now, choosing a cigar with affected deliberation.

"Did Haskett come?" he asked, with his back to her.

"Oh, yes—he came."

"You didn't see him, of course?"

She hesitated a moment. "I let the nurse see him."

That was all. There was nothing more to ask. He swung round toward her, applying a match to his cigar. Well, the thing was over for a week, at any rate. He would try not to think of it. She looked up at him, a trifle rosier than usual, with a smile in her eyes.

"Ready for your coffee, dear?"

He leaned against the mantelpiece, watching her as she lifted the coffee-pot. The lamplight struck a gleam from her bracelets and tipped her soft hair with brightness. How light and slender she was, and how each gesture flowed into the next! She seemed a creature all compact of harmonies. As the thought of Haskett receded, Waythorn felt himself yielding again to the joy of possessorship. They were his, those white hands with their flitting motions, his the light haze of hair, the lips and eyes. . . .

She set down the coffeepot, and reaching for the decanter of cognac, measured off a liqueur glass and poured it into his cup.

Waythorn uttered a sudden exclamation.

"What is the matter?" she said, startled.

"Nothing; only—I don't take cognac in my coffee."

"Oh, how stupid of me," she cried.

Their eyes met, and she blushed a sudden agonized red.

III

Ten days later, Mr. Sellers, still housebound, asked Waythorn to call on his way downtown.

The senior partner, with his swaddled foot propped up by the fire, greeted his associate with an air of embarrassment.

"I'm sorry, my dear fellow; I've got to ask you to do an awkward thing for me."

Waythorn waited, and the other went on, after a pause apparently given to the arrangement of his phrases: "The fact is, when I was knocked out I had just gone into a rather complicated piece of business for—Gus Varick."

"Well?" said Waythorn, with an attempt to put him at his ease.

"Well—it's this way: Varick came to me the day before my attack. He had evidently had an inside tip from somebody, and had made about a hundred thousand. He came to me for advice, and I suggested his going in with Vanderlyn."

"Oh, the deuce!" Waythorn exclaimed. He saw in a flash what had happened. The investment was an alluring one, but required negotiation. He listened quietly while Sellers put the case before him, and, the statement ended, he said: "You think I ought to see Varick?"

"I'm afraid I can't as yet. The doctor is obdurate. And this thing can't wait. I hate to ask you, but no one else in the office knows the ins and outs of it."

Waythorn stood silent. He did not care a farthing for the success of Varick's venture, but the honor of the office was to be considered, and he could hardly refuse to oblige his partner.

"Very well," he said, "I'll do it."

That afternoon, apprised by telephone, Varick called at the office. Waythorn, waiting in his private room, wondered what the others thought of it. The newspapers, at the time of Mrs. Waythorn's marriage, had acquainted their readers with every detail of her previous matrimonial ventures, and Waythorn could fancy the clerks smiling behind Varick's back as he was ushered in.

Varick bore himself admirably. He was easy without being undignified, and Waythorn was conscious of cutting a much less impressive figure. Varick had no experience of business, and the talk prolonged itself for nearly an hour while Waythorn set forth with scrupulous precision the details of the proposed transaction.

"I'm awfully obliged to you," Varick said as he rose. "The fact is I'm not used to having much money to look after, and I don't want to make an ass of myself—" He smiled, and Waythorn could not help noticing that there was something pleasant about his smile. "It feels uncommonly queer to have enough cash to pay one's bills. I'd have sold my soul for it a few years ago!"

Waythorn winced at the allusion. He had heard it rumored that a lack of funds had been one of the determining causes of the Varick separation, but it did not occur to him that Varick's words were intentional. It seemed more likely that the desire to keep clear of embarrassing topics had fatally drawn him into one. Waythorn did not wish to be outdone in civility.

"We'll do the best we can for you," he said. "I think this is a good thing you're in."

"Oh, I'm sure it's immense. It's awfully good of you—" Varick broke off, embarrassed. "I suppose the thing's settled now—but if—"

"If anything happens before Sellers is about, I'll see you again," said Waythorn quietly. He was glad, in the end, to appear the more self-possessed of the two.

The course of Lily's illness ran smooth, and as the days passed Waythorn grew used to the idea of Haskett's weekly visit. The first time the day came round, he stayed out late, and questioned his wife as to the visit on his return. She replied at once that Haskett had merely seen the nurse downstairs, as the doctor did not wish anyone in the child's sickroom till after the crisis.

The following week Waythorn was again conscious of the recurrence of the day, but had forgotten it by the time he came home to dinner. The crisis of the disease came a few days later, with a rapid decline of fever, and the little girl was pronounced out of danger. In the rejoicing which ensued the thought of Haskett passed out of Waythorn's mind, and one afternoon, letting himself into the house with a latchkey, he went straight to his library without noticing a shabby hat and umbrella in the hall.

In the library he found a small effaced-looking man with a thinnish gray beard sitting on the edge of a chair. The stranger might have been a piano tuner, or one of those mysteriously efficient persons who are summoned in emergencies to adjust some detail of the domestic machinery. He blinked at Waythorn through a pair of gold-rimmed spectacles and said mildly: "Mr. Waythorn, I presume? I am Lily's father."

Waythorn flushed. "Oh—" he stammered uncomfortably. He broke off, disliking to appear rude. Inwardly he was trying to adjust the actual Haskett to the image of him projected by his wife's reminiscences. Waythorn had been allowed to infer that Alice's first husband was a brute.

"I am sorry to intrude," said Haskett, with his over-the-counter politeness.

"Don't mention it," returned Waythorn, collecting himself. "I suppose the nurse has been told?"

"I presume so. I can wait," said Haskett. He had a resigned way of speaking, as though life had worn down his natural powers of resistance.

Waythorn stood on the threshold, nervously pulling off his gloves.

"I'm sorry you've been detained. I will send for the nurse," he said; and as he opened the door he added with an effort: "I'm glad we can give you a good report of Lily." He winced as the *we* slipped out, but Haskett seemed not to notice it.

"Thank you, Mr. Waythorn, It's been an anxious time for me."

"Ah, well, that's past. Soon she'll be able to go to you." Waythorn nodded and passed out.

In his own room he flung himself down with a groan. He hated the womanish sensibility which made him suffer so acutely from the grotesque chances of life. He had known when he married that his wife's former husbands were both living, and that amid the multiplied contacts of modern existence there were a thousand chances to one that he would run against one or the other, yet he found himself as much disturbed by his brief encounter with Haskett as though the law had not obligingly removed all difficulties in the way of their meeting.

Waythorn sprang up and began to pace the room nervously. He had not suffered half as much from his two meetings with Varick. It was Haskett's presence in his own house that made the situation so intolerable. He stood still, hearing steps in the passage.

"This way, please," he heard the nurse say. Haskett was being taken upstairs, then: not a corner of the house but was open to him. Waythorn dropped into another chair, staring vaguely ahead of him. On his dressing table stood a photograph of Alice, taken when he had first known her. She was Alice Varick then—how fine and exquisite he had thought her! Those were Varick's pearls about her neck. At Waythorn's insistence they had been returned before her marriage. Had Haskett ever given her any trinkets—and what had become of them, Waythorn wondered? He realized suddenly that he knew very little of Haskett's past or present situation; but from the man's appearance and manner of speech he could reconstruct with curious precision the surroundings of Alice's first marriage. And it startled him to think that she had, in the background of her life, a phase of existence so different from anything with which he had connected her. Varick, whatever his faults, was a gentleman, in the conventional, traditional sense of the term: the sense which at that moment seemed, oddly enough, to have most meaning to Waythorn. He and Varick had the same social habits, spoke the same language, understood the same allusions. But this other man . . . it was grotesquely uppermost in Waythorn's mind that Haskett had worn a made-up tie attached with an elastic. Why should that ridiculous detail symbolize the whole man? Waythorn was exasperated by his own paltriness, but the fact of the tie expanded, forced itself on him, became as it were the key to Alice's past. He could see her, as Mrs. Haskett, sitting in a "front parlor" furnished in plush, with a pianola, and copy of *Ben-Hur*[2] on the center table. He could see her going to the theater with Haskett—or perhaps even to a "Church Sociable"—she in a "picture hat" and Haskett in a black frock coat, a little creased, with the made-up tie on an elastic. On the way home they would stop and look at the illuminated shop windows, lingering over the photographs of New York actresses. On Sunday afternoons Haskett would take her for a walk, pushing Lily ahead of them in a white enameled perambulator, and Waythorn had a vision of the people they would stop and talk to. He could fancy how pretty Alice must have looked, in a dress adroitly constructed from the hints of a New York fashion paper, and how she must have looked down on the other women, chafing at her life, and secretly feeling that she belonged in a bigger place.

For the moment his foremost thought was one of wonder at the way in which she had shed the phase of existence which her marriage with Haskett implied. It was as if her whole aspect, every gesture, every inflection, every allusion, were a studied negation of that period of her life. If she had denied being married to Haskett she could hardly have stood more convicted of duplicity than in this obliteration of the self which had been his wife.

Waythorn started up, checking himself in the analysis of her motives. What right had he to create a fantastic effigy of her and then pass judgment on it? She had spoken vaguely of her first marriage as unhappy, had hinted, with becoming reticence, that Haskett had wrought havoc among her young illusions. . . . It was a pity for Waythorn's peace of mind that Haskett's very inoffensiveness shed a new light on the nature of those illusions. A man would rather think that his wife has been brutalized by her first husband than that the process has been reversed.

IV

"Mr. Waythorn, I don't like that French governess of Lily's."

Haskett, subdued and apologetic, stood before Waythorn in the library, revolving his shabby hat in his hand.

Waythorn, surprised in his armchair over the evening paper, stared back perplexedly at his visitor.

"You'll excuse my asking to see you," Haskett continued. "But this is my last visit, and I thought if I could have a word with you it would be a better way than writing to Mrs. Waythorn's lawyer."

Waythorn rose uneasily. He did not like the French governess either; but that was irrelevant.

"I am not so sure of that," he returned stiffly; "but since you wish it I will give your message to—my wife." He always hesitated over the possessive pronoun in addressing Haskett.

---

2. *Ben-Hur: A Tale of the Christ* (1880) was an extremely popular novel by Lew Wallace (1827–1905).

The latter sighed. "I don't know as that will help much. She didn't like it when I spoke to her."

Waythorn turned red. "When did you see her?" he asked.

"Not since the first day I came to see Lily—right after she was taken sick. I remarked to her then that I didn't like the governess."

Waythorn made no answer. He remembered distinctly that, after that first visit, he had asked his wife if she had seen Haskett. She had lied to him then, but she had respected his wishes since; and the incident cast a curious light on her character. He was sure she would not have seen Haskett that first day if she had divined that Waythorn would object, and the fact that she did not divine it was almost as disagreeable to the latter as the discovery that she had lied to him.

"I don't like the woman," Haskett was repeating with mild persistency. "She ain't straight, Mr. Waythorn—she'll teach the child to be underhand. I've noticed a change in Lily—she's too anxious to please—and she don't always tell the truth. She used to be the straightest child, Mr. Waythorn—" He broke off, his voice a little thick. "Not but what I want her to have a stylish education," he ended.

Waythorn was touched. "I'm sorry, Mr. Haskett; but frankly, I don't quite see what I can do."

Haskett hesitated. Then he laid his hat on the table, and advanced to the hearthrug, on which Waythorn was standing. There was nothing aggressive in his manner, but he had the solemnity of a timid man resolved on a decisive measure.

"There's just one thing you can do, Mr. Waythorn," he said. "You can remind Mrs. Waythorn that, by the decree of the courts, I am entitled to have a voice in Lily's bringing-up." He paused, and went on more deprecatingly: "I'm not the kind to talk about enforcing my rights, Mr. Waythorn. I don't know as I think a man is entitled to rights he hasn't known how to hold on to; but this business of the child is different. I've never let go there—and I never mean to."

The scene left Waythorn deeply shaken. Shamefacedly, in indirect ways, he had been finding out about Haskett; and all that he had learned was favorable. The little man, in order to be near his daughter, had sold out his share in a profitable business in Utica, and accepted a modest clerkship in a New York manufacturing house. He boarded in a shabby street and had few acquaintances. His passion for Lily filled his life. Waythorn felt that this exploration of Haskett was like groping about with a dark lantern in his wife's past; but he saw now that there were recesses his lantern had not explored. He had never inquired into the exact circumstances of his wife's first matrimonial rupture. On the surface all had been fair. It was she who had obtained the divorce, and the court had given her the child. But Waythorn knew how many ambiguities such a verdict might cover. The mere fact that Haskett retained a right over his daughter implied an unsuspected compromise. Waythorn was an idealist. He always refused to recognize unpleasant contingencies till he found himself confronted with them, and then he saw them followed by a spectral train of consequences. His next days were thus haunted, and he determined to try to lay the ghosts by conjuring them up in his wife's presence.

When he repeated Haskett's request a flame of anger passed over her face; but she subdued it instantly and spoke with a slight quiver of outraged motherhood.

"It is very ungentlemanly of him," she said.

The word grated on Waythorn. "That is neither here nor there. It's a bare question of rights."

She murmured: "It's not as if he could ever be a help to Lily—"

Waythorn flushed. This was even less to his taste. "The question is," he repeated, "what authority has he over her?"

She looked downward, twisting herself a little in her seat. "I am willing to see him—I thought you objected," she faltered.

In a flash he understood that she knew the extent of Haskett's claims. Perhaps it was not the first time she had resisted them.

"My objecting has nothing to do with it," he said coldly; "if Haskett has a right to be consulted you must consult him."

She burst into tears, and he saw that she expected him to regard her as a victim.

Haskett did not abuse his rights. Waythorn had felt miserably sure that he would not. But the governess was dismissed, and from time to time the little man demanded an interview with Alice. After the first outburst she accepted the situation with her usual adaptability. Haskett had once reminded Waythorn of the piano tuner, and Mrs. Waythorn, after a month or two, appeared to class him with that domestic familiar. Waythorn could not but respect the father's tenacity. At first he had tried to cultivate the suspicion that Haskett might be "up to" something, that he had an object in securing a foothold in the house. But in his heart Waythorn was sure of Haskett's single-mindedness; he even guessed in the latter a mild contempt for such advantages as his relation with the Waythorns might offer. Haskett's sincerity of purpose made him invulnerable, and his successor had to accept him as a lien on the property.

Mr. Sellers was sent to Europe to recover from his gout, and Varick's affairs hung on Waythorn's hands. The negotiations were prolonged and complicated; they necessitated frequent conferences between the two men, and the interests of the firm forbade Waythorn's suggesting that his client should transfer his business to another office.

Varick appeared well in the transaction. In moments of relaxation his coarse streak appeared, and Waythorn dreaded his geniality; but in the office he was concise and clear-headed, with a flattering deference to Waythorn's judgment. Their business relations being so affably established, it would have been absurd for the two men to ignore each other in society. The first time they met in a drawing room, Varick took up their intercourse in the same easy key, and his hostess' grateful glance obliged Waythorn to respond to it. After that they ran across each other frequently, and one evening at a ball Waythorn, wandering through the remoter rooms, came upon Varick seated beside his wife. She colored a little, and faltered in what she was saying; but Varick nodded to Waythorn without rising, and the latter strolled on.

In the carriage, on the way home, he broke out nervously: "I didn't know you spoke to Varick."

Her voice trembled a little. "It's the first time—he happened to be standing near me; I didn't know what to do. It's so awkward, meeting everywhere—and he said you had been very kind about some business."

"That's different," said Waythorn.

She paused a moment. "I'll do just as you wish," she returned pliantly. "I thought it would be less awkward to speak to him when we meet."

Her pliancy was beginning to sicken him. Had she really no will of her own—no theory about her relation to these men? She had accepted Haskett—did she mean to accept Varick? It was "less awkward," as she had said, and her instinct was to evade difficulties or to circumvent them. With sudden vividness Waythorn saw how the instinct had developed. She was "as easy as an old shoe"—a shoe that too many feet had worn. Her elasticity was the result of tension in too many different directions. Alice Haskett—Alice Varick—Alice Waythorn—she had been each in turn, and had left hanging to each name a little of her privacy, a little of her personality, a little of the inmost self where the unknown god abides.

"Yes—it's better to speak to Varick," said Waythorn wearily.

V

The winter wore on, and society took advantage of the Waythorns' acceptance of Varick. Harassed hostesses were grateful to them for bridging over a social difficulty, and Mrs. Waythorn was held up as a miracle of good taste. Some experimental spirits could not resist the diversion of throwing Varick and his former wife together, and there were those who thought he found a zest in the propinquity. But Mrs. Waythorn's conduct remained irreproachable. She neither avoided Varick nor sought him out. Even Waythorn could not but admit that she had discovered the solution of the newest social problem.

He had married her without giving much thought to that problem. He had fancied that a woman can shed her past like a man. But now he saw that Alice was bound to hers both by the circumstances which forced her into continued relation with it, and by the traces it had left on her nature. With grim irony Waythorn compared himself to a member of a syndicate. He held so many shares in his wife's personality and his predecessors were his partners in the business. If there had been any element of passion in the transaction he would have felt less deteriorated by it. The fact that Alice took her change of husbands like a change of weather reduced the situation to mediocrity. He could have forgiven her for blunders, for excesses; for resisting Haskett, for yielding to Varick; for anything but her acquiescence and her tact. She reminded him of a juggler tossing knives; but the knives were blunt and she knew they would never cut her.

And then, gradually, habit formed a protecting surface for his sensibilities. If he paid for each day's comfort with the small change of his illusions, he grew daily to value the comfort more and set less store upon the coin. He had drifted into a dulling propinquity with Haskett and Varick and he took refuge in the cheap revenge of satirizing the situation. He even began to reckon up the advantages which accrued from it, to ask himself if it were not better to own a third of a wife who knew how to make a man happy than a whole one who had lacked opportunity to acquire the art. For it *was* an art, and made up, like all others, of concessions, eliminations and embellishments; of lights judiciously thrown and shadows skillfully softened. His wife knew exactly how to manage the lights, and he knew exactly to what training she owed her skill. He even tried to trace the source of his obligations, to discriminate between the influences which had combined to produce his domestic happiness: he perceived that Haskett's commonness had made Alice worship good breeding, while Varick's liberal construction of the marriage bond had taught her to value the conjugal virtues; so that he was directly indebted to his predecessors for the devotion which made his life easy if not inspiring.

From this phase he passed into that of complete acceptance. He ceased to satirize himself because time dulled the irony of the situation and the joke lost its humor with its sting. Even the sight of Haskett's hat on the hall table had ceased to touch the springs of epigram. The hat was often seen there now, for it had been decided that it was better for Lily's father to visit her than for the little girl to go to his boardinghouse. Waythorn, having acquiesced in this arrangement, had been surprised to find how little difference it made. Haskett was never obtrusive, and the few visitors who met him on the stairs were unaware of his identity. Waythorn did not know how often he saw Alice, but with himself Haskett was seldom in contact.

One afternoon, however, he learned on entering that Lily's father was waiting to see him. In the library he found Haskett occupying a chair in his usual provisional way. Waythorn always felt grateful to him for not leaning back.

"I hope you'll excuse me, Mr. Waythorn," he said rising. "I wanted to see Mrs. Waythorn about Lily, and your man asked me to wait here till she came in."

"Of course," said Waythorn, remembering that a sudden leak had that morning given over the drawing room to the plumbers.

He opened his cigar case and held it out to his visitor, and Haskett's acceptance seemed to mark a fresh stage in their intercourse. The spring evening was chilly, and Waythorn invited his guest to draw up his chair to the fire. He meant to find an excuse to leave Haskett in a moment; but he was tired and cold, and after all the little man no longer jarred on him.

The two were enclosed in the intimacy of their blended cigar smoke when the door opened and Varick walked into the room. Waythorn rose abruptly. It was the first time that Varick had come to the house, and the surprise of seeing him, combined with the singular inopportuneness of his arrival, gave a new edge to Waythorn's blunted sensibilities. He stared at his visitor without speaking.

Varick seemed too preoccupied to notice his host's embarrassment.

"My dear fellow," he exclaimed in his most expansive tone, "I must apologize for tumbling in on you in this way, but I was too late to catch you downtown, and so I thought—"

He stopped short, catching sight of Haskett, and his sanguine color deepened to a flush which spread vividly under his scant blond hair. But in a moment he recovered himself and nodded slightly. Haskett returned the bow in silence, and Waythorn was still groping for speech when the footman came in carrying a tea table.

The intrusion offered a welcome vent to Waythorn's nerves. "What the deuce are you bringing this here for?" he said sharply.

"I beg your pardon, sir, but the plumbers are still in the drawing room, and Mrs. Waythorn said she would have tea in the library." The footman's perfectly respectful tone implied a reflection on Waythorn's reasonableness.

"Oh, very well," said the latter resignedly, and the footman proceeded to open the folding tea table and set out its complicated appointments. While this interminable process continued the three men stood motionless, watching it with a fascinated stare, till Waythorn, to break the silence, said to Varick, "Won't you have a cigar?"

He held out the case he had just tendered to Haskett, and Varick helped himself with a smile. Waythorn looked about for a match, and finding none, proffered a light from his own cigar. Haskett, in the background, held his ground mildly, examining his cigar tip now and then, and stepping forward at the right moment to knock its ashes into the fire.

The footman at last withdrew, and Varick immediately began: "If I could just say half a word to you about this business—"

"Certainly," stammered Waythorn; "in the dining room—"

But as he placed his hand on the door it opened from without, and his wife appeared on the threshold.

She came in fresh and smiling, in her street dress and hat, shedding a fragrance from the boa which she loosened in advancing.

"Shall we have tea in here, dear?" she began; and then she caught sight of Varick. Her smile deepened, veiling a slight tremor of surprise.

"Why, how do you do?" she said with a distinct note of pleasure.

As she shook hands with Varick she saw Haskett standing behind him. Her smile faded for a moment, but she recalled it quickly, with a scarcely perceptible side glance at Waythorn.

"How do you do, Mr. Haskett?" she said, and shook hands with him a shade less cordially.

The three men stood awkwardly before her, till Varick, always the most self-possessed, dashed into an explanatory phrase.

"We—I had to see Waythorn a moment on business," he stammered, brick-red from chin to nape.

Haskett stepped forward with his air of mild obstinacy. "I am sorry to intrude; but you appointed five o'clock—" he directed his resigned glance to the timepiece on the mantel.

She swept aside their embarrassment with a charming gesture of hospitality.

"I'm so sorry—I'm always late; but the afternoon was so lovely." She stood drawing off her gloves, propitiatory and graceful, diffusing about her a sense of ease and familiarity in which the situation lost its grotesqueness. "But before talking business," she added brightly, "I'm sure everyone wants a cup of tea."

She dropped into her low chair by the tea table, and the two visitors, as if drawn by her smile, advanced to receive the cups she held out.

She glanced about for Waythorn, and he took the third cup with a laugh.

1904

Roman Fever[1]

I

From the table at which they had been lunching two American ladies of ripe but well-cared-for middle age moved across the lofty terrace of the Roman restaurant and, leaning on its parapet, looked first at each other, and then down on the outspread glories of the Palatine[2] and the Forum, with the same expression of vague but benevolent approval.

As they leaned there a girlish voice echoed up gaily from the stairs leading to the court below. "Well, come along, then," it cried, not to them but to an invisible companion, "and let's leave the young things to their knitting"; and a voice as fresh laughed back: "Oh, look here, Babs, not actually *knitting*—" "Well, I mean figuratively," rejoined the first. "After all, we haven't left our poor parents much else to do. . . ." and at that point the turn of the stairs engulfed the dialogue.

The two ladies looked at each other again, this time with a tinge of smiling embarrassment, and the smaller and paler one shook her head and colored slightly.

"Barbara!" she murmured, sending an unheard rebuke after the mocking voice in the stairway.

The other lady, who was fuller, and higher in color, with a small determined nose supported by vigorous black eyebrows, gave a good-humored laugh. "That's what our daughters think of us!"

Her companion replied by a deprecating gesture. "Not of us individually. We must remember that. It's just the collective modern idea of Mothers. And you see—" Half-guiltily she drew from her handsomely mounted black handbag a twist of crimson silk run through by two fine knitting needles. "One never knows," she murmured. "The new system has certainly given us a good deal of time to kill; and sometimes I get tired just looking—even at this." Her gesture was now addressed to the stupendous scene at their feet.

The dark lady laughed again, and they both relapsed upon the view, contemplating it in silence, with a sort of diffused serenity which might have been borrowed from the spring effulgence of the Roman skies. The luncheon hour was long past, and the two had their end of the vast terrace to themselves. At its opposite extremity a few groups, detained by a lingering look at the outspread city, were gathering up guidebooks and fumbling for tips. The last of them scattered, and the two ladies were alone on the air-washed height.

"Well, I don't see why we shouldn't just stay here," said Mrs. Slade, the lady of the high color and energetic brows. Two derelict basket chairs stood near, and she pushed them into the angle of the parapet, and settled herself in one, her gaze upon the Palatine. "After all, it's still the most beautiful view in the world."

"It always will be, to me," assented her friend Mrs. Ansley, with so slight a stress on the "me" that Mrs. Slade, though she noticed it, wondered if it were not merely accidental, like the random underlinings of old-fashioned letter writers.

---

1. First printed in *Liberty* magazine in 1934.
2. Palatine Hill: a park in the center of Rome, with palatial ruins and historical monuments.

"Grace Ansley was always old-fashioned," she thought; and added aloud, with a retrospective smile: "It's a view we've both been familiar with for a good many years. When we first met here we were younger than our girls are now. You remember?"

"Oh, yes, I remember," murmured Mrs. Ansley, with the same undefinable stress. "There's that headwaiter wondering," she interpolated. She was evidently far less sure than her companion of herself and of her rights in the world.

"I'll cure him of wondering," said Mrs. Slade, stretching her hand toward a bag as discreetly opulent-looking as Mrs. Ansley's. Signing to the headwaiter, she explained that she and her friend were old lovers of Rome, and would like to spend the end of the afternoon looking down on the view—that is, if it did not disturb the service? The headwaiter, bowing over her gratuity, assured her that the ladies were most welcome, and would be still more so if they would condescend to remain for dinner. A full-moon night, they would remember. . . .

Mrs. Slade's black brows drew together, as though references to the moon were out of place and even unwelcome. But she smiled away her frown as the headwaiter retreated. "Well, why not? We might do worse. There's no knowing, I suppose, when the girls will be back. Do you even know back from *where*? I don't!"

Mrs. Ansley again colored slightly. "I think those young Italian aviators we met at the Embassy invited them to fly to Tarquinia[3] for tea. I suppose they'll want to wait and fly back by moonlight."

"Moonlight—moonlight! What a part it still plays. Do you suppose they're as sentimental as we were?"

"I've come to the conclusion that I don't in the least know what they are," said Mrs. Ansley. "And perhaps we didn't know much more about each other."

"No; perhaps we didn't."

Her friend gave her a shy glance. "I never should have supposed you were sentimental, Alida."

"Well, perhaps I wasn't." Mrs. Slade drew her lids together in retrospect; and for a few moments the two ladies, who had been intimate since childhood, reflected how little they knew each other. Each one, of course, had a label ready to attach to the other's name; Mrs. Delphin Slade, for instance, would have told herself, or anyone who asked her, that Mrs. Horace Ansley, twenty-five years ago, had been exquisitely lovely—no, you wouldn't believe it, would you?. . . . though, of course, still charming, distinguished. . . . Well, as a girl she had been exquisite; far more beautiful than her daughter Barbara, though certainly Babs, according to the new standards at any rate, was more effective—had more *edge*, as they say. Funny where she got it, with those two nullities as parents. Yes; Horace Ansley was—well, just the duplicate of his wife. Museum specimens of old New York. Good-looking, irreproachable, exemplary. Mrs. Slade and Mrs. Ansley had lived opposite each other—actually as well as figuratively—for years. When the drawing-room curtains in No. 20 East 73rd Street were renewed, No. 23, across the way, was always aware of it. And of all the movings, buyings, travels, anniversaries, illnesses—the tame chronicle of an estimable pair. Little of it escaped

3. An ancient Etruscan city in the province of Viterbo, Lazio, Italy, famous for resisting Roman rule.

Mrs. Slade. But she had grown bored with it by the time her husband made his big *coup* in Wall Street, and when they bought in upper Park Avenue[4] had already begun to think: "I'd rather live opposite a speakeasy[5] for a change; at least one might see it raided." The idea of seeing Grace raided was so amusing that (before the move) she launched it at a woman's lunch. It made a hit, and went the rounds—she sometimes wondered if it had crossed the street, and reached Mrs. Ansley. She hoped not, but didn't much mind. Those were the days when respectability was at a discount, and it did the irreproachable no harm to laugh at them a little.

A few years later, and not many months apart, both ladies lost their husbands. There was an appropriate exchange of wreaths and condolences, and a brief renewal of intimacy in the half-shadow of their mourning; and now, after another interval, they had run across each other in Rome, at the same hotel, each of them the modest appendage of a salient daughter. The similarity of their lot had again drawn them together, lending itself to mild jokes, and the mutual confession that, if in old days it must have been tiring to "keep up" with daughters, it was now, at times, a little dull not to.

No doubt, Mrs. Slade reflected, she felt her unemployment more than poor Grace ever would. It was a big drop from being the wife of Delphin Slade to being his widow. She had always regarded herself (with a certain conjugal pride) as his equal in social gifts, as contributing her full share to the making of the exceptional couple they were: but the difference after his death was irremediable. As the wife of the famous corporation lawyer, always with an international case or two on hand, every day brought its exciting and unexpected obligation: the impromptu entertaining of eminent colleagues from abroad, the hurried dashes on legal business to London, Paris or Rome, where the entertaining was so handsomely reciprocated; the amusement of hearing in her wake: "What, that handsome woman with the good clothes and the eyes is Mrs. Slade—*the* Slade's wife? Really? Generally the wives of celebrities are such frumps."

Yes; being *the* Slade's widow was a dullish business after that. In living up to such a husband all her faculties had been engaged; now she had only her daughter to live up to, for the son who seemed to have inherited his father's gifts had died suddenly in boyhood. She had fought through that agony because her husband was there, to be helped and to help; now, after the father's death, the thought of the boy had become unbearable. There was nothing left but to mother her daughter; and dear Jenny was such a perfect daughter that she needed no excessive mothering. "Now with Babs Ansley I don't know that I *should* be so quiet," Mrs. Slade sometimes half-enviously reflected; but Jenny, who was younger than her brilliant friend, was that rare accident, an extremely pretty girl who somehow made youth and prettiness seem as safe as their absence. It was all perplexing—and to Mrs. Slade a little boring. She wished that Jenny would fall in love—with the wrong man, even; that she might have to be watched, out-maneuvered, rescued. And instead, it was Jenny who watched her mother, kept her out of drafts, made sure that she had taken her tonic. . . .

---

4. Park Avenue would have been a more expensive and exclusive address.

5. During Prohibition, an establishment that illegally sold alcoholic beverages.

Mrs. Ansley was much less articulate than her friend, and her mental portrait of Mrs. Slade was slighter, and drawn with fainter touches. "Alida Slade's awfully brilliant; but not as brilliant as she thinks," would have summed it up; though she would have added, for the enlightenment of strangers, that Mrs. Slade had been an extremely dashing girl; much more so than her daughter, who was pretty, of course, and clever in a way, but had none of her mother's—well, "vividness," someone had once called it. Mrs. Ansley would take up current words like this, and cite them in quotation marks, as unheard-of audacities. No; Jenny was not like her mother. Sometimes Mrs. Ansley thought Alida Slade was disappointed; on the whole she had had a sad life. Full of failures and mistakes; Mrs. Ansley had always been rather sorry for her. . . .

So these two ladies visualized each other, each through the wrong end of her little telescope.

II

For a long time they continued to sit side by side without speaking. It seemed as though, to both, there was a relief in laying down their somewhat futile activities in the presence of the vast Memento Mori which faced them. Mrs. Slade sat quite still, her eyes fixed on the golden slope of the Palace of the Caesars,[6] and after a while Mrs. Ansley ceased to fidget with her bag, and she too sank into meditation. Like many intimate friends, the two ladies had never before had occasion to be silent together, and Mrs. Ansley was slightly embarrassed by what seemed, after so many years, a new stage in their intimacy, and one with which she did not yet know how to deal.

Suddenly the air was full of that deep clangor of bells which periodically covers Rome with a roof of silver. Mrs. Slade glanced at her wristwatch. "Five o'clock already," she said, as though surprised.

Mrs. Ansley suggested interrogatively: "There's bridge at the Embassy at five." For a long time Mrs. Slade did not answer. She appeared to be lost in contemplation, and Mrs. Ansley thought the remark had escaped her. But after a while she said, as if speaking out of a dream: "Bridge, did you say? Not unless you want to. . . . But I don't think I will, you know."

"Oh, no," Mrs. Ansley hastened to assure her. "I don't care to at all. It's so lovely here; and so full of old memories, as you say." She settled herself in her chair, and almost furtively drew forth her knitting. Mrs. Slade took sideway note of this activity, but her own beautifully cared-for hands remained motionless on her knee.

"I was just thinking," she said slowly, "what different things Rome stands for to each generation of travelers. To our grandmothers, Roman fever;[7] to our mothers, sentimental dangers—how we used to be guarded!—to our daughters, no more dangers than the middle of Main Street. They don't know it—but how much they're missing!"

The long golden light was beginning to pale, and Mrs. Ansley lifted her knitting a little closer to her eyes. "Yes; how we were guarded!"

6. Remains of imperial palaces on the Palatine Hill in Rome. "Memento Mori": "Remember you will die" (Latin); here, the phrase refers to the visible ruins of ancient Rome.
7. Malaria.

"I always used to think," Mrs. Slade continued, "that our mothers had a much more difficult job than our grandmothers. When Roman fever stalked the streets it must have been comparatively easy to gather in the girls at the danger hour; but when you and I were young, with such beauty calling us, and the spice of disobedience thrown in, and no worse risk than catching cold during the cool hour after sunset, the mothers used to be put to it to keep us in—didn't they?"

She turned again toward Mrs. Ansley, but the latter had reached a delicate point in her knitting. "One, two, three—slip two; yes, they must have been," she assented, without looking up.

Mrs. Slade's eyes rested on her with a deepened attention. "She can knit—in the face of *this*! How like her. . . ."

Mrs. Slade leaned back, brooding, her eyes ranging from the ruins which faced her to the long green hollow of the Forum, the fading glow of the church fronts beyond it, and the outlying immensity of the Colosseum.[8] Suddenly she thought: "It's all very well to say that our girls have done away with sentiment and moonlight. But if Babs Ansley isn't out to catch that young aviator—the one who's a Marchese[9]—then I don't know anything. And Jenny has no chance beside her. I know that too. I wonder if that's why Grace Ansley likes the two girls to go everywhere together? My poor Jenny as a foil—!" Mrs. Slade gave a hardly audible laugh, and at the sound Mrs. Ansley dropped her knitting.

"Yes—?"

"I—oh, nothing. I was only thinking how your Babs carries everything before her. That Campolieri boy is one of the best matches in Rome. Don't look so innocent, my dear—you know he is. And I was wondering, ever so respectfully, you understand . . . wondering how two such exemplary characters as you and Horace had managed to produce anything quite so dynamic." Mrs. Slade laughed again, with a touch of asperity.

Mrs. Ansley's hands lay inert across her needles. She looked straight out at the great accumulated wreckage of passion and splendor at her feet. But her small profile was almost expressionless. At length she said: "I think you overrate Babs, my dear."

Mrs. Slade's tone grew easier. "No; I don't. I appreciate her. And perhaps envy you. Oh, my girl's perfect; if I were a chronic invalid I'd—well, I think I'd rather be in Jenny's hands. There must be times . . . but there! I always wanted a brilliant daughter . . . and never quite understood why I got an angel instead."

Mrs. Ansley echoed her laugh in a faint murmur. "Babs is an angel too."

"Of course—of course! But she's got rainbow wings. Well, they're wandering by the sea with their young men; and here we sit . . . and it all brings back the past a little too acutely."

Mrs. Ansley had resumed her knitting. One might almost have imagined (if one had known her less well, Mrs. Slade reflected) that, for her also, too many memories rose from the lengthening shadows of those august ruins. But no; she was simply absorbed in her work. What was there for her to worry about? She knew that Babs would almost certainly come back engaged to the extremely eligible Campolieri. "And she'll sell the New York house, and settle

8. Ancient Roman amphitheater, known for its battles between gladiators and public executions of Christians.
9. That is, a marquis, a member of Italian nobility.

down near them in Rome, and never be in their way . . . she's much too tactful. But she'll have an excellent cook, and just the right people in for bridge
and cocktails . . . and a perfectly peaceful old age among her grandchildren."

Mrs. Slade broke off this prophetic flight with a recoil of self-disgust.
There was no one of whom she had less right to think unkindly than of Grace
Ansley. Would she never cure herself of envying her? Perhaps she had begun
too long ago.

She stood up and leaned against the parapet, filling her troubled eyes with
the tranquilizing magic of the hour. But instead of tranquilizing her the sight
seemed to increase her exasperation. Her gaze turned toward the Colosseum.
Already its golden flank was drowned in purple shadow, and above it the sky
curved crystal clear, without light or color. It was the moment when afternoon and evening hang balanced in mid-heaven.

Mrs. Slade turned back and laid her hand on her friend's arm. The gesture was so abrupt that Mrs. Ansley looked up, startled.

"The sun's set. You're not afraid, my dear?"

"Afraid—?"

"Of Roman fever or pneumonia? I remember how ill you were that winter. As a girl you had a very delicate throat, hadn't you?"

"Oh, we're all right up here. Down below, in the Forum, it does get deathly
cold, all of a sudden . . . but not here."

"Ah, of course you know because you had to be so careful." Mrs. Slade
turned back to the parapet. She thought: "I must make one more effort not
to hate her." Aloud she said: "Whenever I look at the Forum from up here,
I remember that story about a great-aunt of yours, wasn't she? A dreadfully
wicked great-aunt?"

"Oh, yes; great-aunt Harriet. The one who was supposed to have sent her
young sister out to the Forum after sunset to gather a night-blooming flower
for her album. All our great-aunts and grandmothers used to have albums
of dried flowers."

Mrs. Slade nodded. "But she really sent her because they were in love with
the same man—"

"Well, that was the family tradition. They said Aunt Harriet confessed it
years afterward. At any rate, the poor little sister caught the fever and died.
Mother used to frighten us with the story when we were children."

"And you frightened *me* with it, that winter when you and I were here as
girls. The winter I was engaged to Delphin."

Mrs. Ansley gave a faint laugh. "Oh, did I? Really frightened you? I don't
believe you're easily frightened."

"Not often; but I was then. I was easily frightened because I was too happy.
I wonder if you know what that means?"

"I—yes . . ." Mrs. Ansley faltered.

"Well, I suppose that was why the story of your wicked aunt made such
an impression on me. And I thought: 'There's no more Roman fever, but the
Forum is deathly cold after sunset—especially after a hot day. And the Colosseum's even colder and damper'."

"The Colosseum—?"

"Yes. It wasn't easy to get in, after the gates were locked for the night. Far
from easy. Still, in those days it could be managed; it *was* managed, often.
Lovers met there who couldn't meet elsewhere. You knew that?"

"I—I dare say. I don't remember."

"You don't remember? You don't remember going to visit some ruins or other one evening, just after dark, and catching a bad chill? You were supposed to have gone to see the moon rise. People always said that expedition was what caused your illness."

There was a moment's silence; then Mrs. Ansley rejoined: "Did they? It was all so long ago."

"Yes. And you got well again—so it didn't matter. But I suppose it struck your friends—the reason given for your illness, I mean—because everybody knew you were so prudent on account of your throat, and your mother took such care of you. . . . You *had* been out late sight-seeing, hadn't you, that night?"

"Perhaps I had. The most prudent girls aren't always prudent. What made you think of it now?"

Mrs. Slade seemed to have no answer ready. But after a moment she broke out: "Because I simply can't bear it any longer—!"

Mrs. Ansley lifted her head quickly. Her eyes were wide and very pale. "Can't bear what?"

"Why—your not knowing that I've always known why you went."

"Why I went—?"

"Yes. You think I'm bluffing, don't you? Well, you went to meet the man I was engaged to—and I can repeat every word of the letter that took you there."

While Mrs. Slade spoke Mrs. Ansley had risen unsteadily to her feet. Her bag, her knitting and gloves, slid in a panic-stricken heap to the ground. She looked at Mrs. Slade as though she were looking at a ghost.

"No, no—don't," she faltered out.

"Why not? Listen, if you don't believe me. 'My one darling, things can't go on like this. I must see you alone. Come to the Colosseum immediately after dark tomorrow. There will be somebody to let you in. No one whom you need fear will suspect'—but perhaps you've forgotten what the letter said?"

Mrs. Ansley met the challenge with an unexpected composure. Steadying herself against the chair she looked at her friend, and replied: "No; I know it by heart too."

"And the signature? 'Only *your* D.S.' Was that it? I'm right, am I? That was the letter that took you out that evening after dark?"

Mrs. Ansley was still looking at her. It seemed to Mrs. Slade that a slow struggle was going on behind the voluntarily controlled mask of her small quiet face. "I shouldn't have thought she had herself so well in hand," Mrs. Slade reflected, almost resentfully. But at this moment Mrs. Ansley spoke. "I don't know how you knew. I burnt that letter at once."

"Yes; you would, naturally—you're so prudent!" The sneer was open now. "And if you burnt the letter you're wondering how on earth I know what was in it. That's it, isn't it?"

Mrs. Slade waited, but Mrs. Ansley did not speak.

"Well, my dear, I know what was in that letter because I wrote it!"

"You wrote it?"

"Yes."

The two women stood for a minute staring at each other in the last golden light. Then Mrs. Ansley dropped back into her chair. "Oh," she murmured, and covered her face with her hands.

Mrs. Slade waited nervously for another word or movement. None came, and at length she broke out: "I horrify you."

Mrs. Ansley's hands dropped to her knee. The face they uncovered was streaked with tears. "I wasn't thinking of you. I was thinking—it was the only letter I ever had from him!"

"And I wrote it. Yes; I wrote it! But I was the girl he was engaged to. Did you happen to remember that?"

Mrs. Ansley's head drooped again. "I'm not trying to excuse myself . . . I remembered. . . ."

"And still you went?"

"Still I went."

Mrs. Slade stood looking down on the small bowed figure at her side. The flame of her wrath had already sunk, and she wondered why she had ever thought there would be any satisfaction in inflicting so purposeless a wound on her friend. But she had to justify herself.

"You do understand? I'd found out—and I hated you, hated you. I knew you were in love with Delphin—and I was afraid; afraid of you, of your quiet ways, your sweetness . . . your . . . well, I wanted you out of the way, that's all. Just for a few weeks; just till I was sure of him. So in a blind fury I wrote that letter . . . I don't know why I'm telling you now."

"I suppose," said Mrs. Ansley slowly, "it's because you've always gone on hating me."

"Perhaps. Or because I wanted to get the whole thing off my mind." She paused. "I'm glad you destroyed the letter. Of course I never thought you'd die."

Mrs. Ansley relapsed into silence, and Mrs. Slade, leaning above her, was conscious of a strange sense of isolation, of being cut off from the warm current of human communion. "You think me a monster!"

"I don't know. . . . It was the only letter I had, and you say he didn't write it?"

"Ah, how you care for him still!"

"I cared for that memory," said Mrs. Ansley.

Mrs. Slade continued to look down on her. She seemed physically reduced by the blow—as if, when she got up, the wind might scatter her like a puff of dust. Mrs. Slade's jealousy suddenly leapt up again at the sight. All these years the woman had been living on that letter. How she must have loved him, to treasure the mere memory of its ashes! The letter of the man her friend was engaged to. Wasn't it she who was the monster?

"You tried your best to get him away from me, didn't you? But you failed; and I kept him. That's all."

"Yes. That's all."

"I wish now I hadn't told you. I'd no idea you'd feel about it as you do; I thought you'd be amused. It all happened so long ago, as you say; and you must do me the justice to remember that I had no reason to think you'd ever taken it seriously. How could I, when you were married to Horace Ansley two months afterward? As soon as you could get out of bed your mother rushed you off to Florence and married you. People were rather surprised—

they wondered at its being done so quickly; but I thought I knew. I had an idea you did it out of *pique*—to be able to say you'd got ahead of Delphin and me. Girls have such silly reasons for doing the most serious things. And your marrying so soon convinced me that you'd never really cared."

"Yes. I suppose it would," Mrs. Ansley assented.

The clear heaven overhead was emptied of all its gold. Dusk spread over it, abruptly darkening the Seven Hills.[1] Here and there lights began to twinkle through the foliage at their feet. Steps were coming and going on the deserted terrace—waiters looking out of the doorway at the head of the stairs, then reappearing with trays and napkins and flasks of wine. Tables were moved, chairs straightened. A feeble string of electric lights flickered out. Some vases of faded flowers were carried away, and brought back replenished. A stout lady in a dust coat suddenly appeared, asking in broken Italian if anyone had seen the elastic band which held together her tattered Baedeker. She poked with her stick under the table at which she had lunched, the waiters assisting.

The corner where Mrs. Slade and Mrs. Ansley sat was still shadowy and deserted. For a long time neither of them spoke. At length Mrs. Slade began again: "I suppose I did it as a sort of joke—"

"A joke?"

"Well, girls are ferocious sometimes, you know. Girls in love especially. And I remember laughing to myself all that evening at the idea that you were waiting around there in the dark, dodging out of sight, listening for every sound, trying to get in.—Of course I was upset when I heard you were so ill afterward."

Mrs. Ansley had not moved for a long time. But now she turned slowly toward her companion. "But I didn't wait. He'd arranged everything. He was there. We were let in at once," she said.

Mrs. Slade sprang up from her leaning position. "Delphin there? They let you in?—Ah, now you're lying!" she burst out with violence.

Mrs. Ansley's voice grew clearer, and full of surprise. "But of course he was there. Naturally he came—"

"Came? How did he know he'd find you there? You must be raving!"

Mrs. Ansley hesitated, as though reflecting. "But I answered the letter. I told him I'd be there. So he came."

Mrs. Slade flung her hands up to her face. "Oh, God—you answered! I never thought of your answering. . . ."

"It's odd you never thought of it, if you wrote the letter."

"Yes. I was blind with rage."

Mrs. Ansley rose, and drew her fur scarf about her. "It is cold here. We'd better go . . . I'm sorry for you," she said, as she clasped the fur about her throat.

The unexpected words sent a pang through Mrs. Slade. "Yes; we'd better go." She gathered up her bag and cloak. "I don't know why you should be sorry for me," she muttered.

Mrs. Ansley stood looking away from her toward the dusky secret mass of the Colosseum. "Well—because I didn't have to wait that night."

1. The Seven Hills of Rome east of the Tiber River form the heart of the city.

Mrs. Slade gave an unquiet laugh. "Yes; I was beaten there. But I oughtn't to begrudge it to you, I suppose. At the end of all these years. After all, I had everything; I had him for twenty-five years. And you had nothing but that one letter that he didn't write."

Mrs. Ansley was again silent. At length she turned toward the door of the terrace. She took a step, and turned back, facing her companion.

"I had Barbara," she said, and began to move ahead of Mrs. Slade toward the stairway.

1934

SUI SIN FAR (EDITH MAUD EATON)
1865–1914

Writing at a time when Chinese were the target of both official exclusion and unofficial vitriol, Sui Sin Far is believed to be the first author of Chinese descent to publish in English in the United States. The second of sixteen children, fourteen of whom lived to adulthood, Far was born Edith Maud Eaton in Macclesfield, England, to a Chinese mother raised in England and a white English father from a well-to-do family. Her father, Edward Eaton, formerly a merchant, became alienated from his English family not long after his marriage to Grace Trefusus and struggled thereafter to earn a living as a landscape painter. When Far was seven the family moved first to New York State and then to Montreal. The family's fortunes began to decline when Far was eleven, and along with other siblings she was withdrawn from school to help support her parents and the younger children by selling, on the street, her father's paintings and her own crocheted lace. She continued to support family members for the rest of her life, though her income as a stenographer and freelance journalist barely covered her own modest needs, even as her health was always fragile, partly as a result of childhood rheumatic fever.

Sui Sin Far and her sister Winnifred were published while they were teenagers; two other sisters became painters, and another sister became the first Chinese American lawyer in Chicago. Winnifred, who wrote under the Japanese-sounding pseudonym Onoto Watanna, published the first Asian American novel, *Miss Nume of Japan*, in 1899, and was popular for many years as the author of sentimental and melodramatic novels.

Though Sui Sin Far began her writing career in Montreal, it was not until 1896, after she moved back to the United States, that she adopted her pseudonym, a literal translation of the symbol for waterlily as water fairy flower or, more generally, bulbs that can sprout and bloom in water. That same year she published her first story, in the American literary magazine *Fly Leaf*. From 1898 to 1909 she lived chiefly in Seattle, where her work as a journalist took her into the city's thriving Chinatown, a frequent setting for her stories. Far also lived briefly in San Francisco and other western U.S. cities, and she spent the final years of her life in Boston. Her stories, essays, and articles were published in newspapers and magazines throughout the United States, though her correspondence reveals the challenge of negotiating the literary marketplace faced by a Chinese American writer.

"Mrs. Spring Fragrance" was first published in *Hampton's Magazine* in January 1910. In 1912 it became the title story for the only book Sui Sin Far published, containing thirty-seven stories, articles, and sketches focusing on Chinese immigrants in late nineteenth-century America. The stories in *Mrs. Spring Fragrance*, set mainly in Seattle, often involve conflict within well-off merchant immigrant families when members of a family differ over the desirability or even the possibility of cultural assimilation in their new nation. One spouse is usually more devoted to traditional values than the other, while children are typically more eager to assimilate than their parents. As in "Mrs. Spring Fragrance," Far's stories frequently take place against a backdrop of an era when anti-Chinese prejudice was institutionalized through U.S. immigration policy. Like others writing about the pressures of Americanization, Sui Sin Far addresses questions of cultural identity, racism, and intergenerational conflict—all issues that have remained important to Asian American fiction in the century since her work first appeared.

Mrs. Spring Fragrance[1]

I

When Mrs. Spring Fragrance first arrived in Seattle, she was unacquainted with even one word of the American language. Five years later her husband, speaking of her, said: "There are no more American words for her learning." And everyone who knew Mrs. Spring Fragrance agreed with Mr. Spring Fragrance.

Mr. Spring Fragrance, whose business name was Sing Yook, was a young curio merchant. Though conservatively Chinese in many respects, he was at the same time what is called by the Westerners, "Americanized." Mrs. Spring Fragrance was even more "Americanized."

Next door to the Spring Fragrances lived the Chin Yuens. Mrs. Chin Yuen was much older than Mrs. Spring Fragrance; but she had a daughter of eighteen with whom Mrs. Spring Fragrance was on terms of great friendship. The daughter was a pretty girl whose Chinese name was Mai Gwi Far (a rose) and whose American name was Laura. Nearly everybody called her Laura, even her parents and Chinese friends. Laura had a sweetheart, a youth named Kai Tzu. Kai Tzu, who was American-born, and as ruddy and stalwart as any young Westerner, was noted amongst baseball players as one of the finest pitchers on the Coast. He could also sing, "Drink to me only with thine eyes,"[2] to Laura's piano accompaniment.

Now the only person who knew that Kai Tzu loved Laura and that Laura loved Kai Tzu, was Mrs. Spring Fragrance. The reason for this was that, although the Chin Yuen parents lived in a house furnished in American style, and wore American clothes, yet they religiously observed many Chinese customs, and their ideals of life were the ideals of their Chinese forefathers. Therefore, they had betrothed their daughter, Laura, at the age of fifteen, to the eldest son of the Chinese Government school-teacher in San Francisco. The time for the consummation of the betrothal was approaching.

1. The story was first published in the January 1910 *Hampton's Magazine*, based in New York City, and then republished in *Mrs. Spring Fragrance and Other Stories* (Chicago: A. C. McClurg, 1912), from which this text is taken.
2. Popular English folk song, which drew on Ben Jonson's (1572–1637) 1616 poem "Song to Celia."

Laura was with Mrs. Spring Fragrance and Mrs. Spring Fragrance was trying to cheer her.

"I had such a pretty walk today," said she. "I crossed the banks above the beach and came back by the long road. In the green grass the daffodils were blowing, in the cottage gardens the currant bushes were flowering, and in the air was the perfume of the wallflower. I wished, Laura, that you were with me."

Laura burst into tears. "That is the walk," she sobbed, "Kai Tzu and I so love; but never, ah, never, can we take it together again."

"Now, Little Sister," comforted Mrs. Spring Fragrance, "you really must not grieve like that. Is there not a beautiful American poem written by a noble American named Tennyson, which says:

> " 'Tis better to have loved and lost,
> Than never to have loved at all?"[3]

Mrs. Spring Fragrance was unaware that Mr. Spring Fragrance, having returned from the city, tired with the day's business, had thrown himself down on the bamboo settee on the veranda, and that although his eyes were engaged in scanning the pages of the *Chinese World*,[4] his ears could not help receiving the words which were borne to him through the open window.

> " 'Tis better to have loved and lost,
> Than never to have loved at all,"

repeated Mr. Spring Fragrance. Not wishing to hear more of the secret talk of women, he arose and sauntered around the veranda to the other side of the house. Two pigeons circled around his head. He felt in his pocket for a li-chi[5] which he usually carried for their pecking. His fingers touched a little box. It contained a jadestone pendant, which Mrs. Spring Fragrance had particularly admired the last time she was down town. It was the fifth anniversary of Mr. and Mrs. Spring Fragrance's wedding day.

Mr. Spring Fragrance pressed the little box down into the depths of his pocket.

A young man came out of the back door of the house at Mr. Spring Fragrance's left. The Chin Yuen house was at his right.

"Good evening," said the young man. "Good evening," returned Mr. Spring Fragrance. He stepped down from his porch and went and leaned over the railing which separated this yard from the yard in which stood the young man.

"Will you please tell me," said Mr. Spring Fragrance, "the meaning of two lines of an American verse which I have heard?"

"Certainly," returned the young man with a genial smile. He was a star student at the University of Washington, and had not the slightest doubt that he could explain the meaning of all things in the universe.

"Well," said Mr. Spring Fragrance, "it is this:

> " 'Tis better to have loved and lost,
> Than never to have loved at all."

---

3. From the English poet Alfred, Lord Tennyson's (1809–1892) *In Memoriam* (1850), an elegy for his beloved friend Arthur Hallam: "I hold it true, whate'er befall; / I feel it, when I sorrow most; / 'Tis better to have loved and lost / Than never to have loved at all" (canto 27, 13–16).
4. A newspaper published in San Francisco's Chinatown at the time in which the story is set.
5. Commonly spelled "lychee," this edible fruit is native to China.

"Ah!" responded the young man with an air of profound wisdom. "That, Mr. Spring Fragrance, means that it is a good thing to love anyway—even if we can't get what we love, or, as the poet tells us, lose what we love. Of course, one needs experience to feel the truth of this teaching."

The young man smiled pensively and reminiscently. More than a dozen young maidens "loved and lost" were passing before his mind's eye.

"The truth of the teaching!" echoed Mr. Spring Fragrance, a little testily. "There is no truth in it whatever. It is disobedient to reason. Is it not better to have what you do not love than to love what you do not have?"

"That depends," answered the young man, "upon temperament."

"I thank you. Good evening," said Mr. Spring Fragrance. He turned away to muse upon the unwisdom of the American way of looking at things.

Meanwhile, inside the house, Laura was refusing to be comforted.

"Ah, no! no!" cried she. "If I had not gone to school with Kai Tzu, nor talked nor walked with him, nor played the accompaniments to his songs, then I might consider with complacency, or at least without horror, my approaching marriage with the son of Man You. But as it is—oh, as it is—!"

The girl rocked herself to and fro in heartfelt grief.

Mrs. Spring Fragrance knelt down beside her, and clasping her arms around her neck, cried in sympathy:

"Little Sister, oh, Little Sister! Dry your tears—do not despair. A moon has yet to pass before the marriage can take place. Who knows what the stars may have to say to one another during its passing? A little bird has whispered to me—"

For a long time Mrs. Spring Fragrance talked. For a long time Laura listened. When the girl arose to go, there was a bright light in her eyes.

II

Mrs. Spring Fragrance, in San Francisco on a visit to her cousin, the wife of the herb doctor of Clay Street, was having a good time. She was invited everywhere that the wife of an honorable Chinese merchant could go. There was much to see and hear, including more than a dozen babies who had been born in the families of her friends since she last visited the city of the Golden Gate. Mrs. Spring Fragrance loved babies. She had had two herself, but both had been transplanted into the spirit land before the completion of even one moon. There were also many dinners and theatre-parties given in her honor. It was at one of the theatre-parties that Mrs. Spring Fragrance met Ah Oi, a young girl who had the reputation of being the prettiest Chinese girl in San Francisco, and the naughtiest. In spite of gossip, however, Mrs. Spring Fragrance took a great fancy to Ah Oi and invited her to a tête-à-tête picnic on the following day. This invitation Ah Oi joyfully accepted. She was a sort of bird girl and never felt so happy as when out in the park or woods.

On the day after the picnic Mrs. Spring Fragrance wrote to Laura Chin Yuen thus:

> MY PRECIOUS LAURA,—May the bamboo ever wave. Next week I accompany Ah Oi to the beauteous town of San José. There will we be met by the son of the Illustrious Teacher, and in a little Mission, presided over by a benevolent American priest, the little Ah Oi and the son

of the Illustrious Teacher will be joined together in love and harmony—two pieces of music made to complete one another.

The Son of the Illustrious Teacher, having been through an American Hall of Learning, is well able to provide for his orphan bride and fears not the displeasure of his parents, now that he is assured that your grief at his loss will not be inconsolable. He wishes me to waft to you and to Kai Tzu—and the little Ah Oi joins with him—ten thousand rainbow wishes for your happiness.

My respects to your honorable parents, and to yourself, the heart of your loving friend,

JADE SPRING FRAGRANCE

To Mr. Spring Fragrance, Mrs. Spring Fragrance also indited a letter:

GREAT AND HONORED MAN,—Greeting from your plum blossom,[6] who is desirous of hiding herself from the sun of your presence for a week of seven days more. My honorable cousin is preparing for the Fifth Moon Festival, and wishes me to compound for the occasion some American "fudge," for which delectable sweet, made by my clumsy hands, you have sometimes shown a slight prejudice. I am enjoying a most agreeable visit, and American friends, as also our own, strive benevolently for the accomplishment of my pleasure. Mrs. Samuel Smith, an American lady, known to my cousin, asked for my accompaniment to a magniloquent lecture the other evening. The subject was "America, the Protector of China!" It was most exhilarating, and the effect of so much expression of benevolence leads me to beg of you to forget to remember that the barber charges you one dollar for a shave while he humbly submits to the American man a bill of fifteen cents. And murmur no more because your honored elder brother, on a visit to this country, is detained under the roof-tree of this great Government instead of under your own humble roof.[7] Console him with the reflection that he is protected under the wing of the Eagle, the Emblem of Liberty. What is the loss of ten hundred years or ten thousand times ten dollars compared with the happiness of knowing oneself so securely sheltered? All of this I have learned from Mrs. Samuel Smith, who is as brilliant and great of mind as one of your own superior sex.

For me it is sufficient to know that the Golden Gate Park is most enchanting, and the seals on the rock at the Cliff House[8] extremely entertaining and amiable. There is much feasting and merry-making under the lanterns in honor of your Stupid Thorn.

I have purchased for your smoking a pipe with an amber mouth. It is said to be very sweet to the lips and to emit a cloud of smoke fit for the gods to inhale.

6. The plum blossom is the Chinese flower of virtue. It has been adopted by the Japanese, just in the same way as they have adopted the Chinese national flower, the chrysanthemum [Sui Sin Far's note].
7. The Chinese Exclusion Act of 1882 mandated the exclusion of Chinese immigrants, with few exceptions. Even Chinese who claimed U.S. citizenship were frequently held for lengthy detentions when entering the country. The act was repealed in 1943.
8. Famous restaurant on the Pacific shore at Point Lobos in San Francisco; it opened in 1863 and, because of its spectacular setting, became a favorite of locals and visitors.

Awaiting, by the wonderful wire of the telegram message, your gracious permission to remain for the celebration of the Fifth Moon Festival and the making of American "fudge," I continue for ten thousand times ten thousand years,

Your ever loving and obedient woman,

JADE

P.S. Forget not to care for the cat, the birds, and the flowers. Do not eat too quickly nor fan too vigorously now that the weather is warming.

Mrs. Spring Fragrance smiled as she folded this last epistle. Even if he were old-fashioned, there was never a husband so good and kind as hers. Only on one occasion since their marriage had he slighted her wishes. That was when, on the last anniversary of their wedding, she had signified a desire for a certain jadestone pendant, and he had failed to satisfy that desire.

But Mrs Spring Fragrance, being of a happy nature, and disposed to look upon the bright side of things, did not allow her mind to dwell upon the jadestone pendant. Instead, she gazed complacently down upon her bejeweled fingers and folded in with her letter to Mr. Spring Fragrance a bright little sheaf of condensed love.

III

Mr. Spring Fragrance sat on his doorstep. He had been reading two letters, one from Mrs. Spring Fragrance, and the other from an elderly bachelor cousin in San Francisco. The one from the elderly bachelor cousin was a business letter, but contained the following postscript:

Tsen Hing, the son of the Government schoolmaster, seems to be much in the company of your young wife. He is a good-looking youth, and pardon me, my dear cousin; but if women are allowed to stray at will from under their husbands' mulberry roofs, what is to prevent them from becoming butterflies?

"Sing Foon is old and cynical," said Mr. Spring Fragrance to himself. "Why should I pay any attention to him? This is America, where a man may speak to a woman, and a woman listen, without any thought of evil."

He destroyed his cousin's letter and re-read his wife's. Then he became very thoughtful. Was the making of American fudge sufficient reason for a wife to wish to remain a week longer in a city where her husband was not?

The young man who lived in the next house came out to water the lawn.

"Good evening," said he. "Any news from Mrs. Spring Fragrance?"

"She is having a very good time," returned Mr. Spring Fragrance.

"Glad to hear it. I think you told me she was to return the end of this week."

"I have changed my mind about her," said Mr. Spring Fragrance. "I am bidding her remain a week longer, as I wish to give a smoking party during her absence. I hope I may have the pleasure of your company."

"I shall be delighted," returned the young fellow. "But, Mr. Spring Fragrance, don't invite any other white fellows. If you do not I shall be able to get in a scoop. You know, I'm a sort of honorary reporter for the *Gleaner*."[9]

"Very well," absently answered Mr. Spring Fragrance.

"Of course, your friend the Consul will be present. I shall call it 'A high-class Chinese stag party!'"

In spite of his melancholy mood, Mr. Spring Fragrance smiled.

"Everything is 'high-class' in America," he observed.

"Sure!" cheerfully assented the young man. "Haven't you ever heard that all Americans are princes and princesses, and just as soon as a foreigner puts his foot upon our shores, he also becomes of the nobility—I mean, the royal family."

"What about my brother in the Detention Pen?" dryly inquired Mr. Spring Fragrance.

"Now, you've got me," said the young man, rubbing his head. "Well, that is a shame—'a beastly shame,' as the Englishman says. But understand, old fellow, we that are real Americans are up against that—even more than you. It is against our principles."

"I offer the real Americans my consolations that they should be compelled to do that which is against their principles."

"Oh, well, it will all come right some day. We're not a bad sort, you know. Think of the indemnity money returned to the Dragon by Uncle Sam."[1]

Mr. Spring Fragrance puffed his pipe in silence for some moments. More than politics was troubling his mind.

At last he spoke. "Love," said he, slowly and distinctly, "comes before the wedding in this country, does it not?"

"Yes, certainly."

Young Carman knew Mr. Spring Fragrance well enough to receive with calmness his most astounding queries.

"Presuming," continued Mr. Spring Fragrance—"presuming that some friend of your father's, living—presuming—in England—has a daughter that he arranges with your father to be your wife. Presuming that you have never seen that daughter, but that you marry her, knowing her not. Presuming that she marries you, knowing you not.—After she marries you and knows you, will that woman love you?"

"Emphatically, no," answered the young man.

"That is the way it would be in America—that the woman who marries the man like that—would not love him?"

"Yes, that is the way it would be in America. Love, in this country, must be free, or it is not love at all."

"In China, it is different!" mused Mr. Spring Fragrance.

"Oh, yes, I have no doubt that in China it is different."

9. Perhaps a reference to the *Weekly Gleaner*, a Jewish American newspaper in San Francisco that began publication in 1857, but "*Gleaner*" was also the generic name of a number of other newspapers.
1. Historically, the dragon was the symbol of the emperor of China, as Uncle Sam is a symbol of the United States. In the aftermath of the Boxer Rebellion (1898–1901), a protest against Western imperialism, the Chinese government agreed to pay reparations to several foreign powers. The United States returned a portion of what it received in the form of the Boxer Indemnity Scholarship Program, which provided financial support for Chinese students studying in America.

"But the love is in the heart all the same," went on Mr. Spring Fragrance.

"Yes, all the same. Everybody falls in love some time or another. Some"—pensively—"many times."

Mr. Spring Fragrance arose.

"I must go down town," said he.

As he walked down the street he recalled the remark of a business acquaintance who had met his wife and had had some conversation with her: "She is just like an American woman."

He had felt somewhat flattered when this remark had been made. He looked upon it as a compliment to his wife's cleverness; but it rankled in his mind as he entered the telegraph office. If his wife was becoming as an American woman, would it not be possible for her to love as an American woman—a man to whom she was not married? There also floated in his memory the verse which his wife had quoted to the daughter of Chin Yuen. When the telegraph clerk handed him a blank, he wrote this message:

"Remain as you wish, but remember that ' 'Tis better to have loved and lost, than never to have loved at all.'"

When Mrs. Spring Fragrance received this message, her laughter tinkled like falling water. How droll! How delightful! Here was her husband quoting American poetry in a telegram. Perhaps he had been reading her American poetry books since she had left him! She hoped so. They would lead him to understand her sympathy for her dear Laura and Kai Tzu. She need no longer keep from him their secret. How joyful! It had been such a hardship to refrain from confiding in him before. But discreetness had been most necessary, seeing that Mr. Spring Fragrance entertained as old-fashioned notions concerning marriage as did the Chin Yuen parents. Strange that that should be so, since he had fallen in love with her picture before *ever* he had seen her, just as she had fallen in love with his! And when the marriage veil was lifted and each beheld the other for the first time in the flesh, there had been no disillusion—no lessening of the respect and affection, which those who had brought about the marriage had inspired in each young heart.

Mrs. Spring Fragrance began to wish she could fall asleep and wake to find the week flown, and she in her own little home pouring tea for Mr. Spring Fragrance.

IV

Mr. Spring Fragrance was walking to business with Mr. Chin Yuen. As they walked they talked.

"Yes," said Mr. Chin Yuen, "the old order is passing away, and the new order is taking its place, even with us who are Chinese. I have finally consented to give my daughter in marriage to young Kai Tzu."

Mr. Spring Fragrance expressed surprise. He had understood that the marriage between his neighbor's daughter and the San Francisco schoolteacher's son was all arranged.

"So 'twas," answered Mr. Chin Yuen; "but it seems the young renegade, without consultation or advice, has placed his affections upon some untrustworthy female, and is so under her influence that he refuses to fulfil his parents' promise to me for him."

"So!" said Mr. Spring Fragrance. The shadow on his brow deepened.

"But," said Mr. Chin Yuen, with affable resignation, "it is all ordained by Heaven. Our daughter, as the wife of Kai Tzu, for whom she has long had a loving feeling, will not now be compelled to dwell with a mother-in-law and where her own mother is not. For that, we are thankful, as she is our only one and the conditions of life in this Western country are not as in China. Moreover, Kai Tzu, though not so much of a scholar as the teacher's son, has a keen eye for business and that, in America, is certainly much more desirable than scholarship. What do you think?"

"Eh! What!" exclaimed Mr. Spring Fragrance. The latter part of his companion's remarks had been lost upon him.

That day the shadow which had been following Mr. Spring Fragrance ever since he had heard his wife quote, " 'Tis better to have loved," etc., became so heavy and deep that he quite lost himself within it.

At home in the evening he fed the cat, the bird, and the flowers. Then, seating himself in a carved black chair—a present from his wife on his last birthday—he took out his pipe and smoked. The cat jumped into his lap. He stroked it softly and tenderly. It had been much fondled by Mrs. Spring Fragrance, and Mr. Spring Fragrance was under the impression that it missed her. "Poor thing!" said he. "I suppose you want her back!" When he arose to go to bed he placed the animal carefully on the floor, and thus apostrophized it:

"O Wise and Silent One, your mistress returns to you, but her heart she leaves behind her, with the Tommies in San Francisco."

The Wise and Silent One made no reply. He was not a jealous cat.

Mr. Spring Fragrance slept not that night; the next morning he ate not. Three days and three nights without sleep and food went by.

There was a springlike freshness in the air on the day that Mrs. Spring Fragrance came home. The skies overhead were as blue as Puget Sound stretching its gleaming length toward the mighty Pacific, and all the beautiful green world seemed to be throbbing with springing life.

Mrs. Spring Fragrance was never so radiant.

"Oh," she cried light-heartedly, "is it not lovely to see the sun shining so clear, and everything so bright to welcome me?"

Mr. Spring Fragrance made no response. It was the morning after the fourth sleepless night.

Mrs. Spring Fragrance noticed his silence, also his grave face.

"Everything—everyone is glad to see me but you," she declared, half seriously, half jestingly.

Mr. Spring Fragrance set down her valise. They had just entered the house.

"If my wife is glad to see me," he quietly replied, "I also am glad to see her!"

Summoning their servant boy, he bade him look after Mrs. Spring Fragrance's comfort.

"I must be at the store in half an hour," said he, looking at his watch. "There is some very important business requiring attention."

"What is the business?" inquired Mrs. Spring Fragrance, her lip quivering with disappointment.

"I cannot just explain to you," answered her husband.

Mrs. Spring Fragrance looked up into his face with honest and earnest eyes. There was something in his manner, in the tone of her husband's voice, which touched her.

"Yen," said she, "you do not look well. You are not well. What is it?"

Something arose in Mr. Spring Fragrance's throat which prevented him from replying.

"O darling one! O sweetest one!" cried a girl's joyous voice. Laura Chin Yuen ran into the room and threw her arms around Mrs. Spring Fragrance's neck.

"I spied you from the window," said Laura, "and I couldn't rest until I told you. We are to be married next week, Kai Tzu and I. And all through you, all through you—the sweetest jade jewel in the world!"

Mr. Spring Fragrance passed out of the room.

"So the son of the Government teacher and little Happy Love are already married," Laura went on, relieving Mrs. Spring Fragrance of her cloak, her hat, and her folding fan.

Mr. Spring Fragrance paused upon the doorstep.

"Sit down, Little Sister, and I will tell you all about it," said Mrs. Spring Fragrance, forgetting her husband for a moment.

When Laura Chin Yuen had danced away, Mr. Spring Fragrance came in and hung up his hat.

"You got back very soon," said Mrs. Spring Fragrance, covertly wiping away the tears which had begun to fall as soon as she thought herself alone.

"I did not go," answered Mr. Spring Fragrance. "I have been listening to you and Laura."

"But if the business is very important, do not you think you should attend to it?" anxiously queried Mrs. Spring Fragrance.

"It is not important to me now," returned Mr. Spring Fragrance. "I would prefer to hear again about Ah Oi and Man You and Laura and Kai Tzu."

"How lovely of you to say that!" exclaimed Mrs. Spring Fragrance, who was easily made happy. And she began to chat away to her husband in the friendliest and wifeliest fashion possible. When she had finished she asked him if he were not glad to hear that those who loved as did the young lovers whose secrets she had been keeping, were to be united; and he replied that indeed he was; that he would like every man to be as happy with a wife as he himself had ever been and ever would be.

"You did not always talk like that," said Mrs. Spring Fragrance slyly. "You must have been reading my American poetry books!"

"American poetry!" ejaculated Mr. Spring Fragrance almost fiercely, "American poetry is detestable, *abhorrable!*"

"Why! why!" exclaimed Mrs. Spring Fragrance, more and more surprised.

But the only explanation which Mr. Spring Fragrance vouchsafed was a jadestone pendant.

1910   1912

W. E. B. DU BOIS
1868–1963

No writer of the early twentieth century surpasses the influence of W. E. B. Du Bois on how Americans think, study, and talk about race in the United States. Unabashedly intellectual and political, Du Bois modeled practices that shaped the African American intelligentsia of the twentieth century, and his ideas contributed to the vocabulary that we still use to address questions of racial difference and inequality. As a writer, Du Bois was prolific and wide-ranging, and his influence on African American literature, philosophy, and political thought is still visible.

William Edward Burghardt Du Bois was born on February 23, 1868, in Great Barrington, Massachusetts. After his father deserted his family, Du Bois's mother—Mary Burghardt Du Bois—raised him with the help of her extended family. Du Bois attended predominantly white schools and churches as a child, and he later wrote that he did not experience discrimination as a child. In 1885, Du Bois traveled to the South for the first time, to Fisk University in Nashville, Tennessee, earning bachelor's degree in 1888. He then applied to Harvard University, where he earned a second bachelor's degree in 1890 and a master's degree in 1891. Before returning to Harvard to complete his doctorate, he studied at the University of Berlin (1892–94), where his studies influenced his thinking about both race and history. In 1895, he received his Ph.D. from Harvard, and his doctoral dissertation, *The Suppression of the African Slave Trade to the United States of America, 1638–1870*, was published the following year as the first volume in the Harvard Historical Studies series. By the time Du Bois completed his graduate studies his accomplishments were already considerable, but he could not secure an appointment at a major research university. He taught first instead at Wilberforce College in Ohio, at that time a small, poor, black college. There he offered Greek, Latin, German, and English—subjects far removed from his real interest in the emerging field of sociology. After spending a year at the University of Pennsylvania, where he did the research for *The Philadelphia Negro* (1899), considered to be the first sociological monograph on an African American community, Du Bois moved to Atlanta University in 1897. There, over the following thirteen years, he produced a steady stream of important studies of African American life. Dedicated to the rigorous, scholarly examination of the so-called Negro problem, Du Bois increasingly understood his scholarship and his activism to be intertwined. Writing for national publications such as the *Atlantic Monthly* and the *Dial*, Du Bois urged Americans to face the devastation that racial inequality was wreaking on the lives of African Americans.

Collecting several of these essays and adding new material, Du Bois published *The Souls of Black Folk* (1903), a book of signal importance in American intellectual history. The book combines autobiography, social science, political commentary, musicology, and even fiction to explore the implications of its dramatic and prophetic announcement that "the problem of the Twentieth Century is the problem of the color-line." In the first chapter, "Of Our Spiritual Strivings," Du Bois introduces a key concept that would inform his thinking for the rest of his career—the notion of the "twoness" of African Americans. "One ever feels his twoness," Du Bois asserts, "an American, a Negro; two souls, two thoughts, two unreconciled strivings; two warring ideals in one dark body, whose dogged strength alone keeps it from being torn asunder." This foundational observation described what Du Bois named "double-consciousness." Another of Du Bois's important ideas was the "Talented Tenth," the

W. E. B. Du Bois in his office at Atlanta University, c. 1905.

title of an essay he published as the second chapter of *The Negro Problem* (1903). By this phrase he meant a college-educated elite that could provide leadership for African Americans after Reconstruction. In this regard, the chapter in *The Souls of Black Folk* that particularly caused a stir when the volume was first published was the one that challenged—coolly and without rancor—the enormous authority and power that had accumulated in the hands of one black spokesman, Booker T. Washington. Washington had founded Tuskegee Institute in Alabama to train African Americans in basic agricultural and mechanical skills and had gained national prominence with his Atlanta Exposition speech in 1895. His address seemed to many people to accept disenfranchisement and segregation and settle for a low level of education in exchange for white "toleration" and economic cooperation. Although Du Bois had initially joined in the general approval of this kind of racial accommodation, by the early 1900s he had begun to reject Washington's position, and with the publication of *The Souls of Black Folk* his public defiance of Washington put the two men in lasting opposition. The almost immediate repudiation of *The Souls of Black Folk* by Washington's allies reinforced Du Bois's emerging radicalism; he became a leader in the Niagara Movement (1905), which aggressively demanded for African Americans the same civil rights enjoyed by white Americans.

In 1910 Du Bois left Atlanta for New York, where he served for the next quarter of a century as editor of the *Crisis*, the official publication of the newly formed National Association for the Advancement of Colored People (NAACP), an organization he helped create. Through this publication Du Bois reached an increasingly large audience—one hundred thousand by 1919—with powerful messages that argued the need for black development and white social enlightenment. He also continued to write in a variety of genres, including a novel about the southern cotton industry, *The Quest of the Golden Fleece* (1911); a massive historical study of *Black Reconstruction in America* (1935); and a full-length autobiography, *Dusk of Dawn: An Autobiography* (1940).

Frustrated by the lack of fundamental change and progress in the condition of African Americans, after 1920 Du Bois shifted his attention from the reform of race relations in America through research and political legislation to the search for longer-range worldwide economic solutions to the international problems of inequity among the races. He began a steady movement toward Pan-African and socialist perspectives that led to his joining the U.S. Communist Party in 1961 and, in the year of his death, becoming a citizen of Ghana. During these forty years he was extremely active as a politician, organizer, and diplomat, and he continued as a powerful writer of poetry, fiction, autobiography, essays, and scholarly works. When, in his last major speech, Martin Luther King Jr. spoke of Du Bois as "one of the most remarkable men of our time," he was uttering the verdict of history.

From The Souls of Black Folk[1]

The Forethought

Herein lie buried many things which if read with patience may show the strange meaning of being black here in the dawning of the Twentieth Century. This meaning is not without interest to you, Gentle Reader; for the problem of the Twentieth Century is the problem of the color-line.

I pray you, then, receive my little book in all charity, studying my words with me, forgiving mistake and foible for sake of the faith and passion that is in me, and seeking the grain of truth hidden there.

I have sought here to sketch, in vague, uncertain outline, the spiritual world in which ten thousand thousand Americans live and strive. First, in two chapters I have tried to show what Emancipation meant to them, and what was its aftermath. In a third chapter I have pointed out the slow rise of personal leadership, and criticised candidly the leader who bears the chief burden of his race to-day. Then, in two other chapters I have sketched in swift outline the two worlds within and without the Veil, and thus have come to the central problem of training men for life. Venturing now into deeper detail, I have in two chapters studied the struggles of the massed millions of the black peasantry, and in another have sought to make clear the present relations of the sons of master and man.

Leaving, then, the world of the white man, I have stepped within the Veil, raising it that you may view faintly its deeper recesses,—the meaning of its religion, the passion of its human sorrow, and the struggle of its greater souls. All this I have ended with a tale twice told but seldom written.

Some of these thoughts of mine have seen the light before in other guise. For kindly consenting to their republication here, in altered and extended form, I must thank the publishers of *The Atlantic Monthly, The World's Work, The Dial, The New World*, and the *Annals of the American Academy of Political and Social Science*.

Before each chapter, as now printed, stands a bar of the Sorrow Songs,[2]— some echo of haunting melody from the only American music which welled up from black souls in the dark past. And, finally, need I add that I who speak here am bone of the bone and flesh of the flesh of them that live within the Veil?

W. E. B. Du B.

Atlanta, Ga., Feb. 1, 1903.

---

1. *The Souls of Black Folk*, a compilation of nine previously printed and five unpublished essays, appeared first as a book in 1903, the source of the text printed here.
2. Du Bois's term for spirituals composed by southern slaves.

I. Of Our Spiritual Strivings

O water, voice of my heart, crying in the sand,
 All night long crying with a mournful cry,
As I lie and listen, and cannot understand
  The voice of my heart in my side or the voice of the sea,
 O water, crying for rest, is it I, is it I?
  All night long the water is crying to me.

Unresting water, there shall never be rest
 Till the last moon droop and the last tide fail,
And the fire of the end begin to burn in the west;
  And the heart shall be weary and wonder and cry like the sea,
 All life long crying without avail,
  As the water all night long is crying to me.

ARTHUR SYMONS[3]

Between me and the other world there is ever an unasked question: unasked by some through feelings of delicacy; by others through the difficulty of rightly framing it. All, nevertheless, flutter round it. They approach me in a half-hesitant sort of way, eye me curiously or compassionately, and then, instead of saying directly, How does it feel to be a problem? they say, I know an excellent colored man in my town; or, I fought at Mechanicsville;[4] or, Do not these Southern outrages make your blood boil? At these I smile, or am interested, or reduce the boiling to a simmer, as the occasion may require. To the real question, How does it feel to be a problem? I answer seldom a word.

And yet, being a problem is a strange experience,—peculiar even for one who has never been anything else, save perhaps in babyhood and in Europe. It is in the early days of rollicking boyhood that the revelation first bursts upon one, all in a day, as it were. I remember well when the shadow swept across me. I was a little thing, away up in the hills of New England, where the dark Housatonic winds between Hoosac and Taghkanic[5] to the sea. In a wee wooden schoolhouse, something put it into the boys' and girls' heads to buy gorgeous visiting-cards—ten cents a package—and exchange. The exchange was merry, till one girl, a tall newcomer, refused my card,—refused it peremptorily, with a glance. Then it dawned upon me with a certain suddenness that I was different from the others; or like, mayhap, in heart and life and longing, but shut out from their world by a vast veil. I had thereafter no desire to tear down that veil, to creep through; I held all beyond it in

---

3. English poet (1865–1945); the quotation is from "The Crying of Water" (1902). The music is an excerpt from the spiritual "Nobody Knows the Trouble I've Seen."
4. Civil War battle in Virginia, June 26, 1862, resulting in heavy Confederate losses.
5. Mountain ranges partly in western Massachusetts, where Du Bois grew up. The Housatonic is a river in western Massachussetts.

common contempt, and lived above it in a region of blue sky and great wandering shadows. That sky was bluest when I could beat my mates at examination-time, or beat them at a foot-race, or even beat their stringy heads. Alas, with the years all this fine contempt began to fade; for the worlds, I longed for, and all their dazzling opportunities, were theirs, not mine. But they should not keep these prizes, I said; some, all, I would wrest from them. Just how I would do it I could never decide: by reading law, by healing the sick, by telling the wonderful tales that swam in my head,—some way. With other black boys the strife was not so fiercely sunny: their youth shrunk into tasteless sycophancy, or into silent hatred of the pale world about them and mocking distrust of everything white; or wasted itself in a bitter cry, Why did God make me an outcast and a stranger in mine own house? The shades of the prison-house closed round about us all: walls strait and stubborn to the whitest, but relentlessly narrow, tall, and unscalable to sons of night who must plod darkly on in resignation, or beat unavailing palms against the stone, or steadily, half hopelessly, watch the streak of blue above.

After the Egyptian and Indian, the Greek and Roman, the Teuton and Mongolian, the Negro is a sort of seventh son, born with a veil, and gifted with second-sight in this American world,[6]—a world which yields him no true self-consciousness, but only lets him see himself through the revelation of the other world. It is a peculiar sensation, this double-consciousness, this sense of always looking at one's self through the eyes of others, of measuring one's soul by the tape of a world that looks on in amused contempt and pity. One ever feels his two-ness,—an American, a Negro; two souls, two thoughts, two unreconciled strivings; two warring ideals in one dark body, whose dogged strength alone keeps it from being torn asunder.

The history of the American Negro is the history of this strife,—this longing to attain self-conscious manhood, to merge his double self into a better and truer self. In this merging he wishes neither of the older selves to be lost. He would not Africanize America, for America has too much to teach the world and Africa. He would not bleach his Negro soul in a flood of white Americanism, for he knows that Negro blood has a message for the world. He simply wishes to make it possible for a man to be both a Negro and an American, without being cursed and spit upon by his fellows, without having the doors of Opportunity closed roughly in his face.

This, then, is the end of his striving: to be a co-worker in the kingdom of culture, to escape both death and isolation, to husband and use his best powers and his latent genius. These powers of body and mind have in the past been strangely wasted, dispersed, or forgotten. The shadow of a mighty Negro past flits through the tale of Ethiopia the Shadowy and of Egypt the Sphinx. Throughout history, the powers of single black men flash here and there like falling stars, and die sometimes before the world has rightly gauged their brightness. Here in America, in the few days since Emancipation, the black man's turning hither and thither in hesitant and doubtful striving has often made his very strength to lose effectiveness, to seem like absence of power, like weakness. And yet it is not weakness,—it is the contradiction of double aims. The double-aimed struggle of the black artisan—on the one hand to

---

6. In some folk traditions, a baby born with a caul—a membrane covering the face—is thought to be fortunate or to have special powers; likewise, a seventh son is often of special significance in folk traditions.

escape white contempt for a nation of mere hewers of wood and drawers of water, and on the other hand to plough and nail and dig for a poverty-stricken horde—could only result in making him a poor craftsman, for he had but half a heart in either cause. By the poverty and ignorance of his people, the Negro minister or doctor was tempted toward quackery and demagogy; and by the criticism of the other world, toward ideals that made him ashamed of his lowly tasks. The would-be black *savant*[7] was confronted by the paradox that the knowledge his people needed was a twice-told tale to his white neighbors, while the knowledge which would teach the white world was Greek to his own flesh and blood. The innate love of harmony and beauty that set the ruder souls of his people a-dancing and a-singing raised but confusion and doubt in the soul of the black artist; for the beauty revealed to him was the soul-beauty of a race which his larger audience despised, and he could not articulate the message of another people. This waste of double aims, this seeking to satisfy two unreconciled ideals, has wrought sad havoc with the courage and faith and deeds of ten thousand thousand people,—has sent them often wooing false gods and invoking false means of salvation, and at times has even seemed about to make them ashamed of themselves.

Away back in the days of bondage they thought to see in one divine event the end of all doubt and disappointment; few men ever worshipped Freedom with half such unquestioning faith as did the American Negro for two centuries. To him, so far as he thought and dreamed, slavery was indeed the sum of all villainies, the cause of all sorrow, the root of all prejudice; Emancipation was the key to a promised land of sweeter beauty than ever stretched before the eyes of wearied Israelites. In song and exhortation swelled one refrain—Liberty; in his tears and curses the God he implored had Freedom in his right hand. At last it came,—suddenly, fearfully, like a dream. With one wild carnival of blood and passion came the message in his own plaintive cadences:—

> "Shout, O children!
> Shout, you're free!
> For God has bought your liberty!"[8]

Years have passed away since then,—ten, twenty, forty; forty years of national life, forty years of renewal and development, and yet the swarthy spectre sits in its accustomed seat at the Nation's feast. In vain do we cry to this our vastest social problem:—

> "Take any shape but that, and my firm nerves
> Shall never tremble!"[9]

The Nation has not yet found peace from its sins; the freedman has not yet found in freedom his promised land. Whatever of good may have come in these years of change, the shadow of a deep disappointment rests upon the Negro people,—a disappointment all the more bitter because the unattained ideal was unbounded save by the simple ignorance of a lowly people.

The first decade was merely a prolongation of the vain search for freedom, the boon that seemed ever barely to elude their grasp,—like a tantalizing will-o'-the-wisp, maddening and misleading the headless host. The holocaust

---

7. Learned person.
8. Lines from a spiritual; the source has not been identified.
9. Shakespeare, *Macbeth* 3.2.99.

of war, the terrors of the Ku-Klux Klan, the lies of carpetbaggers,[1] the disorganization of industry, and the contradictory advice of friends and foes, left the bewildered serf with no new watchword beyond the old cry for freedom. As the time flew, however, he began to grasp a new idea. The ideal of liberty demanded for its attainment powerful means, and these the Fifteenth Amendment[2] gave him. The ballot, which before he had looked upon as a visible sign of freedom, he now regarded as the chief means of gaining and perfecting the liberty with which war had partially endowed him. And why not? Had not votes made war and emancipated millions? Had not votes enfranchised the freedmen? Was anything impossible to a power that had done all this? A million black men started with renewed zeal to vote themselves into the kingdom. So the decade flew away, the revolution of 1876[3] came, and left the half-free serf weary, wondering, but still inspired. Slowly but steadily, in the following years, a new vision began gradually to replace the dream of political power,—a powerful movement, the rise of another ideal to guide the unguided, another pillar of fire by night after a clouded day. It was the ideal of "book-learning"; the curiosity, born of compulsory ignorance, to know and test the power of the cabalistic[4] letters of the white man, the longing to know. Here at last seemed to have been discovered the mountain path to Canaan;[5] longer than the highway of Emancipation and law, steep and rugged, but straight, leading to heights high enough to overlook life.

Up the new path the advance guard toiled, slowly, heavily, doggedly; only those who have watched and guided the faltering feet, the misty minds, the dull understandings, of the dark pupils of these schools know how faithfully, how piteously, this people strove to learn. It was weary work. The cold statistician wrote down the inches of progress here and there, noted also where here and there a foot had slipped or some one had fallen. To the tired climbers, the horizon was ever dark, the mists were often cold, the Canaan was always dim and far away. If, however, the vistas disclosed as yet no goal, no resting-place, little but flattery and criticism, the journey at least gave leisure for reflection and self-examination; it changed the child of Emancipation to the youth with dawning self-consciousness, self-realization, self-respect. In those sombre forests of his striving his own soul rose before him, and he saw himself,—darkly as through a veil; and yet he saw in himself some faint revelation of his power, of his mission. He began to have a dim feeling that, to attain his place in the world, he must be himself, and not another. For the first time he sought to analyze the burden he bore upon his back, that deadweight of social degradation partially masked behind a half-named Negro problem. He felt his poverty; without a cent, without a home, without land, tools, or savings, he had entered into competition with rich, landed, skilled neighbors. To be a poor man is hard, but to be a poor race in a land of dollars is the very bottom of hardships. He felt the weight of his ignorance,—not simply of letters, but of life, of business, of the humanities; the accumulated

---

1. Used as an epithet in the South to describe Northerners who came to the South during Reconstruction to make money by exploiting conditions created by the devastation of the Civil War. Many carried luggage made of carpet materials. "Ku Klux Klan": a secretive and often violent white supremacist society founded in the South shortly after the Civil War.

2. Amendment to the Constitution passed in 1870 to guarantee and protect the voting rights of African American men.

3. Congressional opposition to the continuation of Reconstruction policies and programs after the national elections of 1876.

4. Indecipherable and mystical.

5. The Promised Land of the Israelites.

sloth and shirking and awkwardness of decades and centuries shackled his hands and feet. Nor was his burden all poverty and ignorance. The red stain of bastardy, which two centuries of systematic legal defilement of Negro women had stamped upon his race, meant not only the loss of ancient African chastity, but also the hereditary weight of a mass of corruption from white adulterers, threatening almost the obliteration of the Negro home.

A people thus handicapped ought not to be asked to race with the world, but rather allowed to give all its time and thought to its own social problems. But alas! while sociologists gleefully count his bastards and his prostitutes, the very soul of the toiling, sweating black man is darkened by the shadow of a vast despair. Men call the shadow prejudice, and learnedly explain it as the natural defence of culture against barbarism, learning against ignorance, purity against crime, the "higher" against the "lower" races. To which the Negro cries Amen! and swears that to so much of this strange prejudice as is founded on just homage to civilization, culture, righteousness, and progress, he humbly bows and meekly does obeisance. But before that nameless prejudice that leaps beyond all this he stands helpless, dismayed, and well-nigh speechless; before that personal disrespect and mockery, the ridicule and systematic humiliation, the distortion of fact and wanton license of fancy, the cynical ignoring of the better and the boisterous welcoming of the worse, the all-pervading desire to inculcate disdain for everything black, from Toussaint[6] to the devil,—before this there rises a sickening despair that would disarm and discourage any nation save that black host to whom "discouragement" is an unwritten word.

But the facing of so vast a prejudice could not but bring the inevitable self-questioning, self-disparagement, and lowering of ideals which ever accompany repression and breed in an atmosphere of contempt and hate. Whisperings and portents came borne upon the four winds: Lo! we are diseased and dying, cried the dark hosts; we cannot write, our voting is vain; what need of education, since we must always cook and serve? And the Nation echoed and enforced this self-criticism, saying: Be content to be servants, and nothing more; what need of higher culture for half-men? Away with the black man's ballot, by force or fraud,—and behold the suicide of a race! Nevertheless, out of the evil came something of good,—the more careful adjustment of education to real life, the clearer perception of the Negroes' social responsibilities, and the sobering realization of the meaning of progress.

So dawned the time of *Sturm und Drang:*[7] storm and stress to-day rocks our little boat on the mad waters of the world-sea; there is within and without the sound of conflict, the burning of body and rending of soul; inspiration strives with doubt, and faith with vain questionings. The bright ideals of the past,—physical freedom, political power, the training of brains and the training of hands,—all these in turn have waxed and waned, until even the last grows dim and overcast. Are they all wrong,—all false? No, not that, but each alone was over-simple and incomplete,—the dreams of a credulous race-childhood, or the fond imaginings of the other world which does not know and does not want to know our power. To be really true, all these ideals must be melted and welded into one. The training of the schools we need to-day more than ever,—

---

6. Toussaint L'Ouverture (1743–1803), slave-born Haitian soldier, patriot, and martyr to the liberation of Haiti from foreign control.
7. Storm and stress (German).

the training of deft hands, quick eyes and ears, and above all the broader, deeper, higher culture of gifted minds and pure hearts. The power of the ballot we need in sheer self-defence,—else what shall save us from a second slavery? Freedom, too, the long-sought, we still seek,—the freedom of life and limb, the freedom to work and think, the freedom to love and aspire. Work, culture, liberty,—all these we need, not singly but together, not successively but together, each growing and aiding each, and all striving toward that vaster ideal that swims before the Negro people, the ideal of human brotherhood, gained through the unifying ideal of Race; the ideal of fostering and developing the traits and talents of the Negro, not in opposition to or contempt for other races, but rather in large conformity to the greater ideals of the American Republic, in order that some day on American soil two world-races may give each to each those characteristics both so sadly lack. We the darker ones come even now not altogether empty-handed: there are to-day no truer exponents of the pure human spirit of the Declaration of Independence than the American Negroes; there is no true American music but the wild sweet melodies of the Negro slave; the American fairy tales and folk-lore are Indian and African; and, all in all, we black men seem the sole oasis of simple faith and reverence in a dusty desert of dollars and smartness. Will America be poorer if she replace her brutal dyspeptic blundering with light-hearted but determined Negro humility? or her coarse and cruel wit with loving jovial good-humor? or her vulgar music with the soul of the Sorrow Songs?

Merely a concrete test of the underlying principles of the great republic is the Negro Problem, and the spiritual striving of the freedmen's sons is the travail of souls whose burden is almost beyond the measure of their strength, but who bear it in the name of an historic race, in the name of this the land of their fathers' fathers, and in the name of human opportunity.

And now what I have briefly sketched in large outline let me on coming pages tell again in many ways, with loving emphasis and deeper detail, that men may listen to the striving in the souls of black folk.

* * *

III. Of Mr. Booker T. Washington and Others[8]

From birth till death enslaved; in word, in deed, unmanned!

• • • • • • • •

Hereditary bondsmen! Know ye not
Who would be free themselves must strike the blow?
—BYRON[9]

Easily the most striking thing in the history of the American Negro since 1876[1] is the ascendancy of Mr. Booker T. Washington. It began at the time when war memories and ideals were rapidly passing; a day of astonishing commercial development was dawning; a sense of doubt and hesitation overtook the freedmen's sons,—then it was that his leading began. Mr. Washington came, with a simple definite programme, at the psychological moment when the nation was a little ashamed of having bestowed so much sentiment on Negroes, and was concentrating its energies on Dollars. His programme of industrial education, conciliation of the South, and submission and silence as to civil and political rights, was not wholly original; the Free Negroes from 1830 up to war-time had striven to build industrial schools, and the American Missionary Association had from the first taught various trades; and Price[2] and others had sought a way of honorable alliance with the best of the Southerners. But Mr. Washington first indissolubly linked these things; he put enthusiasm, unlimited energy, and perfect faith into this programme, and changed it from a by-path into a veritable Way of Life. And the tale of the methods by which he did this is a fascinating study of human life.

It startled the nation to hear a Negro advocating such a programme after many decades of bitter complaint; it startled and won the applause of the South, it interested and won the admiration of the North; and after a confused murmur of protest, it silenced if it did not convert the Negroes themselves.

To gain the sympathy and cooperation of the various elements comprising the white South was Mr. Washington's first task; and this, at the time Tuskegee was founded, seemed, for a black man, well-nigh impossible. And

8. *Of Mr. Booker T. Washington and Others* was first published in *Guardian*, July 27, 1902, and then collected in *The Souls of Black Folk*. Booker T. Washington (1856–1915) founded and helped build Tuskegee Institute, a black college in Alabama, and became a powerful leader of and spokesman for black Americans, especially after his address at the Atlanta Exposition in 1895.
9. The epigraph is from *Childe Harold's Pilgrimage* (1812), Canto 2, 74.710, 76.720–21, by George Gordon, Lord Byron (1758–1824). The music is from the refrain of a black spiritual titled "A Great Camp-Meetin' in de Promised Land" (also called "There's a Great Camp Meeting" and "Walk Together Children"). The words of the refrain set to this music are

Going to mourn and never tire—
mourn and never tire, mourn and never tire.

1. Reconstruction ended in 1876; federal troops were withdrawn from the South, and black political power was essentially destroyed.
2. Joseph Charles Price (1854–1893), influential southern black educator and civil rights leader.

yet ten years later it was done in the word spoken at Atlanta: "In all things purely social we can be as separate as the five fingers, and yet one as the hand in all things essential to mutual progress." This "Atlanta Compromise"[3] is by all odds the most notable thing in Mr. Washington's career. The South interpreted it in different ways: the radicals received it as a complete surrender of the demand for civil and political equality; the conservatives, as a generously conceived working basis for mutual understanding. So both approved it, and to-day its author is certainly the most distinguished Southerner since Jefferson Davis, and the one with the largest personal following.

Next to this achievement comes Mr. Washington's work in gaining place and consideration in the North. Others less shrewd and tactful had formerly essayed to sit on these two stools and had fallen between them; but as Mr. Washington knew the heart of the South from birth and training, so by singular insight he intuitively grasped the spirit of the age which was dominating the North. And so thoroughly did he learn the speech and thought of triumphant commercialism, and the ideals of material prosperity, that the picture of a lone black boy poring over a French grammar amid the weeds and dirt of a neglected home soon seemed to him the acme of absurdities.[4] One wonders what Socrates and St. Francis of Assisi would say to this.

And yet this very singleness of vision and thorough oneness with his age is a mark of the successful man. It is as though Nature must needs make men narrow in order to give them force. So Mr. Washington's cult has gained unquestioning followers, his work has wonderfully prospered, his friends are legion, and his enemies are confounded. To-day he stands as the one recognized spokesman of his ten million fellows, and one of the most notable figures in a nation of seventy millions. One hesitates, therefore, to criticise a life which, beginning with so little, has done so much. And yet the time is come when one may speak in all sincerity and utter courtesy of the mistakes and shortcomings of Mr. Washington's career, as well as of his triumphs, without being thought captious or envious, and without forgetting that it is easier to do ill than well in the world.

The criticism that has hitherto met Mr. Washington has not always been of this broad character. In the South especially has he had to walk warily to avoid the harshest judgments,—and naturally so, for he is dealing with the one subject of deepest sensitiveness to that section. Twice—once when at the Chicago celebration of the Spanish-American War he alluded to the color-prejudice that is "eating away the vitals of the South," and once when he dined with President Roosevelt[5]—has the resulting Southern criticism been violent enough to threaten seriously his popularity. In the North the feeling has several times forced itself into words, that Mr. Washington's

---

3. In a speech at the Atlanta Exposition of 1895, Washington in effect traded political, civil, and social rights for blacks for the promise of vocational-training schools and jobs. His purpose was to reduce racial tension in the South while providing a stable black labor force whose skills would provide job security. The speech appears in chapter XIV of Washington's *Up from Slavery*, reprinted on pages 471–74 of this volume.
4. In Washington's *Up from Slavery* (1901), chapter VIII, "Teaching School in a Stable and a Hen-House," there is a passage on the absurdity of knowledge not practically useful:

In fact, one of the saddest things I saw during the month of travel which I have described was a young man, who had attended some high school, sitting down in a one-room cabin, with grease on his clothing, filth all around him, and weeds in the yard and garden, engaged in studying French grammar.

5. Theodore Roosevelt (1858–1919), twenty-sixth president of the United States (1901–09). Washington's dining with him at the White House in 1901 caused controversy around the country.

counsels of submission overlooked certain elements of true manhood, and that his educational programme was unnecessarily narrow. Usually, however, such criticism has not found open expression, although, too, the spiritual sons of the Abolitionists have not been prepared to acknowledge that the schools founded before Tuskegee,[6] by men of broad ideals and self-sacrificing spirit, were wholly failures or worthy of ridicule. While, then, criticism has not failed to follow Mr. Washington, yet the prevailing public opinion of the land has been but too willing to deliver the solution of a wearisome problem into his hands, and say, "If that is all you and your race ask, take it."

Among his own people, however, Mr. Washington has encountered the strongest and most lasting opposition, amounting at times to bitterness, and even to-day continuing strong and insistent even though largely silenced in outward expression by the public opinion of the nation. Some of this opposition is, of course, mere envy; the disappointment of displaced demagogues and the spite of narrow minds. But aside from this, there is among educated and thoughtful colored men in all parts of the land a feeling of deep regret, sorrow, and apprehension at the wide currency and ascendancy which some of Mr. Washington's theories have gained. These same men admire his sincerity of purpose, and are willing to forgive much to honest endeavor which is doing something worth the doing. They coöperate with Mr. Washington as far as they conscientiously can; and, indeed, it is no ordinary tribute to this man's tact and power that, steering as he must between so many diverse interests and opinions, he so largely retains the respect of all.

But the hushing of the criticism of honest opponents is a dangerous thing. It leads some of the best of the critics to unfortunate silence and paralysis of effort, and others to burst into speech so passionately and intemperately as to lose listeners. Honest and earnest criticism from those whose interests are most nearly touched,—criticism of writers by readers, of government by those governed, of leaders by those led,—this is the soul of democracy and the safeguard of modern society. If the best of the American Negroes receive by outer pressure a leader whom they had not recognized before, manifestly there is here a certain palpable gain. Yet there is also irreparable loss,—a loss of that peculiarly valuable education which a group receives when by search and criticism it finds and commissions its own leaders. The way in which this is done is at once the most elementary and the nicest problem of social growth. History is but the record of such group-leadership; and yet how infinitely changeful is its type and character! And of all types and kinds, what can be more instructive than the leadership of a group within a group?—that curious double movement where real progress may be negative and actual advance be relative retrogression. All this is the social student's inspiration and despair.

Now in the past the American Negro has had instructive experience in the choosing of group leaders, founding thus a peculiar dynasty which in the light of present conditions is worth while studying. When sticks and stones and beasts form the sole environment of a people, their attitude is largely one of determined opposition to and conquest of natural forces. But when to earth and brute is added an environment of men and ideas, then

6. The Tuskegee Institute in Alabama, a school for African Americans that Washington led beginning in 1881.

the attitude of the imprisoned group may take three main forms,—a feeling of revolt and revenge; an attempt to adjust all thought and action to the will of the greater group; or, finally, a determined effort at self-realization and self-development despite environing opinion. The influence of all of these attitudes at various times can be traced in the history of the American Negro, and in the evolution of his successive leaders.

Before 1750, while the fire of African freedom still burned in the veins of the slaves, there was in all leadership or attempted leadership but the one motive of revolt and revenge,—typified in the terrible Maroons, the Danish blacks, and Cato[7] of Stono, and veiling all the Americas in fear of insurrection. The liberalizing tendencies of the latter half of the eighteenth century brought, along with kindlier relations between black and white, thoughts of ultimate adjustment and assimilation. Such aspiration was especially voiced in the earnest songs of Phyllis, in the martyrdom of Attucks, the fighting of Salem and Poor, the intellectual accomplishments of Banneker and Derham, and the political demands of the Cuffes.[8]

Stern financial and social stress after the war cooled much of the previous humanitarian ardor. The disappointment and impatience of the Negroes at the persistence of slavery and serfdom voiced itself in two movements. The slaves in the South, aroused undoubtedly by vague rumors of the Haytian revolt, made three fierce attempts at insurrection,—in 1800 under Gabriel in Virginia, in 1822 under Vesey in Carolina, and in 1831 again in Virginia under the terrible Nat Turner.[9] In the Free States, on the other hand, a new and curious attempt at self-development was made. In Philadelphia and New York color-prescription led to a withdrawal of Negro communicants from white churches and the formation of a peculiar socio-religious institution among the Negroes known as the African Church,—an organization still living and controlling in its various branches over a million of men.

Walker's wild appeal[1] against the trend of the times showed how the world was changing after the coming of the cotton-gin. By 1830 slavery seemed hopelessly fastened on the South, and the slaves thoroughly cowed into submission. The free Negroes of the North, inspired by the mulatto immigrants from the West Indies, began to change the basis of their demands; they recognized the slavery of slaves, but insisted that they themselves were freemen, and sought assimilation and amalgamation with the nation on the same terms with other men.

7. The leader of the Stono, South Carolina, slave revolt of September 9, 1739, in which twenty-five whites were killed. "Maroons": fugitive slaves from the West Indies and Guiana in the 17th and 18th centuries, or their descendants. Many of the slaves in the Danish West Indies revolted in 1733 because of the lack of sufficient food.
8. Paul Cuffe (1759–1817) organized to resettle free blacks in African colonies. A champion of civil rights for free blacks in Massachusetts, he took thirty-eight blacks to Africa in 1815 at his own expense. Phyllis (or Phillis) Wheatley (c. 1753–1784), black slave and poet. Crispus Attucks (c. 1723–1770) was killed in the Boston massacre. Peter Salem (d. 1816), black patriot who killed Major Pitcairn in the battle of Bunker Hill. Salem Poor (b. 1747), a black soldier who fought at Bunker Hill, Valley Forge, and White Plains. Benjamin Banneker (1731–1806), a black mathematician who also studied astronomy.

James Derham (b. 1762), the first recognized black physician in America; born a slave, he learned medicine from his physician master, bought his freedom in 1783, and by 1788 was one of the foremost physicians of New Orleans.
9. A slave (1800–1831), he led the Southampton insurrection in 1831, during which approximately sixty whites and more than a hundred slaves were killed or executed. Gabriel (1775?–1800) conspired to attack Richmond, Virginia, with a thousand other slaves on August 30, 1800; but a storm forced a suspension of the mission and two slaves betrayed the conspiracy. On October 7, Gabriel and fifteen others were hanged. Denmark Vesey (c. 1767–1822) purchased his freedom in 1800; he led an unsuccessful uprising in 1822 and was hanged.
1. A revolutionary and eloquent antislavery pamphlet by the black leader David Walker (1785–1830).

Thus, Forten and Purvis of Philadelphia, Shad of Wilmington, Du Bois of New Haven, Barbadoes[2] of Boston, and others, strove singly and together as men, they said, not as slaves; as "people of color," not as "Negroes." The trend of the times, however, refused them recognition save in individual and exceptional cases, considered them as one with all the despised blacks, and they soon found themselves striving to keep even the rights they formerly had of voting and working and moving as freemen. Schemes of migration and colonization arose among them; but these they refused to entertain, and they eventually turned to the Abolition movement as a final refuge.

Here, led by Remond, Nell, Wells-Brown, and Douglass,[3] a new period of self-assertion and self-development dawned. To be sure, ultimate freedom and assimilation was the ideal before the leaders, but the assertion of the manhood rights of the Negro by himself was the main reliance, and John Brown's raid was the extreme of its logic. After the war and emancipation, the great form of Frederick Douglass, the greatest of American Negro leaders, still led the host. Self-assertion, especially in political lines, was the main programme, and behind Douglass came Elliot, Bruce, and Langston, and the Reconstruction politicians, and, less conspicuous but of greater social significance Alexander Crummell and Bishop Daniel Payne.[4]

Then came the Revolution of 1876, the suppression of the Negro votes, the changing and shifting of ideals, and the seeking of new lights in the great night. Douglass, in his old age, still bravely stood for the ideals of his early manhood,—ultimate assimilation *through* self-assertion, and on no other terms. For a time Price arose as a new leader, destined, it seemed, not to give up, but to re-state the old ideals in a form less repugnant to the white South. But he passed away in his prime. Then came the new leader. Nearly all the former ones had become leaders by the silent suffrage of their fellows, had sought to lead their own people alone, and were usually, save Douglass, little known outside their race. But Booker T. Washington arose as essentially the leader not of one race but of two,—a compromiser between the South, the North, and the Negro. Naturally the Negroes resented, at first bitterly, signs of compromise which surrendered their civil and political rights, even though this was to be exchanged for larger chances of economic development. The rich and dominating North, however, was not only

2. James G. Barbadoes was one of those present at the first National Negro Convention along with Forten, Purvis, Shadd, and others. James Forten (1766–1842), black civic leader and philanthropist. Robert Purvis (1810–1898), abolitionist, helped found the American Anti-Slavery Society in 1833 and was the president of the Underground Railway. Abraham Shadd, abolitionist, was on the first board of managers of the American Anti-Slavery Society, a delegate from Delaware for the first National Negro Convention (1830), and president of the third one in 1833. Alexander Du Bois (1803–1887), paternal grandfather of W. E. B. Du Bois, helped form the Negro Episcopal Parish of St. Luke in 1847 and was the senior warden there.
3. Frederick Douglass (1818–1895), abolitionist and orator and born a slave, was U.S. minister to Haiti and U.S. marshal of the District of Columbia. Charles Lenox Remond (1810–1873), black leader. William Cooper Nell (1816–1874), abolitionist, writer, and first African American to hold office under the government of the United States (clerk in the post office). Through his efforts equal school privileges were obtained for black children in Boston. William Wells Brown (1814–1884) published *Clotel* in 1853, the first novel by a black American, and *The Escape* in 1858, the first play by a black American.
4. Daniel Alexander Payne (1811–1893), bishop of the African Methodist Episcopal church and president of Wilberforce University (1863–76). Robert Brown Elliot (1842–1884), black politician, graduate of Eton, South Carolina congressman in the U.S. House of Representatives. Blanche K. Bruce (1841–1898), born a slave, first black man to serve a full term in the U.S. Senate (1875–81). John Mercer Langston (1829–1897), congressman, lawyer, diplomat, educator, born a slave. Crummell (1819–1898), clergyman of the Protestant Episcopal church, missionary in Liberia for twenty years and then in Washington, D.C.

weary of the race problem, but was investing largely in Southern enterprises, and welcomed any method of peaceful coöperation. Thus, by national opinion, the Negroes began to recognize Mr. Washington's leadership; and the voice of criticism was hushed.

Mr. Washington represents in Negro thought the old attitude of adjustment and submission; but adjustment at such a peculiar time as to make his programme unique. This is an age of unusual economic development, and Mr. Washington's programme naturally takes an economic cast, becoming a gospel of Work and Money to such an extent as apparently almost completely to overshadow the higher aims of life. Moreover, this is an age when the more advanced races are coming in closer contact with the less developed races, and the race-feeling is therefore intensified; and Mr. Washington's programme practically accepts the alleged inferiority of the Negro races. Again, in our own land, the reaction from the sentiment of war time has given impetus to race-prejudice against Negroes, and Mr. Washington withdraws many of the high demands of Negroes as men and American citizens. In other periods of intensified prejudice all the Negro's tendency to self-assertion has been called forth; at this period a policy of submission is advocated. In the history of nearly all other races and peoples the doctrine preached at such crises has been that manly self-respect is worth more than lands and houses, and that a people who voluntarily surrender such respect, or cease striving for it, are not worth civilizing.

In answer to this, it has been claimed that the Negro can survive only through submission. Mr. Washington distinctly asks that black people give up, at least for the present, three things,—

First, political power,

Second, insistence on civil rights,

Third, higher education of Negro youth,—

and concentrate all their energies on industrial education, the accumulation of wealth, and the conciliation of the South. This policy has been courageously and insistently advocated for over fifteen years, and has been triumphant for perhaps ten years. As a result of this tender of the palm-branch, what has been the return? In these years there have occurred:

1. The disfranchisement of the Negro.

2. The legal creation of a distinct status of civil inferiority for the Negro.

3. The steady withdrawal of aid from institutions for the higher training of the Negro.

These movements are not, to be sure, direct results of Mr. Washington's teachings; but his propaganda has, without a shadow of doubt, helped their speedier accomplishment. The question then comes: Is it possible, and probable, that nine millions of men can make effective progress in economic lines if they are deprived of political rights, made a servile caste, and allowed only the most meagre chance for developing their exceptional men? If history and reason give any distinct answer to these questions, it is an emphatic *No.* And Mr. Washington thus faces the triple paradox of his career:

1. He is striving nobly to make Negro artisans business men and property-owners; but it is utterly impossible, under modern competitive methods, for

workingmen and property-owners to defend their rights and exist without the right of suffrage.

2. He insists on thrift and self-respect, but at the same time counsels a silent submission to civic inferiority such as is bound to sap the manhood of any race in the long run.

3. He advocates common-school[5] and industrial training, and depreciates institutions of higher learning; but neither the Negro common-schools, nor Tuskegee itself, could remain open a day were it not for teachers trained in Negro colleges, or trained by their graduates.

This triple paradox in Mr. Washington's position is the object of criticism by two classes of colored Americans. One class is spiritually descended from Toussaint the Savior,[6] through Gabriel, Vesey, and Turner, and they represent the attitude of revolt and revenge; they hate the white South blindly and distrust the white race generally, and so far as they agree on definite action, think that the Negro's only hope lies in emigration beyond the borders of the United States. And yet, by the irony of fate, nothing has more effectually made this programme seem hopeless than the recent course of the United States toward weaker and darker peoples in the West Indies, Hawaii, and the Philippines,—for where in the world may we go and be safe from lying and brute force?

The other class of Negroes who cannot agree with Mr. Washington has hitherto said little aloud. They deprecate the sight of scattered counsels, of internal disagreement; and especially they dislike making their just criticism of a useful and earnest man an excuse for a general discharge of venom from small-minded opponents. Nevertheless, the questions involved are so fundamental and serious that it is difficult to see how men like the Grimkes, Kelly Miller, J. W. E. Bowen[7] and other representatives of this group, can much longer be silent. Such men feel in conscience bound to ask of this nation three things:

1. The right to vote.
2. Civic equality.
3. The education of youth according to ability.

They acknowledge Mr. Washington's invaluable service in counselling patience and courtesy in such demands; they do not ask that ignorant black men vote when ignorant whites are debarred, or that any reasonable restrictions in the suffrage should not be applied; they know that the low social level of the mass of the race is responsible for much discrimination against it, but they also know, and the nation knows, that relentless color-prejudice is more often a cause than a result of the Negro's degradation; they seek the abatement of this relic of barbarism, and not its systematic encouragement and pampering by all agencies of social power from the Associated Press to the Church of Christ. They advocate, with Mr. Washington, a broad system of Negro common schools supplemented by thorough industrial training; but they are surprised that a man of

5. A free free public school offering courses at pre-college level.
6. Toussaint L'Ouverture; see n. 6, p. 566.
7. John Wesley Edward Bowen (1855–?), Methodist clergyman and educator, president of Gammon Theological Seminary of Atlanta.

Archibald Grimké (1849–1930) and Francis Grimké (1850–1937), American civic leaders concerned with African American affairs. Miller (1863–1939), dean of Howard University, lectured on the race problem.

Mr. Washington's insight cannot see that no such educational system ever has rested or can rest on any other basis than that of the well-equipped college and university, and they insist that there is a demand for a few such institutions throughout the South to train the best of the Negro youth as teachers, professional men, and leaders.

This group of men honor Mr. Washington for his attitude of conciliation toward the white South; they accept the "Atlanta Compromise" in its broadest interpretation; they recognize, with him, many signs of promise, many men of high purpose and fair judgment, in this section; they know that no easy task has been laid upon a region already tottering under heavy burdens. But, nevertheless, they insist that the way to truth and right lies in straightforward honesty, not in indiscriminate flattery; in praising those of the South who do well and criticising uncompromisingly those who do ill; in taking advantage of the opportunities at hand and urging their fellows to do the same, but at the same time in remembering that only a firm adherence to their higher ideals and aspirations will ever keep those ideals within the realm of possibility. They do not expect that the free right to vote, to enjoy civic rights, and to be educated, will come in a moment; they do not expect to see the bias and prejudices of years disappear at the blast of a trumpet; but they are absolutely certain that the way for a people to gain their reasonable rights is not by voluntarily throwing them away and insisting that they do not want them; that the way for a people to gain respect is not by continually belittling and ridiculing themselves; that, on the contrary, Negroes must insist continually, in season and out of season, that voting is necessary to modern manhood, that color discrimination is barbarism, and that black boys need education as well as white boys.

In failing thus to state plainly and unequivocally the legitimate demands of their people, even at the cost of opposing an honored leader, the thinking classes of American Negroes would shirk a heavy responsibility,—a responsibility to themselves, a responsibility to the struggling masses, a responsibility to the darker races of men whose future depends so largely on this American experiment, but especially a responsibility to this nation,—this common Fatherland. It is wrong to encourage a man or a people in evil-doing; it is wrong to aid and abet a national crime simply because it is unpopular not to do so. The growing spirit of kindliness and reconciliation between the North and South after the frightful differences of a generation ago ought to be a source of deep congratulation to all, and especially to those whose mistreatment caused the war; but if that reconciliation is to be marked by the industrial slavery and civic death of those same black men, with permanent legislation into a position of inferiority, then those black men, if they are really men, are called upon by every consideration of patriotism and loyalty to oppose such a course by all civilized methods, even though such opposition involves disagreement with Mr. Booker T. Washington. We have no right to sit silently by while the inevitable seeds are sown for a harvest of disaster to our children, black and white.

First, it is the duty of black men to judge the South discriminatingly. The present generation of Southerners are not responsible for the past, and they should not be blindly hated or blamed for it. Furthermore, to no class is the indiscriminate endorsement of the recent course of the South toward Negroes more nauseating than to the best thought of the South. The South is not "solid";[8] it is a land in the ferment of social change, wherein forces of all kinds are fighting for supremacy; and to praise the ill the South is to-day perpetrating is just as wrong as to condemn the good. Discriminating and broad-minded criticism is what the South needs,—needs it for the sake of her own white sons and daughters, and for the insurance of robust, healthy mental and moral development.

To-day even the attitude of the Southern whites toward the blacks is not, as so many assume, in all cases the same; the ignorant Southerner hates the Negro, the workingmen fear his competition, the money-makers wish to use him as a laborer, some of the educated see a menace in his upward development, while others—usually the sons of the masters—wish to help him to rise. National opinion has enabled this last class to maintain the Negro common schools, and to protect the Negro partially in property, life, and limb. Through the pressure of the money-makers, the Negro is in danger of being reduced to semi-slavery, especially in the country districts; the workingmen, and those of the educated who fear the Negro, have united to disfranchise him, and some have urged his deportation; while the passions of the ignorant are easily aroused to lynch and abuse any black man. To praise this intricate whirl of thought and prejudice is nonsense; to inveigh indiscriminately against "the South" is unjust; but to use the same breath in praising Governor Aycock, exposing Senator Morgan, arguing with Mr. Thomas Nelson Page, and denouncing Senator Ben Tillman[9] is not only sane, but the imperative duty of thinking black men.

It would be unjust to Mr. Washington not to acknowledge that in several instances he has opposed movements in the South which were unjust to the Negro; he sent memorials to the Louisiana and Alabama constitutional conventions, he has spoken against lynching, and in other ways has openly or silently set his influence against sinister schemes and unfortunate happenings. Notwithstanding this, it is equally true to assert that on the whole the distinct impression left by Mr. Washington's propaganda is, first, that the South is justified in its present attitude toward the Negro because of the Negro's degradation; secondly, that the prime cause of the Negro's failure to rise more quickly is his wrong education in the past; and, thirdly, that his future rise depends primarily on his own efforts. Each of these propositions is a dangerous half-truth. The supplementary truths must never be lost sight of: first, slavery and race-prejudice are potent if not sufficient causes of the Negro's position; second, industrial and common-school training were necessarily slow in planting because they had to await the black teachers trained by higher institutions,—it being extremely doubtful if any essentially different development was possible, and certainly a Tuskegee was unthinkable

---

8. The "solid South" referred to the supposedly unified support of white Southerners for the Democratic party, offering the Democrats a "solid" voting block. The phrase was popularized during the 1876 election that proved to be the end of Reconstruction.

9. Benjamin Ryan Tillman (1847–1918), governor of South Carolina (1890–94) and U.S. Senator (1895–1918), served as the chairman on the committee on suffrage (during the South Carolina constitutional convention) and framed the article providing for an educational and property qualification for voting, thus eliminating the black vote.

He presented the views of the southern extremists on the race question, justified lynching in cases of rape and the use of force to disenfranchise blacks, and advocated the repeal of the Fifteenth Amendment. Charles Brantley Aycock (1859–1912), governor of North Carolina (1901–05). Edwin Denison Morgan (1811–1883), governor of New York (1859–63) and U.S. senator (1863–69), voted with the minority in President Andrew Johnson's veto of the Freedman's Bureau bill and for Johnson's conviction. Page (1853–1922), American novelist and diplomat, did much to build up romantic legends of the southern plantation.

before 1880; and, third, while it is a great truth to say that the Negro must strive and strive mightily to help himself, it is equally true that unless his striving be not simply seconded, but rather aroused and encouraged, by the initiative of the richer and wiser environing group, he cannot hope for great success.

In his failure to realize and impress this last point, Mr. Washington is especially to be criticised. His doctrine has tended to make the whites, North and South, shift the burden of the Negro problem to the Negro's shoulders and stand aside as critical and rather pessimistic spectators; when in fact the burden belongs to the nation, and the hands of none of us are clean if we bend not our energies to righting these great wrongs.

The South ought to be led, by candid and honest criticism, to assert her better self and do her full duty to the race she has cruelly wronged and is still wronging. The North—her co-partner in guilt—cannot salve her conscience by plastering it with gold. We cannot settle this problem by diplomacy and suaveness, by "policy" alone. If worse come to worst, can the moral fibre of this country survive the slow throttling and murder of nine millions of men?

The black men of America have a duty to perform, a duty stern and delicate,—a forward movement to oppose a part of the work of their greatest leader. So far as Mr. Washington preaches Thrift, Patience, and Industrial Training for the masses, we must hold up his hands and strive with him, rejoicing in his honors and glorying in the strength of this Joshua called of God and of man to lead the headless host. But so far as Mr. Washington apologizes for injustice, North or South, does not rightly value the privilege and duty of voting, belittles the emasculating effects of caste distinctions, and opposes the higher training and ambition of our brighter minds,—so far as he, the South, or the Nation, does this,—we must unceasingly and firmly oppose them. By every civilized and peaceful method we must strive for the rights which the world accords to men, clinging unwaveringly to those great words which the sons of the Fathers would fain forget: "We hold these truths to be self-evident: That all men are created equal; that they are endowed by their Creator with certain unalienable rights; that among these are life, liberty, and the pursuit of happiness."

* * *

1903

Realism and Naturalism

Realism and *naturalism* are closely related terms in American literary history, terms that authors, editors, and critics used in the late nineteenth and early twentieth centuries when debating the purpose of literature, the role of literature in a democratic society, and the future of literary expression. Both terms were used to describe a rejection of the past—to make the claim that writers in the current generation were doing something new and distinct from their predecessors. Because these terms were used so widely, and for such different purposes, they are slippery and elastic. Sometimes they are used interchangeably; sometimes they appear as opposites. Because they are such close cousins, realism and naturalism can be better understood as a set of attitudes and tendencies rather than as clearly distinct literary periods or categories.

In the last two decades of the nineteenth century, realism was commonly identified as an emerging force in American fiction, both novels and short stories. Realism implies a rejection of romantic, heroic, exaggerated, and idealistic views of life in favor of detailed, accurate descriptions of the everyday. The characters are presented as ordinary people involved in the normal moral dilemmas of life. Some proponents of realism (and indeed some of its opponents) understood American realism to be an adaptation that borrowed from the best of European fiction. However, because realism focused on the manners and speech of common people, some also believed that realism could play a special role in the United States by representing a variety of populations with accuracy and sympathy. In this way, literature would both reflect and cultivate a democratic society.

Realism was more of a label of convenience for critics than a coherent movement. The works considered then and now as realist diverge in significant ways. Mark Twain's fiction employed regional and class dialects to comic effect—often with a sharp satiric edge. Henry James extended his dramas of upper-class life into the flow of interior thoughts, pushing realism towards stream of consciousness and other characteristics of literary modernism. In her depiction of coastal Maine, Sarah Orne Jewett emphasized how a way of life could be deeply rooted in a landscape and its history.

In spite of this diversity, naturalists asserted that realists focused too narrowly on the middle and professional classes. They claimed that the lives of the poor and the marginalized required a more dramatic form of literature to depict the powerful forces that were shaping American life at the turn of the twentieth century. Naturalists frequently drew on social interpretations of Darwinian evolution, which they employed as a lens to understand the struggles that they saw around them, particularly economic contests between capital and labor. They were frequently pessimistic about the ability of contemporary society to deliver justice, because they understood the human world as driven by animal instincts that lay barely beneath the surface of polite society. In Dreiser's *Sister Carrie* (1900), the narrator observes, "Our civilisation is still in a middle stage, scarcely beast, in that it is no longer wholly guided by instinct; scarcely human, in that it is not yet wholly guided by reason."

With this interest in the primal forces driving human conflict, naturalist fiction frequently relies on plots with incidents of dramatic violence. Naturalistic subject matter ranges from Stephen Crane's awed and terrified Union soldier in *The Red Badge of Courage* (1895), to Frank Norris's and Upton Sinclair's exposés of the power of capitalism in *The Octopus* (1901) and *The Jungle* (1906), to the portraits of psychopathic characters in Norris's *McTeague* (1899) and Jack London's *The Sea-Wolf* (1904). Like *The Octopus*, London's *The Call of the Wild* (1903) was at once a profoundly naturalistic novel and an intensely romantic fable; in London's fiction, though human nature seems inevitably to go wrong, it may be saved in rugged environments where "civilized" notions such as self-gain are no longer useful. By asking questions about the fundamental laws of humanity and human progress, naturalist fiction provided a means of deep inquiry into the meaning of human existence in a world that could be both hostile and cruel.

WILLIAM DEAN HOWELLS

The influence of William Dean Howells (1837–1920) went far beyond the impact of his own novels. As the editor of the *Atlantic Monthly* and *Harper's Monthly Magazine*, he could select, encourage, and promote those writers he considered to be examples of literary realism, which he called "the only literary movement of our time that has any vitality in it." Howells believed that realism would combine artistic achievement and a sense of ethical purpose, allowing literature to fulfill an important mission by representing true portraits of a society and its people. In particular, Howells described literary realism as an antidote to the sentimental romance, which he believed to be dangerous; romance, he believed, depicted characters making choices that could or should not be replicated by their readers.

Howells also believed that literary realism could help hold together an American society increasingly fractured by social class and ethnicity. Realism would do so through the close observation of speech and habits. Howells's own fiction largely depicted the people he knew best: the white, urban professional class. But as an editor and reviewer he supported regional and local-color writers from throughout the United States, as well as writers from a variety of ethnic and racial backgrounds. "Democracy in literature," Howells wrote, "wishes to know and to tell the truth, confident that consolation and delight are there. . . . Men are more alike than unlike one another: let us make them know one another better, that they may be all humbled and strengthened with a sense of their fraternity."

This section contains selections from Howells's "Editor's Study" column, which he published in *Harper's* from 1886 to 1892. In these columns, Howells surveyed the literary developments of his time, both in the United States and abroad, and championed his own literary values. In these excerpts, Howells takes aim at novels that "flatter the passions" and "weaken the mental fibre" of their readers. The test of literature, he writes, is in its ability to represent the real, not the ideal, in art—an argument he makes, comically, by ridiculing an artist who would prefer an artificial, "romantic card-board grasshopper" to an actual insect found in nature. The time is coming, Howells portends, when readers will judge all literature, both past and present, by its ability to present "the simple, the natural, and the honest."

From Editor's Study[1]

* * *

Without taking them too seriously, it still must be owned that the "gaudy hero and heroine" are to blame for a great deal of harm in the world. That heroine long taught by example, if not precept, that Love, or the passion or fancy she mistook for it, was the chief interest of a life which is really concerned with a great many other things; that it was lasting in the way she knew it; that it was worthy of every sacrifice, and was altogether a finer thing than prudence, obedience, reason; that love alone was glorious and beautiful, and these were mean and ugly in comparison with it. More lately she has begun to idolize and illustrate Duty, and she is hardly less mischievous in this new rôle, opposing duty, as she did love, to prudence, obedience, and reason. The stock hero, whom, if we met him, we could not fail to see was a most deplorable person, has undoubtedly imposed himself upon the victims of the fiction habit as admirable. With him, too, love was and is the great affair, whether in its old romantic phase of chivalrous achievement or manifold suffering for love's sake, or its more recent development of the "virile," the bullying, and the brutal, or its still more recent agonies of self-sacrifice, as idle and useless as the moral experiences of the insane asylums. With his vain posturing and his ridiculous splendor he is really a painted barbarian, the prey of his passions and his delusions, full of obsolete ideals, and the motives and ethics of a savage, which the guilty author of his being does his best—or his worst—in spite of his own light and knowledge, to foist upon the reader as something generous and noble. We are not merely bringing this charge against that sort of fiction which is beneath literature and outside of it, "the shoreless lakes of ditch-water,"[2] whose miasms fill the air below the empyrean where the great ones sit; but we are accusing the work of some of the most famous, who have, in this instance or in that, sinned against the truth, which can alone exalt and purify men. We do not say that they have constantly done so, or even commonly done so; but that they have done so at all marks them as of the past, to be read with the due historical allowance for their epoch and their conditions. For we believe that, while inferior writers will and must continue to imitate them in their foibles and their errors, no one hereafter will be able to achieve greatness who is false to humanity, either in its facts or its duties. The light of civilization has already broken even upon the novel, and no conscientious man can now set about painting an image of life without perpetual question of the verity of his work, and without feeling bound to distinguish so clearly that no reader of his may be misled, between what is right and what is wrong, what is noble and what is base, what is health and what is perdition, in the actions and the characters he portrays.

The fiction that aims merely to entertain—the fiction that is to serious fiction as the opéra bouffe,[3] the ballet, and the pantomime are to the true

---

1. These excerpts from Howells's "Editor's Study" columns first appeared in *Harper's Monthly* in April and December 1887.
2. The quoted phrase comes from the Scottish essayist, historian, and critic Thomas Carlyle (1795–1881), and it refers to historical papers he used in compiling an edition of the letters and speeches of the English soldier and statesman Oliver Cromwell (1599–1658).
3. Comic opera (French), sometimes used to refer to the broader category of light opera.

drama—need not feel the burden of this obligation so deeply; but even such fiction will not be gay or trivial to any reader's hurt, and criticism will hold it to account if it passes from painting to teaching folly.

More and more not only the criticism which prints its opinions, but the infinitely vaster and powerfuler criticism which thinks and feels them merely, will make this demand. For our own part we confess that we do not care to judge any work of the imagination without first of all applying this test to it. We must ask ourselves before we ask anything else, Is it true?—true to the motives, the impulses, the principles that shape the life of actual men and women? This truth, which necessarily includes the highest morality and the highest artistry—this truth given, the book *cannot* be wicked and cannot be weak; and without it all graces of style and feats of invention and cunning of construction are so many superfluities of naughtiness. It is well for the truth to have all these, and shine in them, but for falsehood they are merely meretricious, the bedizenment of the wanton; they atone for nothing, they count for nothing. But in fact they come naturally of truth, and grace it without solicitation; they are added unto it. In the whole range of fiction we know of no *true* picture of life—that is, of human nature—which is not also a masterpiece of literature, full of divine and natural beauty. It may have no touch or tint of this special civilization or of that; it had *better* have this local color well ascertained; but the truth is deeper and finer than aspects, and if the book is true to what men and women know of one another's souls it will be true enough, and it will be great and beautiful. It is the conception of literature as something apart from life, super-finely aloof, which makes it really unimportant to the great mass of mankind, without a message or a meaning for them; and it is the notion that a novel may be false in its portrayal of causes and effects that makes literary art contemptible even to those whom it amuses that forbids them to regard the novelist as a serious or right-minded person. If they do not in some moment of indignation cry out against all novels, as our correspondent does, they remain besotted in the fume of the delusions purveyed to them, with no higher feeling for the author than such maudlin affection as the *habitué* of an opium-joint perhaps knows for the attendant who fills his pipe with the drug.

* * *

The time is coming, we trust, when each new author, each new artist, will be considered, not in his proportion to any other author or artist, but in his relation to the human nature, known to us all, which it is his privilege, his high duty, to interpret. "The true standard of the artist is in every man's power" already, as Burke says; Michelangelo's "light of the piazza," the glance of the common eye, is and always was the best light on a statue; Goethe's "boys and blackbirds"[4] have in all ages been the real connoisseurs of berries; but hitherto the mass of common men have been afraid to apply their own simplicity, naturalness, and honesty to the appreciation of the beauti-

---

4. In *From My Life: Poetry and Truth* (1811–1830), Johann Wolfgang von Goethe (1749–1832) remarks that to know the taste of berries and cherries, one should ask the boys and the birds. "As Burke says": slight misquotation from *A Philosophical Inquiry into the Origin of Our Ideas of the Sublime and Beautiful* (1757) by Edmund Burke (1599–1658). "Light of the piazza": from a comment attributed to the Italian artist Michelangelo (1474–1564), who was advising a fellow sculptor not to worry about how a work appeared in his studio, but to be concerned about how it would look in the public outdoors.

ful. They have always cast about for the instruction of some one who professed to know better, and who browbeat wholesome common-sense into the self-distrust that ends in sophistication. They have fallen generally to the worst of this bad species, and have been "amused and misled" (how pretty that quaint old use of *amuse* is!) "by the false lights" of critical vanity and self-righteousness. They have been taught to compare what they see and what they read, not with the things that they have observed and known, but with the things that some other artist or writer has done. Especially if they have themselves the artistic impulse in any direction they are taught to form themselves, not upon life, but upon the masters who became masters only by forming themselves upon life. The seeds of death are planted in them, and they can produce only the still-born, the academic. They are not told to take their work into the public square and see if it seems true to the chance passer, but to test it by the work of the very men who refused and decried any other test of their own work. The young writer who attempts to report the phrase and carriage of every-day life, who tries to tell just how he has heard men talk and seen them look, is made to feel guilty of something low and unworthy by the stupid people who would like to have him show how Shakespeare's men talked and looked, or Scott's, or Thackeray's, or Balzac's, or Hawthorne's, or Dickens's;[5] he is instructed to idealize his personages, that is, to take the life-likeness out of them, and put the literary-likeness into them. He is approached in the spirit of the wretched pedantry into which learning, much or little, always decays when it withdraws itself and stands apart from experience in an attitude of imagined superiority, and which would say with the same confidence to the scientist: "I see that you are looking at a grasshopper there which you have found in the grass, and I suppose you intend to describe it. Now don't waste your time and sin against culture in *that* way. I've got a grasshopper here, which has been evolved at considerable pains and expense out of the grasshopper in general; in fact, it's a type. It's made up of wire and cardboard, very prettily painted in a conventional tint, and it's perfectly indestructible. It isn't very much like a real grasshopper, but it's a great deal nicer, and it's served to represent the notion of a grasshopper ever since man emerged from barbarism. You may say that it's artificial. Well, it *is* artificial; but then it's ideal too; and what you want to do is to cultivate the ideal. You'll find the books full of my kind of grasshopper, and scarcely a trace of yours in any of them. The thing that you are proposing to do is commonplace; but if you say that it isn't commonplace, for the very reason that it hasn't been done before, you'll have to admit that it's photographic."

As we said, we hope the time is coming when not only the artist, but the common, average man, who always "has the standard of the arts in his power," will have also the courage to apply it, and will reject the ideal grasshopper wherever he finds it, in science, in literature, in art, because it is not "simple, natural, and honest," because it is not like a real grasshopper. But we will own that we think the time is yet far off, and that the people who have been brought up on the ideal grasshopper, the heroic grasshopper, the impassioned

---

5. British novelists Sir Walter Scott (1771–1832), William Makepeace Thackeray (1811–1863), French novelist Honoré de Balzac (1779–1850), American writer Nathaniel Hawthorne (1804–1864), and British novelist Charles Dickens (1812–1870).

grasshopper, the self-devoted, adventureful, good old romantic card-board grasshopper, must die out before the simple, honest, and natural grasshopper can have a fair field. We are in no haste to compass the end of these good people, whom we find in the mean time very amusing. It is delightful to meet one of them, either in print or out of it—some sweet elderly lady or excellent gentleman whose youth was pastured on the literature of thirty or forty years ago—and to witness the confidence with which they preach their favorite authors as all the law and the prophets. They have commonly read little or nothing since, or, if they have, they have judged it by a standard taken from these authors, and never dreamt of judging it by nature; they are destitute of the documents in the case of the later writers; they suppose that Balzac was the beginning of realism, and that Zola[6] is its wicked end; they are quite igno- rant, but they are ready to talk you down, if you differ from them, with an assumption of knowledge sufficient for any occasion. The horror, the resent- ment, with which they receive any question of their very peccable literary saints is to be matched only by the frenzy of the *Saturday Review*[7] in defend- ing the British aristocracy; you descend at once very far in the moral and social scale, and anything short of offensive personality is too good for you; it is expressed to you that you are one to be avoided, and put down even a little lower than you have naturally fallen.

These worthy persons are not to blame; it is part of their intellectual mis- sion to represent the petrifaction of taste, and to preserve an image of a smaller and cruder and emptier world than we now live in, a world which was feeling its way toward the simple, the natural, the honest, but was a good deal "amused and misled" by lights now no longer mistakable for heavenly luminaries. They belong to a time, just passing away, when certain authors were considered authorities in certain kinds, when they must be accepted entire and not questioned in any particular. Now we are beginning to see and to say that no author is an authority except in those moments when he held his ear close to Nature's lips and caught her very accent. These moments are not continuous with any authors in the past, and they are rare with all. Therefore we are not afraid to say now that the greatest classics are some- times not at all great, and that we can profit by them only when we hold them, like our meanest contemporaries, to a strict accounting, and verify their work by the standard of the arts which we all have in our power, the simple, the natural, and the honest.

1887

---

6. French writer Émile Zola (1840–1902), whose work was widely considered the leading example of literary naturalism. Because Zola's fiction depicted working-class subjects and characters such as prostitutes, it was highly controversial.
7. Weekly newspaper published in London.

HENRY JAMES

Perhaps the most famous description of realism in the novel is Henry James's essay "The Art of Fiction," in which James (1843–1916) dismisses all prescriptions for novelistic success. James was writing in response to the English novelist and critic Walter Besant, who had proposed that the good novel had to be overtly moral. James offered a rebuttal that rejected all categorical requirements of the novel: "I am quite at a loss to imagine anything (at any rate in this matter of fiction) that people *ought* to like or to dislike. Selection will be sure to take care of itself, for it has a constant motive behind it. That motive is simply experience." The great novelist, James writes, will be keenly attuned to the environment and able to deduce larger truths by understanding the meaning of small details. Typically, the examples that he cites—the novelist who observes a single Parisian meal, the young man who decides against entering a church—are not "extraordinary or startling incidents." Rather, James's interest is in fine-grained ambiguity; his idea of consciousness—a sort of spiderweb of "the very atmosphere of the mind"—means that the question of the "moral" in a work of fiction is irrelevant. James contends that "the deepest quality of a work of art will always be the quality of the mind of the producer. . . . No good novel will ever proceed from a superficial mind."

From The Art of Fiction[1]

* * *

It goes without saying that you will not write a good novel unless you possess the sense of reality; but it will be difficult to give you a recipe for calling that sense into being. Humanity is immense, and reality has a myriad forms; the most one can affirm is that some of the flowers of fiction have the odour of it, and others have not; as for telling you in advance how your nosegay should be composed, that is another affair. It is equally excellent and inconclusive to say that one must write from experience; to our suppositious aspirant such a declaration might savour of mockery. What kind of experience is intended, and where does it begin and end? Experience is never limited, and it is never complete; it is an immense sensibility, a kind of huge spider-web of the finest silken threads suspended in the chamber of consciousness, and catching every air-borne particle in its tissue. It is the very atmosphere of the mind; and when the mind is imaginative—much more when it happens to be that of a man of genius—it takes to itself the faintest hints of life, it converts the very pulses of the air into revelations. The young lady living in a village has only to be a damsel upon whom nothing is lost to make it quite unfair (as it seems to me) to declare to her that she shall have nothing to say about the military. Greater miracles have been seen than that, imagination assisting, she should speak the truth about some of these gentlemen. I remember an English novelist, a woman of genius, telling me that

1. First published in *Longman's Magazine* 4 (September 1884), then in James's *Partial Portraits* (1888); reprinted in *Selected Literary Criticism* by Henry James (1968), from which this text is taken.

she was much commended for the impression she had managed to give in one of her tales of the nature and way of life of the French Protestant youth. She had been asked where she learned so much about this recondite being, she had been congratulated on her peculiar opportunities. These opportunities consisted in her having once, in Paris, as she ascended a staircase, passed an open door where, in the household of a *pasteur*,[2] some of the young Protestants were seated at table round a finished meal. The glimpse made a picture; it lasted only a moment, but that moment was experience. She had got her direct personal impression, and she turned out her type. She knew what youth was, and what Protestantism; she also had the advantage of having seen what it was to be French, so that she converted these ideas into a concrete image and produced a reality. Above all, however, she was blessed with the faculty which when you give it an inch takes an ell, and which for the artist is a much greater source of strength than any accident of residence or of place in the social scale. The power to guess the unseen from the seen, to trace the implication of things, to judge the whole piece by the pattern, the condition of feeling life in general so completely that you are well on your way to knowing any particular corner of it—this cluster of gifts may almost be said to constitute experience, and they occur in country and in town and in the most differing stages of education. If experience consists of impressions, it may be said that impressions *are* experience, just as (have we not seen it?) they are the very air we breathe. Therefore, if I should certainly say to a novice, 'Write from experience and experience only', I should feel that this was rather a tantalizing monition if I were not careful immediately to add, 'Try to be one of the people on whom nothing is lost!'

* * *

A novel is a living thing, all one and continuous, like any other organism, and in proportion as it lives will it be found, that in each of the parts there is something of each of the other parts. The critic who over the close texture of a finished work shall pretend to trace a geography of items will mark some frontiers as artificial, I fear, as any that have been known to history. There is an old-fashioned distinction between the novel of character and the novel of incident which must have cost many a smile to the intending fabulist who was keen about his work. It appears to me as little to the point as the equally celebrated distinction between the novel and the romance—to answer as little to any reality. There are bad novels and good novels, as there are bad pictures and good pictures; but that is the only distinction in which I see any meaning, and I can as little imagine speaking of a novel of character as I can imagine speaking of a picture of character. When one says picture one says of character, when one says novel one says of incident, and the terms may be transposed at will. What is character but the determination of incident? What is incident but the illustration of character? What is either a picture or a novel that is *not* of character? What else do we seek in it and find in it? It is an incident for a woman to stand up with her hand resting on a table and look out at you in a certain way; or if it be not an incident I think it will be hard to say what it is. At the same time it is an expression of character. If you say you don't see it (character in *that—allons*

2. Minister, pastor (French).

donc!),[3] this is exactly what the artist who has reason of his own for thinking he *does* see it undertakes to show you. When a young man makes up his mind that he has not faith enough after all to enter the church as he intended, that is an incident, though you may not hurry to the end of the chapter to see whether perhaps he doesn't change once more. I do not say that these are extraordinary or startling incidents. I do not pretend to estimate the degree of interest proceeding from them, for this will depend upon the skill of the painter. It sounds almost puerile to say that some incidents are intrinsically much more important than others, and I need not take this precaution after having professed my sympathy for the major ones in remarking that the only classification of the novel that I can understand is into that which has life and that which has it not.

* * *

There is one point at which the moral sense and the artistic sense lie very near together; that is in the light of the very obvious truth that the deepest quality of a work of art will always be the quality of the mind of the producer. In proportion as that intelligence is fine will the novel, the picture, the statue partake of the substance of beauty and truth. To be constituted of such elements is, to my vision, to have purpose enough. No good novel will ever proceed from a superficial mind; that seems to me an axiom which, for the artist in fiction, will cover all needful moral ground: if the youthful aspirant take it to heart it will illuminate for him many of the mysteries of 'purpose'.

* * *

1884

3. Let's go! (French).

FRANK NORRIS

The novelist Frank Norris (1870–1902)—whose career was cut short when he died from a ruptured appendix at the age of thirty-two—was one of the most visible proponents of literary naturalism in the United States. In several essays, he disputed the version of realism that Howells practiced. His chief example of naturalism was the fiction of the French writer Émile Zola, whom Norris believed to be a model in his literary representation of the force and vigor of modern life. In "A Plea for Romantic Fiction," first published in 1901, Norris contended that the realism of Howells was bloodless and dull in its depiction of middle-class life. His characterization of realism as "the drama of a broken teacup" proved to be influential as a way of distinguishing between the literary realists of last two decades of the nineteenth century and the naturalists of the early twentieth. "A Plea for Romantic Fiction" was included in Norris's posthumously published book *The Responsibilities of the Novelist* (1903).

A Plea for Romantic Fiction[1]

Let us at the start make a distinction. Observe that one speaks of Romanticism and not of sentimentalism. One claims that the latter is as distinct from the former as is that other form of art which is called Realism. Romance has been often put upon and overburdened by being forced to bear the onus of abuse that by right should fall to sentiment; but the two should be kept very distinct, for a very high and illustrious place will be claimed for Romance, while sentiment will be handed down the scullery stairs.

Many people today are composing mere sentimentalism, and calling it and causing it to be called Romance, so with those who are too busy to think much upon these subjects, but who none the less love honest literature, Romance has fallen into disrepute. Consider now the cut-and-thrust stories. They are labelled Romances, and it is very easy to get the impression that Romance must be an affair of cloaks and daggers, or moonlight and golden hair. But this is not so at all. The true Romance is a more serious business than this. It is not merely a conjurer's trick box, full of flimsy quackeries, tinsel and clap traps, meant only to amuse, and relying upon deception to do even that. Is it not something better than this? Can we not see in it an instrument, keen, finely tempered, flawless—an instrument with which we may go straight through the clothes and tissues and wrappings of flesh down deep into the red, living heart of things?

Is all this too subtle, too merely speculative and intrinsic, too *précieuse*[2] and nice and "literary"? Devoutly one hopes the contrary. So much is made of so-called Romanticism in present-day fiction, that the subject seems worthy of discussion, and a protest against the misuse of a really noble and honest formula of literature appears to be timely—misuse, that is, in the sense of limited use. Let us suppose for the moment that a Romance can be made out of the cut-and-thrust business. Good Heavens, are there no other things that are romantic, even in this—falsely, falsely called—humdrum world of today? Why should it be that so soon as the novelist addresses himself—seriously—to the consideration of contemporary life he must abandon Romance and take up that harsh, loveless, colorless, blunt tool called Realism?

Now, let us understand at once what is meant by Romance and what by Realism. Romance—I take it—is the kind of fiction that takes cognizance of variations from the type of normal life. Realism is the kind of fiction that confines itself to the type of normal life. According to this definition, then, Romance may even treat of the sordid, the unlovely—as for instance, the novels of M. Zola. (Zola has been dubbed a Realist, but he is, on the contrary, the very head of Romanticists.) Also, Realism, used as it sometimes is as a term of reproach, need not be in the remotest sense or degree offensive, but on the other hand respectable as a church and proper as a deacon—as, for instance, the novels of Mr. Howells.

The reason why one claims so much for Romance, and quarrels so pointedly with Realism, is that Realism stultifies itself. It notes only the surface

1. First published in the *Boston Evening Transcript*, December 18, 1901; reprinted in *McTeague: A Story of San Francisco* by Frank Norris, 2nd ed. (1997), from which this text is taken.
2. Precious (French); overly refined.

of things. For it Beauty is not even skin-deep, but only a geometrical plane, without dimensions of depth, a mere outside. Realism is very excellent so far as it goes, but it goes no farther than the Realist himself can actually see, or actually hear. Realism is minute, it is the drama of a broken teacup, the tragedy of a walk down the block, the excitement of an afternoon call, the adventure of an invitation to dinner. It is the visit to my neighbor's house, a formal visit, from which I may draw no conclusions. I see my neighbor and his friends—very, oh, such very! probable people—and that is all. Realism bows upon the doormat and goes away and says to me, as we link arms on the sidewalk: "That is life." And I say it is not. It is not, as you would very well see if you took Romance with you to call upon your neighbor.

Lately you have been taking Romance a weary journey across the water—ages and the flood of years—and haling her into the fusty, musty, worm-eaten, moth-riddled, rust-corroded "Grandes Salles"[3] of the Middle Ages and the Renaissance, and she has found the drama of a bygone age for you there. But would you take her across the street to your neighbor's front parlor (with the bisque fisher boy[4] on the mantel and the photograph of Niagara Falls on glass hanging in the front window); would you introduce her there? Not you. Would you take a walk with her on Fifth avenue, or Beacon street, or Michigan avenue?[5] No indeed. Would you choose her for a companion of a morning spent in Wall Street, or an afternoon in the Waldorf-Astoria?[6] You just guess you would not.

She would be out of place, you say, inappropriate. She might be awkward in my neighbor's front parlor, and knock over the little bisque fisher boy. Well, she might. If she did, you might find underneath the base of the statuette, hidden away, tucked away—what? God knows. But something which would be a complete revelation of my neighbor's secretest life.

So you think Romance would stop in the front parlor and discuss medicated flannels and mineral waters with the ladies?[7] Not for more than five minutes. She would be off upstairs with you, prying, peeping, peering into the closets of the bedrooms, into the nursery, into the sitting-room; yes, and into that little iron box screwed to the lower shelf of the closet in the library; and into those compartments and pigeonholes of the *secrétaire*[8] in the study. She would find a heartache (maybe) between the pillows of the mistress's bed, and a memory carefully secreted in the master's deedbox.[9] She would come upon a great hope amid the books and papers of the study table of the young man's room, and—perhaps—who knows—an affair, or, great heavens, an intrigue, in the scented ribbons and gloves and hairpins of the young lady's bureau. And she would pick here a little and there a little, making up a bag of hopes and fears, and a package of joys and sorrows—great ones, mind you—and then come down to the front door, and stepping out into the street, hand you the bags and package, and say to you—"That is Life!"

Romance does very well in the castles of the Middle Ages and the Renaissance chateaux, and she has the entrée there and is very well received. That

---

3. Great ballrooms or auditoriums (French).
4. Inexpensive imitation of costly porcelain figurines.
5. Streets in New York City, Boston, and Chicago, respectively.
6. Luxury hotel in New York City.
7. Flannels were used to apply warm liquors to the body for the purpose of easing pain by relaxing the skin. Mineral waters were bathed in or drunk as curatives for many medical conditions at this time.
8. Desk (French).
9. Lockbox for money or valuables.

is all well and good. But let us protest against limiting her to such places and such times. You will find her, I grant you, in the chatelaine's[1] chamber and the dungeon of the man-at-arms; but, if you choose to look for her, you will find her equally at home in the brownstone house on the corner and in the office building downtown. And this very day, in this very hour, she is sitting among the rags and wretchedness, the dirt and despair of the tenements of the East Side[2] of New York

"What?" I hear you say, "look for Romance—the lady of the silken robes and golden crown, our beautiful, chaste maiden of soft voice and gentle eyes—look for her among the vicious ruffians, male and female, of Allen Street and Mulberry Bend?"[3] I tell you she is there, and to your shame be it said you will not know her in those surroundings. You, the aristocrats, who demand the fine linen and the purple in your fiction; you, the sensitive, the delicate, who will associate with your Romance only so long as she wears a silken gown. You will not follow her to the slums, for you believe that Romance should only amuse and entertain you, singing you sweet songs and touching the harp of silver strings with rosy-tipped fingers. If haply she should call to you from the squalor of a dive, or the awful degradation of a disorderly house,[4] crying: "Look! listen! This, too, is life. These, too, are my children, look at them, know them and, knowing, help!" Should she call thus, you would stop your ears; you would avert your eyes, and you would answer, "Come from there, Romance. Your place is not there!" And you would make of her a harlequin, a tumbler,[5] a sword dancer, when, as a matter of fact, she should be by right divine a teacher sent from God.

She will not always wear a robe of silk, the gold crown, the jeweled shoon,[6] will not always sweep the silver harp. An iron note is hers if so she choose, and coarse garments, and stained hands; and, meeting her thus, it is for you to know her as she passes—know her for the same young queen of the blue mantle and lilies.[7] She can teach you, if you will be humble to learn. Teach you by showing. God help you, if at last you take from Romance her mission of teaching, if you do not believe that she has a purpose, a nobler purpose and a mightier than mere amusement, mere entertainment. Let Realism do the entertaining with its meticulous presentation of teacups, rag carpets, wall paper and haircloth sofas, stopping with these, going no deeper than it sees, choosing the ordinary, the untroubled, the commonplace.

But to Romance belongs the wide world for range, and the unplumbed depths of the human heart, and the mystery of sex, and the problems of life, and the black, unsearched penetralia of the soul of man. You, the indolent, must not always be amused. What matter the silken clothes, what matter the prince's houses? Romance, too, is a teacher, and if—throwing aside the purple—she wears the camel's hair and feeds upon the locusts,[8] it is to cry aloud unto the people, "Prepare ye the way of the Lord; make straight his path."

1901

1. Wife of an estate owner (French).
2. A working-class neighborhood in Manhattan identified with its immigrant populations.
3. Streets in Lower Manhattan associated with the "Five Points Slum," known during Norris's time as a center of violence and crime.
4. A house of prostitution.

5. Clown or buffoon; acrobat or gymnast.
6. Archaic plural of "shoe."
7. Details frequently seen in depictions of the Virgin Mary.
8. Reference to John the Baptist's self-imposed exile in the wilderness and prophecies of the future (see especially Matthew 3, 11, 14).

JACK LONDON

Jack London's essay "What Life Means to Me" was published in *Cosmopolitan* in March 1906 as part of a series in which the magazine invited American writers to contribute articles on this theme. London (1876–1916) had been warned by the socialist and poet Edwin Markham that the Hearst Corporation, the powerful publisher that owned *Cosmopolitan*, would never print an attack on American capitalism, but the article appeared as London wrote it. London wryly remarked to Markham that "special writers like myself are paid well for expanding their own untrammeled views," because these views will sell magazines. London's second wife, Charmian Kittredge London, later described this essay as his "most impassioned committal of himself as a rebel toward the shames and uncleanness of the capitalist system." "What Life Means to Me," written during the socialist phase of London's development, is one of his strongest expressions of the relation between the naturalistic elements of his fiction and his gritty origins and struggles for survival within urban poverty and an exploitative class system.

From What Life Means to Me[1]

I was born in the working-class. Early I discovered enthusiasm, ambition, and ideals; and to satisfy these became the problem of my child-life. My environment was crude and rough and raw. I had no outlook, but an uplook rather. My place in society was at the bottom. Here life offered nothing but sordidness and wretchedness, both of the flesh and the spirit; for here flesh and spirit were alike starved and tormented.

Above me towered the colossal edifice of society, and to my mind the only way out was up. Into this edifice I early resolved to climb. Up above, men wore black clothes and boiled shirts, and women dressed in beautiful gowns. Also, there were good things to eat, and there was plenty to eat. This much for the flesh. Then there were the things of the spirit. Up above me, I knew, were unselfishnesses of the spirit, clean and noble thinking, keen intellectual living. I knew all this because I read "Seaside Library" novels,[2] in which, with the exception of the villains and adventuresses, all men and women thought beautiful thoughts, spoke a beautiful tongue, and performed glorious deeds. In short, as I accepted the rising of the sun, I accepted that up above me was all that was fine and noble and gracious, all that gave decency and dignity to life, all that made life worth living and that remunerated one for his travail and misery.

* * *

I was a sailor before the mast, a longshoreman, a roustabout;[3] I worked in canneries, and factories, and laundries; I mowed lawns, and cleaned carpets,

---

1. First published in *Cosmopolitan* 41 (March 1906); reprinted in *Revolution and Other Essays* by Jack London (1909), from which this text is taken.
2. Inexpensive novel series published by George Munro, New York, from 1877 to 1882.
3. Dockworker. "Sailor before the mast": a common seaman; not an officer.

and washed windows. And I never got the full product of my toil. I looked at the daughter of the cannery owner, in her carriage, and knew that it was my muscle, in part, that helped drag along that carriage on its rubber tires. I looked at the son of the factory owner, going to college, and knew that it was my muscle that helped, in part, to pay for the wine and good fellowship he enjoyed.

But I did not resent this. It was all in the game. They were the strong. Very well, I was strong. I would carve my way to a place amongst them and make money out of the muscles of other men. I was not afraid of work. I loved hard work. I would pitch in and work harder than ever and eventually become a pillar of society.

And just then, as luck would have it, I found an employer that was of the same mind. I was willing to work, and he was more than willing that I should work. I thought I was learning a trade. In reality, I had displaced two men. I thought he was making an electrician out of me; as a matter of fact, he was making fifty dollars per month out of me. The two men I had displaced had received forty dollars each per month; I was doing the work of both for thirty dollars per month.

This employer worked me nearly to death. A man may love oysters, but too many oysters will disincline him toward that particular diet. And so with me. Too much work sickened me. I did not wish ever to see work again. I fled from work. I became a tramp, begging my way from door to door, wandering over the United States and sweating bloody sweats in slums and prisons.

I had been born in the working-class, and I was now, at the age of eighteen, beneath the point at which I had started. I was down in the cellar of society, down in the subterranean depths of misery about which it is neither nice nor proper to speak. I was in the pit, the abyss, the human cesspool, the shambles and the charnel-house of our civilization. This is the part of the edifice of society that society chooses to ignore. Lack of space compels me here to ignore it, and I shall say only that the things I there saw gave me a terrible scare.

I was scared into thinking. I saw the naked simplicities of the complicated civilization in which I lived. Life was a matter of food and shelter. In order to get food and shelter men sold things. The merchant sold shoes, the politician sold his manhood, and the representative of the people, with exceptions, of course, sold his trust; while nearly all sold their honor. Women, too, whether on the street or in the holy bond of wedlock, were prone to sell their flesh. All things were commodities, all people bought and sold. The one commodity that labor had to sell was muscle. The honor of labor had no price in the market-place. Labor had muscle, and muscle alone, to sell.

But there was a difference, a vital difference. Shoes and trust and honor had a way of renewing themselves. They were imperishable stocks. Muscle, on the other hand, did not renew. As the shoe merchant sold shoes, he continued to replenish his stock. But there was no way of replenishing the laborer's stock of muscle. The more he sold of his muscle, the less of it remained to him. It was his one commodity, and each day his stock of it diminished. In the end, if he did not die before, he sold out and put up his shutters. He was a muscle bankrupt, and nothing remained to him but to go down into the cellar of society and perish miserably.

I learned, further, that brain was likewise a commodity. It, too, was different from muscle. A brain seller was only at his prime when he was fifty or sixty years old, and his wares were fetching higher prices than ever. But a laborer was worked out or broken down at forty-five or fifty. I had been in the cellar of society, and I did not like the place as a habitation. The pipes and drains were unsanitary, and the air was bad to breathe. If I could not live on the parlor floor of society, I could, at any rate, have a try at the attic. It was true, the diet there was slim, but the air at least was pure. So I resolved to sell no more muscle, and to become a vender of brains.

Then began a frantic pursuit of knowledge. I returned to California and opened the books. While thus equipping myself to become a brain merchant, it was inevitable that I should delve into sociology. There I found, in a certain class of books, scientifically formulated, the simple sociological concepts I had already worked out for myself. Other and greater minds, before I was born, had worked out all that I had thought and a vast deal more. I discovered that I was a socialist.

The socialists were revolutionists, inasmuch as they struggled to overthrow the society of the present, and out of the material to build the society of the future. I, too, was a socialist and a revolutionist. I joined the groups of working-class and intellectual revolutionists, and for the first time came into intellectual living. Here I found keen-flashing intellects and brilliant wits; for here I met strong and alert-brained, withal horny-handed, members of the working-class; unfrocked preachers too wide in their Christianity for any congregation of Mammon-worshippers; professors broken on the wheel of university subservience to the ruling class and flung out because they were quick with knowledge which they strove to apply to the affairs of mankind.

Here I found, also, warm faith in the human, glowing idealism, sweetnesses of unselfishness, renunciation, and martyrdom—all the splendid, stinging things of the spirit. Here life was clean, noble, and alive. Here life rehabilitated itself, became wonderful and glorious; and I was glad to be alive. I was in touch with great souls who exalted flesh and spirit over dollars and cents, and to whom the thin wail of the starved slum child meant more than all the pomp and circumstance of commercial expansion and world empire. All about me were nobleness of purpose and heroism of effort, and my days and nights were sunshine and starshine, all fire and dew, with before my eyes, ever burning and blazing, the Holy Grail, Christ's own Grail, the warm human, long-suffering and maltreated, but to be rescued and saved at the last.

* * *

1906, 1909

CHARLOTTE PERKINS GILMAN

Tired of being rejected by editors and publishers who found her feminist provocations too controversial, Charlotte Perkins Gilman (1860–1935) founded the *Forerunner* magazine in 1909. By that point, she had already published her most famous literary work, "The Yellow Wall-paper" (1892), as well as several important works of nonfiction, including the seminal *Women and Economics* (1898). Gilman published the *Forerunner* as a monthly magazine for seven years, and during that time it was essentially a one-woman operation. It included serialized novels and treatises, as well as commentary, poetry, humor, and even an advice column—all written by Gilman herself. The magazine's circulation was small, but it found readers as far away as Australia and India. "Masculine Literature" appeared as part of a larger work that focused on the damage that men had inflicted on the world through their emphasis on aggression and competition. In her discussion of literature, Gilman contends that literary authors have focused too much on the domain of men, to the detriment of both art and society. Her argument can be understood, in part, as a reaction to the tendency in literary naturalism to focus on virile action and brute force. In calling for literature to represent the lives of women in their full complexity and nuance, Gilman presents her own case for a kind of literary realism.

From Masculine Literature[1]

* * *

If the beehive produced literature, the bee's fiction would be rich and broad, full of the complex tasks of comb-building and filling, the care and feeding of the young, the guardian-service of the queen; and far beyond that it would spread to the blue glory of the summer sky, the fresh winds, the endless beauty and sweetness of a thousand thousand flowers. It would treat of the vast fecundity of motherhood, the educative and selective processes of the group-mothers, and the passion of loyalty, of social service, which holds the hive together.

But if the drones wrote fiction, it would have no subject matter save the feasting, of many; and the nuptial flight, of one.

To the male, as such, this mating instinct is frankly the major interest of life; even the belligerent instincts are second to it. To the male, as such, it is for all its intensity, but a passing interest. In nature's economy, his is but a temporary devotion, hers the slow processes of life's fulfillment.

In humanity we have long since, not outgrown, but overgrown, this stage of feeling. In Human Parentage even the mother's share begins to pale beside that ever-growing Social love and care, which guards and guides the children of to-day.

The art of literature in this main form of fiction is far too great a thing to be wholly governed by one dominant note. As life widened and intensified, the artist, if great enough, has transcended sex; and in the mightier works

1. "Masculine Literature" was published as a chapter of *Our Androcentric Culture; or, The Man-Made World*, which was first serialized in Gilman's monthly magazine the *Forerunner* in 1910 and then published in book form in 1911. The text reprinted here comes from the book publication.

of the real masters, we find fiction treating of life, life in general, in all its complex relationships, and refusing to be held longer to the rigid canons of an androcentric past.

That was the power of Balzac[2]—he took in more than this one field. That was the universal appeal of Dickens;[3] he wrote of people, all kinds of people, doing all kinds of things. As you recall with pleasure some preferred novel of this general favorite, you find yourself looking narrowly for the "love story" in it. It is there—for it is part of life; but it does not dominate the whole scene—any more than it does in life.

The thought of the world is made and handed out to us in the main. The makers of books are the makers of thoughts and feelings for the people in general. Fiction is the most popular form in which this world-food is taken. If it were true, it would teach us life easily, swiftly, truly; teach not by preaching but by truly re-presenting; and we should grow up becoming acquainted with a far wider range of life in books than could even be ours in person. Then meeting life in reality we should be wise—and not be disappointed.

As it is, our great sea of fiction is steeped and dyed and flavored all one way. A young man faces life—the seventy year stretch, remember, and is given book upon book wherein one set of feelings is continually vocalized and overestimated. He reads forever of love, good love and bad love, natural and unnatural, legitimate and illegitimate; with the unavoidable inference that there is nothing else going on.

If he is a healthy young man he breaks loose from the whole thing, despises "love stories" and takes up life as he finds it. But what impression he does receive from fiction is a false one, and he suffers without knowing it from lack of the truer, broader views of life it failed to give him.

A young woman faces life—the seventy year stretch remember; and is given the same books—with restrictions. Remember the remark of Rochefoucauld,[4] "There are thirty good stories in the world and twenty-nine cannot be told to women." There is a certain broad field of literature so grossly androcentric that for very shame men have tried to keep it to themselves. But in a milder form, the spades all named teaspoons, or at the worst appearing as trowels—the young woman is given the same fiction. Love and love and love—from "first sight" to marriage. There it stops—just the fluttering ribbon of announcement—"and lived happily ever after."

Is that kind of fiction any sort of picture of a woman's life? Fiction, under our androcentric culture, has not given any true picture of woman's life, very little of human life, and a disproportioned section of man's life.

As we daily grow more human, both of us, this noble art is changing for the better so fast that a short lifetime can mark the growth. New fields are opening and new laborers are working in them. But it is no swift and easy matter to disabuse the race mind from attitudes and habits inculcated for a thousand years. What we have been fed upon so long we are well used to, what we are used to we like, what we like we think is good and proper.

* * *

1910, 1911

---

2. French novelist Honoré de Balzac (1779–1850).
3. British novelist Charles Dickens (1812–1870).

4. François de La Rochefoucauld (1613–1680), a French author of maxims and other witticisms.

THEODORE DREISER
1871–1945

Theodore Dreiser's uncompromising portraits of American society—including frank discussions of sexuality, money, and social class—earned him a substantial following in the first half of the twentieth century, and they continue to attract a widespread readership. With more than twenty books to his name at the time of his death, Dreiser was a prolific author with a long career that stretched from the turn of the twentieth century through the Great Depression. He remains best known for his novels, which ask readers to consider the precise relationship between their complex characters and the carefully described social environments that they inhabit.

Theodore Herman Albert Dreiser was born in Terre Haute, Indiana, on August 17, 1871, the eleventh of thirteen children. His German-born father was stern, emotionally distant, and unsuccessful in providing for his large family. Dreiser later called him "mentally a little weak" and drew upon him as the prototype for the failed men who appear so frequently in Dreiser's novels. Dreiser's mother, by contrast, was steadfastly devoted to the well-being of her children; she was, Dreiser claimed, the only person who ever loved him enough. She, too, appears in fictionalized form in many of Dreiser's books.

Dreiser's unhappy childhood haunted him throughout his life. The large family moved from house to house in Indiana dogged by poverty, insecurity, and internal divisions. One of his brothers became a famous popular songwriter under the name Paul Dresser, but other siblings lived turbulent lives that not only defied their father's rigid morality but placed them on the margins of respectable society altogether. Dreiser as a youth was ungainly, confused, shy, and full of vague yearnings like those of most of his fictional protagonists, male and female.

From the age of fifteen Dreiser was on his own, earning meager support from a variety of menial jobs. A high school teacher staked him to a year at Indiana University in 1889, but Dreiser's real education began in 1892, when persistence and good luck led to his first newspaper job with the *Chicago Globe*. Over the next decade, as an itinerant journalist for several different newspapers, Dreiser slowly groped his way to authorship. He tested what he had learned, from his experience and his reporting, against what he was learning from his independent reading of, among others, Charles Darwin, Thomas Huxley, and Herbert Spencer, late nineteenth-century scientists and social scientists who lent support to the view that nature and society had no divine sanction. Generally speaking, these thinkers agreed that human beings, just as much as other life-forms, were participants in an evolutionary process in which only those who adapted successfully to their environments survive. Spencer in particular argued that human consciousness was itself a product of evolutionary processes and that it entailed the adaptive capacity for altruism and various forms of social cooperation. This tension between, on the one hand, deterministic "chemisms" (as Dreiser called them) and, on the other, the potential for friendship and the improvement of social institutions appears in Dreiser's fiction throughout his writing career. Early on, Dreiser emphasized the mechanistic side of this tension, while in later phases—in his fiction and in his social writings—he appeared to balance his more pessimistic views with a belief in the possibilities of social justice.

Sister Carrie (1900), Dreiser's first novel, two chapters of which are included here, tells the story of Carrie Meeber, a country girl from Wisconsin who comes to Chicago, attracted by the excitement that rapidly growing urban centers held for so many young people in the late 1800s, but even more by the possibility of supporting herself, especially given the meager opportunities in her small rural town. In Chicago she is seduced first by a traveling salesman, Charles Drouet, then by George Hurstwood, a married middle-aged manager of a stylish saloon patronized by wealthy men. Eager to elope with Carrie, Hurstwood steals ten thousand dollars from the safe in the bar; then he and Carrie flee to New York, where, unable to find a job equivalent to the one he gave up, he deteriorates while she begins a successful career on the stage.

Sister Carrie depicts social transgressions by characters who feel no remorse and largely escape punishment, and it is candid about sexual relationships. The novel was virtually suppressed by its first publisher, who printed but refused to promote the book. Later, in 1907, it was reissued by another publisher, and the novel began finding a wider audience that recognized its achievement. Sister Carrie remains powerful because it addresses so many issues that remain pressing in our contemporary moment: class mobility, immigration, urban life, the challenge facing women who seek independence and control of their sexuality, the pressure to succeed in American society, and celebrity culture.

In the first years of the twentieth century Dreiser suffered a nervous breakdown. With the help of his brother Paul, he recovered and by 1904 was on the way to several successful years as an editor, the last of them as editorial director of the Butterick Publishing Company. In 1910 he resigned to write Jennie Gerhardt (1911), one of his best-known novels and the first of a long succession of books that marked his turn to writing as a full-time career. This novel, about the doomed love between a rich man and a poor woman, takes seriously the reality of gentleness, selflessness, and loyalty, though in the end materialism and the pressures associated with wealth and social position carry the day.

In The Financier (1912), The Titan (1914), and The Stoic (not published until 1947), Dreiser shifted from the pathos of helpless protagonists to the power of those unusual individuals who assume dominant roles in business and society. The protagonist of this "Trilogy of Desire" (as Dreiser described it), Frank Cowperwood, is modeled after the Chicago speculator Charles T. Yerkes. These novels of the businessman as buccaneer incorporated, even more than Sister Carrie, explicit discussions of sexual energy and desire—and how that longing becomes entangled with money and social class.

The power of desire—its force and insatiability—is one of the recurring themes of Dreiser's fiction. In An American Tragedy (1925), Dreiser's best-selling and most acclaimed novel, sexual and financial desires collide. The novel is based on a much-publicized murder in upstate New York in 1906. Clyde Griffiths is a poor boy from the provinces who dreams of a life of luxury and status. When his prospect for marrying the wealthy Sondra Finchley is threatened by the pregnant Roberta Alden, a factory worker with whom he has had a relationship, Clyde plans to murder her. He takes Roberta out boating, but at the last moment finds himself unable to carry out his plan. Then when she approaches him, he physically rebuffs her, causing the boat to capsize and causing her to drown after all. Did he kill her or not? The second half of the book follows Clyde's arrest, his trial, his imprisonment, and his eventual execution. The novel was an immediate best seller and confirmed Dreiser's status as one of the leading writers of his time.

During the last two decades of his life, Dreiser turned to polemical writing as well as other genres—poetry, travel books, and autobiography, including Dawn (1931), the first volume in the projected but uncompleted A History of Myself. He visited the Soviet Union in 1927 and published Dreiser Looks at Russia the following year. In the 1930s, like many American intellectuals and writers, Dreiser was increasingly attracted by the philosophical program of the Communist party. Unable to believe in traditional religious credos, yet unable to give up his strong sense of justice, he continued to seek a way to reconcile his determinism with his compassionate sense of life's mysteries.

From Sister Carrie[1]

Chapter I

When Caroline Meeber boarded the afternoon train for Chicago her total outfit consisted of a small trunk, which was checked in the baggage car, a cheap imitation alligator skin satchel holding some minor details of the toilet, a small lunch in a paper box and a yellow leather snap purse, containing her ticket, a scrap of paper with her sister's address in Van Buren Street,[2] and four dollars in money. It was in August, 1889. She was eighteen years of age, bright, timid and full of the illusions of ignorance and youth. Whatever touch of regret at parting characterized her thoughts it was certainly not for advantages now being given up. A gush of tears at her mother's farewell kiss, a touch in the throat when the cars clacked by the flour mill where her father worked by the day, a pathetic sigh as the familiar green environs of the village passed in review, and the threads which bound her so lightly to girlhood and home were irretrievably broken.

To be sure she was not conscious of any of this. Any change, however great, might be remedied. There was always the next station where one might descend and return. There was the great city, bound more closely by these very trains which came up daily. Columbia City was not so very far away, even once she was in Chicago. What pray is a few hours—a hundred miles? She could go back. And then her sister was there. She looked at the little slip bearing the latter's address and wondered. She gazed at the green landscape now passing in swift review until her swifter thoughts replaced its impression with vague conjectures of what Chicago might be. Since infancy her ears had been full of its fame. Once the family had thought of moving there. If she secured good employment they might come now. Anyhow it was vast. There were lights and sounds and a roar of things. People were rich. There were vast depots. This on-rushing train was merely speeding to get there.

When a girl leaves her home at eighteen, she does one of two things. Either she falls into saving hands and becomes better, or she rapidly assumes the cosmopolitan standard of virtue and becomes worse. Of an intermediate balance, under the circumstances, there is no possibility. The city has its cunning wiles no less than the infinitely smaller and more human tempter. There are large forces which allure, with all the soulfulness of expression possible in the most cultured human. The gleam of a thousand lights is often as effective, to all moral intents and purposes, as the persuasive light in a wooing and fascinating eye. Half the undoing of the unsophisticated and natural mind is accomplished by forces wholly superhuman. A blare of sound, a roar of life, a vast array of human hives appeal to the astonished senses in equivocal terms. Without a counselor at hand to whisper cautious interpretations, what falsehoods may not these things breathe into the unguarded ear! Unrecognized for what they are, their beauty, like music, too often relaxes, then weakens, then perverts the simplest human perceptions.

Caroline, or "Sister Carrie" as she had been half affectionately termed by the family, was possessed of a mind rudimentary in its power of observation

---

1. First published by Doubleday & Page (1900), from which this text is taken.

2. East-west Chicago street that, roughly, divides the city in half.

and analysis. Self-interest with her was high, but not strong. It was never-theless her guiding characteristic. Warm with the fancies of youth, pretty with the insipid prettiness of the formative period, possessed of a figure which tended toward eventual shapeliness and an eye alight with certain native intelligence, she was a fair example of the middle American class—two generations removed from the emigrant. Books were beyond her interest—knowledge a sealed book. In the intuitive graces she was still crude. She could scarcely toss her head gracefully. Her hands were almost ineffec-tual for the same reason. The feet, though small, were set flatly. And yet she was interested in her charms, quick to understand the keener pleasures of life, ambitious to gain in material things. A half-equipped little knight she was, venturing to reconnoitre the mysterious city and dreaming wild dreams of some vague, far-off supremacy which should make it prey and subject, the proper penitent, grovelling at a woman's slipper.

"That," said a voice in her ear, "is one of the prettiest little resorts in Wis-consin."

"Is it?" she answered nervously.

The train was just pulling out of Waukesha.[3] For some time she had been conscious of a man behind. She felt him observing her mass of hair. He had been fidgeting, and with natural intuition she felt a certain interest growing in that quarter. Her maidenly reserve and a certain sense of what was con-ventional under the circumstances called her to forestall and deny this famil-iarity, but the daring and magnetism of the individual, born of past experience and triumphs, prevailed. She answered.

He leaned forward to put his elbows upon the back of her seat and pro-ceeded to make himself volubly agreeable.

"Yes, that's a great resort for Chicago people. The hotels are swell. You are not familiar with this part of the country, are you?"

"Oh yes I am," answered Carrie. "That is, I live at Columbia City. I have never been through here though."

"And so this is your first visit to Chicago," he observed.

All the time she was conscious of certain features out of the side of her eye. Flush, colorful cheeks, a light mustache, a gray fedora hat. She now turned and looked upon him in full, the instincts of self-protection and coquetry mingling confusedly in her brain.

"I didn't say that," she said.

"Oh," he answered in a very pleasing way and with an assumed air of mistake. "I thought you did."

Here was a type of the traveling canvasser for a manufacturing house—a class which at that time was first being dubbed by the slang of the day "drum-mers."[4] He came within the meaning of a still newer term which had sprung into general use among Americans in 1880, and which concisely expressed the thought of one whose dress or manners are such as to impress strongly the fancy, or elicit the admiration, of susceptible young women—a "masher." His clothes were of an impressive character, the suit being cut of a striped and crossed pattern of brown wool, very popular at that time. It was what has since become known as a business suit. The low crotch of the vest

---

3. A city in Wisconsin about 100 miles north of Chicago on Lake Michigan.

4. "Canvassers" and "drummers" are salesmen.

revealed a stiff shirt bosom of white and pink stripes, surmounted by a high white collar about which was fastened a tie of distinct pattern. From his coat sleeves protruded a pair of linen cuffs of the same material as the shirt and fastened with large gold-plate buttons set with the common yellow agates known as "cat's-eyes." His fingers bore several rings, one the ever-enduring heavy seal, and from his vest dangled a neat gold watch chain from which was suspended the secret insignia of the Order of Elks.[5] The whole suit was rather tight-fitting and was finished off with broad-soled tan shoes, highly polished, and the grey felt hat, then denominated "fedora," before mentioned. He was, for the order of intellect represented, attractive; and whatever he had to recommend him, you may be sure was not lost upon Carrie, in this her first glance.

Lest this order of individual should permanently pass, let me put down some of the most striking characteristics of his most successful manner and method. Good clothes of course were the first essential, the things without which he was nothing. A strong physical nature actuated by a keen desire for the feminine was the next. A mind free of any consideration of the problems or forces of the world and actuated not by greed but an insatiable love of variable pleasure—woman—pleasure. His method was always simple. Its principal element was daring, backed of course by an intense desire and admiration for the sex. Let him meet with a young woman twice and upon the third meeting he would walk up and straighten her necktie for her and perhaps address her by her first name. If an attractive woman should deign a glance of interest in passing him upon the street he would run up, seize her by the hand in feigned acquaintanceship and convince her that they had met before, providing of course that his pleasing way interested her in knowing him further. In the great department stores he was at his ease in capturing the attention of some young woman, while waiting for the cash boy to come back with his change. In such cases, by those little wiles common to the type, he would find out the girl's name, her favorite flower, where a note would reach her, and perhaps pursue the delicate task of friendship until it proved unpromising for the one aim in view, when it would be relinquished.

He would do very well with more pretentious women, though the burden of expense was a slight deterrent. Upon entering a parlor car at St. Paul, for instance, he would select a chair next to the most promising bit of femininity and soon inquire if she cared to have the shade lowered. Before the train cleared the yards he would have the porter bring her a footstool. At the next lull in his conversational progress he would find her something to read, and from then on by dint of compliment gently insinuated, personal narrative, exaggeration and service, he would win her tolerance and mayhap regard.

Those who have ever delved into the depths of a woman's conscience must, at some time or other, have come upon that mystery of mysteries—the moral significance, to her, of clothes. A woman should some day write the complete philosophy of that subject. No matter how young she is, it is one of the things she wholly comprehends. There is an indescribably faint line in the matter of man's apparel which somehow divides for her those who are worth

***

5. A fraternal organization.

glancing at and those who are not. Once an individual has passed this faint line on the way downward he will get no glance from her. There is another line at which the dress of a man will cause her to study her own. This line the individual at her elbow now marked for Carrie. She became conscious of an inequality. Her own plain blue dress with its black cotton tape trimmings realized itself to her imagination as shabby. She felt the worn state of her shoes.

He mistook this thought wave, which caused her to withdraw her glance and turn for relief to the landscape outside, for some little gain his grace had brought him.

"Let's see," he went on. "I know quite a number of people in your town—Morgenroth the clothier and Gibson the dry-goods man."

"Oh, do you," she interrupted, aroused by memories of longings the displays in the latter's establishment had cost her.

At last he had a clue to her interest and followed it up deftly. In a few minutes he had come about into her seat. He talked of sales of clothing, his travels, Chicago and the amusements of that city.

"If you are going there you will enjoy it immensely. Have you relatives?"

"I am going to visit my sister," she explained.

"You want to see Lincoln Park," he said, "and Michigan Avenue.[6] They are putting up great buildings there. It's a second New York, great. So much to see—theatres, crowds, fine houses—oh you'll like that."

There was a little ache in her fancy of all he described. Her insignificance in the presence of so much magnificence faintly affected her. She realized that hers was not to be a round of pleasure, and yet there was something promising in all the material prospect he set forth. There was something satisfactory in the attention of this individual with his good clothes. She could not help smiling as he told her of some popular actress she reminded him of. She was not silly and yet attention of this sort had its weight.

"You will be in Chicago some little time, won't you?" he observed, at one turn of the now easy conversation.

"I don't know," said Carrie vaguely—a flash vision of the possibility of her not securing employment rising in her mind.

"Several weeks anyhow," he said, looking steadily into her eyes.

There was much more passing now than the mere words indicated. He recognized the indescribable thing that made for fascination and beauty in her. She realized that she was of interest to him from the one standpoint which a woman both delights in and fears. Her manner was simple, though, for the very reason that she had not yet learned the many little affectations with which women conceal their true feelings—some things she did appeared bold. A clever companion, had she ever had one, would have warned her never to look a man in the eyes so steadily.

"Why do you ask?" she said.

"Well, I'm going to be there several weeks. I'm going to study stock at our place and get new samples. I might show you 'round."

"I don't know whether you can or not—I mean I don't know whether I can. I shall be living with my sister and—"

---

6. A fashionable street of stores, office buildings, and the Art Institute. "Lincoln Park": a large lakefront park, home to a zoo and other attractions.

"Well, if she minds, we'll fix that." He took out his pencil and a little pocket note book, as if it were all settled. "What is your address there?"

She fumbled her purse, which contained the address slip.

He reached down in his hip pocket and took out a fat purse. It was filled with slips of paper, some mileage books, a roll of green-backs and so on. It impressed her deeply. Such a purse had never been carried by any man who had ever been attentive to her before. Indeed a man who traveled, who was brisk and experienced and of the world, had never come within such close range before. The purse, the shiny tan shoes, the smart new suit and the *air* with which he did things built up for her a dim world of fortune around him of which he was the centre. It disposed her pleasantly toward all he might do.

He took out a neat business card on which was engraved "Bartlett, Caryoe and Company," and down in the left-hand corner "Chas. H. Drouet."

"That's me," he said, putting the card in her hand and touching his name. "It's pronounced 'Drew-eh.' Our family was French on my father's side."

She looked at it while he put up his purse. Then he got out a letter from a bunch in his coat pocket.

"This is the house I travel for," he went on, pointing to a picture on it—"corner of State and Lake." There was pride in his voice. He felt that it was something to be connected with such a place, and he made her feel that way.

"What is your address?" he began again, fixing his pencil to write.

She looked at his hand.

"Carrie Meeber," she said slowly, "354 West Van Buren St., care S. C. Hanson."

He wrote it carefully down and got out the purse again. "You'll be at home if I come around Monday night?" he said.

"I think so," she answered.

How true it is that words are but vague shadows of the volumes we mean. Little audible links they are, chaining together great inaudible feelings and purposes. Here were these two, bandying little phrases, drawing purses, looking at cards and both unconscious of how inarticulate all their real feelings were. Neither was wise enough to be sure of the working of the mind of the other. He could not tell how his luring succeeded. She could not realize that she was drifting, until he secured her address. Now she felt that she had yielded something—he, that he had gained a victory. Already they felt that they were somehow associated. Already he took control in directing the conversation. His words were easy. Her manner was relaxed.

They were nearing Chicago. Already the signs were numerous. Trains flashed by them. Across wide stretches of flat open prairie they could see lines of telegraph poles stalking across the fields toward the great city. Away off there were indications of suburban towns, some big smoke stacks towering high in the air. Frequently there were two-story frame houses standing out in the open fields, without fence or trees, outposts of the approaching army of homes.

To the child, the genius with imagination, or the wholly untraveled, the approach to a great city for the first time is a wonderful thing. Particularly if it be evening—that mystic period between the glare and the gloom of the world when life is changing from one sphere or condition to another. Ah, the promise of the night. What does it not hold for the weary. What old illusion of hope is not here forever repeated! Says the soul of the toiler to itself, "I shall soon be free. I shall be in the ways and the hosts of the merry. The streets, the lamp, the lighted chamber set for dining are for me. The theatres, the halls, the parties, the ways of rest and the paths of song—these are mine in the night." Though all humanity be still enclosed in the shops, the thrill runs abroad. It is in the air. The dullest feel something which they may not always express or describe. It is the lifting of the burden of toil.

Sister Carrie gazed out of the window. Her companion, affected by her wonder, so contagious are all things, felt anew some interest in the city and pointed out the marvels. Already vast net-works of tracks—the sign and insignia of Chicago—stretched on either hand. There were thousands of cars and a clangor of engine bells. At the sides of this traffic stream stood dingy houses, smoky mills, tall elevators[7] Through the interstices, evidences of the stretching city could be seen. Street cars waited at crossings for the train to go by. Gatemen toiled at wooden arms which closed the streets. Bells clanged, the rails clacked, whistles sounded afar off.

"This is North-West Chicago," said Drouet. "This is the Chicago River," and he pointed to a little muddy creek, crowded with the huge, masted wanderers from far-off waters nosing the black, posted banks. With a puff, a clang and a clatter of rails it was gone. "Chicago is getting to be a great town," he went on. "It's a wonder. You'll find lots to see here."

She did not hear this very well. Her heart was troubled by a kind of terror. The fact that she was alone, away from home, rushing into a great sea of life and endeavor, began to tell. She could not help but feel a little choked for breath—a little sick as her heart beat so fast. She half closed her eyes and tried to think it was nothing, that Columbia City was only a little way off.

"Chicago!—Chicago!" called the brakeman, slamming open the door. They were rushing into a more crowded yard, alive with the clatter and clang of life. She began to gather up her poor little grip and closed her hand firmly upon her purse. Drouet arose, kicked his legs to straighten his trousers and seized his clean yellow grip.

"I suppose your people will be here to meet you," he said. "Let me carry your grip."

"Oh no," she said. "I'd rather you wouldn't. I'd rather you wouldn't be with me when I meet my sister."

"All right," he said in all kindness. "I'll be near, though, in case she isn't here, and take you out there safely."

"You're so kind," said Carrie, feeling the goodness of such attention in her strange situation.

"Chicago!" called the brakeman, drawing the word out long. They were under a great shadowy train shed, where lamps were already beginning to shine out, with passenger cars all about and the train moving at a snail's pace. The people in the car were all up and crowding about the door.

"Well, here we are," said Drouet, leading the way to the door. "Goodbye," he said, "till I see you Monday."

"Goodbye," she said, taking his proffered hand.

"Remember I'll be looking till you find your sister."

She smiled into his eyes.

---

7. Grain elevators.

They filed out and he affected to take no notice of her. A lean-faced, rather commonplace woman recognized Carrie on the platform and hurried forward.

"Why Sister Carrie!" she began and there was a perfunctory embrace of welcome.

Carrie realized the change of affectional atmosphere at once. Amid all the maze, uproar and novelty, she felt cold reality taking her by the hand. No world of light and merriment. No round of amusement. Her sister carried with her much of the grimness of shift and toil.

"Why, how are all the folks at home"—she began—"how is Father, and Mother?"

Carrie answered, but was looking away. Down the aisle toward the gate leading into the waiting room and the street stood Drouet. He was looking back. When he saw that she saw him and was safe with her sister he turned to go, sending back the shadow of a smile. Only Carrie saw it. She felt something lost to her when he moved away. When he disappeared she felt his absence thoroughly. With her sister she was much alone, a lone figure in a tossing, thoughtless sea.

* * *

Chapter III

Once across the river and into the wholesale district, she glanced about her for some likely door at which to apply. As she contemplated the wide windows and imposing signs, she became conscious of being gazed upon and understood for what she was—a wage-seeker. She had never done this thing before and lacked courage. To avoid conspicuity and a certain indefinable shame she felt at being caught spying about for some place where she might apply for a position, she quickened her steps and assumed an air of indifference supposedly common to one upon an errand. In this way she passed many manufacturing and wholesale houses without once glancing in. At last, after several blocks of walking, she felt that this would not do, and began to look about again, though without relaxing her pace. A little way on she saw a great door which for some reason attracted her attention. It was ornamented by a small brass sign, and seemed to be the entrance to a vast hive of six or seven floors. "Perhaps," she thought, "they may want some one" and crossed over to enter, screwing up her courage to the sticking point as she went. When she came within a score of feet of the desired goal, she observed a young gentleman in a grey check suit, fumbling his watch-charm and looking out. That he had anything to do with the concern she could not tell, but because he happened to be looking in her direction, her weakening heart misgave her and she hurried by, too overcome with shame to enter in. After several blocks of walking, in which the uproar of the streets and the novelty of the situation had time to wear away the effect of this, her first defeat, she again looked about. Over the way stood a great six-story structure labeled "Storm and King," which she viewed with rising hope. It was a wholesale dry goods concern and employed women. She could see them moving about now and then upon the upper floors. This place she decided to enter, no matter what. She crossed over and walked directly toward the entrance. As she did so two men came out and paused in the door. A telegraph messenger in blue dashed past her and up the few steps which graced the entrance and disappeared. Several pedestrians out of the hurrying throng which filled the sidewalks passed about her as she paused, hesitating. She looked helplessly around and then, seeing herself observed, retreated. It was too difficult a task. She could not go past them.

So severe a defeat told sadly upon her nerves. She could scarcely understand her weakness and yet she could not think of gazing inquiringly about upon the surrounding scene. Her feet carried her mechanically forward, every foot of her progress being a satisfactory portion of a flight which she gladly made. Block after block passed by. Upon street lamps at the various corners she read names such as Madison, Monroe, La Salle, Clark, Dearborn, State,[8] and still she went, her feet beginning to tire upon the broad stone flagging. She was pleased in part that the streets were bright and clean. The morning sun shining down with steadily increasing warmth made the shady side of the streets pleasantly cool. She looked at the blue sky overhead with more realization of its charm than had ever come to her before.

Her cowardice began to trouble her in a way. She turned back along the street she had come, resolving to hunt up Storm and King and enter in. On the way she encountered a great wholesale shoe company, through the broad plate windows of which she saw an enclosed executive department, hidden by frosted glass. Without this enclosure, but just within the street entrance, sat a grey-haired gentleman at a small table, with a large open ledger of some kind before him. She walked by this institution several times hesitating, but finding herself unobserved she eventually gathered sufficient courage to falter past the screen door and stand humbly waiting.

"Well, young lady," observed the old gentleman looking at her somewhat kindly—"what is it you wish?"

"I am, that is, do you—I mean, do you need any help?" she stammered.

"Not just at present," he answered smiling. "Not just at present. Come in sometime next week. Occasionally we need some one."

She received the answer in silence and backed awkwardly out. The pleasant nature of her reception rather astonished her. She had expected that it would be more difficult, that something cold and harsh would be said—she knew not what. That she had not been put to shame and made to feel her unfortunate position seemed remarkable. She did not realize that it was just this which made her experience easy, but the result was the same. She felt greatly relieved.

Somewhat encouraged, she ventured into another large structure. It was a clothing company, and more people were in evidence—well-dressed men of forty and more, surrounded by brass railings and employed variously.

An office boy approached her.

"Who is it you wish to see?" he asked.

"I want to see the manager," she returned.

He ran away and spoke to one of a group of three men who were conferring together. One broke off and came towards her.

"Well?" he said, coldly. The greeting drove all courage from her at once.

"Do you need any help?" she stammered.

"No," he replied abruptly and turned upon his heel.

8. Major downtown streets between the Chicago River and Lake Michigan.

She went foolishly out, the office boy deferentially swinging the door for her, and gladly sank into the obscuring crowd. It was a severe set-back to her recently pleased mental state.

Now she walked quite aimlessly for a time, turning here and there, seeing one great company after another but finding no courage to prosecute her single inquiry. High noon came and with it hunger. She hunted out an unassuming restaurant and entered but was disturbed to find that the prices were exorbitant for the size of her purse. A bowl of soup was all that she could feel herself able to afford, and with this quickly eaten she went out again. It restored her strength somewhat and made her moderately bold to pursue the search.

In walking a few blocks to fix upon some probable place she again encountered the firm of Storm and King and this time managed to enter. Some gentlemen were conferring close at hand but took no notice of her. She was left standing, gazing nervously upon the floor, her confusion and mental distress momentarily increasing until at last she was ready to turn and hurry eagerly away. When the limit of her distress had been nearly reached she was beckoned to by a man at one of the many desks within the nearby railing.

"Who is it you wish to see?" he inquired.

"Why any one, if you please," she answered. "I am looking for something to do."

"Oh, you want to see Mr. McManus," he returned. "Sit down!" and he pointed to a chair against the neighboring wall. He went on leisurely writing until after a time a short stout gentleman came in from the street.

"Mr. McManus," called the man at the desk, "this young woman wants to see you."

The short gentleman turned about towards Carrie, and she arose and came forward.

"What can I do for you, Miss," he inquired surveying her curiously.

"I want to know if I can get a position," she inquired.

"As what?" he asked.

"Not as anything in particular," she faltered. "I—"

"Have you ever had any experience in the wholesale dry goods business?" he questioned.

"No sir," she replied.

"Are you a stenographer or typewriter?"

"No sir."

"Well we haven't anything here," he said. "We employ only experienced help."

She began to step backward toward the door, when something about her plaintive face attracted him.

"Have you ever worked at anything before?" he inquired.

"No sir," she said.

"Well now, it's hardly possible that you would get anything to do in a wholesale house of this kind. Have you tried the department stores?"

She acknowledged that she had not.

"Well, if I were you," he said, looking at her rather genially, "I would try the department stores. They often need young women as clerks."

"Thank you," she said, her whole nature relieved by this spark of friendly interest.

"Yes," he said, as she moved toward the door, "you try the department stores," and off he went.

At that time the department store was in its earliest form of successful operation and there were not many. The first three in the United States, established about 1884, were in Chicago. Carrie was familiar with the names of several through the advertisements in the "Daily News," and now proceeded to seek them. The words of Mr. McManus had somehow managed to restore her courage, which had fallen low, and she dared to hope that this new line would offer her something in the way of employment. Some time she spent in wandering up and down thinking to encounter the buildings by chance, so readily is the mind, bent upon prosecuting a hard but needful errand, eased by that self-deception which the semblance of search without the reality gives. At last she inquired of a police officer and was directed to proceed "two blocks up" where she would find The Fair.[9] Following his advice she reached that institution and entered.

The nature of these vast retail combinations, should they ever permanently disappear, will form an interesting chapter in the commercial history of our nation. Such a flowering out of a modest trade principle the world had never witnessed up to that time. They were along the line of the most effective retail organization, with hundreds of stores coordinated into one, and laid out upon the most imposing and economic basis. They were handsome, bustling, successful affairs, with a host of clerks and a swarm of patrons. Carrie passed along the busy aisles, much affected by the remarkable displays of trinkets, dress goods, shoes, stationery, jewelry. Each separate counter was a show place of dazzling interest and attraction. She could not help feeling the claim of each trinket and valuable upon her personally and yet she did not stop. There was nothing there which she could not have used—nothing which she did not long to own. The dainty slippers and stockings, the delicately frilled skirts and petticoats, the laces, ribbons, hair-combs, purses, all touched her with individual desire, and she felt keenly the fact that not any of these things were in the range of her purchase. She was a work-seeker, an outcast without employment, one whom the average employé could tell at a glance was poor and in need of a situation.

It must not be thought that anyone could have mistaken her for a nervous, sensitive, high-strung nature, cast unduly upon a cold, calculating and unpoetic world. Such certainly she was not. But women are peculiarly sensitive to the personal adornment or equipment of their person, even the dullest, and particularly is this true of the young. Your bright-eyed, rosy-cheeked maiden, over whom a poet might well rave for the flowerlike expression of her countenance and the lissome and dainty grace of her body, may reasonably be dead to every evidence of the artistic and poetic in the unrelated evidences of life, and yet not lack in material appreciation. Never, it might be said, does she fail in this. With her the bloom of a rose may pass unappreciated, but the bloom of a fold of silk, never. If nothing in the heavens, or the earth, or the waters, could elicit her fancy or delight her from its spiritual or artistic side, think not that the material would be lost. The glint of a buckle, the hue of a precious stone, the faintest tints of the watered silk, these she would devine and qualify as readily as your poet if not more

9. Discount department store, founded in 1874.

so. The creak, the rustle, the glow—the least and best of the graven or spun—, these she would perceive and appreciate—if not because of some fashionable or hearsay quality, then on account of their true beauty, their innate fitness in any order of harmony, their place in the magical order and sequence of dress.

Not only did Carrie feel the drag of desire for all of this which was new and pleasing in apparel for women, but she noticed, too, with a touch at the heart, the fine ladies who elbowed and ignored her, brushing past in utter disregard of her presence, themselves eagerly enlisted in the materials which the store contained. Carrie was not familiar with the appearance of her more fortunate sisters of the city. Neither had she before known the nature and appearance of the shop girls, with whom she now compared poorly. They were pretty in the main, some even handsome, with a certain independence and toss of indifference which added, in the case of the more favored, a certain piquancy. Their clothes were neat, in many instances fine, and wherever she encountered the eye of one, it was only to recognize in it a keen analysis of her own position—her individual shortcomings of dress and that shadow of *manner* which she thought must hang about her and make clear to all who and what she was. A flame of envy lighted in her heart. She realized in a dim way how much the city held—wealth, fashion, ease—every adornment for women, and she longed for dress and beauty with a whole and fulsome heart.

On the second floor were the managerial offices, to which after some inquiry she was now directed. There she found other girls ahead of her, applicants like herself, but with more of that self-satisfied and independent air which experience of the city lends—girls who scrutinized her in a painful manner. After a wait of perhaps three-quarters of an hour she was called in turn.

"Now," said a sharp, quick-mannered Jew who was sitting at a roll-top desk near the window—"have you ever worked in any other store?"

"No sir," said Carrie.

"Oh, you haven't," he said, eyeing her keenly.

"No sir," she replied.

"Well, we prefer young women just now with some experience. I guess we can't use you."

Carrie stood waiting a moment, hardly certain whether the interview had terminated.

"Don't wait!" he exclaimed. "Remember we are very busy here."

Carrie began to move quickly to the door.

"Hold on," he said, calling her back. "Give me your name and address. We want girls occasionally."

When she had gotten safely out again into the street she could scarcely restrain tears. It was not so much the particular rebuff which she had just experienced, but the whole abashing trend of the day. She was tired and rather over-played upon in the nerves. She abandoned the thought of appealing to the other department stores and now wandered on, feeling a certain safety and relief in mingling with the crowd.

In her indifferent wandering she turned into Jackson Street, not far from the river, and was keeping her way along the south side of that imposing thoroughfare, when a piece of wrapping paper written on with marking ink and tacked upon a door attracted her attention. It read "Girls wanted—wrappers and stitchers." She hesitated for the moment, thinking surely to go in, but upon further consideration the added qualifications of "wrappers and stitchers" deterred her. She had no idea of what that meant. Most probably she would need to be experienced in it. She walked on a little way, mentally balancing as to whether or not to apply. Necessity triumphed however and she returned.

The entrance, which opened into a small hall, led to an elevator shaft, the elevator of which was up. It was a dingy affair, being used both as a freight and passenger entrance, and the woodwork was marked and splintered by the heavy boxes which were tumbled in and out, at intervals. A frowzy-headed German-American, about fourteen years of age, operated the elevator in his shirt sleeves and bare feet. His face was considerably marked with grease and dirt.

When the elevator stopped, the boy leisurely raised a protecting arm of wood and by grace of his superior privilege admitted her.

"Wear do you want go?" he inquired.

"I want to see the manager," she replied.

"Wot manager?" he returned, surveying her caustically.

"Is there more than one?" she asked. "I thought it was all one firm."

"Naw," said the youth. "Der's six different people. Want to see Speigelheim?"

"I don't know," answered Carrie. She colored a little as she began to feel the necessity of explaining. "I want to see whoever put up that sign."

"Dot's Speigelheim," said the boy. "Fort floor." Therewith he proudly turned to his task of pulling the rope, and the elevator ascended.

The firm of Speigelheim and Co., makers of boys' caps, occupied one floor of fifty feet in width and some eighty feet in depth. It was a place rather dingily lighted, the darkest portions having incandescent lights, filled in part with machines and part with workbenches. At the latter labored quite a company of girls and some men. The former were drabby looking creatures, stained in face with oil and dust, clad in thin shapeless cotton dresses, and shod with more or less worn shoes. Many of them had their sleeves rolled up, revealing bare arms, and in some cases, owing to heat, their dresses were open at the neck. They were, a fair type of nearly the lowest order of shop girls,—careless, rather slouchy, and more or less pale from confinement. They were not timid however, were rich in curiosity and strong in daring and slang.

Carrie looked about her, very much disturbed and quite sure that she did not want to work here. Aside from making her uncomfortable by sidelong glances, no one paid her the least attention. She waited until the whole department was aware of her presence. Then some word was sent round and a foreman in an apron and shirt sleeves, the latter rolled up to his shoulders, approached.

"Do you want to see me?" he asked.

"Do you need any help?" said Carrie, already learning directness of address.

"Do you know how to stitch caps?" he returned.

"No sir," she replied.

"Have you ever had any experience at this kind of work?" he inquired.

She owned that she hadn't.

"Well," said the foreman, scratching his ear meditatively, "we do need a stitcher. We like experienced help though. We've hardly got time to break people in." He paused and looked away out of the window. "We might, though, put you at finishing," he concluded reflectively.

"How much do you pay a week?" ventured Carrie, emboldened by a certain softness in the man's manner and his simplicity of address.

"Three and a half," he answered.

"Oh," she was about to exclaim, but checked herself, and allowed her thoughts to die without expression.

"We're not exactly in need of anybody," he went on vaguely, looking her over as one would a package. "You can come Monday morning though," he added, "and I'll put you to work."

"Thank you," said Carrie weakly.

"If you come, bring an apron," he added.

He walked away and left her standing by the elevator, never so much as inquiring her name.

While the appearance of the shop and the announcement of the price paid per week operated very much as a blow to Carrie's fancy, the fact that work of any kind, after so rude a round of experience, was offered her, was gratifying. She could not begin to believe that she would take the place, modest as her aspirations were. She had been used to better than that. Her mere experience and the free out-of-doors life of the country caused her nature to revolt at such confinement. Dirt had never been her share. Her sister's flat was clean. This place was grimy and low; the girls were careless and hardened. They must be bad-minded and -hearted, she imagined. Still a place had been offered her. Surely Chicago was not so bad if she could find one place in one day. She might find another and better later.

Her subsequent experiences were not of a reassuring nature, however. From all the more pleasing or imposing places she was turned away abruptly with the most chilling formality. In others where she applied, only the experienced were required. She met with painful rebuffs, the most trying of which had been in a cloak manufacturing house, where she had gone to the fourth floor to inquire.

"No, no," said the foreman, a rough, heavy-built individual who looked after a miserably lighted work shop, "we don't want anyone. Don't come here."

In another factory she was leered upon by a most sensual-faced individual who endeavored to turn the natural questions of the inquiry into a personal interview, asking all sorts of embarrassing questions and endeavoring to satisfy himself evidently that she was of loose enough morals to suit his purpose. In that case she had been relieved enough to get away and found the busy, indifferent streets to be again a soothing refuge.

With the wane of the afternoon went her hopes, her courage and her strength. She had been astonishingly persistent. So earnest an effort was well deserving of a better reward. On every hand, to her fatigued senses, the great business portion grew larger, harder, more stolid in its indifference. It seemed as if it was all closed to her, that the struggle was too fierce for her to hope to do anything at all. Men and women hurried by in long, shifting lines. She felt the flow of the tide of effort and interest, felt her own helplessness without quite realizing the wisp on the tide that she was. She cast about vainly for some possible place to apply but found no door which she had the courage to enter. It would be the same thing all over. The old humiliation of her pleas rewarded by curt denial. Sick at heart and in body, she turned to the west, the direction of Minnie's flat, which she had now fixed in mind, and began that wearisome, baffled retreat which the seeker for employment at nightfall too often makes. In passing through Fifth Avenue, south towards Van Buren Street, where she intended to take a car, she passed the door of a large wholesale shoe house, through the plate glass window of which she could see a middle-aged gentleman sitting at a small desk. One of those forlorn impulses which often grow out of a fixed sense of defeat, the last sprouting of a baffled and uprooted growth of ideas, seized upon her. She walked deliberately through the door and up to the gentleman who looked at her weary face with partially awakened interest.

"What is it?" he said.

"Can you give me something to do?" asked Carrie.

"Now I really don't know," he said kindly. "What kind of work is it you want—you're not a typewriter, are you?"

"Oh, no," answered Carrie.

"Well, we only employ book keepers and typewriters here. You might go round to the side and inquire upstairs. They did want some help upstairs a few days ago. Ask for Mr. Brown."

She hastened around to the side entrance and was taken up by the elevator to the fourth floor.

"Call Mr. Brown, Willie," said the elevator man to a boy near by.

Willie went off and presently returned with the information that Mr. Brown said she should sit down and that he would be around in a little while.

It was a portion of a stock room which gave no idea of the general character of the floor, and Carrie could form no opinion of the nature of the work.

"So you want something to do," said Mr. Brown, after he inquired concerning the nature of her errand. "Have you ever been employed in a shoe factory before?"

"No sir," said Carrie.

"What is your name?" he inquired, and being informed, "Well, I don't know as I have anything for you. Would you work for four and a half a week?"

Carrie was too worn by defeat not to feel that it was considerable. She had not expected that he would offer her less than six. She acquiesced, however, and he took her name and address.

"Well," he said finally—"you report here at eight o'clock Monday morning. I think I can find something for you to do."

He left her revived by the possibilities, sure that she had found something to do at last. Instantly the blood crept warmly over her body. Her nervous tension relaxed. She walked out into the busy street and discovered a new atmosphere. Behold, the throng was moving with a lightsome step. She noticed that men and women were smiling. Scraps of conversation and notes of laughter floated to her. The air was light. People were already pouring out of the buildings, their labor ended for the day. She noticed that they were pleased, and thoughts of her sister's home, and the meal that would be awaiting her, quickened her steps. She hurried on, tired perhaps, but no longer weary of foot. What would not Minnie say! Ah, long the winter in Chicago—the lights, the crowd, the amusement. This was a great, pleasing metropolis after all. Her new firm was a goodly institution. Its windows were of huge plate glass. She could probably do well there. Thoughts of Drouet returned, of the things he had told her. She now felt that life was better. That it was livelier, sprightlier. She boarded a car in the best of sprits, feeling her blood still flowing pleasantly. She would live in Chicago, her mind kept saying to itself. She would have a better time than she ever had before—she would be happy.

1900

STEPHEN CRANE
1871–1900

S hortly after the death of Stephen Crane at the age of twenty-eight, the future novelist Willa Cather asked, "Was ever so much experience and achievement crowded into such space of time?" Indeed, Crane's brief, hectic career of literary celebrity seems in retrospect to be incomparable in its intensity and contradiction. He eschewed convention and lived the life of a penniless artist, yet he sought the approval of the literary establishment. He was a journalist who could spend months composing a single short story. Crane's attention to the rhythms of speech and quotidian detail earned him the praise of literary realists, while his skepticism of moral judgment would make him a favorite of a later generation of modernists.

Crane was born in 1871 in Newark, New Jersey, the youngest of fourteen children (nine of whom survived to adulthood). His family was rooted in the traditions of reform Christianity. On his mother's side were generations of Methodist ministers, and his father was a Methodist minister as well. Crane would not follow in this tradition, eventually rejecting the religious faith of his family and its moral judgments. He instead developed an interest in the military, shaped in part by stories of ancestors who served in the Revolutionary War and the War of 1812. After his father's death in 1880, Crane attended a Methodist boarding school and considered applying to West Point, the U.S Military Academy. Though he later decided against the military—briefly attending Lafayette College and Syracuse University in a thoroughly undistinguished academic career—his fascination with warfare fueled his imagination.

At the age of nineteen, Crane left college to move to New York, where he divided his time between the seedy apartments of his artist friends and the home of his brother, Edmund, in nearby Lake View, New Jersey. He accepted a variety of journalistic assignments even as he worked on his own sketches of urban life. In 1893, Crane published his first book—*Maggie, A Girl of the Streets (A Story of New York)*—at his own expense, going so far as to hire four men to advertise the book by reading it on the elevated train. The short novel earned praise from both Hamlin Garland and William Dean Howells for its revealing portrayal of the urban poor and its deployment of carefully crafted dialect. The story of Maggie—a tenement girl who

Stephen Crane as a war correspondent in Athens, Greece, 1897, posing for a studio photograph.

seems driven by powerful forces into prostitution—was not a commercial success, however. The book did not sell well in Crane's lifetime, even when it was later republished by a more prestigious publishing house after Crane became better known.

By contrast, Crane's next novel, *The Red Badge of Courage* (1895), made him a literary celebrity. Crane was prompted in part by the vogue in the 1880s and '90s for magazine articles about Civil War battles and generals, articles that emphasized the movements of troops and strategies of war but that frequently said little about the experiences of enlisted men. He reportedly remarked to a friend, "I wonder that *some* of these fellows don't tell how they *felt* in those scraps!" *The Red Badge of Courage* emphasizes that feeling, staging a psychological drama of complexity and ambiguity. The protagonist, Henry Fleming, is as much antihero as hero, a man who experiences neither the glory nor the valor of war but rather profound alienation.

The Red Badge of Courage was first syndicated in newspapers in December 1894 to immediate acclaim, and the same syndication company hired him early in 1895 as a roving reporter in the American West and Mexico, experiences that would give him the material for several of his finest tales, including "The Blue Hotel" (1898). That same year, Crane published his first volume of poetry, *The Black Riders and Other Lines*. Predictably, Garland and Howells responded favorably to Crane's spare, original, unflinchingly honest poetry. Garland, for instance, later remarked that his poems "carried the sting and compression of Emily Dickinson's verse," which had finally in that decade become widely available for the first time. Although Crane's experimental, philosophical verse failed to win a large audience, in the decades after his death reviewers would regard it as a forerunner of the Imagist movement led by Hilda Doolittle, Ezra Pound, and Amy Lowell.

Crane's life took a major turn in the fall of 1896, after the New York *Journal* hired him to report on that city's notorious Tenderloin district, famous for its night life of drugs, prostitution, and corruption. After leaving a hashish parlor, Crane challenged the wrongful arrest of a prostitute—and then appeared in court to defend her. The events made headlines, and the scandal chased Crane from New York. He left the city that winter to report on the insurrection in Cuba, where rebels were fighting for independence from Spain. On his way to Cuba he met Cora Howorth Taylor, the proprietor of a bordello in Jacksonville, Florida, with whom would live for the last three years of his life. Crane successfully arranged transport to Cuba, only to face disaster: on January 2, 1897, Crane's ship, *The Commodore*, sank off the coast of Florida. His report of this harrowing adventure was published a few days later in the *New York Press*. More significantly, the experience led to his composition of one of the best-known and most widely reprinted of all American stories, "The Open Boat." This story, like *The Red Badge of Courage*, reveals Crane's characteristic subject matter—the physical, emotional, and intellectual responses of people under extreme pressure, nature's indifference to the fate of humanity, and the difficulty of arriving at moral judgment. Like *Maggie*, "The Open Boat" locates Crane within the currents of American literary naturalism with Frank Norris, Jack London, and Theodore Dreiser—all contemporaries who were not well known to him.

In stories like "The Open Boat" and "The Blue Hotel," Crane achieved his mature style, one characterized by irony and brevity, qualities later associated with the literary modernism of Sherwood Anderson, Gertrude Stein, and Ernest Hemingway. His career in many ways demonstrates the limits of categories such as realism, naturalism, and modernism. But Crane's writing also offers a way of understanding the continuities among these literary movements. After all, Crane deliberately sought the approbation of figures like Garland and Howells, whom he treated sympathetically in his journalism and who, in turn, esteemed his work highly. At the same time, younger authors like Hemingway—who considered Crane one of the three "good writers" of American literature—could find in Crane seeds of their own literary endeavors.

The final years of Crane's life were a flurry of frenetic activity and financial free-fall. He became a war correspondent, covering first the Greco-Turkish War and then later the U.S. invasion of Cuba in 1898. During the same period, he and Cora Taylor settled in England, where Crane became acquainted with Joseph Conrad, H. G. Wells, and Henry James. Crane suffered from both tuberculosis and chronic debt, and his health rapidly declined while he engaged in furious attempts to earn money through his writing. In 1899 he drafted thirteen stories set in the fictional town Whilomville, and he published his second volume of poetry, *War Is Kind*, as well as the novel *Active Service* and the American edition of *"The Monster" and Other Stories*. "The Monster" is a daring exploration of the hypocrisy and cruelty of racial prejudice. During a Christmas party that year Crane nearly died of a lung hemorrhage. Surviving only a few months, he summoned the strength to write a series of nine articles on great battles and completed the first twenty-five chapters of the novel *The O'Ruddy*. In spite of Cora's hopes for a miraculous cure, and the generous assistance of his friends, Crane died on June 5, 1900, in Badenweiler, Germany.

The Open Boat[1]

A TALE INTENDED TO BE AFTER THE FACT, BEING THE EXPERIENCE OF FOUR
MEN FROM THE SUNK STEAMER COMMODORE

I

None of them knew the color of the sky. Their eyes glanced level, and were fastened upon the waves that swept toward them. These waves were of the hue of slate, save for the tops, which were of foaming white, and all of the men knew the colors of the sea. The horizon narrowed and widened, and dipped and rose, and at all times its edge was jagged with waves that seemed thrust up in points like rocks.

Many a man ought to have a bath-tub larger than the boat which here rode upon the sea. These waves were most wrongfully and barbarously abrupt and tall, and each froth-top was a problem in small boat navigation.

The cook squatted in the bottom and looked with both eyes at the six inches of gunwale which separated him from the ocean. His sleeves were rolled over his fat forearms, and the two flaps of his unbuttoned vest dangled as he bent to bail out the boat. Often he said: "Gawd! That was a narrow clip." As he remarked it he invariably gazed eastward over the broken sea.

The oiler,[2] steering with one of the two oars in the boat, sometimes raised himself suddenly to keep clear of water that swirled in over the stern. It was a thin little oar and it seemed often ready to snap.

The correspondent, pulling at the other oar, watched the waves and wondered why he was there.

The injured captain, lying in the bow, was at this time buried in that profound dejection and indifference which comes, temporarily at least, to even the bravest and most enduring when, willy nilly, the firm fails, the army loses, the ship goes down. The mind of the master of a vessel is rooted deep in the timbers of her, though he command for a day or a decade, and this captain had on him the stern impression of a scene in the grays of dawn of seven turned faces, and later a stump of a top-mast with a white ball on it that slashed to and fro at the waves, went low and lower, and down. Thereafter there was something strange in his voice. Although steady, it was deep with mourning, and of a quality beyond oration or tears.

"Keep'er a little more south, Billie," said he.

"'A little more south,' sir," said the oiler in the stern.

A seat in his boat was not unlike a seat upon a bucking broncho, and, by the same token, a broncho is not much smaller. The craft pranced and reared, and plunged like an animal. As each wave came, and she rose for it, she seemed like a horse making at a fence outrageously high. The manner of

---

1. Crane sailed as a correspondent on the steamer *Commodore*, which, on January 1, 1897, left Jacksonville, Florida, with munitions for the Cuban insurrectionists. Early on the morning of January 2, the steamer sank. With three others, Crane reached Daytona Beach in a ten-foot dinghy on the following morning. Under the title "Stephen Crane's Own Story," the *New York Press* on January 7 carried the details of his nearly fatal experience. In June 1897, he published his fictional account, "The Open Boat," in *Scribner's Magazine*. The story gave the title to *"The Open Boat" and Other Tales of Adventure* (1898). The text here reprints that of the University of Virginia edition of *The Works of Stephen Crane, Vol. 5, Tales of Adventure* (1970).

2. One who oils machinery in the engine room of a ship.

her scramble over these walls of water is a mystic thing, and, moreover, at the top of them were ordinarily these problems in white water, the foam racing down from the summit of each wave, requiring a new leap, and a leap from the air. Then, after scornfully bumping a crest, she would slide, and race, and splash down a long incline and arrive bobbing and nodding in front of the next menace.

A singular disadvantage of the sea lies in the fact that after successfully surmounting one wave you discover that there is another behind it just as important and just as nervously anxious to do something effective in the way of swamping boats. In a ten-foot dingey one can get an idea of the resources of the sea in the line of waves that is not probable to the average experience, which is never at sea in a dingey. As each slaty wall of water approached, it shut all else from the view of the men in the boat, and it was not difficult to imagine that this particular wave was the final outburst of the ocean, the last effort of the grim water. There was a terrible grace in the move of the waves, and they came in silence, save for the snarling of the crests.

In the wan light, the faces of the men must have been gray. Their eyes must have glinted in strange ways as they gazed steadily astern. Viewed from a balcony, the whole thing would doubtlessly have been weirdly picturesque. But the men in the boat had no time to see it, and if they had had leisure there were other things to occupy their minds. The sun swung steadily up the sky, and they knew it was broad day because the color of the sea changed from slate to emerald-green, streaked with amber lights, and the foam was like tumbling snow. The process of the breaking day was unknown to them. They were aware only of this effect upon the color of the waves that rolled toward them.

In disjointed sentences the cook and the correspondent argued as to the difference between a life-saving station and a house of refuge. The cook had said: "There's a house of refuge just north of the Mosquito Inlet Light, and as soon as they see us, they'll come off in their boat and pick us up."

"As soon as who see us?" said the correspondent.

"The crew," said the cook.

"Houses of refuge don't have crews," said the correspondent. "As I understand them, they are only places where clothes and grub are stored for the benefit of shipwrecked people. They don't carry crews."

"Oh, yes, they do," said the cook.

"No, they don't," said the correspondent.

"Well, we're not there yet, anyhow," said the oiler, in the stern.

"Well," said the cook, "perhaps it's not a house of refuge that I'm thinking of as being near Mosquito Inlet Light. Perhaps it's a life-saving station."

"We're not there yet," said the oiler, in the stern.

II

As the boat bounced from the top of each wave, the wind tore through the hair of the hatless men, and as the craft plopped her stern down again the spray slashed past them. The crest of each of these waves was a hill, from the top of which the men surveyed, for a moment, a broad tumultuous expanse, shining and wind-riven. It was probably splendid. It was probably glorious, this play of the free sea, wild with lights of emerald and white and amber.

"Bully good thing it's an on-shore wind," said the cook. "If not, where would we be? Wouldn't have a show."

"That's right," said the correspondent.

The busy oiler nodded his assent.

Then the captain, in the bow, chuckled in a way that expressed humor, contempt, tragedy, all in one. "Do you think we've got much of a show, now, boys?" said he.

Whereupon the three were silent, save for a trifle of hemming and hawing. To express any particular optimism at this time they felt to be childish and stupid, but they all doubtless possessed this sense of the situation in their mind. A young man thinks doggedly at such times. On the other hand, the ethics of their condition was decidedly against any open suggestion of hopelessness. So they were silent.

"Oh, well," said the captain, soothing his children, "we'll get ashore all right."

But there was that in his tone which made them think, so the oiler quoth: "Yes! If this wind holds!"

The cook was bailing. "Yes! If we don't catch hell in the surf."

Canton flannel[3] gulls flew near and far. Sometimes they sat down on the sea, near patches of brown sea-weed that rolled over the waves with a movement like carpets on a line in a gale. The birds sat comfortably in groups, and they were envied by some in the dingey, for the wrath of the sea was no more to them than it was to a covey of prairie chickens a thousand miles inland. Often they came very close and stared at the men with black bead-like eyes. At these times they were uncanny and sinister in their unblinking scrutiny, and the men hooted angrily at them, telling them to be gone. One came, and evidently decided to alight on the top of the captain's head. The bird flew parallel to the boat and did not circle, but made short sidelong jumps in the air in chicken-fashion. His black eyes were wistfully fixed upon the captain's head. "Ugly brute," said the oiler to the bird. "You look as if you were made with a jack-knife." The cook and the correspondent swore darkly at the creature. The captain naturally wished to knock it away with the end of the heavy painter, but he did not dare do it, because anything resembling an emphatic gesture would have capsized this freighted boat, and so with his open hand, the captain gently and carefully waved the gull away. After it had been discouraged from the pursuit the captain breathed easier on account of his hair, and others breathed easier because the bird struck their minds at this time as being somehow grewsome and ominous.

In the meantime the oiler and the correspondent rowed. And also they rowed.

They sat together in the same seat, and each rowed an oar. Then the oiler took both oars; then the correspondent took both oars; then the oiler; then the correspondent. They rowed and they rowed. The very ticklish part of the business was when the time came for the reclining one in the stern to take his turn at the oars. By the very last star of truth, it is easier to steal eggs from under a hen than it was to change seats in the dingey. First the man in the stern slid his hand along the thwart and moved with care, as if he were

---

3. Common name of a lightweight cotton fabric, usually white.

of Sèvres.[4] Then the man in the rowing seat slid his hand along the other thwart. It was all done with the most extraordinary care. As the two sidled past each other, the whole party kept watchful eyes on the coming wave, and the captain cried: "Look out now! Steady there!"

The brown mats of sea-weed that appeared from time to time were like islands, bits of earth. They were travelling, apparently, neither one way nor the other. They were, to all intents, stationary. They informed the men in the boat that it was making progress slowly toward the land.

The captain, rearing cautiously in the bow, after the dingey soared on a great swell, said that he had seen the light-house at Mosquito Inlet. Presently the cook remarked that he had seen it. The correspondent was at the oars, then, and for some reason he too wished to look at the light-house, but his back was toward the far shore and the waves were important, and for some time he could not seize an opportunity to turn his head. But at last there came a wave more gentle than the others, and when at the crest of it he swiftly scoured the western horizon.

"See it?" said the captain.

"No," said the correspondent, slowly, "I didn't see anything."

"Look again," said the captain. He pointed. "It's exactly in that direction."

At the top of another wave, the correspondent did as he was bid, and this time his eyes chanced on a small still thing on the edge of the swaying horizon. It was precisely like the point of a pin. It took an anxious eye to find a light-house so tiny.

"Think we'll make it, Captain?"

"If this wind holds and the boat don't swamp, we can't do much else," said the captain.

The little boat, lifted by each towering sea, and splashed viciously by the crests, made progress that in the absence of sea-weed was not apparent to those in her. She seemed just a wee thing wallowing, miraculously, top-up, at the mercy of five oceans. Occasionally, a great spread of water, like white flames, swarmed into her.

"Bail her, cook," said the captain, serenely.

"All right, Captain," said the cheerful cook.

III

It would be difficult to describe the subtle brotherhood of men that was here established on the seas. No one said that it was so. No one mentioned it. But it dwelt in the boat, and each man felt it warm him. They were a captain, an oiler, a cook, and a correspondent, and they were friends, friends in a more curiously iron-bound degree than may be common. The hurt captain, lying against the water-jar in the bow, spoke always in a low voice and calmly, but he could never command a more ready and swiftly obedient crew than the motley three of the dingey. It was more than a mere recognition of what was best for the common safety. There was surely in it a quality that was personal and heartfelt. And after this devotion to the commander of the boat there was this comradeship that the correspondent, for instance, who

---

4. Fine, often ornately decorated French porcelain.

had been taught to be cynical of men, knew even at the time was the best experience of his life. But no one said that it was so. No one mentioned it.

"I wish we had a sail," remarked the captain. "We might try my overcoat on the end of an oar and give you two boys a chance to rest." So the cook and the correspondent held the mast and spread wide the overcoat. The oiler steered, and the little boat made good way with her new rig. Sometimes the oiler had to scull sharply to keep a sea from breaking into the boat, but otherwise sailing was a success.

Meanwhile the light-house had been growing slowly larger. It had now almost assumed color, and appeared like a little gray shadow on the sky. The man at the oars could not be prevented from turning his head rather often to try for a glimpse of this little gray shadow.

At last, from the top of each wave the men in the tossing boat could see land. Even as the light-house was an upright shadow on the sky, this land seemed but a long black shadow on the sea. It certainly was thinner than paper. "We must be about opposite New Smyrna," said the cook, who had coasted this shore often in schooners. "Captain, by the way, I believe they abandoned that life-saving station there about a year ago."

"Did they?" said the captain.

The wind slowly died away. The cook and the correspondent were not now obliged to slave in order to hold high the oar. But the waves continued their old impetuous swooping at the dingey, and the little craft, no longer under way, struggled woundily over them. The oiler or the correspondent took the oars again.

Shipwrecks are *apropos* of nothing. If men could only train for them and have them occur when the men had reached pink condition, there would be less drowning at sea. Of the four in the dingey none had slept any time worth mentioning for two days and two nights previous to embarking in the dingey, and in the excitement of clambering about the deck of a foundering ship they had also forgotten to eat heartily.

For these reasons, and for others, neither the oiler nor the correspondent was fond of rowing at this time. The correspondent wondered ingenuously how in the name of all that was sane could there be people who thought it amusing to row a boat. It was not an amusement; it was a diabolical punishment, and even a genius of mental aberrations could never conclude that it was anything but a horror to the muscles and a crime against the back. He mentioned to the boat in general how the amusement of rowing struck him, and the weary-faced oiler smiled in full sympathy. Previously to the foundering, by the way, the oiler had worked double-watch in the engine-room of the ship.

"Take her easy, now, boys," said the captain. "Don't spend yourselves. If we have to run a surf you'll need all your strength, because we'll sure have to swim for it. Take your time."

Slowly the land arose from the sea. From a black line it became a line of black and a line of white—trees and sand. Finally, the captain said that he could make out a house on the shore. "That's the house of refuge, sure," said the cook. "They'll see us before long, and come out after us."

The distant light-house reared high. "The keeper ought to be able to make us out now, if he's looking through a glass," said the captain. "He'll notify the life-saving people."

"None of those other boats could have got ashore to give word of the wreck," said the oiler, in a low voice. "Else the life-boat would be out hunting us."

Slowly and beautifully the land loomed out of the sea. The wind came again. It had veered from the northeast to the southeast. Finally, a new sound struck the ears of the men in the boat. It was the low thunder of the surf on the shore. "We'll never be able to make the light-house now," said the captain. "Swing her head a little more north, Billie."

"'A little more north,' sir," said the oiler.

Whereupon the little boat turned her nose once more down the wind, and all but the oarsman watched the shore grow. Under the influence of this expansion doubt and direful apprehension was leaving the minds of the men. The management of the boat was still most absorbing, but it could not prevent a quiet cheerfulness. In an hour, perhaps, they would be ashore.

Their back-bones had become thoroughly used to balancing in the boat and they now rode this wild colt of a dingey like circus men. The correspondent thought that he had been drenched to the skin, but happening to feel in the top pocket of his coat, he found therein eight cigars. Four of them were soaked with seawater; four were perfectly scatheless. After a search, somebody produced three dry matches, and thereupon the four waifs rode impudently in their little boat, and with an assurance of an impending rescue shining in their eyes, puffed at the big cigars and judged well and ill of all men. Everybody took a drink of water.

IV

"Cook," remarked the captain, "there don't seem to be any signs of life about your house of refuge."

"No," replied the cook. "Funny they don't see us!"

A broad stretch of lowly coast lay before the eyes of the men. It was of dunes topped with dark vegetation. The roar of the surf was plain, and sometimes they could see the white lip of a wave as it spun up the beach. A tiny house was blocked out black upon the sky. Southward, the slim light-house lifted its little gray length.

Tide, wind, and waves were swinging the dingey northward. "Funny they don't see us," said the men.

The surf's roar was here dulled, but its tone was, nevertheless, thunderous and mighty. As the boat swam over the great rollers, the men sat listening to this roar. "We'll swamp sure," said everybody.

It is fair to say here that there was not a life-saving station within twenty miles in either direction, but the men did not know this fact and in consequence they made dark and opprobrious remarks concerning the eyesight of the nation's life-savers. Four scowling men sat in the dingey and surpassed records in the invention of epithets.

"Funny they don't see us."

The light-heartedness of a former time had completely faded. To their sharpened minds it was easy to conjure pictures of all kinds of incompetency and blindness and, indeed, cowardice. There was the shore of the populous land, and it was bitter and bitter to them that from it came no sign.

"Well," said the captain, ultimately, "I suppose we'll have to make a try for ourselves. If we stay out here too long, we'll none of us have strength left to swim after the boat swamps."

And so the oiler, who was at the oars, turned the boat straight for the shore. There was a sudden tightening of muscles. There was some thinking.

"If we don't all get ashore—" said the captain. "If we don't all get ashore, I suppose you fellows know where to send news of my finish?"

They then briefly exchanged some addresses and admonitions. As for the reflections of the men, there was a great deal of rage in them. Perchance they might be formulated thus: "If I am going to be drowned—if I am going to be drowned—if I am going to be drowned, why, in the name of the seven mad gods who rule the sea, was I allowed to come thus far and contemplate sand and trees? Was I brought here merely to have my nose dragged away as I was about to nibble the sacred cheese of life? It is preposterous. If this old ninny-woman, Fate, cannot do better than this, she should be deprived of the management of men's fortunes. She is an old hen who knows not her intention. If she has decided to drown me, why did she not do it in the beginning and save me all this trouble. The whole affair is absurd. . . . But, no, she cannot mean to drown me. She dare not drown me. She cannot drown me. Not after all this work." Afterward the man might have had an impulse to shake his fist at the clouds. "Just you drown me, now, and then hear what I call you!"

The billows that came at this time were more formidable. They seemed always just about to break and roll over the little boat in a turmoil of foam. There was a preparatory and long growl in the speech of them. No mind unused to the sea would have concluded that the dingey could ascend these sheer heights in time. The shore was still afar. The oiler was a wily surf-man. "Boys," he said, swiftly, "she won't live three minutes more and we're too far out to swim. Shall I take her to sea again, Captain?"

"Yes! Go ahead!" said the captain.

This oiler, by a series of quick miracles, and fast and steady oarsmanship, turned the boat in the middle of the surf and took her safely to sea again.

There was a considerable silence as the boat bumped over the furrowed sea to deeper water. Then somebody in gloom spoke. "Well, anyhow, they must have seen us from the shore by now."

The gulls went in slanting flight up the wind toward the gray desolate east. A squall, marked by dingy clouds, and clouds brick-red, like smoke from a burning building, appeared from the southeast.

"What do you think of those life-saving people? Ain't they peaches?"

"Funny they haven't seen us."

"Maybe they think we're out here for sport! Maybe they think we're fishin'. Maybe they think we're damned fools."

It was a long afternoon. A changed tide tried to force them southward, but wind and wave said northward. Far ahead, where coast-line, sea, and sky formed their mighty angle, there were little dots which seemed to indicate a city on the shore.

"St. Augustine?"

The captain shook his head. "Too near Mosquito Inlet."

And the oiler rowed, and then the correspondent rowed. Then the oiler rowed. It was a weary business. The human back can become the seat of more aches and pains than are registered in books for the composite anatomy of a regiment. It is a limited area, but it can become the theatre of innumerable muscular conflicts, tangles, wrenches, knots, and other comforts.

"Did you ever like to row, Billie?" asked the correspondent.

"No," said the oiler. "Hang it."

When one exchanged the rowing-seat for a place in the bottom of the boat, he suffered a bodily depression that caused him to be careless of everything save an obligation to wiggle one finger. There was cold sea-water swashing to and fro in the boat, and he lay in it. His head, pillowed on a thwart, was within an inch of the swirl of a wave crest, and sometimes a particularly obstreperous sea came inboard and drenched him once more. But these matters did not annoy him. It is almost certain that if the boat had capsized he would have tumbled comfortably out upon the ocean as if he felt sure that it was a great soft mattress.

"Look! There's a man on the shore!"

"Where?"

"There? See 'im? See 'im?"

"Yes, sure! He's walking along."

"Now he's stopped. Look! He's facing us!"

"He's waving at us!"

"So he is! By thunder!"

"Ah, now, we're all right! Now we're all right! There'll be a boat out here for us in half an hour."

"He's going on. He's running. He's going up to that house there."

The remote beach seemed lower than the sea, and it required a searching glance to discern the little black figure. The captain saw a floating stick and they rowed to it. A bath-towel was by some weird chance in the boat, and, tying this on the stick, the captain waved it. The oarsman did not dare turn his head, so he was obliged to ask questions.

"What's he doing now?"

"He's standing still again. He's looking, I think. . . . There he goes again. Toward the house. . . . Now he's stopped again."

"Is he waving at us?"

"No, not now! he was, though."

"Look! There comes another man!"

"He's running."

"Look at him go, would you."

"Why, he's on a bicycle. Now he's met the other man. They're both waving at us. Look!"

"There comes something up the beach."

"What the devil is that thing?"

"Why, it looks like a boat."

"Why, certainly it's a boat."

"No, it's on wheels."

"Yes, so it is. Well, that must be the life-boat. They drag them along shore on a wagon."

"That's the life-boat, sure."

"No, by——, it's—it's an omnibus."

"I tell you it's a life-boat."

"It is not! It's an omnibus. I can see it plain. See? One of those big hotel omnibuses."

"By thunder, you're right. It's an omnibus, sure as fate. What do you suppose they are doing with an omnibus? Maybe they are going around collecting the life-crew, hey?"

"That's it, likely. Look! There's a fellow waving a little black flag. He's standing on the steps of the omnibus. There come those other two fellows. Now they're all talking together. Look at the fellow with the flag. Maybe he ain't waving it!"

"That ain't a flag, is it? That's his coat. Why, certainly, that's his coat."

"So it is. It's his coat. He's taken it off and is waving it around his head. But would you look at him swing it!"

"Oh, say, there isn't any life-saving station there. That's just a winter resort hotel omnibus that has brought over some of the boarders to see us drown."

"What's that idiot with the coat mean? What's he signaling, anyhow?"

"It looks as if he were trying to tell us to go north. There must be a life-saving station up there."

"No! He thinks we're fishing. Just giving us a merry hand. See? Ah, there, Willie."

"Well, I wish I could make something out of those signals. What do you suppose he means?"

"He don't mean anything. He's just playing."

"Well, if he'd just signal us to try the surf again, or to go to sea and wait, or go north, or go south, or go to hell—there would be some reason in it. But look at him. He just stands there and keeps his coat revolving like a wheel. The ass!"

"There come more people."

"Now there's quite a mob. Look! Isn't that a boat?"

"Where? Oh, I see where you mean. No, that's no boat."

"That fellow is still waving his coat."

"He must think we like to see him do that. Why don't he quit it. It don't mean anything."

"I don't know. I think he is trying to make us go north. It must be that there's a life-saving station there somewhere."

"Say, he ain't tired yet. Look at 'im wave."

"Wonder how long he can keep that up. He's been revolving his coat ever since he caught sight of us. He's an idiot. Why aren't they getting men to bring a boat out. A fishing boat—one of those big yawls—could come out here all right. Why don't he do something?"

"Oh, it's all right, now."

"They'll have a boat out here for us in less than no time, now that they've seen us."

A faint yellow tone came into the sky over the low land. The shadows on the sea slowly deepened. The wind bore coldness with it, and the men began to shiver.

"Holy smoke!" said one, allowing his voice to express his impious mood, "if we keep on monkeying out here! If we've got to flounder out here all night!"

"Oh, we'll never have to stay here all night! Don't you worry. They've seen us now, and it won't be long before they'll come chasing out after us."

The shore grew dusky. The man waving a coat blended gradually into this gloom, and it swallowed in the same manner the omnibus and the group of people. The spray, when it dashed uproariously over the side, made the voyagers shrink and swear like men who were being branded.

"I'd like to catch the chump who waved the coat. I feel like socking him one, just for luck."

"Why? What did he do?"

"Oh, nothing, but then he seemed so damned cheerful."

In the meantime the oiler rowed, and then the correspondent rowed, and then the oiler rowed. Gray-faced and bowed forward, they mechanically, turn by turn, plied the leaden oars. The form of the light-house had vanished from the southern horizon, but finally a pale star appeared, just lifting from the sea. The streaked saffron in the west passed before the all-merging darkness, and the sea to the east was black. The land had vanished, and was expressed only by the low and drear thunder of the surf.

"If I am going to be drowned—if I am going to be drowned—if I am going to be drowned, why, in the name of the seven mad gods who rule the sea, was I allowed to come thus far and contemplate sand and trees? Was I brought here merely to have my nose dragged away as I was about to nibble the sacred cheese of life?"

The patient captain, drooped over the water-jar, was sometimes obliged to speak to the oarsman.

"Keep her head up! Keep her head up!"

"'Keep her head up,' sir." The voices were weary and low.

This was surely a quiet evening. All save the oarsman lay heavily and listlessly in the boat's bottom. As for him, his eyes were just capable of noting the tall black waves that swept forward in a most sinister silence, save for an occasional subdued growl of a crest.

The cook's head was on a thwart, and he looked without interest at the water under his nose. He was deep in other scenes. Finally he spoke. "Billie," he murmured, dreamfully, "what kind of pie do you like best?"

V

"Pie," said the oiler and the correspondent, agitatedly. "Don't talk about those things, blast you!"

"Well," said the cook, "I was just thinking about ham sandwiches, and——"

A night on the sea in an open boat is a long night. As darkness settled finally, the shine of the light, lifting from the sea in the south, changed to full gold. On the northern horizon a new light appeared, a small bluish gleam on the edge of the waters. These two lights were the furniture of the world. Otherwise there was nothing but waves.

Two men huddled in the stern, and distances were so magnificent in the dingey that the rower was enabled to keep his feet partly warmed by thrusting them under his companions. Their legs indeed extended far under the rowing-seat until they touched the feet of the captain forward. Sometimes, despite the efforts of the tired oarsman, a wave came piling into the boat, an icy wave of the night, and the chilling water soaked them anew. They would twist their bodies for a moment and groan, and sleep the dead sleep once more, while the water in the boat gurgled about them as the craft rocked.

The plan of the oiler and the correspondent was for one to row until he lost the ability, and then arouse the other from his sea-water couch in the bottom of the boat.

The oiler plied the oars until his head drooped forward, and the overpowering sleep blinded him. And he rowed yet afterward. Then he touched a man in the bottom of the boat, and called his name. "Will you spell me for a little while?" he said meekly.

"Sure, Billie," said the correspondent, awakening and dragging himself to a sitting position. They exchanged places carefully, and the oiler, cuddling down in the sea-water at the cook's side, seemed to go to sleep instantly.

The particular violence of the sea had ceased. The waves came without snarling. The obligation of the man at the oars was to keep the boat headed so that the tilt of the rollers would not capsize her, and to preserve her from filling when the crests rushed past. The black waves were silent and hard to be seen in the darkness. Often one was almost upon the boat before the oarsman was aware.

In a low voice the correspondent addressed the captain. He was not sure that the captain was awake, although this iron man seemed to be always awake. "Captain, shall I keep her making for that light north, sir?"

The same steady voice answered him. "Yes. Keep it about two points off the port bow."

The cook had tied a life-belt around himself in order to get even the warmth which this clumsy cork contrivance could donate, and he seemed almost stove-like when a rower, whose teeth invariably chattered wildly as soon as he ceased his labor, dropped down to sleep.

The correspondent, as he rowed, looked down at the two men sleeping under foot. The cook's arm was around the oiler's shoulders, and, with their fragmentary clothing and haggard faces, they were the babes of the sea, a grotesque rendering of the old babes in the wood.[5]

Later he must have grown stupid at his work, for suddenly there was a growling of water, and a crest came with a roar and a swash into the boat, and it was a wonder that it did not set the cook afloat in his life-belt. The cook continued to sleep, but the oiler sat up, blinking his eyes and shaking with the new cold.

"Oh, I'm awful sorry, Billie," said the correspondent, contritely.

"That's all right, old boy," said the oiler, and lay down again and was asleep.

Presently it seemed that even the captain dozed, and the correspondent thought that he was the one man afloat on all the oceans. The wind had a voice as it came over the waves, and it was sadder than the end.

There was a long, loud swishing astern of the boat, and a gleaming trail of phosphorescence, like blue flame, was furrowed on the black waters. It might have been made by a monstrous knife.

Then there came a stillness, while the correspondent breathed with the open mouth and looked at the sea.

Suddenly there was another swish and another long flash of bluish light, and this time it was alongside the boat, and might almost have been reached

5. A traditional folktale tells of two babes abandoned in the woods, covered in leaves by birds when they fall asleep.

with an oar. The correspondent saw an enormous fin speed like a shadow through the water, hurling the crystalline spray and leaving the long glowing trail.

The correspondent looked over his shoulder at the captain. His face was hidden, and he seemed to be asleep. He looked at the babes of the sea. They certainly were asleep. So, being bereft of sympathy, he leaned a little way to one side and swore softly into the sea.

But the thing did not then leave the vicinity of the boat. Ahead or astern, on one side or the other, at intervals long or short, fled the long sparkling streak, and there was to be heard the whiroo of the dark fin. The speed and power of the thing was greatly to be admired. It cut the water like a gigantic and keen projectile.

The presence of this biding thing did not affect the man with the same horror that it would if he had been a picnicker. He simply looked at the sea dully and swore in an undertone.

Nevertheless, it is true that he did not wish to be alone with the thing. He wished one of his companions to awaken by chance and keep him company with it. But the captain hung motionless over the water-jar and the oiler and the cook in the bottom of the boat were plunged in slumber.

VI

"If I am going to be drowned—if I am going to be drowned—if I am going to be drowned, why, in the name of the seven mad gods who rule the sea, was I allowed to come thus far and contemplate sand and trees?"

During this dismal night, it may be remarked that a man would conclude that it was really the intention of the seven mad gods to drown him, despite the abominable injustice of it. For it was certainly an abominable injustice to drown a man who had worked so hard, so hard. The man felt it would be a crime most unnatural. Other people had drowned at sea since galleys swarmed with painted sails, but still——

When it occurs to a man that nature does not regard him as important, and that she feels she would not maim the universe by disposing of him, he at first wishes to throw bricks at the temple, and he hates deeply the fact that there are no bricks and no temples. Any visible expression of nature would surely be pelleted with his jeers.

Then, if there be no tangible thing to hoot he feels, perhaps, the desire to confront a personification and indulge in pleas, bowed to one knee, and with hands supplicant, saying: "Yes, but I love myself."

A high cold star on a winter's night is the word he feels that she says to him. Thereafter he knows the pathos of his situation.

The men in the dingey had not discussed these matters, but each had, no doubt, reflected upon them in silence and according to his mind. There was seldom any expression upon their faces save the general one of complete weariness. Speech was devoted to the business of the boat.

To chime the notes of his emotion, a verse mysteriously entered the correspondent's head. He had even forgotten that he had forgotten this verse, but it suddenly was in his mind.

A soldier of the Legion lay dying in Algiers,
There was lack of woman's nursing, there was dearth of woman's tears;
But a comrade stood beside him, and he took that comrade's hand,
And he said: "I never more shall see my own, my native land."[6]

In his childhood, the correspondent had been made acquainted with the fact that a soldier of the Legion lay dying in Algiers, but he had never regarded it as important. Myriads of his school-fellows had informed him of the soldier's plight, but the dinning had naturally ended by making him perfectly indifferent. He had never considered it his affair that a soldier of the Legion lay dying in Algiers, nor had it appeared to him as a matter for sorrow. It was less to him than the breaking of a pencil's point.

Now, however, it quaintly came to him as a human, living thing. It was no longer merely a picture of a few throes in the breast of a poet, meanwhile drinking tea and warming his feet at the grate; it was an actuality—stern, mournful, and fine.

The correspondent plainly saw the soldier. He lay on the sand with his feet out straight and still. While his pale left hand was upon his chest in an attempt to thwart the going of his life, the blood came between his fingers. In the far Algerian distance, a city of low square forms was set against a sky that was faint with the last sunset hues. The correspondent, plying the oars and dreaming of the slow and slower movements of the lips of the soldier, was moved by a profound and perfectly impersonal comprehension. He was sorry for the soldier of the Legion who lay dying in Algiers.

The thing which had followed the boat and waited had evidently grown bored at the delay. There was no longer to be heard the slash of the cut-water, and there was no longer the flame of the long trail. The light in the north still glimmered, but it was apparently no nearer to the boat. Sometimes the boom of the surf rang in the correspondent's ears, and he turned the craft seaward then and rowed harder. Southward, some one had evidently built a watch-fire on the beach. It was too low and too far to be seen, but it made a shimmering, roseate reflection upon the bluff back of it, and this could be discerned from the boat. The wind came stronger, and sometimes a wave suddenly raged out like a mountain-cat and there was to be seen the sheen and sparkle of a broken crest.

The captain, in the bow, moved on his water-jar and sat erect. "Pretty long night," he observed to the correspondent. He looked at the shore. "Those life-saving people take their time."

"Did you see that shark playing around?"

"Yes, I saw him. He was a big fellow, all right."

"Wish I had known you were awake."

Later the correspondent spoke into the bottom of the boat.

"Billie!" There was a slow and gradual disentanglement. "Billie, will you spell me?"

"Sure," said the oiler.

As soon as the correspondent touched the cold comfortable seawater in the bottom of the boat, and had huddled close to the cook's life-belt he was deep in sleep, despite the fact that his teeth played all the popular airs. This

6. The lines are incorrectly quoted from Caroline E. S. Norton's poem "Bingen on the Rhine" (1883).

sleep was so good to him that it was but a moment before he heard a voice call his name in a tone that demonstrated the last stages of exhaustion. "Will you spell me?"

"Sure, Billie."

The light in the north had mysteriously vanished, but the correspondent took his course from the wide-awake captain.

Later in the night they took the boat farther out to sea, and the captain directed the cook to take one oar at the stern and keep the boat facing the seas. He was to call out if he should hear the thunder of the surf. This plan enabled the oiler and the correspondent to get respite together. "We'll give those boys a chance to get into shape again," said the captain. They curled down and, after a few preliminary chatterings and trembles, slept once more the dead sleep. Neither knew they had bequeathed to the cook the company of another shark, or perhaps the same shark.

As the boat caroused on the waves, spray occasionally bumped over the side and gave them a fresh soaking, but this had no power to break their repose. The ominous slash of the wind and the water affected them as it would have affected mummies.

"Boys," said the cook, with the notes of every reluctance in his voice, "she's drifted in pretty close. I guess one of you had better take her to sea again." The correspondent, aroused, heard the crash of the toppled crests.

As he was rowing, the captain gave him some whiskey and water, and this steadied the chills out of him. "If I ever get ashore and anybody shows me even a photograph of an oar—"

At last there was a short conversation.

"Billie. . . . Billie, will you spell me?"

"Sure," said the oiler.

VII

When the correspondent again opened his eyes, the sea and the sky were each of the gray hue of the dawning. Later, carmine and gold was painted upon the waters. The morning appeared finally, in its splendor, with a sky of pure blue, and the sunlight flamed on the tips of the waves.

On the distant dunes were set many little black cottages, and a tall white wind-mill reared above them. No man, nor dog, nor bicycle appeared on the beach. The cottages might have formed a deserted village.

The voyagers scanned the shore. A conference was held in the boat. "Well," said the captain, "if no help is coming, we might better try a run through the surf right away. If we stay out here much longer we will be too weak to do anything for ourselves at all." The others silently acquiesced in this reasoning. The boat was headed for the beach. The correspondent wondered if none ever ascended the tall wind-tower, and if then they never looked seaward. This tower was a giant, standing with its back to the plight of the ants. It represented in a degree, to the correspondent, the serenity of nature amid the struggles of the individual—nature in the wind, and nature in the vision of men. She did not seem cruel to him then, nor beneficent, nor treacherous, nor wise. But she was indifferent, flatly indifferent. It is, perhaps, plausible that a man in this situation, impressed with the unconcern of the universe, should see the innumerable flaws of his life and have them taste wickedly in his mind and wish for another chance. A distinction between right and wrong seems absurdly clear to him, then, in this new ignorance of the grave-edge, and he understands that if he were given another opportunity he would mend his conduct and his words, and be better and brighter during an introduction, or at a tea.

"Now, boys," said the captain, "she is going to swamp sure. All we can do is to work her in as far as possible, and then when she swamps, pile out and scramble for the beach. Keep cool now, and don't jump until she swamps sure."

The oiler took the oars. Over his shoulders he scanned the surf. "Captain," he said, "I think I'd better bring her about, and keep her head-on to the seas and back her in."

"All right, Billie," said the captain. "Back her in." The oiler swung the boat then and, seated in the stern, the cook and the correspondent were obliged to look over their shoulders to contemplate the lonely and indifferent shore.

The monstrous inshore rollers heaved the boat high until the men were again enabled to see the white sheets of water scudding up the slanted beach. "We won't get in very close," said the captain. Each time a man could wrest his attention from the rollers, he turned his glance toward the shore, and in the expression of the eyes during this contemplation there was a singular quality. The correspondent, observing the others, knew that they were not afraid, but the full meaning of their glances was shrouded.

As for himself, he was too tired to grapple fundamentally with the fact. He tried to coerce his mind into thinking of it, but the mind was dominated at this time by the muscles, and the muscles said they did not care. It merely occurred to him that if he should drown it would be a shame.

There were no hurried words, no pallor, no plain agitation. The men simply looked at the shore. "Now, remember to get well clear of the boat when you jump," said the captain.

Seaward the crest of a roller suddenly fell with a thunderous crash, and the long white comber came roaring down upon the boat.

"Steady now," said the captain. The men were silent. They turned their eyes from the shore to the comber and waited. The boat slid up the incline, leaped at the furious top, bounced over it, and swung down the long back of the wave. Some water had been shipped and the cook bailed it out.

But the next crest crashed also. The tumbling boiling flood of white water caught the boat and whirled it almost perpendicular. Water swarmed in from all sides. The correspondent had his hands on the gunwale at this time, and when the water entered at that place he swiftly withdrew his fingers, as if he objected to wetting them.

The little boat, drunken with this weight of water, reeled and snuggled deeper into the sea.

"Bail her out, cook! Bail her out," said the captain.

"All right, Captain," said the cook.

"Now, boys, the next one will do for us, sure," said the oiler. "Mind to jump clear of the boat."

The third wave moved forward, huge, furious, implacable. It fairly swallowed the dingey, and almost simultaneously the men tumbled into the sea. A piece of life-belt had lain in the bottom of the boat, and as the correspondent went overboard he held this to his chest with his left hand.

The January water was icy, and he reflected immediately that it was colder than he had expected to find it off the coast of Florida. This appeared to his dazed mind as a fact important enough to be noted at the time. The coldness of the water was sad; it was tragic. This fact was somehow so mixed and confused with his opinion of his own situation that it seemed almost a proper reason for tears. The water was cold.

When he came to the surface he was conscious of little but the noisy water. Afterward he saw his companions in the sea. The oiler was ahead in the race. He was swimming strongly and rapidly. Off to the correspondent's left, the cook's great white and corked back bulged out of the water, and in the rear the captain was hanging with his one good hand to the keel of the overturned dingey.

There is a certain immovable quality to a shore, and the correspondent wondered at it amid the confusion of the sea.

It seemed also very attractive, but the correspondent knew that it was a long journey, and he paddled leisurely. The piece of life preserver lay under him, and sometimes he whirled down the incline of a wave as if he were on a hand-sled.

But finally he arrived at a place in the sea where travel was beset with difficulty. He did not pause swimming to inquire what manner of current had caught him, but there his progress ceased. The shore was set before him like a bit of scenery on a stage, and he looked at it and understood with his eyes each detail of it.

As the cook passed, much farther to the left, the captain was calling to him, "Turn over on your back, cook! Turn over on your back and use the oar."

"All right, sir." The cook turned on his back, and, paddling with an oar, went ahead as if he were a canoe.

Presently the boat also passed to the left of the correspondent with the captain clinging with one hand to the keel. He would have appeared like a man raising himself to look over a board fence, if it were not for the extraordinary gymnastics of the boat. The correspondent marvelled that the captain could still hold to it.

They passed on, nearer to the shore—the oiler, the cook, the captain— and following them went the water-jar, bouncing gayly over the seas.

The correspondent remained in the grip of this strange new enemy—a current. The shore, with its white slope of sand and its green bluff, topped with little silent cottages, was spread like a picture before him. It was very near to him then, but he was impressed as one who in a gallery looks at a scene from Brittany or Holland.

He thought: "I am going to drown? Can it be possible? Can it be possible? Can it be possible?" Perhaps an individual must consider his own death to be the final phenomenon of nature.

But later a wave perhaps whirled him out of this small deadly current, for he found suddenly that he could again make progress toward the shore. Later still, he was aware that the captain, clinging with one hand to the keel of the dingey, had his face turned away from the shore and toward him, and was calling his name. "Come to the boat! Come to the boat!"

In his struggle to reach the captain and the boat, he reflected that when one gets properly wearied, drowning must really be a comfortable arrangement, a cessation of hostilities accompanied by a large degree of relief, and he was glad of it, for the main thing in his mind for some moments had been horror of the temporary agony. He did not wish to be hurt.

Presently he saw a man running along the shore. He was undressing with most remarkable speed. Coat, trousers, shirt, everything flew magically off him.

"Come to the boat," called the captain.

"All right, Captain." As the correspondent paddled, he saw the captain let himself down to bottom and leave the boat. Then the correspondent performed his one little marvel of the voyage. A large wave caught him and flung him with ease and supreme speed completely over the boat and far beyond it. It struck him even then as an event in gymnastics, and a true miracle of the sea. An overturned boat in the surf is not a plaything to a swimming man.

The correspondent arrived in water that reached only to his waist, but his condition did not enable him to stand for more than a moment. Each wave knocked him into a heap, and the under-tow pulled at him.

Then he saw the man who had been running and undressing, and undressing and running, come bounding into the water. He dragged ashore the cook, and then waded toward the captain, but the captain waved him away, and sent him to the correspondent. He was naked, naked as a tree in winter, but a halo was about his head, and he shone like a saint. He gave a strong pull, and a long drag, and a bully heave at the correspondent's hand. The correspondent schooled in the minor formulæ, said: "Thanks, old man." But suddenly the man cried: "What's that?" He pointed a swift finger. The correspondent said: "Go."

In the shallows, face downward, lay the oiler. His forehead touched sand that was periodically, between each wave, clear of the sea.

The correspondent did not know all that transpired afterward. When he achieved safe ground he fell, striking the sand with each particular part of his body. It was as if he had dropped from a roof, but the thud was grateful to him.

It seems that instantly the beach was populated with men with blankets, clothes, and flasks, and women with coffee-pots and all the remedies sacred to their minds. The welcome of the land to the men from the sea was warm and generous, but a still and dripping shape was carried slowly up the beach, and the land's welcome for it could only be the different and sinister hospitality of the grave.

When it came night, the white waves paced to and fro in the moonlight, and the wind brought the sound of the great sea's voice to the men on shore, and they felt that they could then be interpreters.

1897, 1898

From War Is Kind[1]

I

Do not weep, maiden, for war is kind.
Because your lover threw wild hands toward the sky
And the affrighted steed ran on alone,
Do not weep.
War is kind. 5

    Hoarse, booming drums of the regiment
    Little souls who thirst for fight,
    These men were born to drill and die
    The unexplained glory flies above them
    Great is the battle-god, great, and his kingdom—— 10
    A field where a thousand corpses lie.

Do not weep, babe, for war is kind.
Because your father tumbled in the yellow trenches,
Raged at his breast, gulped and died,
Do not weep. 15
War is kind.

    Swift, blazing flag of the regiment
    Eagle with crest of red and gold,
    These men were born to drill and die
    Point for them the virtue of slaughter 20
    Make plain to them the excellence of killing
    And a field where a thousand corpses lie.

Mother whose heart hung humble as a button
On the bright splendid shroud of your son,
Do not weep. 25
War is kind.

*   *   *

XIX

The chatter of a death-demon from a tree-top.

Blood—blood and torn grass—
Had marked the rise of his agony——
This lone hunter.
The grey-green woods impassive 5
Had watched the threshing of his limbs.

A canoe with flashing paddle
A girl with soft searching eyes,

---

1. First published in *"War Is Kind" and Other Lines* (1899); reprinted in *Stephen Crane: Prose and Poetry* (1984), from which this text is taken.

A call: "John!"

Come, arise, hunter!   10
Can you not hear?

The chatter of a death-demon from a tree-top.

XX

The impact of a dollar upon the heart
Smiles warm red light
Sweeping from the hearth rosily upon the white table,
With the hanging cool velvet shadows
Moving softly upon the door.   5

The impact of a million dollars
Is a crash of flunkeys
And yawning emblems of Persia
Cheeked against oak, France and a sabre,
The outcry of old Beauty   10
Whored by pimping merchants
To submission before wine and chatter.
Silly rich peasants stamp the carpets of men,
Dead men who dreamed fragrance and light
Into their woof, their lives;   15
The rug of an honest bear
Under the feet of a cryptic slave
Who speaks always of baubles
Forgetting place, multitude, work and state,
Champing and mouthing of hats   20
Making ratful squeak of hats,
Hats.

XXI

A man said to the universe:
"Sir, I exist!"
"However," replied the universe,
"The fact has not created in me
"A sense of obligation."   5

XXII

When the prophet, a complacent fat man,
Arrived at the mountain-top
He cried: "Woe to my knowledge!
I intended to see good white lands
And bad black lands,   5
But the scene is grey."

1899

PAUL LAURENCE DUNBAR
1872–1906

Deeply admired by readers and critics, Paul Laurence Dunbar was the most visible African American literary figure of the turn of the twentieth century. Beginning with the publication of *Oak and Ivy* in 1893, he published six volumes of poetry, as well as novels, librettos, songs, and essays. Like Charles Chesnutt, Dunbar learned how to appropriate the regional idiom that dominated the representation of blacks in literature and to use it for his own, more subtle ends. His verse often employed a genial, even breezy tone that belied its complexity. As he wrote in his poem "We Wear the Mask," Dunbar used his pen to "mouth with myriad subtleties" the many challenges facing African Americans in his time.

Dunbar's father, Joshua, who had escaped slavery in Kentucky and moved to Ohio via the Underground Railroad, served in the 55th Massachusetts Regiment of the Union Army during the Civil War. His mother, Matilda Murphy, also a former slave, separated from Joshua when Dunbar was two years old. Throughout his childhood, Matilda encouraged Paul in his education, often depriving herself so that he could continue in school. Though Dunbar first wanted to be a lawyer, he chose instead "to be a worthy singer of the songs of God and nature." As he later explained in a letter, he wanted "to interpret my own people though song and story, and prove to the many that we are more human than African."

Dunbar early on developed an ear for language and a love of English Romantic poetry. Yet upon graduation from Central High School, in Dayton, Ohio, where he had been an excellent student, he found only menial jobs open to him. In 1892 he was invited to read a poem at the Western Association of Writers, which was convening in Dayton. Inspired by this experience, in 1893 he traveled to the Columbian Exposition in Chicago, where he met Frederick Douglass and sold his first poetry collection, *Oak and Ivy*, the publication of which he subsidized, for a dollar per copy. Douglass—the former U.S. minister to Haiti and Commissioner of the Haitian Exhibition—hired him as a clerk.

In 1895 Dunbar published his best-known work, *Lyrics of Lowly Life*, from which most of the selections here are drawn. Committed to rendering authentic voices of black speakers, and inspired by Shakespeare, Shelley, Keats, and Tennyson, Dunbar published in such popular venues as the *New York Times*, *Century*, *Lippincott's Monthly*, and the *Saturday Evening Post*, journals with almost exclusively white readerships. Though he was celebrated by black and white literary leaders in his own time—including Douglass, Booker T. Washington, W. E. B. Du Bois, and William Dean Howells—he was later criticized in the 1920s by Harlem Renaissance writers who saw him as catering to a white audience with stereotyped black folk elements and dialect. Despite this criticism, Dunbar's influence on subsequent African American writers such as James Weldon Johnson and Zora Neale Hurston derives from the fact that he tried to present African American speech and customs with an appreciation of their artistic value.

Dunbar married the writer Alice Moore in 1898; they lived in the Le Droit Park section of Washington, D.C., an area that welcomed the new black middle class and where they enjoyed the company of black intellectuals, activists, and artists. During this time he began to emerge as a fiction writer, publishing four collections of short stories and four novels over the next six years. In the last of his novels, *The Sport of the Gods* (1903), Dunbar chronicles the unhappy circumstances of an African American family moving from the rural South to New York City. A year before the novel was published, Dunbar and his wife separated, in part due to his alcoholism, and Dunbar's poetry increasingly reflects a more somber mood. When he returned to Dayton to live with his mother, he believed that he had failed as a poet. Critical and popular attention to his work continued to grow throughout the twentieth century, however, and Dunbar is now recognized as a major contributor to an African American poetic tradition.

An Ante-Bellum Sermon[1]

We is gathahed hyeah, my brothahs,
    In dis howlin' wildaness,
Fu' to speak some words of comfo't
    To each othah in distress.
An' we chooses fu' ouah subjic'   5
    Dis—we 'll 'splain it by an' by;
"An' de Lawd said, 'Moses, Moses,'
    An' de man said, 'Hyeah am I.'"[2]

Now ole Pher'oh, down in Egypt,
    Was de wuss man evah bo'n,   10
An' he had de Hebrew chillun
    Down dah wukin' in his co'n;
'T well de Lawd got tiahed o' his foolin',
    An' sez he: "I'll let him know—
Look hyeah, Moses, go tell Pher'oh   15
    Fu' to let dem chillun go."

"An' ef he refuse to do it,
    I will make him rue de houah,
Fu' I 'll empty down on Egypt
    All de vials of my powah."   20
Yes, he did—an' Pher'oh's ahmy
    Was n't wuth a ha'f a dime;
Fu' de Lawd will he'p his chilun,
    You kin trust him evah time.

An' yo' enemies may 'sail you   25
    In de back an' in de front;
But de Lawd is all aroun' you,
    Fu' to ba' de battle's brunt.
Dey kin fo'ge yo' chains an' shackles
    F'om de mountains to de sea;   30
But de Lawd will sen' some Moses
    Fu' to set his chillun free.

1. First published in Dunbar's *Lyrics of Lowly Life* (1897) and then in his *Complete Poems* (1903); reprinted in *The Complete Poems of Paul Laurence Dunbar* (1993), from which this text is taken.
2. Here and in the following two stanzas, the poem refers to the events of Exodus.

An' de lan' shall hyeah his thundah,
　　Lak a blas' f'om Gab'el's ho'n,
Fu' de Lawd of hosts is mighty 　　　　　　　　　35
　　When he girds his ahmor on.
But fu' feah some one mistakes me,
　　I will pause right hyeah to say,
Dat I 'm still a-preachin' ancient,
　　I ain't talkin' 'bout to-day. 　　　　　　　　　40

But I tell you, fellah christuns,
　　Things 'll happen mighty strange;
Now, de Lawd done dis fu' Isrul,
　　An' his ways don't nevah change,
An' de love he showed to Isrul 　　　　　　　　45
　　Was n't all on Isrul spent;
Now don't run an' tell yo' mastahs
　　Dat I 's preachin' discontent.

'Cause I is n't; I 'se a-judgin'
　　Bible people by deir ac's; 　　　　　　　　　50
I 'se a-givin' you de Scriptuah,
　　I 'se a-handin' you de fac's.
Cose ole Pher'oh b'lieved in slav'ry,
　　But de Lawd he let him see,
Dat de people he put bref in,— 　　　　　　　55
　　Evah mothah's son was free.

An' dahs othahs thinks lak Pher'oh,
　　But dey calls de Scriptuah liar,
Fu' de Bible says "a servant
　　Is a-worthy of his hire."[3] 　　　　　　　　60
An' you cain't git roun' nor thoo dat,
　　An' you cain't git ovah it,
Fu' whatevah place you git in,
　　Dis hyeah Bible too 'll fit.

So you see de Lawd's intention, 　　　　　　　65
　　Evah sence de worl' began,
Was dat His almighty freedom
　　Should belong to evah man,
But I think it would be bettah,
　　Ef I 'd pause agin to say, 　　　　　　　　　70
Dat I 'm talkin' 'bout ouah freedom
　　In a Bibleistic way.

But de Moses is a-comin',
　　An' he 's comin', suah and fas'
We kin hyeah his feet a-trompin', 　　　　　　75
　　We kin hyeah his trumpit blas'.

3. Biblical mandate against the unethical practice of masters withholding wages from their servants, here used to indict slavery (Leviticus 19.13, Deuteronomy 24.15 and 25).

But I want to wa'n you people,
　　Don't you git too brigity;[4]
An' don't you git to braggin'
　　'Bout dese things, you wait an' see.　　　　　　　　80

But when Moses wif his powah
　　Comes an' sets us chillun free,
We will praise de gracious Mastah
　　Dat has gin us liberty;
An' we 'll shout ouah halleluyahs,　　　　　　　　85
　　On dat mighty reck'nin' day,
When we 'se reco'nised ez citiz'—
　　Huh uh! Chillun, let us pray!

　　　　　　　　　　　　　　　　　　1897

We Wear the Mask[1]

We wear the mask that grins and lies,
It hides our cheeks and shades our eyes,—
This debt we pay to human guile;
With torn and bleeding hearts we smile,
And mouth with myriad subtleties.　　　　　　　　5

Why should the world be overwise,
In counting all our tears and sighs?
Nay, let them only see us, while
　　We wear the mask.

We smile, but, O great Christ, our cries　　　　　　10
To thee from tortured souls arise.
We sing, but oh the clay is vile
Beneath our feet, and long the mile;
But let the world dream otherwise,
　　We wear the mask!　　　　　　　　　　　　15

　　　　　　　　　　　　　　　　　　1897

Sympathy[1]

I know what the caged bird feels, alas!
　　When the sun is bright on the upland slopes;
When the wind stirs soft through the springing grass,

---

4. Brazen, presumptuous, or insolent.
1. First published in Dunbar's *Lyrics of Lowly Life* (1897) and then in his *Complete Poems* (1903); reprinted in *The Complete Poems of Paul Laurence Dunbar* (1993), from which this text is taken.

1. First published in Dunbar's *Lyrics of the Hearthside* (1899) and then in his *Complete Poems* (1903); reprinted in *The Complete Poems of Paul Laurence Dunbar* (1993), from which this text is taken.

And the river flows like a stream of glass;
   When the first bird sings and the first bud opes,   5
And the faint perfume from its chalice steals—
I know what the caged bird feels!

I know why the caged bird beats his wing
   Till its blood is red on the cruel bars;
For he must fly back to his perch and cling   10
When he fain would be on the bough a-swing;
   And a pain still throbs in the old, old scars
And they pulse again with a keener sting—
I know why he beats his wing!

I know why the caged bird sings, ah me,   15
   When his wing is bruised and his bosom sore,—
When he beats his bars and he would be free;
It is not a carol of joy or glee,
   But a prayer that he sends from his heart's deep core,
But a plea, that upward to Heaven he flings—   20
I know why the caged bird sings!

1899

Harriet Beecher Stowe[1]

She told the story, and the whole world wept
   At wrongs and cruelties it had not known
   But for this fearless woman's voice alone.
She spoke to consciences that long had slept:
Her message, Freedom's clear reveille, swept   5
   From heedless hovel to complacent throne.
   Command and prophecy were in the tone
And from its sheath the sword of justice leapt.
Around two peoples swelled a fiery wave,
   But both came forth transfigured from the flame.   10
Blest be the hand that dared be strong to save,
   And blest be she who in our weakness came—
Prophet and priestess! At one stroke she gave
   A race to freedom and herself to fame.

1899

1. First published in Dunbar's *Lyrics of the Hearthside* (1899) and then in his *Complete Poems* (1903); reprinted in *The Complete Poems of Paul Laurence Dunbar* (1993), from which this text is taken. Harriet Beecher Stowe (1811–1896), abolitionist and author of many books, the most famous being *Uncle Tom's Cabin* (1852).

Frederick Douglass[1]

A hush is over all the teeming lists,
    And there is pause, a breath-space in the strife;
A spirit brave has passed beyond the mists
    And vapors that obscure the sun of life.
And Ethiopia, with bosom torn,   5
Laments the passing of her noblest born.

She weeps for him a mother's burning tears—
    She loved him with a mother's deepest love.
He was her champion thro' direful years,
    And held her weal all other ends above.   10
When Bondage held her bleeding in the dust,
He raised her up and whispered, "Hope and Trust."

For her his voice, a fearless clarion, rung
    That broke in warning on the ears of men;
For her the strong bow of his power he strung,   15
    And sent his arrows to the very den
Where grim Oppression held his bloody place
And gloated o'er the mis'ries of a race.

And he was no soft-tongued apologist;
    He spoke straightforward, fearlessly uncowed;   20
The sunlight of his truth dispelled the mist,
    And set in bold relief each dark hued cloud;
To sin and crime he gave their proper hue,
And hurled at evil what was evil's due.

Through good and ill report he cleaved his way   25
    Right onward, with his face set toward the heights,
Nor feared to face the foeman's dread array,—
    The lash of scorn, the sting of petty spites.
He dared the lightning in the lightning's track,
And answered thunder with his thunder back.   30

When men maligned him, and their torrent wrath
    In furious imprecations o'er him broke,
He kept his counsel as he kept his path;
    'T was for his race, not for himself he spoke.
He knew the import of his Master's call,   35
And felt himself too mighty to be small.

No miser in the good he held was he,—
    His kindness followed his horizon's rim.

---

1. First published in Dunbar's *Lyrics of Love and Laughter* (1903), then in *The Complete Poems* (1903); reprinted in *The Complete Poems of Paul Laurence Dunbar* (1993), from which this text is taken. Frederick Douglass (1818–1895) was an anti-slavery activist who became the most visible African American leader of the nineteenth century struggle for racial equality.

His heart, his talents, and his hands were free
   To all who truly needed aught of him.   40
Where poverty and ignorance were rife,
He gave his bounty as he gave his life.

The place and cause that first aroused his might
   Still proved its power until his latest day.
In Freedom's lists and for the aid of Right   45
   Still in the foremost rank he waged the fray;
Wrong lived; his occupation was not gone.
He died in action with his armor on!

We weep for him, but we have touched his hand,
   And felt the magic of his presence nigh,   50
The current that he sent throughout the land,
   The kindling spirit of his battlecry.
O'er all that holds us we shall triumph yet,
And place our banner where his hopes were set!

Oh, Douglass, thou hast passed beyond the shore,   55
   But still thy voice is ringing o'er the gale!
Thou 'st taught thy race how high her hopes may soar,
   And bade her seek the heights, nor faint, nor fail.
She will not fail, she heeds thy stirring cry,
She knows thy guardian spirit will be nigh,   60
And, rising from beneath the chast'ning rod,
She stretches out her bleeding hands to God!

1903

JACK LONDON
1876–1916

John Griffith Chaney was born in San Francisco, California, on January 12, 1876, the son of Flora Wellman Chaney, spiritualist and common-law wife of William H. Chaney, an itinerant astrologer who abandoned Flora on learning of her pregnancy. Nine months after the child's birth, Flora married John London, a Civil War veteran and construction worker who adopted "Johnny." As a child, London escaped some of the unhappiness at home by living on and off with the Prentisses, African American neighbors who called him "Jack" and who served as surrogate parents until, at the age of fifteen, he sailed San Francisco Bay as an oyster pirate, going on to become a member of the California Fish Patrol. Entranced by the sea and its possibilities, he sailed aboard a sealing ship, the *Sophia Sutherland*, returning home in 1893 to publish his prize-winning first story, "Typhoon Off the Coast of Japan," in the San Francisco *Morning Call*.

In 1894, following the Panic of 1893, London marched east with a contingent of Coxey's Army, an organized group of the unemployed planning to agitate for jobs in Washington, D.C. He was arrested as a vagrant at Niagara Falls and did thirty days of hard time in the Erie County Penitentiary in Buffalo, New York. He later described the impact of these experiences in *The Road* (1907). "I have often thought," he writes there, "that to this training of my tramp days is due much of my success as a story-writer. In order to get the food whereby I lived, I was compelled to tell tales that rang true. At the back door, out of inexorable necessity, is developed the convincingness and sincerity laid down by all authorities on the art of the short-story. Also, I quite believe it was my tramp-apprenticeship that made a realist out of me. Realism constitutes the only goods one can exchange at the kitchen door for grub."

Returning home, London vowed to educate himself, and he also turned to socialism. (He later ran twice for mayor of Oakland on the socialist ticket.) At the age of twenty he was accepted to the University of California, but, lacking money, he attended for only one semester. The most important event of London's early life occurred in 1897, when, at age twenty-one, he headed to Alaska to take part in the Klondike gold rush, a migration of tens of thousands of men seeking wealth in a forbidding region. In 1900, the prestigious *Atlantic Monthly* featured his story "An Odyssey of the North" in its January issue; Houghton Mifflin published his first book, *The Son of the Wolf*; and he married Bessie Mae Maddern, with whom he went on to have two daughters before their divorce in 1905 and his marriage to Charmian Kittredge. In these years he also traveled to London, England, to write the sociological exposé *The People of the Abyss* (1903) and to Korea to cover the Russo-Japanese War of 1904, and he bought land in Sonoma County, experimenting with terracing and organic farming. London's international reputation, though, came as a writer of adventure fiction, after he won widespread acclaim with *The Call of the Wild* (1903) and *The Sea-Wolf* (1904). Later, after his extensive South Seas travels and residence in Hawaii, he became modern America's first Pacific Rim writer. In a writing career of only twenty years, London published eighteen novels, 198 short stories, three plays, and hundreds of nonfiction books and articles. Unfortunately, his alcoholism exacerbated other health issues, and he died at his California ranch in 1916.

Though London said that he wrote only for money, he was a disciplined and careful craftsman, drawing from many literary, philosophical, scientific, and other sources, and he wrote on many subjects. The "Realism and Naturalism" cluster of this section includes his reflections on the connection between his writing and his experience in an essay titled "What Life Means to Me" (1906). London's substantial body of work reflects the social and intellectual turbulence of the turn of the twentieth century, including his competing sympathies for socialism, Social Darwinism, and Nietzschean individualism; his combination of urban settings and characters with the pastoral and the exotic; his conflicted ideas about race; his dual identity as a literary writer of the emerging naturalist school and a mass-market phenomenon. For both his adventure writing and his socialist works London was an important influence on later writers such as Ernest Hemingway and Richard Wright. By the time he died in 1916, London was the best-selling author in America and was on his way to becoming the most popular American writer in the world. Paradoxically, for much of the twentieth century this same popularity contributed to a lack of interest in London's fiction by literary critics, who largely considered it to be too lowbrow or sensational to be worthy of their attention. But that trend has changed as literary scholars have begun to reexamine London's body of work, both for its considerable narrative artistry and the complexity of London's depiction of the world that he inhabited.

To Build a Fire[1]

Day had broken cold and gray, exceedingly cold and gray, when the man turned aside from the main Yukon trail and climbed the high earth-bank, where a dim and little-travelled trail led eastward through the fat spruce timberland. It was a steep bank, and he paused for breath at the top, excusing the act to himself by looking at his watch. It was nine o'clock. There was no sun nor hint of sun, though there was not a cloud in the sky. It was a clear day, and yet there seemed an intangible pall over the face of things, a subtle gloom that made the day dark, and that was due to the absence of sun. This fact did not worry the man. He was used to the lack of sun. It had been days since he had seen the sun, and he knew that a few more days must pass before that cheerful orb, due south, would just peep above the sky-line and dip immediately from view.

The man flung a look back along the way he had come. The Yukon lay a mile wide and hidden under three feet of ice. On top of this ice were as many feet of snow. It was all pure white, rolling in gentle undulations where the ice-jams of the freeze-up had formed. North and south, as far as his eye could see, it was unbroken white, save for a dark hair-line that curved and twisted from around the spruce-covered island to the south, and that curved and twisted away into the north, where it disappeared behind another spruce-covered island. This dark hair-line was the trail—the main trail—that led south five hundred miles to the Chilcoot Pass, Dyea, and salt water; and that led north seventy miles to Dawson, and still on to the north a thousand miles to Nulato, and finally to St. Michael on Bering Sea, a thousand miles and half a thousand more.[2]

But all this—the mysterious, far-reaching hair-line trail, the absence of sun from the sky, the tremendous cold, and the strangeness and weirdness of it all—made no impression on the man. It was not because he was long used to it. He was a newcomer in the land, a *chechaquo*,[3] and this was his first winter. The trouble with him was that he was without imagination. He was quick and alert in the things of life, but only in the things, and not in the significances. Fifty degrees below zero meant eighty-odd degrees of frost. Such fact impressed him as being cold and uncomfortable, and that was all. It did not lead him to meditate upon his frailty as a creature of temperature, and upon man's frailty in general, able only to live within certain narrow limits of heat and cold; and from there on it did not lead him to the conjectural field of immortality and man's place in the universe. Fifty degrees

1. First published in the *Youth's Companion* for May 29, 1902, in a version of 2,700 words—"for boys only," according to London. The later, widely anthologized version of 7,235 words, written while London was struggling to survive his South Seas voyage aboard his sailboat the *Snark,* was first published in the *Century Magazine* 76 (August 1908). The text here is that of the 1910 collection *Lost Face.*
2. The narrator surveys a long trail extending across the Klondike gold region in Canada and Alaska, from the steep Chilcoot Pass near Skagway, which prospective miners first scaled in the winter of 1897–98 to enter the Yukon watershed to the north; to Dyea, a shabby settlement where they disembarked onto a swampy beach; to Dawson, the hub of the Klondike gold rush; to Nulato, a settlement on the Yukon River; and finally, to St. Michael on the Bering Sea, a settlement north of the mouth of the Yukon, from which miners would sail for home. In the spring of 1898, after failing to find success prospecting for gold, London floated on the Yukon River from Dawson in a makeshift houseboat and then returned home from St. Michael.
3. A newcomer (Chinook).

below zero stood for a bite of frost that hurt and that must be guarded against by the use of mittens, ear-flaps, warm moccasins, and thick socks. Fifty degrees below zero was to him just precisely fifty degrees below zero. That there should be anything more to it than that was a thought that never entered his head.

As he turned to go on, he spat speculatively. There was a sharp, explosive crackle that startled him. He spat again. And again, in the air, before it could fall to the snow, the spittle crackled. He knew that at fifty below spittle crackled on the snow, but this spittle had crackled in the air. Undoubtedly it was colder than fifty below—how much colder he did not know. But the temperature did not matter. He was bound for the old claim on the left fork of Henderson Creek, where the boys were already. They had come over across the divide from the Indian Creek country, while he had come the roundabout way to take a look at the possibilities of getting out logs in the spring from the islands in the Yukon. He would be in to camp by six o'clock; a bit after dark, it was true, but the boys would be there, a fire would be going, and a hot supper would be ready. As for lunch, he pressed his hand against the protruding bundle under his jacket. It was also under his shirt, wrapped up in a handkerchief and lying against the naked skin. It was the only way to keep the biscuits from freezing. He smiled agreeably to himself as he thought of those biscuits, each cut open and sopped in bacon grease, and each enclosing a generous slice of fried bacon.

He plunged in among the big spruce trees. The trail was faint. A foot of snow had fallen since the last sled had passed over, and he was glad he was without a sled, travelling light. In fact, he carried nothing but the lunch wrapped in the handkerchief. He was surprised, however, at the cold. It certainly was cold, he concluded, as he rubbed his numb nose and cheekbones with his mittened hand. He was a warm-whiskered man, but the hair on his face did not protect the high cheek-bones and the eager nose that thrust itself aggressively into the frosty air.

At the man's heels trotted a dog, a big native husky, the proper wolf-dog, gray-coated and without any visible or temperamental difference from its brother, the wild wolf. The animal was depressed by the tremendous cold. It knew that it was no time for travelling. Its instinct told it a truer tale than was told to the man by the man's judgment. In reality, it was not merely colder than fifty below zero; it was colder than sixty below, than seventy below. It was seventy-five below zero. Since the freezing-point is thirty-two above zero, it meant that one hundred and seven degrees of frost obtained. The dog did not know anything about thermometers. Possibly in its brain there was no sharp consciousness of a condition of very cold such as was in the man's brain. But the brute had its instinct. It experienced a vague but menacing apprehension that subdued it and made it slink along at the man's heels, and that made it question eagerly every unwonted movement of the man as if expecting him to go into camp or to seek shelter somewhere and build a fire. The dog had learned fire, and it wanted fire, or else to burrow under the snow and cuddle its warmth away from the air.

The frozen moisture of its breathing had settled on its fur in a fine powder of frost, and especially were its jowls, muzzle, and eyelashes whitened by its crystalled breath. The man's red beard and mustache were likewise frosted, but more solidly, the deposit taking the form of ice and increasing with every warm, moist breath he exhaled. Also, the man was chewing tobacco, and the muzzle of ice held his lips so rigidly that he was unable to clear his chin when he expelled the juice. The result was that a crystal beard of the color and solidity of amber was increasing its length on his chin. If he fell down it would shatter itself, like glass, into brittle fragments. But he did not mind the appendage. It was the penalty all tobacco-chewers paid in that country, and he had been out before in two cold snaps. They had not been so cold as this, he knew, but by the spirit thermometer at Sixty Mile he knew they had been registered at fifty below and at fifty-five.

He held on through the level stretch of woods for several miles, crossed a wide flat of niggerheads,[4] and dropped down a bank to the frozen bed of a small stream. This was Henderson Creek, and he knew he was ten miles from the forks. He looked at his watch. It was ten o'clock. He was making four miles an hour, and he calculated that he would arrive at the forks at half-past twelve. He decided to celebrate that event by eating his lunch there.

The dog dropped in again at his heels, with a tail drooping discouragement, as the man swung along the creek-bed. The furrow of the old sled-trail was plainly visible, but a dozen inches of snow covered the marks of the last runners. In a month no man had come up or down that silent creek. The man held steadily on. He was not much given to thinking, and just then particularly he had nothing to think about save that he would eat lunch at the forks and that at six o'clock he would be in camp with the boys. There was nobody to talk to; and, had there been, speech would have been impossible because of the ice-muzzle on his mouth. So he continued monotonously to chew tobacco and to increase the length of his amber beard.

Once in a while the thought reiterated itself that it was very cold and that he had never experienced such cold. As he walked along he rubbed his cheek-bones and nose with the back of his mittened hand. He did this automatically, now and again changing hands. But rub as he would, the instant he stopped his cheek-bones went numb, and the following instant the end of his nose went numb. He was sure to frost his cheeks; he knew that, and experienced a pang of regret that he had not devised a nose-strap of the sort Bud wore in cold snaps. Such a strap passed across the cheeks, as well, and saved them. But it didn't matter much, after all. What were frosted cheeks? A bit painful, that was all; they were never serious.

Empty as the man's mind was of thoughts, he was keenly observant, and he noticed the changes in the creek, the curves and bends and timber-jams, and always he sharply noted where he placed his feet. Once, coming around a bend, he shied abruptly, like a startled horse, curved away from the place where he had been walking, and retreated several paces back along the trail. The creek he knew was frozen clear to the bottom,—no creek could contain water in that arctic winter,—but he knew also that there were springs that bubbled out from the hillsides and ran along under the snow and on top the ice of the creek. He knew that the coldest snaps never froze these springs, and he knew likewise their danger. They were traps. They hid pools of water under the snow that might be three inches deep, or three feet. Sometimes a skin of ice half an inch thick covered them, and in turn was covered by the

4. Racist name for a strong dark chewing tobacco of the period; applied here to large hummocks of earth under the snow that are created by centuries of alternate freezing and thawing.

snow. Sometimes there were alternate layers of water and ice-skin, so that when one broke through he kept on breaking through for a while, sometimes wetting himself to the waist.

That was why he had shied in such panic. He had felt the give under his feet and heard the crackle of snow-hidden ice-skin. And to get his feet wet in such a temperature meant trouble and danger. At the very least it meant delay, for he would be forced to stop and build a fire, and under its protection to bare his feet while he dried his socks and moccasins. He stood and studied the creek-bed and its banks, and decided that the flow of water came from the right. He reflected awhile, rubbing his nose and cheeks, then skirted to the left, stepping gingerly and testing the footing for each step. Once clear of the danger, he took a fresh chew of tobacco and swung along at his four-mile gait.

In the course of the next two hours he came upon several similar traps. Usually the snow above the hidden pools had a sunken, candied appearance that advertised the danger. Once again, however, he had a close call; and once, suspecting danger, he compelled the dog to go on in front. The dog did not want to go. It hung back until the man shoved it forward, and then it went quickly across the white, unbroken surface. Suddenly it broke through, floundered to one side, and got away to firmer footing. It had wet its forefeet and legs, and almost immediately the water that clung to it turned to ice. It made quick efforts to lick the ice off its legs, then dropped down in the snow and began to bite out the ice that had formed between the toes. This was a matter of instinct. To permit the ice to remain would mean sore feet. It did not know this. It merely obeyed the mysterious prompting that arose from the deep crypts of its being. But the man knew, having achieved a judgment on the subject, and he removed the mitten from his right hand and helped tear out the ice-particles. He did not expose his fingers more than a minute, and was astonished at the swift numbness that smote them. It certainly was cold. He pulled on the mitten hastily, and beat the hand savagely across his chest.

At twelve o'clock the day was at its brightest. Yet the sun was too far south on its winter journey to clear the horizon. The bulge of the earth intervened between it and Henderson Creek, where the man walked under a clear sky at noon and cast no shadow. At half-past twelve, to the minute, he arrived at the forks of the creek. He was pleased at the speed he had made. If he kept it up, he would certainly be with the boys by six. He unbuttoned his jacket and shirt and drew forth his lunch. The action consumed no more than a quarter of a minute, yet in that brief moment the numbness laid hold of the exposed fingers. He did not put the mitten on, but, instead, struck the fingers a dozen sharp smashes against his leg. Then he sat down on a snow-covered log to eat. The sting that followed upon the striking of his fingers against his leg ceased so quickly that he was startled. He had had no chance to take a bite of biscuit. He struck the fingers repeatedly and returned them to the mitten, baring the other hand for the purpose of eating. He tried to take a mouthful, but the ice-muzzle prevented. He had forgotten to build a fire and thaw out. He chuckled at his foolishness, and as he chuckled he noted the numbness creeping into the exposed fingers. Also, he noted that the stinging which had first come to his toes when he sat down was already passing away. He wondered whether the toes were warm or numb. He moved them inside the moccasins and decided that they were numb.

He pulled the mitten on hurriedly and stood up. He was a bit frightened. He stamped up and down until the stinging returned into the feet. It certainly was cold, was his thought. That man from Sulphur Creek[5] had spoken the truth when telling how cold it sometimes got in the country. And he had laughed at him at the time! That showed one must not be too sure of things. There was no mistake about it, it *was* cold. He strode up and down, stamping his feet and threshing his arms, until reassured by the returning warmth. Then he got out matches and proceeded to make a fire. From the under-growth, where high water of the previous spring had lodged a supply of seasoned twigs, he got his fire-wood. Working carefully from a small beginning, he soon had a roaring fire, over which he thawed the ice from his face and in the protection of which he ate his biscuits. For the moment the cold of space was outwitted. The dog took satisfaction in the fire, stretching out close enough for warmth and far enough away to escape being singed.

When the man had finished, he filled his pipe and took his comfortable time over a smoke. Then he pulled on his mittens, settled the ear-flaps of his cap firmly about his ears, and took the creek trail up the left fork. The dog was disappointed and yearned back toward the fire. This man did not know cold. Possibly all the generations of his ancestry had been ignorant of cold, of real cold, of cold one hundred and seven degrees below freezing-point. But the dog knew; all its ancestry knew, and it had inherited the knowledge. And it knew that it was not good to walk abroad in such fearful cold. It was the time to lie snug in a hole in the snow and wait for a curtain of cloud to be drawn across the face of outer space whence this cold came. On the other hand, there was no keen intimacy between the dog and the man. The one was the toil-slave of the other, and the only caresses it had ever received were the caresses of the whip-lash and of harsh and menacing throat-sounds that threatened the whip-lash. So the dog made no effort to communicate its apprehension to the man. It was not concerned in the welfare of the man; it was for its own sake that it yearned back toward the fire. But the man whistled, and spoke to it with the sound of whip-lashes, and the dog swung in at the man's heels and followed after.

The man took a chew of tobacco and proceeded to start a new amber beard. Also, his moist breath quickly powdered with white his mustache, eyebrows, and lashes. There did not seem to be so many springs on the left fork of the Henderson, and for half an hour the man saw no signs of any. And then it happened. At a place where there were no signs, where the soft, unbroken snow seemed to advertise solidity beneath, the man broke through. It was not deep. He wet himself halfway to the knees before he floundered out to the firm crust.

He was angry, and cursed his luck aloud. He had hoped to get into camp with the boys at six o'clock, and this would delay him an hour, for he would have to build a fire and dry out his foot-gear. This was imperative at that low temperature—he knew that much; and he turned aside to the bank, which he climbed. On top, tangled in the underbrush about the trunks of several small spruce trees, was a high-water deposit of dry fire-wood—sticks and twigs, principally, but also larger portions of seasoned branches and fine,

5. Mining area between the towns of Dawson and Granville.

dry, last-year's grasses. He threw down several large pieces on top of the snow. This served for a foundation and prevented the young flame from drowning itself in the snow it otherwise would melt. The flame he got by touching a match to a small shred of birch-bark that he took from his pocket. This burned even more readily than paper. Placing it on the foundation, he fed the young flame with wisps of dry grass and with the tiniest dry twigs.

He worked slowly and carefully, keenly aware of his danger. Gradually, as the flame grew stronger, he increased the size of the twigs with which he fed it. He squatted in the snow, pulling the twigs out from their entanglement in the brush and feeding directly to the flame. He knew there must be no failure. When it is seventy-five below zero, a man must not fail in his first attempt to build a fire—that is, if his feet are wet. If his feet are dry, and he fails, he can run along the trail for half a mile and restore his circulation. But the circulation of wet and freezing feet cannot be restored by running when it is seventy-five below. No matter how fast he runs, the wet feet will freeze the harder.

All this the man knew. The old-timer on Sulphur Creek had told him about it the previous fall, and now he was appreciating the advice. Already all sensation had gone out of his feet. To build the fire he had been forced to remove his mittens, and the fingers had quickly gone numb. His pace of four miles an hour had kept his heart pumping blood to the surface of his body and to all the extremities. But the instant he stopped, the action of the pump eased down. The cold of space smote the unprotected tip of the planet, and he, being on that unprotected tip, received the full force of the blow. The blood of his body recoiled before it. The blood was alive, like the dog, and like the dog it wanted to hide away and cover itself up from the fearful cold. So long as he walked four miles an hour, he pumped that blood, willy-nilly, to the surface; but now it ebbed away and sank down into the recesses of his body. The extremities were the first to feel its absence. His wet feet froze the faster, and his exposed fingers numbed the faster, though they had not yet begun to freeze. Nose and cheeks were already freezing, while the skin of all his body chilled as it lost its blood.

But he was safe. Toes and nose and cheeks would be only touched by the frost, for the fire was beginning to burn with strength. He was feeding it with twigs the size of his finger. In another minute he would be able to feed it with branches the size of his wrist, and then he could remove his wet footgear, and, while it dried, he could keep his naked feet warm by the fire, rubbing them at first, of course, with snow. The fire was a success. He was safe. He remembered the advice of the old-timer on Sulphur Creek, and smiled. The old-timer had been very serious in laying down the law that no man must travel alone in the Klondike after fifty below. Well, here he was; he had had the accident; he was alone; and he had saved himself. Those old-timers were rather womanish, some of them, he thought. All a man had to do was to keep his head, and he was all right. Any man who was a man could travel alone. But it was surprising, the rapidity with which his cheeks and nose were freezing. And he had not thought his fingers could go lifeless in so short a time. Lifeless they were, for he could scarcely make them move together to grip a twig, and they seemed remote from his body and from him. When he touched a twig, he had to look and see whether or not he had hold of it. The wires were pretty well down between him and his finger-ends.

All of which counted for little. There was the fire, snapping and crackling and promising life with every dancing flame. He started to untie his moccasins. They were coated with ice; the thick German socks were like sheaths of iron halfway to the knees; and the moccasin strings were like rods of steel all twisted and knotted as by some conflagration. For a moment he tugged with his numb fingers, then, realizing the folly of it, he drew his sheath-knife.

But before he could cut the strings, it happened. It was his own fault or, rather, his mistake. He should not have built the fire under the spruce tree. He should have built it in the open. But it had been easier to pull the twigs from the brush and drop them directly on the fire. Now the tree under which he had done this carried a weight of snow on its boughs. No wind had blown for weeks, and each bough was fully freighted. Each time he had pulled a twig he had communicated a slight agitation to the tree—an imperceptible agitation, so far as he was concerned, but an agitation sufficient to bring about the disaster. High up in the tree one bough capsized its load of snow. This fell on the boughs beneath, capsizing them. This process continued, spreading out and involving the whole tree. It grew like an avalanche, and it descended without warning upon the man and the fire, and the fire was blotted out! Where it had burned was a mantle of fresh and disordered snow.

The man was shocked. It was as though he had just heard his own sentence of death. For a moment he sat and stared at the spot where the fire had been. Then he grew very calm. Perhaps the old-timer on Sulphur Creek was right. If he had only had a trail-mate he would have been in no danger now. The trail-mate could have built the fire. Well, it was up to him to build the fire over again, and this second time there must be no failure. Even if he succeeded, he would most likely lose some toes. His feet must be badly frozen by now, and there would be some time before the second fire was ready.

Such were his thoughts, but he did not sit and think them. He was busy all the time they were passing through his mind. He made a new foundation for a fire, this time in the open, where no treacherous tree could blot it out. Next, he gathered dry grasses and tiny twigs from the high-water flotsam. He could not bring his fingers together to pull them out, but he was able to gather them by the handful. In this way he got many rotten twigs and bits of green moss that were undesirable, but it was the best he could do. He worked methodically, even collecting an armful of the larger branches to be used later when the fire gathered strength. And all the while the dog sat and watched him, a certain yearning wistfulness in its eyes, for it looked upon him as the fire-provider, and the fire was slow in coming.

When all was ready, the man reached in his pocket for a second piece of birch-bark. He knew the bark was there, and, though he could not feel it with his fingers, he could hear its crisp rustling as he fumbled for it. Try as he would, he could not clutch hold of it. And all the time, in his consciousness, was the knowledge that each instant his feet were freezing. This thought tended to put him in a panic, but he fought against it and kept calm. He pulled on his mittens with his teeth, and threshed his arms back and forth, beating his hands with all his might against his sides. He did this sitting down, and he stood up to do it; and all the while the dog sat in the snow, its wolf-brush of a tail curled around warmly over its forefeet, its sharp wolf-ears pricked forward intently as it watched the man. And the man, as he beat and threshed with his arms and hands, he felt a great surge of envy as he regarded the creature that was warm and secure in its natural covering.

After a time he was aware of the first faraway signals of sensation in his beaten fingers. The faint tingling grew stronger till it evolved into a stinging ache that was excruciating, but which the man hailed with satisfaction. He stripped the mitten from his right hand and fetched forth the birch-bark. The exposed fingers were quickly going numb again. Next he brought out his bunch of sulphur matches. But the tremendous cold had already driven the life out of his fingers. In his effort to separate one match from the others, the whole bunch fell in the snow. He tried to pick it out of the snow, but failed. The dead fingers could neither touch nor clutch. He was very careful. He drove the thought of his freezing feet, and nose, and cheeks, out of his mind, devoting his whole soul to the matches. He watched, using the sense of vision in place of that of touch, and when he saw his fingers on each side the bunch, he closed them—that is, he willed to close them, for the wires were down, and the fingers did not obey. He pulled the mitten on the right hand, and beat it fiercely against his knee. Then, with both mittened hands, he scooped the bunch of matches, along with much snow, into his lap. Yet he was no better off.

After some manipulation he managed to get the bunch between the heels of his mittened hands. In this fashion he carried it to his mouth. The ice crackled and snapped when by a violent effort he opened his mouth. He drew the lower jaw in, curled the upper lip out of the way, and scraped the bunch with his upper teeth in order to separate a match. He succeeded in getting one, which he dropped on his lap. He was no better off. He could not pick it up. Then he devised a way. He picked it up in his teeth and scratched it on his leg. Twenty times he scratched before he succeeded in lighting it. As it flamed he held it with his teeth to the birch-bark. But the burning brimstone went up his nostrils and into his lungs, causing him to cough spasmodically. The match fell into the snow and went out.

The old-timer on Sulphur Creek was right, he thought in the moment of controlled despair that ensued: after fifty below, a man should travel with a partner. He beat his hands, but failed in exciting any sensation. Suddenly he bared both hands, removing the mittens with his teeth. He caught the whole bunch between the heels of his hands. His arm-muscles not being frozen enabled him to press the hand-heels tightly against the matches. Then he scratched the bunch along his leg. It flared into flame, seventy sulphur matches at once! There was no wind to blow them out. He kept his head to one side to escape the strangling fumes, and held the blazing bunch to the birch-bark. As he so held it, he became aware of sensation in his hand. His flesh was burning. He could smell it. Deep down below the surface he could feel it. The sensation developed into pain that grew acute. And still he endured it, holding the flame of the matches clumsily to the bark that would not light readily because his own burning hands were in the way, absorbing most of the flame.

At last, when he could endure no more, he jerked his hands apart. The blazing matches fell sizzling into the snow, but the birch-bark was alight. He began laying dry grasses and the tiniest twigs on the flame. He could not pick and choose, for he had to lift the fuel between the heels of his hands. Small pieces of rotten wood and green moss clung to the twigs, and

"As he looked apathetically about him, his eyes chanced on the dog." Illustration by Frank E. Schoonover for the publication of "To Build a Fire" in *Century Illustrated Monthly Magazine*, October 1908.

he bit them off as well as he could with his teeth. He cherished the flame carefully and awkwardly. It meant life, and it must not perish. The withdrawal of blood from the surface of his body now made him begin to shiver, and he grew more awkward. A large piece of green moss fell squarely on the little fire. He tried to poke it out with his fingers, but his shivering frame made him poke too far, and he disrupted the nucleus of the little fire, the burning grasses and tiny twigs separating and scattering. He tried to poke them together again, but in spite of the tenseness of the effort, his shivering got away with him, and the twigs were hopelessly scattered. Each twig gushed a puff of smoke and went out. The fire-provider had failed. As he looked apathetically about him, his eyes chanced on the dog, sitting across the ruins of the fire from him, in the snow, making restless, hunching movements, slightly lifting one forefoot and then the other, shifting its weight back and forth on them with wistful eagerness.

The sight of the dog put a wild idea into his head. He remembered the tale of the man, caught in a blizzard, who killed a steer and crawled inside the carcass, and so was saved. He would kill the dog and bury his hands in the warm body until the numbness went out of them. Then he could build another fire. He spoke to the dog, calling it to him; but in his voice was a strange note of fear that frightened the animal, who had never known the man to speak in such way before. Something was the matter, and its suspicious nature sensed danger—it knew not what danger, but somewhere, somehow, in its brain arose an apprehension of the man. It flattened its ears down at the sound of the man's voice, and its restless, hunching movements and the liftings and shiftings of its forefeet became more pronounced; but it would not come to the man. He got on his hands and knees and crawled toward the dog. This unusual posture again excited suspicion, and the animal sidled mincingly away.

The man sat up in the snow for a moment and struggled for calmness. Then he pulled on his mittens, by means of his teeth, and got upon his feet. He glanced down at first in order to assure himself that he was really standing up, for the absence of sensation in his feet left him unrelated to the earth. His erect position in itself started to drive the webs of suspicion from the dog's mind; and when he spoke peremptorily, with the sound of whip-lashes in his voice, the dog rendered its customary allegiance and came to him. As it came within reaching distance, the man lost his control. His arms flashed out to the dog, and he experienced genuine surprise when he discovered that his hands could not clutch, that there was neither bend nor feeling in the fingers. He had forgotten for the moment that they were frozen and that they were freezing more and more. All this happened quickly, and before the animal could get away, he encircled its body with his arms. He sat down in the snow, and in this fashion held the dog, while it snarled and whined and struggled.

But it was all he could do, hold its body encircled in his arms and sit there. He realized that he could not kill the dog. There was no way to do it. With his helpless hands he could neither draw nor hold his sheath-knife nor throttle the animal. He released it, and it plunged wildly away, with tail between its legs, and still snarling. It halted forty feet away and surveyed him curiously, with ears sharply pricked forward. The man looked down at his hands in order to locate them, and found them hanging on the ends of his arms. It struck him as curious that one should have to use his eyes in order to find out where his hands were. He began threshing his arms back and forth, beating the mittened hands against his sides. He did this for five minutes, violently, and his heart pumped enough blood up to the surface to put a stop to his shivering. But no sensation was aroused in the hands. He had an impression that they hung like weights on the ends of his arms, but when he tried to run the impression down, he could not find it.

A certain fear of death, dull and oppressive, came to him. This fear quickly became poignant as he realized that it was no longer a mere matter of freezing his fingers and toes, or of losing his hands and feet, but that it was a matter of life and death with the chances against him. This threw him into a panic, and he turned and ran up the creek-bed along the old, dim trail. The dog joined in behind and kept up with him. He ran blindly, without intention, in fear such as he had never known in his life. Slowly, as he ploughed and floundered through the snow, he began to see things again— the banks of the creek, the old timber-jams, the leafless aspens, and the sky. The running made him feel better. He did not shiver. Maybe, if he ran on, his feet would thaw out; and, anyway, if he ran far enough, he would reach camp and the boys. Without doubt he would lose some fingers and toes and some of his face; but the boys would take care of him, and save the rest of him when he got there. And at the same time there was another thought in his mind that said he would never get to the camp and the boys; that it was too many miles away, that the freezing had too great a start on him, and that he would soon be stiff and dead. This thought he kept in the background and refused to consider. Sometimes it pushed itself forward and demanded to be heard, but he thrust it back and strove to think of other things.

It struck him as curious that he could run at all on feet so frozen that he could not feel them when they struck the earth and took the weight of his body. He seemed to himself to skim along above the surface, and to have no connection with the earth. Somewhere he had once seen a winged Mercury[6] and he wondered if Mercury felt as he felt when skimming over the earth.

His theory of running until he reached camp and the boys had one flaw in it: he lacked the endurance. Several times he stumbled, and finally he tottered, crumpled up, and fell. When he tried to rise, he failed. He must sit and rest, he decided, and next time he would merely walk and keep on going. As he sat and regained his breath, he noted that he was feeling quite warm and comfortable. He was not shivering, and it even seemed that a warm glow had come to his chest and trunk. And yet, when he touched his nose or cheeks, there was no sensation. Running would not thaw them out. Nor would it thaw out his hands and feet. Then the thought came to him that the frozen portions of his body must be extending. He tried to keep this thought down, to forget it, to think of something else; he was aware of the panicky feeling that it caused, and he was afraid of the panic. But the thought asserted itself, and persisted, until it produced a vision of his body totally frozen. This was too much, and he made another wild run along the trail. Once he slowed down to a walk, but the thought of the freezing extending itself made him run again.

And all the time the dog ran with him, at his heels. When he fell down a second time, it curled its tail over its forefeet and sat in front of him, facing him, curiously eager and intent. The warmth and security of the animal angered him, and he cursed it till it flattened down its ears appeasingly. This time the shivering came more quickly upon the man. He was losing in his battle with the frost. It was creeping into his body from all sides. The thought of it drove him on, but he ran no more than a hundred feet, when he staggered and pitched headlong. It was his last panic. When he had recovered his breath and control, he sat up and entertained in his mind the conception of meeting death with dignity. However, the conception did not come to him in such terms. His idea of it was that he had been making a fool of himself, running around like a chicken with its head cut off—such was the simile that occurred to him. Well, he was bound to freeze anyway, and he might as well take it decently. With this new-found peace of mind came the first glimmerings of drowsiness. A good idea, he thought, to sleep off to death. It was like taking an anaesthetic. Freezing was not so bad as people thought. There were lots worse ways to die.

He pictured the boys finding his body next day. Suddenly he found himself with them, coming along the trail and looking for himself. And, still with them, he came around a turn in the trail and found himself lying in the snow. He did not belong with himself any more, for even then he was out of himself, standing with the boys and looking at himself in the snow. It certainly was cold, was his thought. When he got back to the States he could tell the folks what real cold was. He drifted on from this to a vision of the old-timer on Sulphur Creek. He could see him quite clearly, warm and comfortable, and smoking a pipe.

---

6. Mercury is the Roman god of messengers, thieves, and storytellers; he flew between heaven and earth wearing winged sandals. He is also the god of healing and the courier of souls to the Underworld.

"You were right, old hoss; you were right," the man mumbled to the old-timer of Sulphur Creek.

Then the man drowsed off into what seemed to him the most comfortable and satisfying sleep he had ever known. The dog sat facing him and waiting. The brief day drew to a close in a long, slow twilight. There were no signs of a fire to be made, and, besides, never in the dog's experience had it known a man to sit like that in the snow and make no fire. As the twilight drew on, its eager yearning for the fire mastered it, and with a great lifting and shifting of forefeet, it whined softly, then flattened its ears down in anticipation of being chidden by the man. But the man remained silent. Later, the dog whined loudly. And still later it crept close to the man and caught the scent of death. This made the animal bristle and back away. A little longer it delayed, howling under the stars that leaped and danced and shone brightly in the cold sky. Then it turned and trotted up the trail in the direction of the camp it knew, where were the other food-providers and fire-providers.

1902, 1908

ZITKALA-ŠA (GERTRUDE SIMMONS BONNIN)
1876–1938

Gertrude Simmons was born in 1876 on the Yankton Sioux Reservation in South Dakota. Her mother was Tate Iyohi Win, or "Reaches the Wind Woman," otherwise known as Ellen Simmons, and her father was probably a white man named Felker who left his wife before the child's birth. Her mother later married another white man, John H. Simmons, whose surname was given to the child. Gertrude Simmons today is usually referred to as Zitkala-Ša (pronounced *sha*), or Red Bird, a name she chose for herself. Zitkala-Ša was an influential Native American writer, orator, and debater; a singer, pianist, and violinist;—and an activist on behalf of women's and Native American rights.

The year of Zitkala-Ša's birth, 1876, was the year in which George Armstrong Custer's Seventh Cavalry was defeated by a coalition of Lakota Sioux and Cheyenne warriors on the Little Bighorn River in Montana, after which the federal government finally drove both tribes onto reservations. In 1890, the U.S. Department of the Census declared the closing of the frontier, meaning that no more "free land" remained open for settlement; the United States had achieved its "manifest destiny," extending its dominion from "sea to shining sea." As an adult, then, Zitkala-Ša lived in what has been called the "transitional" period in Native American history, a difficult time for Indian peoples, when the U.S. government pursued an official policy of "detribalization" and land-hungry whites sought access to tribal domains.

At the age of eight, Zitkala-Ša declared her intention to learn the white man's ways—or, as she puts it in her autobiographical "Impressions of an Indian Childhood" (1900), she wanted to taste the "big red apples" missionaries promised Indian children if they would attend boarding school. She began her schooling at White's Manual Institute, a Quaker school in Indiana. As her autobiography details it, her introduction to "civilization" subjected her and the other Indian children to having their long hair cut, to having the clothing in which they had arrived discarded, and, perhaps most painful, to being forbidden from speaking their Native languages. As Richard Henry Pratt, the headmaster of the Carlisle Indian Institute, put it, this form of education was intended to "Kill the Indian and save the man." Zitkala-Ša was intimately familiar with this precept and the human costs that it extracted from students and their families.

From White's Manual Institute, Zitkala-Ša went on to Earlham College, also in Indiana, where she began to demonstrate a wide range of talents. In the last section of "Impressions of an Indian Childhood," she tells of her appearance as the representative of the college in 1896 at a statewide oratorical competition, where some "rowdies," as she puts it, "threw out a large white flag, with a drawing of a most forlorn Indian girl on it," along with, "in bold black letters words that ridiculed the college which was represented by a 'squaw.'" This slight was somewhat assuaged by her winning second prize overall.

The following year, Zitkala-Ša became "the latest addition to our force of workers," as the Carlisle Institute's publication, the *Indian Helper*, announced in its July 1897 number. At Carlisle, Zitkala-Ša led the glee club, played the piano and violin, and became engaged to Thomas Marshall, a Sioux from the Pine Ridge Agency, a devout Christian convert, "without a peer among our students," who died suddenly from an undiagnosed illness. Soon after Marshall's death, Zitkala-Ša began to publish autobiography and fiction. (She also wrote poetry.) In addition to publications that catered to those interested in Indian education, her writing appeared in magazines such as *Atlantic Monthly* and *Harper's*. Her first book, *Old Indian Legends*, was published in 1901, and a chapter of this book of traditional stories is included in the "Voices from Native America" section elsewhere in this volume. Zitkala-Ša's other writings did not appear in book form until 1921, with the publication of her autobiographical *American Indian Stories*. Her writing introduced a wide readership to the difficulty that American Indians faced in negotiating the pressures of religious conversion and cultural assimilation. Indeed, many of the concerns that she raises echo the writing of turn-of-the-century immigrants from Europe and Asia, even though as a Native of North America, Zitkala-Ša never voluntarily migrated to a new country. Zitkala-Ša's writing also generated controversy. Her story "The Soft-Hearted Sioux" (1901), in which the protagonist's Christianity and "civilization" have unfitted him for any relation to his traditional parents, was pronounced "morally bad" on the front page of the Carlisle Institute newspaper.

In May 1902, Zitkala-Ša married Raymond Bonnin, also a Yankton Sioux, and an employee of the U.S. Indian Service (later the Bureau of Indian Affairs). Although she would occasionally publish stories and poems thereafter, and wrote the libretto for an opera, *Sun Dance*, the bulk of Zitkala-Ša's writing over the second half of her life derived from her active engagement in Indian affairs. After years of work on the Uintah Ouray Ute Agency in Utah, the family moved to Washington, D.C., in 1916 so that Zitkala-Ša could take up her elected position as secretary of the Society of the American Indian (SAI), an organization dedicated to improving the condition of Native people. When the SAI broke up in 1920, Zitkala-Ša began working with the General Federation of Women's Clubs, which established an Indian Welfare Committee in 1921 at her urging. One of the committee's achievements was an inquiry into the treatment of some of the tribes in Oklahoma, which led to the publication, in 1924, of a study of the graft, corruption, and exploitation of the tribes and which spurred the formation under President Hoover of the Merriam Commission in 1928 to study these matters. In 1926, Zitkala-Ša had founded her own organization, the National Council of American Indians, of which she was president, with her husband serving as counselor general, secretary-treasurer, and executive secretary.

Zitkala-Ša's writing reveals the complex pressures that American Indian intellectuals faced at the turn of the twentieth century. Even as many Americans expressed

Carlisle School: "Before" and "After." The Carlisle Indian School produced a considerable number of "before" and "after" photos, representing the difference in appearance between new Indian arrivals to the school and its graduates. Zitkala-Ša came to teach at Carlisle in 1897, at the age of only twenty-one, and she might have known some of these graduates, photographed the year of her arrival—several of whom were older than she was.

a deep fascination with Native American stories, ceremonies, and artwork, the policies of the U.S. government and several other institutions aimed to dispossess tribal peoples of their communally held land, their indigenous languages, and many of their cultural practices. The success of Zitkala-Ša as both an author and an activist offers a remarkable example of how one woman navigated this challenging terrain.

From Impressions of an Indian Childhood[1]

I. My Mother

A wigwam of weather-stained canvas stood at the base of some irregularly ascending hills. A footpath wound its way gently down the sloping land till it reached the broad river bottom; creeping through the long swamp grasses that bent over it on either side, it came out on the edge of the Missouri.

Here, morning, noon, and evening, my mother came to draw water from the muddy stream for our household use. Always, when my mother started for the river, I stopped my play to run along with her. She was only of medium height. Often she was sad and silent, at which times her full arched lips were compressed into hard and bitter lines, and shadows fell under her black eyes. Then I clung to her hand and begged to know what made the tears fall.

"Hush; my little daughter must never talk about my tears"; and smiling through them, she patted my head and said, "Now let me see how fast you can run to-day." Whereupon I tore away at my highest possible speed, with my long black hair blowing in the breeze.

I was a wild little girl of seven. Loosely clad in a slip of brown buckskin, and light-footed with a pair of soft moccasins on my feet, I was as free as the wind that blew my hair, and no less spirited than a bounding deer. These were my mother's pride,—my wild freedom and overflowing spirits. She taught me no fear save that of intruding myself upon others.

Having gone many paces ahead I stopped, panting for breath, and laughing with glee as my mother watched my every movement. I was not wholly conscious of myself, but was more keenly alive to the fire within. It was as if I were the activity, and my hands and feet were only experiments for my spirit to work upon.

Returning from the river, I tugged beside my mother, with my hand upon the bucket I believed I was carrying. One time, on such a return, I remember a bit of conversation we had. My grown-up cousin, Warca-Ziwin (Sunflower), who was then seventeen, always went to the river alone for water for her mother. Their wigwam was not far from ours; and I saw her daily going to and from the river. I admired my cousin greatly. So I said: "Mother, when I am tall as my cousin Warca-Ziwin, you shall not have to come for water. I will do it for you."

With a strange tremor in her voice which I could not understand, she answered, "If the paleface does not take away from us the river we drink."

"Mother, who is this bad paleface?" I asked.

---

1. "Impressions of an Indian Childhood" first appeared in the *Atlantic Monthly* in January 1900, the source of the text printed here. It was later included in *American Indian Stories* (1921).

"My little daughter, he is a sham,—a sickly sham! The bronzed Dakota is the only real man."

I looked up into my mother's face while she spoke; and seeing her bite her lips, I knew she was unhappy. This aroused revenge in my small soul. Stamping my foot on the earth, I cried aloud, "I hate the paleface that makes my mother cry!"

Setting the pail of water on the ground, my mother stooped, and stretching her left hand out on the level with my eyes, she placed her other arm about me; she pointed to the hill where my uncle and my only sister lay buried.

"There is what the paleface has done! Since then your father too has been buried in a hill nearer the rising sun. We were once very happy. But the paleface has stolen our lands and driven us hither. Having defrauded us of our land, the paleface forced us away.

"Well, it happened on the day we moved camp that your sister and uncle were both very sick. Many others were ailing, but there seemed to be no help. We traveled many days and nights; not in the grand happy way that we moved camp when I was a little girl, but we were driven, my child, driven like a herd of buffalo. With every step, your sister, who was not as large as you are now, shrieked with the painful jar until she was hoarse with crying. She grew more and more feverish. Her little hands and cheeks were burning hot. Her little lips were parched and dry, but she would not drink the water I gave her. Then I discovered that her throat was swollen and red. My poor child, how I cried with her because the Great Spirit had forgotten us!

"At last, when we reached this western country, on the first weary night your sister died. And soon your uncle died also, leaving a widow and an orphan daughter, your cousin Warca-Ziwin. Both your sister and uncle might have been happy with us to-day, had it not been for the heartless paleface."

My mother was silent the rest of the way to our wigwam. Though I saw no tears in her eyes, I knew that was because I was with her. She seldom wept before me.

II. The Legends

During the summer days, my mother built her fire in the shadow of our wigwam.

In the early morning our simple breakfast was spread upon the grass west of our tepee. At the farthest point of the shade my mother sat beside her fire, toasting a savory piece of dried meat. Near her, I sat upon my feet, eating my dried meat with unleavened bread, and drinking strong black coffee.

The morning meal was our quiet hour, when we two were entirely alone. At noon, several who chanced to be passing by stopped to rest, and to share our luncheon with us, for they were sure of our hospitality.

My uncle, whose death my mother ever lamented, was one of our nation's bravest warriors. His name was on the lips of old men when talking of the proud feats of valor; and it was mentioned by younger men, too, in connection with deeds of gallantry. Old women praised him for his kindness toward them; young women held him up as an ideal to their sweethearts. Every one loved him, and my mother worshiped his memory. Thus it happened that even strangers were sure of welcome in our lodge, if they but asked a favor in my uncle's name.

Though I heard many strange experiences related by these wayfarers, I loved best the evening meal, for that was the time old legends were told. I was always glad when the sun hung low in the west, for then my mother sent me to invite the neighboring old men and women to eat supper with us. Running all the way to the wigwams, I halted shyly at the entrances. Sometimes I stood long moments without saying a word. It was not any fear that made me so dumb when out upon such a happy errand; nor was it that I wished to withhold the invitation, for it was all I could do to observe this very proper silence. But it was a sensing of the atmosphere, to assure myself that I should not hinder other plans. My mother used to say to me, as I was almost bounding away for the old people: "Wait a moment before you invite any one. If other plans are being discussed, do not interfere, but go elsewhere."

The old folks knew the meaning of my pauses; and often they coaxed my confidence by asking, "What do you seek, little granddaughter?"

"My mother says you are to come to our tepee this evening," I instantly exploded, and breathed the freer afterwards.

"Yes, yes, gladly, gladly I shall come!" each replied. Rising at once and carrying their blankets across one shoulder, they flocked leisurely from their various wigwams toward our dwelling.

My mission done, I ran back, skipping and jumping with delight. All out of breath, I told my mother almost the exact words of the answers to my invitation. Frequently she asked, "What were they doing when you entered their tepee?" This taught me to remember all I saw at a single glance. Often I told my mother my impressions without being questioned.

While in the neighboring wigwams sometimes an old Indian woman asked me, "What is your mother doing?" Unless my mother had cautioned me not to tell, I generally answered her questions without reserve.

At the arrival of our guests I sat close to my mother, and did not leave her side without first asking her consent. I ate my supper in quiet, listening patiently to the talk of the old people, wishing all the time that they would begin the stories I loved best. At last, when I could not wait any longer, I whispered in my mother's ear, "Ask them to tell an Iktomi story,[2] mother."

Soothing my impatience, my mother said aloud, "My little daughter is anxious to hear your legends." By this time all were through eating, and the evening was fast deepening into twilight.

As each in turn began to tell a legend, I pillowed my head in my mother's lap; and lying flat upon my back, I watched the stars as they peeped down upon me, one by one. The increasing interest of the tale aroused me, and I sat up eagerly listening for every word. The old women made funny remarks, and laughed so heartily that I could not help joining them.

The distant howling of a pack of wolves or the hooting of an owl in the river bottom frightened me, and I nestled into my mother's lap. She added some dry sticks to the fire, and the bright flames heaped up into the faces of the old folks as they sat around in a great circle.

On such an evening, I remember the glare of the fire shone on a tattooed star upon the brow of the old warrior who was telling a story. I watched him curiously as he made his unconscious gestures. The blue star upon his bronzed forehead was a puzzle to me. Looking about, I saw two parallel lines

---

2. A story about the Sioux trickster.

on the chin of one of the old women. The rest had none. I examined my mother's face, but found no sign there.

After the warrior's story was finished, I asked the old woman the meaning of the blue lines on her chin, looking all the while out of the corners of my eyes at the warrior with the star on his forehead. I was a little afraid that he would rebuke me for my boldness.

Here the old woman began: "Why, my grandchild, they are signs,—secret signs I dare not tell you. I shall, however, tell you a wonderful story about a woman who had a cross tattooed upon each of her cheeks."

It was a long story of a woman whose magic power lay hidden behind the marks upon her face. I fell asleep before the story was completed.

Ever after that night I felt suspicious of tattooed people. Wherever I saw one I glanced furtively at the mark and round about it, wondering what terrible magic power was covered there.

It was rarely that such a fearful story as this one was told by the camp fire. Its impression was so acute that the picture still remains vividly clear and pronounced.

*   *   *

VII. *The Big Red Apples*

The first turning away from the easy, natural flow of my life occurred in an early spring. It was in my eighth year; in the month of March, I afterward learned. At this age I knew but one language, and that was my mother's native tongue.

From some of my playmates I heard that two paleface missionaries were in our village. They were from that class of white men who wore big hats and carried large hearts, they said. Running direct to my mother, I began to question her why these two strangers were among us. She told me, after I had teased much, that they had come to take away Indian boys and girls to the East. My mother did not seem to want me to talk about them. But in a day or two, I gleaned many wonderful stories from my playfellows concerning the strangers.

"Mother, my friend Judéwin is going home with the missionaries. She is going to a more beautiful country than ours; the palefaces told her so!" I said wistfully, wishing in my heart that I too might go.

Mother sat in a chair, and I was hanging on her knee. Within the last two seasons my big brother Dawée had returned from a three years' education in the East, and his coming back influenced my mother to take a farther step from her native way of living. First it was a change from the buffalo skin to the white man's canvas that covered our wigwam. Now she had given up her wigwam of slender poles, to live, a foreigner, in a home of clumsy logs.

"Yes, my child, several others besides Judéwin are going away with the palefaces. Your brother said the missionaries had inquired about his little sister," she said, watching my face very closely.

My heart thumped so hard against my breast, I wondered if she could hear it.

"Did he tell them to take me, mother?" I asked, fearing lest Dawée had forbidden the palefaces to see me, and that my hope of going to the Wonderland would be entirely blighted.

With a sad, slow smile, she answered: "There! I knew you were wishing to go, because Judéwin has filled your ears with the white men's lies. Don't believe a word they say! Their words are sweet, but, my child, their deeds are bitter. You will cry for me, but they will not even soothe you. Stay with me, my little one! Your brother Dawée says that going East, away from your mother, is too hard an experience for his baby sister."

Thus my mother discouraged my curiosity about the lands beyond our eastern horizon; for it was not yet an ambition for Letters that was stirring me. But on the following day the missionaries did come to our very house. I spied them coming up the footpath leading to our cottage. A third man was with them, but he was not my brother Dawée. It was another, a young interpreter, a paleface who had a smattering of the Indian language. I was ready to run out to meet them, but I did not dare to displease my mother. With great glee, I jumped up and down on our ground floor. I begged my mother to open the door, that they would be sure to come to us. Alas! They came, they saw, and they conquered!

Judéwin had told me of the great tree where grew red, red apples; and how we could reach out our hands and pick all the red apples we could eat. I had never seen apple trees. I had never tasted more than a dozen red apples in my life; and when I heard of the orchards of the East, I was eager to roam among them. The missionaries smiled into my eyes, and patted my head. I wondered how mother could say such hard words against them.

"Mother, ask them if little girls may have all the red apples they want, when they go East," I whispered aloud, in my excitement.

The interpreter heard me, and answered: "Yes, little girl, the nice red apples are for those who pick them; and you will have a ride on the iron horse if you go with these good people."

I had never seen a train, and he knew it.

"Mother, I'm going East! I like big red apples, and I want to ride on the iron horse! Mother, say yes!" I pleaded.

My mother said nothing. The missionaries waited in silence; and my eyes began to blur with tears, though I struggled to choke them back. The corners of my mouth twitched, and my mother saw me.

"I am not ready to give you any word," she said to them. "To-morrow I shall send you my answer by my son."

With this they left us. Alone with my mother, I yielded to my tears, and cried aloud, shaking my head so as not to hear what she was saying to me. This was the first time I had ever been so unwilling to give up my own desire that I refused to hearken to my mother's voice.

There was a solemn silence in our home that night. Before I went to bed I begged the Great Spirit to make my mother willing I should go with the missionaries.

The next morning came, and my mother called me to her side. "My daughter, do you still persist in wishing to leave your mother?" she asked.

"Oh, mother, it is not that I wish to leave you, but I want to see the wonderful Eastern land," I answered.

My dear old aunt came to our house that morning, and I heard her say, "Let her try it."

I hoped that, as usual, my aunt was pleading on my side. My brother Dawée came for mother's decision. I dropped my play, and crept close to my aunt.

"Yes, Dawée, my daughter, though she does not understand what it all means, is anxious to go. She will need an education when she is grown, for then there will be fewer real Dakotas, and many more palefaces. This tearing her away, so young, from her mother is necessary, if I would have her an educated woman. The palefaces, who owe us a large debt for stolen lands, have begun to pay a tardy justice in offering some education to our children. But I know my daughter must suffer keenly in this experiment. For her sake, I dread to tell you my reply to the missionaries. Go, tell them that they may take my little daughter, and that the Great Spirit shall not fail to reward them according to their hearts."

Wrapped in my heavy blanket, I walked with my mother to the carriage that was soon to take us to the iron horse. I was happy. I met my playmates, who were also wearing their best thick blankets. We showed one another our new beaded moccasins, and the width of the belts that girdled our new dresses. Soon we were being drawn rapidly away by the white man's horses. When I saw the lonely figure of my mother vanish in the distance, a sense of regret settled heavily upon me. I felt suddenly weak, as if I might fall limp to the ground. I was in the hands of strangers whom my mother did not fully trust. I no longer felt free to be myself, or to voice my own feelings. The tears trickled down my cheeks, and I buried my face in the folds of my blanket. Now the first step, parting me from my mother, was taken, and all my belated tears availed nothing.

Having driven thirty miles to the ferryboat, we crossed the Missouri in the evening. Then riding again a few miles eastward, we stopped before a massive brick building. I looked at it in amazement, and with a vague misgiving, for in our village I had never seen so large a house. Trembling with fear and distrust of the palefaces, my teeth chattering from the chilly ride, I crept noiselessly in my soft moccasins along the narrow hall, keeping very close to the bare wall. I was as frightened and bewildered as the captured young of a wild creature.

1900

The Soft-Hearted Sioux[1]

I

Beside the open fire I sat within our tepee. With my red blanket wrapped tightly about my crossed legs, I was thinking of the coming season, my sixteenth winter. On either side of the wigwam were my parents. My father was whistling a tune between his teeth while polishing with his bare hand a red stone pipe he had recently carved. Almost in front of me, beyond the center fire, my old grandmother sat near the entranceway.

She turned her face toward her right and addressed most of her words to my mother. Now and then she spoke to me, but never did she allow her eyes to rest upon her daughter's husband, my father. It was only upon rare occasions that my grandmother said anything to him. Thus his ears were open

---

1. "The Soft-Hearted Sioux" first appeared in *Harper's Monthly* in March 1901, the source of the text printed here. It was later included in *American Indian Stories* (1921).

and ready to catch the smallest wish she might express. Sometimes when my grandmother had been saying things which pleased him, my father used to comment upon them. At other times, when he could not approve of what was spoken, he used to work or smoke silently.

On this night my old grandmother began her talk about me. Filling the bowl of her red stone pipe with dry willow bark, she looked across at me.

"My grandchild, you are tall and are no longer a little boy." Narrowing her old eyes, she asked, "My grandchild, when are you going to bring here a handsome young woman?" I stared into the fire rather than meet her gaze. Waiting for my answer, she stooped forward and through the long stem drew a flame into the red stone pipe.

I smiled while my eyes were still fixed upon the bright fire, but I said nothing in reply. Turning to my mother, she offered her the pipe. I glanced at my grandmother. The loose buckskin sleeve fell off at her elbow and showed a wrist covered with silver bracelets. Holding up the fingers of her left hand, she named off the desirable young women of our village.

"Which one, my grandchild, which one?" she questioned.

"Hoh!" I said, pulling at my blanket in confusion. "Not yet!" Here my mother passed the pipe over the fire to my father. Then she, too, began speaking of what I should do.

"My son, be always active. Do not dislike a long hunt. Learn to provide much buffalo meat and many buckskins before you bring home a wife." Presently my father gave the pipe to my grandmother, and he took his turn in the exhortations.

"Ho, my son, I have been counting in my heart the bravest warriors of our people. There is not one of them who won his title in his sixteenth winter. My son, it is a great thing for some brave of sixteen winters to do."

Not a word had I to give in answer. I knew well the fame of my warrior father. He had earned the right of speaking such words, though even he himself was a brave only at my age. Refusing to smoke my grandmother's pipe because my heart was too much stirred by their words, and sorely troubled with a fear lest I should disappoint them, I arose to go. Drawing my blanket over my shoulders, I said, as I stepped toward the entranceway: "I go to hobble my pony. It is now late in the night."

II

Nine winters' snows had buried deep that night when my old grandmother, together with my father and mother, designed my future with the glow of a camp fire upon it.

Yet I did not grow up the warrior, huntsman, and husband I was to have been. At the mission school I learned it was wrong to kill. Nine winters I hunted for the soft heart of Christ, and prayed for the huntsmen who chased the buffalo on the plains.

In the autumn of the tenth year I was sent back to my tribe to preach Christianity to them. With the white man's Bible in my hand, and the white man's tender heart in my breast, I returned to my own people.

Wearing a foreigner's dress, I walked, a stranger, into my father's village.

Asking my way, for I had not forgotten my native tongue, an old man led me toward the tepee where my father lay. From my old companion I learned that my father had been sick many moons. As we drew near the tepee, I heard the chanting of a medicine-man within it. At once I wished to enter in and drive from my home the sorcerer of the plains, but the old warrior checked me. "Ho, wait outside until the medicine-man leaves your father," he said. While talking he scanned me from head to feet. Then he retraced his steps toward the heart of the camping-ground.

My father's dwelling was on the outer limits of the round-faced village. With every heartthrob I grew more impatient to enter the wigwam.

While I turned the leaves of my Bible with nervous fingers, the medicine-man came forth from the dwelling and walked hurriedly away. His head and face were closely covered with the loose robe which draped his entire figure.

He was tall and large. His long strides I have never forgot. They seemed to me then the uncanny gait of eternal death. Quickly pocketing my Bible, I went into the tepee.

Upon a mat lay my father, with furrowed face and gray hair. His eyes and cheeks were sunken far into his head. His sallow skin lay thin upon his pinched nose and high cheekbones. Stooping over him, I took his fevered hand. "How, Ate?"[2] I greeted him. A light flashed from his listless eyes and his dried lips parted. "My son!" he murmured, in a feeble voice. Then again the wave of joy and recognition receded. He closed his eyes, and his hand dropped from my open palm to the ground.

Looking about, I saw an old woman sitting with bowed head. Shaking hands with her, I recognized my mother. I sat down between my father and mother as I used to do, but I did not feel at home. The place where my old grandmother used to sit was now unoccupied. With my mother I bowed my head. Alike our throats were choked and tears were streaming from our eyes; but far apart in spirit our ideas and faiths separated us. My grief was for the soul unsaved; and I thought my mother wept to see a brave man's body broken by sickness.

Useless was my attempt to change the faith in the medicine-man to that abstract power named God. Then one day I became righteously mad with anger that the medicine-man should thus ensnare my father's soul. And when he came to chant his sacred songs I pointed toward the door and bade him go! The man's eyes glared upon me for an instant. Slowly gathering his robe about him, he turned his back upon the sick man and stepped out of our wigwam. "Ha, ha, ha! my son, I cannot live without the medicine-man!" I heard my father cry when the sacred man was gone.

III

On a bright day, when the winged seeds of the prairie-grass were flying hither and thither, I walked solemnly toward the centre of the camping-ground. My heart beat hard and irregularly at my side. Tighter I grasped the sacred book I carried under my arm. Now was the beginning of life's work.

Though I knew it would be hard, I did not once feel that failure was to be my reward. As I stepped unevenly on the rolling ground, I thought of the warriors soon to wash off their war-paints and follow me.

2. Hello, Father (Lakota).

At length I reached the place where the people had assembled to hear me preach. In a large circle men and women sat upon the dry red grass. Within the ring I stood, with the white man's Bible in my hand. I tried to tell them of the soft heart of Christ.

In silence the vast circle of bareheaded warriors sat under an afternoon sun. At last, wiping the wet from my brow, I took my place in the ring. The hush of the assembly filled me with great hope.

I was turning my thoughts upward to the sky in gratitude, when a stir called me to earth again.

A tall, strong man arose. His loose robe hung in folds over his right shoulder. A pair of snapping black eyes fastened themselves like the poisonous fangs of a serpent upon me. He was the medicine-man. A tremor played about my heart and a chill cooled the fire in my veins.

Scornfully he pointed a long forefinger in my direction and asked:

"What loyal son is he who, returning to his father's people, wears a foreigner's dress?" He paused a moment, and then continued: "The dress of that foreigner of whom a story says he bound a native of our land, and heaping dry sticks around him, kindled a fire at his feet!" Waving his hand toward me, he exclaimed, "Here is the traitor to his people!"

I was helpless. Before the eyes of the crowd the cunning magician turned my honest heart into a vile nest of treachery. Alas! the people frowned as they looked upon me.

"Listen!" he went on. "Which one of you who have eyed the young man can see through his bosom and warn the people of the nest of young snakes hatching there? Whose ear was so acute that he caught the hissing of snakes whenever the young man opened his mouth? This one has not only proven false to you, but even to the Great Spirit who made him. He is a fool! Why do you sit here giving ear to a foolish man who could not defend his people because he fears to kill, who could not bring venison to renew the life of his sick father? With his prayers, let him drive away the enemy! With his soft heart, let him keep off starvation! We shall go elsewhere to dwell upon an untainted ground."

With this he disbanded the people. When the sun lowered in the west and the winds were quiet, the village of cone-shaped tepees was gone. The medicine-man had won the hearts of the people.

Only my father's dwelling was left to mark the fighting-ground.

IV

From a long night at my father's bedside I came out to look upon the morning. The yellow sun hung equally between the snow-covered land and the cloudless blue sky. The light of the new day was cold. The strong breath of winter crusted the snow and fitted crystal shells over the rivers and lakes. As I stood in front of the tepee, thinking of the vast prairies which separated us from our tribe, and wondering if the high sky likewise separated the soft-hearted Son of God from us, the icy blast from the North blew through my hair and skull. My neglected hair had grown long and fell upon my neck.

My father had not risen from his bed since the day the medicine-man led the people away. Though I read from the Bible and prayed beside him upon my knees, my father would not listen. Yet I believed my prayers were not unheeded in heaven.

"Ha, ha, ha! my son," my father groaned upon the first snowfall. "My son, our food is gone. There is no one to bring me meat! My son, your soft heart has unfitted you for everything!" Then covering his face with the buffalo-robe, he said no more. Now while I stood out in that cold winter morning, I was starving. For two days I had not seen any food. But my own cold and hunger did not harass my soul as did the whining cry of the sick old man.

Stepping again into the tepee, I untied my snow-shoes, which were fastened to the tent-poles.

My poor mother, watching by the sick one, and faithfully heaping wood upon the centre fire, spoke to me:

"My son, do not fail again to bring your father meat, or he will starve to death."

"How, Ina,"[3] I answered, sorrowfully. From the tepee I started forth again to hunt food for my aged parents. All day I tracked the white level lands in vain. Nowhere, nowhere were there any other footprints but my own! In the evening of this third fast-day I came back without meat. Only a bundle of sticks for the fire I brought on my back. Dropping the wood outside, I lifted the door-flap and set one foot within the tepee.

There I grew dizzy and numb. My eyes swam in tears. Before me lay my old gray-haired father sobbing like a child. In his horny hands he clutched the buffalo-robe, and with his teeth he was gnawing off the edges. Chewing the dry stiff hair and buffalo-skin, my father's eyes sought my hands. Upon seeing them empty, he cried out:

"My son, your soft heart will let me starve before you bring me meat! Two hills eastward stand a herd of cattle. Yet you will see me die before you bring me food!"

Leaving my mother lying with covered head upon her mat, I rushed out into the night.

With a strange warmth in my heart and swiftness in my feet, I climbed over the first hill, and soon the second one. The moonlight upon the white country showed me a clear path to the white man's cattle. With my hand upon the knife in my belt, I leaned heavily against the fence while counting the herd.

Twenty in all I numbered. From among them I chose the best-fattened creature. Leaping over the fence, I plunged my knife into it.

My long knife was sharp, and my hands, no more fearful and slow, slashed off choice chunks of warm flesh. Bending under the meat I had taken for my starving father, I hurried across the prairie.

Toward home I fairly ran with the life-giving food I carried upon my back. Hardly had I climbed the second hill when I heard sounds coming after me. Faster and faster I ran with my load for my father, but the sounds were gaining upon me. I heard the clicking of snowshoes and the squeaking of the leather straps at my heels; yet I did not turn to see what pursued me, for I was intent upon reaching my father. Suddenly like thunder an angry voice shouted curses and threats into my ear! A rough hand wrenched my shoulder and took the meat from me! I stopped struggling to run. A deafening

---

3. Hello, Mother (Lakota).

whir filled my head. The moon and stars began to move. Now the white prairie was sky, and the stars lay under my feet. Now again they were turning. At last the starry blue rose up into place. The noise in my ears was still. A great quiet filled the air. In my hand I found my long knife dripping with blood. At my feet a man's figure lay prone in blood-red snow. The horrible scene about me seemed a trick of my senses, for I could not understand it was real. Looking long upon the blood-stained snow, the load of meat for my starving father reached my recognition at last. Quickly I tossed it over my shoulder and started again homeward.

Tired and haunted I reached the door of the wigwam. Carrying the food before me, I entered with it into the tepee.

"Father, here is food!" I cried, as I dropped the meat near my mother. No answer came. Turning about, I beheld my gray-haired father dead! I saw by the unsteady firelight an old gray-haired skeleton lying rigid and stiff.

Out into the open I started, but the snow at my feet became bloody.

V

On the day after my father's death, having led my mother to the camp of the medicine-man, I gave myself up to those who were searching for the murderer of the paleface.

They bound me hand and foot. Here in this cell I was placed four days ago.

The shrieking winter winds have followed me hither. Rattling the bars, they howl unceasingly: "Your soft heart! your soft heart will see me die before you bring me food!" Hark! something is clanking the chain on the door. It is being opened. From the dark night without a black figure crosses the threshold. It is the guard. He comes to warn me of my fate. He tells me that tomorrow I must die. In his stern face I laugh aloud. I do not fear death.

Yet I wonder who shall come to welcome me in the realm of strange sight. Will the loving Jesus grant me pardon and give my soul a soothing sleep? or will my warrior father greet me and receive me as his son? Will my spirit fly upward to a happy heaven? or shall I sink into the bottomless pit, an outcast from a God of infinite love?

Soon, soon I shall know, for now I see the east is growing red. My heart is strong. My face is calm. My eyes are dry and eager for new scenes. My hands hang quietly at my side. Serene and brave, my soul awaits the men to perch me on the gallows for another flight. I go.

1901

American Literature
1914–1945

THE TWO WARS AS HISTORICAL MARKERS

The conflict eventually known as World War I broke out in Europe in 1914, with Great Britain, France, and Russia fighting against Germany. The United States, which belatedly entered the war in 1917, on the side of Britain and France, had ended its last full-scale conflict, the Civil War, some fifty years previously. In the interval, the country's industrial power had grown immensely. So had its major cities, swelled on the Eastern seaboard by immigrants increasingly from southern and eastern Europe, and on the West Coast, from Asia. In 1914 the country's network of transcontinental railroads linked its productive farms, small towns, and industry to urban centers. Henry Ford had begun the transformation of the automobile from an exotic luxury technology into a consumer good with the 1908 introduction of the Model T, and by 1912 an American entrepreneur had dreamed up the first transcontinental highway. Aviation pioneers were rapidly building on the Wright brothers' first successful powered airplane flights of 1903. Like the Civil War, World War I would mobilize the country's industries and technologies, spur their development, and uproot both soldiers and civilians. On an even larger scale, World War II would do the same.

These events were momentous both in themselves and as harbingers of transformations to come. At the end of World War I, however, the United States was still in the main a nation of small farms and small towns, with about two-thirds of its population living in rural districts or towns of fewer than twenty-five thousand inhabitants. Although several waves of immigration had altered the makeup of the population, the

Night Hawks (detail), Edward Hopper, 1942. For more information about this painting, see the color insert in this volume.

NAACP—Silent March, 1917. On July 28, 1917, under the leadership of the National Association for the Advancement of Colored People, some ten thousand African Americans marched down New York City's Fifth Avenue to protest the race riots of that summer in East Saint Louis, during which an estimated one hundred black citizens were lynched and thousands of others were left homeless.

majority of Americans were still of English or German ancestry and about one American in ten was of African descent. The majority was deeply distrustful of international politics, and after the war ended, many attempted to steer the nation back to prewar modes of life. In 1924 Congress enacted a sweeping exclusionary immigration act, extending the reach of previous restrictions. The act prohibited all Asian immigration and effectively set quotas for other countries at 2 percent of their existing U.S. immigrant populations in 1890, intending thereby to restore the ethnic makeup of the United States to what it had been more than a quarter century earlier (and indeed the proportion of Americans born outside the United States did decline markedly from the 1920s to 1940). The immediate postwar years also saw the so-called Red Scare, when labor union headquarters were raided and immigrant radicals were deported by a government fearful of the influence of the newly Communist Soviet Union (formerly tsarist Russia).

For other Americans, however, the war helped accelerate long-sought changes in the forms of political and social life. The long struggle to win American women the vote—given a final push by women's work as nurses and ambulance drivers during the war—ended in 1920 with the passage of the Nineteenth Amendment to the Constitution. The National Association for the Advancement of Colored People (NAACP), founded in 1909, successfully argued during World War I for the commissioning of black officers in the U.S. armed forces; as they would again after World War II,

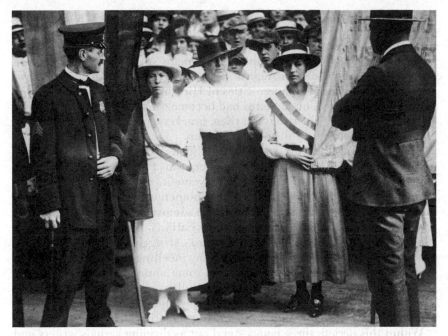

Suffragettes Picket the White House, 1917. Members of the National Woman's Party regularly demonstrated in front of the White House during Woodrow Wilson's administration. After the U.S. entry into World War I heightened concerns for domestic order, pro-suffrage picketers were arrested and jailed.

African Americans who fought abroad returned to fight for their rights at home. Despite the government's restrictions on leftist political activity, many Americans—among them writers and intellectuals as well as labor activists and urban immigrants—looked to the Soviet Union and the international Communist movement for a model in combating inequality and fostering workers' rights in the United States. Other Americans went abroad, for shorter or longer stretches of time, in order to taste the expatriate life (made cheaper in war-ravaged economies by the solid American dollar) in Europe's battered but still vibrant cities and countryside. Some Americans traveled physical and social distances almost as great within the boundaries of the United States, as African Americans began to migrate in large numbers out of the segregated South and young people everywhere increasingly attended college away from home and moved to the cities. African Americans, emancipated urban women, and the restless young faced off against rural and urban traditionalists over the question of who, exactly, was truly "American."

These conflicts over the shape of the future acquired new urgency when the stock market crashed in 1929 and led to an economic depression with a 25 percent unemployment rate—a percentage even larger in its impact, by present-day standards, because women in general were not in the workforce. Known as the Great Depression, this period of economic hardship did not fully end until the United States entered World War II, following the Japanese attack on the American fleet at Pearl Harbor on December 7, 1941. Japan's ally Germany also declared war on the United States, thus involving the country in another European conflict. The war unified the country politically; revitalized industry, which devoted itself to goods needed for the war effort; and put people to work, including women who went into the labor force in unprecedented numbers. Germany surrendered in the spring of 1945. The war ended in August 1945 following the detonation of two atomic bombs over the Japanese cities of Hiroshima and Nagasaki. Europe was in ruins and the United States had become the world's major industrial and political power. The two wars, then, bracket a period during which the United States became a fully modern nation.

In the arena of literature and culture, the period demarcated by the two world wars is known as the era of modernism. Far too broad and widespread to be understood as a single movement, *modernism* nevertheless names a recognizable international phenomenon, a wave of challenges mounted against traditional authority in almost every realm—the arts, religion, science, politics, and social conventions. American literature in these decades registers all sides of the era's struggles and debates, while sharing a commitment to explore the many meanings of modernity. Some writers rejoiced while others lamented; some anticipated future utopias and others believed that civilization had collapsed; but the period's most influential voices, believing that old forms would not work for new times, were inspired by the possibility of creating something entirely new.

Within this period, three issues stand out as dividing various writers and schools of writers, all of them related to the accelerating transformations and conflicts of modernity. One issue centered on the uses of literary tradition. To some, a work registering its allegiance to literary history—through allusion to canonical works of the past, or by using traditional poetic forms and poetic language, or by relying on traditional forms of narrative authority—seemed imitative and old-fashioned. To others, a work failing to honor literary tradition was simply bad or incompetent writing. For still others, literary history was best appreciated oppositionally: modernist works often allude to previous literature ironically, or deliberately fracture traditional literary formulas. A related issue involved the place of popular culture in serious literature. Throughout the era, popular culture gained momentum and influence. Some writers regarded it as crucial for the future of literature that popular art forms, such as film and jazz, be embraced; to others, serious literature by definition had to reject what they saw as the cynical commercialism of popular culture.

Another issue was the question of how far literature should engage itself in political and social struggle. Should art be a domain unto itself, exploring aesthetic questions and enunciating transcendent truths, or should art participate in the politics of the times? For some, a work that was political in aim counted as propaganda, not art; others thought that apolitical literature was evasive and irresponsible; some viewed the call to keep art out of politics as covertly political, a conservative mandate to preserve the status quo, even if it did not acknowledge itself as such.

CHANGING TIMES

The transformations of the first half of the twentieth century were driven both by ideas and by changes in the economic and technological underpinnings of daily life. Much social energy in the 1920s went into enlarging the boundaries for acceptable self-expression. Adherents of small-town values such as the work ethic, social conformity, duty, and respectability clashed ideologically not only with internationally minded radicals but also with newly affluent young people who argued for more diverse, permissive, and tolerant styles of life. To some extent this debate recapitulated the long-standing American conflict between the claims of the individual and those of society, a conflict going back to the seventeenth-century religious conflicts over autonomy of conscience that were later epitomized in Ralph Waldo Emerson's call, in the 1840s: "Whosoever would be a man, must be a non-conformist."

The 1920s saw significant changes in sexual mores, with increasing numbers of young people no longer under the watchful eyes of their small-town elders. These social changes found their most influential theorist in the Austrian psychiatrist Sigmund Freud (1858–1939), inventor of the practice of psychoanalysis. According to Freud, many modern neuroses could be traced to repression and inhibition. Freud developed the idea of the self as grounded in an "unconscious," where forbidden desires, traumas, and unacceptable emotions—mostly sexual in nature and derived from childhood experiences—were stored. Freudian analysis aimed at helping people become aware of their repressed feelings and so less likely to reenact in the present the traumas of the past. Americanized Freudian ideas provided the psychological underpinning for much literature of the interwar era, whether the focus was the individual trapped in a repressive culture or the repressive culture itself.

The middle-class double sexual standard had, in fact, always granted considerable sexual freedom to men; now, however, women—enfranchised and liberated by automobiles and job possibilities away from home—began to demand similar freedom for themselves. Women's demands went well beyond the erotic, however, encompassing education, professional work, mobility, and whatever else seemed like social goods hitherto reserved for men. Female dress changed: long, heavy, restricting garments gave way to short, lightweight, easily worn store-bought clothing. The combination of expanding urban life with new psychologies oriented to self-expression also brought into being new social possibilities for women and men whose sexual desires did not conform to traditional patterns. Freud was only one of a number of thinkers in the period who urged a measure of toleration for sexual minorities, especially homosexuals—a term that entered specialized English usage in the 1890s and came into wider circulation in the years following World War I. Although the legal risks and social stigma borne by homosexuals remained very much in force, gay enclaves became more visible in American life and gay lives became more imaginable as a theme in American literature.

African Americans, like women, became mobile in these years as never before. Around 1915, as a direct result of the industrial needs of World War I, opportunities opened for African Americans in the factories of the North, and what became known as the Great Migration out of the South began. Not only did migration give the lie to southern white claims that African Americans were content with southern segregationist practices, but it also damaged the South's economy by draining off an important segment of its

Lenox Avenue, Sargent Claude Johnson, 1938. Johnson's lithograph pays tribute to the clubs, ballrooms, and bars of New York City's Lenox Avenue, hub of the Harlem Renaissance. During the Great Depression, the Federal Art Project enlisted many notable artists to create graphic works celebrating American cultural and natural landmarks.

working population. Even though African Americans faced racism, segregation, and racial violence in the North, a black American presence soon became powerfully visible in American cultural life. Harlem, a section of New York City, attained an almost wholly black population of over 150,000 by the mid-1920s; from this "city within a city," African Americans wrote, performed, composed, and painted. Here as well they founded two major journals of opinion and culture, *The Crisis* (in 1910) and *Opportunity* (in 1923). This cultural outpouring influenced writers, painters, and musicians of other ethnicities and became known collectively as the Harlem Renaissance.

The famous black intellectual W. E. B. Du Bois had argued in *The Souls of Black Folk* (1903) that African Americans had a kind of double consciousness—of themselves as Americans and as blacks. This doubleness contributed to debates within the African American cultural community. The Harlem Renaissance sparked arguments between those who wanted to claim membership in the culture at large and those who wanted to stake out a separate artistic domain; between those who wanted to celebrate rural African American folkways and those committed to urban intellectuality; between those who wanted to join the American mainstream and those who, disgusted by American race prejudice, aligned themselves with worldwide revolutionary movements; between those who celebrated a "primitive" African heritage and those who rejected the idea as a degrading stereotype. African American women, as Nella Larsen's novel *Passing* (1929) testifies, could experience these divisions with special intensity. Women were very much called on in efforts to "uplift," advance, and educate the black community, but these communal obligations could be felt as constraints on individual freedom and exploration; meanwhile the white social world, given to exoticizing or sexualizing black women, offered few alternatives.

Class inequality, as well as American racial divisions, continued to generate intellectual and artistic debate in the interwar years. The nineteenth-century United States had been host to many radical movements—labor activism, utopianism, socialism, anarchism—inspired by diverse sources. In the twentieth century, especially following the rise of the Soviet Union, the American left increasingly drew its intellectual and political program from the Marxist tradition. The German philosopher Karl Marx (1818–1883) located the roots of human behavior in economics. He claimed that industrializing societies were structurally divided into two antagonistic classes based on different relations to the means of production—capital versus labor. The Industrial Revolution arose from the accumulation of surplus capital by industrialists paying the least possible amount to workers; the next stage in world history would be when workers took control of the means of production for themselves. Because, to Marx, the ideas and ideals of any particular society could represent the interests of only its dominant class, he derided individualism as a middle-class or "bourgeois" value that could only discourage worker solidarity.

Marx's ideas formed the basis for Communist political parties across Europe. In 1917, a Communist revolution in Russia led by Vladimir Ilyich Lenin (1870–1914) overthrew the tsarist regime, instituted the "dictatorship of the proletariat" that Marx had called for, and engineered the development of communism as a unified international movement. Americans who thought of themselves as Marxists in the 1920s and 1930s were usually connected with the Communist Party and subjected to government surveillance and occasional violence, as were socialists, anarchists, union organizers, and others who opposed unfettered American capitalism and marketplace competition. Although politics directed from outside the national boundaries was, almost by definition, "un-American," many adherents of these movements hoped to make the United States conform to its stated ideals, guaranteeing liberty and justice for all.

A defining conflict between American ideals and American realities for writers of the 1920s was the Sacco-Vanzetti case. Nicola Sacco and Bartolomeo Vanzetti were Italian immigrants, not Communists but avowed anarchists; on April 15, 1920, they were arrested near Boston after a murder during a robbery. They were accused of that crime, then tried and condemned to death in 1921; but it was widely believed that they had not received a fair trial and that their political beliefs had been held against them. After a number of appeals, they were executed in 1927, maintaining their innocence to the end. John Dos Passos and Katherine Anne Porter were among the many writers and intellectuals who demonstrated in their defense; several were arrested and jailed. It is estimated that well over a hundred poems (including works by William Carlos Williams, Edna St. Vincent Millay, and Carl Sandburg) along with six plays and eight novels of the time treated the incident from a sympathetic perspective.

Like the Sacco-Vanzetti case in the 1920s, the Scottsboro case in the 1930s brought many American writers and intellectuals, black and white, together in a cause—here, the struggle against racial bias in the justice system. In 1931 nine black youths were indicted in Scottsboro, Alabama, for the alleged rape of two white women in a railroad freight car. They were all found guilty, and some were sentenced to death. The U.S. Supreme Court reversed convictions twice; in a second trial one of the alleged victims retracted her testimony; in 1937 charges against five of the defendants were dropped. But four went to jail, in many people's view unfairly. American

Communists were especially active in the Scottsboro defense; but people across the political spectrum saw the case as crucial to the question of whether black people could receive fair trials in the American South. The unfair trial of an African American man became a literary motif in much writing of the period and beyond, including Richard Wright's *Native Son* (1940), William Faulkner's *Intruder in the Dust* (1948), and Harper Lee's *To Kill a Mockingbird* (1960).

SCIENCE AND TECHNOLOGY

Technology played a vital, although often invisible, role in all these events, because it linked places and spaces, contributing to the shaping of culture as a national phenomenon rather than a series of local manifestations. Without new modes of production, transportation, and communication, modern America in all its complexity could not have existed. Electricity for lights and appliances, along with the telephone—nineteenth-century inventions—expanded into American homes during these years, improving life for many but widening the gap between those plugged into the new networks and those outside them. The phonograph record and the record player (early devices for recording and playing music), the motion picture (which acquired sound in 1929), and the radio brought mass popular culture into being. Although the nineteenth-century dream of forging a scattered population into a single nation could now be realized more instantaneously and directly than was ever possible with print media, many intellectuals suspected that mass culture would create a robotic, passive population vulnerable to demagoguery.

The most powerful technological innovation, however, the automobile, encouraged activity, not passivity. Automobiles put Americans on the road, dramatically reshaped the structure of American industry and occupations, and altered the national topography as well. Along with work in automobile factories themselves, millions of other jobs—in steel mills, parts factories, highway construction and maintenance, gas stations, machine shops, roadside restaurants, motels—depended on the automobile. The road itself became—and has remained—a potent symbol of the United States and of modernity as well. Cities grew, suburbs came into being, small towns died, and new towns arose, all according to the placement of highways, which rapidly supplanted the railroad in shaping the patterns of twentieth-century American urban expansion. The United States had become a nation of migrants as much as or more than it was a nation of immigrants.

In tandem with the impact of technological change on daily life, one of the most important developments in the interwar period was the growth of modern "big" science. At the end of the nineteenth century and beginning of the twentieth, scientists discovered that the atom was not the smallest possible unit of matter, that matter was not indestructible, that both time and space were relative to an observer's position, that some phenomena were so small that attempts at measurement would alter them, that some outcomes could be predicted only in terms of statistical probability, that the universe might be infinite in size and yet infinitely expanding; hence, much of the commonsense basis of nineteenth-century science had to be put aside in favor of far more powerful but also far less commonsensical theories. Among many results, scientists and literary intellectuals became less able to communicate with each other, and their worldviews began to diverge. Writers responded with ambivalence to the new science, sometimes drawing on scientific images and ideas—"the imagination uses the phraseology of science," wrote the poet (and physician) William Carlos Williams—sometimes deploring the lost authority of traditional, humanistic explanations of the concrete, experienced world and felt human life. Gertrude Stein's radical literary experiments were partly inspired by her laboratory experiences in neuroanatomy at Harvard University and the Johns Hopkins Medical School. Poets like Ezra Pound, T. S. Eliot, and Wallace Stevens, however, along with many of their readers, questioned the capacity of science to provide accounts of subjective experience and moral issues, and they elevated the metaphorical language of poetry over the supposed literal accuracy of scientific description. The increased specialization of intellectual activity divided educated people into what the British novelist and physicist C. P. Snow was later to call the "two cultures"—science versus letters.

THE 1930s

The Great Depression was a worldwide phenomenon and fostered social unrest that led to the rise of fascist dictatorships in Europe, including those of Francisco Franco in Spain, Benito Mussolini in Italy, and Adolf Hitler in Germany. Hitler's program, which was to make Germany rich and strong by conquering the rest of Europe, led inexorably to World War II.

In the United States, the Depression made politics and economics the salient issues of public life and overrode questions of individual freedom with fear of mass collapse. Free-enterprise capitalism had always justified itself by arguing that the system not only made a small number of individuals immensely wealthy, but also guaranteed better lives for all. This assurance now rang hollow. The suicides of millionaire bankers

The Bread Line, New York, Clare Leighton, 1932. Leighton, who was born in England and became a U.S. citizen in 1939, made her reputation as an illustrator of rural life and work. This wood engraving's line of idled men dwarfed by their urban surroundings represents Depression-era New York City as the dark antithesis of Leighton's traditional subjects.

Towards Los Angeles, Dorothea Lange 1937. During the Great Depression, the Farm Security Administration (FSA)—one of many new government agencies created in response to the economic emergency—employed a number of well-known documentary photographers. Lange produced memorable portraits of migrants displaced by the Dust Bowl under the FSA's sponsorship.

and stockbrokers made the headlines, but more compelling was the enormous toll among ordinary people who lost their homes, jobs, farms, and life savings in the stock market crash. Conservatives advised waiting until things got better; radicals espoused immediate social revolution. In this polarized atmosphere, the election of Franklin Delano Roosevelt to the presidency in 1932 was a victory for American pragmatism; his series of liberal reforms—Social Security, programs creating jobs in the public sector, welfare, and unemployment insurance—cushioned the worst effects of the Depression and avoided the civil strife that many had thought inevitable.

The terrible economic situation in the United States produced a significant increase in Communist Party membership and prestige in the 1930s. Numerous intellectuals allied themselves with its causes, even if they did not actually become party members. An old radical journal, *The Masses*, later *The New Masses*, became the official literary voice of the party, and various other radical groups founded journals to represent their viewpoints. Visitors to the Soviet Union returned with glowing reports about a true workers' democracy and prosperity for all. The appeal of communism was significantly enhanced by its claim to be an opponent of fascism. Communists fought against Franco in the Spanish Civil War of 1936 and 1937. Hitler's nightmare policies of genocide and racial superiority, and his plans for a general European war to secure more room for the superior German "folk," became increasingly evident as European refugees began to flee to the United States in the 1930s, and many believed that the USSR would be the only country able to withstand the German war machine. But Soviet communism showed another side to Americans when American Communists were ordered to break up the meetings of other radical groups; when Josef Stalin, the Soviet dictator, instituted a series of brutal purges in the Soviet Union, beginning in 1936; and when in 1939 he signed a pact promising not to go to war against Germany. The disillusionment and betrayal felt by many radicals over these acts led many 1930s left-wing activists to become staunch anti-Communists after World War II.

AMERICAN VERSIONS OF MODERNISM

In English-language literary contexts, *modernism* is sometimes used as a catchall term for any kind of literary production in the interwar period that deals with the modern world. More narrowly, it refers to work that represents the transformation of traditional society under the pressures of modernity, and that breaks down traditional literary forms in doing so. Much modernist literature of this kind, which critics increasingly now set apart as "high modernism," is in a sense antimodern: it interprets modernity as an experience of loss. As its title underlines, T. S. Eliot's *The Waste Land*—the great poem of high modernism—represents the modern world as a scene of ruin.

Scholars of international modernism frequently trace its rise back to the later nineteenth century, citing the works of French symbolists in literature, Friedrich Nietzsche in philosophy, and Charles Darwin in science as examples of radically antitraditional modes of thought and artistic practice. As an artistic movement, however, modernism reached a defining level of international coherence and momentum in response to World War I, which was far more devastating to the Continent than it was to the United States. Modernism involved other art forms—sculpture, painting, dance—as well as literature. The poetry of William Butler Yeats; James Joyce's *Ulysses* (1922); Marcel Proust's *Remembrance of Things Past* (1913–27); Thomas Mann's novels and short stories, including *The Magic Mountain* (1927)— these were only a few of the literary products of this movement in England and on the Continent. In painting, artists like Pablo Picasso, Juan Gris, and Georges Braque invented cubism; in the 1920s the surrealistic movement known as Dadaism emerged. The American public was introduced to modern art at the famous New York Armory Show of 1913, which featured cubist paintings and caused an uproar. Marcel Duchamp's *Nude Descending a Staircase*, which, to the untrained eye, looked like a mass of crudely drawn rectangles, was especially provocative. Composers like Igor Stravinsky similarly produced music in a "modern" mode, featuring dissonance and discontinuity rather than neat formal structure and appealing tonal harmonies. His composition *The Rite of Spring* (1913) provoked a riot in the Paris concert hall where it was premiered.

At the heart of the high modernist aesthetic lay the conviction that the previously sustaining structures of human life, whether social, political, religious, or artistic, had been destroyed or shown up as falsehoods or, at best, arbitrary and fragile human constructions. Order, sequence, and unity in works of art might well express human desires for coherence rather than reliable intuitions of reality. Generalization, abstraction, and high-flown writing might conceal rather than convey the real. The traditional form of a story, with its beginnings, complications, and resolutions, might be an artifice imposed on the flux and fragmentation of experience. To the extent that art falsely presented such an order as given or natural, it had to be renovated.

Thus a key formal characteristic typical of high modernist works, whether in painting, sculpture, or musical composition, is its construction out of fragments—fragments of myth or history, fragments of experience or perception, fragments of previous artistic works. Modernist literature is often notable for what it omits: the explanations, interpretations, connections, summaries, and distancing that provide continuity, perspective, and security in earlier literatures. A modernist work may seem to begin arbitrarily, to advance without explanation, and to end without resolution, consisting of vivid segments juxtaposed without cushioning or integrating transitions. There may be abrupt shifts in perspective, voice, and tone. Its rhetoric may be understated, ironic. It may suggest rather than assert, making use of symbols and images instead of statements. Its elements may be drawn from disparate areas of experience. The effect may be shocking and unsettling; the experience of reading will be challenging and difficult. Faced with intuiting connections left unstated, the reader of a modernist work is often said to participate in the creative work of making the poem or story.

Some high modernist works, however, order their discontinuous elements into conspicuous larger patterns, patterns often drawn from world literature, mythologies, and religions. As its title advertises, Joyce's *Ulysses* maps the lives of its modern characters onto Homer's *Odyssey*; Eliot's *The Waste Land* layers the Christian narrative of death and resurrection over a broad range of quest myths. The question for readers lies in the meaning of these borrowed structures and mythic parallels: do they reveal profound similarities or ironic contrasts between the modern world and earlier times? For some writers and readers, the adaptability of ancient stories to modern circumstances testified to their deep truth, underlying the surface buzz and confusion of modernity; for others, such parallels indicated Christianity to be only a myth, one of many human constructions aimed at creating order out of, and finding purpose in, history's flux.

If meaning is a human construction, then meaning cannot be separated from the difficult process of its making; if meaning lies obscured deep underneath the ruins of modern life, then it must be effortfully sought out. Modernist literature therefore tended to foreground the search for meaning over didactic statement, and the subject matter of modernist writing often became, by extension, the literary work itself. While there have long been paintings about painting and poems about poetry, high modernist writing was especially self-reflexive, concerned with its own nature as art and with its questioning of previous traditions of literature. Ironically—because this subject matter was motivated by deep concern about the interrelation of literature and life—this subject often had the effect of limiting the audience for a modernist work; high modernism demanded of its ideal readers an encyclopedic knowledge of the traditions it fragmented or ironized. Nevertheless, over time, the principles of modernism became increasingly influential.

Modernist techniques transformed fiction as well as poetry in this period. Prose writers strove for directness, compression, and vividness. They were often sparing of words. The average novel became quite a bit shorter than it had been in the nineteenth century, when a novel was expected to fill two or even three volumes. The modernist aesthetic gave a new significance to the short story, which had previously been thought of as a relatively slight artistic form. (Poems too became shorter, as narrative poems lost ground to lyrics and the repetitive patterns of rhyme and meter that had helped sustain long poems in previous centuries lost ground to free verse.) Victorian or realistic fiction achieved its effects by accumulation and saturation; modern fiction preferred suggestion. Victorian fiction often featured an authoritative narrator; modern fiction tended to be written in the first person or to limit the reader to one character's point of view on the action. This limitation accorded with the modernist sense that truth does not exist objectively but is the product of the mind's interaction with reality. The selected point of view is often that of a naive or marginal person—a child or an outsider—to convey better the reality of confusion and dissent rather than the myth of certainty and consensus. In both poetry and fiction, modernists tended to emphasize the concrete sensory image or detail over general statement. Allusions to literary, historical, philosophical, or religious details of the past often keep company, in modernist works, with vignettes of contemporary life, chunks of popular culture, dream imagery, and symbolism drawn from the author's private repertory of life experiences. A work built from these various materials may move across time and space, shift from the public to the personal, and open up literature as a field for every sort of concern. The inclusion of material previously deemed "unliterary" in works of high seriousness extended to language that might previously have been thought improper, including representations of the speech of the uneducated and the inarticulate, the colloquial, slangy, and the popular. Traditional realistic fiction had incorporated colloquial and dialect speech, often to comic effect, in its representation of the broad tapestry of social life; but such speakers were usually framed by a narrator's educated literary voice, conveying truth and authority over subordinate voices. In modernist writing like William Faulkner's *As I Lay Dying*, these voices assume the full burden of the narrative's authority; this is what Ernest Hemingway had in mind when he asserted that the American literary tradition began with *Huckleberry Finn*.

"Serious" literature between the two world wars thus found itself in a difficult relationship with the culture at large. If it attacked the old-style ideals of polite literature, it felt itself attacked in turn by the ever-growing industry of popular literature. The reading audience in America was vast, but it preferred kinds of books different from those turned out by literary high modernists; tales of romance or adventure, historical novels, crime fiction, and Westerns became popular modes, enjoying a success that most serious writers could only dream of. The problem was that often they did dream of it; unrealistically, perhaps, the Ezra Pounds and Nathanael Wests of the era imagined themselves having an audience of millions. When, on occasion, this dream came true—as it did for F. Scott Fitzgerald and Ernest Hemingway—writers often accused themselves, and were accused by others, of having sold out.

Serious writers in these years were, in fact, being published and read as writers had not been in earlier times. Modernist works were widely reviewed and referred to in magazines and newspapers of general circulation, where experimental writers like Gertrude Stein enjoyed a notoriety much in excess of their sales. Outside the mass periodical market, the number of so-called little magazines—that is, magazines of very small circulations devoted to the publication of works for a small audience (sometimes the works of a specific group of authors)—was in the hundreds. *Poetry: A Magazine of Verse* began in 1912. *The Little Review* followed in 1914. Then came the *Seven Arts* in 1916, the *Dial* in 1917, the *Frontier* in 1920, *Reviewer* and *Broom* in 1921, *Fugitive* in 1922, *This Quarter* in 1925, *Transition* and *Hound and Horn* in 1927, and many more. The culture that did not listen attentively to serious writers or make them rich still gave them plenty of opportunity to be read, and it allowed them (in such neighborhoods as Greenwich Village in New York City) a freedom in lifestyle that was new in American history. In addition, such major publishers as New Directions, Random House, Scribner, and Harper, and such stylish periodicals as *Vanity Fair*, were actively looking for serious fiction and poetry to feature alongside best sellers like *Gone with the Wind* (1936) and *Anthony Adverse* (1933). Some writers in the period were able to use these opportunities to cross over the hierarchies separating high modernism from middlebrow and popular culture.

Broom Magazine Cover, Enrico Prampolini, 1922. *Broom* was among the most internationally ambitious of modernism's little magazines, publishing authors such as Gertrude Stein, Wallace Stevens, and Jean Toomer alongside work by artists like Man Ray and Picasso. This cover complemented an essay by Harold Loeb, *Broom's* editor, that celebrated the modernist beauty of engines, motors, and airplanes.

Vanity Fair published Gertrude Stein, E. E. Cummings, Sherwood Anderson, and Edna St. Vincent Millay. By the 1930s, American literary modernism had its recognized celebrities in authors like Stein, Fitzgerald, and Hemingway, and a substantial supporting community of publishers, critics, and readers.

MODERNISM ABROAD AND ON NATIVE GROUNDS

The profession of authorship in the United States has always defined itself in part as a patriotic enterprise aimed at developing a cultural life for the nation and embodying national values. High modernism, however, was a self-consciously international movement, and the leading American exponents of high modernism tended to be permanent expatriates, such as Gertrude Stein, Ezra Pound, H.D., and T. S. Eliot. These writers left the United States because they found the country lacking in a tradition of high culture and indifferent, if not actively hostile, to artistic achievement. They also believed that a national culture could never be more than parochial. In London in the first two decades of the twentieth century and in Paris during the 1920s, they found a vibrant community of dedicated artists and a society that respected them and allowed them a great deal of personal freedom. Yet they seldom thought of themselves as deserting their nation, and only Eliot gave up American citizenship (sometimes, too, the traffic went in the other direction, as when the British-born poet Mina Loy became an American citizen). They thought of themselves as bringing the United States into the larger context of European culture. The ranks of these permanent expatriates were swelled by American writers who lived abroad for some part of the period, among them Ernest Hemingway, Sherwood Anderson, F. Scott Fitzgerald, Claude McKay, Katherine Anne Porter, Nella Larsen, Robert Frost, and Eugene O'Neill.

Those writers who came back, however, and those who never left took seriously the task of integrating modernist ideas and methods with American subject matter. Not every experimental modernist writer disconnected literary ambitions from national belonging: Hart Crane, Marianne Moore, and William Carlos Williams, for example, all wanted to write overtly "American" works. Some writers—as the title of John Dos Passos's *U.S.A.* clearly shows—attempted to speak for the nation as a whole. Crane's long poem *The Bridge* and Williams's *Paterson* both take an American city as symbol and expand it to the nation, following the model established by Walt Whitman. F. Scott Fitzgerald's *The Great Gatsby* is similarly ambitious, and many writers addressed the whole nation in individual works—for example, E. E. Cummings's "next to of course god america i" and Claude McKay's "America." And a profoundly modern writer like William Faulkner cannot be extricated from his commitment to writing about his native South.

Like Faulkner, many writers of the period chose to identify themselves with the American scene and to root their work in a specific region, continuing a tradition of regionalist American writing that burgeoned in the years following the American Civil War. Their perspectives on their various regions were sometimes celebratory and sometimes critical. Carl Sandburg, Edgar Lee Masters, Sherwood Anderson, and Willa Cather worked with the Midwest; Cather grounded her later work in the Southwest; John Steinbeck wrote about California; Edwin Arlington Robinson and Robert Frost identified their work with New England. An especially strong center of regional literary activity emerged in the South, which had a weak literary tradition up to the Civil War. Thomas Wolfe's was an Appalachian South of hardy mountain people. Katherine Anne Porter wrote about her native Texas as a heterogeneous combination of frontier, plantation, and Hispanic cultures. Zora Neale Hurston drew on her childhood memories of the all-black town of Eatonville, Florida, for much of her best-known fiction, including her novel *Their Eyes Were Watching God*. William Faulkner depicted a South at once grounded in his native state of Mississippi and also expanded into a mythic region anguished by racial and historical conflict.

As the pairing of Hurston and Faulkner suggests, the history of race in the United States was central to the specifically national subject matter to which many American modernists remained committed. Although race as a subject potentially implicated all American writers, it was African Americans whose contributions most signally differentiated American modernism from that of Europe. The numerous writers associated with the Harlem Renaissance made it impossible ever to think of a national literature without the work of black Americans. Countee Cullen, Langston Hughes, and Zora Neale Hurston attained particular prominence at the time; but others, including Claude McKay and Nella Larsen, were also well known. All were influenced by the values of modernism: both Hughes, for example, with his incorporation of blues rhythms into poetry, and Hurston, with her poetic depictions of folk culture, applied modernist techniques to represent twentieth-century African American lives. Writers associated with the Renaissance expressed protest and anger—Hughes, in particular, wrote a number of powerful antilynching and anticapitalist poems; but the movement's writers also articulated the hopes of racial uplift and, like Hurston, focused on the vitality of black culture more than on the burdens of racism. At least part of this approach was strategic—the bulk of the readership for Harlem authors was white. The note of pure anger was not expressed until Richard Wright, who had come to literary maturity in Chicago, published *Native Son* in 1940. Contributions to the Harlem Renaissance came from artists in many media; an influence equal to or greater than that of the writers came from musicians. Jazz and blues, African American in origin, are felt by many to be the most authentically American art forms the nation has ever produced. African American singers and musicians in this period achieved worldwide reputations and were often much more highly regarded abroad than in the United States.

American literary women had been active on the national scene from Anne Bradstreet forward. Their increasing prominence in the nineteenth century generated a backlash from some male modernists, who asserted their own artistic seriousness by identifying women writers with the didactic, popular writing against which they rebelled. But women refused to stay on the sidelines and associated themselves with all the important literary trends of the era: H.D. and Amy Lowell with imagism, Marianne Moore and Gertrude Stein with high modernism, Willa Cather with mythic regionalism, Zora Neale Hurston and Nella Larsen with the Harlem Renaissance, Katherine Anne Porter with psychological fiction, Edna St. Vincent

Millay with social and sexual liberation. Many of these writers concentrated on depictions of women characters or women's thoughts and experiences. Yet few labeled themselves feminists. The passage of the suffrage amendment in 1920 had taken some of the energy out of feminism that would not return until the 1960s. Some women writers found social causes like labor and racism more important than women's rights; others focused their energies on struggles less amenable to public, legal remedies, as when Mina Loy's "Feminist Manifesto" sought to represent motherhood as compatible with an energetic vision of female sexuality. Nevertheless, these literary women were clearly pushing back the boundaries of the permissible, demanding new cultural freedom for women and taking positions on public causes.

MODERN LITERATURE ON STAGE AND SCREEN

Drama in America was slow to develop as a self-conscious literary form. It was not until 1920 (the year of Eugene O'Neill's *Beyond the Horizon*) that the United States produced a world-class playwright. This is not to say that *theater*—productions and performances—was new to American life. After the American Revolution, theaters—at first with itinerant English actors and companies, then with American—opened throughout the East; among early centers were Boston and Philadelphia as well as New York City. As the country expanded westward, so did its theater, together with other kinds of performance: burlesques, showboats on the Mississippi, minstrel shows, pantomimes. As the nineteenth century went on, the activity became centered more and more in New York—especially within the few blocks known as Broadway. Managers originated plays there and then sent them out to tour through the rest of the country, as Eugene O'Neill's father did with his *Count of Monte Cristo*.

Innovations in American theater are often launched in reaction against Broadway, a pattern observable as early as 1915 with the formation of the Washington Square Players and the Provincetown Players (organized by Susan Glaspell and others), both located in New York's Greenwich Village and both dedicated to the production of plays that more conservative managers refused. The Provincetown Players produced the first works of Glaspell and Eugene O'Neill. These fledgling companies, and others like them, often knew better what they opposed than what they wanted. European influence was important to them. By 1915, Henrik Ibsen in Europe and George Bernard Shaw in England had shown that the theater could be an arena for serious ideas; meanwhile the psychological dramas of August Strindberg, the symbolic work of Maurice Maeterlinck, and the sophisticated criticism of Arthur Schnitzler provided other models. The American tours of European companies, in particular the Moscow Art Theatre in 1923, further exposed Americans to the theatrical avant-garde.

Just as his contemporaries in poetry and fiction were changing and questioning their forms, so Eugene O'Neill sought to refine his. He experimented less in language than in dramatic structure and in new production methods available through technology (e.g., lighting) or borrowed from the stylized realism of German expressionism. Playwrights such as Sidney Howard

Eugene O'Neill and the Provincetown Players, 1916. O'Neill (on ladder) and members of the company preparing the stage for *Bound East for Cardiff*, O'Neill's first play produced by the players, at the company's first New York City theater, on Macdougal Street in Greenwich Village.

(1891–1939), Lillian Hellman (1905–1984), and Robert Sherwood (1896–1955) wrote serious realistic plays. George Kaufman and his many collaborators, especially Moss Hart, invented a distinctively American form, the wisecracking domestic and social comedy, while S. N. Behrman and Philip Barry wrote higher comedies of ideas. The musical comedy was another distinctively American invention: beginning as a revue of jokes, songs, and dances, it progressed steadily toward an integration of its various elements, reaching new heights with the work of George and Ira Gershwin in the 1920s and 1930s and of Oscar Hammerstein, in collaboration with Jerome Kern or Richard Rodgers, from the 1920s on into the 1950s.

Social commentary and satire had been conspicuous in American drama since the early 1920s, beginning, perhaps, with Elmer Rice's fiercely expressionistic play about a rebellious nonentity, *The Adding Machine* (1923). During the Depression social criticism became a much more important dramatic theme, with political plays performed by many radical groups. Among the most significant was Clifford Odets's *Waiting for Lefty* (1935), which dramatized a taxi drivers' strike meeting and turned the stage into a platform for argument. The Federal Theatre Project of 1935–39, established by President Franklin Roosevelt's administration to provide employment to theater artists of all kinds during the Great Depression, produced plays by Odets, O'Neill, and other contemporary authors, alongside new productions of Shakespeare and Aristophanes. The Negro Theatre Unit, a major creative arm of the project, produced works by African American writers, like W. E. B. Du Bois's *Haiti* (1938), as well as innovative productions with black casts, most famously the all-black version of Shakespeare's *Macbeth* adapted by Orson Welles in 1936.

With the rise of the film industry, many popular playwrights and authors of fiction found new outlets for their work in Hollywood. Robert Sherwood became a screenwriter and had a number of his plays adapted into films; Sidney Howard won the Academy Award in 1940 for his adaptation of *Gone with the Wind*. Where writers like William Faulkner and F. Scott Fitzgerald experienced Hollywood as a graveyard of serious literary ambition, Katherine Anne Porter found in the film industry not only financial rewards but also a springboard to wider critical and popular appreciation for her work as a whole. The motion picture industry in turn provided American writers with important new subject matter: Hollywood-based novels of the period include Fitzgerald's *The Last Tycoon* (completed after his death and published in 1941), Nathanael West's *The Day of the Locust* (newly added to this volume), and Budd Schulberg's *What Makes Sammy Run?* (1941)—all of which were later turned into films. The adaptation of literary works from one medium to another accelerated in the first half of the twentieth century. Writers explored the commercial and artistic possibilities emerging in the new relationships among literature's printed page, the stage, and the screen in ways that look forward to the hyperreal, media-saturated generic experimentation that would characterize much American literature in the second half of the twentieth century.

TEXTS	CONTEXTS
1910 Edwin Arlington Robinson, **"Miniver Cheevy"**	
1914 Robert Frost, "Home Burial" • Carl Sandburg, "Chicago"	1914–18 World War I
1915 Edgar Lee Masters, *Spoon River Anthology* • Ezra Pound begins *Cantos*	1915 Great Migration of African Americans from the rural South to northern industrial cities
1916 Susan Glaspell, *Trifles* • Robert Frost, **"Birches"**	
	1917 United States declares war on Germany • revolution in Russia brings Communist Party to power
1918 Willa Cather, *My Ántonia* • Carl Sandburg, **"Grass"**	1918 Daylight Savings Time instituted to allow more daylight for war production
1919 Sherwood Anderson, **Winesburg, Ohio** • Amy Lowell, **"Madonna of the Evening Flowers"**	1919 Senate limits U.S. participation in League of Nations; does not ratify Versailles Treaty to end World War I
1920 Pound, "Hugh Selwyn Mauberley"	1920 18th Amendment prohibits the manufacture, sale, and transportation of alcoholic beverages • 19th Amendment gives women the vote
	1920–27 Sacco-Vanzetti trial
1921 T. S. Eliot, ***The Waste Land*** • Claude McKay, **"Africa," "America"** • Marianne Moore, **"Poetry"** • Langston Hughes, "The Negro Speaks of Rivers"	
	1922 Fascism rises in Europe; Mussolini becomes dictator of Italy
1923 Wallace Stevens, **"Sunday Morning"** • Jean Toomer, *Cane*	
1924 H.D. (Hilda Doolittle), **"Helen"**	1924 Exclusionary immigration act bars Asians from the United States
1925 Countee Cullen, **"Heritage"** • Gertrude Stein, ***The Making of Americans*** • Alain Locke publishes *The New Negro*, leading anthology of the Harlem Renaissance	
1926 Ernest Hemingway, *The Sun Also Rises* • Hart Crane, *The Bridge*	
1927 Zora Neale Hurston, "The Eatonville Anthology"	1927 *The Jazz Singer*, first full-length "talkie," is released
1929 Nella Larsen, *Passing*	1929 Stock market crashes; Great Depression begins

Boldface titles indicate works in the anthology.

TEXTS	CONTEXTS
1930 Katherine Anne Porter, "Flowering Judas"	1930 Sinclair Lewis is first American to win Nobel Prize for literature
1931 E. E. Cummings, "i sing of Olaf glad and big" • F. Scott Fitzgerald, "Babylon Revisited"	1931 Scottsboro trial
1932 Sterling Brown, "He Was a Man"	1932 Franklin Delano Roosevelt's New Deal introduces Social Security, welfare, and unemployment insurance
1933 Gertrude Stein, *The Autobiography of Alice B. Toklas*	1933 Adolf Hitler's Nationalist Socialist (Nazi) Party comes to power in Germany • 18th Amendment repealed
1934 William Carlos Williams, "This Is Just to Say"	1934 Wheeler-Howard (Indian Reorganization) Act passed, ending Dawes era
1936 Ernest Hemingway, "The Snows of Kilimanjaro"	1936 Hitler begins armed occupation of Europe
	1936–39 Spanish Civil War: U.S. volunteers among those fighting against General Franco, who becomes dictator of Spain
1937 Thomas Wolfe, "The Lost Boy"	1937 Stalin's purges
1938 John Dos Passos, *U.S.A.* • William Faulkner, "Barn Burning"	
1939 Richard Wright, "The Man Who Was Almost a Man" • Nathanael West, *The Day of the Locust*	1939–45 World War II • the Holocaust
1940 Eugene O'Neill, *Long Day's Journey into Night*	
	1941 Japan bombs Pearl Harbor, Hawaii • United States enters war against Japan and its allies, Germany and Italy
1942 Wallace Stevens, "Of Modern Poetry"	1942 President Roosevelt orders internment of Japanese Americans in camps
1943 Langston Hughes, "Madam and Her Madam"	
1944 H.D. (Hilda Doolittle), *The Walls Do Not Fall* • Marianne Moore, "In Distrust of Merits"	1944 D Day; Allied invasion of Normandy
	1945 German forces surrender in spring; Japan surrenders in August following explosion of two nuclear bombs over Japanese cities

EDWIN ARLINGTON ROBINSON
1869–1935

Surveying Edwin Arlington Robinson's poetry after his death, Robert Frost observed that Robinson "could make lyric talk like drama." Like Frost, Robinson made his name as a New England regional poet. Along with Edgar Lee Masters and Sherwood Anderson, Robinson focused his most compelling work on wasted or impoverished lives played out in a small-town setting. His brief narrative and portrait poems, composed in traditionally rhymed and metered forms, often represent these blighted lives from the communal viewpoint of a tragic chorus, as in "Richard Cory" and "Eros Turannos"—a collective *we* bearing ironic witness to forms of suffering it cannot fully comprehend.

Robinson was raised in Gardiner, Maine, which became "Tilbury Town" in his poems. His father's lumber business and land speculations failed during the Great Panic of 1893. One of his brothers, a physician, became a drug addict; the other, a businessman, became an alcoholic. Robinson, by nature a scholar and book lover, was able to afford just two years at Harvard, where he continued an ambitious program of largely self-directed reading that included classical works in many languages as well as such American writers as Hawthorne, Whitman, Emerson, and Henry James. He was also drawn to the bleak vision of the British novelist Thomas Hardy. These influences were distilled in the gloomy, austere, yet sonorous verse of his second book, *The Children of the Night* (1897)—*The Torrent and the Night Before* had been published the previous year, at his own expense.

Robinson moved from Gardiner to New York City shortly after *The Children of the Night* appeared. The volume came to the attention of no less a patron than President Theodore Roosevelt, whose son Kermit urged him to find a way of relieving Robinson's financial anxieties. Like Nathaniel Hawthorne and Herman Melville before him, Robinson in 1905 reluctantly accepted a political appointment in the U.S. Customs Service, which he resigned with Roosevelt's departure from office in 1909. *The Town Down River* (1910) and *The Man against the Sky* (1916) brought Robinson increasing numbers of readers and critical notice. His *Collected Poems* (1921) won the first of his three Pulitzer Prizes.

By this time Robinson was over fifty and feeling increasingly distanced from the free verse of his modernist contemporaries. His own efforts turned in the direction of narrative poems, including a trilogy of long poems in imitation of medieval narratives that began with *Merlin* (1917) and ended with *Tristram* (1927), another Pulitzer Prize winner. These works found popular audiences, but many critics and fellow poets were less enthusiastic to see Robinson embrace without irony the romantic nostalgia he had satirized in "Miniver Cheevy." The prizes and honors of Robinson's final decades represented, to a large extent, belated recognition of his earlier poetry. Reviewing his *Collected Poems* in 1922, the poet and critic Yvor Winters praised Robinson for inheriting and extending the twisted, hard, epigrammatic New England tradition of Emerson and Emily Dickinson: to that tradition, Winters wrote, Robinson contributed his own "polished stoniness of mind."

The text of the poems included here is that of *Collected Poems of Edwin Arlington Robinson* (1921, 1937).

Richard Cory

Whenever Richard Cory went down town,
We people on the pavement looked at him:
He was a gentleman from sole to crown,
Clean favored, and imperially slim.

And he was always quietly arrayed,   5
And he was always human when he talked;
But still he fluttered pulses when he said,
"Good-morning," and he glittered when he walked.

And he was rich—yes, richer than a king,—
And admirably schooled in every grace: 10
In fine, we thought that he was everything
To make us wish that we were in his place.

So on we worked, and waited for the light,
And went without the meat, and cursed the bread;
And Richard Cory, one calm summer night,   15
Went home and put a bullet through his head.

1896

Miniver Cheevy

Miniver Cheevy, child of scorn,
    Grew lean while he assailed the seasons;
He wept that he was ever born,
    And he had reasons.

Miniver loved the days of old   5
    When swords were bright and steeds were prancing;
The vision of a warrior bold
    Would set him dancing.

Miniver sighed for what was not,
    And dreamed, and rested from his labors;   10
He dreamed of Thebes and Camelot,[1]
    And Priam's neighbors.[2]

Miniver mourned the ripe renown
    That made so many a name so fragrant;
He mourned Romance, now on the town,   15
    And Art, a vagrant.

1. Thebes was an ancient city in Boeotia, rival
of Athens and Sparta for supremacy in Greece
and the setting of Sophocles's tragedies about
Oedipus. Camelot is the legendary court of King
Arthur and the knights of the Round Table.
2. The neighbors of King Priam in Homer's *Iliad*
are his heroic compatriots in the doomed city
of Troy.

Miniver loved the Medici,[3]
  Albeit he had never seen one;
He would have sinned incessantly
  Could he have been one.   20

Miniver cursed the commonplace
  And eyed a khaki suit with loathing;
He missed the mediæval grace
  Of iron clothing.

Miniver scorned the gold he sought,   25
  But sore annoyed was he without it;
Miniver thought, and thought, and thought,
  And thought about it.

Miniver Cheevy, born too late,
  Scratched his head and kept on thinking;   30
Miniver coughed, and called it fate,
  And kept on drinking.

                          1910

Eros Turannos[1]

She fears him, and will always ask
  What fated her to choose him;
She meets in his engaging mask
  All reasons to refuse him;
But what she meets and what she fears   5
Are less than are the downward years,
Drawn slowly to the foamless weirs
  Of age, were she to lose him.

Between a blurred sagacity
  That once had power to sound him,   10
And Love, that will not let him be
  The Judas[2] that she found him,
Her pride assuages her almost,
As if it were alone the cost.—
He sees that he will not be lost,   15
  And waits and looks around him.

A sense of ocean and old trees
  Envelops and allures him;
Tradition, touching all he sees,
  Beguiles and reassures him;   20

3. Family of wealthy merchants, politicians, churchmen, and art patrons in 16th-century Florence.

1. Love, the tyrant (Latin).
2. One of the twelve apostles in the New Testament; he betrayed Jesus Christ.

And all her doubts of what he says
Are dimmed with what she knows of days—
Till even prejudice delays
   And fades, and she secures him.

The falling leaf inaugurates   25
   The reign of her confusion;
The pounding wave reverberates
   The dirge of her illusion;
And home, where passion lived and died,
Becomes a place where she can hide,   30
While all the town and harbor side
   Vibrate with her seclusion.

We tell you, tapping on our brows,
   The story as it should be,—
As if the story of a house   35
   Were told, or ever could be;
We'll have no kindly veil between
Her visions and those we have seen,—
As if we guessed what hers have been,
   Or what they are or would be.   40

Meanwhile we do no harm; for they
   That with a god have striven,
Not hearing much of what we say,
   Take what the god has given;
Though like waves breaking it may be   45
Or like a changed familiar tree,
Or like a stairway to the sea
   Where down the blind are driven.

                                1914, 1921

WILLA CATHER
1873–1947

Willa Cather was born in Virginia, the oldest child of Charles and Mary Virginia Cather, who moved with their family to the Nebraska Divide when she was nine years old. After a year of farming, they relocated to the town of Red Cloud, and her father went into the real estate business. At sixteen, Cather moved on her own to Lincoln, the state capital and seat of the University of Nebraska; she attended preparatory school for one year and graduated from the university in 1895. In college she studied the classics and participated in the lively contemporary cultural life of the city by reviewing books, plays, and musical performances. Following graduation, she eked out a year as a journalist in Red Cloud and Lincoln before moving to Pittsburgh, Pennsylvania, to work as an editor of a women's magazine, the *Home Monthly,* a position she left five years later to teach high-school English and Latin. During this time she also wrote poems and stories, gathering poems into *April Twilights,* in 1903, and stories (including the early version of "The Sculptor's Funeral") into *The Troll Garden,* in 1905. Also in Pittsburgh, in 1899, she met Isabelle McClung, from a prominent, wealthy family. She lived in the McClung home from 1901 to 1906, when she moved to New York City to write for the journal *McClure's.* Throughout her life, Cather remained devoted to McClung, experiencing her marriage in 1916 as a severe personal loss and being devastated by her death in 1938.

Having long wished to write novels, Cather took a leave of absence from *McClure's* in 1911, and wrote *Alexander's Bridge* (1912). This novel was successful, but it was the next three that made her reputation. Each focused on a western heroine: Alexandra Bergson in *O Pioneers!* (1913), Thea Kronborg in *The Song of the Lark* (1915), and Ántonia Shimerda in *My Ántonia* (1918). While Alexandra is extraordinary as the most successful farmer—the only woman farmer—on the Nebraska Divide, and Thea is extraordinary as a gifted opera singer, Ántonia has no unusual gifts; for Cather and the novel's many readers she stands for the entire experience of European settlement of the Great Plains. These three novels also manifest Cather's lyrical yet understated prose writing; they contain a wealth of detail about the lives of Nebraska settlers—Bohemian Czech, German, Danish, Swedish, Norwegian, French, Russian, and "Americans" from the East—as they learned to farm on the prairie and built communities in which their various ethnicities met and mingled. Cather's is no melting pot ethos, however; rather she sees the frontier as a shifting kaleidoscope of overlapping social groups and individuals. Recognizing that even by the second decade of the twentieth century this period in U.S. history had disappeared, Cather approached her characters with deep respect for what they had endured and accomplished.

Whether these novels (or any of Cather's other work) reflect a lesbian sensibility has been a matter of much critical debate. Her *Selected Letters* (2013), long withheld from publication, confirm that Cather's central emotional involvements in her life were with women; in 1908 she began to share an apartment with Edith Lewis, a Nebraskan whom she had met in 1903, and they lived together until Cather's death. (They lived mostly in New York City, but Cather also traveled a great deal: to Europe, to New England, to the Southwest, and back to Red Cloud to visit her family.) Estrangement from conventional sexuality and sex roles is typical of many of her main characters, male and female; but heterosexual romance and sexual behavior is equally present in her novels. It seems fair to say that close friendship, much more than romantic or sexual love, is the great ideal in her fiction.

Around 1922, according to Cather, the world broke in two; she suffered from the combined effects of poor health, dissatisfaction with the progress of her career, and alarm at the increasing mechanization and mass-produced quality of American life. She joined the Episcopal Church, and her novels took a new direction. Although her books had always celebrated alternative values to the material and conventional, this theme became much more urgent, while the motif of heroic womanhood—which had led many to call her a feminist, though Cather herself kept aloof from all movements—receded. Important books from her "middle period" include *A Lost Lady* (1923) and *The Professor's House* (1925), which deal with spiritual and cultural crises in the lives of the main characters.

Published in 1927, the novel *Death Comes for the Archbishop* initiated another stage. Like many other writers and artists in the 1920s, Cather had become entranced with the American Southwest—especially New Mexico; her first trip to the region in 1912 figured in her depiction (in *The Song of the Lark*) of Thea Kron-

Illustration for *My Ántonia*, W. T. Benda. For the first edition of *My Ántonia*, Cather commissioned a set of drawings by Wladyslaw T. Benda, a Polish immigrant who was part of the New York City art scene. Known to Cather through his work for *McClure's*, Benda simplified his often dramatic visual style to match Cather's spare narration.

borg finding spiritual renewal in this landscape. *Death Comes for the Archbishop,* partly written at Mary Austin's home in Santa Fe, is based on the career of Jean Baptiste Lamy (1814–1888), archbishop of New Mexico, and the priest Joseph Marchebeuf, his close friend and collaborator. Another historical novel, *Shadows on the Rock* (1931) is set even further back in time, in seventeenth-century Quebec. In both books, a composite image of high French culture, ceremonial spirituality, and the American landscape contrasts with the material trivia and empty banality of contemporary life.

Inspired by the classical Latin works that she loved so much, Cather believed in the ideas of art and the artist and strove to attain an artistic height from which she might survey the entire human scene. She tried to imbue the particularities of her stories with what she thought of as universal significance. In *My Ántonia,* which continues to be the favorite novel for most Cather readers, Jim Burden reflects on the aspirations of the poet Virgil to bring the muse to his own country for the first time; by country, Virgil means "not a nation or even a province, but the little rural neighborhood" where he was born. This is clearly what is intended in *My Ántonia;* the idea of combining artistic transcendence with local, especially rural, specificity, speaks to Cather's own goals. It is a measure of her ambition that she thinks of her work in Virgilian terms, since Virgil was the greatest of the Latin poets. This aim was also Cather's in stories of Nebraska such as "Neighbour Rosicky." But a story like "The Sculptor's Funeral" shows her awareness that the neighborhood may not appreciate the artists who put it on the cultural map.

Politically, culturally, and aesthetically, Cather was in many respects deeply conservative as well as conflicted—a sophisticated populist, an agrarian urbanite. She believed in high art and superior people, but also thought great human gifts were more often found among the obscure and ordinary than among those with great advantages. Her vision of the United States seldom focused on Native Americans and African Americans; yet she preferred immigrants from Europe to migrants from the East Coast. She appreciated popular legends and folktales, which appear along with classical myth and allusion in her work. Her subtle experiments with formal structure include the retrospective narrative of *My Ántonia,* the imbedded Southwestern story of Tom Outland in *The Professor's House,* and the seemingly unplotted, episodic chronicle form of *Death Comes for the Archbishop.* She once described her work as deliberately "unfurnished," meaning that it was cut down to only those details absolutely necessary; "suggestion rather than enumeration" was another way she described her goal (see "The Novel Démeublé," p. 812). The resulting spareness and clarity of her fiction puts it in the modernist tradition.

The text of "The Sculptor's Funeral" is that published in *Youth and the Bright Medusa* (1920); that of "Neighbour Rosicky" is from *Obscure Destinies* (1932).

Neighbour Rosicky

I

When Doctor Burleigh told neighbour Rosicky he had a bad heart, Rosicky protested.

"So? No, I guess my heart was always pretty good. I got a little asthma, maybe. Just a awful short breath when I was pitchin' hay last summer, dat's all."

"Well, now, Rosicky, if you know more about it than I do, what did you come to me for? It's your heart that makes you short of breath, I tell you. You're sixty-five years old, and you've always worked hard, and your heart's tired. You've got to be careful from now on, and you can't do heavy work any more. You've got five boys at home to do it for you."

The old farmer looked up at the Doctor with a gleam of amusement in his queer triangular-shaped eyes. His eyes were large and lively, but the lids were caught up in the middle in a curious way, so that they formed a triangle. He did not look like a sick man. His brown face was creased but not wrinkled, he had a ruddy colour in his smooth-shaven cheeks and in his lips, under his long brown moustache. His hair was thin and ragged around his ears, but very little grey. His forehead, naturally high and crossed by deep parallel lines, now ran all the way up to his pointed crown. Rosicky's face had the habit of looking interested,—suggested a contented disposition and a reflective quality that was gay rather than grave. This gave him a certain detachment, the easy manner of an onlooker and observer.

"Well, I guess you ain't got no pills fur a bad heart, Doctor Ed. I guess the only thing is fur me to git me a new one."

Doctor Burleigh swung round in his desk-chair and frowned at the old farmer.

"I think if I were you I'd take a little care of the old one, Rosicky."

Rosicky shrugged. "Maybe I don't know how. I expect you mean fur me not to drink my coffee no more."

"I wouldn't, in your place. But you'll do as you choose about that. I've never yet been able to separate a Bohemian[1] from his coffee or his pipe. I've quit trying. But the sure thing is you've got to cut out farm work. You can feed the stock and do chores about the barn, but you can't do anything in the fields that makes you short of breath."

"How about shelling corn?"

"Of course not!"

Rosicky considered with puckered brows.

"I can't make my heart go no longer'n it wants to, can I, Doctor Ed?"

"I think it's good for five or six years yet, maybe more, if you'll take the strain off it. Sit around the house and help Mary. If I had a good wife like yours, I'd want to stay around the house."

His patient chuckled. "It ain't no place fur a man. I don't like no old man hanging round the kitchen too much. An' my wife, she's a awful hard worker her own self."

---

1. Native of Bohemia, in the Czech Republic.

"That's it; you can help her a little. My Lord, Rosicky, you are one of the few men I know who has a family he can get some comfort out of; happy dispositions, never quarrel among themselves, and they treat you right. I want to see you live a few years and enjoy them."

"Oh, they're good kids, all right," Rosicky assented.

The Doctor wrote him a prescription and asked him how his oldest son, Rudolph, who had married in the spring, was getting on. Rudolph had struck out for himself, on rented land. "And how's Polly? I was afraid Mary mightn't like an American daughter-in-law, but it seems to be working out all right."

"Yes, she's a fine girl. Dat widder woman bring her daughters up very nice. Polly got lots of spunk, an' she got some style, too. Da's nice, for young folks to have some style." Rosicky inclined his head gallantly. His voice and his twinkly smile were an affectionate compliment to his daughter-in-law.

"It looks like a storm, and you'd better be getting home before it comes. In town in the car?" Doctor Burleigh rose.

"No, I'm in de wagon. When you got five boys, you ain't got much chance to ride round in de Ford. I ain't much for cars, noway."

"Well, it's a good road out to your place; but I don't want you bumping around in a wagon much. And never again on a hay-rake, remember!"

Rosicky placed the Doctor's fee delicately behind the desk-telephone, looking the other way, as if this were an absent-minded gesture. He put on his plush cap and his corduroy jacket with a sheepskin collar, and went out.

The Doctor picked up his stethoscope and frowned at it as if he were seriously annoyed with the instrument. He wished it had been telling tales about some other man's heart, some old man who didn't look the Doctor in the eye so knowingly, or hold out such a warm brown hand when he said good-bye. Doctor Burleigh had been a poor boy in the country before he went away to medical school; he had known Rosicky almost ever since he could remember, and he had a deep affection for Mrs. Rosicky.

Only last winter he had had such a good breakfast at Rosicky's, and that when he needed it. He had been out all night on a long, hard confinement case at Tom Marshall's—a big rich farm where there was plenty of stock and plenty of feed and a great deal of expensive farm machinery of the newest model, and no comfort whatever. The woman had too many children and too much work, and she was no manager. When the baby was born at last, and handed over to the assisting neighbour woman, and the mother was properly attended to, Burleigh refused any breakfast in that slovenly house, and drove his buggy—the snow was too deep for a car—eight miles to Anton Rosicky's place. He didn't know another farm-house where a man could get such a warm welcome, and such good strong coffee with rich cream. No wonder the old chap didn't want to give up his coffee!

He had driven in just when the boys had come back from the barn and were washing up for breakfast. The long table, covered with a bright oil-cloth, was set out with dishes waiting for them, and the warm kitchen was full of the smell of coffee and hot biscuit and sausage. Five big handsome boys, running from twenty to twelve, all with what Burleigh called natural good manners—they hadn't a bit of the painful self-consciousness he himself had to struggle with when he was a lad. One ran to put his horse away, another helped him off with his fur coat and hung it up, and Josephine, the youngest child and the only daughter, quickly set another place under her mother's direction.

With Mary, to feed creatures was the natural expression of affection—her chickens, the calves, her big hungry boys. It was a rare pleasure to feed a young man whom she seldom saw and of whom she was as proud as if he belonged to her. Some country housekeepers would have stopped to spread a white cloth over the oilcloth, to change the thick cups and plates for their best china, and the wooden-handled knives for plated ones. But not Mary.

"You must take us as you find us, Doctor Ed. I'd be glad to put out my good things for you if you was expected, but I'm glad to get you any way at all."

He knew she was glad—she threw back her head and spoke out as if she were announcing him to the whole prairie. Rosicky hadn't said anything at all; he merely smiled his twinkling smile, put some more coal on the fire, and went into his own room to pour the Doctor a little drink in a medicine glass. When they were all seated, he watched his wife's face from his end of the table and spoke to her in Czech. Then, with the instinct of politeness which seldom failed him, he turned to the doctor and said slyly: "I was just tellin' her not to ask you no questions about Mrs. Marshall till you eat some breakfast. My wife, she's terrible fur to ask questions."

The boys laughed, and so did Mary. She watched the Doctor devour her biscuit and sausage, too much excited to eat anything herself. She drank her coffee and sat taking in everything about her visitor. She had known him when he was a poor country boy, and was boastfully proud of his success, always saying: "What do people go to Omaha for, to see a doctor, when we got the best one in the State right here?" If Mary liked people at all, she felt physical pleasure in the sight of them, personal exultation in any good fortune that came to them. Burleigh didn't know many women like that, but he knew she was like that.

When his hunger was satisfied, he did, of course, have to tell them about Mrs. Marshall, and he noticed what a friendly interest the boys took in the matter.

Rudolph, the oldest one (he was still living at home then), said: "The last time I was over there, she was lifting them big heavy milk-cans, and I knew she oughtn't to be doing it."

"Yes, Rudolph told me about that when he come home, and I said it wasn't right," Mary put in warmly. "It was all right for me to do them things up to the last, for I was terrible strong, but that woman's weakly. And do you think she'll be able to nurse it, Ed?" She sometimes forgot to give him the title she was so proud of. "And to think of your being up all night and then not able to get a decent breakfast! I don't know what's the matter with such people."

"Why, Mother," said one of the boys, "if Doctor Ed had got breakfast there, we wouldn't have him here. So you ought to be glad."

"He knows I'm glad to have him, John, any time. But I'm sorry for that poor woman, how bad she'll feel the Doctor had to go away in the cold without his breakfast."

"I wish I had been in practice when these were getting born." The Doctor looked down the row of close-clipped heads. "I missed some good breakfasts by not being."

The boys began to laugh at their mother because she flushed so red, but she stood her ground and threw up her head. "I don't care, you wouldn't have got away from this house without breakfast. No doctor ever did. I'd have had something ready fixed that Anton could warm up for you."

The boys laughed harder than ever, and exclaimed at her: "I'll bet you would!" "She would, that!"

"Father, did you get breakfast for the Doctor when we were born?"

"Yes, and he used to bring me my breakfast, too, mighty nice. I was always awful hungry!" Mary admitted with a guilty laugh.

While the boys were getting the Doctor's horse, he went to the window to examine the house plants. "What do you do to your geraniums to keep them blooming all winter, Mary? I never pass this house that from the road I don't see your windows full of flowers."

She snapped off a dark red one, and a ruffled new green leaf, and put them in his buttonhole. "There, that looks better. You look too solemn for a young man, Ed. Why don't you git married? I'm worried about you. Settin' at breakfast, I looked at you real hard, and I seen you've got some grey hairs already."

"Oh, yes! They're coming. Maybe they'd come faster if I married."

"Don't talk so. You'll ruin your health eating at the hotel. I could send your wife a nice loaf of nut bread, if you only had one. I don't like to see a young man getting grey. I'll tell you something, Ed; you make some strong black tea and keep it handy in a bowl, and every morning just brush it into your hair, an' it'll keep the grey from showin' much. That's the way I do!"

Sometimes the Doctor heard the gossipers in the drug-store wondering why Rosicky didn't get on faster. He was industrious, and so were his boys, but they were rather free and easy, weren't pushers, and they didn't always show good judgment. They were comfortable, they were out of debt, but they didn't get much ahead. Maybe, Doctor Burleigh reflected, people as generous and warm-hearted and affectionate as the Rosickys never got ahead much; maybe you couldn't enjoy your life and put it into the bank, too.

II

When Rosicky left Doctor Burleigh's office, he went into the farm-implement store to light his pipe and put on his glasses and read over the list Mary had given him. Then he went into the general merchandise place next door and stood about until the pretty girl with the plucked eyebrows, who always waited on him, was free. Those eyebrows, two thin India-ink strokes, amused him, because he remembered how they used to be. Rosicky always prolonged his shopping by a little joking; the girl knew the old fellow admired her, and she liked to chaff with him.

"Seems to me about every other week you buy ticking, Mr. Rosicky, and always the best quality," she remarked as she measured off the heavy bolt with red stripes.

"You see, my wife is always makin' goose-fedder pillows, an' de thin stuff don't hold in dem little down-fedders."

"You must have lots of pillows at your home."

"Sure. She makes quilts of dem, too. We sleeps easy. Now she's makin' a fedder quilt for my son's wife. You know Polly, that married my Rudolph. How much my bill, Miss Pearl?"

"Eight eighty-five."

"Chust make it nine, and put in some candy fur de women."

"As usual. I never did see a man buy so much candy for his wife. First thing you know, she'll be getting too fat."

"I'd like that. I ain't much fur all dem slim women like what de style is now."

"That's one for me, I suppose, Mr. Bohunk!"[2] Pearl sniffed and elevated her India-ink strokes.

When Rosicky went out to his wagon, it was beginning to snow,—the first snow of the season, and he was glad to see it. He rattled out of town and along the highway through a wonderfully rich stretch of country, the finest farms in the county. He admired this High Prairie, as it was called, and always liked to drive through it. His own place lay in a rougher territory, where there was some clay in the soil and it was not so productive. When he bought his land, he hadn't the money to buy on High Prairie; so he told his boys, when they grumbled, that if their land hadn't some clay in it, they wouldn't own it at all. All the same, he enjoyed looking at these fine farms, as he enjoyed looking at a prize bull.

After he had gone eight miles, he came to the graveyard, which lay just at the edge of his own hay-land. There he stopped his horses and sat still on his wagon seat, looking about at the snowfall. Over yonder on the hill he could see his own house, crouching low, with the clump of orchard behind and the windmill before, and all down the gentle hill-slope the rows of pale gold cornstalks stood out against the white field. The snow was falling over the cornfield and the pasture and the hay-land, steadily, with very little wind—a nice dry snow. The graveyard had only a light wire fence about it and was all overgrown with long red grass. The fine snow, settling into this red grass and upon the few little evergreens and the head-stones, looked very pretty.

It was a nice graveyard, Rosicky reflected, sort of snug and homelike, not cramped or mournful,—a big sweep all round it. A man could lie down in the long grass and see the complete arch of the sky over him, hear the wagons go by; in summer the mowing-machine rattled right up to the wire fence. And it was so near home. Over there across the cornstalks his own roof and wind-mill looked so good to him that he promised himself to mind the Doctor and take care of himself. He was awful fond of his place, he admitted. He wasn't anxious to leave it. And it was a comfort to think that he would never have to go farther than the edge of his own hayfield. The snow, falling over his barn-yard and the graveyard, seemed to draw things together like. And they were all old neighbours in the graveyard, most of them friends; there was nothing to feel awkward or embarrassed about. Embarrassment was the most dis-agreeable feeling Rosicky knew. He didn't often have it,—only with certain people whom he didn't understand at all.

Well, it was a nice snowstorm; a fine sight to see the snow falling so qui-etly and graciously over so much open country. On his cap and shoulders,

2. Bohemian (slang); here used affectionately.

on the horses' backs and manes, light, delicate, mysterious it fell; and with it a dry cool fragrance was released into the air. It meant rest for vegetation and men and beasts, for the ground itself; a season of long nights for sleep, leisurely breakfasts, peace by the fire. This and much more went through Rosicky's mind, but he merely told himself that winter was coming, clucked to his horses, and drove on.

When he reached home, John, the youngest boy, ran out to put away his team for him, and he met Mary coming up from the outside cellar with her apron full of carrots. They went into the house together. On the table, covered with oilcloth figured with clusters of blue grapes, a place was set, and he smelled hot coffee-cake of some kind. Anton never lunched in town; he thought that extravagant, and anyhow he didn't like the food. So Mary always had something ready for him when he got home.

After he was settled in his chair, stirring his coffee in a big cup, Mary took out of the oven a pan of *kolache*[3] stuffed with apricots, examined them anxiously to see whether they had got too dry, put them beside his plate, and then sat down opposite him.

Rosicky asked her in Czech if she wasn't going to have any coffee.

She replied in English, as being somehow the right language for transacting business: "Now what did Doctor Ed say, Anton? You tell me just what."

"He said I was to tell you some compliments, but I forgot 'em." Rosicky's eyes twinkled.

"About you, I mean. What did he say about your asthma?"

"He says I ain't got no asthma." Rosicky took one of the little rolls in his broad brown fingers. The thickened nail of his right thumb told the story of his past.

"Well, what is the matter? And don't try to put me off."

"He don't say nothing much, only I'm a little older, and my heart ain't so good like it used to be."

Mary started and brushed her hair back from her temples with both hands as if she were a little out of her mind. From the way she glared, she might have been in a rage with him.

"He says there's something the matter with your heart? Doctor Ed says so?"

"Now don't yell at me like I was a hog in de garden, Mary. You know I always did like to hear a woman talk soft. He didn't say anything de matter wid my heart, only it ain't so young like it used to be, an' he tell me not to pitch hay or run de corn-sheller."

Mary wanted to jump up, but she sat still. She admired the way he never under any circumstances raised his voice or spoke roughly. He was city-bred, and she was country-bred; she often said she wanted her boys to have their papa's nice ways.

"You never have no pain there, do you? It's your breathing and your stomach that's been wrong. I wouldn't believe nobody but Doctor Ed about it. I guess I'll go see him myself. Didn't he give you no advice?"

"Chust to take it easy like, an' stay round de house dis winter. I guess you got some carpenter work for me to do. I kin make some new shelves for you, and I want dis long time to build a closet in de boys' room and make dem two little fellers keep dere clo'es hung up."

3. Or kolacky, a sweet bun with fruit filling.

Rosicky drank his coffee from time to time, while he considered. His moustache was of the soft long variety and came down over his mouth like the teeth of a buggy-rake over a bundle of hay. Each time he put down his cup, he ran his blue handkerchief over his lips. When he took a drink of water, he managed very neatly with the back of his hand.

Mary sat watching him intently, trying to find any change in his face. It is hard to see anyone who has become like your own body to you. Yes, his hair had got thin, and his high forehead had deep lines running from left to right. But his neck, always clean-shaved except in the busiest seasons, was not loose or baggy. It was burned a dark reddish brown, and there were deep creases in it, but it looked firm and full of blood. His cheeks had a good colour. On either side of his mouth there was a half-moon down the length of his cheek, not wrinkles, but two lines that had come there from his habitual expression. He was shorter and broader than when she married him; his back had grown broad and curved, a good deal like the shell on an old turtle, and his arms and legs were short.

He was fifteen years older than Mary, but she had hardly ever thought about it before. He was her man, and the kind of man she liked. She was rough, and he was gentle—city-bred, as she always said. They had been ship-mates on a rough voyage and had stood by each other in trying times. Life had gone well with them because, at bottom, they had the same ideas about life. They agreed, without discussion, as to what was most important and what was secondary. They didn't often exchange opinions, even in Czech—it was as if they had thought the same thought together. A good deal had to be sacrificed and thrown overboard in a hard life like theirs, and they had never disagreed as to the things that could go. It had been a hard life, and a soft life, too. There wasn't anything brutal in the short, broad-backed man with the three-cornered eyes and the forehead that went on to the top of his skull. He was a city man, a gentle man, and though he had married a rough farm girl, he had never touched her without gentleness.

They had been at one accord not to hurry through life, not to be always skimping and saving. They saw their neighbours buy more land and feed more stock than they did, without discontent. Once when the creamery agent came to the Rosickys to persuade them to sell him their cream, he told them how much money the Fasslers, their nearest neighbours, had made on their cream last year.

"Yes," said Mary, "and look at them Fassler children! Pale, pinched little things, they look like skimmed milk. I had rather put some colour into my children's faces than put money into the bank."

The agent shrugged and turned to Anton.
"I guess we'll do like she says," said Rosicky.

III

Mary very soon got into town to see Doctor Ed, and then she had a talk with her boys and set a guard over Rosicky. Even John, the youngest, had his father on his mind. If Rosicky went to throw hay down from the loft, one of the boys ran up the ladder and took the fork from him. He sometimes complained that though he was getting to be an old man, he wasn't an old woman yet.

That winter he stayed in the house in the afternoons and carpentered, or sat in the chair between the window full of plants and the wooden bench where the two pails of drinking-water stood. This spot was called "Father's corner," though it was not a corner at all. He had a shelf there, where he kept his Bohemian papers and his pipes and tobacco, and his shears and needles and thread and tailor's thimble. Having been a tailor in his youth, he couldn't bear to see a woman patching at his clothes, or at the boys'. He liked tailoring, and always patched all the overalls and jackets and work shirts. Occasionally he made over a pair of pants one of the older boys had outgrown, for the little fellow.

While he sewed, he let his mind run back over his life. He had a good deal to remember, really; life in three countries. The only part of his youth he didn't like to remember was the two years he had spent in London, in Cheapside, working for a German tailor who was wretchedly poor. Those days, when he was nearly always hungry, when his clothes were dropping off him for dirt, and the sound of a strange language kept him in continual bewilderment, had left a sore spot in his mind that wouldn't bear touching.

He was twenty when he landed at Castle Garden in New York, and he had a protector who got him work in a tailor shop in Vesey Street, down near the Washington Market. He looked upon that part of his life as very happy. He became a good workman, he was industrious, and his wages were increased from time to time. He minded his own business and envied nobody's good fortune. He went to night school and learned to read English. He often did overtime work and was well paid for it, but somehow he never saved anything. He couldn't refuse a loan to a friend, and he was self-indulgent. He liked a good dinner, and a little went for beer, a little for tobacco; a good deal went to the girls. He often stood through an opera on Saturday nights; he could get standing-room for a dollar. Those were the great days of opera in New York, and it gave a fellow something to think about for the rest of the week. Rosicky had a quick ear, and a childish love of all the stage splendour; the scenery, the costumes, the ballet. He usually went with a chum, and after the performance they had beer and maybe some oysters somewhere. It was a fine life; for the first five years or so it satisfied him completely. He was never hungry or cold or dirty, and everything amused him: a fire, a dog fight, a parade, a storm, a ferry ride. He thought New York the finest, richest, friendliest city in the world.

Moreover, he had what he called a happy home life. Very near the tailor shop was a small furniture-factory, where an old Austrian, Loeffler, employed a few skilled men and made unusual furniture, most of it to order, for the rich German housewives uptown. The top floor of Loeffler's five-storey factory was a loft, where he kept his choice lumber and stored the old pieces of furniture left on his hands. One of the young workmen he employed was a Czech, and he and Rosicky became fast friends. They persuaded Loeffler to let them have a sleeping-room in one corner of the loft. They bought good beds and bedding and had their pick of the furniture kept up there. The loft was low-pitched, but light and airy, full of windows, and good-smelling by reason of the fine lumber put up there to season. Old

Loeffler used to go down to the docks and buy wood from South America and the East from the sea captains. The young men were as foolish about their house as a bridal pair. Zichec, the young cabinet-maker, devised every sort of convenience, and Rosicky kept their clothes in order. At night and on Sundays, when the quiver of machinery underneath was still, it was the quietest place in the world, and on summer nights all the sea winds blew in. Zichec often practised on his flute in the evening. They were both fond of music and went to the opera together. Rosicky thought he wanted to live like that for ever.

But as the years passed, all alike, he began to get a little restless. When spring came round, he would begin to feel fretted, and he got to drinking. He was likely to drink too much of a Saturday night. On Sunday he was languid and heavy, getting over his spree. On Monday he plunged into work again. So he never had time to figure out what ailed him, although he knew something did. When the grass turned green in Park Place, and the lilac hedge at the back of Trinity churchyard put out its blossoms, he was tormented by a longing to run away. That was why he drank too much; to get a temporary illusion of freedom and wide horizons.

Rosicky, the old Rosicky, could remember as if it were yesterday the day when the young Rosicky found out what was the matter with him. It was on a Fourth of July afternoon, and he was sitting in Park Place in the sun. The lower part of New York was empty. Wall Street, Liberty Street, Broadway, all empty. So much stone and asphalt with nothing going on, so many empty windows. The emptiness was intense, like the stillness in a great factory when the machinery stops and the belts and bands cease running. It was too great a change, it took all the strength out of one. Those blank buildings, without the stream of life pouring through them, were like empty jails. It struck young Rosicky that this was the trouble with big cities; they built you in from the earth itself, cemented you away from any contact with the ground. You lived in an unnatural world, like the fish in an aquarium, who were probably much more comfortable than they ever were in the sea.

On that very day he began to think seriously about the articles he had read in the Bohemian papers, describing prosperous Czech farming communities in the West. He believed he would like to go out there as a farm hand; it was hardly possible that he could ever have land of his own. His people had always been workmen, his father and grandfather had worked in shops. His mother's parents had lived in the country, but they rented their farm and had a hard time to get along. Nobody in his family had ever owned any land,—that belonged to a different station of life altogether. Anton's mother died when he was little, and he was sent into the country to her parents. He stayed with them until he was twelve, and formed those ties with the earth and the farm animals and growing things which are never made at all unless they are made early. After his grandfather died, he went back to live with his father and stepmother, but she was very hard on him, and his father helped him to get passage to London.

After that Fourth of July day in Park Place, the desire to return to the country never left him. To work on another man's farm would be all he asked; to see the sun rise and set and to plant things and watch them grow. He was a very simple man. He was like a tree that has not many roots, but one taproot that goes down deep. He subscribed for a Bohemian paper printed in

Chicago, then for one printed in Omaha. His mind got farther and farther west. He began to save a little money to buy his liberty. When he was thirty-five, there was a great meeting in New York of Bohemian athletic societies, and Rosicky left the tailor shop and went home with the Omaha delegates to try his fortune in another part of the world.

IV

Perhaps the fact that his own youth was well over before he began to have a family was one reason why Rosicky was so fond of his boys. He had almost a grandfather's indulgence for them. He had never had to worry about any of them—except, just now, a little about Rudolph.

On Saturday night the boys always piled into the Ford, took little Josephine, and went to town to the moving-picture show. One Saturday morning they were talking at the breakfast table about starting early that evening, so that they would have an hour or so to see the Christmas things in the stores before the show began. Rosicky looked down the table.

"I hope you boys ain't disappointed, but I want you to let me have de car tonight. Maybe some of you can go in with de neighbours."

Their faces fell. They worked hard all week, and they were still like children. A new jack-knife or a box of candy pleased the older ones as much as the little fellow.

"If you and mother are going to town," Frank said, "maybe you could take a couple of us along with you, anyway.'"

"No, I want to take de car down to Rudolph's, and let him an' Polly go in to de show. She don't git into town enough, an' I'm afraid she's gettin' lonesome, an' he can't afford no car yet."

That settled it. The boys were a good deal dashed. Their father took another piece of apple-cake and went on: "Maybe next Saturday night de two little fellers can go along wid dem."

"Oh, is Rudolph going to have the car every Saturday night?"

Rosicky did not reply at once; then he began to speak seriously: "Listen, boys; Polly ain't lookin' so good. I don't like to see nobody lookin' sad. It comes hard fur a town girl to be a farmer's wife. I don't want no trouble to start in Rudolph's family. When it starts, it ain't so easy to stop. An American girl don't git used to our ways all at once. I like to tell Polly she and Rudolph can have the car every Saturday night till after New Year's, if it's all right with you boys."

"Sure, it's all right, papa," Mary cut in. "And it's good you thought about that. Town girls is used to more than country girls. I lay awake nights, scared she'll make Rudolph discontented with the farm."

The boys put as good a face on it as they could. They surely looked forward to their Saturday nights in town. That evening Rosicky drove the car the half-mile down to Rudolph's new, bare little house.

Polly was in a short-sleeved gingham dress, clearing away the supper dishes. She was a trim, slim little thing, with blue eyes and shingled yellow hair, and her eyebrows were reduced to a mere brush-stroke, like Miss Pearl's.

"Good-evening, Mr. Rosicky. Rudolph's at the barn, I guess." She never called him father, or Mary mother. She was sensitive about having married a foreigner. She never in the world would have done it if Rudolph hadn't been such a handsome, persuasive fellow and such a gallant lover. He had graduated in her class in the high school in town, and their friendship began in the ninth grade.

Rosicky went in, though he wasn't exactly asked. "My boys ain't goin' to town tonight, an' I brought de car over fur you two to go in to de picture show."

Polly, carrying dishes to the sink, looked over her shoulder at him. "Thank you. But I'm late with my work tonight, and pretty tired. Maybe Rudolph would like to go in with you."

"Oh, I don't go to de shows! I'm too old-fashioned. You won't feel so tired after you ride in de air a ways. It's a nice clear night, an' it ain't cold. You go an' fix yourself up, Polly, an' I'll wash de dishes an' leave everything nice fur you."

Polly blushed and tossed her bob. "I couldn't let you do that, Mr. Rosicky, I wouldn't think of it."

Rosicky said nothing. He found a bib apron on a nail behind the kitchen door. He slipped it over his head and then took Polly by her two elbows and pushed her gently toward the door of her own room. "I washed up de kitchen many times for my wife, when de babies was sick or somethin'. You go an' make yourself look nice. I like you to look prettier'n any of dem town girls when you go in. De young folks must have some fun, an' I'm goin' to look out fur you, Polly."

That kind, reassuring grip on her elbows, the old man's funny bright eyes, made Polly want to drop her head on his shoulder for a second. She restrained herself, but she lingered in his grasp at the door of her room, murmuring tearfully: "You always lived in the city when you were young, didn't you? Don't you ever get lonesome out here?"

As she turned round to him, her hand fell naturally into his, and he stood holding it and smiling into her face with his peculiar, knowing, indulgent smile without a shadow of reproach in it. "Dem big cities is all right fur de rich, but dey is terrible hard fur de poor."

"I don't know. Sometimes I think I'd like to take a chance. You lived in New York, didn't you?"

"An' London. Da's bigger still. I learned my trade dere. Here's Rudolph comin', you better hurry."

"Will you tell me about London some time?"

"Maybe. Only I ain't no talker, Polly. Run an' dress yourself up."

The bedroom door closed behind her, and Rudolph came in from the outside, looking anxious. He had seen the car and was sorry any of his family should come just then. Supper hadn't been a very pleasant occasion. Halting in the doorway, he saw his father in a kitchen apron, carrying dishes to the sink. He flushed crimson and something flashed in his eye. Rosicky held up a warning finger.

"I brought de car over fur you an' Polly to go to de picture show, an' I made her let me finish here so you won't be late. You go put on a clean shirt, quick!"

"But don't the boys want the car, Father?"

"Not tonight dey don't." Rosicky fumbled under his apron and found his pants pocket. He took out a silver dollar and said in a hurried whisper: "You go an' buy dat girl some ice cream an' candy tonight, like you was courtin'. She's awful good friends wid me."

Rudolph was very short of cash, but he took the money as if it hurt him. There had been a crop failure all over the country. He had more than once been sorry he'd married this year.

In a few minutes the young people came out, looking clean and a little stiff. Rosicky hurried them off, and then he took his own time with the dishes. He scoured the pots and pans and put away the milk and swept the kitchen. He put some coal in the stove and shut off the draughts, so the place would be warm for them when they got home late at night. Then he sat down and had a pipe and listened to the clock tick.

Generally speaking, marrying an American girl was certainly a risk. A Czech should marry a Czech. It was lucky that Polly was the daughter of a poor widow woman; Rudolph was proud, and if she had a prosperous family to throw up at him, they could never make it go. Polly was one of four sisters, and they all worked; one was book-keeper in the bank, one taught music, and Polly and her younger sister had been clerks, like Miss Pearl. All four of them were musical, had pretty voices, and sang in the Methodist choir, which the eldest sister directed.

Polly missed the sociability of a store position. She missed the choir, and the company of her sisters. She didn't dislike housework, but she disliked so much of it. Rosicky was a little anxious about this pair. He was afraid Polly would grow so discontented that Rudy would quit the farm and take a factory job in Omaha. He had worked for a winter up there, two years ago, to get money to marry on. He had done very well, and they would always take him back at the stockyards. But to Rosicky that meant the end of everything for his son. To be a landless man was to be a wage-earner, a slave, all your life; to have nothing, to be nothing.

Rosicky thought he would come over and do a little carpentering for Polly after the New Year. He guessed she needed jollying. Rudolph was a serious sort of chap, serious in love and serious about his work.

Rosicky shook out his pipe and walked home across the fields. Ahead of him the lamplight shone from his kitchen windows. Suppose he were still in a tailor shop on Vesey Street, with a bunch of pale, narrow-chested sons working on machines, all coming home tired and sullen to eat supper in a kitchen that was a parlour also; with another crowded, angry family quarrelling just across the dumb-waiter shaft, and squeaking pulleys at the windows where dirty washings hung on dirty lines above a court full of old brooms and mops and ash-cans . . .

He stopped by the windmill to look up at the frosty winter stars and draw a long breath before he went inside. That kitchen with the shining windows was dear to him; but the sleeping fields and bright stars and the noble darkness were dearer still.

V

On the day before Christmas the weather set in very cold; no snow, but a bitter, biting wind that whistled and sang over the flat land and lashed one's face like fine wires. There was baking going on in the Rosicky kitchen all day, and Rosicky sat inside, making over a coat that Albert had outgrown into an overcoat for John. Mary had a big red geranium in bloom for Christmas, and a row of Jerusalem cherry trees, full of berries. It was the first year she had ever grown these; Doctor Ed brought her the seeds from Omaha when he went to some medical convention. They reminded Rosicky of plants he had seen in England; and all afternoon, as he stitched, he sat thinking about those two years in London, which his mind usually shrank from even after all this while.

He was a lad of eighteen when he dropped down into London, with no money and no connexions except the address of a cousin who was supposed to be working at a confectioner's. When he went to the pastry shop, however, he found that the cousin had gone to America. Anton tramped the streets for several days, sleeping in doorways and on the Embankment, until he was in utter despair. He knew no English, and the sound of the strange language all about him confused him. By chance he met a poor German tailor who had learned his trade in Vienna, and could speak a little Czech. This tailor, Lifschnitz, kept a repair shop in a Cheapside basement, underneath a cobbler. He didn't much need an apprentice, but he was sorry for the boy and took him in for no wages but his keep and what he could pick up. The pickings were supposed to be coppers given you when you took work home to a customer. But most of the customers called for their clothes themselves, and the coppers that came Anton's way were very few. He had, however, a place to sleep. The tailor's family lived upstairs in three rooms; a kitchen, a bedroom, where Lifschnitz and his wife and five children slept, and a living-room. Two corners of this living room were curtained off for lodgers; in one Rosicky slept on an old horsehair sofa, with a feather quilt to wrap himself in. The other corner was rented to a wretched, dirty boy, who was studying the violin. He actually practised there. Rosicky was dirty, too. There was no way to be anything else. Mrs. Lifschnitz got the water she cooked and washed with from a pump in a brick court, four flights down. There were bugs in the place, and multitudes of fleas, though the poor woman did the best she could. Rosicky knew she often went empty to give another potato or a spoonful of dripping to the two hungry, sad-eyed boys who lodged with her. He used to think he would never get out of there, never get a clean shirt to his back again. What would he do, he wondered, when his clothes actually dropped to pieces and the worn cloth wouldn't hold patches any longer?

It was still early when the old farmer put aside his sewing and his recollections. The sky had been a dark grey all day, with not a gleam of sun, and the light failed at four o'clock. He went to shave and change his shirt while the turkey was roasting. Rudolph and Polly were coming over for supper.

After supper they sat round in the kitchen, and the younger boys were saying how sorry they were it hadn't snowed. Everybody was sorry. They wanted a deep snow that would lie long and keep the wheat warm, and leave the ground soaked when it melted.

"Yes, sir!" Rudolph broke out fiercely; "if we have another dry year like last year, there's going to be hard times in this country."

Rosicky filled his pipe. "You boys don't know what hard times is. You don't owe nobody, you got plenty to eat an' keep warm, an' plenty water to keep clean. When you got them, you can't have it very hard."

Rudolph frowned, opened and shut his big right hand, and dropped it clenched upon his knee. "I've got to have a good deal more than that, father, or I'll quit this farming gamble. I can always make good wages railroading, or at the packing house, and be sure of my money."

"Maybe so," his father answered dryly.

Mary, who had just come in from the pantry and was wiping her hands on the roller towel, thought Rudy and his father were getting too serious. She brought her darning-basket and sat down in the middle of the group.

"I ain't much afraid of hard times, Rudy," she said heartily. "We've had a plenty, but we've always come through. Your father wouldn't never take nothing very hard, not even hard times. I got a mind to tell you a story on him. Maybe you boys can't hardly remember the year we had that terrible hot wind, that burned everything up on the Fourth of July? All the corn an' the gardens. An' that was in the days when we didn't have alfalfa yet,—I guess it wasn't invented.

"Well, that very day your father was out cultivatin' corn, and I was here in the kitchen makin' plum preserves. We had bushels of plums that year. I noticed it was terrible hot, but it's always hot in the kitchen when you're preservin', an' I was too busy with my plums to mind. Anton come in from the field about three o'clock, an' I asked him what was the matter.

"'Nothin',' he says, 'but it's pretty hot an' I think I won't work no more to-day.' He stood round for a few minutes, an' then he says: 'Ain't you near through? I want you should git up a nice supper for us tonight. It's Fourth of July.'

"I told him to git along, that I was right in the middle of preservin', but the plums would taste good on hot biscuit. 'I'm goin' to have fried chicken, too,' he says, and he went off an' killed a couple. You three oldest boys was little fellers, playin' round outside, real hot an' sweaty, an' your father took you to the horse tank down by the windmill an' took off your clothes an' put you in. Them two box-elder trees were little then, but they made shade over the tank. Then he took off all his own clothes, an' got in with you. While he was playin' in the water with you, the Methodist preacher drove into our place to say how all the neighbours was goin' to meet at the schoolhouse that night, to pray for rain. He drove right to the windmill, of course, and there was your father and you three with no clothes on. I was in the kitchen door, an' I had to laugh, for the preacher acted like he ain't never seen a naked man before. He surely was embarrassed, an' your father couldn't git to his clothes; they was all hangin' up on the windmill to let the sweat dry out of 'em. So he laid in the tank where he was, an' put one of you boys on top of him to cover him up a little, an' talked to the preacher.

"When you got through playin' in the water, he put clean clothes on you and a clean shirt on himself, an' by that time I'd begun to get supper. He says: 'It's too hot in here to eat comfortable. Let's have a picnic in the orchard. We'll eat our supper behind the mulberry hedge, under them linden trees.'

"So he carried our supper down, an' a bottle of my wild-grape wine, an' everything tasted good, I can tell you. The wind got cooler as the sun was goin' down, and it turned out pleasant, only I noticed how the leaves was curled up on the linden trees. That made me think, an' I asked your father if that hot wind all day hadn't been terrible hard on the gardens an' the corn.

"'Corn,' he says, 'there ain't no corn.'

"'What you talkin' about?' I said. 'Ain't we got forty acres?'

"'We ain't got an ear,' he says, 'nor nobody else ain't got none. All the corn in this country was cooked by three o'clock today, like you'd roasted it in an oven.'

"'You mean you won't get no crop at all?' I asked him. I couldn't believe it, after he'd worked so hard.

"'No crop this year,' he says. 'That's why we're havin' a picnic. We might as well enjoy what we got.'

"An' that's how your father behaved, when all the neighbours was so discouraged they couldn't look you in the face. An' we enjoyed ourselves that year, poor as we was, an' our neighbours wasn't a bit better off for bein' miserable. Some of 'em grieved till they got poor digestions and couldn't relish what they did have."

The younger boys said they thought their father had the best of it. But Rudolph was thinking that, all the same, the neighbours had managed to get ahead more, in the fifteen years since that time. There must be something wrong about his father's way of doing things. He wished he knew what was going on in the back of Polly's mind. He knew she liked his father, but he knew, too, that she was afraid of something. When his mother sent over coffee-cake or prune tarts or a loaf of fresh bread, Polly seemed to regard them with a certain suspicion. When she observed to him that his brothers had nice manners, her tone implied that it was remarkable they should have. With his mother she was stiff and on her guard. Mary's hearty frankness and gusts of good humour irritated her. Polly was afraid of being unusual or conspicuous in any way, of being 'ordinary' as she said!

When Mary had finished her story, Rosicky laid aside his pipe.

"You boys like me to tell you about some of dem hard times I been through in London?" Warmly encouraged, he sat rubbing his forehead along the deep creases. It was bothersome to tell a long story in English (he nearly always talked to the boys in Czech), but he wanted Polly to hear this one.

"Well, you know about dat tailor shop I worked in in London? I had one Christmas dere I ain't never forgot. Times was awful bad before Christmas; de boss ain't got much work, an' have it awful hard to pay his rent. It ain't so much fun, bein' poor in a big city like London, I'll say! All de windows is full of good t'ings to eat, an' all de pushcarts in de streets is full, an' you smell 'em all de time, an' you ain't got no money—not a damn bit. I didn't mind de cold so much, though I didn't have no overcoat, chust a short jacket I'd outgrowed so it wouldn't meet on me, an' my hands was chapped raw. But I always had a good appetite, like you all know, an' de sight of dem pork pies in de windows was awful fur me!

"Day before Christmas was terrible foggy dat year, an' dat fog gits into your bones and makes you all damp like. Mrs. Lifschnitz didn't give us nothin' but a little bread an' drippin' for supper, because she was savin' to try for to give us a good dinner on Christmas Day. After supper de boss say I go an' enjoy myself, so I went into de streets to listen to de Christmas singers. Dey sing old songs an' make very nice music, an' I run round after dem a good ways, till I got awful hungry. I t'ink maybe if I go home, I can sleep till morning an' forget my belly.

"I went into my corner real quiet, and roll up in my fedder quilt. But I ain't got my head down, till I smell somet'ing good. Seem like it git stronger an' stronger, an' I can't git to sleep noway. I can't understand dat smell. Dere was a gas light in a hall across de court, dat always shine in at my window a little. I got up an' look round. I got a little wooden box in my corner fur a stool, 'cause I ain't got no chair. I picks up dat box, and under it dere is a roast goose on a platter! I can't believe my eyes. I carry it to de window where de light comes in, an' touch it and smell it to find out, an' den I taste it to be sure. I say, I will eat chust one little bite of dat goose, so I can go to sleep, and tomorrow I won't eat none at all. But I tell you, boys, when I stop, one half of dat goose was gone!"

The narrator bowed his head, and the boys shouted. But little Josephine slipped behind his chair and kissed him on the neck beneath his ear.

"Poor little Papa, I don't want him to be hungry!"

"Da's long ago, child. I ain't never been hungry since I had your mudder to cook fur me."

"Go on and tell us the rest, please," said Polly.

"Well, when I come to realize what I done, of course, I felt terrible. I felt better in de stomach, but very bad in de heart. I set on my bed wid dat platter on my knees, an' it all come to me; how hard dat poor woman save to buy dat goose, and how she get some neighbour to cook it dat got more fire, an' how she put it in my corner to keep it away from dem hungry children. Dere was a old carpet hung up to shut my corner off, an' de children wasn't allowed to go in dere. An' I know she put it in my corner because she trust me more'n she did de violin boy. I can't stand it to face her after I spoil de Christmas. So I put on my shoes and go out into de city. I tell myself I better throw myself in de river; but I guess I ain't dat kind of a boy.

"It was after twelve o'clock, an' terrible cold, an' I start out to walk about London all night. I walk along de river awhile, but dey was lots of drunks all along; men, and women too. I chust move along to keep away from de police. I git onto de Strand, an' den over to New Oxford Street, where dere was a big German restaurant on de ground floor, wid big windows all fixed up fine, an' I could see de people havin' parties inside. While I was lookin' in, two men and two ladies come out, laughin' and talkin' and feelin' happy about all dey been eatin' an' drinkin', and dey was speakin' Czech—not like de Austrians, but like de home folks talk it.

"I guess I went crazy, an' I done what I ain't never done before nor since. I went right up to dem gay people an' begun to beg dem: 'Fellow countrymen, for God's sake give me money enough to buy a goose!'

"Dey laugh, of course, but de ladies speak awful kind to me, an' dey take me back into de restaurant and give me hot coffee and cakes, an' make me tell all about how I happened to come to London, an' what I was doin' dere. Dey take my name and where I work down on paper, an' both of dem ladies give me ten shillings.

"De big market at Covent Garden[4] ain't very far away, an' by dat, time it was open. I go dere an buy a big goose an' some pork pies, an' potatoes and onions, an' cakes an' oranges fur de children—all I could carry! When I git home, everybody is still asleep. I pile all I bought on de kitchen table, an' go in an' lay down on my bed, an I ain't waken up till I hear dat woman scream when she come out into her kitchen. My goodness, but she was surprise!

4. Square in London, site of a famous flower and vegetable market and of the Covent Garden opera house.

She laugh an' cry at de same time, an' hug me and waken all de children. She ain't stop fur no breakfast; she git de Christmas dinner ready dat morning, and we all sit down an' eat all we can hold. I ain't never seen dat violin boy have all he can hold before.

"Two-three days after dat, de two men come to hunt me up, an' dey ask my boss, and he give me a good report an' tell dem I was a steady boy all right. One of dem Bohemians was very smart an' run a Bohemian newspaper in New York, an' de odder was a rich man, in de importing business, an' dey been travelling togedder. Dey told me how t'ings was easier in New York, an' offered to pay my passage when dey was goin' home soon on a boat. My boss say to me: 'You go. You ain't got no chance here, an' I like to see you git ahead, fur you always been a good boy to my woman, and fur dat fine Christmas dinner you give us all.' An' da's how I got to New York."

That night when Rudolph and Polly, arm in arm, were running home across the fields with the bitter wind at their backs, his heart leaped for joy when she said she thought they might have his family come over for supper on New Year's Eve. "Let's get up a nice supper, and not let your mother help at all; make her be company for once."

"That would be lovely of you, Polly," he said humbly. He was a very simple, modest boy, and he, too, felt vaguely that Polly and her sisters were more experienced and worldly than his people.

The winter turned out badly for farmers. It was bitterly cold, and after the first light snows before Christmas there was no snow at all—and no rain. March was as bitter as February. On those days when the wind fairly punished the country, Rosicky sat by his window. In the fall he and the boys had put in a big wheat planting, and now the seed had frozen in the ground. All that land would have to be ploughed up and planted over again, planted in corn. It had happened before, but he was younger then, and he never worried about what had to be. He was sure of himself and of Mary; he knew they could bear what they had to bear, that they would always pull through somehow. But he was not so sure about the young ones, and he felt troubled because Rudolph and Polly were having such a hard start.

Sitting beside his flowering window while the panes rattled and the wind blew in under the door, Rosicky gave himself to reflection as he had not done since those Sundays in the loft of the furniture factory in New York, long ago. Then he was trying to find what he wanted in life for himself; now he was trying to find what he wanted for his boys, and why it was he so hungered to feel sure they would be here, working this very land, after he was gone.

They would have to work hard on the farm, and probably they would never do much more than make a living. But if he could think of them as staying here on the land, he wouldn't have to fear any great unkindness for them. Hardships, certainly; it was a hardship to have the wheat freeze in the ground when seed was so high; and to have to sell your stock because you had no feed. But there would be other years when everything came along right, and you caught up. And what you had was your own. You didn't have to choose between bosses and strikers, and go wrong either way. You didn't have to do with dishonest and cruel people. They were the only things in his experience he had found terrifying and horrible: the look in the eyes of a dishonest and crafty man, of a scheming and rapacious woman.

In the country, if you had a mean neighbour, you could keep off his land and make him keep off yours. But in the city, all the foulness and misery and brutality of your neighbours was part of your life. The worst things he had come upon in his journey through the world were human,—depraved and poisonous specimens of man. To this day he could recall certain terrible faces in the London streets. There were mean people everywhere, to be sure, even in their own country town here. But they weren't tempered, hardened, sharpened, like the treacherous people in cities who live by grinding or cheating or poisoning their fellow-men. He had helped to bury two of his fellow-workmen in the tailoring trade, and he was distrustful of the organized industries that see one out of the world in big cities. Here, if you were sick, you had Doctor Ed to look after you; and if you died, fat Mr. Haycock, the kindest man in the world, buried you.

It seemed to Rosicky that for good, honest boys like his, the worst they could do on the farm was better than the best they would be likely to do in the city. If he'd had a mean boy, now, one who was crooked and sharp and tried to put anything over on his brothers, then town would be the place for him. But he had no such boy. As for Rudolph, the discontented one, he would give the shirt off his back to anyone who touched his heart. What Rosicky really hoped for his boys was that they could get through the world without ever knowing much about the cruelty of human beings. "Their mother and me ain't prepared them for that," he sometimes said to himself.

These thoughts brought him back to a grateful consideration of his own case. What an escape he had had, to be sure! He, too, in his time, had had to take money for repair work from the hand of a hungry child who let it go so wistfully; because it was money due his boss. And now, in all these years, he had never had to take a cent from anyone in bitter need—never had to look at the face of a woman become like a wolf's from struggle and famine. When he thought of these things, Rosicky would put on his cap and jacket and slip down to the barn and give his work-horses a little extra oats, letting them eat it out of his hand in their slobbery fashion. It was his way of expressing what he felt, and made him chuckle with pleasure.

The spring came warm, with blue skies,—but dry, dry as bone. The boys began ploughing up the wheat-fields to plant them over in corn. Rosicky would stand at the fence corner and watch them, and the earth was so dry it blew up in clouds of brown dust that hid the horses and the sulky plough and the driver. It was a bad outlook.

The big alfalfa-field that lay between the home place and Rudolph's came up green, but Rosicky was worried because during that open windy winter a great many Russian thistle plants had blown in there and lodged. He kept asking the boys to rake them out; he was afraid their seed would root and "take the alfalfa." Rudolph said that was nonsense. The boys were working so hard planting corn, their father felt he couldn't insist about the thistles, but he set great store by that big alfalfa-field. It was a feed you could depend on,—and there was some deeper reason, vague, but strong. The peculiar green of that clover woke early memories in old Rosicky, went back to something in his childhood in the old world. When he was a little boy, he had played in fields of that strong blue-green colour.

One morning, when Rudolph had gone to town in the car, leaving a work-team idle in his barn, Rosicky went over to his son's place, put the horses to the buggy-rake, and set about quietly taking up those thistles. He behaved with guilty caution, and rather enjoyed stealing a march on Doctor Ed, who was just then taking his first vacation in seven years of practice and was attending a clinic in Chicago. Rosicky got the thistles raked up, but did not stop to burn them. That would take some time, and his breath was pretty short, so he thought he had better get the horses back to the barn.

He got them into the barn and to their stalls, but the pain had come on so sharp in his chest that he didn't try to take the harness off. He started for the house, bending lower with every step. The cramp in his chest was shutting him up like a jack-knife. When he reached the windmill, he swayed and caught at the ladder. He saw Polly coming down the hill, running with the swiftness of a slim greyhound. In a flash she had her shoulder under his armpit.

"Lean on me, Father, hard! Don't be afraid. We can get to the house all right."

Somehow they did, though Rosicky became blind with pain; he could keep on his legs, but he couldn't steer his course. The next thing he was conscious of was lying on Polly's bed, and Polly bending over him wringing out bath-towels in hot water and putting them on his chest. She stopped only to throw coal into the stove, and she kept the tea-kettle and the black pot going. She put these hot applications on him for nearly an hour, she told him afterwards, and all that time he was drawn up stiff and blue, with the sweat pouring off him.

As the pain gradually loosed its grip, the stiffness went out of his jaws, the black circles round his eyes disappeared, and a little of his natural colour came back. When his daughter-in-law buttoned his shirt over his chest at last, he sighed.

"Da's fine, de way I feel now, Polly. It was a awful bad spell, an' I was so sorry it all come on you like it did."

Polly was flushed and excited. "Is the pain really gone? Can I leave you long enough to telephone over to your place?"

Rosicky's eyelids fluttered. "Don't telephone, Polly. It ain't no use to scare my wife. It's nice and quiet here, an' if I ain't too much trouble to you, just let me lay still till I feel like myself. I ain't got no pain now. It's nice here."

Polly bent over him and wiped the moisture from his face. "Oh, I'm so glad it's over!" she broke out impulsively. "It just broke my heart to see you suffer so, Father."

Rosicky motioned her to sit down on the chair where the tea-kettle had been, and looked up at her with that lively affectionate gleam in his eyes. "You was awful good to me, I won't never forget dat. I hate it to be sick on you like dis. Down at de barn I say to myself, dat young girl ain't had much experience in sickness, I don't want to scare her, an' maybe she's got a baby comin' or somet'ing."

Polly took his hand. He was looking at her so intently and affectionately and confidingly; his eyes seemed to caress her face, to regard it with pleasure. She frowned with her funny streaks of eyebrows, and then smiled back at him.

"I guess maybe there is something of that kind going to happen. But I haven't told anyone yet, not my mother or Rudolph. You'll be the first to know."

His hand pressed hers. She noticed that it was warm again. The twinkle in his yellow-brown eyes seemed to come nearer.

"I like mighty well to see dat little child, Polly," was all he said. Then he closed his eyes and lay half-smiling. But Polly sat still, thinking hard. She had a sudden feeling that nobody in the world, not her mother, not Rudolph, or anyone, really loved her as much as old Rosicky did. It perplexed her. She sat frowning and trying to puzzle it out. It was as if Rosicky had a special gift for loving people, something that was like an ear for music or an eye for colour. It was quiet, unobtrusive; it was merely there. You saw it in his eyes,—perhaps that was why they were merry. You felt it in his hands, too. After he dropped off to sleep, she sat holding his warm, broad, flexible brown hand. She had never seen another in the least like it. She wondered if it wasn't a kind of gipsy hand, it was so alive and quick and light in its communications,—very strange in a farmer. Nearly all the farmers she knew had huge lumps of fists, like mauls, or they were knotty and bony and uncomfortable-looking, with stiff fingers. But Rosicky's was like quicksilver, flexible, muscular, about the colour of a pale cigar, with deep, deep creases across the palm. It wasn't nervous, it wasn't a stupid lump; it was a warm brown human hand, with some cleverness in it, a great deal of generosity, and something else which Polly could only call "gypsy-like"—something nimble and lively and sure, in the way that animals are.

Polly remembered that hour long afterwards; it had been like an awakening to her. It seemed to her that she had never learned so much about life from anything as from old Rosicky's hand. It brought her to herself; it communicated some direct and untranslatable message.

When she heard Rudolph coming in the car, she ran out to meet him.

"Oh, Rudy, your father's been awful sick! He raked up those thistles he's been worrying about, and afterward he could hardly get to the house. He suffered so I was afraid he was going to die."

Rudolph jumped to the ground. "Where is he now?"

"On the bed. He's asleep. I was terribly scared, because, you know, I'm so fond of your father." She slipped her arm through his and they went into the house. That afternoon they took Rosicky home and put him to bed, though he protested that he was quite well again.

The next morning he got up and dressed and sat down to breakfast with his family. He told Mary that his coffee tasted better than usual to him, and he warned the boys not to bear any tales to Doctor Ed when he got home. After breakfast he sat down by his window to do some patching and asked Mary to thread several needles for him before she went to feed her chickens,— her eyes were better than his, and her hands steadier. He lit his pipe and took up John's overalls. Mary had been watching him anxiously all morning, and as she went out of the door with her bucket of scraps, she saw that he was smiling. He was thinking, indeed, about Polly, and how he might never have known what a tender heart she had if he hadn't got sick over there. Girls nowadays didn't wear their heart on their sleeve. But now he knew Polly would make a fine woman after the foolishness wore off. Either a woman had that sweetness at her heart or she hadn't. You couldn't always tell by the look of them; but if they had that, everything came out right in the end.

After he had taken a few stitches, the cramp began in his chest, like yesterday. He put his pipe cautiously down on the window-sill and bent over to ease the pull. No use,—he had better try to get to his bed if he could. He rose and groped his way across the familiar floor, which was rising and falling like the deck of a ship. At the door he fell. When Mary came in, she found him lying there, and the moment she touched him she knew that he was gone.

Doctor Ed was away when Rosicky died, and for the first few weeks after he got home he was harddriven. Every day he said to himself that he must get out to see that family that had lost their father. One soft, warm moonlight night in early summer he started for the farm. His mind was on other things, and not until his road ran by the graveyard did he realize that Rosicky wasn't over there on the hill where the red lamplight shone, but here, in the moonlight. He stopped his car, shut off the engine, and sat there for a while.

A sudden hush had fallen on his soul. Everything here seemed strangely moving and significant, though signifying what, he did not know. Close by the wire fence stood Rosicky's mowing-machine, where one of the boys had been cutting hay that afternoon; his own work-horses had been going up and down there. The new-cut hay perfumed all the night air. The moonlight silvered the long, billowy grass that grew over the graves and hid the fence; the few little evergreens stood out black in it, like shadows in a pool. The sky was very blue and soft, the stars rather faint because the moon was full.

For the first time it struck Doctor Ed that this was really a beautiful graveyard. He thought of city cemeteries; acres of shrubbery and heavy stone, so arranged and lonely and unlike anything in the living world. Cities of the dead, indeed; cities of the forgotten, of the "put away." But this was open and free, this little square of long grass which the wind for ever stirred. Nothing but the sky overhead, and the many-coloured fields running on until they met that sky. The horses worked here in summer; the neighbours passed on their way to town; and over yonder, in the cornfield, Rosicky's own cattle would be eating fodder as winter came on. Nothing could be more undeath-like than this place; nothing could be more right for a man who had helped to do the work of great cities and had always longed for the open country and had got to it at last. Rosicky's life seemed to him complete and beautiful.

1928, 1932

The Sculptor's Funeral

A group of the townspeople stood on the station siding of a little Kansas town, awaiting the coming of the night train, which was already twenty minutes overdue. The snow had fallen thick over everything; in the pale starlight the line of bluffs across the wide, white meadows south of the town made soft, smoke-colored curves against the clear sky. The men on the siding stood first on one foot and then on the other, their hands thrust deep into their trousers pockets, their overcoats open, their shoulders screwed up with the cold; and they glanced from time to time toward the southeast, where the railroad track wound along the river shore. They conversed in low tones and moved about restlessly, seeming uncertain as to what was expected of them. There was but one of the company who looked as if he knew exactly why he was there, and he kept conspicuously apart; walking to the far end of the platform, returning to the station door, then pacing up the track again, his chin sunk in the high collar of his overcoat, his burly shoulders drooping forward, his gait heavy and dogged. Presently he was approached by a tall, spare, grizzled man clad in a faded Grand Army suit,[1] who shuffled out from the group and advanced with a certain deference, craning his neck forward until his back made the angle of a jack-knife three-quarters open.

"I reckon she's a goin' to be pretty late again tonight, Jim," he remarked in a squeaky falsetto. "S'pose it's the snow?"

"I don't know," responded the other man with a shade of annoyance, speaking from out an astonishing cataract of red beard that grew fiercely and thickly in all directions.

The spare man shifted the quill toothpick he was chewing to the other side of his mouth. "It ain't likely that anybody from the East will come with the corpse, I s'pose," he went on reflectively.

"I don't know," responded the other, more curtly than before.

"It's too bad he didn't belong to some lodge or other. I like an order funeral[2] myself. They seem more appropriate for people of some repytation," the spare man continued, with an ingratiating concession in his shrill voice, as he carefully placed his toothpick in his vest pocket. He always carried the flag at the G.A.R. funerals in the town.

The heavy man turned on his heel, without replying, and walked up the siding. The spare man rejoined the uneasy group. "Jim's ez full ez a tick, ez ushel," he commented commiseratingly.

Just then a distant whistle sounded, and there was a shuffling of feet on the platform. A number of lanky boys, of all ages, appeared as suddenly and slimily as eels wakened by the crack of thunder; some came from the waiting-room, where they had been warming themselves by the red stove, or half asleep on the slat benches; others uncoiled themselves from baggage trucks or slid out of express wagons. Two clambered down from the driver's seat of a hearse that stood backed up against the siding. They straightened their stooping shoulders and lifted their heads, and a flash of momentary animation kindled their dull eyes at that cold, vibrant scream, the world-wide call for men. It stirred them like the note of a trumpet; just as it had often stirred the man who was coming home tonight, in his boyhood.

The night express shot, red as a rocket, from out the eastward marsh lands and wound along the river shore under the long lines of shivering

---

1. Quasi-military, uniform-inspired suit worn by members of the Grand Army of the Republic (G.A.R.), a fraternal organization for northern veterans of the Civil War founded in 1866.
2. Lodge, order: fraternal organizations.

poplars that sentinelled the meadows, the escaping steam hanging in gray masses against the pale sky and blotting out the Milky Way. In a moment the red glare from the headlight streamed up the snow-covered track before the siding and glittered on the wet, black rails. The burly man with the disheveled red beard walked swiftly up the platform toward the approaching train, uncovering his head as he went. The group of men behind him hesitated, glanced questioningly at one another, and awkwardly followed his example. The train stopped, and the crowd shuffled up to the express car just as the door was thrown open, the man in the G.A.R. suit thrusting his head forward with curiosity. The express messenger appeared in the doorway, accompanied by a young man in a long ulster and travelling cap.

"Are Mr. Merrick's friends here?" inquired the young man.

The group on the platform swayed uneasily. Philip Phelps, the banker, responded with dignity: "We have come to take charge of the body. Mr. Merrick's father is very feeble and can't be about."

"Send the agent out here," growled the express messenger, "and tell the operator to lend a hand."

The coffin was got out of its rough-box and down on the snowy platform. The townspeople drew back enough to make room for it and then formed a close semicircle about it, looking curiously at the palm leaf which lay across the black cover. No one said anything. The baggage man stood by his truck, waiting to get at the trunks. The engine panted heavily, and the fireman dodged in and out among the wheels with his yellow torch and long oil-can, snapping the spindle boxes. The young Bostonian, one of the dead sculptor's pupils who had come with the body, looked about him helplessly. He turned to the banker, the only one of that black, uneasy, stoop-shouldered group who seemed enough of an individual to be addressed.

"None of Mr. Merrick's brothers are here?" he asked uncertainly.

The man with the red beard for the first time stepped up and joined the others. "No, they have not come yet; the family is scattered. The body will be taken directly to the house." He stooped and took hold of one of the handles of the coffin.

"Take the long hill road up, Thompson, it will be easier on the horses," called the liveryman as the undertaker snapped the door of the hearse and prepared to mount to the driver's seat.

Laird, the red-bearded lawyer, turned again to the stranger: "We didn't know whether there would be any one with him or not," he explained. "It's a long walk, so you'd better go up in the hack." He pointed to a single battered conveyance, but the young man replied stiffly: "Thank you, but I think I will go up with the hearse. If you don't object," turning to the undertaker, "I'll ride with you."

They clambered up over the wheels and drove off in the starlight up the long, white hill toward the town. The lamps in the still village were shining from under the low, snow-burdened roofs; and beyond, on every side, the plains reached out into emptiness, peaceful and wide as the soft sky itself, and wrapped in a tangible, white silence.

When the hearse backed up to a wooden sidewalk before a naked, weather-beaten frame house, the same composite, ill-defined group that had stood upon the station siding was huddled about the gate. The front yard was an icy swamp, and a couple of warped planks, extending from the sidewalk to the door, made a sort of rickety footbridge. The gate hung on one hinge, and was opened wide with difficulty. Steavens, the young stranger, noticed that something black was tied to the knob of the front door.

The grating sound made by the casket, as it was drawn from the hearse, was answered by a scream from the house; the front door was wrenched open, and a tall, corpulent woman rushed out bare-headed into the snow and flung herself upon the coffin, shrieking: "My boy, my boy! And this is how you've come home to me!"

As Steavens turned away and closed his eyes with a shudder of unutterable repulsion, another woman, also tall, but flat and angular, dressed entirely in black, darted out of the house and caught Mrs. Merrick by the shoulders, crying sharply: "Come, come, mother; you mustn't go on like this!" Her tone changed to one of obsequious solemnity as she turned to the banker: "The parlour is ready, Mr. Phelps."

The bearers carried the coffin along the narrow boards, while the undertaker ran ahead with the coffin-rests. They bore it into a large, unheated room that smelled of dampness and disuse and furniture polish, and set it down under a hanging lamp ornamented with jingling glass prisms and before a "Rogers group" of John Alden and Priscilla, wreathed with smilax.[3] Henry Steavens stared about him with the sickening conviction that there had been a mistake, and that he had somehow arrived at the wrong destination. He looked at the clover-green Brussels,[4] the fat plush upholstery, among the hand-painted china placques and panels and vases, for some mark of identification,—for something that might once conceivably have belonged to Harvey Merrick. It was not until he recognized his friend in the crayon portrait of a little boy in kilts and curls, hanging above the piano, that he felt willing to let any of these people approach the coffin.

"Take the lid off, Mr. Thompson; let me see my boy's face," wailed the elder woman between her sobs. This time Steavens looked fearfully, almost beseechingly into her face, red and swollen under its masses of strong, black, shiny hair. He flushed, dropped his eyes, and then, almost incredulously, looked again. There was a kind of power about her face—a kind of brutal handsomeness, even; but it was scarred and furrowed by violence, and so colored and coarsened by fiercer passions that grief seemed never to have laid a gentle finger there. The long nose was distended and knobbed at the end, and there were deep lines on either side of it; her heavy, black brows almost met across her forehead, her teeth were large and square, and set far apart—teeth that could tear. She filled the room; the men were obliterated, seemed tossed about like twigs in an angry water, and even Steavens felt himself being drawn into the whirlpool.

The daughter—the tall, raw-boned woman in crêpe, with a mourning comb in her hair which curiously lengthened her long face—sat stiffly upon the sofa, her hands, conspicuous for their large knuckles, folded in her lap,

3. A flowering vine; also the name of a nymph turned into the flower in Greek mythology. "Rogers group": plaster figurines of literary and historical subjects, mass-produced by John Rogers from 1859 to 1892. John Alden and Priscilla were Pilgrims on the *Mayflower* whose love was treated in Henry Wadsworth Longfellow's best-selling 1858 narrative poem *The Courtship of Miles Standish*.
4. Carpeting developed in Europe and mass-produced in the United States beginning in the mid-19th century.

her mouth and eyes drawn down, solemnly awaiting the opening of the coffin. Near the door stood a mulatto woman, evidently a servant in the house, with a timid bearing and an emaciated face pitifully sad and gentle. She was weeping silently, the corner of her calico apron lifted to her eyes, occasionally suppressing a long, quivering sob. Steavens walked over and stood beside her.

Feeble steps were heard on the stairs, and an old man, tall and frail, odorous of pipe smoke, with shaggy, unkept gray hair and a dingy beard, tobacco stained about the mouth, entered uncertainly. He went slowly up to the coffin and stood rolling a blue cotton handkerchief between his hands, seeming so pained and embarrassed by his wife's orgy of grief that he had no consciousness of anything else.

"There, there, Annie, dear, don't take on so," he quavered timidly, putting out a shaking hand and awkwardly patting her elbow. She turned and sank upon his shoulder with such violence that he tottered a little. He did not even glance toward the coffin, but continued to look at her with a dull, frightened, appealing expression, as a spaniel looks at the whip. His sunken cheeks slowly reddened and burned with miserable shame. When his wife rushed from the room, her daughter strode after her with set lips. The servant stole up to the coffin, bent over it for a moment, and then slipped away to the kitchen, leaving Steavens, the lawyer, and the father to themselves. The old man stood looking down at his dead son's face. The sculptor's splendid head seemed even more noble in its rigid stillness than in life. The dark hair had crept down upon the wide forehead; the face seemed strangely long, but in it there was not that repose we expect to find in the faces of the dead. The brows were so drawn that there were two deep lines above the beaked nose, and the chin was thrust forward defiantly. It was as though the strain of life had been so sharp and bitter that death could not at once relax the tension and smooth the countenance into perfect peace—as though he were still guarding something precious, which might even yet be wrested from him.

The old man's lips were working under his stained beard. He turned to the lawyer with timid deference: "Phelps and the rest are comin' back to set up with Harve, ain't they?" he asked. "Thank 'ee, Jim, thank 'ee." He brushed the hair back gently from his son's forehead. "He was a good boy, Jim; always a good boy. He was ez gentle ez a child and the kindest of 'em all—only we didn't none of us ever onderstand him." The tears trickled slowly down his beard and dropped upon the sculptor's coat.

"Martin, Martin! Oh, Martin! come here," his wife wailed from the top of the stairs. The old man started timorously: "Yes, Annie, I'm coming." He turned away, hesitated, stood for a moment in miserable indecision; then reached back and patted the dead man's hair softly, and stumbled from the room.

"Poor old man, I didn't think he had any tears left. Seems as if his eyes would have gone dry long ago. At his age nothing cuts very deep," remarked the lawyer.

Something in his tone made Steavens glance up. While the mother had been in the room, the young man had scarcely seen any one else; but now, from the moment he first glanced into Jim Laird's florid face and bloodshot eyes, he knew that he had found what he had been heartsick at not finding before—the feeling, the understanding, that must exist in some one, even here.

The man was red as his beard, with features swollen and blurred by dissipation, and a hot, blazing blue eye. His face was strained—that of a man who is controlling himself with difficulty—and he kept plucking at his beard with a sort of fierce resentment. Steavens, sitting by the window, watched him turn down the glaring lamp, still its jangling pendants with an angry gesture, and then stand with his hands locked behind him, staring down into the master's face. He could not help wondering what link there had been between the porcelain vessel and so sooty a lump of potter's clay.

From the kitchen an uproar was sounding; when the dining-room door opened, the import of it was clear. The mother was abusing the maid for having forgotten to make the dressing for the chicken salad which had been prepared for the watchers. Steavens had never heard anything in the least like it; it was injured, emotional, dramatic abuse, unique and masterly in its excruciating cruelty, as violent and unrestrained as had been her grief of twenty minutes before. With a shudder of disgust the lawyer went into the dining-room and closed the door into the kitchen.

"Poor Roxy's getting it now," he remarked when he came back. "The Merricks took her out of the poor-house years ago; and if her loyalty would let her, I guess the poor old thing could tell tales that would curdle your blood. She's the mulatto woman who was standing in here a while ago, with her apron to her eyes. The old woman is a fury; there never was anybody like her. She made Harvey's life a hell for him when he lived at home; he was so sick ashamed of it. I never could see how he kept himself sweet."

"He was wonderful," said Steavens slowly, "wonderful; but until tonight I have never known how wonderful."

"That is the eternal wonder of it, anyway; that it can come even from such a dung heap as this," the lawyer cried, with a sweeping gesture which seemed to indicate much more than the four walls within which they stood.

"I think I'll see whether I can get a little air. The room is so close I am beginning to feel rather faint," murmured Steavens, struggling with one of the windows. The sash was stuck, however, and would not yield, so he sat down dejectedly and began pulling at his collar. The lawyer came over, loosened the sash with one blow of his red fist and sent the window up a few inches. Steavens thanked him, but the nausea which had been gradually climbing into his throat for the last half hour left him with but one desire—a desperate feeling that he must get away from this place with what was left of Harvey Merrick. Oh, he comprehended well enough now the quiet bitterness of the smile that he had seen so often on his master's lips!

Once when Merrick returned from a visit home, he brought with him a singularly feeling and suggestive bas-relief[5] of a thin, faded old woman, sitting and sewing something pinnned to her knee; while a full-lipped, full-blooded little urchin, his trousers held up by a single gallows,[6] stood beside her, impatiently twitching her gown to call her attention to a butterfly he had caught. Steavens, impressed by the tender and delicate modelling of the thin, tired face, had asked him if it were his mother. He remembered the dull flush that had burned up in the sculptor's face.

---

5. Low relief (French); a sculpture in which an image is slightly raised against a background.

6. I.e., a single suspender.

The lawyer was sitting in a rocking-chair beside the coffin, his head thrown back and his eyes closed. Steavens looked at him earnestly, puzzled at the line of the chin, and wondering why a man should conceal a feature of such distinction under that disfiguring shock of beard. Suddenly, as though he felt the young sculptor's keen glance, Jim Laird opened his eyes.

"Was he always a good deal of an oyster?" he asked abruptly. "He was terribly shy as a boy."

"Yes, he was an oyster, since you put it so," rejoined Steavens. "Although he could be very fond of people, he always gave one the impression of being detached. He disliked violent emotion; he was reflective, and rather distrustful of himself—except, of course, as regarded his work. He was sure enough there. He distrusted men pretty thoroughly and women even more, yet somehow without believing ill of them. He was determined, indeed, to believe the best; but he seemed afraid to investigate."

"A burnt dog dreads the fire," said the lawyer grimly, and closed his eyes.

Steavens went on and on, reconstructing that whole miserable boyhood. All this raw, biting ugliness had been the portion of the man whose mind was to become an exhaustless gallery of beautiful impressions—so sensitive that the mere shadow of a poplar leaf flickering against a sunny wall would be etched and held there for ever. Surely, if ever a man had the magic word in his finger tips, it was Merrick. Whatever he touched, he revealed its holiest secret; liberated it from enchantment and restored it to its pristine loveliness. Upon whatever he had come in contact with, he had left a beautiful record of the experience—a sort of ethereal signature; a scent, a sound, a color that was his own.

Steavens understood now the real tragedy of his master's life; neither love nor wine, as many had conjectured; but a blow which had fallen earlier and cut deeper than anything else could have done—a shame not his, and yet so unescapably his, to hide in his heart from his very boyhood. And without—the frontier warfare; the yearning of a boy, cast ashore upon a desert of newness and ugliness and sordidness, for all that is chastened and old, and noble with traditions.

At eleven o'clock the tall, flat woman in black announced that the watchers were arriving, and asked them to "step into the dining-room." As Steavens rose, the lawyer said dryly: "You go on—it'll be a good experience for you. I'm not equal to that crowd tonight; I've had twenty years of them."

As Steavens closed the door after him he glanced back at the lawyer, sitting by the coffin in the dim light, with his chin resting on his hand.

The same misty group that had stood before the door of the express car shuffled into the dining-room. In the light of the kerosene lamp they separated and became individuals. The minister, a pale, feeble-looking man with white hair and blond chin-whiskers, took his seat beside a small side table and placed his Bible upon it. The Grand Army man sat down behind the stove and tilted his chair back comfortably against the wall, fishing his quill toothpick from his waistcoat pocket. The two bankers, Phelps and Elder, sat off in a corner behind the dinner-table, where they could finish their discussion of the new usury law and its effect on chattel security loans.[7] The

---

7. Loans backed by the debtor's personal property. Kansas revised its laws regulating interest on loans and prohibiting usury (excessive interest) in 1889.

real estate agent, an old man with a smiling, hypocritical face, soon joined them. The coal and lumber dealer and the cattle shipper sat on opposite sides of the hard coal-burner, their feet on the nickel-work.[8] Steavens took a book from his pocket and began to read. The talk around him ranged through various topics of local interest while the house was quieting down. When it was clear that the members of the family were in bed, the Grand Army man hitched his shoulders and, untangling his long legs, caught his heels on the rounds of his chair.

"S'pose there'll be a will, Phelps?" he queried in his weak falsetto.

The banker laughed disagreeably, and began trimming his nails with a pearl-handled pocket-knife.

"There'll scarcely be any need for one, will there?" he queried in his turn.

The restless Grand Army man shifted his position again, getting his knees still nearer his chin. "Why, the ole man says Harve's done right well lately," he chirped.

The other banker spoke up. "I reckon he means by that Harve ain't asked him to mortgage any more farms lately, so as he could go on with his education."

"Seems like my mind don't reach back to a time when Harve wasn't bein' edycated," tittered the Grand Army man.

There was a general chuckle. The minister took out his handkerchief and blew his nose sonorously. Banker Phelps closed his knife with a snap. "It's too bad the old man's sons didn't turn out better," he remarked with reflective authority. "They never hung together. He spent money enough on Harve to stock a dozen cattle-farms, and he might as well have poured it into Sand Creek. If Harve had stayed at home and helped nurse what little they had, and gone into stock on the old man's bottom farm, they might all have been well fixed. But the old man had to trust everything to tenants and was cheated right and left."

"Harve never could have handled stock none," interposed the cattleman. "He hadn't it in him to be sharp. Do you remember when he bought Sander's mules for eight-year olds, when everybody in town knew that Sander's father-in-law give 'em to his wife for a wedding present eighteen years before, an' they was full-grown mules then?"

The company laughed discreetly, and the Grand Army man rubbed his knees with a spasm of childish delight.

"Harve never was much account for anything practical, and he shore was never fond of work," began the coal and lumber dealer. "I mind the last time he was home; the day he left, when the old man was out to the barn helpin' his hand hitch up to take Harve to the train, and Cal Moots was patchin' up the fence; Harve, he come out on the step and sings out, in his ladylike voice: 'Cal Moots, Cal Moots! please come cord my trunk.'"

"That's Harve for you," approved the Grand Army man. "I kin hear him howlin' yet, when he was a big feller in long pants and his mother used to whale him with a rawhide in the barn for lettin' the cows git foundered in the cornfield when he was drivin' 'em home from pasture. He killed a cow of mine that-a-way onct—a pure Jersey and the best milker I had, an' the ole

---

8. Cast-iron stoves were often finished with nickel trim work, sometimes including footrests.

man had to put up for her. Harve, he was watchin' the sun set acrost the marshes when the anamile got away."

"Where the old man made his mistake was in sending the boy East to school," said Phelps, stroking his goatee and speaking in a deliberate, judicial tone. "There was where he got his head full of nonsense. What Harve needed, of all people, was a course in some first-class Kansas City business college."

The letters were swimming before Steavens's eyes. Was it possible that these men did not understand, that the palm on the coffin meant nothing to them? The very name of their town would have remained for ever buried in the postal guide had it not been now and again mentioned in the world in connection with Harvey Merrick's. He remembered what his master had said to him on the day of his death, after the congestion of both lungs had shut off any probability of recovery, and the sculptor had asked his pupil to send his body home. "It's not a pleasant place to be lying while the world is moving and doing and bettering," he had said with a feeble smile, "but it rather seems as though we ought to go back to the place we came from, in the end. The townspeople will come in for a look at me; and after they have had their say, I shan't have much to fear from the judgment of God!"

The cattleman took up the comment. "Forty's young for a Merrick to cash in; they usually hang on pretty well. Probably he helped it along with whisky."

"His mother's people were not long lived, and Harvey never had a robust constitution," said the minister mildly. He would have liked to say more. He had been the boy's Sunday-school teacher, and had been fond of him; but he felt that he was not in a position to speak. His own sons had turned out badly, and it was not a year since one of them had made his last trip home in the express car, shot in a gambling-house in the Black Hills.

"Nevertheless, there is no disputin' that Harve frequently looked upon the wine when it was red, also variegated, and it shore made an oncommon fool of him," moralized the cattleman.

Just then the door leading into the parlour rattled loudly and every one started involuntarily, looking relieved when only Jim Laird came out. The Grand Army man ducked his head when he saw the spark in his blue, blood-shot eye. They were all afraid of Jim; he was a drunkard, but he could twist the law to suit his client's needs as no other man in all western Kansas could do, and there were many who tried. The lawyer closed the door behind him, leaned back against it and folded his arms, cocking his head a little to one side. When he assumed this attitude in the court-room, ears were always pricked up, as it usually foretold a flood of withering sarcasm.

"I've been with you gentlemen before," he began in a dry, even tone, "when you've sat by the coffins of boys born and raised in this town; and, if I remember rightly, you were never any too well satisfied when you checked them up. What's the matter, anyhow? Why is it that reputable young men are as scarce as millionaires in Sand City? It might almost seem to a stranger that there was some way something the matter with your progressive town. Why did Ruben Sayer, the brightest young lawyer you ever turned out, after he had come home from the university as straight as a die, take to drinking and forge a check and shoot himself? Why did Bill Merrit's son die of the shakes in a saloon in Omaha? Why was Mr. Thomas's son, here, shot in a gambling-house? Why did young Adams burn his mill to beat the insurance companies and go to the pen?"

The lawyer paused and unfolded his arms, laying one clenched fist quietly on the table. "I'll tell you why. Because you drummed nothing but money and knavery into their ears from the time they wore knickerbockers; because you carped away at them as you've been carping here tonight, holding our friends Phelps and Elder up to them for their models, as our grandfathers held up George Washington and John Adams. But the boys were young, and raw at the business you put them to, and how could they match coppers with such artists as Phelps and Elder? You wanted them to be successful rascals; they were only unsuccessful ones—that's all the difference. There was only one boy ever raised in this borderland between ruffianism and civilization who didn't come to grief, and you hated Harvey Merrick more for winning out than you hated all the other boys who got under the wheels. Lord, Lord, how you hate him! Phelps, here, is fond of saying that he could buy and sell us all out any time he's a mind to; but he knew Harve wouldn't have given a tinker's damn for his bank and all his cattlefarms put together; and a lack of appreciation, that way, goes hard with Phelps.

"Old Nimrod thinks Harve drank too much; and this from such as Nimrod and me!

"Brother Elder says Harve was too free with the old man's money—fell short in filial consideration, maybe. Well, we can all remember the very tone in which brother Elder swore his own father was a liar, in the county court; and we all know that the old man came out of that partnership with his son as bare as a sheared lamb. But maybe I'm getting personal, and I'd better be driving ahead at what I want to say."

The lawyer paused a moment, squared his heavy shoulders, and went on: "Harvey Merrick and I went to school together, back East. We were dead in earnest, and we wanted you all to be proud of us some day. We meant to be great men. Even I, and I haven't lost my sense of humor, gentlemen, I meant to be a great man. I came back here to practice, and I found you didn't in the least want me to be a great man. You wanted me to be a shrewd lawyer—oh, yes! Our veteran here wanted me to get him an increase of pension, because he had dyspepsia; Phelps wanted a new county survey that would put the widow Wilson's little bottom farm inside his south line; Elder wanted to lend money at 5 per cent a month, and get it collected; and Stark here wanted to wheedle old women up in Vermont into investing their annuities in real-estate mortgages that are not worth the paper they are written on. Oh, you needed me hard enough, and you'll go on needing me!

"Well, I came back here and became the damned shyster you wanted me to be. You pretend to have some sort of respect for me; and yet you'll stand up and throw mud at Harvey Merrick, whose soul you couldn't dirty and whose hands you couldn't tie. Oh, you're a discriminating lot of Christians! There have been times when the sight of Harvey's name in some Eastern paper has made me hang my head like a whipped dog; and, again, times when I liked to think of him off there in the world, away from all this hog-wallow, climbing the big, clean up-grade he'd set for himself.

"And we? Now that we've fought and lied and sweated and stolen, and hated as only the disappointed strugglers in a bitter, dead little Western town know how to do, what have we got to show for it? Harvey Merrick wouldn't have given one sunset over your marshes for all you've got put together, and you know it. It's not for me to say why, in the inscrutable wisdom of God, a genius should ever have been called from this place of hatred and bitter waters; but I want this Boston man to know that the drivel he's been hearing here tonight is the only tribute any truly great man could have from such a lot of sick, side-tracked, burnt-dog, land-poor sharks as the here-present financiers of Sand City—upon which town may God have mercy!"

The lawyer thrust out his hand to Steavens as he passed him, caught up his overcoat in the hall, and had left the house before the Grand Army man had had time to lift his ducked head and crane his long neck about at his fellows.

Next day Jim Laird was drunk and unable to attend the funeral services. Steavens called twice at his office, but was compelled to start East without seeing him. He had a presentiment that he would hear from him again, and left his address on the lawyer's table; but if Laird found it, he never acknowledged it. The thing in him that Harvey Merrick had loved must have gone under ground with Harvey Merrick's coffin; for it never spoke again, and Jim got the cold he died of driving across the Colorado mountains to defend one of Phelps's sons who had got into trouble out there by cutting government timber.

1905, 1920

AMY LOWELL
1874–1925

Born in Brookline, Massachusetts, the fifth and last child, twelve years younger than her nearest sibling, Amy Lowell hailed from one of Boston's wealthiest and most prestigious and powerful families. The first Lowell arrived at Massachusetts Bay Colony in 1639; from the revolutionary years on, when a Lowell was made a judge by George Washington, no era was without one or more Lowells prominent in the intellectual, religious, political, philanthropic, and commercial life of New England. In the early nineteenth century her paternal grandfather and his brothers established the Lowell textile mills in Lowell, Massachusetts—the town itself had been founded by the Lowells in 1653. The success of these mills changed the economy of New England. Profits were invested in utilities, highways, railroads, and banks. In the same generation her maternal grandfather, Abbot Lawrence, established a second New England textile dynasty. All the Lowell men went to Harvard. Traditionally, those who were not in business became Unitarian ministers or scholars—the poet James Russell Lowell was her great-uncle; her father, Augustus, was important to the founding of the Massachusetts Institute of Technology; her brother Percival was a pioneering scholar of Japanese and Korean civilization and an astronomer (he founded the Lowell Observatory); her brother Abbot Lawrence was president of Harvard from 1909 to 1933.

But none of the millionaires, manufacturers, philanthropists, statesmen, ambassadors, judges, and scholars in Amy Lowell's background could give this energetic and unusually intelligent young woman a model to follow. They were all men, and the rules for Lowell women were different. Women in the family were expected to marry well, imbue their children with a strong sense of family pride, oversee the running of several homes, and participate in upper-class Boston's busy social world. None of this interested Lowell in the least. Yet she believed in the importance of her heritage and shared the self-confidence and drive to contribute notably to public life characteristic of Lowell men.

Resisting the kind of formal education available to women of her class at the time, she attended school only between the ages of ten and seventeen. She educated herself through the use of her family's extensive private library as well as the resources of the Boston Athenaeum, a dues-paying library club founded by one of her ancestors early in the nineteenth century. She had enjoyed writing from childhood on, but did not venture into professional authorship until 1912, at the age of thirty-eight. In that year, her first book of poems—A Dome of Many-Coloured Glass—achieved both popular and critical success.

The year 1912 was the year that Harriet Monroe launched her influential little magazine, Poetry, and when in January 1913 Lowell read H.D.'s imagistic poetry she was converted to this new style. She decided to devote her popularity and social prominence to popularizing imagism and with characteristic energy and self-confidence journeyed to England to meet H.D., Ezra Pound, D. H. Lawrence, Richard Aldington, and other participants in the informal movement. When Pound abandoned imagism for vorticism, Lowell became the chief spokesperson for the movement, editing several imagist anthologies. Two volumes of original criticism by Lowell—Six French Poets (1915) and Tendencies in Modern American Poetry (1917)—also forwarded the cause. Pound, upstaged as a publicist, enviously renamed the movement "Amygism." Lowell retorted that "it was not until I entered the arena and Ezra dropped out that Imagism had to be considered seriously."

Lowell's own poetry—published in Sword Blades and Poppy Seed (1914), Men, Women, and Ghosts (1916), Can Grande's Castle (1918), Pictures of the Floating World (1919), and Legends (1921)—was never exclusively imagistic but included long historical narrative poems and journalistic prose poems and used standard verse patterns, blank verse, and a Whitmanesque free verse resembling the open line developed by Carl Sandburg. Her best poems tend to enclose sharp imagistic representation within this relatively fluid line, thereby achieving an effect of simultaneous compactness and flexibility. Like many women poets, she worked with a symbolic vocabulary of flowers and color.

Lowell enjoyed her success and cheerfully went on the lecture circuit as a celebrity, making innumerable close friendships as a result of her warmth and generosity. Despite health problems that plagued her for most of her life, she remained full of energy and zest. She depended for support on the companionship of Ada Dwyer Russell, a former actress, for whom she wrote many of her most moving appreciations of female beauty. Although she traveled widely in Europe, she was ultimately committed to New England and the Lowell heritage, both of which fused in an attachment to her home, Sevenels, in Brookline. A devotee of Romantic poetry and especially of Keats, she had begun to collect Keats manuscripts in 1905; these now form the basis of the great collection at Harvard University. In addition to all her other activities in the 1920s, she worked on a two-volume biography of Keats that greatly extended the published information about the poet when it appeared in 1925, although its psychological approach offended many traditional critics.

Lowell was just fifty-one when she died. Despite continued sniping from the high modernist poets who thought her work was too accessible, her poetry continued to be both popular and critically esteemed until the 1950s, when scholars focused the canon on a very small number of writers. The efforts of feminists to rediscover and republicize the work of neglected women authors as well as the researches of literary historians into the whole picture of American literary achievement have together brought her work back into the spotlight that it occupied during her lifetime.

The texts printed here are from Lowell's *Complete Poems* (1955).

The Captured Goddess

Over the housetops,
Above the rotating chimney-pots,
I have seen a shiver of amethyst,
And blue and cinnamon have flickered
A moment,   5
At the far end of a dusty street.

Through sheeted rain
Has come a lustre of crimson,
And I have watched moonbeams
Hushed by a film of palest green.   10

It was her wings,
Goddess!
Who stepped over the clouds,
And laid her rainbow feathers
Aslant on the currents of the air.   15
I followed her for long,
With gazing eyes and stumbling feet.
I cared not where she led me,
My eyes were full of colors:
Saffrons, rubies, the yellows of beryls,   20
And the indigo-blue of quartz;
Flights of rose, layers of chrysoprase,
Points of orange, spirals of vermilion,
The spotted gold of tiger-lily petals,
The loud pink of bursting hydrangeas.   25
I followed,
And watched for the flashing of her wings.

In the city I found her,
The narrow-streeted city.
In the market-place I came upon her,   30
Bound and trembling.
Her fluted wings were fastened to her sides with cords,
She was naked and cold,
For that day the wind blew
Without sunshine.   35

Men chaffered for her,
They bargained in silver and gold,

In copper, in wheat,
And called their bids across the market-place.

The Goddess wept.   40

Hiding my face I fled,
And the grey wind hissed behind me,
Along the narrow streets.

                                                                        1914

Venus Transiens

Tell me,
Was Venus more beautiful
Than you are,
When she topped
The crinkled waves,   5
Drifting shoreward
On her plaited shell?
Was Botticelli's[1] vision
Fairer than mine;
And were the painted rosebuds   10
He tossed his lady,
Of better worth
Than the words I blow about you
To cover your too great loveliness
As with a gauze   15
Of misted silver?

For me,
You stand poised
In the blue and buoyant air,
Cinctured by bright winds,   20
Treading the sunlight.
And the waves which precede you
Ripple and stir
The sands at my feet.

                                                                        1919

Madonna of the Evening Flowers

All day long I have been working,
Now I am tired.
I call: "Where are you?"
But there is only the oak tree rustling in the wind.

---

1. Sandro Botticelli (c. 1440–1510), Italian Renaissance painter among whose works is the *Birth of Venus,*
depicting the Greek goddess of love and beauty rising from the ocean on a seashell.

The house is very quiet,   5
The sun shines in on your books,
On your scissors and thimble just put down,
But you are not there.
Suddenly I am lonely:
Where are you?   10
I go about searching.

Then I see you,
Standing under a spire of pale blue larkspur,
With a basket of roses on your arm.
You are cool, like silver,   15
And you smile.
I think the Canterbury bells[1] are playing little tunes.

You tell me that the peonies need spraying,
That the columbines have overrun all bounds,
That the pyrus japonica should be cut back and rounded.   20
You tell me these things.
But I look at you, heart of silver,
White heart-flame of polished silver,
Burning beneath the blue steeples of the larkspur,
And I long to kneel instantly at your feet,   25
While all about us peal the loud, sweet *Te Deums* of the
        Canterbury bells.

                                                                              1919

September, 1918

This afternoon was the colour of water falling through sunlight;
The trees glittered with the tumbling of leaves;
The sidewalks shone like alleys of dropped maple leaves;
And the houses ran along them laughing out of square, open
        windows.
Under a tree in the park,   5
Two little boys, lying flat on their faces,
Were carefully gathering red berries
To put in a pasteboard box.

Some day there will be no war.
Then I shall take out this afternoon   10
And turn it in my fingers,
And remark the sweet taste of it upon my palate,
And note the crisp variety of its flights of leaves.
To-day I can only gather it

---

1. Little bell-shaped blue flowers. Lowell puns on the bells of Canterbury Cathedral in England pealing
out religious music.

And put it into my lunch-box,   15
For I have time for nothing
But the endeavour to balance myself
Upon a broken world.

1919

GERTRUDE STEIN
1874–1946

Among modernists active between the wars, Gertrude Stein was more radically experimental than most. She pushed language to its limits—and kept on pushing. Her work was sometimes literal nonsense, often funny, and always exciting to those who thought of writing as a craft and language as a medium. As Sherwood Anderson wrote, "she is laying word against word, relating sound to sound, feeling for the taste, the smell, the rhythm of the individual word. She is attempting to do something for the writers of our English speech that may be better understood after a time, and she is not in a hurry."

Stein's grandparents were well-off German Jewish immigrants who, at the time of her birth, were established in business in Baltimore. Born in Allegheny, Pennsylvania, she was the youngest of seven children; the family lived abroad from 1875 to 1879 and then settled in northern California. Her parents died when she was an adolescent, leaving their five surviving children well provided for. Stein made a family with her favorite brother, Leo, for many years. When he went to Harvard in 1892 she followed and was admitted to Harvard's "annex for women"—later Radcliffe College. She studied there with the great psychologist William James; some of her early writings—for example, *Three Lives* (1909) and *The Making of Americans*, which she completed in 1908 but did not publish until 1925—are probably trying to apply his theories of consciousness: consciousness as unique to each individual, as an ongoing stream, a perpetual present. In *Three Lives*, also, Stein set herself the difficult task of representing the consciousnesses of three ordinary, working-class women whose lives and minds were not the conventional material of serious literature.

When Leo moved on to Johns Hopkins to study biology, Stein followed, enrolling in the medical school. At the end of her fourth year, she failed intentionally, for several reasons: Leo had become interested in art and decided to go to Europe, she had begun to write, and she had become erotically involved with two women (the story of this triangle formed the basis of her novel *Q.E.D.*, published posthumously in 1950). In early 1903 Leo settled in Paris; Stein joined him that fall. They began to collect modern art and became good friends with many of the brilliant aspiring painters of the day, including Pablo Picasso, Georges Braque, and Henri Matisse. Stein's friendship with the painters was extremely important for her development, for she reproduced some of their experiments in the very different medium of words. Because of them, she came to think of words as tangible entities in themselves as well as vehicles conveying meaning or representing reality. The cubist movement in painting also affected her. Painters like Picasso and Braque believed that so-called repre-

Gertrude Stein and Picasso's Portrait, Man Ray, 1922. Man Ray, one of the most important of modernist photographers, posed Stein at home in front of her 1906 portrait by Pablo Picasso. Stein in her turn composed many "portraits" in writing of her artist friends, including Picasso and Henri Matisse.

sentational paintings conveyed not what people actually saw but rather what they had learned to *think* they saw. The cubists wanted to reproduce a pure visual experience unmediated by cultural ideas. To see a "person" is to see a cultural construct. So they painted a human form reduced to various geometrical shapes as they might be seen from different angles when the form moved or the observer changed position. The degree to which their paintings shocked an audience measured, to Picasso and Braque, the degree to which that audience had lost its original perceiving power.

In 1909 the long companionship of Stein and her brother was complicated when Alice B. Toklas joined the household as Gertrude Stein's lover; she became her secretary, housekeeper, typist, editor, and lifelong companion. Leo moved out in 1913, and the art collection was divided, but the apartment at 27 rue de Fleurus continued to serve as a gathering place for French artists and intellectuals, American expatriates, and American visitors. Without much expectation that her work would achieve any wide audience, Stein continued to write and to advise younger writers like Ernest Hemingway and F. Scott Fitzgerald. "A great deal of description," she said about a draft of Hemingway's first novel, "and not particularly good description. Begin over again and concentrate." The need to concentrate and distill—the idea that description was too often an indulgence—was a lesson the younger writer took to heart.

In the 1920s Stein and Toklas began spending summers in the south of France, where they bought a small house in 1929. They lived there during the war, when they could not return to Paris. Devoted to their adopted country, Stein and Toklas did what they could for France during both world wars. They visited and entertained American soldiers, many of whom continued to write to the couple for years after they had returned to the United States and some of whom visited when they had occasion to return to France. Even though Stein returned to the United States only once, in 1934, on what turned into a very successful lecture tour, she and Toklas always thought of themselves as Americans.

Being American is one topic of investigation that threads itself throughout Stein's body of experimental writing; the other is love. *The Making of Americans*, the most ambitious work of Stein's early career, linked these two concerns by wrenching a familiar novelistic form, that of the multigenerational family saga, into a strange and monumental new shape. Stein called the story of Martha Hersland and her family "a decent family progress," but it is a progress built on repetition—not only the repetition of human character from one generation to the next but also repetition in the words and sentences of Stein's prose. *The Making of Americans* identifies repeating with loving, with the process of writing, with human history, and with the rhythms of life itself: "Repeating is a wonderful thing in living being."

Stein's 1914 *Tender Buttons*, a cubist prose-poem presenting verbal collages of domestic objects, also celebrated her loving relationship with Alice B. Toklas. From its title forward, the work incorporates semiprivate erotic wordplay into its playful catalog of Stein and Toklas's shared life. *Tender Buttons* looked forward to Stein's innovative work of the 1920s, in which she treated words as things, ignoring or defying the connection between words and meanings, continually undercutting expectations about order, coherence, and associations.

In the 1930s Stein turned her writing toward more accessible forms and more public purposes—including self-promotion. Her gossipy, intimate, irreverent autobiography, written as *The Autobiography of Alice B. Toklas* (1933), was serialized in the *Atlantic Monthly* and became a best seller in the United States. In 1934 the opera *Four Saints in Three Acts*, for which she had written a libretto set to music by the American composer Virgil Thomson (1896–1989), opened on Broadway, with an all-black cast daringly chosen to portray Stein's roster of white European saints. *Everybody's Autobiography* (1937) recounted Stein's triumphant American lecture tour of 1934–35. Stein returned to American history for one of her last major works, the libretto to *The Mother of Us All* (set to music once again by Virgil Thomson and premiered in 1947), which centered on the life and work of the suffragist Susan B. Anthony (1820–1906).

By the time of her death Stein had become a public personality. In the later twentieth century, the women's and gay liberation movements contributed to a new appreciation of her radical individualism. Avant-garde American writing and art, such as the L=A=N=G=U=A=G=E school of contemporary poetry and the hypnotically repetitive operas of Philip Glass, continue to register the influence of Stein's experimental work.

The text of *The Making of Americans* is from the first edition (1925).

From The Making of Americans[1]

[INTRODUCTION]

Once an angry man dragged his father along the ground through his own orchard. "Stop!" cried the groaning old man at last, "Stop! I did not drag my father beyond this tree."

It is hard living down the tempers we are born with. We all begin well, for in our youth there is nothing we are more intolerant of than our own sins writ large in others and we fight them fiercely in ourselves; but we grow old and we

---

1. This long book—over nine hundred pages—tells the story of Martha Hersland, who represents Stein herself, and her family. *Making* refers both to family history and to making the book.

see that these our sins are of all sins the really harmless ones to own, nay that they give a charm to any character, and so our struggle with them dies away.

I am writing for myself and strangers. This is the only way that I can do it. Everybody is a real one to me, everybody is like some one else too to me. No one of them that I know can want to know it and so I write for myself and strangers.

Every one is always busy with it, no one of them then ever want to know it that every one looks like some one else and they see it. Mostly every one dislikes to hear it. It is very important to me to always know it, to always see it which one looks like others and to tell it. I write for myself and strangers. I do this for my own sake and for the sake of those who know I know it that they look like other ones, that they are separate and yet always repeated.[2] There are some who like it that I know they are like many others and repeat it, there are many who never can really like it.

There are many that I know and they know it. They are all of them repeating and I hear it. I love it and I tell it, I love it and now I will write it. This is now the history of the way some of them are it.

I write for myself and strangers. No one who knows me can like it. At least they mostly do not like it that every one is of a kind of men and women and I see it. I love it and I write it.

I want readers so strangers must do it. Mostly no one knowing me can like it that I love it that every one is a kind of men and women, that always I am looking and comparing and classifying of them, always I am seeing their repeating. Always more and more I love repeating, it may be irritating to hear from them but always more and more I love it of them. More and more I love it of them, the being in them, the mixing in them, the repeating in them, the deciding the kinds of them every one is who has human being.

This is now a little of what I love and how I write it. Later there will be much more of it.

There are many ways of making kinds of men and women. Now there will be descriptions of every kind of way every one can be a kind of men and women.

This is now a history of Martha Hersland. This is now a history of Martha and of every one who came to be of her living.

There will then be soon much description of every way one can think of men and women, in their beginning, in their middle living, and their ending.[3]

Every one then is an individual being. Every one then is like many others always living, there are many ways of thinking of every one, this is now a description of all of them. There must then be a whole history of each one of them. There must then now be a description of all repeating. Now I will tell all the meaning to me in repeating, the loving there is in me for repeating.

Every one is one inside them, every one reminds some one of some other one who is or was or will be living. Every one has it to say of each one he is like such a one I see it in him, every one has it to say of each one she is like

2. Differences within basic similarities among people correspond to the differences within similar sentences employed as the chief experimental technique of *The Making of Americans*.

3. Here Stein expands her intention to encompass every variation of human life. The repetition of present participles (*-ing*) emphasizes current action, present time.

some one else I can tell by remembering. So it goes on always in living, every one is always remembering some one who is resembling to the one at whom they are then looking. So they go on repeating, every one is themselves inside them and every one is resembling to others, and that is always interesting. There are many ways of making kinds of men and women. In each way of making kinds of them there is a different system of finding them resembling. Sometime there will be here every way there can be of seeing kinds of men and women. Sometime there will be then a complete history of each one. Every one always is repeating the whole of them and so sometime some one who sees them will have a complete history of every one. Sometime some one will know all the ways there are for people to be resembling, some one sometime then will have a completed history of every one.

Soon now there will be a history of the way repeating comes out of them comes out of men and women when they are young, when they are children, they have then their own system of being resembling; this will soon be a description of the men and women in beginning, the being young in them, the being children.

There is then now and here the loving repetition, this is then, now and here, a description of the loving of repetition and then there will be a description of all the kinds of ways there can be seen to be kinds of men and women. Then there will be realised the complete history of every one, the fundamental character of every one, the bottom nature in them, the mixtures in them, the strength and weakness of everything they have inside them, the flavor of them, the meaning in them, the being in them, and then you have a whole history then of each one. Everything then they do in living is clear to the completed understanding, their living, loving, eating, pleasing, smoking, thinking, scolding, drinking, working, dancing, walking, talking, laughing, sleeping, everything in them. There are whole beings then, they are themselves inside them, repeating coming out of them makes a history of each one of them.

Always from the beginning there was to me all living as repeating. This is now a description of my feeling. As I was saying listening to repeating is often irritating,[4] always repeating is all of living, everything in a being is always repeating, more and more listening to repeating gives to me completed understanding. Each one slowly comes to be a whole one to me. Each one slowly comes to be a whole one in me. Soon then it commences to sound through my ears and eyes and feelings the repeating that is always coming out from each one, that is them, that makes then slowly of each one of them a whole one. Repeating then comes slowly then to be to one who has it to have loving repeating as natural being comes to be a full sound telling all the being in each one such a one is ever knowing. Sometimes it takes many years of knowing some one before the repeating that is that one gets to be a steady sounding to the hearing of one who has it as a natural being to love repeating that slowly comes out from every one. Sometimes it takes many years of knowing some one before the repeating in that one comes to be a clear history of such a one. Natures sometimes are so mixed up in some one that steady repeating in them is mixed up with changing. Soon then there will be a completed

---

4. Stein is aware that her techniques may irritate readers, just as human sameness may cause people to be irritated with each other.

history of each one. Sometimes it is difficult to know it in some, for what these are saying is repeating in them is not the real repeating of them, is not the complete repeating for them. Sometimes many years of knowing some one pass before repeating of all being in them comes out clearly from them. As I was saying it is often irritating to listen to the repeating they are doing, always then that one that has it as being to love repeating that is the whole history of each one, such a one has it then that this irritation passes over into patient completed understanding. Loving repeating is one way of being. This is now a description of such feeling.

There are many that I know and they know it. They are all of them repeating and I hear it. I love it and I tell it. I love it and now I will write it. This is now a history of my love of it. I hear it and I love it and I write it. They repeat it. They live it and I see it and I hear it. They live it and I hear it and I see it and I love it and now and always I will write it. There are many kinds of men and women and I know it. They repeat it and I hear it and I love it. This is now a history of the way they do it. This is now a history of the way I love it.[5]

Now I will tell of the meaning to me in repeating, of the loving there is in me for repeating.

Sometimes every one becomes a whole one to me. Sometimes every one has a completed history for me. Slowly each one is a whole one to me, with some, all their living is passing before they are a whole one to me. There is a completed history of them to me then when there is of them a completed understanding of the bottom nature in them of the nature or natures mixed up in them with the bottom nature of them or separated in them. There is then a history of the things they say and do and feel, and happen to them. There is then a history of the living in them. Repeating is always in all of them. Repeating in them comes out of them, slowly making clear to any one that looks closely at them the nature and the natures mixed up in them. This sometime comes to be clear in every one.

Often as I was saying repeating is very irritating to listen to from them and then slowly it settles into a completed history of them. Repeating is a wonderful thing in living being. Sometime then the nature of every one comes to be clear to some one listening to the repeating coming out of each one.

This is then now to be a little description of the loving feeling for understanding of the completed history of each one that comes to one who listens always steadily to all repeating. This is the history then of the loving feeling in me of repeating, the loving feeling in me for completed understanding of the completed history of every one as it slowly comes out in every one as patiently and steadily I hear it and see it as repeating in them. This is now a little a description of this loving feeling. This is now a little a history of it from the beginning.

* * *

1906–08   1925

---

5. In telling about others with such care, Stein shows her love for them; hence the tale is about her love as well as their lives.

ROBERT FROST
1874-1963

Although he identified himself with New England, Robert Frost was born in California and lived there until his father died, when Frost was eleven. The family then moved to New England, where his mother supported them by teaching school. Frost graduated from high school in 1891 in Lawrence, Massachusetts, sharing the post of valedictorian with Elinor White, whom he married three years later. Occasional attendance at Dartmouth College and Harvard, and a variety of different jobs including an attempt to run a farm in Derry, New Hampshire, marked the next twenty years. Frost made a new start in 1912, taking his family, which included four children, to England. There he worked on his poetry and found a publisher for his first book, *A Boy's Will* (1913). Ezra Pound reviewed it favorably, excited (as he put it in a letter) by this "VURRY Amur'k'n talent." Pound recommended Frost's poems to American editors and helped get his second book, *North of Boston*, published in 1914. *North of Boston* was widely praised by critics in America and England when it appeared; the favorable reception persuaded Frost to return home. He bought another farm in New Hampshire and prospered financially through sales of his books and papers, along with teaching and lecturing at various colleges. The success he enjoyed for the rest of his life, however, came too late to cancel the bitterness left by his earlier struggles. Moreover, he endured personal tragedy: a son committed suicide, and a daughter had a complete mental collapse.

The clarity of Frost's diction, the colloquial rhythms, the simplicity of his images, and above all the folksy speaker—these are intended to make the poems look natural, unplanned. In the context of the modernist movement, however, they can be seen as a thoughtful reply to high modernism's fondness for obscurity and difficulty. In addition, by investing in the New England terrain, Frost rejected modernist internationalism and revitalized the tradition of New England regionalism. Readers who accepted Frost's persona and his setting as typically American accepted the powerful myth that rural New England was the heart of America.

Frost played the rhythms of ordinary speech against formal patterns of line and verse and contained them within traditional poetic forms. The interaction of colloquial diction with blank verse is especially central to his dramatic monologues. To Frost traditional forms were the essence of poetry, material with which poets responded to flux and disorder (what, adopting scientific terminology, he called "decay") by forging something permanent. Poetry, he wrote, was "one step backward taken," resisting time—a "momentary stay against confusion."

Throughout the 1920s Frost's poetic practice changed very little; later books—including *Mountain Interval* (1916), *New Hampshire* (1923), and *West-Running Brook* (1928)—confirmed the impression he had created in *North of Boston*. Most of his poems fall into a few types. Nature lyrics describing or commenting on a scene or event—like "Stopping by Woods on a Snowy Evening," "Birches," and "After Apple-Picking"—are probably the best known. There are also dramatic narratives in blank verse about country people, like "The Death of the Hired Man," and poems of commentary or generalization, like "The Gift Outright," which he read at John F. Kennedy's presidential inauguration in 1961. He could also be humorous or sardonic, as in "Fire and Ice." In the nature lyrics, a comparison often emerges between the outer scene and the psyche, a comparison of what Frost in one poem called "outer and inner weather."

Because he presented himself as a New Englander reading a New England landscape, Frost is often interpreted as an ideological descendent of the nineteenth-century American Transcendentalists. But he is far less affirmative about the universe than they; for where they, looking at nature, discerned a benign creator, he saw "no expression, nothing to express." Frost did share with Emerson and Thoreau, however, the belief that collective enterprises could do nothing but weaken the individual self. He avoided political movements precisely because they were movements, group undertakings. In the 1930s he parted company with many American writers by opposing both the social programs of Franklin Roosevelt's New Deal and artistic programs similarly aimed, he thought, at the lessening of social grievances rather than the exploration of enduring human grief. In *A Further Range* (1936), for which he won the third of his four Pulitzer Prizes, Frost invited readers "to a one-man revolution"—the "only revolution that is coming," he declared. Left-leaning critics replied by denouncing the volume's "reactionary" constriction of Frost's poetic voice to that of a head-shaking Yankee skeptic. Frost deeply resented this criticism and responded to it with a newly didactic kind of poetry. In the last twenty years of his life, Frost increased his activities as a teacher and lecturer—at Amherst, at Dartmouth, at Harvard, at the Bread Loaf School of English at Middlebury College in Vermont, and in poetry readings and talks around the country.

The text of the poems included here is that of *The Poetry of Robert Frost* (1969).

The Pasture

I'm going out to clean the pasture spring;
I'll only stop to rake the leaves away
(And wait to watch the water clear, I may):
I shan't be gone long.—You come too.
I'm going out to fetch the little calf   5
That's standing by the mother. It's so young
It totters when she licks it with her tongue.
I shan't be gone long.—You come too.

1913

Mowing

There was never a sound beside the wood but one,
And that was my long scythe whispering to the ground.
What was it it whispered? I knew not well myself;
Perhaps it was something about the heat of the sun,
Something, perhaps, about the lack of sound—   5
And that was why it whispered and did not speak.
It was no dream of the gift of idle hours,
Or easy gold at the hand of fay or elf:
Anything more than the truth would have seemed too weak
To the earnest love that laid the swale[1] in rows,   10

---

1. Grasses in a marshy meadow.

Not without feeble-pointed spikes of flowers
(Pale orchises), and scared a bright green snake.
The fact is the sweetest dream that labor knows.
My long scythe whispered and left the hay to make.

1913

Mending Wall

Something there is that doesn't love a wall,
That sends the frozen-ground-swell under it,
And spills the upper boulders in the sun,
And makes gaps even two can pass abreast.
The work of hunters is another thing: 5
I have come after them and made repair
Where they have left not one stone on a stone,
But they would have the rabbit out of hiding,
To please the yelping dogs. The gaps I mean,
No one has seen them made or heard them made,   10
But at spring mending-time we find them there.
I let my neighbor know beyond the hill;
And on a day we meet to walk the line
And set the wall between us once again.
We keep the wall between us as we go.   15
To each the boulders that have fallen to each.
And some are loaves and some so nearly balls
We have to use a spell to make them balance:
"Stay where you are until our backs are turned!"
We wear our fingers rough with handling them.   20
Oh, just another kind of outdoor game,
One on a side. It comes to little more:
There where it is we do not need the wall:
He is all pine and I am apple orchard.
My apple trees will never get across   25
And eat the cones under his pines, I tell him.
He only says, "Good fences make good neighbors."
Spring is the mischief in me, and I wonder
If I could put a notion in his head:
"*Why* do they make good neighbors? Isn't it   30
Where there are cows? But here there are no cows.
Before I built a wall I'd ask to know
What I was walling in or walling out,
And to whom I was like to give offense.
Something there is that doesn't love a wall,   35
That wants it down." I could say "Elves" to him,
But it's not elves exactly, and I'd rather
He said it for himself. I see him there
Bringing a stone grasped firmly by the top
In each hand, like an old-stone savage armed.   40
He moves in darkness as it seems to me,

Not of woods only and the shade of trees.
He will not go behind his father's saying,
And he likes having thought of it so well
He says again, "Good fences make good neighbors."   45

1914

The Death of the Hired Man

Mary sat musing on the lamp-flame at the table
Waiting for Warren. When she heard his step,
She ran on tip-toe down the darkened passage
To meet him in the doorway with the news
And put him on his guard. "Silas is back."   5
She pushed him outward with her through the door
And shut it after her. "Be kind," she said.
She took the market things from Warren's arms
And set them on the porch, then drew him down
To sit beside her on the wooden steps.   10

"When was I ever anything but kind to him?
But I'll not have the fellow back," he said.
"I told him so last haying, didn't I?
If he left then, I said, that ended it.
What good is he? Who else will harbor him   15
At his age for the little he can do?
What help he is there's no depending on.
Off he goes always when I need him most.
He thinks he ought to earn a little pay,
Enough at least to buy tobacco with,   20
So he won't have to beg and be beholden.
'All right,' I say, 'I can't afford to pay
Any fixed wages, though I wish I could.'
'Someone else can.' 'Then someone else will have to.'
I shouldn't mind his bettering himself   25
If that was what it was. You can be certain,
When he begins like that, there's someone at him
Trying to coax him off with pocket-money,—
In haying time, when any help is scarce.
In winter he comes back to us. I'm done."   30

"Sh! not so loud: he'll hear you," Mary said.

"I want him to: he'll have to soon or late."

"He's worn out. He's asleep beside the stove.
When I came up from Rowe's I found him here,
Huddled against the barn-door fast asleep,   35
A miserable sight, and frightening, too—

You needn't smile—I didn't recognize him—
I wasn't looking for him—and he's changed.
Wait till you see."

      "Where did you say he'd been?"   40

"He didn't say. I dragged him to the house,
And gave him tea and tried to make him smoke.
I tried to make him talk about his travels.
Nothing would do: he just kept nodding off."

"What did he say? Did he say anything?"   45

"But little."

     "Anything? Mary, confess
He said he'd come to ditch the meadow for me."

"Warren!"

    "But did he? I just want to know."   50

"Of course he did. What would you have him say?
Surely you wouldn't grudge the poor old man
Some humble way to save his self-respect.
He added, if you really care to know,
He meant to clear the upper pasture, too.   55
That sounds like something you have heard before?
Warren, I wish you could have heard the way
He jumbled everything. I stopped to look
Two or three times—he made me feel so queer—
To see if he was talking in his sleep.   60
He ran on Harold Wilson—you remember—
The boy you had in haying four years since.
He's finished school, and teaching in his college.
Silas declares you'll have to get him back.
He says they two will make a team for work: 65
Between them they will lay this farm as smooth!
The way he mixed that in with other things.
He thinks young Wilson a likely lad, though daft
On education—you know how they fought
All through July under the blazing sun,   70
Silas up on the cart to build the load,
Harold along beside to pitch it on."

"Yes, I took care to keep well out of earshot."

"Well, those days trouble Silas like a dream.
You wouldn't think they would. How some things linger!   75
Harold's young college-boy's assurance piqued him.
After so many years he still keeps finding

Good arguments he sees he might have used.
I sympathize. I know just how it feels
To think of the right thing to say too late.   80
Harold's associated in his mind with Latin.
He asked me what I thought of Harold's saying
He studied Latin, like the violin,
Because he liked it—that an argument!
He said he couldn't make the boy believe   85
He could find water with a hazel prong—
Which showed how much good school had ever done him.
He wanted to go over that. But most of all
He thinks if he could have another chance
To teach him how to build a load of hay—"   90

"I know, that's Silas' one accomplishment.
He bundles every forkful in its place,
And tags and numbers it for future reference,
So he can find and easily dislodge it
In the unloading. Silas does that well.   95
He takes it out in bunches like big birds' nests.
You never see him standing on the hay
He's trying to lift, straining to lift himself."

"He thinks if he could teach him that, he'd be
Some good perhaps to someone in the world.   100
He hates to see a boy the fool of books.
Poor Silas, so concerned for other folk,
And nothing to look backward to with pride,
And nothing to look forward to with hope,
So now and never any different."   105

Part of a moon was falling down the west,
Dragging the whole sky with it to the hills.
Its light poured softly in her lap. She saw it
And spread her apron to it. She put out her hand
Among the harplike morning-glory strings,   110
Taut with the dew from garden bed to eaves,
As if she played unheard some tenderness
That wrought on him beside her in the night.
"Warren," she said, "he has come home to die:
You needn't be afraid he'll leave you this time."   115

"Home," he mocked gently.

                              "Yes, what else but home?
It all depends on what you mean by home.
Of course he's nothing to us, any more
Than was the hound that came a stranger to us   120
Out of the woods, worn out upon the trail."

"Home is the place where, when you have to go there,
They have to take you in."

                    "I should have called it
Something you somehow haven't to deserve."   125

Warren leaned out and took a step or two,
Picked up a little stick, and brought it back
And broke it in his hand and tossed it by.
"Silas has better claim on us you think
Than on his brother? Thirteen little miles   130
As the road winds would bring him to his door.
Silas has walked that far no doubt today.
Why doesn't he go there? His brother's rich,
A somebody—director in the bank."

"He never told us that."   135

                    "We know it though."

"I think his brother ought to help, of course.
I'll see to that if there is need. He ought of right
To take him in, and might be willing to—
He may be better than appearances.   140
But have some pity on Silas. Do you think
If he had any pride in claiming kin
Or anything he looked for from his brother,
He'd keep so still about him all this time?"

"I wonder what's between them."   145

                    "I can tell you.
Silas is what he is—we wouldn't mind him—
But just the kind that kinsfolk can't abide.
He never did a thing so very bad.
He don't know why he isn't quite as good   150
As anybody. Worthless though he is,
He won't be made ashamed to please his brother."

"I can't think Si ever hurt anyone."

"No, but he hurt my heart the way he lay
And rolled his old head on that sharp-edged chair-back.   155
He wouldn't let me put him on the lounge.
You must go in and see what you can do.
I made the bed up for him there tonight.
You'll be surprised at him—how much he's broken.
His working days are done; I'm sure of it."   160

"I'd not be in a hurry to say that."

"I haven't been. Go, look, see for yourself.
But, Warren, please remember how it is:
He's come to help you ditch the meadow.
He has a plan. You mustn't laugh at him.   165

He may not speak of it, and then he may.
I'll sit and see if that small sailing cloud
Will hit or miss the moon."

         It hit the moon.
Then there were three there, making a dim row,   170
The moon, the little silver cloud, and she.
Warren returned—too soon, it seemed to her,
Slipped to her side, caught up her hand and waited.

"Warren?" she questioned.

            "Dead," was all he answered.   175

                         1914

After Apple-Picking

My long two-pointed ladder's sticking through a tree
Toward heaven still,
And there's a barrel that I didn't fill
Beside it, and there may be two or three
Apples I didn't pick upon some bough.   5
But I am done with apple-picking now.
Essence of winter sleep is on the night,
The scent of apples: I am drowsing off.
I cannot rub the strangeness from my sight
I got from looking through a pane of glass   10
I skimmed this morning from the drinking trough
And held against the world of hoary grass.
It melted, and I let it fall and break.
But I was well
Upon my way to sleep before it fell,   15
And I could tell
What form my dreaming was about to take.
Magnified apples appear and disappear,
Stem end and blossom end,
And every fleck of russet showing clear.   20
My instep arch not only keeps the ache,
It keeps the pressure of a ladder-round.
I feel the ladder sway as the boughs bend.
And I keep hearing from the cellar bin
The rumbling sound   25
Of load on load of apples coming in.
For I have had too much
Of apple-picking: I am overtired
Of the great harvest I myself desired.
There were ten thousand thousand fruit to touch,   30
Cherish in hand, lift down, and not let fall.
For all
That struck the earth,

No matter if not bruised or spiked with stubble,
Went surely to the cider-apple heap 35
As of no worth.
One can see what will trouble
This sleep of mine, whatever sleep it is.
Were he not gone,
The woodchuck could say whether it's like his 40
Long sleep, as I describe its coming on,
Or just some human sleep.

1914

The Wood-Pile

Out walking in the frozen swamp one gray day,
I paused and said, "I will turn back from here.
No, I will go on farther—and we shall see."
The hard snow held me, save where now and then
One foot went through. The view was all in lines 5
Straight up and down of tall slim trees
Too much alike to mark or name a place by
So as to say for certain I was here
Or somewhere else: I was just far from home.
A small bird flew before me. He was careful 10
To put a tree between us when he lighted,
And say no word to tell me who he was
Who was so foolish as to think what *he* thought.
He thought that I was after him for a feather—
The white one in his tail; like one who takes 15
Everything said as personal to himself.
One flight out sideways would have undeceived him.
And then there was a pile of wood for which
I forgot him and let his little fear
Carry him off the way I might have gone, 20
Without so much as wishing him good-night.
He went behind it to make his last stand.
It was a cord of maple, cut and split
And piled—and measured, four by four by eight.
And not another like it could I see. 25
No runner tracks in this year's snow looped near it.
And it was older sure than this year's cutting,
Or even last year's or the year's before.
The wood was gray and the bark warping off it
And the pile somewhat sunken. Clematis 30
Had wound strings round and round it like a bundle.
What held it, though, on one side was a tree
Still growing, and on one a stake and prop,
These latter about to fall. I thought that only
Someone who lived in turning to fresh tasks 35
Could so forget his handiwork on which

He spent himself, the labor of his ax,
And leave it there far from a useful fireplace
To warm the frozen swamp as best it could
With the slow smokeless burning of decay.   40

                                                          1914

The Road Not Taken

Two roads diverged in a yellow wood,
And sorry I could not travel both
And be one traveler, long I stood
And looked down one as far as I could
To where it bent in the undergrowth;   5

Then took the other, as just as fair,
And having perhaps the better claim,
Because it was grassy and wanted wear;
Though as for that, the passing there
Had worn them really about the same,   10

And both that morning equally lay
In leaves no step had trodden black.
Oh, I kept the first for another day!
Yet knowing how way leads on to way,
I doubted if I should ever come back.   15

I shall be telling this with a sigh
Somewhere ages and ages hence:
Two roads diverged in a wood, and I—
I took the one less traveled by,
And that has made all the difference.   20

                                                          1916

Birches

When I see birches bend to left and right
Across the lines of straighter darker trees,
I like to think some boy's been swinging them.
But swinging doesn't bend them down to stay
As ice storms do. Often you must have seen them   5
Loaded with ice a sunny winter morning
After a rain. They click upon themselves
As the breeze rises, and turn many-colored
As the stir cracks and crazes their enamel.
Soon the sun's warmth makes them shed crystal shells   10
Shattering and avalanching on the snow crust—
Such heaps of broken glass to sweep away

You'd think the inner dome of heaven had fallen.
They are dragged to the withered bracken by the load,
And they seem not to break; though once they are bowed   15
So low for long, they never right themselves:
You may see their trunks arching in the woods
Years afterwards, trailing their leaves on the ground
Like girls on hands and knees that throw their hair
Before them over their heads to dry in the sun.   20
But I was going to say when Truth broke in
With all her matter of fact about the ice storm,
I should prefer to have some boy bend them
As he went out and in to fetch the cows—
Some boy too far from town to learn baseball,   25
Whose only play was what he found himself,
Summer or winter, and could play alone.
One by one he subdued his father's trees
By riding them down over and over again
Until he took the stiffness out of them,   30
And not one but hung limp, not one was left
For him to conquer. He learned all there was
To learn about not launching out too soon
And so not carrying the tree away
Clear to the ground. He always kept his poise   35
To the top branches, climbing carefully
With the same pains you use to fill a cup
Up to the brim, and even above the brim.
Then he flung outward, feet first, with a swish,
Kicking his way down through the air to the ground.   40
So was I once myself a swinger of birches.
And so I dream of going back to be.
It's when I'm weary of considerations,
And life is too much like a pathless wood
Where your face burns and tickles with the cobwebs   45
Broken across it, and one eye is weeping
From a twig's having lashed across it open.
I'd like to get away from earth awhile
And then come back to it and begin over.
May no fate willfully misunderstand me   50
And half grant what I wish and snatch me away
Not to return. Earth's the right place for love:
I don't know where it's likely to go better.
I'd like to go by climbing a birch tree,
And climb black branches up a snow-white trunk   55
Toward heaven, till the tree could bear no more,
But dipped its top and set me down again.
That would be good both going and coming back.
One could do worse than be a swinger of birches.

1916

"Out, Out—"[1]

The buzz saw snarled and rattled in the yard
And made dust and dropped stove-length sticks of wood,
Sweet-scented stuff when the breeze drew across it.
And from there those that lifted eyes could count
Five mountain ranges one behind the other   5
Under the sunset far into Vermont.
And the saw snarled and rattled, snarled and rattled,
As it ran light, or had to bear a load.
And nothing happened: day was all but done.
Call it a day, I wish they might have said   10
To please the boy by giving him the half hour
That a boy counts so much when saved from work.
His sister stood beside them in her apron
To tell them "Supper." At the word, the saw,
As if to prove saws knew what supper meant,   15
Leaped out at the boy's hand, or seemed to leap—
He must have given the hand. However it was,
Neither refused the meeting. But the hand!
The boy's first outcry was a rueful laugh,
As he swung toward them holding up the hand,   20
Half in appeal, but half as if to keep
The life from spilling. Then the boy saw all—
Since he was old enough to know, big boy
Doing a man's work, though a child at heart—
He saw all spoiled. "Don't let him cut my hand off—   25
The doctor, when he comes. Don't let him, sister!"
So. But the hand was gone already.
The doctor put him in the dark of ether.
He lay and puffed his lips out with his breath.
And then—the watcher at his pulse took fright.   30
No one believed. They listened at his heart.
Little—less—nothing!—and that ended it.
No more to build on there. And they, since they
Were not the one dead, turned to their affairs.

1916

Fire and Ice

Some say the world will end in fire,
Some say in ice.
From what I've tasted of desire
I hold with those who favor fire.
But if it had to perish twice,   5

---

1. From Shakespeare's *Macbeth* 5.5.23–24: "Out, out, brief candle! / Life's but a walking shadow."

I think I know enough of hate
To say that for destruction ice
Is also great
And would suffice.

1923

Nothing Gold Can Stay

Nature's first green is gold,
Her hardest hue to hold.
Her early leaf's a flower;
But only so an hour.
Then leaf subsides to leaf.   5
So Eden sank to grief,
So dawn goes down to day.
Nothing gold can stay.

1923

Stopping by Woods on a Snowy Evening

Whose woods these are I think I know.
His house is in the village, though;
He will not see me stopping here
To watch his woods fill up with snow.

My little horse must think it queer   5
To stop without a farmhouse near
Between the woods and frozen lake
The darkest evening of the year.

He gives his harness bells a shake
To ask if there is some mistake.   10
The only other sound's the sweep
Of easy wind and downy flake.

The woods are lovely, dark, and deep,
But I have promises to keep,
And miles to go before I sleep.   15
And miles to go before I sleep.

1923

Desert Places

Snow falling and night falling fast, oh, fast
In a field I looked into going past,
And the ground almost covered smooth in snow,
But a few weeds and stubble showing last.

The woods around it have it—it is theirs.   5
All animals are smothered in their lairs.
I am too absent-spirited to count;
The loneliness includes me unawares.

And lonely as it is, that loneliness
Will be more lonely ere it will be less—   10
A blanker whiteness of benighted snow
With no expression, nothing to express.

They cannot scare me with their empty spaces
Between stars—on stars where no human race is.
I have it in me so much nearer home   15
To scare myself with my own desert places.

                                                            1936

Design

I found a dimpled spider, fat and white,
On a white heal-all,[1] holding up a moth
Like a white piece of rigid satin cloth—
Assorted characters of death and blight
Mixed ready to begin the morning right,   5
Like the ingredients of a witches' broth—
A snow-drop spider, a flower like a froth,
And dead wings carried like a paper kite.

What had that flower to do with being white,
The wayside blue and innocent heal-all?   10
What brought the kindred spider to that height,
Then steered the white moth thither in the night?
What but design of darkness to appall?—
If design govern in a thing so small.

                                                      1922, 1936

Neither Out Far Nor In Deep

The people along the sand
All turn and look one way.
They turn their back on the land.
They look at the sea all day.

As long as it takes to pass   5
A ship keeps raising its hull;
The wetter ground like glass
Reflects a standing gull.

1. Common wildflower whose blossom is normally violet or blue.

The land may vary more;
But wherever the truth may be—   10
The water comes ashore,
And the people look at the sea.

They cannot look out far.
They cannot look in deep.
But when was that ever a bar   15
To any watch they keep?

1936

Directive

Back out of all this now too much for us,
Back in a time made simple by the loss
Of detail, burned, dissolved, and broken off
Like graveyard marble sculpture in the weather,
There is a house that is no more a house   5
Upon a farm that is no more a farm
And in a town that is no more a town.
The road there, if you'll let a guide direct you
Who only has at heart your getting lost,
May seem as if it should have been a quarry—   10
Great monolithic knees the former town
Long since gave up pretense of keeping covered.
And there's a story in a book about it:
Besides the wear of iron wagon wheels
The ledges show lines ruled southeast-northwest,   15
The chisel work of an enormous Glacier
That braced his feet against the Arctic Pole.
You must not mind a certain coolness from him
Still said to haunt this side of Panther Mountain.
Nor need you mind the serial ordeal   20
Of being watched from forty cellar holes
As if by eye pairs out of forty firkins.[1]
As for the woods' excitement over you
That sends light rustle rushes to their leaves,
Charge that to upstart inexperience.   25
Where were they all not twenty years ago?
They think too much of having shaded out
A few old pecker-fretted[2] apple trees.
Make yourself up a cheering song of how
Someone's road home from work this once was,   30
Who may be just ahead of you on foot
Or creaking with a buggy load of grain.
The height of the adventure is the height

1. Small wooden tubs for butter or lard.   2. Marked up with small holes by woodpeckers.

Of country where two village cultures faded
Into each other. Both of them are lost.   35
And if you're lost enough to find yourself
By now, pull in your ladder road behind you
And put a sign up closed to all but me.
Then make yourself at home. The only field
Now left's no bigger than a harness gall.[3]   40
First there's the children's house of make-believe,
Some shattered dishes underneath a pine,
The playthings in the playhouse of the children.
Weep for what little things could make them glad.
Then for the house that is no more a house,   45
But only a belilaced cellar hole,
Now slowly closing like a dent in dough.
This was no playhouse but a house in earnest.
Your destination and your destiny's
A brook that was the water of the house,   50
Cold as a spring as yet so near its source,
Too lofty and original to rage.
(We know the valley streams that when aroused
Will leave their tatters hung on barb and thorn.)
I have kept hidden in the instep arch   55
Of an old cedar at the waterside
A broken drinking goblet like the Grail[4]
Under a spell so the wrong ones can't find it,
So can't get saved, as Saint Mark[5] says they mustn't.
(I stole the goblet from the children's playhouse.)   60
Here are your waters and your watering place.
Drink and be whole again beyond confusion.

1947

3. Sore on a horse's skin caused by the rubbing of the harness.
4. The cup used by Jesus at the Last Supper. According to legend, the Grail later disappeared from its keepers because of their moral impurity, and various knights, including those of King Arthur's Round Table, went in quest of it. From this, the quest for the Grail has come to symbolize any spiritual search.
5. A reference to Mark 4.11–12; see also Mark 16.16.

SUSAN GLASPELL
1876–1948

S usan Glaspell—journalist, novelist, short-story writer, playwright, theatrical producer and director, actor—was a multitalented professional who eventually published more than fifty short stories, nine novels, and fourteen plays. Feminist rediscovery of *Trifles*, her first play—written and produced in 1916 and turned into a prize-winning short story, "A Jury of Her Peers," in 1917—has made this her best-known work today.

Born and raised in Davenport, Iowa, Glaspell worked for a year on the Davenport *Morning Republican* after high school graduation, then attended Drake University in Des Moines from 1895 to 1899. In college she wrote for the campus newspaper as well as various Des Moines papers; after graduation she worked for two years on the Des Moines *Daily News*. In 1901 she abandoned journalism, returning to Davenport with a plan to earn her living as a fiction writer. Her early stories, combining regional midwestern settings with romantic plots, found favor with the editors of such popular magazines as *Harper's*, the *Ladies' Home Journal*, the *American Magazine*, and the *Woman's Home Companion*. In 1909 she published her first novel, *The Glory of the Conquered*.

In 1913 she married the recently divorced George Cram Cook, a Harvard-educated native of Davenport, who was a writer and theatrical director much interested in modernist experimentation. The two moved to the East Coast, traveled widely, and collaborated on many projects. They helped found both the Washington Square Players in 1914 and the group that came to be known as the Provincetown Players in 1916.

The Provincetown Players, named for the New England seaport town where many of the members spent their summers, aimed to foster an American theater by producing plays by American playwrights only. Eugene O'Neill became the best-known dramatist of the group; Glaspell was a close second. She not only wrote plays but also acted in them, directed them, and helped produce them. From 1916 to 1922 she wrote nine plays, including *Trifles*, for the Provincetown Players; in 1922 Cook and Glaspell withdrew from the group, finding that it had become too commercially successful to suit their experimental aims.

Cook died in 1924; a later close relationship, with the novelist and playwright Norman Matson, ended in 1932. Throughout the 1930s and 1940s, Glaspell, now a year-round resident of Provincetown, continued to write and publish. Her novel *Judd Rankin's Wife* (1928) was made into a movie. She won the 1930 Pulitzer Prize for drama for *Alison's Room*, a play loosely based on the life of Emily Dickinson. Her last novel, *Judd Rankin's Daughter*, appeared in 1945, three years before she died at the age of seventy-two.

For Glaspell, the influence of such European playwrights as Henrik Ibsen and August Strindberg opened the door to much grimmer writing in a play like *Trifles* than in her popular short stories, with their formulaic happy endings. Her realism—her unsparing depiction of women's narrow, thwarted, isolated, and subjugated lives in rural, regional settings—produces effects unlike the nostalgic celebrations of woman-centered societies often associated with women regionalists. The efficiently plotted *Trifles* also features a formal device found in other Glaspell works, including *Alison's Room*: the main character at its center never appears.

The text is from *Plays by Susan Glaspell* (1987).

Trifles

CHARACTERS

GEORGE HENDERSON, *County Attorney*
HENRY PETERS, *Sheriff*
LEWIS HALE, *a Neighboring Farmer*
MRS PETERS
MRS HALE

SCENE: *The kitchen in the now abandoned farmhouse of* John Wright, *a gloomy kitchen, and left without having been put in order—unwashed pans under the sink, a loaf of bread outside the bread-box, a dish-towel on the table—other signs of incompleted work. At the rear the outer door opens and the* SHERIFF *comes in followed by the* COUNTY ATTORNEY *and* HALE. *The* SHERIFF *and* HALE *are men in middle life, the* COUNTY ATTORNEY *is a young man; all are much bundled up and go at once to the stove. They are followed by the two women—the* SHERIFF'S *wife first; she is a slight wiry woman, a thin nervous face.* MRS HALE *is larger and would ordinarily be called more comfortable looking, but she is disturbed now and looks fearfully about as she enters. The women have come in slowly, and stand close together near the door.*

COUNTY ATTORNEY [*rubbing his hands*]   This feels good. Come up to the fire, ladies.

MRS PETERS [*after taking a step forward*]   I'm not—cold.

SHERIFF [*unbuttoning his overcoat and stepping away from the stove as if to mark the beginning of official business*]   Now, Mr Hale, before we move things about, you explain to Mr Henderson just what you saw when you came here yesterday morning.

COUNTY ATTORNEY   By the way, has anything been moved? Are things just as you left them yesterday?

SHERIFF [*looking about*]   It's just the same. When it dropped below zero last night I thought I'd better send Frank out this morning to make a fire for us—no use getting pneumonia with a big case on, but I told him not to touch anything except the stove—and you know Frank.

COUNTY ATTORNEY   Somebody should have been left here yesterday.

SHERIFF   Oh—yesterday. When I had to send Frank to Morris Center for that man who went crazy—I want you to know I had my hands full yesterday. I knew you could get back from Omaha by today and as long as I went over everything here myself—

COUNTY ATTORNEY   Well, Mr Hale, tell just what happened when you came here yesterday morning.

HALE   Harry and I had started to town with a load of potatoes. We came along the road from my place and as I got here I said, 'I'm going to see if I can't get John Wright to go in with me on a party telephone.'[1] I spoke to Wright about it once before and he put me off, saying folks talked too much anyway, and all he asked was peace and quiet—I guess you know about how much he talked himself; but I thought maybe if I went to the house and talked about it before his wife, though I said to Harry that I didn't know as what his wife wanted made much difference to John—

COUNTY ATTORNEY   Let's talk about that later, Mr Hale. I do want to talk about that, but tell now just what happened when you got to the house.

HALE   I didn't hear or see anything; I knocked at the door, and still it was all quiet inside. I knew they must be up, it was past eight o'clock. So I knocked again, and I thought I heard somebody say, 'Come in.' I wasn't sure. I'm not sure yet, but I opened the door—this door [*indicating the door by which the two women are still standing*] and there in that rocker— [*pointing to it*] sat Mrs Wright.
    [*They all look at the rocker.*]

---

1. A single telephone line shared by several households.

COUNTY ATTORNEY What—was she doing?

HALE She was rockin' back and forth. She had her apron in her hand and was kind of—pleating it.

COUNTY ATTORNEY And how did she—look?

HALE Well, she looked queer.

COUNTY ATTORNEY How do you mean—queer?

HALE Well, as if she didn't know what she was going to do next. And kind of done up.

COUNTY ATTORNEY How did she seem to feel about your coming?

HALE Why, I don't think she minded—one way or other. She didn't pay much attention. I said. 'How do. Mrs Wright it's cold, ain't it?' And she said, 'Is it?'—and went on kind of pleating at her apron. Well, I was surprised: she didn't ask me to come up to the stove, or to set down, but just sat there, not even looking at me, so I said, 'I want to see John.' And then she—laughed. I guess you would call it a laugh. I thought of Harry and the team outside, so I said a little sharp: 'Can't I see John?' 'No,' she says, kind o' dull like. 'Ain't he home?' says I. 'Yes,' says she, 'he's home.' 'Then why can't I see him?' I asked her, out of patience. ''Cause he's dead,' says she. '*Dead?*' says I. She just nodded her head, not getting a bit excited, but rockin' back and forth. 'Why—where is he?' says I, not knowing what to say. She just pointed upstairs—like that [*himself pointing to the room above*] I got up, with the idea of going up there. I walked from there to here—then I says, 'Why, what did he die of?' 'He died of a rope round his neck,' says she, and just went on pleatin' at her apron. Well, I went out and called Harry. I thought I might—need help. We went upstairs and there he was lyin'—

COUNTY ATTORNEY I think I'd rather have you go into that upstairs, where you can point it all out. Just go on now with the rest of the story.

HALE Well, my first thought was to get that rope off. It looked . . . [*stops, his face twitches*] . . . but Harry, he went up to him, and he said, 'No, he's dead all right, and we'd better not touch anything.' So we went back down stairs. She was still sitting that same way. 'Has anybody been notified?' I asked. 'No,' says she unconcerned. 'Who did this, Mrs Wright?' said Harry. He said it business-like—and she stopped pleatin' of her apron. 'I don't know,' she says. 'You don't *know*?' says Harry. 'No,' says she. 'Weren't you sleepin' in the bed with him?' says Harry. 'Yes,' says she, 'but I was on the inside.' 'Somebody slipped a rope round his neck and strangled him and you didn't wake up?' says Harry. 'I didn't wake up,' she said after him. We must 'a looked as if we didn't see how that could be, for after a minute she said, 'I sleep sound.' Harry was going to ask her more questions but I said maybe we ought to let her tell her story first to the coroner, or the sheriff, so Harry went fast as he could to Rivers' place, where there's a telephone.

COUNTY ATTORNEY And what did Mrs Wright do when she knew that you had gone for the coroner?

HALE She moved from that chair to this one over here [*pointing to a small chair in the corner*] and just sat there with her hands held together and looking down. I got a feeling that I ought to make some conversation, so I said I had come in to see if John wanted to put in a telephone, and at that she started to laugh, and then she stopped and looked at me—scared. [*the* COUNTY ATTORNEY, *who has had his notebook out, makes a note*] I dunno, maybe it wasn't scared. I wouldn't like to say it was. Soon Harry got back, and then Dr Lloyd came, and you, Mr Peters, and so I guess that's all I know that you don't.

COUNTY ATTORNEY [*looking around*] I guess we'll go upstairs first—and then out to the barn and around there. [*to the* SHERIFF] You're convinced that there was nothing important here—nothing that would point to any motive.

SHERIFF Nothing here but kitchen things.

> [*The* COUNTY ATTORNEY, *after again looking around the kitchen, opens the door of a cupboard closet. He gets up on a chair and looks on a shelf. Pulls his hand away, sticky.*]

COUNTY ATTORNEY Here's a nice mess.

> [*The women draw nearer.*]

MRS PETERS [*to the other woman*] Oh, her fruit: it did freeze. [*to the* LAWYER] She worried about that when it turned so cold. She said the fire'd go out and her jars would break.

SHERIFF Well, can you beat the women! Held for murder and worryin' about her preserves.

COUNTY ATTORNEY I guess before we're through she may have something more serious than preserves to worry about.

HALE Well, women are used to worrying over trifles.

> [*The two women move a little closer together.*]

COUNTY ATTORNEY [*with the gallantry of a young politician*] And yet, for all their worries, what would we do without the ladies? [*the women do not unbend. He goes to the sink, takes a dipperful of water from the pail and pouring it into a basin, washes his hands. Starts to wipe them on the roller-towel, turns it for a cleaner place*] Dirty towels! [*kicks his foot against the pans under the sink*] Not much of a housekeeper, would you say, ladies?

MRS HALE [*stiffly*] There's a great deal of work to be done on a farm.

COUNTY ATTORNEY To be sure. And yet [*with a little bow to her*] I know there are some Dickson county farmhouses which do not have such roller towels.

> [*He gives it a pull to expose its length again.*]

MRS HALE Those towels get dirty awful quick. Men's hands aren't always as clean as they might be.

COUNTY ATTORNEY Ah, loyal to your sex. I see. But you and Mrs Wright were neighbors. I suppose you were friends, too.

MRS HALE [*shaking her head*] I've not seen much of her of late years. I've not been in this house—it's more than a year.

COUNTY ATTORNEY And why was that? You didn't like her?

MRS HALE I liked her all well enough. Farmers' wives have their hands full, Mr Henderson. And then—

COUNTY ATTORNEY Yes—?

MRS HALE [*looking about*] It never seemed a very cheerful place.

COUNTY ATTORNEY No—it's not cheerful. I shouldn't say she had the homemaking instinct.

MRS HALE Well, I don't know as Wright had, either.

COUNTY ATTORNEY You mean that they didn't get on very well?

MRS HALE   No. I don't mean anything. But I don't think a place'd be any cheerfuller for John Wright's being in it.

COUNTY ATTORNEY   I'd like to talk more of that a little later. I want to get the lay of things upstairs now.

[*He goes to the left, where three steps lead to a stair door.*]

SHERIFF   I suppose anything Mrs Peters does'll be all right. She was to take in some clothes for her, you know, and a few little things. We left in such a hurry yesterday.

COUNTY ATTORNEY   Yes, but I would like to see what you take, Mrs Peters, and keep an eye out for anything that might be of use to us.

MRS PETERS   Yes, Mr Henderson.

[*The women listen to the men's steps on the stairs, then look about the kitchen.*]

MRS HALE   I'd hate to have men coming into my kitchen, snooping around and criticising.

[*She arranges the pans under sink which the* lawyer *had shoved out of place.*]

MRS PETERS   Of course it's no more than their duty.

MRS HALE   Duty's all right, but I guess that deputy sheriff that came out to make the fire might have got a little of this on. [*gives the roller towel a pull*] Wish I'd thought of that sooner. Seems mean to talk about her for not having things slicked up when she had to come away in such a hurry.

MRS PETERS [*who has gone to a small table in the left rear corner of the room, and lifted one end of a towel that covers a pan*]   She had bread set. [*Stands still.*]

MRS HALE [*eyes fixed on a loaf of bread beside the bread-box, which is on a low shelf at the other side of the room. Moves slowly toward it*]   She was going to put this in there. [*picks up loaf, then abruptly drops it. In a manner of returning to familiar things*] It's a shame about her fruit. I wonder if it's all gone. [*gets up on the chair and looks*] I think there's some here that's all right, Mrs Peters. Yes—here; [*holding it toward the window*] this is cherries, too. [*looking again*] I declare I believe that's the only one. [*gets down, bottle in her hand. Goes to the sink and wipes it off on the outside*] She'll feel awful bad after all her hard work in the hot weather. I remember the afternoon I put up my cherries last summer.

[*She puts the bottle on the big kitchen table, center of the room. With a sigh, is about to sit down in the rocking-chair. Before she is seated realizes what chair it is; with a slow look at it, steps back. The chair which she has touched rocks back and forth.*]

MRS PETERS   Well, I must get those things from the front room closet. [*she goes to the door at the right, but after looking into the other room, steps back*] You coming with me, Mrs Hale? You could help me carry them.

[*They go in the other room; reappear,* MRS PETERS *carrying a dress and skirt,* MRS HALE *following with a pair of shoes.*]

MRS PETERS   My, it's cold in there.

[*She puts the clothes on the big table and hurries to the stove.*]

MRS HALE [*examining the skirt*]   Wright was close.[2] I think maybe that's why she kept so much to herself. She didn't even belong to the Ladies Aid.

2. Miserly.

I suppose she felt she couldn't do her part, and then you don't enjoy things when you feel shabby. She used to wear pretty clothes and be lively, when she was Minnie Foster, one of the town girls singing in the choir. But that—oh, that was thirty years ago. This all you was to take in?

MRS PETERS   She said she wanted an apron. Funny thing to want, for there isn't much to get you dirty in jail, goodness knows. But I suppose just to make her feel more natural. She said they was in the top drawer in this cupboard. Yes, here. And then her little shawl that always hung behind the door. [*opens stair door and looks*] Yes, here it is.
   [*Quickly shuts door leading upstairs.*]

MRS HALE [*abruptly moving toward her*]   Mrs Peters?

MRS PETERS   Yes, Mrs Hale?

MRS HALE   Do you think she did it?

MRS PETERS [*in a frightened voice*]   Oh, I don't know.

MRS HALE   Well, I don't think she did. Asking for an apron and her little shawl. Worrying about her fruit.

MRS PETERS [*starts to speak, glances up, where footsteps are heard in the room above. In a low voice*]   Mr Peters says it looks bad for her. Mr Henderson is awful sarcastic in a speech and he'll make fun of her sayin' she didn't wake up.

MRS HALE   Well, I guess John Wright didn't wake when they was slipping that rope under his neck.

MRS PETERS   No, it's strange. It must have been done awful crafty and still. They say it was such a—funny way to kill a man, rigging it all up like that.

MRS HALE   That's just what Mr Hale said. There was a gun in the house. He says that's what he can't understand.

MRS PETERS   Mr Henderson said coming out that what was needed for the case was a motive; something to show anger, or—sudden feeling.

MRS HALE [*who is standing by the table*]   Well, I don't see any signs of anger around here. [*she puts her hand on the dish-towel which lies on the table, stands looking down at table, one half of which is clean, the other half messy*] It's wiped to here. [*makes a move as if to finish work, then turns and looks at loaf of bread outside the bread-box. Drops towel. In that voice of coming back to familiar things.*] Wonder how they are finding things upstairs. I hope she had it a little more red-up[3] up there. You know, it seems kind of *sneaking*. Locking her up in town and then coming out here and trying to get her own house to turn against her!

MRS PETERS   But Mrs Hale, the law is the law.

MRS HALE   I s'pose 'tis. [*unbuttoning her coat*] Better loosen up your things, Mrs Peters. You won't feel them when you go out.
   [MRS PETERS *takes off her fur tippet,[4] goes to hang it on hook at back of room, stands looking at the under part of the small corner table.*]

MRS PETERS   She was piecing a quilt.
   [*She brings the large sewing basket and they look at the bright pieces.*]

MRS HALE   It's log cabin pattern. Pretty, isn't it? I wonder if she was goin' to quilt it or just knot it?

---

3. Tidy.

4. Short cape, falling just below the shoulders.

[*Footsteps have been heard coming down the stairs. The* SHERIFF *enters followed by* HALE *and the* COUNTY ATTORNEY.]

SHERIFF   They wonder if she was going to quilt it or just knot it!

[*The men laugh, the women look abashed.*]

COUNTY ATTORNEY [*rubbing his hands over the stove*]   Frank's fire didn't do much up there, did it? Well, let's go out to the barn and get that cleared up.

[*The men go outside.*]

MRS HALE [*resentfully*]   I don't know as there's anything so strange, our takin' up our time with little things while we're waiting for them to get the evidence. [*she sits down at the big table smoothing out a block with decision*] I don't see as it's anything to laugh about.

MRS PETERS [*apologetically*]   Of course they've got awful important things on their minds.

[*Pulls up a chair and joins* MRS HALE *at the table.*]

MRS HALE [*examining another block*]   Mrs Peters, look at this one. Here, this is the one she was working on, and look at the sewing! All the rest of it has been so nice and even. And look at this! It's all over the place! Why, it looks as if she didn't know what she was about!

[*After she has said this they look at each other, then start to glance back at the door. After an instant* MRS HALE *has pulled at a knot and ripped the sewing.*]

MRS PETERS   Oh, what are you doing, Mrs Hale?

MRS HALE [*mildly*]   Just pulling out a stitch or two that's not sewed very good. [*threading a needle*] Bad sewing always made me fidgety.

MRS PETERS [*nervously*]   I don't think we ought to touch things.

MRS HALE   I'll just finish up this end. [*suddenly stopping and leaning forward*] Mrs Peters?

MRS PETERS   Yes, Mrs Hale?

MRS HALE   What do you suppose she was so nervous about?

MRS PETERS   Oh—I don't know. I don't know as she was nervous. I sometimes sew awful queer when I'm just tired. [MRS HALE *starts to say something, looks at* MRS PETERS, *then goes on sewing*] Well I must get these things wrapped up. They may be through sooner than we think. [*putting apron and other things together*] I wonder where I can find a piece of paper, and string.

MRS HALE   In that cupboard, maybe.

MRS PETERS [*looking in cupboard*]   Why, here's a bird-cage. [*holds it up*] Did she have a bird, Mrs Hale?

MRS HALE   Why, I don't know whether she did or not—I've not been here for so long. There was a man around last year selling canaries cheap, but I don't know as she took one; maybe she did. She used to sing real pretty herself.

MRS PETERS [*glancing around*]   Seems funny to think of a bird here. But she must have had one, or why would she have a cage? I wonder what happened to it.

MRS HALE   I s'pose maybe the cat got it.

MRS PETERS   No, she didn't have a cat. She's got that feeling some people have about cats—being afraid of them. My cat got in her room and she was real upset and asked me to take it out.

MRS HALE   My sister Bessie was like that. Queer, ain't it?

MRS PETERS [*examining the cage*]   Why, look at this door. It's broke. One hinge is pulled apart.

MRS HALE [*looking too*]   Looks as if someone must have been rough with it.

MRS PETERS   Why, yes.

[*She brings the cage forward and puts it on the table.*]

MRS HALE   I wish if they're going to find any evidence they'd be about it. I don't like this place.

MRS PETERS   But I'm awful glad you came with me, Mrs Hale. It would be lonesome for me sitting here alone.

MRS HALE   It would, wouldn't it? [*dropping her sewing*] But I tell you what I do wish, Mrs Peters. I wish I had come over sometimes when *she* was here. I—[*looking around the room*]—wish I had.

MRS PETERS   But of course you were awful busy. Mrs Hale—your house and your children.

MRS HALE   I could've come. I stayed away because it weren't cheerful—and that's why I ought to have come. I—I've never liked this place. Maybe because it's down in a hollow and you don't see the road. I dunno what it is, but it's a lonesome place and always was. I wish I had come over to see Minnie Foster sometimes. I can see now—[*shakes her head*]

MRS PETERS   Well, you mustn't reproach yourself, Mrs Hale. Somehow we just don't see how it is with other folks until—something comes up.

MRS HALE   Not having children makes less work—but it makes a quiet house, and Wright out to work all day, and no company when he did come in. Did you know John Wright, Mrs Peters?

MRS PETERS   Not to know him; I've seen him in town. They say he was a good man.

MRS HALE   Yes—good; he didn't drink, and kept his word as well as most, I guess, and paid his debts. But he was a hard man, Mrs Peters. Just to pass the time of day with him—[*shivers*] Like a raw wind that gets to the bone. [*pauses, her eye falling on the cage*] I should think she would a wanted a bird. But what do you suppose went with it?

MRS PETERS   I don't know, unless it got sick and died.

[*She reaches over and swings the broken door, swings it again, both women watch it.*]

MRS HALE   You weren't raised round here, were you? [MRS PETERS *shakes her head*] You didn't know—her?

MRS PETERS   Not till they brought her yesterday.

MRS HALE   She—come to think of it, she was kind of like a bird herself—real sweet and pretty, but kind of timid and—fluttery. How—she—did—change. [*silence: then as if struck by a happy thought and relieved to get back to everyday things*] Tell you what, Mrs Peters, why don't you take the quilt in with you? It might take up her mind.

MRS PETERS   Why, I think that's a real nice idea, Mrs Hale. There couldn't possibly be any objection to it, could there? Now, just what would I take? I wonder if her patches are in here—and her things.

[*They look in the sewing basket.*]

MRS HALE   Here's some red. I expect this has got sewing things in it. [*brings out a fancy box*] What a pretty box. Looks like something somebody would give you. Maybe her scissors are in here. [*Opens box. Suddenly puts her hand to her nose*] Why—[MRS PETERS *bends nearer, then turns her face away*] There's something wrapped up in this piece of silk.

MRS PETERS   Why, this isn't her scissors.

MRS HALE [*lifting the silk*]   Oh, Mrs Peters—it's—
    [MRS PETERS *bends closer.*]

MRS PETERS   It's the bird.

MRS HALE [*jumping up*]   But, Mrs Peters—look at it! It's neck! Look at its neck! It's all—other side *to*.

MRS PETERS   Somebody—wrung—its—neck.
    [*Their eyes meet. A look of growing comprehension, of horror. Steps are heard outside.* MRS HALE *slips box under quilt pieces, and sinks into her chair. Enter* SHERIFF *and* COUNTY ATTORNEY. MRS PETERS *rises.*]

COUNTY ATTORNEY [*as one turning from serious things to little pleasantries*]   Well ladies, have you decided whether she was going to quilt it or knot it?

MRS PETERS   We think she was going to—knot it.

COUNTY ATTORNEY   Well, that's interesting, I'm sure. [*seeing the bird-cage*] Has the bird flown?

MRS HALE [*putting more quilt pieces over the box*]   We think the—cat got it.

COUNTY ATTORNEY [*preoccupied*]   Is there a cat?
    [MRS HALE *glances in a quick covert way at* MRS PETERS.]

MRS PETERS   Well, not *now*. They're superstitious, you know. They leave.

COUNTY ATTORNEY [*to* SHERIFF PETERS, *continuing an interrupted conversation*]   No sign at all of anyone having come from the outside. Their own rope. Now let's go up again and go over it piece by piece. [*they start upstairs*] It would have to have been someone who knew just the—
    [MRS PETERS *sits down. The two women sit there not looking at one another, but as if peering into something and at the same time holding back. When they talk now it is in the manner of feeling their way over strange ground, as if afraid of what they are saying, but as if they can not help saying it.*]

MRS HALE   She liked the bird. She was going to bury it in that pretty box.

MRS PETERS [*in a whisper*]   When I was a girl—my kitten—there was a boy took a hatchet, and before my eyes—and before I could get there—[*covers her face an instant*] If they hadn't held me back I would have—[*catches herself, looks upstairs where steps are heard, falters weakly*]—hurt him.

MRS HALE [*with a slow look around her*]   I wonder how it would seem never to have had any children around. [*pause*] No, Wright wouldn't like the bird—a thing that sang. She used to sing. He killed that, too.

MRS PETERS [*moving uneasily*]   We don't know who killed the bird.

MRS HALE   I knew John Wright.

MRS PETERS   It was an awful thing was done in this house that night, Mrs Hale. Killing a man while he slept, slipping a rope around his neck that choked the life out of him.

MRS HALE   His neck. Choked the life out of him.
    [*Her hand goes out and rests on the bird-cage.*]

MRS PETERS [*with rising voice*]   We don't know who killed him. We don't *know*.

MRS HALE [*her own feeling not interrupted*] If there'd been years and years of nothing, then a bird to sing to you, it would be awful—still, after the bird was still.

MRS PETERS [*something within her speaking*] I know what stillness is. When we homesteaded in Dakota, and my first baby died—after he was two years old, and me with no other then—

MRS HALE [*moving*] How soon do you suppose they'll be through, looking for the evidence?

MRS PETERS I know what stillness is. [*pulling herself back*] The law has got to punish crime, Mrs Hale.

MRS HALE [*not as if answering that*] I wish you'd seen Minnie Foster when she wore a white dress with blue ribbons and stood up there in the choir and sang. [*a look around the room*] Oh, I *wish* I'd come over here once in a while! That was a crime! That was a crime! Who's going to punish that?

MRS PETERS [*looking upstairs*] We mustn't—take on.

MRS HALE I might have known she needed help! I know how things can be—for women. I tell you, it's queer. Mrs Peters. We live close together and we live far apart. We all go through the same things—it's all just a different kind of the same thing. [*brushes her eyes, noticing the bottle of fruit, reaches out for it*] If I was you, I wouldn't tell her her fruit was gone. Tell her it *ain't*. Tell her it's all right. Take this in to prove it to her. She—she may never know whether it was broke or not.

MRS PETERS [*takes the bottle, looks about for something to wrap it in; takes petticoat from the clothes brought from the other room, very nervously begins winding this around the bottle. In a false voice*] My, it's a good thing the men couldn't hear us. Wouldn't they just laugh! Getting all stirred up over a little thing like a—dead canary. As if that could have anything to do with—with—wouldn't they *laugh!*

[*The men are heard coming down stairs.*]

MRS HALE [*under her breath*] Maybe they would—maybe they wouldn't.

COUNTY ATTORNEY No, Peters, it's all perfectly clear except a reason for doing it. But you know juries when it comes to women. If there was some definite thing. Something to show—something to make a story about—a thing that would connect up with this strange way of doing it—

[*The women's eyes meet for an instant. Enter* HALE *from outer door.*]

HALE Well. I've got the team around. Pretty cold out there.

COUNTY ATTORNEY I'm going to stay here a while by myself. [*to the* SHERIFF] You can send Frank out for me, can't you? I want to go over everything. I'm not satisfied that we can't do better.

SHERIFF Do you want to see what Mrs Peters is going to take in?

[*The* LAWYER *goes to the table, picks up the apron, laughs.*]

COUNTY ATTORNEY Oh, I guess they're not very dangerous things the ladies have picked out. [*Moves a few things about, disturbing the quilt pieces which cover the box. Steps back*] No, Mrs Peters doesn't need supervising. For that matter, a sheriff's wife is married to the law. Ever think of it that way, Mrs Peters?

MRS PETERS Not—just that way.

SHERIFF [*chuckling*]   Married to the law. [*moves toward the other room*] I just want you to come in here a minute, George. We ought to take a look at these windows.

COUNTY ATTORNEY [*scoffingly*]   Oh, windows!

SHERIFF   We'll be right out, Mr Hale.

> [HALE *goes outside. The* SHERIFF *follows the* COUNTY ATTORNEY *into the other room. Then* MRS HALE *rises, hands tight together, looking intensely at* MRS PETERS, *whose eyes make a slow turn, finally meeting* MRS HALE's. *A moment* MRS HALE *holds her, then her own eyes point the way to where the box is concealed. Suddenly* MRS PETERS *throws back quilt pieces and tries to put the box in the bag she is wearing. It is too big. She opens box, starts to take bird out, cannot touch it, goes to pieces, stands there helpless. Sound of a knob turning in the other room.* MRS HALE *snatches the box and puts it in the pocket of her big coat. Enter* COUNTY ATTORNEY *and* SHERIFF.]

COUNTY ATTORNEY [*facetiously*]   Well, Henry, at least we found out that she was not going to quilt it. She was going to—what is it you call it, ladies?

MRS HALE [*her hand against her pocket*]   We call it—knot it, Mr Henderson.

CURTAIN

1916

SHERWOOD ANDERSON
1876–1941

S herwood Anderson was approaching middle age when he abandoned a successful business career to become a writer. Living in Chicago, New Orleans, and Paris, meeting literary people, he worked furiously to make up for his late start, producing novels, short stories, essays, and an autobiography. His short fiction provided a model for younger writers, whose careers he encouraged by literary advice and by practical help in getting published as well. *Winesburg, Ohio,* which appeared in 1919 when he was forty-three years old, remains a major work of experimental fiction and was in its time a bold treatment of small-town life in the American Midwest in the tradition of Edgar Lee Masters's *Spoon River Anthology.*

Anderson was born in southern Ohio, the third of seven children in a family headed by a father whose training and skill as a harness maker were becoming useless in the new world of the automobile. Anderson's father kept his family on the move in search of work; the stamina and tenderness of his mother supplied coherence and security in this nomadic life. Not until 1892, when Anderson was sixteen, did they settle down in the town of Clyde, Ohio, which became the model for Winesburg. Anderson never finished high school. He held a variety of jobs, living in Chicago with an older brother in 1896 and again in 1900 when he worked as an advertising copywriter.

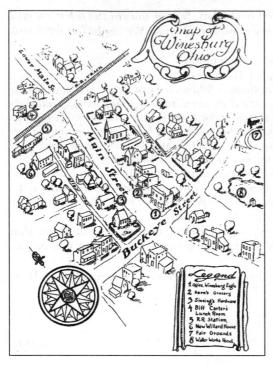

Winesburg, Ohio, Harald Toksvig, 1919. Toksvig's map was printed in the first edition of *Winesburg, Ohio.*

His first wife came from a successful Ohio business family; the couple settled in Ohio where Anderson managed a mail-order house as well as two paint firms. But he found increasingly that the need to write conflicted with his career. In 1912 he left his business and his marriage, returning to Chicago, where he met the writers and artists whose activities were creating the Chicago Renaissance. These included the novelists Floyd Dell and Theodore Dreiser; the poets Edgar Lee Masters, Vachel Lindsay, and Carl Sandburg; and the editors Harriet Monroe of *Poetry* and Margaret C. Anderson of the *Little Review.* His first major publication was *Windy McPherson's Son* (1916), the story of a man who runs away from a small Iowa town in futile search for life's meaning; his second was *Marching Men* (1917), about a charismatic lawyer who tries—unsuccessfully—to reorganize the factory system in a small town. These books reveal three of Anderson's preoccupations: the individual quest for self and social betterment, the small-town environment, and the distrust of modern industrial society. Missing, however, is the interest in human psychology and the sense of conflict between inner and outer worlds that appear in *Winesburg* and later works.

In 1916 Anderson began writing and publishing the tales that were brought together in *Winesburg, Ohio.* The formal achievement of the book lay in its articulation of individual tales to a loose but coherent structure. The lives of a number of people living in the town of Winesburg are observed by the naïve adolescent George Willard, a reporter for the local newspaper. Their stories contribute to his understanding of life and to his preparation for a career as a writer. The book ends when his mother dies and he leaves Winesburg. With the help of the narrator, whose vision is larger than George's, the reader can see how the lives of the characters have been profoundly distorted by the frustration and suppression of so many of their desires. Anderson calls these characters "grotesques," but the intention of *Winesburg, Ohio* is to show that life in all American small towns is grotesque in the same way. Anderson's attitude toward the characters mixes compassion for the individual with dismay at a social order that can do so much damage. His criticism is not specifically political, however; he is measuring society by a utopian standard of free emotional and sensual expression.

Stylistically Anderson strove for the simplest possible prose, using brief or at least uncomplex sentences and an unsophisticated vocabulary appropriate to the muffled awareness and limited resources of his typical characters. Structurally, his stories build toward a moment when the character breaks out in some frenzied gesture of release that is revelatory of a hidden inner life. In both style and structure Anderson's works were important influences on other writers: he encouraged simplicity and directness of style, made attractive the use of the point of view of outsider characters as a way of criticizing conventional society, and gave the craft of the short story a decided push toward stories presenting a slice of life or a significant moment as opposed to panorama and summary.

Winesburg, Ohio appeared near the beginning of Anderson's literary career, and although he continued writing for two decades, he never repeated its success. His best later work was in short stories, published in three volumes: *The Triumph of the Egg* (1921), *Horses and Men* (1923), and *Death in the Woods and Other Stories* (1933). He also wrote a number of novels, including *Poor White* (1920), *Many Marriages* (1923), *Beyond Desire* (1932), and *Kit Brandon* (1936), as well as free verse, prose poems, plays, and essays. A series of autobiographical volumes advertised his career, attempted to define the writer's vocation in America, and discussed his impact on other writers. The more he claimed, however, the less other writers were willing to allow him; both Hemingway and Faulkner, for example, whom he had met in Chicago and New Orleans, respectively, satirized his cult of the simple and thereby disavowed his influence. (In fact, he *had* stimulated and helped both of them—stimulated Hemingway in his quest for stylistic simplicity, Faulkner in his search for the proper subject matter.) During the 1930s Anderson, along with many other writers, was active in liberal causes, and he died at sea on the way to South America while on a goodwill mission for the State Department.

The text is that of *Winesburg, Ohio* (1919).

From Winesburg, Ohio

Hands

Upon the half decayed veranda of a small frame house that stood near the edge of a ravine near the town of Winesburg, Ohio, a fat little old man walked nervously up and down. Across a long field that had been seeded for clover but that had produced only a dense crop of yellow mustard weeds, he could see the public highway along which went a wagon filled with berry pickers returning from the fields. The berry pickers, youths and maidens, laughed and shouted boisterously. A boy clad in a blue shirt leaped from the wagon and attempted to drag after him one of the maidens who screamed and protested shrilly. The feet of the boy in the road kicked up a cloud of dust that floated across the face of the departing sun. Over the long field came a thin girlish voice. "Oh, you Wing Biddlebaum, comb your hair, it's falling into your eyes," commanded the voice to the man, who was bald and whose nervous little hands fiddled about the bare white forehead as though arranging a mass of tangled locks.

Wing Biddlebaum, forever frightened and beset by a ghostly band of doubts, did not think of himself as in any way a part of the life of the town where he had lived for twenty years. Among all the people of Winesburg but one had come close to him. With George Willard, son of Tom Willard, the proprietor of the new Willard House, he had formed something like a friendship. George Willard was the reporter on the *Winesburg Eagle* and sometimes in the evenings he walked out along the highway to Wing Biddlebaum's house. Now as the old man walked up and down on the veranda, his hands moving nervously about, he was hoping that George Willard would come and spend the evening with him. After the wagon containing the berry pickers had passed, he went across the field through the tall mustard weeds and climbing a rail fence peered anxiously along the road to the town. For a moment he stood thus, rubbing his hands together and looking up and down the road, and then, fear overcoming him, ran back to walk again upon the porch on his own house.

In the presence of George Willard, Wing Biddlebaum, who for twenty years had been the town mystery, lost something of his timidity, and his shadowy personality, submerged in a sea of doubts, came forth to look at the world. With the young reporter at his side, he ventured in the light of day into Main Street or strode up and down on the rickety front porch of his own house, talking excitedly. The voice that had been low and trembling became shrill and loud. The bent figure straightened. With a kind of wriggle, like a fish returned to the brook by the fisherman, Biddlebaum the silent began to talk, striving to put into words the ideas that had been accumulated by his mind during long years of silence.

Wing Biddlebaum talked much with his hands. The slender expressive fingers, forever active, forever striving to conceal themselves in his pockets or behind his back, came forth and became the piston rods of his machinery of expression.

The story of Wing Biddlebaum is a story of hands. Their restless activity, like unto the beating of the wings of an imprisoned bird, had given him his name. Some obscure poet of the town had thought of it. The hands alarmed their owner. He wanted to keep them hidden away and looked with amazement at the quiet inexpressive hands of other men who worked beside him in the fields, or passed, driving sleepy teams on country roads.

When he talked to George Willard, Wing Biddlebaum closed his fists and beat with them upon a table or on the walls of his house. The action made him more comfortable. If the desire to talk came to him when the two were walking in the fields, he sought out a stump or the top board of a fence and with his hands pounding busily talked with renewed ease.

The story of Wing Biddlebaum's hands is worth a book in itself. Sympathetically set forth it would tap many strange, beautiful qualities in obscure men. It is a job for a poet. In Winesburg the hands had attracted attention merely because of their activity. With them Wing Biddlebaum had picked as high as a hundred and forty quarts of strawberries in a day. They became his distinguishing feature, the source of his fame. Also they made more grotesque an already grotesque and elusive individuality. Winesburg was proud of the hands of Wing Biddlebaum in the same spirit in which it was proud of Banker White's new stone house and Wesley Moyer's bay stallion, Tony Tip, that had won the two-fifteen trot at the fall races in Cleveland.

As for George Willard, he had many times wanted to ask about the hands. At times an almost overwhelming curiosity had taken hold of him. He felt that there must be a reason for their strange activity and their inclination to keep hidden away and only a growing respect for Wing Biddlebaum kept him from blurting out the questions that were often in his mind.

Once he had been on the point of asking. The two were walking in the fields on a summer afternoon and had stopped to sit upon a grassy bank. All afternoon Wing Biddlebaum had talked as one inspired. By a fence he had stopped and beating like a giant woodpecker upon the top board had shouted at George Willard, condemning his tendency to be too much influenced by the people about him. "You are destroying yourself," he cried. "You have the inclination to be alone and to dream and you are afraid of dreams. You want to be like others in town here. You hear them talk and you try to imitate them."

On the grassy bank Wing Biddlebaum had tried again to drive his point home. His voice became soft and reminiscent, and with a sigh of contentment he launched into a long rambling talk, speaking as one lost in a dream.

Out of the dream Wing Biddlebaum made a picture for George Willard. In the picture men lived again in a kind of pastoral golden age. Across a green open country came clean-limbed young men, some afoot, some mounted upon horses. In crowds the young men came to gather about the feet of an old man who sat beneath a tree in a tiny garden and who talked to them.[1]

Wing Biddlebaum became wholly inspired. For once he forgot the hands. Slowly they stole forth and lay upon George Willard's shoulders. Something new and bold came into the voice that talked. "You must try to forget all you have learned," said the old man. "You must begin to dream. From this time on you must shut your ears to the roaring of the voices."

Pausing in his speech, Wing Biddlebaum looked long and earnestly at George Willard. His eyes glowed. Again he raised the hands to caress the boy and then a look of horror swept over his face.

With a convulsive movement of his body, Wing Biddlebaum sprang to his feet and thrust his hands deep into his trousers pockets. Tears came to his eyes. "I must be getting along home. I can talk no more with you," he said nervously.

Without looking back, the old man had hurried down the hillside and across a meadow, leaving George Willard perplexed and frightened upon the grassy slope. With a shiver of dread the boy arose and went along the road toward town. "I'll not ask him about his hands," he thought, touched by the memory of the terror he had seen in the man's eyes. "There's something wrong, but I don't want to know what it is. His hands have something to do with his fear of me and of everyone."

And George Willard was right. Let us look briefly into the story of the hands. Perhaps our talking of them will arouse the poet who will tell the hidden wonder story of the influence for which the hands were but fluttering pennants of promise.

In his youth Wing Biddlebaum had been a school teacher in a town in Pennsylvania. He was not then known as Wing Biddlebaum, but went by the less euphonic name of Adolph Myers.[2] As Adolph Myers he was much loved by the boys of his school.

Adolph Myers was meant by nature to be a teacher of youth. He was one of those rare, little-understood men who rule by a power so gentle that it passes as a lovable weakness. In their feeling for the boys under their charge such men are not unlike the finer sort of women in their love of men.

---

1. Biddlebaum's picture invokes ideals of the Greek Golden Age generally, and more particularly the image of the Athenian philosopher Socrates (469–399 B.C.E) teaching young Greek aristocrats.

2. Both his adopted surname and his original one underline Biddlebaum's foreignness by labeling him as German and, probably, Jewish.

And yet that is but crudely stated. It needs the poet there. With the boys of his school, Adolph Myers had walked in the evening or had sat talking until dusk upon the schoolhouse steps lost in a kind of dream. Here and there went his hands, caressing the shoulders of the boys, playing about the tousled heads. As he talked his voice became soft and musical. There was a caress in that also. In a way the voice and the hands, the stroking of the shoulders and the touching of the hair was a part of the schoolmaster's effort to carry a dream into the young minds. By the caress that was in his fingers he expressed himself. He was one of those men in whom the force that creates life is diffused, not centralized. Under the caress of his hands doubt and disbelief went out of the minds of the boy and they began also to dream.

And then the tragedy. A half-witted boy of the school became enamored of the young master. In his bed at night he imagined unspeakable things and in the morning went forth to tell his dreams as facts. Strange, hideous accusations fell from his loose-hung lips. Through the Pennsylvania town went a shiver. Hidden, shadowy doubts that had been in men's minds concerning Adolph Myers were galvanized into beliefs.

The tragedy did not linger. Trembling lads were jerked out of bed and questioned. "He put his arms about me," said one. "His fingers were always playing in my hair," said another.

One afternoon a man of the town, Henry Bradford, who kept a saloon, came to the schoolhouse door. Calling Adolph Myers into the school yard he began to beat him with his fists. As his hard knuckles beat down into the frightened face of the schoolmaster, his wrath became more and more terrible. Screaming with dismay, the children ran here and there like disturbed insects "I'll teach you to put your hands on my boy, you beast," roared the saloon keeper, who, tired of beating the master, had begun to kick him about the yard.

Adolph Myers was driven from the Pennsylvania town in the night. With lanterns in their hands a dozen men came to the door of the house where he lived alone and commanded that he dress and come forth. It was raining and one of the men had a rope in his hands. They had intended to hang the schoolmaster, but something in his figure, so small, white, and pitiful, touched their hearts and they let him escape. As he ran away into the darkness they repented of their weakness and ran after him, swearing and throwing sticks and great balls of soft mud at the figure that screamed and ran faster and faster into the darkness.

For twenty years Adolph Myers had lived alone in Winesburg. He was but forty but looked sixty-five. The name of Biddlebaum he got from a box of goods seen at a freight station as he hurried through an eastern Ohio town. He had an aunt in Winesburg, a black-toothed old woman who raised chickens, and with her he lived until she died. He had been ill for a year after the experience in Pennsylvania, and after his recovery worked as a day laborer in the fields, going timidly about and striving to conceal his hands. Although he did not understand what had happened he felt that the hands must be to blame. Again and again the fathers of the boys had talked of the hands. "Keep your hands to yourself," the saloon keeper had roared, dancing with fury in the schoolhouse yard.

Upon the veranda of his house by the ravine, Wing Biddlebaum continued to walk up and down until the sun had disappeared and the road beyond the field was lost in the grey shadows. Going into his house he cut slices of bread and spread honey upon them. When the rumble of the evening train that took away the express cars loaded with the day's harvest of berries had passed and restored the silence of the summer night, he went again to walk upon the veranda. In the darkness he could not see the hands and they became quiet. Although he still hungered for the presence of the boy, who was the medium through which he expressed his love of man, the hunger became again a part of his loneliness and his waiting. Lighting a lamp, Wing Biddlebaum washed the few dishes soiled by his simple meal and, setting up a folding cot by the screen door that led to the porch, prepared to undress for the night. A few stray white bread crumbs lay on the cleanly washed floor by the table; putting the lamp upon a low stool he began to pick up the crumbs, carrying them to his mouth one by one with unbelievable rapidity. In the dense blotch of light beneath the table, the kneeling figure looked like a priest engaged in some service of his church. The nervous expressive fingers, flashing in and out of the light, might well have been mistaken for the fingers of the devotee going swiftly through decade after decade of his rosary.[3]

Mother

Elizabeth Willard, the mother of George Willard, was tall and gaunt and her face was marked with smallpox scars. Although she was but forty-five, some obscure disease had taken the fire out of her figure. Listlessly she went about the disorderly old hotel looking at the faded wall-paper and the ragged carpets and, when she was able to be about, doing the work of a chambermaid among beds soiled by the slumbers of fat traveling men. Her husband, Tom Willard, a slender, graceful man with square shoulders, a quick military step, and a black mustache, trained to turn sharply up at the ends, tried to put the wife out of his mind. The presence of the tall ghostly figure, moving slowly through the halls, he took as a reproach to himself. When he thought of her he grew angry and swore. The hotel was unprofitable and forever on the edge of failure and he wished himself out of it. He thought of the old house and the woman who lived there with him as things defeated and done for. The hotel in which he had begun life so hopefully was now a mere ghost of what a hotel should be. As he went spruce and businesslike through the streets of Winesburg, he sometimes stopped and turned quickly about as though fearing that the spirit of the hotel and of the woman would follow him even into the streets. "Damn such a life, damn it!" he sputtered aimlessly.

Tom Willard had a passion for village politics and for years had been the leading Democrat in a strongly Republican community. Some day, he told himself, the tide of things political will turn in my favor and the years of ineffectual service count big in the bestowal of rewards. He dreamed of going to Congress and even of becoming governor. Once when a younger member of the party arose at a political conference and began to boast of his faithful ser-

3. String of beads used by Roman Catholics to keep track of prayers, divided into sections ("decades") of ten beads.

vice, Tom Willard grew white with fury. "Shut up, you," he roared, glaring about. "What do you know of service? What are you but a boy? Look at what I've done here! I was a Democrat here in Winesburg when it was a crime to be a Democrat. In the old days they fairly hunted us with guns."

Between Elizabeth and her one son George there was a deep unexpressed bond of sympathy, based on a girlhood dream that had long ago died. In the son's presence she was timid and reserved, but sometimes while he hurried about town intent upon his duties as a reporter, she went into his room and closing the door knelt by a little desk, made of a kitchen table, that sat near a window. In the room by the desk she went through a ceremony that was half a prayer, half a demand, addressed to the skies. In the boyish figure she yearned to see something half forgotten that had once been a part of herself recreated. The prayer concerned that. "Even though I die, I will in some way keep defeat from you," she cried, and so deep was her determination that her whole body shook. Her eyes glowed and she clenched her fists. "If I am dead and see him becoming a meaningless drab figure like myself, I will come back," she declared. "I ask God now to give me that privilege. I demand it. I will pay for it. God may beat me with his fists. I will take any blow that may befall if but this my boy be allowed to express something for us both." Pausing uncertainly, the woman stared about the boy's room. "And do not let him become smart and successful either," she added vaguely.

The communion between George Willard and his mother was outwardly a formal thing without meaning. When she was ill and sat by the window in her room he sometimes went in the evening to make her a visit. They sat by a window that looked over the roof of a small frame building into Main Street. By turning their heads they could see, through another window, along an alleyway that ran behind the Main Street stores and into the back door of Abner Groff's bakery. Sometimes as they sat thus a picture of village life presented itself to them. At the back door of his shop appeared Abner Groff with a stick or an empty milk bottle in his hand. For a long time there was a feud between the baker and a grey cat that belonged to Sylvester West, the druggist. The boy and his mother saw the cat creep into the door of the bakery and presently emerge followed by the baker who swore and waved his arms about. The baker's eyes were small and red and his black hair and beard were filled with flour dust. Sometimes he was so angry that, although the cat had disappeared, he hurled sticks, bits of broken glass, and even some of the tools of his trade about. Once he broke a window at the back of Sinning's Hardware Store. In the alley the grey cat crouched behind barrels filled with torn paper and broken bottles above which flew a black swarm of flies. Once when she was alone, and after watching a prolonged and ineffectual outburst on the part of the baker, Elizabeth Willard put her head down on her long white hands and wept. After that she did not look along the alleyway any more, but tried to forget the contest between the bearded man and the cat. It seemed like a rehearsal of her own life, terrible in its vividness.

In the evening when the son sat in the room with his mother, the silence made them both feel awkward. Darkness came on and the evening train came in at the station. In the street below feet tramped up and down upon a board sidewalk. In the station yard, after the evening train had gone, there was a heavy silence. Perhaps Skinner Leason, the express agent, moved a truck the length of the station platform. Over on Main Street sounded a man's voice, laughing. The door of the express office banged. George Willard arose and crossing the room fumbled for the doorknob. Sometimes he knocked against a chair, making it scrape along the floor. By the window sat the sick woman, perfectly still, listless. Her long hands, white and bloodless, could be seen drooping over the ends of the arms of the chair. "I think you had better be out among the boys. You are too much indoors," she said, striving to relieve the embarrassment of the departure. "I thought I would take a walk," replied George Willard, who felt awkward and confused.

One evening in July, when the transient guests who made the New Willard House their temporary homes had become scarce, and the hallways, lighted only by kerosene lamps turned low, were plunged in gloom, Elizabeth Willard had an adventure. She had been ill in bed for several days and her son had not come to visit her. She was alarmed. The feeble blaze of life that remained in her body was blown into a flame by her anxiety and she crept out of bed, dressed and hurried along the hallway toward her son's room, shaking with exaggerated fears. As she went along she steadied herself with her hand, slipped along the papered walls of the hall and breathed with difficulty. The air whistled through her teeth. As she hurried forward she thought how foolish she was. "He is concerned with boyish affairs," she told herself. "Perhaps he has now begun to walk about in the evening with girls."

Elizabeth Willard had a dread of being seen by guests in the hotel that had once belonged to her father and the ownership of which still stood recorded in her name in the county courthouse. The hotel was continually losing patronage because of its shabbiness and she thought of herself as also shabby. Her own room was in an obscure corner and when she felt able to work she voluntarily worked among the beds, preferring the labor that could be done when the guests were abroad seeking trade among the merchants of Winesburg.

By the door of her son's room the mother knelt upon the floor and listened for some sound from within. When she heard the boy moving about and talking in low tones a smile came to her lips. George Willard had a habit of talking aloud to himself and to hear him doing so had always given his mother a peculiar pleasure. The habit in him, she felt, strengthened the secret bond that existed between them. A thousand times she had whispered to herself of the matter. "He is groping about, trying to find himself," she thought. "He is not a dull clod, all words and smartness. Within him there is a secret something that is striving to grow. It is the thing I let be killed in myself."

In the darkness in the hallway by the door the sick woman arose and started again toward her own room. She was afraid that the door would open and the boy come upon her. When she had reached a safe distance and was about to turn a corner into a second hallway she stopped and bracing herself with her hands waited, thinking to shake off a trembling fit of weakness that had come upon her. The presence of the boy in the room had made her happy. In her bed, during the long hours alone, the little fears that had visited her had become giants. Now they were all gone. "When I get back to my room I shall sleep," she murmured gratefully.

But Elizabeth Willard was not to return to her bed and to sleep. As she stood trembling in the darkness the door of her son's room opened and the boy's father, Tom Willard, stepped out. In the light that streamed out at the door he stood with the knob in his hand and talked. What he said infuriated the woman.

Tom Willard was ambitious for his son. He had always thought of himself as a successful man, although nothing he had ever done had turned out successfully. However, when he was out of sight of the New Willard House and had no fear of coming upon his wife, he swaggered and began to dramatize himself as one of the chief men of the town. He wanted his son to succeed. He it was who had secured for the boy the position on the *Winesburg Eagle*. Now, with a ring of earnestness in his voice, he was advising concerning some course of conduct. "I tell you what, George, you've got to wake up," he said sharply. "Will Henderson has spoken to me three times concerning the matter. He says you go along for hours not hearing when you are spoken to and acting like a gawky girl. What ails you?" Tom Willard laughed good-naturedly. "Well, I guess you'll get over it," he said. "I told Will that. You're not a fool and you're not a woman. You're Tom Willard's son and you'll wake up. I'm not afraid. What you say clears things up. If being a newspaper man had put the notion of becoming a writer into your mind that's all right. Only I guess you'll have to wake up to do that too, eh?"

Tom Willard went briskly along the hallway and down a flight of stairs to the office. The woman in the darkness could hear him laughing and talking with a guest who was striving to wear away a dull evening by dozing in a chair by the office door. She returned to the door of her son's room. The weakness had passed from her body as by a miracle and she stepped boldly along. A thousand ideas raced through her head. When she heard the scraping of a chair and the sound of a pen scratching upon paper, she again turned and went back along the hallway to her own room.

A definite determination had come into the mind of the defeated wife of the Winesburg Hotel keeper. The determination was the result of long years of quiet and rather ineffectual thinking. "Now," she told herself, "I will act. There is something threatening my boy and I will ward it off." The fact that the conversation between Tom Willard and his son had been rather quiet and natural, as though an understanding existed between them, maddened her. Although for years she had hated her husband, her hatred had always before been a quite impersonal thing. He had been merely a part of something else that she hated. Now, and by the few words at the door, he had become the thing personified. In the darkness of her own room she clenched her fists and glared about. Going to a cloth bag that hung on a nail by the wall she took out a long pair of sewing scissors and held them in her hand like a dagger. "I will stab him," she said aloud. "He has chosen to be the voice of evil and I will kill him. When I have killed him something will snap within myself and I will die also. It will be a release for all of us."

In her girlhood and before her marriage with Tom Willard, Elizabeth had borne a somewhat shaky reputation in Winesburg. For years she had been what is called "stage-struck" and had paraded through the streets with traveling men guests at her father's hotel, wearing loud clothes and urging them to tell her of life in the cities out of which they had come. Once she startled the town by putting on men's clothes and riding a bicycle down Main Street.

In her own mind the tall girl had been in those days much confused. A great restlessness was in her and it expressed itself in two ways. First there was an uneasy desire for change, for some big definite movement to her life. It was this feeling that had turned her mind to the stage. She dreamed of joining some company and wandering over the world, seeing always new faces and giving something out of herself to all people. Sometimes at night she was quite beside herself with the thought, but when she tried to talk of the matter to the members of the theatrical companies that came to Winesburg and stopped at her father's hotel, she got nowhere. They did not seem to know what she meant, or if she did get something of her passion expressed, they only laughed. "It's not like that," they said. "It's as dull and uninteresting as this here. Nothing comes of it."

With the traveling men when she walked about with them, and later with Tom Willard, it was quite different. Always they seemed to understand and sympathize with her. On the side streets of the village, in the darkness under the trees, they took hold of her hand and she thought that something unexpressed in herself came forth and became a part of an unexpressed something in them.

And then there was the second expression of her restlessness. When that came she felt for a time released and happy. She did not blame the men who walked with her and later she did not blame Tom Willard. It was always the same, beginning with kisses and ending, after strange wild emotions, with peace and then sobbing repentance. When she sobbed she put her hand upon the face of the man and had always the same thought. Even though he were large and bearded she thought he had become suddenly a little boy. She wondered why he did not sob also.

In her room, tucked away in a corner of the old Willard House, Elizabeth Willard lighted a lamp and put it on a dressing table that stood by the door. A thought had come into her mind and she went to a closet and brought out a small square box and set it on the table. The box contained material for make-up and had been left with other things by a theatrical company that had once been stranded in Winesburg. Elizabeth Willard had decided that she would be beautiful. Her hair was still black and there was a great mass of it braided and coiled about her head. The scene that was to take place in the office below began to grow in her mind. No ghostly worn-out figure should confront Tom Willard, but something quite unexpected and startling. Tall and with dusky cheeks and hair that fell in a mass from her shoulders, a figure should come striding down the stairway before the startled loungers in the hotel office. The figure would be silent—it would be swift and terrible. As a tigress whose cub had been threatened would she appear, coming out of the shadows, stealing noiselessly along and holding the long wicked scissors in her hand.

With a little broken sob in her throat Elizabeth Willard blew out the light that stood upon the table and stood weak and trembling in the darkness. The strength that had been a miracle in her body left and she half reeled across the floor, clutching at the back of the chair in which she had spent so many long days staring out over the tin roofs into the main street of Winesburg. In the hallway there was the sound of footsteps and George Willard came in at the door. Sitting in a chair beside his mother he began to talk. "I'm going to get out of here," he said. "I don't know where I shall go or what I shall do but I am going away."

The woman in the chair waited and trembled. An impulse came to her. "I suppose you had better wake up," she said. "You think that? You will go to the city and make money, eh? It will be better for you, you think, to be a business man, to be brisk and smart and alive?" She waited and trembled.

The son shook his head. "I suppose I can't make you understand, but oh, I wish I could," he said earnestly. "I can't even talk to father about it. I don't try. There isn't any use. I don't know what I shall do. I just want to go away and look at people and think."

Silence fell upon the room where the boy and woman sat together. Again, as on the other evenings, they were embarrassed. After a time the boy tried again to talk. "I suppose it won't be for a year or two but I've been thinking about it," he said, rising and going toward the door. "Something father said makes it sure that I shall have to go away." He fumbled with the door knob. In the room the silence became unbearable to the woman. She wanted to cry out with joy because of the words that had come from the lips of her son, but the expression of joy had become impossible to her. "I think you had better go out among the boys. You are too much indoors," she said. "I thought I would go for a little walk," replied the son stepping awkwardly out of the room and closing the door.

CARL SANDBURG
1878–1967

S on of an immigrant Swedish blacksmith who had settled in Galesburg, Illinois, Carl Sandburg was an active populist and socialist, a journalist, and an important figure in the Chicago Renaissance of arts and letters. During the 1920s and 1930s he was one of the most widely read poets in the nation. His poetic aim was to celebrate the working people of America in poems that they could understand. He wrote sympathetically and affirmatively of the masses, using a long verse line unfettered by rhyme or regular meter, a line deriving from Whitman but with cadences closer to the rhythms of ordinary speech. "Simple poems for simple people," he said.

Sandburg's irregular schooling included brief attendance at Lombard College, but he was too restless to work through to a degree. He held a variety of jobs before moving to Chicago in 1913; he was in the army during the Spanish–American War, served as a war correspondent for the Galesburg *Evening Mail*, worked for the Social Democratic Party in Wisconsin, was secretary to the Socialist mayor of Milwaukee, and wrote editorials for the Milwaukee *Leader*. He had long been writing poetry but achieved success with the 1914 publication of his poem "Chicago" in *Poetry* magazine.

Poetry was one element in a surge of artistic activity in Chicago following the 1893 World's Fair. Such midwesterners as the architect Frank Lloyd Wright; the novelists Theodore Dreiser, Henry Blake Fuller, and Floyd Dell; and the poets Edgar Lee Masters and Vachel Lindsay believed not only that Chicago was a great city but that, since the Midwest was America's heartland, it was in this region that the cultural life of the nation ought to center. Two literary magazines—*Poetry*, founded in 1912 by Harriet Monroe, and the *Little Review,* founded by Margaret C. Anderson in 1914—helped bring this informal movement to international attention. Nothing could be more apt to local interests than a celebratory poem called "Chicago."

Four volumes of poetry by Sandburg appeared in the next ten years: *Chicago Poems* (1914), *Cornhuskers* (1918), *Smoke and Steel* (1920), and *Slabs of the Sunburnt West* (1922). These present a panorama of America, concentrating on the prairies and cities of the Midwest. Like Whitman, Sandburg was aware that American life was increasingly urban, and he had little interest in the small town and its conventional middle class. The cities of the Midwest seemed to display both the vitality of the masses and their exploitation in an inequitable class system. Unlike many radicals whose politics were formed after the turn of the twentieth century, Sandburg believed that the people themselves, rather than a cadre of intellectuals acting on behalf of the people, would ultimately shape their own destiny. His political poems express appreciation for the people's energy and outrage at the injustices they suffer. They also balance strong declarative statements with passages of precise description. Other poems show Sandburg working in more lyrical or purely imagistic modes.

If the early "Chicago" is his best-known poem, his most ambitious is the book-length *The People, Yes* (1936), a collage of prose vignettes, anecdotes, and poetry, making use of his researches into American folk song. Sandburg had published these researches in *The American Songbag* in 1927, and he also composed a multivolume biography of Abraham Lincoln between 1926 and 1939. The purpose of this painstaking work was to present Lincoln as an authentic folk hero, a great man who had risen from among the people of the American heartland and represented its best values. He wrote features, editorials, and columns for the *Chicago Daily News* between 1922 and 1930, and pursued other literary projects as well. After World War II, when it became common for poets to read their works at campuses around the country, he enjoyed bringing his old-style populist radicalism to college students.

The text of the poems here is that of *The Complete Poems of Carl Sandburg* (1970).

Chicago

    Hog Butcher for the World,
    Tool Maker, Stacker of Wheat,
    Player with Railroads and the Nation's Freight Handler;
    Stormy, husky, brawling,
    City of the Big Shoulders: 5

They tell me you are wicked and I believe them, for I have seen
    your painted women under the gas lamps luring the farm
    boys.
And they tell me you are crooked and I answer: Yes, it is true I
    have seen the gunman kill and go free to kill again.
And they tell me you are brutal and my reply is: On the faces of
    women and children I have seen the marks of wanton hunger.
And having answered so I turn once more to those who sneer at
    this my city, and I give them back the sneer and say to them:
Come and show me another city with lifted head singing so
    proud to be alive and coarse and strong and cunning.   10
Flinging magnetic curses amid the toil of piling job on job, here
    is a tall bold slugger set vivid against the little soft cities;

Fierce as a dog with tongue lapping for action, cunning as a
    savage pitted against the wilderness,
        Bareheaded,
        Shoveling,
        Wrecking,   15
        Planning,
        Building, breaking, rebuilding,
Under the smoke, dust all over his mouth, laughing with white
    teeth,
Under the terrible burden of destiny laughing as a young man
    laughs,
Laughing even as an ignorant fighter laughs who has never lost
    a battle,   20
Bragging and laughing that under his wrist is the pulse, and
    under his ribs the heart of the people,
        Laughing!
Laughing the stormy, husky, brawling laughter of Youth, half-
    naked, sweating, proud to be Hog Butcher, Tool Maker,
    Stacker of Wheat, Player with Railroads and Freight
    Handler to the Nation.

                                                   1914, 1916

Fog

    The fog comes
    on little cat feet.

    It sits looking
    over harbor and city
    on silent haunches   5
    and then moves on.

                                                    1916

Grass[1]

    Pile the bodies high at Austerlitz and Waterloo.
    Shovel them under and let me work—
                I am the grass; I cover all.

    And pile them high at Gettysburg
    And pile them high at Ypres and Verdun.   5
    Shovel them under and let me work.

---

1. The proper names in this poem are all famous battlefields in the Napoleonic Wars, the American
Civil War, and World War I.

> Two years, ten years, and passengers ask the conductor:
> What place is this?
> Where are we now?

> I am the grass.   10
> Let me work.

1918

WALLACE STEVENS
1879–1955

Wallace Stevens was raised in Reading, Pennsylvania, and attended Harvard for three years as a special student before leaving in 1900 to find a career. His father, a self-made lawyer and businessman, advised Stevens to approach his Harvard studies both broadly and practically. Cautioning Stevens that "you are not out on a pic-nic—but really preparing for the campaign of life—where self sustenance is essential and where everything depends upon yourself," he also encouraged his son's pursuit of a wide-ranging liberal education. Anticipating that Stevens's "power of painting pictures in words" might one day make him famous, his father suggested that he "Paint truth but not always in drab clothes"—"A little romance is essential to ecstasy." As a young man, Stevens wrestled with both sides of his father's values. Drawn equally to a life of aesthetic dreaming and practical work, Stevens admonished himself "not to be a dilettante—half dream, half deed. I must be all dream or all deed." Ultimately, however, he straddled these worlds more successfully than perhaps any other American poet of the twentieth century.

After moving to New York City for a brief attempt at journalism, Stevens went to law school. He started publishing in little magazines in 1914 and frequented literary gatherings in New York, becoming friends with William Carlos Williams and Marianne Moore, among others. In 1916 he began to work for the Hartford Accident and Indemnity Company and moved with his wife to Hartford, Connecticut. They made that city their lifelong home, Stevens writing his poetry at night and during summers. Visiting Florida frequently on business from 1922 onward, he experienced the contrast between the South's lush tropical climate and the chilly austerity of New England that he would turn into a metaphor for opposing ways of imagining the world in poems like "The Snow Man" and "Sunday Morning." A good businessman, Stevens by the mid-1930s was prosperous. He continued to work for the same company until his death, eventually becoming a vice president.

Stevens's first volume of poetry, *Harmonium*, appeared in 1923. The poems in that book are dazzling in their wit, imagery, and color; they found Stevens an audience, although some critics saw in them so much display as to make their "seriousness" questionable. But Stevens's purpose in part was to show that display was a valid poetic exercise—that poetry existed to illuminate the world's surfaces as well as its depths. Anything but drab, the poems of *Harmonium* abound in allusions to music and painting; are packed with sense images, especially of sound and color; and are elegant and unexpectedly funny. Consider the surprise and humor in the titles of the selections printed here as well as these: "Floral Decorations for Bananas,"

"Palace of the Babies," "The Bird with the Coppery, Keen Claws," "Frogs Eat Butterflies, Snakes Eat Frogs, Hogs Eat Snakes, Men Eat Hogs." Stevens's line is simple—either blank verse or brief stanzas, sparsely rhymed—so that the reader's attention is directed to vocabulary and imagery more often than prosody. Invented words are frequent, some employed simply for the pleasure of their sound effects.

Harmonium interspersed brief lyrics with more extended meditative poems, some of which became in the following decades not only landmarks of Stevens's career but also touchstones for critics attempting to define the ambitions of twentieth-century poetry more broadly. "Peter Quince at the Clavier" along with "Sunday Morning" articulated Stevens's paradoxical belief that the only immortal beauty is that found in earthly nature and mortal human life. In "Sunday Morning," the speaker replies to human yearnings for "imperishable bliss" by asserting that the annual return of "April's green" will outlast every human myth or image of permanence, including Christianity's faith in the resurrection of Christ.

Stevens thought of the twentieth century as "an age of disbelief," and he did not much regret the loss. "To see the gods dispelled in mid-air and dissolve like clouds is one of the great human experiences," he wrote near the end of his life. Stevens's hope that with the fading of traditional religion poetry might become the forger of new faiths coincided with the convictions of such other modernist poets as T. S. Eliot (before his conversion to Anglo-Catholicism) and Ezra Pound. From the beginning of his career to the end, Stevens played variations on the proposition that poetry gestures toward a "supreme fiction," embraced without the need of final belief. All gods, Stevens thought, borrowed their power from the human world. The modern poet's role was to return that borrowed glory to its origins and, in doing so, to provide men and women with "a style of bearing themselves in reality."

Reality was an important word for Stevens throughout his career, often paired with *imagination*. Stevens inherited the central conviction of the nineteenth-century British romantic poets and American transcendentalists, that reality comes to human beings through acts of perception and imaginative ordering that at least half create—as the poet William Wordsworth (1770–1850) famously phrased it—what we experience. Placing a jar on a hill in Tennessee ("Anecdote of the Jar") reorders the world perceived around it; the singer's voice (as in "The Idea of Order at Key West") creates the world for her and her audience.

In the six years following the appearance of *Harmonium* Stevens published little new work. During the years leading up to World War II, however, Stevens's concern for the pressures of reality deepened, and his style altered. New volumes and major works began appearing with *Ideas of Order* in 1935, *Owl's Clover* in 1936, *The Man with a Blue Guitar* in 1937, and *Parts of a World* in 1942. The poems became increasingly discursive and philosophical; the conspicuous effects diminished, the diction became plainer. Although he would always remain distanced from political movements, World War II drew Stevens to articulate his own distinctive concern for the active role that poetry might play in the world: "It has to think about war / And it has to find what will suffice" ("Of Modern Poetry").

After World War II, long poems in this discursive, philosophical style became increasingly central to Stevens's work. "Notes Toward a Supreme Fiction" anchored *Transport to Summer* (1947), and *An Ordinary Evening in New Haven* (1950) included "The Auroras of Autumn" and "An Ordinary Evening in New Haven." A book collecting his occasional lectures appeared as *The Necessary Angel* in 1951. A final collection, *The Rock* (1954) appeared in the same year as his *Collected Poems*. Circling around the image of a rock covered with fallen leaves (a pun, among other things, on the leaves of a book), these last poems explored both "an end of the imagination" and the unending work of reclothing the world in images.

Stevens had always been something of a late bloomer as a poet—*Harmonium* appeared when he was forty-four—and his reputation rose steeply in the last decade of his life. He received the Bollingen Prize for lifetime achievement in poetry in

1950 and the National Book Award for *Auroras of Autumn* in 1951. His *Collected Poems* (1954) was recognized with the Pulitzer Prize as well as a second National Book Award in 1955, and has been celebrated as one of the most important books of American poetry in the twentieth century.

The text of the poems included here is that of *The Collected Poems of Wallace Stevens* (1954).

The Snow Man

One must have a mind of winter
To regard the frost and the boughs
Of the pine-trees crusted with snow;

And have been cold a long time
To behold the junipers shagged with ice,   5
The spruces rough in the distant glitter

Of the January sun; and not to think
Of any misery in the sound of the wind,
In the sound of a few leaves,

Which is the sound of the land   10
Full of the same wind
That is blowing in the same bare place

For the listener, who listens in the snow,
And, nothing himself, beholds
Nothing that is not there and the nothing that is.   15

1931

A High-Toned Old Christian Woman

Poetry is the supreme fiction, madame.
Take the moral law and make a nave[1] of it
And from the nave build haunted heaven. Thus,
The conscience is converted into palms,
Like windy citherns[2] hankering for hymns.   5
We agree in principle. That's clear. But take
The opposing law and make a peristyle,[3]
And from the peristyle project a masque[4]
Beyond the planets. Thus, our bawdiness,
Unpurged by epitaph, indulged at last,   10

1. Main body of a church building, especially the vaulted central portion of a Christian Gothic church.
2. I.e., citterns; pear-shaped guitars.
3. Colonnade surrounding a building, especially the cells or main chamber of an ancient Greek temple—an "opposing law" to a Christian church.
4. Spectacle or entertainment consisting of music, dancing, mime, and often poetry.

Is equally converted into palms,
Squiggling like saxophones. And palm for palm,
Madame, we are where we began. Allow,
Therefore, that in the planetary scene
Your disaffected flagellants, well-stuffed,   15
Smacking their muzzy[5] bellies in parade,
Proud of such novelties of the sublime,
Such tink and tank and tunk-a-tunk-tunk,
May, merely may, madame, whip from themselves
A jovial hullabaloo among the spheres.   20
This will make widows wince. But fictive things
Wink as they will. Wink most when widows wince.

1923

The Emperor of Ice-Cream

Call the roller of big cigars,
The muscular one, and bid him whip
In kitchen cups concupiscent curds.
Let the wenches dawdle in such dress
As they are used to wear, and let the boys   5
Bring flowers in last month's newspapers.
Let be be finale of seem.
The only emperor is the emperor of ice-cream.

Take from the dresser of deal,[1]
Lacking the three glass knobs, that sheet   10
On which she embroidered fantails[2] once
And spread it so as to cover her face.
If her horny feet protrude, they come
To show how cold she is, and dumb.
Let the lamp affix its beam.   15
The only emperor is the emperor of ice-cream.

1923

Disillusionment of Ten O'Clock

The houses are haunted
By white night-gowns.
None are green,
Or purple with green rings,
Or green with yellow rings,   5
Or yellow with blue rings.
None of them are strange,
With socks of lace

5. Sodden with drunkenness.
1. Plain, unfinished wood.

2. Stevens explained that "the word fantails does not mean fan, but fantail pigeons."

And beaded ceintures.
People are not going   10
To dream of baboons and periwinkles.
Only, here and there, an old sailor,
Drunk and asleep in his boots,
Catches tigers
In red weather.   15

1931

Sunday Morning[1]

I

Complacencies of the peignoir, and late
Coffee and oranges in a sunny chair,
And the green freedom of a cockatoo
Upon a rug mingle to dissipate
The holy hush of ancient sacrifice.   5
She dreams a little, and she feels the dark
Encroachment of that old catastrophe,
As a calm darkens among water-lights.
The pungent oranges and bright, green wings
Seem things in some procession of the dead,   10
Winding across wide water, without sound.
The day is like wide water, without sound,
Stilled for the passing of her dreaming feet
Over the seas, to silent Palestine,
Dominion of the blood and sepulchre.   15

II

Why should she give her bounty to the dead?
What is divinity if it can come
Only in silent shadows and in dreams?
Shall she not find in comforts of the sun,
In pungent fruit and bright, green wings, or else   20
In any balm or beauty of the earth,
Things to be cherished like the thought of heaven?
Divinity must live within herself:
Passions of rain, or moods in falling snow;
Grievings in loneliness, or unsubdued   25
Elations when the forest blooms; gusty
Emotions on wet roads on autumn nights;
All pleasures and all pains, remembering
The bough of summer and the winter branch.
These are the measures destined for her soul.   30

1. This poem was first published in *Poetry* magazine in 1915; the editor, Harriet Monroe, printed
only five of its eight stanzas but arranged them
in the order Stevens suggested when consenting to
the deletions (I, VIII, IV, V, and VII); he restored
the deleted stanzas and the original sequence in
subsequent printings.

III

Jove[2] in the clouds had his inhuman birth.
No mother suckled him, no sweet land gave
Large-mannered motions to his mythy mind.
He moved among us, as a muttering king,
Magnificent, would move among his hinds,   35
Until our blood, commingling, virginal,
With heaven, brought such requital to desire
The very hinds[3] discerned it, in a star.
Shall our blood fail? Or shall it come to be
The blood of paradise? And shall the earth   40
Seem all of paradise that we shall know?
The sky will be much friendlier then than now,
A part of labor and a part of pain,
And next in glory to enduring love,
Not this dividing and indifferent blue.   45

IV

She says, "I am content when wakened birds,
Before they fly, test the reality
Of misty fields, by their sweet questionings;
But when the birds are gone, and their warm fields
Return no more, where, then, is paradise?"   50
There is not any haunt of prophecy,
Nor any old chimera[4] of the grave,
Neither the golden underground, nor isle
Melodious, where spirits gat them home,
Nor visionary south, nor cloudy palm   55
Remote on heaven's hill,[5] that has endured
As April's green endures; or will endure
Like her remembrance of awakened birds,
Or her desire for June and evening, tipped
By the consummation of the swallow's wings.   60

V

She says, "But in contentment I still feel
The need of some imperishable bliss."
Death is the mother of beauty; hence from her,
Alone, shall come fulfillment to our dreams
And our desires. Although she strews the leaves   65
Of sure obliteration on our paths,
The path sick sorrow took, the many paths
Where triumph rang its brassy phrase, or love
Whispered a little out of tenderness,
She makes the willow shiver in the sun   70

---

2. Supreme god in Roman mythology.
3. Farmhands; an allusion to the shepherds who saw the star of Bethlehem that signaled the birth of Jesus.
4. In Greek mythology, a monster with a lion's head, goat's body, and serpent's tail.
5. Versions of Paradise in diverse world religions.

For maidens who were wont to sit and gaze
Upon the grass, relinquished to their feet.
She causes boys to pile new plums and pears
On disregarded plate. The maidens taste
And stray impassioned in the littering leaves.   75

VI

Is there no change of death in paradise?
Does ripe fruit never fall? Or do the boughs
Hang always heavy in that perfect sky,
Unchanging, yet so like our perishing earth,
With rivers like our own that seek for seas   80
They never find, the same receding shores
That never touch with inarticulate pang?
Why set the pear upon those river-banks
Or spice the shores with odors of the plum?
Alas, that they should wear our colors there,   85
The silken weavings of our afternoons,
And pick the strings of our insipid lutes!
Death is the mother of beauty, mystical,
Within whose burning bosom we devise
Our earthly mothers waiting, sleeplessly.   90

VII

Supple and turbulent, a ring of men
Shall chant in orgy on a summer morn
Their boisterous devotion to the sun,
Not as a god, but as a god might be,
Naked among them, like a savage source.   95
Their chant shall be a chant of paradise,
Out of their blood, returning to the sky;
And in their chant shall enter, voice by voice,
The windy lake wherein their lord delights,
The trees, like serafin,[6] and echoing hills,   100
That choir among themselves long afterward.
They shall know well the heavenly fellowship
Of men that perish and of summer morn.
And whence they came and whither they shall go
The dew upon their feet shall manifest.   105

VIII

She hears, upon that water without sound,
A voice that cries, "The tomb in Palestine
Is not the porch of spirits lingering.
It is the grave of Jesus, where he lay."
We live in an old chaos of the sun,   110
Or old dependency of day and night,
Or island solitude, unsponsored, free,
Of that wide water, inescapable.

6. I.e., seraphim; angels.

Deer walk upon our mountains, and the quail
Whistle about us their spontaneous cries;   115
Sweet berries ripen in the wilderness;
And, in the isolation of the sky,
At evening, casual flocks of pigeons make
Ambiguous undulations as they sink,
Downward to darkness, on extended wings.   120

1915, 1923

Anecdote of the Jar

I placed a jar in Tennessee,
And round it was, upon a hill.
It made the slovenly wilderness
Surround that hill.

The wilderness rose up to it,   5
And sprawled around, no longer wild.
The jar was round upon the ground
And tall and of a port in air.

It took dominion everywhere.
The jar was gray and bare.   10
It did not give of bird or bush,
Like nothing else in Tennessee.

1923

Thirteen Ways of Looking at a Blackbird

I

Among twenty snowy mountains,
The only moving thing
Was the eye of the blackbird.

II

I was of three minds,
Like a tree   5
In which there are three blackbirds.

III

The blackbird whirled in the autumn winds.
It was a small part of the pantomime.

IV

A man and a woman
Are one.   10
A man and a woman and a blackbird
Are one.

V

I do not know which to prefer,
The beauty of inflections
Or the beauty of innuendoes,   15
The blackbird whistling
Or just after.

VI

Icicles filled the long window
With barbaric glass.
The shadow of the blackbird   20
Crossed it, to and fro.
The mood
Traced in the shadow
An indecipherable cause.

VII

O thin men of Haddam,[1]   25
Why do you imagine golden birds?
Do you not see how the blackbird
Walks around the feet
Of the women about you?

VIII

I know noble accents   30
And lucid, inescapable rhythms;
But I know, too,
That the blackbird is involved
In what I know.

IX

When the blackbird flew out of sight,   35
It marked the edge
Of one of many circles.

X

At the sight of blackbirds
Flying in a green light,
Even the bawds of euphony   40
Would cry out sharply.

---

1. A city in Connecticut.

XI

He rode over Connecticut
In a glass coach.
Once, a fear pierced him,
In that he mistook   45
The shadow of his equipage
For blackbirds.

XII

The river is moving.
The blackbird must be flying.

XIII

It was evening all afternoon.   50
It was snowing
And it was going to snow.
The blackbird sat
In the cedar-limbs.

1931

The Idea of Order at Key West[1]

She sang beyond the genius of the sea.
The water never formed to mind or voice,
Like a body wholly body, fluttering
Its empty sleeves; and yet its mimic motion
Made constant cry, caused constantly a cry,   5
That was not ours although we understood,
Inhuman, of the veritable ocean.

The sea was not a mask. No more was she.
The song and water were not medleyed sound
Even if what she sang was what she heard,   10
Since what she sang was uttered word by word.
It may be that in all her phrases stirred
The grinding water and the gasping wind;
But it was she and not the sea we heard.

For she was the maker of the song she sang.   15
The ever-hooded, tragic-gestured sea
Was merely a place by which she walked to sing.
Whose spirit is this? we said, because we knew
It was the spirit that we sought and knew
That we should ask this often as she sang.   20

---

1. One of the islands off the southern coast of Florida, where Stevens vacationed. The poem begins with the scene of a woman walking by the sea and singing.

If it was only the dark voice of the sea
That rose, or even colored by many waves;
If it was only the outer voice of sky
And cloud, of the sunken coral water-walled,
However clear, it would have been deep air,   25
The heaving speech of air, a summer sound
Repeated in a summer without end
And sound alone. But it was more than that,
More even than her voice, and ours, among
The meaningless plungings of water and the wind,   30
Theatrical distances, bronze shadows heaped
On high horizons, mountainous atmospheres
Of sky and sea.
                It was her voice that made
The sky acutest at its vanishing.   35
She measured to the hour its solitude.
She was the single artificer of the world
In which she sang. And when she sang, the sea,
Whatever self it had, became the self
That was her song, for she was the maker. Then we,   40
As we beheld her striding there alone,
Knew that there never was a world for her
Except the one she sang and, singing, made.

Ramon Fernandez,[2] tell me, if you know,
Why, when the singing ended and we turned   45
Toward the town, tell why the glassy lights,
The lights in the fishing boats at anchor there,
As the night descended, tilting in the air,
Mastered the night and portioned out the sea,
Fixing emblazoned zones and fiery poles,   50
Arranging, deepening, enchanting night.

Oh! Blessed rage for order, pale Ramon,
The maker's rage to order words of the sea,
Words of the fragrant portals, dimly-starred,
And of ourselves and of our origins,   55
In ghostlier demarcations, keener sounds.

                        1936

Of Modern Poetry

The poem of the mind in the act of finding
What will suffice. It has not always had
To find: the scene was set; it repeated what
Was in the script.
                Then the theatre was changed   5

---

2. A French literary critic and essayist (1894–1944). Stevens said that he had invented the name and that its coincidence with a real person was accidental.

To something else. Its past was a souvenir.
It has to be living, to learn the speech of the place.
It has to face the men of the time and to meet
The women of the time. It has to think about war
And it has to find what will suffice. It has   10
To construct a new stage. It has to be on that stage
And, like an insatiable actor, slowly and
With meditation, speak words that in the ear,
In the delicatest ear of the mind, repeat,
Exactly, that which it wants to hear, at the sound   15
Of which, an invisible audience listens,
Not to the play, but to itself, expressed
In an emotion as of two people, as of two
Emotions becoming one. The actor is
A metaphysician in the dark, twanging   20
An instrument, twanging a wiry string that gives
Sounds passing through sudden rightnesses, wholly
Containing the mind, below which it cannot descend,
Beyond which it has no will to rise.
                                        It must   25
Be the finding of a satisfaction, and may
Be of a man skating, a woman dancing, a woman
Combing. The poem of the act of the mind.

                                                        1942

WILLIAM CARLOS WILLIAMS
1883–1963

A modernist known for his disagreements with all the other modernists, William Carlos Williams thought of himself as the most underrated poet of his generation. His reputation has risen dramatically since World War II as a younger generation of poets testified to the influence of his work on their idea of what poetry should be. The simplicity of his verse forms, the matter-of-factness of both his subject matter and his means of describing it, seemed to bring poetry into natural relation with everyday life. He is now judged to be among the most important poets writing between the wars. His career continued into the 1960s, taking new directions as he produced, along with shorter lyrics, his epic five-part poem *Paterson*.

He was born in 1883 in Rutherford, New Jersey, a town near the city of Paterson. His maternal grandmother, an Englishwoman deserted by her husband, had come to America with her son, married again, and moved to Puerto Rico. Her son—Williams's father—married a woman descended on one side from French Basque people, on the other from Dutch Jews. This mix of origins always fascinated Williams and made him feel that he was different from what he thought of as mainstream Americans—that is, northeasterners or midwesterners of English descent. After the family moved to

New Jersey, Williams's father worked as a salesman for a perfume company; in childhood his father was often away from home, and the two women—mother and grandmother—were the most important adults to him.

Except for a year in Europe, Williams attended local schools. He entered the School of Dentistry at the University of Pennsylvania directly after graduating from high school but soon switched to medicine. In college he met and became friends with Ezra Pound; Hilda Doolittle, later to become known as the poet H.D.; and the painter Charles Demuth. These friendships did much to steer him toward poetry, and even as he completed his medical work, interned in New York City, and did postgraduate study in Leipzig, Germany, he was reconceiving his commitment to medicine as a means of self-support in the more important enterprise of becoming a poet. Although he never lost his sense that he was a doctor in order to be a poet, his patients knew him as a dedicated old-fashioned physician, who made house calls, listened to people's problems, and helped them through life's crises. Pediatrics was his specialty; and in the course of his career, he delivered more than two thousand babies.

In 1912, after internship and study abroad, Williams married his fiancée of several years, Florence Herman. Despite strains in their relationship caused by Williams's continuing interest in other women, the marriage lasted and became, toward the end of Williams's life, the subject of some beautiful love poetry, including "Asphodel, that Greeny Flower." In the meantime women and the mixed belittlement—adoration accorded them by men (including the poet) were persistent themes in his work. The couple settled in Rutherford, where Williams opened his practice. Except for a trip to Europe in 1924, when he saw Pound and met James Joyce, among others, and trips for lectures and poetry readings later in his career, Williams remained in Rutherford all his life, continuing his medical practice until poor health forced him to retire. He wrote at night, and spent weekends in New York City with friends who were writers and artists—the avant-garde painters Marcel Duchamp and Francis Picabia, the poets Marianne Moore and Wallace Stevens, and others. At their gatherings he acquired a reputation for outspoken hostility to most of the "-isms" of the day.

The characteristic Williams style emerged clearly in the landmark volume of mixed prose and poetry *Spring and All* (1923; see pp. 790–91 and 814–15). This book demonstrates that the gesture of staying at home was more for him than a practical assessment of his chances of self-support. Interested, like his friend Ezra Pound, in making a new kind of poetry, Williams also wanted always to speak as an American within an American context. He staked this claim in the title of one of his books of essays, *In the American Grain* (1925), and in his choice of his own region as the setting and subject of *Paterson* (1946–58), a long poem about his native city incorporating a great variety of textual fragments—letters, newspaper accounts, poetry—in a modernist collage.

Williams detested Eliot's *The Waste Land*, describing its popularity as a "catastrophe" and deploring not only its internationalism but also its pessimism and deliberate obscurity. To him these characteristics were un-American. Yet Williams was not a sentimental celebrant of American life. He objected to Robert Frost's homespun poetry—which might be thought of as similar to his own work—for nostalgically evoking a bygone rural America rather than engaging with what he saw as the real American present. His America was made up of small cities like Paterson, with immigrants, factories, and poor working-class people struggling to get by. The sickness and suffering he saw as a physician entered into his poetry, as did his personal life; but the overall impact of his poetry is social rather than autobiographical.

The social aspect of Williams's poetry rises from its accumulation of detail; he opposed the use of poetry for general statements and abstract critique. "No ideas but in things," he wrote—a line that became one of the most influential mottos of twentieth-century American poetry. "Not ideas about the thing but the thing itself," echoed Wallace Stevens; yet there is a world of difference between Williams's plainspoken and often opinionated writing and Stevens's cool elegance. Williams drew his vocabulary from up-to-date local speech and searched for a poetic line derived from the cadences of street talk. But he rejected "free verse" as an absurdity; rhythm within the line, and linking one line to another, was the heart of poetic craft to him. While working on *Paterson*, he invented the "triadic" or "stepped line," a long line broken into three segments, which he used in many poems, including several of the selections printed here.

Williams published fiction and essays as well as poetry, especially during the 1930s. Books of short stories (*The Edge of the Knife*, 1932, and *Life along the Passaic River*, 1938) and novels (*White Mule*, 1937, and *In the Money*, 1940) appeared in these years. He was also involved with others in the establishment of several little magazines, each designed to promulgate counterstatements to the powerful influences of Pound, Eliot, and the New Critics. All the time he remained active in his community and in political events; in the 1930s and 1940s he aligned himself with liberal Democratic and, on occasion, leftist issues but always from the vantage point of an unreconstructed individualism. Some of his affiliations were held against him in the McCarthy era and to his great distress he was deprived in 1948 of the post of consultant in poetry at the Library of Congress.

It was also in 1948 that he had a heart attack, and in 1951 the first of a series of strokes required him to turn over his medical practice to one of his two sons and made writing increasingly difficult. Nevertheless, he persevered in his work on *Paterson*, whose five books were published in 1946, 1948, 1949, 1951, and 1958. *The Desert Music* (1954) and *Pictures from Brueghel* (1962), containing new poetry, also appeared; but by 1961 Williams had to stop writing. By the time of his death a host of younger poets, including Allen Ginsberg, Denise Levertov, Charles Olson, and Robert Creeley, had been inspired by his example. He won the National Book Award in 1950, the Bollingen Prize in 1953, and the Pulitzer Prize in 1962.

The texts of the poems included here are those of *The Collected Poems of William Carlos Williams*, Volume 1: *1909–1939* (1986), edited by A. Walton Litz and Christopher MacGowan, and *The Collected Poems of William Carlos Williams*, Volume 2: *1939–1962* (1988), edited by Christopher MacGowan.

The Young Housewife

At ten A.M. the young housewife
moves about in negligee behind
the wooden walls of her husband's house.
I pass solitary in my car.

Then again she comes to the curb   5
to call the ice-man, fish-man, and stands
shy, uncorseted, tucking in
stray ends of hair, and I compare her
to a fallen leaf.

The noiseless wheels of my car   10
rush with a crackling sound over
dried leaves as I bow and pass smiling.

1916, 1917

Portrait of a Lady

Your thighs are appletrees
whose blossoms touch the sky.
Which sky? The sky
where Watteau[1] hung a lady's
slipper. Your knees   5
are a southern breeze—or
a gust of snow. Agh! what
sort of man was Fragonard?[2]
—as if that answered
anything. Ah, yes—below   10
the knees, since the tune
drops that way, it is
one of those white summer days,
the tall grass of your ankles
flickers upon the shore—   15
Which shore?—
the sand clings to my lips—
Which shore?
Agh, petals maybe. How
should I know?   20
Which shore? Which shore?
I said petals from an appletree.

             1920, 1934

Queen-Anne's-Lace[1]

Her body is not so white as
anemone petals nor so smooth—nor
so remote a thing. It is a field
of the wild carrot taking
the field by force; the grass   5
does not raise above it.
Here is no question of whiteness,
white as can be, with a purple mole
at the center of each flower.
Each flower is a hand's span   10
of her whiteness. Wherever
his hand has lain there is
a tiny purple blemish. Each part
is a blossom under his touch
to which the fibres of her being   15

1. Jean Antoine Watteau (1684–1721), French artist who painted elegantly dressed lovers in idealized rustic settings.
2. Jean Honoré Fragonard (1732–1806), French painter who depicted fashionable lovers in paintings more wittily and openly erotic than Watteau's. Fragonard's *The Swing* depicts a girl who has kicked her slipper into the air.
1. A common wildflower whose white bloom is composed of numerous tiny blossoms, each with a dark spot at the center, joined to the stalk by fibrous stems.

stem one by one, each to its end,
until the whole field is a
white desire, empty, a single stem,
a cluster, flower by flower,
a pious wish to whiteness gone over—   20
or nothing.

1921

The Widow's Lament in Springtime

Sorrow is my own yard
where the new grass
flames as it has flamed
often before but not
with the cold fire   5
that closes round me this year.
Thirtyfive years
I lived with my husband.
The plumtree is white today
with masses of flowers.   10
Masses of flowers
load the cherry branches
and color some bushes
yellow and some red
but the grief in my heart   15
is stronger than they
for though they were my joy
formerly, today I notice them
and turn away forgetting.
Today my son told me   20
that in the meadows,
at the edge of the heavy woods
in the distance, he saw
trees of white flowers.
I feel that I would like   25
to go there
and fall into those flowers
and sink into the marsh near them.

1921

Spring and All[1]

By the road to the contagious hospital[2]
under the surge of the blue

1. In the volume *Spring and All* (as originally published, 1923), prose statements were interspersed through the poems, which were identified by roman numerals. Williams added titles later and used the volume's title for the opening poem. For examples of the prose sections of *Spring and All*, see "Modernist Manifestos," p. 814.
2. I.e., a hospital for treating contagious diseases.

mottled clouds driven from the
northeast—a cold wind. Beyond, the
waste of broad, muddy fields   5
brown with dried weeds, standing and fallen

patches of standing water
the scattering of tall trees

All along the road the reddish
purplish, forked, upstanding, twiggy   10
stuff of bushes and small trees
with dead, brown leaves under them
leafless vines—

Lifeless in appearance, sluggish
dazed spring approaches—   15

They enter the new world naked,
cold, uncertain of all
save that they enter. All about them
the cold, familiar wind—

Now the grass, tomorrow   20
the stiff curl of wildcarrot leaf

One by one objects are defined—
It quickens: clarity, outline of leaf

But now the stark dignity of
entrance—Still, the profound change   25
has come upon them: rooted, they
grip down and begin to awaken

1923

To Elsie[1]

The pure products of America
go crazy—
mountain folk from Kentucky

or the ribbed north end of
Jersey   5
with its isolate lakes and

valleys, its deaf-mutes, thieves
old names
and promiscuity between

---

1. In *Spring and All,* this poem was originally numbered XVIII. Elsie, from the State Orphanage, worked for the Williams family as a nursemaid.

devil-may-care men who have taken   10
to railroading
out of sheer lust of adventure—

and young slatterns, bathed
in filth
from Monday to Saturday   15

to be tricked out that night
with gauds
from imaginations which have no

peasant traditions to give them
character   20
but flutter and flaunt

sheer rags—succumbing without
emotion
save numbed terror

under some hedge of choke-cherry   25
or viburnum—
which they cannot express—

Unless it be that marriage
perhaps
with a dash of Indian blood   30

will throw up a girl so desolate
so hemmed round
with disease or murder

that she'll be rescued by an
agent—   35
reared by the state and

sent out at fifteen to work in
some hard-pressed
house in the suburbs—

some doctor's family, some Elsie—   40
voluptuous water
expressing with broken

brain the truth about us—
her great
ungainly hips and flopping breasts   45

addressed to cheap
jewelry
and rich young men with fine eyes

as if the earth under our feet
were   50
an excrement of some sky

and we degraded prisoners
destined
to hunger until we eat filth

while the imagination strains   55
after deer
going by fields of goldenrod in

the stifling heat of September
Somehow
it seems to destroy us   60

It is only in isolate flecks that
something
is given off

No one
to witness   65
and adjust, no one to drive the car

                                                            1923

The Red Wheelbarrow[1]

so much depends
upon

a red wheel
barrow

glazed with rain   5
water

beside the white
chickens

                                                            1923

This Is Just to Say

I have eaten
the plums
that were in
the icebox

1. Numbered XXII in *Spring and All*.

and which   5
you were probably
saving
for breakfast

Forgive me
they were delicious   10
so sweet
and so cold

                                1934

A Sort of a Song

Let the snake wait under
his weed
and the writing
be of words, slow and quick, sharp
to strike, quiet to wait,   5
sleepless.

—through metaphor to reconcile
the people and the stones.
Compose. (No ideas
but in things) Invent!   10
Saxifrage is my flower that splits
the rocks.

                                1944

The Dance

In Brueghel's great picture, The Kermess,[1]
the dancers go round, they go round and
around, the squeal and the blare and the
tweedle of bagpipes, a bugle and fiddles
tipping their bellies (round as the thick-   5
sided glasses whose wash they impound)
their hips and their bellies off balance
to turn them. Kicking and rolling about
the Fair Grounds, swinging their butts, those
shanks must be sound to bear up under such   10
rollicking measures, prance as they dance
in Brueghel's great picture, The Kermess.

                                1944

---

1. *The Wedding Dance* by the Flemish painter Pieter Brueghel (or Breughel) the Elder (c. 1525–1569).

Landscape with the Fall of Icarus[1]

According to Brueghel[2]
when Icarus fell
it was spring

a farmer was ploughing
his field   5
the whole pageantry

of the year was
awake tingling
near

the edge of the sea   10
concerned
with itself

sweating in the sun
that melted
the wings' wax   15

unsignificantly
off the coast
there was

a splash quite unnoticed
this was   20
Icarus drowning

1962

1. In Greek mythology, a young man whose father made wings for him with feathers held together by wax. Icarus flew too close to the sun, the wax melted, and he fell into the sea and drowned.

2. A landscape by Flemish painter Pieter Brueghel the Elder (c. 1525–1569) in which Icarus is depicted by a tiny leg sticking out of the sea in one corner of the picture.

EZRA POUND
1885–1972

Ezra Loomis Pound was born in Hailey, Idaho. When he was still an infant his parents settled in a comfortable suburb near Philadelphia where his father was an assayer at the regional branch of the U.S. Mint. "I knew at fifteen pretty much what I wanted to do," he wrote in 1913; what he wanted was to become a poet. He had this goal in mind as an undergraduate at the University of Pennsylvania (where he met and became lifelong friends with William Carlos Williams and had a romance with Hilda Doolittle, who was later to become the poet H.D.) and at Hamilton College; it also motivated his graduate studies in languages—French, Italian, Old English, and Latin—at the University of Pennsylvania, where he received an M.A. in 1906. He planned to support himself as a college teacher while writing.

The poetry that he had in mind in these early years was in vogue at the turn of the twentieth century—melodious in versification and diction, romantic in themes, world-weary in tone—poetry for which the term *decadent* was used. A particular image of the poet went with such poetry: the poet committed to art for its own sake, careless of convention, and continually shocking the respectable middle class. A rebellious and colorful personality, Pound delighted in this role but quickly found that it was not compatible with the sober behavior expected from professors of language. He lost his first teaching job, at Wabash College in Indiana, in fewer than six months.

Convinced that his country had no place for him—and that a country with no place for him had no place for art—he went to Europe in 1908. He settled in London and quickly became involved in its literary life, and especially prominent in movements to revolutionize poetry and identify good new poets. He supported himself by teaching and reviewing for several journals. For a while he acted as secretary to the great Irish poet William Butler Yeats. He married Dorothy Shakespear, daughter of a close friend of Yeats, in 1914. Ten years later he became involved with the American expatriate Olga Rudge and maintained relationships with both women thereafter.

As an advocate of the new, he found himself propagandizing against the very poetry that had made him want to be a poet at the start, and this contradiction remained throughout his life: on the one hand, a desire to "make it new"; on the other, a deep attachment to the old. Many of his critical essays were later collected and published in books such as *Make It New* (1934), *The ABC of Reading* (1934), *Polite Essays* (1937), and *Literary Essays* (1954). He was generous in his efforts to assist other writers in their work and in their attempts to get published; he was helpful to H.D., T. S. Eliot, James Joyce, William Carlos Williams, Robert Frost, Ernest Hemingway, and Marianne Moore, to name just a few.

Pound first campaigned for "imagism," his name for a new kind of poetry. Rather than describing something—an object or situation—and then generalizing about it, imagist poets attempted to present the object directly, avoiding the ornate diction and complex but predictable verse forms of traditional poetry. Any significance to be derived from the image had to appear inherent in its spare, clean presentation. "Go in fear of abstractions," Pound wrote (see "A Retrospect," p. 809–11). Elaborate grammatical constructions seemed artificial; hence this new poetry tended to work by juxtaposition of fragments. Although imagism lasted only briefly as a formal movement, most subsequent twentieth-century poetry showed its influence. Pound soon moved on to "vorticism," which, although still espousing direct and bare presentation, sought for some principle of dynamism and energy in the image. In his imagist phase Pound was connected with H.D. and Richard Aldington, a British poet who became H.D.'s husband; as a vorticist he was allied with the iconoclastic writer and artist Wyndham Lewis.

Pound thought of the United States as a culturally backward nation and longed to produce a sophisticated, worldly poetry on behalf of his country. Walt Whitman was his symbol of American poetic narrowness. His major works during his London years consisted of free translations from languages unknown to most Westerners: Provençal, Chinese, Japanese. He also experimented with the dramatic monologue form developed by the English Victorian poet Robert Browning. Poems from these years appeared in his volumes *A Lume Spento* (By the spent light; Italian), which appeared in 1908, *A Quinzaine for This Yule* (1908), and *Personae* (1910). *Persona* means "mask," and the poems in this last volume developed the dramatic monologue as a means for the poet to assume various identities and to engage in acts of historical reconstruction and empathy.

Although the imagist view of poetry would seem to exclude the long poem as a workable form, Pound could not overcome the traditional belief that a really great poem had to be long. He hoped to write such a poem himself, a poem for his time, which would unite biography and history by representing the total content of his mind and memory. To this end he began working on his *Cantos* in 1915. The cantos were separate poems of varying lengths, combining reminiscence, meditation, description, and transcriptions from books Pound was reading, all of which were to be forged into unity by the heat of the poet's imagination. Ultimately, he produced 116 cantos, whose intricate obscurities continue to fascinate and challenge critics. The London period came to a close with two poems of disillusionment, "Hugh Selwyn Mauberley (Life and Contacts)" and "Mauberley," which described the decay of Western civilization in the aftermath of the Great War.

Looking for an explanation of what had gone wrong, Pound came upon the "social credit" theories of Major Clifford Hugh Douglas, a social economist who attributed all the ills of civilization to the interposition of money between human exchanges of goods. At this point, poetry and politics fused in Pound's work, and he began to search for a society in which art was protected from money and to record this search in poems and essays. This became a dominant theme in the *Cantos*. Leaving England for good in 1920, he lived on the Mediterranean Sea, in Paris for a time, and then settled in the small Italian town of Rapallo in 1925. His survey of history having persuaded him that the ideal society was a hierarchy with a strong leader and an agricultural economy, he greeted the Italian Fascist dictator Benito Mussolini as a deliverer. He looked for other strong leaders in world history and idealized them in the *Cantos*. During World War II he voluntarily served the Italian government by making numerous English-language radio broadcasts beamed at England and the United States in which he vilified Jews, President Franklin D. Roosevelt, and American society in general. When the U.S. Army occupied Italy, Pound was arrested, held for weeks in an open-air cage at the prison camp near Pisa, and finally brought to the United States to be tried for treason. The trial did not take place, however, because the court accepted a psychiatric report to the effect that Pound was "insane and mentally unfit to be tried." From 1946 to 1958 he was a patient and a prisoner in St. Elizabeth's Hospital for the criminally insane in Washington, D.C. During those years he received visits, wrote letters, composed cantos, and continued his polemic against American society.

In 1948 the *Pisan Cantos* (LXXIV–LXXXIV) won the Library of Congress's newly established Bollingen Prize for poetry, an event that provoked tremendous debate about Pound's stature as a poet as well as a citizen. Ten years later the efforts of a committee of writers succeeded in winning Pound's release; he returned to Italy, where he died at the age of eighty-seven. He remains one of the most controversial poets of the era.

The texts of the poems included here are those of *Personae: The Collected Poems* (rev., 1949) and *The Cantos* (1976).

To Whistler, American[1]

On the loan exhibit of his paintings at the Tate Gallery.

You also, our first great
Had tried all ways;
Tested and pried and worked in many fashions,
And this much gives me heart to play the game.

1. James Abbott McNeill Whistler (1834–1903), expatriate American painter.

Here is a part that's slight, and part gone wrong,   5
And much of little moment, and some few
Perfect as Dürer![2]
"In the Studio" and these two portraits,[3] if I had my choice!
And then these sketches in the mood of Greece?

You had your searches, your uncertainties,   10
And this is good to know—for us, I mean,
Who bear the brunt of our America
And try to wrench her impulse into art.

You were not always sure, not always set
To hiding night or tuning "symphonies";[4]   15
Had not one style from birth, but tried and pried
And stretched and tampered with the media.

You and Abe Lincoln from that mass of dolts
Show us there's chance at least of winning through.

                                              1912, 1949

Portrait d'une Femme[1]

Your mind and you are our Sargasso Sea,[2]
London has swept about you this score years
And bright ships left you this or that in fee:
Ideas, old gossip, oddments of all things,
Strange spars of knowledge and dimmed wares of price.   5
Great minds have sought you—lacking someone else.
You have been second always. Tragical?
No. You preferred it to the usual thing:
One dull man, dulling and uxorious,
One average mind—with one thought less, each year.   10
Oh, you are patient, I have seen you sit
Hours, where something might have floated up.
And now you pay one. Yes, you richly pay.
You are a person of some interest, one comes to you
And takes strange gain away: 15
Trophies fished up; some curious suggestion;
Fact that leads nowhere; and a tale or two,
Pregnant with mandrakes,[3] or with something else
That might prove useful and yet never proves,
That never fits a corner or shows use,   20

2. Albrecht Dürer (1471–1528), German painter
and engraver.
3. "'Brown and Gold—de Race,' 'Grenat et Or—
Le Petit Cardinal' ('Garnet and Gold—The Little Cardinal')" [Pound's note]. Titles and subjects
of the portraits.
4. Whistler painted many night scenes and
titled many paintings "symphonies."

1. Portrait of a lady (French).
2. Sea in the North Atlantic where boats were
becalmed; named for its large masses of floating
seaweed.
3. Herb used as a cathartic; believed in legend
to have human properties, to shriek when pulled
from the ground, and to promote pregnancy.

Or finds its hour upon the loom of days:
The tarnished, gaudy, wonderful old work;
Idols and ambergris and rare inlays,
These are your riches, your great store; and yet
For all this sea-hoard of deciduous things,   25
Strange woods half sodden, and new brighter stuff:
In the slow float of differing light and deep,
No! there is nothing! In the whole and all,
Nothing that's quite your own.
     Yet this is you.   30

              1912

A Pact

I make a pact with you, Walt Whitman—
I have detested you long enough.
I come to you as a grown child
Who has had a pig-headed father;
I am old enough now to make friends.   5
It was you that broke the new wood,
Now is a time for carving.
We have one sap and one root—
Let there be commerce between us.

           1913, 1916

In a Station of the Metro[1]

The apparition of these faces in the crowd;
Petals on a wet, black bough.

           1913, 1916

The River-Merchant's Wife: A Letter[1]

While my hair was still cut straight across my forehead
I played about the front gate, pulling flowers.
You came by on bamboo stilts, playing horse,
You walked about my seat, playing with blue plums.
And we went on living in the village of Chŭkan: 5
Two small people, without dislike or suspicion.

At fourteen I married My Lord you.
I never laughed, being bashful.

---

1. Paris subway.
1. Adaptation from the Chinese of Li Po (701–762), named Rihaku in Japanese, from the papers of Ernest Fenollosa, an American scholar whose widow gave his papers on Japan and China to Pound.

Lowering my head, I looked at the wall.
Called to, a thousand times, I never looked back.   10

At fifteen I stopped scowling,
I desired my dust to be mingled with yours
Forever and forever and forever.
Why should I climb the look out?

At sixteen you departed,   15
You went into far Ku-tŭ-en, by the river of swirling eddies,
And you have been gone five months.
The monkeys make sorrowful noise overhead.

You dragged your feet when you went out.
By the gate now, the moss is grown, the different mosses, 20
Too deep to clear them away!
The leaves fall early this autumn, in wind.
The paired butterflies are already yellow with August
Over the grass in the West garden;
They hurt me. I grow older.   25
If you are coming down through the narrows of the river Kiang,
Please let me know beforehand,
And I will come out to meet you
          As far as Chŭ-fū-Sa.

By Rihaku

1915

From The Cantos

I[1]

And then went down to the ship,
Set keel to breakers, forth on the godly sea, and
We set up mast and sail on that swart ship,
Bore sheep aboard her, and our bodies also
Heavy with weeping, and winds from sternward   5
Bore us out onward with bellying canvas,
Circe's[2] this craft, the trim-coifed goddess.
Then sat we amidships, wind jamming the tiller,
Thus with stretched sail, we went over sea till day's end.
Sun to his slumber, shadows o'er all the ocean,   10
Came we then to the bounds of deepest water,
To the Kimmerian[3] lands, and peopled cities

---

1. Lines 1–68 are an adaptation of book 11 of Homer's *Odyssey*, which recounts Odysseus's voyage to Hades, the underworld of the dead. Odysseus was a native of Ithaca, in Greece.
2. Odysseus lived for a year with Circe before he determined to return to Ithaca. She instructed him to get directions for his trip home by visiting the Theban prophet Tiresias in the underworld.
3. Mythical people living in a foggy region at the edge of the earth.

Covered with close-webbed mist, unpierced ever
With glitter of sun-rays
Nor with stars stretched, nor looking back from heaven   15
Swartest night stretched over wretched men there
The ocean flowing backward, came we then to the place
Aforesaid by Circe.
Here did they rites, Perimedes and Eurylochus,[4]
And drawing sword from my hip   20
I dug the ell-square pitkin;[5]
Poured we libations unto each the dead,
First mead then sweet wine, water mixed with white flour.
Then prayed I many a prayer to the sickly death's-heads;
As set in Ithaca, sterile bulls of the best   25
For sacrifice, heaping the pyre with goods,
A sheep to Tiresias only, black and a bell-sheep.[6]
Dark blood flowed in the fosse,[7]
Souls out of Erebus,[8] cadaverous dead, of brides
Of youths and of the old who had borne much;   30
Souls stained with recent tears, girls tender,
Men many, mauled with bronze lance heads,
Battle spoil, bearing yet dreory[9] arms,
These many crowded about me; with shouting,
Pallor upon me, cried to my men for more beasts;   35
Slaughtered the herds, sheep slain of bronze;
Poured ointment, cried to the gods,
To Pluto the strong, and praised Proserpine;[1]
Unsheathed the narrow sword,
I sat to keep off the impetuous impotent dead,   40
Till I should hear Tiresias.
But first Elpenor[2] came, our friend Elpenor,
Unburied, cast on the wide earth,
Limbs that we left in the house of Circe,
Unwept, unwrapped in sepulchre, since toils urged other.   45
Pitiful spirit. And I cried in hurried speech:
"Elpenor, how art thou come to this dark coast?
"Cam'st thou afoot, outstripping seamen?"
       And he in heavy speech:
"Ill fate and abundant wine. I slept in Circe's ingle.[3]   50
"Going down the long ladder unguarded,
"I fell against the buttress,
"Shattered the nape-nerve, the soul sought Avernus.[4]
"But thou, O King, I bid remember me, unwept, unburied,
"Heap up mine arms, be tomb by sea-bord, and inscribed: 55
"*A man of no fortune, and with a name to come.*
"And set my oar up, that I swung mid fellows."

4. Two of Odysseus's companions.
5. Small pit, one ell (forty-five inches) on each side.
6. The prophet Tiresias is likened to a sheep that leads the herd.
7. Ditch, trench.
8. Land of the dead, Hades.
9. Bloody.

1. Goddess of regeneration and wife of Pluto, god of the underworld.
2. Odysseus's companion who fell to his death from the roof of Circe's house and was left unburied by his friends.
3. Corner, house.
4. Lake near Naples, the entrance to Hades.

And Anticlea[5] came, whom I beat off, and then Tiresias Theban,
Holding his golden wand, knew me, and spoke first:
"A second time?[6] why? man of ill star,   60
"Facing the sunless dead and this joyless region?
"Stand from the fosse, leave me my bloody bever[7]
"For soothsay."
            And I stepped back,
And he strong with the blood, said then: "Odysseus   65
"Shalt return through spiteful Neptune,[8] over dark seas,
"Lose all companions." And then Anticlea came.
Lie quiet Divus. I mean, that is Andreas Divus,
In officina Wecheli, 1538, out of Homer.[9]
And he sailed, by Sirens and thence outward and away   70
And unto Circe.
            Venerandam,[1]
In the Cretan's phrase, with the golden crown, Aphrodite,
Cypri munimenta sortita est,[2] mirthful, orichalchi,[3] with golden
Girdles and breast bands, thou with dark eyelids   75
Bearing the golden bough of Argicida.[4] So that:

                                                                        1925

---

5. Odysseus's mother. In the *Odyssey,* Odysseus weeps at the sight of her but obeys Circe's instructions to speak to no one until Tiresias has first drunk the libation of blood that will enable him to speak.
6. They met once before on earth.
7. Libation.
8. God of the sea, who was to delay Odysseus's return by a storm at sea.
9. Pound acknowledges using the Renaissance Latin translation of Homer, produced in the workshop ("officina") of Wechel in Paris in 1538, by Andreas Divus.
1. Commanding reverence; a phrase describing Aphrodite, the goddess of love, in the Latin trans-lation of the second Homeric Hymn by Georgius Dartona Cretensis (the "Cretan" in line 73).
2. The fortresses of Cyprus were her appointed realm (Latin).
3. Of copper (Latin); a reference to gifts presented to Aphrodite in the second Homeric Hymn.
4. Aeneas offered the Golden Bough to Proserpine before descending to the underworld. Pound associates Persephone with Aphrodite, goddess of love and slayer of the Greeks (Argi) during the Trojan War, and associates the Golden Bough, sacred to the goddess Diana, with the magic wand of the god Hermes, slayer of the many-eyed Argus ("Argicida") and liberator of Io.

Modernist Manifestos

As an artistic movement, or set of movements, given to asserting its breaks with past traditions, modernism in the early twentieth century often proclaimed itself in the writing of manifestos. The modernist manifesto is a public declaration of artistic convictions, relatively brief, often highly stylized or epigrammatic in the mode of other forms of modernist writing, and almost always an aggressively self-conscious declaration of artistic independence.

The word *manifesto*, derived from Latin and meaning "to make public," first entered English usage in the seventeenth century to describe printed declarations of belief and advocacy. Early manifestos tended to be weapons forged by dissenting groups in religious and political struggles, a tradition that continued into the nineteenth century with perhaps the most famous political manifesto of the era, Karl Marx's *Communist Manifesto* (1848). In the nineteenth century, artistic groups also began to issue manifestos. The preface to the second edition of *Lyrical Ballads* (1800) by the poets William Wordsworth and Samuel Taylor Coleridge, for example, defended their "experiment" with a new kind of poetry; in the United States, Ralph Waldo Emerson's *Nature* (1836), the founding document of American transcendentalism, called for spiritual and artistic renewal; inspired partly by Emerson's example, Margaret Fuller's "The Great Lawsuit: MAN *versus* MEN. WOMAN *versus* WOMEN" (1843) linked women's pursuit of political rights to their pursuit of artistic expression and intellectual independence. In late-nineteenth-century Paris, the "Symbolist Manifesto" (1886), by the poet Jean Moréas, turned the genre of the manifesto in some of its characteristically high modernist directions. Attacking not so much oppressive social conditions as oppressive conceptions of literature, the symbolists declared their hostility to realism's "plain meanings, declamations, false sentimentality and matter-of-fact description" in order to claim for poetry a freer, less moralizing play of verbal imagination.

The writers of manifestos did not have one particular audience in mind; it was enough for them to get their positions into the public realm. But manifestos also worked to bring like-minded people together; a poet might publish a manifesto in a journal of poetry, a political radical in a radical journal, and so on. In the modernist period, manifestos increasingly reached an international community of self-consciously avant-garde, cosmopolitan artists. The Italian writer F. T. Marinetti published his "Manifesto of Futurism" in French; Ezra Pound's "A Retrospect" ranged freely over his contemporaries in British and American modernist poetry as well as over Pound's admired writers of the past in several languages—Dante, Goethe, Shakespeare; Willa Cather similarly juxtaposed American fiction with French, Russian, and British works in "The Novel Démeublé."

Hostility is often a rhetorical tool of the manifesto, and it was especially so in the modernist period. Modernist manifestos often tried to grab their audiences by the lapels, to separate not only the new from the old but also a creative *us* from a "vulgar" or hidebound *them*. The us–them divide was intended to offend traditionalists as well as to unite the believers in new artistic movements, and it often succeeded in both aims. Marinetti's "Manifesto of Futurism" set the tone in 1909 by declaring that "No work without an aggressive character can be a masterpiece" and exalting "scorn for women" along with modern technology. By 1918, Ezra Pound in "A Retrospect" could manage to insult in one sentence both traditional poetic forms and would-be imitators of his own free verse: "The actual language and phrasing" of the new poetry, Pound complained, "is often as bad as that of our elders without even the excuse that the words are shoveled in to fill a metric pattern or to complete the noise of a rhyme-sound." The modernist boundary between *us* and *them*, Pound's "Retrospect" implies, will always be in motion, always pushing forward and leaving someone behind.

At the same time, however, the very aggression of some high modernist manifestos encouraged some members of their audience to talk back with equal vigor. Marinetti denounced advocates of women's suffrage but recognized a counterpart to his own aggressive tactics in London's most radical suffragettes, to the point of joining them on a march that was broken up by mounted police. The Anglo-American poet Mina Loy wrote and privately circulated her "Feminist Manifesto" as an enthusiastic member of Marinetti's circle; his take-no-prisoners example licensed her rhetoric of destruction and demolition, which she aimed not only at the institutions of sexism but also at less confrontational versions of feminism.

Other influential modernist manifestos were more measured in their language or more subtle in their explorations of the relationship between modernist destruction and cultural production. William Carlos Williams's exuberant prose interludes in *Spring and All* asserted, with the aid of language borrowed from evolutionary biology, that modernism's sudden "SPRING" into the new was the explosive culmination of many small, repeated movements in the past. The title metaphor of Willa Cather's "The Novel Démeublé"—the novel "unfurnished"—suggested that modernism might prune the decorative excesses of nineteenth-century realism without abandoning its basic structure. And Langston Hughes, although he railed against "the mountain standing in the way of any true Negro art in America," ultimately envisioned the mountain—the internal and external struggles of black Americans to cast off white denigrations of African American culture—as the foundation of a higher and broader modernist art: "We build our temples for tomorrow, strong as we know how, and we stand on top of the mountain, free within ourselves."

F. T. MARINETTI

Marinetti (1876–1944) published two obscure volumes of poetry in his native Italian before "The Founding and Manifesto of Futurism" appeared in *Le Figaro,* an influential Parisian journal, in February 1909. The futurist manifesto attracted an international circle of artists and writers into Marinetti's orbit, including painters, architects, poets, sculptors, playwrights, and film directors. Across all the arts, futurism scorned traditional standards of artistic beauty, celebrated modern technologies of speed, and aimed to shock audiences: futurist painters adopted the mixed perspectives of cubism to celebrate speeding trains, and futurist theater drew on cabaret, variety shows, and circuses in staging free-form events that violated traditional theater's boundary between actors and audience. Futurism's aesthetic of aggression had unsettling political implications as well: true to his manifesto's declaration that war is "the only hygiene" of the world, Marinetti welcomed the technologically enhanced slaughter of World War I and supported the rise of Mussolini's Italian fascism.

From Manifesto of Futurism

1. We intend to sing the love of danger, the habit of energy and fearlessness.

2. Courage, audacity, and revolt will be essential elements of our poetry.

3. Up to now literature has exalted a pensive immobility, ecstasy, and sleep. We intend to exalt aggressive action, a feverish insomnia, the racer's stride, the mortal leap, the punch and the slap.

4. We say that the world's magnificence has been enriched by a new beauty; the beauty of speed. A racing car whose hood is adorned with great pipes, like serpents of explosive breath—a roaring car that seems to ride on grapeshot—is more beautiful than the *Victory of Samothrace*.[1]

5. We want to hymn the man at the wheel, who hurls the lance of his spirit across the Earth, along the circle of its orbit.

6. The poet must spend himself with ardor, splendor, and generosity, to swell the enthusiastic fervor of the primordial elements.

7. Except in struggle, there is no more beauty. No work without an aggressive character can be a masterpiece. Poetry must be conceived as a violent attack on unknown forces, to reduce and prostrate them before man.

8. We stand on the last promontory of the centuries! . . . Why should we look back, when what we want is to break down the mysterious doors of the Impossible? Time and Space died yesterday. We already live in the absolute, because we have created eternal, omnipresent speed.

9. We will glorify war—the world's only hygiene—militarism, patriotism, the destructive gesture of freedom-bringers, beautiful ideas worth dying for, and scorn for woman.

10. We will destroy the museums, libraries, academies of every kind, will fight moralism, feminism, every opportunistic or utilitarian cowardice.

11. We will sing of great crowds excited by work, by pleasure, and by riot; we will sing of the multicolored, polyphonic tides of revolution in the modern capitals; we will sing of the vibrant nightly fervor of arsenals and shipyards blazing with violent electric moons; greedy railway stations that devour smoke-plumed serpents; factories hung on clouds by the crooked lines of their smoke; bridges that stride the rivers like giant gymnasts, flashing in the sun with a glitter of knives; adventurous steamers that sniff the horizon; deep-chested locomotives whose wheels paw the tracks like the hooves of enormous steel horses bridled by tubing; and the sleek flight of planes whose propellers chatter in the wind like banners and seem to cheer like an enthusiastic crowd.

* * *

1909

---

1. Famous Greek statue of Nike, the winged goddess of victory, from the 2nd or 3rd century B.C.E.; discovered on the island of Samothrace in 1863, it became an icon of 19th-century high artistic taste.

MINA LOY

"**F**eminist Manifesto" was written during Loy's association with F. T. Marinetti but never published during her lifetime (1882–1966); it survives in a copy sent to a friend, the writer Mabel Dodge Luhan, in 1914. Loy's central demand is sexual freedom, the end of the divide between "the mistress" and "the mother," and the destruction of women's attachment to ideals of their own purity. Loy's modernist call for women's free sexual expression appeals to elite women's sense of race and class privilege: echoing nineteenth-century alarms that granting women life choices beyond marriage and childbearing would lead to white "race suicide," Loy urges "superior" women to embrace maternity as both a responsibility and an aspect of their own sexual development.

Feminist Manifesto

The feminist movement as at present instituted is
Inadequate

Women if you want to realise yourselves—you are on the eve of a devastating psychological upheaval—all your pet illusions must be unmasked—the lies of centuries have got to go— are you prepared for the **Wrench**—? There is no half- measure—NO scratching on the surface of the rubbish heap of tradition, will bring about **Reform**, the only method is
Absolute Demolition

Cease to place your confidence in economic legislation, vice- crusades & uniform education[1]—you are glossing over
Reality.
Professional & commercial careers are opening up for you—
Is that all you want ?

1. Securing women's legal right to own property, gaining access to education for women (especially higher education) on the same terms as men, and suppressing prostitution were all important goals of 19th- and early 20th-century feminist move- ments.

And if you honestly desire to find your level without prejudice—be **Brave** & deny at the outset—that pathetic clap-trap war cry **Woman is the
equal of man—**

She is **NOT!**   for

The man who lives a life in which his activities conform to a
social code which is a protectorate of the feminine element—
——is no longer **masculine**
The women who adapt themselves to a theoretical valuation of
their sex as a **relative impersonality**, are not yet
Feminine
Leave off looking to men to find out what you are **not** —seek
within yourselves to find out what you **are**
As conditions are at present constituted—you have the choice
between **Parasitism, & Prostitu-
tion** —or Negation

Men & women are enemies, with the enmity of the exploited
for the parasite, the parasite for the exploited—at present they
are at the mercy of the advantage that each can take of the
others sexual dependence—. The only point at which the
interests of the sexes merge—is the sexual embrace.

The first illusion it is to your interest to demolish is the
division of women into two classes   **the mistress,
& the mother** every well-balanced & developed woman
knows that is not true, Nature has endowed the complete
woman with a faculty for expressing herself through **all** her
functions—there are **no restrictions** the woman who is
so incompletely evolved as to be un-self-conscious in sex, will
prove a restrictive influence on the temperamental expansion
of the next generation; the woman who is a poor mistress will
be an incompetent mother—an inferior mentality—& will
enjoy an inadequate apprehension of **Life** .

To obtain results you must make sacrifices & the first &
greatest sacrifice you have to make is of your "<u>virtue</u>"
The fictitious value of woman as identified with her physical
purity—is too easy a stand-by——rendering her lethargic in
the acquisition of intrinsic merits of character by which she
could obtain a concrete value—therefore, the first self-
enforced law for the female sex, as a protection against the
man made bogey of virtue—which is the principle instrument
of her subjection, would be the <u>unconditional</u> surgical
<u>destruction</u> <u>of</u> <u>virginity</u> through-out the female population at
puberty—.

The value of man is assessed entirely according to his use or
interest to the community, the value of woman, depends
entirely on <u>chance</u>, her success or insuccess in manoeuvering
a man into taking the life-long responsibility of her—
The advantages of marriage of too ridiculously ample—
compared to all other trades—for under modern conditions a
woman can accept preposterously luxurious support from a
man (with-out return of any sort—even offspring)—as a thank
offering for her virginity
The woman who has not succeeded in striking that
advantageous bargain—is prohibited from any but
surreptitious re-action to Life-stimuli—& entirely
<u>debarred</u> <u>maternity.</u>
Every woman has a right to maternity—
Every woman of superior intelligence should realize her race-
responsibility, in producing children in adequate proportion to
the unfit or degenerate members of her sex—

Each child of a superior woman should be the result of a
definite period of psychic development in her life—& not
necessarily of a possibly irksome & outworn continuance of an
alliance—spontaneously adapted for vital creation in the
beginning but not necessarily harmoniously balanced as the
parties to it—follow their individual lines of personal
evolution—

For the harmony of the race, each individual should be the
expression of an easy & ample interpenetration of the male &
female temperaments—free of stress
Woman must become more responsible for the child than
man—
Women must destroy in themselves, the desire to be loved—

The feeling that it is a personal insult when a man transfers
his attentions from her to another woman
The desire for comfortable protection instead of an intelligent
curiosity & courage in meeting & resisting the pressure of life
sex or so called love must be reduced to its initial element,
honour, grief, sentimentality, pride & consequently jealousy
must be detached from it.
Woman for her happiness must retain her deceptive fragility of
appearance, combined with indomitable will, irreducible
courage, & abundant health the outcome of sound nerves—
Another great illusion that woman must use all her
introspective clear-sightedness & unbiassed bravery to
destroy—for the sake of her self respect is the impurity of sex
the realisation in defiance of superstition that there is nothing
impure in sex—except in the mental attitude to it—will
constitute an incalculable & wider social regeneration than it
is possible for our generation to imagine.

1914   1982

EZRA POUND

"A Retrospect" summarizes Pound's (1885–1972) early declarations of the principles of Imagism. His famous list of "Don'ts," originally published in 1913,
cautioned poets against superfluous words, rigid metrical rhythms, and the use of
abstract rhetoric rather than "direct treatment" of poetic subjects. Pound's own
poetry by 1918 was taking a turn away from Imagism's characteristic emphasis on
representing "an intellectual and emotional complex in an instant of time" and
toward longer poems, more engaged with history and the inherited materials of art.

From A Retrospect

There has been so much scribbling about a new fashion in poetry, that I may perhaps be pardoned this brief recapitulation and retrospect.

In the spring or early summer of 1912, "H. D.," Richard Aldington and myself decided[1] that we were agreed upon the three principles following:

1. Direct treatment of the 'thing' whether subjective or objective.
2. To use absolutely no word that does not contribute to the presentation.
3. As regarding rhythm: to compose in the sequence of the musical phrase, not in sequence of a metronome.

Upon many points of taste and of predilection we differed, but agreeing upon these three positions we thought we had as much right to a group name, at least as much right, as a number of French "schools" proclaimed by Mr Flint in the August number of Harold Monro's[2] magazine for 1911.

This school has since been "joined" or "followed" by numerous people who, whatever their merits, do not show any signs of agreeing with the second specification. Indeed *vers libre*[3] has become as prolix and as verbose as any of the flaccid varieties that preceded it. It has brought faults of its own. The actual language and phrasing is often as bad as that of our elders without even the excuse that the words are shovelled in to fill a metric pattern or to complete the noise of a rhyme-sound. Whether or no the phrases followed by the followers are musical must be left to the reader's decision. At times I can find a marked metre in "vers libres," as stale and hackneyed as any pseudo-Swinburnian,[4] at times the writers seem to follow no musical structure whatever. But it is, on the whole, good that the field should be ploughed. Perhaps a few good poems have come from the new method, and if so it is justified.

Criticism is not a circumscription or a set of prohibitions. It provides fixed points of departure. It may startle a dull reader into alertness. That little of it which is good is mostly in stray phrases; or if it be an older artist helping a younger it is in great measure but rules of thumb, cautions gained by experience.

I set together a few phrases on practical working about the time the first remarks on imagisme were published. The first use of the word "Imagiste" was in my note to T.E. Hulme's[5] five poems, printed at the end of my "Ripostes" in the autumn of 1912. I reprint my cautions from *Poetry* for March, 1913.

A FEW DON'TS

An "Image" is that which presents an intellectual and emotional complex in an instant of time. I use the term "complex" rather in the technical sense employed by the newer psychologists, such as Hart,[6] though we might not agree absolutely in our application.

1. H.D. and the British poet Richard Aldington (1892–1962), who married H.D. in 1913, were among the first poets designated "Imagistes" by Pound.
2. Scottish poet and critic Harold Munro founded the *Poetry Review* in 1911. The British poet and translator Frank Stuart Flint (1885–1960) was a friend of Pound's and another Imagist.
3. Free verse (French); poetry without a fixed pattern of rhyme or meter.

4. The British Victorian poet Algernon Swinburne (1837–1909) was famous for using elaborate poetic forms.
5. Thomas Ernest Hulme (1883–1917), British poet and critic who, with Pound, formulated early statements of Imagism.
6. British psychologist Bernard Hart (1879–1960), influenced by the theories of Sigmund Freud, popularized the idea of the "complex" as an "emotional system of ideas."

It is the presentation of such a "complex" instantaneously which gives that sense of sudden liberation; that sense of freedom from time limits and space limits; that sense of sudden growth, which we experience in the presence of the greatest works of art.

It is better to present one Image in a lifetime than to produce voluminous works.

All this, however, some may consider open to debate. The immediate necessity is to tabulate A LIST OF DON'TS for those beginning to write verses. I can not put all of them into Mosaic[7] negative.

To begin with, consider the three propositions (demanding direct treatment, economy of words, and the sequence of the musical phrase), not as dogma—never consider anything as dogma—but as the result of long contemplation, which, even if it is some one else's contemplation, may be worth consideration.

Pay no attention to the criticism of men who have never themselves written a notable work. Consider the discrepancies between the actual writing of the Greek poets and dramatists, and the theories of the Graeco-Roman grammarians, concocted to explain their metres.

LANGUAGE

Use no superfluous word, no adjective which does not reveal something.

Don't use such an expression as "dim lands *of peace*." It dulls the image. It mixes an abstraction with the concrete. It comes from the writer's not realizing that the natural object is always the *adequate* symbol.

Go in fear of abstractions. Do not retell in mediocre verse what has already been done in good prose. Don't think any intelligent person is going to be deceived when you try to shirk all the difficulties of the unspeakably difficult art of good prose by chopping your composition into line lengths.

What the expert is tired of today the public will be tired of tomorrow.

Don't imagine that the art of poetry is any simpler than the art of music, or that you can please the expert before you have spent at least as much effort on the art of verse as the average piano teacher spends on the art of music.

Be influenced by as many great artists as you can, but have the decency either to acknowledge the debt outright, or to try to conceal it.

Don't allow "influence" to mean merely that you mop up the particular decorative vocabulary of some one or two poets whom you happen to admire. A Turkish war correspondent was recently caught red-handed babbling in his despatches of "dove-grey" hills, or else it was "pearl-pale," I can not remember.

Use either no ornament or good ornament.

1918

---

7. Referring to the "Thou shalt not . . ." formula of the Ten Commandments of Moses (Exodus 20.1–17).

WILLA CATHER

"The Novel Démeublé" strikes many familiar high modernist themes: distrust of mass production, the importance of distinguishing popular entertainment from serious art, and disdain for nineteenth-century realism with its consumerist catalogs of material objects. In this essay, however, Cather (1873–1947) sifts through the nineteenth-century heritage rather than rejecting it wholesale; she finds a precursor for her own ideal of the "unfurnished" modernist novel in Hawthorne's *The Scarlet Letter*.

From The Novel Démeublé

The novel, for a long while, has been over-furnished. The property-man has been so busy on its pages, the importance of material objects and their vivid presentation have been so stressed, that we take it for granted whoever can observe, and can write the English language, can write a novel. Often the latter qualification is considered unnecessary.

In any discussion of the novel, one must make it clear whether one is talking about the novel as a form of amusement, or as a form of art; since they serve very different purposes and in very different ways. One does not wish the egg one eats for breakfast, or the morning paper, to be made of the stuff of immortality. The novel manufactured to entertain great multitudes of people must be considered exactly like a cheap soap or a cheap perfume, or cheap furniture. Fine quality is a distinct disadvantage in articles made for great numbers of people who do not want quality but quantity, who do not want a thing that "wears," but who want change,—a succession of new things that are quickly thread-bare and can be lightly thrown away. Does anyone pretend that if the Woolworth store windows were piled high with Tanagra figurines at ten cents, they could for a moment compete with Kewpie brides[1] in the popular esteem? Amusement is one thing; enjoyment of art is another.

* * *

There is a popular superstition that "realism" asserts itself in the cataloguing of a great number of material objects, in explaining mechanical processes, the methods of operating manufactories and trades, and in minutely and unsparingly describing physical sensations. But is not realism, more than it is anything else, an attitude of mind on the part of the writer toward his material, a vague indication of the sympathy and candour with which he accepts, rather than chooses, his theme? Is the story of a

1. Kewpie dolls, enormously popular from their introduction in the 1910s, were manufactured in ceramic and, later, plastic. Named for their resemblance to images of Cupid, they were often distributed in bride and groom sets. "Woolworth's": American chain store founded in the late 19th century and noted for inexpensive merchandise. "Tanagra figurines": miniature terracotta statues, usually of fashionably dressed women, mass produced in Greece at the end of the 4th century B.C.E.

banker who is unfaithful to his wife and who ruins himself by speculation in trying to gratify the caprices of his mistresses, at all reinforced by a masterly exposition of banking, our whole system of credits, the methods of the Stock Exchange? Of course, if the story is thin, these things do reinforce it in a sense,—any amount of red meat thrown into the scale to make the beam dip. But are the banking system and the Stock Exchange worth being written about at all? Have such things any proper place in imaginative art?

* * *

If the novel is a form of imaginative art, it cannot be at the same time a vivid and brilliant form of journalism. Out of the teeming, gleaming stream of the present it must select the eternal material of art. There are hopeful signs that some of the younger writers are trying to break away from mere verisimilitude, and, following the development of modern painting, to interpret imaginatively the material and social investiture of their characters; to present their scene by suggestion rather than by enumeration. The higher processes of art are all processes of simplification. The novelist must learn to write, and then he must unlearn it; just as the modern painter learns to draw, and then learns when utterly to disregard his accomplishment, when to subordinate it to a higher and truer effect. In this direction only, it seems to me, can the novel develop into anything more varied and perfect than all the many novels that have gone before.

One of the very earliest American romances might well serve as a suggestion to later writers. In *The Scarlet Letter* how truly in the spirit of art is the mise-en-scène[2] presented. That drudge, the theme-writing high-school student, could scarcely be sent there for information regarding the manners and dress and interiors of Puritan society. The material investiture of the story is presented as if unconsciously; by the reserved, fastidious hand of an artist, not by the gaudy fingers of a showman or the mechanical industry of a department-store window-dresser. As I remember it, in the twilight melancholy of that book, in its consistent mood, one can scarcely ever see the actual surroundings of the people; one feels them, rather, in the dusk.

Whatever is felt upon the page without being specifically named there— that, one might say, is created. It is the inexplicable presence of the thing not named, of the overtone divined by the ear but not heard by it, the verbal mood, the emotional aura of the fact or the thing or the deed, that gives high quality to the novel or the drama, as well as to poetry itself.

* * *

How wonderful it would be if we could throw all the furniture out of the window; and along with it, all the meaningless reiterations concerning physical sensations, all the tiresome old patterns, and leave the room as bare as the stage of a Greek theatre, or as that house into which the glory of Pentecost[3] descended; leave the scene bare for the play of emotions, great and little—for the nursery tale, no less than the tragedy, is killed by tasteless

---

2. Stage setting (French). *The Scarlet Letter* (1850), by American novelist Nathaniel Hawthorne (1804–1864).
3. Christian festival marking the descent of the

Holy Spirit to Christ's disciples after his death and resurrection (Acts 2.1–4); often painted as described in the Bible, with the disciples at a table in a closed room.

amplitude. The elder Dumas[4] enunciated a great principle when he said that to make a drama, a man needed one passion, and four walls.

1922

WILLIAM CARLOS WILLIAMS

Williams's 1923 *Spring and All* interspersed untitled short poems (many of them, like "Spring and All" and "The Red Wheelbarrow," now familiar to readers as free-standing lyrics) with sections of manifesto-style prose. *Spring and All* dramatizes repeatedly what Williams (1883–1963) calls "the leap from prose to the process of imagination," charting the rhythmic ebb and flow of imagination's force. Although the poems in *Spring and All* are numbered consecutively, the headings of the prose interludes frequently, as here, play with typographical conventions of numbering.

From Spring and All

CHAPTER VI

Now, in the imagination, all flesh, all human flesh has been dead upon the earth for ten million, billion years. The bird has turned into a stone within whose heart an egg, unlaid, remained hidden.

It is spring! but miracle of miracles a miraculous miracle has gradually taken place during these seemingly wasted eons. Through the orderly sequences of unmentionable time EVOLUTION HAS REPEATED ITSELF FROM THE BEGINNING.

Good God!

Every step once taken in the first advance of the human race, from the amoeba to the highest type of intelligence, has been duplicated, every step exactly paralleling the one that preceded in the dead ages gone by. A perfect plagiarism results. Everything is and is new. Only the imagination is undeceived.

At this point the entire complicated and laborious process begins to near a new day. (More of this in Chapter XIX) But for the moment everything is fresh, perfect, recreated.

In fact now, for the first time, everything IS new. Now at last the perfect effect is being witlessly discovered. The terms "veracity" "actuality" "real" "natural" "sincere" are being discussed at length, every word in the discus-

---

4. Alexandre Dumas (1802–1870), popular French novelist, author of *The Three Musketeers* (1844).

sion being evolved from an identical discussion which took place the day before yesterday.

Yes, the imagination, drunk with prohibitions, has destroyed and recreated everything afresh in the likeness of that which it was. Now indeed men look about in amazement at each other with a full realization of the meaning of "art."

CHAPTER 2

It is spring: life again begins to assume its normal appearance as of "today." Only the imagination is undeceived. The volcanos are extinct. Coal is beginning to be dug again where the fern forests stood last night. (If an error is noted here, pay no attention to it.)

CHAPTER XIX

I realize that the chapters are rather quick in their sequence and that nothing much is contained in any one of them but no one should be surprised at this today.

THE TRADITIONALISTS OF PLAGIARISM

It is spring. That is to say, it is approaching THE BEGINNING.

In that huge and microscopic career of time, as it were a wild horse racing in an illimitable pampa[1] under the stars, describing immense and microscopic circles with his hoofs on the solid turf, running without a stop for the millionth part of a second until he is aged and worn to a heap of skin, bones and ragged hoofs—In that majestic progress of life, that gives the exact impression of Phidias' frieze,[2] the men and beasts of which, though they seem of the rigidity of marble are not so but move, with blinding rapidity, though we do not have the time to notice it, their legs advancing a millionth part of an inch every fifty thousand years—In that progress of life which seems stillness itself in the mass of its movements—at last SPRING is approaching.

In that colossal surge toward the finite and the capable life has now arrived for the second time at that exact moment when in the ages past the destruction of the species *Homo sapiens* occurred.

Now at last that process of miraculous verisimilitude, that great copying which evolution has followed, repeating move for move every move that it made in the past—is approaching the end.

Suddenly it is at an end. THE WORLD IS NEW.[3]

1923

1. Extensive grassy plains of central Argentina (Spanish, *la pampa*).
2. The most important sculptor of classical Athens, Phidias (c. 500–c. 432 B.C.E.) or his students executed the frieze (a long band of relief sculpture surmounting columns) decorating the Par-

thenon in Athens. The frieze depicts a festival procession of men and horses.
3. In the original publication, the poem "Spring and All" ("By the road to the contagious hospital"; see p. 790) directly followed this section.

LANGSTON HUGHES

Where Willa Cather, along with many other modernists, sought to divide high art from popular entertainment, Langston Hughes (1902–1967) urged African American artists to embrace black popular culture, epitomized for Hughes and many other observers of the 1920s by the innovations of jazz. "The Negro Artist and the Racial Mountain," published at the height of the Harlem Renaissance, takes aim at white audiences who looked to black artists for easy, stereotypical entertainment. Hughes's essay reserves most of its anger, however, for black elites who—he charged—preferred their artists to imitate white standards.

From The Negro Artist and the Racial Mountain

One of the most promising of the young Negro poets said to me once, "I want to be a poet—not a Negro poet," meaning, I believe, "I want to write like a white poet"; meaning subconsciously, "I would like to be a white poet"; meaning behind that, "I would like to be white." And I was sorry the young man said that, for no great poet has ever been afraid of being himself. And I doubted then that, with his desire to run away spiritually from his race, this boy would ever be a great poet. But this is the mountain standing in the way of any true Negro art in America—this urge within the race toward whiteness, the desire to pour racial individuality into the mold of American standardization, and to be as little Negro and as much American as possible.

* * *

The Negro artist works against an undertow of sharp criticism and misunderstanding from his own group and unintentional bribes from the whites. "O, be respectable, write about nice people, show how good we are," say the Negroes. "Be stereotyped, don't go too far, don't shatter our illusions about you, don't amuse us too seriously. We will pay you," say the whites. Both would have told Jean Toomer not to write "Cane."[1] The colored people did not praise it. The white people did not buy it. Most of the colored people who did read "Cane" hate it. They are afraid of it. Although the critics gave it good reviews the public remained indifferent. Yet (excepting the work of Du Bois[2]) "Cane" contains the finest prose written by a Negro in America. And like the singing of Robeson,[3] it is truly racial.

* * *

1. Jean Toomer's *Cane* combines prose and poems in a modernist dual portrait of rural Georgia and the urban black community of Washington, D.C.; see p. 967.
2. W. E. B. Du Bois (1868–1963), author of *The Souls of Black Folk* (1903) and other works on African American life and history.
3. Paul Robeson (1898–1976), African American actor and singer; in 1925 he made his concert debut in New York City with a program of black spirituals.

Most of my own poems are racial in theme and treatment, derived from the life I know. In many of them I try to grasp and hold some of the meanings and rhythms of jazz. I am sincere as I know how to be in these poems and yet after every reading I answer questions like these from my own people: Do you think Negroes should always write about Negroes? I wish you wouldn't read some of your poems to white folks. How do you find anything interesting in a place like a cabaret? Why do you write about black people? You aren't black. What makes you do so many jazz poems?

But jazz to me is one of the inherent expressions of Negro life in America: the eternal tom-tom beating in the Negro soul—the tom-tom of revolt against weariness in a white world, a world of subway trains, and work, work, work; the tom-tom of joy and laughter, and pain swallowed in a smile. Yet the Philadelphia clubwoman is ashamed to say that her race created it and she does not like me to write about it. The old subconscious "white is best" runs through her mind. Years of study under white teachers, a lifetime of white books, pictures, and papers, and white manners, morals, and Puritan standards made her dislike the spirituals. And now she turns up her nose at jazz and all its manifestations—likewise almost everything else distinctly racial. She doesn't care for the Winold Reiss[4] portraits of Negroes because they are "too Negro." She does not want a true picture of herself from anybody. She wants the artist to flatter her, to make the white world believe that all Negroes are as smug and as near white in soul as she wants to be. But, to my mind, it is the duty of the younger Negro artist, if he accepts any duties at all from outsiders, to change through the force of his art that old whispering "I want to be white," hidden in the aspirations of his people, to "Why should I want to be white? I am a Negro—and beautiful!"

So I am ashamed for the black poet who says, "I want to be a poet, not a Negro poet," as though his own racial world were not as interesting as any other world. I am ashamed, too, for the colored artist who runs from the painting of Negro faces to the painting of sunsets after the manner of the academicians because he fears the strange un-whiteness of his own features. An artist must be free to choose what he does, certainly, but he must also never be afraid to do what he might choose.

Let the blare of Negro Jazz bands and the bellowing voice of Bessie Smith singing Blues penetrate the closed ears of the colored near-intellectuals until they listen and perhaps understand. Let Paul Robeson singing Water Boy, and Rudolph Fisher writing about the streets of Harlem, and Jean Toomer holding the heart of Georgia in his hands, and Aaron Douglas[5] drawing strange black fantasies cause the smug Negro middle class to turn from their white, respectable, ordinary books and papers to catch a glimmer of their own beauty. We younger Negro artists who create now intend to express our individual dark-skinned selves without fear or shame. If white people are pleased we are glad. If they are not, it doesn't matter. We know we are beautiful. And ugly too. The tom-tom cries and the tom-tom laughs. If colored people are pleased we are glad. If they are not, their displeasure

4. German-born artist (1886–1953), known for his portraits of figures from the Harlem Renaissance.
5. Painter and muralist (1899–1979), who studied with Reiss and who became the first head of the Harlem Artists' Guild. Bessie Smith (1894?–1937), noted blues singer at the height of her fame in the 1920s. Rudolph Fisher (1897–1934), Harlem Renaissance author and musician who arranged songs for Robeson's 1925 New York concert debut.

doesn't matter either. We build our temples for tomorrow, strong as we know how, and we stand on top of the mountain, free within ourselves.

1926

H.D. (HILDA DOOLITTLE)
1886–1961

I n January 1913, Harriet Monroe's influential little magazine, *Poetry,* printed three vivid poems by an unknown "H.D., Imagiste." These spare, elegant lyrics were among the first important products of the "Imagist" movement: poems devoid of explanation and declamation, unrhymed and lacking regular beat, depending on the power of an image to arrest attention and convey emotion. The poet's pen name, the movement's name, and the submission to the magazine were all the work of Ezra Pound, poet and tireless publicist for anything new in the world of poetry. The poems themselves had been written by his friend Hilda Doolittle. In later years, H.D. would look back at these events as epitomizing her dilemma: how to be a woman poet speaking in a world where women were spoken for and about by men. It is, perhaps, a symbol of her sense of difficulty that, though she strove for a voice that could be recognized as clearly feminine, she continued to publish under the name that Pound had devised for her.

She was born in Bethlehem, Pennsylvania, one girl in a family of five boys. Her mother was a musician and music teacher, active in the Moravian church to which many in Bethlehem belonged. The symbols and rituals of this group, along with its tradition of secrecy created in response to centuries of oppression, had much to do with H.D.'s interest in images and her attraction in later life to occult and other symbol systems: the cabala, numerology, the tarot, and psychoanalysis.

When her father, an astronomer and mathematician, was appointed director of the observatory at the University of Pennsylvania, the family moved to a suburb of Philadelphia. There, when she was fifteen years old, H.D. met Ezra Pound, a student at the university, already dedicated to poetry and acting the poet's role with dramatic intensity. The two were engaged for a while, but Pound's influence continued long after each had gone on to other partners. H.D. attended college at Bryn Mawr for two years; in 1911 she made a bold move to London, where Pound had gone some years earlier. She married a member of his circle, the English poet Richard Aldington, in 1913. With Aldington she studied Greek and read the classics, but the marriage was not a success and was destroyed by their separation during World War I when Aldington went into the army and served in France.

The years 1918–19 were terrible for H.D.: her brother Gilbert was killed in the fighting in France, her father died soon thereafter, her marriage broke up, close friendships with Pound and with D. H. Lawrence came to an end, she had a nearly fatal case of flu, and amid all this gave birth to a daughter who Aldington said was not his child. But she was rescued from the worst of her emotional and financial troubles by Winifred Ellerman, whose father, a shipping magnate, was one of the wealthiest men in England. Ellerman, a writer who had adopted the pen name

Bryher, had initially been attracted by H.D.'s poetry; their relationship developed first as a love affair and then into a lifelong friendship.

In 1923, H.D. settled in Switzerland. With Bryher's financial help she raised her daughter and cared for her ailing mother, who had joined her household. During 1933 and 1934 she spent time in Vienna, where she underwent analysis by Sigmund Freud, hoping to understand both her writer's block and what she called her "two loves" of women and men. Freud's theory of the unconscious and the disguised ways in which it reaches expression accorded well with H.D.'s understanding of how the unexplained images in a poem could be significant; the images were coded personal meanings. H.D.'s religious mysticism clashed with Freud's materialism, however, and she had mixed reactions to Freud's developing theory that women's unhappiness was determined by their sense of biological inferiority to men. But H.D. was instrumental (with Bryher's help) in getting Freud, who was Jewish, safely to London when the Nazi regime took over in Austria. When World War II broke out H.D. went back to London to share England's fate in crisis.

During the 1930s she worked mostly in prose forms and composed several auto-biographical pieces (some of which remain unpublished). Like many major poets of the era, H.D. came in time to feel the need to write longer works; the bombardment of London inspired three long related poems about World War II, *The Walls Do Not Fall* (1944), *Tribute to the Angels* (1945), and *The Flowering of the Rod* (1946), which appeared together as *Trilogy*. In them she combined layers of historical and personal experience; wars going back to the Trojan War all fused in one image of humankind forever imposing and enduring violence.

The personal and the historical had always been one to her, and she became increasingly attracted to the image of Helen, the so-called cause of the Trojan War, as an image of herself. According to Homer's *Iliad,* Helen's beauty led Paris, a Tro-jan prince, to steal her from her Greek husband, Menelaus; and all the Greek war-riors made common cause to get her back. After ten years' encampment before the walls of Troy, they found a devious way to enter the city and destroy it. H.D. was struck by the fact that the legend was related entirely from the male point of view; Helen never had a chance to speak. The object of man's acts and the subject of their poems, she was herself always silent. If Helen tried to speak, would she even have a voice or a point of view? Out of these broodings, and helped by her study of sym-bols, H.D. wrote her meditative epic of more than fourteen hundred lines, *Helen in Egypt*. The poem, composed between 1951 and 1955, consists of three books of interspersed verse and prose commentary, which follow Helen's quest. "She herself is the writing" that she seeks to understand, the poet observes.

H.D.'s Imagist poetry, for which she was known during her lifetime, represents the Imagist credo with its vivid phrasing, compelling imagery, free verse, short poetic line, and avoidance of abstraction and generalization. She followed Pound's example in producing many translations of poetry from older literature, especially from her favorite Greek poets. Her natural images are influenced by her early immersion in astronomy as well as by Greek poetry's Mediterranean settings. Austere landscapes of sea, wind, stars, and sand are contrasted with sensual figures of jewels, honey, and shells. Traditional metaphorical resources of earlier women's poetry, such as flow-ers and birds, are absorbed into modernism's aesthetic of "fiery tempered steel." As when her "Oread" calls upon the sea to "splash your great pines / on our rocks," H.D.'s best-known poems embody high modernism's goal of condensing forces at once lush and shattering, violent and creative, into a single arresting image.

The texts of the poems included here are those of *Collected Poems 1912–1944,* edited by Louis L. Martz (1983).

Mid-day

The light beats upon me.
I am startled—
a split leaf crackles on the paved floor—
I am anguished—defeated.

A slight wind shakes the seed-pods—   5
my thoughts are spent
as the black seeds.
My thoughts tear me,
I dread their fever.
I am scattered in its whirl.   10
I am scattered like
the hot shrivelled seeds.

The shrivelled seeds
are split on the path—
the grass bends with dust,   15
the grape slips
under its crackled leaf:
yet far beyond the spent seed-pods,
and the blackened stalks of mint,
the poplar is bright on the hill,   20
the poplar spreads out,
deep-rooted among trees.

O poplar, you are great
among the hill-stones,
while I perish on the path   25
among the crevices of the rocks.

                                        1916

Oread[1]

Whirl up, sea—
whirl your pointed pines,
splash your great pines
on our rocks,
hurl your green over us,   5
cover us with your pools of fir.

                                  1914, 1924

1. A nymph of mountains and hills.

Leda[1]

Where the slow river
meets the tide,
a red swan lifts red wings
and darker beak,
and underneath the purple down   5
of his soft breast
uncurls his coral feet.

Through the deep purple
of the dying heat
of sun and mist,   10
the level ray of sun-beam
has caressed
the lily with dark breast,
and flecked with richer gold
its golden crest.   15

Where the slow lifting
of the tide,
floats into the river
and slowly drifts
among the reeds,   20
and lifts the yellow flags,
he floats
where tide and river meet.

Ah kingly kiss—
no more regret   25
nor old deep memories
to mar the bliss;
where the low sedge is thick,
the gold day-lily
outspreads and rests   30
beneath soft fluttering
of red swan wings
and the warm quivering
of the red swan's breast.

1919, 1921

---

1. In Greek mythology, Leda is the mortal raped by Zeus, in the guise of a swan. Helen of Troy was her daughter.

Helen[1]

All Greece hates
the still eyes in the white face,
the lustre as of olives
where she stands,
and the white hands.   5

All Greece reviles
the wan face when she smiles,
hating it deeper still
when it grows wan and white,
remembering past enchantments   10
and past ills.

Greece sees unmoved,
God's daughter, born of love,
the beauty of cool feet
and slenderest knees,   15
could love indeed the maid,
only if she were laid,
white ash amid funereal cypresses.

1924

1. In Greek legend, the wife of Menelaus. Her kidnapping by the Trojan prince Paris started the Trojan War. She was the daughter of the god Zeus, the product of his rape, when disguised as a swan, of the mortal Leda.

MARIANNE MOORE
1887–1972

Marianne Moore was a radically inventive modernist, greatly admired by other poets of her generation, and a powerful influence on such later writers as Robert Lowell, Randall Jarrell, and Richard Wilbur. Like her forerunner Emily Dickinson, she made of the traditional and constraining "woman's place" a protected space to do her own work, but unlike Dickinson, she was a deliberate professional, publishing her poems regularly, in touch with the movements and artists of her time. She was famous for the statement that poetry, though departing from the real world, re-created that world within its forms: poems were "imaginary gardens with real toads in them." Her earlier work is distinguished by great precision of observation and language, ornate diction, and complex stanza and prosodic patterns. Her later work is much less ornate; and in revising her poetry, she tended to simplify and shorten.

She was born in Kirkwood, Missouri, a suburb of St. Louis. In her childhood, the family was abandoned by her father; they moved to Carlisle, Pennsylvania, where—in a pattern common among both men and women writers of this period—her mother supported them by teaching school. She went to Bryn Mawr College, graduating in 1909; traveled with her mother in England and France in 1911; and returned to Carlisle to teach at the U.S. Indian School between 1911 and 1915. Having begun to write poetry in college, she was first published in 1915 and 1916 in such little magazines as the *Egoist* (an English magazine with which Ezra Pound was associated), *Poetry,* and *Others* (a journal for experimental writing with which William Carlos Williams was associated, founded by Alfred Kreymbourg, a New York poet and playwright). Through these magazines she entered the avant-garde and modernist world. She never married; in 1916 she and her mother merged their household with that of Moore's brother, a Presbyterian minister, and they moved with him to a parish in Brooklyn, New York. There Moore was close to literary circles and Ebbets Field, where the Dodgers, then a Brooklyn baseball team, had their home stadium. Moore was a lifelong fan.

While holding jobs in schools and libraries, Moore worked at her poetry. A volume called simply *Poems* was brought out in London in 1921 without her knowledge through the efforts of two women friends who were writers, H.D. (whom she had met at Bryn Mawr) and Bryher. A long and ambitious poem, "Marriage," appeared in the little magazine *Manikan* in 1923. Another book, *Observations,* appeared in 1924 and won the Dial Award; William Carlos Williams praised it as "a break *through* all preconceptions of poetic form and mood and pace." In 1925 she began to work as editor of the *Dial,* continuing in this influential position until the magazine was disbanded in 1929. Her reviews and editorial judgments were greatly respected, although her preference for elegance and decorum over sexual frankness was not shared by some of the writers—Hart Crane and James Joyce among them—whose work she rejected or published only after they revised it. As a critic, Moore was prolific; her collected prose makes a larger book than her collected poetry.

Moore believed that poets usually undervalued prose; "precision, economy of statement, logic" were features of good prose that could "liberate" the imagination, she wrote, and she often found these qualities in scientific and historical description. Her poems were an amalgam of her own observation and her wide reading, which she acknowledged by quotation marks and often by footnotes as well. Many of her quotations are obscure or inexact, and some have no identifiable sources. Moore's poetry rarely incorporates direct quotations from or allusions to other poets, the kinds of reference by which poets conventionally invoke a great tradition and assert their own place in it. She prefers to juxtapose disparate areas of human knowledge and to combine the elevated with the ordinary. Moore's notebooks suggest, for example, that the image of the kiwi bird in "The Mind Is an Enchanting Thing" emerged from a sketch Moore made of a shoe-polish tin; she praises the human mind both for its capacity to be mesmerized by the small facets of its environment and for its changeful, self-undoing freedom.

Against the exactitude and "unbearable accuracy" (as she put it) of her language, Moore counterpointed a complex texture of stanza form and versification. Pound worked with the clause, Williams with the line, H.D. with the image, Stevens and Stein with the word; Moore, unlike these modernist contemporaries, for the most part used the entire stanza as the unit of her poetry. Her stanzas are composed of regular lines counted by syllables, instead of by stress, and rhymes often occur at unaccented syllables and in the middle of a line or even a word. The effects she achieves are complex and subtle; she was often called the "poet's poet" of her day because the reader needed to pay close attention to appreciate the audacity of her formal experiments.

Nevertheless, her poetry also had a thematic, declarative edge, which the outbreak of World War II led her to expand. In "The Paper Nautilus," she drew on her characteristic vein of natural observation in order to will that a threatened civilization be protected by love. At the same time, Moore was keenly aware of her distance, as a civilian and a woman, from direct experience of combat; "In Distrust of Merits," her most famous poem of the war, reflects Moore's struggle (like Dickinson's during the Civil War) to adopt an ethically responsible relationship toward the fighting she could know only through newsreels and photographs.

Moore received the Bollingen, National Book, and Pulitzer awards for *Collected Poems* in 1951. Throughout her lifetime she continued to revise, expand, cut, and select, so that from volume to volume a poem with the same name may be a very different work. Her *Complete Poems* of 1967 represented her poetry as she wanted it remembered, but a full understanding of Moore calls for reading all of the versions of her changing work.

Poetry[1]

I, too, dislike it: there are things that are important beyond all
      this fiddle.
   Reading it, however, with a perfect contempt for it, one
      discovers in
it after all, a place for the genuine.
    Hands that can grasp, eyes
      that can dilate, hair that can rise   5
        if it must, these things are important not because a

high-sounding interpretation can be put upon them but because
      they are
   useful. When they become so derivative as to become
      unintelligible,
   the same thing may be said for all of us, that we
      do not admire what   10
      we cannot understand: the bat
        holding on upside down or in quest of something to

eat, elephants pushing, a wild horse taking a roll, a tireless wolf
      under
   a tree, the immovable critic twitching his skin like a horse
      that feels a flea, the base-
ball fan, the statistician—   15
      nor is it valid
        to discriminate against "business documents and

school-books";[2] all these phenomena are important. One must
      make a distinction
   however: when dragged into prominence by half poets, the
      result is not poetry,
   nor till the poets among us can be   20
      "literalists of

1. The version printed here follows the text and format of *Selected Poems* (1935).
2. Diary of Tolstoy (Dutton), p. 84. "Where the boundary between prose and poetry lies, I shall never be able to understand. The question is raised in manuals of style, yet the answer to it lies beyond me. Poetry is verse; prose is not verse. Or else poetry is everything with the exception of business documents and school books" [Moore's note].

the imagination"[3]—above
insolence and triviality and can present

for inspection, "imaginary gardens with real toads in them," shall
we have
it. In the meantime, if you demand on the one hand,   25
the raw material of poetry in
all its rawness and
that which is on the other hand
genuine, then you are interested in poetry.

1921, 1935

To a Snail[1]

If "compression is the first grace of style,"[2]
you have it. Contractility is a virtue
as modesty is a virtue.
It is not the acquisition of any one thing
that is able to adorn,   5
or the incidental quality that occurs
as a concomitant of something well said,
that we value in style,
but the principle that is hid:
in the absence of feet, "a method of conclusions";   10
"a knowledge of principles,"
in the curious phenomenon of your occipital horn.

1924

The Paper Nautilus[1]

For authorities whose hopes
are shaped by mercenaries?
Writers entrapped by
teatime fame and by
commuters' comforts? Not for these   5
the paper nautilus
constructs her thin glass shell.

Giving her perishable
souvenir of hope, a dull

---

3. Yeats's *Ideas of Good and Evil* (A.H. Bullen),
p. 182. "The limitation of his view was from the
very intensity of his vision; he was a too literal
realist of imagination, as others are of nature;
and because he believed that the figures seen by
the mind's eye, when exalted by inspiration, were
'eternal existences,' symbols of divine essences,
he hated every grace of style that might obscure

their lineaments" [Moore's note].
1. The text is from *Complete Poems* (1967).
2. "The very first grace of style is that which
comes from compression." *Demetrius on Style*
translated by W. Hamilton Fyfe. Heinemann,
1932 [Moore's note].
1. The text is from *Complete Poems* (1967).

white outside and smooth   10
edged inner surface
glossy as the sea, the watchful
maker of it guards it
day and night; she scarcely

eats until the eggs are hatched.   15
Buried eight-fold in her eight
arms, for she is in
a sense a devil
fish, her glass ram'shorn-cradled freight
is hid but is not crushed;   20
as Hercules,[2] bitten

by a crab loyal to the hydra,
was hindered to succeed,
the intensively
watched eggs coming from   25
the shell free it when they are freed,—
leaving its wasp-nest flaws
of white on white, and close

laid Ionic[3] chiton-folds
like the lines in the mane of   30
a Parthenon[4] horse,
round which the arms had
wound themselves as if they knew love
is the only fortress
strong enough to trust to.   35

                                                              1941, 1967

The Mind Is an Enchanting Thing[1]

is an enchanted thing
        like the glaze on a
katydid-wing
            subdivided by sun
            till the nettings are legion.   5
Like Gieseking playing Scarlatti;[2]

like the apteryx[3] awl
        as a beak, or the
kiwi's rain-shawl

2. Hero of Greek myth, who performed numerous exploits including battle with the hydra,
a many-headed monster.
3. Classical Greek, specifically Athenian.
4. Temple in Athens decorated by a carved marble band of sculptures, including processions of
horses.

1. The text is from Complete Poems (1967).
2. Walter Wilhelm Gieseking (1895–1956),
French-born German pianist, known for his ren-
ditions of compositions by the Italian composer
Domenico Scarlatti (1685–1757).
3. A flightless New Zealand bird, related to the
kiwi, with a beak shaped like an awl.

of haired feathers, the mind 10
feeling its way as though blind,
walks along with its eyes on the ground.

It has memory's ear
that can hear without
having to hear. 15
Like the gyroscope's fall,
truly unequivocal
because trued by regnant certainty,

it is a power of
strong enchantment. It 20
is like the dove
neck animated by
sun; it is memory's eye;
it's conscientious inconsistency.

It tears off the veil; tears 25
the temptation, the
mist the heart wears,
from its eye—if the heart
has a face; it takes apart
dejection. It's fire in the dove-neck's 30

iridescence; in the
inconsistencies
of Scarlatti.
Unconfusion submits
its confusion to proof; it's 35
not a Herod's[4] oath that cannot change.

1944

4. Herod Antipas (d. 39 C.E.), ruler of Judea under the Romans. He had John the Baptist beheaded to fulfill a promise to Salome (Mark 6.22–27).

T. S. ELIOT
1888–1965

The publication in 1922 of *The Waste Land* in the British little magazine *Criterion* and the American *Dial* was a cultural and literary event. The poem's title and the view it incorporated of modern civilization seemed, to many, to catch precisely the state of culture and society after World War I. The war, supposedly fought to save European civilization, had been the most brutal and destructive in Western history: what kind of civilization could have allowed it to take place? The long, fragmented structure of *The Waste Land*, too, contained so many technical innovations that ideas of what poetry was and how it worked seemed fundamentally changed. A generation of poets either imitated or resisted it.

The author of this poem was an American living in London, T. S. Eliot. Eliot had a comfortable upbringing in St. Louis: his mother was involved in cultural and charitable activities and wrote poetry; his father was a successful businessman. His grandfather Eliot had been a New England Unitarian minister who, moving to St. Louis, had founded Washington University. Eliot was thus a product of that New England–based "genteel tradition" that shaped the nation's cultural life after the Civil War. He attended Harvard for both undergraduate (1906–10) and graduate (1911–14) work. He studied at the Sorbonne in Paris from 1910 to 1911 and at Oxford from 1915 to 1916, writing a dissertation on the idealistic philosophy of the English logician and metaphysician F. H. Bradley (1846–1924). The war prevented Eliot from returning to Harvard for the oral defense of his doctoral degree, and this delay became the occasion of his turning to a life in poetry and letters rather than in academics.

Eliot had begun writing traditional poetry as a college student. In 1908, however, he read Arthur Symons's *The Symbolist Movement in Literature* (1899) and learned about Jules LaForgue and other French Symbolist poets. Symons's book altered Eliot's view of poetry, as "The Love Song of J. Alfred Prufrock" (published in *Poetry* in 1915) and "Preludes" (published in *Blast* in the same year) showed; in these poems Eliot took Symons's "revolt against exteriority, against rhetoric" in the direction of associative, oblique free verse. His fellow expatriate and poet Ezra Pound, reading this work, began enthusiastically introducing Eliot in literary circles as a young American who had "trained himself *and* modernized himself *on his own*." Pound helped Eliot over several years to get financially established. In addition, he was a perceptive reader and critic of Eliot's draft poems.

Eliot settled in England, marrying Vivian Haigh-Wood in 1915. Separated in 1932, they never divorced; Haigh-Wood died in a mental institution in 1947. After marrying, Eliot worked in London, first as a teacher and then from 1917 to 1925 in the foreign department of Lloyd's Bank, hoping to find time to write poetry and literary essays. His criticism was published in the *Egoist* and then in the little magazine that he founded, *Criterion*, which was published from 1922 to 1939. His persuasive style, a mixture of advocacy and judiciousness, effectively counterpointed Pound's aggressive, confrontational approach; the two together had a tremendous effect on how the poetry of the day was written and how the poetry of the past was evaluated. More than any other Americans they defined what is now thought of as "high" modernism.

Eliot began working on *The Waste Land* in 1921 and finished it in a Swiss sanatorium while recovering from a mental collapse brought on by overwork, marital problems, and general depression. He accepted some alterations suggested by his wife and cut huge chunks out of the poem on Pound's advice. Although Pound's work on the poem was all excision, so different was the manuscript before and after Pound's suggestions were incorporated that some critics suggest we should think of *The Waste Land* as jointly authored. The poem as published in *Criterion* and the *Dial* had no footnotes; these were appended for its publication in book form and added yet another layer (possibly self-mocking) to the complex texture of the poem.

The Waste Land consists of five discontinuous segments, each composed of fragments incorporating multiple voices and characters, literary and historical allusions and quotations, vignettes of contemporary life, surrealistic images, myths and legends. "These fragments I have shored against my ruins," the poet writes, asking whether he can form any coherent structure from the splinters of civilization. The poem's discontinuous elements are organized by recurrent allusions to the myth of seasonal death, burial, and rebirth that, according to much anthropological thinking of the time, underlay all religions. In Sir James Frazer's multivolume *The Golden Bough* (1890–1915) and Jessie Weston's *From Ritual to Romance* (1920), Eliot found a repertory of myths through which he could invoke, without specifically naming any religion, the story of a desert land brought to life by a king's sacrifice. Although it gestures toward religious belief, *The Waste Land* concludes with the outcome of the quest for regeneration uncertain in a cacophonous, desolate landscape.

Many readers saw *The Waste Land* as the definitive cultural statement of its time, but it was not definitive for Eliot. The poem may have been Eliot's indirect confession of personal discord, for which he sought resolution in social orders beyond those of poetry. In 1927 he became a British citizen; in a preface to the collection of essays *For Lancelot Andrewes* (1928), he declared himself a "classicist in literature, royalist in politics, and anglo-catholic in religion."

Eliot inspecting manuscripts at his desk.

After "The Hollow Men" and the "Sweeney" poems, which continue *The Waste Land*'s critique of modern civilization, he turned increasingly to poems of religious doubt and reconciliation. "The Journey of the Magi" and "Ash Wednesday" are poems about the search for a faith desperately needed, yet difficult to sustain. The *Four Quartets*, begun with "Burnt Norton" in 1934 and completed in 1943, are not so much reports of secure faith as dramatizations of the difficult process of arriving at belief. The *Four Quartets* move away from the fragmentary quotation and collage techniques of *The Waste Land* in favor of plainer expository statement grounded in particular times and places—the England of Eliot's chosen citizenship and the America of his origins—while aspiring to a timeless religious faith.

An emphasis on order, hierarchy, and racial homogeneity emerged in Eliot's social essays of the later 1920s and 1930s; a strain of crude anti-Semitism had appeared in the earlier Sweeney poems. As European politics became increasingly turbulent, the stability promised by totalitarian regimes appealed to some observers, Eliot included. The Communist rejection of all religion also tended to drive the more traditionally religious modernists into the opposing camp of fascism. Pound's and Eliot's Fascist sympathies in the 1930s, together with their immense influence on poetry, linked high modernism with reactionary politics in the public's perception, even while individual modernists in these years embraced political movements ranging from the far left to the extreme right, maintained centrist or liberal allegiances, or despised politics completely.

During the 1930s and 1940s, Eliot's criticism and poetry became increasingly important to the group of writers—many of them poets and academics in the United States—whose work became known collectively as the "New Criticism." In his influential essay "Tradition and the Individual Talent," Eliot had defined the English and European poetic tradition as a self-sufficient organic whole, an elastic equilibrium that constantly reformed itself to accommodate new poets. What makes poems matter, in Eliot's definition of tradition, is their effect on other poems, not their capacity to act upon the world outside of poetry. Poets contribute to the tradition, he argued, not through the direct expression of individual emotion but through a difficult process of distancing "the man who suffers" from "the mind which creates"; readers, therefore, should focus on the feeling embodied in the poem itself rather than reading the poem through the life of the poet. In other essays, Eliot denigrated didactic, expository, or narrative poets like Milton and the Victorians while applauding the verbally complex, paradoxical, indirect, symbolic work of seventeenth-century Metaphysical poets like John Donne and George Herbert. Through the New Criticism, Eliot's "impersonal" approach to poetry had a powerful role in shaping the literary curriculum in American colleges and universities, especially following World War II.

For the New Criticism, which analyzed poems for imagery, allusion, ambiguity, and irony, Eliot's essays provided theory, his poetry opportunities for practical criticism. But when critics used Eliot's preference for difficult indirection to judge literary quality and made interpretation the main task of readers, they often overlooked the lyricism, obvious didacticism, and humor of Eliot's own poetry. And they minimized the poems' cultural, historical, and autobiographical content.

However elitist his pronouncements, however hostile to modernity he claimed to be, Eliot drew heavily on popular forms and longed to have wide cultural influence. There are vaudeville turns throughout *The Waste Land*. He admired Charlie Chaplin and wanted "as large and miscellaneous an audience as possible." He pursued this ambition by writing verse plays. *Murder in the Cathedral* (1935) was a church pageant; *The Family Reunion* (1939), *The Cocktail Party* (1949), *The Confidential Clerk* (1953), and *The Elder Statesman* (1959), all religious in theme, were successfully produced in London and on Broadway. He never became a popular poet, however, despite his tremendous impact on the teaching and writing of poetry. Although Eliot remained a resident of England, he returned to the United States frequently to lecture and to give readings of his poems. He married his assistant, Valerie Fletcher, in 1957. By the time of his death he had become a social and cultural institution.

The text of the poems is that of *The Complete Poems and Plays of T. S. Eliot* (1969).

The Love Song of J. Alfred Prufrock

S'io credessi che mia risposta fosse
a persona che mai tornasse al mondo,
questa fiamma staria senza più scosse.
Ma per ciò che giammai di questo fondo
non tornò vivo alcun, s'i'odo il vero,
senza tema d'infamia ti rispondo.[1]

Let us go then, you and I,
When the evening is spread out against the sky
Like a patient etherised upon a table;
Let us go, through certain half-deserted streets,
The muttering retreats   5
Of restless nights in one-night cheap hotels
And sawdust restaurants with oyster-shells:
Streets that follow like a tedious argument
Of insidious intent

---

1. If I thought that my reply would be to one who would ever return to the world, this flame would stay without further movement; but since none has ever returned alive from this depth, if what I hear is true, I answer you without fear of infamy (Italian; Dante's *Inferno* 27.61–66). The speaker, Guido da Montefeltro, consumed in flame as punishment for giving false counsel, confesses his shame without fear of its being reported since he believes Dante cannot return to earth.

To lead you to an overwhelming question . . .   10
Oh, do not ask, 'What is it?'
Let us go and make our visit.

In the room the women come and go
Talking of Michelangelo.

The yellow fog that rubs its back upon the window-panes,   15
The yellow smoke that rubs its muzzle on the window-panes,
Licked its tongue into the corners of the evening,

Lingered upon the pools that stand in drains,
Let fall upon its back the soot that falls from chimneys,
Slipped by the terrace, made a sudden leap,   20
And seeing that it was a soft October night,
Curled once about the house, and fell asleep.

And indeed there will be time[2]
For the yellow smoke that slides along the street
Rubbing its back upon the window-panes;   25
There will be time, there will be time
To prepare a face to meet the faces that you meet;
There will be time to murder and create,
And time for all the works and days[3] of hands
That lift and drop a question on your plate;   30
Time for you and time for me,
And time yet for a hundred indecisions,
And for a hundred visions and revisions,
Before the taking of a toast and tea.

In the room the women come and go   35
Talking of Michelangelo.

And indeed there will be time
To wonder, 'Do I dare?' and, 'Do I dare?'
Time to turn back and descend the stair,
With a bald spot in the middle of my hair—   40
(They will say: 'How his hair is growing thin!')
My morning coat, my collar mounting firmly to the chin,
My necktie rich and modest, but asserted by a simple pin—
(They will say: 'But how his arms and legs are thin!')
Do I dare   45
Disturb the universe?
In a minute there is time
For decisions and revisions which a minute will reverse.

For I have known them all already, known them all—
Have known the evenings, mornings, afternoons,   50

---

2. An echo of Andrew Marvell, "To His Coy Mistress" (1681): "Had we but world enough and time."

3. *Works and Days* is a didactic poem about farming by the Greek poet Hesiod (8th century B.C.E.).

I have measured out my life with coffee spoons;
I know the voices dying with a dying fall[4]
Beneath the music from a farther room.
   So how should I presume?

And I have known the eyes already, known them all—   55
The eyes that fix you in a formulated phrase,
And when I am formulated, sprawling on a pin,
When I am pinned and wriggling on the wall,
Then how should I begin
To spit out all the butt-ends of my days and ways?   60
   And how should I presume?
And I have known the arms already, known them all—
Arms that are braceleted and white and bare
(But in the lamplight, downed with light brown hair!)
Is it perfume from a dress   65
That makes me so digress?
Arms that lie along a table, or wrap about a shawl.
   And should I then presume?
   And how should I begin?
   . . . . . .
Shall I say, I have gone at dusk through narrow streets   70
And watched the smoke that rises from the pipes
Of lonely men in shirt-sleeves, leaning out of windows? . . .

I should have been a pair of ragged claws
Scuttling across the floors of silent seas.
   . . . . . .

And the afternoon, the evening, sleeps so peacefully!   75
Smoothed by long fingers,
Asleep . . . tired . . . or it malingers,
Stretched on the floor, here beside you and me.
Should I, after tea and cakes and ices,
Have the strength to force the moment to its crisis?   80
But though I have wept and fasted, wept and prayed,
Though I have seen my head (grown slightly bald) brought in
     upon a platter,[5]
I am no prophet—and here's no great matter;
I have seen the moment of my greatness flicker,
And I have seen the eternal Footman hold my coat, and snicker,   85
And in short, I was afraid.

And would it have been worth it, after all,
After the cups, the marmalade, the tea,
Among the porcelain, among some talk of you and me,
Would it have been worth while,   90
To have bitten off the matter with a smile,

---

4. Echo of Duke Orsino's invocation of music in Shakespeare's *Twelfth Night* 1.1.4: "If music be the food of love, play on. . . . That strain again! It had a dying fall."

5. The head of the prophet John the Baptist, who was killed at the behest of Princess Salome, was brought to her on a platter (see Mark 6.17–20, Matthew 14.3–11).

To have squeezed the universe into a ball
To roll it towards some overwhelming question,
To say: 'I am Lazarus,[6] come from the dead,
Come back to tell you all, I shall tell you all'—   95
If one, settling a pillow by her head,
    Should say: 'That is not what I meant at all.
    That is not it, at all.'

And would it have been worth it, after all,
Would it have been worth while,   100
After the sunsets and the dooryards and the sprinkled streets,
After the novels, after the teacups, after the skirts that trail
    along the floor—
And this, and so much more?—
It is impossible to say just what I mean!
But as if a magic lantern threw the nerves in patterns on a screen: 105
Would it have been worth while
If one, settling a pillow or throwing off a shawl,
And turning toward the window, should say:
    'That is not it at all,
    That is not what I meant, at all.'   110
  . . . . . .

No! I am not Prince Hamlet, nor was meant to be;
Am an attendant lord, one that will do
To swell a progress,[7] start a scene or two,
Advise the prince; no doubt, an easy tool,
Deferential, glad to be of use,   115
Politic, cautious, and meticulous;
Full of high sentence,[8] but a bit obtuse;
At times, indeed, almost ridiculous—
Almost, at times, the Fool.

I grow old . . . I grow old . . .   120
I shall wear the bottoms of my trousers rolled.

Shall I part my hair behind? Do I dare to eat a peach?
I shall wear white flannel trousers, and walk upon the beach.
I have heard the mermaids singing, each to each.

I do not think that they will sing to me.   125

I have seen them riding seaward on the waves
Combing the white hair of the waves blown back
When the wind blows the water white and black.

We have lingered in the chambers of the sea
By sea-girls wreathed with seaweed red and brown   130
Till human voices wake us, and we drown.

1915, 1917

---

6. The resurrection of Lazarus is recounted in John 11.1–44; see also Luke 16.19–31.
7. A journey or procession made by royal courts and often portrayed on Elizabethan stages.
8. Opinions, sententiousness.

The Waste Land[1]

"Nam Sibyllam quidem Cumis ego ipse oculis meis vidi in ampulla pendere, et cum illi pueri dicerent: Σίβυλα τί θέλεις respondebat illa: ἀποθανεῖν θέλω."[2]

FOR EZRA POUND
IL MIGLIOR FABBRO.[3]

I. The Burial of the Dead[4]

April is the cruellest month, breeding
Lilacs out of the dead land, mixing
Memory and desire, stirring
Dull roots with spring rain.
Winter kept us warm, covering   5
Earth in forgetful snow, feeding
A little life with dried tubers.
Summer surprised us, coming over the Starnbergersee[5]
With a shower of rain; we stopped in the colonnade,
And went on in sunlight, into the Hofgarten,[6]   10
And drank coffee, and talked for an hour.
Bin gar keine Russin, stamm' aus Litauen, echt deutsch.[7]
And when we were children, staying at the arch-duke's,
My cousin's, he took me out on a sled,
And I was frightened. He said, Marie,   15
Marie, hold on tight. And down we went.
In the mountains, there you feel free.
I read, much of the night, and go south in the winter.

What are the roots that clutch, what branches grow
Out of this stony rubbish? Son of man,[8]   20
You cannot say, or guess, for you know only
A heap of broken images, where the sun beats,
And the dead tree gives no shelter, the cricket no relief,[9]

1. Eliot's notes for the first hardcover edition of *The Waste Land* opened with his acknowledgment that "not only the title, but the plan and a good deal of the incidental symbolism of the poem" were suggested by Jessie L. Weston's book on the Grail Legend, *From Ritual to Romance* (1920), and that he was indebted also to James G. Frazer's *The Golden Bough* (1890–1915), "especially the two volumes *Adonis, Attis, Osiris*," which deal with vegetation myths and fertility rites. Eliot's notes are incorporated in the footnotes to this text. Many critics believe that the notes were added in a spirit of parody. The numerous and extensive literary quotations add to the multivocal effect of the poem.
2. A quotation from Petronius's *Satyricon* (1st century C.E.) about the Sibyl (prophetess) of Cumae, blessed with eternal life by Apollo but doomed to perpetual old age, who guided Aeneas through Hades in Virgil's *Aeneid*: "For once I myself saw with my own eyes the Sibyl at Cumae hanging in a cage, and when the boys said to her

'Sibyl, what do you want?' she replied, 'I want to die.'"
3. "The better maker," the tribute in Dante's *Purgatorio* 26.117 to the Provençal poet Arnaut Daniel.
4. The title of the Anglican burial service.
5. A lake near Munich. Lines 8–16 were suggested by the Countess Marie Larisch's memoir, *My Past* (1913).
6. A public park in Munich, with cafés; former grounds of a Bavarian palace.
7. I am certainly not Russian; I come from Lithuania, a true German (German).
8. "Cf. Ezekiel II, i" [Eliot's note]. There God addresses the prophet Ezekiel as "Son of man" and declares: "stand upon thy feet, and I will speak unto thee."
9. "Cf. Ecclesiastes XII, v" [Eliot's note]. There the preacher describes the bleakness of old age when "the grasshopper shall be a burden, and desire shall fail."

And the dry stone no sound of water. Only
There is shadow under this red rock,[1]   25
(Come in under the shadow of this red rock),
And I will show you something different from either
Your shadow at morning striding behind you
Or your shadow at evening rising to meet you;
I will show you fear in a handful of dust.   30

       Frisch weht der Wind
       Der Heimat zu
       Mein Irisch Kind,
       Wo weilest du?[2]

'You gave me hyacinths first a year ago;   35
'They called me the hyacinth girl.'
—Yet when we came back, late, from the hyacinth[3] garden,
Your arms full, and your hair wet, I could not
Speak, and my eyes failed, I was neither
Living nor dead, and I knew nothing,   40
Looking into the heart of light, the silence.
Oed' und leer das Meer.[4]

Madame Sosostris,[5] famous clairvoyante,
Had a bad cold, nevertheless
Is known to be the wisest woman in Europe,   45
With a wicked pack of cards.[6] Here, said she,
Is your card, the drowned Phoenician Sailor,[7]
(Those are pearls that were his eyes.[8] Look!)
Here is Belladonna,[9] the Lady of the Rocks,
The lady of situations.   50
Here is the man with three staves, and here the Wheel,
And here is the one-eyed merchant,[1] and this card,
Which is blank, is something he carries on his back,
Which I am forbidden to see. I do not find

1. Cf. Isaiah 32.1–2 and the prophecy that the reign of the Messiah "shall be . . . as rivers of water in a dry place, as the shadow of a great rock in a weary land."
2. "V. [see] *Tristan und Isolde*, I, verses 5–8" [Eliot's note]. In Wagner's opera, a sailor aboard Tristan's ship recalls his love back in Ireland: "Fresh blows the wind to the homeland; my Irish child, where are you waiting?"
3. The boy in Ovid's *Metamorphoses* 10, who was beloved by Apollo but slain by a jealous rival. The Greeks celebrated his festival in May.
4. "III, verse 24" [Eliot's note]. In *Tristan*, III, verse 24, the dying Tristan, awaiting the ship that carries his beloved Isolde, is told that "Empty and barren is the sea."
5. Eliot derived the name from "Sesostris, the Sorceress of Ectabana," the pseudo-Egyptian name assumed by a woman who tells fortunes in Aldous Huxley's novel *Chrome Yellow* (1921). Sesostris was a 12th-dynasty Egyptian king.
6. The tarot deck of cards. Eliot's note to this passage reads: "I am not familiar with the exact constitution of the Tarot pack of cards, from which I have obviously departed to suit my own convenience. The Hanged Man, a member of the tra-

ditional pack, fits my purpose in two ways: because he is associated in my mind with the Hanged God of Frazer, and because I associate him with the hooded figure in the passage of the disciples to Emmaus in Part V. The Phoenician Sailor and the Merchant appear later; also the 'crowds of people,' and Death by Water is executed in Part IV. The Man with Three Staves (an authentic member of the Tarot pack) I associate, quite arbitrarily, with the Fisher King himself."
7. A symbolic figure that includes "Mr. Eugenides, the Smyrna merchant" in Part III and "Phlebas the Phoenician" in Part IV. The ancient Phoenicians were seagoing merchants who spread Egyptian fertility cults throughout the Mediterranean.
8. The line is a quotation from Ariel's song in Shakespeare's *Tempest* 1.2.398. Prince Ferdinand, disconsolate because he thinks his father has drowned in the storm, is consoled when Ariel sings of a miraculous sea change that has transformed death into "something rich and strange."
9. Literally "beautiful lady"; the name of both the poisonous plant deadly nightshade and a cosmetic.
1. These three figures are from the Tarot deck.

The Hanged Man. Fear death by water. 55
I see crowds of people, walking round in a ring.
Thank you. If you see dear Mrs. Equitone,
Tell her I bring the horoscope myself:
One must be so careful these days.

Unreal City,[2] 60
Under the brown fog of a winter dawn,
A crowd flowed over London Bridge, so many,
I had not thought death had undone so many.[3]
Sighs, short and infrequent, were exhaled,[4]
And each man fixed his eyes before his feet. 65
Flowed up the hill and down King William Street,
To where Saint Mary Woolnoth kept the hours
With a dead sound on the final stroke of nine.[5]
There I saw one I knew, and stopped him, crying: 'Stetson![6]
'You who were with me in the ships at Mylae![7] 70
'That corpse you planted last year in your garden,
'Has it begun to sprout? Will it bloom this year?
'Or has the sudden frost disturbed its bed?
'O keep the Dog far hence, that's friend to men,
'Or with his nails he'll dig it up again![8] 75
'You! hypocrite lecteur!—mon semblable,—mon frère!'[9]

II. A Game of Chess[1]

The Chair she sat in, like a burnished throne,[2]
Glowed on the marble, where the glass
Held up by standards wrought with fruited vines
From which a golden Cupidon peeped out 80
(Another hid his eyes behind his wing)

2. "Cf. Baudelaire: 'Fourmillante cité, cité pleine de rêves, / Où le spectre en plein jour raccroche le passant'" [Eliot's note]. The lines are quoted from "Les Sept Vieillards" (The seven old men), poem 93 of Les Fleurs du Mal (The flowers of evil, 1857) by the French Symbolist Charles Baudelaire (1821–1867), and may be translated from the French: "Swarming city, city full of dreams, / Where the specter in broad daylight accosts the passerby."
3. "Cf. Inferno III, 55–57" [Eliot's note]. The note continues to quote Dante's lines, which may be translated: "So long a train of people, / That I should never have believed / That death had undone so many."
4. "Cf. Inferno IV, 25–27" [Eliot's note]. Dante describes, in Limbo, the virtuous pagan dead, who, living before Christ, could not hope for salvation. The lines read: "Here, so far as I could tell by listening, / There was no lamentation except sighs, / which caused the eternal air to tremble."
5. "A phenomenon which I have often noticed" [Eliot's note]. The church named is in the financial district of London.
6. A hat manufacturer.
7. The battle of Mylae (260 B.C.E.) was a victory for Rome against Carthage.
8. "Cf. the dirge in Webster's White Devil"

[Eliot's note]. In the play by John Webster (d. 1625), a crazed woman fears that the corpses of her decadent and murdered relatives might be disinterred: "But keep the wolf far thence, that's foe to men, / For with his nails he'll dig them up again." In echoing the lines Eliot altered "foe" to "friend" and the "wolf" to "Dog," invoking the brilliant Dog Star, Sirius, whose rise in the heavens accompanied the flooding of the Nile and promised the return of fertility to Egypt.
9. "V. Baudelaire, Preface to Fleurs du Mal" [Eliot's note]. The last line of the introductory poem to Les Fleurs du Mal. "Au Lecteur" (To the reader) may be translated from the French: "Hypocrite reader!—my likeness—my brother!
1. The title suggests two plays by Thomas Middleton: A Game of Chess (1627), about a marriage of political expediency, and Women Beware Women (1657), containing a scene in which a mother-in-law is engrossed in a chess game while her daughter-in-law is seduced nearby. Eliot's note to line 118 refers readers to this play. It is now believed that much of this section reflects Eliot's disintegrating marriage.
2. "Cf. Antony and Cleopatra, II, ii. 190" [Eliot's note]. In Shakespeare's play, Enobarbus's description of Cleopatra begins: "The barge she sat in, like a burnish'd throne, / Burn'd on the water."

Doubled the flames of sevenbranched candelabra
Reflecting light upon the table as
The glitter of her jewels rose to meet it,
From satin cases poured in rich profusion.   85
In vials of ivory and coloured glass
Unstoppered, lurked her strange synthetic perfumes,
Unguent, powdered, or liquid—troubled, confused
And drowned the sense in odours; stirred by the air
That freshened from the window, these ascended   90
In fattening the prolonged candle-flames,
Flung their smoke into the laquearia,³
Stirring the pattern on the coffered ceiling.
Huge sea-wood fed with copper
Burned green and orange, framed by the coloured stone,   95
In which sad light a carvèd dolphin swam.
Above the antique mantel was displayed
As though a window gave upon the sylvan scene⁴
The change of Philomel, by the barbarous king
So rudely forced; yet there the nightingale   100
Filled all the desert with inviolable voice
And still she cried, and still the world pursues,
'Jug Jug'⁵ to dirty ears.
And other withered stumps of time
Were told upon the walls; staring forms   105
Leaned out, leaning, hushing the room enclosed.
Footsteps shuffled on the stair.
Under the firelight, under the brush, her hair
Spread out in fiery points
Glowed into words, then would be savagely still.   110

'My nerves are bad to-night. Yes, bad. Stay with me.
'Speak to me. Why do you never speak. Speak.
    'What are you thinking of? What thinking? What?
'I never know what you are thinking. Think.'

I think we are in rats' alley⁶   115
Where the dead men lost their bones.

'What is that noise?'
                        The wind under the door.⁷
'What is that noise now? What is the wind doing?'

---

3. "Laquearia, V. *Aeneid,* I, 726" [Eliot's note].
Eliot quotes the passage containing the term
laquearia ("paneled ceiling") and describing the
banquet hall where Queen Dido welcomed Aeneas
to Carthage. It reads: "Blazing torches hang from
the gilded paneled ceiling, and torches conquer
the night with flames." Aeneas became Dido's
lover but abandoned her to continue his journey
to found Rome, and she committed suicide.
4. Eliot's notes for lines 98–99 refer the reader
to "Milton, *Paradise Lost,* IV, 140" for the phrase
"sylvan scene" and to "Ovid, *Metamorphoses,* VI,
Philomela." The lines splice the setting of Eve's
temptation in the Garden of Eden, first described

through Satan's eyes, with the rape of Philomela
by her sister's husband, King Tereus, and her
transformation into the nightingale. Eliot's note
for line 100 refers the reader ahead to the nightingale's song in Part III, line 204, of his own poem.
5. The conventional rendering of the nightingale's song in Elizabethan poetry.
6. Eliot's note refers readers to "Part III, l. 195."
7. "Cf. Webster: 'Is the wind in that door still?'"
[Eliot's note]. In John Webster's *The Devil's Law
Case* (1623) 3.2.162, a duke is cured of an infection by a wound intended to kill him; a surprised
surgeon asks the quoted question, meaning, "Is
he still alive?"

Nothing again nothing.   120
                                                    'Do
'You know nothing? Do you see nothing? Do you remember
'Nothing?'

            I remember
Those are pearls that were his eyes.   125
'Are you alive, or not? Is there nothing in your head?'
                                              But
O O O O that Shakespeherian Rag—
It's so elegant
So intelligent   130
'What shall I do now? What shall I do?'
'I shall rush out as I am, and walk the street
'With my hair down, so. What shall we do tomorrow?
'What shall we ever do?'
                        The hot water at ten.   135
And if it rains, a closed car at four.
And we shall play a game of chess,
Pressing lidless eyes and waiting for a knock upon the door.

When Lil's husband got demobbed,[8] I said—
I didn't mince my words, I said to her myself,   140
HURRY UP PLEASE ITS TIME[9]
Now Albert's coming back, make yourself a bit smart.
He'll want to know what you done with that money he gave you
To get yourself some teeth. He did, I was there.
You have them all out, Lil, and get a nice set,   145
He said, I swear, I can't bear to look at you.
And no more can't I, I said, and think of poor Albert,
He's been in the army four years, he wants a good time,
And if you don't give it him, there's others will, I said.
Oh is there, she said. Something o' that, I said.   150
Then I'll know who to thank, she said, and give me a straight look.
HURRY UP PLEASE ITS TIME
If you don't like it you can get on with it, I said.
Others can pick and choose if you can't.
But if Albert makes off, it won't be for lack of telling. 155
You ought to be ashamed, I said, to look so antique.
(And her only thirty-one.)
I can't help it, she said, pulling a long face,
It's them pills I took, to bring it off, she said.
(She's had five already, and nearly died of young George.) 160
The chemist[1] said it would be all right, but I've never been the same.
You *are* a proper fool, I said.
Well, if Albert won't leave you alone, there it is, I said,
What you get married for if you don't want children?
HURRY UP PLEASE ITS TIME   165

8. Slang for "demobilized," discharged from the   pub at closing time.
army.   1. Pharmacist.
9. Routine call of British bartenders to clear the

Well, that Sunday Albert was home, they had a hot gammon,[2]
And they asked me in to dinner, to get the beauty of it hot—
HURRY UP PLEASE ITS TIME
HURRY UP PLEASE ITS TIME
Goonight Bill, Goonight Lou. Goonight May. Goonight.   170
Ta ta. Goonight. Goonight.
Good night, ladies, good night, sweet ladies, good night, good night.[3]

III. The Fire Sermon[4]

The river's tent is broken; the last fingers of leaf
Clutch and sink into the wet bank. The wind
Crosses the brown land, unheard. The nymphs are departed.   175
Sweet Thames, run softly, till I end my song.[5]
The river bears no empty bottles, sandwich papers,
Silk handkerchiefs, cardboard boxes, cigarette ends
Or other testimony of summer nights. The nymphs are departed.
And their friends, the loitering heirs of City directors;   180
Departed, have left no addresses.
By the waters of Leman I sat down and wept[6] . . .
Sweet Thames, run softly till I end my song,
Sweet Thames, run softly, for I speak not loud or long.
But at my back in a cold blast I hear[7]   185
The rattle of the bones, and chuckle spread from ear to ear.

A rat crept softly through the vegetation
Dragging its slimy belly on the bank
While I was fishing in the dull canal
On a winter evening round behind the gashouse   190
Musing upon the king my brother's wreck[8]
And on the king my father's death before him.
White bodies naked on the low damp ground
And bones cast in a little low dry garret,
Rattled by the rat's foot only, year to year.   195
But at my back from time to time I hear
The sound of horns and motors, which shall bring
Sweeney to Mrs. Porter in the spring.[9]

---

2. Ham or bacon.
3. A double echo of the popular song "Good night ladies, we're going to leave you now" and mad Ophelia's farewell before drowning, in Shakespeare, *Hamlet* 4.5.72.
4. I.e., Buddha's Fire Sermon. See p. 843, n. 8.
5. "V. Spenser, *Prothalamion*" [Eliot's note]. The line is the refrain of the marriage song by Edmund Spenser (1552–1599), a pastoral celebration of marriage set along the Thames River near London.
6. The phrasing recalls Psalms 137.1, in which the exiled Jews mourn for their homeland: "By the rivers of Babylon, there we sat down, yea, we wept, when we remembered Zion." Lake Leman is another name for Lake Geneva, location of the sanatorium where Eliot wrote the bulk of *The Waste Land*. The archaic term *leman*, for "illicit mistress," led to the phrase "waters of leman"

signifying lusts.
7. This line and line 196 echo Andrew Marvell (1621–1678), *To His Coy Mistress*, lines 21–24: "But at my back I always hear / Time's wingèd chariot hurrying near; / And yonder all before us lie / Deserts of vast eternity."
8. "Cf. *The Tempest*, I, ii" [Eliot's note]. Another allusion to Shakespeare's play, 1.2.389–90, where Prince Ferdinand, thinking his father dead, describes himself as "Sitting on a bank, / Weeping again the King my father's wrack."
9. "Cf. Day, *Parliament of Bees*: 'When of the sudden, listening, you shall hear, / A noise of horns and hunting, which shall bring / Actaeon to Diana in the spring, / Where all shall see her naked skin'" [Eliot's note]. Actaeon was changed into a stag and hunted to death as punishment for seeing Diana, goddess of chastity, bathing. John Day (1574–c. 1640), English poet.

O the moon shone bright on Mrs. Porter
And on her daughter   200
They wash their feet in soda water[1]
Et, O ces voix d'enfants, chantant dans la coupole!;[2]

Twit twit twit
Jug jug jug jug jug jug

So rudely forc'd.   205
Tereu[3]

Unreal City
Under the brown fog of a winter noon
Mr. Eugenides, the Smyrna merchant
Unshaven, with a pocket full of currants   210
C.i.f.[4] London: documents at sight,
Asked me in demotic French
To luncheon at the Cannon Street Hotel
Followed by a weekend at the Metropole.

At the violet hour, when the eyes and back   215
Turn upward from the desk, when the human engine waits
Like a taxi throbbing waiting,
I Tiresias,[5] though blind, throbbing between two lives,
Old man with wrinkled female breasts, can see
At the violet hour, the evening hour that strives   220
Homeward, and brings the sailor home from sea,[6]

1. "I do not know the origin of the ballad from which these lines are taken: it was reported to me from Sydney, Australia" [Eliot's note]. The bawdy song was popular among World War I troops.
2. "V. Verlaine, *Parsifal*" [Eliot's note]. The last line of the sonnet "Parsifal" by the French Symbolist Paul Verlaine (1844–1896) reads: "And O those children's voices singing in the cupola." In Wagner's opera, the feet of Parsifal, the questing knight, are washed before he enters the sanctuary of the Grail.
3. Alludes to Tereus, who raped Philomela, and like *jug* is a conventional Elizabethan term for the nightingale's song; also a slang pronunciation of *true*.
4. "The currants were quoted at a price 'carriage and insurance free to London'; and the Bill of Lading, etc. were to be handed to the buyer upon payment of the sight draft" [Eliot's note]. Some have suggested another possibility for the phrase "carriage and insurance free": "cost, insurance and freight."
5. Eliot's note reads: "Tiresias, although a mere spectator and not indeed a 'character,' is yet the most important personage in the poem, uniting all the rest. Just as the one-eyed merchant, seller of currants, melts into the Phoenician Sailor, and the latter is not wholly distinct from Ferdinand Prince of Naples, so all the women are one woman, and the two sexes meet in Tiresias. What Tiresias *sees*, in fact, is the substance of the poem. The whole passage from Ovid is of great anthropological interest." The note quotes the Latin passage from Ovid, *Metamorphoses* 2.421–43, which may be translated: "Jove [very drunk] said jokingly to Juno: 'You women have greater pleasure in love than that enjoyed by men.' She denied it. So they decided to refer the question to wise Tiresias who knew love from both points of view. For once, with a blow of his staff, he had separated two huge snakes who were copulating in the forest, and miraculously was changed instantly from a man into a woman and remained so for seven years. In the eighth year he saw the snakes again and said: 'If a blow against you is so powerful that it changes the sex of the author of it, now I shall strike you again.' With these words he struck them, and his former shape and masculinity were restored. As referee in the sportive quarrel, he supported Jove's claim. Juno, overly upset by the decision, condemned the arbitrator to eternal blindness. But the all-powerful father (inasmuch as no god can undo what has been done by another god) gave him the power of prophecy, with this honor compensating him for the loss of sight."
6. "This may not appear as exact as Sappho's lines, but I had in mind the 'longshore' or 'dory' fisherman, who returns at nightfall" [Eliot's note]. Fragment 149, by the female Greek poet Sappho (fl. 600 B.C.E.), celebrates the Evening Star who "brings homeward all those / Scattered by the dawn, / The sheep to fold . . . / The children to their mother's side." A more familiar echo is "Home is the sailor, home from sea" in "Requiem" by Robert Louis Stevenson (1850–1894).

The typist home at teatime, clears her breakfast, lights
Her stove, and lays out food in tins.
Out of the window perilously spread
Her drying combinations touched by the sun's last rays,   225
On the divan are piled (at night her bed)
Stockings, slippers, camisoles, and stays.
I Tiresias, old man with wrinkled dugs
Perceived the scene, and foretold the rest—
I too awaited the expected guest.   230
He, the young man carbuncular, arrives,
A small house agent's clerk, with one bold stare,
One of the low on whom assurance sits
As a silk hat on a Bradford[7] millionaire.
The time is now propitious, as he guesses,   235
The meal is ended, she is bored and tired,
Endeavours to engage her in caresses
Which still are unreproved, if undesired.
Flushed and decided, he assaults at once;
Exploring hands encounter no defence;   240
His vanity requires no response,
And makes a welcome of indifference.
(And I Tiresias have foresuffered all
Enacted on this same divan or bed;
I who have sat by Thebes below the wall[8]   245
And walked among the lowest of the dead.)
Bestows one final patronising kiss,
And gropes his way, finding the stairs unlit . . .

She turns and looks a moment in the glass,
Hardly aware of her departed lover;   250
Her brain allows one half-formed thought to pass:
'Well now that's done: and I'm glad it's over.'
When lovely woman stoops to folly and
Paces about her room again, alone,
She smoothes her hair with automatic hand,   255
And puts a record on the gramophone.[9]

'This music crept by me upon the waters'[1]
And along the Strand, up Queen Victoria Street.
O City city, I can sometimes hear
Beside a public bar in Lower Thames Street,   260
The pleasant whining of a mandoline
And a clatter and a chatter from within

7. A Yorkshire, England, manufacturing town where fortunes were made during World War I.
8. Tiresias prophesied in the marketplace below the wall of Thebes, witnessed the tragedies of Oedipus and Creon in that city, and retained his prophetic powers in the underworld.
9. Eliot's note refers to the novel *The Vicar of Wakefield* (1766) by Oliver Goldsmith (1728–1774) and the song sung by Olivia when she revisits the scene of her seduction: "When lovely woman stoops to folly / And finds too late that men betray / What charm can soothe her melancholy, / What art can wash her guilt away? / The only art her guilt to cover, / To hide her shame from every eye, / To give repentance to her lover / And wring his bosom—is to die."
1. Eliot's note refers to Shakespeare's *The Tempest*, the scene where Ferdinand listens to Ariel's song telling of his father's miraculous sea change: "This music crept by me on the waters, / Allaying both their fury and my passion / With its sweet air" (1.2.391–93).

Where fishmen lounge at noon: where the walls
Of Magnus Martyr[2] hold
Inexplicable splendour of Ionian white and gold.   265

       The river sweats[3]
       Oil and tar
       The barges drift
       With the turning tide
       Red sails   270
       Wide
       To leeward, swing on the heavy spar.
       The barges wash
       Drifting logs
       Down Greenwich reach   275
       Past the Isle of Dogs.[4]
            Weialala leia
            Wallala leialala

       Elizabeth and Leicester[5]
       Beating oars   280
       The stern was formed
       A gilded shell
       Red and gold
       The brisk swell
       Rippled both shores   285
       Southwest wind
       Carried down stream
       The peal of bells
       White towers
            Weialala leia   290
            Wallala leialala

Trams and dusty trees.
Highbury bore me. Richmond and Kew
Undid me.[6] By Richmond I raised my knees
Supine on the floor of a narrow canoe.'   295
'My feet are at Moorgate, and my heart
Under my feet. After the event
He wept. He promised "a new start."
I made no comment. What should I resent?'

2. "The interior of St. Magnus Martyr is to my mind one of the finest among [Christopher] Wren's interiors" [Eliot's note].
3. "The Song of the (three) Thames-daughters begins here. From line 292 to 306 inclusive they speak in turn. V. *Götterdämmerung*, III, i: the Rhine-daughters" [Eliot's note]. Lines 277–78 and 290–91 are from the lament of the Rhine maidens for the lost beauty of the Rhine River in the opera by Richard Wagner (1813–1883), *Götterdämmerung* (The twilight of the gods, 1876).
4. A peninsula in the Thames opposite Greenwich, a borough of London and the birthplace of Queen Elizabeth I. Throughout this section Eliot has named places along the Thames River.

5. Reference to the romance between Queen Elizabeth I and the earl of Leicester. Eliot's note refers to the historian James A. Froude, "*Elizabeth*, Vol. I. ch. iv, letter of [bishop] De Quadra [the ambassador] to Philip of Spain: 'In the afternoon we were in a barge, watching the games on the river. (The queen) was alone with Lord Robert and myself on the poop, when they began to talk nonsense, and went so far that Lord Robert at last said, as I was on the spot there was no reason why they should not be married if the queen pleased.'"
6. "Cf. *Purgatorio*, V, 133" [Eliot's note]. Eliot parodies Dante's lines, which may be translated: "Remember me, who am La Pia. / Siena made me, Maremma undid me."

'On Margate Sands,   300
I can connect
Nothing with nothing.
The broken fingernails of dirty hands.
My people humble people who expect
Nothing.'   305
        la la

To Carthage then I came[7]

Burning burning burning burning[8]
O Lord Thou pluckest me out[9]
O Lord Thou pluckest   310

burning

IV. Death by Water

Phlebas the Phoenician, a fortnight dead,
Forgot the cry of gulls, and the deep sea swell
And the profit and loss.
                 A current under sea   315
Picked his bones in whispers. As he rose and fell
He passed the stages of his age and youth
Entering the whirlpool.
               Gentile or Jew
O you who turn the wheel and look to windward,   320
Consider Phlebas, who was once handsome and tall as you.

V. What the Thunder Said[1]

After the torchlight red on sweaty faces
After the frosty silence in the gardens
After the agony in stony places
The shouting and the crying   325
Prison and palace and reverberation
Of thunder of spring over distant mountains
He who was living is now dead
We who were living are now dying
With a little patience[2]   330

---

7. "V. St. Augustine's *Confessions*: 'to Carthage then I came, where a cauldron of unholy loves sang all about mine ears'" [Eliot's note]. Augustine here recounts his licentious youth.

8. Eliot's note to lines 307–09 refers to "Buddha's Fire Sermon (which corresponds in importance to the Sermon on the Mount)" and "St. Augustine's Confessions." The "collocation of these two representatives of eastern and western asceticism, as the culmination of this part of the poem, is not an accident."

9. The line is from Augustine's *Confessions* and echoes also Zechariah 3.2, where Jehovah, rebuking Satan, calls the high priest Joshua "a brand plucked out of the fire."

1. "In the first part of Part V three themes are employed: the journey to Emmaus, the approach to the Chapel Perilous (see Miss Weston's book) and the present decay of eastern Europe" [Eliot's note]. During his disciples' journey to Emmaus, after his Crucifixion and Resurrection, Jesus walked alongside and conversed with them, but they did not recognize him (Luke 24.13–34).

2. The opening nine lines allude to Christ's imprisonment and trial, to his agony in the garden of Gethsemane, and to his Crucifixion on Golgotha (Calvary) and burial.

Here is no water but only rock
Rock and no water and the sandy road
The road winding above among the mountains
Which are mountains of rock without water
If there were water we should stop and drink   335
Amongst the rock one cannot stop or think
Sweat is dry and feet are in the sand
If there were only water amongst the rock
Dead mountain mouth of carious teeth that cannot spit
Here one can neither stand nor lie nor sit   340
There is not even silence in the mountains
But dry sterile thunder without rain
There is not even solitude in the mountains
But red sullen faces sneer and snarl
From doors of mudcracked houses   345
                        If there were water

    And no rock
    If there were rock
    And also water
    And water   350
    A spring
    A pool among the rock
    If there were the sound of water only
    Not the cicada[3]
    And dry grass singing   355
    But sound of water over a rock
    Where the hermit-thrush[4] sings in the pine trees
    Drip drop drip drop drop drop drop
    But there is no water

Who is the third who walks always beside you?[5]   360
When I count, there are only you and I together
But when I look ahead up the white road
There is always another one walking beside you
Gliding wrapt in a brown mantle, hooded
I do not know whether a man or a woman   365
—But who is that on the other side of you?

What is that sound high in the air[6]
Murmur of maternal lamentation
Who are those hooded hordes swarming

---

3. Grasshopper. Cf. line 23 and see p. 834, n. 9.
4. "This is . . . the hermit-thrush which I have heard in Quebec Province. Chapman says (*Handbook of Birds of Eastern North America*) 'it is most at home in secluded woodland and thickety retreats.' . . . Its 'water dripping song' is justly celebrated" [Eliot's note].
5. "The following lines were stimulated by the account of one of the Antarctic expeditions (I forget which, but I think one of Shackleton's): it was related that the party of explorers, at the extremity of their strength, had the constant delusion that there was *one more member* than could actually be counted" [Eliot's note].
6. Eliot's note quotes a passage in German from *Blick ins Chaos* (1920) by Hermann Hesse (1877–1962), which may be translated: "Already half of Europe, already at least half of Eastern Europe, on the way to Chaos, drives drunk in sacred infatuation along the edge of the precipice, since drunkenly, as though hymn-singing, as Dimitri Karamazov sang in [the novel] *The Brothers Karamazov* [1882] by Feodor Dostoevsky [1821–1881]. The offended bourgeois laughs at the songs; the saint and the seer hear them with tears."

Over endless plains, stumbling in cracked earth 370
Ringed by the flat horizon only
What is the city over the mountains
Cracks and reforms and bursts in the violet air
Falling towers
Jerusalem Athens Alexandria 375
Vienna London
Unreal

A woman drew her long black hair out tight
And fiddled whisper music on those strings
And bats with baby faces in the violet light 380
Whistled, and beat their wings
And crawled head downward down a blackened wall
And upside down in air were towers
Tolling reminiscent bells, that kept the hours
And voices singing out of empty cisterns and exhausted wells. 385

In this decayed hole among the mountains
In the faint moonlight, the grass is singing
Over the tumbled graves, about the chapel
There is the empty chapel, only the wind's home.
It has no windows, and the door swings, 390
Dry bones can harm no one.
Only a cock stood on the rooftree
Co co rico co co rico[7]
In a flash of lightning. Then a damp gust
Bringing rain 395

Ganga[8] was sunken, and the limp leaves
Waited for rain, while the black clouds
Gathered far distant, over Himavant.[9]
The jungle crouched, humped in silence.
Then spoke the thunder 400
Da[1]
Datta: what have we given?
My friend, blood shaking my heart
The awful daring of a moment's surrender
Which an age of prudence can never retract 405
By this, and this only, we have existed
Which is not to be found in our obituaries
Or in memories draped by the beneficent spider[2]

7. A cock's crow in folklore signaled the departure of ghosts (as in Shakespeare's *Hamlet* 1.1.157ff.); in Matthew 26.34 and 74, a cock crowed, as Christ predicted, when Peter denied him three times.
8. The Indian river Ganges.
9. A mountain in the Himalayas.
1. "'Datta, dayadhvam, damyata' (Give, sympathise, control). The fable of the meaning of the Thunder is found in the *Brihadaranyaka—Upanishad*, 5, 1" [Eliot's note]. In the Hindu legend, the injunction of Prajapati (supreme deity) is *Da*, which is interpreted in three different ways by gods, men, and demons, to mean "control ourselves," "give alms," and "have compassion." Prajapati assures them that when "the divine voice, The Thunder," repeats the syllable it means all three things and that therefore "one should practice . . . Self-Control, Alms-giving, and Compassion."
2. Eliot's note refers to Webster's *The White Devil* 5.6: "they'll remarry / Ere the worm pierce your winding-sheet, ere the spider / Make a thin curtain for your epitaphs."

Or under seals broken by the lean solicitor
In our empty rooms   410
DA
Dayadhvam: I have heard the key[3]
Turn in the door once and turn once only
We think of the key, each in his prison
Thinking of the key, each confirms a prison   415
Only at nightfall, aethereal rumours
Revive for a moment a broken Coriolanus[4]
DA
Damyata: The boat responded
Gaily, to the hand expert with sail and oar   420
The sea was calm, your heart would have responded
Gaily, when invited, beating obedient
To controlling hands

                  I sat upon the shore
Fishing,[5] with the arid plain behind me   425
Shall I at least set my lands in order?[6]
London Bridge is falling down falling down falling down
Poi s'ascose nel foco che gli affina[7]
Quando fiam uti chelidon[8]—O swallow swallow
Le Prince d'Aquitaine à la tour abolie[9]   430
These fragments I have shored against my ruins
Why then Ile fit you. Hieronymo's mad againe.[1]
Datta. Dayadhvam. Damyata.
            Shantih   shantih   shantih[2]

1921   1922

---

3. "Cf. *Inferno*, XXXIII, 46" [Eliot's note]. At this point Ugolino recalls his imprisonment with his children, where they starved to death: "And I heard below the door of the horrible tower being locked up." Eliot's note continues: "Also F. H. Bradley, *Appearance and Reality*, p.346. 'My external sensations are no less private to myself than are my thoughts or my feelings. In either case my experience falls within my own circle, a circle closed on the outside; and, with all its elements alike, every sphere is opaque to the others which surround it. . . . In brief, regarded as an existence which appears in a soul, the whole world for each is peculiar and private to that soul.'"
4. Roman patrician who defiantly chose self-exile when threatened with banishment by the leaders of the populace. He is the tragic protagonist in Shakespeare's *Coriolanus* (1608).
5. "V. Weston: *From Ritual to Romance*; chapter on the Fisher King" [Eliot's note].
6. Cf. Isaiah 38.1: "Thus saith the Lord, Set thine house in order: for thou shalt die, and not live."
7. Eliot's note to *Purgatorio* 26 quotes in Italian the passage (lines 145–48) where the Provençal poet Arnaut Daniel, recalling his lusts, addresses Dante: "I pray you now, by the Goodness that guides you to the summit of this staircase, reflect in due season on my suffering." Then, in the line quoted in *The Waste Land*, "he hid himself in the fire that refines them."
8. Eliot's note refers to the *Pervigilium Veneris* (The Vigil of Venus), an anonymous Latin poem, and suggests a comparison with "Philomela in Parts II and III" of *The Waste Land*. The last stanzas of the *Pervigilium* recreate the myth of the nightingale in the image of a swallow, and the poet listening to the bird speaks the quoted line, "When shall I be as the swallow," and adds: "that I may cease to be silent." "O Swallow, Swallow" are the opening words of one of the songs interspersed in Tennyson's narrative poem *The Princess* (1847).
9. "V. Gerard de Nerval, Sonnet *El Desdichado*" [Eliot's note]. The line reads: "The Prince of Aquitaine in the ruined tower."
1. Eliot's note refers to Thomas Kyd's revenge play, *The Spanish Tragedy*, subtitled *Hieronymo's Mad Againe* (1594). In it Hieronymo is asked to write a court play and he answers, "I'll fit you," in the double sense of "oblige" and "get even." He manages, although mad, to kill the murderers of his son by acting in the play and assigning parts appropriately, then commits suicide.
2. "Shantih. Repeated as here, a formal ending to an Upanishad. 'The peace which passeth understanding' is our equivalent to this word" [Eliot's note]. The Upanishad is a Vedic treatise, a sacred Hindu text.

The Hollow Men

Mistah Kurtz—he dead.[1]
                                A penny for the Old Guy[2]

I

We are the hollow men
We are the stuffed men
Leaning together
Headpiece filled with straw. Alas!
Our dried voices, when   5
We whisper together
Are quiet and meaningless
As wind in dry grass
Or rats' feet over broken glass
In our dry cellar   10

Shape without form, shade without colour,
Paralysed force, gesture without motion;

Those who have crossed
With direct eyes, to death's other Kingdom
Remember us—if at all—not as lost   15
Violent souls, but only
As the hollow men
The stuffed men.

II

Eyes I dare not meet in dreams
In death's dream kingdom   20
These do not appear:
There, the eyes are
Sunlight on a broken column
There, is a tree swinging
And voices are   25
In the wind's singing
More distant and more solemn
Than a fading star.

Let me be no nearer
In death's dream kingdom   30
Let me also wear

---

1. Quotation from *Heart of Darkness*, by Joseph Conrad (1857–1924). Kurtz went into the African jungle as an official of a trading company and degenerated into an evil, tyrannical man. His dying words were "the horror!"
2. Guy Fawkes led a group of conspirators who planned to blow up the English House of Commons in 1605; he was caught and executed before the plan was carried out. On the day of his execution (November 5) children make straw effigies of the "guy" and beg for pennies for fireworks.

Such deliberate disguises
Rat's coat, crowskin, crossed staves
In a field
Behaving as the wind behaves   35
No nearer—

Not that final meeting
In the twilight kingdom

III

This is the dead land
This is cactus land   40
Here the stone images
Are raised, here they receive
The supplication of a dead man's hand
Under the twinkle of a fading star.

Is it like this   45
In death's other kingdom
Waking alone
At the hour when we are
Trembling with tenderness
Lips that would kiss   50
Form prayers to broken stone.

IV

The eyes are not here
There are no eyes here
In this valley of dying stars
In this hollow valley   55
This broken jaw of our lost kingdoms

In this last of meeting places
We grope together
And avoid speech
Gathered on this beach of the tumid river   60

Sightless, unless
The eyes reappear
As the perpetual star
Multifoliate rose³
Of death's twilight kingdom   65
The hope only
Of empty men.

---

3. Part 3 of *The Divine Comedy*, by Dante Alighieri (1265–1321), is a vision of Paradise. The souls of the saved in heaven range themselves around the deity in the figure of a "multifoliate rose" (*Paradiso* 28.30).

V

Here we go round the prickly pear
Prickly pear prickly pear
Here we go round the prickly pear   70
At five o'clock in the morning.[4]

Between the idea
And the reality
Between the motion
And the act   75
Falls the Shadow

                              For Thine is the Kingdom[5]

Between the conception
And the creation
Between the emotion   80
And the response
Falls the Shadow

                                        Life is very long

Between the desire
And the spasm   85
Between the potency
And the existence
Between the essence
And the descent
Falls the Shadow   90

                              For Thine is the Kingdom

For Thine is
Life is
For Thine is the

This is the way the world ends   95
This is the way the world ends
This is the way the world ends
Not with a bang but a whimper.

                                                       1925

---

4. Allusion to a children's rhyming game, "Here we go round the mulberry bush," substituting a prickly pear cactus for the mulberry bush.
5. Part of a line from the Lord's Prayer.

FROM FOUR QUARTETS

Burnt Norton[1]

τοῦ λόγον δ'εόντος ξυνοῦ ζώουσιν οἱ πολλοί
ὡς ἰδίαν ἔχοντες φρόνησιν.
                                    I. p.77. Fr. 2.
ὁδὸς ἄνω κάτω μία καί ὠυτή.
                                    I. p.89. Fr. 60.[2]
                    —Diels: *Die Fragmente der Vorsokratiker*
                                    (Herakleitos)

I

Time present and time past
Are both perhaps present in time future,
And time future contained in time past.[3]
If all time is eternally present
All time is unredeemable.   5
What might have been is an abstraction
Remaining a perpetual possibility
Only in a world of speculation.
What might have been and what has been
Point to one end, which is always present.   10
Footfalls echo in the memory
Down the passage which we did not take
Towards the door we never opened
Into the rose-garden.[4] My words echo
Thus, in your mind.   15
                    But to what purpose
Disturbing the dust on a bowl of rose-leaves
I do not know.
                    Other echoes
Inhabit the garden. Shall we follow?   20
Quick, said the bird, find them, find them,
Round the corner. Through the first gate,
Into our first world, shall we follow
The deception of the thrush? Into our first world.

1. Eliot made "Burnt Norton," published originally as a separate poem, the basis and formal
model for "East Coker" (1940), "The Dry Salvages"
(1941), and "Little Gidding" (1942). Together they
make up *Four Quartets* (1943). The *Quartets* seeks
to capture those rare moments when eternity
"intersects" the temporal continuum, while treating also the relations between those moments and
the flux of time. Central to "Burnt Norton" is the
idea of the Spanish mystic St. John of the Cross
(1542–1591) that the ascent of a soul to union
with God is facilitated by memory and disciplined
meditation but that meditation is superseded by a
"dark night of the soul" that deepens paradoxically
the nearer one approaches the light of God. Burnt
Norton is a manor house in Gloucestershire,
England.
2. The Greek epigraphs are from the pre-Socratic
philosopher Heraclitus (540?–475 B.C.E.) and may
be translated: "But although the Word is common
to all, the majority of people live as though they
had each an understanding peculiarly his own"
and "The way up and the way down are one and
the same."
3. The opening lines echo Ecclesiastes 3.15:
"That which hath been is now; and that which is
to be hath already been."
4. The rose is a symbol of sexual and spiritual
love; in Christian traditions it is associated with
the harmony of religious truth and with the Virgin Mary. The memory may be personal as well.

There they were, dignified, invisible,   25
Moving without pressure, over the dead leaves,
In the autumn heat, through the vibrant air,
And the bird called, in response to
The unheard music hidden in the shrubbery,
And the unseen eyebeam crossed, for the roses   30
Had the look of flowers that are looked at.
There they were as our guests, accepted and accepting.
So we moved, and they, in a formal pattern,
Along the empty alley, into the box circle,[5]
To look down into the drained pool.   35
Dry the pool, dry concrete, brown edged,
And the pool was filled with water out of sunlight,
And the lotos rose, quietly, quietly,
The surface glittered out of heart of light,[6]
And they were behind us, reflected in the pool.   40
Then a cloud passed, and the pool was empty.
Go, said the bird, for the leaves were full of children,
Hidden excitedly, containing laughter.
Go, go, go, said the bird: human kind
Cannot bear very much reality.   45
Time past and time future
What might have been and what has been.
Point to one end, which is always present.

                                    II

Garlic and sapphires in the mud
Clot the bedded axle-tree.   50
The trilling wire in the blood
Sings below inveterate scars
Appeasing long forgotten wars.
The dance along the artery
The circulation of the lymph   55
Are figured in the drift of stars
Ascend to summer in the tree
We move above the moving tree
In light upon the figured leaf[7]
And hear upon the sodden floor   60
Below, the boarhound and the boar
Pursue their pattern as before
But reconciled among the stars.

At the still point of the turning world. Neither flesh nor fleshless;
Neither from nor towards; at the still point, there the dance is,   65
But neither arrest nor movement. And do not call it fixity,
Where past and future are gathered. Neither movement from
        nor towards,

5. Evergreen boxwood shrubs, planted in a circle.
6. An echo of Dante, *Paradiso* 12.28–29: "From out of the heart of one of the new lights there moved a voice."
7. An echo of the description of death in Tennyson, *In Memoriam* (1850) 43.10–12: "So that still garden of the souls / In many a figured leaf enrolls / The total world since life began."

Neither ascent nor decline. Except for the point, the still point,
There would be no dance and there is only the dance.
I can only say, *there* we have been: but I cannot say where.   70
And I cannot say, how long, for that is to place it in time.
The inner freedom from the practical desire,
The release from action and suffering, release from the inner
And the outer compulsion, yet surrounded
By a grace of sense, a white light still and moving,   75
Erhebung[8] without motion, concentration
Without elimination, both a new world
And the old made explicit, understood
In the completion of its partial ecstasy,
The resolution of its partial horror.   80
Yet the enchainment of past and future
Woven in the weakness of the changing body,
Protects mankind from heaven and damnation
Which flesh cannot endure.
                         Time past and time future   85
Allow but a little consciousness.
To be conscious is not to be in time
But only in time can the moment in the rose-garden,
The moment in the arbour where the rain beat,
The moment in the draughty church at smokefall   90
Be remembered; involved with past and future.
Only through time time is conquered.

III

Here is a place of disaffection
Time before and time after
In a dim light: neither daylight   95
Investing form with lucid stillness
Turning shadow into transient beauty
With slow rotation suggesting permanence
Nor darkness to purify the soul
Emptying the sensual with deprivation   100
Cleansing affection from the temporal.
Neither plenitude nor vacancy. Only a flicker
Over the strained time-ridden faces
Distracted from distraction by distraction
Filled with fancies and empty of meaning   105
Tumid apathy with no concentration
Men and bits of paper, whirled by the cold wind
That blows before and after time,
Wind in and out of unwholesome lungs
Time before and time after.   110
Eructation of unhealthy souls
Into the faded air, the torpid
Driven on the wind that sweeps the gloomy hills of London,

8. Exaltation (German).

Hampstead and Clerkenwell, Campden and Putney,
Highgate, Primrose and Ludgate.⁹ Not here   115
Not here the darkness, in this twittering world.

Descend lower, descend only
Into the world of perpetual solitude,
World not world, but that which is not world,
Internal darkness, deprivation   120
And destitution of all property,
Desiccation of the world of sense,
Evacuation of the world of fancy,
Inoperancy of the world of spirit;
This is the one way, and the other   125
Is the same, not in movement
But abstention from movement; while the world moves
In appetency, on its metalled ways
Of time past and time future.

IV

Time and the bell have buried the day,   130
The black cloud carries the sun away.
Will the sunflower turn to us, will the clematis
Stray down, bend to us; tendril and spray
Clutch and cling?
Chill   135
Fingers of yew be curled
Down on us? After the kingfisher's wing
Has answered light to light, and is silent, the light is still
At the still point of the turning world.

V

Words move, music moves   140
Only in time; but that which is only living
Can only die. Words, after speech, reach
Into the silence. Only by the form, the pattern,
Can words or music reach
The stillness, as a Chinese jar still   145
Moves perpetually in its stillness.
Not the stillness of the violin, while the note lasts,
Not that only, but the co-existence,
Or say that the end precedes the beginning,
And the end and the beginning were always there   150
Before the beginning and after the end.
And all is always now. Words strain,
Crack and sometimes break, under the burden,
Under the tension, slip, slide, perish,
Decay with imprecision, will not stay in place,   155

---

9. Districts and neighborhoods in London.

Will not stay still. Shrieking voices
Scolding, mocking, or merely chattering,
Always assail them. The Word in the desert[1]
Is most attacked by voices of temptation,
The crying shadow in the funeral dance,   160
The loud lament of the disconsolate chimera.[2]
The detail of the pattern is movement,
As in the figure of the ten stairs.[3]
Desire itself is movement
Not in itself desirable;   165
Love is itself unmoving,
Only the cause and end of movement,
Timeless, and undesiring
Except in the aspect of time
Caught in the form of limitation   170
Between un-being and being.
Sudden in a shaft of sunlight
Even while the dust moves
There rises the hidden laughter
Of children in the foliage   175
Quick, now, here, now always—
Ridiculous the waste sad time
Stretching before and after.

                                                              1936, 1943

1. An allusion to Christ's temptation in the wilderness (Luke 4.1–4).
2. A monster in Greek mythology and a symbol
of fantasies and delusions.

3. An allusion to St. John of the Cross's figure
for the soul's ascent to God: "The Ten Degrees of
the Mystical Ladder of Divine Love."

EUGENE O'NEILL
1888–1953

E ugene O'Neill, the nation's first major playwright, was born in a New York City
hotel on Broadway on October 16, 1888. His father was James O'Neill, an
actor who abandoned his early success in Shakespearean roles to make a fortune
playing the lead role in a dramatization of Alexander Dumas's swashbuckling
novel *The Count of Monte Cristo* (1844–45), which he performed on tour more
than five thousand times. O'Neill's mother, Ella Quinlan, the daughter of a successful Irish immigrant businessman in Cincinnati, hated backstage life and
became addicted to morphine. An older brother, James Jr., had been born in 1878
and during most of Eugene's childhood was away at various boarding schools. Later
"Jamie," Eugene's idol, became an actor and an alcoholic.

During O'Neill's childhood, his parents toured for part of every year, lived in New
York City hotels for another part, and spent summers at their home in New London,

Connecticut. O'Neill went to good preparatory schools and started college at Princeton in 1906. Suspended after his freshman year for missing classes and exams, O'Neill found work in New York City, where he met Kathleen Jenkins; when she became pregnant, the two eloped. With his father's help, he shipped out to sea and went searching for gold in South America, leaving his wife behind; it would be eleven years before he met their son, Eugene Jr., born in 1910. O'Neill drank and drifted, alternating sea voyages with sojourns in Greenwich Village, an area of lower Manhattan that was becoming home to artists and political radicals. After nearly dying of tuberculosis in 1912, O'Neill decided to curtail his drinking and write plays. In 1914 his father subsidized the publication of *Thirst*, a collection of five one-act plays; fortified by this accomplishment, O'Neill applied and was accepted as a special student at Harvard in the playwriting class of Professor George Pierce Baker—the first such class offered at an American university. O'Neill's real entry into the contemporary theater, though, came through his Greenwich Village friends: he joined a new experimental theater group called the Provincetown Players—in the summer its members staged plays on a wharf in Provincetown, Massachusetts. For the rest of the year they used a small theater in the Village. They produced O'Neill's one-act play *Bound East for Cardiff* in the summer of 1916.

The Provincetown group gave O'Neill his forum, and—working closely with playwright Susan Glaspell—he gave them a place in American theater history. Play followed play in these early years: five of his plays were staged in 1917, and he wrote another six in 1918. The works with likely appeal for general audiences were moved uptown from the Village to Broadway, making O'Neill both famous and financially successful. Many of these early plays, with crude and slangy dialogue that departed strikingly from the stage rhetoric of the day, were grim one-acts based on his experiences at sea. Instead of the elegant witticisms of drawing-room comedy or the flowery eloquence of historical drama, audiences were faced with ships' holds and sailors' bars. An exaggerated realism, veering toward expressionism, was the mode of these earliest works.

Around 1920, O'Neill's plays became longer and less realistic, and his aims more ambitious. He began to experiment with techniques to convey inner emotions not expressible in dramatic action—the world of the mind, of memories and fears. He ignored standard play divisions of scenes and acts; made his characters wear masks; split one character between two actors; and reintroduced ghosts, choruses, and Shakespearean-style monologues and direct addresses to the audience. The political radicalism of his Greenwich Village circles was reflected in the themes of many of these plays, although O'Neill would always be more drawn to the deep-lived emotions of social conflicts than to organized political movements aimed at resolving them. In *The Emperor Jones* (1920), a former Pullman porter uses the lessons of Wall Street ("Dere's little stealin' like you does, and dere's big stealin' like I does") to oppress the inhabitants of a Caribbean island; their revolt sends Jones into flight, pursued by the ghosts of New World slavery. In *The Hairy Ape* (1922), a sailor, becoming aware of how he is viewed by the upper class, degenerates into what he is perceived to be. *Desire under the Elms* (1924) links family conflict to lust after property and control as well as to erotic desire; *The Great God Brown* (1926) drew on O'Neill's full array of experimental techniques to expose the inner life of a business magnate. Centered on the turbulent emotional life of a beautiful woman, *Strange Interlude* (1928), despite its audacious nine-act length, won the Pulitzer Prize, was made into a Hollywood film, and became O'Neill's greatest commercial success.

O'Neill's father had died in 1920, his mother in 1921, his brother in 1923. During the mid-1920s, O'Neill became interested in dramatizing the complicated pattern of his family's life. He was influenced by the popularization of Sigmund Freud's ideas: the power of irrational drives; the existence of a subconscious; the roles of repression and inhibition in the formation of personality and in adult suffering; the importance of sex; and above all the lifelong influence of parents. With Freud, he saw the family as a locus of intense and irresolvable conflicting feelings: as Edmund observes of his mother in *Long Day's Journey into Night*, "it's as if, in spite of loving us, she hated us." But where Freud's famous case histories explore the conflicts of an individual, O'Neill's dramatic method came to focus on the family, rather than the person, as the fundamental human unit. He found inspiration and confirmation for this approach in classical Greek drama, which had always centered on families. His 1931 *Mourning Becomes Electra*, based on the *Oresteia* cycle of the classical Greek playwright Aeschylus, situated the ancient story of family murder and divine retribution in Civil War America with great success.

Twice married after the annulment of his early elopement, O'Neill began to suffer from a series of health problems in the 1930s, was diagnosed with Parkinson's disease in 1941, and lived in relative seclusion for the last twenty years of his life. Following the production of *Mourning Becomes Electra* in 1931, his output slowed. Much of his work from the 1930s and 1940s remained in manuscript until after his death, and there was a twelve-year gap in the staging of his plays between *Days without End* (1934), which failed on Broadway, and *The Iceman Cometh*, in 1946, which also did poorly. During this interval O'Neill set out and revised increasingly ambitious plans for cycles of plays that would encompass American history through the stories of several families. Recalling the conflicting immigrant experiences of his own parents—the prosperous assimilation of his mother's family contrasted with his Irish-born father's famine-driven economic insecurity and greed—sharpened O'Neill's sense of American history as a family drama of possession and dispossession.

Three years after O'Neill's death, *Iceman* was successfully revived, and O'Neill's work reattained prominence. His widow, the former actress Carlotta Monterey, whom O'Neill had married in 1929, released other plays, which were widely acclaimed in posthumous productions. Among such stagings were parts of a projected nine- or eleven-play sequence (critics differ in the interpretation of the surviving manuscript material) about an Irish family in America named the Melody family and some obviously autobiographical dramas about a family named the Tyrones. The Melody plays produced after O'Neill's death include *A Touch of the Poet*, produced in 1957, and *More Stately Mansions*, which was staged in 1967; the Tyrone plays include *Long Day's Journey into Night*, produced in 1956, and *A Moon for the Misbegotten*, produced in 1957.

In inscribing the manuscript of *Long Day's Journey* to Carlotta, O'Neill wrote that he had faced his dead in this play, writing "with deep pity and understanding and forgiveness for *all* the four haunted Tyrones." His treatment made it impossible to blame any of the characters for the suffering they inflicted on the others; each Tyrone was both a victim and an oppressor. The Tyrones are at the mercy of the past, and the word *ghosts* recurs throughout the play: ghosts of those they remember, those who influenced them, their younger selves, their dreams and ambitions, and their disappointments. O'Neill handled the emotionalism of his theme with rigorous dramatic formalism, designing the play as a series of encounters—each character is placed with one, two, or three of the others, until every combination is worked through. *Long Day's Journey* observes the classical dramatic unities of time and space, following the family's various configurations through one day, from the pretense of conventional family life in the morning to the tragic truth of their night. The audience thus witnesses a literal day in the lives of the Tyrones, as well as the journey through life toward death.

Romantic, realistic, naturalistic, melodramatic, sentimental, cynical, poetic—O'Neill's work in general is all of these. Even while he made his characters espouse philosophical positions, O'Neill was not trying to write philosophical drama. He wanted to make plays conveying emotions of such intensity and complexity that the theater would become a vital force in American life. In all his works, the spectacle of emotional intensity was meant to produce emotional response in an audience—what

Aristotle, in his *Poetics*, had called "catharsis." O'Neill's plays have been translated and staged all over the world; he won the Pulitzer Prize four times and the Nobel Prize in 1936, the first and so far only American dramatist to do so.

The text is that of the Yale University Press Edition (1956).

Long Day's Journey into Night

CHARACTERS

JAMES TYRONE
MARY CAVAN TYRONE, *his wife*
JAMES TYRONE, JR., *their elder son*
EDMUND TYRONE, *their younger son*
CATHLEEN, *second girl*[1]

SCENES

ACT 1   *Living room of the Tyrones' summer home 8:30 A.M. of a day in August,* 1912
ACT 2   SCENE 1   *The same, around* 12:45
            SCENE 2   *The same, about a half hour later*
ACT 3   *The same, around* 6:30 *that evening*
ACT 4   *The same, around midnight*

Act 1

SCENE—*Living room of* JAMES TYRONE's *summer home on a morning in August,* 1912.

At rear are two double doorways with portieres. The one at right leads into a front parlor with the formally arranged, set appearance of a room rarely occupied. The other opens on a dark, windowless back parlor, never used except as a passage from living room to dining room. Against the wall between the doorways is a small bookcase, with a picture of Shakespeare above it, containing novels by Balzac, Zola, Stendhal, philosophical and sociological works by Schopenhauer, Nietzsche, Marx, Engels, Kropotkin, Max Sterner, plays by Ibsen, Shaw, Strindberg, poetry by Swinburne, Rossetti, Wilde, Ernest Dowson, Kipling, etc.[2]

In the right wall, rear, is a screen door leading out on the porch which extends halfway around the house. Farther forward, a series of three windows looks over the front lawn to the harbor and the avenue that runs along the water front. A small wicker table and an ordinary oak desk are against the wall, flanking the windows.

In the left wall, a similar series of windows looks out on the grounds in back of the house. Beneath them is a wicker couch with cushions, its head toward rear. Farther back is a large, glassed-in bookcase with sets of Dumas, Victor

---

1. A servant.
2. A variety of 19th-century (especially late-19th-century) authors are cited. Nobody in the audience would be able to read the titles and authors

on these books—an example of O'Neill's novelistic approach to theatrical detail, also seen in the minute physical descriptions he provides of the characters' appearance and behavior throughout.

Hugo, Charles Lever, three sets of Shakespeare, The World's Best Literature in fifty large volumes, Hume's History of England, Thiers' History of the Consulate and Empire, Smollett's History of England, Gibbon's Roman Empire and miscellaneous volumes of old plays, poetry, and several histories of Ireland. The astonishing thing about these sets is that all the volumes have the look of having been read and reread.

The hardwood floor is nearly covered by a rug, inoffensive in design and color. At center is a round table with a green shaded reading lamp, the cord plugged in one of the four sockets in the chandelier above. Around the table within reading-light range are four chairs, three of them wicker armchairs, the fourth (at right front of table) a varnished oak rocker with leather bottom.

It is around 8:30. Sunshine comes through the windows at right.

As the curtain rises, the family have just finished breakfast. MARY TYRONE and her husband enter together from the back parlor, coming from the dining room.

MARY is fifty-four, about medium height. She still has a young, graceful figure, a trifle plump, but showing little evidence of middle-aged waist and hips, although she is not tightly corseted. Her face is distinctly Irish in type. It must once have been extremely pretty, and is still striking. It does not match her healthy figure but is thin and pale with the bone structure prominent. Her nose is long and straight, her mouth wide with full, sensitive lips. She uses no rouge or any sort of make-up. Her high forehead is framed by thick, pure white hair. Accentuated by her pallor and white hair, her dark brown eyes appear black. They are unusually large and beautiful, with black brows and long curling lashes.

What strikes one immediately is her extreme nervousness. Her hands are never still. They were once beautiful hands, with long, tapering fingers, but rheumatism has knotted the joints and warped the fingers, so that now they have an ugly crippled look. One avoids looking at them, the more so because one is conscious she is sensitive about their appearance and humiliated by her inability to control the nervousness which draws attention to them.

She is dressed simply but with a sure sense of what becomes her. Her hair is arranged with fastidious care. Her voice is soft and attractive. When she is merry, there is a touch of Irish lilt in it.

Her most appealing quality is the simple, unaffected charm of a shy convent-girl youthfulness she has never lost—an innate unworldly innocence.

JAMES TYRONE is sixty-five but looks ten years younger. About five feet eight, broad-shouldered and deep-chested, he seems taller and slenderer because of his bearing, which has a soldierly quality of head up, chest out, stomach in, shoulders squared. His face has begun to break down but he is still remarkably good looking—a big, finely shaped head, a handsome profile, deep-set light-brown eyes. His grey hair is thin with a bald spot like a monk's tonsure.

The stamp of his profession is unmistakably on him. Not that he indulges in any of the deliberate temperamental posturings of the stage star. He is by nature and preference a simple, unpretentious man, whose inclinations are still close to his humble beginnings and his Irish farmer forebears. But the actor shows in all his unconscious habits of speech, movement and gesture. These have the quality of belonging to a studied technique. His voice is remarkably fine, resonant and flexible, and he takes great pride in it.

His clothes, assuredly, do not costume any romantic part. He wears a threadbare, ready-made, grey sack suit and shineless black shoes, a collar-less shirt with a thick white handkerchief knotted loosely around his throat. There is nothing *picturesquely careless about this get-up. It is commonplace shabby. He believes in wearing his clothes to the limit of usefulness, is dressed now for gardening, and doesn't give a damn how he looks.*

He has never been really sick a day in his life. He has no nerves. There is a lot of stolid, earthy peasant in him, mixed with streaks of sentimental melancholy and rare flashes of intuitive sensibility.

TYRONE's *arm is around his wife's waist as they appear from the back parlor. Entering the living room he gives her a playful hug.*

TYRONE   You're a fine armful now, Mary, with those twenty pounds you've gained.

MARY [*smiles affectionately*]   I've gotten too fat, you mean, dear. I really ought to reduce.

TYRONE   None of that, my lady! You're just right. We'll have no talk of reducing. Is that why you ate so little breakfast?

MARY   So little? I thought I ate a lot.

TYRONE   You didn't. Not as much as I'd like to see, anyway.

MARY [*teasingly*]   Oh you! You expect everyone to eat the enormous breakfast you do. No one else in the world could without dying of indigestion. [*She comes forward to stand by the right of table.*]

TYRONE [*following her*]   I hope I'm not as big a glutton as that sounds. [*with hearty satisfaction*] But thank God, I've kept my appetite and I've the digestion of a young man of twenty, if I am sixty-five.

MARY   You surely have, James. No one could deny that.
[*She laughs and sits in the wicker armchair at right rear of table. He comes around in back of her and selects a cigar from a box on the table and cuts off the end with a little clipper. From the dining room* JAMIE's *and* EDMUND's *voices are heard. Mary turns her head that way.*]
Why did the boys stay in the dining room, I wonder? Cathleen must be waiting to clear the table.

TYRONE [*jokingly but with an undercurrent of resentment*]   It's a secret confab they don't want me to hear, I suppose. I'll bet they're cooking up some new scheme to touch the Old Man.
[*She is silent on this, keeping her head turned toward their voices. Her hands appear on the table top, moving restlessly. He lights his cigar and sits down in the rocker at right of table, which is his chair, and puffs contentedly.*]
There's nothing like the first after-breakfast cigar, if it's a good one, and this new lot have the right mellow flavor. They're a great bargain, too. I got them dead cheap. It was McGuire put me on to them.

MARY [*a trifle acidly*]   I hope he didn't put you on to any new piece of property at the same time. His real estate bargains don't work out so well.

TYRONE [*defensively*]   I wouldn't say that, Mary. After all, he was the one who advised me to buy that place on Chestnut Street and I made a quick turnover on it for a fine profit.

MARY [*smiles now with teasing affection*]   I know. The famous one stroke of good luck. I'm sure McGuire never dreamed—[*Then she pats his hand.*] Never mind, James. I know it's a waste of breath trying to convince you you're not a cunning real estate speculator.

TYRONE [*huffily*]   I've no such idea. But land is land, and it's safer than the stocks and bonds of Wall Street swindlers. [*then placatingly*] But let's not argue about business this early in the morning.

[*A pause. The boys' voices are again heard and one of them has a fit of coughing.* MARY *listens worriedly. Her fingers play nervously on the table top.*]

MARY   James, it's Edmund you ought to scold for not eating enough. He hardly touched anything except coffee. He needs to eat to keep up his strength. I keep telling him that but he says he simply has no appetite. Of course, there's nothing takes away your appetite like a bad summer cold.

TYRONE   Yes, it's only natural. So don't let yourself get worried—

MARY [*quickly*]   Oh, I'm not. I know he'll be all right in a few days if he takes care of himself. [*as if she wanted to dismiss the subject but can't*] But it does seem a shame he should have to be sick right now.

TYRONE   Yes, it is bad luck. [*He gives her a quick, worried look.*] But you mustn't let it upset you, Mary. Remember, you've got to take care of yourself, too.

MARY [*quickly*]   I'm not upset. There's nothing to be upset about. What makes you think I'm upset?

TYRONE   Why, nothing, except you've seemed a bit high-strung the past few days.

MARY [*forcing a smile*]   I have? Nonsense, dear. It's your imagination. [*with sudden tenseness*] You really must not watch me all the time, James. I mean, it makes me self-conscious.

TYRONE [*putting a hand over one of her nervously playing ones*]   Now, now, Mary. That's your imagination. If I've watched you it was to admire how fat and beautiful you looked. [*His voice is suddenly moved by deep feeling.*] I can't tell you the deep happiness it gives me, darling, to see you as you've been since you came back to us, your dear old self again. [*He leans over and kisses her cheek impulsively—then turning back adds with a constrained air*] So keep up the good work, Mary.

MARY [*has turned her head away*]   I will, dear. [*She gets up restlessly and goes to the windows at right.*] Thank heavens, the fog is gone. [*She turns back.*] I do feel out of sorts this morning. I wasn't able to get much sleep with that awful foghorn going all night long.

TYRONE   Yes, it's like having a sick whale in the back yard. It kept me awake, too.

MARY [*affectionately amused*]   Did it? You had a strange way of showing your restlessness. You were snoring so hard I couldn't tell which was the foghorn! [*She comes to him, laughing, and pats his cheek playfully.*] Ten foghorns couldn't disturb you. You haven't a nerve in you. You've never had.

TYRONE [*his vanity piqued—testily*]   Nonsense. You always exaggerate about my snoring.

MARY   I couldn't. If you could only hear yourself once—

[*A burst of laughter comes from the dining room. She turns her head, smiling.*]

What's the joke, I wonder?

TYRONE [*grumpily*]   It's on me. I'll bet that much. It's always on the Old Man.

MARY [*teasingly*]   Yes, it's terrible the way we all pick on you, isn't it? You're so abused! [*She laughs—then with a pleased, relieved air*] Well, no matter what the joke is about, it's a relief to hear Edmund laugh. He's been so down in the mouth lately.

TYRONE [*ignoring this—resentfully*]   Some joke of Jamie's, I'll wager. He's forever making sneering fun of somebody, that one.

MARY   Now don't start in on poor Jamie, dear. [*without conviction*] He'll turn out all right in the end, you wait and see.

TYRONE   He'd better start soon, then. He's nearly thirty-four.

MARY [*ignoring this*]   Good heavens, are they going to stay in the dining room all day? [*She goes to the back parlor doorway and calls*] Jamie! Edmund! Come in the living room and give Cathleen a chance to clear the table.

[EDMUND *calls back,* "We're coming, Mama." *She goes back to the table.*]

TYRONE [*grumbling*]   You'd find excuses for him no matter what he did.

MARY [*sitting down beside him, pats his hand*]   Shush.

Their sons JAMES, JR., *and* EDMUND *enter together from the back parlor. They are both grinning, still chuckling over what had caused their laughter, and as they come forward they glance at their father and their grins grow broader.*

JAMIE, *the elder, is thirty-three. He has his father's broad-shouldered, deep-chested physique, is an inch taller and weighs less, but appears shorter and stouter because he lacks* TYRONE's *bearing and graceful carriage. He also lacks his father's vitality. The signs of premature disintegration are on him. His face is still good looking, despite marks of dissipation, but it has never been handsome like* TYRONE's, *although* JAMIE *resembles him rather than his mother. He has fine brown eyes, their color midway between his father's lighter and his mother's darker ones. His hair is thinning and already there is indication of a bald spot like* TYRONE's. *His nose is unlike that of any other member of the family, pronouncedly aquiline. Combined with his habitual expression of cynicism it gives his countenance a Mephistophelian cast. But on the rare occasions when he smiles without sneering, his personality possesses the remnant of a humorous, romantic, irresponsible Irish charm—that of the beguiling ne'er-do-well, with a strain of the sentimentally poetic, attractive to women and popular with men.*

He is dressed in an old sack suit, not as shabby as TYRONE's, *and wears a collar and tie. His fair skin is sunburned a reddish, freckled tan.*

EDMUND *is ten years younger than his brother, a couple of inches taller, thin and wiry. Where* JAMIE *takes after his father, with little resemblance to his mother,* EDMUND *looks like both his parents, but is more like his mother. Her big, dark eyes are the dominant feature in his long, narrow Irish face. His mouth has the same quality of hypersensitiveness hers possesses. His high fore-head is hers accentuated, with dark brown hair, sunbleached to red at the ends, brushed straight back from it. But his nose is his father's and his face in profile recalls* TYRONE's. EDMUND's *hands are noticeably like his mother's, with the same exceptionally long fingers. They even have to a minor degree the same nervousness. It is in the quality of extreme nervous sensibility that the likeness of* EDMUND *to his mother is most marked.*

He is plainly in bad health. Much thinner than he should be, his eyes appear feverish and his cheeks are sunken. His skin, in spite of being sunburned a deep brown, has a parched sallowness. He wears a shirt, collar and tie, no coat, old flannel trousers, brown sneakers.

MARY [*turns smilingly to them, in a merry tone that is a bit forced*]   I've been teasing your father about his snoring. [*to* TYRONE] I'll leave it to the boys, James. They must have heard you. No, not you, Jamie. I could hear you down the hall almost as bad as your father. You're like him. As soon as your head touches the pillow you're off and ten foghorns couldn't wake you. [*She stops abruptly, catching* JAMIE's *eyes regarding her with an uneasy, probing look. Her smile vanishes and her manner becomes self-conscious.*] Why are you staring, Jamie? [*Her hands flutter up to her hair.*] Is my hair coming down? It's hard for me to do it up properly now. My eyes are getting so bad and I never can find my glasses.

JAMIE [*looks away guiltily*]   Your hair's all right, Mama. I was only thinking how well you look.

TYRONE [*heartily*]   Just what I've been telling her, Jamie. She's so fat and sassy, there'll soon be no holding her.

EDMUND   Yes, you certainly look grand, Mama. [*She is reassured and smiles at him lovingly. He winks with a kidding grin.*] I'll back you up about Papa's snoring. Gosh, what a racket!

JAMIE   I heard him, too. [*He quotes, putting on a ham-actor manner*] "The Moor, I know his trumpet."[3]

   [*His mother and brother laugh.*]

TYRONE [*scathingly*]   If it takes my snoring to make you remember Shakespeare instead of the dope sheet on the ponies, I hope I'll keep on with it.

MARY   Now, James! You mustn't be so touchy.

   [JAMIE *shrugs his shoulders and sits down in the chair on her right.*]

EDMUND [*irritably*]   Yes, for Pete's sake, Papa! The first thing after breakfast! Give it a rest, can't you? [*He slumps down in the chair at left of table next to his brother. His father ignores him.*]

MARY [*reprovingly*]   Your father wasn't finding fault with you. You don't have to always take Jamie's part. You'd think you were the one ten years older.

JAMIE [*boredly*]   What's all the fuss about? Let's forget it.

TYRONE [*contemptuously*]   Yes, forget! Forget everything and face nothing! It's a convenient philosophy if you've no ambition in life except to—

MARY   James, do be quiet. [*She puts an arm around his shoulder—coaxingly*] You must have gotten out of the wrong side of the bed this morning. [*to the boys, changing the subject*] What were you two grinning about like Cheshire cats when you came in? What was the joke?

TYRONE [*with a painful effort to be a good sport*]   Yes, let us in on it, lads. I told your mother I knew damned well it would be one on me, but never mind that, I'm used to it.

JAMIE [*dryly*]   Don't look at me. This is the Kid's story.

EDMUND [*grins*]   I meant to tell you last night, Papa, and forgot it. Yesterday when I went for a walk I dropped in at the Inn—

MARY [*worriedly*]   You shouldn't drink now, Edmund.

---

3. Shakespeare's *Othello* 2.1.180.

EDMUND [*ignoring this*]   And who do you think I met there, with a beautiful bun on,[4] but Shaughnessy, the tenant on that farm of yours.

MARY [*smiling*]   That dreadful man! But he is funny.

TYRONE [*scowling*]   He's not so funny when you're his landlord. He's a wily Shanty Mick, that one. He could hide behind a corkscrew. What's he complaining about now, Edmund—for I'm damned sure he's complaining. I suppose he wants his rent lowered. I let him have the place for almost nothing, just to keep someone on it, and he never pays that till I threaten to evict him.

EDMUND   No, he didn't beef about anything. He was so pleased with life he even bought a drink, and that's practically unheard of. He was delighted because he'd had a fight with your friend, Harker, the Standard Oil millionaire, and won a glorious victory.

MARY [*with amused dismay*]   Oh, Lord! James, you'll really have to do something—

TYRONE   Bad luck to Shaughnessy, anyway!

JAMIE [*maliciously*]   I'll bet the next time you see Harker at the Club and give him the old respectful bow, he won't see you.

EDMUND   Yes. Harker will think you're no gentleman for harboring a tenant who isn't humble in the presence of a king of America.

TYRONE   Never mind the Socialist gabble. I don't care to listen—

MARY [*tactfully*]   Go on with your story, Edmund.

EDMUND [*grins at his father provocatively*]   Well, you remember, Papa, the ice pond on Harker's estate is right next to the farm, and you remember Shaughnessy keeps pigs. Well, it seems there's a break in the fence and the pigs have been bathing in the millionaire's ice pond, and Harker's foreman told him he was sure Shaughnessy had broken the fence on purpose to give his pigs a free wallow.

MARY [*shocked and amused*]   Good heavens!

TYRONE [*sourly, but with a trace of admiration*]   I'm sure he did, too, the dirty scallywag. It's like him.

EDMUND   So Harker came in person to rebuke Shaughnessy. [*He chuckles.*] A very bonehead play! If I needed any further proof that our ruling plutocrats, especially the ones who inherited their boodle, are not mental giants, that would clinch it.

TYRONE [*with appreciation, before he thinks*]   Yes, he'd be no match for Shaughnessy. [*then he growls*] Keep your damned anarchist remarks to yourself. I won't have them in my house. [*But he is full of eager anticipation.*] What happened?

EDMUND   Harker had as much chance as I would with Jack Johnson.[5] Shaughnessy got a few drinks under his belt and was waiting at the gate to welcome him. He told me he never gave Harker a chance to open his mouth. He began by shouting that he was no slave Standard Oil could trample on. He was a King of Ireland, if he had his rights, and scum was scum to him, no matter how much money it had stolen from the poor.

MARY   Oh, Lord! [*But she can't help laughing.*]

---

4. I.e., drunk.
5. Famous prizefighter, the first African American heavyweight boxing champion of the world.

EDMUND Then he accused Harker of making his foreman break down the fence to entice the pigs into the ice pond in order to destroy them. The poor pigs, Shaughnessy yelled, had caught their death of cold. Many of them were dying of pneumonia, and several others had been taken down with cholera from drinking the poisoned water. He told Harker he was hiring a lawyer to sue him for damages. And he wound up by saying that he had to put up with poison ivy, ticks, potato bugs, snakes and skunks on his farm, but he was an honest man who drew the line somewhere, and he'd be damned if he'd stand for a Standard Oil thief trespassing. So would Harker kindly remove his dirty feet from the premises before he sicked the dog on him. And Harker did! [*He and* JAMIE *laugh.*]

MARY [*shocked but giggling*] Heavens, what a terrible tongue that man has!

TYRONE [*admiringly before he thinks*] The damned old scoundrel! By God, you can't beat him! [*He laughs—then stops abruptly and scowls.*] The dirty blackguard! He'll get me in serious trouble yet. I hope you told him I'd be mad as hell—

EDMUND I told him you'd be tickled to death over the great Irish victory, and so you are. Stop faking, Papa.

TYRONE Well, I'm not tickled to death.

MARY [*teasingly*] You are, too, James. You're simply delighted!

TYRONE No, Mary, a joke is a joke, but—

EDMUND I told Shaughnessy he should have reminded Harker that a Standard Oil millionaire ought to welcome the flavor of hog in his ice water as an appropriate touch.

TYRONE The devil you did! [*frowning*] Keep your damned Socialist anarchist sentiments out of my affairs!

EDMUND Shaughnessy almost wept because he hadn't thought of that one, but he said he'd include it in a letter he's writing to Harker, along with a few other insults he'd overlooked. [*He and* JAMIE *laugh.*]

TYRONE What are you laughing at? There's nothing funny—A fine son you are to help that blackguard get me into a lawsuit!

MARY Now, James, don't lose your temper.

TYRONE [*turns on* JAMIE] And you're worse than he is, encouraging him. I suppose you're regretting you weren't there to prompt Shaughnessy with a few nastier insults. You've a fine talent for that, if for nothing else.

MARY James! There's no reason to scold Jamie.
    [JAMIE *is about to make some sneering remark to his father, but he shrugs his shoulders.*]

EDMUND [*with sudden nervous exasperation*] Oh, for God's sake, Papa! If you're starting that stuff again, I'll beat it. [*He jumps up.*] I left my book upstairs, anyway. [*He goes to the front parlor, saying disgustedly*] God, Papa, I should think you'd get sick of hearing yourself—
    [*He disappears.* TYRONE *looks after him angrily.*]

MARY You musn't mind Edmund, James. Remember he isn't well.
    [EDMUND *can be heard coughing as he goes upstairs. She adds nervously*] A summer cold makes anyone irritable.

JAMIE [*genuinely concerned*] It's not just a cold he's got. The Kid is damned sick.
    [*His father gives him a sharp warning look but he doesn't see it.*]

MARY [*turns on him resentfully*] Why do you say that? It *is* just a cold! Anyone can tell that! You always imagine things!

TYRONE [*with another warning glance at* JAMIE—*easily*] All Jamie meant was Edmund might have a touch of something else, too, which makes his cold worse.

JAMIE Sure, Mama. That's all I meant.

TYRONE Doctor Hardy thinks it might be a bit of malarial fever he caught when he was in the tropics. If it is, quinine will soon cure it.

MARY [*a look of contemptuous hostility flashes across her face*] Doctor Hardy! I wouldn't believe a thing he said, if he swore on a stack of Bibles! I know what doctors are. They're all alike. Anything, they don't care what, to keep you coming to them. [*She stops short, overcome by a fit of acute self-consciousness as she catches their eyes fixed on her. Her hands jerk nervously to her hair. She forces a smile.*] What is it? What are you looking at? Is my hair—?

TYRONE [*puts his arm around her—with guilty heartiness, giving her a playful hug*] There's nothing wrong with your hair. The healthier and fatter you get, the vainer you become. You'll soon spend half the day primping before the mirror.

MARY [*half reassured*] I really should have new glasses. My eyes are so bad now.

TYRONE [*with Irish blarney*] Your eyes are beautiful, and well you know it. [*He gives her a kiss. Her face lights up with a charming, shy embarrassment. Suddenly and startlingly one sees in her face the girl she had once been, not a ghost of the dead, but still a living part of her.*]

MARY You mustn't be so silly, James. Right in front of Jamie!

TYRONE Oh, he's on to you, too. He knows this fuss about eyes and hair is only fishing for compliments. Eh, Jamie?

JAMIE [*his face has cleared, too, and there is an old boyish charm in his loving smile at his mother*] Yes, You can't kid us, Mama.

MARY [*laughs and an Irish lilt comes into her voice*] Go along with both of you! [*then she speaks with a girlish gravity*] But I did truly have beautiful hair once, didn't I, James?

TYRONE The most beautiful in the world!

MARY It was a rare shade of reddish brown and so long it came down below my knees. You ought to remember it, too, Jamie. It wasn't until after Edmund was born that I had a single grey hair. Then it began to turn white. [*The girlishness fades from her face.*]

TYRONE [*quickly*] And that made it prettier than ever.

MARY [*again embarrassed and pleased*] Will you listen to your father, Jamie—after thirty-five years of marriage! He isn't a great actor for nothing, is he? What's come over you, James? Are you pouring coals of fire on my head for teasing you about snoring? Well, then, I take it all back. It must have been only the foghorn I heard. [*She laughs, and they laugh with her. Then she changes to a brisk businesslike air.*] But I can't stay with you any longer, even to hear compliments. I must see the cook about dinner and the day's marketing. [*She gets up and sighs with humorous exaggeration.*] Bridget is so lazy. And so sly. She begins telling me about her relatives so I can't get a word in edgeways and scold her. Well, I might as well get it over. [*She goes to the back-parlor doorway, then turns, her face worried again.*] You mustn't make Edmund work on the grounds with you, James, remember. [*again with the strange obstinate set to her face*] Not that he isn't strong enough, but he'd perspire and he might catch more cold.

> [*She disappears through the back parlor.* TYRONE *turns on* JAMIE *condemningly.*]

TYRONE   You're a fine lunkhead! Haven't you any sense? The one thing to avoid is saying anything that would get her more upset over Edmund.

JAMIE [*shrugging his shoulders*]   All right. Have it your way. I think it's the wrong idea to let Mama go on kidding yourself. It will only make the shock worse when she has to face it. Anyway, you can see she's deliberately fooling herself with that summer cold talk. She knows better.

TYRONE   Knows? Nobody knows yet.

JAMIE   Well, I do. I was with Edmund when he went to Doc Hardy on Monday. I heard him pull that touch of malaria stuff. He was stalling. That isn't what he thinks any more. You know it as well as I do. You talked to him when you went uptown yesterday, didn't you?

TYRONE   He couldn't say anything for sure yet. He's to phone me today before Edmund goes to him.

JAMIE [*slowly*]   He thinks it's consumption,[6] doesn't he, Papa?

TYRONE [*reluctantly*]   He said it might be.

JAMIE [*moved, his love for his brother coming out*]   Poor kid! God damn it! [*He turns on his father accusingly.*] It might never have happened if you'd sent him to a real doctor when he first got sick.

TYRONE   What's the matter with Hardy? He's always been our doctor up here.

JAMIE   Everything's the matter with him! Even in this hick burg he's rated third class! He's a cheap old quack!

TYRONE   That's right! Run him down! Run down everybody! Everyone is a fake to you!

JAMIE [*contemptuously*]   Hardy only charges a dollar. That's what makes you think he's a fine doctor!

TYRONE [*stung*]   That's enough! You're not drunk now! There's no excuse— [*He controls himself—a bit defensively*] If you mean I can't afford one of the fine society doctors who prey on the rich summer people—

JAMIE   Can't afford? You're one of the biggest property owners around here.

TYRONE   That doesn't mean I'm rich. It's all mortgaged—

JAMIE   Because you always buy more instead of paying off mortgages. If Edmund was a lousy acre of land you wanted, the sky would be the limit!

TYRONE   That's a lie! And your sneers against Doctor Hardy are lies! He doesn't put on frills, or have an office in a fashionable location, or drive around in an expensive automobile. That's what you pay for with those other five-dollars-to-look-at-your-tongue fellows, not their skill.

JAMIE [*with a scornful shrug of his shoulders*]   Oh, all right. I'm a fool to argue. You can't change the leopard's spots.

TYRONE [*with rising anger*]   No, you can't. You've taught me that lesson only too well. I've lost all hope you will ever change yours. You dare tell

6. Tuberculosis.

The Gross Clinic (Portrait of Professor Gross), Thomas Eakins, 1875

Over the course of his career, Eakins (1844–1916) was profoundly interested in both the human body and the lives of professional men. In *The Gross Clinic,* he combines these two subjects. The painting is at once a portrait of the Philadelphia surgeon Dr. Samuel D. Gross and an exhibition of his professional skill. As Gross stands in a teaching amphitheater, light illuminates his brow and the leg of the patient, inviting the viewer to consider the relationship of mind to body. The calm of Gross's posture contrasts with the recoil of the female viewer, possibly a relative of the patient, on the lower left. Eakins inserts himself into the picture at the far right, where he holds a pad of paper and pencil, observing the scene as part of his own professional practice. Because of his attention to concrete detail and veracity, Eakins is commonly regarded as a realist painter, in much the same way that William Dean Howells and others are regarded as realist writers.

Children Sleeping in Mulberry Street, Jacob Riis, 1890

Riis (1825–1914) was a Danish immigrant who worked as a New York police reporter. His photographs of the Irish and Italian immigrant poor appeared in his influential book *How the Other Half Lives* (1890). Riis's composition articulates the position of homeless slum children: they sleep where they can, bunched up below street level. The photograph emphasizes their reliance on each other— they huddle together—but also shows that the space they inhabit is not safe: the stones behind the boys seem overwhelming and the iron railing and drainpipe make it seem as if they are in a subterranean prison. Riis was photographing immigrant life in New York during the same period when Stephen Crane and Abraham Cahan were writing about similar subjects, and well after Horatio Alger had popularized the rags-to-riches story of *Ragged Dick.*

Custer's Last Fight, Otto Becker, 1895

In 1876, George Armstrong Custer and his Seventh Cavalry were defeated by Lakota Sioux and Cheyenne Indians at the Battle of the Little Bighorn. Nearly twenty years later, the Anheuser-Busch brewing company commissioned Otto Becker to produce *Custer's Last Fight* and distributed the lithograph to barrooms across the nation. The image of Custer, saber aloft, surrounded by hordes of Indians was historically inaccurate, but the lithograph was widely seen as the United States prepared to enter the Spanish-American War. Such images, with their negative depictions of Indian warriors, created challenges for Native American authors writing in the aftermath of the Plains Indian Wars.

Women Watching a Sun Dance, Amos Bad Heart Bull, undated

In the years 1890 to 1913 Amos Bad Heart Bull (1869–1913), an Oglala Lakota Sioux, produced 415 paintings and drawings. Many depict aspects of the Battle of the Little Bighorn, as well as other important events in the history and culture of his people. This painting depicts women watching a Sun Dance through a pine-bough barricade. The horseshoe shape of each woman's head, black except for the part at the center, is conventional in the art of the Plains people.

Nampeyo Decorating Pottery, Edward S. Curtis, 1900

Photography was an important medium for the representation of American Indians at the turn of the twentieth century, and Curtis (1868–1952) was perhaps the most significant photographer of Native subjects during this time. His portraits struck an elegiac tone, based on the premise that American Indians were vanishing. At the same time, his work showed the remarkable artistry of Native peoples, as in this photograph of the renowned Hopi-Tewa ceramicist Nampeyo (c. 1856–1942). As anthropologists and tourists began studying the indigenous peoples of the Southwest in the late nineteenth century, Nampeyo became known as a master of pottery, and her designs remain influential to this day.

Madame X (Madame Pierre Gautreau), John Singer Sargent, 1884

Born in Italy to American parents, Sargent (1856–1925) became the most famous portraitist of his day. He was especially known for his portraits of upper-class women, but he also painted U.S. presidents and business tycoons. Similar in some ways to Henry James and Edith Wharton in their fiction, Sargent depicted the sophistication of his subjects but also conveyed the complicated lives beneath the surface. Madame Pierre Gautreau was originally named Virginie Amélie Avegno; she was born in Louisiana and traveled to Paris with her mother after her father was killed in the Civil War. There, she married a wealthy banker and became a celebrated social figure. When Sargent displayed the painting in 1884, his depiction of the sexual allure of this young, married woman—with bare shoulders and a barely visible ring on her left hand—provoked scandalized responses. Sargent had captured something dangerous, and he would not sell the painting for more than thirty years.

The Banjo Lesson, Henry Ossawa Tanner, 1893

Tanner (1859–1937) studied with Thomas Eakins at the Philadelphia Academy of Fine Arts and then in Paris. As an African American painter, he encountered many of the same challenges that faced authors like Paul Laurence Dunbar, Charles W. Chesnutt, and Pauline Hopkins. In *The Banjo Lesson,* Tanner confronts the powerful stereotype of African Americans as strutting, high-stepping performers. The golden light that enters from the side of the painting conveys dignity to the two figures and illuminates the careful brushstrokes of their features. The banjo links generations, as both the teacher and his pupil concentrate on the craft of musicianship.

Scribner's for June, Charles Dana Gibson, 1895

In the 1890s, illustrator Charles Dana Gibson (1867–1944) began to depict American women in a manner that became known as the "Gibson girl"—a style of white womanhood that combined femininity with virility. With her upswept hair and hourglass figure, the Gibson girl became recognizable at a time when the "New American Woman" was a subject of frequent commentary in the popular press. In some illustrations, Gibson's urbane subjects seem to be conforming to the social expectations of their gender and class, but in others they challenge the conventions of female behavior. On this cover of the popular *Scribner's* magazine, the subject confidently rides directly into the gaze of the viewer. Her nipped waist and perfect posture suggest traditional feminine manners; however, she wears bloomers, a garment associated with female independence and strength in the nineteenth century. Because it signified mobility and modernity, the bicycle was a favorite symbol of both those who celebrated and those who mocked the efforts of women to achieve greater autonomy.

Both Members of This Club, George Bellows, 1909

Bellows (1882–1925) was a member of the Ashcan school, a group of artists who advocated representing American society in all its forms, especially the lives of the working classes, much like the naturalist writers of the time. Bellows's paintings of boxing matches are characterized by thick brushstrokes on a dark background and emphasize the motion of human figures within the confines of the ring. *Both Members of This Club* was composed at a time when many white boxers refused to enter the ring against black opponents. In the painting, Bellows creates an atmosphere of athleticism and spectacle, with both boxers performing for a grotesquely leering crowd.

Manhattan's Misty Sunset, Frederick Childe Hassam, 1911

Hassam (1850–1935), an American Impressionist, was the premier painter of New York City. *Manhattan's Misty Sunset* captures the romantic attraction of New York as a place of both tremendous opportunity and uncertainty and mystery. Hassam's limited color palette is organized around cool tones, as shades of green generalize the shapes of Brooklyn warehouses across the East River from Hassam's studio, punctuated by barely visible streetlights; the drizzle and fog suggest an ambivalence toward industrial America.

1914–1945

Nude Descending a Staircase, No. 2, Marcel Duchamp, 1912

Rejected by Duchamp's fellow French modernists when he submitted it to the annual Salon des Indépendants (the annual exhibition of France's Society of Independent Artists) in 1912, *Nude Descending a Staircase* went on to become the most controversial work shown at the 1913 International Exhibition of Modern Art in New York City—the Armory Show, as it became known, after its site in a National Guard armory. Featuring paintings and sculpture by European avant-garde artists as well as a scattering of Americans, including Edward Hopper and Charles Sheeler, the Armory Show brought modernist art to the attention of a broad American public. *Nude Descending a Staircase* links Cubism's technique of representing objects in multiple perspectives with the innovations of late nineteenth-century multiple-exposure photography, the precursor to motion pictures.

Portrait of a German Officer, Marsden Hartley, 1914

Born in Lewiston, Maine, Hartley immersed himself in European modernist painting at Gertrude Stein's Paris salon during a 1912 trip financed by the photographer Alfred Stieglitz. Hartley's abstract "portrait," completed on his second European trip to Berlin and before the United States entered World War I, represents its wartime subject in fragments of ribbons, uniforms, and flags. The painting memorializes Hartley's friend Karl von Freyburg, a German cavalry officer who had been killed in combat. Hartley's *Portrait* is deliberately far removed from the kind of traditional memorial art that might have idealized an officer on his horse. Among the elements incorporated into the painting are Freyburg's initials (K v. F) and the age at which he died (24). Like T. S. Eliot's *The Waste Land* (p. 834), this work registers a world blown to pieces.

Hollywood, Thomas Hart Benton, 1937–38

The Missouri-born painter Thomas Hart Benton studied at the Art Institute of Chicago and then, like other American artists of his generation, traveled to Paris for further education and immersion in avant-garde circles. On returning to the United States, Benton worked as a painter of backdrops for early silent movies being filmed in Fort Lee, New Jersey. His service in the U.S. Navy during World War I introduced him to still another use for painting, as camouflage for warships. But after the war, Benton declared himself "an enemy of modernism" and turned toward a more realistic style. During the Great Depression, he earned a national reputation by producing several series of murals on subjects from American regional life and history, including controversial topics like slavery and the Ku Klux Klan. In 1937 *Life* magazine sent Benton to Los Angeles to cover the film industry; his large canvas *Hollywood* was the result. Like many famous paintings in Western art, *Hollywood* centers the viewer's gaze on a nearly nude female body, a modern-day goddess in the process of creation. Surrounding this body are not cupids and angels but managers and technicians of an industrial workplace—one of many American work settings that Benton painted. Like Nathanael West in *The Day of the Locust*, Benton in *Hollywood* focuses on the unnamed and invisible laborers supporting the film industry.

Black Belt, Archibald J. Motley, 1934

Motley attended the School of the Art Institute of Chicago and later studied European art on a Guggenheim fellowship in Paris, where he was drawn to Renaissance and nineteenth-century realistic portraiture. During the 1930s his painting was supported by the federal Works Progress Administration. *Black Belt* captures the social breadth and vitality of Chicago's South Side and other emerging African American urban centers, using a stylized realism of vivid colors and flat perspective. His men and women include well-dressed couples; a matronly, homeward-bound woman; and the stoic, downcast worker in the foreground. In the middle background a man in a suit and hat glances warily over his shoulder toward the viewer; in his poem about the South Side (p. 1041), Langston Hughes explicitly challenged outsiders looking in on black life.

River Rouge Plant, Charles Sheeler, 1932

This painting of a Ford Motor Company factory near Detroit grew out of a series of photographs that Sheeler took for an advertising agency. Along with other "precisionist" painters of the 1920s and 1930s, Sheeler was influenced by Futurism's celebration of the machine and by Cubism's breaking of traditional unified perspective into multiple flat planes. Sheeler's painterly style, however, remained realistic; he sought the broken planes and angles of Cubism in the objects themselves (here, the multiple white planes of the factory and its reflection) and avoided calling attention to the medium of paint—its texture and brushwork, the surface of the canvas—over what it represented. Like the poet Hart Crane, Sheeler found the materials for a modernist art in the American industrial landscape.

From the Faraway, Nearby, Georgia O'Keeffe, 1937

O'Keeffe found inspiration in the landscapes of the American Southwest. Noted in the 1920s for her large, vivid paintings of flowers "with great sexy involutions" (as *Life* magazine observed), O'Keeffe in the 1930s began painting the bones she found scattered about the New Mexico desert. In this almost surrealist image, the sharp lines of the elk antlers floating in the foreground are echoed in softer form by the hills; the painting's perspective collapses the middle distance to put the faraway and the nearby on top of one another. O'Keeffe's paintings became modernist icons of the American landscape; the bones of the Southwest, she wrote, opened her work up to "the wideness and wonder of the world as I live in it."

We Can Do It! ("Rosie the Riveter"), J. Howard Miller, c. 1942

World War II drew many women out of traditional roles in the home and into the industrial labor force and various forms of war-related work. Miller's poster *We Can Do It!*, produced by the defense contractor Westinghouse for the War Production Co-ordinating Committee, uses the bright colors and clean, simple lines of advertising to make the dislocations of traditional gender patterns familiar and acceptable, at least for the duration of the war. The worker's pert face and feminine grooming balance her assertively flexed bicep. A popular wartime song, "Rosie the Riveter," gave Miller's anonymous heroine her familiar nickname.

Night Hawks, Edward Hopper, 1942

Born in Nyack, New York, and trained at the New York Institute of Design, Hopper sold his first painting at the 1913 Armory show and lived in New York's Greenwich Village for most of his career. Hopper's painting represents the night life of loners in the city. Its stylized realism preserves traditional perspective, accentuated by the deep view through the restaurant's large plate-glass window, but simplifies both realistic detail and painterly brushwork. In both style and subject, Hopper's painting is often compared to the work of writers like Ernest Hemingway and to the visual style of 1940s *film noir* (literally, "dark film"). *Night Hawks* depicts a clean, well-lighted restaurant against a dark urban background of uncertain danger or promise. The customer with his back to the viewer, like one of the "private eye" characters of *film noir*, keeps to himself but stands in for the viewer's anonymous perspective on the scene.

1945 to the Present

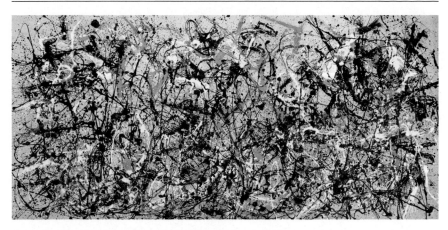

Autumn Rhythm (Number 30), Jackson Pollock, 1950

With Abstract Expressionism, the style of post–World War II American painting that had international impact, the canvas became less a surface upon which to represent than an arena in which to act. Jackson Pollock (1912–1956) was the most noteworthy of the so-called action painters. One of his favorite methods, working above a canvas stretched on the ground, dancing over and around it, dripping and swirling paint, was dramatic enough to be captured in photographs and film documentaries.

James Baldwin,
September 13, 1955, Carl Van Vechten

This portrait is one of a series that Van Vechten took of Baldwin using different backdrops, drapes, and lighting. The photographer captured many of the era's writers and artists in rich color images, working in the medium from 1939 until his death in 1964. This image juxtaposes Baldwin's thoughtful expression—he gazes to his left at something outside the frame—with the images of stylized white women on the poster behind him, whose gazes are similarly distant. All three faces are contemplative, even while they become subjects for the viewer's own contempla-tion. Baldwin commented throughout his life on what he called his "ugliness" and doodled fashionable white women's faces like those behind him on the backs of his earliest manuscripts. Even while he unpacked the racist norms of beauty in his writing, he thus remained in some ways fascinated by those norms. Van Vechten, revealing Baldwin's classically symmetrical features and rich skin tones in contrast—and parallel—to the faces behind him, offered a different view—a view of Baldwin's beauty.

Blam, Roy Lichtenstein, 1962

Roy Lichtenstein (1923–1997) helped to launch the Pop Art movement. Lichtenstein used bold outlines, vivid colors, and the technique of Benday dots, popular in commercial printing, to simulate with painting the process of mechanical reproduction. This aesthetic clearly defied the expressionist practices of abstract painters like Jackson Pollock. The cartoon style of *Blam* (in fact, Lichtenstein took this image from a comic book) and its onomatopoetic lettering are typical of Lichtenstein's work. The literally explosive image—a fighter plane being blown apart in the air—also suggests the way in which Pop Art sought to explode boundaries between an original and a copy, a unique image and one that is reproduced, and between high and low culture more generally. Fiction writers like Donald Barthelme, poets like John Ashbery, and comic book artists like Art Spiegelman are all indebted in different ways to Pop Art.

Estate, Robert Rauschenberg, 1963

Few artworks reflect the social and aesthetic nature of their times as boldly as the combines and assemblages of Robert Rauschenberg (b. 1925). Self-consciousness about his medium combines with sociopolitical awareness in works that address both concerns and make them the viewers' own.

Estate employs brushwork, silk-screening, photography, and photocopying to interrogate its audience as well as itself. Most important, every image in this collage remains recognizable, even as the expressive manner of combination (including several brushstrokes and color actions worthy of Abstract Expressionism) emphasizes the artist's creative act.

Campbell's Soup 1 (Tomato), Andy Warhol, 1968

For the Pop artist Andy Warhol (1928–1987), an object as banal as a Campbell's soup can could evoke the spirit of the American 1960s. While both representational and abstract painting had conventionally been dedicated to matters of great importance, whether in the subject portrayed or in the activity of putting paint to canvas, Warhol's soup can undercut the premises of both styles while commenting on the materialism underlying the business of producing and selling art. Creativity was now a matter of selection, in this case of lavishing the artist's considerable talent and technique on (and commanding a high price for) such an everyday object. From this decade onward, literary artists would find success by doing much the same thing.

*Earthrise and Lunar Horizon
from* Apollo 8, 1968

The photo of "Earthrise" over the
lunar horizon was taken by the
Apollo 8 crew, astronauts Frank
Borman (b. 1928), James Lovell
(b. 1928), and William Anders (b.
1933), who were the first humans
to leave Earth's orbit, entering
into lunar orbit on Christmas Eve,
1968. The photograph showed the
Earth for the first time as it
appears from deep space. The
philosopher Hannah Arendt, in
her book *The Human Condition*
(1958), anticipated the significance of this image when she
wrote that a shift from seeing men
and women as earthbound creatures to seeing them as dwellers of
the universe would be a radical
change in understanding the
human condition, as revolutionary
as the invention of the telescope.

The American Indian
Fritz Scholder, 1970

The American Indian by Fritz Scholder
(1937–2005), a Luiseño Indian,
belongs to a series of paintings that
blew open the doors of "acceptable"
Indian imagery and undermined
clichés and stereotypes of the stoic
"noble savage." Rather than traditional
Indian regalia, the figure wears a judicial
robe fashioned from the American
flag, as if to suggest that only being
wrapped in the symbol of the colonists
will certify him as "American." But the
whitened face and skeletal rendering
of the figure's mouth suggest what
colonization cost him. The single feather
in his hair, the necklace, and the
tomahawk may suggest how the
expectations of tourists also shape his
depiction.

Untitled, Cindy
Sherman, 1981

This photograph by the
artist Cindy Sherman
(b. 1954) is number 96
of her "Centerfold"
series (1981). Like
Sherman's earlier,
black-and-white "Film
Stills," this series
consists of "self-
portraits" in which the
artist explores
representations of
women by dressing in a
variety of costumes and adopting a variety of poses. Sherman's role as both photographer and
subject reverses the traditional power of the male gaze, and here she examines and subverts the
objectified images of women displayed in magazine centerfolds. Rather than signaling availability,
this cropped, color-saturated photograph is enigmatic. Sherman's girlish clothing, evoking the
1950s, conceals more than it reveals, and she holds in her hand a largely unreadable scrap torn
from a newspaper. Her gaze, vacant and interior, is also unreadable. Her distinctly unrevealing
sweater and the flush on her face become part of the color pattern—oranges and browns forming
a series of grids and checks—rather than erotic signs.

Vietnam Veterans
Memorial, Maya Lin,
1982

Located on the mall in
Washington, D.C., the
Vietnam Veterans
Memorial is a
246-foot-long, v-shaped
sunken wall of black
granite. It is engraved
with more than
fifty-eight thousand
names of those who died
in the Vietnam conflict.
The names are listed in
chronological order, and
to locate a particular
name a visitor walks
along the wall searching for it. The polished surface of the granite reflects the sky, the surrounding landscape, and the visitor. Considerable controversy attended the design, by the Chinese
American architect Maya Lin (b. 1959), some objecting to its abstraction in place of the realistic
statuary of most war memorials, and some finding it too somber. Lin has said she wanted a
structure that would carve out a space for the public display of grief and loss, and the memorial
has a powerful elegiac quality. Dedicated on Veterans Day, 1982, it has become the most widely
visited monument in Washington.

Sonny's Quilt, Faith Ringgold, 1986

In *Sonny's Quilt*, an acrylic painting on canvas with a pieced fabric border, Faith Ringgold (b. 1930) unites two African American art forms: jazz and the quilt. This quilt depicts the jazz saxophonist Theodore Walter "Sonny" Rollins poised high on an imagined intersection of the Williamsburg Bridge, which runs across the quilt, and the Brooklyn Bridge, which recedes into the visual field of the quilt below him. Ringgold's depiction of the two bridges evokes the iconic status of the Brooklyn Bridge in American painting, photography, and literature, while honoring the fact that Rollins chose the Williamsburg Bridge as his favored place to practice.

After "Invisible Man" by Ralph Ellison, the Prologue, Jeff Wall, 2000

Ralph Ellison's masterwork, the novel *Invisible Man*, has inspired several prominent photographers to enter its imaginative world. In the introduction to this section, readers will find an image from Gordon Parks's photo essay on the novel, which appeared in *Life* magazine in 1952, a series that included an image based, like the one above, on the novel's famous scene of the unnamed protagonist in his basement apartment, flooded with the light of over a thousand bulbs. While Parks's photograph is abstract in composition, Jeff Wall creates an elaborately staged but naturalistic space for his version of the scene, directing attention away from the symbolic significance of the bulbs—the sense that no amount of light can make the protagonist socially visible as a human being. Instead, his back is turned to the viewer, and he is dwarfed by the textured clutter of his space.

World Trade Center Burning, Peter Morgan, September 11, 2001

"A screaming comes across the sky." This opening sentence of Thomas Pynchon's 1973 novel *Gravity's Rainbow* had for decades impressed readers with the terrors of modern warfare, in which military technologies at the far edge of human inventiveness were turned against people at home. That Pynchon's scene was London, under attack from German V-2 rockets near the end of World War II, may have allayed readers' most personal fears. Yet on September 11, 2001, another such screaming awoke not just the United States but the whole world to the reality that wholesale destruction was an ever-present possibility. After half a century of Cold War rhetoric that had made such catastrophes unthinkable, the unthinkable happened. Two jet airliners were crashed into the twin towers of New York's World Trade Center in an event witnessed within minutes by television viewers all over the Earth. By the time the buildings collapsed, the whole world was watching. What in normal terms might be a line in a novel or a scene in a movie was now most horribly real.

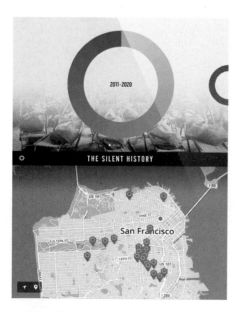

Screenshot from *The Silent History*, by Eli Horowitz, Kevin Moffett, and Matthew Derby, with app design by Russell Quinn, 2012

The Silent History, the first novel built fully into a mobile app, was released in daily installments to subscribers in 2012 and was thereafter sold as a complete novel through the Apple App Store. A paper version was published in 2014. In the original app format, parts of the novel called "Field Reports" are available only in specific geographic locations tracked by a mobile device's GPS. Horowitz's vision was to create a novel you could "explore" in a physical sense, blending the imaginative world of the story with the reader's presence in real-world locations. *The Silent History* demonstrates how formal innovations in contemporary literature arise as traditional story-telling genres, such as the novel, migrate into ever-changing electronic media.

me what I can afford? You've never known the value of a dollar and never will! You've never saved a dollar in your life! At the end of each season you're penniless! You've thrown your salary away every week on whores and whiskey!

JAMIE   My salary! Christ!

TYRONE   It's more than you're worth, and you couldn't get that if it wasn't for me. If you weren't my son, there isn't a manager in the business who would give you a part, your reputation stinks so. As it is, I have to humble my pride and beg for you, saying you've turned over a new leaf, although I know it's a lie!

JAMIE   I never wanted to be an actor. You forced me on the stage.

TYRONE   That's a lie! You made no effort to find anything else to do. You left it to me to get you a job and I have no influence except in the theater. Forced you! You never wanted to do anything except loaf in barrooms! You'd have been content to sit back like a lazy lunk and sponge on me for the rest of your life! After all the money I'd wasted on your education, and all you did was get fired in disgrace from every college you went to!

JAMIE   Oh, for God's sake, don't drag up that ancient history!

TYRONE   It's not ancient history that you have to come home every summer to live on me.

JAMIE   I earn my board and lodging working on the grounds. It saves you hiring a man.

TYRONE   Bah! You have to be driven to do even that much! [*His anger ebbs into a weary complaint.*] I wouldn't give a damn if you ever displayed the slightest sign of gratitude. The only thanks is to have you sneer at me for a dirty miser, sneer at my profession, sneer at every damned thing in the world—except yourself.

JAMIE [*wryly*]   That's not true, Papa. You can't hear me talking to myself, that's all.

TYRONE [*stares at him puzzledly, then quotes mechanically*]   "Ingratitude, the vilest weed that grows"![7]

JAMIE   I could see that line coming! God, how many thousand times—! [*He stops, bored with their quarrel, and shrugs his shoulders.*] All right, Papa. I'm a bum. Anything you like, so long as it stops the argument.

TYRONE [*with indignant appeal now*]   If you'd get ambition in your head instead of folly! You're young yet. You could still make your mark. You had the talent to become a fine actor! You have it still. You're my son—!

JAMIE [*boredly*]   Let's forget me. I'm not interested in the subject. Neither are you. [TYRONE *gives up.* JAMIE *goes on casually.*] What started us on this? Oh, Doc Hardy. When is he going to call you up about Edmund?

TYRONE   Around lunch time. [*He pauses—then defensively*] I couldn't have sent Edmund to a better doctor. Hardy's treated him whenever he was sick up here, since he was knee high. He knows his constitution as no other doctor could. It's not a question of my being miserly, as you'd like to make out. [*bitterly*] And what could the finest specialist in America do for Edmund, after he's deliberately ruined his health by the mad life he's led ever since he was fired from college? Even before that when he was in prep school, he began dissipating and playing the Broadway

7. Shakespeare's *King Lear* 1.4.

sport to imitate you, when he's never had your constitution to stand it. You're a healthy hulk like me—or you were at his age—but he's always been a bundle of nerves like his mother. I've warned him for years his body couldn't stand it, but he wouldn't heed me, and now it's too late.

JAMIE [*sharply*]   What do you mean, too late? You talk as if you thought—

TYRONE [*guiltily explosive*]   Don't be a damned fool! I meant nothing but what's plain to anyone! His health has broken down and he may be an invalid for a long time.

JAMIE [*stares at his father, ignoring his explanation*]   I know it's an Irish peasant idea consumption is fatal. It probably is when you live in a hovel on a bog, but over here, with modern treatment—

TYRONE   Don't I know that! What are you gabbing about, anyway? And keep your dirty tongue off Ireland, with your sneers about peasants and bogs and hovels! [*accusingly*] The less you say about Edmund's sickness, the better for your conscience! You're more responsible than anyone!

JAMIE [*stung*]   That's a lie! I won't stand for that, Papa!

TYRONE   It's the truth! You've been the worst influence for him. He grew up admiring you as a hero! A fine example you set him! If you ever gave him advice except in the ways of rottenness, I've never heard of it! You made him old before his time, pumping him full of what you consider worldly wisdom, when he was too young to see that your mind was so poisoned by your own failure in life, you wanted to believe every man was a knave with his soul for sale, and every woman who wasn't a whore was a fool!

JAMIE [*with a defensive air of weary indifference again*]   All right. I did put Edmund wise to things, but not until I saw he'd started to raise hell, and knew he'd laugh at me if I tried the good advice, older brother stuff. All I did was make a pal of him and be absolutely frank so he'd learn from my mistakes that—[*He shrugs his shoulders—cynically*] Well, that if you can't be good you can at least be careful.

[*His father snorts contemptuously. Suddenly* JAMIE *becomes really moved.*]

That's a rotten accusation, Papa. You know how much the Kid means to me, and how close we've always been—not like the usual brothers! I'd do anything for him.

TYRONE [*impressed—mollifyingly*]   I know you may have thought it was for the best, Jamie. I didn't say you did it deliberately to harm him.

JAMIE   Besides it's damned rot! I'd like to see anyone influence Edmund more than he wants to be. His quietness fools people into thinking they can do what they like with him. But he's stubborn as hell inside and what he does is what he wants to do, and to hell with anyone else! What had I to do with all the crazy stunts he's pulled in the last few years— working his way all over the map as a sailor and all that stuff. I thought that was a damned fool idea, and I told him so. You can't imagine me getting fun out of being on the beach in South America, or living in filthy dives, drinking rotgut, can you? No, thanks! I'll stick to Broadway, and a room with a bath, and bars that serve bonded Bourbon.

TYRONE   You and Broadway! It's made you what you are! [*with a touch of pride*] Whatever Edmund's done, he's had the guts to go off on his own, where he couldn't come whining to me the minute he was broke.

JAMIE [*stung into sneering jealousy*]   He's always come home broke finally, hasn't he? And what did his going away get him? Look at him now! [*He is suddenly shamefaced.*] Christ! That's a lousy thing to say. I don't mean that.

TYRONE [*decides to ignore this*]   He's been doing well on the paper. I was hoping he'd found the work he wants to do at last.

JAMIE [*sneering jealously again*]   A hick town rag! Whatever bull they hand you, they tell me he's a pretty bum reporter. If he weren't your son—[*ashamed again*] No, that's not true! They're glad to have him, but it's the special stuff that gets him by. Some of the poems and parodies he's written are damned good. [*grudgingly again*] Not that they'd ever get him anywhere on the big time. [*hastily*] But he's certainly made a damned good start.

TYRONE   Yes. He's made a start. You used to talk about wanting to become a newspaper man but you were never willing to start at the bottom. You expected—

JAMIE   Oh, for Christ's sake, Papa! Can't you lay off me!

TYRONE [*stares at him—then looks away—after a pause*]   It's damnable luck Edmund should be sick right now. It couldn't have come at a worse time for him. [*He adds, unable to conceal an almost furtive uneasiness*] Or for your mother. It's damnable she should have this to upset her, just when she needs peace and freedom from worry. She's been so well in the two months since she came home. [*His voice grows husky and trembles a little.*] It's been heaven to me. This home has been a home again. But I needn't tell you, Jamie.

[*His son looks at him, for the first time with an understanding sympathy. It is as if suddenly a deep bond of common feeling existed between them in which their antagonisms could be forgotten.*]

JAMIE [*almost gently*]   I've felt the same way, Papa.

TYRONE   Yes, this time you can see how strong and sure of herself she is. She's a different woman entirely from the other times. She has control of her nerves—or she had until Edmund got sick. Now you can feel her growing tense and frightened underneath. I wish to God we could keep the truth from her, but we can't if he has to be sent to a sanatorium. What makes it worse is her father died of consumption. She worshiped him and she's never forgotten. Yes, it will be hard for her. But she can do it! She has the will power now! We must help her, Jamie, in every way we can!

JAMIE [*moved*]   Of course, Papa. [*hesitantly*] Outside of nerves, she seems perfectly all right this morning.

TYRONE [*with hearty confidence now*]   Never better. She's full of fun and mischief. [*Suddenly he frowns at* JAMIE *suspiciously.*] Why do you say, seems? Why shouldn't she be all right? What the hell do you mean?

JAMIE   Don't start jumping down my throat! God, Papa, this ought to be one thing we can talk over frankly without a battle.

TYRONE   I'm sorry, Jamie. [*tensely*] But go on and tell me—

JAMIE   There's nothing to tell. I was all wrong. It's just that last night—Well, you know how it is, I can't forget the past. I can't help being suspicious. Any more than you can. [*bitterly*] That's the hell of it. And makes it hell for Mama! She watches us watching her—

TYRONE [*sadly*] I know. [*tensely*] Well, what was it! Can't you speak out!

JAMIE Nothing, I tell you. Just my damned foolishness. Around three o'clock this morning, I woke up and heard her moving around in the spare room. Then she went to the bathroom. I pretended to be asleep. She stopped in the hall to listen, as if she wanted to make sure I was.

TYRONE [*with forced scorn*] For God's sake, is that all? She told me herself the foghorn kept her awake all night, and every night since Edmund's been sick she's been up and down, going to his room to see how he was.

JAMIE [*eagerly*] Yes, that's right, she did stop to listen outside his room. [*hesitantly again*] It was her being in the spare room that scared me. I couldn't help remembering that when she starts sleeping alone in there, it has always been a sign—

TYRONE It isn't this time! It's easily explained. Where else could she go last night to get away from my snoring? [*He gives way to a burst of resentful anger.*] By God, how you can live with a mind that sees nothing but the worst motives behind everything is beyond me!

JAMIE [*stung*] Don't pull that! I've just said I was all wrong. Don't you suppose I'm as glad of that as you are!

TYRONE [*mollifyingly*] I'm sure you are, Jamie. [*A pause. His expression becomes somber. He speaks slowly with a superstitious dread.*] It would be like a curse she can't escape if worry over Edmund—It was her long sickness after bringing him into the world that she first—

JAMIE She didn't have anything to do with it!

TYRONE I'm not blaming her.

JAMIE [*bitingly*] Then who are you blaming? Edmund, for being born?

TYRONE You damned fool! No one was to blame.

JAMIE The bastard of a doctor was! From what Mama's said, he was another cheap quack like Hardy! You wouldn't pay for a first-rate—

TYRONE That's a lie! [*furiously*] So I'm to blame! That's what you're driving at, is it? You evil-minded loafer!

JAMIE [*warningly as he hears his mother in the dining room*] Ssh!
[TYRONE *gets hastily to his feet and goes to look out the windows at right.* JAMIE *speaks with a complete change of tone.*]
Well, if we're going to cut the front hedge today, we'd better go to work.
[MARY *comes in from the back parlor. She gives a quick, suspicious glance from one to the other, her manner nervously self-conscious.*]

TYRONE [*turns from the window—with an actor's heartiness*] Yes, it's too fine a morning to waste indoors arguing. Take a look out the window, Mary. There's no fog in the harbor. I'm sure the spell of it we've had is over now.

MARY [*going to him*] I hope so, dear. [*to* JAMIE, *forcing a smile*] Did I actually hear you suggesting work on the front hedge, Jamie? Wonders will never cease! You must want pocket money badly.

JAMIE [*kiddingly*] When don't I? [*He winks at her, with a derisive glance at his father.*] I expect a salary of at least one large iron man[8] at the end of the week—to carouse on!

---

8. Dollar (slang).

MARY [*does not respond to his humor—her hands fluttering over the front of her dress*]   What were you two arguing about?

JAMIE [*shrugs his shoulders*]   The same old stuff.

MARY   I heard you say something about a doctor, and your father accusing you of being evil-minded.

JAMIE [*quickly*]   Oh, that. I was saying again Doc Hardy isn't my idea of the world's greatest physician.

MARY [*knows he is lying—vaguely*]   Oh. No, I wouldn't say he was either. [*changing the subject—forcing a smile*] That Bridget! I thought I'd never get away. She told me about her second cousin on the police force in St. Louis. [*then with nervous irritation*] Well, if you're going to work on the hedge why don't you go? [*hastily*] I mean, take advantage of the sunshine before the fog comes back. [*strangely, as if talking aloud to herself*] Because I know it will. [*Suddenly she is self-consciously aware that they are both staring fixedly at her—flurriedly, raising her hands*] Or I should say, the rheumatism in my hands knows. It's a better weather prophet than you are, James. [*She stares at her hands with fascinated repulsion.*] Ugh! How ugly they are! Who'd ever believe they were once beautiful?

[*They stare at her with a growing dread.*]

TYRONE [*takes her hands and gently pushes them down*]   Now, now, Mary. None of that foolishness. They're the sweetest hands in the world.

[*She smiles, her face lighting up, and kisses him gratefully. He turns to his son.*]

Come on Jamie. Your mother's right to scold us. The way to start work is to start work. The hot sun will sweat some of that booze fat off your middle.

[*He opens the screen door and goes out on the porch and disappears down a flight of steps leading to the ground. JAMIE rises from his chair and, taking off his coat, goes to the door. At the door he turns back but avoids looking at her, and she does not look at him.*]

JAMIE [*with an awkward, uneasy tenderness*]   We're all so proud of you, Mama, so darned happy.

[*She stiffens and stares at him with a frightened defiance. He flounders on.*]

But you've still got to be careful. You mustn't worry so much about Edmund. He'll be all right.

MARY [*with a stubborn, bitterly resentful look*]   Of course, he'll be all right. And I don't know what you mean, warning me to be careful.

JAMIE [*rebuffed and hurt, shrugs his shoulders*]   All right, Mama. I'm sorry I spoke.

[*He goes out on the porch. She waits rigidly until he disappears down the steps. Then she sinks down in the chair he had occupied, her face betraying a frightened, furtive desperation, her hands roving over the table top, aimlessly moving objects around. She hears EDMUND descending the stairs in the front hall. As he nears the bottom he has a fit of coughing. She springs to her feet, as if she wanted to run away from the sound, and goes quickly to the windows at right. She is looking out, apparently calm, as he enters from the front parlor, a book in one hand. She turns to him, her lips set in a welcoming, motherly smile.*]

MARY   Here you are. I was just going upstairs to look for you.

EDMUND   I waited until they went out. I don't want to mix up in any arguments. I feel too rotten.

MARY [*almost resentfully*]   Oh, I'm sure you don't feel half as badly as you make out. You're such a baby. You like to get us worried so we'll make a fuss over you. [*hastily*] I'm only teasing, dear. I know how miserably uncomfortable you must be. But you feel better today, don't you? [*worriedly, taking his arm*] All the same, you've grown much too thin. You need to rest all you can. Sit down and I'll make you comfortable. [*He sits down in the rocking chair and she puts a pillow behind his back.*] There, How's that?

EDMUND   Grand. Thanks, Mama.

MARY [*kisses him—tenderly*]   All you need is your mother to nurse you. Big as you are, you're still the baby of the family to me, you know.

EDMUND [*takes her hand—with deep seriousness*]   Never mind me. You take care of yourself. That's all that counts.

MARY [*evading his eyes*]   But I am, dear. [*forcing a laugh*] Heavens, don't you see how fat I've grown! I'll have to have all my dresses let out. [*She turns away and goes to the windows at right. She attempts a light, amused tone.*] They've started clipping the hedge. Poor Jamie! How he hates working in front where everyone passing can see him. There go the Chatfields in their new Mercedes. It's a beautiful car, isn't it? Not like our secondhand Packard. Poor Jamie! He bent almost under the hedge so they wouldn't notice him. They bowed to your father and he bowed back as if he were taking a curtain call. In that filthy old suit I've tried to make him throw away. [*Her voice has grown bitter.*] Really, he ought to have more pride than to make such a show of himself.

EDMUND   He's right not to give a damn what anyone thinks. Jamie's a fool to care about the Chatfields. For Pete's sake, who ever heard of them outside this hick burg?

MARY [*with satisfaction*]   No one. You're quite right, Edmund. Big frogs in a small puddle. It is stupid of Jamie. [*She pauses, looking out the window— then with an undercurrent of lonely yearning*] Still, the Chatfields and people like them stand for something. I mean they have decent, presentable homes they don't have to be ashamed of. They have friends who entertain them and whom they entertain. They're not cut off from everyone. [*She turns back from the window.*] Not that I want anything to do with them. I've always hated this town and everyone in it. You know that. I never wanted to live here in the first place, but your father liked it and insisted on building this house, and I've had to come here every summer.

EDMUND   Well, it's better than spending the summer in a New York hotel, isn't it? And this town's not so bad. I like it well enough. I suppose because it's the only home we've had.

MARY   I've never felt it was my home. It was wrong from the start. Everything was done in the cheapest way. Your father would never spend the money to make it right. It's just as well we haven't any friends here. I'd be ashamed to have them step in the door. But he's never wanted family friends. He hates calling on people, or receiving them. All he likes is to hobnob with men at the Club or in a barroom. Jamie and you are the same way, but you're not to blame. You've never had a chance to meet decent people here. I know you both would have been so different if you'd been able to associate with nice girls instead of—You'd never have disgraced yourselves as you have, so that now no respectable parents will let their daughters be seen with you.

EDMUND [irritably] Oh, Mama, forget it! Who cares? Jamie and I would be bored stiff. And about the Old Man, what's the use of talking? You can't change him.

MARY [mechanically rebuking] Don't call your father the Old Man. You should have more respect. [then dully] I know it's useless to talk. But sometimes I feel so lonely. [Her lips quiver and she keeps her head turned away.]

EDMUND Anyway, you've got to be fair, Mama. It may have been all his fault in the beginning, but you know that later on, even if he'd wanted to, we couldn't have had people here—[He flounders guiltily.] I mean, you wouldn't have wanted them.

MARY [wincing—her lips quivering pitifully] Don't. I can't bear having you remind me.

EDMUND Don't take it that way! Please, Mama! I'm trying to help. Because it's bad for you to forget. The right way is to remember. So you'll always be on your guard. You know what's happened before. [miserably] God, Mama, you know I hate to remind you. I'm doing it because it's been so wonderful having you home the way you've been, and it would be terrible—

MARY [strickenly] Please, dear. I know you mean it for the best, but—[A defensive uneasiness comes into her voice again.] I don't understand why you should suddenly say such things. What put it in your mind this morning?

EDMUND [evasively] Nothing. Just because I feel rotten and blue, I suppose.

MARY Tell me the truth. Why are you so suspicious all of a sudden?

EDMUND I'm not!

MARY Oh, yes you are. I can feel it. Your father and Jamie, too—particularly Jamie.

EDMUND Now don't start imagining things, Mama.

MARY [her hands fluttering] It makes it so much harder, living in this atmosphere of constant suspicion, knowing everyone is spying on me, and none of you believe in me, or trust me.

EDMUND That's crazy, Mama. We do trust you.

MARY If there was only some place I could go to get away for a day, or even an afternoon, some woman friend I could talk to—not about anything serious, simply laugh and gossip and forget for a while—someone besides the servants—that stupid Cathleen!

EDMUND [gets up worriedly and puts his arm around her] Stop it, Mama. You're getting yourself worked up over nothing.

MARY Your father goes out. He meets his friends in barrooms or at the Club. You and Jamie have the boys you know. You go out. But I am alone. I've always been alone.

EDMUND [soothingly] Come now! You know that's a fib. One of us always stays around to keep you company, or goes with you in the automobile when you take a drive.

MARY [*bitterly*]   Because you're afraid to trust me alone! [*She turns on him—sharply.*] I insist you tell me why you act so differently this morning—why you felt you had to remind me—

EDMUND [*hesitates—then blurts out guiltily*]   It's stupid. It's just that I wasn't asleep when you came in my room last night. You didn't go back to your and Papa's room. You went in the spare room for the rest of the night.

MARY   Because your father's snoring was driving me crazy! For heaven's sake, haven't I often used the spare room as my bedroom? [*bitterly*] But I see what you thought. That was when—

EDMUND [*too vehemently*]   I didn't think anything!

MARY   So you pretended to be asleep in order to spy on me!

EDMUND   No! I did it because I knew if you found out I was feverish and couldn't sleep, it would upset you.

MARY   Jamie was pretending to be asleep, too, I'm sure, and I suppose your father—

EDMUND   Stop it, Mama!

MARY   Oh, I can't bear it, Edmund, when even you—! [*Her hands flutter up to pat her hair in their aimless, distracted way. Suddenly a strange undercurrent of revengefulness comes into her voice.*] It would serve all of you right if it was true!

EDMUND   Mama! Don't say that! That's the way you talk when—

MARY   Stop suspecting me! Please, dear! You hurt me! I couldn't sleep because I was thinking about you. That's the real reason! I've been so worried ever since you've been sick. [*She puts her arms around him and hugs him with a frightened, protective tenderness.*]

EDMUND [*soothingly*]   That's foolishness. You know it's only a bad cold.

MARY   Yes, of course, I know that!

EDMUND   But listen, Mama. I want you to promise me that even if it should turn out to be something worse, you'll know I'll soon be all right again, anyway, and you won't worry yourself sick, and you'll keep on taking care of yourself—

MARY [*frightenedly*]   I won't listen when you're so silly! There's absolutely no reason to talk as if you expected something dreadful! Of course, I promise you. I give you my sacred word of honor! [*then with a sad bitterness*] But I suppose you're remembering I've promised before on my word of honor.

EDMUND   No!

MARY [*her bitterness receding into a resigned helplessness*]   I'm not blaming you, dear. How can you help it? How can any one of us forget? [*strangely*] That's what makes it so hard—for all of us. We can't forget.

EDMUND [*grabs her shoulder*]   Mama! Stop it!

MARY [*forcing a smile*]   All right, dear. I didn't mean to be so gloomy. Don't mind me. Here. Let me feel your head. Why, it's nice and cool. You certainly haven't any fever now.

EDMUND   Forget! It's you—

MARY   But I'm quite all right, dear. [*with a quick, strange, calculating, almost sly glance at him*] Except I naturally feel tired and nervous this morning, after such a bad night. I really ought to go upstairs and lie down until lunch time and take a nap.

[*He gives her an instinctive look of suspicion—then, ashamed of himself, looks quickly away. She hurries on nervously.*]

What are you going to do? Read here? It would be much better for you to go out in the fresh air and sunshine. But don't get overheated, remember. Be sure and wear a hat.

[*She stops, looking straight at him now. He avoids her eyes. There is a tense pause. Then she speaks jeeringly.*]

Or are you afraid to trust me alone?

EDMUND [*tormentedly*]   No! Can't you stop talking like that! I think you ought to take a nap. [*He goes to the screen door—forcing a joking tone*] I'll go down and help Jamie bear up. I love to lie in the shade and watch him work.

[*He forces a laugh in which she makes herself join. Then he goes out on the porch and disappears down the steps. Her first reaction is one of relief. She appears to relax. She sinks down in one of the wicker armchairs at rear of table and leans her head back, closing her eyes. But suddenly she grows terribly tense again. Her eyes open and she strains forward, seized by a fit of nervous panic. She begins a desperate battle with herself. Her long fingers, warped and knotted by rheumatism, drum on the arms of the chair, driven by an insistent life of their own, without her consent.*]

CURTAIN

Act 2

SCENE 1

SCENE—*The same. It is around quarter to one. No sunlight comes into the room now through the windows at right. Outside the day is still fine but increasingly sultry, with a faint haziness in the air which softens the glare of the sun.*

EDMUND *sits in the armchair at left of table, reading a book. Or rather he is trying to concentrate on it but cannot. He seems to be listening for some sound from upstairs. His manner is nervously apprehensive and he looks more sickly than in the previous act.*

The second girl, CATHLEEN, *enters from the back parlor. She carries a tray on which is a bottle of bonded Bourbon, several whiskey glasses and a pitcher of ice water. She is a buxom Irish peasant, in her early twenties, with a red-cheeked comely face, black hair and blue eyes—amiable, ignorant, clumsy, and possessed by a dense, well-meaning stupidity. She puts the tray on the table.* EDMUND *pretends to be so absorbed in his book he does not notice her, but she ignores this.*

CATHLEEN [*with garrulous familiarity*]   Here's the whiskey. It'll be lunch time soon. Will I call your father and Mister Jamie, or will you?

EDMUND [*without looking up from his book*]   You do it.

CATHLEEN   It's a wonder your father wouldn't look at his watch once in a while. He's a divil for making the meals late, and then Bridget curses me as if I was to blame. But he's a grand handsome man, if he is old. You'll never see the day you're as good looking—nor Mister Jamie, either. [*She chuckles.*] I'll wager Mister Jamie wouldn't miss the time to stop work and have his drop of whiskey if he had a watch to his name!

EDMUND [*gives up trying to ignore her and grins*] You win that one.

CATHLEEN And here's another I'd win, that you're making me call them so you can sneak a drink before they come.

EDMUND Well, I hadn't thought of that—

CATHLEEN Oh no, not you! Butter wouldn't melt in your mouth, I suppose.

EDMUND But now you suggest it—

CATHLEEN [*suddenly primly virtuous*] I'd never suggest a man or a woman touch drink, Mister Edmund. Sure, didn't it kill an uncle of mine in the old country. [*relenting*] Still, a drop now and then is no harm when you're in low spirits, or have a bad cold.

EDMUND Thanks for handing me a good excuse. [*then with forced casualness*] You'd better call my mother, too.

CATHLEEN What for? She's always on time without any calling. God bless her, she has some consideration for the help.

EDMUND She's been taking a nap.

CATHLEEN She wasn't asleep when I finished my work upstairs a while back. She was lying down in the spare room with her eyes wide open. She'd a terrible headache, she said.

EDMUND [*his casualness more forced*] Oh well then, just call my father.

CATHLEEN [*goes to the screen door, grumbling good-naturedly*] No wonder my feet kill me each night. I won't walk out in this heat and get sunstroke. I'll call from the porch.

[*She goes out on the side porch, letting the screen door slam behind her, and disappears on her way to the front porch. A moment later she is heard shouting.*]

Mister Tyrone! Mister Jamie! It's time!

[EDMUND, *who has been staring frightenedly before him, forgetting his book, springs to his feet nervously.*]

EDMUND God, what a wench!

[*He grabs the bottle and pours a drink, adds ice water and drinks. As he does so, he hears someone coming in the front door. He puts the glass hastily on the tray and sits down again, opening his book.* JAMIE *comes in from the front parlor, his coat over his arm. He has taken off collar and tie and carries them in his hand. He is wiping sweat from his forehead with a handkerchief.* EDMUND *looks up as if his reading was interrupted.* JAMIE *takes one look at the bottle and glasses and smiles cynically.*]

JAMIE Sneaking one, eh? Cut out the bluff, Kid. You're a rottener actor than I am.

EDMUND [*grins*] Yes, I grabbed one while the going was good.

JAMIE [*puts a hand affectionately on his shoulder*] That's better. Why kid me? We're pals, aren't we?

EDMUND I wasn't sure it was you coming.

JAMIE I made the Old Man look at his watch. I was halfway up the walk when Cathleen burst into song. Our wild Irish lark! She ought to be a train announcer.

EDMUND That's what drove me to drink. Why don't you sneak one while you've got a chance?

JAMIE I was thinking of that little thing. [*He goes quickly to the window at right.*] The Old Man was talking to old Captain Turner. Yes, he's still at it. [*He comes back and takes a drink.*] And now to cover up from his eagle eye. [*He measures two drinks of water and pours them in the whiskey bottle and shakes it up.*] There. That fixes it. [*He pours water in the glass and sets it on the table by* EDMUND.] And here's the water you've been drinking.

EDMUND   Fine! You don't think it will fool him, do you?

JAMIE   Maybe not, but he can't prove it. [*Putting on his collar and tie.*] I hope he doesn't forget lunch listening to himself talk. I'm hungry. [*He sits across the table from* EDMUND—*irritably*] That's what I hate about working down in front. He puts on an act for every damned fool that comes along.

EDMUND [*gloomily*]   You're in luck to be hungry. The way I feel I don't care if I ever eat again.

JAMIE [*gives him a glance of concern*]   Listen, Kid. You know me. I've never lectured you, but Doctor Hardy was right when he told you to cut out the redeye.

EDMUND   Oh, I'm going to after he hands me the bad news this afternoon. A few before then won't make any difference.

JAMIE [*hesitates—then slowly*]   I'm glad you've got your mind prepared for bad news. It won't be such a jolt. [*He catches* EDMUND *staring at him.*] I mean, it's a cinch you're really sick, and it would be wrong dope to kid yourself.

EDMUND [*disturbed*]   I'm not. I know how rotten I feel, and the fever and chills I get at night are no joke. I think Doctor Hardy's last guess was right. It must be the damned malaria come back on me.

JAMIE   Maybe, but don't be too sure.

EDMUND   Why? What do you think it is?

JAMIE   Hell, how would I know? I'm no Doc. [*abruptly*] Where's Mama?

EDMUND   Upstairs.

JAMIE [*looks at him sharply*]   When did she go up?

EDMUND   Oh, about the time I came down to the hedge, I guess. She said she was going to take a nap.

JAMIE   You didn't tell me—

EDMUND [*defensively*]   Why should I? What about it? She was tired out. She didn't get much sleep last night.

JAMIE   I know she didn't.

[*A pause. The brothers avoid looking at each other.*]

EDMUND   That damned foghorn kept me awake, too.

[*Another pause.*]

JAMIE   She's been upstairs alone all morning, eh? You haven't seen her?

EDMUND   No. I've been reading here. I wanted to give her a chance to sleep.

JAMIE   Is she coming down to lunch?

EDMUND   Of course.

JAMIE [*dryly*]   No of course about it. She might not want any lunch. Or she might start having most of her meals alone upstairs. That's happened, hasn't it?

EDMUND [*with frightened resentment*]   Cut it out, Jamie! Can't you think anything but—? [*persuasively*] You're all wrong to suspect anything. Cathleen saw her not long ago. Mama didn't tell her she wouldn't be down to lunch.

JAMIE   Then she wasn't taking a nap?

EDMUND   Not right then, but she was lying down, Cathleen said.

JAMIE   In the spare room?

EDMUND   Yes. For Pete's sake, what of it?

JAMIE [*bursts out*]   You damned fool! Why did you leave her alone so long? Why didn't you stick around?

EDMUND   Because she accused me—and you and Papa—of spying on her all the time and not trusting her. She made me feel ashamed. I know how rotten it must be for her. And she promised on her sacred word of honor—

JAMIE [*with a bitter weariness*]   You ought to know that doesn't mean anything.

EDMUND   It does this time!

JAMIE   That's what we thought the other times. [*He leans over the table to give his brother's arm an affectionate grasp.*] Listen, Kid, I know you think I'm a cynical bastard, but remember I've seen a lot more of this game than you have. You never knew what was really wrong until you were in prep-school. Papa and I kept it from you. But I was wise ten years or more before we had to tell you. I know the game backwards and I've been thinking all morning of the way she acted last night when she thought we were asleep. I haven't been able to think of anything else. And now you tell me she got you to leave her alone upstairs all morning.

EDMUND   She didn't! You're crazy!

JAMIE [*placatingly*]   All right, Kid. Don't start a battle with me. I hope as much as you do I'm crazy. I've been as happy as hell because I'd really begun to believe that this time—[*He stops—looking through the front parlor toward the hall—lowering his voice, hurriedly*] She's coming downstairs. You win on that. I guess I'm a damned suspicious louse.

   [*They grow tense with a hopeful, fearful expectancy. JAMIE mutters*]
Damn! I wish I'd grabbed another drink.

EDMUND   Me, too.

   [*He coughs nervously and this brings on a real fit of coughing. JAMIE glances at him with worried pity. MARY enters from the front parlor. At first one notices no change except that she appears to be less nervous, to be more as she was when we first saw her after breakfast, but then one becomes aware that her eyes are brighter, and there is a peculiar detachment in her voice and manner, as if she were a little withdrawn from her words and actions.*]

MARY [*goes worriedly to EDMUND and puts her arm around him*]   You mustn't cough like that. It's bad for your throat. You don't want to get a sore throat on top of your cold.

   [*She kisses him. He stops coughing and gives her a quick apprehensive glance, but if his suspicions are aroused her tenderness makes him renounce them and he believes what he wants to believe for the moment. On the other hand, JAMIE knows after one probing look at her that his suspicions are justified. His eyes fall to stare at the floor, his face sets in an expression of embittered, defensive cynicism. MARY goes on, half sitting on the arm of EDMUND's chair, her arm around him, so her face is above and behind his and he cannot look into her eyes.*]

But I seem to be always picking on you, telling you don't do this and don't do that. Forgive me, dear. It's just that I want to take care of you.

EDMUND   I know, Mama. How about you? Do you feel rested?

MARY   Yes, ever so much better. I've been lying down ever since you went out. It's what I needed after such a restless night. I don't feel nervous now.

EDMUND   That's fine.

[*He pats her hand on his shoulder.* JAMIE *gives him a strange, almost contemptuous glance, wondering if his brother can really mean this.* EDMUND *does not notice but his mother does.*]

MARY   [*in a forced teasing tone*]   Good heavens, how down in the mouth you look, Jamie. What's the matter now?

JAMIE   [*without looking at her*]   Nothing.

MARY   Oh, I'd forgotten you've been working on the front hedge. That accounts for your sinking into the dumps, doesn't it?

JAMIE   If you want to think so, Mama.

MARY   [*keeping her tone*]   Well, that's the effect it always has, isn't it? What a big baby you are! Isn't he, Edmund?

EDMUND   He's certainly a fool to care what anyone thinks.

MARY   [*strangely*]   Yes, the only way is to make yourself not care.

[*She catches* JAMIE *giving her a bitter glance and changes the subject.*] Where is your father? I heard Cathleen call him.

EDMUND   Gabbing with old Captain Turner, Jamie says. He'll be late, as usual.

[JAMIE *gets up and goes to the windows at right, glad of an excuse to turn his back.*]

MARY   I've told Cathleen time and again she must go wherever he is and tell him. The idea of screaming as if this were a cheap boardinghouse!

JAMIE   [*looking out the window*]   She's down there now. [*sneeringly*] Interrupting the famous Beautiful Voice! She should have more respect.

MARY   [*sharply—letting her resentment toward him come out*]   It's you who should have more respect. Stop sneering at your father! I won't have it! You ought to be proud you're his son! He may have his faults. Who hasn't? But he's worked hard all his life. He made his way up from ignorance and poverty to the top of his profession! Everyone else admires him and you should be the last one to sneer—you, who, thanks to him, have never had to work hard in your life!

[*Stung,* JAMIE *has turned to stare at her with accusing antagonism. Her eyes waver guiltily and she adds in a tone which begins to placate*] Remember your father is getting old, Jamie. You really ought to show more consideration.

JAMIE   I ought to?

EDMUND   [*uneasily*]   Oh, dry up, Jamie!

[JAMIE *looks out the window again.*]

And, for Pete's sake, Mama, why jump on Jamie all of a sudden?

MARY   [*bitterly*]   Because he's always sneering at someone else, always looking for the worst weakness in everyone. [*then with a strange, abrupt change to a detached, impersonal tone*] But I suppose life has made him like that, and he can't help it. None of us can help the things life has done to us. They're done before you realize it, and once they're done they make you do other things until at last everything comes between you and what you'd like to be, and you've lost your true self forever.

[EDMUND *is made apprehensive by her strangeness. He tries to look up in her eyes but she keeps them averted.* JAMIE *turns to her—then looks quickly out of the window again.*]

JAMIE [*dully*]   I'm hungry. I wish the Old Man would get a move on. It's a rotten trick the way he keeps meals waiting, and then beefs because they're spoiled.

MARY [*with a resentment that has a quality of being automatic and on the surface while inwardly she is indifferent*]   Yes, it's very trying, Jamie. You don't know how trying. You don't have to keep house with summer servants who don't care because they know it isn't a permanent position. The really good servants are all with people who have homes and not merely summer places. And your father won't even pay the wages the best summer help ask. So every year I have stupid, lazy greenhorns to deal with. But you've heard me say this a thousand times. So has he, but it goes in one ear and out the other. He thinks money spent on a home is money wasted. He's lived too much in hotels. Never the best hotels, of course. Second-rate hotels. He doesn't understand a home. He doesn't feel at home in it. And yet, he wants a home. He's even proud of having this shabby place. He loves it here. [*She laughs—a hopeless and yet amused laugh.*] It's really funny, when you come to think of it. He's a peculiar man.

EDMUND [*again attempting uneasily to look up in her eyes*]   What makes you ramble on like that, Mama?

MARY [*quickly casual—patting his cheek*]   Why, nothing in particular, dear. It *is* foolish.

[*As she speaks,* CATHLEEN *enters from the back parlor.*]

CATHLEEN [*volubly*]   Lunch is ready, Ma'am, I went down to Mister Tyrone, like you ordered, and he said he'd come right away, but he kept on talking to that man, telling him of the time when—

MARY [*indifferently*]   All right, Cathleen. Tell Bridget I'm sorry but she'll have to wait a few minutes until Mister Tyrone is here.

[CATHLEEN *mutters,* "Yes, Ma'am," *and goes off through the back parlor, grumbling to herself.*]

JAMIE   Damn it! Why don't you go ahead without him? He told us to.

MARY [*with a remote, amused smile*]   He doesn't mean it. Don't you know your father yet? He'd be so terribly hurt.

EDMUND [*jumps up—as if he was glad of an excuse to leave*]   I'll make him get a move on.

[*He goes out on the side porch. A moment later he is heard calling from the porch exasperatedly.*]

Hey! Papa! Come on! We can't wait all day!

[MARY *has risen from the arm of the chair. Her hands play restlessly over the table top. She does not look at* JAMIE *but she feels the cynically appraising glance he gives her face and hands.*]

MARY [*tensely*]   Why do you stare like that?

JAMIE   You know. [*He turns back to the window.*]

MARY   I don't know.

JAMIE   Oh, for God's sake, do you think you can fool me, Mama? I'm not blind.

MARY [*looks directly at him now, her face set again in an expression of blank, stubborn denial*]   I don't know what you're talking about.

JAMIE   No? Take a look at your eyes in the mirror!

EDMUND [*coming in from the porch*]   I got Papa moving. He'll be here in a minute. [*with a glance from one to the other, which his mother avoids—uneasily*] What happened? What's the matter, Mama?

MARY [*disturbed by his coming, gives way to a flurry of guilty, nervous excitement*]   Your brother ought to be ashamed of himself. He's been insinuating I don't know what.

EDMUND [*turns on* JAMIE]   God damn you!
[*He takes a threatening step toward him.* JAMIE *turns his back with a shrug and looks out the window.*]

MARY [*more upset, grabs* EDMUND's *arm—excitedly*]   Stop this at once, do you hear me? How dare you use such language before me! [*Abruptly her tone and manner change to the strange detachment she has shown before.*] It's wrong to blame your brother. He can't help being what the past has made him. Any more than your father can. Or you. Or I.

EDMUND [*frightenedly—with a desperate hoping against hope*]   He's a liar! It's a lie, isn't it, Mama?

MARY [*keeping her eyes averted*]   What is a lie? Now you're talking in riddles like Jamie. [*Then her eyes meet his stricken, accusing look. She stammers*] Edmund! Don't! [*She looks away and her manner instantly regains the quality of strange detachment—calmly*] There's your father coming up the steps now. I must tell Bridget.
[*She goes through the back parlor.* EDMUND *moves slowly to his chair. He looks sick and hopeless.*]

JAMIE [*from the window, without looking around*]   Well?

EDMUND [*refusing to admit anything to his brother yet—weakly defiant*]   Well, what? You're a liar.
[JAMIE *again shrugs his shoulders. The screen door on the front porch is heard closing.* EDMUND *says dully*]
Here's Papa. I hope he loosens up with the old bottle.
[TYRONE *comes in through the front parlor. He is putting on his coat.*]

TYRONE   Sorry I'm late. Captain Turner stopped to talk and once he starts gabbing you can't get away from him.

JAMIE [*without turning—dryly*]   You mean once he starts listening.
[*His father regards him with dislike. He comes to the table with a quick measuring look at the bottle of whiskey. Without turning,* JAMIE *senses this.*]
It's all right. The level in the bottle hasn't changed.

TYRONE   I wasn't noticing that. [*He adds caustically*] As if it proved anything with you around. I'm on to your tricks.

EDMUND [*dully*]   Did I hear you say, let's all have a drink?

TYRONE [*frowns at him*]   Jamie is welcome after his hard morning's work, but I won't invite you. Doctor Hardy—

EDMUND   To hell with Doctor Hardy! One isn't going to kill me. I feel—all in, Papa.

TYRONE [*with a worried look at him—putting on a fake heartiness*]   Come along, then. It's before a meal and I've always found that good whiskey, taken in moderation as an appetizer, is the best of tonics.
[EDMUND *gets up as his father passes the bottle to him. He pours a big drink.* TYRONE *frowns admonishingly.*]
I said, in moderation.
[*He pours his own drink and passes the bottle to* JAMIE, *grumbling.*]

It'd be a waste of breath mentioning moderation to you.

[*Ignoring the hint,* JAMIE *pours a big drink. His father scowls—then, giving it up, resumes his hearty air, raising his glass.*]

Well, here's health and happiness!

[EDMUND *gives a bitter laugh.*]

EDMUND   That's a joke!

TYRONE   What is?

EDMUND   Nothing. Here's how. [*They drink.*]

TYRONE [*becoming aware of the atmosphere*]   What's the matter here? There's gloom in the air you could cut with a knife. [*turns on* JAMIE *resentfully*] You got the drink you were after, didn't you? Why are you wearing that gloomy look on your mug?

JAMIE [*shrugging his shoulders*]   You won't be singing a song yourself soon.

EDMUND   Shut up, Jamie.

TYRONE [*uneasy now—changing the subject*]   I thought lunch was ready. I'm hungry as a hunter. Where is your mother?

MARY [*returning through the back parlor, calls*]   Here I am.

[*She comes in. She is excited and self-conscious. As she talks, she glances everywhere except at any of their faces.*]

I've had to calm down Bridget. She's in a tantrum over your being late again, and I don't blame her. If your lunch is dried up from waiting in the oven, she said it served you right, you could like it or leave it for all she cared. [*with increasing excitement*] Oh, I'm so sick and tired of pretending this is a home! You won't help me! You won't put yourself out the least bit! You don't know how to act in a home! You don't really want one! You never have wanted one—never since the day we were married! You should have remained a bachelor and lived in second-rate hotels and entertained your friends in barrooms! [*She adds strangely, as if she were now talking aloud to herself rather than to* TYRONE] Then nothing would ever have happened.

[*They stare at her.* TYRONE *knows now. He suddenly looks a tired, bitterly sad old man.* EDMUND *glances at his father and sees that he knows, but he still cannot help trying to warn his mother.*]

EDMUND   Mama! Stop talking. Why don't we go in to lunch.

MARY [*Starts and at once the quality of unnatural detachment settles on her face again. She even smiles with an ironical amusement to herself.*]   Yes, it is inconsiderate of me to dig up the past, when I know your father and Jamie must be hungry. [*putting her arm around* EDMUND'S *shoulder—with a fond solicitude which is at the same time remote*] I do hope you have an appetite, dear. You really must eat more [*Her eyes become fixed on the whiskey glass on the table beside him—sharply*] Why is that glass there? Did you take a drink? Oh, how can you be such a fool? Don't you know it's the worst thing? [*She turns on* TYRONE.] You're to blame, James. How could you let him? Do you want to kill him? Don't you remember my father? He wouldn't stop after he was stricken. He said doctors were fools! He thought, like you, that whiskey is a good tonic! [*A look of terror comes into her eyes and she stammers*] But, of course, there's no comparison at all. I don't know why I—Forgive me for scolding you, James. One small drink won't hurt Edmund. It might be good for him, if it gives him an appetite.

[*She pats* EDMUND'S *cheek playfully, the strange detachment again in her manner. He jerks his head away. She seems not to notice, but she moves instinctively away.*]

JAMIE [*roughly, to hide his tense nerves*] For God's sake, let's eat. I've been working in the damned dirt under the hedge all morning. I've earned my grub.

> [*He comes around in back of his father, not looking at his mother, and grabs* EDMUND's *shoulder.*]

Come on, Kid. Let's put on the feed bag.

> [EDMUND *gets up, keeping his eyes averted from his mother. They pass her, heading for the back parlor.*]

TYRONE [*dully*] Yes, you go in with your mother, lads. I'll join you in a second.

> [*But they keep on without waiting for her. She looks at their backs with a helpless hurt and, as they enter the back parlor, starts to follow them.* TYRONE's *eyes are on her, sad and condemning. She feels them and turns sharply without meeting his stare.*]

MARY Why do you look at me like that? [*Her hands flutter up to pat her hair.*] Is it my hair coming down? I was so worn out from last night, I thought I'd better lie down this morning. I drowsed off and had a nice refreshing nap. But I'm sure I fixed my hair again when I woke up. [*forcing a laugh*] Although, as usual, I couldn't find my glasses. [*sharply*] Please stop staring! One would think you were accusing me—[*then pleadingly*] James! You don't understand!

TYRONE [*with dull anger*] I understand that I've been a God-damned fool to believe in you!

> [*He walks away from her to pour himself a big drink.*]

MARY [*her face again sets in stubborn defiance*] I don't know what you mean by "believing in me." All I've felt was distrust and spying and suspicion. [*then accusingly*] Why are you having another drink? You never have more than one before lunch. [*bitterly*] I know what to expect. You will be drunk tonight. Well, it won't be the first time, will it—or the thousandth? [*again she bursts out pleadingly*] Oh, James, please! You don't understand! I'm worried about Edmund! I'm so afraid he—

TYRONE I don't want to listen to excuses, Mary.

MARY [*strickenly*] Excuses? You mean—? Oh, you can't believe that of me! You mustn't believe that, James! [*then slipping away into her strange detachment—quite casually*] Shall we not go into lunch dear? I don't want anything but I know you're hungry.

> [*He walks slowly to where she stands in the doorway. He walks like an old man. As he reaches her she bursts out piteously.*]

James! I tried so hard! I tried so hard! Please believe—!

TYRONE [*moved in spite of himself—helplessly*] I suppose you did, Mary. [*then grief-strickenly*] For the love of God, why couldn't you have the strength to keep on?

MARY [*her face setting into that stubborn denial again*] I don't know what you're talking about. Have the strength to keep on what?

TYRONE [*hopelessly*] Never mind. It's no use now.

> [*He moves on and she keeps beside him as they disappear in the back parlor.*]

CURTAIN

Act 2

SCENE 2

SCENE—*The same, about a half hour later. The tray with the bottle of whiskey has been removed from the table. The family are returning from lunch as the curtain rises.* MARY *is the first to enter from the back parlor. Her husband follows. He is not with her as he was in the similar entrance after breakfast at the opening of Act One. He avoids touching her or looking at her. There is condemnation in his face, mingled now with the beginning of an old weary, helpless resignation.* JAMIE *and* EDMUND *follow their father.* JAMIE's *face is hard with defensive cynicism.* EDMUND *tries to copy this defense but without success. He plainly shows he is heartsick as well as physically ill.*

MARY *is terribly nervous again, as if the strain of sitting through lunch with them had been too much for her. Yet at the same time, in contrast to this, her expression shows more of that strange aloofness which seems to stand apart from her nerves and the anxieties which harry them.*

She is talking as she enters—a stream of words that issues casually, in a routine of family conversation, from her mouth. She appears indifferent to the fact that their thoughts are not on what she is saying any more than her own are. As she talks, she comes to the left of the table and stands, facing front, one hand fumbling with the bosom of her dress, the other playing over the table top. TYRONE *lights a cigar and goes to the screen door, staring out.* JAMIE *fills a pipe from a jar on top of the bookcase at rear. He lights it as he goes to look out the window at right.* EDMUND *sits in a chair by the table, turned half away from his mother so he does not have to watch her.*

MARY   It's no use finding fault with Bridget. She doesn't listen. I can't threaten her, or she'd threaten she'd leave. And she does do her best at times. It's too bad they seem to be just the times you're sure to be late, James. Well, there's this consolation: it's difficult to tell from her cooking whether she's doing her best or her worst. [*She gives a little laugh of detached amusement—indifferently*] Never mind. The summer will soon be over, thank goodness. Your season will open again and we can go back to second-rate hotels and trains. I hate them, too, but at least I don't expect them to be like a home, and there's no housekeeping to worry about. It's unreasonable to expect Bridget or Cathleen to act as if this was a home. They know it isn't as well as we know it. It never has been and it never will be.

TYRONE [*bitterly without turning around*]   No, it never can be now. But it was once, before you—

MARY [*her face instantly set in blank denial*]   Before I what? [*There is dead silence. She goes on with a return of her detached air.*] No, no. Whatever you mean, it isn't true, dear. It was never a home. You've always preferred the Club or barroom. And for me it's always been as lonely as a dirty room in a one-night stand hotel. In a real home one is never lonely. You forget I know from experience what a home is like. I gave up one to marry you—my father's home. [*At once, through an association of ideas she turns to* EDMUND. *Her manner becomes tenderly solicitous, but there is the strange quality of detachment in it.*] I'm worried about you,

Edmund. You hardly touched a thing at lunch. That's no way to take care of yourself. It's all right for me not to have an appetite. I've been growing too fat. But you must eat. [*coaxingly maternal*] Promise me you will, dear, for my sake.

EDMUND [*dully*]   Yes, Mama.

MARY [*pats his cheek as he tries not to shrink away*]   That's a good boy.
   [*There is another pause of dead silence. Then the telephone in the front hall rings and all of them stiffen startledly.*]

TYRONE [*hastily*]   I'll answer. McGuire said he'd call me. [*He goes out through the front parlor.*]

MARY [*indifferently*]   McGuire. He must have another piece of property on his list that no one would think of buying except your father. It doesn't matter any more, but it's always seemed to me your father could afford to keep on buying property but never to give me a home.
   [*She stops to listen as* TYRONE's *voice is heard from the hall.*]

TYRONE   Hello. [*with forced heartiness*] Oh, how are you, Doctor?
   [JAMIE *turns from the window.* MARY's *fingers play more rapidly on the table top.* TYRONE's *voice, trying to conceal, reveals that he is hearing bad news.*]
I see—[*hurriedly*] Well, you'll explain all about it when you see him this afternoon. Yes, he'll be in without fail. Four o'clock. I'll drop in myself and have a talk with you before that. I have to go uptown on business, anyway. Goodbye, Doctor.

EDMUND [*dully*]   That didn't sound like glad tidings.
   [JAMIE *gives him a pitying glance—then looks out the window again.* MARY's *face is terrified and her hands flutter distractedly.* TYRONE *comes in. The strain is obvious in his casualness as he addresses* EDMUND.]

TYRONE   It was Doctor Hardy. He wants you to be sure and see him at four.

EDMUND [*dully*]   What did he say? Not that I give a damn now.

MARY [*bursts out excitedly*]   I wouldn't believe him if he swore on a stack of Bibles. You mustn't pay attention to a word he says, Edmund.

TYRONE [*sharply*]   Mary!

MARY [*more excitedly*]   Oh, we all realize why you like him, James! Because he's cheap! But please don't try to tell me! I know all about Doctor Hardy. Heaven knows I ought to after all these years. He's an ignorant fool! There should be a law to keep men like him from practicing. He hasn't the slightest idea—When you're in agony and half insane, he sits and holds your hand and delivers sermons on will power! [*Her face is drawn in an expression of intense suffering by the memory. For the moment, she loses all caution. With bitter hatred*] He deliberately humiliates you! He makes you beg and plead! He treats you like a criminal! He understands nothing! And yet it was exactly the same type of cheap quack who first gave you the medicine—and you never knew what it was until too late! [*passionately*] I hate doctors! They'll sell their souls! What's worse, they'll sell yours, and you never know it till one day you find yourself in hell!

EDMUND   Mama! For God's sake, stop talking.

TYRONE [*shakily*]   Yes, Mary, it's no time—

MARY [*suddenly is overcome by guilty confusion—stammers*]   I—Forgive me, dear. You're right. It's useless to be angry now. [*There is again a pause of dead silence. When she speaks again, her face has cleared and is calm, and the quality of uncanny detachment is in her voice and manner.*] I'm going upstairs for a moment, if you'll excuse me. I have to fix my hair. [*she adds smilingly*] That is if I can find my glasses. I'll be right down.

TYRONE [*as she starts through the doorway—pleading and rebuking*]   Mary!

MARY [*turns to stare at him calmly*]   Yes, dear? What is it?

TYRONE [*helplessly*]   Nothing.

MARY [*with a strange derisive smile*]   You're welcome to come up and watch me if you're so suspicious.

TYRONE   As if that could do any good! You'd only postpone it. And I'm not your jailor. This isn't a prison.

MARY   No. I know you can't help thinking it's a home. [*She adds quickly with a detached contrition*] I'm sorry, dear. I don't mean to be bitter. It's not your fault.

> [*She turns and disappears through the back parlor. The three in the room remain silent. It is as if they were waiting until she got upstairs before speaking.*]

JAMIE [*cynically brutal*]   Another shot in the arm!

EDMUND [*angrily*]   Cut out that kind of talk!

TYRONE   Yes! Hold your foul tongue and your rotten Broadway loafer's lingo! Have you no pity or decency? [*losing his temper*] You ought to be kicked out in the gutter! But if I did it, you know damned well who'd weep and plead for you, and excuse you and complain till I let you come back.

JAMIE [*a spasm of pain crosses his face*]   Christ, don't I know that? No pity? I have all the pity in the world for her. I understand what a hard game to beat she's up against—which is more than you ever have! My lingo didn't mean I had no feeling. I was merely putting bluntly what we all know, and have to live with now, again. [*bitterly*] The cures are no damned good except for a while. The truth is there is no cure and we've been saps to hope—[*cynically*] They never come back!

EDMUND [*scornfully parodying his brother's cynicism*]   They never come back! Everything is in the bag! It's all a frame-up! We're all fall guys and suckers and we can't beat the game! [*disdainfully*] Christ, if I felt the way you do—!

JAMIE [*stung for a moment—then shrugging his shoulders, dryly*]   I thought you did. Your poetry isn't very cheery. Nor the stuff you read and claim to admire. [*He indicates the small bookcase at rear.*] Your pet with the unpronounceable name, for example.

EDMUND   Nietzsche. You don't know what you're talking about. You haven't read him.

JAMIE   Enough to know it's a lot of bunk!

TYRONE   Shut up, both of you! There's little choice between the philosophy you learned from Broadway loafers, and the one Edmund got from his books. They're both rotten to the core. You've both flouted the faith you were born and brought up in—the one true faith of the Catholic Church—and your denial has brought nothing but self-destruction!

> [*His two sons stare at him contemptuously. They forget their quarrel and are as one against him on this issue.*]

EDMUND   That's the bunk, Papa!

JAMIE   We don't pretend, at any rate. [*caustically*] I don't notice you've worn any holes in the knees of your pants going to Mass.

TYRONE   It's true I'm a bad Catholic in the observance, God forgive me. But I believe! [*angrily*] And you're a liar! I may not go to church but every night and morning of my life I get on my knees and pray!

EDMUND   [*bitingly*]   Did you pray for Mama?

TYRONE   I did. I've prayed to God these many years for her.

EDMUND   Then Nietzsche must be right. [*He quotes from* Thus Spake Zarathustra.] "God is dead: of His pity for man hath God died."

TYRONE   [*ignores this*]   If your mother had prayed, too—She hasn't denied her faith, but she's forgotten it, until now there's no strength of the spirit left in her to fight against her curse. [*then dully resigned*] But what's the good of talk? We've lived with this before and now we must again. There's no help for it. [*bitterly*] Only I wish she hadn't led me to hope this time. By God, I never will again!

EDMUND   That's a rotten thing to say, Papa! [*defiantly*] Well, I'll hope! She's just started. It can't have got a hold on her yet. She can still stop. I'm going to talk to her.

JAMIE   [*shrugs his shoulders*]   You can't talk to her now. She'll listen but she won't listen. She'll be here but she won't be here. You know the way she gets.

TYRONE   Yes, that's the way the poison acts on her always. Every day from now on, there'll be the same drifting away from us until by the end of each night—

EDMUND   [*miserably*]   Cut it out, Papa! [*He jumps up from his chair.*] I'm going to get dressed. [*bitterly, as he goes*] I'll make so much noise she can't suspect I've come to spy on her.

    [*He disappears through the front parlor and can be heard stamping noisily upstairs.*]

JAMIE   [*after a pause*]   What did Doc Hardy say about the Kid?

TYRONE   [*dully*]   It's what you thought. He's got consumption.

JAMIE   God damn it!

TYRONE   There is no possible doubt, he said.

JAMIE   He'll have to go to a sanatorium.

TYRONE   Yes, and the sooner the better, Hardy said, for him and everyone around him. He claims that in six months to a year Edmund will be cured, if he obeys orders. [*He sighs—gloomily and resentfully*] I never thought a child of mine—It doesn't come from my side of the family. There wasn't one of us that didn't have lungs as strong as an ox.

JAMIE   Who gives a damn about that part of it! Where does Hardy want to send him?

TYRONE   That's what I'm to see him about.

JAMIE   Well, for God's sake, pick out a good place and not some cheap dump!

TYRONE   [*stung*]   I'll send him wherever Hardy thinks best!

JAMIE   Well, don't give Hardy your old over-the-hills-to-the-poorhouse song about taxes and mortgages.

TYRONE   I'm no millionaire who can throw money away! Why shouldn't I tell Hardy the truth?

JAMIE Because he'll think you want him to pick a cheap dump, and because he'll know it isn't the truth—especially if he hears afterwards you've seen McGuire and let that flannel-mouth, gold-brick merchant sting you with another piece of bum property!

TYRONE Keep your nose out of my business!

JAMIE This is Edmund's business. What I'm afraid of is, with your Irish bog trotter idea that consumption is fatal, you'll figure it would be a waste of money to spend any more than you can help.

TYRONE You liar!

JAMIE All right. Prove I'm a liar. That's what I want. That's why I brought it up.

TYRONE [*his rage still smoldering*] I have every hope Edmund will be cured. And keep your dirty tongue off Ireland! You're a fine one to sneer, with the map of it on your face!

JAMIE Not after I wash my face. [*Then before his father can react to this insult to the Old Sod he adds dryly, shrugging his shoulders*] Well, I've said all I have to say. It's up to you. [*abruptly*] What do you want me to do this afternoon, now you're going uptown? I've done all I can do on the hedge until you cut more of it. You don't want me to go ahead with your clipping, I know that.

TYRONE No. You'd get it crooked, as you get everything else.

JAMIE Then I'd better go uptown with Edmund. The bad news coming on top of what's happened to Mama may hit him hard.

TYRONE [*forgetting his quarrel*] Yes, go with him, Jamie. Keep up his spirits, if you can. [*He adds caustically*] If you can without making it an excuse to get drunk!

JAMIE What would I use for money? The last I heard they were still selling booze, not giving it away. [*He starts for the front-parlor doorway.*] I'll get dressed.

  [*He stops in the doorway as he sees his mother approaching from the hall, and moves aside to let her come in. Her eyes look brighter, and her manner is more detached. This change becomes more marked as the scene goes on.*]

MARY [*vaguely*] You haven't seen my glasses anywhere, have you, Jamie?

  [*She doesn't look at him. He glances away, ignoring her question but she doesn't seem to expect an answer. She comes forward, addressing her husband without looking at him.*]

You haven't seen them, have you, James?

  [*Behind her* JAMIE *disappears through the front parlor.*]

TYRONE [*turns to look out the screen door*] No, Mary.

MARY What's the matter with Jamie? Have you been nagging at him again? You shouldn't treat him with such contempt all the time. He's not to blame. If he'd been brought up in a real home, I'm sure he would have been different. [*She comes to the windows at right—lightly*] You're not much of a weather prophet, dear. See how hazy it's getting. I can hardly see the other shore.

TYRONE [*trying to speak naturally*] Yes, I spoke too soon. We're in for another night of fog, I'm afraid.

MARY Oh, well, I won't mind it tonight.

TYRONE No, I don't imagine you will, Mary.

MARY [*flashes a glance at him—after a pause*] I don't see Jamie going down to the hedge. Where did he go?

TYRONE He's going with Edmund to the Doctor's. He went up to change his clothes. [*then, glad of an excuse to leave her*] I'd better do the same or I'll be late for my appointment at the Club.

> [*He makes a move toward the front-parlor doorway, but with a swift impulsive movement she reaches out and clasps his arm.*]

MARY [*a note of pleading in her voice*] Don't go yet, dear. I don't want to be alone. [*hastily*] I mean, you have plenty of time. You know you boast you can dress in one-tenth the time it takes the boys. [*vaguely*] There is something I wanted to say. What is it? I've forgotten. I'm glad Jamie is going uptown. You didn't give him any money, I hope.

TYRONE I did not.

MARY He'd only spend it on drink and you know what a vile, poisonous tongue he has when he's drunk. Not that I would mind anything he said tonight, but he always manages to drive you into a rage, especially if you're drunk, too, as you will be.

TYRONE [*resentfully*] I won't. I never get drunk.

MARY [*teasing indifferently*] Oh, I'm sure you'll hold it well. You always have. It's hard for a stranger to tell, but after thirty-five years of marriage—

TYRONE I've never missed a performance in my life. That's the proof! [*then bitterly*] If I did get drunk it is not you who should blame me. No man has ever had a better reason.

MARY Reason? What reason? You always drink too much when you go to the Club, don't you? Particularly when you meet McGuire. He sees to that. Don't think I'm finding fault, dear. You must do as you please. I won't mind.

TYRONE I know you won't. [*He turns toward the front parlor, anxious to escape.*] I've got to get dressed.

MARY [*again she reaches out and grasps his arm—pleadingly*] No, please wait a little while, dear. At least, until one of the boys comes down. You will all be leaving me so soon.

TYRONE [*with bitter sadness*] It's you who are leaving us, Mary.

MARY I? That's a silly thing to say, James. How could I leave? There is nowhere I could go. Who would I go to see? I have no friends.

TYRONE It's your own fault—[*He stops and sighs helplessly—persuasively*] There's surely one thing you can do this afternoon that will be good for you, Mary. Take a drive in the automobile. Get away from the house. Get a little sun and fresh air. [*injuredly*] I bought the automobile for you. You know I don't like the damned things. I'd rather walk any day, or take a trolley. [*with growing resentment*] I had it here waiting for you when you came back from the sanatorium. I hoped it would give you pleasure and distract your mind. You used to ride in it every day, but you've hardly used it at all lately. I paid a lot of money I couldn't afford, and there's the chauffeur I have to board and lodge and pay high wages whether he drives you or not. [*bitterly*] Waste! The same old waste that will land me in the poorhouse in my old age! What good did it do you? I might as well have thrown the money out the window.

MARY [*with detached calm*] Yes, it was a waste of money, James. You shouldn't have bought a secondhand automobile. You were swindled again as you always are, because you insist on secondhand bargains in everything.

TYRONE It's one of the best makes! Everyone says it's better than any of the new ones!

MARY [*ignoring this*] It was another waste to hire Smythe, who was only a helper in a garage and had never been a chauffeur. Oh, I realize his wages are less than a real chauffeur's, but he more than makes up for that, I'm sure, by the graft he gets from the garage on repair bills. Something is always wrong. Smythe sees to that, I'm afraid.

TYRONE I don't believe it! He may not be a fancy millionaire's flunky but he's honest! You're as bad as Jamie, suspecting everyone!

MARY You mustn't be offended, dear. I wasn't offended when you gave me the automobile. I knew you didn't mean to humiliate me. I knew that was the way you had to do everything. I was grateful and touched. I knew buying the car was a hard thing for you to do, and it proved how much you loved me, in your way, especially when you couldn't really believe it would do me any good.

TYRONE Mary! [*He suddenly hugs her to him—brokenly*] Dear Mary! For the love of God, for my sake and the boys' sake and your own, won't you stop now?

MARY [*stammers in guilty confusion for a second*] I—James! Please! [*Her strange, stubborn defense comes back instantly.*] Stop what? What are you talking about?

[*He lets his arm fall to his side brokenly. She impulsively puts her arm around him.*]

James! We've loved each other! We always will! Let's remember only that, and not try to understand what we cannot understand, or help things that cannot be helped—the things life has done to us we cannot excuse or explain.

TYRONE [*as if he hadn't heard—bitterly*] You won't even try?

MARY [*her arms drop hopelessly and she turns away—with detachment*] Try to go for a drive this afternoon, you mean? Why, yes, if you wish me to, although it makes me feel lonelier than if I stayed here. There is no one I can invite to drive with me, and I never know where to tell Smythe to go. If there was a friend's house where I could drop in and laugh and gossip awhile. But, of course, there isn't. There never has been. [*her manner becoming more and more remote*] At the Convent I had so many friends. Girls whose families lived in lovely homes. I used to visit them and they'd visit me in my father's home. But, naturally, after I married an actor—you know how actors were considered in those days—a lot of them gave me the cold shoulder. And then, right after we were married, there was the scandal of that woman who had been your mistress, suing you. From then on, all my old friends either pitied me or cut me dead. I hated the ones who cut me much less than the pitiers.

TYRONE [*with guilty resentment*] For God's sake, don't dig up what's long forgotten. If you're that far gone in the past already, when it's only the beginning of the afternoon, what will you be tonight?

MARY [*stares at him defiantly now*] Come to think of it, I do have to drive uptown. There's something I must get at the drugstore.

TYRONE [*bitterly scornful*] Leave it to you to have some of the stuff hidden, and prescriptions for more! I hope you'll lay in a good stock ahead so we'll never have another night like the one when you screamed for it, and ran out of the house in your nightdress half crazy, to try and throw yourself off the dock!

MARY [*tries to ignore this*] I have to get tooth powder and toilet soap and cold cream—[*She breaks down pitiably.*] James! You mustn't remember! You mustn't humiliate me so!

TYRONE [*ashamed*] I'm sorry. Forgive me, Mary!

MARY [*defensively detached again*] It doesn't matter. Nothing like that ever happened. You must have dreamed it.

> [*He stares at her hopelessly. Her voice seems to drift farther and farther away.*]

I was so healthy before Edmund was born. You remember, James. There wasn't a nerve in my body. Even traveling with you season after season, with week after week of one-night stands, in trains without Pullmans, in dirty rooms of filthy hotels, eating bad food, bearing children in hotel rooms, I still kept healthy. But bearing Edmund was the last straw. I was so sick afterwards, and that ignorant quack of a cheap hotel doctor—All he knew was I was in pain. It was easy for him to stop the pain.

TYRONE Mary! For God's sake, forget the past!

MARY [*with strange objective calm*] Why? How can I? The past is the present, isn't it? It's the future, too. We all try to lie out of that but life won't let us. [*going on*] I blame only myself. I swore after Eugene died I would never have another baby. I was to blame for his death. If I hadn't left him with my mother to join you on the road, because you wrote telling me you missed me and were so lonely, Jamie would never have been allowed, when he still had measles, to go in the baby's room. [*her face hardening*] I've always believed Jamie did it on purpose. He was jealous of the baby. He hated him. [*as TYRONE starts to protest*] Oh, I know Jamie was only seven, but he was never stupid. He'd been warned it might kill the baby. He knew. I've never been able to forgive him for that.

TYRONE [*with bitter sadness*] Are you back with Eugene now? Can't you let our dead baby rest in peace?

MARY [*as if she hadn't heard him*] It was my fault. I should have insisted on staying with Eugene and not have let you persuade me to join you, just because I loved you. Above all, I shouldn't have let you insist I have another baby to take Eugene's place, because you thought that would make me forget his death. I knew from experience by then that children should have homes to be born in, if they are to be good children, and women need homes, if they are to be good mothers. I was afraid all the time I carried Edmund. I knew something terrible would happen. I knew I'd proved by the way I'd left Eugene that I wasn't worthy to have another baby, and that God would punish me if I did. I never should have borne Edmund.

TYRONE [*with an uneasy glance through the front parlor*] Mary! Be careful with your talk. If he heard you he might think you never wanted him. He's feeling bad enough already without—

MARY [*violently*]   It's a lie! I did want him! More than anything in the world! You don't understand! I meant, for his sake. He has never been happy. He never will be. Nor healthy. He was born nervous and too sensitive, and that's my fault. And now, ever since he's been so sick I've kept remembering Eugene and my father and I've been so frightened and guilty—[*then, catching herself, with an instant change to stubborn denial*] Oh, I know it's foolish to imagine dreadful things when there's no reason for it. After all, everyone has colds and gets over them.

   [TYRONE *stares at her and sighs helplessly. He turns away toward the front parlor and sees* EDMUND *coming down the stairs in the hall.*]

TYRONE [*sharply, in a low voice*]   Here's Edmund. For God's sake try and be yourself—at least until he goes! You can do that much for him!

   [*He waits, forcing his face into a pleasantly paternal expression. She waits frightenedly, seized again by a nervous panic, her hands fluttering over the bosom of her dress, up to her throat and hair, with a distracted aimlessness. Then, as* EDMUND *approaches the doorway, she cannot face him. She goes swiftly away to the windows at left and stares out with her back to the front parlor.* EDMUND *enters. He has changed to a ready-made blue serge suit, high stiff collar and tie, black shoes. With an actor's heartiness*]

Well! You look spic and span. I'm on my way up to change, too. [*He starts to pass him.*]

EDMUND [*dryly*]   Wait a minute, Papa. I hate to bring up disagreeable topics, but there's the matter of carfare. I'm broke.

TYRONE [*starts automatically on a customary lecture*]   You'll always be broke until you learn the value—[*checks himself guiltily, looking at his son's sick face with worried pity*] But you've been learning, lad. You worked hard before you took ill. You've done splendidly. I'm proud of you.

   [*He pulls out a small roll of bills from his pants pocket and carefully selects one.* EDMUND *takes it. He glances at it and his face expresses astonishment. His father again reacts customarily—sarcastically*]

Thank you. [*He quotes*] "How sharper than a serpent's tooth it is—"

EDMUND   "To have a thankless child."[9] I know. Give me a chance, Papa. I'm knocked speechless. This isn't a dollar. It's a ten spot.

TYRONE [*embarrassed by his generosity*]   Put it in your pocket. You'll probably meet some of your friends uptown and you can't hold your end up and be sociable with nothing in your jeans.

EDMUND   You meant it? Gosh, thank you, Papa. [*He is genuinely pleased and grateful for a moment—then he stares at his father's face with uneasy suspicion.*] But why all of a sudden—? [*cynically*] Did Doc Hardy tell you I was going to die? [*Then he sees his father is bitterly hurt.*] No! That's a rotten crack. I was only kidding, Papa. [*He puts an arm around his father impulsively and gives him an affectionate hug.*] I'm very grateful. Honest, Papa.

TYRONE [*touched, returns his hug*]   You're welcome, lad.

MARY [*suddenly turns to them in a confused panic of frightened anger*]   I won't have it! [*She stamps her foot.*] Do you hear, Edmund! Such morbid nonsense! Saying you're going to die! It's the books you read! Nothing

9. Shakespeare's *King Lear* 1.4.312.

but sadness and death! Your father shouldn't allow you to have them. And some of the poems you've written yourself are even worse! You'd think you didn't want to live! A boy of your age with everything before him! It's just a pose you get out of books! You're not really sick at all!

TYRONE   Mary! Hold your tongue!

MARY [*instantly changing to a detached tone*]   But, James, it's absurd of Edmund to be so gloomy and make such a great to-do about nothing. [*turning to* EDMUND *but avoiding his eyes—teasingly affectionate*] Never mind, dear. I'm on to you. [*She comes to him.*] You want to be petted and spoiled and made a fuss over, isn't that it? You're still such a baby. [*She puts her arm around him and hugs him. He remains rigid and unyielding. Her voice begins to tremble.*] But please don't carry it too far, dear. Don't say horrible things. I know it's foolish to take them seriously but I can't help it. You've got me—so frightened.

   [*She breaks and hides her face on his shoulder, sobbing.* EDMUND *is moved in spite of himself. He pats her shoulder with an awkward tenderness.*]

EDMUND   Don't, mother. [*His eyes meet his father's.*]

TYRONE [*huskily—clutching at hopeless hope*]   Maybe if you asked your mother now what you said you were going to—[*He fumbles with his watch.*] By God, look at the time! I'll have to shake a leg.

   [*He hurries away through the front parlor.* MARY *lifts her head. Her manner is again one of detached motherly solicitude. She seems to have forgotten the tears which are still in her eyes.*]

MARY   How do you feel, dear? [*She feels his forehead.*] Your head is a little hot, but that's just from going out in the sun. You look ever so much better than you did this morning. [*taking his hand*] Come and sit down. You mustn't stand on your feet so much. You must learn to husband your strength.

   [*She gets him to sit and she sits sideways on the arm of his chair, an arm around his shoulder, so he cannot meet her eyes.*]

EDMUND [*starts to blurt out the appeal he now feels is quite hopeless*]   Listen, Mama—

MARY [*interrupting quickly*]   Now, now! Don't talk. Lean back and rest. [*persuasively*] You know, I think it would be much better for you if you stayed home this afternoon and let me take care of you. It's such a tiring trip uptown in the dirty old trolley on a hot day like this. I'm sure you'd be much better off here with me.

EDMUND [*dully*]   You forget I have an appointment with Hardy. [*trying again to get his appeal started*] Listen, Mama—

MARY [*quickly*]   You can telephone and say you don't feel well enough. [*excitedly*] It's simply a waste of time and money seeing him. He'll only tell you some lie. He'll pretend he's found something serious the matter because that's his bread and butter. [*She gives a hard sneering little laugh.*] The old idiot! All he knows about medicine is to look solemn and preach will power!

EDMUND [*trying to catch her eyes*]   Mama! Please listen! I want to ask you something! You—You're only just started. You can still stop. You've got the will power! We'll all help you. I'll do anything! Won't you, Mama?

MARY [*stammers pleadingly*]   Please don't—talk about things you don't understand!

EDMUND [*dully*]   All right, I give up. I knew it was no use.

MARY [*in blank denial now*]   Anyway, I don't know what you're referring to. But I do know you should be the last one—Right after I returned from the sanatorium, you began to be ill. The doctor there had warned me I must have peace at home with nothing to upset me, and all I've done is worry about you. [*then distractedly*] But that's no excuse! I'm only trying to explain. It's not an excuse! [*She hugs him to her—pleadingly*] Promise me, dear, you won't believe I made you an excuse.

EDMUND [*bitterly*]   What else can I believe?

MARY [*slowly takes her arm away—her manner remote and objective again*] Yes, I suppose you can't help suspecting that.

EDMUND [*ashamed but still bitter*]   What do you expect?

MARY   Nothing, I don't blame you. How could you believe me—when I can't believe myself? I've become such a liar. I never lied about anything once upon a time. Now I have to lie, especially to myself. But how can you understand, when I don't myself. I've never understood anything about it, except that one day long ago I found I could no longer call my soul my own. [*She pauses—then lowering her voice to a strange tone of whispered confidence*] But some day, dear, I will find it again— some day when you're all well, and I see you healthy and happy and successful, and I don't have to feel guilty any more—some day when the Blessed Virgin Mary forgives me and gives me back the faith in Her love and pity I used to have in my convent days, and I can pray to Her again—when She sees no one in the world can believe in me even for a moment any more, then She will believe in me, and with Her help it will be so easy. I will hear myself scream with agony, and at the same time I will laugh because I will be so sure of myself. [*then as EDMUND remains hopelessly silent, she adds sadly*] Of course, you can't believe that, either. [*She rises from the arm of his chair and goes to stare out the windows at right with her back to him—casually*] Now I think of it, you might as well go uptown. I forgot I'm taking a drive. I have to go to the drugstore. You would hardly want to go there with me. You'd be so ashamed.

EDMUND [*brokenly*]   Mama! Don't!

MARY   I suppose you'll divide that ten dollars your father gave you with Jamie. You always divide with each other, don't you? Like good sports. Well, I know what he'll do with his share. Get drunk someplace where he can be with the only kind of woman he understands or likes. [*She turns to him, pleading frightenedly*] Edmund! Promise me you won't drink! It's so dangerous! You know Doctor Hardy told you—

EDMUND [*bitterly*]   I thought he was an old idiot. Anyway, by tonight, what will you care?

MARY [*pitifully*]   Edmund!

[JAMIE's *voice is heard from the front hall,* "Come on, Kid, let's beat it." MARY's *manner at once becomes detached again.*]

Go on, Edmund. Jamie's waiting. [*She goes to the front-parlor doorway.*] There comes your father downstairs, too.

[TYRONE's *voice calls,* "Come on, Edmund."]

EDMUND [*jumping up from his chair*]   I'm coming.

[*He stops beside her—without looking at her.*]

Goodbye, Mama.

MARY [*kisses him with detached affection*]   Goodbye, dear. If you're coming home for dinner, try not to be late. And tell your father. You know what Bridget is.

[*He turns and hurries away.* TYRONE *calls from the hall,* "Goodbye, Mary," *and then* JAMIE, "Goodbye, Mama." *She calls back*]

Goodbye. [*The front screen door is heard closing after them. She comes and stands by the table, one hand drumming on it, the other fluttering up to pat her hair. She stares about the room with frightened, forsaken eyes and whispers to herself.*] It's so lonely here. [*Then her face hardens into bitter self-contempt.*] You're lying to yourself again. You wanted to get rid of them. Their contempt and disgust aren't pleasant company. You're glad they're gone. [*She gives a little despairing laugh.*] Then Mother of God, why do I feel so lonely?

CURTAIN

Act 3

SCENE—*The same. It is around half past six in the evening. Dusk is gathering in the living room, an early dusk due to the fog which has rolled in from the Sound and is like a white curtain drawn down outside the windows. From a lighthouse beyond the harbor's mouth, a foghorn is heard at regular intervals, moaning like a mournful whale in labor, and from the harbor itself, intermittently, comes the warning ringing of bells on yachts at anchor.*

The tray with the bottle of whiskey, glasses, and pitcher of ice water is on the table, as it was in the pre-luncheon scene of the previous act. MARY *and the second girl,* CATHLEEN, *are discovered. The latter is standing at left of table. She holds an empty whiskey glass in her hand as if she'd forgotten she had it. She shows the effects of drink. Her stupid, good-humored face wears a pleased and flattered simper.*

MARY *is paler than before and her eyes shine with unnatural brilliance. The strange detachment in her manner has intensified. She has hidden deeper within herself and found refuge and release in a dream where present reality is but an appearance to be accepted and dismissed unfeelingly—even with a hard cynicism—or entirely ignored. There is at times an uncanny gay, free youthfulness in her manner, as if in spirit she were released to become again, simply and without self-consciousness, the naive, happy, chattering schoolgirl of her convent days. She wears the dress into which she had changed for her drive to town, a simple, fairly expensive affair, which would be extremely becoming if it were not for the careless, almost slovenly way she wears it. Her hair is no longer fastidiously in place. It has a slightly disheveled, lopsided look. She talks to* CATHLEEN *with a confiding familiarity, as if the second girl were an old, intimate friend. As the curtain rises, she is standing by the screen door looking out. A moan of the foghorn is heard.*

MARY [*amused—girlishly*]   That foghorn! Isn't it awful, Cathleen?

CATHLEEN [*talks more familiarly than usual but never with intentional impertinence because she sincerely likes her mistress*]   It is indeed, Ma'am. It's like a banshee.

MARY [*Goes on as if she hadn't heard. In nearly all the following dialogue there is the feeling that she has* CATHLEEN *with her merely as an excuse to keep talking.*] I don't mind it tonight. Last night it drove me crazy. I lay awake worrying until I couldn't stand it any more.

CATHLEEN Bad cess to it.[1] I was scared out of my wits riding back from town. I thought that ugly monkey, Smythe, would drive us in a ditch or against a tree. You couldn't see your hand in front of you. I'm glad you had me sit in back with you, Ma'am. If I'd been in front with that monkey—He can't keep his dirty hands to himself. Give him half a chance and he's pinching me on the leg or you-know-where—asking your pardon, Ma'am, but it's true.

MARY [*dreamily*] It wasn't the fog I minded, Cathleen, I really love fog.

CATHLEEN They say it's good for the complexion.

MARY It hides you from the world and the world from you. You feel that everything has changed, and nothing is what it seemed to be. No one can find or touch you any more.

CATHLEEN I wouldn't care so much if Smythe was a fine, handsome man like some chauffeurs I've seen—I mean, if it was all in fun, for I'm a decent girl. But for a shriveled runt like Smythe—! I've told him, you must think I'm hard up that I'd notice a monkey like you. I've warned him, one day I'll give a clout that'll knock him into next week. And so I will!

MARY It's the foghorn I hate. It won't let you alone. It keeps reminding you, and warning you, and calling you back. [*She smiles strangely.*] But it can't tonight. It's just an ugly sound. It doesn't remind me of anything. [*She gives a teasing, girlish laugh.*] Except, perhaps, Mr. Tyrone's snores. I've always had such fun teasing him about it. He has snored ever since I can remember, especially when he's had too much to drink, and yet he's like a child, he hates to admit it. [*She laughs, coming to the table.*] Well, I suppose I snore at times, too, and I don't like to admit it. So I have no right to make fun of him, have I? [*She sits in the rocker at right of table.*]

CATHLEEN Ah, sure, everybody healthy snores. It's a sign of sanity, they say. [*then, worriedly*] What time is it, Ma'am? I ought to go back in the kitchen. The damp is in Bridget's rheumatism and she's like a raging divil. She'll bite my head off.

[*She puts her glass on the table and makes a movement toward the back parlor.*]

MARY [*with a flash of apprehension*] No, don't go, Cathleen. I don't want to be alone, yet.

CATHLEEN You won't be for long. The Master and the boys will be home soon.

MARY I doubt if they'll come back for dinner. They have too good an excuse to remain in the barrooms where they feel at home.

[CATHLEEN *stares at her, stupidly puzzled.* MARY *goes on smilingly*] Don't worry about Bridget. I'll tell her I kept you with me, and you can take a big drink of whiskey to her when you go. She won't mind then.

CATHLEEN [*grins—at her ease again*] No, Ma'am. That's the one thing can make her cheerful. She loves her drop.

MARY Have another drink yourself, if you wish, Cathleen.

1. Bad luck to it (Irish).

CATHLEEN I don't know if I'd better, Ma'am. I can feel what I've had already. [*reaching for the bottle*] Well, maybe one more won't harm. [*She pours a drink.*] Here's your good health, Ma'am. [*She drinks without bothering about a chaser.*]

MARY [*dreamily*] I really did have good health once, Cathleen. But that was long ago.

CATHLEEN [*worried again*] The Master's sure to notice what's gone from the bottle. He has the eye of a hawk for that.

MARY [*amusedly*] Oh, we'll play Jamie's trick on him. Just measure a few drinks of water and pour them in.

CATHLEEN [*does this—with a silly giggle*] God save me, it'll be half water. He'll know by the taste.

MARY [*indifferently*] No, by the time he comes home he'll be too drunk to tell the difference. He has such a good excuse, he believes, to drown his sorrows.

CATHLEEN [*philosophically*] Well, it's a good man's failing. I wouldn't give a trauneen[2] for a teetotaler. They've no high spirits. [*then, stupidly puzzled*] Good excuse? You mean Master Edmund, Ma'am? I can tell the Master is worried about him.

MARY [*stiffens defensively—but in a strange way the reaction has a mechanical quality, as if it did not penetrate to real emotion*] Don't be silly, Cathleen. Why should he be? A touch of grippe is nothing. And Mr. Tyrone never is worried about anything, except money and property and the fear he'll end his days in poverty. I mean, deeply worried. Because he cannot really understand anything else. [*She gives a little laugh of detached, affectionate amusement.*] My husband is a very peculiar man, Cathleen.

CATHLEEN [*vaguely resentful*] Well, he's a fine, handsome, kind gentleman just the same, Ma'am. Never mind his weakness.

MARY Oh, I don't mind. I've loved him dearly for thirty-six years. That proves I know he's lovable at heart and can't help being what he is, doesn't it?

CATHLEEN [*hazily reassured*] That's right. Ma'am. Love him dearly, for any fool can see he worships the ground you walk on. [*fighting the effect of her last drink and trying to be soberly conversational*] Speaking of acting, Ma'am, how is it you never went on the stage?

MARY [*resentfully*] I? What put that absurd notion in your head? I was brought up in a respectable home and educated in the best convent in the Middle West. Before I met Mr. Tyrone I hardly knew there was such a thing as a theater. I was a very pious girl. I even dreamed of becoming a nun. I've never had the slightest desire to be an actress.

CATHLEEN [*bluntly*] Well, I can't imagine you a holy nun, Ma'am. Sure, you never darken the door of a church, God forgive you.

MARY [*ignores this*] I've never felt at home in the theater. Even though Mr. Tyrone has made me go with him on all his tours, I've had little to do with the people in his company, or with anyone on the stage. Not that I have anything against them. They have always been kind to me, and I to them. But I've never felt at home with them. Their life is not my life. It has always stood between me and—[*She gets up—abruptly*] But let's not

---

2. Coin of very low value (Irish).

talk of old things that couldn't be helped. [*She goes to the porch door and stares out.*] How thick the fog is. I can't see the road. All the people in the world could pass by and I would never know. I wish it was always that way. It's getting dark already. It will soon be night, thank goodness. [*She turns back—vaguely*] It was kind of you to keep me company this afternoon, Cathleen. I would have been lonely driving uptown alone.

CATHLEEN   Sure, wouldn't I rather ride in a fine automobile than stay here and listen to Bridget's lies about her relations? It was like a vacation, Ma'am. [*She pauses—then stupidly*] There was only one thing I didn't like.

MARY [*vaguely*]   What was that, Cathleen?

CATHLEEN   The way the man in the drugstore acted when I took in the prescription for you. [*indignantly*] The impidence[3] of him!

MARY [*with stubborn blankness*]   What are you talking about? What drugstore? What prescription? [*then hastily, as* CATHLEEN *stares in stupid amazement*] Oh, of course, I'd forgotten. The medicine for the rheumatism in my hands. What did the man say? [*then with indifference*] Not that it matters, as long as he filled the prescription.

CATHLEEN   It mattered to me, then! I'm not used to being treated like a thief. He gave me a long look and says insultingly, "Where did you get hold of this?" and I says, "It's none of your damned business, but if you must know, it's for the lady I work for, Mrs. Tyrone, who's sitting out in the automobile." That shut him up quick. He gave a look out at you and said, "Oh," and went to get the medicine.

MARY [*vaguely*]   Yes, he knows me. [*She sits in the armchair at right rear of table. She adds in a calm, detached voice*] It's a special kind of medicine. I have to take it because there is no other that can stop the pain—*all* the pain—I mean, in my hands. [*She raises her hands and regards them with melancholy sympathy. There is no tremor in them now.*] Poor hands! You'd never believe it, but they were once one of my good points, along with my hair and eyes, and I had a fine figure, too. [*Her tone has become more and more far-off and dreamy.*] They were a musician's hands. I used to love the piano. I worked so hard at my music in the Convent—if you can call it work when you do something you love. Mother Elizabeth and my music teacher both said I had more talent than any student they remembered. My father paid for special lessons. He spoiled me. He would do anything I asked. He would have sent me to Europe to study after I graduated from the Convent. I might have gone—if I hadn't fallen in love with Mr. Tyrone. Or I might have become a nun. I had two dreams. To be a nun, that was the more beautiful one. To become a concert pianist, that was the other. [*She pauses, regarding her hands fixedly.* CATHLEEN *blinks her eyes to fight off drowsiness and a tipsy feeling.*] I haven't touched a piano in so many years. I couldn't play with such crippled fingers, even if I wanted to. For a time after my marriage I tried to keep up my music. But it was hopeless. One-night stands, cheap hotels, dirty trains, leaving children, never having a home—[*She stares at her hands with fascinated disgust.*] See, Cathleen, how ugly they are! So maimed and crippled! You would think they'd been through some horrible accident! [*She gives a*

---

3. Impudence.

strange little laugh.] So they have, come to think of it. [*She suddenly thrusts her hands behind her back.*] I won't look at them. They're worse than the foghorn for reminding me—[*then with defiant self-assurance*] But even they can't touch me now. [*She brings her hands from behind her back and deliberately stares at them—calmly*] They're far away. I see them, but the pain has gone.

CATHLEEN [*stupidly puzzled*] You've taken some of the medicine? It made you act funny, Ma'am. If I didn't know better, I'd think you'd a drop taken.

MARY [*dreamily*] It kills the pain. You go back until at last you are beyond its reach. Only the past when you were happy is real. [*She pauses—then as if her words had been an evocation which called back happiness she changes in her whole manner and facial expression. She looks younger. There is a quality of an innocent convent girl about her, and she smiles shyly.*] If you think Mr. Tyrone is handsome now, Cathleen, you should have seen him when I first met him. He had the reputation of being one of the best looking men in the country. The girls in the Convent who had seen him act, or seen his photographs, used to rave about him. He was a great matinee idol then, you know. Women used to wait at the stage door just to see him come out. You can imagine how excited I was when my father wrote me he and James Tyrone had become friends, and that I was to meet him when I came home for Easter vacation. I showed the letter to all the girls, and how envious they were! My father took me to see him act first. It was a play about the French Revolution and the leading part was a nobleman. I couldn't take my eyes off him. I wept when he was thrown in prison—and then was so mad at myself because I was afraid my eyes and nose would be red. My father had said we'd go backstage to his dressing room right after the play, and so we did. [*She gives a little excited, shy laugh.*] I was so bashful all I could do was stammer and blush like a little fool. But he didn't seem to think I was a fool. I know he liked me the first moment we were introduced. [*coquettishly*] I guess my eyes and nose couldn't have been red, after all. I was really very pretty then, Cathleen. And he was handsomer than my wildest dream, in his make-up and his nobleman's costume that was so becoming to him. He was different from all ordinary men, like someone from another world. At the same time he was simple, and kind, and unassuming, not a bit stuck-up or vain. I fell in love right then. So did he, he told me afterwards. I forgot all about becoming a nun or a concert pianist. All I wanted was to be his wife. [*She pauses, staring before her with unnaturally bright, dreamy eyes, and a rapt, tender, girlish smile.*] Thirty-six years ago, but I can see it as clearly as if it were tonight! We've loved each other ever since. And in all those thirty-six years, there has never been a breath of scandal about him. I mean, with any other woman. Never since he met me. That has made me very happy, Cathleen. It has made me forgive so many other things.

CATHLEEN [*fighting tipsy drowsiness—sentimentally*] He's a fine gentleman and you're a lucky woman. [*then, fidgeting*] Can I take the drink to Bridget, Ma'am? It must be near dinnertime and I ought to be in the kitchen helping her. If she don't get something to quiet her temper, she'll be after me with the cleaver.

MARY [*with a vague exasperation at being brought back from her dream*] Yes, yes, go. I don't need you now.

CATHLEEN [*with relief*] Thank you, Ma'am. [*She pours out a big drink and starts for the back parlor with it.*] You won't be alone long. The Master and the boys—

MARY [*impatiently*] No, no, they won't come. Tell Bridget I won't wait. You can serve dinner promptly at half past six. I'm not hungry but I'll sit at the table and we'll get it over with.

CATHLEEN You ought to eat something, Ma'am. It's a queer medicine if it takes away your appetite.

MARY [*has begun to drift into dreams again—reacts mechanically*] What medicine? I don't know what you mean. [*in dismissal*] You better take the drink to Bridget.

CATHLEEN Yes, Ma'am.

[*She disappears through the back parlor.* MARY *waits until she hears the pantry door close behind her. Then she settles back in relaxed dreaminess, staring fixedly at nothing. Her arms rest limply along the arms of the chair, her hands with long, warped, swollen-knuckled, sensitive fingers drooping in complete calm. It is growing dark in the room. There is a pause of dead quiet. Then from the world outside comes the melancholy moan of the foghorn, followed by a chorus of bells, muffled by the fog, from the anchored craft in the harbor.* MARY's *face gives no sign she has heard, but her hands jerk and the fingers automatically play for a moment on the air. She frowns and shakes her head mechanically as if a fly had walked across her mind. She suddenly loses all the girlish quality and is an aging, cynically sad, embittered woman.*]

MARY [*bitterly*] You're a sentimental fool. What is so wonderful about that first meeting between a silly romantic schoolgirl and a matinee idol? You were much happier before you knew he existed, in the Convent when you used to pray to the Blessed Virgin. [*longingly*] If I could only find the faith I lost, so I could pray again! [*She pauses—then begins to recite the Hail Mary in a flat, empty tone.*] "Hail, Mary, full of grace! The Lord is with Thee; blessed art Thou among women." [*sneeringly*] You expect the Blessed Virgin to be fooled by a lying dope fiend reciting words! You can't hide from her! [*She springs to her feet. Her hands fly up to pat her hair distractedly.*] I must go upstairs. I haven't taken enough. When you start again you never know exactly how much you need. [*She goes toward the front parlor—then stops in the doorway as she hears the sound of voices from the front path. She starts guiltily.*] That must be them—[*She hurries back to sit down. Her face sets in stubborn defensiveness—resentfully*] Why are they coming back? They don't want to. And I'd much rather be alone. [*Suddenly her whole manner changes. She becomes pathetically relieved and eager.*] Oh, I'm so glad they've come! I've been so horribly lonely!

[*The front door is heard closing and* TYRONE *calls uneasily from the hall.*]

TYRONE Are you there, Mary?

[*The light in the hall is turned on and shines through the front parlor to fall on* MARY.]

MARY [*rises from her chair, her face lighting up lovingly—with excited eagerness*] I'm here, dear. In the living room. I've been waiting for you.

[TYRONE *comes in through the front parlor.* EDMUND *is behind him.* TYRONE *has had a lot to drink but beyond a slightly glazed look in his eyes and a trace of blur in his speech, he does not show it.* EDMUND *has also had more than a few drinks without much apparent effect, except that his sunken cheeks are flushed and his eyes look bright and feverish. They stop in the doorway to stare appraisingly at her. What they see fulfills their worst expectations. But for the moment MARY is unconscious of their condemning eyes. She kisses her husband and then EDMUND. Her manner is unnaturally effusive. They submit shrinkingly. She talks excitedly.*]

I'm so happy you've come. I had given up hope. I was afraid you wouldn't come home. It's such a dismal, foggy evening. It must be much more cheerful in the barrooms uptown, where there are people you can talk and joke with. No, don't deny it. I know how you feel. I don't blame you a bit. I'm all the more grateful to you for coming home. I was sitting here so lonely and blue. Come and sit down.

[*She sits at left rear of table,* EDMUND *at left of table, and* TYRONE *in the rocker at right of it.*]

Dinner won't be ready for a minute. You're actually a little early. Will wonders never cease. Here's the whiskey, dear. Shall I pour a drink for you? [*Without waiting for a reply she does so.*] And you, Edmund? I don't want to encourage you, but one before dinner, as an appetizer, can't do any harm.

[*She pours a drink for him. They make no move to take the drinks. She talks on as if unaware of their silence.*]

Where's Jamie? But, of course, he'll never come home so long as he has the price of a drink left. [*She reaches out and clasps her husband's hand—sadly*] I'm afraid Jamie has been lost to us for a long time, dear. [*Her face hardens.*] But we mustn't allow him to drag Edmund down with him, as he'd like to do. He's jealous because Edmund has always been the baby—just as he used to be of Eugene. He'll never be content until he makes Edmund as hopeless a failure as he is.

EDMUND [*miserably*]   Stop talking, Mama.

TYRONE [*dully*]   Yes, Mary, the less you say now—[*then to Edmund, a bit tipsily*] All the same there's truth in your mother's warning. Beware of that brother of yours, or he'll poison life for you with his damned sneering serpent's tongue!

EDMUND [*as before*]   Oh, cut it out, Papa.

MARY [*goes on as if nothing had been said*]   It's hard to believe, seeing Jamie as he is now, that he was ever my baby. Do you remember what a healthy, happy baby he was, James? The one-night stands and filthy trains and cheap hotels and bad food never made him cross or sick. He was always smiling or laughing. He hardly ever cried. Eugene was the same, too, happy and healthy, during the two years he lived before I let him die through my neglect.

TYRONE   Oh, for the love of God! I'm a fool for coming home!

EDMUND   Papa! Shut up!

MARY [*smiles with detached tenderness at* EDMUND]   It was Edmund who was the crosspatch when he was little, always getting upset and frightened about nothing at all. [*She pats his hand—teasingly*] Everyone used to say, dear, you'd cry at the drop of a hat.

EDMUND [*cannot control his bitterness*]   Maybe I guessed there was a good reason not to laugh.

TYRONE [*reproving and pitying*]   Now, now, lad. You know better than to pay attention—

MARY [*as if she hadn't heard—sadly again*] Who would have thought Jamie would grow up to disgrace us. You remember, James, for years after he went to boarding school, we received such glowing reports. Everyone liked him. All his teachers told us what a fine brain he had, and how easily he learned his lessons. Even after he began to drink and they had to expel him, they wrote us how sorry they were, because he was so likable and such a brilliant student. They predicted a wonderful future for him if he would only learn to take life seriously. [*She pauses— then adds with a strange, sad detachment*] It's such a pity. Poor Jamie! It's hard to understand—[*Abruptly a change comes over her. Her face hardens and she stares at her husband with accusing hostility.*] No, it isn't at all. You brought him up to be a boozer. Since he first opened his eyes, he's seen you drinking. Always a bottle on the bureau in the cheap hotel rooms! And if he had a nightmare when he was little, or a stomach-ache, your remedy was to give him a teaspoonful of whiskey to quiet him.

TYRONE [*stung*] So I'm to blame because that lazy hulk has made a drunken loafer of himself? Is that what I came home to listen to? I might have known! When you have the poison in you, you want to blame everyone but yourself!

EDMUND Papa! You told me not to pay attention. [*then, resentfully*] Anyway it's true. You did the same thing with me. I can remember that teaspoonful of booze every time I woke up with a nightmare.

MARY [*in a detached reminiscent tone*] Yes, you were continually having nightmares as a child. You were born afraid. Because I was so afraid to bring you into the world. [*She pauses—then goes on with the same detachment*] Please don't think I blame your father, Edmund. He didn't know any better. He never went to school after he was ten. His people were the most ignorant kind of poverty-stricken Irish. I'm sure they honestly believed whiskey is the healthiest medicine for a child who is sick or frightened.

[TYRONE *is about to burst out in angry defense of his family but* EDMUND *intervenes.*]

EDMUND [*sharply*] Papa! [*changing the subject*] Are we going to have this drink, or aren't we?

TYRONE [*controlling himself—dully*] You're right. I'm a fool to take notice. [*He picks up his glass listlessly.*] Drink hearty, lad.

[EDMUND *drinks but* TYRONE *remains staring at the glass in his hand.* EDMUND *at once realizes how much the whiskey has been watered. He frowns, glancing from the bottle to his mother—starts to say something but stops.*]

MARY [*in a changed tone—repentantly*] I'm sorry if I sounded bitter, James. I'm not. It's all so far away. But I did feel a little hurt when you wished you hadn't come home. I was so relieved and happy when you came, and grateful to you. It's very dreary and sad to be here alone in the fog with night falling.

TYRONE [*moved*] I'm glad I came, Mary, when you act like your real self.

MARY I was so lonesome I kept Cathleen with me just to have someone to talk to. [*Her manner and quality drift back to the shy convent girl again.*] Do you know what I was telling her, dear? About the night my father took me to your dressing room and I first fell in love with you. Do you remember?

TYRONE [*deeply moved—his voice husky*]   Can you think I'd ever forget, Mary?

[EDMUND *looks away from them, sad and embarrassed.*]

MARY [*tenderly*]   No. I know you still love me, James, in spite of everything.

TYRONE [*His face works and he blinks back tears—with quiet intensity*] Yes! As God is my judge! Always and forever, Mary!

MARY   And I love you, dear, in spite of everything.

[*There is a pause in which* EDMUND *moves embarrassedly. The strange detachment comes over her manner again as if she were speaking impersonally of people seen from a distance.*]

But I must confess, James, although I couldn't help loving you, I would never have married you if I'd known you drank so much. I remember the first night your barroom friends had to help you up to the door of our hotel room, and knocked and then ran away before I came to the door. We were still on our honeymoon, do you remember?

TYRONE [*with guilty vehemence*]   I don't remember! It wasn't on our honeymoon! And I never in my life had to be helped to bed, or missed a performance!

MARY [*as though he hadn't spoken*]   I had waited in that ugly hotel room hour after hour. I kept making excuses for you. I told myself it must be some business connected with the theater. I knew so little about the theater. Then I became terrified. I imagined all sorts of horrible accidents. I got on my knees and prayed that nothing had happened to you— and then they brought you up and left you outside the door. [*She gives a little, sad sigh.*] I didn't know how often that was to happen in the years to come, how many times I was to wait in ugly hotel rooms. I became quite used to it.

EDMUND [*bursts out with a look of accusing hate at his father*]   Christ! No wonder—! [*He controls himself—gruffly*] When is dinner, Mama? It must be time.

TYRONE [*overwhelmed by shame which he tries to hide, fumbles with his watch*]   Yes. It must be. Let's see. [*He stares at his watch without seeing it—pleadingly*] Mary! Can't you forget—?

MARY [*with detached pity*]   No, dear. But I forgive. I always forgive you. So don't look so guilty. I'm sorry I remembered out loud. I don't want to be sad, or to make you sad. I want to remember only the happy part of the past. [*Her manner drifts back to the shy, gay convent girl.*] Do you remember our wedding, dear? I'm sure you've completely forgotten what my wedding gown looked like. Men don't notice such things. They don't think they're important. But it was important to me, I can tell you! How I fussed and worried! I was so excited and happy! My father told me to buy anything I wanted and never mind what it cost. The best is none too good, he said. I'm afraid he spoiled me dreadfully. My mother didn't. She was very pious and strict. I think she was a little jealous. She didn't approve of my marrying—especially an actor. I think she hoped I would become a nun. She used to scold my father. She'd grumble, "You never tell me, never mind what it costs, when I buy anything! You've spoiled that girl so, I pity her husband if she ever marries. She'll expect him to give her the moon. She'll never make a good wife." [*She laughs affection-*

ately.] Poor mother! [*She smiles at* TYRONE *with a strange, incongruous coquetry.*] But she was mistaken, wasn't she, James? I haven't been such a bad wife, have I?

TYRONE [*huskily, trying to force a smile*] I'm not complaining, Mary.

MARY [*a shadow of vague guilt crosses her face*] At least, I've loved you dearly, and done the best I could—under the circumstances. [*The shadow vanishes and her shy, girlish expression returns.*] That wedding gown was nearly the death of me and the dressmaker, too! [*She laughs.*] I was so particular. It was never quite good enough. At last she said she refused to touch it any more or she might spoil it, and I made her leave so I could be alone to examine myself in the mirror. I was so pleased and vain. I thought to myself, "Even if your nose and mouth and ears are a trifle too large, your eyes and hair and figure, and your hands, make up for it. You're just as pretty as any actress he's ever met, and you don't have to use paint." [*She pauses, wrinkling her brow in an effort of memory.*] Where is my wedding gown now, I wonder? I kept it wrapped up in tissue paper in my trunk. I used to hope I would have a daughter and when it came time for her to marry—She couldn't have bought a lovelier gown, and I knew, James, you'd never tell her, never mind the cost. You'd want her to pick up something at a bargain. It was made of soft, shimmering satin, trimmed with wonderful old duchesse lace, in tiny ruffles around the neck and sleeves, and worked in with the folds that were draped round in a bustle effect at the back. The basque[4] was boned and very tight. I remember I held my breath when it was fitted, so my waist would be as small as possible. My father even let me have duchesse lace on my white satin slippers, and lace with orange blossoms in my veil. Oh, how I loved that gown! It was so beautiful! Where is it now, I wonder? I used to take it out from time to time when I was lonely, but it always made me cry, so finally a long while ago—[*She wrinkles her forehead again.*] I wonder where I hid it? Probably in one of the old trunks in the attic. Some day I'll have to look.

> [*She stops, staring before her.* TYRONE *sighs, shaking his head hope-lessly, and attempts to catch his son's eye, looking for sympathy, but* EDMUND *is staring at the floor.*]

TYRONE [*forces a casual tone*] Isn't it dinner time, dear? [*with a feeble attempt at teasing*] You're forever scolding me for being late, but now I'm on time for once, it's dinner that's late.

> [*She doesn't appear to hear him. He adds, still pleasantly*]

Well, if I can't eat yet, I can drink. I'd forgotten I had this.

> [*He drinks his drink.* EDMUND *watches him.* TYRONE *scowls and looks at his wife with sharp suspicion—roughly*]

Who's been tampering with my whiskey? The damned stuff is half water! Jamie's been away and he wouldn't overdo his trick like this, anyway. Any fool could tell—Mary, answer me! [*with angry disgust*] I hope to God you haven't taken to drink on top of—

EDMUND Shut up, Papa! [*to his mother, without looking at her*] You treated Cathleen and Bridget, isn't that it, Mama?

MARY [*with indifferent casualness*] Yes, of course. They work hard for poor wages. And I'm the housekeeper, I have to keep them from leaving.

---

4. Tight-fitting bodice.

Besides, I wanted to treat Cathleen because I had her drive uptown with me, and sent her to get my prescription filled.

EDMUND For God's sake, Mama! You can't trust her! Do you want everyone on earth to know?

MARY [*her face hardening stubbornly*] Know what? That I suffer from rheumatism in my hands and have to take medicine to kill the pain? Why should I be ashamed of that? [*turns on* EDMUND *with a hard, accusing antagonism—almost a revengeful enmity*] I never knew what rheumatism was before you were born! Ask your father!

[EDMUND *looks away, shrinking into himself.*]

TYRONE Don't mind her, lad. It doesn't mean anything. When she gets to the stage where she gives the old crazy excuse about her hands she's gone far away from us.

MARY [*turns on him—with a strangely triumphant, taunting smile*] I'm glad you realize that, James! Now perhaps you'll give up trying to remind me, you and Edmund! [*abruptly, in a detached, matter-of-fact tone*] Why don't you light the light, James? It's getting dark. I know you hate to, but Edmund has proved to you that one bulb burning doesn't cost much. There's no sense letting your fear of the poorhouse make you too stingy.

TYRONE [*reacts mechanically*] I never claimed one bulb cost much! It's having them on, one here and one there, that makes the Electric Light Company rich. [*He gets up and turns on the reading lamp—roughly*] But I'm a fool to talk reason to you. [*to* EDMUND] I'll get a fresh bottle of whiskey, lad, and we'll have a real drink. [*He goes through the back parlor.*]

MARY [*with detached amusement*] He'll sneak around to the outside cellar door so the servants won't see him. He's really ashamed of keeping his whiskey padlocked in the cellar. Your father is a strange man, Edmund. It took many years before I understood him. You must try to understand and forgive him, too, and not feel contempt because he's close-fisted. His father deserted his mother and their six children a year or so after they came to America. He told them he had a premonition he would die soon, and he was homesick for Ireland, and wanted to go back there to die. So he went and he did die. He must have been a peculiar man, too. Your father had to go to work in a machine shop when he was only ten years old.

EDMUND [*protests dully*] Oh, for Pete's sake, Mama. I've heard Papa tell that machine shop story ten thousand times.

MARY Yes, dear, you've had to listen, but I don't think you've ever tried to understand.

EDMUND [*ignoring this—miserably*] Listen, Mama! You're not so far gone yet you've forgotten everything. You haven't asked me what I found out this afternoon. Don't you care a damn?

MARY [*shakenly*] Don't say that! You hurt me, dear!

EDMUND What I've got is serious, Mama. Doc Hardy knows for sure now.

MARY [*stiffens into scornful, defensive stubbornness*] That lying old quack! I warned you he'd invent—!

EDMUND [*miserably dogged*] He called in a specialist to examine me, so he'd be absolutely sure.

MARY [*ignoring this*] Don't tell me about Hardy! If you heard what the doctor at the sanatorium, who really knows something, said about how he'd treated me! He said he ought to be locked up! He said it was a wonder I hadn't gone mad! I told him I had once, that time I ran down in my nightdress to throw myself off the dock. You remember that, don't you? And yet you want me to pay attention to what Doctor Hardy says. Oh, no!

EDMUND [*bitterly*] I remember, all right. It was right after that Papa and Jamie decided they couldn't hide it from me any more. Jamie told me. I called him a liar! I tried to punch him in the nose. But I knew he wasn't lying. [*His voice trembles, his eyes begin to fill with tears.*] God, it made everything in life seem rotten!

MARY [*pitiably*] Oh, don't. My baby! You hurt me so dreadfully!

EDMUND [*dully*] I'm sorry, Mama. It was you who brought it up. [*then with a bitter, stubborn persistence*] Listen, Mama. I'm going to tell you whether you want to hear or not. I've got to go to a sanatorium.

MARY [*dazedly, as if this was something that had never occurred to her*] Go away? [*violently*] No! I won't have it! How dare Doctor Hardy advise such a thing without consulting me! How dare your father allow him! What right has he? You are my baby! Let him attend to Jamie! [*more and more excited and bitter*] I know why he wants you sent to a sanatorium. To take you from me! He's always tried to do that. He's been jealous of every one of my babies! He kept finding ways to make me leave them. That's what caused Eugene's death. He's been jealous of you most of all. He knew I loved you most because—

EDMUND [*miserably*] Oh, stop talking crazy, can't you, Mama! Stop trying to blame him. And why are you so against my going away now? I've been away a lot, and I've never noticed it broke your heart!

MARY [*bitterly*] I'm afraid you're not very sensitive, after all. [*sadly*] You might have guessed, dear, that after I knew you knew—about me—I had to be glad whenever you were where you couldn't see me.

EDMUND [*brokenly*] Mama! Don't! [*He reaches out blindly and takes her hand—but he drops it immediately, overcome by bitterness again.*] All this talk about loving me—and you won't even listen when I try to tell you how sick—

MARY [*with an abrupt transformation into a detached bullying motherliness*] Now, now. That's enough! I don't care to hear because I know it's nothing but Hardy's ignorant lies.

[*He shrinks back into himself. She keeps on in a forced, teasing tone but with an increasing undercurrent of resentment.*]

You're so like your father, dear. You love to make a scene out of nothing so you can be dramatic and tragic. [*with a belittling laugh*] If I gave you the slightest encouragement, you'd tell me next you were going to die—

EDMUND People do die of it. Your own father—

MARY [*sharply*] Why do you mention him? There's no comparison at all with you. He had consumption. [*angrily*] I hate you when you become gloomy and morbid! I forbid you to remind me of my father's death, do you hear me?

EDMUND [*his face hard—grimly*] Yes, I hear you, Mama. I wish to God I didn't! [*He gets up from his chair and stands staring condemningly at her—bitterly*] It's pretty hard to take at times, having a dope fiend for a mother!

[*She winces—all life seeming to drain from her face, leaving it with the appearance of a plaster cast. Instantly* EDMUND *wishes he could take back what he has said. He stammers miserably.*]

Forgive me, Mama. I was angry. You hurt me.

[*There is a pause in which the foghorn and the ships' bells are heard.*]

MARY [*goes slowly to the windows at right like an automaton—looking out, a blank, far-off quality in her voice*]   Just listen to that awful foghorn. And the bells. Why is it fog makes everything sound so sad and lost, I wonder?

EDMUND [*brokenly*]   I—I can't stay here. I don't want any dinner.

[*He hurries away through the front parlor. She keeps staring out the window until she hears the front door close behind him. Then she comes back and sits in her chair, the same blank look on her face.*]

MARY [*vaguely*]   I must go upstairs. I haven't taken enough. [*She pauses—then longingly*] I hope, sometime, without meaning it, I will take an overdose. I never could do it deliberately. The Blessed Virgin would never forgive me, then.

[*She hears* TYRONE *returning and turns as he comes in, through the back parlor, with a bottle of whiskey he has just uncorked. He is fuming.*]

TYRONE [*wrathfully*]   The padlock is all scratched. That drunken loafer has tried to pick the lock with a piece of wire, the way he's done before. [*with satisfaction, as if this was a perpetual battle of wits with his elder son*] But I've fooled him this time. It's a special padlock a professional burglar couldn't pick. [*He puts the bottle on the tray and suddenly is aware of* EDMUND's *absence.*] Where's Edmund?

MARY [*with a vague far-away air*]   He went out. Perhaps he's going uptown again to find Jamie. He still has some money left, I suppose, and it's burning a hole in his pocket. He said he didn't want any dinner. He doesn't seem to have any appetite these days. [*then stubbornly*] But it's just a summer cold.

[TYRONE *stares at her and shakes his head helplessly and pours himself a big drink and drinks it. Suddenly it is too much for her and she breaks out and sobs.*]

Oh, James, I'm so frightened! [*She gets up and throws her arms around him and hides her face on his shoulder—sobbingly*] I know he's going to die!

TYRONE   Don't say that! It's not true! They promised me in six months he'd be cured.

MARY   You don't believe that! I can tell when you're acting! And it will be my fault. I should never have borne him. It would have been better for his sake. I could never hurt him then. He wouldn't have had to know his mother was a dope fiend—and hate her!

TYRONE [*his voice quivering*]   Hush, Mary, for the love of God! He loves you. He knows it was a curse put on you without your knowing or willing it. He's proud you're his mother! [*abruptly as he hears the pantry door opening*] Hush, now! Here comes Cathleen. You don't want her to see you crying.

[*She turns quickly away from him to the windows at right, hastily wiping her eyes. A moment later* CATHLEEN *appears in the back-parlor doorway. She is uncertain in her walk and grinning woozily.*]

CATHLEEN [*starts guiltily when she sees* TYRONE—*with dignity*]   Dinner is served, Sir. [*raising her voice unnecessarily*] Dinner is served, Ma'am. [*She forgets her dignity and addresses* TYRONE *with good-natured familiarity*] So you're here, are you? Well, well. Won't Bridget be in a rage! I told her the Madame said you wouldn't be home. [*then reading accusation in his eye*] Don't be looking at me that way. If I've a drop taken, I didn't steal it. I was invited.

   [*She turns with huffy dignity and disappears through the back parlor.*]

TYRONE [*sighs—then summoning his actor's heartiness*]   Come along, dear. Let's have our dinner. I'm hungry as a hunter.

MARY [*comes to him—her face is composed in plaster again and her tone is remote*]   I'm afraid you'll have to excuse me, James. I couldn't possibly eat anything. My hands pain me dreadfully. I think the best thing for me is to go to bed and rest. Good night dear.

   [*She kisses him mechanically and turns toward the front parlor.*]

TYRONE [*harshly*]   Up to take more of that God-damned poison, is that it? You'll be like a mad ghost before the night's over!

MARY [*starts to walk away—blankly*]   I don't know what you're talking about, James. You say such mean, bitter things when you've drunk too much. You're as bad as Jamie or Edmund.

   [*She moves off through the front parlor. He stands a second as if not knowing what to do. He is a sad, bewildered, broken old man. He walks wearily off through the back parlor toward the dining room.*]

CURTAIN

Act 4

SCENE—*The same. It is around midnight. The lamp in the front hall has been turned out, so that now no light shines through the front parlor. In the living room only the reading lamp on the table is lighted. Outside the windows the wall of fog appears denser than ever. As the curtain rises, the foghorn is heard, followed by the ships' bells from the harbor.*

   TYRONE *is seated at the table. He wears his pince-nez⁵ and is playing soli-taire. He has taken off his coat and has on an old brown dressing gown. The whiskey bottle on the tray is three-quarters empty. There is a fresh full bottle on the table, which he has brought from the cellar so there will be an ample reserve on hand. He is drunk and shows it by the owlish, deliberate manner in which he peers at each card to make certain of its identity, and then plays it as if he wasn't certain of his aim. His eyes have a misted, oily look and his mouth is slack. But despite all the whiskey in him, he has not escaped, and he looks as he appeared at the close of the preceding act, a sad, defeated old man, possessed by hopeless resignation.*

   As the curtain rises, he finishes a game and sweeps the cards together. He shuffles them clumsily, dropping a couple on the floor. He retrieves them with difficulty, and starts to shuffle again, when he hears someone entering the front door. He peers over his pince-nez through the front parlor.

---

5. Eyeglasses clipped to the nose.

TYRONE [*his voice thick*] Who's that? Is it you, Edmund?

> [EDMUND's *voice answers curtly,* "Yes." *Then he evidently collides with something in the dark hall and can be heard cursing. A moment later the hall lamp is turned on.* TYRONE *frowns and calls.*]

Turn that light out before you come in.

> [*But* EDMUND *doesn't. He comes in through the front parlor. He is drunk now, too, but like his father he carries it well, and gives little physical sign of it except in his eyes and a chip-on-the-shoulder aggressiveness in his manner.* TYRONE *speaks, at first with a warm, relieved welcome.*]

I'm glad you've come, lad. I've been damned lonely. [*then resentfully*] You're a fine one to run away and leave me to sit alone here all night when you know—[*with sharp irritation*] I told you to turn out that light! We're not giving a ball. There's no reason to have the house ablaze with electricity at this time of night, burning up money!

EDMUND [*angrily*] Ablaze with electricity! One bulb! Hell, everyone keeps a light on in the front hall until they go to bed. [*He rubs his knee.*] I damned near busted my knee on the hat stand.

TYRONE The light from here shows in the hall. You could see your way well enough if you were sober.

EDMUND If *I* was sober? I like that!

TYRONE I don't give a damn what other people do. If they want to be wasteful fools, for the sake of show, let them be!

EDMUND One bulb! Christ, don't be such a cheap skate! I've proved by figures if you left the light bulb on all night it wouldn't be as much as one drink!

TYRONE To hell with your figures! The proof is in the bills I have to pay!

EDMUND [*sits down opposite his father—contemptuously*] Yes, facts don't mean a thing, do they? What you want to believe, that's the only truth! [*derisively*] Shakespeare was an Irish Catholic, for example.

TYRONE [*stubbornly*] So he was. The proof is in his plays.

EDMUND Well he wasn't, and there's no proof of it in his plays, except to you! [*jeeringly*] The Duke of Wellington, there was another good Irish Catholic!

TYRONE I never said he was a good one. He was a renegade but a Catholic just the same.

EDMUND Well, he wasn't. You just want to believe no one but an Irish Catholic general could beat Napoleon.

TYRONE I'm not going to argue with you. I asked you to turn out that light in the hall.

EDMUND I heard you, and as far as I'm concerned it stays on.

TYRONE None of your damned insolence! Are you going to obey me or not?

EDMUND Not! If you want to be a crazy miser put it out yourself!

TYRONE [*with threatening anger*] Listen to me! I've put up with a lot from you because from the mad things you've done at times I've thought you weren't quite right in your head. I've excused you and never lifted my hand to you. But there's a straw that breaks the camel's back. You'll obey me and put out that light or, big as you are, I'll give you a thrashing that'll teach you—! [*Suddenly he remembers* EDMUND's *illness and instantly becomes guilty and shamefaced.*] Forgive me, lad. I forgot—You shouldn't goad me into losing my temper.

EDMUND [*ashamed himself now*]   Forget it, Papa. I apologize, too. I had no right being nasty about nothing. I am a bit soused, I guess. I'll put out the damned light. [*He starts to get up.*]

TYRONE   No, stay where you are. Let it burn.

> [*He stands up abruptly—and a bit drunkenly—and begins turning on the three bulbs in the chandelier, with a childish, bitterly dramatic self-pity.*]
>
> We'll have them all on! Let them burn! To hell with them! The poorhouse is the end of the road, and it might as well be sooner as later! [*He finishes turning on the lights.*]

EDMUND [*has watched this proceeding with an awakened sense of humor—now he grins, teasing affectionately*]   That's a grand curtain. [*He laughs.*] You're a wonder, Papa.

TYRONE [*sits down sheepishly—grumbles pathetically*]   That's right, laugh at the old fool! The poor old ham! But the final curtain will be in the poorhouse just the same, and that's not comedy! [*Then as* EDMUND *is still grinning, he changes the subject.*] Well, well, let's not argue. You've got brains in that head of yours, though you do your best to deny them. You'll live to learn the value of a dollar. You're not like your damned tramp of a brother. I've given up hope he'll ever get sense. Where is he, by the way?

EDMUND   How would I know?

TYRONE   I thought you'd gone back uptown to meet him.

EDMUND   No. I walked out to the beach. I haven't seen him since this afternoon.

TYRONE   Well, if you split the money I gave you with him, like a fool—

EDMUND   Sure I did. He's always staked me when he had anything.

TYRONE   Then it doesn't take a soothsayer to tell he's probably in the whorehouse.

EDMUND   What of it if he is? Why not?

TYRONE [*contemptuously*]   Why not, indeed. It's the fit place for him. If he's ever had a loftier dream than whores and whiskey, he's never shown it.

EDMUND   Oh, for Pete's sake, Papa! If you're going to start that stuff, I'll beat it. [*He starts to get up.*]

TYRONE [*placatingly*]   All right, all right, I'll stop. God knows, I don't like the subject either. Will you join me in a drink?

EDMUND   Ah! Now you're talking!

TYRONE [*passes the bottle to him—mechanically*]   I'm wrong to treat you. You've had enough already.

EDMUND [*pouring a big drink—a bit drunkenly*]   Enough is *not* as good as a feast. [*He hands back the bottle.*]

TYRONE   It's too much in your condition.

EDMUND   Forget my condition! [*He raises his glass.*] Here's how.

TYRONE   Drink hearty. [*They drink.*] If you walked all the way to the beach you must be damp and chilled.

EDMUND   Oh, I dropped in at the Inn on the way out and back.

TYRONE   It's not a night I'd pick for a long walk.

EDMUND   I loved the fog. It was what I needed. [*He sounds more tipsy and looks it.*]

TYRONE   You should have more sense than to risk—

EDMUND   To hell with sense! We're all crazy. What do we want with sense? [*He quotes from Dowson*[6] *sardonically.*]

> "They are not long, the weeping and the laughter,
> Love and desire and hate:
> I think they have no portion in us after
> We pass the gate.
>
> They are not long, the days of wine and roses:
> Out of a misty dream
> Our path emerges for a while, then closes
> Within a dream."

[*staring before him*] The fog was where I wanted to be. Halfway down the path you can't see this house. You'd never know it was here. Or any of the other places down the avenue. I couldn't see but a few feet ahead. I didn't meet a soul. Everything looked and sounded unreal. Nothing was what it is. That's what I wanted—to be alone with myself in another world where truth is untrue and life can hide from itself. Out beyond the harbor, where the road runs along the beach, I even lost the feeling of being on land. The fog and the sea seemed part of each other. It was like walking on the bottom of the sea. As if I had drowned long ago. As if I was a ghost belonging to the fog, and the fog was the ghost of the sea. It felt damned peaceful to be nothing more than a ghost within a ghost. [*He sees his father staring at him with mingled worry and irritated disapproval. He grins mockingly.*] Don't look at me as if I'd gone nutty. I'm talking sense. Who wants to see life as it is, if they can help it? It's the three Gorgons[7] in one. You look in their faces and turn to stone. Or it's Pan.[8] You see him and you die—that is, inside you—and have to go on living as a ghost.

TYRONE [*impressed and at the same time revolted*]   You have a poet in you but it's a damned morbid one! [*forcing a smile*] Devil take your pessimism. I feel low-spirited enough. [*He sighs.*] Why can't you remember your Shakespeare and forget the third-raters. You'll find what you're trying to say in him—as you'll find everything else worth saying. [*He quotes, using his fine voice*] "We are such stuff as dreams are made on, and our little life is rounded with a sleep."[9]

EDMUND [*ironically*]   Fine! That's beautiful. But I wasn't trying to say that. We are such stuff as manure is made on, so let's drink up and forget it. That's more my idea.

TYRONE [*disgustedly*]   Ach! Keep such sentiments to yourself. I shouldn't have given you that drink.

EDMUND   It did pack a wallop, all right. On you, too. [*He grins with affectionate teasing.*] Even if you've never missed a performance! [*aggressively*] Well, what's wrong with being drunk? It's what we're after, isn't it? Let's not kid each other, Papa. Not tonight. We know what we're trying to forget. [*hurriedly*] But let's not talk about it. It's no use now.

TYRONE [*dully*]   No. All we can do is try to be resigned—again.

---

6. Ernest Dowson (1867–1900), English poet.
7. In Greek mythology, three monstrous sisters so ugly that the sight of them turned one to stone.

8. Greek god of woods, fields, and flocks, half man and half goat, associated with wildness.
9. Shakespeare's *The Tempest* 4.1.156–58.

EDMUND   Or be so drunk you can forget. [*He recites, and recites well, with bitter, ironical passion, the Symons' translation of Baudelaire's*[1] *prose poem.*] "Be always drunken. Nothing else matters: that is the only question. If you would not feel the horrible burden of Time weighing on your shoulders and crushing you to the earth, be drunken continually.

"Drunken with what? With wine, with poetry, or with virtue, as you will. But be drunken.

"And if sometimes, on the stairs of a palace, or on the green side of a ditch, or in the dreary solitude of your own room, you should awaken and the drunkenness be half or wholly slipped away from you, ask of the wind, or of the wave, or of the star, or of the bird, or of the clock, of whatever flies, or sighs, or rocks, or sings, or speaks, ask what hour it is; and the wind, wave, star, bird, clock, will answer you: 'It is the hour to be drunken! Be drunken, if you would not be martyred slaves of Time; be drunken continually! With wine, with poetry, or with virtue, as you will.'" [*He grins at his father provocatively.*]

TYRONE   [*thickly humorous*]   I wouldn't worry about the virtue part of it, if I were you. [*then disgustedly*] Pah! It's morbid nonsense! What little truth is in it you'll find nobly said in Shakespeare. [*then appreciatively*] But you recited it well, lad. Who wrote it?

EDMUND   Baudelaire.

TYRONE   Never heard of him.

EDMUND   [*grins provocatively*]   He also wrote a poem about Jamie and the Great White Way.

TYRONE   That loafer! I hope to God he misses the last car and has to stay uptown!

EDMUND   [*goes on, ignoring this*]   Although he was French and never saw Broadway and died before Jamie was born, he knew him and Little Old New York just the same. [*He recites the Symons' translation of Baudelaire's "Epilogue."*]

> "With heart at rest I climbed the citadel's
> Steep height, and saw the city as from a tower,
> Hospital, brothel, prison, and such hells,
>
> Where evil comes up softly like a flower.
> Thou knowest, O Satan, patron of my pain,
> Not for vain tears I went up at that hour;
>
> But like an old sad faithful lecher, fain
> To drink delight of that enormous trull
> Whose hellish beauty makes me young again.
>
> Whether thou sleep, with heavy vapours full,
> Sodden with day, or, new apparelled, stand
> In gold-laced veils of evening beautiful,
>
> I love thee, infamous city! Harlots and
> Hunted have pleasures of their own to give,
> The vulgar herd can never understand."

---

1. Charles Baudelaire (1821–1867), French poet. Arthur Symons (1865–1945), English poet and literary critic.

TYRONE [*with irritable disgust*]   Morbid filth! Where the hell do you get your taste in literature? Filth and despair and pessimism! Another atheist, I suppose. When you deny God, you deny hope. That's the trouble with you. If you'd get down on your knees—

EDMUND [*as if he hadn't heard—sardonically*]   It's a good likeness of Jamie, don't you think, hunted by himself and whiskey, hiding in a Broadway hotel room with some fat tart—he likes them fat—reciting Dowson's Cynara to her. [*He recites derisively, but with deep feeling*]

> "All night upon mine heart I felt her warm heart beat,
> Night-long within mine arms in love and sleep she lay;
> Surely the kisses of her bought red mouth were sweet;
> But I was desolate and sick of an old passion,
> When I awoke and found the dawn was gray:
> I have been faithful to thee, Cynara! in my fashion."

[*jeeringly*] And the poor fat burlesque queen doesn't get a word of it, but suspects she's being insulted! And Jamie never loved any Cynara, and was never faithful to a woman in his life, even in his fashion! But he lies there, kidding himself he is superior and enjoys pleasures "the vulgar herd can never understand"! [*He laughs.*] It's nuts—completely nuts!

TYRONE [*vaguely—his voice thick*]   It's madness, yes. If you'd get on your knees and pray. When you deny God, you deny sanity.

EDMUND [*ignoring this*]   But who am I to feel superior? I've done the same damned thing. And it's no more crazy than Dowson himself, inspired by an absinthe hangover, writing it to a dumb barmaid, who thought he was a poor crazy souse, and gave him the gate to marry a waiter! [*He laughs—then soberly, with genuine sympathy*] Poor Dowson. Booze and consumption got him. [*He starts and for a second looks miserable and frightened. Then with defensive irony*] Perhaps it would be tactful of me to change the subject.

TYRONE [*thickly*]   Where you get your taste in authors—That damned library of yours! [*He indicates the small bookcase at rear.*] Voltaire, Rousseau, Schopenhauer, Nietzsche, Ibsen! Atheists, fools, and madmen! And your poets! This Dowson, and this Baudelaire, and Swinburne and Oscar Wilde, and Whitman and Poe! Whore-mongers and degenerates! Pah! When I've three good sets of Shakespeare there [*he nods at the large bookcase*] you could read.

EDMUND [*provocatively*]   They say he was a souse, too.

TYRONE   They lie! I don't doubt he liked his glass—it's a good man's failing—but he knew how to drink so it didn't poison his brain with morbidness and filth. Don't compare him with the pack you've got in there. [*He indicates the small bookcase again.*] Your dirty Zola! And your Dante Gabriel Rossetti who was a dope fiend! [*He starts and looks guilty.*]

EDMUND [*with defensive dryness*]   Perhaps it would be wise to change the subject. [*a pause*] You can't accuse me of not knowing Shakespeare. Didn't I win five dollars from you once when you bet me I couldn't learn a leading part of his in a week, as you used to do in stock in the old days. I learned Macbeth and recited it letter perfect, with you giving me the cues.

TYRONE [*approvingly*]   That's true. So you did. [*He smiles teasingly and sighs.*] It was a terrible ordeal, I remember, hearing you murder the lines. I kept wishing I'd paid over the bet without making you prove it.

> [*He chuckles and* EDMUND *grins. Then he starts as he hears a sound from upstairs—with dread*]

Did you hear? She's moving around. I was hoping she'd gone to sleep.

EDMUND   Forget it! How about another drink?

> [*He reaches out and gets the bottle, pours a drink and hands it back. Then with a strained casualness, as his father pours a drink*]

When did Mama go to bed?

TYRONE   Right after you left. She wouldn't eat any dinner. What made you run away?

EDMUND   Nothing. [*Abruptly raising his glass.*]   Well, here's how.

TYRONE [*mechanically*]   Drink hearty, lad. [*They drink.* TYRONE *again listens to sounds upstairs—with dread*] She's moving around a lot. I hope to God she doesn't come down.

EDMUND [*dully*]   Yes. She'll be nothing but a ghost haunting the past by this time. [*He pauses—then miserably*] Back before I was born—

TYRONE   Doesn't she do the same with me? Back before she ever knew me. You'd think the only happy days she's ever known were in her father's home, or at the Convent, praying and playing the piano. [*jealous resentment in his bitterness*] As I've told you before, you must take her memories with a grain of salt. Her wonderful home was ordinary enough. Her father wasn't the great, generous, noble Irish gentleman she makes out. He was a nice enough man, good company and a good talker. I liked him and he liked me. He was prosperous enough, too, in his wholesale grocery business, an able man. But he had his weakness. She condemns my drinking but she forgets his. It's true he never touched a drop till he was forty, but after that he made up for lost time. He became a steady champagne drinker, the worst kind. That was his grand pose, to drink only champagne. Well, it finished him quick—that and the consumption— [*He stops with a guilty glance at his son.*]

EDMUND [*sardonically*]   We don't seem able to avoid unpleasant topics, do we?

TYRONE [*sighs sadly*]   No. [*then with a pathetic attempt at heartiness*] What do you say to a game or two of Casino, lad?

EDMUND   All right.

TYRONE [*shuffling the cards clumsily*]   We can't lock up and go to bed till Jamie comes on the last trolley—which I hope he won't—and I don't want to go upstairs, anyway, till she's asleep.

EDMUND   Neither do I.

TYRONE [*keeps shuffling the cards fumblingly, forgetting to deal them*]   As I was saying, you must take her tales of the past with a grain of salt. The piano playing and her dream of becoming a concert pianist. That was put in her head by the nuns flattering her. She was their pet. They loved her for being so devout. They're innocent women, anyway, when it comes to the world. They don't know that not one in a million who shows promise ever rises to concert playing. Not that your mother didn't play well for a schoolgirl, but that's no reason to take it for granted she could have—

EDMUND [*sharply*]   Why don't you deal, if we're going to play.

TYRONE   Eh? I am. [*dealing with very uncertain judgment of distance*] And the idea she might have become a nun. That's the worst. Your mother was one of the most beautiful girls you could ever see. She knew it, too. She was a bit of a rogue and a coquette, God bless her, behind all her shyness and blushes. She was never made to renounce the world. She was bursting with health and high spirits and the love of loving.

EDMUND   For God's sake, Papa! Why don't you pick up your hand?

TYRONE [*picks it up—dully*]   Yes, let's see what I have here.

[*They both stare at their cards unseeingly. Then they both start.* TYRONE *whispers*]

Listen!

EDMUND   She's coming downstairs.

TYRONE [*hurriedly*]   We'll play our game. Pretend not to notice and she'll soon go up again.

EDMUND [*staring through the front parlor—with relief*]   I don't see her. She must have started down and then turned back.

TYRONE   Thank God.

EDMUND   Yes. It's pretty horrible to see her the way she must be now. [*with bitter misery*] The hardest thing to take is the blank wall she builds around her. Or it's more like a bank of fog in which she hides and loses herself. Deliberately, that's the hell of it! You know something in her does it deliberately—to get beyond our reach, to be rid of us, to forget we're alive! It's as if, in spite of loving us, she hated us!

TYRONE [*remonstrates gently*]   Now, now, lad. It's not her. It's the damned poison.

EDMUND [*bitterly*]   She takes it to get that effect. At least, I know she did this time! [*abruptly*] My play, isn't it? Here. [*He plays a card.*]

TYRONE [*plays mechanically—gently reproachful*]   She's been terribly frightened about your illness, for all her pretending. Don't be too hard on her, lad. Remember she's not responsible. Once that cursed poison gets a hold on anyone—

EDMUND [*his face grows hard and he stares at his father with bitter accusation*]   It never should have gotten a hold on her! I know damned well she's not to blame! And I know who is! You are! Your damned stinginess! If you'd spent money for a decent doctor when she was so sick after I was born, she'd never have known morphine existed! Instead you put her in the hands of a hotel quack who wouldn't admit his ignorance and took the easiest way out, not giving a damn what happened to her afterwards! All because his fee was cheap! Another one of your bargains!

TYRONE [*stung—angrily*]   Be quiet! How dare you talk of something you know nothing about! [*trying to control his temper*] You must try to see my side of it, too, lad. How was I to know he was that kind of a doctor? He had a good reputation—

EDMUND   Among the souses in the hotel bar, I suppose!

TYRONE   That's a lie! I asked the hotel proprietor to recommend the best—

EDMUND   Yes! At the same time crying poorhouse and making it plain you wanted a cheap one! I know your system! By God, I ought to after this afternoon!

TYRONE [*guiltily defensive*]   What about this afternoon?

EDMUND   Never mind now. We're talking about Mama! I'm saying no matter how you excuse yourself you know damned well your stinginess is to blame—

TYRONE   And I say you're a liar! Shut your mouth right now, or—

EDMUND [*ignoring this*]   After you found out she'd been made a morphine addict, why didn't you send her to a cure then, at the start, while she still had a chance? No, that would have meant spending some money! I'll bet you told her all she had to do was use a little will power! That's what you still believe in your heart, in spite of what doctors, who really know something about it, have told you!

TYRONE   You lie again! I know better than that now! But how was I to know then? What did I know of morphine? It was years before I discovered what was wrong. I thought she'd never got over her sickness, that's all. Why didn't I send her to a cure, you say? [*bitterly*] Haven't I? I've spent thousands upon thousands in cures! A waste. What good have they done her? She always started again.

EDMUND   Because you've never given her anything that would help her want to stay off it! No home except this summer dump in a place she hates and you've refused even to spend money to make this look decent, while you keep buying more property, and playing sucker for every con man with a gold mine, or a silver mine, or any kind of get-rich-quick swindle! You've dragged her around on the road, season after season, on one-night stands, with no one she could talk to, waiting night after night in dirty hotel rooms for you to come back with a bun on after the bars closed! Christ, is it any wonder she didn't want to be cured. Jesus, when I think of it I hate your guts!

TYRONE [*strickenly*]   Edmund! [*then in a rage*] How dare you talk to your father like that, you insolent young cub! After all I've done for you.

EDMUND   We'll come to that, what you're doing for me!

TYRONE [*looking guilty again—ignores this*]   Will you stop repeating your mother's crazy accusations, which she never makes unless it's the poison talking? I never dragged her on the road against her will. Naturally, I wanted her with me. I loved her. And she came because she loved me and wanted to be with me. That's the truth, no matter what she says when she's not herself. And she needn't have been lonely. There was always the members of my company to talk to, if she'd wanted. She had her children, too, and I insisted, in spite of the expense, on having a nurse to travel with her.

EDMUND [*bitterly*]   Yes, your one generosity, and that because you were jealous of her paying too much attention to us, and wanted us out of your way! It was another mistake, too! If she'd had to take care of me all by herself, and had that to occupy her mind, maybe she'd have been able—

TYRONE [*goaded into vindictiveness*]   Or for that matter, if you insist in judging things by what she says when she's not in her right mind, if you hadn't been born she'd never—[*He stops ashamed.*]

EDMUND [*suddenly spent and miserable*]   Sure. I know that's what she feels, Papa.

TYRONE [*protests penitently*]   She doesn't! She loves you as dearly as ever mother loved a son! I only said that because you put me in such a God-damned rage, raking up the past, and saying you hate me—

EDMUND [*dully*]   I didn't mean it, Papa. [*He suddenly smiles—kidding a bit drunkenly*] I'm like Mama, I can't help liking you, in spite of everything.

TYRONE [*grins a bit drunkenly in return*]   I might say the same of you. You're no great shakes as a son. It's a case of "A poor thing but mine own."[2] [*They both chuckle with real, if alcoholic, affection.* TYRONE *changes the subject.*] What's happened to our game? Whose play is it?

EDMUND   Yours, I guess.

> [TYRONE *plays a card which* EDMUND *takes and the game gets forgotten again.*]

TYRONE   You mustn't let yourself be too downhearted, lad, by the bad news you had today. Both the doctors promised me, if you obey orders at this place you're going, you'll be cured in six months, or a year at most.

EDMUND [*his face hard again*]   Don't kid me. You don't believe that.

TYRONE [*too vehemently*]   Of course I believe it! Why shouldn't I believe it when both Hardy and the specialist—?

EDMUND   You think I'm going to die.

TYRONE   That's a lie! You're crazy!

EDMUND [*more bitterly*]   So why waste money? That's why you're sending me to a state farm—

TYRONE [*in guilty confusion*]   What state farm? It's the Hilltown Sanatorium, that's all I know, and both doctors said it was the best place for you.

EDMUND [*scathingly*]   For the money! That is, for nothing, or practically nothing. Don't lie, Papa! You know damned well Hilltown Sanatorium is a state institution! Jamie suspected you'd cry poorhouse to Hardy and he wormed the truth out of him.

TYRONE [*furiously*]   That drunken loafer! I'll kick him out in the gutter! He's poisoned your mind against me ever since you were old enough to listen!

EDMUND   You can't deny it's the truth about the state farm, can you?

TYRONE   It's not true the way you look at it! What if it is run by the state? That's nothing against it. The state has the money to make a better place than any private sanatorium. And why shouldn't I take advantage of it? It's my right—and yours. We're residents. I'm a property owner. I help to support it. I'm taxed to death—

EDMUND [*with bitter irony*]   Yes, on property valued at a quarter of a million.

TYRONE   Lies! It's all mortgaged!

EDMUND   Hardy and the specialist know what you're worth. I wonder what they thought of you when they heard you moaning poorhouse and showing you wanted to wish me on charity!

TYRONE   It's a lie! All I told them was I couldn't afford any millionaire's sanatorium because I was land poor. That's the truth!

EDMUND   And then you went to the Club to meet McGuire and let him stick you with another bum piece of property! [*as* TYRONE *starts to deny*] Don't lie about it! We met McGuire in the hotel bar after he left you. Jamie kidded him about hooking you, and he winked and laughed!

TYRONE [*lying feebly*]   He's a liar if he said—

---

2. Shakespeare's *As You Like It* 5.4.60.

EDMUND   Don't lie about it! [*with gathering intensity*] God, Papa, ever since I went to sea and was on my own, and found out what hard work for little pay was, and what it felt like to be broke, and starve, and camp on park benches because I had no place to sleep, I've tried to be fair to you because I knew what you'd been up against as a kid. I've tried to make allowances. Christ, you have to make allowances in this damned family or go nuts! I have tried to make allowances for myself when I remember all the rotten stuff I've pulled! I've tried to feel like Mama that you can't help being what you are where money is concerned. But God Almighty, this last stunt of yours is too much! It makes me want to puke! Not because of the rotten way you're treating me. To hell with that! I've treated you rottenly, in my way, more than once. But to think when it's a question of your son having consumption, you can show yourself up before the whole town as such a stinking old tightwad! Don't you know Hardy will talk and the whole damned town will know! Jesus, Papa, haven't you any pride or shame? [*bursting with rage*] And don't think I'll let you get away with it! I won't go to any damned state farm just to save you a few lousy dollars to buy more bum property with! You stinking old miser—! [*He chokes huskily, his voice trembling with rage, and then is shaken by a fit of coughing.*]

TYRONE [*has shrunk back in his chair under this attack, his guilty contrition greater than his anger—he stammers*]   Be quiet! Don't say that to me! You're drunk! I won't mind you. Stop coughing, lad. You've got yourself worked up over nothing. Who said you had to go to this Hilltown place? You can go anywhere you like. I don't give a damn what it costs. All I care about is to have you get well. Don't call me a stinking miser, just because I don't want doctors to think I'm a millionaire they can swindle.

> [EDMUND *has stopped coughing. He looks sick and weak. His father stares at him frightenedly.*]

You look weak, lad. You'd better take a bracer.

EDMUND [*grabs the bottle and pours his glass brimfull—weakly*]   Thanks. [*He gulps down the whiskey.*]

TYRONE [*pours himself a big drink, which empties the bottle, and drinks it; his head bows and he stares dully at the cards on the table—vaguely*] Whose play is it? [*He goes on dully, without resentment.*] A stinking old miser. Well, maybe you're right. Maybe I can't help being, although all my life since I had anything I've thrown money over the bar to buy drinks for everyone in the house, or loaned money to sponges I knew would never pay it back—[*with a loose-mouthed sneer of self-contempt*] But, of course, that was in barrooms, when I was full of whiskey. I can't feel that way about it when I'm sober in my home. It was at home I first learned the value of a dollar and the fear of the poorhouse. I've never been able to believe in my luck since. I've always feared it would change and everything I had would be taken away. But still, the more property you own, the safer you think you are. That may not be logical, but it's the way I have to feel. Banks fail, and your money's gone, but you think you can keep land beneath your feet. [*Abruptly his tone becomes scornfully superior.*] You said you realized what I'd been up against as a boy. The hell you do! How could you? You've had everything—nurses, schools, college, though you didn't stay there. You've had food, clothing. Oh, I know you had a fling of hard work with your back and hands, a bit of being homeless and penniless in a foreign land, and I respect you for it. But it was a game of romance and adventure to you. It was play.

EDMUND [*dully sarcastic*]   Yes, particularly the time I tried to commit suicide at Jimmie the Priest's, and almost did.

TYRONE   You weren't in your right mind. No son of mine would ever—You were drunk.

EDMUND   I was stone cold sober. That was the trouble. I'd stopped to think too long.

TYRONE [*with drunken peevishness*]   Don't start your damned atheist morbidness again! I don't care to listen. I was trying to make plain to you— [*scornfully*] What do you know of the value of a dollar? When I was ten my father deserted my mother and went back to Ireland to die. Which he did soon enough, and deserved to, and I hope he's roasting in hell. He mistook rat poison for flour, or sugar, or something. There was gossip it wasn't by mistake but that's a lie. No one in my family ever—

EDMUND   My bet is, it wasn't by mistake.

TYRONE   More morbidness! Your brother put that in your head. The worst he can suspect is the only truth for him. But never mind. My mother was left, a stranger in a strange land, with four small children, me and a sister a little older and two younger than me. My two older brothers had moved to other parts. They couldn't help. They were hard put to it to keep themselves alive. There was no damned romance in our poverty. Twice we were evicted from the miserable hovel we called home, with my mother's few sticks of furniture thrown out in the street, and my mother and sisters crying. I cried, too, though I tried hard not to, because I was the man of the family. At ten years old! There was no more school for me. I worked twelve hours a day in a machine shop, learning to make files. A dirty barn of a place where rain dripped through the roof, where you roasted in summer, and there was no stove in winter, and your hands got numb with cold, where the only light came through two small filthy windows, so on grey days I'd have to sit bent over with my eyes almost touching the files in order to see! You talk of work! And what do you think I got for it? Fifty cents a week! It's the truth! Fifty cents a week! And my poor mother washed and scrubbed for the Yanks by the day, and my older sister sewed, and my two younger stayed at home to keep the house. We never had clothes enough to wear, nor enough food to eat. Well I remember one Thanksgiving, or maybe it was Christmas, when some Yank in whose house mother had been scrubbing gave her a dollar extra for a present, and on the way home she spent it all on food. I can remember her hugging and kissing us and saying with tears of joy running down her tired face: "Glory be to God, for once in our lives we'll have enough for each of us!" [*He wipes tears from his eyes.*] A fine, brave, sweet woman. There never was a braver or finer.

EDMUND [*moved*]   Yes, she must have been.

TYRONE   Her one fear was she'd get old and sick and have to die in the poorhouse. [*He pauses—then adds with grim humor*] It was in those days I learned to be a miser. A dollar was worth so much then. And once you've learned a lesson, it's hard to unlearn it. You have to look for bargains. If

I took this state farm sanatorium for a good bargain, you'll have to forgive me. The doctors did tell me it's a good place. You must believe that, Edmund. And I swear I never meant you to go there if you didn't want to. [*vehemently*] You can choose any place you like! Never mind what it costs! Any place I can afford. Any place you like—within reason.

> [*At this qualification, a grin twitches* EDMUND'S *lips. His resentment has gone. His father goes on with an elaborately offhand, casual air.*]

There was another sanatorium the specialist recommended. He said it had a record as good as any place in the country. It's endowed by a group of millionaire factory owners, for the benefit of their workers principally, but you're eligible to go there because you're a resident. There's such a pile of money behind it, they don't have to charge much. It's only seven dollars a week but you get ten times that value. [*hastily*] I don't want to persuade you to anything, understand. I'm simply repeating what I was told.

EDMUND [*concealing his smile—casually*]   Oh, I know that. It sounds like a good bargain to me. I'd like to go there. So that settles that. [*Abruptly he is miserably desperate again—dully*] It doesn't matter a damn now, anyway. Let's forget it! [*changing the subject*] How about our game? Whose play is it?

TYRONE [*mechanically*]   I don't know. Mine, I guess. No, it's yours.

> [EDMUND *plays a card. His father takes it. Then about to play from his hand, he again forgets the game.*]

Yes, maybe life overdid the lesson for me, and made a dollar worth too much, and the time came when that mistake ruined my career as a fine actor. [*sadly*] I've never admitted this to anyone before, lad, but tonight I'm so heartsick I feel at the end of everything, and what's the use of fake pride and pretense. That God-damned play I bought for a song and made such a great success in—a great money success—it ruined me with its promise of an easy fortune. I didn't want to do anything else, and by the time I woke up to the fact I'd become a slave to the damned thing and did try other plays, it was too late. They had identified me with that one part, and didn't want me in anything else. They were right, too. I'd lost the great talent I once had through years of easy repetition, never learning a new part, never really working hard. Thirty-five to forty thousand dollars net profit a season like snapping your fingers! It was too great a temptation. Yet before I bought the damned thing I was considered one of the three or four young actors with the greatest artistic promise in America. I'd worked like hell. I'd left a good job as a machinist to take supers'[3] parts because I loved the theater. I was wild with ambition. I read all the plays ever written. I studied Shakespeare as you'd study the Bible. I educated myself. I got rid of an Irish brogue you could cut with a knife. I loved Shakespeare. I would have acted in any of his plays for nothing, for the joy of being alive in his great poetry. And I acted well in him. I felt inspired by him. I could have been a great Shakespearean actor, if I'd kept on. I know that! In 1874 when Edwin Booth[4] came to the theater in Chicago where I was leading man, I played Cassius to his Brutus one

3. Supernumeraries, extras.
4. Edwin Booth (1833–1893), American actor and theatrical manager.

night, Brutus to his Cassius the next, Othello to his Iago, and so on. The first night I played Othello, he said to our manager. "That young man is playing Othello better than I ever did!" [*proudly*] That from Booth, the greatest actor of his day or any other! And it was true! And I was only twenty-seven years old! As I look back on it now, that night was the high spot in my career. I had life where I wanted it! And for a time after that I kept on upward with ambition high. Married your mother. Ask her what I was like in those days. Her love was an added incentive to ambition. But a few years later my good bad luck made me find the big money-maker. It wasn't that in my eyes at first. It was a great romantic part I knew I could play better than anyone. But it was a great box office success from the start—and then life had me where it wanted me—at from thirty-five to forty thousand net profit a season! A fortune in those days—or even in these. [*bitterly*] What the hell was it I wanted to buy, I wonder, that was worth—Well, no matter. It's a late day for regrets. [*He glances vaguely at his cards.*] My play, isn't it?

EDMUND [*moved, stares at his father with understanding—slowly*]   I'm glad you've told me this, Papa. I know you a lot better now.

TYRONE [*with a loose, twisted smile*]   Maybe I shouldn't have told you. Maybe you'll only feel more contempt for me. And it's a poor way to convince you of the value of a dollar. [*Then as if this phrase automatically aroused an habitual association in his mind, he glances up at the chandelier disapprovingly.*] The glare from those extra lights hurts my eyes. You don't mind if I turn them out, do you? We don't need them, and there's no use making the Electric Company rich.

EDMUND [*controlling a wild impulse to laugh—agreeably*]   No, sure not. Turn them out.

TYRONE [*gets heavily and a bit waveringly to his feet and gropes uncertainly for the lights—his mind going back to its line of thought*]   No, I don't know what the hell it was I wanted to buy. [*He clicks out one bulb.*] On my solemn oath, Edmund, I'd gladly face not having an acre of land to call my own, nor a penny in the bank—[*He clicks out another bulb.*] I'd be willing to have no home but the poorhouse in my old age if I could look back now on having been the fine artist I might have been.

> [*He turns out the third bulb, so only the reading lamp is on, and sits down again heavily.* EDMUND *suddenly cannot hold back a burst of strained, ironical laughter.* TYRONE *is hurt.*]

What the devil are you laughing at?

EDMUND   Not at you, Papa. At life. It's so damned crazy.

TYRONE [*growls*]   More of your morbidness! There's nothing wrong with life. It's we who—[*He quotes*] "The fault, dear Brutus, is not in our stars, but in ourselves that we are underlings."[5] [*He pauses—then sadly*] The praise Edwin Booth gave my Othello. I made the manager put down his exact words in writing. I kept it in my wallet for years. I used to read it every once in a while until finally it made me feel so bad I didn't want to face it any more. Where is it now, I wonder? Somewhere in this house. I remember I put it away carefully—

---

5. Shakespeare's *Julius Caesar* 1.2.134.

EDMUND [*with a wry ironical sadness*]   It might be in an old trunk in the attic, along with Mama's wedding dress. [*Then as his father stares at him, he adds quickly*] For Pete's sake, if we're going to play cards, let's play.

> [*He takes the card his father had played and leads. For a moment, they play the game, like mechanical chess players. Then* TYRONE *stops, listening to a sound upstairs.*]

TYRONE   She's still moving around. God knows when she'll go to sleep.

EDMUND [*pleads tensely*]   For Christ's sake, Papa, forget it!

> [*He reaches out and pours a drink.* TYRONE *starts to protest, then gives it up.* EDMUND *drinks. He puts down the glass. His expression changes. When he speaks it is as if he were deliberately giving way to drunkenness and seeking to hide behind a maudlin manner.*]

Yes, she moves above and beyond us, a ghost haunting the past, and here we sit pretending to forget, but straining our ears listening for the slightest sound, hearing the fog drip from the eaves like the uneven tick of a rundown, crazy clock—or like the dreary tears of a trollop spattering in a puddle of stale beer on a honky-tonk table top! [*He laughs with maudlin appreciation.*] Not so bad, that last, eh? Original, not Baudelaire. Give me credit! [*then with alcoholic talkativeness*] You've just told me some high spots in your memories. Want to hear mine? They're all connected with the sea. Here's one. When I was on the Squarehead square rigger, bound for Buenos Aires. Full moon in the Trades. The old hooker driving fourteen knots. I lay on the bowsprit, facing astern, with the water foaming into spume under me, the masts with every sail white in the moonlight, towering high above me. I became drunk with the beauty and singing rhythm of it, and for a moment I lost myself—actually lost my life. I was set free! I dissolved in the sea, became white sails and flying spray, became beauty and rhythm, became moonlight and the ship and the high dim-starred sky! I belonged, without past or future, within peace and unity and a wild joy, within something greater than my own life, or the life of Man, to Life itself! To God, if you want to put it that way. Then another time, on the American Line, when I was lookout on the crow's nest in the dawn watch. A calm sea, that time. Only a lazy ground swell and a slow drowsy roll of the ship. The passengers asleep and none of the crew in sight. No sound of man. Black smoke pouring from the funnels behind and beneath me. Dreaming, not keeping lookout, feeling alone, and above, and apart, watching the dawn creep like a painted dream over the sky and sea which slept together. Then the moment of ecstatic freedom came. The peace, the end of the quest, the last harbor, the joy of belonging to a fulfillment beyond men's lousy, pitiful, greedy fears and hopes and dreams! And several other times in my life, when I was swimming far out, or lying alone on a beach, I have had the same experience. Became the sun, the hot sand, green seaweed anchored to a rock, swaying in the tide. Like a saint's vision of beatitude. Like the veil of things as they seem drawn back by an unseen hand. For a second you see—and seeing the secret, are the secret. For a second there is meaning! Then the hand lets the veil fall and you are alone, lost in the fog again, and you stumble on toward nowhere, for no good reason! [*He grins wryly.*] It was a great mistake, my being born a man, I would have been much more successful as a sea gull or a fish. As it is,

I will always be a stranger who never feels at home, who does not really want and is not really wanted, who can never belong, who must always be a little in love with death!

TYRONE [*stares at him—impressed*]   Yes, there's the makings of a poet in you all right. [*then protesting uneasily*] But that's morbid craziness about not being wanted and loving death.

EDMUND [*sardonically*]   The *makings* of a poet. No, I'm afraid I'm like the guy who is always panhandling for a smoke. He hasn't even got the makings. He's got only the habit. I couldn't touch what I tried to tell you just now. I just stammered. That's the best I'll ever do. I mean, if I live. Well, it will be faithful realism, at least. Stammering is the native eloquence of us fog people.

[*A pause. Then they both jump startledly as there is a noise from outside the house, as if someone had stumbled and fallen on the front steps. EDMUND grins.*]

Well, that sounds like the absent brother. He must have a peach of a bun on.

TYRONE [*scowling*]   That loafer! He caught the last car, bad luck to it. [*He gets to his feet.*] Get him to bed, Edmund. I'll go out on the porch. He has a tongue like an adder when he's drunk. I'd only lose my temper.

[*He goes out the door to the side porch as the front door in the hall bangs shut behind JAMIE. EDMUND watches with amusement JAMIE's wavering progress through the front parlor. JAMIE comes in. He is very drunk and woozy on his legs. His eyes are glassy, his face bloated, his speech blurred, his mouth slack like his father's, a leer on his lips.*]

JAMIE [*swaying and blinking in the doorway—in a loud voice*]   What ho! What ho!

EDMUND [*sharply*]   Nix on the loud noise!

JAMIE [*blinks at him*]   Oh, hello, Kid. [*with great seriousness*] I'm as drunk as a fiddler's bitch.

EDMUND [*dryly*]   Thanks for telling me your great secret.

JAMIE [*grins foolishly*]   Yes. Unneshesary information Number One, eh? [*He bends and slaps at the knees of his trousers.*] Had serious accident. The front steps tried to trample on me. Took advantage of fog to waylay me. Ought to be a lighthouse out there. Dark in here, too. [*scowling*] What the hell is this, the morgue? Lesh have some light on subject. [*He sways forward to the table, reciting Kipling*[6]]

"Ford, ford, ford o' Kabul river,
Ford o' Kabul river in the dark!
Keep the crossing-stakes beside you, an' they
will surely guide you
'Cross the ford o' Kabul river in the dark."

[*He fumbles at the chandelier and manages to turn on the three bulbs.*] Thash more like it. The hell with old Gaspard.[7] Where is the old tightwad?

EDMUND   Out on the porch.

---

6. Rudyard Kipling (1865–1936), English author.
7. Jamie's contemptuous name for his father, drawn from a character in the popular drama *The Bells*.

JAMIE   Can't expect us to live in the Black Hole of Calcutta.[8] [*His eyes fix on the full bottle of whiskey.*] Say! Have I got the d.t.'s?[9] [*He reaches out fumblingly and grabs it.*] By God, it's real. What's matter with the Old Man tonight? Must be ossified to forget he left this out. Grab opportunity by the forelock. Key to my success. [*He slops a big drink into a glass.*]

EDMUND   You're stinking now. That will knock you stiff.

JAMIE   Wisdom from the mouth of babes. Can the wise stuff, Kid. You're still wet behind the ears. [*He lowers himself into a chair, holding the drink carefully aloft.*]

EDMUND   All right. Pass out if you want to.

JAMIE   Can't, that's trouble. Had enough to sink a ship, but can't sink. Well, here's hoping. [*He drinks.*]

EDMUND   Shove over the bottle. I'll have one, too.

JAMIE   [*with sudden, big-brotherly solicitude, grabbing the bottle*]   No, you don't. Not while I'm around. Remember doctor's orders. Maybe no one else gives a damn if you die, but I do. My kid brother. I love your guts, Kid. Everything else is gone. You're all I've got left. [*pulling bottle closer to him*] So no booze for you, if I can help it. [*Beneath his drunken sentimentality there is a genuine sincerity.*]

EDMUND   [*irritably*]   Oh, lay off it.

JAMIE   [*is hurt and his face hardens*]   You don't believe I care, eh? Just drunken bull. [*He shoves the bottle over.*] All right. Go ahead and kill yourself.

EDMUND   [*seeing he is hurt—affectionately*]   Sure I know you care, Jamie, and I'm going on the wagon. But tonight doesn't count. Too many damned things have happened today. [*He pours a drink.*] Here's how. [*He drinks.*]

JAMIE   [*sobers up momentarily and with a pitying look*]   I know, Kid. It's been a lousy day for you. [*then with sneering cynicism*] I'll bet old Gaspard hasn't tried to keep you off booze. Probably give you a case to take with you to the state farm for pauper patients. The sooner you kick the bucket, the less expense. [*with contemptuous hatred*] What a bastard to have for a father! Christ, if you put him in a book, no one would believe it!

EDMUND   [*defensively*]   Oh, Papa's all right, if you try to understand him— and keep your sense of humor.

JAMIE   [*cynically*]   He's been putting on the old sob act for you, eh? He can always kid you. But not me. Never again. [*then slowly*] Although, in a way, I do feel sorry for him about one thing. But he has even that coming to him. He's to blame. [*hurriedly*] But to hell with that. [*He grabs the bottle and pours another drink, appearing very drunk again.*] That lash drink's getting me. This one ought to put the lights out. Did you tell Gaspard I got it out of Doc Hardy this sanatorium is a charity dump?

EDMUND   [*reluctantly*]   Yes. I told him I wouldn't go there. It's all settled now. He said I can go anywhere I want. [*He adds, smiling without resentment*] Within reason, of course.

JAMIE   [*drunkenly imitating his father*]   Of course, lad. Anything within reason. [*sneering*] That means another cheap dump. Old Gaspard, the miser in "The Bells," that's a part he can play without make-up.

---

8. Small dungeon in Calcutta, India, where, on June 20, 1756, 123 of 146 British prisoners died of suffocation. Hence, any small, cramped space.
9. Delirium tremens.

EDMUND [*irritably*]   Oh, shut up, will you. I've heard that Gaspard stuff a
million times.

JAMIE [*shrugs his shoulders—thickly*]   Aw right, if you're shatisfied—let
him get away with it. It's your funeral—I mean, I hope it won't be.

EDMUND [*changing the subject*]   What did you do uptown tonight? Go to
Mamie Burns?

JAMIE [*very drunk, his head nodding*]   Sure thing. Where else could I find
suitable feminine companionship? And love. Don't forget love. What is
a man without a good woman's love? A God-damned hollow shell.

EDMUND [*chuckles tipsily, letting himself go now and be drunk*]   You're
a nut.

JAMIE [*quotes with gusto from Oscar Wilde's[1] "The Harlot's House"*]

"Then, turning to my love, I said,
'The dead are dancing with the dead,
The dust is whirling with the dust.'

But she—she heard the violin,
And left my side and entered in:
Love passed into the house of lust.

Then suddenly the tune went false,
The dancers wearied of the waltz . . ."

[*He breaks off, thickly*] Not strictly accurate. If my love was with me, I
didn't notice it. She must have been a ghost. [*He pauses.*] Guess which
one of Mamie's charmers I picked to bless me with her woman's love.
It'll hand you a laugh, Kid. I picked Fat Violet.

EDMUND [*laughs drunkenly*]   No, honest? Some pick! God, she weighs a
ton. What the hell for, a joke?

JAMIE   No joke. Very serious. By the time I hit Mamie's dump I felt very
sad about myself and all the other poor bums in the world. Ready for a
weep on any old womanly bosom. You know how you get when John Barleycorn turns on the soft music inside you. Then, soon as I got in the
door, Mamie began telling me all her troubles. Beefed how rotten business was, and she was going to give Fat Violet the gate. Customers didn't
fall for Vi. Only reason she'd kept her was she could play the piano. Lately
Vi's gone on drunks and been too boiled to play, and was eating her out of
house and home, and although Vi was a goodhearted dumbbell, and she
felt sorry for her because she didn't know how the hell she'd make a living, still business was business, and she couldn't afford to run a house for
fat tarts. Well, that made me feel sorry for Fat Violet, so I squandered two
bucks of your dough to escort her upstairs. With no dishonorable intentions whatever. I like them fat, but not that fat. All I wanted was a little
heart-to-heart talk concerning the infinite sorrow of life.

EDMUND [*chuckles drunkenly*]   Poor Vi! I'll bet you recited Kipling and
Swinburne and Dowson and gave her "I have been faithful to thee,
Cynara, in my fashion."

JAMIE [*grins loosely*]   Sure—with the Old Master, John Barleycorn, playing soft music. She stood it for a while. Then she got good and sore.

---

1. Irish author (1854–1900).

Got the idea I took her upstairs for a joke. Gave me a grand bawling out. Said she was better than a drunken bum who recited poetry. Then she began to cry. So I had to say I loved her because she was fat, and she wanted to believe that, and I stayed with her to prove it, and that cheered her up, and she kissed me when I left, and said she'd fallen hard for me, and we both cried a little more in the hallway, and everything was fine, except Mamie Burns thought I'd gone bughouse.

EDMUND [*quotes derisively*]

> "Harlots and
> Hunted have pleasures of their own to give,
> The vulgar herd can never understand."

JAMIE [*nods his head drunkenly*]   Egzactly! Hell of a good time, at that. You should have stuck around with me, Kid. Mamie Burns inquired after you. Sorry to hear you were sick. She meant it, too. [*He pauses— then with maudlin humor, in a ham-actor tone*] This night has opened my eyes to a great career in store for me, my boy! I shall give the art of acting back to the performing seals, which are its most perfect expression. By applying my natural God-given talents in their proper sphere, I shall attain the pinnacle of success! I'll be the lover of the fat woman in Barnum and Bailey's circus! [EDMUND *laughs.* JAMIE's *mood changes to arrogant disdain.*] Pah! Imagine me sunk to the fat girl in a hick town hooker shop! Me! Who have made some of the best-lookers on Broadway sit up and beg! [*He quotes from Kipling's "Sestina of the Tramp-Royal"*]

> "Speakin' in general, I 'ave tried 'em all,
> The 'appy roads that take you o'er the world."

[*with sodden melancholy*] Not so apt. Happy roads is bunk. Weary roads is right. Get you nowhere fast. That's where I've got—nowhere. Where everyone lands in the end, even if most of the suckers won't admit it.

EDMUND [*derisively*]   Can it! You'll be crying in a minute.

JAMIE [*starts and stares at his brother for a second with bitter hostility— thickly*]   Don't get—too damned fresh. [*then abruptly*] But you're right. To hell with repining! Fat Violet's a good kid. Glad I stayed with her. Christian act. Cured her blues. Hell of a good time. You should have stuck with me, Kid. Taken your mind off your troubles. What's the use coming home to get the blues over what can't be helped. All over— finished now—not a hope! [*He stops, his head nodding drunkenly, his eyes closing—then suddenly he looks up, his face hard, and quotes jeeringly.*]

> "If I were hanged on the highest hill,
> Mother o' mine, O mother o' mine!
> I know whose love would follow me still . . ."

EDMUND [*violently*]   Shut up!

JAMIE [*in a cruel, sneering tone with hatred in it*]   Where's the hophead? Gone to sleep?

> [EDMUND *jerks as if he'd been struck. There is a tense silence.* EDMUND's *face looks stricken and sick. Then in a burst of rage he springs from his chair.*]

EDMUND   You dirty bastard!

[*He punches his brother in the face, a blow that glances off the cheekbone. For a second* JAMIE *reacts pugnaciously and half rises from his chair to do battle, but suddenly he seems to sober up to a shocked realization of what he has said and he sinks back limply.*]

JAMIE [*miserably*] Thanks, Kid. I certainly had that coming. Don't know what made me—booze talking—You know me, Kid.

EDMUND [*his anger ebbing*] I know you'd never say that unless—But God, Jamie, no matter how drunk you are, it's no excuse! [*He pauses—miserably*] I'm sorry I hit you. You and I never scrap—that bad. [*He sinks back on his chair.*]

JAMIE [*huskily*] It's all right. Glad you did. My dirty tongue. Like to cut it out. [*He hides his face in his hands—dully*] I suppose it's because I feel so damned sunk. Because this time Mama had me fooled. I really believed she had it licked. She thinks I always believe the worst, but this time I believed the best. [*His voice flutters.*] I suppose I can't forgive her—yet. It meant so much. I'd begun to hope, if she'd beaten the game, I could, too. [*He begins to sob, and the horrible part of his weeping is that it appears sober, not the maudlin tears of drunkenness.*]

EDMUND [*blinking back tears himself*] God, don't I know how you feel! Stop it, Jamie!

JAMIE [*trying to control his sobs*] I've known about Mama so much longer than you. Never forget the first time I got wise. Caught her in the act with a hypo. Christ, I'd never dreamed before that any women but whores took dope! [*He pauses.*] And then this stuff of you getting consumption. It's got me licked. We've been more than brothers. You're the only pal I've ever had. I love your guts. I'd do anything for you.

EDMUND [*reaches out and pats his arm*] I know that, Jamie.

JAMIE [*his crying over—drops his hands from his face—with a strange bitterness*] Yet I'll bet you've heard Mama and old Gaspard spill so much bunk about my hoping for the worst, you suspect right now I'm thinking to myself that Papa is old and can't last much longer, and if you were to die, Mama and I would get all he's got, and so I'm probably hoping—

EDMUND [*indignantly*] Shut up, you damned fool! What the hell put that in your nut? [*He stares at his brother accusingly.*] Yes, that's what I'd like to know. What put that in your mind?

JAMIE [*confusedly—appearing drunk again*] Don't be a dumbbell! What I said! Always suspected of hoping for the worst. I've got so I can't help— [*then drunkenly resentful*] What are you trying to do, accuse me? Don't play the wise guy with me! I've learned more of life than you'll ever know! Just because you've read a lot of highbrow junk, don't think you can fool me! You're only an overgrown kid! Mama's baby and Papa's pet! The family White Hope! You've been getting a swelled head lately. About nothing! About a few poems in a hick town newspaper! Hell, I used to write better stuff for the Lit magazine in college! You better wake up! You're setting no rivers on fire! You let hick town boobs flatter you with bunk about your future—

[*Abruptly his tone changes to disgusted contrition.* EDMUND *has looked away from him, trying to ignore this tirade.*]

Hell, Kid, forget it. That goes for Sweeny. You know I don't mean it. No one hopes more than I do you'll knock 'em all dead. No one is prouder you've started to make good. [*drunkenly assertive*] Why shouldn't I be proud? Hell, it's purely selfish. You reflect credit on me. I've had more to do with bringing you up than anyone. I wised you up about women, so you'd never be a fall guy, or make any mistakes you didn't want to make! And who steered you on to reading poetry first? Swinburne,[2] for example? I did! And because I once wanted to write, I planted it in your mind that someday you'd write! Hell, you're more than my brother. I made you! You're my Frankenstein![3]

> [*He has risen to a note of drunken arrogance.* EDMUND *is grinning with amusement now.*]

EDMUND   All right, I'm your Frankenstein. So let's have a drink. [*He laughs.*] You crazy nut!

JAMIE [*thickly*]   I'll have a drink. Not you. Got to take care of you. [*He reaches out with a foolish grin of doting affection and grabs his brother's hand.*] Don't be scared of this sanatorium business. Hell, you can beat that standing on your head. Six months and you'll be in the pink. Probably haven't got consumption at all. Doctors lot of fakers. Told me years ago to cut out booze or I'd soon be dead—and here I am. They're all con men. Anything to grab your dough. I'll bet this state farm stuff is political graft game. Doctors get a cut for every patient they send.

EDMUND [*disgustedly amused*]   You're the limit! At the Last Judgment, you'll be around telling everyone it's in the bag.

JAMIE   And I'll be right. Slip a piece of change to the Judge and be saved, but if you're broke you can go to hell!

> [*He grins at this blasphemy and* EDMUND *has to laugh.* JAMIE *goes on.*]

"Therefore put money in thy purse."[4] That's the only dope. [*mockingly*] The secret of my success! Look what it's got me!

> [*He lets* EDMUND's *hand go to pour a big drink, and gulps it down. He stares at his brother with bleary affection—takes his hand again and begins to talk thickly but with a strange, convincing sincerity.*]

Listen, Kid, you'll be going away. May not get another chance to talk. Or might not be drunk enough to tell you truth. So got to tell you now. Something I ought to have told you long ago—for your own good.

> [*He pauses—struggling with himself.* EDMUND *stares, impressed and uneasy. Jamie blurts out*]

Not drunken bull, but "in vino veritas"[5] stuff. You better take it seriously. Want to warn you—against me. Mama and Papa are right. I've been rotten bad influence. And worst of it is, I did it on purpose.

EDMUND [*uneasily*]   Shut up! I don't want to hear—

JAMIE   Nix, Kid! You listen! Did it on purpose to make a bum of you. Or part of me did. A big part. That part that's been dead so long. That hates life. My putting you wise so you'd learn from my mistakes. Believed that myself at times, but it's a fake. Made my mistakes look good. Made getting drunk romantic. Made whores fascinating vampires instead of poor, stupid, diseased slobs they really are. Made fun of work as sucker's game. Never wanted you to succeed and make me look even worse

---

2. Algernon Charles Swinburne (1837–1909), English poet and critic.
3. In the novel *Frankenstein* by the English author Mary Shelley (1797–1851), the scientist Dr. Frankenstein creates a monster. Jamie confuses the scientist with his creation, although it is possible that the mistake is O'Neill's.
4. Shakespeare's *Othello* 1.3.354.
5. In wine there is truth (Latin).

by comparison. Wanted you to fail. Always jealous of you. Mama's baby, Papa's pet! [*He stares at* EDMUND *with increasing enmity.*] And it was your being born that started Mama on dope. I know that's not your fault, but all the same, God damn you, I can't help hating your guts—!

EDMUND [*almost frightenedly*]   Jamie! Cut it out! You're crazy!

JAMIE   But don't get wrong idea, Kid. I love you more than I hate you. My saying what I'm telling you now proves it. I run the risk you'll hate me— and you're all I've got left. But I didn't mean to tell you that last stuff—go that far back. Don't know what made me. What I wanted to say is, I'd like to see you become the greatest success in the world. But you'd better be on your guard. Because I'll do my damnedest to make you fail. Can't help it. I hate myself. Got to take revenge. On everyone else. Especially you. Oscar Wilde's "Reading Gaol" has the dope twisted. The man was dead and so he had to kill the thing he loved. That's what it ought to be. The dead part of me hopes you won't get well. Maybe he's even glad the game has got Mama again! He wants company, he doesn't want to be the only corpse around the house! [*He gives a hard, tortured laugh.*]

EDMUND   Jesus, Jamie! You really have gone crazy!

JAMIE   Think it over and you'll see I'm right. Think it over when you're away from me in the sanatorium. Make up your mind you've got to tie a can to me—get me out of your life—think of me as dead—tell people, "I had a brother, but he's dead." And when you come back, look out for me. I'll be waiting to welcome you with that "my old pal" stuff, and give you the glad hand, and at the first good chance I get stab you in the back.

EDMUND   Shut up! I'll be God-damned if I'll listen to you any more—

JAMIE [*as if he hadn't heard*]   Only don't forget me. Remember I warned you—for your sake. Give me credit. Greater love hath no man than this, that he saveth his brother from himself. [*very drunkenly, his head bobbing*] That's all. Feel better now. Gone to confession. Know you absolve me, don't you, Kid? You understand. You're a damned fine kid. Ought to be. I made you. So go and get well. Don't die on me. You're all I've got left. God bless you, Kid. [*His eyes close. He mumbles*] That last drink— the old K.O.

   [*He falls into a drunken doze, not completely asleep.* EDMUND *buries his face in his hands miserably.* TYRONE *comes in quietly through the screen door from the porch, his dressing gown wet with fog, the collar turned up around his throat. His face is stern and disgusted but at the same time pitying.* EDMUND *does not notice his entrance.*]

TYRONE [*in a low voice*]   Thank God he's asleep.

   [EDMUND *looks up with a start.*]

I thought he'd never stop talking. [*He turns down the collar of his dressing gown.*] We'd better let him stay where he is and sleep it off.

   [EDMUND *remains silent.* TYRONE *regards him—then goes on*]

I heard the last part of his talk. It's what I've warned you. I hope you'll heed the warning, now it comes from his own mouth.

   [EDMUND *gives no sign of having heard.* TYRONE *adds pityingly*]

But don't take it too much to heart, lad. He loves to exaggerate the worst of himself when he's drunk. He's devoted to you. It's the one good thing left in him. [*He looks down on* JAMIE *with a bitter sadness.*] A sweet spectacle for me! My first-born, who I hoped would bear my name in honor and dignity, who showed such brilliant promise!

EDMUND [*miserably*]   Keep quiet, can't you, Papa?

TYRONE [*pours a drink*]   A waste! A wreck, a drunken hulk, done with and finished!

> [*He drinks.* JAMIE *has become restless, sensing his father's presence, struggling up from his stupor. Now he gets his eyes open to blink up at* TYRONE. *The latter moves back a step defensively, his face growing hard.*]

JAMIE [*suddenly points a finger at him and recites with dramatic emphasis*]

> "Clarence is come, false, fleeting, perjured Clarence,
> That stabbed me in the field by Tewksbury.
> Seize on him, Furies, take him into torment."[6]

[*then resentfully*] What the hell are you staring at? [*He recites sardonically from Rossetti*[7]]

> "Look in my face. My name is Might-Have-Been;
> I am also called No More, Too Late, Farewell."

TYRONE   I'm well aware of that, and God knows I don't want to look at it.

EDMUND   Papa! Quit it!

JAMIE [*derisively*]   Got a great idea for you, Papa. Put on revival of "The Bells" this season. Great part in it you can play without make-up. Old Gaspard, the miser!

> [TYRONE *turns away, trying to control his temper.*]

EDMUND   Shut up, Jamie!

JAMIE [*jeeringly*]   I claim Edwin Booth never saw the day when he could give as good a performance as a trained seal. Seals are intelligent and honest. They don't put up any bluffs about the Art of Acting. They admit they're just hams earning their daily fish.

TYRONE [*stung, turns on him in a rage*]   You loafer!

EDMUND   Papa! Do you want to start a row that will bring Mama down? Jamie, go back to sleep! You've shot off your mouth too much already.

> [TYRONE *turns away.*]

JAMIE [*thickly*]   All right, Kid. Not looking for argument. Too damned sleepy.

> [*He closes his eyes, his head nodding.* TYRONE *comes to the table and sits down, turning his chair so he won't look at* JAMIE. *At once he becomes sleepy, too.*]

TYRONE [*heavily*]   I wish to God she'd go to bed so that I could, too. [*drowsily*] I'm dog tired. I can't stay up all night like I used to. Getting old—old and finished. [*with a bone-cracking yawn*] Can't keep my eyes open. I think I'll catch a few winks. Why don't you do the same, Edmund? It'll pass the time until she—

> [*His voice trails off. His eyes close, his chin sags, and he begins to breathe heavily through his mouth.* EDMUND *sits tensely. He hears something and jerks nervously forward in his chair, staring through the front parlor into the hall. He jumps up with a hunted, distracted expression. It seems for a second he is going to hide in the back parlor. Then he sits down again and waits, his eyes averted, his hands gripping the arms of his chair. Suddenly all five bulbs of the chandelier in the front parlor are turned*

---

6. Shakespeare's *Richard III* 1.4.55–57.
7. Dante Gabriel Rossetti (1821–1882), English poet and painter.

*on from a wall switch, and a moment later someone starts playing the
piano in there—the opening of one of Chopin's[8] simpler waltzes, done
with a forgetful, stiff-fingered groping, as if an awkward schoolgirl
were practicing it for the first time.* TYRONE *starts to wide-awakeness
and sober dread, and* JAMIE'S *head jerks back and his eyes open. For a
moment they listen frozenly. The playing stops as abruptly as it began,
and* MARY *appears in the doorway. She wears a sky-blue dressing gown
over her nightdress, dainty slippers and pompons on her bare feet. Her
face is paler than ever. Her eyes look enormous. They glisten like polished black jewels. The uncanny thing is that her face now appears so
youthful. Experience seems ironed out of it. It is a marble mask of girlish
innocence, the mouth caught in a shy smile. Her white hair is braided in
two pigtails which hang over her breast. Over one arm, carried neglect-
fully, trailing on the floor, as if she had forgotten she held it, is an old-
fashioned white satin wedding gown, trimmed with duchesse lace. She
hesitates in the doorway, glancing round the room, her forehead puckered puzzledly, like someone who has come to a room to get something
but has become absent-minded on the way and forgotten what it was.
They stare at her. She seems aware of them merely as she is aware of
other objects in the room, the furniture, the windows, familiar things she
accepts automatically as naturally belonging there but which she is too
preoccupied to notice.*]

JAMIE [*breaks the cracking silence—bitterly, self-defensively sardonic*]   The
Mad Scene. Enter Ophelia![9]

[*His father and brother both turn on him fiercely.* EDMUND *is quicker.
He slaps* JAMIE *across the mouth with the back of his hand.*]

TYRONE [*his voice trembling with suppressed fury*]   Good boy, Edmund.
The dirty blackguard! His own mother!

JAMIE [*mumbles guiltily, without resentment*]   All right, Kid. Had it coming. But I told you how much I'd hoped—[*He puts his hands over his face
and begins to sob.*]

TYRONE   I'll kick you out in the gutter tomorrow, so help me God. [*But
JAMIE'S sobbing breaks his anger, and he turns and shakes his shoulder,
pleading*] Jamie, for the love of God, stop it!

[*Then* MARY *speaks, and they freeze into silence again, staring at her.
She has paid no attention whatever to the incident. It is simply a part of
the familiar atmosphere of the room, a background which does not
touch her preoccupation; and she speaks aloud to herself, not to them.*]

MARY   I play so badly now. I'm all out of practice. Sister Theresa will give
me a dreadful scolding. She'll tell me it isn't fair to my father when he
spends so much money for extra lessons. She's quite right, it isn't fair,
when he's so good and generous, and so proud of me. I'll practice every
day from now on. But something horrible has happened to my hands.
The fingers have gotten so stiff—[*She lifts her hands to examine them
with a frightened puzzlement.*] The knuckles are all swollen. They're so
ugly. I'll have to go to the Infirmary and show Sister Martha. [*with a
sweet smile of affectionate trust*] She's old and a little cranky, but I love
her just the same, and she has things in her medicine chest that'll cure
anything. She'll give me something to rub on my hands, and tell me to

---

8. Frederic Chopin (1810–1849), Polish composer famous for works for the piano.

9. An allusion to Shakespeare's *Hamlet.*

pray to the Blessed Virgin, and they'll be well again in no time. [*She forgets her hands and comes into the room, the wedding gown trailing on the floor. She glances around vaguely, her forehead puckered again.*] Let me see. What did I come here to find? It's terrible, how absent-minded I've become. I'm always dreaming and forgetting.

TYRONE [*in a stifled voice*]   What's that she's carrying, Edmund?

EDMUND [*dully*]   Her wedding gown, I suppose.

TYRONE   Christ! [*He gets to his feet and stands directly in her path—in anguish*] Mary! Isn't it bad enough—? [*controlling himself—gently persuasive*] Here, let me take it, dear. You'll only step on it and tear it and get it dirty dragging it on the floor. Then you'd be sorry afterwards.
[*She lets him take it, regarding him from somewhere far away within herself, without recognition, without either affection or animosity.*]

MARY [*with the shy politeness of a well-bred young girl toward an elderly gentleman who relieves her of a bundle*]   Thank you. You are very kind. [*She regards the wedding gown with a puzzled interest.*] It's a wedding gown. It's very lovely, isn't it? [*A shadow crosses her face and she looks vaguely uneasy.*] I remember now. I found it in the attic hidden in a trunk. But I don't know what I wanted it for. I'm going to be a nun— that is, if I can only find—[*She looks around the room, her forehead puckered again.*] What is it I'm looking for? I know it's something I lost. [*She moves back from* TYRONE, *aware of him now only as some obstacle in her path.*]

TYRONE [*in hopeless appeal*]   Mary!
[*But it cannot penetrate her preoccupation. She doesn't seem to hear him. He gives up helplessly, shrinking into himself, even his defensive drunkenness taken from him, leaving him sick and sober. He sinks back on his chair, holding the wedding gown in his arms with an unconscious clumsy, protective gentleness.*]

JAMIE [*drops his hand from his face, his eyes on the table top. He has suddenly sobered up, too—dully*]   It's no good, Papa. [*He recites from Swinburne's "A Leave-taking" and does it well, simply but with a bitter sadness.*]

> "Let us rise up and part; she will not know.
> Let us go seaward as the great winds go,
> Full of blown sand and foam; what help is here?
> There is no help, for all these things are so,
> And all the world is bitter as a tear.
> And how these things are, though ye strove to show,
> She would not know."

MARY [*looking around her*]   Something I miss terribly. It can't be altogether lost. [*She starts to move around in back of* JAMIE's *chair.*]

JAMIE [*turns to look up into her face—and cannot help appealing pleadingly in his turn*]   Mama!
[*She does not seem to hear. He looks away hopelessly.*]
Hell! What's the use? It's no good. [*He recites from "A Leave-taking" again with increased bitterness.*]

> "Let us go hence, my songs; she will not hear.
> Let us go hence together without fear;

Keep silence now, for singing-time is over,
And over all old things and all things dear.
She loves not you nor me as all we love her.
Yea, though we sang as angels in her ear,
She would not hear."

MARY [*looking around her*]   Something I need terribly. I remember when
I had it I was never lonely nor afraid. I can't have lost it forever, I would
die if I thought that. Because then there would be no hope.
[*She moves like a sleepwalker, around the back of* JAMIE's *chair, then
forward toward left front, passing behind* EDMUND.]
EDMUND [*turns impulsively and grabs her arm. As he pleads he has the quality of a bewilderedly hurt little boy.*]   Mama! It isn't a summer cold! I've
got consumption!
MARY [*For a second he seems to have broken through to her. She trembles
and her expression becomes terrified. She calls distractedly, as if giving a
command to herself.*]   No! [*And instantly she is far away again. She murmurs gently but impersonally*] You must not try to touch me. You must
not try to hold me. It isn't right, when I am hoping to be a nun.
[*He lets his hand drop from her arm. She moves left to the front end of
the sofa beneath the windows and sits down, facing front, her hands
folded in her lap, in a demure school-girlish pose.*]
JAMIE [*gives Edmund a strange look of mingled pity and jealous gloating*]
You damned fool. It's no good. [*He recites again from the Swinburne
poem.*]

"Let us go hence, go hence; she will not see.
Sing all once more together; surely she,
She too, remembering days and words that were,
Will turn a little toward us, sighing; but we,
We are hence, we are gone, as though we had not been there.
Nay, and though all men seeing had pity on me,
She would not see."

TYRONE [*trying to shake off his hopeless stupor*]   Oh, we're fools to pay
any attention. It's the damned poison. But I've never known her to
drown herself in it as deep as this. [*gruffly*] Pass me that bottle, Jamie.
And stop reciting that damned morbid poetry. I won't have it in my
house!
[JAMIE *pushes the bottle toward him. He pours a drink without disar-
ranging the wedding gown he holds carefully over his other arm and on
his lap, and shoves the bottle back.* JAMIE *pours his and passes the bottle
to* EDMUND, *who, in turn, pours one.* TYRONE *lifts his glass and his sons
follow suit mechanically, but before they can drink* MARY *speaks and
they slowly lower their drinks to the table, forgetting them.*]
MARY [*staring dreamily before her. Her face looks extraordinarily youthful
and innocent. The shyly eager, trusting smile is on her lips as she talks aloud
to herself.*] I had a talk with Mother Elizabeth. She is so sweet and good.
A saint on earth. I love her dearly. It may be sinful of me but I love her
better than my own mother. Because she always understands, even before
you say a word. Her kind blue eyes look right into your heart. You can't
keep any secrets from her. You couldn't deceive her, even if you were
mean enough to want to. [*She gives a little rebellious toss of her head—*

with girlish pique] All the same, I don't think she was so understanding this time. I told her I wanted to be a nun. I explained how sure I was of my vocation, that I had prayed to the Blessed Virgin to make me sure, and to find me worthy. I told Mother I had had a true vision when I was praying in the shrine of Our Lady of Lourdes, on the little island in the lake. I said I knew, as surely as I knew I was kneeling there, that the Blessed Virgin had smiled and blessed me with her consent. But Mother Elizabeth told me I must be more sure than that, even, that I must prove it wasn't simply my imagination. She said, if I was so sure, then I wouldn't mind putting myself to a test by going home after I graduated, and living as other girls lived, going out to parties and dances and enjoying myself; and then if after a year or two I still felt sure, I could come back to see her and we would talk it over again. [*She tosses her head—indignantly*] I never dreamed Holy Mother would give me such advice! I was really shocked. I said, of course, I would do anything she suggested, but I knew it was simply a waste of time. After I left her, I felt all mixed up, so I went to the shrine and prayed to the Blessed Virgin and found peace again because I knew she heard my prayer and would always love me and see no harm ever came to me so long as I never lost my faith in her. [*She pauses and a look of growing uneasiness comes over her face. She passes a hand over her forehead as if brushing cobwebs from her brain—vaguely*] That was in the winter of senior year. Then in the spring something happened to me. Yes, I remember. I fell in love with James Tyrone and was so happy for a time. [*She stares before her in a sad dream.* TYRONE *stirs in his chair.* EDMUND *and* JAMIE *remain motionless.*]

CURTAIN

1940

CLAUDE McKAY
1889–1948

One of his biographers aptly calls Claude McKay a lifelong wanderer, a "sojourner" in the Harlem Renaissance. A Jamaican by birth, he did not become an American citizen until 1940; he left Harlem just when the Renaissance was getting started; he criticized leading black intellectuals like W. E. B. Du Bois and Alain Locke (who, in turn, criticized him). Nevertheless, *Harlem Shadows*, his 1922 book of poetry, is generally considered the book that initiated the Harlem Renaissance; his *Home to Harlem* (1928) was the only best-selling African American novel of the decade. Whether the Harlem Renaissance was a unified movement or a resonant label encompassing artists with diverse aims, whether McKay was an American Harlemite or a man of the world, he was unquestionably one of the most important black writers of the 1920s. As well as influencing African American literature, he has had a major impact on writing by West Indians and Africans.

Claude McKay (Festus Claudius McKay) was born in Sunny Ville, a rural village in central Jamaica. This village, with its setting of spectacular natural beauty, became in later years his symbol of a lost golden age. McKay's grandfather, a West African Ashanti, had been brought to the island as a slave, and McKay's father passed on to his son what he remembered of Ashanti values and rituals. Economic necessity led the young McKay to Kingston (Jamaica's principal city) in 1909, where he was apprenticed to a cabinetmaker and wheelwright. Combining his emerging literary ambitions with an interest in Jamaican folkways, McKay published two ground-breaking books of dialect poetry—*Songs of Jamaica* and *Constab Ballads*—in 1912. Prize money from these books took him to the United States to study agriculture, but his literary ambitions drew him to New York City after two years in school (first at the Tuskegee Institute, then at Kansas State College). He married his Jamaican sweetheart, Eulalie Imelda Lewars, in 1914; the couple had a daughter, but the marriage did not last. Supporting himself in jobs like restaurant kitchen helper and Pullman railroad waiter, he began to publish in avant-garde journals; by 1917 he was appearing in *The Seven Arts, Pearson's*, and the prominent left-wing *Liberator*, edited by Max Eastman. *The Liberator* published his famous poem "If We Must Die" in 1919. His poetry, much of it written in strict sonnet form, braided racial subject matter, radical politics, and poetic technique into compelling statements that were also good poetry according to traditional standards.

McKay's radical politics, already formed in Jamaica, rose from his belief that racism was inseparable from capitalism, which he saw as a structure designed to perpetuate economic inequality. To him, attacking capitalism was attacking racial injustice. Before the publication of *Harlem Shadows*, McKay had spent 1919–21 in England; in 1923 he went to Moscow, where he was welcomed as a celebrity. His connections to the Communist regime in Russia made him a target for the FBI, which issued orders to keep him from returning to the United States. He stayed in Europe until 1934, living mainly in France but also in Spain and Morocco. *Home to Harlem* (1928), written mostly in France, was an episodic guide to Harlem's artistic, popular, and intellectual life. Later events turned it into one of the movement's last statements; retrenchment in the publishing industry after the stock market crash of 1929, the emergence of younger African American writers with different values, and dissension among Harlem artists themselves combined to bring an end to the Harlem Renaissance and altered the character of life in Harlem itself.

When McKay was finally able to return to the United States in 1934, the nation was deep in the Great Depression. With general unemployment at over 25 percent, paid literary work was extremely hard to come by. In 1935 he joined the New York City branch of the Federal Writers' Project, a New Deal organization giving work to unemployed writers. Except for his important autobiography, *A Long Way from Home* (1937), he did little creative work, and his health failed. Through his friendship with Ellen Tarry, a young African American writer who was a Catholic, he received medical care from Friendship House, a Catholic lay organization in Harlem. In the later years of his life, appalled by Stalin's purges, McKay repudiated his earlier Communist sympathies. He began to work at Friendship House and, after moving to Chicago, worked for the Catholic Youth Organization. He converted to Catholicism in 1944 and died in Chicago four years later.

All texts are from *Harlem Shadows* (1922).

The Harlem Dancer

Applauding youths laughed with young prostitutes
And watched her perfect, half-clothed body sway;
Her voice was like the sound of blended flutes
Blown by black players upon a picnic day.
She sang and danced on gracefully and calm,   5
The light gauze hanging loose about her form;
To me she seemed a proudly-swaying palm
Grown lovelier for passing through a storm.
Upon her swarthy neck black shiny curls
Luxuriant fell; and tossing coins in praise,   10
The wine-flushed, bold-eyed boys, and even the girls,
Devoured her shape with eager, passionate gaze;
But looking at her falsely-smiling face,
I knew her self was not in that strange place.

1917, 1922

Harlem Shadows

I hear the halting footsteps of a lass
   In Negro Harlem when the night lets fall
Its veil. I see the shapes of girls who pass
   To bend and barter at desire's call.
Ah, little dark girls who in slippered feet   5
Go prowling through the night from street to street!

Through the long night until the silver break
   Of day the little gray feet know no rest;
Through the lone night until the last snow-flake
   Has dropped from heaven upon the earth's white breast,   10
The dusky, half-clad girls of tired feet
Are trudging, thinly shod, from street to street.

Ah, stern harsh world, that in the wretched way
   Of poverty, dishonor and disgrace,
Has pushed the timid little feet of clay,   15
   The sacred brown feet of my fallen race!
Ah, heart of me, the weary, weary feet
In Harlem wandering from street to street.

1918, 1922

The Lynching

His Spirit in smoke ascended to high heaven.
His father, by the cruelest way of pain,
Had bidden him to his bosom once again;
The awful sin remained still unforgiven.
All night a bright and solitary star   5
(Perchance the one that ever guided him,
Yet gave him up at last to Fate's wild whim)
Hung pitifully o'er the swinging char.
Day dawned, and soon the mixed crowds came to view
The ghastly body swaying in the sun   10
The women thronged to look, but never a one
Showed sorrow in her eyes of steely blue;
And little lads, lynchers that were to be,
Danced round the dreadful thing in fiendish glee.

1919, 1922

If We Must Die

If we must die, let it not be like hogs
Hunted and penned in an inglorious spot,
While round us bark the mad and hungry dogs,
Making their mock at our accursèd lot.
If we must die, O let us nobly die,   5
So that our precious blood may not be shed
In vain; then even the monsters we defy
Shall be constrained to honor us though dead!
O kinsmen! we must meet the common foe!
Though far outnumbered let us show us brave,   10
And for their thousand blows deal one deathblow!
What though before us lies the open grave?
Like men we'll face the murderous, cowardly pack,
Pressed to the wall, dying, but fighting back!

1919, 1922

Africa

The sun sought thy dim bed and brought forth light,
The sciences were sucklings at thy breast;
When all the world was young in pregnant night
Thy slaves toiled at thy monumental best.
Thou ancient treasure-land, thou modern prize,   5
New peoples marvel at thy pyramids!
The years roll on, thy sphinx of riddle eyes

Watches the mad world with immobile lids.
The Hebrews humbled them at Pharaoh's name.
Cradle of Power! Yet all things were in vain!   10
Honor and Glory, Arrogance and Fame!
They went. The darkness swallowed thee again.
Thou art the harlot, now thy time is done,
Of all the mighty nations of the sun.

                                        1921, 1922

America

Although she feeds me bread of bitterness,
And sinks into my throat her tiger's tooth,
Stealing my breath of life, I will confess
I love this cultured hell that tests my youth!
Her vigor flows like tides into my blood,   5
Giving me strength erect against her hate.
Her bigness sweeps my being like a flood.
Yet as a rebel fronts a king in state,
I stand within her walls with not a shred
Of terror, malice, not a word of jeer.   10
Darkly I gaze into the days ahead,
And see her might and granite wonders there,
Beneath the touch of Time's unerring hand,
Like priceless treasures sinking in the sand.

                                        1921, 1922

KATHERINE ANNE PORTER
1890–1980

Over a long writing life Katherine Anne Porter produced only four books of stories and one novel, *Ship of Fools*, which did not appear until she was over seventy. Her reputation as a prose writer did not depend on quantity; each story was technically skilled, emotionally powerful, combining traditional narration with new symbolic techniques and contemporary subject matter.

Callie Porter—she changed the name to Katherine Anne when she became a writer—was born in the small settlement of Indian Creek, Texas; her mother died soon after giving birth to her fourth child, when Porter was not quite two years old. Her father moved them all to his mother's home in Kyle, Texas, where the paternal grandmother raised the family in extreme poverty. The father gave up all attempts to support them either financially or emotionally; the security provided by the strong, loving, but pious and stern grandmother ended with her death when Porter was eleven. Porter married to leave home immediately after her sixteenth birthday, only to find that rooted domesticity was not for her. Long before her divorce in 1915, she had separated from her first husband and begun a life of travel, activity, and changes of jobs.

She started writing in 1916 as a reporter for a Dallas newspaper. In 1917 she moved to Denver, the next year to New York City's Greenwich Village. Between 1918 and 1924 she lived mainly in Mexico, freelancing, meeting artists and intellectuals, and becoming involved in revolutionary politics. In Mexico she found the resources of journalism inadequate to her ambitions; using an anecdote she had heard from an archaeologist as a kernel, she wrote her first story, "María Concepción," which was published in the prestigious *Century* magazine in 1922. Like all her stories, it dealt with powerful emotions and had a strong sense of locale. Critics praised her as a major talent.

Although she considered herself a serious writer from this time on, Porter was distracted from fiction by many crosscurrents. A self-supporting woman with expensive tastes, she hesitated to give up lucrative freelance offers. She enjoyed travel and gladly took on jobs that sent her abroad. She became involved in political causes, including the Sacco-Vanzetti case. She was married four times.

Porter planned each story meticulously—taking extensive notes, devising scenarios, roughing out dialogue, and revising many times, sometimes over a period of years. She did not write confessional or simple autobiographical fiction, but each story originated in an important experience of her life. Although not a feminist, Porter devoted much of her work to exploring the tensions in women's lives in the modern era. The story that made her famous for life, so that everything else she published thereafter was looked on as a literary event, was "Flowering Judas" (1929), set in Mexico and dealing with revolutionary politics, lust, and betrayal. The reality of mixed motives and the difference between pure idealism and egotistical opportunism as they are encountered in revolutionary politics are among the themes in this deceptively simple narrative. It appeared in the little magazine *Hound and Horn*. The collections *Flowering Judas* and *Noon Wine* came out in 1930 and 1937. In 1930 Porter went back to Mexico and the following year to Europe on a Guggenheim fellowship; she lived in Berlin, Paris, and Basel before returning to the United States in 1936. Two more collections of stories and novellas appeared in 1939 (*Pale Horse, Pale Rider*) and in 1944 (*The Leaning Tower*). These later collections feature several stories about Miranda Gay, a character who is partly autobiographical and partly an idealized image of the southern belle facing the modern world. *Pale Horse, Pale Rider* narrates Miranda's World War I romance with a soldier in the highly charged political climate of the American home front.

Soon after arriving in Europe in 1931 Porter began working on a novel, but it was not until 1962 that *Ship of Fools*, which runs to almost five hundred pages, appeared. Set on an ocean liner crossing the Atlantic to Germany in August 1931, it explores the characters and developing relationships of a large number of passengers; the ship, as Porter wrote in a preface, stands for "this world on its voyage to eternity." As in "Flowering Judas" and *Pale Horse, Pale Rider* the personal and the political intersect in *Ship of Fools*, since the coming of Nazism in Germany frames the interlinked stories of the travelers. In its film version, *Ship of Fools* brought Porter a great deal of money. Capitalizing on the publicity, her publishers brought out the *Collected Stories* in 1965, from which followed the National Book Award, the Pulitzer Prize, the Gold Medal for fiction of the National Institute of Arts and Letters, and election to the American Academy of Letters, all in the next two years. The happiest occasions in her later years—she lived to be ninety—were connected with endowing and establishing the Katherine Anne Porter Room at the University of Maryland, not far from her last home near Washington, D.C.

The texts are from the *Collected Stories* (1965).

Flowering Judas[1]

Braggioni sits heaped upon the edge of a straight-backed chair much too small for him, and sings to Laura in a furry, mournful voice. Laura has begun to find reasons for avoiding her own house until the latest possible moment, for Braggioni is there almost every night. No matter how late she is, he will be sitting there with a surly, waiting expression, pulling at his kinky yellow hair, thumbing the strings of his guitar, snarling a tune under his breath. Lupe the Indian maid meets Laura at the door, and says with a flicker of a glance towards the upper room, "He waits."

Laura wishes to lie down, she is tired of her hairpins and the feel of her long tight sleeves, but she says to him, "Have you a new song for me this evening?" If he says yes, she asks him to sing it. If he says no, she remembers his favorite one, and asks him to sing it again. Lupe brings her a cup of chocolate and a plate of rice, and Laura eats at the small table under the lamp, first inviting Braggioni, whose answer is always the same: "I have eaten, and besides, chocolate thickens the voice."

Laura says, "Sing, then," and Braggioni heaves himself into song. He scratches the guitar familiarly as though it were a pet animal, and sings passionately off key, taking the high notes in a prolonged painful squeal. Laura, who haunts the markets listening to the ballad singers, and stops every day to hear the blind boy playing his reed-flute in Sixteenth of September Street,[2] listens to Braggioni with pitiless courtesy, because she dares not smile at his miserable performance. Nobody dares to smile at him. Braggioni is cruel to everyone, with a kind of specialized insolence, but he is so vain of his talents, and so sensitive to slights, it would require a cruelty and vanity greater than his own to lay a finger on the vast cureless wound of his self-esteem. It would require courage, too, for it is dangerous to offend him, and nobody has this courage.

Braggioni loves himself with such tenderness and amplitude and eternal charity that his followers—for he is a leader of men, a skilled revolutionist, and his skin has been punctured in honorable warfare—warm themselves in the reflected glow, and say to each other: "He has a real nobility, a love of humanity raised above mere personal affections." The excess of this self-love has flowed out, inconveniently for her, over Laura, who, with so many others, owes her comfortable situation and her salary to him. When he is in a very good humor, he tells her, "I am tempted to forgive you for being a *gringa*. *Gringita!*"[3] and Laura, burning, imagines herself leaning forward suddenly, and with a sound back-handed slap wiping the suety smile from his face. If he notices her eyes at these moments he gives no sign.

She knows what Braggioni would offer her, and she must resist tenaciously without appearing to resist, and if she could avoid it she would not admit even to herself the slow drift of his intention. During these long evenings which have spoiled a long month for her, she sits in her deep chair

1. One of a genus of trees and shrubs with purplish rosy flowers. According to legend, Judas Iscariot, betrayer of Jesus, hanged himself from such a tree.
2. A street in Morelia, a city in western Mexico where the story is set.
3. A young female foreigner, non-Mexican girl; a patronizing term meaning "cute little foreign girl." Diminutive of *gringa*, which is used pejoratively, especially for an American.

with an open book on her knees, resting her eyes on the consoling rigidity of the printed page when the sight and sound of Braggioni singing threaten to identify themselves with all her remembered afflictions and to add their weight to her uneasy premonitions of the future. The gluttonous bulk of Braggioni has become a symbol of her many disillusions, for a revolutionist should be lean, animated by heroic faith, a vessel of abstract virtues. This is nonsense, she knows it now and is ashamed of it. Revolution must have leaders, and leadership is a career for energetic men. She is, her comrades tell her, full of romantic error, for what she defines as cynicism in them is merely "a developed sense of reality." She is almost too willing to say, "I am wrong, I suppose I don't really understand the principles," and afterward she makes a secret truce with herself, determined not to surrender her will to such expedient logic. But she cannot help feeling that she has been betrayed irreparably by the disunion between her way of living and her feeling of what life should be, and at times she is almost contented to rest in this sense of grievance as a private store of consolation. Sometimes she wishes to run away, but she stays. Now she longs to fly out of this room, down the narrow stairs, and into the street where the houses lean together like conspirators under a single mottled lamp, and leave Braggioni singing to himself.

Instead she looks at Braggioni, frankly and clearly, like a good child who understands the rules of behavior. Her knees cling together under sound blue serge, and her round white collar is not purposely nun-like. She wears the uniform of an idea, and has renounced vanities. She was born Roman Catholic, and in spite of her fear of being seen by someone who might make a scandal of it, she slips now and again into some crumbling little church, kneels on the chilly stone, and says a Hail Mary on the gold rosary she bought in Tehuantepec. It is no good and she ends by examining the altar with its tinsel flowers and ragged brocades, and feels tender about the battered doll-shape of some male saint whose white, lace-trimmed drawers hang limply around his ankles below the hieratic dignity of his velvet robe. She has encased herself in a set of principles derived from her early training, leaving no detail of gesture or of personal taste untouched, and for this reason she will not wear lace made on machines. This is her private heresy, for in her special group the machine is sacred, and will be the salvation of the workers. She loves fine lace, and there is a tiny edge of fluted cobweb on this collar, which is one of twenty precisely alike, folded in blue tissue paper in the upper drawer of her clothes chest.

Braggioni catches her glance solidly as if he had been waiting for it, leans forward, balancing his paunch between his spread knees, and sings with tremendous emphasis, weighing his words. He has, the song relates, no father and no mother, nor even a friend to console him; lonely as a wave of the sea he comes and goes, lonely as a wave. His mouth opens round and yearns sideways, his balloon cheeks grow oily with the labor of song. He bulges marvelously in his expensive garments. Over his lavender collar, crushed upon a purple necktie, held by a diamond hoop: over his ammunition belt of tooled leather worked in silver, buckled cruelly around his gasping middle: over the tops of his glossy yellow shoes Braggioni swells with ominous ripeness, his mauve silk hose stretched taut, his ankles bound with the stout leather thongs of his shoes.

When he stretches his eyelids at Laura she notes again that his eyes are the true tawny yellow cat's eyes. He is rich, not in money, he tells her, but in power, and this power brings with it the blameless ownership of things, and the right to indulge his love of small luxuries. "I have a taste for the elegant refinements," he said once, flourishing a yellow silk handkerchief before her nose. "Smell that? It is Jockey Club, imported from New York." Nonetheless he is wounded by life. He will say so presently. "It is true everything turns to dust in the hand, to gall on the tongue." He sighs and his leather belt creaks like a saddle girth. "I am disappointed in everything as it comes. Everything." He shakes his head. "You, poor thing, you will be disappointed too. You are born for it. We are more alike than you realize in some things. Wait and see. Some day you will remember what I have told you, you will know that Braggioni was your friend."

Laura feels a slow chill, a purely physical sense of danger, a warning in her blood that violence, mutilation, a shocking death, wait for her with lessening patience. She has translated this fear into something homely, immediate, and sometimes hesitates before crossing the street. "My personal fate is nothing, except as the testimony of a mental attitude," she reminds herself, quoting from some forgotten philosophic primer, and is sensible enough to add, "Anyhow, I shall not be killed by an automobile if I can help it."

"It may be true I am as corrupt, in another way, as Braggioni," she thinks in spite of herself, "as callous, as incomplete," and if this is so, any kind of death seems preferable. Still she sits quietly, she does not run. Where could she go? Uninvited she has promised herself to this place; she can no longer imagine herself as living in another country, and there is no pleasure in remembering her life before she came here.

Precisely what is the nature of this devotion, its true motives, and what are its obligations? Laura cannot say. She spends part of her days in Xochimilco, near by, teaching Indian children to say in English, "The cat is on the mat." When she appears in the classroom they crowd about her with smiles on their wise, innocent, clay-colored faces, crying, "Good morning, my titcher!" in immaculate voices, and they make of her desk a fresh garden of flowers every day.

During her leisure she goes to union meetings and listens to busy important voices quarreling over tactics, methods, internal politics. She visits the prisoners of her own political faith in their cells, where they entertain themselves with counting cockroaches, repenting of their indiscretions, composing their memoirs, writing out manifestoes and plans for their comrades who are still walking about free, hands in pockets, sniffing fresh air. Laura brings them food and cigarettes and a little money, and she brings messages disguised in equivocal phrases from the men outside who dare not set foot in the prison for fear of disappearing into the cells kept empty for them. If the prisoners confuse night and day, and complain, "Dear little Laura, time doesn't pass in this infernal hole, and I won't know when it is time to sleep unless I have a reminder," she brings them their favorite narcotics, and says in a tone that does not wound them with pity, "Tonight will really be night for you," and though her Spanish amuses them, they find her comforting, useful. If they lose patience and all faith, and curse the slowness of their friends in coming to their rescue with money and influence, they trust her not to repeat everything, and if she inquires, "Where do you think we can find money, or influence?" they are certain to answer, "Well, there is Braggioni, why doesn't he do something?"

She smuggles letters from headquarters to men hiding from firing squads in back streets in mildewed houses, where they sit in tumbled beds and talk bitterly as if all Mexico were at their heels, when Laura knows positively they might appear at the band concert in the Alameda[4] on Sunday morning, and no one would notice them. But Braggioni says, "Let them sweat a little. The next time they may be careful. It is very restful to have them out of the way for a while." She is not afraid to knock on any door in any street after midnight, and enter in the darkness, and say to one of these men who is really in danger: "They will be looking for you—seriously—tomorrow morning after six. Here is some money from Vicente. Go to Vera Cruz and wait."

She borrows money from the Roumanian agitator to give to his bitter enemy the Polish agitator. The favor of Braggioni is their disputed territory, and Braggioni holds the balance nicely, for he can use them both. The Polish agitator talks love to her over café tables, hoping to exploit what he believes is her secret sentimental preference for him, and he gives her misinformation which he begs her to repeat as the solemn truth to certain persons. The Roumanian is more adroit. He is generous with his money in all good causes, and lies to her with an air of ingenuous candor, as if he were her good friend and confidant. She never repeats anything they may say. Braggioni never asks questions. He has other ways to discover all that he wishes to know about them.

Nobody touches her, but all praise her gray eyes, and the soft, round under lip which promises gayety, yet is always grave, nearly always firmly closed: and they cannot understand why she is in Mexico. She walks back and forth on her errands, with puzzled eyebrows, carrying her little folder of drawings and music and school papers. No dancer dances more beautifully than Laura walks, and she inspires some amusing, unexpected ardors, which cause little gossip, because nothing comes of them. A young captain who had been a soldier in Zapata's[5] army attempted, during a horseback ride near Cuernavaca, to express his desire for her with the noble simplicity befitting a rude folk-hero: but gently, because he was gentle. This gentleness was his defeat, for when he alighted, and removed her foot from the stirrup, and essayed to draw her down into his arms, her horse, ordinarily a tame one, shied fiercely, reared and plunged away. The young hero's horse careered blindly after his stable-mate, and the hero did not return to the hotel until rather late that evening. At breakfast he came to her table in full charro dress,[6] gray buckskin jacket and trousers with strings of silver buttons down the leg, and he was in a humorous, careless mood. "May I sit with you?" and "You are a wonderful rider. I was terrified that you might be thrown and dragged. I should never have forgiven myself. But I cannot admire you enough for your riding!"

"I learned to ride in Arizona," said Laura.

---

4. Public promenade bordered with trees.
5. Emiliano Zapata (c. 1879–1919), Mexican peasant revolutionary general whose movement, *zapatismo*, combined agrarian and Mexican Indian cultural aspirations; one of the most significant figures in Mexico from 1910 to 1919, when he was murdered.
6. Costume worn by a peasant horseman of special status.

"If you will ride with me again this morning, I promise you a horse that will not shy with you," he said. But Laura remembered that she must return to Mexico City at noon.

Next morning the children made a celebration and spent their playtime writing on the blackboard, "We lov ar ticher," and with tinted chalks they drew wreaths of flowers around the words. The young hero wrote her a letter: "I am a very foolish, wasteful, impulsive man. I should have first said I love you, and then you would not have run away. But you shall see me again." Laura thought, "I must send him a box of colored crayons," but she was trying to forgive herself for having spurred her horse at the wrong moment.

A brown, shock-haired youth came and stood in her patio one night and sang like a lost soul for two hours, but Laura could think of nothing to do about it. The moonlight spread a wash of gauzy silver over the clear spaces of the garden, and the shadows were cobalt blue. The scarlet blossoms of the Judas tree were dull purple, and the names of the colors repeated themselves automatically in her mind, while she watched not the boy, but his shadow, fallen like a dark garment across the fountain rim, trailing in the water. Lupe came silently and whispered expert counsel in her ear: "If you will throw him one little flower, he will sing another song or two and go away." Laura threw the flower, and he sang a last song and went away with the flower tucked in the band of his hat. Lupe said, "He is one of the organizers of the Typographers Union, and before that he sold corridos[7] in the Merced market, and before that, he came from Guanajuato, where I was born. I would not trust any man, but I trust least those from Guanajuato."

She did not tell Laura that he would be back again the next night, and the next, nor that he would follow her at a certain fixed distance around the Merced market, through the Zócolo, up Francisco I. Madero Avenue, and so along the Paseo de la Reforma to Chapultepec Park, and into the Philosopher's Footpath, still with that flower withering in his hat, and an indivisible attention in his eyes.

Now Laura is accustomed to him, it means nothing except that he is nineteen years old and is observing a convention with all propriety, as though it were founded on a law of nature, which in the end it might well prove to be. He is beginning to write poems which he prints on a wooden press, and he leaves them stuck like handbills in her door. She is pleasantly disturbed by the abstract, unhurried watchfulness of his black eyes which will in time turn easily towards another object. She tells herself that throwing the flower was a mistake, for she is twenty-two years old and knows better; but she refuses to regret it, and persuades herself that her negation of all external events as they occur is a sign that she is gradually perfecting herself in the stoicism she strives to cultivate against that disaster she fears, though she cannot name it.

She is not at home in the world. Every day she teaches children who remain strangers to her, though she loves their tender round hands and their charming opportunist savagery. She knocks at unfamiliar doors not knowing whether a friend or a stranger shall answer, and even if a known face emerges from the sour gloom of that unknown interior, still it is the face of a stranger. No matter what this stranger says to her, nor what her message to him, the

7. Popular ballads.

very cells of her flesh reject knowledge and kinship in one monotonous word. No. No. No. She draws her strength from this one holy talismanic word which does not suffer her to be led into evil. Denying everything, she may walk anywhere in safety, she looks at everything without amazement.

No, repeats this firm unchanging voice of her blood; and she looks at Braggioni without amazement. He is a great man, he wishes to impress this simple girl who covers her great round breasts with thick dark cloth, and who hides long, invaluably beautiful legs under a heavy skirt. She is almost thin except for the incomprehensible fullness of her breasts, like a nursing mother's, and Braggioni, who considers himself a judge of women, speculates again on the puzzle of her notorious virginity, and takes the liberty of speech which she permits without a sign of modesty, indeed, without any sort of sign, which is disconcerting.

"You think you are so cold, *gringita!* Wait and see. You will surprise yourself some day! May I be there to advise you!" He stretches his eyelids at her, and his ill-humored cat's eyes waver in a separate glance for the two points of light marking the opposite ends of a smoothly drawn path between the swollen curve of her breasts. He is not put off by that blue serge, nor by her resolutely fixed gaze. There is all the time in the world. His cheeks are bellying with the wind of song. "O girl with the dark eyes," he sings, and reconsiders. "But yours are not dark. I can change all that. O girl with the green eyes, you have stolen my heart away!" then his mind wanders to the song, and Laura feels the weight of his attention being shifted elsewhere. Singing thus, he seems harmless, he is quite harmless, there is nothing to do but sit patiently and say "No," when the moment comes. She draws a full breath, and her mind wanders also, but not far. She dares not wander too far.

Not for nothing has Braggioni taken pains to be a good revolutionist and a professional lover of humanity. He will never die of it. He has the malice, the cleverness, the wickedness, the sharpness of wit, the hardness of heart, stipulated for loving the world profitably. *He will never die of it.* He will live to see himself kicked out from his feeding trough by other hungry world-saviors. Traditionally he must sing in spite of his life which drives him to bloodshed, he tells Laura, for his father was a Tuscany[8] peasant who drifted to Yucatan and married a Maya woman: a woman of race, an aristocrat. They gave him the love and knowledge of music, thus: and under the rip of his thumbnail, the strings of the instrument complain like exposed nerves.

Once he was called Delgadito by all the girls and married women who ran after him; he was so scrawny all his bones showed under his thin cotton clothing, and he could squeeze his emptiness to the very backbone with his two hands. He was a poet and the revolution was only a dream then; too many women loved him and sapped away his youth, and he could never find enough to eat anywhere, anywhere! Now he is a leader of men, crafty men who whisper in his ear, hungry men who wait for hours outside his office for a word with him, emaciated men with wild faces who waylay him at the street gate with a timid, "Comrade, let me tell you . . ." and they blow the foul breath from their empty stomachs in his face.

He is always sympathetic. He gives them handfuls of small coins from his own pocket, he promises them work, there will be demonstrations, they

8. A region in north-central Italy.

must join the unions and attend the meetings, above all they must be on the watch for spies. They are closer to him than his own brothers, without them he can do nothing—until tomorrow, comrade!

Until tomorrow. "They are stupid, they are lazy, they are treacherous, they would cut my throat for nothing," he says to Laura. He has good food and abundant drink, he hires an automobile and drives in the Paseo on Sunday morning, and enjoys plenty of sleep in a soft bed beside a wife who dares not disturb him; and he sits pampering his bones in easy billows of fat, singing to Laura, who knows and thinks these things about him. When he was fifteen, he tried to drown himself because he loved a girl, his first love, and she laughed at him. "A thousand women have paid for that," and his tight little mouth turns down at the corners. Now he perfumes his hair with Jockey Club, and confides to Laura: "One woman is really as good as another for me, in the dark. I prefer them all."

His wife organizes unions among the girls in the cigarette factories, and walks in picket lines, and even speaks at meetings in the evening. But she cannot be brought to acknowledge the benefits of true liberty. "I tell her I must have my freedom, net. She does not understand my point of view." Laura has heard this many times. Braggioni scratches the guitar and meditates. "She is an instinctively virtuous woman, pure gold, no doubt of that. If she were not, I should lock her up, and she knows it."

His wife, who works so hard for the good of the factory girls, employs part of her leisure lying on the floor weeping because there are so many women in the world, and only one husband for her, and she never knows where nor when to look for him. He told her: "Unless you can learn to cry when I am not here, I must go away for good." That day he went away and took a room at the Hotel Madrid.

It is this month of separation for the sake of higher principles that has been spoiled not only for Mrs. Braggioni, whose sense of reality is beyond criticism, but for Laura, who feels herself bogged in a nightmare. Tonight Laura envies Mrs. Braggioni, who is alone, and free to weep as much as she pleases about a concrete wrong. Laura has just come from a visit to the prison, and she is waiting for tomorrow with a bitter anxiety as if tomorrow may not come, but time may be caught immovably in this hour, with herself transfixed, Braggioni singing on forever, and Eugenio's body not yet discovered by the guard.

Braggioni says: "Are you going to sleep?" Almost before she can shake her head, he begins telling her about the May-day disturbances coming on in Morelia, for the Catholics hold a festival in honor of the Blessed Virgin, and the Socialists celebrate their martyrs on that day. "There will be two independent processions, starting from either end of town, and they will march until they meet, and the rest depends . . ." He asks her to oil and load his pistols. Standing up, he unbuckles his ammunition belt, and spreads it laden across her knees. Laura sits with the shells slipping through the cleaning cloth dipped in oil, and he says again he cannot understand why she works so hard for the revolutionary idea unless she loves some man who is in it. "Are you not in love with someone?" "No," says Laura. "And no one is in love with you?" "No." "Then it is your own fault. No woman need go begging. Why, what is the matter with you? The legless beggar woman in the Alameda has a perfectly faithful lover. Did you know that?"

Laura peers down the pistol barrel and says nothing, but a long, slow faintness rises and subsides in her; Braggioni curves his swollen fingers around the throat of the guitar and softly smothers the music out of it, and when she hears him again he seems to have forgotten her, and is speaking in the hypnotic voice he uses when talking in small rooms to a listening, close-gathered crowd. Some day this world, now seemingly so composed and eternal, to the edges of every sea shall be merely a tangle of gaping trenches, of crashing walls and broken bodies. Everything must be torn from its accustomed place where it has rotted for centuries, hurled skyward and distributed, cast down again clean as rain, without separate identity. Nothing shall survive that the stiffened hands of poverty have created for the rich and no one shall be left alive except the elect spirits destined to procreate a new world cleansed of cruelty and injustice, ruled by benevolent anarchy: "Pistols are good, I love them, cannon are even better, but in the end I pin my faith to good dynamite," he concludes, and strokes the pistol lying in her hands. "Once I dreamed of destroying this city, in case it offered resistance to General Ortíz, but it fell into his hands like an overripe pear."

He is made restless by his own words, rises and stands waiting. Laura holds up the belt to him: "Put that on, and go kill somebody in Morelia, and you will be happier," she says softly. The presence of death in the room makes her bold. "Today, I found Eugenio going into a stupor. He refused to allow me to call the prison doctor. He had taken all the tablets I brought him yesterday. He said he took them because he was bored."

"He is a fool, and his death is his own business," says Braggioni, fastening his belt carefully.

"I told him if he had waited only a little while longer, you would have got him set free," says Laura. "He said he did not want to wait."

"He is a fool and we are well rid of him," says Braggioni, reaching for his hat.

He goes away. Laura knows his mood has changed, she will not see him any more for a while. He will send word when he needs her to go on errands into strange streets, to speak to the strange faces that will appear, like clay masks with the power of human speech, to mutter their thanks to Braggioni for his help. Now she is free, and she thinks, I must run while there is time. But she does not go.

Braggioni enters his own house where for a month his wife has spent many hours every night weeping and tangling her hair upon her pillow. She is weeping now, and she weeps more at the sight of him, the cause of all her sorrows. He looks about the room. Nothing is changed, the smells are good and familiar, he is well acquainted with the woman who comes toward him with no reproach except grief on her face. He says to her tenderly: "You are so good, please don't cry any more, you dear good creature." She says, "Are you tired, my angel? Sit here and I will wash your feet." She brings a bowl of water, and kneeling, unlaces his shoes, and when from her knees she raises her sad eyes under her blackened lids, he is sorry for everything, and bursts into tears. "Ah, yes, I am hungry, I am tired, let us eat something together," he says, between sobs. His wife leans her head on his arm and says, "Forgive me!" and this time he is refreshed by the solemn, endless rain of her tears.

Laura takes off her serge dress and puts on a white linen nightgown and goes to bed. She turns her head a little to one side, and lying still, reminds herself that it is time to sleep. Numbers tick in her brain like little clocks, soundless doors close of themselves around her. If you would sleep, you must not remember anything, the children will say tomorrow, good morning, my teacher, the poor prisoners who come every day bringing flowers to their jailor. 1-2-3-4-5—it is monstrous to confuse love with revolution, night with day, life with death—ah, Eugenio!

The tolling of the midnight bell is a signal, but what does it mean? Get up, Laura, and follow me: come out of your sleep, out of your bed, out of this strange house. What are you doing in this house? Without a word, without fear she rose and reached for Eugenio's hand, but he eluded her with a sharp, sly smile and drifted away. This is not all, you shall see—Murderer, he said, follow me, I will show you a new country, but it is far away and we must hurry. No, said Laura, not unless you take my hand, no; and she clung first to the stair rail, and then to the topmost branch of the Judas tree that bent down slowly and set her upon the earth, and then to the rocky ledge of a cliff, and then to the jagged wave of a sea that was not water but a desert of crumbling stone. Where are you taking me, she asked in wonder but without fear. To death, and it is a long way off, and we must hurry, said Eugenio. No, said Laura, not unless you take my hand. Then eat these flowers, poor prisoner, said Eugenio in a voice of pity, take and eat: and from the Judas tree he stripped the warm bleeding flowers, and held them to her lips. She saw that his hand was fleshless, a cluster of small white petrified branches, and his eye sockets were without light, but she ate the flowers greedily for they satisfied both hunger and thirst. Murderer! said Eugenio, and Cannibal! This is my body and my blood. Laura cried No! and at the sound of her own voice, she awoke trembling, and was afraid to sleep again.

1929, 1930

ZORA NEALE HURSTON
1891–1960

Zora Neale Hurston was born in 1891 in Notasulga, Alabama, and moved with her family in 1892 to Eatonville, Florida, an all-black town. Her father, a Baptist preacher of considerable eloquence, was not a family man and made life difficult for his wife and eight children. The tie between mother and daughter was strong; Lucy Hurston was a driving force and strong support for all her children. But her death when Zora Hurston was about eleven left the child with little home life. Hitherto, the town of Eatonville had been like an extended family to her, and her early childhood was protected from racism because she encountered no white people. With her mother's death, Hurston's wanderings and her initiation into American racism began. The early security had given her the core of self-confidence she needed to survive. She moved from one relative's home to another until she was old enough to support herself, and with her earnings she began slowly to pursue an education.

Although she had never finished grade school in Eatonville she was able to enter and complete college. In the early 1920s at Howard University in Washington, D.C. (the nation's leading African American university at that time), she studied with the great black educator Alain Locke, who was to make history with his anthology *The New Negro* in 1925. After a short story, "Drenched in Light," appeared in the New York African American magazine *Opportunity*, she decided to move to Harlem and pursue a literary career there.

As her biographer, Robert Hemenway, writes, "Zora Hurston was an extraordinarily witty woman, and she acquired an instant reputation in New York for her high spirits and side-splitting tales of Eatonville life. She could walk into a room of strangers . . . and almost immediately gather people, charm, amuse, and impress them." The Eatonville vignettes printed here convey the flavor of this

Zora Neale Hurston, as photographed by Carl Van Vechten in 1938.

discourse. Generous, outspoken, high spirited, an interesting conversationalist, she worked as a personal secretary for the politically liberal novelist Fannie Hurst and entered Barnard College. Her career took two simultaneous directions: at Barnard she studied with the famous anthropologist Franz Boas and developed an interest in black folk traditions, and in Harlem she became well known as a storyteller, an informal performing artist. Thus she was doubly committed to oral narrative, and her work excels in its representation of people talking.

When she graduated from Barnard in 1927 she received a fellowship to return to Florida and study the oral traditions of Eatonville. From then on, she strove to achieve a balance between focusing on the folk and her origins and focusing on herself as an individual. After the fellowship money ran out, Hurston was supported by Mrs. R. Osgood Mason, an elderly white patron of the arts. Mason had firm ideas about what she wanted her protégés to produce; she required them all to get her permission before publishing any of the work that she had subsidized. In this relationship, Hurston experienced a difficulty that all the black artists of the Harlem Renaissance had to face—the fact that well-off white people were the sponsors of, and often expected to be the chief audience for, their work.

Hurston's work was not entirely popular with the male intellectual leaders of the Harlem community. She quarreled especially with Langston Hughes; she rejected the idea that a black writer's chief concern should be how blacks were being portrayed to the white reader. She did not write to "uplift her race," either; because in her view it was already uplifted, she (like Claude McKay) was not embarrassed to present her characters as mixtures of good and bad, strong and weak. Some of the other Harlem writers thought her either naive or egotistical, but Hurston argued that freedom could only mean freedom from all coercion, no matter what the source.

The Great Depression brought an end to the structure that had undergirded Hurston's fieldwork, and she turned fully to writing. Unfortunately her most important work appeared in the mid-1930s when there was little interest in it, or in African American writing in general. She published *Jonah's Gourd Vine* in 1934 (a novel whose main character is based on her father); *Mules and Men* in 1935 (based on material from her field trips in Florida—this was her best-selling book, but it earned a total of only $943.75); and *Their Eyes Were Watching God*, in 1937. This novel about an African American woman's quest for selfhood has become a popular and critical favorite, both a woman's story, and a descriptive critique of southern African American folk society, showing its divisions and diversity. Technically, it is a loosely organized, highly metaphorical novel, with passages of broad folk humor and of extreme artistic compression. Other books followed in 1938 and 1939, and she wrote an autobiography—*Dust Tracks on a Road*—which appeared in 1942, with its occasional expression of antiwhite sentiments removed by her editors. At this point, however, Hurston had no audience. For the last decade of her life she lived in Florida, working from time to time as a maid.

Sweat[1]

It was eleven o'clock of a Spring night in Florida. It was Sunday. Any other night, Delia Jones would have been in bed for two hours by this time. But she was a washwoman, and Monday morning meant a great deal to her. So she collected the soiled clothes on Saturday when she returned the clean things. Sunday night after church, she sorted them and put the white things to soak. It saved her almost a half day's start. A great hamper in the bedroom held the clothes that she brought home. It was so much neater than a number of bundles lying around.

She squatted in the kitchen floor beside the great pile of clothes, sorting them into small heaps according to color, and humming a song in a mournful key, but wondering through it all where Sykes, her husband, had gone with her horse and buckboard.

Just then something long, round, limp and black fell upon her shoulders and slithered to the floor beside her. A great terror took hold of her. It softened her knees and dried her mouth so that it was a full minute before she could cry out or move. Then she saw that it was the big bull whip her husband liked to carry when he drove.

She lifted her eyes to the door and saw him standing there bent over with laughter at her fright. She screamed at him.

"Sykes, what you throw dat whip on me like dat? You know it would skeer me—looks just like a snake, an' you knows how skeered Ah is of snakes."

"Course Ah knowed it! That's how come Ah done it." He slapped his leg with his hand and almost rolled on the ground in his mirth. "If you such a big fool dat you got to have a fit over a earth worm or a string, Ah don't keer how bad Ah skeer you."

"You aint got no business doing it. Gawd knows it's a sin. Some day Ah'm gointuh drop dead from some of yo' foolishness. 'Nother thing, where you been wid mah rig? Ah feeds dat pony. He aint fuh you to be drivin' wid no bull whip."

1. The text is that of the first printing in *Fire!!* (1926).

"You sho is one aggravatin' nigger woman!" he declared and stepped into the room. She resumed her work and did not answer him at once. "Ah done tole you time and again to keep them white folks' clothes outa dis house."

He picked up the whip and glared down at her. Delia went on with her work. She went out into the yard and returned with a galvanized tub and sat it on the washbench. She saw that Sykes had kicked all of the clothes together again, and now stood in her way truculently, his whole manner hoping, *praying*, for an argument. But she walked calmly around him and commenced to re-sort the things.

"Next time, Ah'm gointer kick 'em outdoors," he threatened as he struck a match along the leg of his corduroy breeches.

Delia never looked up from her work, and her thin, stooped shoulders sagged further.

"Ah aint for no fuss t'night, Sykes. Ah just come from taking sacrament at the church house."

He snorted scornfully. "Yeah, you just come from de church house on a Sunday night, but heah you is gone to work on them clothes. You ain't nothing but a hypocrite. One of them amen-corner Christians—sing, whoop, and shout, then come home and wash white folks clothes on the Sabbath."

He stepped roughly upon the whitest pile of things, kicking them helter-skelter as he crossed the room. His wife gave a little scream of dismay, and quickly gathered them together again.

"Sykes, you quit grindin' dirt into these clothes! How can Ah git through by Sat'day if Ah don't start on Sunday?"

"Ah don't keer if you never git through. Anyhow, Ah done promised Gawd and a couple of other men, Ah aint gointer have it in mah house. Don't gimme no lip neither, else Ah'll throw 'em out and put mah fist up side yo' head to boot."

Delia's habitual meekness seemed to slip from her shoulders like a blown scarf. She was on her feet; her poor little body, her bare knuckly hands bravely defying the strapping hulk before her.

"Looka heah, Sykes, you done gone too fur. Ah been married to you fur fifteen years, and Ah been takin' in washin' fur fifteen years. Sweat, sweat, sweat! Work and sweat, cry and sweat, pray and sweat!"

"What's that got to do with me?" he asked brutally.

"What's it got to do with you, Sykes? Mah tub of suds is filled yo' belly with vittles more times than yo' hands is filled it. Mah sweat is done paid for this house and Ah reckon Ah kin keep on sweatin' in it."

She seized the iron skillet from the stove and struck a defensive pose, which act surprised him greatly, coming from her. It cowed him and he did not strike her as he usually did.

"Naw you won't," she panted, "that ole snaggle-toothed black woman you runnin' with aint comin' heah to pile up on *mah* sweat and blood. You aint paid for nothin' on this place, and Ah'm gointer stay right heah till Ah'm toted out foot foremost."

"Well, you better quit gittin' me riled up, else they'll be totin' you out sooner than you expect. Ah'm so tired of you Ah don't know whut to do. Gawd! how Ah hates skinny wimmen!"

A little awed by this new Delia, he sidled out of the door and slammed the back gate after him. He did not say where he had gone, but she knew too well. She knew very well that he would not return until nearly daybreak also. Her work over, she went on to bed but not to sleep at once. Things had come to a pretty pass!

She lay awake, gazing upon the debris that cluttered their matrimonial trail. Not an image left standing along the way. Anything like flowers had long ago been drowned in the salty stream that had been pressed from her heart. Her tears, her sweat, her blood. She had brought love to the union and he had brought a longing after the flesh. Two months after the wedding, he had given her the first brutal beating. She had the memory of his numerous trips to Orlando with all of his wages when he had returned to her penniless, even before the first year had passed. She was young and soft then, but now she thought of her knotty, muscled limbs, her harsh knuckly hands, and drew herself up into an unhappy little ball in the middle of the big feather bed. Too late now to hope for love, even if it were not Bertha it would be someone else. This case differed from the others only in that she was bolder than the others. Too late for everything except her little home. She had built it for her old days, and planted one by one the trees and flowers there. It was lovely to her, lovely.

Somehow, before sleep came, she found herself saying aloud: "Oh well, whatever goes over the Devil's back, is got to come under his belly. Sometime or ruther, Sykes, like everybody else, is gointer reap his sowing." After that she was able to build a spiritual earthworks against her husband. His shells could no longer reach her. *Amen.* She went to sleep and slept until he announced his presence in bed by kicking her feet and rudely snatching the cover away.

"Gimme some kivah heah, an' git yo' damn foots over on yo' own side! Ah oughter mash you in yo' mouf fuh drawing dat skillet on me."

Delia went clear to the rail without answering him. A triumphant indifference to all that he was or did.

The week was as full of work for Delia as all other weeks, and Saturday found her behind her little pony, collecting and delivering clothes.

It was a hot, hot day near the end of July. The village men on Joe Clarke's porch even chewed cane listlessly. They did not hurl the cane-knots as usual. They let them dribble over the edge of the porch. Even conversation had collapsed under the heat.

"Heah come Delia Jones," Jim Merchant said, as the shaggy pony came 'round the bend of the road toward them. The rusty buckboard was heaped with baskets of crisp, clean laundry.

"Yep," Joe Lindsay agreed. "Hot or col', rain or shine, jes ez reg'lar ez de weeks roll roun' Delia carries 'em an' fetches 'em on Sat'day."

"She better if she wanter eat," said Moss. "Sykes Jones aint wuth de shot an' powder hit would tek tuh kill 'em. Not to *huh* he aint."

"He sho' aint," Walter Thomas chimed in. "It's too bad, too, cause she wuz a right pritty li'l trick when he got huh. Ah'd uh mah'ied huh mahseff if he hadnter beat me to it."

Delia nodded briefly at the men as she drove past.

"Too much knockin' will ruin *any* 'oman. He done beat huh 'nough tuh kill three women, let 'lone change they looks," said Elijah Moseley. "How Sykes kin stommuck dat big black greasy Mogul he's layin' roun' wid, gits me. Ah swear dat eight-rock couldn't kiss a sardine can Ah done thowed out de back do' 'way las' yeah."

"Aw, she's fat, thass how come. He's allus been crazy 'bout fat women," put in Merchant. "He'd a' been tied up wid one long time ago if he could a' found one tuh have him. Did Ah tell yuh 'bout him come sidlin' roun' *mah* wife—bringin' her a basket uh pee-cans outa his yard fuh a present? Yessir, mah wife! She tol' him tuh take 'em right straight back home, cause Delia works so hard ovah dat washtub she reckon everything on de place taste lak sweat an' soapsuds. Ah jus' wisht Ah'd a' caught 'im 'roun' dere! Ah'd a' made his hips ketch on fiah down dat shell road."

"Ah know he done it, too. Ah sees 'im grinnin' at every 'oman dat passes," Walter Thomas said. "But even so, he useter eat some mighty big hunks uh humble pie tuh git dat lil' 'oman he got. She wuz ez pretty ez a speckled pup! Dat wuz fifteen yeahs ago. He useter be so skeered uh losin' huh, she could make him do some parts of a husband's duty. Dey never wuz de same in de mind."

"There oughter be a law about him," said Lindsay. "He aint fit tuh carry guts tuh a bear."

Clarke spoke for the first time. "Taint no law on earth dat kin make a man be decent if it aint in 'im. There's plenty men dat takes a wife lak dey do a joint uh sugar-cane. It's round, juicy an' sweet when dey gits it. But dey squeeze an' grind, squeeze an' grind an' wring tell dey wring every drop uh pleasure dat's in 'em out. When dey's satisfied dat dey is wrung dry, dey treats 'em jes lak dey do a cane-chew. Dey thows 'em away. Dey knows whut dey is doin' while dey is at it, an' hates theirselves fuh it but they keeps on hangin' after huh tell she's empty. Den dey hates huh fuh bein' a cane-chew an' in de way."

"We oughter take Sykes an' dat stray 'oman uh his'n down in Lake Howell swamp an' lay on de rawhide till they cain't say 'Lawd a' mussy.' He allus wuz uh ovahbearin' niggah, but since dat white 'oman from up north done teached 'im how to run a automobile, he done got too biggety to live—an' we oughter kill 'im," Old Man Anderson advised.

A grunt of approval went around the porch. But the heat was melting their civic virtue and Elijah Moseley began to bait Joe Clarke.

"Come on, Joe, git a melon outa dere an' slice it up for yo' customers. We'se all sufferin' wid de heat. De bear's done got *me!*"

"Thass right, Joe, a watermelon is jes' whut Ah needs tuh cure de eppizu-dicks." Walter Thomas joined forces with Moseley. "Come on dere, Joe. We all is steady customers an' you aint set us up in a long time. Ah chooses dat long, bowlegged Floridy favorite."

"A god, an' be dough. You all gimme twenty cents and slice away," Clarke retorted. "Ah needs a col' slice m'self. Heah, everybody chip in. Ah'll lend y'all mah meat knife."

The money was quickly subscribed and the huge melon brought forth. At that moment, Sykes and Bertha arrived. A determined silence fell on the porch and the melon was put away again.

Merchant snapped down the blade of his jack-knife and moved toward the store door.

"Come on in, Joe, an' gimme a slab uh sow belly an' uh pound uh coffee—almost fuhgot 'twas Sat'day. Got to git on home." Most of the men left also.

Just then Delia drove past on her way home, as Sykes was ordering magnificently for Bertha. It pleased him for Delia to see.

"Git whutsoever yo' heart desires, Honey. Wait a minute, Joe. Give huh two botles uh strawberry soda-water, uh quart uh parched ground-peas, an a block uh chewin' gum."

With all this they left the store, with Sykes reminding Bertha that this was his town and she could have it if she wanted it.

The men returned soon after they left, and held their watermelon feast.

"Where did Sykes Jones git dat 'oman from nohow?" Lindsay asked.

"Ovah Apopka. Guess dey musta been cleanin' out de town when she lef'. She don't look lak a thing but a hunk uh liver wid hair on it."

"Well, she sho' kin squall," Dave Carter contributed. "When she gits ready tuh laff, she jes' opens huh mouf an' latches it back tuh de las' notch. No ole grandpa alligator down in Lake Bell aint got nothin' on huh."

Bertha had been in town three months now. Sykes was still paying her room rent at Della Lewis'—the only house in town that would have taken her in. Sykes took her frequently to Winter Park to "stomps." He still assured her that he was the swellest man in the state.

"Sho' you kin have dat lil' ole house soon's Ah kin git dat 'oman outa dere. Everything b'longs tuh me an' you sho' kin have it. Ah sho' 'bominates uh skinny 'oman. Lawdy, you sho' is got one portly shape on you! You kin git *anything* you wants. Dis is *mah* town an' you sho' kin have it."

Delia's work-worn knees crawled over the earth in Gethsemane and up the rocks of Calvary many, many times during these months. She avoided the villagers and meeting places in her efforts to be blind and deaf. But Bertha nullified this to a degree, by coming to Delia's house to call Sykes out to her at the gate.

Delia and Sykes fought all the time now with no peaceful interludes. They slept and ate in silence. Two or three times Delia had attempted a timid friendliness, but she was repulsed each time. It was plain that the breaches must remain agape.

The sun had burned July to August. The heat streamed down like a million hot arrows, smiting all things living upon the earth. Grass withered, leaves browned, snakes went blind in shedding and men and dogs went mad. Dog days!

Delia came home one day and found Sykes there before her. She wondered, but started to go on into the house without speaking, even though he was standing in the kitchen door and she must either stoop under his arm or ask him to move. He made no room for her. She noticed a soap box beside the steps, but paid no particular attention to it, knowing that he must have brought it there. As she was stooping to pass under his outstretched arm, he suddenly pushed her backward, laughingly.

"Look in de box dere Delia, Ah done brung yuh somethin'!"

She nearly fell upon the box in her stumbling, and when she saw what it held, she all but fainted outright.

"Sykes! Sykes, mah Gawd! You take dat rattlesnake 'way from heah! You *gottuh*. Oh, Jesus, have mussy!"

"Ah aint gut tuh do nuthin' uh de kin'—fact is Ah aint got tuh do nothin' but die. Taint no use uh you puttin' on airs makin' out lak you skeered uh dat snake—he's gointer stay right heah tell he die. He wouldn't bite me cause Ah knows how tuh handle 'im. Nohow he wouldn't risk breakin' out his fangs 'gin *yo'* skinny laigs."

"Naw, now Sykes, don't keep dat thing 'roun' heah tuh skeer me tuh death. You knows Ah'm even feared uh earth worms. Thass de biggest snake Ah evah did see. Kill 'im Sykes, please."

"Doan ast me tuh do nothin' fuh yuh. Goin' 'roun' tryin' tuh be so damn astorperious. Naw, Ah aint gonna kill it. Ah think uh damn sight mo' uh him dan you! Dat's a nice snake an' anybody doan lak 'im kin jes' hit de grit."

The village soon heard that Sykes had the snake, and came to see and ask questions.

"How de hen-fire did you ketch dat six-foot rattler, Sykes?" Thomas asked.

"He's full uh frogs so he caint hardly move, thass how Ah eased up on 'm. But Ah'm a snake charmer an' knows how tuh handle 'em. Shux, dat aint nothin'. Ah could ketch one eve'y day if Ah so wanted tuh."

"Whut he needs is a heavy hick'ry club leaned real heavy on his head. Dat's de bes 'way tuh charm a rattlesnake."

"Naw, Walt, y'all jes' don't understand dese diamon' backs lak Ah do," said Sykes in a superior tone of voice.

The village agreed with Walter, but the snake stayed on. His box remained by the kitchen door with its screen wire covering. Two or three days later it had digested its meal of frogs and literally came to life. It rattled at every movement in the kitchen or the yard. One day as Delia came down the kitchen steps she saw his chalky-white fangs curved like scimitars hung in the wire meshes. This time she did not run away with averted eyes as usual. She stood for a long time in the doorway in a red fury that grew bloodier for every second that she regarded the creature that was her torment.

That night she broached the subject as soon as Sykes sat down to the table.

"Sykes, Ah wants you tuh take dat snake 'way fum heah. You done starved me an' Ah put up widcher, you done beat me an Ah took dat, but you done kilt all mah insides bringin' dat varmint heah."

Sykes poured out a saucer full of coffee and drank it deliberately before he answered her.

"A whole lot Ah keer 'bout how you feels inside uh out. Dat snake aint goin' no damn wheah till Ah gits ready fuh 'im tuh go. So fur as beatin' is concerned, yuh aint took near all dat you gointer take ef yuh stay 'roun' *me*."

Delia pushed back her plate and got up from the table. "Ah hates you, Sykes," she said calmly. "Ah hates you tuh de same degree dat Ah useter love yuh. Ah done took an' took till mah belly is full up tuh mah neck. Dat's de reason Ah got mah letter fum de church an' moved mah membership tuh Woodbridge—so Ah don't haftuh take no sacrament wid yuh. Ah don't wan-tuh see yuh 'roun' me a-tall. Lay 'roun' wid dat 'oman all yuh wants tuh, but gwan 'way fum me an' mah house. Ah hates yuh lak uh suck-egg dog."

Sykes almost let the huge wad of corn bread and collard greens he was chewing fall out of his mouth in amazement. He had a hard time whipping himself up to the proper fury to try to answer Delia.

"Well, Ah'm glad you does hate me. Ah'm sho' tiahed uh you hangin' ontuh me. Ah don't want yuh. Look at yuh stringey ole neck! Yo' rawbony laigs an' arms is enough tuh cut uh man tuh death. You looks jes' lak de devvul's doll-baby tuh *me*. You cain't hate me no worse dan Ah hates you. Ah been hatin' *you* fuh years."

"Yo' ole black hide don't look lak nothin' tuh me, but uh passel uh wrinkled up rubber, wid yo' big ole yeahs flappin' on each side lak uh paih uh buzzard wings. Don't think Ah'm gointuh be run way fum mah house neither. Ah'm goin' tuh de white folks bout *you*, mah young man, de very nex' time you lay yo' han's on me. Mah cup is done run ovah." Delia said this with no signs of fear and Sykes departed from the house, threatening her, but made not the slightest move to carry out any of them.

That night he did not return at all, and the next day being Sunday, Delia was glad that she did not have to quarrel before she hitched up her pony and drove the four miles to Woodbridge.

She stayed to the night service—"love feast"—which was very warm and full of spirit. In the emotional winds her domestic trials were borne far and wide so that she sang as she drove homeward,

> *Jurden water, black an' col'*
> *Chills de body, not de soul*
> *An' Ah wantah cross Jurden in uh calm time.*

She came from the barn to the kitchen door and stopped.

"Whut's de mattah, ol' satan, you aint kickin' up yo' racket?" She addressed the snake's box. Complete silence. She went on into the house with a new hope in its birth struggles. Perhaps her threat to go to the white folks had frightened Sykes! Perhaps he was sorry! Fifteen years of misery and suppression had brought Delia to the place where she would hope *anything* that looked towards a way over or through her wall of inhibitions.

She felt in the match safe behind the stove at once for a match. There was only one there.

"Dat niggah wouldn't fetch nothin' heah tuh save his rotten neck, but he kin run thew whut Ah brings quick enough. Now he done toted off nigh on tuh haff uh box uh matches. He done had dat 'oman heah in mah house, too."

Nobody but a woman could tell how she knew this even before she struck the match. But she did and it put her into a new fury.

Presently she brought in the tubs to put the white things to soak. This time she decided she need not bring the hamper out of the bedroom; she would go in there and do the sorting. She picked up the pot-bellied lamp and went in. The room was small and the hamper stood hard by the foot of the white iron bed. She could sit and reach through the bedposts—resting as she worked.

"Ah wantah cross Jurden in uh calm time." She was singing again. The mood of the "love feast" had returned. She threw back the lid of the basket almost gaily. Then, moved by both horror and terror, she sprung back toward the door. *There lay the snake in the basket!* He moved sluggishly at first, but even as she turned round and round, jumped up and down in an insanity of fear, he began to stir vigorously. She saw him pouring his awful beauty from the basket upon the bed, then she seized the lamp and ran as fast as she could to the kitchen. The wind from the open door blew out the light and the darkness added to her terror. She sped to the darkness of the yard, slamming the door after her before she thought to set down the lamp. She did not feel safe even on the ground, so she climbed up in the hay barn.

There for an hour or more she lay sprawled upon the hay a gibbering wreck.

Finally she grew quiet, and after that, coherent thought. With this, stalked through her a cold, bloody rage. Hours of this. A period of introspection, a space of retrospection, then a mixture of both. Out of this an awful calm.

"Well, Ah done de bes' Ah could. If things aint right, Gawd knows taint mah fault."

She went to sleep—a twitchy sleep—and woke up to a faint gray sky. There was a loud hollow sound below. She peered out. Sykes was at the wood-pile, demolishing a wire-covered box.

He hurried to the kitchen door, but hung outside there some minutes before he entered, and stood some minutes more inside before he closed it after him.

The gray in the sky was spreading. Delia descended without fear now, and crouched beneath the low bedroom window. The drawn shade shut out the dawn, shut in the night. But the thin walls held back no sound.

"Dat ol' scratch is woke up now!" She mused at the tremendous whirr inside, which every woodsman knows, is one of the sound illusions. The rattler is a ventriloquist. His whirr sounds to the right, to the left, straight ahead, behind, close under foot—everywhere but where it is. Woe to him who guesses wrong unless he is prepared to hold up his end of the argument! Sometimes he strikes without rattling at all.

Inside, Skyes heard nothing until he knocked a pot lid off the stove while trying to reach the match safe in the dark. He had emptied his pockets at Bertha's.

The snake seemed to wake up under the stove and Skyes made a quick leap into the bedroom. In spite of the gin he had had, his head was clearing now.

"Mah Gawd!" he chattered, "ef Ah could on'y strack uh light!"

The rattling ceased for a moment as he stood paralyzed. He waited. It seemed that the snake waited also.

"Oh fuh de light! Ah thought he'd be too sick"—Skyes was muttering to himself when the whirr began again, closer, right underfoot this time. Long before this, Skyes' ability to think had been flattened down to primitive instinct and he leaped—onto the bed.

Outside Delia heard a cry that might have come from a maddened chimpanzee, a stricken gorilla. All the terror, all the horror, all the rage that man possibly could express, without a recognizable human sound.

A tremendous stir inside there, another series of animal screams, the intermittent whirr of the reptile. The shade torn violently down from the window, letting in the red dawn, a huge brown hand seizing the window stick, great dull blows upon the wooden floor punctuating the gibberish of sound long after the rattle of the snake had abruptly subsided. All this Delia could see and hear from her place beneath the window, and it made her ill. She crept over to the four-o'clocks and stretched herself on the cool earth to recover.

She lay there. "Delia, Delia!" She could hear Skyes calling in a most despairing tone as one who expected no answer. The sun crept on up, and he called. Delia could not move—her legs were gone flabby. She never moved, he called, and the sun kept rising.

"Mah Gawd!" she heard him moan. "Mah Gawd fum Heben!" She heard him stumbling about and got up from her flower-bed. The sun was growing warm. As she approached the door she heard him call out hopefully, "Delia, is dat you Ah heah?"

She saw him on his hands and knees as soon as she reached the door. He crept an inch or two toward her—all that he was able, and she saw his horribly swollen neck and his one open eye shining with hope. A surge of pity too strong to support bore her away from that eye that must, could not, fail to see the tubs. He would see the lamp. Orlando with its doctors was too far. She could scarcely reach the Chinaberry tree, where she waited in the growing heat while inside she knew the cold river was creeping up and up to extinguish that eye which must know by now that she knew.

1926

How It Feels to Be Colored Me[1]

I am colored but I offer nothing in the way of extenuating circumstances except the fact that I am the only Negro in the United States whose grandfather on the mother's side was *not* an Indian chief.

I remember the very day that I became colored. Up to my thirteenth year I lived in the little Negro town of Eatonville, Florida. It is exclusively a colored town. The only white people I knew passed through the town going to or coming from Orlando. The native whites rode dusty horses, the Northern tourists chugged down the sandy village road in automobiles. The town knew the Southerners and never stopped cane chewing when they passed. But the Northerners were something else again. They were peered at cautiously from behind the curtains by the timid. The more venturesome would come out on the porch to watch them go past and got just as much pleasure out of the tourists as the tourists got out of the village.

The front porch might seem a daring place for the rest of the town, but it was a gallery seat for me. My favorite place was atop the gate-post. Proscenium box[2] for a born first-nighter. Not only did I enjoy the show, but I didn't mind the actors knowing that I liked it. I usually spoke to them in passing. I'd wave at them and when they returned my salute, I would say something like this: "Howdy-do-well-I-thank-you-where-you-goin'?" Usually automobile or the horse paused at this, and after a queer exchange of compliments, I would probably "go a piece of the way" with them, as we say in farthest

---

1. The text is that of *I Love Myself When I Am Laughing . . . and Then Again When I Am Looking Mean and Impressive* (1979), edited by Alice Walker.
2. Box at the front of the auditorium, closest to the stage.

Florida. If one of my family happened to come to the front in time to see me, of course negotiations would be rudely broken off. But even so, it is clear that I was the first "welcome-to-our-state" Floridian, and I hope the Miami Chamber of Commerce will please take notice.

During this period, white people differed from colored to me only in that they rode through town and never lived there. They liked to hear me "speak pieces" and sing and wanted to see me dance the parse-me-la, and gave me generously of their small silver for doing these things, which seemed strange to me for I wanted to do them so much that I needed bribing to stop. Only they didn't know it. The colored people gave no dimes. They deplored any joyful tendencies in me, but I was their Zora nevertheless. I belonged to them, to the nearby hotels, to the county—everybody's Zora.

But changes came in the family when I was thirteen, and I was sent to school in Jacksonville. I left Eatonville, the town of the oleanders, as Zora. When I disembarked from the river-boat at Jacksonville, she was no more. It seemed that I had suffered a sea change. I was not Zora of Orange County any more, I was now a little colored girl. I found it out in certain ways. In my heart as well as in the mirror, I became a fast brown—warranted not to rub nor run.

But I am not tragically colored. There is no great sorrow dammed up in my soul, nor lurking behind my eyes. I do not mind at all. I do not belong to the sobbing school of Negrohood who hold that nature somehow has given them a lowdown dirty deal and whose feelings are all hurt about it. Even in the helter-skelter skirmish that is my life, I have seen that the world is to the strong regardless of a little pigmentation more or less. No, I do not weep at the world—I am too busy sharpening my oyster knife.

Someone is always at my elbow reminding me that I am the granddaughter of slaves. It fails to register depression with me. Slavery is sixty years in the past. The operation was successful and the patient is doing well, thank you. The terrible struggle that made me an American out of a potential slave said "On the line!" The Reconstruction said "Get set!"; and the generation before said "Go!" I am off to a flying start and I must not halt in the stretch to look behind and weep. Slavery is the price I paid for civilization, and the choice was not with me. It is a bully adventure and worth all that I have paid through my ancestors for it. No one on earth ever had a greater chance for glory. The world to be won and nothing to be lost. It is thrilling to think—to know that for any act of mine, I shall get twice as much praise or twice as much blame. It is quite exciting to hold the center of the national stage, with the spectators not knowing whether to laugh or to weep.

The position of my white neighbor is much more difficult. No brown specter pulls up a chair beside me when I sit down to eat. No dark ghost thrusts its leg against mine in bed. The game of keeping what one has is never so exciting as the game of getting.

I do not always feel colored. Even now I often achieve the unconscious Zora of Eatonville before the Hegira.[3] I feel most colored when I am thrown against a sharp white background.

---

3. Forced march of Muhammad from Mecca to Medina in 622 C.E.; hence any forced flight or journey for safety.

For instance at Barnard. "Besides the waters of the Hudson" I feel my race. Among the thousand white persons, I am a dark rock surged upon, and overswept, but through it all, I remain myself. When covered by the waters, I am; and the ebb but reveals me again.

Sometimes it is the other way around. A white person is set down in our midst, but the contrast is just as sharp for me. For instance, when I sit in the drafty basement that is The New World Cabaret[4] with a white person, my color comes. We enter chatting about any little nothing that we have in common and are seated by the jazz waiters. In the abrupt way that jazz orchestras have, this one plunges into a number. It loses no time in circumlocutions, but gets right down to business. It constricts the thorax and splits the heart with its tempo and narcotic harmonies. This orchestra grows rambunctious, rears on its hind legs and attacks the tonal veil with primitive fury, rending it, clawing it until it breaks through to the jungle beyond. I follow those heathen—follow them exultingly. I dance wildly inside myself; I yell within, I whoop; I shake my assegai[5] above my head, I hurl it true to the mark yeeeeooww! I am in the jungle and living in the jungle way. My face is painted red and yellow and my body is painted blue. My pulse is throbbing like a war drum. I want to slaughter something—give pain, give death to what, I do not know. But the piece ends. The men of the orchestra wipe their lips and rest their fingers. I creep back slowly to the veneer we call civilization with the last tone and find the white friend sitting motionless in his seat smoking calmly.

"Good music they have here," he remarks, drumming the table with his fingertips.

Music. The great blobs of purple and red emotion have not touched him. He has only heard what I felt. He is far away and I see him but dimly across the ocean and the continent that have fallen between us. He is so pale with his whiteness then and I am so colored.

At certain times I have no race, I am me. When I set my hat at a certain angle and saunter down Seventh Avenue, Harlem City, feeling as snooty as the lions in front of the Forty-Second Street Library, for instance. So far as my feelings are concerned, Peggy Hopkins Joyce on the Boule Mich[6] with her gorgeous raiment, stately carriage, knees knocking together in a most aristocratic manner, has nothing on me. The cosmic Zora emerges. I belong to no race nor time. I am the eternal feminine with its string of beads.

I have no separate feeling about being an American citizen and colored. I am merely a fragment of the Great Soul that surges within the boundaries. My country, right or wrong.

Sometimes, I feel discriminated against, but it does not make me angry. It merely astonishes me. How can any deny themselves the pleasure of my company? It's beyond me.

But in the main, I feel like a brown bag of miscellany propped against a wall. Against a wall in company with other bags, white, red and yellow. Pour

---

4. Popular Harlem nightclub in the 1920s.
5. A slender spear used by some South African peoples.
6. Boulevard St. Michel, a street on the Left Bank of Paris running through the Latin Quarter. It is lined with cafés that were—and still are—frequented by Americans. Joyce was a much-photographed socialite and heiress.

out the contents, and there is discovered a jumble of small things priceless and worthless. A first-water diamond, an empty spool, bits of broken glass, lengths of string, a key to a door long since crumbled away, a rusty knife-blade, old shoes saved for a road that never was and never will be, a nail bent under the weight of things too heavy for any nail, a dried flower or two still a little fragrant. In your hand is the brown bag. On the ground before you is the jumble it held—so much like the jumble in the bags, could they be emptied, that all might be dumped in a single heap and the bags refilled without altering the content of any greatly. A bit of colored glass more or less would not matter. Perhaps that is how the Great Stuffer of Bags filled them in the first place—who knows?

1928

E. E. CUMMINGS
1894–1962

Beginning in the 1920s and 1930s, Edward Estlin Cummings built a reputation as author of a particularly agreeable kind of modernist poetry, distinguished by clever formal innovation, a tender lyricism, and the thematic celebration of individuals against mass society. These qualities were evident in his first literary success, a zesty prose account of his experience in a French prison camp during World War I, *The Enormous Room* (1922). He and a friend had joined the ambulance corps in France the day after the United States entered the war; their disdain for the bureaucracy, expressed in outspoken letters home, aroused antagonism among French officials and they were imprisoned. To be made a prisoner by one's own side struck Cummings as outrageous and yet funny; from the experience he produced an ironic, profane celebration of the ordinary soldier and an attack on bureaucracy. His poetry continued the attack on depersonalized, commercial, exploitative mass culture and celebrated loners, lovers, and nonconformists.

He was born in Cambridge, Massachusetts. His father was a Congregationalist minister and teacher at Harvard; the family was close knit and Cummings, a much-loved son. While a student at Harvard (he graduated in 1915 and took an M.A. in 1916) he began to write poetry based on the intricate stanza patterns of the pre-Raphaelite and Metaphysical writers he was reading in English literature classes. When he began to innovate—as he did after discovering the poetry of Ezra Pound—he was able to build (like Pound himself) from a firm apprenticeship in traditional techniques.

After the war, Cummings established a life that included a studio in Greenwich Village, travel and sojourns in France, and summers at the family home in New Hampshire. He was a painter as well as a poet; simple living and careful management of a small allowance from his mother, along with prizes, royalties, and commissions, enabled him to work full time as an artist. He published four volumes of well-received poetry in the 1920s and a book of collected poems toward the end of the 1930s. In the 1950s he visited and read at many college campuses, where students

E. E. Cummings, self-portrait, 1939. Cummings showed his early abstract paintings at modernist exhibitions like that of New York's Society of Independent Artists; his later work, like this self-portrait, became more realistic and figurative.

enjoyed his tricks of verse and vocabulary and appreciated his tender yet earthy poetry. He received a special citation by the National Book Award committee in 1955 and the Bollingen Prize in 1957.

In his attempts to reshape poetry Cummings was also concerned with being widely accessible. Cummings's verse is characterized by common speech and attention to the visual form of the poem—that is, the poem as it appears on the page as distinguished from its sound when read aloud. Experiments with capitalization or lack of it, punctuation, line breaks, hyphenation, and verse shapes were all carried out for the reader's eyes as well as ears. To express his sense that life was always in process, he wrote untitled poems without beginnings and endings, consisting of fragmentary lines. There is always humor in his poetry, and his outrage at cruelty and exploitation is balanced with gusto and celebration of the body.

The text of the poems included here is that of *Complete Poems* (1991).

in Just-

in Just-
spring   when the world is mud-
luscious the little
lame balloonman

whistles   far   and wee   5

and eddieandbill come
running from marbles and
piracies and it's
spring

when the world is puddle-wonderful   10

the queer
old balloonman whistles

far   and   wee
and bettyandisbel come dancing

from hop-scotch and jump-rope and   15

it's
spring
and
    the

        goat-footed   20

balloonMan   whistles
far
and
wee

                                1920, 1923

O sweet spontaneous

O sweet spontaneous
earth how often have
the
doting

        fingers of   5
prurient philosophers pinched
and
poked

thee
,has the naughty thumb   10
of science prodded
thy

    beauty   .how
often have religions taken
thee upon their scraggy knees   15
squeezing and

buffeting thee that thou mightest conceive
gods
        (but
true   20

to the incomparable
couch of death thy
rhythmic
lover

thou answerest   25

them only with

spring)

1920, 1923

Buffalo Bill 's

Buffalo Bill 's[1]
defunct
          who used to
          ride a watersmooth-silver
                                        stallion   5
and break onetwothreefourfive pigeonsjustlikethat
                                                    Jesus

he was a handsome man
                          and what i want to know is
how do you like your blueeyed boy   10
Mister Death

1920, 1923

"next to of course god america i

"next to of course god america i
love you land of the pilgrims' and so forth oh
say can you see by the dawn's early my
country 'tis of centuries come and go
and are no more what of it we should worry   5
in every language even deafanddumb
thy sons acclaim your glorious name by gorry
by jingo by gee by gosh by gum
why talk of beauty what could be more beautiful than these heroic happy dead   10
who rushed like lions to the roaring slaughter
they did not stop to think they died instead
then shall the voice of liberty be mute?"

He spoke.   And drank rapidly a glass of water

1926

1. William F. Cody (1846–1917), American scout and Wild West showman.

i sing of Olaf glad and big

i sing of Olaf glad and big
whose warmest heart recoiled at war:
a conscientious object-or

his wellbelovéd colonel(trig
westpointer[1] most succinctly bred)   5
took erring Olaf soon in hand;
but—though an host of overjoyed
noncoms[2](first knocking on the head
him)do through icy waters roll
that helplessness which others stroke   10
with brushes recently employed
anent this muddy toiletbowl,
while kindred intellects evoke
allegiance per blunt instruments—
Olaf(being to all intents   15
a corpse and wanting any rag
upon what God unto him gave)
responds,without getting annoyed
"I will not kiss your fucking flag"

straightway the silver bird[3] looked grave   20
(departing hurriedly to shave)

but—though all kinds of officers
(a yearning nation's blueeyed pride)
their passive prey did kick and curse
until for wear their clarion   25
voices and boots were much the worse,
and egged the firstclassprivates on
his rectum wickedly to tease
by means of skilfully applied
bayonets roasted hot with heat—   30
Olaf(upon what were once knees)
does almost ceaselessly repeat
"there is some shit I will not eat"

our president,being of which
assertions duly notified   35
threw the yellowsonofabitch
into a dungeon,where he died

Christ(of His mercy infinite)
i pray to see; and Olaf,too

1. Graduate of the U.S. Military Academy at
West Point, New York.

2. Noncommissioned officers.
3. Insignia of a colonel.

preponderatingly because 40
unless statistics lie he was
more brave than me:more blond than you.

1931

somewhere i have never travelled,gladly beyond

somewhere i have never travelled,gladly beyond
any experience,your eyes have their silence:
in your most frail gesture are things which enclose me,
or which i cannot touch because they are too near

your slightest look easily will unclose me 5
though i have closed myself as fingers,
you open always petal by petal myself as Spring opens
(touching skilfully,mysteriously)her first rose

or if your wish be to close me,iand
my life will shut very beautifully,suddenly, 10
as when the heart of this flower imagines
the snow carefully everywhere descending;

nothing which we are to perceive in this world equals
the power of your intense fragility:whose texture
compels me with the colour of its countries, 15
rendering death and forever with each breathing

(i do not know what it is about you that closes
and opens;only something in me understands
the voice of your eyes is deeper than all roses)
nobody,not even the rain,has such small hands 20

1931

anyone lived in a pretty how town

anyone lived in a pretty how town
(with up so floating many bells down)
spring summer autumn winter
he sang his didn't he danced his did.

Women and men(both little and small) 5
cared for anyone not at all
they sowed their isn't they reaped their same
sun moon stars rain

children guessed(but only a few
and down they forgot as up they grew 10

autumn winter spring summer)
that noone loved him more by more

when by now and tree by leaf
she laughed his joy she cried his grief
bird by snow and stir by still   15
anyone's any was all to her

someones married their everyones
laughed their cryings and did their dance
(sleep wake hope and then)they
said their nevers they slept their dream   20

stars rain sun moon
(and only the snow can begin to explain
how children are apt to forget to remember
with up so floating many bells down)

one day anyone died i guess   25
(and noone stooped to kiss his face)
busy folk buried them side by side
little by little and was by was

all by all and deep by deep
and more by more they dream their sleep   30
noone and anyone earth by april
wish by spirit and if by yes.

Women and men(both dong and ding)
summer autumn winter spring
reaped their sowing and went their came   35
sun moon stars rain

1940

JEAN TOOMER
1894–1967

Jean Toomer's *Cane*, the author's contribution to Harlem Renaissance literature, received immediate acclaim when it appeared in 1923. Toomer described African American communities from Chicago and Washington, D.C., to small-town Georgia through the analytic filter of a modernist, urban literary style. William Stanley Braithwaite, in the NAACP-sponsored *Crisis*, praised him as the first to "write about the Negro without the surrender or the compromise of the author's vision." Sherwood Anderson recognized *Cane* as the work of an artistic peer, and other readers compared it favorably to Anderson's *Winesburg, Ohio*.

Born in Washington, D.C., Toomer never knew his father. He grew up with his grandfather, who had been an important Louisiana politician during the Reconstruction era, and his mother. After high school graduation, he attended several colleges—the University of Wisconsin, the Massachusetts College of Agriculture, the American College of Physical Training in Chicago, the University of Chicago, and the City College of New York—without completing a degree. He held numerous short-term jobs in various parts of the country, including four months in 1921 as superintendent of a small black school in Sparta, Georgia. This encounter with black Americans in the rural South formed the basis of *Cane*.

Toomer began writing when he was in his middle twenties, publishing poems and stories in avant-garde magazines such as *Broom*, the *Little Review*, and *Prairie*. He also published in the major political and artistic journals of the Harlem Renaissance such as the *Liberator, Crisis*, and *Opportunity*. Composed as an assemblage of short stories, sketches, poems, and even a play, *Cane* brought together many of Toomer's published magazine pieces.

Part I of *Cane*, set in rural Georgia, depicts a black community based in the rhythms of cotton culture, charged with sexual desire, and menaced by white violence. Part II shows black life in Washington, D.C., and Chicago, the fast-paced urban hives of money and ambition. The autobiographical third part describes an African American intellectual teaching in the South, trying to put down roots in an unfamiliar setting that he struggles to recognize as the source of his own artistic ambitions. This three-part structure is held together by a narrator who alternately steps forward in a first-person voice and recedes into third-person narration, poetry, or drama. *Cane*'s shifting voices explore whether a northern, urban African American can understand himself and his vocation by immersion in a black folk heritage that he has never known. The work is distinguished by its poetic, imagistic, evocative prose; its linguistic innovativeness; and its experimental construction.

Toomer spent much of the last forty years of his life looking for a spiritual community; he had difficulty finding publishers for the writing he produced during these decades. For a while he was a disciple of the Russian mystic George I. Gurdjieff. In the late 1940s he became a committed Quaker. At his death he left many unpublished short stories, as well as novels, plays, and an autobiography.

The text is that of the first edition (1923) as corrected in 1973.

From Cane[1]

Georgia Dusk

The sky, lazily disdaining to pursue
    The setting sun, too indolent to hold
    A lengthened tournament for flashing gold,
Passively darkens for night's barbecue,

A feast of moon and men and barking hounds,   5
    An orgy for some genius of the South
    With blood-hot eyes and cane-lipped scented mouth,
Surprised in making folk-songs from soul sounds.

1. Of the book's three sections, the first and the last are Georgia scenes. "Fern" appears in the first section after the poem "Georgia Dusk." "Portrait in Georgia" concludes the first section. "Seventh Street" is the first sketch in the second section, which is devoted to Washington, D.C., and Chicago.

The sawmill blows its whistle, buzz-saws stop,
 And silence breaks the bud of knoll and hill,   10
 Soft settling pollen where plowed lands fulfill
Their early promise of a bumper crop.

Smoke from the pyramidal sawdust pile
 Curls up, blue ghosts of trees, tarrying low
 Where only chips and stumps are left to show   15
The solid proof of former domicile.

Meanwhile, the men, with vestiges of pomp,
 Race memories of king and caravan,
 High-priests, an ostrich, and a juju-man,[2]
Go singing through the footpaths of the swamp.   20

Their voices rise . . the pine trees are guitars,
 Strumming, pine-needles fall like sheets of rain . .
 Their voices rise . . the chorus of the cane
Is caroling a vesper to the stars . .

O singers, resinous and soft your songs   25
 Above the sacred whisper of the pines,
 Give virgin lips to cornfield concubines,
Bring dreams of Christ to dusky cane-lipped throngs.

Fern

Face flowed into her eyes. Flowed in soft cream foam and plaintive ripples, in such a way that wherever your glance may momentarily have rested, it immediately thereafter wavered in the direction of her eyes. The soft suggestion of down slightly darkened, like the shadow of a bird's wing might, the creamy brown color of her upper lip. Why, after noticing it, you sought her eyes, I cannot tell you. Her nose was aquiline, Semitic. If you have heard a Jewish cantor[3] sing, if he has touched you and made your own sorrow seem trivial when compared with his, you will know my feeling when I follow the curves of her profile, like mobile rivers, to their common delta. They were strange eyes. In this, that they sought nothing—that is, nothing that was obvious and tangible and that one could see, and they gave the impression that nothing was to be denied. When a woman seeks, you will have observed, her eyes deny. Fern's eyes desired nothing that you could give her; there was no reason why they should withhold. Men saw her eyes and fooled themselves. Fern's eyes said to them that she was easy. When she was young, a few men took her, but got no joy from it. And then, once done, they felt bound to her (quite unlike their hit and run with other girls), felt as though it would take them a lifetime to fulfill an obligation which they could find no name for. They became attached to her, and hungered after finding the barest trace of what she might desire. As she grew up, new men who came to town felt as almost

2. West African tribesman who controls the magical fetish or charm, or "juju."

3. Singer in religious services.

everyone did who ever saw her: that they would not be denied. Men were everlastingly bringing her their bodies. Something inside of her got tired of them, I guess, for I am certain that for the life of her she could not tell why or how she began to turn them off. A man in fever is no trifling thing to send away. They began to leave her, baffled and ashamed, yet vowing to themselves that some day they would do some fine thing for her: send her candy every week and not let her know whom it came from, watch out for her wedding-day and give her a magnificent something with no name on it, buy a house and deed it to her, rescue her from some unworthy fellow who had tricked her into marrying him. As you know, men are apt to idolize or fear that which they cannot understand, especially if it be a woman. She did not deny them, yet the fact was that they were denied. A sort of superstition crept into their consciousness of her being somehow above them. Being above them meant that she was not to be approached by anyone. She became a virgin. Now a virgin in a small southern town is by no means the usual thing, if you will believe me. That the sexes were made to mate is the practice of the South. Particularly, black folks were made to mate. And it is black folks whom I have been talking about thus far. What white men thought of Fern I can arrive at only by analogy. They let her alone.

Anyone, of course, could see her, could see her eyes. If you walked up the Dixie Pike most any time of day, you'd be most like to see her resting listless-like on the railing of her porch, back propped against a post, head tilted a little forward because there was a nail in the porch post just where her head came which for some reason or other she never took the trouble to pull out. Her eyes, if it were sunset, rested idly where the sun, molten and glorious, was pouring down between the fringe of pines. Or maybe they gazed at the gray cabin on the knoll from which an evening folk-song was coming. Perhaps they followed a cow that had been turned loose to roam and feed on cotton-stalks and corn leaves. Like as not they'd settle on some vague spot above the horizon, though hardly a trace of wistfulness would come to them. If it were dusk, then they'd wait for the search-light of the evening train which you could see miles up the track before it flared across the Dixie Pike, close to her home. Wherever they looked, you'd follow them and then waver back. Like her face, the whole countryside seemed to flow into her eyes. Flowed into them with the soft listless cadence of Georgia's South. A young Negro, once, was looking at her, spellbound, from the road. A white man passing in a buggy had to flick him with his whip if he was to get by without running him over. I first saw her on her porch. I was passing with a fellow whose crusty numbness (I was from the North and suspected of being prejudiced and stuck-up) was melting as he found me warm. I asked him who she was. "That's Fern," was all that I could get from him. Some folks already thought that I was given to nosing around; I let it go at that, so far as questions were concerned. But at first sight of her I felt as if I heard a Jewish cantor sing. As if his singing rose above the unheard chorus of a folk-song. And I felt bound to her. I too had my dreams: something I would do for her. I have knocked about from town to town too much not to know the futility of mere change of place. Besides, picture if you can, this cream-colored solitary girl sitting at a tenement window looking down on the indifferent throngs of Harlem. Better that she listen to folk-songs at dusk in Georgia, you would say, and so would I. Or, suppose she came up North and married. Even a doctor or a lawyer, say, one who would be sure to get along—that is, make money. You and I know, who have had experience in such things, that love is not a thing like prejudice which can be bettered by changes of town. Could men in Washington, Chicago, or New York, more than the men of Georgia, bring her something left vacant by the bestowal of their bodies? You and I who know men in these cities will have to say, they could not. See her out and out a prostitute along State Street in Chicago. See her move into a southern town where white men are more aggressive. See her become a white man's concubine . . . Something I must do for her. There was myself. What could I do for her? Talk, of course. Push back the fringe of pines upon new horizons. To what purpose? and what for? Her? Myself? Men in her case seem to lose their selfishness. I lost mine before I touched her. I ask you, friend (it makes no difference if you sit in the Pullman or the Jim Crow[4] as the train crosses her road), what thoughts would come to you—that is, after you'd finished with the thoughts that leap into men's minds at the sight of a pretty woman who will not deny them; what thoughts would come to you, had you seen her in a quick flash, keen and intuitively, as she sat there on her porch when your train thundered by? Would you have got off at the next station and come back for her to take her where? Would you have completely forgotten her as soon as you reached Macon, Atlanta, Augusta, Pasadena, Madison, Chicago, Boston, or New Orleans? Would you tell your wife or sweetheart about a girl you saw? Your thoughts can help me, and I would like to know. Something I would do for her . . .

One evening I walked up the Pike on purpose, and stopped to say hello. Some of her family were about, but they moved away to make room for me. Damn if I knew how to begin. Would you? Mr. and Miss So-and-So, people, the weather, the crops, the new preacher, the frolic, the church benefit, rabbit and possum hunting, the new soft drink they had at old Pap's store, the schedule of the trains, what kind of town Macon was, Negro's migration north, bollweevils, syrup, the Bible—to all these things she gave a yassur or nassur, without further comment. I began to wonder if perhaps my own emotional sensibility had played one of its tricks on me. "Lets take a walk," I at last ventured. The suggestion, coming after so long an isolation, was novel enough, I guess, to surprise. But it wasnt that. Something told me that men before me had said just that as a prelude to the offering of their bodies. I tried to tell her with my eyes. I think she understood. The thing from her that made my throat catch, vanished. Its passing left her visible in a way I'd thought, but never seen. We walked down the Pike with people on all the porches gaping at us. "Doesnt it make you mad?" She meant the row of petty gossiping people. She meant the world. Through a canebrake that was ripe for cutting, the branch was reached. Under a sweet-gum tree, and where reddish leaves had dammed the creek a little, we sat down. Dusk, suggesting the almost imperceptible procession of giant trees, settled with a purple haze about the cane. I felt strange, as I always do in Georgia, particularly at dusk. I felt that things unseen to men were tangibly immediate. It would not

<hr />

4. In the segregated South, black persons were required to sit in the "Jim Crow" section of railway cars and were not allowed as passengers in the first-class "Pullman" lounges, or sleeping cars.

have surprised me had I had vision. People have them in Georgia more often than you would suppose. A black woman once saw the mother of Christ and drew her in charcoal on the courthouse wall . . . When one is on the soil of one's ancestors, most anything can come to one . . . From force of habit, I suppose, I held Fern in my arms—that is, without at first noticing it. Then my mind came back to her. Her eyes, unusually weird and open, held me. Held God. He flowed in as I've seen the countryside flow in. Seen men. I must have done something—what, I don't know, in the confusion of my emotion. She sprang up. Rushed some distance from me. Fell to her knees, and began swaying, swaying. Her body was tortured with something it could not let out. Like boiling sap it flooded arms and fingers till she shook them as if they burned her. It found her throat, and spattered inarticulately in plaintive, convulsive sounds, mingled with calls to Christ Jesus. And then she sang, brokenly. A Jewish cantor singing with a broken voice. A child's voice, uncertain, or an old man's. Dusk hid her; I could hear only her song. It seemed to me as though she were pounding her head in anguish upon the ground. I rushed at her. She fainted in my arms.

There was talk about her fainting with me in the canefield. And I got one or two ugly looks from town men who'd set themselves up to protect her. In fact, there was talk of making me leave town. But they never did. They kept a watch-out for me, though. Shortly after, I came back North. From the train window I saw her as I crossed her road. Saw her on her porch, head tilted a little forward where the nail was, eyes vaguely focused on the sunset. Saw her face flow into them, the countryside and something that I call God, flowing into them . . . Nothing ever really happened. Nothing ever came to Fern, not even I. Something I would do for her. Some fine unnamed thing . . . And, friend, you? She is still living, I have reason to know. Her name, against the chance that you might happen down that way, is Fernie May Rosen.

* * *

Portrait in Georgia

Hair—braided chestnut,
    coiled like a lyncher's rope,
Eyes—fagots,
Lips—old scars, or the first red blisters,
Breath—the last sweet scent of cane,
And her slim body, white as the ash
    of black flesh after flame.

* * *

Seventh Street

Money burns the pocket, pocket hurts,
Bootleggers in silken shirts,
Ballooned, zooming Cadillacs,
Whizzing, whizzing down the street-car tracks.

Seventh Street is a bastard of Prohibition and the War.[5] A crude-boned, soft-skinned wedge of nigger life breathing its loafer air, jazz songs and love, thrusting unconscious rhythms, black reddish blood into the white and whitewashed wood of Washington. Stale soggy wood of Washington. Wedges rust in soggy wood . . . Split it! In two! Again! Shred it! . . the sun. Wedges are brilliant in the sun; ribbons of wet wood dry and blow away. Black reddish blood. Pouring for crude-boned soft-skinned life, who set you flowing? Blood suckers of the War would spin in a frenzy of dizziness if they drank your blood. Prohibition would put a stop to it. Who set you flowing? White and whitewash disappear in blood. Who set you flowing? Flowing down the smooth asphalt of Seventh Street, in shanties, brick office buildings, theaters, drug stores, restaurants, and cabarets? Eddying on the corners? Swirling like a blood-red smoke up where the buzzards fly in heaven? God would not dare to suck black red blood. A Nigger God! He would duck his head in shame and call for the Judgment Day. Who set you flowing?

> Money burns the pocket, pocket hurts,
> Bootleggers in silken shirts,
> Ballooned, zooming Cadillacs,
> Whizzing, whizzing down the street-car tracks.

1923

5. World War I.

F. SCOTT FITZGERALD
1896–1940

In the 1920s and 1930s F. Scott Fitzgerald was equally famous as a writer and as a celebrity author whose lifestyle seemed to symbolize the two decades; in the 1920s he stood for all-night partying, drinking, and the pursuit of pleasure, while in the 1930s he stood for the gloomy aftermath of excess. "Babylon Revisited," written immediately after the stock market crash, is simultaneously a personal and a national story.

Fitzgerald was born in a middle-class neighborhood in St. Paul, Minnesota, descended on his father's side from southern colonial landowners and legislators, on his mother's from Irish immigrants. Much of his boyhood was spent in Buffalo and Syracuse, New York. The family was not prosperous and it took an aunt's support to send him to a Catholic boarding school in New Jersey in 1911. Two years later he entered Princeton University, where he participated in extracurricular literary and dramatic activities, forming friendships with campus intellectuals, like the prominent critic Edmund Wilson, who were to help him in later years. But he failed to make the football team and felt the disappointment for years. After three years of college Fitzgerald quit to join the army, but the war ended before he saw active service. Stationed in Montgomery, Alabama, he met and courted Zelda Sayre, a local belle who rejected him. In 1919 he went to New York City, determined to make a fortune and win Zelda. Amazingly, he succeeded. A novel he had begun in college, revised, and published in 1920 as *This Side of Paradise* became an immediate best-seller, making its author rich and famous at the age of twenty-four. As one of the earliest examples of a novel about college life, *This Side of Paradise* was accepted as the voice of the younger generation in a society increasingly oriented toward youth. He combined the traditional narrative and rhetorical gifts of a good fiction writer, it appeared, with a thoroughly modern sensibility. A week after the novel appeared, Scott and Zelda were married. Living extravagantly in New York City and St. Paul, and on Long Island, they more than spent the money Fitzgerald made from two collections of short stories—*Flappers and Philosophers* (1920) and *Tales of the Jazz Age* (1922)—and a second novel, *The Beautiful and Damned* (1922). Their only child, a daughter, was born in 1921.

In 1924, the Fitzgeralds moved to Europe to live more cheaply. They made friends with American expatriates: Hemingway, Stein, and Pound among others. During this time Fitzgerald published his best-known and most successful novel, *The Great Gatsby* (1925), and another book of short stories, *All the Sad Young Men* (1926). *The Great Gatsby* tells the story of a self-made young man whose dream of success, personified in a rich and beautiful young woman named Daisy, turns out to be a fantasy in every sense: Daisy belongs to a corrupt society, Gatsby corrupts himself in the quest for her, and above all, the rich have no intention of sharing their privileges. The novel is narrated from the point of view of Nick Carraway, an onlooker who is both moved and repelled by the tale he tells and whose responses form a sort of subplot: this experiment in narrative point of view was widely imitated. The structure of *The Great Gatsby* is compact; the style dazzling; and its images of automobiles, parties, and garbage heaps seem to capture the contradictions of a consumer society. The novel became an instant classic and remains so to this day.

Fitzgerald wrote dozens of short stories during the twenties; many were published in the mass-circulation weekly the *Saturday Evening Post*, which paid extremely well. Despite the pace at which he worked—in all he wrote 178 short stories—the Fitzgeralds could not get out of debt. Scott became an alcoholic, and Zelda had a mental breakdown in 1930 and spent most of the rest of her life institutionalized. In 1931 Fitzgerald reestablished himself permanently in the United States, living at first near Baltimore, where his wife was hospitalized. A fourth novel, *Tender Is the Night*, appeared in 1934. The novel follows the emotional decline of a young American psychiatrist whose personal energies are sapped and his career corroded equally by his marriage to a beautiful and wealthy patient and his own weakness of character ("character" was one of Fitzgerald's favorite concepts). As in *The Great Gatsby*, the character begins as a disciple of the work ethic and turns into a pursuer of wealth, and the American Dream accordingly turns into a nightmare. Unlike *Gatsby*, whose characters never really connect with each other, *Tender Is the Night* shows a range of intimacies, none of them successful. The novel did not sell well. In 1937 Fitzgerald turned to Hollywood screenwriting; toward the end of the decade things were looking up for him, and he planned to revive his career as a fiction writer. But his health had been ruined by heavy drinking; he died of a heart attack in Hollywood at the age of forty-four, leaving an unfinished novel about a film mogul, *The Last Tycoon*, which was brought out by Edmund Wilson in 1941. Wilson also successfully promoted Fitzgerald's posthumous reputation by editing a collection of his writings, which he called *The Crack-Up*, in 1945.

The text of "Winter Dreams" is from *Metropolitan* magazine (1922); that of "Babylon Revisited" is from *Stories of F. Scott Fitzgerald* (1951).

Winter Dreams

Some of the caddies were poor as sin and lived in one-room houses with a neurasthenic cow in the front yard, but Dexter Green's father owned the second best grocery store in Dillard—the best one was "The Hub," patronized by the wealthy people from Lake Erminie—and Dexter caddied only for pocket-money.

In the fall when the days became crisp and grey and the long Minnesota winter shut down like the white lid of a box, Dexter's skis moved over the snow that hid the fairways of the golf course. At these times the country gave him a feeling of profound melancholy—it offended him that the links should lie in enforced fallowness, haunted by ragged sparrows for the long season. It was dreary, too, that on the tees where the gay colors fluttered in summer there were now only the desolate sand-boxes knee-deep in crusted ice. When he crossed the hills the wind blew cold as misery, and if the sun was out he tramped with his eyes squinted up against the hard dimensionless glare.

In April the winter ceased abruptly. The snow ran down into Lake Erminie scarcely tarrying for the early golfers to brave the season with red and black balls. Without elation, without an interval of moist glory the cold was gone.

Dexter knew that there was something dismal about this northern spring, just as he knew there was something gorgeous about the fall. Fall made him clench his hands and tremble and repeat idiotic sentences to himself and make brisk abrupt gestures of command to imaginary audiences and armies. October filled him with hope which November raised to a sort of ecstatic triumph, and in this wood the fleeting brilliant impressions of the summer at Lake Erminie were ready grist to his will. He became a golf champion and defeated Mr. T. A. Hedrick in a marvelous match played over a hundred times in the fairways of his imagination, a match each detail of which he changed about untiringly—sometimes winning with almost laughable ease, sometimes coming up magnificently from behind. Again, stepping from a Pierce-Arrow automobile, like Mr. Mortimer Jones, he strolled frigidly into the lounge of the Erminie Golf Club—or perhaps, surrounded by an admiring crowd, he gave an exhibition of fancy diving from the springboard of the Erminie Club raft. . . . Among those most impressed was Mr. Mortimer Jones.

And one day it came to pass that Mr. Jones, himself and not his ghost, came up to Dexter, almost with tears in his eyes and said that Dexter was the —— best caddy in the club and wouldn't he decide not to quit if Mr. Jones made it worth his while, because every other —— caddy in the club lost one ball a hole for him—regularly—

"No, sir," said Dexter, decisively, "I don't want to caddy any more." Then, after a pause, "I'm too old."

"You're—why, you're not more than fourteen. Why did you decide just this morning that you wanted to quit? You promised that next week you'd go over to the state tournament with me."

"I decided I was too old."

Dexter handed in his "A Class" badge, collected what money was due him from the caddy master and caught the train for Dillard.

"The best —— caddy I ever saw," shouted Mr. Mortimer Jones over a drink that afternoon. "Never lost a ball! Willing! Intelligent! Quiet! Honest! Grateful!—"

The little girl who had done this was eleven—beautifully ugly as little girls are apt to be who are destined after a few years to be inexpressably lovely and bring no end of misery to a great number of men. The spark, however, was perceptible. There was a general ungodliness in the way her lips twisted down at the corners when she smiled and in the—Heaven help us!—in the almost passionate quality of her eyes. Vitality is born early in such women. It was utterly in evidence now, shining through her thin frame in a sort of glow.

She had come eagerly out on to the course at nine o'clock with a white linen nurse and five small new golf clubs in a white canvas bag which the nurse was carrying. When Dexter first saw her she was standing by the caddy house, rather ill-at-ease and trying to conceal the fact by engaging her nurse in an obviously unnatural conversation illumined by startling and irrevelant smiles from herself.

"Well, it's certainly a nice day, Hilda," Dexter heard her say, then she drew down the corners of her mouth, smiled and glanced furtively around, her eyes in transit falling for an instant on Dexter.

Then to the nurse:

"Well, I guess there aren't very many people out here this morning, are there?"

The smile again radiant, blatantly artificial—convincing.

"I don't know what we're supposed to do now," said the nurse, looking nowhere in particular.

"Oh, that's all right"—the smile—"I'll fix it up."

Dexter stood perfectly still, his mouth faintly ajar. He knew that if he moved forward a step his stare would be in her line of vision—if he moved backward he would lose his full view of her face—For a moment he had not realized how young she was. Now he remembered having seen her several times the year before—in bloomers.

Suddenly, involuntarily, he laughed, a short abrupt laugh—then, startled by himself, he turned and began to walk quickly away.

"Boy!"

Dexter stopped.

"Boy—"

Beyond question he was addressed. Not only that, but he was treated to that absurd smile, that preposterous smile—the memory of which at least half a dozen men were to carry to the grave.

"Boy, do you know where the golf teacher is?"

"He's giving a lesson."

"Well, do you know where the caddy-master is?"

"He's not here yet this morning."

"Oh." For a moment this baffled her. She stood alternately on her right and left foot.

"We'd like to get a caddy," said the nurse. "Mrs. Mortimer Jones sent us out to play golf and we don't know how without we get a caddy."

Here she was stopped by an ominous glance from Miss Jones, followed immediately by the smile.

"There aren't any caddies here except me," said Dexter to the nurse. "And I got to stay here in charge until the caddy-master gets here."

"Oh."

Miss Jones and her retinue now withdrew and at a proper distance from Dexter became involved in a heated conversation. The conversation was concluded by Miss Jones taking one of the clubs and hitting it on the ground with violence. For further emphasis she raised it again and was about to bring it down smartly upon the nurse's bosom, when the nurse seized the club and twisted it from her hands.

"You darn *fool!*" cried Miss Jones wildly.

Another argument ensued. Realizing that the elements of the comedy were implied in the scene, Dexter several times began to smile but each time slew the smile before it reached maturity. He could not resist the monstrous conviction that the little girl was justified in beating the nurse.

The situation was resolved by the fortuitous appearance of the caddy-master who was appealed to immediately by the nurse.

"Miss Jones is to have a little caddy and this one says he can't go."

"Mr. McKenna said I was to wait here till you came," said Dexter quickly.

"Well, he's here now." Miss Jones smiled cheerfully at the caddy-master. Then she dropped her bag and set off at a haughty mince toward the first tee.

"Well?" The caddy-master turned to Dexter. "What you standing there like a dummy for? Go pick up the young lady's clubs."

"I don't think I'll go out today," said Dexter.

"You don't—"

"I think I'll quit."

The enormity of his decision frightened him. He was a favorite caddy and the thirty dollars a month he earned through the summer were not to be made elsewhere in Dillard. But he had received a strong emotional shock and his perturbation required a violent and immediate outlet.

It is not so simple as that, either. As so frequently would be the case in the future, Dexter was unconsciously dictated to by his winter dreams.

Now, of course, the quality and the seasonability of these winter dreams varied, but the stuff of them remained. They persuaded Dexter several years later to pass up a business course at the State University—his father, prospering now, would have paid his way—for the precarious advantage of attending an older and more famous university in the East, where he was bothered by his scanty funds. But do not get the impression, because his winter dreams happened to be concerned at first with musings on the rich, that there was anything shoddy in the boy. He wanted not association with glittering things and glittering people—he wanted the glittering things themselves. Often he reached out for the best without knowing why he wanted it—and sometimes he ran up against the mysterious denials and prohibitions in which life indulges. It is with one of those denials and not with his career as a whole that this story deals.

He made money. It was rather amazing. After college he went to the city from which Lake Erminie draws its wealthy patrons. When he was only twenty-three and had been there not quite two years, there were already people who liked to say, "Now *there's* a boy—" All about him rich men's sons were peddling bonds precariously, or investing patrimonies precariously, or plodding through the two dozen volumes of canned rubbish in the "George Washington Commercial Course," but Dexter borrowed a thousand dollars on his college degree and his steady eyes, and bought a partnership in a *laundry*.

It was a small laundry when he went into it. Dexter made a specialty of learning how the English washed fine woolen golf stockings without shrinking them. Inside of a year he was catering to the trade who wore knickerbockers. Men were insisting that their shetland hose and sweaters go to his laundry just as they had insisted on a caddy who could find golf balls. A little later he was doing their wives' lingerie as well—and running five branches in different parts of the city. Before he was twenty-seven he owned the largest string of laundries in his section of the country. It was then that he sold out and went to New York. But the part of his story that concerns us here goes back to when he was making his first big success.

When he was twenty-three Mr. W. L. Hart, one of the grey-haired men who like to say "Now there's a boy"—gave him a guest card to the Lake Erminie Club for over a week-end. So he signed his name one day on the register, and that afternoon played golf in a foursome with Mr. Hart and Mr. Sandwood and Mr. T. A. Hedrick. He did not consider it necessary to remark that he had once carried Mr. Hart's bag over this same links and that he knew every trap and gully with his eyes shut—but he found himself glancing at the four caddies who trailed them, trying to catch a gleam or gesture that would remind him of himself, that would lessen the gap which lay between his past and his future.

It was a curious day, slashed abruptly with fleeting, familiar impressions. One minute he had the sense of being a trespasser—in the next he was impressed by the tremendous superiority he felt toward Mr. T. A. Hedrick, who was a bore and not even a good golfer any more.

Then, because of a ball Mr. Hart lost near the fifteenth green an enormous thing happened. While they were searching the stiff grasses of the rough there was a clear call of "Fore!" from behind a hill in their rear. And as they all turned abruptly from their search a bright new ball sliced abruptly over the hill and caught Mr. T. A. Hedrick rather neatly in the stomach.

Mr. T. A. Hedrick grunted and cursed.

"By Gad!" cried Mr. Hedrick, "they ought to put some of these crazy women off the course. It's getting to be outrageous."

A head and a voice came up together over the hill:

"Do you mind if we go through?"

"You hit me in the stomach!" thundered Mr. Hedrick.

"Did I?" The girl approached the group of men. "I'm sorry. I yelled 'Fore!'"

Her glance fell casually on each of the men. She nodded to Sandwood and then scanned the fairway for her ball.

"Did I bounce off into the rough?"

It was impossible to determine whether this question was ingenuous or malicious. In a moment, however, she left no doubt, for as her partner came up over the hill she called cheerfully.

"Here I am! I'd have gone on the green except that I hit something."

As she took her stance for a short mashie shot, Dexter looked at her closely. She wore a blue gingham dress, rimmed at throat and shoulders with a white edging that accentuated her tan. The quality of exaggeration, of thinness that had made her passionate eyes and down turning mouth absurd at eleven was gone now. She was arrestingly beautiful. The color in her cheeks was centered like the color in a picture—it was not a "high" color, but a sort of fluctuating and feverish warmth, so shaded that it seemed at any moment it would recede and disappear. This color and the mobility of her mouth gave a continual impression of flux, of intense life, of passionate vitality—balanced only partially by the sad luxury of her eyes.

She swung her mashie impatiently and without interest, pitching the ball into a sandpit on the other side of the green. With a quick insincere smile and a careless "Thank you!" she went on after it.

"That Judy Jones!" remarked Mr. Hedrick on the next tee, as they waited—some moments—for her to play on ahead. "All she needs is to be turned up and spanked for six months and then to be married off to an old-fashioned cavalry captain."

"Gosh, she's good looking!" said Mr. Sandwood, who was just over thirty.

"Good-looking!" cried Mr. Hedrick contemptuously. "She always looks as if she wanted to be kissed! Turning those big cow-eyes on every young calf in town!"

It is doubtful if Mr. Hedrick intended a reference to the maternal instinct.

"She'd play pretty good golf if she'd try," said Mr. Sandwood.

"She has no form," said Mr. Hedrick solemnly.

"She has a nice figure," said Mr. Sandwood.

"Better thank the Lord she doesn't drive a swifter ball," said Mr. Hart, winking at Dexter. "Come on. Let's go."

Later in the afternoon the sun went down with a riotous swirl of gold and varying blues and scarlets, and left the dry rustling night of western summer. Dexter watched from the verandah of the Erminie Club, watched the even overlap of the waters in the little wind, silver molasses under the harvest moon. Then the moon held a finger to her lips and the lake became a clear pool, pale and quiet. Dexter put on his bathing suit and swam out to the farthest raft, where he stretched dripping on the wet canvas of the spring board.

There was a fish jumping and a star shining and the lights around the lake were gleaming. Over on a dark peninsula a piano was playing the songs of last summer and of summers before that—songs from "The Pink Lady" and "The Chocolate Soldier" and "Mlle. Modiste"—and because the sound of a piano over a stretch of water had always seemed beautiful to Dexter he lay perfectly quiet and listened.

The tune the piano was playing at that moment had been gay and new five years before when Dexter was a sophomore at college. They had played it at a prom once and because he could not afford the luxury of proms in those days he had stood outside the gymnasium and listened. The sound of the tune and the splash of the fish jumping precipitated in him a sort of ecstasy and it was with that ecstasy he viewed what happened to him now. The ecstasy was a gorgeous appreciation. It was his sense that, for once, he was magnificently atune to life and that everything about him was radiating a brightness and a glamor he might never know again.

A low pale oblong detached itself suddenly from the darkness of the peninsula, spitting forth the reverberate sound of a racing motorboat. Two white streamers of cleft water rolled themselves out behind it and almost immediately the boat was beside him, drowning out the hot tinkle of the piano in the drone of its spray. Dexter raising himself on his arms was aware of a figure standing at the wheel, of two dark eyes regarding him over the lengthening space of water—then the boat had gone by and was sweeping in an immense and purposeless circle of spray round and round in the middle of the lake. With equal eccentricity one of the circles flattened out and headed back toward the raft.

"Who's that?" she called, shutting off the motor. She was so near now that Dexter could see her bathing suit, which consisted apparently of pink rompers. "Oh—you're one of the men I hit in the stomach."

The nose of the boat bumped the raft. After an inexpert struggle, Dexter managed to twist the line around a two-by-four. Then the raft tilted rakishly as she sprung on.

"Well, kiddo," she said huskily, "do you"—she broke off. She had sat herself upon the springboard, found it damp and jumped up quickly,—"do you want to go surf-board riding?"

He indicated that he would be delighted.

"The name is Judy Jones. Ghastly reputation but enormously popular." She favored him with an absurd smirk—rather, what tried to be a smirk, for, twist her mouth as she might, it was not grotesque, it was merely beautiful. "See that house over on the peninsula?"

"No."

"Well, there's a house there that I live in only you can't see it because it's too dark. And in that house there is a fella waiting for me. When he drove up by the door I drove out by the dock because he has watery eyes and asks me if I have an ideal."

There was a fish jumping and a star shining and the lights around the lake were gleaming. Dexter sat beside Judy Jones and she explained how her boat was driven. Then she was in the water, swimming to the floating surf-board with exquisite crawl. Watching her was as without effort to the eye as watching a branch waving or a sea-gull flying. Her arms, burned to butternut, moved sinuously among the dull platinum ripples, elbow appearing first, casting the forearm back with a cadence of falling water, then reaching out and down stabbing a path ahead.

They moved out into the lake and, turning, Dexter saw that she was kneeling on the low rear of the now up-tilted surf-board.

"Go faster," she called, "fast as it'll go."

Obediently he jammed the lever forward and the white spray mounted at the bow. When he looked around again the girl was standing up on the rushing board, her arms spread ecstatically, her eyes lifted toward the moon.

"It's awful cold, kiddo," she shouted. "What's your name anyways?"

"The name is Dexter Green. Would it amuse you to know how good you look back there?"

"Yes," she shouted, "it would amuse me. Except that I'm too cold. Come to dinner tomorrow night."

He kept thinking how glad he was that he had never caddied for this girl. The damp gingham clinging made her like a statue and turned her intense mobility to immobility at last.

"—At seven o'clock," she shouted, "Judy Jones, Girl, who hit man in stomach. Better write it down,"—and then, "Faster—oh, faster!"

Had he been as calm inwardly as he was in appearance, Dexter would have had time to examine his surroundings in detail. He received, however, an enduring impression that the house was the most elaborate he had ever seen. He had known for a long time that it was the finest on Lake Erminie, with a Pompeiian swimming pool and twelve acres of lawn and garden. But what gave it an air of breathless intensity was the sense that it was inhabited by Judy Jones—that it was as casual a thing to her as the little house in the village had once been to Dexter. There was a feeling of mystery in it, of bedrooms upstairs more beautiful and strange than other bedrooms, of gay and radiant activities taking place through these deep corridors and of romances that were not musty and laid already in lavender, but were fresh and breathing and set forth in rich motor cars and in great dances whose flowers were scarcely withered. They were more real because he could feel them all about him, pervading the air with the shades and echoes of still vibrant emotion.

And so while he waited for her to appear he peopled the soft deep summer room and the sun porch that opened from it with the men who had already loved Judy Jones. He knew the sort of men they were—the men who when he first went to college had entered from the great prep-schools with graceful clothes and the deep tan of healthy summer, who did nothing or anything with the same debonaire ease.

Dexter had seen that, in one sense, he was better than these men. He was newer and stronger. Yet in acknowledging to himself that he wished his children to be like them he was admitting that he was but the rough, strong stuff from which this graceful aristocracy eternally sprang.

When, a year before, the time had come when he could wear good clothes, he had known who were the best tailors in America, and the best tailor in America had made him the suit he wore this evening. He had acquired that particular reserve peculiar to his university, that set it off from other universities. He recognized the value to him of such a mannerism and he had adopted it; he knew that to be careless in dress and manner required more confidence than to be careful. But carelessness was for his children. His mother's name had been Krimslich. She was a Bohemian[1] of the peasant class and she had talked broken English to the end of her days. Her son must keep to the set patterns.

He waited for Judy Jones in her house, and he saw these other young men around him. It excited him that many men had loved her. It increased her value in his eyes.

At a little after seven Judy Jones came downstairs. She wore a blue silk afternoon dress. He was disappointed at first that she had not put on something more elaborate, and this feeling was accentuated when, after a brief greeting, she went to the door of a butler's pantry and pushing it open called: "You can have dinner, Martha." He had rather expected that a butler would announce dinner, that there would be a cocktail perhaps. It even offended him that she should know the maid's name.

Then he put these thoughts behind him as they sat down together on a chintz-covered lounge.

"Father and mother won't be here," she said.

---

1. Native of Bohemia, in the Czech Republic.

"Ought I to be sorry?"

"They're really quite nice," she confessed, as if it had just occurred to her. "I think my father's the best looking man of his age I've ever seen. And mother looks about thirty."

He remembered the last time he had seen her father, and found he was glad the parents were not to be here tonight. They would wonder who he was. He had been born in Keeble, a Minnesota village fifty miles farther north and he always gave Keeble as his home instead of Dillard. Country towns were well enough to come from if they weren't inconveniently in sight and used as foot-stools by fashionable lakes.

Before dinner he found the conversation unsatisfactory. The beautiful Judy seemed faintly irritable—as much so as it was possible to be with a comparative stranger. They discussed Lake Erminie and its golf course, the surf-board riding of the night before and the cold she had caught, which made her voice more husky and charming than ever. They talked of his university which she had visited frequently during the past two years, and of the nearby city which supplied Lake Erminie with its patrons and whither Dexter would return next day to his prospering laundries.

During dinner she slipped into a moody depression which gave Dexter a feeling of guilt. Whatever petulance she uttered in her throaty voice worried him. Whatever she smiled at—at him, at a silver fork, at nothing—, it disturbed him that her smile could have no root in mirth, or even in amusement. When the red corners of her lips curved down, it was less a smile than an invitation to a kiss.

Then, after dinner, she led him out on the dark sun-porch and deliberately changed the atmosphere.

"Do I seem gloomy?" she demanded.

"No, but I'm afraid I'm boring you," he answered quickly.

"You're not. I like you. But I've just had rather an unpleasant afternoon. There was a—man I cared about. He told me out of a clear sky that he was poor as a church-mouse. He'd never even hinted it before. Does this sound horribly mundane?"

"Perhaps he was afraid to tell you."

"I suppose he was," she answered thoughtfully. "He didn't start right. You see, if I'd thought of him as poor—well, I've been mad about loads of poor men, and fully intended to marry them all. But in this case, I hadn't thought of him that way and my interest in him wasn't strong enough to survive the shock."

"I know. As if a girl calmly informed her fiancé that she was a widow. He might not object to widows, but——"

"Let's start right," she suggested suddenly. "Who are you, anyhow?"

For a moment Dexter hesitated. There were two versions of his life that he could tell. There was Dillard and his caddying and his struggle through college, or——

"I'm nobody," he announced. "My career is largely a matter of futures."

"Are you poor?"

"No," he said frankly, "I'm probably making more money than any man my age in the northwest. I know that's an obnoxious remark, but you advised me to start right."

There was a pause. She smiled, and with a touch of amusement.

"You sound like a man in a play."

"It's your fault. You tempted me into being assertive."

Suddenly she turned her dark eyes directly upon him and the corners of her mouth drooped until her face seemed to open like a flower. He dared scarcely to breathe, he had the sense that she was exerting some force upon him; making him overwhelmingly conscious of the youth and mystery that wealth imprisons and preserves, the freshness of many clothes, of cool rooms and gleaming things, safe and proud above the hot struggles of the poor.

The porch was bright with the bought luxury of starshine. The wicker of the settee squeaked fashionably when he put his arm around her, commanded by her eyes. He kissed her curious and lovely mouth and committed himself to the following of a grail.

It began like that—and continued, with varying shades of intensity, on such a note right up to the dénouement. Dexter surrendered a part of himself to the most direct and unprincipled personality with which he had ever come in contact. Whatever the beautiful Judy Jones desired, she went after with the full pressure of her charm. There was no divergence of method, no jockeying for position or premeditation of effects—there was very little mental quality in any of her affairs. She simply made men conscious to the highest degree of her physical loveliness.

Dexter had no desire to change her. Her deficiencies were knit up with a passionate energy that transcended and justified them.

When, as Judy's head lay against his shoulder that first night, she whispered:

"I don't know what's the matter with me. Last night I thought I was in love with a man and tonight I think I'm in love with you—"

—it seemed to him a beautiful and romantic thing to say. It was the exquisite excitability that for the moment he controlled and owned. But a week later he was compelled to view this same quality in a different light. She took him in her roadster to a picnic supper and after supper she disappeared, likewise in her roadster, with another man. Dexter became enormously upset and was scarcely able to be decently civil to the other people present. When she assured him that she had not kissed the other man he knew she was lying—yet he was glad that she had taken the trouble to lie to him.

He was, as he found before the summer ended, one of a dozen, a varying dozen, who circulated about her. Each of them had at one time been favored above all others—about half of them still basked in the solace of occasional sentimental revivals. Whenever one showed signs of dropping out through long neglect she granted him a brief honeyed hour which encouraged him to tag along for a year or so longer. Judy made these forays upon the helpless and defeated without malice, indeed half unconscious that there was anything mischievous in what she did.

When a new man came to town everyone dropped out—dates were automatically cancelled.

The helpless part of trying to do anything about it was that she did it all herself. She was not a girl who could be "won" in the kinetic sense—she was proof against cleverness, she was proof against charm, if any of these assailed her too strongly she would immediately resolve the affair to a physical basis and under the magic of her physical splendor the strong as well as the brilliant played her game and not their own. She was entertained only by the gratification of her desires and by the direct exercise of her own charm. Perhaps from so much youthful love, so many youthful lovers she had come, in self defense, to nourish herself wholly from within.

Succeeding Dexter's first exhilaration came restlessness and dissatisfaction. The helpless ecstasy of losing himself in her charm was a powerful opiate rather than a tonic. It was fortunate for his work during the winter that those moments of ecstasy came infrequently. Early in their acquaintance it had seemed for a while that there was a deep and spontaneous mutual attraction—that first August for example—three days of long evenings on her dusky verandah, of strange wan kisses through the late afternoon, in shadowy alcoves or behind the protecting trellises of the garden arbors, of mornings when she was fresh as a dream and almost shy at meeting him in the clarity of the rising day. There was all the ecstasy of an engagement about it, sharpened by his realization that there was no engagement. It was during those three days that, for the first time, he had asked her to marry him. She said "maybe some day," she said "kiss me," she said "I'd like to marry you," she said "I love you,"—she said—nothing.

The three days were interrupted by the arrival of a New York man who visited the Jones' for half September. To Dexter's agony, rumor engaged them. The man was the son of the president of a great trust company. But at the end of a month it was reported that Judy was yawning. At a dance one night she sat all evening in a motor boat with an old beau, while the New Yorker searched the club for her frantically. She told the old beau that she was bored with her visitor and two days later he left. She was seen with him at the station and it was reported that he looked very mournful indeed.

On this note the summer ended. Dexter was twenty-four and he found himself increasingly in a position to do as he wished. He joined two clubs in the city and lived at one of them. Though he was by no means an integral part of the stag-lines at these clubs he managed to be on hand at dances where Judy Jones was likely to appear. He could have gone out socially as much as he liked—he was an eligible young man, now, and popular with downtown fathers. His confessed devotion to Judy Jones had rather solidified his position. But he had no social aspirations and rather despised the dancing men who were always on tap for the Thursday or Saturday parties and who filled in at dinners with the younger married set. Already he was playing with the idea of going East to New York. He wanted to take Judy Jones with him. No disillusion as to the world in which she had grown up could cure his illusion as to her desirability.

Remember that—for only in the light of it can what he did for her be understood.

Eighteen months after he first met Judy Jones he became engaged to another girl. Her name was Irene Scheerer and her father was one of the men who had always believed in Dexter. Irene was light haired and sweet and honorable and a little stout and she had two beaus whom she pleasantly relinquished when Dexter formally asked her to marry him.

Summer, fall, winter, spring, another summer, another fall—so much he had given of his active life to the curved lips of Judy Jones. She had treated him with interest, with encouragement, with malice, with indifference, with

contempt. She had inflicted on him the innumerable little slights and indig-
nities possible in such a case—as if in revenge for having ever cared for him
at all. She had beckoned him and yawned at him and beckoned him again
and he had responded often with bitterness and narrowed eyes. She had
brought him ecstatic happiness and intolerable agony of spirit. She had
caused him untold inconvenience and not a little trouble. She had insulted
him and she had ridden over him and she had played his interest in her
against his interest in his work—for fun. She had done everything to him
except to criticize him—this she had not done—it seemed to him only
because it might have sullied the utter indifference she manifested and sincerely felt toward him.

When autumn had come and gone again it occurred to him that he could
not have Judy Jones. He had to beat this into his mind but he convinced
himself at last. He lay awake at night for a while and argued it over. He told
himself the trouble and the pain she had caused him, he enumerated her
glaring deficiencies as a wife. Then he said to himself that he loved her and
after a while he fell asleep. For a week, lest he imagine her husky voice over
the telephone or her eyes opposite him at lunch, he worked hard and late
and at night he went to his office and plotted out his years.

At the end of a week he went to a dance and cut in on her once. For almost
the first time since they had met he did not ask her to sit out with him or tell
her that she was lovely. It hurt him that she did not miss these things—that
was all. He was not jealous when he saw that there was a new man tonight.
He had been hardened against jealousy long before.

He stayed late at the dance. He sat for an hour with Irene Scheerer and
talked about books and about music. He knew very little about either. But
he was beginning to be master of his own time now and he had a rather
priggish notion that he—the young and already fabulously successful Dexter Green—should know more about such things.

That was in October when he was twenty-five. In January Dexter and
Irene became engaged. It was to be announced in June and they were to be
married three months later.

The Minnesota winter prolonged itself interminably and it was almost May
when the winds came soft and the snow ran down into Lake Erminie at last.
For the first time in over a year Dexter was enjoying a certain tranquility
of spirit. Judy Jones had been in Florida and afterwards in Hot Springs and
somewhere she had been engaged and somewhere she had broken it off. At
first, when Dexter had definitely given her up, it had made him sad that people still linked them together and asked for news of her, but when he began to
be placed at dinner next to Irene Scheerer people didn't ask him about her
any more—they told him about her. He ceased to be an authority on her.

May at last. Dexter walked the streets at night when the darkness was
damp as rain, wondering that so soon, with so little done, so much of ecstasy
had gone from him. May one year back had been marked by Judy's poignant,
unforgivable, yet forgiven turbulence—it had been one of those rare times
when he fancied she had grown to care for him. That old penny's worth of
happiness he had spent for this bushel of content. He knew that Irene would
be no more than a curtain spread behind him, a hand moving among gleaming tea cups, a voice calling to children . . . fire and loveliness were gone,

magic of night and the hushed wonder of the hours and seasons . . . slender lips, down turning, dropping to his lips like poppy petals, bearing him up into a heaven of eyes . . . a haunting gesture, light of a warm lamp on her hair. The thing was deep in him. He was too strong, too alive for it to die lightly.

In the middle of May when the weather balanced for a few days on the thin bridge that led to deep summer he turned in one night at Irene's house. Their engagement was to be announced in a week now—no one would be surprised at it. And tonight they would sit together on the lounge at the College Club and look on for an hour at the dancers. It gave him a sense of solidity to go with her—. She was so sturdily popular, so intensely a "good egg."

He mounted the steps of the brown stone house and stepped inside.

"Irene," he called.

Mrs. Scheerer came out of the living room to meet him.

"Dexter," she said. "Irene's gone upstairs with a splitting headache. She wanted to go with you but I made her go to bed."

"Nothing serious I—"

"Oh, no. She's going to play golf with you in the morning. You can spare her for just one night, can't you, Dexter?"

Her smile was kind. She and Dexter liked each other. In the living room he talked for a moment before he said goodnight.

Returning to the College Club, where he had rooms, he stood in the doorway for a moment and watched the dancers. He leaned against the door post, nodded at a man or two—yawned.

"Hello, kiddo."

The familiar voice at his elbow startled him. Judy Jones had left a man and crossed the room to him—Judy Jones, a slender enamelled doll in cloth of gold, gold in a band at her head, gold in two slipper points at her dress's hem. The fragile glow of her face seemed to blossom as she smiled at him. A breeze of warmth and light blew through the room. His hands in the pockets of his dinner jacket tightened spasmodically. He was filled with a sudden excitement.

"When did you get back?" he asked casually.

"Come here and I'll tell you about it."

She turned and he followed her. She had been away—he could have wept at the wonder of her return. She had passed through enchanted streets, doing young things that were like plaintive music. All mysterious happenings, all fresh and quickening hopes, had gone away with her, come back with her now.

She turned in the doorway.

"Have you a car here? If you haven't I have."

"I have a coupé."

In then, with a rustle of golden cloth. He slammed the door. Into so many cars she had stepped—like this—like that—her back against the leather, so—her elbow resting on the door—waiting. She would have been soiled long since had there been anything to soil her,—except herself—but these things were all her own outpouring.

With an effort he forced himself to start the car and avoiding her surprised glance backed into the street. This was nothing, he must remember. She had done this before and he had put her behind him, as he would have slashed a bad account from his books.

He drove slowly downtown and affecting a disinterested abstraction traversed the deserted streets of the business section, peopled here and there, where a movie was giving out its crowd or where consumptive or pugilistic youth lounged in front of pool halls. The clink of glasses and the slap of hands on the bars issued from saloons, cloisters of glazed glass and dirty yellow light.

She was watching him closely and the silence was embarrassing yet in this crisis he could find no casual word with which to profane the hour. At a convenient turning he began to zig-zag back toward the College Club.

"Have you missed me?" she asked suddenly.

"Everybody missed you."

He wondered if she knew of Irene Scheerer. She had been back only a day—her absence had been almost contemporaneous with his engagement.

"What a remark!" Judy laughed sadly—without sadness. She looked at him searchingly. He became absorbed for a moment in the dashboard.

"You're handsomer than you used to be," she said thoughtfully. "Dexter, you have the most rememberable eyes."

He could have laughed at this, but he did not laugh. It was the sort of thing that was said to sophomores. Yet it stabbed at him.

"I'm awfully tired of everything, kiddo." She called everyone kiddo, endowing the obsolete slang with careless, individual camaraderie. "I wish you'd marry me."

The directness of this confused him. He should have told her now that he was going to marry another girl but he could not tell her. He could as easily have sworn that he had never loved her.

"I think we'd get along," she continued, on the same note, "unless probably you've forgotten me and fallen in love with another girl."

Her confidence was obviously enormous. She had said, in effect, that she found such a thing impossible to believe, that if it were true he had merely committed a childish indiscretion—and probably to show off. She would forgive him, because it was not a matter of any moment but rather something to be brushed aside lightly.

"Of course you could never love anybody but me," she continued. "I like the way you love me. Oh, Dexter, have you forgotten last year?"

"No, I haven't forgotten."

"Neither have I!"

Was she sincerely moved—or was she carried along by the wave of her own acting?

"I wish we could be like that again," she said, and he forced himself to answer:

"I don't think we can."

"I suppose not. . . . I hear you're giving Irene Scheerer a violent rush."

There was not the faintest emphasis on the name, yet Dexter was suddenly ashamed.

"Oh, take me home," cried Judy suddenly. "I don't want to go back to that idiotic dance—with those children."

Then, as he turned up the street that led to the residence district, Judy began to cry quietly to herself. He had never seen her cry before.

The dark street lightened, the dwellings of the rich loomed up around them, he stopped his coupé in front of the great white bulk of the Mortimer

Jones' house, somnolent, gorgeous, drenched with the splendor of the damp moonlight. Its solidity startled him. The strong walls, the fine steel of the girders, the breadth and beam and pomp of it were there only to bring out the contrast with the young beauty beside him. It was sturdy to accentuate her slightness—as if to show what a breeze could be generated by a butterfly's wing.

He sat perfectly quiet, his nerves in wild clamor, afraid that if he moved he would find her irresistibly in his arms. Two tears had rolled down her wet face and trembled on her upper lip.

"I'm more beautiful than anybody else," she said brokenly, "why can't I be happy?" Her moist eyes tore at his stability—mouth turned slowly downward with an exquisite sadness. "I'd like to marry you if you'll have me, Dexter. I suppose you think I'm not worth having but I'll be so beautiful for you, Dexter."

A million phrases of anger, of pride, of passion, of hatred, of tenderness fought on his lips. Then a perfect wave of emotion washed over him, carrying off with it a sediment of wisdom, of convention, of doubt, of honor. This was his girl who was speaking, his own, his beautiful, his pride.

"Won't you come in?" he heard her draw in her breath sharply.

Waiting.

"All right," his voice was trembling, "I'll come in."

It seems strange to say that neither when it was over nor a long time afterward did he regret that night. Looking at it from the perspective of ten years, the fact that Judy's flare for him endured just one month seemed of little importance. Nor did it matter that by his yielding he subjected himself to a deeper agony in the end and gave serious hurt to Irene Scheerer and to Irene's parents who had befriended him. There was nothing sufficiently pictorial about Irene's grief to stamp itself on his mind.

Dexter was at bottom hard-minded. The attitude of the city on his action was of no importance to him, not because he was going to leave the city, but because any outside attitude on the situation seemed superficial. He was completely indifferent to popular opinion. Nor, when he had seen that it was no use, that he did not possess in himself the power to move fundamentally or to hold Judy Jones, did he bear any malice toward her. He loved her and he would love her until the day he was too old for loving—but he could not have her. So he tasted the deep pain that is reserved only for the strong, just as he had tasted for a little while the deep happiness.

Even the ultimate falsity of the grounds upon which Judy terminated the engagement—that she did not want to "take him away" from Irene, that it—was on her conscience—did not revolt him. He was beyond any revulsion or any amusement.

He went east in February with the intention of selling out his laundries and settling in New York—but the war[2] came to America in March and changed his plans. He returned to the west, handed over the management of the business to his partner and went into the first officers' training camp in late April. He was one of those young thousands who greeted the war

2. World War I, which the United States entered in 1917.

with a certain amount of relief, welcoming the liberation from webs of tangled emotion.

This story is not his biography, remember, although things creep into it which have nothing to do with those dreams he had when he was young. We are almost done with them and with him now. There is only one more incident to be related here and it happens seven years farther on.

It took place in New York, where he had done well—so well that there were no barriers too high for him now. He was thirty-two years old, and, except for one flying trip immediately after the war, he had not been west in seven years. A man named Devlin from Detroit came into his office to see him in a business way, and then and there this incident occurred, and closed out, so to speak, this particular side of his life.

"So you're from the middle west," said the man Devlin with careless curiosity. "That's funny—I thought men like you were probably born and raised on Wall Street. You know—wife of one of my best friends in Detroit came from your city. I was an usher at the wedding."

Dexter waited with no apprehension of what was coming. There was a magic that his city would never lose for him. Just as Judy's house had always seemed to him more mysterious and gay than other houses, so his dream of the city itself, now that he had gone from it, was pervaded with a melancholy beauty.

"Judy Simms," said Devlin with no particular interest, "Judy Jones she was once."

"Yes. I knew her." A dull impatience spread over him. He had heard, of course, that she was married,—perhaps deliberately he had heard no more.

"Awfully nice girl," brooded Devlin, meaninglessly, "I'm sort of sorry for her."

"Why?" Something in Dexter was alert, receptive, at once.

"Oh, Joe Simms has gone to pieces in a way. I don't mean he beats her, you understand, or anything like that. But he drinks and runs around—"

"Doesn't she run around?"

"No. Stays at home with her kids."

"Oh."

"She's a little too old for him," said Devlin.

"Too old!" cried Dexter, "why man, she's only twenty-seven."

He was possessed with a wild notion of rushing out into the streets and taking a train to Detroit. He rose to his feet, spasmodically, involuntarily.

"I guess you're busy," Devlin apologized quickly. "I didn't realize—"

"No, I'm not busy," said Dexter, steadying his voice. "I'm not busy at all. Not busy at all. Did you say she was—twenty-seven. No, I said she was twenty-seven."

"Yes, you did," agreed Devlin drily.

"Go on, then. Go on."

"What do you mean?"

"About Judy Jones."

Devlin looked at him helplessly.

"Well, that's—I told you all there is to it. He treats her like the devil. Oh, they're not going to get divorced or anything. When he's particularly outrageous she forgives him. In fact, I'm inclined to think she loves him. She was a pretty girl when she first came to Detroit."

A pretty girl! The phrase struck Dexter as ludicrous.

"Isn't she—a pretty girl any more?"

"Oh, she's all right."

"Look here," said Dexter, sitting down suddenly, "I don't understand. You say she was a 'pretty girl' and now you say she's 'all right.' I don't understand what you mean—Judy Jones wasn't a pretty girl, at all. She was a great beauty. Why, I knew her, I knew her. She was—"

Devlin laughed pleasantly.

"I'm not trying to start a row," he said. "I think Judy's a nice girl and I like her. I can't understand how a man like Joe Simms could fall madly in love with her, but he did." Then he added, "Most of the women like her."

Dexter looked closely at Devlin, thinking wildly that there must be a reason for this, some insensitivity in the man or some private malice.

"Lots of women fade just-like-*that*." Devlin snapped his fingers. "You must have seen it happen. Perhaps I've forgotten how pretty she was at her wedding. I've seen her so much since then, you see. She has nice eyes."

A sort of dullness settled down upon Dexter. For the first time in his life he felt like getting very drunk. He knew that he was laughing loudly at something Devlin had said but he did not know what it was or why it was funny. When Devlin went, in a few minutes, he lay down on his lounge and looked out the window at the New York skyline into which the sun was sinking in dully lovely shades of pink and gold.

He had thought that having nothing else to lose he was invulnerable at last—but he knew that he had just lost something more, as surely as if he had married Judy Jones and seen her fade away before his eyes.

The dream was gone. Something had been taken from him. In a sort of panic he pushed the palms of his hands into his eyes and tried to bring up a picture of the waters lapping at Lake Erminie and the moonlit verandah, and gingham on the golf links and the dry sun and the gold color of her neck's soft down. And her mouth damp to his kisses and her eyes plaintive with melancholy and her freshness like new fine linen in the morning. Why these things were no longer in the world. They had existed and they existed no more.

For the first time in years the tears were streaming down his face. But they were for himself now. He did not care about mouth and eyes and moving hands. He wanted to care and he could not care. For he had gone away and he could never go back any more. The gates were closed, the sun was gone down and there was no beauty but the grey beauty of steel that withstands all time. Even the grief he could have borne was left behind in the country of illusion, of youth, of the richness of life, where his winter dreams had flourished.

"Long ago," he said, "long ago, there was something in me, but now that thing is gone. Now that thing is gone, that thing is gone. I cannot cry. I cannot care. That thing will come back no more."

1922

Babylon Revisited[1]

"And where's Mr. Campbell?" Charlie asked.

"Gone to Switzerland. Mr. Campbell's a pretty sick man, Mr. Wales."

"I'm sorry to hear that. And George Hardt?" Charlie inquired.

"Back in America, gone to work."

"And where is the Snow Bird?"

"He was in here last week. Anyway, his friend, Mr. Schaeffer, is in Paris."

Two familiar names from the long list of a year and a half ago. Charlie scribbled an address in his notebook and tore out the page.

"If you see Mr. Schaeffer, give him this," he said. "It's my brother-in-law's address. I haven't settled on a hotel yet."

He was not really disappointed to find Paris was so empty. But the still-ness in the Ritz bar was strange and portentous. It was not an American bar any more—he felt polite in it, and not as if he owned it. It had gone back into France. He felt the stillness from the moment he got out of the taxi and saw the doorman, usually in a frenzy of activity at this hour, gossiping with a *chasseur*[2] by the servants' entrance.

Passing through the corridor, he heard only a single, bored voice in the once-clamorous women's room. When he turned into the bar he traveled the twenty feet of green carpet with his eyes fixed straight ahead by old habit; and then, with his foot firmly on the rail, he turned and surveyed the room, encountering only a single pair of eyes that fluttered up from a news-paper in the corner. Charlie asked for the head barman, Paul, who in the latter days of the bull market had come to work in his own custom-built car—disembarking, however, with due nicety at the nearest corner. But Paul was at his country house today and Alix giving him information.

"No, no more," Charlie said, "I'm going slow these days."

Alix congratulated him: "You were going pretty strong a couple of years ago."

"I'll stick to it all right," Charlie assured him. "I've stuck to it for over a year and a half now."

"How do you find conditions in America?"

"I haven't been to America for months. I'm in business in Prague, repre-senting a couple of concerns there. They don't know about me down there."

Alix smiled.

"Remember the night of George Hardt's bachelor dinner here?" said Charlie. "By the way, what's become of Claude Fessenden?"

Alix lowered his voice confidentially: "He's in Paris, but he doesn't come here any more. Paul doesn't allow it. He ran up a bill of thirty thousand francs, charging all his drinks and his lunches, and usually his dinner, for more than a year. And when Paul finally told him he had to pay, he gave him a bad check."

Alix shook his head sadly.

---

1. Babylon was an ancient, prosperous city in Mesopotamia, associated by the Hebrews and Greeks with materialism and sensual pleasure; here, the reference is to Paris, where the story is set in the aftermath of the stock market crash of 1929.

2. Messenger-boy, errand runner (French).

"I don't understand it, such a dandy fellow. Now he's all bloated up—" He made a plump apple of his hands.

Charlie watched a group of strident queens installing themselves in a corner.

"Nothing affects them," he thought. "Stocks rise and fall, people loaf or work, but they go on forever." The place oppressed him. He called for the dice and shook with Alix for the drink.

"Here for long, Mr. Wales?"

"I'm here for four or five days to see my little girl."

"Oh-h! You have a little girl?"

Outside, the fire-red, gas-blue, ghost-green signs shone smokily through the tranquil rain. It was late afternoon and the streets were in movement; the *bistros*[3] gleamed. At the corner of the Boulevard des Capucines he took a taxi. The Place de la Concorde moved by in pink majesty; they crossed the logical Seine, and Charlie felt the sudden provincial quality of the left bank.[4]

Charlie directed his taxi to the Avenue de l'Opera, which was out of his way. But he wanted to see the blue hour spread over the magnificent façade, and imagine that the cab horns, playing endlessly the first few bars of *Le Plus que Lent*,[5] were the trumpets of the Second Empire. They were closing the iron grill in front of Brentano's Book-store, and people were already at dinner behind the trim little bourgeois hedge of Duval's. He had never eaten at a really cheap restaurant in Paris. Five-course dinner, four francs fifty, eighteen cents, wine included. For some odd reason he wished that he had.

As they rolled on to the Left Bank and he felt its sudden provincialism, he thought, "I spoiled this city for myself. I didn't realize it, but the days came along one after another, and then two years were gone, and everything was gone, and I was gone."

He was thirty-five, and good to look at. The Irish mobility of his face was sobered by a deep wrinkle between his eyes. As he rang his brother-in-law's bell in the Rue Palatine, the wrinkle deepened till it pulled down his brows; he felt a cramping sensation in his belly. From behind the maid who opened the door darted a lovely little girl of nine who shrieked "Daddy!" and flew up, struggling like a fish, into his arms. She pulled his head around by one ear and set her cheek against his.

"My old pie," he said.

"Oh, daddy, daddy, daddy, daddy, dads, dads, dads!"

She drew him into the salon, where the family waited, a boy and a girl his daughter's age, his sister-in-law and her husband. He greeted Marion with his voice pitched carefully to avoid either feigned enthusiasm or dislike, but her response was more frankly tepid, though she minimized her expression of unalterable distrust by directing her regard toward his child. The two men clasped hands in a friendly way and Lincoln Peters rested his for a moment on Charlie's shoulder.

---

3. Small, informal restaurants.
4. Paris is divided by the Seine River; the grander buildings and broader streets are on the Right Bank. To Charlie, the Left Bank is more like a town than a city.

5. I.e., *La Plus que Lente* (More than slow), piano composition by French composer Claude Debussy (1862–1918).

The room was warm and comfortably American. The three children moved intimately about, playing through the yellow oblongs that led to other rooms; the cheer of six o'clock spoke in the eager smacks of the fire and the sounds of French activity in the kitchen. But Charlie did not relax; his heart sat up rigidly in his body and he drew confidence from his daughter, who from time to time came close to him, holding in her arms the doll he had brought.

"Really extremely well," he declared in answer to Lincoln's question. "There's a lot of business there that isn't moving at all, but we're doing even better than ever. In fact, damn well. I'm bringing my sister over from America next month to keep house for me. My income last year was bigger than it was when I had money. You see, the Czechs—"

His boasting was for a specific purpose; but after a moment, seeing a faint restiveness in Lincoln's eye, he changed the subject:

"Those are fine children of yours, well brought up, good manners."

"We think Honoria's a great little girl too."

Marion Peters came back from the kitchen. She was a tall woman with worried eyes, who had once possessed a fresh American loveliness. Charlie had never been sensitive to it and was always surprised when people spoke of how pretty she had been. From the first there had been an instinctive antipathy between them.

"Well, how do you find Honoria?" she asked.

"Wonderful. I was astonished how much she's grown in ten months. All the children are looking well."

"We haven't had a doctor for a year. How do you like being back in Paris?"

"It seems very funny to see so few Americans around."

"I'm delighted," Marion said vehemently. "Now at least you can go into a store without their assuming you're a millionaire. We've suffered like everybody, but on the whole it's a good deal pleasanter."

"But it was nice while it lasted," Charlie said. "We were a sort of royalty, almost infallible, with a sort of magic around us. In the bar this afternoon"—he stumbled, seeing his mistake—"there wasn't a man I knew."

She looked at him keenly. "I should think you'd have had enough of bars."

"I only stayed a minute. I take one drink every afternoon, and no more."

"Don't you want a cocktail before dinner?" Lincoln asked.

"I take only one drink every afternoon, and I've had that."

"I hope you keep to it," said Marion.

Her dislike was evident in the coldness with which she spoke, but Charlie only smiled; he had larger plans. Her very aggressiveness gave him an advantage, and he knew enough to wait. He wanted them to initiate the discussion of what they knew had brought him to Paris.

At dinner he couldn't decide whether Honoria was most like him or her mother. Fortunate if she didn't combine the traits of both that had brought them to disaster. A great wave of protectiveness went over him. He thought he knew what to do for her. He believed in character; he wanted to jump back a whole generation and trust in character again as the eternally valuable element. Everything else wore out.

He left soon after dinner, but not to go home. He was curious to see Paris by night with clearer and more judicious eyes than those of other days. He bought a *strapontin* for the Casino and watched Josephine Baker[6] go through her chocolate arabesques.

After an hour he left and strolled toward Montmartre, up the Rue Pigalle into the Place Blanche. The rain had stopped and there were a few people in evening clothes disembarking from taxis in front of cabarets, and *cocottes*[7] prowling singly or in pairs, and many Negroes. He passed a lighted door from which issued music, and stopped with the sense of familiarity; it was Bricktop's, where he had parted with so many hours and so much money. A few doors farther on he found another ancient rendezvous and incautiously put his head inside. Immediately an eager orchestra burst into sound, a pair of professional dancers leaped to their feet and a maître d'hôtel swooped toward him, crying, "Crowd just arriving, sir!" But he withdrew quickly.

"You have to be damn drunk," he thought.

Zelli's was closed, the bleak and sinister cheap hotels surrounding it were dark; up in the Rue Blanche there was more light and a local, colloquial French crowd. The Poet's Cave had disappeared, but the two great mouths of the Café of Heaven and the Café of Hell still yawned—even devoured, as he watched, the meager contents of a tourist bus—a German, a Japanese, and an American couple who glanced at him with frightened eyes.

So much for the effort and ingenuity of Montmartre. All the catering to vice and waste was on an utterly childish scale, and he suddenly realized the meaning of the word "dissipate"—to dissipate into thin air; to make nothing out of something. In the little hours of the night every move from place to place was an enormous human jump, an increase of paying for the privilege of slower and slower motion.

He remembered thousand-franc notes given to an orchestra for playing a single number, hundred-franc notes tossed to a doorman for calling a cab.

But it hadn't been given for nothing.

It had been given, even the most wildly squandered sum, as an offering to destiny that he might not remember the things most worth remembering, the things that now he would always remember—his child taken from his control, his wife escaped to a grave in Vermont.

In the glare of a *brasserie*[8] a woman spoke to him. He bought her some eggs and coffee, and then, eluding her encouraging stare, gave her a twenty-franc note and took a taxi to his hotel.

II

He woke upon a fine fall day—football weather. The depression of yesterday was gone and he liked the people on the streets. At noon he sat opposite Honoria at Le Grand Vatel, the only restaurant he could think of not reminiscent of champagne dinners and long luncheons that began at two and ended in a blurred and vague twilight.

"Now, how about vegetables? Oughtn't you to have some vegetables?"

"Well, yes."

---

6. African American jazz singer and dancer (1906–1975) who arrived in Paris with a vaudeville troupe in 1925 and remained as a star entertainer. *"Strapontin"*: folding seat.

7. Coquettes (French, literal trans.); prostitutes.
8. Large, plain restaurant specializing in simple meals and beer.

"Here's *épinards* and *chou-fleur* and carrots and *haricots*."[9]

"I'd like *chou-fleur*."

"Wouldn't you like to have two vegetables?"

"I usually only have one at lunch."

The waiter was pretending to be inordinately fond of children. *"Qu'elle est mignonne la petite! Elle parle exactement comme une Française."*[1]

"How about dessert? Shall we wait and see?"

The waiter disappeared. Honoria looked at her father expectantly.

"What are we going to do?"

"First, we're going to that toy store in the Rue Saint-Honoré and buy you anything you like. And then we're going to the vaudeville at the Empire."

She hesitated. "I like it about the vaudeville, but not the toy store."

"Why not?"

"Well, you brought me this doll." She had it with her. "And I've got lots of things. And we're not rich any more, are we?"

"We never were. But today you are to have anything you want."

"All right," she agreed resignedly.

When there had been her mother and a French nurse he had been inclined to be strict; now he extended himself, reached out for a new tolerance; he must be both parents to her and not shut any of her out of communication.

"I want to get to know you," he said gravely. "First let me introduce myself. My name is Charles J. Wales, of Prague."

"Oh, daddy!" her voice cracked with laughter.

"And who are you, please?" he persisted, and she accepted a rôle immediately: "Honoria Wales, Rue Palatine, Paris."

"Married or single?"

"No, not married. Single."

He indicated the doll. "But I see you have a child, madame."

Unwilling to disinherit it, she took it to her heart and thought quickly: "Yes, I've been married, but I'm not married now. My husband is dead."

He went on quickly, "And the child's name?"

"Simone. That's after my best friend at school."

"I'm very pleased that you're doing so well at school."

"I'm third this month," she boasted. "Elsie"—that was her cousin—"is only about eighteenth, and Richard is about at the bottom."

"You like Richard and Elsie, don't you?"

"Oh, yes. I like Richard quite well and I like her all right."

Cautiously and casually he asked: "And Aunt Marion and Uncle Lincoln—which do you like best?"

"Oh, Uncle Lincoln, I guess."

He was increasingly aware of her presence. As they came in, a murmur of ". . . adorable" followed them, and now the people at the next table bent all their silences upon her, staring as if she were something no more conscious than a flower.

"Why don't I live with you?" she asked suddenly. "Because mamma's dead?"

---

9. Green beans (French). *"Épinards"*: spinach. *"Chou-fleur"*: cauliflower.
1. How cute she is! She speaks exactly like a French girl (French).

"You must stay here and learn more French. It would have been hard for daddy to take care of you so well."

"I don't really need much taking care of any more. I do everything for myself."

Going out of the restaurant, a man and a woman unexpectedly hailed him.

"Well, the old Wales!"

"Hello there, Lorraine. . . . Dunc."

Sudden ghosts out of the past: Duncan Schaeffer, a friend from college. Lorraine Quarrles, a lovely, pale blonde of thirty; one of a crowd who had helped them make months into days in the lavish times of three years ago.

"My husband couldn't come this year," she said, in answer to his question. "We're poor as hell. So he gave me two hundred a month and told me I could do my worst on that. . . . This your little girl?"

"What about coming back and sitting down?" Duncan asked.

"Can't do it." He was glad for an excuse. As always, he felt Lorraine's passionate, provocative attraction, but his own rhythm was different now.

"Well, how about dinner?" she asked.

"I'm not free. Give me your address and let me call you."

"Charlie, I believe you're sober," she said judicially. "I honestly believe he's sober, Dunc. Pinch him and see if he's sober."

Charlie indicated Honoria with his head. They both laughed.

"What's your address?" said Duncan skeptically.

He hesitated, unwilling to give the name of his hotel.

"I'm not settled yet. I'd better call you. We're going to see the vaudeville at the Empire."

"There! That's what I want to do," Lorraine said. "I want to see some clowns and acrobats and jugglers. That's just what we'll do, Dunc."

"We've got to do an errand first," said Charlie. "Perhaps we'll see you there."

"All right, you snob. . . . Good-by, beautiful little girl."

"Good-by."

Honoria bobbed politely.

Somehow, an unwelcome encounter. They liked him because he was functioning, because he was serious; they wanted to see him, because he was stronger than they were now, because they wanted to draw a certain sustenance from his strength.

At the Empire, Honoria proudly refused to sit upon her father's folded coat. She was already an individual with a code of her own, and Charlie was more and more absorbed by the desire of putting a little of himself into her before she crystallized utterly. It was hopeless to try to know her in so short a time.

Between the acts they came upon Duncan and Lorraine in the lobby where the band was playing.

"Have a drink?"

"All right, but not up at the bar. We'll take a table."

"The perfect father."

Listening abstractedly to Lorraine, Charlie watched Honoria's eyes leave their table, and he followed them wistfully about the room, wondering what they saw. He met her glance and she smiled.

"I liked that lemonade," she said.

What had she said? What had he expected? Going home in a taxi afterward, he pulled her over until her head rested against his chest.

"Darling, do you ever think about your mother?"

"Yes, sometimes," she answered vaguely.

"I don't want you to forget her. Have you got a picture of her?"

"Yes, I think so. Anyhow, Aunt Marion has. Why don't you want me to forget her?"

"She loved you very much."

"I loved her too."

They were silent for a moment.

"Daddy, I want to come and live with you," she said suddenly.

His heart leaped; he had wanted it to come like this.

"Aren't you perfectly happy?"

"Yes, but I love you better than anybody. And you love me better than anybody, don't you, now that mummy's dead?"

"Of course I do. But you won't always like me best, honey. You'll grow up and meet somebody your own age and go marry him and forget you ever had a daddy."

"Yes, that's true," she agreed tranquilly.

He didn't go in. He was coming back at nine o'clock and he wanted to keep himself fresh and new for the thing he must say then.

"When you're safe inside, just show yourself in that window."

"All right. Good-by, dads, dads, dads, dads."

He waited in the dark street until she appeared, all warm and glowing, in the window above and kissed her fingers out into the night.

III

They were waiting. Marion sat behind the coffee service in a dignified black dinner dress that just faintly suggested mourning. Lincoln was walking up and down with the animation of one who had already been talking. They were as anxious as he was to get into the question. He opened it almost immediately:

"I suppose you know what I want to see you about—why I really came to Paris."

Marion played with the black stars on her necklace and frowned.

"I'm awfully anxious to have a home," he continued. "And I'm awfully anxious to have Honoria in it. I appreciate your taking in Honoria for her mother's sake, but things have changed now"—he hesitated and then continued more forcibly—"changed radically with me, and I want to ask you to reconsider the matter. It would be silly for me to deny that about three years ago I was acting badly—"

Marion looked up at him with hard eyes.

"—but all that's over. As I told you, I haven't had more than a drink a day for over a year, and I take that drink deliberately, so that the idea of alcohol won't get too big in my imagination. You see the idea?"

"No," said Marion succinctly.

"It's a sort of stunt I set myself. It keeps the matter in proportion."

"I get you," said Lincoln. "You don't want to admit it's got any attraction for you."

"Something like that. Sometimes I forget and don't take it. But I try to take it. Anyhow, I couldn't afford to drink in my position. The people I represent are more than satisfied with what I've done, and I'm bringing my sister over from Burlington to keep house for me, and I want awfully to have Honoria too. You know that even when her mother and I weren't getting along well we never let anything that happened touch Honoria. I know she's fond of me and I know I'm able to take care of her and—well, there you are. How do you feel about it?"

He knew that now he would have to take a beating. It would last an hour or two hours, and it would be difficult, but if he modulated his inevitable resentment to the chastened attitude of the reformed sinner, he might win his point in the end.

Keep your temper, he told himself. You don't want to be justified. You want Honoria.

Lincoln spoke first: "We've been talking it over ever since we got your letter last month. We're happy to have Honoria here. She's a dear little thing, and we're glad to be able to help her, but of course that isn't the question—"

Marion interrupted suddenly. "How long are you going to stay sober, Charlie?" she asked.

"Permanently, I hope."

"How can anybody count on that?"

"You know I never did drink heavily until I gave up business and came over here with nothing to do. Then Helen and I began to run around with—"

"Please leave Helen out of it. I can't bear to hear you talk about her like that."

He stared at her grimly; he had never been certain how fond of each other the sisters were in life.

"My drinking only lasted about a year and a half—from the time we came over until I—collapsed."

"It was time enough."

"It was time enough," he agreed.

"My duty is entirely to Helen," she said. "I try to think what she would have wanted me to do. Frankly, from the night you did that terrible thing you haven't really existed for me. I can't help that. She was my sister."

"Yes."

"When she was dying she asked me to look out for Honoria. If you hadn't been in a sanitarium then, it might have helped matters."

He had no answer.

"I'll never in my life be able to forget the morning when Helen knocked at my door, soaked to the skin and shivering and said you'd locked her out."

Charlie gripped the sides of the chair. This was more difficult than he expected; he wanted to launch out into a long expostulation and explanation, but he only said: "The night I locked her out—" and she interrupted, "I don't feel up to going over that again."

After a moment's silence Lincoln said: "We're getting off the subject. You want Marion to set aside her legal guardianship and give you Honoria. I think the main point for her is whether she has confidence in you or not."

"I don't blame Marion," Charlie said slowly, "but I think she can have entire confidence in me. I had a good record up to three years ago. Of course, it's within human possibilities I might go wrong any time. But if we wait much longer I'll lose Honoria's childhood and my chance for a home." He shook his head, "I'll simply lose her, don't you see?"

"Yes, I see," said Lincoln.

"Why didn't you think of all this before?" Marion asked.

"I suppose I did, from time to time, but Helen and I were getting along badly. When I consented to the guardianship, I was flat on my back in a sanitarium and the market had cleaned me out. I knew I'd acted badly, and I thought if it would bring any peace to Helen, I'd agree to anything. But now it's different. I'm functioning, I'm behaving damn well, so far as—"

"Please don't swear at me," Marion said.

He looked at her, startled. With each remark the force of her dislike became more and more apparent. She had built up all her fear of life into one wall and faced it toward him. This trivial reproof was possibly the result of some trouble with the cook several hours before. Charlie became increasingly alarmed at leaving Honoria in this atmosphere of hostility against himself; sooner or later it would come out, in a word here, a shake of the head there, and some of that distrust would be irrevocably implanted in Honoria. But he pulled his temper down out of his face and shut it up inside him; he had won a point, for Lincoln realized the absurdity of Marion's remark and asked her lightly since when she had objected to the word "damn."

"Another thing," Charlie said: "I'm able to give her certain advantages now. I'm going to take a French governess to Prague with me. I've got a lease on a new apartment—"

He stopped, realizing that he was blundering. They couldn't be expected to accept with equanimity the fact that his income was again twice as large as their own.

"I suppose you can give her more luxuries than we can," said Marion. "When you were throwing away money we were living along watching every ten francs. . . . I suppose you'll start doing it again."

"Oh, no," he said. "I've learned. I worked hard for ten years, you know—until I got lucky in the market, like so many people. Terribly lucky. It won't happen again."

There was a long silence. All of them felt their nerves straining, and for the first time in a year Charlie wanted a drink. He was sure now that Lincoln Peters wanted him to have his child.

Marion shuddered suddenly; part of her saw that Charlie's feet were planted on the earth now, and her own maternal feeling recognized the naturalness of his desire; but she had lived for a long time with a prejudice—a prejudice founded on a curious disbelief in her sister's happiness, and which, in the shock of one terrible night, had turned to hatred for him. It had all happened at a point in her life where the discouragement of ill health and adverse circumstances made it necessary for her to believe in tangible villainy and a tangible villain.

"I can't help what I think!" she cried out suddenly. "How much you were responsible for Helen's death, I don't know. It's something you'll have to square with your own conscience."

An electric current of agony surged through him; for a moment he was almost on his feet, an unuttered sound echoing in his throat. He hung on to himself for a moment, another moment.

"Hold on there," said Lincoln uncomfortably. "I never thought you were responsible for that."

"Helen died of heart trouble," Charlie said dully.

"Yes, heart trouble." Marion spoke as if the phrase had another meaning for her.

Then, in the flatness that followed her outburst, she saw him plainly and she knew he had somehow arrived at control over the situation. Glancing at her husband, she found no help from him, and as abruptly as if it were a matter of no importance, she threw up the sponge.

"Do what you like!" she cried, springing up from her chair. "She's your child. I'm not the person to stand in your way. I think if it were my child I'd rather see her—" She managed to check herself. "You two decide it. I can't stand this. I'm sick. I'm going to bed."

She hurried from the room; after a moment Lincoln said:

"This has been a hard day for her. You know how strongly she feels—" His voice was almost apologetic: "When a woman gets an idea in her head."

"Of course."

"It's going to be all right. I think she sees now that you—can provide for the child, and so we can't very well stand in your way or Honoria's way."

"Thank you, Lincoln."

"I'd better go along and see how she is."

"I'm going."

He was still trembling when he reached the street, but a walk down the Rue Bonaparte to the *quais*[2] set him up, and as he crossed the Seine, fresh and new by the *quai* lamps, he felt exultant. But back in his room he couldn't sleep. The image of Helen haunted him. Helen whom he had loved so until they had senselessly begun to abuse each other's love, tear it into shreds. On that terrible February night that Marion remembered so vividly, a slow quarrel had gone on for hours. There was a scene at the Florida, and then he attempted to take her home, and then she kissed young Webb at a table; after that there was what she had hysterically said. When he arrived home alone he turned the key in the lock in wild anger. How could he know she would arrive an hour later alone, that there would be a snowstorm in which she wandered about in slippers, too confused to find a taxi? Then the aftermath, her escaping pneumonia by a miracle, and all the attendant horror. They were "reconciled," but that was the beginning of the end, and Marion, who had seen with her own eyes and who imagined it to be one of many scenes from her sister's martyrdom, never forgot.

Going over it again brought Helen nearer, and in the white, soft light that steals upon half sleep near morning he found himself talking to her again. She said that he was perfectly right about Honoria and that she wanted Honoria to be with him. She said she was glad he was being good and doing better. She said a lot of other things—very friendly things—but she was in a swing in a white dress, and swinging faster and faster all the time, so that at the end he could not hear clearly all that she said.

2. Quays (French); a section of the Left Bank is lined with quays, or walking places along the river.

IV

He woke up feeling happy. The door of the world was open again. He made plans, vistas, futures for Honoria and himself, but suddenly he grew sad, remembering all the plans he and Helen had made. She had not planned to die. The present was the thing—work to do and someone to love. But not to love too much, for he knew the injury that a father can do to a daughter or a mother to a son by attaching them too closely: afterward, out in the world, the child would seek in the marriage partner the same blind tenderness and, failing probably to find it, turn against love and life.

It was another bright, crisp day. He called Lincoln Peters at the bank where he worked and asked if he could count on taking Honoria when he left for Prague. Lincoln agreed that there was no reason for delay. One thing—the legal guardianship. Marion wanted to retain that a while longer. She was upset by the whole matter, and it would oil things if she felt that the situation was still in her control for another year. Charlie agreed, wanting only the tangible, visible child.

Then the question of a governess. Charles sat in a gloomy agency and talked to a cross Béarnaise and to a buxom Breton peasant,[3] neither of whom he could have endured. There were others whom he would see tomorrow.

He lunched with Lincoln Peters at Griffons, trying to keep down his exultation.

"There's nothing quite like your own child," Lincoln said. "But you understand how Marion feels too."

"She's forgotten how hard I worked for seven years there," Charlie said. "She just remembers one night."

"There's another thing." Lincoln hesitated. "While you and Helen were tearing around Europe throwing money away, we were just getting along. I didn't touch any of the prosperity because I never got ahead enough to carry anything but my insurance. I think Marion felt there was some kind of injustice in it—you not even working toward the end, and getting richer and richer."

"It went just as quick as it came," said Charlie.

"Yes, a lot of it stayed in the hands of *chasseurs* and saxophone players and maîtres d'hôtel—well, the big party's over now. I just said that to explain Marion's feeling about those crazy years. If you drop in about six o'clock tonight before Marion's too tired, we'll settle the details on the spot."

Back at his hotel, Charlie found a *pneumatique* that had been redirected from the Ritz bar where Charlie had left his address for the purpose of finding a certain man.

"DEAR CHARLIE: You were so strange when we saw you the other day that I wondered if I did something to offend you. If so, I'm not conscious of it. In fact, I have thought about you too much for the last year, and it's always been in the back of my mind that I might see you if I came over here. We *did* have such good times that crazy spring, like the

---

3. Béarn and Breton are two French provincial regions. The implication is that Charlie wants a higher-class (preferably Parisian) governess.

night you and I stole the butcher's tricycle, and the time we tried to call on the president and you had the old derby rim and the wire cane. Everybody seems so old lately, but I don't feel old a bit. Couldn't we get together some time today for old time's sake? I've got a vile hang-over for the moment, but will be feeling better this afternoon and will look for you about five in the sweatshop at the Ritz.

> "Always devotedly,
> LORRAINE."

His first feeling was one of awe that he had actually, in his mature years, stolen a tricycle and pedaled Lorraine all over the Étoile between the small hours and dawn. In retrospect it was a nightmare. Locking out Helen didn't fit in with any other act of his life, but the tricycle incident did—it was one of many. How many weeks or months of dissipation to arrive at that condition of utter irresponsibility?

He tried to picture how Lorraine had appeared to him then—very attractive; Helen was unhappy about it, though she said nothing. Yesterday, in the restaurant, Lorraine had seemed trite, blurred, worn away. He emphatically did not want to see her, and he was glad Alix had not given away his hotel address. It was a relief to think, instead, of Honoria, to think of Sundays spent with her and of saying good morning to her and of knowing she was there in his house at night, drawing her breath in the darkness.

At five he took a taxi and bought presents for all the Peters—a piquant cloth doll, a box of Roman soldiers, flowers for Marion, big linen handkerchiefs for Lincoln.

He saw, when he arrived in the apartment, that Marion had accepted the inevitable. She greeted him now as though he were a recalcitrant member of the family, rather than a menacing outsider. Honoria had been told she was going; Charlie was glad to see that her tact made her conceal her excessive happiness. Only on his lap did she whisper her delight and the question "When?" before she slipped away with the other children.

He and Marion were alone for a minute in the room, and on an impulse he spoke out boldly:

"Family quarrels are bitter things. They don't go according to any rules. They're not like aches or wounds; they're more like splits in the skin that won't heal because there's not enough material. I wish you and I could be on better terms."

"Some things are hard to forget," she answered. "It's a question of confidence." There was no answer to this and presently she asked, "When do you propose to take her?"

"As soon as I can get a governess. I hoped the day after tomorrow."

"That's impossible. I've got to get her things in shape. Not before Saturday."

He yielded. Coming back into the room, Lincoln offered him a drink.

"I'll take my daily whisky," he said.

It was warm here, it was a home, people together by a fire. The children felt very safe and important; the mother and father were serious, watchful. They had things to do for the children more important than his visit here. A spoonful of medicine was, after all, more important than the strained relations between Marion and himself. They were not dull people, but they were very much in the grip of life and circumstances. He wondered if he couldn't do something to get Lincoln out of his rut at the bank.

A long peal at the door-bell; the *bonne à tout faire*[4] passed through and went down the corridor. The door opened upon another long ring, and then voices, and the three in the salon looked up expectantly; Richard moved to bring the corridor within his range of vision, and Marion rose. Then the maid came back along the corridor, closely followed by the voices, which developed under the light into Duncan Schaeffer and Lorraine Quarrles.

They were gay, they were hilarious, they were roaring with laughter. For a moment Charlie was astounded; unable to understand how they ferreted out the Peters' address.

"Ah-h-h!" Duncan wagged his finger roguishly at Charlie. "Ah-h-h!"

They both slid down another cascade of laughter. Anxious and at a loss, Charlie shook hands with them quickly and presented them to Lincoln and Marion. Marion nodded, scarcely speaking. She had drawn back a step toward the fire; her little girl stood beside her, and Marion put an arm about her shoulder.

With growing annoyance at the intrusion, Charlie waited for them to explain themselves. After some concentration Duncan said:

"We came to invite you out to dinner. Lorraine and I insist that all this shishi, cagy business 'bout your address got to stop."

Charlie came closer to them, as if to force them backward down the corridor.

"Sorry, but I can't. Tell me where you'll be and I'll phone you in half an hour."

This made no impression. Lorraine sat down suddenly on the side of a chair, and focusing her eyes on Richard, cried, "Oh, what a nice little boy! Come here, little boy." Richard glanced at his mother, but did not move. With a perceptible shrug of her shoulders, Lorraine turned back to Charlie:

"Come and dine. Sure your cousins won' mine. See you so sel'om. Or solemn."

"I can't," said Charlie sharply. "You two have dinner and I'll phone you."

Her voice became suddenly unpleasant. "All right, we'll go. But I remember once when you hammered on my door at four A.M. I was enough of a good sport to give you a drink. Come on, Dunc."

Still in slow motion, with blurred, angry faces, with uncertain feet, they retired along the corridor.

"Good night," Charlie said.

"Good night!" responded Lorraine emphatically.

When he went back into the salon Marion had not moved, only now her son was standing in the circle of her other arm. Lincoln was still swinging Honoria back and forth like a pendulum from side to side.

"What an outrage!" Charlie broke out. "What an absolute outrage!"

Neither of them answered. Charlie dropped into an armchair, picked up his drink, set it down again and said:

---

4. Maid of all work (French). The Peters family cannot afford to hire several servants with specialized tasks.

"People I haven't seen for two years having the colossal nerve—"

He broke off. Marion had made the sound "Oh!" in one swift, furious breath, turned her body from him with a jerk and left the room.

Lincoln set down Honoria carefully.

"You children go in and start your soup," he said, and when they obeyed, he said to Charlie:

"Marion's not well and she can't stand shocks. That kind of people make her really physically sick."

"I didn't tell them to come here. They wormed your name out of somebody. They deliberately—"

"Well, it's too bad. It doesn't help matters. Excuse me a minute."

Left alone, Charlie sat tense in his chair. In the next room he could hear the children eating, talking in monosyllables, already oblivious to the scene between their elders. He heard a murmur of conversation from a farther room and then the ticking bell of a telephone receiver picked up, and in a panic he moved to the other side of the room and out of earshot.

In a minute Lincoln came back. "Look here, Charlie. I think we'd better call off dinner for tonight. Marion's in bad shape."

"Is she angry with me?"

"Sort of," he said, almost roughly. "She's not strong and—"

"You mean she's changed her mind about Honoria?"

"She's pretty bitter right now. I don't know. You phone me at the bank tomorrow."

"I wish you'd explain to her I never dreamed these people would come here. I'm just as sore as you are."

"I couldn't explain anything to her now."

Charlie got up. He took his coat and hat and started down the corridor. Then he opened the door of the dining room and said in a strange voice, "Good night, children."

Honoria rose and ran around the table to hug him.

"Good night, sweetheart," he said vaguely, and then trying to make his voice more tender, trying to conciliate something, "Good night, dear children."

V

Charlie went directly to the Ritz bar with the furious idea of finding Lorraine and Duncan, but they were not there, and he realized that in any case there was nothing he could do. He had not touched his drink at the Peters, and now he ordered a whisky-and-soda. Paul came over to say hello.

"It's a great change," he said sadly. "We do about half the business we did. So many fellows I hear about back in the States lost everything, maybe not in the first crash, but then in the second. Your friend George Hardt lost every cent, I hear. Are you back in the States?"

"No, I'm in business in Prague."

"I heard that you lost a lot in the crash."

"I did," and he added grimly, "but I lost everything I wanted in the boom."

"Selling short."

"Something like that."

Again the memory of those days swept over him like a nightmare—the people they had met travelling; then people who couldn't add a row of figures or speak a coherent sentence. The little man Helen had consented to dance with at the ship's party, who had insulted her ten feet from the table; the women and girls carried screaming with drink or drugs out of public places—

—The men who locked their wives out in the snow, because the snow of twenty-nine wasn't real snow. If you didn't want it to be snow, you just paid some money.

He went to the phone and called the Peters' apartment; Lincoln answered.

"I called up because this thing is on my mind. Has Marion said anything definite?"

"Marion's sick," Lincoln answered shortly. "I know this thing isn't altogether your fault, but I can't have her go to pieces about it. I'm afraid we'll have to let it slide for six months; I can't take the chance of working her up to this state again."

"I see."

"I'm sorry, Charlie."

He went back to his table. His whisky glass was empty, but he shook his head when Alix looked at it questioningly. There wasn't much he could do now except send Honoria some things; he would send her a lot of things tomorrow. He thought rather angrily that this was just money—he had given so many people money. . . .

"No, no more," he said to another waiter. "What do I owe you?"

He would come back some day; they couldn't make him pay forever. But he wanted his child, and nothing was much good now, beside that fact. He wasn't young any more, with a lot of nice thoughts and dreams to have by himself. He was absolutely sure Helen wouldn't have wanted him to be so alone.

1931

WILLIAM FAULKNER
1897–1962

Between 1929 and 1936 William Faulkner published novels about childhood, families, sex, race, obsessions, time, the past, his native South, and the modern world. He invented voices for characters ranging from sages to children, criminals, the insane, even the dead—sometimes all within one book. He developed, beyond this ventriloquism, his own unmistakable narrative voice: urgent, intense, highly rhetorical. He experimented with narrative chronology and with techniques for representing mind and memory. He invented an entire southern county and wrote its history.

He was a native Mississippian, born near Oxford, where his parents moved when he was about five. His great-grandfather had been a local legend: a colonel in the Civil War, lawyer, railroad builder, financier, politician, writer, and public figure who was shot and killed by a business and political rival in 1889. Faulkner's grandfather carried on some of the family enterprises, and his father worked first for the railroad (the Gulf and Chicago) and later as business manager of the University of Mississippi. His father was a reclusive man who loved to hunt, drink, and swap stories with his hunting friends; the mother, ambitious, sensitive, and literary, was a more profound influence on Faulkner, her favorite of four sons. In Faulkner's childhood his maternal grandmother also lived with them; she was a high-spirited, independent, and imaginative old lady whose death in 1907 seems to have affected Faulkner deeply.

Faulkner dropped out of high school in 1915 and had no further formal education beyond a year (1919–20) as a special student at the University of Mississippi. Through family connections, various jobs were made for him, but he was unhappy in all of them. In 1918 Estelle Oldham, his high school love, married someone else; Faulkner briefly left Oxford. First he went to New Haven, where his best friend and informal tutor, Phil Stone, was attending law school at Yale; then he enlisted in the British Royal Flying Corps and was sent to Canada to train. World War I ended before he saw active service; nevertheless, when he returned to Oxford in 1919 he was limping from what he claimed was a war wound.

Back at home, Faulkner drifted from one job to another and wrote poetry that was a mélange of Shakespearean, pastoral, Victorian, and Edwardian modes, with an overlay of French Symbolism, which he published in *The Marble Faun*, in 1924. In 1925 he went to New Orleans where, for the first time, he met and mingled with literary people, including Sherwood Anderson, who encouraged Faulkner to develop his own style, to concentrate on prose, and to use his region for material.

Faulkner wrote his first novel, *Soldier's Pay*, in New Orleans, and Anderson recommended it to his own publisher, Liveright; it appeared in 1926. He also published in the New Orleans magazine *The Double Dealer* and the newspaper *The Times Picayune*. He learned about the experimental writing of James Joyce and the ideas of Sigmund Freud. After a trip to Europe at the end of the same year, he returned to Oxford. In 1929 he married Estelle Oldham, who had been divorced and had returned to Oxford with her two children. They bought a ruined mansion, Rowan Oak, in 1930 and began to restore it to its antebellum appearance. A daughter born in 1931 died in infancy; a second daughter, Jill, was born in 1933.

Faulkner's second novel was a satire on New Orleans intellectuals called *Mosquitos* (1927). His more typical subject matter emerged with his rejected novel *Flags in the Dust*, and the shortened version of it that appeared in 1929 as *Sartoris*. In this work Faulkner focused on the interconnections between a prominent southern family and the local community: the Sartoris family as well as many other characters appeared in later works, and the region, renamed Yoknapatawpha County, was to become the locale of Faulkner's imaginative world.

The social and historical emphasis in *Sartoris* was not directly followed up in the works Faulkner wrote next. *The Sound and the Fury* (1929)—Faulkner's favorite novel—and *As I Lay Dying* (1930) were dramatically experimental attempts to articulate the inexpressible aspects of individual psychology. *The Sound and the Fury* has four sections, each with a different narrator, each supplying a different piece of the plot. Three of the narrators are brothers: Benjy, the idiot; Quentin, the suicide; and Jason, the business failure. Each of them, for different reasons, mourns the loss of their sister, Caddie. While the story moves out to the disintegration of the old southern family to which these brothers belong, its focus is on the private obsessions of the brothers, and it invents an entirely different style for each narrator. Only the last section, told from a traditionally omniscient point of view, provides a sequential narration; the other three jump freely in time and space. The structure of *As I Lay Dying* is even more complex. Like *The Sound and the Fury*, it is organized around the loss of a beloved woman. The precipitating event in the novel is the death of a mother. The story moves forward in chronological time as the "poor white" Bundren family takes her body to the town of Jefferson for burial. Its narration is divided into fifty-nine sections of interior monologue by fifteen characters, each with a different perception of the action and a different way of relating to reality. The family's adventures and misadventures on the road are comic, tragic, grotesque, absurd, and deeply moving.

Neither these books nor Faulkner's early short stories were very popular. *Sanctuary*, a sensational work about sex, gangsters, official corruption, and urban violence, attracted considerable attention, however. Published in 1931, it took its place in the large amount of hard-boiled fiction that appeared in the decade, notably by such authors as Dashiell Hammett and Raymond Chandler. During four different intervals— 1932–37, 1942–45, 1951, and 1954—Faulkner spent time in Hollywood or on contract as a scriptwriter. He worked well with the director Howard Hawks and wrote the scripts for two famous movies, an adaptation of Ernest Hemingway's *To Have and Have Not* and an adaptation of Raymond Chandler's *The Big Sleep*, both starring Humphrey Bogart and Lauren Bacall.

He continued to produce brilliant and inventive novels during these years. *Light in August* (1932) counterpointed a comic pastoral about the pregnant earth-mother figure Lena Grove with a grim tragedy about the embittered outcast Joe Christmas, who may or may not be racially mixed; it interrelated individual psychology and cultural pathology. *Absalom, Absalom!*, which followed in 1936, is thought by many to be Faulkner's masterpiece. The story of Thomas Sutpen, the ruthless would-be founder of a southern dynasty after the Civil War, is related by four different speakers, each trying to find "the meaning" of the story. The reader, observing how the story changes in each telling, comes to see that making stories is the human way of making meaning. Like Faulkner's earlier novels, *Absalom* is thus simultaneously about an individual, about the South, and about itself as a work of fic-

To Have and Have Not, movie poster, 1944. Faulkner coauthored the screenplay that adapted Hemingway's 1937 novel as a romantic vehicle for Humphrey Bogart and the newcomer Lauren Bacall.

tion. But its emphasis shifts from the private psychology that dominated in earlier work to social psychology: to the collective mind of the South.

With World War II, Faulkner's work became more traditional and less difficult. He began to write about the rise, in Yoknapatawpha County, of the poor white family named Snopes—this family had appeared in earlier works (like "Barn Burning")—and the simultaneous decline of the region's "aristocratic" families. *The Hamlet* (1940) was the first of three novels devoted to the Snopeses. Because all his works had been set in Yoknapatawpha County and were interconnected, the region and its people began to take on an existence independent of any one book in which they appeared.

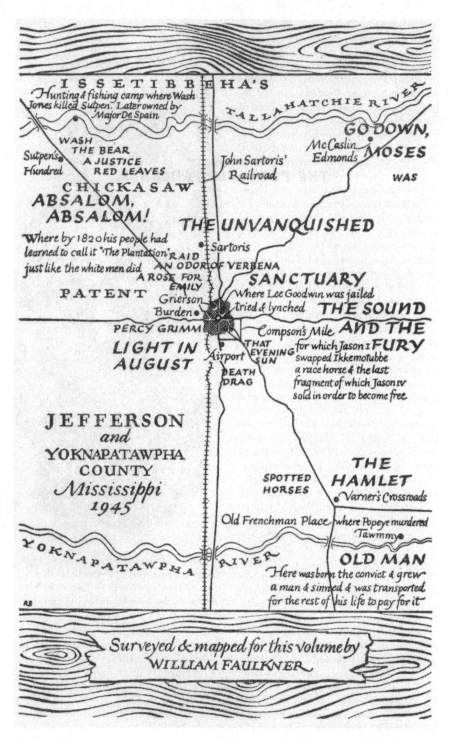

Yoknapatawpha County. Faulkner drew this map of his fictional world for Malcolm Cowley's 1946 collection *The Portable Faulkner*.

Faulkner's national reputation soared after the publication in 1946 of an anthology of his writings, *The Portable Faulkner*, edited by the critic Malcolm Cowley. He already had a major reputation abroad, especially in France, where his work in translation was a powerful influence on the French so-called new novel and its practitioners such as Michel Butor and Alain Robbe-Grillet. His antiracist *Intruder in the Dust* (1948) occasioned the award of the Nobel Prize in 1950. In the 1950s Faulkner visited many college campuses. His writing took on more of the air of an old-fashioned yarn; he dealt with more legendary and local color materials; he rounded out the Snopes saga with *The Town* (1957) and *The Mansion* (1959). At the age of sixty-five he died of a heart attack.

The texts included here are those of *Collected Stories* (1950).

A Rose for Emily

I

When Miss Emily Grierson died, our whole town went to her funeral: the men through a sort of respectful affection for a fallen monument, the women mostly out of curiosity to see the inside of her house, which no one save an old manservant—a combined gardener and cook—had seen in at least ten years.

It was a big, squarish frame house that had once been white, decorated with cupolas and spires and scrolled balconies in the heavily lightsome style of the seventies, set on what had once been our most select street. But garages and cotton gins had encroached and obliterated even the august names of that neighborhood; only Miss Emily's house was left, lifting its stubborn and coquettish decay above the cotton wagons and the gasoline pumps—an eyesore among eyesores. And now Miss Emily had gone to join the representatives of those august names where they lay in the cedar-bemused cemetery among the ranked and anonymous graves of Union and Confederate soldiers who fell at the battle of Jefferson.

Alive, Miss Emily had been a tradition, a duty, and a care; a sort of hereditary obligation upon the town, dating from that day in 1894 when Colonel Sartoris, the mayor—he who fathered the edict that no Negro woman should appear on the streets without an apron—remitted her taxes, the dispensation dating from the death of her father on into perpetuity. Not that Miss Emily would have accepted charity. Colonel Sartoris invented an involved tale to the effect that Miss Emily's father had loaned money to the town, which the town, as a matter of business, preferred this way of repaying. Only a man of Colonel Sartoris' generation and thought could have invented it, and only a woman could have believed it.

When the next generation, with its more modern ideas, became mayors and aldermen, this arrangement created some little dissatisfaction. On the first of the year they mailed her a tax notice. February came, and there was no reply. They wrote her a formal letter, asking her to call at the sheriff's office at her convenience. A week later the mayor wrote her himself, offering to call or to send his car for her, and received in reply a note on paper of an archaic shape, in a thin, flowing calligraphy in faded ink, to the effect that she no longer went out at all. The tax notice was also enclosed, without comment.

They called a special meeting of the Board of Aldermen. A deputation waited upon her, knocked at the door through which no visitor had passed since she ceased giving china-painting lessons eight or ten years earlier. They were admitted by the old Negro into a dim hall from which a stairway mounted into still more shadow. It smelled of dust and disuse—a close, dank smell. The Negro led them into the parlor. It was furnished in heavy, leather-covered furniture. When the Negro opened the blinds of one window, they could see that the leather was cracked; and when they sat down, a faint dust rose sluggishly about their thighs, spinning with slow motes in the single sunray. On a tarnished gilt easel before the fireplace stood a crayon portrait of Miss Emily's father.

They rose when she entered—a small, fat woman in black, with a thin gold chain descending to her waist and vanishing into her belt, leaning on an ebony cane with a tarnished gold head. Her skeleton was small and spare; perhaps that was why what would have been merely plumpness in another was obesity in her. She looked bloated, like a body long submerged in motionless water, and of that pallid hue. Her eyes, lost in the fatty ridges of her face, looked like two small pieces of coal pressed into a lump of dough as they moved from one face to another while the visitors stated their errand.

She did not ask them to sit. She just stood in the door and listened quietly until the spokesman came to a stumbling halt. Then they could hear the invisible watch ticking at the end of the gold chain.

Her voice was dry and cold. "I have no taxes in Jefferson. Colonel Sartoris explained it to me. Perhaps one of you can gain access to the city records and satisfy yourselves."

"But we have. We are the city authorities, Miss Emily. Didn't you get a notice from the sheriff, signed by him?"

"I received a paper, yes," Miss Emily said. "Perhaps he considers himself the sheriff . . . . . . I have no taxes in Jefferson."

"But there is nothing on the books to show that, you see. We must go by the—"

"See Colonel Sartoris. I have no taxes in Jefferson."

"But, Miss Emily—"

"See Colonel Sartoris." (Colonel Sartoris had been dead almost ten years.) "I have no taxes in Jefferson. Tobe!" The Negro appeared. "Show these gentlemen out."

II

So she vanquished them, horse and foot, just as she had vanquished their fathers thirty years before about the smell. That was two years after her father's death and a short time after her sweetheart—the one we believed would marry her—had deserted her. After her father's death she went out very little; after her sweetheart went away, people hardly saw her at all. A few of the ladies had the temerity to call, but were not received, and the only sign of life about the place was the Negro man—a young man then—going in and out with a market basket.

"Just as if a man—any man—could keep a kitchen properly," the ladies said; so they were not surprised when the smell developed. It was another link between the gross, teeming world and the high and mighty Griersons.

A neighbor, a woman, complained to the mayor, Judge Stevens, eighty years old.

"But what will you have me do about it, madam?" he said.

"Why, send her word to stop it," the woman said. "Isn't there a law?"

"I'm sure that won't be necessary," Judge Stevens said. "It's probably just a snake or a rat that nigger of hers killed in the yard. I'll speak to him about it."

The next day he received two more complaints, one from a man who came in diffident deprecation. "We really must do something about it, Judge. I'd be the last one in the world to bother Miss Emily, but we've got to do something." That night the Board of Aldermen met—three gray-beards and one younger man, a member of the rising generation.

"It's simple enough," he said. "Send her word to have her place cleaned up. Give her a certain time to do it in, and if she don't . . . . . ."

"Dammit, sir," Judge Stevens said, "will you accuse a lady to her face of smelling bad?"

So the next night, after midnight, four men crossed Miss Emily's lawn and slunk about the house like burglars, sniffing along the base of the brickwork and at the cellar openings while one of them performed a regular sowing motion with his hand out of a sack slung from his shoulder. They broke open the cellar door and sprinkled lime there, and in all the outbuildings. As they recrossed the lawn, a window that had been dark was lighted and Miss Emily sat in it, the light behind her, and her upright torso motionless as that of an idol. They crept quietly across the lawn and into the shadow of the locusts that lined the street. After a week or two the smell went away.

That was when people had begun to feel really sorry for her. People in our town, remembering how old lady Wyatt, her great-aunt, had gone completely crazy at last, believed that the Griersons held themselves a little too high for what they really were. None of the young men were quite good enough for Miss Emily and such. We had long thought of them as a tableau; Miss Emily a slender figure in white in the background, her father a spraddled silhouette in the foreground, his back to her and clutching a horsewhip, the two of them framed by the back-flung front door. So when she got to be thirty and was still single, we were not pleased exactly, but vindicated; even with insanity in the family she wouldn't have turned down all of her chances if they had really materialized.

When her father died, it got about that the house was all that was left to her; and in a way, people were glad. At last they could pity Miss Emily. Being left alone, and a pauper, she had become humanized. Now she too would know the old thrill and the old despair of a penny more or less.

The day after his death all the ladies prepared to call at the house and offer condolence and aid, as is our custom. Miss Emily met them at the door, dressed as usual and with no trace of grief on her face. She told them that her father was not dead. She did that for three days, with the ministers calling on her, and the doctors, trying to persuade her to let them dispose of the body. Just as they were about to resort to law and force, she broke down, and they buried her father quickly.

We did not say she was crazy then. We believed she had to do that. We remembered all the young men her father had driven away, and we knew that with nothing left, she would have to cling to that which had robbed her, as people will.

III

She was sick for a long time. When we saw her again, her hair was cut short, making her look like a girl, with a vague resemblance to those angels in colored church windows—sort of tragic and serene.

The town had just let the contracts for paving the sidewalks, and in the summer after her father's death they began to work. The construction company came with niggers and mules and machinery, and a foreman named Homer Barron, a Yankee—a big, dark, ready man, with a big voice and eyes lighter than his face. The little boys would follow in groups to hear him cuss the niggers, and the niggers singing in time to the rise and fall of picks. Pretty soon he knew everybody in town. Whenever you heard a lot of laughing anywhere about the square, Homer Barron would be in the center of the group. Presently we began to see him and Miss Emily on Sunday afternoons driving in the yellow-wheeled buggy and the matched team of bays from the livery stable.

At first we were glad that Miss Emily would have an interest, because the ladies all said, "Of course a Grierson would not think seriously of a Northerner, a day laborer." But there were still others, older people, who said that even grief could not cause a real lady to forget *noblesse oblige*—without calling it *noblesse oblige*. They just said, "Poor Emily. Her kinsfolk should come to her." She had some kin in Alabama; but years ago her father had fallen out with them over the estate of old lady Wyatt, the crazy woman, and there was no communication between the two families. They had not even been represented at the funeral.

And as soon as the old people said, "Poor Emily," the whispering began. "Do you suppose it's really so?" they said to one another. "Of course it is. What else could . . . . . ." This behind their hands; rustling of craned silk and satin behind jalousies closed upon the sun of Sunday afternoon as the thin, swift clop-clop-clop of the matched team passed: "Poor Emily."

She carried her head high enough—even when we believed that she was fallen. It was as if she demanded more than ever the recognition of her dignity as the last Grierson; as if it had wanted that touch of earthiness to reaffirm her imperviousness. Like when she bought the rat poison, the arsenic. That was over a year after they had begun to say "Poor Emily," and while the two female cousins were visiting her.

"I want some poison," she said to the druggist. She was over thirty then, still a slight woman, though thinner than usual, with cold, haughty black eyes in a face the flesh of which was strained across the temples and about the eyesockets as you imagine a lighthouse-keeper's face ought to look. "I want some poison," she said.

"Yes, Miss Emily. What kind? For rats and such? I'd recom—"

"I want the best you have. I don't care what kind."

The druggist named several. "They'll kill anything up to an elephant. But what you want is—"

"Arsenic," Miss Emily said. "Is that a good one?"

"Is . . . . . . arsenic? Yes ma'am. But what you want—"

"I want arsenic."

The druggist looked down at her. She looked back at him, erect, her face like a strained flag. "Why, of course," the druggist said. "If that's what you want. But the law requires you to tell what you are going to use it for."

Miss Emily just stared at him, her head tilted back in order to look him eye for eye, until he looked away and went and got the arsenic and wrapped it up. The Negro delivery boy brought her the package; the druggist didn't come back. When she opened the package at home there was written on the box, under the skull and bones: "For rats."

IV

So the next day we all said, "She will kill herself"; and we said it would be the best thing. When she had first begun to be seen with Homer Barron, we had said, "She will marry him." Then we said, "She will persuade him yet," because Homer himself had remarked—he liked men, and it was known that he drank with the younger men in the Elks' Club—that he was not a marrying man. Later we said, "Poor Emily," behind the jalousies as they passed on Sunday afternoon in the glittering buggy, Miss Emily with her head high and Homer Barron with his hat cocked and a cigar in his teeth, reins and whip in a yellow glove.

Then some of the ladies began to say that it was a disgrace to the town and a bad example to the young people. The men did not want to interfere, but at last the ladies forced the Baptist minister—Miss Emily's people were Episcopal—to call upon her. He would never divulge what happened during that interview, but he refused to go back again. The next Sunday they again drove about the streets, and the following day the minister's wife wrote to Miss Emily's relations in Alabama.

So she had blood-kin under her roof again and we sat back to watch developments. At first nothing happened. Then we were sure that they were to be married. We learned that Miss Emily had been to the jeweler's and ordered a man's toilet set in silver, with the letters H. B. on each piece. Two days later we learned that she had bought a complete outfit of men's clothing, including a nightshirt, and we said, "They are married." We were really glad. We were glad because the two female cousins were even more Grierson than Miss Emily had ever been.

So we were not surprised when Homer Barron—the streets had been finished some time since—was gone. We were a little disappointed that there was not a public blowing-off, but we believed that he had gone on to prepare for Miss Emily's coming, or to give her a chance to get rid of the cousins. (By that time it was a cabal, and we were all Miss Emily's allies to help circumvent the cousins.) Sure enough, after another week they departed. And, as we had expected all along, within three days Homer Barron was back in town. A neighbor saw the Negro man admit him at the kitchen door at dusk one evening.

And that was the last we saw of Homer Barron. And of Miss Emily for some time. The Negro man went in and out with the market basket, but the front door remained closed. Now and then we would see her at a window for a moment, as the men did that night when they sprinkled the lime, but for almost six months she did not appear on the streets. Then we knew that this was to be expected too; as if that quality of her father which had thwarted her woman's life so many times had been too virulent and too furious to die.

When we next saw Miss Emily, she had grown fat and her hair was turning gray. During the next few years it grew grayer and grayer until it attained an even pepper-and-salt iron-gray, when it ceased turning. Up to the day of her death at seventy-four it was still that vigorous iron-gray, like the hair of an active man.

From that time on her front door remained closed, save for a period of six or seven years, when she was about forty, during which she gave lessons in china-painting. She fitted up a studio in one of the downstairs rooms, where the daughters and granddaughters of Colonel Sartoris' contemporaries were sent to her with the same regularity and in the same spirit that they were sent on Sundays with a twenty-five-cent piece for the collection plate. Meanwhile her taxes had been remitted.

Then the newer generation became the backbone and the spirit of the town, and the painting pupils grew up and fell away and did not send their children to her with boxes of color and tedious brushes and pictures cut from the ladies' magazines. The front door closed upon the last one and remained closed for good. When the town got free postal delivery Miss Emily alone refused to let them fasten the metal numbers above her door and attach a mailbox to it. She would not listen to them.

Daily, monthly, yearly we watched the Negro grow grayer and more stooped, going in and out with the market basket. Each December we sent her a tax notice, which would be returned by the post office a week later, unclaimed. Now and then we would see her in one of the downstairs windows—she had evidently shut up the top floor of the house—like the carven torso of an idol in a niche, looking or not looking at us, we could never tell which. Thus she passed from generation to generation—dear, inescapable, impervious, tranquil, and perverse.

And so she died. Fell ill in the house filled with dust and shadows, with only a doddering Negro man to wait on her. We did not even know she was sick; we had long since given up trying to get any information from the Negro. He talked to no one, probably not even to her, for his voice had grown harsh and rusty, as if from disuse.

She died in one of the downstairs rooms, in a heavy walnut bed with a curtain, her gray head propped on a pillow yellow and moldy with age and lack of sunlight.

V

The Negro met the first of the ladies at the front door and let them in, with their hushed, sibilant voices and their quick, curious glances, and then he disappeared. He walked right through the house and out the back and was not seen again.

The two female cousins came at once. They held the funeral on the second day, with the town coming to look at Miss Emily beneath a mass of bought flowers, with the crayon face of her father musing profoundly above the bier and the ladies sibilant and macabre; and the very old men—some in their brushed Confederate uniforms—on the porch and the lawn, talking of Miss

Emily as if she had been a contemporary of theirs, believing that they had danced with her and courted her perhaps, confusing time with its mathematical progression, as the old do, to whom all the past is not a diminishing road, but, instead, a huge meadow which no winter ever quite touches, divided from them now by the narrow bottle-neck of the most recent decade of years.

Already we knew that there was one room in that region above stairs which no one had seen in forty years, and which would have to be forced. They waited until Miss Emily was decently in the ground before they opened it.

The violence of breaking down the door seemed to fill this room with pervading dust. A thin, acrid pall as of the tomb seemed to lie everywhere upon this room decked and furnished as for a bridal: upon the valance curtains of faded rose color, upon the rose-shaded lights, upon the dressing table, upon the delicate array of crystal and the man's toilet things backed with tarnished silver, silver so tarnished that the monogram was obscured. Among them lay a collar and tie, as if they had just been removed, which, lifted, left upon the surface a pale crescent in the dust. Upon a chair hung the suit, carefully folded; beneath it the two mute shoes and the discarded socks.

The man himself lay in the bed.

For a long while we just stood there, looking down at the profound and fleshless grin. The body had apparently once lain in the attitude of an embrace, but now the long sleep that outlasts love, that conquers even the grimace of love, had cuckolded him. What was left of him, rotted beneath what was left of the nightshirt, had become inextricable from the bed in which he lay; and upon him and upon the pillow beside him lay that even coating of the patient and biding dust.

Then we noticed that in the second pillow was the indentation of a head. One of us lifted something from it, and leaning forward, that faint and invisible dust dry and acrid in the nostrils, we saw a long strand of iron-gray hair.

1931

Barn Burning

The store in which the Justice of the Peace's court was sitting smelled of cheese. The boy, crouched on his nail keg at the back of the crowded room, knew he smelled cheese, and more: from where he sat he could see the ranked shelves close-packed with the solid, squat, dynamic shapes of tin cans whose labels his stomach read, not from the lettering which meant nothing to his mind but from the scarlet devils and the silver curve of fish—this, the cheese which he knew he smelled and the hermetic meat which his intestines believed he smelled coming in intermittent gusts momentary and brief between the other constant one, the smell and sense just a little of fear because mostly of despair and grief, the old fierce pull of blood. He could not see the table where the Justice sat and before which his father and his father's enemy (*our enemy* he thought in that despair; *ourn! mine and hisn both! He's my father!*) stood, but he could hear them, the two of them that is, because his father had said no word yet:

"But what proof have you, Mr. Harris?"

"I told you. The hog got into my corn. I caught it up and sent it back to him. He had no fence that would hold it. I told him so, warned him. The next time I put the hog in my pen. When he came to get it I gave him enough wire to patch up his pen. The next time I put the hog up and kept it. I rode down to his house and saw the wire I gave him still rolled on to the spool in his yard. I told him he could have the hog when he paid me a dollar pound fee. That evening a nigger came with the dollar and got the hog. He was a strange nigger. He said, 'He say to tell you wood and hay kin burn.' I said, 'What?' 'That whut he say to tell you,' the nigger said. 'Wood and hay kin burn.' That night my barn burned. I got the stock out but I lost the barn."

"Where is the nigger? Have you got him?"

"He was a strange nigger, I tell you. I don't know what became of him."

"But that's not proof. Don't you see that's not proof?"

"Get that boy up here. He knows." For a moment the boy thought too that the man meant his older brother until Harris said, "Not him. The little one. The boy," and, crouching, small for his age, small and wiry like his father, in patched and faded jeans even too small for him, with straight, uncombed, brown hair and eyes gray and wild as storm scud, he saw the men between himself and the table part and become a lane of grim faces, at the end of which he saw the Justice, a shabby, collarless, graying man in spectacles, beckoning him. He felt no floor under his bare feet; he seemed to walk beneath the palpable weight of the grim turning faces. His father, stiff in his black Sunday coat donned not for the trial but for the moving, did not even look at him. *He aims for me to lie*, he thought, again with that frantic grief and despair. *And I will have to do hit.*

"What's your name, boy?" the Justice said.

"Colonel Sartoris Snopes,"[1] the boy whispered.

"Hey?" the Justice said. "Talk louder. Colonel Sartoris? I reckon anybody named for Colonel Sartoris in this country can't help but tell the truth, can they?" The boy said nothing. *Enemy! Enemy!* he thought; for a moment he could not even see, could not see that the Justice's face was kindly nor discern that his voice was troubled when he spoke to the man named Harris: "Do you want me to question this boy?" But he could hear, and during those subsequent long seconds while there was absolutely no sound in the crowded little room save that of quiet and intent breathing it was as if he had swung outward at the end of a grape vine, over a ravine, and at the top of the swing had been caught in a prolonged instant of mesmerized gravity, weightless in time.

"No!" Harris said violently, explosively. "Damnation! Send him out of here!" Now time, the fluid world, rushed beneath him again, the voices coming to him again through the smell of cheese and sealed meat, the fear and despair and the old grief of blood:

"This case is closed. I can't find against you, Snopes, but I can give you advice. Leave this country and don't come back to it."

---

1. The boy is named for Colonel Sartoris, a leading citizen of Jefferson (the fictional town that Faulkner based on his hometown of Oxford, Mississippi) and an officer in the Confederate Army. The Snopeses are a poor white family from the same area. Both families appear in other works by Faulkner.

His father spoke for the first time, his voice cold and harsh, level, without emphasis: "I aim to. I don't figure to stay in a country among people who . . ." he said something unprintable and vile, addressed to no one.

"That'll do," the Justice said. "Take your wagon and get out of this country before dark. Case dismissed."

His father turned, and he followed the stiff black coat, the wiry figure walking a little stiffly from where a Confederate provost's man's musket ball had taken him in the heel on a stolen horse thirty years ago, followed the two backs now, since his older brother had appeared from somewhere in the crowd, no taller than the father but thicker, chewing tobacco steadily, between the two lines of grim-faced men and out of the store and across the worn gallery and down the sagging steps and among the dogs and half-grown boys in the mild May dust, where as he passed a voice hissed:

"Barn burner!"

Again he could not see, whirling; there was a face in a red haze, moonlike, bigger than the full moon, the owner of it half again his size, he leaping in the red haze toward the face, feeling no blow, feeling no shock when his head struck the earth, scrabbling up and leaping again, feeling no blow this time either and tasting no blood, scrabbling up to see the other boy in full flight and himself already leaping into pursuit as his father's hand jerked him back, the harsh, cold voice speaking above him: "Go get in the wagon."

It stood in a grove of locusts and mulberries across the road. His two hulking sisters in their Sunday dresses and his mother and her sister in calico and sunbonnets were already in it, sitting on and among the sorry residue of the dozen and more movings which even the boy could remember—the battered stove, the broken beds and chairs, the clock inlaid with mother-of-pearl, which would not run, stopped at some fourteen minutes past two o'clock of a dead and forgotten day and time, which had been his mother's dowry. She was crying, though when she saw him she drew her sleeve across her face and began to descend from the wagon. "Get back," the father said.

"He's hurt. I got to get some water and wash his . . ."

"Get back in the wagon," his father said. He got in too, over the tail-gate. His father mounted to the seat where the older brother already sat and struck the gaunt mules two savage blows with the peeled willow, but without heat. It was not even sadistic; it was exactly that same quality which in later years would cause his descendants to over-run the engine before putting a motor car into motion, striking and reining back in the same movement. The wagon went on, the store with its quiet crowd of grimly watching men dropped behind; a curve in the road hid it. *Forever* he thought. *Maybe he's done satisfied now, now that he has* . . . stopping himself, not to say it aloud even to himself. His mother's hand touched his shoulder.

"Does hit hurt?" she said.

"Naw," he said. "Hit don't hurt. Lemme be."

"Can't you wipe some of the blood off before hit dries?"

"I'll wash to-night," he said. "Lemme be, I tell you."

The wagon went on. He did not know where they were going. None of them ever did or ever asked, because it was always somewhere, always a house of sorts waiting for them a day or two days or even three days away. Likely his father had already arranged to make a crop on another farm before he . . . Again he had to stop himself. He (the father) always did. There was something about his wolflike independence and even courage when the advantage was at least neutral which impressed strangers, as if they got from his latent ravening ferocity not so much a sense of dependability as a feeling that his ferocious conviction in the rightness of his own actions would be of advantage to all whose interest lay with his.

That night they camped, in a grove of oaks and beeches where a spring ran. The nights were still cool and they had a fire against it, of a rail lifted from a nearby fence and cut into lengths—a small fire, neat, niggard almost, a shrewd fire; such fires were his father's habit and custom always, even in freezing weather. Older, the boy might have remarked this and wondered why not a big one; why should not a man who had not only seen the waste and extravagance of war, but who had in his blood an inherent voracious prodigality with material not his own, have burned everything in sight? Then he might have gone a step farther and thought that that was the reason: that niggard blaze was the living fruit of nights passed during those four years in the woods hiding from all men, blue or gray, with his strings of horses (captured horses, he called them). And older still, he might have divined the true reason: that the element of fire spoke to some deep mainspring of his father's being, as the element of steel or of powder spoke to other men, as the one weapon for the preservation of integrity, else breath were not worth the breathing, and hence to be regarded with respect and used with discretion.

But he did not think this now and he had seen those same niggard blazes all his life. He merely ate his supper beside it and was already half asleep over his iron plate when his father called him, and once more he followed the stiff back, the stiff and ruthless limp, up the slope and on to the starlit road where, turning, he could see his father against the stars but without face or depth—a shape black, flat, and bloodless as though cut from tin in the iron folds of the frockcoat which had not been made for him, the voice harsh like tin and without heat like tin:

"You were fixing to tell them. You would have told him." He didn't answer. His father struck him with the flat of his hand on the side of the head, hard but without heat, exactly as he had struck the two mules at the store, exactly as he would strike either of them with any stick in order to kill a horse fly, his voice still without heat or anger: "You're getting to be a man. You got to learn. You got to learn to stick to your own blood or you ain't going to have any blood to stick to you. Do you think either of them, any man there this morning, would? Don't you know all they wanted was a chance to get at me because they knew I had them beat? Eh?" Later, twenty years later, he was to tell himself, "If I had said they wanted only truth, justice, he would have hit me again." But now he said nothing. He was not crying. He just stood there. "Answer me," his father said.

"Yes," he whispered. His father turned.

"Get on to bed. We'll be there to-morrow."

To-morrow they were there. In the early afternoon the wagon stopped before a paintless two-room house identical almost with the dozen others it had stopped before even in the boy's ten years, and again, as on the other dozen occasions, his mother and aunt got down and began to unload the wagon, although his two sisters and his father and brother had not moved.

"Likely hit ain't fitten for hawgs," one of the sisters said.

"Nevertheless, fit it will and you'll hog it and like it," his father said. "Get out of them chairs and help your Ma unload."

The two sisters got down, big, bovine, in a flutter of cheap ribbons; one of them drew from the jumbled wagon bed a battered lantern, the other a worn broom. His father handed the reins to the older son and began to climb stiffly over the wheel. "When they get unloaded, take the team to the barn and feed them." Then he said, and at first the boy thought he was still speaking to his brother: "Come with me."

"Me?" he said.

"Yes," his father said. "You."

"Abner," his mother said. His father paused and looked back—the harsh level stare beneath the shaggy, graying, irascible brows.

"I reckon I'll have a word with the man that aims to begin to-morrow owning me body and soul for the next eight months."

They went back up the road. A week ago—or before last night, that is—he would have asked where they were going, but not now. His father had struck him before last night but never before had he paused afterward to explain why; it was as if the blow and the following calm, outrageous voice still rang, repercussed, divulging nothing to him save the terrible handicap of being young, the light weight of his few years, just heavy enough to prevent his soaring free of the world as it seemed to be ordered but not heavy enough to keep him footed solid in it, to resist it and try to change the course of its events.

Presently he could see the grove of oaks and cedars and the other flowering trees and shrubs where the house would be, though not the house yet. They walked beside a fence massed with honeysuckle and Cherokee roses and came to a gate swinging open between two brick pillars, and now, beyond a sweep of drive, he saw the house for the first time and at that instant he forgot his father and the terror and despair both, and even when he remembered his father again (who had not stopped) the terror and despair did not return. Because, for all the twelve movings, they had sojourned until now in a poor country, a land of small farms and fields and houses, and he had never seen a house like this before. *Hit's big as a courthouse* he thought quietly, with a surge of peace and joy whose reason he could not have thought into words, being too young for that: *They are safe from him. People whose lives are a part of this peace and dignity are beyond his touch, he no more to them than a buzzing wasp: capable of stinging for a little moment but that's all; the spell of this peace and dignity rendering even the barns and stable and cribs which belong to it impervious to the puny flames he might contrive* . . . this, the peace and joy, ebbing for an instant as he looked again at the stiff black back, the stiff and implacable limp of the figure which was not dwarfed by the house, for the reason that it had never looked big anywhere and which now, against the serene columned backdrop, had more than ever that impervious quality of something cut ruthlessly from tin, depthless, as though, sidewise to the sun, it would cast no shadow. Watching him, the boy remarked the absolutely undeviating course which his father held and saw the stiff foot come squarely down in a pile of fresh droppings where a horse had stood in the drive and which his father could have avoided by a simple change of stride. But it ebbed only for a moment, though he could not have thought this into words either, walking on in the spell of the house, which he could even want but without envy, without sorrow, certainly never with that ravening and jealous rage which unknown to him walked in the ironlike black coat before him: *Maybe he will feel it too. Maybe it will even change him now from what maybe he couldn't help but be.*

They crossed the portico. Now he could hear his father's stiff foot as it came down on the boards with clocklike finality, a sound out of all proportion to the displacement of the body it bore and which was not dwarfed either by the white door before it, as though it had attained to a sort of vicious and ravening minimum not to be dwarfed by anything—the flat, wide, black hat, the formal coat of broadcloth which had once been black but which had now that friction-glazed greenish cast of the bodies of old house flies, the lifted sleeve which was too large, the lifted hand like a curled claw. The door opened so promptly that the boy knew the Negro must have been watching them all the time, an old man with neat grizzled hair, in a linen jacket, who stood barring the door with his body, saying, "Wipe yo foots, white man, fo you come in here. Major ain't home nohow."

"Get out of my way, nigger," his father said, without heat too, flinging the door back and the Negro also and entering, his hat still on his head. And now the boy saw the prints of the stiff foot on the doorjamb and saw them appear on the pale rug behind the machinelike deliberation of the foot which seemed to bear (or transmit) twice the weight which the body compassed. The Negro was shouting "Miss Lula! Miss Lula!" somewhere behind them, then the boy, deluged as though by a warm wave by a suave turn of carpeted stair and a pendant glitter of chandeliers and a mute gleam of gold frames, heard the swift feet and saw her too, a lady—perhaps he had never seen her like before either—in a gray, smooth gown with lace at the throat and an apron tied at the waist and the sleeves turned back, wiping cake or biscuit dough from her hands with a towel as she came up the hall, looking not at his father at all but at the tracks on the blond rug with an expression of incredulous amazement.

"I tried," the Negro cried. "I tole him to . . ."

"Will you please go away?" she said in a shaking voice. "Major de Spain is not at home. Will you please go away?"

His father had not spoken again. He did not speak again. He did not even look at her. He just stood stiff in the center of the rug, in his hat, the shaggy iron-gray brows twitching slightly above the pebble-colored eyes as he appeared to examine the house with brief deliberation. Then with the same deliberation he turned; the boy watched him pivot on the good leg and saw the stiff foot drag round the arc of the turning, leaving a final long and fading smear. His father never looked at it, he never once looked down at the rug. The Negro held the door. It closed behind them, upon the hysteric and indistinguishable woman-wail. His father stopped at the top of the steps and scraped his boot clean on the edge of it. At the gate he stopped again. He stood for a moment, planted stiffly on the stiff foot, looking back at the house. "Pretty and white, ain't it?" he said. "That's sweat. Nigger sweat. Maybe it ain't white enough yet to suit him. Maybe he wants to mix some white sweat with it."

Two hours later the boy was chopping wood behind the house within which his mother and aunt and the two sisters (the mother and aunt, not the two girls, he knew that; even at this distance and muffled by walls the flat loud voices of the two girls emanated an incorrigible idle inertia) were setting up the stove to prepare a meal, when he heard the hooves and saw the linen-clad man on a fine sorrel mare, whom he recognized even before he saw the rolled rug in front of the Negro youth following on a fat bay carriage horse—a suffused, angry face vanishing, still at full gallop, beyond the corner of the house where his father and brother were sitting in the two tilted chairs; and a moment later, almost before he could have put the axe down, he heard the hooves again and watched the sorrel mare go back out of the yard, already galloping again. Then his father began to shout one of the sisters' names, who presently emerged backward from the kitchen door dragging the rolled rug along the ground by one end while the other sister walked behind it.

"If you ain't going to tote, go on and set up the wash pot," the first said.

"You, Sarty!" the second shouted. "Set up the wash pot!" His father appeared at the door, framed against that shabbiness, as he had been against that other bland perfection, impervious to either, the mother's anxious face at his shoulder.

"Go on," the father said. "Pick it up." The two sisters stooped, broad, lethargic; stooping, they presented an incredible expanse of pale cloth and a flutter of tawdry ribbons.

"If I thought enough of a rug to have to git hit all the way from France I wouldn't keep hit where folks coming in would have to tromp on hit," the first said. They raised the rug.

"Abner," the mother said. "Let me do it."

"You go back and git dinner," his father said. "I'll tend to this."

From the woodpile through the rest of the afternoon the boy watched them, the rug spread flat in the dust beside the bubbling wash-pot, the two sisters stooping over it with that profound and lethargic reluctance, while the father stood over them in turn, implacable and grim, driving them though never raising his voice again. He could smell the harsh homemade lye they were using; he saw his mother come to the door once and look toward them with an expression not anxious now but very like despair; he saw his father turn, and he fell to with the axe and saw from the corner of his eye his father raise from the ground a flattish fragment of field stone and examine it and return to the pot, and this time his mother actually spoke: "Abner. Abner. Please don't. Please, Abner."

Then he was done too. It was dusk; the whippoorwills had already begun. He could smell coffee from the room where they would presently eat the cold food remaining from the mid-afternoon meal, though when he entered the house he realized they were having coffee again probably because there was a fire on the hearth, before which the rug now lay spread over the backs of the two chairs. The tracks of his father's foot were gone. Where they had been were now long, water-cloudy scoriations resembling the sporadic course of a lilliputian mowing machine.

It still hung there while they ate the cold food and then went to bed, scattered without order or claim up and down the two rooms, his mother in one bed, where his father would later lie, the older brother in the other, himself, the aunt, and the two sisters on pallets on the floor. But his father was not in bed yet. The last thing the boy remembered was the depthless, harsh silhouette of the hat and coat bending over the rug and it seemed to him that he had not even closed his eyes when the silhouette was standing over him, the fire almost dead behind it, the stiff foot prodding him awake. "Catch up the mule," his father said.

When he returned with the mule his father was standing in the black door, the rolled rug over his shoulder. "Ain't you going to ride?" he said.

"No. Give me your foot."

He bent his knee into his father's hand, the wiry, surprising power flowed smoothly, rising, he rising with it, on to the mule's bare back (they had owned a saddle once; the boy could remember it though not when or where) and with the same effortlessness his father swung the rug up in front of him. Now in the starlight they retraced the afternoon's path, up the dusty road rife with honeysuckle, through the gate and up the black tunnel of the drive to the lightless house, where he sat on the mule and felt the rough warp of the rug drag across his thighs and vanish.

"Don't you want me to help?" he whispered. His father did not answer and now he heard again that stiff foot striking the hollow portico with that wooden and clocklike deliberation, that outrageous overstatement of the weight it carried. The rug, hunched, not flung (the boy could tell that even in the darkness) from his father's shoulder, struck the angle of wall and floor with a sound unbelievably loud, thunderous, then the foot again, unhurried and enormous; a light came on in the house and the boy sat, tense, breathing steadily and quietly and just a little fast, though the foot itself did not increase its beat at all, descending the steps now; now the boy could see him.

"Don't you want to ride now?" he whispered. "We kin both ride now," the light within the house altering now, flaring up and sinking. *He's coming down the stairs now,* he thought. He had already ridden the mule up beside the horse block; presently his father was up behind him and he doubled the reins over and slashed the mule across the neck, but before the animal could begin to trot the hard, thin arm came round him, the hard, knotted hand jerking the mule back to a walk.

In the first red rays of the sun they were in the lot, putting plow gear on the mules. This time the sorrel mare was in the lot before he heard it at all, the rider collarless and even bareheaded, trembling, speaking in a shaking voice as the woman in the house had done, his father merely looking up once before stooping again to the hame he was buckling, so that the man on the mare spoke to his stooping back:

"You must realize you have ruined that rug. Wasn't there anybody here, any of your women . . ." he ceased, shaking, the boy watching him, the older brother leaning now in the stable door, chewing, blinking slowly and steadily at nothing apparently. "It cost a hundred dollars. But you never had a hundred dollars. You never will. So I'm going to charge you twenty bushels of corn against your crop. I'll add it in your contract and when you come to the commissary you can sign it. That won't keep Mrs. de Spain quiet but maybe it will teach you to wipe your feet off before you enter her house again."

Then he was gone. The boy looked at his father, who still had not spoken or even looked up again, who was now adjusting the logger-head in the hame.

"Pap," he said. His father looked at him—the inscrutable face, the shaggy brows beneath which the gray eyes glinted coldly. Suddenly the boy went toward him, fast, stopping as suddenly. "You done the best you could!" he cried. "If he wanted hit done different why didn't he wait and tell you how?

He won't git no twenty bushels! He won't git none! We'll gether hit and hide hit! I kin watch . . ."

"Did you put the cutter back in that straight stock like I told you?"

"No, sir," he said.

"Then go do it."

That was Wednesday. During the rest of that week he worked steadily, at what was within his scope and some which was beyond it, with an industry that did not need to be driven nor even commanded twice; he had this from his mother, with the difference that some at least of what he did he liked to do, such as splitting wood with the half-size axe which his mother and aunt had earned, or saved money somehow, to present him with at Christmas. In company with the two older women (and on one afternoon, even one of the sisters), he built pens for the shoat and the cow which were a part of his father's contract with the landlord, and one afternoon, his father being absent, gone somewhere on one of the mules, he went to the field.

They were running a middle buster now, his brother holding the plow straight while he handled the reins, and walking beside the straining mule, the rich black soil shearing cool and damp against his bare ankles, he thought *Maybe this is the end of it. Maybe even that twenty bushels that seems hard to have to pay for just a rug will be a cheap price for him to stop forever and always from being what he used to be*; thinking, dreaming now, so that his brother had to speak sharply to him to mind the mule: *Maybe he even won't collect the twenty bushels. Maybe it will all add up and balance and vanish—corn, rug, fire; the terror and grief, the being pulled two ways like between two teams of horses—gone, done with for ever and ever.*

Then it was Saturday; he looked up from beneath the mule he was harnessing and saw his father in the black coat and hat. "Not that," his father said. "The wagon gear." And then, two hours later, sitting in the wagon bed behind his father and brother on the seat, the wagon accomplished a final curve, and he saw the weathered paintless store with its tattered tobacco- and patent-medicine posters and the tethered wagons and saddle animals below the gallery. He mounted the gnawed steps behind his father and brother, and there again was the lane of quiet, watching faces for the three of them to walk through. He saw the man in spectacles sitting at the plank table and he did not need to be told this was a Justice of the Peace; he sent one glare of fierce, exultant, partisan defiance at the man in collar and cravat now, whom he had seen but twice before in his life, and that on a galloping horse, who now wore on his face an expression not of rage but of amazed unbelief which the boy could not have known was at the incredible circumstance of being sued by one of his own tenants, and came and stood against his father and cried at the Justice: "He ain't done it! He ain't burnt . . ."

"Go back to the wagon," his father said.

"Burnt?" the Justice said. "Do I understand this rug was burned too?"

"Does anybody here claim it was?" his father said. "Go back to the wagon." But he did not, he merely retreated to the rear of the room, crowded as that other had been, but not to sit down this time, instead, to stand pressing among the motionless bodies, listening to the voices:

"And you claim twenty bushels of corn is too high for the damage you did to the rug?"

"He brought the rug to me and said he wanted the tracks washed out of it. I washed the tracks out and took the rug back to him."

"But you didn't carry the rug back to him in the same condition it was in before you made the tracks on it."

His father did not answer, and now for perhaps half a minute there was no sound at all save that of breathing, the faint, steady suspiration of complete and intent listening.

"You decline to answer that, Mr. Snopes?" Again his father did not answer. "I'm going to find against you, Mr. Snopes. I'm going to find that you were responsible for the injury to Major de Spain's rug and hold you liable for it. But twenty bushels of corn seems a little high for a man in your circumstances to have to pay. Major de Spain claims it cost a hundred dollars. October corn will be worth about fifty cents. I figure that if Major de Spain can stand a ninety-five-dollar loss on something he paid cash for, you can stand a five-dollar loss you haven't earned yet. I hold you in damages to Major de Spain to the amount of ten bushels of corn over and above your contract with him, to be paid to him out of your crop at gathering time. Court adjourned."

It had taken no time hardly, the morning was but half begun. He thought they would return home and perhaps back to the field, since they were late, far behind all other farmers. But instead his father passed on behind the wagon, merely indicating with his hand for the older brother to follow with it, and crossed the road toward the blacksmith shop opposite, pressing on after his father, overtaking him, speaking, whispering up at the harsh, calm face beneath the weathered hat: "He won't git no ten bushels neither. He won't git one. We'll . . ." until his father glanced for an instant down at him, the face absolutely calm, the grizzled eyebrows tangled above the cold eyes, the voice almost pleasant, almost gentle:

"You think so? Well, we'll wait till October anyway."

The matter of the wagon—the setting of a spoke or two and the tightening of the tires—did not take long either, the business of the tires accomplished by driving the wagon into the spring branch behind the shop and letting it stand there, the mules nuzzling into the water from time to time, and the boy on the seat with the idle reins, looking up the slope and through the sooty tunnel of the shed where the slow hammer rang and where his father sat on an upended cypress bolt, easily, either talking or listening, still sitting there when the boy brought the dripping wagon up out of the branch and halted it before the door.

"Take them on to the shade and hitch," his father said. He did so and returned. His father and the smith and a third man squatting on his heels inside the door were talking, about crops and animals; the boy, squatting too in the ammoniac dust and hoof-parings and scales of rust, heard his father tell a long and unhurried story out of the time before the birth of the older brother even when he had been a professional horsetrader. And then his father came up beside him where he stood before a tattered last year's circus poster on the other side of the store, gazing rapt and quiet at the scarlet horses, the incredible poisings and convolutions of tulle and tights and the painted leers of comedians, and said "It's time to eat."

But not at home. Squatting beside his brother against the front wall, he watched his father emerge from the store and produce from a paper sack a segment of cheese and divide it carefully and deliberately into three with his pocket knife and produce crackers from the same sack. They all three squatted on the gallery and ate, slowly, without talking; then in the store again, they drank from a tin dipper tepid water smelling of the cedar bucket and of living beech trees. And still they did not go home. It was a horse lot this time, a tall rail fence upon and along which men stood and sat and out of which one by one horses were led, to be walked and trotted and then cantered back and forth along the road while the slow swapping and buying went on and the sun began to slant westward, they—the three of them—watching and listening, the older brother with his muddy eyes and his steady, inevitable tobacco, the father commenting now and then on certain of the animals, to no one in particular.

It was after sundown when they reached home. They ate supper by lamplight, then, sitting on the doorstep, the boy watched the night fully accomplish, listening to the whippoorwills and the frogs, when he heard his mother's voice: "Abner! No! No! Oh, God. Oh, God. Abner!" and he rose, whirled, and saw the altered light through the door where a candle stub now burned in a bottle neck on the table and his father, still in the hat and coat, at once formal and burlesque as though dressed carefully for some shabby and ceremonial violence, emptying the reservoir of the lamp back into the five-gallon kerosene can from which it had been filled, while the mother tugged at his arm until he shifted the lamp to the other hand and flung her back, not savagely or viciously, just hard, into the wall, her hands flung out against the wall for balance, her mouth open and in her face the same quality of hopeless despair as had been in her voice. Then his father saw him standing in the door.

"Go to the barn and get that can of oil we were oiling the wagon with," he said. The boy did not move. Then he could speak.

"What . . ." he cried. "What are you . . ."

"Go get that oil," his father said. "Go."

Then he was moving, running, outside the house, toward the stable: this is the old habit, the old blood which he had not been permitted to choose for himself, which had been bequeathed him willy nilly and which had run for so long (and who knew where, battening on what of outrage and savagery and lust) before it came to him. *I could keep on,* he thought. *I could run on and on and never look back, never need to see his face again. Only I can't. I can't,* the rusted can in his hand now, the liquid sploshing in it as he ran back to the house and into it, into the sound of his mother's weeping in the next room, and handed the can to his father.

"Ain't you going to even send a nigger?" he cried. "At least you sent a nigger before!"

This time his father didn't strike him. The hand came even faster than the blow had, the same hand which had set the can on the table with almost excruciating care flashing from the can toward him too quick for him to follow it, gripping him by the back of his shirt and on to tiptoe before he had seen it quit the can, the face stooping at him in breathless and frozen ferocity, the cold, dead voice speaking over him to the older brother who leaned against the table, chewing with that steady, curious, sidewise motion of cows:

"Empty the can into the big one and go on. I'll catch up with you."

"Better tie him up to the bedpost," the brother said.

"Do like I told you," the father said. Then the boy was moving, his bunched shirt and the hard, bony hand between his shoulder-blades, his toes just touching the floor, across the room and into the other one, past the sisters sitting with spread heavy thighs in the two chairs over the cold hearth, and to where his mother and aunt sat side by side on the bed, the aunt's arms about his mother's shoulders.

"Hold him," the father said. The aunt made a startled movement. "Not you," the father said. "Lennie. Take hold of him. I want to see you do it." His mother took him by the wrist. "You'll hold him better than that. If he gets loose don't you know what he is going to do? He will go up yonder." He jerked his head toward the road. "Maybe I'd better tie him."

"I'll hold him," his mother whispered.

"See you do then." Then his father was gone, the stiff foot heavy and measured upon the boards, ceasing at last.

Then he began to struggle. His mother caught him in both arms, he jerking and wrenching at them. He would be stronger in the end, he knew that. But he had no time to wait for it. "Lemme go!" he cried. "I don't want to have to hit you!"

"Let him go!" the aunt said. "If he don't go, before God, I am going there myself!"

"Don't you see I can't!" his mother cried. "Sarty! Sarty! No! No! Help me, Lizzie!"

Then he was free. His aunt grasped at him but it was too late. He whirled, running, his mother stumbled forward on to her knees behind him, crying to the nearer sister: "Catch him, Net! Catch him!" But that was too late too, the sister (the sisters were twins, born at the same time, yet either of them now gave the impression of being, encompassing as much living meat and volume and weight as any other two of the family) not yet having begun to rise from the chair, her head, face, alone merely turned, presenting to him in the flying instant an astonishing expanse of young female features untroubled by any surprise even, wearing only an expression of bovine interest. Then he was out of the room, out of the house, in the mild dust of the starlit road and the heavy rifeness of honeysuckle, the pale ribbon unspooling with terrific slowness under his running feet, reaching the gate at last and turning in, running, his heart and lungs drumming, on up the drive toward the lighted house, the lighted door. He did not knock, he burst in, sobbing for breath, incapable for the moment of speech; he saw the astonished face of the Negro in the linen jacket without knowing when the Negro had appeared.

"De Spain!" he cried, panted. "Where's . . ." then he saw the white man too emerging from a white door down the hall. "Barn!" he cried. "Barn!"

"What?" the white man said. "Barn?"

"Yes!" the boy cried. "Barn!"

"Catch him!" the white man shouted.

But it was too late this time too. The Negro grasped his shirt, but the entire sleeve, rotten with washing, carried away, and he was out that door too and in the drive again, and had actually never ceased to run even while he was screaming into the white man's face.

Behind him the white man was shouting, "My horse! Fetch my horse!" and he thought for an instant of cutting across the park and climbing the fence into the road, but he did not know the park nor how high the vine-massed fence might be and he dared not risk it. So he ran on down the drive, blood and breath roaring; presently he was in the road again though he could not see it. He could not hear either: the galloping mare was almost upon him before he heard her, and even then he held his course, as if the very urgency of his wild grief and need must in a moment more find him wings, waiting until the ultimate instant to hurl himself aside and into the weed-choked roadside ditch as the horse thundered past and on, for an instant in furious silhouette against the stars, the tranquil early summer night sky which, even before the shape of the horse and rider vanished, stained abruptly and violently upward: a long, swirling roar incredible and soundless, blotting the stars, and he springing up and into the road again, running again, knowing it was too late yet still running even after he heard the shot and, an instant later, two shots, pausing now without knowing he had ceased to run, crying "Pap! Pap!", running again before he knew he had begun to run, stumbling, tripping over something and scrabbling up again without ceasing to run, looking backward over his shoulder at the glare as he got up, running on among the invisible trees, panting, sobbing, "Father! Father!"

At midnight he was sitting on the crest of a hill. He did not know it was midnight and he did not know how far he had come. But there was no glare behind him now and he sat now, his back toward what he had called home for four days anyhow, his face toward the dark woods which he would enter when breath was strong again, small, shaking steadily in the chill darkness, hugging himself into the remainder of his thin, rotten shirt, the grief and despair now no longer terror and fear but just grief and despair. *Father. My father,* he thought. "He was brave!" he cried suddenly, aloud but not loud, no more than a whisper: "He was! He was in the war! He was in Colonel Sartoris' cav'ry!" not knowing that his father had gone to that war a private in the fine old European sense, wearing no uniform, admitting the authority of and giving fidelity to no man or army or flag, going to war as Malbrouck[2] himself did: for booty—it meant nothing and less than nothing to him if it were enemy booty or his own.

The slow constellations wheeled on. It would be dawn and then sun-up after a while and he would be hungry. But that would be to-morrow and now he was only cold, and walking would cure that. His breathing was easier now and he decided to get up and go on, and then he found that he had been asleep because he knew it was almost dawn, the night almost over. He could tell that from the whippoorwills. They were everywhere now among the dark trees below him, constant and inflectioned and ceaseless, so that, as the instant for giving over to the day birds drew nearer and nearer, there was no interval at all between them. He got up. He was a little stiff, but walking would cure that too as it would the cold, and soon there would be the sun. He went on down the hill, toward the dark woods within which the liquid silver voices of the birds called unceasing—the rapid and urgent beating of the urgent and quiring heart of the late spring night. He did not look back.

1938

2. Figure in an 18th-century French ballad, "Malbrouck Has Gone to the War," popularly identified with John Churchill, First Duke of Marlborough (1650–1722), who rose through the ranks from private to become a famous commander. Despite his military genius, he was often accused of greed and disloyalty.

HART CRANE
1899–1932

B efore his suicide at the age of thirty-two, Hart Crane led a life of extremes: he wrote poetry of frequently ecstatic intensity, drank uncontrollably, had bitterly ambivalent relations with his quarreling parents; he relished the comparative erotic freedom of post–World War I Greenwich Village while enduring his literary friends' disapproval of his homosexuality. Born and raised in Ohio, Crane went to New York City in 1917, ostensibly to prepare for college but in fact to investigate the possibility of a literary career. Returning to Cleveland for four years (1919–23), he tried unsuccessfully to enter business as a means of financing an after-hours literary life. During these years he read widely and developed a large circle of intellectual friends and correspondents. He also published some of the poems that made his early reputation: "My Grandmother's Love Letters" in 1920, "Chaplinesque" in 1921, and "For the Marriage of Faustus and Helen" in 1922. He also began work on the love sequence *Voyages*. By 1923, believing himself ready to succeed as a writer, he moved back to New York City.

His most productive years came between 1923 and 1927. He completed *Voyages* in 1924, published his first collection, *White Buildings,* in 1926, and composed ten of the fifteen poems that were to make up *The Bridge* in 1926. He held occasional jobs, but received most of his support from his parents, friends, and above all from the patronage of a banker, Otto Kahn. Crane defined himself as a follower of Walt Whitman in the visionary, prophetic, affirmative American tradition, aiming at nothing less than to master the techniques of modernism while reversing its direction— to make it positive, celebratory, and deeply meshed with contemporary American life without sacrificing technical complexity or richness.

Crane's practice centered on metaphor—the device that, in his view, represented the difference between poetry and expository prose. He believed that metaphor had preceded logic in the development of human thought and that it still remained the primary mode in which human knowledge was acquired and through which experience was connected to mind. In Charlie Chaplin's silent movie character "The Tramp," Crane found a repertory of metaphors for the poet's loving posture towards the modern world; "At Melville's Tomb" pushes metaphor to the breaking point of logic in its homage to the earlier American author, whose reputation in the 1920s was just beginning to revive following years of neglect. Like his model Whitman, Crane wrote from the paradoxical, conflicted position of the outsider claiming to speak from and for the very center of America.

The text of the poems included here is that of *Complete Poems of Hart Crane,* edited by Marc Simon (1993).

Chaplinesque[1]

We make our meek adjustments,
Contented with such random consolations

---

1. Crane wrote of seeing Charlie Chaplin's film *The Kid* (1921) and said that he aimed "to put in words some of the Chaplin pantomime, so beauti- ful, and so full of eloquence, and so modern." The film "made me feel myself, as a poet, as being 'in the same boat' with him," Crane wrote.

As the wind deposits
In slithered and too ample pockets.

For we can still love the world, who find   5
A famished kitten on the step, and know
Recesses for it from the fury of the street,
Or warm torn elbow coverts.

We will sidestep, and to the final smirk
Dally the doom of that inevitable thumb   10
That slowly chafes its puckered index toward us,
Facing the dull squint with what innocence
And what surprise!

And yet these fine collapses are not lies
More than the pirouettes of any pliant cane;   15
Our obsequies[2] are, in a way, no enterprise.
We can evade you, and all else but the heart:
What blame to us if the heart live on.

The game enforces smirks; but we have seen
The moon in lonely alleys make   20
A grail of laughter of an empty ash can,
And through all sound of gaiety and quest
Have heard a kitten in the wilderness.

                                                          1921, 1926

At Melville's Tomb[1]

Often beneath the wave, wide from this ledge
The dice of drowned men's bones he saw bequeath
An embassy. Their numbers as he watched,
Beat on the dusty shore and were obscured.[2]

And wrecks passed without sound of bells,   5
The calyx of death's bounty giving back

---

2. In the double sense of "funeral rites" and "obsequiousness."
1. This poem was published in *Poetry* magazine
only after Crane provided the editor, Harriet
Monroe, with a detailed explanation of its
images. His letter and Monroe's inquiries and
comments were published with the poem.
Crane's detailed comments in the letter are
incorporated in the notes to the poem. Herman
Melville (1819–1891), American author.
2. "Dice bequeath an embassy, in the first place,

by being ground (in this connection only, of
course) in little cubes from the bones of drowned
men by the action of the sea, and are finally
thrown up on the sand, having 'numbers' but no
identification. These being the bones of dead men
who never completed their voyage, it seems legitimate to refer to them as the only surviving evidence of certain messages undelivered, mute
evidence of certain things. . . . Dice as a symbol of
chance and circumstance is also implied" [Crane's
note].

A scattered chapter, livid hieroglyph,
The portent wound in corridors of shells.[3]

Then in the circuit calm of one vast coil,
Its lashings charmed and malice reconciled,   10
Frosted eyes there were that lifted altars;[4]
And silent answers crept across the stars.

Compass, quadrant and sextant contrive
No farther tides[5] . . . High in the azure steeps
Monody shall not wake the mariner.   15
This fabulous shadow only the sea keeps.

                                                        1926

3. "This calyx refers in a double ironic sense both to a cornucopia and the vortex made by a sinking vessel. As soon as the water has closed over a ship this whirlpool sends up broken spars, wreckage, etc., which can be alluded to as livid *hieroglyphs,* making a *scattered chapter* so far as any complete record of the recent ship and crew is concerned. In fact, about as much definite knowledge might come from all this as anyone might gain from the roar of his own veins, which is easily heard (haven't you ever done it?) by holding a shell close to one's ear" [Crane's note]. A calyx is a whorl of leaves forming the outer casing of the bud of a plant.
4. "Refers simply to a conviction that a man, not knowing perhaps a definite god yet being endowed with a reverence for deity—such a man naturally postulates a deity somehow, and the altar of that deity by the very *action* of the eyes *lifted* in searching" [Crane's note].
5. "Hasn't it often occurred that instruments originally invented for record and computation have inadvertently so extended the concepts of the entity they were invented to measure (concepts of space, etc.) in the mind and imagination that employed them, that they may metaphorically be said to have extended the original boundaries of the entity measured? This little bit of 'relativity' ought not to be discredited in poetry now that scientists are proceeding to measure the universe on principles of pure *ratio,* quite as metaphorical, so far as previous standards of scientific methods extended, as some of the axioms in *Job*" [Crane's note].

ERNEST HEMINGWAY
1899–1961

The narrator in Ernest Hemingway's *A Farewell to Arms,* reflecting on his war experiences, observes at one point, "I was always embarrassed by the words sacred, glorious, and sacrifice and the expression in vain. . . . I had seen nothing sacred, and the things that were glorious had no glory and the sacrifices were like the stockyards at Chicago if nothing was done with the meat except to bury it. There were many words that you could not stand to hear." Hemingway's aim and achievement as a novelist and short-story writer were to convey his concerns in a prose style built from what was left after eliminating all the words one "could not stand to hear." As flamboyant in his personal style as he was severe in his writing, Hemingway became an international celebrity after the publication in 1926 of his first novel, *The Sun Also Rises.* At the time of his death, he was probably the most famous writer in the world.

    He was born and raised in Oak Park, Illinois, one of six children. His mother was a music teacher, director of the church choir, and a lover of high culture who had contemplated a career as an opera singer. His father was a successful physician, prone to depression, who enjoyed hunting, fishing, and cooking and who shared in household responsibilities more than most men of his era. The family spent summers at their cottage in northern Michigan, where many of Hemingway's stories are set. After high school, Hemingway took a job on the *Kansas City Star*. When the United States entered the war in 1917, Hemingway was eager to go. An eye problem barred him from the army, so he joined the ambulance corps. Within three weeks he was wounded by shrapnel. After six months in the hospital Hemingway went home as a decorated hero: when wounded, he had carried a comrade more badly hurt than he to safety. He found readjustment difficult and became increasingly estranged from his family, especially his mother. Years later, when his father committed suicide, Hemingway blamed his mother for that death.

In 1920 he married Hadley Richardson and went to Paris. Supported partly by her money and partly by his journalism, Hemingway worked at becoming a writer. He came to know Gertrude Stein, Sherwood Anderson, Ezra Pound, F. Scott Fitzgerald, and others in the large community of expatriate artistic and literary Americans. Besides reading his manuscripts and advising him, Fitzgerald and Anderson, better known than he, used their influence to get his book of short stories *In Our Time* published in the United States in 1925. In this book, stories about the adolescent Nick Adams as he grows up in northern Michigan alternate with very brief, powerful vignettes of war and crime.

In 1926 his novel *The Sun Also Rises* appeared; it presents the stripped-down "Hemingway style" at its finest. "I always try to write on the principle of the iceberg," he told an interviewer. "There is seven-eighths of it under water for every part that shows." Narrated by Jake Barnes, whose World War I wounds have left him sexually impotent, *The Sun Also Rises* depicts Jake's efforts to live according to a self-conscious code of dignity, of "grace under pressure," in the midst of a circle of self-seeking American and English expatriates in Paris—the "lost generation," as Gertrude Stein dubbed them. He finds an ideal in the rich tradition of Spanish peasant life, especially as epitomized in bullfighting and the bullfighter. *The Sun Also Rises* was directly responsible for a surge of American tourism to Pamplona, Spain, where the novel's bullfights are set.

In 1927 Hemingway brought out his second collection of stories, *Men without Women*. Adapting journalistic techniques in telegraphic prose that minimized narrator commentary and depended heavily on uncontextualized dialogue, these stories developed the modern, speeded-up, streamlined style exemplified in "Hills Like White Elephants." His second novel, *A Farewell to Arms*, appeared in 1929. It described a romance between an American army officer, Frederic Henry, and a British nurse, Catherine Barkley. The two run away from war, trying to make "a separate peace," but their idyll is shattered when Catherine dies in childbirth. Hemingway's work has been much criticized for its depictions of women. The wholly good Catherine lives for Frederic Henry alone; and Maria, in his Spanish Civil War novel (*For Whom the Bell Tolls*, 1940), is a fantasy figure of total submissiveness. Characters like Brett Ashley in *The Sun Also Rises* and Pilar in *For Whom the Bell Tolls*, however, are strong, complex figures. Overall, Hemingway identified the rapid change in women's status after World War I and the general blurring of sex roles that accompanied the new sexual freedom as aspects of modernity that men were simultaneously attracted to and found hard to deal with. More recently, especially in light of the themes of some of his posthumously published writings, critics have begun to reinterpret Hemingway's work as preoccupied with the cultural and psychological meanings of masculinity in a way that bespeaks considerable sexual ambivalence.

As Hemingway aged, his interest in exclusively masculine forms of self-assertion and self-definition became more pronounced. War, hunting, and similar pursuits that he had used at first to show men manifesting dignity in the face of certain defeat increasingly became depicted (in his life as well as his writing) as occasions for competitive masculine display and triumph. Soon after the publication of *The Sun Also Rises*, his first marriage broke up; in all he was married four times. In the 1930s and 1940s he adopted the style of life of a celebrity. Some of his best-known work from these years, such as "The Snows of Kilimanjaro" (1936), treats the theme of the successful writer losing his talent in an atmosphere of success, adulation, and wealth.

A political loner distrustful of all ideological abstractions, Hemingway was nevertheless drawn into antifascist politics by the Spanish Civil War. In *To Have and Have Not* (1937), the earliest of his political novels, the good characters are working-class people and the antagonists are idle rich. *For Whom the Bell Tolls* draws on Hemingway's experiences in Spain as a war correspondent, celebrating both the peasant antifascists and the Americans who fought on their behalf. Hemingway's opposition to fascism did not, however, keep him from viewing the pro-Loyalist communists, who were also active in the Spanish Civil War, with considerable skepticism. His one play, *The Fifth Column*—which was printed along with his collected stories in 1938 and staged in 1940—specifically blames the communists for betraying the cause.

Hemingway was fiercely anti-Nazi during World War II. As well as working as a war correspondent, work that sent him often to Europe, he used his fishing boat to keep watch for German submarines off the coast of Cuba, where he had a home. After the war ended, he continued his travels and was badly hurt in Africa in January 1954 in the crash of a small plane. He had already published his allegorical fable *The Old Man and the Sea* (1952), in the mass-circulation weekly magazine *Life;* this, his last major work published during his lifetime, won a Pulitzer Prize in 1953 and was central to his winning the Nobel Prize in 1954. The plane crash had damaged his mental and physical health, and he never fully recovered. Subject increasingly to depression and an incapacitating paranoia—afflictions that seem to have run in his family— he was hospitalized several times before killing himself in 1961. Yet it does appear that some of his suspicions about being watched by U.S. government agents may have been justified. Many writers associated with radical causes had dossiers compiled on them by the FBI. Several books have been published posthumously based on the voluminous manuscript collections he left. These include a book of reminiscences about his life in 1920s Paris, *A Moveable Feast* (1964); a novel about literary fame and sexual ambiguity constructed from several unfinished drafts, *The Garden of Eden* (1986); and *The Nick Adams Stories* (1972), a collection that added eight previously unpublished stories to the group.

Hills Like White Elephants[1]

The hills across the valley of the Ebro[2] were long and white. On this side there was no shade and no trees and the station was between two lines of rails in the sun. Close against the side of the station there was the warm shadow of the building and a curtain, made of strings of bamboo beads, hung across the open door into the bar, to keep out flies. The American and the girl with him sat at a table in the shade, outside the building. It was very hot and the express from Barcelona would come in forty minutes. It stopped at this junction for two minutes and went on to Madrid.

"What should we drink?" the girl asked. She had taken off her hat and put it on the table.

"It's pretty hot," the man said.

"Let's drink beer."

"Dos cervezas,"[3] the man said into the curtain.

"Big ones?" a woman asked from the doorway.

1. The text is from *Men without Women* (1927), published by Charles Scribner's Sons.
2. Spain's largest river.
3. Two beers (Spanish).

"Yes. Two big ones."

The woman brought two glasses of beer and two felt pads. She put the felt pads and the beer glasses on the table and looked at the man and the girl. The girl was looking off at the line of hills. They were white in the sun and the country was brown and dry.

"They look like white elephants," she said.

"I've never seen one," the man drank his beer.

"No, you wouldn't have."

"I might have," the man said. "Just because you say I wouldn't have doesn't prove anything."

The girl looked at the bead curtain. "They've painted something on it," she said. "What does it say?"

"Anis del Toro.[4] It's a drink."

"Could we try it?"

The man called "Listen" through the curtain. The woman came out from the bar.

"Four reales."[5]

"We want two Anis del Toro."

"With water?"

"Do you want it with water?"

"I don't know," the girl said. "Is it good with water?"

"It's all right."

"You want them with water?" asked the woman.

"Yes, with water."

"It tastes like licorice," the girl said and put the glass down.

"That's the way with everything."

"Yes," said the girl. "Everything tastes of licorice. Especially all the things you've waited so long for, like absinthe."[6]

"Oh, cut it out."

"You started it," the girl said. "I was being amused. I was having a fine time."

"Well, let's try and have a fine time."

"All right. I was trying. I said the mountains looked like white elephants. Wasn't that bright?"

"That was bright."

"I wanted to try this new drink. That's all we do, isn't it—look at things and try new drinks?"

"I guess so."

The girl looked across at the hills.

"They're lovely hills," she said. "They don't really look like white elephants. I just meant the coloring of their skin through the trees."

"Should we have another drink?"

"All right."

The warm wind blew the bead curtain against the table.

"The beer's nice and cool," the man said.

"It's lovely," the girl said.

---

4. Bull's anisette (Spanish, literal trans.); a brand of anise-flavored liqueur.
5. Small Spanish coins. In 1925, 4 reales were worth about 15 cents in U.S. money.

6. Anise- and herb-flavored, highly alcoholic spirit, associated with Parisian life and banned in the United States in 1912.

"It's really an awfully simple operation, Jig," the man said. "It's not really an operation at all."

The girl looked at the ground the table legs rested on.

"I know you wouldn't mind it, Jig. It's really not anything. It's just to let the air in."

The girl did not say anything.

"I'll go with you and I'll stay with you all the time. They just let the air in and then it's all perfectly natural."

"Then what will we do afterward?"

"We'll be fine afterward. Just like we were before."

"What makes you think so?"

"That's the only thing that bothers us. It's the only thing that's made us unhappy."

The girl looked at the bead curtain, put her hand out and took hold of two of the strings of beads.

"And you think then we'll be all right and be happy."

"I know we will. You don't have to be afraid. I've known lots of people that have done it."

"So have I," said the girl. "And afterward they were all so happy."

"Well," the man said, "if you don't want to you don't have to. I wouldn't have you do it if you didn't want to. But I know it's perfectly simple."

"And you really want to?"

"I think it's the best thing to do. But I don't want you to do it if you don't really want to."

"And if I do it you'll be happy and things will be like they were and you'll love me?"

"I love you now. You know I love you."

"I know. But if I do it, then it will be nice again if I say things are like white elephants, and you'll like it?"

"I'll love it. I love it now but I just can't think about it. You know how I get when I worry."

"If I do it you won't ever worry?"

"I won't worry about that because it's perfectly simple."

"Then I'll do it. Because I don't care about me."

"What do you mean?"

"I don't care about me."

"Well, I care about you."

"Oh, yes. But I don't care about me. And I'll do it and then everything will be fine."

"I don't want you to do it if you feel that way."

The girl stood up and walked to the end of the station. Across, on the other side, were fields of grain and trees along the banks of the Ebro. Far away, beyond the river, were mountains. The shadow of a cloud moved across the field of grain and she saw the river through the trees.

"And we could have all this," she said. "And we could have everything and every day we make it more impossible."

"What did you say?"

"I said we could have everything."

"We can have everything."

"No, we can't."

"We can have the whole world."

"No, we can't."

"We can go everywhere."

"No, we can't. It isn't ours any more."

"It's ours."

"No, it isn't. And once they take it away, you never get it back."

"But they haven't taken it away."

"We'll wait and see."

"Come on back in the shade," he said. "You mustn't feel that way."

"I don't feel any way," the girl said. "I just know things."

"I don't want you to do anything that you don't want to do——"

"Nor that isn't good for me," she said. "I know. Could we have another beer?"

"All right. But you've got to realize——"

"I realize," the girl said. "Can't we maybe stop talking?"

They sat down at the table and the girl looked across at the hills on the dry side of the valley and the man looked at her and at the table.

"You've got to realize," he said, "that I don't want you to do it if you don't want to. I'm perfectly willing to go through with it if it means anything to you."

"Doesn't it mean anything to you? We could get along."

"Of course it does. But I don't want anybody but you. I don't want any one else. And I know it's perfectly simple."

"Yes, you know it's perfectly simple."

"It's all right for you to say that, but I do know it."

"Would you do something for me now?"

"I'd do anything for you."

"Would you please please please please please please please stop talking?"

He did not say anything but looked at the bags against the wall of the station. There were labels on them from all the hotels where they had spent nights.

"But I don't want you to," he said, "I don't care anything about it."

"I'll scream," the girl said.

The woman came out through the curtains with two glasses of beer and put them down on the damp felt pads. "The train comes in five minutes," she said.

"What did she say?" asked the girl.

"That the train is coming in five minutes."

The girl smiled brightly at the woman, to thank her.

"I'd better take the bags over to the other side of the station," the man said. She smiled at him.

"All right. Then come back and we'll finish the beer."

He picked up the two heavy bags and carried them around the station to the other tracks. He looked up the tracks but could not see the train. Coming back, he walked through the barroom, where people waiting for the train were drinking. He drank an Anis at the bar and looked at the people. They were all waiting reasonably for the train. He went out through the bead curtain. She was sitting at the table and smiled at him.

"Do you feel better?" he asked.

"I feel fine," she said. "There's nothing wrong with me. I feel fine."

1927

LANGSTON HUGHES
1902–1967

angston Hughes was the most popular and versatile of the many writers connected with the Harlem Renaissance. Along with Zora Neale Hurston, and in contrast to Jean Toomer and Countee Cullen (who wanted to work with the patterns of written literary forms, whether traditional or experimental), he wanted to capture the oral and improvisatory traditions of black culture in written form.

Hughes was born in Joplin, Missouri; as a child, since his parents were separated, he lived mainly with his maternal grandmother in Lawrence, Kansas. He did, however, live intermittently both with his mother in Detroit and Cleveland, where he finished high school and began to write poetry, and with his father, who, disgusted with American racism, had gone to Mexico. Like other poets in this era—T. S. Eliot, Hart Crane, Edgar Lee Masters, and Robert Frost—Hughes had a mother sympathetic to his poetic ambitions and a businesslike father with whom he was in deep, scarring conflict.

Hughes entered Columbia University in 1920 but left after a year. Traveling and drifting, he shipped out as a merchant seaman and worked at a nightclub in Paris (France) and as a busboy in Washington, D.C. All this time he was writing and publishing poetry, chiefly in the two important African American periodicals *Opportunity* and the *Crisis*. Eleven of Hughes's poems were published in Alain Locke's pioneering anthology, *The New Negro* (1925), and he was also well represented in Countee Cullen's 1927 anthology, *Caroling Dusk*. Carl Van Vechten, one of the white patrons of African American writing, helped get *The Weary Blues,* Hughes's first volume of poems, published in 1926. It was in this year, too, that his important essay "The Negro Artist and the Racial Mountain" appeared in the *Nation* (see p. 816); in that essay Hughes described the immense challenges to be faced by the serious black artist "who would produce a racial art" but insisted on the need for courageous artists to make the attempt. Other patrons appeared: Amy Spingarn financed his college education at Lincoln University (Pennsylvania), and Charlotte Mason subsidized him in New York City between 1928 and 1930. The publication of his novel *Not without Laughter* in 1930 solidified his reputation and sales, enabling him to support himself. By the 1930s he was being called "the bard of Harlem."

The Great Depression brought an abrupt end to much African American literary activity, but Hughes was already a public figure. In the activist 1930s he was much absorbed in radical politics. Hughes and other blacks were drawn by the American Communist Party, which made racial justice an important plank in its platform, promoting an image of working-class solidarity that nullified racial boundaries. He visited the Soviet Union in 1932 and produced a significant amount of radical writing up to the eve of World War II. He covered the Spanish civil war for the *Baltimore Afro-American* in 1937. By the end of the decade he had also been involved in drama and screenplay writing and had begun an autobiography, all the while publishing poetry. In 1943 he invented the folksy, streetwise character Jesse B. Semple, whose commonsense prose monologues on race were eventually collected in four volumes, and Alberta K. Johnson, Semple's female equivalent, in his series of "Madam" poems.

In the 1950s and 1960s Hughes published a variety of anthologies for children and adults, including *First Book of Negroes* (1952), *The First Book of Jazz* (1955), and *The Book of Negro Folklore* (1958). In 1953 he was called to testify before Senator Joseph McCarthy's committee on subversive activities in connection with his 1930s radicalism. The FBI listed him as a security risk until 1959; and during these years, when he could not travel outside the United States because he would not have been allowed to reenter the country, Hughes worked to rehabilitate his reputation as a good American by producing patriotic poetry. From 1960 to the end of his life he was again on the international circuit.

Within the spectrum of artistic possibilities open to writers of the Harlem Renaissance—drawing on African American rural folk forms; on literary traditions and forms that entered the United States from Europe and Great Britain; or on the new cultural forms of blacks in American cities—Hughes chose to focus his work on modern, urban black life. He modeled his stanza forms on the improvisatory rhythms of jazz music and adapted the vocabulary of everyday black speech to poetry. He also acknowledged finding inspiration for his writing in the work of white American poets who preceded him. Like Walt Whitman he heard America singing, and he asserted his right to sing America back; he also learned from Carl Sandburg's earlier attempts to work jazz into poetry. Hughes did not confuse his pride in African American culture with complacency toward the material deprivations of black life in the United States. He was keenly aware that the modernist "vogue in things Negro" among white Americans was potentially exploitative and voyeuristic; he confronted such racial tourists with the misery as well as the jazz of Chicago's South Side. Early and late, Hughes's poems demanded that African Americans be acknowledged as owners of the culture they gave to the United States and as fully enfranchised American citizens.

The source of the poems printed here is *Collected Poems* (1994).

The Negro Speaks of Rivers

I've known rivers:
I've known rivers ancient as the world and older than the
       flow of human blood in human veins.

My soul has grown deep like the rivers.

I bathed in the Euphrates when dawns were young.
I built my hut near the Congo and it lulled me to sleep.   5
I looked upon the Nile and raised the pyramids above it.
I heard the singing of the Mississippi when Abe Lincoln
       went down to New Orleans, and I've seen its
       muddy bosom turn all golden in the sunset

I've known rivers:
Ancient, dusky rivers.

My soul has grown deep like the rivers.   10

1921, 1926

Mother to Son

Well, son, I'll tell you:
Life for me ain't been no crystal stair.

It's had tacks in it,
And splinters,
And boards torn up,   5
And places with no carpet on the floor—
Bare.
But all the time
I'se been a-climbin' on,
And reachin' landin's,   10
And turnin' corners,
And sometimes goin' in the dark
Where there ain't been no light.
So boy, don't you turn back.
Don't you set down on the steps   15
'Cause you finds it's kinder hard.
Don't you fall now—
For I'se still goin', honey,
I'se still climbin',
And life for me ain't been no crystal stair.   20

                                              1922, 1926

I, Too

I, too, sing America.

I am the darker brother.
They send me to eat in the kitchen
When company comes,
But I laugh,   5
And eat well,
And grow strong.

Tomorrow,
I'll be at the table
When company comes.   10
Nobody'll dare
Say to me,
"Eat in the kitchen,"
Then.

Besides,   15
They'll see how beautiful I am
And be ashamed—

I, too, am America.

                                              1925, 1959

The Weary Blues

Droning a drowsy syncopated tune,
Rocking back and forth to a mellow croon,
   I heard a Negro play.
Down on Lenox Avenue the other night
By the pale dull pallor of an old gas light   5
   He did a lazy sway. . . .
   He did a lazy sway. . . .
To the tune o' those Weary Blues.
With his ebony hands on each ivory key.
He made that poor piano moan with melody.   10
   O Blues!
Swaying to and fro on his rickety stool
He played that sad raggy tune like a musical fool.
   Sweet Blues!
Coming from a black man's soul.   15
   O Blues!
In a deep song voice with a melancholy tone
I heard that Negro sing, that old piano moan—
   "Ain't got nobody in all this world,
   Ain't got nobody but ma self.   20
   I's gwine to quit ma frownin'
   And put ma troubles on de shelf."
Thump, thump, thump, went his foot on the floor.
He played a few chords then he sang some more—
   "I got de Weary Blues   25
   And I can't be satisfied.
   Got de Weary Blues
   And can't be satisfied—
   I ain't happy no mo'
   And I wish that I had died."   30
And far into the night he crooned that tune.
The stars went out and so did the moon.
The singer stopped playing and went to bed
While the Weary Blues echoed through his head.
He slept like a rock or a man that's dead.   35

                         1925

Mulatto

I am your son, white man!

Georgia dusk
And the turpentine woods.
One of the pillars of the temple fell.

    You are my son!   5
    Like hell!

The moon over the turpentine woods.
The Southern night
Full of stars,
Great big yellow stars.   10
   What's a body but a toy?
    Juicy bodies
    Of nigger wenches
    Blue black
    Against black fences.   15
    O, you little bastard boy,
    What's a body but a toy?
The scent of pine wood stings the soft night air.
    What's the body of your mother?
Silver moonlight everywhere.   20

    What's the body of your mother?
Sharp pine scent in the evening air.
     A nigger night,
     A nigger joy,
     A little yellow   25
     Bastard boy.

    Naw, you ain't my brother.
    Niggers ain't my brother.
    Not ever.
    Niggers ain't my brother.   30
The Southern night is full of stars,
Great big yellow stars.
     O, sweet as earth,
     Dusk dark bodies
     Give sweet birth   35
To little yellow bastard boys.

    Git on back there in the night,
    You ain't white.

The bright stars scatter everywhere.
Pine wood scent in the evening air.   40
     A nigger night,
     A nigger joy.

   I am your son, white man!

     A little yellow
     Bastard boy.   45

1927

Song for a Dark Girl

Way Down South in Dixie[1]
    (Break the heart of me)
They hung my black young lover
    To a cross roads tree.

Way Down South in Dixie
    (Bruised body high in air)
I asked the white Lord Jesus
    What was the use of prayer.

Way Down South in Dixie
    (Break the heart of me)
Love is a naked shadow
    On a gnarled and naked tree.

                1927

Visitors to the Black Belt

You can talk about
Across the railroad tracks—
To me it's *here*
On this side of the tracks.

You can talk about
Up in Harlem—
To me it's *here*
In Harlem.

You can say
Jazz on the South Side[1]—
To me it's hell
On the South Side:

    Kitchenettes
    With no heat
    And garbage
    In the halls.

Who're you, outsider?

Ask me who am I.

                1940, 1943

---

1. Last line of "Dixie," the popular minstrel song, probably composed by Daniel D. Emmett (1815–1904).

1. African American neighborhood in Chicago. See also Archibald J. Motley's 1934 painting, *Black Belt*, in the color insert to this volume.

Note on Commercial Theatre

You've taken my blues and gone—
You sing 'em on Broadway
And you sing 'em in Hollywood Bowl,[1]
And you mixed 'em up with symphonies
And you fixed 'em   5
So they don't sound like me.
Yep, you done taken my blues and gone.

You also took my spirituals and gone.
You put me in *Macbeth* and *Carmen Jones*[2]
And all kinds of *Swing Mikados*[3]   10
And in everything but what's about me—
But someday somebody'll
Stand up and talk about me,
And write about me—

Black and beautiful—   15
And sing about me,
And put on plays about me!

I reckon it'll be
Me myself!

Yes, it'll be me.   20

1940, 1959

Democracy

Democracy will not come
Today, this year
      Nor ever
Through compromise and fear.

I have as much right   5
As the other fellow has
      To stand
On my two feet
And own the land.

---

1. Outdoor concert amphitheater constructed in the 1920s.
2. An all-black musical (1943), loosely based on the opera *Carmen* by French composer George Bizet (1838–1875), focused on African American life during World War II. An all-black production of Shakespeare's *Macbeth* (1606), set in Haiti, was a Broadway success in 1936.
3. During 1939, two different all-black versions of *The Mikado* (1885), a comic opera by the British team of W. S. Gilbert (1836–1911) and Arthur Sullivan (1842–1900), competed on Broadway: *The Swing Mikado* (which premiered in Chicago in 1938) and *The Hot Mikado*.

I tire so of hearing people say,   10
Let things take their course.
Tomorrow is another day.
I do not need my freedom when I'm dead.
I cannot live on tomorrow's bread.

Freedom   15
Is a strong seed
Planted
In a great need.
I live here, too.
I want freedom   20
Just as you.

1949

Theme for English B

The instructor said,

Go home and write
a page tonight.
And let that page come out of you—
Then, it will be true.   5

I wonder if it's that simple?
I am twenty-two, colored, born in Winston-Salem.
I went to school there, then Durham, then here
to this college on the hill above Harlem.[1]
I am the only colored student in my class.   10
The steps from the hill lead down into Harlem,
through a park, then I cross St. Nicholas,
Eighth Avenue, Seventh, and I come to the Y,
the Harlem Branch Y, where I take the elevator
up to my room, sit down, and write this page: 15

It's not easy to know what is true for you or me
at twenty-two, my age. But I guess I'm what
I feel and see and hear, Harlem, I hear you:
hear you, hear me—we two—you, me, talk on this page.
(I hear New York, too.) Me—who?   20
Well, I like to eat, sleep, drink, and be in love.
I like to work, read, learn, and understand life.
I like a pipe for a Christmas present,
or records—Bessie, bop, or Bach.[2]
I guess being colored doesn't make me *not* like   25

1. The City College of the City University of New York. Winston-Salem and Durham are cities in North Carolina.
2. Johann Sebastian Bach (1685–1750), German composer of the Baroque era. Bessie Smith (1894–1937), noted blues singer. "Bop": jazz form developed in Harlem during World War II.

the same things other folks like who are other races.
So will my page be colored that I write?
Being me, it will not be white.
But it will be
a part of you, instructor.   30
You are white—
yet a part of me, as I am a part of you.
That's American.
Sometimes perhaps you don't want to be a part of me.
Nor do I often want to be a part of you.   35
But we are, that's true!
As I learn from you,
I guess you learn from me—
although you're older—and white—
and somewhat more free.   40

This is my page for English B.

1949

JOHN STEINBECK
1902–1968

M ost of John Steinbeck's best writing is set in the region of California that he
called home, the Salinas Valley and Monterey peninsula of California, where
visitors today will find official remembrances of him everywhere. Steinbeck believed
in the American promise of opportunity for all, but believed also that social injustices and economic inequalities had put opportunity beyond reach for many. His
work merged literary modernism with literary realism, celebrated traditional rural
communities along with social outcasts and immigrant cultures, and endorsed conservative values and radical politics at the same time.

Steinbeck's father managed a flour mill and later became treasurer of Monterey
County; his mother, who had taught school before marriage, was active in local civic
affairs. Their home was full of books, and Steinbeck read avidly from an early age.
After graduating from Salinas High School in 1919, he began to study at Stanford
University but took time off for a variety of short-term jobs at local mills, farms, and
estates. During this period he developed an abiding respect for people who worked
on farms and in factories, and committed his literary abilities to their cause. He left
college for good in 1925, having completed less than three years of coursework, and
continued his roving life.

With financial help from his father, Steinbeck spent most of 1929 writing. He
moved to the seaside town of Pacific Grove, on the Monterey coast, and in 1930 was
married (the first of three times). In 1935 he achieved commercial success with his
third novel, *Tortilla Flat,* a celebration of the Mexican-American culture of the "*pai-
sanos*" who lived in the Monterey hills. Steinbeck's next novel, *In Dubious Battle*
(1936), contrasted the decency of striking migratory farm workers both to the cynicism of landowners and their vigilantes, and to the equal cynicism of Communist

labor union organizers who exploit the workers' plight for their own purposes. Sympathy for the underdog appears again in *Of Mice and Men* (1937), a best-selling short novel about two itinerant ranch hands, and yet again in *The Grapes of Wrath* (1939), his most famous and most ambitious novel. *The Long Valley* (1938) brought together a number of his stories set in the Salinas Valley, including "The Chrysanthemums."

Inspired by the devastating 1930s drought in the southern plains states and the exodus of thousands of farmers from their homes in the so-called Dust Bowl, *The Grapes of Wrath* told the story of the Joad family, who, after losing their land in Oklahoma, migrated westward to California on U.S. Highway 66 looking for, but not finding, a better life. Because of its supposed radicalism, the novel was banned or burned in several states, but even so, it became the nation's number one best seller and won a Pulitzer Prize in 1940. *Cannery Row* (1945), a local-color novel about workers in the sardine canneries of Monterey, also became a best seller.

During and after World War II, the film industry began paying serious attention to Steinbeck's writing. *Of Mice and Men* was adapted as a film in 1939, and *The Grapes of Wrath* followed in 1940. The family saga *East of Eden* (1952), Steinbeck's longest novel, was filmed in 1955 with the electric young actor James Dean (1931–1955) in a starring role. The qualities that made Steinbeck's fiction so adaptable to the screen were also those for which he won the Nobel Prize in 1962; the prize committee praised his work for "combining sympathetic humour and keen social perception."

The text of "The Chrysanthemums" is that of its first printing, in *Harper's* (1937).

The Chrysanthemums

The high grey-flannel fog of winter closed off the Salinas Valley from the sky and from all the rest of the world. On every side it sat like a lid on the mountains and made of the great valley a closed pot. On the broad, level land floor the gang plows[1] bit deep and left the black earth shining like metal where the shares had cut. On the foothill ranches across the Salinas River, the yellow stubble fields seemed to be bathed in pale cold sunshine, but there was no sunshine in the valley now in December. The thick willow scrub along the river flamed with sharp and positive yellow leaves.

It was a time of quiet and of waiting. The air was cold and tender. A light wind blew up from the southwest so that the farmers were mildly hopeful of a good rain before long; but fog and rain do not go together.

Across the river, on Henry Allen's foothill ranch there was little work to be done, for the hay was cut and stored and the orchards were plowed up to receive the rain deeply when it should come. The cattle on the higher slopes were becoming shaggy and rough-coated.

Elisa Allen, working in her flower garden, looked down across the yard and saw Henry, her husband, talking to two men in business suits. The three of them stood by the tractor shed, each man with one foot on the side of the little Fordson.[2] They smoked cigarettes and studied the machine as they talked.

Elisa watched them for a moment and then went back to her work. She was thirty-five. Her face was lean and strong and her eyes were as clear as

1. Plows with multiple plowshares, or plowing blades.
2. Brand of tractor made by the Ford Motor Company.

water. Her figure looked blocked and heavy in her gardening costume, a man's black hat pulled low down over her eyes, clodhopper shoes, a figured print dress almost completely covered by a big corduroy apron with four big pockets to hold the snips, the trowel and scratcher, the seeds and the knife she worked with. She wore heavy leather gloves to protect her hands while she worked.

She was cutting down the old year's chrysanthemum stalks with a pair of short and powerful scissors. She looked down toward the men by the tractor shed now and then. Her face was eager and mature and handsome; even her work with the scissors was over-eager, over-powerful. The chrysanthemum stems seemed too small and easy for her energy.

She brushed a cloud of hair out of her eyes with the back of her glove, and left a smudge of earth on her cheek in doing it. Behind her stood the neat white farm house with red geraniums close-banked around it as high as the windows. It was a hard-swept looking little house with hard-polished windows, and a clean mud-mat on the front steps.

Elisa cast another glance toward the tractor shed. The strangers were getting into their Ford coupe.[3] She took off a glove and put her strong fingers down into the forest of new green chrysanthemum sprouts that were growing around the old roots. She spread the leaves and looked down among the close-growing stems. No aphids were there, no sowbugs or snails or cutworms. Her terrier fingers destroyed such pests before they could get started.

Elisa started at the sound of her husband's voice. He had come near quietly, and he leaned over the wire fence that protected her flower garden from cattle and dogs and chickens.

"At it again," he said. "You've got a strong new crop coming."

Elisa straightened her back and pulled on the gardening glove again. "Yes. They'll be strong this coming year." In her tone and on her face there was a little smugness.

"You've got a gift with things," Henry observed. "Some of those yellow chrysanthemums you had this year were ten inches across. I wish you'd work out in the orchard and raise some apples that big."

Her eyes sharpened. "Maybe I could do it, too. I've a gift with things, all right. My mother had it. She could stick anything in the ground and make it grow. She said it was having planters' hands that knew how to do it."

"Well, it sure works with flowers," he said.

"Henry, who were those men you were talking to?"

"Why, sure, that's what I came to tell you. They were from the Western Meat Company. I sold those thirty head of three-year-old steers. Got nearly my own price, too."

"Good," she said. "Good for you."

"And I thought," he continued, "I thought how it's Saturday afternoon, and we might go into Salinas for dinner at a restaurant, and then to a picture show—to celebrate, you see."

"Good," she repeated. "Oh, yes. That will be good."

Henry put on his joking tone. "There's fights tonight. How'd you like to go to the fights?"

---

3. Closed-roof, two-door automobile.

"Oh, no," she said breathlessly. "No, I wouldn't like fights."

"Just fooling, Elisa. We'll go to a movie. Let's see. It's two now. I'm going to take Scotty and bring down those steers from the hill. It'll take us maybe two hours. We'll go in town about five and have dinner at the Cominos Hotel. Like that?"

"Of course I'll like it. It's good to eat away from home."

"All right, then. I'll go get up a couple of horses."

She said, "I'll have plenty of time to transplant some of these sets, I guess."

She heard her husband calling Scotty down by the barn. And a little later she saw the two men ride up the pale yellow hillside in search of the steers.

There was a little square sandy bed kept for rooting the chrysanthemums. With her trowel she turned the soil over and over, and smoothed it and patted it firm. Then she dug ten parallel trenches to receive the sets. Back at the chrysanthemum bed she pulled out the little crisp shoots, trimmed off the leaves of each one with her scissors and laid it on a small orderly pile.

A squeak of wheels and plod of hoofs came from the road. Elisa looked up. The country road ran along the dense bank of willows and cottonwoods that bordered the river, and up this road came a curious vehicle, curiously drawn. It was an old spring-wagon, with a round canvas top on it like the cover of a prairie schooner. It was drawn by an old bay horse and a little grey-and-white burro. A big stubble-bearded man sat between the cover flaps and drove the crawling team. Underneath the wagon, between the hind wheels, a lean and rangy mongrel dog walked sedately. Words were painted on the canvas, in clumsy, crooked letters. "Pots, pans, knives, sisors, lawn mores, Fixed." Two rows of articles, and the triumphantly definitive "Fixed" below. The black paint had run down in little sharp points beneath each letter.

Elisa, squatting on the ground, watched to see the crazy, loose-jointed wagon pass by. But it didn't pass. It turned into the farm road in front of her house, crooked old wheels skirling and squeaking. The rangy dog darted from between the wheels and ran ahead. Instantly the two ranch shepherds flew out at him. Then all three stopped, and with stiff and quivering tails, with taut straight legs, with ambassadorial dignity, they slowly circled, sniffing daintily. The caravan pulled up to Elisa's wire fence and stopped. Now the newcomer dog, feeling out-numbered, lowered his tail and retired under the wagon with raised hackles and bared teeth.

The man on the wagon seat called out, "That's a bad dog in a fight when he gets started."

Elisa laughed. "I see he is. How soon does he generally get started?"

The man caught up her laughter and echoed it heartily. "Sometimes not for weeks and weeks," he said. He climbed stiffly down, over the wheel. The horse and the donkey drooped like unwatered flowers.

Elisa saw that he was a very big man. Although his hair and beard were greying, he did not look old. His worn black suit was wrinkled and spotted with grease. The laughter had disappeared from his face and eyes the moment his laughing voice ceased. His eyes were dark, and they were full of the brooding that gets in the eyes of teamsters and of sailors. The calloused hands he rested on the wire fence were cracked, and every crack was a black line. He took off his battered hat.

"I'm off my general road, ma'am," he said. "Does this dirt road cut over across the river to the Los Angeles highway?"

Elisa stood up and shoved the thick scissors in her apron pocket. "Well, yes, it does, but it winds around and then fords the river. I don't think your team could pull through the sand."

He replied with some asperity, "It might surprise you what them beasts can pull through."

"When they get started?" she asked.

He smiled for a second. "Yes. When they get started."

"Well," said Elisa, "I think you'll save time if you go back to the Salinas road and pick up the highway there."

He drew a big finger down the chicken wire and made it sing. "I ain't in any hurry, ma'am. I go from Seattle to San Diego and back every year. Takes all my time. About six months each way. I aim to follow nice weather."

Elisa took off her gloves and stuffed them in the apron pocket with the scissors. She touched the under edge of her man's hat, searching for fugitive hairs. "That sounds like a nice kind of a way to live," she said.

He leaned confidentially over the fence. "Maybe you noticed the writing on my wagon. I mend pots and sharpen knives and scissors. You got any of them things to do?"

"Oh, no," she said quickly. "Nothing like that." Her eyes hardened with resistance.

"Scissors is the worst thing," he explained. "Most people just ruin scissors trying to sharpen 'em, but I know how. I got a special tool. It's a little bobbit kind of thing, and patented. But it sure does the trick."

"No. My scissors are all sharp."

"All right, then. Take a pot," he continued earnestly, "a bent pot, or a pot with a hole. I can make it like new so you don't have to buy no new ones. That's a saving for you."

"No," she said shortly. "I tell you I have nothing like that for you to do."

His face fell to an exaggerated sadness. His voice took on a whining undertone. "I ain't had a thing to do today. Maybe I won't have no supper tonight. You see I'm off my regular road. I know folks on the highway clear from Seattle to San Diego. They save their things for me to sharpen up because they know I do it so good and save them money."

"I'm sorry," Elisa said irritably. "I haven't anything for you to do."

His eyes left her face and fell to searching the ground. They roamed about until they came to the chrysanthemum bed where she had been working. "What's them plants, ma'am?"

The irritation and resistance melted from Elisa's face. "Oh, those are chrysanthemums, giant whites and yellows. I raise them every year, bigger than anybody around here."

"Kind of a long-stemmed flower? Looks like a quick puff of colored smoke?" he asked.

"That's it. What a nice way to describe them."

"They smell kind of nasty till you get used to them," he said.

"It's a good bitter smell," she retorted, "not nasty at all."

He changed his tone quickly. "I like the smell myself."

"I had ten-inch blooms this year," she said.

The man leaned farther over the fence. "Look. I know a lady down the road a piece, has got the nicest garden you ever seen. Got nearly every kind of flower but no chrysantheums. Last time I was mending a copper-bottom washtub for her (that's a hard job but I do it good), she said to me, 'If you ever run acrost some nice chrysantheums I wish you'd try to get me a few seeds.' That's what she told me."

Elisa's eyes grew alert and eager. "She couldn't have known much about chrysanthemums. You *can* raise them from seed, but it's much easier to root the little sprouts you see there."

"Oh," he said. "I s'pose I can't take none to her, then."

"Why yes you can," Elisa cried. "I can put some in damp sand, and you can carry them right along with you. They'll take root in the pot if you keep them damp. And then she can transplant them."

"She'd sure like to have some, ma'am. You say they're nice ones?"

"Beautiful," she said. "Oh, beautiful." Her eyes shone. She tore off the battered hat and shook out her dark pretty hair. "I'll put them in a flower pot, and you can take them right with you. Come into the yard."

While the man came through the picket gate Elisa ran excitedly along the geranium-bordered path to the back of the house. And she returned carrying a big red flower pot. The gloves were forgotten now. She kneeled on the ground by the starting bed and dug up the sandy soil with her fingers and scooped it into the bright new flower pot. Then she picked up the little pile of shoots she had prepared. With her strong fingers she pressed them into the sand and tamped around them with her knuckles. The man stood over her. "I'll tell you what to do," she said. "You remember so you can tell the lady."

"Yes, I'll try to remember."

"Well, look. These will take root in about a month. Then she must set them out, about a foot apart in good rich earth like this, see?" She lifted a handful of dark soil for him to look at. "They'll grow fast and tall. Now remember this: In July tell her to cut them down, about eight inches from the ground."

"Before they bloom?" he asked.

"Yes, before they bloom." Her face was tight with eagerness. "They'll grow right up again. About the last of September the buds will start."

She stopped and seemed perplexed. "It's the budding that takes the most care," she said hesitantly. "I don't know how to tell you." She looked deep into his eyes, searchingly. Her mouth opened a little, and she seemed to be listening. "I'll try to tell you," she said. "Did you ever hear of planting hands?"

"Can't say I have, ma'am."

"Well, I can only tell you what it feels like. It's when you're picking off the buds you don't want. Everything goes right down into your fingertips. You watch your fingers work. They do it themselves. You can feel how it is. They pick and pick the buds. They never make a mistake. They're with the plant. Do you see? Your fingers and the plant. You can feel that, right up your arm. They know. They never make a mistake. You can feel it. When you're like that you can't do anything wrong. Do you see that? Can you understand that?"

She was kneeling on the ground looking up at him. Her breast swelled passionately.

The man's eyes narrowed. He looked away self-consciously. "Maybe I know," he said. "Sometimes in the night in the wagon there—"

Elisa's voice grew husky. She broke in on him, "I've never lived as you do, but I know what you mean. When the night is dark—why, the stars are sharp-pointed, and there's quiet. Why, you rise up and up! Every pointed star gets driven into your body. It's like that. Hot and sharp and—lovely."

Kneeling there, her hand went out toward his legs in the greasy black trousers. Her hesitant fingers almost touched the cloth. Then her hand dropped to the ground. She crouched low like a fawning dog.

He said, "It's nice, just like you say. Only when you don't have no dinner, it ain't."

She stood up then, very straight, and her face was ashamed. She held the flower pot out to him and placed it gently in his arms. "Here. Put it in your wagon, on the seat, where you can watch it. Maybe I can find something for you to do."

At the back of the house she dug in the can pile and found two old and battered aluminum saucepans. She carried them back and gave them to him. "Here, maybe you can fix these."

His manner changed. He became professional. "Good as new I can fix them." At the back of his wagon he set a little anvil, and out of an oily tool box dug a small machine hammer. Elisa came through the gate to watch him while he pounded out the dents in the kettles. His mouth grew sure and knowing. At a difficult part of the work he sucked his under-lip.

"You sleep right in the wagon?" Elisa asked.

"Right in the wagon, ma'am. Rain or shine I'm dry as a cow in there."

"It must be nice," she said. "It must be very nice. I wish women could do such things."

"It ain't the right kind of a life for a woman."

Her upper lip raised a little, showing her teeth. "How do you know? How can you tell?" she said.

"I don't know, ma'am," he protested. "Of course I don't know. Now here's your kettles, done. You don't have to buy no new ones."

"How much?"

"Oh, fifty cents'll do. I keep my prices down and my work good. That's why I have all them satisfied customers up and down the highway."

Elisa brought him a fifty-cent piece from the house and dropped it in his hand. "You might be surprised to have a rival some time. I can sharpen scissors, too. And I can beat the dents out of little pots. I could show you what a woman might do."

He put his hammer back in the oily box and shoved the little anvil out of sight. "It would be a lonely life for a woman, ma'am, and a scary life, too, with animals creeping under the wagon all night." He climbed over the single-tree, steadying himself with a hand on the burro's white rump. He settled himself in the seat, picked up the lines. "Thank you kindly, ma'am," he said. "I'll do like you told me; I'll go back and catch the Salinas road."

"Mind," she called, "if you're long in getting there, keep the sand damp."

"Sand, ma'am? . . . Sand? Oh, sure. You mean around the chrysanthemums. Sure I will." He clucked his tongue. The beasts leaned luxuriously into their collars. The mongrel dog took his place between the back wheels. The wagon turned and crawled out the entrance road and back the way it had come, along the river.

Elisa stood in front of her wire fence watching the slow progress of the caravan. Her shoulders were straight, her head thrown back, her eyes half-closed, so that the scene came vaguely into them. Her lips moved silently, forming the words "Good-bye—good-bye." Then she whispered, "That's a bright direction. There's a glowing there." The sound of her whisper startled her. She shook herself free and looked about to see whether anyone had been listening. Only the dogs had heard. They lifted their heads toward her from their sleeping in the dust, and then stretched out their chins and settled asleep again. Elisa turned and ran hurriedly into the house.

In the kitchen she reached behind the stove and felt the water tank. It was full of hot water from the noonday cooking. In the bathroom she tore off her soiled clothes and flung them into the corner. And then she scrubbed herself with a little block of pumice, legs and thighs, loins and chest and arms, until her skin was scratched and red. When she had dried herself she stood in front of a mirror in her bedroom and looked at her body. She tightened her stomach and threw out her chest. She turned and looked over her shoulder at her back.

After a while she began to dress, slowly. She put on her newest underclothing and her nicest stockings and the dress which was the symbol of her prettiness. She worked carefully on her hair, penciled her eyebrows and rouged her lips.

Before she was finished she heard the little thunder of hoofs and the shouts of Henry and his helper as they drove the red steers into the corral. She heard the gate bang shut and set herself for Henry's arrival.

His step sounded on the porch. He entered the house calling, "Elisa, where are you?"

"In my room, dressing. I'm not ready. There's hot water for your bath. Hurry up. It's getting late."

When she heard him splashing in the tub, Elisa laid his dark suit on the bed, and shirt and socks and tie beside it. She stood his polished shoes on the floor beside the bed. Then she went to the porch and sat primly and stiffly down. She looked toward the river road where the willow-line was still yellow with frosted leaves so that under the high grey fog they seemed a thin band of sunshine. This was the only color in the grey afternoon. She sat unmoving for a long time. Her eyes blinked rarely.

Henry came banging out of the door, shoving his tie inside his vest as he came. Elisa stiffened and her face grew tight. Henry stopped short and looked at her. "Why—why, Elisa. You look so nice!"

"Nice? You think I look nice? What do you mean by 'nice'?"

Henry blundered on. "I don't know. I mean you look different, strong and happy."

"I am strong? Yes, strong. What do you mean 'strong'?"

He looked bewildered. "You're playing some kind of a game," he said helplessly. "It's a kind of a play. You look strong enough to break a calf over your knee, happy enough to eat it like a watermelon."

For a second she lost her rigidity. "Henry! Don't talk like that. You didn't know what you said." She grew complete again. "I'm strong," she boasted. "I never knew before how strong."

Henry looked down toward the tractor shed, and when he brought his eyes back to her, they were his own again. "I'll get out the car. You can put on your coat while I'm starting."

Elisa went into the house. She heard him drive to the gate and idle down his motor, and then she took a long time to put on her hat. She pulled it here and pressed it there. When Henry turned the motor off she slipped into her coat and went out.

The little roadster bounced along on the dirt road by the river, raising the birds and driving the rabbits into the brush. Two cranes flapped heavily over the willow-line and dropped into the river-bed.

Far ahead on the road Elisa saw a dark speck. She knew.

She tried not to look as they passed it, but her eyes would not obey. She whispered to herself sadly, "He might have thrown them off the road. That wouldn't have been much trouble, not very much. But he kept the pot," she explained. "He had to keep the pot. That's why he couldn't get them off the road."

The roadster turned a bend and she saw the caravan ahead. She swung full around toward her husband so she could not see the little covered wagon and the mismatched team as the car passed them.

In a moment it was over. The thing was done. She did not look back.

She said loudly, to be heard above the motor, "It will be good, tonight, a good dinner."

"Now you've changed again," Henry complained. He took one hand from the wheel and patted her knee. "I ought to take you in to dinner oftener. It would be good for both of us. We get so heavy out on the ranch."

"Henry," she asked, "could we have wine at dinner?"

"Sure we could. Say! That will be fine."

She was silent for a while; then she said, "Henry, at those prize fights, do the men hurt each other very much?"

"Sometimes a little, not often. Why?"

"Well, I've read how they break noses, and blood runs down their chests. I've read how the fighting gloves get heavy and soggy with blood."

He looked around at her. "What's the matter, Elisa? I didn't know you read things like that." He brought the car to a stop, then turned to the right over the Salinas River bridge.

"Do any women ever go to the fights?" she asked.

"Oh, sure, some. What's the matter, Elisa? Do you want to go? I don't think you'd like it, but I'll take you if you really want to go."

She relaxed limply in the seat. "Oh, no. No. I don't want to go. I'm sure I don't." Her face was turned away from him. "It will be enough if we can have wine. It will be plenty." She turned up her coat collar so he could not see that she was crying weakly—like an old woman.

1937

COUNTEE CULLEN
1903–1946

More than most poets of the Harlem Renaissance, Countee Cullen valued traditional poetic forms in English—the sonnet, rhymed couplets, and quatrains—over modernist free verse or rhythms suggested by jazz and popular culture. Never one to shy away from controversy, Cullen prefaced his important anthology of African American poetry, *Caroling Dusk* (1927), with the assertion, "As heretical as it may sound, there is the probability that Negro poets, dependent as they are on the English language, may have more to gain from the rich background of English and American poetry than from any nebulous atavistic yearnings toward an African inheritance." Cullen demanded that black poets be considered as American poets, ultimately without any special racial designation. Nevertheless, the titles of his books of poetry—*Color* (1925), *Copper Sun* (1927), *The Ballad of the Brown Girl* (1928)—showed that, like Claude MacKay and Jean Toomer, he felt a responsibility to write about being black even if he did so in modes outside of black folk traditions. Although he clashed with a number of his contemporaries in the Harlem Renaissance, Cullen could also be generous to black writers whose poetics differed from his. What mattered to Cullen was appreciating the full range of black literary writing, a range as great, he insisted, as that found among white poets in English, and resisting every "attempt to corral the ebony muse into some definite mold" to which all black writers should conform.

Although Cullen's birthplace and early years are obscure, he was adopted at some point in his childhood by a Harlem-based minister and given a good education, first in New York public schools and then at New York University, where he received his B.A. in 1925, and at Harvard, where he took an M.A. in 1926. His first book of poems, *Color*, appeared in his senior year at college; it established him as the "black Keats," a prodigy.

From 1926 to 1928, Cullen was assistant editor at the important black journal *Opportunity*, for which he also wrote a feature column, "The Dark Tower." In 1928 he married Nina Yolande Du Bois, the daughter of W. E. B. Du Bois, and won a Guggenheim fellowship that took him to Paris and enabled him to complete another book of poems, *The Black Christ* (1929). His marriage quickly disintegrated, however, over Cullen's attraction to men, and the couple was divorced in 1930. Neither *The Black Christ* nor the novel that followed, *One Way to Heaven* (1932), earned the acclaim of Cullen's earlier books. He spent the last years of his life teaching at New York's Frederick Douglass Junior High School, where his pupils included the future novelist James Baldwin. With the revival of scholarly interest in the Harlem Renaissance, Cullen's distinctive combination of traditionalist poetic skill with acerbic self-questioning on matters of racism and racial identity has once again brought his poetry to critical attention.

The text of the poems included here is that of *Color* (1925).

Yet Do I Marvel

I doubt not God is good, well-meaning, kind,
And did He stoop to quibble could tell why
The little buried mole continues blind,
Why flesh that mirrors Him must some day die,
Make plain the reason tortured Tantalus   5
Is baited by the fickle fruit, declare
If merely brute caprice dooms Sisyphus[1]
To struggle up a never-ending stair.
Inscrutable His ways are, and immune
To catechism by a mind too strewn   10
With petty cares to slightly understand
What awful brain compels His awful hand.
Yet do I marvel at this curious thing:
To make a poet black, and bid him sing!

                                                           1925

Incident

Once riding in old Baltimore,
    Heart-filled, head-filled with glee,
I saw a Baltimorean
    Keep looking straight at me.

Now I was eight and very small,   5
    And he was no whit bigger,
And so I smiled, but he poked out
    His tongue, and called me, "Nigger."

I saw the whole of Baltimore
    From May until December;   10
Of all the things that happened there
    That's all that I remember.

                                                           1925

Heritage

What is Africa to me:
Copper sun or scarlet sea,
Jungle star or jungle track,

---

1. Tantalus and Sisyphus are figures in Greek mythology who were punished in Hades. Tantalus was offered food and water that was then instantly snatched away. Sisyphus had to roll a heavy stone to the top of a hill and, after it rolled back down, repeat the ordeal perpetually.

Strong bronzed men, or regal black
Women from whose loins I sprang   5
When the birds of Eden sang?
One three centuries removed
From the scenes his fathers loved,
Spicy grove, cinnamon tree,
What is Africa to me?   10

So I lie, who all day long
Want no sound except the song
Sung by wild barbaric birds
Goading massive jungle herds,
Juggernauts[1] of flesh that pass   15
Trampling tall defiant grass
Where young forest lovers lie,
Plighting troth beneath the sky.
So I lie, who always hear,
Though I cram against my ear   20
Both my thumbs, and keep them there,
Great drums throbbing through the air.
So I lie, whose fount of pride,
Dear distress, and joy allied,
Is my somber flesh and skin,   25
With the dark blood dammed within
Like great pulsing tides of wine
That, I fear, must burst the fine
Channels of the chafing net
Where they surge and foam and fret.   30

Africa? A book one thumbs
Listlessly, till slumber comes.
Unremembered are her bats
Circling through the night, her cats
Crouching in the river reeds,   35
Stalking gentle flesh that feeds
By the river brink; no more
Does the bugle-throated roar
Cry that monarch claws have leapt
From the scabbards where they slept.   40
Silver snakes that once a year
Doff the lovely coats you wear,
Seek no covert in your fear
Lest a mortal eye should see;
What's your nakedness to me?   45
Here no leprous flowers rear
Fierce corollas[2] in the air;
Here no bodies sleek and wet,

1. The juggernaut is a sacred Hindu idol dragged on a huge car in the path of which devotees were believed to throw themselves—hence any power demanding blind sacrifice, here spliced with the image of elephants.
2. The whorl of petals forming the inner envelope of a flower.

Dripping mingled rain and sweat,
Tread the savage measures of   50
Jungle boys and girls in love.
What is last year's snow to me,[3]
Last year's anything? The tree
Budding yearly must forget
How its past arose or set—   55
Bough and blossom, flower, fruit,
Even what shy bird with mute
Wonder at her travail there,
Meekly labored in its hair.
One three centuries removed   60
From the scenes his fathers loved,
Spicy grove, cinnamon tree,
What is Africa to me?

So I lie, who find no peace
Night or day, no slight release   65
From the unremittant beat
Made by cruel padded feet
Walking through my body's street.
Up and down they go, and back,
Treading out a jungle track.   70
So I lie, who never quite
Safely sleep from rain at night—
I can never rest at all
When the rain begins to fall;
Like a soul gone mad with pain   75
I must match its weird refrain;
Ever must I twist and squirm,
Writhing like a baited worm,
While its primal measures drip
Through my body, crying, "Strip!   80
Doff this new exuberance.
Come and dance the Lover's Dance!"
In an old remembered way
Rain works on me night and day.

Quaint, outlandish heathen gods   85
Black men fashion out of rods,
Clay, and brittle bits of stone,
In a likeness like their own,
My conversion came high-priced;
I belong to Jesus Christ,   90
Preacher of humility;
Heathen gods are naught to me.

Father, Son, and Holy Ghost,
So I make an idle boast;

3. An echo of the lament "Where are the snows of yesteryear?" from "Grand Testament" by the 15th-century French poet François Villon.

Jesus of the twice-turned cheek[4]   95
Lamb of God, although I speak
With my mouth thus, in my heart
Do I play a double part.
Ever at Thy glowing altar
Must my heart grow sick and falter,   100
Wishing He I served were black,
Thinking then it would not lack
Precedent of pain to guide it,
Let who would or might deride it;
Surely then this flesh would know   105
Yours had borne a kindred woe.
Lord, I fashion dark gods, too,
Daring even to give You
Dark despairing features where,
Crowned with dark rebellious hair,   110
Patience wavers just so much as
Mortal grief compels, while touches
Quick and hot, of anger, rise
To smitten cheek and weary eyes.
Lord, forgive me if my need   115
Sometimes shapes a human creed.
All day long and all night through,
One thing only must I do:
Quench my pride and cool my blood,
Lest I perish in the flood.   120
Lest a hidden ember set
Timber that I thought was wet
Burning like the dryest flax,
Melting like the merest wax,
Lest the grave restore its dead.   125
Not yet has my heart or head
In the least way realized
They and I are civilized.

1925

---

4. In his Sermon on the Mount (Matthew 5.39), Jesus declared that when struck on the cheek, one should turn the other cheek rather than strike back.

RICHARD WRIGHT

1908–1960

With the 1940 publication of *Native Son* by the Book-of-the-Month Club, Richard Wright became the most famous African American author of his time. *Native Son* is an uncompromising study of an African American underclass youth who is goaded to brutal violence by the oppression, hatred, and incomprehension of the white world. The sensational story disregarded conventional wisdom about how black authors should approach a white reading audience. Bigger Thomas, the main character, embodied everything that such an audience might fear and detest, but by situating the point of view within this character's consciousness Wright forced readers to see the world through Bigger's eyes and thus to understand him. The novel was structured like a hard-boiled detective story, contained layers of literary allusion and symbol, and combined Marxist social analysis with existential philosophy—in brief, it was at once a powerful social statement and a complex work of literary art.

Wright was born near Natchez, Mississippi. When he was five, his father abandoned the family—Wright, his younger brother, and his mother—and for the next ten years Wright was raised by a series of relatives in Mississippi. By 1925, when he went to Memphis on his own, he had moved twenty times. Extreme poverty, a constantly interrupted education that never went beyond junior high school, and the religious fundamentalism of his grandmother, along with the constant experiences of humiliation and hatred in a racially segregated South: all these contributed to Wright's growing sense that the hidden anger of black people was justified and that only by acknowledging and expressing it could they grapple with it. The title of *Native Son* made the point that the United States is as much the country of black as of white; the story showed that blacks had been deprived of their inheritance.

Two years after moving to Memphis, Wright went north to Chicago. There he took a series of odd jobs and then joined the WPA Writers' Project (a government project of the Depression years to help support authors) as a writer of guidebooks and as a director of the Federal Negro Theater. He began to study Marxist theory, contributing poetry to leftist literary magazines and joining the Communist Party in 1932. By 1935 he had become the center of a group of African American Chicago writers and had started to write fiction. He was influenced by the naturalistic fiction of James T. Farrell, whose study of sociology at the University of Chicago had helped give structure to his popular Studs Lonigan trilogy about working people of Irish descent.

Wright moved to New York in 1937 to write for the New York Writers' Project and as a reporter on the communist *Daily Worker*. In 1938 he published *Uncle Tom's Children*, a collection of four short stories. (An earlier novel, *Lawd Today*, was not published until after his death.) Set in the rural South, the stories center on racial conflict and physical violence. Wright's theme of the devastating effect of relentless, institutionalized hatred and humiliation on the black male's psyche was paramount in all of them.

After *Native Son*, Wright turned to autobiographical writings that eventuated in *Black Boy*, published in 1945. Many consider this to be his best book, and such writers as Ralph Ellison and James Baldwin took it as a model for their own work in the 1950s and 1960s. A communist activist in the early 1940s, Wright became increasingly disillusioned and broke completely with the party in 1944. Visiting France in

1946, he was warmly received by leading writers and philosophers. In 1947 he settled permanently in that country, where he was perceived from the first as one of the important experimental modernist prose writers and was ranked on a level with Hemingway, Fitzgerald, and Faulkner. An existential novel, *The Outsider* (1953), was followed by five more books: two novels and three collections of lectures, travel writings, and sociopolitical commentary. The collection *Eight Men,* from which the story printed here is taken, was the last literary project he worked on, and it appeared the year after his death.

Wright's immersion in Marxist doctrine gave him tools for representing society as divided into antagonistic classes and run for the benefit of the few. But in each of his works he portrays individuals who, no matter how they are deformed and brutalized by oppression and exploitation, retain a transcendent spark of selfhood. Ultimately, it is in this spark that Wright put his faith. His writing from first to last affirmed the dignity and humanity of society's outcasts without romanticizing them, and indicted those who had cast them out. As Ralph Ellison expressed it, Wright's example "converted the American Negro impulse toward self-annihilation and 'going underground' into a will to confront the world" and to "throw his findings unashamedly into the guilty conscience of America."

The text was first published in *Harper's Bazaar* (1939) under the title "Almos' a Man." Under its present title it appeared in *Eight Men* (1961), a posthumous collection of Wright's short fiction.

The Man Who Was Almost a Man

Dave struck out across the fields, looking homeward through paling light. Whut's the use talkin wid em niggers in the field? Anyhow, his mother was putting supper on the table. Them niggers can't understan nothing. One of these days he was going to get a gun and practice shooting, then they couldn't talk to him as though he were a little boy. He slowed, looking at the ground. Shucks, Ah ain scareda them even ef they are biggern me! Aw, Ah know whut Ahma do. Ahm going by ol Joe's sto n git that Sears Roebuck catlog n look at them guns. Mebbe Ma will lemme buy one when she gits mah pay from ol man Hawkins. Ahma beg her t gimme some money. Ahm ol ernough to hava gun. Ahm seventeen. Almost a man. He strode, feeling his long loose-jointed limbs. Shucks, a man oughta hava little gun aftah he done worked hard all day.

He came in sight of Joe's store. A yellow lantern glowed on the front porch. He mounted steps and went through the screen door, hearing it bang behind him. There was a strong smell of coal oil and mackerel fish. He felt very confident until he saw fat Joe walk in through the rear door, then his courage began to ooze.

"Howdy, Dave! Whutcha want?"

"How yuh, Mistah Joe? Aw, Ah don wanna buy nothing. Ah jus wanted t see ef yuhd lemme look at tha catlog erwhile."

"Sure! You wanna see it here?"

"Nawsuh. Ah wans t take it home wid me. Ah'll bring it back termorrow when Ah come in from the fiels."

"You plannin on buying something?"

"Yessuh."

"Your ma lettin you have your own money now?"

"Shucks. Mistah Joe, Ahm gittin t be a man like anybody else!"

Joe laughed and wiped his greasy white face with a red bandanna.

"Whut you plannin on buyin?"

Dave looked at the floor, scratched his head, scratched his thigh, and smiled. Then he looked up shyly.

"Ah'll tell yuh, Mistah Joe, ef yuh promise yuh won't tell."

"I promise."

"Waal, Ahma buy a gun."

"A gun? What you want with a gun?"

"Ah wanna keep it."

"You ain't nothing but a boy. You don't need a gun."

"Aw, lemme have the catlog, Mistah Joe. Ah'll bring it back."

Joe walked through the rear door. Dave was elated. He looked around at barrels of sugar and flour. He heard Joe coming back. He craned his neck to see if he were bringing the book. Yeah, he's got it. Gawddog, he's got it!

"Here, but be sure you bring it back. It's the only one I got."

"Sho, Mistah Joe."

"Say, if you wanna buy a gun, why don't you buy one from me? I gotta gun to sell."

"Will it shoot?"

"Sure it'll shoot."

"Whut kind is it?"

"Oh, it's kinda old . . . a left-hand Wheeler. A pistol. A big one."

"Is it got bullets in it?"

"It's loaded."

"Kin Ah see it?"

"Where's your money?"

"What yuh wan fer it?"

"I'll let you have it for two dollars."

"Just two dollahs? Shucks, Ah could buy tha when Ah git mah pay."

"I'll have it here when you want it."

"Awright, suh. Ah be in fer it."

He went through the door, hearing it slam again behind him. Ahma git some money from Ma n buy me a gun! Only two dollahs! He tucked the thick catalogue under his arm and hurried.

"Where yuh been, boy?" His mother held a steaming dish of black-eyed peas.

"Aw, Ma, Ah just stopped down the road t talk wid the boys."

"Yuh know bettah t keep suppah waitin."

He sat down, resting the catalogue on the edge of the table.

"Yuh git up from there and git to the well n wash yosef! Ah ain feedin no hogs in mah house!"

She grabbed his shoulder and pushed him. He stumbled out of the room, then came back to get the catalogue.

"Whut this?"

"Aw, Ma, it's jusa catlog."

"Who yuh git it from?"

"From Joe, down at the sto."

"Waal, thas good. We kin use it in the outhouse."

"Naw, Ma." He grabbed for it. "Gimme ma catlog, Ma."

She held onto it and glared at him.

"Quit hollerin at me! Whut's wrong wid yuh? Yuh crazy?"

"But Ma, please. It ain mine! It's Joe's! He tol me t bring it back t im termorrow."

She gave up the book. He stumbled down the back steps, hugging the thick book under his arm. When he had splashed water on his face and hands, he groped back to the kitchen and fumbled in a corner for the towel. He bumped into a chair; it clattered to the floor. The catalogue sprawled at his feet. When he had dried his eyes he snatched up the book and held it again under his arm. His mother stood watching him.

"Now, ef yuh gonna act a fool over that ol book, Ah'll take it n burn it up."

"Naw, Ma, please."

"Waal, set down n be still!"

He sat down and drew the oil lamp close. He thumbed page after page, unaware of the food his mother set on the table. His father came in. Then his small brother.

"Whutcha got there, Dave?" his father asked.

"Jusa catlog," he answered, not looking up.

"Yeah, here they is!" His eyes glowed at blue-and-black revolvers. He glanced up, feeling sudden guilt. His father was watching him. He eased the book under the table and rested it on his knees. After the blessing was asked, he ate. He scooped up peas and swallowed fat meat without chewing. Buttermilk helped to wash it down. He did not want to mention money before his father. He would do much better by cornering his mother when she was alone. He looked at his father uneasily out of the edge of his eye.

"Boy, how come yuh don quit foolin wid tha book n eat yo suppah?"

"Yessuh."

"How you n ol man Hawkins gitten erlong?"

"Suh?"

"Can't yuh hear? Why don yuh lissen? Ah ast yu how wuz yuh n ol man Hawkins gittin erlong?"

"Oh, swell, Pa. Ah plows mo lan than anybody over there."

"Waal, yuh oughta keep yo mind on whut yuh doin."

"Yessuh."

He poured his plate full of molasses and sopped it up slowly with a chunk of cornbread. When his father and brother had left the kitchen, he still sat and looked again at the guns in the catalogue, longing to muster courage enough to present his case to his mother. Lawd, ef Ah only had tha pretty one! He could almost feel the slickness of the weapon with his fingers. If he had a gun like that he would polish it and keep it shining so it would never rust. N Ah'd keep it loaded, by Gawd!

"Ma?" His voice was hesitant.

"Hunh?"

"Ol man Hawkins give yuh mah money yit?"

"Yeah, but ain no usa yuh thinking bout throwin nona it erway. Ahm keepin tha money sos yuh kin have cloes t go to school this winter."

He rose and went to her side with the open catalogue in his palms. She was washing dishes, her head bent low over a pan. Shyly he raised the book. When he spoke, his voice was husky, faint.

"Ma, Gawd knows Ah wans one of these."

"One of whut?" she asked, not raising her eyes.

"One of these," he said again, not daring even to point. She glanced up at the page, then at him with wide eyes.

"Nigger, is yuh gone plumb crazy?"

"Aw, Ma."

"Git outta here! Don yuh talk t me bout no gun! Yuh a fool!"

"Ma, Ah kin buy one fer two dollahs."

"Not ef Ah knows it, yuh ain!"

"But yuh promised me one."

"Ah don care whut Ah promised! Yuh ain nothing but a boy yit!"

"Ma, ef yuh lemme buy one Ah'll *never* ast yuh fer nothing no mo."

"Ah tol yuh t git outta here! Yuh ain gonna toucha penny of tha money fer no gun! Thas how come Ah has Mistah Hawkins t pay yo wages t me, cause Ah knows yuh ain got no sense."

"But, Ma, we needa gun. Pa ain got no gun. We needa gun in the house. Yuh kin never tell whut might happen."

"Now don yuh try to maka fool outta me, boy! Ef we did hava gun, yuh wouldn't have it!"

He laid the catalogue down and slipped his arm around her waist.

"Aw, Ma, Ah done worked hard alla summer n ain ast yuh fer nothin, is Ah, now?"

"Thas whut yuh spose t do!"

"But Ma, Ah wans a gun. Yuh kin lemme have two dollahs outta mah money. Please, Ma. I kin give it to Pa . . . Please, Ma! Ah loves yuh, Ma."

When she spoke her voice came soft and low.

"What yuh wan wida gun, Dave? Yuh don need no gun. Yuh'll git in trouble. N ef yo pa jus thought Ah let yuh have money t buy a gun he'd hava fit."

"Ah'll hide it, Ma. It ain but two dollahs."

"Lawd, chil, whut's wrong wid yuh?"

"Ain nothing wrong, Ma. Ahm almos a man now. Ah wans a gun."

"Who gonna sell yuh a gun?"

"Ol Joe at the sto."

"N it don cos but two dollahs?"

"Thas all, Ma. Just two dollahs. Please, Ma."

She was stacking the plates away; her hands moved slowly, reflectively. Dave kept an anxious silence. Finally, she turned to him.

"Ah'll let yuh git tha gun ef yuh promise me one thing."

"Whut's tha, Ma?"

"Yuh bring it straight back t me, yuh hear? It be fer Pa."

"Yessum! Lemme go now, Ma."

She stooped, turned slightly to one side, raised the hem of her dress, rolled down the top of her stocking, and came up with a slender wad of bills.

"Here," she said. "Lawd knows yuh don need no gun. But yer pa does. Yuh bring it right back t me, yuh hear? Ahma put it up. Now ef yuh don, Ahma have yuh pa pick yuh so hard yuh won fergit it."

"Yessum."

He took the money, ran down the steps, and across the yard.

"Dave! Yuuuuuh Daaaaave!"

He heard, but he was not going to stop now. "Naw, Lawd!"

The first movement he made the following morning was to reach under his pillow for the gun. In the gray light of dawn he held it loosely, feeling a sense of power. Could kill a man with a gun like this. Kill anybody, black or white. And if he were holding his gun in his hand, nobody could run over him; they would have to respect him. It was a big gun, with a long barrel and a heavy handle. He raised and lowered it in his hand, marveling at its weight.

He had not come straight home with it as his mother had asked; instead he had stayed out in the fields, holding the weapon in his hand, aiming it now and then at some imaginary foe. But he had not fired it; he had been afraid that his father might hear. Also he was not sure he knew how to fire it.

To avoid surrendering the pistol he had not come into the house until he knew that they were all asleep. When his mother had tiptoed to his bedside late that night and demanded the gun, he had first played possum; then he had told her that the gun was hidden outdoors, that he would bring it to her in the morning. Now he lay turning it slowly in his hands. He broke it, took out the cartridges, felt them, and then put them back.

He slid out of bed, got a long strip of old flannel from a trunk, wrapped the gun in it, and tied it to his naked thigh while it was still loaded. He did not go in to breakfast. Even though it was not yet daylight, he started for Jim Hawkins' plantation. Just as the sun was rising he reached the barns where the mules and plows were kept.

"Hey! That you, Dave?"

He turned. Jim Hawkins stood eying him suspiciously.

"What're yuh doing here so early?"

"Ah didn't know Ah wuz gittin up so early, Mistah Hawkins. Ah wuz fixin t hitch up ol Jenny n take her t the fiels."

"Good. Since you're so early, how about plowing that stretch down by the woods?"

"Suits me, Mistah Hawkins."

"O.K. Go to it!"

He hitched Jenny to a plow and started across the fields. Hot dog! This was just what he wanted. If he could get down by the woods, he could shoot his gun and nobody would hear. He walked behind the plow, hearing the traces creaking, feeling the gun tied tight to his thigh.

When he reached the woods, he plowed two whole rows before he decided to take out the gun. Finally, he stopped, looked in all directions, then untied the gun and held it in his hand. He turned to the mule and smiled.

"Know whut this is, Jenny? Naw, yuh wouldn know! Yuhs jusa ol mule! Anyhow, this is a gun, n it kin shoot, by Gawd!"

He held the gun at arm's length. Whut t hell, Ahma shoot this thing! He looked at Jenny again.

"Lissen here, Jenny! When Ah pull this ol trigger, Ah don wan yuh t run n acka fool now!"

Jenny stood with head down, her short ears pricked straight. Dave walked off about twenty feet, held the gun far out from him at arm's length, and turned his head. Hell, he told himself, Ah ain afraid. The gun felt loose in his fingers; he waved it wildly for a moment. Then he shut his eyes and tightened his forefinger. Bloom! A report half deafened him and he thought his right hand was torn from his arm. He heard Jenny whinnying and galloping over the field, and he found himself on his knees, squeezing his fingers hard between his legs. His hand was numb; he jammed it into his mouth, trying to warm it, trying to stop the pain. The gun lay at his feet. He did not quite know what had happened. He stood up and stared at the gun as though it were a living thing. He gritted his teeth and kicked the gun. Yuh almos broke mah arm! He turned to look for Jenny; she was far over the fields, tossing her head and kicking wildly.

"Hol on there, ol mule!"

When he caught up with her she stood trembling, walling her big white eyes at him. The plow was far away; the traces had broken. Then Dave stopped short, looking, not believing. Jenny was bleeding. Her left side was red and wet with blood. He went closer. Lawd, have mercy! Wondah did Ah shoot this mule? He grabbed for Jenny's mane. She flinched, snorted, whirled, tossing her head.

"Hol on now! Hol on."

Then he saw the hole in Jenny's side, right between the ribs. It was round, wet, red. A crimson stream streaked down the front leg, flowing fast. Good Gawd! Ah wuzn't shootin at tha mule. He felt panic. He knew he had to stop that blood, or Jenny would bleed to death. He had never seen so much blood in all his life. He chased the mule for a half a mile, trying to catch her. Finally she stopped, breathing hard, stumpy tail half arched. He caught her mane and led her back to where the plow and gun lay. Then he stooped and grabbed handfuls of damp black earth and tried to plug the bullet hole. Jenny shuddered, whinnied, and broke from him.

"Hol on! Hol on now!"

He tried to plug it again, but blood came anyhow. His fingers were hot and sticky. He rubbed dirt into his palms, trying to dry them. Then again he attempted to plug the bullet hole, but Jenny shied away, kicking her heels high. He stood helpless. He had to do something. He ran at Jenny; she dodged him. He watched a red stream of blood flow down Jenny's leg and form a bright pool at her feet.

"Jenny . . . Jenny," he called weakly.

His lips trembled. She's bleeding t death! He looked in the direction of home, wanting to go back, wanting to get help. But he saw the pistol lying in the damp black clay. He had a queer feeling that if he only did something, this would not be; Jenny would not be there bleeding to death.

When he went to her this time, she did not move. She stood with sleepy, dreamy eyes; and when he touched her she gave a low-pitched whinny and knelt to the ground, her front knees slopping in blood.

"Jenny . . . Jenny . . ." he whispered.

For a long time she held her neck erect; then her head sank, slowly. Her ribs swelled with a mighty heave and she went over.

Dave's stomach felt empty, very empty. He picked up the gun and held it gingerly between his thumb and forefinger. He buried it at the foot of a tree. He took a stick and tried to cover the pool of blood with dirt—but what was the use? There was Jenny lying with her mouth open and her eyes walled and glassy. He could not tell Jim Hawkins he had shot his mule. But he had to tell something. Yeah, Ah'll tell em Jenny started gittin wil n fell on the joint of the plow. . . . But that would hardly happen to a mule. He walked across the field slowly, head down.

It was sunset. Two of Jim Hawkins' men were over near the edge of the woods digging a hole in which to bury Jenny. Dave was surrounded by a knot of people, all of whom were looking down at the dead mule.

"I don't see how in the world it happened," said Jim Hawkins for the tenth time.

The crowd parted and Dave's mother, father, and small brother pushed into the center.

"Where Dave?" his mother called.

"There he is," said Jim Hawkins.

His mother grabbed him.

"Whut happened, Dave? Whut yuh done?"

"Nothin."

"C mon, boy, talk," his father said.

Dave took a deep breath and told the story he knew nobody believed.

"Waal," he drawled. "Ah brung ol Jenny down here sos Ah could do mah plowin. Ah plowed bout two rows, just like yuh see." He stopped and pointed at the long rows of upturned earth. "Then somethin musta been wrong wid ol Jenny. She wouldn ack right a-tall. She started snortin n kickin her heels. Ah tried t hol her, but she pulled erway, rearin n goin in. Then when the point of the plow was stickin up in the air, she swung erroun n twisted herself back on it . . . She stuck herself n started t bleed. N fo Ah could do anything, she wuz dead."

"Did you ever hear of anything like that in all your life?" asked Jim Hawkins.

There were white and black standing in the crowd. They murmured. Dave's mother came close to him and looked hard into his face. "Tell the truth, Dave," she said.

"Looks like a bullet hole to me," said one man.

"Dave, whut yuh do wid the gun?" his mother asked.

The crowd surged in, looking at him. He jammed his hands into his pockets, shook his head slowly from left to right, and backed away. His eyes were wide and painful.

"Did he hava gun?" asked Jim Hawkins.

"By Gawd, Ah tol yuh tha wu a gun wound," said a man, slapping his thigh.

His father caught his shoulders and shook him till his teeth rattled.

"Tell whut happened, yuh rascal! Tell whut . . ."

Dave looked at Jenny's stiff legs and began to cry.

"Whut yuh do wid tha gun?" his mother asked.

"Whut wuz he doin wida gun?" his father asked.

"Come on and tell the truth," said Hawkins. "Ain't nobody going to hurt you . . ."

His mother crowded close to him.

"Did yuh shoot tha mule, Dave?"

Dave cried, seeing blurred white and black faces.

"Ahh ddinn gggo tt sshooot hher . . . Ah ssswear ffo Gawd Ahh ddin. . . . Ah wuz a-tryin t sssee ef the old gggun would sshoot."

"Where yuh git the gun from?" his father asked.

"Ah got it from Joe, at the sto."

"Where yuh git the money?"

"Ma give it t me."

"He kept worryin me, Bob. Ah had t. Ah tol im t bring the gun right back to me . . . It was fer yuh, the gun."

"But how yuh happen to shoot that mule?" asked Jim Hawkins.

"Ah wuzn shootin at the mule, Mistah Hawkins. The gun jumped when Ah pulled the trigger . . . N fo Ah knowed anythin Jenny was there a-bleedin."

Somebody in the crowd laughed. Jim Hawkins walked close to Dave and looked into his face.

"Well, looks like you have bought you a mule, Dave."

"Ah swear fo Gawd, Ah didn go t kill the mule, Mistah Hawkins!"

"But you killed her!"

All the crowd was laughing now. They stood on tiptoe and poked heads over one another's shoulders.

"Well, boy, looks like yuh done bought a dead mule! Hahaha!"

"Ain tha ershame."

"Hohohohoho."

Dave stood, head down, twisting his feet in the dirt.

"Well, you needn't worry about it, Bob," said Jim Hawkins to Dave's father. "Just let the boy keep on working and pay me two dollars a month."

"Whut yuh wan fer yo mule, Mistah Hawkins?"

Jim Hawkins screwed up his eyes.

"Fifty dollars."

"Whut yuh do wid tha gun?" Dave's father demanded.

Dave said nothing.

"Yuh wan me t take a tree n beat yuh till yuh talk!"

"Nawsuh!"

"Whut yuh do wid it?"

"Ah throwed it erway."

"Where?"

"Ah . . . Ah throwed it in the creek."

"Waal, c mon home. N firs thing in the mawnin git to tha creek n fin tha gun."

"Yessuh."

"Whut yuh pay fer it?"

"Two dollahs."

"Take tha gun n git yo money back n carry it t Mistah Hawkins, yuh hear? N don fergit Ahma lam you black bottom good fer this! Now march yosef on home, suh!"

Dave turned and walked slowly. He heard people laughing. Dave glared, his eyes welling with tears. Hot anger bubbled in him. Then he swallowed and stumbled on.

That night Dave did not sleep. He was glad that he had gotten out of killing the mule so easily, but he was hurt. Something hot seemed to turn over inside him each time he remembered how they had laughed. He tossed on his bed, feeling his hard pillow. N Pa says he's gonna beat me . . . He remembered other beatings, and his back quivered. Naw, naw, Ah sho don wan im t beat me tha way no mo. Dam em all! Nobody ever gave him anything. All he did was work. They treat me like a mule, n then they beat me. He gritted his teeth. N Ma had t tell on me.

Well, if he had to, he would take old man Hawkins that two dollars. But that meant selling the gun. And he wanted to keep that gun. Fifty dollars for a dead mule.

He turned over, thinking how he had fired the gun. He had an itch to fire it again. Ef other men kin shoota gun, by Gawd, Ah kin! He was still, listening. Mebbe they all sleepin now. The house was still. He heard the soft breathing of his brother. Yes, now! He would go down and get that gun and see if he could fire it! He eased out of bed and slipped into overalls.

The moon was bright. He ran almost all the way to the edge of the woods. He stumbled over the ground, looking for the spot where he had buried the gun. Yeah, here it is. Like a hungry dog scratching for a bone, he pawed it up. He puffed his black cheeks and blew dirt from the trigger and barrel. He broke it and found four cartridges unshot. He looked around; the fields were filled with silence and moonlight. He clutched the gun stiff and hard in his fingers. But, as soon as he wanted to pull the trigger, he shut his eyes and turned his head. Naw, An can't shoot wid mah eyes closed n mah head turned. With effort he held his eyes open; then he squeezed. *Bloooom!* He was stiff, not breathing. The gun was still in his hands. Dammit, he'd done it! He fired again. *Blooooom!* He smiled. *Blooooom! Bloooom! Click, click.* There! It was empty. If anybody could shoot a gun, he could. He put the gun into his hip pocket and started across the fields.

When he reached the top of a ridge he stood straight and proud in the moonlight, looking at Jim Hawkins' big white house, feeling the gun sagging in his pocket. Lawd, ef Ah had just one mo bullet Ah'd taka shot at tha house. Ah'd like t scare ol man Hawkins jusa little . . . Jusa enough t let im know Dave Saunders is a man.

To his left the road curved, running to the tracks of the Illinois Central. He jerked his head, listening. From far off came a faint *hoooof-hoooof; hoooof-hoooof; hoooof-hoooof.* . . . He stood rigid. Two dollahs a mont. Les see now . . . Tha means it'll take bout two years. Shucks! Ah'll be dam!

He started down the road, toward the tracks. Yeah, here she comes! He stood beside the track and held himself stiffly. Here she comes, erroun the ben . . . C mon, yuh slow poke! C mon! He had his hand on his gun; something quivered in his stomach. Then the train thundered past, the gray and brown box cars rumbling and clinking. He gripped the gun tightly; then he jerked his hand out of his pocket. Ah betcha Bill wouldn't do it! Ah betcha. . . . The cars slid past, steel grinding upon steel. Ahm ridin yuh ternight, so hep me Gawd! He was hot all over. He hesitated just a moment; then he grabbed, pulled atop of a car, and lay flat. He felt his pocket; the gun was still there. Ahead the long rails were glinting in the moonlight, stretching away, away to somewhere, somewhere where he could be a man . . .

1939, 1961

American Literature since 1945

H ow do we tell the story of American literature in our own time? In one version of that story, we are led into the twenty-first century by an unlikely hero named Oscar Wao, the creation of novelist and short-story writer Junot Díaz in *The Brief Wondrous Life of Oscar Wao* (2008). Oscar is a nerdy, overweight devotee of fantasy fiction and comics, dreaming of becoming the Dominican American J. R. R. Tolkien, author of Oscar's favorite novels, the Lord of the Rings trilogy. Failing at exercise, dating, and the college social scene, Oscar leaves New Jersey for an extended stay with relatives in the Dominican Republic. There he achieves the romantic fulfillment that eluded him at home, but his refugee family's tragic history comes full circle, too, as Oscar's life is changed forever by his unwitting entanglement with the Dominican Republic's brutal political regime. This, Díaz tells us, is *fuku*, a curse that wreaks havoc the world over, anywhere we find those hungry for power crushing the freedom, and the bodies, of the weak.

Díaz's hero and the novel that brings him to life embody what feels truly new in American writing of the twenty-first century. When we read *Oscar Wao*—or virtually any of Díaz's stories, such as "Drown," reprinted in this volume—we plug into an electric, multilingual English renewed by Spanish, African, and Latin American borrowings. What has been called a *mestizo* language was practiced, described, and theorized by the writer Gloria Anzaldúa decades before (see her essay "How to Tame a Wild Tongue," also in this volume). Building on the work of Anzaldúa and others, a writer of Díaz's generation need not justify the hybrid, but can simply inhabit it, using new language to reach new regions of human experience and

---

Blam, Roy Lichtenstein, 1962. For more information about this painting, see the color insert in this volume.

American culture. Following Díaz's allusions in *Oscar Wao*, readers are led to genre fiction, superhero comics, film, fashion, pop music, arts, religious ritual, modern sexuality, and mass entertainment—a cultural milieu that stretches from New Jersey to Santo Domingo. But Díaz's headlong prose also brings references to more traditionally literary writers such as William Shakespeare, Herman Melville, and the Latin American novelist Gabriel García Márquez, alongside the terms and ideas of literary criticism, history, philosophy, gender theory, and critiques of political power. Twenty-first-century readers have been more than ready to embrace Díaz's capacious literary and cultural vision. They have been willing to wrestle with what is difficult in his writing while they revel in his brilliant, loving use of the lowbrow and the popular. Do readers have to choose between the academic and the popular, between "serious" and "entertaining"? Junot Díaz says no. What do the X-Men comics have to say about theories of dictatorship? *Oscar Wao* explains—in a footnote, no less. Twenty-first-century readers live these intersections daily, code-shifting as they move among family, friends, school, work, nations, and cultures. The fiction of Junot Díaz seems to speak all these languages and more.

Junot Díaz took eleven years to write *The Brief Wondrous Life of Oscar Wao*. He had to invent the hybrid language from which to spin the strands of his story. The Pulitzer Prize committee—known for honoring epic novels that sum up something important about American life—chose *Oscar Wao* for the 2008 prize, marking the arrival in literature of a vision of America already lived by many of its citizens. At the beginning of the twenty-first century, *Oscar Wao* did just what the poet Ezra Pound exhorted ambitious writers to do at the start of the twentieth century: "Make it new." In doing so, of course, Díaz joined a literary tradition even as he broke its molds.

The vitality of contemporary American literature, evident throughout the most recent selections in this volume, is fueled by two great engines, one artistic and one demographic. The artistic urge to experiment galvanized writers inspired by, or reacting against, the influential modernist writers of the first half of the twentieth century who themselves experimented ceaselessly with literary form and with the subjects and stories that could be spoken through poetry, drama, and fiction. At the same time, the demographics of American education and immigration were changing radically, beginning in the middle of the twentieth century. These forces transformed the cast of American high- and middlebrow culture: who participated in American culture, and who was taught the reading and writing skills essential to the creation of modern literature. As an interest in experiment surged through a nation of new readers and writers, the basic elements of literary culture were renewed once more.

NEW READERS, NEW WRITERS, NEW HEROES

Addressing American college students in 1950, the Russian émigré author Vladimir Nabokov gave his audience a multiple-choice quiz: What makes a reader a *good* reader? The options included joining a book club, identifying with characters, and reading a story for what it had to say about society. These were, for Nabokov, trick answers: they were common ways of reading then, as now, but he disparaged them. He wanted readers to take a different approach. The correct answers, he told the students, were owning a dictionary, possessing a good memory, and having imagination. Both the "wrong" answers and the ones Nabokov thought were right tell us a great deal about what the new generation of American readers was looking for when they turned to literature.

These readers—more diverse and better educated than ever before, faced with more choices than ever before—would help to define American and world literature over the next half century. Many of those regularly encountering literary works in the second half of the twentieth century were, or had been, servicemen. Quality paperbacks at low prices were suddenly everywhere, and the format was no longer the province solely of lowbrow "pulp" fiction. Millions of pocket-sized paperbacks had been sent abroad during World War II, given away by publishers through the Armed Services Editions series. Mysteries, Westerns, domestic novels, and works by Charles Dickens and Shakespeare all found their way overseas. *The Great Gatsby*, which had faded from public consciousness by the 1940s, was made popular again by servicemen and their paperbacks. While these books carried aspects of American and British culture into the barracks and bivouacs of soldiers in the theaters of war, those soldiers were also encountering the languages and cultures of Europe, North Africa, India, and Japan in the course of their service, broadening their cultural education in ways not specifically American. Coming back to the United States after 1945, veterans were greeted by an entitlement that dramatically changed American society: the benefits of the GI Bill—the Servicemen's Readjustment Act of 1944—signed into law by President Roosevelt. Under its provisions the government provided money so that veterans could buy homes and attend school, receiving tuition and a

Army Special Services librarian and soldiers in the Philippines, 1946.

The GI Bill (1944), which provided federal subsidies to support college education for returning World War II veterans, democratized American higher education. Shown here, veterans and other students at New York University in January 1945.

stipend for up to four years of college or other professional training. For the first time, men from immigrant, poor, and working-class families, whose parents had little education, were attending college in droves. In 1947, the program's peak year, 49 percent of students admitted to college were veterans. By the time the original version of the law had run its course in 1956, 7.8 million out of the 16 million World War II veterans had benefited from its education and training provisions. Combined with a booming American economy, plentiful jobs, and the widespread urge to start adult lives delayed by military deployment, the entitlement helped to lift millions of individuals and families into the middle class.

That demographic change transformed the demographics of reading and writing for the rest of the century. American readers' increasing sophistication about aesthetic and cultural matters was fueled by their professors' desire to teach the formally complex works promoted by the international modernist writers they admired from the early twentieth century. An influx of writers and scholars fleeing Europe just prior to the outbreak of war had given American intellectuals renewed contact with the literary currents of French, German, and Russian literature. "The New Criticism"—a modernist-inspired method of critical interpretation grounded in reading the text "closely"—was popular in literature classrooms just about everywhere, enshrined in textbooks such as Cleanth Brooks and Robert Penn Warren's *Understanding Poetry* (1938) and *Understanding Fiction* (1943; the writer Flannery O'Connor called *Understanding Fiction* her "Bible"). The method put students from varied backgrounds on an equal footing as readers and helped them to see how literary works were crafted, benefits that explain why students and teachers still practice "close reading" today.

Nabokov's recommended reading practices would serve students well as they encountered complex literary works, European influences, and the challenge of reading closely—and they would serve the future readers of his morally edgy novel *Lolita* (1955), too. *Lolita* is about a gentlemanly and intellectual European pedophile in love with a brash American preteen girl.

Initially banned in the United States, once *Lolita* became available freely to the American public in 1958, it became a best seller even as it tested readers' moral tolerance and aesthetic sophistication. Ironically, then, while Nabokov strove to teach American college students a kind of literary appreciation fostered by his aristocratic European education, the practices he in turn discouraged were too deeply embedded in American history to be set aside by the new college students filling the lecture halls and classrooms where he taught. Literature's capacity to change the culture by encouraging readers to think about their society through the lens of a story had already had significant effects in the nation's history. Nineteenth-century readers identifying with the characters in Harriet Beecher Stowe's *Uncle Tom's Cabin* or turning to Frederick Douglass's autobiography to understand slavery fueled the abolitionist movement that in turn fueled the Civil War. The African American characters that northern white readers identified with or listened to in fiction and autobiography reached them in ways their social lives otherwise prevented.

In the second half of the twentieth century, a new generation read not only for the "aesthetic bliss" Nabokov celebrated and for the formal features of language that "close reading" and an appreciation of international modernism could reveal, but also in order to remake themselves and their society. Those socially engaged acts of reading ensured that writers catering to them would make their mark both on the development of fiction, poetry, and drama as art forms and on politics, commerce, religion, medicine, and domestic life. By the mid-twentieth century, one could already point to a long history of black writers in the United States who used their skills on the page to fight the philosophy, psychology, and policies of white supremacy. The burgeoning civil rights movement and, later, the Black Arts movement, brought many more black writers into publication. While African American members of the armed services were in Europe, James Baldwin—who did not qualify for the service because of the effects of childhood malnutrition—was working in the War Information Office in New York, but he was also honing his craft as a fiction writer, joining a distinguished generation of black writers that included Ralph Ellison, Richard Wright, Langston Hughes, Ann Petry, and others who enjoyed wide audiences in the United States before, during, and after the war. Although James Baldwin left the United States in 1949 and spent most of the rest of his life in Europe, he would become one of the most canny commentators on race to address a mass readership in the postwar period. The essays contained in his well-received 1965 volume, *The Fire Next Time*, are even more direct than the critique to be found in *Black Boy*, the memoir that his mentor Richard Wright had published just twenty years earlier. This was partly due to the genre Baldwin chose: Baldwin's essays were not stories or memoirs, but cultural criticism. He provided a pointed psychological, spiritual, sexual, and practical analysis of racism in America that was as important to the civil rights movement's intellectual evolution as sit-ins and boycotts were to its political success. Baldwin's fiction—such as the story "Sonny's Blues," found in this volume—matched this social analysis with storytelling that could make readers feel the human cost of poverty and addiction in black communities—the outgrowths of the racist society Baldwin's essays lay bare.

"A Man Becomes Invisible." One of a set of images created by photographer Gordon Parks for a photo essay on Ralph Ellison's *Invisible Man*. The essay was published in *Life* magazine on August 25, 1952.

Drawing energy from the newly educated readers and writers of the mid-twentieth century, American fiction and drama in the postwar period frequently celebrated nonconforming outsiders like Baldwin's Sonny: the philosophical character, often a writer or an artist, usually male, who suffers social rejection for his ideals or simply for his identity. The social liberation movements of the second half of the twentieth century—not only the civil rights movement, but also the later Black Power movement, the American Indian Movement (AIM, founded in 1968), the women's liberation movement (which gained momentum in the early 1970s), and the movement for gay rights (which began with a protest at the Stonewall Inn in Greenwich Village, New York City, in 1969, and entered a new phase with the AIDS crisis in the mid-1980s)—inspired content for this infinitely flexible dramatic setup. Notable examples of the outsider character would include the nameless narrator of Ralph Ellison's *Invisible Man* (1952); Augie in Saul Bellow's *The Adventures of Augie March* (1953); the autobiographical narrator of Maxine Hong Kingston's stories in *The Woman Warrior* (1979); Toni Morrison's Milkman Dead and Guitar Bains (*Song of Soloman*, 1979); Don DeLillo's Jack Gladney (*White Noise*, 1985); Sherman Alexie's Junior in his acclaimed young adult novel, *The Absolutely True Diary of a Part-Time Indian* (2007); Junot Díaz's Oscar Wao (*The Brief Wondrous Life of Oscar Wao*, 2007); and Philip Roth's many Jewish protagonists who belong neither in their Jewish communities nor in the Protestant-dominated culture around them, the kind of character central to the story "Defender of the Faith" and embodied perhaps most memorably in Coleman Silk—the contemporary black man who lives out his life as a Jew in Roth's *The Human Stain* (2000). There were limits to American optimism about the prospects for outsiders' lives: like Willy Loman in Arthur Miller's play *Death of a*

Salesman, the outsider trying to reenter society's circle of norms can fail, sometimes spectacularly. These misfit characters can be heroes and antiheroes, weak men or rebels, and their stories can end in tragedy or triumph.

Such outsider characters were related to the rise of a new readership looking for characters with whom they could identify, but they were also inspired by discontent with mass culture in the United States and its perceived insistence on social conformity. That discontent sent young people in the postwar period searching for meaning and identity—beyond the desire for upward mobility, marriage and children, a house in the suburbs, and the sturdy work ethic of their fathers and mothers. The satirical and sometimes simply resistant attitude toward intellectual, cultural, reli-

Toni Morrison in 1970 at Random House, where she worked as an editor.

gious, and political authority cultivated among the coterie of so-called beatniks in the late 1940s and 1950s—a group that included Allen Ginsberg, Gary Snyder, Jack Kerouac, and William Burroughs—had become a popular movement among the generation born in the decade after the war. In the 1970s, many important women writers whom readers will find in this anthology—such as Jamaica Kincaid, Anne Sexton, Elizabeth Bishop, Toni Morrison, and Leslie Marmon Silko—also resisted conformities of race, education, religion, and gender that they perceived had circumscribed the lives of the women and men around them. Some, like Bishop, found artistic and personal solidarity among artists with whom they shared an aesthetic vision and a common set of cultural touchstones (later in this volume readers can see Bishop among a roomful of male writers at New York's Gotham Book Mart in a group photograph included alongside the selections from poet Randall Jarrell). Others, like Bambara, cultivated a diverse solidarity of women through collective projects and mutual support—as in Bambara's significant gathering of writers in the volume she edited, *The Black Woman: An Anthology* (1970). Toni Morrison spent twenty years as an editor at Random House, the job she held before becoming a full-time writer, where she ensured that black writers received the attention they deserved. And some writers resisted norms by arguing for new ones, as demonstrated in Silko's lifelong advocacy for politically engaged Native American art, which led her to criticize sharply white writers (famously, the poet Gary Snyder) for appropriating Native American sources as well as Native writers (such as fellow fiction writer Louise Erdrich) for being insufficiently committed to Native American

Levittown. Construction and aerial views of housing development in Levittown, PA, built by Levitt & Sons between 1951 and 1957. Levittown was the prototype for similar developments built all over the country in the 1950s and 1960s. They offered largely identical single-family homes for a generation of upwardly mobile middle-class Americans who wanted to move out of cities.

materials. Silko's admonishments to writers regarding the subjects and cultural materials that they should or should not write about suggests how nonconformity with the mainstream could sometimes place different forms of expectation or restraint upon writers. Do writers have to turn to their own heritage for inspiration? Sometimes it has seemed that writers of color are expected to do so, and white writers are free to choose not to. Language itself is a form of conformity and restraint. In the fiction of George Saunders—such as his story "CivilWarLand in Bad Decline," included here—the characters resist (and are sometimes overcome by) the stifling, dystopian worlds of American business where the euphemisms of customer service and "total quality management" jargon make it nearly impossible to describe, or even to perceive, the world beyond capitalist enterprise. Noncomformity had its most theatrical moment in the 1960s youth counterculture, epitomized by LSD advocate Timothy Leary's exhortation to "turn on, tune in, drop out." "Turning on" to the exploration of consciousness through psychedelic drugs such as LSD was meant to expand the mind beyond the limits of conventional thought and perception. For Leary and many in the counterculture, to "tune in" meant that one would seek to be open to the world spiritually, intellectually, and sensually; to "drop out" was to reject social conventions and free the mind of the unconscious limits that accompanied those conventions. The writer Joan Didion turned a critical eye on the counterculture in her essay "Slouching Towards Bethlehem," excerpted below in the "Creative Nonfiction" cluster, but the counterculture was artistically enabling for many, including Didion herself, whose practice of reportage looked little like the conventional journalism of her day. Didion waxed personal in her reporting—breaking the rules of objectivity—as the counterculture around her took to heart the adage that "the personal is political."

"Dropping out" was the 1960s incarnation of an old impulse in American culture, one that can be traced back at least to Henry David Thoreau, alone in his cabin on Walden Pond writing essays about civil disobedience, who was jailed briefly upon his return to town for refusing to pay taxes that supported slavery and the war against Mexico. But this aspect of the counterculture was not as politically engaged as the model of Thoreau might suggest. The ethic of "dropping out" was perhaps most famously embodied by novelist Ken Kesey. Kesey became famous when he published *One Flew Over the Cuckoo's Nest* (1962), a best-selling novel that told the story of a man sent to a mental institution and, finally, lobotomized, because he would not conform to society's expectations. The money Kesey earned from this book supported him and a group of followers call-

The Merry Pranksters atop their bus, "Further."

ing themselves "The Merry Pranksters," who experimented with drugs, music, art, meditation, macrobiotic diets, and unusual social, sexual, and leadership arrangements. The Pranksters' compound in the redwood groves of La Honda, California, and their converted schoolbus, called "Further" and piloted by Neal Cassady, the model for Jack Kerouac's hero in *On the Road* (1957), became the symbols of the counterculture's ideals and excesses. Kesey's world was described in Thomas Wolfe's book *The Electric Kool-Aid Acid Test* (1968), an early example of a genre that came to be called "creative nonfiction." Like Hunter S. Thompson's "gonzo" journalism—in which the journalist immerses him- or herself in extreme experience in order to report on it vividly—this new genre of writing used literary language (in these cases, the high-energy poetic prose style of the Beat writers) to report on real people and events. Wolfe and Thompson crafted their styles to match—and to make the reader feel that she had somehow experienced—their wild subjects.

Testifying to the broadly shared celebration of the outsider in American prose writing, we can look back to Holden Caulfield in J. D. Salinger's *The Catcher in the Rye* (1951) and to the melancholy, misfit suburbanites of John Cheever's and John Updike's stories to round out the fellowship of nonconforming heroes. This was a durable narrative and thematic convention that long accompanied protest and cultural transformation but also had its politically quietist side. Nabokov, who told his college student audience they should not identify with characters, would not approve: America's newly expanded and diverse reading public embraced these figures and, yes, *identified* with them as culture heroes and fellow-travelers. That they still speak to readers today—many can be met in the pages of this volume of *The Norton Anthology of American Literature*—reveals how unconventionality itself can become a fertile and endlessly engaging convention.

LITERATURE AND AMERICAN MEDIA

While education, immigration, and political and cultural unrest had an enormous impact on America's readers and writers during the second half of the twentieth century, the medium of writing itself was suddenly surrounded by a rich and shifting context of new media. Many would say that writing—fiction, poetry, and plays especially—had to *compete* with other media in new ways, but that would oversimplify the matter. For the new media that developed after World War II and through into the twenty-first century are closely related to literature and together take up themes and ideas rooted in literature's longer history.

Two major developments dominate our sense of the media landscape of the late twentieth and early twenty-first centuries: first, the rise of television after the Second World War, and second, the invention of the Internet in the 1990s. These two forms of media—and of course, the second is better understood as a whole constellation of media, including text, moving and still images, and sound—fascinated not only their mass publics but also writers and dramatists whose very vocations made them highly aware of the powers and effects of different media. The very first "media theorist" was a trained literary critic, a Canadian-born professor named Marshall McLuhan, whose best-known book, *Understanding Media* (1964), consciously echoed the titles of the much-used literary textbooks of the New Criticism. Famous for his dictum that "the medium is the message," he argued that *how* something is communicated is sometimes the very essence of *what* it communicates. Television shows and print advertising were often the targets of his analyses, but he also wrote lovingly of medieval life, of a time before Gutenberg's printing press, when oral storytelling, music, and traveling dramatic productions constituted the public media of the day. McLuhan's attention to the material medium at the expense of content sometimes seemed absurd to his critics, but his emphasis reflected the public's sense that television in particular was changing American mass culture less because of what was said on television than because of how it delivered a culture of performance into living rooms across the country. The television networks took types of programs already well established in radio and on the vaudeville stage of the early twentieth century—such as the variety show, the interview or advice show, and cowboy and detective stories—and made them come alive every night on screens in American homes. In 1947, about 6,000 sets could be found in those homes; by 1951, the number was over 12 million. McLuhan's prolific writing and speaking about television made him a celebrity. When appointed by Fordham University to hold the prestigious Albert Schweitzer Chair, he was one of the highest paid English professors in the country (with a salary of $100,000 in 1967). He was so well known that Woody Allen gave him an amusing cameo in his film *Annie Hall* (1977): Allen's character pulls McLuhan out from behind a billboard in the lobby of a movie theater in order to refute an annoying man spouting media criticism while waiting in line for tickets. McLuhan lamented the passivity with which viewers received television. Allen makes the scene in which McLuhan appears a commentary on passivity. Allen breaks character and addresses the film's audience: "If life were only like this!" he says to the audience, as McLuhan gives the obnoxious moviegoer an intellectual dressing-down.

Media critic Marshall McLuhan (far right) and, addressing the audience, film-maker Woody Allen (center) in *Annie Hall* (1977).

The problem of passivity in the face of spectacle is something that television made urgent and that modern uses of drama highlight in the twentieth and twenty-first centuries. Television made Americans nightly spectators to realities that were far from entertaining. Images of violence against peaceful civil rights protesters and, in the late 1960s and '70s, images of the war in Vietnam—which many term the first "televised war"—galvanized national issues that might otherwise have seemed too local or too far away to engage people throughout the country. Viewers found their passivity challenged: What should they do with the violence or injustice that they saw in front of them on the screen? How did watching something implicate them as participants in what they watched? How did performance in social life constrain them—to norms of gender or race, for example? How might performance free them?

In twentieth- and twenty-first-century drama, playwrights experimented—as Woody Allen does in *Annie Hall*—with the so-called fourth wall, the side of the stage that faces the audience. They explored what would happen when a play broke through that wall, treating the whole theater, including the audience, as its staging area. Even public spaces—parks, streets, and museums—were treated as stages that could include random passersby. The term *fourth wall* comes from the eighteenth-century French playwright Denis Diderot; engaging the audience was routine in Shakespearean drama, and the audience is always crucial to comedy—we have to laugh in order for comedy to work. And in classical Greek drama, the fourth wall is broken whenever the chorus addresses the audience directly and comments on the action. Among the plays included in this volume, for instance, August Wilson's *Fences* (1983) provokes audiences to think about barriers and spheres of action, to consider how enclosures determine human beings' powers of expression. The stage, in every play, fences things in, and, therefore, fences things out. The counterculture experimented with "happenings" that moved performance out to public spaces where the question of what is fenced in or out becomes particularly acute. A description of one such performance appears in the excerpt from Didion's "Slouching Towards Bethlehem" in the Creative Nonfiction cluster in this volume: a performance by the San Francisco Mime Troupe in the section of Golden Gate Park known as the "Panhandle." Disturbingly, the troupe uses the racist tradition of blackface theater to goad people into resisting racist political structures; Didion implicitly asks the reader to consider whether such a performance finally undermines or reinforces racial stereotyping.

Avant-garde theater invites readers to think of theater as a place where such questions can be explored and where the real-life social roles that people perform can be experimented with. Even realist theater was tending toward this kind of self-conscious meditation on spectatorship. "Reality TV" in the twenty-first century, with its confession booths and "real" people, pushes right through the fourth wall, even as it gives the viewer an uncomfortable voyeuristic feeling as he or she passively consumes, as entertainment, the tears and abuses of the people on the show. What seemed in the early twentieth century like artificiality—the artwork's own acknowledgment that it is fictional—became the ultimate stamp of a certain kind of realism in the twenty-first century.

Poetry was affected, too, by the rising interest in theatricality that the new medium of television stimulated. One of the signal changes in poetic practice, starting with the Beat poets in the middle of the twentieth century, was the growing popularity of public poetry readings. Perhaps the most famous reading of the twentieth century occurred on October 7, 1955, at the Six Gallery in San Francisco—a converted garage with a toilet adjoining the stage area. Jack Kerouac passed the wine jug while Allen Ginsberg read *Howl*, which had not been heard before that night. After using the toilet with the door ajar in front of the audience, Ginsberg pulled up his pants, walked out, and read a tour de force poem that seemed to expose the bodies and the anguish of, as the poem put it, "the best minds of my generation." Joined that night by the poets of what came to be called the "San Francisco Renaissance," Ginsberg's performance reminded the world that poetry was an oral medium, an art of sound—a fact that had faded from view (rightly or wrongly) as readers absorbed the most famous poems of the early twentieth century, including T. S. Eliot's footnoted *The Waste Land* (1922), considered by some the ultimate modernist example of the art form. Readings such as the one at the Six Gallery treated poetry like jazz performance—an experience of musicality, improvisation, and blues-inspired rhythm and emotion. Robert Lowell explained that part of his own dramatic change of poetic style from formalism to free verse forms in the 1950s came from the realization that his more traditional poems would not make

ComCo (Communications Company) poster for a poetry reading by LeRoi Jones (1967). Chester Anderson Papers, Bancroft Library, University of California.

much of a splash at a reading. Sylvia Plath read "Daddy" on BBC radio shortly before her suicide in 1963, her flat, elegant tone playing like a chill wind on the surface of tightly controlled anger. Again and again the poets in this volume turn to music, from Theodore Roethke's "My Papa's Waltz," to the jazz-inspired poetry of Michael Harper, to the dancing figures and film scores in Tracy K. Smith's "Thirst" and "The Universe: Original Motion Picture Soundtrack."

While fiction, like poetry, began to be read onstage regularly during the period covered by this volume, it was not drama or live performance but film that intersected most broadly with narrative: Patricia Highsmith and Philip K. Dick wrote stories that were adapted regularly into popular Hollywood films; film features in Don DeLillo's stories almost as often as television does; and the crosscuts and dialogue of film can be discerned in fictional forms and settings throughout the period. Still-image media such as photography and painting interface with literature, too. Natasha Trethewey's poetry meditates on both these media. For her, they represent the deceptions and the truths of history that the poet must confront. Like Marshall McLuhan, Trethewey reveals messages inherent to different media, such as the oppressive racial spectatorship implicit in much photography, even—or especially—when it is used to reveal the beauty of the downtrodden. What does writing accomplish, then, that television, film, music, photography, and painting cannot quite achieve? Readers will find many answers among the selections here. Writers throughout the period wrestle with, borrow from, and sometimes engulf the media of their times as they reimagine what literature can be and do.

EXPERIMENT AND PLAY IN TWENTIETH- AND TWENTY-FIRST-CENTURY LITERATURE

What is "postmodern"? In contemporary parlance, this is an endlessly useful term that can describe practically anything aesthetically edgy or off-kilter, anything that bends genres or cultural registers, anything that comments on the welter of media in contemporary culture. Students coming to the study of the literature of this period for the first time might well use *postmodern* to define the works that were most influential in the second half of the twentieth century. The term suggests a variety of ideas and styles. Don DeLillo's *White Noise* (1985) has been considered one of the best fictional descriptions of life in postmodern America. Postmodern life is imagined by DeLillo as a heap of fragments, a babble of incessant voices flowing from modern media (radio, television, film, and cyberspace) to penetrate our perceptions and thoughts. In DeLillo's America, material consumption and entertainment become the goals of domestic and professional life, and his stories are crammed with cars, stores, fast food, breaking news, tourist attractions, screens, and sports. The human beings caught up in these pursuits, though, always suspect there is something beyond all these glittery attractions. In the face of such a world, the protagonist of *White Noise*, Jack Gladney, seeks genuine transcendence, looking variously to data, psychotropic drugs, mystical sound, and spiritual mantras in his search for meaning. The enchanting words Jack hears muttered by his sleeping daughter turn out to be the name of a car—"Toyota Celica." Is DeLillo suggesting that it is impossible to reclaim the soul in modern, commercial America? Or, rather, is transcendence available to us in all human culture, no matter how banal? Or is Jack's mistake simply funny? This sort of ambiguity and uncertainty, and the way DeLillo shifts between satire and sincerity, suggests what is so inviting to readers in the literature typically called "postmodern." Readers of fiction have found such openness to interpretation especially appealing in the exuberant satires of Thomas Pynchon, George Saunders, Lydia Davis, and Ishmael Reed, to name a few.

In poetry, writers embraced the task of re-enchanting the material, commercial world—a task that poets have been called to since the ancient Greek poet Hesiod celebrated human labor in "Works and Days." In "A Supermarket in California," Allen Ginsberg's speaker, walking and thinking of the nineteenth-century American poet Walt Whitman, looks at the grocery aisles with new wonder: "What peaches and what penumbras!" He catches earthy Walt squeezing the produce and eyeing the handsome grocery boys. Others felt it was poetry's job to probe the material properties of language itself. The poets known as the "L=A=N=G=U=A=G=E" school, and their experimentalist precursor, John Ashbery, questioned the basic expectations of meaning. What can language do and become if it is freed from the requirement that it steadily refer to the world? Perhaps poems should represent the distracted mind as it writes the poem, rather than some object that can discipline the poet's unruly attention. Such poetry can seem difficult—indeed, it *is* difficult to follow meaning and sense if these are not the underlying threads holding a poem together. And yet, like the ambiguous satires of the story writers, postmodern poetry most often wants to play *with* readers, not against them. Ashbery was inspired by mid-century abstract painting—by artists such as Jackson Pollock and Mark Rothko. Readers can take pleasure in the color, texture, feeling, connotations, and shapes of language even if its meanings remain elusive.

Writing in the second half of the twentieth century was not experimental only in matters of form. For many writers, the imperative to create challenging or innovative forms—be they poetic, narrative, or dramatic—paled in significance next to the social changes they, and the world around them, were experiencing. Realism, in whatever genre, could respond to the shocks of contemporary life. When the forms of modernist literature seemed too heady, too abstract, or too intellectual, realism offered a mode suited to the autobiographical and the personal. The poet Robert Lowell lived this transition in his own work: the poems in his first book, *Lord Weary's Castle* (1946), were formally intricate, lyrically beautiful, and concerned with large subjects—the Protestant legacy in commercial life, the spiritual condition of the nation. But in fact these concerns grew from Lowell's own past, from his distinguished, old New England Protestant family, a family from which he dissented when he converted to Catholicism in 1940. *Life Studies* (1959), Lowell's second volume of poetry, changed tack, driving straight for the autobiographical core of his art with freer forms, more direct language, and candid accounts of his ruined loves and his struggles with alcoholism, depression, and mania. Breaking with both social decorum and poetic form, a prose section acknowledges a possibly Jewish ancestor in the poet's white-Anglo-Saxon-Protestant family tree. Alongside work by other poets who used the so-called confessional approach to poetry—including Frank O'Hara, Anne Sexton, Sylvia Plath, Adrienne Rich, and Sharon Olds—Lowell's experiments with subject and form brought newly accessible urgency and emotion to lyric poetry in the decades after World War II. Billy Collins's popular contemporary poetry must be read in this context: the poem "I Chop Some Parsley While Listening to Art Blakey's Version of 'Three Blind Mice'" (1998) uses an immediately personal and ordinary (not to mention humorous) occasion to transcribe the poet's thoughts on the effects of music. This is a different kind of confession—there is no deep trauma remembered here, no scandal or lost love. And the poem doesn't push the boundaries of socially acceptable topics in the manner of confessional poetry. Rather, it pushes the boundaries of poetic relevance—chopping parsley? chopping onions? speculations about the three blind mice of nursery rhyme fame? But the poem's accessible realism and its unapologetic emotion owe a debt to the generation of poets that began with Lowell.

"From the modernism you choose you get the postmodernism you deserve." So declared the critic David Antin in his 1972 essay "Modernism and Postmodernism." Given the wide variety of aesthetic strategies people refer to when they use the word *postmodernism*, Antin is surely correct. While writers who have been called "postmodern" sometimes rejected or reacted against the early-twentieth-century writers and artists who have been called "modernists," their techniques and concerns are often continuous with those of these earlier practitioners. The writers of the early twentieth century took up socially taboo topics, were inspired by other artistic media, and wove high and low culture into their work. They wrestled with profound social changes and with a brutal, seemingly pointless war. And so when late-twentieth-century writers reacted against modernism, they had also decided what the movement meant. From the longer perspective of the twenty-first century, it's clear that the aesthetic epoch reflected in much of this section could just as well be termed "long modernism." Like their early-twentieth-century precursors, many of the writers included here experiment with literary form and subject as an antidote to what they see as the violent, empty, fragmented, and soul-crushingly conventional forms of modern life.

What is truly *post*modern, then? Writers such as Natasha Trethewey, Patricia Highsmith, and George Saunders turn to personal history, to lowbrow visual media, to the new languages of business, and to genres such as horror and science fiction for sources of inspiration and provocation that were not typical for writers of the early twentieth century. Consider, for instance, how a lesbian pulp novel such as *The Fear and the Guilt* (1954), by Wilene Shaw (the pen name of Virginia M. Harrison), sports its genre conventions on its cover: Ruby brings her lover, Christy, to her southern home, where Christy is seduced by Ruby's father (and agrees to marry him). By contrast, Highsmith's carefully crafted realist novel, *The Price of Salt* (1952), upended such pulp conventions. It is a love story between two women with an unprecedented happy ending for the couple. Though some critics have noted how its narrative artistry seems to have inspired the cross-

Cover of original 1952 edition of *The Price of Salt*, by Patricia Highsmith, publishing under the pseudonym Claire Morgan. The book's imagery and format placed it in the company of lowbrow erotic genre fiction such as the example on the right, *The Fear and the Guilt* (1954).

country car chase in Nabokov's *Lolita*, and while it is clear that Highsmith learned much from the great modern novelist Henry James, *The Price of Salt* wore a paperback cover and looked as steamy as its pulp sisters. Harkening back to the literature of the nineteenth century, writers understood as postmodern in this sense seek to make readers *feel* something even while they revel in satire and irony, while (for all their confessional force) the writers of "long modernism" can be suspicious of sentiment. Rejecting or reimagining what "elite" literature might look like, writers looking for alternatives to a dominant and elite modernism likewise reimagine their readers and pave the way for the innovations of a writer like Junot Díaz.

LITERATURE NOW

In the United States alone, over 50,000 novels are published each year. Worldwide, the number is well over 200,000. It is cheaper and easier than ever to make written works available to readers. Writing programs have made the professional lives of poets and other writers sustainable, even when their work doesn't turn a profit in the publishing market. The Association of Writers and Writing Programs reports that in 1975 there were a total of 79 programs granting creative writing degrees ranging from the

Author **Grace Paley** teaching writing at Sarah Lawrence College.

associate's degree to the Ph.D. In 2012 that number was 880. The teaching now done by many writers not only allows them to continue writing but also trains new writers, whose work can in turn be found in the ever-increasing numbers of creative writing journals and websites, as well as in the blogs, posts, and Twitter feeds generated daily to keep Web content fresh. If the ranks of readers and writers expanded dramatically in the United States in the wake of World War II, how much more has the audience for writing of all kinds expanded—but also fragmented—in the wake of the Internet? The rise of digital culture and of global publishing has made the ubiquity of writing, and of English, suddenly obvious.

One argument about what literature looks like now is that it is defined by its global audience, massive production, and transnational use of English. The literary critic Rebecca Walkowitz notes that many of the most successful writers now labor with the knowledge that their work will instantly be translated into multiple languages. She argues that this fact has driven a resurgence in literary experimentation with plot and character, elements of fiction that "survive" translation in ways that more material aspects of language—grammar, sound, etymology—cannot. Others point to the way that the migration of literary works to unexpected new contexts changes the interpretation and social meaning of those works. Critics have tracked, for instance, how the southern novelist William Faulkner was received in Japan in the twentieth century, or how the movie *Shrek* has been remade and repurposed by digital film artists in Iran. And Web formats privilege some forms of writing over others: fiction with short (that is, easily scrollable) chapters or sections translates better to online contexts than narratives made up of longer blocks of text. Poetry, by contrast, translates beautifully to the screen. In turn, poetry and fiction appearing in traditional print form sometimes borrow styles from texting, posts, and tweets. Readers should be sure to explore the Poetry Foundation's excellent website, which provides additional poems and readings by virtually every poet in this anthology.

What does all the writing sparked by the rise of the Internet tell us about literature today? Crucially, it reminds us that language itself is a living thing, an artistic medium that changes in the very hands of the writers and speakers who use it. Physical and virtual migrations of people and their writing in the contemporary world are driven by economic, political, religious, and personal forces—forces that call out now, as they always have, for a response in art. As Junot Díaz, Gloria Anzaldúa, Maxine Hong Kingston, Tracy K. Smith, and other writers fold multiple languages into their literary works, they recraft the English we have at our disposal. African immigration, the rise of Spanish as an American language (just as German was in the American West in the nineteenth century), and immigrations yet to come will continually reshape the literary landscape. Today, writing flourishes at the grass roots, much of it thriving apart from major publishers, advertisers, and reviewing venues even as the most admired of the writers in the last half-century become the touchstones of an evolving tradition. While this overabundance has unsettled any shared sense of what merits readers' attention, it also indicates the extraordinary energy and possibility in American literature now. Intrepid readers who go exploring will find as-yet-undiscovered wonders.

AMERICAN LITERATURE SINCE 1945

TEXTS	CONTEXTS
1941 Eudora Welty, **"Petrified Man"**	
1945 Randall Jarrell, **"The Death of the Ball Turret Gunner"**	1945 U.S. drops atomic bombs on Hiroshima and Nagasaki; Japan surrenders, ending World War II • Cold War begins
1947 Tennesse Williams, *A Streetcar Named Desire*	1947 Jackie Robinson becomes the first black Major League ballplayer
1948 Theodore Roethke, *The Lost Son*	
1949 Arthur Miller, *Death of a Salesman*	
1950 Richard Wilbur, "A World without Objects Is a Sensible Emptiness" • Charles Olson, "Projective Verse"	1950 Senator Joseph McCarthy begins attacks on supposed Communist influence on U.S. government
	1950–53 Korean War
1952 Ralph Ellison, *Invisible Man*	
1953 Saul Bellow, *The Adventures of Augie March*	1953 House Concurrent Resolution 108 dictates government's intention to "terminate" its treaty relations with Native American tribes
	1954 *Brown v. Board of Education* declares segregated schools unconstitutional • Beat Generation poets begin to gather at San Francisco's City Lights Bookshop
1955 Flannery O'Connor, **"Good Country People"**	
1955–68 John Berryman composes *The Dream Songs* (pub. 1964, 1968, 1977)	
1956 Allen Ginsberg, *Howl*	1956 Martin Luther King Jr. leads bus boycott in Montgomery, Alabama
1957 Jack Kerouac, *On the Road*	
1958 Bernard Malamud, "The Magic Barrel"	
1959 Philip Roth, **"Defender of the Faith"** • Robert Lowell, *Life Studies* • Frank O'Hara, "Personism"	1959 Fidel Castro becomes Communist leader of Cuba
1960 Thomas Pynchon, **"Entropy"** • Gwendolyn Brooks, **"We Real Cool"**	1960 Woolworth lunch counter sit-in in Greensboro, North Carolina, marks beginning of civil rights movement
1961 Denise Levertov, **"The Jacob's Ladder"**	
1962 Robert Hayden, **"Middle Passage"**	1962 United States and Soviet Union come close to war over Russian missiles based in Cuba; missiles withdrawn
1963 James Wright, "A Blessing"	1963 Martin Luther King Jr. delivers "I Have a Dream" speech • black church in Birmingham, Alabama, bombed, killing four girls • President John F. Kennedy assassinated

Boldface titles indicate works in the anthology.

TEXTS	CONTEXTS
1964 John Cheever, **"The Swimmer"** • Amiri Baraka (LeRoi Jones), **"An Agony. As Now."** • Frank O'Hara, "A Step Away from Them" • Philip K. Dick, "Precious Artifact"	
1965 James Baldwin, **"Going to Meet the Man"** • A. R. Ammons, "Corson's Inlet"	**1965** Riots break out in Watts section of Los Angeles • Malcolm X assassinated • hippie culture flourishes in San Francisco
	1965–73 Vietnam War
1966 James Merrill, "The Broken Home" • Sylvia Plath, *Ariel*	**1966** National Organization for Women (NOW) founded • Hayden and Brooks criticized at Black Writers' Conference, Fisk University, for composing "academic" poetry
1967 A. R. Ammons, "A Poem Is a Walk" • W. S. Merwin, "For a Coming Extinction" • Patricia Highsmith, **"The Quest for *Blank Claveringi*"**	
1968 Donald Barthelme, "The Balloon" • Edward Abbey, *Desert Solitaire* • Joan Didion, **"Slouching Towards Bethlehem"**	**1968** Martin Luther King Jr. assassinated • Senator Robert F. Kennedy assassinated • photo of Earthrise by Apollo 8
1969 N. Scott Momaday, *The Way to Rainy Mountain* • Kurt Vonnegut, *Slaughterhouse-Five* • Galway Kinnell, "The Porcupine" • Robert Penn Warren, *Audubon*	**1969** U.S. astronauts land on the moon • Stonewall riots in New York City initiate gay liberation movement • Woodstock Festival held near Bethel, New York
1970 Ishmael Reed, "Neo-HooDoo Manifesto"	**1970** National Guard kills four students during antiwar demonstration at Kent State University, Ohio
1971 Audre Lorde, **"Black Mother Woman"**	
1972 Rudolfo Anaya, *Bless Me, Ultima* • Anne Sexton, *The Death of the Fathers*	**1972** Watergate scandal • military draft ends
1973 Alice Walker, **"Everyday Use"** • Adrienne Rich, *Diving into the Wreck*	**1973** *Roe v. Wade* legalizes abortion • American Indian Movement members occupy Wounded Knee, South Dakota
1974 Grace Paley, "A Conversation with My Father" • Annie Dillard, *Pilgrim at Tinker Creek*	**1974** President Richard Nixon resigns in wake of Watergate, avoiding impeachment
1975 John Updike, **"Separating"** • John Ashbery, "Self-Portrait in a Convex Mirror" • Michael S. Harper, "Nightmare Begins Responsibility"	
1976 Elizabeth Bishop, *Geography III* • Maxine Hong Kingston, **"No Name Woman"** • Barry Lopez, *Desert Notes*	**1976** U.S. bicentennial
1977 Audre Lorde, "Poetry Is Not a Luxury"	
1978 Ann Beattie, "Weekend" • Jamaica Kincaid, **"Girl"**	
1979 Philip Levine, "Starlight" • Mary Oliver, "The Black Snake"	

TEXTS	CONTEXTS
1980 Toni Cade Bambara, "Medley" • Sam Shepard, *True West*	
1981 Leslie Marmon Silko, **"Lullaby"** • James Dickey, "Falling" • Simon J. Ortiz, "From Sand Creek"	
1982 Raymond Carver, **"Cathedral"** • David Mamet, *Glengarry Glen Ross*	**1982** Equal Rights Amendment defeated • antinuclear movement protests manufacture of nuclear weapons • AIDS officially identified in the United States
1983 Toni Morrison, **"Recitatif"** • Joy Harjo, **"Call It Fear"**	
1984 Louise Erdrich, **"Dear John Wayne"**	
1985 Ursula K. Le Guin, "She Unnames Them" • Don DeLillo, ***White Noise***	**1985** Introduction of first desktop publishing software, Aldus pagemaker
1986 Lydia Davis, "Break It Down" • Art Spiegelman, *Maus I* • Rita Dove, *Thomas and Beulah* • Li-Young Lee, **"Eating Together"**	
1987 Gloria Anzaldúa, *Borderlands/La Frontera* • Sharon Olds, "I Go Back to May 1937"	
1988 Yusef Komunyakaa, **"Facing It"**	
1989 Amy Tan, *The Joy Luck Club*	**1989** Soviet Union collapses; Cold War ends • oil tanker *Exxon Valdez* runs aground in Alaska
1990 Robert Pinsky, "The Want Bone" • Frank Bidart, "Ellen West"	**1990** Congress passes Native American Graves Protection and Repatriation Act
1991 Sandra Cisneros, ***Woman Hollering Creek***	**1991** United States enters Persian Gulf War • World Wide Web introduced
1992 Edward P. Jones, "The First Day"	
1993 Gary Snyder, "Ripples on the Surface" • A. R. Ammons, *Garbage* • Sherman Alexie, "This Is What It Means to Say Phoenix, Arizona"	
	1995 Federal building in Oklahoma City bombed in a terrorist attack
1996 W. S. Merwin, "Lament for the Makers" • Sherman Alexie, "The Exaggeration of Despair" • Junot Díaz, **"Drown"** • George Saunders, **"CivilWar-Land in Bad Decline"**	
	1997 *Mars Pathfinder* robot explores Mars
1998 Billy Collins, "I Chop Some Parsley While Listening to Art Blakey's Version of 'Three Blind Mice'"	

TEXTS	CONTEXTS
1999 Jhumpa Lahiri, **"Sexy"** • Charles Simic, "Arriving Celebrities"	
2000 Lucille Clifton, "Moonchild"	
	2001 Execution of Timothy McVeigh, convicted of 1995 Oklahoma City bombing • September 11 terrorist attacks on Pentagon and World Trade Center
	2003 United States and Great Britain invade Iraq
2004 Louise Glück, "October" • David Foster Wallace, **"Consider the Lobster"**	
2006 Natasha Trethewey, *Native Guard*	
2007 Edwidge Danticat, *Brother, I'm Dying* • Junot Díaz, *The Brief Wondrous Life of Oscar Wao*	2007 Advent of worst economic recession since the Great Depression.
	2009 Inauguration of Barack Obama as U.S. president
	2010 Massive oil spill in the Gulf of Mexico
2011 Tracy K. Smith, "My God, It's Full of Stars"	2011 Death of terrorist leader Osama bin Laden, architect of 9/11 attacks
	2013 Second inauguration of Barack Obama as U.S. president
	2014 Police shooting of an unarmed black teenager named Michael Brown in Ferguson, Missouri, touches off nationwide protests
	2015 U.S. Supreme Court rules that state bans on same-sex marriage are unconstitutional • hundreds of thousands of migrants from Syria and other areas in the Middle East cross into Europe

THEODORE ROETHKE
1908–1963

Theodore Roethke had the kind of childhood a poet might have invented. He was born in Saginaw, Michigan, where both his German grandfather and his father kept greenhouses for a living. The greenhouse world, he later said, represented for him "both heaven and hell, a kind of tropics created in the savage climate of Michigan, where austere German Americans turned their love of order and their terrifying efficiency into something truly beautiful." Throughout his life he was haunted both by the ordered, protected world of the greenhouse—the constant activity of growth, the cultivated flowers—and by the desolate landscape of his part of Michigan. "The marsh, the mire, the Void, is always there, immediate and terrifying. It is a splendid place for schooling the spirit. It is America."

Roethke's poetry often reenacted this "schooling" of the spirit by revisiting the landscapes of his childhood: the nature poems that make up the largest part of his early work try to bridge the distance between a child's consciousness and the adult mysteries presided over by his father. Roethke arranged and rearranged these poems to give the sense of a spiritual autobiography, especially in preparing the volumes *The Lost Son and Other Poems* (1948), *Praise to the End!* (1951), and *The Waking* (1953). In what are known as "the greenhouse poems," the greenhouse world emerged as a "reality harsher than reality," the cultivator's activity pulsating and threatening. Its overseers, like "Frau Bauman, Frau Schmidt, and Frau Schwartze" (the title of one poem) emerge as gods, fates, muses, and witches all in one. By focusing on the minute processes of botanical growth—the rooting, the budding—the poet found a way of participating in the mysteries of this once alien world, whether he was deep in the subterranean root cellar or, as a child, perched high on top of the greenhouse.

In his books *The Lost Son* and *Praise to the End!* Roethke explored the regenerative possibilities of prerational speech (like children's riddles) in which language as sound recaptures nonlogical states of being. In these poems, his most dazzling and original work, Roethke opened up the possibilities of language. The title of one section of the long poem *The Lost Son* is "The Gibber," a pun because the word means both a meaningless utterance and the pouch at the base of a flower's calyx. The pun identifies principles of growth with the possibilities of speech freed from logical meanings, and the sequence as a whole suggests the power of both nature and language to revive the spirit of an adult life: "A lively understandable spirit / Once entertained you. / It will come again. / Be still. / Wait."

If the nature poems of Roethke's first four books explore the anxieties within him since childhood, his later love poems show him in periods of release and momentary pleasure: "And I dance round and round, / A fond and foolish man, / And see and suffer myself / In another being at last." The love poems, many included in *Words for the Wind* (1958) and *The Far Field* (1964), are among the most appealing in modern American verse. His beautiful and tender "Elegy for Jane" should be included in this category. These poems stand in sharp relief to the suffering Roethke experienced in other areas of his personal life—several mental breakdowns and periods of alcoholism—which led to a premature death. *The Far Field*, a posthumous volume, includes fierce, strongly rhymed lyrics in which Roethke tried "bare, even terrible statement," pressing toward the threshold of spiritual insight: "A man goes far to find out what he is— / Death of the self in a long, tearless night, / All natural shapes blazing unnatural light." The nature poems of this last volume, gathered as "The North American Sequence," use extended landscape to find natural analogies for the human passage toward the dark unknown, hoping "in their rhythms to catch the very movement of mind itself."

Roethke is remembered as one of the great teachers of poetry, especially by those young poets and critics who studied with him at the University of Washington from 1948 until the time of his death. James Wright, David Wagoner, and Richard Hugo, among others, attended his classes. He was noted for his mastery of sound and metrics. Although his own poetry was intensely personal, his starting advice to students always deemphasized undisciplined self-expression. "Write like someone else," he instructed beginners. In Roethke's own career, however, this advice had its costs. His apprenticeship to Yeats, in particular, endangered his own poetic voice; in some late poems the echo of this great predecessor makes Roethke all but inaudible.

Roethke was much honored later in his career: a Pulitzer Prize for *The Waking* (1953); a National Book Award and Bollingen Prize for the collected poems, *Words for the Wind* (1958); and a posthumous National Book Award for *The Far Field* (1964).

Cuttings

Sticks-in-a-drowse droop over sugary loam,
Their intricate stem-fur dries;
But still the delicate slips keep coaxing up water;
The small cells bulge;

One nub of growth   5
Nudges a sand-crumb loose,
Pokes through a musty sheath
Its pale tendrilous horn.

1948

Cuttings

(later)

This urge, wrestle, resurrection of dry sticks,
Cut stems struggling to put down feet,
What saint strained so much,
Rose on such lopped limbs to a new life?

I can hear, underground, that sucking and sobbing,   5
In my veins, in my bones I feel it,—
The small waters seeping upward,
The tight grains parting at last.
When sprouts break out,
Slippery as fish   10
I quail, lean to beginnings, sheath-wet.

1948

My Papa's Waltz

The whiskey on your breath
Could make a small boy dizzy;
But I hung on like death:
Such waltzing was not easy.

We romped until the pans   5
Slid from the kitchen shelf;
My mother's countenance
Could not unfrown itself.

The hand that held my wrist
Was battered on one knuckle;   10
At every step you missed
My right ear scraped a buckle.

You beat time on my head
With a palm caked hard by dirt,
Then waltzed me off to bed   15
Still clinging to your shirt.

                                                        1948

Dolor

I have known the inexorable sadness of pencils,
Neat in their boxes, dolor of pad and paper-weight,
All the misery of manilla folders and mucilage,
Desolation in immaculate public places,
Lonely reception room, lavatory, switchboard,   5
The unalterable pathos of basin and pitcher,
Ritual of multigraph, paper-clip, comma,
Endless duplication of lives and objects.
And I have seen dust from the walls of institutions,
Finer than flour, alive, more dangerous than silica,   10
Sift, almost invisible, through long afternoons of tedium,
Dropping a fine film on nails and delicate eyebrows,
Glazing the pale hair, the duplicate grey standard faces.

                                                        1948

The Waking

I wake to sleep, and take my waking slow.
I feel my fate in what I cannot fear.
I learn by going where I have to go.

We think by feeling. What is there to know?
I hear my being dance from ear to ear.   5
I wake to sleep, and take my waking slow.

Of those so close beside me, which are you?
God bless the Ground! I shall walk softly there,
And learn by going where I have to go.

Light takes the Tree; but who can tell us how?   10
The lowly worm climbs up a winding stair;
I wake to sleep, and take my waking slow.

Great Nature has another thing to do
To you and me; so take the lively air,
And, lovely, learn by going where to go.   15

This shaking keeps me steady. I should know.
What falls away is always. And is near.
I wake to sleep, and take my waking slow.
I learn by going where I have to go.

                                                                    1953

Elegy for Jane

My Student, Thrown by a Horse

I remember the neckcurls, limp and damp as tendrils;
And her quick look, a sidelong pickerel smile;
And how, once startled into talk, the light syllables leaped for her,
And she balanced in the delight of her thought,
A wren, happy, tail into the wind,   5
Her song trembling the twigs and small branches.
The shade sang with her;
The leaves, their whispers turned to kissing;
And the mold sang in the bleached valleys under the rose.

Oh, when she was sad, she cast herself down into such a pure depth, 10
Even a father could not find her:
Scraping her cheek against straw;
Stirring the clearest water.

My sparrow, you are not here,
Waiting like a fern, making a spiny shadow.   15
The sides of wet stones cannot console me,
Nor the moss, wound with the last light.

If only I could nudge you from this sleep,
My maimed darling, my skittery pigeon.
Over this damp grave I speak the words of my love: 20
I, with no rights in this matter,
Neither father nor lover.

                                                                    1953

I Knew a Woman

I knew a woman, lovely in her bones,
When small birds sighed, she would sigh back at them;
Ah, when she moved, she moved more ways than one:
The shapes a bright container can contain!
Of her choice virtues only gods should speak,   5
Or English poets who grew up on Greek
(I'd have them sing in chorus, cheek to cheek).

How well her wishes went! She stroked my chin,
She taught me Turn, and Counter-turn, and Stand;[1]
She taught me Touch, that undulant white skin;   10
I nibbled meekly from her proffered hand;
She was the sickle; I, poor I, the rake,
Coming behind her for her pretty sake
(But what prodigious mowing we did make).

Love likes a gander, and adores a goose: 15
Her full lips pursed, the errant note to seize;
She played it quick, she played it light and loose;
My eyes, they dazzled at her flowing knees;
Her several parts could keep a pure repose,
Or one hip quiver with a mobile nose   20
(She moved in circles, and those circles moved).

Let seed be grass, and grass turn into hay:
I'm martyr to a motion not my own;
What's freedom for? To know eternity.
I swear she cast a shadow white as stone.   25
But who would count eternity in days?
These old bones live to learn her wanton ways:
(I measure time by how a body sways).

1958

---

1. The triadic parts of a Pindaric ode, a ceremonious poem in the manner of the Greek lyric poet Pindar (c. 522–c. 438 B.C.E.).

EUDORA WELTY
1909–2001

I n her essay "Place in Fiction," Eudora Welty spoke of her work as filled with the spirit of place: "Location is the ground conductor of all the currents of emotion and belief and moral conviction that charge out from the story in its course." Both her outwardly uneventful life and her writing are most intimately connected to the topography and atmosphere, the season and the soil of Mississippi, her lifelong home.

Born in Jackson to parents who came from the North, and raised in comfortable circumstances (her father headed an insurance company), she attended Mississippi State College for Women, then graduated from the University of Wisconsin in 1929. After a course in advertising at the Columbia University School of Business, she returned to Mississippi, working first as a radio writer and newspaper society editor, then for the Depression-era Works Progress Administration, taking photographs of and interviewing local residents. Those travels would be reflected in her fiction and also in a book of her photographs, *One Time and Place*, published in 1971.

She began writing fiction after her return to Mississippi in 1931 and five years later published her first story, "Death of a Traveling Salesman," in a small magazine. Over the next two years six of her stories were published in the *Southern Review*, a serious literary magazine one of whose editors was the poet and novelist Robert Penn Warren. She also received strong support from Katherine Anne Porter, who contributed an introduction to Welty's first book of stories, *A Curtain of Green* (1941). That introduction hailed the arrival of another gifted southern fiction writer, and in fact the volume contained some of the best stories she ever wrote, such as "Petrified Man." Her profusion of metaphor and the difficult surface of her narrative—often oblique and indirect in its effect—were in part a mark of her admiration for modern writers like Virginia Woolf and (as with any young southern writer) William Faulkner. Although Welty's stories were as shapely as those of her mentor, Porter, they were more richly idiomatic and comic in their inclination. A second collection, *The Wide Net*, appeared two years later; and her first novel, *The Robber Bridegroom*, was published in 1942.

In that year and the next she was awarded the O. Henry Memorial Prize for the best piece of short fiction, and from then on she received a steady stream of awards and prizes, including the Pulitzer Prize for her novel *The Optimist's Daughter* (1972). Her most ambitious and longest piece of fiction is *Losing Battles* (1970), in which she aimed to compose a narrative made up almost wholly out of her characters' voices in mainly humorous interplay. Like Robert Frost, Welty loved gossip in all its actuality and intimacy, and if that love failed in the novels to produce compelling, extended sequences, it did result in many lively and entertaining pages. Perhaps her finest single book after *A Curtain of Green* was *The Golden Apples* (1949), a sequence of tales about a fabulous, invented, small Mississippi community named Morgana. Her characters appear and reappear in these related stories and come together most memorably in the brilliant "June Recital," perhaps her masterpiece.

Throughout her fiction Welty's wonderfully sharp sense of humor is strongly evident. Although her characters often consist of involuted southern families, physically handicapped, mentally retarded, or generally unstable kinfolk—and although her narratives are shot through with undercurrents of death, violence, and degradation—Welty transforms everything with an entertaining twist. No matter how desperate a situation may be, she makes us listen to the way a character talks about it; we pay attention to style rather than information. And although her attitude toward human folly is satiric, her satire is devoid of the wish to undermine and mock her characters. Instead, the vivid realizations of her prose give them irresistible life and a memorable expressiveness. Yet she remarked in an essay that "fine story writers seem to be in a sense obstructionists," and Welty's narratives unfold through varied repetitions or reiterations that have, she once claimed, the function of a deliberate double exposure in photography. By making us pay close attention to who is speaking and the implications of that speech, by asking us to imagine the way in which a silent character is responding to that speech, and by making us read behind the deceptively simple response she gives to that character, she makes us active readers, playfully engaged in a typically complicated scene. "Why I Live at the P.O.," "Keela, the Outcast Indian Maiden," "Powerhouse," "June Recital," "Petrified Man," and many others demonstrate the strength and the joy of her art. And although she has been called a "regional" writer, she has noted the condescending nature of that term, which she calls an "outsider's term; it has no meaning for the insider who is doing the writing, because as far as he knows he is simply writing about life" (*On Writing*). So it is with Eudora Welty's fiction.

The text is from *A Curtain of Green* (1941).

Petrified Man

"Reach in my purse and git me a cigarette without no powder in it if you kin, Mrs. Fletcher, honey," said Leota to her ten o'clock shampoo-and-set customer. "I don't like no perfumed cigarettes."

Mrs. Fletcher gladly reached over to the lavender shelf under the lavender-framed mirror, shook a hair net loose from the clasp of the patent-leather bag, and slapped her hand down quickly on a powder puff which burst out when the purse was opened.

"Why, look at the peanuts, Leota!" said Mrs. Fletcher in her marvelling voice.

"Honey, them goobers has been in my purse a week if they's been in it a day. Mrs. Pike bought them peanuts."

"Who's Mrs. Pike?" asked Mrs. Fletcher, settling back. Hidden in this den of curling fluid and henna[1] packs, separated by a lavender swing-door from the other customers, who were being gratified in other booths, she could give her curiosity its freedom. She looked expectantly at the black part in Leota's yellow curls as she bent to light the cigarette.

"Mrs. Pike is this lady from New Orleans," said Leota, puffing, and pressing into Mrs. Fletcher's scalp with strong red-nailed fingers. "A friend, not a customer. You see, like maybe I told you last time, me and Fred and Sal and Joe all had us a fuss, so Sal and Joe up and moved out, so we didn't do a thing but rent out their room. So we rented it to Mrs. Pike. And Mr. Pike." She flicked an ash into the basket of dirty towels. "Mrs. Pike is a very decided blonde. *She* bought me the peanuts."

"She must be cute," said Mrs. Fletcher.

"Honey, 'cute' ain't the word for what she is. I'm tellin' you, Mrs. Pike is attractive. She has her a good time. She's got a sharp eye out, Mrs. Pike has."

---

1. Reddish brown dye for tinting hair.

She dashed the comb through the air, and paused dramatically as a cloud of Mrs. Fletcher's hennaed hair floated out of the lavender teeth like a small storm-cloud.

"Hair fallin'."

"Aw, Leota."

"Uh-huh, commencin' to fall out," said Leota, combing again, and letting fall another cloud.

"Is it any dandruff in it?" Mrs. Fletcher was frowning, her hair-line eyebrows diving down toward her nose, and her wrinkled, beady-lashed eyelids batting with concentration.

"Nope." She combed again. "Just fallin' out."

"Bet it was that last perm'nent you gave me that did it," Mrs. Fletcher said cruelly. "Remember you cooked me fourteen minutes."

"You had fourteen minutes comin' to you," said Leota with finality.

"Bound to be somethin'," persisted Mrs. Fletcher. "Dandruff, dandruff. I couldn't of caught a thing like that from Mr. Fletcher, could I?"

"Well," Leota answered at last, "you know what I heard in here yestiddy, one of Thelma's ladies was settin' over yonder in Thelma's booth gittin' a machineless, and I don't mean to insist or insinuate or anything, Mrs. Fletcher, but Thelma's lady just happ'med to throw out—I forgotten what she was talkin' about at the time—that you was p-r-e-g., and lots of times that'll make your hair do awful funny, fall out and God knows what all. It just ain't our fault, is the way I look at it."

There was a pause. The women stared at each other in the mirror.

"Who was it?" demanded Mrs. Fletcher.

"Honey, I really couldn't say," said Leota. "Not that you look it."

"Where's Thelma? I'll get it out of her," said Mrs. Fletcher.

"Now, honey, I wouldn't go and git mad over a little thing like that," Leota said, combing hastily, as though to hold Mrs. Fletcher down by the hair. "I'm sure it was somebody didn't mean no harm in the world. How far gone are you?"

"Just wait," said Mrs. Fletcher, and shrieked for Thelma, who came in and took a drag from Leota's cigarette.

"Thelma, honey, throw your mind back to yestiddy if you kin," said Leota, drenching Mrs. Fletcher's hair with a thick fluid and catching the overflow in a cold wet towel at her neck.

"Well, I got my lady half wound for a spiral," said Thelma doubtfully.

"This won't take but a minute," said Leota. "Who is it you got in there, old Horse Face? Just cast your mind back and try to remember who your lady was yestiddy who happ'm to mention that my customer was pregnant, that's all. She's dead to know."

Thelma drooped her blood-red lips and looked over Mrs. Fletcher's head into the mirror. "Why, honey, I ain't got the faintest," she breathed. "I really don't recollect the faintest. But I'm sure she meant no harm. I declare, I forgot my hair finally got combed and thought it was a stranger behind me."

"Was it that Mrs. Hutchinson?" Mrs. Fletcher was tensely polite.

"Mrs. Hutchinson? Oh, Mrs. Hutchinson." Thelma batted her eyes. "Naw, precious, she come on Thursday and didn't ev'm mention your name. I doubt if she ev'm knows you're on the way."

"Thelma!" cried Leota staunchly.

"All I know is, whoever it is 'll be sorry some day. Why, I just barely knew it myself!" cried Mrs. Fletcher. "Just let her wait!"

"Why? What're you gonna do to her?"

It was a child's voice, and the women looked down. A little boy was making tents with aluminum wave pinchers[2] on the floor under the sink.

"Billy Boy, hon, mustn't bother nice ladies," Leota smiled. She slapped him brightly and behind her back waved Thelma out of the booth. "Ain't Billy Boy a sight? Only three years old and already just nuts about the beauty-parlor business."

"I never saw him here before," said Mrs. Fletcher, still unmollified.

"He ain't been here before, that's how come," said Leota. "He belongs to Mrs. Pike. She got her a job but it was Fay's Millinery. He oughtn't to try on those ladies' hats, they come down over his eyes like I don't know what. They just git to look ridiculous, that's what, an' of course he's gonna put 'em on: hats. They tole Mrs. Pike they didn't appreciate him hangin' around there. Here, he couldn't hurt a thing."

"Well! I don't like children that much," said Mrs. Fletcher.

"Well!" said Leota moodily.

"Well! I'm almost tempted not to have this one," said Mrs. Fletcher. "That Mrs. Hutchinson! Just looks straight through you when she sees you on the street and then spits at you behind your back."

"Mr. Fletcher would beat you on the head if you didn't have it now," said Leota reasonably. "After going this far."

Mrs. Fletcher sat up straight. "Mr. Fletcher can't do a thing with me."

"He can't!" Leota winked at herself in the mirror.

"No, siree, he can't. If he so much as raises his voice against me, he knows good and well I'll have one of my sick headaches, and then I'm just not fit to live with. And if I really look that pregnant already—"

"Well, now, honey, I just want you to know—I habm't told any of my ladies and I ain't goin' to tell 'em—even that you're losin' your hair. You just get you one of those Stork-a-Lure dresses and stop worryin'. What people don't know don't hurt nobody, as Mrs. Pike says."

"Did you tell Mrs. Pike?" asked Mrs. Fletcher sulkily.

"Well, Mrs. Fletcher, look, you ain't ever goin' to lay eyes on Mrs. Pike or her lay eyes on you, so what diffunce does it make in the long run?"

"I knew it!" Mrs. Fletcher deliberately nodded her head so as to destroy a ringlet Leota was working on behind her ear. "Mrs. Pike!"

Leota sighed. "I reckon I might as well tell you. It wasn't any more Thelma's lady tole me you was pregnant than a bat."

"Not Mrs. Hutchinson?"

"Naw, Lord! It was Mrs. Pike."

"Mrs. Pike!" Mrs. Fletcher could only sputter and let curling fluid roll into her ear. "How could Mrs. Pike possibly know I was pregnant or otherwise, when she doesn't even know me? The nerve of some people!"

"Well, here's how it was. Remember Sunday?"

"Yes," said Mrs. Fletcher.

---

2. Clips used to form and hold (or set) hair curl or wave.

"Sunday, Mrs. Pike an' me was all by ourself. Mr. Pike and Fred had gone over to Eagle Lake, sayin' they was goin' to catch 'em some fish, but they didn't a course. So we was gettin' in Mrs. Pike's car, it's a 1939 Dodge—"

"1939, eh," said Mrs. Fletcher.

"—An' we was gettin' us a Jax beer apiece—that's the beer that Mrs. Pike says is made right in N.O., so she won't drink no other kind. So I seen you drive up to the drugstore an' run in for just a secont, leavin' I reckon Mr. Fletcher in the car, an' come runnin' out with looked like a perscription. So I says to Mrs. Pike, just to be makin' talk, 'Right yonder's Mrs. Fletcher, and I reckon that's Mr. Fletcher—she's one of my regular customers,' I says."

"I had on a figured print," said Mrs. Fletcher tentatively.

"You sure did," agreed Leota. "So Mrs. Pike, she give you a good look— she's very observant, a good judge of character, cute as a minute, you know— and she says, 'I bet you another Jax that lady's three months on the way.'"

"What gall!" said Mrs. Fletcher. "Mrs. Pike!"

"Mrs. Pike ain't goin' to bite you," said Leota. "Mrs. Pike is a lovely girl, you'd be crazy about her, Mrs. Fletcher. But she can't sit still a minute. We went to the travellin' freak show yestiddy after work. I got through early— nine o'clock. In the vacant store next door. What, you ain't been?"

"No, I despise freaks," declared Mrs. Fletcher.

"Aw. Well, honey, talkin' about bein' pregnant an' all, you ought to see those twins in a bottle, you really owe it to yourself."

"What twins?" asked Mrs. Fletcher out of the side of her mouth.

"Well, honey, they got these two twins in a bottle, see? Born joined plumb together—dead a course." Leota dropped her voice into a soft lyrical hum. "They was about this long—pardon—must of been full time, all right, wouldn't you say?—an' they had these two heads an' two faces an' four arms an' four legs, all kind of joined *here*. See, this face looked this-a-way, and the other face looked that-a-way, over their shoulder, see. Kinda pathetic."

"Glah!" said Mrs. Fletcher disapprovingly.

"Well, ugly? Honey, I mean to tell you—their parents was first cousins and all like that. Billy Boy, git me a fresh towel from off Teeny's stack—this 'n's wringin' wet—an' quit ticklin' my ankles with that curler. I declare! He don't miss nothin'."

"Me and Mr. Fletcher aren't one speck of kin, or he could never of had me," said Mrs. Fletcher placidly.

"Of course not!" protested Leota. "Neither is me an' Fred, not that we know of. Well, honey, what Mrs. Pike liked was the pygmies. They've got these pygmies down there, too, an' Mrs. Pike was just wild about 'em. You know, the teeniniest men in the universe? Well, honey, they can just rest back on their little bohunkus an' roll around an' you can't hardly tell if they're sittin' or standin'. That'll give you some idea. They're about forty-two years old. Just suppose it was your husband!"

"Well, Mr. Fletcher is five foot nine and one half," said Mrs. Fletcher quickly.

"Fred's five foot ten," said Leota, "but I tell him he's still a shrimp, account of I'm so tall." She made a deep wave over Mrs. Fletcher's other temple with the comb. "Well, these pygmies are a kind of a dark brown, Mrs. Fletcher. Not bad lookin' for what they are, you know."

"I wouldn't care for them," said Mrs. Fletcher. "What does that Mrs. Pike see in them?"

"Aw, I don't know," said Leota. "She's just cute, that's all. But they got this man, this petrified man, that ever'thing ever since he was nine years old, when it goes through his digestion, see, somehow Mrs. Pike says it goes to his joints and has been turning to stone."

"How awful!" said Mrs. Fletcher.

"He's forty-two too. That looks like a bad age."

"Who said so, that Mrs. Pike? I bet she's forty-two," said Mrs. Fletcher.

"Naw," said Leota, "Mrs. Pike's thirty-three, born in January, an Aquarian. He could move his head—like this. A course his head and mind ain't a joint, so to speak, and I guess his stomach ain't, either—not yet, anyways. But see—his food, he eats it, and it goes down, see, and then he digests it"— Leota rose on her toes for an instant—"and it goes out to his joints and before you can say 'Jack Robinson,' it's stone—pure stone. He's turning to stone. How'd you liked to be married to a guy like that? All he can do, he can move his head just a quarter of an inch. A course he *looks* just *terrible*."

"I should think he would," said Mrs. Fletcher frostily. "Mr. Fletcher takes bending exercises every night of the world. I make him."

"All Fred does is lay around the house like a rug. I wouldn't be surprised if he woke up some day and couldn't move. The petrified man just sat there moving his quarter of an inch though," said Leota reminiscently.

"Did Mrs. Pike like the petrified man?" asked Mrs. Fletcher.

"Not as much as she did the others," said Leota deprecatingly. "And then she likes a man to be a good dresser, and all that."

"Is Mr. Pike a good dresser?" asked Mrs. Fletcher sceptically.

"Oh, well, yeah," said Leota, "but he's twelve or fourteen years older'n her. She ast Lady Evangeline about him."

"Who's Lady Evangeline?" asked Mrs. Fletcher.

"Well, it's this mind reader they got in the freak show," said Leota. "Was real good. Lady Evangeline is her name, and if I had another dollar I wouldn't do a thing but have my other palm read. She had what Mrs. Pike said was the 'sixth mind' but she had the worst manicure I ever saw on a living person."

"What did she tell Mrs. Pike?" asked Mrs. Fletcher.

"She told her Mr. Pike was as true to her as he could be and besides, would come into some money."

"Humph!" said Mrs. Fletcher. "What does he do?"

"I can't tell," said Leota, "because he don't work. Lady Evangeline didn't tell me enough about my nature or anything. And I would like to go back and find out some more about this boy. Used to go with this boy until he got married to this girl. Oh, shoot, that was about three and a half years ago, when you was still goin' to the Robert E. Lee Beauty Shop in Jackson. He married her for her money. Another fortune-teller tole me that at the time. So I'm not in love with him anymore, anyway, besides being married to Fred, but Mrs. Pike thought, just for the hell of it, see, to ask Lady Evangeline was he happy."

"Does Mrs. Pike know everything about you already?" asked Mrs. Fletcher unbelievingly. "Mercy!"

"Oh, yeah, I tole her ever'thing about ever'thing, from now on back to I don't know when—to when I first started goin' out," said Leota. "So I ast Lady Evangeline for one of my questions, was he happily married, and she says, just like she was glad I ask her, 'Honey,' she says, 'naw, he idn't. You write down this day, March 8, 1941,' she says, 'and mock it down: three years from today him and her won't be occupyin' the same bed.' There it is, up on the wall with them other dates—see, Mrs. Fletcher? And she says, 'Child, you ought to be glad you didn't git him, because he's so mercenary.' So I'm glad I married Fred. He sure ain't mercenary, money don't mean a thing to him. But I sure would like to go back and have my other palm read."

"Did Mrs. Pike believe in what the fortune-teller said?" asked Mrs. Fletcher in a superior tone of voice.

"Lord, yes, she's from New Orleans. Ever'body in New Orleans believes ever'thing spooky. One of 'em in New Orleans before it was raided says to Mrs. Pike one summer she was goin' to go from State to State and meet some grey-headed men, and, sure enough, she says she went on a beautician convention up to Chicago. . . ."

"Oh!" said Mrs. Fletcher. "Oh, is Mrs. Pike a beautician too?"

"Sure she is," protested Leota. "She's a beautician. I'm goin' to git her in here if I can. Before she married. But it don't leave you. She says sure enough, there was three men who was a very large part of making her trip what it was, and they all three had grey in their hair and they went in six States. Got Christmas cards from 'em. Billy Boy, go see if Thelma's got any dry cotton. Look how Mrs. Fletcher's a-drippin'.'"

"Where did Mrs. Pike meet Mr. Pike?" asked Mrs. Fletcher primly.

"On another train," said Leota.

"I met Mr. Fletcher, or rather he met me, in a rental library," said Mrs. Fletcher with dignity, as she watched the net come down over her head.

"Honey, me an' Fred, we met in a rumble seat[3] eight months ago and we was practically on what you might call the way to the altar inside of half an hour," said Leota in a guttural voice, and bit a bobby pin open. "Course it don't last. Mrs. Pike says nothin' like that ever lasts."

"Mr. Fletcher and myself are as much in love as the day we married," said Mrs. Fletcher belligerently as Leota stuffed cotton into her ears.

"Mrs. Pike says it don't last," repeated Leota in a louder voice. "Now go git under the dryer. You can turn yourself on, can't you? I'll be back to comb you out. Durin' lunch I promised to give Mrs. Pike a facial. You know— free. Her bein' in the business, so to speak."

"I bet she needs one," said Mrs. Fletcher, letting the swing-door fly back against Leota. "Oh, pardon me."

A week later, on time for her appointment, Mrs. Fletcher sank heavily into Leota's chair after first removing a drug-store rental book, called *Life Is Like That*, from the seat. She stared in a discouraged way into the mirror.

"You can tell it when I'm sitting down, all right," she said.

Leota seemed preoccupied and stood shaking out a lavender cloth. She began to pin it around Mrs. Fletcher's neck in silence.

"I said you sure can tell it when I'm sitting straight on and coming at you this way," Mrs. Fletcher said.

"Why, honey, naw you can't," said Leota gloomily. "Why, I'd never know. If somebody was to come up to me on the street and say, 'Mrs. Fletcher is pregnant!' I'd say, 'Heck, she don't look it to me.'"

---

3. Folding seat at the rear of an automobile.

"If a certain party hadn't found it out and spread it around, it wouldn't be too late even now," said Mrs. Fletcher frostily, but Leota was almost choking her with the cloth, pinning it so tight, and she couldn't speak clearly. She paddled her hands in the air until Leota wearily loosened her.

"Listen, honey, you're just a virgin compared to Mrs. Montjoy," Leota was going on, still absent-minded. She bent Mrs. Fletcher back in the chair and, sighing, tossed liquid from a teacup on to her head and dug both hands into her scalp. "You know Mrs. Montjoy—her husband's that premature-greyheaded fella?"

"She's in the Trojan Garden Club, is all I know," said Mrs. Fletcher.

"Well, honey," said Leota, but in a weary voice, "she come in here not the week before and not the day before she had her baby—she come in here the very selfsame day, I mean to tell you. Child, we was all plumb scared to death. There she was! Come for her shampoo an' set. Why, Mrs. Fletcher, in an hour an' twenty minutes she was layin' up there in the Babtist Hospital with a seb'm-pound son. It was that close a shave. I declare, if I hadn't been so tired I would of drank up a bottle of gin that night."

"What gall," said Mrs. Fletcher. "I never knew her at all well."

"See, her husband was waitin' outside in the car, and her bags was all packed an' in the back seat, an' she was all ready, 'cept she wanted her shampoo an' set. An' havin' one pain right after another. Her husband kep' comin' in here, scared-like, but couldn't do nothin' with her a course. She yelled bloody murder, too, but she always yelled her head off when I give her a perm'nent."

"She must of been crazy," said Mrs. Fletcher. "How did she look?"

"Shoot!" said Leota.

"Well, I can guess," asid Mrs. Fletcher. "Awful."

"Just wanted to look pretty while she was havin' her baby, is all," said Leota airily. "Course, we was glad to give the lady what she was after—that's our motto—but I bet a hour later she wasn't payin' no mind to them little end curls. I bet she wasn't thinkin' about she ought to have on a net. It wouldn't of done her no good if she had."

"No, I don't suppose it would," said Mrs. Fletcher.

"Yeah man! She was a-yellin'. Just like when I give her perm'nent."

"Her husband ought to make her behave. Don't it seem that way to you?" asked Mrs. Fletcher. "He ought to put his foot down."

"Ha," said Leota. "A lot he could do. Maybe some women is soft."

"Oh, you mistake me, I don't mean for her to get soft—far from it! Women have to stand up for themselves, or there's just no telling. But now you take me—I ask Mr. Fletcher's advice now and then, and he appreciates it, especially on something important, like is it time for a permanent—not that I've told him about the baby. He says, 'Why, dear, go ahead!' Just ask their *advice*."

"Huh! If I ever ast Fred's advice we'd be floatin' down the Yazoo River on a houseboat or somethin' by this time," said Leota. "I'm sick of Fred. I told him to go over to Vicksburg."

"Is he going?" demanded Mrs. Fletcher.

"Sure. See, the fortune-teller—I went back and had my other palm read, since we've got to rent the room agin—said my lover was goin' to work in Vicksburg, so I don't know who she could mean, unless she meant Fred. And Fred ain't workin' here—that much is so."

"Is he going to work in Vicksburg?" asked Mrs. Fletcher. "And—"

"Sure. Lady Evangeline said so. Said the future is going to be brighter than the present. He don't want to go, but I ain't gonna put up with nothin' like that. Lays around the house an' bulls—did bull—with that good-for-nothin' Mr. Pike. He says if he goes who'll cook, but I says I never get to eat anyway— not meals. Billy Boy, take Mrs. Grover that *Screen Secrets* and leg it."

Mrs. Fletcher heard stamping feet go out the door.

"Is that that Mrs. Pike's little boy here again?" she asked, sitting up gingerly.

"Yeah, that's still him." Leota stuck out her tongue.

Mrs. Fletcher could hardly believe her eyes. "Well! How's Mrs. Pike, your attractive new friend with the sharp eyes who spreads it around town that perfect strangers are pregnant?" she asked in a sweetened tone.

"Oh, Mizziz Pike." Leota combed Mrs. Fletcher's hair with heavy strokes.

"You act like you're tired," said Mrs. Fletcher.

"Tired? Feel like it's four o'clock in the afternoon already," said Leota. "I ain't told you the awful luck we had, me and Fred? It's the worst thing you ever heard of. Maybe *you* think Mrs. Pike's got sharp eyes. Shoot, there's a limit! Well, you know, we rented out our room to this Mr. and Mrs. Pike from New Orleans when Sal an' Joe Fentress got mad at us 'cause they drank up some home-brew we had in the closet—Sal an' Joe did. So, a week ago Sat'-day Mr. and Mrs. Pike moved in. Well, I kinda fixed up the room, you know—put a sofa pillow on the couch and picked some ragged robbins and put in a vase, but they never did say they appreciated it. Anyway, then I put some old magazines on the table."

"I think that was lovely," said Mrs. Fletcher.

"Wait. So, come night 'fore last, Fred and this Mr. Pike, who Fred just took up with, was back from they said they was fishin', bein' as neither one of 'em has got a job to his name, and we was all settin' around their room. So Mrs. Pike was settin' there, readin' a old *Startling G-Man Tales* that was mine, mind you, I'd bought it myself, and all of a sudden she jumps!—into the air— you'd 'a' thought she'd set on a spider—an' says, 'Canfield'—ain't that silly, that's Mr. Pike—'Canfield, my God A'mighty,' she says, 'honey,' she says, 'we're rich, and you won't have to work.' Not that he turned one hand anyway. Well, me and Fred rushes over to her, and Mr. Pike, too, and there she sets, pointin' her finger at a photo in my copy of *Startling G-Man*. 'See that man?' yells Mrs. Pike. 'Remember him, Canfield?' 'Never forget a face,' says Mr. Pike. 'It's Mr. Petrie, that we stayed with him in the apartment next to ours in Tou- louse Street in N.O. for six weeks. Mr. Petrie.' 'Well,' says Mrs. Pike, like she can't hold out one secont longer, 'Mr. Petrie is wanted for five hundred dollars cash, for rapin' four women in California, and I know where he is.'"

"Mercy!" said Mrs. Fletcher. "Where was he?"

At some time Leota had washed her hair and now she yanked her up by the back locks and sat her up.

"Know where he was?"

"I certainly don't," Mrs. Fletcher said. Her scalp hurt all over.

Leota flung a towel around the top of her customer's head. "Nowhere else but in that freak show! I saw him just as plain as Mrs. Pike. *He* was the petrified man!"

"Who would ever have thought that!" cried Mrs. Fletcher sympathetically.

"So Mr. Pike says, 'Well whatta you know about that', an' he looks real hard at the photo and whistles. And she starts dancin' and singin' about their good luck. She meant our bad luck! I made a point of tellin' that fortune-teller the next time I saw her. I said, 'Listen, that magazine was layin' around the house for a month, and there was the freak show runnin' night an' day, not two steps away from my own beauty parlor, with Mr. Petrie just settin' there waitin'. An' it had to be Mr. and Mrs. Pike, almost perfect strangers.'"

"What gall," said Mrs. Fletcher. She was only sitting there, wrapped in a turban, but she did not mind.

"Fortune-tellers don't care. And Mrs. Pike, she goes around actin' like she thinks she was Mrs. God," said Leota. "So they're goin' to leave tomorrow, Mr. and Mrs. Pike. And in the meantime I got to keep that mean, bad little ole kid here, gettin' under my feet ever' minute of the day an' talkin' back too."

"Have they gotten the five hundred dollars' reward already?" asked Mrs. Fletcher.

"Well," said Leota, "at first Mr. Pike didn't want to do anything about it. Can you feature that? Said he kinda liked that ole bird and said he was real nice to 'em, lent 'em money or somethin'. But Mrs. Pike simply tole him he could just go to hell, and I can see her point. She says, 'You ain't worked a lick in six months, and here I make five hundred dollars in two seconts, and what thanks do I get for it? You go to hell, Canfield,' she says. So," Leota went on in a despondent voice, "they called up the cops and they caught the ole bird, all right, right there in the freak show where I saw him with my own eyes, thinkin' he was petrified. He's the one. Did it under his real name—Mr. Petrie. Four women in California, all in the month of August. So Mrs. Pike gits five hundred dollars. And my magazine, and right next door to my beauty parlor. I cried all night, but Fred said it wasn't a bit of use and to go to sleep, because the whole thing was just a sort of coincidence—you know: can't do nothin' about it. He says it put him clean out of the notion of goin' to Vicksburg for a few days till we rent out the room agin—no tellin' who we'll git this time."

"But can you imagine anybody knowing this old man, that's raped four women?" persisted Mrs. Fletcher, and she shuddered audibly. "Did Mrs. Pike *speak* to him when she met him in the freak show?"

Leota had begun to comb Mrs. Fletcher's hair. "I says to her, I says, 'I didn't notice you fallin' on his neck when he was the petrified man—don't tell me you didn't recognize your fine friend?' And she says, 'I didn't recognize him with that white powder all over his face. He just looked familiar,' Mrs. Pike says, 'and lots of people look familiar.' But she says that ole petrified man did put her in mind of somebody. She wondered who it was! Kep' her awake, which man she'd ever knew it reminded her of. So when she seen the photo, it all come to her. Like a flash. Mr. Petrie. The way he'd turn his head and look at her when she took him in his breakfast."

"Took him in his breakfast!" shrieked Mrs. Fletcher. "Listen—don't tell me. I'd 'a' felt something."

"Four women. I guess those women didn't have the faintest notion at the time they'd be worth a hundred an' twenty-five bucks apiece some day to Mrs. Pike. We ast her how old the fella was then, an's she says he musta had one foot in the grave, at least. Can you beat it?"

"Not really petrified at all, of course," said Mrs. Fletcher meditatively. She drew herself up. "I'd 'a' felt something," she said proudly.

"Shoot! I did feel somethin'," said Leota. "I tole Fred when I got home I felt so funny. I said, 'Fred, that ole petrified man sure did leave me with a funny feelin'.' He says, 'Funny-haha or funny-peculiar?' and I says, 'Funny-peculiar.'" She pointed her comb into the air emphatically.

"I'll bet you did," said Mrs. Fletcher.

They both heard a crackling noise.

Leota screamed, "Billy Boy! What you doin' in my purse?"

"Aw, I'm just eatin' these ole stale peanuts up," said Billy Boy.

"You come here to me!" screamed Leota, recklessly flinging down the comb, which scattered a whole ashtray full of bobby pins and knocked down a row of Coca-Cola bottles. "This is the last straw!"

"I caught him! I caught him!" giggled Mrs. Fletcher. "I'll hold him on my lap. You bad, bad boy, you! I guess I better learn how to spank little old bad boys," she said.

Leota's eleven o'clock customer pushed open the swing-door upon Leota's paddling him heartily with the brush, while he gave angry but belittling screams which penetrated beyond the booth and filled the whole curious beauty parlor. From everywhere ladies began to gather round to watch the paddling. Billy Boy kicked both Leota and Mrs. Fletcher as hard as he could, Mrs. Fletcher with her new fixed smile.

Billy Boy stomped through the group of wild-haired ladies and went out the door, but flung back the words, "If you're so smart, why ain't you rich?"

1941

ELIZABETH BISHOP
1911–1979

"The enormous power of reticence," the poet Octavio Paz said in a tribute, "—that is the great lesson of Elizabeth Bishop." Bishop's reticence originates in a temperament indistinguishable from her style; her remarkable formal gifts allowed her to create ordered and lucid structures that hold strong feelings in place. Chief among these feelings was a powerful sense of loss. Born in Worcester, Massachusetts, she was eight months old when her father died. Her mother suffered a series of breakdowns and was permanently institutionalized when Elizabeth was five. "I've never concealed this," Bishop once wrote, "although I don't like to make too much of it. But of course it is an important fact, to me. I didn't see her again." Her understatement is characteristic. When Bishop wrote about her early life—as she first did in several poems and stories in the 1950s and last did in her extraordinary final book, *Geography III* (1976)—she resisted sentimentality and self-pity. It was as if she could look at the events of her own life with the same unflinching gaze she turned on the landscapes that so consistently compelled her. The deep feeling in her poems rises out of direct and particular description, but Bishop does more than simply observe. Whether writing about her childhood landscape of Nova Scotia or her adopted Brazil, she often opens a poem with long perspectives on time, with landscapes that dwarf the merely human, emphasizing the dignified frailty of a human observer.

Examining her own case, she traces the observer's instinct to early childhood. "In the Waiting Room," a poem written in the early 1970s, probes the sources of her interest in details. Using an incident from when she was seven—a little girl waits for her aunt in the dentist's anteroom—Bishop shows how in the course of the episode she became aware, as if wounded, of the utter strangeness and engulfing power of the world. The spectator in that poem hangs on to details as a kind of life jacket; she observes because she has to.

After her father's death, Bishop and her mother lived with Bishop's maternal grandparents in Great Village, Nova Scotia. She remained there for several years after her mother was institutionalized, until she was removed ("kidnapped," as she says in one of her stories) by her paternal grandparents and taken to live in Worcester, Massachusetts. This experience was followed by a series of illnesses (eczema, bronchitis, and asthma), which plagued her for years. Bishop later lived with an aunt and attended Walnut Hill School, a private high school. In 1934 she graduated from Vassar College, where she had been introduced to Marianne Moore. Moore's meticulous taste for fact was to influence Bishop's poetry, but more immediately Moore's independent life as a poet seemed an alternative to Bishop's vaguer intentions to attend medical school. Bishop lived in New York City and in Key West, Florida; a traveling fellowship took her to Brazil, where she met Lotade Macedo Soares, an architect with whom she lived for sixteen years. Lota committed suicide in 1967, a loss registered in Bishop's late villanelle "One Art" (1976).

Exile and travel were always at the heart of Bishop's poems. The title of her first book, *North & South* (1946), looks backward to the northern seas of Nova Scotia and forward to the tropical worlds of Brazil. Her poems are set among these landscapes, where she can stress the sweep and violence of encircling and eroding geological powers or, in the case of Brazil, a bewildering botanical plenty. *Questions of Travel* (1965), her third volume, constitutes a sequence of poems initiating her, with her botanist-geologist-anthropologist's curiosity, into Brazilian life and the mysteries of what questions a traveler-exile should ask. In this series with its increasing penetration of a new country, a process is at work similar to one Bishop identifies in the great English naturalist Charles Darwin, of whom Bishop once said: "One admires the beautiful solid case being built up out of his endless, heroic observations, almost unconscious or automatic—and then comes a sudden relaxation, a forgetful phrase, and one feels the strangeness of his undertaking, sees the lonely young man, his eyes fixed on facts and minute details, sinking or sliding giddily off into the unknown."

In 1969 Bishop's *Complete Poems* appeared, an ironic title in light of the fact that she continued to publish new poetry. *Geography III* contains some of her best work, poems that, from the perspective of her return to the United States, look back on the appetite for exploration apparent in her earlier verse. The influence of her long friendship with the poet Robert Lowell, and their high regard for one another's work, may be felt in the way *Geography III* explores the memory and autobiography more directly than does her earlier work. Bishop, however, believed that there were limits on the ways in which poems could use the materials of a life. In a well-known 1972 letter to Lowell, she discusses these limits. Having left Brazil, Bishop lived in Boston from 1970 and taught at Harvard University until 1977. She received the Pulitzer Prize for the combined volume *North & South and A Cold Spring* (1955) and the National Book Award for *The Complete Poems*, and in 1976 was the first woman and the first American to receive the Books Abroad Neustadt International Prize for Literature. Since Bishop's death, most of her published work has been gathered in two volumes: *The Complete Poems 1929–1979* and *The Collected Prose*. An edition of her unpublished poems and drafts, *Edgar Allan Poe & The Juke-Box*, was published to some controversy in 2006.

The Fish

I caught a tremendous fish
and held him beside the boat
half out of water, with my hook
fast in a corner of his mouth.
He didn't fight.   5
He hadn't fought at all.
He hung a grunting weight,
battered and venerable
and homely. Here and there
his brown skin hung in strips   10
like ancient wallpaper,
and its pattern of darker brown
was like wallpaper:
shapes like full-blown roses
stained and lost through age.   15
He was speckled with barnacles,
fine rosettes of lime,
and infested
with tiny white sea-lice,
and underneath two or three   20
rags of green weed hung down.
While his gills were breathing in
the terrible oxygen
—the frightening gills,
fresh and crisp with blood,   25
that can cut so badly—
I thought of the coarse white flesh
packed in like feathers,
the big bones and the little bones,
the dramatic reds and blacks   30
of his shiny entrails,
and the pink swim-bladder
like a big peony.
I looked into his eyes
which were far larger than mine   35
but shallower, and yellowed,
the irises backed and packed
with tarnished tinfoil
seen through the lenses
of old scratched isinglass.[1]   40
They shifted a little, but not
to return my stare.
—It was more like the tipping
of an object toward the light.
I admired his sullen face,   45
the mechanism of his jaw,
and then I saw

---

1. A whitish, semitransparent substance, originally obtained from the swim bladders of some fresh-water fish and occasionally used for windows.

that from his lower lip
—if you could call it a lip—
grim, wet, and weaponlike,   50
hung five old pieces of fish-line,
or four and a wire leader
with the swivel still attached,
with all their five big hooks
grown firmly in his mouth.   55
A green line, frayed at the end
where he broke it, two heavier lines,
and a fine black thread
still crimped from the strain and snap
when it broke and he got away.   60
Like medals with their ribbons
frayed and wavering,
a five-haired beard of wisdom
trailing from his aching jaw.
I stared and stared   65
and victory filled up
the little rented boat,
from the pool of bilge
where oil had spread a rainbow
around the rusted engine   70
to the bailer rusted orange,
the sun-cracked thwarts,
the oarlocks on their strings,
the gunnels—until everything
was rainbow, rainbow, rainbow!   75
And I let the fish go.

                                                    1946

At the Fishhouses

Although it is a cold evening,
down by one of the fishhouses
an old man sits netting,
his net, in the gloaming almost invisible
a dark purple-brown,   5
and his shuttle worn and polished.
The air smells so strong of codfish
it makes one's nose run and one's eyes water.
The five fishhouses have steeply peaked roofs
and narrow, cleated gangplanks slant up   10
to storerooms in the gables
for the wheelbarrows to be pushed up and down on.
All is silver: the heavy surface of the sea,
swelling slowly as if considering spilling over,
is opaque, but the silver of the benches,   15
the lobster pots, and masts, scattered
among the wild jagged rocks,

is of an apparent translucence
like the small old buildings with an emerald moss
growing on their shoreward walls. 20
The big fish tubs are completely lined
with layers of beautiful herring scales
and the wheelbarrows are similarly plastered
with creamy iridescent coats of mail,
with small iridescent flies crawling on them. 25
Up on the little slope behind the houses,
set in the sparse bright sprinkle of grass,
is an ancient wooden capstan,[1]
cracked, with two long bleached handles
and some melancholy stains, like dried blood, 30
where the ironwork has rusted.
The old man accepts a Lucky Strike.[2]
He was a friend of my grandfather.
We talk of the decline in the population
and of codfish and herring 35
while he waits for a herring boat to come in.
There are sequins on his vest and on his thumb.
He has scraped the scales, the principal beauty,
from unnumbered fish with that black old knife,
the blade of which is almost worn away. 40

Down at the water's edge, at the place
where they haul up the boats, up the long ramp
descending into the water, thin silver
tree trunks are laid horizontally
across the gray stones, down and down 45
at intervals of four or five feet.

Cold dark deep and absolutely clear,
element bearable to no mortal,
to fish and to seals . . . One seal particularly
I have seen here evening after evening. 50
He was curious about me. He was interested in music;
like me a believer in total immersion,[3]
so I used to sing him Baptist hymns.
I also sang "A Mighty Fortress Is Our God."
He stood up in the water and regarded me 55
steadily, moving his head a little.
Then he would disappear, then suddenly emerge
almost in the same spot, with a sort of shrug
as if it were against his better judgment.
Cold dark deep and absolutely clear, 60
the clear gray icy water . . . Back, behind us,
the dignified tall firs begin.
Bluish, associating with their shadows,
a million Christmas trees stand

---

1. Cylindrical drum around which rope is wound, used for winching or hoisting the anchor of a ship.
2. Brand of cigarettes.
3. Form of baptism favored by Baptists.

waiting for Christmas. The water seems suspended 65
above the rounded gray and blue-gray stones.
I have seen it over and over, the same sea, the same,
slightly, indifferently swinging above the stones,
icily free above the stones,
above the stones and then the world. 70
If you should dip your hand in,
your wrist would ache immediately,
your bones would begin to ache and your hand would burn
as if the water were a transmutation of fire
that feeds on stones and burns with a dark gray flame. 75
If you tasted it, it would first taste bitter,
then briny, then surely burn your tongue.
It is like what we imagine knowledge to be:
dark, salt, clear, moving, utterly free,
drawn from the cold hard mouth 80
of the world, derived from the rocky breasts
forever, flowing and drawn, and since
our knowledge is historical, flowing, and flown.

1955

The Armadillo

for Robert Lowell

This is the time of year
when almost every night
the frail, illegal fire balloons appear.
Climbing the mountain height,

rising toward a saint 5
still honored in these parts,
the paper chambers flush and fill with light
that comes and goes, like hearts.

Once up against the sky it's hard
to tell them from the stars— 10
planets, that is—the tinted ones:
Venus going down, or Mars,

or the pale green one. With a wind,
they flare and falter, wobble and toss;
but if it's still they steer between 15
the kite sticks of the Southern Cross,

receding, dwindling, solemnly
and steadily forsaking us,
or, in the downdraft from a peak,
suddenly turning dangerous. 20

Last night another big one fell.
It splattered like an egg of fire
against the cliff behind the house.
The flame ran down. We saw the pair

of owls who nest there flying up   25
and up, their whirling black-and-white
stained bright pink underneath, until
they shrieked up out of sight.

The ancient owls' nest must have burned.
Hastily, all alone,   30
a glistening armadillo left the scene,
rose-flecked, head down, tail down,

and then a baby rabbit jumped out,
short-eared, to our surprise.
So soft!—a handful of intangible ash   35
with fixed, ignited eyes.

Too pretty, dreamlike mimicry!
O falling fire and piercing cry
and panic, and a weak mailed fist[1]
clenched ignorant against the sky!   40

1965

Sestina[1]

September rain falls on the house.
In the failing light, the old grandmother
sits in the kitchen with the child
beside the Little Marvel Stove,
reading the jokes from the almanac,   5
laughing and talking to hide her tears.

She thinks that her equinoctial tears
and the rain that beats on the roof of the house
were both foretold by the almanac,
but only known to a grandmother.   10
The iron kettle sings on the stove.
She cuts some bread and says to the child,

It's time for tea now; but the child
is watching the teakettle's small hard tears
dance like mad on the hot black stove,   15
the way the rain must dance on the house.

1. The armadillo, curled tight and protected
against everything but fire.
1. A fixed verse form in which the end words of the first six-line stanza must be used at the ends of the lines in the following stanzas in a rotating order; the final three lines must contain all six words.

Tidying up, the old grandmother
hangs up the clever almanac

on its string. Birdlike, the almanac
hovers half open above the child,   20
hovers above the old grandmother
and her teacup full of dark brown tears.
She shivers and says she thinks the house
feels chilly, and puts more wood in the stove.

It was to be, says the Marvel Stove.   25
I know what I know, says the almanac.
With crayons the child draws a rigid house
and a winding pathway. Then the child
puts in a man with buttons like tears
and shows it proudly to the grandmother.   30

But secretly, while the grandmother
busies herself about the stove,
the little moons fall down like tears
from between the pages of the almanac
into the flower bed the child   35
has carefully placed in the front of the house.

Time to plant tears, says the almanac.
The grandmother sings to the marvellous stove
and the child draws another inscrutable house.

                                                          1965

In the Waiting Room

In Worcester, Massachusetts,
I went with Aunt Consuelo
to keep her dentist's appointment
and sat and waited for her
in the dentist's waiting room.   5
It was winter. It got dark
early. The waiting room
was full of grown-up people,
arctics and overcoats,
lamps and magazines.   10
My aunt was inside
what seemed like a long time
and while I waited I read
the *National Geographic*
(I could read) and carefully   15
studied the photographs:
the inside of a volcano,
black, and full of ashes;
then it was spilling over

in rivulets of fire.   20
Osa and Martin Johnson[1]
dressed in riding breeches,
laced boots, and pith helmets.
A dead man slung on a pole
—"Long Pig,"[2] the caption said.   25
Babies with pointed heads
wound round and round with string;
black, naked women with necks
wound round and round with wire
like the necks of light bulbs.   30
Their breasts were horrifying.
I read it right straight through.
I was too shy to stop.
And then I looked at the cover:
the yellow margins, the date.   35

Suddenly, from inside,
came an *oh!* of pain
—Aunt Consuelo's voice—
not very loud or long.
I wasn't at all surprised;   40
even then I knew she was
a foolish, timid woman.
I might have been embarrassed,
but wasn't. What took me
completely by surprise   45
was that it was *me*:
my voice, in my mouth.
Without thinking at all
I was my foolish aunt,
I—we—were falling, falling,   50
our eyes glued to the cover
of the *National Geographic*,
February, 1918.

I said to myself: three days
and you'll be seven years old.   55
I was saying it to stop
the sensation of falling off
the round, turning world
into cold, blue-black space.
But I felt: you are an *I*,   60
you are an *Elizabeth*,
you are one of *them*.
Why should you be one, too?
I scarcely dared to look.
to see what it was I was.   65
I gave a sidelong glance

1. Famous explorers and travel writers.
2. Polynesian cannibals' name for the human carcass.

—I couldn't look any higher—
at shadowy gray knees,
trousers and skirts and boots
and different pairs of hands   70
lying under the lamps.
I knew that nothing stranger
had ever happened, that nothing
stranger could ever happen.
Why should I be my aunt,   75
or me, or anyone?
What similarities—
boots, hands, the family voice
I felt in my throat, or even
the *National Geographic*   80
and those awful hanging breasts—
held us all together
or made us all just one?
How—I didn't know any
word for it—how "unlikely" . . .   85
How had I come to be here,
like them, and overhear
a cry of pain that could have
got loud and worse but hadn't?

The waiting room was bright   90
and too hot. It was sliding
beneath a big black wave,
another, and another.

Then I was back in it.
The War was on. Outside,   95
in Worcester, Massachusetts,
were night and slush and cold,
and it was still the fifth
of February, 1918.

                                        1976

One Art

The art of losing isn't hard to master;
so many things seem filled with the intent
to be lost that their loss is no disaster.

Lose something every day. Accept the fluster
of lost door keys, the hour badly spent.   5
The art of losing isn't hard to master.

Then practice losing farther, losing faster:
places, and names, and where it was you meant
to travel. None of these will bring disaster.

I lost my mother's watch. And look! my last, or 10
next-to-last, of three loved houses went.
The art of losing isn't hard to master.

I lost two cities, lovely ones. And, vaster,
some realms I owned, two rivers, a continent.
I miss them, but it wasn't a disaster. 15

—Even losing you (the joking voice, a gesture
I love) I shan't have lied. It's evident
the art of losing's not too hard to master
though it may look like (*Write* it!) like disaster.

1976

TENNESSEE WILLIAMS
1911–1983

Speaking of Blanche DuBois, the heroine of *A Streetcar Named Desire*, Tennessee Williams once said, "She was a demonic creature; the size of her feeling was too great for her to contain." In Williams's plays—he wrote and rewrote more than twenty full-length dramas as well as screenplays and shorter works—his characters are driven by the size of their feelings, much as Williams felt driven to write about them.

He was born Thomas Lanier Williams in Columbus, Mississippi. His mother, "Miss Edwina," the daughter of an Episcopalian minister, was repressed and genteel, very much the southern belle in her youth. His father, Cornelius, was a traveling salesman, often away from his family and often violent and drunk when at home. As a child, Williams was sickly and overly protected by his mother; he was closely attached to his sister, Rose, repelled by the roughhouse world of boys, and alienated from his father. The family's move from Mississippi to St. Louis, where Cornelius became a sales manager of the shoe company he had traveled for, was a shock to Mrs. Williams and her young children, used to living in small southern towns where a minister's daughter was an important person. Yet Mrs. Williams could take care of herself; she was a "survivor."

Williams went to the University of Missouri but left after two years; his father then found him a job in the shoe-factory warehouse. He worked there for nearly three years, writing feverishly at night. (His closest friend at the time was a burly coworker, easygoing and attractive to women, named Stanley Kowalski, whose name and characteristics Williams would borrow for *A Streetcar Named Desire*.) Williams found the life so difficult, however, that he succumbed to a nervous breakdown. After recovering at the home of his beloved grandparents, he went on to further studies, finally graduating at the age of twenty-seven. Earlier, Rose had been suffering increasing mental imbalance; the final trauma was apparently brought on by one of Cornelius's alcoholic rages, in which he beat Edwina and, trying to calm Rose, made a gesture that she took to be sexual. Shortly thereafter Edwina signed the papers allowing Rose to be "tragically becalmed" by a prefrontal lobotomy. Rose spent most of her life in sanatoriums, except when Williams brought her out for visits.

The next year, Williams left for New Orleans, the first of many temporary homes; it would provide the setting for *A Streetcar Named Desire*. In New Orleans he changed his name to "Tennessee," later giving—as often when discussing his life—various romantic reasons for doing so. There also he actively entered the homosexual world.

Williams had had plays produced at local theaters and in 1939 he won a prize for a collection of one-act plays, *American Blues*. The next year *Battle of Angels* failed (in 1957 he would rewrite it as *Orpheus Descending*). His first success was *The Glass Menagerie* (1945). Williams called it a "memory play," seen through the recollections of the writer, Tom, who talks to the audience about himself and about the scenes depicting his mother, Amanda, poverty-stricken but genteelly living on memories of her southern youth and her "gentlemen callers"; his crippled sister, Laura, who finds refuge in her "menagerie" of little glass animals; and the traumatic effect of a modern "gentleman caller" on them. While there are similarities between Edwina, Rose, and Tennessee on the one hand, and Amanda, Laura, and Tom on the other, there are also differences: the play is not literally autobiographical.

The financial success of *Menagerie* proved exhilarating, then debilitating. Williams fled to Mexico to work full-time on an earlier play, *The Poker Night*. It had begun as *The Moth*; its first image, as Williams's biographer, Donald Spoto, tells us, was "simply that of a woman, sitting with folded hands near a window, while moonlight streamed in and she awaited in vain the arrival of her boyfriend": named Blanche, she was at first intended as a young Amanda. During rehearsals of *Menagerie*, Williams had asked members of the stage crew to teach him to play poker, and he began to visualize his new play as a series of confrontations between working-class poker players and two refined southern women.

As the focus of his attention changed from Stanley to Blanche, *The Poker Night* turned into *A Streetcar Named Desire*. Upon opening in 1947, it was an even greater success than *The Glass Menagerie*, and it won the Pulitzer Prize. Williams was able to travel and to buy a home in Key West, Florida, where he did much of his ensuing work. At about this time his "transitory heart" found "a home at last" in a young man named Frank Merlo.

For more than a decade thereafter a new Williams play appeared almost every two years. Among the most successful were *The Rose Tattoo* (1950), in which the tempestuous heroine, Serafina, worshiping the memory of her dead husband, finds love again; the Pulitzer Prize–winning *Cat on a Hot Tin Roof* (1955), which portrays the conflict of the dying Big Daddy and his impotent son, Brick, watched and controlled by Brick's wife, "Maggie the Cat"; and *The Night of the Iguana* (1961), which brings a varied group of tormented people together at a rundown hotel on the Mexican coast. His plays were produced widely abroad and also became equally successful films. Yet some of the ones now regarded as the best of this period were commercial failures: *Summer and Smoke* (1948), for example, and the surrealistic and visionary *Camino Real* (1953).

For years Williams had depended on a wide variety of drugs, especially to help him sleep and to keep him awake in the early mornings, when he invariably worked. In the 1960s the drugs began to take a real toll. Other factors contributed to the decline of his later years: Frank Merlo's death, the emergence of younger playwrights of whom he felt blindly jealous, and the violent nature of the 1960s, which seemed both to mirror his inner chaos and to leave him behind.

Yet despite Broadway failures, critical disparagements, and a breakdown for which he was hospitalized, he valiantly kept working. Spoto notes that in Williams's late work, Rose was "the source and inspiration of everything he wrote, either directly—with a surrogate character representing her—or indirectly, in the situation of romanticized mental illness or unvarnished verisimilitude." This observation is certainly true of his last Broadway play, the failed *Clothes for a Summer Hotel* (1980), ostensibly about the ghosts of Scott and Zelda Fitzgerald, and of the play he obsessively wrote and rewrote, *The Two Character Play*, which chronicles the descent of a brother and sister, who are also lovers, into madness and death.

A game of seven-card stud poker continues as the action of *A Streetcar Named Desire* concludes. Original Broadway production, 1947.

Despite Williams's self-destructiveness, in his writing and in his social life, the work of his great years was now being seriously studied and often revived by regional and community theaters. Critics began to see that he was one of America's best and most dedicated playwrights. And he kept on working. He was collaborating on a film of two stories about Rose when he died, apparently having choked to death on the lid of a pill bottle.

Always reluctant to talk about his work (likening it to a "bird that will be startled away, as by a hawk's shadow"), Williams did not see himself in a tradition of American dramaturgy. He acknowledged the influence of Anton Chekhov, the nineteenth-century Russian writer of dramas with lonely, searching characters; of D. H. Lawrence, the British novelist who emphasized the theme of a sexual life force; and above all of the American Hart Crane, homosexual *poète maudit*, who, he said, "touched fire that burned [himself] alive," adding that "perhaps it is only through self-immolation of such a nature that we living beings can offer to you the entire truth of ourselves." Such a statement indicates the deeply confessional quality of Williams's writing, even in plays not directly autobiographical.

Although he never acknowledged any debt to the American playwright Eugene O'Neill, Williams shared with O'Neill an impatience over the theatrical conventions of realism. *The Glass Menagerie*, for example, uses screened projections, lighting effects, and music to emphasize that it takes place in Tom's memory. *A Streetcar Named Desire* moves in and out of the house on Elysian Fields, while music and lighting reinforce all the major themes. Williams also relies on the effects of language, especially of a vivid and colloquial Southern speech that may be compared with that of William Faulkner, Eudora Welty, or Flannery O'Connor. Rhythms of language become almost a musical indication of character, distinguishing Blanche from other characters. Reading or seeing his plays, we become aware of how symbolic repetitions—in Blanche's and Stanley's turns of phrase, the naked light bulb and the paper lantern, the Mexican woman selling flowers for the dead, the "Varsouviana" waltz and the reverberating voices—produce a heightening of reality: what Williams called "poetic realism."

More than a half century later, does the destruction of Blanche, the "lady," still have the power to move us? Elia Kazan, in his director's notes, calls her "an outdated creature, approaching extinction . . . like a dinosaur." But Blythe Danner, who played Blanche in a 1988 revival, acutely observes that Williams "was attached to the things that were going to destroy him" and that Blanche, similarly, is attracted to and repelled by Stanley: "It's Tennessee fighting, fighting, fighting what he doesn't want to get into, what is very prevalent in his mind. That incredible contradiction in so many people is what he captures better than any other playwright."

Contemporary criticisms of Williams's plays focused on their violence and their obsession with sexuality, which in some of the later work struck some commentators as an almost morbid preoccupation with "perversion"—murder, rape, drugs, incest, nymphomania. The shriller voices making such accusations were attacking Williams for his homosexuality, which could not be publicly spoken of in this country until comparatively recently. These taboo topics, however, figure as instances of Williams's deeper subjects: desire and loneliness. As he said in an interview, "Desire is rooted in a longing for companionship, a release from the loneliness that haunts every individual." Loneliness and desire propel his characters into extreme behavior, no doubt, but such behavior literally dramatizes the plight that Williams saw as universal.

The following text is from *The Theatre of Tennessee Williams*, volume 1 (1971).

A Streetcar Named Desire

And so it was I entered the broken world
To trace the visionary company of love, its voice
An instant in the wind (I know not whither hurled)
But not for long to hold each desperate choice.
     —*"The Broken Tower"* by Hart Crane[1]

THE CHARACTERS

BLANCHE	PABLO
STELLA	A NEGRO WOMAN
STANLEY	A DOCTOR
MITCH	A NURSE
EUNICE	A YOUNG COLLECTOR
STEVE	A MEXICAN WOMAN

Scene One

The exterior of a two-story corner building on a street in New Orleans which is named Elysian Fields and runs between the L & N tracks and the river.[2] The section is poor but, unlike corresponding sections in other American cities, it has a raffish charm. The houses are mostly white frame, weathered grey, with rickety outside stairs and galleries and quaintly ornamented gables. This building contains two flats, upstairs and down. Faded white stairs ascend to the entrances of both.

1. American poet (1899–1932).
2. Elysian Fields is a New Orleans street at the northern tip of the French Quarter, between the Louisville & Nashville railroad tracks and the Mississippi River. In Greek mythology the Elysian Fields are the abode of the blessed in the afterlife.

It is first dark of an evening early in May. The sky that shows around the dim white building is a peculiarly tender blue, almost a turquoise, which invests the scene with a kind of lyricism and gracefully attenuates the atmosphere of decay. You can almost feel the warm breath of the brown river beyond the river warehouses with their faint redolences of bananas and coffee. A corresponding air is evoked by the music of Negro entertainers at a barroom around the corner. In this part of New Orleans you are practically always just around the corner, or a few doors down the street, from a tinny piano being played with the infatuated fluency of brown fingers. This "Blue Piano" expresses the spirit of the life which goes on here.

Two women, one white and one colored, are taking the air on the steps of the building. The white woman is EUNICE, *who occupies the upstairs flat; the colored woman a neighbor, for New Orleans is a cosmopolitan city where there is a relatively warm and easy intermingling of races in the old part of town.*

Above the music of the "Blue Piano" the voices of people on the street can be heard overlapping.

[*Two men come around the corner,* STANLEY KOWALSKI *and* MITCH. *They are about twenty-eight or thirty years old, roughly dressed in blue denim work clothes.* STANLEY *carries his bowling jacket and a red-stained package from a butcher's. They stop at the foot of the steps.*]

STANLEY [*bellowing*]   Hey there! Stella, baby!

[STELLA *comes out on the first floor landing, a gentle young woman, about twenty-five, and of a background obviously quite different from her husband's.*]

STELLA [*mildly*]   Don't holler at me like that. Hi, Mitch.

STANLEY   Catch!

STELLA   What?

STANLEY   Meat!

[*He heaves the package at her. She cries out in protest but manages to catch it: then she laughs breathlessly. Her husband and his companion have already started back around the corner.*]

STELLA [*calling after him*]   Stanley! Where are you going?

STANLEY   Bowling!

STELLA   Can I come watch?

STANLEY   Come on. [*He goes out.*]

STELLA   Be over soon. [*to the white woman*] Hello, Eunice. How are you?

EUNICE   I'm all right. Tell Steve to get him a poor boy's sandwich 'cause nothing's left here.

[*They all laugh; the colored woman does not stop.* STELLA *goes out.*]

COLORED WOMAN   What was that package he th'ew at 'er? [*She rises from steps, laughing louder.*]

EUNICE   You hush, now!

NEGRO WOMAN   Catch *what!*

[*She continues to laugh.* BLANCHE *comes around the corner, carrying a valise. She looks at a slip of paper, then at the building, then again at the slip and again at the building. Her expression is one of shocked disbelief. Her appearance is incongruous to this setting. She is daintily dressed in a white suit with a fluffy bodice, necklace and earrings of pearl, white gloves and hat, looking as if she were arriving at a summer tea or cocktail party in the garden district. She is about five years older than* STELLA. *Her delicate beauty must avoid a strong light. There is something about her uncertain manner, as well as her white clothes, that suggests a moth.*]

EUNICE [*finally*]   What's the matter, honey? Are you lost?

BLANCHE [*with faintly hysterical humor*]   They told me to take a street-car named Desire, and then transfer to one called Cemeteries[3] and ride six blocks and get off at—Elysian Fields!

EUNICE   That's where you are now.

BLANCHE   At Elysian Fields?

EUNICE   This here is Elysian Fields.

BLANCHE   They mustn't have—understood—what number I wanted . . .

EUNICE   What number you lookin' for?

[BLANCHE *wearily refers to the slip of paper.*]

BLANCHE   Six thirty-two.

EUNICE   You don't have to look no further.

BLANCHE [*uncomprehendingly*]   I'm looking for my sister, Stella DuBois, I mean—Mrs. Stanley Kowalski.

EUNICE   That's the party.—You just did miss her, though.

BLANCHE   This—can this be—her home?

EUNICE   She's got the downstairs here and I got the up.

BLANCHE   Oh. She's—out?

EUNICE   You noticed that bowling alley around the corner?

BLANCHE   I'm—not sure I did.

EUNICE   Well, that's where she's at, watchin' her husband bowl. [*There is a pause.*] You want to leave your suitcase here an' go find her?

BLANCHE   No.

NEGRO WOMAN   I'll go tell her you come.

BLANCHE   Thanks.

NEGRO WOMAN   You welcome. [*She goes out.*]

EUNICE   She wasn't expecting you?

BLANCHE   No. No, not tonight.

EUNICE   Well, why don't you just go in and make yourself at home till they get back.

BLANCHE   How could I—do that?

EUNICE   We own this place so I can let you in.

[*She gets up and opens the downstairs door. A light goes on behind the blind, turning it light blue.* BLANCHE *slowly follows her into the down-stairs flat. The surrounding areas dim out as the interior is lighted. Two rooms can be seen, not too clearly defined. The one first entered is primar-ily a kitchen but contains a folding bed to be used by* BLANCHE. *The room beyond this is a bedroom. Off this room is a narrow door to a bathroom.*]

EUNICE [*defensively, noticing* BLANCHE's *look*]   It's sort of messed up right now but when it's clean it's real sweet.

BLANCHE   Is it?

EUNICE   Uh-huh, I think so. So you're Stella's sister?

BLANCHE   Yes. [*wanting to get rid of her*] Thanks for letting me in.

EUNICE   *Por nada*,[4] as the Mexicans say, *por nada!* Stella spoke of you.

BLANCHE   Yes?

EUNICE   I think she said you taught school.

BLANCHE   Yes.

EUNICE   And you're from Mississippi, huh?

3. The end of a streetcar line that stopped at a cemetery. Desire is a New Orleans street.
4. It's nothing (Spanish).

BLANCHE   Yes.

EUNICE   She showed me a picture of your home-place, the plantation.

BLANCHE   Belle Reve?[5]

EUNICE   A great big place with white columns.

BLANCHE   Yes . . .

EUNICE   A place like that must be awful hard to keep up.

BLANCHE   If you will excuse me, I'm just about to drop.

EUNICE   Sure, honey. Why don't you set down?

BLANCHE   What I meant was I'd like to be left alone.

EUNICE [*offended*]   Aw. I'll make myself scarce, in that case.

BLANCHE   I didn't meant to be rude, but—

EUNICE   I'll drop by the bowling alley an' hustle her up. [*She goes out the door.*]
   [BLANCHE *sits in a chair very stiffly with her shoulders slightly hunched
   and her legs pressed close together and her hands tightly clutching her
   purse as if she were quite cold. After a while the blind look goes out of her
   eyes and she begins to look slowly around. A cat screeches. She catches
   her breath with a startled gesture. Suddenly she notices something in a
   half opened closet. She springs up and crosses to it, and removes a whiskey bottle. She pours a half tumbler of whiskey and tosses it down. She
   carefully replaces the bottle and washes out the tumbler at the sink. Then
   she resumes her seat in front of the table.*]

BLANCHE [*faintly to herself*]   I've got to keep hold of myself! [STELLA
   *comes quickly around the corner of the building and runs to the door of
   the downstairs flat.*]

STELLA [*calling out joyfully*]   Blanche!
   [*For a moment they stare at each other. Then* BLANCHE *springs up and
   runs to her with a wild cry.*]

BLANCHE   Stella, oh, Stella, Stella! Stella for Star!
   [*She begins to speak with feverish vivacity as if she feared for either of
   them to stop and think. They catch each other in a spasmodic embrace.*]

BLANCHE   Now, then, let me look at you. But don't you look at me, Stella,
   no, no, no, not till later, not till I've bathed and rested! And turn that
   over-light off! Turn that off! I won't be looked at in this merciles glare!
   [STELLA *laughs and complies.*] Come back here now! Oh, my baby! Stella!
   Stella for Star! [*She embraces her again.*] I thought you would never come
   back to this horrible place! What am I saying? I didn't mean to say that.
   I meant to be nice about it and say—Oh, what a convenient location and
   such—Ha-a-ha! Precious lamb! You haven't said a *word* to me.

STELLA   You haven't given me a chance to, honey! [*She laughs, but her
   glance at* BLANCHE *is a little anxious.*]

BLANCHE   Well, now you talk. Open your pretty mouth and talk while I
   look around for some liquor! I know you must have some liquor on the
   place! Where could it be, I wonder? Oh, I spy, I spy!
   [*She rushes to the closet and removes the bottle; she is shaking all over
   and panting for breath as she tries to laugh. The bottle nearly slips from
   her grasp.*]

STELLA [*noticing*]   Blanche, you sit down and let me pour the drinks. I
   don't know what we've got to mix with. Maybe a coke's in the icebox.
   Look'n see, honey, while I'm—

5. Beautiful Dream (French).

BLANCHE   No coke, honey, not with my nerves tonight! Where—where—where is—?

STELLA   Stanley? Bowling! He loves it. They're having a—found some soda!—tournament . . .

BLANCHE   Just water, baby, to chase it! Now don't get worried, your sister hasn't turned into a drunkard, she's just all shaken up and hot and tired and dirty! You sit down, now, and explain this place to me! What are you doing in a place like this?

STELLA   Now, Blanche—

BLANCHE   Oh, I'm not going to be hypocritical, I'm going to be honestly critical about it! Never, never, never in my worst dreams could I picture—Only Poe! Only Mr. Edgar Allan Poe!—could do it justice! Out there I suppose is the ghoul-haunted woodland of Weir![6] [*She laughs.*]

STELLA   No, honey, those are the L & N tracks.

BLANCHE   No, now seriously, putting joking aside. Why didn't you tell me, why didn't you write me, honey, why didn't you let me know?

STELLA   [*carefully, pouring herself a drink*]   Tell you what, Blanche?

BLANCHE   Why, that you had to live in these conditions!

STELLA   Aren't you being a little intense about it? It's not that bad at all! New Orleans isn't like other cities.

BLANCHE   This has got nothing to do with New Orleans. You might as well say—forgive me, blessed baby! [*She suddenly stops short.*] The subject is closed!

STELLA   [*a little drily*]   Thanks.

[*During the pause,* BLANCHE *stares at her. She smiles at* BLANCHE.]

BLANCHE   [*looking down at her glass, which shakes in her hand*]   You're all I've got in the world, and you're not glad to see me!

STELLA   [*sincerely*]   Why, Blanche, you know that's not true.

BLANCHE   No?—I'd forgotten how quiet you were.

STELLA   You never did give me a chance to say much, Blanche. So I just got in the habit of being quiet around you.

BLANCHE   [*vaguely*]   A good habit to get into . . . [*then, abruptly*] You haven't asked me how I happened to get away from the school before the spring term ended.

STELLA   Well, I thought you'd volunteer that information—if you wanted to tell me.

BLANCHE   You thought I'd been fired?

STELLA   No, I—thought you might have—resigned . . .

BLANCHE   I was so exhausted by all I'd been through my—nerves broke. [*nervously tamping cigarette*] I was on the verge of—lunacy, almost! So Mr. Graves—Mr. Graves is the high school superintendent—he suggested I take a leave of absence. I couldn't put all of those details into the wire . . . [*She drinks quickly.*] Oh, this buzzes right through me and feels so *good*!

STELLA   Won't you have another?

BLANCHE   No, one's my limit.

STELLA   Sure?

BLANCHE   You haven't said a word about my appearance.

---

6. From the refrain of Poe's gothic ballad "Ulalume" (1847).

STELLA   You look just fine.

BLANCHE   God love you for a liar! Daylight never exposed so total a ruin! But you—you've put on some weight, yes, you're just as plump as a little partridge! And it's so becoming to you!

STELLA   Now, Blanche—

BLANCHE   Yes, it is, it is or I wouldn't say it! You just have to watch around the hips a little. Stand up.

STELLA   Not now.

BLANCHE   You hear me? I said stand up! [STELLA *complies reluctantly.*] You messy child, you, you've spilt something on that pretty white lace collar! About your hair—you ought to have it cut in a feather bob with your dainty features. Stella, you have a maid, don't you?

STELLA   No. With only two rooms it's—

BLANCHE   What? *Two* rooms, did you say?

STELLA   This one and— [*She is embarrassed.*]

BLANCHE   The other one? [*She laughs sharply. There is an embarrassed silence.*]

BLANCHE   I am going to take just one little tiny nip more, sort of to put the stopper on, so to speak. . . . Then put the bottle away so I won't be tempted. [*She rises.*] I want you to look at *my* figure! [*She turns around.*] You know I haven't put on one ounce in ten years, Stella? I weigh what I weighed the summer you left Belle Reve. The summer Dad died and you left us . . .

STELLA   [*a little wearily*]   It's just incredible, Blanche, how well you're looking.

BLANCHE   [*They both laugh uncomfortably.*]   But, Stella, there's only two rooms, I don't see where you're going to put me!

STELLA   We're going to put you in here.

BLANCHE   What kind of bed's this—one of those collapsible things? [*She sits on it.*]

STELLA   Does it feel all right?

BLANCHE   [*dubiously*]   Wonderful, honey. I don't like a bed that gives much. But there's no door between the two rooms, and Stanley—will it be decent?

STELLA   Stanley is Polish, you know.

BLANCHE   Oh, yes. They're something like Irish, aren't they?

STELLA   Well—

BLANCHE   Only not so—highbrow? [*They both laugh again in the same way.*] I brought some nice clothes to meet all your lovely friends in.

STELLA   I'm afraid you won't think they are lovely.

BLANCHE   What are they like?

STELLA   They're Stanley's friends.

BLANCHE   Polacks?

STELLA   They're a mixed lot, Blanche.

BLANCHE   Heterogeneous—types?

STELLA   Oh, yes. Yes, types is right!

BLANCHE   Well—anyhow—I brought nice clothes and I'll wear them. I guess you're hoping I'll say I'll put up at a hotel, but I'm not going to put up at a hotel. I want to be *near* you, got to be *with* somebody, I *can't* be *alone*! Because—as you must have noticed—I'm—*not* very *well*. . . . [*Her voice drops and her look is frightened.*]

STELLA You seem a little bit nervous or overwrought or something.

BLANCHE Will Stanley like me, or will I be just a visiting in-law, Stella? I couldn't stand that.

STELLA You'll get along fine together, if you'll just try not to—well—compare him with men that we went out with at home.

BLANCHE Is he so—different?

STELLA Yes. A different species.

BLANCHE In what way; what's he like?

STELLA Oh, you can't describe someone you're in love with! Here's a picture of him! [*She hands a photograph to* BLANCHE.]

BLANCHE An officer?

STELLA A Master Sergeant in the Engineers' Corps. Those are decorations!

BLANCHE He had those on when you met him?

STELLA I assure you I wasn't just blinded by all the brass.

BLANCHE That's not what I—

STELLA But of course there were things to adjust myself to later on.

BLANCHE Such as his civilian background! [STELLA *laughs uncertainly*.] How did he take it when you said I was coming?

STELLA Oh, Stanley doesn't know yet.

BLANCHE [*frightened*] You—haven't told him?

STELLA He's on the road a good deal.

BLANCHE Oh. Travels?

STELLA Yes.

BLANCHE Good. I mean—isn't it?

STELLA [*half to herself*] I can hardly stand it when he is away for a night . . .

BLANCHE Why, Stella!

STELLA When he's away for a week I nearly go wild!

BLANCHE Gracious!

STELLA And when he comes back I cry on his lap like a baby . . . [*She smiles to herself.*]

BLANCHE I guess that is what is meant by being in love . . . [STELLA *looks up with a radiant smile.*] Stella—

STELLA What?

BLANCHE [*in an uneasy rush*] I haven't asked you the things you probably thought I was going to ask. And so I'll expect you to be understanding about what *I* have to tell *you*.

STELLA What, Blanche? [*Her face turns anxious.*]

BLANCHE Well, Stella—you're going to reproach me, I know that you're bound to reproach me—but before you do—take into consideration—you left! I stayed and struggled! You came to New Orleans and looked out for yourself! *I* stayed at *Belle Reve* and tried to hold it together! I'm not meaning this in any reproachful way, but *all* the burden descended on *my* shoulders.

STELLA The best I could do was make my own living, Blanche.

[BLANCHE *begins to shake again with intensity.*]

BLANCHE I know, I know. But you are the one that abandoned Belle Reve, not I! I stayed and fought for it, bled for it, almost died for it!

STELLA Stop this hysterical outburst and tell me what's happened? What do you mean fought and bled? What kind of—

BLANCHE   I knew you would, Stella. I knew you would take this attitude about it!

STELLA   About—what?—please!

BLANCHE [*slowly*]   The loss—the loss . . .

STELLA   Belle Reve? Lost, is it? No!

BLANCHE   Yes, Stella.

> [*They stare at each other across the yellow-checked linoleum of the table.* BLANCHE *slowly nods her head and* STELLA *looks slowly down at her hands folded on the table. The music of the "Blue Piano" grows louder.* BLANCHE *touches her handkerchief to her forehead.*]

STELLA   But how did it go? What happened?

BLANCHE [*springing up*]   You're a fine one to ask me how it went!

STELLA   Blanche!

BLANCHE   You're a fine one to sit there *accusing me* of it!

STELLA   *Blanche!*

BLANCHE   I, I, *I* took the blows in my face and my body! All of those deaths! The long parade to the graveyard! Father, mother! Margaret, that dreadful way! So big with it, it couldn't be put in a coffin! But had to be burned like rubbish! You just came home in time for the funerals, Stella. And funerals are pretty compared to deaths. Funerals are quiet, but deaths—not always. Sometimes their breathing is hoarse, and sometimes it rattles, and sometimes they even cry out to you, "Don't let me go!" Even the old, sometimes, say, "Don't let me go." As if you were able to stop them! But funerals are quiet, with pretty flowers. And, oh, what gorgeous boxes they pack them away in! Unless you were there at the bed when they cried out, "Hold me!" you'd never suspect there was the struggle for breath and bleeding. You didn't dream, but I saw! *Saw! Saw!* And now you sit there telling me with your eyes that I let the place go! How in hell do you think all that sickness and dying was paid for? Death is expensive, Miss Stella! And old Cousin Jessie's right after Margaret's, hers! Why, the Grim Reaper had put up his tent on our doorstep! . . . Stella. Belle Reve was his headquarters! Honey— that's how it slipped through my fingers! Which of them left us a fortune? Which of them left a cent of insurance even? Only poor Jessie—one hundred to pay for her coffin. That was all, Stella! And I with my pitiful salary at the school. Yes, accuse me! Sit there and stare at me, thinking I let the place go! *I* let the place go? Where were *you*! In bed with your—Polack!

STELLA [*springing*]   Blanche! You be still! That's enough! [*She starts out.*]

BLANCHE   Where are you going?

STELLA   I'm going into the bathroom to wash my face.

BLANCHE   Oh, Stella, Stella, you're crying!

STELLA   Does that surprise you?

BLANCHE   Forgive me—I didn't mean to—

> [*The sound of men's voices is heard.* STELLA *goes into the bathroom, closing the door behind her. When the men appear, and* BLANCHE *realizes it must be* STANLEY *returning, she moves uncertainly from the bathroom door to the dressing table, looking apprehensively toward the front door.* STANLEY *enters, followed by* STEVE *and* MITCH. STANLEY *pauses near his door,* STEVE *by the foot of the spiral stair, and* MITCH *is slightly above and to the right of them, about to go out. As the men enter, we hear some of the following dialogue.*]

STANLEY   Is that how he got it?

STEVE   Sure that's how he got it. He hit the old weather-bird for 300 bucks on a six-number-ticket.

MITCH   Don't tell him those things; he'll believe it.
   [*Mitch starts out.*]

STANLEY [*restraining Mitch*]   Hey, Mitch—come back here.
   [BLANCHE, *at the sound of voices, retires in the bedroom. She picks up* STANLEY's *photo from dressing table, looks at it, puts it down. When* STANLEY *enters the apartment, she darts and hides behind the screen at the head of bed.*]

STEVE [*to* STANLEY *and* MITCH]   Hey, are we playin' poker tomorrow?

STANLEY   Sure—at Mitch's.

MITCH [*hearing this, returns quickly to the stair rail*]   No—not at my place. My mother's still sick!

STANLEY   Okay, at my place . . . [MITCH *starts out again.*] But you bring the beer!
   [MITCH *pretends not to hear—calls out "Good night, all," and goes out, singing.* EUNICE's *voice is heard, above.*]

EUNICE   Break it up down there! I made the spaghetti dish and ate it myself.

STEVE [*going upstairs*]   I told you and phoned you we was playing. [*to the men*] Jax beer![7]

EUNICE   You never phoned me once.

STEVE   I told you at breakfast—and phoned you at lunch . . .

EUNICE   Well, never mind about that. You just get yourself home here once in a while.

STEVE   You want it in the papers?
   [*More laughter and shouts of parting come from the men.* STANLEY *throws the screen door of the kitchen open and comes in. He is of medium height, about five feet eight or nine, and strongly, compactly built. Animal joy in his being is implicit in all his movements and attitudes. Since earliest manhood the center of his life has been pleasure with women, the giving and taking of it, not with weak indulgence, dependently, but with the power and pride of a richly feathered male bird among hens. Branching out from this complete and satisfying center are all the auxiliary channels of his life, such as his heartiness with men, his appreciation of rough humor, his love of good drink and food and games, his car, his radio, everything that is his, that bears his emblem of the gaudy seed-bearer. He sizes women up at a glance, with sexual classifications, crude images flashing into his mind and determining the way he smiles at them.*]

BLANCHE [*drawing involuntarily back from his stare*]   You must be Stanley. I'm Blanche.

STANLEY   Stella's sister?

BLANCHE   Yes.

STANLEY   H'lo. Where's the little woman?

BLANCHE   In the bathroom.

STANLEY   Oh. Didn't know you were coming in town.

BLANCHE   I—uh—

STANLEY   Where you from, Blanche?

7. A local brand.

BLANCHE   Why, I—live in Laurel.
        [*He has crossed to the closet and removed the whiskey bottle.*]
STANLEY   In Laurel, huh? Oh, yeah. Yeah, in Laurel, that's right. Not in my
    territory. Liquor goes fast in hot weather. [*He holds the bottle to the light
    to observe its depletion.*] Have a shot?
BLANCHE   No, I—rarely touch it.
STANLEY   Some people rarely touch it, but it touches them often.
BLANCHE [*faintly*]   Ha-ha.
STANLEY   My clothes're stickin' to me. Do you mind if I make myself com-
    fortable? [*He starts to remove his shirt.*]
BLANCHE   Please, please do.
STANLEY   Be comfortable is my motto.
BLANCHE   It's mine, too. It's hard to stay looking fresh. I haven't washed
    or even powdered my face and—here you are!
STANLEY   You know you can catch cold sitting around in damp things,
    especially when you been exercising hard like bowling is. You're a teacher,
    aren't you?
BLANCHE   Yes.
STANLEY   What do you teach, Blanche?
BLANCHE   English.
STANLEY   I never was a very good English student. How long you here for,
    Blanche?
BLANCHE   I—don't know yet.
STANLEY   You going to shack up here?
BLANCHE   I thought I would if it's not inconvenient for you all.
STANLEY   Good.
BLANCHE   Traveling wears me out.
STANLEY   Well, take it easy.
        [*A cat screeches near the window,* BLANCHE *springs up.*]
BLANCHE   What's that?
STANLEY   Cats . . . Hey, Stella!
STELLA [*faintly, from the bathroom*]   Yes, Stanley.
STANLEY   Haven't fallen in, have you? [*He grins at* BLANCHE. *She tries
    unsuccessfully to smile back. There is a silence.*] I'm afraid I'll strike you
    as being the unrefined type. Stella's spoke of you a good deal. You were
    married once, weren't you?
        [*The music of the polka rises up, faint in the distance.*]
BLANCHE   Yes. When I was quite young.
STANLEY   What happened?
BLANCHE   The boy—the boy died. [*She sinks back down.*] I'm afraid I'm—
    going to be sick! [*Her head falls on her arms.*]

Scene Two

It is six o'clock the following evening. BLANCHE *is bathing.* STELLA *is completing
her toilette.* BLANCHE's *dress, a flowered print, is laid out on* STELLA's *bed.*
    STANLEY *enters the kitchen from outside, leaving the door open on the perpet-
ual "Blue Piano" around the corner.*

STANLEY What's all this monkey doings?

STELLA Oh, Stan! [*She jumps up and kisses him, which he accepts with lordly composure.*] I'm taking Blanche to Galatoire's[8] for supper and then to a show, because it's your poker night.

STANLEY How about my supper, huh? I'm not going to no Galatoire's for supper!

STELLA I put you a cold plate on ice.

STANLEY Well, isn't that just dandy!

STELLA I'm going to try to keep Blanche out till the party breaks up because I don't know how she would take it. So we'll go to one of the little places in the Quarter afterward and you'd better give me some money.

STANLEY Where is she?

STELLA She's soaking in a hot tub to quiet her nerves. She's terribly upset.

STANLEY Over what?

STELLA She's been through such an ordeal.

STANLEY Yeah?

STELLA Stan, we've—lost Belle Reve!

STANLEY The place in the country?

STELLA Yes.

STANLEY How?

STELLA [*vaguely*] Oh, it had to be—sacrificed or something. [*There is a pause while* STANLEY *considers.* STELLA *is changing into her dress.*] When she comes in be sure to say something nice about her appearance. And, oh! Don't mention the baby. I haven't said anything yet, I'm waiting until she gets in a quieter condition.

STANLEY [*ominously*] So?

STELLA And try to understand her and be nice to her, Stan.

BLANCHE [*singing in the bathroom*] "From the land of the sky blue water, They brought a captive maid!"

STELLA She wasn't expecting to find us in such a small place. You see I'd tried to gloss things over a little in my letters.

STANLEY So?

STELLA And admire her dress and tell her she's looking wonderful. That's important with Blanche. Her little weakness!

STANLEY Yeah. I get the idea. Now let's skip back a little to where you said the country place was disposed of.

STELLA Oh!—yes . . .

STANLEY How about that? Let's have a few more details on that subjeck.

STELLA It's best not to talk much about it until she's calmed down.

STANLEY So that's the deal, huh? Sister Blanche cannot be annoyed with business details right now!

STELLA You saw how she was last night.

STANLEY Uh-hum, I saw how she was. Now let's have a gander at the bill of sale.

STELLA I haven't seen any.

STANLEY She didn't show you no papers, no deed of sale or nothing like that, huh?

---

8. Renowned fancy restaurant with traditional New Orleans cuisine.

STELLA   It seems like it wasn't sold.

STANLEY   Well, what in hell was it then, give away? To charity?

STELLA   Shhh! She'll hear you.

STANLEY   I don't care if she hears me. Let's see the papers!

STELLA   There weren't any papers, she didn't show any papers, I don't care about papers.

STANLEY   Have you ever heard of the Napoleonic code?[9]

STELLA   No, Stanley, I haven't heard of the Napoleonic code and if I have, I don't see what it—

STANLEY   Let me enlighten you on a point or two, baby.

STELLA   Yes?

STANLEY   In the state of Louisiana we have the Napoleonic code according to which what belongs to the wife belongs to the husband and vice versa. For instance if I had a piece of property, or you had a piece of property—

STELLA   My head is swimming!

STANLEY   All right. I'll wait till she gets through soaking in a hot tub and then I'll inquire if *she* is acquainted with the Napoleonic code. It looks to me like you have been swindled, baby, and when you're swindled under the Napoleonic code I'm swindled *too*. And I don't like to be *swindled*.

STELLA   There's plenty of time to ask her questions later but if you do now she'll go to pieces again. I don't understand what happened to Belle Reve but you don't know how ridiculous you are being when you suggest that my sister or I or anyone of our family could have perpetrated a swindle on anyone else.

STANLEY   Then where's the money if the place was sold?

STELLA   Not sold—*lost, lost!*
   [*He stalks into bedroom, and she follows him.*]
   Stanley!
   [*He pulls open the wardrobe trunk standing in middle of room and jerks out an armful of dresses.*]

STANLEY   Open your eyes to this stuff! You think she got them out of a teacher's pay?

STELLA   Hush!

STANLEY   Look at these feathers and furs that she come here to preen herself in! What's this here? A solid-gold dress, I believe! And this one! What is these here? Fox-pieces! [*He blows on them.*] Genuine fox fur-pieces, a half a mile long! Where are your fox-pieces, Stella? Bushy snow-white ones, no less! Where are your white fox-pieces?

STELLA   Those are inexpensive summer furs that Blanche has had a long time.

STANLEY   I got an acquaintance who deals in this sort of merchandise. I'll have him in here to appraise it. I'm willing to bet you there's thousands of dollars invested in this stuff here!

STELLA   Don't be such an idiot, Stanley!
   [*He hurls the furs to the day bed. Then he jerks open a small drawer in the trunk and pulls up a fistful of costume jewelry.*]

STANLEY   And what have we here? The treasure chest of a pirate!

9. This codification of French law (1802), made by Napoleon as emperor, is the basis for Louisiana's civil law.

STELLA   Oh, Stanley!

STANLEY   Pearls! Ropes of them! What is this sister of yours, a deep-sea diver? Bracelets of solid gold, too! Where are your pearls and gold bracelets?

STELLA   Shhh! Be still, Stanley!

STANLEY   And diamonds! A crown for an empress!

STELLA   A rhinestone tiara she wore to a costume ball.

STANLEY   What's rhinestone?

STELLA   Next door to glass.

STANLEY   Are you kidding? I have an acquaintance that works in a jewelry store. I'll have him in here to make an appraisal of this. Here's your plantation, or what was left of it, here!

STELLA   You have no idea how stupid and horrid you're being! Now close that trunk before she comes out of the bathroom!

[*He kicks the trunk partly closed and sits on the kitchen table.*]

STANLEY   The Kowalskis and the DuBoises have different notions.

STELLA [*angrily*]   Indeed they have, thank heavens!—*I'm* going outside. [*She snatches up her white hat and gloves and crosses to the outside door.*] You come out with me while Blanche is getting dressed.

STANLEY   Since when do you give me orders?

STELLA   Are you going to stay here and insult her?

STANLEY   You're damn tootin' I'm going to stay here.

[STELLA *goes out to the porch.* BLANCHE *comes out of the bathroom in a red satin robe.*]

BLANCHE [*airily*]   Hello, Stanley! Here I am, all freshly bathed and scented, and feeling like a brand new human being!

[*He lights a cigarette.*]

STANLEY   That's good.

BLANCHE [*drawing the curtains at the windows*]   Excuse me while I slip on my pretty new dress!

STANLEY   Go right ahead, Blanche.

[*She closes the drapes between the rooms.*]

BLANCHE   I understand there's to be a little card party to which we ladies are cordially *not* invited!

STANLEY [*ominously*]   Yeah?

[BLANCHE *throws off her robe and slips into a flowered print dress.*]

BLANCHE   Where's Stella?

STANLEY   Out on the porch.

BLANCHE   I'm going to ask a favor of you in a moment.

STANLEY   What could that be, I wonder?

BLANCHE   Some buttons in back! You may enter! [*He crosses through drapes with a smoldering look.*] How do I look?

STANLEY   You look all right.

BLANCHE   Many thanks! Now the buttons!

STANLEY   I can't do nothing with them.

BLANCHE   You men with your big clumsy fingers. May I have a drag on your cig?

STANLEY   Have one for yourself.

BLANCHE   Why, thanks! . . . It looks like my trunk has exploded.

STANLEY   Me an' Stella were helping you unpack.

BLANCHE   Well, you certainly did a fast and thorough job of it!

STANLEY   It looks like you raided some stylish shops in Paris.

BLANCHE   Ha-ha! Yes—clothes are my passion!

STANLEY   What does it cost for a string of fur-pieces like that?

BLANCHE   Why, those were a tribute from an admirer of mine!

STANLEY   He must have had a lot of—admiration!

BLANCHE   Oh, in my youth I excited some admiration. But look at me now! [*She smiles at him radiantly.*] Would you think it possible that I was once considered to be—attractive?

STANLEY   Your looks are okay.

BLANCHE   I was fishing for a compliment, Stanley.

STANLEY   I don't go in for that stuff.

BLANCHE   What—stuff?

STANLEY   Compliments to women about their looks. I never met a woman that didn't know if she was good-looking or not without being told, and some of them give themselves credit for more than they've got. I once went out with a doll who said to me, "I am the glamorous type, I am the glamorous type!" I said, "So what?"

BLANCHE   And what did she say then?

STANLEY   She didn't say nothing. That shut her up like a clam.

BLANCHE   Did it end the romance?

STANLEY   It ended the conversation—that was all. Some men are took in by this Hollywood glamor stuff and some men are not.

BLANCHE   I'm sure you belong in the second category.

STANLEY   That's right.

BLANCHE   I cannot imagine any witch of a woman casting a spell over you.

STANLEY   That's—right.

BLANCHE   You're simple, straightforward and honest, a little bit on the primitive side I should think. To interest you a woman would have to— [*She pauses with an indefinite gesture.*]

STANLEY [*slowly*]   Lay . . . her cards on the table.

BLANCHE [*smiling*]   Well, I never cared for wishy-washy people. That was why, when you walked in here last night, I said to myself—"My sister has married a man!"—Of course that was all that I could tell about you.

STANLEY [*booming*]   Now let's cut the re-bop![1]

BLANCHE [*pressing hands to her ears*]   Ouuuuu!

STELLA [*calling from the steps*]   Stanley! You come out here and let Blanche finish dressing!

BLANCHE   I'm through dressing, honey.

STELLA   Well, you come out, then.

STANLEY   Your sister and I are having a little talk.

BLANCHE [*lightly*]   Honey, do me a favor. Run to the drugstore and get me a lemon Coke with plenty of chipped ice in it!—Will you do that for me, sweetie?

STELLA [*uncertainly*]   Yes. [*She goes around the corner of the building.*]

BLANCHE   The poor little thing was out there listening to us, and I have an idea she doesn't understand you as well as I do. . . . All right; now,

---

1. Nonsense (from "bebop," a form of jazz).

Mr. Kowalski, let us proceed without any more double-talk. I'm ready to answer all questions. I've nothing to hide. What is it?

STANLEY   There is such a thing in this state of Louisiana as the Napoleonic code, according to which whatever belongs to my wife is also mine—and vice versa.

BLANCHE   My, but you have an impressive judicial air!
  [*She sprays herself with her atomizer; then playfully sprays him with it. He seizes the atomizer and slams it down on the dresser. She throws back her head and laughs.*]

STANLEY   If I didn't know that you was my wife's sister I'd get ideas about you!

BLANCHE   Such as what!

STANLEY   Don't play so dumb. You know what!

BLANCHE [*she puts the atomizer on the table*]   All right. Cards on the table. That suits me. [*She turns to* STANLEY.] I know I fib a good deal. After all, a woman's charm is fifty per cent illusion, but when a thing is important I tell the truth, and this is the truth: I haven't cheated my sister or you or anyone else as long as I have lived.

STANLEY   Where's the papers? In the trunk?

BLANCHE   Everything that I own is in that trunk.
  [STANLEY *crosses to the trunk, shoves it roughly open and begins to open compartments.*]

BLANCHE   What in the name of heaven are you thinking of! What's in the back of that little boy's mind of yours? That I am absconding with something, attempting some kind of treachery on my sister?—Let me do that! It will be faster and simpler . . . [*She crosses to the trunk and takes out a box.*] I keep my papers mostly in this tin box. [*She opens it.*]

STANLEY   What's them underneath? [*He indicates another sheaf of paper.*]

BLANCHE   These are love-letters, yellowing with antiquity, all from one boy.
  [*He snatches them up. She speaks fiercely.*] Give those back to me!

STANLEY   I'll have a look at them first!

BLANCHE   The touch of your hands insults them!

STANLEY   Don't pull that stuff!
  [*He rips off the ribbon and starts to examine them.* BLANCHE *snatches them from him, and they cascade to the floor.*]

BLANCHE   Now that you've touched them I'll burn them!

STANLEY [*staring, baffled*]   What in hell are they?

BLANCHE [*on the floor gathering them up*]   Poems a dead boy wrote. I hurt him the way that you would like to hurt me, but you can't! I'm not young and vulnerable any more. But my young husband was and I—never mind about that! Just give them back to me!

STANLEY   What do you mean by saying you'll have to burn them?

BLANCHE   I'm sorry, I must have lost my head for a moment. Everyone has something he won't let others touch because of their—intimate nature . . .
  [*She now seems faint with exhaustion and she sits down with the strong box and puts on a pair of glasses and goes methodically through a large stack of papers.*]
  Ambler & Ambler. Hmmmmm. . . . Crabtree. . . . More Ambler & Ambler.

STANLEY   What is Ambler & Ambler?

BLANCHE   A firm that made loans on the place.

STANLEY   Then it *was* lost on a mortgage?

BLANCHE [*touching her forehead*]   That must've been what happened.

STANLEY   I don't want no ifs, ands or buts! What's all the rest of them papers?
[*She hands him the entire box. He carries it to the table and starts to examine the paper.*]

BLANCHE [*picking up a large envelope containing more papers*]   There are thousands of papers, stretching back over hundreds of years, affecting Belle Reve as, piece by piece, our improvident grandfathers and father and uncles and brothers exchanged the land for their epic fornications—to put it plainly! [*She removes her glasses with an exhausted laugh.*] The four-letter word deprived us of our plantation, till finally all that was left—and Stella can verify that!—was the house itself and about twenty acres of ground, including a graveyard, to which now all but Stella and I have retreated. [*She pours the contents of the envelope on the table.*] Here all of them are, all papers! I hereby endow you with them! Take them, peruse them—commit them to memory, even! I think it's wonderfully fitting that Belle Reve should finally be this bunch of old papers in your big, capable hands! . . . I wonder if Stella's come back with my lemon Coke . . . [*She leans back and closes her eyes.*]

STANLEY   I have a lawyer acquaintance who will study these out.

BLANCHE   Present them to him with a box of aspirin tablets.

STANLEY [*becoming somewhat sheepish*]   You see, under the Napoleonic code—a man has to take an interest in his wife's affairs—especially now that she's going to have a baby.
[BLANCHE *opens her eyes. The "Blue Piano" sounds louder.*]

BLANCHE   Stella? Stella going to have a baby? [*dreamily*] I didn't know she was going to have a baby!
[*She gets up and crosses to the outside door.* STELLA *appears around the corner with a carton from the drugstore.* STANLEY *goes into the bedroom with the envelope and the box. The inner rooms fade to darkness and the outside wall of the house is visible,* BLANCHE *meets* STELLA *at the foot of the steps to the sidewalk.*]

BLANCHE   Stella, Stella for star! How lovely to have a baby! It's all right. Everything's all right.

STELLA   I'm sorry he did that to you.

BLANCHE   Oh, I guess he's just not the type that goes for jasmine perfume, but maybe he's what we need to mix with our blood now that we've lost Belle Reve. We thrashed it out. I feel a bit shaky, but I think I handled it nicely, I laughed and treated it all as a joke. [STEVE *and* PABLO *appear, carrying a case of beer.*] I called him a little boy and laughed and flirted. Yes, I was flirting with your husband! [*as the men approach*] The guests are gathering for the poker party. [*The two men pass between them, and enter the house.*] Which way do we go now, Stella—this way?

STELLA   No, this way. [*She leads* BLANCHE *away.*]

BLANCHE [*laughing*]   The blind are leading the blind!
[*A tamale* VENDOR *is heard calling.*]

VENDOR'S VOICE   Red-hot!

Scene Three

THE POKER NIGHT[2]

*There is a picture of Van Gogh's[3] of a billiard-parlor at night. The kitchen now suggests that sort of lurid nocturnal brilliance, the raw colors of childhood's spectrum. Over the yellow linoleum of the kitchen table hangs an electric bulb with a vivid green glass shade. The poker players—*STANLEY, STEVE, MITCH *and* PABLO—*wear colored shirts, solid blues, a purple, a red-and-white check, a light green, and they are men at the peak of their physical manhood, as coarse and direct and powerful as the primary colors. There are vivid slices of watermelon on the table, whiskey bottles and glasses. The bedroom is relatively dim with only the light that spills between the portieres and through the wide window on the street.*

For a moment, there is absorbed silence as a hand is dealt.

STEVE   Anything wild this deal?

PABLO   One-eyed jacks are wild.

STEVE   Give me two cards.

PABLO   You, Mitch?

MITCH   I'm out.

PABLO   One.

MITCH   Anyone want a shot?

STANLEY   Yeah. Me.

PABLO   Why don't somebody go to the Chinaman's and bring back a load of chop suey?

STANLEY   When I'm losing you want to eat! Ante up! Openers? Openers! Get y'r ass off the table, Mitch. Nothing belongs on a poker table but cards, chips and whiskey.
   [*He lurches up and tosses some watermelon rinds to the floor.*]

MITCH   Kind of on your high horse, ain't you?

STANLEY   How many?

STEVE   Give me three.

STANLEY   One.

MITCH   I'm out again. I oughta go home pretty soon.

STANLEY   Shut up.

MITCH   I gotta sick mother. She don't go to sleep until I come in at night.

STANLEY   Then why don't you stay home with her?

MITCH   She says to go out, so I go, but I don't enjoy it. All the while I keep wondering how she is.

STANLEY   Aw, for the sake of Jesus, go home, then!

PABLO   What've you got?

STEVE   Spade flush.

MITCH   You all are married. But I'll be alone when she goes.—I'm going to the bathroom.

STANLEY   Hurry back and we'll fix you a sugar-tit.

MITCH   Aw, go rut. [*He crosses through the bedroom into the bathroom.*]

STEVE [*dealing a hand*]   Seven card stud.[4] [*telling his joke as he deals*] This ole farmer is out in back of his house sittin' down th'owing corn to the

---

2. Williams's first title for *A Streetcar Named Desire* (see headnote).
3. *The Night Café*, by the Dutch Postimpression-

ist painter Vincent van Gogh (1853–1890).
4. An adventurous and risky variant of poker.

chickens when all at once he hears a loud cackle and this young hen comes lickety split around the side of the house with the rooster right behind her and gaining on her fast.

STANLEY [*impatient with the story*]   Deal!

STEVE   But when the rooster catches sight of the farmer th'owing the corn he puts on the brakes and lets the hen get away and starts pecking corn. And the old farmer says, "Lord God, I hopes I never gits *that* hongry!"

    [STEVE *and* PABLO *laugh. The sisters appear around the corner of the building.*]

STELLA   The game is still going on.

BLANCHE   How do I look?

STELLA   Lovely, Blanche.

BLANCHE   I feel so hot and frazzled. Wait till I powder before you open the door. Do I look done in?

STELLA   Why no. You are as fresh as a daisy.

BLANCHE   One that's been picked a few days.

    [STELLA *opens the door and they enter.*]

STELLA   Well, well, well. I see you boys are still at it?

STANLEY   Where you been?

STELLA   Blanche and I took in a show. Blanche, this is Mr. Gonzales and Mr. Hubbell.

BLANCHE   Please don't get up.

STANLEY   Nobody's going to get up, so don't be worried.

STELLA   How much longer is this game going to continue?

STANLEY   Till we get ready to quit.

BLANCHE   Poker is so fascinating. Could I kibitz?

STANLEY   You could not. Why don't you women go up and sit with Eunice?

STELLA   Because it is nearly two-thirty. [BLANCHE *crosses into the bedroom and partially closes the portieres.*] Couldn't you call it quits after one more hand?

    [*A chair scrapes.* STANLEY *gives a loud whack of his hand on her thigh.*]

STELLA [*sharply*]   That's not fun, Stanley.

    [*The men laugh,* STELLA *goes into the bedroom.*]

STELLA   It makes me so mad when he does that in front of people.

BLANCHE   I think I will bathe.

STELLA   Again?

BLANCHE   My nerves are in knots. Is the bathroom occupied?

STELLA   I don't know.

    [BLANCHE *knocks,* MITCH *opens the door and comes out, still wiping his hands on a towel.*]

BLANCHE   Oh!—good evening.

MITCH   Hello. [*He stares at her.*]

STELLA   Blanche, this is Harold Mitchell. My sister, Blanche DuBois.

MITCH [*with awkward courtesy*]   How do you do, Miss DuBois.

STELLA   How is your mother now, Mitch?

MITCH   About the same, thanks. She appreciated your sending over that custard.—Excuse me, please.

    [*He crosses slowly back into the kitchen, glancing back at* BLANCHE *and coughing a little shyly. He realizes he still has the towel in his hands and with an embarrassed laugh hands it to* STELLA. BLANCHE *looks after him with a certain interest.*]

BLANCHE   That one seems—superior to the others.

STELLA   Yes, he is.

BLANCHE   I thought he had a sort of sensitive look.

STELLA   His mother is sick.

BLANCHE   Is he married?

STELLA   No.

BLANCHE   Is he a wolf?

STELLA   Why, Blanche! [BLANCHE *laughs.*] I don't think he would be.

BLANCHE   What does—what does he do? [*She is unbuttoning her blouse.*]

STELLA   He's on the precision bench in the spare parts department. At the plant Stanley travels for.

BLANCHE   Is that something much?

STELLA   No. Stanley's the only one of his crowd that's likely to get anywhere.

BLANCHE   What makes you think Stanley will?

STELLA   Look at him.

BLANCHE   I've looked at him.

STELLA   Then you should know.

BLANCHE   I'm sorry, but I haven't noticed the stamp of genius even on Stanley's forehead.

> [*She takes off the blouse and stands in her pink silk brassiere and white skirt in the light through the portieres. The game has continued in undertones.*]

STELLA   It isn't on his forehead and it isn't genius.

BLANCHE   Oh. Well, what is it, and where? I would like to know.

STELLA   It's a drive that he has. You're standing in the light, Blanche!

BLANCHE   Oh, am I!

> [*She moves out of the yellow streak of light.* STELLA *has removed her dress and put on a light blue satin kimona.*]

STELLA   [*with girlish laughter*]   You ought to see their wives.

BLANCHE   [*laughingly*]   I can imagine. Big, beefy things, I suppose.

STELLA   You know that one upstairs? [*more laughter*] One time [*laughing*] the plaster—[*laughing*] cracked—

STANLEY   You hens cut out that conversation in there!

STELLA   You can't hear us.

STANLEY   Well, you can hear me and I said to hush up!

STELLA   This is my house and I'll talk as much as I want to!

BLANCHE   Stella, don't start a row.

STELLA   He's half drunk!—I'll be out in a minute.

> [*She goes into the bathroom,* BLANCHE *rises and crosses leisurely to a small white radio and turns it on.*]

STANLEY   Awright, Mitch, you in?

MITCH   What? Oh!—No, I'm out!

> [BLANCHE *moves back into the streak of light. She raises her arms and stretches, as she moves indolently back to the chair. Rhumba music comes over the radio.* MITCH *rises at the table.*]

STANLEY   Who turned that on in there?

BLANCHE   I did. Do you mind?

STANLEY   Turn it off!

STEVE   Aw, let the girls have their music.

PABLO   Sure, that's good, leave it on!

STEVE   Sounds like Xavier Cugat!⁵

> [STANLEY *jumps up and, crossing to the radio, turns it off. He stops short at the sight of* BLANCHE *in the chair. She returns his look without flinching. Then he sits again at the poker table. Two of the men have started arguing hotly.*]

STEVE   I didn't hear you name it.

PABLO   Didn't I name it, Mitch?

MITCH   I wasn't listenin'.

PABLO   What were you doing, then?

STANLEY   He was looking through them drapes. [*He jumps up and jerks roughly at curtains to close them.*] Now deal the hand over again and let's play cards or quit. Some people get ants when they win.

> [MITCH *rises as* STANLEY *returns to his seat.*]

STANLEY [*yelling*]   Sit down!

MITCH   I'm going to the "head." Deal me out.

PABLO   Sure he's got ants now. Seven five-dollar bills in his pants pocket folded up tight as spitballs.

STEVE   Tomorrow you'll see him at the cashier's window getting them changed into quarters.

STANLEY   And when he goes home he'll deposit them one by one in a piggy bank his mother give him for Christmas. [*dealing*] This game is Spit in the Ocean.⁶

> [MITCH *laughs uncomfortably and continues through the portieres. He stops just inside.*]

BLANCHE [*softly*]   Hello! The Little Boys' Room is busy right now.

MITCH   We've—been drinking beer.

BLANCHE   I hate beer.

MITCH   It's—a hot weather drink.

BLANCHE   Oh, I don't think so; it always makes me warmer. Have you got any cigs? [*She has slipped on the dark red satin wrapper.*]

MITCH   Sure.

BLANCHE   What kind are they?

MITCH   Luckies.

BLANCHE   Oh, good. What a pretty case. Silver?

MITCH   Yes. Yes; read the inscription.

BLANCHE   Oh, is there an inscription? I can't make it out. [*He strikes a match and moves closer.*] Oh! [*reading with feigned difficulty*] "And if God choose, / I shall but love thee better—after—death!" Why, that's from my favorite sonnet by Mrs. Browning.⁷

MITCH   You know it?

BLANCHE   Certainly I do!

MITCH   There's a story connected with that inscription.

BLANCHE   It sounds like a romance.

MITCH   A pretty sad one.

BLANCHE   Oh?

MITCH   The girl's dead now.

---

5. Cuban bandleader (1900–1990), well known for composing and playing rhumbas.
6. Another variant of poker.
7. Elizabeth Barrett Browning (1806–1861), British poet, most famous for her sequence of love poems, *Sonnets from the Portuguese*. The quotation here is from sonnet 43, better known by its first line, "How do I love thee?"

BLANCHE [*in a tone of deep sympathy*]   Oh!

MITCH   She knew she was dying when she give me this. A very strange girl, very sweet—very!

BLANCHE   She must have been fond of you. Sick people have such deep, sincere attachments.

MITCH   That's right, they certainly do.

BLANCHE   Sorrow makes for sincerity, I think.

MITCH   It sure brings it out in people.

BLANCHE   The little there is belongs to people who have experienced some sorrow.

MITCH   I believe you are right about that.

BLANCHE   I'm positive that I am. Show me a person who hasn't known any sorrow and I'll show you a shuperficial—Listen to me! My tongue is a little—thick! You boys are responsible for it. The show let out at eleven and we couldn't come home on account of the poker game so we had to go somewhere and drink. I'm not accustomed to having more than one drink. Two is the limit—and *three*! [*She laughs.*] Tonight I had three.

STANLEY   Mitch!

MITCH   Deal me out. I'm talking to Miss—

BLANCHE   DuBois.

MITCH   Miss DuBois?

BLANCHE   It's a French name. It means woods and Blanche means white, so the two together mean white woods. Like an orchard in spring! You can remember it by that.

MITCH   You're French?

BLANCHE   We are French by extraction. Our first American ancestors were French Huguenots.

MITCH   You are Stella's sister, are you not?

BLANCHE   Yes, Stella is my precious little sister. I call her little in spite of the fact she's somewhat older than I. Just slightly. Less than a year. Will you do something for me?

MITCH   Sure. What?

BLANCHE   I bought this adorable little colored paper lantern at a Chinese shop on Bourbon. Put it over the light bulb! Will you, please?

MITCH   Be glad to.

BLANCHE   I can't stand a naked light bulb, any more than I can a rude remark or a vulgar action.

MITCH [*adjusting the lantern*]   I guess we strike you as being a pretty rough bunch.

BLANCHE   I'm very adaptable—to circumstances.

MITCH   Well, that's a good thing to be. You are visiting Stanley and Stella?

BLANCHE   Stella hasn't been so well lately, and I came down to help her for a while. She's very run down.

MITCH   You're not—?

BLANCHE   Married? No, no. I'm an old maid schoolteacher!

MITCH   You may teach school but you're certainly not an old maid.

BLANCHE   Thank you, sir! I appreciate your gallantry!

MITCH   So you are in the teaching profession?

BLANCHE   Yes. Ah, yes . . .

MITCH   Grade school or high school or—

STANLEY [*bellowing*]   Mitch!

MITCH   Coming!

BLANCHE   Gracious, what lung-power! . . . I teach high school. In Laurel.

MITCH   What do you teach? What subject?

BLANCHE   Guess!

MITCH   I bet you teach art or music? [BLANCHE *laughs delicately.*] Of course I could be wrong. You might teach arithmetic.

BLANCHE   Never arithmetic, sir; never arithmetic! [*with a laugh*] I don't even know my multiplication tables! No, I have the misfortune of being an English instructor. I attempt to instill a bunch of bobby-soxers and drugstore Romeos with reverence for Hawthorne and Whitman and Poe!

MITCH   I guess that some of them are more interested in other things.

BLANCHE   How very right you are! Their literary heritage is not what most of them treasure above all else! But they're sweet things! And in the spring, it's touching to notice them making their first discovery of love! As if nobody had ever known it before!

[*The bathroom door opens and* STELLA *comes out.* BLANCHE *continues talking to* MITCH.]

Oh! Have you finished? Wait—I'll turn on the radio.

[*She turns the knobs on the radio and it begins to play "Wien, Wien, nur du allein."*[8] BLANCHE *waltzes to the music with romantic gestures,* MITCH *is delighted and moves in awkward imitation like a dancing bear.* STANLEY *stalks fiercely through the portieres into the bedroom. He crosses to the small white radio and snatches it off the table. With a shouted oath, he tosses the instrument out the window.*]

STELLA   Drunk—drunk—animal thing, you! [*She rushes through to the poker table.*] All of you—please go home! If any of you have one spark of decency in you—

BLANCHE [*wildly*]   Stella, watch out, he's—

[STANLEY *charges after* STELLA.]

MEN [*feebly*]   Take it easy, Stanley. Easy, fellow.—Let's all—

STELLA   You lay your hands on me and I'll—

[*She backs out of sight. He advances and disappears. There is the sound of a blow.* STELLA *cries out.* BLANCHE *screams and runs into the kitchen. The men rush forward and there is grappling and cursing. Something is overturned with a crash.*]

BLANCHE [*shrilly*]   My sister is going to have a baby!

MITCH   This is terrible.

BLANCHE   Lunacy, absolute lunacy!

MITCH   Get him in here, men.

[STANLEY *is forced, pinioned by the two men, into the bedroom. He nearly throws them off. Then all at once he subsides and is limp in their grasp. They speak quietly and lovingly to him and he leans his face on one of their shoulders.*]

STELLA [*in a high, unnatural voice, out of sight*]   I want to go away, I want to go away!

MITCH   Poker shouldn't be played in a house with women.

[BLANCHE *rushes into the bedroom.*]

BLANCHE   I want my sister's clothes! We'll go to that woman's upstairs!

---

8. Vienna, Vienna, you are my only (German); a waltz from an operetta by Franz Lehár (1870–1948).

MITCH   Where is the clothes?

BLANCHE [*opening the closet*]   I've got them! [*She rushes through to* STELLA.]
Stella, Stella, precious! Dear, dear little sister, don't be afraid!
[*With her arm around* STELLA, BLANCHE *guides her to the outside door
and upstairs.*]

STANLEY [*dully*]   What's the matter; what's happened?

MITCH   You just blew your top, Stan.

PABLO   He's okay, now.

STEVE   Sure, my boy's okay!

MITCH   Put him on the bed and get a wet towel.

PABLO   I think coffee would do him a world of good, now.

STANLEY [*thickly*]   I want water.

MITCH   Put him under the shower!
[*The men talk quietly as they lead him to the bathroom.*]

STANLEY   Let the rut go of me, you sons of bitches!
[*Sounds of blows are heard. The water goes on full tilt.*]

STEVE   Let's get quick out of here!
[*They rush to the poker table and sweep up their winnings on their way
out.*]

MITCH [*sadly but firmly*]   Poker should not be played in a house with
women.
[*The door closes on them and the place is still. The Negro entertainers
in the bar around the corner play "Paper Doll"*[9] *slow and blue. After a
moment* STANLEY *comes out of the bathroom dripping water and still in
his clinging wet polka dot drawers.*]

STANLEY   Stella! [*There is a pause.*] My baby doll's left me!
[*He breaks into sobs. Then he goes to the phone and dials, still shuddering with sobs.*]
Eunice? I want my baby! [*He waits a moment; then he hangs up and dials
again.*] Eunice! I'll keep on ringin' until I talk with my baby!
[*An indistinguishable shrill voice is heard. He hurls phone to floor. Dissonant brass and piano sounds as the rooms dim out to darkness and the
outer walls appear in the night light. The "Blue Piano" plays for a brief
interval. Finally,* STANLEY *stumbles half-dressed out to the porch and
down the wooden steps to the pavement before the building. There he
throws back his head like a baying hound and bellows his wife's name:
"Stella! Stella, sweetheart! Stella!"*]

STANLEY   Stell-*lahhhhh*!

EUNICE [*calling down from the door of her upper apartment*]   Quit that
howling out there an' go back to bed!

STANLEY   I want my baby down here. Stella, Stella!

EUNICE   She ain't comin' down so you quit! Or you'll git th' law on you!

STANLEY   Stella!

EUNICE   You can't beat on a woman an' then call 'er back! She won't come!
And her goin' t' have a baby! . . . You stinker! You whelp of a Polack, you!
I hope they do haul you in and turn the fire hose on you, same as the last
time!

STANLEY [*humbly*]   Eunice, I want my girl to come down with me!

EUNICE   Hah! [*She slams her door.*]

---

9. Popular song of the early 1940s by Johnny Black.

STANLEY [*with heaven-splitting violence*] *STELL-LAHHHHH!*
>[*The low-tone clarinet moans. The door upstairs opens again.* STELLA *slips down the rickety stairs in her robe. Her eyes are glistening with tears and her hair loose about her throat and shoulders. They stare at each other. Then they come together with low, animal moans. He falls to his knees on the steps and presses his face to her belly, curving a little with maternity. Her eyes go blind with tenderness as she catches his head and raises him level with her. He snatches the screen door open and lifts her off her feet and bears her into the dark flat.* BLANCHE *comes out the upper landing in her robe and slips fearfully down the steps.*]

BLANCHE Where is my little sister? Stella? Stella?
>[*She stops before the dark entrance of her sister's flat. Then catches her breath as if struck. She rushes down to the walk before the house. She looks right and left as if for a sanctuary. The music fades away,* MITCH *appears from around the corner.*]

MITCH Miss DuBois?

BLANCHE Oh!

MITCH All quiet on the Potomac now?

BLANCHE She ran downstairs and went back in there with him.

MITCH Sure she did.

BLANCHE I'm terrified!

MITCH Ho-ho! There's nothing to be scared of. They're crazy about each other.

BLANCHE I'm not used to such—

MITCH Naw, it's a shame this had to happen when you just got here. But don't take it serious.

BLANCHE Violence! Is so—

MITCH Set down on the steps and have a cigarette with me.

BLANCHE I'm not properly dressed.

MITCH That don't make no difference in the Quarter.

BLANCHE Such a pretty silver case.

MITCH I showed you the inscription, didn't I?

BLANCHE Yes. [*During the pause, she looks up at the sky.*] There's so much— so much confusion in the world . . . [*He coughs diffidently.*] Thank you for being so kind! I need kindness now.

Scene Four

It is early the following morning. There is a confusion of street cries like a choral chant.

STELLA *is lying down in the bedroom. Her face is serene in the early morning sunlight. One hand rests on her belly, rounding slightly with new maternity. From the other dangles a book of colored comics. Her eyes and lips have that almost narcotized tranquility that is in the faces of Eastern idols.*

The table is sloppy with remains of breakfast and the debris of the preceding night, and STANLEY's *gaudy pyjamas lie across the threshold of the bathroom. The outside door is slightly ajar on a sky of summer brilliance.*

BLANCHE *appears at this door. She has spent a sleepless night and her appearance entirely contrasts with* STELLA's. *She presses her knuckles nervously to her lips as she looks through the door, before entering.*

BLANCHE   Stella?

STELLA [*stirring lazily*]   Hmmh?

[BLANCHE *utters a moaning cry and runs into the bedroom, throwing herself down beside* STELLA *in a rush of hysterical tenderness.*]

BLANCHE   Baby, my baby sister!

STELLA [*drawing away from her*]   Blanche, what is the matter with you?

[BLANCHE *straightens up slowly and stands beside the bed looking down at her sister with knuckles pressed to her lips.*]

BLANCHE   He's left?

STELLA   Stan? Yes.

BLANCHE   Will he be back?

STELLA   He's gone to get the car greased. Why?

BLANCHE   Why! I've been half crazy, Stella! When I found out you'd been insane enough to come back in here after what happened—I started to rush in after you!

STELLA   I'm glad you didn't.

BLANCHE   What were you thinking of? [STELLA *makes an indefinite gesture.*] Answer me! What? What?

STELLA   Please, Blanche! Sit down and stop yelling.

BLANCHE   All right, Stella. I will repeat the question quietly now. How could you come back in this place last night? Why, you must have slept with him!

[STELLA *gets up in a calm and leisurely way.*]

STELLA   Blanche, I'd forgotten how excitable you are. You're making much too much fuss about this.

BLANCHE   Am I?

STELLA   Yes, you are, Blanche. I know how it must have seemed to you and I'm awful sorry it had to happen, but it wasn't anything as serious as you seem to take it. In the first place, when men are drinking and playing poker anything can happen. It's always a powder-keg. He didn't know what he was doing. . . . He was as good as a lamb when I came back and he's really very, very ashamed of himself.

BLANCHE   And that—that makes it all right?

STELLA   No, it isn't all right for anybody to make such a terrible row, but—people do sometimes. Stanley's always smashed things. Why, on our wedding night—soon as we came in here—he snatched off one of my slippers and rushed about the place smashing light bulbs with it.

BLANCHE   He did—*what*?

STELLA   He smashed all the light bulbs with the heel of my slipper! [*She laughs.*]

BLANCHE   And you—you *let* him? Didn't *run*, didn't *scream*?

STELLA   I was—sort of—thrilled by it. [*She waits for a moment.*] Eunice and you had breakfast?

BLANCHE   Do you suppose I wanted any breakfast?

STELLA   There's some coffee left on the stove.

BLANCHE   You're so—matter of fact about it, Stella.

STELLA   What other can I be? He's taken the radio to get it fixed. It didn't land on the pavement so only one tube was smashed.

BLANCHE   And you are standing there smiling!

STELLA   What do you want me to do?

BLANCHE   Pull yourself together and face the facts.

STELLA   What are they, in your opinion?

BLANCHE   In my opinion? You're married to a madman!

STELLA   No!

BLANCHE   Yes, you are, your fix is worse than mine is! Only you're not being sensible about it. I'm going to *do* something. Get hold of myself and make myself a new life!

STELLA   Yes?

BLANCHE   But you've given in. And that isn't right, you're not old! You can get out.

STELLA   [*slowly and emphatically*]   I'm not in anything I want to get out of.

BLANCHE   [*incredulously*]   What—Stella?

STELLA   I said I am not in anything that I have a desire to get out of. Look at the mess in this room! And those empty bottles! They went through two cases last night! He promised this morning that he was going to quit having these poker parties, but you know how long such a promise is going to keep. Oh, well, it's his pleasure, like mine is movies and bridge. People have got to tolerate each other's habits, I guess.

BLANCHE   I don't understand you. [STELLA *turns toward her.*] I don't understand your indifference. Is this a Chinese philosophy you've—cultivated?

STELLA   Is what—what?

BLANCHE   This—shuffling about and mumbling—'One tube smashed—beer bottles—mess in the kitchen!'—as if nothing out of the ordinary has happened! [STELLA *laughs uncertainly and picking up the broom, twirls it in her hands.*]

BLANCHE   Are you deliberately shaking that thing in my face?

STELLA   No.

BLANCHE   Stop it. Let go of that broom. I won't have you cleaning up for him!

STELLA   Then who's going to do it? Are you?

BLANCHE   I? I!

STELLA   No, I didn't think so.

BLANCHE   Oh, let me think, if only my mind would function! We've got to get hold of some money, that's the way out!

STELLA   I guess that money is always nice to get hold of.

BLANCHE   Listen to me. I have an idea of some kind. [*Shakily she twists a cigarette into her holder.*] Do you remember Shep Huntleigh? [STELLA *shakes her head.*] Of course you remember Shep Huntleigh. I went out with him at college and wore his pin for a while. Well—

STELLA   Well?

BLANCHE   I ran into him last winter. You know I went to Miami during the Christmas holidays?

STELLA   No.

BLANCHE   Well, I did. I took the trip as an investment, thinking I'd meet someone with a million dollars.

STELLA   Did you?

BLANCHE   Yes. I ran into Shep Huntleigh—I ran into him on Biscayne Boulevard, on Christmas Eve, about dusk . . . getting into his car—Cadillac convertible; must have been a block long!

STELLA   I should think it would have been—inconvenient in traffic!

BLANCHE   You've heard of oil wells?

STELLA Yes—remotely.

BLANCHE He has them, all over Texas. Texas is literally spouting gold in his pockets.

STELLA My, my.

BLANCHE Y'know how indifferent I am to money. I think of money in terms of what it does for you. But he could do it, he could certainly do it!

STELLA Do what, Blanche?

BLANCHE Why—set us up in a—shop!

STELLA What kind of a shop?

BLANCHE Oh, a—shop of some kind! He could do it with half what his wife throws away at the races.

STELLA He's married?

BLANCHE Honey, would I be here if the man weren't married? [STELLA *laughs a little.* BLANCHE *suddenly springs up and crosses to phone. She speaks shrilly.*] How do I get Western Union?—Operator! Western Union!

STELLA That's a dial phone, honey.

BLANCHE I can't dial, I'm too—

STELLA Just dial O.

BLANCHE O?

STELLA Yes, "O" for Operator! [BLANCHE *considers a moment; then she puts the phone down.*]

BLANCHE Give me a pencil. Where is a slip of paper? I've got to write it down first—the message, I mean . . . [*She goes to the dressing table, and grabs up a sheet of Kleenex and an eyebrow pencil for writing equipment.*] Let me see now . . . [*She bites the pencil.*] 'Darling Shep. Sister and I in desperate situation.'

STELLA I beg your pardon!

BLANCHE 'Sister and I in desperate situation. Will explain details later. Would you be interested in—?' [*She bites the pencil again.*] 'Would you be—interested—in . . .' [*She smashes the pencil on the table and springs up.*] You never get anywhere with direct appeals!

STELLA [*with a laugh*] Don't be so ridiculous, darling!

BLANCHE But I'll think of something, I've *got* to think of—*some*thing! Don't laugh at me, Stella! Please, please don't—I—I want you to look at the contents of my purse! Here's what's in it! [*She snatches her purse open.*] Sixty-five measly cents in coin of the realm!

STELLA [*crossing to bureau*] Stanley doesn't give me a regular allowance, he likes to pay bills himself, but—this morning he gave me ten dollars to smooth things over. You take five of it, Blanche, and I'll keep the rest.

BLANCHE Oh, no. No, Stella.

STELLA [*insisting*] I know how it helps your morale just having a little pocket-money on you.

BLANCHE No, thank you—I'll take to the streets!

STELLA Talk sense! How did you happen to get so low on funds?

BLANCHE Money just goes—it goes places. [*She rubs her forehead.*] Sometime today I've got to get hold of a Bromo![1]

STELLA I'll fix you one now.

BLANCHE Not yet—I've got to keep thinking!

1. Short for Bromo-Seltzer, a headache and heartburn remedy.

STELLA   I wish you'd just let things go, at least for a—while . . .

BLANCHE   Stella, I can't live with him! You can, he's your husband. But how could I stay here with him, after last night, with just those curtains between us?

STELLA   Blanche, you saw him at his worst last night.

BLANCHE   On the contrary, I saw him at his best! What such a man has to offer is animal force and he gave a wonderful exhibition of that! But the only way to live with such a man is to—go to bed with him! And that's your job—not mine!

STELLA   After you've rested a little, you'll see it's going to work out. You don't have to worry about anything while you're here. I mean—expenses . . .

BLANCHE   I have to plan for us both, to get us both—out!

STELLA   You take it for granted that I am in something that I want to get out of.

BLANCHE   I take it for granted that you still have sufficient memory of Belle Reve to find this place and these poker players impossible to live with.

STELLA   Well, you're taking entirely too much for granted.

BLANCHE   I can't believe you're in earnest.

STELLA   No?

BLANCHE   I understand how it happened—a little. You saw him in uniform, an officer, not here but—

STELLA   I'm not sure it would have made any difference where I saw him.

BLANCHE   Now don't say it was one of those mysterious electric things between people! If you do I'll laugh in your face.

STELLA   I am not going to say anything more at all about it!

BLANCHE   All right, then, don't!

STELLA   But there are things that happen between a man and a woman in the dark—that sort of make everything else seem—unimportant. [*Pause.*]

BLANCHE   What you are talking about is brutal desire—just—Desire!— the name of that rattle-trap streetcar that bangs through the Quarter, up one old narrow street and down another . . .

STELLA   Haven't you ever ridden on that streetcar?

BLANCHE   It brought me here.—Where I'm not wanted and where I'm ashamed to be . . .

STELLA   Then don't you think your superior attitude is a bit out of place?

BLANCHE   I am not being or feeling at all superior, Stella. Believe me I'm not! It's just this. This is how I look at it. A man like that is someone to go out with—once—twice—three times when the devil is in you. But live with? Have a child by?

STELLA   I have told you I love him.

BLANCHE   Then I *tremble* for you! I just—*tremble* for you. . . .

STELLA   I can't help your trembling if you insist on trembling!
   [*There is a pause.*]

BLANCHE   May I—speak—*plainly?*

STELLA   Yes, do. Go ahead. As plainly as you want to.
   [*Outside, a train approaches. They are silent till the noise subsides. They are both in the bedroom. Under cover of the train's noise* STANLEY *enters from outside. He stands unseen by the women, holding some packages in his arms, and overhears their following conversation. He wears an undershirt and grease-stained seersucker pants.*]

BLANCHE   Well—if you'll forgive me—he's *common*!

STELLA   Why, yes, I suppose he is.

BLANCHE   Suppose! You can't have forgotten that much of our bringing up, Stella, that you just *suppose* that any part of a gentleman's in his nature! *Not one particle, no!* Oh, if he was just—*ordinary*! Just *plain*— but good and wholesome, but—*no*. There's something downright—*bestial*—about him! You're hating me saying this, aren't you?

STELLA   [*coldly*]   Go on and say it all, Blanche.

BLANCHE   He acts like an animal, has an animal's habits! Eats like one, moves like one, talks like one! There's even something—sub-human— something not quite to the stage of humanity yet! Yes, something—ape- like about him, like one of those pictures I've seen in—anthropological studies! Thousands and thousands of years have passed him right by, and there he is—Stanley Kowalski—survivor of the Stone Age! Bearing the raw meat home from the kill in the jungle! And you—*you* here— *waiting* for him! Maybe he'll strike you or maybe grunt and kiss you! That is, if kisses have been discovered yet! Night falls and the other apes gather! There in the front of the cave, all grunting like him, and swill- ing and gnawing and hulking! His poker night! you call it—this party of apes! Somebody growls—some creature snatches at something—the fight is on! *God!* Maybe we are a long way from being made in God's image, but Stella—my sister—there has been *some* progress since then! Such things as art—as poetry and music—such kinds of new light have come into the world since then! In some kinds of people some tenderer feelings have had some little beginning! That we have got to make *grow*! And *cling* to, and hold as our flag! In this dark march toward whatever it is we're approaching. . . . *Don't—don't hang back with the brutes!*

[*Another train passes outside.* STANLEY *hesitates, licking his lips. Then suddenly he turns stealthily about and withdraws through front door. The women are still unaware of his presence. When the train has passed he calls through the closed front door.*]

STANLEY   Hey! Hey, Stella!

STELLA   [*who has listened gravely to* BLANCHE]   Stanley!

BLANCHE   Stell, I—

[*But* STELLA *has gone to the front door.* STANLEY *enters casually with his packages.*]

STANLEY   Hiyuh, Stella. Blanche back?

STELLA   Yes, she's back.

STANLEY   Hiyuh, Blanche. [*He grins at her.*]

STELLA   You must've got under the car.

STANLEY   Them darn mechanics at Fritz's don't know their ass fr'm—*Hey!*

[STELLA *has embraced him with both arms, fiercely, and full in the view of* BLANCHE. *He laughs and clasps her head to him. Over her head he grins through the curtains at* BLANCHE. *As the lights fade away, with a lingering brightness on their embrace, the music of the "Blue Piano" and trumpet and drums is heard.*]

Scene Five

BLANCHE *is seated in the bedroom fanning herself with a palm leaf as she reads over a just-completed letter. Suddenly she bursts into a peal of laughter.* STELLA *is dressing in the bedroom.*

STELLA   What are you laughing at, honey?

BLANCHE   Myself, myself, for being such a liar! I'm writing a letter to Shep. [*She picks up the letter.*] "Darling Shep. I am spending the summer on the wing, making flying visits here and there. And who knows, perhaps I shall take a sudden notion to *swoop* down on *Dallas!* How would you feel about that? Ha-ha! [*She laughs nervously and brightly, touching her throat as if actually talking to* SHEP.] Forewarned is forearmed, as they say!"— How does that sound?

STELLA   Uh-huh . . .

BLANCHE [*going on nervously*]   "Most of my sister's friends go north in the summer but some have homes on the Gulf and there has been a continued round of entertainments, teas, cocktails, and luncheons—"
    [*A disturbance is heard upstairs at the Hubbells' apartment.*]

STELLA   Eunice seems to be having some trouble with Steve.
    [EUNICE'S *voice shouts in terrible wrath.*]

EUNICE   I heard about you and that blonde!

STEVE   That's a damn lie!

EUNICE   You ain't pulling the wool over my eyes! I wouldn't mind if you'd stay down at the Four Deuces, but you always going up.

STEVE   Who ever seen me up?

EUNICE   I seen you chasing her 'round the balcony—I'm gonna call the vice squad!

STEVE   Don't you throw that at me!

EUNICE [*shrieking*]   You hit me! I'm gonna call the police!
    [*A clatter of aluminum striking a wall is heard, followed by a man's angry roar, shouts and overturned furniture. There is a crash; then a relative hush.*]

BLANCHE [*brightly*]   Did he *kill* her?
    [EUNICE *appears on the steps in daemonic disorder.*]

STELLA   No! She's coming downstairs.

EUNICE   Call the police, I'm going to call the police! [*She rushes around the corner.*]
    [*They laugh lightly.* STANLEY *comes around the corner in his green and scarlet silk bowling shirt. He trots up the steps and bangs into the kitchen.* BLANCHE *registers his entrance with nervous gestures.*]

STANLEY   What's a matter with Eun-uss?

STELLA   She and Steve had a row. Has she got the police?

STANLEY   Naw. She's gettin' a drink.

STELLA   That's much more practical!
    [STEVE *comes down nursing a bruise on his forehead and looks in the door.*]

STEVE   She here?

STANLEY   Naw, naw. At the Four Deuces.

STEVE   That rutting hunk! [*He looks around the corner a bit timidly, then turns with affected boldness and runs after her.*]

BLANCHE   I must jot that down in my notebook. Ha-ha! I'm compiling a notebook of quaint little words and phrases I've picked up here.

STANLEY   You won't pick up nothing here you ain't heard before.

BLANCHE   Can I count on that?

STANLEY   You can count on it up to five hundred.

BLANCHE   That's a mighty high number. [*He jerks open the bureau drawer, slams it shut and throws shoes in a corner. At each noise* BLANCHE *winces slightly. Finally she speaks.*] What sign were you born under?

STANLEY [*while he is dressing*]   Sign?

BLANCHE   Astrological sign. I bet you were born under Aries. Aries people are forceful and dynamic. They dote on noise! They love to bang things around! You must have had lots of banging around in the army and now that you're out, you make up for it by treating inanimate objects with such a fury!

[STELLA *has been going in and out of closet during this scene. Now she pops her head out of the closet.*]

STELLA   Stanley was born just five minutes after Christmas.

BLANCHE   Capricorn—the Goat!

STANLEY   What sign were *you* born under?

BLANCHE   Oh, my birthday's next month, the fifteenth of September; that's under Virgo.

STANLEY   What's Virgo?

BLANCHE   Virgo is the Virgin.

STANLEY [*contemptuously*]   Hah! [*He advances a little as he knots his tie.*] Say, do you happen to know somebody named Shaw?

[*Her face expresses a faint shock. She reaches for the cologne bottle and dampens her handkerchief as she answers carefully.*]

BLANCHE   Why, everybody knows somebody named Shaw!

STANLEY   Well, this somebody named Shaw is under the impression he met you in Laurel, but I figure he must have got you mixed up with some other party because this other party is someone he met at a hotel called the Flamingo.

[BLANCHE *laughs breathlessly as she touches the cologne-dampened handkerchief to her temples.*]

BLANCHE   I'm afraid he does have me mixed up with this "other party." The Hotel Flamingo is not the sort of establishment I would dare to be seen in!

STANLEY   You know of it?

BLANCHE   Yes, I've seen it and smelled it.

STANLEY   You must've got pretty close if you could smell it.

BLANCHE   The odor of cheap perfume is penetrating.

STANLEY   That stuff you use is expensive?

BLANCHE   Twenty-five dollars an ounce! I'm nearly out. That's just a hint if you want to remember my birthday! [*She speaks lightly but her voice has a note of fear.*]

STANLEY   Shaw must've got you mixed up. He goes in and out of Laurel all the time so he can check on it and clear up any mistake.

[*He turns away and crosses to the portieres.* BLANCHE *closes her eyes as if faint. Her hand trembles as she lifts the handkerchief again to her forehead.* STEVE *and* EUNICE *come around corner.* STEVE'S *arm is around*

EUNICE's *shoulder and she is sobbing luxuriously and he is cooing love-words. There is a murmur of thunder as they go slowly upstairs in a tight embrace.*]

STANLEY [*to* STELLA] I'll wait for you at the Four Deuces!

STELLA Hey! Don't I rate one kiss?

STANLEY Not in front of your sister.
[*He goes out.* BLANCHE *rises from her chair. She seems faint; looks about her with an expression of almost panic.*]

BLANCHE Stella! What have you heard about me?

STELLA Huh?

BLANCHE What have people been telling you about me?

STELLA Telling?

BLANCHE You haven't heard any—unkind—gossip about me?

STELLA Why, no, Blanche, of course not!

BLANCHE Honey, there was—a good deal of talk in Laurel.

STELLA About *you*, Blanche?

BLANCHE I wasn't so good the last two years or so, after Belle Reve had started to slip through my fingers.

STELLA All of us do things we—

BLANCHE I never was hard or self-sufficient enough. When people are soft—soft people have got to shimmer and glow—they've got to put on soft colors, the colors of butterfly wings, and put a—paper lantern over the light. . . . It isn't enough to be soft. You've got to be soft *and attractive*. And I—I'm fading now! I don't know how much longer I can turn the trick.
[*The afternoon has faded to dusk.* STELLA *goes into the bedroom and turns on the light under the paper lantern. She holds a bottled soft drink in her hand.*]

BLANCHE Have you been listening to me?

STELLA I don't listen to you when you are being morbid! [*She advances with the bottled Coke.*]

BLANCHE [*with abrupt change to gaiety*] Is that Coke for me?

STELLA Not for anyone else!

BLANCHE Why, you precious thing, you! Is it just Coke?

STELLA [*turning*] You mean you want a shot in it!

BLANCHE Well, honey, a shot never does a Coke any harm! Let me! You mustn't wait on me!

STELLA I like to wait on you, Blanche. It makes it seem more like home.
[*She goes into the kitchen, finds a glass and pours a shot of whiskey into it.*]

BLANCHE I have to admit I love to be waited on . . .
[*She rushes into the bedroom.* STELLA *goes to her with the glass.* BLANCHE *suddenly clutches* STELLA's *free hand with a moaning sound and presses the hand to her lips.* STELLA *is embarrassed by her show of emotion.* BLANCHE *speaks in a choked voice.*]
You're—you're—so *good* to me! And I—

STELLA Blanche.

BLANCHE I know, I won't! You hate me to talk sentimental! But honey, *believe* I feel things more than I *tell* you! I *won't* stay long! I won't, I promise I—

STELLA Blanche!

BLANCHE [*hysterically*] I won't, I promise, *I'll* go! Go *soon*! I will *really*! I *won't* hang around until he—throws me out . . .

STELLA Now will you stop talking foolish?

BLANCHE Yes, honey. Watch how you pour—that fizzy stuff foams over!
[BLANCHE *laughs shrilly and grabs the glass, but her hand shakes so it almost slips from her grasp.* STELLA *pours the Coke into the glass. It foams over and spills.* BLANCHE *gives a piercing cry.*]

STELLA [*shocked by the cry*] Heavens!

BLANCHE Right on my pretty white skirt!

STELLA Oh . . . Use my hanky. Blot gently.

BLANCHE [*slowly recovering*] I know—gently—gently . . .

STELLA Did it stain?

BLANCHE Not a bit. Ha-ha! Isn't that lucky? [*She sits down shakily, taking a grateful drink. She holds the glass in both hands and continues to laugh a little.*]

STELLA Why did you scream like that?

BLANCHE I don't know why I screamed! [*continuing nervously*] Mitch—Mitch is coming at seven. I guess I am just feeling nervous about our relations. [*She begins to talk rapidly and breathlessly.*] He hasn't gotten a thing but a good-night kiss, that's all I have given him, Stella. I want his respect. And men don't want anything they get too easy. But on the other hand men lose interest quickly. Especially when the girl is over—thirty. They think a girl over thirty ought to—the vulgar term is—"put out." . . . And I—I'm not "putting out." Of course he—he doesn't know—I mean I haven't informed him—of my real age!

STELLA Why are you sensitive about your age?

BLANCHE Because of hard knocks my vanity's been given. What I mean is—he thinks I'm sort of—prim and proper, you know! [*She laughs out sharply.*] I want to *deceive* him enough to make him—want me . . .

STELLA Blanche, do you want *him*?

BLANCHE I want to *rest*! I want to breathe quietly again! Yes—I *want* Mitch . . . *very badly*! Just think! If it happens! I can leave here and not be anyone's problem . . .
[STANLEY *comes around the corner with a drink under his belt.*]

STANLEY [*bawling*] Hey, Steve! Hey, Eunice! Hey, Stella!
[*There are joyous calls from above. Trumpet and drums are heard from around the corner.*]

STELLA [*kissing* BLANCHE *impulsively*] It *will* happen!

BLANCHE [*doubtfully*] It will?

STELLA It *will*! [*She goes across into the kitchen, looking back at* BLANCHE.] It will, honey, it will. . . . But don't take another drink! [*Her voice catches as she goes out the door to meet her husband.*]
[BLANCHE *sinks faintly back in her chair with her drink.* EUNICE *shrieks with laughter and runs down the steps.* STEVE *bounds after her with goatlike screeches and chases her around corner.* STANLEY *and* STELLA *twine arms as they follow, laughing. Dusk settles deeper. The music from the Four Deuces is slow and blue.*]

BLANCHE Ah, me, ah, me, ah, me . . .
[*Her eyes fall shut and the palm leaf fan drops from her fingers. She slaps her hand on the chair arm a couple of times. There is a little glimmer of*

lightning about the building. A YOUNG MAN *comes along the street and rings the bell.*]

BLANCHE   Come in.

[*The* YOUNG MAN *appears through the portieres. She regards him with interest.*]

BLANCHE   Well, well! What can I do for *you*?

YOUNG MAN   I'm collecting for *The Evening Star.*

BLANCHE   I didn't know that stars took up collections.

YOUNG MAN   It's the paper.

BLANCHE   I know, I was joking—feebly! Will you—have a drink?

YOUNG MAN   No, ma'am. No, thank you. I can't drink on the job.

BLANCHE   Oh, well, now, let's see. . . . No, I don't have a dime! I'm not the lady of the house. I'm her sister from Mississippi. I'm one of those poor relations you've heard about.

YOUNG MAN   That's all right. I'll drop by later. [*He starts to go out. She approaches a little.*]

BLANCHE   Hey! [*He turns back shyly. She puts a cigarette in a long holder.*] Could you give me a light? [*She crosses toward him. They meet at the door between the two rooms.*]

YOUNG MAN   Sure. [*He takes out a lighter.*] This doesn't always work.

BLANCHE   It's temperamental? [*It flares.*] Ah!—thank you. [*He starts away again.*] Hey! [*He turns again, still more uncertainly. She goes close to him.*] Uh—what time is it?

YOUNG MAN   Fifteen of seven, ma'am.

BLANCHE   So late? Don't you just love these long rainy afternoons in New Orleans when an hour isn't just an hour—but a little piece of eternity dropped into your hands—and who knows what to do with it? [*She touches his shoulders.*] You—uh—didn't get wet in the rain?

YOUNG MAN   No, ma'am. I stepped inside.

BLANCHE   In a drugstore? And had a soda?

YOUNG MAN   Uh-huh.

BLANCHE   Chocolate?

YOUNG MAN   No, ma'am. Cherry.

BLANCHE [*laughing*]   Cherry!

YOUNG MAN   A cherry soda.

BLANCHE   You make my mouth water. [*She touches his cheek lightly, and smiles. Then she goes to the trunk.*]

YOUNG MAN   Well, I'd better be going—

BLANCHE [*stopping him*]   Young man!

[*He turns. She takes a large, gossamer scarf from the trunk and drapes it about her shoulders. In the ensuing pause, the "Blue Piano" is heard. It continues through the rest of this scene and the opening of the next. The young man clears his throat and looks yearningly at the door.*]

Young man! Young, young, young man! Has anyone ever told you that you look like a young Prince out of the Arabian Nights?

[*The* YOUNG MAN *laughs uncomfortably and stands like a bashful kid.* BLANCHE *speaks softly to him.*]

Well, you do, honey lamb! Come here. I want to kiss you, just once, softly and sweetly on your mouth!

[*Without waiting for him to accept, she crosses quickly to him and presses her lips to his.*]

Now run along, now, quickly! It would be nice to keep you, but I've got to be good—and keep my hands off children.

[*He stares at her a moment. She opens the door for him and blows a kiss at him as he goes down the steps with a dazed look. She stands there a little dreamily after he has disappeared. Then* MITCH *appears around the corner with a bunch of roses.*]

BLANCHE [*gaily*]   Look who's coming! My Rosenkavalier! Bow to me first . . . now present them! *Ahhhh—Merciiii!*[2]

[*She looks at him over them, coquettishly pressing them to her lips. He beams at her self-consciously.*]

Scene Six

It is about two A.M *on the same evening. The outer wall of the building is visible.* BLANCHE *and* MITCH *come in. The utter exhaustion which only a neurasthenic personality can know is evident in* BLANCHE'*s voice and manner.* MITCH *is stolid but depressed. They have probably been out to the amusement park on Lake Pontchartrain, for* MITCH *is bearing, upside down, a plaster statuette of Mae West, the sort of prize won at shooting galleries and carnival games of chance.*

BLANCHE [*stopping lifelessly at the steps*]   Well— [MITCH *laughs uneasily.*] Well . . .

MITCH   I guess it must be pretty late—and you're tired.

BLANCHE   Even the hot tamale man has deserted the street, and he hangs on till the end. [MITCH *laughs uneasily again.*] How will you get home?

MITCH   I'll walk over to Bourbon and catch an owl-car.

BLANCHE [*laughing grimly*]   Is that streetcar named Desire still grinding along the tracks at this hour?

MITCH [*heavily*]   I'm afraid you haven't gotten much fun out of this evening, Blanche.

BLANCHE   I spoiled it for *you.*

MITCH   No, you didn't, but I felt all the time that I wasn't giving you much—entertainment.

BLANCHE   I simply couldn't rise to the occasion. That was all. I don't think I've ever tried so hard to be gay and made such a dismal mess of it. I get ten points for trying!—I *did* try.

MITCH   Why did you try if you didn't feel like it, Blanche?

BLANCHE   I was just obeying the law of nature.

MITCH   Which law is that?

BLANCHE   The one that says the lady must entertain the gentleman—or no dice! See if you can locate my door key in this purse. When I'm so tired my fingers are all thumbs!

MITCH [*rooting in her purse*]   This it?

BLANCHE   No, honey, that's the key to my trunk which I must soon be packing.

MITCH   You mean you are leaving here soon?

BLANCHE   I've outstayed my welcome.

MITCH   This it?

2. "Merci": thank you (French). "My Rosenkavalier": Knight of the Rose (German); title of a romantic opera (1911) by Richard Strauss.

[*The music fades away.*]

BLANCHE   Eureka! Honey, you open the door while I take a last look at the sky. [*She leans on the porch rail. He opens the door and stands awkwardly behind her.*] I'm looking for the Pleiades, the Seven Sisters, but these girls are not out tonight. Oh, yes they are, there they are! God bless them! All in a bunch going home from their little bridge party. . . . Y' get the door open? Good boy! I guess you—want to go now . . .

[*He shuffles and coughs a little.*]

MITCH   Can I—uh—kiss you—good night?

BLANCHE   Why do you always ask me if you may?

MITCH   I don't know whether you want me to or not.

BLANCHE   Why should you be so doubtful?

MITCH   That night when we parked by the lake and I kissed you, you—

BLANCHE   Honey, it wasn't the kiss I objected to. I liked the kiss very much. It was the other little—familiarity—that I—felt obliged to—discourage. . . . I didn't resent it! Not a bit in the world! In fact, I was somewhat flattered that you—desired me! But, honey, you know as well as I do that a single girl, a girl alone in the world, has got to keep a firm hold on her emotions or she'll be lost!

MITCH [*solemnly*]   Lost?

BLANCHE   I guess you are used to girls that like to be lost. The kind that get lost immediately, on the first date!

MITCH   I like you to be exactly the way that you are, because in all my—experience—I have never known anyone like you.

[BLANCHE *looks at him gravely; then she bursts into laughter and then claps a hand to her mouth.*]

MITCH   Are you laughing at me?

BLANCHE   No, honey. The lord and lady of the house have not yet returned, so come in. We'll have a nightcap. Let's leave the lights off. Shall we?

MITCH   You just—do what you want to.

[BLANCHE *precedes him into the kitchen. The outer wall of the building disappears and the interiors of the two rooms can be dimly seen.*]

BLANCHE [*remaining in the first room*]   The other room's more comfortable—go on in. This crashing around in the dark is my search for some liquor.

MITCH   You want a drink?

BLANCHE   I want *you* to have a drink! You have been so anxious and solemn all evening, and so have I; we have both been anxious and solemn and now for these few last remaining moments of our lives together—I want to create—*joie de vivre*! I'm lighting a candle.

MITCH   That's good.

BLANCHE   We are going to be very Bohemian. We are going to pretend that we are sitting in a little artists' cafe on the Left Bank in Paris! [*She lights a candle stub and puts it in a bottle.*] Je suis la Dame aux Camellias! Vous êtes—Armand!*[3]* Understand French?

MITCH [*heavily*]   Naw. Naw, I—

3. I am the Lady of the Camellias! You are—Armand! (French). Both are characters in the popular romantic play *La Dame aux Camélias* (1852), by the French author Alexandre Dumas *fils*; she is a courtesan who gives up her true love, Armand.

BLANCHE *Voulez-vous couchez avec moi ce soir? Vous ne comprenez pas? Ah, quelle dommage!*[4]—I mean it's a damned good thing. . . . I've found some liquor! Just enough for two shots without any dividends, honey . . .

MITCH [*heavily*] That's—good.

[*She enters the bedroom with the drinks and the candle.*]

BLANCHE Sit down! Why don't you take off your coat and loosen your collar?

MITCH I better leave it on.

BLANCHE No. I want you to be comfortable.

MITCH I am ashamed of the way I perspire. My shirt is sticking to me.

BLANCHE Perspiration is healthy. If people didn't perspire they would die in five minutes. [*She takes his coat from him.*] This is a nice coat. What kind of material is it?

MITCH They call that stuff alpaca.

BLANCHE Oh. Alpaca.

MITCH It's very light-weight alpaca.

BLANCHE Oh. Light-weight alpaca.

MITCH I don't like to wear a wash-coat even in summer because I sweat through it.

BLANCHE Oh.

MITCH And it don't look neat on me. A man with a heavy build has got to be careful of what he puts on him so he don't look too clumsy.

BLANCHE You are not too heavy.

MITCH You don't think I am?

BLANCHE You are not the delicate type. You have a massive bone-structure and a very imposing physique.

MITCH Thank you. Last Christmas I was given a membership to the New Orleans Athletic Club.

BLANCHE Oh, good.

MITCH It was the finest present I ever was given. I work out there with the weights and I swim and I keep myself fit. When I started there, I was getting soft in the belly but now my belly is hard. It is so hard now that a man can punch me in the belly and it don't hurt me. Punch me! Go on! See?

[*She pokes lightly at him.*]

BLANCHE Gracious. [*Her hand touches her chest.*]

MITCH Guess how much I weigh, Blanche?

BLANCHE Oh, I'd say in the vicinity of—one hundred and eighty?

MITCH Guess again.

BLANCHE Not that much?

MITCH No. More.

BLANCHE Well, you're a tall man and you can carry a good deal of weight without looking awkward.

MITCH I weigh two hundred and seven pounds and I'm six feet one and one half inches tall in my bare feet—without shoes on. And that is what I weigh stripped.

BLANCHE Oh, my goodness, me! It's awe-inspiring.

---

4. Would you like to sleep with me this evening? You don't understand? Ah, what a pity! (French).

MITCH [*embarrassed*]   My weight is not a very interesting subject to talk about. [*He hesitates for a moment.*] What's yours?

BLANCHE   My weight?

MITCH   Yes.

BLANCHE   Guess!

MITCH   Let me lift you.

BLANCHE   Samson![5] Go on, lift me. [*He comes behind her and puts his hands on her waist and raises her lightly off the ground.*] Well?

MITCH   You are light as a feather.

BLANCHE   Ha-ha! [*He lowers her but keeps his hands on her waist.* BLANCHE *speaks with an affectation of demureness.*] You may release me now.

MITCH   Huh?

BLANCHE [*gaily*]   I said unhand me, sir. [*He fumblingly embraces her. Her voice sounds gently reproving.*] Now, Mitch. Just because Stanley and Stella aren't at home is no reason why you shouldn't behave like a gentleman.

MITCH   Just give me a slap whenever I step out of bounds.

BLANCHE   That won't be necessary. You're a natural gentleman, one of the very few that are left in the world. I don't want you to think that I am severe and old maid school-teacherish or anything like that. It's just—well—

MITCH   Huh?

BLANCHE   I guess it is just that I have—old-fashioned ideals! [*She rolls her eyes, knowing he cannot see her face.* MITCH *goes to the front door. There is a considerable silence between them.* BLANCHE *sighs and* MITCH *coughs self-consciously.*]

MITCH [*finally*]   Where's Stanley and Stella tonight?

BLANCHE   They have gone out. With Mr. and Mrs. Hubbell upstairs.

MITCH   Where did they go?

BLANCHE   I think they were planning to go to a midnight prevue at Loew's State.

MITCH   We should all go out together some night.

BLANCHE   No. That wouldn't be a good plan.

MITCH   Why not?

BLANCHE   You are an old friend of Stanley's?

MITCH   We was together in the Two-Forty-First.[6]

BLANCHE   I guess he talks to you frankly?

MITCH   Sure.

BLANCHE   Has he talked to you about me?

BLANCHE   Oh—not very much.

BLANCHE   The way you say that, I suspect that he has.

MITCH   No, he hasn't said much.

BLANCHE   But what he *has* said. What would you say his attitude toward me was?

MITCH   Why do you want to ask that?

BLANCHE   Well—

MITCH   Don't you get along with him?

5. Legendary strong man in the Bible's Book of Judges; he is captured by the Philistines after he reveals the secret of his strength, his long hair, to the temptress Delilah.
6. Engineering battalion in World War II.

BLANCHE   What do you think?

MITCH   I don't think he understands you.

BLANCHE   That is putting it mildly. If it weren't for Stella about to have a baby, I wouldn't be able to endure things here.

MITCH   He isn't—nice to you?

BLANCHE   He is insufferably rude. Goes out of his way to offend me.

MITCH   In what way, Blanche?

BLANCHE   Why, in every conceivable way.

MITCH   I'm surprised to hear that.

BLANCHE   Are you?

MITCH   Well, I—don't see how anybody could be rude to you.

BLANCHE   It's really a pretty frightful situation. You see, there's no privacy here. There's just these portieres between the two rooms at night. He stalks through the rooms in his underwear at night. And I have to ask him to close the bathroom door. That sort of commonness isn't necessary. You probably wonder why I don't move out. Well, I'll tell you frankly. A teacher's salary is barely sufficient for her living expenses. I didn't save a penny last year and so I had to come here for the summer. That's why I have to put up with my sister's husband. And he has to put up with me, apparently so much against his wishes. . . . Surely he must have told you how much he hates me!

MITCH   I don't think he hates you.

BLANCHE   He hates me. Or why would he insult me? The first time I laid eyes on him I thought to myself, that man is my executioner! That man will destroy me, unless——

MITCH   Blanche—

BLANCHE   Yes, honey?

MITCH   Can I ask you a question?

BLANCHE   Yes. What?

MITCH   How old are you?
   [*She makes a nervous gesture.*]

BLANCHE   Why do you want to know?

MITCH   I talked to my mother about you and she said, "How old is Blanche?" And I wasn't able to tell her. [*There is another pause.*]

BLANCHE   You talked to your mother about me?

MITCH   Yes.

BLANCHE   Why?

MITCH   I told my mother how nice you were, and I liked you.

BLANCHE   Were you sincere about that?

MITCH   You know I was.

BLANCHE   Why did your mother want to know my age?

MITCH   Mother is sick.

BLANCHE   I'm sorry to hear it. Badly?

MITCH   She won't live long. Maybe just a few months.

BLANCHE   Oh.

MITCH   She worries because I'm not settled.

BLANCHE   Oh.

MITCH   She wants me to be settled down before she— [*His voice is hoarse and he clears his throat twice, shuffling nervously around with his hands in and out of his pockets.*]

BLANCHE   You love her very much, don't you?

MITCH   Yes.

BLANCHE   I think you have a great capacity for devotion. You will be lonely when she passes on, won't you? [MITCH *clears his throat and nods.*] I understand what that is.

MITCH   To be lonely?

BLANCHE   I loved someone, too, and the person I loved I lost.

MITCH   Dead? [*She crosses to the window and sits on the sill, looking out. She pours herself another drink.*] A man?

BLANCHE   He was a boy, just a boy, when I was a very young girl. When I was sixteen, I made the discovery—love. All at once and much, much too completely. It was like you suddenly turned a blinding light on something that had always been half in shadow, that's how it struck the world for me. But I was unlucky. Deluded. There was something different about the boy, a nervousness, a softness and tenderness which wasn't like a man's, although he wasn't the least bit effeminate looking—still—that thing was there. . . . He came to me for help. I didn't know that. I didn't find out anything till after our marriage when we'd run away and come back and all I knew was I'd failed him in some mysterious way and wasn't able to give the help he needed but couldn't speak of! He was in the quicksands and clutching at me—but I wasn't holding him out, I was slipping in with him! I didn't know that. I didn't know anything except I loved him unendurably but without being able to help him or help myself. Then I found out. In the worst of all possible ways. By coming suddenly into a room that I thought was empty—which wasn't empty, but had two people in it . . . the boy I had married and an older man who had been his friend for years . . .

> [*A locomotive is heard approaching outside. She claps her hands to her ears and crouches over. The headlight of the locomotive glares into the room as it thunders past. As the noise recedes she straightens slowly and continues speaking.*]

Afterward we pretended that nothing had been discovered. Yes, the three of us drove out to Moon Lake Casino, very drunk and laughing all the way.

> [*Polka music sounds, in a minor key faint with distance.*]

We danced the Varsouviana![7] Suddenly in the middle of the dance the boy I had married broke away from me and ran out of the casino. A few moments later—a shot!

> [*The polka stops abruptly. BLANCHE rises stiffly. Then, the polka resumes in a major key.*]

I ran out—all did!—all ran and gathered about the terrible thing at the edge of the lake! I couldn't get near for the crowding. Then somebody caught my arm. "Don't go any closer! Come back! You don't want to see!" See? See what! Then I heard voices say—Allan! Allan! The Grey boy! He'd stuck the revolver into his mouth, and fired—so that the back of his head had been—blown away!

> [*She sways and covers her face.*]

It was because—on the dance floor—unable to stop myself—I'd suddenly said—"I saw! I know! You disgust me . . ." And then the search-

---

7. Fast Polish waltz, similar to the polka.

light which had been turned on the world was turned off again and never for one moment since has there been any light that's stronger than this—kitchen—candle . . .

> [MITCH *gets up awkwardly and moves toward her a little. The polka music increases.* MITCH *stands beside her.*]

MITCH [*drawing her slowly into his arms*]   You need somebody. And I need somebody, too. Could it be—you and me, Blanche?

> [*She stares at him vacantly for a moment. Then with a soft cry huddles in his embrace. She makes a sobbing effort to speak but the words won't come. He kisses her forehead and her eyes and finally her lips. The Polka tune fades out. Her breath is drawn and released in long, grateful sobs.*]

BLANCHE   Sometimes—there's God—so quickly!

Scene Seven

It is late afternoon in mid-September.

The portieres are open and a table is set for a birthday supper, with cake and flowers.

STELLA *is completing the decorations as* STANLEY *comes in.*

STANLEY   What's all this stuff for?

STELLA   Honey, it's Blanche's birthday.

STANLEY   She here?

STELLA   In the bathroom.

STANLEY [*mimicking*]   "Washing out some things"?

STELLA   I reckon so.

STANLEY   How long she been in there?

STELLA   All afternoon.

STANLEY [*mimicking*]   "Soaking in a hot tub"?

STELLA   Yes.

STANLEY   Temperature 100 on the nose, and she soaks herself in a hot tub.

STELLA   She says it cools her off for the evening.

STANLEY   And you run out an' get her cokes, I suppose? And serve 'em to Her Majesty in the tub? [STELLA *shrugs.*] Set down here a minute.

STELLA   Stanley, I've got things to do.

STANLEY   Set down! I've got th' dope on your big sister, Stella.

STELLA   Stanley, stop picking on Blanche.

STANLEY   That girl calls *me* common!

STELLA   Lately you been doing all you can think of to rub her the wrong way, Stanley, and Blanche is sensitive and you've got to realize that Blanche and I grew up under very different circumstances than you did.

STANLEY   So I been told. And told and told and told! You know she's been feeding us a pack of lies here?

STELLA   No, I don't, and—

STANLEY   Well, she has, however. But now the cat's out of the bag! I found out some things!

STELLA   What—things?

STANLEY   Things I already suspected. But now I got proof from the most reliable sources—which I have checked on!

> [BLANCHE *is singing in the bathroom a saccharine popular ballad which is used contrapuntally with* STANLEY's *speech.*]

STELLA [*to* STANLEY]   Lower your voice!

STANLEY   Some canary bird, huh!

STELLA   Now please tell me quietly what you think you've found out about my sister.

STANLEY   Lie Number One: All this squeamishness she puts on! You should just know the line she's been feeding to Mitch. He thought she had never been more than kissed by a fellow! But Sister Blanche is no lily! Ha-ha! Some lily she is!

STELLA   What have you heard and who from?

STANLEY   Our supply-man down at the plant has been going through Laurel for years and he knows all about her and everybody else in the town of Laurel knows all about her. She is as famous in Laurel as if she was the President of the United States, only she is not respected by any party! This supply-man stops at a hotel called the Flamingo.

BLANCHE [*singing blithely*]   "Say, it's only a paper moon, Sailing over a cardboard sea—But it wouldn't be make-believe If you believed in me!"[8]

STELLA   What about the—Flamingo?

STANLEY   She stayed there, too.

STELLA   My sister lived at Belle Reve.

STANLEY   This is after the home-place had slipped through her lily-white fingers! She moved to the Flamingo! A second-class hotel which has the advantage of not interfering in the private social life of the personalities there! The Flamingo is used to all kinds of goings-on. But even the management of the Flamingo was impressed by Dame Blanche! In fact they was so impressed by Dame Blanche that they requested her to turn in her room key—for permanently! This happened a couple of weeks before she showed here.

BLANCHE [*singing*]   "It's a Barnum and Bailey world, Just as phony as it can be—But it wouldn't be make-believe If you believed in me!"

STELLA   What—contemptible—lies!

STANLEY   Sure, I can see how you would be upset by this. She pulled the wool over your eyes as much as Mitch's!

STELLA   It's pure invention! There's not a word of truth in it and if I were a man and this creature had dared to invent such things in my presence—

BLANCHE [*singing*]   "Without your love, It's a honky-tonk parade! Without your love, It's a melody played In a penny arcade . . ."

STANLEY   Honey, I told you I thoroughly checked on these stories! Now wait till I finished. The trouble with Dame Blanche was that she couldn't put on her act any more in Laurel! They got wised up after two or three dates with her and then they quit, and she goes on to another, the same old line, same old act, same old hooey! But the town was too small for this to go on forever! And as time went by she became a town character. Regarded as not just different but downright loco—nuts. [STELLA *draws back.*] And for the last year or two she has been washed up like poison. That's why she's here this summer, visiting royalty, putting on all this act—because she's practically told by the mayor to get out of town! Yes,

---

8. From "It's Only a Paper Moon" (1933), a popular song by Harold Arlen.

did you know there was an army camp near Laurel and your sister's was one of the places called "Out-of-Bounds"?

BLANCHE "It's only a paper moon, Just as phony as it can be—But it wouldn't be make-believe If you believed in me!"

STANLEY Well, so much for her being such a refined and particular type of girl. Which brings us to Lie Number Two.

STELLA I don't want to hear any more!

STANLEY She's not going back to teach school! In fact I am willing to bet you that she never had no idea of returning to Laurel! She didn't resign temporarily from the high school because of her nerves! No, siree, Bob! She didn't. They kicked her out of that high school before the spring term ended—and I hate to tell you the reason that step was taken! A seventeen-year-old boy—she'd gotten mixed up with!

BLANCHE "It's a Barnum and Bailey world, Just as phony as it can be—"
[*In the bathroom the water goes on loud; little breathless cries and peals of laughter are heard as if a child were frolicking in the tub.*]

STELLA This is making me—sick!

STANLEY The boy's dad learned about it and got in touch with the high school superintendent. Boy, oh, boy, I'd like to have been in that office when Dame Blanche was called on the carpet! I'd like to have seen her trying to squirm out of that one! But they had her on the hook good and proper that time and she knew that the jig was all up! They told her she better move on to some fresh territory. Yep, it was practickly a town ordinance passed against her!
[*The bathroom door is opened and* BLANCHE *thrusts her head out, holding a towel about her hair.*]

BLANCHE Stella!

STELLA [*faintly*] Yes, Blanche?

BLANCHE Give me another bath-towel to dry my hair with. I've just washed it.

STELLA Yes, Blanche. [*She crosses in a dazed way from the kitchen to the bathroom door with a towel.*]

BLANCHE What's the matter, honey?

STELLA Matter? Why?

BLANCHE You have such a strange expression on your face!

STELLA Oh— [*she tries to laugh*] I guess I'm a little tired!

BLANCHE Why don't you bathe, too, soon as I get out?

STANLEY [*calling from the kitchen*] How soon is that going to be?

BLANCHE Not so terribly long! Possess your soul in patience!

STANLEY It's not my soul, it's my kidneys I'm worried about!
[BLANCHE *slams the door.* STANLEY *laughs harshly.* STELLA *comes slowly back into the kitchen.*]

STANLEY Well, what do you think of it?

STELLA I don't believe all of those stories and I think your supply-man was mean and rotten to tell them. It's possible that some of the things he said are partly true. There are things about my sister I don't approve of—things that caused sorrow at home. She was always—flighty!

STANLEY Flighty!

STELLA But when she was young, very young, she married a boy who wrote poetry. . . . He was extremely good-looking. I think Blanche didn't just love him but worshipped the ground he walked on! Adored him and thought him almost too fine to be human! But then she found out—

STANLEY   What?

STELLA   This beautiful and talented young man was a degenerate. Didn't your supply-man give you that information?

STANLEY   All we discussed was recent history. That must have been a pretty long time ago.

STELLA   Yes, it was—a pretty long time ago . . .

[STANLEY *comes up and takes her by the shoulders rather gently. She gently withdraws from him. Automatically she starts sticking little pink candles in the birthday cake.*]

STANLEY   How many candles you putting in that cake?

STELLA   I'll stop at twenty-five.

STANLEY   Is company expected?

STELLA   We asked Mitch to come over for cake and ice-cream.

[STANLEY *looks a little uncomfortable. He lights a cigarette from the one he has just finished.*]

STANLEY   I wouldn't be expecting Mitch over tonight.

[STELLA *pauses in her occupation with candles and looks slowly around at* STANLEY.]

STELLA   Why?

STANLEY   Mitch is a buddy of mine. We were in the same outfit together— Two-forty-first Engineers. We work in the same plant and now on the same bowling team. You think I could face him if—

STELLA   Stanley Kowalski, did you—did you repeat what that—?

STANLEY   You're goddam right I told him! I'd have that on my conscience the rest of my life if I knew all that stuff and let my best friend get caught!

STELLA   Is Mitch through with her?

STANLEY   Wouldn't you be if—?

STELLA   I said, *Is Mitch through with her?*

[BLANCHE'*s voice is lifted again, serenely as a bell. She sings* "But it wouldn't be make-believe If you believed in me."]

STANLEY   No, I don't think he's necessarily through with her—just wised up!

STELLA   Stanley, she thought Mitch was—going to—going to marry her. I was hoping so, too.

STANLEY   Well, he's not going to marry her. Maybe he *was*, but he's not going to jump in a tank with a school of sharks—now! [*He rises.*] Blanche! Oh, Blanche! Can I please get in my bathroom? [*There is a pause.*]

BLANCHE   Yes, indeed, sir! Can you wait one second while I dry?

STANLEY   Having waited one hour I guess one second ought to pass in a hurry.

STELLA   And she hasn't got her job? Well, what will she do!

STANLEY   She's not stayin' here after Tuesday. You know that, don't you? Just to make sure I bought her ticket myself. A bus ticket.

STELLA   In the first place, Blanche wouldn't go on a bus.

STANLEY   She'll go on a bus and like it.

STELLA   No, she won't, no, she won't, Stanley!

STANLEY   *She'll go!* Period. P.S. She'll go *Tuesday*!

STELLA [*slowly*]   What'll—she—do? What on earth will she—*do*!

STANLEY   Her future is mapped out for her.

STELLA   What do you mean?

[BLANCHE *sings*.]

STANLEY   Hey, canary bird! Toots! Get *OUT* of the *BATHROOM!*

[*The bathroom door flies open and* BLANCHE *emerges with a gay peal of laughter, but as* STANLEY *crosses past her, a frightened look appears in her face, almost a look of panic. He doesn't look at her but slams the bathroom door shut as he goes in.*]

BLANCHE [*snatching up a hairbrush*]   Oh, I feel so good after my long, hot bath, I feel so good and cool and—rested!

STELLA [*sadly and doubtfully from the kitchen*]   Do you, Blanche?

BLANCHE [*snatching up a hairbrush*]   Yes, I do, so refreshed! [*She tinkles her highball glass.*] A hot bath and a long, cold drink always give me a brand new outlook on life! [*She looks through the portieres at* STELLA, *standing between them, and slowly stops brushing.*] Something has happened!—What is it?

STELLA [*turning away quickly*]   Why, nothing has happened, Blanche.

BLANCHE   You're lying! Something has!

[*She stares fearfully at* STELLA, *who pretends to be busy at the table. The distant piano goes into a hectic breakdown.*]

Scene Eight

Three quarters of an hour later.

The view through the big windows is fading gradually into a still-golden dusk. A torch of sunlight blazes on the side of a big water-tank or oil-drum across the empty lot toward the business district which is now pierced by pinpoints of lighted windows or windows reflecting the sunset.

The three people are completing a dismal birthday supper. STANLEY *looks sullen.* STELLA *is embarrassed and sad.*

BLANCHE *has a tight, artificial smile on her drawn face. There is a fourth place at the table which is left vacant.*

BLANCHE [*suddenly*]   Stanley, tell us a joke, tell us a funny story to make us all laugh. I don't know what's the matter, we're all so solemn. Is it because I've been stood up by my beau?

[STELLA *laughs feebly.*]

It's the first time in my entire experience with men, and I've had a good deal of all sorts, that I've actually been stood up by anybody! Ha-ha! I don't know how to take it. . . . Tell us a funny little story, Stanley! Something to help us out.

STANLEY   I didn't think you liked my stories, Blanche.

BLANCHE   I like them when they're amusing but not indecent.

STANLEY   I don't know any refined enough for your taste.

BLANCHE   Then let me tell one.

STELLA   Yes, you tell one, Blanche. You used to know lots of good stories.

[*The music fades.*]

BLANCHE   Let me see, now. . . . I must run through my repertoire! Oh, yes—I love parrot stories! Do you all like parrot stories? Well, this one's about the old maid and the parrot. This old maid, she had a parrot that cursed a blue streak and knew more vulgar expressions than Mr. Kowalski!

STANLEY   Huh.

BLANCHE   And the only way to hush the parrot up was to put the cover back on its cage so it would think it was night and go back to sleep. Well, one morning the old maid had just uncovered the parrot for the day— when who should she see coming up the front walk but the preacher! Well, she rushed back to the parrot and slipped the cover back on the cage and then she let in the preacher. And the parrot was perfectly still, just as quiet as a mouse, but just as she was asking the preacher how much sugar he wanted in his coffee—the parrot broke the silence with a loud—[*She whistles.*]—and said—"God *damn,* but that was a short day!"

> [*She throws back her head and laughs.* STELLA *also makes an ineffectual effort to seem amused.* STANLEY *pays no attention to the story but reaches way over the table to spear his fork into the remaining chop which he eats with his fingers.*]

BLANCHE   Apparently Mr. Kowalski was not amused.

STELLA   Mr. Kowalski is too busy making a pig of himself to think of anything else!

STANLEY   That's right, baby.

STELLA   Your face and your fingers are disgustingly greasy. Go and wash up and then help me clear the table.

> [*He hurls a plate to the floor.*]

STANLEY   That's how I'll clear the table! [*He seizes her arm.*] Don't ever talk that way to me! "Pig—Polack—disgusting—vulgar—greasy!"—them kind of words have been on your tongue and your sister's too much around here! What do you two think you are? A pair of queens? Remember what Huey Long[9] said—"Every Man is a King!" And I am the king around here, so don't forget it! [*He hurls a cup and saucer to the floor.*] My place is cleared! You want me to clear your places?

> [STELLA *begins to cry weakly.* STANLEY *stalks out on the porch and lights a cigarette. The Negro entertainers around the corner are heard.*]

BLANCHE   What happened while I was bathing? What did he tell you, Stella?

STELLA   Nothing, nothing, nothing!

BLANCHE   I think he told you something about Mitch and me! You know why Mitch didn't come but you won't tell me! [STELLA *shakes her head helplessly.*] I'm going to call him!

STELLA   I wouldn't call him, Blanche.

BLANCHE   I am, I'm going to call him on the phone.

STELLA [*miserably*]   I wish you wouldn't.

BLANCHE   I intend to be given some explanation from someone!

> [*She rushes to the phone in the bedroom.* STELLA *goes out on the porch and stares reproachfully at her husband. He grunts and turns away from her.*]

STELLA   I hope you're pleased with your doings. I never had so much trouble swallowing food in my life, looking at that girl's face and the empty chair! [*She cries quietly.*]

BLANCHE [*at the phone*]   Hello. Mr. Mitchell, please. . . . Oh. . . . I would like to leave a number if I may. Magnolia 9047. And say it's important to call. . . . Yes, very important. . . . Thank you.

---

9. Demagogic Louisiana political leader, governor, and senator (1893–1935).

[*She remains by the phone with a lost, frightened look.* STANLEY *turns slowly back toward his wife and takes her clumsily in his arms.*]

STANLEY   Stell, it's gonna be all right after she goes and after you've had the baby. It's gonna be all right again between you and me the way that it was. You remember the way that it was? Them nights we had together? God, honey, it's gonna be sweet when we can make noise in the night the way that we used to and get the colored lights going with nobody's sister behind the curtains to hear us!

[*Their upstairs neighbors are heard in bellowing laughter at something.* STANLEY *chuckles.*]

Steve an' Eunice . . .

STELLA   Come on back in. [*She returns to the kitchen and starts lighting the candles on the white cake.*] Blanche?

BLANCHE   Yes. [*She returns from the bedroom to the table in the kitchen.*] Oh, those pretty, pretty little candles! Oh, don't burn them, Stella.

STELLA   I certainly will.

[STANLEY *comes back in.*]

BLANCHE   You ought to save them for baby's birthdays. Oh, I hope candles are going to glow in his life and I hope that his eyes are going to be like candles, like two blue candles lighted in a white cake!

STANLEY [*sitting down*]   What poetry!

BLANCHE [*she pauses reflectively for a moment*]   I shouldn't have called him.

STELLA   There's lots of things could have happened.

BLANCHE   There's no excuse for it, Stella. I don't have to put up with insults. I won't be taken for granted.

STANLEY   Goddamn, it's hot in here with the steam from the bathroom.

BLANCHE   I've said I was sorry three times. [*The piano fades out.*] I take hot baths for my nerves. Hydrotherapy, they call it. You healthy Polack, without a nerve in your body, of course you don't know what anxiety feels like!

STANLEY   I am not a Polack. People from Poland are Poles, not Polacks. But what I am is a one-hundred-per-cent American, born and raised in the greatest country on earth and proud as hell of it, so don't ever call me a Polack.

[*The phone rings.* BLANCHE *rises expectantly.*]

BLANCHE   Oh, that's for me, I'm sure.

STANLEY   *I'm* not sure. Keep your seat. [*He crosses leisurely to phone.*] H'lo. Aw, yeh, hello, Mac.

[*He leans against wall, staring insultingly in at* BLANCHE. *She sinks back in her chair with a frightened look.* STELLA *leans over and touches her shoulder.*]

BLANCHE   Oh, keep your hands off me, Stella. What is the matter with you? Why do you look at me with that pitying look?

STANLEY [*bawling*]   QUIET IN THERE!—We've got a noisy woman on the place.—Go on, Mac. At Riley's? No, I don't wanta bowl at Riley's. I had a little trouble with Riley last week. I'm the team captain, ain't I? All right, then, we're not gonna bowl at Riley's, we're gonna bowl at the West Side or the Gala! All right, Mac. See you!

[*He hangs up and returns to the table.* BLANCHE *fiercely controls herself, drinking quickly from her tumbler of water. He doesn't look at her but reaches in a pocket. Then he speaks slowly and with false amiability.*]

Sister Blanche, I've got a little birthday remembrance for you.

BLANCHE   Oh, have you, Stanley? I wasn't expecting any, I—I don't know why Stella wants to observe my birthday! I'd much rather forget it—when you—reach twenty-seven! Well—age is a subject that you'd prefer to—ignore!

STANLEY   Twenty-seven?

BLANCHE [*quickly*]   What is it? Is it for *me*?

[*He is holding a little envelope toward her.*]

STANLEY   Yes, I hope you like it!

BLANCHE   Why, why—Why, it's a—

STANLEY   Ticket! Back to Laurel! On the Greyhound! Tuesday!

[*The Varsouviana music steals in softly and continues playing.* STELLA *rises abruptly and turns her back.* BLANCHE *tries to smile. Then she tries to laugh. Then she gives both up and springs from the table and runs into the next room. She clutches her throat and then runs into the bathroom. Coughing, gagging sounds are heard.*]

Well!

STELLA   You didn't need to do that.

STANLEY   Don't forget all that I took off her.

STELLA   You needn't have been so cruel to someone alone as she is.

STANLEY   Delicate piece she is.

STELLA   She is. She was. You didn't know Blanche as a girl. Nobody, nobody, was tender and trusting as she was. But people like you abused her, and forced her to change.

[*He crosses into the bedroom, ripping off his shirt, and changes into a brilliant silk bowling shirt. She follows him.*]

Do you think you're going bowling now?

STANLEY   Sure.

STELLA   You're not going bowling. [*She catches hold of his shirt.*] Why did you do this to her?

STANLEY   I done nothing to no one. Let go of my shirt. You've torn it.

STELLA   I want to know why. Tell me why.

STANLEY   When we first met, me and you, you thought I was common. How right you was, baby. I was common as dirt. You showed me the snapshot of the place with the columns. I pulled you down off them columns and how you loved it, having them colored lights going! And wasn't we happy together, wasn't it all okay till she showed here?

[STELLA *makes a slight movement. Her look goes suddenly inward as if some interior voice had called her name. She begins a slow, shuffling progress from the bedroom to the kitchen, leaning and resting on the back of the chair and then on the edge of a table with a blind look and listening expression.* STANLEY, *finishing with his shirt, is unaware of her reaction.*]

And wasn't we happy together? Wasn't it all okay? Till she showed here. Hoity-Toity, describing me as an ape. [*He suddenly notices the change in* STELLA.] Hey, what is it, Stel? [*He crosses to her.*]

STELLA [*quietly*]   Take me to the hospital.

[*He is with her now, supporting her with his arm, murmuring indistinguishably as they go outside.*]

Scene Nine

A while later that evening. BLANCHE *is seated in a tense hunched position in a bedroom chair that she has recovered with diagonal green and white stripes. She has on her scarlet satin robe. On the table beside chair is a bottle of liquor and a glass. The rapid, feverish polka tune, the "Varsouviana," is heard. The music is in her mind; she is drinking to escape it and the sense of disaster closing in on her, and she seems to whisper the words of the song. An electric fan is turning back and forth across her.*

MITCH *comes around the corner in work clothes: blue denim shirt and pants. He is unshaven. He climbs the steps to the door and rings.* BLANCHE *is startled.*

BLANCHE   Who is it, please?

MITCH [*hoarsely*]   Me. Mitch.
[*The polka tune stops.*]

BLANCHE   Mitch!—Just a minute.
[*She rushes about frantically, hiding the bottle in a closet, crouching at the mirror and dabbing her face with cologne and powder. She is so excited that her breath is audible as she dashes about. At last she rushes to the door in the kitchen and lets him in.*]
Mitch!—Y'know, I really shouldn't let you in after the treatment I have received from you this evening! So utterly uncavalier! But hello, beautiful!
[*She offers him her lips. He ignores it and pushes past her into the flat. She looks fearfully after him as he stalks into the bedroom.*]
My, my, what a cold shoulder! And such uncouth apparel! Why, you haven't even shaved! The unforgivable insult to a lady! But I forgive you. I forgive you because it's such a relief to see you. You've stopped that polka tune that I had caught in my head. Have you ever had anything caught in your head? No, of course you haven't, you dumb angel-puss, you'd never get anything awful caught in your head!
[*He stares at her while she follows him while she talks. It is obvious that he has had a few drinks on the way over.*]

MITCH   Do we have to have that fan on?

BLANCHE   No!

MITCH   I don't like fans.

BLANCHE   Then let's turn it off, honey. I'm not partial to them!
[*She presses the switch and the fan nods slowly off. She clears her throat uneasily as* MITCH *plumps himself down on the bed in the bedroom and lights a cigarette.*]
I don't know what there is to drink. I—haven't investigated.

MITCH   I don't want Stan's liquor.

BLANCHE   It isn't Stan's. Everything here isn't Stan's. Some things on the premises are actually mine! How is your mother? Isn't your mother well?

MITCH   Why?

BLANCHE   Something's the matter tonight, but never mind. I won't cross-examine the witness. I'll just—[*She touches her forehead vaguely. The polka tune starts up again.*]—pretend I don't notice anything different about you! That—music again . . .

MITCH   What music?

BLANCHE The "Varsouviana"! The polka tune they were playing when Allan—Wait!

[*A distant revolver shot is heard.* BLANCHE *seems relieved.*]

There now, the shot! It always stops after that.

[*The polka music dies out again.*]

Yes, now it's stopped.

MITCH Are you boxed out of your mind?

BLANCHE I'll go and see what I can find in the way of— [*She crosses into the closet, pretending to search for the bottle.*] Oh, by the way, excuse me for not being dressed. But I'd practically given you up! Had you forgotten your invitation to supper?

MITCH I wasn't going to see you any more.

BLANCHE Wait a minute. I can't hear what you're saying and you talk so little that when you do say something, I don't want to miss a single syllable of it. . . . What am I looking around here for? Oh, yes—liquor! We've had so much excitement around here this evening that I *am* boxed out of my mind! [*She pretends suddenly to find the bottle. He draws his foot up on the bed and stares at her contemptuously.*] Here's something. Southern Comfort! What is that, I wonder?

MITCH If you don't know, it must belong to Stan.

BLANCHE Take your foot off the bed. It has a light cover on it. Of course you boys don't notice things like that. I've done so much with this place since I've been here.

MITCH I bet you have.

BLANCHE You saw it before I came. Well, look at it now! This room is almost—dainty! I want to keep it that way. I wonder if this stuff ought to be mixed with something? Ummm, it's sweet, so sweet! It's terribly, terribly sweet! Why, it's a *liqueur*, I believe! Yes, that's what it *is*, a liqueur! [MITCH *grunts.*] I'm afraid you won't like it, but try it, and maybe you will.

MITCH I told you already I don't want none of his liquor and I mean it. You ought to lay off his liquor. He says you been lapping it up all summer like a wild cat!

BLANCHE What a fantastic statement! Fantastic of him to say it, fantastic of you to repeat it! I won't descend to the level of such cheap accusations to answer them, even!

MITCH Huh.

BLANCHE What's in your mind? I see something in your eyes!

MITCH [*getting up*] It's dark in here.

BLANCHE I like it dark. The dark is comforting to me.

MITCH I don't think I ever seen you in the light. [BLANCHE *laughs breathlessly.*] That's a fact!

BLANCHE Is it?

MITCH I've never seen you in the afternoon.

BLANCHE Whose fault is that?

MITCH You never want to go out in the afternoon.

BLANCHE Why, Mitch, you're at the plant in the afternoon!

MITCH Not Sunday afternoon. I've asked you to go out with me sometimes on Sundays but you always make an excuse. You never want to go out till after six and then it's always some place that's not lighted much.

BLANCHE   There is some obscure meaning in this but I fail to catch it.

MITCH   What it means is I've never had a real good look at you, Blanche. Let's turn the light on here.

BLANCHE [*fearfully*]   Light? Which light? What for?

MITCH   This one with the paper thing on it. [*He tears the paper lantern off the light bulb. She utters a frightened gasp.*]

BLANCHE   What did you do that for?

MITCH   So I can take a look at you good and plain!

BLANCHE   Of course you don't really mean to be insulting!

MITCH   No, just realistic.

BLANCHE   I don't want realism. I want magic! [MITCH *laughs.*] Yes, yes, magic! I try to give that to people. I misrepresent things to them. I don't tell truth, I tell what *ought* to be truth. And if that is sinful, then let me be damned for it!—*Don't turn the light on!*

> [MITCH *crosses to the switch. He turns the light on and stares at her. She cries out and covers her face. He turns the lights off again.*]

MITCH [*slowly and bitterly*]   I don't mind you being older than what I thought. But all the rest of it—Christ! That pitch about your ideals being so old-fashioned and all the malarkey that you've dished out all summer. Oh, I knew you weren't sixteen any more. But I was a fool enough to believe you was straight.

BLANCHE   Who told you I wasn't—"straight"? My loving brother-in-law. And you believed him.

MITCH   I called him a liar at first. And then I checked on the story. First I asked our supply-man who travels through Laurel. And then I talked directly over long-distance to this merchant.

BLANCHE   Who is this merchant?

MITCH   Kiefaber.

BLANCHE   The merchant Kiefaber of Laurel! I know the man. He whistled at me. I put him in his place. So now for revenge he makes up stories about me.

MITCH   Three people, Kiefaber, Stanley and Shaw, swore to them!

BLANCHE   Rub-a-dub-dub, three men in a tub! And such a filthy tub!

MITCH   Didn't you stay at a hotel called The Flamingo?

BLANCHE   Flamingo? No! Tarantula was the name of it! I stayed at a hotel called The Tarantula Arms!

MITCH [*stupidly*]   Tarantula?

BLANCHE   Yes, a big spider! That's where I brought my victims. [*She pours herself another drink.*] Yes, I had many intimacies with strangers. After the death of Allan—intimacies with strangers was all I seemed able to fill my empty heart with. . . . I think it was panic, just panic, that drove me from one to another, hunting for some protection—here and there, in the most—unlikely places—even, at last, in a seventeen-year-old boy but—somebody wrote the superintendent about it—"This woman is morally unfit for her position!"

> [*She throws back her head with convulsive, sobbing laughter. Then she repeats the statement, gasps, and drinks.*]

True? Yes, I suppose—unfit somehow—anyway. . . . So I came here. There was nowhere else I could go. I was played out. You know what played out is? My youth was suddenly gone up the water-spout, and—I met you. You said you needed somebody. Well, I needed somebody, too. I thanked God for you, because you seemed to be gentle—a cleft in the rock of the world that I could hide in! But I guess I was asking, hoping—too much! Kiefaber, Stanley and Shaw have tied an old tin can to the tail of the kite.

[*There is a pause.* MITCH *stares at her dumbly.*]

MITCH   You lied to me, Blanche.

BLANCHE   Don't say I lied to you.

MITCH   Lies, lies, inside and out, all lies.

BLANCHE   Never inside, I didn't lie in my heart . . .

[*A* VENDOR *comes around the corner. She is a blind* MEXICAN WOMAN *in a dark shawl, carrying bunches of those gaudy tin flowers that lower-class Mexicans display at funerals and other festive occasions. She is calling barely audibly. Her figure is only faintly visible outside the building.*]

MEXICAN WOMAN   Flores. Flores, Flores para los muertos.[1] Flores. Flores.

BLANCHE   What? Oh! Somebody outside . . . [*She goes to the door, opens it and stares at the* MEXICAN WOMAN.]

MEXICAN WOMAN [*she is at the door and offers* BLANCHE *some of her flowers*] Flores? Flores para los muertos?

BLANCHE [*frightened*]   No, no! Not now! Not now!

[*She darts back into the apartment, slamming the door.*]

MEXICAN WOMAN [*she turns away and starts to move down the street*]   Flores para los muertos.

[*The polka tune fades in.*]

BLANCHE [*as if to herself*]   Crumble and fade and—regrets—recriminations . . . "If you'd done this, it wouldn't've cost me that!"

MEXICAN WOMAN   Corones para los muertos.[2] Corones . . .

BLANCHE   Legacies! Huh. . . . And other things such as bloodstained pillow-slips—"Her linen needs changing"—"Yes, Mother. But couldn't we get a colored girl to do it?" No, we couldn't of course. Everything gone but the—

MEXICAN WOMAN   Flores.

BLANCHE   Death—I used to sit here and she used to sit over there and death was as close as you are. . . . We didn't dare even admit we had ever heard of it!

MEXICAN WOMAN   Flores para los muertos, flores—flores . . .

BLANCHE   The opposite is desire. So do you wonder? How could you possibly wonder! Not far from Belle Reve, before we had lost Belle Reve, was a camp where they trained young soldiers. On Sunday nights they would go in town to get drunk—

MEXICAN WOMAN [*softly*]   Corones . . .

BLANCHE   —and on the way back they would stagger onto my lawn and call—"Blanche! Blanche!"—the deaf old lady remaining suspected nothing. But sometimes I slipped outside to answer their calls. . . . Later the paddy-wagon would gather them up like daisies . . . the long way home . . .

[*The* MEXICAN WOMAN *turns slowly and drifts back off with her soft mournful cries.* BLANCHE *goes to the dresser and leans forward on it. After a moment,* MITCH *rises and follows her purposefully. The polka music fades away. He places his hands on her waist and tries to turn her about.*]

---

1. Flowers for the dead (Spanish).   2. Wreaths for the dead (Spanish).

BLANCHE   What do you want?

MITCH [*fumbling to embrace her*]   What I been missing all summer.

BLANCHE   Then marry me, Mitch!

MITCH   I don't think I want to marry you anymore.

BLANCHE   No?

MITCH [*dropping his hands from her waist*]   You're not clean enough to bring in the house with my mother.

BLANCHE   Go away, then. [*He stares at her.*] Get out of here quick before I start screaming fire! [*Her throat is tightening with hysteria.*] Get out of here quick before I start screaming fire.

> [*He still remains staring. She suddenly rushes to the big window with its pale blue square of the soft summer light and cries wildly.*]

Fire! Fire! Fire!

> [*With a startled gasp, MITCH turns and goes out the outer door, clatters awkwardly down the steps and around the corner of the building. BLANCHE staggers back from the window and falls to her knees. The distant piano is slow and blue.*]

Scene Ten

It is a few hours later that night.

> BLANCHE *has been drinking fairly steadily since* MITCH *left. She has dragged her wardrobe trunk into the center of the bedroom. It hangs open with flowery dresses thrown across it. As the drinking and packing went on, a mood of hysterical exhilaration came into her and she has decked herself out in a somewhat soiled and crumpled white satin evening gown and a pair of scuffed silver slippers with brilliants set in their heels.*

> *Now she is placing the rhinestone tiara on her head before the mirror of the dressing-table and murmuring excitedly as if to a group of spectral admirers.*

BLANCHE   How about taking a swim, a moonlight swim at the old rock-quarry? If anyone's sober enough to drive a car! Ha-ha! Best way in the world to stop your head buzzing! Only you've got to be careful to dive where the deep pool is—if you hit a rock you don't come up till tomorrow . . .

> [*Tremblingly she lifts the hand mirror for a closer inspection. She catches her breath and slams the mirror face down with such violence that the glass cracks. She moans a little and attempts to rise.* STANLEY *appears around the corner of the building. He still has on the vivid green silk bowling shirt. As he rounds the corner the honky-tonk music is heard. It continues softly throughout the scene. He enters the kitchen, slamming the door. As he peers in at* BLANCHE *he gives a low whistle. He has had a few drinks on the way and has brought some quart beer bottles home with him.*]

BLANCHE   How is my sister?

STANLEY   She is doing okay.

BLANCHE   And how is the baby?

STANLEY [*grinning amiably*]   The baby won't come before morning so they told me to go home and get a little shut-eye.

BLANCHE   Does that mean we are to be alone in here?

STANLEY   Yep. Just me and you, Blanche. Unless you got somebody hid under the bed. What've you got on those fine feathers for?

BLANCHE   Oh, that's right. You left before my wire came.

STANLEY   You got a wire?

BLANCHE   I received a telegram from an old admirer of mine.

STANLEY   Anything good?

BLANCHE   I think so. An invitation.

STANLEY   What to? A fireman's ball?

BLANCHE   [throwing back her head]   A cruise of the Caribbean on a yacht!

STANLEY   Well, well. What do you know?

BLANCHE   I have never been so surprised in my life.

STANLEY   I guess not.

BLANCHE   It came like a bolt from the blue!

STANLEY   Who did you say it was from?

BLANCHE   An old beau of mine.

STANLEY   The one that give you the white fox-pieces?

BLANCHE   Mr. Shep Huntleigh. I wore his ATO pin my last year at college. I hadn't seen him again until last Christmas. I ran in to him on Biscayne Boulevard. Then—just now—this wire—inviting me on a cruise of the Caribbean! The problem is clothes. I tore into my trunk to see what I have that's suitable for the tropics!

STANLEY   And come up with that—gorgeous—diamond—tiara?

BLANCHE   This old relic? Ha-ha! It's only rhinestones.

STANLEY   Gosh. I thought it was Tiffany diamonds. [He unbuttons his shirt.]

BLANCHE   Well, anyhow, I shall be entertained in style.

STANLEY   Uh-huh. It goes to show, you never know what is coming.

BLANCHE   Just when I thought my luck had begun to fail me—

STANLEY   Into the picture pops this Miami millionaire.

BLANCHE   This man is not from Miami. This man is from Dallas.

STANLEY   This man is from Dallas?

BLANCHE   Yes, this man is from Dallas where gold spouts out of the ground!

STANLEY   Well, just so he's from somewhere! [He starts removing his shirt.]

BLANCHE   Close the curtains before you undress any further.

STANLEY   [amiably]   This is all I'm going to undress right now. [He rips the sack off a quart beer bottle] Seen a bottle-opener?

   [She moves slowly toward the dresser, where she stands with her hands knotted together.]

I used to have a cousin who could open a beer bottle with his teeth. [pounding the bottle cap on the corner of table] That was his only accomplishment, all he could do—he was just a human bottle-opener. And then one time, at a wedding party, he broke his front teeth off! After that he was so ashamed of himself he used t' sneak out of the house when company came . . .

   [The bottle cap pops off and a geyser of foam shoots up. Stanley laughs happily, holding up the bottle over his head.]

Ha-ha! Rain from heaven! [He extends the bottle toward her] Shall we bury the hatchet and make it a loving-cup? Huh?

BLANCHE   No, thank you.

STANLEY   Well, it's a red-letter night for us both. You having an oil millionaire and me having a baby.

   [He goes to the bureau in the bedroom and crouches to remove something from the bottom drawer.]

BLANCHE [*drawing back*] What are you doing in here?

STANLEY Here's something I always break out on special occasions like this. The silk pyjamas I wore on my wedding night!

BLANCHE Oh.

STANLEY When the telephone rings and they say, "You've got a son!" I'll tear this off and wave it like a flag! [*He shakes out a brilliant pyjama coat.*] I guess we are both entitled to put on the dog. [*He goes back to the kitchen with the coat over his arm.*]

BLANCHE When I think of how divine it is going to be to have such a thing as privacy once more—I could weep with joy!

STANLEY This millionaire from Dallas is not going to interfere with your privacy any?

BLANCHE It won't be the sort of thing you have in mind. This man is a gentleman and he respects me. [*improvising feverishly*] What he wants is my companionship. Having great wealth sometimes makes people lonely! A cultivated woman, a woman of intelligence and breeding, can enrich a man's life—immeasurably! I have those things to offer, and this doesn't take them away. Physical beauty is passing. A transitory possession. But beauty of the mind and richness of the spirit and tenderness of the heart—and I have all of those things—aren't taken away, but grow! Increase with the years! How strange that I should be called a destitute woman! When I have all of these treasures locked in my heart. [*A choked sob comes from her.*] I think of myself as a very, very rich woman! But I have been foolish—casting my pearls before swine!

STANLEY Swine, huh?

BLANCHE Yes, swine! Swine! And I'm thinking not only of you but of your friend, Mr. Mitchell. He came to see me tonight. He dared to come here in his work clothes! And to repeat slander to me, vicious stories that he had gotten from you! I gave him his walking papers . . .

STANLEY You did, huh?

BLANCHE But then he came back. He returned with a box of roses to beg my forgiveness! He implored my forgiveness. But some things are not forgivable. Deliberate cruelty is not forgivable. It is the one unforgivable thing in my opinion and it is the one thing of which I have never, never been guilty. And so I told him, I said to him, "Thank you," but it was foolish of me to think that we could ever adapt ourselves to each other. Our ways of life are too different. Our attitudes and our backgrounds are incompatible. We have to be realistic about such things. So farewell, my friend! And let there be no hard feelings . . .

STANLEY Was this before or after the telegram came from the Texas oil millionaire?

BLANCHE What telegram? No! No, after! As a matter of fact, the wire came just as—

STANLEY As a matter of fact there wasn't no wire at all!

BLANCHE Oh, oh!

STANLEY There isn't no millionaire! And Mitch didn't come back with roses 'cause I know where he is—

BLANCHE Oh!

STANLEY There isn't a goddam thing but imagination!

BLANCHE Oh!

STANLEY And lies and conceit and tricks!

BLANCHE Oh!

STANLEY And look at yourself! Take a look at yourself in that worn-out Mardi Gras outfit, rented for fifty cents from some rag-picker! And with the crazy crown on! What queen do you think you are?

BLANCHE Oh—God . . .

STANLEY I've been on to you from the start! Not once did you pull any wool over this boy's eyes! You come in here and sprinkle the place with powder and spray perfume and cover the light-bulb with a paper lantern, and lo and behold the place has turned into Egypt and you are the Queen of the Nile! Sitting on your throne and swilling down my liquor! I say—*Ha!—Ha!* Do you hear me? *Ha—ha—ha!* [*He walks into the bedroom.*]

BLANCHE Don't come in here!

[*Lurid reflections appear on the walls around* BLANCHE. *The shadows are of a grotesque and menacing form. She catches her breath, crosses to the phone and jiggles the hook.* STANLEY *goes into the bathroom and closes the door.*]

Operator, operator! Give me long-distance, please. . . . I want to get in touch with Mr. Shep Huntleigh of Dallas. He's so well known he doesn't require any address. Just ask anybody who—Wait!!—No, I couldn't find it right now. . . . Please understand, I—No! No, wait!. . . . One moment! Someone is—Nothing! Hold on, please!

[*She sets the phone down and crosses warily into the kitchen. The night is filled with inhuman voices like cries in a jungle. The shadows and lurid reflections move sinuously as flames along the wall spaces. Through the back wall of the rooms, which have become transparent, can be seen the sidewalk. A prostitute has rolled a drunkard. He pursues her along the walk, overtakes her and there is a struggle. A policeman's whistle breaks it up. The figures disappear. Some moments later the Negro Woman appears around the corner with a sequined bag which the prostitute had dropped on the walk. She is rooting excitedly through it.* BLANCHE *presses her knuckles to her lips and returns slowly to the phone. She speaks in a hoarse whisper.*]

BLANCHE Operator! Operator! Never mind long-distance. Get Western Union. There isn't time to be—Western—Western Union!

[*She waits anxiously.*]

Western Union? Yes! I—want to—Take down this message! "In desperate, desperate circumstances! Help me! Caught in a trap. Caught in—" Oh!

[*The bathroom door is thrown open and* STANLEY *comes out in the brilliant silk pyjamas. He grins at her as he knots the tasseled sash about his waist. She gasps and backs away from the phone. He stares at her for a count of ten. Then a clicking becomes audible from the telephone, steady and rasping.*]

STANLEY You left th' phone off th' hook.

[*He crosses to it deliberately and sets it back on the hook. After he has replaced it, he stares at her again, his mouth slowly curving into a grin, as he weaves between* BLANCHE *and the outer door. The barely audible "Blue Piano" begins to drum up louder. The sound of it turns into the roar of an approaching locomotive.* BLANCHE *crouches, pressing her fists to her ears until it has gone by.*]

BLANCHE [*finally straightening*]   Let me—let me get by you!

STANLEY   Get by me? Sure. Go ahead. [*He moves back a pace in the door-way.*]

BLANCHE   You—you stand over there! [*She indicates a further position.*]

STANLEY [*grinning*]   You got plenty of room to walk by me now.

BLANCHE   Not with you there! But I've got to get out somehow!

STANLEY   You think I'll interfere with you? Ha-ha!

> [*The "Blue Piano" goes softly. She turns confusedly and makes a faint gesture. The inhuman jungle voices rise up. He takes a step toward her, biting his tongue which protrudes between his lips.*]

STANLEY [*softly*]   Come to think of it—maybe you wouldn't be bad to—interfere with . . .

> [BLANCHE *moves backward through the door into the bedroom.*]

BLANCHE   Stay back! Don't you come toward me another step or I'll—

STANLEY   What?

BLANCHE   Some awful thing will happen! It will!

STANLEY   What are you putting on now?

> [*They are now both inside the bedroom.*]

BLANCHE   I warn you, don't, I'm in danger!

> [*He takes another step. She smashes a bottle on the table and faces him, clutching the broken top.*]

STANLEY   What did you do that for?

BLANCHE   So I could twist the broken end in your face!

STANLEY   I bet you would do that!

BLANCHE   I would! I will if you—

STANLEY   Oh! So you want some roughhouse! All right, let's have some roughhouse!

> [*He springs toward her, overturning the table. She cries out and strikes at him with the bottle top but he catches her wrist.*]

Tiger—tiger! Drop the bottle-top! Drop it! We've had this date with each other from the beginning!

> [*She moans. The bottle-top falls. She sinks to her knees: He picks up her inert figure and carries her to the bed. The hot trumpet and drums from the Four Deuces sound loudly.*]

Scene Eleven

It is some weeks later. STELLA *is packing* BLANCHE's *things. Sounds of water can be heard running in the bathroom.*

*The portieres are partly open on the poker players—*STANLEY, STEVE, MITCH *and* PABLO—*who sit around the table in the kitchen. The atmosphere of the kitchen is now the same raw, lurid one of the disastrous poker night.*

The building is framed by the sky of turquoise. STELLA *has been crying as she arranges the flowery dresses in the open trunk.*

EUNICE *comes down the steps from her flat above and enters the kitchen. There is an outburst from the poker table.*

STANLEY   Drew to an inside straight and made it, by God.

PABLO   *Maldita sea tu suerto!*

STANLEY   Put it in English, greaseball.

PABLO   I am cursing your rutting luck.

STANLEY [*prodigiously elated*]   You know what luck is? Luck is believing you're lucky. Take at Salerno.[3] I believed I was lucky. I figured that 4 out of 5 would not come through but I would . . . and I did. I put that down as a rule. To hold front position in this rat-race you've got to believe you are lucky.

MITCH   You . . . you . . . you . . . Brag . . . brag . . . bull . . . bull.

[STELLA *goes into the bedroom and starts folding a dress.*]

STANLEY   What's the matter with him?

EUNICE [*walking past the table*]   I always did say that men are callous things with no feelings, but this does beat anything. Making pigs of yourselves. [*She comes through the portieres into the bedroom.*]

STANLEY   What's the matter with her?

STELLA   How is my baby?

EUNICE   Sleeping like a little angel. Brought you some grapes. [*She puts them on a stool and lowers her voice.*] Blanche?

STELLA   Bathing.

EUNICE   How is she?

STELLA   She wouldn't eat anything but asked for a drink.

EUNICE   What did you tell her?

STELLA   I—just told her that—we'd made arrangements for her to rest in the country. She's got it mixed in her mind with Shep Huntleigh.

[BLANCHE *opens the bathroom door slightly.*]

BLANCHE   Stella.

STELLA   Yes, Blanche.

BLANCHE   If anyone calls while I'm bathing take the number and tell them I'll call right back.

STELLA   Yes.

BLANCHE   That cool yellow silk—the bouclé. See if it's crushed. If it's not too crushed I'll wear it and on the lapel that silver and turquoise pin in the shape of a seahorse. You will find them in the heart-shaped box I keep my accessories in. And Stella . . . Try and locate a bunch of artificial violets in that box, too, to pin with the seahorse on the lapel of the jacket.

[*She closes the door.* STELLA *turns to* EUNICE.]

STELLA   I don't know if I did the right thing.

EUNICE   What else could you do?

STELLA   I couldn't believe her story and go on living with Stanley.

EUNICE   Don't ever believe it. Life has got to go on. No matter what happens, you've got to keep on going.

[*The bathroom door opens a little.*]

BLANCHE [*looking out*]   Is the coast clear?

STELLA   Yes, Blanche. [*to* EUNICE] Tell her how well she's looking.

BLANCHE   Please close the curtains before I come out.

STELLA   They're closed.

STANLEY   —How many for you?

PABLO   Two.

STEVE   Three.

3. Important beachhead in the Allied invasion of Italy in World War II.

[BLANCHE *appears in the amber light of the door. She has a tragic radiance in her red satin robe following the sculptural lines of her body. The "Varsouviana" rises audibly as* BLANCHE *enters the bedroom.*]

BLANCHE [*with faintly hysterical vivacity*]   I have just washed my hair.

STELLA   Did you?

BLANCHE   I'm not sure I got the soap out.

EUNICE   Such fine hair!

BLANCHE [*accepting the compliment*]   It's a problem. Didn't I get a call?

STELLA   Who from, Blanche?

BLANCHE   Shep Huntleigh . . .

STELLA   Why, not yet, honey!

BLANCHE   How strange! I—

[*At the sound of* BLANCHE's *voice* MITCH's *arm supporting his cards has sagged and his gaze is dissolved into space.* STANLEY *slaps him on the shoulder.*]

STANLEY   Hey, Mitch, come to!

[*The sound of this new voice shocks* BLANCHE. *She makes a shocked gesture, forming his name with her lips.* STELLA *nods and looks quickly away.* BLANCHE *stands quite still for some moments—the silver-backed mirror in her hand and a look of sorrowful perplexity as though all human experience shows on her face.* BLANCHE *finally speaks but with sudden hysteria.*]

BLANCHE   What's going on here?

[*She turns from* STELLA *to* EUNICE *and back to* STELLA. *Her rising voice penetrates the concentration of the game.* MITCH *ducks his head lower but* STANLEY *shoves back his chair as if about to rise.* STEVE *places a restraining hand on his arm.*]

BLANCHE [*continuing*]   What's happened here? I want an explanation of what's happened here.

STELLA [*agonizingly*]   Hush! Hush!

EUNICE   Hush! Hush! Honey.

STELLA   Please, Blanche.

BLANCHE   Why are you looking at me like that? Is something wrong with me?

EUNICE   You look wonderful, Blanche. Don't she look wonderful?

STELLA   Yes.

EUNICE   I understand you are going on a trip.

STELLA   Yes, Blanche *is.* She's going on a vacation.

EUNICE   I'm green with envy.

BLANCHE   Help me, help me get dressed!

STELLA [*handing her dress*]   Is this what you—

BLANCHE   Yes, it will do! I'm anxious to get out of here—this place is a trap!

EUNICE   What a pretty blue jacket.

STELLA   It's lilac colored.

BLANCHE   You're both mistaken. It's Della Robbia blue.[4] The blue of the robe in the old Madonna pictures. Are these grapes washed?

[*She fingers the bunch of grapes which* EUNICE *had brought in.*]

EUNICE   Huh?

---

4. A shade of light blue seen in terra cottas made by the Della Robbia family during the Italian Renaissance.

BLANCHE   Washed, I said. Are they washed?

EUNICE   They're from the French Market.

BLANCHE   That doesn't mean they've been washed. [*The cathedral bells chime.*] Those cathedral bells—they're the only clean thing in the Quarter. Well, I'm going now. I'm ready to go.

EUNICE [*whispering*]   She's going to walk out before they get here.

STELLA   Wait, Blanche.

BLANCHE   I don't want to pass in front of those men.

EUNICE   Then wait'll the game breaks up.

STELLA   Sit down and . . .

   [BLANCHE *turns weakly, hesitantly about. She lets them push her into a chair.*]

BLANCHE   I can smell the sea air. The rest of my time I'm going to spend on the sea. And when I die, I'm going to die on the sea. You know what I shall die of [*She plucks a grape.*] I shall die of eating an unwashed grape one day out on the ocean. I will die—with my hand in the hand of some nice-looking ship's doctor, a very young one with a small blond mustache and a big silver watch. "Poor lady," they'll say, "the quinine did her no good. That unwashed grape has transported her soul to heaven." [*The cathedral chimes are heard.*] And I'll be buried at sea sewn up in a clean white sack and dropped overboard—at noon—in the blaze of summer— and into an ocean as blue as [*chimes again*] my first lover's eyes!

   [A DOCTOR *and a* MATRON *have appeared around the corner of the building and climbed the steps to the porch. The gravity of their profession is exaggerated—the unmistakable aura of the state institution with its cynical detachment. The* DOCTOR *rings the doorbell. The murmur of the game is interrupted.*]

EUNICE [*whispering to* STELLA]   That must be them.

   [STELLA *presses her fists to her lips.*]

BLANCHE [*rising slowly*]   What is it?

EUNICE [*affectedly casual*]   Excuse me while I see who's at the door.

STELLA   Yes.

   [EUNICE *goes into the kitchen.*]

BLANCHE [*tensely*]   I wonder if it's for me.

   [*A whispered colloquy takes place at the door.*]

EUNICE [*returning, brightly*]   Someone is calling for Blanche.

BLANCHE   It *is* for me, then! [*She looks fearfully from one to the other and then to the portieres. The "Varsouviana" faintly plays.*] Is it the gentleman I was expecting from Dallas?

EUNICE   I think it is, Blanche.

BLANCHE   I'm not quite ready.

STELLA   Ask him to wait outside.

BLANCHE   I . . .

   [EUNICE *goes back to the portieres. Drums sound very softly.*]

STELLA   Everything packed?

BLANCHE   My silver toilet articles are still out.

STELLA   Ah!

EUNICE [*returning*]   They're waiting in front of the house.

BLANCHE   They! Who's "they"?

EUNICE   There's a lady with him.

BLANCHE   I cannot imagine who this "lady" could be! How is she dressed?

EUNICE   Just—just a sort of a—plain-tailored outfit.

BLANCHE   Possibly she's— [*Her voice dies out nervously.*]

STELLA   Shall we go, Blanche?

BLANCHE   Must we go through that room?

STELLA   I will go with you.

BLANCHE   How do I look?

STELLA   Lovely.

EUNICE [*echoing*]   Lovely.

> [BLANCHE *moves fearfully to the portieres.* EUNICE *draws them open for her.* BLANCHE *goes into the kitchen.*]

BLANCHE [*to the men*]   Please don't get up. I'm only passing through.

> [*She crosses quickly to outside door.* STELLA *and* EUNICE *follow. The poker players stand awkwardly at the table—all except* MITCH *who remains seated, looking down at the table.* BLANCHE *steps out on a small porch at the side of the door. She stops short and catches her breath.*]

DOCTOR   How do you do?

BLANCHE   You are not the gentleman I was expecting. [*She suddenly gasps and starts back up the steps. She stops by* STELLA, *who stands just outside the door, and speaks in a frightening whisper.*] That man isn't Shep Huntleigh.

> [*The "Varsouviana" is playing distantly.* STELLA *stares back at* BLANCHE. EUNICE *is holding* STELLA'S *arm. There is a moment of silence—no sound but that of* STANLEY *steadily shuffling the cards.* BLANCHE *catches her breath again and slips back into the flat. She enters the flat with a peculiar smile, her eyes wide and brilliant. As soon as her sister goes past her,* STELLA *closes her eyes and clenches her hands.* EUNICE *throws her arms comfortingly about her. Then she starts up to her flat.* BLANCHE *stops just inside the door.* MITCH *keeps staring down at his hands on the table, but the other men look at her curiously. At last she starts around the table toward the bedroom. As she does,* STANLEY *suddenly pushes back his chair and rises as if to block her way. The* MATRON *follows her into the flat.*]

STANLEY   Did you forget something?

BLANCHE [*shrilly*]   Yes! Yes, I forgot something!

> [*She rushes past him into the bedroom. Lurid reflections appear on the walls in odd, sinuous shapes. The "Varsouviana" is filtered into a weird distortion, accompanied by the cries and noises of the jungle.* BLANCHE *seizes the back of a chair as if to defend herself.*]

STANLEY [*sotto voce*][5]   Doc, you better go in.

DOCTOR [*sotto voce, motioning to the* MATRON]   Nurse, bring her out.

> [*The* MATRON *advances on one side,* STANLEY *on the other. Divested of all the softer properties of womanhood, the* MATRON *is a peculiarly sinister figure in her severe dress. Her voice is bold and toneless as a firebell.*]

MATRON   Hello, Blanche.

> [*The greeting is echoed and re-echoed by other mysterious voices behind the walls, as if reverberated through a canyon of rock.*]

STANLEY   She says that she forgot something.

> [*The echo sounds in threatening whispers.*]

MATRON   That's all right.

STANLEY   What did you forget, Blanche?

BLANCHE   I—I—

---

5. In an undertone [Italian].

MATRON   It don't matter. We can pick it up later.

STANLEY   Sure. We can send it along with the trunk.

BLANCHE [*retreating in panic*]   I don't know you—I don't know you. I want to be—left alone—please!

MATRON   Now, Blanche!

ECHOES [*rising and falling*]   Now, Blanche—now, Blanche—now, Blanche!

STANLEY   You left nothing here but spilt talcum and old empty perfume bottles—unless it's the paper lantern you want to take with you. You want the lantern?

> [*He crosses to dressing table and seizes the paper lantern, tearing it off the light bulb, and extends it toward her. She cries out as if the lantern was herself. The* MATRON *steps boldly toward her. She screams and tries to break past the* MATRON. *All the men spring to their feet.* STELLA *runs out to the porch, with* EUNICE *following to comfort her, simultaneously with the confused voices of the men in the kitchen.* STELLA *rushes into* EUNICE's *embrace on the porch.*]

STELLA   Oh, my God, Eunice help me! Don't let them do that to her, don't let them hurt her! Oh, God, oh, please God, don't hurt her! What are they doing to her? What are they doing? [*She tries to break from* EUNICE's *arms.*]

EUNICE   No, honey, no, no, honey. Stay here. Don't go back in there. Stay with me and don't look.

STELLA   What have I done to my sister? Oh, God, what have I done to my sister?

EUNICE   You done the right thing, the only thing you could do. She couldn't stay here; there wasn't no other place for her to go.

> [*While* STELLA *and* EUNICE *are speaking on the porch the voices of the men in the kitchen overlap them.* MITCH *has started toward the bedroom.* STANLEY *crosses to block him.* STANLEY *pushes him aside.* MITCH *lunges and strikes at* STANLEY. STANLEY *pushes* MITCH *back.* MITCH *collapses at the table, sobbing. During the preceding scenes, the* MATRON *catches hold of* BLANCHE's *arm and prevents her flight.* BLANCHE *turns wildly and scratches at the* MATRON. *The heavy woman pinions her arms.* BLANCHE *cries out hoarsely and slips to her knees.*]

MATRON   These fingernails have to be trimmed. [*The* DOCTOR *comes into the room and she looks at him.*] Jacket, Doctor?

DOCTOR   Not unless necessary.

> [*He takes off his hat and now he becomes personalized. The unhuman quality goes. His voice is gentle and reassuring as he crosses to* BLANCHE *and crouches in front of her. As he speaks her name, her terror subsides a little. The lurid reflections fade from the walls, the inhuman cries and noises die out and her own hoarse crying is calmed.*]

DOCTOR   Miss DuBois.

> [*She turns her face to him and stares at him with desperate pleading. He smiles; then he speaks to the* MATRON.]

It won't be necessary.

BLANCHE [*faintly*]   Ask her to let go of me.

DOCTOR [*to the* MATRON]   Let go.

> [*The* MATRON *releases her.* BLANCHE *extends her hands toward the* DOCTOR. *He draws her up gently and supports her with his arm and leads her through the portieres.*]

BLANCHE [*holding tight to his arm*] Whoever you are—I have always depended on the kindness of strangers.

[*The poker players stand back as* BLANCHE *and the* DOCTOR *cross the kitchen to the front door. She allows him to lead her as if she were blind. As they go out on the porch,* STELLA *cries out her sister's name from where she is crouched a few steps up on the stairs.*]

STELLA Blanche! Blanche, Blanche!

[BLANCHE *walks on without turning, followed by the* DOCTOR *and the* MATRON. *They go around the corner of the building.* EUNICE *descends to* STELLA *and places the child in her arms. It is wrapped in a pale blue blanket.* STELLA *accepts the child, sobbingly.* EUNICE *continues downstairs and enters the kitchen where the men, except for* STANLEY, *are returning silently to their places about the table.* STANLEY *has gone out on the porch and stands at the foot of the steps looking at* STELLA.]

STANLEY [*a bit uncertainly*] Stella?

[*She sobs with inhuman abandon. There is something luxurious in her complete surrender to crying now that her sister is gone.*]

STANLEY [*voluptuously, soothingly*] Now, honey. Now, love. Now, now, love. [*He kneels beside her and his fingers find the opening of her blouse.*] Now, now, love. Now, love. . . .

[*The luxurious sobbing, the sensual murmur fade away under the swelling music of the "Blue Piano" and the muted trumpet.*]

STEVE This game is seven-card stud.

CURTAIN

1947

JOHN CHEEVER
1912–1982

" It seems to me that man's inclination toward light, toward brightness, is very nearly botanical—and I mean spiritual light. One not only needs it, one struggles for it." These sentences from an interview with John Cheever, conducted by the novelist John Hersey, at first glance look strange coming from a "*New Yorker* writer" of entertaining stories in which harried, well-to-do, white middle-class suburbanites conduct their lives. "Our Chekhov of the exurbs," he was dubbed by the reviewer John Leonard, with reference to the mythical community of Shady Hill (which Cheever created along the lines of existing ones in Fairfield, Connecticut, or Westchester County, New York). Yet Chekhov's own characters, living in darkness, aspire toward "spiritual light," with a similarly "botanical" inclination. Trapped in their beautifully appointed houses and neighborhoods but carried along by the cool, effortless prose of their creator, Cheever's characters are viewed with a sympathetic irony, well-seasoned by sadness.

Cheever's early years were not notably idyllic, and he displays little nostalgia for a lost childhood. Born in Quincy, Massachusetts, he grew up in what he describes as shabby gentility, with his father departing the family when his son was fifteen. (Cheever had an older brother, Fred, with whom he formed a strong but troubled relationship.) Two years later his father lost the family's money in the crash of 1929, and by that time Cheever had been expelled from Thayer Academy, in Braintree. The expulsion marked the end of his formal education and the beginning of his career as a writer; for, remarkably, he wrote a short story about the experience, titled it "Expelled," and sent it to the *New Republic*, where Malcolm Cowley (who would become a lifelong friend) published it.

During the 1930s Cheever lived in New York City, in impoverished circumstances, taking odd jobs to support himself and winning a fellowship to the writer's colony at Yaddo, in Saratoga Springs, New York. His New York life would provide the material for many of his early stories, whose protagonists are rather frequently in desperate economic situations. With the coming of World War II, Cheever joined the armed forces and served in the Pacific theater but saw no combat. In 1941 he married Mary Winternitz. About the marriage, which produced three children and lasted through four decades, Cheever said, "That two people—both of us tempermental, quarrelsome, and intensely ambitious—could have gotten along for such a vast period of time is for me a very good example of the boundlessness of human nature." Meanwhile, with the help of Malcolm Cowley, he began to publish in the *New Yorker*, and in 1943, while he was serving in the military, his first book of stories (*The Way Some People Live*) was published to favorable reviews. Over the decades to follow the stories continued to appear, largely in the *New Yorker*, where he became—along with J. D. Salinger and John Updike—a recurrent phenomenon. Five further volumes of short fiction were published, and in 1978 *The Stories of John Cheever* gathered those he wished to be remembered for.

Although he is praised for his skill as a realist depictor of suburban manners and morals, Cheever's art cannot be adequately understood in such terms alone. As Stephen C. Moore has pointed out, "His best stories move from a base in a mimetic presentation of surface reality—the *scenery* of apparently successful American middle class life—to fables of heroism." Cheever's embattled heroes express themselves in taking up challenges that are essentially fabulous, and foolhardy: swimming home

across the backyard pools of Westchester ("The Swimmer," printed here); performing feats of physical daredeviltry in suburban living rooms ("O Youth and Beauty");
or dealing with the myriad demands and temptations that beset the hero who, having
escaped death in an airplane, returns home to more severe trials ("The Country
Husband"). Whatever the specific narrative, we are always aware of the storyteller's
art, shaping ordinary life into the odder, more willful figures of fantasy and romance.

While Cheever will be remembered primarily as a short-story writer, his output
includes a respectable number of novels. In 1957 he won a National Book Award for
his first one, *The Wapshot Chronicle* (it was followed by *The Wapshot Scandal*, in
1964), notable for its New England seacoast setting and domestic flavor, if less so for a
continuously engaging narrative line. Perhaps his most gripping novel is *Bullet Park*
(1969), which, like the best of the stories, is both realistic and fabulous. The suburban
milieu, seen from the 5:42 train from New York, has never been depicted more accurately, even lovingly, by Cheever. And as is to be expected, his protagonist's carefully
built, pious suburban existence turns out to be a mess. The novel provoked interesting
disagreement about its merits (some critics felt the narrative manipulations both ruthless and sentimental), but there was no disagreement about the vivid quality of its
represented life, on the commuter train or at the cocktail party. In the years just previous to his death, and after a bout with alcohol and drug addiction, Cheever published
his two final novels, *Falconer* (1978) and *Oh What a Paradise It Seems* (1980), the former receiving much praise for its harrowing rendering of prison life. (Farragut, the
novel's hero, is sent to Falconer Prison for killing his brother; Cheever lived in Ossin-
ing, New York, home of Sing Sing Prison, during his later years.)

From the beginning to the end of his career he was and remained a thoroughly
professional writer, wary of pronouncing on the world at large (there is a noticeable
absence of politics and ideology in his work) or on the meaning and significance of
his own art. As one sees from his *Journals* (1991), he agonized over the disruptive
facts of his alcoholism and his homosexuality. But he remained a private man,
seemingly untouched by experiments—or fads—in fiction writing. Whether or not,
as T. S. Eliot said about Henry James, he had a mind so fine that no idea could vio-
late it, Cheever remained firmly resistant to ideas of all sorts. This insular tendency
is probably a reason why his work makes less than a "major" claim on us, but it is
also the condition responsible for his devoted and scrupulous attention to the particularities of middle-class life at the far edge of its promised dream.

This text of "The Swimmer" is from *The Brigadier and the Golf Widow* (1964).

The Swimmer

It was one of those midsummer Sundays when everyone sits around saying: "I
drank too much last night." You might have heard it whispered by the parish-
ioners leaving church, heard it from the lips of the priest himself, struggling
with his cassock in the *vestiarium*,[1] heard it from the golf links and the tennis
courts, heard it from the wildlife preserve where the leader of the Audubon
group was suffering from a terrible hangover. "I *drank* too much," said Donald Westerhazy. "We all *drank* too much," said Lucinda Merrill. "It must have
been the wine," said Helen Westerhazy. "I *drank* too much of that claret."

This was at the edge of the Westerhazys' pool. The pool, fed by an arte-
sian well with a high iron content, was a pale shade of green. It was a fine
day. In the west there was a massive stand of cumulus cloud so like a city

---

1. Cloakroom for religious vestments adjacent to a church's sanctuary.

seen from a distance—from the bow of an approaching ship—that it might have had a name. Lisbon. Hackensack.[2] The sun was hot. Neddy Merrill sat by the green water, one hand in it, one around a glass of gin. He was a slender man—he seemed to have the especial slenderness of youth—and while he was far from young he had slid down his banister that morning and given the bronze backside of Aphrodite[3] on the hall table a smack, as he jogged toward the smell of coffee in his dining room. He might have been compared to a summer's day, particularly the last hours of one, and while he lacked a tennis racket or a sail bag the impression was definitely one of youth, sport, and clement weather. He had been swimming and now he was breathing deeply, stertorously as if he could gulp into his lungs the components of that moment, the heat of the sun, the intenseness of his pleasure. It all seemed to flow into his chest. His own house stood in Bullet Park,[4] eight miles to the south, where his four beautiful daughters would have had their lunch and might be playing tennis. Then it occurred to him that by taking a dogleg to the southwest he could reach his home by water.

His life was not confining and the delight he took in this observation could not be explained by its suggestion of escape. He seemed to see, with a cartographer's eye, that string of swimming pools, that quasi-subterranean stream that curved across the county. He had made a discovery, a contribution to modern geography; he would name the stream Lucinda after his wife. He was not a practical joker nor was he a fool but he was determinedly original and had a vague and modest idea of himself as a legendary figure. The day was beautiful and it seemed to him that a long swim might enlarge and celebrate its beauty.

He took off a sweater that was hung over his shoulders and dove in. He had an inexplicable contempt for men who did not hurl themselves into pools. He swam a choppy crawl, breathing either with every stroke or every fourth stroke and counting somewhere well in the back of his mind the one-two one-two of a flutter kick. It was not a serviceable stroke for long distances but the domestication of swimming had saddled the sport with some customs and in his part of the world a crawl was customary. To be embraced and sustained by the light green water was less a pleasure, it seemed, than the resumption of a natural condition, and he would have liked to swim without trunks, but this was not possible, considering his project. He hoisted himself up on the far curb—he never used the ladder—and started across the lawn. When Lucinda asked where he was going he said he was going to swim home.

The only maps and charts he had to go by were remembered or imaginary but these were clear enough. First there were the Grahams, the Hammers, the Lears, the Howlands, and the Crosscups. He would cross Ditmar Street to the Bunkers and come, after a short portage, to the Levys, the Welchers, and the public pool in Lancaster. Then there were the Hallorans, the Sachses, the Biswangers, Shirley Adams, the Gilmartins, and the Clydes. The day was lovely, and that he lived in a world so generously supplied with water seemed like a clemency, a beneficence. His heart was high and he ran across the grass. Making his way home by an uncommon route gave him

2. A town in New Jersey. Lisbon is the capital of Portugal.
3. Greek goddess of love and beauty.

4. Fictive suburb used as a location for many of Cheever's stories and novels.

the feeling that he was a pilgrim, an explorer, a man with a destiny, and he knew that he would find friends all along the way; friends would line the banks of the Lucinda River.

He went through a hedge that separated the Westerhazys' land from the Grahams', walked under some flowering apple trees, passed the shed that housed their pump and filter, and came out at the Grahams' pool. "Why, Neddy," Mrs. Graham said, "what a marvelous surprise. I've been trying to get you on the phone all morning. Here, let me get you a drink." He saw then, like any explorer, that the hospitable customs and traditions of the natives would have to be handled with diplomacy if he was ever going to reach his destination. He did not want to mystify or seem rude to the Grahams nor did he have the time to linger there. He swam the length of their pool and joined them in the sun and was rescued, a few minutes later, by the arrival of two carloads of friends from Connecticut. During the uproarious reunions he was able to slip away. He went down by the front of the Grahams' house, stepped over a thorny hedge, and crossed a vacant lot to the Hammers'. Mrs. Hammer, looking up from her roses, saw him swim by although she wasn't quite sure who it was. The Lears heard him splashing past the open windows of their living room. The Howlands and the Crosscups were away. After leaving the Howlands' he crossed Ditmar Street and started for the Bunkers', where he could hear, even at that distance, the noise of a party.

The water refracted the sound of voices and laughter and seemed to suspend it in midair. The Bunkers' pool was on a rise and he climbed some stairs to a terrace where twenty-five or thirty men and women were drinking. The only person in the water was Rusty Towers, who floated there on a rubber raft. Oh how bonny and lush were the banks of the Lucinda River! Prosperous men and women gathered by the sapphire-colored waters while caterer's men in white coats passed them cold gin. Overhead a red de Haviland trainer was circling around and around and around in the sky with something like the glee of a child in a swing. Ned felt a passing affection for the scene, a tenderness for the gathering, as if it was something he might touch. In the distance he heard thunder. As soon as Enid Bunker saw him she began to scream: "Oh look who's here! What a marvelous surprise! When Lucinda said that you couldn't come I thought I'd *die*." She made her way to him through the crowd, and when they had finished kissing she led him to the bar, a progress that was slowed by the fact that he stopped to kiss eight or ten other women and shake the hands of as many men. A smiling bartender he had seen at a hundred parties gave him a gin and tonic and he stood by the bar for a moment, anxious not to get stuck in any conversation that would delay his voyage. When he seemed about to be surrounded he dove in and swam close to the side to avoid colliding with Rusty's raft. At the far end of the pool he bypassed the Tomlinsons with a broad smile and jogged up the garden path. The gravel cut his feet but this was the only unpleasantness. The party was confined to the pool, and as he went toward the house he heard the brilliant, watery sound of voices fade, heard the noise of a radio from the Bunkers' kitchen, where someone was listening to a ballgame. Sunday afternoon. He made his way through the parked cars and down the grassy border of their driveway to Alewives' Lane. He did not want to be seen on the road in his bathing trunks but there was no traffic and he made the short distance to the Levys' driveway, marked with a private property sign and a green tube for the *New York Times*. All the doors and windows of the big house were open but there were no signs of life; not even a dog barked. He went around the side of the house to the pool and saw that the Levys had only recently left. Glasses and bottles and dishes of nuts were on a table at the deep end, where there was a bathhouse or gazebo, hung with Japanese lanterns. After swimming the pool he got himself a glass and poured a drink. It was his fourth or fifth drink and he had swum nearly half the length of the Lucinda River. He felt tired, clean, and pleased at that moment to be alone; pleased with everything.

It would storm. The stand of cumulus cloud—that city—had risen and darkened, and while he sat there he heard the percussiveness of thunder again. The de Haviland trainer was still circling overhead and it seemed to Ned that he could almost hear the pilot laugh with pleasure in the afternoon; but when there was another peal of thunder he took off for home. A train whistle blew and he wondered what time it had gotten to be. Four? Five? He thought of the provincial station at that hour, where a waiter, his tuxedo concealed by a raincoat, a dwarf with some flowers wrapped in newspaper, and a woman who had been crying would be waiting for the local. It was suddenly growing dark; it was that moment when the pin-headed birds seem to organize their song into some acute and knowledgeable recognition of the storm's approach. Then there was a fine noise of rushing water from the crown of an oak at his back, as if a spigot there had been turned. Then the noise of fountains came from the crowns of all the tall trees. Why did he love storms, what was the meaning of his excitement when the door sprang open and the rain wind fled rudely up the stairs, why had the simple task of shutting the windows of an old house seemed fitting and urgent, why did the first watery notes of a storm wind have for him the unmistakable sound of good news, cheer, glad tidings? Then there was an explosion, a smell of cordite, and rain lashed the Japanese lanterns that Mrs. Levy had bought in Kyoto the year before last, or was it the year before that?

He stayed in the Levys' gazebo until the storm had passed. The rain had cooled the air and he shivered. The force of the wind had stripped a maple of its red and yellow leaves and scattered them over the grass and the water. Since it was midsummer the tree must be blighted, and yet he felt a peculiar sadness at this sign of autumn. He braced his shoulders, emptied his glass, and started for the Welchers' pool. This meant crossing the Lindleys' riding ring and he was surprised to find it overgrown with grass and all the jumps dismantled. He wondered if the Lindleys had sold their horses or gone away for the summer and put them out to board. He seemed to remember having heard something about the Lindleys and their horses but the memory was unclear. On he went, barefoot through the wet grass, to the Welchers', where he found their pool was dry.

This breach in his chain of water disappointed him absurdly, and he felt like some explorer who seeks a torrential headwater and finds a dead stream. He was disappointed and mystified. It was common enough to go away for the summer but no one ever drained his pool. The Welchers had definitely gone away. The pool furniture was folded, stacked, and covered with a tarpaulin. The bathhouse was locked. All the windows of the house were shut, and when he went around to the driveway in front he saw a for-sale sign nailed to a tree. When had he last heard from the Welchers—when, that is, had he and Lucinda last regretted an invitation to dine with them? It seemed only a week or so ago. Was his memory failing or had he so disciplined it in the repression of unpleasant facts that he had damaged his sense of the truth? Then in the distance he heard the sound of a tennis game. This cheered him, cleared away all his apprehensions and let him regard the overcast sky and the cold air with indifference. This was the day that Neddy Merrill swam across the county. That was the day! He started off then for his most difficult portage.

Had you gone for a Sunday afternoon ride that day you might have seen him, close to naked, standing on the shoulders of route 424, waiting for a chance to cross. You might have wondered if he was the victim of foul play, had his car broken down, or was he merely a fool. Standing barefoot in the deposits of the highway—beer cans, rags, and blowout patches—exposed to all kinds of ridicule, he seemed pitiful. He had known when he started that this was a part of his journey—it had been on his maps—but confronted with the lines of traffic, worming through the summery light, he found himself unprepared. He was laughed at, jeered at, a beer can was thrown at him, and he had no dignity or humor to bring to the situation. He could have gone back, back to the Westerhazys', where Lucinda would still be sitting in the sun. He had signed nothing, vowed nothing, pledged nothing, not even to himself. Why, believing as he did, that all human obduracy was susceptible to common sense, was he unable to turn back? Why was he determined to complete his journey even if it meant putting his life in danger? At what point had this prank, this joke, this piece of horseplay become serious? He could not go back, he could not even recall with any clearness the green water at the Westerhazys', the sense of inhaling the day's components, the friendly and relaxed voices saying that they had *drunk* too much. In the space of an hour, more or less, he had covered a distance that made his return impossible.

An old man, tooling down the highway at fifteen miles an hour, let him get to the middle of the road, where there was a grass divider. Here he was exposed to the ridicule of the northbound traffic, but after ten or fifteen minutes he was able to cross. From here he had only a short walk to the Recreation Center at the edge of the Village of Lancaster, where there were some handball courts and a public pool.

The effect of the water on voices, the illusion of brilliance and suspense, was the same here as it had been at the Bunkers' but the sounds here were louder, harsher, and more shrill, and as soon as he entered the crowded enclosure he was confronted with regimentation. "ALL SWIMMERS MUST TAKE A SHOWER BEFORE USING THE POOL. ALL SWIMMERS MUST USE THE FOOTBATH. ALL SWIMMERS MUST WEAR THEIR IDENTIFICATION DISKS." He took a shower, washed his feet in a cloudy and bitter solution and made his way to the edge of the water. It stank of chlorine and looked to him like a sink. A pair of life-guards in a pair of towers blew police whistles at what seemed to be regular intervals and abused the swimmers through a public address system. Neddy remembered the sapphire water at the Bunkers' with longing and thought that he might contaminate himself—damage his own prosperousness and charm—by swimming in this murk, but he reminded himself that he was an explorer, a pilgrim, and that this was merely a stagnant bend in the Lucinda River. He dove, scowling with distaste, into the chlorine and had to swim with his head above water to avoid collisions, but even so he was bumped into, splashed and jostled. When he got to the shallow end both lifeguards were shouting at him: "Hey, you, you without the identification disk, get outa the water." He did, but they had no way of pursuing him and he went through the reek of suntan oil and chlorine out through the hurricane fence and passed the handball courts. By crossing the road he entered the wooded part of the Halloran estate. The woods were not cleared and the footing was treacherous and difficult until he reached the lawn and the clipped beech hedge that encircled their pool.

The Hallorans were friends, an elderly couple of enormous wealth who seemed to bask in the suspicion that they might be Communists. They were zealous reformers but they were not Communists, and yet when they were accused, as they sometimes were, of subversion, it seemed to gratify and excite them. Their beech hedge was yellow and he guessed this had been blighted like the Levys' maple. He called hullo, hullo, to warn the Hallorans of his approach, to palliate his invasion of their privacy. The Hallorans, for reasons that had never been explained to him, did not wear bathing suits. No explanations were in order, really. Their nakedness was a detail in their uncompromising zeal for reform and he stepped politely out of his trunks before he went through the opening in the hedge.

Mrs. Halloran, a stout woman with white hair and a serene face, was reading the *Times*. Mr. Halloran was taking beech leaves out of the water with a scoop. They seemed not surprised or displeased to see him. Their pool was perhaps the oldest in the county, a fieldstone rectangle, fed by a brook. It had no filter or pump and its waters were the opaque gold of the stream.

"I'm swimming across the county," Ned said.

"Why, I didn't know one could," exclaimed Mrs. Halloran.

"Well, I've made it from the Westerhazys'," Ned said. "That must be about four miles."

He left his trunks at the deep end, walked to the shallow end, and swam this stretch. As he was pulling himself out of the water he heard Mrs. Halloran say: "We've been *terribly* sorry to hear about all your misfortunes, Neddy."

"My misfortunes?" Ned asked. "I don't know what you mean."

"Why, we heard that you'd sold the house and that your poor children . . ."

"I don't recall having sold the house," Ned said, "and the girls are at home."

"Yes," Mrs. Halloran sighed. "Yes . . ." Her voice filled the air with an unseasonable melancholy and Ned spoke briskly. "Thank you for the swim."

"Well, have a nice trip," said Mrs. Halloran.

Beyond the hedge he pulled on his trunks and fastened them. They were loose and he wondered if, during the space of an afternoon, he could have lost some weight. He was cold and he was tired and the naked Hallorans and their dark water had depressed him. The swim was too much for his strength but how could he have guessed this, sliding down the banister that morning and sitting in the Westerhazys' sun? His arms were lame. His legs felt rubbery and ached at the joints. The worst of it was the cold in his bones and the feeling that he might never be warm again. Leaves were falling down around him and he smelled woodsmoke on the wind. Who would be burning wood at this time of year?

He needed a drink. Whiskey would warm him, pick him up, carry him through the last of his journey, refresh his feeling that it was original and valorous to swim across the county. Channel swimmers took brandy. He needed a stimulant. He crossed the lawn in front of the Hallorans' house and went down a little path to where they had built a house for their only daughter Helen and her husband Eric Sachs. The Sachses' pool was small and he found Helen and her husband there.

"Oh, *Neddy*," Helen said. "Did you lunch at Mother's?"

"Not *really*," Ned said. "I *did* stop to see your parents." This seemed to be explanation enough. "I'm terribly sorry to break in on you like this but I've taken a chill and I wonder if you'd give me a drink."

"Why, I'd *love* to," Helen said, "but there hasn't been anything in this house to drink since Eric's operation. That was three years ago."

Was he losing his memory, had his gift for concealing painful facts let him forget that he had sold his house, that his children were in trouble, and that his friend had been ill? His eyes slipped from Eric's face to his abdomen, where he saw three pale, sutured scars, two of them at least a foot long. Gone was his navel, and what, Neddy thought, would the roving hand, bed-checking one's gifts at 3 A.M. make of a belly with no navel, no link to birth, this breach in the succession?

"I'm sure you can get a drink at the Biswangers'," Helen said. "They're having an enormous do. You can hear it from here. Listen!"

She raised her head and from across the road, the lawns, the gardens, the woods, the fields, he heard again the brilliant noise of voices over water. "Well, I'll get wet," he said, still feeling that he had no freedom of choice about his means of travel. He dove into the Sachses' cold water and, gasping, close to drowning, made his way from one end of the pool to the other. "Lucinda and I want *terribly* to see you," he said over his shoulder, his face set toward the Biswangers'. "We're sorry it's been so long and we'll call you *very* soon."

He crossed some fields to the Biswangers' and the sounds of revelry there. They would be honored to give him a drink, they would be happy to give him a drink, they would in fact be lucky to give him a drink. The Biswangers invited him and Lucinda for dinner four times a year, six weeks in advance. They were always rebuffed and yet they continued to send out their invitations, unwilling to comprehend the rigid and undemocratic realities of their society. They were the sort of people who discussed the price of things at cocktails, exchanged market tips during dinner, and after dinner told dirty stories to mixed company. They did not belong to Neddy's set—they were not even on Lucinda's Christmas card list. He went toward their pool with feelings of indifference, charity, and some unease, since it seemed to be getting dark and these were the longest days of the year. The party when he joined it was noisy and large. Grace Biswanger was the kind of hostess who asked the optometrist, the veterinarian, the real-estate dealer and the dentist. No one was swimming and the twilight, reflected on the water of the pool, had a wintry gleam. There was a bar and he started for this. When Grace Biswanger saw him she came toward him, not affectionately as he had every right to expect, but bellicosely.

"Why, this party has everything," she said loudly, "including a gate crasher."

She could not deal him a social blow—there was no question about this and he did not flinch. "As a gate crasher," he asked politely, "do I rate a drink?"

"Suit yourself," she said. "You don't seem to pay much attention to invitations."

She turned her back on him and joined some guests, and he went to the bar and ordered a whiskey. The bartender served him but he served him rudely. His was a world in which the caterer's men kept the social score, and to be rebuffed by a part-time barkeep meant that he had suffered some loss of social esteem. Or perhaps the man was new and uninformed. Then he heard Grace at his back say: "They went for broke overnight—nothing but income—and he showed up drunk one Sunday and asked us to loan him five thousand dollars. . . ." She was always talking about money. It was worse than eating your peas off a knife. He dove into the pool, swam its length and went away.

The next pool on his list, the last but two, belonged to his old mistress, Shirley Adams. If he had suffered any injuries at the Biswangers' they would be cured here. Love—sexual roughhouse in fact—was the supreme elixir, the painkiller, the brightly colored pill that would put the spring back into his step, the joy of life in his heart. They had had an affair last week, last month, last year. He couldn't remember. It was he who had broken it off, his was the upper hand, and he stepped through the gate of the wall that surrounded her pool with nothing so considered as self-confidence. It seemed in a way to be his pool as the lover, particularly the illicit lover, enjoys the possessions of his mistress with an authority unknown to holy matrimony. She was there, her hair the color of brass, but her figure, at the edge of the lighted, cerulean water, excited in him no profound memories. It had been, he thought, a lighthearted affair, although she had wept when he broke it off. She seemed confused to see him and he wondered if she was still wounded. Would she, God forbid, weep again?

"What do you want?" she asked.

"I'm swimming across the county."

"Good Christ. Will you ever grow up?"

"What's the matter?"

"If you've come here for money," she said, "I won't give you another cent."

"You could give me a drink."

"I could but I won't. I'm not alone."

"Well, I'm on my way."

He dove in and swam the pool, but when he tried to haul himself up onto the curb he found that the strength in his arms and his shoulders had gone, and he paddled to the ladder and climbed out. Looking over his shoulder he saw, in the lighted bathhouse, a young man. Going out onto the dark lawn he smelled chrysanthemums or marigolds—some stubborn autumnal fragrance—on the night air, strong as gas. Looking overhead he saw that the stars had come out, but why should he seem to see Andromeda, Cepheus, and Cassiopeia? What had become of the constellations of midsummer? He began to cry.

It was probably the first time in his adult life that he had ever cried, certainly the first time in his life that he had ever felt so miserable, cold, tired, and bewildered. He could not understand the rudeness of the caterer's barkeep or the rudeness of a mistress who had come to him on her knees and showered his trousers with tears. He had swum too long, he had been immersed too long, and his nose and his throat were sore from the water. What he needed then was a drink, some company, and some clean dry clothes, and while he could have cut directly across the road to his home he went on to the Gilmartins' pool. Here, for the first time in his life, he did not dive but went down the steps into the icy water and swam a hobbled side stroke that he might have learned as a youth. He staggered with fatigue on his way to the Clydes' and paddled the length of their pool, stopping again and again with his hand on the curb to rest. He climbed up the ladder and wondered if he had the strength to get home. He had done what he wanted, he had swum the county, but he was so stupefied with exhaustion that his triumph seemed vague. Stooped, holding onto the gateposts for support, he turned up the driveway of his house.

The place was dark. Was it so late that they had all gone to bed? Had Lucinda stayed at the Westerhazys' for supper? Had the girls joined her there or gone someplace else? Hadn't they agreed, as they usually did on Sunday, to regret all their invitations and stay at home? He tried the garage doors to see what cars were in but the doors were locked and rust came off the handles onto his hands. Going toward the house, he saw that the force of the thunderstorm had knocked one of the rain gutters loose. It hung down over the front door like an umbrella rib, but it could be fixed in the morning. The house was locked, and he thought that the stupid cook or the stupid maid must have locked the place up until he remembered that it had been some time since they had employed a maid or a cook. He shouted, pounded on the door, tried to force it with his shoulder, and then, looking in at the windows, saw that the place was empty.

1964

ROBERT HAYDEN
1913–1980

" Hayden is by far the best chronicler and rememberer of the African American heritage in these Americas that I know of," the poet Michael Harper, whose own sense of history is indebted to Robert Hayden's work, has said. Hayden's poems save what has vanished, what has been lost to standard histories, like a 1920s prizefighter from the Midwest ("Free Fantasia: Tiger Flowers") or a miner trapped in Crystal Cave ("Beginnings, V"). He records the loss of what others never noticed as missing, and in their recovery he discovers a significance in the passing moment, the passed-over figure, the inarticulate gesture, which lasts through time. Always, in his words, "opposed to the chauvinistic and the doctrinaire" in art, he cherished the freedom of the poet to write about whatever seized the imagination. But his imagination was in its nature elegiac and historical. As he remembers and re-creates the African American heritage, he speaks to the struggles of the individual spirit for freedom and to painful self-divisions known to the people of many times and places. But if the circumstances he confronts in his poems are often harsh, his work captures the energy and joyfulness that make survival possible.

Born in Detroit, Michigan, Hayden grew up in a poor neighborhood called by its inhabitants, with affectionate irony, "Paradise Valley." His powerful sequence *Elegies for Paradise Valley* (1978) resurrects the neighborhood in its racial and ethnic mix. Memory for Hayden is an act of love that leads to self-awareness; in this sequence and in poems like "Those Winter Sundays," he writes about his own past, confronts its pain, and preserves its sustaining moments of happiness.

Hayden had a deep understanding of the conflicts that divide the self. His family history gave him an early acquaintance with such self-division: his parents' marriage ended when he was young, and his mother left him in the care of foster parents (whose surname he adopted) when she left Detroit to look for work. He remained with the Haydens even after his mother returned to Detroit when he was a teenager and lived for a period with his foster family until conflict arose between her and his foster mother. "I lived in the midst of so much turmoil all the time I didn't know if I loved or hated," he once said. As an African American and as a poet Hayden also lived between worlds. He courageously maintained his sense of vocation through years of critical neglect and amid the demands of full-time teaching at Fisk University from 1946 to 1968. He published his first book, *Heart-Shape in the Dust,* in 1940, but his mature work did not appear in quantity until his volume *Ballad of Remembrance* (1962). At the same time his belief that the poet should not be restricted by any set of themes, racial or otherwise, and the highly formal quality of his work led to criticism by some young African American writers in the 1960s. But Hayden never abandoned his belief in the power of art to speak universally. In a 1974 interview he told Dennis Gendron of rereading Yeats's poem "Easter 1916" in the wake of the riots in Detroit—"that is the kind of poetry I want to write," he said, in admiration of the ways Yeats conceived a particular historical and political moment so that it speaks across time and place.

In fact, Hayden did himself write that kind of poetry. His most famous poem, "Middle Passage," demonstrates his transfiguring imagination and the knowledge of historical documents, which began early in his career. In 1936, after leaving college because of increasingly difficult economic conditions, Hayden joined the Federal Writers Project of the Works Progress Administration, and for two years he researched the history of abolition movements and the Underground Railroad in Michigan. "Middle Passage" is a collage of accounts of the slave ships that transported men and women from Africa into slavery in the New World. Through the multiple voices in the poem, Hayden lets the accounts of those who participated in (and profited from) the slave trade reveal the evidence of their own damnation. The blindness that attacks one of the ships becomes a symbol of the devastating suffering of those transported into slavery and of the moral blindness everywhere evident in the traders' accounts. The collage technique allows Hayden to suggest the fragmentation of the story; the silences in the poem evoke the missing voices of those who suffered and died on the voyages or in the intolerable conditions of slavery. At the heart of the poem is the account of a rebellion led by one of the slaves (Cinquez) on the ship *Amistad.* Cinquez is one of several figures in Hayden's poems who dramatize "The deep immortal human wish / the timeless will" ("Middle Passage") that for Hayden is the indomitable yearning for freedom. This "timeless will" and struggle also appear in his poems about Harriet Tubman ("Runagate Runagate"), Nat Turner, Frederick Douglass, Phillis Wheatley, and the later figures Paul Robeson and Bessie Smith.

Hayden's experiment with collage technique in "Middle Passage" connects him to modernist poets like T. S. Eliot and William Carlos Williams and to an African American tradition acutely aware of the power of voice. He continued to experiment with poetic form and with the creation of different voices, always testing the possibilities of craft and forging a language to express what he knew and felt. His sequences *Beginnings* and *Elegies for Paradise Valley* demonstrate his formal originality, as does his late poem "American Journal," with its long lines and its approximation to prose. Hayden loved language and was unafraid to be lushly descriptive as well as to be precisely imagistic. His work summons us to notice the world as we had not before and offers us candor, clearsightedness, and a transforming gaiety.

From 1968 until his death, Hayden was professor of English at the University of Michigan at Ann Arbor. In 1976 he became the first African American to be appointed poetry consultant to the Library of Congress, the position now known as poet laureate of the United States.

Middle Passage[1]

I

Jesús, Estrella, Esperanza, Mercy[2]

Sails flashing to the wind like weapons,
sharks following the moans the fever and the dying;
horror the corposant and compass rose.[3]

Middle Passage: 5
      voyage through death
             to life upon these shores.

"10 April 1800—
Blacks rebellious. Crew uneasy. Our linguist says
their moaning is a prayer for death,   10
ours and their own. Some try to starve themselves.
Lost three this morning leaped with crazy laughter
to the waiting sharks, sang as they went under."

Desire, Adventure, Tartar, Ann:

Standing to America, bringing home   15
black gold, black ivory, black seed.

      Deep in the festering hold thy father lies,
      of his bones New England pews are made,
      those are altar lights that were his eyes.[4]

Jesus   Saviour   Pilot   Me   20
Over   Life's   Tempestuous   Sea[5]

We pray that Thou wilt grant, O Lord,
safe passage to our vessels bringing
heathen souls unto Thy chastening.

Jesus   Saviour   25

      "8 bells. I cannot sleep, for I am sick
with fear, but writing eases fear a little
since still my eyes can see these words take shape
upon the page & so I write, as one
would turn to exorcism. 4 days scudding,   30
but now the sea is calm again. Misfortune
follows in our wake like sharks (our grinning
tutelary gods). Which one of us

---

1. Main route for the slave trade in the Atlantic between Africa and the West Indies.
2. Names of slave ships. (*Estrella* and *Esperanza* are Spanish for "Star" and "Hope," respectively.)
3. Circle printed on a map showing compass directions. "Corposant": a fiery luminousness that can appear on the decks of ships during electrical storms.
4. "Full fathom five thy father lies; / Of his bones are coral made; / Those are pearls that were his eyes" (Shakespeare's *Tempest* 1.2.400–402). The sprite Ariel is singing about the supposed death by drowning of the king of Naples.
5. Words from a Protestant hymn.

has killed an albatross?[6] A plague among
our blacks—Ophthalmia: blindness—& we   35
have jettisoned the blind to no avail.
It spreads, the terrifying sickness spreads.
Its claws have scratched sight from the Capt.'s eyes
& there is blindness in the fo'c'sle[7]
& we must sail 3 weeks before we come   40
to port."

What port awaits us, Davy Jones'
or home? I've heard of slavers drifting, drifting,
playthings of wind and storm and chance, their crews
gone blind, the jungle hatred   45
crawling up on deck.

Thou   Who   Walked   On   Galilee

"Deponent further sayeth *The Bella J*
left the Guinea Coast
with cargo of five hundred blacks and odd   50
for the barracoons[8] of Florida:

"That there was hardly room 'tween-decks for half
the sweltering cattle stowed spoon-fashion there;
that some went mad of thirst and tore their flesh
and sucked the blood: 55

"That Crew and Captain lusted with the comeliest
of the savage girls kept naked in the cabins;
that there was one they called The Guinea Rose
and they cast lots and fought to lie with her:

"That when the Bo's'n piped all hands,[9] the flames   60
spreading from starboard already were beyond
control, the negroes howling and their chains
entangled with the flames:

"That the burning blacks could not be reached,
that the Crew abandoned ship,   65
leaving their shrieking negresses behind,
that the Captain perished drunken with the wenches:

"Further Deponent sayeth not."

Pilot   Oh   Pilot   Me

6. A bird of good omen; to kill one is an unlucky
and impious act (as in Samuel Taylor Coleridge's
Rime of the Ancient Mariner).
7. Short for forecastle, the place in a ship where
sailors are quartered.
8. Barracks or enclosures for slaves.
9. I.e., when the boatswain (petty officer aboard
a ship) signaled to summon all the crew on deck.

II

Aye, lad, and I have seen those factories,   70
Gambia, Rio Pongo, Calabar;[1]
have watched the artful mongos[2] baiting traps
of war wherein the victor and the vanquished

Were caught as prizes for our barracoons.
Have seen the nigger kings whose vanity   75
and greed turned wild black hides of Fellatah,
Mandingo, Ibo, Kru[3] to gold for us.

And there was one—King Anthracite we named him—
fetish face beneath French parasols
of brass and orange velvet, impudent mouth   80
whose cups were carven skulls of enemies:

He'd honor us with drum and feast and conjo[4]
and palm-oil-glistening wenches deft in love,
and for tin crowns that shone with paste,
red calico and German-silver trinkets   85

Would have the drums talk war and send
his warriors to burn the sleeping villages
and kill the sick and old and lead the young
in coffles[5] to our factories.

Twenty years a trader, twenty years,   90
for there was wealth aplenty to be harvested
from those black fields, and I'd be trading still
but for the fevers melting down my bones.

III

Shuttles in the rocking loom of history,
the dark ships move, the dark ships move,   95
their bright ironical names
like jests of kindness on a murderer's mouth;
plough through thrashing glister toward
fata morgana's lucent melting shore,
weave toward New World littorals[6] that are   100
mirage and myth and actual shore.

Voyage through death,
                    voyage whose chartings are unlove.

A charnel stench, effluvium of living death
spreads outward from the hold,   105

---

1. A city in southeast Nigeria. Gambia is a river
and nation in West Africa. Rio Pongo is a watercourse, dry for most of the year, in East Africa.
2. I.e., Africans.

3. African tribes.
4. Dance.
5. Train of slaves fastened together.
6. Coastal regions. "Fata morgana": mirage.

where the living and the dead, the horribly dying,
lie interlocked, lie foul with blood and excrement.

Deep in the festering hold thy father lies,
the corpse of mercy rots with him,
rats eat love's rotten gelid eyes.   110

But, oh, the living look at you
with human eyes whose suffering accuses you,
whose hatred reaches through the swill of dark
to strike you like a leper's claw.

You cannot stare that hatred down   115
or chain the fear that stalks the watches
and breathes on you its fetid scorching breath;
cannot kill the deep immortal human wish,
the timeless will.

"But for the storm that flung up barriers   120
of wind and wave, *The Amistad*,[7] señores,
would have reached the port of Príncipe in two,
three days at most; but for the storm we should
have been prepared for what befell.
Swift as the puma's leap it came. There was   125
that interval of moonless calm filled only
with the water's and the rigging's usual sounds,
then sudden movement, blows and snarling cries
and they had fallen on us with machete
and marlinspike. It was as though the very   130
air, the night itself were striking us.
Exhausted by the rigors of the storm,
we were no match for them. Our men went down
before the murderous Africans. Our loyal
Celestino ran from below with gun   135
and lantern and I saw, before the cane-
knife's wounding flash, Cinquez,
that surly brute who calls himself a prince,
directing, urging on the ghastly work.[8]
He hacked the poor mulatto down, and then   140
he turned on me. The decks were slippery
when daylight finally came. It sickens me
to think of what I saw, of how these apes
threw overboard the butchered bodies of
our men, true Christians all, like so much jetsam.   145
Enough, enough. The rest is quickly told:
Cinquez was forced to spare the two of us

---

7. A Spanish ship—the name means "Friendship"—that carried fifty-three illegally obtained
slaves out of Havana, Cuba, in July 1839. The
slaves revolted and seized the ship.

8. During the mutiny the Africans, led by a man
called Cinqué, or Cinquez, killed the captain,
his slave Celestino, and the mate, but spared the
two slave owners.

you see to steer the ship to Africa,
and we like phantoms doomed to rove the sea
voyaged east by day and west by night,   150
deceiving them, hoping for rescue,
prisoners on our own vessel, till
at length we drifted to the shores of this
your land, America, where we were freed
from our unspeakable misery. Now we   155
demand, good sirs, the extradition of
Cinquez and his accomplices to La
Havana.⁹ And it distresses us to know
there are so many here who seem inclined
to justify the mutiny of these blacks.   160
We find it paradoxical indeed
that you whose wealth, whose tree of liberty
are rooted in the labor of your slaves
should suffer the august John Quincy Adams
to speak with so much passion of the right   165
of chattel slaves to kill their lawful masters
and with his Roman rhetoric weave a hero's
garland for Cinquez.¹ I tell you that
we are determined to return to Cuba
with our slaves and there see justice done. Cinquez—   170
or let us say 'the Prince'—Cinquez shall die."

The deep immortal human wish,
the timeless will:

Cinquez its deathless primaveral image,
life that transfigures many lives.   175

Voyage through death
            to life upon these shores.

                                                                    1962

Homage to the Empress of the Blues¹

Because there was a man somewhere in a candystripe silk shirt,
gracile and dangerous as a jaguar and because a woman moaned for him
in sixty-watt gloom and mourned him Faithless Love
Twotiming Love Oh Love Oh Careless Aggravating Love,

9. After two months the *Amistad* reached Long Island Sound, where it was detained by the American ship *Washington*, the slaves were imprisoned, and the owners were freed. The owners began litigation to return the slaves to Havana to be tried for murder.
1. The case reached the Supreme Court in 1841; the Africans were defended by former president John Quincy Adams, and the court released the thirty-seven survivors to return to Africa.
1. Bessie Smith (1895–1937), one of the greatest American blues singers. Her flamboyant style, which grew out of the black vaudeville tradition, made her popular in the 1920s.

She came out on the stage in yards of pearls, emerging like   5
a favorite scenic view, flashed her golden smile and sang.

Because grey laths began somewhere to show from underneath
torn hurdygurdy² lithographs of dollfaced heaven;
and because there were those who feared alarming fists of snow
on the door and those who feared the riot-squad of statistics,   10

She came out on the stage in ostrich feathers, beaded satin,
and shone that smile on us and sang.

1962

Those Winter Sundays

Sundays too my father got up early
and put his clothes on in the blueblack cold,
then with cracked hands that ached
from labor in the weekday weather made
banked fires blaze. No one ever thanked him.   5

I'd wake and hear the cold splintering, breaking.
When the rooms were warm, he'd call,
and slowly I would rise and dress,
fearing the chronic angers of that house,

Speaking indifferently to him,   10
who had driven out the cold
and polished my good shoes as well.
What did I know, what did I know
of love's austere and lonely offices?

1962

---

2. A disreputable kind of dance hall, so called because of the hurdy-gurdies (barrel organs) that provided the music for dancing. "Laths": the strips of wood that form a backing for wall plaster.

RANDALL JARRELL
1914–1965

" M onstrously knowing and monstrously innocent. . . . A Wordsworth with the obsession of a Lewis Carroll"—so Robert Lowell once described his friend and fellow poet Randall Jarrell. Jarrell was a teacher and a critic as well as a poet, and for many writers of his generation—Lowell, Delmore Schwartz, and John Berryman among them—he was the critic whose taste was most unerring, who seemed to know instantly what was genuine and what was not. An extraordinary teacher, he loved the activity of teaching, both in and out of the classroom; "the gods who had taken away the poet's audience had given him students," he once said. The novelist Peter Taylor recalls that when he came to Vanderbilt University as a freshman in the mid-1930s, Jarrell, then a graduate student, had already turned the literary students into disciples; he held court discussing Chekhov on the sidelines of touch football games. For all his brilliance Jarrell was, at heart, democratic. Believing that poetry belongs to every life, his teaching, his literary criticism, and his poetry aimed to recapture and reeducate a general audience lost to poetry in an age of specialization. Jarrell's interests were democratic as well, and he had a lifelong fascination with popular culture. Witty and incisive, Jarrell could be intimidating; at the same time he remained deeply in touch with childhood's mystery and enchantment. It was as if, his close friend the philosopher Hannah Arendt once said, he "had emerged from the enchanted forests." He loved fairy tales, translated a number of them, and wrote several books for children, among them *The Bat-Poet* (1964). The childlike quality of the person informs Jarrell's poems as well; he is unembarrassed by the adult heart still in thrall to childhood's wishes.

Jarrell was born in Nashville, Tennessee, but spent much of his childhood in Long Beach, California. After his parents divorced when he was eleven, he remained for a year with his grandparents in Hollywood, then returned to live with his mother in Nashville. He majored in psychology at Vanderbilt and stayed on there to do graduate work in English. In 1937 he left Nashville to teach at Kenyon College (Gambier, Ohio) at the invitation of his old Vanderbilt professor John Crowe Ransom, the New Critic and Fugitive poet. From that time on Jarrell almost always had some connection with a university: after Kenyon, the University of Texas, Sarah Lawrence College, and from 1947 until his death, the Women's College of the University of North Carolina at Greensboro. But, as suggested by his novel *Pictures from an Institution* (1954) with its mixed satiric and tender views of academic life, he was never satisfied with a cloistered education. As poetry editor of *The Nation* (1946), and then in a series of essays and reviews collected as *Poetry and the Age* (1953), he introduced readers to the work of his contemporaries—Elizabeth Bishop, Robert Lowell, John Berryman, the William Carlos Williams of *Paterson*—and influentially reassessed the reputations of Walt Whitman and Robert Frost.

Among the poets who emerged after World War II, Jarrell stands out for his colloquial plainness. While others—Richard Wilbur and the early Robert Lowell, for example—were writing highly structured poems with complicated imagery, Jarrell's work feels and sounds close to what he calls in one poem the "dailiness of life" ("Well Water"). He is master of the everyday heartbreak and identifies with ordinary forms of loneliness. Jarrell's gift of imaginative sympathy appears in the treatment of soldiers in his war poems, the strongest to come out of World War II. He had been trained as an Army Air Force pilot and after that as a control operator,

The Gotham Book Mart. This midtown Manhattan store was famous for its literary
eminences. A December 1948 party drew a roomful of midcentury writers, including,
clockwise, W. H. Auden on the ladder, Elizabeth Bishop, Delmore Schwartz, Randall
Jarrell, Charles Henri Ford, William Rose Benét, Stephen Spender, Marya Zaturenska,
Horace Gregory, Tennessee Williams, Richard Eberhart, Gore Vidal, and José Garcia Villa.

and he had a sense of the war's special casualties. With their understanding of soldiers as both destructive and innocent at the same time, these poems make his
volumes *Little Friend, Little Friend* (1945) and *Losses* (1948) powerful and moving.
Jarrell also empathized with the dreams, loneliness, and disappointments of
women, whose perspective he often adopted, as in the title poem of his collection
The Woman at the Washington Zoo (1960) and his poem "Next Day."

Against the blasted or unrealized possibilities of adult life Jarrell often poised the
rich mysteries of childhood. The title poem of his last book, *The Lost World* (1965),
looks back to his Los Angeles playtime, the movie sets and plaster dinosaurs and
pterodactyls against whose eternal lighthearted presence he measures his own
aging. The poem has Jarrell's characteristic sense of loss but also his capacity for a
mysterious happiness, which animates the poem even as he holds "nothing" in his
hands.

Jarrell suffered a nervous breakdown in February 1965, but returned to teaching
that fall. In October he was struck by a car and died. His *Complete Poems* were
published posthumously (1969), as were a translation of Goethe's *Faust*, Part I, in
preparation at his death, and two books of essays, *The Third Book of Criticism*
(1969) and *Kipling, Auden & Co.* (1980).

The Death of the Ball Turret Gunner[1]

From my mother's sleep I fell into the State,
And I hunched in its belly till my wet fur froze.
Six miles from earth, loosed from its dream of life,
I woke to black flak[2] and the nightmare fighters.
When I died they washed me out of the turret with a hose.   5

1945

Second Air Force

Far off, above the plain the summer dries,
The great loops of the hangars sway like hills.
Buses and weariness and loss, the nodding soldiers
Are wire, the bare frame building, and a pass
To what was hers; her head hides his square patch   5
And she thinks heavily: My son is grown.
She sees a world: sand roads, tar-paper barracks,
The bubbling asphalt of the runways, sage,
The dunes rising to the interminable ranges,
The dim flights moving over clouds like clouds.   10
The armorers in their patched faded green,
Sweat-stiffened, banded with brass cartridges,
Walk to the line; their Fortresses,[1] all tail,
Stand wrong and flimsy on their skinny legs,
And the crews climb to them clumsily as bears.   15
The head withdraws into its hatch (a boy's),
The engines rise to their blind laboring roar,
And the green, made beasts run home to air.
Now in each aspect death is pure.
(At twilight they wink over men like stars   20
And hour by hour, through the night, some see
The great lights floating in—from Mars, from Mars.)
How emptily the watchers see them gone.

They go, there is silence; the woman and her son
Stand in the forest of the shadows, and the light   25
Washes them like water. In the long-sunken city
Of evening, the sunlight stills like sleep
The faint wonder of the drowned; in the evening,
In the last dreaming light, so fresh, so old,

1. A ball turret was a plexiglass sphere set into the belly of a B-17 or B-24 [bomber], and inhabited by two .50 caliber machine-guns and one man, a short, small man. When this gunner tracked with his machine-guns a fighter attacking his bomber from below, he revolved with the turret; hunched upside-down in his little sphere, he looked like the foetus in the womb. The fighters which attacked him were armed with cannon firing explosive shells. The hose was a steam hose [Jarrell's note].
2. Antiaircraft fire.
1. B-17 Flying Fortresses, an American bomber in World War II.

The soldiers pass like beasts, unquestioning,   30
And the watcher for an instant understands
What there is then no need to understand;
But she wakes from her knowledge, and her stare,
A shadow now, moves emptily among
The shadows learning in their shadowy fields   35
The empty missions.
                 Remembering,
She hears the bomber calling, *Little Friend!*[2]
To the fighter hanging in the hostile sky,
And sees the ragged flame eat, rib by rib,   40
Along the metal of the wing into her heart:
The lives stream out, blossom, and float steadily
To the flames of the earth, the flames
That burn like stars above the lands of men.

She saves from the twilight that takes everything   45
A squadron shipping, in its last parade—
Its dogs run by it, barking at the band—
A gunner walking to his barracks, half-asleep,
Starting at something, stumbling (above, invisible,
The crews in the steady winter of the sky   50
Tremble in their wired fur); and feels for them
The love of life for life. The hopeful cells
Heavy with someone else's death, cold carriers
Of someone else's victory, grope past their lives
Into her own bewilderment: The years meant *this*?   55

But for them the bombers answer everything.

                                 1945

Thinking of the Lost World

This spoonful of chocolate tapioca
Tastes like—like peanut butter, like the vanilla
Extract Mama told me not to drink.
Swallowing the spoonful, I have already traveled
Through time to my childhood. It puzzles me   5
That age is like it.
               Come back to that calm country
Through which the stream of my life first meandered,
My wife, our cat, and I sit here and see

2. In "Second Air Force" the woman visiting her son remembers what she has read on the front page of her newspaper the week before, a conversation between a bomber, in flames over Germany, and one of the fighters protecting it: "Then I heard the bomber call me in: 'Little Friend, Little Friend, I got two engines on fire. Can you see me, Little Friend?' I said, 'I'm crossing right over you. Let's go home'" [Jarrell's note].

Squirrels quarreling in the feeder, a mockingbird   10
Copying our chipmunk, as our end copies
Its beginning.
              Back in Los Angeles, we missed
Los Angeles. The sunshine of the Land
Of Sunshine is a gray mist now, the atmosphere   15
Of some factory planet: when you stand and look
You see a block or two, and your eyes water.
The orange groves are all cut down . . . My bow
Is lost, all my arrows are lost or broken,
My knife is sunk in the eucalyptus tree   20
Too far for even Pop to get it out,
And the tree's sawed down. It and the stair-sticks
And the planks of the tree house are all firewood
Burned long ago; its gray smoke smells of Vicks.[1]

Twenty Years After, thirty-five years after,   25
Is as good as ever—better than ever,
Now that D'Artagnan[2] is no longer old—
Except that it is unbelievable.
I say to my old self: "I believe. Help thou
Mine unbelief."   30
              I believe the dinosaur
Or pterodactyl's married the pink sphinx
And lives with those Indians in the undiscovered
Country between California and Arizona
That the mad girl told me she was princess of—   35
Looking at me with the eyes of a lion,
Big, golden, without human understanding,
As she threw paper-wads from the back seat
Of the car in which I drove her with her mother
From the jail in Waycross to the hospital   40
In Daytona. If I took my eyes from the road
And looked back into her eyes, the car would—I'd be—

Or if only I could find a crystal set[3]
Sometimes, surely, I could still hear their chief
Reading to them from Dumas or *Amazing Stories*;   45
If I could find in some Museum of Cars
Mama's dark blue Buick, Lucky's electric,
Couldn't I be driven there? Hold out to them,
The paraffin half picked out, Tawny's dewclaw—
And have walk to me from among their wigwams   50
My tall brown aunt, to whisper to me: "Dead?
They told you I was dead?"
                          As if you could die!
If I never saw you, never again
Wrote to you, even, after a few years,   55

1. A remedy for colds.
2. Hero of *The Three Musketeers* (1844), by Alexandre Dumas *père*; its sequel was *Twenty Years*
After (1845).
3. Old-fashioned radio receiver, often built by
children in the 1920s and '30s.

How often you've visited me, having put on,
As a mermaid puts on her sealskin, another face
And voice, that don't fool me for a minute—
That are yours for good . . . All of them are gone
Except for me; and for me nothing is gone—   60
The chicken's body is still going round
And round in widening circles, a satellite
From which, as the sun sets, the scientist bends
A look of evil on the unsuspecting earth.
Mama and Pop and Dandeen are still there   65
In the Gay Twenties.
                          The Gay Twenties! You say
The Gay Nineties . . . But it's all right: they *were* gay,
O so gay! A certain number of years after,
Any time is Gay, to the new ones who ask: 70
"Was that the first World War or the second?"
Moving between the first world and the second,
I hear a boy call, now that my beard's gray:
"Santa Claus! Hi, Santa Claus!" It *is* miraculous
To have the children call you Santa Claus.   75
I wave back. When my hand drops to the wheel,
It is brown and spotted, and its nails are ridged
Like Mama's. Where's my own hand? My smooth
White bitten-fingernailed one? I seem to see
A shape in tennis shoes and khaki riding-pants   80
Standing there empty-handed; I reach out to it
Empty-handed, my hand comes back empty,
And yet my emptiness is traded for its emptiness,
I have found that Lost World in the Lost and Found
Columns whose gray illegible advertisements   85
My soul has memorized world after world:
LOST—NOTHING. STRAYED FROM NOWHERE. NO REWARD.
I hold in my own hands, in happiness,
Nothing: the nothing for which there's no reward.

                                                      1965

JOHN BERRYMAN
1914–1972

From a generation whose ideal poem was short, self-contained, and ironic, John Berryman emerged as the author of two extended and passionate works: "Homage to Mistress Bradstreet" and the lyric sequence *The Dream Songs*. It was as if Berryman needed more space than the single lyric provided—a larger theater in which to play out an unrelenting psychic drama. He had written shorter poems—songs and sonnets—but his discovery of large-scale dramatic situations and strange new voices astonished his contemporaries.

Berryman seemed fated to intense suffering and self-preoccupation. His father, a banker, shot himself outside his son's window when the boy was twelve. The suicide haunted Berryman to the end of his own life, which also came by suicide. Berryman, who was born John Smith, took a new name from his stepfather, also a banker. His childhood was a series of displacements: ten years near McAlester, Oklahoma, then Tampa, Florida, and after his father's suicide, Gloucester, Massachusetts, and New York City. His mother's second marriage ended in divorce, but his stepfather sent him to private school in Connecticut. Berryman graduated from Columbia College in 1936 and won a fellowship to Clare College, Cambridge, England.

He was later to say of himself, "I masquerade as a writer. Actually I am a scholar." However misleading this may be about his poetry, it reminds us that throughout his life Berryman drew nourishment from teaching—at Wayne State, at Harvard (1940–43), then off and on at Princeton, and from 1955 until his death, at the University of Minnesota. He chose to teach not creative writing but literature and the "history of civilization," and he claimed that such teaching forced him into areas in which he would not otherwise have done detailed work. A mixture of bookishness and wildness characterizes all his writing: five years of research lay behind the intensities of "Homage to Mistress Bradstreet," while an important constituent of "huffy Henry's" personality in *The Dream Songs* is his professorial awkwardness and exhibitionism.

Berryman seemed drawn to borrowing identities in his poetry. In his first important volume, *The Dispossessed* (1948), he had experimented with various dramatic voices in the short poems "Nervous Songs: The Song of the Demented Priest," "A Professor's Song," "The Song of the Tortured Girl," and "The Song of the Man Forsaken and Obsessed." The *dispossession* of the book's title had two opposite and urgent meanings for him: "the miserable, *put out of one's own*, and the relieved, saved, undevilled, de-spelled." Taking on such roles was for Berryman both a revelation of his cast-out, fatherless state and an exorcism of it. It was perhaps in that spirit that he entered into an imaginary dialogue with what he felt as the kindred nature of the Puritan poet Anne Bradstreet. "Both of our worlds unhanded us." What started out to be a poem of fifty lines emerged as the fifty-seven stanzas of "Homage to Mistress Bradstreet" (1956), a work so absorbing that after completing it Berryman claimed to be "a ruin for two years." It was not Bradstreet's poetry that engaged him. Quite the contrary: he was fascinated by the contrast between her "bald abstract rime" and her life of passionate suffering. The poem explores the kinship between Bradstreet and Berryman as figures of turbulence and rebellion.

Berryman took literary encouragement from another American poet of the past, Stephen Crane, about whom he wrote a book-length critical study in 1950. Crane's poems, he said, have "the character of a 'dream,' something seen naively in a new relation." Berryman's attraction to a poetry that accommodated the nightmare antics of the dream world became apparent in his own long work, *The Dream Songs*. It was modeled, he claimed, on "the greatest American poem," Whitman's "Song of Myself," in which the speaker assumes a fluid, ever-changing persona. *77 Dream Songs* was published in 1964. Additional poems, to a total of 385, appeared in *His Toy, His Dream, His Rest* (1968). (Some uncollected dream songs were published posthumously in *Henry's Fate*, 1977, and drafts of others remained in manuscript.) Obvious links exist between Berryman and other so-called confessional writers such as Robert Lowell, Sylvia Plath, and Anne Sexton. But the special autobiographical flavor of *The Dream Songs* is that of a psychic vaudeville; as in dreams, the poet represents himself through a fluid series of alter egos, whose voices often flow into one another in single poems. One of these voices is that of a blackface minstrel, and Berryman's appropriation of this dialect prompted Michael Harper's poem "Tongue-Tied in Black and White," written both as homage to Berryman and as part of Harper's quarrel with the use of "that needful black idiom offending me" ("Tongue-Tied in Black and White"). Despite the suffering that these poems enact, Berryman seemed to find a secret strength through the staginess, variety, resourcefulness, and renewals of these poems.

 The Dream Songs brought Berryman a success that was not entirely beneficial. The collection *Love and Fame* (1970) shows him beguiled by his own celebrity and wrestling with some of its temptations. In an unfinished, posthumously published novel, *Recovery*, he portrays himself as increasingly prey to alcoholism. Berryman had been married twice before, and his hospitalization for drinking and for periods of insanity had put a strain on his third marriage. He came to distrust his poetry as a form of exhibitionism, and in his use of the discipline of prose and in the prayers that crowd his last two volumes of poetry (*Delusions, Etc.* appeared posthumously), he was clearly in search of some new and humbling style. Having been raised a strict Catholic and fallen away from the church, he tried to return to it in his last years, speaking of his need for a "God of rescue." On January 7, 1972, Berryman committed suicide by leaping from a Minneapolis bridge.

From The Dream Songs[1]

1

Huffy Henry hid   the day,
unappeasable Henry sulked.
I see his point,—a trying to put things over.
It was the thought that they thought
they could *do* it made Henry wicked & away.   5
But he should have come out and talked.

---

1. These poems were written over a period of thirteen years. (*77 Dream Songs* was published in 1964, and the remaining poems appeared in *His Toy, His Dream, His Rest* in 1968. Some uncollected dream songs were included in the volume *Henry's Fate*, which appeared five years after Berryman committed suicide in 1972.) Berryman placed an introductory note at the head of *His Toy, His Dream, His Rest*: "The poem then, whatever its wide cast of characters, is essentially about an imaginary character (not the poet, not me) named Henry, a white American in early middle age sometimes in blackface, who has suffered an irreversible loss and talks about himself sometimes in the first person, sometimes in the third, sometimes even in the second; he has a friend, never named, who addresses him as Mr. Bones and variants thereof. Requiescant in pace." (The final sentence here is Latin for "Rest in peace.")

All the world like a woolen lover
once did seem on Henry's side.
Then came a departure.
Thereafter nothing fell out as it might or ought.   10
I don't see how Henry, pried
open for all the world to see, survived.

What he has now to say is a long
wonder the world can bear & be.
Once in a sycamore I was glad   15
all at the top, and I sang.
Hard on the land wears the strong sea
and empty grows every bed.

14

Life, friends, is boring. We must not say so.
After all, the sky flashes, the great sea yearns,
we ourselves flash and yearn,
and moreover my mother told me as a boy
(repeatedly) 'Ever to confess you're bored   5
means you have no

Inner Resources.' I conclude now I have no
inner resources, because I am heavy bored.
Peoples bore me,
literature bores me, especially great literature,   10
Henry bores me, with his plights & gripes
as bad as achilles,[2]

who loves people and valiant art, which bores me.
And the tranquil hills, & gin, look like a drag
and somehow a dog   15
has taken itself & its tail considerably away
into mountains or sea or sky, leaving
behind: me, wag.

29

There sat down, once, a thing on Henry's heart
so heavy, if he had a hundred years
& more, & weeping, sleepless, in all them time
Henry could not make good.
Starts again always in Henry's ears   5
the little cough somewhere, an odour, a chime.

2. Greek hero of Homer's *Iliad*, who, angry at slights against his honor, sulked in his tent and refused
to fight against the Trojans.

And there is another thing he has in mind
like a grave Sienese face[3] a thousand years
would fail to blur the still profiled reproach of. Ghastly,
with open eyes, he attends, blind.   10
All the bells say: too late. This is not for tears;
thinking.

But never did Henry, as he thought he did,
end anyone and hacks her body up
and hide the pieces, where they may be found.   15
He knows: he went over everyone, & nobody's missing.
Often he reckons, in the dawn, them up.
Nobody is ever missing.

384

The marker slants, flowerless, day's almost done,
I stand above my father's grave with rage,
often, often before
I've made this awful pilgrimage to one
who cannot visit me, who tore his page   5
out: I come back for more,

I spit upon this dreadful banker's grave
who shot his heart out in a Florida dawn
O ho alas alas
When will indifference come, I moan & rave   10
I'd like to scrabble till I got right down
away down under the grass

and ax the casket open ha to see
just how he's taking it, which he sought so hard
we'll tear apart   15
the mouldering grave clothes ha & then Henry
will heft the ax once more, his final card,
and fell it on the start.

                                                                           1968

3. Allusion to the somber, austere mosaiclike religious portraits by the Italian painters who worked in Siena during the 13th and 14th centuries.

RALPH ELLISON
1914–1994

When Ralph Waldo Ellison began writing what would become *Invisible Man* (1952), American readers and critics were skeptical that black experience could rise to the level of "universal" significance that defined high literary ambition at the time. Asked in 1953 whether he thought "the Negro writer" could "escape provincialism when his literature is concerned with a minority," Ellison stressed the universality of the individual human being. Ellison was true to the experience, thoughts, imagination, and inner truth of the individual in his fiction. He consciously departed from the model of his mentor, Richard Wright, setting aside the social realism perfected by Wright—and thereafter expected of black writers—in favor of the styles and techniques of Modernism. Inspired by Melville, Hemingway, Joyce, and others, he stepped away from realism to reconsider humanity through the eyes of an unnamed black narrator described only as "invisible."

Ellison was born and raised in Oklahoma, won a state scholarship, and attended the Tuskegee Institute, where he was a music major, his instrument the trumpet. He embraced both the Western classical repertoire and the world of Kansas City jazz then just reaching its heyday. Befriending the blues singer Jimmy Rushing and other members of what would be the great Count Basie band of the 1930s, Ellison saw in this "deep, rowdy stream of jazz" the power and control that constituted art. His abiding love of music is found in some of the essays in his collection *Shadow and Act* (1964). Ellison also immersed himself in the visual arts, admiring the African American sculptor Richmond Barthé, with whom he studied for a short time after he arrived in New York City in the early 1940s. He invoked Picasso as a master artist who could transform folk content into universal form, and he was inspired by the photography in Richard Wright's *Twelve Million Black Voices* (1941). Ellison collected art throughout his life, and readers of his fiction have noted that visual elements such as framing, color, shape, pigment, and the image of the canvas recur in his work as often as the more commonly noted elements of sound and music.

Ellison created *Invisible Man* through an arduous, seven-year process of planning and revision, inspired by his Modernist literary models and informed by his knowledge of music and the visual arts. When the novel was published in 1952, he was criticized for being less political than he should be as a black writer. The most prominent of these critics, Irving Howe, took the author to task for not following Wright's lead and devoting his fiction to the "Negro cause". Howe believed that African Americans should write social protest novels about the tragedy of black ghetto life. But Ellison's intellectual sphere was much broader, and in his life he crossed and recrossed what W. E. B. Du Bois called "the color line." He married a white woman at a time when this was against the law in several states, and he enjoyed an artistic circle that included not only the artists, writers, and musicians of the Harlem Renaissance but also the thriving Yiddish language writers in New York (an acquaintance reported that he was nearly fluent in Yiddish). Ellison wrote parts of *Invisible Man* at the office of a Jewish friend on Fifth Avenue, and in a letter he noted that white people at Radio City Music Hall looking through his windows as he typed seemed to think he was doing something obscene. For a short time he lived in the Hudson Valley with Saul Bellow, also featured in this volume, who was the son of Russian Jewish parents. Both Bellow and Ellison aspired to be great *American* writers.

"I wasn't, and am not, *primarily* concerned with injustice, but with art," Ellison declared. And yet he saw the novel as a driver of social change. "Serious literature" engaged what Ellison described as the "moral core" of a society; for Ellison, this meant the values of democracy and equality. Ellison called *Invisible Man* an "attempt to return to the mood of personal moral responsibility for democracy which typified the best of our nineteenth-century fiction." Readers may note that the narrator is told by a wealthy trustee to read Ralph Waldo Emerson (Ellison's namesake); the speech in "Battle Royal" sounds Emersonian, and references to Emerson and Melville can be found throughout the narrative. Ellison believed that in devoting himself to the novel as an art form, he took on "the responsibilities inherited by those who practice the craft in the U.S."—those of "describing for all that fragment of the huge diverse American experience which I know best" and of "shaping . . . the culture as I should like it to be." "The American novel," Ellison explained, "is in this sense a conquest of the frontier; as it describes our experience, it creates it."

Invisible Man won the National Book Award, and Ellison subsequently received a number of awards and lectureships. He taught at the Salzburg Seminar, Bard College, and the University of Chicago. In 1970 he was named Albert Schweitzer Professor of the Humanities at New York University, where he taught until his retirement. Always humble, Ellison called *Invisible Man* "an attempt" at a great novel, and he wondered whether it would "be around in 20 years." Ellison's self-critical habits of mind kept him from completing another book after *Invisible Man*; when he died in 1994 he left a mass of notes and manuscript material meant for several novels. Editors assembled the late novel *Juneteenth* (1999) from over 2,000 manuscript pages. A version of the novel Ellison worked on right after *Invisible Man*, titled *Three Days Before the Shooting . . .* , was similarly pieced together and published in 2010.

"Battle Royal," the excerpt from *Invisible Man* reprinted here, was originally published as a stand-alone story called "Invisible Man" in a 1947 issue of Cyril Connolly's *Horizon*, a leading British art and literature journal. It appeared in a special double issue titled "Art on the American *Horizon*," alongside contributions from the American poets Wallace Stevens, Marianne Moore, and E.E. Cummings; art critic Clement Greenberg; and media critic Marshall McLuhan. It was republished in the United States in 1948 as "Battle Royal" in *'48: The Magazine of the Year*. Because many readers assumed that black writers drew only from personal experience, the story was received as if it were fact. Ellison had to insist that the story was "an imaginative re-creation of certain aspects of our American life and the effect these have upon our personality. As such," he advised, "it is to be read as a near allegory or an extended metaphor. . . . The facts themselves are of no moment, are, for me, even amusing."

From Invisible Man

Chapter I

[BATTLE ROYAL]

It goes a long way back, some twenty years. All my life I had been looking for something, and everywhere I turned someone tried to tell me what it was. I accepted their answers too, though they were often in contradiction and even self-contradictory. I was naïve. I was looking for myself and asking everyone except myself questions which I, and only I, could answer. It took me a long time and much painful boomeranging of my expectations to achieve a realization everyone else appears to have been born with: That I am nobody but myself. But first I had to discover that I am an invisible man!

And yet I am no freak of nature, nor of history. I was in the cards, other things having been equal (or unequal) eighty-five years ago. I am not ashamed of my grandparents for having been slaves. I am only ashamed of myself for having at one time been ashamed. About eighty-five years ago they were told that they were free, united with others of our country in everything pertaining to the common good, and, in everything social, separate like the fingers of the hand. And they believed it. They exulted in it. They stayed in their place, worked hard, and brought up my father to do the same. But my grandfather is the one. He was an odd old guy, my grandfather, and I am told I take after him. It was he who caused the trouble. On his deathbed he called my father to him and said, "Son, after I'm gone I want you to keep up the good fight. I never told you, but our life is a war and I have been a traitor all my born days, a spy in the enemy's country ever since I give up my gun back in the Reconstruction. Live with your head in the lion's mouth. I want you to overcome 'em with yeses, undermine 'em with grins, agree 'em to death and destruction, let 'em swoller you till they vomit or bust wide open." They thought the old man had gone out of his mind. He had been the meekest of men. The younger children were rushed from the room, the shades drawn and the flame of the lamp turned so low that it sputtered on the wick like the old man's breathing. "Learn it to the younguns," he whispered fiercely; then he died.

But my folks were more alarmed over his last words than over his dying. It was as though he had not died at all, his words caused so much anxiety. I was warned emphatically to forget what he had said and, indeed, this is the first time it has been mentioned outside the family circle. It had a tremendous effect upon me, however. I could never be sure of what he meant. Grandfather had been a quiet old man who never made any trouble, yet on his deathbed he had called himself a traitor and a spy, and he had spoken of his meekness as a dangerous activity. It became a constant puzzle which lay unanswered in the back of my mind. And whenever things went well for me I remembered my grandfather and felt guilty and uncomfortable. It was as though I was carrying out his advice in spite of myself. And to make it worse, everyone loved me for it. I was praised by the most lily-white men of the town. I was considered an example of desirable conduct—just as my grandfather had been. And what puzzled me was that the old man had defined it as *treachery*. When I was praised for my conduct I felt a guilt that in some way I was doing something that was really against the wishes of the white folks, that if they had understood they would have desired me to act just the opposite, that I should have been sulky and mean, and that that really would have been what they wanted, even though they were fooled and thought they wanted me to act as I did. It made me afraid that some day they would look upon me as a traitor and I would be lost. Still I was more afraid to act any other way because they didn't like that at all. The old man's words were like a curse. On my graduation day I delivered an oration in which I showed that humility was the secret, indeed, the very essence of progress. (Not that I believed this—how could I, remembering my grandfather?—I only believed that it worked.) It was a great success. Everyone praised me and I was invited to give the speech at a gathering of the town's leading white citizens. It was a triumph for our whole community.

It was in the main ballroom of the leading hotel. When I got there I discovered that it was on the occasion of a smoker, and I was told that since I was to be there anyway I might as well take part in the battle royal to be fought by some of my schoolmates as part of the entertainment. The battle royal came first.

All of the town's big shots were there in their tuxedoes, wolfing down the buffet foods, drinking beer and whiskey and smoking black cigars. It was a large room with a high ceiling. Chairs were arranged in neat rows around three sides of a portable boxing ring. The fourth side was clear, revealing a gleaming space of polished floor. I had some misgivings over the battle royal, by the way. Not from a distaste for fighting, but because I didn't care too much for the other fellows who were to take part. They were tough guys who seemed to have no grandfather's curse worrying their minds. No one could mistake their toughness. And besides, I suspected that fighting a battle royal might detract from the dignity of my speech. In those pre-invisible days I visualized myself as a potential Booker T. Washington.[1] But the other fellows didn't care too much for me either, and there were nine of them. I felt superior to them in my way, and I didn't like the manner in which we were all crowded together into the servants' elevator. Nor did they like my being there. In fact, as the warmly lighted floors flashed past the elevator we had words over the fact that I, by taking part in the fight, had knocked one of their friends out of a night's work.

We were led out of the elevator through a rococo hall into an anteroom and told to get into our fighting togs. Each of us was issued a pair of boxing gloves and ushered out into the big mirrored hall, which we entered looking cautiously about us and whispering, lest we might accidentally be heard above the noise of the room. It was foggy with cigar smoke. And already the whiskey was taking effect. I was shocked to see some of the most important men of the town quite tipsy. They were all there—bankers, lawyers, judges, doctors, fire chiefs, teachers, merchants. Even one of the more fashionable pastors. Something we could not see was going on up front. A clarinet was vibrating sensuously and the men were standing up and moving eagerly forward. We were a small tight group, clustered together, our bare upper bodies touching and shining with anticipatory sweat; while up front the big shots were becoming increasingly excited over something we still could not see. Suddenly I heard the school superintendent, who had told me to come, yell, "Bring up the shines, gentlemen! Bring up the little shines!"

We were rushed up to the front of the ballroom, where it smelled even more strongly of tobacco and whiskey. Then we were pushed into place. I almost wet my pants. A sea of faces, some hostile, some amused, ringed around us, and in the center, facing us, stood a magnificent blonde—stark naked. There was dead silence. I felt a blast of cold air chill me. I tried to back away, but they were behind me and around me. Some of the boys stood with lowered heads, trembling. I felt a wave of irrational guilt and fear. My teeth chattered, my skin turned to goose flesh, my knees knocked. Yet I was strongly attracted and looked in spite of myself. Had the price of looking been blindness, I would have looked. The hair was yellow like that of a circus kewpie doll, the face heavily powdered and rouged, as though to form an abstract mask, the eyes hollow and smeared a cool blue, the color of a baboon's butt. I felt a desire to spit upon her as my eyes brushed slowly over her body. Her

1. African American author and educator (1856–1915).

breasts were firm and round as the domes of East Indian temples, and I stood so close as to see the fine skin texture and beads of pearly perspiration glistening like dew around the pink and erected buds of her nipples. I wanted at one and the same time to run from the room, to sink through the floor, or go to her and cover her from my eyes and the eyes of the others with my body; to feel the soft thighs, to caress her and destroy her, to love her and murder her, to hide from her, and yet to stroke where below the small American flag tattooed upon her belly her thighs formed a capital V. I had a notion that of all in the room she saw only me with her impersonal eyes.

And then she began to dance, a slow sensuous movement; the smoke of a hundred cigars clinging to her like the thinnest of veils. She seemed like a fair bird-girl girdled in veils calling to me from the angry surface of some gray and threatening sea. I was transported. Then I became aware of the clarinet playing and the big shots yelling at us. Some threatened us if we looked and others if we did not. On my right I saw one boy faint. And now a man grabbed a silver pitcher from a table and stepped close as he dashed ice water upon him and stood him up and forced two of us to support him as his head hung and moans issued from his thick bluish lips. Another boy began to plead to go home. He was the largest of the group, wearing dark red fighting trunks much too small to conceal the erection which projected from him as though in answer to the insinuating low-registered moaning of the clarinet. He tried to hide himself with his boxing gloves.

And all the while the blonde continued dancing, smiling faintly at the big shots who watched her with fascination, and faintly smiling at our fear. I noticed a certain merchant who followed her hungrily, his lips loose and drooling. He was a large man who wore diamond studs in a shirtfront which swelled with the ample paunch underneath, and each time the blonde swayed her undulating hips he ran his hand through the thin hair of his bald head and, with his arms upheld, his posture clumsy like that of an intoxicated panda, wound his belly in a slow and obscene grind. This creature was completely hypnotized. The music had quickened. As the dancer flung herself about with a detached expression on her face, the men began reaching out to touch her. I could see their beefy fingers sink into the soft flesh. Some of the others tried to stop them and she began to move around the floor in graceful circles, as they gave chase, slipping and sliding over the polished floor. It was mad. Chairs went crashing, drinks were spilt, as they ran laughing and howling after her. They caught her just as she reached a door, raised her from the floor, and tossed her as college boys are tossed at a hazing, and above her red, fixed-smiling lips I saw the terror and disgust in her eyes, almost like my own terror and that which I saw in some of the other boys. As I watched, they tossed her twice and her soft breasts seem to flatten against the air and her legs flung wildly as she spun. Some of the more sober ones helped her to escape. And I started off the floor, heading for the anteroom with the rest of the boys.

Some were still crying and in hysteria. But as we tried to leave we were stopped and ordered to get into the ring. There was nothing to do but what we were told. All ten of us climbed under the ropes and allowed ourselves to be blindfolded with broad bands of white cloth. One of the men seemed to feel a bit sympathetic and tried to cheer us up as we stood with our backs against the ropes. Some of us tried to grin. "See that boy over there?" one of the men said. "I want you to run across at the bell and give it to him right in the belly. If you don't get him, I'm going to get you. I don't like his looks." Each of us was told the same. The blindfolds were put on. Yet even then I had been going over my speech. In my mind each word was as bright as flame. I felt the cloth pressed into place, and frowned so that it would be loosened when I relaxed.

But now I felt a sudden fit of blind terror. I was unused to darkness. It was as though I had suddenly found myself in a dark room filled with poisonous cottonmouths. I could hear the bleary voices yelling insistently for the battle royal to begin.

"Get going in there!"

"Let me at that big nigger!"

I strained to pick up the school superintendent's voice, as though to squeeze some security out of that slightly more familiar sound.

"Let me at those black sonsabitches!" someone yelled.

"No, Jackson, no!" another voice yelled. "Here, somebody, help me hold Jack."

"I want to get at that ginger-colored nigger. Tear him limb from limb," the first voice yelled.

I stood against the ropes trembling. For in those days I was what they called ginger-colored, and he sounded as though he might crunch me between his teeth like a crisp ginger cookie.

Quite a struggle was going on. Chairs were being kicked about and I could hear voices grunting as with a terrific effort. I wanted to see, to see more desperately than ever before. But the blindfold was tight as a thick skin-puckering scab and when I raised my gloved hands to push the layers of white aside a voice yelled, "Oh, no you don't, black bastard! Leave that alone!"

"Ring the bell before Jackson kills him a coon!" someone boomed in the sudden silence. And I heard the bell clang and the sound of the feet scuffling forward.

A glove smacked against my head. I pivoted, striking out stiffly as someone went past, and felt the jar ripple along the length of my arm to my shoulder. Then it seemed as though all nine of the boys had turned upon me at once. Blows pounded me from all sides while I struck out as best I could. So many blows landed upon me that I wondered if I were not the only blindfolded fighter in the ring, or if the man called Jackson hadn't succeeded in getting me after all.

Blindfolded, I could no longer control my motions. I had no dignity. I stumbled about like a baby or a drunken man. The smoke had become thicker and with each new blow it seemed to sear and further restrict my lungs. My saliva became like hot bitter glue. A glove connected with my head, filling my mouth with warm blood. It was everywhere. I could not tell if the moisture I felt upon my body was sweat or blood. A blow landed hard against the nape of my neck. I felt myself going over, my head hitting the floor. Streaks of blue light filled the black world behind the blindfold. I lay prone, pretending that I was knocked out, but felt myself seized by hands and yanked to my feet. "Get going, black boy! Mix it up!" My arms were like lead, my head smarting from blows. I managed to feel my way to the ropes and held on, trying to catch my breath. A glove landed in my mid-section and I went over again, feeling as though the smoke had become a knife jabbed into my guts. Pushed this way and that by the legs milling around me, I finally pulled erect and discovered that I could see the black, sweat-washed forms weaving in the smoky-blue atmosphere like drunken dancers weaving to the rapid drum-like thuds of blows.

Everyone fought hysterically. It was complete anarchy. Everybody fought everybody else. No group fought together for long. Two, three, four, fought one, then turned to fight each other, were themselves attacked. Blows landed below the belt and in the kidney, with the gloves open as well as closed, and with my eye partly opened now there was not so much terror. I moved carefully, avoiding blows, although not too many to attract attention, fighting from group to group. The boys groped about like blind, cautious crabs crouching to protect their mid-sections, their heads pulled in short against their shoulders, their arms stretched nervously before them, with their fists testing the smoke-filled air like the knobbed feelers of hypersensitive snails. In one corner I glimpsed a boy violently punching the air and heard him scream in pain as he smashed his hand against a ring post. For a second I saw him bent over holding his hand, then going down as a blow caught his unprotected head. I played one group against the other, slipping in and throwing a punch then stepping out of range while pushing the others into the melee to take the blows blindly aimed at me. The smoke was agonizing and there were no rounds, no bells at three minute intervals to relieve our exhaustion. The room spun around me, a swirl of lights, smoke, sweating bodies surrounded by tense white faces. I bled from both nose and mouth, the blood spattering upon my chest.

The men kept yelling, "Slug him, black boy! Knock his guts out!"

"Uppercut him! Kill him! Kill that big boy!"

Taking a fake fall, I saw a boy going down heavily beside me as though we were felled by a single blow, saw a sneaker-clad foot shoot into his groin as the two who had knocked him down stumbled upon him. I rolled out of range, feeling a twinge of nausea.

The harder we fought the more threatening the men became. And yet, I had begun to worry about my speech again. How would it go? Would they recognize my ability? What would they give me?

I was fighting automatically when suddenly I noticed that one after another of the boys was leaving the ring. I was surprised, filled with panic, as though I had been left alone with an unknown danger. Then I understood. The boys had arranged it among themselves. It was the custom for the two men left in the ring to slug it out for the winner's prize. I discovered this too late. When the bell sounded two men in tuxedoes leaped into the ring and removed the blindfold. I found myself facing Tatlock, the biggest of the gang. I felt sick at my stomach. Hardly had the bell stopped ringing in my ears than it clanged again and I saw him moving swiftly toward me. Thinking of nothing else to do I hit him smash on the nose. He kept coming, bringing the rank sharp violence of stale sweat. His face was a black blank of a face, only his eyes alive—with hate of me and aglow with a feverish terror from what had happened to us all. I became anxious. I wanted to deliver my speech and he came at me as though he meant to beat it out of me. I smashed him again and again, taking his blows as they came. Then on a sudden impulse I struck him lightly and as we clinched, I whispered, "Fake like I knocked you out, you can have the prize."

"I'll break your behind," he whispered hoarsely.

"For *them?*"

"For *me*, sonofabitch!"

They were yelling for us to break it up and Tatlock spun me half around with a blow, and as a joggled camera sweeps in a reeling scene, I saw the howling red faces crouching tense beneath the cloud of blue-gray smoke. For a moment the world wavered, unraveled, flowed, then my head cleared and Tatlock bounced before me. That fluttering shadow before my eyes was his jabbing left hand. Then falling forward, my head against his damp shoulder, I whispered,

"I'll make it five dollars more."

"Go to hell!"

But his muscles relaxed a trifle beneath my pressure and I breathed, "Seven?"

"Give it to your ma," he said, ripping me beneath the heart.

And while I still held him I butted him and moved away. I felt myself bombarded with punches. I fought back with hopeless desperation. I wanted to deliver my speech more than anything else in the world, because I felt that only these men could judge truly my ability, and now this stupid clown was ruining my chances. I began fighting carefully now, moving in to punch him and out again with my greater speed. A lucky blow to his chin and I had him going too—until I heard a loud voice yell, "I got my money on the big boy."

Hearing this, I almost dropped my guard. I was confused: Should I try to win against the voice out there? Would not this go against my speech, and was not this a moment for humility, for nonresistance? A blow to my head as I danced about sent my right eye popping like a jack-in-the-box and settled my dilemma. The room went red as I fell. It was a dream fall, my body languid and fastidious as to where to land, until the floor became impatient and smashed up to meet me. A moment later I came to. An hypnotic voice said FIVE emphatically. And I lay there, hazily watching a dark red spot of my own blood shaping itself into a butterfly, glistening and soaking into the soiled gray world of the canvas.

When the voice drawled TEN I was lifted up and dragged to a chair. I sat dazed. My eye pained and swelled with each throb of my pounding heart and I wondered if now I would be allowed to speak. I was wringing wet, my mouth still bleeding. We were grouped along the wall now. The other boys ignored me as they congratulated Tatlock and speculated as to how much they would be paid. One boy whimpered over his smashed hand. Looking up front, I saw attendants in white jackets rolling the portable ring away and placing a small square rug in the vacant space surrounded by chairs. Perhaps, I thought, I will stand on the rug to deliver my speech.

Then the M.C. called to us, "Come on up here boys and get your money."

We ran forward to where the men laughed and talked in their chairs, waiting. Everyone seemed friendly now.

"There it is on the rug," the man said. I saw the rug covered with coins of all dimensions and a few crumpled bills. But what excited me, scattered here and there, were the gold pieces.

"Boys, it's all yours," the man said. "You get all you grab."

"That's right, Sambo," a blond man said, winking at me confidentially.

I trembled with excitement, forgetting my pain. I would get the gold and the bills, I thought. I would use both hands. I would throw my body against the boys nearest me to block them from the gold.

"Get down around the rug now," the man commanded, "and don't anyone touch it until I give the signal."

"This ought to be good," I heard.

As told, we got around the square rug on our knees. Slowly the man raised his freckled hand as we followed it upward with our eyes.

I heard, "These niggers look like they're about to pray!"

Then, "Ready," the man said. "Go!"

I lunged for a yellow coin lying on the blue design of the carpet, touching it and sending a surprised shriek to join those rising around me. I tried frantically to remove my hand but could not let go. A hot, violent force tore through my body, shaking me like a wet rat. The rug was electrified. The hair bristled up on my head as I shook myself free. My muscles jumped, my nerves jangled, writhed. But I saw that this was not stopping the other boys. Laughing in fear and embarrassment, some were holding back and scooping up the coins knocked off by the painful contortions of the others. The men roared above us as we struggled.

"Pick it up, goddamnit, pick it up!" someone called like a bass-voiced parrot. "Go on, get it!"

I crawled rapidly around the floor, picking up the coins, trying to avoid the coppers and to get greenbacks and the gold. Ignoring the shock by laughing, as I brushed the coins off quickly, I discovered that I could contain the electricity—a contradiction, but it works. Then the men began to push us onto the rug. Laughing embarrassedly, we struggled out of their hands and kept after the coins. We were all wet and slippery and hard to hold. Suddenly I saw a boy lifted into the air, glistening with sweat like a circus seal, and dropped, his wet back landing flush upon the charged rug, heard him yell and saw him literally dance upon his back, his elbows beating a frenzied tattoo upon the floor, his muscles twitching like the flesh of a horse stung by many flies. When he finally rolled off, his face was gray and no one stopped him when he ran from the floor amid booming laughter.

"Get the money," the M.C. called. "That's good hard American cash!"

And we snatched and grabbed, snatched and grabbed. I was careful not to come too close to the rug now, and when I felt the hot whiskey breath descend upon me like a cloud of foul air I reached out and grabbed the leg of a chair. It was occupied and I held on desperately.

"Leggo, nigger! Leggo!"

The huge face wavered down to mine as he tried to push me free. But my body was slippery and he was too drunk. It was Mr. Colcord, who owned a chain of movie houses and "entertainment palaces." Each time he grabbed me I slipped out of his hands. It became a real struggle. I feared the rug more than I did the drunk, so I held on, surprising myself for a moment by trying to topple *him* upon the rug. It was such an enormous idea that I found myself actually carrying it out. I tried not to be obvious, yet when I grabbed his leg, trying to tumble him out of the chair, he raised up roaring with laughter, and, looking at me with soberness dead in the eye, kicked me viciously in the chest. The chair leg flew out of my hand and I felt myself going and rolled. It was as though I had rolled through a bed of hot coals. It seemed a whole century would pass before I would roll free, a century in which I was seared through the deepest levels of my body to the fearful breath within me and the breath seared and heated to the point of explosion. It'll all be over in a flash, I thought as I rolled clear. It'll all be over in a flash.

But not yet, the men on the other side were waiting, red faces swollen as though from apoplexy as they bent forward in their chairs. Seeing their fingers coming toward me I rolled away as a fumbled football rolls off the receiver's fingertips, back into the coals. That time I luckily sent the rug sliding out of place and heard the coins ringing against the floor and the boys scuffling to pick them up and the M.C. calling, "All right, boys, that's all. Go get dressed and get your money."

I was limp as a dish rag. My back felt as though it had been beaten with wires.

When we had dressed the M.C. came in and gave us each five dollars, except Tatlock, who got ten for being last in the ring. Then he told us to leave. I was not to get a chance to deliver my speech, I thought. I was going out into the dim alley in despair when I was stopped and told to go back. I returned to the ballroom, where the men were pushing back their chairs and gathering in groups to talk.

The M.C. knocked on a table for quiet. "Gentlemen," he said, "we almost forgot an important part of the program. A most serious part, gentlemen. This boy was brought here to deliver a speech which he made at his graduation yesterday . . ."

"Bravo!"

"I'm told that he is the smartest boy we've got out there in Greenwood. I'm told that he knows more big words than a pocket-sized dictionary."

Much applause and laughter.

"So now, gentlemen, I want you to give him your attention."

There was still laughter as I faced them, my mouth dry, my eye throbbing. I began slowly, but evidently my throat was tense, because they began shouting, "Louder! Louder!"

"We of the younger generation extol the wisdom of that great leader and educator," I shouted, "who first spoke these flaming words of wisdom: 'A ship lost at sea for many days suddenly sighted a friendly vessel. From the mast of the unfortunate vessel was seen a signal: "Water, water; we die of thirst!" The answer from the friendly vessel came back: "Cast down your bucket where you are." The captain of the distressed vessel, at last heeding the injunction, cast down his bucket, and it came up full of fresh sparkling water from the mouth of the Amazon River.' And like him I say, and in his words, 'To those of my race who depend upon bettering their condition in a foreign land, or who underestimate the importance of cultivating friendly relations with the Southern white man, who is his next-door neighbor, I would say: "Cast down your bucket where you are"—cast it down in making friends in every manly way of the people of all races by whom we are surrounded . . .'"

I spoke automatically and with such fervor that I did not realize that the men were still talking and laughing until my dry mouth, filling up with blood from the cut, almost strangled me. I coughed, wanting to stop and go to one of the tall brass, sand-filled spittoons to relieve myself, but a few of the men, especially the superintendent, were listening and I was afraid. So I gulped it down, blood, saliva and all, and continued. (What powers of endurance I had during those days! What enthusiasm! What a belief in the lightness of things!) I spoke even louder in spite of the pain. But still they talked and still they laughed, as though deaf with cotton in dirty ears. So I spoke with greater emotional emphasis. I closed my ears and swallowed blood until I was nauseated. The speech seemed a hundred times as long as before, but I could not leave out a single word. All had to be said, each memorized nuance considered, rendered. Nor was that all. Whenever I uttered a word of three or more syllables a group of voices would yell for me to repeat it. I used the phrase "social responsibility," and they yelled:

"What's that word you say, boy?"

"Social responsibility," I said.

"What?"

"Social . . ."

"Louder."

". . . responsibility."

"More!"

"Respon—"

"Repeat!"

"—sibility."

The room filled with the uproar of laughter until, no doubt, distracted by having to gulp down my blood, I made a mistake and yelled a phrase I had often seen denounced in newspaper editorials, heard debated in private.

"Social . . ."

"What?" they yelled.

". . . equality—"

The laughter hung smokelike in the sudden stillness. I opened my eyes, puzzled. Sounds of displeasure filled the room. The M.C. rushed forward. They shouted hostile phrases at me. But I did not understand.

A small dry mustached man in the front row blared out, "Say that slowly, son!"

"What, sir?"

"What you just said!"

"Social responsibility, sir," I said.

"You weren't being smart, were you, boy?" he said, not unkindly.

"No, sir!"

"You sure that about 'equality' was a mistake?"

"Oh, yes, sir," I said. "I was swallowing blood."

"Well, you had better speak more slowly so we can understand. We mean to do right by you, but you've got to know your place at all times. All right, now, go on with your speech."

I was afraid. I wanted to leave but I wanted also to speak and I was afraid they'd snatch me down.

"Thank you, sir," I said, beginning where I had left off, and having them ignore me as before.

Yet when I finished there was a thunderous applause. I was surprised to see the superintendent come forth with a package wrapped in white tissue paper, and, gesturing for quiet, address the men.

"Gentlemen, you see that I did not overpraise the boy. He makes a good speech and some day he'll lead his people in the proper paths. And I don't have to tell you that that is important in these days and times. This is a good, smart boy, and so to encourage him in the right direction, in the name of the Board of Education I wish to present him a prize in the form of this . . ."

He paused, removing the tissue paper and revealing a gleaming calfskin brief case.

". . . in the form of this first-class article from Shad Whitmore's shop."

"Boy," he said, addressing me, "take this prize and keep it well. Consider it a badge of office. Prize it. Keep developing as you are and some day it will be filled with important papers that will help shape the destiny of your people."

I was so moved that I could hardly express my thanks. A rope of bloody saliva forming a shape like an undiscovered continent drooled upon the leather and I wiped it quickly away. I felt an importance that I had never dreamed.

"Open it and see what's inside," I was told.

My fingers a-tremble, I complied, smelling the fresh leather and finding an official-looking document inside. It was a scholarship to the state college for Negroes. My eyes filled with tears and I ran awkwardly off the floor.

I was overjoyed; I did not even mind when I discovered that the gold pieces I had scrambled for were brass pocket tokens advertising a certain make of automobile.

When I reached home everyone was excited. Next day the neighbors came to congratulate me. I even felt safe from grandfather, whose deathbed curse usually spoiled my triumphs. I stood beneath his photograph with my brief case in hand and smiled triumphantly into his stolid black peasant's face. It was a face that fascinated me. The eyes seemed to follow everywhere I went.

That night I dreamed I was at a circus with him and that he refused to laugh at the clowns no matter what they did. Then later he told me to open my brief case and read what was inside and I did, finding an official envelope stamped with the state seal; and inside the envelope I found another and another, endlessly, and I thought I would fall of weariness. "Them's years," he said. "Now open that one." And I did and in it I found an engraved document containing a short message in letters of gold. "Read it," my grandfather said. "Out loud!"

"To Whom It May Concern," I intoned. "Keep This Nigger-Boy Running."

I awoke with the old man's laughter ringing in my ears.

(It was a dream I was to remember and dream again for many years after. But at that time I had no insight into its meaning. First I had to attend college.)

1952

ARTHUR MILLER
1915-2005

For much modern American drama the family is the central subject, as the anthology selections show. In *Long Day's Journey into Night* Eugene O'Neill studied his own family through the Tyrones; in Tennessee Williams's *A Streetcar Named Desire* the Kowalskis are one family, which Blanche invades, while Blanche and Stella, as sisters, are another. Most of Arthur Miller's plays, as well, concentrate on the family and envision an ideal world as, perhaps, an enlarged family. Often the protagonist's sense of family draws him into conflict with—and eventual doom in—the outside world. Yet Miller recognized that an ideal is sometimes a rationalization. Joe Keller insists in *All My Sons* (1947) that during the war he shipped damaged airplane parts to support his family, but a desire for commercial success was part of his motive. Eddie Carbone in *A View from the Bridge* (1955) accepts death because of his sense of responsibility to his niece, but married man though he is, he may also be in love with that same niece. In *Death of a Salesman* (1949) Willy Loman's delusions and self-deceptions derive from, and return to, his image of himself as family provider, an image he cannot live up to; driven by his desire to be "well liked," a successful social personality, he fails to connect with either of his sons and neglects his wife. Thus Miller's treatment of the family leads to a treatment both of personal ideals and of the society within which families have to operate.

Miller was born into a German Jewish family in Manhattan; his father was a well-to-do but almost illiterate clothing manufacturer, his mother an avid reader. When his father's business collapsed after the stock market crash in 1929, the family moved to Brooklyn, where Miller graduated from high school. His subsequent two years of work in an automobile-parts warehouse to earn money for college tuition are warmly recalled in his play *A Memory of Two Mondays* (1955). At the University of Michigan he enrolled as a journalism student. These were the years of the Spanish Civil War, the rise of fascism, and the attraction of Marxism as a way out of the Depression, and here Miller formed his political views. He also began to write plays, which won prizes at the university and in New York. He then went to work for the Federal Theater Project, wrote radio plays, toured army camps to gather material for a film, and married Mary Slattery, the first of his three wives.

In 1947 Miller enjoyed his first Broadway success, *All My Sons*. (*The Man Who Had All the Luck* had failed in 1944.) This strongly realistic portrayal of a family divided because of the father's insistence on business as usual during World War II drew the attention of audiences and theater critics. *Death of a Salesman*, his masterpiece, was produced two years later and won the Pulitzer Prize. An adaptation of Ibsen's *An Enemy of the People* followed in 1951. It was suggested to him by the actors Fredric March and Florence Eldridge, but Miller was clearly drawn by Ibsen's hero, Dr. Stockmann, who leads a fight against pollution with strong but confused idealism.

In the early 1950s, the hysterical search for supposed Communist infiltration of American life reached its height as Senator Joseph McCarthy summoned suspect after suspect to hearings in Washington. Miller later said that at this time he was reading a book about the Salem witch trials and saw that "the main point of the hearings, precisely as in seventeenth-century Salem, was that the accused make public confession, damn his confederates as well as his Devil master, and guarantee his sterling new allegiance by breaking disgusting old vows—whereupon he was let loose to rejoin the society of extremely decent people." Out of this insight

Actor Lee J. Cobb as Willy Loman being restrained by actors Arthur Kennedy (left) and Cameron Mitchell (right) as his sons Biff and Hap, respectively, in the 1949 original Broadway production of *Death of a Salesman*.

came *The Crucible* (1953), in which the hero, John Proctor, allows himself to be executed rather than sign away his name and his children's respect. Hysteria touched Miller personally when he was denied a passport and in 1957 was convicted of contempt of Congress for refusing to name suspected Communists (this conviction was unanimously overturned by the Supreme Court the following year).

Miller had long been looking for a way to dramatize what he had earlier learned about mob control of the Brooklyn waterfront and finally did so in the one-act play *A View from the Bridge*, produced with *A Memory of Two Mondays* in 1955; later he would rework *View* into a full-length play. Meanwhile, he had met the glamorous movie actress Marilyn Monroe; they married in 1956, after he divorced his first wife. He wrote the screenplay *The Misfits* for Monroe, but in their private life, their complex natures were ill-sorted. The marriage ended in divorce in 1961, and a year later he married the photographer Ingeborg Morath, with whom he collaborated on several books of photographs and essays.

In 1964 two plays opened: *After the Fall* (in which the protagonist is a thinly disguised Miller investigating his family, his responsibilities, and his wives) and *Incident at Vichy* (about Jews and Nazis in Vichy, France). While these were by no means as successful as *Salesman*, they returned him seriously to the stage. Among later plays are *The Price* (1968), *The Creation of the World and Other Business* (1972), *The Archbishop's Ceiling* (1977), and two one-act plays under the title *Danger: Memory!* (1986). These last fared poorly in New York, but found successful productions elsewhere in the world.

Miller in his later years was something of an activist. In the late 1960s he was asked to become president of PEN (Poets, Essayists, Novelists), the international writers' group. By opening this organization to writers in what were then Iron Curtain countries and speaking out for those repressed by totalitarian regimes, he became a respected champion of human rights.

Like his contemporary Tennessee Williams, Miller rejected the influence of "mawkish twenties slang" and "deadly repetitiveness." Again like Williams, Miller was impatient with prosy dialogue and well-made structures. As he explained, the success of *A Streetcar Named Desire* in 1947 helped him write *Death of a Salesman*:

> With *Streetcar*, Tennessee had printed a license to speak at full throat, and it helped strengthen me as I turned to Willy Loman, a salesman always full of words, and better yet, a man who could never cease trying, like Adam, to name himself and the world's wonders. I had known all along that this play could not be encompassed by conventional realism, and for one integral reason: in Willy the past was as alive as what was happening at the moment, sometimes even crashing in to completely overwhelm his mind. I wanted precisely the same fluidity of form.

In *Salesman* the action moves effortlessly from the present—the last twenty-four hours of Willy's life—into moments in his memory, symbolized in the stage setting by the idyllic leaves around his house that, in these past moments, block out the threatening apartment houses. The successful realization of this fluidity on the stage was greatly aided by Miller's director, Elia Kazan, and his stage designer, Jo Mielziner, both of whom had worked with Williams two years earlier on *Streetcar*. A striking difference between Williams and Miller, however, is the latter's overt moralizing, which adds a didactic element to his plays not to be found in those of Williams.

The text is from *Arthur Miller's Collected Plays* (1957).

Death of a Salesman

Certain Private Conversations in Two Acts and a Requiem

THE CHARACTERS

WILLY LOMAN	THE WOMAN	JENNY
LINDA	CHARLEY	STANLEY
BIFF	UNCLE BEN	MISS FORSYTHE
HAPPY	HOWARD WAGNER	LETTA
BERNARD		

The action takes place in WILLY LOMAN'S *house and yard and in various places he visits in the New York and Boston of today.*

Act One

A melody is heard, playing upon a flute. It is small and fine, telling of grass and trees and the horizon. The curtain rises.

Before us is the Salesman's house. We are aware of towering, angular shapes behind it, surrounding it on all sides. Only the blue light of the sky falls upon the house and forestage; the surrounding area shows an angry flow of orange. As more light appears, we see a solid vault of apartment houses around the small, fragile-seeming home. An air of the dream clings to the place, a dream rising out of reality. The kitchen at center seems actual enough, for there is a kitchen table with three chairs, and a refrigerator. But no other fixtures are seen. At the back of the kitchen there is a draped entrance, which leads to the living-room. To the right of the kitchen, on a level raised two feet, is a bedroom furnished only with a brass bedstead and a straight chair. On a shelf over the bed a silver athletic trophy stands. A window opens onto the apartment house at the side.

Behind the kitchen, on a level raised six and a half feet, is the boys' bedroom, at present barely visible. Two beds are dimly seen, and at the back of the room a dormer window. (This bedroom is above the unseen living-room.) At the left a stairway curves up to it from the kitchen.

The entire setting is wholly or, in some places, partially transparent. The roofline of the house is one-dimensional; under and over it we see the apartment buildings. Before the house lies an apron, curving beyond the forestage into the orchestra. This forward area serves as the back yard as well as the locale of all WILLY's *imaginings and of his city scenes. Whenever the action is in the present the actors observe the imaginary wall-lines, entering the house only through its door at the left. But in the scenes of the past these boundaries are broken, and characters enter or leave a room by stepping "through" a wall onto the forestage.*

From the right, WILLY LOMAN, *the Salesman, enters, carrying two large sample cases. The flute plays on. He hears but is not aware of it. He is past sixty years of age, dressed quietly. Even as he crosses the stage to the doorway of the house, his exhaustion is apparent. He unlocks the door, comes into the kitchen, and thankfully lets his burden down, feeling the soreness of his palms. A word-sigh escapes his lips—it might be "Oh, boy, oh, boy." He closes the door, then carries his cases out into the living-room, through the draped kitchen doorway.*

LINDA, *his wife, has stirred in her bed at the right. She gets out and puts on a robe, listening. Most often jovial, she has developed an iron repression of her exceptions to* WILLY's *behavior—she more than loves him, she admires him, as though his mercurial nature, his temper, his massive dreams and little cruelties, served her only as sharp reminders of the turbulent longings within him, longings which she shares but lacks the temperament to utter and follow to their end.*

LINDA [*hearing* WILLY *outside the bedroom, calls with some trepidation*] Willy!

WILLY   It's all right. I came back.

LINDA   Why? What happened? [*slight pause*] Did something happen, Willy?

WILLY   No, nothing happened.

LINDA   You didn't smash the car, did you?

WILLY [*with casual irritation*]   I said nothing happened. Didn't you hear me?

LINDA   Don't you feel well?

WILLY   I'm tired to the death. [*The flute has faded away. He sits on the bed beside her, a little numb.*] I couldn't make it. I just couldn't make it, Linda.

LINDA [*very carefully, delicately*]   Where were you all day? You look terrible.

WILLY   I got as far as a little above Yonkers. I stopped for a cup of coffee. Maybe it was the coffee.

LINDA   What?

WILLY [*after a pause*]   I suddenly couldn't drive any more. The car kept going off onto the shoulder, y'know?

LINDA [*helpfully*]   Oh. Maybe it was the steering again. I don't think Angelo knows the Studebaker.

WILLY   No, it's me, it's me. Suddenly I realize I'm goin' sixty miles an hour and I don't remember the last five minutes. I'm—I can't seem to—keep my mind to it.

LINDA   Maybe it's your glasses. You never went for your new glasses.

WILLY   No, I see everything. I came back ten miles an hour. It took me nearly four hours from Yonkers.

LINDA [*resigned*]   Well, you'll just have to take a rest, Willy, you can't continue this way.

WILLY   I just got back from Florida.

LINDA   But you didn't rest your mind. Your mind is overactive, and the mind is what counts, dear.

WILLY   I'll start out in the morning. Maybe I'll feel better in the morning. [*She is taking off his shoes.*] These goddam arch supports are killing me.

LINDA   Take an aspirin. Should I get you an aspirin? It'll soothe you.

WILLY [*with wonder*]   I was driving along, you understand? And I was fine. I was even observing the scenery. You can imagine, me looking at scenery, on the road every week of my life. But it's so beautiful up there, Linda, the trees are so thick, and the sun is warm. I opened the windshield and just let the warm air bathe over me. And then all of a sudden I'm goin' off the road! I'm tellin' ya, I absolutely forgot I was driving. If I'd've gone the other way over the white line I might've killed somebody. So I went on again—and five minutes later I'm dreamin' again, and I nearly— [*He presses two fingers against his eyes.*] I have such thoughts, I have such strange thoughts.

LINDA   Willy, dear. Talk to them again. There's no reason why you can't work in New York.

WILLY   They don't need me in New York. I'm the New England man. I'm vital in New England.

LINDA   But you're sixty years old. They can't expect you to keep traveling every week.

WILLY   I'll have to send a wire to Portland. I'm supposed to see Brown and Morrison tomorrow morning at ten o'clock to show the line. Goddammit, I could sell them! [*He starts putting on his jacket.*]

LINDA [*taking the jacket from him*]   Why don't you go down to the place tomorrow and tell Howard you've simply got to work in New York? You're too accommodating, dear.

WILLY   If old man Wagner was alive I'd been in charge of New York now! That man was a prince, he was a masterful man. But that boy of his, that Howard, he don't appreciate. When I went north the first time, the Wagner Company didn't know where New England was!

LINDA   Why don't you tell those things to Howard, dear?

WILLY [*encouraged*]   I will, I definitely will. Is there any cheese?

LINDA   I'll make you a sandwich.

WILLY   No, go to sleep. I'll take some milk. I'll be up right away. The boys in?

LINDA   They're sleeping. Happy took Biff on a date tonight.

WILLY [*interested*]   That so?

LINDA   It was so nice to see them shaving together, one behind the other, in the bathroom. And going out together. You notice? The whole house smells of shaving lotion.

WILLY   Figure it out. Work a lifetime to pay off a house. You finally own it, and there's nobody to live in it.

LINDA   Well, dear, life is a casting off. It's always that way.

WILLY   No, no, some people—some people accomplish something. Did Biff say anything after I went this morning?

LINDA   You shouldn't have criticized him, Willy, especially after he just got off the train. You mustn't lose your temper with him.

WILLY   When the hell did I lose my temper? I simply asked him if he was making any money. Is that a criticism?

LINDA   But, dear, how could he make any money?

WILLY [*worried and angered*]   There's such an undercurrent in him. He became a moody man. Did he apologize when I left this morning?

LINDA   He was crestfallen, Willy. You know how he admires you. I think if he finds himself, then you'll both be happier and not fight any more.

WILLY   How can he find himself on a farm? Is that a life? A farmhand? In the beginning, when he was young, I thought, well, a young man, it's good for him to tramp around, take a lot of different jobs. But it's more than ten years now and he has yet to make thirty-five dollars a week?

LINDA   He's finding himself, Willy.

WILLY   Not finding yourself at the age of thirty-four is a disgrace!

LINDA   Shh!

WILLY   The trouble is he's lazy, goddammit!

LINDA   Willy, please!

WILLY   Biff is a lazy bum!

LINDA   They're sleeping. Get something to eat. Go on down.

WILLY   Why did he come home? I would like to know what brought him home.

LINDA   I don't know. I think he's still lost, Willy. I think he's very lost.

WILLY   Biff Loman is lost. In the greatest country in the world a young man with such—personal attractiveness, gets lost. And such a hard worker. There's one thing about Biff—he's not lazy.

LINDA   Never.

WILLY [*with pity and resolve*]   I'll see him in the morning; I'll have a nice talk with him. I'll get him a job selling. He could be big in no time. My God! Remember how they used to follow him around in high school? When he smiled at one of them their faces lit up. When he walked down the street . . . [*He loses himself in reminiscences.*]

LINDA [*trying to bring him out of it*]   Willy, dear, I got a new kind of American-type cheese today. It's whipped.

WILLY   Why do you get American when I like Swiss?

LINDA   I just thought you'd like a change—

WILLY I don't want a change! I want Swiss cheese. Why am I always being contradicted?

LINDA [*with a covering laugh*] I thought it would be a surprise.

WILLY Why don't you open a window in here, for God's sake?

LINDA [*with infinite patience*] They're all open, dear.

WILLY The way they boxed us in here. Bricks and windows, windows and bricks.

LINDA We should've bought the land next door.

WILLY The street is lined with cars. There's not a breath of fresh air in the neighborhood. The grass don't grow any more, you can't raise a carrot in the back yard. They should've had a law against apartment houses. Remember those two beautiful elm trees out there? When I and Biff hung the swing between them?

LINDA Yeah, like being a million miles from the city.

WILLY They should've arrested the builder for cutting those down. They massacred the neighborhood. [*lost*] More and more I think of those days, Linda. This time of year it was lilac and wisteria. And then the peonies would come out, and the daffodils. What fragrance in this room!

LINDA Well, after all, people had to move somewhere.

WILLY No, there's more people now.

LINDA I don't think there's more people. I think—

WILLY There's more people! That's what's ruining this country! Population is getting out of control. The competition is maddening! Smell the stink from that apartment house! And another one on the other side . . . How can they whip cheese?

[*On* WILLY's *last line,* BIFF *and* HAPPY *raise themselves up in their beds, listening.*]

LINDA Go down, try it. And be quiet.

WILLY [*turning to* LINDA, *guiltily*] You're not worried about me, are you, sweetheart?

BIFF What's the matter?

HAPPY Listen!

LINDA You've got too much on the ball to worry about.

WILLY You're my foundation and my support, Linda.

LINDA Just try to relax, dear. You make mountains out of molehills.

WILLY I won't fight with him any more. If he wants to go back to Texas, let him go.

LINDA He'll find his way.

WILLY Sure. Certain men just don't get started till later in life. Like Thomas Edison, I think. Or B. F. Goodrich. One of them was deaf. [*He starts for the bedroom doorway.*] I'll put my money on Biff.

LINDA And Willy—if it's warm Sunday we'll drive in the country. And we'll open the windshield, and take lunch.

WILLY No, the windshields don't open on the new cars.

LINDA But you opened it today.

WILLY Me? I didn't. [*He stops.*] Now isn't that peculiar! Isn't that a remarkable—[*He breaks off in amazement and fright as the flute is heard distantly.*]

LINDA What, darling?

WILLY That is the most remarkable thing.

LINDA   What, dear?

WILLY   I was thinking of the Chevvy. [*slight pause*] Nineteen twenty-eight . . . when I had that red Chevvy—[*breaks off*] That funny? I coulda sworn I was driving that Chevvy today.

LINDA   Well, that's nothing. Something must've reminded you.

WILLY   Remarkable. Ts. Remember those days? The way Biff used to simonize that car? The dealer refused to believe there was eighty thousand miles on it. [*He shakes his head.*] Heh! [*to* LINDA] Close your eyes, I'll be right up. [*He walks out of the bedroom.*]

HAPPY [*to* BIFF]   Jesus, maybe he smashed up the car again!

LINDA [*calling after* WILLY]   Be careful on the stairs, dear! The cheese is on the middle shelf! [*She turns, goes over to the bed, takes his jacket, and goes out of the bedroom.*]

> [*Light has risen on the boys' room. Unseen,* WILLY *is heard talking to himself, "Eighty thousand miles," and a little laugh.* BIFF *gets out of bed, comes downstage a bit, and stands attentively.* BIFF *is two years older than his brother* HAPPY, *well built, but in these days bears a worn air and seems less self-assured. He has succeeded less, and his dreams are stronger and less acceptable than* HAPPY'S. HAPPY *is tall, powerfully made. Sexuality is like a visible color on him, or a scent that many women have discovered. He, like his brother, is lost, but in a different way, for he has never allowed himself to turn his face toward defeat and is thus more confused and hard-skinned, although seemingly more content.*]

HAPPY [*getting out of bed*]   He's going to get his license taken away if he keeps that up. I'm getting nervous about him, y'know, Biff?

BIFF   His eyes are going.

HAPPY   No, I've driven with him. He sees all right. He just doesn't keep his mind on it. I drove into the city with him last week. He stops at a green light and then it turns red and he goes. [*He laughs.*]

BIFF   Maybe he's color-blind.

HAPPY   Pop? Why he's got the finest eye for color in the business. You know that.

BIFF [*sitting down on his bed*]   I'm going to sleep.

HAPPY   You're not still sour on Dad, are you Biff?

BIFF   He's all right, I guess.

WILLY [*underneath them, in the living-room*]   Yes, sir, eighty thousand miles—eighty-two thousand!

BIFF   You smoking?

HAPPY [*holding out a pack of cigarettes*]   Want one?

BIFF [*taking a cigarette*]   I can never sleep when I smell it.

WILLY   What a simonizing job, heh!

HAPPY [*with deep sentiment*]   Funny, Biff, y'know? Us sleeping in here again? The old beds. [*He pats his bed affectionately.*] All the talk that went across those two beds, huh? Our whole lives.

BIFF   Yeah. Lotta dreams and plans.

HAPPY [*with a deep and masculine laugh*]   About five hundred women would like to know what was said in this room.

> [*They share a soft laugh.*]

BIFF   Remember that big Betsy something—what the hell was her name—over on Bushwick Avenue?

HAPPY [*combing his hair*]   With the collie dog!

BIFF   That's the one. I got you in there, remember?

HAPPY   Yeah, that was my first time—I think. Boy, there was a pig! [*They laugh, almost crudely.*] You taught me everything I know about women. Don't forget that.

BIFF   I bet you forgot how bashful you used to be. Especially with girls.

HAPPY   Oh, I still am, Biff.

BIFF   Oh, go on.

HAPPY   I just control it, that's all. I think I got less bashful and you got more so. What happened, Biff? Where's the old humor, the old confidence? [*He shakes* BIFF's *knee.* BIFF *gets up and moves restlessly about the room.*] What's the matter?

BIFF   Why does Dad mock me all the time?

HAPPY   He's not mocking you, he—

BIFF   Everything I say there's a twist of mockery on his face. I can't get near him.

HAPPY   He just wants you to make good, that's all. I wanted to talk to you about Dad for a long time, Biff. Something's—happening to him. He— talks to himself.

BIFF   I noticed that this morning. But he always mumbled.

HAPPY   But not so noticeable. It got so embarrassing I sent him to Florida. And you know something? Most of the time he's talking to you.

BIFF   What's he say about me?

HAPPY   I can't make it out.

BIFF   What's he say about me?

HAPPY   I think the fact that you're not settled, that you're still kind of up in the air . . .

BIFF   There's one or two other things depressing him, Happy.

HAPPY   What do you mean?

BIFF   Never mind. Just don't lay it all to me.

HAPPY   But I think if you just got started—I mean—is there any future for you out there?

BIFF   I tell ya, Hap, I don't know what the future is. I don't know—what I'm supposed to want.

HAPPY   What do you mean?

BIFF   Well, I spent six or seven years after high school trying to work myself up. Shipping clerk, salesman, business of one kind or another. And it's a measly manner of existence. To get on that subway on the hot mornings in summer. To devote your whole life to keeping stock, or making phone calls, or selling or buying. To suffer fifty weeks of the year for the sake of a two-week vacation, when all you really desire is to be outdoors, with your shirt off. And always to have to get ahead of the next fella. And still—that's how you build a future.

HAPPY   Well, you really enjoy it on a farm? Are you content out there?

BIFF [*with rising agitation*]   Hap, I've had twenty or thirty different kinds of jobs since I left home before the war, and it always turns out the same. I just realized it lately. In Nebraska when I herded cattle, and the Dakotas, and Arizona, and now in Texas. It's why I came home now, I guess, because I realized it. This farm I work on, it's spring there now, see? And they've got about fifteen new colts. There's nothing more inspiring or—

beautiful than the sight of a mare and a new colt. And it's cool there now, see? Texas is cool now, and it's spring. And whenever spring comes to where I am, I suddenly get the feeling, my God, I'm not gettin' anywhere! What the hell am I doing, playing around with horses, twenty-eight dollars a week! I'm thirty-four years old. I oughta be makin' my future. That's when I come running home. And now, I get here, and I don't know what to do with myself. [*after a pause*] I've always made a point of not wasting my life, and everytime I come back here I know that all I've done is to waste my life.

HAPPY   You're a poet, you know that, Biff? You're a—you're an idealist!

BIFF   No, I'm mixed up very bad. Maybe I oughta get married. Maybe I oughta get stuck into something. Maybe that's my trouble. I'm like a boy. I'm not married. I'm not in business, I just—I'm like a boy. Are you content, Hap? You're a success, aren't you? Are you content?

HAPPY   Hell, no!

BIFF   Why? You're making money, aren't you?

HAPPY   [*moving about with energy, expressiveness*]   All I can do now is wait for the merchandise manager to die. And suppose I get to be merchandise manager? He's a good friend of mine, and he just built a terrific estate on Long Island. And he lived there about two months and sold it, and now he's building another one. He can't enjoy it once it's finished. And I know that's just what I would do. I don't know what the hell I'm workin' for. Sometimes I sit in my apartment—all alone. And I think of the rent I'm paying. And it's crazy. But then, it's what I always wanted. My own apartment, a car, and plenty of women. And still, goddammit, I'm lonely.

BIFF   [*with enthusiasm*]   Listen why don't you come out West with me?

HAPPY   You and I, heh?

BIFF   Sure, maybe we could buy a ranch. Raise cattle, use our muscles. Men built like we are should be working out in the open.

HAPPY   [*avidly*]   The Loman Brothers, heh?

BIFF   [*with vast affection*]   Sure, we'd be known all over the counties!

HAPPY   [*enthralled*]   That's what I dream about, Biff. Sometimes I want to just rip my clothes off in the middle of the store and outbox that goddam merchandise manager. I mean I can outbox, outrun, and outlift anybody in that store, and I have to take orders from those common, petty sons-of-bitches till I can't stand it any more.

BIFF   I'm tellin' you, kid, if you were with me I'd be happy out there.

HAPPY   [*enthused*]   See, Biff, everybody around me is so false that I'm constantly lowering my ideals . . .

BIFF   Baby, together we'd stand up for one another, we'd have someone to trust.

HAPPY   If I were around you—

BIFF   Hap, the trouble is we weren't brought up to grub for money. I don't know how to do it.

HAPPY   Neither can I!

BIFF   Then let's go!

HAPPY   The only thing is—what can you make out there?

BIFF   But look at your friend. Builds an estate and then hasn't the peace of mind to live in it.

HAPPY   Yeah, but when he walks into the store the waves part in front of him. That's fifty-two thousand dollars a year coming through the revolving door, and I got more in my pinky finger than he's got in his head.

BIFF   Yeah, but you just said—

HAPPY   I gotta show some of those pompous, self-important executives over there that Hap Loman can make the grade. I want to walk into the store the way he walks in. Then I'll go with you, Biff. We'll be together yet, I swear. But take those two we had tonight. Now weren't they gorgeous creatures?

BIFF   Yeah, yeah, most gorgeous I've had in years.

HAPPY   I get that any time I want, Biff. Whenever I feel disgusted. The only trouble is, it gets like bowling or something. I just keep knockin' them over and it doesn't mean anything. You still run around a lot?

BIFF   Naa. I'd like to find a girl—steady, somebody with substance.

HAPPY   That's what I long for.

BIFF   Go on! You'd never come home.

HAPPY   I would! Somebody with character, with resistance! Like Mom, y'know? You're gonna call me a bastard when I tell you this. That girl Charlotte I was with tonight is engaged to be married in five weeks. [He tries on his new hat.]

BIFF   No kiddin'!

HAPPY   Sure, the guy's in line for the vice-presidency of the store. I don't know what gets into me, maybe I just have an overdeveloped sense of competition or something, but I went and ruined her, and furthermore I can't get rid of her. And he's the third executive I've done that to. Isn't that a crummy characteristic? And to top it all, I go to their weddings! [indignantly, but laughing] Like I'm not supposed to take bribes. Manufacturers offer me a hundred-dollar bill now and then to throw an order their way. You know how honest I am, but it's like this girl, see. I hate myself for it. Because I don't want the girl, and, still, I take it and—I love it!

BIFF   Let's go to sleep.

HAPPY   I guess we didn't settle anything, heh?

BIFF   I just got one idea that I think I'm going to try.

HAPPY   What's that?

BIFF   Remember Bill Oliver?

HAPPY   Sure, Oliver is very big now. You want to work for him again?

BIFF   No, but when I quit he said something to me. He put his arm on my shoulder, and he said, "Biff, if you ever need anything, come to me."

HAPPY   I remember that. That sounds good.

BIFF   I think I'll go to see him. If I could get ten thousand or even seven or eight thousand dollars I could buy a beautiful ranch.

HAPPY   I bet he'd back you. 'Cause he thought highly of you, Biff. I mean, they all do. You're well liked, Biff. That's why I say to come back here, and we both have the apartment. And I'm tellin' you, Biff, any babe you want . . .

BIFF   No, with a ranch I could do the work I like and still be something. I just wonder though. I wonder if Oliver still thinks I stole that carton of basketballs.

HAPPY   Oh, he probably forgot that long ago. It's almost ten years. You're too sensitive. Anyway, he didn't really fire you.

BIFF   Well, I think he was going to. I think that's why I quit. I was never sure whether he knew or not. I know he thought the world of me, though. I was the only one he'd let lock up the place.

WILLY [*below*]   You gonna wash the engine, Biff?

HAPPY   Shh!

> [BIFF *looks at* HAPPY, *who is gazing down, listening.* WILLY *is mumbling in the parlor.*]

HAPPY   You hear that?

> [*They listen.* WILLY *laughs warmly.*]

BIFF [*growing angry*]   Doesn't he know Mom can hear that?

WILLY   Don't get your sweater dirty, Biff!

> [*A look of pain crosses* BIFF's *face.*]

HAPPY   Isn't that terrible? Don't leave again, will you? You'll find a job here. You gotta stick around. I don't know what to do about him, it's getting embarrassing.

WILLY   What a simonizing job!

BIFF   Mom's hearing that!

WILLY   No kiddin', Biff, you got a date? Wonderful!

HAPPY   Go on to sleep. But talk to him in the morning, will you?

BIFF [*reluctantly getting into bed*]   With her in the house. Brother!

HAPPY [*getting into bed*]   I wish you'd have a good talk with him.

> [*The light on their room begins to fade.*]

BIFF [*to himself in bed*]   That selfish, stupid . . .

HAPPY   Sh . . . Sleep, Biff.

> [*Their light is out. Well before they have finished speaking,* WILLY's *form is dimly seen below in the darkened kitchen. He opens the refrigerator, searches in there, and takes out a bottle of milk. The apartment houses are fading out, and the entire house and surroundings become covered with leaves. Music insinuates itself as the leaves appear.*]

WILLY   Just wanna be careful with those girls, Biff, that's all. Don't make any promises. No promises of any kind. Because a girl, y'know, they always believe what you tell 'em, and you're very young, Biff, you're too young to be talking seriously to girls.

> [*Light rises on the kitchen.* WILLY, *talking, shuts the refrigerator door and comes downstage to the kitchen table. He pours milk into a glass. He is totally immersed in himself, smiling faintly.*]

WILLY   Too young entirely, Biff. You want to watch your schooling first. Then when you're all set, there'll be plenty of girls for a boy like you. [*He smiles broadly at a kitchen chair.*] That so? The girls pay for you? [*He laughs.*] Boy, you must really be makin' a hit.

> [WILLY *is gradually addressing—physically—a point offstage, speaking through the wall of the kitchen, and his voice has been rising in volume to that of a normal conversation.*]

WILLY   I been wondering why you polish the car so careful. Ha! Don't leave the hubcaps, boys. Get the chamois to the hubcaps. Happy, use newspaper on the windows, it's the easiest thing. Show him how to do it, Biff! You see, Happy? Pad it up, use it like a pad. That's it, that's it, good work. You're doin' all right, Hap. [*He pauses, then nods in approbation for a few seconds, then looks upward.*] Biff, first thing we gotta do when we get time is clip that big branch over the house. Afraid it's gonna fall in a storm and hit the roof. Tell you what. We get a rope and sling her around, and then we climb up there with a couple of saws and take her down. Soon as you finish the car, boys, I wanna see ya. I got a surprise for you, boys.

BIFF [*offstage*] Whatta ya got, Dad?

WILLY No, you finish first. Never leave a job till you're finished— remember that, [*looking toward the "big trees"*] Biff, up in Albany I saw a beautiful hammock. I think I'll buy it next trip, and we'll hang it right between those two elms. Wouldn't that be something? Just swingin' there under those branches. Boy, that would be . . .

> [YOUNG BIFF *and* YOUNG HAPPY *appear from the direction* WILLY *was addressing.* HAPPY *carries rags and a pail of water.* BIFF, *wearing a sweater with a block "S," carries a football.*]

BIFF [*pointing in the direction of the car offstage*] How's that, Pop, professional?

WILLY Terrific. Terrific job, boys. Good work, Biff.

HAPPY Where's the surprise, Pop?

WILLY In the back seat of the car.

HAPPY Boy! [*He runs off.*]

BIFF What is it, Dad? Tell me, what'd you buy?

WILLY [*laughing, cuffs him*] Never mind, something I want you to have.

BIFF [*turns and starts off*] What is it, Hap?

HAPPY [*offstage*] It's a punching bag!

BIFF Oh, Pop!

WILLY It's got Gene Tunney's[1] signature on it!

> [HAPPY *runs onstage with a punching bag.*]

BIFF Gee, how'd you know we wanted a punching bag?

WILLY Well, it's the finest thing for the timing.

HAPPY [*lies down on his back and pedals with his feet*] I'm losing weight, you notice, Pop?

WILLY [*to* HAPPY] Jumping rope is good too.

BIFF Did you see the new football I got?

WILLY [*examining the ball*] Where'd you get a new ball?

BIFF The coach told me to practice my passing.

WILLY That so? And he gave you the ball, heh?

BIFF Well, I borrowed it from the locker room. [*He laughs confidentially.*]

WILLY [*laughing with him at the left*] I want you to return that.

HAPPY I told you he wouldn't like it!

BIFF [*angrily*] Well, I'm bringing it back!

WILLY [*stopping the incipient argument, to* HAPPY] Sure, he's gotta practice with a regulation ball, doesn't he? [*to* BIFF] Coach'll probably congratulate you on your initiative!

BIFF Oh, he keeps congratulating my initiative all the time, Pop.

WILLY That's because he likes you. If somebody else took that ball there'd be an uproar. So what's the report, boys, what's the report?

BIFF Where'd you go this time, Dad? Gee we were lonesome for you.

WILLY [*pleased, puts an arm around each boy and they come down to the apron*] Lonesome, heh?

---

1. World heavyweight boxing champion from 1926 to 1928.

BIFF Missed you every minute.

WILLY Don't say? Tell you a secret, boys. Don't breathe it to a soul. Some-day I'll have my own business, and I'll never have to leave home any more.

HAPPY Like Uncle Charley, heh?

WILLY Bigger than Uncle Charley! Because Charley is not—liked. He's liked, but he's not—well liked.

BIFF Where'd you go this time, Dad?

WILLY Well, I got on the road, and I went north to Providence. Met the Mayor.

BIFF The Mayor of Providence!

WILLY He was sitting in the hotel lobby.

BIFF What'd he say?

WILLY He said, "Morning!" And I said, "You got a fine city here, Mayor." And then he had coffee with me. And then I went to Waterbury. Water-bury is a fine city. Big clock city, the famous Waterbury clock. Sold a nice bill there. And then Boston—Boston is the cradle of the Revolution. A fine city. And a couple of other towns in Mass., and on to Portland and Bangor and straight home!

BIFF Gee, I'd love to go with you sometime, Dad.

WILLY Soon as summer comes.

HAPPY Promise?

WILLY You and Hap and I, and I'll show you all the towns. America is full of beautiful towns and fine, upstanding people. And they know me, boys, they know me up and down New England. The finest people. And when I bring you fellas up, there'll be open sesame for all of us, 'cause one thing, boys: I have friends. I can park my car in any street in New England, and the cops protect it like their own. This summer, heh?

BIFF and HAPPY [*together*] Yeah! You bet!

WILLY We'll take our bathing suits.

HAPPY We'll carry your bags, Pop!

WILLY Oh, won't that be something! Me comin' into the Boston stores with you boys carryin' my bags. What a sensation!

[BIFF *is prancing around, practicing passing the ball.*]

WILLY You nervous, Biff, about the game?

BIFF Not if you're gonna be there.

WILLY What do they say about you in school, now that they made you captain?

HAPPY There's a crowd of girls behind him everytime the classes change.

BIFF [*taking* WILLY'S *hand*] This Saturday, Pop, this Saturday—just for you, I'm going to break through for a touchdown.

HAPPY You're supposed to pass.

BIFF I'm takin' one play for Pop. You watch me, Pop, and when I take off my helmet, that means I'm breakin' out. Then you watch me crash through that line!

WILLY [*kisses* BIFF] Oh, wait'll I tell this in Boston!

[BERNARD *enters in knickers. He is younger than* BIFF, *earnest and loyal, a worried boy.*]

BERNARD Biff, where are you? You're supposed to study with me today.

WILLY Hey, looka Bernard. What're you lookin' so anemic about, Bernard?

BERNARD He's gotta study, Uncle Willy. He's got Regents[2] next week.

HAPPY [*tauntingly, spinning* BERNARD *around*] Let's box, Bernard!

BERNARD Biff! [*He gets away from* HAPPY.] Listen, Biff, I heard Mr. Birnbaum say that if you don't start studyin' math he's gonna flunk you, and
you won't graduate. I heard him!

WILLY You better study with him, Biff. Go ahead now.

BERNARD I heard him!

BIFF Oh, Pop, you didn't see my sneakers! [*He holds up a foot for* WILLY *to
look at.*]

WILLY Hey, that's a beautiful job of printing!

BERNARD [*wiping his glasses*] Just because he printed University of Virginia
on his sneakers doesn't mean they've got to graduate him, Uncle Willy!

WILLY [*angrily*] What're you talking about? With scholarships to three
universities they're gonna flunk him?

BERNARD But I heard Mr. Birnbaum say—

WILLY Don't be a pest, Bernard! [*to his boys*] What an anemic!

BERNARD Okay, I'm waiting for you in my house, Biff.

[BERNARD *goes off. The Lomans laugh.*]

WILLY Bernard is not well liked, is he?

BIFF He's liked, but he's not well liked.

HAPPY That's right, Pop.

WILLY That's just what I mean. Bernard can get the best marks in school,
y'understand, but when he gets out in the business world, y'understand,
you are going to be five times ahead of him. That's why I thank Almighty
God you're both built like Adonises.[3] Because the man who makes an
appearance in the business world, the man who creates personal interest, is the man who gets ahead. Be liked and you will never want. You
take me, for instance. I never have to wait in line to see a buyer. "Willy
Loman is here!" That's all they have to know, and I go right through.

BIFF Did you knock them dead, Pop?

WILLY Knocked 'em cold in Providence, slaughtered 'em in Boston.

HAPPY [*on his back, pedaling again*] I'm losing weight, you notice, Pop?

[LINDA *enters, as of old, a ribbon in her hair, carrying a basket of washing.*]

LINDA [*with youthful energy*] Hello, dear!

WILLY Sweetheart!

LINDA How'd the Chevvy run?

WILLY Chevrolet, Linda, is the greatest car ever built. [*to the boys*] Since
when do you let your mother carry wash up the stairs?

BIFF Grab hold there, boy!

HAPPY Where to, Mom?

LINDA Hang them up on the line. And you better go down to your friends,
Biff. The cellar is full of boys. They don't know what to do with themselves.

BIFF Ah, when Pop comes home they can wait!

WILLY [*laughs appreciatively*] You better go down and tell them what to
do, Biff.

---

2. Compulsory statewide high school examinations in New York.
3. In Greek mythology Adonis was a beautiful youth favored by Aphrodite, the goddess of love.

BIFF   I think I'll have them sweep out the furnace room.

WILLY   Good work, Biff.

BIFF   [*goes through wall-line of kitchen to doorway at back and calls down*] Fellas! Everybody sweep out the furnace room! I'll be right down!

VOICES   All right! Okay, Biff.

BIFF   George and Sam and Frank, come out back! We're hangin' up the wash! Come on, Hap, on the double!

     [*He and* HAPPY *carry out the basket.*]

LINDA   The way they obey him!

WILLY   Well, that training, the training. I'm tellin' you, I was sellin' thousands and thousands, but I had to come home.

LINDA   Oh, the whole block'll be at that game. Did you sell anything?

WILLY   I did five hundred gross in Providence and seven hundred gross in Boston.

LINDA   No! Wait a minute, I've got a pencil. [*She pulls pencil and paper out of her apron pocket.*] That makes your commission . . . Two hundred— my God! Two hundred and twelve dollars!

WILLY   Well, I didn't figure it yet, but . . .

LINDA   How much did you do?

WILLY   Well, I—I did—about a hundred and eighty gross in Providence. Well, no—it came to—roughly two hundred gross on the whole trip.

LINDA   [*without hesitation*]   Two hundred gross. That's . . . [*She figures.*]

WILLY   The trouble was that three of the stores were half closed for inventory in Boston. Otherwise I woulda broke records.

LINDA   Well, it makes seventy dollars and some pennies. That's very good.

WILLY   What do we owe?

LINDA   Well, on the first there's sixteen dollars on the refrigerator—

WILLY   Why sixteen?

LINDA   Well, the fan belt broke, so it was a dollar eighty.

WILLY   But it's brand new.

LINDA   Well, the man said that's the way it is. Till they work themselves in, y'know.

     [*They move through the wall-line into the kitchen.*]

WILLY   I hope we didn't get stuck on that machine.

LINDA   They got the biggest ads of any of them!

WILLY   I know, it's a fine machine. What else?

LINDA   Well, there's nine-sixty for the washing machine. And for the vacuum cleaner there's three and a half due on the fifteenth. Then the roof, you got twenty-one dollars remaining.

WILLY   It don't leak, does it?

LINDA   No, they did a wonderful job. Then you owe Frank for the carburetor.

WILLY   I'm not going to pay that man! That goddam Chevrolet, they ought to prohibit the manufacture of that car!

LINDA   Well, you owe him three and a half. And odds and ends, comes to around a hundred and twenty dollars by the fifteenth.

WILLY   A hundred and twenty dollars! My God, if business don't pick up I don't know what I'm gonna do!

LINDA   Well, next week you'll do better.

WILLY   Oh, I'll knock 'em dead next week. I'll go to Hartford. I'm very well liked in Hartford. You know, the trouble is, Linda, people don't seem to take to me.
[*They move onto the forestage.*]

LINDA   Oh, don't be foolish.

WILLY   I know it when I walk in. They seem to laugh at me.

LINDA   Why? Why would they laugh at you? Don't talk that way, Willy.
[WILLY *moves to the edge of the stage.* LINDA *goes into the kitchen and starts to darn stockings.*]

WILLY   I don't know the reason for it, but they just pass me by. I'm not noticed.

LINDA   But you're doing wonderful, dear. You're making seventy to a hundred dollars a week.

WILLY   But I gotta be at it ten, twelve hours a day. Other men—I don't know—they do it easier. I don't know why—I can't stop myself—I talk too much. A man oughta come in with a few words. One thing about Charley. He's a man of few words, and they respect him.

LINDA   You don't talk too much, you're just lively.

WILLY   [*smiling*]   Well, I figure, what the hell, life is short, a couple of jokes. [*to himself*] I joke too much! [*The smiles goes.*]

LINDA   Why? You're—

WILLY   I'm fat. I'm very—foolish to look at, Linda. I didn't tell you, but Christmas time I happened to be calling on F. H. Stewarts, and a salesman I know, as I was going in to see the buyer I heard him say something about—walrus. And I—I cracked him right across the face. I won't take that. I simply will not take that. But they do laugh at me. I know that.

LINDA   Darling . . .

WILLY   I gotta overcome it. I know I gotta overcome it. I'm not dressing to advantage, maybe.

LINDA   Willy, darling, you're the handsomest man in the world—

WILLY   Oh, no, Linda.

LINDA   To me you are. [*slight pause*] The handsomest.
[*From the darkness is heard the laughter of a woman.* WILLY *doesn't turn to it, but it continues through* LINDA's *lines.*]

LINDA   And the boys, Willy. Few men are idolized by their children the way you are.
[*Music is heard as behind a scrim,*[4] *to the left of the house,* THE WOMAN, *dimly seen, is dressing.*]

WILLY   [*with great feeling*]   You're the best there is, Linda, you're a pal, you know that? On the road—on the road I want to grab you sometimes and just kiss the life outa you.
[*The laughter is loud now, and he moves into a brightening area at the left, where* THE WOMAN *has come from behind the scrim and is standing, putting on her hat, looking into a "mirror" and laughing.*]

WILLY   'Cause I get so lonely—especially when business is bad and there's nobody to talk to. I get the feeling that I'll never sell anything again, that I won't make a living for you, or a business, a business for the boys.

---

4. Part of a stage set; a painted gauze curtain that becomes transparent when lighted from the back.

[*He talks through* THE WOMAN's *subsiding laughter;* THE WOMAN *primps at the "mirror."*] There's so much I want to make for—

THE WOMAN   Me? You didn't make me, Willy. I picked you.

WILLY [*pleased*]   You picked me?

THE WOMAN [*who is quite proper-looking,* WILLY's *age*]   I did. I've been sitting at that desk watching all the salesmen go by, day in, day out. But you've got such a sense of humor, and we do have such a good time together, don't we?

WILLY   Sure, sure. [*He takes her in his arms.*] Why do you have to go now?

THE WOMAN   It's two o'clock . . .

WILLY   No, come on in! [*He pulls her.*]

THE WOMAN   . . . my sisters'll be scandalized. When'll you be back?

WILLY   Oh, two weeks about. Will you come up again?

THE WOMAN   Sure thing. You do make me laugh. It's good for me. [*She squeezes his arm, kisses him.*] And I think you're a wonderful man.

WILLY   You picked me, heh?

THE WOMAN   Sure. Because you're so sweet. And such a kidder.

WILLY   Well, I'll see you next time I'm in Boston.

THE WOMAN   I'll put you right through to the buyers.

WILLY [*slapping her bottom*]   Right. Well, bottoms up!

THE WOMAN [*slaps him gently and laughs*]   You just kill me, Willy. [*He suddenly grabs her and kisses her roughly.*] You kill me. And thanks for the stockings. I love a lot of stockings. Well, good night.

WILLY   Good night. And keep your pores open!

THE WOMAN   Oh, Willy!

[THE WOMAN *bursts out laughing, and* LINDA's *laughter blends in.* THE WOMAN *disappears into the dark. Now the area at the kitchen table brightens.* LINDA *is sitting where she was at the kitchen table, but now is mending a pair of her silk stockings.*]

LINDA   You are, Willy. The handsomest man. You've got no reason to feel that—

WILLY [*coming out of* THE WOMAN's *dimming area and going over to* LINDA]   I'll make it all up to you, Linda. I'll—

LINDA   There's nothing to make up, dear. You're doing fine, better than—

WILLY [*noticing her mending*]   What's that?

LINDA   Just mending my stockings. They're so expensive—

WILLY [*angrily, taking them from her*]   I won't have you mending stockings in this house! Now throw them out!

[LINDA *puts the stockings in her pocket.*]

BERNARD [*entering on the run*]   Where is he? If he doesn't study!

WILLY [*moving to the forestage, with great agitation*]   You'll give him the answers!

BERNARD   I do, but I can't on a Regents! That's a state exam! They're liable to arrest me!

WILLY   Where is he? I'll whip him, I'll whip him!

LINDA   And he'd better give back that football, Willy, it's not nice.

WILLY   Biff! Where is he? Why is he taking everything?

LINDA   He's too rough with the girls, Willy. All the mothers are afraid of him!

WILLY   I'll whip him!

BERNARD   He's driving the car without a license!

[THE WOMAN's *laugh is heard.*]

WILLY   Shut up!

LINDA   All the mothers—

WILLY   Shut up!

BERNARD [*backing quietly away and out*]   Mr. Birnbaum says he's stuck up.

WILLY   Get outa here!

BERNARD   If he doesn't buckle down he'll flunk math! [*He goes off.*]

LINDA   He's right, Willy, you've gotta—

WILLY [*exploding at her*]   There's nothing the matter with him! You want him to be a worm like Bernard? He's got spirit, personality . . .

[*As he speaks,* LINDA, *almost in tears, exits into the living-room.* WILLY *is alone in the kitchen, wilting and staring. The leaves are gone. It is night again, and the apartment houses look down from behind.*]

WILLY   Loaded with it. Loaded! What is he stealing? He's giving it back, isn't he? Why is he stealing? What did I tell him? I never in my life told him anything but decent things.

[HAPPY *in pajamas has come down the stairs;* WILLY *suddenly becomes aware of* HAPPY's *presence.*]

HAPPY   Let's go now, come on.

WILLY [*sitting down at the kitchen table*]   Huh! Why did she have to wax the floors herself? Everytime she waxes the floors she keels over. She knows that!

HAPPY   Shh! Take it easy. What brought you back tonight?

WILLY   I got an awful scare. Nearly hit a kid in Yonkers. God! Why didn't I go to Alaska with my brother Ben that time! Ben! That man was a genius, that man was success incarnate! What a mistake! He begged me to go.

HAPPY   Well, there's no use in—

WILLY   You guys! There was a man started with the clothes on his back and ended up with diamond mines!

HAPPY   Boy, someday I'd like to know how he did it.

WILLY   What's the mystery? The man knew what he wanted and went out and got it! Walked into a jungle, and comes out, the age of twenty-one, and he's rich! The world is an oyster, but you don't crack it open on a mattress!

HAPPY   Pop, I told you I'm gonna retire you for life.

WILLY   You'll retire me for life on seventy goddam dollars a week? And your women and your car and your apartment, and you'll retire me for life! Christ's sake, I couldn't get past Yonkers today! Where are you guys, where are you? The woods are burning! I can't drive a car!

[CHARLEY *has appeared in the doorway. He is a large man, slow of speech, laconic, immovable. In all he says, despite what he says, there is pity, and, now, trepidation. He has a robe over pajamas, slippers on his feet. He enters the kitchen.*]

CHARLEY   Everything all right?

HAPPY   Yeah, Charley, everything's . . .

WILLY   What's the matter?

CHARLEY   I heard some noise. I thought something happened. Can't we do something about the walls? You sneeze in here, and in my house hats blow off.

HAPPY   Let's go to bed, Dad. Come on.
   [CHARLEY *signals to* HAPPY *to go.*]
WILLY   You go ahead, I'm not tired at the moment.
HAPPY [*to* WILLY]   Take it easy, huh? [*He exits.*]
WILLY   What're you doin' up?
CHARLEY [*sitting down at the kitchen table opposite* WILLY]   Couldn't sleep
   good. I had a heartburn.
WILLY   Well, you don't know how to eat.
CHARLEY   I eat with my mouth.
WILLY   No, you're ignorant. You gotta know about vitamins and things
   like that.
CHARLEY   Come on, let's shoot. Tire you out a little.
WILLY [*hesitantly*]   All right. You got cards?
CHARLEY [*taking a deck from his pocket*]   Yeah, I got them. Someplace.
   What is it with those vitamins?
WILLY [*dealing*]   They build up your bones. Chemistry.
CHARLEY   Yeah, but there's no bones in a heartburn.
WILLY   What are you talkin' about? Do you know the first thing about it?
CHARLEY   Don't get insulted.
WILLY   Don't talk about something you don't know anything about.
   [*They are playing. Pause.*]
CHARLEY   What're you doin' home?
WILLY   A little trouble with the car.
CHARLEY   Oh. [*pause*] I'd like to take a trip to California.
WILLY   Don't say.
CHARLEY   You want a job?
WILLY   I got a job, I told you that. [*after a slight pause*] What the hell are
   you offering me a job for?
CHARLEY   Don't get insulted.
WILLY   Don't insult me.
CHARLEY   I don't see no sense in it. You don't have to go on this way.
WILLY   I got a good job. [*slight pause*] What do you keep comin' in here
   for?
CHARLEY   You want me to go?
WILLY [*after a pause, withering*]   I can't understand it. He's going back to
   Texas again. What the hell is that?
CHARLEY   Let him go.
WILLY   I got nothin' to give him, Charley, I'm clean, I'm clean.
CHARLEY   He won't starve. None a them starve. Forget about him.
WILLY   Then what have I got to remember?
CHARLEY   You take it too hard. To hell with it. When a deposit bottle is
   broken you don't get your nickel back.
WILLY   That's easy enough for you to say.
CHARLEY   That ain't easy for me to say.
WILLY   Did you see the ceiling I put up in the living-room?
CHARLEY   Yeah, that's a piece of work. To put up a ceiling is a mystery to
   me. How do you do it?
WILLY   What's the difference?
CHARLEY   Well, talk about it.

WILLY   You gonna put up a ceiling?

CHARLEY   How could I put up a ceiling?

WILLY   Then what the hell are you bothering me for?

CHARLEY   You're insulted again.

WILLY   A man who can't handle tools is not a man. You're disgusting.

CHARLEY   Don't call me disgusting, Willy.

> [UNCLE BEN, *carrying a valise and an umbrella, enters the forestage from around the right corner of the house. He is a stolid man, in his sixties, with a mustache and an authoritative air. He is utterly certain of his destiny, and there is an aura of far places about him. He enters exactly as* WILLY *speaks.*]

WILLY   I'm getting awfully tired, Ben.

> [BEN's *music is heard.* BEN *looks around at everything.*]

CHARLEY   Good, keep playing; you'll sleep better. Did you call me Ben?

> [BEN *looks at his watch.*]

WILLY   That's funny. For a second there you reminded me of my brother Ben.

BEN   I only have a few minutes. [*He strolls, inspecting the place.* WILLY *and* CHARLEY *continue playing.*]

CHARLEY   You never heard from him again, heh? Since that time?

WILLY   Didn't Linda tell you? Couple of weeks ago we got a letter from his wife in Africa. He died.

CHARLEY   That so.

BEN [*chuckling*]   So this is Brooklyn, eh?

CHARLEY   Maybe you're in for some of his money.

WILLY   Naa, he had seven sons. There's just one opportunity I had with that man . . .

BEN   I must make a train, William. There are several properties I'm looking at in Alaska.

WILLY   Sure, sure! If I'd gone with him to Alaska that time, everything would've been totally different.

CHARLEY   Go on, you'd froze to death up there.

WILLY   What're you talking about?

BEN   Opportunity is tremendous in Alaska, William. Surprised you're not up there.

WILLY   Sure, tremendous.

CHARLEY   Heh?

WILLY   There was the only man I ever met who knew the answers.

CHARLEY   Who?

BEN   How are you all?

WILLY [*taking a pot, smiling*]   Fine, fine.

CHARLEY   Pretty sharp tonight.

BEN   Is Mother living with you?

WILLY   No, she died a long time ago.

CHARLEY   Who?

BEN   That's too bad. Fine specimen of a lady, Mother.

WILLY [*to* CHARLEY]   Heh?

BEN   I'd hoped to see the old girl.

CHARLEY   Who died?

BEN   Heard anything from Father, have you?

WILLY [*unnerved*]   What do you mean, who died?

CHARLEY [*taking a pot*]   What're you talkin' about?

BEN [*looking at his watch*]   William, it's half-past eight!

WILLY [*as though to dispel his confusion he angrily stops* CHARLEY's *hand*] That's my build!

CHARLEY   I put the ace—

WILLY   If you don't know how to play the game I'm not gonna throw my money away on you!

CHARLEY [*rising*]   It was my ace, for God's sake!

WILLY   I'm through, I'm through!

BEN   When did Mother die?

WILLY   Long ago. Since the beginning you never knew how to play cards.

CHARLEY [*picks up the cards and goes to the door*]   All right! Next time I'll bring a deck with five aces.

WILLY   I don't play that kind of game!

CHARLEY [*turning to him*]   You ought to be ashamed of yourself!

WILLY   Yeah?

CHARLEY   Yeah! [*He goes out.*]

WILLY [*slamming the door after him*]   Ignoramus!

BEN [*as* WILLY *comes toward him through the wall-line of the kitchen*]   So you're William.

WILLY [*shaking* BEN's *hand*]   Ben! I've been waiting for you so long! What's the answer? How did you do it?

BEN   Oh, there's a story in that.

[LINDA *enters the forestage, as of old, carrying the wash basket.*]

LINDA   Is this Ben?

BEN [*gallantly*]   How do you do, my dear.

LINDA   Where've you been all these years? Willy's always wondered why you—

WILLY [*pulling* BEN *away from her impatiently*]   Where is Dad? Didn't you follow him? How did you get started?

BEN   Well, I don't know how much you remember.

WILLY   Well, I was just a baby, of course, only three or four years old—

BEN   Three years and eleven months.

WILLY   What a memory, Ben!

BEN   I have many enterprises, William, and I have never kept books.

WILLY   I remember I was sitting under the wagon in—was it Nebraska?

BEN   It was South Dakota, and I gave you a bunch of wild flowers.

WILLY   I remember you walking away down some open road.

BEN [*laughing*]   I was going to find Father in Alaska.

WILLY   Where is he?

BEN   At that age I had a very faulty view of geography, William. I discovered after a few days that I was heading due south, so instead of Alaska, I ended up in Africa.

LINDA   Africa!

WILLY   The Gold Coast!

BEN   Principally diamond mines.

LINDA   Diamond mines!

BEN Yes, my dear. But I've only a few minutes—

WILLY No! Boys! Boys! [YOUNG BIFF and HAPPY appear.] Listen to this. This is your Uncle Ben, a great man! Tell my boys, Ben!

BEN Why, boys, when I was seventeen I walked into the jungle, and when I was twenty-one I walked out. [He laughs.] And by God I was rich.

WILLY [to the boys] You see what I been talking about? The greatest things can happen!

BEN [glancing at his watch] I have an appointment in Ketchikan Tuesday week.

WILLY No, Ben! Please tell about Dad. I want my boys to hear. I want them to know the kind of stock they spring from. All I remember is a man with a big beard, and I was in Mamma's lap, sitting around a fire, and some kind of high music.

BEN His flute. He played the flute.

WILLY Sure, the flute, that's right!

[New music is heard, a high, rollicking tune.]

BEN Father was a very great and a very wild-hearted man. We would start in Boston, and he'd toss the whole family into the wagon, and then he'd drive the team right across the country; through Ohio, and Indiana, Michigan, Illinois, and all the Western states. And we'd stop in the towns and sell the flutes that he'd made on the way. Great inventor, Father. With one gadget he made more in a week than a man like you could make in a lifetime.

WILLY That's just the way I'm bringing them up, Ben—rugged, well liked, all-around.

BEN Yeah? [to BIFF] Hit that, boy—hard as you can. [He pounds his stomach.]

BIFF Oh, no, sir!

BEN [taking boxing stance] Come on, get to me! [He laughs.]

WILLY Go to it, Biff! Go ahead, show him!

BIFF Okay! [He cocks his fist and starts in.]

LINDA [to WILLY] Why must he fight, dear?

BEN [sparring with BIFF] Good boy! Good boy!

WILLY How's that, Ben, heh?

HAPPY Give him the left, Biff!

LINDA Why are you fighting?

BEN Good boy! [Suddenly comes in, trips BIFF, and stands over him, the point of his umbrella poised over BIFF's eye.]

LINDA Look out, Biff!

BIFF Gee!

BEN [patting BIFF's knee] Never fight fair with a stranger, boy. You'll never get out of the jungle that way. [taking LINDA's hand and bowing] It was an honor and a pleasure to meet you, Linda.

LINDA [withdrawing her hand coldly, frightened] Have a nice—trip.

BEN [to WILLY] And good luck with your—what do you do?

WILLY Selling.

BEN Yes. Well . . . [He raises his hand in farewell to all.]

WILLY No, Ben, I don't want you to think . . . [He takes BEN's arm to show him.] It's Brooklyn, I know, but we hunt too.

BEN Really, now.

WILLY   Oh, sure, there's snakes and rabbits and—that's why I moved out here. Why, Biff can fell any one of these trees in no time! Boys! Go right over to where they're building the apartment house and get some sand. We're gonna rebuild the entire front stoop right now! Watch this, Ben!

BIFF   Yes, sir! On the double, Hap!

HAPPY [*as he and* BIFF *run off*]   I lost weight, Pop, you notice?

[CHARLEY *enters in knickers, even before the boys are gone.*]

CHARLEY   Listen, if they steal any more from that building the watchman'll put the cops on them!

LINDA [*to* WILLY]   Don't let Biff . . .

[BEN *laughs lustily.*]

WILLY   You shoulda seen the lumber they brought home last week. At least a dozen six-by-tens worth all kinds a money.

CHARLEY   Listen, if that watchman—

WILLY   I gave them hell, understand. But I got a couple of fearless characters there.

CHARLEY   Willy, the jails are full of fearless characters.

BEN [*clapping* WILLY *on the back, with a laugh at* CHARLEY]   And the stock exchange, friend!

WILLY [*joining in* BEN'S *laughter*]   Where are the rest of your pants?

CHARLEY   My wife bought them.

WILLY   Now all you need is a golf club and you can go upstairs and go to sleep. [*to* BEN] Great athlete! Between him and his son Bernard they can't hammer a nail!

BERNARD [*rushing in*]   The watchman's chasing Biff!

WILLY [*angrily*]   Shut up! He's not stealing anything!

LINDA [*alarmed, hurrying off left*]   Where is he? Biff, dear! [*She exits.*]

WILLY [*moving toward the left, away from* BEN]   There's nothing wrong. What's the matter with you?

BEN   Nervy boy. Good!

WILLY [*laughing*]   Oh, nerves of iron, that Biff!

CHARLEY   Don't know what it is. My New England man comes back and he's bleedin', they murdered him up there.

WILLY   It's contacts, Charley, I got important contacts!

CHARLEY [*sarcastically*]   Glad to hear it, Willy. Come in later, we'll shoot a little casino. I'll take some of your Portland money. [*He laughs at* WILLY *and exits.*]

WILLY [*turning to* BEN]   Business is bad, it's murderous. But not for me, of course.

BEN   I'll stop by on my way back to Africa.

WILLY [*longingly*]   Can't you stay a few days? You're just what I need, Ben, because I—I have a fine position here, but I—well, Dad left when I was such a baby and I never had a chance to talk to him and I still feel— kind of temporary about myself.

BEN   I'll be late for my train.

[*They are at opposite ends of the stage.*]

WILLY   Ben, my boys—can't we talk? They'd go into the jaws of hell for me, see, but I—

BEN   William, you're being first-rate with your boys. Outstanding, manly chaps!

WILLY [*hanging on to his words*]   Oh, Ben, that's good to hear! Because sometimes I'm afraid that I'm not teaching them the right kind of—Ben, how should I teach them?

BEN [*giving great weight to each word, and with a certain vicious audacity*]   William, when I walked into the jungle, I was seventeen. When I walked out I was twenty-one. And, by God, I was rich! [*He goes off into darkness around the right corner of the house.*]

WILLY   . . . was rich! That's just the spirit I want to imbue them with! To walk into a jungle! I was right! I was right! I was right!

[BEN *is gone, but* WILLY *is still speaking to him as* LINDA, *in nightgown and robe, enters the kitchen, glances around for* WILLY, *then goes to the door of the house, looks out and sees him. Comes down to his left. He looks at her.*]

LINDA   Willy, dear? Willy?

WILLY   I was right!

LINDA   Did you have some cheese? [*He can't answer.*] It's very late, darling. Come to bed, heh?

WILLY [*looking straight up*]   Gotta break your neck to see a star in this yard.

LINDA   You coming in?

WILLY   Whatever happened to that diamond watch fob? Remember? When Ben came from Africa that time? Didn't he give me a watch fob with a diamond in it?

LINDA   You pawned it, dear. Twelve, thirteen years ago. For Biff's radio correspondence course.

WILLY   Gee, that was a beautiful thing. I'll take a walk.

LINDA   But you're in your slippers.

WILLY [*starting to go around the house at the left*]   I was right! I was! [*half to* LINDA, *as he goes, shaking his head*] What a man! There was a man worth talking to. I was right!

LINDA [*calling after* WILLY]   But in your slippers, Willy!

[WILLY *is almost gone when* BIFF, *in his pajamas, comes down the stairs and enters the kitchen.*]

BIFF   What is he doing out there?

LINDA   Sh!

BIFF   God Almighty, Mom, how long has he been doing this?

LINDA   Don't, he'll hear you.

BIFF   What the hell is the matter with him?

LINDA   It'll pass by morning.

BIFF   Shouldn't we do anything?

LINDA   Oh, my dear, you should do a lot of things, but there's nothing to do so go to sleep.

[HAPPY *comes down the stairs and sits on the steps.*]

HAPPY   I never heard him so loud, Mom.

LINDA   Well, come around more often; you'll hear him. [*She sits down at the table and mends the lining of* WILLY's *jacket.*]

BIFF   Why didn't you ever write me about this, Mom?

LINDA   How would I write to you? For over three months you had no address.

BIFF   I was on the move. But you know I thought of you all the time. You know that, don't you, pal?

LINDA   I know, dear, I know. But he likes to have a letter. Just to know that there's still a possibility for better things.

BIFF   He's not like this all the time, is he?

LINDA   It's when you come home he's always the worst.

BIFF   When I come home?

LINDA   When you write you're coming, he's all smiles, and talks about the future, and—he's just wonderful. And then the closer you seem to come, the more shaky he gets, and then, by the time you get here, he's arguing, and he seems angry at you. I think it's just that maybe he can't bring himself to—to open up to you. Why are you so hateful to each other? Why is that?

BIFF [*evasively*]   I'm not hateful, Mom.

LINDA   But you no sooner come in the door than you're fighting!

BIFF   I don't know why. I mean to change. I'm tryin', Mom, you understand?

LINDA   Are you home to stay now?

BIFF   I don't know. I want to look around, see what's doin'.

LINDA   Biff, you can't look around all your life, can you?

BIFF   I just can't take hold, Mom. I can't take hold of some kind of a life.

LINDA   Biff, a man is not a bird, to come and go with the springtime.

BIFF   Your hair . . . [*He touches her hair.*] Your hair got so gray.

LINDA   Oh, it's been gray since you were in high school. I just stopped dyeing it, that's all.

BIFF   Dye it again, will ya? I don't want my pal looking old. [*He smiles.*]

LINDA   You're such a boy! You think you can go away for a year and . . . You've got to get it into your head now that one day you'll knock on this door and there'll be strange people here—

BIFF   What are you talking about? You're not even sixty, Mom.

LINDA   But what about your father?

BIFF [*lamely*]   Well, I meant him too.

HAPPY   He admires Pop.

LINDA   Biff, dear, if you don't have any feeling for him, then you can't have any feeling for me.

BIFF   Sure I can, Mom.

LINDA   No. You can't just come to see me, because I love him. [*with a threat, but only a threat, of tears*] He's the dearest man in the world to me, and I won't have anyone making him feel unwanted and low and blue. You've got to make up your mind now, darling, there's no leeway any more. Either he's your father and you pay him that respect, or else you're not to come here. I know he's not easy to get along with—nobody knows that better than me—but . . .

WILLY [*from the left, with a laugh*]   Hey, hey, Biffo!

BIFF [*starting to go out after* WILLY]   What the hell is the matter with him? [HAPPY *stops him.*]

LINDA   Don't—don't go near him!

BIFF   Stop making excuses for him! He always, always wiped the floor with you. Never had an ounce of respect for you.

HAPPY   He's always had respect for—

BIFF   What the hell do you know about it?

HAPPY [*surlily*]   Just don't call him crazy!

BIFF   He's got no character—Charley wouldn't do this. Not in his own house—spewing out that vomit from his mind.

HAPPY   Charley never had to cope with what he's got to.

BIFF   People are worse off than Willy Loman. Believe me, I've seen them!

LINDA   Then make Charley your father, Biff. You can't do that, can you? I don't say he's a great man. Willy Loman never made a lot of money. His name was never in the paper. He's not the finest character that ever lived. But he's a human being, and a terrible thing is happening to him. So attention must be paid. He's not to be allowed to fall into his grave like an old dog. Attention, attention must be finally paid to such a person. You called him crazy—

BIFF   I didn't mean—

LINDA   No, a lot of people think he's lost his—balance. But you don't have to be very smart to know what his trouble is. The man is exhausted.

HAPPY   Sure!

LINDA   A small man can be just as exhausted as a great man. He works for a company thirty-six years this March, opens up unheard-of territories to their trademark, and now in his old age they take his salary away.

HAPPY [*indignantly*]   I didn't know that, Mom.

LINDA   You never asked, my dear! Now that you get your spending money someplace else you don't trouble your mind with him.

HAPPY   But I gave you money last—

LINDA   Christmas time, fifty dollars! To fix the hot water it cost ninety-seven fifty! For five weeks he's been on straight commission, like a beginner, an unknown!

BIFF   Those ungrateful bastards!

LINDA   Are they any worse than his sons? When he brought them business, when he was young, they were glad to see him. But now his old friends, the old buyers that loved him so and always found some order to hand him in a pinch—they're all dead, retired. He used to be able to make six, seven calls a day in Boston. Now he takes his valises out of the car and puts them back and takes them out again and he's exhausted. Instead of walking he talks now. He drives seven hundred miles, and when he gets there no one knows him any more, no one welcomes him. And what goes through a man's mind, driving seven hundred miles home without having earned a cent? Why shouldn't he talk to himself? Why? When he has to go to Charley and borrow fifty dollars a week and pretend to me that it's his pay? How long can that go on? How long? You see what I'm sitting here and waiting for? And you tell me he has no character? The man who never worked a day but for your benefit? When does he get the medal for that? Is this his reward—to turn around at the age of sixty-three and find his sons, who he loved better than his life, one a philandering bum—

HAPPY   Mom!

LINDA   That's all you are, my baby! [*to* BIFF] And you! What happened to the love you had for him? You were such pals! How you used to talk to him on the phone every night! How lonely he was till he could come home to you!

BIFF   All right, Mom. I'll live here in my room, and I'll get a job. I'll keep away from him, that's all.

LINDA   No, Biff. You can't stay here and fight all the time.

BIFF   He threw me out of this house, remember that.

LINDA   Why did he do that? I never knew why.

BIFF   Because I know he's a fake and he doesn't like anybody around who knows!

LINDA   Why a fake? In what way? What do you mean?

BIFF   Just don't lay it all at my feet. It's between me and him—that's all I have to say. I'll chip in from now on. He'll settle for half my pay check. He'll be all right. I'm going to bed. [*He starts for the stairs.*]

LINDA   He won't be all right.

BIFF   [*turning on the stairs, furiously*]   I hate this city and I'll stay here. Now what do you want?

LINDA   He's dying, Biff.

        [HAPPY *turns quickly to her, shocked.*]

BIFF   [*after a pause*]   Why is he dying?

LINDA   He's been trying to kill himself.

BIFF   [*with great horror*]   How?

LINDA   I live from day to day.

BIFF   What're you talking about?

LINDA   Remember I wrote you that he smashed up the car again? In February?

BIFF   Well?

LINDA   The insurance inspector came. He said that they have evidence. That all these accidents in the last year—weren't—weren't—accidents.

HAPPY   How can they tell that? That's a lie.

LINDA   It seems there's a woman . . . [*she takes a breath as*]

⎧BIFF   [*sharply but contained*]   What woman?
⎩LINDA   [*simultaneously*]   . . . and this woman . . .

LINDA   What?

BIFF   Nothing. Go ahead.

LINDA   What did you say?

BIFF   Nothing. I just said what woman?

HAPPY   What about her?

LINDA   Well, it seems she was walking down the road and saw his car. She says that he wasn't driving fast at all, and that he didn't skid. She says he came to that little bridge, and then deliberately smashed into the railing, and it was only the shallowness of the water that saved him.

BIFF   Oh, no, he probably just fell asleep again.

LINDA   I don't think he fell asleep.

BIFF   Why not?

LINDA   Last month . . . [*with great difficulty*] Oh, boys, it's so hard to say a thing like this! He's just a big stupid man to you, but I tell you there's more good in him than in many other people. [*She chokes, wipes her eyes.*] I was looking for a fuse. The lights blew out, and I went down the cellar.

And behind the fuse box—it happened to fall out—was a length of rubber pipe—just short.

HAPPY   No kidding?

LINDA   There's a little attachment on the end of it. I knew right away. And sure enough, on the bottom of the water heater there's a new little nipple on the gas pipe.

HAPPY [*angrily*]   That—jerk.

BIFF   Did you have it taken off?

LINDA   I'm—I'm ashamed to. How can I mention it to him? Every day I go down and take away that little rubber pipe. But, when he comes home, I put it back where it was. How can I insult him that way? I don't know what to do. I live from day to day, boys. I tell you, I know every thought in his mind. It sounds so old-fashioned and silly, but I tell you he put his whole life into you and you've turned your backs on him. [*She is bent over in the chair, weeping, her face in her hands.*] Biff, I swear to God! Biff, his life is in your hands!

HAPPY [*to* BIFF]   How do you like that damned fool!

BIFF [*kissing her*]   All right, pal, all right. It's all settled now. I've been remiss. I know that, Mom. But now I'll stay, and I swear to you, I'll apply myself. [*kneeling in front of her, in a fever of self-reproach*] It's just—you see, Mom, I don't fit in business. Not that I won't try. I'll try, and I'll make good.

HAPPY   Sure you will. The trouble with you in business was you never tried to please people.

BIFF   I know, I—

HAPPY   Like when you worked for Harrison's. Bob Harrison said you were tops, and then you go and do some damn fool thing like whistling whole songs in the elevator like a comedian.

BIFF [*against* HAPPY]   So what? I like to whistle sometimes.

HAPPY   You don't raise a guy to a responsible job who whistles in the elevator!

LINDA   Well, don't argue about it now.

HAPPY   Like when you'd go off and swim in the middle of the day instead of taking the line around.

BIFF [*his resentment rising*]   Well, don't you run off? You take off sometimes, don't you? On a nice summer day?

HAPPY   Yeah, but I cover myself!

LINDA   Boys!

HAPPY   If I'm going to take a fade the boss can call any number where I'm supposed to be and they'll swear to him that I just left. I'll tell you something that I hate to say, Biff, but in the business world some of them think you're crazy.

BIFF [*angered*]   Screw the business world!

HAPPY   All right, screw it! Great, but cover yourself!

LINDA   Hap, Hap!

BIFF   I don't care what they think! They've laughed at Dad for years, and you know why? Because we don't belong in this nuthouse of a city! We should be mixing cement on some open plain, or—or carpenters. A carpenter is allowed to whistle!

[WILLY *walks in from the entrance of the house, at left.*]

WILLY   Even your grandfather was better than a carpenter. [*Pause. They watch him.*] You never grew up. Bernard does not whistle in the elevator, I assure you.

BIFF [*as though to laugh* WILLY *out of it*]   Yeah, but you do, Pop.

WILLY   I never in my life whistled in an elevator! And who in the business world thinks I'm crazy?

BIFF   I didn't mean it like that, Pop. Now don't make a whole thing out of it, will ya?

WILLY   Go back to the West! Be a carpenter, a cowboy, enjoy yourself!

LINDA   Willy, he was just saying—

WILLY   I heard what he said!

HAPPY [*trying to quiet* WILLY]   Hey, Pop, come on now . . .

WILLY [*continuing over* HAPPY'*s line*]   They laugh at me, heh? Go to Filene's, go to the Hub, go to Slattery's, Boston. Call out the name Willy Loman and see what happens! Big Shot!

BIFF   All right, Pop.

WILLY   Big!

BIFF   All right!

WILLY   Why do you always insult me?

BIFF   I didn't say a word. [*to* LINDA] Did I say a word?

LINDA   He didn't say anything, Willy.

WILLY [*going to the doorway of the living-room*]   All right, good night, good night.

LINDA   Willy, dear, he just decided . . .

WILLY [*to* BIFF]   If you get tired hanging around tomorrow, paint the ceiling I put up in the living-room.

BIFF   I'm leaving early tomorrow.

HAPPY   He's going to see Bill Oliver, Pop.

WILLY [*interestedly*]   Oliver? For what?

BIFF [*with reserve, but trying, trying*]   He always said he'd stake me. I'd like to go into business, so maybe I can take him up on it.

LINDA   Isn't that wonderful?

WILLY   Don't interrupt. What's wonderful about it? There's fifty men in the City of New York who'd stake him. [*to* BIFF] Sporting goods?

BIFF   I guess so. I know something about it and—

WILLY   He knows something about it! You know sporting goods better than Spalding, for God's sake! How much is he giving you?

BIFF   I don't know, I didn't even see him yet, but—

WILLY   Then what're you talkin' about?

BIFF [*getting angry*]   Well, all I said was I'm gonna see him, that's all!

WILLY [*turning away*]   Ah, you're counting your chickens again.

BIFF [*starting left for the stairs*]   Oh, Jesus, I'm going to sleep!

WILLY [*calling after him*]   Don't curse in this house!

BIFF [*turning*]   Since when did you get so clean?

HAPPY [*trying to stop them*]   Wait a . . .

WILLY   Don't use that language to me! I won't have it!

HAPPY [*grabbing* BIFF, *shouts*]   Wait a minute! I got an idea. I got a feasible idea. Come here, Biff, let's talk this over now, let's talk some sense here. When I was down in Florida last time, I thought of a great idea to sell sporting goods. It just came back to me. You and I, Biff—we have a line, the Loman Line. We train a couple of weeks, and put on a couple of exhibitions, see?

WILLY That's an idea!

HAPPY Wait! We form two basketball teams, see? Two water-polo teams. We play each other. It's a million dollars' worth of publicity. Two brothers, see? The Loman Brothers. Displays in the Royal Palms—all the hotels. And banners over the ring and the basketball court: "Loman Brothers." Baby, we could sell sporting goods!

WILLY That is a one-million-dollar idea!

LINDA Marvelous!

BIFF I'm in great shape as far as that's concerned.

HAPPY And the beauty of it is, Biff, it wouldn't be like a business. We'd be out playin' ball again . . .

BIFF [enthused] Yeah, that's . . .

WILLY Million-dollar . . .

HAPPY And you wouldn't get fed up with it, Biff. It'd be the family again. There'd be the old honor, and comradeship, and if you wanted to go off for a swim or somethin'—well, you'd do it! Without some smart cooky gettin' up ahead of you!

WILLY Lick the world! You guys together could absolutely lick the civilized world.

BIFF I'll see Oliver tomorrow. Hap, if we could work that out . . .

LINDA Maybe things are beginning to—

WILLY [wildly enthused, to LINDA] Stop interrupting! [to BIFF] But don't wear sport jacket and slacks when you see Oliver.

BIFF No, I'll—

WILLY A business suit, and talk as little as possible, and don't crack any jokes.

BIFF He did like me. Always liked me.

LINDA He loved you!

WILLY [to LINDA] Will you stop! [to BIFF] Walk in very serious. You are not applying for a boy's job. Money is to pass. Be quiet, fine, and serious. Everybody likes a kidder, but nobody lends him money.

HAPPY I'll try to get some myself, Biff. I'm sure I can.

WILLY I see great things for you kids, I think your troubles are over. But remember, start big and you'll end big. Ask for fifteen. How much you gonna ask for?

BIFF Gee, I don't know—

WILLY And don't say "Gee." "Gee" is a boy's word. A man walking in for fifteen thousand dollars does not say "Gee!"

BIFF Ten, I think, would be top though.

WILLY Don't be so modest. You always started too low. Walk in with a big laugh. Don't look worried. Start off with a couple of your good stories to lighten things up. It's not what you say, it's how you say it—because personality always wins the day.

LINDA Oliver always thought the highest of him—

WILLY Will you let me talk?

BIFF Don't yell at her, Pop, will ya?

WILLY [*angrily*] I was talking, wasn't I?

BIFF I don't like you yelling at her all the time, and I'm tellin' you, that's all.

WILLY What're you, takin' over this house?

LINDA Willy—

WILLY [*turning on her*] Don't take his side all the time, goddammit!

BIFF [*furiously*] Stop yelling at her!

WILLY [*suddenly pulling on his cheek, beaten down, guilt ridden*] Give my best to Bill Oliver—he may remember me. [*He exits through the living-room doorway.*]

LINDA [*her voice subdued*] What'd you have to start that for? [BIFF *turns away.*] You see how sweet he was as soon as you talked hopefully? [*She goes over to* BIFF.] Come up and say good night to him. Don't let him go to bed that way.

HAPPY Come on, Biff, let's buck him up.

LINDA Please, dear. Just say good night. It takes so little to make him happy. Come. [*She goes through the living-room doorway, calling upstairs from within the living-room*] Your pajamas are hanging in the bathroom, Willy!

HAPPY [*looking toward where* LINDA *went out*] What a woman! They broke the mold when they made her. You know that, Biff?

BIFF He's off salary. My God, working on commission!

HAPPY Well, let's face it: he's no hot-shot selling man. Except that sometimes, you have to admit, he's a sweet personality.

BIFF [*deciding*] Lend me ten bucks, will ya? I want to buy some new ties.

HAPPY I'll take you to a place I know. Beautiful stuff. Wear one of my striped shirts tomorrow.

BIFF She got gray. Mom got awful old. Gee, I'm gonna go in to Oliver tomorrow and knock him for a—

HAPPY Come on up. Tell that to Dad. Let's give him a whirl. Come on.

BIFF [*steamed up*] You know, with ten thousand bucks, boy!

HAPPY [*as they go into the living-room*] That's the talk, Biff, that's the first time I've heard the old confidence out of you! [*from within the living-room, fading off*] You're gonna live with me, kid, and any babe you want just say the word . . . [*The last lines are hardly heard. They are mounting the stairs to their parents' bedroom.*]

LINDA [*entering her bedroom and addressing* WILLY, *who is in the bathroom. She is straightening the bed for him.*] Can you do anything about the shower? It drips.

WILLY [*from the bathroom*] All of a sudden everything falls to pieces! Goddam plumbing, oughta be sued, those people. I hardly finished putting it in and the thing . . . [*His words rumble off.*]

LINDA I'm just wondering if Oliver will remember him. You think he might?

WILLY [*coming out of the bathroom in his pajamas*] Remember him? What's the matter with you, you crazy? If he'd've stayed with Oliver he'd be on top by now! Wait'll Oliver gets a look at him. You don't know the average caliber any more. The average young man today—[*he is getting into bed*]—is got a caliber of zero. Greatest thing in the world for him was to bum around.

[BIFF *and* HAPPY *enter the bedroom. Slight pause.*]

WILLY [*stops short, looking at* BIFF]   Glad to hear it, boy.

HAPPY   He wanted to say good night to you, sport.

WILLY [*to* BIFF]   Yeah. Knock him dead, boy. What'd you want to tell me?

BIFF   Just take it easy, Pop. Good night. [*He turns to go.*]

WILLY [*unable to resist*]   And if anything falls off the desk while you're talking to him—like a package or something—don't you pick it up. They have office boys for that.

LINDA   I'll make a big breakfast—

WILLY   Will you let me finish? [*to* BIFF] Tell him you were in the business in the West. Not farm work.

BIFF   All right, Dad.

LINDA   I think everything—

WILLY [*going right through her speech*]   And don't undersell yourself. No less than fifteen thousand dollars.

BIFF [*unable to bear him*]   Okay. Good night, Mom. [*He starts moving.*]

WILLY   Because you got a greatness in you, Biff, remember that. You got all kinds a greatness . . . [*He lies back, exhausted.* BIFF *walks out.*]

LINDA [*calling after* BIFF]   Sleep well, darling!

HAPPY   I'm gonna get married, Mom. I wanted to tell you.

LINDA   Go to sleep, dear.

HAPPY [*going*]   I just wanted to tell you.

WILLY   Keep up the good work. [HAPPY *exits.*] God . . . remember that Ebbets Field[5] game? The championship of the city?

LINDA   Just rest. Should I sing to you?

WILLY   Yeah. Sing to me. [LINDA *hums a soft lullaby.*] When that team came out—he was the tallest, remember?

LINDA   Oh, yes. And in gold.
[BIFF *enters the darkened kitchen, takes a cigarette, and leaves the house. He comes downstage into a golden pool of light. He smokes, staring at the night.*]

WILLY   Like a young god. Hercules[6]—something like that. And the sun, the sun all around him. Remember how he waved to me? Right up from the field, with the representatives of three colleges standing by? And the buyers I brought, and the cheers when he came out—Loman, Loman, Loman! God Almighty, he'll be great yet. A star like that, magnificent, can never really fade away!
[*The light on* WILLY *is fading. The gas heater begins to glow through the kitchen wall, near the stairs, a blue flame beneath red coils.*]

LINDA [*timidly*]   Willy dear, what has he got against you?

WILLY   I'm so tired. Don't talk any more.
[BIFF *slowly returns to the kitchen. He stops, stares toward the heater.*]

LINDA   Will you ask Howard to let you work in New York?

WILLY   First thing in the morning. Everything'll be all right.
[BIFF *reaches behind the heater and draws out a length of rubber tubing. He is horrified and turns his head toward* WILLY'S *room, still dimly lit, from which the strains of* LINDA'S *desperate but monotonous humming rise.*]

---

5. Brooklyn sports stadium.
6. In Greek and Roman mythology the son of the chief god (Zeus, Jupiter), famous for his great strength.

WILLY [*staring through the window into the moonlight*]   Gee, look at the moon moving between the buildings!

[BIFF *wraps the tubing around his hand and quickly goes up the stairs.*]

CURTAIN

Act Two

Music is heard, gay and bright. The curtain rises as the music fades away. WILLY, *in shirt sleeves, is sitting at the kitchen table, sipping coffee, his hat in his lap.* LINDA *is filling his cup when she can.*

WILLY   Wonderful coffee. Meal in itself.

LINDA   Can I make you some eggs?

WILLY   No. Take a breath.

LINDA   You look so rested, dear.

WILLY   I slept like a dead one. First time in months. Imagine, sleeping till ten on a Tuesday morning. Boys left nice and early, heh?

LINDA   They were out of here by eight o'clock.

WILLY   Good work!

LINDA   It was so thrilling to see them leaving together. I can't get over the shaving lotion in this house!

WILLY [*smiling*]   Mmm—

LINDA   Biff was very changed this morning. His whole attitude seemed to be hopeful. He couldn't wait to get downtown to see Oliver.

WILLY   He's heading for a change. There's no question, there simply are certain men that take longer to get—solidified. How did he dress?

LINDA   His blue suit. He's so handsome in that suit. He could be a— anything in that suit!

[WILLY *gets up from the table.* LINDA *holds his jacket for him.*]

WILLY   There's no question, no question at all. Gee, on the way home tonight I'd like to buy some seeds.

LINDA [*laughing*]   That'd be wonderful. But not enough sun gets back there. Nothing'll grow any more.

WILLY   You wait, kid, before it's all over we're gonna get a little place out in the country, and I'll raise some vegetables, a couple of chickens . . .

LINDA   You'll do it yet, dear.

[WILLY *walks out of his jacket.* LINDA *follows him.*]

WILLY   And they'll get married, and come for a weekend. I'd build a little guest house. 'Cause I got so many fine tools, all I'd need would be a little lumber and some peace of mind.

LINDA [*joyfully*]   I sewed the lining . . .

WILLY   I could build two guest houses, so they'd both come. Did he decide how much he's going to ask Oliver for?

LINDA [*getting him into the jacket*]   He didn't mention it, but I imagine ten or fifteen thousand. You going to talk to Howard today?

WILLY   Yeah. I'll put it to him straight and simple. He'll just have to take me off the road.

LINDA   And Willy, don't forget to ask for a little advance, because we've got the insurance premium. It's the grace period now.

WILLY   That's a hundred . . . ?

LINDA   A hundred and eight, sixty-eight. Because we're a little short again.

WILLY   Why are we short?

LINDA   Well, you had the motor job on the car . . .

WILLY   That goddam Studebaker!

LINDA   And you got one more payment on the refrigerator . . .

WILLY   But it just broke again!

LINDA   Well, it's old, dear.

WILLY   I told you we should've bought a well-advertised machine. Charley bought a General Electric and it's twenty years old and it's still good, that son-of-a-bitch.

LINDA   But, Willy—

WILLY   Whoever heard of a Hastings refrigerator? Once in my life I would like to own something outright before it's broken! I'm always in a race with the junkyard! I just finished paying for the car and it's on its last legs. The refrigerator consumes belts like a goddam maniac. They time those things. They time them so when you finally paid for them, they're used up.

LINDA   [buttoning up his jacket as he unbuttons it]   All told, about two hundred dollars would carry us, dear. But that includes the last payment on the mortgage. After this payment, Willy, the house belongs to us.

WILLY   It's twenty-five years!

LINDA   Biff was nine years old when we bought it.

WILLY   Well, that's a great thing. To weather a twenty-five year mortgage is—

LINDA   It's an accomplishment.

WILLY   All the cement, the lumber, the reconstruction I put in this house! There ain't a crack to be found in it anymore.

LINDA   Well, it served its purpose.

WILLY   What purpose? Some stranger'll come along, move in, and that's that. If only Biff would take this house, and raise a family . . . [He starts to go.] Good-by, I'm late.

LINDA   [suddenly remembering]   Oh, I forgot! You're supposed to meet them for dinner.

WILLY   Me?

LINDA   At Frank's Chop House on Forty-eighth near Sixth Avenue.

WILLY   Is that so! How about you?

LINDA   No, just the three of you. They're gonna blow you to a big meal!

WILLY   Don't say! Who thought of that?

LINDA   Biff came to me this morning, Willy, and he said, "Tell Dad, we want to blow him to a big meal." Be there six o'clock. You and your two boys are going to have dinner.

WILLY   Gee whiz! That's really somethin'. I'm gonna knock Howard for a loop, kid. I'll get an advance, and I'll come home with a New York job. Goddammit, now I'm gonna do it!

LINDA   Oh, that's the spirit, Willy!

WILLY   I will never get behind a wheel the rest of my life!

LINDA   It's changing, Willy, I can feel it changing!

WILLY   Beyond a question. G'by, I'm late. [He starts to go again.]

LINDA   [calling after him as she runs to the kitchen table for a handkerchief] You got your glasses?

WILLY [*feels for them, then comes back in*]   Yeah, yeah, got my glasses.

LINDA [*giving him the handkerchief*]   And a handkerchief.

WILLY   Yeah, handkerchief.

LINDA   And your saccharine?

WILLY   Yeah, my saccharine.

LINDA   Be careful on the subway stairs.
[*She kisses him, and a silk stocking is seen hanging from her hand.* WILLY *notices it.*]

WILLY   Will you stop mending stockings? At least while I'm in the house. It gets me nervous. I can't tell you. Please.
[LINDA *hides the stocking in her hand as she follows* WILLY *across the forestage in front of the house.*]

LINDA   Remember, Frank's Chop House.

WILLY [*passing the apron*]   Maybe beets would grow out there.

LINDA [*laughing*]   But you tried so many times.

WILLY   Yeah. Well, don't work hard today. [*He disappears around the right corner of the house.*]

LINDA   Be careful!
[*As* WILLY *vanishes,* LINDA *waves to him. Suddenly the phone rings. She runs across the stage and into the kitchen and lifts it.*]

LINDA   Hello? Oh, Biff! I'm so glad you called, I just . . . Yes, sure, I just told him. Yes, he'll be there for dinner at six o'clock, I didn't forget. Listen, I was just dying to tell you. You know that little rubber pipe I told you about? That he connected to the gas heater? I finally decided to go down the cellar this morning and take it away and destroy it. But it's gone! Imagine? He took it away himself, it isn't there! [*She listens.*] When? Oh, then you took it. Oh—nothing, it's just that I'd hoped he'd taken it away himself. Oh, I'm not worried, darling, because this morning he left in such high spirits, it was like the old days! I'm not afraid any more. Did Mr. Oliver see you? . . . Well, you wait there then. And make a nice impression on him, darling. Just don't perspire too much before you see him. And have a nice time with Dad. He may have big news too! . . . That's right, a New York job. And be sweet to him tonight, dear. Be loving to him. Because he's only a little boat looking for a harbor. [*She is trembling with sorrow and joy.*] Oh, that's wonderful, Biff, you'll save his life. Thanks, darling. Just put your arm around him when he comes into the restaurant. Give him a smile. That's the boy . . . Good-by, dear. . . . You got your comb? . . . That's fine. Good-by, Biff dear.
[*In the middle of her speech,* HOWARD WAGNER, *thirty-six, wheels in a small typewriter table on which is a wire-recording machine and proceeds to plug it in. This is on the left forestage. Light slowly fades on* LINDA *as it rises on* HOWARD. HOWARD *is intent on threading the machine and only glances over his shoulder as* WILLY *appears.*]

WILLY   Pst! Pst!

HOWARD   Hello, Willy, come in.

WILLY   Like to have a little talk with you, Howard.

HOWARD   Sorry to keep you waiting. I'll be with you in a minute.

WILLY   What's that, Howard?

HOWARD   Didn't you ever see one of these? Wire recorder.

WILLY   Oh. Can we talk a minute?

HOWARD Records things. Just got delivery yesterday. Been driving me crazy, the most terrific machine I ever saw in my life. I was up all night with it.

WILLY What do you do with it?

HOWARD I bought it for dictation, but you can do anything with it. Listen to this. I had it home last night. Listen to what I picked up. The first one is my daughter. Get this. [*He flicks the switch and "Roll out the Barrel" is heard being whistled.*] Listen to that kid whistle.

WILLY That is lifelike, isn't it?

HOWARD Seven years old. Get that tone.

WILLY Ts, ts. Like to ask a little favor if you . . .
        [*The whistling breaks off, and the voice of* HOWARD'*s daughter is heard.*]

HIS DAUGHTER "Now you, Daddy."

HOWARD She's crazy for me! [*Again the same song is whistled.*] That's me! Ha! [*He winks.*]

WILLY You're very good!
        [*The whistling breaks off again. The machine runs silent for a moment.*]

HOWARD Sh! Get this now, this is my son.

HIS SON "The capital of Alabama is Montgomery; the capital of Arizona is Phoenix; the capital of Arkansas is Little Rock; the capital of California is Sacramento . . ." [*and on, and on*]

HOWARD [*holding up five fingers*] Five years old, Willy!

WILLY He'll make an announcer some day!

HIS SON [*continuing*] "The capital . . ."

HOWARD Get that—alphabetical order! [*The machine breaks off suddenly.*] Wait a minute. The maid kicked the plug out.

WILLY It certainly is a—

HOWARD Sh, for God's sake!

HIS SON "It's nine o'clock, Bulova watch time. So I have to go to sleep."

WILLY That really is—

HOWARD Wait a minute! The next is my wife.
        [*They wait.*]

HOWARD'S VOICE "Go on, say something." [*pause*] "Well, you gonna talk?"

HIS WIFE "I can't think of anything."

HOWARD'S VOICE "Well, talk—it's turning."

HIS WIFE [*shyly, beaten*] "Hello." [*silence*] "Oh, Howard, I can't talk into this . . ."

HOWARD [*snapping the machine off*] That was my wife.

WILLY That is a wonderful machine. Can we—

HOWARD I tell you, Willy, I'm gonna take my camera, and my handsaw, and all my hobbies, and out they go. This is the most fascinating relaxation I ever found.

WILLY I think I'll get one myself.

HOWARD Sure, they're only a hundred and a half. You can't do without it. Supposing you wanna hear Jack Benny,[7] see? But you can't be at home at that hour. So you tell the maid to turn the radio on when Jack Benny comes on, and this automatically goes on with the radio . . .

---

7. Vastly popular radio comedian of the 1930s and 1940s.

WILLY   And when you come home you . . .

HOWARD   You can come home twelve o'clock, one o'clock, any time you like, and you get yourself a Coke and sit yourself down, throw the switch, and there's Jack Benny's program in the middle of the night!

WILLY   I'm definitely going to get one. Because lots of time I'm on the road, and I think to myself, what I must be missing on the radio!

HOWARD   Don't you have a radio in the car?

WILLY   Well, yeah, but who ever thinks of turning it on?

HOWARD   Say, aren't you supposed to be in Boston?

WILLY   That's what I want to talk to you about, Howard. You got a minute? [He draws a chair in from the wing.]

HOWARD   What happened? What're you doing here?

WILLY   Well . . .

HOWARD   You didn't crack up again, did you?

WILLY   Oh, no. No . . .

HOWARD   Geez, you had me worried there for a minute. What's the trouble?

WILLY   Well, tell you the truth, Howard. I've come to the decision that I'd rather not travel any more.

HOWARD   Not travel! Well, what'll you do?

WILLY   Remember, Christmas time, when you had the party here? You said you'd try to think of some spot for me here in town.

HOWARD   With us?

WILLY   Well, sure.

HOWARD   Oh, yeah, yeah. I remember. Well, I couldn't think of anything for you, Willy.

WILLY   I tell ya, Howard. The kids are all grown up, y'know. I don't need much any more. If I could take home—well, sixty-five dollars a week, I could swing it.

HOWARD   Yeah, but Willy, see I—

WILLY   I tell ya why, Howard. Speaking frankly and between the two of us, y'know—I'm just a little tired.

HOWARD   Oh, I could understand that, Willy. But you're a road man, Willy, and we do a road business. We've only got a half-dozen salesmen on the floor here.

WILLY   God knows, Howard, I never asked a favor of any man. But I was with the firm when your father used to carry you in here in his arms.

HOWARD   I know that, Willy, but—

WILLY   Your father came to me the day you were born and asked me what I thought of the name of Howard, may he rest in peace.

HOWARD   I appreciate that, Willy, but there just is no spot here for you. If I had a spot I'd slam you right in, but I just don't have a single solitary spot.

    [He looks for his lighter. WILLY has picked it up and gives it to him. Pause.]

WILLY [with increasing anger]   Howard, all I need to set my table is fifty dollars a week.

HOWARD   But where am I going to put you, kid?

WILLY   Look, it isn't a question of whether I can sell merchandise, is it?

HOWARD   No, but it's a business, kid, and everybody's gotta pull his own weight.

WILLY [desperately]   Just let me tell you a story, Howard—

HOWARD   'Cause you gotta admit, business is business.

WILLY [*angrily*]   Business is definitely business, but just listen for a minute. You don't understand this. When I was a boy—eighteen, nineteen—I was already on the road. And there was a question in my mind as to whether selling had a future for me. Because in those days I had a yearning to go to Alaska. See, there were three gold strikes in one month in Alaska, and I felt like going out. Just for the ride, you might say.

HOWARD [*barely interested*]   Don't say.

WILLY   Oh, yeah, my father lived many years in Alaska. He was an adventurous man. We've got quite a little streak of self-reliance in our family. I thought I'd go out with my older brother and try to locate him, and maybe settle in the North with the old man. And I was almost decided to go, when I met a salesman in the Parker House. His name was Dave Singleman. And he was eighty-four years old, and he'd drummed merchandise in thirty-one states. And old Dave, he'd go up to his room, y'understand, put on his green velvet slippers—I'll never forget—and pick up his phone and call the buyers, and without ever leaving his room, at the age of eighty-four, he made a living. And when I saw that, I realized that selling was the greatest career a man could want. 'Cause what could be more satisfying than to be able to go, at the age of eighty-four, into twenty or thirty different cities, and pick up a phone, and be remembered and loved and helped by so many different people? Do you know? when he died—and by the way he died the death of a salesman, in his green velvet slippers in the smoker of the New York, New Haven and Hartford, going into Boston—when he died, hundreds of salesmen and buyers were at his funeral. Things were sad on a lotta trains for months after that. [*He stands up.* HOWARD *has not looked at him.*] In those days there was personality in it, Howard. There was respect, and comradeship, and gratitude in it. Today, it's all cut and dried, and there's no chance for bringing friendship to bear—or personality. You see what I mean? They don't know me anymore.

HOWARD [*moving away, toward the right*]   That's just the thing, Willy.

WILLY   If I had forty dollars a week—that's all I'd need. Forty dollars, Howard.

HOWARD   Kid, I can't take blood from a stone, I—

WILLY [*desperation is on him now*]   Howard, the year Al Smith[8] was nominated, your father came to me and—

HOWARD [*starting to go off*]   I've got to see some people, kid.

WILLY [*stopping him*]   I'm talking about your father! There were promises made across this desk! You mustn't tell me you've got people to see—I put thirty-four years into this firm, Howard, and now I can't pay my insurance! You can't eat the orange and throw the peel away—a man is not a piece of fruit! [*after a pause*] Now pay attention. Your father—in 1928 I had a big year. I averaged a hundred and seventy dollars a week in commissions.

HOWARD [*impatiently*]   Now, Willy, you never averaged—

WILLY [*banging his hand on the desk*]   I averaged a hundred and seventy dollars a week in the year of 1928! And your father came to me—or

---

8. Democratic candidate for president in 1928.

rather, I was in the office here—it was right over this desk—and he put his hand on my shoulder—

HOWARD [*getting up*]   You'll have to excuse me, Willy, I gotta see some people. Pull yourself together. [*going out*] I'll be back in a little while.

[*On* HOWARD's *exit, the light on his chair grows very bright and strange.*]

WILLY   Pull myself together! What the hell did I say to him? My God, I was yelling at him! How could I! [WILLY *breaks off, staring at the light, which occupies the chair, animating it. He approaches this chair, standing across the desk from it.*] Frank, Frank, don't you remember what you told me that time? How you put your hand on my shoulder, and Frank . . . [*He leans on the desk and as he speaks the dead man's name he accidentally switches on the recorder, and instantly*]

HOWARD'S SON   ". . . of New York is Albany. The capital of Ohio is Cincinnati, the capital of Rhode Island is . . ." [*The recitation continues.*]

WILLY [*leaping away with fright, shouting*]   Ha! Howard! Howard! Howard!

HOWARD [*rushing in*]   What happened?

WILLY [*pointing at the machine, which continues nasally, childishly, with the capital cities*]   Shut it off! Shut it off!

HOWARD [*pulling the plug out*]   Look, Willy . . .

WILLY [*pressing his hands to his eyes*]   I gotta get myself some coffee. I'll get some coffee . . .

[WILLY *starts to walk out.* HOWARD *stops him.*]

HOWARD [*rolling up the cord*]   Willy, look . . .

WILLY   I'll go to Boston.

HOWARD   Willy, you can't go to Boston for us.

WILLY   Why can't I go?

HOWARD   I don't want you to represent us. I've been meaning to tell you for a long time now.

WILLY   Howard, are you firing me?

HOWARD   I think you need a good long rest, Willy.

WILLY   Howard—

HOWARD   And when you feel better, come back, and we'll see if we can work something out.

WILLY   But I gotta earn money, Howard. I'm in no position to—

HOWARD   Where are your sons? Why don't your sons give you a hand?

WILLY   They're working on a very big deal.

HOWARD   This is no time for false pride, Willy. You go to your sons and you tell them that you're tired. You've got two great boys, haven't you?

WILLY   Oh, no question, no question, but in the meantime . . .

HOWARD   Then that's that, heh?

WILLY   All right, I'll go to Boston tomorrow.

HOWARD   No, no.

WILLY   I can't throw myself on my sons. I'm not a cripple!

HOWARD   Look, kid, I'm busy, I'm busy this morning.

WILLY [*grasping* HOWARD's *arm*]   Howard, you've got to let me go to Boston!

HOWARD [*hard, keeping himself under control*]   I've got a line of people to see this morning. Sit down, take five minutes, and pull yourself together, and then go home, will ya? I need the office, Willy. [*He starts to go, turns, remembering the recorder, starts to push off the table holding the recorder.*]

Oh, yeah. Whenever you can this week, stop by and drop off the samples. You'll feel better, Willy, and then come back and we'll talk. Pull yourself together, kid, there's people outside.

[HOWARD *exits, pushing the table off left.* WILLY *stares into space, exhausted. Now the music is heard—*BEN's *music—first distantly, then closer, closer. As* WILLY *speaks,* BEN *enters from the right. He carries valise and umbrella.*]

WILLY   Oh, Ben, how did you do it? What is the answer? Did you wind up the Alaska deal already?

BEN   Doesn't take much time if you know what you're doing. Just a short business trip. Boarding ship in an hour. Wanted to say good-by.

WILLY   Ben, I've got to talk to you.

BEN [*glancing at his watch*]   Haven't the time, William.

WILLY [*crossing the apron to* BEN]   Ben, nothing's working out. I don't know what to do.

BEN   Now, look here, William. I've bought timberland in Alaska and I need a man to look after things for me.

WILLY   God, timberland! Me and my boys in those grand outdoors!

BEN   You've a new continent at your doorstep, William. Get out of these cities, they're full of talk and time payments and courts of law. Screw on your fists and you can fight for a fortune up there.

WILLY   Yes, yes! Linda, Linda!

[LINDA *enters as of old, with the wash.*]

LINDA   Oh, you're back?

BEN   I haven't much time.

WILLY   No, wait! Linda, he's got a proposition for me in Alaska.

LINDA   But you've got— [*to* BEN] He's got a beautiful job here.

WILLY   But in Alaska, kid, I could—

LINDA   You're doing well enough, Willy!

BEN [*to* LINDA]   Enough for what, my dear?

LINDA [*frightened of* BEN *and angry at him*]   Don't say those things to him! Enough to be happy right here, right now. [*to* WILLY, *while* BEN *laughs*] Why must everybody conquer the world? You're well liked, and the boys love you, and someday—[*to* BEN]—why, old man Wagner told him just the other day that if he keeps it up he'll be a member of the firm, didn't he, Willy?

WILLY   Sure, sure. I am building something with this firm, Ben, and if a man is building something he must be on the right track, mustn't he?

BEN   What are you building? Lay your hand on it. Where is it?

WILLY [*hesitantly*]   That's true, Linda, there's nothing.

LINDA   Why? [*to* BEN] There's a man eighty-four years old—

WILLY   That's right, Ben, that's right. When I look at that man I say, what is there to worry about?

BEN   Bah!

WILLY   It's true, Ben. All he has to do is go into any city, pick up the phone, and he's making his living and you know why?

BEN [*picking up his valise*]   I've got to go.

WILLY [*holding* BEN *back*]   Look at this boy!

[BIFF, *in his high school sweater, enters carrying suitcase.* HAPPY *carries* BIFF's *shoulder guards, gold helmet, and football pants.*]

WILLY   Without a penny to his name, three great universities are begging for him, and from there the sky's the limit, because it's not what you do, Ben. It's who you know and the smile on your face! It's contacts, Ben, contacts! The whole wealth of Alaska passes over the lunch table at the Commodore Hotel, and that's the wonder, the wonder of this country, that a man can end with diamonds here on the basis of being liked! [*He turns to* BIFF.] And that's why when you get out on that field today it's important. Because thousands of people will be rooting for you and loving you. [*to* BEN, *who has again begun to leave*] And Ben! when he walks into a business office his name will sound out like a bell and all the doors will open to him! I've seen it, Ben, I've seen it a thousand times! You can't feel it with your hand like timber, but it's there!

BEN   Good-by, William.

WILLY   Ben, am I right? Don't you think I'm right? I value your advice.

BEN   There's a new continent at your doorstep, William. You could walk out rich. Rich! [*He is gone.*]

WILLY   We'll do it here, Ben! You hear me? We're gonna do it here!
      [*Young* BERNARD *rushes in. The gay music of the Boys is heard.*]

BERNARD   Oh, gee, I was afraid you left already!

WILLY   Why? What time is it?

BERNARD   It's half-past one!

WILLY   Well, come on, everybody! Ebbets Field next stop! Where's the pennants? [*He rushes through the wall-line of the kitchen and out into the living-room.*]

LINDA [*to* BIFF]   Did you pack fresh underwear?

BIFF [*who has been limbering up*]   I want to go!

BERNARD   Biff, I'm carrying your helmet, ain't I?

HAPPY   No, I'm carrying the helmet.

BERNARD   Oh, Biff, you promised me.

HAPPY   I'm carrying the helmet.

BERNARD   How am I going to get in the locker room?

LINDA   Let him carry the shoulder guards. [*She puts her coat and hat on in the kitchen.*]

BERNARD   Can I, Biff? 'Cause I told everybody I'm going to be in the locker room.

HAPPY   In Ebbets Field it's the clubhouse.

BERNARD   I meant the clubhouse. Biff!

HAPPY   Biff!

BIFF [*grandly, after a slight pause*]   Let him carry the shoulder guards.

HAPPY [*as he gives* BERNARD *the shoulder guards*]   Stay close to us now.
      [WILLY *rushes in with the pennants.*]

WILLY [*handing them out*]   Everybody wave when Biff comes out on the field. [HAPPY *and* BERNARD *run off.*] You set now, boy?
      [*The music has died away.*]

BIFF   Ready to go, Pop. Every muscle is ready.

WILLY [*at the edge of the apron*]   You realize what this means?

BIFF   That's right, Pop.

WILLY [*feeling* BIFF'*s muscles*]   You're comin' home this afternoon captain of the All-Scholastic Championship Team of the City of New York.

BIFF I got it, Pop. And remember, pal, when I take off my helmet, that touchdown is for you.

WILLY Let's go! [*He is starting out, with his arm around* BIFF, *when* CHARLEY *enters, as of old, in knickers.*] I got no room for you, Charley.

CHARLEY Room? For what?

WILLY In the car.

CHARLEY You goin' for a ride? I wanted to shoot some casino.

WILLY [*furiously*] Casino! [*incredulously*] Don't you realize what today is?

LINDA Oh, he knows, Willy. He's just kidding you.

WILLY That's nothing to kid about!

CHARLEY No, Linda, what's goin' on?

LINDA He's playing in Ebbets Field.

CHARLEY Baseball in this weather?

WILLY Don't talk to him. Come on, come on! [*He is pushing them out.*]

CHARLEY Wait a minute, didn't you hear the news?

WILLY What?

CHARLEY Don't you listen to the radio? Ebbets Field just blew up.

WILLY You go to hell! [CHARLEY *laughs. Pushing them out*] Come on, come on! We're late.

CHARLEY [*as they go*] Knock a homer, Biff, knock a homer!

WILLY [*the last to leave, turning to* CHARLEY] I don't think that was funny, Charley. This is the greatest day of his life.

CHARLEY Willy, when are you going to grow up?

WILLY Yeah, heh? When this game is over, Charley, you'll be laughing out of the other side of your face. They'll be calling him another Red Grange.[9] Twenty-five thousand a year.

CHARLEY [*kidding*] Is that so?

WILLY Yeah, that's so.

CHARLEY Well, then, I'm sorry, Willy. But tell me something.

WILLY What?

CHARLEY Who is Red Grange?

WILLY Put up your hands. Goddam you, put up your hands!
[CHARLEY, *chuckling, shakes his head and walks away, around the left corner of the stage.* WILLY *follows him. The music rises to a mocking frenzy.*]

WILLY Who the hell do you think you are, better than everybody else? You don't know everything, you big, ignorant, stupid . . . Put up your hands!
[*Light rises, on the right side of the forestage, on a small table in the reception room of* CHARLEY's *office. Traffic sounds are heard.* BERNARD, *now mature, sits whistling to himself. A pair of tennis rackets and an overnight bag are on the floor beside him.*]

WILLY [*offstage*] What are you walking away for? Don't walk away! If you're going to say something say it to my face! I know you laugh at me behind my back. You'll laugh out of the other side of your goddam face after this game. Touchdown! Touchdown! Eighty thousand people! Touchdown! Right between the goal posts.

---

9. Harold Edward Grange (1903–1991), all-American halfback at the University of Illinois from 1923 to 1925, who then played professionally for the Chicago Bears.

[BERNARD *is a quiet, earnest, but self-assured young man.* WILLY'S *voice is coming from right upstage now.* BERNARD *lowers his feet off the table and listens.* JENNY, *his father's secretary, enters.*]

JENNY [*distressed*] Say, Bernard, will you go out in the hall?

BERNARD What is that noise? Who is it?

JENNY Mr. Loman. He just got off the elevator.

BERNARD [*getting up*] Who's he arguing with?

JENNY Nobody. There's nobody with him. I can't deal with him any more, and your father gets all upset everytime he comes. I've got a lot of typing to do, and your father's waiting to sign it. Will you see him?

WILLY [*entering*] Touchdown! Touch— [*He sees* JENNY.] Jenny, Jenny, good to see you. How're ya? Workin'? Or still honest?

JENNY Fine. How've you been feeling?

WILLY Not much any more, Jenny. Ha, ha! [*He is surprised to see the rackets.*]

BERNARD Hello, Uncle Willy.

WILLY [*almost shocked*] Bernard! Well, look who's here! [*He comes quickly, guiltily to* BERNARD *and warmly shakes his hand.*]

BERNARD How are you? Good to see you.

WILLY What are you doing here?

BERNARD Oh, just stopped by to see Pop. Get off my feet till my train leaves. I'm going to Washington in a few minutes.

WILLY Is he in?

BERNARD Yes, he's in his office with the accountant. Sit down.

WILLY [*sitting down*] What're you going to do in Washington?

BERNARD Oh, just a case I've got there, Willy.

WILLY That so? [*indicating the rackets*] You going to play tennis there?

BERNARD I'm staying with a friend who's got a court.

WILLY Don't say. His own tennis court. Must be fine people, I bet.

BERNARD They are, very nice. Dad tells me Biff's in town.

WILLY [*with a big smile*] Yeah, Biff's in. Working on a very big deal, Bernard.

BERNARD What's Biff doing?

WILLY Well, he's been doing very big things in the West. But he decided to establish himself here. Very big. We're having dinner. Did I hear your wife had a boy?

BERNARD That's right. Our second.

WILLY Two boys! What do you know!

BERNARD What kind of a deal has Biff got?

WILLY Well, Bill Oliver—very big sporting-goods man—he wants Biff very badly. Called him in from the West. Long distance, carte blanche, special deliveries. Your friends have their own private tennis court?

BERNARD You still with the old firm, Willy?

WILLY [*after a pause*] I'm—I'm overjoyed to see how you made the grade, Bernard, overjoyed. It's an encouraging thing to see a young man really— really—Looks very good for Biff—very—[*He breaks off, then*] Bernard— [*He is so full of emotion, he breaks off again.*]

BERNARD What is it, Willy?

WILLY [*small and alone*] What—what's the secret?

BERNARD What secret?

WILLY   How—how did you? Why didn't he ever catch on?

BERNARD   I wouldn't know that, Willy.

WILLY [*confidentially, desperately*]   You were his friend, his boyhood friend. There's something I don't understand about it. His life ended after that Ebbets Field game. From the age of seventeen nothing good ever happened to him.

BERNARD   He never trained himself for anything.

WILLY   But he did, he did. After high school he took so many correspondence courses. Radio mechanics; television; God knows what, and never made the slightest mark.

BERNARD [*taking off his glasses*]   Willy, do you want to talk candidly?

WILLY [*rising, faces* BERNARD]   I regard you as a very brilliant man, Bernard. I value your advice.

BERNARD   Oh, the hell with the advice, Willy. I couldn't advise you. There's just one thing I've always wanted to ask you. When he was supposed to graduate, and the math teacher flunked him—

WILLY   Oh, that son-of-a-bitch ruined his life.

BERNARD   Yeah, but, Willy, all he had to do was go to summer school and make up that subject.

WILLY   That's right, that's right.

BERNARD   Did you tell him not to go to summer school?

WILLY   Me? I begged him to go. I ordered him to go!

BERNARD   Then why wouldn't he go?

WILLY   Why? Why! Bernard, that question has been trailing me like a ghost for the last fifteen years. He flunked the subject, and laid down and died like a hammer hit him!

BERNARD   Take it easy, kid.

WILLY   Let me talk to you—I got nobody to talk to. Bernard, Bernard, was it my fault? Y'see? It keeps going around in my mind, maybe I did something to him. I got nothing to give him.

BERNARD   Don't take it so hard.

WILLY   Why did he lay down? What is the story there? You were his friend!

BERNARD   Willy, I remember, it was June, and our grades came out. And he'd flunked math.

WILLY   That son-of-a-bitch!

BERNARD   No, it wasn't right then. Biff just got very angry, I remember, and he was ready to enroll in summer school.

WILLY [*surprised*]   He was?

BERNARD   He wasn't beaten by it at all. But then, Willy, he disappeared from the block for almost a month. And I got the idea that he'd gone up to New England to see you. Did he have a talk with you then?

[WILLY *stares in silence.*]

BERNARD   Willy?

WILLY [*with a strong edge of resentment in his voice*]   Yeah, he came to Boston. What about it?

BERNARD   Well, just that when he came back—I'll never forget this, it always mystifies me. Because I'd thought so well of Biff, even though he'd always taken advantage of me. I loved him, Willy, y'know? And he came back after that month and took his sneakers—remember those sneakers with "University of Virginia" printed on them? He was so proud of those, wore them every day. And he took them down in the cellar, and burned them up in the furnace. We had a fist fight. It lasted at least half an hour. Just the two of us, punching each other down the cellar, and crying right through it. I've often thought of how strange it was that I knew he'd given up his life. What happened in Boston, Willy?

[WILLY *looks at him as at an intruder.*]

BERNARD   I just bring it up because you asked me.

WILLY [*angrily*]   Nothing. What do you mean, "What happened?" What's that got to do with anything?

BERNARD   Well, don't get sore.

WILLY   What are you trying to do, blame it on me? If a boy lays down is that my fault?

BERNARD   Now, Willy, don't get—

WILLY   Well, don't—don't talk to me that way! What does that mean, "What happened?"

[CHARLEY *enters. He is in his vest, and he carries a bottle of bourbon.*]

CHARLEY   Hey, you're going to miss that train. [*He waves the bottle.*]

BERNARD   Yeah, I'm going. [*He takes the bottle.*] Thanks, Pop. [*He picks up his rackets and bag.*] Good-by, Willy, and don't worry about it. You know, "If at first you don't succeed . . ."

WILLY   Yes, I believe in that.

BERNARD   But sometimes, Willy, it's better for a man just to walk away.

WILLY   Walk away?

BERNARD   That's right.

WILLY   But if you can't walk away?

BERNARD [*after a slight pause*]   I guess that's when it's tough. [*extending his hand*] Good-by, Willy.

WILLY [*shaking* BERNARD's *hand*]   Good-by, boy.

CHARLEY [*an arm on* BERNARD's *shoulder*]   How do you like this kid? Gonna argue a case in front of the Supreme Court.

BERNARD [*protesting*]   Pop!

WILLY [*genuinely shocked, pained, and happy*]   No! The Supreme Court!

BERNARD   I gotta run. 'By, Dad!

CHARLEY   Knock 'em dead, Bernard!

[BERNARD *goes off.*]

WILLY [*as* CHARLEY *takes out his wallet*]   The Supreme Court! And he didn't even mention it!

CHARLEY [*counting out money on the desk*]   He don't have to—he's gonna do it.

WILLY   And you never told him what to do, did you? You never took any interest in him.

CHARLEY   My salvation is that I never took any interest in anything. There's some money—fifty dollars. I got an accountant inside.

WILLY   Charley, look . . . [*with difficulty*] I got my insurance to pay. If you can manage it—I need a hundred and ten dollars.

[CHARLEY *doesn't reply for a moment; merely stops moving.*]

WILLY   I'd draw it from my bank but Linda would know, and I . . .

CHARLEY   Sit down, Willy.

WILLY [*moving toward the chair*]   I'm keeping an account of everything, remember. I'll pay every penny back. [*He sits.*]

CHARLEY   Now listen to me, Willy.

WILLY   I want you to know I appreciate . . .

CHARLEY [*sitting down on the table*]   Willy, what're you doin'? What the hell is goin' on in your head?

WILLY   Why? I'm simply . . .

CHARLEY   I offered you a job. You can make fifty dollars a week. And I won't send you on the road.

WILLY   I've got a job.

CHARLEY   Without pay? What kind of job is a job without pay? [*He rises.*] Now, look kid, enough is enough. I'm no genius but I know when I'm being insulted.

WILLY   Insulted!

CHARLEY   Why don't you want to work for me?

WILLY   What's the matter with you? I've got a job.

CHARLEY   Then what're you walkin' in here every week for?

WILLY [*getting up*]   Well, if you don't want me to walk in here—

CHARLEY   I am offering you a job!

WILLY   I don't want your goddam job!

CHARLEY   When the hell are you going to grow up?

WILLY [*furiously*]   You big ignoramus, if you say that to me again I'll rap you one! I don't care how big you are! [*He's ready to fight. Pause.*]

CHARLEY [*kindly, going to him*]   How much do you need, Willy?

WILLY   Charley, I'm strapped, I'm strapped. I don't know what to do. I was just fired.

CHARLEY   Howard fired you?

WILLY   That snotnose. Imagine that? I named him. I named him Howard.

CHARLEY   Willy, when're you gonna realize that them things don't mean anything? You named him Howard, but you can't sell that. The only thing you got in this world is what you can sell. And the funny thing is that you're a salesman, and you don't know that.

WILLY   I've always tried to think otherwise. I guess. I always felt that if a man was impressive, and well liked, that nothing—

CHARLEY   Why must everybody like you? Who liked J. P. Morgan?[1] Was he impressive? In a Turkish bath he'd look like a butcher. But with his pockets on he was very well liked. Now listen, Willy, I know you don't like me, and nobody can say I'm in love with you, but I'll give you a job because—just for the hell of it, put it that way. Now what do you say?

WILLY   I—I just can't work for you, Charley.

CHARLEY   What're you, jealous of me?

WILLY   I can't work for you, that's all, don't ask me why.

CHARLEY [*angered, takes out more bills*]   You been jealous of me all your life, you damned fool! Here, pay your insurance. [*He puts the money in* WILLY's *hand.*]

WILLY   I'm keeping strict accounts.

---

1. John Pierpont Morgan (1837–1913), American banker and philanthropist famed for his enormous wealth.

CHARLEY   I've got some work to do. Take care of yourself. And pay your insurance.

WILLY [*moving to the right*]   Funny, y'know? After all the highways, and the trains, and the appointments, and the years, you end up worth more dead than alive.

CHARLEY   Willy, nobody's worth nothin' dead. [*after a slight pause*] Did you hear what I said?

[WILLY *stands still, dreaming.*]

CHARLEY   Willy!

WILLY   Apologize to Bernard for me when you see him. I didn't mean to argue with him. He's a fine boy. They're all fine boys, and they'll end up big—all of them. Someday they'll all play tennis together. Wish me luck, Charley. He saw Bill Oliver today.

CHARLEY   Good luck.

WILLY [*on the verge of tears*]   Charley, you're the only friend I got. Isn't that a remarkable thing? [*He goes out.*]

CHARLEY   Jesus!

[CHARLEY *stares after him a moment and follows. All light blacks out. Suddenly raucous music is heard, and a red glow rises behind the screen at right.* STANLEY, *a young waiter, appears, carrying a table, followed by* HAPPY, *who is carrying two chairs.*]

STANLEY [*putting the table down*]   That's all right, Mr. Loman, I can handle it myself. [*He turns and takes the chairs from* HAPPY *and places them at the table.*]

HAPPY [*glancing around*]   Oh, this is better.

STANLEY   Sure, in the front there you're in the middle of all kinds a noise. Whenever you got a party. Mr. Loman, you just tell me and I'll put you back here. Y'know, there's a lotta people they don't like it private, because when they go out they like to see a lotta action around them because they're sick and tired to stay in the house by theirself. But I know you, you ain't from Hackensack. You know what I mean?

HAPPY [*sitting down*]   So how's it coming, Stanley?

STANLEY   Ah, it's a dog life. I only wish during the war they'd a took me in the Army. I coulda been dead by now.

HAPPY   My brother's back, Stanley.

STANLEY   Oh, he come back, heh? From the Far West.

HAPPY   Yeah, big cattle man, my brother, so treat him right. And my father's coming too.

STANLEY   Oh, your father too!

HAPPY   You got a couple of nice lobsters?

STANLEY   Hundred per cent, big.

HAPPY   I want them with the claws.

STANLEY   Don't worry, I don't give you no mice. [HAPPY *laughs.*] How about some wine? It'll put a head on the meal.

HAPPY   No. You remember, Stanley, that recipe I brought you from overseas? With the champagne in it?

STANLEY   Oh, yeah, sure. I still got it tacked up yet in the kitchen. But that'll have to cost a buck apiece anyways.

HAPPY   That's all right.

STANLEY   What'd you, hit a number or somethin'?

HAPPY   No, it's a little celebration. My brother is—I think he pulled off a big deal today. I think we're going into business together.

STANLEY   Great! That's the best for you. Because a family business, you know what I mean?—that's the best.

HAPPY   That's what I think.

STANLEY   'Cause what's the difference? Somebody steals? It's in the family. Know what I mean? [*sotto voce*][2] Like this bartender here. The boss is goin' crazy what kinda leak he's got in the cash register. You put it in but it don't come out.

HAPPY [*raising his head*]   Sh!

STANLEY   What?

HAPPY   You notice I wasn't lookin' right or left, was I?

STANLEY   No.

HAPPY   And my eyes are closed.

STANLEY   So what's the—?

HAPPY   Strudel's comin'.

STANLEY [*catching on, looks around*]   Ah, no, there's no—
      [*He breaks off as a furred, lavishly dressed girl enters and sits at the next table. Both follow her with their eyes.*]

STANLEY   Geez, how'd ya know?

HAPPY   I got radar or something. [*staring directly at her profile*] Oooooooo . . . Stanley.

STANLEY   I think that's for you, Mr. Loman.

HAPPY   Look at that mouth. Oh, God. And the binoculars.

STANLEY   Geez, you got a life, Mr. Loman.

HAPPY   Wait on her.

STANLEY [*going to the girl's table*]   Would you like a menu, ma'am?

GIRL   I'm expecting someone, but I'd like a—

HAPPY   Why don't you bring her—excuse me, miss, do you mind? I sell champagne, and I'd like you to try my brand. Bring her a champagne, Stanley.

GIRL   That's awfully nice of you.

HAPPY   Don't mention it. It's all company money. [*He laughs.*]

GIRL   That's a charming product to be selling, isn't it?

HAPPY   Oh, gets to be like everything else. Selling is selling, y'know.

GIRL   I suppose.

HAPPY   You don't happen to sell, do you?

GIRL   No, I don't sell.

HAPPY   Would you object to a compliment from a stranger? You ought to be on a magazine cover.

GIRL [*looking at him a little archly*]   I have been.
      [STANLEY *comes in with a glass of champagne.*]

HAPPY   What'd I say before, Stanley? You see? She's a cover girl.

STANLEY   Oh, I could see, I could see.

HAPPY [*to the* GIRL]   What magazine?

GIRL   Oh, a lot of them. [*She takes the drink.*] Thank you.

HAPPY   You know what they say in France, don't you? "Champagne is the drink of the complexion"—Hya, Biff!

---

2. In an undertone [Italian].

[BIFF *has entered and sits with* HAPPY.]

BIFF   Hello, kid. Sorry I'm late.

HAPPY   I just got here. Uh, Miss—?

GIRL   Forsythe.

HAPPY   Miss Forsythe, this is my brother.

BIFF   Is Dad here?

HAPPY   His name is Biff. You might've heard of him. Great football player.

GIRL   Really? What team?

HAPPY   Are you familiar with football?

GIRL   No, I'm afraid I'm not.

HAPPY   Biff is quarterback with the New York Giants.

GIRL   Well, that's nice, isn't it? [*She drinks.*]

HAPPY   Good health.

GIRL   I'm happy to meet you.

HAPPY   That's my name. Hap. It's really Harold, but at West Point they called me Happy.

GIRL   [*now really impressed*]   Oh, I see. How do you do? [*She turns her profile.*]

BIFF   Isn't Dad coming?

HAPPY   You want her?

BIFF   Oh, I could never make that.

HAPPY   I remember the time that idea would never come into your head. Where's the old confidence, Biff?

BIFF   I just saw Oliver—

HAPPY   Wait a minute. I've got to see that old confidence again. Do you want her? She's on call.

BIFF   Oh, no. [*He turns to look at the* GIRL.]

HAPPY   I'm telling you. Watch this. [*turning to the* GIRL] Honey? [*She turns to him.*] Are you busy?

GIRL   Well, I am . . . but I could make a phone call.

HAPPY   Do that, will you, honey? And see if you can get a friend. We'll be here for a while. Biff is one of the greatest football players in the country.

GIRL   [*standing up*]   Well, I'm certainly happy to meet you.

HAPPY   Come back soon.

GIRL   I'll try.

HAPPY   Don't try, honey, try hard.

[*The* GIRL *exits.* STANLEY *follows, shaking his head in bewildered admiration.*]

HAPPY   Isn't that a shame now? A beautiful girl like that? That's why I can't get married. There's not a good woman in a thousand. New York is loaded with them, kid!

BIFF   Hap, look—

HAPPY   I told you she was on call!

BIFF   [*strangely unnerved*]   Cut it out, will ya? I want to say something to you.

HAPPY   Did you see Oliver?

BIFF   I saw him all right. Now look, I want to tell Dad a couple of things and I want you to help me.

HAPPY   What? Is he going to back you?

BIFF   Are you crazy? You're out of your goddam head, you know that?

HAPPY   Why? What happened?

BIFF   [*breathlessly*]   I did a terrible thing today, Hap. It's been the strangest day I ever went through. I'm all numb, I swear.

HAPPY   You mean he wouldn't see you?

BIFF   Well, I waited six hours for him, see? All day. Kept sending my name in. Even tried to date his secretary so she'd get me to him, but no soap.

HAPPY   Because you're not showin' the old confidence, Biff. He remembered you, didn't he?

BIFF   [*stopping* HAPPY *with a gesture*]   Finally, about five o'clock, he comes out. Didn't remember who I was or anything. I felt like such an idiot, Hap.

HAPPY   Did you tell him my Florida idea?

BIFF   He walked away. I saw him for one minute. I got so mad I could've torn the walls down! How the hell did I ever get the idea I was a salesman there? I even believed myself that I'd been a salesman for him! And then he gave me one look and—I realized what a ridiculous lie my whole life has been! We've been talking in a dream for fifteen years. I was a shipping clerk.

HAPPY   What'd you do?

BIFF   [*with great tension and wonder*]   Well, he left, see. And the secretary went out. I was all alone in the waiting-room. I don't know what came over me, Hap. The next thing I know I'm in his office—paneled walls, everything. I can't explain it. I—Hap, I took his fountain pen.

HAPPY   Geez, did he catch you?

BIFF   I ran out. I ran down all eleven flights. I ran and ran and ran.

HAPPY   That was an awful dumb—what'd you do that for?

BIFF   [*agonized*]   I don't know, I just—wanted to take something, I don't know. You gotta help me, Hap, I'm gonna tell Pop.

HAPPY   You crazy? What for?

BIFF   Hap, he's got to understand that I'm not the man somebody lends that kind of money to. He thinks I've been spiting him all these years and it's eating him up.

HAPPY   That's just it. You tell him something nice.

BIFF   I can't.

HAPPY   Say you got a lunch date with Oliver tomorrow.

BIFF   So what do I do tomorrow?

HAPPY   You leave the house tomorrow and come back at night and say Oliver is thinking it over. And he thinks it over for a couple of weeks, and gradually it fades away and nobody's the worse.

BIFF   But it'll go on forever!

HAPPY   Dad is never so happy as when he's looking forward to something!
   [WILLY *enters.*]

HAPPY   Hello, scout!

WILLY   Gee, I haven't been here in years!
   [STANLEY *has followed* WILLY *in and sets a chair for him.* STANLEY *starts off but* HAPPY *stops him.*]

HAPPY   Stanley!
   [STANLEY *stands by, waiting for an order.*]

BIFF [*going to* WILLY *with guilt, as to an invalid*]   Sit down, Pop. You want a drink?

WILLY   Sure, I don't mind.

BIFF   Let's get a load on.

WILLY   You look worried.

BIFF   N-no. [*to* STANLEY] Scotch all around. Make it doubles.

STANLEY   Doubles, right. [*He goes.*]

WILLY   You had a couple already, didn't you?

BIFF   Just a couple, yeah.

WILLY   Well, what happened, boy? [*nodding affirmatively, with a smile*] Everything go all right?

BIFF   [*takes a breath, then reaches out and grasps* WILLY's *hand*]   Pal . . . [*He is smiling bravely, and* WILLY *is smiling too.*] I had an experience today.

HAPPY   Terrific, Pop.

WILLY   That so? What happened?

BIFF   [*high, slightly alcoholic, above the earth*]   I'm going to tell you everything from first to last. It's been a strange day. [*Silence. He looks around, composes himself as best he can, but his breath keeps breaking the rhythm of his voice.*] I had to wait quite a while for him, and—

WILLY   Oliver?

BIFF   Yeah, Oliver. All day, as a matter of cold fact. And a lot of—instances—facts, Pop, facts about my life came back to me. Who was it, Pop? Who ever said I was a salesman with Oliver?

WILLY   Well, you were.

BIFF   No, Dad, I was a shipping clerk.

WILLY   But you were practically—

BIFF   [*with determination*]   Dad, I don't know who said it first, but I was never a salesman for Bill Oliver.

WILLY   What're you talking about?

BIFF   Let's hold on to the facts tonight, Pop. We're not going to get anywhere bullin' around. I was a shipping clerk.

WILLY   [*angrily*]   All right, now listen to me—

BIFF   Why don't you let me finish?

WILLY   I'm not interested in stories about the past or any crap of that kind because the woods are burning, boys, you understand? There's a big blaze going on all around. I was fired today.

BIFF   [*shocked*]   How could you be?

WILLY   I was fired, and I'm looking for a little good news to tell your mother, because the woman has waited and the woman has suffered. The gist of it is that I haven't got a story left in my head, Biff. So don't give me a lecture about facts and aspects. I am not interested. Now what've you got to say to me?

[STANLEY *enters with three drinks. They wait until he leaves.*]

WILLY   Did you see Oliver?

BIFF   Jesus, Dad!

WILLY   You mean you didn't go up there?

HAPPY   Sure he went up there.

BIFF   I did. I—saw him. How could they fire you?

WILLY   [*on the edge of his chair*]   What kind of a welcome did he give you?

BIFF   He won't even let you work on commission?

WILLY   I'm out! [*driving*] So tell me, he gave you a warm welcome?

HAPPY   Sure, Pop, sure!

BIFF [*driven*]   Well, it was kind of—

WILLY   I was wondering if he'd remember you. [*to* HAPPY] Imagine, man doesn't see him for ten, twelve years and gives him that kind of a welcome!

HAPPY   Damn right!

BIFF [*trying to return to the offensive*]   Pop, look—

WILLY   You know why he remembered you, don't you? Because you impressed him in those days.

BIFF   Let's talk quietly and get this down to the facts, huh?

WILLY [*as though* BIFF *had been interrupting*]   Well, what happened? It's great news, Biff. Did he take you into his office or'd you talk in the waiting-room?

BIFF   Well, he came in, see, and—

WILLY [*with a big smile*]   What'd he say? Betcha he threw his arm around you.

BIFF   Well, he kinda—

WILLY   He's a fine man. [*to* HAPPY] Very hard man to see, y'know.

HAPPY [*agreeing*]   Oh, I know.

WILLY [*to* BIFF]   Is that where you had the drinks?

BIFF   Yeah, he gave me a couple of—no, no!

HAPPY [*cutting in*]   He told him my Florida idea.

WILLY   Don't interrupt. [*to* BIFF] How'd he react to the Florida idea?

BIFF   Dad, will you give me a minute to explain?

WILLY   I've been waiting for you to explain since I sat down here! What happened? He took you into his office and what?

BIFF   Well—I talked. And—he listened, see.

WILLY   Famous for the way he listens, y'know. What was his answer?

BIFF   His answer was— [*He breaks off, suddenly angry.*] Dad, you're not letting me tell you what I want to tell you!

WILLY [*accusing, angered*]   You didn't see him, did you?

BIFF   I did see him!

WILLY   What'd you insult him or something? You insulted him, didn't you?

BIFF   Listen, will you let me out of it, will you just let me out of it!

HAPPY   What the hell!

WILLY   Tell me what happened!

BIFF [*to* HAPPY]   I can't talk to him!

> [*A single trumpet note jars the ear. The light of green leaves stains the house, which holds the air of night and a dream.* YOUNG BERNARD *enters and knocks on the door of the house.*]

YOUNG BERNARD [*frantically*]   Mrs. Loman, Mrs. Loman!

HAPPY   Tell him what happened!

BIFF [*to* HAPPY]   Shut up and leave me alone!

WILLY   No, no. You had to go and flunk math!

BIFF   What math? What're you talking about?

YOUNG BERNARD   Mrs. Loman, Mrs. Loman!

> [LINDA *appears in the house, as of old.*]

WILLY [*wildly*]   Math, math, math!

BIFF   Take it easy, Pop!

YOUNG BERNARD   Mrs. Loman!

WILLY [*furiously*]   If you hadn't flunked you'd've been set by now!

BIFF   Now, look, I'm gonna tell you what happened, and you're going to listen to me.

YOUNG BERNARD   Mrs. Loman!

BIFF   I waited six hours—

HAPPY   What the hell are you saying?

BIFF   I kept sending in my name but he wouldn't see me. So finally he . . . [*He continues unheard as light fades low on the restaurant.*]

YOUNG BERNARD   Biff flunked math!

LINDA   No!

YOUNG BERNARD   Birnbaum flunked him! They won't graduate him!

LINDA   But they have to. He's gotta go to the university. Where is he? Biff! Biff!

YOUNG BERNARD   No, he left. He went to Grand Central.

LINDA   Grand—You mean he went to Boston!

YOUNG BERNARD   Is Uncle Willy in Boston?

LINDA   Oh, maybe Willy can talk to the teacher. Oh, the poor, poor boy! [*Light on house area snaps out.*]

BIFF [*at the table, now audible, holding up a gold fountain pen*]   . . . so I'm washed up with Oliver, you understand? Are you listening to me?

WILLY [*at a loss*]   Yeah, sure. If you hadn't flunked—

BIFF   Flunked what? What're you talking about?

WILLY   Don't blame everything on me! I didn't flunk math—you did! What pen?

HAPPY   That was awful dumb, Biff, a pen like that is worth—

WILLY [*seeing the pen for the first time*]   You took Oliver's pen?

BIFF [*weakening*]   Dad, I just explained it to you.

WILLY   You stole Bill Oliver's fountain pen!

BIFF   I didn't exactly steal it! That's just what I've been explaining to you!

HAPPY   He had it in his hand and just then Oliver walked in, so he got nervous and stuck it in his pocket!

WILLY   My God, Biff!

BIFF   I never intended to do it, Dad!

OPERATOR'S VOICE   Standish Arms, good evening!

WILLY [*shouting*]   I'm not in my room!

BIFF [*frightened*]   Dad, what's the matter? [*He and* HAPPY *stand up.*]

OPERATOR   Ringing Mr. Loman for you!

WILLY   I'm not there, stop it!

BIFF [*horrified, gets down on one knee before* WILLY]   Dad, I'll make good, I'll make good. [WILLY *tries to get to his feet.* BIFF *holds him down.*] Sit down now.

WILLY   No, you're no good, you're no good for anything.

BIFF   I am, Dad, I'll find something else, you understand? Now don't worry about anything. [*He holds up* WILLY's *face.*] Talk to me, Dad.

OPERATOR   Mr. Loman does not answer. Shall I page him?

WILLY [*attempting to stand, as though to rush and silence the* OPERATOR] No, no, no!

HAPPY   He'll strike something, Pop.

WILLY   No, no . . .

BIFF [*desperately, standing over* WILLY] Pop, listen! Listen to me! I'm telling you something good. Oliver talked to his partner about the Florida
idea. You listening? He—he talked to his partner, and he came to me . . .
I'm going to be all right, you hear? Dad, listen to me, he said it was just
a question of the amount!

WILLY Then you . . . got it?

HAPPY He's gonna be terrific, Pop!

WILLY [*trying to stand*] Then you got it, haven't you? You got it! You got it!

BIFF [*agonized, holds* WILLY *down*] No, no. Look, Pop. I'm supposed to
have lunch with them tomorrow. I'm just telling you this so you'll know
that I can still make an impression, Pop. And I'll make good somewhere,
but I can't go tomorrow, see?

WILLY Why not? You simply—

BIFF But the pen, Pop!

WILLY You give it to him and tell him it was an oversight!

HAPPY Sure, have lunch tomorrow!

BIFF I can't say that—

WILLY You were doing a crossword puzzle and accidentally used his pen!

BIFF Listen, kid, I took those balls years ago, now I walk in with his
fountain pen? That clinches it, don't you see? I can't face him like that!
I'll try elsewhere.

PAGE'S VOICE Paging Mr. Loman!

WILLY Don't you want to be anything?

BIFF Pop, how can I go back?

WILLY You don't want to be anything, is that what's behind it?

BIFF [*now angry at* WILLY *for not crediting his sympathy*] Don't take it that
way! You think it was easy walking into that office after what I'd done to
him? A team of horses couldn't have dragged me back to Bill Oliver!

WILLY Then why'd you go?

BIFF Why did I go? Why did I go! Look at you! Look at what's become of
you!
[*Off left,* THE WOMAN *laughs.*]

WILLY Biff, you're going to go to that lunch tomorrow, or—

BIFF I can't go. I've got no appointment!

HAPPY Biff for . . . !

WILLY Are you spiting me?

BIFF Don't take it that way! Goddammit!

WILLY [*strikes* BIFF *and falters away from the table*] You rotten little louse!
Are you spiting me?

THE WOMAN Someone's at the door, Willy!

BIFF I'm no good, can't you see what I am?

HAPPY [*separating them*] Hey, you're in a restaurant! Now cut it out, both
of you? [*The girls enter.*] Hello, girls, sit down.
[THE WOMAN *laughs, off left.*]

MISS FORSYTHE I guess we might as well. This is Letta.

THE WOMAN Willy, are you going to wake up?

BIFF [*ignoring* WILLY] How're ya, miss, sit down. What do you drink?

MISS FORSYTHE Letta might not be able to stay long.

LETTA I gotta get up early tomorrow. I got jury duty. I'm so excited! Were
you fellows ever on a jury?

BIFF   No, but I been in front of them! [*The girls laugh.*] This is my father.

LETTA   Isn't he cute? Sit down with us, Pop.

HAPPY   Sit him down, Biff!

BIFF [*going to him*]   Come on, slugger, drink us under the table. To hell with it! Come on, sit down, pal.
>   [*On* BIFF*'s last insistence,* WILLY *is about to sit.*]

THE WOMAN [*now urgently*]   Willy, are you going to answer the door!
>   [THE WOMAN*'s call pulls* WILLY *back. He starts right, befuddled.*]

BIFF   Hey, where are you going?

WILLY   Open the door.

BIFF   The door?

WILLY   The washroom . . . the door . . . where's the door?

BIFF [*leading* WILLY *to the left*]   Just go straight down.
>   [WILLY *moves left.*]

THE WOMAN   Willy, Willy, are you going to get up, get up, get up, get up?
>   [WILLY *exits left.*]

LETTA   I think it's sweet you bring your daddy along.

MISS FORSYTHE   Oh, he isn't really your father!

BIFF [*at left, turning to her resentfully*]   Miss Forsythe, you've just seen a prince walk by. A fine, troubled prince. A hard-working, unappreciated prince. A pal, you understand? A good companion. Always for his boys.

LETTA   That's so sweet.

HAPPY   Well, girls, what's the program? We're wasting time. Come on, Biff. Gather round. Where would you like to go?

BIFF   Why don't you do something for him?

HAPPY   Me!

BIFF   Don't you give a damn for him, Hap?

HAPPY   What're you talking about? I'm the one who—

BIFF   I sense it, you don't give a good goddam about him. [*He takes the rolled-up hose from his pocket and puts it on the table in front of* HAPPY.] Look what I found in the cellar, for Christ's sake. How can you bear to let it go on?

HAPPY   Me? Who goes away? Who runs off and—

BIFF   Yeah, but he doesn't mean anything to you. You could help him—I can't! Don't you understand what I'm talking about? He's going to kill himself, don't you know that?

HAPPY   Don't I know it! Me!

BIFF   Hap, help him! Jesus . . . help him . . . Help me, help me, I can't bear to look at his face! [*Ready to weep, he hurries out, up right.*]

HAPPY [*starting after him*]   Where are you going?

MISS FORSYTHE   What's he so mad about?

HAPPY   Come on, girls, we'll catch up with him.

MISS FORSYTHE [*as* HAPPY *pushes her out*]   Say, I don't like that temper of his!

HAPPY   He's just a little overstrung, he'll be all right!

WILLY [*off left, as* THE WOMAN *laughs*]   Don't answer! Don't answer!

LETTA   Don't you want to tell your father—

HAPPY   No, that's not my father. He's just a guy. Come on, we'll catch Biff, and, honey, we're going to paint this town! Stanley, where's the check! Hey, Stanley!

[*They exit.* STANLEY *looks toward left.*]

STANLEY [*calling to* HAPPY *indignantly*] Mr. Loman! Mr. Loman!

    [STANLEY *picks up a chair and follows them off. Knocking is heard off left.* THE WOMAN *enters, laughing.* WILLY *follows her. She is in a black slip; he is buttoning his shirt. Raw, sensuous music accompanies their speech.*]

WILLY Will you stop laughing? Will you stop?

THE WOMAN Aren't you going to answer the door? He'll wake the whole hotel.

WILLY I'm not expecting anybody.

THE WOMAN Whyn't you have another drink, honey, and stop being so damn self-centered?

WILLY I'm so lonely.

THE WOMAN You know you ruined me, Willy? From now on, whenever you come to the office, I'll see that you go right through to the buyers. No waiting at my desk any more, Willy. You ruined me.

WILLY That's nice of you to say that.

THE WOMAN Gee, you are self-centered! Why so sad? You are the saddest, self-centeredest soul I ever did see-saw. [*She laughs. He kisses her.*] Come on inside, drummer boy. It's silly to be dressing in the middle of the night. [*As knocking is heard*] Aren't you going to answer the door?

WILLY They're knocking on the wrong door.

THE WOMAN But I felt the knocking. And he heard us talking in here. Maybe the hotel's on fire!

WILLY [*his terror rising*] It's a mistake.

THE WOMAN Then tell them to go away!

WILLY There's nobody there.

THE WOMAN It's getting on my nerves, Willy. There's somebody standing out there and it's getting on my nerves!

WILLY [*pushing her away from him*] All right, stay in the bathroom here, and don't come out. I think there's a law in Massachusetts about it, so don't come out. It may be that new room clerk. He looked very mean. So don't come out. It's a mistake, there's no fire.

    [*The knocking is heard again. He takes a few steps away from her, and she vanishes into the wing. The light follows him, and now he is facing* YOUNG BIFF, *who carries a suitcase.* BIFF *steps toward him. The music is gone.*]

BIFF Why didn't you answer?

WILLY Biff! What are you doing in Boston?

BIFF Why didn't you answer? I've been knocking for five minutes, I called you on the phone—

WILLY I just heard you. I was in the bathroom and had the door shut. Did anything happen home?

BIFF Dad—I let you down.

WILLY What do you mean?

BIFF Dad . . .

WILLY Biffo, what's this about? [*putting his arm around* BIFF] Come on, let's go downstairs and get you a malted.

BIFF Dad, I flunked math.

WILLY Not for the term?

BIFF   The term. I haven't got enough credits to graduate.

WILLY   You mean to say Bernard wouldn't give you the answers?

BIFF   He did, he tried, but I only got a sixty-one.

WILLY   And they wouldn't give you four points?

BIFF   Birnbaum refused absolutely. I begged him, Pop, but he won't give me those points. You gotta talk to him before they close the school. Because if he saw the kind of man you are, and you just talked to him in your way, I'm sure he'd come through for me. The class came right before practice, see, and I didn't go enough. Would you talk to him? He'd like you, Pop. You know the way you could talk.

WILLY   You're on. We'll drive right back.

BIFF   Oh, Dad, good work! I'm sure he'll change for you!

WILLY   Go downstairs and tell the clerk I'm checkin' out. Go right down.

BIFF   Yes, sir! See, the reason he hates me, Pop—one day he was late for class so I got up at the blackboard and imitated him. I crossed my eyes and talked with a lithp.

WILLY [*laughing*]   You did? The kids like it?

BIFF   They nearly died laughing!

WILLY   Yeah? What'd you do?

BIFF   The thquare root of thixty twee is . . . [WILLY *bursts out laughing;* BIFF *joins him.*] And in the middle of it he walked in!

    [WILLY *laughs and* THE WOMAN *joins in offstage.*]

WILLY [*without hesitation*]   Hurry downstairs and—

BIFF   Somebody in there?

WILLY   No, that was next door.

    [THE WOMAN *laughs offstage.*]

BIFF   Somebody got in your bathroom!

WILLY   No, it's the next room, there's a party—

THE WOMAN [*enters laughing. She lisps this*]   Can I come in? There's something in the bathtub, Willy, and it's moving!

    [WILLY *looks at* BIFF, *who is staring open-mouthed and horrified at* THE WOMAN.]

WILLY   Ah—you better go back to your room. They must be finished painting by now. They're painting her room so I let her take a shower here. Go back, go back . . . [*He pushes her.*]

THE WOMAN [*resisting*]   But I've got to get dressed, Willy, I can't—

WILLY   Get out of here! Go back, go back . . . [*suddenly striving for the ordinary*] This is Miss Francis, Biff, she's a buyer. They're painting her room. Go back, Miss Francis, go back . . .

THE WOMAN   But my clothes, I can't go out naked in the hall!

WILLY [*pushing her offstage*]   Get outa here! Go back, go back!

    [BIFF *slowly sits down on his suitcase as the argument continues offstage.*]

THE WOMAN   Where's my stockings? You promised me stockings, Willy!

WILLY   I have no stockings here!

THE WOMAN   You had two boxes of size nine sheers for me, and I want them!

WILLY   Here, for God's sake, will you get outa here!

THE WOMAN [*enters holding a box of stockings*]   I just hope there's nobody in the hall. That's all I hope. [*to* BIFF] Are you football or baseball?

BIFF   Football.

THE WOMAN [*angry, humiliated*]   That's me too. G'night. [*She snatches her clothes from* WILLY, *and walks out.*]

WILLY [*after a pause*]   Well, better get going. I want to get to the school first thing in the morning. Get my suits out of the closet. I'll get my valise. [BIFF *doesn't move.*] What's the matter? [BIFF *remains motionless, tears falling.*] She's a buyer. Buys for J. H. Simmons. She lives down the hall— they're painting. You don't imagine— [*He breaks off. After a pause*] Now listen, pal, she's just a buyer. She sees merchandise in her room and they have to keep it looking just so . . . [*Pause. Assuming command*] All right, get my suits. [BIFF *doesn't move.*] Now stop crying and do as I say. I gave you an order. Biff, I gave you an order! Is that what you do when I give you an order? How dare you cry! [*putting his arm around* BIFF] Now look, Biff, when you grow up you'll understand about these things. You mustn't—you mustn't overemphasize a thing like this. I'll see Birnbaum first thing in the morning.

BIFF   Never mind.

WILLY [*getting down beside* BIFF]   Never mind! He's going to give you those points. I'll see to it.

BIFF   He wouldn't listen to you.

WILLY   He certainly will listen to me. You need those points for the U. of Virginia.

BIFF   I'm not going there.

WILLY   Heh? If I can't get him to change that mark you'll make it up in summer school. You've got all summer to—

BIFF [*his weeping breaking from him*]   Dad . . .

WILLY [*infected by it*]   Oh, my boy . . .

BIFF   Dad . . .

WILLY   She's nothing to me, Biff. I was lonely, I was terribly lonely.

BIFF   You—you gave her Mama's stockings! [*His tears break through and he rises to go.*]

WILLY [*grabbing for* BIFF]   I gave you an order!

BIFF   Don't touch me, you—liar!

WILLY   Apologize for that!

BIFF   You fake! You phony little fake! You fake! [*Overcome, he turns quickly and weeping fully goes out with his suitcase,* WILLY *is left on the floor on his knees.*]

WILLY   I gave you an order! Biff, come back here or I'll beat you! Come back here! I'll whip you!

[STANLEY *comes quickly in from the right and stands in front of* WILLY.]

WILLY [*shouts at* STANLEY]   I gave you an order . . .

STANLEY   Hey, let's pick it up, pick it up, Mr. Loman. [*He helps* WILLY *to his feet.*] Your boys left with the chippies. They said they'll see you home.

[*A second waiter watches some distance away.*]

WILLY   But we were supposed to have dinner together.

[*Music is heard,* WILLY's *theme.*]

STANLEY   Can you make it?

WILLY   I'll—sure, I can make it. [*suddenly concerned about his clothes*] Do I—I look all right?

STANLEY   Sure, you look all right. [*He flicks a speck off* WILLY's *lapel.*]

WILLY   Here—here's a dollar.

STANLEY   Oh, your son paid me. It's all right.

WILLY [*putting it in* STANLEY's *hand*]   No, take it. You're a good boy.

STANLEY   Oh, no, you don't have to . . .

WILLY   Here—here's some more, I don't need it any more. [*after a slight pause*] Tell me—is there a seed store in the neighborhood?

STANLEY   Seeds? You mean like to plant?

    [*As* WILLY *turns,* STANLEY *slips the money back into his jacket pocket.*]

WILLY   Yes. Carrots, peas . . .

STANLEY   Well, there's hardware stores on Sixth Avenue, but it may be too late now.

WILLY [*anxiously*]   Oh, I'd better hurry. I've got to get some seeds. [*He starts off to the right.*] I've got to get some seeds, right away. Nothing's planted. I don't have a thing in the ground.

    [WILLY *hurries out as the light goes down.* STANLEY *moves over to the right after him, watches him off. The other waiter has been staring at* WILLY.]

STANLEY [*to the waiter*]   Well, whatta you looking at?

    [*The waiter picks up the chairs and moves off right.* STANLEY *takes the table and follows him. The light fades on this area. There is a long pause, the sound of the flute coming over. The light gradually rises on the kitchen, which is empty.* HAPPY *appears at the door of the house, followed by* BIFF. HAPPY *is carrying a large bunch of long-stemmed roses. He enters the kitchen, looks around for* LINDA. *Not seeing her, he turns to* BIFF, *who is just outside the house door, and makes a gesture with his hands, indicating "Not here, I guess." He looks into the living-room and freezes. Inside,* LINDA, *unseen, is seated,* WILLY's *coat on her lap. She rises ominously and quietly and moves toward* HAPPY, *who backs up into the kitchen, afraid.*]

HAPPY   Hey, what're you doing up? [LINDA *says nothing but moves toward him implacably.*] Where's Pop? [*He keeps backing to the right, and now* LINDA *is in full view in the doorway to the living-room.*] Is he sleeping?

LINDA   Where were you?

HAPPY [*trying to laugh it off*]   We met two girls, Mom, very fine types. Here, we brought you some flowers. [*offering them to her*] Put them in your room, Ma.

    [*She knocks them to the floor at* BIFF's *feet. He has now come inside and closed the door behind him. She stares at* BIFF, *silent.*]

HAPPY   Now what'd you do that for? Mom, I want you to have some flowers—

LINDA [*cutting* HAPPY *off, violently to* BIFF]   Don't you care whether he lives or dies?

HAPPY [*going to the stairs*]   Come upstairs, Biff.

BIFF [*with a flare of disgust, to* HAPPY]   Go away from me! [*to* LINDA] What do you mean, lives or dies? Nobody's dying around here, pal.

LINDA   Get out of my sight! Get out of here!

BIFF   I wanna see the boss.

LINDA   You're not going near him!

BIFF   Where is he? [*He moves into the living-room and* LINDA *follows.*]

LINDA [*shouting after* BIFF]   You invite him for dinner. He looks forward to it all day—[BIFF *appears in his parents' bedroom, looks around and exits*]—and then you desert him there. There's no stranger you'd do that to!

HAPPY   Why? He had a swell time with us. Listen, when I—[LINDA *comes back into the kitchen*]—desert him I hope I don't outlive the day!

LINDA   Get out of here!

HAPPY   Now look, Mom . . .

LINDA   Did you have to go to women tonight? You and your lousy rotten whores!

> [BIFF *re-enters the kitchen.*]

HAPPY   Mom, all we did was follow Biff around trying to cheer him up! [*to* BIFF] Boy, what a night you gave me!

LINDA   Get out of here, both of you, and don't come back! I don't want you tormenting him any more. Go on now, get your things together! [*to* BIFF] You can sleep in his apartment. [*She starts to pick up the flowers and stops herself.*] Pick up this stuff, I'm not your maid any more. Pick it up, you bum, you!

> [HAPPY *turns his back to her in refusal.* BIFF *slowly moves over and gets down on his knees, picking up the flowers.*]

LINDA   You're a pair of animals! Not one, not another living soul would have had the cruelty to walk out on that man in a restaurant!

BIFF [*not looking at her*]   Is that what he said?

LINDA   He didn't have to say anything. He was so humiliated he nearly limped when he came in.

HAPPY   But, Mom, he had a great time with us—

BIFF [*cutting him off violently*]   Shut up!

> [*Without another word,* HAPPY *goes upstairs.*]

LINDA   You! You didn't even go in to see if he was all right!

BIFF [*still on the floor in front of* LINDA, *the flowers in his hand; with self-loathing*]   No. Didn't. Didn't do a damned thing. How do you like that, heh? Left him babbling in a toilet.

LINDA   You louse. You . . .

BIFF   Now you hit it on the nose! [*He gets up, throws the flowers in the waste-basket.*] The scum of the earth, and you're looking at him!

LINDA   Get out of here!

BIFF   I gotta talk to the boss, Mom. Where is he?

LINDA   You're not going near him. Get out of this house!

BIFF [*with absolute assurance, determination*]   No. We're gonna have an abrupt conversation, him and me.

LINDA   You're not talking to him!

> [*Hammering is heard from outside the house, off right.* BIFF *turns toward the noise.*]

LINDA [*suddenly pleading*]   Will you please leave him alone?

BIFF   What's he doing out there?

LINDA   He's planting the garden!

BIFF [*quietly*]   Now? Oh, my God!

> [BIFF *moves outside,* LINDA *following. The light dies down on them and comes up on the center of the apron as* WILLY *walks into it. He is carrying a flashlight, a hoe, and a handful of seed packets. He raps the top of the hoe sharply to fix it firmly, and then moves to the left, measuring off the distance with his foot. He holds the flashlight to look at the seed packets, reading off the instructions. He is in the blue of night.*]

WILLY   Carrots . . . quarter-inch apart. Rows . . . one-foot rows. [*He measures it off.*] One foot. [*He puts down a package and measures off.*] Beets.

[*He puts down another package and measures again.*] Lettuce. [*He reads the package, puts it down.*] One foot— [*He breaks off as* BEN *appears at the right and moves slowly down to him.*] What a proposition, ts, ts. Terrific, terrific. 'Cause she's suffered, Ben, the woman has suffered. You understand me? A man can't go out the way he came in, Ben, a man has got to add up to something. You can't, you can't— [BEN *moves toward him as though to interrupt.*] You gotta consider, now. Don't answer so quick. Remember, it's a guaranteed twenty-thousand-dollar proposition. Now look, Ben, I want you to go through the ins and outs of this thing with me. I've got nobody to talk to, Ben, and the woman has suffered, you hear me?

BEN [*standing still, considering*]   What's the proposition?

WILLY   It's twenty thousand dollars on the barrelhead. Guaranteed, gilt-edged, you understand?

BEN   You don't want to make a fool of yourself. They might not honor the policy.

WILLY   How can they dare refuse? Didn't I work like a coolie to meet every premium on the nose? And now they don't pay off! Impossible!

BEN   It's called a cowardly thing, William.

WILLY   Why? Does it take more guts to stand here the rest of my life ringing up a zero?

BEN [*yielding*]   That's a point, William. [*He moves, thinking, turns.*] And twenty thousand—that *is* something one can feel with the hand, it is there.

WILLY [*now assured, with rising power*]   Oh, Ben, that's the whole beauty of it! I see it like a diamond, shining in the dark, hard and rough, that I can pick up and touch in my hand. Not like—like an appointment! This would not be another damned-fool appointment, Ben, and it changes all the aspects. Because he thinks I'm nothing, see, and so he spites me. But the funeral— [*straightening up*] Ben, that funeral will be massive! They'll come from Maine, Massachusetts, Vermont, New Hampshire! All the old-timers with the strange license plates—that boy will be thunderstruck, Ben, because he never realized—I am known! Rhode Island, New York, New Jersey—I am known, Ben, and he'll see it with his eyes once and for all. He'll see what I am, Ben! He's in for a shock, that boy!

BEN [*coming down to the edge of the garden*]   He'll call you a coward.

WILLY [*suddenly fearful*]   No, that would be terrible.

BEN   Yes. And a damned fool.

WILLY   No, no, he mustn't, I won't have that! [*He is broken and desperate.*]

BEN   He'll hate you, William.

[*The gay music of the Boys is heard.*]

WILLY   Oh, Ben, how do we get back to all the great times? Used to be so full of light, and comradeship, the sleigh-riding in winter, and the ruddiness on his cheeks. And always some kind of good news coming up, always something nice coming up ahead. And never even let me carry the valises in the house, and simonizing, simonizing that little red car! Why, why can't I give him something and not have him hate me?

BEN   Let me think about it. [*He glances at his watch.*] I still have a little time. Remarkable proposition, but you've got to be sure you're not making a fool of yourself.

[BEN *drifts off upstage and goes out of sight.* BIFF *comes down from the left.*]

WILLY [*suddenly conscious of* BIFF, *turns and looks up at him, then begins picking up the packages of seeds in confusion*]   Where the hell is that seed? [*indignantly*] You can't see nothing out here! They boxed in the whole goddam neighborhood!

BIFF   There are people all around here. Don't you realize that?

WILLY   I'm busy. Don't bother me.

BIFF [*taking the hoe from* WILLY]   I'm saying good-by to you, Pop. [WILLY *looks at him, silent, unable to move.*] I'm not coming back any more.

WILLY   You're not going to see Oliver tomorrow?

BIFF   I've got no appointment, Dad.

WILLY   He put his arm around you, and you've got no appointment?

BIFF   Pop, get this now, will you? Everytime I've left it's been a fight that sent me out of here. Today I realized something about myself and I tried to explain it to you and I—I think I'm just not smart enough to make any sense out of it for you. To hell with whose fault it is or anything like that. [*He takes* WILLY'S *arm.*] Let's just wrap it up, heh? Come on in, we'll tell Mom. [*He gently tries to pull* WILLY *to left.*]

WILLY [*frozen, immobile, with guilt in his voice*]   No, I don't want to see her.

BIFF   Come on! [*He pulls again, and* WILLY *tries to pull away.*]

WILLY [*highly nervous*]   No, no, I don't want to see her.

BIFF [*tries to look into* WILLY'S *face, as if to find the answer there*]   Why don't you want to see her?

WILLY [*more harshly now*]   Don't bother me, will you?

BIFF   What do you mean, you don't want to see her? You don't want them calling you yellow, do you? This isn't your fault; it's me, I'm a bum. Now come inside! [WILLY *strains to get away.*] Did you hear what I said to you?

[WILLY *pulls away and quickly goes by himself into the house.* BIFF *follows.*]

LINDA [*to* WILLY]   Did you plant, dear?

BIFF [*at the door, to* LINDA]   All right, we had it out. I'm going and I'm not writing any more.

LINDA [*going to* WILLY *in the kitchen*]   I think that's the best way, dear. 'Cause there's no use drawing it out, you'll just never get along.

[WILLY *doesn't respond.*]

BIFF   People ask where I am and what I'm doing, you don't know, and you don't care. That way it'll be off your mind and you can start brightening up again. All right? That clears it, doesn't it? [WILLY *is silent, and* BIFF *goes to him.*] You gonna wish me luck, scout? [*He extends his hand.*] What do you say?

LINDA   Shake his hand, Willy.

WILLY [*turning to her, seething with hurt*]   There's no necessity to mention the pen at all, y'know.

BIFF [*gently*]   I've got no appointment, Dad.

WILLY [*erupting fiercely*]   He put his arm around . . . ?

BIFF   Dad, you're never going to see what I am, so what's the use of arguing? If I strike oil I'll send you a check. Meantime forget I'm alive.

WILLY [*to* LINDA]   Spite, see?

BIFF Shake hands, Dad.

WILLY Not my hand.

BIFF I was hoping not to go this way.

WILLY Well, this is the way you're going. Good-by.

[BIFF *looks at him a moment, then turns sharply and goes to the stairs.*]

WILLY [*stops him with*] May you rot in hell if you leave this house!

BIFF [*turning*] Exactly what is it that you want from me?

WILLY I want you to know, on the train, in the mountains, in the valleys, wherever you go, that you cut down your life for spite!

BIFF No, no.

WILLY Spite, spite, is the word of your undoing! And when you're down and out, remember what did it. When you're rotting somewhere beside the railroad tracks, remember, and don't you dare blame it on me!

BIFF I'm not blaming it on you!

WILLY I won't take the rap for this, you hear?

[HAPPY *comes down the stairs and stands on the bottom step, watching.*]

BIFF That's just what I'm telling you!

WILLY [*sinking into a chair at the table, with full accusation*] You're trying to put a knife in me—don't think I don't know what you're doing!

BIFF All right, phony! Then let's lay it on the line. [*He whips the rubber tube out of his pocket and puts it on the table.*]

HAPPY You crazy—

LINDA Biff! [*She moves to grab the hose, but* BIFF *holds it down with his hand.*]

BIFF Leave it there! Don't move it!

WILLY [*not looking at it*] What is that?

BIFF You know goddam well what that is.

WILLY [*caged, wanting to escape*] I never saw that.

BIFF You saw it. The mice didn't bring it into the cellar! What is this supposed to do, make a hero out of you? This supposed to make me sorry for you?

WILLY Never heard of it.

BIFF There'll be no pity for you, you hear it? No pity!

WILLY [*to* LINDA] You hear the spite!

BIFF No, you're going to hear the truth—what you are and what I am!

LINDA Stop it!

WILLY Spite!

HAPPY [*coming down toward* BIFF] You cut it now!

BIFF [*to* HAPPY] The man don't know who we are! The man is gonna know! [*to* WILLY] We never told the truth for ten minutes in this house!

HAPPY We always told the truth!

BIFF [*turning on him*] You big blow, are you the assistant buyer? You're one of the two assistants to the assistant, aren't you?

HAPPY Well, I'm practically—

BIFF You're practically full of it! We all are! And I'm through with it. [*to* WILLY] Now hear this, Willy, this is me.

WILLY I know you!

BIFF You know why I had no address for three months? I stole a suit in Kansas City and I was in jail. [*to* LINDA, *who is sobbing*] Stop crying. I'm through with it.

[LINDA *turns away from them, her hands covering her face.*]

WILLY   I suppose that's my fault!

BIFF   I stole myself out of every good job since high school!

WILLY   And whose fault is that?

BIFF   And I never got anywhere because you blew me so full of hot air I could never stand taking orders from anybody! That's whose fault it is!

WILLY   I hear that!

LINDA   Don't, Biff!

BIFF   It's goddam time you heard that! I had to be boss big shot in two weeks, and I'm through with it!

WILLY   Then hang yourself! For spite, hang yourself!

BIFF   No! Nobody's hanging himself, Willy! I ran down eleven flights with a pen in my hand today. And suddenly I stopped, you hear me? And in the middle of that office building, do you hear this? I stopped in the middle of that building and I saw—the sky. I saw the things that I love in this world. The work and the food and time to sit and smoke. And I looked at the pen and said to myself, what the hell am I grabbing this for? Why am I trying to become what I don't want to be? What am I doing in an office, making a contemptuous, begging fool of myself, when all I want is out there, waiting for me the minute I say I know who I am! Why can't I say that, Willy? [*He tries to make* WILLY *face him, but* WILLY *pulls away and moves to the left.*]

WILLY [*with hatred, threateningly*]   The door of your life is wide open!

BIFF   Pop! I'm a dime a dozen, and so are you!

WILLY [*turning on him now in an uncontrolled outburst*]   I am not a dime a dozen! I am Willy Loman, and you are Biff Loman!

[BIFF *starts for* WILLY, *but is blocked by* HAPPY. *In his fury,* BIFF *seems on the verge of attacking his father.*]

BIFF   I am not a leader of men, Willy, and neither are you. You were never anything but a hard-working drummer who landed in the ash can like all the rest of them! I'm one dollar an hour, Willy! I tried seven states and couldn't raise it. A buck an hour! Do you gather my meaning? I'm not bringing home any prizes any more, and you're going to stop waiting for me to bring them home!

WILLY [*directly to* BIFF]   You vengeful, spiteful mut!

[BIFF *breaks from* HAPPY. WILLY, *in fright, starts up the stairs.* BIFF *grabs him.*]

BIFF [*at the peak of his fury*]   Pop, I'm nothing! I'm nothing, Pop. Can't you understand that? There's no spite in it any more. I'm just what I am, that's all.

[BIFF's *fury has spent itself, and he breaks down, sobbing, holding on to* WILLY, *who dumbly fumbles for* BIFF's *face.*]

WILLY [*astonished*]   What're you doing? What're you doing? [*to* LINDA] Why is he crying?

BIFF [*crying, broken*]   Will you let me go, for Christ's sake? Will you take that phony dream and burn it before something happens? [*Struggling to contain himself, he pulls away and moves to the stairs.*] I'll go in the morning. Put him—put him to bed. [*Exhausted,* BIFF *moves up the stairs to his room.*]

WILLY [*after a long pause, astonished, elevated*]   Isn't that—isn't that remarkable? Biff—he likes me!

LINDA   He loves you, Willy!

HAPPY [*deeply moved*]   Always did, Pop.

WILLY   Oh, Biff! [*staring wildly*] He cried! Cried to me. [*He is choking with his love, and now cries out his promise.*] That boy—that boy is going to be magnificent!

[BEN *appears in the light just outside the kitchen.*]

BEN   Yes, outstanding, with twenty thousand behind him.

LINDA [*sensing the racing of his mind, fearfully, carefully*]   Now come to bed, Willy. It's all settled now.

WILLY [*finding it difficult not to rush out of the house*]   Yes, we'll sleep. Come on. Go to sleep, Hap.

BEN   And it does take a great kind of a man to crack the jungle.

[*In accents of dread,* BEN's *idyllic music starts up.*]

HAPPY [*his arm around* LINDA]   I'm getting married, Pop, don't forget it. I'm changing everything. I'm gonna run that department before the year is up. You'll see, Mom. [*He kisses her.*]

BEN   The jungle is dark but full of diamonds, Willy.

[WILLY *turns, moves, listening to* BEN.]

LINDA   Be good. You're both good boys, just act that way, that's all.

HAPPY   'Night, Pop. [*He goes upstairs.*]

LINDA [*to* WILLY]   Come, dear.

BEN [*with greater force*]   One must go in to fetch a diamond out.

WILLY [*to* LINDA, *as he moves slowly along the edge of the kitchen, toward the door*]   I just want to get settled down, Linda. Let me sit alone for a little.

LINDA [*almost uttering her fear*]   I want you upstairs.

WILLY [*taking her in his arms*]   In a few minutes, Linda. I couldn't sleep right now. Go on, you look awful tired. [*He kisses her.*]

BEN   Not like an appointment at all. A diamond is rough and hard to the touch.

WILLY   Go on now. I'll be right up.

LINDA   I think this is the only way, Willy.

WILLY   Sure, it's the best thing.

BEN   Best thing!

WILLY   The only way. Everything is gonna be—go on, kid, get to bed. You look so tired.

LINDA   Come right up.

WILLY   Two minutes.

[LINDA *goes into the living-room, then reappears in her bedroom.* WILLY *moves just outside the kitchen door.*]

WILLY   Loves me. [*wonderingly*] Always loved me. Isn't that a remarkable thing? Ben, he'll worship me for it!

BEN [*with promise*]   It's dark there, but full of diamonds.

WILLY   Can you imagine that magnificence with twenty thousand dollars in his pocket?

LINDA [*calling from her room*]   Willy! Come up!

WILLY [*calling into the kitchen*]   Yes! Yes. Coming! It's very smart, you realize that, don't you, sweetheart? Even Ben sees it. I gotta go, baby. 'By! 'By! [*going over to* BEN, *almost dancing*] Imagine? When the mail comes he'll be ahead of Bernard again!

BEN   A perfect proposition all around.

WILLY   Did you see how he cried to me? Oh, if I could kiss him, Ben!

BEN   Time, William, time!

WILLY   Oh, Ben, I always knew one way or another we were gonna make it, Biff and I!

BEN   [*looking at his watch*]   The boat. We'll be late. [*He moves slowly off into the darkness.*]

WILLY   [*elegiacally, turning to the house*]   Now when you kick off, boy, I want a seventy-yard boot, and get right down the field under the ball, and when you hit, hit low and hit hard, because it's important, boy. [*He swings around and faces the audience.*] There's all kinds of important people in the stands, and the first thing you know . . . [*suddenly realizing he is alone*] Ben! Ben, where do I . . . ? [*He makes a sudden movement of search.*] Ben, how do I . . . ?

LINDA   [*calling*]   Willy, you coming up?

WILLY   [*uttering a gasp of fear, whirling about as if to quiet her*]   Sh! [*He turns around as if to find his way; sounds, faces, voices, seem to be swarming in upon him and he flicks at them, crying,*] Sh! Sh! [*Suddenly music, faint and high, stops him. It rises in intensity, almost to an unbearable scream. He goes up and down on his toes, and rushes off around the house.*] Shhh!

LINDA   Willy?
   [*There is no answer.* LINDA *waits.* BIFF *gets up off his bed. He is still in his clothes.* HAPPY *sits up.* BIFF *stands listening.*]

LINDA   [*with real fear*]   Willy, answer me! Willy!
   [*There is the sound of a car starting and moving away at full speed.*]

LINDA   No!

BIFF   [*rushing down the stairs*]   Pop!
   [*As the car speeds off, the music crashes down in a frenzy of sound, which becomes the soft pulsation of a single cello string.* BIFF *slowly returns to his bedroom. He and* HAPPY *gravely don their jackets.* LINDA *slowly walks out of her room. The music has developed into a dead march. The leaves of day are appearing over everything.* CHARLEY *and* BERNARD *somberly dressed, appear and knock on the kitchen door.* BIFF *and* HAPPY *slowly descend the stairs to the kitchen as* CHARLEY *and* BERNARD *enter. All stop a moment when* LINDA, *in clothes of mourning, bearing a little bunch of roses, comes through the draped doorway into the kitchen. She goes to* CHARLEY *and takes his arm. Now all move toward the audience, through the wall-line of the kitchen. At the limit of the apron,* LINDA *lays down the flowers, kneels, and sits back on her heels. All stare down at the grave.*]

Requiem

CHARLEY   It's getting dark, Linda.
   [LINDA *doesn't react. She stares at the grave.*]

BIFF   How about it, Mom? Better get some rest, heh? They'll be closing the gate soon.
   [LINDA *makes no move. Pause.*]

HAPPY   [*deeply angered*]   He had no right to do that. There was no necessity for it. We would've helped him.

CHARLEY   [*grunting*]   Hmmm.

BIFF   Come along, Mom.

LINDA   Why didn't anybody come?

CHARLEY   It was a very nice funeral.

LINDA   But where are all the people he knew? Maybe they blame him.

CHARLEY   Naa. It's a rough world, Linda. They wouldn't blame him.

LINDA   I can't understand it. At this time especially. First time in thirty-five years we were just about free and clear. He only needed a little salary. He was even finished with the dentist.

CHARLEY   No man only needs a little salary.

LINDA   I can't understand it.

BIFF   There were a lot of nice days. When he'd come home from a trip; or on Sundays, making the stoop; finishing the cellar; putting on the new porch; when he built the extra bathroom; and put up the garage. You know something, Charley, there's more of him in that front stoop than in all the sales he ever made.

CHARLEY   Yeah. He was a happy man with a batch of cement.

LINDA   He was so wonderful with his hands.

BIFF   He had the wrong dreams. All, all, wrong.

HAPPY [almost ready to fight BIFF]   Don't say that!

BIFF   He never knew who he was.

CHARLEY [stopping HAPPY's movement and reply. To BIFF]   Nobody dast blame this man. You don't understand: Willy was a salesman. And for a salesman, there is no rock bottom to the life. He don't put a bolt to a nut, he don't tell you the law or give you medicine. He's a man way out there in the blue, riding on a smile and a shoeshine. And when they start not smiling back—that's an earthquake. And then you get yourself a couple of spots on your hat, and you're finished. Nobody dast blame this man. A salesman is got to dream, boy. It comes with the territory.

BIFF   Charley, the man didn't know who he was.

HAPPY [infuriated]   Don't say that!

BIFF   Why don't you come with me, Happy?

HAPPY   I'm not licked that easily. I'm staying right in this city, and I'm gonna beat this racket! [He looks at BIFF, his chin set.] The Loman Brothers!

BIFF   I know who I am, kid.

HAPPY   All right, boy. I'm gonna show you and everybody else that Willy Loman did not die in vain. He had a good dream. It's the only dream you can have—to come out number-one man. He fought it out here, and this is where I'm gonna win it for him.

BIFF [with a hopeless glance at HAPPY, bends toward his mother]   Let's go, Mom.

LINDA   I'll be with you in a minute. Go on, Charley. [He hesitates.] I want to, just for a minute. I never had a chance to say good-by.

[CHARLEY moves away, followed by HAPPY. BIFF remains a slight distance up and left of LINDA. She sits there, summoning herself. The flute begins, not far away, playing behind her speech.]

LINDA   Forgive me, dear. I can't cry. I don't know what it is, but I can't cry. I don't understand it. Why did you ever do that? Help me, Willy, I can't cry. It seems to me that you're just on another trip. I keep expecting you. Willy, dear, I can't cry. Why did you do it? I search and search and I search, and I can't understand it, Willy. I made the last payment on the house today. Today, dear. And there'll be nobody home. [A sob rises in her

throat.] We're free and clear. [*Sobbing more fully, released*] We're free.
[BIFF *comes slowly toward her.*] We're free . . . We're free . . .

> [BIFF *lifts her to her feet and moves out up right with her in his arms.*
> LINDA *sobs quietly.* BERNARD *and* CHARLEY *come together and follow
> them, followed by* HAPPY. *Only the music of the flute is left on the dark-
> ening stage as over the house the hard towers of the apartment buildings
> rise into sharp focus, and*]

CURTAIN

1949

ROBERT LOWELL
1917–1977

I n "North Haven," her poem in memory of Robert Lowell, Elizabeth Bishop translates the birdsong as Lowell seemed to hear it: "repeat, repeat, repeat, revise,
revise, revise." Repeatedly, even obsessively, Lowell returned to certain subjects in his
poems. Each return confirmed an existing pattern even as it opened the possibility
for revision. In fact, Lowell's life was full of revision. Descended from Protestant
New Englanders, he converted to Catholicism, then fell away from it; he married
three times; and he changed his poetic style more than once. In the later part of his
career Lowell revised even his published poems and did so repeatedly. "Revision is
inspiration," he once said, "no reading of the finished work as exciting as writing-in
the last changes." Revision allowed for Lowell's love of stray events, his attraction to
the fluidity of life (in this, he resembles Wallace Stevens). But Lowell also wanted to
organize life into formal patterns, to locate the random moment in the design of an
epic history (his Catholicism can be seen, in part, as an expression of this desire).
History offered plot and repetition: just as patterns of his childhood recurred in
adult life, the sins of his New England ancestors were reenacted by contemporary
America. Lowell's vision of history leaned toward apocalypse, toward the revelation
of a prior meaning that the poet agonized to determine, and yet he cherished the
freedom of "human chances," with all their indeterminacy. His poems had to accommodate these opposing impulses. Concerning the sequence of poems in *Notebook
1967–1968*, begun as a poetic diary, he said: "Accident threw up the subject and the
plot swallowed them—famished for human chances." If Lowell often swallowed up
the casual, the random, the ordinary, and the domestic into the forms of his poems,
his best plots have a spontaneity whose meanings cannot be fixed.

The burden of family history was substantial for Lowell, whose ancestors included
members of Boston's patrician families. His grandfather was a well-known Episcopal
minister and head of the fashionable St. Mark's School, which the poet was later to
attend. His great-granduncle James Russell Lowell had been a poet and the ambas-
sador to England. The family's light note was provided by the poet Amy Lowell, "big
and a scandal, as if Mae West were a cousin." In the context of this history Lowell's
father, who fared badly in business after his retirement from service as a naval officer, appeared as a diminished figure.

Lowell's first act of revising family history was to leave New England after two years at Harvard (1935–37) in order to study at Ohio's Kenyon College with John Crowe Ransom, the poet and critic. The move brought him in closer touch with the New Criticism and its predilections for "formal difficult poems," the wit and irony of English Metaphysical writers such as John Donne. He also, through Ransom and the poet Allen Tate, came into contact with (although he never formally joined) the Fugitive movement, whose members were southern agrarians opposed to what they regarded as the corrupting values of northern industrialism.

Two of the acts that most decisively separated Lowell from family history were his conversion to Roman Catholicism (1940) and his resistance to American policies in World War II. Although he tried to enlist in the navy, he refused to be drafted into the army. He opposed the saturation bombing of Hamburg and the Allied policy of unconditional surrender and was as a result sentenced to a year's confinement in New York City's West Street jail. The presiding judge at his hearing admonished him for "marring" his family traditions. In his first book, *Lord Weary's Castle* (1946), his Catholicism provided a set of symbols and a distanced platform from which to express his violent antagonism to Protestant mercantile Boston. The stunning, apocalyptic conclusions of these early poems ("the Lord survives the rainbow of his will" or "The blue kingfisher dives on you in fire") render the devastating judgment of the eternal on the fallen history of the individual and the nation.

Alongside these poems drawing on Old Testament anger in *Lord Weary's Castle* were poems, such as "Mr. Edwards and the Spider," that explored from within the nervous intensity that underlay Puritan revivalism. Later dramatic narratives with modern settings, such as "The Mills of the Kavanaghs" and "Falling Asleep over the Aeneid," reveal his psychological interest in and obsession with ruined New England families.

In *Life Studies* (1959) Lowell changed his style dramatically. His subjects became explicitly autobiographical, his language more open and direct. In 1957 he gave readings in California, where Allen Ginsberg and the other Beats had just made their strongest impact in San Francisco. In contrast to their candid, breezy writing, Lowell felt his own seemed "distant, symbol-ridden, and willfully difficult. . . . I felt my old poems hid what they were really about, and many times offered a stiff, humorless, and even impenetrable surface." Although more controlled and severe than Beat writers, he was stimulated by Ginsberg's self-revelations to write more openly than he had about his parents and grandparents, about the mental breakdowns he suffered in the 1950s, and about the difficulties of marriage. (Lowell divorced his first wife, the novelist Jean Stafford, and married the critic Elizabeth Hardwick in 1949.)

Life Studies, by and large, records his ambivalence toward the New England where he resettled after the war, on Boston's "hardly passionate Marlborough Street." Revising his stance toward New England and family history, he no longer denounces the city of his fathers as if he were a privileged outsider. In complicated psychological portraits of his childhood and his relation to his parents and his wives, he assumes a portion of the weakness and vulnerability for himself.

In 1960 Lowell left Boston to live in New York City. *For the Union Dead* (1964), the book that followed, continued the autobiographical vein of *Life Studies*. Lowell called it a book about "witheredness . . . lemony, soured and dry, the drouth I had touched with my own hands." These poems seem more carefully controlled than his earlier *Life Studies*. Often they organize key images from the past into a pattern that illuminates the present. The book includes a number of poems that fuse private and public themes, such as "Fall 1961" and the volume's title poem.

In 1969 Lowell published *Notebook 1967–1968* and then revised these poems for a second, augmented edition, called simply *Notebook* (1970). In 1973, in a characteristic act, he once more revised, rearranged, and expanded *Notebook*'s poems and published them in two separate books. The more personal poems, recording the breakup of his second marriage and his separation from his wife and daughter, were published as *For Lizzie and Harriet*. Those dealing more with public subjects, past and present, were published as *History*. These two books show Lowell once again engaged with the relations between the random event, or the moment in a personal life, and an epic design. In these unrhymed, loosely blank-verse revisions of the sonnet, Lowell responded to the books he was reading, to the events of his personal life, and to the Vietnam War, of which he was an outspoken critic. "Things I felt or saw, or read were drift in the whirlpool."

At the same time a new collection of sonnets, *The Dolphin* (1973), appeared, recording his marriage to Lady Caroline Blackwood. (Lowell's friend the poet Elizabeth Bishop objected to his use of Blackwood's letters in the volume.) He divided his time between Blackwood's home in England and periods of teaching writing and literature at Harvard—a familiar pattern for him, in which the old tensions between New England and "elsewhere" were being constantly explored and renewed. His last book, *Day by Day* (1977), records those stresses as well as new marital difficulties. It also contains some of his most powerful poems about his childhood.

For those who cherish the work of the early Lowell, with its manic, rhythmic energy and its enjambed lines building to fierce power, or those who admire the passionate engagement of *Life Studies* or *For the Union Dead*, the poems of his last four books can be disappointing. At times flat and dispirited, they can seem worked up rather than fully imagined. Yet the later Lowell demonstrates his substantial gifts in a quieter mode.

Lowell's career included an interest in the theater, for which he wrote a version of *Prometheus Bound*, a translation of Racine's *Phaedra*, and adaptations of Melville and Hawthorne stories gathered as *The Old Glory*. He also translated from modern European poetry and the classics, often freely as "imitations," which brought important poetic voices into English currency. His *Selected Poems* (his own choices) appeared in 1976. When he died suddenly at the age of sixty, he was the dominant and most honored poet of his generation—not only for his ten volumes of verse but for his broad activity as a man of letters. He took upon himself the role of poet as public figure, sometimes at great personal cost. He was with the group of writers who led Vietnam War protesters against the Pentagon in 1967, where Norman Mailer, a fellow protester, observed that "Lowell gave off at times the unwilling haunted saintliness of a man who was repaying the moral debts of ten generations of ancestors."

The Quaker Graveyard in Nantucket

[*For Warren Winslow*,[1] *Dead at Sea*]

> Let man have dominion over the fishes of the sea and the fowls of the air and the beasts of the whole earth, and every creeping creature that moveth upon the earth.[2]

I

A brackish reach of shoal off Madaket[3]—
The sea was still breaking violently and night
Had steamed into our North Atlantic Fleet,
When the drowned sailor clutched the drag-net. Light

---

1. A cousin of Lowell's who died in the sinking of a naval vessel during World War II.
2. From Genesis 1.26, the account of the cre-
ation of humankind.
3. On Nantucket Island.

Flashed from his matted head and marble feet,   5
He grappled at the net
With the coiled, hurdling muscles of his thighs:
The corpse was bloodless, a botch of reds and whites,
Its open, staring eyes
Were lustreless dead-lights[4]   10
Or cabin-windows on a stranded hulk
Heavy with sand. We weight the body, close
Its eyes and heave it seaward whence it came,
Where the heel-headed dogfish barks its nose
On Ahab's[5] void and forehead; and the name   15
Is blocked in yellow chalk.
Sailors, who pitch this portent at the sea
Where dreadnaughts shall confess
Its hell-bent deity,
When you are powerless   20
To sand-bag this Atlantic bulwark, faced
By the earth-shaker, green, unwearied, chaste
In his steel scales: ask for no Orphean lute
To pluck life back.[6] The guns of the steeled fleet
Recoil and then repeat   25
The hoarse salute.

II

Whenever winds are moving and their breath
Heaves at the roped-in bulwarks of this pier,
The terns and sea-gulls tremble at your death
In these home waters. Sailor, can you hear   30
The Pequod's[7] sea wings, beating landward, fall
Headlong and break on our Atlantic wall
Off 'Sconset, where the yawing S-boats[8] splash
The bellbuoy, with ballooning spinnakers,
As the entangled, screeching mainsheet clears   35
The blocks: off Madaket, where lubbers[9] lash
The heavy surf and throw their long lead squids
For blue-fish? Sea-gulls blink their heavy lids
Seaward. The winds' wings beat upon the stones,
Cousin, and scream for you and the claws rush   40
At the sea's throat and wring it in the slush
Of this old Quaker graveyard where the bones
Cry out in the long night for the hurt beast
Bobbing by Ahab's whaleboats in the East.

4. Shutters over portholes to keep out water in a storm. The images in lines 4–11 come from "The Shipwreck," the opening chapter of *Cape Cod*, by Henry David Thoreau (1817–1862).
5. Protagonist of the novel *Moby-Dick*, by Herman Melville (1819–1891); he drowns as the culmination of his obsessive hunt for the white whale. Melville uses Ahab's forehead as an emblem of his monomaniac passion.
6. In Greek mythology Orpheus, through his music, tried to win the freedom of his bride, Eurydice, from the Underworld. "Earth-shaker": an epithet for Poseidon, the Greek god of the oceans and of earthquakes.
7. Ahab's ship, destroyed by Moby-Dick.
8. Type of large racing sailboats. "Yawing": steering wildly in heavy seas.
9. Sailor's term for clumsy crew members.

III

All you recovered from Poseidon died   45
With you, my cousin, and the harrowed brine
Is fruitless on the blue beard of the god,
Stretching beyond us to the castles in Spain,
Nantucket's westward haven. To Cape Cod
Guns, cradled on the tide,   50
Blast the eelgrass about a waterclock
Of bilge and backwash, roil the salt and sand
Lashing earth's scaffold, rock
Our warships in the hand
Of the great God, where time's contrition blues   55
Whatever it was these Quaker[1] sailors lost
In the mad scramble of their lives. They died
When time was open-eyed,
Wooden and childish; only bones abide
There, in the nowhere, where their boats were tossed   60
Sky-high, where mariners had fabled news
Of IS,[2] the whited monster. What it cost
Them is their secret. In the sperm-whale's slick
I see the Quakers drown and hear their cry:
"If God himself had not been on our side,   65
If God himself had not been on our side,
When the Atlantic rose against us, why,
Then it had swallowed us up quick."

IV

This is the end of the whaleroad[3] and the whale
Who spewed Nantucket bones on the thrashed swell   70
And stirred the troubled waters to whirlpools
To send the Pequod packing off to hell:
This is the end of them, three-quarters fools,
Snatching at straws to sail
Seaward and seaward on the turntail whale,   75
Spouting out blood and water as it rolls,
Sick as a dog to these Atlantic shoals:
Clamavimus,[4] O depths. Let the sea-gulls wail

For water, for the deep where the high tide
Mutters to its hurt self, mutters and ebbs.   80
Waves wallow in their wash, go out and out,
Leave only the death-rattle of the crabs,
The beach increasing, its enormous snout
Sucking the ocean's side.
This is the end of running on the waves;   85
We are poured out like water. Who will dance

---

1. The whaling population of Nantucket
included many Quakers.
2. The white whale is here imagined as a force
like the God of Exodus 3.14, who, when asked his
name by Moses, replies, "I AM THAT I AM." Also an
abbreviation of Iesu Salvator, Latin for Jesus, savior of men.
3. An Anglo-Saxon epithet for the sea.
4. We have called (Latin), adapting the opening
of Psalm 130: "Out of the depths have I cried unto
thee, O Lord."

The mast-lashed master of Leviathans
Up from this field of Quakers in their unstoned graves?

V

When the whale's viscera go and the roll
Of its corruption overruns this world   90
Beyond tree-swept Nantucket and Woods Hole[5]
And Martha's Vineyard, Sailor, will your sword
Whistle and fall and sink into the fat?
In the great ash-pit of Jehoshaphat[6]
The bones cry for the blood of the white whale,   95
The fat flukes arch and whack about its ears,
The death-lance churns into the sanctuary, tears
The gun-blue swingle,[7] heaving like a flail,
And hacks the coiling life out: it works and drags
And rips the sperm-whale's midriff into rags,   100
Gobbets of blubber spill to wind and weather,
Sailor, and gulls go round the stoven timbers
Where the morning stars sing out together
And thunder shakes the white surf and dismembers
The red flag hammered in the mast-head.[8] Hide,   105
Our steel, Jonas Messias, in Thy side.[9]

VI. OUR LADY OF WALSINGHAM[1]

There once the penitents took off their shoes
And then walked barefoot the remaining mile;
And the small trees, a stream and hedgerows file
Slowly along the munching English lane,   110
Like cows to the old shrine, until you lose
Track of your dragging pain.
The stream flows down under the druid tree,
Shiloah's[2] whirlpools gurgle and make glad
The castle of God. Sailor, you were glad   115
And whistled Sion by that stream. But see:

Our Lady, too small for her canopy,
Sits near the altar. There's no comeliness
At all or charm in that expressionless
Face with its heavy eyelids. As before,   120
This face, for centuries a memory,
Non est species, neque decor,[3]

---

5. On the coast of Massachusetts, near the island of Martha's Vineyard.
6. "The day of judgment. The world, according to some prophets, will end in fire" [Lowell's note]. In Joel 3, the Last Judgment takes place in the valley of Jehoshaphat.
7. Knifelike wooden instrument for beating flax (into fiber for spinning).
8. At the end of *Moby-Dick*, the arm of the American Indian Tashtego appears from the waves and nails Ahab's flag to the sinking mast.

9. Because he emerged alive from the belly of a whale, the prophet Jonah is often linked with the messiah as a figure of salvation.
1. Lowell took these details from E. I. Watkin's *Catholic Art and Culture* (1942), which includes a description of the medieval shrine of the Virgin at Walsingham.
2. The stream that flows past God's Temple on Mount Sion (Isaiah 8.6). In Isaiah 51.11 the redeemed come "singing into Zion."
3. There is no ostentation or elegance (Latin).

Expressionless, expresses God: it goes
Past castled Sion. She knows what God knows,
Not Calvary's Cross nor crib at Bethlehem   125
Now, and the world shall come to Walsingham.

VII

The empty winds are creaking and the oak
Splatters and splatters on the cenotaph,
The boughs are trembling and a gaff
Bobs on the untimely stroke   130
Of the greased wash exploding on a shoal-bell
In the old mouth of the Atlantic. It's well;
Atlantic, you are fouled with the blue sailors,
Sea-monsters, upward angel, downward fish:
Unmarried and corroding, spare of flesh   135
Mart once of supercilious, wing'd clippers,
Atlantic, where your bell-trap guts its spoil
You could cut the brackish winds with a knife
Here in Nantucket, and cast up the time
When the Lord God formed man from the sea's slime   140
And breathed into his face the breath of life,
And blue-lung'd combers lumbered to the kill.
The Lord survives the rainbow[4] of His will.

                                                            1946

Mr. Edwards and the Spider[1]

I saw the spiders marching through the air,
Swimming from tree to tree that mildewed day
    In latter August when the hay
    Came creaking to the barn. But where
        The wind is westerly,   5
Where gnarled November makes the spiders fly
Into the apparitions of the sky,
    They purpose nothing but their ease and die
Urgently beating east to sunrise and the sea;

What are we in the hands of the great God?   10
It was in vain you set up thorn and briar
    In battle array against the fire
    And treason crackling in your blood;
        For the wild thorns grow tame
And will do nothing to oppose the flame;   15
    Your lacerations tell the losing game

4. Alluding to God's covenant with Noah after
the Flood. The rainbow symbolized the fact that
humanity would never again be destroyed by flood
(Genesis 9.11).
1. Jonathan Edwards (1703–1758), Puritan

preacher and theologian. Lowell quotes his writings throughout. The details of the first stanza
come from his youthful essay "Of Insects" ("The
Habits of Spiders").

You play against a sickness past your cure.
How will the hands be strong? How will the heart endure?[2]

A very little thing, a little worm,
Or hourglass-blazoned spider,[3] it is said,   20
   Can kill a tiger. Will the dead
   Hold up his mirror and affirm
     To the four winds the smell
And flash of his authority? It's well
If God who holds you to the pit of hell,   25
Much as one holds a spider, will destroy,
Baffle and dissipate your soul. As a small boy

On Windsor Marsh,[4] I saw the spider die
When thrown into the bowels of fierce fire:
   There's no long struggle, no desire   30
   To get up on its feet and fly—
     It stretches out its feet
And dies. This is the sinner's last retreat;
Yes, and no strength exerted on the heat
Then sinews the abolished will, when sick   35
And full of burning, it will whistle on a brick.

But who can plumb the sinking of that soul?
Josiah Hawley,[5] picture yourself cast
   Into a brick-kiln where the blast
   Fans your quick vitals to a coal—   40
     If measured by a glass,
How long would it seem burning! Let there pass
A minute, ten, ten trillion; but the blaze
Is infinite, eternal: this is death,
To die and know it. This is the Black Widow, death.   45

1946

Skunk Hour

for Elizabeth Bishop

Nautilus Island's[1] hermit
heiress still lives through winter in her Spartan cottage;
her sheep still graze above the sea.
Her son's a bishop. Her farmer
is first selectman in our village;   5
she's in her dotage.

2. This stanza draws on Edwards's sermon "Sinners in the Hands of an Angry God," whose point of departure is Ezekiel 22.14: "Can thine heart endure or can thine hands be strong in the days that I shall deal with thee?" (cf. line 18).
3. The poisonous black widow spider has, on the underside of its abdomen, a red marking that resembles an hourglass.
4. East Windsor, Connecticut, Edwards's childhood home.
5. Edwards's uncle, Joseph Hawley.
1. The poem is set in Castine, Maine, where Lowell had a summer house.

Thirsting for
the hierarchic privacy
of Queen Victoria's century,
she buys up all   10
the eyesores facing her shore,
and lets them fall.

The season's ill—
we've lost our summer millionaire,
who seemed to leap from an L. L. Bean   15
catalogue.[2] His nine-knot yawl
was auctioned off to lobstermen.
A red fox stain covers Blue Hill.

And now our fairy
decorator brightens his shop for fall;   20
his fishnet's filled with orange cork,
orange, his cobbler's bench and awl;
there is no money in his work,
he'd rather marry.

One dark night,   25
my Tudor Ford climbed the hill's skull;
I watched for love-cars. Lights turned down,
they lay together, hull to hull,
where the graveyard shelves on the town. . . .
My mind's not right.   30

A car radio bleats,
"Love, O careless Love. . . ." I hear
my ill-spirit sob in each blood cell,
as if my hand were at its throat. . . .
I myself am hell;[3]   35
nobody's here—

only skunks, that search
in the moonlight for a bite to eat.
They march on their soles up Main Street:
white stripes, moonstruck eyes' red fire   40
under the chalk-dry and spar spire
of the Trinitarian Church.

I stand on top
of our back steps and breathe the rich air—
a mother skunk with her column of kittens swills the garbage pail.   45
She jabs her wedge-head in a cup
of sour cream, drops her ostrich tail,
and will not scare.

1959

2. From a mail-order house in Maine that primarily sells sporting goods and clothing to the
wealthy and upper middle class.

3. "Which way I fly is Hell, myself am Hell"
(Satan in Milton's *Paradise Lost* 4.75).

For the Union Dead[1]

"Relinquunt Omnia Servare Rem Publicam."[2]

The old South Boston Aquarium stands
in a Sahara of snow now. Its broken windows are boarded.
The bronze weathervane cod has lost half its scales.
The airy tanks are dry.

Once my nose crawled like a snail on the glass;   5
my hand tingled
to burst the bubbles
drifting from the noses of the cowed, compliant fish.

My hand draws back. I often sigh still
for the dark downward and vegetating kingdom   10
of the fish and reptile. One morning last March,
I pressed against the new barbed and galvanized

fence on the Boston Common. Behind their cage,
yellow dinosaur steamshovels were grunting
as they cropped up tons of mush and grass   15
to gouge their underworld garage.

Parking spaces luxuriate like civic
sandpiles in the heart of Boston.
A girdle of orange, Puritan-pumpkin colored girders
braces the tingling Statehouse,   20

shaking over the excavations, as it faces Colonel Shaw
and his bell-cheeked Negro infantry
on St. Gaudens' shaking Civil War relief,
propped by a plank splint against the garage's earthquake.

Two months after marching through Boston,   25
half the regiment was dead;
at the dedication
William James[3] could almost hear the bronze Negroes breathe.

Their monument sticks like a fishbone
in the city's throat.   30
Its Colonel is as lean
as a compass-needle.

1. First published as "Colonel Shaw and the Massachusetts' 54th" in a paperback edition of *Life Studies* (1960). It became the title poem of *For the Union Dead* (1964).
2. Robert Gould Shaw (1837–1863) led the first all–African American regiment in the Union army during the Civil War. He was killed in the attack against Fort Wagner, South Carolina. A bronze relief by the sculptor Augustus Saint-Gaudens (1848–1897), dedicated in 1897, standing opposite the Massachusetts State House on Boston Common, commemorates the deaths. A Latin inscription on the monument reads *Omnia Reliquit Servare Rem Publicam* ("He leaves all behind to save the Republic"). Lowell's epigraph alters the inscription slightly, changing the third-person singular (*he*) to the third-person plural: "*They* give up everything to save the Republic."
3. Philosopher and psychologist (1842–1910) who taught at Harvard.

He has an angry wrenlike vigilance,
a greyhound's gentle tautness;
he seems to wince at pleasure,   35
and suffocate for privacy.

He is out of bounds now. He rejoices in man's lovely,
peculiar power to choose life and die—
when he leads his black soldiers to death,
he cannot bend his back.   40

On a thousand small town New England greens,
the old white churches hold their air
of sparse, sincere rebellion; frayed flags
quilt the graveyards of the Grand Army of the Republic.

The stone statues of the abstract Union Soldier   45
grow slimmer and younger each year—
wasp-waisted, they doze over muskets
and muse through their sideburns . . .

Shaw's father wanted no monument
except the ditch,   50
where his son's body was thrown[4]
and lost with his "niggers."

The ditch is nearer.
There are no statues for the last war[5] here;
on Boylston Street,[6] a commercial photograph   55
shows Hiroshima boiling[7]

over a Mosler Safe, the "Rock of Ages"[8]
that survived the blast. Space is nearer.
When I crouch to my television set,
the drained faces of Negro school-children rise like balloons.[9]   60

Colonel Shaw
is riding on his bubble,
he waits
for the blessed break.

The Aquarium is gone. Everywhere,   65
giant finned cars nose forward like fish;
a savage servility
slides by on grease.

1960, 1964

4. By the Confederate soldiers at Fort Wagner.
5. World War II.
6. In Boston, where the poem is set.
7. On August 6, 1945, the United States dropped
an atomic bomb on this Japanese city.
8. Biblical reference to an indestructible and
supernatural rock, the foundation of an everlasting kingdom. Used as an advertising slogan by
Mosler Safes.
9. Probably news photographs connected with
contemporary civil rights demonstrations to
secure desegregation of schools in the South.

GWENDOLYN BROOKS
1917-2000

" If there was ever a born poet," the writer Alice Walker once said in an interview, "I think it is Brooks." A passionate sense of language and an often daring use of formal structures are hallmarks of Gwendolyn Brooks's poetry. She used these gifts in a career characterized by dramatic evolution, a career that linked two very different generations of African American poets. "Until 1967," Brooks said, "my own Blackness did not confront me with a shrill spelling of itself." She then grouped herself with militant black writers and defined her work as belonging primarily to the African American community. In her earlier work, however, Brooks followed the example of the older writers of the Harlem Renaissance, Langston Hughes and Countee Cullen among them, who honored the ideal of an integrated society. In that period her work received support largely from white audiences. But Brooks's changing sense of her commitments should not obscure her persistent, underlying concerns. She never lacked political awareness, and in remarkably versatile poems, both early and late, she wrote about black experience and black rage, with a particular awareness of the complex lives of black women.

Brooks was born in Topeka, Kansas; she grew up in Chicago and is closely identified with the energies and problems of its black community. She went to Chicago's Englewood High School and graduated from Wilson Junior College. Brooks remembered writing poetry from the time she was seven and keeping poetry note books from the time she was eleven. She got her education in the moderns—poets such as Pound and Eliot—under the guidance of a rich Chicago socialite, Inez Cunningham Stark, who was a reader for *Poetry* magazine and taught a poetry class at the Southside Community Art Center. Her first book, *A Street in Bronzeville* (1945), took its title from the name journalists gave to Chicago's black ghetto. Her poems portrayed the waste and loss that are the inevitable result of what Langston Hughes called the "dream deferred." With her second book of poems, *Annie Allen* (1949), Brooks became the first African American to receive the Pulitzer Prize for poetry.

In *Annie Allen* and in her Bronzeville poems (*Bronzeville Boys and Girls*, 1956, continued the work begun in *A Street in Bronzeville*), Brooks concentrated on portraits of what Hughes called "the ordinary aspects of black life," stressing the vitality and the often subversive morality of ghetto figures. She portrayed the good girls who want to be bad; the bored children of hardworking, pious mothers; the laments of women, some of them mothers, abandoned by their men. Brooks's diction was a combination of street talk, the florid biblical speech of black Protestant preachers, and the traditional vocabulary of English and American verse. She wrote vigorous, strongly accented, and strongly rhymed lines with a great deal of alliteration. She also cultivated traditional lyric forms; for example, she was one of the few modern poets to write extensively in the sonnet form.

A great change in Brooks's life came at Fisk University in 1967 with the Second Black Writers' Conference, in whose charged activist atmosphere she encountered many of the new young black poets. After this, Brooks tested the possibility of writing poetry exclusively for black audiences. She drew closer to militant political groups as a result of conducting poetry workshops for some members of the Blackstone Rangers, a teenage gang in Chicago. In autobiographical writings such as her prose *Report from Part One* (1972), Brooks became more self-conscious about her own potential role as a leader of black feminists. She left her New York publisher to have her work printed by African American publishers, especially the Broadside Press. Brooks's poetry, too, changed, in both its focus and its technique. Her subjects tended to be more explicitly political and to deal with questions of revolutionary violence and issues of African American identity. Stylistically, her work evolved out of the concentrated imagery and narratives of her earlier writing, with its often formal diction, and moved toward an increased use of the energetic, improvisatory rhythms of jazz, the combinations of African chants, and an emphatically spoken language. The resulting poetry constantly revises itself and its sense of the world, open to change but evoking history. "How does one convey the influence Gwendolyn Brooks has had on generations—not only writers but people from all walks of life?" the poet Rita Dove has remarked, remembering how, as a young woman, she was "struck by these poems . . . that weren't afraid to take language and swamp it, twist it, and engage it so that it shimmered and dashed and lingered."

FROM A STREET IN BRONZEVILLE

to David and Keziah Brooks

kitchenette building

We are things of dry hours and the involuntary plan,
Grayed in, and gray. "Dream" makes a giddy sound, not strong
Like "rent," "feeding a wife," "satisfying a man."

But could a dream send up through onion fumes
Its white and violet, fight with fried potatoes   5
And yesterday's garbage ripening in the hall,
Flutter, or sing an aria down these rooms

Even if we were willing to let it in,
Had time to warm it, keep it very clean,
Anticipate a message, let it begin?   10

We wonder. But not well! not for a minute!
Since Number Five is out of the bathroom now,
We think of lukewarm water, hope to get in it.

                                                              1945

the mother

Abortions will not let you forget.
You remember the children you got that you did not get,
The damp small pulps with a little or with no hair,

The singers and workers that never handled the air.
You will never neglect or beat   5
Them, or silence or buy with a sweet.
You will never wind up the sucking-thumb
Or scuttle off ghosts that come.
You will never leave them, controlling your luscious sigh,
Return for a snack of them, with gobbling mother-eye.   10

I have heard in the voices of the wind the voices of my dim
        killed children.
I have contracted. I have eased
My dim dears at the breasts they could never suck.
I have said, Sweets, if I sinned, if I seized
Your luck   15
And your lives from your unfinished reach,
If I stole your births and your names,
Your straight baby tears and your games,
Your stilted or lovely loves, your tumults, your marriages, aches,
        and your deaths,
If I poisoned the beginnings of your breaths,   20
Believe that even in my deliberateness I was not deliberate.
Though why should I whine,
Whine that the crime was other than mine?—
Since anyhow you are dead.
Or rather, or instead,   25
You were never made.

But that too, I am afraid,
Is faulty: oh, what shall I say, how is the truth to be said?
You were born, you had body, you died.
It is just that you never giggled or planned or cried.   30

Believe me, I loved you all.
Believe me, I knew you, though faintly, and I loved, I loved you
All.

                                                                1945

the white troops had their orders but the
Negroes looked like men

They had supposed their formula was fixed.
They had obeyed instructions to devise
A type of cold, a type of hooded gaze.
But when the Negroes came they were perplexed.
These Negroes looked like men. Besides, it taxed   5
Time and the temper to remember those
Congenital iniquities that cause
Disfavor of the darkness. Such as boxed
Their feelings properly, complete to tags—
A box for dark men and a box for Other—   10

Would often find the contents had been scrambled.
Or even switched. Who really gave two figs?
Neither the earth nor heaven ever trembled.
And there was nothing startling in the weather.

1945

We Real Cool

THE POOL PLAYERS.
SEVEN AT THE GOLDEN SHOVEL.

We real cool. We
Left school. We

Lurk late. We
Strike straight. We

Sing sin. We   5
Thin gin. We

Jazz June. We
Die soon.

1960

The Last Quatrain of the Ballad of Emmett Till[1]

after the murder,
after the burial

Emmett's mother is a pretty-faced thing;
      the tint of pulled taffy.
She sits in a red room,   5
      drinking black coffee.
She kisses her killed boy.
      And she is sorry.
Chaos in windy grays
      through a red prairie.   10

1960

---

1. A fourteen-year-old African American boy lynched in Mississippi in 1955 for allegedly "leering" at a white woman.

To the Diaspora[1]

you did not know you were Afrika

When you set out for Afrika
you did not know you were going.
Because
you did not know you were Afrika.
You did not know the Black continent   5
that had to be reached
was you.

I could not have told you then that some sun
would come,
somewhere over the road,   10
would come evoking the diamonds
of you, the Black continent—
somewhere over the road.
You would not have believed my mouth.

When I told you, meeting you somewhere close   15
to the heat and youth of the road,
liking my loyalty, liking belief,
you smiled and you thanked me but very little believed me.

Here is some sun. Some.
Now off into the places rough to reach.   20
Though dry, though drowsy, all unwillingly a-wobble,
into the dissonant and dangerous crescendo.
Your work, that was done, to be done to be done to be done.

1981

1. People settled far from their ancestral homelands.

PATRICIA HIGHSMITH
1921–1995

Patricia Highsmith's career is connected to the most popular entertainments of the late twentieth century. Born in 1921 in Fort Worth, Texas, Highsmith worked in a comic book studio during World War II, writing heroic, jingoistic comic books with titles like "The Destroyer" and "The Fighting Yank." The influences of comics, crime and detective fiction, science fiction, horror, and Hollywood film are all palpable in her work, even as she consistently invoked such canonical European writers as Fyodor Dostoyevsky and André Gide when discussing her primary influences. The premise of one of her most famous novels, *The Talented Mr. Ripley* (1955), was inspired by Henry James's great novel *The Ambassadors* (1903), which features a naïve American man sent to retrieve the scion of a wealthy American family who has fallen prey to the seductions of Europe. Highsmith won prizes for detective and crime fiction throughout her life, in both Europe and America, but more traditional literary honors were elusive.

Highsmith's blend of the popular and the highbrow, of the visceral and the intellectual, distinguishes her work and has startled readers for over half a century. She died in 1995, just days before the publication of her thirtieth work of fiction. She had also written, in 1966, a handbook for writing suspense stories, and two additional story collections were published in the years following her death. Because Highsmith deftly combined the suspense plots of genre fiction with knotty philosophical questions and unforgettable characters, her work found a natural outlet in the movies. Her first novel, *Strangers on a Train* (1950), was adapted by Alfred Hitchcock in 1951. Later film adaptations of *The Talented Mr. Ripley* (in France in 1960 and in the United States in 1999) and *The Price of Salt* (1952; adapted as *Carol* in 2015) have helped to keep Highsmith's fiction steadily in front of audiences.

Highsmith's most famous work—the five-novel Ripley series that began with *The Talented Mr. Ripley* and ended with *Ripley Under Water* (1991)—dared readers to sympathize with Tom Ripley, murderer of his rich friend, Dickie Greenleaf. Tom impersonates Greenleaf for a time after the murder, eventually taking over Dickie's clothes, possessions, relationships, and trust fund. Inheriting Dickie's money, Tom reverts to his own identity and goes on to lead a life of wealth and intrigue in subsequent novels. Readers found themselves rooting for Tom to succeed as Highsmith skillfully drew on class resentments, the dynamics of homophobia and homoerotic attraction, and the American tradition of the self-made man to craft her unlikely hero. As recent criticism points out, readers could understand Ripley as deviating from a 1950s repressive society, but in his materialism and upper-class strivings, they could also think of him as a model American citizen. Highsmith so identified with Tom Ripley that she would sign letters "Pat H, alias Ripley," and said that she often had the feeling that Ripley was writing the novels and she was "merely typing" them.

Murder and eroticism were linked in Highsmith's mind: "Murder is a kind of making love, a kind of possessing," she wrote in her journal, reflecting upon a woman she became attracted to while working at Bloomingdale's. That attraction inspired Highsmith's other major literary accomplishment: the novel *The Price of Salt*, published under the pseudonym Claire Morgan. The novel is widely regarded as the first lesbian love story with a happy ending. In it, the young protagonist, Therese, a set designer, meets Carol, a beautiful and married older woman. The experienced Carol seduces Therese, Therese subsequently leaves her fiancé, and the two women set out on a road trip, followed by a private detective hired by Carol's husband. Carol faces the agonizing choice of abandoning Therese or giving up her child in divorce proceedings. Carol eventually chooses Therese, and they live happily together in an apartment in New York City.

In her short fiction, Highsmith explored human relationships with animals, a theme that drives "The Quest for *Blank Claveringi*," the story reprinted here, in which an aging scientist seeks to crown his life's work by documenting and then naming after himself a species of giant snails. The story is typical Highsmith in that she was particularly attracted to animals that were not usual human companions. In the 1960s, she kept a collection of over 300 beloved snails, pets she would bring out at dinner parties to slither around the table. In many stories, especially those contained in *The Animal-Lover's Book of Beastly Murder* (1975), she imagined animals of all kinds taking violent revenge on human beings for acts of abuse. Highsmith's ability— and willingness—to enter into the minds of creatures operating far from human social norms (whether those creatures were mammal, reptile, human, or otherwise) makes her fiction both daring and strange, reminding us of the work of writers such as Franz Kafka, who famously imagined a man transformed into a dung beetle, or the playwright Eugene Ionesco, who in 1959 staged a play in which the inhabitants of a French town turn into rhinoceroses.

Highsmith moved to Europe permanently in 1963 to be near women who were romantically important to her; her work has been much appreciated there. Late in her life, her fiction reflected the topics of her times—including the Israeli-Arab conflict, fundamentalist Christianity, and the AIDS crisis. She became increasingly and publicly anti-Semitic as she aged, losing some of her public admiration as a consequence. Today her reputation stands on the unique qualities and literary strength of her first two decades as a writer. Her fiction brings news of humanity's darkest, strangest, and most fundamental elements.

The Quest for *Blank Claveringi*

Avery Clavering, a professor of zoology at a California university, heard of the giant snails of Kuwa in a footnote of a book on molluscs. His sabbatical had been coming up in three months when he read the few lines:

> It is said by Matusas Islands natives that snails even larger than this exist on the uninhabited island of Kuwa, twenty-five miles distant from the Matusas. The Matusans claim that these snails have a shell diameter of twenty feet and that they are man-eating. Dr. Wm. J. Stead, now living in the Matusas, visited Kuwa in 1949 without finding any snails at all, but the legend persists.

The item aroused Professor Clavering's interest, because he very much wanted to discover some animal, bird, reptile or even mollusc to which he could give his name. *Something-or-other Claveringi.*[1] The professor was forty-eight. His time, perhaps, was not growing short, but he had achieved no particular renown. The discovery of a new species would win him immortality in his field.

The Matusas, the professor saw on a map, were three small islands arranged like the points of an isosceles triangle not far from Hawaii. He wrote a letter to Dr. Stead and received the following reply, written on an abominable typewriter, so many words pale, he could scarcely read it:

April 8th, 19—

Dear Professor Clavering:
I have long heard of the giant snails of Kuwa, but before you make a trip of such length, I must tell you that the natives here assure me a group of them went about twenty years ago to Kuwa to exterminate these so-called man-eating snails which they imagined could swim the ocean between Kuwa and the Matusas and do some damage to the latter islands. They claim to have killed off the whole community of them

---

1. In scientific naming (called "binomial nomenclature"), each species of animal is given two Latin names, designating first the genus, or group, to which an animal belongs, and, second, the animal's particular species. Species may be named after the person who first records the animal's existence in modern scientific classification. In this case, the person's name is given a Latin ending. Prof. Clavering does not know the genus to which a giant snail may belong ("*Something-or-other*"), but he plans to name the species after himself, "*Claveringi.*"

except for one old fellow they could not kill. This is typical of native stories—there's always one that got away. I haven't much doubt the snails were no bigger than three feet across and that they were not * * * * (here a word was illegible, due both to the pale ribbon and a squashed insect). You say you read of my effort in 1949 to find the giant snails. What the footnote did not say is that I have made several trips since to find them. I retired to the Matusas, in fact, for that purpose. I now believe the snails to be mere folklore, a figment of the natives' imagination. If I were you, I would not waste time or money on an expedition.

Yours sincerely,
Wm. J. Stead, M.D.

Professor Clavering had the money and the time. He detected a sourness in Dr. Stead's letter. Maybe Dr. Stead had just had bad luck. By post, Professor Clavering hired a thirty-foot sailboat with an auxiliary motor from Hawaii. He wanted to make the trip alone from the Matusas. *Blank Claveringi*. Regardless of the size, the snail was apt to be different from any known snail, because of its isolation—if it existed. He planned to go one month ahead of his wife and to join her and their twenty-year-old daughter Wanda in Hawaii for a more orthodox holiday after he had visited Kuwa. A month would give him plenty of time to find the snail, even if there were only one, to take photographs, and make notes.

It was late June when Professor Clavering, equipped with water tanks, tinned beef, soup and milk, biscuits, writing materials, camera, knife, hatchet, and a Winchester .22[2] which he hardly knew how to use, set forth from one of the Matusas bound for Kuwa. Dr. Stead, who had been his host for a few days, saw him off. Dr. Stead was seventy-five, he said, but he looked older, due perhaps to the ravages of drink and the apparently aimless life he led now. He had not looked for the giant snail in two years, he said.

"I've given the last third of my life to looking for this snail, you might say," Dr Stead added. "But that's man's fate, I suppose, the pursuit of the nonexistent. Well—good luck to you, Professor Clavering!" He waved his old American straw hat as the *Samantha* left the dock under motor power.

Professor Clavering had made out to Stead that if he did find snails, he would come back at once, get some natives to accompany him, and return to Kuwa with materials to make crates for the snails. Stead had expressed doubt whether he could persuade any natives to accompany him, if the snail or snails were really large. But then, Dr. Stead had been negative about everything pertaining to Professor Clavering's quest. Professor Clavering was glad to get away from him.

After about an hour, Professor Clavering cut the motor and tentatively hoisted some sail. The wind was favorable, but he knew little about sails, and he paid close attention to his compass. At last, Kuwa came into view, a tan hump on a sea of blue. He was quite close before he saw any greenery, and this was only the tops of some trees. Already, he was looking for anything resembling a giant snail, and regretting he had not brought binoculars, but the island was only three miles long and one mile broad. He

---

2. A small-bore rifle used largely for target shooting and small game.

decided to aim for a small beach. He dropped anchor, two of them, in water so clear he could see the sand under it. He stood for a few minutes on the deck.

The only life he saw was a few birds in the tops of trees, brightly colored, crested birds, making cries he had never heard before. There was no low-lying vegetation whatsoever, none of the grass and reeds that might have been expected on an island such as this—much like the Matusas in soil color—and this augured well of the presence of snails that might have devoured everything green within their reach. It was only a quarter to two. Professor Clavering ate part of a papaya, two boiled eggs, and brewed coffee on his alcohol burner, as he had had nothing to eat since 6 a.m. Then with his hunting knife and hatchet in the belt of his khaki shorts, and his camera around his neck, he lowered himself into the water. The *Samantha* carried no rowboat.

He sank up to his neck, but he could walk on the bottom. He held the camera high. He emerged panting, as he was some twenty pounds over-weight. Professor Clavering was to regret every one of those pounds before the day was over, but as he got his breath and looked around him, and felt himself drying off in the warm sunlight, he was happy. He wiped his hatchet and knife with dry sand, then walked inland, alert for the rounded form of a snail's shell, moving or stationary, anywhere. But as snails were more or less noctur-nal, he thought any snails might well be sleeping in some cave or crevice with no idea of emerging until nightfall.

He decided to cross the island first, then follow the coast to right or left and circle the island. He had not gone a quarter of a mile, when his heart gave a leap. Ten yards before him, he saw three bent saplings with their top leaves chewed off. The young trees were four inches in diameter at their bases. It would have taken a considerable weight to bend them down, something like a hundred pounds. The professor looked on the trees and the ground for the glaze left by snails, but found none. But rain could have washed it away. A snail whose shell was three feet in diameter would not weigh enough to bend such a tree, so Professor Clavering now hoped for something bigger. He pushed on.

He arrived at the other side of the island. The sea had eaten a notch into the shore, forming a mostly dry gulley of a hundred yards' length and a depth of thirty feet. The land here was sandy but moist, and there was, he saw, a little vegetation in the form of patchy grass. But here, the lower branches of all the trees had been divested of their leaves, and so long ago that the branches had dried and fallen off. All this bespoke the presence of land snails. Professor Clavering stooped and looked down into the gulley. He saw, just over the edge of his side of the crevice, the pink-tan curve of something that was neither rock nor sand. If it was a snail, it was monstrous. Involun-tarily, he took a step backward, scattering pebbles down the gulley.

The professor ran round the gulley to have a better look. It was a snail, and its shell was about fifteen feet high. He had a view of its left side, the side without the spiral. It resembled a peach-colored sail filled with wind, and the sunlight made nacreous,[3] silvery patches gleam and twinkle as the great

---

3. Resembling the iridescent coating from which pearls are formed and that lines the inside of shells.

thing stirred. The little rain of pebbles had aroused it, the professor realized. If the shell was fifteen or eighteen feet in diameter, he reckoned that the snail's body or foot would be something like six yards long when extended. Rooted to the spot, the professor stood, thrilled as much by the (as yet) empty phrase *Blank Claveringi* which throbbed in his head as by the fact he was looking upon something no man had seen before, or at least no scientist. The crate would have to be bigger than he had thought, but the *Samantha* would be capable of taking it on her forward deck.

The snail was backing to pull its head from the narrow part of the gulley. The moist body, the color of tea with milk, came into view with the slowness of an enormous snake awakening from slumber. All was silent, except for pebbles dropping from the snail's underside as it lifted its head, except for the professor's constrained breathing. The snail's head, facing inland, rose higher and higher, and its antennae, with which it saw, began to extend. Professor Clavering realized he had disturbed it from its diurnal sleep, and a brief terror caused him to retreat again, sending more pebbles down the slope.

The snail heard this, and slowly turned its enormous head toward him.

The professor felt paralyzed. A gigantic face regarded him, a face with drooping, scalloped cheeks or lips, with antennae six feet long now, the eyes on the ends of them scrutinizing him at his own level and scarcely ten feet away, with the disdain of a Herculean lorgnette,[4] with the unknown potency of a pair of oversized telescopes. The snail reared so high, it had to arch its antennae to keep him in view. Six yards long? It would be more like eight or ten yards. The snail turned itself to move toward him.

Still, the professor did not budge. He knew about snails' teeth, the twenty-odd thousand pairs of them even in a small garden snail, set in comblike structures, the upper front teeth visible, moving up and down constantly just under transparent flesh. A snail of this size, with proportionate teeth, could chew through a tree as quickly as a woodsman's axe, the professor thought. The snail was advancing up the bank with monumental confidence. He had to stand still for a few seconds simply to admire it. *His* snail! The professor opened his camera and took a picture, just as the snail was hauling its shell over the edge of the quarry.

"You are magnificent!" Professor Clavering said in a soft and awestruck voice. Then he took a few steps backward.

It was pleasant to think he could skip nimbly about, comparatively speaking, observing the snail from all angles, while the snail could only creep toward him at what seemed the rate of one yard in ten seconds. The professor thought to watch the snail for an hour or so, then go back to the *Samantha* and write some notes. He would sleep aboard the boat, take some more photographs tomorrow morning, then start under engine power back to the Matusas. He trotted for twenty yards, then turned to watch the snail approach.

The snail travelled with its head lifted three feet above the ground, keeping the professor in the focus of its eyes. It was moving faster. Professor

4. Of the size of the Greek hero, Hercules, renowned for his strength. A lorgnette is a pair of glasses or opera glasses held in front of the eyes by a long side handle.

Clavering retreated sooner than he intended, and before he could get another picture.

Now Professor Clavering looked around for a mate of the snail. He was rather glad not to see another snail, but he cautioned himself not to rule out the possibility of a mate. It wouldn't be pleasant to be cornered by two snails, yet the idea excited him. Impossible to think of a situation in which he could not escape from two slow, lumbering creatures like the—the what? *Amygdalus Persica* (his mind stuck on peaches, because of the beautiful color of the shell) *Carnivora*[5] (perhaps) *Claveringi*. That could be improved upon, the professor thought as he walked backward, watching.

A little grove of trees gave him an idea. If he stood in the grove, the snail could not reach him, and he would also have a close view. The professor took a stand amid twelve or fifteen trees, all about twenty feet high. The snail did not slacken its speed, but began to circle the grove, still watching the professor. Finding no opening big enough between two trees, the snail raised its head higher, fifteen feet high, and began to creep up on the trees. Branches cracked, and one tree snapped.

Professor Clavering ducked and retreated. He had a glimpse of a great belly gliding unhurt over a jagged tree trunk, of a circular mouth two feet across, open and showing the still wider upper band of teeth like shark's teeth, munching automatically up and down. The snail cruised gently down over the tree tops, some of which sprang back into position as the snail's weight left them.

Click! went the professor's camera.

What a sight that had been! Something like a slow hurdle. He imagined entertaining friends with an account of it, substantiated by the photograph, once he got back to California. Old Professor McIlroy of the biology department had laughed at him for spending seven thousand dollars on an effort he predicted would be futile!

Professor Clavering was tiring, so he cut directly for the *Samantha*. He noticed that the snail veered also in a direction that would intercept him, if they kept on at their steady though different speeds, and the professor chuckled and trotted for a bit. The snail also picked up speed, and the professor remembered the wide, upward rippling of the snail's body as it had hurdled the trees. It would be interesting to see how fast the snail could go on a straight course. Such a test would have to wait for America.

He reached the water and saw his beach a few yards away to his right, but no ship was there. He'd made a mistake, he thought, and his beach was on the other side of the island. Then he caught sight of the *Samantha* half a mile out on the ocean, drifting away.

'Damn!' Professor Clavering said aloud. He'd done something wrong with the anchors. Did he dare try to swim to it? The distance frightened him, and it was growing wider every moment.

A rattle of pebbles behind him made him turn. The snail was hardly twenty feet away.

The professor trotted down toward the beach. There was bound to be some slit on the coast, a cave however small, where he could be out of reach of the snail. He wanted to rest for a while. What really annoyed him now

---

5. The genus comprising carnivores, or meat-eaters. "*Amygdalus Persica*": scientific name for the peach tree.

was the prospect of a chilly night without blankets or food. The Matusas natives had been right: there was nothing to eat on Kuwa.

Professor Clavering stopped dead, his shoes sliding on sand and pebbles. Before him, not fifty feet away on the beach, was another snail as big as the one following him, and somewhat lighter in colour. Its tail was in the sea, and its muzzle dripped water as it reared itself to get a look at him.

It was this snail, the professor realized, that had chewed through the hemp ropes and let the boat go free. Was there something about new hemp ropes that appealed to snails? This question he put out of his mind for the nonce. He had a snail before and behind him. The professor trotted on along the shore. The only crevice of shelter he was sure existed was the gulley on the other side of the island. He forced himself to walk at a moderate pace for a while, to breathe normally, then he sat down and treated himself to a rest.

The first snail was the first to appear, and as it had lost sight of him, it lifted its head and looked slowly to right and left, though without slackening its progress. The professor sat motionless, bare head lowered, hoping the snail would not see him. But he was not that lucky. The snail saw him and altered its course to a straight line for him. Behind it came the second snail—its wife? its husband?—the professor could not tell and there was no way of telling.

Professor Clavering had to leave his resting place. The weight of his hatchet reminded him that he at least had a weapon. A good scare, he thought, a minor wound might discourage them. He knew they were hungry, that their teeth could tear his flesh more easily than they tore trees, and that alive or dead, he would be eaten by these snails if he permitted it to happen. He drew his hatchet and faced them, conscious that he cut a not very formidable figure with his slight paunch, his pale, skinny legs, his height of five feet seven, about a third the snails' height, but his brows above his glasses were set with a determination to defend his life.

The first snail reared when it was ten feet away. The professor advanced and swung the hatchet at the projecting mantle on the snail's left side. He had not dared get close enough, his aim was inches short, and the weight of the hatchet pulled the professor off balance. He staggered and fell under the raised muzzle, and had just time to roll himself from under the descending mouth before it touched the ground where he had been. Angry now, he circled the snail and swung a blow at the nacreous shell, which turned the blade. The hatchet took an inch-deep chip, but nothing more. The professor swung again, higher this time and in the center of the shell's posterior, trying for the lung valve beneath, but the valve was still higher, he knew, ten feet from the ground, and once more his hatchet took only a chip. The snail began to turn itself to face him.

The professor then confronted the second snail, rushed at it and swung the hatchet, cutting it in the cheek. The hatchet sank up to its wooden handle, and he had to tug to get it out, and then had to run a few yards, as the snail put on speed and reared its head for a biting attack. Glancing back, the professor saw that no liquid (he had not, of course, expected blood) came from the cut in the snail's cheek, and in fact he couldn't see the cut. And the blow had certainly been no discouragement to the snail's advance.

Professor Clavering began to walk at a sensible pace straight for the snails' lair on the other side of the island. By the time he scrambled down the side of the gulley, he was winded and his legs hurt. But he saw to his relief that the gulley narrowed to a sharp V. Wedged in that, he would be safe. Professor Clavering started into the V, which had an overhanging top rather like a cave, when he saw that what he had taken for some rounded rocks were moving—at least some of them were. They were baby snails! They were larger than good-sized beach balls. And the professor saw, from the way a couple of them were devouring grass blades, that they were hungry.

A snail's head appeared high on his left. The giant parent snail began to descend the gulley. A crepitation,[6] a pair of antennae against the sky on his right, heralded the arrival of the second snail. He had nowhere to turn except the sea, which was not a bad idea, he thought, as these were land snails. The professor waded out and turned left, walking waist-deep in water. It was slow going, and a snail was coming after him. He got closer to the land and ran in thigh-deep water.

The first snail, the darker one, entered the water boldly and crept along in a depth of several inches, showing signs of being willing to go into deeper water when it got abreast of Professor Clavering. The professor hoped the other snail, maybe the mother, had stayed with the young. But it hadn't. It was following along the land, and accelerating. The professor plunged wildly for the shore where he would be able to move faster.

Now, thank goodness, he saw rocks. Great igneous masses of rocks covered a sloping hill down to the sea. There was bound to be a niche, some place there where he could take shelter. The sun was sinking into the ocean, it would be dark soon, and there was no moon, he knew. The professor was thirsty. When he reached the rocks, he flung himself like a corpse into a trough made by four or five scratchy boulders, which caused him to lie in a curve. The rocks rose two feet above his body, and the trough was hardly a foot wide. A snail couldn't, he reasoned, stick its head down here and bite him.

The peachy curves of the snails' shells appeared, and one, the second, drew closer.

'I'll strike it with my hatchet if it comes!' the professor swore to himself. 'I'll cut its face to ribbons with my knife!' He was now reconciled to killing both adults, because he could take back a pair of the young ones, and in fact more easily because they were smaller.

The snail seemed to sniff like a dog, though inaudibly, as its muzzle hovered over the professor's hiding place. Then with majestic calm it came down on the rocks between which the professor lay. Its slimy foot covered the aperture and within seconds had blocked out almost all the light.

Professor Clavering drew his hunting knife in anger and panic, and plunged it several times into the snail's soft flesh. The snail seemed not even to wince. A few seconds later, it stopped moving, though the professor knew that it was not only not dead, as the stabs hadn't touched any vital organs, but that it had fastened itself over his trench in the firmest possible way. No slit of light showed. The professor was only grateful that the irregularity of the rocks must afford a supply of air. Now he pressed frantically

6. A crackling sound.

with his palms against the snail's body, and felt his hands slip and scrape against rock. The firmness of the snail, his inability to budge it, made him feel slightly sick for a moment.

An hour passed. The professor almost slept, but the experience was more like a prolonged hallucination. He dreamed, or feared, that he was being chewed by twenty thousand pairs of teeth into a heap of mince,[7] which the two giant snails shared with their offspring. To add to his misery, he was cold and hungry. The snail's body gave no warmth, and was even cool.

Some hours later, the professor awoke and saw stars above him. The snail had departed. It was pitch dark. He stood up cautiously, trying not to make a sound, and stepped out of the crevice. He was free! On a sandy stretch of beach a few yards away, Professor Clavering lay down, pressed against a vertical face of rock. Here he slept the remaining hours until dawn.

He awakened just in time, and perhaps not the dawn but a sixth sense had awakened him. The first snail was coming toward him and was only ten feet away. The professor got up on trembling legs, and trotted inland, up a slope. An idea came to him: if he could push a boulder of, say, five hundred pounds— possible with a lever—onto an adult snail in the gulley, and smash the spot below which its lung lay, then he could kill it. Otherwise, he could think of no other means at his disposal that could inflict a fatal injury. His gun might, but the gun was on the *Samantha*. He had already estimated that it might be a week, or never, that help would come from the Matusas. The *Samantha* would not necessarily float back to the Matusas, would not necessarily be seen by any other ship for days, and even if it was seen, would it be apparent she was drifting? And if so, would the spotters make a beeline for the Matusas to report it? Not necessarily. The professor bent quickly and licked some dew from a leaf. The snails were twenty yards behind him now.

The trouble is, I'm becoming exhausted, he said to himself.

He was even more tired at noon. Only one snail pursued him, but the professor imagined the other resting or eating a tree top, in order to be fresh later. The professor could trot a hundred yards, find a spot to rest in, but he dared not shut his eyes for long, lest he sleep. And he was definitely weak from lack of food.

So the day passed. His idea of dropping a rock down the gulley was thwarted by two factors: the second snail was guarding the gulley now, at the top of its V, and there was no such rock as he needed within a hundred yards.

When dusk came, the professor could not find the hill where the igneous rocks were. Both snails had him in their sight now. His watch said a quarter to seven. Professor Clavering took a deep breath and faced the fact that he must make an attempt to kill one or both snails before dark. Almost without thinking, or planning—he was too spent for that—he chopped down a slender tree and hacked off its branches. The leaves of these branches were devoured by the two snails five minutes after the branches had fallen to the ground. The professor dragged his tree several yards inland, and sharpened one end of it with the hatchet. It was too heavy a weapon for one hand to wield, but in two hands, it made a kind of battering ram, or giant spear.

---

7. Ground food, especially meat.

At once, Professor Clavering turned and attacked, running with the spear pointed slightly upward. He aimed for the first snail's mouth, but struck too low, and the tree end penetrated about four inches into the snail's chest—or the area below its face. No vital organ here, except the long, straight esophagus, which in these giant snails would be set deeper than four inches. He had nothing for his trouble but lacerated hands. His spear hung for a few seconds in the snail's flesh, then fell out onto the ground. The professor retreated, pulling his hatchet from his belt. The second snail, coming up abreast of the other, paused to chew off a few inches of the tree stump, then joined its mate in giving attention to Professor Clavering. There was something contemptuous, something absolutely assured, about the snails' slow progress toward him, as if they were thinking, "Escape us a hundred, a thousand times, we shall finally reach you and devour every trace of you."

The professor advanced once more, circled the snail he had just hit with the tree spear, and swung his hatchet at the rear of its shell. Desperately, he attacked the same spot with five or six direct hits, for now he had a plan. His hacking operation had to be halted, because the second snail was coming up behind him. Its snout and an antenna even brushed the professor's legs moistly and staggered him, before he could step out of its way. Two more hatchet blows the professor got in, and then he stopped, because his right arm hurt. He had by no means gone through the shell, but he had no strength for more effort with the hatchet. He went back for his spear. His target was a small one, but he ran toward it with desperate purpose.

The blow landed. It even broke through.

The professor's hands were further torn, but he was oblivious of them. His success made him as joyous as if he had killed both his enemies, as if a rescue ship with food, water, and a bed were even then sailing into Kuwa's beach.

The snail was twisting and rearing up with pain.

Professor Clavering ran forward, lifted the drooping spear and pushed it with all his might farther into the snail, pointing it upward to go as close as possible to the lung. Whether the snail died soon or not, it was hors de combat,[8] the professor saw. And he himself experienced something like physical collapse an instant after seeing the snail's condition. He was quite incapable of taking on the other snail in the same manner, and the other snail was coming after him. The professor tried to walk in a straight line away from both snails, but he weaved with fatigue and faintness. He looked behind him. The unhurt snail was thirty feet away. The wounded snail faced him, but was motionless, half in and half out of its shell, suffering in silence some agony of asphyxiation. Professor Clavering walked on.

Quite by accident, just as it was growing dark, he came upon his field of rocks. Among them he took shelter for the second time. The snail's snout probed the trench in which he lay, but could not quite reach him. Would it not be better to remain in the trench tomorrow, to hope for rain for water? He fell asleep before he could come to any decision.

Again, when the professor awakened at dawn, the snail had departed. His hands throbbed. Their palms were encrusted with dried blood and sand. He thought it wise to go to the sea and wash them in salt water.

---

8. "Out of action" because of injury in battle (French).

The giant snail lay between him and the sea, and at his approach, the snail very slowly began to creep toward him. Professor Clavering made a wobbling detour and continued on his way toward the water. He dipped his hands and moved them rapidly back and forth, at last lifted water to his face, longed to wet his dry mouth, warned himself that he should not, and yielded anyway, spitting out the water almost at once. Land snails hated salt and could be killed by salt crystals. The professor angrily flung handfuls of water at the snail's face. The snail only lifted its head higher, out of the professor's range. Its form was slender now, and it had, oddly, the grace of a horned gazelle, of some animal of the deer family. The snail lowered its snout, and the professor trudged away, but not quickly enough: the snail came down on his shoulder and the suctorial[9] mouth clamped.

The professor screamed. *My God*, he thought, as a piece of his shirt, a piece of flesh and possibly bone was torn from his left shoulder, *why was I such an ass as to linger?* The snail's weight pushed him under, but it was shallow here, and he struggled to his feet and walked toward the land. Blood streamed hotly down his side. He could not bear to look at his shoulder to see what had happened, and would not have been surprised if his left arm had dropped off in the next instant. The professor walked on aimlessly in shallow water near the land. He was still going faster than the snail.

Then he lifted his eyes to the empty horizon, and saw a dark spot in the water in the mid-distance. He stopped, wondering if it were real or a trick of his eyes: but now he made out the double body of a catamaran,[1] and he thought he saw Dr. Stead's straw hat. They had come from the Matusas!

"Hello!" The professor was shocked at the hoarseness, the feebleness of his voice. Not a chance that he had been heard.

But with hope now, the professor's strength increased. He headed for a little beach—not his beach, a smaller one—and when he got there he stood in its center, his good arm raised, and shouted, "Dr. *Stead*! This way!—On the beach!" He could definitely see Dr. Stead's hat and four dark heads.

There was no answering shout. Professor Clavering could not tell if they had heard him or not. And the accursed snail was only thirty feet away now! He'd lost his hatchet, he realized. And the camera that had been under water with him was now ruined, and so were the two pictures in it. No matter. He would live.

"*Here!*" he shouted, again lifting his arm.

The natives heard this. Suddenly all heads in the catamaran turned to him.

Dr. Stead pointed to him and gesticulated, and dimly Professor Clavering heard the good doctor urging the boatman to make for the shore. He saw Dr. Stead half stand up in the catamaran.

The natives gave a whoop—at first Professor Clavering thought it a whoop of joy, or of recognition, but almost at once a wild swing of the sail, a splash of a couple of oars, told him that the natives were trying to change their course.

Pebbles crackled. The snail was near. And this of course was what the natives had seen—the giant snail.

---

9. Adapted for sucking.   1. A boat with two hulls.

"*Please—Here!*" the professor screamed. He plunged again into the water. "*Please!*"

Dr. Stead was trying, that the professor could see. But the natives were rowing, paddling with hands even, and their sail was carrying them obliquely away.

The snail made a splash as it entered the sea. To drown or to be eaten alive? the professor wondered. He was waist-deep when he stumbled, waist-deep but head under when the snail crashed down upon him, and he realized as the thousands of pairs of teeth began to gnaw at his back, that his fate was both to drown and to be chewed to death.

1967, 1970

JACK KEROUAC
1922–1969

Like many trailblazing writers, Jack Kerouac led a life filled with contradictions. Regarded as a liberator of prose and champion of idiomatic American expression, he did not start learning English until grade school and did not feel comfortable speaking it until he finished high school (his parents were French Canadian, and French was the family's language at home in Lowell, Massachusetts; his given name was "Jean-Louis"). Having won a football scholarship to Columbia University, he rejected the athletic crowd to join the literary innovators gathering at the college neighborhood's popular West End Bar, among them Allen Ginsberg and William S. Burroughs, who would achieve fame as a poet and a novelist, respectively. Not famous himself until the late 1950s, when a wave of interest in the Beat Movement installed him as its unwilling leader, Kerouac rode the crest of the counterculture's growing fascination with Eastern religions, most notably Zen Buddhism, while never rejecting the Catholicism of his childhood. Even adulatory responses to his work risked contradiction. Critics praised his most famous novel, *On the Road* (1957), for its seeming embrace of expansive westward energies reminiscent of America's Manifest Destiny myth, even though the book in fact moves from the West Coast to the East. The final chapter is set in New York City.

Kerouac's ambitions were monumental, but his heavy drinking killed him by age forty-seven. His several marriages, until the last one, ended in annulment, desertion, or divorce. His greatest loyalty as an adult was to his widowed mother, in later years an invalid, for whom he cared until his death. Wartime service in the merchant marine had given Kerouac skills useful during the wanderings that characterized his life; railroad brakeman and forest-fire lookout were among the jobs he took during the late 1940s and early 1950s. Once royalties from *On the Road* could sustain the transient life he preferred, he spent his time visiting friends and writing as inspiration struck. "Home" was a series of addresses in Massachusetts, New York (on Long Island), and Florida, most of them chosen for his mother's convenience.

Kerouac is known for a writing practice he called "spontaneous prose," reminiscent of jazz improvisation in its emphasis on rhythms, inflections, and freewheeling references. A rejection of what he and other Beat writers saw as the overly formal and elite style of the Modernist literary works that then dominated the high-cultural landscape, the practice of spontaneous prose sought to eliminate the gap between thought and word, between experience and voice, between life and art. Asked by his friends Ginsberg and Burroughs in 1953 to explain how he wrote his novel *The Subterraneans* in three days flat, he composed a manifesto called "The Essentials of Spontaneous Prose," which he then taped above his desk. (It was published in the *Black Mountain Review* in 1957.) Among its tenets are these: "No time for poetry but exactly what is"; "Remove literary grammatical and syntactical inhibition"; "Bookmovie is the movie in words, the visual American form." He advocated "not 'selectivity' of expression but following free deviation (association) of mind into limitless blow-on-subject seas of thought, swimming in sea of English with no discipline other than rhythms of rhetorical exhalation and expostulated statement, like a fist coming down on a table with each complete utterance, bang!" After his first book, *The Town and the City* (1950), a social novel in a realistic mode, he composed all his novels in the exuberant form of prose he perfected.

"My work comprises one vast book like [Marcel] Proust's except that my remembrances are written on the run instead of afterwards in a sick bed," Kerouac observes at the start of his novel *Big Sur* (1962), comparing his project to the French modernist Proust's seven-volume *Remembrance of Things Past* (1913–27). Though Kerouac's canon consists of more than a dozen novels published during his lifetime and others recovered from manuscript and issued after his death, the author had seen them as one grand project, the parts of which he intended to revise, integrate, and present to readers as a single massive narrative. Neither writing nor publishing them in the order in which he had conceived their action, Kerouac did

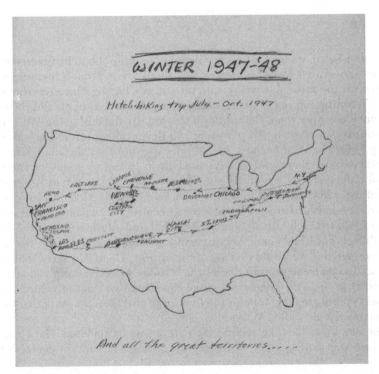

Jack Kerouac's hand-drawn map of his travels in the summer and fall of 1947.

not live long enough to begin his intended synthesis. But he named the project "the Duluoz Legend," from the name of his protagonist in *Big Sur* and other works. Central to the legend is Kerouac's close friendship with legendary counterculture and Beat figure Neal Cassady (fictionalized as Dean Moriarity in *On the Road* and as Cody Pomeray in *Visions of Cody*, 1972). Their relationship had been the motivation for both the author's wanderings and his impulsive, sometimes explosive manner of writing.

On the Road, the first and last chapters of which are reprinted here, was written in 1951, though by then Kerouac had been thinking about writing a road novel for several years. He composed much of it on a single scroll of typing paper in a three-week rush fueled by wine, coffee, and Benzedrine. In the opening chapter, the Kerouac figure and narrator, Sal Paradise, describes Dean Moriarty's kinetic speech and the foundations of their remarkable friendship. Readers meet "Carlo Marx," based on Allen Ginsberg; "Old Bull Lee" and "Jane," based on William and Jane Burroughs; and "Elmer Hassel," based on Kerouac's friend from his Columbia days, Herbert Huncke. In the book's final chapter, Sal has returned to New York disillusioned after Dean abandoned him in Mexico, where Sal was broke and suffering from a fever. Dean's too-little, too-late show of friendship—traveling cross-country by bus and hitching rides, apparently just to see Sal for a day or two and meet Sal's new girlfriend—confounds Sal. But for Kerouac, Dean's return leads to the book's famous final sentence, honoring Dean as the muse for a new, ecstatic prose.

From On the Road

Part One

I

I first met Dean not long after my wife and I split up. I had just gotten over a serious illness that I won't bother to talk about, except that it had something to do with the miserably weary split-up and my feeling that everything was dead. With the coming of Dean Moriarty began the part of my life you could call my life on the road. Before that I'd often dreamed of going West to see the country, always vaguely planning and never taking off. Dean is the perfect guy for the road because he actually was born on the road, when his parents were passing through Salt Lake City in 1926, in a jalopy, on their way to Los Angeles. First reports of him came to me through Chad King, who'd shown me a few letters from him written in a New Mexico reform school. I was tremendously interested in the letters because they so naïvely and sweetly asked Chad to teach him all about Nietzsche[1] and all the wonderful intellectual things that Chad knew. At one point Carlo and I talked about the letters and wondered if we would ever meet the strange Dean Moriarty. This is all far back, when Dean was not the way he is today, when he was a young jailkid shrouded in mystery. Then news came that Dean was out of reform school and was coming to New York for the first time; also there was talk that he had just married a girl called Marylou.

One day I was hanging around the campus and Chad and Tim Gray told me Dean was staying in a cold-water pad[2] in East Harlem, the Spanish Har-

---

1. Friedrich Nietzsche (1844–1900), German philosopher.

2. A cheap apartment with no running hot water.

lem. Dean had arrived the night before, the first time in New York, with his beautiful little sharp chick Marylou; they got off the Greyhound bus at 50th Street and cut around the corner looking for a place to eat and went right in Hector's, and since then Hector's cafeteria has always been a big symbol of New York for Dean. They spent money on beautiful big glazed cakes and creampuffs.

All this time Dean was telling Marylou things like this: "Now, darling, here we are in New York and although I haven't quite told you everything that I was thinking about when we crossed Missouri and especially at the point when we passed the Boonville reformatory which reminded me of my jail problem, it is absolutely necessary now to postpone all those leftover things concerning our personal lovethings and at once begin thinking of specific worklife plans . . ." and so on in the way that he had in those early days.

I went to the cold-water flat with the boys, and Dean came to the door in his shorts. Marylou was jumping off the couch; Dean had dispatched the occupant of the apartment to the kitchen, probably to make coffee, while he proceeded with his love-problems, for to him sex was the one and only holy and important thing in life, although he had to sweat and curse to make a living and so on. You saw that in the way he stood bobbing his head, always looking down, nodding, like a young boxer to instructions, to make you think he was listening to every word, throwing in a thousand "Yeses" and "That's rights." My first impression of Dean was of a young Gene Autry[3]—trim, thin-hipped, blue-eyed, with a real Oklahoma accent—a sideburned hero of the snowy West. In fact he'd just been working on a ranch, Ed Wall's in Colorado, before marrying Marylou and coming East. Marylou was a pretty blonde with immense ringlets of hair like a sea of golden tresses; she sat there on the edge of the couch with her hands hanging in her lap and her smoky blue country eyes fixed in a wide stare because she was in an evil gray New York pad that she'd heard about back West, and waiting like a longbodied emaciated Modigliani[4] surrealist woman in a serious room. But, outside of being a sweet little girl, she was awfully dumb and capable of doing horrible things. That night we all drank beer and pulled wrists and talked till dawn, and in the morning, while we sat around dumbly smoking butts from ashtrays in the gray light of a gloomy day, Dean got up nervously, paced around, thinking, and decided the thing to do was to have Marylou make breakfast and sweep the floor. "In other words we've got to get on the ball, darling, what I'm saying, otherwise it'll fluctuating and lack of true knowledge or crystallization of our plans." Then I went away.

During the following week he confided in Chad King that he absolutely had to learn how to write from him; Chad said I was a writer and he should come to me for advice. Meanwhile Dean had gotten a job in a parking lot, had a fight with Marylou in their Hoboken apartment—God knows why they went there—and she was so mad and so down deep vindictive that she reported to the police some false trumped-up hysterical crazy charge, and Dean had to lam[5] from Hoboken. So he had no place to live. He came right out to Paterson, New Jersey, where I was living with my aunt, and one night while I was

3. American actor and singer (1907–1998), known for his cowboy roles in popular Westerns.
4. Amedeo Modigliani (1884–1920), modernist Italian painter and sculptor, known for his elon-gated human forms, lived and worked in Paris after 1906.
5. To escape or live on the run, usually to evade legal troubles.

studying there was a knock on the door, and there was Dean, bowing, shuffling obsequiously in the dark of the hall, and saying, "Hel-lo, you remember me—Dean Moriarty? I've come to ask you to show me how to write."

"And where's Marylou?" I asked, and Dean said she'd apparently whored a few dollars together and gone back to Denver—"the whore!" So we went out to have a few beers because we couldn't talk like we wanted to talk in front of my aunt, who sat in the living room reading her paper. She took one look at Dean and decided that he was a madman.

In the bar I told Dean, "Hell, man, I know very well you didn't come to me only to want to become a writer, and after all what do I really know about it except you've got to stick to it with the energy of a benny addict."[6] And he said, "Yes, of course, I know exactly what you mean and in fact all those problems have occurred to me, but the thing that I want is the realization of those factors that should one depend on Schopenhauer's[7] dichotomy for any inwardly realized . . ." and so on in that way, things I understood not a bit and he himself didn't. In those days he really didn't know what he was talking about; that is to say, he was a young jailkid all hung-up on the wonderful possibilities of becoming a real intellectual, and he liked to talk in the tone and using the words, but in a jumbled way, that he had heard from "real intellectuals"—although, mind you, he wasn't so naïve as that in all other things, and it took him just a few months with Carlo Marx to become completely *in there* with all the terms and jargon. Nonetheless we understood each other on other levels of madness, and I agreed that he could stay at my house till he found a job and furthermore we agreed to go out West sometime. That was the winter of 1947.

One night when Dean ate supper at my house—he already had the parking-lot job in New York—he leaned over my shoulder as I typed rapidly away and said, "Come on man, those girls won't wait, make it fast."

I said, "Hold on just a minute, I'll be right with you soon as I finish this chapter," and it was one of the best chapters in the book. Then I dressed and off we flew to New York to meet some girls. As we rode in the bus in the weird phosphorescent void of the Lincoln Tunnel we leaned on each other with fingers waving and yelled and talked excitedly, and I was beginning to get the bug like Dean. He was simply a youth tremendously excited with life, and though he was a con-man, he was only conning because he wanted so much to live and to get involved with people who would otherwise pay no attention to him. He was conning me and I knew it (for room and board and "how-to-write," etc.), and he knew I knew (this has been the basis of our relationship), but I didn't care and we got along fine—no pestering, no catering; we tiptoed around each other like heartbreaking new friends. I began to learn from him as much as he probably learned from me. As far as my work was concerned he said, "Go ahead, everything you do is great." He watched over my shoulder as I wrote stories, yelling, "Yes! That's right! Wow! Man!" and "Phew!" and wiped his face with his handkerchief. "Man, wow, there's so many things to do, so many things to write! How to even *begin* to get it all down and without modified restraints and all hung-up on like literary inhibitions and grammatical fears . . ."

---

6. Benzedrine, a form of amphetamine, typically makes its users hyperactive.

7. Artur Schopenhauer (1788–1860), German Romantic philosopher.

"That's right, man, now you're talking." And a kind of holy lightning I saw flashing from his excitement and his visions, which he described so torrentially that people in buses looked around to see the "overexcited nut." In the West he'd spent a third of his time in the poolhall, a third in jail, and a third in the public library. They'd seen him rushing eagerly down the winter streets, bareheaded, carrying books to the poolhall, or climbing trees to get into the attics of buddies where he spent days reading or hiding from the law.

We went to New York—I forget what the situation was, two colored girls—there were no girls there; they were supposed to meet him in a diner and didn't show up. We went to his parking lot where he had a few things to do—change his clothes in the shack in back and spruce up a bit in front of a cracked mirror and so on, and then we took off. And that was the night Dean met Carlo Marx. A tremendous thing happened when Dean met Carlo Marx. Two keen minds that they are, they took to each other at the drop of a hat. Two piercing eyes glanced into two piercing eyes—the holy con-man with the shining mind, and the sorrowful poetic con-man with the dark mind that is Carlo Marx. From that moment on I saw very little of Dean, and I was a little sorry too. Their energies met head-on, I was a lout compared, I couldn't keep up with them. The whole mad swirl of everything that was to come began then; it would mix up all my friends and all I had left of my family in a big dust cloud over the American Night. Carlo told him of Old Bull Lee, Elmer Hassel, Jane: Lee in Texas growing weed, Hassel on Riker's Island, Jane wandering on Times Square in a benzedrine hallucination, with her baby girl in her arms and ending up in Bellevue.[8] And Dean told Carlo of unknown people in the West like Tommy Snark, the clubfooted poolhall rotation shark and cardplayer and queer saint. He told him of Roy Johnson, Big Ed Dunkel, his boyhood buddies, his street buddies, his innumerable girls and sex-parties and pornographic pictures, his heroes, heroines, adventures. They rushed down the street together, digging everything in the early way they had, which later became so much sadder and perceptive and blank. But then they danced down the streets like dingledodies,[9] and I shambled after as I've been doing all my life after people who interest me, because the only people for me are the mad ones, the ones who are mad to live, mad to talk, mad to be saved, desirous of everything at the same time, the ones who never yawn or say a commonplace thing, but burn, burn, burn like fabulous yellow roman candles exploding like spiders across the stars and in the middle you see the blue centerlight pop and everybody goes "Awww!" What did they call such young people in Goethe's[1] Germany? Wanting dearly to learn how to write like Carlo, the first thing you know, Dean was attacking him with a great amorous soul such as only a con-man can have. "Now, Carlo, let *me* speak—here's what *I'm* saying . . ." I didn't see them for about two weeks, during which time they cemented their relationship to fiendish allday-allnight-talk proportions.

Then came spring, the great time of traveling, and everybody in the scattered gang was getting ready to take one trip or another. I was busily at work on my novel and when I came to the halfway mark, after a trip down South with my aunt to visit my brother Rocco, I got ready to travel West for the very first time.

Dean had already left. Carlo and I saw him off at the 34th Street Greyhound station. Upstairs they had a place where you could make pictures for a quarter. Carlo took off his glasses and looked sinister. Dean made a profile shot and looked coyly around. I took a straight picture that made me look like a thirty-year-old Italian who'd kill anybody who said anything against his mother. This picture Carlo and Dean neatly cut down the middle with a razor and saved a half each in their wallets. Dean was wearing a real Western business suit for his big trip back to Denver; he'd finished his first fling in New York. I say fling, but he only worked like a dog in parking lots. The most fantastic parking-lot attendant in the world, he can back a car forty miles an hour into a tight squeeze and stop at the wall, jump out, race among fenders, leap into another car, circle it fifty miles an hour in a narrow space, back swiftly into tight spot, *hump*, snap the car with the emergency so that you see it bounce as he flies out; then clear to the ticket shack, sprinting like a track star, hand a ticket, leap into a newly arrived car before the owner's half out, leap literally under him as he steps out, start the car with the door flapping, and roar off to the next available spot, arc, pop in, brake, out, run; working like that without pause eight hours a night, evening rush hours and after-theater rush hours, in greasy wino pants with a frayed fur-lined jacket and beat[2] shoes that flap. Now he'd bought a new suit to go back in; blue with pencil stripes, vest and all—eleven dollars on Third Avenue, with a watch and watch chain, and a portable typewriter with which he was going to start writing in a Denver rooming house as soon as he got a job there. We had a farewell meal of franks and beans in a Seventh Avenue Riker's,[3] and then Dean got on the bus that said Chicago and roared off into the night. There went our wrangler. I promised myself to go the same way when spring really bloomed and opened up the land.

And this was really the way that my whole road experience began, and the things that were to come are too fantastic not to tell.

Yes, and it wasn't only because I was a writer and needed new experiences that I wanted to know Dean more, and because my life hanging around the campus had reached the completion of its cycle and was stultified, but because, somehow in spite of our difference in character, he reminded me of some long-lost brother; the sight of his suffering bony face with the long sideburns and his straining muscular sweating neck made me remember my boyhood in those dye-dumps and swim-holes and riversides of Paterson and the Passaic.[4] His dirty workclothes clung to him so gracefully, as though you couldn't buy a better fit from a custom tailor but only earn it from the Natural Tailor of Natural Joy, as Dean had, in his stresses. And in his excited way of speaking I heard again the voices of old companions and brothers under the bridge, among the motorcycles, along the wash-lined neighborhood

2. Worn, beaten-down; Kerouac adopted this usage of *beat* to describe his postwar generation of disaffected writers, artists, and intellectuals.
3. Popular chain of New York City cafeterias.

(The name is unrelated to that of the Riker's Island jail complex.)
4. Paterson is a city in northern New Jersey; the Passaic River runs through the region.

and drowsy doorsteps of afternoon where boys played guitars while their older brothers worked in the mills. All my other current friends were "intellectuals"—Chad the Nietzschean anthropologist, Carlo Marx and his nutty surrealist low-voiced serious staring talk, Old Bull Lee and his critical anti-everything drawl—or else they were slinking criminals like Elmer Hassel, with that hip sneer; Jane Lee the same, sprawled on the Oriental cover of her couch, sniffing at the *New Yorker*. But Dean's intelligence was every bit as formal and shining and complete, without the tedious intellectualness. And his "criminality" was not something that sulked and sneered; it was a wild yea-saying overburst of American joy; it was Western, the west wind, an ode from the Plains, something new, long prophesied, long a-coming (he only stole cars for joy rides). Besides, all my New York friends were in the negative, nightmare position of putting down society and giving their tired bookish or political or psychoanalytical reasons, but Dean just raced in society, eager for bread and love; he didn't care one way or the other, "so long's I can get that lil ole gal with that lil sumpin down there tween her legs, boy," and "so long's we can *eat*, son, y'ear me? I'm *hungry*, I'm *starving*, let's *eat right now!*"—and off we'd rush to *eat*, whereof, as saith Ecclesiastes,[5] "It is your portion under the sun."

A western kinsman of the sun, Dean. Although my aunt warned me that he would get me in trouble, I could hear a new call and see a new horizon, and believe it at my young age; and a little bit of trouble or even Dean's eventual rejection of me as a buddy, putting me down, as he would later, on starving sidewalks and sickbeds—what did it matter? I was a young writer and I wanted to take off.

Somewhere along the line I knew there'd be girls, visions, everything; somewhere along the line the pearl would be handed to me.

Part Five

Dean drove from Mexico City and saw Victor again in Gregoria and pushed that old car all the way to Lake Charles, Louisiana, before the rear end finally dropped on the road as he had always known it would. So he wired Inez for airplane fare and flew the rest of the way. When he arrived in New York with the divorce papers in his hands, he and Inez immediately went to Newark and got married; and that night, telling her everything was all right and not to worry, and making logics where there was nothing but inestimable sorrowful sweats, he jumped on a bus and roared off again across the awful continent to San Francisco to rejoin Camille and the two baby girls. So now he was three times married, twice divorced, and living with his second wife.[6]

In the fall I myself started back home from Mexico City and one night just over Laredo border in Dilley, Texas, I was standing on the hot road

5. One of the 24 books of the Hebrew Bible, Ecclesiastes meditates on life's transitory nature.
6. Dean is shuttling between coasts and women. Camille, who lives in San Francisco, is Dean's second wife and mother of his two children; though they are in the process of divorcing, Dean remains attached to her. Inez, who lives in Newark, New Jersey, becomes Dean's third wife. Sal and Dean had last been together in Mexico City, where Dean had abandoned Sal while Sal was sick.

underneath an arc-lamp with the summer moths smashing into it when I heard the sound of footsteps from the darkness beyond, and lo, a tall old man with flowing white hair came clomping by with a pack on his back, and when he saw me as he passed, he said, "*Go moan for man*," and clomped on back to his dark. Did this mean that I should at last go on my pilgrimage on foot on the dark roads around America? I struggled and hurried to New York, and one night I was standing in a dark street in Manhattan and called up to the window of a loft where I thought my friends were having a party. But a pretty girl stuck her head out the window and said, "Yes? Who is it?"

"Sal Paradise," I said, and heard my name resound in the sad and empty street.

"Come on up," she called. "I'm making hot chocolate." So I went up and there she was, the girl with the pure and innocent dear eyes that I had always searched for and for so long. We agreed to love each other madly. In the winter we planned to migrate to San Francisco, bringing all our beat furniture and broken belongings with us in a jalopy panel truck. I wrote to Dean and told him. He wrote back a huge letter eighteen thousand words long, all about his young years in Denver, and said he was coming to get me and personally select the old truck himself and drive us home. We had six weeks to save up the money for the truck and began working and counting every cent. And suddenly Dean arrived anyway, five and a half weeks in advance, and nobody had any money to go through with the plan.

I was taking a walk in the middle of the night and came back to my girl to tell her what I thought about during my walk. She stood in the dark little pad with a strange smile. I told her a number of things and suddenly I noticed the hush in the room and looked around and saw a battered book on the radio. I knew it was Dean's high-eternity-in-the-afternoon Proust.[7] As in a dream I saw him tiptoe in from the dark hall in his stocking feet. He couldn't talk any more. He hopped and laughed, he stuttered and fluttered his hands and said, "Ah—ah—you must listen to hear." We listened, all ears. But he forgot what he wanted to say. "Really listen—ahem. Look, dear Sal—sweet Laura—I've come—I'm gone—but wait—ah yes." And he stared with rocky sorrow into his hands. "Can't talk no more—do you understand that it is—or might be—But listen!" We all listened. He was listening to sounds in the night. "Yes!" he whispered with awe. "But you see—no need to talk any more—and further."

"But why did you come so soon, Dean?"

"Ah," he said, looking at me as if for the first time, "so soon, yes. We—we'll know—that is, I don't know. I came on the railroad pass—cabooses—old hard-bench coaches—Texas—played flute and wooden sweet potato[8] all the way." He took out his new wooden flute. He played a few squeaky notes on it and jumped up and down in his stocking feet. "See?" he said. "But of course, Sal, I can talk as soon as ever and have many things to say to you in

---

7. Marcel Proust (1871–1922), French novelist, author of the dreamy, semi-autobiographical seven-volume novel, *À la recherche du temps perdu* (translated as *Rememberance of Things Past or In Search of Lost Time*).
8. A kind of ocarina, a hollow wooden wind instrument shaped like a sweet potato.

fact with my own little bangtail mind I've been reading and reading this gone[9] Proust all the way across the country and digging a great number of things I'll never have TIME to tell you about and we STILL haven't talked of Mexico and our parting there in fever—but no need to talk. Absolutely, now, yes?"

"All right, we won't talk." And he started telling the story of what he did in LA on the way over in every possible detail, how he visited a family, had dinner, talked to the father, the sons, the sisters—what they looked like, what they ate, their furnishings, their thoughts, their interests, their very souls; it took him three hours of detailed elucidation, and having concluded this he said, "Ah, but you see what I wanted to REALLY tell you—much later—Arkansas, crossing on train—playing flute—play cards with boys, my dirty deck—won money, blew sweet-potato solo—for sailors. Long long awful trip five days and five nights just to SEE you, Sal."

"What about Camille?"

"Gave permission of course—waiting for me. Camille and I all straight forever-and-ever . . ."

"And Inez?"

"I—I—I want her to come back to Frisco with me live other side of town— don't you think? Don't know why I came." Later he said in a sudden moment of gaping wonder, "Well and yes, of course. I wanted to see your sweet girl and you—glad of you—love you as ever." He stayed in New York three days and hastily made preparations to get back on the train with his railroad passes and again recross the continent, five days and five nights in dusty coaches and hard-bench crummies, and of course we had no money for a truck and couldn't go back with him. With Inez he spent one night explaining and sweating and fighting, and she threw him out. A letter came for him, care of me. I saw it. It was from Camille. "My heart broke when I saw you go across the tracks with your bag. I pray and pray you get back safe. . . . I do want Sal and his friend to come and live on the same street. . . . I know you'll make it but I can't help worrying—now that we've decided everything. . . . Dear Dean, it's the end of the first half of the century. Welcome with love and kisses to spend the other half with us. We all wait for you. [Signed] Camille, Amy, and Little Joanie." So Dean's life was settled with his most constant, most embittered, and best-knowing wife Camille, and I thanked God for him.

The last time I saw him it was under sad and strange circumstances. Remi Boncœur had arrived in New York after having gone around the world several times in ships. I wanted him to meet and know Dean. They did meet, but Dean couldn't talk any more and said nothing, and Remi turned away. Remi had gotten tickets for the Duke Ellington[1] concert at the Metropolitan Opera and insisted Laura and I come with him and his girl. Remi was fat and sad now but still the eager and formal gentleman, and he wanted to do things the *right way*, as he emphasized. So he got his bookie to drive us to the concert in a Cadillac. It was a cold winter night. The Cadillac was parked and ready to go. Dean stood outside the windows with his bag, ready to go to Penn Station and on across the land.

---

9. Slang for "great" or "fine."
1. Edward Kennedy "Duke" Ellington (1899–1974), leading American jazz composer, pianist, and band leader.

"Good-by, Dean," I said. "I sure wish I didn't have to go to the concert."

"D'you think I can ride to Fortieth Street with you?" he whispered. "Want to be with you as much as possible, m'boy, and besides it's so durned cold in this here New Yawk . . ." I whispered to Remi. No, he wouldn't have it, he liked me but he didn't like my idiot friends. I wasn't going to start all over again ruining his planned evenings as I had done at Alfred's in San Francisco in 1947 with Roland Major.

"Absolutely out of the question, Sal!" Poor Remi, he had a special necktie made for this evening; on it was painted a replica of the concert tickets, and the names Sal and Laura and Remi and Vicki, the girl, together with a series of sad jokes and some of his favorite sayings such as "You can't teach the old maestro a new tune."

So Dean couldn't ride uptown with us and the only thing I could do was sit in the back of the Cadillac and wave at him. The bookie at the wheel also wanted nothing to do with Dean. Dean, ragged in a motheaten overcoat he brought specially for the freezing temperatures of the East, walked off alone, and the last I saw of him he rounded the corner of Seventh Avenue, eyes on the street ahead, and bent to it again. Poor little Laura, my baby, to whom I'd told everything about Dean, began almost to cry.

"Oh, we shouldn't let him go like this. What'll we do?"

Old Dean's gone, I thought, and out loud I said, "He'll be all right." And off we went to the sad and disinclined concert for which I had no stomach whatever and all the time I was thinking of Dean and how he got back on the train and rode over three thousand miles over that awful land and never knew why he had come anyway, except to see me.

So in America when the sun goes down and I sit on the old broken-down river pier watching the long, long skies over New Jersey and sense all that raw land that rolls in one unbelievable huge bulge over to the West Coast, and all that road going, all the people dreaming in the immensity of it, and in Iowa I know by now the children must be crying in the land where they let the children cry, and tonight the stars'll be out, and don't you know that God is Pooh Bear? the evening star must be drooping and shedding her sparkler dims on the prairie, which is just before the coming of complete night that blesses the earth, darkens all rivers, cups the peaks and folds the final shore in, and nobody, nobody knows what's going to happen to anybody besides the forlorn rags of growing old, I think of Dean Moriarty, I even think of Old Dean Moriarty the father we never found, I think of Dean Moriarty.

1957

DENISE LEVERTOV
1923–1997

Denise Levertov once wrote of her predecessor, the poet H. D.: "She showed a way to penetrate mystery; which means, not to flood darkness with light so that darkness is destroyed, but to *enter into* darkness, mystery, so that it is experienced." Along with Robert Duncan, Levertov carried out in her own distinctive way H. D.'s tradition of visionary poetry. More grounded than her predecessor in observing the natural world and in appreciating daily life, Levertov connected the concrete to the invisible, as suggested by the image of *The Jacob's Ladder* (1961), the title of her fifth book. She desired that a poem be "hard as a floor, sound as a bench" but also that it be "mysterious" ("Illustrious Ancestors"), and in her poems ordinary events open into the unknown. The origins of Levertov's magical sense of the world are not difficult to trace. She was born in England and wrote of her parents: "My mother was descended from the Welsh tailor and mystic Angel Jones of Mold, my father from the noted Hasid, Schneour Zaiman [d. 1831], the 'Rav of Northern White Russia.'" In "Illustrious Ancestors" Levertov claimed a connection to her forefathers, both mystical and Hasidic: "some line still taut between me and them." Hasidism, a sect of Judaism that emphasizes the soul's communion with God rather than formal religious observance and encourages what Levertov called "a wonder at creation," was an important influence on her father, Paul Philip Levertoff. He had converted to Christianity as a student and later became an Anglican priest, but he retained his interest in Judaism and told Hasidic legends to Levertov and her older sister, Olga, throughout their childhoods. From her mother, Beatrice Spooner-Jones, Levertov learned to look closely at the world around her, and we might say of her work what she said of her mother: "with how much gazing / her life had paid tribute to the world's body" ("The 90th Year").

In 1947 Levertov married an American, Mitchell Goodman (they later divorced), and moved to the United States. She described this move as crucial to her development as a poet; it "necessitated the finding of new rhythms in which to write, in accordance with new rhythms of life and speech." In this discovery of a new idiom the stylistic influence of William Carlos Williams was especially important to her; without it, she said, "I could not have developed from a British Romantic with an almost Victorian background to an American poet of any vitality." Levertov embraced Williams's interest in an organic poetic form, growing out of the poet's relation to her subject, and like Duncan and Robert Creeley, she actively explored the relations between the line and the unit of breath as they control rhythm, melody, and emphasis. But if Levertov became the poet she was by becoming an American poet, her European heritage also enriched her sense of influence. Although her poem "September 1961" acknowledges her link to "the old great ones" (Ezra Pound, Williams, and H. D.), she was as at home with the German lyric poet Rainer Maria Rilke as with the American Transcendentalist Ralph Waldo Emerson. And in the United States she discovered the work of the Jewish theologian and philosopher Martin Buber, which renewed her interest "in the Hasidic ideas with which I was dimly acquainted as a child." Her eclecticism let her move easily between plain and richly descriptive language, between a vivid perception of the "thing itself" and the often radiant mystery that, for Levertov, arose from such seeing.

From 1956 to 1959 Levertov lived with her husband and son in Mexico. They were joined there by her mother, who, after her daughter's departure, remained in Mexico for the final eighteen years of her life (she died in 1977). Several moving poems in Levertov's collection *Life in the Forest* (1978), among them "The 90th Year" and "Death in Mexico," address her mother's last years. In the late 1960s the political crisis prompted by the Vietnam War turned Levertov's work more directly to public woes, as reflected in her following four books. Not all the poems in these books explicitly concern political issues ("The Sorrow Dance," for example, contains her sequence in memory of her sister, Olga, one of her finest, most powerful poems); nonetheless, many poems originated in a need for public testimony. Her overtly political poems are not often among her best, however; their very explicitness restricted her distinctive strengths as a poet, which included a feeling for the inexplicable, a language lyrical enough to express wish and desire, and a capacity for playfulness. But it is a mistake to separate too rigidly the political concerns in her work from a larger engagement with the world. As she wrote: "If a degree of intimacy is a condition of lyric expression, surely—at times when events make feelings run high—that intimacy between writer and political belief does exist, and is as intense as other emotions."

The power of Levertov's poems depends on her capacity to balance, however precariously, her two-sided vision, to keep alive both terms of what one critic called her "magical realism." At its best her work seems to spring from experience deep within her, stirred into being by a source beyond herself (as "Caedmon" is suddenly "affrighted" by an angel, or the poet at the age of sixteen dreams deeply, "sunk in the well"). Her finest poems render the inexplicable nature of our ordinary lives and their capacity for unexpected beauty. But Levertov's capacity for pleasure in the world never strays too far from the knowledge that the very landscapes that delight us contain places "that can pull you / down" ("Zeroing In"), as our inner landscapes also contain places "'that are bruised forever, that time / never assuages, never.'"

Levertov published several collections of prose, including *The Poet in the World* (1973), *Light Up the Cave* (1981), and *New and Selected Essays* (1992). In 1987 she published her fifteenth book of poems, *Breathing the Water*. This book contains a long sequence, "The Showings: Lady Julian of Norwich, 1342–1416," which continues the link between Levertov's work and a visionary tradition. She published three subsequent collections: *A Door in the Hive* (1989), *Evening Train* (1992), and *Tesserae* (1995). Levertov taught widely and from 1982 until her death was professor of English at Stanford University, where she was an important teacher for a younger generation of writers.

To the Snake

Green Snake, when I hung you round my neck
and stroked your cold, pulsing throat
     as you hissed to me, glinting
arrowy gold scales, and I felt
     the weight of you on my shoulders,   5
and the whispering silver of your dryness
     sounded close at my ears—
Green Snake—I swore to my companions that certainly
     you were harmless! But truly
I had no certainty, and no hope, only desiring   10
     to hold you, for that joy,
                which left
a long wake of pleasure, as the leaves moved

and you faded into the pattern
of grass and shadows, and I returned   15
smiling and haunted, to a dark morning.

                                                                1960

The Jacob's Ladder[1]

The stairway is not
a thing of gleaming strands
a radiant evanescence
for angels' feet that only glance in their tread, and need not
touch the stone.   5

It is of stone.
A rosy stone that takes
a glowing tone of softness
only because behind it the sky is a doubtful, a doubting
night gray.   10

A stairway of sharp
angles, solidly built.
One sees that the angels must spring
down from one step to the next, giving a little
lift of the wings: 15

and a man climbing
must scrape his knees, and bring
the grip of his hands into play. The cut stone
consoles his groping feet. Wings brush past him.
The poem ascends.   20

                                                                1961

In Mind

There's in my mind a woman
of innocence, unadorned but

fair-featured, and smelling of
apples or grass. She wears

a utopian smock or shift, her hair   5
is light brown and smooth, and she

is kind and very clean without
ostentation—

---

1. Jacob dreamed of "a ladder set up on the earth, and the top of it reached to heaven: and behold the angels of God ascending and descending on it" (Genesis 28.12).

but she has
no imagination.   10

And there's a
turbulent moon-ridden girl

or old woman, or both,
dressed in opals and rags, feathers

and torn taffeta,   15
who knows strange songs—

but she is not kind.

1964

JAMES BALDWIN
1924–1987

I n the early 1940s, the African American writer James Baldwin was once refused
service at a restaurant in New Jersey, and he reacted with anger, finally throwing a
water glass at the waitress. He fled, pursued by police. Reflecting later on the experience in his essay "Notes of a Native Son" (1955), Baldwin wrote that he was struck
by two facts, "both equally difficult for the imagination to grasp, and one was that I
could have been murdered. But the other was that I had been ready to commit murder." Baldwin's ability to speak honestly about race in America—in widely read
essays as well as in fiction—and to analyze the inner dynamics of race in a way that
was both gripping and intellectual made him a key figure in the history of civil rights
in America from the 1940s right up to his death in 1987. Though he mainly lived
abroad in Paris and other European cities from 1949 onward, his voice was heard
back home, distinguished by an emphasis on shared humanity and the possibility of
love across racial lines.

Baldwin was brought up in a poor and strictly religious household in Harlem with
an authoritarian father—later revealed to be his stepfather—his beloved mother, and
eight siblings. His reading began at home, where he read and reread the Bible and
Harriet Beecher Stowe's *Uncle Tom's Cabin*. He attended public schools in New York
City alongside black Harlem neighbors and Jewish, Irish, and Eastern European
immigrants from other parts of the city. A theater teacher at his middle school introduced him to the writings of Charles Dickens and took him to see Shakespeare plays
in the city. He then attended DeWitt Clinton High School, which reached a peak
enrollment of twelve thousand students in the 1930s and was reputed to be the
largest high school in the world; the photographer Richard Avedon was a classmate.
At DeWitt Clinton he met remarkable teachers—including the poet Countee
Cullen—who further opened the worlds of literature and intellectual life to the
young James. Baldwin briefly became a child preacher at the age of fourteen. When
he abandoned preaching he also left the church, but the church never left him. Its

message of love, suffering, and redemption in a violent world remained rooted in his imagination; its lyrical cadences, found in scripture, oratory, and ecstatic music, recur as both the themes and the models for his prose.

Starting in the late 1940s, Baldwin published essays on topics ranging from art and literature to history to black life in Harlem, Atlanta, and Paris. His fame grew when he found a voice in fiction, publishing the critically acclaimed realist novel *Go Tell It on the Mountain* in 1953, a story about the teenage son of a black preacher in Harlem that hewed closely to his own biography. *Go Tell It on the Mountain* was followed by a play, *Amen Corner*, which was staged once in 1955 by the Howard University Players and was not produced again for over a decade. It was published in full in 1968. A second novel, *Giovanni's Room* (1956), departed from the subject of black life in Harlem. Baldwin did not want to be pigeonholed as the new "Negro writer" on the scene. *Giovanni's Room* was a tragic love story about a white American named David and his relationship with Giovanni, the beautiful and doomed lover he meets in Paris. Written by a black writer through the first-person perspective of a white gay man, and openly sympathetic to the plight of its central characters, *Giovanni's Room* was both a professionally risky and a beautifully crafted novel. But Baldwin would soon become too indispensible a participant in the evolving civil rights movement to be dismissed by readers who found gay subject matter offensive. His essays on the experience of being black in the United States and in postwar Europe had already established him as a serious thinker about race. In his notable 1962 essay "Letter from a Region of my Mind," he analyzed religion's relationship to race as well as the fraught psychology of black-white relations in America, using terms that explored the sexualized emotional dependency of white America on black inferiority. The *New Yorker* featured the essay, cementing Baldwin's reputation as the writer who seemed best able to explain black and white America to itself.

Baldwin continued to write fiction and essays throughout his life. In novels and short stories, his preoccupations were remarkably consistent: doomed black and white men, strong but tired black women, jazz or church musicians, preachers and hustlers, brothers and mothers and sons, the experience of racial violence and the lives of expatriates. Having lived a bravely open homosexual life since his teens, Baldwin stood out for his humane representations of masculine gay men and for his candid reflections on love between men of different races.

He ultimately published six novels, two plays, and a collection of short stories. The early novels, including *Another Country* (1962), are regarded as his best. His nonfiction was collected in *Notes of a Native Son* (1955), *The Price of the Ticket* (1985), and various other volumes, including *Collected Essays* (1998) and *The Cross of Redemption* (2010).

The stories reprinted here represent high points in his literary oeuvre. In "Going to Meet the Man" (1965), Baldwin dares to write from the perspectives of a white deputy sheriff and his young son and thus to fully engage the horror of lynching. Baldwin shocks the reader with racist language and sexualized violence while showing how easily a young boy becomes complicit with a racist culture. "Sonny's Blues" (1957) is a classic Baldwin story, imagining music as a source of redemption within the black community, despite the realities of poverty, incarceration, and addiction.

Going to Meet the Man

"What's the matter?" she asked.

"I don't know," he said, trying to laugh, "I guess I'm tired."

"You've been working too hard," she said. "I keep telling you."

"Well, goddammit, woman," he said, "it's not my fault!" He tried again; he wretchedly failed again. Then he just lay there, silent, angry, and helpless. Excitement filled him like a toothache, but it refused to enter his flesh. He stroked her breast. This was his wife. He could not ask her to do just a little thing for him, just to help him out, just for a little while, the way he could ask a nigger girl to do it. He lay there, and he sighed. The image of a black girl caused a distant excitement in him, like a far-away light; but, again, the excitement was more like pain; instead of forcing him to act, it made action impossible.

"Go to sleep," she said, gently, "you got a hard day tomorrow."

"Yeah," he said, and rolled over on his side, facing her, one hand still on one breast. "Goddamn the niggers. The black stinking coons. You'd think they'd learn. Wouldn't you think they'd learn? I mean, *wouldn't* you?"

"They going to be out there tomorrow," she said, and took his hand away, "get some sleep."

He lay there, one hand between his legs, staring at the frail sanctuary of his wife. A faint light came from the shutters; the moon was full. Two dogs, far away, were barking at each other, back and forth, insistently, as though they were agreeing to make an appointment. He heard a car coming north on the road and he half sat up, his hand reaching for his holster, which was on a chair near the bed, on top of his pants. The lights hit the shutters and seemed to travel across the room and then went out. The sound of the car slipped away, he heard it hit gravel, then heard it no more. Some liver-lipped students, probably, heading back to that college—but coming from where? His watch said it was two in the morning. They could be coming from anywhere, from out of state most likely, and they would be at the courthouse tomorrow. The niggers were getting ready. Well, they would be ready, too.

He moaned. He wanted to let whatever was in him out; but it wouldn't come out. Goddamn! he said aloud, and turned again, on his side, away from Grace, staring at the shutters. He was a big, healthy man and he had never had any trouble sleeping. And he wasn't old enough yet to have any trouble getting it up—he was only forty-two. And he was a good man, a God-fearing man, he had tried to do his duty all his life, and he had been a deputy sheriff for several years. Nothing had ever bothered him before, certainly not getting it up. Sometimes, sure, like any other man, he knew that he wanted a little more spice than Grace could give him and he would drive over yonder and pick up a black piece or arrest her, it came to the same thing, but he couldn't do that now, no more. There was no telling what might happen once your ass was in the air. And they were low enough to kill a man then, too, every one of them, or the girl herself might do it, right while she was making believe you made her feel so good. The niggers. What had the good Lord Almighty had in mind when he made the niggers? Well. They were pretty good at that, all right. Damn. Damn. Goddamn.

This wasn't helping him to sleep. He turned again, toward Grace again, and moved close to her warm body. He felt something he had never felt before. He felt that he would like to hold her, hold her, hold her, and be buried in her like a child and never have to get up in the morning again and go downtown to face those faces, good Christ, they were ugly! and never have to enter that jailhouse again and smell that smell and hear that singing; never again feel that filthy, kinky, greasy hair under his hand, never again watch those black breasts leap against the leaping cattle prod, never hear those moans again or watch that blood run down or the fat lips split or the sealed eyes struggle open. They were animals, they were no better than animals, what could be done with people like that? Here they had been in a civilized country for years and they still lived like animals. Their houses were dark, with oil cloth or cardboard in the windows, the smell was enough to make you puke your guts out, and there they sat, a whole tribe, pumping out kids, it looked like, every damn five minutes, and laughing and talking and playing music like they didn't have a care in the world, and he reckoned they didn't, neither, and coming to the door, into the sunlight, just standing there, just looking foolish, not thinking of anything but just getting back to what they were doing, saying, Yes suh, Mr. Jesse. I surely will, Mr. Jesse. Fine weather, Mr. Jesse. Why, I thank you, Mr. Jesse. He had worked for a mail-order house for a while and it had been his job to collect the payments for the stuff they bought. They were too dumb to know that they were being cheated blind, but that was no skin off his ass—he was just supposed to do his job. They would be late—they didn't have the sense to put money aside; but it was easy to scare them, and he never really had any trouble. Hell, they all liked him, the kids used to smile when he came to the door. He gave them candy, sometimes, or chewing gum, and rubbed their rough bullet heads—maybe the candy should have been poisoned. Those kids were grown now. He had had trouble with one of them today.

"There was this nigger today," he said; and stopped; his voice sounded peculiar. He touched Grace. "You awake?" he asked. She mumbled something, impatiently, she was probably telling him to go to sleep. It was all right. He knew that he was not alone.

"What a funny time," he said, "to be thinking about a thing like that—you listening?" She mumbled something again. He rolled over on his back. "This nigger's one of the ringleaders. We had trouble with him before. We must have had him out there at the work farm three or four times. Well, Big Jim C. and some of the boys really had to whip that nigger's ass today." He looked over at Grace; he could not tell whether she was listening or not; and he was afraid to ask again. "They had this line you know, to register"—he laughed, but she did not—"and they wouldn't stay where Big Jim C. wanted them, no, they had to start blocking traffic all around the courthouse so couldn't nothing or nobody get through, and Big Jim C. told them to disperse and they wouldn't move, they just kept up that singing, and Big Jim C. figured that the others would move if this nigger would move, him being the ringleader, but he wouldn't move and he wouldn't let the others move, so they had to beat him and a couple of the others and they threw them in the wagon—but I didn't see this nigger till I got to the jail. They were still singing and I was supposed to make them stop. Well, I couldn't make them stop for me but I knew he could make them stop. He was lying on the ground jerking and moaning, they had threw him in a cell by himself, and blood was coming out his ears from where Big Jim C. and his boys had whipped him. Wouldn't you think they'd learn? I put the prod to him and he jerked some more and he kind of screamed—but he didn't have much voice left. 'You make them stop that singing,' I said to him, 'you hear me? You make them stop that singing.' He acted like he didn't hear me and I put it to him again, under his arms, and he just rolled around on the floor and blood started coming from his mouth. He'd pissed his pants already." He paused. His mouth felt dry and his throat was as rough as sandpaper; as he talked, he began to hurt all over with that peculiar excitement which refused to be released. "You all are going to stop your singing, I said to him, and you are going to stop coming down to the courthouse and disrupting traffic and molesting the people and keeping us from our duties and keeping doctors from getting to sick white women and getting all them Northerners in this town to give our town a bad name—!" As he said this, he kept prodding the boy, sweat pouring from beneath the helmet he had not yet taken off. The boy rolled around in his own dirt and water and blood and tried to scream again as the prod hit his testicles, but the scream did not come out, only a kind of rattle and a moan. He stopped. He was not supposed to kill the nigger. The cell was filled with a terrible odor. The boy was still. "You hear me?" he called. "You had enough?" The singing went on. "You had enough?" His foot leapt out, he had not known it was going to, and caught the boy flush on the jaw. *Jesus,* he thought, *this ain't no nigger, this is a goddamn bull,* and he screamed again, "You had enough? You going to make them stop that singing now?"

But the boy was out. And now he was shaking worse than the boy had been shaking. He was glad no one could see him. At the same time, he felt very close to a very peculiar, particular joy; something deep in him and deep in his memory was stirred, but whatever was in his memory eluded him. He took off his helmet. He walked to the cell door.

"White man," said the boy, from the floor, behind him.

He stopped. For some reason, he grabbed his privates.

"You remember Old Julia?"

The boy said, from the floor, with his mouth full of blood, and one eye, barely open, glaring like the eye of a cat in the dark, "My grandmother's name was Mrs. Julia Blossom. *Mrs.* Julia Blossom. You going to call our women by their right names yet.—And those kids ain't going to stop singing. We going to keep on singing until every one of you miserable white mothers go stark raving out of your minds." Then he closed the one eye; he spat blood; his head fell back against the floor.

He looked down at the boy, whom he had been seeing, off and on, for more than a year, and suddenly remembered him: Old Julia had been one of his mail-order customers, a nice old woman. He had not seen her for years, he supposed that she must be dead.

He had walked into the yard, the boy had been sitting in a swing. He had smiled at the boy, and asked, "Old Julia home?"

The boy looked at him for a long time before he answered. "Don't no Old Julia live here."

"This is her house. I know her. She's lived here for years."

The boy shook his head. "You might know a Old Julia someplace else, white man. But don't nobody by that name live here."

He watched the boy; the boy watched him. The boy certainly wasn't more than ten. *White man.* He didn't have time to be fooling around with some crazy kid. He yelled, "Hey! Old Julia!"

But only silence answered him. The expression on the boy's face did not change. The sun beat down on them both, still and silent; he had the feeling that he had been caught up in a nightmare, a nightmare dreamed by a child; perhaps one of the nightmares he himself had dreamed as a child. It had that feeling—everything familiar, without undergoing any other change, had been subtly and hideously displaced: the trees, the sun, the patches of grass in the yard, the leaning porch and the weary porch steps and the cardboard in the windows and the black hole of the door which looked like the entrance to a cave, and the eyes of the pickaninny, all, all, were charged with malevolence. *White man.* He looked at the boy. "She's gone out?"

The boy said nothing.

"Well," he said, "tell her I passed by and I'll pass by next week." He started to go; he stopped. "You want some chewing gum?"

The boy got down from the swing and started for the house. He said, "I don't want nothing you got, white man." He walked into the house and closed the door behind him.

Now the boy looked as though he were dead. Jesse wanted to go over to him and pick him up and pistol whip him until the boy's head burst open like a melon. He began to tremble with what he believed was rage, sweat, both cold and hot, raced down his body, the singing filled him as though it were a weird, uncontrollable, monstrous howling rumbling up from the depths of his own belly, he felt an icy fear rise in him and raise him up, and he shouted, he howled, "You lucky we *pump* some white blood into you every once in a while—your women! Here's what I got for all the black bitches in the world—!" Then he was, abruptly, almost too weak to stand; to his bewilderment, his horror, beneath his own fingers, he felt himself violently stiffen—with no warning at all; he dropped his hands and he stared at the boy and he left the cell.

"All that singing they do," he said. "All that singing." He could not remember the first time he had heard it; he had been hearing it all his life. It was the sound with which he was most familiar—though it was also the sound of which he had been least conscious—and it had always contained an obscure comfort. They were singing to God. They were singing for mercy and they hoped to go to heaven, and he had even sometimes felt, when looking into the eyes of some of the old women, a few of the very old men, that they were singing for mercy for his soul, too. Of course he had never thought of their heaven or of what God was, or could be, for them; God was the same for everyone, he supposed, and heaven was where good people went—he supposed. He had never thought much about what it meant to be a good person. He tried to be a good person and treat everybody right: it wasn't his fault if the niggers had taken it into their heads to fight against God and go against the rules laid down in the Bible for everyone to read! Any preacher would tell you that. He was only doing his duty: protecting white people from the niggers and the niggers from themselves. And there were still lots of good niggers around—he had to remember that; they weren't all like that boy this afternoon; and the good niggers must be mighty sad to see what was happening to their people. They would thank him when this was over. In that way they had, the best of them, not quite looking him in the eye, in a low voice, with a little smile: We surely thanks you, Mr. Jesse. From the bottom of our hearts, we thanks you. He smiled. They hadn't all gone crazy. This trouble would pass.—He knew that the young people had changed some of the words to the songs. He had scarcely listened to the words before and he did not listen to them now; but he knew that the words were different; he could hear that much. He did not know if the faces were different, he had never, before this trouble began, watched them as they sang, but he certainly did not like what he saw now. They hated him, and this hatred was blacker than their hearts, blacker than their skins, redder than their blood, and harder, by far, than his club. Each day, each night, he felt worn out, aching, with their smell in his nostrils and filling his lungs, as though he were drowning—drowning in niggers; and it was all to be done again when he awoke. It would never end. It would never end. Perhaps this was what the singing had meant all along. They had not been singing black folks into heaven, they had been singing white folks into hell.

Everyone felt this black suspicion in many ways, but no one knew how to express it. Men much older than he, who had been responsible for law and order much longer than he, were now much quieter than they had been, and the tone of their jokes, in a way that he could not quite put his finger on, had changed. These men were his models, they had been friends to his father, and they had taught him what it meant to be a man. He looked to them for courage now. It wasn't that he didn't know that what he was doing was right—he knew that, nobody had to tell him that; it was only that he missed the ease of former years. But they didn't have much time to hang out with each other these days. They tended to stay close to their families every free minute because nobody knew what might happen next. Explosions rocked the night of their tranquil town. Each time each man wondered silently if perhaps this time the dynamite had not fallen into the wrong hands. They thought that they knew where all the guns were; but they could not possibly know every move that was made in that secret place where the darkies lived. From time to time it was suggested that they form a posse and search the home of every nigger, but they hadn't done it yet. For one thing, this might have brought the bastards from the North down on their backs; for another, although the niggers were scattered throughout the town— down in the hollow near the railroad tracks, way west near the mills, up on the hill, the well-off ones, and some out near the college—nothing seemed to happen in one part of town without the niggers immediately knowing it in the other. This meant that they could not take them by surprise. They rarely mentioned it, but they *knew* that some of the niggers had guns. It stood to reason, as they said, since, after all, some of them had been in the Army. There were niggers in the Army right now and God knows they wouldn't have had any trouble stealing this half-assed government blind—the whole world was doing it, look at the European countries and all those countries in Africa. They made jokes about it—bitter jokes; and they cursed the government in Washington, which had betrayed them; but they had not yet formed a posse. Now, if their town had been laid out like some towns in the North, where all the niggers lived together in one locality, they could have gone down and set fire to the houses and brought about peace that way. If the niggers had all lived in one place, they could have kept the fire in one place. But the way this town was laid out, the fire could hardly be controlled. It would spread all over town—and the niggers would probably be helping it to spread. Still, from time to time, they spoke of doing it, anyway; so that now there was a real fear among them that somebody might go crazy and light the match.

They rarely mentioned anything not directly related to the war that they were fighting, but this had failed to establish between them the unspoken communication of soldiers during a war. Each man, in the thrilling silence which sped outward from their exchanges, their laughter, and their anecdotes, seemed wrestling, in various degrees of darkness, with a secret which he could not articulate to himself, and which, however directly it related to the war, related yet more surely to his privacy and his past. They could no longer be sure, after all, that they had all done the same things. They had never dreamed that their privacy could contain any element of terror, could threaten, that is, to reveal itself, to the scrutiny of a judgment day, while remaining unreadable and inaccessible to themselves; nor had they dreamed that the past, while certainly refusing to be forgotten, could yet so stubbornly refuse to be remembered. They felt themselves mysteriously set at naught, as no longer entering into the real concerns of other people—while here they were, out-numbered, fighting to save the civilized world. They had thought that people would care—people didn't care; not enough, anyway, to help them. It would have been a help, really, or at least a relief, even to have been forced to surrender. Thus they had lost, probably forever, their old and easy connection with each other. They were forced to depend on each other more and, at the same time, to trust each other less. Who could tell when one of them might not betray them all, for money, or for the ease of confession? But no one dared imagine what there might be to confess. They were soldiers fighting a war, but their relationship to each other was that of accomplices in a crime. They all had to keep their mouths shut.

I stepped in the river at Jordan.

Out of the darkness of the room, out of nowhere, the line came flying up at him, with the melody and the beat. He turned wordlessly toward his sleeping wife. *I stepped in the river at Jordan.* Where had he heard that song?

"Grace," he whispered. "You awake?"

She did not answer. If she was awake, she wanted him to sleep. Her breathing was slow and easy, her body slowly rose and fell.

I stepped in the river at Jordan.

The water came to my knees.

He began to sweat. He felt an overwhelming fear, which yet contained a curious and dreadful pleasure.

I stepped in the river at Jordan.

The water came to my waist.

It had been night, as it was now, he was in the car between his mother and his father, sleepy, his head in his mother's lap, sleepy, and yet full of excitement. The singing came from far away, across the dark fields. There were no lights anywhere. They had said good-bye to all the others and turned off on this dark dirt road. They were almost home.

I stepped in the river at Jordan,

The water came over my head,

I looked way over to the other side,

He was making up my dying bed!

"I guess they singing for him," his father said, seeming very weary and subdued now. "Even when they're sad, they sound like they just about to go and tear off a piece." He yawned and leaned across the boy and slapped his wife lightly on the shoulder, allowing his hand to rest there for a moment. "Don't they?"

"Don't talk that way," she said.

"Well, that's what we going to do," he said, "you can make up your mind to that." He started whistling. "You see? When I begin to feel it, I gets kind of musical, too."

Oh, Lord! Come on and ease my troubling mind!

He had a black friend, his age, eight, who lived nearby. His name was Otis. They wrestled together in the dirt. Now the thought of Otis made him sick. He began to shiver. His mother put her arm around him.

"He's tired," she said.

"We'll be home soon," said his father. He began to whistle again.

"We didn't see Otis this morning," Jesse said. He did not know why he said this. His voice, in the darkness of the car, sounded small and accusing.

"You haven't seen Otis for a couple of mornings," his mother said.

That was true. But he was only concerned about *this* morning.

"No," said his father, "I reckon Otis's folks was afraid to let him show himself this morning."

"But Otis didn't do nothing!" Now his voice sounded questioning.

"Otis *can't* do nothing," said his father, "he's too little." The car lights picked up their wooden house, which now solemnly approached them, the lights falling around it like yellow dust. Their dog, chained to a tree, began to bark.

"We just want to make sure Otis *don't* do nothing," said his father, and stopped the car. He looked down at Jesse. "And you tell him what your Daddy said, you hear?"

"Yes sir," he said.

His father switched off the lights. The dog moaned and pranced, but they ignored him and went inside. He could not sleep. He lay awake, hearing the night sounds, the dog yawning and moaning outside, the sawing of the crickets, the cry of the owl, dogs barking far away, then no sounds at all, just the heavy, endless buzzing of the night. The darkness pressed on his eyelids like a scratchy blanket. He turned, he turned again. He wanted to call his mother, but he knew his father would not like this. He was terribly afraid. Then he heard his father's voice in the other room, low, with a joke in it; but this did not help him, it frightened him more, he knew what was going to happen. He put his head under the blanket, then pushed his head out again, for fear, staring at the dark window. He heard his mother's moan, his father's sigh; he gritted his teeth. Then their bed began to rock. His father's breathing seemed to fill the world.

That morning, before the sun had gathered all its strength, men and women, some flushed and some pale with excitement, came with news. Jesse's father seemed to know what the news was before the first jalopy stopped in the yard, and he ran out, crying, "They got him, then? They got him?"

The first jalopy held eight people, three men and two women and three children. The children were sitting on the laps of the grown-ups. Jesse knew two of them, the two boys; they shyly and uncomfortably greeted each other. He did not know the girl.

"Yes, they got him," said one of the women, the older one, who wore a wide hat and a fancy, faded blue dress. "They found him early this morning."

"How far had he got?" Jesse's father asked.

"He hadn't got no further than Harkness," one of the men said. "Look like he got lost up there in all them trees—or maybe he just got so scared he couldn't move." They all laughed.

"Yes, and you know it's near a graveyard, too," said the younger woman, and they laughed again.

"Is that where they got him now?" asked Jesse's father.

By this time there were three cars piled behind the first one, with everyone looking excited and shining, and Jesse noticed that they were carrying food. It was like a Fourth of July picnic.

"Yeah, that's where he is," said one of the men, "declare, Jesse, you going to keep us here all day long, answering your damn fool questions. Come on, we ain't got no time to waste."

"Don't bother putting up no food," cried a woman from one of the other cars, "we got enough. Just come on."

"Why, thank you," said Jesse's father, "we be right along, then."

"I better get a sweater for the boy," said his mother, "in case it turns cold."

Jesse watched his mother's thin legs cross the yard. He knew that she also wanted to comb her hair a little and maybe put on a better dress, the dress she wore to church. His father guessed this, too, for he yelled behind her, "Now don't you go trying to turn yourself into no movie star. You just come on." But he laughed as he said this, and winked at the men; his wife was younger and prettier than most of the other women. He clapped Jesse on the head and started pulling him toward the car. "You all go on," he said, "I'll be right behind you. Jesse, you go tie up that there dog while I get this car started."

The cars sputtered and coughed and shook; the caravan began to move; bright dust filled the air. As soon as he was tied up, the dog began to bark. Jesse's mother came out of the house, carrying a jacket for his father and a sweater for Jesse. She had put a ribbon in her hair and had an old shawl around her shoulders.

"Put these in the car, son," she said, and handed everything to him. She bent down and stroked the dog, looked to see if there was water in his bowl, then went back up the three porch steps and closed the door.

"Come on," said his father, "ain't nothing in there for nobody to steal." He was sitting in the car, which trembled and belched. The last car of the caravan had disappeared but the sound of singing floated behind them.

Jesse got into the car, sitting close to his father, loving the smell of the car, and the trembling, and the bright day, and the sense of going on a great and unexpected journey. His mother got in and closed the door and the car began to move. Not until then did he ask, "Where are we going? Are we going on a picnic?"

He had a feeling that he knew where they were going, but he was not sure.

"That's right," his father said, "we're going on a picnic. You won't ever forget *this* picnic—!"

"Are we," he asked, after a moment, "going to see the bad nigger—the one that knocked down old Miss Standish?"

"Well, I reckon," said his mother, "that we *might* see him."

He started to ask, *Will a lot of niggers be there? Will Otis be there?*—but he did not ask his question, to which, in a strange and uncomfortable way, he already knew the answer. Their friends, in the other cars, stretched up the road as far as he could see; other cars had joined them; there were cars behind them. They were singing. The sun seemed suddenly very hot, and he was at once very happy and a little afraid. He did not quite understand what was happening, and he did not know what to ask—he had no one to ask. He had grown accustomed, for the solution of such mysteries, to go to Otis. He felt that Otis knew everything. But he could not ask Otis about this. Anyway, he had not seen Otis for two days; he had not seen a black face anywhere for more than two days; and he now realized, as they began chugging up the long hill which eventually led to Harkness, that there were no black faces on the road this morning, no black people anywhere. From the houses in which they lived, all along the road, no smoke curled, no life stirred— maybe one or two chickens were to be seen, that was all. There was no one at the windows, no one in the yard, no one sitting on the porches, and the doors were closed. He had come this road many a time and seen women washing in the yard (there were no clothes on the clotheslines), men working in the fields, children playing in the dust; black men passed them on the road other mornings, other days, on foot, or in wagons, sometimes in cars, tipping their hats, smiling, joking, their teeth a solid white against their skin, their eyes as warm as the sun, the blackness of their skin like dull fire against the white or the blue or the grey of their torn clothes. They passed the nigger church—dead-white, desolate, locked up; and the graveyard, where no one knelt or walked, and he saw no flowers. He wanted to ask, *Where are they? Where are they all?* But he did not dare. As the hill grew steeper, the sun grew colder. He looked at his mother and his father. They looked straight ahead, seeming to be listening to the singing which echoed and echoed in this graveyard silence. They were strangers to him now. They were looking at something he could not see. His father's lips had a strange, cruel curve, he wet his lips from time to time, and swallowed. He was terribly aware of his father's tongue, it was as though he had never seen it before. And his father's body suddenly seemed immense, bigger than a mountain. His eyes, which were grey-green, looked yellow in the sunlight; or at least there was a light in them which he had never seen before. His mother patted her hair and adjusted the ribbon, leaning forward to look into the car mirror. "You look all right," said his father, and laughed. "When that nigger looks at you, he's going to swear he throwed his life away for nothing. Wouldn't be surprised if he don't come back to haunt you." And he laughed again.

The singing now slowly began to cease; and he realized that they were nearing their destination. They had reached a straight, narrow, pebbly road, with trees on either side. The sunlight filtered down on them from a great height, as though they were underwater; and the branches of the trees scraped against the cars with a tearing sound. To the right of them, and beneath them, invisible now, lay the town; and to the left, miles of trees which led to the high mountain range which his ancestors had crossed in order to settle in this valley. Now, all was silent, except for the bumping of the tires against the rocky road, the sputtering of motors, and the sound of a crying child. And they seemed to move more slowly. They were beginning to climb again. He watched the cars ahead as they toiled patiently upward, disappearing into the sunlight of the clearing. Presently, he felt their vehicle also rise, heard his father's changed breathing, the sunlight hit his face, the trees moved away from them, and they were there. As their car crossed the clearing, he looked around. There seemed to be millions, there were certainly hundreds of people in the clearing, staring toward something he could not see. There was a fire. He could not see the flames, but he smelled the smoke. Then they were on the other side of the clearing, among the trees again. His father drove off the road and parked the car behind a great many other cars. He looked down at Jesse.

"You all right?" he asked.

"Yes sir," he said.

"Well, come on, then," his father said. He reached over and opened the door on his mother's side. His mother stepped out first. They followed her into the clearing. At first he was aware only of confusion, of his mother and father greeting and being greeted, himself being handled, hugged, and patted, and told how much he had grown. The wind blew the smoke from the fire across the clearing into his eyes and nose. He could not see over the backs of the people in front of him. The sounds of laughing and cursing and wrath—and something else—rolled in waves from the front of the mob to the back. Those in front expressed their delight at what they saw, and this delight rolled backward, wave upon wave, across the clearing, more acrid than the smoke. His father reached down suddenly and sat Jesse on his shoulders.

Now he saw the fire—of twigs and boxes, piled high; flames made pale orange and yellow and thin as a veil under the steadier light of the sun; grey-blue smoke rolled upward and poured over their heads. Beyond the shifting curtain of fire and smoke, he made out first only a length of gleaming chain, attached to a great limb of the tree; then he saw that this chain bound two black hands together at the wrist, dirty yellow palm facing dirty yellow palm. The smoke poured up; the hands dropped out of sight; a cry went up from the crowd. Then the hands slowly came into view again, pulled upward by the chain. This time he saw the kinky, sweating, bloody head—he had never before seen a head with so much hair on it, hair so black and so tangled that it seemed like another jungle. The head was hanging. He saw the forehead, flat and high, with a kind of arrow of hair in the center, like he had, like his father had; they called it a widow's peak; and the mangled eyebrows, the wide nose, the closed eyes, and the glinting eyelashes and the hanging lips, all streaming with blood and sweat. His hands were straight above his head. All his weight pulled downward from his hands; and he was a big man, a bigger man than his father, and black as an African jungle cat, and naked. Jesse pulled upward; his father's hands held him firmly by the ankles. He wanted to say something, he did not know what, but nothing he said could have been heard, for now the crowd roared again as a man stepped forward and put more wood on the fire. The flames leapt up. He thought he heard the hanging man scream, but he was not sure. Sweat was pouring from the hair in his armpits, poured down his sides, over his chest, into his navel and his groin. He was lowered again; he was raised again. Now Jesse knew that he heard him scream. The head went back, the mouth wide open, blood bubbling from the mouth; the veins of the neck jumped out; Jesse clung to his father's neck in terror as the cry rolled over the crowd. The cry of all the people rose to answer the dying man's cry. He wanted death to come quickly. They wanted to make death wait: and it was they who held death, now, on a leash which they lengthened little by little. *What did he do?* Jesse wondered. *What did the man do? What did he do?*—but he could not ask his father. He was seated on his father's shoulders, but his father was far away. There were two older men, friends of his father's, raising and lowering the chain; everyone, indiscriminately, seemed to be responsible for the fire. There was no hair left on the nigger's privates, and the eyes, now, were wide open, as white as the eyes of a clown or a doll. The smoke now carried a terrible odor across the clearing, the odor of something burning which was both sweet and rotten.

He turned his head a little and saw the field of faces. He watched his mother's face. Her eyes were very bright, her mouth was open: she was more beautiful than he had ever seen her, and more strange. He began to feel a joy he had never felt before. He watched the hanging, gleaming body, the most beautiful and terrible object he had ever seen till then. One of his father's friends reached up and in his hands he held a knife: and Jesse wished that he had been that man. It was a long, bright knife and the sun seemed to catch it, to play with it, to caress it—it was brighter than the fire. And a wave of laughter swept the crowd. Jesse felt his father's hands on his ankles slip and tighten. The man with the knife walked toward the crowd, smiling slightly; as though this were a signal, silence fell; he heard his mother cough. Then the man with the knife walked up to the hanging body. He turned and smiled again. Now there was a silence all over the field. The hanging head looked up. It seemed fully conscious now, as though the fire had burned out terror and pain. The man with the knife took the nigger's privates in his hand, one hand, still smiling, as though he were weighing them. In the cradle of the one white hand, the nigger's privates seemed as remote as meat being weighed in the scales; but seemed heavier, too, much heavier, and Jesse felt his scrotum tighten; and huge, huge, much bigger than his father's, flaccid, hairless, the largest thing he had ever seen till then, and the blackest. The white hand stretched them, cradled them, caressed them. Then the dying man's eyes looked straight into Jesse's eyes—it could not have been as long as a second, but it seemed longer than a year. Then Jesse screamed, and the crowd screamed as the knife flashed, first up, then down, cutting the dreadful thing away, and the blood came roaring down. Then the crowd rushed forward, tearing at the body with their hands, with knives, with rocks, with stones, howling and cursing. Jesse's head, of its own weight, fell downward toward his father's head. Someone stepped forward and drenched the body with kerosene. Where the man had been, a great sheet of flame appeared. Jesse's father lowered him to the ground.

"Well, I told you," said his father, "you wasn't never going to forget *this* picnic." His father's face was full of sweat, his eyes were very peaceful. At that moment Jesse loved his father more than he had ever loved him. He felt that his father had carried him through a mighty test, had revealed to him a great secret which would be the key to his life forever.

"I reckon," he said. "I reckon."

Jesse's father took him by the hand and, with his mother a little behind them, talking and laughing with the other women, they walked through the crowd, across the clearing. The black body was on the ground, the chain which had held it was being rolled up by one of his father's friends. Whatever the fire had left undone, the hands and the knives and the stones of the people had accomplished. The head was caved in, one eye was torn out, one ear was hanging. But one had to look carefully to realize this, for it was, now, merely, a black charred object on the black, charred ground. He lay spread-eagled with what had been a wound between what had been his legs.

"They going to leave him here, then?" Jesse whispered.

"Yeah," said his father, "they'll come and get him by and by. I reckon we better get over there and get some of that food before it's all gone."

"I reckon," he muttered now to himself, "I reckon." Grace stirred and touched him on the thigh: the moonlight covered her like glory. Something bubbled up in him, his nature again returned to him. He thought of the boy in the cell; he thought of the man in the fire; he thought of the knife and grabbed himself and stroked himself and a terrible sound, something between a high laugh and a howl, came out of him and dragged his sleeping wife up on one elbow. She stared at him in a moonlight which had now grown cold as ice. He thought of the morning and grabbed her, laughing and crying, crying and laughing, and he whispered, as he stroked her, as he took her, "Come on, sugar, I'm going to do you like a nigger, just like a nigger, come on, sugar, and love me just like you'd love a nigger." He thought of the morning as he labored and she moaned, thought of morning as he labored harder than he ever had before, and before his labors had ended, he heard the first cock crow and the dogs begin to bark, and the sound of tires on the gravel road.

1965

Sonny's Blues

I read about it in the paper, in the subway, on my way to work. I read it, and I couldn't believe it, and I read it again. Then perhaps I just stared at it, at the newsprint spelling out his name, spelling out the story. I stared at it in the swinging lights of the subway car, and in the faces and bodies of the people, and in my own face, trapped in the darkness which roared outside.

It was not to be believed and I kept telling myself that, as I walked from the subway station to the high school. And at the same time I couldn't doubt it. I was scared, scared for Sonny. He became real to me again. A great block of ice got settled in my belly and kept melting there slowly all day long, while I taught my classes algebra. It was a special kind of ice. It kept melting, sending trickles of ice water all up and down my veins, but it never got less. Sometimes it hardened and seemed to expand until I felt my guts were going to come spilling out or that I was going to choke or scream. This would always be at a moment when I was remembering some specific thing Sonny had once said or done.

When he was about as old as the boys in my classes his face had been bright and open, there was a lot of copper in it; and he'd had wonderfully direct brown eyes, and great gentleness and privacy. I wondered what he looked like now. He had been picked up, the evening before, in a raid on an apartment downtown, for peddling and using heroin.

I couldn't believe it: but what I mean by that is that I couldn't find any room for it anywhere inside me. I had kept it outside me for a long time. I hadn't wanted to know. I had had suspicions, but I didn't name them, I kept putting them away. I told myself that Sonny was wild, but he wasn't crazy. And he'd always been a good boy, he hadn't ever turned hard or evil or disrespectful, the way kids can, so quick, so quick, especially in Harlem. I didn't want to believe that I'd ever see my brother going down, coming to nothing, all that light in his face gone out, in the condition I'd already seen so many others. Yet it had happened and here I was, talking about algebra to a lot of boys who might, every one of them for all I knew, be popping off needles every time they went to the head.[1] Maybe it did more for them than algebra could.

I was sure that the first time Sonny had ever had horse,[2] he couldn't have been much older than these boys were now. These boys, now, were living as we'd been living then, they were growing up with a rush and their heads bumped abruptly against the low ceiling of their actual possibilities. They were filled with rage. All they really knew were two darknesses, the darkness of their lives, which was now closing in on them, and the darkness of the movies, which had blinded them to that other darkness, and in which they now, vindictively, dreamed, at once more together than they were at any other time, and more alone.

When the last bell rang, the last class ended, I let out my breath. It seemed I'd been holding it for all that time. My clothes were wet—I may have looked as though I'd been sitting in a steam bath, all dressed up, all afternoon. I sat alone in the classroom a long time. I listened to the boys outside, downstairs, shouting and cursing and laughing. Their laughter struck me for perhaps the first time. It was not the joyous laughter which—God knows why—one associates with children. It was mocking and insular, its intent was to denigrate. It was disenchanted, and in this, also, lay the authority of their curses. Perhaps I was listening to them because I was thinking about my brother and in them I heard my brother. And myself.

One boy was whistling a tune, at once very complicated and very simple, it seemed to be pouring out of him as though he were a bird, and it sounded very cool and moving through all that harsh, bright air, only just holding its own through all those other sounds.

I stood up and walked over to the window and looked down into the courtyard. It was the beginning of the spring and the sap was rising in the boys. A teacher passed through them every now and again, quickly, as though he or she couldn't wait to get out of that courtyard, to get those boys out of their sight and off their minds. I started collecting my stuff. I thought I'd better get home and talk to Isabel.

The courtyard was almost deserted by the time I got downstairs. I saw this boy standing in the shadow of a doorway, looking just like Sonny. I almost called his name. Then I saw that it wasn't Sonny, but somebody we used to know, a boy from around our block. He'd been Sonny's friend. He'd never been mine, having been too young for me, and, anyway, I'd never liked him. And now, even though he was a grown-up man, he still hung around that block, still spent hours on the street corners, was always high and raggy. I used to run into him from time to time and he'd often work around to asking me for a quarter or fifty cents. He always had some real good excuse, too, and I always gave it to him, I don't know why.

But now, abruptly, I hated him. I couldn't stand the way he looked at me, partly like a dog, partly like a cunning child. I wanted to ask him what the hell he was doing in the school courtyard.

He sort of shuffled over to me, and he said, "I see you got the papers. So you already know about it."

1. Lavatory.　　　　　2. Slang term for heroin.

"You mean about Sonny? Yes, I already know about it. How come they didn't get you?"

He grinned. It made him repulsive and it also brought to mind what he'd looked like as a kid. "I wasn't there. I stay away from them people."

"Good for you." I offered him a cigarette and I watched him through the smoke. "You come all the way down here just to tell me about Sonny?"

"That's right." He was sort of shaking his head and his eyes looked strange, as though they were about to cross. The bright sun deadened his damp dark brown skin and it made his eyes look yellow and showed up the dirt in his kinked hair. He smelled funky. I moved a little away from him and I said, "Well, thanks. But I already know about it and I got to get home."

"I'll walk you a little ways," he said. We started walking. There were a couple of kids still loitering in the courtyard and one of them said good-night to me and looked strangely at the boy beside me.

"What're you going to do?" he asked me. "I mean, about Sonny?"

"Look. I haven't seen Sonny for over a year, I'm not sure I'm going to do anything. Anyway, what the hell _can_ I do?"

"That's right," he said quickly, "ain't nothing you can do. Can't much help old Sonny no more, I guess."

It was what I was thinking and so it seemed to me he had no right to say it.

"I'm surprised at Sonny, though," he went on—he had a funny way of talking, he looked straight ahead as though he were talking to himself—"I thought Sonny was a smart boy, I thought he was too smart to get hung."[3]

"I guess he thought so too," I said sharply, "and that's how he got hung. And how about you? You're pretty goddamn smart, I bet."

Then he looked directly at me, just for a minute. "I ain't smart," he said. "If I was smart, I'd have reached for a pistol a long time ago."

"Look. Don't tell _me_ your sad story, if it was up to me, I'd give you one." Then I felt guilty—guilty, probably, for never having supposed that the poor bastard _had_ a story of his own, much less a sad one, and I asked, quickly, "What's going to happen to him now?"

He didn't answer this. He was off by himself some place. "Funny thing," he said, and from his tone we might have been discussing the quickest way to get to Brooklyn, "when I saw the papers this morning, the first thing I asked myself was if I had anything to do with it. I felt sort of responsible."

I began to listen more carefully. The subway station was on the corner, just before us, and I stopped. He stopped, too. We were in front of a bar and he ducked slightly, peering in, but whoever he was looking for didn't seem to be there. The juke box was blasting away with something black and bouncy and I half watched the barmaid as she danced her way from the juke box to her place behind the bar. And I watched her face as she laughingly responded to something someone said to her, still keeping time to the music. When she smiled one saw the little girl, one sensed the doomed, still-struggling woman beneath the battered face of the semi-whore.

"I never _give_ Sonny nothing," the boy said finally, "but a long time ago I come to school high and Sonny asked me how it felt." He paused, I couldn't bear to watch him, I watched the barmaid, and I listened to the music

3. Become an addict.

which seemed to be causing the pavement to shake. "I told him it felt great."
The music stopped, the barmaid paused and watched the juke box until the
music began again. "It did."

All this was carrying me some place I didn't want to go. I certainly didn't
want to know how it felt. It filled everything, the people, the houses, the music,
the dark, quicksilver barmaid, with menace; and this menace was their reality.

"What's going to happen to him now?" I asked again.

"They'll send him away some place and they'll try to cure him." He shook
his head. "Maybe he'll even think he's kicked the habit. Then they'll let him
loose"—he gestured, throwing his cigarette into the gutter. "That's all."

"What do you mean, that's *all*?"

But I knew what he meant.

"I *mean*, that's *all*." He turned his head and looked at me, pulling down
the corners of his mouth. "Don't you know what I mean?" he asked,
softly.

"How the hell *would* I know what you mean?" I almost whispered it, I
don't know why.

"That's right," he said to the air, "how would *he* know what I mean?" He
turned toward me again, patient and calm, and yet I somehow felt him
shaking, shaking as though he were going to fall apart. I felt that ice in my
guts again, the dread I'd felt all afternoon; and again I watched the barmaid, moving about the bar, washing glasses, and singing. "Listen. They'll
let him out and then it'll just start all over again. That's what I mean."

"You mean—they'll let him out. And then he'll just start working his
way back in again. You mean he'll never kick the habit. Is that what you
mean?"

"That's right," he said, cheerfully. "*You* see what I mean."

"Tell me," I said at last, "why does he want to die? He must want to die,
he's killing himself, why does he want to die?"

He looked at me in surprise. He licked his lips. "He don't want to die. He
wants to live. Don't nobody want to die, ever."

Then I wanted to ask him—too many things. He could not have answered,
or if he had, I could not have borne the answers. I started walking. "Well, I
guess it's none of my business."

"It's going to be rough on old Sonny," he said. We reached the subway station. "This is your station?" he asked. I nodded. I took one step down. "Damn!"
he said, suddenly. I looked up at him. He grinned again. "Damn it if I didn't
leave all my money home. You ain't got a dollar on you, have you? Just for a
couple of days, is all."

All at once something inside gave and threatened to come pouring out of
me. I didn't hate him anymore. I felt that in another moment I'd start crying like a child.

"Sure," I said. "Don't sweat." I looked in my wallet and didn't have a dollar, I only had a five. "Here," I said. "That hold you?"

He didn't look at it—he didn't want to look at it. A terrible, closed look
came over his face, as though he were keeping the number on the bill a
secret from him and me. "Thanks," he said, and now he was dying to see me
go. "Don't worry about Sonny. Maybe I'll write him or something."

"Sure," I said. "You do that. So long."

"Be seeing you," he said. I went on down the steps.

And I didn't write Sonny or send him anything for a long time. When I finally did, it was just after my little girl died, he wrote me back a letter which made me feel like a bastard.

Here's what he said:

> Dear brother,
>
> You don't know how much I needed to hear from you. I wanted to write you many a time but I dug how much I must have hurt you and so I didn't write. But now I feel like a man who's been trying to climb up out of some deep, real deep and funky hole and just saw the sun up there, outside. I got to get outside.
>
> I can't tell you much about how I got here. I mean I don't know how to tell you. I guess I was afraid of something or I was trying to escape from something and you know I have never been very strong in the head (smile). I'm glad Mama and Daddy are dead and can't see what's happened to their son and I swear if I'd known what I was doing I would never have hurt you so, you and a lot of other fine people who were nice to me and who believed in me.
>
> I don't want you to think it had anything to do with me being a musician. It's more than that. Or maybe less than that. I can't get anything straight in my head down here and I try not to think about what's going to happen to me when I get outside again. Sometime I think I'm going to flip and *never* get outside and sometime I think I'll come straight back. I tell you one thing, though, I'd rather blow my brains out than go through this again. But that's what they all say, so they tell me. If I tell you when I'm coming to New York and if you could meet me, I sure would appreciate it. Give my love to Isabel and the kids and I was sure sorry to hear about little Gracie. I wish I could be like Mama and say the Lord's will be done, but I don't know it seems to me that trouble is the one thing that never does get stopped and I don't know what good it does to blame it on the Lord. But maybe it does some good if you believe it.
>
> Your brother,
> Sonny

Then I kept in constant touch with him and I sent him whatever I could and I went to meet him when he came back to New York. When I saw him many things I thought I had forgotten came flooding back to me. This was because I had begun, finally, to wonder about Sonny, about the life that Sonny lived inside. This life, whatever it was, had made him older and thinner and it had deepened the distant stillness in which he had always moved. He looked very unlike my baby brother. Yet, when he smiled, when we shook hands, the baby brother I'd never known looked out from the depths of his private life, like an animal waiting to be coaxed into the light.

"How you been keeping?" he asked me.

"All right. And you?"

"Just fine." He was smiling all over his face. "It's good to see you again."

"It's good to see you."

The seven years' difference in our ages lay between us like a chasm: I wondered if these years would ever operate between us as a bridge. I was remembering, and it made it hard to catch my breath, that I had been there when he was born; and I had heard the first words he had ever spoken. When he started to walk, he walked from our mother straight to me. I caught him just before he fell when he took the first steps he ever took in this world.

"How's Isabel?"

"Just fine. She's dying to see you."

"And the boys?"

"They're fine, too. They're anxious to see their uncle."

"Oh, come on. You know they don't remember me."

"Are you kidding? Of course they remember you."

He grinned again. We got into a taxi. We had a lot to say to each other, far too much to know how to begin.

As the taxi began to move, I asked, "You still want to go to India?"

He laughed. "You still remember that. Hell, no. This place is Indian enough for me."

"It used to belong to them,"[4] I said.

And he laughed again. "They damn sure knew what they were doing when they got rid of it."

Years ago, when he was around fourteen, he'd been all hipped on the idea of going to India. He read books about people sitting on rocks, naked, in all kinds of weather, but mostly bad, naturally, and walking barefoot through hot coals and arriving at wisdom. I used to say that it sounded to me as though they were getting away from wisdom as fast as they could. I think he sort of looked down on me for that.

"Do you mind," he asked, "if we have the driver drive alongside the park?[5] On the west side—I haven't seen the city in so long."

"Of course not," I said. I was afraid that I might sound as though I were humoring him, but I hoped he wouldn't take it that way.

So we drove along, between the green of the park and the stony, lifeless elegance of hotels and apartment buildings, toward the vivid, killing streets of our childhood. These streets hadn't changed, though housing projects jutted up out of them now like rocks in the middle of a boiling sea. Most of the houses in which we had grown up had vanished, as had the stores from which we had stolen, the basements in which we had first tried sex, the rooftops from which we had hurled tin cans and bricks. But houses exactly like the houses of our past yet dominated the landscape, boys exactly like the boys we once had been found themselves smothering in these houses, came down into the streets for light and air and found themselves encircled by disaster. Some escaped the trap, most didn't. Those who got out always left something of themselves behind, as some animals amputate a leg and leave it in the trap. It might be said, perhaps, that I had escaped, after all, I was a school teacher; or that Sonny had, he hadn't lived in Harlem for years. Yet, as the cab moved uptown through streets which seemed, with a rush, to darken with dark people, and as I covertly studied Sonny's face, it came to me that what we both were seeking through our separate cab windows was that part of ourselves which had been left behind. It's always at the hour of trouble and confrontation that the missing member aches.

---

4. Manhattan Island, in the center of New York City, was purchased by Dutch settlers from the

Lenape tribe, circa 1626.

5. Central Park.

We hit 110th Street and started rolling up Lenox Avenue. And I'd known this avenue all my life, but it seemed to me again, as it had seemed on the day I'd first heard about Sonny's trouble, filled with a hidden menace which was its very breath of life.

"We almost there," said Sonny.

"Almost." We were both too nervous to say anything more.

We live in a housing project. It hasn't been up long. A few days after it was up it seemed uninhabitably new, now, of course, it's already rundown. It looks like a parody of the good, clean, faceless life—God knows the people who live in it do their best to make it a parody. The beat-looking grass lying around isn't enough to make their lives green, the hedges will never hold out the streets, and they know it. The big windows fool no one, they aren't big enough to make space out of no space. They don't bother with the windows, they watch the TV screen instead. The playground is most popular with the children who don't play at jacks, or skip rope, or roller skate, or swing, and they can be found in it after dark. We moved in partly because it's not too far from where I teach, and partly for the kids; but it's really just like the houses in which Sonny and I grew up. The same things happen, they'll have the same things to remember. The moment Sonny and I started into the house I had the feeling that I was simply bringing him back into the danger he had almost died trying to escape.

Sonny has never been talkative. So I don't know why I was sure he'd be dying to talk to me when supper was over the first night. Everything went fine, the oldest boy remembered him, and the youngest boy liked him, and Sonny had remembered to bring something for each of them; and Isabel, who is really much nicer than I am, more open and giving, had gone to a lot of trouble about dinner and was genuinely glad to see him. And she's always been able to tease Sonny in a way that I haven't. It was nice to see her face so vivid again and to hear her laugh and watch her make Sonny laugh. She wasn't, or, anyway, she didn't seem to be, at all uneasy or embarrassed. She chatted as though there were no subject which had to be avoided and she got Sonny past his first, faint stiffness. And thank God she was there, for I was filled with that icy dread again. Everything I did seemed awkward to me, and everything I said sounded freighted with hidden meaning. I was trying to remember everything I'd heard about dope addiction and I couldn't help watching Sonny for signs. I wasn't doing it out of malice. I was trying to find out something about my brother. I was dying to hear him tell me he was safe.

"Safe!" my father grunted, whenever Mama suggested trying to move to a neighborhood which might be safer for children. "Safe, hell! Ain't no place safe for kids, nor nobody."

He always went on like this, but he wasn't, ever, really as bad as he sounded, not even on weekends, when he got drunk. As a matter of fact, he was always on the lookout for "something a little better," but he died before he found it. He died suddenly, during a drunken weekend in the middle of the war, when Sonny was fifteen. He and Sonny hadn't ever got on too well. And this was partly because Sonny was the apple of his father's eye. It was because he loved Sonny so much and was frightened for him, that he was always fighting with him. It doesn't do any good to fight with Sonny. Sonny just moves back, inside himself, where he can't be reached. But the principal reason that they never hit it off is that they were so much alike. Daddy was big and rough and loud-talking, just the opposite of Sonny, but they both had—that same privacy.

Mama tried to tell me something about this, just after Daddy died. I was home on leave from the army.

This was the last time I ever saw my mother alive. Just the same, this picture gets all mixed up in my mind with pictures I had of her when she was younger. The way I always see her is the way she used to be on a Sunday afternoon, say, when the old folks were talking after the big Sunday dinner. I always see her wearing pale blue. She'd be sitting on the sofa. And my father would be sitting in the easy chair, not far from her. And the living room would be full of church folks and relatives. There they sit, in chairs all around the living room, and the night is creeping up outside, but nobody knows it yet. You can see the darkness growing against the windowpanes and you hear the street noises every now and again, or maybe the jangling beat of a tambourine from one of the churches close by, but it's real quiet in the room. For a moment nobody's talking, but every face looks darkening, like the sky outside. And my mother rocks a little from the waist, and my father's eyes are closed. Everyone is looking at something a child can't see. For a minute they've forgotten the children. Maybe a kid is lying on the rug, half asleep. Maybe somebody's got a kid in his lap and is absent-mindedly stroking the kid's head. Maybe there's a kid, quiet and big-eyed, curled up in a big chair in the corner. The silence, the darkness coming, and the darkness in the faces frightens the child obscurely. He hopes that the hand which strokes his forehead will never stop—will never die. He hopes that there will never come a time when the old folks won't be sitting around the living room, talking about where they've come from, and what they've seen, and what's happened to them and their kinfolk.

But something deep and watchful in the child knows that this is bound to end, is already ending. In a moment someone will get up and turn on the light. Then the old folks will remember the children and they won't talk anymore that day. And when light fills the room, the child is filled with darkness. He knows that every time this happens he's moved just a little closer to that darkness outside. The darkness outside is what the old folks have been talking about. It's what they've come from. It's what they endure. The child knows that they won't talk anymore because if he knows too much about what's happened to *them*, he'll know too much too soon, about what's going to happen to *him*.

The last time I talked to my mother, I remember I was restless. I wanted to get out and see Isabel. We weren't married then and we had a lot to straighten out between us.

There Mama sat, in black, by the window. She was humming an old church song, *Lord, you brought me from a long ways off*. Sonny was out somewhere. Mama kept watching the streets.

"I don't know," she said, "if I'll ever see you again, after you go off from here. But I hope you'll remember the things I tried to teach you."

"Don't talk like that," I said, and smiled. "You'll be here a long time yet."

She smiled, too, but she said nothing. She was quiet for a long time. And I said, "Mama, don't you worry about nothing. I'll be writing all the time, and you be getting the checks. . . ."

"I want to talk to you about your brother," she said, suddenly. "If anything happens to me he ain't going to have nobody to look out for him."

"Mama," I said, "ain't nothing going to happen to you *or* Sonny. Sonny's all right. He's a good boy and he's got good sense."

"It ain't a question of his being a good boy," Mama said, "nor of his having good sense. It ain't only the bad ones, nor yet the dumb ones that gets sucked under." She stopped, looking at me. "Your Daddy once had a brother," she said, and she smiled in a way that made me feel she was in pain. "You didn't never know that, did you?"

"No," I said, "I never knew that," and I watched her face.

"Oh, yes," she said, "your Daddy had a brother." She looked out of the window again. "I know you never saw your Daddy cry. But *I* did—many a time, through all these years."

I asked her, "What happened to his brother? How come nobody's ever talked about him?"

This was the first time I ever saw my mother look old.

"His brother got killed," she said, "when he was just a little younger than you are now. I knew him. He was a fine boy. He was maybe a little full of the devil, but he didn't mean nobody no harm."

Then she stopped and the room was silent, exactly as it had sometimes been on those Sunday afternoons. Mama kept looking out into the streets.

"He used to have a job in the mill," she said, "and, like all young folks, he just liked to perform Saturday nights. Saturday nights, him and your father would drift around to different places, go to dances and things like that, or just sit around with people they knew, and your father's brother would sing, he had a fine voice, and play along with himself on his guitar. Well, this particular Saturday night, him and your father was coming home from some place, and they were both a little drunk and there was a moon that night, it was bright like day. Your father's brother was feeling kind of good, and he was whistling to himself, and he had his guitar slung over his shoulder. They was coming down a hill and beneath them was a road that turned off from the highway. Well, your father's brother, being always kind of frisky, decided to run down this hill, and he did, with that guitar banging and clanging behind him, and he ran across the road, and he was making water behind a tree. And your father was sort of amused at him and he was still coming down the hill, kind of slow. Then he heard a car motor and that same minute his brother stepped from behind the tree, into the road, in the moonlight. And he started to cross the road. And your father started to run down the hill, he says he don't know why. This car was full of white men. They was all drunk, and when they seen your father's brother they let out a great whoop and holler and they aimed the car straight at him. They was having fun, they just wanted to scare him, the way they do sometimes, you know. But they was drunk. And I guess the boy, being drunk, too, and scared, kind of lost his head. By the time he jumped it was too late. Your father says he heard his brother scream when the car rolled over him, and he heard the wood of that guitar when it give, and he heard them strings go flying, and he heard them white men shouting, and the car kept on a-going and it ain't stopped till this day. And, time your father got down the hill, his brother weren't nothing but blood and pulp."

Tears were gleaming on my mother's face. There wasn't anything I could say.

"He never mentioned it," she said, "because I never let him mention it before you children. Your Daddy was like a crazy man that night and for many a night thereafter. He says he never in his life seen anything as dark as that road after the lights of that car had gone away. Weren't nothing, weren't nobody on that road, just your Daddy and his brother and that busted guitar. Oh, yes. Your Daddy never did really get right again. Till the day he died he weren't sure but that every white man he saw was the man that killed his brother."

She stopped and took out her handkerchief and dried her eyes and looked at me.

"I ain't telling you all this," she said, "to make you scared or bitter or to make you hate nobody. I'm telling you this because you got a brother. And the world ain't changed."

I guess I didn't want to believe this. I guess she saw this in my face. She turned away from me, toward the window again, searching those streets.

"But I praise my Redeemer," she said at last, "that He called your Daddy home before me. I ain't saying it to throw no flowers at myself, but, I declare, it keeps me from feeling too cast down to know I helped your father get safely through this world. Your father always acted like he was the roughest, strongest man on earth. And everybody took him to be like that. But if he hadn't had *me* there—to see his tears!"

She was crying again. Still, I couldn't move. I said, "Lord, Lord, Mama, I didn't know it was like that."

"Oh, honey," she said, "there's a lot that you don't know. But you are going to find it out." She stood up from the window and came over to me. "You got to hold on to your brother," she said, "and don't let him fall, no matter what it looks like is happening to him and no matter how evil you gets with him. You going to be evil with him many a time. But don't you forget what I told you, you hear?"

"I won't forget," I said. "Don't you worry, I won't forget. I won't let nothing happen to Sonny."

My mother smiled as though she were amused at something she saw in my face. Then, "You may not be able to stop nothing from happening. But you got to let him know you's *there*."

Two days later I was married, and then I was gone. And I had a lot of things on my mind and I pretty well forgot my promise to Mama until I got shipped home on a special furlough for her funeral.

And, after the funeral, with just Sonny and me alone in the empty kitchen, I tried to find out something about him.

"What do you want to do?" I asked him.

"I'm going to be a musician," he said.

For he had graduated, in the time I had been away, from dancing to the juke box to finding out who was playing what, and what they were doing with it, and he had bought himself a set of drums.

"You mean, you want to be a drummer?" I somehow had the feeling that being a drummer might be all right for other people but not for my brother Sonny.

"I don't think," he said, looking at me very gravely, "that I'll ever be a good drummer. But I think I can play a piano."

I frowned. I'd never played the role of the older brother quite so seriously before, had scarcely ever, in fact, *asked* Sonny a damn thing. I sensed myself in the presence of something I didn't really know how to handle, didn't understand. So I made my frown a little deeper as I asked: "What kind of musician do you want to be?"

He grinned. "How many kinds do you think there are?"

"Be *serious*," I said.

He laughed, throwing his head back, and then looked at me. "I *am* serious."

"Well, then, for Christ's sake, stop kidding around and answer a serious question. I mean, do you want to be a concert pianist, you want to play classical music and all that, or—or what?" Long before I finished he was laughing again. "For Christ's *sake*, Sonny!"

He sobered, but with difficulty. "I'm sorry. But you sound so—*scared!*" and he was off again.

"Well, you may think it's funny now, baby, but it's not going to be so funny when you have to make your living at it, let me tell you *that*." I was furious because I knew he was laughing at me and I didn't know why.

"No," he said, very sober now, and afraid, perhaps, that he'd hurt me, "I don't want to be a classical pianist. That isn't what interests me. I mean"—he paused, looking hard at me, as though his eyes would help me to understand, and then gestured helplessly, as though perhaps his hand would help—"I mean, I'll have a lot of studying to do, and I'll have to study *everything*, but, I mean, I want to play *with*—jazz musicians." He stopped. "I want to play jazz," he said.

Well, the word had never before sounded as heavy, as real, as it sounded that afternoon in Sonny's mouth. I just looked at him and I was probably frowning a real frown by this time. I simply couldn't see why on earth he'd want to spend his time hanging around nightclubs, clowning around on bandstands, while people pushed each other around a dance floor. It seemed—beneath him, somehow. I had never thought about it before, had never been forced to, but I suppose I had always put jazz musicians in a class with what Daddy called "good-time people."

"Are you *serious*?"

"Hell, *yes*, I'm serious."

He looked more helpless than ever, and annoyed, and deeply hurt.

I suggested, helpfully: "You mean—like Louis Armstrong?"[6]

His face closed as though I'd struck him. "No. I'm not talking about none of that old-time, down-home crap."

"Well, look, Sonny, I'm sorry, don't get mad. I just don't altogether get it, that's all. Name somebody—you know, a jazz musician you admire."

"Bird."

"Who?"

"Bird! Charlie Parker![7] Don't they teach you nothing in the goddamn army?"

I lit a cigarette. I was surprised and then a little amused to discover that I was trembling. "I've been out of touch," I said. "You'll have to be patient with me. Now. Who's this Parker character?"

6. American jazz trumpeter (1901–1971).
7. Charles Christopher Parker Jr. (1920–1955), nicknamed "Yardbird" or simply "Bird," American jazz saxophonist credited with inventing the experimental "bebop" style of jazz. He died from the effects of long-term heroin addiction.

"He's just one of the greatest jazz musicians alive," said Sonny, sullenly, his hands in his pockets, his back to me. "Maybe *the* greatest," he added, bitterly, "that's probably why *you* never heard of him."

"All right," I said, "I'm ignorant. I'm sorry. I'll go out and buy all the cat's records right away, all right?"

"It don't," said Sonny, with dignity, "make any difference to me. I don't care what you listen to. Don't do me no favors."

I was beginning to realize that I'd never seen him so upset before. With another part of my mind I was thinking that this would probably turn out to be one of those things kids go through and that I shouldn't make it seem important by pushing it too hard. Still, I didn't think it would do any harm to ask: "Doesn't all this take a lot of time? Can you make a living at it?"

He turned back to me and half leaned, half sat, on the kitchen table. "Everything takes time," he said, "and—well, yes, sure, I can make a living at it. But what I don't seem to be able to make you understand is that it's the only thing I want to do."

"Well, Sonny," I said, gently, "you know people can't always do exactly what they *want* to do—"

"*No*, I don't know that," said Sonny, surprising me. "I think people *ought* to do what they want to do, what else are they alive for?"

"You getting to be a big boy," I said desperately, "it's time you started thinking about your future."

"I'm thinking about my future," said Sonny, grimly. "I think about it all the time."

I gave up. I decided, if he didn't change his mind, that we could always talk about it later. "In the meantime," I said, "you got to finish school." We had already decided that he'd have to move in with Isabel and her folks. I knew this wasn't the ideal arrangement because Isabel's folks are inclined to be dicty[8] and they hadn't especially wanted Isabel to marry me. But I didn't know what else to do. "And we have to get you fixed up at Isabel's."

There was a long silence. He moved from the kitchen table to the window. "That's a terrible idea. You know it yourself."

"Do you have a *better* idea?"

He just walked up and down the kitchen for a minute. He was as tall as I was. He had started to shave. I suddenly had the feeling that I didn't know him at all.

He stopped at the kitchen table and picked up my cigarettes. Looking at me with a kind of mocking, amused defiance, he put one between his lips. "You mind?"

"You smoking already?"

He lit the cigarette and nodded, watching me through the smoke. "I just wanted to see if I'd have the courage to smoke in front of you." He grinned and blew a great cloud of smoke to the ceiling. "It was easy." He looked at my face. "Come on, now. I bet you was smoking at my age, tell the truth."

I didn't say anything but the truth was on my face, and he laughed. But now there was something very strained in his laugh. "Sure. And I bet that ain't all you was doing."

___

8. Slang for "snobbish."

He was frightening me a little. "Cut the crap," I said. "We already decided that you was going to go and live at Isabel's. Now what's got into you all of a sudden?"

"*You* decided it," he pointed out. "*I* didn't decide nothing." He stopped in front of me, leaning against the stove, arms loosely folded. "Look, brother. I don't want to stay in Harlem no more, I really don't." He was very earnest. He looked at me, then over toward the kitchen window. There was something in his eyes I'd never seen before, some thoughtfulness, some worry all his own. He rubbed the muscle of one arm. "It's time I was getting out of here."

"Where do you want to *go*, Sonny?"

"I want to join the army. Or the navy, I don't care. If I say I'm old enough, they'll believe me."

Then I got mad. It was because I was so scared. "You must be crazy. You goddamn fool, what the hell do you want to go and join the *army* for?"

"I just told you. To get out of Harlem."

"Sonny, you haven't even finished *school*. And if you really want to be a musician, how do you expect to study if you're in the *army*?"

He looked at me, trapped, and in anguish. "There's ways. I might be able to work out some kind of deal. Anyway, I'll have the G.I. Bill[9] when I come out."

"*If* you come out." We stared at each other. "Sonny, please. Be reasonable. I know the setup is far from perfect. But we got to do the best we can."

"I ain't learning nothing in school," he said. "Even when I go." He turned away from me and opened the window and threw his cigarette out into the narrow alley. I watched his back. "At least, I ain't learning nothing you'd want me to learn." He slammed the window so hard I thought the glass would fly out, and turned back to me. "And I'm sick of the stink of these garbage cans!"

"Sonny," I said, "I know how you feel. But if you don't finish school now, you're going to be sorry later that you didn't." I grabbed him by the shoulders. "And you only got another year. It ain't so bad. And I'll come back and I swear I'll help you do *whatever* you want to do. Just try to put up with it till I come back. Will you please do that? For me?"

He didn't answer and he wouldn't look at me.

"Sonny. You hear me?"

He pulled away. "I hear you. But you never hear anything *I* say."

I didn't know what to say to that. He looked out of the window and then back at me. "OK," he said, and sighed. "I'll try."

Then I said, trying to cheer him up a little, "They got a piano at Isabel's. You can practice on it."

And as a matter of fact, it did cheer him up for a minute. "That's right," he said to himself. "I forgot that." His face relaxed a little. But the worry, the thoughtfulness, played on it still, the way shadows play on a face which is staring into the fire.

But I thought I'd never hear the end of that piano. At first, Isabel would write me, saying how nice it was that Sonny was so serious about his music

---

9. The Servicemen's Readjustment Act (1944), known as the G.I. Bill, provided educational and other benefits to World War II veterans.

and how, as soon as he came in from school, or wherever he had been when he was supposed to be at school, he went straight to that piano and stayed there until suppertime. And, after supper, he went back to that piano and stayed there until everybody went to bed. He was at the piano all day Saturday and all day Sunday. Then he bought a record player and started playing records. He'd play one record over and over again, all day long sometimes, and he'd improvise along with it on the piano. Or he'd play one section of the record, one chord, one change, one progression, then he'd do it on the piano. Then back to the record. Then back to the piano.

Well, I really don't know how they stood it. Isabel finally confessed that it wasn't like living with a person at all, it was like living with sound. And the sound didn't make any sense to her, didn't make any sense to any of them—naturally. They began, in a way, to be afflicted by this presence that was living in their home. It was as though Sonny were some sort of god, or monster. He moved in an atmosphere which wasn't like theirs at all. They fed him and he ate, he washed himself, he walked in and out of their door; he certainly wasn't nasty or unpleasant or rude, Sonny isn't any of those things; but it was as though he were all wrapped up in some cloud, some fire, some vision all his own; and there wasn't any way to reach him.

At the same time, he wasn't really a man yet, he was still a child, and they had to watch out for him in all kinds of ways. They certainly couldn't throw him out. Neither did they dare to make a great scene about that piano because even they dimly sensed, as I sensed, from so many thousands of miles away, that Sonny was at that piano playing for his life.

But he hadn't been going to school. One day a letter came from the school board and Isabel's mother got it—there had, apparently, been other letters but Sonny had torn them up. This day, when Sonny came in, Isabel's mother showed him the letter and asked where he'd been spending his time. And she finally got it out of him that he'd been down in Greenwich Village,[1] with musicians and other characters, in a white girl's apartment. And this scared her and she started to scream at him and what came up, once she began— though she denies it to this day—was what sacrifices they were making to give Sonny a decent home and how little he appreciated it.

Sonny didn't play the piano that day. By evening, Isabel's mother had calmed down but then there was the old man to deal with, and Isabel herself. Isabel says she did her best to be calm but she broke down and started crying. She says she just watched Sonny's face. She could tell, by watching him, what was happening with him. And what was happening was that they penetrated his cloud, they had reached him. Even if their fingers had been a thousand times more gentle than human fingers ever are, he could hardly help feeling that they had stripped him naked and were spitting on that nakedness. For he also had to see that his presence, that music, which was life or death to him, had been torture for them and that they had endured it, not at all for his sake, but only for mine. And Sonny couldn't take that. He can take it a little better today than he could then but he's still not very good at it and, frankly, I don't know anybody who is.

---

1. Neighborhood in Lower Manhattan where artists, musicians, writers, and intellectuals gathered in the mid-20th century.

The silence of the next few days must have been louder than the sound of all the music ever played since time began. One morning, before she went to work, Isabel was in his room for something and she suddenly realized that all of his records were gone. And she knew for certain that he was gone. And he was. He went as far as the navy would carry him. He finally sent me a postcard from some place in Greece and that was the first I knew that Sonny was still alive. I didn't see him anymore until we were both back in New York and the war had long been over.

He was a man by then, of course, but I wasn't willing to see it. He came by the house from time to time, but we fought almost every time we met. I didn't like the way he carried himself, loose and dreamlike all the time, and I didn't like his friends, and his music seemed to be merely an excuse for the life he led. It sounded just that weird and disordered.

Then we had a fight, a pretty awful fight, and I didn't see him for months. By and by I looked him up, where he was living, in a furnished room in the Village, and I tried to make it up. But there were lots of other people in the room and Sonny just lay on his bed, and he wouldn't come downstairs with me, and he treated these other people as though they were his family and I weren't. So I got mad and then he got mad, and then I told him that he might just as well be dead as live the way he was living. Then he stood up and he told me not to worry about him anymore in life, that he *was* dead as far as I was concerned. Then he pushed me to the door and the other people looked on as though nothing were happening, and he slammed the door behind me. I stood in the hallway, staring at the door. I heard somebody laugh in the room and then the tears came to my eyes. I started down the steps, whistling to keep from crying, I kept whistling to myself, *You going to need me, baby, one of these cold, rainy days.*[2]

I read about Sonny's trouble in the spring. Little Grace died in the fall. She was a beautiful little girl. But she only lived a little over two years. She died of polio and she suffered. She had a slight fever for a couple of days, but it didn't seem like anything and we just kept her in bed. And we would certainly have called the doctor, but the fever dropped, she seemed to be all right. So we thought it had just been a cold. Then, one day, she was up, playing, Isabel was in the kitchen fixing lunch for the two boys when they'd come in from school, and she heard Grace fall down in the living room. When you have a lot of children you don't always start running when one of them falls, unless they start screaming or something. And, this time, Grace was quiet. Yet, Isabel says that when she heard that *thump* and then that silence, something happened in her to make her afraid. And she ran to the living room and there was little Grace on the floor, all twisted up, and the reason she hadn't screamed was that she couldn't get her breath. And when she did scream, it was the worst sound, Isabel says, that she'd ever heard in all her life, and she still hears it sometimes in her dreams. Isabel will sometimes wake me up with a low, moaning, strangled sound and I have to be quick to awaken her and hold her to me and where Isabel is weeping against me seems a mortal wound.

2. Possibly based on Bertha "Chippie" Hill's 1928 recording of the song "Some Cold Rainy Day."

I think I may have written Sonny the very day that little Grace was buried. I was sitting in the living room in the dark, by myself, and I suddenly thought of Sonny. My trouble made his real.

One Saturday afternoon, when Sonny had been living with us, or, anyway, been in our house, for nearly two weeks, I found myself wandering aimlessly about the living room, drinking from a can of beer, and trying to work up the courage to search Sonny's room. He was out, he was usually out whenever I was home, and Isabel had taken the children to see their grandparents. Suddenly I was standing still in front of the living room window, watching Seventh Avenue. The idea of searching Sonny's room made me still. I scarcely dared to admit to myself what I'd be searching for. I didn't know what I'd do if I found it. Or if I didn't.

On the sidewalk across from me, near the entrance to a barbecue joint, some people were holding an old-fashioned revival meeting. The barbecue cook, wearing a dirty white apron, his conked[3] hair reddish and metallic in the pale sun, and a cigarette between his lips, stood in the doorway, watching them. Kids and older people paused in their errands and stood there, along with some older men and a couple of very tough-looking women who watched everything that happened on the avenue, as though they owned it, or were maybe owned by it. Well, they were watching this, too. The revival was being carried on by three sisters in black, and a brother. All they had were their voices and their Bibles and a tambourine. The brother was testifying and while he testified two of the sisters stood together, seeming to say, amen, and the third sister walked around with the tambourine outstretched and a couple of people dropped coins into it. Then the brother's testimony ended and the sister who had been taking up the collection dumped the coins into her palm and transferred them to the pocket of her long black robe. Then she raised both hands, striking the tambourine against the air, and then against one hand, and she started to sing. And the two other sisters and the brother joined in.

It was strange, suddenly, to watch, though I had been seeing these street meetings all my life. So, of course, had everybody else down there. Yet, they paused and watched and listened and I stood still at the window. "*Tis the old ship of Zion,*" they sang, and the sister with the tambourine kept a steady, jangling beat, "*it has rescued many a thousand!*"[4] Not a soul under the sound of their voices was hearing this song for the first time, not one of them had been rescued. Nor had they seen much in the way of rescue work being done around them. Neither did they especially believe in the holiness of the three sisters and the brother, they knew too much about them, knew where they lived, and how. The woman with the tambourine, whose voice dominated the air, whose face was bright with joy, was divided by very little from the woman who stood watching her, a cigarette between her heavy, chapped lips, her hair a cuckoo's nest, her face scarred and swollen from many beatings, and her black eyes glittering like coal. Perhaps they both knew this, which was why, when, as rarely, they addressed each other, they addressed each other as Sister. As the singing filled the air the watching, listening

---

3. Chemically straightened.
4. From the song "The Old Ship of Zion," a 19th-century Christian spiritual.

faces underwent a change, the eyes focusing on something within; the music seemed to soothe a poison out of them; and time seemed, nearly, to fall away from the sullen, belligerent, battered faces, as though they were fleeing back to their first condition, while dreaming of their last. The barbecue cook half shook his head and smiled, and dropped his cigarette and disappeared into his joint. A man fumbled in his pockets for change and stood holding it in his hand impatiently, as though he had just remembered a pressing appointment further up the avenue. He looked furious. Then I saw Sonny, standing on the edge of the crowd. He was carrying a wide, flat notebook with a green cover, and it made him look, from where I was standing, almost like a schoolboy. The coppery sun brought out the copper in his skin, he was very faintly smiling, standing very still. Then the singing stopped, the tambourine turned into a collection plate again. The furious man dropped in his coins and vanished, so did a couple of the women, and Sonny dropped some change in the plate, looking directly at the woman with a little smile. He started across the avenue, toward the house. He has a slow, loping walk, something like the way Harlem hipsters walk, only he's imposed on this his own half-beat. I had never really noticed it before.

I stayed at the window, both relieved and apprehensive. As Sonny disappeared from my sight, they began singing again. And they were still singing when his key turned in the lock.

"Hey," he said.

"Hey, yourself. You want some beer?"

"No. Well, maybe." But he came up to the window and stood beside me, looking out. "What a warm voice," he said.

They were singing *If I could only hear my mother pray again!*[5]

"Yes," I said, "and she can sure beat that tambourine."

"But what a terrible song," he said, and laughed. He dropped his notebook on the sofa and disappeared into the kitchen. "Where's Isabel and the kids?"

"I think they went to see their grandparents. You hungry?"

"No." He came back into the living room with his can of beer. "You want to come some place with me tonight?"

I sensed, I don't know how, that I couldn't possibly say no. "Sure. Where?"

He sat down on the sofa and picked up his notebook and started leafing through it. "I'm going to sit in with some fellows in a joint in the Village."

"You mean, you're going to play, tonight?"

"That's right." He took a swallow of his beer and moved back to the window. He gave me a sidelong look. "If you can stand it."

"I'll try," I said.

He smiled to himself and we both watched as the meeting across the way broke up. The three sisters and the brother, heads bowed, were singing *God be with you till we meet again.*[6] The faces around them were very quiet. Then the song ended. The small crowd dispersed. We watched the three women and the lone man walk slowly up the avenue.

5. Traditional Christian spiritual.
6. Christian spiritual by Jeremiah E. Rankin (1828–1904).

"When she was singing before," said Sonny, abruptly, "her voice reminded me for a minute of what heroin feels like sometimes—when it's in your veins. It makes you feel sort of warm and cool at the same time. And distant. And—and sure." He sipped his beer, very deliberately not looking at me. I watched his face. "It makes you feel—in control. Sometimes you've got to have that feeling."

"Do you?" I sat down slowly in the easy chair.

"Sometimes." He went to the sofa and picked up his notebook again. "Some people do."

"In order," I asked, "to play?" And my voice was very ugly, full of contempt and anger.

"Well"—he looked at me with great troubled eyes, as though, in fact, he hoped his eyes would tell me things he could never otherwise say—"they *think* so. And *if* they think so—!"

"And what do *you* think?" I asked.

He sat on the sofa and put his can of beer on the floor. "I don't know," he said, and I couldn't be sure if he were answering my question or pursuing his thoughts. His face didn't tell me. "It's not so much to *play*. It's to *stand* it, to be able to make it at all. On any level." He frowned and smiled: "In order to keep from shaking to pieces."

"But these friends of yours," I said, "they seem to shake themselves to pieces pretty goddamn fast."

"Maybe." He played with the notebook. And something told me that I should curb my tongue, that Sonny was doing his best to talk, that I should listen. "But of course you only know the ones that've gone to pieces. Some don't—or at least they haven't *yet* and that's just about all *any* of us can say." He paused. "And then there are some who just live, really, in hell, and they know it and they see what's happening and they go right on. I don't know." He sighed, dropped the notebook, folded his arms. "Some guys, you can tell from the way they play, they on something *all* the time. And you can see that, well, it makes something real for them. But of course," he picked up his beer from the floor and sipped it and put the can down again, "they *want* to, too, you've got to see that. Even some of them that say they don't—*some*, not all."

"And what about you?" I asked—I couldn't help it. "What about you? Do *you* want to?"

He stood up and walked to the window and remained silent for a long time. Then he sighed. "Me," he said. Then: "While I was downstairs before, on my way here, listening to that woman sing, it struck me all of a sudden how much suffering she must have had to go through—to sing like that. It's *repulsive* to think you have to suffer that much."

I said: "But there's no way not to suffer—is there, Sonny?"

"I believe not," he said and smiled, "but that's never stopped anyone from trying." He looked at me. "Has it?" I realized, with this mocking look, that there stood between us, forever, beyond the power of time or forgiveness, the fact that I had held silence—so long!—when he had needed human speech to help him. He turned back to the window. "No, there's no way not to suffer. But you try all kinds of ways to keep from drowning in it, to keep on top of it, and to make it seem—well, like *you*. Like you did something, all right, and now you're suffering for it. You know?" I said nothing. "Well you know," he said, impatiently, "why *do* people suffer? Maybe it's better to do something to give it a reason, *any* reason."

"But we just agreed," I said, "that there's no way not to suffer. Isn't it better, then, just to—take it?"

"But nobody just takes it," Sonny cried, "that's what I'm telling you! *Everybody* tries not to. You're just hung up on the *way* some people try—it's not *your* way!"

The hair on my face began to itch, my face felt wet. "That's not true," I said, "that's not true. I don't give a damn what other people do, I don't even care how they suffer. I just care how *you* suffer." And he looked at me. "Please believe me," I said, "I don't want to see you—die—trying not to suffer."

"I won't," he said, flatly, "die trying not to suffer. At least, not any faster than anybody else."

"But there's no need," I said, trying to laugh, "is there? in killing yourself."

I wanted to say more, but I couldn't. I wanted to talk about willpower and how life could be—well, beautiful. I wanted to say that it was all within; but was it? or, rather, wasn't that exactly the trouble? And I wanted to promise that I would never fail him again. But it would all have sounded—empty words and lies.

So I made the promise to myself and prayed that I would keep it.

"It's terrible sometimes, inside," he said, "that's what's the trouble. You walk these streets, black and funky and cold, and there's not really a living ass to talk to, and there's nothing shaking, and there's no way of getting it out—that storm inside. You can't talk it and you can't make love with it, and when you finally try to get with it and play it, you realize *nobody's* listening. So *you've* got to listen. You got to find a way to listen."

And then he walked away from the window and sat on the sofa again, as though all the wind had suddenly been knocked out of him. "Sometimes you'll do *anything* to play, even cut your mother's throat." He laughed and looked at me. "Or your brother's." Then he sobered. "Or your own." Then: "Don't worry. I'm all right now and I think I'll *be* all right. But I can't forget—where I've been. I don't mean just the physical place I've been, I mean where I've *been*. And *what* I've been."

"What have you been, Sonny?" I asked.

He smiled—but sat sideways on the sofa, his elbow resting on the back, his fingers playing with his mouth and chin, not looking at me. "I've been something I didn't recognize, didn't know I could be. Didn't know anybody could be." He stopped, looking inward, looking helplessly young, looking old. "I'm not talking about it now because I feel *guilty* or anything like that— maybe it would be better if I did, I don't know. Anyway, I can't really talk about it. Not to you, not to anybody," and now he turned and faced me. "Sometimes, you know, and it was actually when I was most *out* of the world, I felt that I was in it, that I was *with* it, really, and I could play or I didn't really have to *play*, it just came out of me, it was there. And I don't know how I played, thinking about it now, but I know I did awful things, those times, sometimes, to people. Or it wasn't that I *did* anything to them—it was that they weren't real." He picked up the beer can; it was empty; he rolled it between his palms: "And other times—well, I needed a fix, I needed to find a place to lean, I needed to clear a space to *listen*—and I couldn't find it, and

I—went crazy, I did terrible things to *me*, I was terrible *for* me." He began pressing the beer can between his hands, I watched the metal begin to give. It glittered, as he played with it, like a knife, and I was afraid he would cut himself, but I said nothing. "Oh well. I can never tell you. I was all by myself at the bottom of something, stinking and sweating and crying and shaking, and I smelled it, you know? *my* stink, and I thought I'd die if I couldn't get away from it and yet, all the same, I knew that everything I was doing was just locking me in with it. And I didn't know," he paused, still flattening the beer can, "I didn't know, I still *don't* know, something kept telling me that maybe it was good to smell your own stink, but I didn't think that *that* was what I'd been trying to do—and—who can stand it?" and he abruptly dropped the ruined beer can, looking at me with a small, still smile, and then rose, walking to the window as though it were the lodestone rock.[7] I watched his face, he watched the avenue. "I couldn't tell you when Mama died—but the reason I wanted to leave Harlem so bad was to get away from drugs. And then, when I ran away, that's what I was running from—really. When I came back, nothing had changed, I hadn't changed, I was just—older." And he stopped, drumming with his fingers on the windowpane. The sun had vanished, soon darkness would fall. I watched his face. "It can come again," he said, almost as though speaking to himself. Then he turned to me. "It can come again," he repeated. "I just want you to know that."

"All right," I said, at last. "So it can come again. All right."

He smiled, but the smile was sorrowful. "I had to try to tell you," he said.

"Yes," I said. "I understand that."

"You're my brother," he said, looking straight at me, and not smiling at all.

"Yes," I repeated, "yes. I understand that."

He turned back to the window, looking out. "All that hatred down there," he said, "all that hatred and misery and love. It's a wonder it doesn't blow the avenue apart."

We went to the only nightclub on a short, dark street, downtown. We squeezed through the narrow, chattering, jam-packed bar to the entrance of the big room, where the bandstand was. And we stood there for a moment, for the lights were very dim in this room and we couldn't see. Then, "Hello, boy," said a voice and an enormous black man, much older than Sonny or myself, erupted out of all that atmospheric lighting and put an arm around Sonny's shoulder. "I been sitting right here," he said, "waiting for you."

He had a big voice, too, and heads in the darkness turned toward us.

Sonny grinned and pulled a little away, and said, "Creole, this is my brother. I told you about him."

Creole shook my hand. "I'm glad to meet you, son," he said, and it was clear that he was glad to meet me *there*, for Sonny's sake. And he smiled, "You got a real musician in *your* family," and he took his arm from Sonny's shoulder and slapped him, lightly, affectionately, with the back of his hand.

"Well. Now I've heard it all," said a voice behind us. This was another musician, and a friend of Sonny's, a coal-black, cheerful-looking man, built close to the ground. He immediately began confiding to me, at the top of his

7. Naturally magnetized rock.

lungs, the most terrible things about Sonny, his teeth gleaming like a light-house and his laugh coming up out of him like the beginning of an earth-quake. And it turned out that everyone at the bar knew Sonny, or almost everyone; some were musicians, working there, or nearby, or not working, some were simply hangers-on, and some were there to hear Sonny play. I was introduced to all of them and they were all very polite to me. Yet, it was clear that, for them, I was only Sonny's brother. Here, I was in Sonny's world. Or, rather: his kingdom. Here, it was not even a question that his veins bore royal blood.

They were going to play soon and Creole installed me, by myself, at a table in a dark corner. Then I watched them, Creole, and the little black man, and Sonny, and the others, while they horsed around, standing just below the bandstand. The light from the bandstand spilled just a little short of them and, watching them laughing and gesturing and moving about, I had the feeling that they, nevertheless, were being most careful not to step into that circle of light too suddenly: that if they moved into the light too suddenly, without thinking, they would perish in flame. Then, while I watched, one of them, the small, black man, moved into the light and crossed the bandstand and started fooling around with his drums. Then—being funny and being, also, extremely ceremonious—Creole took Sonny by the arm and led him to the piano. A woman's voice called Sonny's name and a few hands started clapping. And Sonny, also being funny and being ceremonious, and so touched, I think, that he could have cried, but neither hiding it nor showing it, riding it like a man, grinned, and put both hands to his heart and bowed from the waist.

Creole then went to the bass fiddle and a lean, very bright-skinned brown man jumped up on the bandstand and picked up his horn. So there they were, and the atmosphere on the bandstand and in the room began to change and tighten. Someone stepped up to the microphone and announced them. Then there were all kinds of murmurs. Some people at the bar shushed others. The waitress ran around, frantically getting in the last orders, guys and chicks got closer to each other, and the lights on the bandstand, on the quartet, turned to a kind of indigo. Then they all looked different there. Creole looked about him for the last time, as though he were making certain that all his chickens were in the coop, and then he—jumped and struck the fiddle. And there they were.

All I know about music is that not many people ever really hear it. And even then, on the rare occasions when something opens within, and the music enters, what we mainly hear, or hear corroborated, are personal, pri-vate, vanishing evocations. But the man who creates the music is hearing something else, is dealing with the roar rising from the void and imposing order on it as it hits the air. What is evoked in him, then, is of another order, more terrible because it has no words, and triumphant, too, for that same reason. And his triumph, when he triumphs, is ours. I just watched Sonny's face. His face was troubled, he was working hard, but he wasn't with it. And I had the feeling that, in a way, everyone on the bandstand was waiting for him, both waiting for him and pushing him along. But as I began to watch Creole, I realized that it was Creole who held them all back. He had them on a short rein. Up there, keeping the beat with his whole body, wailing on the fiddle, with his eyes half closed, he was listening to everything, but he was listening to Sonny. He was having a dialogue with Sonny. He wanted Sonny to leave the shoreline and strike out for the deep water. He was Sonny's witness that deep water and drowning were not the same thing— he had been there, and he knew. And he wanted Sonny to know. He was waiting for Sonny to do the things on the keys which would let Creole know that Sonny was in the water.

And, while Creole listened, Sonny moved, deep within, exactly like someone in torment. I had never before thought of how awful the relationship must be between the musician and his instrument. He has to fill it, this instrument, with the breath of life, his own. He has to make it do what he wants it to do. And a piano is just a piano. It's made out of so much wood and wires and little hammers and big ones, and ivory. While there's only so much you can do with it, the only way to find this out is to try; to try and make it do everything.

And Sonny hadn't been near a piano for over a year. And he wasn't on much better terms with his life, not the life that stretched before him now. He and the piano stammered, started one way, got scared, stopped; started another way, panicked, marked time, started again; then seemed to have found a direction, panicked again, got stuck. And the face I saw on Sonny I'd never seen before. Everything had been burned out of it, and, at the same time, things usually hidden were being burned in, by the fire and fury of the battle which was occurring in him up there.

Yet, watching Creole's face as they neared the end of the first set, I had the feeling that something had happened, something I hadn't heard. Then they finished, there was scattered applause, and then, without an instant's warning, Creole started into something else, it was almost sardonic, it was *Am I Blue.*[8] And, as though he commanded, Sonny began to play. Something began to happen. And Creole let out the reins. The dry, low, black man said something awful on the drums, Creole answered, and the drums talked back. Then the horn insisted, sweet and high, slightly detached perhaps, and Creole listened, commenting now and then, dry, and driving, beautiful and calm and old. Then they all came together again, and Sonny was part of the family again. I could tell this from his face. He seemed to have found, right there beneath his fingers, a damn brand-new piano. It seemed that he couldn't get over it. Then, for awhile, just being happy with Sonny, they seemed to be agreeing with him that brand-new pianos certainly were a gas.

Then Creole stepped forward to remind them that what they were playing was the blues. He hit something in all of them, he hit something in me, myself, and the music tightened and deepened, apprehension began to beat the air. Creole began to tell us what the blues were all about. They were not about anything very new. He and his boys up there were keeping it new, at the risk of ruin, destruction, madness, and death, in order to find new ways to make us listen. For, while the tale of how we suffer, and how we are delighted, and how we may triumph is never new, it always must be heard. There isn't any other tale to tell, it's the only light we've got in all this darkness.

And this tale, according to that face, that body, those strong hands on those strings, has another aspect in every country, and a new depth in

8. Jazz standard by Harry Akst and Grant Clarke (1929).

every generation. Listen, Creole seemed to be saying, listen. Now these are Sonny's blues. He made the little black man on the drums know it, and the bright, brown man on the horn. Creole wasn't trying any longer to get Sonny in the water. He was wishing him Godspeed. Then he stepped back, very slowly, filling the air with the immense suggestion that Sonny speak for himself.

Then they all gathered around Sonny and Sonny played. Every now and again one of them seemed to say, amen. Sonny's fingers filled the air with life, his life. But that life contained so many others. And Sonny went all the way back, he really began with the spare, flat statement of the opening phrase of the song. Then he began to make it his. It was very beautiful because it wasn't hurried and it was no longer a lament. I seemed to hear with what burning he had made it his, with what burning we had yet to make it ours, how we could cease lamenting. Freedom lurked around us and I understood, at last, that he could help us to be free if we would listen, that he would never be free until we did. Yet, there was no battle in his face now. I heard what he had gone through, and would continue to go through until he came to rest in earth. He had made it his: that long line, of which we knew only Mama and Daddy. And he was giving it back, as everything must be given back, so that, passing through death, it can live forever. I saw my mother's face again, and felt, for the first time, how the stones of the road she had walked on must have bruised her feet. I saw the moonlit road where my father's brother died. And it brought something else back to me, and carried me past it, I saw my little girl again and felt Isabel's tears again, and I felt my own tears begin to rise. And I was yet aware that this was only a moment, that the world waited outside, as hungry as a tiger, and that trouble stretched above us, longer than the sky.

Then it was over. Creole and Sonny let out their breath, both soaking wet, and grinning. There was a lot of applause and some of it was real. In the dark, the girl came by and I asked her to take drinks to the bandstand. There was a long pause, while they talked up there in the indigo light and after awhile I saw the girl put a Scotch and milk on top of the piano for Sonny. He didn't seem to notice it, but just before they started playing again, he sipped from it and looked toward me, and nodded. Then he put it back on top of the piano. For me, then, as they began to play again, it glowed and shook above my brother's head like the very cup of trembling.[9]

1957

---

9. See Isaiah 51.22: "Thus saith thy lord the LORD, and thy God that pleadeth the cause of his people, Behold, I have taken out of thine hand the cup of trembling, even the dregs of the cup of my fury; thou shalt no more drink it again."

FLANNERY O'CONNOR
1925–1964

F lannery O'Connor, one of the twentieth century's finest short-story writers, was born in Savannah, Georgia; lived with her mother in Milledgeville, Georgia, for much of her life; and died before her fortieth birthday—a victim of lupus, which had also killed her father. Her life and fiction thus tracked a southern orbit, and she was considered an important figure among the southern writers who have grown popular since the 1930s, including novelist William Faulkner, the poet and novelist Robert Penn Warren, and novelists Katherine Ann Porter, Carson McCullers, Harper Lee, and Caroline Gordon (O'Connor's longtime mentor), to name a few. But O'Connor was also one of the early graduates of the Iowa Writers Workshop, completing her M.F.A. degree there in 1947. What she learned at the Workshop about the craft and discipline of story writing informed her practice for the rest of her life. One textbook she encountered there—Cleanth Brooks and Robert Penn Warren's *Understanding Fiction* (1943)—became, as she said, her "Bible," and, indeed, teachers have often turned to O'Connor's work to illustrate key elements of the short story. Her story "A Good Man Is Hard to Find" (1955) was ultimately included as a model in the 1959 edition of *Understanding Fiction*.

To call a textbook scripture speaks, in O'Connor's case, to the weight of a third influence that shapes her work, alongside southern culture and the literary formalism she learned at Iowa: Roman Catholicism. She sought, as she said, to write "Christian realism," where the ugly, the stubborn, and the sinful take center stage in dramas of violence and redemption, played out on a small scale to universal consequences. Her stories are often dark comedies; O'Connor's understanding of divine mercy included a generous irony that she turned on villains and heroes alike. She turned that irony on herself, too. As a result of her lupus, O'Connor had to use crutches from 1955 onward; she remarked, apropos of a trip to the healing waters at Lourdes, France, "I had the best-looking crutches in Europe." She refused to indulge either in pity or in self-pity in the face of what she saw as pervasive human imperfection in a fallen world.

O'Connor published two novels, *Wise Blood* (1952) and *The Violent Bear It Away* (1960). They are weighty with religious symbolism, dense with cultural observation, and ingeniously contrived in the black-humored manner of Nathanael West, her American predecessor in this mode. But her most memorable characters and plots can be found in the stories, which are extremely funny, sometimes unbearably so. O'Connor often leaves readers wondering just what they are laughing at. Upon consideration, the jokes appear dreadful, as with Manley Pointer's treatment of Joy Hopewell's artificial leg in "Good Country People" or Mr. Shiftlet's of his bride in "The Life You Save May Be Your Own." A typical Flannery O'Connor story consists at its most vital level of people talking, clucking their clichés about life, death, and the universe. These clichés are captured with beautiful accuracy by an artist who had spent her life listening to them, lovingly and maliciously keeping track until she could put them to use. Early in her life she hoped to be a cartoonist, and there is cartoonlike mastery in her vivid renderings of character through speech and gesture. O'Connor's art lies partly in making it impossible for us merely to scorn the banalities of expression and behavior by which these people get through their lives. Critics have called her a maker of grotesques, a label that like other ones— regionalist, southern lady, or Roman Catholic writer—might have annoyed her if it didn't obviously amuse her, too. She once remarked tartly that "anything that comes out of the South is going to be called grotesque by the Northern reader, unless it is grotesque, in which case it is going to be called realistic."

Although O'Connor's stories are filled with religious allusions and parodies, they do not preach. One of her best is titled "Revelation," but O'Connor seldom concludes any story with a simple, unambiguous sense of what has been revealed. "A Good Man Is Hard to Find," reprinted here, has famously flummoxed readers in this regard ever since its publication. The stories included in this selection are from her collection *A Good Man Is Hard to Find* (1955).

Good Country People

Besides the neutral expression that she wore when she was alone, Mrs. Freeman had two others, forward and reverse, that she used for all her human dealings. Her forward expression was steady and driving like the advance of a heavy truck. Her eyes never swerved to left or right but turned as the story turned as if they followed a yellow line down the center of it. She seldom used the other expression because it was not often necessary for her to retract a statement, but when she did, her face came to a complete stop, there was an almost imperceptible movement of her black eyes, during which they seemed to be receding, and then the observer would see that Mrs. Freeman, though she might stand there as real as several grain sacks thrown on top of each other, was no longer there in spirit. As for getting anything across to her when this was the case, Mrs. Hopewell had given it up. She might talk her head off. Mrs. Freeman could never be brought to admit herself wrong on any point. She would stand there and if she could be brought to say anything, it was something like, "Well, I wouldn't of said it was and I wouldn't of said it wasn't," or letting her gaze range over the top kitchen shelf where there was an assortment of dusty bottles, she might remark, "I see you ain't ate many of them figs you put up last summer."

They carried on their important business in the kitchen at breakfast. Every morning Mrs. Hopewell got up at seven o'clock and lit her gas heater and Joy's. Joy was her daughter, a large blonde girl who had an artificial leg. Mrs. Hopewell thought of her as a child though she was thirty-two years old and highly educated. Joy would get up while her mother was eating and lumber into the bathroom and slam the door, and before long, Mrs. Freeman would arrive at the back door. Joy would hear her mother call, "Come on in," and then they would talk for a while in low voices that were indistinguishable in the bathroom. By the time Joy came in, they had usually finished the weather report and were on one or the other of Mrs. Freeman's daughters, Glynese or Carramae. Joy called them Glycerin and Caramel. Glynese, a redhead, was eighteen and had many admirers; Carramae, a blonde, was only fifteen but already married and pregnant. She could not keep anything on her stomach. Every morning Mrs. Freeman told Mrs. Hopewell how many times she had vomited since the last report.

Mrs. Hopewell liked to tell people that Glynese and Carramae were two of the finest girls she knew and that Mrs. Freeman was a *lady* and that she was never ashamed to take her anywhere or introduce her to anybody they might meet. Then she would tell how she had happened to hire the Freemans in the first place and how they were a godsend to her and how she had had them four years. The reason for her keeping them so long was that they were not trash. They were good country people. She had telephoned the man whose name they had given as a reference and he had told her that Mr. Free-man was a good farmer but that his wife was the nosiest woman ever to walk the earth. "She's got to be into everything," the man said. "If she don't get there before the dust settles, you can bet she's dead, that's all. She'll want to know all your business. I can stand him real good," he had said, "but me nor my wife neither could have stood that woman one more minute on this place." That had put Mrs. Hopewell off for a few days.

She had hired them in the end because there were no other applicants but she had made up her mind beforehand exactly how she would handle the woman. Since she was the type who had to be into everything, then, Mrs. Hopewell had decided, she would not only let her be into everything, she would *see to it* that she was into everything—she would give her the responsibility of everything, she would put her in charge. Mrs. Hopewell had no bad qualities of her own but she was able to use other people's in such a constructive way that she never felt the lack. She had hired the Freemans and she had kept them four years.

Nothing is perfect. This was one of Mrs. Hopewell's favorite sayings. Another was: that is life! And still another, the most important, was: well, other people have their opinions too. She would make these statements, usually at the table, in a tone of gentle insistence as if no one held them but her, and the large hulking Joy, whose constant outrage had obliterated every expression from her face, would stare just a little to the side of her, her eyes icy blue, with the look of someone who has achieved blindness by an act of will and means to keep it.

When Mrs. Hopewell said to Mrs. Freeman that life was like that, Mrs. Freeman would say, "I always said so myself." Nothing had been arrived at by anyone that had not first been arrived at by her. She was quicker than Mr. Freeman. When Mrs. Hopewell said to her after they had been on the place a while, "You know, you're the wheel behind the wheel," and winked, Mrs. Freeman had said, "I know it. I've always been quick. It's some that are quicker than others."

"Everybody is different," Mrs. Hopewell said.

"Yes, most people is," Mrs. Freeman said.

"It takes all kinds to make the world."

"I always said it did myself."

The girl was used to this kind of dialogue for breakfast and more of it for dinner; sometimes they had it for supper too. When they had no guest they ate in the kitchen because that was easier. Mrs. Freeman always managed to arrive at some point during the meal and to watch them finish it. She would stand in the doorway if it were summer but in the winter she would stand with one elbow on top of the refrigerator and look down on them, or she would stand by the gas heater, lifting the back of her skirt slightly. Occasionally she would stand against the wall and roll her head from side to side. At no time was she in any hurry to leave. All this was very trying on Mrs. Hopewell but she was a woman of great patience. She realized that nothing is perfect and that in the Freemans she had good country people and that if, in this day and age, you get good country people, you had better hang onto them.

She had had plenty of experience with trash. Before the Freemans she had averaged one tenant family a year. The wives of these farmers were not the kind you would want to be around you for very long. Mrs. Hopewell, who had divorced her husband long ago, needed someone to walk over the fields with her; and when Joy had to be impressed for these services, her remarks were usually so ugly and her face so glum that Mrs. Hopewell would say, "If you can't come pleasantly, I don't want you at all," to which the girl, standing square and rigid-shouldered with her neck thrust slightly forward, would reply, "If you want me, here I am—LIKE I AM."

Mrs. Hopewell excused this attitude because of the leg (which had been shot off in a hunting accident when Joy was ten). It was hard for Mrs. Hopewell to realize that her child was thirty-two now and that for more than twenty years she had had only one leg. She thought of her still as a child because it tore her heart to think instead of the poor stout girl in her thirties who had never danced a step or had any *normal* good times. Her name was really Joy but as soon as she was twenty-one and away from home, she had had it legally changed. Mrs. Hopewell was certain that she had thought and thought until she had hit upon the ugliest name in any language. Then she had gone and had the beautiful name, Joy, changed without telling her mother until after she had done it. Her legal name was Hulga.

When Mrs. Hopewell thought the name, Hulga, she thought of the broad blank hull of a battleship. She would not use it. She continued to call her Joy to which the girl responded but in a purely mechanical way.

Hulga had learned to tolerate Mrs. Freeman who saved her from taking walks with her mother. Even Glynese and Carramae were useful when they occupied attention that might otherwise have been directed at her. At first she had thought she could not stand Mrs. Freeman for she had found that it was not possible to be rude to her. Mrs. Freeman would take on strange resentments and for days together she would be sullen but the source of her displeasure was always obscure; a direct attack, a positive leer, blatant ugliness to her face—these never touched her. And without warning one day, she began calling her Hulga.

She did not call her that in front of Mrs. Hopewell who would have been incensed but when she and the girl happened to be out of the house together, she would say something and add the name Hulga to the end of it, and the big spectacled Joy-Hulga would scowl and redden as if her privacy had been intruded upon. She considered the name her personal affair. She had arrived at it first purely on the basis of its ugly sound and then the full genius of its fitness had struck her. She had a vision of the name working like the ugly sweating Vulcan who stayed in the furnace and to whom, presumably, the goddess had to come when called.[1] She saw it as the name of her highest creative act. One of her major triumphs was that her mother had not been able to turn her dust into Joy, but the greater one was that she had been able to turn it herself into Hulga. However, Mrs. Freeman's relish for using the name only irritated her. It was as if Mrs. Freeman's beady steel-pointed eyes had penetrated far enough behind her face to reach some secret fact. Something about her seemed to fascinate Mrs. Freeman and then one day Hulga

---

1. Vulcan was the Greek god of fire, whom Venus, goddess of love, "presumably" obeyed as her consort.

realized that it was the artificial leg. Mrs. Freeman had a special fondness for the details of secret infections, hidden deformities, assaults upon children. Of diseases, she preferred the lingering or incurable. Hulga had heard Mrs. Hopewell give her the details of the hunting accident, how the leg had been literally blasted off, how she had never lost consciousness. Mrs. Freeman could listen to it any time as if it had happened an hour ago.

When Hulga stumped into the kitchen in the morning (she could walk without making the awful noise but she made it—Mrs. Hopewell was certain—because it was ugly-sounding), she glanced at them and did not speak. Mrs. Hopewell would be in her red kimono with her hair tied around her head in rags. She would be sitting at the table, finishing her breakfast and Mrs. Freeman would be hanging by her elbow outward from the refrigerator, looking down at the table. Hulga always put her eggs on the stove to boil and then stood over them with her arms folded, and Mrs. Hopewell would look at her—a kind of indirect gaze divided between her and Mrs. Freeman—and would think that if she would only keep herself up a little, she wouldn't be so bad looking. There was nothing wrong with her face that a pleasant expression wouldn't help. Mrs. Hopewell said that people who looked on the bright side of things would be beautiful even if they were not.

Whenever she looked at Joy this way, she could not help but feel that it would have been better if the child had not taken the Ph.D. It had certainly not brought her out any and now that she had it, there was no more excuse for her to go to school again. Mrs. Hopewell thought it was nice for girls to go to school to have a good time but Joy had "gone through." Anyhow, she would not have been strong enough to go again. The doctors had told Mrs. Hopewell that with the best of care, Joy might see forty-five. She had a weak heart. Joy had made it plain that if it had not been for this condition, she would be far from these red hills and good country people. She would be in a university lecturing to people who knew what she was talking about. And Mrs. Hopewell could very well picture her there, looking like a scarecrow and lecturing to more of the same. Here she went about all day in a six-year-old skirt and a yellow sweat shirt with a faded cowboy on a horse embossed on it. She thought this was funny; Mrs. Hopewell thought it was idiotic and showed simply that she was still a child. She was brilliant but she didn't have a grain of sense. It seemed to Mrs. Hopewell that every year she grew less like other people and more like herself—bloated, rude, and squint-eyed. And she said such strange things! To her own mother she had said—without warning, without excuse, standing up in the middle of a meal with her face purple and her mouth half full—"Woman! do you ever look inside? Do you ever look inside and see what you are *not*? God!" she had cried sinking down again and staring at her plate, "Malebranche[2] was right: we are not our own light. We are not our own light!" Mrs. Hopewell had no idea to this day what brought that on. She had only made the remark, hoping Joy would take it in, that a smile never hurt anyone.

The girl had taken the Ph.D. in philosophy and this left Mrs. Hopewell at a complete loss. You could say, "My daughter is a nurse," or "My daughter is a school teacher," or even, "My daughter is a chemical engineer." You could

---

2. Nicolas Malebranche (1638–1715), French philosopher.

not say, "My daughter is a philosopher." That was something that had ended with the Greeks and Romans. All day Joy sat on her neck in a deep chair, reading. Sometimes she went for walks but she didn't like dogs or cats or birds or flowers or nature or nice young men. She looked at nice young men as if she could smell their stupidity.

One day Mrs. Hopewell had picked up one of the books the girl had just put down and opening it at random, she read, "Science, on the other hand, has to assert its soberness and seriousness afresh and declare that it is concerned solely with what-is. Nothing—how can it be for science anything but a horror and a phantasm? If science is right, then one thing stands firm: science wishes to know nothing of nothing. Such is after all the strictly scientific approach to Nothing. We know it by wishing to know nothing of Nothing." These words had been underlined with a blue pencil and they worked on Mrs. Hopewell like some evil incantation in gibberish. She shut the book quickly and went out of the room as if she were having a chill.

This morning when the girl came in, Mrs. Freeman was on Carramae. "She thrown up four times after supper," she said, "and was up twict in the night after three o'clock. Yesterday she didn't do nothing but ramble in the bureau drawer. All she did. Stand up there and see what she could run up on."

"She's got to eat," Mrs. Hopewell muttered, sipping her coffee, while she watched Joy's back at the stove. She was wondering what the child had said to the Bible salesman. She could not imagine what kind of a conversation she could possibly have had with him.

He was a tall gaunt hatless youth who had called yesterday to sell them a Bible. He had appeared at the door, carrying a large black suitcase that weighted him so heavily on one side that he had to brace himself against the door facing. He seemed on the point of collapse but he said in a cheerful voice, "Good morning, Mrs. Cedars!" and set the suitcase down on the mat. He was not a bad-looking young man though he had on a bright blue suit and yellow socks that were not pulled up far enough. He had prominent face bones and a streak of sticky-looking brown hair falling across his forehead.

"I'm Mrs. Hopewell," she said.

"Oh!" he said, pretending to look puzzled but with his eyes sparkling, "I saw it said 'The Cedars' on the mailbox so I thought you was Mrs. Cedars!" and he burst out in a pleasant laugh. He picked up the satchel and under cover of a pant, he fell forward into her hall. It was rather as if the suitcase had moved first, jerking him after it. "Mrs. Hopewell!" he said and grabbed her hand. "I hope you are well!" and he laughed again and then all at once his face sobered completely. He paused and gave her a straight earnest look and said, "Lady, I've come to speak of serious things."

"Well, come in," she muttered, none too pleased because her dinner was almost ready. He came into the parlor and sat down on the edge of a straight chair and put the suitcase between his feet and glanced around the room as if he were sizing her up by it. Her silver gleamed on the two sideboards; she decided he had never been in a room as elegant as this.

"Mrs. Hopewell," he began, using her name in a way that sounded almost intimate, "I know you believe in Chrustian service."

"Well yes," she murmured.

"I know," he said and paused, looking very wise with his head cocked on one side, "that you're a good woman. Friends have told me."

Mrs. Hopewell never liked to be taken for a fool. "What are you selling?" she asked.

"Bibles," the young man said and his eye raced around the room before he added, "I see you have no family Bible in your parlor, I see that is the one lack you got!"

Mrs. Hopewell could not say, "My daughter is an atheist and won't let me keep the Bible in the parlor." She said, stiffening slightly, "I keep my Bible by my bedside." This was not the truth. It was in the attic somewhere.

"Lady," he said, "the word of God ought to be in the parlor."

"Well, I think that's a matter of taste," she began. "I think . . ."

"Lady," he said, "for a Christian, the word of God ought to be in every room in the house besides in his heart. I know you're a Christian because I can see it in every line of your face."

She stood up and said, "Well, young man, I don't want to buy a Bible and I smell my dinner burning."

He didn't get up. He began to twist his hands and looking down at them, he said softly, "Well lady, I'll tell you the truth—not many people want to buy one nowadays and besides, I know I'm real simple. I don't know how to say a thing but to say it. I'm just a country boy." He glanced up into her unfriendly face. "People like you don't like to fool with country people like me!"

"Why!" she cried, "good country people are the salt of the earth! Besides, we all have different ways of doing, it takes all kinds to make the world go 'round. That's life!"

"You said a mouthful," he said.

"Why, I think there aren't enough good country people in the world!" she said, stirred. "I think that's what's wrong with it!"

His face had brightened. "I didn't inraduce myself," he said. "I'm Manley Pointer from out in the country around Willohobie, not even from a place, just from near a place."

"You wait a minute," she said. "I have to see about my dinner." She went out to the kitchen and found Joy standing near the door where she had been listening.

"Get rid of the salt of the earth," she said, "and let's eat."

Mrs. Hopewell gave her a pained look and turned the heat down under the vegetables. "I can't be rude to anybody," she murmured and went back into the parlor.

He had opened the suitcase and was sitting with a Bible on each knee.

"You might as well put those up," she told him. "I don't want one."

"I appreciate your honesty," he said. "You don't see any more real honest people unless you go way out in the country."

"I know," she said, "real genuine folks!" Through the crack in the door she heard a groan.

"I guess a lot of boys come telling you they're working their way through college," he said, "but I'm not going to tell you that. Somehow," he said, "I don't want to go to college. I want to devote my life to Christian service. See," he said, lowering his voice, "I got this heart condition. I may not live long. When you know it's something wrong with you and you may not live long, well then, lady . . ." He paused, with his mouth open, and stared at her.

He and Joy had the same condition! She knew that her eyes were filling with tears but she collected herself quickly and murmured, "Won't you stay for dinner? We'd love to have you!" and was sorry the instant she heard herself say it.

"Yes mam," he said in an abashed voice, "I would sher love to do that!"

Joy had given him one look on being introduced to him and then throughout the meal had not glanced at him again. He had addressed several remarks to her, which she had pretended not to hear. Mrs. Hopewell could not understand deliberate rudeness, although she lived with it, and she felt she had always to overflow with hospitality to make up for Joy's lack of courtesy. She urged him to talk about himself and he did. He said he was the seventh child of twelve and that his father had been crushed under a tree when he himself was eight years old. He had been crushed very badly, in fact, almost cut in two and was practically not recognizable. His mother had got along the best she could by hard working and she had always seen that her children went to Sunday School and that they read the Bible every evening. He was now nineteen years old and he had been selling Bibles for four months. In that time he had sold seventy-seven Bibles and had the promise of two more sales. He wanted to become a missionary because he thought that was the way you could do most for people. "He who losest his life shall find it," he said simply and he was so sincere, so genuine and earnest that Mrs. Hopewell would not for the world have smiled. He prevented his peas from sliding onto the table by blocking them with a piece of bread which he later cleaned his plate with. She could see Joy observing sidewise how he handled his knife and fork and she saw too that every few minutes, the boy would dart a keen appraising glance at the girl as if he were trying to attract her attention.

After dinner Joy cleared the dishes off the table and disappeared and Mrs. Hopewell was left to talk with him. He told her again about his childhood and his father's accident and about various things that had happened to him. Every five minutes or so she would stifle a yawn. He sat for two hours until finally she told him she must go because she had an appointment in town. He packed his Bibles and thanked her and prepared to leave, but in the doorway he stopped and wrung her hand and said that not on any of his trips had he met a lady as nice as her and he asked if he could come again. She had said she would always be happy to see him.

Joy had been standing in the road, apparently looking at something in the distance, when he came down the steps toward her, bent to the side with his heavy valise. He stopped where she was standing and confronted her directly. Mrs. Hopewell could not hear what he said but she trembled to think what Joy would say to him. She could see that after a minute Joy said something and that then the boy began to speak again, making an excited gesture with his free hand. After a minute Joy said something else at which the boy began to speak once more. Then to her amazement, Mrs. Hopewell saw the two of them walk off together, toward the gate. Joy had walked all the way to the gate with him and Mrs. Hopewell could not imagine what they had said to each other, and she had not yet dared to ask.

Mrs. Freeman was insisting upon her attention. She had moved from the refrigerator to the heater so that Mrs. Hopewell had to turn and face her in order to seem to be listening. "Glynese gone out with Harvey Hill again last night," she said. "She had this sty."

"Hill," Mrs. Hopewell said absently, "is that the one who works in the garage?"

"Nome, he's the one that goes to chiropracter school," Mrs. Freeman said. "She had this sty. Been had it two days. So she says when he brought her in the other night he says, 'Lemme get rid of that sty for you,' and she says, 'How?' and he says, 'You just lay yourself down acrost the seat of that car and I'll show you.' So she done it and he popped her neck. Kept on a-popping it several times until she made him quit. This morning," Mrs. Freeman said, "she ain't got no sty. She ain't got no traces of a sty."

"I never heard of that before," Mrs. Hopewell said.

"He ast her to marry him before the Ordinary,"[3] Mrs. Freeman went on, "and she told him she wasn't going to be married in no *office*."

"Well, Glynese is a fine girl," Mrs. Hopewell said. "Glynese and Carramae are both fine girls."

"Carramae said when her and Lyman was married Lyman said it sure felt sacred to him. She said he said he wouldn't take five hundred dollars for being married by a preacher."

"How much would he take?" the girl asked from the stove.

"He said he wouldn't take five hundred dollars," Mrs. Freeman repeated.

"Well we all have work to do," Mrs. Hopewell said.

"Lyman said it just felt more sacred to him," Mrs. Freeman said. "The doctor wants Carramae to eat prunes. Says instead of medicine. Says them cramps is coming from pressure. You know where I think it is?"

"She'll be better in a few weeks," Mrs. Hopewell said.

"In the tube," Mrs. Freeman said. "Else she wouldn't be as sick as she is."

Hulga had cracked her two eggs into a saucer and was bringing them to the table along with a cup of coffee that she had filled too full. She sat down carefully and began to eat, meaning to keep Mrs. Freeman there by questions if for any reason she showed an inclination to leave. She could perceive her mother's eye on her. The first round-about question would be about the Bible salesman and she did not wish to bring it on. "How did he pop her neck?" she asked.

Mrs. Freeman went into a description of how he had popped her neck. She said he owned a '55 Mercury but that Glynese said she would rather marry a man with only a '36 Plymouth who would be married by a preacher. The girl asked what if he had a '32 Plymouth and Mrs. Freeman said what Glynese had said was a '36 Plymouth.

Mrs. Hopewell said there were not many girls with Glynese's common sense. She said what she admired in those girls was their common sense. She said that reminded her that they had had a nice visitor yesterday, a young man selling Bibles. "Lord," she said, "he bored me to death but he was so sincere and genuine I couldn't be rude to him. He was just good country people, you know," she said, "—just the salt of the earth."

"I seen him walk up," Mrs. Freeman said, "and then later—I seen him walk off," and Hulga could feel the slight shift in her voice, the slight insinuation, that he had not walked off alone, had he? Her face remained expressionless but the color rose into her neck and she seemed to swallow it down with the next spoonful of egg. Mrs. Freeman was looking at her as if they had a secret together.

---

3. Justice of the peace who performs the marriage ceremony in chambers rather than in public.

"Well, it takes all kinds of people to make the world go 'round," Mrs. Hopewell said. "It's very good we aren't all alike."

"Some people are more alike than others," Mrs. Freeman said.

Hulga got up and stumped, with about twice the noise that was necessary, into her room and locked the door. She was to meet the Bible salesman at ten o'clock at the gate. She had thought about it half the night. She had started thinking of it as a great joke and then she had begun to see profound implications in it. She had lain in bed imagining dialogues for them that were insane on the surface but that reached below to depths that no Bible salesman would be aware of. Their conversation yesterday had been of this kind.

He had stopped in front of her and had simply stood there. His face was bony and sweaty and bright, with a little pointed nose in the center of it, and his look was different from what it had been at the dinner table. He was gazing at her with open curiosity, with fascination, like a child watching a new fantastic animal at the zoo, and he was breathing as if he had run a great distance to reach her. His gaze seemed somehow familiar but she could not think where she had been regarded with it before. For almost a minute he didn't say anything. Then on what seemed an insuck of breath, he whispered, "You ever ate a chicken that was two days old?"

The girl looked at him stonily. He might have just put this question up for consideration at the meeting of a philosophical association. "Yes," she presently replied as if she had considered it from all angles.

"It must have been mighty small!" he said triumphantly and shook all over with little nervous giggles, getting very red in the face, and subsiding finally into his gaze of complete admiration, while the girl's expression remained exactly the same.

"How old are you?" he asked softly.

She waited some time before she answered. Then in a flat voice she said, "Seventeen."

His smiles came in succession like waves breaking on the surface of a little lake. "I see you got a wooden leg," he said. "I think you're brave. I think you're real sweet."

The girl stood blank and solid and silent.

"Walk to the gate with me," he said. "You're a brave sweet little thing and I liked you the minute I seen you walk in the door."

Hulga began to move forward.

"What's your name?" he asked, smiling down on the top of her head.

"Hulga," she said.

"Hulga," he murmured, "Hulga. Hulga. I never heard of anybody name Hulga before. You're shy, aren't you, Hulga?" he asked.

She nodded, watching his large red hand on the handle of the giant valise.

"I like girls that wear glasses," he said. "I think a lot. I'm not like these people that a serious thought don't ever enter their heads. It's because I may die."

"I may die too," she said suddenly and looked up at him. His eyes were very small and brown, glittering feverishly.

"Listen," he said, "don't you think some people was meant to meet on account of what all they got in common and all? Like they both think serious thoughts and all?" He shifted the valise to his other hand so that the hand nearest her was free. He caught hold of her elbow and shook it a little.

"I don't work on Saturday," he said. "I like to walk in the woods and see what Mother Nature is wearing. O'er the hills and far away. Pic-nics and things. Couldn't we go on a pic-nic tomorrow? Say yes, Hulga," he said and gave her a dying look as if he felt his insides about to drop out of him. He had even seemed to sway slightly toward her.

During the night she had imagined that she seduced him. She imagined that the two of them walked on the place until they came to the storage barn beyond the two back fields and there, she imagined, that things came to such a pass that she very easily seduced him and that then, of course, she had to reckon with his remorse. True genius can get an idea across even to an inferior mind. She imagined that she took his remorse in hand and changed it into a deeper understanding of life. She took all his shame away and turned it into something useful.

She set off for the gate at exactly ten o'clock, escaping without drawing Mrs. Hopewell's attention. She didn't take anything to eat, forgetting that food is usually taken on a picnic. She wore a pair of slacks and a dirty white shirt, and as an afterthought, she had put some Vapex on the collar of it since she did not own any perfume. When she reached the gate no one was there.

She looked up and down the empty highway and had the furious feeling that she had been tricked, that he had only meant to make her walk to the gate after the idea of him. Then suddenly he stood up, very tall, from behind a bush on the opposite embankment. Smiling, he lifted his hat which was new and wide-brimmed. He had not worn it yesterday and she wondered if he had bought it for the occasion. It was toast-colored with a red and white band around it and was slightly too large for him. He stepped from behind the bush still carrying the black valise. He had on the same suit and the same yellow socks sucked down in his shoes from walking. He crossed the highway and said, "I knew you'd come!"

The girl wondered acidly how he had known this. She pointed to the valise and asked, "Why did you bring your Bibles?"

He took her elbow, smiling down on her as if he could not stop. "You can never tell when you'll need the word of God, Hulga," he said. She had a moment in which she doubted that this was actually happening and then they began to climb the embankment. They went down into the pasture toward the woods. The boy walked lightly by her side, bouncing on his toes. The valise did not seem to be heavy today; he even swung it. They crossed half the pasture without saying anything and then, putting his hand easily on the small of her back, he asked softly, "Where does your wooden leg join on?"

She turned an ugly red and glared at him and for an instant the boy looked abashed. "I didn't mean you no harm," he said. "I only meant you're so brave and all. I guess God takes care of you."

"No," she said, looking forward and walking fast, "I don't even believe in God."

At this he stopped and whistled. "No!" he exclaimed as if he were too astonished to say anything else.

She walked on and in a second he was bouncing at her side, fanning with his hat. "That's very unusual for a girl," he remarked, watching her out of the corner of his eye. When they reached the edge of the wood, he put his hand on her back again and drew her against him without a word and kissed her heavily.

The kiss, which had more pressure than feeling behind it, produced that extra surge of adrenalin in the girl that enables one to carry a packed trunk out of a burning house, but in her, the power went at once to the brain. Even before he released her, her mind, clear and detached and ironic anyway, was regarding him from a great distance, with amusement but with pity. She had never been kissed before and she was pleased to discover that it was an unexceptional experience and all a matter of the mind's control. Some people might enjoy drain water if they were told it was vodka. When the boy, looking expectant but uncertain, pushed her gently away, she turned and walked on, saying nothing as if such business, for her, were common enough.

He came along panting at her side, trying to help her when he saw a root that she might trip over. He caught and held back the long swaying blades of thorn vine until she had passed beyond them. She led the way and he came breathing heavily behind her. Then they came out on a sunlit hillside, sloping softly into another one a little smaller. Beyond, they could see the rusted top of the old barn where the extra hay was stored.

The hill was sprinkled with small pink weeds. "Then you ain't saved?" he asked suddenly, stopping.

The girl smiled. It was the first time she had smiled at him at all. "In my economy," she said, "I'm saved and you are damned but I told you I didn't believe in God."

Nothing seemed to destroy the boy's look of admiration. He gazed at her now as if the fantastic animal at the zoo had put its paw through the bars and given him a loving poke. She thought he looked as if he wanted to kiss her again and she walked on before he had the chance.

"Ain't there somewheres we can sit down sometime?" he murmured, his voice softening toward the end of the sentence.

"In that barn," she said.

They made for it rapidly as if it might slide away like a train. It was a large two-story barn, cool and dark inside. The boy pointed up the ladder that led into the loft and said, "It's too bad we can't go up there."

"Why can't we?" she asked.

"Yer leg," he said reverently.

The girl gave him a contemptuous look and putting both hands on the ladder, she climbed it while he stood below, apparently awestruck. She pulled herself expertly through the opening and then looked down at him and said, "Well, come on if you're coming," and he began to climb the ladder, awkwardly bringing the suitcase with him.

"We won't need the Bible," she observed.

"You never can tell," he said, panting. After he had got into the loft, he was a few seconds catching his breath. She had sat down in a pile of straw. A wide sheath of sunlight, filled with dust particles, slanted over her. She lay back against a bale, her face turned away, looking out the front opening of the barn where hay was thrown from a wagon into the loft. The two pink-speckled hillsides lay back against a dark ridge of woods. The sky was cloudless and cold blue. The boy dropped down by her side and put one arm under her and the other over her and began methodically kissing her face, making little noises like a fish. He did not remove his hat but it was pushed far enough back not to interfere. When her glasses got in his way, he took them off of her and slipped them into his pocket.

The girl at first did not return any of the kisses but presently she began to and after she had put several on his cheek, she reached his lips and remained there, kissing him again and again as if she were trying to draw all the breath out of him. His breath was clear and sweet like a child's and the kisses were sticky like a child's. He mumbled about loving her and about knowing when he first seen her that he loved her, but the mumbling was like the sleepy fretting of a child being put to sleep by his mother. Her mind, throughout this, never stopped or lost itself for a second to her feelings. "You ain't said you loved me none," he whispered finally, pulling back from her. "You got to say that."

She looked away from him off into the hollow sky and then down at a black ridge and then down farther into what appeared to be two green swelling lakes. She didn't realize he had taken her glasses but this landscape could not seem exceptional to her for she seldom paid any close attention to her surroundings.

"You got to say it," he repeated. "You got to say you love me."

She was always careful how she committed herself. "In a sense," she began, "if you use the word loosely, you might say that. But it's not a word I use. I don't have illusions. I'm one of those people who see *through* to nothing."

The boy was frowning. "You got to say it. I said it and you got to say it," he said.

The girl looked at him almost tenderly. "You poor baby," she murmured. "It's just as well you don't understand," and she pulled him by the neck, facedown against her. "We are all damned," she said, "but some of us have taken off our blindfolds and see that there's nothing to see. It's a kind of salvation."

The boy's astonished eyes looked blankly through the ends of her hair. "Okay," he almost whined, "but do you love me or don'tcher?"

"Yes," she said and added, "in a sense. But I must tell you something. There mustn't be anything dishonest between us." She lifted his head and looked him in the eye. "I am thirty years old," she said. "I have a number of degrees."

The boy's look was irritated but dogged. "I don't care," he said. "I don't care a thing about what all you done. I just want to know if you love me or don'tcher?" and he caught her to him and wildly planted her face with kisses until she said, "Yes, yes."

"Okay then," he said, letting her go. "Prove it."

She smiled, looking dreamily out on the shifty landscape. She had seduced him without even making up her mind to try. "How?" she asked, feeling that he should be delayed a little.

He leaned over and put his lips to her ear. "Show me where your wooden leg joins on," he whispered.

The girl uttered a sharp little cry and her face instantly drained of color. The obscenity of the suggestion was not what shocked her. As a child she had sometimes been subject to feelings of shame but education had removed the last traces of that as a good surgeon scrapes for cancer; she would no more have felt it over what he was asking than she would have believed in his Bible. But she was as sensitive about the artificial leg as a peacock about his tail. No one ever touched it but her. She took care of it as someone else would his soul, in private and almost with her own eyes turned away. "No," she said.

"I known it," he muttered, sitting up. "You're just playing me for a sucker."

"Oh no no!" she cried. "It joins on at the knee. Only at the knee. Why do you want to see it?"

The boy gave her a long penetrating look. "Because," he said, "it's what makes you different. You ain't like anybody else."

She sat staring at him. There was nothing about her face or her round freezing-blue eyes to indicate that this had moved her; but she felt as if her heart had stopped and left her mind to pump her blood. She decided that for the first time in her life she was face to face with real innocence. This boy, with an instinct that came from beyond wisdom, had touched the truth about her. When after a minute, she said in a hoarse high voice, "All right," it was like surrendering to him completely. It was like losing her own life and finding it again, miraculously, in his.

Very gently he began to roll the slack leg up. The artificial limb, in a white sock and brown flat shoe, was bound in a heavy material like canvas and ended in an ugly jointure where it was attached to the stump. The boy's face and his voice were entirely reverent as he uncovered it and said, "Now show me how to take it off and on."

She took it off for him and put it back on again and then he took it off himself, handling it as tenderly as if it were a real one. "See!" he said with a delighted child's face. "Now I can do it myself!"

"Put it back on," she said. She was thinking that she would run away with him and that every night he would take the leg off and every morning put it back on again. "Put it back on," she said.

"Not yet," he murmured, setting it on its foot out of her reach. "Leave it off for a while. You got me instead."

She gave a cry of alarm but he pushed her down and began to kiss her again. Without the leg she felt entirely dependent on him. Her brain seemed to have stopped thinking altogether and to be about some other function that it was not very good at. Different expressions raced back and forth over her face. Every now and then the boy, his eyes like two steel spikes, would glance behind him where the leg stood. Finally she pushed him off and said, "Put it back on me now."

"Wait," he said. He leaned the other way and pulled the valise toward him and opened it. It had a pale blue spotted lining and there were only two Bibles in it. He took one of these out and opened the cover of it. It was hollow and contained a pocket flask of whiskey, a pack of cards, and a small blue box with printing on it. He laid these out in front of her one at a time in an evenly-spaced row, like one presenting offerings at the shrine of a goddess. He put the blue box in her hand. THIS PRODUCT TO BE USED ONLY FOR THE PREVENTION OF DISEASE, she read, and dropped it. The boy was unscrewing the top of the flask. He stopped and pointed, with a smile, to the deck of cards. It was not an ordinary deck but one with an obscene picture on the back of each card. "Take a swig," he said, offering her the bottle first. He held it in front of her, but like one mesmerized, she did not move.

Her voice when she spoke had an almost pleading sound. "Aren't you," she murmured, "aren't you just good country people?"

The boy cocked his head. He looked as if he were just beginning to understand that she might be trying to insult him. "Yeah," he said, curling his lip slightly, "but it ain't held me back none. I'm as good as you any day in the week."

"Give me my leg," she said.

He pushed it farther away with his foot. "Come on now, let's begin to have us a good time," he said coaxingly. "We ain't got to know one another good yet."

"Give me my leg!" she screamed and tried to lunge for it but he pushed her down easily.

"What's the matter with you all of a sudden?" he asked, frowning as he screwed the top on the flask and put it quickly back inside the Bible. "You just a while ago said you didn't believe in nothing. I thought you was some girl!"

Her face was almost purple. "You're a Christian!" she hissed. "You're a fine Christian! You're just like them all—say one thing and do another. You're a perfect Christian, you're . . ."

The boy's mouth was set angrily. "I hope you don't think," he said in a lofty indignant tone, "that I believe in that crap! I may sell Bibles but I know which end is up and I wasn't born yesterday and I know where I'm going!"

"Give me my leg!" she screeched. He jumped up so quickly that she barely saw him sweep the cards and the blue box into the Bible and throw the Bible into the valise. She saw him grab the leg and then she saw it for an instant slanted forlornly across the inside of the suitcase with a Bible at either side of its opposite ends. He slammed the lid shut and snatched up the valise and swung it down the hole and then stepped through himself.

When all of him had passed but his head, he turned and regarded her with a look that no longer had any admiration in it. "I've gotten a lot of interesting things," he said. "One time I got a woman's glass eye this way. And you needn't to think you'll catch me because Pointer ain't really my name. I use a different name at every house I call at and don't stay nowhere long. And I'll tell you another thing, Hulga," he said, using the name as if he didn't think much of it, "you ain't so smart. I been believing in nothing every since I was born!" and then the toast-colored hat disappeared down the hole and the girl was left, sitting on the straw in the dusty sunlight. When she turned her churning face toward the opening, she saw his blue figure struggling successfully over the green speckled lake.

Mrs. Hopewell and Mrs. Freeman, who were in the back pasture, digging up onions, saw him emerge a little later from the woods and head across the meadow toward the highway. "Why, that looks like that nice dull young man that tried to sell me a Bible yesterday," Mrs. Hopewell said, squinting. "He must have been selling them to the Negroes back in there. He was so simple," she said, "but I guess the world would be better off if we were all that simple."

Mrs. Freeman's gaze drove forward and just touched him before he disappeared under the hill. Then she returned her attention to the evil-smelling onion shoot she was lifting from the ground. "Some can't be that simple," she said. "I know I never could."

1955

A Good Man Is Hard to Find

The grandmother didn't want to go to Florida. She wanted to visit some of her connections in east Tennessee and she was seizing at every chance to change Bailey's mind. Bailey was the son she lived with, her only boy. He was sitting on the edge of his chair at the table, bent over the orange sports section of the *Journal*. "Now look here, Bailey," she said, "see here, read this," and she stood with one hand on her thin hip and the other rattling the newspaper at his bald head. "Here this fellow that calls himself The Misfit is aloose from the Federal Pen[1] and headed toward Florida and you read here what it says he did to these people. Just you read it. I wouldn't take my children in any direction with a criminal like that aloose in it. I couldn't answer to my conscience if I did."

Bailey didn't look up from his reading so she wheeled around then and faced the children's mother, a young woman in slacks, whose face was as broad and innocent as a cabbage and was tied around with a green head-kerchief that had two points on the top like a rabbit's ears. She was sitting on the sofa, feeding the baby his apricots out of a jar. "The children have been to Florida before," the old lady said. "You all ought to take them somewhere else for a change so they would see different parts of the world and be broad. They never have been to east Tennessee."

The children's mother didn't seem to hear her but the eight-year-old boy, John Wesley, a stocky child with glasses, said, "If you don't want to go to Florida, why dontcha stay at home?" He and the little girl, June Star, were reading the funny papers[2] on the floor.

"She wouldn't stay at home to be queen for a day,"[3] June Star said without raising her yellow head.

"Yes and what would you do if this fellow, The Misfit, caught you?" the grandmother asked.

"I'd smack his face," John Wesley said.

"She wouldn't stay at home for a million bucks," June Star said. "Afraid she'd miss something. She has to go everywhere we go."

"All right, Miss," the grandmother said. "Just remember that the next time you want me to curl your hair."

June Star said her hair was naturally curly.

The next morning the grandmother was the first one in the car, ready to go. She had her big black valise that looked like the head of a hippopotamus in one corner, and underneath it she was hiding a basket with Pitty Sing, the cat, in it. She didn't intend for the cat to be left alone in the house for three days because he would miss her too much and she was afraid he might brush against one of the gas burners and accidentally asphyxiate himself. Her son, Bailey, didn't like to arrive at a motel with a cat.

She sat in the middle of the back seat with John Wesley and June Star on either side of her. Bailey and the children's mother and the baby sat in front

---

1. Federal Penitentiary.
2. Comics.
3. Reference to a long-running radio and then television program, *Queen for a Day*, in which women competed to tell the most heartbreaking stories of personal hardship in order to be crowned "Queen for a Day" and win valuable prizes.

and they left Atlanta at eight forty-five with the mileage on the car at 55890. The grandmother wrote this down because she thought it would be interesting to say how many miles they had been when they got back. It took them twenty minutes to reach the outskirts of the city.

The old lady settled herself comfortably, removing her white cotton gloves and putting them up with her purse on the shelf in front of the back window. The children's mother still had on slacks and still had her head tied up in a green kerchief, but the grandmother had on a navy blue straw sailor hat with a bunch of white violets on the brim and a navy blue dress with a small white dot in the print. Her collars and cuffs were white organdy trimmed with lace and at her neckline she had pinned a purple spray of cloth violets containing a sachet. In case of an accident, anyone seeing her dead on the highway would know at once that she was a lady.

She said she thought it was going to be a good day for driving, neither too hot nor too cold, and she cautioned Bailey that the speed limit was fifty-five miles an hour and that the patrolmen hid themselves behind billboards and small clumps of trees and sped out after you before you had a chance to slow down. She pointed out interesting details of the scenery: Stone Mountain; the blue granite that in some places came up to both sides of the highway; the brilliant red clay banks slightly streaked with purple; and the various crops that made rows of green lace-work on the ground. The trees were full of silver-white sunlight and the meanest of them sparkled. The children were reading comic magazines and their mother had gone back to sleep.

"Let's go through Georgia fast so we won't have to look at it much," John Wesley said.

"If I were a little boy," said the grandmother, "I wouldn't talk about my native state that way. Tennessee has the mountains and Georgia has the hills."

"Tennessee is just a hillbilly dumping ground," John Wesley said, "and Georgia is a lousy state too."

"You said it," June Star said.

"In my time," said the grandmother, folding her thin veined fingers, "children were more respectful of their native states and their parents and everything else. People did right then. Oh look at the cute little pickaninny[4]!" she said and pointed to a Negro child standing in the door of a shack. "Wouldn't that make a picture, now?" she asked and they all turned and looked at the little Negro out of the back window. He waved.

"He didn't have any britches on," June Star said.

"He probably didn't have any," the grandmother explained. "Little niggers in the country don't have things like we do. If I could paint, I'd paint that picture," she said.

The children exchanged comic books.

The grandmother offered to hold the baby and the children's mother passed him over the front seat to her. She set him on her knee and bounced him and told him about the things they were passing. She rolled her eyes and screwed up her mouth and stuck her leathery thin face into his smooth bland one. Occasionally he gave her a faraway smile. They passed a large cotton field with five or six graves fenced in the middle of it, like a small

---

4. Derogatory term for an African American child.

island. "Look at the graveyard!" the grandmother said, pointing it out. "That was the old family burying ground. That belonged to the plantation."

"Where's the plantation?" John Wesley asked.

"Gone with the Wind,"[5] said the grandmother. "Ha. Ha."

When the children finished all the comic books they had brought, they opened the lunch and ate it. The grandmother ate a peanut butter sandwich and an olive and would not let the children throw the box and the paper napkins out the window. When there was nothing else to do they played a game by choosing a cloud and making the other two guess what shape it suggested. John Wesley took one the shape of a cow and June Star guessed a cow and John Wesley said, no, an automobile, and June Star said he didn't play fair, and they began to slap each other over the grandmother.

The grandmother said she would tell them a story if they would keep quiet. When she told a story, she rolled her eyes and waved her head and was very dramatic. She said once when she was a maiden lady she had been courted by a Mr. Edgar Atkins Teagarden from Jasper, Georgia. She said he was a very good-looking man and a gentleman and that he brought her a watermelon every Saturday afternoon with his initials cut in it, E. A. T. Well, one Saturday, she said, Mr. Teagarden brought the watermelon and there was nobody at home and he left it on the front porch and returned in his buggy to Jasper, but she never got the watermelon, she said, because a nigger boy ate it when he saw the initials, E. A. T.! This story tickled John Wesley's funny bone and he giggled and giggled but June Star didn't think it was any good. She said she wouldn't marry a man that just brought her a watermelon on Saturday. The grandmother said she would have done well to marry Mr. Teagarden because he was a gentleman and had bought Coca-Cola stock when it first came out and that he had died only a few years ago, a very wealthy man.

They stopped at The Tower for barbecued sandwiches. The Tower was a part stucco and part wood filling station and dance hall set in a clearing outside of Timothy. A fat man named Red Sammy Butts ran it and there were signs stuck here and there on the building and for miles up and down the highway saying, TRY RED SAMMY'S FAMOUS BARBECUE. NONE LIKE FAMOUS RED SAMMY'S! RED SAM! THE FAT BOY WITH THE HAPPY LAUGH! A VETERAN! RED SAMMY'S YOUR MAN!

Red Sammy was lying on the bare ground outside The Tower with his head under a truck while a gray monkey about a foot high, chained to a small chinaberry tree, chattered nearby. The monkey sprang back into the tree and got on the highest limb as soon as he saw the children jump out of the car and run toward him.

Inside, The Tower was a long dark room with a counter at one end and tables at the other and dancing space in the middle. They all sat down at a board table next to the nickelodeon[6] and Red Sam's wife, a tall burnt-brown woman with hair and eyes lighter than her skin, came and took their order. The children's mother put a dime in the machine and played "The Tennessee Waltz," and the grandmother said that tune always made her want to dance. She asked Bailey if he would like to dance but he only glared at her.

5. Margaret Mitchell's 1936 southern romance novel, *Gone with the Wind*, won the Pulitzer Prize and was made into a popular 1939 film starring Clark Gable and Vivien Leigh.
6. Jukebox.

He didn't have a naturally sunny disposition like she did and trips made him nervous. The grandmother's brown eyes were very bright. She swayed her head from side to side and pretended she was dancing in her chair. June Star said play something she could tap to so the children's mother put in another dime and played a fast number and June Star stepped out onto the dance floor and did her tap routine.

"Ain't she cute?" Red Sam's wife said, leaning over the counter. "Would you like to come be my little girl?"

"No I certainly wouldn't," June Star said. "I wouldn't live in a broken-down place like this for a million bucks!" and she ran back to the table.

"Ain't she cute?" the woman repeated, stretching her mouth politely.

"Aren't you ashamed?" hissed the grandmother.

Red Sam came in and told his wife to quit lounging on the counter and hurry up with these people's order. His khaki trousers reached just to his hip bones and his stomach hung over them like a sack of meal swaying under his shirt. He came over and sat down at a table nearby and let out a combination sigh and yodel. "You can't win," he said. "You can't win," and he wiped his sweating red face off with a gray handkerchief. "These days you don't know who to trust," he said. "Ain't that the truth?"

"People are certainly not nice like they used to be," said the grandmother.

"Two fellers come in here last week," Red Sammy said, "driving a Chrysler. It was a old beat-up car but it was a good one and these boys looked all right to me. Said they worked at the mill and you know I let them fellers charge[7] the gas they bought? Now why did I do that?"

"Because you're a good man!" the grandmother said at once.

"Yes'm, I suppose so," Red Sam said as if he were struck with this answer.

His wife brought the orders, carrying the five plates all at once without a tray, two in each hand and one balanced on her arm. "It isn't a soul in this green world of God's that you can trust," she said. "And I don't count nobody out of that, not nobody," she repeated, looking at Red Sammy.

"Did you read about that criminal, The Misfit, that's escaped?" asked the grandmother.

"I wouldn't be a bit surprised if he didn't attack this place right here," said the woman. "If he hears about it being here, I wouldn't be none surprised to see him. If he hears it's two cent in the cash register, I wouldn't be a tall surprised if he . . ."

"That'll do," Red Sam said. "Go bring these people their Co'-Colas," and the woman went off to get the rest of the order.

"A good man is hard to find," Red Sammy said. "Everything is getting terrible. I remember the day you could go off and leave your screen door unlatched. Not no more."

He and the grandmother discussed better times. The old lady said that in her opinion Europe was entirely to blame for the way things were now. She said the way Europe acted you would think we were made of money and Red Sam said it was no use talking about it, she was exactly right.[8] The children ran outside into the white sunlight and looked at the monkey in the lacy

7. To buy with a promise to pay the shopkeeper later.
8. Referring to money supplied by the United States for the reconstruction of Europe after World War II.

chinaberry tree. He was busy catching fleas on himself and biting each one carefully between his teeth as if it were a delicacy.

They drove off again into the hot afternoon. The grandmother took cat naps and woke up every few minutes with her own snoring. Outside of Toombsboro she woke up and recalled an old plantation that she had visited in this neighborhood once when she was a young lady. She said the house had six white columns across the front and that there was an avenue of oaks leading up to it and two little wooden trellis arbors on either side in front where you sat down with your suitor after a stroll in the garden. She recalled exactly which road to turn off to get to it. She knew that Bailey would not be willing to lose any time looking at an old house, but the more she talked about it, the more she wanted to see it once again and find out if the little twin arbors were still standing. "There was a secret panel in this house," she said craftily, not telling the truth but wishing that she were, "and the story went that all the family silver was hidden in it when Sherman[9] came through but it was never found . . ."

"Hey!" John Wesley said. "Let's go see it! We'll find it! We'll poke all the woodwork and find it! Who lives there? Where do you turn off at? Hey Pop, can't we turn off there?"

"We never have seen a house with a secret panel!" June Star shrieked. "Let's go to the house with the secret panel! Hey Pop, can't we go see the house with the secret panel!"

"It's not far from here, I know," the grandmother said. "It wouldn't take over twenty minutes."

Bailey was looking straight ahead. His jaw was as rigid as a horseshoe. "No," he said.

The children began to yell and scream that they wanted to see the house with the secret panel. John Wesley kicked the back of the front seat and June Star hung over her mother's shoulder and whined desperately into her ear that they never had any fun even on their vacation, that they could never do what THEY wanted to do. The baby began to scream and John Wesley kicked the back of the seat so hard that his father could feel the blows in his kidney.

"All right!" he shouted and drew the car to a stop at the side of the road. "Will you all shut up? Will you all just shut up for one second? If you don't shut up, we won't go anywhere."

"It would be very educational for them," the grandmother murmured.

"All right," Bailey said, "but get this: this is the only time we're going to stop for anything like this. This is the one and only time."

"The dirt road that you have to turn down is about a mile back," the grandmother directed. "I marked it when we passed."

"A dirt road," Bailey groaned.

After they had turned around and were headed toward the dirt road, the grandmother recalled other points about the house, the beautiful glass over the front doorway and the candle-lamp in the hall. John Wesley said that the secret panel was probably in the fireplace.

---

9. William Tecumseh Sherman (1820–1891), commander of the Union army that devastated much of Georgia during the American Civil War (1861–65).

"You can't go inside this house," Bailey said. "You don't know who lives there."

"While you all talk to the people in front, I'll run around behind and get in a window," John Wesley suggested.

"We'll all stay in the car," his mother said.

They turned onto the dirt road and the car raced roughly along in a swirl of pink dust. The grandmother recalled the times when there were no paved roads and thirty miles was a day's journey. The dirt road was hilly and there were sudden washes in it and sharp curves on dangerous embankments. All at once they would be on a hill, looking down over the blue tops of trees for miles around, then the next minute, they would be in a red depression with the dust-coated trees looking down on them.

"This place had better turn up in a minute," Bailey said, "or I'm going to turn around."

The road looked as if no one had traveled on it in months.

"It's not much farther," the grandmother said and just as she said it, a horrible thought came to her. The thought was so embarrassing that she turned red in the face and her eyes dilated and her feet jumped up, upsetting her valise in the corner. The instant the valise moved, the newspaper top she had over the basket under it rose with a snarl and Pitty Sing, the cat, sprang onto Bailey's shoulder.

The children were thrown to the floor and their mother, clutching the baby, was thrown out the door onto the ground; the old lady was thrown into the front seat. The car turned over once and landed right-side-up in a gulch off the side of the road. Bailey remained in the driver's seat with the cat—gray-striped with a broad white face and an orange nose—clinging to his neck like a caterpillar.

As soon as the children saw they could move their arms and legs, they scrambled out of the car, shouting, "We've had an ACCIDENT!" The grandmother was curled up under the dashboard, hoping she was injured so that Bailey's wrath would not come down on her all at once. The horrible thought she had had before the accident was that the house she had remembered so vividly was not in Georgia but in Tennessee.

Bailey removed the cat from his neck with both hands and flung it out the window against the side of a pine tree. Then he got out of the car and started looking for the children's mother. She was sitting against the side of the red gutted ditch, holding the screaming baby, but she only had a cut down her face and a broken shoulder. "We've had an ACCIDENT!" the children screamed in a frenzy of delight.

"But nobody's killed," June Star said with disappointment as the grandmother limped out of the car, her hat still pinned to her head but the broken front brim standing up at a jaunty angle and the violet spray hanging off the side. They all sat down in the ditch, except the children, to recover from the shock. They were all shaking.

"Maybe a car will come along," said the children's mother hoarsely.

"I believe I have injured an organ," said the grandmother, pressing her side, but no one answered her. Bailey's teeth were clattering. He had on a yellow sport shirt with bright blue parrots designed in it and his face was as yellow as the shirt. The grandmother decided that she would not mention that the house was in Tennessee.

The road was about ten feet above and they could see only the tops of the trees on the other side of it. Behind the ditch they were sitting in there were more woods, tall and dark and deep. In a few minutes they saw a car, some distance away on top of a hill, coming slowly as if the occupants were watching them. The grandmother stood up and waved both arms dramatically to attract their attention. The car continued to come on slowly, disappeared around a bend and appeared again, moving even slower, on top of the hill they had gone over. It was a big black battered hearse-like automobile. There were three men in it.

It came to a stop just over them and for some minutes, the driver looked down with a steady expressionless gaze to where they were sitting, and didn't speak. Then he turned his head and muttered something to the other two and they got out. One was a fat boy in black trousers and a red sweat shirt with a silver stallion embossed on the front of it. He moved around on the right side of them and stood staring, his mouth partly open in a kind of loose grin. The other had on khaki pants and a blue striped coat and a gray hat pulled down very low, hiding most of his face. He came around slowly on the left side. Neither spoke.

The driver got out of the car and stood by the side of it, looking down at them. He was an older man than the other two. His hair was just beginning to gray and he wore silver-rimmed spectacles that gave him a scholarly look. He had a long creased face and didn't have on any shirt or undershirt. He had on blue jeans that were too tight for him and was holding a black hat and a gun. The two boys also had guns.

"We've had an ACCIDENT!" the children screamed.

The grandmother had the peculiar feeling that the bespectacled man was someone she knew. His face was as familiar to her as if she had known him all her life but she could not recall who he was. He moved away from the car and began to come down the embankment, placing his feet carefully so that he wouldn't slip. He had on tan and white shoes and no socks, and his ankles were red and thin. "Good afternoon," he said. "I see you all had you a little spill."

"We turned over twice!" said the grandmother.

"Oncet," he corrected. "We seen it happen. Try their car and see will it run, Hiram," he said quietly to the boy with the gray hat.

"What you got that gun for?" John Wesley asked. "Whatcha gonna do with that gun?"

"Lady," the man said to the children's mother, "would you mind calling them children to sit down by you? Children make me nervous. I want all you all to sit down right together there where you're at."

"What are you telling US what to do for?" June Star asked.

Behind them the line of woods gaped like a dark open mouth. "Come here," said their mother.

"Look here now," Bailey began suddenly, "we're in a predicament! We're in . . ."

The grandmother shrieked. She scrambled to her feet and stood staring. "You're The Misfit!" she said. "I recognized you at once!"

"Yes'm," the man said, smiling slightly as if he were pleased in spite of himself to be known, "but it would have been better for all of you, lady, if you hadn't of reckernized me."

Bailey turned his head sharply and said something to his mother that shocked even the children. The old lady began to cry and The Misfit reddened.

"Lady," he said, "don't you get upset. Sometimes a man says things he don't mean. I don't reckon he meant to talk to you thataway."

"You wouldn't shoot a lady, would you?" the grandmother said and removed a clean handkerchief from her cuff and began to slap at her eyes with it.

The Misfit pointed the toe of his shoe into the ground and made a little hole and then covered it up again. "I would hate to have to," he said.

"Listen," the grandmother almost screamed, "I know you're a good man. You don't look a bit like you have common blood. I know you must come from nice people!"

"Yes mam," he said, "finest people in the world." When he smiled he showed a row of strong white teeth. "God never made a finer woman than my mother and my daddy's heart was pure gold," he said. The boy with the red sweat shirt had come around behind them and was standing with his gun at his hip. The Misfit squatted down on the ground. "Watch them children, Bobby Lee," he said. "You know they make me nervous." He looked at the six of them huddled together in front of him and he seemed to be embarrassed as if he couldn't think of anything to say. "Ain't a cloud in the sky," he remarked, looking up at it. "Don't see no sun but don't see no cloud neither."

"Yes, it's a beautiful day," said the grandmother. "Listen," she said, "you shouldn't call yourself The Misfit because I know you're a good man at heart. I can just look at you and tell."

"Hush!" Bailey yelled. "Hush! Everybody shut up and let me handle this!" He was squatting in the position of a runner about to sprint forward but he didn't move.

"I pre-chate that, lady," The Misfit said and drew a little circle in the ground with the butt of his gun.

"It'll take a half a hour to fix this here car," Hiram called, looking over the raised hood of it.

"Well, first you and Bobby Lee get him and that little boy to step over yonder with you," The Misfit said, pointing to Bailey and John Wesley. "The boys want to ast you something," he said to Bailey. "Would you mind stepping back in them woods there with them?"

"Listen," Bailey began, "we're in a terrible predicament! Nobody realizes what this is," and his voice cracked. His eyes were as blue and intense as the parrots in his shirt and he remained perfectly still.

The grandmother reached up to adjust her hat brim as if she were going to the woods with him but it came off in her hand. She stood staring at it and after a second she let it fall on the ground. Hiram pulled Bailey up by the arm as if he were assisting an old man. John Wesley caught hold of his father's hand and Bobby Lee followed. They went off toward the woods and just as they reached the dark edge, Bailey turned and supporting himself against a gray naked pine trunk, he shouted, "I'll be back in a minute, Mamma, wait on me!"

"Come back this instant!" his mother shrilled but they all disappeared into the woods.

"Bailey Boy!" the grandmother called in a tragic voice but she found she was looking at The Misfit squatting on the ground in front of her. "I just know you're a good man," she said desperately. "You're not a bit common!"

"Nome, I ain't a good man," The Misfit said after a second as if he had considered her statement carefully, "but I ain't the worst in the world neither. My daddy said I was a different breed of dog from my brothers and sisters. 'You know,' Daddy said, 'it's some that can live their whole life out without asking about it and it's others has to know why it is, and this boy is one of the latters. He's going to be into everything!'" He put on his black hat and looked up suddenly and then away deep into the woods as if he were embarrassed again. "I'm sorry I don't have on a shirt before you ladies," he said, hunching his shoulders slightly. "We buried our clothes that we had on when we escaped and we're just making do until we can get better. We borrowed these from some folks we met," he explained.

"That's perfectly all right," the grandmother said. "Maybe Bailey has an extra shirt in his suitcase."

"I'll look and see terrectly," The Misfit said.

"Where are they taking him?" the children's mother screamed.

"Daddy was a card[1] himself," The Misfit said. "You couldn't put anything over on him. He never got in trouble with the Authorities though. Just had the knack of handling them."

"You could be honest too if you'd only try," said the grandmother. "Think how wonderful it would be to settle down and live a comfortable life and not have to think about somebody chasing you all the time."

The Misfit kept scratching in the ground with the butt of his gun as if he were thinking about it. "Yes'm, somebody is always after you," he murmured.

The grandmother noticed how thin his shoulder blades were just behind his hat because she was standing up looking down on him. "Do you ever pray?" she asked.

He shook his head. All she saw was the black hat wiggle between his shoulder blades. "Nome," he said.

There was a pistol shot from the woods, followed closely by another. Then silence. The old lady's head jerked around. She could hear the wind move through the tree tops like a long satisfied insuck of breath. "Bailey Boy!" she called.

"I was a gospel singer for a while," The Misfit said. "I been most everything. Been in the arm service, both land and sea, at home and abroad, been twict married, been an undertaker, been with the railroads, plowed Mother Earth, been in a tornado, seen a man burnt alive oncet," and looked up at the children's mother and the little girl who were sitting close together, their faces white and their eyes glassy; "I even seen a woman flogged," he said.

"Pray, pray," the grandmother began, "pray, pray . . ."

"I never was a bad boy that I remember of," The Misfit said in an almost dreamy voice, "but somewheres along the line I done something wrong and got sent to the penitentiary. I was buried alive," and he looked up and held her attention to him by a steady stare.

"That's when you should have started to pray," she said. "What did you do to get sent to the penitentiary that first time?"

"Turn to the right, it was a wall," The Misfit said, looking up again at the cloudless sky. "Turn to the left, it was a wall. Look up it was a ceiling, look

1. A clever man.

down it was a floor. I forget what I done, lady. I set there and set there, trying to remember what it was I done and I ain't recalled it to this day. Oncet in a while, I would think it was coming to me, but it never come."

"Maybe they put you in by mistake," the old lady said vaguely.

"Nome," he said. "It wasn't no mistake. They had the papers on me."

"You must have stolen something," she said.

The Misfit sneered slightly. "Nobody had nothing I wanted," he said. "It was a head-doctor[2] at the penitentiary said what I had done was kill my daddy but I known that for a lie. My daddy died in nineteen ought nineteen of the epidemic flu and I never had a thing to do with it. He was buried in the Mount Hopewell Baptist churchyard and you can go there and see for yourself."

"If you would pray," the old lady said, "Jesus would help you."

"That's right," The Misfit said.

"Well then, why don't you pray?" she asked trembling with delight suddenly.

"I don't want no hep," he said. "I'm doing all right by myself."

Bobby Lee and Hiram came ambling back from the woods. Bobby Lee was dragging a yellow shirt with bright blue parrots in it.

"Thow me that shirt, Bobby Lee," The Misfit said. The shirt came flying at him and landed on his shoulder and he put it on. The grandmother couldn't name what the shirt reminded her of. "No, lady," The Misfit said while he was buttoning it up, "I found out the crime don't matter. You can do one thing or you can do another, kill a man or take a tire off his car, because sooner or later you're going to forget what it was you done and just be punished for it."

The children's mother had begun to make heaving noises as if she couldn't get her breath. "Lady," he asked, "would you and that little girl like to step off yonder with Bobby Lee and Hiram and join your husband?"

"Yes, thank you," the mother said faintly. Her left arm dangled helplessly and she was holding the baby, who had gone to sleep, in the other. "Hep that lady up, Hiram," The Misfit said as she struggled to climb out of the ditch, "and Bobby Lee, you hold onto that little girl's hand."

"I don't want to hold hands with him," June Star said. "He reminds me of a pig."

The fat boy blushed and laughed and caught her by the arm and pulled her off into the woods after Hiram and her mother.

Alone with The Misfit, the grandmother found that she had lost her voice. There was not a cloud in the sky nor any sun. There was nothing around her but woods. She wanted to tell him that he must pray. She opened and closed her mouth several times before anything came out. Finally she found herself saying, "Jesus, Jesus," meaning, Jesus will help you, but the way she was saying it, it sounded as if she might be cursing.

"Yes'm," The Misfit said as if he agreed. "Jesus thown everything off balance. It was the same case with Him as with me except He hadn't committed any crime and they could prove I had committed one because they had the papers on me. Of course," he said, "they never shown me my papers. That's

---

2. A psychiatrist.

why I sign myself now. I said long ago, you get you a signature and sign every-thing you do and keep a copy of it. Then you'll know what you done and you can hold up the crime to the punishment and see do they match and in the end you'll have something to prove you ain't been treated right. I call myself The Misfit," he said, "because I can't make what all I done wrong fit what all I gone through in punishment."

There was a piercing scream from the woods, followed closely by a pistol report. "Does it seem right to you, lady, that one is punished a heap and another ain't punished at all?"

"Jesus!" the old lady cried. "You've got good blood! I know you wouldn't shoot a lady! I know you come from nice people! Pray! Jesus, you ought not to shoot a lady. I'll give you all the money I've got!"

"Lady," The Misfit said, looking beyond her far into the woods, "there never was a body that give the undertaker a tip."

There were two more pistol reports and the grandmother raised her head like a parched old turkey hen crying for water and called, "Bailey Boy, Bailey Boy!" as if her heart would break.

"Jesus was the only One that ever raised the dead."[3] The Misfit continued, "and He shouldn't have done it. He thrown everything off balance. If He did what He said, then it's nothing for you to do but throw away everything and follow Him, and if He didn't, then it's nothing for you to do but enjoy the few minutes you got left the best way you can—by killing somebody or burning down his house or doing some other meanness to him. No pleasure but meanness," he said and his voice had become almost a snarl.

"Maybe He didn't raise the dead," the old lady mumbled, not knowing what she was saying and feeling so dizzy that she sank down in the ditch with her legs twisted under her.

"I wasn't there so I can't say He didn't," The Misfit said. "I wisht I had of been there," he said, hitting the ground with his fist. "It ain't right I wasn't there because if I had of been there I would of known. Listen lady," he said in a high voice, "if I had of been there I would of known and I wouldn't be like I am now." His voice seemed about to crack and the grandmother's head cleared for an instant. She saw the man's face twisted close to her own as if he were going to cry and she murmured, "Why you're one of my babies. You're one of my own children!" She reached out and touched him on the shoulder. The Misfit sprang back as if a snake had bitten him and shot her three times through the chest. Then he put his gun down on the ground and took off his glasses and began to clean them.

Hiram and Bobby Lee returned from the woods and stood over the ditch, looking down at the grandmother who half sat and half lay in a puddle of blood with her legs crossed under her like a child's and her face smiling up at the cloudless sky.

Without his glasses, The Misfit's eyes were red-rimmed and pale and defenseless-looking. "Take her off and throw her where you thrown the others," he said, picking up the cat that was rubbing itself against his leg.

"She was a talker, wasn't she?" Bobby Lee said, sliding down the ditch with a yodel.

---

3. Chapter 11 of the Gospel of John tells of Jesus bringing a man named Lazarus back to life four days after Lazarus had died.

"She would of been a good woman," The Misfit said, "if it had been some-body there to shoot her every minute of her life."

"Some fun!" Bobby Lee said.

"Shut up, Bobby Lee," The Misfit said. "It's no real pleasure in life."

1953

ALLEN GINSBERG
1926–1997

" H old back the edges of your gowns, Ladies, we are going through hell." William Carlos Williams's introduction to Allen Ginsberg's *Howl* (1956) was probably the most auspicious public welcome from one poet to another since, one hundred years before, the American Transcendentalist Ralph Waldo Emerson had hailed the unknown Walt Whitman in a letter that Whitman used as a preface to the second edition of *Leaves of Grass*. *Howl* combined apocalyptic criticism of the dull, prosperous Eisenhower years with exuberant celebration of an emerging counterculture. It was the best-known and most widely circulated book of poems of its time, and with its appearance Ginsberg became part of the history of publicity as well as the history of poetry. *Howl* and Jack Kerouac's novel *On the Road* (1957) were the pocket Bibles of the generation whose name Kerouac had coined—"Beat," with its punning overtones of "beaten down" and "beatified."

Ginsberg was the son of Louis Ginsberg, a poet and schoolteacher in New Jersey, and of Naomi Ginsberg, a Russian émigré, whose madness and eventual death her son memorialized in "Kaddish" (1959). His official education took place at Columbia University, but for him as for Kerouac the presence of William Burroughs in New York was equally influential. Burroughs (1914–1997), later the author of *Naked Lunch* (1959), one of the most inventive experiments in American prose, was at that time a drug addict about to embark on an expatriate life in Mexico and Tangier. He helped Ginsberg discover modern writers: Kafka, Yeats, Céline, Rimbaud. Ginsberg responded to Burroughs's liberated kind of life, to his comic-apocalyptic view of American society, and to his bold literary use of autobiography, as when writing about his own experience with addicts and addiction in *Junkie*, whose chapters Ginsberg was reading in manuscript form in 1950.

Ginsberg's New York career has passed into mythology for a generation of poets and readers. In 1945, his sophomore year, he was expelled from Columbia: he had sketched some obscene drawings and phrases in the dust of his dormitory window to draw the attention of a neglectful cleaning woman to the grimy state of his room. Then, living periodically with Burroughs and Kerouac, he shipped out for short trips as a messman on merchant tankers and worked in addition as a welder, a night porter, and a dishwasher.

One summer, in a Harlem apartment, Ginsberg underwent what he always represented as the central conversion experience of his life. He had an "auditory vision" of the English poet William Blake reciting his poems: first "Ah! Sunflower," and then a few minutes later the same oracular voice intoning "The Sick Rose." It was "like hearing the doom of the whole universe, and at the same time the inevitable beauty of that doom." Ginsberg was convinced that the presence of "this big god over all . . . and that the whole purpose of being born was to wake up to Him."

Ginsberg eventually finished Columbia in 1948 with high grades but under a legal cloud. Herbert Huncke, a colorful but irresponsible addict friend, had been using Ginsberg's apartment as a storage depot for the goods he stole to support his drug habit. To avoid prosecution as an accomplice, Ginsberg had to plead insanity and spent eight months in the Columbia Psychiatric Institute.

After more odd jobs and considerable success as a market researcher in San Francisco, Ginsberg left the straight, nine-to-five world for good. He was drawn to San Francisco, he said, by its "long honorable . . . tradition of Bohemian—Buddhist—Wobbly [the I.W.W., an early radical labor movement]—mystical—anarchist social involvement." In the years after 1954 he met San Francisco poets such as Robert Duncan, Kenneth Rexroth, Gary Snyder (who was studying Chinese and Japanese at Berkeley), and Lawrence Ferlinghetti, whose City Lights Bookshop became the publisher of *Howl*. The night Ginsberg read the new poem aloud at the Six Gallery has been called "the birth trauma of the Beat Generation."

The spontaneity of surface in *Howl* conceals but grows out of Ginsberg's care and self-consciousness about rhythm and meter. Under the influence of William Carlos Williams, who had befriended him in Paterson after he left the mental hospital, Ginsberg had started carrying around a notebook to record the rhythms of voices around him. Kerouac's *On the Road* gave him further examples of "frank talk" and, in addition, of an "oceanic" prose "sometimes as sublime as epic line." Under Kerouac's influence Ginsberg began the long tumbling lines that were to become his trademark. He carefully explained that all of *Howl and Other Poems* was an experiment in what could be done with the long line, the longer unit of breath that seemed natural for him. "My feeling is for a big long clanky statement," one that accommodates "not the way you would *say* it, a thought, but the way you would think it—i.e., we think rapidly,

Ginsberg reading *Howl* in New York City in 1966, nine years after the court ruling finding it of redeeming social value and declaring it not obscene.

in visual images as well as words, and if each successive thought were transcribed in its confusion . . . you get a slightly different prosody than if you were talking slowly."

Ginsberg learned the long line as well from biblical rhetoric, from the eighteenth-century English poet Christopher Smart, and above all, from Whitman and Blake. His first book pays tribute to both of these latter poets. "A Supermarket in California," with its movement from exclamations to sad questioning, is Ginsberg's melancholy reminder of what has become, after a century, of Whitman's vision of American plenty. In "Sunflower Sutra" he celebrates the battered nobility beneath our industrial "skin of grime." Ginsberg at his best gives a sense of doom and beauty, whether in the denunciatory impatient prophecies of Howl or in the catalog of suffering in "Kaddish." His disconnected phrases can accumulate as narrative shrieks or, at other moments, can build as a litany of praise.

By the end of the 1960s Ginsberg was widely known and widely traveled. He had conducted publicly his own pursuit of inner peace during a long stay with Buddhist instructors in India and at home served as a kind of guru for many young people disoriented by the Vietnam War. Ginsberg read his poetry and held "office hours" in universities all over America, a presence at everything from "be-ins"—mass outdoor festivals of chanting, costumes, and music—to antiwar protests. He was a gentle and persuasive presence at hearings for many kinds of reform: revision of severe drug laws and laws against homosexuality. Ginsberg had lived for years with the poet Peter Orlovsky and wrote frankly about their relationship. His poems record his drug experiences as well, and "The Change," written in Japan in 1963, marks his decision to keep away from what he considered the nonhuman domination of drugs and to lay new stress on "living in and inhabiting the human form."

In The Fall of America (1972) Ginsberg created an "epic" that included history and registered the ups and downs of his travels across the United States. These "transit" poems sometimes seem like tape-recorded random lists of sights, sounds, and names, but at their best they give a sense of how far America has fallen, by measuring the provisional and changing world of nuclear America against the traces of nature still visible in our landscape and place-names. With Ginsberg's death, contemporary American poetry lost one of its most definitive and revolutionary figures. Happily, the poems endure.

Howl

for Carl Solomon[1]

I

I saw the best minds of my generation destroyed by madness, starving
    hysterical naked,
dragging themselves through the negro streets at dawn looking for an angry
    fix,
angelheaded hipsters burning for the ancient heavenly connection[2] to the
    starry dynamo in the machinery of night,

1. Ginsberg met Solomon (1928–1993) while both were patients at the Columbia Psychiatric Institute in 1949 and called him "an intuitive Bronx Dadaist and prose-poet." Many details in Howl come from the "apocryphal history" that Solomon told Ginsberg in 1949. In "More Mis- haps" (1968) Solomon admits that these adventures were "compounded partly of truth, but for the most [of] raving self-justification, crypto-bohemian boasting . . . effeminate prancing and esoteric aphorisms."
2. In one sense, a person who can supply drugs.

who poverty and tatters and hollow-eyed and high sat up smoking in the
supernatural darkness of cold-water flats floating across the tops of
cities contemplating jazz,

who bared their brains to Heaven under the El and saw Mohammedan[3]
angels staggering on tenement roofs illuminated,

who passed through universities with radiant cool eyes hallucinating
Arkansas and Blake-light[4] tragedy among the scholars of war,

who were expelled from the academies for crazy & publishing obscene odes
on the windows of the skull,

who cowered in unshaven rooms in underwear, burning their money in
wastebaskets and listening to the Terror through the wall,

who got busted in their pubic beards returning through Laredo with a belt
of marijuana for New York,

who ate fire in paint hotels or drank turpentine in Paradise Alley,[5] death, or
purgatoried their torsos night after night

with dreams, with drugs, with waking nightmares, alcohol and cock and
endless balls,

incomparable blind streets of shuddering cloud and lightning in the mind
leaping toward poles of Canada & Paterson,[6] illuminating all the
motionless world of Time between,

Peyote solidities of halls, backyard green tree cemetery dawns, wine
drunkenness over the rooftops, storefront boroughs of teahead joyride
neon blinking traffic light, sun and moon and tree vibrations in the
roaring winter dusks of Brooklyn, ashcan rantings and kind king light
of mind,

who chained themselves to subways for the endless ride from Battery to
holy Bronx[7] on benzedrine until the noise of wheels and children
brought them down shuddering mouth-wracked and battered bleak of
brain all drained of brilliance in the drear light of Zoo,

who sank all night in submarine light of Bickford's floated out and sat
through the stale beer afternoon in desolate Fugazzi's,[8] listening to the
crack of doom on the hydrogen jukebox,

who talked continuously seventy hours from park to pad to bar to Bellevue[9]
to museum to the Brooklyn Bridge,

a lost battalion of platonic conversationalists jumping down the stoops off
fire escapes off windowsills off Empire State out of the moon,

yacketayakking screaming vomiting whispering facts and memories and
anecdotes and eyeball kicks and shocks of hospitals and jails and wars,

whole intellects disgorged in total recall for seven days and nights with
brilliant eyes, meat for the Synagogue cast on the pavement,

---

3. An English term for a Muslim, commonly used
in Western literature until the mid-twentieth century; now considered offensive by many Muslims
because it implies that they worship the prophet
Mohammed (or Muhammad) in the same way
that Christians worship Christ. "The El": the elevated railway in New York City; also a Hebrew
word for God.
4. Refers to Ginsberg's apocalyptic vision of the
English poet William Blake (1757–1827).
5. A tenement courtyard in New York's East Village; setting of Kerouac's *The Subterraneans*
(1958).

6. Ginsberg's hometown; also the town celebrated by William Carlos Williams in his long
poem *Paterson* (1946–58).
7. Opposite ends of a New York subway line
running from the Battery (the southern tip of
Manhattan) to the Bronx Zoo as its northern
terminus.
8. New York bar that was a hipster hangout in the
1950s and 1960s. "Bickford's": a line of restaurants and cafeterias in the New York area from
the 1920s to the 1960s.
9. New York public hospital to which psychiatric
patients may be committed.

who vanished into nowhere Zen New Jersey leaving a trail of ambiguous
    picture postcards of Atlantic City Hall,   20

suffering Eastern sweats and Tangerian bone-grindings and migraines of
    China[1] under junk-withdrawal in Newark's bleak furnished room,

who wandered around and around at midnight in the railroad yard
    wondering where to go, and went, leaving no broken hearts,

who lit cigarettes in boxcars boxcars boxcars racketing through snow
    toward lonesome farms in grandfather night,

who studied Plotinus Poe St. John of the Cross[2] telepathy and bop kaballah[3]
    because the cosmos instinctively vibrated at their feet in Kansas,

who loned it through the streets of Idaho seeking visionary indian angels
    who were visionary indian angels,   25

who thought they were only mad when Baltimore gleamed in supernatural
    ecstasy,

who jumped in limousines with the Chinaman of Oklahoma on the impulse
    of winter midnight streetlight smalltown rain,

who lounged hungry and lonesome through Houston seeking jazz or sex or
    soup, and followed the brilliant Spaniard to converse about America
    and Eternity, a hopeless task, and so took ship to Africa,

who disappeared into the volcanoes of Mexico leaving behind nothing but
    the shadow of dungarees and the lava and ash of poetry scattered in
    fireplace Chicago,

who reappeared on the West Coast investigating the FBI in beards and
    shorts with big pacifist eyes sexy in their dark skin passing out
    incomprehensible leaflets,   30

who burned cigarette holes in their arms protesting the narcotic tobacco
    haze of Capitalism,

who distributed Supercommunist pamphlets in Union Square weeping and
    undressing while the sirens of Los Alamos[4] wailed them down, and
    wailed down Wall,[5] and the Staten Island ferry also wailed,

who broke down crying in white gymnasiums naked and trembling before
    the machinery of other skeletons,

who bit detectives in the neck and shrieked with delight in policecars for
    committing no crime but their own wild cooking pederasty and
    intoxication,

who howled on their knees in the subway and were dragged off the roof
    waving genitals and manuscripts,   35

who let themselves be fucked in the ass by saintly motorcyclists, and
    screamed with joy,

who blew and were blown by those human seraphim, the sailors, caresses
    of Atlantic and Caribbean love,

who balled in the morning in the evenings in rosegardens and the grass of
    public parks and cemeteries scattering their semen freely to whomever
    come who may,

1. African and Asian sources of drugs.
2. Spanish visionary and poet (1542–1591), author of *The Dark Night of the Soul*. Plotinus (205–270), visionary Roman philosopher. Edgar Allan Poe (1809–1849), American poet and author of supernatural tales.
3. A mystical tradition of interpreting Hebrew scripture. "Bop": jazz style of the 1940s.
4. New Mexico center for the development of the atomic bomb. In New York in the 1930s Union Square was a gathering place for radical speakers.
5. Wall Street; but also alludes to the Wailing Wall, a place of public lamentation and prayer in Jerusalem.

who hiccupped endlessly trying to giggle but wound up with a sob behind a
partition in a Turkish Bath when the blonde & naked angel came to
pierce them with a sword,[6]

who lost their loveboys to the three old shrews of fate[7] the one eyed shrew
of the heterosexual dollar the one eyed shrew that winks out of the
womb and the one eyed shrew that does nothing but sit on her ass and
snip the intellectual golden threads of the craftsman's loom,   40

who copulated ecstatic and insatiate with a bottle of beer a sweetheart a
package of cigarettes a candle and fell off the bed, and continued
along the floor and down the hall and ended fainting on the wall with
a vision of ultimate cunt and come eluding the last gyzym of
consciousness,

who sweetened the snatches of a million girls trembling in the sunset, and
were red eyed in the morning but prepared to sweeten the snatch of
the sunrise, flashing buttocks under barns and naked in the lake,

who went out whoring through Colorado in myriad stolen nightcars, N.C.,[8]
secret hero of these poems, cocksman and Adonis of Denver—joy to
the memory of his innumerable lays of girls in empty lots & diner
backyards, moviehouses' rickety rows, on mountaintops in caves or
with gaunt waitresses in familiar roadside lonely petticoat upliftings &
especially secret gas-station solipsisms of johns, & hometown alleys
too,

who faded out in vast sordid movies, were shifted in dreams, woke on a
sudden Manhattan, and picked themselves up out of basements
hungover with heartless Tokay[9] and horrors of Third Avenue iron
dreams & stumbled to unemployment offices,

who walked all night with their shoes full of blood on the snowbank docks
waiting for a door in the East River to open to a room full of steamheat
and opium,   45

who created great suicidal dramas on the apartment cliff-banks of the
Hudson under the wartime blue floodlight of the moon & their heads
shall be crowned with laurel in oblivion,

who ate the lamb stew of the imagination or digested the crab at the muddy
bottom of the rivers of Bowery,[1]

who wept at the romance of the streets with their pushcarts full of onions
and bad music,

who sat in boxes breathing in the darkness under the bridge, and rose up to
build harpsichords in their lofts,

who coughed on the sixth floor of Harlem crowned with flame under the
tubercular sky surrounded by orange crates of theology,   50

who scribbled all night rocking and rolling over lofty incantations which
in the yellow morning were stanzas of gibberish,

who cooked rotten animals lung heart feet tail borsht & tortillas dreaming
of the pure vegetable kingdom,

who plunged themselves under meat trucks looking for an egg,

---

6. An allusion to *The Ecstasy of St. Teresa*, a
sculpture by Lorenzo Bernini (1598–1680) based
on St. Teresa of Ávila's (1515–1582) distinctly
erotic description of a religious vision.
7. In Greek mythology, goddesses who determine
a mortal's life by spinning out a length of thread
and cutting it at the time of death.

8. Neal Cassady, hip companion of Jack Kerouac and the original Dean Moriarty, one of the
leading figures in *On the Road*.
9. A naturally sweet wine made in Hungary.
1. Southern extension of Third Avenue in New
York City; traditional haunt of derelicts and
alcoholics.

who threw their watches off the roof to cast their ballot for Eternity outside
    of Time, & alarm clocks fell on their heads every day for the next
    decade,
who cut their wrists three times successively unsuccessfully, gave up and
    were forced to open antique stores where they thought they were
    growing old and cried,   55
who were burned alive in their innocent flannel suits on Madison Avenue[2]
    amid blasts of leaden verse & the tanked-up clatter of the iron
    regiments of fashion & the nitroglycerine shrieks of the fairies of
    advertising & the mustard gas of sinister intelligent editors, or were
    run down by the drunken taxicabs of Absolute Reality,
who jumped off the Brooklyn Bridge this actually happened and walked
    away unknown and forgotten into the ghostly daze of Chinatown soup
    alleyways & firetrucks, not even one free beer,
who sang out of their windows in despair, fell out of the subway window,
    jumped in the filthy Passaic,[3] leaped on negroes, cried all over the
    street, danced on broken wineglasses barefoot smashed phonograph
    records of nostalgic European 1930's German jazz finished the
    whiskey and threw up groaning into the bloody toilet, moans in their
    ears and the blast of colossal steamwhistles,
who barreled down the highways of the past journeying to each other's
    hotrod-Golgotha[4] jail-solitude watch or Birmingham jazz incarnation,
who drove crosscountry seventytwo hours to find out if I had a vision or you
    had a vision or he had a vision to find out Eternity,   60
who journeyed to Denver, who died in Denver, who came back to Denver &
    waited in vain, who watched over Denver & brooded & loned in
    Denver and finally went away to find out the Time, & now Denver is
    lonesome for her heroes,
who fell on their knees in hopeless cathedrals praying for each other's
    salvation and light and breasts, until the soul illuminated its hair for a
    second,
who crashed through their minds in jail waiting for impossible criminals
    with golden heads and the charm of reality in their hearts who sang
    sweet blues to Alcatraz,
who retired to Mexico to cultivate a habit, or Rocky Mount to tender
    Buddha or Tangiers to boys or Southern Pacific to the black
    locomotive or Harvard to Narcissus to Woodlawn[5] to the daisychain or
    grave,
who demanded sanity trials accusing the radio of hypnotism & were left
    with their insanity & their hands & a hung jury,   65
who threw potato salad at CCNY lecturers on Dadaism[6] and subsequently
    presented themselves on the granite steps of the madhouse with
    shaven heads and harlequin speech of suicide, demanding
    instantaneous lobotomy,

---

2. Center of New York advertising agencies.
3. River flowing past Paterson, New Jersey.
4. The place just outside the walls of Jerusalem where Jesus was believed to have been crucified; also known as Calvary.
5. A cemetery in the Bronx. The Southern Pacific is a railroad company. The references in

this line are to the lives of Kerouac, Cassady, and William Burroughs (an author and fellow Beat).
6. Artistic cult of absurdity (c. 1916–20). "CCNY": City College of New York. This and the following incidents probably derived from the "apocryphal history of my adventures" related by Solomon to Ginsberg.

and who were given instead the concrete void of insulin metrasol electricity
hydrotherapy psychotherapy occupational therapy pingpong &
amnesia,
who in humorless protest overturned only one symbolic pingpong table,
resting briefly in catatonia,
returning years later truly bald except for a wig of blood, and tears and
fingers, to the visible madman doom of the wards of the madtowns of
the East,
Pilgrim State's Rockland's and Greystone's[7] foetid halls, bickering with the
echoes of the soul, rocking and rolling in the midnight solitude-bench
dolmen-realms of love, dream of life a nightmare, bodies turned to
stone as heavy as the moon,   70
with mother finally*******, and the last fantastic book flung out of the
tenement window, and the last door closed at 4 AM and the last
telephone slammed at the wall in reply and the last furnished room
emptied down to the last piece of mental furniture, a yellow paper rose
twisted on a wire hanger in the closet, and even that imaginary,
nothing but a hopeful little bit of hallucination—
ah, Carl,[8] while you are not safe I am not safe, and now you're really in the
total animal soup of time—
and who therefore ran through the icy streets obsessed with a sudden flash
of the alchemy of the use of the ellipse the catalog the meter & the
vibrating plane,
who dreamt and made incarnate gaps in Time & Space through images
juxtaposed, and trapped the archangel of the soul between 2 visual
images and joined the elemental verbs and set the noun and dash of
consciousness together jumping with sensation of Pater Omnipotens
Aeterna Deus[9]
to recreate the syntax and measure of poor human prose and stand before
you speechless and intelligent and shaking with shame, rejected yet
confessing out the soul to conform to the rhythm of thought in his
naked and endless head,   75
the madman bum and angel beat in Time, unknown, yet putting down
here what might be left to say in time come after death,
and rose reincarnate in the ghostly clothes of jazz in the goldhorn shadow
of the band and blew the suffering of America's naked mind for love
into an eli eli lamma lamma sabacthani[1] saxophone cry that shivered
the cities down to the last radio
with the absolute heart of the poem of life butchered out of their own
bodies good to eat a thousand years.

II

What sphinx of cement and aluminum bashed open their skulls and ate up
their brains and imagination?

7. Three psychiatric hospitals near New York.
Solomon was institutionalized at Pilgrim State
and Rockland; Ginsberg's mother, Naomi, was
permanently institutionalized at Greystone after
years of suffering hallucinations and paranoid
attacks. She died there in 1956, the year after
Howl was written.
8. Solomon.
9. All-Powerful Father, Eternal God (Latin). An
allusion to a phrase used by the French painter
Paul Cézanne (1839–1906), in a 1904 letter
describing the effects of nature. In an interview,
Ginsberg compared his own method of sharply
juxtaposed images with Cézanne's foreshorten-
ing of perspective in landscape painting.
1. Christ's last words on the Cross: My God, my
God, why have you forsaken me? (Aramaic).

Moloch![2] Solitude! Filth! Ugliness! Ashcans and unobtainable dollars!
Children screaming under the stairways! Boys sobbing in armies! Old
men weeping in the parks! 80
Moloch! Moloch! Nightmare of Moloch! Moloch the loveless! Mental
Moloch! Moloch the heavy judger of men!
Moloch the incomprehensible prison! Moloch the crossbone soulless
jailhouse and Congress of sorrows! Moloch whose buildings are
judgment! Moloch the vast stone of war! Moloch the stunned
governments!
Moloch whose mind is pure machinery! Moloch whose blood is running
money! Moloch whose fingers are ten armies! Moloch whose breast is
a cannibal dynamo! Moloch whose ear is a smoking tomb!
Moloch whose eyes are a thousand blind windows! Moloch whose
skyscrapers stand in the long streets like endless Jehovahs! Moloch
whose factories dream and croak in the fog! Moloch whose
smokestacks and antennae crown the cities!
Moloch whose love is endless oil and stone! Moloch whose soul is
electricity and banks! Moloch whose poverty is the specter of genius!
Moloch whose fate is a cloud of sexless hydrogen! Moloch whose
name is the Mind! 85
Moloch in whom I sit lonely! Moloch in whom I dream Angels! Crazy in
Moloch! Cocksucker in Moloch! Lacklove and manless in Moloch!
Moloch who entered my soul early! Moloch in whom I am a consciousness
without a body! Moloch who frightened me out of my natural ecstasy!
Moloch whom I abandon! Wake up in Moloch! Light streaming out of
the sky!
Moloch! Moloch! Robot apartments! invisible suburbs! skeleton treasuries!
blind capitals! demonic industries! spectral nations! invincible
madhouses! granite cocks! monstrous bombs!
They broke their backs lifting Moloch to Heaven! Pavements, trees, radios,
tons! lifting the city to Heaven which exists and is everywhere about
us!
Visions! omens! hallucinations! miracles! ecstasies! gone down the Ameri-
can river! 90
Dreams! adorations! illuminations! religions! the whole boatload of
sensitive bullshit!
Breakthroughs! over the river! flips and crucifixions! gone down the flood!
Highs! Epiphanies! Despairs! Ten years' animal screams and suicides!
Minds! New loves! Mad generation! down on the rocks of Time!
Real holy laughter in the river! They saw it all! the wild eyes! the holy yells!
They bade farewell! They jumped off the roof! to solitude! waving!
carrying flowers! Down to the river! into the street!

III

Carl Solomon! I'm with you in Rockland
where you're madder than I am 95
I'm with you in Rockland
where you must feel very strange

2. Ginsberg's own annotation in the facsimile edition of the poem reads: "'Moloch': or Molech, the
Canaanite fire god, whose worship was marked by
parents' burning their children as proprietary sacrifice. 'And thou shalt not let any of thy seed pass
through the fire to Molech' [Leviticus 18:21]."

I'm with you in Rockland
 where you imitate the shade of my mother
I'm with you in Rockland   100
 where you've murdered your twelve secretaries
I'm with you in Rockland
 where you laugh at this invisible humor
I'm with you in Rockland
 where we are great writers on the same dreadful typewriter   105
I'm with you in Rockland
 where your condition has become serious and is reported on the radio
I'm with you in Rockland
 where the faculties of the skull no longer admit the worms of the
 senses
I'm with you in Rockland   110
 where you drink the tea of the breasts of the spinsters of Utica[3]
I'm with you in Rockland
 where you pun on the bodies of your nurses the harpies of the Bronx
I'm with you in Rockland
 where you scream in a straightjacket that you're losing the game of
 the actual pingpong of the abyss   115
I'm with you in Rockland
 where you bang on the catatonic piano the soul is innocent and
 immortal it should never die ungodly in an armed madhouse
I'm with you in Rockland
 where fifty more shocks will never return your soul to its body again
 from its pilgrimage to a cross in the void
I'm with you in Rockland   120
 where you accuse your doctors of insanity and plot the Hebrew
 socialist revolution against the fascist national Golgotha
I'm with you in Rockland
 where you will split the heavens of Long Island and resurrect your
 living human Jesus from the superhuman tomb
I'm with you in Rockland
 where there are twenty five thousand mad comrades all together
 singing the final stanzas of the Internationale[4]   125
I'm with you in Rockland
 where we hug and kiss the United States under our bedsheets the
 United States that coughs all night and won't let us sleep
I'm with you in Rockland
 where we wake up electrified out of the coma by our own souls'
 airplanes roaring over the roof they've come to drop angelic bombs
 the hospital illuminates itself   imaginary walls collapse   O skinny
 legions run outside   O starry-spangled shock of mercy the eternal
 war is here   O victory forget your underwear we're free
I'm with you in Rockland   130
 in my dreams you walk dripping from a sea-journey on the highway
 across America in tears to the door of my cottage in the Western night

San Francisco, 1955–56   1956

---

3. Town in central New York.
4. Former socialist and Communist song; the official Soviet anthem until 1944.

Footnote to Howl

Holy ! Holy ! Holy ! Holy ! Holy ! Holy ! Holy ! Holy ! Holy ! Holy ! Holy !
    Holy ! Holy ! Holy ! Holy !
The world is holy ! The soul is holy ! The skin is holy ! The nose is holy !
    The tongue and cock and hand and asshole holy !
Everything is holy ! everybody's holy ! everywhere is holy ! everyday is in
    eternity ! Everyman's an angel !
The bum's as holy as the seraphim ! the madman is holy as you my soul are
    holy !
The typewriter is holy the poem is holy the voice is holy the hearers are
    holy the ecstasy is holy !   5
Holy Peter holy Allen holy Solomon holy Lucien holy Kerouac holy Huncke
    holy Burroughs holy Cassady[1] holy the unknown buggered and
    suffering beggars holy the hideous human angels !
Holy my mother in the insane asylum ! Holy the cocks of the grandfathers
    of Kansas !
Holy the groaning saxophone ! Holy the bop apocalypse ! Holy the
    jazzbands marijuana hipsters peace & junk & drums !
Holy the solitudes of skyscrapers and pavements ! Holy the cafeterias filled
    with the millions ! Holy the mysterious rivers of tears under the
    streets !
Holy the lone juggernaut ! Holy the vast lamb of the middle-class ! Holy the
    crazy shepherds of rebellion ! Who digs Los Angeles IS Los Angeles !   10
Holy New York Holy San Francisco Holy Peoria & Seattle Holy Paris Holy
    Tangiers Holy Moscow Holy Istanbul !
Holy time in eternity holy eternity in time holy the clocks in space holy the
    fourth dimension holy the fifth International holy the Angel in
    Moloch !

1955–56   1956, 1959

A Supermarket in California

What thoughts I have of you tonight, Walt Whitman,[1] for I walked down
the sidestreets under the trees with a headache self-conscious looking at
the full moon.
    In my hungry fatigue, and shopping for images, I went into the neon
fruit supermarket, dreaming of your enumerations!

1. All the figures mentioned here are Americans who shared or inspired a literary bohemia of the time. "Peter": Peter Orlovsky (1933–2010), Beat poet and Ginsberg's partner for four decades. "Allen": Ginsberg. "Solomon": Carl Solomon (1928–1993), whom Ginsberg met at the psychiatric hospital where Ginsberg's mother was being treated and to whom Ginsberg dedicated "Howl." "Lucien": Lucien Carr (1923–2005), one of the Beats and Ginsberg's roommate at Columbia University in the 1940s. "Kerouac": Jack Kerouac (1922–1969), novelist and founding figure of the Beat generation. "Huncke": Herbert Huncke (1915–1996), writer who influenced Ginsberg and who introduced Ginsberg and Kerouac to the term "beat." "Burroughs": William Burroughs (1914–1997), writer, spoken-word performer, and social critic most famous for the novel *Naked Lunch* (1959). "Cassady": Neal Cassady (1926–1968), an icon of the Beat generation and the inspiration for the character Dean Moriarty in Kerouac's best-known work, *On the Road* (1957).
1. American poet (1819–1892), author of *Leaves of Grass*, against whose homosexuality and vision of American plenty Ginsberg measures himself.

What peaches and what penumbras![2] Whole families shopping at night!
Aisles full of husbands! Wives in the avocados, babies in the tomatoes!—
and you, Garcia Lorca,[3] what were you doing down by the watermelons?

I saw you, Walt Whitman, childless, lonely old grubber, poking among
the meats in the refrigerator and eyeing the grocery boys.
I heard you asking questions of each: Who killed the pork chops? What
price bananas? Are you my Angel?   5
I wandered in and out of the brilliant stacks of cans following you, and
followed in my imagination by the store detective.
We strode down the open corridors together in our solitary fancy tasting
artichokes, possessing every frozen delicacy, and never passing the cashier.

Where are we going, Walt Whitman? The doors close in an hour. Which
way does your beard point tonight?
(I touch your book and dream of our odyssey in the supermarket and
feel absurd.)
Will we walk all night through solitary streets? The trees add shade to
shade, lights out in the houses, we'll both be lonely.   10

Will we stroll dreaming of the lost America of love past blue automobiles in driveways, home to our silent cottage?
Ah, dear father, graybeard, lonely old courage-teacher, what America
did you have when Charon quit poling his ferry and you got out on a
smoking bank and stood watching the boat disappear on the black waters
of Lethe?[4]

Berkeley, 1955   1956

2. Partial shadows.
3. Federico García Lorca (1898–1936), Spanish
poet and dramatist and author of "A Poet in New
York," whose work is characterized by surrealist
and homoerotic inspiration.
4. Forgetfulness. In Greek mythology, one of the
rivers of Hades, the Underworld. Charon was
the boatman who ferried the dead to Hades.

JOHN ASHBERY
1927–2017

John Ashbery described his writing this way: "I think that any one of my poems
might be considered to be a snapshot of whatever is going on in my mind at the
time—first of all the desire to write a poem, after that wondering if I've left the
oven on or thinking about where I must be in the next hour." Ashbery developed a
style hospitable to quicksilver changes in tone and attention. His work often moves
freely between different modes of discourse, between a language of popular culture and commonplace experience and a heightened rhetoric often associated with
poetic vision. Ashbery's poems show an awareness of the various linguistic codes
(including clichés and conventional public speech) by which we live and through

which we define ourselves. This awareness includes an interest in what he called "prose voices," and he often wrote in a way that challenges the supposed boundaries between poetry and prose.

Ashbery's poetry was not always so open to contradictory notions and impulses. His early books rejected the mere surfaces of realism and the momentary in order to get at "remoter areas of consciousness." The protagonist of "Illustration" (from his first book, *Some Trees*) is a cheerful nun about to leave behind the irrelevancies of the world by leaping from a skyscraper. Her act implies "Much that is beautiful must be discarded / So that we may resemble a taller / impression of ourselves." To reach the "remoter areas of consciousness," Ashbery tried various technical experiments. He used highly patterned forms such as the sestina in "Some Trees" and "The Tennis Court Oath" (1962) not with any show of mechanical brilliance but to explore: "I once told somebody that writing a sestina was rather like riding downhill on a bicycle and having the pedals push your feet. I wanted my feet to be pushed into places they wouldn't normally have taken."

Ashbery was born in Rochester, New York. He attended Deerfield Academy and Harvard, from which he graduated in 1949. He received an M.A. in English from Columbia in 1951. After a preliminary stay in France as a Fulbright scholar, he returned in 1958 for eight years and was art critic for the European edition of the *New York Herald Tribune* and reported the European shows and exhibitions for *Art News* and *Arts International*. He returned to New York in 1965 to be executive editor of *Art News*, a position he held until 1972. He taught creative writing at Brooklyn College, Bard College, Wesleyan University, and other institutions over his long career.

Ashbery's interest in art played a formative role in his poetry. He is often associated with Frank O'Hara, James Schuyler, and Kenneth Koch as part of the "New York school" of poets. The name refers to their common interest in the New York school of abstract painters of the 1940s and 1950s, some of whose techniques they wished to adapt to poetry. These painters avoided realism in order to stress the work of art as a representation of the creative act that produced it—as in the action paintings of Jackson Pollock. Ashbery's long poem *Self-Portrait in a Convex Mirror* gives as much attention to the rapidly changing feelings of the poet in the act of writing his poem as it does to the Renaissance painting that inspired him. The poem moves back and forth between the distracted energies that feed a work of art and the completed composition, which the artist feels as both a triumph and a falsification of complex feelings. Ashbery shares with O'Hara a sense of the colloquial brilliance of daily life in New York and sets this in tension with the concentration and stasis of art.

Ashbery published prolifically after his first collection, *Self-Portrait in a Convex Mirror*, appeared in 1975. His important book-length poem, *Flow Chart*, appeared in 1991. His entertaining and provocative *Other Traditions* (2000) is a collection of his Norton Lectures on poetry at Harvard. Ashbery's work, especially his earlier, more highly experimental poems, was particularly influential for a younger generation identified as "Language" poets, such as Charles Bernstein, Lyn Hejinian, and Susan Howe. They were attracted to the linguistic playfulness of Ashbery's poetry and to its resistance to being read as a single, personal voice. Exposing and sometimes breaking through the world's dominant uses of language, Ashbery's poems open new possibilities of meaning: "We are all talkers / It is true, but underneath the talk lies / The moving and not wanting to be moved, the loose / Meaning, untidy and simple like the threshing floor" ("Soonest Mended").

Illustration

I

A novice[1] was sitting on a cornice
High over the city. Angels

Combined their prayers with those
Of the police, begging her to come off it.

One lady promised to be her friend.   5
"I do not want a friend," she said.

A mother offered her some nylons
Stripped from her very legs. Others brought

Little offerings of fruit and candy,
The blind man all his flowers. If any   10

Could be called successful, these were,
For that the scene should be a ceremony

Was what she wanted. "I desire
Monuments," she said. "I want to move

Figuratively, as waves caress   15
The thoughtless shore. You people I know

Will offer me every good thing
I do not want. But please remember

I died accepting them." With that, the wind
Unpinned her bulky robes, and naked   20

As a roc's[2] egg, she drifted softly downward
Out of the angels' tenderness and the minds of men.

II

Much that is beautiful must be discarded
So that we may resemble a taller

Impression of ourselves. Moths climb in the flame,   25
Alas, that wish only to be the flame:

They do not lessen our stature.
We twinkle under the weight

---

1. Student in the first stage of instruction to be a nun.
2. Legendary bird of prey.

Of indiscretions. But how could we tell
That of the truth we know, she was   30

The somber vestment? For that night, rockets sighed
Elegantly over the city, and there was feasting:

There is so much in that moment!
So many attitudes toward that flame,

We might have soared from earth, watching her glide   35
Aloft, in her peplum[3] of bright leaves.

But she, of course, was only an effigy
Of indifference, a miracle

Not meant for us, as the leaves are not
Winter's because it is the end.   40

                                                                   1956

Soonest Mended

Barely tolerated, living on the margin
In our technological society, we were always having to be rescued
On the brink of destruction, like heroines in *Orlando Furioso*[1]
Before it was time to start all over again.
There would be thunder in the bushes, a rustling of coils,   5
And Angelica, in the Ingres painting,[2] was considering
The colorful but small monster near her toe, as though wondering
      whether forgetting
The whole thing might not, in the end, be the only solution.
And then there always came a time when
Happy Hooligan[3] in his rusted green automobile   10
Came plowing down the course, just to make sure everything was O.K.,
Only by that time we were in another chapter and confused
About how to receive this latest piece of information.
Was it information? Weren't we rather acting this out
For someone else's benefit, thoughts in a mind   15
With room enough and to spare for our little problems (so they began
      to seem),
Our daily quandary about food and the rent and bills to be paid?
To reduce all this to a small variant,
To step free at last, minuscule on the gigantic plateau—
This was our ambition: to be small and clear and free.   20
Alas, the summer's energy wanes quickly.

3. In ancient Greece, a drapery about the upper
part of the body.
1. Fantastical epic poem by Ludovico Ariosto
(1474–1533), whose romantic heroine Angelica
is constantly being rescued from imminent perils such as monsters and storms at sea.

2. *Roger Delivering Angelica* (1819), a painting
based on a scene from Ariosto, by French artist
Jean-Auguste-Dominique Ingres (1780–1867).
3. The good-natured, simple title character of a
popular comic strip of the 1920s and 1930s.

A moment and it is gone. And no longer
May we make the necessary arrangements, simple as they are.
Our star was brighter perhaps when it had water in it.
Now there is no question even of that, but only   25
Of holding on to the hard earth so as not to get thrown off,
With an occasional dream, a vision: a robin flies across
The upper corner of the window, you brush your hair away
And cannot quite see, or a wound will flash
Against the sweet faces of the others, something like: 30
This is what you wanted to hear, so why
Did you think of listening to something else? We are all talkers
It is true, but underneath the talk lies
The moving and not wanting to be moved, the loose
Meaning, untidy and simple like a threshing floor.[4]   35

These then were some hazards of the course,
Yet though we knew the course *was* hazards and nothing else
It was still a shock when, almost a quarter of a century later,
The clarity of the rules dawned on you for the first time.
They were the players, and we who had struggled at the game   40
Were merely spectators, though subject to its vicissitudes
And moving with it out of the tearful stadium, borne on shoulders,
        at last.
Night after night this message returns, repeated
In the flickering bulbs of the sky, raised past us, taken away from us,
Yet ours over and over until the end that is past truth,   45
The being of our sentences, in the climate that fostered them,
Not ours to own, like a book, but to be with, and sometimes
To be without, alone and desperate.
But the fantasy makes it ours, a kind of fence-sitting
Raised to the level of an esthetic ideal. These were moments, years,   50
Solid with reality, faces, namable events, kisses, heroic acts,
But like the friendly beginning of a geometrical progression
Not too reassuring, as though meaning could be cast aside some day
When it had been outgrown. Better, you said, to stay cowering
Like this in the early lessons, since the promise of learning   55
Is a delusion, and I agreed, adding that
Tomorrow would alter the sense of what had already been learned,
That the learning process is extended in this way, so that from this
        standpoint
None of us ever graduates from college,
For time is an emulsion,[5] and probably thinking not to grow up   60
Is the brightest kind of maturity for us, right now at any rate.
And you see, both of us were right, though nothing
Has somehow come to nothing; the avatars[6]
Of our conforming to the rules and living
Around the home have made—well, in a sense, "good citizens" of us,   65
Brushing the teeth and all that, and learning to accept
The charity of the hard moments as they are doled out,

4. Used at harvest time to separate the wheat
from the chaff, which is to be discarded.
5. A chemical solution in which the particles of

one liquid are suspended in another.
6. Incarnations.

For this is action, this not being sure, this careless
Preparing, sowing the seeds crooked in the furrow,
Making ready to forget, and always coming back   70
To the mooring of starting out, that day so long ago.

1970

Myrtle

How funny your name would be
if you could follow it back to where
the first person thought of saying it,
naming himself that, or maybe
some other persons thought of it   5
and named that person. It would
be like following a river to its source,
which would be impossible. Rivers have no source.
They just automatically appear at a place
where they get wider, and soon a real   10
river comes along, with fish and debris,
regal as you please, and someone
has already given it a name: St. Benno[1]
(saints are popular for this purpose) or, or
some other name, the name of his   15
long-lost girlfriend, who comes
at long last to impersonate that river,
on a stage, her voice clanking
like its bed, her clothing of sand
and pasted paper, a piece of real technology,   20
while all along she is thinking, I can
do what I want to do. But I want to stay here.

1996

1. St. Benno of Meissen (1010–1106), patron of angling.

ANNE SEXTON
1928–1974

Anne Sexton's first book of poems, *To Bedlam and Part Way Back* (1960), was published at a time when the label "confessional" came to be attached to poems more frankly autobiographical than had been usual in American verse. For Sexton the term is particularly apt. Although she had abandoned the Roman Catholicism into which she was born, her poems enact something analogous to preparing for and receiving religious absolution.

Sexton's confessions were to be made in terms more startling than the traditional Catholic images of her childhood. The purpose of her poems was not to analyze or explain behavior but to make it palpable in all its ferocity of feeling. Poetry "should be a shock to the senses. It should also hurt." This is apparent in both her themes and the ways in which she exhibits her subjects. Sexton writes about sex, illegitimacy, guilt, madness, and suicide. *To Bedlam* portrays her breakdown, her time in a mental hospital, her efforts at reconciliation with her daughter and husband when she returns. Her second book, *All My Pretty Ones* (1962), takes its title from Shakespeare's *Macbeth* and refers to the deaths of both her parents within three months of one another. Later books—*Live or Die* (1966), *The Death Notebooks* (1974), and *The Awful Rowing toward God* (1975; posthumous)—act out a debate about suicide and prefigure Sexton's taking of her own life. And yet, as the poet's tender address to her daughter in "Little Girl, My String Bean, My Lovely Woman" suggests, Sexton's work ranges beyond an obsession with death.

Sexton spoke of images as "the heart of poetry. Images come from the unconscious. Imagination and the unconscious are one and the same." Powerful images substantiate the strangeness of feelings and through them the poet attempts to redefine experiences so as to gain understanding, absolution, or revenge. Sexton's poems, poised between, as her titles suggest, life and death or "bedlam and part way back," are efforts at establishing a middle ground of self-assertion, substituting surreal images for the reductive versions of life visible to the exterior eye.

Sexton was born in 1928 in Newton, Massachusetts, and attended Garland Junior College. She came to poetry fairly late—when she was twenty-eight, after seeing the critic I. A. Richards lecturing about the sonnet on television. In the late 1950s she attended poetry workshops in the Boston area, including Robert Lowell's poetry seminars at Boston University. One of her fellow students was Sylvia Plath, whose suicide she commemorated in a poem, "Sylvia's Death." Sexton claimed that she was less influenced by Lowell's *Life Studies* than by W. D. Snodgrass's autobiographical *Heart's Needle* (1959), but certainly Lowell's support and the association with Plath left their mark on her and made it possible for her to publish. Although her career was relatively brief, she received several major literary prizes, including the Pulitzer Prize for *Live or Die* and an American Academy of Arts and Letters traveling fellowship. Her suicide came after a series of mental breakdowns.

The Starry Night

That does not keep me from having a terrible
need of—shall I say the word—religion.
Then I go out at night to paint the stars.
—Vincent Van Gogh[1]
in a letter to his brother

The town does not exist
except where one black-haired tree slips
up like a drowned woman into the hot sky.
The town is silent. The night boils with eleven stars.
Oh starry starry night! This is how   5
I want to die.

---

1. Dutch painter (1853–1890) who in his thirties committed suicide. This letter to his brother—his only confidant—was written in September 1888. At the time he was painting *Starry Night on the Rhône*.

It moves. They are all alive.
Even the moon bulges in its orange irons
to push children, like a god, from its eye.
The old unseen serpent swallows up the stars.   10
Oh starry starry night! This is how
I want to die:

into that rushing beast of the night,
sucked up by that great dragon, to split
from my life with no flag,   15
no belly,
no cry.

                                                          1962

Sylvia's Death

for Sylvia Plath[1]

Oh Sylvia, Sylvia,
with a dead box of stones and spoons,

with two children, two meteors
wandering loose in the tiny playroom,

with your mouth into the sheet,   5
into the roofbeam, into the dumb prayer,

(Sylvia, Sylvia,
where did you go
after you wrote me
from Devonshire   10
about raising potatoes
and keeping bees?)

what did you stand by,
just how did you lie down into?

Thief!—   15
how did you crawl into,

crawl down alone
into the death I wanted so badly and for so long,

the death we said we both outgrew,
the one we wore on our skinny breasts,   20

---

1. American poet (1932–1963) and friend of Sexton's who committed suicide. Plath was living in
England with her children, having separated from her husband, the poet Ted Hughes.

the one we talked of so often each time
we downed three extra dry martinis in Boston,

the death that talked of analysts and cures,
the death that talked like brides with plots,

the death we drank to,   25
the motives and then the quiet deed?

(In Boston
the dying
ride in cabs,
yes death again,   30
that ride home
with *our* boy.)

O Sylvia, I remember the sleepy drummer
who beat on our eyes with an old story,

how we wanted to let him come   35
like a sadist or a New York fairy

to do his job,
a necessity, a window in a wall or a crib,

and since that time he waited
under our heart, our cupboard,   40

and I see now that we store him up
year after year, old suicides

and I know at the news of your death,
a terrible taste for it, like salt.

(And me,   45
me too.
And now, Sylvia,
you again
with death again,
that ride home   50
with *our* boy.)

And I say only
with my arms stretched out into that stone place,

what is your death
but an old belonging,   55

a mole that fell out
of one of your poems?

　　　　(O friend,
　　　　while the moon's bad,
　　　　and the king's gone,　　　　　　　　　　　　　　　　60
　　　　and the queen's at her wit's end
　　　　the bar fly ought to sing!)

　　　　O tiny mother,
　　　　you too!
　　　　O funny duchess!　　　　　　　　　　　　　　　　65
　　　　O blonde thing!

February 17, 1963　　　　　　　　　　　　　　　　　　　1966

Little Girl, My String Bean, My Lovely Woman

My daughter, at eleven
(almost twelve), is like a garden.

Oh darling! Born in that sweet birthday suit
and having owned it and known it for so long,
now you must watch high noon enter—　　　　　　　　5
noon, that ghost hour.
Oh, funny little girl—this one under a blueberry sky,
this one! How can I say that I've known
just what you know and just where you are?

It's not a strange place, this odd home　　　　　　　10
where your face sits in my hand
so full of distance,
so full of its immediate fever.
The summer has seized you,
as when, last month in Amalfi,[1] I saw　　　　　　　15
lemons as large as your desk-side globe—
that miniature map of the world—
and I could mention, too,
the market stalls of mushrooms
and garlic buds all engorged.　　　　　　　　　　　　20
Or I think even of the orchard next door,
where the berries are done
and the apples are beginning to swell.
And once, with our first backyard,
I remember I planted an acre of yellow beans　　　　25
we couldn't eat.

Oh, little girl,
my stringbean,
how do you grow?
You grow this way.　　　　　　　　　　　　　　　30
You are too many to eat.

---

1. A seaport town in Campania, Italy.

I hear
as in a dream
the conversation of the old wives
speaking of *womanhood*.   35
I remember that I heard nothing myself.
I was alone.
I waited like a target.

Let high noon enter—
the hour of the ghosts.   40
Once the Romans believed
that noon was the ghost hour,
and I can believe it, too,
under that startling sun,
and someday they will come to you,   45
someday, men bare to the waist, young Romans
at noon where they belong,
with ladders and hammers
while no one sleeps.

But before they enter   50
I will have said,
Your bones are lovely,
and before their strange hands
there was always this hand that formed.

Oh, darling, let your body in,   55
let it tie you in,
in comfort.
What I want to say, Linda,
is that women are born twice.

If I could have watched you grow   60
as a magical mother might,
if I could have seen through my magical transparent belly,
there would have been such ripening within:
your embryo,
the seed taking on its own,   65
life clapping the bedpost,
bones from the pond,
thumbs and two mysterious eyes,
the awfully human head,
the heart jumping like a puppy,   70
the important lungs,
the becoming—
while it becomes!
as it does now,
a world of its own,   75
a delicate place.

I say hello
to such shakes and knockings and high jinks,
such music, such sprouts,

such dancing-mad-bears of music,   80
such necessary sugar,
such goings-on!

Oh, little girl,
my stringbean,
how do you grow?   85
You grow this way.
You are too many to eat.

What I want to say, Linda,
is that there is nothing in your body that lies.
All that is new is telling the truth.   90
I'm here, that somebody else,
an old tree in the background.

Darling,
stand still at your door,
sure of yourself, a white stone, a good stone—   95
as exceptional as laughter
you will strike fire,
that new thing!

July 14, 1964   1966

ADRIENNE RICH
1929–2012

A childhood of reading and hearing poems taught Adrienne Rich to love the sound of words; her adult life taught her that poetry must "consciously situate itself amid political conditions." Over the years she conducted a passionate struggle to honor these parts of herself, in her best poems brilliantly mixing what she called "the poetry of the actual world with the poetry of sound." Extending a dialogue—between art and politics—that she first discovered in W. B. Yeats, whose poems she read as an undergraduate at Radcliffe, her work addresses with particular power the experiences of women, experiences often omitted from history and misrepresented in literature. Our culture, she believes, is "split at the root" (to adapt the title of one of her essays); art is separated from politics, and the poet's identity as a woman is separated from her art. Rich's work seeks a language that will expose and integrate these divisions in the self and in the world. To do this she wrote "directly and overtly as a woman, out of a woman's body and experience," for "to take women's existence seriously as theme and source for art, was something I had been hungering to do, needing to do, all my writing life."

Rich's first book was published in the Yale Younger Poets series, a prize particularly important for poets of her generation (others in the series have included James Wright, John Ashbery, and W. S. Merwin). W. H. Auden, the judge for the series in the 1950s, said of Rich's volume *A Change of World* (1951) that her poems "were neatly and modestly dressed . . . respect their elders, but are not cowed by them and do not tell fibs." Rich, looking back at that period from the vantage point of 1972, renders a more complicated sense of things. In an influential essay, "When We Dead Awaken," she recalls this period as one in which the chief models for poetry were men; from those models she first learned her craft. Even in reading the poetry of older women writers she found herself "looking . . . for the same things I found in the poetry of men . . . , to be equal was still confused with sounding the same." Twenty years and five volumes after *A Change of World* she published *The Will to Change*, taking its title from the opening line of Charles Olson's *The Kingfishers*: "What does not change / is the will to change." The shift of emphasis in Rich's titles signals an important turn in her work—from acceptance of change as a way of the world to an active sense of change as willed or desired.

In 1953 Rich married and in her twenties gave birth to three children within four years—"a radicalizing experience," she said. It was during this time that Rich experienced most severely that gap between what she calls the "energy of creation" and the "energy of relation. . . . In those early years I always felt the conflict as a failure of love in myself." In her later work Rich came to identify the source of that conflict not as individual but as social, and in 1976 she published a book of prose, *Of Woman Born: Motherhood as Experience and Institution*, in which she contrasts the actual experience of bearing and raising children with the myths fostered by our medical, social, and political institutions.

With her third and fourth books, *Snapshots of a Daughter-in-Law* (1963) and *Necessities of Life* (1966), Rich began explicitly to treat problems that engaged her throughout her writing life. The title poem of *Snapshots* exposes the gap between literary versions of women's experience and the day-to-day truths of their lives.

Rich's poems aim at self-definition, at establishing boundaries of the self, but they also fight off the notion that insights remain solitary and unshared. Many of her poems proceed by means of intimate argument, sometimes with externalized parts of herself, as if to dramatize the way identity forms from the self's movement beyond fixed boundaries. In some of her most powerful later poems she pushes her imagination to recognize the multiple aspects of the self ("My selves," she calls them in her poem "Integrity"); in "Transcendental Etude," she writes: *"I am the lover and the loved, / home and wanderer, she who splits / firewood and she who knocks, a stranger / in the storm."* In other important later poems she carried out a dialogue with lives similar to and different from her own, as in the generous and powerful title poem of her collection *An Atlas of the Difficult World* (1991). As she writes in the essay "Blood, Bread, and Poetry," in her development as a poet she came to feel "more and more urgently the dynamic between poetry as language and poetry as a kind of action, probing, burning, stripping, placing itself in dialogue with others."

After Rich and her husband moved to New York City in 1966 they became increasingly involved in radical politics, especially in the opposition to the Vietnam War. These concerns are reflected in the poems of *Leaflets* (1969) and *The Will to Change* (1971). Along with new subject matter came equally important changes in style. Rich's poems throughout the 1960s moved away from formal verse patterns to more jagged utterance. Devices such as sentence fragments, lines of varying length, and irregular spacing to mark off phrases emphasized a voice of greater urgency. With "Snapshots of a Daughter-in-Law" Rich began dating her poems, as if to mark each one as provisional, true to the moment but an instrument of passage, like an entry in a journal in which feelings are subject to continual revision.

In the 1970s Rich dedicated herself increasingly to feminism. Her work as a poet, a prose writer, and a public speaker took on a new unity and intensity. The continuing task was to see herself—as she put it in 1984—as neither "unique nor universal, but a person in history, a woman and not a man, a white and also Jewish inheritor of a particular Western consciousness, from the making of which most women have been excluded." She says in "Planetarium": "I am an instrument in the shape / of a woman trying to translate pulsations / into images for the relief of the body / and the reconstruction of the mind."

Rich's collections of prose—*Of Woman Born*; *On Lies, Secrets, and Silences: Selected Prose 1966–1978*; *Blood, Bread, and Poetry: Selected Prose 1979–1985*; *What Is Found There: Notebooks on Poetry and Politics* (1993); and *Arts of the Possible* (2001)—provide an important context for her poems. In these works she addresses issues of women's education and their literary traditions, Jewish identity, the relations between poetry and politics, and what she has called "the erasure of lesbian existence." As a young woman Rich had been stirred by James Baldwin's comment that "any real change implies the breakup of the world as one has always known it, the loss of all that gave one an identity, the end of safety." In many ways her essays, like her poems, track the forces that resist such change and the human conditions that require it. Her essay "Compulsory Heterosexuality and Lesbian Existence" is an important example of such an examination.

Although Rich's individual poems do not consistently succeed in expressing a political vision without sacrificing "intensity of language," her work is best read as a continuous process. The books have an air of ongoing, pained investigation, almost scientific in intention but with an ardor suggested by their titles: *The Dream of a Common Language* (1977), *A Wild Patience Has Taken Me This Far* (1981), *The Fact of a Doorframe* (1984), and *Your Native Land, Your Life* (1986). Rich's later books, *Time's Power* (1989), *An Atlas of the Difficult World* (1991), *Dark Fields of the Republic: Poems 1991–1995* (1995), *Midnight Salvage: Poems 1995–1998* (1999), *Fox* (2001), and *The School Among the Ruins* (2004), demonstrate an ongoing power of language and deepening poetic vision. *Telephone Ringing in the Labyrinth* (2007) collects poems from 2004–06. Late in her life, Rich published *A Human Eye: Essays on Art in Society, 1997–2008*, *Tonight No Poetry Will Serve: Poems 2007–2010*, and *Later Poems: Selected and New, 1971–2012*. Reading through her poems we may sometimes wish for more relaxation and playfulness, for a liberating comic sense of self almost never present in her work. What we find, however, is invaluable—a poet whose imagination confronts and resists the harsh necessities of our times and keeps alive a vision of what is possible: "a whole new poetry beginning here" ("Transcendental Etude").

Snapshots of a Daughter-in-Law

1

You, once a belle in Shreveport,
with henna-colored hair, skin like a peachbud,
still have your dresses copied from that time,
and play a Chopin prelude
called by Cortot: *"Delicious recollections*   5
float like perfume through the memory."[1]

Your mind now, moldering like wedding-cake,
heavy with useless experience, rich
with suspicion, rumor, fantasy,

---

1. A remark made by Alfred Cortot (1877–1962), a well-known French pianist, in his *Chopin: 24 Preludes* (1930); he is referring specifically to Chopin's Prelude No. 7, Andantino, A Major.

crumbling to pieces under the knife-edge 10
of mere fact. In the prime of your life.

Nervy, glowering, your daughter
wipes the teaspoons, grows another way.

2

Banging the coffee-pot into the sink
she hears the angels chiding, and looks out 15
past the raked gardens to the sloppy sky.
Only a week since They said: *Have no patience.*

The next time it was: *Be insatiable.*
Then: *Save yourself; others you cannot save.*
Sometimes she's let the tapstream scald her arm, 20
a match burn to her thumbnail,

or held her hand above the kettle's snout
right in the woolly steam. They are probably angels,
since nothing hurts her anymore, except
each morning's grit blowing into her eyes. 25

3

A thinking woman sleeps with monsters.[2]
The beak that grips her, she becomes. And Nature,
that sprung-lidded, still commodious
steamer-trunk of *tempora* and *mores*[3]
gets stuffed with it all: the mildewed orange-flowers, 30
the female pills, the terrible breasts
of Boadicea[4] beneath flat foxes' heads and orchids.

Two handsome women, gripped in argument,
each proud, acute, subtle, I hear scream
across the cut glass and majolica 35
like Furies[5] cornered from their prey:
The argument *ad feminam*,[6] all the old knives
that have rusted in my back, I drive in yours,
ma semblable, ma soeur![7]

2. A reference to W. B. Yeats's "Leda and the Swan," a poem about the rape of a maiden by Zeus in the form of a giant bird. The poem ends: "Did she put on his knowledge with his power / Before the indifferent beak could let her drop?"
3. Times and customs (Latin), an allusion to the Roman orator Cicero's famous phrase "O Tempora! O Mores!" ("Alas for the degeneracy of our times and the low standard of our morals!").
4. British queen in the time of the Emperor Nero; she led her people in a large, ultimately unsuccessful revolt against Roman rule. "Female pills": remedies for menstrual pain.

5. Greek goddesses of vengeance. "Majolica": a kind of earthenware with a richly colored glaze.
6. Feminine version of the Latin phrase *ad hominem* (literally, "to the man"), referring to an argument directed not to reason but to personal prejudices and emotions.
7. The last line of Charles Baudelaire's French poem "Au Lecteur" addresses *"Hypocrite lecteur!—mon semblable—mon frère!"* (Hypocrite reader, like me, my brother!); Rich here instead addresses *"ma soeur"* (my sister). See also T. S. Eliot, "The Waste Land," line 76.

4

Knowing themselves too well in one another: 40
their gifts no pure fruition, but a thorn,
the prick filed sharp against a hint of scorn . . .
Reading while waiting
for the iron to heat,
writing, *My Life had stood—a Loaded Gun*[8]—   45
in that Amherst pantry while the jellies boil and scum,
or, more often,
iron-eyed and beaked and purposed as a bird,
dusting everything on the whatnot every day of life.

5

Dulce ridens, dulce loquens,[9]   50
she shaves her legs until they gleam
like petrified mammoth-tusk.

6

When to her lute Corinna sings[1]
neither words nor music are her own;
only the long hair dipping   55
over her cheek, only the song
of silk against her knees
and these
adjusted in reflections of an eye.

Poised, trembling and unsatisfied, before   60
an unlocked door, that cage of cages,
tell us, you bird, you tragical machine—
is this *fertilisante douleur?*[2] Pinned down
by love, for you the only natural action,
are you edged more keen   65
to prise the secrets of the vault? has Nature shown
her household books to you, daughter-in-law,
that her sons never saw?

7

*"To have in this uncertain world some stay
which cannot be undermined, is   70
of the utmost consequence."*[3]

---

8. *"Emily Dickinson, Complete Poems,* ed. T. H. Johnson, 1960, p. 369" [Rich's note]; this is the poem numbered 754 in the Johnson edition. Amherst, Massachusetts, is the town where Dickinson lived her entire life (1830–1886).
9. Sweetly laughing, sweetly speaking (Latin, from Horace, *Odes,* 22.23–24).
1. First line of a lyric poem by Thomas Campion

(1567–1620) about the extent to which a courtier is moved by Corinna's beautiful music.
2. Fertilizing (or life-giving) sorrow (French).
3. "From Mary Wollstonecraft, *Thoughts on the Education of Daughters,* London, 1787" [Rich's note]. Wollstonecraft (1759–1797), one of the first feminist thinkers, is best-known for her "Vindication of the Rights of Woman."

Thus wrote
a woman, partly brave and partly good,
who fought with what she partly understood.
Few men about her would or could do more,   75
hence she was labeled harpy, shrew and whore.

8

"You all die at fifteen," said Diderot,[4]
and turn part legend, part convention.
Still, eyes inaccurately dream
behind closed windows blankening with steam.   80
Deliciously, all that we might have been,
all that we were—fire, tears,
wit, taste, martyred ambition—
stirs like the memory of refused adultery
the drained and flagging bosom of our middle years.   85

9

Not that it is done well, but
that it is done at all?[5] Yes, think
of the odds! or shrug them off forever.
This luxury of the precocious child,
Time's precious chronic invalid,—   90
would we, darlings, resign it if we could?
Our blight has been our sinecure:
mere talent was enough for us—
glitter in fragments and rough drafts.

Sigh no more, ladies.   95
                    Time is male
and in his cups drinks to the fair.
Bemused by gallantry, we hear
our mediocrities over-praised,
indolence read as abnegation,   100
slattern thought styled intuition,
every lapse forgiven, our crime
only to cast too bold a shadow
or smash the mold straight off.

For that, solitary confinement,   105
tear gas, attrition shelling.
Few applicants for that honor.

---

4. Denis Diderot (1713–1784), French philosopher, encyclopedist, playwright, and critic. "'You all die at fifteen': 'Vous mourez toutes à quinze ans,' from the *Lettres à Sophie Volland*, quoted by Simone de Beauvoir in *Le Deuxième Sexe*, Vol. II, pp. 123–24" [Rich's note].

5. An allusion to Samuel Johnson's remark to James Boswell: "Sir, a woman's preaching is like a dog's walking on his hinder legs. It is not done well; but you are surprised to find it done at all" (July 31, 1763).

10

                    Well,
she's long about her coming, who must be
more merciless to herself than history.   110
Her mind full to the wind, I see her plunge
breasted and glancing through the currents,
taking the light upon her
at least as beautiful as any boy
or helicopter,[6]   115
                    poised, still coming,
her fine blades making the air wince

but her cargo
no promise then:
delivered   120
palpable
ours.

1958–60   1963

A Valediction Forbidding Mourning[1]

My swirling wants. Your frozen lips.
The grammar turned and attacked me.
Themes, written under duress.
Emptiness of the notations.

They gave me a drug that slowed the healing of wounds.   5

I want you to see this before I leave:
the experience of repetition as death
the failure of criticism to locate the pain
the poster in the bus that said:
my bleeding is under control.   10

A red plant in a cemetery of plastic wreaths.

A last attempt: the language is a dialect called metaphor.
These images go unglossed: hair, glacier, flashlight.
When I think of a landscape I am thinking of a time.
When I talk of taking a trip I mean forever.   15

---

6. "She comes down from the remoteness of
ages, from Thebes, from Crete, from Chichén-
Itzá; and she is also the totem set deep in the
African jungle; she is a helicopter and she is a
bird; and there is this, the greatest wonder of all:
under her tinted hair the forest murmur becomes
a thought, and words issue from her breasts"
(Simone de Beauvoir, *The Second Sex*, trans.
H. M. Parshley [New York, 1953], 729). (A translation of the passage from *Le Deuxième Sexe*,
Vol. II, 574, cited in French by Rich.)
1. Title of a famous poem by John Donne (1572–
1631) in which the English poet forbids his wife to
lament his departure for a trip to the Continent.

I could say: those mountains have a meaning
but further than that I could not say.

To do something very common, in my own way.

1970   1971

Diving into the Wreck

First having read the book of myths,
and loaded the camera,
and checked the edge of the knife-blade,
I put on
the body-armor of black rubber   5
the absurd flippers
the grave and awkward mask.
I am having to do this
not like Cousteau[1] with his
assiduous team   10
aboard the sun-flooded schooner
but here alone.

There is a ladder.
The ladder is always there
hanging innocently   15
close to the side of the schooner.
We know what it is for,
we who have used it.
Otherwise
it's a piece of maritime floss   20
some sundry equipment.

I go down.
Rung after rung and still
the oxygen immerses me
the blue light   25
the clear atoms
of our human air.
I go down.
My flippers cripple me,
I crawl like an insect down the ladder   30
and there is no one
to tell me when the ocean
will begin.

First the air is blue and then
it is bluer and then green and then   35

1. Jacques-Yves Cousteau (1910–1997), French underwater explorer and author.

black I am blacking out and yet
my mask is powerful
it pumps my blood with power
the sea is another story
the sea is not a question of power   40
I have to learn alone
to turn my body without force
in the deep element.

And now: it is easy to forget
what I came for   45
among so many who have always
lived here
swaying their crenellated fans
between the reefs
and besides   50
you breathe differently down here.

I came to explore the wreck.
The words are purposes.
The words are maps.
I came to see the damage that was done   55
and the treasures that prevail.
I stroke the beam of my lamp
slowly along the flank
of something more permanent
than fish or weed   60

the thing I came for:
the wreck and not the story of the wreck
the thing itself and not the myth
the drowned face[2] always staring
toward the sun   65
the evidence of damage
worn by salt and sway into this threadbare beauty
the ribs of the disaster
curving their assertion
among the tentative haunters.   70

This is the place.
And I am here, the mermaid whose dark hair
streams black, the merman in his armored body
We circle silently
about the wreck   75
we dive into the hold.
I am she: I am he

whose drowned face sleeps with open eyes
whose breasts still bear the stress
whose silver, copper, vermeil cargo lies   80

---

2. Referring to the ornamental female figurehead that formed the prow of many old sailing ships.

obscurely inside barrels
half-wedged and left to rot
we are the half-destroyed instruments
that once held to a course
the water-eaten log 85
the fouled compass

We are, I am, you are
by cowardice or courage
the one who find our way
back to this scene 90
carrying a knife, a camera
a book of myths
in which
our names do not appear.

1972   1973

Transcendental Etude[1]

for Michelle Cliff

This August evening I've been driving
over backroads fringed with queen anne's lace
my car startling young deer in meadows—one
gave a hoarse intake of her breath and all
four fawns sprang after her 5
into the dark maples.
Three months from today they'll be fair game
for the hit-and-run hunters, glorying
in a weekend's destructive power,
triggers fingered by drunken gunmen, sometimes 10
so inept as to leave the shattered animal
stunned in her blood. But this evening deep in summer
the deer are still alive and free,
nibbling apples from early-laden boughs
so weighted, so englobed 15
with already yellowing fruit
they seem eternal, Hesperidean[2]
in the clear-tuned, cricket-throbbing air.

Later I stood in the dooryard,
my nerves singing the immense 20
fragility of all this sweetness,
this green world already sentimentalized, photographed,
advertised to death. Yet, it persists
stubbornly beyond the fake Vermont

---

1. "Etude": a piece of music played for the practice of a point of technique or a composition built
on technique but played for its artistic value.

2. I.e., like the golden apples of the tree guarded
by the Hesperides, daughters of Atlas, in Greek
mythology.

of antique barnboards glazed into discothèques,   25
artificial snow, the sick Vermont of children
conceived in apathy, grown to winters
of rotgut violence,
poverty gnashing its teeth like a blind cat at their lives.
Still, it persists. Turning off onto a dirt road   30
from the raw cuts bulldozed through a quiet village
for the tourist run to Canada,
I've sat on a stone fence above a great, soft, sloping field
of musing heifers, a farmstead
slanting its planes calmly in the calm light,   35
a dead elm raising bleached arms
above a green so dense with life,
minute, momentary life—slugs, moles, pheasants, gnats,
spiders, moths, hummingbirds, groundhogs, butterflies—
a lifetime is too narrow   40
to understand it all, beginning with the huge
rockshelves that underlie all that life.

No one ever told us we had to study our lives,
make of our lives a study, as if learning natural history
or music, that we should begin   45
with the simple exercises first
and slowly go on trying
the hard ones, practicing till strength
and accuracy became one with the daring
to leap into transcendence, take the chance   50
of breaking down in the wild arpeggio
or faulting the full sentence of the fugue.[3]
—And in fact we can't live like that: we take on
everything at once before we've even begun
to read or mark time, we're forced to begin   55
in the midst of the hardest movement,
the one already sounding as we are born.
At most we're allowed a few months
of simply listening to the simple line
of a woman's voice singing a child   60
against her heart. Everything else is too soon,
too sudden, the wrenching-apart, that woman's heartbeat
heard ever after from a distance,
the loss of that ground-note echoing
whenever we are happy, or in despair.   65

Everything else seems beyond us,
we aren't ready for it, nothing that was said
is true for us, caught naked in the argument,
the counterpoint, trying to sightread
what our fingers can't keep up with, learn by heart   70

---

3. Musical piece characterized by the interweaving of several voices. "Arpeggio": production of a chord's tones in succession.

what we can't even read. And yet
it *is* this we were born to. We aren't virtuosi
or child prodigies, there are no prodigies
in this realm, only a half-blind, stubborn
cleaving to the timbre, the tones of what we are   75
—even when all the texts describe it differently.

And we're not performers, like Liszt,[4] competing
against the world for speed and brilliance
(the 79-year-old pianist said, when I asked her
What makes a virtuoso?—Competitiveness.)   80
The longer I live the more I mistrust
theatricality, the false glamour cast
by performance, the more I know its poverty beside
the truths we are salvaging from
the splitting-open of our lives.   85
The woman who sits watching, listening,
eyes moving in the darkness
in rehearsing in her body, hearing-out in her blood
a score touched off in her perhaps
by some words, a few chords, from the stage: 90
a tale only she can tell.

But there come times—perhaps this is one of them—
when we have to take ourselves more seriously or die;
when we have to pull back from the incantations,
rhythms we've moved to thoughtlessly,   95
and disenthrall ourselves, bestow
ourselves to silence, or a severer listening, cleansed
of oratory, formulas, choruses, laments, static
crowding the wires. We cut the wires,
find ourselves in free-fall, as if   100
our true home were the undimensional
solitudes, the rift
in the Great Nebula.[5]
No one who survives to speak
new language, has avoided this: 105
the cutting-away of an old force that held her
rooted to an old ground
the pitch of utter loneliness
where she herself and all creation
seem equally dispersed, weightless, her being a cry   110
to which no echo comes or can ever come.

But in fact we were always like this,
rootless, dismembered: knowing it makes the difference.
Birth stripped our birthright from us,

4. Franz Liszt (1811–1886), Hungarian composer
and pianist noted for his virtuoso performances.
5. A nebula is an immense body of rarefied gas
or dust in interstellar space. Rich may be referring to the Great Nebula in the Orion constellation or to a body of dark nebulae, usually called
the "Great Rift," which in photographs appears
to divide the Milky Way.

tore us from a woman, from women, from ourselves   115
so early on
and the whole chorus throbbing at our ears
like midges, told us nothing, nothing
of origins, nothing we needed
to know, nothing that could re-member us.   120

Only: that it is unnatural,
the homesickness for a woman, for ourselves,
for that acute joy at the shadow her head and arms
cast on a wall, her heavy or slender
thighs on which we lay, flesh against flesh,   125
eyes steady on the face of love; smell of her milk, her sweat,
terror of her disappearance, all fused in this hunger
for the element they have called most dangerous, to be
lifted breathtaken on her breast, to rock within her
—even if beaten back, stranded against, to apprehend   130
in a sudden brine-clear thought
trembling like the tiny, orbed, endangered
egg-sac of a new world:
This is what she was to me, and this
is how I can love myself—   135
as only a woman can love me.

*Homesick for myself, for her—*as, after the heatwave
breaks, the clear tones of the world
manifest: cloud, bough, wall, insect, the very soul of light:
homesick as the fluted vault of desire   140
articulates itself: *I am the lover and the loved,*
home and wanderer, she who splits
firewood and she who knocks, a stranger
in the storm, two women, eye to eye
measuring each other's spirit, each other's   145
limitless desire,
                      a whole new poetry beginning here.

Vision begins to happen in such a life
as if a woman quietly walked away
from the argument and jargon in a room   150
and sitting down in the kitchen, began turning in her lap
bits of yarn, calico and velvet scraps,
laying them out absently on the scrubbed boards
in the lamplight, with small rainbow-colored shells
sent in cotton-wool from somewhere far away,   155
and skeins of milkweed from the nearest meadow—
original domestic silk, the finest findings—
and the darkblue petal of the petunia,
and the dry darkbrown lace of seaweed;
not forgotten either, the shed silver   160
whisker of the cat,
the spiral of paper-wasp-nest curling

beside the finch's yellow feather.
Such a composition has nothing to do with eternity,
the striving for greatness, brilliance—   165
only with the musing of a mind
one with her body, experienced fingers quietly pushing
dark against bright, silk against roughness,
pulling the tenets of a life together
with no mere will to mastery,   170
only care for the many-lived, unending
forms in which she finds herself,
becoming now the sherd of broken glass
slicing light in a corner, dangerous
to flesh, now the plentiful, soft leaf   175
that wrapped round the throbbing finger, soothes the wound;
and now the stone foundation, rockshelf further
forming underneath everything that grows.

1977   1978

TONI MORRISON
1931–2019

The 1993 Nobel Laureate in literature, Toni Morrison was a novelist of great importance in her own right and was the central figure in putting fiction by and about
African American women at the forefront of the late-twentieth-century literary
canon. Whereas the legacy of slavery had obscured a usable tradition, and critical
stereotypes at times restricted such writers' range, Morrison's fiction served as a
model for reconstructing a culturally empowering past. She joined the great
American tradition of self-invention: her example and her editorial work figured
importantly in the careers of other writers, such as Toni Cade Bambara and Gayl
Jones.

Morrison was born in Lorain, Ohio, where much of her fiction is set (a departure
from earlier African American narratives typically located in the rural South or urban
North). Having earned a B.A. from Howard University with a major in English and a
minor in classics, and an M.A. from Cornell University (with a thesis on suicide in the
novels of Virginia Woolf and William Faulkner), Morrison began a teaching career in
1955 that reached from Texas Southern University back to Howard, where her students included the future activist Stokeley Carmichael and the future critic Houston
A. Baker Jr. At this time she married Harold Morrison, a Jamaican architect, with
whom she had two children before ending their marriage in 1964. Already writing, she
took a job with the publishing firm Random House and eventually settled in New York
City, where she worked until 1983. During these same years she held visiting teaching
appointments at institutions including Yale University and Bard College.

As a first novel, *The Bluest Eye* (1970) is uncommonly mature for its confident
use of various narrative voices. Throughout her career Morrison was dedicated to

constructing a practical cultural identity of a race and a gender whose self-images had been obscured or denied by dominating forces, and in *The Bluest Eye* she already shows that narrative strategy is an important element in such construction. A girl's need to be loved generates the novel's action, action that involves displaced and alienated affections (and eventually incestuous rape); the family's inability to produce a style of existence in which love can be born and thrive leads to just such a devastating fate for Morrison's protagonist. Love is also denied in *Sula* (1974), in which relationships extend in two directions: between contemporaries (Sula and her friend Nel) and with previous generations.

With *Song of Solomon* (1977) Morrison seeks a more positive redemption of her characters. Turning away from his parents' loveless marriage, Milkman Dead makes a physical and mental journey to his ancestral roots. Here he discovers a more useful legacy in communal tales about Grandmother and Great-Grandfather, each long dead but infusing the local culture with emotionally sustaining lore. Milkman uses this lore to learn how the spiritual guidance offered by his aunt Pilate eclipses the material concerns of his parents' world.

Allegory becomes an important strategy in *Tar Baby* (1981), drawing on the strong folk culture of Haiti, where two contrasting persons form a troubled relationship based on their distinct searches for and rejections of a heritage. Yet it is in a rebuilding of history, rather than allegory or myth, that Morrison achieved her great strength as a novelist in *Beloved* (1987), the winner of her first major award, the Pulitzer Prize. Set in the middle 1870s, when race relations in America were at their most crucial juncture (slavery having ended and the course of the South's Reconstruction not yet fully determined), this novel shows a mother (Sethe) being haunted and eventually destroyed by the ghost of a daughter (Beloved) whom she had killed eighteen years earlier rather than allow her to be taken by a vicious slavemaster. This novel is central to Morrison's canon because it involves so many important themes and techniques, from love and guilt to history's role in clarifying the past's influence on the present, all told in an experimental style of magical realism that draws upon techniques from both oral storytelling and modernist fiction.

Paradise (1988) takes a nineteenth-century utopia and reexamines its ideals in the face of 1970s realities—a reminder of how neither past nor present can be insulated from the other. *Jazz* (1992) finds Morrison modeling her narrative voice on the progression of a jazz solo to demonstrate how improvisation with detail can change the nature of what is expressed. Present and past weave together in her characters' lives as the narrative seeks to understand the jealousies of love and the sometimes macabre manifestations of hatred. *Love* (2003), with its murder, arson, pedophilia, and several rapes punctuating a narrative in which arguments over a legacy dislodge awkward elements of the past, is a reminder of how disturbing Morrison's fiction can be. *A Mercy* (2008) explores the contradictions between American and pastoral ideals and the realities of Native American extermination and African American slavery. Her last novel was *God Help the Child* (2015).

From 1989 to 2006, Morrison served as Goheen Professor of the Humanities at Princeton University. Together with her Nobel lecture, her essays collected as *Playing in the Dark: Whiteness and the Literary Imagination* (1992) challenge stereotypes in white critical thinking about black literature. Her short story "Recitatif," written for *Confirmation*, the 1983 anthology edited by Amiri and Amina Baraka, directly addresses the issues of individual and family, past and present, and race and its effacements that motivate the larger sense of her work. A "recitatif" is a vocal performance in which a narrative is not stated but sung. In her work Morrison's voice sings proudly of a past that in the artistic nature of its reconstruction puts all Americans in touch with a more positively usable heritage.

The following text is from *Confirmation*.

Recitatif

My mother danced all night and Roberta's was sick. That's why we were taken to St. Bonny's. People want to put their arms around you when you tell them you were in a shelter, but it really wasn't bad. No big long room with one hundred beds like Bellevue.[1] There were four to a room, and when Roberta and me came, there was a shortage of state kids, so we were the only ones assigned to 406 and could go from bed to bed if we wanted to. And we wanted to, too. We changed beds every night and for the whole four months we were there we never picked one out as our own permanent bed.

It didn't start out that way. The minute I walked in and the Big Bozo introduced us, I got sick to my stomach. It was one thing to be taken out of your own bed early in the morning—it was something else to be stuck in a strange place with a girl from a whole other race. And Mary, that's my mother, she was right. Every now and then she would stop dancing long enough to tell me something important and one of the things she said was that they never washed their hair and they smelled funny. Roberta sure did. Smell funny, I mean. So when the Big Bozo (nobody ever called her Mrs. Itkin, just like nobody ever said St. Bonaventure)—when she said, "Twyla, this is Roberta. Roberta, this is Twyla. Make each other welcome." I said, "My mother won't like you putting me in here."

"Good," said Bozo. "Maybe then she'll come and take you home."

How's that for mean? If Roberta had laughed I would have killed her, but she didn't. She just walked over to the window and stood with her back to us.

"Turn around," said the Bozo. "Don't be rude. Now Twyla. Roberta. When you hear a loud buzzer, that's the call for dinner. Come down to the first floor. Any fights and no movie." And then, just to make sure we knew what we would be missing, "The Wizard of Oz."[2]

Roberta must have thought I meant that my mother would be mad about my being put in the shelter. Not about rooming with her, because as soon as Bozo left she came over to me and said, "Is your mother sick too?"

"No," I said. "She just likes to dance all night."

"Oh," she nodded her head and I liked the way she understood things so fast. So for the moment it didn't matter that we looked like salt and pepper standing there and that's what the other kids called us sometimes. We were eight years old and got F's all the time. Me because I couldn't remember what I read or what the teacher said. And Roberta because she couldn't read at all and didn't even listen to the teacher. She wasn't good at anything except jacks, at which she was a killer: pow scoop pow scoop pow scoop.

We didn't like each other all that much at first, but nobody else wanted to play with us because we weren't real orphans with beautiful dead parents in the sky. We were dumped. Even the New York City Puerto Ricans and the upstate Indians ignored us. All kinds of kids were in there, black ones, white ones, even two Koreans. The food was good, though. At least I thought so. Roberta hated it and left whole pieces of things on her plate: Spam, Salisbury

---

1. Bellevue Hospital in New York City is known for its psychiatric ward. St. Bonaventure's offers the services of a youth shelter and school.

2. The 1939 film based on the 1900 children's book by the American writer L. Frank Baum (1856–1919).

steak—even jello with fruit cocktail in it, and she didn't care if I ate what she wouldn't. Mary's idea of supper was popcorn and a can of Yoo-Hoo.[3] Hot mashed potatoes and two weenies was like Thanksgiving for me.

It really wasn't bad, St. Bonny's. The big girls on the second floor pushed us around now and then. But that was all. They wore lipstick and eyebrow pencil and wobbled their knees while they watched TV. Fifteen, sixteen, even, some of them were. They were put-out girls, scared runaways most of them. Poor little girls who fought their uncles off but looked tough to us, and mean. God did they look mean. The staff tried to keep them separate from the younger children, but sometimes they caught us watching them in the orchard where they played radios and danced with each other. They'd light out after us and pull our hair or twist our arms. We were scared of them, Roberta and me, but neither of us wanted the other one to know it. So we got a good list of dirty names we could shout back when we ran from them through the orchard. I used to dream a lot and almost always the orchard was there. Two acres, four maybe, of these little apple trees. Hundreds of them. Empty and crooked like beggar women when I first came to St. Bonny's but fat with flowers when I left. I don't know why I dreamt about that orchard so much. Nothing really happened there. Nothing all that important, I mean. Just the big girls dancing and playing the radio. Roberta and me watching. Maggie fell down there once. The kitchen woman with legs like parentheses. And the big girls laughed at her. We should have helped her up, I know, but we were scared of those girls with lipstick and eyebrow pencil. Maggie couldn't talk. The kids said she had her tongue cut out, but I think she was just born that way: mute. She was old and sandy-colored and she worked in the kitchen. I don't know if she was nice or not. I just remember her legs like parentheses and how she rocked when she walked. She worked from early in the morning till two o'clock, and if she was late, if she had too much cleaning and didn't get out till two-fifteen or so, she'd cut through the orchard so she wouldn't miss her bus and have to wait another hour. She wore this really stupid little hat—a kid's hat with ear flaps—and she wasn't much taller than we were. A really awful little hat. Even for a mute, it was dumb—dressing like a kid and never saying anything at all.

"But what about if somebody tries to kill her?" I used to wonder about that. "Or what if she wants to cry? Can she cry?"

"Sure," Roberta said. "But just tears. No sounds come out."

"She can't scream?"

"Nope. Nothing."

"Can she hear?"

"I guess."

"Let's call her," I said. And we did.

"Dummy! Dummy!" She never turned her head.

"Bow legs! Bow legs!" Nothing. She just rocked on, the chin straps of her baby-boy hat swaying from side to side. I think we were wrong. I think she could hear and didn't let on. And it shames me even now to think there was somebody in there after all who heard us call her those names and couldn't tell on us.

We got along all right, Roberta and me. Changed beds every night, got F's in civics and communication skills and gym. The Bozo was disappointed

---

3. A chocolate soft drink.

in us, she said. Out of 130 of us state cases, 90 were under twelve. Almost all were real orphans with beautiful dead parents in the sky. We were the only ones dumped and the only ones with F's in three classes including gym. So we got along—what with her leaving whole pieces of things on her plate and being nice about not asking questions.

I think it was the day before Maggie fell down that we found out our mothers were coming to visit us on the same Sunday. We had been at the shelter twenty-eight days (Roberta twenty-eight and a half) and this was their first visit with us. Our mothers would come at ten o'clock in time for chapel, then lunch with us in the teachers' lounge. I thought if my dancing mother met her sick mother it might be good for her. And Roberta thought her sick mother would get a big bang out of a dancing one. We got excited about it and curled each other's hair. After breakfast we sat on the bed watching the road from the window. Roberta's socks were still wet. She washed them the night before and put them on the radiator to dry. They hadn't, but she put them on anyway because their tops were so pretty—scalloped in pink. Each of us had a purple construction-paper basket that we had made in craft class. Mine had a yellow crayon rabbit on it. Roberta's had eggs with wiggly lines of color. Inside were cellophane grass and just the jelly beans because I'd eaten the two marshmallow eggs they gave us. The Big Bozo came herself to get us. Smiling she told us we looked very nice and to come downstairs. We were so surprised by the smile we'd never seen before, neither of us moved.

"Don't you want to see your mommies?"

I stood up first and spilled the jelly beans all over the floor. Bozo's smile disappeared while we scrambled to get the candy up off the floor and put it back in the grass.

She escorted us downstairs to the first floor, where the other girls were lining up to file into the chapel. A bunch of grown-ups stood to one side. Viewers mostly. The old biddies who wanted servants and the fags who wanted company looking for children they might want to adopt. Once in a while a grandmother. Almost never anybody young or anybody whose face wouldn't scare you in the night. Because if any of the real orphans had young relatives they wouldn't be real orphans. I saw Mary right away. She had on those green slacks I hated and hated even more now because didn't she know we were going to chapel? And that fur jacket with the pocket linings so ripped she had to pull to get her hands out of them. But her face was pretty—like always, and she smiled and waved like she was the little girl looking for her mother—not me.

I walked slowly, trying not to drop the jelly beans and hoping the paper handle would hold. I had to use my last Chiclet because by the time I finished cutting everything out, all the Elmer's was gone. I am left-handed and the scissors never worked for me. It didn't matter, though; I might just as well have chewed the gum. Mary dropped to her knees and grabbed me, mashing the basket, the jelly beans, and the grass into her ratty fur jacket.

"Twyla, baby. Twyla, baby!"

I could have killed her. Already I heard the big girls in the orchard the next time saying, "Twyyyyyla, baby!" But I couldn't stay mad at Mary while she was smiling and hugging me and smelling of Lady Esther dusting powder. I wanted to stay buried in her fur all day.

To tell the truth I forgot about Roberta. Mary and I got in line for the traipse into chapel and I was feeling proud because she looked so beautiful even in those ugly green slacks that made her behind stick out. A pretty mother on earth is better than a beautiful dead one in the sky even if she did leave you all alone to go dancing.

I felt a tap on my shoulder, turned, and saw Roberta smiling. I smiled back, but not too much lest somebody think this visit was the biggest thing that ever happened in my life. Then Roberta said, "Mother, I want you to meet my roommate, Twyla. And that's Twyla's mother."

I looked up it seemed for miles. She was big. Bigger than any man and on her chest was the biggest cross I'd ever seen. I swear it was six inches long each way. And in the crook of her arm was the biggest Bible ever made.

Mary, simple-minded as ever, grinned and tried to yank her hand out of the pocket with the raggedy lining—to shake hands, I guess. Roberta's mother looked down at me and then looked down at Mary too. She didn't say anything, just grabbed Roberta with her Bible-free hand and stepped out of line, walking quickly to the rear of it. Mary was still grinning because she's not too swift when it comes to what's really going on. Then this light bulb goes off in her head and she says "That bitch!" really loud and us almost in the chapel now. Organ music whining; the Bonny Angels singing sweetly. Everybody in the world turned around to look. And Mary would have kept it up—kept calling names if I hadn't squeezed her hand as hard as I could. That helped a little, but she still twitched and crossed and uncrossed her legs all through service. Even groaned a couple of times. Why did I think she would come there and act right? Slacks. No hat like the grandmothers and viewers, and groaning all the while. When we stood for hymns she kept her mouth shut. Wouldn't even look at the words on the page. She actually reached in her purse for a mirror to check her lipstick. All I could think of was that she really needed to be killed. The sermon lasted a year, and I knew the real orphans were looking smug again.

We were supposed to have lunch in the teachers' lounge, but Mary didn't bring anything, so we picked fur and cellophane grass off the mashed jelly beans and ate them. I could have killed her. I sneaked a look at Roberta. Her mother had brought chicken legs and ham sandwiches and oranges and a whole box of chocolate-covered grahams. Roberta drank milk from a thermos while her mother read the Bible to her.

Things are not right. The wrong food is always with the wrong people. Maybe that's why I got into waitress work later—to match up the right people with the right food. Roberta just let those chicken legs sit there, but she did bring a stack of grahams up to me later when the visit was over. I think she was sorry that her mother would not shake my mother's hand. And I liked that and I liked the fact that she didn't say a word about Mary groaning all the way through the service and not bringing any lunch.

Roberta left in May when the apple trees were heavy and white. On her last day we went to the orchard to watch the big girls smoke and dance by the radio. It didn't matter that they said, "Twyyyyyla, baby." We sat on the ground and breathed. Lady Esther. Apple blossoms. I still go soft when I smell one or the other. Roberta was going home. The big cross and the big Bible was coming to get her and she seemed sort of glad and sort of not. I thought I would die in that room of four beds without her and I knew Bozo had plans to move some other dumped kid in there with me. Roberta promised to write every day, which was really sweet of her because she couldn't read a lick so how could she write anybody. I would have drawn pictures and sent them to her but she never gave me her address. Little by little she faded. Her wet socks with the pink scalloped tops and her big serious-looking eyes—that's all I could catch when I tried to bring her to mind.

I was working behind the counter at the Howard Johnson's on the Thruway just before the Kingston exit. Not a bad job. Kind of a long ride from Newburgh,[4] but okay once I got there. Mine was the second night shift—eleven to seven. Very light until a Greyhound checked in for breakfast around six-thirty. At that hour the sun was all the way clear of the hills behind the restaurant. The place looked better at night—more like shelter—but I loved it when the sun broke in, even if it did show all the cracks in the vinyl and the speckled floor looked dirty no matter what the mop boy did.

It was August and a bus crowd was just unloading. They would stand around a long while: going to the john, and looking at gifts and junk-for-sale machines, reluctant to sit down so soon. Even to eat. I was trying to fill the coffee pots and get them all situated on the electric burners when I saw her. She was sitting in a booth smoking a cigarette with two guys smothered in head and facial hair. Her own hair was so big and wild I could hardly see her face. But the eyes. I would know them anywhere. She had on a powder-blue halter and shorts outfit and earrings the size of bracelets. Talk about lipstick and eyebrow pencil. She made the big girls look like nuns. I couldn't get off the counter until seven o'clock, but I kept watching the booth in case they got up to leave before that. My replacement was on time for a change, so I counted and stacked my receipts as fast as I could and signed off. I walked over to the booth, smiling and wondering if she would remember me. Or even if she wanted to remember me. Maybe she didn't want to be reminded of St. Bonny's or to have anybody know she was ever there. I know I never talked about it to anybody.

I put my hands in my apron pockets and leaned against the back of the booth facing them.

"Roberta? Roberta Fisk?"

She looked up. "Yeah?"

"Twyla."

She squinted for a second and then said, "Wow."

"Remember me?"

"Sure. Hey. Wow."

"It's been a while," I said, and gave a smile to the two hairy guys.

"Yeah. Wow. You work here?"

"Yeah," I said. "I live in Newburgh."

"Newburgh? No kidding?" She laughed then a private laugh that included the guys but only the guys, and they laughed with her. What could I do but laugh too and wonder why I was standing there with my knees showing out from under that uniform. Without looking I could see the blue and white triangle on my head, my hair shapeless in a net, my ankles thick in white oxfords. Nothing could have been less sheer than my stockings. There was this silence that came down right after I laughed. A silence it was her turn to fill up. With introductions, maybe, to her boyfriends or an invitation to sit down and have a Coke. Instead she lit a cigarette off the one she'd just

---

4. A city beside the Hudson River, located eighty miles north of New York City.

finished and said, "We're on our way to the Coast. He's got an appointment with Hendrix."[5] She gestured casually toward the boy next to her.

"Hendrix? Fantastic," I said. "Really fantastic. What's she doing now?"

Roberta coughed on her cigarette and the two guys rolled their eyes up at the ceiling.

"Hendrix. Jimi Hendrix, asshole. He's only the biggest—Oh, wow. Forget it."

I was dismissed without anyone saying goodbye, so I thought I would do it for her.

"How's your mother?" I asked. Her grin cracked her whole face. She swallowed. "Fine," she said. "How's yours?"

"Pretty as a picture," I said and turned away. The backs of my knees were damp. Howard Johnson's really was a dump in the sunlight.

James is as comfortable as a house slipper. He liked my cooking and I liked his big loud family. They have lived in Newburgh all of their lives and talk about it the way people do who have always known a home. His grandmother is a porch swing older than his father and when they talk about streets and avenues and buildings they call them names they no longer have. They still call the A & P[6] Rico's because it stands on property once a mom and pop store owned by Mr. Rico. And they call the new community college Town Hall because it once was. My mother-in-law puts up jelly and cucumbers and buys butter wrapped in cloth from a dairy. James and his father talk about fishing and baseball and I can see them all together on the Hudson in a raggedy skiff. Half the population of Newburgh is on welfare now, but to my husband's family it was still some upstate paradise of a time long past. A time of ice houses and vegetable wagons, coal furnaces and children weeding gardens. When our son was born my mother-in-law gave me the crib blanket that had been hers.

But the town they remembered had changed. Something quick was in the air. Magnificent old houses, so ruined they had become shelter for squatters and rent risks, were bought and renovated. Smart IBM people[7] moved out of their suburbs back into the city and put shutters up and herb gardens in their backyards. A brochure came in the mail announcing the opening of a Food Emporium. Gourmet food it said—and listed items the rich IBM crowd would want. It was located in a new mall at the edge of town and I drove out to shop there one day—just to see. It was late in June. After the tulips were gone and the Queen Elizabeth roses were open everywhere. I trailed my cart along the aisle tossing in smoked oysters and Robert's sauce and things I knew would sit in my cupboard for years. Only when I found some Klondike ice cream bars did I feel less guilty about spending James's fireman's salary so foolishly. My father-in-law ate them with the same gusto little Joseph did.

Waiting in the check-out line I heard a voice say, "Twyla!"

The classical music piped over the aisles had affected me and the woman leaning toward me was dressed to kill. Diamonds on her hand, a smart white summer dress. "I'm Mrs. Benson," I said.

5. Jimi Hendrix (1942–1970), African American musician and rock star.
6. Supermarket, part of a national chain once called the Great Atlantic and Pacific Tea Company.
7. High-salaried employees of the International Business Machine Corporation, headquartered in the suburbs north of New York City.

"Ho. Ho. The Big Bozo," she sang.

For a split second I didn't know what she was talking about. She had a bunch of asparagus and two cartons of fancy water.

"Roberta!"

"Right."

"For heaven's sake. Roberta."

"You look great," she said.

"So do you. Where are you? Here? In Newburgh?"

"Yes. Over in Annandale."

I was opening my mouth to say more when the cashier called my attention to her empty counter.

"Meet you outside." Roberta pointed her finger and went into the express line.

I placed the groceries and kept myself from glancing around to check Roberta's progress. I remembered Howard Johnson's and looking for a chance to speak only to be greeted with a stingy "wow." But she was waiting for me and her huge hair was sleek now, smooth around a small, nicely shaped head. Shoes, dress, everything lovely and summery and rich. I was dying to know what happened to her, how she got from Jimi Hendrix to Annandale, a neighborhood full of doctors and IBM executives. Easy, I thought. Everything is so easy for them. They think they own the world.

"How long," I asked her. "How long have you been here?"

"A year. I got married to a man who lives here. And you, you're married too, right? Benson, you said."

"Yeah. James Benson."

"And is he nice?"

"Oh, is he nice?"

"Well, is he?" Roberta's eyes were steady as though she really meant the question and wanted an answer.

"He's wonderful, Roberta. Wonderful."

"So you're happy."

"Very."

"That's good," she said and nodded her head. "I always hoped you'd be happy. Any kids? I know you have kids."

"One. A boy. How about you?"

"Four."

"Four?"

She laughed. "Step kids. He's a widower."

"Oh."

"Got a minute? Let's have a coffee."

I thought about the Klondikes melting and the inconvenience of going all the way to my car and putting the bags in the trunk. Served me right for buying all that stuff I didn't need. Roberta was ahead of me.

"Put them in my car. It's right here."

And then I saw the dark blue limousine.

"You married a Chinaman?"

"No," she laughed. "He's the driver."

"Oh, my. If the Big Bozo could see you now."

We both giggled. Really giggled. Suddenly, in just a pulse beat, twenty years disappeared and all of it came rushing back. The big girls (whom we called gar girls—Roberta's misheard word for the evil stone faces described in a civics class) there dancing in the orchard, the ploppy mashed potatoes, the double weenies, the Spam with pineapple. We went into the coffee shop holding on to one another and I tried to think why we were glad to see each other this time and not before. Once, twelve years ago, we passed like strangers. A black girl and a white girl meeting in a Howard Johnson's on the road and having nothing to say. One in a blue and white triangle waitress hat—the other on her way to see Hendrix. Now we were behaving like sisters separated for much too long. Those four short months were nothing in time. Maybe it was the thing itself. Just being there, together. Two little girls who knew what nobody else in the world knew—how not to ask questions. How to believe what had to be believed. There was politeness in that reluctance and generosity as well. Is your mother sick too? No, she dances all night. Oh—and an understanding nod.

We sat in a booth by the window and fell into recollection like veterans.

"Did you ever learn to read?"

"Watch." She picked up the menu. "Special of the day. Cream of corn soup. Entrées. Two dots and a wriggly line. Quiche. Chef salad, scallops . . ."

I was laughing and applauding when the waitress came up.

"Remember the Easter baskets?"

"And how we tried to *introduce* them?"

"Your mother with that cross like two telephone poles."

"And yours with those tight slacks."

We laughed so loudly heads turned and made the laughter harder to suppress.

"What happened to the Jimi Hendrix date?"

Roberta made a blow-out sound with her lips.

"When he died I thought about you."

"Oh, you heard about him finally?"

"Finally. Come on, I was a small-town country waitress."

"And I was a small-town country dropout. God, were we wild. I still don't know how I got out of there alive."

"But you did."

"I did. I really did. Now I'm Mrs. Kenneth Norton."

"Sounds like a mouthful."

"It is."

"Servants and all?"

Roberta held up two fingers.

"Ow! What does he do?"

"Computers and stuff. What do I know?"

"I don't remember a hell of a lot from those days, but Lord, St. Bonny's is as clear as daylight. Remember Maggie? The day she fell down and those gar girls laughed at her?"

Roberta looked up from her salad and stared at me. "Maggie didn't fall," she said.

"Yes, she did. You remember."

"No, Twyla. They knocked her down. Those girls pushed her down and tore her clothes. In the orchard."

"I don't—that's not what happened."

"Sure it is. In the orchard. Remember how scared we were?"

"Wait a minute. I don't remember any of that."

"And Bozo was fired."

"You're crazy. She was there when I left. You left before me."

"I went back. You weren't there when they fired Bozo."

"What?"

"Twice. Once for a year when I was about ten, another for two months when I was fourteen. That's when I ran away."

"You ran away from St. Bonny's?"

"I had to. What do you want? Me dancing in that orchard?"

"Are you sure about Maggie?"

"Of course I'm sure. You've blocked it, Twyla. It happened. Those girls had behavior problems, you know."

"Didn't they, though. But why can't I remember the Maggie thing?"

"Believe me. It happened. And we were there."

"Who did you room with when you went back?" I asked her as if I would know her. The Maggie thing was troubling me.

"Creeps. They tickled themselves in the night."

My ears were itching and I wanted to go home suddenly. This was all very well but she couldn't just comb her hair, wash her face and pretend everything was hunky-dory. After the Howard Johnson's snub. And no apology. Nothing.

"Were you on dope or what that time at Howard Johnson's?" I tried to make my voice sound friendlier than I felt.

"Maybe, a little. I never did drugs much. Why?"

"I don't know; you acted sort of like you didn't want to know me then."

"Oh, Twyla, you know how it was in those days: black—white. You know how everything was."

But I didn't know. I thought it was just the opposite. Busloads of blacks and whites came into Howard Johnson's together. They roamed together then: students, musicians, lovers, protesters. You got to see everything at Howard Johnson's and blacks were very friendly with whites in those days. But sitting there with nothing on my plate but two hard tomato wedges wondering about the melting Klondikes it seemed childish remembering the slight. We went to her car, and with the help of the driver, got my stuff into my station wagon.

"We'll keep in touch this time," she said.

"Sure," I said. "Sure. Give me a call."

"I will," she said, and then just as I was sliding behind the wheel, she leaned into the window. "By the way. Your mother. Did she ever stop dancing?"

I shook my head. "No. Never."

Roberta nodded.

"And yours? Did she ever get well?"

She smiled a tiny sad smile. "No. She never did. Look, call me, okay?"

"Okay," I said, but I knew I wouldn't. Roberta had messed up my past somehow with that business about Maggie. I wouldn't forget a thing like that. Would I?

Strife came to us that fall. At least that's what the paper called it. Strife. Racial strife. The word made me think of a bird—a big shrieking bird out of 1,000,000,000 B.C. Flapping its wings and cawing. Its eye with no lid always bearing down on you. All day it screeched and at night it slept on the rooftops. It woke you in the morning and from the *Today* show to the eleven o'clock news it kept you an awful company. I couldn't figure it out from one day to the next. I knew I was supposed to feel something strong, but I didn't know what, and James wasn't any help. Joseph was on the list of kids to be transferred from the junior high school to another one at some far-out-of-the-way place and I thought it was a good thing until I heard it was a bad thing. I mean I didn't know. All the schools seemed dumps to me, and the fact that one was nicer looking didn't hold much weight. But the papers were full of it and then the kids began to get jumpy. In August, mind you. Schools weren't even open yet. I thought Joseph might be frightened to go over there, but he didn't seem scared so I forgot about it, until I found myself driving along Hudson Street out there by the school they were trying to integrate and saw a line of women marching. And who do you suppose was in line, big as life, holding a sign in front of her bigger than her mother's cross? MOTHERS HAVE RIGHTS TOO! it said.

I drove on, and then changed my mind. I circled the block, slowed down, and honked my horn.

Roberta looked over and when she saw me she waved. I didn't wave back, but I didn't move either. She handed her sign to another woman and came over to where I was parked.

"Hi."

"What are you doing?"

"Picketing. What's it look like?"

"What for?"

"What do you mean 'What for?' They want to take my kids and send them out of the neighborhood. They don't want to go."

"So what if they go to another school? My boy's being bussed too, and I don't mind. Why should you?"

"It's not about us, Twyla. Me and you. It's about our kids."

"What's more *us* than that?"

"Well, it is a free country."

"Not yet, but it will be."

"What the hell does that mean? I'm not doing anything to you."

"You really think that?"

"I know it."

"I wonder what made me think you were different."

"I wonder what made me think you were different."

"Look at them," I said. "Just look. Who do they think they are? Swarming all over the place like they own it. And now they think they can decide where my child goes to school. Look at them, Roberta. They're Bozos."

Roberta turned around and looked at the women. Almost all of them were standing still now, waiting. Some were even edging toward us. Roberta looked at me out of some refrigerator behind her eyes. "No, they're not. They're just mothers."

"And what am I? Swiss cheese?"

"I used to curl your hair."

"I hated your hands in my hair."

The women were moving. Our faces looked mean to them of course and they looked as though they could not wait to throw themselves in front of a police car, or better yet, into my car and drag me away by my ankles. Now they surrounded my car and gently, gently began to rock it. I swayed back and forth like a sideways yo-yo. Automatically I reached for Roberta, like the old days in the orchard when they saw us watching them and we had to get out of there, and if one of us fell the other pulled her up and if one of us was caught the other stayed to kick and scratch, and neither would leave the other behind. My arm shot out of the car window but no receiving hand was there. Roberta was looking at me sway from side to side in the car and her face was still. My purse slid from the car seat down under the dashboard. The four policemen who had been drinking Tab[8] in their car finally got the message and strolled over, forcing their way through the women. Quietly, firmly they spoke. "Okay, ladies. Back in line or off the streets."

Some of them went away willingly; others had to be urged away from the car doors and the hood. Roberta didn't move. She was looking steadily at me. I was fumbling to turn on the ignition, which wouldn't catch because the gearshift was still in drive. The seats of the car were a mess because the swaying had thrown my grocery coupons all over it and my purse was sprawled on the floor.

"Maybe I am different now, Twyla. But you're not. You're the same little state kid who kicked a poor old black lady when she was down on the ground. You kicked a black lady and you have the nerve to call me a bigot."

The coupons were everywhere and the guts of my purse were bunched under the dashboard. What was she saying? Black? Maggie wasn't black.

"She wasn't black," I said.

"Like hell she wasn't, and you kicked her. We both did. You kicked a black lady who couldn't even scream."

"Liar!"

"You're the liar! Why don't you just go on home and leave us alone, huh?"

She turned away and I skidded away from the curb.

The next morning I went into the garage and cut the side out of the carton our portable TV had come in. It wasn't nearly big enough, but after a while I had a decent sign: red spray-painted letters on a white background—AND SO DO CHILDREN * * * *. I meant just to go down to the school and tack it up somewhere so those cows on the picket line across the street could see it, but when I got there, some ten or so others had already assembled—protesting the cows across the street. Police permits and everything. I got in line and we strutted in time on our side while Roberta's group strutted on theirs. That first day we were all dignified, pretending the other side didn't exist. The second day there was name calling and finger gestures. But that was about all. People changed signs from time to time, but Roberta never did and neither did I. Actually my sign didn't make sense without Roberta's. "And so do children what?" one of the women on my side asked me. Have rights, I said, as though it was obvious.

Roberta didn't acknowledge my presence in any way and I got to thinking maybe she didn't know I was there. I began to pace myself in the line, jostling people one minute and lagging behind the next, so Roberta and I could reach the end of our respective lines at the same time and there would be a moment in our turn when we would face each other. Still, I couldn't tell

8. A diet soda.

whether she saw me and knew my sign was for her. The next day I went early before we were scheduled to assemble. I waited until she got there before I exposed my new creation. As soon as she hoisted her MOTHERS HAVE RIGHTS TOO I began to wave my new one, which said, HOW WOULD YOU KNOW? I know she saw that one, but I had gotten addicted now. My signs got crazier each day, and the women on my side decided that I was a kook. They couldn't make heads or tails out of my brilliant screaming posters.

I brought a painted sign in queenly red with huge black letters that said, IS YOUR MOTHER WELL? Roberta took her lunch break and didn't come back for the rest of the day or any day after. Two days later I stopped going too and couldn't have been missed because nobody understood my signs anyway.

It was a nasty six weeks. Classes were suspended and Joseph didn't go to anybody's school until October. The children—everybody's children—soon got bored with that extended vacation they thought was going to be so great. They looked at TV until their eyes flattened. I spent a couple of mornings tutoring my son, as the other mothers said we should. Twice I opened a text from last year that he had never turned in. Twice he yawned in my face. Other mothers organized living room sessions so the kids would keep up. None of the kids could concentrate so they drifted back to *The Price Is Right* and *The Brady Bunch*.[9] When the school finally opened there were fights once or twice and some sirens roared through the streets every once in a while. There were a lot of photographers from Albany. And just when ABC was about to send up a news crew, the kids settled down like nothing in the world had happened. Joseph hung my HOW WOULD YOU KNOW? sign in his bedroom. I don't know what became of AND SO DO CHILDREN * * * *. I think my father-in-law cleaned some fish on it. He was always puttering around in our garage. Each of his five children lived in Newburgh and he acted as though he had five extra homes.

I couldn't help looking for Roberta when Joseph graduated from high school, but I didn't see her. It didn't trouble me much what she had said to me in the car. I mean the kicking part. I know I didn't do that, I couldn't do that. But I was puzzled by her telling me Maggie was black. When I thought about it I actually couldn't be certain. She wasn't pitch-black, I knew, or I would have remembered that. What I remember was the kiddie hat, and the semicircle legs. I tried to reassure myself about the race thing for a long time until it dawned on me that the truth was already there, and Roberta knew it. I didn't kick her; I didn't join in with the gar girls and kick that lady, but I sure did want to. We watched and never tried to help her and never called for help. Maggie was my dancing mother. Deaf, I thought, and dumb. Nobody inside. Nobody who would hear you if you cried in the night. Nobody who could tell you anything important that you could use. Rocking, dancing, swaying as she walked. And when the gar girls pushed her down, and started roughhousing, I knew she wouldn't scream, couldn't—just like me—and I was glad about that.

We decided not to have a tree, because Christmas would be at my mother-in-law's house, so why have a tree at both places? Joseph was at SUNY New

---

Paltz[1] and we had to economize, we said. But at the last minute, I changed my mind. Nothing could be that bad. So I rushed around town looking for a tree, something small but wide. By the time I found a place, it was snowing and very late. I dawdled like it was the most important purchase in the world and the tree man was fed up with me. Finally I chose one and had it tied onto the trunk of the car. I drove away slowly because the sand trucks were not out yet and the streets could be murder at the beginning of a snowfall. Downtown the streets were wide and rather empty except for a cluster of people coming out of the Newburgh Hotel. The one hotel in town that wasn't built out of cardboard and Plexiglas. A party, probably. The men huddled in the snow were dressed in tails and the women had on furs. Shiny things glittered from underneath their coats. It made me tired to look at them. Tired, tired, tired. On the next corner was a small diner with loops and loops of paper bells in the window. I stopped the car and went in. Just for a cup of coffee and twenty minutes of peace before I went home and tried to finish everything before Christmas Eve.

"Twyla?"

There she was. In a silvery evening gown and dark fur coat. A man and another woman were with her, the man fumbling for change to put in the cigarette machine. The woman was humming and tapping on the counter with her fingernails. They all looked a little bit drunk.

"Well. It's you."

"How are you?"

I shrugged. "Pretty good. Frazzled. Christmas and all."

"Regular?" called the woman from the counter.

"Fine," Roberta called back and then, "Wait for me in the car."

She slipped into the booth beside me. "I have to tell you something, Twyla. I made up my mind if I ever saw you again, I'd tell you."

"I'd just as soon not hear anything, Roberta. It doesn't matter now, anyway."

"No," she said. "Not about that."

"Don't be long," said the woman. She carried two regulars to go and the man peeled his cigarette pack as they left.

"It's about St. Bonny's and Maggie."

"Oh, please."

"Listen to me. I really did think she was black. I didn't make that up. I really thought so. But now I can't be sure. I just remember her as old, so old. And because she couldn't talk—well, you know, I thought she was crazy. She'd been brought up in an institution like my mother was and like I thought I would be too. And you were right. We didn't kick her. It was the gar girls. Only them. But, well, I wanted to. I really wanted them to hurt her. I said we did it, too. You and me, but that's not true. And I don't want you to carry that around. It was just that I wanted to do it so bad that day—wanting to is doing it."

Her eyes were watery from the drinks she'd had, I guess. I know it's that way with me. One glass of wine and I start bawling over the littlest thing.

"We were kids, Roberta."

"Yeah. Yeah. I know, just kids."

"Eight."

1. A campus in the State University of New York system, located 70 miles north of New York City.

"Eight."

"And lonely."

"Scared, too."

She wiped her cheeks with the heel of her hand and smiled. "Well, that's all I wanted to say."

I nodded and couldn't think of any way to fill the silence that went from the diner past the paper bells on out into the snow. It was heavy now. I thought I'd better wait for the sand trucks before starting home.

"Thanks, Roberta."

"Sure."

"Did I tell you? My mother, she never did stop dancing."

"Yes. You told me. And mine, she never got well." Roberta lifted her hands from the tabletop and covered her face with her palms. When she took them away she really was crying. "Oh shit, Twyla. Shit, shit, shit. What the hell happened to Maggie?"

1983

SYLVIA PLATH
1932–1963

I n an introduction to Sylvia Plath's *Ariel* (1965), published two years after her suicide in London, Robert Lowell wrote: "In these poems . . . Sylvia Plath becomes herself, becomes something imaginary, newly, wildly, and subtly created— . . . one of those super-real, hypnotic great classical heroines." Lowell had first met Plath in 1958, during her regular visits to his poetry seminar at Boston University, where he remembered her "air of maddening docility." Later, writing his introduction, he recognized her astonishing creation of a poetic self. The poems of *Ariel* were written at white heat, two or three a day, in the last months of Plath's life, but there is nothing hurried in their language or structure. When they are taken together with the poems posthumously published in *Crossing the Water* (1971) and *Winter Trees* (1972), a coherent persona emerges: larger than life, operatic in feeling. Although this focus on the self often excludes attention to the larger world, it generates the dynamic energy of her work. Plath appropriates a centrally American tradition, the heroic ego confronting the sublime, but she brilliantly revises this tradition by turning what the American Transcendentalist Ralph Waldo Emerson called the "great and crescive self" into a heroine instead of a hero. Seizing a mythic power, the Plath of the poems transmutes the domestic and the ordinary into the hallucinatory, the utterly strange. Her revision of the romantic ego dramatizes its tendency toward disproportion and excess, and she is fully capable of both using and mocking this heightened sense of self, as she does in her poem "Lady Lazarus."

Plath's well-known autobiographical novel, *The Bell Jar* (1963), has nothing of the brilliance of her poems, but it effectively dramatizes the stereotyping of women's roles in the 1950s and the turmoil of a young woman only partly aware that her gifts and ambitions greatly exceed the options available to her. In the novel Plath uses her experience as a guest editor of a young-women's magazine (in real life, *Mademoiselle*) and then, in an abrupt shift, presents her heroine's attempted suicide and hospitalization. Plath herself had suffered a serious breakdown and attempted suicide between her junior and senior years in college. The popularity of *The Bell Jar* may be one reason why attention to Plath's life has sometimes obscured the accomplishments of her art. While her poems often begin in autobiography, their success depends on Plath's imaginative transformations of experience into myth, as in a number of her poems (such as "Daddy") where the figure of her Prussian father is transformed into an emblem for masculine authority. Otto Plath was an entomologist and the author of a treatise on bumblebees. His death in 1940 from gangrene (the consequence of a diabetic condition he refused to treat), when Plath was eight, was the crucial event of her childhood. After his death her mother, Aurelia, while struggling to support two small children, encouraged her daughter's literary ambitions.

In many ways Plath embodied the bright, young, middle-class woman of the 1950s. She went to Smith College on a scholarship and graduated summa cum laude. On a Fulbright grant she studied in England at Cambridge University, where she met and married the poet Ted Hughes. On the face of it her marriage must have seemed the perfect fate for such a young woman; it combined romance, two poets beginning careers together (Plath's first book, *The Colossus*, appeared in 1960, three years after Hughes's first collection, *The Hawk in the Rain*), and two children (Frieda, born in 1960, and Nicholas, born in 1962), with a country house in Devon, England. In her poems, however, we find the strains of such a life; the work is galvanized by suffering, by a terrible constriction against which she unlooses "The lioness, / The shriek in the bath, / The cloak of holes" ("Purdah"). In articulating a dark vision of domestic life, Plath adopted the license of Robert Lowell and Anne Sexton, a fellow student in Lowell's poetry seminar, to write about "private and taboo subjects."

While still living in Devon, Plath wrote most of the poems that were to make up *Ariel* (by Christmas 1962, she had gathered them in a black binder and arranged them in a careful sequence). The marriage broke up in the summer of 1962, and at the beginning of the new year Plath found herself with two small children, living in a London flat during one of the coldest winters in recent British history. There she began new poems, writing furiously until February 1963, when she took her own life. The *Ariel* collection published by Hughes in 1965 does not follow Plath's intended sequence; it omits what Hughes called "some of the more personally aggressive poems from 1962" and includes the dozen or so poems Plath wrote in the months before her death and that she had envisioned as the beginnings of a third book. Nonetheless, the powerful, angry poems of *Ariel*, mining a limited range of deep feeling, are Plath's best-known work. Fueled by an anger toward her husband and her father, she speaks in these poems as one whose feelings are more than her own; it is as if she were the character in George Eliot's *Daniel Deronda* (1876) who appears suddenly before the novel's heroine and says, "I am a woman's life." Other poems, however, demonstrate her ability to render a wider variety of emotion; they include poems about her children (such as "Morning Song," "Child," and "Parliament Hill Fields") and a number of arresting poems about the natural world. In the vastness of natural processes the Romantic ego finds something as large as itself, and Plath's response to nature is intense, often uncanny. Her poems offer an eccentric vision where (as in "Blackberrying") the appearance of the natural world is never separable from the consciousness of the one who sees it.

For all her courting of excess Plath is a remarkably controlled writer; her lucid stanzas, her clear diction, and her dazzling alterations of sound all display that control. The imaginative intensity of her poems is her own triumphant creation out of the difficult circumstances of her life. She once remarked, "I cannot sympathize with those cries from the heart that are informed by nothing except a needle or a knife. . . . I believe that one should be able to control and manipulate experiences, even the most terrifying . . . with an informed and intelligent mind." The influence of her style, and of the persona she created, continues to be felt in the work of a wide variety of contemporary poets.

Morning Song

Love set you going like a fat gold watch.
The midwife slapped your footsoles, and your bald cry
Took its place among the elements.

Our voices echo, magnifying your arrival. New statue.
In a drafty museum, your nakedness   5
Shadows our safety. We stand round blankly as walls.

I'm no more your mother
Than the cloud that distills a mirror to reflect its own slow
Effacement at the wind's hand.

All night your moth-breath   10
Flickers among the flat pink roses. I wake to listen:
A far sea moves in my ear.

One cry, and I stumble from bed, cow-heavy and floral
In my Victorian nightgown.
Your mouth opens clean as a cat's. The window square   15

Whitens and swallows its dull stars. And now you try
Your handful of notes;
The clear vowels rise like balloons.

1961   1966

Lady Lazarus[1]

I have done it again.
One year in every ten
I manage it—

A sort of walking miracle, my skin
Bright as a Nazi lampshade,[2]   5
My right foot

A paperweight,
My face a featureless, fine
Jew linen.

Peel off the napkin   10
O my enemy.
Do I terrify?——

1. Lazarus was raised from the dead by Jesus   2. In the Nazi death camps, the victims' skins
(John 11.1–45).   were sometimes used to make lampshades.

The nose, the eye pits, the full set of teeth?
The sour breath
Will vanish in a day.   15

Soon, soon the flesh
The grave cave ate will be
At home on me

And I a smiling woman.
I am only thirty.   20
And like the cat I have nine times to die.

This is Number Three.
What a trash
To annihilate each decade.

What a million filaments.   25
The peanut-crunching crowd
Shoves in to see

Them unwrap me hand and foot——
The big strip tease.
Gentlemen, ladies   30

These are my hands
My knees.
I may be skin and bone,

Nevertheless, I am the same, identical woman.
The first time it happened I was ten.   35
It was an accident.

The second time I meant
To last it out and not come back at all.
I rocked shut

As a seashell.   40
They had to call and call
And pick the worms off me like sticky pearls.

Dying
Is an art, like everything else.
I do it exceptionally well.   45

I do it so it feels like hell.
I do it so it feels real.
I guess you could say I've a call.

It's easy enough to do it in a cell.
It's easy enough to do it and stay put.   50
It's the theatrical

Comeback in broad day
To the same place, the same face, the same brute
Amused shout:

'A miracle!'   55
That knocks me out.
There is a charge

For the eyeing of my scars, there is a charge
For the hearing of my heart——
It really goes.   60

And there is a charge, a very large charge
For a word or a touch
Or a bit of blood

Or a piece of my hair or my clothes.
So, so, Herr[3] Doktor.   65
So, Herr Enemy.

I am your opus,
I am your valuable,
The pure gold baby

That melts to a shriek.   70
I turn and burn.
Do not think I underestimate your great concern.

Ash, ash——
You poke and stir.
Flesh, bone, there is nothing there——   75

A cake of soap,
A wedding ring,
A gold filling.[4]

Herr God, Herr Lucifer
Beware   80
Beware.

Out of the ash[5]
I rise with my red hair
And I eat men like air.

1962   1966

---

3. Mr. (German).
4. The Nazis used human remains in the making
of soap and scavenged corpses for jewelry and
gold teeth.

5. An allusion to the phoenix, a mythical bird
that dies by fire and is reborn out of its own
ashes.

Daddy

You do not do, you do not do
Any more, black shoe
In which I have lived like a foot
For thirty years, poor and white,
Barely daring to breathe or Achoo.

Daddy, I have had to kill you.
You died before I had time——
Marble-heavy, a bag full of God,
Ghastly statue with one grey toe[1]
Big as a Frisco seal

And a head in the freakish Atlantic
Where it pours bean green over blue
In the waters of beautiful Nauset.[2]
I used to pray to recover you.
Ach, du.[3]

In the German tongue, in the Polish town[4]
Scraped flat by the roller
Of wars, wars, wars.
But the name of the town is common.
My Polack friend

Says there are a dozen or two.
So I never could tell where you
Put your foot, your root,
I never could talk to you.
The tongue stuck in my jaw.

It stuck in a barb wire snare.
Ich,[5] ich, ich, ich,
I could hardly speak.
I thought every German was you.
And the language obscene

An engine, an engine
Chuffing me off like a Jew.
A Jew to Dachau, Auschwitz, Belsen.[6]
I began to talk like a Jew.
I think I may well be a Jew.

5

10

15

20

25

30

35

1. Plath's father's toe turned black from gangrene, a complication of diabetes.
2. Massachusetts beach.
3. Ah, you (German): the first of a series of references to her father's German origins.

4. The poet's father, of German descent, was born in Grabow, Poland.
5. I (German).
6. German concentration camps, where millions of Jews were murdered during World War II.

The snows of the Tyrol,[7] the clear beer of Vienna
Are not very pure or true.
With my gypsy ancestress and my weird luck
And my Taroc[8] pack and my Taroc pack
I may be a bit of a Jew.   40

I have always been scared of *you*,
With your Luftwaffe,[9] your gobbledygoo.
And your neat mustache
And your Aryan eye, bright blue.
Panzer[1]-man, panzer-man, O You——   45

Not God but a swastika
So black no sky could squeak through.
Every woman adores a Fascist,
The boot in the face, the brute
Brute heart of a brute like you.   50

You stand at the blackboard, daddy,
In the picture I have of you,
A cleft in your chin instead of your foot
But no less a devil for that, no not
And less the black man who   55

Bit my pretty red heart in two.
I was ten when they buried you.
At twenty I tried to die
And get back, back, back to you.
I thought even the bones would do.   60

But they pulled me out of the sack,
And they stuck me together with glue.[2]
And then I knew what to do.
I made a model of you,
A man in black with a Meinkampf[3] look   65

And a love of the rack and the screw.
And I said I do, I do.
So daddy, I'm finally through.
The black telephone's off at the root,
The voices just can't worm through.   70

If I've killed one man, I've killed two——
The vampire who said he was you
And drank my blood for a year,

---

7. Austrian Alpine region.
8. Variation of Tarot, ancient fortune-telling cards. Gypsies, like Jews, were objects of Nazi genocidal ambition; many died in the concentration camps.
9. The German air force.
1. Armor (German); refers to the German army's tank corps in World War II. Hitler preached the

superiority of the Aryans—people of German stock with blond hair and blue eyes.
2. An allusion to Plath's first suicide attempt.
3. A reference to Hitler's political autobiography, *Mein Kampf* (*My Struggle*), written and published before his rise to power, in which the future dictator outlined his plans for world conquest.

Seven years, if you want to know.
Daddy, you can lie back now.   75

There's a stake in your fat black heart
And the villagers never liked you.
They are dancing and stamping on you.
They always *knew* it was you.
Daddy, daddy, you bastard, I'm through.   80

1962   1966

Blackberrying

Nobody in the lane, and nothing, nothing but blackberries,
Blackberries on either side, though on the right mainly,
A blackberry alley, going down in hooks, and a sea
Somewhere at the end of it, heaving. Blackberries
Big as the ball of my thumb, and dumb as eyes   5
Ebon in the hedges, fat
With blue-red juices. These they squander on my fingers.
I had not asked for such a blood sisterhood; they must love me.
They accommodate themselves to my milkbottle, flattening their sides.

Overhead go the choughs[1] in black, cacophonous flocks—   10
Bits of burnt paper wheeling in a blown sky.
Theirs is the only voice, protesting, protesting.
I do not think the sea will appear at all.
The high, green meadows are glowing, as if lit from within.
I come to one bush of berries so ripe it is a bush of flies,   15
Hanging their bluegreen bellies and their wing panes in a Chinese screen.
The honey-feast of the berries has stunned them; they believe in heaven.
One more hook, and the berries and bushes end.

The only thing to come now is the sea.
From between two hills a sudden wind funnels at me,   20
Slapping its phantom laundry in my face.
These hills are too green and sweet to have tasted salt.
I follow the sheep path between them. A last hook brings me
To the hills' northern face, and the face is orange rock
That looks out on nothing, nothing but a great space   25
Of white and pewter lights, and a din like silversmiths
Beating and beating at an intractable metal.

1961   1971

---

1. Small, chattering birds of the crow family.

Child

Your clear eye is the one absolutely beautiful thing.
I want to fill it with color and ducks,
The zoo of the new

Whose names you meditate—
April snowdrop, Indian pipe,   5
Little

Stalk without wrinkle,
Pool in which images
Should be grand and classical

Not this troublous   10
Wringing of hands, this dark
Ceiling without a star.

1963   1972

JOHN UPDIKE
1932–2009

"To transcribe middleness with all its grits, bumps and anonymities, in its
fullness of satisfaction and mystery: is it possible . . . or worth doing?" John
Updike's novels and stories give a positive answer to the question he asks in his
early memoir, *The Dogwood Tree: A Boyhood*; for he is arguably the most significant
transcriber, or creator rather, of "middleness" in American writing since William
Dean Howells (about whom he has written appreciatively) a century earlier. Falling
in love in high school, meeting a college roommate, going to the eye doctor or dentist, eating supper on Sunday night, visiting your mother with your wife and son—
these activities are made to yield up their possibilities to a writer as responsively
curious in imagination and delicately precise in his literary expression as Updike
showed himself to be.

Born in Shillington, Pennsylvania, John Updike was an only child. He was
gifted at drawing and caricature, and after graduating summa cum laude from
Harvard in 1954, he spent a year studying art in England, then returned to America and went to work for the *New Yorker*, where his first stories appeared and to
which he contributed regularly for five decades. When later in the 1950s he left
the magazine, he also left New York City and with his wife and children settled in
Ipswich, Massachusetts. There he pursued "his solitary trade as methodically as
the dentist practiced his," resisting the temptations of university teaching as successfully as he did the blandishments of media talk shows. His ample output was
achieved through dedicated, steady work; his books are the fruit of patience, leisure, and craft.

Since 1959, when his first novel, *The Poorhouse Fair*, appeared, Updike published not only many novels and stories but also eight books of poetry, a play, and a vast store of book reviews and other prose writings. He is most admired by some readers as the author of the "Olinger" stories (included in *The Early Stories: 1953–1975*, 2003) about life in an imaginary Pennsylvania town that takes on its colors from the real Shillington of his youth. The heroes of these stories are adolescents straining to break out of their fast-perishing environments, as they grow up and as their small town turns into something else. Updike treats them with a blend of affection and ironic humor that is wonderfully assured in its touch, although his sense of place, of growing up during the Depression and the years of World War II, is always vividly present. Like Howells (whose fine memoir of his youthful days in Ohio, *A Boy's Town*, is an ancestor of Updike's *The Dogwood Tree*), he shows how one's spirit takes on its coloration from the material circumstances—houses, clothes, landscape, food, parents—one is bounded by.

This sense of place, which is also a sense of life, is found in the stories and in the novels, too, although Updike found it harder to invent convincing forms in which to tell longer tales. His most ambitious novel is probably *The Centaur* (1964), memorable for its portrayal of three days of confusion and error in the life of an American high school teacher seen through his son's eyes, but the book is also burdened with an elaborate set of mythical trappings that seem less than inevitable. *Couples* (1968), a novel that gained him a good deal of notoriety as a chronicler of sexual relationships, both marital and adulterous, is jammed with much interesting early-1960s lore about suburban life but seems uncertain whether it is an exercise in realism or a creative fantasy, as does *Marry Me* (1976).

In the four "Rabbit" novels, Updike found his most congenial and engaging subject for longer fiction. In each book he rendered the sense of an era—the 1950s in *Rabbit, Run*; the late 1960s in *Rabbit Redux*; the great gasoline crisis of 1979 in *Rabbit Is Rich*; the end of the Reagan era (and the end of Rabbit) in *Rabbit at Rest* (1990)—through the eyes of a hero who both is and is not like his creator. Harry "Rabbit" Angstrom, ex–high school basketball star, perpetually prey to nostalgia and in love with his own past, lives in a present he can't abide. *Rabbit, Run* shows him trying to escape from his town, his job, his wife, and his child by a series of disastrously sentimental and humanly irresponsible actions; yet Updike makes us feel Rabbit's yearnings even as we judge the painful consequences of yielding to them. Ten years later the fading basketball star has become a fortyish, dispirited printer with a wayward wife and a country that is both landing on the moon and falling to pieces. *Rabbit Redux* is masterly in presenting a small town rotting away from its past certainties; it also attempts to deal with the Vietnam War and the black revolution. *Rabbit Is Rich* is a gentler, sadder chronicling of the hero's settling into grandfatherhood as he draws ever closer to death; while *Rabbit at Rest*, the longest and richest of the four novels, brings him to a moving conclusion. Rabbit's coda is presented in the reflections of his son and illegitimate daughter in "Rabbit Remembered," collected in *Licks of Love* (2000). In *Roger's Version* (1986) and *S* (1988), Updike adopted—or permitted his protagonists to adopt—a more broadly, sometimes a harsher, satiric view of contemporary religion, computer technology, feminism, and other forms of "liberation." Still, for all his virtuosity as a novelist, his best work may be found in the stories and in his short novel *Of the Farm* (1965). In "Separating" (printed here) the boy from "The Happiest I've Been" (*The Same Door*, 1959) has grown up, married, and fathered children and is now about to leave them as he moves into divorce. It is a beautiful example of Updike's careful, poised sense of how things work, a sense that can also be observed in the poem "Dog's Death" and in his memoir *Self-Consciousness* (1989).

Near the end of "The Dogwood Tree," he summarized his boyish dream of becoming an artist:

He saw art—between drawing and writing he ignorantly made no distinction—as a method of riding a thin pencil out of Shillington, out of time altogether, into an infinity of unseen and even unborn hearts. He pictured this infinity as radiant. How innocent!

Most writers would name that innocence only to deplore it. Updike maintained instead that, as with the Christian faith he professed, succeeding years gave him no better assumptions with which to replace it. In any case, his fine sense of fact protected him from fashionable extravagances in black humor and experimental narratives, while enabling him to be both a satirist and a celebrator of our social and domestic conditions. In the last decade of his life a fabulative, almost magical atmosphere appeared in some works, as with his 2000 novel, *Gertrude and Claudius*. Yet even here John Updike showed himself to be our era's most sensitive craftsman of personal and societal manners, as he did in the generational family saga based on spiritual perceptions, *In the Beauty of the Lilies* (1996), in *Villages* (2004), a bildungsroman about a protagonist's marriages, careers, and communities, and in the sociopolitical challenge of *Terrorist* (2006).

The following text is from the *New Yorker* (June 23, 1975).

Separating

The day was fair. Brilliant. All that June the weather had mocked the Maples' internal misery with solid sunlight—golden shafts and cascades of green in which their conversations had wormed unseeing, their sad murmuring selves the only stain in Nature. Usually by this time of the year they had acquired tans; but when they met their elder daughter's plane on her return from a year in England they were almost as pale as she, though Judith was too dazzled by the sunny opulent jumble of her native land to notice. They did not spoil her homecoming by telling her immediately. Wait a few days, let her recover from jet lag, had been one of their formulations, in that string of gray dialogues—over coffee, over cocktails, over Cointreau—that had shaped the strategy of their dissolution, while the earth performed its annual stunt of renewal unnoticed beyond their closed windows. Richard had thought to leave at Easter; Joan had insisted they wait until the four children were at last assembled, with all exams passed and ceremonies attended, and the bauble of summer to console them. So he had drudged away, in love, in dread, repairing screens, getting the mowers sharpened, rolling and patching their new tennis court.

The court, clay, had come through its first winter pitted and windswept bare of redcoat. Years ago the Maples had observed how often, among their friends, divorce followed a dramatic home improvement, as if the marriage were making one last twitchy effort to live; their own worst crisis had come amid the plaster dust and exposed plumbing of a kitchen renovation. Yet, a summer ago, as canary-yellow bulldozers gaily churned a grassy, daisy-dotted knoll into a muddy plateau, and a crew of pigtailed young men raked and tamped clay into a plane, this transformation did not strike them as ominous, but festive in its impudence; their marriage could rend the earth for fun. The next spring, waking each day at dawn to a sliding sensation as if the bed were being tipped, Richard found the barren tennis court, its net and tapes still rolled in the barn, an environment congruous with his mood of purposeful desolation, and the crumbling of handfuls of clay into cracks and holes (dogs had frolicked on the court in a thaw; rivulets had evolved trenches) an activity suitably elemental and interminable. In his sealed heart he hoped the day would never come.

Now it was here. A Friday. Judith was reacclimated; all four children were assembled, before jobs and camps and visits again scattered them. Joan thought they should be told one by one. Richard was for making an announcement at the table. She said, "I think just making an announcement is a cop-out. They'll start quarrelling and playing to each other instead of focussing. They're each individuals, you know, not just some corporate obstacle to your freedom."

"O.K., O.K. I agree." Joan's plan was exact. That evening, they were giving Judith a belated welcome-home dinner, of lobster and champagne. Then, the party over, they, the two of them, who nineteen years before would push her in a baby carriage along Tenth Street to Washington Square,[1] were to walk her out of the house, to the bridge across the salt creek, and tell her, swearing her to secrecy. Then Richard Jr., who was going directly from work to a rock concert in Boston, would be told, either late when he returned on the train or early Saturday morning before he went off to his job; he was seventeen and employed as one of a golf-course maintenance crew. Then the two younger children, John and Margaret, could, as the morning wore on, be informed.

"Mopped up, as it were," Richard said.

"Do you have any better plan? That leaves you the rest of Saturday to answer any questions, pack, and make your wonderful departure."

"No," he said, meaning he had no better plan, and agreed to hers, though it had an edge of false order, a plea for control in the semblance of its achievement, like Joan's long chore lists and financial accountings and, in the days when he first knew her, her too copious lecture notes. Her plan turned one hurdle for him into four—four knife-sharp walls, each with a sheer blind drop on the other side.

All spring he had been morbidly conscious of insides and outsides, of barriers and partitions. He and Joan stood as a thin barrier between the children and the truth. Each moment was a partition, with the past on one side and the future on the other, a future containing this unthinkable *now*. Beyond four knifelike walls a new life for him waited vaguely. His skull cupped a secret, a white face, a face both frightened and soothing, both strange and known, that he wanted to shield from tears, which he felt all about him, solid as the sunlight. So haunted, he had become obsessed with battening down the house against his absence, replacing screens and sash cords, hinges and latches—a Houdini[2] making things snug before his escape.

The lock. He had still to replace a lock on one of the doors of the screened porch. The task, like most such, proved more difficult than he had imagined. The old lock, aluminum frozen by corrosion, had been deliberately rendered obsolete by manufacturers. Three hardware stores had nothing that even approximately matched the mortised hole its removal (surprisingly easy) left. Another hole had to be gouged, with bits too small and saws too big,

1. In Greenwich Village, an area in lower Manhattan, New York City.
2. Harry Houdini (1874–1926), American magician and escape artist.

and the old hole fitted with a block of wood—the chisels dull, the saw rusty, his fingers thick with lack of sleep. The sun poured down, beyond the porch, on a world of neglect. The bushes already needed pruning, the windward side of the house was shedding flakes of paint, rain would get in when he was gone, insects, rot, death. His family, all those he would lose, filtered through the edges of his awareness as he struggled with screw holes, splinters, opaque instructions, minutiae of metal.

Judith sat on the porch, a princess returned from exile. She regaled them with stories of fuel shortages, of bomb scares in the Underground, of Pakistani workmen loudly lusting after her as she walked past on her way to dance school. Joan came and went, in and out of the house, calmer than she should have been, praising his struggles with the lock as if this were one more and not the last of their chain of shared chores. The younger of his sons, John, now at fifteen suddenly, unwittingly handsome, for a few minutes held the rickety screen door while his father clumsily hammered and chiselled, each blow a kind of sob in Richard's ears. His younger daughter, having been at a slumber party, slept on the porch hammock through all the noise—heavy and pink, trusting and forsaken. Time, like the sunlight, continued relentlessly; the sunlight slowly slanted. Today was one of the longest days. The lock clicked, worked. He was through. He had a drink; he drank it on the porch, listening to his daughter. "It was so sweet," she was saying, "during the worst of it, how all the butcher's and bakery shops kept open by candlelight. They're all so plucky and cute. From the papers, things sounded so much worse here—people shooting people in gas lines, and everybody freezing."

Richard asked her, "Do you still want to live in England forever?" *Forever*: the concept, now a reality upon him, pressed and scratched at the back of his throat.

"No," Judith confessed, turning her oval face to him, its eyes still childishly far apart, but the lips set as over something succulent and satisfactory. "I was anxious to come home. I'm an American." She was a woman. They had raised her; he and Joan had endured together to raise her, alone of the four. The others had still some raising left in them. Yet it was the thought of telling Judith—the image of her, their first baby, walking between them arm in arm to the bridge—that broke him. The partition between himself and the tears broke. Richard sat down to the celebratory meal with the back of his throat aching; the champagne, the lobster seemed phases of sunshine; he saw them and tasted them through tears. He blinked, swallowed, croakily joked about hay fever. The tears would not stop leaking through; they came not through a hole that could be plugged but through a permeable spot in a membrane, steadily, purely, endlessly, fruitfully. They became his tears, a shield for himself against these others—their faces, the fact of their assembly, a last time as innocents, at a table where he sat the last time as head. Tears dropped from his nose as he broke the lobster's back; salt flavored his champagne as he sipped it; the raw clench at the back of his throat was delicious. He could not help himself.

His children tried to ignore his tears. Judith on his right, lit a cigarette, gazed upward in the direction of her too energetic, too sophisticated exhalation; on her other side, John earnestly bent his face to the extraction of the last morsels—legs, tail segments—from the scarlet corpse. Joan, at the opposite end of the table, glanced at him surprised, her reproach displaced by a quick grimace, of forgiveness, or of salute to his superior gift of strategy. Between them, Margaret, no longer called Bean, thirteen and large for her age, gazed from the other side of his pane of tears as if into a shopwindow at something she coveted—at her father, a crystalline heap of splinters and memories. It was not she, however, but John who, in the kitchen, as they cleared the plates and carapaces away, asked Joan the question: *"Why is Daddy crying?"*

Richard heard the question but not the murmured answer. Then he heard Bean cry, "Oh, no-oh!"—the faintly dramatized exclamation of one who had long expected it.

John returned to the table carrying a bowl of salad. He nodded tersely at his father and his lips shaped the conspiratorial words "She told."

"Told what?" Richard asked aloud, insanely.

The boy sat down as if to rebuke his father's distraction with the example of his own good manners and said quietly, "The separation."

Joan and Margaret returned; the child, in Richard's twisted vision, seemed diminished in size, and relieved, relieved to have had the boogey-man at last proved real. He called out to her—the distances at the table had grown immense—"You knew, you always knew," but the clenching at the back of his throat prevented him from making sense of it. From afar he heard Joan talking, levelly, sensibly, reciting what they had prepared: it was a separation for the summer, an experiment. She and Daddy both agreed it would be good for them; they needed space and time to think; they liked each other but did not make each other happy enough, somehow.

Judith, imitating her mother's factual tone, but in her youth off-key, too cool, said, "I think it's silly. You should either live together or get divorced."

Richard's crying, like a wave that has crested and crashed, had become tumultuous; but it was overtopped by another tumult, for John, who had been so reserved, now grew larger and larger at the table. Perhaps his younger sister's being credited with knowing set him off. "Why didn't you *tell* us?" he asked, in a large round voice quite unlike his own. "You should have *told* us you weren't getting along."

Richard was startled into attempting to force words through his tears. "We *do* get along, that's the trouble, so it doesn't show even to us—" "That we do not love each other" was the rest of the sentence; he couldn't finish it.

Joan finished for him, in her style. "And we've always, *especially*, loved our children."

John was not mollified. "What do you care about *us*?" he boomed. "We're just little things you *had*." His sisters' laughing forced a laugh from him, which he turned hard and parodistic: "Ha ha *ha*." Richard and Joan realized simultaneously that the child was drunk, on Judith's homecoming champagne. Feeling bound to keep the center of the stage, John took a cigarette from Judith's pack, poked it into his mouth, let it hang from his lower lip, and squinted like a gangster.

"You're not little things we had," Richard called to him. "You're the whole point. But you're grown. Or almost."

The boy was lighting matches. Instead of holding them to his cigarette (for they had never seen him smoke; being "good" had been his way of setting himself apart), he held them to his mother's face, closer and closer, for her to blow out. Then he lit the whole folder—a hiss and then a torch, held against his mother's face. Prismed by tears, the flame filled Richard's vision; he didn't know how it was extinguished. He heard Margaret say, "Oh stop showing off," and saw John, in response, break the cigarette in two and put the halves entirely into his mouth and chew, sticking out his tongue to display the shreds to his sister.

Joan talked to him, reasoning—a fountain of reason, unintelligible. "Talked about it for years . . . our children must help us . . . Daddy and I both want . . ." As the boy listened, he carefully wadded a paper napkin into the leaves of his salad, fashioned a ball of paper and lettuce, and popped it into his mouth, looking around the table for the expected laughter. None came. Judith said, "Be mature," and dismissed a plume of smoke.

Richard got up from this stifling table and led the boy outside. Though the house was in twilight, the outdoors still brimmed with light, the long waste light of high summer. Both laughing, he supervised John's spitting out the lettuce and paper and tobacco into the pachysandra.[3] He took him by the hand—a square gritty hand, but for its softness a man's. Yet, it held on. They ran together up into the field, past the tennis court. The raw banking left by the bulldozers was dotted with daisies. Past the court and a flat stretch where they used to play family baseball stood a soft green rise glorious in the sun, each weed and species of grass distinct as illumination on parchment. "I'm sorry, so sorry," Richard cried. "You were the only one who ever tried to help me with all the goddam jobs around this place."

Sobbing, safe within his tears and the champagne, John explained, "It's not just the separation, it's the whole crummy year, I *hate* that school, you can't make any friends, the history teacher's a scud."[4]

They sat on the crest of the rise, shaking and warm from their tears but easier in their voices, and Richard tried to focus on the child's sad year— the weekdays long with homework, the weekends spent in his room with model airplanes, while his parents murmured down below, nursing their separation. How selfish, how blind, Richard thought; his eyes felt scoured. He told his son, "We'll think about getting you transferred. Life's too short to be miserable."

They had said what they could, but did not want the moment to heal, and talked on, about the school, about the tennis court, whether it would ever again be as good as it had been that first summer. They walked to inspect it and pressed a few more tapes more firmly down. A little stiltedly, perhaps trying to make too much of the moment, to prolong it, Richard led the boy to the spot in the field where the view was best, of the metallic blue river, the emerald marsh, the scattered islands velvet with shadow in the low light, the white bits of beach far away. "See," he said. "It goes on being beautiful. It'll be here tomorrow."

"I know," John answered, impatiently. The moment had closed.

Back in the house, the others had opened some white wine, the champagne being drunk, and still sat at the table, the three females, gossiping.

3. Green, leafy plant, frequently used as ground cover.
4. Dull, disagreeable, objectionable person.

Where Joan sat had become the head. She turned, showing him a tearless face, and asked, "All right?"

"We're fine," he said, resenting it, though relieved, that the party went on without him.

In bed she explained, "I couldn't cry I guess because I cried so much all spring. It really wasn't fair. It's your idea, and you made it look as though I was kicking you out."

"I'm sorry," he said. "I couldn't stop. I wanted to but couldn't."

"You *didn't* want to. You loved it. You were having your way, making a general announcement."

"I love having it over," he admitted. "God, those kids were great. So brave and funny." John, returned to the house, had settled to a model airplane in his room, and kept shouting down to them, "I'm O.K. No sweat." "And the way," Richard went on, cozy in his relief, "they never questioned the reasons we gave. No thought of a third person. Not even Judith."

"That *was* touching," Joan said.

He gave her a hug. "You were great too. Thank you." Guiltily, he realized he did not feel separated.

"You still have Dickie to do," she told him. These words set before him a black mountain in the darkness; its cold breath, its near weight affected his chest. Of the four children Dickie was most nearly his conscience. Joan did not need to add, "That's one piece of your dirty work I won't do for you."

"I know. I'll do it. You go to sleep."

Within minutes, her breathing slowed, became oblivious and deep. It was quarter to midnight. Dickie's train from the concert would come in at one-fourteen. Richard set the alarm for one. He had slept atrociously for weeks. But whenever he closed his lids some glimpse of the last hours scorched them—Judith exhaling toward the ceiling in a kind of aversion, Bean's mute staring, the sunstruck growth of the field where he and John had rested. The mountain before him moved closer, moved within him; he was huge, momentous. The ache at the back of his throat felt stale. His wife slept as if slain beside him. When, exasperated by his hot lids, his crowded heart, he rose from bed and dressed, she awoke enough to turn over. He told her then, "If I could undo it all, I would."

"Where would you begin?" she asked. There was no place. Giving him courage, she was always giving him courage. He put on shoes without socks in the dark. The children were breathing in their rooms, the downstairs was hollow. In their confusion they had left lights burning. He turned off all but one, the kitchen overhead. The car started. He had hoped it wouldn't. He met only moonlight on the road; it seemed a diaphanous companion, flickering in the leaves along the roadside, haunting his rearview mirror like a pursuer, melting under his headlights. The center of town, not quite deserted, was eerie at this hour. A young cop in uniform kept company with a gang of T-shirted kids on the steps of the bank. Across from the railroad station, several bars kept open. Customers, mostly young, passed in and out of the warm night, savoring summer's novelty. Voices shouted from cars as they passed; an immense conversation seemed in progress. Richard parked and in his weariness put his head on the passenger seat, out of the commotion and wheeling lights. It was as when, in the movies, an assassin grimly carries his mission through the jostle of a carnival—except the movies cannot show the precipitous, palpable slope you cling to within. You cannot climb back down; you can only fall. The synthetic fabric of the car seat, warmed by his cheek, confided to him an ancient, distant scent of vanilla.

A train whistle caused him to lift his head. It was on time; he had hoped it would be late. The slender drawgates descended. The bell of approach tingled happily. The great metal body, horizontally fluted, rocked to a stop, and sleepy teen-agers disembarked, his son among them. Dickie did not show surprise that his father was meeting him at this terrible hour. He sauntered to the car with two friends, both taller than he. He said "Hi" to his father and took the passenger's seat with an exhausted promptness that expressed gratitude. The friends got into the back, and Richard was grateful; a few more minutes' postponement would be won by driving them home.

He asked, "How was the concert?"

"Groovy," one boy said from the back seat.

"It bit," the other said.

"It was O.K.," Dickie said, moderate by nature, so reasonable that in his childhood the unreason of the world had given him headaches, stomach aches, nausea. When the second friend had been dropped off at his dark house, the boy blurted, "Dad, my eyes are killing me with hay fever! I'm out there cutting that mothering grass all day!"

"Do we still have those drops?"

"They didn't do any good last summer."

"They might this." Richard swung a U-turn on the empty street. The drive home took a few minutes. The mountain was here, in his throat. "Richard," he said, and felt the boy, slumped and rubbing his eyes, go tense at his tone, "I didn't come to meet you just to make your life easier. I came because your mother and I have some news for you, and you're a hard man to get ahold of these days. It's sad news."

"That's O.K." The reassurance came out soft, but quick, as if released from the tip of a spring.

Richard had feared that his tears would return and choke him, but the boy's manliness set an example, and his voice issued forth steady and dry. "It's sad news, but it needn't be tragic news, at least for you. It should have no practical effect on your life, though it's bound to have an emotional effect. You'll work at your job, and go back to school in September. Your mother and I are really proud of what you're making of your life; we don't want that to change at all."

"Yeah," the boy said lightly, on the intake of his breath, holding himself up. They turned the corner; the church they went to loomed like a gutted fort. The home of the woman Richard hoped to marry stood across the green. Her bedroom light burned.

"Your mother and I," he said, "have decided to separate. For the summer. Nothing legal, no divorce yet. We want to see how it feels. For some years now, we haven't been doing enough for each other, making each other as happy as we should be. Have you sensed that?"

"No," the boy said. It was an honest, unemotional answer: true or false in a quiz.

Glad for the factual basis, Richard pursued, even garrulously, the details. His apartment across town, his utter accessibility, the split vacation arrangements, the advantages to the children, the added mobility and variety of the summer. Dickie listened, absorbing. "Do the others know?"

Richard described how they had been told.

"How did they take it?"

"The girls pretty calmly. John flipped out; he shouted and ate a cigarette and made a salad out of his napkin and told us how much he hated school."

His brother chuckled. "He did?"

"Yeah. The school issue was more upsetting for him than Mom and me. He seemed to feel better for having exploded."

"He did?" The repetition was the first sign that he was stunned.

"Yes. Dickie, I want to tell you something. This last hour, waiting for your train to get in, has been about the worst of my life. I hate this. *Hate* it. My father would have died before doing it to me." He felt immensely lighter, saying this. He had dumped the mountain on the boy. They were home. Moving swiftly as a shadow, Dickie was out of the car, through the bright kitchen. Richard called after him, "Want a glass of milk or anything?"

"No thanks."

"Want us to call the course tomorrow and say you're too sick to work?"

"No, that's all right." The answer was faint, delivered at the door to his room; Richard listened for the slam of a tantrum. The door closed normally. The sound was sickening.

Joan had sunk into that first deep trough of sleep and was slow to awake. Richard had to repeat, "I told him."

"What did he say?"

"Nothing much. Could you go say good night to him? Please."

She left their room, without putting on a bathrobe. He sluggishly changed back into his pajamas and walked down the hall. Dickie was already in bed, Joan was sitting beside him, and the boy's bedside clock radio was murmuring music. When she stood, an inexplicable light—the moon?—outlined her body through the nightie. Richard sat on the warm place she had indented on the child's narrow mattress. He asked him, "Do you want the radio on like that?"

"It always is."

"Doesn't it keep you awake? It would me."

"No."

"Are you sleepy?"

"Yeah."

"Good. Sure you want to get up and go to work? You've had a big night."

"I want to."

Away at school this winter he had learned for the first time that you can go short of sleep and live. As an infant he had slept with an immobile, sweating intensity that had alarmed his babysitters. As the children aged, he became the first to go to bed, earlier for a time than his younger brother and sister. Even now, he would go slack in the middle of a television show, his sprawled legs hairy and brown. "O.K. Good boy. Dickie, listen. I love you so much, I never knew how much until now. No matter how this works out, I'll always be with you. Really."

Richard bent to kiss an averted face but his son, sinewy, turned and with wet cheeks embraced him and gave him a kiss, on the lips, passionate as a woman's. In his father's ear he moaned one word, the crucial, intelligent word: *"Why?"*

Why. It was a whistle of wind in a crack, a knife thrust, a window thrown open on emptiness. The white face was gone, the darkness was featureless. Richard had forgotten why.

1975

PHILIP ROTH
1933–2018

From the moment Philip Roth's collection of stories *Goodbye, Columbus* won the Houghton Mifflin Literary Fellowship for 1959, his career received the ambiguous reward of much anxious concern from critics, centered on whether he would develop the promise displayed in this first book. Ten years later, with *Portnoy's Complaint*, Roth became overnight the famous author of a "dirty" bestseller, yet his success only made his critics more uneasy. Was this gifted portrayer of Jewish middle-class life really more interested in scoring points off caricatures than in creating and exploring characters? Did his very facility with words inhibit the exercise of deeper sympathies and more humanly generous purposes?

Roth grew up in Newark, New Jersey, attended the branch of Rutgers University there, graduated from Bucknell University, took an M.A. in English literature at the University of Chicago, then served in the army. Over the years he taught at a number of universities while receiving many awards and fellowships. Like John Barth, another "university" writer, Roth is an ironic humorist, although the impulse behind his early stories is darker and less playful. *Goodbye, Columbus* is about Jews on the verge of being or already having been assimilated into the larger American culture, and the stories confidently take the measure of their embattled heroes, as in "The Conversion of the Jews" or "Epstein" or the long title story. "Defender of the Faith" (printed here), arguably the best piece in the collection, is distinguished for the way Roth explores rather than exploits the conflict between personal feelings and religious loyalties as they are felt by Nathan Marx, a U.S. Army sergeant in a Missouri training company near the end of World War II. Throughout *Goodbye, Columbus* the narrator's voice is centrally important: in some stories it is indistinguishable from that of a campus wiseguy; in others it reaches out to a calmer and graver sense of disparities between promises and performance.

Roth's first two novels, *Letting Go* (1962) and *When She Was Good* (1967), markedly extended the territory charted in *Goodbye, Columbus* and showed him eager and equipped to write about people other than Jews. *Letting Go* is conventional in technique and in its subjects—love, marriage, university life—but Roth's easy mastery of the look and feel of places and things is everywhere evident. F. Scott Fitzgerald is the American writer whose presence in these early novels is most strongly felt; in particular, the section from *Letting Go* told in the first person by a graduate student in English betrays its indebtedness to Fitzgerald's Nick Carraway, the narrator of *The Great Gatsby*. This Fitzgeraldian atmosphere, with its nostalgic evocation of adolescence and early romantic visions, is even more evident in *When She Was Good*, which is strong in its rendering of middle-American living rooms and kitchens, the flushed atmosphere of late-night 1950s sex in parked cars, or the lyrics of popular songs—bits of remembered trivia that Roth, like his predecessor, has a genius for bringing to life.

The less-than-overwhelming reception of his second novel probably helped Roth move away from relatively sober realism; certainly *Portnoy's Complaint* (1969) is a louder and more virtuoso performance than the earlier books. Alexander Portnoy's recollections of early childhood miseries are really a pretext for Roth to perform a succession of clever numbers in the inventive mode of a stand-up comic. Memories of growing up in New Jersey, listening to radio programs, playing softball, ogling girls at the ice-skating rink, or (most sensationally) masturbating in outlandish ways add up to an entertaining narrative that is sometimes crude but more often delicate and precise.

After *Portnoy* Roth moved toward fantasy and further showmanly operations: *Our Gang* (1970) attempted to do for Richard Nixon and his associates what actual events were to do one better; *The Breast* (1971) is a rather unamusing fable about a man's metamorphosis into that object; *The Great American Novel* (1973) threatened to sink under its weight of baseball lore dressed up in tall tales and sick jokes. But in *My Life as a Man* (1974) and *The Professor of Desire* (1977) he returned to matters that have traditionally preoccupied the social novelist and that inform his own best work: marriage, divorce, the family, Jewishness, and psychoanalysis—the pressures of civilization and the resultant individual discontents.

His finest work is to be found in the Zuckerman novels, beginning with *Zuckerman Bound* (1985) and its successor, *The Counterlife* (1987). In these novels Roth created a hero-as-novelist whose experience parallels in important ways that of his creator. A scandalous novel, *Carnovsky*, recalls *Portnoy's Complaint*; a critic named Milton Appel is a stand-in for the real critic Irving Howe, who once subjected Roth's work to hostile criticism. Yet for all the dangers of self-pity or self-absorption such autobiographical reference involves, the novels add up to something much deeper, more comic and touching, than self-advertisement and complaint. Scenes like the death of Zuckerman's father in a Florida hospital and the subsequent return of the son to the vanished Newark where he grew up are moving expressions of the generous purposes and human sympathies we find in Roth's work at its best. And those purposes and sympathies are also evident in his autobiographical writing: in *The Facts* (1988) and especially in *Patrimony* (1991), a poignant memoir of his father.

In the 1990s and into the twenty-first century, Roth developed his art of impersonation into audacious and sometimes excessive forms. *Operation Shylock* (1993) poses a presumably real Philip Roth who encounters an impostor; *Sabbath's Theater* (1995) recasts his typical protagonist as a puppeteer who manipulates women in much the same way; *American Pastoral* (1997) brings back Nathan Zuckerman for a high school reunion and the investigation of a "more ordinary" classmate's life. Zuckerman remains on hand for *I Married a Communist* (1998) and *The Human Stain* (2000), while David Kepesh (who had turned into a female breast in the author's much earlier fantasy) reappears as a professor who seduces his students in *The Dying Animal* (2001). Further seduction takes place in *Everyman* (2006), although the author's most disturbing projections are reserved for *The Plot against America* (2004), in which a fictive Charles A. Lindbergh becomes president and initiates repression of American Jews. *Exit Ghost* (2007) has Nathan Zuckerman return to New York City and reencounter characters from previous novels. *Indignation* (2008) sets a young man's maturation against the looming threat of military service in the Korean War. *The Humbling* (2009) projects Roth's late-life anxieties as a writer onto the career of an actor in decline. *Nemesis* (2010), his final novel, expands the author's concerns with human morality (and the role of a God who allows such suffering) to encompass a polio epidemic in the Newark of his childhood. Throughout his work, Roth's emphasis remains on invention, reminding readers that the writerly self is a virtually inexhaustible resource for the imagination. Nevertheless, in 2012 Roth announced his retirement from writing, saying he had "done my best with what I had."

The following text is from *Goodbye, Columbus* (1959).

Defender of the Faith

In May of 1945, only a few weeks after the fighting had ended in Europe, I was rotated back to the States, where I spent the remainder of the war with a training company at Camp Crowder, Missouri. We had been racing across Germany so swiftly during the late winter and spring that when I boarded the plane that drizzly morning in Berlin, I couldn't believe our destination lay to the west. My mind might inform me otherwise, but there was an inertia of the spirit that told me we were flying to a new front where we would disembark and continue our push eastward—eastward until we'd circled the globe, marching through villages along whose twisting, cobbled streets crowds of the enemy would watch us take possession of what up till then they'd considered their own. I had changed enough in two years not to mind the trembling of the old people, the crying of the very young, the uncertain fear in the eyes of the once-arrogant. After two years I had been fortunate enough to develop an infantryman's heart which, like his feet, at first aches and swells, but finally grows horny enough for him to travel the weirdest paths without feeling a thing.

Captain Paul Barrett was to be my C.O. at Camp Crowder. The day I reported for duty he came out of his office to shake my hand. He was short, gruff, and fiery, and indoors or out he wore his polished helmet liner[1] down on his little eyes. In Europe he had received a battlefield commission and a serious chest wound, and had been returned to the States only a few months before. He spoke easily to me, but was, I thought, unnecessarily abusive towards the troops. At the evening formation, he introduced me.

"Gentlemen," he called. "Sergeant Thurston, as you know, is no longer with this Company. Your new First Sergeant is Sergeant Nathan Marx here. He is a veteran of the European theater and consequently will take no shit."

I sat up late in the orderly room that evening, trying halfheartedly to solve the riddle of duty rosters, personnel forms, and morning reports. The CQ[2] slept with his mouth open on a mattress on the floor. A trainee stood reading the next day's duty roster, which was posted on the bulletin board directly inside the screen door. It was a warm evening and I could hear the men's radios playing dance music over in the barracks.

The trainee, who I knew had been staring at me whenever I looked groggily into the forms, finally took a step in my direction.

"Hey, Sarge—we having a G.I. party tomorrow night?" A G.I. party is a barracks-cleaning.

"You usually have them on Friday nights?"

"Yes," and then he added mysteriously, "that's the whole thing."

"Then you'll have a G.I. party."

He turned away and I heard him mumbling. His shoulders were moving and I wondered if he was crying.

"What's your name, soldier?" I asked.

---

1. Plastic liner worn under a helmet to prevent chafing and bruising.
2. Noncommissioned officer in charge of quarters at night or on weekends.

He turned, not crying at all. Instead his green-speckled eyes, long and narrow, flashed like fish in the sun. He walked over to me and sat on the edge of my desk.

He reached out a hand. "Sheldon," he said.

"Stand on your own two feet, Sheldon."

Climbing off the desk, he said, "Sheldon Grossbart." He smiled wider at the intimacy into which he'd led me.

"You against cleaning the barracks Friday night, Grossbart? Maybe we shouldn't have G.I. parties—maybe we should get a maid." My tone startled me: I felt like a Charlie McCarthy, with every top sergeant I had ever known as my Edgar Bergen.[3]

"No, Sergeant." He grew serious, but with a seriousness that seemed only to be the stifling of a smile. "It's just G.I. parties on Friday night, of all nights . . ."

He slipped up to the corner of the desk again—not quite sitting, but not quite standing either. He looked at me with those speckled eyes flashing and then made a gesture with his hand. It was very slight, no more than a rotation back and forth of the wrist, and yet it managed to exclude from our affairs everything else in the orderly room, to make the two of us the center of the world. It seemed, in fact, to exclude everything about the two of us except our hearts. "Sergeant Thurston was one thing," he whispered, an eye flashing to the sleeping CQ, "but we thought with you here, things might be a little different."

"We?"

"The Jewish personnel."

"Why?" I said, harshly.

He hesitated a moment, and then, uncontrollably, his hand went up to his mouth. "I mean . . ." he said.

"What's on your mind?" Whether I was still angry at the "Sheldon" business or something else, I hadn't a chance to tell—but clearly I was angry.

". . . we thought you . . . Marx, you know, like Karl Marx. The Marx brothers. Those guys are all . . . M-A-R-X, isn't that how you spell it, Sergeant?"

"M-A-R-X."

"Fishbein said—" He stopped. "What I mean to say, Sergeant—" His face and neck were red, and his mouth moved but no words came out. In a moment, he raised himself to attention, gazing down at me. It was as though he had suddenly decided he could expect no more sympathy from me than from Thurston, the reason being that I was of Thurston's faith and not his. The young man had managed to confuse himself as to what my faith really was, but I felt no desire to straighten him out. Very simply, I didn't like him.

When I did nothing but return his gaze, he spoke, in an altered tone. "You see, Sergeant," he explained to me, "Friday nights, Jews are supposed to go to services."

"Did Sergeant Thurston tell you you couldn't go to them when there was a G.I. party?"

"No."

"Did he say you had to stay and scrub the floors?"

---

3. A ventriloquist who, with Charlie McCarthy, his dummy, was a popular radio comedian.

"No, Sergeant."

"Did the Captain say you had to stay and scrub the floors?"

"That isn't it, Sergeant. It's the other guys in the barracks." He leaned toward me. "They think we're goofing off. But we're not. That's when Jews go to services, Friday night. We have to."

"Then go."

"But the other guys make accusations. They have no right."

"That's not the Army's problem, Grossbart. It's a personal problem you'll have to work out yourself."

"But it's un*fair*."

I got up to leave. "There's nothing I can do about it," I said.

Grossbart stiffened in front of me. "But this is a matter of *religion*, sir."

"Sergeant."

"I mean 'Sergeant,' " he said, almost snarling.

"Look, go see the chaplain. The I.G.[4] You want to see Captain Barrett, I'll arrange an appointment."

"No, no. I don't want to make trouble, Sergeant. That's the first thing they throw up to you. I just want my rights!"

"Damn it, Grossbart, stop whining. You have your rights. You can stay and scrub floors or you can go to *shul*[5]—"

The smile swam in again. Spittle gleamed at the corners of his mouth. "You mean church, Sergeant."

"I mean *shul*, Grossbart!" I walked past him and outside. Near me I heard the scrunching of a guard's boots on gravel. In the lighted windows of the barracks the young men in T-shirts and fatigue pants were sitting on their bunks, polishing their rifles. Suddenly there was a light rustling behind me. I turned and saw Grossbart's dark frame fleeing back to the barracks, racing to tell his Jewish friends that they were right—that like Karl and Harpo, I was one of them.

The next morning, while chatting with the Captain, I recounted the incident of the previous evening, as if to unburden myself of it. Somehow in the telling it seemed to the Captain that I was not so much explaining Grossbart's position as defending it.

"Marx, I'd fight side by side with a nigger if the fellow proved to me he was a man. I pride myself," the Captain said looking out the window, "that I've got an open mind. Consequently, Sergeant, nobody gets special treatment here, for the good *or* the bad. All a man's got to do is prove himself. A man fires well on the range, I give him a weekend pass. He scores high in PT, he gets a weekend pass. He *earns* it." He turned from the window and pointed a finger at me. "You're a Jewish fellow, am I right, Marx?"

"Yes, sir."

"And I admire you. I admire you because of the ribbons on your chest, not because you had a hem stitched on your dick before you were old enough to even know you had one. I judge a man by what he shows me on the field of battle, Sergeant. It's what he's got *here*," he said, and then, though I

4. Inspector general, who, apart from the chaplain, provided the only route by which complaints could be registered.

5. Synagogue (Yiddish).

expected he would point to his heart, he jerked a thumb towards the buttons straining to hold his blouse across his belly. "Guts," he said.

"Okay, sir, I only wanted to pass on to you how the men felt."

"Mr. Marx, you're going to be old before your time if you worry about how the men feel. Leave that stuff to the Chaplain—pussy, the clap, church picnics with the little girls from Joplin, that's all his business, not yours. Let's us train these fellas to shoot straight. If the Jewish personnel feels the other men are accusing them of goldbricking . . . well, I just don't know. Seems awful funny how suddenly the Lord is calling so loud in Private Grossman's ear he's just got to run to church."

"Synagogue," I said.

"Synagogue is right, Sergeant. I'll write that down for handy reference. Thank you for stopping by."

That evening, a few minutes before the company gathered outside the orderly room for the chow formation, I called the CQ, Corporal Robert LaHill, in to see me. LaHill was a dark burly fellow whose hair curled out of his clothes wherever it could. He carried a glaze in his eyes that made one think of caves and dinosaurs. "LaHill," I said, "when you take the formation, remind the men that they're free to attend church services *whenever* they are held, provided they report to the orderly room before they leave the area."

LaHill didn't flicker; he scratched his wrist, but gave no indication that he'd heard or understood.

"LaHill," I said, "*church*. You remember? Church, priest, Mass, confession . . ."

He curled one lip into a ghastly smile; I took it for a signal that for a second he had flickered back up into the human race.

"Jewish personnel who want to attend services this evening are to fall out in front of the orderly room at 1900." And then I added, "By order of Captain Barrett."

A little while later, as a twilight softer than any I had seen that year dropped over Camp Crowder, I heard LaHill's thick, inflectionless voice outside my window: "Give me your ears, troopers. Toppie says for me to tell you that at 1900 hours all Jewish personnel is to fall out in front here if they wants to attend the Jewish Mass."

At seven o'clock, I looked out of the orderly-room window and saw three soldiers in starched khakis standing alone on the dusty quadrangle. They looked at their watches, and fidgeted while they whispered back and forth. It was getting darker, and alone on the deserted field they looked tiny. When I walked to the door I heard the noises of the G.I. party coming from the surrounding barracks—bunks being pushed to the wall, faucets pounding water into buckets, brooms whisking at the wooden floors. In the windows big puffs of cloth moved round and round, cleaning the dirt away for Saturday's inspection. I walked outside and the moment my foot hit the ground I thought I heard Grossbart, who was now in the center, call to the other two, "Ten-*hut!*" Or maybe when they all three jumped to attention, I imagined I heard the command.

At my approach, Grossbart stepped forward. "Thank you, sir," he said.

"Sergeant, Grossbart," I reminded him. "You call officers 'Sir.' I'm not an officer. You've been in the Army three weeks—you know that."

He turned his palms out at his sides to indicate that, in truth, he and I lived beyond convention. "Thank you, anyway," he said.

"Yes," the tall boy behind him said. "Thanks a lot."

And the third whispered, "Thank you," but his mouth barely fluttered so that he did not alter by more than a lip's movement, the posture of attention.

"For what?" I said.

Grossbart snorted, happily. "For the announcement before. The Corporal's announcement. It helped. It made it . . ."

"Fancier." It was the tall boy finishing Grossbart's sentence.

Grossbart smiled. "He means formal, sir. Public," he said to me. "Now it won't seem as though we're just taking off, goldbricking, because the work has begun."

"It was by order of Captain Barrett," I said.

"Ahh, but you pull a little weight . . ." Grossbart said. "So we thank you." Then he turned to his companions. "Sergeant Marx, I want you to meet Larry Fishbein."

The tall boy stepped forward and extended his hand. I shook it. "You from New York?" he asked.

"Yes."

"Me too." He had a cadaverous face that collapsed inward from his cheekbone to his jaw, and when he smiled—as he did at the news of our communal attachment—revealed a mouthful of bad teeth. He blinked his eyes a good deal, as though he were fighting back tears. "What borough?" he asked.

I turned to Grossbart. "It's five after seven. What time are services?"

"*Shul*," he smiled, "is in ten minutes. I want you to meet Mickey Halpern. This is Nathan Marx, our Sergeant."

The third boy hopped forward. "Private Michael Halpern." He saluted.

"Salute officers, Halpern." The boy dropped his hand, and in his nervousness checked to see if his shirt pockets were buttoned on the way down.

"Shall I march them over, sir?" Grossbart asked, "or are you coming along?"

From behind Grossbart, Fishbein piped up. "Afterwards they're having refreshments. A Ladies' Auxiliary from St. Louis, the rabbi told us last week."

"The chaplain," whispered Halpern.

"You're welcome to come along," Grossbart said.

To avoid his plea, I looked away, and saw, in the windows of the barracks, a cloud of faces staring out at the four of us.

"Look, hurry out of here, Grossbart."

"Okay, then," he said. He turned to the others. "Double time, *march!*" and they started off, but ten feet away Grossbart spun about, and running backwards he called to me, "Good *shabus*,[6] sir." And then the three were swallowed into the Missouri dusk.

Even after they'd disappeared over the parade grounds, whose green was now a deep twilight blue, I could hear Grossbart singing the double-time cadence, and as it grew dimmer and dimmer it suddenly touched some deep

6. Sabbath (Yiddish).

memory—as did the slant of light—and I was remembering the shrill sounds of a Bronx playground, where years ago, beside the Grand Concourse,[7] I had played on long spring evenings such as this. Those thin fading sounds . . . It was a pleasant memory for a young man so far from peace and home, and it brought so very many recollections with it that I began to grow exceedingly tender about myself. In fact, I indulged myself to a reverie so strong that I felt within as though a hand had opened and was reaching down inside. It had to reach so very far to touch me. It had to reach past those days in the forests of Belgium and the dying I'd refused to weep over; past the nights in those German farmhouses whose books we'd burned to warm us, and which I couldn't bother to mourn; past those endless stretches when I'd shut off all softness I might feel for my fellows, and managed even to deny myself the posture of a conqueror—the swagger that I, as a Jew, might well have worn as my boots whacked against the rubble of Münster, Braunschweig, and finally Berlin.

But now one night noise, one rumor of home and time past, and memory plunged down through all I had anesthetized and came to what I suddenly remembered to be myself. So it was not altogether curious that in search of more of me I found myself following Grossbart's tracks to Chapel No. 3 where the Jewish services were being held.

I took a seat in the last row, which was empty. Two rows in front sat Grossbart, Fishbein, and Halpern, each holding a little white dixie cup. Fishbein was pouring the contents of his cup into Grossbart's, and Grossbart looked mirthful as the liquid drew a purple arc between his hand and Fishbein's. In the glary yellow light, I saw the chaplain on the pulpit chanting the first line of the responsive reading. Grossbart's prayerbook remained closed on his lap; he swished the cup around. Only Halpern responded in prayer. The fingers of his right hand were spread wide across the cover of the book, and his cap was pulled down low onto his brow so that it was round like a *yarmulke*[8] rather than long and pointed. From time to time, Grossbart wet his lips at the cup's edge; Fishbein, his long yellow face, a dying light bulb, looked from here to there, leaning forward at the neck to catch sight of the faces down the row, in front—then behind. He saw me and his eyelids beat a tattoo. His elbow slid into Grossbart's side, his neck inclined towards his friend, and then, when the congregation responded, Grossbart's voice was among them. Fishbein looked into his book now too; his lips, however, didn't move.

Finally it was time to drink the wine. The chaplain smiled down at them as Grossbart swigged in one long gulp, Halpern sipped, meditating, and Fishbein faked devotion with an empty cup.

At last the chaplain spoke: "As I look down amongst the congregation—" he grinned at the word, "this night, I see many new faces, and I want to welcome you to Friday night services here at Camp Crowder. I am Major Leo Ben Ezra, your chaplain . . ." Though an American, the chaplain spoke English very deliberately, syllabically almost, as though to communicate, above all, to the lip-readers in the audience. "I have only a few words to say before we adjourn to the refreshment room where the kind ladies of the Temple Sinai, St. Louis, Missouri, have a nice setting for you."

---

7. Avenue in the Bronx, New York.   8. Skullcap (Yiddish).

Applause and whistling broke out. After a momentary grin, the chaplain raised his palms to the congregation, his eyes flicking upward a moment, as if to remind the troops where they were and Who Else might be in attendance. In the sudden silence that followed, I thought I heard Grossbart's cackle—"Let the goyim[9] clean the floors!" Were those the words? I wasn't sure, but Fishbein, grinning, nudged Halpern. Halpern looked dumbly at him, then went back to his prayerbook, which had been occupying him all through the rabbi's talk. One hand tugged at the black kinky hair that stuck out under his cap. His lips moved.

The rabbi continued. "It is about the food that I want to speak to you for a moment. I know, I know, I know," he intoned, wearily, "how in the mouths of most of you the trafe[1] food tastes like ashes. I know how you gag, some of you, and how your parents suffer to think of their children eating foods unclean and offensive to the palate. What can I tell you? I can only say close your eyes and swallow as best you can. Eat what you must to live and throw away the rest. I wish I could help more. For those of you who find this impossible, may I ask that you try and try, but then come to see me in private where, if your revulsion is such, we will have to seek aid from those higher up."

A round of chatter rose and subsided; then everyone sang "Ain Kelohanoh," after all those years I discovered I still knew the words.

Suddenly, the service over, Grossbart was upon me. "Higher up? He means the General?"

"Hey, Shelly," Fishbein interrupted, "he means God." He smacked his face and looked at Halpern. "How high can you go!"

"Shhh!" Grossbart said. "What do you think, Sergeant?"

"I don't know. You better ask the chaplain."

"I'm going to. I'm making an appointment to see him in private. So is Mickey."

Halpern shook his head. "No, no, Sheldon . . ."

"You have rights, Mickey. They can't push us around."

"It's okay. It bothers my mother, not me . . ."

Grossbart looked at me. "Yesterday he threw up. From the hash. It was all ham and God knows what else."

"I have a cold—that was why," Halpern said. He pushed his yamalkah back into a cap.

"What about you, Fishbein?" I asked. "You kosher too?"

He flushed, which made the yellow more gray than pink. "A little. But I'll let it ride. I have a very strong stomach. And I don't eat a lot anyway . . ." I continued to look at him, and he held up his wrist to re-enforce what he'd just said. His watch was tightened to the last hole and he pointed that out to me. "So I don't mind."

"But services are important to you?" I asked him.

He looked at Grossbart. "Sure, sir."

"Sergeant."

"Not so much at home," said Grossbart, coming between us, "but away from home it gives one a sense of his Jewishness."

"We have to stick together," Fishbein said.

---

9. Gentiles (Yiddish).   1. Unkosher—unfit to eat (Yiddish).

I started to walk towards the door; Halpern stepped back to make way for me.

"That's what happened in Germany," Grossbart was saying, loud enough for me to hear. "They didn't stick together. They let themselves get pushed around."

I turned. "Look, Grossbart, this is the Army, not summer camp."

He smiled. "So?" Halpern tried to sneak off, but Grossbart held his arm. "So?" he said again.

"Grossbart," I asked, "how old are you?"

"Nineteen."

"And you?" I said to Fishbein.

"The same. The same month even."

"And what about him?" I pointed to Halpern, who'd finally made it safely to the door.

"Eighteen," Grossbart whispered. "But he's like he can't tie his shoes or brush his teeth himself. I feel sorry for him."

"I feel sorry for all of us, Grossbart, but just act like a man. Just don't overdo it."

"Overdo what, sir?"

"The sir business. Don't overdo that," I said, and I left him standing there. I passed by Halpern but he did not look up. Then I was outside, black surrounded me—but behind I heard Grossbart call, "Hey, Mickey, *lieb-schen*,[2] come on back. Refreshments!"

Liebschen! My grandmother's word for me!

One morning, a week later, while I was working at my desk, Captain Barrett shouted for me to come into his office. When I entered, he had his helmet liner squashed down so that I couldn't even see his eyes. He was on the phone, and when he spoke to me, he cupped one hand over the mouthpiece.

"Who the fuck is Grossbart?"

"Third platoon, Captain," I said. "A trainee."

"What's all this stink about food? His mother called a goddam congress-man about the food . . ." He uncovered the mouthpiece and slid his helmet up so I could see the curl of his bottom eyelash. "Yes, sir," he said into the phone. "Yes, sir. I'm still here, sir. I'm asking Marx here right now . . ."

He covered the mouthpiece again and looked back to me. "Lightfoot Har-ry's on the phone," he said, between his teeth. "This congressman calls General Lyman who calls Colonel Sousa who calls the Major who calls me. They're just dying to stick this thing on me. What's a matter," he shook the phone at me, "I don't feed the troops? What the hell is this?"

"Sir, Grossbart is strange . . ." Barrett greeted that with a mockingly indulgent smile. I altered my approach. "Captain, he's a very orthodox Jew and so he's only allowed to eat certain foods."

"He throws up, the congressman said. Every time he eats something his mother says he throws up!"

"He's accustomed to observing the dietary laws, Captain."

"So why's his old lady have to call the White House!"

2. Darling (German).

"Jewish parents, sir, they're apt to be more protective than you expect. I mean Jews have a very close family life. A boy goes away from home, sometimes the mother is liable to get very upset. Probably the boy *mentioned* something in a letter and his mother misinterpreted."

"I'd like to punch him one right in the mouth. There's a goddam war on and he wants a silver platter!"

"I don't think the boy's to blame, sir. I'm sure we can straighten it out by just asking him. Jewish parents worry—"

"*All* parents worry, for Christ sake. But they don't get on their high horse and start pulling strings—"

I interrupted, my voice higher, tighter than before. "The home life, Captain, is so very important . . . but you're right, it may sometimes get out of hand. It's a very wonderful thing, Captain, but because it's so close, this kind of thing—"

He didn't listen any longer to my attempt to present both myself and Lightfoot Harry with an explanation for the letter. He turned back to the phone. "Sir?" he said. "Sir, Marx here tells me Jews have a tendency to be pushy. He says he thinks he can settle it right here in the Company . . . Yes, sir . . . I *will* call back, sir, soon as I can . . ." He hung up. "Where are the men, Sergeant?"

"On the range."

With a whack on the top, he crushed his helmet over his eyes, and charged out of his chair. "We're going for a ride."

The Captain drove and I sat beside him. It was a hot spring day and under my newly starched fatigues it felt as though my armpits were melting down onto my sides and chest. The roads were dry and by the time we reached the firing range, my teeth felt gritty with dust though my mouth had been shut the whole trip. The Captain slammed the brakes on and told me to get the hell out and find Grossbart.

I found him on his belly, firing wildly at the 500 feet target. Waiting their turns behind him were Halpern and Fishbein. Fishbein, wearing a pair of rimless G.I. glasses I hadn't seen on him before, gave the appearance of an old peddler who would gladly have sold you the rifle and cartridges that were slung all over him. I stood back by the ammo boxes, waiting for Grossbart to finish spraying the distant targets. Fishbein straggled back to stand near me.

"Hello, Sergeant Marx."

"How are you?" I mumbled.

"Fine, thank you. Sheldon's really a good shot."

"I didn't notice."

"I'm not so good, but I think I'm getting the hang of it now . . . Sergeant, I don't mean to, you know, ask what I shouldn't . . . ." The boy stopped. He was trying to speak intimately but the noise of the shooting necessitated that he shout at me.

"What is it?" I asked. Down the range I saw Captain Barrett standing up in the jeep, scanning the line for me and Grossbart.

"My parents keep asking and asking where we're going. Everybody says the Pacific. I don't care, but my parents . . . If I could relieve their minds I think I could concentrate more on my shooting."

"I don't know where, Fishbein. Try to concentrate anyway."

"Sheldon says you might be able to find out—"

"I don't know a thing, Fishbein. You just take it easy, and don't let Sheldon—"

"*I'm* taking it easy, Sergeant. It's at home—"

Grossbart had just finished on the line and was dusting his fatigues with one hand. I left Fishbein's sentence in the middle.

"Grossbart, the Captain wants to see you."

He came toward us. His eyes blazed and twinkled. "Hi!"

"Don't point that goddam rifle!"

"I wouldn't shoot you, Sarge." He gave me a smile wide as a pumpkin as he turned the barrel aside.

"Damn you, Grossbart—this is no joke! Follow me."

I walked ahead of him and had the awful suspicion that behind me Grossbart was *marching*, his rifle on his shoulder, as though he were a one-man detachment.

At the jeep he gave the Captain a rifle salute. "Private Sheldon Grossbart, sir."

"At ease, Grossman." The Captain slid over to the empty front seat, and crooking a finger, invited Grossbart closer.

"Bart, sir. Sheldon Gross*bart*. It's a common error." Grossbart nodded to me—*I* understand, he indicated. I looked away, just as the mess truck pulled up to the range, disgorging a half dozen K.P.'s with rolled-up sleeves. The mess sergeant screamed at them while they set up the chow line equipment.

"Grossbart, your mama wrote some congressman that we don't feed you right. Do you know that?" the Captain said.

"It was my father, sir. He wrote to Representative Franconi that my religion forbids me to eat certain foods."

"What religion is that, Grossbart?"

"Jewish."

"Jewish, *sir*," I said to Grossbart.

"Excuse me, sir. 'Jewish, sir.'"

"What have you been living on?" the Captain asked. "You've been in the Army a month already. You don't look to me like you're falling to pieces."

"I eat because I have to, sir. But Sergeant Marx will testify to the fact that I don't eat one mouthful more than I need to in order to survive."

"Marx," Barrett asked, "is that so?"

"I've never seen Grossbart eat, sir," I said.

"But you heard the rabbi," Grossbart said. "He told us what to do, and I listened."

The Captain looked at me. "Well, Marx?"

"I still don't know what he eats and doesn't eat, sir."

Grossbart raised his rifle, as though to offer it to me. "But, Sergeant—"

"Look, Grossbart, just answer the Captain's questions!" I said sharply.

Barrett smiled at me and I resented it. "All right, Grossbart," he said, "What is it you want? The little piece of paper? You want out?"

"No, sir. Only to be allowed to live as a Jew. And for the others, too."

"What others?"

"Fishbein, sir, and Halpern."

"They don't like the way we serve either?"

"Halpern throws up, sir. I've seen it."

"I thought *you* threw up."

"Just once, sir. I didn't know the sausage was sausage."

"We'll give menus, Grossbart. We'll show training films about the food, so you can identify when we're trying to poison you."

Grossbart did not answer. Out before me, the men had been organized into two long chow lines. At the tail end of one I spotted Fishbein—or rather, his glasses spotted me. They winked sunlight back at me like a friend. Halpern stood next to him, patting inside his collar with a khaki handkerchief. They moved with the line as it began to edge up towards the food. The mess sergeant was still screaming at the K.P.'s, who stood ready to ladle out the food, bewildered. For a moment I was actually terrorized by the thought that somehow the mess sergeant was going to get involved in Grossbart's problem.

"Come over here, Marx," the Captain said to me. "Marx, you're a Jewish fella, am I right?"

I played straight man. "Yes, sir."

"How long you been in the Army? Tell this boy."

"Three years and two months."

"A year in combat, Grossbart. Twelve goddam months in combat all through Europe. I admire this man," the Captain said, snapping a wrist against my chest. But do you hear him peeping about the food? Do you? I want an answer, Grossbart. Yes or no."

"No, sir."

"And why not? He's a Jewish fella."

"Some things are more important to some Jews than other things to other Jews."

Barrett blew up. "Look, Grossbart, Marx here is a good man, a goddam *hero.* When you were sitting on your sweet ass in high school, Sergeant Marx was killing Germans. Who does more for the Jews, you by throwing up over a lousy piece of sausage, a piece of firstcut meat—or Marx by killing those Nazi bastards? If I was a Jew, Grossbart, I'd kiss this man's feet. He's a goddam hero, you know that? And *he* eats what we give him. Why do you have to cause trouble is what I want to know! What is it you're buckin' for, a discharge?"

"No, sir."

"I'm talking to a *wall!* Sergeant, get him out of my way." Barrett pounced over to the driver's seat. "I'm going to see the chaplain!" The engine roared, the jeep spun around, and then, raising a whirl of dust, the Captain was headed back to camp.

For a moment, Grossbart and I stood side by side, watching the jeep. Then he looked at me and said, "I don't want to start trouble. That's the first thing they toss up to us."

When he spoke I saw that his teeth were white and straight, and the sight of them suddenly made me understand that Grossbart actually did have parents: that once upon a time someone had taken little Sheldon to the dentist. He was someone's son. Despite all the talk about his parents, it was hard to believe in Grossbart as a child, an heir—as related by blood to anyone, mother, father, or, above all, to me. This realization led me to another.

"What does your father do, Grossbart?" I asked, as we started to walk back towards the chow line.

"He's a tailor."

"An American?"

"Now, yes. A son in the Army," he said, jokingly.

"And your mother?" I asked.

He winked. "A *ballabusta*[3]—she practically sleeps with a dustcloth in her hand."

"She's also an immigrant?"

"All she talks is Yiddish, still."

"And your father too?"

"A little English. 'Clean,' 'Press,' 'Take the pants in . . .' That's the extent of it. But they're good to me . . ."

"Then, Grossbart—" I reached out and stopped him. He turned towards me and when our eyes met his seemed to jump back, shiver in their sockets. He looked afraid. "Grossbart, then you were the one who wrote that letter, weren't you?"

It took only a second or two for his eyes to flash happy again. "Yes." He walked on, and I kept pace. "It's what my father *would* have written if he had known how. It was his name, though. *He* signed it. He even mailed it. I sent it home. For the New York postmark."

I was astonished, and he saw it. With complete seriousness, he thrust his right arm in front of me. "Blood is blood, Sergeant," he said, pinching the blue vein in his wrist.

"What the hell *are* you trying to do, Grossbart? I've seen you eat. Do you know that? I told the Captain I don't know what you eat, but I've seen you eat like a hound at chow."

"We work hard, Sergeant. We're in training. For a furnace to work, you've got to feed it coal."

"If you wrote the letter, Grossbart, then why did you say you threw up all the time?"

"I was really talking about Mickey there. But he would never write, Sergeant, though I pleaded with him. He'll waste away to nothing if I don't help. Sergeant, I used my name, my father's name, but it's Mickey and Fishbein too I'm watching out for."

"You're a regular Messiah,[4] aren't you?"

We were at the chow line now.

"That's a good one, Sergeant." He smiled. "But who knows? Who can tell? Maybe you're the Messiah . . . a little bit. What Mickey says is the Messiah is a collective idea. He went to Yeshivah,[5] Mickey, for a while. He says *together* we're the Messiah. Me a little bit, you a little bit . . . You should hear that kid talk, Sergeant, when he gets going."

"Me a little bit, you a little bit. You'd like to believe that, wouldn't you, Grossbart? That makes everything so clean for you."

"It doesn't seem too bad a thing to believe, Sergeant. It only means we should all give a little, is all . . ."

I walked off to eat my rations with the other noncoms.[6]

Two days later a letter addressed to Captain Barrett passed over my desk. It had come through the chain of command—from the office of Congressman

---

3. Good housekeeper (Yiddish).
4. The deliverer who will rule over the people of Israel at the end of time.
5. Jewish institution of learning.
6. Noncommissioned officers.

Franconi, where it had been received, to General Lyman, to Colonel Sousa, to Major Lamont, to Captain Barrett. I read it over twice while the Captain was at the officers' mess. It was dated May 14th, the day Barrett had spoken with Grossbart on the rifle range.

Dear Congressman:

First let me thank you for your interest in behalf of my son, Private Sheldon Grossbart. Fortunately, I was able to speak with Sheldon on the phone the other night, and I think I've been able to solve our problem. He is, as I mentioned in my last letter, a very religious boy, and it was only with the greatest difficulty that I could persuade him that the religious thing to do— what God Himself would want Sheldon to do—would be to suffer the pangs of religious remorse for the good of his country and all mankind. It took some doing, Congressman, but finally he saw the light. In fact, what he said (and I wrote down the words on a scratch pad so as never to forget), what he said was, "I guess you're right, Dad. So many millions of my fellow Jews gave up their lives to the enemy, the least I can do is live for a while minus a bit of my heritage so as to help end this struggle and regain for all the children of God dignity and humanity." That, Congressman, would make any father proud.

By the way, Sheldon wanted me to know—and to pass on to you—the name of a soldier who helped him reach this decision: SERGEANT NATHAN MARX. Sergeant Marx is a combat veteran who is Sheldon's First Sergeant. This man has helped Sheldon over some of the first hurdles he's had to face in the Army, and is in part responsible for Sheldon's changing his mind about the dietary laws. I know Sheldon would appreciate any recognition Marx could receive.

Thank you and good luck. I look forward to seeing your name on the next election ballot.

Respectfully,
Samuel E. Grossbart

Attached to the Grossbart communiqué was a communiqué addressed to General Marshall Lyman, the post commander, and signed by Representative Charles E. Franconi of the House of Representatives. The communiqué informed General Lyman that Sergeant Nathan Marx was a credit to the U.S. Army and the Jewish people.

What was Grossbart's motive in recanting? Did he feel he'd gone too far? Was the letter a strategic retreat—a crafty attempt to strengthen what he considered our alliance? Or had he actually changed his mind, via an imaginary dialogue between Grossbart *père* and *fils*?[7] I was puzzled, but only for a few days—that is, only until I realized that whatever his reasons, he had actually decided to disappear from my life: he was going to allow himself to become just another trainee. I saw him at inspection but he never winked; at chow formations but he never flashed me a sign; on Sundays, with the other trainees, he would sit around watching the noncoms' softball team, for whom I pitched, but not once did he speak an unnecessary or unusual word to me. Fishbein and Halpern retreated from sight too, at Grossbart's command I was sure. Apparently he'd seen that wisdom lay in

7. Father and son (French).

turning back before he plunged us over into the ugliness of privilege unde-
served. Our separation allowed me to forgive him our past encounters, and,
finally, to admire him for his good sense.

Meanwhile, free of Grossbart, I grew used to my job and my administrative
tasks. I stepped on a scale one day and discovered I had truly become a non-
combatant: I had gained seven pounds. I found patience to get past the first
three pages of a book. I thought about the future more and more, and wrote
letters to girls I'd known before the war—I even got a few answers. I sent away
to Columbia for a Law School catalogue. I continued to follow the war in the
Pacific, but it was not my war and I read of bombings and battles like a civilian. I thought I could see the end in sight and sometimes at night I dreamed
that I was walking on the streets of Manhattan—Broadway, Third Avenue,
and 116th Street, where I had lived those three years I'd attended Columbia
College. I curled myself around these dreams and I began to be happy.

And then one Saturday when everyone was away and I was alone in the
orderly room reading a month-old copy of the *Sporting News*, Grossbart
reappeared.

"You a baseball fan, Sergeant?"

I looked up. "How are you?"

"Fine," Grossbart said. "They're making a soldier out of me."

"How are Fishbein and Halpern?"

"Coming along," he said. "We've got no training this afternoon. They're
at the movies."

"How come you're not with them?"

"I wanted to come over and say hello."

He smiled—a shy, regular-guy smile, as though he and I well knew that
our friendship drew its sustenance from unexpected visits, remembered
birthdays, and borrowed lawnmowers. At first it offended me, and then the
feeling was swallowed by the general uneasiness I felt at the thought that
everyone on the post was locked away in a dark movie theater and I was
here alone with Grossbart. I folded my paper.

"Sergeant," he said, "I'd like to ask a favor. It is a favor and I'm making no
bones about it."

He stopped, allowing me to refuse him a hearing—which, of course,
forced me into a courtesy I did not intend. "Go ahead."

"Well, actually it's two favors."

I said nothing.

"The first one's about these rumors. Everybody says we're going to the
Pacific."

"As I told your friend Fishbein, I don't know. You'll just have to wait to
find out. Like everybody else."

"You think there's a chance of any of us going East?"

"Germany," I said, "maybe."

"I meant New York."

"I don't think so, Grossbart. Offhand."

"Thanks for the information, Sergeant," he said.

"It's not information, Grossbart. Just what I surmise."

"It certainly would be good to be near home. My parents . . . you know."
He took a step towards the door and then turned back. "Oh the other thing.
May I ask the other?"

"What is it?"

"The other thing is—I've got relatives in St. Louis and they say they'll give me a whole Passover dinner if I can get down there. God, Sergeant, that'd mean an awful lot to me."

I stood up. "No passes during basic, Grossbart."

"But we're off from now till Monday morning, Sergeant. I could leave the post and no one would even know."

"I'd know. You'd know."

"But that's all. Just the two of us. Last night I called my aunt and you should have heard her. 'Come, come,' she said. 'I got gefilte fish, *chrain*,[8] the works!' Just a day, Sergeant, I'd take the blame if anything happened."

"The captain isn't here to sign a pass."

"You could sign."

"Look, Grossbart—"

"Sergeant, for two months practically I've been eating *trafe* till I want to die."

"I thought you'd made up your mind to live with it. To be minus a little bit of heritage."

He pointed a finger at me. "You!" he said. "That wasn't for you to read!"

"I read it. So what."

"That letter was addressed to a congressman."

"Grossbart, don't feed me any crap. You *wanted* me to read it."

"Why are you persecuting me, Sergeant?"

"Are you kidding!"

"I've run into this before," he said, "but never from my own!"

"Get out of here, Grossbart! Get the hell out of my sight!"

He did not move. "Ashamed, that's what you are. So you take it out on the rest of us. They say Hitler himself was half a Jew. Seeing this, I wouldn't doubt it!"

"What are you trying to do with me, Grossbart? What are you after? You want me to give you special privileges, to change the food, to find out about your orders, to give you weekend passes."

"You even talk like a goy!" Grossbart shook his fist. "Is this a weekend pass I'm asking for? Is a Seder[9] sacred or not?"

Seder! It suddenly occurred to me that Passover had been celebrated weeks before. I confronted Grossbart with the fact.

"That's right," he said. "Who says no? A month ago, and *I* was in the field eating hash! And now all I ask is a simple favor—a Jewish boy I thought would understand. My aunt's willing to go out of her way—to make a Seder a month later—" He turned to go, mumbling.

"Come back here!" I called. He stopped and looked at me. "Grossbart, why can't you be like the rest? Why do you have to stick out like a sore thumb? Why do you beg for special treatment?"

"Because I'm a Jew, Sergeant. I *am* different. Better, maybe not. But different."

"This is a war, Grossbart. For the time being *be* the same."

"I refuse."

---

8. Horseradish, traditionally eaten as part of the Passover meal.
9. Ceremonial dinner on the first evening of Passover.

"What?"

"I refuse. I can't stop being me, that's all there is to it." Tears came to his eyes. "It's a hard thing to be a Jew. But now I see what Mickey says—it's a harder thing to stay one." He raised a hand sadly toward me. "Look at you."

"Stop crying!"

"Stop this, stop that, stop the other thing! You stop, Sergeant. Stop closing your heart to your own!" And wiping his face with his sleeve, he ran out the door. "The least we can do for one another . . . the least . . ."

An hour later I saw Grossbart headed across the field. He wore a pair of starched khakis and carried only a little leather ditty bag. I went to the door and from the outside felt the heat of the day. It was quiet—not a soul in sight except over by the mess hall four K.P.'s sitting round a pan, sloped forward from the waists, gabbing and peeling potatoes in the sun.

"Grossbart!" I called.

He looked toward me and continued walking.

"Grossbart, get over here!"

He turned and stepped into his long shadow. Finally he stood before me.

"Where are you going?" I said.

"St. Louis. I don't care."

"You'll get caught without a pass."

"So I'll get caught without a pass."

"You'll go to the stockade."

"I'm in the stockade." He made an about-face and headed off.

I let him go only a step: "Come back here," I said, and he followed me into the office, where I typed out a pass and signed the Captain's name and my own initials after it.

He took the pass from me and then, a moment later, he reached out and grabbed my hand. "Sergeant, you don't know how much this means to me."

"Okay. Don't get in any trouble."

"I wish I could show you how much this means to me."

"Don't do me any favors. Don't write any more congressmen for citations."

Amazingly, he smiled. "You're right. I won't. But let me do something."

"Bring me a piece of that gefilte fish. Just get out of here."

"I will! With a slice of carrot and a little horseradish. I won't forget."

"All right. Just show your pass at the gate. And don't tell *anybody*."

"I won't. It's a month late, but a good Yom Tov[1] to you."

"Good Yom Tov, Grossbart," I said.

"You're a good Jew, Sergeant. You like to think you have a hard heart, but underneath you're a fine decent man. I mean that."

Those last three words touched me more than any words from Grossbart's mouth had the right to. "All right, Grossbart. Now call me 'sir' and get the hell out of here."

He ran out the door and was gone. I felt very pleased with myself—it was a great relief to stop fighting Grossbart. And it had cost me nothing. Barrett would never find out, and if he did, I could manage to invent some excuse. For a while I sat at my desk, comfortable in my decision. Then the screen door flew back and Grossbart burst in again. "Sergeant!" he said. Behind

---

1. Holiday (Yiddish).

him I saw Fishbein and Halpern, both in starched khakis, both carrying ditty bags exactly like Grossbart's.

"Sergeant, I caught Mickey and Larry coming out of the movies. I almost missed them."

"Grossbart, did I say tell no one?"

"But my aunt said I could bring friends. That I should, in fact."

"I'm the Sergeant, Grossbart—not your aunt!"

Grossbart looked at me in disbelief; he pulled Halpern up by his sleeve. "Mickey, tell the Sergeant what this would mean to you."

"Grossbart, for God's sake, spare us—"

"Tell him what you told me, Mickey. How much it would mean."

Halpern looked at me and, shrugging his shoulders, made his admission. "A lot."

Fishbein stepped forward without prompting. "This would mean a great deal to me and my parents, Sergeant Marx."

"No!" I shouted.

Grossbart was shaking his head. "Sergeant, I could see you denying me, but how you can deny Mickey, a Yeshivah boy, that's beyond me."

"I'm not denying Mickey anything. You just pushed a little too hard, Grossbart. *You* denied him."

"I'll give him my pass, then," Grossbart said. "I'll give him my aunt's address and a little note. At least let him go."

In a second he had crammed the pass into Halpern's pants' pocket. Halpern looked at me, Fishbein too. Grossbart was at the door, pushing it open. "Mickey, bring me a piece of gefilte fish at least." And then he was outside again.

The three of us looked at one another and then I said, "Halpern, hand that pass over."

He took it from his pocket and gave it to me. Fishbein had now moved to the doorway, where he lingered. He stood there with his mouth slightly open and then pointed to himself. "And me?" he asked.

His utter ridiculousness exhausted me. I slumped down in my seat and I felt pulses knocking at the back of my eyes. "Fishbein," I said, "you understand I'm not trying to deny you anything, don't you? If it was my Army I'd serve gefilte fish in the mess hall. I'd sell kugel[2] in the PX, honest to God."

Halpern smiled.

"You understand, don't you, Halpern?"

"Yes, Sergeant."

"And you, Fishbein? I don't want enemies. I'm just like you—I want to serve my time and go home. I miss the same things you miss."

"Then, Sergeant," Fishbein interrupted, "Why don't you come too?"

"Where?"

"To St. Louis. To Shelley's aunt. We'll have a regular Seder. Play hide-the-matzah." He gave a broad, black-toothed smile.

I saw Grossbart in the doorway again, on the other side of the screen.

"Pssst!" He waved a piece of paper. "Mickey, here's the address. Tell her I couldn't get away."

---

2. Baked pudding of noodles or potatoes.

Halpern did not move. He looked at me and I saw the shrug moving up his arms into his shoulders again. I took the cover off my typewriter and made out passes for him and Fishbein. "Go," I said, "the three of you."

I thought Halpern was going to kiss my hand.

That afternoon, in a bar in Joplin, I drank beer and listened with half an ear to the Cardinal game. I tried to look squarely at what I'd become involved in, and began to wonder if perhaps the struggle with Grossbart wasn't as much my fault as his. What was I that I had to *muster* generous feelings? Who was I to have been feeling so grudging, so tight-hearted? After all, I wasn't being asked to move the world. Had I a right, then, or a reason, to clamp down on Grossbart, when that meant clamping down on Halpern, too? And Fishbein, that ugly agreeable soul, wouldn't he suffer in the bargain also? Out of the many recollections that had tumbled over me these past few days, I heard from some childhood moment my grandmother's voice: "What are you making a *tsimas*?"[3] It was what she would ask my mother when, say, I had cut myself with a knife and her daughter was busy bawling me out. I would need a hug and a kiss and my mother would moralize! But my grandmother knew—mercy overrides justice. I should have known it, too. Who was Nathan Marx to be such a pennypincher with kindness? Surely, I thought, the Messiah himself—if he should ever come—won't niggle over nickels and dimes. God willing, he'll hug and kiss.

The next day, while we were playing softball over on the Parade Grounds, I decided to ask Bob Wright, who was noncom in charge over at Classification and Assignment, where he thought our trainees would be sent when their cycle ended in two weeks. I asked casually, between innings, and he said, "They're pushing them all into the Pacific. Shulman cut the orders on your boys the other day."

The news shocked me, as though I were father to Halpern, Fishbein, and Grossbart.

That night I was just sliding into sleep when someone tapped on the door. "What is it?"

"Sheldon."

He opened the door and came in. For a moment I felt his presence without being able to see him. "How was it?" I asked, as though to the darkness.

He popped into sight before me. "Great, Sergeant." I felt my springs sag; Grossbart was sitting on the edge of the bed. I sat up.

"How about you?" he asked. "Have a nice weekend?"

"Yes."

He took a deep paternal breath. "The others went to sleep . . ." We sat silently for a while, as a homey feeling invaded my ugly little cubicle: the door was locked, the cat out, the children safely in bed.

"Sergeant, can I tell you something? Personal?"

I did not answer and he seemed to know why. "Not about me. About Mickey. Sergeant, I never felt for anybody like I feel for him. Last night I

---

3. Fuss (Yiddish, literal trans.); here a side dish made of mixed cooked vegetables and fruit.

heard Mickey in the bed next to me. He was crying so, it could have broken your heart. Real sobs."

"I'm sorry to hear that."

"I had to talk to him to stop him. He held my hand, Sergeant—he wouldn't let it go. He was almost hysterical. He kept saying if he only knew where we were going. Even if he knew it *was* the Pacific, that would be better than nothing. Just to know."

Long ago, someone had taught Grossbart the sad law that only lies can get the truth. Not that I couldn't believe in Halpern's crying—his eyes *always* seemed red-rimmed. But, fact or not, it became a lie when Grossbart uttered it. He was entirely strategic. But then—it came with the force of indictment—so was I! There are strategies of aggression, but there are strategies of retreat, as well. And so, recognizing that I myself, had not been without craft and guile, I told him what I knew. "It is the Pacific."

He let out a small gasp, which was not a lie. "I'll tell him. I wish it was otherwise."

"So do I."

He jumped on my words. "You mean you think you could do something? A change maybe?"

"No, I couldn't do a thing."

"Don't you know anybody over at C & A?"

"Grossbart, there's nothing I can do. If your orders are for the Pacific then it's the Pacific."

"But Mickey."

"Mickey, you, me—everybody, Grossbart. There's nothing to be done. Maybe the war'll end before you go. Pray for a miracle."

"But—"

"Good night, Grossbart." I settled back, and was relieved to feel the springs upbend again as Grossbart rose to leave. I could see him clearly now; his jaw had dropped and he looked like a dazed prizefighter. I noticed for the first time a little paper bag in his hand.

"Grossbart"—I smiled—"my gift?"

"Oh, yes, Sergeant. Here, from all of us." He handed me the bag. "It's egg roll."

"Egg roll?" I accepted the bag and felt a damp grease spot on the bottom. I opened it, sure that Grossbart was joking.

"We thought you'd probably like it. You know, Chinese egg roll. We thought you'd probably have a taste for—"

"Your aunt served egg roll?"

"She wasn't home."

"Grossbart, she invited you. You told me she invited you and your friends."

"I know. I just reread the letter. *Next* week."

I got out of bed and walked to the window. It was black as far off as I could see. "Grossbart," I said. But I was not calling him.

"What?"

"What are you, Grossbart? Honest to God, what are you?"

I think it was the first time I'd asked him a question for which he didn't have an immediate answer.

"How can you do this to people?" I asked.

"Sergeant, the day away did us all a world of good. Fishbein, you should see him, he *loves* Chinese food."

"But the Seder," I said.

"We took second best, Sergeant."

Rage came charging at me. I didn't sidestep—I grabbed it, pulled it in, hugged it to my chest.

"Grossbart, you're a liar! You're a schemer and a crook! You've got no respect for anything! Nothing at all! Not for me, for the truth, not even for poor Halpern! You use us all—"

"Sergeant, Sergeant, I feel for Mickey, honest to God, I do. I *love* Mickey. I try—"

"You try! You feel!" I lurched towards him and grabbed his shirt front. I shook him furiously. "Grossbart, get out. Get out and stay the hell away from me! Because if I see you, I'll make your life miserable. *You understand that?*"

"Yes."

I let him free, and when he walked from the room I wanted to spit on the floor where he had stood. I couldn't stop the fury from rising in my heart. It engulfed me, owned me, till it seemed I could only rid myself of it with tears or an act of violence. I snatched from the bed the bag Grossbart had given me and with all my strength threw it out the window. And the next morning, as the men policed the area around the barracks, I heard a great cry go up from one of the trainees who'd been anticipating only his morning handful of cigarette butts and candy wrappers. "Egg roll!" he shouted. "Holy Christ, Chinese goddam egg roll!"

A week later, when I read the orders that had come down from C & A, I couldn't believe my eyes. Every single trainee was to be shipped to Camp Stoneham, California, and from there to the Pacific. Every trainee but one: Private Sheldon Grossbart was to be sent to Fort Monmouth, New Jersey. I read the mimeographed sheet several times. Dee, Farrell, Fishbein, Fuselli, Fylypowycz, Glinicki, Gromke, Gucwa, Halpern, Hardy, Helebrandt . . . right down to Anton Zygadlo, all were to be headed West before the month was out. All except Grossbart. He had pulled a string and I wasn't it.

I lifted the phone and called C & A.

The voice on the other end said smartly, "Corporal Shulman, sir."

"Let me speak to Sergeant Wright."

"Who is this calling, sir?"

"Sergeant Marx."

And to my surprise, the voice said, "*Oh.*" Then: "Just a minute, Sergeant."

Shulman's *oh* stayed with me while I waited for Wright to come to the phone. Why *oh*? Who was Shulman? And then, so simply, I knew I'd discovered the string Grossbart had pulled. In fact, I could hear Grossbart the day he'd discovered Shulman, in the PX, or the bowling alley, or maybe even at services. "Glad to meet you. Where you from? Bronx? Me too. Do you know so-and-so? And so-and-so? Me too! You work at C & A? Really? Hey, how's chances of getting East? Could you do something? Change something? Swindle, cheat, lie? We gotta help each other, you know . . . if the Jews in Germany . . ."

At the other end Bob Wright answered. "How are you, Nate? How's the pitching arm?"

"Good. Bob, I wonder if you could do me a favor." I heard clearly my own words and they so reminded me of Grossbart that I dropped more easily than I could have imagined into what I had planned. "This may sound crazy, Bob, but I got a kid here on orders to Monmouth who wants them changed. He had a brother killed in Europe and he's hot to go to the Pacific. Says he'd feel like a coward if he wound up stateside. I don't know, Bob, can anything be done? Put somebody else in the Monmouth slot?"

"Who?" he asked cagily.

"Anybody. First guy on the alphabet. I don't care. The kid just asked if something could be done."

"What's his name?"

"Grossbart, Sheldon."

Wright didn't answer.

"Yeah," I said, "he's a Jewish kid, so he thought I could help him out. You know."

"I guess I can do something," he finally said. "The Major hasn't been around here for weeks—TDY[4] to the golf course. I'll try, Nate that's all I can say."

"I'd appreciate it, Bob. See you Sunday," and I hung up, perspiring.

And the following day the corrected orders appeared: Fishbein, Fuselli, Fylypowycz, Glinicki, Grossbart, Gucwa, Halpern, Hardy . . . Lucky Private Harley Alton was to go to Fort Monmouth, New Jersey, where for some reason or other, they wanted an enlisted man with infantry training.

After chow that night I stopped back at the orderly room to straighten out the guard duty roster. Grossbart was waiting for me. He spoke first.

"You son of a bitch!"

I sat down at my desk and while he glared down at me I began to make the necessary alterations in the duty roster.

"What do you have against me?" he cried. "Against my family? Would it kill you for me to be near my father, God knows how many months he has left to him."

"Why?"

"His heart," Grossbart said. "He hasn't had enough troubles in a lifetime, you've got to add to them. I curse the day I ever met you, Marx! Shulman told me what happened over there. There's no limit to your anti-Semitism, is there! The damage you've done here isn't enough. You have to make a special phone call! You really want me dead!"

I made the last few notations in the duty roster and got up to leave. "Good night, Grossbart."

"You owe me an explanation!" He stood in my path.

"Sheldon, you're the one who owes explanations."

He scowled. "To *you?*"

"To me, I think so, yes. Mostly to Fishbein and Halpern."

"That's right, twist things around. I owe nobody nothing, I've done all I could do for them. Now I think I've got the right to watch out for myself."

"For each other we have to learn to watch out, Sheldon. You told me yourself."

"You call this watching out for me, what you did?"

"No. For all of us."

---

4. Temporary Duty, an army orders term used ironically here.

I pushed him aside and started for the door. I heard his furious breathing behind me, and it sounded like steam rushing from the engine of his terrible strength.

"You'll be all right," I said from the door. And, I thought, so would Fishbein and Halpern be all right, even in the Pacific, if only Grossbart could continue to see in the obsequiousness of the one, the soft spirituality of the other, some profit for himself.

I stood outside the orderly room, and I heard Grossbart weeping behind me. Over in the barracks, in the lighted windows, I could see the boys in their T-shirts sitting on their bunks talking about their orders, as they'd been doing for the past two days. With a kind of quiet nervousness, they polished shoes, shined belt buckles, squared away underwear, trying as best they could to accept their fate. Behind me, Grossbart swallowed hard, accepting his. And then, resisting with all my will an impulse to turn and seek pardon for my vindictiveness, I accepted my own.

1959

AMIRI BARAKA (LEROI JONES)
1934–2014

When in 1967 LeRoi Jones assumed the Bantuized Muslim name Amiri Baraka (meaning Prince, a Blessed One), he was undergoing one of several changes in his progression as a maker of literature. Born Everett Leroy Jones, he was the child of middle-class African American parents in Newark, New Jersey, where his scholastic abilities took him to the best schools available; as Baraka recalls in his autobiography, his classmates were more often white suburbanites than inner-city children of his own race. He restyled his name as "LeRoi" during his undergraduate years at Howard University (a traditionally African American institution), to which he had transferred from the mostly white campus of Rutgers University (where he had won a scholarship). After leaving Howard in 1954 and serving in the U.S. Air Force, from which he was discharged for unapproved political activities, Jones moved to New York City's Greenwich Village and became prominent on the avant-garde poetry scene. His friends were white innovators—Gilbert Sorrentino, Diane DiPrima, and Frank O'Hara among them—with whom he worked on the magazine Kulchur in addition to editing and publishing his own journal, Yugen. Married to Hettie Cohen, he began an interracial family and wrote record reviews for mainstream jazz magazines.

Jones was well established in the more intellectually elite quarters of New York's world of poetry, art, and music. Yet as racial tensions mounted, with the assassination of Medgar Evers, fatal church bombings in Alabama, and the murder of civil rights workers James Chaney, Andrew Goodman, and Michael Schwerner in Mississippi, Jones's life underwent major changes as well. In 1965, following the assassination of Malcolm X, he left his wife and children and moved to Harlem, where as a newly declared black cultural nationalist he founded the Black Arts Repertory

Theater, dedicated to taking socially militant drama directly to the people it represented.

Poetry as a vehicle of popular encouragement remained central to Baraka's belief. He may well have agreed with the judge who once convicted him of incitement to riot that his poems could motivate people to act (whether such influence or intent had been proven in legal form is another matter, and his incitement conviction was later overturned on appeal). As opposed to his very first work, which conveyed a personal anguish for which the poet projected no political solution ("I am inside someone / who hates me, I look / out from his eyes") and whose collective title conveys little hope other than in the act of expression (*Preface to a Twenty Volume Suicide Note*, 1961), his later work is replete with exhortations, capitalized imperatives for action, and chant-like repetitions designed to arouse a fury for action and then direct it toward the achievement of specific social goals. Much like his drama, this poetry is overtly presentational, declaring what the reader needs to think about and then providing the stimulus to act. Yet all the while the personal nature of Baraka stands behind it, making clear that a deep and complex imagination has been brought to bear on the issues. The range and intensity of Baraka's poetry is evident in his 1995 collection, *Trans-bluesency: The Selected Poems of Amiri Baraka/LeRoi Jones (1961–1995)*. His 2004 collection, *Somebody Blew Up America & Other Poems*, contains Baraka's controversial poem of the same name, written after 9/11, during a period in which he was New Jersey's poet laureate. After the poem's publication, public outcry became so great that the governor of New Jersey took action to abolish the position. Although Baraka sued, the United States Court of Appeals eventually ruled that state officials were immune from such lawsuits. Baraka never feared controversy; he remained an influence for many younger writers both as a major poet and as a cultural and political leader.

Beginning in the 1980s Baraka taught in the African Studies Department at the State University of New York, Stony Brook. In addition to poetry and drama, he continued to write essays on social subjects and on jazz.

An Agony. As Now.

I am inside someone
who hates me. I look
out from his eyes. Smell
what fouled tunes come in
to his breath. Love his   5
wretched women.

Slits in the metal, for sun. Where
my eyes sit turning, at the cool air
the glance of light, or hard flesh
rubbed against me, a woman, a man,   10
without shadow, or voice, or meaning.

This is the enclosure (flesh,
where innocence is a weapon. An
abstraction. Touch. (Not mine,
Or yours, if you are the soul I had   15
and abandoned when I was blind and had
my enemies carry me as a dead man
(if he is beautiful, or pitied.

It can be pain. (As now, as all his
flesh hurts me.) It can be that. Or   20
pain. As when she ran from me into
that forest.
        Or pain, the mind
silver spiraled whirled against the
sun, higher than even old men thought   25
God would be. Or pain. And the other. The
yes. (Inside his books, his fingers. They
are withered yellow flowers and were never
beautiful.) The yes. You will, lost soul, say
'beauty.' Beauty, practiced, as the tree. The   30
slow river. A white sun in its wet sentences.

Or, the cold men in their gale. Ecstasy. Flesh
or soul. The yes. (Their robes blown. Their bowls
empty. They chant at my heels, not at yours.) Flesh
or soul, as corrupt. Where the answer moves too quickly.   35
Where the God is a self, after all.)

Cold air blown through narrow blind eyes. Flesh,
white hot metal. Glows as the day with its sun.
It is a human love, I live inside. A bony skeleton
you recognize as words or simple feeling.   40

But it has no feeling. As the metal, is hot, it is not,
given to love.

It burns the thing
inside it. And that thing
screams.   45

                                        1964

A Poem for Willie Best[1]

I

The face sings, alone
at the top
        of the body. All
flesh, all song, aligned. For hell
is silent, at those cracked lips   5
flakes of skin and mind
twist and whistle softly
as they fall.
        It was your own death
you saw. Your own face, stiff   10
and raw. This
without sound, or

---

1. Willie Best was a negro character actor whose Hollywood name was Sleep'n'eat [Baraka's note].

movement. Sweet afton,[2] the
dead beggar bleeds
yet. His blood, for a time   15
alive, and huddled in a door
way, struggling to sing. Rain
washes it into cracks. Pits
whose bottoms are famous. Whose sides
are innocent broadcasts   20
of another life.

II

At this point, neither
front nor back. A point, the
dimensionless line. The top
of a head, seen from Christ's   25
heaven, stripped of history
or desire.
      Fixed, perpendicular
to shadow. (Even speech, vertical,
leaves no trace. Born in to death   30
held fast to it, where
the lover spreads his arms, the line
he makes to threaten Gods with history.
The fingers stretch to emptiness. At
each point, after flesh, even light   35
is speculation. But an end, his end,
failing a beginning.

2

A cross. The gesture, symbol, line
arms held stiff, nailed stiff, with
no sign, of what gave them strength.   40
The point, become a line, a cross, or
the man, and his material, driven in
the ground. If the head rolls back
and the mouth opens, screamed into
existence, there will be perhaps   45
only the slightest hint of movement
a smear; no help will come. No one
will turn to that station again.

III

At a cross roads, sits the
player. No drum, no umbrella, even   50
though it's raining. Again, and we

---

2. "Flow Gently Sweet Afton," a poem by the Scottish poet Robert Burns (1759–1796), refers to the river Afton in Ayrshire, Scotland.

are somehow less miserable because
here is a hero, used to being wet.
One road is where you are standing now
(reading this, the other, crosses then   55
rushes into a wood.

        5 lbs neckbones.
        5 lbs hog innards.
        10 bottles cheap wine.
                 (the contents   60
of a paper bag, also shoes, with holes
for the big toe, and several rusted
knives. This is a literature, of
symbols. And it is his gift, as the
bag is.   65
        (The contents
again, holy saviours,
           300 men on horseback
           75 bibles
           the quietness   70
of a field. A rich
man, though wet through
by the rain.
        I said,
           47 howitzers[3]   75
           7 polished horse jaws
           a few trees being waved
softly back under
the black night
        All this should be   80
invested.

IV

Where
ever,
he has gone. Who ever
mourns   85
or sits silent
to remember

There is nothing of pity
here. Nothing
of sympathy.   90

V

This is the dance of the raised
leg. Of the hand on the knee
quickly.
        As a dance it punishes

---

3. Short, relatively light cannons for the high-angle firing of shells at a low velocity.

speech. 'The house burned. The   95
old man killed.'
                  As a dance it
is obscure.

VI

This is the song
of the highest C.   100
                  The falsetto. An elegance
that punishes silence. This is the song
of the toes pointed inward, the arms swung, the
hips, moved, for fucking, slow, from side
to side. He is quoted   105
saying, "My father was
never a jockey,
                  but
   he did teach me
                  how to ride."   110

VII

The balance.
                  (Rushed in, swarmed of dark, cloaks,
and only red lights pushed a message
to the street. Rub.
                  This is the lady,   115
I saw you with.
This is your mother.
This is the lady I wanted
some how to sleep with.
                  As a dance, or   120
our elegant song. Sun red and grown
from trees, fences, mud roads in dried out
river beds. This is for me, with no God
but what is given. Give me
                  Something more   125
than what is here. I must tell you
my body hurts.

The balance.
                  Can you hear? Here
I am again. Your boy, dynamite. Can   130
you hear? My soul is moved. The soul
you gave me. I say, my soul, and it
is moved. That soul
you gave me.
                  Yes, I'm sure   135
this is the lady. You
slept with her. Witness, your boy,
here, dynamite. Hear?
                  I mean

can you?   140
The balance.
                    He was tired of losing. (And
his walking buddies tired
of walking.
                    Bent slightly,   145
at the waist. Left hand low, to flick
quick showy jabs ala Sugar.[4] The right
cocked, to complete,
                          any combination.
                    He was   150
tired of losing, but he was fighting
a big dumb "farmer."
                    Such a blue bright
afternoon, and only a few hundred yards
from the beach. He said, I'm tired   155
of losing.
          "I *got* ta cut'cha."

VIII

A renegade
behind the mask. And even
the mask, a renegade   160
disguise. Black skin
and hanging lip.
                    Lazy
                    Frightened
                    Thieving   165
                    Very potent sexually
                    Scars
                    Generally inferior
                          (but natural
rhythms.   170

His head is
at the window. The only
part
     that sings.
(The word he used   175
               (we are passing St. Mark's place[5]
               and those crazy jews who fuck)
                                   to provoke
in neon, still useful
in the rain,   180
          to provoke
some meaning, where before
there was only hell. I said
silence, at his huddled blood.

---

4. Sugar Ray Robinson (1921–1989), American boxer.
5. Street in New York City's East Village.

It is an obscene invention.   185
A white sticky discharge.
"Jism," in white chalk
on the back of Angel's garage.
Red jackets with the head of
Hobbes[6] staring into space. "Jasm"   190
the name the leader took, had it
stenciled on his chest.
                                    And he sits
wet at the crossroads, remembering distinctly
each weightless face that eases by. (Sun at   195
the back door, and that hideous mindless grin.
                        (Hear?

                                            1964

6. Thomas Hobbes (1588–1679), English philosopher who believed a "social contract" was necessary
between rulers and the ruled. Here he represents the Western, white, materialist tradition.

AUDRE LORDE
1934–1992

Audre Lorde's poetry wages what she called "a war against the tyrannies of silence"; it articulates what has been passed over out of fear or discomfort, what has been kept hidden and secret. Reading her we feel the violence inherent in breaking a silence, perhaps most often as she probes the experience of anger—the anger of black toward white or white toward black, a woman's anger at men and other women, and men's anger toward women. "My Black woman's anger," she wrote in her collection of essays, *Sister Outsider*, "is a molten pond at the core of me, my most fiercely guarded secret." Having admitted this secret into her poems, Lorde transforms our expectations of what is a fit subject for the lyric. Her work is often deliberately disturbing, the powerful voice of the poem cutting through denial, politeness, and fear. In developing this voice Lorde drew on African resources, especially the matriarchal mythology and history of West Africa. Her seventh book, *The Black Unicorn* (1978), reflects the time she spent in Africa studying, in particular, Yoruba mythology and reclaiming her connection to the rich African cultures. The African presence is evident in one of her last books, *Our Dead Behind Us* (1986), as well. Lorde's work suggests that she always connected poetry to the speaking voice, but her study of African materials deepened her connection to oral traditions (like the chant or the call) and taught her the power of voice to cut across time and place. From African writers, she said, she learned that "we live in accordance with, in a kind of correspondence with, the rest of the world as a whole." A powerful voice informed by personal and cultural history creates the possibility, for Lorde, of bridging the differences her work does not seek to erase. "It is not difference that immobilizes us," she wrote, "but silence."

Her work celebrates difference and confounds it. In Adrienne Rich's words, Lorde wrote "as a Black woman, a mother, a daughter, a Lesbian, a feminist, a visionary." Her poem "Coal" affirms an *I* that is "the total black, being spoken / from the earth's inside." This total blackness was, for her, also associated with Eros and with creativity; she celebrated this source as what she called "woman's place of power within each of us," which is "neither white nor surface; it is dark, it is ancient; and it is deep." Her best work calls on the deepest places of her own life—on the pain she experienced, on her rage (her second book, in 1972, was titled *Cables to Rage*), on her longing and desire. One of the silences her poems broke concerns love between women, and she wrote a number of poems that are erotic, precise, and true to both the power and delicacy of feeling. Unafraid of anger, she was also capable of tenderness; this is perhaps most clear not only in her love poems but in poems that address a younger generation.

Lorde was born in New York City and lived in New York almost all her life. Her parents were West Indian, and her mother was light skinned. "I grew up in a genuine confusion / between grass and weeds and flowers / and what colored meant," Lorde wrote in her poem "Outside." Part of that confusion was the conflict represented by her father's blackness and her mother's desire for whiteness (in "Black Mother Woman" Lorde speaks of the mother as "split with deceitful longings"). Lorde's understanding of identity forged out of conflict began for her, then, in her own family history with its legacy of "conflicting rebellions" ("Black Mother Woman"). In 1961 she received a B.A. from Hunter College and later a Master's of Library Science from Columbia University. The following year she married and the marriage produced a daughter and a son (she divorced in 1970). In 1968 she became poet-in-residence for a year at Tougaloo College in Mississippi, her first experience in the American South. Thereafter she knew her work to be that of a writer and teacher; she taught at John Jay College of Criminal Justice in New York City and, from 1981, was professor of English at Hunter College. In the last years of her life Lorde traveled extensively, not only to Africa but to Australia (where she met with aborigine women) and Germany. During her last years she lived much of the time in St. Croix.

"I have come to believe over and over again," Lorde said, "that what is most important to me must be spoken, made verbal and shared, even at the risk of having it bruised or misunderstood." (Her essay "Poetry Is Not a Luxury" [1977] makes the case for poetry's essential speaking of what is otherwise unnamed and unthought. The drive toward expression made Lorde a prolific writer and led her to compose several prose works in which she shared experiences often restricted to privacy: *The Cancer Journals* (1980), an account of her struggle with breast cancer, and *Zami: A New Spelling of My Name* (1982), a "biomythography" of her growing up and her emergent lesbian identity. The urgency Lorde felt to make experience "verbal and shared," however, sometimes overrode a distinction crucial to her work: that between poetry and rhetoric. She preserved this distinction in her best work by listening and responding to other voices in herself and in the world around her. With their combination of pain, anger, and tenderness, her finest poems are poetry as illumination, poetry in which, as she said, "we give name to those ideas which are—until the poem—nameless, formless, about to be birthed, but already felt."

Coal

I
is the total black, being spoken
from the earth's inside.
There are many kinds of open
how a diamond comes into a knot of flame   5
how sound comes into a word, coloured
by who pays what for speaking.

Some words are open like a diamond
on glass windows
singing out within the passing crash of sun   10
Then there are words like stapled wagers
in a perforated book,—buy and sign and tear apart—
and come whatever wills all chances
the stub remains
an ill-pulled tooth with a ragged edge.   15
Some words live in my throat
breeding like adders. Others know sun
seeking like gypsies over my tongue
to explode through my lips
like young sparrows bursting from shell.   20
Some words
bedevil me.

Love is a word, another kind of open.
As the diamond comes into a knot of flame
I am Black because I come from the earth's inside   25
now take my word for jewel in the open light.

1968

The Woman Thing

The hunters are back from beating the winter's face
in search of a challenge or task
in search of food
making fresh tracks for their children's hunger
they do not watch the sun   5
they cannot wear its heat for a sign
of triumph or freedom;
The hunters are treading heavily homeward
through snow that is marked
with their own bloody footprints.   10
emptyhanded, the hunters return
snow-maddened, sustained by their rages.

In the night after food they may seek
young girls for their amusement. But now
the hunters are coming   15
and the unbaked girls flee from their angers.
All this day I have craved
food for my child's hunger
Emptyhanded the hunters come shouting
injustices drip from their mouths   20
like stale snow melted in sunlight.

Meanwhile
the woman thing my mother taught me

bakes off its covering of snow
like a rising blackening sun.   25

1968

Black Mother Woman

I cannot recall you gentle
yet through your heavy love
I have become
an image of your once delicate flesh
split with deceitful longings.   5

When strangers come and compliment me
your aged spirit takes a bow
jingling with pride
but once you hid that secret
in the center of furies   10
hanging me
with deep breasts and wiry hair
with your own split flesh
and long suffering eyes
buried in myths of little worth.   15

But I have peeled away your anger
down to the core of love
and look mother
I Am
a dark temple where your true spirit rises   20
beautiful
and tough as chestnut
stanchion[1] against your nightmare of weakness
and if my eyes conceal
a squadron of conflicting rebellions   25
I learned from you
to define myself
through your denials.

1971

---

1. Upright bar or post (for supporting, e.g., a railing).

LUCILLE CLIFTON
1936–2010

ucille Clifton seemed able to lift the poem off the page and return it to the air we breathe. Like the work of Langston Hughes or William Carlos Williams, her poems allow us to hear the language of our daily lives as poetry and to experience the poetry in our ordinary lives. Although a closer look reveals the subtle craft of her poems (for example, the slant rhymes and the carefully paced repetitions), they appear deceptively simple. Their frankness and directness close the distance between poet and reader, especially when these poems are read aloud. Clifton emphasized the informality in her work through the lowercase letters she preferred and through her frequent omission of titles. The language of her poems reflects her identity; "I am a black woman poet," she said, "and I sound like one." Grounded in realistic details, her poems do not shy away from what is harsh and painful, including incest, suicide, mental illness, and the effects of poverty and racism. But while Clifton's anger fueled many poems, her imagination found beauty and humor in unexpected places; indeed, she seemed able to make poetry out of anything. In this she resembles the African American quilters who rework the materials of ordinary experience into distinctive and compelling designs. Indeed, she titled one of her books *Quilting* (1991) and borrowed its section headings from the names of traditional quilt patterns.

Born in Depew, New York, to a father who worked in the steel mills and a mother who was a launderer and a homemaker (and who wrote poems but burned them), Clifton was the first person in her family to attend college. "I had a very regular life, the life of a poor black person," Clifton once said; but her background and her gifts sometimes made her feel that "there is no planet stranger / than the one I'm from" ("note, passed to superman"). At sixteen she began her studies at Howard University in Washington, D.C., and she later attended Fredonia State Teachers College in New York State. She went on to work as a claims clerk in the New York State Division of Employment (1958–60) and as a literature assistant at the Office of Education in Washington (1960–71). Clifton never formally studied creative writing, but she wrote poems and thought of herself as a poet from a young age. However, her work did not receive public recognition until she was in her thirties. In 1969 she sent a poem to the poet Robert Hayden at the National Endowment for the Arts. Hayden had left the NEA, but his successor, Carolyn Kizer, read the work and submitted it to the YW-YMHA Poetry Center Discovery Award competition in New York City. Clifton won the competition and at the award ceremony, after she read her poems, an editor from Random House in the audience offered to publish her first book, *Good Times* (1969). *Good Times* appeared when she was thirty-three, a wife and mother with six children under the age of eleven. During these years her method of composition followed those writers, many of them women, who compose lines of poetry in the mind until there is time to write them down.

Clifton came from a line of African American storytellers extending from her great-grandmother, Caroline Donald, who was born in Dahomey, Africa, sold into slavery, and taken to America. Clifton's memoir, *Generations* (1976), chronicles the history of her family, including the genealogy and the tradition of strong women passed down to Clifton through her father's stories. In much of her work, Clifton consciously sought to recover an African American past that has too often been

omitted from standard histories and to retell history from previously unacknowl-
edged points of view.

In a poem beginning "the light that came to Lucille Clifton," a voice from "the
non-dead past" speaks this message to her: "You might as well open the door, my
child / for truth is furiously knocking." Throughout her long and productive career
as a poet, and as a writer of memoirs and children's books, she transmitted the
voices of a living past. Like Toni Morrison's fiction, Clifton's poems are full of ghosts:
her mother and father, her unborn children, her ancestors, and sometimes mythical
and biblical figures. These presences in her work bear witness to a legacy of pain,
wisdom, and survival. As a writer brave enough to open the door to the truths of her
life and her world, Clifton possessed a "gift of understanding" that put her in touch
with the suffering of the "holy lost" ("Wild Blessing"), but the spiritual dimension
of her work also reveals the possibility of joy and transformation, evident in "blessing the boats."

Clifton's books include *Good News about the Earth* (1972) and *Two-Headed
Woman* (1980), which received the University of Massachusetts Juniper Prize. Both
of these volumes were nominated for the Pulitzer Prize. Subsequent collections
include *Next* (1987), *The Book of Light* (1993), *Blessing the Boats: New and Selected
Poems 1988–2000* (2000), *Mercy* (2004), and *Voices* (2008). Clifton's work for children includes *The Black BCs* (1970), *The Times They Used to Be* (1974), and an
award-winning series of books featuring events in the life of Everett Anderson, a
young black boy. In 1999 she was elected a chancellor of the Academy of American
Poets. She served as poet laureate for the State of Maryland and as distinguished
professor of humanities at St. Mary's College in Maryland.

miss rosie

```
              when i watch you
              wrapped up like garbage
              sitting, surrounded by the smell
              of too old potato peels
              or                                                    5
              when i watch you
              in your old man's shoes
              with the little toe cut out
              sitting, waiting for your mind
              like next week's grocery                            10
              i say
              when i watch you
              you wet brown bag of a woman
              who used to be the best looking gal in georgia
              used to be called the Georgia Rose                  15
              i stand up
              through your destruction
              i stand up
```

1969   1987

the lost baby poem

the time i dropped your almost body down
down to meet the waters under the city
and run one with the sewage to the sea
what did i know about waters rushing back
what did i know about drowning   5
or being drowned

you would have been born into winter
in the year of the disconnected gas
and no car   we would have made the thin
walk over genesee hill[1] into the canada wind   10
to watch you slip like ice into strangers' hands
you would have fallen naked as snow into winter
if you were here i could tell you these
and some other things

if i am ever less than a mountain   15
for your definite brothers and sisters
let the rivers pour over my head
let the sea take me for a spiller
of seas   let black men call me stranger
always   for your never named sake   20

                                            1972

homage to my hips

these hips are big hips
they need space to
move around in.
they don't fit into little
petty places, these hips.   5
are free hips.
they don't like to be held back.
these hips have never been enslaved,
they go where they want to go
they do what they want to do.   10
these hips are mighty hips.
these hips are magic hips.
i have known them
to put a spell on a man and
spin him like a top!   15

                                            1980

---

1. Genesee County is in western New York State.

wild blessings

licked in the palm of my hand
by an uninvited woman, so i have held
in that hand the hand of a man who
emptied into his daughter, the hand
of a girl who threw herself   5
from a tenement window, the trembling
junkie hand of a priest, of a boy who
shattered across viet nam
someone resembling his mother,
and more, and more.   10
do not ask me to thank the tongue
that circled my fingers
or pride myself on the attentions
of the holy lost.
i am grateful for many blessings   15
but the gift of understanding,
the wild one, maybe not.

                                                    1991

wishes for sons

i wish them cramps.
i wish them a strange town
and the last tampon.
i wish them no 7–11.

i wish them one week early   5
and wearing a white skirt.
i wish them one week late.

later i wish them hot flashes
and clots like you
wouldn't believe.   let the   10
flashes come when they
meet someone special.
let the clots come
when they want to.

let them think they have accepted   15
arrogance in the universe,
then bring them to gynecologists
not unlike themselves.

                                                    1991

the mississippi river empties into the gulf

and the gulf enters the sea and so forth,
none of them emptying anything,
all of them carrying yesterday
forever on their white tipped backs,
all of them dragging forward tomorrow.   5
it is the great circulation
of the earth's body, like the blood
of the gods, this river in which the past
is always flowing, every water
is the same water coming round.   10
everyday someone is standing on the edge
of this river, staring into time,
whispering mistakenly:
only here, only now.

                                        1996

[oh antic God]

oh antic God
return to me
my mother in her thirties[1]
leaned across the front porch
the huge pillow of her breasts   5
pressing against the rail
summoning me in for bed.

I am almost the dead woman's age times two.

I can barely recall her song
the scent of her hands   10
though her wild hair scratches my dreams
at night.   return to me, oh Lord of then
and now, my mother's calling,
her young voice humming my name.

                                        2004

---

1. Thelma Moore Sayles, Clifton's mother, died at age forty-four.

DON DeLILLO
b. 1936

D on DeLillo's best-known novels evoke twentieth- and twenty-first-century American culture and global history on its grandest scale. Encompassing big-league sports, atomic bombs, space exploration, the 9/11 attacks, international business, environmental disasters, huge art installations, and glittering supermar-kets, his sixteen novels have captured the preoccupations of his times. Not histori-cal novels in the traditional sense, DeLillo's works allow readers to hear how people of all ages speak, think, and experience the world as massive forces bear down upon them. He observes modern experience with an eye that is both critical and loving. Touched always with humor that makes the reader see cultural absurdities in a new light, his attention to the human dimensions of mass culture has made his work popular since his breakthrough novel, *White Noise*, was published in 1985.

"The future belongs to crowds." The narrator of *Mao II* makes this prophecy on the heels of a prologue describing the mass wedding of 13,000 followers of the Rev-erend Sun Myung Moon in Yankee Stadium. This kind of spectacle appears fre-quently in DeLillo's work. His millennial novel, *Underworld* (1998), begins with one of his best-known crowd scenes, set at the Polo Grounds baseball stadium in New York: it is 1951, the famous playoff game between two New York City teams, the Giants and the Dodgers. In the stands we find power brokers and celebrities and thousands of ordinary New Yorkers. In *Libra* (1988), DeLillo conjures up the mass of humanity lining the presidential motorcade route in Dallas, Texas, on November 22, 1963, a scene the reader experiences through the eyes of President Kennedy's assas-sin, Lee Harvey Oswald.

DeLillo's crowds reflect the vibrant city where the author has lived throughout his life. "New York made me," he once declared. "There's a sensibility, a sense of humor, an approach, a sort of dark approach to things that's part New York, and maybe part growing up Catholic, and that . . . shapes my work far more than anything I read." Born in New York City in 1936 and raised in a tight-knit Southern Italian neighbor-hood in the Bronx, DeLillo attended Catholic schools, graduating from Fordham University in the late fifties. In Catholic ritual, and in the modern art and jazz he discovered in the city in the sixties, he found his most enduring preoccupations as a writer of fiction.

For all their fascination with crowds, DeLillo's novels are grounded in the lives of their characters. In any DeLillo crowd scene, the reader will find individuals the novel will follow closely. *Underworld*, DeLillo's most massive novel, follows Cotter, a black child from the projects, as he jumps the stiles to see the Giants-Dodgers play-off game. The boy later escapes from the stands with the game-winning homerun ball off Bobby Thompson's bat, and the ball becomes a precious object that carries characters' stories and American history along with it to the start of the new century five decades later. Through such characters, DeLillo ushers readers into the place where recorded history gives way to the novelist's imagination. Shuttling between mass culture and the private lives contained in crowds, DeLillo's fiction diagrams the machinery of transcendence: How does an immigrant or outcast become an American? How does a soldier decide to assassinate a president? How does a believer connect to the cosmos? How does a wildly diverse city become a human community? And how do the decisions of individuals add up to History?

DeLillo is renowned for understanding how media of all kinds penetrate deep into modern life. That wisdom has resonated steadily with readers as the Internet age dawned and flourished over the course of his writing career. His characters strive for authentic human connection within the flow of advertising, television, film, radio, gossip, misinformation, and mass hysteria that swirls around their living rooms, bedrooms, cars, and kitchen tables. Children have a special role in countering these forces. In *The Names* (1982), a child writes mystical stories filled with misspellings. His estranged parents and their friends make the plot run—the novel follows a cult that is methodically committing murders in small villages along the Mediterranean coast of Greece—but the novel's transcendent passages come from the boy's pen. Through him DeLillo presents an innocent, authentic, and nonviolent mysticism that counters the cult's murderous rituals. A toddler in *White Noise* gradually gives up words in favor of more-visceral forms of human communication—he cries steadily for twenty-four hours and then stops. These strange speakers, or nonspeakers, draw others beyond ordinary language to a deeper experience of the human condition.

The form and style of DeLillo's novels reflect his shifts in scale from the crowd to the individual, from panoramic scenes to family bedrooms. His epic novels are built from multiple individual stories that braid together into a broad view of an era, a nation, or even the whole globe. Within each story DeLillo's fine-tuned ear for dialogue allows the reader to hear the very words through which his characters put their lives together. As the digital age took hold in the early twenty-first century, even his early novels seemed both prophetic and redemptive to contemporary readers looking to find coherent stories that could hold their own within the torrent of words and pictures flowing over us every day.

When *White Noise* was published, DeLillo was considered a practitioner of the "paranoid school" of American fiction: part of a group of writers, including Thomas Pynchon, John Barth, William Gaddis, and Richard Powers, whose novels represented massive institutions or conspiracies in which characters could not hope to shape their own lives. The novel's funny, satirical picture of fragmented American family life in a leafy suburb seemed to capture what was "postmodern" in middle-class life—the way television seemed to generate reality, the encompassing aura of consumer culture, the morphing domestic scene shaped by divorce, remarriage, international careers, and blended families. DeLillo's dark humor cast a critical light on middle-class achievements—the main character of *White Noise* is a failing professor of "Hitler Studies" who, try as he might, cannot learn German. But for all the novel's satire and fragmentation, classic moments of transcendence and community emerge from *White Noise*. Such elements return in all of DeLillo's major novels and set him apart from his paranoid peers, putting him ultimately closer to a school of religiously inflected American novelists that would include secular Jewish writers, American Catholic novelists, and those Protestant writers who reserve a place for mysticism and grace.

DeLillo has garnered several major prizes in his long career, starting with the National Book Award for *White Noise*, later followed by the Jerusalem Prize and the William Dean Howells Medal for *Underworld*. In 2013 he was awarded the first Library of Congress Prize for American Fiction, which honors "strong, unique, enduring voices that—throughout long, consistently accomplished careers—have told us something about the American experience." Receiving news of the award, DeLillo said that his "first thoughts were of my mother and father, who came to this country the hard way, as young people confronting a new language and culture." The prize, he said, "is the culmination of their efforts and a tribute to their memory."

In the selection from *White Noise* that follows, the main character, Professor Jack Gladney, and his family have been evacuated from their home, joining the mass of humanity converging upon a school gym to shelter from an environmental disaster that the media have dubbed the "Airborne Toxic Event." Arriving at the gym in the family car, Gladney, his wife, Babette, and their four children are suddenly thrown out of their suburban security. Each must find a place in the unfolding American spectacle.

From White Noise

Part II: Airborne Toxic Event

Small crowds collected around certain men. Here were the sources of information and rumor. One person worked in a chemical plant, another had overheard a remark, a third was related to a clerk in a state agency. True, false, and other kinds of news radiated through the dormitory from these dense clusters.

It was said that we would be allowed to go home first thing in the morning; that the government was engaged in a cover-up; that a helicopter had entered the toxic cloud and never reappeared; that the dogs had arrived from New Mexico, parachuting into a meadow in a daring night drop; that the town of Farmington would be uninhabitable for forty years.

Remarks existed in a state of permanent flotation. No one thing was either more or less plausible than any other thing. As people jolted out of reality, we were released from the need to distinguish.

Some families chose to sleep in their cars, others were forced to do so because there was no room for them in the seven or eight buildings on the grounds. We were in a large barracks, one of three such buildings at the camp, and with the generator now working we were fairly comfortable. The Red Cross had provided cots, portable heaters, sandwiches and coffee. There were kerosene lamps to supplement the existing overhead lights. Many people had radios, extra food to share with others, blankets, beach chairs, extra clothing. The place was crowded, still quite cold, but the sight of nurses and volunteer workers made us feel the children were safe, and the presence of other stranded souls, young women with infants, old and infirm people, gave us a certain staunchness and will, a selfless bent that was pronounced enough to function as a common identity. This large gray area, dank and bare and lost to history just a couple of hours ago, was an oddly agreeable place right now, filled with an eagerness of community and voice.

Seekers of news moved from one cluster of people to another, tending to linger at the larger groups. In this way I moved slowly through the barracks. There were nine evacuation centers, I learned, including this one and the Kung Fu Palace. Iron City had not been emptied out; nor had most of the other towns in the area. It was said that the governor was on his way from the capitol in an executive helicopter. It would probably set down in a bean field outside a deserted town, allowing the governor to emerge, square-jawed and confident, in a bush jacket, within camera range, for ten or fifteen seconds, as a demonstration of his imperishability.

What a surprise it was to ease my way between people at the outer edges of one of the largest clusters and discover that my own son was at the center of things, speaking in his new-found voice, his tone of enthusiasm for runaway calamity. He was talking about the airborne toxic event in a technical way, although his voice all but sang with prophetic disclosure. He pronounced the name itself, Nyodene Derivative,[1] with an unseemly relish, taking morbid delight in the very sound. People listened attentively to this adolescent boy in a field jacket and cap, with binoculars strapped around his neck and an Instamatic[2] fastened to his belt. No doubt his listeners were influenced by his age. He would be truthful and earnest, serving no special interest; he would have an awareness of the environment; his knowledge of chemistry would be fresh and up-to-date.

I heard him say, "The stuff they sprayed on the big spill at the train yard was probably soda ash. But it was a case of too little too late. My guess is they'll get some crop dusters up in the air at daybreak and bombard the toxic cloud with lots more soda ash, which could break it up and scatter it into a million harmless puffs. Soda ash is the common name for sodium carbonate, which is used in the manufacture of glass, ceramics, detergents, and soaps. It's also what they use to make bicarbonate of soda, something a lot of you have probably guzzled after a night on the town."

People moved in closer, impressed by the boy's knowledgeability and wit. It was remarkable to hear him speak so easily to a crowd of strangers. Was he finding himself, learning how to determine his worth from the reactions of others? Was it possible that out of the turmoil and surge of this dreadful event he would learn to make his way in the world?

"What you're probably all wondering is what exactly is this Nyodene D. we keep hearing about? A good question. We studied it in school, we saw movies of rats having convulsions and so on. So, okay, it's basically simple. Nyodene D. is a whole bunch of things thrown together that are byproducts of the manufacture of insecticide. The original stuff kills roaches, the byproducts kill everything left over. A little joke our teacher made."

He snapped his fingers, let his left leg swing a bit.

"In powder form it's colorless, odorless, and very dangerous, except no one seems to know exactly what it causes in humans or in the offspring of humans. They tested for years and either they don't know for sure or they know and aren't saying. Some things are too awful to publicize."

He arched his brows and began to twitch comically, his tongue lolling in a corner of his mouth. I was astonished to hear people laugh.

"Once it seeps into the soil, it has a life span of forty years. This is longer than a lot of people. After five years you'll notice various kinds of fungi appearing between your regular windows and storm windows as well as in your clothes and food. After ten years your screens will turn rusty and begin to pit and rot. Siding will warp. There will be glass breakage and trauma to pets. After twenty years you'll probably have to seal yourself in the attic and just wait and see. I guess there's a lesson in all this. Get to know your chemicals."

I didn't want him to see me there. It would make him self-conscious, remind him of his former life as a gloomy and fugitive boy. Let him bloom, if that's what he was doing, in the name of mischance, dread, and random disaster. So I slipped away, passing a man who wore snow boots wrapped in

1. Fictional toxic substance; elsewhere in the novel it is referred to as "Nyodene D." and is said to be "packed with chlorides, benzines, phenols, hydrocarbons."
2. Inexpensive and popular point-and-shoot camera made by Kodak between 1963 and 1988.

plastic, and headed for the far end of the barracks, where we'd earlier made camp.

We were next to a black family of Jehovah's Witnesses.[3] A man and woman with a boy about twelve. Father and son were handing out tracts to people nearby and seemed to have no trouble finding willing recipients and listeners.

The woman said to Babette, "Isn't this something?"

"Nothing surprises me anymore," Babette said.

"Isn't that the truth."

"What would surprise me would be if there were no surprises."

"That sounds about right."

"Or if there were little bitty surprises. That would be a surprise. Instead of things like this."

"God Jehovah's got a bigger surprise in store than this," the woman said.

"God Jehovah?"

"That's the one."

Steffie and Wilder were asleep in one of the cots. Denise sat at the other end engrossed in the *Physicians' Desk Reference*. Several air mattresses were stacked against the wall. There was a long line at the emergency telephone, people calling relatives or trying to reach the switchboard at one or another radio call-in show. The radios here were tuned mainly to just such shows. Babette sat in a camp chair, going through a canvas bag full of snack thins and other provisions. I noticed jars and cartons that had been sitting in the refrigerator or cabinet for months.

"I thought this would be a good time to cut down on fatty things," she said.

"Why now especially?"

"This is a time for discipline, mental toughness. We're practically at the edge."

"I think it's interesting that you regard a possible disaster for yourself, your family, and thousands of other people as an opportunity to cut down on fatty foods."

"You take discipline where you can find it," she said. "If I don't eat my yogurt now, I may as well stop buying the stuff forever. Except I think I'll skip the wheat germ."

The brand name was foreign-looking. I picked up the jar of wheat germ and examined the label closely.

"It's German," I told her. "Eat it."

There were people in pajamas and slippers. A man with a rifle slung over his shoulder. Kids crawling into sleeping bags. Babette gestured, wanting me to lean closer.

"Let's keep the radio turned off," she whispered. "So the girls can't hear. They haven't gotten beyond *déjà vu*. I want to keep it that way."

"What if the symptoms are real?"

"How could they be real?"

"Why couldn't they be real?"

---

3. Christian denomination founded in America by Charles Taze Russell in the 1870s. Practitioners are known for their door-to-door evangelism and belief that the end of the world is near.

"They get them only when they're broadcast," she whispered.

"Did Steffie hear about *déjà vu* on the radio?"

"She must have."

"How do you know? Were you with her when it was broadcast?"

"I'm not sure."

"Think hard."

"I can't remember."

"Do you remember telling her what *déjà vu* means?"

She spooned some yogurt out of the carton, seemed to pause, deep in thought.

"This happened before," she said finally.

"What happened before?"

"Eating yogurt, sitting here, talking about *déjà vu*."

"I don't want to hear this."

"The yogurt was on my spoon. I saw it in a flash. The whole experience. Natural, whole-milk, low-fat."

The yogurt was still on the spoon. I watched her put the spoon to her mouth, thoughtfully, trying to measure the action against the illusion of a matching original. From my squatting position I motioned her to lean closer.

"Heinrich seems to be coming out of his shell," I whispered.

"Where is he? I haven't seen him."

"See that knot of people? He's right in the middle. He's telling them what he knows about the toxic event."

"What does he know?"

"Quite a lot, it turns out."

"Why didn't he tell us?" she whispered.

"He's probably tired of us. He doesn't think it's worth his while to be funny and charming in front of his family. That's the way sons are. We represent the wrong kind of challenge."

"Funny and charming?"

"I guess he had it in him all the while. It was a question of finding the right time to exercise his gifts."

She moved closer, our heads almost touching.

"Don't you think you ought to go over there?" she said. "Let him see you in the crowd. Show him that his father is present at his big moment."

"He'll only get upset if he sees me in the crowd."

"Why?"

"I'm his father."

"So if you go over there, you'll ruin things by embarrassing him and cramping his style because of the father-son thing. And if you don't go over, he'll never know you saw him in his big moment and he'll think he has to behave in your presence the way he's always behaved, sort of peevishly and defensive, instead of in this new, delightful, and expansive manner."

"It's a double bind."

"What if I went over?" she whispered.

"He'll think I sent you."

"Would that be so awful?"

"He thinks I use you to get him to do what I want."

"There may be some truth in that, Jack. But then what are stepparents for if they can't be used in little skirmishes between blood relatives?"

I moved still closer, lowered my voice even more.

"Just a Life Saver,"[4] I said.

"What?"

"Just some saliva that you didn't know what to do with."

"It was a Life Saver," she whispered, making an O with her thumb and index finger.

"Give me one."

"It was the last one."

"What flavor—*quick*."

"Cherry."

I puckered my lips and made little sucking sounds. The black man with the tracts came over and squatted next to me. We engaged in an earnest and prolonged handshake. He studied me openly, giving the impression that he had traveled this rugged distance, uprooting his family, not to escape the chemical event but to find the one person who would understand what he had to say.

"It's happening everywhere, isn't it?"

"More or less," I said.

"And what's the government doing about it?"

"Nothing."

"You said it, I didn't. There's only one word in the language to describe what's being done and you found it exactly. I'm not surprised at all. But when you think about it, what *can* they do? Because what is coming is definitely coming. No government in the world is big enough to stop it. Does a man like yourself know the size of India's standing army?"

"One million."

"I didn't say it, you did. One million soldiers and they can't stop it. Do you know who's got the biggest standing army in the world?"

"It's either China or Russia, although the Vietnamese ought to be mentioned."

"Tell me this," he said. "Can the Vietnamese stop it?"

"No."

"It's here, isn't it? People feel it. We know in our bones. God's kingdom is coming."

He was a rangy man with sparse hair and a gap between his two front teeth. He squatted easily, seemed loose-jointed and comfortable. I realized he was wearing a suit and tie with running shoes.

"Are these great days?" he said.

I studied his face, trying to find a clue to the right answer.

"Do you feel it coming? Is it on the way? Do you *want* it to come?"

He bounced on his toes as he spoke.

"Wars, famines, earthquakes, volcanic eruptions. It's all beginning to jell. In your own words, is there anything that can stop it from coming once it picks up momentum?"

"No."

"You said it, I didn't. Floods, tornados, epidemics of strange new diseases. Is it a sign? Is it the truth? Are you ready?"

---

4. Jack had caught Babette taking an experimental pill meant to cure the fear of death; she claimed she was swallowing a Life Saver candy or saliva. Jack also wants a supply of these pills.

"Do people really feel it in their bones?" I said.

"Good news travels fast."

"Do people talk about it? On your door-to-door visits, do you get the impression they want it?"

"It's not do they want it. It's where do I go to sign up. It's get me out of here right now. People ask, 'Is there seasonal change in God's kingdom?' They ask, 'Are there bridge tolls and returnable bottles?' In other words I'm saying they're getting right down to it."

"You feel it's a ground swell."

"A sudden gathering. Exactly put. I took one look and I knew. This is a man who understands."

"Earthquakes are not up, statistically."

He gave me a condescending smile. I felt it was richly deserved, although I wasn't sure why. Maybe it was prissy to be quoting statistics in the face of powerful beliefs, fears, desires.

"How do you plan to spend your resurrection?" he said, as though asking about a long weekend coming up.

"We all get one?"

"You're either among the wicked or among the saved. The wicked get to rot as they walk down the street. They get to feel their own eyes slide out of their sockets. You'll know them by their stickiness and lost parts. People tracking slime of their own making. All the flashiness of Armageddon is in the rotting. The saved know each other by their neatness and reserve. He doesn't have showy ways is how you know a saved person."

He was a serious man, he was matter-of-fact and practical, down to his running shoes. I wondered about his eerie self-assurance, his freedom from doubt. Is this the point of Armageddon? No ambiguity, no more doubt. He was ready to run into the next world. He was forcing the next world to seep into my consciousness, stupendous events that seemed matter-of-fact to him, self-evident, reasonable, imminent, true. I did not feel Armageddon in my bones but I worried about all those people who did, who were ready for it, wishing hard, making phone calls and bank withdrawals. If enough people want it to happen, will it happen? How many people are enough people? Why are we talking to each other from this aboriginal crouch?

He handed me a pamphlet called "Twenty Common Mistakes About the End of the World." I struggled out of the squatting posture, feeling dizziness and back-pain. At the front of the hall a woman was saying something about exposure to toxic agents. Her small voice was almost lost in the shuffling roar of the barracks, the kind of low-level rumble that humans routinely make in large enclosed places. Denise had put down her reference work and was giving me a hard-eyed look. It was the look she usually saved for her father and his latest loss of foothold.

"What's wrong?" I said to her.

"Didn't you hear what the voice said?"

"Exposure."

"That's right," she said sharply.

"What's that got to do with us?"

"Not us," she said. "You."

"Why me?"

"Aren't you the one who got out of the car to fill the gas tank?"

"Where was the airborne event when I did that?"

"Just ahead of us. Don't you remember? You got back in the car and we went a little ways and then there it was in all those lights."

"You're saying when I got out of the car, the cloud may have been close enough to rain all over me."

"It's not your fault," she said impatiently, "but you were practically right in it for about two and a half minutes."

I made my way up front. Two lines were forming. A to M and N to Z. At the end of each line was a folding table with a microcomputer on it. Technicians milled about, men and women with lapel badges and color-coded armbands. I stood behind the life-jacket-wearing family. They looked bright, happy, and well-drilled. The thick orange vests did not seem especially out of place even though we were on more or less dry land, well above sea level, many miles from the nearest ominous body of water. Stark upheavals bring out every sort of quaint aberration by the very suddenness of their coming. Dashes of color and idiosyncrasy marked the scene from beginning to end.

The lines were not long. When I reached the A-to-M desk, the man seated there typed out data on his keyboard. My name, age, medical history, so on. He was a gaunt young man who seemed suspicious of conversation that strayed outside certain unspecified guidelines. Over the left sleeve on his khaki jacket he wore a green armband bearing the word SIMUVAC.

I related the circumstances of my presumed exposure.

"How long were you out there?"

"Two and a half minutes," I said. "Is that considered long or short?"

"Anything that puts you in contact with actual emissions means we have a situation."

"Why didn't the drifting cloud disperse in all that wind and rain?"

"This is not your everyday cirrus. This is a high-definition event. It is packed with dense concentrations of byproduct. You could almost toss a hook in there and tow it out to sea, which I'm exaggerating to make a point."

"What about people in the car? I had to open the door to get out and get back in."

"There are known degrees of exposure. I'd say their situation is they're minimal risks. It's the two and a half minutes standing right in it that makes me wince. Actual skin and orifice contact. This is Nyodene D. A whole new generation of toxic waste. What we call state of the art. One part per million million can send a rat into a permanent state."

He regarded me with the grimly superior air of a combat veteran. Obviously he didn't think much of people whose complacent and overprotected lives did not allow for encounters with brain-dead rats. I wanted this man on my side. He had access to data. I was prepared to be servile and fawning if it would keep him from dropping casually shattering remarks about my degree of exposure and chances for survival.

"That's quite an armband you've got there. What does SIMUVAC mean? Sounds important."

"Short for simulated evacuation. A new state program they're still battling over funds for."

"But this evacuation isn't simulated. It's real."

"We know that. But we thought we could use it as a model."

"A form of practice? Are you saying you saw a chance to use the real event in order to rehearse the simulation?"

"We took it right into the streets."

"How is it going?" I said.

"The insertion curve isn't as smooth as we would like. There's a probability excess. Plus which we don't have our victims laid out where we'd want them if this was an actual simulation. In other words we're forced to take our victims as we find them. We didn't get a jump on computer traffic. Suddenly it just spilled out, three-dimensionally, all over the landscape. You have to make allowances for the fact that everything we see tonight is real. There's a lot of polishing we still have to do. But that's what this exercise is all about."

"What about the computers? Is that real data you're running through the system or is it just practice stuff?"

"You watch," he said.

He spent a fair amount of time tapping on the keys and then studying coded responses on the data screen—a considerably longer time, it seemed to me, than he'd devoted to the people who'd preceded me in line. In fact I began to feel that others were watching me. I stood with my arms folded, trying to create a picture of an impassive man, someone in line at a hardware store waiting for the girl at the register to ring up his heavy-duty rope. It seemed the only way to neutralize events, to counteract the passage of computerized dots that registered my life and death. Look at no one, reveal nothing, remain still. The genius of the primitive mind is that it can render human helplessness in noble and beautiful ways.

"You're generating big numbers," he said, peering at the screen.

"I was out there only two and a half minutes. That's how many seconds?"

"It's not just you were out there so many seconds. It's your whole data profile. I tapped into your history. I'm getting bracketed numbers with pulsing stars."

"What does that mean?"

"You'd rather not know."

He made a silencing gesture as if something of particular morbid interest was appearing on the screen. I wondered what he meant when he said he'd tapped into my history. Where was it located exactly? Some state or federal agency, some insurance company or credit firm or medical clearinghouse? What history was he referring to? I'd told him some basic things. Height, weight, childhood diseases. What else did he know? Did he know about my wives, my involvement with Hitler, my dreams and fears?[5]

He had a skinny neck and jug-handle ears to go with his starved skull—the innocent prewar look of a rural murderer.

"Am I going to die?"

"Not as such," he said.

"What do you mean?"

"Not in so many words."

"How many words does it take?"

"It's not a question of words. It's a question of years. We'll know more in fifteen years. In the meantime we definitely have a situation."

---

5. Jack has been married five times to four different women; his academic field is called Hitler Studies.

"What will we know in fifteen years?"

"If you're still alive at the time, we'll know that much more than we do now. Nyodene D. has a life span of thirty years. You'll have made it halfway through."

"I thought it was forty years."

"Forty years in the soil. Thirty years in the human body."

"So, to outlive this substance, I will have to make it into my eighties. Then I can begin to relax."

"Knowing what we know at this time."

"But the general consensus seems to be that we don't know enough at this time to be sure of anything."

"Let me answer like so. If I was a rat I wouldn't want to be anywhere within a two hundred mile radius of the airborne event."

"What if you were a human?"

He looked at me carefully. I stood with my arms folded, staring over his head toward the front door of the barracks. To look at him would be to declare my vulnerability.

"I wouldn't worry about what I can't see or feel," he said. "I'd go ahead and live my life. Get married, settle down, have kids. There's no reason you can't do these things, knowing what we know."

"But you said we have a situation."

"I didn't say it. The computer did. The whole system says it. It's what we call a massive data-base tally. Gladney, J. A. K. I punch in the name, the substance, the exposure time and then I tap into your computer history. Your genetics, your personals, your medicals, your psychologicals, your police-and-hospitals. It comes back pulsing stars. This doesn't mean anything is going to happen to you as such, at least not today or tomorrow. It just means you are the sum total of your data. No man escapes that."

"And this massive so-called tally is not a simulation despite that armband you're wearing. It is real."

"It is real," he said.

I stood absolutely still. If they thought I was already dead, they might be inclined to leave me alone. I think I felt as I would if a doctor had held an X-ray to the light showing a star-shaped hole at the center of one of my vital organs. Death has entered. It is inside you. You are said to be dying and yet are separate from the dying, can ponder it at your leisure, literally see on the X-ray photograph or computer screen the horrible alien logic of it all. It is when death is rendered graphically, is televised so to speak, that you sense an eerie separation between your condition and yourself. A network of symbols has been introduced, an entire awesome technology wrested from the gods. It makes you feel like a stranger in your own dying.

I wanted my academic gown[6] and dark glasses.

When I got back to the other end of the barracks, the three younger children were asleep, Heinrich was making notations on a road map and Babette was seated some distance away with Old Man Treadwell and a number of other blind people. She was reading to them from a small and brightly colored stack of supermarket tabloids.

---

6. The ceremonial robe whose color and style indicates the level, subject, and often the place, of the wearer's education; the robes are worn by scholars during commencement and other ritual occasions.

I needed a distraction. I found a camp chair and set it near the wall behind Babette. There were four blind people, a nurse and three sighted people arranged in a semicircle facing the reader. Others occasionally paused to listen to an item or two, then moved on. Babette employed her storytelling voice, the same sincere and lilting tone she used when she read fairy tales to Wilder or erotic passages to her husband in their brass bed high above the headlong traffic hum.

She reported a front-page story. "Life After Death Guaranteed with Bonus Coupons." Then turned to the designated page.

"Scientists at Princeton's famed Institute for Advanced Studies have stunned the world by presenting absolute and undeniable proof of life after death. A researcher at the world-renowned Institute has used hypnosis to induce hundreds of people to recall their previous-life experiences as pyramid-builders, exchange students, and extraterrestrials."

Babette changed her voice to do dialogue.

"'In the last year alone,' declares reincarnation hypnotist Ling Ti Wan, 'I have helped hundreds to regress to previous lives under hypnosis. One of my most amazing subjects was a woman who was able to recall her life as a hunter-gatherer in the Mesolithic era ten thousand years ago. It was remarkable to hear this tiny senior citizen in polyester slacks describe her life as a hulking male chieftain whose band inhabited a peat bog and hunted wild boar with primitive bow and arrow. She was able to identify features of that era which only a trained archaeologist could know about. She even spoke several phrases in the language of that day, a tongue remarkably similar to modern-day German.'"

Babette's voice resumed its tone of straight narration.

"Dr. Shiv Chatterjee, fitness guru and high-energy physicist, recently stunned a live TV audience by relating the well-documented case of two women, unknown to each other, who came to him for regression in the same week, only to discover that they had been twin sisters in the lost city of Atlantis fifty thousand years ago. Both women describe the city, before its mysterious and catastrophic plunge into the sea, as a clean and well-run municipality where you could walk safely almost any time of day or night. Today they are food stylists for NASA.[7]

"Even more startling is the case of five-year-old Patti Weaver who has made convincing claims to Dr. Chatterjee that in her previous-life experience she was the secret KGB[8] assassin responsible for the unsolved murders of famed personalities Howard Hughes, Marilyn Monroe, and Elvis Presley. Known in international espionage circles as 'the Viper' for the deadly and untraceable venom he injected into the balls of the feet of his celebrity victims, the assassin died in a fiery Moscow helicopter crash just hours before little Patti Weaver was born in Popular Mechanics, Iowa. She not only has the same bodily markings as the Viper but seems to have a remarkable knack for picking up Russian words and phrases.

"'I regressed this subject at least a dozen times,' says Dr. Chatterjee. 'I used the toughest professional techniques to get her to contradict herself.

7. National Aeronautics and Space Administration, the government agency responsible for space exploration.
8. Komitet Gosudarstvennoy Bezopasnosti (KGB)

or "Committee for State Security," the Soviet Union's secretive national spy and security agency, in operation from the 1950s through the 1980s.

But her story is remarkably consistent. It is a tale of the good that can come from evil.' Says little Patti, 'At the moment of my death as the Viper, I saw a glowing circle of light. It seemed to welcome me, to beckon. It was a warm spiritual experience. I just walked right toward it. I was not sad at all.'"

Babette did the voices of Dr. Chatterjee and Patti Weaver. Her Chatterjee was a warm and mellow Indian-accented English, with clipped phrasing. She did Patti as a child-hero in a contemporary movie, the only person on screen who is unawed by mysterious throbbing phenomena.

"In a further startling development it was revealed by little Patti that the three supercelebrities were murdered for the same astonishing reason. Each of them at the time of his or her death was in secret possession of the Holy Shroud of Turin,[9] famed for its sacred curative powers. Entertainers Elvis and Marilyn were drink-and-drug nightmare victims and secretly hoped to restore spiritual and bodily calm to their lives by actually drying themselves with the Holy Shroud after pore-cleansing sessions in the sauna. Multifaceted billionaire Howard Hughes suffered from stop-action blink syndrome, a bizarre condition which prevented his eyes from reopening for hours after a simple blink, and he obviously hoped to utilize the amazing power of the Shroud until the Viper intervened with a swift injection of phantom venom. Patti Weaver has further revealed under hypnosis that the KGB has long sought possession of the Shroud of Turin on behalf of the rapidly aging and pain-racked members of the Politburo, the famed executive committee of the Communist Party. Possession of the Shroud is said to be the real motive behind the attempted assassination of Pope John Paul II at the Vatican—an attempt that failed only because the Viper had already died in a horror helicopter crash and been reborn as a freckle-faced girl in Iowa.

"The no-risk bonus coupon below gives you guaranteed access to dozens of documented cases of life after death, everlasting life, previous-life experiences, posthumous life in outer space, transmigration of souls, and personalized resurrection through stream-of-consciousness computer techniques."

I studied the faces in the semicircle. No one seemed amazed by this account. Old Man Treadwell lit a cigarette, impatient with his own trembling hand, forced to shake out the flame before it burned him. There was no interest shown in discussion, The story occupied some recess of passive belief. There it was, familiar and comforting in its own strange way, a set of statements no less real than our daily quota of observable household fact. Even Babette in her tone of voice betrayed no sign of skepticism or condescension. Surely I was in no position to feel superior to these elderly listeners, blind or sighted. Little Patti's walk toward the warm welcoming glow found me in a weakened and receptive state. I wanted to believe at least this part of the tale.

Babette read an ad. The Stanford Linear Accelerator 3-Day Particle-Smashing Diet.

She picked up another tabloid. The cover story concerned the country's leading psychics and their predictions for the coming year. She read the items slowly.

---

9. A linen cloth, bearing the likeness of the front and back of a man's face and body marked with the wounds of crucifixion, that is believed by some to be the cloth that wrapped the body of Jesus following his death on the cross.

"Squadrons of UFOs will invade Disney World and Cape Canaveral.[1] In a startling twist, the attack will be revealed as a demonstration of the folly of war, leading to a nuclear test-ban treaty between the U.S. and Russia.

"The ghost of Elvis Presley will be seen taking lonely walks at dawn around Graceland, his musical mansion.

"A Japanese consortium will buy Air Force One[2] and turn it into a luxury flying condominium with midair refueling privileges and air-to-surface missile capability.

"Bigfoot will appear dramatically at a campsite in the rugged and scenic Pacific Northwest. The hairy, upright man-beast, who stands eight feet tall and may be evolution's missing link, will gently welcome tourists to gather around him, revealing himself to be an apostle of peace.

"UFOs will raise the lost city of Atlantis from its watery grave in the Caribbean by telekinetic means and the help of powerful cables with properties not known in earthlike materials. The result will be a 'city of peace' where money and passports are totally unknown.

"The spirit of Lyndon B. Johnson[3] will contact CBS executives to arrange an interview on live TV in order to defend itself against charges made in recent books.

"Beatle assassin Mark David Chapman[4] will legally change his name to John Lennon and begin a new career as a rock lyricist from his prison cell on murderer's row.

"Members of an air-crash cult will hijack a jumbo jet and crash it into the White House in an act of blind devotion to their mysterious and reclusive leader, known only as Uncle Bob. The President and First Lady will miraculously survive with minor cuts, according to close friends of the couple.

"Dead multibillionaire Howard Hughes will mysteriously appear in the sky over Las Vegas.

"Wonder drugs mass-produced aboard UFO pharmaceutical labs in the weightless environment of space will lead to cures for anxiety, obesity, and mood swings.

"From beyond the grave, dead living legend John Wayne will communicate telepathically with President Reagan[5] to help frame U.S. foreign policy. Mellowed by death, the strapping actor will advocate a hopeful policy of peace and love.

"Sixties superkiller Charles Manson will break out of prison and terrorize the California countryside for weeks before negotiating a surrender on live TV in the offices of International Creative Management.[6]

"Earth's only satellite, the moon, will explode on a humid night in July, playing havoc with tides and raining dirt and debris over much of our

1. Cape Canaveral, Florida; location of the John F. Kennedy Space Center.
2. The plane that carries the president of the United States.
3. Lyndon B. Johnson (1908–1973), 36th president of the United States (1963–69).
4. Mark David Chapman shot and killed the musician John Lennon, founding member of the Beatles, outside Lennon's apartment in New York City on December 8, 1980.
5. Ronald Reagan (1911–2004), 40th president of the United States (1981–89). He had been a well-known film and television actor from the 1930s to the late '60s. John Wayne (1907–1979), American movie actor famed for his roles in Westerns.
6. A talent agency with offices in Los Angeles, New York, Washington, D.C., and London. "Manson": Charles Manson (b. 1934), leader of the Manson Family, a cult he founded in California in the late 1960s. Manson was convicted in 1971 of conspiracy to murder seven people; these and other murders were carried out on his orders by members of his cult.

planet. But UFO cleanup crews will help avert a worldwide disaster, signalling an era of peace and harmony."

I watched the audience. Folded arms, heads slightly tilted. The predictions did not seem reckless to them. They were content to exchange brief and unrelated remarks, as during a break for a commercial on TV. The tabloid future, with its mechanism of a hopeful twist to apocalyptic events, was perhaps not so very remote from our own immediate experience. Look at us, I thought. Forced out of our homes, sent streaming into the bitter night, pursued by a toxic cloud, crammed together in makeshift quarters, ambiguously death-sentenced. We'd become part of the public stuff of media disaster. The small audience of the old and blind recognized the predictions of the psychics as events so near to happening that they had to be shaped in advance to our needs and wishes. Out of some persistent sense of large-scale ruin, we kept inventing hope.

Babette read an ad for diet sunglasses. The old people listened with interest. I went back to our area. I wanted to be near the children, watch them sleep. Watching children sleep makes me feel devout, part of a spiritual system. It is the closest I can come to God. If there is a secular equivalent of standing in a great spired cathedral with marble pillars and streams of mystical light slanting through two-tier Gothic windows, it would be watching children in their little bedrooms fast asleep. Girls especially.

Most of the lights were out now. The barracks roar had subsided. People were settling in. Heinrich was still awake, sitting on the floor, fully dressed, his back to the wall, reading a Red Cross resuscitation manual. He was not, in any case, a child whose lustrous slumber brought me peace. A restless, teeth-grinding, and erratic sleeper, the boy sometimes fell from his bed, to be found in a fetal bundle by early light, shivering on the hardwood floor.

"They seem to have things under control," I said.

"Who?"

"Whoever's in charge out there."

"Who's in charge?"

"Never mind."

"It's like we've been flung back in time," he said. "Here we are in the Stone Age, knowing all these great things after centuries of progress but what can we do to make life easier for the Stone Agers? Can we make a refrigerator? Can we even explain how it works? What is electricity? What is light? We experience these things every day of our lives but what good does it do if we find ourselves hurled back in time and we can't even tell people the basic principles much less actually make something that would improve conditions. Name one thing you could make. Could you make a simple wooden match that you could strike on a rock to make a flame? We think we're so great and modern. Moon landings, artificial hearts. But what if you were hurled into a time warp and came face to face with the ancient Greeks. The Greeks invented trigonometry. They did autopsies and dissections. What could you tell an ancient Greek that he couldn't say, 'Big deal.' Could you tell him about the atom? Atom is a Greek word. The Greeks knew that the major events in the universe can't be seen by the eye of man. It's waves, it's rays, it's particles."

"We're doing all right."

"We're sitting in this huge moldy room. It's like we're flung back."

"We have heat, we have light."

"These are Stone Age things. They had heat and light. They had fire. They rubbed flints together and made sparks. Could you rub flints together? Would you know a flint if you saw one? If a Stoner Ager asked you what a nucleotide is, could you tell him? How do we make carbon paper?[7] What is glass? If you came awake tomorrow in the Middle Ages and there was an epidemic raging, what could you do to stop it, knowing what you know about the progress of medicines and diseases? Here it is practically the twenty-first century and you've read hundreds of books and magazines and seen a hundred TV shows about science and medicine. Could you tell those people one little crucial thing that might save a million and a half lives?"

"'Boil your water,' I'd tell them."

"Sure. What about 'Wash behind your ears.' That's about as good."

"I still think we're doing fairly well. There was no warning. We have food, we have radios."

"What is a radio? What is the principle of a radio? Go ahead, explain. You're sitting in the middle of this circle of people. They use pebble tools. They eat grubs. Explain a radio."

"There's no mystery. Powerful transmitters send signals. They travel through the air, to be picked up by receivers."

"They travel through the air. What, like birds? Why not tell them magic? They travel through the air in magic waves. What is a nucleotide? You don't know, do you? Yet these are the building blocks of life. What good is knowledge if it just floats in the air? It goes from computer to computer. It changes and grows every second of every day. But nobody actually knows anything."

"You know something. You know about Nyodene D. I saw you with those people."

"That was a one-time freak," he told me.

He went back to his reading. I decided to get some air. Outside there were several groups of people standing around fires in fifty-five-gallon drums. A man sold soft drinks and sandwiches from an open-sided vehicle. Parked nearby were school buses, motorcycles, smallish vans called ambulettes. I walked around a while. There were people asleep in cars, others pitching tents. Beams of light swung slowly through the woods, searching out sounds, calm voices calling. I walked past a carload of prostitutes from Iron City. The interior light was on, the faces occupied the windows. They resembled the checkout women at the supermarket, blondish, double-chinned, resigned. A man leaned against the front door on the driver's side, speaking through a small opening in the window, his breath showing white. A radio said: "Hog futures[8] have declined in sympathy, adding bearishness to that market."

I realized the man talking to the prostitutes was Murray Jay Siskind. I walked over there, waited for him to finish his sentence before addressing him. He took off his right glove to shake my hand. The car window went up.

"I thought you were in New York for the term break."

"I came back early to look at car-crash movies. Alfonse arranged a week of screenings to help me prepare for my seminar. I was on the airport bus

---

7. A special kind of paper coated on one side with solid ink, used for making copies of documents produced on a typewriter.
8. Financial contract in which the price of a certain good (hogs) is agreed upon today, with the sale taking place in the future at the agreed-upon price. Profits depend upon what happens to the good's value between contract and sale.

heading in from Iron City when sirens started blowing. The driver didn't have much choice but to follow the traffic out here."

"Where are you spending the night?"

"The whole bus was assigned to one of the outbuildings. I heard a rumor about painted women and came out to investigate. One of them is dressed in leopard loungewear under her coat. She showed me. Another one says she has a snap-off crotch. What do you think she means by that? I'm a little worried, though, about all these outbreaks of life-style diseases. I carry a reinforced ribbed condom at all times. One size fits all. But I have a feeling it's not much protection against the intelligence and adaptability of the modern virus."

"The women don't seem busy," I said.

"I don't think this is the kind of disaster that leads to sexual abandon. One or two fellows might come skulking out eventually but there won't be an orgiastic horde, not tonight anyway."

"I guess people need time to go through certain stages."

"It's obvious," he said.

I told him I'd spent two and a half minutes exposed to the toxic cloud. Then I summarized the interview I'd had with the SIMUVAC man.

"That little breath of Nyodene has planted a death in my body. It is now official, according to the computer. I've got death inside me. It's just a question of whether or not I can outlive it. It has a life span of its own. Thirty years. Even if it doesn't kill me in a direct way, it will probably outlive me in my own body. I could die in a plane crash and the Nyodene D. would be thriving as my remains were laid to rest."

"This is the nature of modern death," Murray said. "It has a life independent of us. It is growing in prestige and dimension. It has a sweep it never had before. We study it objectively. We can predict its appearance, trace its path in the body. We can take cross-section pictures of it, tape its tremors and waves. We've never been so close to it, so familiar with its habits and attitudes. We know it intimately. But it continues to grow, to acquire breadth and scope, new outlets, new passages and means. The more we learn, the more it grows. Is this some law of physics? Every advance in knowledge and technique is matched by a new kind of death, a new strain. Death adapts, like a viral agent. Is it a law of nature? Or some private superstition of mine? I sense that the dead are closer to us than ever. I sense that we inhabit the same air as the dead. Remember Lao Tse.[9] There is no difference between the quick and the dead. They are one channel of vitality.' He said this six hundred years before Christ. It is true once again, perhaps more true than ever."

He placed his hands on my shoulders and looked sadly into my face. He told me in the simplest words how sorry he was about what had happened. He talked to me about the likelihood of a computer error. Computers make mistakes, he said. Carpet static can cause a mistake. Some lint or hair in the circuits. He didn't believe this and neither did I. But he spoke convincingly, his eyes filled with spontaneous emotion, a broad and profound feeling. I felt oddly rewarded. His compassion was equal to the occasion, an impressive pity and grief. The bad news was almost worth it.

"Ever since I was in my twenties, I've had the fear, the dread. Now it's been realized. I feel enmeshed, I feel deeply involved. It's no wonder they

---

9. Chinese Taoist poet and philosopher (571–531 B.C.E.).

call this thing the airborne toxic event. It's an event all right. It marks the end of uneventful things. This is just the beginning. Wait and see."

A talk-show host said: "You are on the air." The fires burned in the oil drums. The sandwich vendor closed down his van.

"Any episodes of *déjà vu* in your group?"

"Wife and daughter," I said.

"There's a theory about *déjà vu*."

"I don't want to hear it."

"Why do we think these things happened before? Simple. They did happen before, in our minds, as visions of the future. Because these are precognitions, we can't fit the material into our system of consciousness as it is now structured. This is basically supernatural stuff. We're seeing into the future but haven't learned how to process the experience. So it stays hidden until the precognition comes true, until we come face to face with the event. Now we are free to remember it, to experience it as familiar material."

"Why are so many people having these episodes now?"

"Because death is in the air," he said gently. "It is liberating suppressed material. It is getting us closer to things we haven't learned about ourselves. Most of us have probably seen our own death but haven't known how to make the material surface. Maybe when we die, the first thing we'll say is, 'I know this feeling. I was here before.'"

He put his hands back on my shoulders, studied me with renewed and touching sadness. We heard the prostitutes call out to someone.

"I'd like to lose interest in myself," I told Murray. "Is there any chance of that happening?"

"None. Better men have tried."

"I guess you're right."

"It's obvious."

"I wish there was something I could do. I wish I could out-think the problem."

"Work harder on your Hitler," he said.

I looked at him. How much did he know?

The car window opened a crack. One of the women said to Murray, "All right, I'll do it for twenty-five."

"Have you checked with your representative?" he said.

She rolled down the window to peer at him. She had the opaque look of a hair-curlered woman on the evening news whose house had been buried in mud.

"You know who I mean," Murray said. "The fellow who sees to your emotional needs in return for one hundred percent of your earnings. The fellow you depend on to beat you up when you're bad."

"Bobby? He's in Iron City, keeping out of the cloud. He doesn't like to expose himself unless it's absolutely necessary."

The women laughed, six heads bobbing. It was insider's laughter, a little overdone, meant to identify them as people bound together in ways not easily appreciated by the rest of us.

A second window opened half an inch, a bright mouth appeared. "The type pimp Bobby is, he likes to use his mind."

A second round of laughter. We weren't sure whether it was at Bobby's expense, or ours, or theirs. The windows went up.

"It's none of my business," I said, "but what is it she's willing to do with you for twenty-five dollars?"

"The Heimlich maneuver."[1]

I studied the part of his face that lay between the touring cap and beard. He seemed deep in thought, gazing at the car. The windows were fogged, the women's heads capped in cigarette smoke.

"Of course we'd have to find a vertical space," he said absently.

"You don't really expect her to lodge a chunk of food in her windpipe."

He looked at me, half startled. "What? No, no, that won't be necessary. As long as she makes gagging and choking sounds. As long as she sighs deeply when I jolt the pelvis. As long as she collapses helplessly backward into my life-saving embrace."

He took off his glove to shake my hand. Then he went over to the car to work out details with the woman in question. I watched him knock on the rear door. After a moment it opened and he squeezed into the back seat. I walked over to one of the oil drums. Three men and a woman stood around the fire, passing rumors back and forth.

Three of the live deer at the Kung Fu Palace were dead. The governor was dead, his pilot and co-pilot seriously injured after a crash landing in a shopping mall. Two of the men at the switching yard were dead, tiny acid burns visible in their Mylex suits. Packs of German shepherds, the Nyodene-sniffing dogs, had shed their parachutes and were being set loose in the affected communities. There was a rash of UFO sightings in the area. There was widespread looting by men in plastic sheets. Two looters were dead. Six National Guardsmen were dead, killed in a firefight that broke out after a racial incident. There were reports of miscarriages, babies born prematurely. There were sightings of additional billowing clouds.

The people who relayed these pieces of unverified information did so with a certain respectful dread, bouncing on their toes in the cold, arms crossed on their chests. They were fearful that the stories might be true but at the same time impressed by the dramatic character of things. The toxic event had released a spirit of imagination. People spun tales, others listened spellbound. There was a growing respect for the vivid rumor, the most chilling tale. We were no closer to believing or disbelieving a given story than we had been earlier. But there was a greater appreciation now. We began to marvel at our own ability to manufacture awe.

German shepherds. That was the reassuring news I took inside with me. The sturdy body, dense and darkish coat, fierce head, long lapping tongue. I pictured them prowling the empty streets, heavy-gaited, alert. Able to hear sounds we couldn't hear, able to sense changes in the flow of information. I saw them in our house, snouting into closets, tall ears pointed, a smell about them of heat and fur and stored power.

In the barracks almost everyone was sleeping. I made my way along a dim wall. The massed bodies lay in heavy rest, seeming to emit a single nasal sigh. Figures stirred; a wide-eyed Asian child watched me step among a dozen clustered sleeping bags. Colored lights skipped past my right ear. I heard a toilet flush.

---

1. First-aid technique for dislodging an obstruction from the windpipe of someone who is choking.

Babette was curled on an air mattress, covered in her coat. My son slept sitting in a chair like some boozed commuter, head rolling on his chest. I carried a camp chair over to the cot where the younger children were. Then I sat there, leaning forward, to watch them sleep.

A random tumble of heads and dangled limbs. In those soft warm faces was a quality of trust so absolute and pure that I did not want to think it might be misplaced. There must be something, somewhere, large and grand and redoubtable enough to justify this shining reliance and implicit belief. A feeling of desperate piety swept over me. It was cosmic in nature, full of yearnings and reachings. It spoke of vast distances, awesome but subtle forces. These sleeping children were like figures in an ad for the Rosicrucians,[2] drawing a powerful beam of light from somewhere off the page. Steffie turned slightly, then muttered something in her sleep. It seemed important that I know what it was. In my current state, bearing the death impression of the Nyodene cloud, I was ready to search anywhere for signs and hints, intimations of odd comfort. I pulled my chair up closer. Her face in pouchy sleep might have been a structure designed solely to protect the eyes, those great, large and apprehensive things, prone to color phases and a darting alertness, to a perception of distress in others. I sat there watching her. Moments later she spoke again. Distinct syllables this time, not some dreamy murmur—but a language not quite of this world. I struggled to understand. I was convinced she was saying something, fitting together units of stable meaning. I watched her face, waited. Ten minutes passed. She uttered two clearly audible words, familiar and elusive at the same time, words that seemed to have a ritual meaning, part of a verbal spell or ecstatic chant.

Toyota Celica.

A long moment passed before I realized this was the name of an automobile. The truth only amazed me more. The utterance was beautiful and mysterious, gold-shot with looming wonder. It was like the name of an ancient power in the sky, tablet-carved in cuneiform.[3] It made me feel that something hovered. But how could this be? A simple brand name, an ordinary car. How could these near-nonsense words, murmured in a child's restless sleep, make me sense a meaning, a presence? She was only repeating some TV voice. Toyota Corolla, Toyota Celica, Toyota Cressida. Supranational names, computer-generated, more or less universally pronounceable. Part of every child's brain noise, the substatic regions too deep to probe. Whatever its source, the utterance struck me with the impact of a moment of splendid transcendence.

I depend on my children for that.

I sat a while longer, watching Denise, watching Wilder, feeling selfless and spiritually large. There was an empty air mattress on the floor but I wanted to share Babette's and eased myself next to her body, a dreaming mound. Her hands, feet, and face were drawn under the sheltering coat; only a burst of hair remained. I fell at once into marine oblivion, a deep-dwelling crablike consciousness, silent and dreamless.

1985

2. Originally a secretive anti-Catholic philosophical society, founded in Germany in the 17th century. Modern branches of the Rosicrucians, both Christian and Masonic, continue to propound secret knowledge and to recruit followers.
3. System of writing used in ancient Mesopotamia, with characters pressed into clay tablets.

THOMAS PYNCHON
b. 1937

Thomas Pynchon has remained the most private of contemporary American writers, without so much as a photograph of him in circulation. A few facts are known: born on Long Island, graduated from Cornell University—where he was a student in Vladimir Nabokov's European literature course—in the late 1950s, served a term in the navy, and now lives—it is said—in southern (or is it northern?) California. He appeared twice as a character with a paper bag over his head on the cartoon comedy show *The Simpsons*, in 2004, voicing himself. Beyond that, silence, which has been broken only by eight strange and distinctive novels, plus a few short stories.

"Entropy," one of Pynchon's first publications (1960), is printed here as an introduction to his work. Its thematics of an elusive order within radical disorder anticipates his first novel, *V.* (1963), particularly in its reference to modern physics. That complex novel cannot be understood by reference to convenient fictional signposts. Although it showed an indebtedness to Faulkner and Joyce (an indebtedness shared by most serious American novelists), Pynchon's style was already wholly his own. In writing that was by turns labyrinthine, eloquent, and colloquial, he showed a particular fondness for imitating and parodying various styles. But instead of disparaging or minimizing their subjects, these imitations and parodies radiated a generous exuberance that extended to the many characters who inhabit *V.* and whose individual paranoias—Pynchon's word to characterize attempts to make connections between events—propel them into unbelievably complicated and absurd plots. The interest of *V.* was largely in the inventiveness with which Pynchon developed those plots, which might involve anything from diplomatic spy stories in nineteenth-century Africa to the bombing of Malta during World War II to the surgical reconstruction of a young woman's nose to a hunt for alligators in New York City sewers.

The comic talent shown in various New York episodes from *V.* was also evident in *The Crying of Lot 49* (1966). This short, perfectly controlled novel teases us and itself with questions about the meaning of our American heritage, as embodied in the form of the mysterious legacy left to its heroine, Oedipa Maas. (The jokey yet portentous name exemplifies Pynchon's way of playing at "significance.") What is the connection between this legacy and the mysterious alternative to the U.S. Postal System on which Oedipa believes she has stumbled? Is there a secret network of alienated citizens carrying on their lives outside the ordinary systems and institutions of American life? Or is it all Oedipa's delusion, her private paranoia? These questions are considered through a style that continually surprises and unsettles us, though it is less discontinuous than *V.*'s. In Pynchon's world everything serious has its silly aspects (inspired by the Marx Brothers and countless other comic acts), while bits of trivia and foolery are suddenly elevated, through the style, into objects of sublime contemplation—as at the novel's end, when Oedipa thinks of "squatters" who "slept in junkyards in the stripped shells of wrecked Plymouths, or even, daring, spent the night up some pole in a lineman's tent like caterpillars, swung among a web of telephone wires, living in the very copper rigging and secular miracle of communication, untroubled by the dumb voltages flickering their miles, the night long, in the thousands of unheard messages." Often Pynchon's sentences enact the daring freedom he admires, in contrast to the institutions of a technological society.

Pynchon's longest and most daring and exhaustive effort came with the publication, in 1973, of *Gravity's Rainbow*. This encyclopedic fantasy operates through brilliant improvisations, tall tales, obscene parables, and burlesque stage routines, all of which work together into a story of supersonic capabilities and annihilative retributions. A huge cast of characters, each with a crazy name and a plot to unravel, is located all over the map, but mainly in World War II London and in postwar Germany. As the four main and the countless subsidiary plots take shape, characters—and the reader—attempt to "read" the messages flickering, the dumb intent to communicate, in the most casual as well as the most portentous sign. Pynchon's knowingness and fascination with popular culture are overwhelmingly evident in *Gravity's Rainbow*, as is his preoccupation with the lore of theoretical science, of obscure historical tales, and of contemporary comic books. No one denies the formidably encyclopedic nature of this astonishing effort; the question is, as Warner Berthoff has asked, whether that effort may not also be "encyclopedically monotonous and static." More readers begin *Gravity's Rainbow* than finish it.

After 1973, except for the publication in 1984 of some of his early stories (in *Slow Learner*), all was silent on the Pynchon front until *Vineland* appeared in 1990, followed by *Mason & Dixon* in 1997 and *Against the Day* in 2006. *Vineland* is wonderful on the California terrain and has much freewheeling and funny inventiveness; at other times Pynchon seems to be flogging his material and repeating himself. *Mason & Dixon*, about the plotters of the line that would differentiate the American North and South, is written in the manner of his more ambitious works, a massive "mega-novel" that by its very excesses of character, plot, and references to history (arcane and otherwise) seeks to overwhelm the reader with its display of authority. *Against the Day* (2006) and *Inherent Vice* (2009) have more conventional subjects—family-revenge drama and crime solving, respectively—yet the author still dotes on fantastic inventions and overwritten prose. *Bleeding Edge* (2013) was a National Book Award finalist; it is a detective story set in New York City in the early days of the Internet and during the months prior to the attacks of September 11. Although there is still no consensus on his stature as an enduring American writer, there is general recognition of the quirky, uncanny exactitude of his imagination, evident across his oeuvre. Pynchon's theatrical spellbindings as a man of metaphor, and his feats of association (in Robert Frost's phrase), are employed on subjects—like the rocket in *Gravity's Rainbow*—that were thought to be beyond words. For daring, wit, and exuberance, no contemporary writer excels him.

The following text is from *Slow Learner* (1984).

Entropy

> Boris has just given me a summary of his views. He is a weather prophet. The weather will continue bad, he says. There will be more calamities, more death, more despair. Not the slightest indication of a change anywhere. . . . We must get into step, a lockstep toward the prison of death. There is no escape. The weather will not change.
>
> —*Tropic of Cancer*[1]

Downstairs, Meatball Mulligan's lease-breaking party was moving into its 40th hour. On the kitchen floor, amid a litter of empty champagne fifths, were Sandor Rojas and three friends, playing spit in the ocean and staying

---

1. Novel (1934) by the American writer Henry Miller (1891–1980).

awake on Heidseck[2] and benzedrine pills. In the living room Duke, Vincent, Krinkles and Paco sat crouched over a 15-inch speaker which had been bolted into the top of a wastepaper basket, listening to 27 watts' worth of *The Heroes' Gate at Kiev*.[3] They all wore hornrimmed sunglasses and rapt expressions, and smoked funny-looking cigarettes which contained not, as you might expect, tobacco, but an adulterated form of *cannabis sativa*.[4] This group was the Duke di Angelis quartet. They recorded for a local label called Tambú and had to their credit one 10' LP entitled *Songs of Outer Space*. From time to time one of them would flick the ashes from his cigarette into the speaker cone to watch them dance around. Meatball himself was sleeping over by the window, holding an empty magnum to his chest as if it were a teddy bear. Several government girls, who worked for people like the State Department and NSA, had passed out on couches, chairs and in one case the bathroom sink.

This was in early February of '57 and back then there were a lot of American expatriates around Washington, D.C., who would talk, every time they met you, about how someday they were going to go over to Europe for real but right now it seemed they were working for the government. Everyone saw a fine irony in this. They would stage, for instance, polyglot parties where the newcomer was sort of ignored if he couldn't carry on simultaneous conversations in three or four languages. They would haunt Armenian delicatessens for weeks at a stretch and invite you over for bulghour and lamb in tiny kitchens whose walls were covered with bullfight posters. They would have affairs with sultry girls from Andalucía or the Midi[5] who studied economics at Georgetown. Their Dôme was a collegiate Rathskeller out on Wisconsin Avenue called the Old Heidelberg and they had to settle for cherry blossoms instead of lime trees when spring came, but in its lethargic way their life provided, as they said, kicks.

At the moment, Meatball's party seemed to be gathering its second wind. Outside there was rain. Rain splatted against the tar paper on the roof and was fractured into a fine spray off the noses, eyebrows and lips of wooden gargoyles under the eaves, and ran like drool down the windowpanes. The day before, it had snowed and the day before that there had been winds of gale force and before that the sun had made the city glitter bright as April, though the calendar read early February. It is a curious season in Washington, this false spring. Somewhere in it are Lincoln's Birthday and the Chinese New Year, and a forlornness in the streets because cherry blossoms are weeks away still and, as Sarah Vaughan has put it, spring will be a little late this year. Generally crowds like the one which would gather in the Old Heidelberg on weekday afternoons to drink Würtzburger and to sing Lili Marlene (not to mention The Sweetheart of Sigma Chi) are inevitably and incorrigibly Romantic. And as every good Romantic knows, the soul (*spiritus, ruach, pneuma*)[6] is nothing, substantially, but air; it is only natural that warpings in the atmosphere should be recapitulated in those who breathe it. So that over and above the public components—holidays,

---

2. A very dry champagne. "Spit in the ocean": a form of poker.
3. Music by the Russian composer Modest Mussorgsky (1839–1881) from his *Pictures at an Exhibition*.

4. Marijuana.
5. Regions of Spain and France, respectively.
6. "Soul" (and also "breath") in, respectively, Latin, Hebrew, and Greek.

The Gerry Mulligan Quartet premiered in Los Angeles in 1952 with Mulligan on baritone saxophone, Chet Baker on trumpet, Bob Whitlock on bass, and Chico Hamilton on drums. There was no pianist, an innovation for small ensemble jazz, leaving harmonic silences for the other instruments to fill.

tourist attractions—there are private meanderings, linked to the climate as if this spell were a *stretto* passage in the year's fugue: haphazard weather, aimless loves, unpredicted commitments: months one can easily spend *in* fugue, because oddly enough, later on, winds, rains, passions of February and March are never remembered in that city, it is as if they had never been.

The last bass notes of *The Heroes' Gate* boomed up through the floor and woke Callisto from an uneasy sleep. The first thing he became aware of was a small bird he had been holding gently between his hands, against his body. He turned his head sidewise on the pillow to smile down at it, at its blue hunched-down head and sick, lidded eyes, wondering how many more nights he would have to give it warmth before it was well again. He had been holding the bird like that for three days: it was the only way he knew to restore its health. Next to him the girl stirred and whimpered, her arm thrown across her face. Mingled with the sounds of the rain came the first tentative, querulous morning voices of the other birds, hidden in philodendrons and small fan palms: patches of scarlet, yellow and blue laced through this Rousseau-like[7] fantasy, this hothouse jungle it had taken him seven years to weave together. Hermetically sealed, it was a tiny enclave of regularity in the city's chaos, alien to the vagaries of the weather, of national politics, of any civil disorder. Through trial-and-error Callisto had perfected its ecological balance, with the help of the girl its artistic harmony, so that the swayings of its plant life, the stirrings of its birds and human inhabitants

---

7. Henri Rousseau (1844–1910), French primitive painter of exotic landscapes.

were all as integral as the rhythms of a perfectly-executed mobile. He and the girl could no longer, of course, be omitted from that sanctuary; they had become necessary to its unity. What they needed from outside was delivered. They did not go out.

"Is he all right," she whispered. She lay like a tawny question mark facing him, her eyes suddenly huge and dark and blinking slowly. Callisto ran a finger beneath the feathers at the base of the bird's neck; caressed it gently. "He's going to be well, I think. See: he hears his friends beginning to wake up." The girl had heard the rain and the birds even before she was fully awake. Her name was Aubade: she was part French and part Annamese, and she lived on her own curious and lonely planet, where the clouds and the odor of poincianas, the bitterness of wine and the accidental fingers at the small of her back or feathery against her breasts came to her reduced inevitably to the terms of sound: of music which emerged at intervals from a howling darkness of discordancy. "Aubade," he said, "go see." Obedient, she arose; padded to the window, pulled aside the drapes and after a moment said: "It is 37. Still 37." Callisto frowned. "Since Tuesday, then," he said. "No change." Henry Adams,[8] three generations before his own, had stared aghast at Power; Callisto found himself now in much the same state over Thermodynamics, the inner life of that power, realizing like his predecessor that the Virgin and the dynamo stand as much for love as for power; that the two are indeed identical; and that love therefore not only makes the world go round but also makes the boccie ball spin, the nebula precess. It was this latter or sidereal element which disturbed him. The cosmologists had predicted an eventual heat-death for the universe (something like Limbo: form and motion abolished, heat-energy identical at every point in it); the meteorologists, day-to-day, staved it off by contradicting with a reassuring array of varied temperatures.

But for three days now, despite the changeful weather, the mercury had stayed at 37 degrees Fahrenheit. Leery at omens of apocalypse, Callisto shifted beneath the covers. His fingers pressed the bird more firmly, as if needing some pulsing or suffering assurance of an early break in the temperature.

It was that last cymbal crash that did it. Meatball was hurled wincing into consciousness as the synchronized wagging of heads over the wastebasket stopped. The final hiss remained for an instant in the room, then melted into the whisper of rain outside. "Aarrgghh," announced Meatball in the silence, looking at the empty magnum. Krinkles, in slow motion, turned, smiled and held out a cigarette. "Tea time, man," he said. "No, no," said Meatball. "How many times I got to tell you guys. Not at my place. You ought to know, Washington is lousy with Feds." Krinkles looked wistful. "Jeez, Meatball," he said, "you don't want to do nothing no more." "Hair of dog," said Meatball. "Only hope. Any juice left?" He began to crawl toward the kitchen. "No champagne, I don't think," Duke said. "Case of tequila behind the icebox." They put on an Earl Bostic[9] side. Meatball paused at the kitchen door, glowering at Sandor Rojas. "Lemons," he said after some thought. He crawled to the refrigerator and got out three lemons and some cubes, found

8. American historian and man of letters (1838–1918) whose writings explore the nature of power, cultural figurations of which ranged from the Virgin Mary to the modern dynamo engine.
9. American jazz musician (1913–1965) who also recorded rhythm-and-blues material.

the tequila and set about restoring order to his nervous system. He drew blood once cutting the lemons and had to use two hands squeezing them and his foot to crack the ice tray but after about ten minutes he found himself, through some miracle, beaming down into a monster tequila sour. "That looks yummy," Sandor Rojas said. "How about you make me one." Meatball blinked at him. "*Kitchi lofass a shegithe*,"[1] he replied automatically, and wandered away into the bathroom. "I say," he called out a moment later to no one in particular. "I say, there seems to be a girl or something sleeping in the sink." He took her by the shoulders and shook. "Wha," she said. "You don't look too comfortable," Meatball said. "Well," she agreed. She stumbled to the shower, turned on the cold water and sat down crosslegged in the spray. "That's better," she smiled.

"Meatball," Sandor Rojas yelled from the kitchen. "Somebody is trying to come in the window. A burglar, I think. A second-story man." "What are you worrying about," Meatball said. "We're on the third floor." He loped back into the kitchen. A shaggy woebegone figure stood out on the fire escape, raking his fingernails down the windowpane. Meatball opened the window. "Saul," he said.

"Sort of wet out," Saul said. He climbed in, dripping. "You heard, I guess."

"Miriam left you," Meatball said, "or something, is all I heard."

There was a sudden flurry of knocking at the front door. "Do come in," Sandor Rojas called. The door opened and there were three coeds from George Washington, all of whom were majoring in philosophy. They were each holding a gallon of Chianti. Sandor leaped up and dashed into the living room. "We heard there was a party," one blonde said. "Young blood," Sandor shouted. He was an ex-Hungarian freedom fighter who had easily the worst chronic case of what certain critics of the middle class have called Don Giovannism in the District of Columbia. *Purchè porti la gonnella, voi sapete quel che fa.*[2] Like Pavlov's dog: a contralto voice or a whiff of Arpège and Sandor would begin to salivate. Meatball regarded the trio blearily as they filed into the kitchen; he shrugged. "Put the wine in the icebox," he said, "and good morning."

Aubade's neck made a golden bow as she bent over the sheets of foolscap, scribbling away in the green murk of the room. "As a young man at Princeton," Callisto was dictating, nestling the bird against the gray hairs of his chest, "Callisto had learned a mnemonic device for remembering the Laws of Thermodynamics: you can't win, things are going to get worse before they get better, who says they're going to get better. At the age of 54, confronted with Gibbs'[3] notion of the universe, he suddenly realized that undergraduate cant had been oracle, after all. That spindly maze of equations became, for him, a vision of ultimate, cosmic heat-death. He had known all along, of course, that nothing but a theoretical engine or system ever runs at 100% efficiency; and about the theorem of Clausius, which states that the entropy of an isolated system always continually increases. It was not,

1. Little horse prick in your asshole (Hungarian).
2. As long as she wears a skirt, you know what he does (Italian); from Lorenzo da Ponte's libretto to Mozart's opera *Don Giovanni* (1787).

3. Josiah Willard Gibbs (1839–1903), American physicist and chemist, a founder of statistical mechanics.

however, until Gibbs and Boltzmann[4] brought to this principle the methods of statistical mechanics that the horrible significance of it all dawned on him: only then did he realize that the isolated system—galaxy, engine, human being, culture, whatever—must evolve spontaneously toward the Condition of the More Probable. He was forced, therefore, in the sad dying fall of middle age, to a radical reëvaluation of everything he had learned up to then; all the cities and seasons and casual passions of his days had now to be looked at in a new and elusive light. He did not know if he was equal to the task. He was aware of the dangers of the reductive fallacy and, he hoped, strong enough not to drift into the graceful decadence of an enervated fatalism. His had always been a vigorous, Italian sort of pessimism: like Machiavelli, he allowed the forces of *virtù* and *fortuna*[5] to be about 50/50; but the equations now introduced a random factor which pushed the odds to some unutterable and indeterminate ratio which he found himself afraid to calculate." Around him loomed vague hothouse shapes; the pitifully small heart fluttered against his own. Counterpointed against his words the girl heard the chatter of birds and fitful car honkings scattered along the wet morning and Earl Bostic's alto rising in occasional wild peaks through the floor. The architectonic purity of her world was constantly threatened by such hints of anarchy: gaps and excrescences and skew lines, and a shifting or tilting of planes to which she had continually to readjust lest the whole structure shiver into a disarray of discrete and meaningless signals. Callisto had described the process once as a kind of "feedback": she crawled into dreams each night with a sense of exhaustion, and a desperate resolve never to relax that vigilance. Even in the brief periods when Callisto made love to her, soaring above the bowing of taut nerves in haphazard double-stops would be the one singing string of her determination.

"Nevertheless," continued Callisto, "he found in entropy or the measure of disorganization for a closed system an adequate metaphor to apply to certain phenomena in his own world. He saw, for example, the younger generation responding to Madison Avenue with the same spleen his own had once reserved for Wall Street: and in American 'consumerism' discovered a similar tendency from the least to the most probable, from differentiation to sameness, from ordered individuality to a kind of chaos. He found himself, in short, restating Gibbs' prediction in social terms, and envisioned a heat-death for his culture in which ideas, like heat-energy, would no longer be transferred, since each point in it would ultimately have the same quantity of energy; and intellectual motion would, accordingly, cease." He glanced up suddenly. "Check it now," he said. Again she rose and peered out at the thermometer. "37," she said. "The rain has stopped." He bent his head quickly and held his lips against a quivering wing. "Then it will change soon," he said, trying to keep his voice firm.

Sitting on the stove Saul was like any big rag doll that a kid has been taking out some incomprehensible rage on. "What happened," Meatball said. "If you feel like talking, I mean."

"Of course I feel like talking," Saul said. "One thing I did, I slugged her."

4. Ludwig Boltzmann (1844–1906), Austrian physicist who studied how atoms determine visual properties of matter. Rudolf Clausius (1822–1888), German physicist, developer of the science of thermodynamics.

5. Niccolò Machiavelli (1469–1527), Florentine statesman and writer on government, contrasted virtuous behavior (*virtù*) with good luck (*fortuna*).

"Discipline must be maintained."

"Ha, ha. I wish you'd been there. Oh Meatball, it was a lovely fight. She ended up throwing a *Handbook of Chemistry and Physics* at me, only it missed and went through the window, and when the glass broke I reckon something in her broke too. She stormed out of the house crying, out in the rain. No raincoat or anything."

"She'll be back."

"No."

"Well!" Soon Meatball said: "It was something earthshattering, no doubt. Like who is better, Sal Mineo or Ricky Nelson."[6]

"What it was about," Saul said, "was communication theory. Which of course makes it very hilarious."

"I don't know anything about communication theory."

"Neither does my wife. Come right down to it, who does? That's the joke."

When Meatball saw the kind of smile Saul had on his face he said: "Maybe you would like tequila or something."

"No. I mean, I'm sorry. It's a field you can go off the deep end in, is all. You get where you're watching all the time for security cops: behind bushes, around corners. MUFFET is top secret."

"Wha."

"Multi-unit factorial field electronic tabulator."

"You were fighting about that."

"Miriam has been reading science fiction again. That and *Scientific American*. It seems she is, as we say, bugged at this idea of computers acting like people. I made the mistake of saying you can just as well turn that around, and talk about human behavior like a program fed into an IBM machine."

"Why not," Meatball said.

"Indeed, why not. In fact it is sort of crucial to communication, not to mention information theory. Only when I said that she hit the roof. Up went the balloon. And I can't figure out *why*. If anybody should know why, I should. I refuse to believe the government is wasting taxpayers' money on me, when it has so many bigger and better things to waste it on."

Meatball made a moue. "Maybe she thought you were acting like a cold, dehumanized amoral scientist type."

"My god," Saul flung up an arm. "Dehumanized. How much more human can I get? I worry, Meatball, I do. There are Europeans wandering around North Africa these days with their tongues torn out of their heads because those tongues have spoken the wrong words. Only the Europeans thought they were the right words."

"Language barrier," Meatball suggested.

Saul jumped down off the stove. "That," he said, angry, "is a good candidate for sick joke of the year. No, ace, it is *not* a barrier. If it is anything it's a kind of leakage. Tell a girl: 'I love you.' No trouble with two-thirds of that, it's a closed circuit. Just you and she. But that nasty four-letter word in the middle, *that's* the one you have to look out for. Ambiguity. Redundance. Irrelevance, even. Leakage. All this is noise. Noise screws up your signal, makes for disorganization in the circuit."

---

6. Contemporary figures from film and television who were icons of bad and good teenage behavior, respectively.

Meatball shuffled around. "Well, now, Saul," he muttered, "you're sort of, I don't know, expecting a lot from people. I mean, you know. What it is is, most of the things we say, I guess, are mostly noise."

"Ha! Half of what you just said, for example."

"Well, you do it too."

"I know." Saul smiled grimly. "It's a bitch, ain't it."

"I bet that's what keeps divorce lawyers in business. Whoops."

"Oh I'm not sensitive. Besides," frowning, "you're right. You find I think that most 'successful' marriages—Miriam and me, up to last night—are sort of founded on compromises. You never run at top efficiency, usually all you have is a minimum basis for a workable thing. I believe the phrase is Togetherness."

"Aarrgghh."

"Exactly. You find that one a bit noisy, don't you. But the noise content is different for each of us because you're a bachelor and I'm not. Or wasn't. The hell with it."

"Well sure," Meatball said, trying to be helpful, "you were using different words. By 'human being' you meant something that you can look at like it was a computer. It helps you think better on the job or something. But Miriam meant something entirely—"

"The hell with it."

Meatball fell silent. "I'll take that drink," Saul said after a while.

The card game had been abandoned and Sandor's friends were slowly getting wasted on tequila. On the living room couch, one of the coeds and Krinkles were engaged in amorous conversation. "No," Krinkles was saying, "no, I can't put Dave *down*. In fact I give Dave a lot of credit, man. Especially considering his accident and all." The girl's smile faded. "How terrible," she said. "What accident?" "Hadn't you heard?" Krinkles said. "When Dave was in the army, just a private E-2, they sent him down to Oak Ridge on special duty. Something to do with the Manhattan Project.[7] He was handling hot stuff one day and got an overdose of radiation. So now he's got to wear lead gloves all the time." She shook her head sympathetically. "What an awful break for a piano player."

Meatball had abandoned Saul to a bottle of tequila and was about to go to sleep in a closet when the front door flew open and the place was invaded by five enlisted personnel of the U.S. Navy, all in varying stages of abomination. "This is the place," shouted a fat, pimply seaman apprentice who had lost his white hat. "This here is the hoorhouse that chief was telling us about." A stringy-looking 3rd class boatswain's mate pushed him aside and cased the living room. "You're right, Slab," he said. "But it don't look like much, even for Stateside. I seen better tail in Naples, Italy." "How much, hey," boomed a large seaman with adenoids, who was holding a Mason jar full of white lightning. "Oh, my god," said Meatball.

Outside the temperature remained constant at 37 degrees Fahrenheit. In the hothouse Aubade stood absently caressing the branches of a young mimosa, hearing a motif of sap-rising, the rough and unresolved anticipatory theme of those fragile pink blossoms which, it is said, insure fertility.

---

7. The research program that developed the atomic bomb for use at the end of World War II.

That music rose in a tangled tracery: arabesques of order competing fugally with the improvised discords of the party downstairs, which peaked sometimes in cusps and ogees of noise. That precious signal-to-noise ratio, whose delicate balance required every calorie of her strength, seesawed inside the small tenuous skull as she watched Callisto, sheltering the bird. Callisto was trying to confront any idea of the heat-death now, as he nuzzled the feathery lump in his hands. He sought correspondences. Sade, of course. And Temple Drake, gaunt and hopeless in her little park in Paris, at the end of *Sanctuary*.[8] Final equilibrium. *Nightwood*.[9] And the tango. Any tango, but more than any perhaps the sad sick dance in Stravinsky's *L'Histoire du Soldat*.[1] He thought back: what had tango music been for them after the war, what meanings had he missed in all the stately coupled automatons in the *cafés'-dansants*,[2] or in the metronomes which had ticked behind the eyes of his own partners? Not even the clean constant winds of Switzerland could cure the *grippe espagnole*.[3] Stravinsky had had it, they all had had it. And how many musicians were left after Passchendaele, after the Marne?[4] It came down in this case to seven: violin, double-bass. Clarinet, bassoon. Cornet, trombone. Tympani. Almost as if any tiny troupe of saltimbanques had set about conveying the same information as a full pit-orchestra. There was hardly a full complement left in Europe. Yet with violin and tympani Stravinsky had managed to communicate in that tango the same exhaustion, the same airlessness one saw in the slicked-down youths who were trying to imitate Vernon Castle, and in their mistresses, who simply did not care. *Ma maîtresse*.[5] Celeste. Returning to Nice after the second war he had found that café replaced by a perfume shop which catered to American tourists. And no secret vestige of her in the cobblestones or in the old pension next door; no perfume to match her breath heavy with the sweet Spanish wine she always drank. And so instead he had purchased a Henry Miller novel and left for Paris,[6] and read the book on the train so that when he arrived he had been given at least a little forewarning. And saw that Celeste and the others and even Temple Drake were not all that had changed. "Aubade," he said, "my head aches." The sound of his voice generated in the girl an answering scrap of melody. Her movement toward the kitchen, the towel, the cold water, and his eyes following her formed a weird and intricate canon; as she placed the compress on his forehead his sigh of gratitude seemed to signal a new subject, another series of modulations.

"No," Meatball was still saying, "no, I'm afraid not. This is not a house of ill repute. I'm sorry, really I am." Slab was adamant. "But the chief said," he kept repeating. The seaman offered to swap the moonshine for a good piece. Meatball looked around frantically, as if seeking assistance. In the middle of the room, the Duke di Angelis quartet were engaged in a historic moment. Vincent was seated and the others standing: they were going

8. Sexually notorious novel published in 1931 by the American writer William Faulkner (1897–1962).
9. Novel published in 1936 by the American expatriate writer Djuna Barnes (1892–1982).
1. "The Story of the Soldier" (French), a 1918 work by the Russian composer Igor Stravinsky (1882–1971).

2. Café dancers (French).
3. Spanish flu (French).
4. Battle sites in World War I noted for their extremely high casualties.
5. My mistress (French).
6. Miller was famous for his overtly sexual novels written in Paris during the 1930s.

through the motions of a group having a session, only without instruments. "I say," Meatball said. Duke moved his head a few times, smiled faintly, lit a cigarette, and eventually caught sight of Meatball. "Quiet, man," he whispered. Vincent began to fling his arms around, his fists clenched; then, abruptly, was still, then repeated the performance. This went on for a few minutes while Meatball sipped his drink moodily. The navy had withdrawn to the kitchen. Finally at some invisible signal the group stopped tapping their feet and Duke grinned and said, "At least we ended together."

Meatball glared at him. "I say," he said. "I have this new conception, man," Duke said. "You remember your namesake. You remember Gerry."

"No," said Meatball. "I'll remember April, if that's any help."

"As a matter of fact," Duke said, "it was Love for Sale. Which shows how much you know. The point is, it was Mulligan, Chet Baker[7] and that crew, way back then, out yonder. You dig?"

"Baritone sax," Meatball said. "Something about a baritone sax."

"But no piano, man. No guitar. Or accordion. You know what that means."

"Not exactly," Meatball said.

"Well first let me just say, that I am no Mingus, no John Lewis.[8] Theory was never my strong point. I mean things like reading were always difficult for me and all—"

"I know," Meatball said drily. "You got your card taken away because you changed key on Happy Birthday at a Kiwanis Club picnic."

"Rotarian. But it occurred to me, in one of these flashes of insight, that if that first quartet of Mulligan's had no piano, it could only mean one thing."

"No chords," said Paco, the baby-faced bass.

"What he is trying to say," Duke said, "is no root chords. Nothing to listen to while you blow a horizontal line. What one does in such a case is, one *thinks* the roots."

A horrified awareness was dawning on Meatball. "And the next logical extension," he said.

"Is to think everything," Duke announced with simple dignity. "Roots, line, everything."

Meatball looked at Duke, awed. "But," he said.

"Well," Duke said modestly, "there are a few bugs to work out."

"But," Meatball said.

"Just listen," Duke said. "You'll catch on." And off they went again into orbit, presumably somewhere around the asteroid belt. After a while Krinkles made an embouchure and started moving his fingers and Duke clapped his hand to his forehead. "Oaf!" he roared. "The new head we're using, you remember, I wrote last night?" "Sure," Krinkles said, "the new head. I come in on the bridge. All your heads I come in then." "Right," Duke said. "So why—" "Wha," said Krinkles, "16 bars, I wait, I come in—" "16?" Duke said. "No. No, Krinkles. Eight you waited. You want me to sing it? A cigarette that bears a lipstick's traces, an airline ticket to romantic places."

---

7. In 1952 the American jazz musicians Gerry Mulligan (1927–1996) and Chet Baker (1929–1988) became famous for their revolutionary pianoless quartet.

8. Charles Mingus (1922–1979) and John Lewis (1920–2001), American jazz musicians noted for their compositions.

Krinkles scratched his head. "These Foolish Things, you mean." "Yes," Duke said, "yes, Krinkles. Bravo." "Not I'll Remember April," Krinkles said. *"Minghe morte,"*[9] said Duke. "I *figured* we were playing it a little slow," Krinkles said. Meatball chuckled. "Back to the old drawing board," he said. "No, man," Duke said, "back to the airless void." And they took off again, only it seemed Paco was playing in G sharp while the rest were in E flat, so they had to start all over.

In the kitchen two of the girls from George Washington and the sailors were singing Let's All Go Down and Piss on the Forrestal.[1] There was a two-handed, bilingual *morra*[2] game on over by the icebox. Saul had filled several paper bags with water and was sitting on the fire escape, dropping them on passersby in the street. A fat government girl in a Bennington sweatshirt, recently engaged to an ensign attached to the Forrestal, came charging into the kitchen, head lowered, and butted Slab in the stomach. Figuring this was as good an excuse for a fight as any, Slab's buddies piled in. The *morra* players were nose-to-nose, screaming *trois, sette* at the tops of their lungs. From the shower the girl Meatball had taken out of the sink announced that she was drowning. She had apparently sat on the drain and the water was now up to her neck. The noise in Meatball's apartment had reached a sustained, ungodly crescendo.

Meatball stood and watched, scratching his stomach lazily. The way he figured, there were only about two ways he could cope: (a) lock himself in the closet and maybe eventually they would all go away, or (b) try to calm everybody down, one by one. (a) was certainly the more attractive alternative. But then he started thinking about that closet. It was dark and stuffy and he would be alone. He did not feature being alone. And then this crew off the good ship Lollipop[3] or whatever it was might take it upon themselves to kick down the closet door, for a lark. And if that happened he would be, at the very least, embarrassed. The other way was more a pain in the neck, but probably better in the long run.

So he decided to try and keep his lease-breaking party from deteriorating into total chaos: he gave wine to the sailors and separated the *morra* players; he introduced the fat government girl to Sandor Rojas, who would keep her out of trouble; he helped the girl in the shower to dry off and get into bed; he had another talk with Saul; he called a repairman for the refrigerator, which someone had discovered was on the blink. This is what he did until nightfall, when most of the revellers had passed out and the party trembled on the threshold of its third day.

Upstairs Callisto, helpless in the past, did not feel the faint rhythm inside the bird begin to slacken and fail. Aubade was by the window, wandering the ashes of her own lovely world; the temperature held steady, the sky had become a uniform darkening gray. Then something from downstairs—a girl's scream, an overturned chair, a glass dropped on the floor, he would never know what exactly—pierced that private time-warp and he became aware of the faltering, the constriction of muscles, the tiny tossings of the

---

9. Dead prick (Italian).
1. Aircraft carrier in the U.S. Navy.
2. Finger game originally played by Italians. The commands are numbers; below, three (*trois,*

French) and seven (*sette,* Italian).
3. The subject of film and song popularized in the 1930s by the American child actress Shirley Temple (1928–2014).

bird's head; and his own pulse began to pound more fiercely, as if trying to compensate. "Aubade," he called weakly, "he's dying." The girl, flowing and rapt, crossed the hothouse to gaze down at Callisto's hands. The two remained like that, poised, for one minute, and two, while the heartbeat ticked a graceful diminuendo down at last into stillness. Callisto raised his head slowly. "I held him," he protested, impotent with the wonder of it, "to give him the warmth of my body. Almost as if I were communicating life to him, or a sense of life. What has happened? Has the transfer of heat ceased to work? Is there no more . . ." He did not finish.

"I was just at the window," she said. He sank back, terrified. She stood a moment more, irresolute; she had sensed his obsession long ago, realized somehow that that constant 37 was now decisive. Suddenly then, as if seeing the single and unavoidable conclusion to all this she moved swiftly to the window before Callisto could speak; tore away the drapes and smashed out the glass with two exquisite hands which came away bleeding and glistening with splinters; and turned to face the man on the bed and wait with him until the moment of equilibrium was reached, when 37 degrees Fahrenheit should prevail both outside and inside, and forever, and the hovering, curious dominant of their separate lives should resolve into a tonic of darkness and the final absence of all motion.

1984

RAYMOND CARVER
1938–1988

Minimal fiction; designer fiction; even "dirty fiction," a phrase the British magazine *Granta* used to characterize the new style of American writing that was supposedly polluting the realistic short story with unconventional, irrealistic techniques—these terms were tossed around by critics of an abruptly new style of work that at times seemed to dominate the 1980s. Popularized by Bobbie Ann Mason, Ann Beattie, Frederick Barthelme, and Barry Hannah as well, its chief practitioner was a master of fine arts graduate from the University of Iowa's Writers Workshop, Raymond Carver, whose collections *Will You Please Be Quiet, Please?* (1976), *What We Talk About When We Talk About Love* (1981), and *Cathedral* (1983) set the most imitated style of their generation. Moved to put some order to these many definitions, writer John Barth—whose nonrealistic, innovative work had helped characterize the writing of the decades before—coined the term Post-Alcoholic Blue-Collar Minimalist Hyperrealism to describe the school Carver may have inadvertently founded. A recovering alcoholic, Carver had worked as a janitor, sawmill hand, delivery person, and sales representative, suggesting the profile Barth had in mind. But more pertinent to the style of his fiction was his training at Iowa and teaching in creative writing programs at universities around the country. By the time of his death, his became the most accepted style in such academic programs and in the literary magazines they generated.

This style's success is important. With conventions of literary realism having been challenged and theorists questioning all such previously stable assumptions, readers of Barth, Donald Barthelme, Kurt Vonnegut, and other such experimenters may have felt that simple realism was no longer an up-to-date way in which to write. Raymond Carver proved that it was, and that previous challenges to realistic tradition had only made it all the more effective, especially when those challenges are incorporated in the new style. Carver's patient narration does not strive for a reader's suspension of disbelief. Rather, as in the introduction of the bizarre situation experienced in "Cathedral" (printed here), its plain, even flat statement presents matter unadorned by devices meant to persuade or convince. So a blind man wants to learn what the architecture of a cathedral suggests? Here it is, Carver's story says: what you see is what there is; take it or leave it; if you are blind, he will help you feel your way through, but never as a direction to meaning, only to an apprehension of the facts. Carver's characters are usually working-class people somewhat down on their luck. Often, alcohol figures in their lives, less as a stimulant than as a further depressant. Totally unexceptional, their failures, like their hopes, are small, even puny. But from such stripped-down essentials the author is able to write in a plain, simple manner, sticking to the absolute minimum so that no one can accuse him of trying to create illusions.

Much was made of Raymond Carver's alcoholism and recovery. He made no apologies for his hard, sometimes abusive life, the rigors of which contributed to ill health and an early death. His stories and poems have the same quiet toughness to them, not flamboyant in confrontation with life's meanness but dedicated to holding on against time's slowly destructive friction with a grittiness all their own.

The following text is from *Cathedral* (1983).

Cathedral

This blind man, an old friend of my wife's, he was on his way to spend the night. His wife had died. So he was visiting the dead wife's relatives in Connecticut. He called my wife from his in-laws'. Arrangements were made. He would come by train, a five-hour trip, and my wife would meet him at the station. She hadn't seen him since she worked for him one summer in Seattle ten years ago. But she and the blind man had kept in touch. They made tapes and mailed them back and forth. I wasn't enthusiastic about his visit. He was no one I knew. And his being blind bothered me. My idea of blindness came from the movies. In the movies, the blind moved slowly and never laughed. Sometimes they were led by seeing-eye dogs. A blind man in my house was not something I looked forward to.

That summer in Seattle she had needed a job. She didn't have any money. The man she was going to marry at the end of the summer was in officers' training school. He didn't have any money, either. But she was in love with the guy, and he was in love with her, etc. She'd seen something in the paper: HELP WANTED—*Reading to Blind Man*, and a telephone number. She phoned and went over, was hired on the spot. She'd worked with this blind man all summer. She read stuff to him, case studies, reports, that sort of thing. She helped him organize his little office in the county social-service department. They'd become good friends, my wife and the blind man. How do I know these things? She told me. And she told me something else. On her last day in the office, the blind man asked if he could touch her face. She agreed to this. She told me he touched his fingers to every part of her face, her nose—even her neck! She never forgot it. She even tried to write a poem about it. She was always trying to write a poem. She wrote a poem or two every year, usually after something really important had happened to her.

When we first started going out together, she showed me the poem. In the poem, she recalled his fingers and the way they had moved around over her face. In the poem, she talked about what she had felt at the time, about what went through her mind when the blind man touched her nose and lips. I can remember I didn't think much of the poem. Of course, I didn't tell her that. Maybe I just don't understand poetry. I admit it's not the first thing I reach for when I pick up something to read.

Anyway, this man who'd first enjoyed her favors, the officer-to-be, he'd been her childhood sweetheart. So okay. I'm saying that at the end of the summer she let the blind man run his hands over her face, said goodbye to him, married her childhood etc., who was now a commissioned officer, and she moved away from Seattle. But they'd kept in touch, she and the blind man. She made the first contact after a year or so. She called him up one night from an Air Force base in Alabama. She wanted to talk. They talked. He asked her to send him a tape and tell him about her life. She did this. She sent the tape. On the tape, she told the blind man about her husband and about their life together in the military. She told the blind man she loved her husband but she didn't like it where they lived and she didn't like it that he was a part of the military-industrial thing. She told the blind man she'd written a poem and he was in it. She told him that she was writing a poem about what it was like to be an Air Force officer's wife. The poem wasn't finished yet. She was still writing it. The blind man made a tape. He sent her the tape. She made a tape. This went on for years. My wife's officer was posted to one base and then another. She sent tapes from Moody AFB,[1] McGuire, McConnell, and finally Travis, near Sacramento, where one night she got to feeling lonely and cut off from people she kept losing in that moving-around life. She got to feeling she couldn't go it another step. She went in and swallowed all the pills and capsules in the medicine chest and washed them down with a bottle of gin. Then she got into a hot bath and passed out.

But instead of dying, she got sick. She threw up. Her officer—why should he have a name? he was the childhood sweetheart, and what more does he want?—came home from somewhere, found her, and called the ambulance. In time, she put it all on a tape and sent the tape to the blind man. Over the years, she put all kinds of stuff on tapes and sent the tapes off lickety-split. Next to writing a poem every year, I think it was her chief means of recreation. On one tape, she told the blind man she'd decided to live away from her officer for a time. On another tape, she told him about her divorce. She and I began going out, and of course she told her blind man about it. She told him everything, or so it seemed to me. Once she asked me if I'd like to hear the latest tape from the blind man. This was a year ago. I was on the tape, she said. So I said okay, I'd listen to it. I got us drinks and we settled down in the living room. We made ready to listen. First she inserted the

---

1. Air force base. Names of other air force bases follow.

tape into the player and adjusted a couple of dials. Then she pushed a lever. The tape squeaked and someone began to talk in this loud voice. She lowered the volume. After a few minutes of harmless chitchat, I heard my own name in the mouth of this stranger, this blind man I didn't even know! And then this: "From all you've said about him, I can only conclude—" But we were interrupted, a knock at the door, something, and we didn't ever get back to the tape. Maybe it was just as well. I'd heard all I wanted to.

Now this same blind man was coming to sleep in my house.

"Maybe I could take him bowling," I said to my wife. She was at the draining board doing scalloped potatoes. She put down the knife she was using and turned around.

"If you love me," she said, "you can do this for me. If you don't love me, okay. But if you had a friend, any friend, and the friend came to visit, I'd make him feel comfortable." She wiped her hands with the dish towel.

"I don't have any blind friends," I said.

"You don't have *any* friends," she said. "Period. Besides," she said, "goddam it, his wife's just died! Don't you understand that? The man's lost his wife!"

I didn't answer. She'd told me a little about the blind man's wife. Her name was Beulah. Beulah! That's a name for a colored woman.

"Was his wife a Negro?" I asked.

"Are you crazy?" my wife said. "Have you just flipped or something?" She picked up a potato. I saw it hit the floor, then roll under the stove. "What's wrong with you?" she said. "Are you drunk?"

"I'm just asking," I said.

Right then my wife filled me in with more detail than I cared to know. I made a drink and sat at the kitchen table to listen. Pieces of the story began to fall into place.

Beulah had gone to work for the blind man the summer after my wife had stopped working for him. Pretty soon Beulah and the blind man had themselves a church wedding. It was a little wedding—who'd want to go to such a wedding in the first place?—just the two of them, plus the minister and the minister's wife. But it was a church wedding just the same. It was what Beulah had wanted, he'd said. But even then Beulah must have been carrying the cancer in her glands. After they had been inseparable for eight years—my wife's word, *inseparable*—Beulah's health went into a rapid decline. She died in a Seattle hospital room, the blind man sitting beside the bed and holding on to her hand. They'd married, lived and worked together, slept together—had sex, sure—and then the blind man had to bury her. All this without his having ever seen what the goddamned woman looked like. It was beyond my understanding. Hearing this, I felt sorry for the blind man for a little bit. And then I found myself thinking what a pitiful life this woman must have led. Imagine a woman who could never see herself as she was seen in the eyes of her loved one. A woman who could go on day after day and never receive the smallest compliment from her beloved. A woman whose husband could never read the expression on her face, be it misery or something better. Someone who could wear makeup or not—what difference to him? She could, if she wanted, wear green eyeshadow around one eye, a straight pin in her nostril, yellow slacks and purple shoes, no matter. And then to slip off into death, the blind man's hand on her hand, his blind eyes streaming tears—I'm imagining now—her last thought maybe this: that he never even knew what she looked like, and she on an express to the grave. Robert was left with a small insurance policy and half of a twenty-peso Mexican coin. The other half of the coin went into the box with her. Pathetic.

So when the time rolled around, my wife went to the depot to pick him up. With nothing to do but wait—sure, I blamed him for that—I was having a drink and watching the TV when I heard the car pull into the drive. I got up from the sofa with my drink and went to the window to have a look.

I saw my wife laughing as she parked the car. I saw her get out of the car and shut the door. She was still wearing a smile. Just amazing. She went around to the other side of the car to where the blind man was already starting to get out. This blind man, feature this, he was wearing a full beard! A beard on a blind man! Too much, I say. The blind man reached into the back seat and dragged out a suitcase. My wife took his arm, shut the car door, and, talking all the way, moved him down the drive and then up the steps to the front porch. I turned off the TV. I finished my drink, rinsed the glass, dried my hands. Then I went to the door.

My wife said, "I want you to meet Robert. Robert, this is my husband. I've told you all about him." She was beaming. She had this blind man by his coat sleeve.

The blind man let go of his suitcase and up came his hand.

I took it. He squeezed hard, held my hand, and then he let it go.

"I feel like we've already met," he boomed.

"Likewise," I said. I didn't know what else to say. Then I said, "Welcome. I've heard a lot about you." We began to move then, a little group, from the porch into the living room, my wife guiding him by the arm. The blind man was carrying his suitcase in his other hand. My wife said things like, "To your left here, Robert. That's right. Now watch it, there's a chair. That's it. Sit down right here. This is the sofa. We just bought this sofa two weeks ago."

I started to say something about the old sofa. I'd liked that old sofa. But I didn't say anything. Then I wanted to say something else, small-talk, about the scenic ride along the Hudson. How going *to* New York, you should sit on the right-hand side of the train, and coming *from* New York, the left-hand side.

"Did you have a good train ride?" I said. "Which side of the train did you sit on, by the way?"

"What a question, which side!" my wife said. "What's it matter which side?" she said.

"I just asked," I said.

"Right side," the blind man said. "I hadn't been on a train in nearly forty years. Not since I was a kid. With my folks. That's been a long time. I'd nearly forgotten the sensation. I have winter in my beard now," he said. "So I've been told, anyway. Do I look distinguished, my dear?" the blind man said to my wife.

"You look distinguished, Robert," she said. "Robert," she said. "Robert, it's just so good to see you."

My wife finally took her eyes off the blind man and looked at me. I had the feeling she didn't like what she saw. I shrugged.

I've never met, or personally known, anyone who was blind. This blind man was late forties, a heavy-set, balding man with stooped shoulders, as if he carried a great weight there. He wore brown slacks, brown shoes, a light-brown shirt, a tie, a sports coat. Spiffy. He also had this full beard. But he didn't use a cane and he didn't wear dark glasses. I'd always thought dark glasses were a must for the blind. Fact was, I wished he had a pair. At first glance, his eyes looked like anyone else's eyes. But if you looked close, there was something different about them. Too much white in the iris, for one thing, and the pupils seemed to move around in the sockets without his knowing it or being able to stop it. Creepy. As I stared at his face, I saw the left pupil turn in toward his nose while the other made an effort to keep in one place. But it was only an effort, for that eye was on the roam without his knowing it or wanting it to be.

I said, "Let me get you a drink. What's your pleasure? We have a little of everything. It's one of our pastimes."

"Bub, I'm a Scotch man myself," he said fast enough in this big voice.

"Right," I said. Bub! "Sure you are. I knew it."

He let his fingers touch his suitcase, which was sitting alongside the sofa. He was taking his bearings. I didn't blame him for that.

"I'll move that up to your room," my wife said.

"No, that's fine," the blind man said loudly. "It can go up when I go up."

"A little water with the Scotch?" I said.

"Very little," he said.

"I knew it," I said.

He said, "Just a tad. The Irish actor, Barry Fitzgerald?[2] I'm like that fellow. When I drink water, Fitzgerald said, I drink water. When I drink whiskey, I drink whiskey." My wife laughed. The blind man brought his hand up under his beard. He lifted his beard slowly and let it drop.

I did the drinks, three big glasses of Scotch with a splash of water in each. Then we made ourselves comfortable and talked about Robert's travels. First the long flight from the West Coast to Connecticut, we covered that. Then from Connecticut up here by train. We had another drink concerning that leg of the trip.

I remembered having read somewhere that the blind didn't smoke because, as speculation had it, they couldn't see the smoke they exhaled. I thought I knew that much and that much only about blind people. But this blind man smoked his cigarette down to the nubbin and then lit another one. This blind man filled his ashtray and my wife emptied it.

When we sat down at the table for dinner, we had another drink. My wife heaped Robert's plate with cube steak, scalloped potatoes, green beans. I buttered him up two slices of bread. I said, "Here's bread and butter for you." I swallowed some of my drink. "Now let us pray," I said, and the blind man lowered his head. My wife looked at me, her mouth agape. "Pray the phone won't ring and the food doesn't get cold," I said.

We dug in. We ate everything there was to eat on the table. We ate like there was no tomorrow. We didn't talk. We ate. We scarfed. We grazed that table. We were into serious eating. The blind man had right away located

2. Noted for his stock characterizations of Irish figures (often priests) in American films of the 1940s and 1950s.

his foods, he knew just where everything was on his plate. I watched with admiration as he used his knife and fork on the meat. He'd cut two pieces of meat, fork the meat into his mouth, and then go all out for the scalloped potatoes, the beans next, and then he'd tear off a hunk of buttered bread and eat that. He'd follow this up with a big drink of milk. It didn't seem to bother him to use his fingers once in a while, either.

We finished everything, including half a strawberry pie. For a few moments, we sat as if stunned. Sweat beaded on our faces. Finally, we got up from the table and left the dirty plates. We didn't look back. We took ourselves into the living room and sank into our places again. Robert and my wife sat on the sofa. I took the big chair. We had us two or three more drinks while they talked about the major things that had come to pass for them in the past ten years. For the most part, I just listened. Now and then I joined in. I didn't want him to think I'd left the room, and I didn't want her to think I was feeling left out. They talked of things that had happened to them—to them!—these past ten years. I waited in vain to hear my name on my wife's sweet lips: "And then my dear husband came into my life"— something like that. But I heard nothing of the sort. More talk of Robert. Robert had done a little of everything, it seemed, a regular blind jack-of-all-trades. But most recently he and his wife had had an Amway[3] distributorship, from which, I gathered, they'd earned their living, such as it was. The blind man was also a ham radio operator. He talked in his loud voice about conversations he'd had with fellow operators in Guam, in the Philippines, in Alaska, and even in Tahiti. He said he'd have a lot of friends there if he ever wanted to go visit those places. From time to time, he'd turn his blind face toward me, put his hand under his beard, ask me something. How long had I been in my present position? (Three years.) Did I like my work? (I didn't.) Was I going to stay with it? (What were the options?) Finally, when I thought he was beginning to run down, I got up and turned on the TV.

My wife looked at me with irritation. She was heading toward a boil. Then she looked at the blind man and said, "Robert, do you have a TV?"

The blind man said, "My dear, I have two TVs. I have a color set and a black-and-white thing, an old relic. It's funny, but if I turn the TV on, and I'm always turning it on, I turn on the color set. It's funny, don't you think?"

I didn't know what to say to that. I had absolutely nothing to say to that. No opinion. So I watched the news program and tried to listen to what the announcer was saying.

"This is a color TV," the blind man said. "Don't ask me how, but I can tell."

"We traded up a while ago," I said.

The blind man had another taste of his drink. He lifted his beard, sniffed it, and let it fall. He leaned forward on the sofa. He positioned his ashtray on the coffee table, then put the lighter to his cigarette. He leaned back on the sofa and crossed his legs at the ankles.

My wife covered her mouth, and then she yawned. She stretched. She said, "I think I'll go upstairs and put on my robe. I think I'll change into something else. Robert, you make yourself comfortable," she said.

---

3. A retail sales business operated by selling directly to consumers in their homes.

"I'm comfortable," the blind man said.

"I want you to feel comfortable in this house," she said.

"I am comfortable," the blind man said.

After she'd left the room, he and I listened to the weather report and then to the sports roundup. By that time, she'd been gone so long I didn't know if she was going to come back. I thought she might have gone to bed. I wished she'd come back downstairs. I didn't want to be left alone with a blind man. I asked him if he wanted another drink, and he said sure. Then I asked if he wanted to smoke some dope with me. I said I'd just rolled a number. I hadn't, but I planned to do so in about two shakes.

"I'll try some with you," he said.

"Damn right," I said. "That's the stuff."

I got our drinks and sat down on the sofa with him. Then I rolled us two fat numbers. I lit one and passed it. I brought it to his fingers. He took it and inhaled.

"Hold it as long as you can," I said. I could tell he didn't know the first thing.

My wife came back downstairs wearing her pink robe and her pink slippers.

"What do I smell?" she said.

"We thought we'd have us some cannabis," I said.

My wife gave me a savage look. Then she looked at the blind man and said, "Robert, I didn't know you smoked."

He said, "I do now, my dear. There's a first time for everything. But I don't feel anything yet."

"This stuff is pretty mellow," I said. "This stuff is mild. It's dope you can reason with," I said. "It doesn't mess you up."

"Not much it doesn't, bub," he said, and laughed.

My wife sat on the sofa between the blind man and me. I passed her the number. She took it and toked and then passed it back to me. "Which way is this going?" she said. Then she said, "I shouldn't be smoking this. I can hardly keep my eyes open as it is. That dinner did me in. I shouldn't have eaten so much."

"It was the strawberry pie," the blind man said. "That's what did it," he said, and he laughed his big laugh. Then he shook his head.

"There's more strawberry pie," I said.

"Do you want some more, Robert?" my wife said.

"Maybe in a little while," he said.

We gave our attention to the TV. My wife yawned again. She said, "Your bed is made up when you feel like going to bed, Robert. I know you must have had a long day. When you're ready to go to bed, say so." She pulled his arm. "Robert?"

He came to and said, "I've had a real nice time. This beats tapes, doesn't it?"

I said, "Coming at you," and I put the number between his fingers. He inhaled, held the smoke, and then let it go. It was like he'd been doing it since he was nine years old.

"Thanks, bub," he said. "But I think this is all for me. I think I'm beginning to feel it," he said. He held the burning roach out for my wife.

"Same here," she said. "Ditto. Me, too." She took the roach and passed it to me. "I may just sit here for a while between you two guys with my eyes closed. But don't let me bother you, okay? Either one of you. If it bothers you, say so. Otherwise, I may just sit here with my eyes closed until you're ready to go to bed," she said. "Your bed's made up, Robert, when you're ready. It's right next to our room at the top of the stairs. We'll show you up when you're ready. You wake me up now, you guys, if I fall asleep." She said that and then she closed her eyes and went to sleep.

The news program ended. I got up and changed the channel. I sat back down on the sofa. I wished my wife hadn't pooped out. Her head lay across the back of the sofa, her mouth open. She'd turned so that her robe had slipped away from her legs, exposing a juicy thigh. I reached to draw her robe back over her, and it was then that I glanced at the blind man. What the hell! I flipped the robe open again.

"You say when you want some strawberry pie," I said.

"I will," he said.

I said, "Are you tired? Do you want me to take you up to your bed? Are you ready to hit the hay?"

"Not yet," he said. "No, I'll stay up with you, bub. If that's all right. I'll stay up until you're ready to turn in. We haven't had a chance to talk. Know what I mean? I feel like me and her monopolized the evening." He lifted his beard and he let it fall. He picked up his cigarettes and his lighter.

"That's all right," I said. Then I said, "I'm glad for the company."

And I guess I was. Every night I smoked dope and stayed up as long as I could before I fell asleep. My wife and I hardly ever went to bed at the same time. When I did go to sleep, I had these dreams. Sometimes I'd wake up from one of them, my heart going crazy.

Something about the church and the Middle Ages was on the TV. Not your run-of-the-mill TV fare. I wanted to watch something else. I turned to the other channels. But there was nothing on them, either. So I turned back to the first channel and apologized.

"Bub, it's all right," the blind man said. "It's fine with me. Whatever you want to watch is okay. I'm always learning something. Learning never ends. It won't hurt me to learn something tonight. I got ears," he said.

We didn't say anything for a time. He was leaning forward with his head turned at me, his right ear aimed in the direction of the set. Very disconcerting. Now and then his eyelids drooped and then they snapped open again. Now and then he put his fingers into his beard and tugged, like he was thinking about something he was hearing on the television.

On the screen, a group of men wearing cowls was being set upon and tormented by men dressed in skeleton costumes and men dressed as devils. The men dressed as devils wore devil masks, horns, and long tails. This pageant was part of a procession. The Englishman who was narrating the thing said it took place in Spain once a year. I tried to explain to the blind man what was happening.

"Skeletons," he said. "I know about skeletons," he said, and he nodded.

The TV showed this one cathedral. Then there was a long, slow look at another one. Finally, the picture switched to the famous one in Paris, with its flying buttresses and its spires reaching up to the clouds. The camera pulled away to show the whole of the cathedral rising above the skyline.

There were times when the Englishman who was telling the thing would shut up, would simply let the camera move around over the cathedrals. Or else the camera would tour the countryside, men in fields walking behind oxen. I waited as long as I could. Then I felt I had to say something. I said, "They're showing the outside of this cathedral now. Gargoyles. Little statues carved to look like monsters. Now I guess they're in Italy. Yeah, they're in Italy. There's paintings on the walls of this one church."

"Are those fresco paintings, bub?" he asked, and he sipped from his drink.

I reached for my glass. But it was empty. I tried to remember what I could remember. "You're asking me are those frescoes?" I said. "That's a good question. I don't know."

The camera moved to a cathedral outside Lisbon. The differences in the Portuguese cathedral compared with the French and Italian were not that great. But they were there. Mostly the interior stuff. Then something occurred to me, and I said, "Something has occurred to me. Do you have any idea what a cathedral is? What they look like, that is? Do you follow me? If somebody says cathedral to you, do you have any notion what they're talking about? Do you know the difference between that and a Baptist church, say?"

He let the smoke dribble from his mouth. "I know they took hundreds of workers fifty or a hundred years to build," he said. "I just heard the man say that, of course. I know generations of the same families worked on a cathedral. I heard him say that, too. The men who began their life's work on them, they never lived to see the completion of their work. In that wise, bub, they're no different from the rest of us, right?" He laughed. Then his eyelids drooped again. His head nodded. He seemed to be snoozing. Maybe he was imagining himself in Portugal. The TV was showing another cathedral now. This one was in Germany. The Englishman's voice droned on. "Cathedrals," the blind man said. He sat up and rolled his head back and forth. "If you want the truth, bub, that's about all I know. What I just said. What I heard him say. But maybe you could describe one to me? I wish you'd do it. I'd like that. If you want to know, I really don't have a good idea."

I stared hard at the shot of the cathedral on the TV. How could I even begin to describe it? But say my life depended on it. Say my life was being threatened by an insane guy who said I had to do it or else.

I stared some more at the cathedral before the picture flipped off into the countryside. There was no use. I turned to the blind man and said, "To begin with, they're very tall." I was looking around the room for clues. "They reach way up. Up and up. Toward the sky. They're so big, some of them, they have to have these supports. To help hold them up, so to speak. These supports are called buttresses. They remind me of viaducts, for some reason. But maybe you don't know viaducts, either? Sometimes the cathedrals have devils and such carved into the front. Sometimes lords and ladies. Don't ask me why this is," I said.

He was nodding. The whole upper part of his body seemed to be moving back and forth.

"I'm not doing so good, am I?" I said.

He stopped nodding and leaned forward on the edge of the sofa. As he listened to me, he was running his fingers through his beard. I wasn't getting through to him, I could see that. But he waited for me to go on just the same. He nodded, like he was trying to encourage me. I tried to think what else to say. "They're really big," I said. "They're massive. They're built of stone. Marble, too, sometimes. In those olden days, when they built cathedrals, men wanted to be close to God. In those olden days, God was an important part of everyone's life. You could tell this from their cathedral-building. I'm sorry," I said, "but it looks like that's the best I can do for you. I'm just no good at it."

"That's all right, bub," the blind man said. "Hey, listen. I hope you don't mind my asking you. Can I ask you something? Let me ask you a simple question, yes or no. I'm just curious and there's no offense. You're my host. But let me ask if you are in any way religious? You don't mind my asking?"

I shook my head. He couldn't see that, though. A wink is the same as a nod to a blind man. "I guess I don't believe in it. In anything. Sometimes it's hard. You know what I'm saying?"

"Sure, I do," he said.

"Right," I said.

The Englishman was still holding forth. My wife sighed in her sleep. She drew a long breath and went on with her sleeping.

"You'll have to forgive me," I said. "But I can't tell you what a cathedral looks like. It just isn't in me to do it. I can't do any more than I've done."

The blind man sat very still, his head down, as he listened to me.

I said, "The truth is, cathedrals don't mean anything special to me. Nothing. Cathedrals. They're something to look at on late-night TV. That's all they are."

It was then that the blind man cleared his throat. He brought something up. He took a handkerchief from his back pocket. Then he said, "I get it, bub. It's okay. It happens. Don't worry about it," he said. "Hey, listen to me. Will you do me a favor? I got an idea. Why don't you find us some heavy paper? And a pen. We'll do something. We'll draw one together. Get us a pen and some heavy paper. Go on, bub, get the stuff," he said.

So I went upstairs. My legs felt like they didn't have any strength in them. They felt like they did after I'd done some running. In my wife's room, I looked around. I found some ballpoints in a little basket on her table. And then I tried to think where to look for the kind of paper he was talking about.

Downstairs, in the kitchen, I found a shopping bag with onion skins in the bottom of the bag. I emptied the bag and shook it. I brought it into the living room and sat down with it near his legs. I moved some things, smoothed the wrinkles from the bag, spread it out on the coffee table.

The blind man got down from the sofa and sat next to me on the carpet.

He ran his fingers over the paper. He went up and down the sides of the paper. The edges, even the edges. He fingered the corners.

"All right," he said. "All right, let's do her."

He found my hand, the hand with the pen. He closed his hand over my hand. "Go ahead, bub, draw," he said. "Draw. You'll see. I'll follow along with you. It'll be okay. Just begin now like I'm telling you. You'll see. Draw," the blind man said.

So I began. First I drew a box that looked like a house. It could have been the house I lived in. Then I put a roof on it. At either end of the roof, I drew spires. Crazy.

"Swell," he said. "Terrific. You're doing fine," he said. "Never thought anything like this could happen in your lifetime, did you, bub? Well, it's a strange life, we all know that. Go on now. Keep it up."

I put in windows with arches. I drew flying buttresses. I hung great doors. I couldn't stop. The TV station went off the air. I put down the pen and closed and opened my fingers. The blind man felt around over the paper. He moved the tips of his fingers over the paper, all over what I had drawn, and he nodded.

"Doing fine," the blind man said.

I took up the pen again, and he found my hand. I kept at it. I'm no artist. But I kept drawing just the same.

My wife opened up her eyes and gazed at us. She sat up on the sofa, her robe hanging open. She said, "What are you doing? Tell me, I want to know."

I didn't answer her.

The blind man said, "We're drawing a cathedral. Me and him are working on it. Press hard," he said to me. "That's right. That's good," he said. "Sure. You got it, bub. I can tell. You didn't think you could. But you can, can't you? You're cooking with gas now. You know what I'm saying? We're going to really have us something here in a minute. How's the old arm?" he said. "Put some people in there now. What's a cathedral without people?"

My wife said, "What's going on? Robert, what are you doing? What's going on?"

"It's all right," he said to her. "Close your eyes now," the blind man said to me.

I did it. I closed them just like he said.

"Are they closed?" he said. "Don't fudge."

"They're closed," I said.

"Keep them that way," he said. He said, "Don't stop now. Draw."

So we kept on with it. His fingers rode my fingers as my hand went over the paper. It was like nothing else in my life up to now.

Then he said, "I think that's it. I think you got it," he said. "Take a look. What do you think?"

But I had my eyes closed. I thought I'd keep them that way for a little longer. I thought it was something I ought to do.

"Well?" he said. "Are you looking?"

My eyes were still closed. I was in my house. I knew that. But I didn't feel like I was inside anything.

"It's really something," I said.

1983

MAXINE HONG KINGSTON
b. 1940

axine Hong Kingston was born in Stockton, California, to Chinese immigrant parents. Before they emigrated from China, Kingston's father had been a schoolteacher and a poet; her mother had been a rural doctor in a profession consisting almost entirely of men. In America they took on quite different identities: her father, at times unemployed, worked in a gambling house and a laundry; her mother raised six children, of whom Kingston was the eldest.

Kingston graduated from the University of California at Berkeley, studying there in the turbulent middle sixties. Her debut as a writer was auspicious: in 1976, an unknown, she published her first and most widely read book, *The Woman Warrior*, and was catapulted to literary fame. Subtitled "Memoirs of a Girlhood among Ghosts," it combines autobiographical fact with legends, especially Asian ones, to make a distinct imaginative creation. Reviews of the book, almost universally laudatory, emphasized its poetic and lyric beauty. *The Woman Warrior* is about the cultural conflicts Chinese Americans must confront. Still, what remains in the mind is its quality of vivid particularity, as for example at the beginning of "Shaman," the book's third section:

> Once in a long while, four times so far for me, my mother brings out the metal tube that holds her medical diploma. On the tube are gold circles crossed with seven red lines each—"joy" ideographs in abstract. There are also little flowers that look like gears for a gold machine. . . . When I open it the smell of China flies out, a thousand-year-old bat flying heavy-handed out of the Chinese caverns where bats are as white as dust, a smell that comes from long ago, far back in my brain.

Although *The Woman Warrior* received the National Book Critics' Circle award for general nonfiction, there is nothing "general" in the richness of its language.

The importance of storytelling to Kingston's enterprise in *The Woman Warrior* and its successor, *China Men* (1980), cannot be overemphasized. In an interview with Bill Moyers on public television, Kingston said that her attempt was to push the account toward "form" by giving it a "redemptive" meaning, making it a "beautiful" story rather than a sordid one. As is typically the case with her practice as a writer, her effort is to mediate between present and past: "I think that my stories have a constant breaking in and out of the present and past. So the reader might be walking along very well in the present, but the past breaks through and changes and enlightens the present and vice versa."

Kingston had originally conceived of *The Woman Warrior* and *China Men* as one long book, but decided to preserve an overall division by gender: *Warrior* is about her female antecedents; while *China Men*, which won the 1980 National Book Award for nonfiction, deals with her relation to her father and complements that relation by providing epic-like biographies of earlier male forebears, especially those Chinese who came to America and worked on building the railroads. In a final section she writes about her brother who served in the U.S. Navy during the Vietnam War. As she discusses in the interview with Moyers, her father annotated both of these memoir-meditations, carrying further the conversation between the generations.

Tripmaster Monkey (1989), presented more deliberately as a novel, is an exercise as excessive as the young fifth-generation American hero, Wittman Ah Sing, who is portrayed there. Subtitled "His Fake Book," the novel is an extended, picaresque account of Wittman's adventures as an aspiring playwright who imagines himself to be an incarnation of the legendary Monkey King—a trickster hero said to have brought the Buddha's teaching to China. Combining magic, realism, and black humor, *Tripmaster Monkey* is about a young man's search for a community in America. Although Kingston's myth-laden narratives have been called "exotic," she dislikes the word, since she has dedicated her art to exploring what it means to be a human being in American society. In fact, she thinks of her books as more American than Chinese, sees the American poet William Carlos Williams's *In the American Grain* as a true prose predecessor, and probably would be happy to think of the hero of *Tripmaster Monkey* as a later, different version of Huck Finn (in Mark Twain's novel) or Augie March (in Saul Bellow's). As the critic Jennie Wang explains in even larger dimensions, Kingston's Wittman Ah Sing, "the maker/magician . . . conceived in the mind's fancy of a metafictionist," joins in his multiculturalism American and postmodern ambitions.

In 2011 Kingston celebrated her sixty-fifth birthday by publishing a memoir, *I Love a Broad Margin to My Life*. Written in verse form, this work engages issues of aging as the writer recalls incidents in her marriage, her career, and her involvement with social causes. She considers imaginative elements as well, including the ultimate fate of her Woman Warrior and the experiences of her protagonist in *Tripmaster Monkey* in a projected visit to China.

The following text is from *The Woman Warrior* (1976).

From The Woman Warrior

No Name Woman

"You must not tell anyone," my mother said, "what I am about to tell you. In China your father had a sister who killed herself. She jumped into the family well. We say that your father has all brothers because it is as if she had never been born.

"In 1924 just a few days after our village celebrated seventeen hurry-up weddings—to make sure that every young man who went 'out on the road' would responsibly come home—your father and his brothers and your grandfather and his brothers and your aunt's new husband sailed for America, the Gold Mountain. It was your grandfather's last trip. Those lucky enough to get contracts waved good-bye from the decks. They fed and guarded the stowaways and helped them off in Cuba, New York, Bali, Hawaii. 'We'll meet in California next year,' they said. All of them sent money home.

"I remember looking at your aunt one day when she and I were dressing; I had not noticed before that she had such a protruding melon of a stomach. But I did not think, 'She's pregnant,' until she began to look like other pregnant women, her shirt pulling and the white tops of her black pants showing. She could not have been pregnant, you see, because her husband had been gone for years. No one said anything. We did not discuss it. In early summer she was ready to have the child, long after the time when it could have been possible.

"The village had also been counting. On the night the baby was to be born the villagers raided our house. Some were crying. Like a great saw, teeth strung with lights, files of people walked zigzag across our land, tearing the rice. Their lanterns doubled in the disturbed black water, which drained away through the broken bunds.[1] As the villagers closed in, we could see that some of them, probably men and women we knew well, wore white masks. The people with long hair hung it over their faces. Women with short hair made it stand up on end. Some had tied white bands around their foreheads, arms, and legs.

"At first they threw mud and rocks at the house. Then they threw eggs and began slaughtering our stock. We could hear the animals scream their deaths—the roosters, the pigs, a last great roar from the ox. Familiar wild heads flared in our night windows; the villagers encircled us. Some of the faces stopped to peer at us, their eyes rushing like searchlights. The hands flattened against the panes, framed heads, and left red prints.

"The villagers broke in the front and the back doors at the same time, even though we had not locked the doors against them. Their knives dripped with the blood of our animals. They smeared blood on the doors and walls. One woman swung a chicken, whose throat she had slit, splattering blood in red arcs about her. We stood together in the middle of our house, in the family hall with the pictures and tables of the ancestors around us, and looked straight ahead.

"At that time the house had only two wings. When the men came back, we would build two more to enclose our courtyard and a third one to begin a second courtyard. The villagers pushed through both wings, even your grandparents' rooms, to find your aunt's, which was also mine until the men returned. From this room a new wing for one of the younger families would grow. They ripped up her clothes and shoes and broke her combs, grinding them underfoot. They tore her work from the loom. They scattered the cooking fire and rolled the new weaving in it. We could hear them in the kitchen breaking our bowls and banging the pots. They overturned the great waisthigh earthenware jugs; duck eggs, pickled fruits, vegetables burst out and mixed in acrid torrents. The old woman from the next field swept a broom through the air and loosed the spirits-of-the-broom over our heads. 'Pig,' 'Ghost.' 'Pig,' they sobbed and scolded while they ruined our house.

"When they left, they took sugar and oranges to bless themselves. They cut pieces from the dead animals. Some of them took bowls that were not broken and clothes that were not torn. Afterward we swept up the rice and sewed it back up into sacks. But the smells from the spilled preserves lasted. Your aunt gave birth in the pigsty that night. The next morning when I went for the water, I found her and the baby plugging up the family well.

"Don't let your father know that I told you. He denies her. Now that you have started to menstruate, what happened to her could happen to you. Don't humiliate us. You wouldn't like to be forgotten as if you had never been born. The villagers are watchful."

Whenever she had to warn us about life, my mother told stories that ran like this one, a story to grow up on. She tested our strength to establish realities. Those in the emigrant generations who could not reassert brute survival died young and far from home. Those of us in the first American

---

1. Embankments built to enclose rice paddies and control the flow of irrigation water.

generations have had to figure out how the invisible world the emigrants built around our childhoods fits in solid America.

The immigrants confused the gods by diverting their curses, misleading them with crooked streets and false names. They must try to confuse their offspring as well, who, I suppose, threaten them in similar ways—always trying to get things straight, always trying to name the unspeakable. The Chinese I know hide their names; sojourners take new names when their lives change and guard their real names with silence.

Chinese-Americans, when you try to understand what things in you are Chinese, how do you separate what is peculiar to childhood, to poverty, insanities, one family, your mother who marked your growing with stories, from what is Chinese? What is Chinese tradition and what is the movies?

If I want to learn what clothes my aunt wore, whether flashy or ordinary, I would have to begin. "Remember Father's drowned-in-the-well sister?" I cannot ask that. My mother has told me once and for all the useful parts. She will add nothing unless powered by Necessity, a riverbank that guides her life. She plants vegetable gardens rather than lawns, she carries the odd-shaped tomatoes home from the fields and eats food left for the gods.

Whenever we did frivolous things, we used up energy, we flew high kites. We children came up off the ground over the melting cones our parents brought home from work and the American movie on New Year's Day—*Oh, You Beautiful Doll* with Betty Grable one year, and *She Wore a Yellow Ribbon* with John Wayne another year. After the one carnival ride each, we paid in guilt; our tired father counted his change on the dark walk home.

Adultery is extravagance. Could people who hatch their own chicks and eat the embryos and the heads for delicacies and boil the feet in vinegar for party food, leaving only the gravel, eating even the gizzard lining—could such people engender a prodigal aunt? To be a woman, to have a daughter in starvation time was a waste enough. My aunt could not have been the lone romantic who gave up everything for sex. Women in the old China did not choose. Some man had commanded her to lie with him and be his secret evil. I wonder whether he masked himself when he joined the raid on her family.

Perhaps she had encountered him in the fields or on the mountain where the daughters-in-law collected fuel. Or perhaps he first noticed her in the marketplace. He was not a stranger because the village housed no strangers. She had to have dealings with him other than sex. Perhaps he worked an adjoining field, or he sold her the cloth for the dress she sewed and wore. His demand must have surprised, then terrified her. She obeyed him; she always did as she was told.

When the family found a young man in the next village to be her husband, she had stood tractably beside the best rooster, his proxy,[2] and promised before they met that she would be his forever. She was lucky that he was her age and she would be the first wife, an advantage secure now. The night she first saw him, he had sex with her. Then he left for America. She had almost forgotten what he looked like. When she tried to envision him, she only saw

---

2. Someone or something that has the power to substitute or act for another.

the black and white face in the group photograph the men had had taken before leaving.

The other man was not, after all, much different from her husband. They both gave orders: she followed. "If you tell your family, I'll beat you. I'll kill you. Be here again next week." No one talked sex, ever. And she might have separated the rapes from the rest of living if only she did not have to buy her oil from him or gather wood in the same forest. I want her fear to have lasted just as long as rape lasted so that the fear could have been contained. No drawnout fear. But women at sex hazarded birth and hence lifetimes. The fear did not stop but permeated everywhere. She told the man, "I think I'm pregnant." He organized the raid against her.

On nights when my mother and father talked about their life back home, sometimes they mentioned an "outcast table" whose business they still seemed to be settling, their voices tight. In a commensal tradition,[3] where food is precious, the powerful older people made wrongdoers eat alone. Instead of letting them start separate new lives like the Japanese, who could become samurais and geishas,[4] the Chinese family, faces averted but eyes glowering sideways, hung on to the offenders and fed them leftovers. My aunt must have lived in the same house as my parents and eaten at an out-cast table. My mother spoke about the raid as if she had seen it, when she and my aunt, a daughter-in-law to a different household, should not have been living together at all. Daughters-in-law lived with their husbands' parents, not their own; a synonym for marriage in Chinese is "taking a daughter-in-law." Her husband's parents could have sold her, mortgaged her, stoned her. But they had sent her back to her own mother and father, a mysterious act hinting at disgraces not told me. Perhaps they had thrown her out to deflect the avengers.

She was the only daughter; her four brothers went with her father, hus-band, and uncles "out on the road" and for some years became western men. When the goods were divided among the family, three of the brothers took land, and the youngest, my father, chose an education. After my grandparents gave their daughter away to her husband's family, they had dispensed all the adventure and all the property. They expected her alone to keep the traditional ways, which her brothers, now among the barbarians, could fumble without detection. The heavy, deep-rooted women were to maintain the past against the flood, safe for returning. But the rare urge west had fixed upon our family, and so my aunt crossed boundaries not delineated in space.

The work of preservation demands that the feelings playing about in one's guts not be turned into action. Just watch their passing like cherry blossoms. But perhaps my aunt, my forerunner, caught in a slow life, let dreams grow and fade and after some months or years went toward what persisted. Fear at the enormities of the forbidden kept her desires delicate, wire and bone. She looked at a man because she liked the way the hair was tucked behind his ears, or she liked the question-mark line of a long torso curving at the shoul-der and straight at the hip. For warm eyes or a soft voice or a slow walk— that's all—a few hairs, a line, a brightness, a sound, a pace, she gave up

---

3. A tradition in which people eat together at the same table.
4. In Japanese society, women trained to entertain men. "Samurai": the Japanese warrior elite.

family. She offered us up for a charm that vanished with tiredness, a pigtail that didn't toss when the wind died. Why, the wrong lighting could erase the dearest thing about him.

It could very well have been, however, that my aunt did not take subtle enjoyment of her friend, but, a wild woman, kept rollicking company. Imagining her free with sex doesn't fit, though. I don't know any women like that, or men either. Unless I see her life branching into mine, she gives me no ancestral help.

To sustain her being in love, she often worked at herself in the mirror, guessing at the colors and shapes that would interest him, changing them frequently in order to hit on the right combination. She wanted him to look back.

On a farm near the sea, a woman who tended her appearance reaped a reputation for eccentricity. All the married women blunt-cut their hair in flaps about their ears or pulled it back in tight buns. No nonsense. Neither style blew easily into heart-catching tangles. And at their weddings they displayed themselves in their long hair for the last time. "It brushed the backs of my knees," my mother tells me. "It was braided, and even so, it brushed the backs of my knees."

At the mirror my aunt combed individuality into her bob. A bun could have been contrived to escape into black streamers blowing in the wind or in quiet wisps about her face, but only the older women in our picture album wear buns. She brushed her hair back from her forehead, tucking the flaps behind her ears. She looped a piece of thread, knotted into a circle between her index fingers and thumbs, and ran the double strand across her forehead. When she closed her fingers as if she were making a pair of shadow geese bite, the string twisted together catching the little hairs. Then she pulled the thread away from her skin, ripping the hair out neatly, her eyes watering from the needles of pain. Opening her fingers, she cleaned the thread, then rolled it along her hairline and the tops of her eyebrows. My mother did the same to me and my sisters and herself. I used to believe that the expression "caught by the short hairs" meant a captive held with a depilatory string. It especially hurt at the temples, but my mother said we were lucky we didn't have to have our feet bound when we were seven. Sisters used to sit on their beds and cry together, she said, as their mothers or their slave removed the bandages for a few minutes each night and let the blood gush back into their veins. I hope that the man my aunt loved appreciated a smooth brow, that he wasn't just a tits-and-ass man.

Once my aunt found a freckle on her chin, at a spot that the almanac said predestined her for unhappiness. She dug it out with a hot needle and washed the wound with peroxide.

More attention to her looks than these pullings of hairs and pickings at spots would have caused gossip among the villagers. They owned work clothes and good clothes, and they wore good clothes for feasting the new seasons. But since a woman combing her hair hexes beginnings, my aunt rarely found an occasion to look her best. Women looked like great sea snails—the corded wood, babies, and laundry they carried were the whorls on their backs. The Chinese did not admire a bent back; goddesses and warriors stood straight. Still there must have been a marvelous freeing of beauty when a worker laid down her burden and stretched and arched.

Such commonplace loveliness, however, was not enough for my aunt. She dreamed of a lover for the fifteen days of New Year's, the time for families to exchange visits, money, and food. She plied her secret comb. And sure enough she cursed the year, the family, the village, and herself.

Even as her hair lured her imminent lover, many other men looked at her. Uncles, cousins, nephews, brothers would have looked, too, had they been home between journeys. Perhaps they had already been restraining their curiosity, and they left, fearful that their glances, like a field of nesting birds, might be startled and caught. Poverty hurt, and that was their first reason for leaving. But another, final reason for leaving the crowded house was the never-said.

She may have been unusually beloved, the precious only daughter, spoiled and mirror gazing because of the affection the family lavished on her. When her husband left, they welcomed the chance to take her back from the in-laws; she could live like the little daughter for just a while longer. There are stories that my grandfather was different from other people, "crazy ever since the little Jap bayoneted him in the head." He used to put his naked penis on the dinner table, laughing. And one day he brought home a baby girl, wrapped up inside his brown western-style greatcoat.[5] He had traded one of his sons, probably my father, the youngest, for her. My grandmother made him trade back. When he finally got a daughter of his own, he doted on her. They must have all loved her, except perhaps my father, the only brother who never went back to China, having once been traded for a girl.

Brothers and sisters, newly men and women, had to efface their sexual color and present plain miens. Disturbing hair and eyes, a smile like no other, threatened the ideal of five generations living under one roof. To focus blurs, people shouted face to face and yelled from room to room. The immigrants I know have loud voices, unmodulated to American tones even after years away from the village where they called their friendships out across the fields. I have not been able to stop my mother's screams in public libraries or over telephones. Walking erect (knees straight, toes pointed forward, not pigeon-toed, which is Chinese-feminine) and speaking in an inaudible voice, I have tried to turn myself American-feminine. Chinese communication was loud, public. Only sick people had to whisper. But at the dinner table, where the family members came nearest one another, no one could talk, not the outcasts nor any eaters. Every word that falls from the mouth is a coin lost. Silently they gave and accepted food with both hands. A preoccupied child who took his bowl with one hand got a sideways glare. A complete moment of total attention is due everyone alike. Children and lovers have no singularity here, but my aunt used a secret voice, a separate attentiveness.

She kept the man's name to herself throughout her labor and dying; she did not accuse him that he be punished with her. To save her inseminator's name she gave silent birth.

He may have been somebody in her own household, but intercourse with a man outside the family would have been no less abhorrent. All the village were kinsmen, and the titles shouted in loud country voices never let kinship be forgotten. Any man within visiting distance would have been neutralized

5. A heavy overcoat.

as a lover—"brother," "younger brother," "older brother"—one hundred and fifteen relationship titles. Parents researched birth charts probably not so much to assure good fortune as to circumvent incest in a population that has but one hundred surnames. Everybody has eight million relatives. How useless then sexual mannerisms, how dangerous.

As if it came from an atavism[6] deeper than fear, I used to add "brother" silently to boys' names. It hexed the boys, who would or would not ask me to dance, and made them less scary and as familiar and deserving of benevolence as girls.

But, of course, I hexed myself also—no dates. I should have stood up, both arms waving, and shouted out across libraries, "Hey, you! Love me back." I had no idea, though, how to make attraction selective, how to control its direction and magnitude. If I made myself American-pretty so that the five or six Chinese boys in the class fell in love with me, everyone else—the Caucasian, Negro, and Japanese boys—would too. Sisterliness, dignified and honorable, made much more sense.

Attraction eludes control so stubbornly that whole societies designed to organize relationships among people cannot keep order, not even when they bind people to one another from childhood and raise them together. Among the very poor and the wealthy, brothers married their adopted sisters, like doves. Our family allowed some romance, paying adult brides' prices and providing dowries so that their sons and daughters could marry strangers. Marriage promises to turn strangers into friendly relatives—a nation of siblings.

In the village structure, spirits shimmered among the live creatures, balanced and held in equilibrium by time and land. But one human being flaring up into violence could open up a black hole; a maelstrom[7] that pulled in the sky. The frightened villagers, who depended on one another to maintain the real, went to my aunt to show her a personal, physical representation of the break she had made in the "roundness." Misallying couples snapped off the future, which was to be embodied in true offspring. The villagers punished her for acting as if she could have a private life, secret and apart from them.

If my aunt had betrayed the family at a time of large grain yields and peace, when many boys were born, and wings were being built on many houses, perhaps she might have escaped such severe punishment. But the men— hungry, greedy, tired of planting in dry soil—had been forced to leave the village in order to send food-money home. There were ghost plagues, bandit plagues, wars with the Japanese, floods. My Chinese brother and sister had died of an unknown sickness. Adultery, perhaps only a mistake during good times, became a crime when the village needed food.

The round moon cakes and round doorways, the round tables of graduated size that fit one roundness inside another, round windows and rice bowls—these talismans had lost their power to warn this family of the law: a family must be whole, faithfully keeping the descent line by having sons to feed the old and the dead, who in turn look after the family. The villagers came to show my aunt and her lover in hiding a broken house. The villagers were speeding up the circling of events because she was too shortsighted to

6. A trait with origins further back than the preceding generation; a throwback.
7. A powerful, violent whirlpool.

see that her infidelity had already harmed the village, that waves of consequences would return unpredictably, sometimes in disguise, as now, to hurt
her. This roundness had to be made coin-sized so that she would see its circumference: punish her at the birth of her baby. Awaken her to the inexorable.
People who refused fatalism because they could invent small resources
insisted on culpability. Deny accidents and wrest fault from the stars.

After the villagers left, their lanterns now scattering in various directions
toward home, the family broke their silence and cursed her. "Aiaa, we're
going to die. Death is coming. Death is coming. Look what you've done.
You've killed us. Ghost! Dead ghost! Ghost! You've never been born." She
ran out into the fields, far enough from the house so that she could no longer hear their voices, and pressed herself against the earth, her own land no
more. When she felt the birth coming, she thought that she had been hurt.
Her body seized together. "They've hurt me too much," she thought. "This
is gall, and it will kill me." With forehead and knees against the earth, her
body convulsed and then relaxed. She turned on her back, lay on the
ground. The black well of sky and stars went out and out and out forever;
her body and her complexity seemed to disappear. She was one of the stars,
a bright dot in blackness, without home, without a companion, in eternal
cold and silence. An agoraphobia[8] rose in her, speeding higher and higher,
bigger and bigger; she would not be able to contain it; there would be no
end to fear.

Flayed, unprotected against space, she felt pain return, focusing her
body. This pain chilled her—a cold, steady kind of surface pain. Inside,
spasmodically, the other pain, the pain of the child, heated her. For hours
she lay on the ground, alternately body and space. Sometimes a vision of
normal comfort obliterated reality: she saw the family in the evening gambling at the dinner table, the young people massaging their elder's backs.
She saw them congratulating one another, high joy on the mornings the
rice shoots came up. When these pictures burst, the stars drew yet further
apart. Black space opened.

She got to her feet to fight better and remembered that old-fashioned
women gave birth in their pigsties to fool the jealous, pain-dealing gods, who
do not snatch piglets. Before the next spasms could stop her, she ran to the
pigsty, each step a rushing out into emptiness. She climbed over the fence
and knelt in the dirt. It was good to have a fence enclosing her, a tribal person
alone.

Laboring, this woman who had carried her child as a foreign growth that
sickened her every day, expelled it at last. She reached down to touch the
hot, wet, moving mass, surely smaller than anything human, and could feel
that it was human after all—fingers, toes, nails, nose. She pulled it up on to
her belly, and it lay curled there, but in the air, feet precisely tucked one
under the other. She opened her loose shirt and buttoned the child inside.
After resting, it squirmed and thrashed and she pushed it up to her breast.
It turned its head this way and that until it found her nipple. There, it made
little snuffling noises. She clenched her teeth at its preciousness, lovely as a
young calf, a piglet, a little dog.

---

8. An abnormal fear of open space.

She may have gone to the pigsty as a last act of responsibility: she would protect this child as she had protected its father. It would look after her soul, leaving supplies on her grave. But how would this tiny child without family find her grave when there would be no marker for her anywhere, neither in the earth nor the family hall? No one would give her a family hall name. She had taken the child with her into the wastes. At its birth the two of them had felt the same raw pain of separation, a wound that only the family pressing tight could close. A child with no descent line would not soften her life but only trail after her, ghostlike, begging her to give it purpose. At dawn the villagers on their way to the fields would stand around the fence and look.

Full of milk, the little ghost slept. When it awoke, she hardened her breasts against the milk that crying loosens. Toward morning she picked up the baby and walked to the well.

Carrying the baby to the well shows loving. Otherwise abandon it. Turn its face into the mud. Mothers who love their children take them along. It was probably a girl; there is some hope of forgiveness for boys.

"Don't tell anyone you had an aunt. Your father does not want to hear her name. She has never been born." I have believed that sex was unspeakable and words so strong and fathers so frail that "aunt" would do my father mysterious harm. I have thought that my family, having settled among immigrants who had also been their neighbors in the ancestral land, needed to clean their name, and a wrong word would incite the kinspeople even here. But there is more to this silence: they want me to participate in her punishment. And I have.

In the twenty years since I heard this story I have not asked for details nor said my aunt's name; I do not know it. People who can comfort the dead can also chase after them to hurt them further—a reverse ancestor worship. The real punishment was not the raid swiftly inflicted by the villagers, but the family's deliberately forgetting her. Her betrayal so maddened them, they saw to it that she would suffer forever, even after death. Always hungry, always needing, she would have to beg food from other ghosts, snatch and steal it from those whose living descendants give them gifts. She would have to fight the ghosts massed at crossroads for the buns a few thoughtful citizens leave to decoy her away from village and home so that the ancestral spirits could feast unharassed. At peace, they could act like gods, not ghosts, their descent lines providing them with paper suits and dresses, spirit money, paper houses, paper automobiles, chicken, meat, and rice[9] into eternity—essences delivered up in smoke and flames, steam and incense rising from each rice bowl. In an attempt to make the Chinese care for people outside the family, Chairman Mao[1] encourages us now to give our paper replicas to the spirits of outstanding soldiers and workers, no matter whose ancestors they may be. My aunt remains forever hungry. Goods are not distributed evenly among the dead.

My aunt haunts me—her ghost drawn to me because now, after fifty years of neglect, I alone devote pages of paper to her, though not origamied

9. Traditionally, offerings left at the graves of ancestors.
1. Mao Zedong (1893–1976), head of the Chinese Communist Party and leader of China from 1949 to 1976.

into houses and clothes. I do not think she always means me well. I am telling on her, and she was a spite suicide, drowning herself in the drinking water. The Chinese are always very frightened of the drowned one, whose weeping ghost, wet hair hanging and skin bloated, waits silently by the water to pull down a substitute.

1976

BILLY COLLINS
b. 1941

The voice in a Billy Collins poem is so intimate and immediate that we feel we are in the same room with the poet. Collins imagines poet and reader sitting together at a breakfast table: "I will lean forward, / elbows on the table, / with something to tell you / and you will look up, as always, / your spoon dripping with milk, ready to listen" ("A Portrait of the Reader with a Bowl of Cereal"). The colloquial voice in his poems charms us with its air of spontaneous expression, its modesty, its humor. If some of his poems coast on charm alone, Collins's best work takes us on a surprising ride: its strange and unexpected associations deepen the familiar into the mysterious or make the mysterious familiar.

Describing the structures of his poetry, Collins says, "We are attempting, all the time, to create a logical, rational path through the day. To the left and right there are an amazing set of distractions that we can't afford to follow. But the poet is willing to stop anywhere." His poems often proceed as accounts of a day and its distractions, as in "Tuesday, June 4, 1991." At the same time the formal shapeliness of Collins's work endows ordinary activity with a strange and pleasing formality and turns it, line by measured line and stanza by stanza, into a ritual including both the pleasures and the pathos of life. These poems present a humorous self-awareness about the speaker's dramatizing and obsessive love of distraction—anything, no matter how insignificant, can carry off his attention—and one thing that is so welcome about Collins's poems is that they are funny. Only on later readings do we realize that they are also sad. When he looks over the edges of domestic life there is blankness; unlike the work of a Jorie Graham or a Charles Wright, a Collins poem evokes no metaphysical structures that might sustain this fragile world. Yet (in the Irish poet William Butler Yeats's phrase) Collins loves "what vanishes"—the day in June, the good meal, even one's memories. This knowledge of how things large and small disappear is a great equalizer. The humor in Collins's poetry puts this equalizing principle to work; he deflates the grandiose and subjects large statements of truth to the test of the particular. Collins's titles, imaginative and playful, suggest the way he alights on small, usually trivial instances in which life's strangeness and mystery flash out: "Weighing the Dog," "I Chop Some Parsley While Listening to Art Blakey's Version of 'Three Blind Mice.'" Other titles signal the way he grounds the improbable within the everyday: "Taking Off Emily Dickinson's Clothes," "Shoveling Snow with Buddha."

Collins's collections of poems include *Questions about Angels* (1977), *The Art of Drowning* (1995), *Picnic, Lightning* (1998), *Sailing Alone Around the World: New and Selected Poems* (2001), *Nine Horses* (2003), *The Trouble with Poetry and*

Other Poems (2005), Ballistics (2008), Horoscopes for the Dead (2011), and Aimless Love: New and Selected Poems (2013). He served as poet laureate of the United States from 2001 to 2003. Born in New York City (in a hospital where, as he likes to note, William Carlos Williams worked as a pediatric resident), Collins teaches at Lehman College of the City University. Walking the city streets animates him and inflects some of his poems in a way that recalls the work of Frank O'Hara, with whom Collins shares an idiomatic American voice, colloquial and understated, shaped by jazz and the blues. Collins's work often plays with the melody of a pentameter line as a jazz musician plays on and off the melody of a song; the pentameter is an undertone from which a more idiosyncratic rhythm moves around and away. While the rhythms of Collins's poetry often enforce a slowing-down, a tender lingering over everyday life, their breezy tone and quick humor seem to suggest that nothing too serious is going on. It is as if Collins were fending off the large, prophetic claims made by visionary poets (early in his career he earned a Ph.D. at the University of California at Riverside, specializing in the Romantic period), even as some of his poems are riffs on the Romantic tradition. Such Collins poems as "Keats's Handwriting" and "Lines Composed Over Three Thousand Miles from Tintern Abbey" deflate the romantic sublime and substitute for it a vision self-deprecating and humorous. Thus when we hear nightingales in a Collins poem, they're a group singing on the gospel radio station ("Sunday Morning with the Sensational Nightingales").

Collins's modest claims for poetry and the fact that his work is so appealing and accessible can lead us to underestimate the necessity and reward of rereading him. The best of his poems open up a moment like a series of nested boxes; if we read too quickly, we miss the pleasure and surprise of intricate connections and deepening discoveries. A Collins poem has a spontaneity that yields immediate pleasure, but only when we listen again more attentively do we recognize the art that makes itself look easy.

Forgetfulness

The name of the author is the first to go
followed obediently by the title, the plot,
the heartbreaking conclusion, the entire novel
which suddenly becomes one you have never read, never even heard of,

as if, one by one, the memories you used to harbor   5
decided to retire to the southern hemisphere of the brain,
to a little fishing village where there are no phones.

Long ago you kissed the names of the nine Muses goodbye,
and watched the quadratic equation pack its bag,
and even now as you memorize the order of the planets,   10

something else is slipping away, a state flower perhaps,
the address of an uncle, the capital of Paraguay.

Whatever it is you are struggling to remember
it is not poised on the tip of your tongue,
not even lurking in some obscure corner of your spleen.   15

It has floated away down a dark mythological river
whose name begins with an *L* as far as you can recall,[1]
well on your own way to oblivion where you will join those
who have even forgotten how to swim and how to ride a bicycle.

No wonder you rise in the middle of the night   20
to look up the date of a famous battle in a book on war.
No wonder the moon in the window seems to have drifted
out of a love poem that you used to know by heart.

                                                        1991

I Chop Some Parsley While Listening to Art Blakey's[1] Version of "Three Blind Mice"

And I start wondering how they came to be blind.
If it was congenital, they could be brothers and sisters,
and I think of the poor mother
brooding over her sightless young triplets.

Or was it a common accident, all three caught   5
in a searing explosion, a fireworks perhaps?
If not,
if each came to his or her blindness separately,

how did they ever manage to find one another?
Would it not be difficult for a blind mouse   10
to locate even one fellow mouse with vision
let alone two other blind ones?

And how, in their tiny darkness,
could they possibly have run after a farmer's wife
or anyone else's wife for that matter?   15
Not to mention why.

Just so she could cut off their tails
with a carving knife, is the cynic's answer,
but the thought of them without eyes
and now without tails to trail through the moist grass   20

or slip around the corner of a baseboard
has the cynic who always lounges within me
up off his couch and at the window
trying to hide the rising softness that he feels.

---

1. In Greek mythology, Lethe is the river of forgetfulness in Hades.

1. Jazz drummer and bandleader (1919–1990).

Art Blakey on the drums.

By now I am on to dicing an onion   25
which might account for the wet stinging
in my own eyes, though Freddie Hubbard's
mournful trumpet on "Blue Moon,"

which happens to be the next cut,[2]
cannot be said to be making matters any better.   30

1998

The Night House

Every day the body works in the fields of the world
mending a stone wall
or swinging a sickle through the tall grass—
the grass of civics, the grass of money—
and every night the body curls around itself   5
and listens for the soft bells of sleep.

---

2. The next song (or "cut" on a vinyl record) on *Three Blind Mice, Vol. 1,* a 1962 live recording by Art Blakey's Jazz Messengers, which included Freddie Hubbard (1938–2008).

But the heart is restless and rises
from the body in the middle of the night,
leaves the trapezoidal bedroom
with its thick, pictureless walls   10
to sit by herself at the kitchen table
and heat some milk in a pan.

And the mind gets up too, puts on a robe
and goes downstairs, lights a cigarette,
and opens a book on engineering.   15
Even the conscience awakens
and roams from room to room in the dark,
darting away from every mirror like a strange fish.

And the soul is up on the roof
in her nightdress, straddling the ridge,   20
singing a song about the wildness of the sea
until the first rip of pink appears in the sky.
Then, they all will return to the sleeping body
the way a flock of birds settles back into a tree,

resuming their daily colloquy,   25
talking to each other or themselves
even through the heat of the long afternoons.
Which is why the body—that house of voices—
sometimes puts down its metal tongs, its needle, or its pen
to stare into the distance,   30

to listen to all its names being called
before bending again to its labor.

1998

GLORIA ANZALDÚA
1942–2004

The term "Chicano" was originally pejorative, used on both sides of the border to identify Mexican Americans of the lowest social class. Just as the once demeaning label "black" was appropriated and revalued by African Americans during the civil rights, black power, and black arts movements of the 1960s, so "Chicano" was embraced by Hispanic activists as a badge of pride, especially among university students and farm workers. By 1987, when the first edition of Gloria Anzaldúa's *Borderlands / La Frontera: The New Mestiza* appeared, two more politically sensitive terms had been added to the sociocultural lexicon: "Chicana," specifically identifying Mexican American women, particularly in light of their announced aims and the general interests of the Chicano movement, and "mestiza," describing Chicana women who are especially concerned with a heritage that is both Chicana and Native American. Together with Cherríe Moraga, her coeditor on *This Bridge Called My Back: Writings by Radical Women of Color* (1981), Anzaldúa emerged as a pioneer in both the writing and the study of Chicana literature.

The daughter of ranchers in Jesus Maria of the Valley, Texas, Anzaldúa labored as a migrant fieldworker before earning a B.A. from Pan American University (1969) and an M.A. from the University of Texas at Austin (1973); she did further graduate study at the University of California at Santa Cruz. She taught creative writing, Chicano studies, and feminist studies at major universities from Texas to California. She published the novel *La Prieta* (Spanish for "the dark one," 1997), other anthologies, and a series of children's books, the most notable of which—*Prietita and the Ghost Woman / Prietita y La Llorona* (1996)—introduces young readers to an important figure in Chicana culture.

La Llorona is one of the three principal representations of women in Mexican culture: *La Virgen de Guadalupe*, a vision of the Virgin Mary who appeared to an Indian, Juan Diego, in 1531 on a hillside outside Mexico City that was sacred to the worship of Tonantzín, the Indian "Mother of Heaven"; *La Chingada*, incorrectly translated as "The Raped One" but whom Anzaldúa insists be accurately identified as "The Fucked One," the deposed Aztec princess (also known as La Malinche, Doña Marina, and Malintzín Tenepal) who served the Spanish military leader Hernan Cortés as translator and lover during his consolidation of colonial power between 1519 and 1522; and *La Llorona*, "The Woman Who Cries," a spurned mistress of Mexican legend who drowned her children and was fated to eternally seek their recovery. Each of these representations metaphorically controls a certain distinct realm of possibility for Chicanas. At the core of Anzaldúa's work is the belief that because metaphors structure the way we think, the metaphorical influences of these types of women must be reshaped so that Chicanas can escape the binary constraint of being judged as either a virgin or a whore (and nothing else). *Borderlands/La Frontera* is Anzaldúa's most comprehensive effort toward that restructuring.

Although written mainly in English, the essay printed here reflects another key part of Anzaldúa's art: not only did she wish to write in Spanish from time to time but she did not always translate that Spanish into English. When she did not provide such a translation in a piece primarily in English, she wanted to speak directly to those who either could not or chose not to communicate in English. This practice, much like her blending of fiction, poetry, social commentary, and personal memoir, helps create the narrative richness that characterizes her work.

The following text is from the second edition of *Borderlands/La Frontera* (1999).

How to Tame a Wild Tongue

"We're going to have to control your tongue," the dentist says, pulling out all the metal from my mouth. Silver bits plop and tinkle into the basin. My mouth is a motherlode.

The dentist is cleaning out my roots. I get a whiff of the stench when I gasp. "I can't cap that tooth yet, you're still draining," he says.

"We're going to have to do something about your tongue," I hear the anger rising in his voice. My tongue keeps pushing out the wads of cotton, pushing back the drills, the long thin needles. "I've never seen anything as strong or as stubborn," he says. And I think, how do you tame a wild tongue, train it to be quiet, how do you bridle and saddle it? How do you make it lie down?

> "Who is to say that robbing a people of
> its language is less violent than war?"
> —Ray Gwyn Smith[1]

I remember being caught speaking Spanish at recess—that was good for three licks on the knuckles with a sharp ruler. I remember being sent to the corner of the classroom for "talking back" to the Anglo teacher when all I was trying to do was tell her how to pronounce my name. "If you want to be American, speak 'American.' If you don't like it, go back to Mexico where you belong."

"I want you to speak English. *Pa'hallar buen trabajo tienes que saber hablar el inglés bien. Qué vale toda tu educación si todavía hablas inglés con un 'accent,'*" my mother would say, mortified that I spoke English like a Mexican. At Pan American University, I, and all Chicano students were required to take two speech classes. Their purpose: to get rid of our accents.

Attacks on one's form of expression with the intent to censor are a violation of the First Amendment. *El Anglo con cara de inocente nos arrancó la lengua.* Wild tongues can't be tamed, they can only be cut out.

Overcoming the Tradition of Silence

Ahogadas, escupimos el oscuro.
Peleando con nuestra propia sombra
el silencio nos sepulta.

En boca cerrada no entran moscas. "Flies don't enter a closed mouth" is a saying I kept hearing when I was a child. *Ser habladora* was to be a gossip and a liar, to talk too much. *Muchachitas bien criadas*, well-bred girls don't answer back. *Es una falta de respeto* to talk back to one's mother or father. I remember one of the sins I'd recite to the priest in the confession box the few times I went to confession: talking back to my mother, *hablar pa' 'trás, repelar. Hocicona, repelona, chismosa*, having a big mouth, questioning, carrying tales are all signs of being *mal criada*. In my culture they are all words that are derogatory if applied to women—I've never heard them applied to men.

The first time I heard two women, a Puerto Rican and a Cuban, say the word *"nosotras,"* I was shocked. I had not known the word existed. Chicanas use *nosotros* whether we're male or female. We are robbed of our female being by the masculine plural. Language is a male discourse.

> And our tongues have become
> dry   the wilderness has
> dried out our tongues   and
> we have forgotten speech.
> —Irena Klepfisz[2]

1. Ray Gwyn Smith [(b. 1944), Welsh painter and art educator active in the United States], *Moorland Is Cold Country*, unpublished book [Anzaldúa's note].
2. Irena Klepfisz [(b. 1941), North American critic], *"Di rayze aheym / The Journey Home,"* in *The Tribe of Dina: A Jewish Women's Anthology*, Melanie Kaye/Kantrowitz and Irena Klepfisz, eds. (Montpelier, VT: Sinister Wisdom Books, 1986), 49 [Anzaldúa's note].

Even our own people, other Spanish speakers *nos quieren poner candados en la boca.* They would hold us back with their bag of *reglas de academia.*

Oyé como ladra: el lenguaje de la frontera

Quien tiene boca se equivoca.
—Mexican saying

"*Pocho,*[3] cultural traitor, you're speaking the oppressor's language by speaking English, you're ruining the Spanish language," I have been accused by various Latinos and Latinas. Chicano Spanish is considered by the purist and by most Latinos deficient, a mutilation of Spanish.

But Chicano Spanish is a border tongue which developed naturally. Change, *evolución, enriquecimiento de palabras nuevas por invención o adopción* have created variants of Chicano Spanish, *un nuevo lenguaje. Un lenguaje que corresponde a un modo de vivir.* Chicano Spanish is not incorrect, it is a living language.

For a people who are neither Spanish nor live in a country in which Spanish is the first language; for a people who live in a country in which English is the reigning tongue but who are not Anglo; for a people who cannot entirely identify with either standard (formal, Castillian) Spanish nor standard English, what recourse is left to them but to create their own language? A language which they can connect their identity to, one capable of communicating the realities and values true to themselves—a language with terms that are neither *español ni inglés,* but both. We speak a patois, a forked tongue, a variation of two languages.

Chicano Spanish sprang out of the Chicanos' need to identify ourselves as a distinct people. We needed a language with which we could communicate with ourselves, a secret language. For some of us, language is a homeland closer than the Southwest—for many Chicanos today live in the Midwest and the East. And because we are a complex, heterogeneous people, we speak many languages. Some of the languages we speak are:

1. Standard English
2. Working class and slang English
3. Standard Spanish
4. Standard Mexican Spanish
5. North Mexican Spanish dialect
6. Chicano Spanish (Texas, New Mexico, Arizona and California have regional variations)
7. Tex-Mex
8. *Pachuco* (called *caló*)

My "home" tongues are the languages I speak with my sister and brothers, with my friends. They are the last five listed, with 6 and 7 being closest to my heart. From school, the media and job situations, I've picked up standard and working class English. From Mamagrande Locha and from reading Spanish and Mexican literature, I've picked up Standard Spanish and Standard Mexican Spanish. From *los recién llegados,* Mexican immigrants, and *braceros,* I

---

3. An anglicized Mexican or American of Mexican origin who speaks Spanish with an accent characteristic of North Americans and who distorts and reconstructs the language according to the influence of English. Anzaldúa offers a definition later in this selection.

learned the North Mexican dialect. With Mexicans I'll try to speak either Standard Mexican Spanish or the North Mexican dialect. From my parents and Chicanos living in the Valley,[4] I picked up Chicano Texas Spanish, and I speak it with my mom; younger brother (who married a Mexican and who rarely mixes Spanish with English), aunts and older relatives.

With Chicanas from *Nuevo México* or *Arizona* I will speak Chicano Spanish a little, but often they don't understand what I'm saying. With most California Chicanas I speak entirely in English (unless I forget). When I first moved to San Francisco, I'd rattle off something in Spanish, unintentionally embarrassing them. Often it is only with another Chicana *tejana* that I can talk freely.

Words distorted by English are known as anglicisms or *pochismos*. The *pocho* is an anglicized Mexican or American of Mexican origin who speaks Spanish with an accent characteristic of North Americans and who distorts and reconstructs the language according to the influence of English.[5] Tex-Mex, or Spanglish, comes most naturally to me. I may switch back and forth from English to Spanish in the same sentence or in the same word. With my sister and my brother Nune and with Chicano *tejano* contemporaries I speak in Tex-Mex.

From kids and people my own age I picked up *Pachuco*. *Pachuco* (the language of the zoot suiters) is a language of rebellion, both against Standard Spanish and Standard English. It is a secret language. Adults of the culture and outsiders cannot understand it. It is made up of slang words from both English and Spanish. *Ruca* means girl or woman, *vato* means guy or dude, *chale* means no, *simón* means yes, *churo* is sure, talk is *periquiar*, *pigionear* means petting, *que gacho* means how nerdy, *ponte águila* means watch out, death is called *la pelona*. Through lack of practice and not having others who can speak it, I've lost most of the *Pachuco* tongue.

Chicano Spanish

Chicanos, after 250 years of Spanish/Anglo colonization have developed significant differences in the Spanish we speak. We collapse two adjacent vowels into a single syllable and sometimes shift the stress in certain words such as *maíz / maiz, cohete / cuete*. We leave out certain consonants when they appear between vowels: *lado/lao, mojado/mojao*. Chicanos from South Texas pronounced *f* as *j* as in *jue* (*fue*). Chicanos use "archaisms," words that are no longer in the Spanish language, words that have been evolved out. We say *semos, truje, haiga, ansina,* and *naiden*. We retain the "archaic" *j*, as in *jalar*, that derives from an earlier *h*, (the French *halar* or the Germanic *halon* which was lost to standard Spanish in the 16th century), but which is still found in several regional dialects such as the one spoken in South Texas. (Due to geography, Chicanos from the Valley of South Texas were cut off linguistically from other Spanish speakers. We tend to use words that the Spaniards brought over from Medieval Spain. The majority of the Spanish

4. I.e., of the Rio Grande in southern Texas, bordering Mexico.
5. R. C. Ortega, *Dialectología Del Barrio*, trans. Hortencia S. Alwan (Los Angeles, CA: R. C. Ortega Publisher & Bookseller, 1977), 132 [Anzaldúa's note].

colonizers in Mexico and the Southwest came from Extremadura—Hernán Cortés was one of them—and Andalucía.[6] Andalucians pronounce *ll* like a *y*, and their *d*'s tend to be absorbed by adjacent vowels: *tirado* becomes *tirao*. They brought *el lenguaje popular, dialectos y regionalismos*.)[7]

Chicanos and other Spanish speakers also shift *ll* to *y* and *z* to *s*.[8] We leave out initial syllables, saying *tar* for *estar*, *toy* for *estoy*; *hora* for *ahora* (*cubanos* and *puertorriqueños* also leave out initial letters of some words.) We also leave out the final syllable such as *pa* for *para*. The intervocalic *y*, the *ll* as in *tortilla, ella, botella*, gets replaced by *tortia* or *tortiya, ea, botea*. We add an additional syllable at the beginning of certain words: *atocar* for *tocar, agastar* for *gastar*. Sometimes we'll say *lavaste las vacijas*, other times *lavates* (substituting the *ates* verb endings for the *aste*).

We use anglicisms, words borrowed from English: *bola* from ball, *carpeta* from carpet, *máchina de lavar* (instead of *lavadora*) from washing machine. Tex-Mex argot, created by adding a Spanish sound at the beginning or end of an English word such as *cookiar* for cook, *watchar* for watch, *parkiar* for park, and *rapiar* for rape, is the result of the pressures on Spanish speakers to adapt to English.

We don't use the word *vosotros/as* or its accompanying verb form. We don't say *claro* (to mean yes), *imagínate*, or *me emociona*, unless we picked up Spanish from Latinas, out of a book, or in a classroom. Other Spanish-speaking groups are going through the same, or similar, development in their Spanish.

Linguistic Terrorism

> *Deslenguadas. Somos los del español deficiente.* We are your linguistic nightmare, your linguistic aberration, your linguistic *mestizaje*, the subject of your *burla*. Because we speak with tongues of fire we are culturally crucified. Racially, culturally and linguistically *somos huérfanos*—we speak an orphan tongue.

Chicanas who grew up speaking Chicano Spanish have internalized the belief that we speak poor Spanish. It is illegitimate, a bastard language. And because we internalize how our language has been used against us by the dominant culture, we use our language differences against each other.

Chicana feminists often skirt around each other with suspicion and hesitation. For the longest time I couldn't figure it out. Then it dawned on me. To be close to another Chicana is like looking into the mirror. We are afraid of what we'll see there. *Pena*. Shame. Low estimation of self. In childhood we are told that our language is wrong. Repeated attacks on our native tongue diminish our sense of self. The attacks continue throughout our lives.

Chicanas feel uncomfortable talking in Spanish to Latinas, afraid of their censure. Their language was not outlawed in their countries. They had a whole lifetime of being immersed in their native tongue; generations,

---

6. Region in southern Spain. Extremadura is a city in central Spain. Cortés (1485–1547), Spanish soldier and explorer who conquered the Aztecs and claimed Mexico for Spain.
7. Eduardo Hernández-Chávez, Andrew D. Cohen, and Anthony F. Beltramo, *El Lenguaje de los Chicanos: Regional and Social Characteristics of Language Used by Mexican Americans* (Arlington, VA: Center for Applied Linguistics, 1975), 39 [Anzaldúa's note].
8. Hernández-Chávez, xvii [Anzaldúa's note].

centuries in which Spanish was a first language, taught in school, heard on radio and TV, and read in the newspaper.

If a person, Chicana or Latina, has a low estimation of my native tongue, she also has a low estimation of me. Often with *mexicanas y latinas* we'll speak English as a neutral language. Even among Chicanas we tend to speak English at parties or conferences. Yet, at the same time, we're afraid the other will think we're *agringadas* because we don't speak Chicano Spanish. We oppress each other trying to out-Chicano each other, vying to be the "real" Chicanas, to speak like Chicanos. There is no one Chicano language just as there is no one Chicano experience. A monolingual Chicana whose first language is English or Spanish is just as much a Chicana as one who speaks several variants of Spanish. A Chicana from Michigan or Chicago or Detroit is just as much a Chicana as one from the Southwest. Chicano Spanish is as diverse linguistically as it is regionally.

By the end of this century, Spanish speakers will comprise the biggest minority group in the U.S., a country where students in high schools and colleges are encouraged to take French classes because French is considered more "cultured." But for a language to remain alive it must be used.[9] By the end of this century English, and not Spanish, will be the mother tongue of most Chicanos and Latinos.

So, if you want to really hurt me, talk badly about my language. Ethnic identity is twin skin to linguistic identity—I am my language. Until I can take pride in my language, I cannot take pride in myself. Until I can accept as legitimate Chicano Texas Spanish, Tex-Mex and all the other languages I speak, I cannot accept the legitimacy of myself. Until I am free to write bilingually and to switch codes without having always to translate, while I still have to speak English or Spanish when I would rather speak Spanglish, and as long as I have to accommodate the English speakers rather than having them accommodate me, my tongue will be illegitimate.

I will no longer be made to feel ashamed of existing. I will have my voice: Indian, Spanish, white. I will have my serpent's tongue—my woman's voice, my sexual voice, my poet's voice. I will overcome the tradition of silence.

> My fingers
> move sly against your palm
> Like women everywhere, we speak in code. . . .
> —Melanie Kaye/Kantrowitz[1]

"Vistas," corridos, y comida: My Native Tongue

In the 1960s, I read my first Chicano novel. It was *City of Night* by John Rechy[2] a gay Texan, son of a Scottish father and a Mexican mother. For days I walked around in stunned amazement that a Chicano could write

---

9. Irena Klepfisz, "Secular Jewish Identity: Yidishkayt in America," in *The Tribe of Dina*, Kaye/Kantrowitz, eds., 43 [Anzaldúa's note].
1. Melanie Kaye/Kantrowitz, "Sign," in *We Speak in Code: Poems and Other Writings* (Pitts-burgh, PA: Motheroot Publications, Inc., 1980), 85 [Anzaldúa's note].
2. American novelist (b. 1931). The book was published in 1963.

and could get published. When I read *I Am Joaquín*[3] I was surprised to see a bilingual book by a Chicano in print. When I saw poetry written in Tex-Mex for the first time, a feeling of pure joy flashed through me. I felt like we really existed as a people. In 1971, when I started teaching High School English to Chicano students, I tried to supplement the required texts with works by Chicanos, only to be reprimanded and forbidden to do so by the principal. He claimed that I was supposed to teach "American" and English literature. At the risk of being fired, I swore my students to secrecy and slipped in Chicano short stories, poems, a play. In graduate school, while working toward a Ph.D., I had to "argue" with one advisor after the other, semester after semester, before I was allowed to make Chicano literature an area of focus.

Even before I read books by Chicanos or Mexicans, it was the Mexican movies I saw at the drive-in—the Thursday night special of $1.00 a carload—that gave me a sense of belonging. *"Vámonos a las vistas,"* my mother would call out and we'd all—grandmother, brothers, sister and cousins—squeeze into the car. We'd wolf down cheese and bologna white bread sandwiches while watching Pedro Infante in melodramatic tear-jerkers like *Nosotros los pobres*,[4] the first "real" Mexican movie (that was not an imitation of European movies). I remember seeing *Cuando los hijos se van*[5] and surmising that all Mexican movies played up the love a mother has for her children and what ungrateful sons and daughters suffer when they are not devoted to their mothers. I remember the singing-type "westerns" of Jorge Negrete and Miguel Aceves Mejía.[6] When watching Mexican movies, I felt a sense of homecoming as well as alienation. People who were to amount to something didn't go to Mexican movies, or *bailes* or tune their radios to *bolero, rancherita*, and *corrido* music.

The whole time I was growing up, there was *norteño* music sometimes called North Mexican border music, or Tex-Mex music, or Chicano music, or *cantina* (bar) music. I grew up listening to *conjuntos*, three- or four-piece bands made up of folk musicians playing guitar, *bajo sexto*,[7] drums and button accordion, which Chicanos had borrowed from the German immigrants who had come to Central Texas and Mexico to farm and build breweries. In the Rio Grande Valley, Steve Jordan and Little Joe Hernández were popular, and Flaco Jiménez[8] was the accordion king. The rhythms of Tex-Mex music are those of the polka, also adapted from the Germans, who in turn had borrowed the polka from the Czechs and Bohemians.

I remember the hot, sultry evenings when *corridos*—songs of love and death on the Texas-Mexican borderlands—reverberated out of cheap amplifiers from the local *cantinas* and wafted in through my bedroom window.

Corridos first became widely used along the South Texas / Mexican border during the early conflict between Chicanos and Anglos. The *corridos*

---

3. Rodolfo Gonzales [(1928–2005), Chicano novelist], *I Am Joaquín Yo Soy Joaquín* (New York, NY: Bantam Books, 1972). It was first published in 1967 [Anzaldúa's note].
4. A 1947 film. Infante (1917–1957), Mexican film actor and singer.
5. A 1941 film.

6. Mexican singer and film actor (1916–2006). Negrete (1911–1953), Mexican singing actor.
7. Twelve-string guitar tuned one octave lower than normal.
8. Mexican American musicians. Esteban Jordán (1939–2010). José María De Leon Hérnandez (b. 1940), Leonardo "Flaco" Jiménez (b. 1939).

are usually about Mexican heroes who do valiant deeds against the Anglo oppressors. Pancho Villa's song, *"La cucaracha,"* is the most famous one. *Corridos* of John F. Kennedy[9] and his death are still very popular in the Valley. Older Chicanos remember Lydia Mendoza,[1] one of the great border *corrido* singers who was called *la Gloria de Tejas*. Her *"El tango negre,"* sung during the Great Depression, made her a singer of the people. The everpresent *corridos* narrated one hundred years of border history, bringing news of events as well as entertaining. These folk musicians and folk songs are our chief cultural mythmakers, and they made our hard lives seem bearable.

I grew up feeling ambivalent about our music. Country-western and rock-and-roll had more status. In the 50s and 60s, for the slightly educated and *agringado* Chicanos, there existed a sense of shame at being caught listening to our music. Yet I couldn't stop my feet from thumping to the music, could not stop humming the words, nor hide from myself the exhilaration I felt when I heard it.

There are more subtle ways that we internalize identification, especially in the forms of images and emotions. For me food and certain smells are tied to my identity, to my homeland. Woodsmoke curling up to an immense blue sky; woodsmoke perfuming my grandmother's clothes, her skin. The stench of cow manure and the yellow patches on the ground; the crack of a .22 rifle and the reek of cordite. Homemade white cheese sizzling in a pan, melting inside a folded *tortilla*. My sister Hilda's hot, spicy *menudo*[2] *chile colorado* making it deep red, pieces of *panza* and hominy floating on top. My brother Carito barbecuing *fajitas* in the backyard. Even now and 3,000 miles away, I can see my mother spicing the ground beef, pork and venison with *chile*. My mouth salivates at the thought of the hot steaming *tamales* I would be eating if I were home.

> *Si le preguntas a mi mamá, "¿Qué eres?"*

> "Identity is the essential core of who
> we are as individuals, the conscious
> experience of the self inside."
> —Kaufman[3]

Nosotros los Chicanos straddle the borderlands. On one side of us, we are constantly exposed to the Spanish of the Mexicans, on the other side we hear the Anglos' incessant clamoring so that we forget our language. Among ourselves we don't say *nosotros los americanos, o nosotros los españoles, o nosotros los hispanos*. We say *nosotros los mexicanos* (by *mexicanos* we do not mean citizens of Mexico; we do not mean a national identity, but a racial one). We distinguish between *mexicanos del otro lado* and *mexicanos de este*

9. Thirty-fifth U.S. president (1917–1963), assassinated in Dallas, Texas. Villa (ca. 1877–1923), born Doroteo Arango, Mexican revolutionary leader.
1. Mexican American singer, songwriter, and musician (1916–2007).
2. Mexican soup made of simmered tripe, onion,

garlic, chili, and hominy.
3. Gershen Kaufman [(b. 1943), American psychologist], *Shame: The Power of Caring* (Cambridge: Schenkman Books, Inc. 1980), 68. This book was instrumental in my understanding of shame [from Anzaldúa's note].

lado. Deep in our hearts we believe that being Mexican has nothing to do with which country one lives in. Being Mexican is a state of soul—not one of mind, not one of citizenship. Neither eagle nor serpent,[4] but both. And like the ocean, neither animal respects borders.

> *Dime con quien andas y te diré quien eres.*
> (Tell me who your friends are and I'll tell you who
> you are.)
> —Mexican saying

Si le preguntas a mi mamá, "¿Qué eres?" te dirá, "Soy mexicana." My brothers and sister say the same. I sometimes will answer *"soy mexicana"* and at others will say *"soy Chicana" o "soy tejana."* But I identified as *"Raza"* before I ever identified as *"mexicana"* or "Chicana."

As a culture, we call ourselves Spanish when referring to ourselves as a linguistic group and when copping out. It is then that we forget our predominant Indian genes. We are 70 to 80 percent Indian.[5] We call ourselves Hispanic[6] or Spanish-American or Latin American or Latin when linking ourselves to other Spanish-speaking peoples of the Western hemisphere and when copping out. We call ourselves Mexican-American[7] to signify we are neither Mexican nor American, but more the noun "American" than the adjective "Mexican" (and when copping out).

Chicanos and other people of color suffer economically for not acculturating. This voluntary (yet forced) alienation makes for psychological conflict, a kind of dual identity—we don't identify with the Anglo-American cultural values and we don't totally identify with the Mexican cultural values. We are a synergy of two cultures with various degrees of Mexicanness or Angloness. I have so internalized the borderland conflict that sometimes I feel like one cancels out the other and we are zero, nothing, no one. *A veces no soy nada ni nadie. Pero hasta cuando no lo soy, lo soy.*

When not copping out, when we know we are more than nothing, we call ourselves Mexican, referring to race and ancestry; *mestizo* when affirming both our Indian and Spanish (but we hardly ever own our Black ancestry); Chicano when referring to a politically aware people born and/or raised in the U.S.; *Raza* when referring to Chicanos; *tejanos* when we are Chicanos from Texas.

Chicanos did not know we were a people until 1965 when Cesar Chavez[8] and the farmworkers united and *I Am Joaquín* was published and *la Raza Unida* party[9] was formed in Texas. With that recognition, we became a distinct people. Something momentous happened to the Chicano soul—we became aware of our reality and acquired a name and a language (Chicano Spanish) that reflected that reality. Now that we had a name, some of the fragmented pieces began to fall together—who we were, what we were, how

---

4. Respectively, male and female cultural figurations.
5. John R. Chávez [(b. 1949), American scholar and educator], *The Lost Land: The Chicano Images of the Southwest* (Albuquerque, NM: University of New Mexico Press, 1984), 88–90 [from Anzaldúa's note].
6. "Hispanic" is derived from Hispanis (*España*, a name given to the Iberian Peninsula in

ancient times when it was a part of the Roman Empire) and is a term designated by the U.S. government to make it easier to handle us on paper [Anzaldúa's note].
7. The Treaty of Guadalupe Hidalgo created the Mexican-American in 1848 [Anzaldúa's note].
8. Chicano union organizer (1927–1993).
9. Known in America as the United Farm Workers; founded in 1962.

we had evolved. We began to get glimpses of what we might eventually become.

Yet the struggle of identities continues, the struggle of borders is our reality still. One day the inner struggle will cease and a true integration take place. In the meantime, *tenemos que hacerla lucha. ¿Quién está protegiendo los ranchos de mi gente? ¿Quién está tratando de cerrar la fisura entre la india y el bianco en nuestra sangre? El Chicano, sí, el Chicano que anda como un ladrón en su propia casa.*[1]

Los Chicanos, how patient we seem, how very patient. There is the quiet of the Indian about us. We know how to survive. When other races have given up their tongue, we've kept ours. We know what it is to live under the hammer blow of the dominant *norteamericano* culture. But more than we count the blows, we count the days the weeks the years the centuries the eons until the white laws and commerce and customs will rot in the deserts they've created, lie bleached. *Humildes* yet proud, *quietos* yet wild, *nosotros los mexicanos* Chicanos will walk by the crumbling ashes as we go about our business. Stubborn, persevering, impenetrable as stone, yet possessing a malleability that renders us unbreakable, we, the *mestizas* and *mestizos*, will remain.

1987

1. Anglos, in order to alleviate their guilt for dispossessing the Chicano, stressed the Spanish part of us and perpetrated the myth of the Spanish Southwest. We have accepted the fiction that we are Hispanic, that is Spanish, in order to accommodate ourselves to the dominant culture and its abhorrence of Indians. Chávez, 88–91 [Anzaldúa's note].

ALICE WALKER
b. 1944

Of the two daughters at odds over family heirlooms in the story "Everyday Use" (included here), Alice Walker resembles each one. Like the burned Maggie, she spent a childhood even more limited than her family's rural poverty dictated, for as a little girl she was shot in the eye with a BB gun; the disfigurement plagued her until it was corrected during her college years. Like Dee, she was able to attend college—first Spelman College and then Sarah Lawrence College on a scholarship—and acquire urban sophistication from the North. Many of Walker's characters become adept in the new cultural language of the Black Arts and black power movements to which the author contributed as a young writer—and all of them are subjected to the same dismay Dee's mother feels at having to rule against this daughter's wishes. Like the mother, therefore, Walker is given to seeing both sides of a situation; and when it comes to choosing between her characters' opposing positions, she tends to be critical of her own personality first and extremely sparing in her judgment of others.

From her native Eatonton, Georgia, Walker gained an understanding of the rural South. In her essay "Beyond the Peacock," Walker evaluates both the older white writer Flannery O'Connor, who lived in nearby Milledgeville, and the perspectives from which readers see the region and its heritage. Visitors to O'Connor's home, for example, often romanticize the house's handmade bricks; Walker points out that the slaves who made those bricks surely suffered in the process. As the educated child of sharecroppers, Walker can critically reexamine the myths in and around O'Connor's life while doing justice to the complexity of O'Connor's work.

After college Walker returned to the South, first to work in the civil rights movement against segregation and then to teach at Jackson State College in Mississippi. Her first novel, *The Third Life of Grange Copeland* (1970), follows its protagonist through three generations of domestic experience. In *Meridian* (1976), Walker presents fragmentary recollections of the 1960s among characters trying to make sense of their recent past. This novel reflects many of the topics treated in the author's short-story collection, *In Love & Trouble* (1973), in which a range of African American women almost always have unhappy relationships with men. Walker's third novel, *The Color Purple* (1982), makes her strongest narrative statement, formulated from what she calls a "womanist" (as opposed to strictly feminist) perspective. This approach draws on the black folk expression "womanish," which in a mother-to-daughter context signifies a call to adult, mature, responsible (and courageous) behavior. Such behavior benefits women and men and is necessary, Walker argues, for the survival of all African Americans by keeping creativity alive. The plot and the style of *The Color Purple* show how this happens, as the young black woman Celie draws on her sister's letters (written from Africa) for her own letters to God. Though Celie's life by any other terms could be considered disastrous (including rape, incest, and the killing of her babies by her father, and both physical and psychological abuse by her husband), her actions and her ability to express herself give her status as an individual. To everyone who will listen, Celie says: "I am here."

Walker has continued to publish novels, short stories, poetry, and essays. In *The Same River Twice* (1996) she writes about how the filming of *The Color Purple* challenged and changed her life. As a sociocultural critic she has examined the atrocity of female genital mutilation in parts of Africa, also incorporating her conclusions in her novel *Possessing the Secret of Joy* (1992), and as a literary critic she has spoken for a richer and more complete understanding of Zora Neale Hurston, whose employment of folk materials in narrative anticipates Walker's. Throughout her career she has spoken about the need for strength from African American women, and her writing seeks workable models for such strength.

The following text is from *In Love & Trouble* (1973).

Everyday Use

For Your Grandmama

I will wait for her in the yard that Maggie and I made so clean and wavy yesterday afternoon. A yard like this is more comfortable than most people know. It is not just a yard. It is like an extended living room. When the hard clay is swept clean as a floor and the fine sand around the edges lined with tiny, irregular grooves, anyone can come and sit and look up into the elm tree and wait for the breezes that never come inside the house.

Maggie will be nervous until after her sister goes: she will stand hopelessly in corners, homely and ashamed of the burn scars down her arms and legs, eyeing her sister with a mixture of envy and awe. She thinks her sister has held life always in the palm of one hand, that "no" is a word the world never learned to say to her.

You've no doubt seen those TV shows where the child who has "made it" is confronted, as a surprise, by her own mother and father, tottering in weakly from backstage. (A pleasant surprise, of course: What would they do if parent and child came on the show only to curse out and insult each other?) On TV mother and child embrace and smile into each other's faces. Sometimes the mother and father weep, the child wraps them in her arms and leans across the table to tell how she would not have made it without their help. I have seen these programs.

Sometimes I dream a dream in which Dee and I are suddenly brought together on a TV program of this sort. Out of a dark and soft-seated limousine I am ushered into a bright room filled with many people. There I meet a smiling, gray, sporty man like Johnny Carson who shakes my hand and tells me what a fine girl I have. Then we are on the stage and Dee is embracing me with tears in her eyes. She pins on my dress a large orchid, even though she has told me once that she thinks orchids are tacky flowers.

In real life I am a large, big-boned woman with rough, man-working hands. In the winter I wear flannel nightgowns to bed and overalls during the day. I can kill and clean a hog as mercilessly as a man. My fat keeps me hot in zero weather. I can work outside all day, breaking ice to get water for washing; I can eat pork liver cooked over the open fire minutes after it comes steaming from the hog. One winter I knocked a bull calf straight in the brain between the eyes with a sledge hammer and had the meat hung up to chill before nightfall. But of course all this does not show on television. I am the way my daughter would want me to be: a hundred pounds lighter, my skin like an uncooked barley pancake. My hair glistens in the hot bright lights. Johnny Carson has much to do to keep up with my quick and witty tongue.

But that is a mistake. I know even before I wake up. Who ever knew a Johnson with a quick tongue? Who can even imagine me looking a strange white man in the eye? It seems to me I have talked to them always with one foot raised in flight, with my head turned in whichever way is farthest from them. Dee, though. She would always look anyone in the eye. Hesitation was no part of her nature.

"How do I look, Mama?" Maggie says, showing just enough of her thin body enveloped in pink skirt and red blouse for me to know she's there, almost hidden by the door.

"Come out into the yard," I say.

Have you ever seen a lame animal, perhaps a dog run over by some careless person rich enough to own a car, sidle up to someone who is ignorant enough to be kind to them? That is the way my Maggie walks. She has been like this, chin on chest, eyes on ground, feet in shuffle, ever since the fire that burned the other house to the ground.

Dee is lighter than Maggie, with nicer hair and a fuller figure. She's a woman now, though sometimes I forget. How long ago was it that the other house burned? Ten, twelve years? Sometimes I can still hear the flames and feel Maggie's arms sticking to me, her hair smoking and her dress falling off her in little black papery flakes. Her eyes seemed stretched open, blazed open by the flames reflected in them. And Dee. I see her standing off under the sweet gum tree she used to dig gum out of; a look of concentration on her face as she watched the last dingy gray board of the house fall in toward the red-hot brick chimney. Why don't you do a dance around the ashes? I'd wanted to ask her. She had hated the house that much.

I used to think she hated Maggie, too. But that was before we raised the money, the church and me, to send her to Augusta to school. She used to read to us without pity; forcing words, lies, other folks' habits, whole lives upon us two, sitting trapped and ignorant underneath her voice. She washed us in a river of make-believe, burned us with a lot of knowledge we didn't necessarily need to know. Pressed us to her with the serious way she read, to shove us away at just the moment, like dimwits, we seemed about to understand.

Dee wanted nice things. A yellow organdy dress to wear to her graduation from high school; black pumps to match a green suit she'd made from an old suit somebody gave me. She was determined to stare down any disaster in her efforts. Her eyelids would not flicker for minutes at a time. Often I fought off the temptation to shake her. At sixteen she had a style of her own: and knew what style was.

I never had an education myself. After second grade the school was closed down. Don't ask me why: in 1927 colored asked fewer questions than they do now. Sometimes Maggie reads to me. She stumbles along good-naturedly but can't see well. She knows she is not bright. Like good looks and money, quickness passed her by. She will marry John Thomas (who has mossy teeth in an earnest face) and then I'll be free to sit here and I guess just sing church songs to myself. Although I never was a good singer. Never could carry a tune. I was always better at a man's job. I used to love to milk till I was hooked in the side in '49. Cows are soothing and slow and don't bother you, unless you try to milk them the wrong way.

I have deliberately turned my back on the house. It is three rooms, just like the one that burned, except the roof is tin; they don't make shingle roofs any more. There are no real windows, just some holes cut in the sides, like the portholes in a ship, but not round and not square, with rawhide holding the shutters up on the outside. This house is in a pasture, too, like the other one. No doubt when Dee sees it she will want to tear it down. She wrote me once that no matter where we "choose" to live, she will manage to come see us. But she will never bring her friends. Maggie and I thought about this and Maggie asked me, "Mama, when did Dee ever *have* any friends?"

She had a few. Furtive boys in pink shirts hanging about on washday after school. Nervous girls who never laughed. Impressed with her they worshiped the well-turned phrase, the cute shape, the scalding humor that erupted like bubbles in lye. She read to them.

When she was courting Jimmy T she didn't have much time to pay to us, but turned all her faultfinding power on him. He *flew* to marry a cheap city girl from a family of ignorant flashy people. She hardly had time to recompose herself.

When she comes I will meet—but there they are!

Maggie attempts to make a dash for the house, in her shuffling way, but I stay her with my hand. "Come back here," I say. And she stops and tries to dig a well in the sand with her toe.

It is hard to see them clearly through the strong sun. But even the first glimpse of leg out of the car tells me it is Dee. Her feet were always neat-looking, as if God himself had shaped them with a certain style. From the other side of the car comes a short, stocky man. Hair is all over his head a foot long and hanging from his chin like a kinky mule tail. I hear Maggie suck in her breath. "Uhnnnh," is what it sounds like. Like when you see the wriggling end of a snake just in front of your foot on the road. "Uhnnnh."

Dee next. A dress down to the ground, in this hot weather. A dress so loud it hurts my eyes. There are yellows and oranges enough to throw back the light of the sun. I feel my whole face warming from the heat waves it throws out. Earrings gold, too, and hanging down to her shoulders. Bracelets dangling and making noises when she moves her arm up to shake the folds of the dress out of her armpits. The dress is loose and flows, and as she walks closer, I like it. I hear Maggie go "Uhnnnh" again. It is her sister's hair. It stands straight up like the wool on a sheep. It is black as night and around the edges are two long pigtails that rope about like small lizards disappearing behind her ears.

"Wa-su-zo-Tean-o!" she says, coming on in that gliding way the dress makes her move. The short stocky fellow with the hair to his navel is all grinning and he follows up with "Asalamalakim, my mother and sister!" He moves to hug Maggie but she falls back, right up against the back of my chair. I feel her trembling there and when I look up I see the perspiration falling off her chin.

"Don't get up," says Dee. Since I am stout it takes something of a push. You can see me trying to move a second or two before I make it. She turns, showing white heels through her sandals, and goes back to the car. Out she peeks next with a Polaroid. She stoops down quickly and lines up picture after picture of me sitting there in front of the house with Maggie cowering behind me. She never takes a shot without making sure the house is included. When a cow comes nibbling around the edge of the yard she snaps it and me and Maggie *and* the house. Then she puts the Polaroid in the back seat of the car, and comes up and kisses me on the forehead.

Meanwhile Asalamalakim is going through motions with Maggie's hand. Maggie's hand is as limp as a fish, and probably as cold, despite the sweat, and she keeps trying to pull it back. It looks like Asalamalakim wants to shake hands but wants to do it fancy. Or maybe he don't know how people shake hands. Anyhow, he soon gives up on Maggie.

"Well," I say. "Dee."

"No, Mama," she says. "Not 'Dee,' Wangero Leewanika Kemanjo!"

"What happened to 'Dee'?" I wanted to know.

"She's dead," Wangero said. "I couldn't bear it any longer, being named after the people who oppress me."

"You know as well as me you was named after your aunt Dicie," I said. Dicie is my sister. She named Dee. We called her "Big Dee" after Dee was born.

"But who was *she* named after?" asked Wangero.

"I guess after Grandma Dee," I said.

"And who was she named after?" asked Wangero.

"Her mother," I said, and saw Wangero was getting tired. "That's about as far back as I can trace it," I said. Though, in fact, I probably could have carried it back beyond the Civil War through the branches.

"Well," said Asalamalakim, "there you are."

"Uhnnnh," I heard Maggie say.

"There I was not," I said, "before 'Dicie' cropped up in our family, so why should I try to trace it that far back?"

He just stood there grinning, looking down on me like somebody inspecting a Model A car.[1] Every once in a while he and Wangero sent eye signals over my head.

"How do you pronounce this name?" I asked.

"You don't have to call me by it if you don't want to," said Wangero.

"Why shouldn't I?" I asked. "If that's what you want us to call you, we'll call you."

"I know it might sound awkward at first," said Wangero.

"I'll get used to it," I said. "Ream it out again."

Well, soon we got the name out of the way. Asalamalakim had a name twice as long and three times as hard. After I tripped over it two or three times he told me to just call him Hakim-a-barber. I wanted to ask him was he a barber, but I didn't really think he was, so I didn't ask.

"You must belong to those beef-cattle peoples down the road," I said. They said "Asalamalakim" when they met you, too, but they didn't shake hands. Always too busy: feeding the cattle, fixing the fences, putting up salt-lick shelters, throwing down hay. When the white folks poisoned some of the herd the men stayed up all night with rifles in their hands. I walked a mile and a half just to see the sight.

Hakim-a-barber said, "I accept some of their doctrines, but farming and raising cattle is not my style." (They didn't tell me, and I didn't ask, whether Wangero (Dee) had really gone and married him.)

We sat down to eat and right away he said he didn't eat collards and pork was unclean. Wangero, though, went on through the chitlins and corn bread, the greens and everything else. She talked a blue streak over the sweet potatoes. Everything delighted her. Even the fact that we still used the benches her daddy made for the table when we couldn't afford to buy chairs.

"Oh, Mama!" she cried. Then turned to Hakim-a-barber. "I never knew how lovely these benches are. You can feel the rump prints," she said, running her hands underneath her and along the bench. Then she gave a sigh and her hand closed over Grandma Dee's butter dish. "That's it!" she said. "I knew there was something I wanted to ask you if I could have." She jumped up from the table and went over in the corner where the churn stood, the milk in it clabber by now. She looked at the churn and looked at it.

"This churn top is what I need," she said. "Didn't Uncle Buddy whittle it out of a tree you all used to have?"

"Yes," I said.

"Uh huh," she said happily. "And I want the dasher, too."

"Uncle Buddy whittle that, too?" asked the barber.

Dee (Wangero) looked up at me.

"Aunt Dee's first husband whittled the dash," said Maggie so low you almost couldn't hear her. "His name was Henry, but they called him Stash."

"Maggie's brain is like an elephant's," Wangero said, laughing. "I can use the churn top as a centerpiece for the alcove table," she said, sliding a plate over the churn, "and I'll think of something artistic to do with the dasher."

---

1. Popular model of Ford automobile introduced in 1928.

When she finished wrapping the dasher the handle stuck out. I took it for a moment in my hands. You didn't even have to look close to see where hands pushing the dasher up and down to make butter had left a kind of sink in the wood. In fact, there were a lot of small sinks; you could see where thumbs and fingers had sunk into the wood. It was beautiful light yellow wood, from a tree that grew in the yard where Big Dee and Stash had lived.

After dinner Dee (Wangero) went to the trunk at the foot of my bed and started rifling through it. Maggie hung back in the kitchen over the dishpan. Out came Wangero with two quilts. They had been pieced by Grandma Dee and then Big Dee and me had hung them on the quilt frames on the front porch and quilted them. One was in the Lone Star pattern. The other was Walk Around the Mountain. In both of them were scraps of dresses Grandma Dee had worn fifty and more years ago. Bits and pieces of Grandpa Jarrell's Paisley shirts. And one teeny faded blue piece, about the size of a penny matchbox, that was from Great Grandpa Ezra's uniform that he wore in the Civil War.

"Mama," Wangero said sweet as a bird. "Can I have these old quilts?"

I heard something fall in the kitchen, and a minute later the kitchen door slammed.

"Why don't you take one or two of the others?" I asked. "These old things was just done by me and Big Dee from some tops your grandma pieced before she died."

"No," said Wangero. "I don't want those. They are stitched around the borders by machine."

"That'll make them last better," I said.

"That's not the point," said Wangero. "These are all pieces of dresses Grandma used to wear. She did all this stitching by hand. Imagine!" She held the quilts securely in her arms, stroking them.

"Some of the pieces, like those lavender ones, come from old clothes her mother handed down to her," I said, moving up to touch the quilts. Dee (Wangero) moved back just enough so that I couldn't reach the quilts. They already belonged to her.

"Imagine!" she breathed again, clutching them closely to her bosom.

"The truth is," I said, "I promised to give them quilts to Maggie, for when she marries John Thomas."

She gasped like a bee had stung her.

"Maggie can't appreciate these quilts!" she said. "She'd probably be backward enough to put them to everyday use."

"I reckon she would," I said. "God knows I been saving 'em for long enough with nobody using 'em. I hope she will!" I didn't want to bring up how I had offered Dee (Wangero) a quilt when she went away to college. Then she had told me they were old-fashioned, out of style.

"But they're *priceless*!" she was saying now, furiously; for she has a temper. "Maggie would put them on the bed and in five years they'd be in rags. Less than that!"

"She can always make some more," I said. "Maggie knows how to quilt."

Dee (Wangero) looked at me with hatred. "You just will not understand. The point is these quilts, *these* quilts!"

"Well," I said, stumped. "What would *you* do with them?"

"Hang them," she said. As if that was the only thing you *could* do with quilts.

Maggie by now was standing in the door. I could almost hear the sound her feet made as they scraped over each other.

"She can have them, Mama," she said, like somebody used to never winning anything, or having anything reserved for her. "I can 'member Grandma Dee without the quilts."

I looked at her hard. She had filled her bottom lip with checkerberry snuff and it gave her face a kind of dopey, hangdog look. It was Grandma Dee and Big Dee who taught her how to quilt herself. She stood there with her scarred hands hidden in the folds of her skirt. She looked at her sister with something like fear but she wasn't mad at her. This was Maggie's portion. This was the way she knew God to work.

When I looked at her like that something hit me in the top of my head and ran down to the soles of my feet. Just like when I'm in church and the spirit of God touches me and I get happy and shout. I did something I never had done before: hugged Maggie to me, then dragged her on into the room, snatched the quilts out of Miss Wangero's hands and dumped them into Maggie's lap. Maggie just sat there on my bed with her mouth open.

"Take one or two of the others," I said to Dee.

But she turned without a word and went out to Hakim-a-barber.

"You just don't understand," she said, as Maggie and I came out to the car.

"What don't I understand?" I wanted to know.

"Your heritage," she said. And then she turned to Maggie, kissed her, and said, "You ought to try to make something of yourself, too, Maggie. It's really a new day for us. But from the way you and Mama still live you'd never know it."

She put on some sunglasses that hid everything above the tip of her nose and her chin.

Maggie smiled; maybe at the sunglasses. But a real smile, not scared. After we watched the car dust settle I asked Maggie to bring me a dip of snuff. And then the two of us sat there just enjoying, until it was time to go in the house and go to bed.

1973

YUSEF KOMUNYAKAA
b. 1947

The excavation of lost names is one of the driving impulses of Yusef Komunyakaa's work. His poems recover and reanimate figures from history such as the African American elevator operator, Thomas McKeller, who appears in a stunning portrait by John Singer Sargent ("Nude Study"). In researching the portrait, Komunyakaa learned that it had been "unearthed in Sargent's studio after his death" and that "McKeller's image had been cannibalized to depict [the ancient Greek and Roman god] Apollo and a bas-relief of [the ancient Greek poet and musician] Arion—other heads and lines grafted onto his classical physique." Komunyakaa's work continually questions and revises both the cultural contradictions projected onto the black body and the erasure of black presence from history and culture. Significantly, he adopted the lost surname of a Trinidadian grandfather who came to the United States as a child, "smuggled in like a sack of papaya / On a banana boat." As the poet recounts in "Mismatched Shoes," his grandfather's "true name" disappeared in the process of assimilation. After his death his grandson "slipped into his skin" and took back the name "Komunyakaa," in what the poet calls "an affirmation of my heritage and its ambiguity."

Komunyakaa was born in Bogalusa, Louisiana, seventy miles northeast of New Orleans. Bogalusa means "Magic City" (a phrase that became the title of his 1992 collection of poems), and a lush, semitropical landscape informs many of his poems. But as the oldest of six children, and as the son of a carpenter who could write only his name, Komunyakaa grew up in an impoverished neighborhood and experienced a racial inequity that coexisted with natural beauty. At a young age, he has said, he decided that "imagination could serve as a choice of weapons."

Because the military seemed to offer a way into a larger world, Komunyakaa enlisted in the army and was sent to Vietnam, where he served as a war correspondent and editor of the military newspaper, writing accounts of what he witnessed in combat. For his work he was awarded the Bronze Star. While in Vietnam he carried with him several anthologies of poetry, but only after his military service ended did he begin to write poems, studying at the University of Colorado and then at the University of California at Irvine, where his teachers included Charles Wright and C. K. Williams. In 1984, fourteen years after his tour of duty ended, Komunyakaa began to write poems about his war experience. From his father he had learned to build and renovate houses; as he works, he has said, he keeps a pad of paper close by. While renovating a house in New Orleans he began to write down images and lines about Vietnam and so began the first in what became a series of poems about his Vietnam experience. These were collected in *Dien Cai Dau* (1988), whose title (meaning "crazy") is a Vietnamese phrase used to describe American soldiers. In one of these poems, "Facing It," he sees his own "clouded reflection" in the "black granite" of the Vietnam War Memorial designed by Maya Lin, an image of which appears in the color insert of this anthology.

To write about his surreal wartime experiences Komunyakaa drew on the work of surrealists like the French poet and critic André Breton. Komunyakaa shares with these writers and artists an emphasis on the image as linked to the unconscious, and his poems often work through a series of short lines whose quick, associative images bypass logic. A surrealist impulse to distort the familiar and juxtapose beauty and violence appears in Komunyakaa's Vietnam poems and in the racial and erotic tensions of poems like "Jasmine" (from *The Pleasure Dome*, 2001). An emphasis on the dreamlike, irrational, and fantastic was already apparent in his first two books, *Copacetic* (1984) and *I Apologize for the Eyes in My Head* (1986), both of which also reflect the musical influences of his native Louisiana.

Growing up so close to New Orleans brought Komunyakaa in early contact with jazz and the blues. The title of his first book, *Copacetic*, is a term adapted by jazz musicians from the African American tap dancer Bill "Bojangles" Robinson; in jazz it refers to especially pleasing and mellow music. Like Langston Hughes, Komunyakaa explores throughout his work the power of music—blues, jazz, and poetry—to address and, in part, to heal the pain of living in a racially divided society. The rapid energy of poems like "Facing It" and "Slam, Dunk, & Hook" belong to what the poet calls a "felt and lived syncopation," a rhythm of shifting beats that bears the influence of musicians like Charlie Parker, John Coltrane, and Miles Davis. Komunyakaa also works in tighter formal structures, whose exactness and precision suggest the careful measuring and fitting of carpentry. The quatrains of *Talking Dirty to the Gods* (2000) and the three-line stanzas of *Taboo* (2004) provide what the poet calls "an illusion of control" over volatile and complicated social and psychic material. They reflect Komunyakaa's preferred poetic strategy of "insinuation and nuance." Although his work often looks unflinchingly at what otherwise is hidden or denied, the social, racial, or erotic context of a poem often emerges in details or images, rather than in direct description. *Warhorses* (2008) continues this poet's ongoing investigation of war and violence.

Komunyakaa coedited with J. A. Sascha Feinstein a two-volume collection, *The Jazz Poetry Anthology* (1991) and *Second Set* (1996), and has also been extensively involved in collaborations with jazz musicians and vocalists. His poetry has received numerous awards, among them both the Pulitzer Prize and the Kingsley Tuft Poetry Award for *Neon Vernacular: New and Selected Poems 1977–1989* (1994). He is a professor in the Council of Humanities and Creative Writing Program at Princeton University.

Facing It

My black face fades,
hiding inside the black granite.
I said I wouldn't
dammit: No tears.
I'm stone. I'm flesh.   5
My clouded reflection eyes me
like a bird of prey, the profile of night
slanted against morning. I turn
this way—the stone lets me go.
I turn that way—I'm inside   10
the Vietnam Veterans Memorial[1]
again, depending on the light
to make a difference.
I go down the 58,022 names,
half-expecting to find   15
my own in letters like smoke.
I touch the name Andrew Johnson;
I see the booby trap's white flash.
Names shimmer on a woman's blouse
but when she walks away   20
the names stay on the wall.
Brushstrokes flash, a red bird's
wings cutting across my stare.
The sky. A plane in the sky.
A white vet's image floats   25
closer to me, then his pale eyes
look through mine. I'm a window.
He's lost his right arm
inside the stone. In the black mirror
a woman's trying to erase names: 30
No, she's brushing a boy's hair.

1988

1. An image of the Vietnam War Memorial in Washington, D.C., designed by the architect Maya Lin and dedicated in 1982, appears in the color insert of this anthology.

My Father's Love Letters

On Fridays he'd open a can of Jax[1]
After coming home from the mill,
& ask me to write a letter to my mother
Who sent postcards of desert flowers
Taller than men. He would beg,   5
Promising to never beat her
Again. Somehow I was happy
She had gone, & sometimes wanted
To slip in a reminder, how Mary Lou
Williams' "Polka Dots & Moonbeams"[2]   10
Never made the swelling go down.
His carpenter's apron always bulged
With old nails, a claw hammer
Looped at his side & extension cords
Coiled around his feet.   15
Words rolled from under the pressure
Of my ballpoint: Love,
Baby, Honey, Please.
We sat in the quiet brutality
Of voltage meters & pipe threaders,   20
Lost between sentences . . .
The gleam of a five-pound wedge
On the concrete floor
Pulled a sunset
Through the doorway of his toolshed.   25
I wondered if she laughed
& held them over a gas burner.
My father could only sign
His name, but he'd look at blueprints
& say how many bricks   30
Formed each wall. This man,
Who stole roses & hyacinth
For his yard, would stand there
With eyes closed & fists balled,
Laboring over a simple word, almost   35
Redeemed by what he tried to say.

1992

---

1. A beer originally brewed in New Orleans, Louisiana.
2. The American jazz pianist Mary Lou Williams (1910–1981) performed with and composed for many of the great jazz artists of the 1940s and 1950s. The song "Polka Dots and Moonbeams" (1940) was composed by Jimmy Van Heusen (1913–1990) and Johnny Burke (1908–1964).

Slam, Dunk, & Hook

Fast breaks. Lay ups. With Mercury's
Insignia[1] on our sneakers,
We outmaneuvered to footwork
Of bad angels. Nothing but a hot
Swish of strings like silk   5
Ten feet out. In the roundhouse
Labyrinth our bodies
Created, we could almost
Last forever, poised in midair
Like storybook sea monsters.   10
A high note hung there
A long second. Off
The rim. We'd corkscrew
Up & dunk balls that exploded
The skullcap of hope & good   15
Intention. Lanky, all hands
& feet . . . sprung rhythm.[2]
We were metaphysical when girls
Cheered on the sidelines.
Tangled up in a falling,   20
Muscles were a bright motor
Double-flashing to the metal hoop
Nailed to our oak.
When Sonny Boy's mama died
He played nonstop all day, so hard   25
Our backboard splintered.
Glistening with sweat,
We rolled the ball off
Our fingertips. Trouble
Was there slapping a blackjack[3]   30
Against an open palm.
Dribble, drive to the inside,
& glide like a sparrow hawk.[4]
Lay ups. Fast breaks.
We had moves we didn't know   35
We had. Our bodies spun
On swivels of bone & faith,
Through a lyric slipknot
Of joy, & we knew we were
Beautiful & dangerous.   40

1992

---

1. Mercury, the messenger of the ancient Greek gods, is depicted wearing winged sandals.
2. "Sprung rhythm" is a term used by the English poet Gerard Manley Hopkins (1844–1889) to describe a poetic meter with a variable rather than fixed number of syllables in each poetic foot.
3. A small leather-covered bludgeon.
4. One of the best-known, handsomest, and smallest North American hawks.

When Dusk Weighs Daybreak

I want Catullus[1]
In every line, a barb
The sun plays for good
Luck. I need to know if iron

Tastes like laudanum[2]   5
Or a woman. I already sense
What sleeps in the same flesh,
Ariadne & her half brother[3]

Caught in the other's dream.
I want each question to fit me   10
Like a shiny hook, a lure
In the gullet. What it is

To look & know how much muscle
It takes to lift a green slab.
I need a Son House blues[4]   15
To wear out my tongue.

2000

1. Gaius Valerius Catullus (c. 86–c. 54 B.C.E.),
Roman poet who wittily expressed love and hate
in some of the finest lyric poetry of his time.
2. An opium-based painkiller.
3. In Greek mythology Ariadne was the daughter of Pasiphaë and the Cretan king, Minos. She
fell in love with the Athenian hero Theseus and
helped him escape the Labyrinth after he slew
her half-brother, the Minotaur, a beast half bull
and half man.
4. Eddie James House Jr. (1902–1988), better
known as "Son," American blues singer and guitarist regarded as an epitome of the Delta blues
tradition.

LESLIE MARMON SILKO
b. 1948

Born in Albuquerque, New Mexico, Leslie Marmon Silko was raised in Old
Laguna, a village fifty miles west of Albuquerque. The Spaniards had founded a
mission there early in the eighteenth century, but Old Laguna had been formed centuries earlier by cattle-keeping Pueblos who successfully repelled raids on them by
the Navajos and the Apaches. Writing of the unchanging character of Pueblo religious practices over the centuries, the historian Joe S. Sando notes that "the tradition of religious beliefs permeates every aspect of the people's life; it determines
man's relation with the natural world and with his fellow man. Its basic concern is
continuity of a harmonious relationship with the world in which man lives."

Silko's work addresses such matters. Her own heritage is complicated in that her
great-grandfather Robert Marmon was white, whereas her mother was a mixed-

blood Plains Indian who kept her daughter on the traditional cradle board during her first year of infancy. (Her ancestry also includes some Mexican blood.) Silko has made this heritage a source of strength. She writes: "I suppose at the core of my writing is the attempt to identify what it is to be a half-breed or mixed-blooded person; what it is to grow up neither white nor fully traditional Indian." At the same time she insists that "what I know is Laguna. This place I am from is everything I am as a writer and human being." An active child, Silko had a horse of her own by age eight, and by thirteen she owned a rifle, with which she took part in deer hunts. Commuting to Albuquerque, she attended Catholic schools, earned a B.A. at the University of New Mexico, then began law school under a special program for Native Americans, though she soon gave it up to become a writer and teacher.

Her first published story, "The Man to Send Rain Clouds" (1969), came out of a writing assignment in college. She had heard, in Laguna, of an old man who died in a sheep camp and was given a traditional native burial—a fact resented by the Catholic priest who was not called in. The story she wrote about this situation, published in the *New Mexico Quarterly*, put her on the road to success as a writer. In 1974 a selection of her poems was published in the volume *Laguna Woman*, and in 1977 her novel *Ceremony* brought her recognition as a leading voice among Native American writers. *Ceremony* shows the dark aspects of modern American Indian life, focusing on a World War II veteran who is in acute physical and emotional straits as the novel begins, but who manages to survive by reestablishing contact with his native roots. Silko has insisted that the book is not just or even mainly about characters: "This novel is essentially about the powers inherent in the process of storytelling. . . . The chanting or telling of ancient stories to effect certain cures or protect from illness and harm has always been a part of the Pueblo's curing ceremonies." So this story of a family represents an attempt "to search for a ceremony to deal with despair"—the despair that has led to the "suicide, the alcoholism, and the violence which occur in so many Indian communities today."

Thus a strong moral connection exists between Silko's purely aesthetic delight in the writing of a story and the therapeutic, functional uses she hopes the story will play in the Native American community. In *Ceremony*, the aptly titled 1981 collection *Storyteller* (which also contains poems and photographs), and her epic 1991 novel, *Almanac of the Dead*, Silko's prose is an expressive, active presence, sympathetically creating landscape as well as animals and human beings. Plants assume narrative status in her third novel, *Gardens in the Dunes* (1999), which looks back to late-nineteenth-century events to underscore a basic theme: that myth and history do not coincide.

The following text is from *Storyteller* (1981).

Lullaby

The sun had gone down but the snow in the wind gave off its own light. It came in thick tufts like new wool—washed before the weaver spins it. Ayah reached out for it like her own babies had, and she smiled when she remembered how she had laughed at them. She was an old woman now, and her life had become memories. She sat down with her back against the wide cottonwood tree, feeling the rough bark on her back bones; she faced east and listened to the wind and snow sing a high-pitched Yeibechei[1] song. Out of the wind she felt warmer, and she could watch the wide fluffy snow fill in her tracks, steadily, until the direction she had come from was gone. By the

---

1. Navajo dance.

light of the snow she could see the dark outline of the big arroyo[2] a few feet away. She was sitting on the edge of Cebolleta Creek, where in the spring-time the thin cows would graze on grass already chewed flat to the ground. In the wide deep creek bed where only a trickle of water flowed in the summer, the skinny cows would wander, looking for new grass along winding paths splashed with manure.

Ayah pulled the old Army blanket over her head like a shawl. Jimmie's blanket—the one he had sent to her. That was a long time ago and the green wool was faded, and it was unraveling on the edges. She did not want to think about Jimmie. So she thought about the weaving and the way her mother had done it. On the wall wooden loom set into the sand under a tamarack tree for shade. She could see it clearly. She had been only a little girl when her grandma gave her the wooden combs to pull the twigs and burrs from the raw, freshly washed wool. And while she combed the wool, her grandma sat beside her, spinning a silvery strand of yarn around the smooth cedar spindle. Her mother worked at the loom with yarns dyed bright yellow and red and gold. She watched them dye the yarn in boiling black pots full of bee-weed petals, juniper berries, and sage. The blankets her mother made were soft and woven so tight that rain rolled off them like birds' feathers. Ayah remembered sleeping warm on cold windy nights, wrapped in her mother's blankets on the hogan's[3] sandy floor.

The snow drifted now, with the northwest wind hurling it in gusts. It drifted up around her black overshoes—old ones with little metal buckles. She smiled at the snow which was trying to cover her little by little. She could remember when they had no black rubber overshoes; only the high buck-skin leggings that they wrapped over their elkhide moccasins. If the snow was dry or frozen, a person could walk all day and not get wet; and in the evenings the beams of the ceiling would hang with lengths of pale buckskin leggings, drying out slowly.

She felt peaceful remembering. She didn't feel cold any more. Jimmie's blanket seemed warmer than it had ever been. And she could remember the morning he was born. She could remember whispering to her mother, who was sleeping on the other side of the hogan, to tell her it was time now. She did not want to wake the others. The second time she called to her, her mother stood up and pulled on her shoes; she knew. They walked to the old stone hogan together, Ayah walking a step behind her mother. She waited alone, learning the rhythms of the pains while her mother went to call the old woman to help them. The morning was already warm even before dawn and Ayah smelled the bee flowers blooming and the young willow growing at the springs. She could remember that so clearly, but his birth merged into the births of the other children and to her it became all the same birth. They named him for the summer morning and in English they called him Jimmie.

It wasn't like Jimmie died. He just never came back, and one day a dark blue sedan with white writing on its doors pulled up in front of the boxcar shack where the rancher let the Indians live. A man in a khaki uniform trimmed in gold gave them a yellow piece of paper and told them that Jimmie was dead. He said the Army would try to get the body back and then

---

2. Gully carved by water.   3. Navajo dwelling usually made of logs and mud.

it would be shipped to them; but it wasn't likely because the helicopter had burned after it crashed. All of this was told to Chato because he could understand English. She stood inside the doorway holding the baby while Chato listened. Chato spoke English like a white man and he spoke Spanish too. He was taller than the white man and he stood straighter too. Chato didn't explain why; he just told the military man they could keep the body if they found it. The white man looked bewildered; he nodded his head and he left. Then Chato looked at her and shook his head, and then he told her, "Jimmie isn't coming home anymore," and when he spoke, he used the words to speak of the dead. She didn't cry then, but she hurt inside with anger. And she mourned him as the years passed, when a horse fell with Chato and broke his leg, and the white rancher told them he wouldn't pay Chato until he could work again. She mourned Jimmie because he would have worked for his father then; he would have saddled the big bay horse and ridden the fence lines each day, with wire cutters and heavy gloves, fixing the breaks in the barbed wire and putting the stray cattle back inside again.

She mourned him after the white doctors came to take Danny and Ella away. She was at the shack alone that day they came. It was back in the days before they hired Navajo women to go with them as interpreters. She recognized one of the doctors. She had seen him at the children's clinic at Cañoncito about a month ago. They were wearing khaki uniforms and they waved papers at her and a black ball-point pen, trying to make her understand their English words. She was frightened by the way they looked at the children, like the lizard watches the fly. Danny was swinging on the tire swing on the elm tree behind the rancher's house, and Ella was toddling around the front door, dragging the broomstick horse Chato made for her. Ayah could see they wanted her to sign the papers, and Chato had taught her to sign her name. It was something she was proud of. She only wanted them to go, and to take their eyes away from her children.

She took the pen from the man without looking at his face and she signed the papers in three different places he pointed to. She stared at the ground by their feet and waited for them to leave. But they stood there and began to point and gesture at the children. Danny stopped swinging. Ayah could see his fear. She moved suddenly and grabbed Ella into her arms; the child squirmed, trying to get back to her toys. Ayah ran with the baby toward Danny; she screamed for him to run and then she grabbed him around his chest and carried him too. She ran south into the foothills of juniper trees and black lava rock. Behind her she heard the doctors running, but they had been taken by surprise, and as the hills became steeper and the cholla cactus were thicker, they stopped. When she reached the top of the hill, she stopped to listen in case they were circling around her. But in a few minutes she heard a car engine start and they drove away. The children had been too surprised to cry while she ran with them. Danny was shaking and Ella's little fingers were gripping Ayah's blouse.

She stayed up in the hills for the rest of the day, sitting on a black lava boulder in the sunshine where she could see for miles all around her. The sky was light blue and cloudless, and it was warm for late April. The sun warmth relaxed her and took the fear and anger away. She lay back on the rock and watched the sky. It seemed to her that she could walk into the sky, stepping through clouds endlessly. Danny played with little pebbles and stones, pretending they were birds eggs and then little rabbits. Ella sat at her feet and dropped fistfuls of dirt into the breeze, watching the dust and particles of sand intently. Ayah watched a hawk soar high above them, dark wings gliding; hunting or only watching, she did not know. The hawk was patient and he circled all afternoon before he disappeared around the high volcanic peak the Mexicans called Guadalupe.

Late in the afternoon, Ayah looked down at the gray boxcar shack with the paint all peeled from the wood; the stove pipe on the roof was rusted and crooked. The fire she had built that morning in the oil drum stove had burned out. Ella was asleep in her lap now and Danny sat close to her, complaining that he was hungry; he asked when they would go to the house. "We will stay up here until your father comes," she told him, "because those white men were chasing us." The boy remembered then and he nodded at her silently.

If Jimmie had been there he could have read those papers and explained to her what they said. Ayah would have known then, never to sign them. The doctors came back the next day and they brought a BIA[4] policeman with them. They told Chato they had her signature and that was all they needed. Except for the kids. She listened to Chato sullenly; she hated him when he told her it was the old woman who died in the winter, spitting blood; it was her old grandma who had given the children this disease. "They don't spit blood," she said coldly. "The whites lie." She held Ella and Danny close to her, ready to run to the hills again. "I want a medicine man first," she said to Chato, not looking at him. He shook his head. "It's too late now. The policeman is with them. You signed the paper." His voice was gentle.

It was worse than if they had died: to lose the children and to know that somewhere, in a place called Colorado, in a place full of sick and dying strangers, her children were without her. There had been babies that died soon after they were born, and one that died before he could walk. She had carried them herself, up to the boulders and great pieces of the cliff that long ago crashed down from Long Mesa; she laid them in the crevices of sandstone and buried them in fine brown sand with round quartz pebbles that washed down the hills in the rain. She had endured it because they had been with her. But she could not bear this pain. She did not sleep for a long time after they took her children. She stayed on the hill where they had fled the first time, and she slept rolled up in the blanket Jimmie had sent her. She carried the pain in her belly and it was fed by everything she saw: the blue sky of their last day together and the dust and pebbles they played with; the swing in the elm tree and broomstick horse choked life from her. The pain filled her stomach and there was no room for food or for her lungs to fill with air. The air and the food would have been theirs.

She hated Chato, not because he let the policeman and doctors put the screaming children in the government car, but because he had taught her to sign her name. Because it was like the old ones always told her about learning their language or any of their ways: it endangered you. She slept alone on the hill until the middle of November when the first snows came. Then she made a bed for herself where the children had slept. She did not lie down beside Chato again until many years later, when he was sick and shivering and only her body could keep him warm. The illness came after

---

4. Bureau of Indian Affairs, an agency of the U.S. government charged with assisting the tribal authorities of reservations.

the white rancher told Chato he was too old to work for him anymore, and Chato and his old woman should be out of the shack by the next afternoon because the rancher had hired new people to work there. That had satisfied her. To see how the white man repaid Chato's years of loyalty and work. All of Chato's fine-sounding English talk didn't change things.

It snowed steadily and the luminous light from the snow gradually diminished into the darkness. Somewhere in Cebolleta a dog barked and other village dogs joined with it. Ayah looked in the direction she had come, from the bar where Chato was buying the wine. Sometimes he told her to go on ahead and wait; and then he never came. And when she finally went back looking for him, she would find him passed out at the bottom of the wooden steps to Azzie's Bar. All the wine would be gone and most of the money too, from the pale blue check that came to them once a month in a government envelope. It was then that she would look at his face and his hands, scarred by ropes and the barbed wire of all those years, and she would think, this man is a stranger; for forty years she had smiled at him and cooked his food, but he remained a stranger. She stood up again, with the snow almost to her knees, and she walked back to find Chato.

It was hard to walk in the deep snow and she felt the air burn in her lungs. She stopped a short distance from the bar to rest and readjust the blanket. But this time he wasn't waiting for her on the bottom step with his old Stetson hat pulled down and his shoulders hunched up in his long wool overcoat.

She was careful not to slip on the wooden steps. When she pushed the door open, warm air and cigarette smoke hit her face. She looked around slowly and deliberately, in every corner, in every dark place that the old man might find to sleep. The bar owner didn't like Indians in there, especially Navajos, but he let Chato come in because he could talk Spanish like he was one of them. The men at the bar stared at her, and the bartender saw that she left the door open wide. Snowflakes were flying inside like moths and melting into a puddle on the oiled wood floor. He motioned to her to close the door, but she did not see him. She held herself straight and walked across the room slowly, searching the room with every step. The snow in her hair melted and she could feel it on her forehead. At the far corner of the room, she saw red flames at the mica window of the old stove door; she looked behind the stove just to make sure. The bar got quiet except for the Spanish polka music playing on the jukebox. She stood by the stove and shook the snow from her blanket and held it near the stove to dry. The wet wool smell reminded her of new-born goats in early March, brought inside to warm near the fire. She felt calm.

In past years they would have told her to get out. But her hair was white now and her face was wrinkled. They looked at her like she was a spider crawling slowly across the room. They were afraid; she could feel the fear. She looked at their faces steadily. They reminded her of the first time the white people brought her children back to her that winter. Danny had been shy and hid behind the thin white woman who brought them. And the baby had not known her until Ayah took her into her arms, and then Ella had nuzzled close to her as she had when she was nursing. The blonde woman was nervous and kept looking at a dainty gold watch on her wrist. She sat on the bench near the small window and watched the dark snow clouds gather around the mountains; she was worrying about the unpaved road. She was frightened by what she saw inside too: the strips of venison drying on a rope across the ceiling and the children jabbering excitedly in a language she did not know. So they stayed for only a few hours. Ayah watched the government car disappear down the road and she knew they were already being weaned from these lava hills and from this sky. The last time they came was in early June, and Ella stared at her the way the men in the bar were now staring. Ayah did not try to pick her up; she smiled at her instead and spoke cheerfully to Danny. When he tried to answer her, he could not seem to remember and he spoke English words with the Navajo. But he gave her a scrap of paper that he had found somewhere and carried in his pocket; it was folded in half, and he shyly looked up at her and said it was a bird. She asked Chato if they were home for good this time. He spoke to the white woman and she shook her head. "How much longer?" he asked, and she said she didn't know; but Chato saw how she stared at the box-car shack. Ayah turned away then. She did not say good-bye.

She felt satisfied that the men in the bar feared her. Maybe it was her face and the way she held her mouth with teeth clenched tight, like there was nothing anyone could do to her now. She walked north down the road, searching for the old man. She did this because she had the blanket, and there would be no place for him except with her and the blanket in the old adobe barn near the arroyo. They always slept there when they came to Cebolleta. If the money and the wine were gone, she would be relieved because then they could go home again; back to the old hogan with a dirt roof and rock walls where she herself had been born. And the next day the old man could go back to the few sheep they still had, to follow along behind them, guiding them, into dry sandy arroyos where sparse grass grew. She knew he did not like walking behind old ewes when for so many years he rode big quarter horses and worked with cattle. But she wasn't sorry for him; he should have known all along what would happen.

There had not been enough rain for their garden in five years; and that was when Chato finally hitched a ride into the town and brought back brown boxes of rice and sugar and big tin cans of welfare peaches. After that, at the first of the month they went to Cebolleta to ask the postmaster for the check; and then Chato would go to the bar and cash it. They did this as they planted the garden every May, not because anything would survive the summer dust, but because it was time to do this. The journey passed the days that smelled silent and dry like the caves above the canyon with yellow painted buffaloes on their walls.

He was walking along the pavement when she found him. He did not stop or turn around when he heard her behind him. She walked beside him and she noticed how slowly he moved now. He smelled strongly of woodsmoke and urine. Lately he had been forgetting. Sometimes he called her by his sister's name and she had been gone for a long time. Once she had found him wandering on the road to the white man's ranch, and she asked him why he was going that way; he laughed at her and said, "You know they can't run that ranch without me," and he walked on determined, limping on the leg that had been crushed many years before. Now he looked at her curiously, as if for the first time, but he kept shuffling along, moving slowly along the side of the highway. His gray hair had grown long and spread out on the shoulders of the long overcoat. He wore the old felt hat pulled down over his ears. His boots were worn out at the toes and he had stuffed pieces of an old red shirt in the holes. The rags made his feet look like little animals up to their ears in snow. She laughed at his feet; the snow muffled the sound of her laugh. He stopped and looked at her again. The wind had quit blowing and the snow was falling straight down; the southeast sky was beginning to clear and Ayah could see a star.

"Let's rest awhile," she said to him. They walked away from the road and up the slope to the giant boulders that had tumbled down from the red sandrock mesa throughout the centuries of rainstorms and earth tremors. In a place where the boulders shut out the wind, they sat down with their backs against the rock. She offered half of the blanket to him and they sat wrapped together.

The storm passed swiftly. The clouds moved east. They were massive and full, crowding together across the sky. She watched them with the feeling of horses—steely blue-gray horses startled across the sky. The powerful haunches pushed into the distances and the tail hairs streamed white mist behind them. The sky cleared. Ayah saw that there was nothing between her and the stars. The light was crystalline. There was no shimmer, no distortion through earth haze. She breathed the clarity of the night sky; she smelled the purity of the half moon and the stars. He was lying on his side with his knees pulled up near his belly for warmth. His eyes were closed now, and in the light from the stars and the moon, he looked young again.

She could see it descend out of the night sky: an icy stillness from the edge of the thin moon. She recognized the freezing. It came gradually, sinking snowflake by snowflake until the crust was heavy and deep. It had the strength of the stars in Orion, and its journey was endless. Ayah knew that with the wine he would sleep. He would not feel it. She tucked the blanket around him, remembering how it was when Ella had been with her; and she felt the rush so big inside her heart for the babies. And she sang the only song she knew to sing for babies. She could not remember if she had ever sung it to her children, but she knew that her grandmother had sung it and her mother had sung it:

> The earth is your mother,
>   she holds you.
> The sky is your father,
>   he protects you.
> Sleep,
> sleep.
> Rainbow is your sister,
>   she loves you.
> The winds are your brothers,
>   they sing to you.
> Sleep,
> sleep.
> We are together always
> We are together always
> There never was a time
> when this
> was not so.

1981

ART SPIEGELMAN
b. 1948

Comic panels have existed since the end of the nineteeth century, beginning with Richard F. Outcault's *The Yellow Kid* in 1895. By the 1920s panels had evolved into strips—George Herriman's *Krazy Kat* was the most famous—and by the end of the 1930s these strips had grown into comic books, most successfully with the *Superman* series produced by Jerry Siegel and Joe Schuster. It would take the cultural transformations of the 1960s, however, for this trend of interweaving visual elements with an expanding sense of narrative to achieve literary form. As opposed to simple entertainment, literature involves, on a genuinely cultural level, both expression and reflection, comprising the beliefs and practices of a people. In the 1960s, as long-established beliefs and practices were challenged and to some extent changed, comic-book art found itself uniquely positioned as an underground form ready to disrupt a traditional, more conservative order.

How underground comics became graphic novels is apparent from Art Spiegelman's career. A college dropout, Spiegelman found his first work in the most elemental form of cartoon humor, the illustrations for cards and stickers packaged with bubblegum and marketed as Wacky Packages and Garbage Pail Kids, a basely satirical form of 1960s counterculture created in the New York design studios of Topps and other novelty companies. When in 1970 Spiegelman moved from New York to San Francisco, his work progressed from novelty to subversion—of the comic-strip form and of larger cultural themes. Cartoonist R. Crumb had recently developed *Zap Comix* as a way of replacing convention with creation, both in the way comics were drawn and in the subjects they treated. Spiegelman's affinity was with the second wave of this movement, including the Zippy comics drawn by Bill Griffin, in which sequential art pushed common limits to be boldly experimental. Here older practices were turned against themselves, with action breaking out of frames, narratives interrogating themselves, and characters challenging all standards of social acceptability.

Spiegelman's return to New York prompted the key development in his work and emergence as a graphic novelist. Married to the artist and designer Françoise Mouly in 1977 and beginning a family, Spiegelman paid new attention to his father's stories about the signal event in the elder Spiegelmans' lives, the Holocaust. As Polish Jews who had been persecuted and imprisoned at Auschwitz, where their first son died, the Spiegelmans had emigrated first to Sweden (where Art was born three years after the war's end) and then to the United States, settling in the Rego Park neighborhood of Queens, New York City, and becoming naturalized American citizens. His parents' cultural transformation was greater than any Spiegelman had experienced in the 1960s, and he sought the artistic tools to represent it. In 1978 Will Eisner had taken comic books to a new level of expression by arguing theological matters in *A Contract with God*—the type of work that could be sold in bookstores rather than just on newsstands. But by applying his cartoonist's serial-narrative skills to his father's experiences, Siegelman gave the graphic novel literary importance.

Maus I (1986) and *Maus II* (1991) are complex creations, enfolding not just the father's tale but also his act of telling it, both of which are measured by the son's reception. Their handling of the Holocaust, a subject of countless previous treatments and certain to endure as one of humanity's major stories, as a cartoon adds great imaginative dimension. Thanks to a suggestive set of references, with Jews as mice (victims of prey), Germans as cats (predators of mice), French as frogs (a reminder of the self-conscious vulgarity of older comic strips), and Poles as pigs (a dietary contrast with Jews, but also a calculated insult), graphic representation gives new facets to a familiar story. Cartooning by nature involves a great amount of artistic license. Parameters of taste are much more elastic than those for fiction, poetry, and all but the most performative of drama, while the form's roots in popular culture continue to show despite the bleachings of high taste.

Even in becoming a countercultural icon, Spiegelman has maintained a sense of humor about himself. No matter how serious his subject matter (including his 2004 treatment of the 9/11 attacks, *In the Shadow of No Towers*), the cartoonist is always the fall guy, enduring his father's occasional impatience and the terrors of life. In this sense Spiegelman's mature works echo the sentiments of his first publications, *The Complete Mr. Infinity* (1970) and *The Viper Vicar of Vice, Villany, and Vickedness* (1972), both expressive of the 1960s counterculture and older comic-book tradition that a new generation of readers would accept as illustrative of their own sensibilities.

The following text is from *Maus I and II* (1997).

From Maus

C H A P T E R   S I X

JANINA LIVES OVER THERE.

RICHIEU'S GOVERNESS ALWAYS OFFERED SHE WOULD HELP US.

WE CAME TO HER HOUSE NEAR TOWN...

OPEN UP, JANINA! QUICK!

W-WHO'S THERE?

MY GOD! IT'S THE SPIEGELMANS!

YOU'LL BRING TROUBLE! GO AWAY! *QUICKLY!*

SLAM

I'M FRIGHTENED, VLADEK.

MAYBE WE SHOULD TRY MY FATHER'S OLD HOUSE. THE JANITOR HAS KNOWN OUR FAMILY FOR YEARS.

LET'S TRY. WE'VE **GOT** TO GET OFF THE STREETS BEFORE DAWN!

I WAS A LITTLE SAFE. I HAD A COAT AND BOOTS, SO LIKE A GESTAPO WORE WHEN HE WAS NOT IN SERVICE. BUT ANJA—HER APPEARANCE—YOU COULD SEE MORE *EASY* SHE WAS JEWISH. I WAS AFRAID FOR HER.

WAKE UP, MR. LUKOWSKI. LET US IN. *PLEASE!!*

HUH? W-WHO IS IT?

ANJA! ANJA ZYLBERBERG!

WHAT ARE YOU DOING HERE, CHILD? IT ISN'T SAFE! WAIT— I'LL UNLOCK THE GATE.

I WALKED SLOW...

CLIK CLIK

BEHIND ME ALSO WALKED SLOW.

IF I WALKED FAST...

CLIK

BEHIND ME ALSO WALKED FAST.

WE WERE ALONE. HE SPOKE...

AMCHA?

IN HEBREW HE SAID TO ME, "OUR NATION?"

HAD I TO ANSWER HIM, OR NO?

A-AMCHA.

I THOUGHT YOU WERE A JEW.

... I'M JEWISH TOO! THERE ARE VERY FEW OF US LEFT...

MY WIFE AND I HAVE BEEN HIDING IN SOSNOWIEC FOR OVER A YEAR.

I'M WITH MY WIFE TOO. WE'RE HUNGRY AND WE NEED A PLACE TO HIDE!

GO TO THE BLACK MARKET ON DE-KERTA STREET, NUMBER 8.

SO I LEFT HIM AND WENT RIGHT AWAY TO DEKERTA 8. THERE IT WAS A BIG COURTYARD...

?

ALL AROUND I LOOKED, BUT IT WAS NOBODY.

PSSST!

!

WANNA BUY SOME FOOD WITHOUT COUPONS, MISTER?

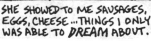

SHE SHOWED TO ME SAUSAGES, EGGS, CHEESE ...THINGS I ONLY WAS ABLE TO DREAM ABOUT.

I BOUGHT AND WENT QUICK BACK TO ANJA.

GOOD MORNING.

VLADEK! YOU WERE GONE SO LONG.

I HAD TO GET BREAKFAST!... WANT SOME SAUSAGES? ...OR EGGS?...OR WOULD YOU PREFER CHOCOLATE?

WHAT?

IT'S A *MIRACLE!* HOW DID YOU MANAGE IT?

I'M A MAGICIAN! HAVE SOME MILK.

I WENT AGAIN BACK TO DEKERTA. THERE I COULD CHANGE JEWELRY FOR MARKS—AND MARKS FOR FOOD, OR A PLACE TO STAY.

THIS TIME IT WAS MORE PEOPLE...THERE EVEN, I SAW SOME JEWISH BOYS I KNEW FROM BEFORE THE WAR.

VLADEK SPIEGELMAN?! I HARDLY RECOGNIZED YOU, SO YOU'RE STILL ALIVE, EH?

LEO? YES. I'M WITH ANJA.

WE NEED A HIDING PLACE.

HOW ABOUT MRS. KAWKA?

SHE HAS A SMALL FARM ON THE OUTSKIRTS OF TOWN...

SHE MIGHT TAKE YOU IN, IF YOU CAN PAY.

IT WAS NOT SO FAR TO GO TO KAWKA'S FARM...

ALRIGHT THEN, MR. SPIEGELMAN. YOU AND YOUR WIFE CAN STAY IN MY BARN.

WE'LL COME LATE TONIGHT.

BUT, REMEMBER—IF YOU'RE FOUND THERE, I DON'T KNOW YOU! ... YOU MUST SAY THAT THE BARN DOOR WAS OPEN AND YOU JUST SNEAKED IN.

DON'T WORRY...WE WON'T BETRAY YOU!

IT'S ALMOST DAWN—WHEN MRS. KAWKA COMES TO MILK HER COW, SHE'LL BRING YOU SOME COFFEE.

WHERE ARE YOU GOING?

TO DEKERTA.

DON'T LEAVE ME ALONE AGAIN. I'M TERRIFIED WHILE YOU'RE GONE.

AND SO WE CAME THERE TO LIVE WITH KAWKA'S COW.

DON'T WORRY, ANJA. I'LL BE SAFE. IF I DIDN'T GO OUT WE WOULDN'T HAVE FOOD...WE WOULDN'T HAVE THIS PLACE!..

AND WE'VE GOT TO FIND A WARMER PLACE FOR THE WINTER...AWAY FROM SOSNOWIEC IF POSSIBLE...

I—I'LL BE OKAY. COME BACK QUICK.

I TRAVELED OFTEN WITH THE STREETCAR TO TOWN.

IT WAS TWO CARS. ONE WAS ONLY GERMANS AND OFFICIALS. THE SECOND, IT WAS ONLY THE POLES.

ALWAYS I WENT STRAIGHT IN THE OFFICIAL CAR....

HEIL HITLER.

THE GERMANS PAID NO ATTENTION OF ME.... IN THE PO-LISH CAR THEY COULD SMELL IF A POLISH JEW CAME IN.

AT THE BLACK MARKET I SAW SEVERAL TIMES A NICE WOMAN, WHAT I MADE A LITTLE FRIENDS WITH HER...

GOOD MORNING, MR. SPIEGELMAN.

HOW DO YOU DO, MRS. MOTONOWA! WHAT DO YOU HAVE IN YOUR BASKET TODAY?

HOW ABOUT A LOAF OF FRESH BREAD?

FINE, FINE,

OH, I'M SORRY. I DON'T HAVE ANY CHANGE.

IT'S OKAY... KEEP IT FOR YOUR LITTLE BOY.

ARE YOU AND YOUR WIFE STILL LIVING IN A BARN?

WE HAVEN'T FOUND ANYTHING BETTER.

I'VE BEEN THINKING ABOUT IT... WHY DON'T YOU BOTH MOVE IN WITH MY SON AND ME?

WHAT ABOUT YOUR HUSBAND?

HE WORKS IN GERMANY, AND ONLY COMES HOME FOR 10 DAYS EVERY 3 MONTHS... I'LL KEEP YOU HIDDEN IN THE CELLAR WHEN HE'S AROUND.

IT SOUNDS GOOD TO ME, BUT IT'S OVER 20 KILOMETERS TO YOUR HOUSE IN SZOPIENICE. MY WIFE WILL BE AFRAID TO GO!

DON'T WORRY. I'LL ESCORT YOU!

THE NEXT EVENING SHE CAME WITH HER 7-YEARS-OLD BOY TO KAWKA'S FARMHOUSE...

I WALKED WITH MOTONOWA AS IF SHE WAS MY WIFE.

AND ANJA, LIKE A GOVERNESS, WENT WITH THE LITTLE BOY BEHIND. AND NOBODY EVEN LOOKED ON US.

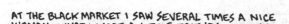

WE HAD HERE A LITTLE COMFORTABLE... WE HAD WHERE TO SIT.

REMEMBER, LITTLE ONE — NEVER TELL ANYBODY THERE ARE JEWS HERE. THEY'LL SHOOT US ALL!

YES, AUNT ANJA.

THE LITTLE BOY WAS VERY SMART AND HE LOVED VERY MUCH ANJA.

YOU HAD TO PAY MRS. MOTONOWA TO KEEP YOU, RIGHT?

OF COURSE I PAID... AND WELL I PAID.

...WHAT YOU THINK? SOMEONE WILL RISK THEIR LIFE FOR NOTHING?

...I PAID ALSO FOR THE FOOD WHAT SHE GAVE TO US FROM HER SMUGGLING BUSINESS.

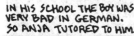

BUT, ONE TIME I MISSED A FEW COINS TO THE BREAD...

I'LL PAY YOU THE REST TOMORROW, AFTER I GO OUT AND CASH SOME VALUABLES.

SORRY... I WASN'T ABLE TO FIND ANY BREAD TODAY.

ALWAYS SHE GOT BREAD, SO I DIDN'T BELIEVE... BUT, STILL, SHE WAS A GOOD WOMAN.

IN HIS SCHOOL THE BOY WAS VERY BAD IN GERMAN. SO ANJA TUTORED TO HIM.

ICH BIN... DU BIST... ER IST...

SHE KNEW GERMAN LIKE AN EXPERT.

AND SOON HE CAME OUT WITH VERY GOOD GRADES.

MY TEACHER ASKED ME HOW I IMPROVED SO MUCH...

SO I TOLD HIM MY MOTHER WAS HELPING ME.

WHEW

HE WAS REALLY A CLEVER BOY.

BUT IT WAS A FEW THINGS HERE NOT SO GOOD... HER HOME WAS VERY SMALL AND IT WAS ON THE GROUND FLOOR ...

BE SURE TO KEEP AWAY FROM THE WINDOW — YOU MIGHT BE SEEN!

NOK NOK

ONE MINUTE!

(QUICK — GET IN THE CLOSET!)

IF SOMEBODY CAME, WE HAD FAST TO HIDE.

A LETTER FROM YOUR HUSBAND, MRS. MOTONOWA.

THANKS.

BUT I HAD SOMETHING ALLERGIC IN THE CLOSET.

AAH-

OR MAYBE IT WAS A COLD — I CAN'T REMEMBER ...

-CHMF

BUT ALWAYS I HAD TO SNEEZE.

STILL, EVERYTHING HERE WAS FINE, UNTIL ONE SATURDAY MOTONOWA RAN VERY EARLY BACK FROM HER BLACK MARKET WORK...

THIS IS TERRIBLE!

THE GESTAPO JUST SEARCHED ME — THEY TOOK MY GOODS!

THEY MAY COME SEARCH HERE ANY MINUTE! YOU'VE GOT TO LEAVE!

WHAT?

BUT WHERE CAN WE GO?

I DON'T KNOW. BUT YOU MUST GET OUT NOW!

OH MY GOD... THIS IS THE END!

ANJA STARTED TO CRY... BUT WE HAD NOT A CHOICE.

WE'LL WALK TOWARD SOS-NOWIEC—AT LEAST WE'LL KNOW OUR WAY AROUND.

ANJA WAS SO AFRAID SHE WAS SHAKING.

STAY CALM—WALK AS IF WE'RE JUST STROLLING... AND *SPEAK GERMAN.*

FOR HOURS WE WALKED.

B-BESUCHEN WIR DOCH FRAU KAWKA.

GUTE IDEE.

VLADEK·WE'RE BEING FOLLOWED.

RELAX

BUT IF WE TURNED A COR-NER, THEY ALSO TURNED.

ES IST KALT.

JA. JA.

OF COURSE I WAS RIGHT—THEY DIDN'T MEAN ANYTHING ON US.

WOOSH

THEY JUST WERE WALKING.

STAYING ON THE STREET ALL NIGHT IS TOO DANGEROUS... MAYBE WE CAN HIDE IN THAT CONSTRUCTION SITE.

GOOD—I'M EXHAUSTED.

HERE WAS A FOUNDATION MADE VERY DEEP DOWN IN THE GROUND..

BE CAREFUL!

I JUMPED FIRST IN, AND I PULLED OVER BRICKS FOR ANJA TO STEP DOWN.

AND HERE WE WAITED A COLD FEW HOURS FOR THE DAY.

IT STARTED TO BE LIGHT...

COME. WE WON'T BE NOTICED IF WE MIX WITH PEOPLE OUT ON THE STREET.

I'M SO TIRED AND COLD...

WE CAN REST NOW.

WE CAME FINALLY AGAIN TO THIS PLACE WITH THE COW AND WENT INSIDE.

LATER, KAWKA CAME IN...

W-WHO'S IN HERE?

THE SPIEGEL-MANS... WE HAD NOWHERE ELSE TO GO.

WELL... I GUESS YOU CAN STAY. BUT, REMEMBER: I DON'T KNOW YOU'RE HERE!

WHY, MRS. SPIEGELMAN, YOU'RE SHIVERING!

YOU CAN COME INTO MY HOUSE FOR AN HOUR OR SO, 'TIL YOU WARM UP.

SHE TOOK ANJA INSIDE AND BROUGHT TO ME SOME FOOD... IN THOSE DAYS I WAS SO STRONG I COULD SIT EVEN IN THE SNOW ALL NIGHT.

THINGS CAN'T BE THIS BAD EVERYWHERE! I'D GIVE ANYTHING TO GET OUT OF POLAND!

YOU KNOW, BEFORE I TOOK YOU IN, I HAD A YOUNG MAN AND HIS SON HERE...

TWO PEOPLE I KNOW SMUG-GLED THEM INTO HUNGARY. I HEARD HE AND HIS BOY WERE DOING WELL THERE.

HUNGARY! REALLY?! I'D LIKE TO MEET THOSE SMUGGLERS!

 SHE TOLD ME THESE TWO ACQUAINTANCES VISITED OFTEN TO HER ON THURSDAY EVENINGS.... TODAY WAS MAYBE A MONDAY...

 I DON'T GET IT... WASN'T HUNGARY AS DANGEROUS AS POLAND?

 NO. FOR A LONGER TIME IT WAS *BETTER* THERE IN HUNGARY FOR THE JEWS.... BUT THEN, NEAR THE VERY FINISH OF THE WAR, THEY ALL GOT PUT *ALSO* TO AUSCHWITZ.

 I WAS THERE, AND I SAW IT. THOUSANDS—HUNDREDS OF THOUSANDS OF JEWS FROM HUNGARY...

 SO MANY, IT WASN'T EVEN ROOM ENOUGH TO BURY THEM ALL IN THE OVENS.

 BUT AT THAT TIME, WHEN I WAS THERE WITH KAWKA, WE COULDN'T *KNOW* THEN.

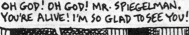 SO... I WENT NEXT DAY TO DEKERTA STREET TO BUY FOOD...

OH GOD! OH GOD! MR. SPIEGELMAN. YOU'RE ALIVE! I'M SO GLAD TO SEE YOU!

MRS. MOTONOWA!

I WANTED TO FIND A NEW CONNECTION TO HIDE US. BUT *REALLY* I DIDN'T THINK TO FIND AGAIN *HER*.

 PRAISE MARY, YOU'RE SAFE! I COULDN'T *SLEEP,* I FELT SO GUILTY ABOUT CHASING YOU AND YOUR WIFE OUT.

 THE GESTAPO NEVER EVEN CAME TO MY HOUSE. I JUST PANICKED FOR NOTHING. PLEASE COME BACK AGAIN.

 ANJA WAS GLAD OF GOING BACK. AND MOTONOWA ALSO—ALWAYS I PAID HER NICELY.

 AND THAT SAME NIGHT WE SAID GOODBYE TO KAWKA AND WENT AGAIN TO SZOPIENICE.

AFTER WE WERE BACK ONLY A SHORT TIME...

WELL, MY HUSBAND WRITES THAT HE'S COMING HOME FOR HIS 10-DAY VACATION.

IF HE KNEW YOU WERE HERE HE'D THROW US ALL OUT. BUT, DON'T WORRY... YOU'LL BE ALL RIGHT IN MY CELLAR.

...I SET UP A MATTRESS... I'LL COME DOWN WHENEVER I CAN.

SO EACH DAY AND NIGHT WE SAT IN SUCH A STORAGE LOCKER...

IN THE DAYS WE WERE AFRAID TO BREATHE— PEOPLE CAME DOWN OFTEN TO *THEIR* LOCKERS.

AT NIGHT WE COULD MOVE AROUND A LITTLE, BUT IT WAS SOMETHING ELSE DOWN THERE..

AIEEE!

WH-WHAT IS IT?

TH-THERE ARE **RATS** DOWN HERE!

SHH- CALM DOWN, STOP SCREAMING.

THOSE AREN'T RATS. THEY'RE VERY SMALL. ONE RAN OVER MY HAND BEFORE. THEY'RE JUST **MICE!**

OF COURSE, IT **WAS** REALLY RATS. BUT I WANTED ANJA TO FEEL MORE EASY.

BUT, THEN, MOTONOWA STOPPED TO COME DOWN.

IT'S BEEN 3 DAYS SINCE SHE BROUGHT ANY FOOD.

HERE... HAVE ANOTHER CANDY...

I HAD STILL CANDIES I ORGANIZED ON DEKERTA. ONLY *THIS* WE HAD TO EAT.

ALSO, HERE WE HAD NO PLACE WHERE TO WASH, SO ANJA GOT ON ALL HER SKIN A TERRIBLE RASH.

I DON'T KNOW WHAT'S WORSE— THE HUNGER OR THE ITCHING.

DON'T SCRATCH! IT ONLY— SHH!

CLIK

THE DOOR.

I'M SORRY I COULDN'T GET DOWN BEFORE—MY HUSBAND IS GETTING SUSPICIOUS.

HE ASKED WHY I GO TO THE CELLAR SO OFTEN. HE EVEN ASKED IF I WAS HIDING JEWS HERE! ...HE WAS JOKING, BUT STILL...

ARE YOU ALL RIGHT HERE?

THERE ARE *RATS*, GIANT RATS! THEY'RE HORRIBLE!

WELL—YOU'RE BETTER OFF WITH THE RATS THAN WITH THE GESTAPO... AT LEAST THE RATS WON'T *KILL* YOU!

MMM...

AND SHE WAS RIGHT. WE WERE HAPPY EVEN TO HAVE *THESE* CONDITIONS.

AFTER THE TEN DAYS HER HUSBAND LEFT, AND SHE TOOK US BACK.

IT'S GOOD TO BE "HOME," EH, VLADEK!

IT'S A LOT NICER THAN THAT CELLAR.

BUT I DIDN'T FEEL SAFE HERE. IT WAS TOO MANY WAYS SOMEBODY COULD FIND US OUT. I WANTED TO GO BETTER TO HUNGARY.

SO, WHEN IT CAME THURSDAY, I WENT IN THE DIRECTION TO TAKE A STREETCAR TO SEE KAWKA IN SOSNOWIEC.

LOOK!

I HAD TO PASS WHERE SOME CHILDREN WERE PLAYING.

A JEW! A JEW!

THEY RAN SCREAMING HOME.

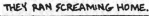

HELP! MOMMY! A JEW!!

A JEW!

QUICK, THE MOTHERS CAME OUTSIDE TO SEE WHAT WAS!

THE MOTHERS ALWAYS TOLD SO: "BE CAREFUL! A JEW WILL CATCH YOU TO A BAG AND EAT YOU!" ... SO THEY TAUGHT TO THEIR CHILDREN.

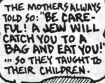

I APPROACHED OVER TO THEM...

HEIL HITLER.

IF I RAN AWAY THEY, WOULD SEE: "YES, IT *IS* A JEW HERE."

DON'T BE AFRAID, LITTLE ONES. I'M NOT A JEW. I WON'T HURT YOU.

SORRY, MISTER. YOU KNOW HOW KIDS ARE... HEIL HITLER.

SO I CAME OUT WELL FROM THIS...

BUT THE EXPERIENCE COST ME REALLY A LOT OF HAIRS.

1986

JOY HARJO
b. 1951

J oy Harjo was born in Tulsa, Oklahoma, to a mother of mixed Cherokee, French, and Irish blood. She has described her father's family, members of the Creek (also known as Muscogee) tribe, as "rebels and speakers," among them a Baptist minister (Harjo's paternal grandfather), two painters (her grandmother and aunt), and a great-great-grandfather who in 1832 led a Creek rebellion against their forced removal from Alabama into Oklahoma. As the critic Laura Coltelli has pointed out, the work of many contemporary Native American writers (a large number of whom are of mixed blood) enacts a quest to reenvision identity by confronting the historical, cultural, and political realities that shape lives experienced between different worlds. Drawing on a family tradition of powerful speaking, Harjo participates in a search to reimagine and repair painful fractures in contemporary experience: between past and present, between person and landscape, and between parts of the self. Thus traveling is a mythic activity in her poems, enacting this search for community and historical connectedness. As in the work of James Welch, Simon J. Ortiz, and Leslie Marmon Silko, the theme of traveling in Harjo's poems resonates with the historical displacements and migrations of native peoples (especially the forced removal of the Creeks). She has called herself the wanderer in her family, and her poems often map her journeys, whether on foot, by car, or in a plane. Perhaps Harjo thinks of herself as the family wanderer because she left Oklahoma to attend high school at the Institute of American Indian Arts in Santa Fe, New Mexico ("in a way it saved my life," she has said). Since receiving a B.A. from the University of New Mexico in 1976 and an MFA from the University of Iowa, she has taught at the Institute of American Indian Arts, Arizona State University, the University of Colorado, the University of Arizona, and the University of New Mexico.

Harjo's vision of the interrelatedness of all things is common to Native American storytelling. The ethic that emerges from this worldview stresses reciprocity between people and various sources of power, including tradition and the natural world. Harjo's poems bring together mythic, feminist, and cultural perspectives and also unite contemporary urban experience with Native American myth and legend. In her collection *She Had Some Horses* (1983) this integration seeks to assuage the loneliness and desperation of those on the margin who populate much of the volume: a woman raising her mixed-blood children alone, a friend who threatens suicide, a woman who threatens to drop from a thirteenth-story window. The collection *In Mad Love and War* (1990) exhibits anger at the separations caused by dispossession and violence, as in an elegy for Anna Mae Pictou Aquash, a young Micmac woman shot dead on the Pine Ridge Reservation. Poems such as this recall the passion for social justice in the works of James Wright, Audre Lorde, and Leslie Marmon Silko; indeed, the spirit of Harjo's rebel great-great-grandfather is never far from her work.

Harjo has been a leading figure in the adaptation of oral traditions into written forms, consciously using the written word in her poems in a way that duplicates certain oral and ceremonial techniques. Her poems extensively and emphatically use repetition, of both words and units of thought, as mnemonic and structuring devices. For example, her poem "When the World As We Knew It Ended," written in response to the events of September 11, 2001, begins a series of stanzas with the repetition and variation of "We saw it," "We heard it," "We knew it. . . ." Reflecting the understanding that Native American tradition is not fixed but evolves and changes, Harjo has fearlessly experimented, adapting new musical and poetic forms to Native American traditions. She has long drawn on reggae, rock, Creek Stomp Dance songs, country, and African music and has integrated performance and dance into her poetry. A musician and songwriter, she has released several CD collections, including *Letter from the End of the Twentieth Century* (1997), *Native Joy for Real* (2005), and a musical version of *She Had Some Horses* (2006). Harjo plays the saxophone, which is not a traditional Native American instrument, but, she has said, "Someday it may be."

Metamorphosis, common in Native American storytelling, is central to Harjo's vision, where the world is constituted by change and constancy. Her collection *The Woman Who Fell from the Sky* (1994) embodies metamorphosis in its structure—the retelling of contemporary experience through traditional myths—and metamorphosis recurs in its stories. Various Native American traditions tell the story of a sky woman who falls through the void of space and creates the human universe. In the title poem of this volume, a group of women ("angry at their inattentive husbands") run off with stars; one of these women dares to look back at Earth and falls from the sky. In Harjo's hands this myth becomes the story of two lovers who were children together at an Indian boarding school. Adrift in an urban landscape, they are reunited, their narrative characterized by fracture and repair. In the same collection, "Flood" renders a young girl's sexuality and imaginative power through the myth of the water monster. The prose poems that form much of this book remind us that Native American storytelling, an oral tradition, does not distinguish between poetry and prose. For all Harjo's anguished sense of the warring factions in our world and our selves, her works consistently engage in a process of healing and regeneration, themes that continue in her collection *A Map to the Next World* (2000). Like the kitchen table in her poem "Perhaps the World Ends Here," Harjo's poems are a space where "we sing with joy, with sorrow. We pray of suffering and remorse. We give thanks."

Harjo has also written screenplays and the text for Stephen Strom's photographs of the Southwestern landscape, *Secrets from the Center of the World* (1989), and she has edited an anthology of tribal women's writings from around the world. A collection of interviews, *The Spiral of Memory* (1996), edited by Laura Coltelli, is a valuable accompaniment to her poems. *How We Became Human* (2003) presents a selection from Harjo's earlier work, including poems from hard-to-find chapbooks, as well as newer work. In 2013 she published a memoir, *Crazy Brave*.

Call It Fear

There is this edge where shadows
and bones of some of us walk
                backwards.
Talk backwards. There is this edge
call it an ocean of fear of the dark. Or   5
name it with other songs. Under our ribs
our hearts are bloody stars. Shine on
shine on, and horses in their galloping flight
strike the curve of ribs.
                     Heartbeat   10
and breathe back sharply. Breathe
                     backwards.
There is this edge within me
           I saw it once
an August Sunday morning when the heat hadn't   15
left this earth. And Goodluck

sat sleeping next to me in the truck.
We had never broken through the edge of the
singing at four a.m.
                We had only wanted to talk, to hear   20
any other voice to stay alive with.
              And there was this edge—
not the drop of sandy rock cliff
bones of volcanic earth into
                   Albuquerque.   25
Not that,
        but a string of shadow horses kicking
and pulling me out of my belly,
           not into the Rio Grande[1] but into the music
barely coming through   30
              Sunday church singing
from the radio. Battery worn-down but the voices
talking backwards.

                                    1983

White Bear

She begins to board the flight
   to Albuquerque. Late night.
But stops in the corrugated tunnel,
   a space between leaving and staying,
where the night sky catches   5

        her whole life

she has felt like a woman
   balancing on a wooden nickle heart
approaching herself from here to
   there, Tulsa or New York   10
with knives or corn meal.

The last flight someone talked
   about how coming from Seattle
the pilot flew a circle
   over Mt. St. Helens,[1] she sat   15
quiet. (But had seen the eruption
   as the earth beginning
to come apart, as in birth
   out of violence.)

She watches the yellow lights   20
   of towns below the airplane flicker,
fade and fall backwards. Somewhere,

---

1. River flowing from southern Colorado through New Mexico and then forming the boundary between Texas and Mexico.

1. A volcanic peak in Washington State; it erupted in 1980.

she dreamed, there is the white bear

moving down from the north, motioning her paws
    like a long arctic night, that kind   25
of circle and the whole world balanced in
    between carved of ebony and ice

        oh so hard

the clear black nights
    like her daughter's eyes, and the white   30
bear moon, cupped like an ivory rocking
cradle, tipping back it could go
either way
        all darkness
                is open to all light.   35

1983

RITA DOVE
b. 1952

What she has called the "friction" between the beauty of a poetic form and a difficult or painful subject appeals to Rita Dove. Her own formal control and discipline create a beautiful design and a haunting music in "Parsley," a poem based on a murderous event: in 1957 the dictator of the Dominican Republic, Rafael Trujillo, ordered twenty thousand black Haitians killed because they could not pronounce the letter "r" in *perejil*, the Spanish word for parsley. What compels Dove in this poem is the way a "single, beautiful word" has the power of life and death. More astonishing is that she writes from the perspectives of both the Haitians in the cane fields and General Trujillo in his palace. When asked in an interview about her capacity to imagine Trujillo, Dove responded, "I frankly don't believe anyone who says they've never felt any evil, that they cannot understand that process of evil. It was important to me to try to understand that arbitrary quality of his cruelty. . . . Making us get into his head may shock us all into seeing what the human being is capable of, because if we can go that far into his head, we're halfway there ourselves." An ability to enter into different points of view in a single poem is characteristic of Dove's disinterested imagination. Her method is to avoid commentary, to let the imagined person or object, the suggestive detail, speak for itself. Often her work suggests what the English poet John Keats called "negative capability," the gift of the poet to become what he or she is not.

Born in Akron, Dove attended Miami University of Ohio and, after her graduation, studied modern European literature as a Fulbright/Hays fellow at the University of Tübingen in Germany. When she returned from Europe she earned an MFA at the University of Iowa (in 1977). Later she taught creative writing at Arizona State University before joining the University of Virginia, where she is now Commonwealth Professor of English. Since her Fulbright year she has repeatedly chosen to live abroad, in Ireland, Israel, France, and especially Germany. Her travel in Europe and elsewhere suggests part of the imperative she feels as a poet: to range widely through fields of experience, to cross boundaries of space as well as time. Her first book, *The Yellow House on the Corner* (1980), is notable for its intense poems about adolescence; her second book, *Museum* (1983), dramatically extends the range of her work. "When I started *Museum*," she has said, "I was in Europe, and I had a way of looking back on America and distancing myself from my experience." As well as for several fine poems about her father (a subject that may also have needed distance), the book is remarkable for the way distance allowed Dove to move out of her immediate experience, freed her to imagine widely different lives.

As if to show that it is also possible to travel widely while staying at home, Dove's *Thomas and Beulah* (1986) is an extended sequence based on her grandparents' lives. Her continuing fascination with imagining different perspectives on the same event is evident in this sequence. Dove has described the book's origins this way:

> My grandmother had told me a story that had happened to my grandfather when he was young, coming up on a riverboat to Akron, Ohio, my hometown. But that was all I had, basically. And the story so fascinated me that I tried to write about it. I started off writing stories about my grandfather and soon, because I ran out of real fact, in order to keep going, I made up facts for this character, Thomas. . . . Then this poem "Dusting" appeared, really out of nowhere. I didn't realize this was Thomas's wife saying, "I want to talk. And you can't do his side without my side. . . ."

This is the story, in part, of a marriage and of a black couple's life in the industrial Midwest in the period from 1900 to 1960. Thomas's point of view controls the poems of the book's first section, while the second part imagines his wife's. The larger framework of the sequence links family history to social history. Thomas's journey from the rural South to the industrial city of Akron (where he finds employment in the Goodyear Zeppelin factory until the Depression puts him out of work) is part of the larger social movement of African Americans from the South into Northern industrial cities in the first part of the twentieth century. The individual lyrics of Dove's sequence create and sustain the story through distinct and often ordinary moments in which each life is vividly portrayed. It is part of Dove's gift that she can render the apparently unimportant moments that inform a life and set them against a background of larger historical forces, as do Robert Hayden in *Elegies for Paradise Valley* and Robert Lowell in *Notebook*.

Many of the figures in Dove's poems are displaced, on the border between different worlds: for example, Thomas and Beulah, and the biracial violin prodigy, George Bridgetower (1780–1860), who is the focus of her volume *Sonata Mulattica* (2009). The experience of displacement, of what she has called living in "two different worlds, seeing things with double vision," consistently compels this poet's imagination. It takes both detachment and control to maintain (and to live with) such doubleness. This may be why Dove's rich sense of language and her love of sound are joined to a disciplined formal sense. The forms of her poems often hold in place difficult or ambiguous feelings and keep the expression of feeling understated. While restraint is one strength of Dove's poems, her work can sometimes seem austere. Such careful control recalls Elizabeth Bishop's early work, also highly controlled and even, at times, guarded. As Bishop grew to relax her restraints, to open into an extraordinary expressiveness, so Dove's career shows a similar growth. Her collections *Grace Notes* (1989), *Mother Love* (1995), and *American Smooth* (2004) suggest just such a relaxing of the poet's guard, while *On the Bus with Rosa Parks* (2000) demonstrates an ongoing ability to unite social conscience with a transformative sense of language and form. With each book she asks something more from herself, and she has now become one of our indispensable poets. Dove was poet laureate of the United States from 1993 to 1995.

Adolescence—I

In water-heavy nights behind grandmother's porch
We knelt in the tickling grasses and whispered:
Linda's face hung before us, pale as a pecan,
And it grew wise as she said:
    "A boy's lips are soft,   5
      As soft as baby's skin."
The air closed over her words.
A firefly whirred near my ear, and in the distance
I could hear streetlamps ping
Into miniature suns   10
Against a feathery sky.

          1980

Adolescence—II

Although it is night, I sit in the bathroom, waiting.
Sweat prickles behind my knees, the baby-breasts are alert.
Venetian blinds slice up the moon; the tiles quiver in pale strips.

Then they come, the three seal men with eyes as round
As dinner plates and eyelashes like sharpened tines.   5
They bring the scent of licorice. One sits in the washbowl,

One on the bathtub edge; one leans against the door.
"Can you feel it yet?" they whisper.
I don't know what to say, again. They chuckle,

Patting their sleek bodies with their hands.   10
"Well, maybe next time." And they rise,
Glittering like pools of ink under moonlight,

And vanish. I clutch at the ragged holes
They leave behind, here at the edge of darkness.
Night rests like a ball of fur on my tongue.   15

          1980

Parsley[1]

1. The Cane[2] Fields

There is a parrot imitating spring
in the palace, its feathers parsley green.
Out of the swamp the cane appears

to haunt us, and we cut it down. El General
searches for a word; he is all the world   5
there is. Like a parrot imitating spring,

we lie down screaming as rain punches through
and we come up green. We cannot speak an R—
out of the swamp, the cane appears

and then the mountain we call in whispers *Katalina*.[3]   10
The children gnaw their teeth to arrowheads.
There is a parrot imitating spring.

El General has found his word: *perejil.*
Who says it, lives. He laughs, teeth shining
out of the swamp. The cane appears   15

in our dreams, lashed by wind and streaming.
And we lie down. For every drop of blood
there is a parrot imitating spring.
Out of the swamp the cane appears.

2. The Palace

The word the general's chosen is parsley.   20
It is fall, when thoughts turn
to love and death; the general thinks
of his mother, how she died in the fall
and he planted her walking cane at the grave
and it flowered, each spring stolidly forming   25
four-star blossoms. The general

pulls on his boots, he stomps to
her room in the palace, the one without
curtains, the one with a parrot
in a brass ring. As he paces he wonders   30
Who can I kill today. And for a moment
the little knot of screams
is still. The parrot, who has traveled

---

1. On October 2, 1937, Rafael Trujillo (1891–
1961), dictator of the Dominican Republic,
ordered 20,000 blacks killed because they could
not pronounce the letter "r" in *perejil*, the Spanish
word for parsley [Dove's note].
2. I.e., sugar cane.
3. Katarina (because "we cannot speak an R").

all the way from Australia in an ivory
cage, is, coy as a widow, practising   35
spring. Ever since the morning
his mother collapsed in the kitchen
while baking skull-shaped candies
for the Day of the Dead,[4] the general
has hated sweets. He orders pastries   40
brought up for the bird; they arrive

dusted with sugar on a bed of lace.
The knot in his throat starts to twitch;
he sees his boots the first day in battle
splashed with mud and urine   45
as a soldier falls at his feet amazed—
how stupid he looked!—at the sound
of artillery. *I never thought it would sing*
the soldier said, and died. Now

the general sees the fields of sugar   50
cane, lashed by rain and streaming.
He sees his mother's smile, the teeth
gnawed to arrowheads. He hears
the Haitians sing without R's
as they swing the great machetes: 55
Katalina, they sing, *Katalina*,

mi madle, mi amol en muelte.[5] God knows
his mother was no stupid woman; she
could roll an R like a queen. Even
a parrot can roll an R! In the bare room   60
the bright feathers arch in a parody
of greenery, as the last pale crumbs
disappear under the blackened tongue. Someone

calls out his name in a voice
so like his mother's, a startled tear   65
splashes the tip of his right boot.
My mother, my love in death.
The general remembers the tiny green sprigs
men of his village wore in their capes
to honor the birth of a son. He will   70
order many, this time, to be killed

for a single, beautiful word.

1983

4. All Soul's Day, November 2. An Aztec festival for the spirits of the dead that coincides with the Catholic calendar. In Latin America and the Caribbean, people move in processions to cemeteries, bearing candles, flowers, and food, all of which may be shaped to resemble symbols of death, such as skulls or coffins.
5. I.e., *mi madre, mi amor en muerte*—"my mother, my love in death."

Rosa[1]

How she sat there,
the time right inside a place
so wrong it was ready.

That trim name with
its dream of a bench   5
to rest on. Her sensible coat.

Doing nothing was the doing:
the clean flame of her gaze
carved by a camera flash.

How she stood up   10
when they bent down to retrieve
her purse. That courtesy.

2000

1. Rosa Parks (1913–2005). From a series of poems titled *On the Bus with Rosa Parks*. On December 1, 1955, in Montgomery, Alabama, Parks, an African American seamstress and secretary of the local National Association for the Advancement of Colored People (NAACP), was arrested and taken to jail for refusing to yield her seat on a bus to a white passenger. Her arrest prompted a boycott of the city bus system and inspired the civil rights movement in the late 1950s and the 1960s.

SANDRA CISNEROS
b. 1954

Sandra Cisneros began writing at age ten, much like the young Chicana narrator of *The House on Mango Street* (1984), the volume of interrelated vignettes from a child's perspective that brought Cisneros her first major attention. In brief, sharply drawn segments, the narrator, Esperanza, conveys the ambience of growing up in Chicago's Mexican American community. The social bond of this neighborhood eases the contrast between Esperanza's nurturing family and the more hostile forces of poverty and racism. Cisneros cultivates a sense of warmth and naïve humor for her protagonists, qualities that are evident in introductory parts to *Woman Hollering Creek* (1991), a short-story collection that also focuses on young women facing hostile forces. Without sentimentalizing or idealizing her narrator's perspective, Cisneros presents glimpses of a world full of adult challenges and multicultural complexities. Sex is a topic in all Cisneros's work, including her poetry collected as *My Wicked Wicked Ways* (1987) and *Loose Woman* (1994)—sometimes gentle and even silly, other times brutally assaultive. What remains constant is the author's view that by romanticizing sexual relations women cooperate with a male view that can be oppressive, even physically destructive. As has been said of the protagonist of her 2002 novel, *Caramelo*, Cisneros is "caught between here and there." Yet "here" and "there" are not as dichotomous as young versus old, female versus male, or Mexico versus the United States. Instead, the flow of experience between these poles yields her work's subject: people finding their own lifestyles in the space between fixed boundaries. Because this intervening space is so rich in creative potential, Cisneros can balance unhappiness with humor and find personal victories where others might see social defeat.

Born in Chicago, the child of a Mexican father and a Mexican American mother, Cisneros spent parts of her childhood in Texas and Mexico as well. Her Catholic-school background led to a B.A. degree from Chicago's Loyola University, after which she earned a graduate degree in creative writing from the University of Iowa's Writers Workshop. Teaching in San Antonio, Texas, she used her position as a writer and an educator to champion Chicana feminism, especially as this movement combines cultural issues with women's concerns. In raising controversy by having her house painted very brightly, she openly questioned monocultural "historical districts" and "community covenants." *Whose* history? Cisneros asked. *Which* community sets standards? (Through research she established that her decorating style was in accordance with her home's background and that the standards used to dispute her choice were arbitrary.) A dissatisfaction with the politics of publishing has made her an advocate of small-press dissemination. Most of all, as in the story reprinted here, she is eager to show the rich dynamics of characters existing in the blend of Mexican and American cultures that begins with speaking two languages and extends to almost every aspect of life. Spanish words, Mexican holidays, ethnic foods, and localized religious practices punctuate her narratives; her characters have a facility with cultural play that reflects the bilingual and bicultural life shared by millions of Mexican Americans.

The following text is from *Woman Hollering Creek* (1991).

Woman Hollering Creek

The day Don Serafín gave Juan Pedro Martínez Sánchez permission to take Cleófilas Enriqueta DeLeón Hernández as his bride, across her father's threshold, over several miles of dirt road and several miles of paved, over one border and beyond to a town *en el otro lado*—on the other side—already did he divine the morning his daughter would raise her hand over her eyes, look south, and dream of returning to the chores that never ended, six good-for-nothing brothers, and one old man's complaints.

He had said, after all, in the hubbub of parting: I am your father, I will never abandon you. He *had* said that, hadn't he, when he hugged and then let her go. But at the moment Cleófilas was busy looking for Chela, her maid of honor, to fulfill their bouquet conspiracy. She would not remember her father's parting words until later. *I am your father, I will never abandon you.*

Only now as a mother did she remember. Now, when she and Juan Pedrito sat by the creek's edge. How when a man and a woman love each other, sometimes that love sours. But a parent's love for a child, a child's for its parents, is another thing entirely.

This is what Cleófilas thought evenings when Juan Pedro did not come home, and she lay on her side of the bed listening to the hollow roar of the interstate, a distant dog barking, the pecan trees rustling like ladies in stiff petticoats—*shh-shh-shh, shh-shh-shh*—soothing her to sleep.

In the town where she grew up, there isn't very much to do except accompany the aunts and godmothers to the house of one or the other to play cards. Or walk to the cinema to see this week's film again, speckled and with one hair quivering annoyingly on the screen. Or to the center of town to order a milk shake that will appear in a day and a half as a pimple on her backside. Or to the girlfriend's house to watch the latest *telenovela*[1] episode and try to copy the way the women comb their hair, wear their makeup.

But what Cleófilas has been waiting for, has been whispering and sighing and giggling for, has been anticipating since she was old enough to lean against the window displays of gauze and butterflies and lace, is passion. Not the kind on the cover of the ¡*Alarma!*[2] magazines, mind you, where the lover is photographed with the bloody fork she used to salvage her good name. But passion in its purest crystalline essence. The kind the books and songs and *telenovelas* describe when one finds, finally, the great love of one's life, and does whatever one can, must do, at whatever the cost.

Tú o Nadie. "You or No One." The title of the current favorite *telenovela*. The beautiful Lucía Méndez having to put up with all kinds of hardships of the heart, separation and betrayal, and loving, always loving no matter what, because *that* is the most important thing, and did you see Lucía Méndez on the Bayer aspirin commercials—wasn't she lovely? Does she dye her hair do you think? Cleófilas is going to go to the *farmacía*[3] and buy a hair rinse; her girlfriend Chela will apply it—it's not that difficult at all.

Because you didn't watch last night's episode when Lucía confessed she loved him more than anyone in her life. In her life! And she sings the song "You or No One" in the beginning and end of the show. *Tú o Nadie.* Somehow one ought to live one's life like that, don't you think? You or no one. Because to suffer for love is good. The pain all sweet somehow. In the end.

Seguín. She had liked the sound of it. Far away and lovely. Not like *Monclova. Coahuia.*[4] Ugly.

Seguín, Tejas. A nice sterling ring to it. The tinkle of money. She would get to wear outfits like the women on the *tele*, like Lucía Méndez. And have a lovely house, and wouldn't Chela be jealous.

And yes, they will drive all the way to Laredo[5] to get her wedding dress. That's what they say. Because Juan Pedro wants to get married right away, without a long engagement since he can't take off too much time from work.

---

1. Serialized TV melodrama (Spanish).
2. Graphic, sensationalistic Mexican magazine published since 1963.
3. Pharmacy, drugstore (Spanish).
4. Respectively a town and state in Mexico, the latter bordering Texas. "Seguín": city in Guadalupe County, south-central Texas.
5. City in southwestern Texas, on the Mexican border.

He has a very important position in Seguin with, with . . . a beer company, I think. Or was it tires? Yes, he has to be back. So they will get married in the spring when he can take off work, and then they will drive off in his new pickup—did you see it?—to their new home in Seguin. Well, not exactly new, but they're going to repaint the house. You know newlyweds. New paint and new furniture. Why not? He can afford it. And later on add maybe a room or two for the children. May they be blessed with many.

Well, you'll see. Cleófilas has always been so good with her sewing machine. A little *rrrr, rrrr, rrrr* of the machine and *¡zas!* Miracles. She's always been so clever, that girl. Poor thing. And without even a mama to advise her on things like her wedding night. Well, may God help her. What with a father with a head like a burro, and those six clumsy brothers. Well, what do you think! Yes, I'm going to the wedding. Of course! The dress I want to wear just needs to be altered a teensy bit to bring it up to date. See, I saw a new style last night that I thought would suit me. Did you watch last night's episode of *The Rich Also Cry*?[6] Well, did you notice the dress the mother was wearing?

La Gritona.[7] Such a funny name for such a lovely *arroyo*.[8] But that's what they called the creek that ran behind the house. Though no one could say whether the woman had hollered from anger or pain. The natives only knew the *arroyo* one crossed on the way to San Antonio, and then once again on the way back, was called Woman Hollering, a name no one from these parts questioned, little less understood. *Pues, allá de los indios, quién sabe*[9]—who knows, the townspeople shrugged, because it was of no concern to their lives how this trickle of water received its curious name.

"What do you want to know for?" Trini the laundromat attendant asked in the same gruff Spanish she always used whenever she gave Cleófilas change or yelled at her for something. First for putting too much soap in the machines. Later, for sitting on a washer. And still later, after Juan Pedrito was born, for not understanding that in this country you cannot let your baby walk around with no diaper and his pee-pee hanging out, it wasn't nice, *¿entiendes? Pues*.[1]

How could Cleófilas explain to a woman like this why the name Woman Hollering fascinated her. Well, there was no sense talking to Trini.

On the other hand there were the neighbor ladies, one on either side of the house they rented near the *arroyo*. The woman Soledad on the left, the woman Dolores on the right.

The neighbor lady Soledad liked to call herself a widow, though how she came to be one was a mystery. Her husband had either died, or run away with an ice-house[2] floozie, or simply gone out for cigarettes one afternoon and never came back. It was hard to say which since Soledad, as a rule, didn't mention him.

In the other house lived *la señora*[3] Dolores, kind and very sweet, but her house smelled too much of incense and candles from the altars that burned continuously in memory of two sons who had died in the last war and one

---

6. First global soap opera (production beginning in Mexico in 1979), exported to Russia, China, the United States, and other countries.
7. The Shouter, Yeller, Hollerer (Spanish).
8. Stream (Spanish).

9. Well, beyond the Indians, who knows (Spanish).
1. Do you understand? Well (Spanish).
2. Tavern.
3. The lady (Spanish).

husband who had died shortly after from grief. The neighbor lady Dolores divided her time between the memory of these men and her garden, famous for its sunflowers—so tall they had to be supported with broom handles and old boards; red red cockscombs, fringed and bleeding a thick menstrual color; and, especially, roses whose sad scent reminded Cleófilas of the dead. Each Sunday *la señora* Dolores clipped the most beautiful of these flowers and arranged them on three modest headstones at the Seguin cemetery.

The neighbor ladies, Soledad, Dolores, they might've known once the name of the *arroyo* before it turned English but they did not know now. They were too busy remembering the men who had left through either choice or circumstance and would never come back.

Pain or rage, Cleófilas wondered when she drove over the bridge the first time as a newlywed and Juan Pedro had pointed it out. *La Gritona*, he had said, and she had laughed. Such a funny name for a creek so pretty and full of happily ever after.

The first time she had been so surprised she didn't cry out or try to defend herself. She had always said she would strike back if a man, any man, were to strike her.

But when the moment came, and he slapped her once, and then again, and again; until the lip split and bled an orchid of blood, she didn't fight back, she didn't break into tears, she didn't run away as she imagined she might when she saw such things in the *telenovelas*.

In her own home her parents had never raised a hand to each other or to their children. Although she admitted she may have been brought up a little leniently as an only daughter—*la consentida*,[4] the princess—there were some things she would never tolerate. Ever.

Instead, when it happened the first time, when they were barely man and wife, she had been so stunned, it left her speechless, motionless, numb. She had done nothing but reach up to the heat on her mouth and stare at the blood on her hand as if even then she didn't understand.

She could think of nothing to say, said nothing. Just stroked the dark curls of the man who wept and would weep like a child, his tears of repentance and shame, this time and each.

The men at the ice house. From what she can tell, from the times during her first year when still a newlywed she is invited and accompanies her husband, sits mute beside their conversation, waits and sips a beer until it grows warm, twists a paper napkin into a knot, then another into a fan, one into a rose, nods her head, smiles, yawns, politely grins, laughs at the appropriate moments, leans against her husband's sleeve, tugs at his elbow, and finally becomes good at predicting where the talk will lead, from this Cleófilas concludes each is nightly trying to find the truth lying at the bottom of the bottle like a gold doubloon on the sea floor.

They want to tell each other what they want to tell themselves. But what is bumping like a helium balloon at the ceiling of the brain never finds its way out. It bubbles and rises, it gurgles in the throat, it rolls across the surface of the tongue, and erupts from the lips—a belch.

4. The spoiled one (Spanish).

If they are lucky, there are tears at the end of the long night. At any given moment, the fists try to speak. They are dogs chasing their own tails before lying down to sleep, trying to find a way, a route, an out, and—finally—get some peace.

In the morning sometimes before he opens his eyes. Or after they have finished loving. Or at times when he is simply across from her at the table putting pieces of food into his mouth and chewing. Cleófilas thinks, This is the man I have waited my whole life for.

Not that he isn't a good man. She has to remind herself why she loves him when she changes the baby's Pampers, or when she mops the bathroom floor, or tries to make the curtains for the doorways without doors, or whiten the linen. Or wonder a little when he kicks the refrigerator and says he hates this shitty house and is going out where he won't be bothered with the baby's howling and her suspicious questions, and her requests to fix this and this and this because if she had any brains in her head she'd realize he's been up before the rooster earning his living to pay for the food in her belly and the roof over her head and would have to wake up again early the next day so why can't you just leave me in peace, woman.

He is not very tall, no, and he doesn't look like the men on the *telenovelas*. His face still scarred from acne. And he has a bit of a belly from all the beer he drinks. Well, he's always been husky.

This man who farts and belches and snores as well as laughs and kisses and holds her. Somehow this husband whose whiskers she finds each morning in the sink, whose shoes she must air each evening on the porch, this husband who cuts his fingernails in public, laughs loudly, curses like a man, and demands each course of dinner be served on a separate plate like at his mother's, as soon as he gets home, on time or late, and who doesn't care at all for music or *telenovelas* or romance or roses or the moon floating pearly over the *arroyo*, or through the bedroom window for that matter, shut the blinds and go back to sleep, this man, this father, this rival, this keeper, this lord, this master, this husband till kingdom come.

A doubt. Slender as a hair. A washed cup set back on the shelf wrong-side-up. Her lipstick, and body talc, and hairbrush all arranged in the bathroom a different way.

No. Her imagination. The house the same as always. Nothing.

Coming home from the hospital with her new son, her husband. Something comforting in discovering her house slippers beneath the bed, the faded housecoat where she left it on the bathroom hook. Her pillow. Their bed.

Sweet sweet homecoming. Sweet as the scent of face powder in the air, jasmine, sticky liquor.

Smudged fingerprint on the door. Crushed cigarette in a glass. Wrinkle in the brain crumpling to a crease.

Sometimes she thinks of her father's house. But how could she go back there? What a disgrace. What would the neighbors say? Coming home like that with one baby on her hip and one in the oven. Where's your husband?

The town of gossips. The town of dust and despair. Which she has traded for this town of gossips. This town of dust, despair. Houses farther apart perhaps, though no more privacy because of it. No leafy *zócalo*[5] in the center of the town, though the murmur of talk is clear enough all the same. No huddled whispering on the church steps each Sunday. Because here the whispering begins at sunset at the ice house instead.

This town with its silly pride for a bronze pecan the size of a baby carriage in front of the city hall. TV repair shop, drugstore, hardware, dry cleaner's, chiropractor's, liquor store, bail bonds, empty storefront, and nothing, nothing, nothing of interest. Nothing one could walk to, at any rate. Because the towns here are built so that you have to depend on husbands. Or you stay home. Or you drive. If you're rich enough to own, allowed to drive, your own car.

There is no place to go. Unless one counts the neighbor ladies. Soledad on one side, Dolores on the other. Or the creek.

Don't go out there after dark, *mi'jita*.[6] Stay near the house. *No es bueno para la salud.*[7] Mala suerte. Bad luck. *Mal aire.*[8] You'll get sick and the baby too. You'll catch a fright wandering about in the dark, and then you'll see how right we were.

The stream sometimes only a muddy puddle in the summer, though now in the springtime, because of the rains, a good-size alive thing, a thing with a voice all its own, all day and all night calling in its high, silver voice. Is it La Llorona,[9] the weeping woman? La Llorona, who drowned her own children. Perhaps La Llorona is the one they named the creek after, she thinks, remembering all the stories she learned as a child.

La Llorona calling to her. She is sure of it. Cleófilas sets the baby's Donald Duck blanket on the grass. Listens. The day sky turning to night. The baby pulling up fistfuls of grass and laughing. La Llorona. Wonders if something as quiet as this drives a woman to the darkness under the trees.

What she needs is . . . and made a gesture as if to yank a woman's buttocks to his groin. Maximiliano, the foul-smelling fool from across the road, said this and set the men laughing, but Cleófilas just muttered. *Grosera*,[1] and went on washing dishes.

She knew he said it not because it was true, but more because it was he who needed to sleep with a woman, instead of drinking each night at the ice house and stumbling home alone.

Maximiliano who was said to have killed his wife in an ice-house brawl when she came at him with a mop. I had to shoot, he had said—she was armed.

Their laughter outside the kitchen window. Her husband's, his friends'. Manolo, Beto, Efraín, el Perico.[2] Maximiliano.

Was Cleófilas just exaggerating as her husband always said? It seemed the newspapers were full of such stories. This woman found on the side of the interstate. This one pushed from a moving car. This one's cadaver, this one unconscious, this one beaten blue. Her ex-husband, her husband, her lover, her father, her brother, her uncle, her friend, her co-worker. Always.

5. Town square (Spanish).
6. My daughter (Spanish).
7. It's not good for one's health (Spanish).
8. Bad air (Spanish).
9. The Woman Who Cries (Spanish), a spurned

mistress of Mexican legend who drowned her children and was fated to eternally seek their recovery.
1. Vulgar, crude (Spanish).
2. The Parakeet (Spanish).

The same grisly news in the pages of the dailies. She dunked a glass under the soapy water for a moment—shivered.

He had thrown a book. Hers. From across the room. A hot welt across the cheek. She could forgive that. But what stung more was the fact it was *her* book, a love story by Corín Tellado,[3] what she loved most now that she lived in the U.S., without a television set, without the *telenovelas*.

Except now and again when her husband was away and she could manage it, the few episodes glimpsed at the neighbor lady Soledad's house because Dolores didn't care for that sort of thing, though Soledad was often kind enough to retell what had happened on what episode of *María de Nadie*,[4] the poor Argentine country girl who had the ill fortune of falling in love with the beautiful son of the Arrocha family, the very family she worked for, whose roof she slept under and whose floors she vacuumed, while in that same house, with the dust brooms and floor cleaners as witnesses, the square-jawed Juan Carlos Arrocha had uttered words of love, I love you, María, listen to me, *mi querida*,[5] but it was she who had to say No, no, we are not of the same class, and remind him it was not his place nor hers to fall in love, while all the while her heart was breaking, can you imagine.

Cleófilas thought her life would have to be like that, like a *telenovela*, only now the episodes got sadder and sadder. And there were no commercials in between for comic relief. And no happy ending in sight. She thought this when she sat with the baby out by the creek behind the house. Celófilas de . . . ? But somehow she would have to change her name to Topazio, or Yesenia, Cristal, Adriana, Stefania, Andrea, something more poetic than Cleófilas. Everything happened to women with names like jewels. But what happened to a Cleófilas? Nothing. But a crack in the face.

Because the doctor has said so. She has to go. To make sure the new baby is all right, so there won't be any problems when he's born, and the appointment card says next Tuesday. Could he please take her. And that's all.

No, she won't mention it. She promises. If the doctor asks she can say she fell down the front steps or slipped when she was out in the backyard, slipped out back, she could tell him that. She has to go back next Tuesday, Juan Pedro, please, for the new baby. For their child.

She could write to her father and ask maybe for money, just a loan, for the new baby's medical expenses. Well then if he'd rather she didn't. All right, she won't. Please don't anymore. Please don't. She knows it's difficult saving money with all the bills they have, but how else are they going to get out of debt with the truck payments? And after the rent and the food and the electricity and the gas and the water and the who-knows-what, well, there's hardly anything left. But please, at least for the doctor visit. She won't ask for anything else. She has to. Why is she so anxious? Because.

Because she is going to make sure the baby is not turned around backward this time to split her down the center. Yes. Next Tuesday at five-thirty. I'll have Juan Pedrito dressed and ready. But those are the only shoes he

---

3. Pseudonym of María del Socorro Tellado López (1927–2009), Spanish novelist.
4. *María of No One* (Spanish), television series produced in Argentina.
5. My dear (Spanish).

has. I'll polish them, and we'll be ready. As soon as you come from work. We won't make you ashamed.

Felice? It's me, Graciela.

No, I can't talk louder. I'm at work.

Look, I need kind of a favor. There's a patient, a lady here who's got a problem.

Well, wait a minute. Are you listening to me or what?

I can't talk real loud 'cause her husband's in the next room.

Well, would you just listen?

I was going to do this sonogram on her—she's pregnant, right?—and she just starts crying on me. *Híjole,*[6] Felice! This poor lady's got black-and-blue marks all over. I'm not kidding.

From her husband. Who else? Another one of those brides from across the border. And her family's all in Mexico.

Shit. You think they're going to help her? Give me a break. This lady doesn't even speak English. She hasn't been allowed to call home or write or nothing. That's why I'm calling you.

She needs a ride.

Not to Mexico, you goof. Just to the Greyhound.[7] In San Anto.

No, just a ride. She's got her own money. All you'd have to do is drop her off in San Antonio on your way home. Come on, Felice. Please? If we don't help her, who will? I'd drive her myself, but she needs to be on that bus before her husband gets home from work. What do you say?

I don't know. Wait.

Right away, tomorrow even.

Well, if tomorrow's no good for you . . .

It's a date, Felice. Thursday. At the Cash N Carry[8] off I-10. Noon. She'll be ready.

Oh, and her name's Cleófilas.

I don't know. One of those Mexican saints, I guess. A martyr or something.

Cleófilas. C-L-E-O-F-I-L-A-S. Cle. O. Fi. Las. Write it down.

Thanks, Felice. When her kid's born she'll have to name her after us, right?

Yeah, you got it. A regular soap opera sometimes. *Qué vida, comadre. Bueno*[9] bye.

All morning that flutter of half-fear, half-doubt. At any moment Juan Pedro might appear in the doorway. On the street. At the Cash N Carry. Like in the dreams she dreamed.

There was that to think about, yes, until the woman in the pickup drove up. Then there wasn't time to think about anything but the pickup pointed toward San Antonio. Put your bags in the back and get in.

But when they drove across the *arroyo,* the driver opened her mouth and let out a yell as loud as any mariachi. Which startled not only Cleófilas, but Juan Pedrito as well.

---

6. Shoot! or Gee! (Spanish).
7. Long-distance bus line.
8. Retail store.
9. What a life, girlfriend, well (Spanish).

Pues,[1] look how cute. I scared you two, right? Sorry. Should've warned you. Every time I cross that bridge I do that. Because of the name, you know. Woman Hollering. *Pues,* I holler. She said this in a Spanish pocked with English and laughed. Did you ever notice, Felice continued, how nothing around here is named after a woman? Really. Unless she's the Virgin. I guess you're only famous if you're a virgin. She was laughing again.

That's why I like the name of that *arroyo*. Makes you want to holler like Tarzan, right?

Everything about this woman, this Felice, amazed Cleófilas. The fact that she drove a pickup. A pickup, mind you, but when Cleófilas asked if it was her husband's, she said she didn't have a husband. The pickup was hers. She herself had chosen it. She herself was paying for it.

I used to have a Pontiac Sunbird.[2] But those cars are for *viejas*.[3] Pussy cars. Now this here is a *real* car.

What kind of talk was that coming from a woman? Cleófilas thought. But then again, Felice was like no woman she'd ever met. Can you imagine, when we crossed the *arroyo* she just started yelling like a crazy, she would say later to her father and brothers. Just like that. Who would've thought?

Who would've? Pain or rage, perhaps, but not a hoot like the one Felice had just let go. Makes you want to holler like Tarzan, Felice had said.

Then Felice began laughing again, but it wasn't Felice laughing. It was gurgling out of her own throat, a long ribbon of laughter, like water.

1991

1. Well (Spanish).   3. Old ladies (Spanish).
2. Compact American automobile.

LOUISE ERDRICH
b. 1954

L ouise Erdrich grew up in the small town of Wahpeton, North Dakota, on the Minnesota border. Her mother was French Chippewa, her maternal grandmother was tribal chairman on the Turtle Mountain Reservation, and both of her parents worked in the Bureau of Indian Affairs boarding school in Wahpeton. She wrote stories as a child, encouraged by her father, who paid her a nickel for each one, but Erdrich's growing up was not marked by a special awareness of her Chippewa background. She has said that she never thought about "what was Native American and what wasn't. . . . There wasn't a political climate at the time about Indian rights." The eldest of seven children, she "grew up just taking it all in as something that was part of me."

In 1972 she entered Dartmouth College, participating in a Native American studies program run by Michael Dorris—himself part American Indian and a writer— whom eventually she would marry (a relationship ending with their separation and his suicide in 1997). In her undergraduate years she won prizes for poetry and fiction and worked at a variety of jobs, such as teaching poetry in prisons, editing a Boston

Indian Council newspaper, and flag-signaling on a construction site. After deciding on a career as a writer, she earned an MFA degree at Johns Hopkins, for which degree she submitted a number of poems—later to appear in her collection *Jacklight* (1984)—and part of a novel. There followed the usual sending out of poems and stories, the rejection slips, eventually the acceptances.

Her first novel, *Love Medicine*, which won the National Book Critics Circle award for 1984, began as a short story. Collaborating with her husband, she not only expanded the story but planned the resulting novel as the first of a tetralogy, ranging over different periods of time and focusing on the lives of two Chippewa families. Her interest in the interaction of quirky, passionate, complex individuals—Native American, mixed blood, German American, or Anglo—lies at the center of her fiction.

Successive chapters of *Love Medicine* jump from 1981 to 1934 to 1948, each chapter told through a particular character's point of view (sometimes we see the same event from succeeding points of view). But each individual chapter is more a discrete whole than is the case with a traditional novel, a technique Erdrich uses in many of her novels, including *Tracks* (1988), the second chapter of which was published as the story "Fleur" (printed here). Like many of Erdrich's narratives, *Tracks* draws context from High Plains Dakotas town life, where Anglo and Native American cultures meet (if not mix).

Erdrich's style is easy, offhand, quietly unostentatious, but her language often has an unpredictability and sense of surprise, as in the first paragraph of "The Red Convertible," whose protagonist, Lyman Lamartine, tells us:

> I was the first one to drive a convertible on my reservation. And of course, it was red, a red Olds. I owned that car along with my brother Henry Junior. We owned it together until his boots filled with water on a windy night and he bought out my share. Now Henry owns the whole car, and his younger brother (that's myself) Lyman walks everywhere he goes.

Such clarity and directness are only part of the story, however, since her style also calls upon lyric resources, notable in the following sentence from her second novel, *The Beet Queen*: "After the miraculous sheets of black ice came the floods, stranding boards and snaky knots of debris high in the branches, leaving brown leeches to dry like raisins on the sidewalks when the water receded, and leaving the smell of river mud, a rotten sweetness, in the backyards and gutters."

Native American oral expression does not distinguish between prose and poetry, and like many Native American writers Erdrich works in several forms. "I began as a poet, writing poetry," she has said. "I began to tell stories in poems." The lyrical descriptions in her fiction resemble the language of her poems, and the characterizations and narratives in her poetry resemble those of her fiction. Her most recent poetry collection, *Original Fire* (2003), presents new poems together with work from two earlier collections, *Jacklight* and *Baptism of Desire* (1989). Among the previously published poems are "The Butcher's Wife," which has close affinities in setting and character to her novels, and "The Potchikoo Stories," a group of prose poems about the mythical Potchikoo's life and afterlife. "Grief," a new poem, suggests the traditions of imagist poetry. But in the end such generic distinctions run counter to Erdrich's fusion of storytelling modes.

Like her fiction, Erdrich's poetry sometimes offers realistic accounts of small-town life and sometimes retells mythical stories. "I was Sleeping Where the Black Oaks Move" exemplifies her lyrical description and her mythical imagination. Many of the poems also reflect Erdrich's awareness of the historical and ongoing devastations of Native American life, what she calls in the poem "Dear John Wayne" "the history that brought us all here." Whatever forms her storytelling takes, its linguistic resources and mixture of grief, humor, anger, and tenderness deepen our understanding of the complexities of experience.

Dear John Wayne[1]

August and the drive-in picture is packed.
We lounge on the hood of the Pontiac
surrounded by the slow-burning spirals they sell
at the window, to vanquish the hordes of mosquitoes.
Nothing works. They break through the smoke screen for blood.   5

Always the lookout spots the Indians first,
spread north to south, barring progress.
The Sioux or some other Plains bunch[2]
in spectacular columns, ICBM missiles,[3]
feathers bristling in the meaningful sunset.   10

The drum breaks. There will be no parlance.
Only the arrows whining, a death-cloud of nerves
swarming down on the settlers
who die beautifully, tumbling like dust weeds
into the history that brought us all here   15
together: this wide screen beneath the sign of the bear.

The sky fills, acres of blue squint and eye
that the crowd cheers. His face moves over us,
a thick cloud of vengeance, pitted
like the land that was once flesh. Each rut,   20
each scar makes a promise: *It is
not over, this fight, not as long as you resist.*

Everything we see belongs to us.

A few laughing Indians fall over the hood
slipping in the hot spilled butter.   25
The eye sees a lot, John, but the heart is so blind.
Death makes us owners of nothing.
He smiles, a horizon of teeth
the credits reel over, and then the white fields

again blowing in the true-to-life dark.   30
The dark films over everything.
We get into the car
scratching our mosquito bites, speechless and small
as people are when the movie is done.
We are back in our skins.   35

---

1. American movie actor (1907–1979) who embodied the image of the strong, taciturn cowboy or soldier, and who in many ways personified the dominant American values of his era. He died of cancer.

2. The Sioux (Lakota) are a North American Plains Indian people.
3. Intercontinental Ballistic Missiles, developed starting in 1971.

How can we help but keep hearing his voice,
the flip side of the sound track, still playing:
Come on, boys, we got them
where we want them, drunk, running.
They'll give us what we want, what we need.   40
Even his disease was the idea of taking everything.
Those cells, burning, doubling, splitting out of their skins.

1984

I Was Sleeping Where the Black Oaks Move

We watched from the house
as the river grew, helpless
and terrible in its unfamiliar body.
Wrestling everything into it,
the water wrapped around trees   5
until their life-hold was broken.
They went down, one by one,
and the river dragged off their covering.

Nests of the herons, roots washed to bones,
snags of soaked bark on the shoreline: 10
a whole forest pulled through the teeth
of the spillway. Trees surfacing
singly, where the river poured off
into arteries for fields below the reservation.

When at last it was over, the long removal,   15
they had all become the same dry wood.
We walked among them, the branches
whitening in the raw sun.
Above us drifted herons,
alone, hoarse-voiced, broken,   20
settling their beaks among the hollows.

Grandpa said, *These are the ghosts of the tree people,*
moving above us, unable to take their rest.

Sometimes now, we dream our way back to the heron dance.
Their long wings are bending the air   25
into circles through which they fall.
They rise again in shifting wheels.
How long must we live in the broken figures
their necks make, narrowing the sky.

1984

Grief

Sometimes you have to take your own hand
as though you were a lost child
and bring yourself stumbling
home over twisted ice.

Whiteness drifts over your house.   5
A page of warm light
falls steady from the open door.

Here is your bed, folded open.
Lie down, lie down, let the blue snow cover you.

                                        2003

Fleur[1]

The first time she drowned in the cold and glassy waters of Lake Turcot, Fleur Pillager was only a girl. Two men saw the boat tip, saw her struggle in the waves. They rowed over to the place she went down, and jumped in. When they dragged her over the gunwales, she was cold to the touch and stiff, so they slapped her face, shook her by the heels, worked her arms back and forth, and pounded her back until she coughed up lake water. She shivered all over like a dog, then took a breath. But it wasn't long afterward that those two men disappeared. The first wandered off and the other, Jean Hat, got himself run over by a cart.

It went to show, my grandma said. It figured to her, all right. By saving Fleur Pillager, those two men had lost themselves.

The next time she fell in the lake, Fleur Pillager was twenty years old and no one touched her. She washed onshore, her skin a dull dead gray, but when George Many Women bent to look closer, he saw her chest move. Then her eyes spun open, sharp black riprock, and she looked at him. "You'll take my place," she hissed. Everybody scattered and left her there, so no one knows how she dragged herself home. Soon after that we noticed Many Women changed, grew afraid, wouldn't leave his house, and would not be forced to go near water. For his caution, he lived until the day that his sons brought him a new tin bathtub. Then the first time he used the tub he slipped, got knocked out, and breathed water while his wife stood in the other room frying breakfast.

Men stayed clear of Fleur Pillager after the second drowning. Even though she was good-looking, nobody dared to court her because it was clear that Misshepeshu, the waterman, the monster, wanted her for himself. He's a devil, that one, love-hungry with desire and maddened for the touch of young girls, the strong and daring especially, the ones like Fleur.

---

1. First published in *Esquire* magazine, August 1986.

Our mothers warn us that we'll think he's handsome, for he appears with green eyes, copper skin, a mouth tender as a child's. But if you fall into his arms, he sprouts horns, fangs, claws, fins. His feet are joined as one and his skin, brass scales, rings to the touch. You're fascinated, cannot move. He casts a shell necklace at your feet, weeps gleaming chips that harden into mica on your breasts. He holds you under. Then he takes the body of a lion or a fat brown worm. He's made of gold. He's made of beach moss. He's a thing of dry foam, a thing of death by drowning, the death a Chippewa cannot survive.

Unless you are Fleur Pillager. We all knew she couldn't swim. After the first time, we thought she'd never go back to Lake Turcot. We thought she'd keep to herself, live quiet, stop killing men off by drowning in the lake. After the first time, we thought she'd keep the good ways. But then, after the second drowning, we knew that we were dealing with something much more serious. She was haywire, out of control. She messed with evil, laughed at the old women's advice, and dressed like a man. She got herself into some half-forgotten medicine, studied ways we shouldn't talk about. Some say she kept the finger of a child in her pocket and a powder of unborn rabbits in a leather thong around her neck. She laid the heart of an owl on her tongue so she could see at night, and went out, hunting, not even in her own body. We know for sure because the next morning, in the snow or dust, we followed the tracks of her bare feet and saw where they changed, where the claws sprang out, the pad broadened and pressed into the dirt. By night we heard her chuffing cough, the bear cough. By day her silence and the wide grin she threw to bring down our guard made us frightened. Some thought that Fleur Pillager should be driven off the reservation, but not a single person who spoke like this had the nerve. And finally, when people were just about to get together and throw her out, she left on her own and didn't come back all summer. That's what this story is about.

During that summer, when she lived a few miles south in Argus, things happened. She almost destroyed that town.

When she got down to Argus in the year of 1920, it was just a small grid of six streets on either side of the railroad depot. There were two elevators, one central, the other a few miles west. Two stores competed for the trade of the three hundred citizens, and three churches quarreled with one another for their souls. There was a frame building for Lutherans, a heavy brick one for Episcopalians, and a long narrow shingled Catholic church. This last had a tall slender steeple, twice as high as any building or tree.

No doubt, across the low, flat wheat, watching from the road as she came near Argus on foot, Fleur saw that steeple rise, a shadow thin as a needle. Maybe in that raw space it drew her the way a lone tree draws lightning. Maybe, in the end, the Catholics are to blame. For if she hadn't seen that sign of pride, that slim prayer, that marker, maybe she would have kept walking.

But Fleur Pillager turned, and the first place she went once she came into town was to the back door of the priest's residence attached to the landmark church. She didn't go there for a handout, although she got that, but to ask for work. She got that too, or the town got her. It's hard to tell which came out worse, her or the men or the town, although the upshot of it all was that Fleur lived.

The four men who worked at the butcher's had carved up about a thousand carcasses between them, maybe half of that steers and the other half pigs, sheep, and game animals like deer, elk, and bear. That's not even mentioning the chickens, which were beyond counting. Pete Kozka owned the place, and employed Lily Veddar, Tor Grunewald, and my stepfather, Dutch James, who had brought my mother down from the reservation the year before she disappointed him by dying. Dutch took me out of school to take her place. I kept house half the time and worked the other in the butcher shop, sweeping floors, putting sawdust down, running a hambone across the street to a customer's bean pot or a package of sausage to the corner. I was a good one to have around because until they needed me, I was invisible. I blended into the stained brown walls, a skinny, big-nosed girl with staring eyes. Because I could fade into a corner or squeeze beneath a shelf, I knew everything, what the men said when no one was around, and what they did to Fleur.

Kozka's Meats served farmers for a fifty-mile area, both to slaughter, for it had a stock pen and chute, and to cure the meat by smoking it or spicing it in sausage. The storage locker was a marvel, made of many thicknesses of brick, earth insulation, and Minnesota timber, lined inside with sawdust and vast blocks of ice cut from Lake Turcot, hauled down from home each winter by horse and sledge.

A ramshackle board building, part slaughterhouse, part store, was fixed to the low, thick square of the lockers. That's where Fleur worked. Kozka hired her for her strength. She could lift a haunch or carry a pole of sausages without stumbling, and she soon learned cutting from Pete's wife, a string-thin blonde who chain-smoked and handled the razor-edged knives with nerveless precision, slicing close to her stained fingers. Fleur and Fritzie Kozka worked afternoons, wrapping their cuts in paper, and Fleur hauled the packages to the lockers. The meat was left outside the heavy oak doors that were only opened at 5:00 each afternoon, before the men ate supper.

Sometimes Dutch, Tor, and Lily stayed at the lockers, and when they did I stayed too, cleaned floors, restoked the fires in the front smokehouses, while the men sat around the squat cast-iron stove spearing slats of herring onto hardtack bread. They played long games of poker or cribbage on a board made from the planed end of a salt crate. They talked and I listened, although there wasn't much to hear since almost nothing ever happened in Argus. Tor was married, Dutch had lost my mother, and Lily read circulars. They mainly discussed about the auctions to come, equipment, or women.

Every so often, Pete Kozka came out front to make a whist, leaving Fritzie to smoke cigarettes and fry raised doughnuts in the back room. He sat and played a few rounds but kept his thoughts to himself. Fritzie did not tolerate him talking behind her back, and the one book he read was the New Testament. If he said something, it concerned weather or a surplus of sheep stomachs, a ham that smoked green or the markets for corn and wheat. He had a good-luck talisman, the opal-white lens of a cow's eye. Playing cards, he rubbed it between his fingers. That soft sound and the slap of cards was about the only conversation.

Fleur finally gave them a subject.

Her cheeks were wide and flat, her hands large, chapped, muscular. Fleur's shoulders were broad as beams, her hips fishlike, slippery, narrow. An old green dress clung to her waist, worn thin where she sat. Her braids were thick like the tails of animals, and swung against her when she moved, deliberately, slowly in her work, held in and half-tamed, but only half. I could tell, but the others never saw. They never looked into her sly brown eyes or noticed her teeth, strong and sharp and very white. Her legs were bare, and since she padded in beadworked moccasins they never saw that her fifth toes were missing. They never knew she'd drowned. They were blinded, they were stupid, they only saw her in the flesh.

And yet it wasn't just that she was a Chippewa, or even that she was a woman, it wasn't that she was good-looking or even that she was alone that made their brains hum. It was how she played cards.

Women didn't usually play with men, so the evening that Fleur drew a chair to the men's table without being so much as asked, there was a shock of surprise.

"What's this," said Lily. He was fat, with a snake's cold pale eyes and precious skin, smooth and lily-white, which is how he got his name. Lily had a dog, a stumpy mean little bull of a thing with a belly drum-tight from eating pork rinds. The dog liked to play cards just like Lily, and straddled his barrel thighs through games of stud, rum poker, vingt-un.[2] The dog snapped at Fleur's arm that first night, but cringed back, its snarl frozen, when she took her place.

"I thought," she said, her voice soft and stroking, "you might deal me in."

There was a space between the heavy bin of spiced flour and the wall where I just fit. I hunkered down there, kept my eyes open, saw her black hair swing over the chair, her feet solid on the wood floor. I couldn't see up on the table where the cards slapped down, so after they were deep in their game I raised myself up in the shadows, and crouched on a sill of wood.

I watched Fleur's hands stack and ruffle, divide the cards, spill them to each player in a blur, rake them up and shuffle again. Tor, short and scrappy, shut one eye and squinted the other at Fleur. Dutch screwed his lips around a wet cigar.

"Gotta see a man," he mumbled, getting up to go out back to the privy. The others broke, put their cards down, and Fleur sat alone in the lamplight that glowed in a sheen across the push of her breasts. I watched her closely, then she paid me a beam of notice for the first time. She turned, looked straight at me, and grinned the white wolf grin a Pillager turns on its victims, except that she wasn't after me.

"Pauline there," she said. "How much money you got?"

We had all been paid for the week that day. Eight cents was in my pocket.

"Stake me," she said, holding out her long fingers. I put the coins in her palm and then I melted back to nothing, part of the walls and tables. It was a long time before I understood that the men would not have seen me no matter what I did, how I moved. I wasn't anything like Fleur. My dress hung loose and my back was already curved, an old woman's. Work had roughened me, reading made my eyes sore, caring for my mother before she died had hardened my face. I was not much to look at, so they never saw me.

When the men came back and sat around the table, they had drawn together. They shot each other small glances, stuck their tongues in their cheeks, burst out laughing at odd moments, to rattle Fleur. But she never minded. They played their vingt-un, staying even as Fleur slowly gained. Those pennies I had given her drew nickels and attracted dimes until there was a small pile in front of her.

Then she hooked them with five card draw, nothing wild. She dealt, discarded, drew, and then she sighed and her cards gave a little shiver. Tor's eye gleamed, and Dutch straightened in his seat.

"I'll pay to see that hand," said Lily Veddar.

Fleur showed, and she had nothing there, nothing at all.

Tor's thin smile cracked open, and he threw his hand in too.

"Well, we know one thing," he said, leaning back in his chair, "the squaw can't bluff."

With that I lowered myself into a mound of swept sawdust and slept. I woke up during the night, but none of them had moved yet, so I couldn't either. Still later, the men must have gone out again, or Fritzie come out to break the game, because I was lifted, soothed, cradled in a woman's arms and rocked so quiet that I kept my eyes shut while Fleur rolled me into a closet of grimy ledgers, oiled paper, balls of string, and thick files that fit beneath me like a mattress.

The game went on after work the next evening. I got my eight cents back five times over, and Fleur kept the rest of the dollar she'd won for a stake. This time they didn't play so late, but they played regular, and then kept going at it night after night. They played poker now, or variations, for one week straight, and each time Fleur won exactly one dollar, no more and no less, too consistent for luck.

By this time, Lily and the other men were so lit with suspense that they got Pete to join the game with them. They concentrated, the fat dog sitting tense in Lily Veddar's lap, Tor suspicious, Dutch stroking his huge square brow, Pete steady. It wasn't that Fleur won that hooked them in so, because she lost hands too. It was rather that she never had a freak hand or even anything above a straight. She only took on her low cards, which didn't sit right. By chance, Fleur should have gotten a full or a flush by now. The irritating thing was she beat with pairs and never bluffed, because she couldn't, and still she ended each night with exactly one dollar. Lily couldn't believe, first of all, that a woman could be smart enough to play cards, but even if she was, that she would then be stupid enough to cheat for a dollar a night. By day I watched him turn the problem over, his hard white face dull, small fingers probing at his knuckles, until he finally thought he had Fleur figured as a bit-time player, caution her game. Raising the stakes would throw her.

More than anything now, he wanted Fleur to come away with something but a dollar. Two bits less or ten more, the sum didn't matter, just so he broke her streak.

Night after night she played, won her dollar, and left to stay in a place that just Fritzie and I knew about. Fleur bathed in the slaughtering tub, then slept in the unused brick smokehouse behind the lockers, a windowless place tarred on the inside with scorched fats. When I brushed against her skin I noticed that she smelled of the walls, rich and woody, slightly burnt. Since that night she put me in the closet I was no longer afraid of her, but followed her close, stayed with her, became her moving shadow that the men never noticed, the shadow that could have saved her.

August, the month that bears fruit, closed around the shop, and Pete and Fritzie left for Minnesota to escape the heat. Night by night, running, Fleur had won thirty dollars, and only Pete's presence had kept Lily at bay. But Pete was gone now, and one payday, with the heat so bad no one could move but Fleur, the men sat and played and waited while she finished work. The cards sweat, limp in their fingers, the table was slick with grease, and even the walls were warm to the touch. The air was motionless. Fleur was in the next room boiling heads.

Her green dress, drenched, wrapped her like a transparent sheet. A skin of lakeweed. Black snarls of veining clung to her arms. Her braids were loose, half unraveled, tied behind her neck in a thick loop. She stood in steam, turning skulls through a vat with a wooden paddle. When scraps boiled to the surface, she bent with a round tin sieve and scooped them out. She'd filled two dishpans.

"Ain't that enough now?" called Lily. "We're waiting." The stump of a dog trembled in his lap, alive with rage. It never smelled me or noticed me above Fleur's smoky skin. The air was heavy in my corner, and pressed me down. Fleur sat with them.

"Now what do you say?" Lily asked the dog. It barked. That was the signal for the real game to start.

"Let's up the ante," said Lily, who had been stalking this night all month. He had a roll of money in his pocket. Fleur had five bills in her dress. The men had each saved their full pay.

"Ante a dollar then," said Fleur, and pitched hers in. She lost, but they let her scrape along, cent by cent. And then she won some. She played unevenly, as if chance were all she had. She reeled them in. The game went on. The dog was stiff now, poised on Lily's knees, a ball of vicious muscle with its yellow eyes slit in concentration. It gave advice, seemed to sniff the lay of Fleur's cards, twitched and nudged. Fleur was up, then down, saved by a scratch. Tor dealt seven cards, three down. The pot grew, round by round, until it held all the money. Nobody folded. Then it all rode on one last card and they went silent. Fleur picked hers up and drew a long breath. The heat lowered like a bell. Her card shook, but she stayed in.

Lily smiled and took the dog's head tenderly between his palms.

"Say Fatso," he said, crooning the words. "You reckon that girl's bluffing?"

The dog whined and Lily laughed. "Me too," he said, "let's show." He swept his bills and coins into the pot and then they turned their cards over.

Lily looked once, looked again, then he squeezed the dog like a fist of dough and slammed it on the table.

Fleur threw out her arms and drew the money over, grinning that same wolf grin that she'd used on me, the grin that had them. She jammed the bills in her dress, scooped the coins up in waxed white paper that she tied with string.

"Let's go another round," said Lily, his voice choked with burrs. But Fleur opened her mouth and yawned, then walked out back to gather slops for the one big hog that was waiting in the stock pen to be killed.

The men sat still as rocks, their hands spread on the oiled wood table. Dutch had chewed his cigar to damp shreds, Tor's eye was dull. Lily's gaze was the only one to follow Fleur. I didn't move. I felt them gathering, saw my stepfather's veins, the ones in his forehead that stood out in anger. The dog rolled off the table and curled in a knot below the counter, where none of the men could touch it.

Lily rose and stepped out back to the closet of ledgers where Pete kept his private stock. He brought back a bottle, uncorked and tipped it between his fingers. The lump in his throat moved, then he passed it on. They drank, quickly felt the whiskey's fire, and planned with their eyes things they couldn't say aloud.

When they left, I followed. I hid out back in the clutter of broken boards and chicken crates beside the stock pen, where they waited. Fleur could not be seen at first, and then the moon broke and showed her, slipping cautiously along the rough board chute with a bucket in her hand. Her hair fell, wild and coarse, to her waist, and her dress was a floating patch in the dark. She made a pig-calling sound, rang the tin pail lightly against the wood, froze suspiciously. But too late. In the sound of the ring Lily moved, fat and nimble, stepped right behind Fleur and put out his creamy hands. At his first touch, she whirled and doused him with the bucket of sour slops. He pushed her against the big fence and the package of coins split, went clinking and jumping, winked against the wood. Fleur rolled over once and vanished into the yard.

The moon fell behind a curtain of ragged clouds, and Lily followed into the dark muck. But he tripped, pitched over the huge flank of the pig, who lay mired to the snout, heavily snoring. I sprang out of the weeds and climbed the side of the pen, stuck like glue. I saw the sow rise to her neat, knobby knees, gain her balance and sway, curious, as Lily stumbled forward. Fleur had backed into the angle of rough wood just beyond, and when Lily tried to jostle past, the sow tipped up on her hind legs and struck, quick and hard as a snake. She plunged her head into Lily's thick side and snatched a mouthful of his shirt. She lunged again, caught him lower, so that he grunted in pained surprise. He seemed to ponder, breathing deep. Then he launched his huge body in a swimmer's dive.

The sow screamed as his body smacked over hers. She rolled, striking out with her knife-sharp hooves, and Lily gathered himself upon her, took her foot-long face by the ears and scraped her snout and cheeks against the trestles of the pen. He hurled the sow's tight skull against an iron post, but instead of knocking her dead, he merely woke her from her dream.

She reared, shrieked, drew him with her so that they posed standing upright. They bowed jerkily to each other, as if to begin. Then his arms swung and flailed. She sank her black fangs into his shoulder, clasping him, dancing him forward and backward through the pen. Their steps picked up pace, went wild. The two dipped as one, box-stepped, tripped one another. She ran her split foot through his hair. He grabbed her kinked tail. They went down and came up, the same shape and then the same color until the men couldn't tell one from the other in that light and Fleur was able to launch herself over the gates, swing down, hit gravel.

The men saw, yelled, and chased her at a dead run to the smokehouse. And Lily too, once the sow gave up in disgust and freed him. That is where I should have gone to Fleur, saved her, thrown myself on Dutch. But I went stiff with fear and couldn't unlatch myself from the trestles or move at all. I closed my eyes and put my head in my arms, tried to hide, so there is nothing to describe but what I couldn't block out, Fleur's hoarse breath, so loud it filled me, her cry in the old language, and my name repeated over and over among the words.

The heat was still dense the next morning when I came back to work. Fleur was gone but the men were there, slack-faced, hung over. Lily was paler and softer than ever, as if his flesh had steamed on his bones. They smoked, took pulls off a bottle. It wasn't noon yet. I worked awhile, waiting shop and sharpening steel. But I was sick, I was smothered, I was sweating so hard that my hands slipped on the knives, and I wiped my fingers clean of the greasy touch of the customers' coins. Lily opened his mouth and roared once, not in anger. There was no meaning to the sound. His boxer dog, sprawled limp beside his foot, never lifted its head. Nor did the other men.

They didn't notice when I stepped outside, hoping for a clear breath. And then I forgot them because I knew that we were all balanced, ready to tip, to fly, to be crushed as soon as the weather broke. The sky was so low that I felt the weight of it like a yoke. Clouds hung down, witch teats, a tornado's green-brown cones, and as I watched one flicked out and became a delicate probing thumb. Even as I picked up my heels and ran back inside, the wind blew suddenly, cold, and then came rain.

Inside, the men had disappeared already and the whole place was trembling as if a huge hand was pinched at the rafters, shaking it. I ran straight through, screaming for Dutch or for any of them, and then I stopped at the heavy doors of the lockers, where they had surely taken shelter. I stood there a moment. Everything went still. Then I heard a cry building in the wind, faint at first, a whistle and then a shrill scream that tore through the walls and gathered around me, spoke plain so I understood that I should move, put my arms out, and slam down the great iron bar that fit across the hasp and lock.

Outside, the wind was stronger, like a hand held against me. I struggled forward. The bushes tossed, the awnings flapped off storefronts, the rails of porches rattled. The odd cloud became a fat snout that nosed along the earth and sniffled, jabbed, picked at things, sucked them up, blew them apart, rooted around as if it was following a certain scent, then stopped behind me at the butcher shop and bored down like a drill.

I went flying, landed somewhere in a ball. When I opened my eyes and looked, stranger things were happening.

A herd of cattle flew through the air like giant birds, dropping dung, their mouths opened in stunned bellows. A candle, still lighted, blew past, and tables, napkins, garden tools, a whole school of drifting eyeglasses, jackets on hangers, hams, a checkerboard, a lampshade, and at last the sow from behind the lockers, on the run, her hooves a blur, set free, swooping, diving, screaming as everything in Argus fell apart and got turned upside down, smashed, and thoroughly wrecked.

Days passed before the town went looking for the men. They were bachelors, after all, except for Tor, whose wife had suffered a blow to the head that made her forgetful. Everyone was occupied with digging out, in high relief because even though the Catholic steeple had been torn off like a peaked cap and sent across five fields, those huddled in the cellar were unhurt. Walls had fallen, windows were demolished, but the stores were intact and so were the bankers and shop owners who had taken refuge in their safes or beneath their cash registers. It was a fair-minded disaster, no one could be said to have suffered much more than the next, at least not until Pete and Fritzie came home.

Of all the businesses in Argus, Kozka's Meats had suffered worst. The boards of the front building had been split to kindling, piled in a huge pyramid, and the shop equipment was blasted far and wide. Pete paced off the distance the iron bathtub had been flung—a hundred feet. The glass candy case went fifty, and landed without so much as a cracked pane. There were other surprises as well, for the back rooms where Fritzie and Pete lived were undisturbed. Fritzie said the dust still coated her china figures, and upon her kitchen table, in the ashtray, perched the last cigarette she'd put out in haste. She lit and finished it, looking through the window. From there, she could see that the old smokehouse Fleur had slept in was crushed to a reddish sand and the stockpens were completely torn apart, the rails stacked helter-skelter. Fritzie asked for Fleur. People shrugged. Then she asked about the others and, suddenly, the town understood that three men were missing.

There was a rally of help, a gathering of shovels and volunteers. We passed boards from hand to hand, stacked them, uncovered what lay beneath the pile of jagged splinters. The lockers, full of meat that was Pete and Fritzie's investment, slowly came into sight, still intact. When enough room was made for a man to stand on the roof, there were calls, a general urge to hack through and see what lay below. But Fritzie shouted that she wouldn't allow it because the meat would spoil. And so the work continued, board by board, until at last the heavy oak doors of the freezer were revealed and people pressed to the entry. Everyone wanted to be the first, but since it was my stepfather lost, I was let go in when Pete and Fritzie wedged through into the sudden icy air.

Pete scraped a match on his boot, lit the lamp Fritzie held, and then the three of us stood still in its circle. Light glared off the skinned and hanging carcasses, the crates of wrapped sausages, the bright and cloudy blocks of lake ice, pure as winter. The cold bit into us, pleasant at first, then numbing. We must have stood there a couple of minutes before we saw the men, or more rightly, the humps of fur, the iced and shaggy hides they wore, the bearskins they had taken down and wrapped about themselves. We stepped closer and Fritzie tilted the lantern beneath the flaps of fur into their faces. The dog was there, perched among them, heavy as a doorstop. The three had hunched around a barrel where the game was still laid out, and a dead lantern and an empty bottle too. But they had thrown down their last hands and hunkered tight, clutching one another, knuckles raw from beating at the door they had also attacked with hooks. Frost stars gleamed off their eyelashes and the stubble of their beards. Their faces were set in concentration, mouths open as if to speak some careful thought, some agreement they'd come to in each other's arms.

Power travels in the bloodlines, handed out before birth. It comes down through the hands, which in the Pillagers were strong and knotted, big, spidery, and rough, with sensitive fingertips good at dealing cards. It comes through the eyes, too, belligerent, darkest brown, the eyes of those in the bear clan, impolite as they gaze directly at a person.

In my dreams, I look straight back at Fleur, at the men. I am no longer the watcher on the dark sill, the skinny girl.

The blood draws us back, as if it runs through a vein of earth. I've come home and, except for talking to my cousins, live a quiet life. Fleur lives quiet too, down on Lake Turcot with her boat. Some say she's married to the waterman, Misshepeshu, or that she's living in shame with white men or windigos, or that she's killed them all. I'm about the only one here who ever goes to visit her. Last winter, I went to help out in her cabin when she bore the child, whose green eyes and skin the color of an old penny made more talk, as no one could decide if the child was mixed blood or what, fathered in a smokehouse, or by a man with brass scales, or by the lake. The girl is bold, smiling in her sleep, as if she knows what people wonder, as if she hears the old men talk, turning the story over. It comes up different every time and has no ending, no beginning. They get the middle wrong too. They only know they don't know anything.

1988

LI-YOUNG LEE
b. 1957

I n his poem "Persimmons" Li-Young Lee remembers his father saying, "Some things never leave a person." Many of the poems in Lee's books—*Rose* (1986), *The City in Which I Love You* (1990), *Book of My Nights* (2001), and *Behind My Eyes* (2008)—testify to a sense of the past, especially his father's past, that never leaves Lee. The father in Lee's poems is personal and mythic; he instructs the poet-son in "the art of memory." Lee's father, born in China, served as a personal physician to Mao Zedong. He later was jailed for nineteen months, a political prisoner of the Indonesian dictator Sukarno. Lee was born in Jakarta, Indonesia. In 1959 the family fled Indonesia and traveled to Hong Kong, Macao, and Japan, finally arriving in America, where Lee's father became a Presbyterian minister in a small town in western Pennsylvania. Many of Lee's poems seek to remember and understand his father's life and to come to terms with Lee's differences from that powerful figure.

Lee's work reminds us about the ancient connections between memory and poetry. In his work memory is often sweet; it draws the poet to the past even when, as in "Eating Alone," that sweetness is as dizzying as the juice of a rotten pear in which a hornet spins. But memory can also be a burden, and its pull is countered in Lee's work by a sensuous apprehension of the present. As in his poem "This Room and Everything in It," the erotic immediacy of the moment can disrupt any effort to fix that moment in the orders of memory. Everywhere in Lee's work is the evidence of hearing, taste, smell, and touch as well as sight. If the poet's bodily presence in the world recalls his great American precursor Walt Whitman, Lee's fluid motion between the physical world and the domain of memory, dream, or vision also carries out Whitman's visionary strain and links Lee to the work of Theodore Roethke, James Wright, and Denise Levertov, among others. The intensity of Lee's poems, however, is often leavened by a subtle and winning humor and playfulness; such qualities are especially valuable in a poet at times too easily seduced by beauty.

Lee studied at the University of Pittsburgh (where one of his teachers was the poet Gerald Stern), the University of Arizona, and the State University of New York College at Brockport. He has since taught at various universities. In 1995 he published a prose memoir, *The Winged Seed: A Remembrance*. His prose, like his poetry, is characterized by his deep sense of connection between an individual life and a powerful past, mediated by his ability to move between plain speech and a lushness evocative of biblical language.

Persimmons

In sixth grade Mrs. Walker
slapped the back of my head
and made me stand in the corner
for not knowing the difference
between *persimmon* and *precision*.   5
How to choose

persimmons. This is precision.
Ripe ones are soft and brown-spotted.
Sniff the bottoms. The sweet one
will be fragrant. How to eat: 10
put the knife away, lay down newspaper.
Peel the skin tenderly, not to tear the meat.
Chew the skin, suck it,
and swallow. Now, eat
the meat of the fruit,   15
so sweet,
all of it, to the heart.

Donna undresses, her stomach is white.
In the yard, dewy and shivering
with crickets, we lie naked,   20
face-up, face-down.
I teach her Chinese.
Crickets: *chiu chiu.* Dew: I've forgotten.
Naked: I've forgotten.
Ni, wo: you and me.   25
I part her legs,
remember to tell her
she is beautiful as the moon.

Other words
that got me into trouble were   30
fight and *fright, wren* and *yarn.*
Fight was what I did when I was frightened,
fright was what I felt when I was fighting.
Wrens are small, plain birds,
yarn is what one knits with.   35
Wrens are soft as yarn.

My mother made birds out of yarn.
I loved to watch her tie the stuff;
a bird, a rabbit, a wee man.

Mrs. Walker brought a persimmon to class   40
and cut it up
so everyone could taste
a *Chinese apple*. Knowing
it wasn't ripe or sweet, I didn't eat
but I watched the other faces.   45

My mother said every persimmon has a sun
inside, something golden, glowing,
warm as my face.

Once, in the cellar, I found two wrapped in newspaper,
forgotten and not yet ripe.   50
I took them and set both on my bedroom windowsill,
where each morning a cardinal
sang, *The sun, the sun.*

Finally understanding
he was going blind,   55
my father sat up all one night
waiting for a song, a ghost.
I gave him the persimmons,
swelled, heavy as sadness,
and sweet as love.   60

This year, in the muddy lighting
of my parents' cellar, I rummage, looking
for something I lost.
My father sits on the tired, wooden stairs,
black cane between his knees,   65
hand over hand, gripping the handle.

He's so happy that I've come home.
I ask how his eyes are, a stupid question.
All gone, he answers.

Under some blankets, I find a box.   70
Inside the box I find three scrolls.
I sit beside him and untie
three paintings by my father:
Hibiscus leaf and a white flower.
Two cats preening.   75
Two persimmons, so full they want to drop from the cloth.

He raises both hands to touch the cloth,
asks, *Which is this?*

This is persimmons, Father.

Oh, the feel of the wolftail on the silk,   80
the strength, the tense
precision in the wrist.
I painted them hundreds of times
eyes closed. These I painted blind.
Some things never leave a person: 85
scent of the hair of one you love,
the texture of persimmons,
in your palm, the ripe weight.

1986

Eating Alone

I've pulled the last of the year's young onions.
The garden is bare now. The ground is cold,
brown and old. What is left of the day flames
in the maples at the corner of my
eye. I turn, a cardinal vanishes.   5
By the cellar door, I wash the onions,
then drink from the icy metal spigot.

Once, years back, I walked beside my father
among the windfall pears. I can't recall
our words. We may have strolled in silence. But   10
I still see him bend, that way—left hand braced
on knee, creaky—to lift and hold to my
eye a rotten pear. In it, a hornet
spun crazily, glazed in slow, glistening juice.

It was my father I saw this morning   15
waving to me from the trees. I almost
called to him, until I came close enough
to see the shovel, leaning where I had
left it, in the flickering, deep green shade.

White rice steaming, almost done. Sweet green peas   20
fried in onions. Shrimp braised in sesame
oil and garlic. And my own loneliness.
What more could I, a young man, want.

1986

Eating Together

In the steamer is the trout
seasoned with slivers of ginger,
two sprigs of green onion, and sesame oil.

We shall eat it with rice for lunch,
brothers, sister, my mother who will   5
taste the sweetest meat of the head,
holding it between her fingers
deftly, the way my father did
weeks ago. Then he lay down
to sleep like a snow-covered road   10
winding through pines older than him,
without any travelers, and lonely for no one.

1986

This Room and Everything in It

Lie still now
while I prepare For my future,
certain hard days ahead,
when I'll need what I know so clearly this moment.

I am making use   5
of the one thing I learned
of all the things my father tried to teach me:
the art of memory.

I am letting this room
and everything in it   10
stand for my ideas about love
and its difficulties.

I'll let your love-cries,
those spacious notes
of a moment ago,   15
stand for distance.

Your scent,
that scent
of spice and a wound,
I'll let stand for mystery.   20

Your sunken belly
is the daily cup
of milk I drank
as a boy before morning prayer.

The sun on the face   25
of the wall
is God, the face
I can't see, my soul,

and so on, each thing
standing for a separate idea,   30

and those ideas forming the constellation
of my greater idea.
And one day, when I need
to tell myself something intelligent
about love,   35

I'll close my eyes
and recall this room and everything in it:
My body is estrangement.
This desire, perfection.
Your closed eyes my extinction.   40
Now I've forgotten my
idea. The book
on the windowsill, riffled by wind . . .
the even-numbered pages are
the past, the odd-   45
numbered pages, the future.
The sun is
God, your body is milk . . .

useless, useless . . .
your cries are song, my body's not me . . .   50
no good . . . my idea
has evaporated . . . your hair is time, your thighs are song . . .
it had something to do
with death . . . it had something
to do with love.   55

1990

Creative Nonfiction

In what is known today as "creative nonfiction," writers report on the world without the pretense of journalistic objectivity or the imperatives of timeliness associated with traditional "news." The novelist David Foster Wallace described his own forays into the genre as a process of "peeling back my skull. You know, welcome to my mind for twenty pages, see through my eyes." "Creative nonfiction" is a relatively new term—it first appeared officially in 1983 as a category for creative writing fellowships in the National Endowment of the Arts—but examples of the form appear much earlier in American literature. If Thoreau and Emerson were publishing their essays today, much of their work would probably be called creative nonfiction. Indeed, travel and nature writing have long been a part of American literature. The term is fluid, suggesting a hybrid that involves facts, research, and information while using the forms and strategies of fiction, poetry, film, drama, biography, autobiography, and even philosophy.

The term is closely allied with what was, in the 1970s, called "the New Journalism" (the writer Tom Wolfe published a combined manifesto and anthology with that title in 1973), in which, instead of simply reporting an event, the writer reports on himself or herself within the event, either as a participant or as an observer (or both). Examples of the "the New Journalism" include Wolfe's *The Kandy-Kolored Tangerine-Flake Streamline Baby* (1965), Truman Capote's *In Cold Blood* (1966), Norman Mailer's *Armies of the Night* (1968), Joan Didion's *Slouching Towards Bethlehem* (1968), Hunter S. Thompson's *Fear and Loathing in Las Vegas* (1972), and Michael Herr's *Dispatches* (1977). The New Journalism was intended by its practitioners to reflect critically on both the novel and journalism. Wolfe, for instance, insisted (as had others since the early twentieth century) that the novel was a dead end. Disconnected from reality, it did not have the relevance that nonfiction might have. The novelist Philip Roth echoed that thought in fiction: in *The Ghost Writer* (1979) he has his protagonist, a writer alter-ego named Nathan Zuckerman, lament, "If only I could invent as presumptuously as real life! If one day I could just *approach* the originality and excitement of what actually goes on!" For many writers, the upheavals of the 1960s—including the civil rights movement, the hippie counterculture, the Cold War, and the war in Vietnam—seemed to exceed what any individual could imagine and demanded an expressive mode that could match the "originality and excitement" of history itself. Wolfe turned to the language of the Beat writers, which he brought to his descriptions of the counterculture. Didion looked to the spare prose of Hemingway, certain that "the seemingly insignificant things that most of us spend our days noticing are really significant, have meaning, and tell us something."

For Capote and Mailer, the novel remained a force to be reckoned with, and they plundered its resources to narrate real dramas. In *Armies of the Night*, which was subtitled "History as a Novel / The Novel as History," Mailer begins by invoking a traditional journalistic account of the 1967 anti–Vietnam War march on the Pentagon, but soon dismisses it: "Now we may leave *Time* in order to find out what happened," he declares. The "novel" that follows presents Mailer as a character, alongside the poets Robert Lowell and Mitchell Goodman, radical activist Jerry Rubin, and other literary and political celebrities, whose escapades make reportage into absurdist modern comedy. Capote, too, found the novel a better tool for telling the story of a quadruple murder in *In Cold Blood*. Novels have always been able to present complex characters and mixed motives, and to show characters evolving over time. Capote's epic account of a real crime draws on that tradition in representing an incident of spectacular violence as well as the psychological and cultural vortex from which it was born.

The New Journalism called into question the traditional objectivity of reporting, addressing—and reveling in—what the physicist Werner Heisenberg called "the uncertainty principle" (a theory the novelist Thomas Pynchon frequently invokes in his work), which asserts that the observer's presence alters the phenomenon being observed. Like all movements, the one that rode under this banner came to an end. By 1975 writers were already asking, in print, "Whatever Happened to the New Journalism?" and by 1981 the writer Joe Nocera declared it dead—its credibility killed, he argued, by Hunter S. Thompson. And in the surest sign of the movement's end, its name has lately been resurrected, in Robert S. Boynton's anthology, as *The New New Journalism* (2005). What remained of the New Journalism, once "creative nonfiction" arose to replace it in the early 1980s, was the focus on narrative drive, inventive language, distinctive voice, and personal observation. Creative nonfiction is open in its aim of merging literary technique with fidelity to fact.

As with all hybrids, the distinctions between it and other forms are slippery. Among the selections here, Thompson and Didion represent the New Journalism, demonstrating how style shapes copious concrete detail into forms that ask readers to reflect on the significance of facts. Today, most memoirs, personal essays, long-form features, and environmental writing are considered to be creative nonfiction, but the writers in this cluster provide especially innovative examples of these forms. Edwidge Danticat mingles autobiography, political analysis, and biography. The environmental writings of Edward Abbey and Barry Lopez combine carefully observed, factual description of landscapes and natural creatures with an equal focus on the writer's feelings and reflections. Wallace's essay on the Maine Lobster Festival grounds itself in entertaining, feature-style magazine reportage but ends with rigorous intellectual inquiry more common to philosophy or science. It is easy to understand why many examples of the form slip back and forth between a variety of categories: among the selections here, Jamaica Kincaid's "Girl" appeared in a book collection advertised as "Stories," and it was featured under the rubric of "Fiction" when it was first published in the *New Yorker*; but many critics and reviewers have since called the work a prose poem or an autobiography.

The term "Creative Nonfiction" is fully at ease with such slippage and happily embraces work that mixes elements of many different genres; whatever the mixture, it's the quality of writing and the use of various techniques that establish the work as "creative." In the twenty-first century, hybridity is a significant cultural modality, and much of contemporary writing is self-consciously hybrid. Mixing poetry and essay, personal reflection and journalism, reportage and critique, nature writing and myth, or inventing other combinations, some of the most vital American writing is now, and always has been, creative nonfiction.

EDWARD ABBEY

A prolific writer, Edward Abbey (1927–1989) was the author of many novels but he is most famous for his personal essays, which have become classics of environmental writing. Born and raised in Pennsylvania, he went west in his teens, and late in the 1950s he worked at Arches National Monument (now Arches National Park) near Moab in eastern Utah, as a seasonal ranger. In the spirit of Thoreau's residence at Walden Pond and Gary Snyder's summers as a fire lookout in Washington State's

North Cascades, Abbey said he sought solitude in an effort to "confront, immediately and directly if possible, the bare bones of existence." His most famous book, *Desert Solitaire* (1968), came out of his journals from this period; the book is a compilation of description, natural history, tall tales, and polemical environmentalism.

One of the most gripping chapters in *Desert Solitaire* focuses on Abbey's time in Havasu, at the base of the Grand Canyon. As he tells it, during a stop at the Grand Canyon with friends en route to Los Angeles he decided on the spur of the moment to descend to the canyon floor ("fourteen miles by trail") to take a look at Havasu Canyon in Arizona, the homeland of the Havasupai Native people. Five weeks later, he emerged to find that his friends had sensibly gone on without him. During the weeks he spent there, Abbey camped and explored the surrounding landscape alone. The selection here focuses on one such day of exploration, when, looking for a short-cut back to his camp, he made a series of potentially fatal decisions.

Havasu

Most of my wandering in the desert I've done alone. Not so much from choice as from necessity—I generally prefer to go into places where no one else wants to go. I find that in contemplating the natural world my pleasure is greater if there are not too many others contemplating it with me, at the same time. However, there are special hazards in traveling alone. Your chances of dying, in case of sickness or accident, are much improved, simply because there is no one around to go for help.

Exploring a side canyon off Havasu Canyon[1] one day, I was unable to resist the temptation to climb up out of it onto what corresponds in that region to the Tonto Bench.[2] Late in the afternoon I realized that I would not have enough time to get back to my camp before dark, unless I could find a much shorter route than the one by which I had come. I looked for a shortcut.

Nearby was another little side canyon which appeared to lead down into Havasu Canyon. It was a steep, shadowy, extremely narrow defile with the usual meandering course and overhanging walls; from where I stood, near its head, I could not tell if the route was feasible all the way down to the floor of the main canyon. I had no rope with me—only my walking stick. But I was hungry and thirsty, as always. I started down.

For a while everything went well. The floor of the little canyon began as a bed of dry sand, scattered with rocks. Farther down a few boulders were wedged between the walls; I climbed over and under them. Then the canyon took on the slickrock[3] character—smooth, sheer, slippery sandstone carved by erosion into a series of scoops and potholes which got bigger as I descended. In some of these basins there was a little water left over from the last flood, warm and fetid water under an oily-looking scum, condensed by prolonged evaporation to a sort of broth, rich in dead and dying organisms. My canteen was empty and I was very thirsty but I felt that I could wait.

1. A canyon with waterfall, forming a side branch of the Grand Canyon, that was once the home of a prehistoric people and has been occupied by the Havasupai, "people of the blue-green waters," for the last 800 years.
2. The long, narrow strip of relatively level land located in the Grand Canyon, separating the inner gorge from the upper canyon and following the course of the Colorado River.
3. A term used in the Southwest to refer to smooth, consolidated, and hardened sand dunes.

I came to a lip on the canyon floor which overhung by twelve feet the largest so far of these stagnant pools. On each side rose the canyon walls, roughly perpendicular. There was no way to continue except by dropping into the pool. I hesitated. Beyond this point there could hardly be any returning, yet the main canyon was still not visible below. Obviously the only sensible thing to do was to turn back. I edged over the lip of stone and dropped feet first into the water.

Deeper than I expected. The warm, thick fluid came up and closed over my head as my feet touched the muck at the bottom. I had to swim to the farther side. And here I found myself on the verge of another drop-off, with one more huge bowl of green soup below.

This drop-off was about the same height as the one before, but not overhanging. It resembled a children's playground slide, concave and S-curved, only steeper, wider, with a vertical pitch in the middle. It did not lead directly into the water but ended in a series of steplike ledges above the pool. Beyond the pool lay another edge, another drop-off into an unknown depth. Again I paused, and for a much longer time. But I no longer had the option of turning around and going back. I eased myself into the chute[4] and let go of everything—except my faithful stick.

I hit rock bottom hard, but without any physical injury. I swam the stinking pond dog-paddle[5] style, pushing the heavy scum away from my face, and crawled out on the far side to see what my fate was going to be.

Fatal. Death by starvation, slow and tedious. For I was looking straight down an overhanging cliff to a rubble pile of broken rocks eighty feet below.

After the first wave of utter panic had passed I began to try to think. First of all I was not going to die immediately, unless another flash flood came down the gorge; there was the pond of stagnant water on hand to save me from thirst and a man can live, they say, for thirty days or more without food. My sun-bleached bones, dramatically sprawled at the bottom of the chasm, would provide the diversion of the picturesque for future wanderers—if any man ever came this way again.

My second thought was to scream for help, although I knew very well there could be no other human being within miles. I even tried it but the sound of that anxious shout, cut short in the dead air within the canyon walls, was so inhuman, so detached as it seemed from myself, that it terrified me and I didn't attempt it again.

I thought of tearing my clothes into strips and plaiting a rope. But what was I wearing?—boots, socks, a pair of old and ragged blue jeans, a flimsy T-shirt, an ancient and rotten sombrero[6] of straw. Not a chance of weaving such a wardrobe into a rope eighty feet long, or even twenty feet long.

How about a signal fire? There was nothing to burn but my clothes; not a tree, not a shrub, not even a weed grew in this stony cul-de-sac. Even if I burned my clothing the chances of the smoke being seen by some Hualapai Indian[7] high on the south rim were very small; and if he did see the smoke, what then? He'd shrug his shoulders, sigh, and take another pull from his

---

4. A waterfall or steep descent in a river.
5. A simple swimming style, often used by children.
6. A broad-brimmed hat common in Spain and Spanish America.
7. "People of the tall pine," the Hualapai are a Native American people living along the pine-clad southern side of the Grand Canyon.

Tokay[8] bottle. Furthermore, without clothes, the sun would soon bake me to death.

There was only one thing I could do. I had a tiny notebook in my hip pocket and a stub of pencil. When these dried out I could at least record my final thoughts. I would have plenty of time to write not only my epitaph but my own elegy.[9]

But not yet.

There were a few loose stones scattered about the edge of the pool. Taking the biggest first, I swam with it back to the foot of the slickrock chute and placed it there. One by one I brought the others and made a shaky little pile about two feet high leaning against the chute. Hopeless, of course, but there was nothing else to do. I stood on the top of the pile and stretched upward, straining my arms to their utmost limit and groped with fingers and fingernails for a hold on something firm. There was nothing. I crept back down. I began to cry. It was easy. All alone, I didn't have to be brave.

Through the tears I noticed my old walking stick lying nearby. I took it and stood it on the most solid stone in the pile, behind the two topmost stones. I took off my boots, tied them together and hung them around my neck, on my back. I got up on the little pile again and lifted one leg and set my big toe on the top of the stick. This could never work. Slowly and painfully, leaning as much of my weight as I could against the sandstone slide, I applied more and more pressure to the stick, pushing my body upward until I was again stretched out full length above it. Again I felt about for a fingerhold. There was none. The chute was smooth as polished marble.

No, not quite that smooth. This was sandstone, soft and porous, not marble, and between it and my wet body and wet clothing a certain friction was created. In addition, the stick had enabled me to reach a higher section of the S-curved chute, where the angle was more favorable. I discovered that I could move upward, inch by inch, through adhesion and with the help of the leveling tendency of the curve. I gave an extra little push with my big toe—the stones collapsed below, the stick clattered down—and crawled rather like a snail or slug, oozing slime, up over the rounded summit of the slide.

The next obstacle, the overhanging spout twelve feet above a deep plunge pool, looked impossible. It *was* impossible, but with the blind faith of despair I slogged into the water and swam underneath the drop-off and floundered around for a while, scrabbling at the slippery rock until my nerves and tiring muscles convinced my numbed brain that *this was not the way*. I swam back to solid ground and lay down to rest and die in comfort.

Far above I could see the sky, an irregular strip of blue between the dark, hard-edged canyon walls that seemed to lean toward each other as they towered above me. Across that narrow opening a small white cloud was passing, so lovely and precious and delicate and forever inaccessible that it broke the heart and made me weep like a woman, like a child. In all my life I had never seen anything so beautiful.

The walls that rose on either side of the drop-off were literally perpendicular. Eroded by weathering, however, and not by the corrasion[1] of rushing

---

8. Tokay is a sweet wine, often cheaply available.
9. An epitaph is a short text inscribed on a tombstone, honoring a deceased person; an elegy is a mournful poem, especially a funeral song or a

lament for the dead.
1. The wearing away of rock by the constant flow of water.

floodwater, they had a rough surface, chipped, broken, cracked. Where the walls joined the face of the overhang they formed almost a square corner, with a number of minute crevices and inch-wide shelves on either side. It might, after all, be possible. What did I have to lose?

When I had regained some measure of nerve and steadiness I got up off my back and tried the wall beside the pond, clinging to the rock with bare toes and fingertips and inching my way crabwise toward the corner. The watersoaked, heavy boots dangling from my neck, swinging back and forth with my every movement, threw me off balance and I fell into the pool. I swam out to the bank, unslung the boots and threw them up over the drop-off, out of sight. They'd be there if I ever needed them again. Once more I attached myself to the wall, tenderly, sensitively, like a limpet,[2] and very slowly, very cautiously, worked my way into the corner. Here I was able to climb upward, a few centimeters at a time, by bracing myself against the opposite sides and finding sufficient niches for fingers and toes. As I neared the top and the overhang became noticeable I prepared for a slip, planning to push myself away from the rock so as to fall into the center of the pool where the water was deepest. But it wasn't necessary. Somehow, with a skill and tenacity I could never have found in myself under ordinary circumstances, I managed to creep straight up that gloomy cliff and over the brink of the drop-off and into the flower of safety. My boots were floating under the surface of the little puddle above. As I poured the stinking water out of them and pulled them on and laced them up I discovered myself bawling again for the third time in three hours, the hot delicious tears of victory. And up above the clouds replied—thunder.

I emerged from that treacherous little canyon at sundown, with an enormous fire in the western sky and lightning overhead. Through sweet twilight and the sudden dazzling flare of lightning a I hiked back along the Tonto Bench, bellowing the *Ode to Joy*.[3] Long before I reached the place where I could descend safely to the main canyon and my camp, however, darkness set in, the clouds opened their bays and the rain poured down. I took shelter under a ledge in a shallow cave about three feet high—hardly room to sit up in. Others had been here before: the dusty floor of the little hole was littered with the droppings of birds, rats, jackrabbits, and coyotes. There were also a few long gray pieces of scat with a curious twist at one tip—cougar? I didn't care. I had some matches with me, sealed in paraffin (the prudent explorer); I scraped together the handiest twigs and animal droppings and built a little fire and waited for the rain to stop.

It didn't stop. The rain came down for hours in alternate waves of storm and drizzle and I very soon had burnt up all the fuel within reach. No matter. I stretched out in the coyote den, pillowed my head on my arm and suffered through the long long night, wet, cold, aching, hungry, wretched, dreaming claustrophobic nightmares. It was one of the happiest nights of my life.

1968

---

2. Common name for numerous kinds of salt-water and freshwater snails.
3. A famous theme in the final movement of German composer and pianist Ludwig van Beethoven's (1770–1827) Ninth Symphony (1824), based on a text by the German poet Friedrich Schiller (1759–1805).

BARRY LOPEZ

B arry Lopez's "The Raven" is a difficult piece of writing to categorize. In its specific
attention to details of the desert landscape and creatures, it belongs to the genre
of nature writing for which Lopez (b. 1945) is so well known (for example, his award-
winning books *Arctic Dreams*, 1986, and *Of Wolves and Men*, 2004). But like much of
Lopez's writing, "The Raven" is clearly not a simple factual description of ravens.
Embedded in the piece are what we might call "raven tales"—fables or stories about
the life and behaviors of a bird whose symbolic importance in indigenous cultures is
widespread. And, in fact, the book in which this piece first appeared, *Desert Notes:
Reflections in the Eye of a Raven* (1976), bore the subtitle "Short Stories." But as Lopez
himself has pointed out, "the distinction between fiction and nonfiction, though logical and even useful, is not as important as the distinction between an authentic and
inauthentic story." "The Raven" is an authentic story about the desert landscape and
its inhabitants and, equally important, a story that creates in the writer and the reader
an authentic sense of wonder. In its presentation of a natural world deeply connected
to myth and storytelling there are clear affinities between this piece and the work of
Native American writers like Louise Erdrich and Sherman Alexie.

Lopez is an intimate observer of the landscape he writes about in "The Raven." He
grew up in rural Southern California and as a child spent time in the Mojave Desert.
His interest in the relationships between landscapes and human culture has taken
him on travels to both remote and populated parts of the world.

The Raven

I am going to have to start at the other end by telling you this: there are no
crows in the desert. What appear to be crows are ravens. You must examine
the crow, however, before you can understand the raven. To forget the crow
completely, as some have tried to do, would be like trying to understand the
one who stayed without talking to the one who left. It is important to make
note of who has left the desert.

To begin with, the crow does nothing alone. He cannot abide silence and
he is prone to stealing things, twigs and bits of straw, from the nests of his
neighbors. It is a game with him. He enjoys tricks. If he cannot make up his
mind the crow will take two or three wives, but this is not a game. The crow
is very accommodating and he admires compulsiveness.

Crows will live in street trees in the residential areas of great cities. They
will walk at night on the roofs of parked cars and peck at the grit; they will
scrape the pinpoints of their talons across the steel and, with their necks
outthrust, watch for frightened children listening in their beds.

Put all this to the raven: he will open his mouth as if to say something.
Then he will look the other way and say nothing. Later, when you have forgotten, he will tell you he admires the crow.

The raven is larger than the crow and has a beard of black feathers at his
throat. He is careful to kill only what he needs. Crows, on the other hand,
will search out the great horned owl, kick and punch him awake, and then,

for roosting too close to their nests, they will kill him. They will come out of the sky on a fat, hot afternoon and slam into the head of a dozing rabbit and go away laughing. They will tear out a whole row of planted corn and eat only a few kernels. They will defecate on scarecrows and go home and sleep with 200,000 of their friends in an atmosphere of congratulation. Again, it is only a game; this should not be taken to mean that they are evil.

There is however this: when too many crows come together on a roost there is a lot of shoving and noise and a white film begins to descend over the crows' eyes and they go blind. They fall from their perches and lie on the ground and starve to death. When confronted with this information, crows will look past you and warn you vacantly that it is easy to be misled.

The crow flies like a pigeon. The raven flies like a hawk He is seen only at a great distance and then not very clearly. This is true of the crow too, but if you are very clever you can trap the crow. The only way to be sure what you have seen is a raven is to follow him until he dies of old age, and then examine the body.

Once there were many crows in the desert. I am told it was like this: you could sit back in the rocks and watch a pack of crows working over the carcass of a coyote. Some would eat, the others would try to squeeze out the vultures. The raven would never be seen. He would be at a distance, alone, perhaps eating a scorpion.

There was, at this time, a small alkaline water hole at the desert's edge. Its waters were bitter. No one but crows would drink there, although they drank sparingly, just one or two sips at a time. One day a raven warned someone about the dangers of drinking the bitter water and was overheard by a crow. When word of this passed among the crows they felt insulted. They jeered and raised insulting gestures to the ravens. They bullied each other into drinking the alkaline water until they had drunk the hole dry and gone blind.

The crows flew into canyon walls and dove straight into the ground at forty miles an hour and broke their necks. The worst of it was their cartwheeling across the desert floor, stiff wings outstretched, beaks agape, white eyes ballooning, surprising rattlesnakes hidden under sage bushes out of the noonday sun. The snakes awoke, struck and held. The wheeling birds strew them across the desert like sprung traps.

When all the crows were finally dead, the desert bacteria and fungi bored into them, burrowed through bone and muscle, through aqueous humor[1] and feathers until they had reduced the stiff limbs of soft black to blue dust.

After that, there were no more crows in the desert. The few who watched from a distance took it as a sign and moved away.

Finally there is this: one morning four ravens sat at the edge of the desert waiting for the sun to rise. They had been there all night and the dew was like beads of quicksilver on their wings. Their eyes were closed and they were as still as the cracks in the desert floor.

The wind came off the snow-capped peaks to the north and ruffled their breath feathers. Their talons arched in the white earth and they smoothed

---

1. The thick watery substance filling the space in the eyeball between the lens and the cornea.

their wings with sleek, dark bills. At first light their bodies swelled and their eyes flashed purple. When the dew dried on their wings they lifted off from the desert floor and flew away in four directions. Crows would never have had the patience for this.

If you want to know more about the raven: bury yourself in the desert so that you have a commanding view of the high basalt[2] cliffs where he lives. Let only your eyes protrude. Do not blink—the movement will alert the raven to your continued presence. Wait until a generation of ravens has passed away. Of the new generation there will be at least one bird who will find you. He will see your eyes staring up out of the desert floor. The raven is cautious, but he is thorough. He will sense your peaceful intentions. Let him have the first word. Be careful: he will tell you he knows nothing.

If you do not have the time for this, scour the weathered desert shacks for some sign of the raven's body. Look under old mattresses and beneath loose floorboards. Look behind the walls. Sooner or later you will find a severed foot. It will be his and it will be well preserved.

Take it out in the sunlight and examine it closely. Notice that there are three fingers that face forward, and a fourth, the longest and like a thumb, that faces to the rear. The instrument will be black but no longer shiny, the back of it sheathed in armor plate and the underside padded like a wolf's foot.

At the end of each digit you will find a black, curved talon. You will see that the talons are not as sharp as you might have suspected. They are made to grasp and hold fast, not to puncture. They are more like the jaws of a trap than a fistful of ice picks. The subtle difference serves the raven well in the desert. He can weather a storm on a barren juniper limb; he can pick up and examine the crow's eye without breaking it.

1976

2. A common volcanic rock, usually fine-grained due to the rapid cooling of lava.

JAMAICA KINCAID

Jamaica Kincaid was born on the island of Antigua in the West Indies in 1949; at seventeen she felt she had to "rescue herself" from an oppressive cultural and family situation and came to New York as an *au pair* (she calls herself "a servant"). Writing, she has said, was for her "a matter of saving my life." In 1973 she changed her birth name of Elaine Cynthia Potter Richardson to Jamaica Kincaid, because, she said, her family disapproved of her writing. After she left Antigua she did not see her mother again for twenty years. When she began a career as a writer she became a regular contributor to the *New Yorker* magazine. Her first book, *Annie John* (1983), is an autobiographical coming-of-age novel, as is *Lucy* (1990), a fictional version of her coming to New York. Her other work includes a book about Antigua (*A Small Place*, 1988), a memoir (*My Brother*, 1998), two books on gardening (one of her passions), and the stylistically innovative novel *See Now Then* (2013).

"Girl," which first appeared in the *New Yorker* in 1978, is one all-but-uninterrupted sentence in which a West Indian mother instructs her daughter on how to be the "proper" young woman she is certain her daughter is not. Although the daughter twice tries to interject, she's unable to change what is essentially monologue into dialogue. Kincaid has said that the voice in the story is "my mother's voice exactly over many years" and that, as a child, "a powerless person," she spoke infrequently. Like the other pieces collected in *At the Bottom of the River* (1983), "Girl" resists classification. Its implicit narrative makes it story; its strong rhythm and vivid images make it poetry. Simultaneously, like an essay it documents issues of gender and power. And, like much of this writer's work, it is rooted in autobiography. "I am so happy to write that I don't care what you call it," she has said. The mother/daughter relationship in "Girl" is one of Kincaid's earliest explorations of her ongoing and self-proclaimed "obsessive theme" as a writer: "the relationship between the powerful and the powerless."

Girl

Wash the white clothes on Monday and put them on the stone heap; wash the color clothes on Tuesday and put them on the clothesline to dry; don't walk barehead in the hot sun; cook pumpkin fritters[1] in very hot sweet oil; soak your little cloths right after you take them off; when buying cotton to make yourself a nice blouse, be sure that it doesn't have gum[2] on it, because that way it won't hold up well after a wash; soak salt fish[3] overnight before you cook it; is it true that you sing benna[4] in Sunday school?; always eat your food in such a way that it won't turn someone else's stomach; on Sundays try to walk like a lady and not like the slut you are so bent on becoming; don't sing benna in Sunday school; you mustn't speak to wharf-rat[5] boys, not even to give directions; don't eat fruits on the street—flies will follow you; *but I don't sing benna on Sundays at all and never in Sunday school*; this is how to sew on a button; this is how to make a buttonhole for the button you have just sewed on; this is how to hem a dress when you see the hem coming down and so to prevent yourself from looking like the slut I know you are so bent on becoming; this is how you iron your father's khaki shirt so that it doesn't have a crease; this is how you iron your father's khaki pants so that they don't have a crease; this is how you grow okra[6]—far from the house, because okra tree harbors red ants; when you are growing dasheen,[7] make sure it gets plenty of water or else it makes your throat itch when you are eating it; this is how you sweep a corner; this is how you sweep a whole house; this is how you sweep a yard; this is how you smile to someone you don't like too much; this is how you smile to someone you don't like at all; this is how you smile to someone you like completely; this is how you set a table for tea; this is how you set a table for dinner; this is how you set a table for dinner with an important guest; this is how you set a table for lunch; this is how you set a table for

1. A Caribbean dish made from fried calabaza, or West Indian pumpkin.
2. A naturally occurring, viscous resin found in the woody parts of plants.
3. A popular West Indian dish of dried and salted codfish sautéed with spices.
4. A calypso-like music characterized by a call-and-response format; it was used as a form of folk communication to spread gossip and other

local news across the islands of the British West Indies in the early 20th century.
5. Regarding an individual who lives by stealing from ships or warehouses near wharves.
6. Vegetable thought to be of African origin, grown in tropical and warm temperate climates, often cooked in soups and stews or served raw.
7. The edible, starchy, tuberous root of taro, a tropical plant.

breakfast; this is how to behave in the presence of men who don't know you very well, and this way they won't recognize immediately the slut I have warned you against becoming; be sure to wash every day, even if it is with your own spit; don't squat down to play marbles—you are not a boy, you know; don't pick people's flowers—you might catch something; don't throw stones at blackbirds; because it might not be a blackbird at all; this is how to make a bread pudding;[8] this is how to make doukona;[9] this is how to make pepper pot;[1] this is how to make a good medicine for a cold; this is how to make a good medicine to throw away a child before it even becomes a child; this is how to catch a fish; this is how to throw back a fish you don't like, and that way something bad won't fall on you; this is how to bully a man; this is how a man bullies you; this is how to love a man, and if this doesn't work there are other ways, and if they don't work don't feel too bad about giving up; this is how to spit up in the air if you feel like it, and this is how to move quick so that it doesn't fall on you; this is how to make ends meet; always squeeze bread to make sure it's fresh; *but what if the baker won't let me feel the bread?*; you mean to say that after all you are really going to be the kind of woman who the baker won't let near the bread?

1978, 1983

8. A dessert made from leftover bread.
9. A Caribbean pudding made from plantain and wrapped in a plantain leaf.

1. A Caribbean meat stew, strongly flavored with cinnamon, hot peppers, and cassareep, a special sauce made from the cassava root.

HUNTER S. THOMPSON

Hunter Stockton Thompson (1937–2005) was born in Louisville, Kentucky. He was a gifted student in literature, but misbehavior at the end of his senior year of high school earned him thirty days in juvenile detention, which prevented his graduation. Joining the air force as a way of getting out of town led to more trouble but also introduced him to the pleasures of life in the Caribbean, where he found work as a newspaper reporter. From there he moved on to feature journalism for such new countercultural magazines as *Scanlan's*, *Ramparts*, and *Rolling Stone*. Early attempts at fiction proved unpublishable until much later in his career, which he fashioned as an extreme style of literary journalism, his method focusing more on the observer's reaction to events than on events themselves (and using the techniques of fiction, such as characterization, imagery, and symbolism, to express those reactions). His most famous books remain his earliest ones: *Hell's Angels* (1967), covering a year he spent riding with this motorcycle gang; *Fear and Loathing in Las Vegas* (1971), an account of his failure to cover a dirt-bike race and a narcotics-law-enforcement convention; and *Fear and Loathing on the Campaign Trail '72* (1973), collecting his presidential campaign reporting as a correspondent for *Rolling Stone*. A self-styled Doctor of Gonzo Journalism, Thompson continued to publish personal reporting about the excesses of American culture until his death from a self-inflicted gunshot.

From Fear and Loathing in Las Vegas

The Circus-Circus[1] is what the whole hep world would be doing on Saturday night if the Nazis had won the war. This is the Sixth Reich.[2] The ground floor is full of gambling tables, like all the other casinos . . . but the place is about four stories high, in the style of a circus tent, and all manner of strange County-Fair/Polish Carnival madness is going on up in this space. Right above the gambling tables the Forty Flying Carazito Brothers are doing a high-wire trapeze act, along with four muzzled Wolverines and the Six Nymphet Sisters from San Diego . . . so you're down on the main floor playing blackjack, and the stakes are getting high when suddenly you chance to look up, and there, right smack above your head is a half-naked fourteen-year-old girl being chased through the air by a snarling wolverine, which is suddenly locked in a death battle with two silver-painted Polacks who come swinging down from opposite balconies and meet in mid-air on the wolverine's neck . . . both Polacks seize the animal as they fall straight down towards the crap tables—but they bounce off the net; they separate and spring back up towards the roof in three different directions, and just as they're about to fall again they are grabbed out of the air by three Korean Kittens and trapezed off to one of the balconies.

This madness goes on and on, but nobody seems to notice. The gambling action runs twenty-four hours a day on the main floor, and the circus never ends. Meanwhile, on all the upstairs balconies, the customers are being hustled by every conceivable kind of bizarre shuck. All kinds of funhouse-type booths. Shoot the pasties off the nipples of a ten-foot bull-dyke and win a cotton-candy goat. Stand in front of this fantastic machine, my friend, and for just 99¢ your likeness will appear, two hundred feet tall, on a screen above downtown Las Vegas. Ninety-nine cents more for a voice message. "Say whatever you want, fella. They'll hear you, don't worry about that. Remember you'll be two hundred feet tall."

Jesus Christ. I could see myself lying in bed in the Mint Hotel, half-asleep and staring idly out the window, when suddenly a vicious nazi drunkard appears two hundred feet tall in the midnight sky, screaming gibberish at the world: *"Woodstock Über Alles!"*[3]

We will close the drapes tonight. A thing like that could send a drug person careening around the room like a ping-pong ball. Hallucinations are bad enough. But after a while you learn to cope with things like seeing your dead grandmother crawling up your leg with a knife in her teeth. Most acid fanciers can handle this sort of thing.

But *nobody* can handle that other trip—the possibility that any freak with $1.98 can walk into the Circus-Circus and suddenly appear in the sky over downtown Las Vegas twelve times the size of God, howling anything that

---

1. Casino and entertainment center that opened in Las Vegas, Nevada, in 1968.
2. The Nazi government in Germany (1933–45) declared itself the Third Reich ("Empire"); there were no Fourth and Fifth Reichs.
3. Woodstock Above All (German); a play on the German National Anthem (*"Das Lied der*

Deutschen," popularly known as *"Deutschland, Deutschland, Über Alles"*), with a reference to Woodstock, the rock festival held August 15–17, 1969, outside Bethel, an area southwest of Woodstock, New York, an event considered the high point of 1960s counterculture.

comes into his head. No, this is not a good town for psychedelic drugs. Reality itself is too twisted.

1971

JOAN DIDION

Joan Didion's collection of essays on the 1960s counterculture, *Slouching Towards Bethlehem* (1968), made her famous and established her as a practitioner of "the New Journalism." Her second essay collection, *The White Album* (1979), mixes autobiography with analyses of cultural events in Los Angeles in the 1960s (the book's title refers to the Beatles' 1968 double album which had no graphics or text on the cover other than the band's name). These widely influential books confirmed Didion's reputation as a shrewd and edgy cultural observer and literary stylist. She has also published several novels, including *Play It As It Lays* (1970) and *Democracy* (1984).

A native Californian, Didion (b. 1934) moved to New York as a young woman, where she worked for *Vogue* magazine and, in 1964, married the novelist John Gregory Dunne. In the mid-1960s they moved to Los Angeles, where they spent the next twenty years. Didion and Dunne collaborated on several screenplays and became a glamorous couple whose talents were sought after in Hollywood. In the 1980s they moved back to New York, where Didion continued her work as a screenwriter, novelist, and nonfiction author. *The Year of Magical Thinking* (2005) is Didion's account of the year following her husband's sudden death from cardiac arrest. Two months before its publication, the couple's daughter, Quintana Roo, whom they adopted in 1966, also died. In the memoir, Didion turned her steely-eyed gaze on herself, using all the tools at her disposal to offer an unsparing description of grief. "We tell stories in order to live," *The White Album* begins; over a quarter century later, Didion remained true to those words.

In this excerpt from the title essay of *Slouching Towards Bethlehem*, Didion presents the chaotic scene of "happenings" in 1960s San Francisco—spontaneous public performances meant to provoke thought and reaction. She penetrates the lives of those who drift through the transient crowds near Golden Gate Park. Coolly noting such details as blackface performers and little children taking LSD, Didion plays journalistic neutrality against what she views as the excesses of the counterculture.

From Slouching Towards Bethlehem

Janis Joplin is singing with Big Brother in the Panhandle and almost everybody is high and it is a pretty nice Sunday afternoon between three and six o'clock, which the activists say are the three hours of the week when something is most likely to happen in the Haight-Ashbury, and who turns up but Peter Berg.[1] He is with his wife and six or seven other people, along with

---

1. American actor, playwright, and activist (1937–2011), cofounder of the Diggers, a radical community action and street theater group operating in San Francisco from 1967 until 1968, and a member of the San Francisco Mime Troupe, a street theater group founded in 1959. "Janis Joplin": rock star (1943–1970) and lead singer of Big Brother and the Holding Company,

San Francisco Mime Troupe performing in Golden Gate Park.

Chester Anderson's associate The Connection,[2] and the first peculiar thing is, they're in blackface.

I mention to Max and Sharon[3] that some members of the Mime Troupe seem to be in blackface.

"It's street theater," Sharon assures me. "It's supposed to be really groovy."

The Mime Troupers get a little closer, and there are some other peculiar things about them. For one thing they are tapping people on the head with dime-store plastic nightsticks, and for another they are wearing signs on their backs. "HOW MANY TIMES YOU BEEN RAPED, YOU LOVE FREAKS?" and "WHO STOLE CHUCK BERRY'S[4] MUSIC?," things like that. Then they are distributing communication company fliers which say:

& this summer thousands of un-white un-suburban boppers are going to want to know why you've given up what they can't get & how you get away with it & how come you not a faggot[5] with hair so long & they want haight street one way or the other. IF YOU DON'T KNOW, BY AUGUST HAIGHT STREET WILL BE A CEMETERY.

Max reads the flier and stands up. "I'm getting bad vibes," he says, and he and Sharon leave.

I have to stay around because I'm looking for Otto so I walk over to where the Mime Troupers have formed a circle around a Negro. Peter Berg is saying if anybody asks that this is street theater, and I figure the curtain is up because what they are doing right now is jabbing the Negro with the nightsticks. They jab, and they bare their teeth, and they rock on the balls of their feet and they wait.

---

a band formed in San Francisco in 1965; "Panhandle": park in San Francisco adjacent to Golden Gate Park; "Haight-Ashbury": San Francisco neighborhood where hippies and thousands of others attracted to the counterculture movement gathered during the 1967 "Summer of Love."

2. Nickname for Claude Hayward, who along with writer and editor Chester Anderson (1932–1991), cofounded the Communications Company (ComCo), which made mimeographed posters for the Diggers, the San Francisco Mime Troupe, and others.

3. Max, Sharon, Otto, Susan, Don, Sue Ann, and others mentioned by first name are people Didion met in San Francisco as she reported on the counterculture.

4. Charles Edward Anderson "Chuck" Berry (1926–2017), African American singer, guitarist, and songwriter who pioneered rock and roll in the mid-twentieth century.

5. Derogatory term for homosexual. "Boppers": slang for fans or players of bebop-style jazz.

"I'm beginning to get annoyed here," the Negro says. "I'm gonna get mad."

By now there are several Negroes around, reading the signs and watching.

"Just beginning to get annoyed, are you?" one of the Mime Troupers says. "Don't you think it's about time?"

"Nobody *stole* Chuck Berry's music, man," says another Negro who has been studying the signs. "Chuck Berry's music belongs to *every*body."

"Yeh?" a girl in blackface says. "Everybody *who?*"

"Why," he says, confused. "Everybody. In America."

"In *America*," the blackface girl shrieks. "Listen to him talk about *America*."

"Listen," he says helplessly. "Listen here."

"What'd *America* ever do for you?" the girl in blackface jeers. "White kids here, they can sit in the Park all summer long, listening to the music they stole, because their bigshot parents keep sending them money. Who ever sends you money?"

"Listen," the Negro says, his voice rising. "You're gonna start something here, this isn't right—".

"You tell us what's right, black boy," the girl says.

The youngest member of the blackface group, an earnest tall kid about nineteen, twenty, is hanging back at the edge of the scene. I offer him an apple and ask what is going on. "Well," he says, "I'm new at this, I'm just beginning to study it, but you see the capitalists are taking over the District, and that's what Peter—well, ask Peter."

I did not ask Peter. It went on for a while. But on that particular Sunday between three and six o'clock everyone was too high and the weather was too good and the Hunter's Point[6] gangs who usually come in between three and six on Sunday afternoon had come in on Saturday instead, and nothing started. While I waited for Otto I asked a little girl I knew slightly what she had thought of it. "It's something groovy they call street theater," she said. I said I had wondered if it might not have political overtones. She was seventeen years old and she worked it around in her mind awhile and finally she remembered a couple of words from somewhere. "Maybe it's some John Birch[7] thing," she said.

When I finally find Otto he says "I got something at my place that'll blow your mind," and when we get there I see a child on the living-room floor, wearing a reefer coat,[8] reading a comic book. She keeps licking her lips in concentration and the only off thing about her is that she's wearing white lipstick.

"Five years old," Otto says. "On acid."[9]

The five-year-old's name is Susan, and she tells me she is in High Kindergarten. She lives with her mother and some other people, just got over the measles, wants a bicycle for Christmas, and particularly likes Coca-Cola,

---

6. African American neighborhood in southeast San Francisco.
7. Anticommunist activist group that opposed the civil rights movement.

8. Short, double-breasted jacket, typically worn by sailors in the navy.
9. Lysergic acid diethylamide (LSD), a powerful hallucinogenic drug.

ice cream, Marty in the Jefferson Airplane, Bob in the Grateful Dead,[1] and the beach. She remembers going to the beach once a long time ago, and wishes she had taken a bucket. For a year now her mother has given her both acid and peyote.[2] Susan describes it as getting stoned.

I start to ask if any of the other children in High Kindergarten get stoned, but I falter at the key words.

"She means do the other kids in your class turn on, *get stoned*," says the friend of her mother's who brought her to Otto's.

"Only Sally and Anne," Susan says.

"What about Lia?" her mother's friend prompts.

"Lia," Susan says, "is not in High Kindergarten."

Sue Ann's three-year-old Michael started a fire this morning before anyone was up, but Don got it out before much damage was done. Michael burned his arm though, which is probably why Sue Ann was so jumpy when she happened to see him chewing on an electric cord. "You'll fry like rice," she screamed. The only people around were Don and one of Sue Ann's macrobiotic friends and somebody who was on his way to a commune in the Santa Lucias, and they didn't notice Sue Ann screaming at Michael because they were in the kitchen trying to retrieve some very good Moroccan hash[3] which had dropped down through a floorboard damaged in the fire.

1967

1. Bob Weir (b. 1947), guitarist for the Grateful Dead, rock band. "Marty": Martin Balin (b. 1942), founder and co–lead singer of the rock band Jefferson Airplane. Both bands were formed in San Francisco in 1965.
2. Small cactus used as a drug for its psychoactive properties. Historically used by Native Americans for spiritual purposes.
3. Abbreviated term for hashish, a drug in the cannabis family. "Macrobiotic": following a diet of unprocessed foods based on Taoist principles of balancing life forces of yin and yang. "Santa Lucias": mountain range along the central coast of California.

DAVID FOSTER WALLACE

Known both for his fiction—particularly his epic novels *Infinite Jest* (1996) and the posthumously published *The Pale King* (2011)—and for his exuberant nonfiction, Wallace represents a maximal style in both genres. Wallace was the son of Midwestern academics, his father a philosophy professor and his mother an English teacher. He grew up in Illinois and was educated at Amherst College, where he majored in philosophy and English, and where he started to study creative writing. He graduated from the MFA program in fiction at the University of Arizona in 1987; eleven years later *Infinite Jest* earned him a MacArthur Foundation "genius grant," which freed him from teaching for a time.

Wallace's intense approach to writing was distinguished by extended research projects—notably on the pornography industry for the essay "Adult World" and on the Internal Revenue Service for *The Pale King*—and a style that was by turns sincere and satirical, self-conscious and arrogant, intellectual and lowbrow. Plagued by manic depression and addiction throughout his adult life, Wallace committed suicide in 2008, inspiring an outpouring of regret and appreciation, as well as a serious biography and a posthumously assembled version of *The Pale King*, which he had been working on when he died. In his nonfiction, Wallace took up a wide array of subjects, from television to politics to tennis, with a verve and curiosity that made a mark on this swiftly evolving genre.

Wallace's appetite for arcane facts and attraction to American kitsch combine with his inward-looking attention to consciousness in this selection from one of his most widely admired essays, "Consider the Lobster." His assignment for *Gourmet* magazine was to report on the 2004 Maine Lobster Festival. Always fascinated by the experience of psychic pain and the ethics of inflicting pain on others, Wallace adopts a relentlessly questioning style that bars readers from simply consuming his description of the lobster's anatomy and passively accepting the ways cooks kill them.

From Consider the Lobster

There happen to be two main criteria that most ethicists agree on for determining whether a living creature has the capacity to suffer and so has genuine interests that it may or may not be our moral duty to consider.[1] One is how much of the neurological hardware required for pain-experience the animal comes equipped with—nociceptors, prostaglandins, neuronal opioid receptors, etc. The other criterion is whether the animal demonstrates behavior associated with pain. And it takes a lot of intellectual gymnastics and behaviorist[2] hairsplitting not to see struggling, thrashing, and lid-clattering as just such pain-behavior. According to marine zoologists, it usually takes lobsters between 35 and 45 seconds to die in boiling water. (No source I could find talks about how long it takes them to die in superheated steam; one rather hopes it's faster.)

There are, of course, other ways to kill your lobster on-site and so achieve maximum freshness. Some cooks' practice is to drive a sharp heavy knife point-first into a spot just above the midpoint between the lobster's eye-stalks (more or less where the Third Eye[3] is in human foreheads). This is alleged either to kill the lobster instantly or to render it insensate, and is said at least to eliminate some of the cowardice involved in throwing a creature into boiling water and then fleeing the room. As far as I can tell from talking to proponents of the knife-in-head method, the idea is that it's more violent but ultimately more merciful, plus that a willingness to exert personal agency and accept responsibility for stabbing the lobster's head honors the lobster somehow and entitles one to eat it (there's often a vague sort

---

1. "Interests" basically means strong and legitimate preferences, which obviously require some degree of consciousness, responsiveness to stimuli, etc. See, for instance, the utilitarian philosopher Peter Singer, whose 1974 *Animal Liberation* is more or less the bible of the modern animal-rights movement:

> It would be nonsense to say that it was not in the interests of a stone to be kicked along the road by a schoolboy. A stone does not have interests because it cannot suffer. Nothing that we can do to it could possibly make any

difference to its welfare. A mouse, on the other hand, does have an interest in not being kicked along the road, because it will suffer if it is [Wallace's note].

2. Adherent of the theory that psychology is best understood by studying the external behavior of individuals.

3. The spiritual inner eye associated with Hindu tradition, represented as an eye or triangle set between the brows, in the middle of the forehead.

of Native American spirituality-of-the-hunt flavor to pro-knife arguments). But the problem with the knife method is basic biology: Lobsters' nervous systems operate off not one but several ganglia, a.k.a. nerve bundles, which are sort of wired in series and distributed all along the lobster's underside, from stem to stern. And disabling only the frontal ganglion does not normally result in quick death or unconsciousness.

Another alternative is to put the lobster in cold saltwater and then very slowly bring it up to a full boil. Cooks who advocate this method are going on the analogy to a frog, which can supposedly be kept from jumping out of a boiling pot by heating the water incrementally. In order to save a lot of research-summarizing, I'll simply assure you that the analogy between frogs and lobsters turns out not to hold—plus, if the kettle's water isn't aerated seawater, the immersed lobster suffers from slow suffocation, although usually not decisive enough suffocation to keep it from still thrashing and clattering when the water gets hot enough to kill it. In fact, lobsters boiled incrementally often display a whole bonus set of gruesome, convulsionlike reactions that you don't see in regular boiling.

Ultimately, the only certain virtues of the home-lobotomy[4] and slow-heating methods are comparative, because there are even worse/crueler ways people prepare lobster. Time-thrifty cooks sometimes microwave them alive (usually after poking several vent-holes in the carapace, which is a precaution most shellfish-microwavers learn about the hard way). Live dismemberment, on the other hand, is big in Europe—some chefs cut the lobster in half before cooking; others like to tear off the claws and tail and toss only these parts into the pot.

And there's more unhappy news respecting suffering-criterion number one. Lobsters don't have much in the way of eyesight or hearing, but they do have an exquisite tactile sense, one facilitated by hundreds of thousands of tiny hairs that protrude through their carapace. "Thus it is," in the words of T. M. Prudden's industry classic *About Lobster*, "that although encased in what seems a solid, impenetrable armor, the lobster can receive stimuli and impressions from without as readily as if it possessed a soft and delicate skin." And lobsters do have nociceptors,[5] as well as invertebrate versions of the prostaglandins and major neurotransmitters via which our own brains register pain.

Lobsters do not, on the other hand, appear to have the equipment for making or absorbing natural opioids like endorphins and enkephalins, which are what more advanced nervous systems use to try to handle intense pain. From this fact, though, one could conclude either that lobsters are maybe even *more* vulnerable to pain, since they lack mammalian nervous systems' built-in analgesia,[6] or, instead, that the absence of natural opioids implies an absence of the really intense pain-sensations that natural opioids are designed to mitigate. I for one can detect a marked upswing in mood as I contemplate this latter possibility. It could be that their lack of endorphin/enkephalin hardware means that lobsters' raw subjective experience of pain is so radically different from mammals' that it may not even

4. Surgery to sever nerves in the prefrontal lobe of the brain.
5. This is the neurological term for special pain-receptors that are "sensitive to potentially damaging extremes of temperature, to mechanical forces, and to chemical substances which are released when body tissues are damaged" [Wallace's note].
6. Ability to block pain.

deserve the term "pain." Perhaps lobsters are more like those frontal-lobotomy patients one reads about who report experiencing pain in a totally different way than you and I. These patients evidently do feel physical pain, neurologically speaking, but don't dislike it—though neither do they like it; it's more that they feel it but don't feel anything *about* it—the point being that the pain is not distressing to them or something they want to get away from. Maybe lobsters, who are also without frontal lobes, are detached from the neurological-registration-of-injury-or-hazard we call pain in just the same way. There is, after all, a difference between (1) pain as a purely neurological event, and (2) actual suffering, which seems crucially to involve an emotional component, an awareness of pain as unpleasant, as something to fear/dislike/want to avoid.

Still, after all the abstract intellection, there remain the facts of the frantically clanking lid, the pathetic clinging to the edge of the pot. Standing at the stove, it is hard to deny in any meaningful way that this is a living creature experiencing pain and wishing to avoid/escape the painful experience. To my lay mind, the lobster's behavior in the kettle appears to be the expression of a *preference*, and it may well be that an ability to form preferences is the decisive criterion for real suffering.[7] The logic of this (preference → suffering) relation may be easiest to see in the negative case. If you cut certain kinds of worms in half, the halves will often keep crawling around and going about their vermiform[8] business as if nothing had happened. When we assert, based on their post-op behavior, that these worms appear not to be suffering, what we're really saying is that there's no sign the worms know anything bad has happened or would *prefer* not to have gotten cut in half.

Lobsters, though, are known to exhibit preferences. Experiments have shown that they can detect changes of only a degree or two in water temperature; one reason for their complex migratory cycles (which can often cover 100-plus miles a year) is to pursue the temperatures they like best.[9] And, as mentioned, they're bottom-dwellers and do not like bright light—if a tank of food-lobsters is out in the sunlight or a store's fluorescence, the lobsters will always congregate in whatever part is darkest. Fairly solitary in the ocean, they also clearly dislike the crowding that's part of their captivity in

---

7. "Preference" is maybe roughly synonymous with "interests," but it is a better term for our purposes because it's less abstractly philosophical—"preference" seems more personal, and it's the whole idea of a living creature's personal experience that's at issue [Wallace's note].

8. Having the form of a worm.

9. Of course, the most common sort of counterargument here would begin by objecting that "like best" is really just a metaphor, and a misleadingly anthropomorphic one at that. The counterarguer would posit that the lobster seeks to maintain a certain optimal ambient temperature out of nothing but unconscious instinct (with a similar explanation for the low-light affinities upcoming in the main text). The thrust of such a counterargument will be that the lobster's thrashings and clankings in the kettle express not unpreferred pain but involuntary reflexes, like your leg shooting out when the doctor hits your knee. Be advised that there are professional scientists, including many researchers who use animals in

experiments, who hold to the view that nonhuman creatures have no real feelings at all, merely "behaviors." Be further advised that this view has a long history that goes all the way back to Descartes, although its modern support comes mostly from behaviorist psychology.

To these what-looks-like-pain-is-really-just-reflexes counterarguments, however, there happen to be all sorts of scientific and pro-animal rights counter-counterarguments. And then further attempted rebuttals and redirects, and so on. Suffice it to say that both the scientific and the philosophical arguments on either side of the animal-suffering issue are involved, abstruse, technical, often informed by self-interest or ideology, and in the end so totally inconclusive that as a practical matter, in the kitchen or restaurant, it all still seems to come down to individual conscience, going with (no pun) your gut [Wallace's note].

tanks, since (as also mentioned) one reason why lobsters' claws are banded on capture is to keep them from attacking one another under the stress of close-quarter storage.

In any event, at the MLF,[1] standing by the bubbling tanks outside the World's Largest Lobster Cooker, watching the fresh-caught lobsters pile over one another, wave their hobbled claws impotently, huddle in the rear corners, or scrabble frantically back from the glass as you approach, it is difficult not to sense that they're unhappy, or frightened, even if it's some rudimentary version of these feelings . . . and, again, why does rudimentariness even enter into it? Why is a primitive, inarticulate form of suffering less urgent or uncomfortable for the person who's helping to inflict it by paying for the food it results in? I'm not trying to give you a PETA-like screed here—at least I don't think so. I'm trying, rather, to work out and articulate some of the troubling questions that arise amid all the laughter and saltation[2] and community pride of the Maine Lobster Festival. The truth is that if you, the festival attendee, permit yourself to think that lobsters can suffer and would rather not, the MLF begins to take on the aspect of something like a Roman circus or medieval torture-fest.

Does that comparison seem a bit much? If so, exactly why? Or what about this one: Is it possible that future generations will regard our present agribusiness and eating practices in much the same way we now view Nero's entertainments or Mengele's[3] experiments? My own initial reaction is that such a comparison is hysterical, extreme—and yet the reason it seems extreme to me appears to be that I believe animals are less morally important than human beings;[4] and when it comes to defending such a belief, even to myself, I have to acknowledge that (a) I have an obvious selfish interest in this belief, since I like to eat certain kinds of animals and want to be able to keep doing it, and (b) I haven't succeeded in working out any sort of personal ethical system in which the belief is truly defensible instead of just selfishly convenient.

Given this article's venue and my own lack of culinary sophistication, I'm curious about whether the reader can identify with any of these reactions and acknowledgments and discomforts. I'm also concerned not to come off as shrill or preachy when what I really am is more like confused. For those *Gourmet* readers who enjoy well-prepared and -presented meals involving beef, veal, lamb, pork, chicken, lobster, etc.: Do you think much about the (possible) moral status and (probable) suffering of the animals involved? If you do, what ethical convictions have you worked out that permit you not just to eat but to savor and enjoy flesh-based viands (since of course refined *enjoyment*, rather than mere ingestion, is the whole point of gastronomy[5])?

1. Maine Lobster Festival.
2. The two relevant meanings are dancing, and spurting forth of blood, both obsolete. "PETA": People for the Ethical Treatment of Animals, an animal-rights activist group.
3. Josef Mengele (1911–1979), German Shutzstaffel (SS) officer and physician who conducted medical experiments on prisoners in the Auschwitz concentration camp in Poland during World War II. "Nero": famously violent Roman emperor (37–68 C.E.), ruling from 54 to 68 C.E.

4. Meaning *a lot* less important, apparently, since the moral comparison here is not the value of one human's life vs. the value of one animal's life, but rather the value of one animal's life vs. the value of one human's taste for a particular kind of protein. Even the most diehard carniphile will acknowledge that it's possible to live and eat well without consuming animals [Wallace's note].
5. The art of choosing, preparing, and eating fine food.

If, on the other hand, you'll have no truck with confusions or convictions and regard stuff like the previous paragraph as just so much fatuous navel-gazing, what makes it feel truly okay, inside, to just dismiss the whole thing out of hand? That is, is your refusal to think about any of this the product of actual thought, or is it just that you don't want to think about it? And if the latter, then why not? Do you ever think, even idly, about the possible reasons for your reluctance to think about it? I am not trying to bait anyone here—I'm genuinely curious. After all, isn't being extra aware and attentive and thoughtful about one's food and its overall context part of what distinguishes a real gourmet? Or is all the gourmet's extra attention and sensibility just supposed to be sensuous? Is it really all just a matter of taste and presentation?

These last few queries, though, while sincere, obviously involve much larger and more abstract questions about the connections (if any) between aesthetics and morality—about what the adjective in a phrase like "The Magazine of Good Living"[6] is really supposed to mean—and these questions lead straightaway into such deep and treacherous waters that it's probably best to stop the public discussion right here. There are limits to what even interested persons can ask of each other.

2004

6. *Gourmet* magazine's slogan.

EDWIDGE DANTICAT

Edwidge Danticat was born in Port-au-Prince, the capital of Haiti, in 1969. Her novels *Breath, Eyes, Memory* (1994) and *The Farming of Bones* (1998), as well as her collection of stories, *Krik? Krak!* (1995—the title comes from a Haitian chant), draw on her experiences as a Haitian American. Danticat was two years old when her father left Haiti to make a better life for the family in the United States; two years later, her mother left to join him. For the next eight years Danticat and her brother remained in Haiti under the care of their uncle Joseph, a Baptist minister who founded his own church and school in Port-au-Prince. She then emigrated to the United States to be reunited with her parents. In 2004, after violence destroyed her uncle's church and put his life in jeopardy, Joseph entered the United States asking for temporary asylum but was detained in Miami by Department of Homeland Security officials suspicious of his plea. During questioning, Joseph collapsed but was refused treatment at the time. The next day he was taken to a Florida hospital where he died. In October 2007 Danticat testified on this issue before the House Judiciary Subcommittee on Immigration, Citizenship Refuges, Border Security, and International Law. Like many creative nonfiction writers, Danticat uses personal narrative to illuminate larger issues: the political and economic situation in Haiti, the challenges facing immigrants to the United States, and the need to reform the practices of immigration detainee medical care.

Brother, I'm Dying is a memoir partly of the writer's childhood in Haiti and, more particularly, of the interconnected lives of her uncle and father, who, after leaving Haiti, ran a car-service business in New York and died from pulmonary fibrosis soon after his brother's death. When the adult Danticat, now pregnant with her first child, listens to her gravely ill father respond to the question "Have you enjoyed your life?" by speaking of his children and family, she recalls living as a child with her uncle when the family would regularly receive letters from her father in the United States. This selection captures Danticat's exploration of what words can and cannot say, a question at the heart of this writer's work.

From Brother, I'm Dying

Listening to my father, I remembered a time when I used to dream of smuggling him words. I was eight years old and Bob and I were living in Haiti with his oldest brother, my uncle Joseph, and his wife. And since they didn't have a telephone at home—few Haitian families did then—and access to the call centers was costly, we had no choice but to write letters. Every other month, my father would mail a half-page, three-paragraph missive addressed to my uncle. Scribbled in his minuscule scrawl, sometimes on plain white paper, other times on lined, hole-punched notebook pages still showing bits of fringe from the spiral binding, my father's letters were composed in stilted French,[1] with the first paragraph offering news of his and my mother's health, the second detailing how to spend the money they had wired for food, lodging, and school expenses for Bob and myself, the third section concluding abruptly after reassuring us that we'd be hearing from him again before long.

Later I would discover in a first-year college composition class that his letters had been written in a diamond sequence, the Aristotelian *Poetics*[2] correspondence, requiring an opening greeting, a middle detail or request, and a brief farewell at the end. The letter-writing process had been such an agonizing chore for my father, one that he'd hurried through while assembling our survival money, that this specific epistolary formula, which he followed unconsciously, had offered him a comforting way of disciplining his emotions.

"I was no writer," he later told me. "What I wanted to tell you and your brother was too big for any piece of paper and a small envelope."

Whatever restraint my father showed in his letters was easily compensated for by Uncle Joseph's reactions to them. First there was the public reading in my uncle's sparsely furnished pink living room, in front of Tante[3] Denise, Bob and me. This was done so there would be no misunderstanding as to how the money my parents sent for me and my brother would be spent. Usually my uncle would read the letters out loud, pausing now and then to ask my help with my father's penmanship, a kindness, I thought, a way to include me a step further. It soon became obvious, however, that my father's handwriting was as clear to me as my own, so I eventually acquired the job of deciphering his letters.

Along with this task came a few minutes of preparation for the reading and thus a few intimate moments with my father's letters, not only the words

---

1. That is, the formal French taught in Haitian schools, rather than the vernacular Creole of everyday life.
2. The earliest surviving work of dramatic and

literary theory, written by Aristotle (384–322 B.C.E.), which analyzes poetry in terms of its essential elements.
3. Aunt (French).

and phrases, which did not vary greatly from month to month, but the vowels and syllables, their tilts and slants, which did. Because he wrote so little, I would try to guess his thoughts and moods from the dotting of his *i*'s and the crossing of his *t*'s, from whether there were actual periods at the ends of his sentences or just faint dots where the tip of his pen had simply landed. Did commas split his streamlined phrases, or were they staccato,[4] like someone speaking too rapidly, out of breath?

For the family readings, I recited my father's letters in a monotone, honoring what I interpreted as a secret between us, that the impersonal style of his letters was due as much to his lack of faith in words and their ability to accurately reproduce his emotions as to his caution with Bob's and my feelings, avoiding too-happy news that might add to the anguish of separation, too-sad news that might worry us, and any hint of judgment or disapproval for my aunt and uncle, which they could have interpreted as suggestions that they were mistreating us. The dispassionate letters were his way of avoiding a minefield, one he could have set off from a distance without being able to comfort the victims.

Given all this anxiety, I'm amazed my father wrote at all. The regularity, the consistency of his correspondence now feels like an act of valor. In contrast, my replies, though less routine—Uncle Joseph did most of the writing— were both painstakingly upbeat and suppliant. In my letters, I bragged about my good grades and requested, as a reward for them, an American doll at Christmas, a typewriter or sewing machine for my birthday, a pair of "real" gold earrings for Easter. But the things I truly wanted I was afraid to ask for, like when I would finally see him and my mother again. However, since my uncle read and corrected all my letters for faulty grammar and spelling, I wrote for his eyes more than my father's, hoping that even after the vigorous editing, my father would still decode the longing in my childish cursive slopes and arches, which were so much like his own.

The words that both my father and I wanted to exchange we never did. These letters were not approved, in his case by him, in my case by my uncle. No matter what the reason, we have always been equally paralyzed by the fear of breaking each other's heart. This is why I could never ask the question Bob did. I also could never tell my father that I'd learned from the doctor that he was dying. Even when they mattered less, there were things he and I were too afraid to say.

2007

---

4. A form of musical articulation, signifying unconnected notes, short and detached.

GEORGE SAUNDERS
b. 1958

F ew writers in the second half of the twentieth century have probed the commercial culture of America with the insight and wit of George Saunders. Saunders's ear tunes to the jargon of business management, the platitudes of marketing, the clichés of popular psychology, and the euphemisms that blind people to violence of all kinds. Within the distilled form of the short story, Saunders creates characters partially trapped in these ways of speaking—and thinking—who struggle to bend their language to more moral or soulful human ends.

Saunders's early life was suffused with the varieties of language so often on display in the stories. His father was in the Air Force, stationed in Amarillo, Texas, when Saunders was born in 1958. The family later moved to Chicago, where his father worked in the insurance and coal businesses, then bought a Chicken Unlimited franchise where the young Saunders worked in high school alongside his mother and sisters. Saunders tells how his father "would bring home books like Machiavelli's *The Prince* or Michael Harrington's *The Other Side of America* or *The Jungle* by Upton Sinclair, and he would just leave them on my bed, saying, 'I think you should take a look at this.'"

Saunders became a writer relatively late in life. He graduated from the Colorado School of Mines and worked in the Sumatran oil fields after college. Stationed at a remote jungle camp, he started reading seriously. After falling sick from swimming in a polluted river, he returned to the United States and took a variety of odd jobs, including, as he says, "doorman, roofer, convenience store clerk" and "knuckle-puller" in a slaughterhouse. Quoting the British Marxist critic Terry Eagleton, Saunders says he came to understand "capitalism as a benign-looking thing that . . . 'plunders the sensuality of the body.'" The sense that modern labor renders people less than human pervades Saunders's work, though he is also a comic writer.

Comic writing, for Saunders, does not always mean funny writing. He has said that "comic, for me, means that there is always a shortfall between what we think of ourselves and what we are. . . . Maybe the most clearly we ever see reality is when it boots us in the ass." He cites the work of Steve Martin, Monty Python, the Marx Brothers, and Dr. Seuss (alongside many literary sources) as influences on his writing. He became a student, and, less than a decade later, in 1996, a professor at the MFA program at Syracuse University. In 2006, he was awarded both Guggenheim and MacArthur Fellowships—the latter known as the "genius grant." He has published four short-story collections, a book of essays titled *The Braindead Megaphone* (2007), an illustrated fable, a children's book, and nonfiction articles for *GQ*, the *New Yorker*, and other publications on topics ranging from the "Minute Men" on the Mexican border to theme hotels in Dubai to a homeless tent city in Fresno, California, where he lived for a time while doing research.

In the story reprinted here, one of his most admired, Saunders meditates on the issues of racism and war in American history, as the Civil War is repackaged as contemporary entertainment but becomes, finally and inescapably, real. His weak hero struggles to find both words and actions to match the persistent nudge of human compassion that prompts him to resist these American legacies.

CivilWarLand in Bad Decline

Whenever a potential big investor comes for the tour the first thing I do is take him to the transplanted Erie Canal Lock.[1] We've got a good ninety feet of actual Canal out there and a well-researched dioramic of a coolie[2] campsite. Were our faces ever red when we found out it was actually the Irish who built the Canal. We've got no budget to correct, so every fifteen minutes or so a device in the bunkhouse gives off the approximate aroma of an Oriental meal.

Today my possible Historical Reconstruction Associate is Mr. Haberstrom, founder of Burn'n' Learn. Burn'n' Learn is national. Their gimmick is a fully stocked library on the premises and as you tan you call out the name of any book you want to these high-school girls on roller skates. As we walk up the trail he's wearing a sweatsuit and smoking a cigar and I tell him I admire his acumen. I tell him some men are dreamers and others are doers. He asks which am I and I say let's face it, I'm basically the guy who leads the dreamers up the trail to view the Canal Segment. He likes that. He says I have a good head on my shoulders. He touches my arm and says he's hot to spend some reflective moments at the Canal because his great-grandfather was a barge guider way back when who got killed by a donkey. When we reach the clearing he gets all emotional and bolts off through the gambling plaster Chinese. Not to be crass but I sense an impending sizable contribution.

When I come up behind him however I see that once again the gangs have been at it with their spray cans, all over my Lock. Haberstrom takes a nice long look. Then he pokes me with the spitty end of his cigar and says not with his money I don't, and storms back down the trail.

I stand there alone a few minutes. The last thing I need is some fat guy's spit on my tie. I think about quitting. Then I think about my last degrading batch of résumés. Two hundred send-outs and no nibbles. My feeling is that prospective employers are put off by the fact that I was a lowly Verisimilitude Inspector for nine years with no promotions. I think of my car payment. I think of how much Marcus and Howie love the little playhouse I'm still paying off. Once again I decide to eat my pride and sit tight.

So I wipe off my tie with a leaf and start down to break the Haberstrom news to Mr. Alsuga.

Mr. A's another self-made man. He cashed in on his love of history by conceptualizing CivilWarLand in his spare time. He started out with just a settler's shack and one Union costume and now has considerable influence in Rotary.[3]

His office is in City Hall. He agrees that the gangs are getting out of hand. Last month they wounded three Visitors and killed a dray horse.[4] Several of them encircled and made fun of Mrs. Dugan in her settler outfit

---

1. Completed in 1825, the Erie Canal runs from the Hudson River in the east to Lake Erie in the west; 35 locks manage water flow between stretches of water at different elevations, allowing two-way traffic.
2. Derogatory term for Asian laborers who came to the United States in the nineteenth century.
3. Founded in 1905, Rotary International is a service organization and social club operating in communities in the United States and around the world.
4. Horse bred to pull heavy loads.

as she was taking her fresh-baked bread over to the simulated Towne Meeting. No way they're paying admission, so they're either tunneling in or coming in over the retaining wall.

Mr. Alsuga believes the solution to the gang problem is Teen Groups. I tell him that's basically what a gang is, a Teen Group. But he says how can it be a Teen Group without an adult mentor with a special skill, like whittling? Mr. Alsuga whittles. Once he gave an Old Tyme Skills Seminar on it in the Blacksmith Shoppe. It was poorly attended. All he got was two widowers and a chess-club type no gang would have wanted anyway. And myself. I attended. Evelyn called me a bootlicker, but I attended. She called me a bootlicker, and I told her she'd better bear in mind which side of the bread her butter was on. She said whichever side it was on it wasn't enough to shake a stick at. She's always denigrating my paystub. I came home from the Seminar with this kind of whittled duck. She threw it away the next day because she said she thought it was an acorn. It looked nothing like an acorn. As far as I'm concerned she threw it away out of spite. It made me livid and twice that night I had to step into a closet and perform my Hatred Abatement Breathing.

But that's neither here nor there.

Mr. Alsuga pulls out the summer stats. We're in the worst attendance decline in ten years. If it gets any worse, staff is going to be let go in droves. He gives me a meaningful look. I know full well I'm not one of his key players. Then he asks who we have that might be willing to fight fire with fire.

I say: I could research it.
He says: Why don't you research it?
So I go research it.

Sylvia Loomis is the queen of info. It's in her personality. She enjoys digging up dirt on people. She calls herself an S&M buff in training. She's still too meek to go whole hog, so when she parties at the Make Me Club on Airport Road she limits herself to walking around talking mean while wearing kiddie handcuffs. But she's good at what she does, which is Security. It was Sylvia who identified the part-timer systematically crapping in the planters in the Gift Acquisition Center and Sylvia who figured out it was Phil in Grounds leaving obscene messages for the Teen Belles on MessageMinder. She has access to all records. I ask can she identify current employees with a history of violence. She says she can if I buy her lunch.

We decide to eat in-Park. We go over to Nate's Saloon. Sylvia says don't spread it around but two of the nine cancan girls are knocked up. Then she pulls out her folder and says that according to her review of the data, we have a pretty tame bunch on our hands. The best she can do is Ned Quinn. His records indicate that while in high school he once burned down a storage shed. I almost die laughing. Quinn's an Adjunct Thespian and a world-class worry-wart. I can't count the times I've come upon him in Costuming, dwelling on the gory details of his Dread Disease Rider.[5] He's a failed actor who won't stop trying. He says this is the only job he could find that would allow him to continue to develop his craft. Because he's ugly as sin he spe-

---

5. A clause added to a life insurance policy, giving the policyholder part of the death benefit in the case that the holder contracts a terminal illness.

cializes in roles that require masks, such as Humpty-Dumpty during Mother Goose Days.

I report back to Mr. Alsuga and he says Quinn may not be much but he's all we've got. Quinn's dirt-poor with six kids and Mr. A says that's a plus, as we'll need someone between a rock and a hard place. What he suggests we do is equip the Desperate Patrol with live ammo and put Quinn in charge. The Desperate Patrol limps along under floodlights as the night's crowning event. We've costumed them to resemble troops who've been in the field too long. We used actual Gettysburg[6] photos. The climax of the Patrol is a re-enacted partial rebellion, quelled by a rousing speech. After the speech the boys take off their hats and put their arms around each other and sing "I Was Born Under a Wandering Star."[7] Then there's fireworks and the Parade of Old-Fashioned Conveyance. Then we clear the place out and go home.

"Why not confab with Quinn?" Mr. A says. "Get his input and feelings."

"I was going to say that," I say.

I look up the Thespian Center's SpeedDial extension and a few minutes later Quinn's bounding up the steps in the Wounded Grizzly suit.

"Desperate Patrol?" Mr. A says as Quinn sits down. "Any interest on your part?"

"Love it," Quinn says. "Excellent." He's been trying to get on Desperate Patrol for years. It's considered the pinnacle by the Thespians because of the wealth of speaking parts. He's so excited he's shifting around in his seat and getting some of his paw blood on Mr. A's nice cane chair.

"The gangs in our park are a damn blight," Mr. A says. "I'm talking about meeting force with force. Something in it for you? Oh yes."

"I'd like to see Quinn give the rousing speech myself," I say.

"Societal order," Mr. A says. "Sustaining the lifeblood of this goddamned park we've all put so much of our hearts into."

"He's not just free-associating," I say.

"I'm not sure I get it," Quinn says.

"What I'm suggesting is live ammo in your weapon only," Mr. A says. "Fire at your discretion. You see an unsavory intruder, you shoot at his feet. Just give him a scare. Nobody gets hurt. An additional two bills a week is what I'm talking."

"I'm an actor," Quinn says.

"Quinn's got kids," I say. "He knows the value of a buck."

"This is acting of the highest stripe," Mr. A says. "Act like a mercenary."

"Go for it on a trial basis," I say.

"I'm not sure I get it," Quinn says. "But jeez, that's good money."

"Superfantastic," says Mr. A.

Next evening Mr. A and I go over the Verisimilitude Irregularities List. We've been having some heated discussions about our bird-species percentages. Mr. Grayson, Staff Ornithologist, has recently recalculated and estimates that to accurately approximate the 1865 bird population we'll need to eliminate a couple hundred orioles or so. He suggests using air guns or

6. The Battle of Gettysburg (July 1–3, 1863), fought between the Union and Confederate armies, caused the highest casualties of any battle in the Civil War.

7. Song by Alan J. Lerner and Frederick Loewe from the musical comedy *Paint Your Wagon*, which premiered on Broadway in 1951.

poison. Mr. A says that, in his eyes, in fiscally troubled times, an ornithologist is a luxury, and this may be the perfect time to send Grayson packing. I like Grayson. He went way overboard on Howie's baseball candy. But I've got me and mine to think of. So I call Grayson in. Mr. A says did you botch the initial calculation or were you privy to new info. Mr. Grayson admits it was a botch. Mr. A sends him out into the hall and we confab.

"You'll do the telling," Mr. A says. "I'm getting too old for cruelty."

He takes his walking stick and beeper and says he'll be in the Great Forest if I need him.

I call Grayson back in and let him go, and hand him Kleenexes and fend off a few blows and almost before I know it he's reeling out the door and I go grab a pita.

Is this the life I envisioned for myself? My God no. I wanted to be a high jumper. But I have two of the sweetest children ever born. I go in at night and look at them in their fairly expensive sleepers and think: There are a couple of kids who don't need to worry about freezing to death or being cast out to the wolves. You should see their little eyes light up when I bring home a treat. They may not know the value of a dollar, but it's my intention to see that they never need to.

I'm filling out Grayson's Employee Retrospective when I hear gunshots from the perimeter. I run out and there's Quinn and a few of his men tied to the cannon. The gang guys took Quinn's pants and put some tiny notches in his penis with their knives. I free Quinn and tell him to get over to the Infirmary to guard against infection. He's absolutely shaking and can hardly walk, so I wrap him up in a Confederate flag and call over a hay cart and load him in.

When I tell Mr. A he says: Garbage in, garbage out, and that we were idiots for expecting a milquetoast[8] to save our rears.

We decide to leave the police out of it because of the possible bad PR. So we give Quinn the rest of the week off and promise to let him play Grant now and then, and that's that.

When Visitors first come in there's this cornball part where they sit in this kind of spaceship and supposedly get blasted into space and travel faster than the speed of light and end up in 1865. The unit's dated. The helmets we distribute look like bowls and all the paint's peeling off. I've argued and argued that we need to update. But in the midst of a budget crunch one can't necessarily hang the moon. When the tape of space sounds is over and the walls stop shaking, we pass out the period costumes. We try not to offend anyone, liability law being what it is. We distribute the slave and Native American roles equitably among racial groups. Anyone is free to request a different identity at any time. In spite of our precautions, there's a Herlicher in every crowd. He's the guy who sued us last fall for making him hangman. He claimed that for weeks afterwards he had nightmares and because he wasn't getting enough sleep botched a big contract by sending an important government buyer a load of torn pool liners. Big deal, is my feeling. But he's suing us for fifty grand for emotional stress because the buyer ridiculed him

8. Weak and timid person.

in front of his co-workers. Whenever he comes in we make him sheriff but he won't back down an inch.

Mr. A calls me into his office and says he's got bad news and bad news, and which do I want first. I say the bad news. First off, he says, the gangs have spraypainted a picture of Quinn's notched penis on the side of the Everly Mansion. Second, last Friday's simulated frontier hunt has got us in hot water, because apparently some of the beef we toughen up to resemble buffalo meat was tainted, and the story's going in the Sunday supplement. And finally, the verdict's come in on the Herlicher case and we owe that goofball a hundred grand instead of fifty because the pinko[9] judge empathized.

I wait for him to say I'm fired but instead he breaks down in tears. I pat his back and mix him a drink. He says why don't I join him. So I join him.

"It doesn't look good," he says, "for men like you and I."

"No it doesn't," I say.

"All I wanted to do," he says, "was to give the public a meaningful perspective on a historical niche I've always found personally fascinating."

"I know what you mean," I say.

At eleven the phone rings. It's Maurer in Refuse Control calling to say that the gangs have set fire to the Anglican Church. That structure cost upwards of ninety thousand to transport from Clydesville and refurbish. We can see the flames from Mr. A's window.

"Oh Christ!" Mr. A says. "If I could kill those kids I would kill those kids. One shouldn't desecrate the dream of another individual in the fashion in which they have mine."

"I know it," I say.

We drink and drink and finally he falls asleep on his office couch.

On the way to my car I keep an eye out for the ghostly McKinnon family. Back in the actual 1860s all this land was theirs. Their homestead's long gone but our records indicate that it was located near present-day Information Hoedown. They probably never saw this many buildings in their entire lives. They don't realize we're chronically slumming, they just think the valley's prospering. Something bad must have happened to them because their spirits are always wandering around at night looking dismayed.

Tonight I find the Mrs. doing wash by the creek. She sees me coming and asks if she can buy my boots. Machine stitching amazes her. I ask how are the girls. She says Maribeth has been sad because no appropriate boy ever died in the valley so she's doomed to loneliness forever. Maribeth is a homely sincere girl who glides around mooning and pining and reading bad poetry chapbooks. Whenever we keep the Park open late for high-school parties, she's in her glory. There was one kid who was able to see her and even got a crush on her, but when he finally tried to kiss her near Hostelry[1] and found out she was spectral it just about killed him. I slipped him a fifty and told him to keep it under wraps. As far as I know he's still in therapy. I realize I should have come forward but they probably would have nut-hutted me, and then where would my family be?

<hr>

9. Slang for a communist sympathizer.   1. Inn.

The Mrs. says what Maribeth needs is choir practice followed by a nice quilting bee. In better times I would have taken the quilting-bee idea and run with it. But now there's no budget. That's basically how I finally moved up from Verisimilitude Inspector to Special Assistant, by lifting ideas from the McKinnons. The Mrs. likes me because after she taught me a few obscure 1800s ballads and I parlayed them into Individual Achievement Awards, I bought her a Rubik's Cube. To her, colored plastic is like something from Venus. The Mr. has kind of warned me away from her a couple of times. He doesn't trust me. He thinks the Rubik's Cube is the devil's work. I've brought him lighters and *Playboys*[2] and once I even dragged out Howie's little synth[2] and the mobile battery pak. I set the synth for carillon and played it from behind a bush. I could tell he was tickled, but he stonewalled. It's too bad I can't make an inroad because he was at Antietam[3] and could be a gold mine of war info. He came back from the war and a year later died in his cornfield, which is now Parking. So he spends most of his time out there calling the cars Beelzebubs[4] and kicking their tires.

Tonight he's walking silently up and down the rows. I get out to my KCar[5] and think oh jeez, I've locked the keys in. The Mr. sits down at the base of the A3 lightpole and asks did I see the fire and do I realize it was divine retribution for my slovenly moral state. I say thank you very much. No way I'm telling him about the gangs. He can barely handle the concept of women wearing trousers. Finally I give up on prying the window down and go call Evelyn for the spare set. While I wait for her I sit on the hood and watch the stars. The Mr. watches them too. He says there are fewer than when he was a boy. He says that even the heavens have fallen into disrepair. I think about explaining smog to him but then Evelyn pulls up.

She's wearing her bathrobe and as soon as she gets out starts with the lip. Howie and Marcus are asleep in the back. The Mr. says it's part and parcel of my fallen state that I allow a woman to speak to me in such a tone. He suggests I throttle her and lock her in the woodshed. Meanwhile she's going on and on so much about my irresponsibility that the kids are waking up. I want to get out before the gangs come swooping down on us. The Parking Area's easy pickings. She calls me a thoughtless oaf and sticks me in the gut with the car keys.

Marcus wakes up all groggy and says: Hey, our daddy.

Evelyn says: Yes, unfortunately he is.

Just after lunch next day a guy shows up at Personnel looking so completely Civil War they immediately hire him and send him out to sit on the porch of the old Kriegal place with a butter churn. His name's Samuel and he doesn't say a word going through Costuming and at the end of the day leaves on a bike. I do the normal clandestine New Employee Observation

---

2. Synthesizer; electronic keyboard. *"Playboy"*: popular adult magazine founded in 1953. "Rubik's Cube": puzzle toy made popular in the 1980s.
3. The Battle of Antietam, in Maryland (September 17, 1862) ended the first Confederate invasion into the North. This was the bloodiest one-day battle in American history; the Union victory led to Abraham Lincoln's preliminary issuance of the Emancipation Proclamation.
4. Devils.
5. Inexpensive sedan manufactured by the Chrysler Corporation, 1981–95.

from the O'Toole gazebo and I like what I see. He seems to have a passable knowledge of how to pretend to churn butter. At one point he makes the mistake of departing from the list of Then-Current Events to discuss the World Series with a Visitor, but my feeling is, we can work with that. All in all he presents a positive and convincing appearance, and I say so in my review.

Sylvia runs her routine check on him and calls me at home that night and says boy do we have a hot prospect on our hands if fucking with the gangs is still on our agenda. She talks like that. I've got her on speakerphone in the rec room and Marcus starts running around the room saying fuck. Evelyn stands there with her arms crossed, giving me a drop-dead look. I wave her off and she flips me the bird.

Sylvia's federal sources indicate that Samuel got kicked out of Vietnam[6] for participating in a bloodbath. Sylvia claims this is oxymoronic. She sounds excited. She suggests I take a nice long look at his marksmanship scores. She says his special combat course listing goes on for pages.

I call Mr. A and he says it sounds like Sam's our man. I express reservations at arming an alleged war criminal and giving him free rein in a family-oriented facility. Mr. A says if we don't get our act together there won't be any family-oriented facility left in a month. Revenues have hit rock bottom and his investors are frothing at the mouth. There's talk of outright closure and liquidation of assets.

He says: Now get off your indefensible high horse and give me Sam's home phone.

So I get off my indefensible high horse and give him Sam's home phone.

Thursday after we've armed Samuel and sent him and the Patrol out, I stop by the Worship Center to check on the Foley baptism. Baptisms are an excellent revenue source. We charge three hundred dollars to rent the Center, which is the former lodge of the Siala utopian free-love community. We trucked it in from downstate, a redbrick building with a nice gold dome. In the old days if one of the Sialians was overeating to the exclusion of others or excessively masturbating, he or she would be publicly dressed down for hours on end in the lodge. Now we put up white draperies and pipe in Stephen Foster[7] and provide at no charge a list of preachers of various denominations.

The Foleys are an overweight crew. The room's full of crying sincere large people wishing the best for a baby. It makes me remember our own sweet beaners in their little frocks. I sit down near the wood-burning heater in the Invalid area and see that Justin in Prep has forgotten to remove the mannequin elderly couple clutching rosaries. Hopefully the Foleys won't notice and withhold payment.

The priest dips the baby's head into the fake marble basin and the door flies open and in comes a racially mixed gang. They stroll up the aisle tousling hair and requisition a Foley niece, a cute redhead of about sixteen.

---

6. That is, the American phase of the war in Vietnam (1955–75).
7. Stephen Collins Foster (1826–1864), American songwriter, famous for patriotic standards such as "My Old Kentucky Home" and "Oh! Susanna" as well as songs used in black-face minstrel shows.

Her dad stands up and gets a blackjack in the head. One of the gang guys pushes her down the aisle with his hands on her breasts. As she passes she looks right at me. The gang guy spits on my shoe and I make my face neutral so he won't get hacked off and drag me into it.

The door slams and the Foleys sit there stunned. Then the baby starts crying and everyone runs shouting outside in time to see the gang dragging the niece into the woods. I panic. I try to think of where the nearest pay phone is. I'm weighing the efficiency of running to Administration and making the call from my cubicle when six fast shots come from the woods. Several of the oldest Foleys assume the worst and drop weeping to their knees in the churchyard.

I don't know the first thing about counseling survivors, so I run for Mr. A.

He's drinking and watching his bigscreen. I tell him what happened and he jumps up and calls the police. Then he says let's go do whatever little we can for these poor people who entrusted us with their sacred family occasion only to have us drop the ball by failing to adequately protect them.

When we get back to the churchyard the Foleys are kicking and upbraiding six gang corpses. Samuel's having a glass of punch with the niece. The niece's dad is hanging all over Sam trying to confirm his daughter's virginity. Sam says it wasn't even close and goes on and on about the precision of his scope.

Then we hear sirens.

Sam says: I'm going into the woods.

Mr. A says: We never saw you, big guy.

The niece's dad says: Bless you, sir.

Sam says: Adios.

Mr. A stands on the hitching post and makes a little speech, the gist of which is, let's blame another gang for killing these dirtbags so Sam can get on with his important work.

The Foleys agree.

The police arrive and we all lie like rugs.

The word spreads on Sam and the gangs leave us alone. For two months the Park is quiet and revenues start upscaling. Then some high-school kid pulls a butter knife on Fred Moore and steals a handful of penny candy from the General Store. As per specs, Fred alerts Mr. A of a Revenue-Impacting Event. Mr. A calls Security and we perform Exit Sealage. We look everywhere, but the kid's gone. Mr. A says what the hell, Unseal, it's just candy, profit loss is minimal. Sam hears the Unseal Tone on the PA and comes out of the woods all mad with his face painted and says that once the word gets out we've gone soft the gangs will be back in a heartbeat. I ask since when do gangs use butter knives. Sam says a properly trained individual can kill a wild boar with a butter knife. Mr. A gives me a look and says why don't we let Sam run this aspect of the operation since he possesses the necessary expertise. Then Mr. A offers to buy him lunch and Sam says no, he'll eat raw weeds and berries as usual.

I go back to my Verisimilitude Evaluation on the Cimarron Brothel. Everything looks super. As per my recommendations they've replaced the young attractive simulated whores with uglier women with a little less on the ball. We were able to move the ex–simulated whores over to the Sweete

Shoppe, so everybody's happy, especially the new simulated whores, who were for the most part middle-aged women we lured away from fast-food places via superior wages.

When I've finished the Evaluation I go back to my office for lunch. I step inside and turn on the fake oil lamp and there's a damn human hand on my chair, holding a note. All around the hand there's penny candy. The note says: Sir, another pig disciplined who won't mess with us anymore and also I need more ammo. It's signed: Samuel the Rectifier.

I call Mr. A and he says Jesus. Then he tells me to bury the hand in the marsh behind Refreshments. I say shouldn't we call the police. He says we let it pass when it was six dead kids, why should we start getting moralistic now over one stinking hand?

I say: But sir, he killed a high-schooler for stealing candy.

He says: That so-called high-schooler threatened Fred Moore, a valued old friend of mine, with a knife.

A butter knife, I say.

He asks if I've seen the droves of unemployed huddled in front of Personnel every morning.

I ask if that's a threat and he says no, it's a reasonable future prognostication.

"What's done is done," he says. "We're in this together. If I take the fall on this, you'll eat the wienie as well. Let's just put this sordid ugliness behind us and get on with the business of providing an enjoyable living for those we love."

I hang up and sit looking at the hand. There's a class ring on it.

Finally I knock it into a garbage sack with my phone and go out to the marsh.

As I'm digging, Mr. McKinnon glides up. He gets down on his knees and starts sniffing the sack. He starts talking about bloody wagon wheels and a boy he once saw sitting in a creek slapping the water with his own severed arm. He tells how the dead looked with rain on their faces and of hearing lunatic singing from all corners of the field of battle and of king-sized rodents gorging themselves on the entrails of his friends.

It occurs to me that the Mr.'s a loon.

I dig down a couple feet and drop the hand in. Then I backfill and get out of there fast. I look over my shoulder and he's rocking back and forth over the hole mumbling to himself.

As I pass a sewer cover the Mrs. rises out of it. Seeing the Mr. enthralled by blood she starts shrieking and howling to beat the band. When she finally calms down she comes to rest in a tree branch. Tears run down her see-through cheeks. She says there's been a horrid violent seed in him since he came home from the war. She says she can see they're going to have to go away. Then she blasts over my head elongate and glowing and full of grief and my hat gets sucked off.

All night I have bad dreams about severed hands. In one I'm eating chili and a hand comes out of my bowl and gives me the thumbs-down. I wake up with a tingling wrist. Evelyn says if I insist on sleeping uneasily would I mind doing it on the couch, since she has a family to care for during the day and this requires a certain amount of rest. I think about confessing to her but then I realize if I do she'll nail me.

The nights when she'd fall asleep with her cheek on my thigh are certainly long past.

I lie there awhile watching her make angry faces in her sleep. Then I go for a walk. As usual Mr. Ebershom's practicing figure-skating moves in his foyer. I sit down by our subdivision's fake creek and think. First of all, burying a hand isn't murder. It doesn't say anywhere thou shalt not bury some guy's hand. By the time I got involved the kid was dead. Where his hand ended up is inconsequential.

Then I think: What am I saying? I did a horrible thing. Even as I sit here I'm an accomplice and an obstructor of justice.

But then I see myself in the penitentiary and the boys waking up scared in the night without me, and right then and there with my feet in the creek I decide to stay clammed up forever and take my lumps in the afterlife.

Halloween's special in the Park. Our brochure says: Lose Yourself in Eerie Autumnal Splendor. We spray cobwebs around the Structures and dress up Staff in ghoul costumes and hand out period-authentic treats. We hide holograph generators in the woods and project images of famous Americans as ghosts. It's always a confusing time for the McKinnons. Last year the Mr. got in a head-to-head with the image of Jefferson Davis.[8] He stood there in the woods yelling at it for hours while the Mrs. and the girls begged him to come away. Finally I had to cut power to the unit.

I drive home at lunch and pick the boys up for trick-or-treating. Marcus is a rancher and Howie's an accountant. He's wearing thick fake lips and carrying a ledger. The Park's the only safe place to trick-or-treat anymore. Last year some wacko in a complex near our house laced his Snickers with a virus. I drove by the school and they were CPRing this little girl in a canary suit. So forget it.

I take them around to the various Structures and they pick up their share of saltwater taffy and hard tasteless frontier candy and wooden whistles and toy soldiers made of soap.

Then just as we start across the Timeless Green a mob of teens bursts out of the Feinstein Memorial Conifer Grove.

"Gangs!" I yell to the boys. "Get down!"

I hear a shot and look up and there's Samuel standing on a stump at tree line. Thank God, I think. He lets loose another round and one of the teens drops. Marcus is down beside me whimpering with his nose in my armpit. Howie's always been the slow one. He stands there with his mouth open, one hand in his plastic pumpkin. A second teen drops. Then Howie drops and his pumpkin goes flying.

I crawl over and beg him to be okay. He says there's no pain. I check him over and check him over and all that's wrong is his ledger's been shot. I'm so relieved I kiss him on the mouth and he yells at me to quit.

Samuel drops a third teen, then runs yipping into the woods.

The ambulance shows up and the paramedics load up the wounded teens. They're all still alive and one's saying a rosary. I take the boys to City Hall and confront Mr. A. I tell him I'm turning Sam in. He asks if I've gone daft

---

8. Davis (1808–1889) was president of the Confederate States of America during the Civil War.

and suggests I try putting food on the table from a jail cell while convicts stand in line waiting to have their way with my rear.

At this point I send the boys out to the foyer.

"He shot Howie," I say. "I want him put away."

"He shot Howie's ledger," Mr. A says. "He shot Howie's ledger in the process of saving Howie's life. But whatever. Let's not mince hairs. If Sam gets put away, we get put away. Does that sound to you like a desirable experience?"

"No," I say.

"What I'm primarily saying," he says, "is that this is a time for knowledge assimilation, not backstabbing. We learned a lesson, you and I. We personally grew. Gratitude for this growth is an appropriate response. Gratitude, and being careful never to make the same mistake twice."

He gets out a Bible and says let's swear on it that we'll never hire a crazed maniac to perform an important security function again. Then the phone rings. Sylvia's cross-referenced today's Admissions data and found that the teens weren't a gang at all but a bird-watching group who made the mistake of being male and adolescent and wandering too far off the trail.

"Ouch," Mr. A says. "This could be a serious negative."

In the foyer the kids are trying to get the loaches in the corporate tank to eat bits of Styrofoam. I phone Evelyn and tell her what happened and she calls me a butcher. She wants to know how on earth I could bring the boys to the Park knowing what I knew. She says she doesn't see how I'm going to live with myself in light of how much they trusted and loved me and how badly I let them down by leaving their fates to chance.

I say I'm sorry and she seems to be thinking. Then she tells me just get them home without putting them in further jeopardy, assuming that's within the scope of my mental powers.

At home she puts them in the tub and sends me out for pizza. I opt for Melvin's Pasta Lair. Melvin's a religious zealot who during the Depression worked five jobs at once. Sometimes I tell him my troubles and he says I should stop whining and count my blessings. Tonight I tell him I feel I should take some responsibility for eliminating the Samuel problem but I'm hesitant because of the discrepancy in our relative experience in violence. He says you mean you're scared. I say not scared, just aware of the likelihood of the possibility of failure. He gives me a look. I say it must have been great to grow up when men were men. He says men have always been what they are now, namely incapable of coping with life without the intervention of God the Almighty. Then in the oven behind him my pizza starts smoking and he says case in point.

He makes me another and urges me to get in touch with my Lord personally. I tell him I will. I always tell him I will.

When I get home they're gone.

Evelyn's note says: I could never forgive you for putting our sons at risk. Goodbye forever, you passive flake. Don't try to find us. I've told the kids you sent us away in order to marry a floozy.

Like an idiot I run out to the street. Mrs. Schmidt is prodding her automatic sprinkler system with a rake, trying to detect leaks in advance. She asks how I am and I tell her not now. I sit on the lawn. The stars are very near. The phone rings. I run inside prepared to grovel, but it's only Mr. A. He says come down to the Park immediately because he's got big horrific news.

When I get there he's sitting in his office half-crocked. He tells me we're unemployed. The investors have gotten wind of the bird-watcher shootings and withdrawn all support. The Park is no more. I tell him about Evelyn and the kids. He says that's the least of his worries because he's got crushing debt. He asks if I have any savings he could have. I say no. He says that just for the record and my own personal development, he's always found me dull and has kept me around primarily for my yes-man capabilities and because sometimes I'm so cautious I'm a hoot.

Then he says: Look, get your ass out, I'm torching this shithole for insurance purposes.

I want to hit or at least insult him, but I need this week's pay to find my kids. So I jog off through the Park. In front of Information Hoedown I see the McKinnons cavorting. I get closer and see that they're not cavorting at all, they've inadvertently wandered too close to their actual death site and are being compelled to act out again and again the last minutes of their lives. The girls are lying side by side on the ground and the Mr. is whacking at them with an invisible scythe. The Mrs. is belly-up with one arm flailing in what must have been the parlor. The shrieking is mind-boggling. When he's killed everyone the Mr. walks out to his former field and mimes blowing out his brains. Then he gets up and starts over. It goes on and on, through five cycles. Finally he sits down in the dirt and starts weeping. The Mrs. and the girls backpedal away. He gets up and follows them, pitifully trying to explain.

Behind us the Visitor Center erupts in flames.

The McKinnons go off down the hill, passing through bushes and trees. He's shouting for forgiveness. He's shouting that he's just a man. He's shouting that hatred and war made him nuts. I start running down the hill agreeing with him. The Mrs. gives me a look and puts her hands over Maribeth's ears. We're all running. The Mrs. starts screaming about the feel of the scythe as it opened her up. The girls bemoan their unborn kids. We make quite a group. Since I'm still alive I keep clipping trees with my shoulders and falling down.

At the bottom of the hill they pass through the retaining wall and I run into it. I wake up on my back in the culvert. Blood's running out of my ears and a transparent boy's kneeling over me. I can tell he's no McKinnon because he's wearing sweatpants.

"Get up now," he says in a gentle voice. "Fire's coming."

"No," I say. "I'm through. I'm done living."

"I don't think so," he says. "You've got amends to make."

"I screwed up," I say. "I did bad things."

"No joke," he says, and holds up his stump.

I roll over into the culvert muck and he grabs me by the collar and sits me up.

"I steal four jawbreakers and a Slim Jim and your friend kills and mutilates me?" he says.

"He wasn't my friend," I say.

"He wasn't your enemy," the kid says.

Then he cocks his head. Through his clear skull I see Sam coming out of the woods. The kid cowers behind me. Even dead he's scared of Sam. He's so scared he blasts straight up in the air shrieking and vanishes over the retaining wall.

Sam comes for me with a hunting knife.

"Don't take this too personal," he says, "but you've got to go. You know a few things I don't want broadcast."

I'm madly framing calming words in my head as he drives the knife in. I can't believe it. Never again to see my kids? Never again to sleep and wake to their liquid high voices and sweet breaths?

Sweet Evelyn, I think, I should have loved you better.

Possessing perfect knowledge I hover above him as he hacks me to bits. I see his rough childhood. I see his mother doing something horrid to him with a broomstick. I see the hate in his heart and the people he has yet to kill before pneumonia gets him at eighty-three. I see the dead kid's mom unable to sleep, pounding her fists against her face in grief at the moment I was burying her son's hand. I see the pain I've caused. I see the man I could have been, and the man I was, and then everything is bright and new and keen with love and I sweep through Sam's body, trying to change him, trying so hard, and feeling only hate and hate, solid as stone.

1996

SHERMAN ALEXIE
b. 1966

Except for one great-grandparent, Sherman Alexie's lineage is entirely Native American: Coeur d'Alene on his father's side; Colville, Flathead, and Spokane on his mother's. The cities of Coeur d'Alene (Idaho) and Spokane (Washington) mark the interior northwest corner of the contiguous forty-eight states, the place where Alexie's poetry, fiction, and cinematic work is sometimes set. Yet his interest in Native American culture ranges widely, to include other tribes such as the Navajo and regions throughout the West and Southwest. Raised on the Spokane reservation at Wellpinit, Washington, Alexie thrived in the cultural immersion that secondary education at Reardan High School, some distance from home, provided—especially the popular culture that would later infuse his work. Hence both words in the designation "Native American" figure prominently in how he sees himself as a writer.

Equal doses of trouble and humor characterize Alexie's work. Having survived hydrocephalus (a cerebrospinal abnormality) as a child and alcoholism as a young adult, he drew on his college experience as an undergraduate at Gonzaga University in Spokane and Washington State University in Pullman to find a literary voice, inspired by writers as diverse as John Steinbeck and the Native American poets included by Joseph Bruchac in the anthology *Songs from This Earth on Turtle's Back* (1983). In 1992 he published his own first work, *The Business of Fancydancing: Stories and Poems*, with one of America's most prominent small presses, Hanging Loose (Brooklyn, New York).

When *The Business of Fancydancing* was published, a review in the *New York Times* called Alexie "one of the major lyric voices of our time." "I was a twenty-five-year-old Spokane Indian guy working as a secretary at a high school exchange program," he has written. "I thought 'Great! Where do I go from here?'"

Alexie has continued telling stories through poetry, fiction, and screenwriting. *Reservation Blues* (1994) was his first novel, followed by *Indian Killer* in 1996. *Flight* (2007) shows the influence of Kurt Vonnegut, from its device of time travel to its reinvention of history from a comparative point of view. Presented broadly, even comically, his stories often draw on simple incidents, as in the story reprinted here. His storytelling offers a tragicomic vision of contemporary Native American life, notably in his National Book Award–winning novel *The Absolutely True Diary of a Part-Time Indian* (2007), in the stories of his several collections, and in his several volumes of poetry. College educated and street-smart ("I'm a rez kid who's gone urban"), irreverent and also dead serious, Alexie resembles the trickster figure of Crow in his poem "Crow Testament."

Alexie's poems have a furious energy. Although some of his work takes traditional forms, most of his poems are open and improvisational, frequently and effectively using repetition and parallelism. The title of Alexie's 2000 collection, *One Stick Song*, offers an apt image for his work; it refers to a gambling game in which sticks function like chips. When down to one stick, he explains, "You're desperate," and a "One Stick Song" is "a desperate celebration, a desperate attempt to save yourself, putting everything you have into one song." The best of Alexie's poems make facing up to grief and anger an act of survival. The intensity of this effort is especially evident when he reads from or recites his work. A brilliant performer, sliding between humor, anger, and pain, he makes a poetry reading a dynamic event. It is no wonder that his interest in performance has extended to stand-up comedy as well.

Popular audiences know Alexie from the 2002 film he wrote and directed, *The Business of Fancydancing*, and especially his 1998 film *Smoke Signals*, a major Hollywood production he scripted from material in his story collection *The Lone Ranger and Tonto Fistfight in Heaven* (1993). These stories and the movies drawn from them cover a broad range of contemporary Native American experience. As one of his characters says, Native Americans have "a way of surviving. But it's almost like Indians can easily survive the big stuff. Mass murder, loss of language and land rights. It's the small things that hurt the most. The white waitress who wouldn't take an order, Tonto, the Washington Redskins."

At Navajo Monument Valley Tribal School

from the photograph
by Skeet McAuley

the football field rises
to meet the mesa. Indian boys
gallop across the grass, against

the beginning of their body.
On those Saturday afternoons,   5
unbroken horses gather to watch

their sons growing larger
in the small parts of the world.
Everyone is the quarterback.

Navajo Monument Valley playing field, where "the football field rises / to meet the mesa." Photograph by Skeet McAuley.

There is no thin man in a big hat   10
writing down all the names
in two columns: winners and losers.

This is the eternal football game,
Indians versus Indians. All the Skins
in the wooden bleachers fancydancing,   15

stomping red dust straight down
into nothing. Before the game is over,
the eighth-grade girls' track team

comes running, circling the field,
their thin and brown legs echoing   20
wild horses, wild horses, wild horses.

1992

Pawn Shop

I walk into the bar, after being gone for a while, and it's empty. The Bartender tells me all the Indians are gone, do I know where they went? I tell him I don't know, and I don't know, so he gives me a beer just for being Indian, small favors, and I wonder where all the Skins disappeared to, and after a while, I leave, searching the streets, searching storefronts,   5 until I walk into a pawn shop, find a single heart beating under glass, and I know who it used to belong to, I know all of them.

1992

Crow Testament[1]

1

Cain lifts Crow, that heavy black bird
and strikes down Abel.[2]

Damn, says Crow, I guess
this is just the beginning.

2

The white man, disguised   5
as a falcon, swoops in
and yet again steals a salmon
from Crow's talons.

Damn, says Crow, if I could swim
I would have fled this country years ago.   10

3

The Crow God as depicted
in all of the reliable Crow bibles
looks exactly like a Crow.

Damn, says Crow, this makes it
so much easier to worship myself.   15

4

Among the ashes of Jericho,[3]
Crow sacrifices his firstborn son.

Damn, says Crow, a million nests
are soaked with blood.

5

When Crows fight Crows   20
the sky fills with beaks and talons.

Damn, says Crow, it's raining feathers.

---

1. Crow, like Raven, is a trickster figure in many Native American cultures.
2. In Genesis, Cain kills his brother, Abel. They are the sons of Adam and Eve.
3. This biblical city, famous for its great walls, was the first town attacked by the Israelites under Joshua, after they crossed the Jordan River.

6

Crow flies around the reservation
and collects empty beer bottles

but they are so heavy   25
he can carry only one at a time.

So, one by one, he returns them
but gets only five cents a bottle.

Damn, says Crow, redemption
is not easy.   30

7

Crow rides a pale horse
into a crowded powwow
but none of the Indians panic.

Damn, says Crow, I guess
they already live near the end of the world.   35

2000

NATASHA TRETHEWEY
b. 1966

Natasha Trethewey has been a significant voice in American poetry since the 1990s. As a young poet she was part of the Dark Room Collective in the 1990s, a group of Boston-based poets of African descent that began meeting first to establish a reading series, later becoming a tightly knit group that toured, read, and shared work together. The group included the poet Kevin Young and several others who went on to have distinguished careers. Trethewey, for her part, won the Pulitzer Prize for her 2006 collection, *Native Guard*, a recognition that significantly broadened the audience for her work, and she was named poet laureate of the United States in 2012.

What new and loyal readers of Trethewey's work find, from collection to collection, is a poet exquisitely attuned to medium: not only the rich medium of poetic language that marries emotion, narrative, and sound, but also multiple visual media. Her 2002 collection, *Bellocq's Ophelia*, contained a series of poems meditating on the photographs of E. J. Bellocq, who made portraits of multiracial women—often called "octoroons" and "quadroons" in the nineteenth century—working in the brothels of New Orleans in 1912. *Thrall*, her 2012 collection, probes the so-called Casta paintings—

The poets of the Dark Room Collective (1996). From left: Natasha Trethewey, Kevin Young, Major Jackson, Nehassaiu deGannes, Thomas Sayers Ellis, Sharan Strange, Adisa Vera Beatty.

eighteenth-century Spanish canvases focused on the representation of skin color. The paintings set out to catalog in aesthetic terms the racial mixtures of colonialism and the transatlantic slave trade—white-skinned Spanish fathers in silk and lace posing with African or Native women and the children of these unions. In lyrics scattered throughout her collections, Trethewey engages photographs and visual environments ranging from family snapshots to museum exhibits. Choosing images at once beautiful and ethically disturbing, Trethewey translates vision—which renders its objects just that, *objects*—into voice. We hear the voices of Bellocq's models, who tell their stories beyond the photograph's frame. We hear the voice of a thinking narrator, who has us see the sumptuous tableaux of mixed races for what they are: the output of a racist hierarchy of beauty, power, sex, and history. And we hear the voice of an autobiographical speaker, a biracial woman addressing, mourning, accusing, and questioning by turns her white father and her black mother.

In Natasha Trethewey's hands poetry is a live wire to the past. In *Native Guard*, she brings readers into the consciousness of a private in the Louisiana Native Guard, a corps of black Union soldiers who guarded Confederate prisoners and died in battle on Trethewey's home ground in southern Mississippi. Alongside that history, Trethewey places a series of elegies for her mother, who was murdered at the hands of an abusive lover when Trethewey was in her twenties. In the most heartbreaking of these elegies, "Graveyard Blues," the familiar themes and rhymes of the blues allow the speaker to remember the act of burying her mother. It is a searing memory somehow comforted by the blues, a form that embodies the pain of generations of Americans of African descent. In the poem we feel both the blues' general sadness and the specific sharp fact of this speaker's story. *Thrall*, too, crosses the personal with the historical: meditations on the speaker's own biracial heritage entwine with the poems about the Casta paintings. Trethewey's poetry has a purchase on American life that is formally flexible, rich in aesthetic resources, keyed to the flow of the continent's violent history. That historical perspective has informed Trethewey's prose writing as well. Moved in the aftermath of Hurricane Katrina to return to her native town of Gulfport, Mississippi, she offers a complicated and very human understanding of natural disaster and its aftermath there, laying out the relationship between poverty, race, and landscape in Mississippi since the experience of Hurricane Camille in the late 1960s.

To date, Trethewey has written four collections of poetry and one book of prose. Since 2001 she has been based in Atlanta, where she was raised, and where she is the Robert W. Woodruff Professor of English and Creative Writing at Emory University. Her perch in academia is fitting, given her erudition, the evidence of which we see especially in her historical poetry. But she is still very much a poet of the people. As poet laureate, Trethewey reinstated the great but lapsed tradition of the poet laureate's "office hours"—time she set aside each week in the Library of Congress to talk about poetry with anyone who wished to come by. In her second year as laureate, her main project was to work with the Public Broadcasting Service (PBS) on a series of films about the meaning and role of poetry in our ordinary lives today.

In keeping with such priorities, readers will find her poetry accessible, humane, and democratic—but it is not therefore safe or easy. Trethewey shows how our practice of art and our conception of beauty have been complicit with racist violence. She shows us how the human body and voice are unmade—and perhaps, ultimately, remade—under the weight of history.

Vignette

—from a photograph
by E. J. Bellocq, circa 1912[1]

They pose the portrait outside
the brothel—Bellocq's black scrim,
a chair for her to sit on. She wears
white, a rhinestone choker, fur,
her dark crown of hair—an elegant image,   5
one she might send to her mother.
Perhaps the others crowd in behind
Bellocq, awaiting their turns, tremors
of laughter in their white throats.
Maybe Bellocq chats, just a little,   10
to put her at ease while he waits
for the right moment, a look on her face
to keep in a gilded frame, the ornate box
he'll put her in. Suppose he tells her

---

1. John Ernest Joseph Bellocq (1873–1949), American photographer.

about a circus coming to town—monkeys   15
and organ music, the high trapeze—but then

she's no longer listening; she's forgotten
he's there. Instead she must be thinking
of her childhood wonder at seeing
the contortionist in a sideshow—how   20
he could make himself small, fit
into cramped spaces, his lungs
barely expanding with each tiny breath.
She thinks of her own shallow breath—
her back straining the stays of a bustier,   25
the weight of a body pressing her down.
Picture her face now as she realizes
that it must have been harder every year,
that the contortionist, too, must have ached
each night in his tent. This is how   30
Bellocq takes her, her brow furrowed
as she looks out to the left, past all of them.
Imagine her a moment later—after
the flash, blinded—stepping out
of the frame, wide-eyed, into her life.   35

2002

Graveyard Blues

It rained the whole time we were laying her down;
Rained from church to grave when we put her down.
The suck of mud at our feet was a hollow sound.

When the preacher called out I held up my hand;
When he called for a witness I raised my hand   5
Death stops the body's work, the soul's a journeyman.

The sun came out when I turned to walk away,
Glared down on me as I turned and walked away—
My back to my mother, leaving her where she lay.

The road going home was pocked with holes,   10
That home-going road's always full of holes;
Though we slow down, time's wheel still rolls.

I wander now among names of the dead:
My mother's name, stone pillow for my head.

2006

Photograph: Ice Storm, 1971

Why the rough edge of beauty? Why
the tired face of a woman, suffering,
made luminous by the camera's eye?

Or the storm that drives us inside
for days, power lines down, food rotting   5
in the refrigerator, while outside

the landscape glistens beneath a glaze
of ice? Why remember anything
but the wonder of those few days,

the iced trees, each leaf in its glassy case?   10
The picture we took that first morning,
the front yard a beautiful, strange place—

why on the back has someone made a list
of our names, the date, the event: nothing
of what's inside—mother, stepfather's fist?   15

2006

Native Guard[1]

*If this war is to be forgotten, I ask in the name of all things
sacred what shall men remember?*
—FREDERICK DOUGLASS

November 1862

Truth be told, I do not want to forget
anything of my former life: the landscape's
song of bondage—dirge in the river's throat
where it churns into the Gulf, wind in trees
choked with vines. I thought to carry with me   5
want of freedom though I had been freed,

---

1. Epigraph from "Address at the Grave of the Unknown Dead" by Frederick Douglass, Arlington, Virginia, May 30, 1871; quoted in *Race and Reunion: The Civil War in American Memory* by David Blight. Cambridge, Mass.: Belknap Press, 2001.

The first regiments of the Louisiana Native Guards were mustered into service in September, October, and November of 1862—the 1st Regiment thus becoming the first officially sanctioned regiment of black soldiers in the Union Army, and the 2nd and 3rd made up of men who had been slaves only months before enlisting. During the war, the fort at Ship Island, Mississippi, called Fort Massachusetts, was maintained as a prison for Confederate soldiers—military convicts and prisoners of war—manned by the 2nd Regiment. Among the 2nd Regiment's officers was Francis E. Dumas—the son of a white Creole father and a mulatto mother—who had inherited slaves when his father died. Although Louisiana law prohibited him from manumitting these slaves, when he joined the Union Army, Dumas freed them and encouraged those men of age to join the Native Guards. (From *The Louisiana Native Guards: The Black Military Experience During the Civil War* by James G. Hollandsworth. Baton Rouge: Louisiana State University Press, 1995.) [Trethewey's note.]

remembrance not constant recollection.
Yes: I was born a slave, at harvest time,
in the Parish of Ascension; I've reached
thirty-three with history of one younger   10
inscribed upon my back. I now use ink
to keep record, a closed book, not the lure
of memory—flawed, changeful—that dulls the lash
for the master, sharpens it for the slave.

December 1862

For the slave, having a master sharpens   15
the bend into work, the way the sergeant
moves us now to perfect battalion drill,
dress parade. Still, we're called supply units—
not infantry—and so we dig trenches,
haul burdens for the army no less heavy   20
than before. I heard the colonel call it
nigger work. Half rations make our work
familiar still. We take those things we need
from the Confederates' abandoned homes:
salt, sugar, even this journal, near full   25
with someone else's words, overlapped now,
crosshatched beneath mine. On every page,
his story intersecting with my own.

January 1863[2]

O how history intersects—my own
berth upon a ship called the *Northern Star*   30
and I'm delivered into a new life,
Fort Massachusetts: a great irony—
both path and destination of freedom
I'd not dared to travel. Here, now, I walk
ankle-deep in sand, fly-bitten, nearly   35
smothered by heat, and yet I can look out
upon the Gulf and see the surf breaking,
tossing the ships, the great gunboats bobbing
on the water. And are we not the same,
slaves in the hands of the master, destiny?   40
—night sky red with the promise of fortune,
dawn pink as new flesh: healing, unfettered.

2. The Union ship *Northern Star* transported seven companies of the 2nd Louisiana Native Guards to Fort Massachusetts, Ship Island, on January 12, 1863. The lines ". . . I can look out / upon the Gulf and see the surf breaking. / tossing the ships, the great gunboats bobbing / on the water. And are we not the same, / slaves in the hands of the master, destiny?" are borrowed, in slightly different form, from *Thank God My Regiment an African One: The Civil War Diary of Colonel Nathan W. Daniels*, edited by C. P. Weaver. Baton Rouge: Louisiana State University Press, 1998. [Trethewey's note.]

January 1863

Today, dawn red as warning. Unfettered
supplies, stacked on the beach at our landing,
washed away in the storm that rose too fast,   45
caught us unprepared. Later, as we worked,
I joined in the low singing someone raised
to pace us, and felt a bond in labor
I had not known. It was then a dark man
removed his shirt, revealed the scars, crosshatched   50
like the lines in this journal, on his back.
It was he who remarked at how the ropes
cracked like whips on the sand, made us take note
of the wild dance of a tent loosed by wind.
We watched and learned. Like any shrewd master,   55
we know now to tie down what we will keep.

February 1863

We know it is our duty now to keep
white men as prisoners—rebel soldiers,
would-be masters. We're all bondsmen here, each
to the other. Freedom has gotten them   60
captivity. For us, a conscription
we have chosen—jailors to those who still
would have us slaves. They are cautious, dreading
the sight of us. Some neither read nor write,
are laid too low and have few words to send   65
but those I give them. Still, they are wary
of a negro writing, taking down letters.
X binds them to the page[3]—a mute symbol
like the cross on a grave. I suspect they fear
I'll listen, put something else down in ink.   70

March 1863

I listen, put down in ink what I know
they labor to say between silences
too big for words: worry for beloveds—
My Dearest, how are you getting along—
what has become of their small plots of land   75
did you harvest enough food to put by?
They long for the comfort of former lives—
I see you as you were, waving goodbye.
Some send photographs—a likeness in case
the body can't return. Others dictate   80
harsh facts of this war: *The hot air carries*
the stench of limbs, rotten in the bone pit.
Flies swarm—a black cloud. We hunger, grow weak.
When men die, we eat their share of hardtack.[4]

3. Illiterate prisoners would sign letters written   4. A durable cracker of flour, water, and salt.
on their behalf with an "X."

April 1863[5]

When men die, we eat their share of hardtack   85
trying not to recall their hollow sockets,
the worm-stitch of their cheeks. Today we buried
the last of our dead from Pascagoula,
and those who died retreating to our ship—
white sailors in blue firing upon us   90
as if we were the enemy. I'd thought
the fighting over, then watched a man fall
beside me, knees-first as in prayer, then
another, his arms outstretched as if borne
upon the cross. Smoke that rose from each gun   95
seemed a soul departing. The Colonel said:
an unfortunate incident; said:
their names shall deck the page of history.

June 1863[6]

Some names shall deck the page of history
as it is written on stone. Some will not.   100
Yesterday, word came of colored troops, dead
on the battlefield at Port Hudson; how
General Banks was heard to say *I have
no dead there*, and left them, unclaimed. Last night,
I dreamt their eyes still open—dim, clouded   105
as the eyes of fish washed ashore, yet fixed—
staring back at me. Still, more come today
eager to enlist. Their bodies—haggard
faces, gaunt limbs—bring news of the mainland.
Starved, they suffer like our prisoners. Dying,   110
they plead for what we do not have to give.
Death makes equals of us all: a fair master.

August 1864

Dumas was a fair master to us all.
He taught me to read and write: I was a man-
servant, if not a man. At my work,   115
I studied natural things—all manner
of plants, birds I draw now in my book: wren,

5. On April 9, 1863, 180 black men and their officers went onto the mainland to meet Confederate troops near Pascagoula, Mississippi. After the skirmish, as the black troops were retreating (having been outnumbered by the Confederates), white Union troops on board the gunboat *Jackson* fired directly at them and not at oncoming Confederates. Several black soldiers were killed or wounded. The phrases *an unfortunate incident* and *their names shall deck the page of history* are also from *Thank God My Regiment an African One: The Civil War Diary of Colonel Nathan W. Daniels.* [Trethewey's note.]

6. During the battle of Port Hudson in May 1863, General Nathaniel P. Banks requested a truce to locate the wounded Union soldiers and bury the dead. His troops, however, ignored the area where the Native Guards had fought, leaving those men unclaimed. When Colonel Shelby, a Confederate officer, asked permission to bury the putrefying bodies in front of his lines, Banks refused, saying that he had no dead in that area. (From *The Louisiana Native Guards: The Black Military Experience During the Civil War.*) [Trethewey's note.]

willet, egret, loon. Tending the gardens,
I thought only to study live things, thought
never to know so much about the dead.   120
Now I tend Ship Island graves, mounds like dunes
that shift and disappear. I record names,
send home simple notes, not much more than how
and when—an official duty. I'm told
it's best to spare most detail, but I know   125
there are things which must be accounted for.

1865[7]

These are things which must be accounted for:
slaughter under the white flag of surrender—
black massacre at Fort Pillow; our new name,
the Corps d'Afrique—words that take the *native*   130
from our claim; mossbacks[8] and freedmen—exiles
in their own homeland; the diseased, the maimed,
every lost limb, and what remains: phantom
ache, memory haunting an empty sleeve;
the hog-eaten at Gettysburg, unmarked   135
in their graves; all the dead letters, unanswered;
untold stories of those that time will render
mute. Beneath battlefields, green again,
the dead molder—a scaffolding of bone
we tread upon, forgetting. Truth be told.   140

2006

Miracle of the Black Leg

*Pictorial representations of the physician-saints Cosmas and
Damian and the myth of the miracle transplant—black donor,
white recipient—date back to the mid-fourteenth century,
appearing much later than written versions of the story.*

1.

Always, the dark body hewn asunder; always
      one man is healed, his sick limb replaced,
placed in the other man's grave: the white leg

7. In April 1864, Confederate troops attacked Fort Pillow, a Union garrison fifty miles north of Memphis. One correspondent, in a dispatch to the *Mobile Advertiser and Register*, reported that, after gaining control of the fort, the Confederates disregarded several individual attempts by the black troops to surrender, and "an indiscriminate slaughter followed" in which Colonel Nathan Bedford Forrest purportedly ordered the black troops "shot down like dogs." (From "The Fort Pillow Massacre: Assessing the Evidence," by John Cimprich, in *Black Soldiers in Blue: African-American Troops in the Civil War Era*, edited by John David Smith. Chapel Hill: University of North Carolina Press, 2002.) [Trethewey's note.]
8. Men who hid to avoid conscription into the Confederate army.

buried beside the corpse or attached as if
it were always there. If not for the dark appendage   5
    you might miss the story beneath this story—
what remains each time the myth changes: how,
    in one version, the doctors harvest the leg
from a man, four days dead, in his tomb at the church
    of a martyr, or—in another—desecrate a body   10
fresh in the graveyard at Saint Peter in Chains:[1]
    there was buried just today an Ethiopian.
Even now, it stays with us: when we mean to uncover
    the truth, we dig, say *unearth.*

2.

Emblematic in paint, a signifier of the body's lacuna,   15
    the black leg is at once a grafted narrative,
a redacted line of text, and in this scene a dark stocking
    pulled above the knee. Here the patient is sleeping,
his head at rest in his hand. Beatific, he looks as if
    he'll wake from a dream. On the floor   20
beside the bed, a dead *Moor*—hands crossed at the groin,
    the swapped limb white and rotting, fused in place.
And in the corner, a question: poised as if to speak
    the syntax of sloughing, a snake's curved form.
It emerges from the mouth of a boy like a tongue—slippery   25
    and rooted in the body as knowledge. For centuries
this is how the myth repeats: the miracle—in words
    or wood or paint—is a record of thought.

3.

See how the story changes: in one painting
    the *Ethiop* is merely a body, featureless in a coffin,   30
so black he has no face. In another, the patient—
    at the top of the frame—seems to writhe in pain,
the black leg grafted to his thigh. Below him
    a mirror of suffering: the *blackamoor*—
his body a fragment—arched across the doctor's lap   35
    as if dying from his wound. If not immanence,
the soul's bright anchor—blood passed from one
    to the other—what knowledge haunts each body,
what history, what phantom ache? One man always
    low, in a grave or on the ground, the other   40
up high, closer to heaven; one man always diseased,
    the other a body in service, plundered.

---

1. Roman Catholic church and basilica in Rome; among the relics preserved there are chains said to have bound Saint Peter when he was held captive in Jerusalem.

4.

Both men are alive in Villoldo's carving.[2]
   In twinned relief, they hold the same posture,
the same pained face, each man reaching to touch   45
   his left leg. The black man, on the floor,
holds his stump. Above him, the doctor restrains
   the patient's arm as if to prevent him touching
the dark amendment of flesh. How not to see it—
   the men bound one to the other, symbiotic—   50
one man rendered expendable, the other worthy
   of this sacrifice? In version after version, even
when the *Ethiopian* isn't there, the leg is a stand-in,
   a black modifier against the white body,
a piece cut off—as in the origin of the word *comma*:   55
   caesura in a story that's still being written.

2012

2. "Miracle of the Black Leg" (1547), by Spanish sculptor Isidro de Villoldo (1500–1556).

JHUMPA LAHIRI
b. 1967

When Jhumpa Lahiri writes, her setting is quite literally the world—focused sometimes here and sometimes there, but always with global implications. This orientation is a factor of her times. Unlike children of earlier immigrant generations, Lahiri did not face the pressures of assimilating into an American society apart from and in some cases above other cultures. Instead, international trade, travel, and communications have made global culture a practical reality. In "Sexy," one of Lahiri's most wide-ranging yet intimate stories, her protagonist listens to a sad tale about a friend's "cousin's husband." The bad news, "a wife's worst nightmare," is being conveyed in Boston, where the friends live, but it involves a flight from Delhi to Montreal stopping at Heathrow Airport outside London. Four locations in two hemispheres an ocean and a continent apart indicate the world that people with family backgrounds in India share when they become Americans. Geographical barriers become much more easily manageable thanks to cell phones and e-mail. Education, employment, friendships, and romantic relationships span the world. Films from India are viewed with American pop songs in mind and Chinese cuisine in the stomach, all, flavorful as they are, seeming as natural as the lives being lived among such givens.

The flavor of Lahiri's fiction defies categorization, other than being dependent on no single national ingredient. A visit to Boston's Mapparium (a giant globe viewed from inside) or Museum of Fine Arts is less a field trip through region and history than a comfortable part of her characters' way of living, a reminder of the larger culture they share.

The author's Bengali parents parted from their large extended family when they moved from Kolkata to London, where Lahiri was born. Following a normal progression in the former British Commonwealth, Lahiri's parents then relocated to the United States, where they worked as educators in Rhode Island while she studied at Barnard College and Boston University, concentrating on literature and creative writing and ending with a Ph.D. Her first stories reflect how much of her family's past had to be conveyed to her via storytelling, such as in "When Mr. Pirzada Came to Dine," where a ten-year-old in America learns about political troubles in India from a visiting family friend. To the youngster, it sounds exotic, but no more so than the situation experienced by a pair of Indian newlyweds, in "This Blessed House," who are alternately intrigued and mystified by fundamentalist Christian curios left behind by the previous tenants of their new home. Much of Lahiri's short fiction, first collected in *Interpreter of Maladies* (1999) and extended in *Unaccustomed Earth* (2008), involves discoveries of this nature, in which she is particularly adept at portraying the learning process of someone acting without monocultural constraint. The curiosity of children or young adults is a hallmark of her style.

In 2003, having married, become a mother, and settled in the Park Slope area of Brooklyn, New York, a neighborhood popular with writers, Lahiri published her novel *The Namesake*. Like her earlier work, it contrasts cultural assimilation with curiosity about the values, beliefs, and practices of a preceding generation. But here a certain amount of anger and confusion come into play, as the protagonist, Gogol Ganguli, is uncomfortable with how the private first name his parents have used for him at home has become his public name as well, all without his understanding its personal (much less literary) significance. Lahiri had been saddled with "Jhumpa" as a first name by her teachers, who found it easier to pronounce than her other two given names, either of which would have been more appropriate for formal use. But while Lahiri's enforced assimilation didn't bother her, Ganguli's does, although much of his discomfort is comic, such as when he assumes that a sociologist's anagrammatical reference to "ABCDs" means not "multiculturals" but "American-born confused deshi" (India countrymen). In fact, Ganguli doesn't even know what "deshi" properly means, just that his parents customarily refer to India as "desh." He "never thinks of India as desh. He thinks of it as Americans do, as India." Other contrasts, such as arranged marriages versus modern ones, are handled with more gravity in this novel, and two fraught marriages structure Lahiri's ambitious 2013 novel, *The Lowland*.

The following text is from *Interpreter of Maladies* (1999).

Sexy

It was a wife's worst nightmare. After nine years of marriage, Laxmi told Miranda, her cousin's husband had fallen in love with another woman. He sat next to her on a plane, on a flight from Delhi to Montreal, and instead of flying home to his wife and son, he got off with the woman at Heathrow.[1] He called his wife, and told her he'd had a conversation that had changed his life, and that he needed time to figure things out. Laxmi's cousin had taken to her bed.

"Not that I blame her," Laxmi said. She reached for the Hot Mix she munched throughout the day, which looked to Miranda like dusty orange cereal. "Imagine. An English girl, half his age." Laxmi was only a few years older than Miranda, but she was already married, and kept a photo of herself and her husband, seated on a white stone bench in front of the Taj Mahal,[2] tacked to the inside of her cubicle, which was next to Miranda's.

---

1. International airport near London.
2. Muslim mausoleum near Agra, India, built on a monumental scale in the mid-17th century by Emperor Shah Jahan for his favorite wife, Mumtaz Mahal.

Laxmi had been on the phone for at least an hour, trying to calm her cousin down. No one noticed; they worked for a public radio station,[3] in the fundraising department, and were surrounded by people who spent all day on the phone, soliciting pledges.

"I feel worst for the boy," Laxmi added. "He's been at home for days. My cousin said she can't even take him to school."

"It sounds awful," Miranda said. Normally Laxmi's phone conversations— mainly to her husband, about what to cook for dinner—distracted Miranda as she typed letters, asking members of the radio station to increase their annual pledge in exchange for a tote bag or an umbrella. She could hear Laxmi clearly, her sentences peppered every now and then with an Indian word, through the laminated wall between their desks. But that afternoon Miranda hadn't been listening. She'd been on the phone herself, with Dev, deciding where to meet later that evening.

"Then again, a few days at home won't hurt him." Laxmi ate some more Hot Mix, then put it away in a drawer. "He's something of a genius. He has a Punjabi mother and a Bengali[4] father, and because he learns French and English at school he already speaks four languages. I think he skipped two grades."

Dev was Bengali, too. At first Miranda thought it was a religion. But then he pointed it out to her, a place in India called Bengal, in a map printed in an issue of *The Economist*.[5] He had brought the magazine specially to her apartment, for she did not own an atlas, or any other books with maps in them. He'd pointed to the city where he'd been born, and another city where his father had been born. One of the cities had a box around it, intended to attract the reader's eye. When Miranda asked what the box indicated, Dev rolled up the magazine, and said, "Nothing you'll ever need to worry about," and he tapped her playfully on the head.

Before leaving her apartment he'd tossed the magazine in the garbage, along with the ends of the three cigarettes he always smoked in the course of his visits. But after she watched his car disappear down Commonwealth Avenue,[6] back to his house in the suburbs, where he lived with his wife, Miranda retrieved it, and brushed the ashes off the cover, and rolled it in the opposite direction to get it to lie flat. She got into bed, still rumpled from their lovemaking, and studied the borders of Bengal. There was a bay below and mountains above. The map was connected to an article about something called the Gramin Bank.[7] She turned the page, hoping for a photograph of the city where Dev was born, but all she found were graphs and grids. Still, she stared at them, thinking the whole while about Dev, about how only fifteen minutes ago he'd propped her feet on top of his shoulders, and pressed her knees to her chest, and told her that he couldn't get enough of her.

She'd met him a week ago, at Filene's.[8] She was there on her lunch break, buying discounted pantyhose in the Basement. Afterward she took the escalator to the main part of the store, to the cosmetics department, where soaps and creams were displayed like jewels, and eye shadows and powders

3. Noncommercial, listener-supported, often oriented toward arts and culture in its broadcasting.
4. Punjab, state in northern India; Bengal, former province of India, now a region that includes Bengal State and East Bengal, the latter part of Bangladesh.
5. Weekly British magazine of news and commentary.

6. Major thoroughfare in Boston.
7. Properly the Grameen Bank, which provides credit to the poorest classes in rural Bangladesh as a means of fighting poverty and promoting social economic development.
8. A department store. Filene's Basement, downstairs, was a renowned discount store.

shimmered like butterflies pinned behind protective glass. Though Miranda had never bought anything other than a lipstick, she liked walking through the cramped, confined maze, which was familiar to her in a way the rest of Boston still was not. She liked negotiating her way past the women planted at every turn, who sprayed cards with perfume and waved them in the air; sometimes she would find a card days afterward, folded in her coat pocket, and the rich aroma, still faintly preserved, would warm her as she waited on cold mornings for the T.[9]

That day, stopping to smell one of the more pleasing cards, Miranda noticed a man standing at one of the counters. He held a slip of paper covered in a precise, feminine hand. A saleswoman took one look at the paper and began to open drawers. She produced an oblong cake of soap in a black case, a hydrating mask, a vial of cell renewal drops, and two tubes of face cream. The man was tanned, with black hair that was visible on his knuckles. He wore a flamingo pink shirt, a navy blue suit, a camel overcoat with gleaming leather buttons. In order to pay he had taken off pigskin gloves. Crisp bills emerged from a burgundy wallet. He didn't wear a wedding ring.

"What can I get you, honey?" the saleswoman asked Miranda. She looked over the tops of her tortoiseshell glasses, assessing Miranda's complexion.

Miranda didn't know what she wanted. All she knew was that she didn't want the man to walk away. He seemed to be lingering, waiting, along with the saleswoman, for her to say something. She stared at some bottles, some short, others tall, arranged on an oval tray, like a family posing for a photograph.

"A cream," Miranda said eventually.

"How old are you?"

"Twenty-two."

The saleswoman nodded, opening a frosted bottle. "This may seem a bit heavier than what you're used to, but I'd start now. All your wrinkles are going to form by twenty-five. After that they just start showing."

While the saleswoman dabbed the cream on Miranda's face, the man stood and watched. While Miranda was told the proper way to apply it, in swift upward strokes beginning at the base of her throat, he spun the lipstick carousel. He pressed a pump that dispensed cellulite gel and massaged it into the back of his ungloved hand. He opened a jar, leaned over, and drew so close that a drop of cream flecked his nose.

Miranda smiled, but her mouth was obscured by a large brush that the saleswoman was sweeping over her face. "This is blusher Number Two," the woman said. "Gives you some color."

Miranda nodded, glancing at her reflection in one of the angled mirrors that lined the counter. She had silver eyes and skin as pale as paper, and the contrast with her hair, as dark and glossy as an espresso bean, caused people to describe her as striking, if not pretty. She had a narrow, egg-shaped head that rose to a prominent point. Her features, too, were narrow, with nostrils so slim that they appeared to have been pinched with a clothespin. Now her face glowed, rosy at the cheeks, smoky below the brow bone. Her lips glistened.

---

9. Metropolitan Transit Authority (MTA), Boston's subway system.

The man was glancing in a mirror, too, quickly wiping the cream from his nose. Miranda wondered where he was from. She thought he might be Spanish, or Lebanese. When he opened another jar, and said, to no one in particular, "This one smells like pineapple," she detected only the hint of an accent.

"Anything else for you today?" the saleswoman asked, accepting Miranda's credit card.

"No thanks."

The woman wrapped the cream in several layers of red tissue. "You'll be very happy with this product." Miranda's hand was unsteady as she signed the receipt. The man hadn't budged.

"I threw in a sample of our new eye gel," the saleswoman added, handing Miranda a small shopping bag. She looked at Miranda's credit card before sliding it across the counter. "Bye-bye, Miranda."

Miranda began walking. At first she sped up. Then, noticing the doors that led to Downtown Crossing,[1] she slowed down.

"Part of your name is Indian," the man said, pacing his steps with hers.

She stopped, as did he, at a circular table piled with sweaters, flanked with pinecones and velvet bows. "Miranda?"

"Mira. I have an aunt named Mira."

His name was Dev. He worked in an investment bank back that way he said, tilting his head in the direction of South Station.[2] He was the first man with a mustache, Miranda decided, she found handsome.

They walked together toward Park Street station,[3] past the kiosks that sold cheap belts and handbags. A fierce January wind spoiled the part in her hair. As she fished for a token in her coat pocket, her eyes fell to his shopping bag. "And those are for her?"

"Who?"

"Your Aunt Mira."

"They're for my wife." He uttered the words slowly, holding Miranda's gaze. "She's going to India for a few weeks." He rolled his eyes. "She's addicted to this stuff."

Somehow, without the wife there, it didn't seem so wrong. At first Miranda and Dev spent every night together, almost. He explained that he couldn't spend the whole night at her place, because his wife called every day at six in the morning, from India, where it was four in the afternoon. And so he left her apartment at two, three, often as late as four in the morning, driving back to his house in the suburbs. During the day he called her every hour, it seemed, from work, or from his cell phone. Once he learned Miranda's schedule he left her a message each evening at five-thirty, when she was on the T coming back to her apartment, just so, he said, she could hear his voice as soon as she walked through the door. "I'm thinking about you," he'd say on the tape. "I can't wait to see you." He told her he liked spending time in her apartment, with its kitchen counter no wider than a breadbox, and scratchy floors that sloped, and a buzzer in the lobby that always made a slightly embarrassing sound when he pressed it. He said he admired her for moving to Boston, where she knew no one, instead of remaining in Michigan, where

---

1. Major interchange of MTA subway lines.
2. MTA commuter hub for lines from the south

suburbs.
3. MTA stop in the business district.

she'd grown up and gone to college. When Miranda told him it was nothing to admire, that she'd moved to Boston precisely for that reason, he shook his head. "I know what it's like to be lonely," he said, suddenly serious, and at that moment Miranda felt that he understood her—understood how she felt some nights on the T, after seeing a movie on her own, or going to a bookstore to read magazines, or having drinks with Laxmi, who always had to meet her husband at Alewife station[4] in an hour or two. In less serious moments Dev said he liked that her legs were longer than her torso, something he'd observed the first time she walked across a room naked. "You're the first," he told her, admiring her from the bed. "The first woman I've known with legs this long."

Dev was the first to tell her that. Unlike the boys she dated in college, who were simply taller, heavier versions of the ones she dated in high school, Dev was the first always to pay for things, and hold doors open, and reach across a table in a restaurant to kiss her hand. He was the first to bring her a bouquet of flowers so immense she'd had to split it up into all six of her drinking glasses, and the first to whisper her name again and again when they made love. Within days of meeting him, when she was at work, Miranda began to wish that there were a picture of her and Dev tacked to the inside of her cubicle, like the one of Laxmi and her husband in front of the Taj Mahal. She didn't tell Laxmi about Dev. She didn't tell anyone. Part of her wanted to tell Laxmi, if only because Laxmi was Indian, too. But Laxmi was always on the phone with her cousin these days, who was still in bed, whose husband was still in London, and whose son still wasn't going to school. "You must eat something," Laxmi would urge. "You mustn't lose your health." When she wasn't speaking to her cousin, she spoke to her husband, shorter conversations, in which she ended up arguing about whether to have chicken or lamb for dinner. "I'm sorry," Miranda heard her apologize at one point. "This whole thing just makes me a little paranoid."

Miranda and Dev didn't argue. They went to movies at the Nickelodeon and kissed the whole time. They ate pulled pork and cornbread in Davis Square,[5] a paper napkin tucked like a cravat into the collar of Dev's shirt. They sipped sangria at the bar of a Spanish restaurant, a grinning pig's head presiding over their conversation. They went to the MFA[6] and picked out a poster of water lilies for her bedroom. One Saturday, following an afternoon concert at Symphony Hall, he showed her his favorite place in the city, the Mapparium[7] at the Christian Science center, where they stood inside a room made of glowing stained-glass panels, which was shaped like the inside of a globe, but looked like the outside of one. In the middle of the room was a transparent bridge, so that they felt as if they were standing in the center of the world. Dev pointed to India, which was red, and far more detailed than the map in *The Economist*. He explained that many of the countries, like Siam and Italian Somaliland,[8] no longer existed in the same way; the names had changed by now. The ocean, as blue as a peacock's breast, appeared in two shades, depending on the depth of the water. He showed her the deepest spot on earth, seven miles deep, above the Mariana Islands.[9] They peered

4. MTA stop in Cambridge, Massachusetts, across the Charles River from Boston.
5. MTA stop near Tufts University in a formerly working-class, now upscale neighborhood.
6. Museum of Fine Arts (Boston).

7. Large walk-through globe that maps the earth as stars and planets would be seen in a planetarium.
8. Presently Thailand and Somalia.
9. Island chain in the western Pacific Ocean.

over the bridge and saw the Antarctic archipelago[1] at their feet, craned their necks and saw a giant metal star overhead. As Dev spoke, his voice bounced wildly off the glass, sometimes loud, sometimes soft, sometimes seeming to land in Miranda's chest, sometimes eluding her ear altogether. When a group of tourists walked onto the bridge, she could hear them clearing their throats, as if through microphones. Dev explained that it was because of the acoustics.

Miranda found London, where Laxmi's cousin's husband was, with the woman he'd met on the plane. She wondered which of the cities in India Dev's wife was in. The farthest Miranda had ever been was to the Bahamas once when she was a child. She searched but couldn't find it on the glass panels. When the tourists left and she and Dev were alone again, he told her to stand at one end of the bridge. Even though they were thirty feet apart, Dev said, they'd be able to hear each other whisper.

"I don't believe you," Miranda said. It was the first time she'd spoken since they'd entered. She felt as if speakers were embedded in her ears.

"Go ahead," he urged, walking backward to his end of the bridge. His voice dropped to a whisper. "Say something." She watched his lips forming the words; at the same time she heard them so clearly that she felt them under her skin, under her winter coat, so near and full of warmth that she felt herself go hot.

"Hi," she whispered, unsure of what else to say.

"You're sexy," he whispered back.

At work the following week, Laxmi told Miranda that it wasn't the first time her cousin's husband had had an affair. "She's decided to let him come to his senses," Laxmi said one evening as they were getting ready to leave the office. "She says it's for the boy. She's willing to forgive him for the boy." Miranda waited as Laxmi shut off her computer. "He'll come crawling back, and she'll let him," Laxmi said, shaking her head. "Not me. If my husband so much as looked at another woman I'd change the locks." She studied the picture tacked to her cubicle. Laxmi's husband had his arm draped over her shoulder, his knees leaning in toward her on the bench. She turned to Miranda. "Wouldn't you?"

She nodded. Dev's wife was coming back from India the next day. That afternoon he'd called Miranda at work, to say he had to go to the airport to pick her up. He promised he'd call as soon as he could.

"What's the Taj Mahal like?" she asked Laxmi.

"The most romantic spot on earth." Laxmi's face brightened at the memory. "An everlasting monument to love."

While Dev was at the airport, Miranda went to Filene's Basement to buy herself things she thought a mistress should have. She found a pair of black high heels with buckles smaller than a baby's teeth. She found a satin slip with scalloped edges and a knee-length silk robe. Instead of the pantyhose she normally wore to work, she found sheer stockings with a seam. She searched through piles and wandered through racks, pressing back hanger after hanger, until she found a cocktail dress made of a slinky silvery material that

---

1. Group of islands northwest of the Antarctic Peninsula.

matched her eyes, with little chains for straps. As she shopped she thought about Dev, and about what he'd told her in the Mapparium. It was the first time a man had called her sexy, and when she closed her eyes she could still feel his whisper drifting through her body, under her skin. In the fitting room, which was just one big room with mirrors on the walls, she found a spot next to an older woman with a shiny face and coarse frosted hair. The woman stood barefoot in her underwear, pulling the black net of a body stocking taut between her fingers.

"Always check for snags," the woman advised.

Miranda pulled out the satin slip with scalloped edges. She held it to her chest.

The woman nodded with approval. "Oh yes."

"And this?" She held up the silver cocktail dress.

"Absolutely," the woman said. "He'll want to rip it right off you."

Miranda pictured the two of them at a restaurant in the South End[2] they'd been to, where Dev had ordered foie gras and a soup made with champagne and raspberries. She pictured herself in the cocktail dress, and Dev in one of his suits, kissing her hand across the table. Only the next time Dev came to visit her, on a Sunday afternoon several days since the last time they'd seen each other, he was in gym clothes. After his wife came back, that was his excuse: on Sundays he drove into Boston and went running along the Charles. The first Sunday she opened the door in the knee-length robe, but Dev didn't even notice it; he carried her over to the bed, wearing sweatpants and sneakers, and entered her without a word. Later, she slipped on the robe when she walked across the room to get him a saucer for his cigarette ashes, but he complained that she was depriving him of the sight of her long legs, and demanded that she remove it. So the next Sunday she didn't bother. She wore jeans. She kept the lingerie at the back of a drawer, behind her socks and everyday underwear. The silver cocktail dress hung in her closet, the tag dangling from the seam. Often, in the morning, the dress would be in a heap on the floor; the chain straps always slipped off the metal hanger.

Still, Miranda looked forward to Sundays. In the mornings she went to a deli and bought a baguette and little containers of things Dev liked to eat, like pickled herring, and potato salad, and tortes of pesto and mascarpone cheese. They ate in bed, picking up the herring with their fingers and ripping the baguette with their hands. Dev told her stories about his childhood, when he would come home from school and drink mango juice served to him on a tray, and then play cricket by a lake, dressed all in white. He told her about how, at eighteen, he'd been sent to a college in upstate New York during something called the Emergency,[3] and about how it took him years to be able to follow American accents in movies, in spite of the fact that he'd had an English-medium education. As he talked he smoked three cigarettes, crushing them in a saucer by the side of her bed. Sometimes he asked her questions, like how many lovers she'd had (three) and how old she'd been the first time (nineteen). After lunch they made love, on sheets covered with

2. Trendy Boston neighborhood.
3. State of internal emergency declared in 1975 by Indira Gandhi (1917–1984), prime minister of India, that allowed her to rule by decree until 1977, when she was defeated in an election.

crumbs, and then Dev took a nap for twelve minutes. Miranda had never known an adult who took naps, but Dev said it was something he'd grown up doing in India, where it was so hot that people didn't leave their homes until the sun went down. "Plus it allows us to sleep together," he murmured mischievously, curving his arm like a big bracelet around her body.

Only Miranda never slept. She watched the clock on her bedside table, or pressed her face against Dev's fingers, intertwined with hers, each with its half-dozen hairs at the knuckle. After six minutes she turned to face him, sighing and stretching, to test if he was really sleeping. He always was. His ribs were visible through his skin as he breathed, and yet he was beginning to develop a paunch. He complained about the hair on his shoulders, but Miranda thought him perfect, and refused to imagine him any other way.

At the end of twelve minutes Dev would open his eyes as if he'd been awake all along, smiling at her, full of a contentment she wished she felt herself. "The best twelve minutes of the week." He'd sigh, running a hand along the backs of her calves. Then he'd spring out of bed, pulling on his sweatpants and lacing up his sneakers. He would go to the bathroom and brush his teeth with his index finger, something he told her all Indians knew how to do, to get rid of the smoke in his mouth. When she kissed him good-bye she smelled herself sometimes in his hair. But she knew that his excuse, that he'd spent the afternoon jogging, allowed him to take a shower when he got home, first thing.

Apart from Laxmi and Dev, the only Indians whom Miranda had known were a family in the neighborhood where she'd grown up, named the Dixits. Much to the amusement of the neighborhood children, including Miranda, but not including the Dixit children, Mr. Dixit would jog each evening along the flat winding streets of their development in his everyday shirt and trousers, his only concession to athletic apparel a pair of cheap Keds. Every weekend, the family—mother, father, two boys, and a girl—piled into their car and went away, to where nobody knew. The fathers complained that Mr. Dixit did not fertilize his lawn properly, did not rake his leaves on time, and agreed that the Dixits' house, the only one with vinyl siding, detracted from the neighborhood's charm. The mothers never invited Mrs. Dixit to join them around the Armstrongs' swimming pool. Waiting for the school bus with the Dixit children standing to one side, the other children would say "The Dixits dig shit," under their breath, and then burst into laughter.

One year, all the neighborhood children were invited to the birthday party of the Dixit girl. Miranda remembered a heavy aroma of incense and onions in the house, and a pile of shoes heaped by the front door. But most of all she remembered a piece of fabric, about the size of a pillowcase, which hung from a wooden dowel at the bottom of the stairs. It was a painting of a naked woman with a red face shaped like a knight's shield. She had enormous white eyes that tilted toward her temples, and mere dots for pupils. Two circles, with the same dots at their centers, indicated her breasts. In one hand she brandished a dagger. With one foot she crushed a struggling man on the ground. Around her body was a necklace composed of bleeding heads, strung together like a popcorn chain. She stuck her tongue out at Miranda.

"It is the goddess Kali,"[4] Mrs. Dixit explained brightly, shifting the dowel slightly in order to straighten the image. Mrs. Dixit's hands were painted with henna, an intricate pattern of zigzags and stars. "Come please, time for cake."

Miranda, then nine years old, had been too frightened to eat the cake. For months afterward she'd been too frightened even to walk on the same side of the street as the Dixits' house, which she had to pass twice daily, once to get to the bus stop, and once again to come home. For a while she even held her breath until she reached the next lawn, just as she did when the school bus passed a cemetery.

It shamed her now. Now, when she and Dev made love, Miranda closed her eyes and saw deserts and elephants, and marble pavilions floating on lakes beneath a full moon. One Saturday, having nothing else to do, she walked all the way to Central Square,[5] to an Indian restaurant, and ordered a plate of tandoori chicken. As she ate she tried to memorize phrases printed at the bottom of the menu, for things like "delicious" and "water" and "check, please." The phrases didn't stick in her mind, and so she began to stop from time to time in the foreign-language section of a bookstore in Kenmore Square,[6] where she studied the Bengali alphabet in the Teach Yourself series. Once she went so far as to try to transcribe the Indian part of her name, "Mira," into her Filofax,[7] her hand moving in unfamiliar directions, stopping and turning and picking up her pen when she least expected to. Following the arrows in the book, she drew a bar from left to right from which the letters hung; one looked more like a number than a letter, another looked like a triangle on its side. It had taken her several tries to get the letters of her name to resemble the sample letters in the book, and even then she wasn't sure if she'd written Mira or Mara. It was a scribble to her, but somewhere in the world, she realized with a shock, it meant something.

During the week it wasn't so bad. Work kept her busy, and she and Laxmi had begun having lunch together at a new Indian restaurant around the corner, during which Laxmi reported the latest status of her cousin's marriage. Sometimes Miranda tried to change the topic; it made her feel the way she once felt in college, when she and her boyfriend at the time had walked away from a crowded house of pancakes without paying for their food, just to see if they could get away with it. But Laxmi spoke of nothing else. "If I were her I'd fly straight to London and shoot them both," she announced one day. She snapped a papadum in half and dipped it into chutney.[8] "I don't know how she can just wait this way."

Miranda knew how to wait. In the evenings she sat at her dining table and coated her nails with clear nail polish, and ate salad straight from the salad bowl, and watched television, and waited for Sunday. Saturdays were the worst because by Saturday it seemed that Sunday would never come. One Saturday when Dev called, late at night, she heard people laughing and talking in the background, so many that she asked him if he was at a concert hall. But he was only calling from his house in the suburbs. "I can't hear you that well," he said. "We have guests. Miss me?" She looked at the

---

4. Hindu goddess of destruction.
5. In Cambridge.
6. In Boston.
7. Loose-leaf personal organizer, manufactured

by the Filofax Company in England.
8. Thick, sweet, spicy sauce used as a condiment. "Papadum": crisp lentil wafer.

television screen, a sitcom that she'd muted with the remote control when the phone rang. She pictured him whispering into his cell phone, in a room upstairs, a hand on the doorknob, the hallway filled with guests. "Miranda, do you miss me?" he asked again. She told him that she did.

The next day, when Dev came to visit, Miranda asked him what his wife looked like. She was nervous to ask, waiting until he'd smoked the last of his cigarettes, crushing it with a firm twist into the saucer. She wondered if they'd quarrel. But Dev wasn't surprised by the question. He told her, spreading some smoked whitefish on a cracker, that his wife resembled an actress in Bombay named Madhuri Dixit.[9]

For an instant Miranda's heart stopped. But no, the Dixit girl had been named something else, something that began with P. Still, she wondered if the actress and the Dixit girl were related. She'd been plain, wearing her hair in two braids all through high school.

A few days later Miranda went to an Indian grocery in Central Square which also rented videos. The door opened to a complicated tinkling of bells. It was dinnertime, and she was the only customer. A video was playing on a television hooked up in a corner of the store: a row of young women in harem pants were thrusting their hips in synchrony on a beach.

"Can I help you?" the man standing at the cash register asked. He was eating a samosa,[1] dipping it into some dark brown sauce on a paper plate. Below the glass counter at his waist were trays of more plump samosas, and what looked like pale, diamond-shaped pieces of fudge covered with foil, and some bright orange pastries floating in syrup. "You like some video?"

Miranda opened up her Filofax, where she had written "Mottery Dixit." She looked up at the videos on the shelves behind the counter. She saw women wearing skirts that sat low on the hips and tops that tied like bandannas between their breasts. Some leaned back against a stone wall, or a tree. They were beautiful, the way the women dancing on the beach were beautiful, with kohl-rimmed eyes and long black hair. She knew then that Madhuri Dixit was beautiful, too.

"We have subtitled versions, miss," the man continued. He wiped his fingertips quickly on his shirt and pulled out three titles.

"No," Miranda said. "Thank you, no." She wandered through the store, studying shelves lined with unlabeled packets and tins. The freezer case was stuffed with bags of pita bread and vegetables she didn't recognize. The only thing she recognized was a rack lined with bags and bags of the Hot Mix that Laxmi was always eating. She thought about buying some for Laxmi, then hesitated, wondering how to explain what she'd been doing in an Indian grocery.

"Very spicy," the man said, shaking his head, his eyes traveling across Miranda's body. "Too spicy for you."

By February, Laxmi's cousin's husband still hadn't come to his senses. He had returned to Montreal, argued bitterly with his wife for two weeks, packed two suitcases, and flown back to London. He wanted a divorce.

---

9. Indian film actress (b. 1967) renowned for her beauty.
1. Deep-fried turnover filled with vegetables or ground meat.

Miranda sat in her cubicle and listened as Laxmi kept telling her cousin that there were better men in the world, just waiting to come out of the woodwork. The next day the cousin said she and her son were going to her parents' house in California, to try to recuperate. Laxmi convinced her to arrange a weekend layover in Boston. "A quick change of place will do you good," Laxmi insisted gently, "besides which, I haven't seen you in years."

Miranda stared at her own phone, wishing Dev would call. It had been four days since their last conversation. She heard Laxmi dialing directory assistance, asking for the number of a beauty salon. "Something soothing," Laxmi requested. She scheduled massages, facials, manicures, and pedicures. Then she reserved a table for lunch at the Four Seasons. In her determination to cheer up her cousin, Laxmi had forgotten about the boy. She rapped her knuckles on the laminated wall.

"Are you busy Saturday?"

The boy was thin. He wore a yellow knapsack strapped across his back, gray herringbone trousers, a red V-necked sweater, and black leather shoes. His hair was cut in a thick fringe over his eyes, which had dark circles under them. They were the first thing Miranda noticed. They made him look haggard, as if he smoked a great deal and slept very little, in spite of the fact that he was only seven years old. He clasped a large sketch pad with a spiral binding. His name was Rohin.

"Ask me a capital," he said, staring up at Miranda.

She stared back at him. It was eight-thirty on a Saturday morning. She took a sip of coffee. "A what?"

"It's a game he's been playing," Laxmi's cousin explained. She was thin like her son, with a long face and the same dark circles under her eyes. A rust-colored coat hung heavy on her shoulders. Her black hair, with a few strands of gray at the temples, was pulled back like a ballerina's. "You ask him a country and he tells you the capital."

"You should have heard him in the car," Laxmi said. "He's already memorized all of Europe."

"It's not a game," Rohin said. "I'm having a competition with a boy at school. We're competing to memorize all the capitals. I'm going to beat him."

Miranda nodded. "Okay. What's the capital of India?"

"That's no good." He marched away, his arms swinging like a toy soldier. Then he marched back to Laxmi's cousin and tugged at a pocket of her overcoat. "Ask me a hard one."

"Senegal," she said.

"Dakar!" Rohin exclaimed triumphantly, and began running in larger and larger circles. Eventually he ran into the kitchen. Miranda could hear him opening and closing the fridge.

"Rohin, don't touch without asking," Laxmi's cousin called out wearily. She managed a smile for Miranda. "Don't worry, he'll fall asleep in a few hours. And thanks for watching him."

"Back at three," Laxmi said, disappearing with her cousin down the hallway. "We're double-parked."

Miranda fastened the chain on the door. She went to the kitchen to find Rohin, but he was now in the living room, at the dining table, kneeling on one of the director's chairs. He unzipped his knapsack, pushed Miranda's basket of manicure supplies to one side of the table, and spread his crayons over the surface. Miranda stood over his shoulder. She watched as he gripped a blue crayon and drew the outline of an airplane.

"It's lovely," she said. When he didn't reply, she went to the kitchen to pour herself more coffee.

"Some for me, please," Rohin called out.

She returned to the living room. "Some what?"

"Some coffee. There's enough in the pot. I saw."

She walked over to the table and sat opposite him. At times he nearly stood up to reach for a new crayon. He barely made a dent in the director's chair.

"You're too young for coffee."

Rohin leaned over the sketch pad, so that his tiny chest and shoulders almost touched it, his head tilted to one side. "The stewardess let me have coffee," he said. "She made it with milk and lots of sugar." He straightened, revealing a woman's face beside the plane, with long wavy hair and eyes like asterisks. "Her hair was more shiny," he decided, adding, "My father met a pretty woman on a plane, too." He looked at Miranda. His face darkened as he watched her sip. "Can't I have just a little coffee? Please?"

She wondered, in spite of his composed, brooding expression, if he were the type to throw a tantrum. She imagined his kicking her with his leather shoes, screaming for coffee, screaming and crying until his mother and Laxmi came back to fetch him. She went to the kitchen and prepared a cup for him as he'd requested. She selected a mug she didn't care for, in case he dropped it.

"Thank you," he said when she put it on the table. He took short sips, holding the mug securely with both hands.

Miranda sat with him while he drew, but when she attempted to put a coat of clear polish on her nails he protested. Instead he pulled out a paperback world almanac from his knapsack and asked her to quiz him. The countries were arranged by continent, six to a page, with the capitals in boldface, followed by a short entry on the population, government, and other statistics. Miranda turned to a page in the Africa section and went down the list.

"Mali," she asked him.

"Bamako," he replied instantly.

"Malawi."

"Lilongwe."

She remembered looking at Africa in the Mapparium. She remembered the fat part of it was green.

"Go on," Rohin said.

"Mauritania."

"Nouakchott."

"Mauritius."

He paused, squeezed his eyes shut, then opened them, defeated. "I can't remember."

"Port Louis," she told him.

"Port Louis." He began to say it again and again, like a chant under his breath.

When they reached the last of the countries in Africa, Rohin said he wanted to watch cartoons, telling Miranda to watch them with him. When the cartoons ended, he followed her to the kitchen, and stood by her side as she made more coffee. He didn't follow her when she went to the bathroom a few minutes later, but when she opened the door she was startled to find him standing outside.

"Do you need to go?"

He shook his head but walked into the bathroom anyway. He put the cover of the toilet down, climbed on top of it, and surveyed the narrow glass shelf over the sink which held Miranda's toothbrush and makeup.

"What's this for?" he asked, picking up the sample of eye gel she'd gotten the day she met Dev.

"Puffiness."

"What's puffiness?"

"Here," she explained, pointing.

"After you've been crying?"

"I guess so."

Rohin opened the tube and smelled it. He squeezed a drop of it onto a finger, then rubbed it on his hand. "It stings." He inspected the back of his hand closely, as if expecting it to change color. "My mother has puffiness. She says it's a cold, but really she cries, sometimes for hours. Sometimes straight through dinner. Sometimes she cries so hard her eyes puff up like bullfrogs."

Miranda wondered if she ought to feed him. In the kitchen she discovered a bag of rice cakes and some lettuce. She offered to go out, to buy something from the deli, but Rohin said he wasn't very hungry, and accepted one of the rice cakes. "You eat one too," he said. They sat at the table, the rice cakes between them. He turned to a fresh page in his sketch pad. "You draw."

She selected a blue crayon. "What should I draw?"

He thought for a moment. "I know," he said. He asked her to draw things in the living room: the sofa, the director's chairs, the television, the telephone. "This way I can memorize it."

"Memorize what?"

"Our day together." He reached for another rice cake.

"Why do you want to memorize it?"

"Because we're never going to see each other, ever again."

The precision of the phrase startled her. She looked at him, feeling slightly depressed. Rohin didn't look depressed. He tapped the page. "Go on."

And so she drew the items as best as she could—the sofa, the director's chairs, the television, the telephone. He sidled up to her, so close that it was sometimes difficult to see what she was doing. He put his small brown hand over hers. "Now me."

She handed him the crayon.

He shook his head. "No, now draw me."

"I can't," she said. "It won't look like you."

The brooding look began to spread across Rohin's face again, just as it had when she'd refused him coffee. "Please?"

She drew his face, outlining his head and the thick fringe of hair. He sat perfectly still, with a formal, melancholy expression, his gaze fixed to one side. Miranda wished she could draw a good likeness. Her hand moved in conjunction with her eyes, in unknown ways, just as it had that day in the bookstore when she'd transcribed her name in Bengali letters. It looked nothing like him. She was in the middle of drawing his nose when he wriggled away from the table.

"I'm bored," he announced, heading toward her bedroom. She heard him opening the door, opening the drawers of her bureau and closing them.

When she joined him he was inside the closet. After a moment he emerged, his hair disheveled, holding the silver cocktail dress. "This was on the floor."

"It falls off the hanger."

Rohin looked at the dress and then at Miranda's body. "Put it on."

"Excuse me?"

"Put it on."

There was no reason to put it on. Apart from in the fitting room at Filene's she had never worn it, and as long as she was with Dev she knew she never would. She knew they would never go to restaurants, where he would reach across a table and kiss her hand. They would meet in her apartment, on Sundays, he in his sweatpants, she in her jeans. She took the dress from Rohin and shook it out, even though the slinky fabric never wrinkled. She reached into the closet for a free hanger.

"Please put it on," Rohin asked, suddenly standing behind her. He pressed his face against her, clasping her waist with both his thin arms. "Please?"

"All right," she said, surprised by the strength of his grip.

He smiled, satisfied, and sat on the edge of her bed.

"You have to wait out there," she said, pointing to the door. "I'll come out when I'm ready."

"But my mother always takes her clothes off in front of me."

"She does?"

Rohin nodded. "She doesn't even pick them up afterward. She leaves them all on the floor by the bed, all tangled.

"One day she slept in my room," he continued. "She said it felt better than her bed, now that my father's gone."

"I'm not your mother," Miranda said, lifting him by the armpits off her bed. When he refused to stand, she picked him up. He was heavier than she expected, and he clung to her, his legs wrapped firmly around her hips, his head resting against her chest. She set him down in the hallway and shut the door. As extra precaution she fastened the latch. She changed into the dress, glancing into the full-length mirror nailed to the back of the door. Her ankle socks looked silly, and so she opened a drawer and found the stockings. She searched through the back of the closet and slipped on the high heels with the tiny buckles. The chain straps of the dress were as light as paper clips against her collarbone. It was a bit loose on her. She could not zip it herself.

Rohin began knocking. "May I come in now?"

She opened the door. Rohin was holding his almanac in his hands, muttering something under his breath. His eyes opened wide at the sight of her. "I need help with the zipper," she said. She sat on the edge of the bed.

Rohin fastened the zipper to the top, and then Miranda stood up and twirled. Rohin put down the almanac. "You're sexy," he declared.

"What did you say?"

"You're sexy."

Miranda sat down again. Though she knew it meant nothing, her heart skipped a beat. Rohin probably referred to all women as sexy. He'd probably heard the word on television, or seen it on the cover of a magazine. She remembered the day in the Mapparium, standing across the bridge from Dev.

At the time she thought she knew what his words meant. At the time they'd made sense.

Miranda folded her arms across her chest and looked Rohin in the eyes. "Tell me something."

He was silent.

"What does it mean?"

"What?"

"That word. 'Sexy.' What does it mean?"

He looked down, suddenly shy. "I can't tell you."

"Why not?"

"It's a secret." He pressed his lips together, so hard that a bit of them went white.

"Tell me the secret. I want to know."

Rohin sat on the bed beside Miranda and began to kick the edge of the mattress with the backs of his shoes. He giggled nervously, his thin body flinching as if it were being tickled.

"Tell me," Miranda demanded. She leaned over and gripped his ankles, holding his feet still.

Rohin looked at her, his eyes like slits. He struggled to kick the mattress again, but Miranda pressed against him. He fell back on the bed, his back straight as a board. He cupped his hands around his mouth, and then he whispered, "It means loving someone you don't know."

Miranda felt Rohin's words under her skin, the same way she'd felt Dev's. But instead of going hot she felt numb. It reminded her of the way she'd felt at the Indian grocery, the moment she knew, without even looking at a picture, that Madhuri Dixit, whom Dev's wife resembled, was beautiful.

"That's what my father did," Rohin continued. "He sat next to someone he didn't know, someone sexy, and now he loves her instead of my mother."

He took off his shoes and placed them side by side on the floor. Then he peeled back the comforter and crawled into Miranda's bed with the almanac. A minute later the book dropped from his hands, and he closed his eyes. Miranda watched him sleep, the comforter rising and falling as he breathed. He didn't wake up after twelve minutes like Dev, or even twenty. He didn't open his eyes as she stepped out of the silver cocktail dress and back into her jeans, and put the high-heeled shoes in the back of the closet, and rolled up the stockings and put them back in her drawer.

When she had put everything away she sat on the bed. She leaned toward him, close enough to see some white powder from the rice cakes stuck to the corners of his mouth, and picked up the almanac. As she turned the pages she imagined the quarrels Rohin had overheard in his house in Montreal. "Is she pretty?" his mother would have asked his father, wearing the same bathrobe she'd worn for weeks, her own pretty face turning spiteful. "Is she sexy?" His father would deny it at first, try to change the subject. "Tell me," Rohin's mother would shriek, "tell me if she's sexy." In the end his father would admit that she was, and his mother would cry and cry, in a bed surrounded by a tangle of clothes, her eyes puffing up like bullfrogs. "How could you," she'd ask, sobbing, "how could you love a woman you don't even know?"

As Miranda imagined the scene she began to cry a little herself. In the Mapparium that day, all the countries had seemed close enough to touch, and Dev's voice had bounced wildly off the glass. From across the bridge, thirty feet away, his words had reached her ears, so near and full of warmth that they'd drifted for days under her skin. Miranda cried harder, unable to stop. But Rohin still slept. She guessed that he was used to it now, to the sound of a woman crying.

On Sunday, Dev called to tell Miranda he was on his way. "I'm almost ready. I'll be there at two."

She was watching a cooking show on television. A woman pointed to a row of apples, explaining which were best for baking. "You shouldn't come today."

"Why not?"

"I have a cold," she lied. It wasn't far from the truth; crying had left her congested. "I've been in bed all morning."

"You do sound stuffed up." There was a pause. "Do you need anything?"

"I'm all set."

"Drink lots of fluids."

"Dev?"

"Yes, Miranda?"

"Do you remember that day we went to the Mapparium?"

"Of course."

"Do you remember how we whispered to each other?"

"I remember," Dev whispered playfully.

"Do you remember what you said?"

There was a pause. "'Let's go back to your place.'" He laughed quietly. "Next Sunday, then?"

The day before, as she'd cried, Miranda had believed she would never forget anything—not even the way her name looked written in Bengali. She'd fallen asleep beside Rohin and when she woke up he was drawing an airplane on the copy of *The Economist* she'd saved, hidden under the bed. "Who's Devajit Mitra?" he had asked, looking at the address label.

Miranda pictured Dev, in his sweatpants and sneakers, laughing into the phone. In a moment he'd join his wife downstairs, and tell her he wasn't going jogging. He'd pulled a muscle while stretching, he'd say, settling down to read the paper. In spite of herself, she longed for him. She would see him one more Sunday, she decided, perhaps two. Then she would tell him the things she had known all along: that it wasn't fair to her, or to his wife, that they both deserved better, that there was no point in it dragging on.

But the next Sunday it snowed, so much so that Dev couldn't tell his wife he was going running along the Charles. The Sunday after that, the snow had melted, but Miranda made plans to go to the movies with Laxmi, and when she told Dev this over the phone, he didn't ask her to cancel them. The third Sunday she got up early and went out for a walk. It was cold but sunny, and so she walked all the way down Commonwealth Avenue, past the restaurants where Dev had kissed her, and then she walked all the way to the Christian Science center. The Mapparium was closed, but she bought a cup of coffee nearby and sat on one of the benches in the plaza outside the church, gazing at its giant pillars and its massive dome, and at the clear-blue sky spread over the city.

1999

JUNOT DÍAZ
b. 1968

The people of two neighborhoods inspire most of Junot Díaz's fiction: those living in Villa Juana, a district of Santo Domingo in the Dominican Republic, and others residing in the London Terrace area of Palin, New Jersey. Born on the last day of 1968, Díaz lived in Villa Juana for his first five years, a time when his father was away working in the United States. Just before his fifth birthday he joined his father in New Jersey. Becoming an American did not mark a division in his life, nor would it as a source for his writing. Instead, Díaz appreciates the rich duality of any immigrant's experience. Narratives set in the Dominican Republic show characters ever mindful of what is happening among their relations on the North American mainland, and the young people in his New Jersey stories speak an English heavily laced with Dominican slang and live in a manner still marked by their Caribbean heritage. Not so much people of two worlds, Díaz's characters are creatures of a new world fashioned by fluid migrations and ultimately shaped by their own ingenuity.

The stories collected in *Drown* (1996) show the influence of two authors whose work Díaz read in college, Sandra Cisneros and Toni Morrison. Majoring in English at Kean College and Rutgers University, Díaz profited from a "living-and-learning" residence hall program that provided an immersion in both creative writing and literary studies. From Cisneros's fiction he learned how a neighborhood, such as the one she depicted in *The House on Mango Street* (1984), can be as vital and vibrant a creation as any character—how the neighborhood itself can be a character in the writer's imagination, a technique Díaz would later develop in his own manner. Morrison's novels popular during Díaz's undergraduate years (1988–92) are especially strong in privileging the novelist as creator of an otherwise unwritten minority history, a theme the younger writer would extend to the immigrant's experience of living in two worlds, neither of which conform to dominant cultural models. At the same time Díaz was paying for his education by working numerous part-time jobs that he recalls as roles customarily reserved for adult Latinos recently arrived in the United States, such as in the service industries (washing dishes, delivering pool tables) and in a steel plant. An MFA in creative writing from Cornell University followed in 1995, by which time Díaz had published many of the stories collected in *Drown*, including several in such prestigious venues as the *New Yorker* and the *Paris Review*. Díaz lives in New York City, where he remains active in the Dominican community; at the Massachusetts Institute of Technology he teaches creative writing in the Program in Writing and Humanistic Studies.

The fact that Díaz's novel, *The Brief Wondrous Life of Oscar Wao* (2007), appeared eleven years after *Drown* is indicative of his painstaking writing method. A winner of both the 2008 Pulitzer Prize for fiction and the National Book Critics Circle Award for the best novel of 2007, *The Brief Wondrous Life of Oscar Wao* presents a character who fulfills Díaz's professed goal of challenging "the type of protagonist that many of the young male Latino writers I knew were writing," as the author told Meghan O'Rourke of *Slate* in the wake of his awards. In a similar discussion with Jaime Perales Contreras of the bilingual *Literal* magazine, Díaz explained that his title character's name was prompted by a young Mexican literature student's pronunciation of Oscar Wilde's name. "Spanglish" is the slang term for such colorful mixtures of Spanish and English, and as a poetry of sorts it contributes to the texture and rhythm of Díaz's narration. As O'Rourke puts it, his fiction "is propelled by its attention to the energetic hybridity of American life," stretching from the questions of identity and inclusion dealt with in the stories of *Drown* to the complexities of a multicultural boyhood depicted in the novel. Throughout Díaz's work "authority" is an ever-present concern, from the memories of Oscar Wao's family suffering under the Trujillo dictatorship in the Dominican Republic to the contested nature of various narrative accounts with which young Oscar struggles in his American high school.

The following text is the title story from the 1996 collection *Drown*.

Drown

My mother tells me Beto's home, waits for me to say something, but I keep watching the TV. Only when she's in bed do I put on my jacket and swing through the neighborhood to see. He's a pato[1] now but two years ago we were friends and he would walk into the apartment without knocking, his heavy voice rousing my mother from the Spanish of her room and drawing me up from the basement, a voice that crackled and made you think of uncles or grandfathers.

We were raging then, crazy the way we stole, broke windows, the way we pissed on people's steps and then challenged them to come out and stop us. Beto was leaving for college at the end of the summer and was delirious from the thought of it—he hated everything about the neighborhood, the break-apart buildings, the little strips of grass, the piles of garbage around the cans, and the dump, especially the dump.

I don't know how you can do it, he said to me. I would just find me a job anywhere and go.

Yeah, I said. I wasn't like him. I had another year to go in high school, no promises elsewhere.

Days we spent in the mall or out in the parking lot playing stickball, but nights were what we waited for. The heat in the apartments was like something heavy that had come inside to die. Families arranged on their porches, the glow from their TVs washing blue against the brick. From my family apartment you could smell the pear trees that had been planted years ago, four to a court, probably to save us all from asphyxiation. Nothing moved fast, even the daylight was slow to fade, but as soon as night settled Beto and I headed down to the community center and sprang the fence into the pool. We were never alone, every kid with legs was there. We lunged from the boards and swam out of the deep end, wrestling and farting around. At around midnight abuelas,[2] with their night hair swirled around spiky rollers, shouted at us from their apartment windows. ¡Sinvergüenzas![3] Go home!

I pass his apartment but the windows are dark; I put my ear to the busted-up door and hear only the familiar hum of the air conditioner. I haven't decided yet if I'll talk to him. I can go back to my dinner and two years will become three.

Even from four blocks off I can hear the racket from the pool—radios too—and wonder if we were ever that loud. Little has changed, not the stink

---

1. Dominican slang (pejorative) for a gay man (literally, "duck" in Spanish).

2. Grandmothers (Spanish).

3. Shameless, brazen ones (Spanish).

of chlorine, not the bottles exploding against the lifeguard station. I hook my fingers through the plastic-coated hurricane fence. Something tells me that he will be here; I hop the fence, feeling stupid when I sprawl on the dandelions and the grass.

Nice one, somebody calls out.

Fuck me, I say. I'm not the oldest motherfucker in the place, but it's close. I take off my shirt and my shoes and then knife in. Many of the kids here are younger brothers of the people I used to go to school with. Two of them swim past, black and Latino, and they pause when they see me, recognizing the guy who sells them their shitty dope. The crackheads have their own man, Lucero, and some other guy who drives in from Paterson,[4] the only full-time commuter in the area.

The water feels good. Starting at the deep end I glide over the slick-tiled bottom without kicking up a spume or making a splash. Sometimes another swimmer churns past me, more a disturbance of water than a body. I can still go far without coming up. While everything above is loud and bright, everything below is whispers. And always the risk of coming up to find the cops stabbing their searchlights out across the water. And then everyone running, wet feet slapping against the concrete, yelling, Fuck you, officers, you puto sucios,[5] fuck you.

When I'm tired I wade through to the shallow end, past some kid who's kissing his girlfriend, watching me as though I'm going to try to cut in, and I sit near the sign that runs the pool during the day. *No Horseplay, No Running, No Defecating, No Urinating, No Expectorating.* At the bottom someone has scrawled in *No Whites, No Fat Chiks* and someone else has provided the missing *c*. I laugh. Beto hadn't known what expectorating meant though he was the one leaving for college. I told him, spitting a greener by the side of the pool.

Shit, he said. Where did you learn that?

I shrugged.

Tell me. He hated when I knew something he didn't. He put his hands on my shoulders and pushed me under. He was wearing a cross and cutoff jeans. He was stronger than me and held me down until water flooded my nose and throat. Even then I didn't tell him; he thought I didn't read, not even dictionaries.

We live alone. My mother has enough for the rent and groceries and I cover the phone bill, sometimes the cable. She's so quiet that most of the time I'm startled to find her in the apartment. I'll enter a room and she'll stir, detaching herself from the cracking plaster walls, from the stained cabinets, and fright will pass through me like a wire. She has discovered the secret to silence: pouring café without a splash, walking between rooms as if gliding on a cushion of felt, crying without a sound. You have traveled to the East and learned many secret things, I've told her. You're like a shadow warrior.

And you're like a crazy, she says. Like a big crazy.

When I come in she's still awake, her hands picking clots of lint from her skirt. I put a towel down on the sofa and we watch television together. We

4. City in northern New Jersey. 5. Dirty whores (Spanish).

settle on the Spanish-language news: drama for her, violence for me. Today a child has survived a seven-story fall, busting nothing but his diaper. The hysterical baby-sitter, about three hundred pounds of her, is head-butting the microphone.

It's a goddamn miraclevilla,[6] she cries.

My mother asks me if I found Beto. I tell her that I didn't look.

That's too bad. He was telling me that he might be starting at a school for business.

So what?

She's never understood why we don't speak anymore. I've tried to explain, all wise-like, that everything changes, but she thinks that sort of saying is only around so you can prove it wrong.

He asked me what you were doing.

What did you say?

I told him you were fine.

You should have told him I moved.

And what if he ran into you?

I'm not allowed to visit my mother?

She notices the tightening of my arms. You should be more like me and your father.

Can't you see I'm watching television?

I was angry at him, wasn't I? But now we can talk to each other.

Am I watching television here or what?

Saturdays she asks me to take her to the mall. As a son I feel I owe her that much, even though neither of us has a car and we have to walk two miles through redneck territory to catch the M15.[7]

Before we head out she drags us through the apartment to make sure the windows are locked. She can't reach the latches so she has me test them. With the air conditioner on we never open windows but I go through the routine anyway. Putting my hand on the latch is not enough—she wants to hear it rattle. This place just isn't safe, she tells me. Lorena got lazy and look what they did to her. They punched her and kept her locked up in her place. Those morenos[8] ate all her food and even made phone calls. Phone calls!

That's why we don't have long-distance, I tell her but she shakes her head. That's not funny, she says.

She doesn't go out much, so when she does it's a big deal. She dresses up, even puts on makeup. Which is why I don't give her lip about taking her to the mall even though I usually make a fortune on Saturdays, selling to those kids going down to Belmar or out to Spruce Run.

I recognize like half the kids on the bus. I keep my head buried in my cap, praying that nobody tries to score. She watches the traffic, her hands somewhere inside her purse, doesn't say a word.

When we arrive at the mall I give her fifty dollars. Buy something, I say, hating the image I have of her, picking through the sale bins, wrinkling

---

6. Slang term for "miraculous" in "Spanglish," an amalgamation of Spanish and English as spoken in some Hispanic communities.

7. Bus route in the New Brunswick area of New Jersey.

8. Dark-skinned persons (Spanish).

everything. Back in the day, my father would give her a hundred dollars at the end of each summer for my new clothes and she would take nearly a week to spend it, even though it never amounted to more than a couple of t-shirts and two pairs of jeans. She folds the bills into a square. I'll see you at three, she says.

I wander through the stores, staying in sight of the cashiers so they won't have reason to follow me. The circuit I make has not changed since my looting days. Bookstore, record store, comic-book shop, Macy's. Me and Beto used to steal like mad from these places, two, three hundred dollars of shit in an outing. Our system was simple—we walked into a store with a shopping bag and came out loaded. Back then security wasn't tight. The only trick was in the exit. We stopped right at the entrance of the store and checked out some worthless piece of junk to stop people from getting suspicious. What do you think? we asked each other. Would she like it? Both of us had seen bad shoplifters at work. All grab and run, nothing smooth about them. Not us. We idled out of the stores slow, like a fat seventies car. At this, Beto was the best. He even talked to mall security, asked them for directions, his bag all loaded up, and me, standing ten feet away, shitting my pants. When he finished he smiled, swinging his shopping bag up to hit me.

You got to stop that messing around, I told him. I'm not going to jail for bullshit like that.

You don't go to jail for shoplifting. They just turn you over to your old man.

I don't know about you, but my pops hits like a motherfucker.

He laughed. You know my dad. He flexed his hands. The nigger's got arthritis.

My mother never suspected, even when my clothes couldn't all fit in my closet, but my father wasn't that easy. He knew what things cost and knew that I didn't have a regular job.

You're going to get caught, he told me one day. Just you wait. When you do I'll show them everything you've taken and then they'll throw your stupid ass away like a bad piece of meat.

He was a charmer, my pop, a real asshole, but he was right. Nobody can stay smooth forever, especially kids like us. One day at the bookstore, we didn't even hide the drops. Four issues of the same *Playboy* for kicks, enough audio books to start our own library. No last-minute juke either. The lady who stepped in front of us didn't look old, even with her white hair. Her silk shirt was half unbuttoned and a silver horn necklace sat on the freckled top of her chest. I'm sorry fellows, but I have to check your bag, she said. I kept moving, and looked back all annoyed, like she was asking us for a quarter or something. Beto got polite and stopped. No problem, he said, slamming the heavy bag into her face. She hit the cold tile with a squawk, her palms slapping the ground. There you go, Beto said.

Security found us across from the bus stop, under a Jeep Cherokee. A bus had come and gone, both of us too scared to take it, imagining a plainclothes waiting to clap the cuffs on. I remember that when the rent-a-cop tapped his nightstick against the fender and said, You little shits better come out here real slow, I started to cry. Beto didn't say a word, his face stretched out and gray, his hand squeezing mine, the bones in our fingers pressing together.

Nights I drink with Alex and Danny. The Malibou Bar is no good, just wash-outs and the sucias[9] we can con into joining us. We drink too much, roar at each other and make the skinny bartender move closer to the phone. On the wall hangs a cork dartboard and a Brunswick Gold Crown[1] blocks the bath-room, its bumpers squashed, the felt pulled like old skin.

When the bar begins to shake back and forth like a rumba, I call it a night and go home, through the fields that surround the apartments. In the distance you can see the Raritan,[2] as shiny as an earthworm, the same river my homeboy goes to school on. The dump has long since shut down, and grass has spread over it like a sickly fuzz, and from where I stand, my right hand directing a colorless stream of piss downward, the landfill might be the top of a blond head, square and old.

In the mornings I run. My mother is already up, dressing for her housecleaning job. She says nothing to me, would rather point to the mangu[3] she has prepared than speak.

I run three miles easily, could have pushed a fourth if I were in the mood. I keep an eye out for the recruiter who prowls around our neighborhood in his dark K-car.[4] We've spoken before. He was out of uniform and called me over, jovial, and I thought I was helping some white dude with directions. Would you mind if I asked you a question?

No.

Do you have a job?

Not right now.

Would you like one? A real career, more than you'll get around here?

I remember stepping back. Depends on what it is, I said.

Son, I know somebody who's hiring. It's the United States government.

Well. Sorry, but I ain't Army material.

That's exactly what I used to think, he said, his ten piggy fingers buried in his carpeted steering wheel. But now I have a house, a car, a gun and a wife. Discipline. Loyalty. Can you say that you have those things? Even one?

He's a southerner, red-haired, his drawl so out of place that the people around here laugh just hearing him. I take to the bushes when I see his car on the road. These days my guts feel loose and cold and I want to be away from here. He won't have to show me his Desert Eagle[5] or flash the photos of the skinny Filipino girls sucking dick. He'll only have to smile and name the places and I'll listen.

When I reach the apartment, I lean against my door, waiting for my heart to slow, for the pain to lose its edge. I hear my mother's voice, a whisper from the kitchen. She sounds hurt or nervous, maybe both. At first I'm terrified that Beto's inside with her but then I look and see the phone cord, swinging lazily. She's talking to my father, something she knows I disapprove of. He's in Florida now, a sad guy who calls her and begs for money. He swears that if she moves down there he'll leave the woman he's living with. These are lies, I've told her, but she still calls him. His words coil inside of her, wrecking her sleep for days. She opens the refrigerator door slightly so that the whir of

9. Sluts (Spanish).
1. Pool table.
2. River in New Jersey.
3. Dominican dish made from plantains with

butter, salt, pepper, and water.
4. A Chrysler Corporation automobile popular as a fleet vehicle.
5. A semi-automatic military pistol.

the compressor masks their conversation. I walk in on her and hang up the phone. That's enough, I say.

She's startled, her hand squeezing the loose folds of her neck. That was him, she says quietly.

On school days Beto and I chilled at the stop together but as soon as that bus came over the Parkwood hill I got to thinking about how I was failing gym and screwing up math and how I hated every single living teacher on the planet.

I'll see *you* in the p.m., I said.

He was already standing on line. I just stood back and grinned, my hands in my pockets. With our bus drivers you didn't have to hide. Two of them didn't give a rat fuck and the third one, the Brazilian preacher, was too busy talking Bible to notice anything but the traffic in front of him.

Being truant without a car was no easy job but I managed. I watched a lot of TV and when it got boring I trooped down to the mall or the Sayreville library, where you could watch old documentaries for free. I always came back to the neighborhood late, so the bus wouldn't pass me on Ernston and nobody could yell Asshole! out the windows. Beto would usually be home or down by the swings, but other times he wouldn't be around at all. Out visiting other neighborhoods. He knew a lot of folks I didn't—a messed-up black kid from Madison Park, two brothers who were into that N.Y. club scene, who spent money on platform shoes and leather backpacks. I'd leave a message with his parents and then watch some more TV. The next day he'd be out at the bus stop, too busy smoking a cigarette to say much about the day before.

You need to learn how to walk the world, he told me. There's a lot out there.

Some nights me and the boys drive to New Brunswick. A nice city, the Raritan so low and silty that you don't have to be Jesus to walk over it. We hit the Melody and the Roxy, stare at the college girls. We drink a lot and then spin out onto the dance floor. None of the chicas[6] ever dance with us, but a glance or a touch can keep us talking shit for hours.

Once the clubs close we go to the Franklin Diner, gorge ourselves on pancakes, and then, after we've smoked our pack, head home. Danny passes out in the back seat and Alex cranks the window down to keep the wind in his eyes. He's fallen asleep in the past, wrecked two cars before this one. The streets have been picked clean of students and townies and we blow through every light, red or green. At the Old Bridge Turnpike we pass the fag bar, which never seems to close. Patos are all over the parking lot, drinking and talking.

Sometimes Alex will stop by the side of the road and say, Excuse me. When somebody comes over from the bar he'll point his plastic pistol at them, just to see if they'll run or shit their pants. Tonight he just puts his head out the window. Fuck you! he shouts and then settles back in his seat, laughing.

That's original, I say.

---

6. Girls (Spanish).

He puts his head out the window again. Eat me, then!

Yeah, Danny mumbles from the back. Eat me.

Twice. That's it.

The first time was at the end of that summer. We had just come back from the pool and were watching a porn video at his parents' apartment. His father was a nut for these tapes, ordering them from wholesalers in California and Grand Rapids. Beto used to tell me how his pop would watch them in the middle of the day, not caring a lick about his moms, who spent the time in the kitchen, taking hours to cook a pot of rice and gandules.[7] Beto would sit down with his pop and neither of them would say a word, except to laugh when somebody caught it in the eye or the face.

We were an hour into the new movie, some vaina[8] that looked like it had been filmed in the apartment next door, when he reached into my shorts. What the fuck are you doing? I asked, but he didn't stop. His hand was dry. I kept my eyes on the television, too scared to watch. I came right away, smearing the plastic sofa covers. My legs started shaking and suddenly I wanted out. He didn't say anything to me as I left, just sat there watching the screen.

The next day he called and when I heard his voice I was cool but I wouldn't go to the mall or anywhere else. My mother sensed that something was wrong and pestered me about it, but I told her to leave me the fuck alone, and my pops, who was home on a visit, stirred himself from the couch to slap me down. Mostly I stayed in the basement, terrified that I would end up abnormal, a fucking pato, but he was my best friend and back then that mattered to me more than anything. This alone got me out of the apartment and over to the pool that night. He was already there, his body pale and flabby under the water. Hey, he said. I was beginning to worry about you.

Nothing to worry about, I said.

We swam and didn't talk much and later we watched a Skytop crew pull a bikini top from a girl stupid enough to hang out alone. Give it, she said, covering herself, but these kids howled, holding it up over her head, the shiny laces flopping just out of reach. When they began to pluck at her arms, she walked away, leaving them to try the top on over their flat pecs.

He put his hand on my shoulder, my pulse a code under his palm. Let's go, he said. Unless of course you're not feeling good.

I'm feeling fine, I said.

Since his parents worked nights we pretty much owned the place until six the next morning. We sat in front of his television, in our towels, his hands bracing against my abdomen and thighs. I'll stop if you want, he said and I didn't respond. After I was done, he laid his head in my lap. I wasn't asleep or awake, but caught somewhere in between, rocked slowly back and forth the way surf holds junk against the shore, rolling it over and over. In three weeks he was leaving. Nobody can touch me, he kept saying. We'd visited the school and I'd seen how beautiful the campus was, with all the students drifting from dorm to class. I thought of how in high school our teachers loved to crowd us into their lounge every time a space shuttle took off from Florida.

---

7. Pigeon peas (Spanish).

8. Dominican slang for "stuff" (Spanish).

One teacher, whose family had two grammar schools named after it, compared us to the shuttles. A few of you are going to make it. Those are the orbiters. But the majority of you are just going to burn out. Going nowhere. He dropped his hand onto his desk. I could already see myself losing altitude, fading, the earth spread out beneath me, hard and bright.

I had my eyes closed and the television was on and when the hallway door crashed open, he jumped up and I nearly cut my dick off struggling with my shorts. It's just the neighbor, he said, laughing. He was laughing, but I was saying, Fuck this, and getting my clothes on.

I believe I see him in his father's bottomed-out Cadillac, heading towards the turnpike, but I can't be sure. He's probably back in school already. I deal close to home, trooping up and down the same dead-end street where the kids drink and smoke. These punks joke with me, pat me down for taps, sometimes too hard. Now that strip malls line Route 9, a lot of folks have part-time jobs; the kids stand around smoking in their aprons, name tags dangling heavily from pockets.

When I get home, my sneakers are filthy so I take an old toothbrush to their soles, scraping the crap into the tub. My mother has thrown open the windows and propped open the door. It's cool enough, she explains. She has prepared dinner—rice and beans, fried cheese, tostones.[9] Look what I bought, she says, showing me two blue t-shirts. They were two for one so I bought you one. Try it on.

It fits tight but I don't mind. She cranks up the television. A movie dubbed into Spanish, a classic, one that everyone knows. The actors throw themselves around, passionate, but their words are plain and deliberate. It's hard to imagine anybody going through life this way. I pull out the plug of bills from my pockets. She takes it from me, her fingers soothing the creases. A man who treats his plata[1] like this doesn't deserve to spend it, she says.

We watch the movie and the two hours together makes us friendly. She puts her hand on mine. Near the end of the film, just as our heroes are about to fall apart under a hail of bullets, she takes off her glasses and kneads her temples, the light of the television flickering across her face. She watches another minute and then her chin lists to her chest. Almost immediately her eyelashes begin to tremble, a quiet semaphore. She is dreaming, dreaming of Boca Raton, of strolling under the jacarandas[2] with my father. You can't be anywhere forever, was what Beto used to say, what he said to me the day I went to see him off. He handed me a gift, a book, and after he was gone I threw it away, didn't even bother to open it and read what he'd written.

I let her sleep until the end of the movie and when I wake her she shakes her head, grimacing. You better check those windows, she says. I promise her I will.

1996

---

9. Flattened fried plantains, a side dish in the Dominican Republic.
1. Slang term for money (literally, "silver" in Spanish).
2. Flowering trees native to the tropics.

Selected Bibliographies

AMERICAN LITERATURE 1865–1914

Reference Works

Many useful sources are now online, including the *International MLA Bibliography*; "A Brief Timeline of American Literature and Events, 1620–1920," www.wsu.edu/~campbelld/amlit/; and "PAL: Perspectives in American Literature—A Research and Reference Guide," archive.csustan.edu/english /reuben/pal/table.html. Author biographies are available in the *Dictionary of Literary Biography*, the *American National Biography*, and Jay Parini's *American Writers: A Collection of Literary Biographies* (2003). General resources for the period include *A Companion to American Fiction, 1865– 1914*, edited by Robert Paul Lamb and G. R. Thompson (2005); *The Oxford Handbook of Nineteenth-Century American Literature*, edited by Russ Castronovo (2012); *A Companion to the Regional Literatures of America*, edited by Charles L. Crow (2003); Sharon M. Harris's *American Women Prose Writers, 1870–1920* (2000), which includes biographical information; Trudier Harris and Thadious M. Davis's *Afro-American Writers before the Harlem Renaissance* (1986); *African American Writers*, 2nd edition, edited by Valerie Smith (2001); Xiao-huang Yin's *Chinese American Literature since the 1850s* (2006), which traces representations of Chinese American identity, especially in tales of interracial marriage in the fiction of Sui Sin Far and others; *The Oxford Handbook of Indigenous American Literature*, edited by James H. Cox and Daniel Heath Justice (2014); *Native American Writers of the United States* (1997), edited by Kenneth Roemer; and *Hispanic Literature of the United States: A Comprehensive Reference*, edited by Nicolás Kannelos (2003). The annual *American Literary Scholarship* (also online) provides critical commentary on a wide range of scholarly books and articles; for guidance to recent books on American literature in this period, see the chapters on "Themes, Topics, Criticism" and "Nineteenth-Century Literature."

Literary Histories

The eight-volume *Cambridge History of American Literature* (Sacvan Bercovitch, general editor, 1995–2006) addresses literary genres and periods. A useful introduction to the novels of this period is volume 6 of *The Oxford History of the Novel in English: The American Novel, 1870–1940* (2014), edited by Michael Elliott and Pricilla Wald; see also the relevant chapters in *The Cambridge History of the American Novel* (2011), edited by Leonard Cassuto, Claire Eby, and Benjamin Reiss, and Gregg Crane's *The Cambridge Introduction to the Nineteenth-Century American Novel* (2007). American poetry is covered in Alan Shucard, Fred Moramarco, and William Sullivan's *Modern American Poetry, 1865–1950* (1989), and Robert Shulman's *Social Criticism and Nineteenth-Century American Poetry, 1865–1950* (1989). A provocative one-volume reference work is *A New Literary History of America* (2009), edited by Greil Marcus and Werner Sollors. Important studies of American literary history and culture during the 1865–1914 period include Edlie Wong's *Racial Reconstruction: Black Inclusion, Chinese Exclusion, and the Fictions of Citizenship* (2015); Nathaniel Cadle's *The Mediating Nation: Late American Realism, Globalization, and the Progressive State* (2014); Susan Goodman's *Republic of Words the Atlantic Monthly and its Writers, 1857–1925* (2011), James Salazar's *Bodies of Reform: The Rhetoric of Character in Gilded-Age America* (2010), Nancy Bentley's *Frantic Panoramas: American Literature and Mass Culture, 1870–1920* (2009), Susan L. Mizruchi's *The Rise of Multicultural America* (2008), Russ Castronovo's *Beautiful Democracy: Aesthetics and Anarchy in a Global Era* (2007), Molly Crumpton Winter's *American Narratives: Multiethnic Writing in the Age of Realism* (2007), James C. Davis's *Commerce in Color: Race, Consumer Culture, and American Literature 1893–1933* (2007), Claudia Stokes's *Writers in Retrospect: The Rise of American Literary History* (2006), Loren Glass's *Authors, Inc.: Literary Celebrity in the Modern United States, 1880–1980* (2004), Robert Dale Parker's *The Invention of Native American Literature* (2003), Gregg D. Crane's *Race, Citizenship, and Law in American Literature* (2002), John Carlos Rowe's *Literary Culture and U.S. Imperialism: From the Revolution to World War II* (2000), Orm Øverland's *Immigrant Minds, American Identities: Making the United States Home, 1870–1930* (2000), and Gavin Jones's *Strange Talk: The Politics of Dialect Literature in Gilded Age America* (1999).

Studies of American women writers include Dale M. Bauer's *Sex Expression and American Women Writers, 1860–1940* (2009); *Before They Could Vote: American Women's Autobiographical Writing, 1819–1919*, edited by Sidonie A. Smith and Julia Watson (2006); Susan S. Williams's *Reclaiming Authorship: Literary Women in America, 1850–1900* (2006); Martha H. Patterson's *Beyond the Gibson Girl: Reimagining the American New Woman, 1895–1915* (2005); Suzanne Bost's *Mulattas and Mestizas: Representing Mixed Identities in the Americas, 1850–2000* (2003); *The Cambridge Companion to Nineteenth-Century American Women's Writing* (2001), edited by Dale M. Bauer and Philip Gould; Elsa Nettels's *Language and Gender in American Fiction: Howells, James, Wharton, and Cather* (1997); and Elizabeth Ammons's *Conflicting Stories: American Women Writers at the Turn into the Twentieth Century* (1992). Hazel V. Carby's *Reconstructing Womanhood: The Emergence of the Afro-American Woman Novelist* (1988) discusses Pauline Hopkins and Ida B. Wells-Barnett. For an introduction to scholarship on African American writers during this period see also Eric Gardner's *Unexpected Places: Relocating Nineteenth-Century African American Literature* (2011); John Ernest's *Chaotic Justice: Rethinking African-American Lit-*

erary History (2009); Gene Andrew Jarrett's *Deans and Truants: Race and Realism in African American Literature* (2007); Jennifer C. James's *A Freedom Bought with Blood: African American War Literature from the Civil War to World War II* (2007); *Post-Bellum, Pre-Harlem: African American Literature and Culture, 1877–1919* (2006), edited by Barbara McCaskill and Caroline Gebhard; Elizabeth McHenry's *Forgotten Readers: Recovering the Lost History of African American Literary Societies* (2002); Eric J. Sundquist's *To Wake the Nations: Race in the Making of American Literature* (1993); and Toni Morrison's *Playing in the Dark: Whiteness and the Literary Imagination* (1992). Peter Nabokov's *Native American Testimony* (1978; rev. and expanded 1991) is an important collection of Native American oratory. David Murray's *Forked Tongues: Speech, Writing, and Representation in North American Indian Texts* (1991) contains excellent commentary on several different speeches, and William Clements's study *Oratory in Native North America* (2002) is also valuable. The best brief study of traditional Native oratory—Indian to Indian speech—is Donald Bahr's "Oratory," an entry in Andrew Wiget's edited volume, *Dictionary of Native American Literature* (1994). Important works addressing Native American writing during this period include *Red on Red: Native American Literary* Separatism (1999), Siobhan Senier's *Voices of American Indian Assimilation and Resistance: Helen Hunt Jackson, Sarah Winnemucca, and Victoria Howard* (2003), Robert Warrior's *The People and the Word: Reading Native Nonfiction* (2005), Scott Lyons's *X-Marks: Native Signatures of Assent* (2010). Also see Philip Deloria's *Indians in Unexpected Places* (2004) for an excellent work on the cultural forces affecting Native peoples in the early twentieth century.

Realism and naturalism are discussed in *The Cambridge Introduction to American Literary Realism*, edited by Phillip Barrish (2011); *The Oxford Handbook of American Literary Naturalism*, edited by Keith Newlin (2012); and *The Cambridge Companion to American Realism and Naturalism: Howells to London*, edited by Donald Pizer (1995). See also Pizer's *American Naturalism and the Jews: Garland, Norris, Dreiser, Wharton, and Cather* (2008) and *Realism and Naturalism in Nineteenth-Century American Literature* (1984), along with his edited collection *Documents of American Realism and Naturalism* (1998). Other important work on realism and naturalism includes Jane F. Thrailkill's *Affecting Fictions: Mind, Body, and Emotion in American Literary Realism* (2007), Jennifer L. Fleissner's *Women, Compulsion, Modernity: The Moment of American Naturalism* (2004), Henry Wonham's *Playing the Races: Ethnic Caricature and American Literary Realism* (2004), Bert Bender's *Evolution and "the Sex Problem": American Narratives during the Eclipse of Darwinism* (2004), Michael A. Elliott's *The Culture Concept: Writing and Difference in the Age of Realism* (2002), Barbara Hochman's *Getting at the Author: Reimagining Books and Reading in the Age of American Realism* (2001), Phillip Barrish's *American Literary Realism, Critical Theory, and Intellectual Prestige, 1880–1990* (2001), Brook Thomas's *American Literary Realism and the Failed Promise of Contract* (1997), David E. Shi's *Facing Facts: Realism in American Thought and Culture, 1850–1920* (1995), Kenneth Warren's *Black and White Strangers: Race and American Literary Realism* (1993), Michael Davitt Bell's *The Problem of American Realism: Studies in the Cultural History of a Literary Idea* (1993), Amy Kaplan's *The Social Construction of American Realism* (1988), Walter Benn Michaels's *The*

Gold Standard and the Logic of Naturalism (1987), June Howard's *Form and History in American Literary Naturalism* (1985), and Warner Berthoff's classic *The Ferment of Realism* (1965).

On regionalism see Philip Joseph's *American Literary Regionalism* (2007); *American Literary Geographies: Spatial Practice and Cultural Production, 1500–1900*, edited by Martin Brückner and Hsuan L. Hsu (2007); Judith Fetterley and Marjorie Pryse's *Writing Out of Place: Regionalism, Women, and American Literary Culture* (2003); Stephanie Foote's *Regional Fictions: Culture and Identity in Nineteenth-Century American Literature* (2001); and Donna M. Campbell's *Resisting Regionalism: Gender and Naturalism in American Fiction, 1885–1915* (1998). On Western writing in particular, see Nina Baym's *Women Writers of the American West, 1833–1927* (2011), Nathaniel Lewis's *Unsettling the Literary West: Authenticity and Authorship* (2003), Noreen Groover Lape's *West of the Border: The Multicultural Literature of the Western American Frontiers* (2000), Bonney MacDonald's *Updating the Literary West* (1997), and Glen A. Love's *New Americans: The Westerner and the Modern Experience in the American Novel* (1982).

Ambrose Bierce

The fullest edition of Bierce's writings is *Collected Works of Ambrose Bierce* (1909–12), edited by Walter Neale. *The Short Fiction of Ambrose Bierce, 3 Volumes: A Comprehensive Edition* (2006), edited by S. T. Joshi, Lawrence I. Berkove, and David E. Schultz, brings together all of Bierce's known short fiction with helpful introductions, extensive annotations, textual variants, and a section of Bierce's prefaces to his published short fiction. Joshi and Schultz also edited *The Fall of the Republic and Other Political Satires* (2000), *The Unabridged Devil's Dictionary* (2000), and *A Much Misunderstood Man: Selected Letters of Ambrose Bierce* (2003). *Phantoms of a Blood-Stained Period: The Complete Civil War Writings of Ambrose Bierce*, is edited by Russell Duncan and David J. Klooster (2002); Robert C. Evans edited *"An Occurrence at Owl Creek Bridge": An Annotated Critical Edition* (2003). Bierce's poetry is collected in *Poems of Ambrose Bierce*, edited by M. E. Grenander (1996). The largest collection of Bierce's letters is available in Bertha C. Pope's edition of *The Letters of Ambrose Bierce* (1921).

Robert L. Gale surveys Bierce's life and work in *An Ambrose Bierce Companion* (2001). S. T. Joshi and David E. Schultz edited *Ambrose Bierce: An Annotated Bibliography of Primary Sources* (1999). Prior to Lawrence I. Berkove's fine critical biography, *A Prescription for Adversity: The Moral Art of Ambrose Bierce* (2002), the standard critical biography had been Paul Fatout's still useful *Ambrose Bierce, the Devil's Lexicographer* (1951). On Bierce and the Civil War, see Roy Morris Jr.'s *Ambrose Bierce: Alone in Bad Company* (1996), Brian Thomenson's *Shadows of Blue & Gray: The Civil War Writings of Ambrose Bierce* (2003),

Donald T. Blume's *Ambrose Bierce's Civilians and Soldiers in Context: A Critical Study* (2004), and David M. Owens's *The Devil's Topographer: Ambrose Bierce and the American War Story* (2006). Dennis Drabelle's *The Great American Railroad War: How Ambrose Bierce and Frank Norris Took on the Notorious Central Pacific Railroad* (2012) discusses Bierce's journalistic career in detail. Cathy N. Davidson's *The Experimental Fictions of Ambrose Bierce: Structuring the Ineffable* (1984) remains an important work; Davidson also edited *Critical Essays on Ambrose Bierce* (1982).

Charles W. Chesnutt

Werner Sollors edited the Library of America's *Charles W. Chesnutt: Stories, Novels and Essays* (2002). *Charles W. Chesnutt: Essays and Speeches*, edited by Joseph R. McElrath Jr., Robert C. Leitz III, and Jesse S. Crisler (1999), presents all of Chesnutt's known nonfiction. McElrath, Leitz, and Crisler have also edited *An Exemplary Citizen: Letters of Charles W. Chesnutt, 1906–1932* (2002). Richard H. Brodhead edited *The Journals of Charles W. Chesnutt* (1993), as well as *The Conjure Woman and Other Conjure Tales* (1993); and William L. Andrews edited *The Collected Stories of Charles W. Chesnutt* (1992). *The Portable Charles W. Chesnutt*, edited by Andrews and Henry Louis Gates Jr., appeared in 2008, and Norton has published a critical edition of *The Conjure Stories: Authoritative Texts, Contexts, Criticism* (2012), edited by Robert B. Stepto and Jennifer Rae Greeson.

Chesnutt's daughter, Helen M. Chesnutt, published the first full-length biography, *Charles Waddell Chesnutt: Pioneer of the Color Line* (1952). William L. Andrews's *The Liter-*

ary Career of Charles W. Chesnutt (1980) is a useful critical biography. Marjorie Pryse and Hortense J. Spillers's Conjuring: Black Women, Fiction, and Literary Tradition (1985) and Jane Campbell's Mythic Black Fiction: The Transformation of History (1986) contain useful contextual material on Chesnutt. A more specialized study is Ernestine Williams Pickens's Charles W. Chesnutt and the Progressive Movement (1994). Eric J. Sundquist's To Wake the Nations (1993) treats Chesnutt at length. Other valuable critical studies include Robert B. Stepto's Charles Chesnutt: The Uncle Julius Stories (1984), Henry Wonham's Charles W. Chesnutt: A Study of the Short Fiction (1998), Charles Duncan's The Absent Man: The Narrative Craft of Charles W. Chesnutt (1998), Dean McWilliams's Charles W. Chesnutt and the Fictions of Race (2002), Matthew Wilson's Whiteness in the Novels of Charles W. Chesnutt (2004), Ryan Simmons's Chesnutt and Realism: A Study of the Novels (2006), and Ernestine Pickens Glass and Susan Prothro's Passing in the Works of Charles W. Chesnutt (2010). Two edited essay collections provide especially good introductions to Chesnutt criticism: Joseph R. McElrath's Critical Essays on Charles W. Chesnutt (1999), and David Garrett Izzo and Maria Orban's Charles Chesnutt Reappraised: Essays on the First Major African American Fiction Writer (2009).

Kate Chopin
Per Seyersted edited The Complete Works of Kate Chopin (1969) in two volumes; he also published Kate Chopin: A Critical Biography (1969). Emily Toth's Unveiling Kate Chopin (1999), which incorporates material from Chopin's later discovered diaries and manuscripts, is now the standard biography. Barbara C. Ewell's Kate Chopin (1986) and Kate Chopin: A Literary Life by Nancy Walker (2001) are good introductions to the life and work. Important essay collections are The Cambridge Companion to Kate Chopin (2008), edited by Janet Beer; Kate Chopin in the Twenty-First Century: New Critical Essays (2008), edited by Heather Ostman; and Awakenings: The Story of the Kate Chopin Revival (2009), edited by Bernard Koloski.

Nancy A. Walker edited Kate Chopin: The Awakening, Complete Authoritative Text with Biographical and Historical Contexts (1993); Margo Culley edited the second edition of the Norton Critical Edition of The Awakening (1994). Susan Disheroon Green, David Caudle, and Emily Toth compiled Kate Chopin: An Annotated Bibliography of Critical Works (1999). Seyersted and Toth edited A Kate Chopin Miscellany (1980), a collection of unpublished short fiction, poems, and letters. Bernard J. Kosloski brought out an edition of

Chopin's two most important collections of short stories, "Bayou Folk" and "A Night in Acadie" (1999).

Critical studies of Chopin's writings include Wendy Martin's edited collection New Essays on The Awakening (1988); Lynda S. Boren and Sara deSaussure's edited collection Kate Chopin Reconsidered: Beyond the Bayou (1992); Joyce Dyer's The Awakening: A Novel of Beginnings (1993); Bernard J. Kosloski's Kate Chopin: A Study of the Short Fiction (1996); Janet Beer's comparative Kate Chopin, Edith Wharton and Charlotte Perkins Gilman: Studies in Short Fiction (2005), and James Nagel's Race and Culture in New Orleans Stories: Kate Chopin, Grace King, Alice Dunbar-Nelson, and George Washington Cable (2014).

Samuel L. Clemens
See Mark Twain.

Stephen Crane
Fredson Bowers is the textual editor of The Works of Stephen Crane (1969–76); J. C. Levenson edited The Library of America volume, Crane: Prose and Poetry (1996). The fourth edition of the Norton Critical Edition of The Red Badge of Courage, edited by Eric Carl Link and Donald Pizer, was published in 2007. R. W. Stallman and Lillian Gilkes's Stephen Crane: Letters (1960) was followed and to some extent superseded by The Correspondence of Stephen Crane (1988), edited by Stanley Wertheim and Paul Sorrentino. Joseph Katz edited both The Portable Stephen Crane (1969) and The Poems of Stephen Crane: A Critical Edition (1966). Patrick K. Dooley compiled Stephen Crane: An Annotated Bibliography of Secondary Scholarship (1992), a research tool now annually updated by Dooley in Stephen Crane Studies. Paul Sorrentino recently published a comprehensive, insightful biography of Crane, Stephen Crane: A Life of Fire (2014). Other useful biographical resources include Linda H. Davis's Badge of Courage: The Life of Stephen Crane (1998); The Crane Log: A Documentary Life of Stephen Crane, 1871–1900 (1994), edited by Wertheim and Sorrentino; and Christopher Benfey's The Double Life of Stephen Crane: A Biography (1992). Sorrentino's Stephen Crane Remembered (2006) collects writings by Crane's friends, colleagues, and contemporaries. Wertheim edited the comprehensive A Stephen Crane Encyclopedia (1997).

Edwin H. Cady's Stephen Crane (1980) provides a good critical introduction to Crane's life and work. Other studies of interest include James Nagel's Stephen Crane and Literary Impressionism (1980), Chester L. Wolford's The Anger of Stephen Crane: Fiction and the Epic Tradition (1983), David Halliburton's The

Color of the Sky: A Study of Stephen Crane (1991), Patrick K. Dooley's *The Pluralistic Philosophy of Stephen Crane* (1993), Michael Robertson's *Stephen Crane, Journalism, and the Making of Modern American Literature* (1997), Bill Brown's *The Material Unconscious: American Amusement, Stephen Crane and the Economics of Play* (1997), George E. Monteiro's *Stephen Crane's Blue Badge of Courage* (2000), Keith Gandal's *Class Representation in Modern Fiction and Film* (2007), and John Fagg's *On the Cusp: Stephen Crane, George Bellow, and Modernism* (2009). Donald Pizer edited and introduced *Critical Essays on Stephen Crane's The Red Badge of Courage* (1990), and Pizer's own essays on Crane have recently been published together as *Writer in Motion: The Major Fiction of Stephen Crane: Collected Critical Essays* (2013).

Emily Dickinson

Three volumes of *The Poems of Emily Dickinson* (1955) were edited by Thomas H. Johnson; and Johnson and Theodora Ward edited three companion volumes of *The Letters of Emily Dickinson* (1958). R. W. Franklin's three-volume *Poems of Emily Dickinson: Variorum Edition* (1998) augments and updates Johnson's three-volume *Poems*. In 1999 Franklin published the one-volume *The Poems of Emily Dickinson: Reading Edition*. Important biographies include Richard B. Sewall's *The Life of Emily Dickinson* (1974), Cynthia Griffin Wolff's *Emily Dickinson* (1986), Alfred Habegger's *My Wars Are Laid Away in Books: The Life of Emily Dickinson* (2001), Brenda Wineapple's *White Heat: The Friendship of Emily Dickinson and Thomas Wentworth Higginson* (2008), and Lyndall Gordon's *Lives Like Loaded Guns: Emily Dickinson and Her Family's Feuds* (2010). Jay Leyda's *The Years and Hours of Emily Dickinson* (1960) provides two volumes of documents, such as excerpts from family letters. Additional documents can be found in Polly Longsworth's *The World of Emily Dickinson* (1990) and Ellen Louise Hart and Martha Nell Smith's *Open Me Carefully: Emily Dickinson's Intimate Letters to Susan Huntington Dickinson* (1998).

Research tools include Joseph Duchac's *The Poems of Emily Dickinson: An Annotated Guide to Commentary Published in English, 1890–1977* (1979), and the continuation (published in 1993) covering 1978–89; Karen Dandurand's *Dickinson Scholarship: An Annotated Bibliography 1969–1985* (1988), and Willis J. Buckingham's *Emily Dickinson's Reception in the 1890s* (1989). Also useful are Jane Donahue Eberwein's *An Emily Dickinson Encyclopedia* (1998) and Sharon Leiter's *Critical Companion to Emily Dickinson: A Literary Reference to Her Life and Work* (2007).

The *Dickinson Electronic Archives* emilydickinson.org, directed by Smith and Marta Werner, offer access to Dickinson's manuscripts, out-of-print volumes about Dickinson, and never-before-published writings by various family members. Other valuable research tools include Martha Nell Smith and Lara Vetter's *Emily Dickinson's Correspondences: A Born-Digital Textual Inquiry* (2008), Amherst College's *Emily Dickinson Collection* acdc.amherst.edu/browse/collection/edu, and Harvard University Press and the Houghton Library's *Emily Dickinson Archive* www.edickinson.org.

Edited collections of critical essays provide an excellent introduction to Dickinson studies. See Judith Farr's *Emily Dickinson: A Collection of Critical Essays* (1996); Gudrun Grabher, Roland Hagenbüchle, and Cristanne Miller's *The Emily Dickinson Handbook* (1998, 2006); Wendy Martin's *The Cambridge Companion to Emily Dickinson* (2002); Vivian R. Pollak's *A Historical Guide to Emily Dickinson* (2004); Martha Nell Smith and Mary Loeffelholz's *A Companion to Emily Dickinson* (2008); Jane Donahue Eberwein and Cindy MacKenzie's *Reading Emily Dickinson's Letters: Critical Essays* (2009), Eliza Richards's *Emily Dickinson in Context* (2013), Jed Deppman, Marianne Noble, and Gary Lee Stonum's *Emily Dickinson and Philosophy* (2013), and Paul Crumbley and Eleanor Elson Heginbotham's *Dickinson's Fascicles: A Spectrum of Possibilities* (2014). Important studies include Paula Bennett's *Emily Dickinson: Woman Poet* (1990), Martha Nell Smith's *Rowing in Eden: Rereading Emily Dickinson* (1992), Sharon Cameron's *Choosing Not Choosing: Dickinson's Fascicles* (1993), Domhnall Mitchell's *Emily Dickinson: Monarch of Perception* (2000), Eleanor Elson Heginbotham's *Reading the Fascicles of Emily Dickinson* (2003), Virginia Jackson's *Dickinson's Misery: A Theory of Lyric Reading* (2005), Jed Deppman's *Trying to Think with Emily Dickinson* (2008), Cristanne Miller's *Reading in Time: Emily Dickinson in the Nineteenth Century* (2012), and Alexandra Socarides's *Dickinson Unbound: Paper, Process, Poetics* (2012). For a lively engagement with Dickinson's poetry from a celebrated close reader, see Helen Vendler's *Dickinson: Poems and Commentaries* (2010).

Theodore Dreiser

There is no complete edition of Dreiser's writings, although the University of Pennsylvania Press began such an edition, publishing volumes that included *Sister Carrie*, edited by John C. Berkey and Alice M. Winters (1981); *American Diaries: 1902–1926*, edited by Thomas P. Riggio (1983); and a restored edition of *Jennie Gerhardt*, edited by West (1992). Important resources include Robert H. Elias's three-volume *Letters of Theodore Dreiser* (1959); Donald Pizer's *Theodore Dreiser: A Selection of Uncollected Prose* (1977); *Theodore Dreiser: Interviews*, edited by Frederick E. Rusch, Pizer, and Riggio (2004); the Norton Critical Edition of *Sister Carrie*, edited by Pizer (2006); Pizer's *A Picture and a Criticism of Life: New Letters* (2008); Riggio's *Letters to Women: New Letters* (2009); and Jude Davies's edition of Dreiser's *Political Writings* (2011). The standard biographies are Jerome Loving's *The Last Titan: A Life of Theodore Dreiser* (2005) and Richard Lingeman's two-volume *Theodore Dreiser: At the Gates of the City, 1891–1907* (1986) and *Theodore Dreiser: An American Journey, 1908–1945* (1990).

Useful critical books include Richard Lehan, *Theodore Dreiser: His World and His Novels* (1974); Donald Pizer, *The Novels of Theodore Dreiser* (1976); Philip Gerber, *Theodore Dreiser Revisited* (1992); Louis J. Zanine, *Mechanism and Mysticism: The Influence of Science on the Thought and Work of Theodore Dreiser* (1993); Clare Virginia Eby, *Dreiser and Veblen: Saboteurs of the Status Quo* (1999); Pizer, *Literary Masters: Theodore Dreiser* (2000); and Mary Hricko, *The Genesis of the Chicago Renaissance: Theodore Dreiser, Langston Hughes, Richard Wright, and James T. Farrell* (2009). See also Miriam Gogol's edited collection *Theodore Dreiser: Beyond Naturalism* (1995), Yoshinobo Hakutani's edited *Theodore Dreiser and American Culture: New Readings* (2000), and Leonard Cassuto and Clare Eby's *The Cambridge Companion to Theodore Dreiser* (2004).

W. E. B. Du Bois

Herbert Aptheker's *The Complete Published Works of W. E. B. Du Bois* (1973–1986), in thirty-six volumes, offers a comprehensive collection of Du Bois's writings. Useful shorter collections include Philip S. Foner's *W. E. B. Du Bois Speaks: Speeches and Addresses* (1970); Eric Sundquist's *The Oxford W. E. B. Du Bois Reader* (1995); and the Library of America volume, *Du Bois: Writings*, edited by Nathan Huggins (1996). Herbert Aptheker edited the three-volume *The Correspondence of W. E. B. Du Bois* (1973–1978), the four-volume *Writings by W. E. B. Du Bois in Periodicals Edited by Others* (1982), *Selections from Phylon* (1980), and the two-volume *Selections from the Crisis* (1972). Other good collections are Phil Zuckerman's *The Social Theory of W. E. B. Du Bois* (2004), Amy Helene Kirschke's *Art in Crisis: W. E. B. Du Bois and the Art of the Crisis Magazine* (2006), Robert Wortham's *W. E. B. Du Bois and the Sociological Imagination: A Reader, 1897–1914*

(2009), and Eugene F. Provenzo and Edmund Kobina Abaka's *W. E. B. Du Bois on Africa* (2012). Important biographies of Du Bois include Arnold Rampersad's *The Art and Imagination of W. E. B. Du Bois* (1976); Jack B. Moore's *W. E. B. Du Bois* (1981); and David Levering Lewis's now standard two-volume *W. E. B. Du Bois: Biography of a Race, 1868–1919* (1993) and *W. E. B. Du Bois: The Fight for Equality and the American Century, 1919–1963* (2000).

The centennial publication of *The Souls of Black Folk* is addressed in Dolan Hubbard's edited collection, *The Souls of Black Folk: One Hundred Years Later* (2003), and in Chester Fontenot and Mary Alice Morgan's edited *W. E. B. Du Bois and Race: Essays Celebrating the Centennial Publication of The Souls of Black Folk* (2001). Critical studies of Du Bois's politics and art include Eric J. Sundquist's *To Wake the Nations: Race in the Making of American Literature* (1993), Adolph L. Reed Jr.'s *W. E. B. Du Bois and American Political Thought* (1995), Shannon Zamir's *W. E. B. Du Bois and American Thought, 1888–1903* (1995), Shawn Michelle Smith's *Photography on the Color Line: W. E. B. Du Bois, Race, and Visual Culture* (2004), Derek Alridge's *The Educational Thought of W. E. B. Du Bois: An Intellectual History* (2008), Jonathon S. Kahn's *Divine Discontent: The Religious Imagination of W. E. B. Du Bois* (2009), and Kwame Anthony Appiah's *Lines of Descent: W. E. B. Du Bois and the Emergence of Identity* (2014). There are also several useful collections of essays on Du Bois, including Mary Keller and Chester J. Fontenot's *Re-Cognizing W. E. B. Du Bois in the 21st Century: Essays on W. E. B. Du Bois* (2007), Susan Gillman and Alys Eve Weinbaum's *Next to the Color Line: Gender, Sexuality, and W. E. B. Du Bois* (2007), Shamoon Zamir's *The Cambridge Companion to W. E. B. Du Bois* (2008), and Amy Helene Kirschke and Phillip Luke Sinitiere's *W.E.B. Du Bois, the Crisis, and American History* (2014).

Paul Laurence Dunbar

Important editions include *The Collected Poetry of Paul Laurence Dunbar* (1993), edited by Joanne M. Braxton, and *The Complete Stories of Paul Laurence Dunbar* (2006), edited by Gene Andrew Jarrett. Also useful is a 1999 reprint of *The Life and Works of Paul Laurence Dunbar: Containing His Complete Poetical Works, His Best Short Stories, Numerous Anecdotes, and a Complete Biography*, originally compiled and introduced by William Dean Howells in 1907. Other useful editions include *In His Own Voice: The Dramatic and Other Uncollected Works of Paul Laurence Dunbar* (2002), edited by Herbert Woodward Martin and Ronald Primeau, with a foreword by Henry

Louis Gates Jr., and *The Collected Novels of Paul Laurence Dunbar* (2009), edited by Herbert Woodward Martin, Ronald Primeau, and Gene Andrew Jarrett. For a good biography, see Felton O. Best's *Crossing the Color Line: A Biography of Paul Laurence Dunbar, 1872–1906* (1996). Illuminating discussions of Dunbar's writings can be found in Gayle Jones's *Liberating Voices* (1991), Keith D. Leonard's *Fettered Genius: The African American Bardic Poet from Slavery to Civil Rights* (2006), and Jennifer C. James's *Freedom Bought with Blood* (2007). Gene Jarrett's *Deans and Truants: Race and Realism in African American Literature* (2007) has an excellent chapter on Dunbar and Howells. A special issue of *African American Review* (summer 2007) marked the centenary of Dunbar's death with a collection of excellent, up-to-date essays on Dunbar's life and art, and *We Wear the Mask: Paul Laurence Dunbar and the Politics of Representative Reality* (2010), edited by Willie J. Harrell Jr., provides another useful introduction to recent criticism.

Sui Sin Far (Edith Maud Eaton)
The only substantial collection of Sui Sin Far's writing is *"Mrs. Spring Fragrance" and Other Writings* (1995), edited by Amy Ling and Annette White-Parks. White-Parks has also published *Sui Sin Far/Edith Maude Eaton: A Literary Biography* (1995), with a chronological listing of her writings. Historical and critical work on Sui Sin Far includes Elaine Kim, *Asian American Literature: An Introduction to the Writings and Their Social Context* (1982); William F. Wu, *The Yellow Peril: Chinese Americans in American Fiction, 1850–1940* (1982); Mary Dearborn, *Pocahontas's Daughters: Gender and Ethnicity in American Culture* (1986); Amy Ling, *Between Worlds: Women Writers of Chinese Ancestry* (1990); and Susan Coultrap-McQuin, *Doing Literary Business: American Women Writers in the Nineteenth Century* (1990). Two books published in 2001 add to the scholarship on Sui Sin Far and her sister: Diana Birchall's *Onoto Watanna: The Story of Winnifred Eaton*, and Dominika Ferens's *Edith and Winnifred Eaton: Chinatown Missions and Japanese Romances*. Elizabeth Ammons's *Conflicting Stories* (1992) has a chapter on "Mrs. Spring Fragrance"; see also the chapters on Sui Sin Far in Molly Crumpton Winter's *American Narratives: Multiethnic Writing in the Age of Realism* (2007) and Mary Chapman's *Making Noise, Making News: Suffrage Print Culture and U.S. Modernism* (2014).

Mary E. Wilkins Freeman
The best collection of Freeman's work is *Selected Stories of Mary E. Wilkins Freeman* (1983), edited and introduced by Marjorie Pryse. Brent L. Kendrick edited *The Infant Sphinx: Collected Letters of Mary E. Wilkins Freeman* (1985); Charles Johanningsmeier edited a 2002 reprinting of Freeman's 1894 novel *Pembroke*; and Mary R. Reichard edited *A Mary Wilkins Freeman Reader* (1997). Perry D. Westbrook's *Mary Wilkins Freeman* (1988) provides a good introduction to Freeman's life and writings; Leah Blatt Glasser's *In a Closet Hidden: The Life and Work of Mary E. Wilkins Freeman* (1996) also contributes to biographical and critical scholarship. Other books with discussions of Freeman include Judith Fetterley and Marjorie Pryse's anthology *American Women Regionalists: 1850–1910* (1992), Reichard's *Mary Wilkins Freeman: A Study of the Short Story* (1998), Reichardt's *A Web of Relationship: Women in the Short Fiction of Mary Wilkins Freeman* (2007), Roxanne Harde's edited *Narratives of Community: Women's Short Story Sequences* (2007), and Jeffrey Weinstock's *Scare Tactics: Supernatural Fiction by American Women* (2008). See also the Mary E. Wilkins Freeman special issue of *American Transcendental Quarterly*, guest edited by Shirley Marchalonis (1999).

Charlotte Perkins Gilman
Editions of Gilman's writings include *The Living of Charlotte Perkins Gilman: An Autobiography*, edited by Ann J. Lane (1975); *Herland*, edited by Lane (1979); *The Charlotte Perkins Gilman Reader*, edited by Lane (1980); *Herland and Selected Stories by Charlotte Perkins Gilman*, edited by Barbara Solomon (1992); *Charlotte Perkins Gilman: Her Progress Toward Utopia with Selected Writings*, edited by Carol Farley Kessler (1994); *Women and Economics: A Study of the Economic Relation Between Men and Women as a Factor in Social Evolution*, edited by Michael Kimmel (1998); and *Charlotte Perkins Gilman's In This Our World and Uncollected Poems*, edited by Denise D. Knight and Gary Scharnhorst (2012). Gary Scharnhorst's *Charlotte Perkins Gilman: A Bibliography* (2003) is indispensable. Cynthia J. Davis's *Charlotte Perkins Gilman: A Biography* (2010) is likely to become the standard biography, though Ann J. Lane's *To Herland and Beyond: The Life and Work of Charlotte Perkins Gilman* (1990) remains quite useful.

Judith Allen's *The Feminism of Charlotte Perkins Gilman: Sexualities, Histories, Progressivism* (2009) is an excellent, comprehensive critical study of the development of Gilman's thought. Other major studies include Denise D. Knight's *Charlotte Perkins Gilman: A Study of the Short Fiction* (1997), Sheryl L. Meyering's *Charlotte Perkins Gilman: The Woman and*

Her Work (1989), Polly Wynn Allen's *Building Domestic Liberty: Charlotte Perkins Gilman's Architectural Feminism* (1988), and Gary Scharnhorst's *Charlotte Perkins Gilman* (1985). There are several insightful essay collections on Gilman: Davis and Knight edited *Charlotte Perkins Gilman and Her Contemporaries: Literary and Intellectual Contexts* (2004); Joanne B. Karpinski edited *Critical Essays on Charlotte Perkins Gilman* (1992); and Jennifer S. Tuttle and Carol Farley Kessler edited *Charlotte Perkins Gilman: New Texts, New Contexts* (2011). For good comparative studies, see Janet Beer's *Kate Chopin, Edith Wharton and Charlotte Perkins Gilman: Studies in Short Fiction* (2005), Beth Sutton-Ramspeck's *Raising the Dust: The Literary Housekeeping of Mary Ward, Sarah Grand, and Charlotte Perkins Gilman* (2004), and Alys Eve Weinbaum's *Wayward Reproductions: Genealogies of Race and Nation in Transatlantic Modern Thought* (2004).

Critical casebooks on "The Yellow Wall-Paper" include Catherine Golden's *The Captive Imagination: A Casebook on "The Yellow Wallpaper"* (1991); Julie Bates Dock's *The Legend of "The Yellow Wallpaper": A Documentary Casebook* (1998); and Dock's *Charlotte Perkins Gilman's "The Yellow Wall-Paper" and the History of Its Publication and Reception: A Critical Edition and Documentary Casebook* (1998).

Bret Harte
The most complete collection is *The Works of Bret Harte* in twenty-five volumes (1914). Harte's poetry may be found in *The Complete Poetical Works of Bret Harte* (1899). Geoffrey Bret Harte edited *The Letters of Bret Harte* (1926); *Selected Letters of Bret Harte* appeared in 1997, edited by Gary Scharnhorst and Robert L. Gale. Scharnhorst also edited Bret Harte's *California* (1990) and coedited (with Lawrence I. Berkove) *The Old West in the Old World: Lost Plays by Bret Harte and Sam Davis* (2006). Scharnhorst's critical biography, *Bret Harte: Opening the American Literary West* (2000), anlayzes Harte's life, career, and reception; Axel Nissen's biography, *Bret Harte: Prince and Pauper* (2000), should also be consulted. The best bibliography is Scharnhorst's *Bret Harte: A Bibliography* (1995). Provocative discussions of Harte can be found in Chis Packard's *Queer Cowboys and Other Erotic Male Friendships in Nineteenth-Century American Literature* (2005) and Joanna Levin's *Bohemia in America, 1858–1920* (2010). Though he is not mentioned in the title, Harte is a central figure in Ben Tarnoff's account of the San Francisco literary scene, *The Bohemians: Mark Twain and the San Francisco Writers Who Reinvented American Literature* (2014).

Pauline E. Hopkins
Editions of Hopkins's works include Ira Dworkin's *Daughter of the Revolution: The Major Nonfiction Works of Pauline E. Hopkins* (2006), which collects essays, speeches, and letters; Richard Yarborough's edition of *Contending Forces: A Romance Illustrative of Negro Life North and South* (1991); and Hazel V. Carby's *The Magazine Novels of Pauline Hopkins* (1990), which reprints *Hagar's Daughter, Winona,* and *Of One Blood.* An excellent biography is Lois Brown's *Pauline Elizabeth Hopkins: Black Daughter of the Revolution* (2008); see also Hanna Wallinger's *Pauline E. Hopkins: A Literary Biography* (2005). Good critical work on Hopkins can be found in Carby's *Reconstructing Womanhood: The Emergence of the Afro-American Woman Novelist* (1987), Claudia Tate's *Domestic Allegories of Political Desire* (1992), Susan Gilman's *Blood Talk: American Race Melodrama and the Culture of the Occult* (2003), Daphne Brooks's *Bodies in Dissent: Spectacular Performances of Race and Freedom, 1850–1910* (2006), Gretchen Murphy's *Shadowing the White Man's Burden: U.S. Imperialism and the Problem of the Color Line* (2010), Alisha R. Knight's *Pauline Hopkins and the American Dream: An African American Writer's (Re)visionary Gospel of Success* (2012), and Kimberly Snyder Manganelli's *Transatlantic Spectacles of Race: The Tragic Mulatta and the Tragic Muse* (2012).

William Dean Howells
Indiana University Press's *A Selected Edition of W. D. Howells* (1968–1993), comprised of over thirty volumes, is the standard edition of his works. Howells's letters can be found in *The Correspondence of Samuel L. Clemens and William Dean Howells, 1972–1910* (1960), edited by Henry Nash Smith and William M. Gibson; *Life in Letters of William Dean Howells* (1928), edited by his daughter Mildred Howells; and the *John Hay-Howells Letters* (1980), edited by George Monteiro and Brenda Murphy. Ruth Bardon's *Selected Short Stories of William Dean Howells* was published in 1997. Other collections include *Interviews with William Dean Howells* (1973), compiled by Ulrich Halfmann; John W. Crowley's *The Mask of Fiction: Essays of W. D. Howells* (1989); *The Early Prose Writings of William Dean Howells* (1990), edited by Thomas Wortham; and *Staging Howells: Plays and Correspondence* (1994), edited by Lawrence Barrett, George Arms, Mary Beth Whidden, and Gary Scharnhorst. The Library of America also published two collections of Howells's novels, edited by Edwin Cady and Don Cook, in 1982 and 1989.

The important early biographies of Howells are Edwin H. Cady's *The Road to Realism: The*

Early Years, 1837–1885 (1956) and The Realist at War: The Mature Years, 1885–1920 (1958); Van Wyck Brooks's Howells: His Life and Work (1959); and Kenneth S Lynn's William Dean Howells: An American Life (1971). More recently, John W. Crowley published The Dean of American Letters: The Late Career of William Dean Howells (2005) and Susan Goodman and Carl Dawson brought out William Dean Howells: A Writer's Life (2005). Useful critical studies of Howells's writings include Crowley's The Black Heart's Truth: The Early Career of W. D. Howells (1985), Amy Kaplan's The Social Construction of American Realism (1988), Edwin H. Cady and Louis Budd's collection On Howells: The Best Articles from American Literature (1993), Gregory J. Stratman's Speaking for Howells: Charting the Dean's Career through the Language of His Characters (2001), Michael A. Elliott's The Culture Concept: Race, Writing, and Difference in the Age of Realism (2002), Susan Goodman's American Novelists and Manners, 1880–1940 (2003), Rob Davidson's The Master and the Dean: The Literary Criticism of Henry James and William Dean Howells (2005), and Dohra Ahmad's Landscapes of Hope: Anti-Colonial Utopianism in America (2009). Howells also figures centrally in Susan Goodman's Republic of Words: The Atlantic Monthly and Its Writers, 1857–1925 (2011).

Henry James

The Novels and Tales of Henry James (The New York Edition), in twenty-six volumes, originally published in 1907–17, was reissued 1962–65. Other collections of James's diverse writings are available in R. P. Blackmur's The Art of the Novel (1935) (which collects James's prefaces to the works in the New York Edition), F. O. Matthiessen and Kenneth B. Murdoch's The Notebooks of Henry James (1947), Leon Edel's The Complete Plays of Henry James (1949), F. W. Dupee's edition of the three volumes of Henry James: Autobiography (1956), Morris Shapiro's Selected Literary Criticism (1963), and Pierre A. Walker's Henry James on Culture: Collected Essays on Politics and the American Social Scene (1999). James's novels, short stories, and literary essays are collected in multiple volumes of the Library of America series. Tales of Henry James (2005) was published as a Norton Critical Edition, edited by Christof Wegelin and Henry B. Wonham, and offers a useful introduction to James's short fiction. Leon Edel is the editor of the five-volume The Letters of Henry James published between 1974 and 1984. Philip Horne has published Henry James: A Life in Letters (1999), with half of the nearly 300 selections previously unpublished, and Susan E. Gunter and Steven H. Jobe have

edited Dearly Beloved Friends: Henry James's Letters to Younger Men (2001), which contains a number of previously unpublished letters. Beginning in 2006, the University of Nebraska Press began publishing The Complete Letters of Henry James, edited by Pierre A. Walker, Gred Zacharias, and Alfred Habegger. Two helpful bibliographies are A Bibliography of Henry James (1999), edited by Edel, Dan H. Laurence, and James Rambeau; and Judith E. Funston's Henry James: A Reference Guide, 1975–1987 (1991). Lawrence Raw's Adapting Henry James to the Screen: Gender, Fiction and Film (2006) offers a detailed history of film adaptations of James's works, twenty-eight in all. John R. Bradley edited Henry James on Stage and Screen (2000), and Susan M. Griffin edited Henry James Goes to the Movies (2001).

Leon Edel's five-volume opus Henry James (1953–72) remains the standard biography. Sheldon N. Novick published Henry James: The Mature Master (2007) as a follow-up to his Henry James: The Young Master (1996), recasting James as an active and engaged artist rather than a lonely observer of life. Fred Kaplan's Henry James: The Imagination of Genius, A Biography (1999) relies almost exclusively on the letters and diaries of James and his associates. Notable books about the entire James family include Philip Fisher's House of Wits (2008), R. W. B. Lewis's The Jameses (1993), and F. O. Matthiessen's The James Family (1947). Other biographical studies include Edwin Sill Fussell's The Catholic Side of Henry James (1993), Kenneth Graham's Henry James: A Literary Life (1995), Carol Holly's Intensely Family: The Inheritance of Family Shame and the Autobiographies of Henry James (1995), and Lyndall Gordon's A Private Life of Henry James: Two Women and His Art (1999), which looks at James's relationships with his cousin Minnie Temple and friend Constance Fenimore Woolson. James's later career is illuminated by Lyall H. Powers's edition of Theodora Bosanquet's memoir, Henry James at Work (2006), originally published in 1924. Among the best of the immense number of critical studies of James are Ruth Bernard Yeazell's Language and Knowledge in the Late Novels of Henry James (1976), Charles Robert Anderson's Person, Place, and Thing in Henry James's Novels (1977), Daniel Mark Fogel's Henry James and the Structure of the Romantic Imagination (1981), John Carlos Rowe's The Theoretical Dimensions of Henry James (1984), Sharon Cameron's Thinking in Henry James (1989), Alfred Habegger's Henry James and the "Woman Business" (1989), Millicent Bell's Meaning in Henry James (1991), Ross Posnock's The Trial of Curiosity: Henry James, William James, and the Challenge of Modernity (1991), Sara Blair's Henry James and the

Writing of Race and Nation (1996), Wendy Graham's *Henry James's Thwarted Love* (1999), Eric Haralson's *Henry James and Queer Modernity* (2003), Leland Person's *Henry James and the Suspense of Masculinity* (2003), J. Hillis Miller's *Literature As Conduct: Speech Acts in Henry James* (2005), Hazel Hutchison's *Seeing and Believing: Henry James and the Spiritual World* (2006), Elaine Pigeon's *Queer Impressions: Henry James's Art of Fiction* (2006), Victoria Coulson's *Henry James, Women and Realism* (2007), Kendall Johnson's *Henry James and the Visual* (2007), Amy Tucker's *The Illustration of the Master: Henry James and the Magazine Revolution* (2010), Michael Gorra's *Portrait of a Novel: Henry James and the Making of an American Masterpiece* (2012), and Miranda El-Rayess's *Henry James and the Culture of Consumption* (2014).

Given the volume of James scholarship, novice scholars may want to begin with one of the many available essay collections. Particularly valuable edited collections include Graham Clark's *Henry James: Critical Assessments* (1991), Daniel Mark Fogel's *A Companion to Henry James Studies* (1993), Peter Rawlings's *Critical Essays on Henry James* (1993), Jonathan Freedman's *The Cambridge Companion to Henry James* (1998), Joseph Dewey's *The Finer Thread, The Tighter Weave: New Essays on the Short Fiction* (2001), Peggy McCormack's *Questioning the Master: Gender and Sexuality in Henry James's Writings* (2000), Greg Zacharias's *A Companion to Henry James* (2008), and John Carlos Rowe and Eric L. Haralson's *Historical Guide to Henry James* (2012)

Sarah Orne Jewett

Jewett's *Stories and Tales* were published in seven volumes in 1910; a selection, *The Best Stories of Sarah Orne Jewett* (1925), was edited in two volumes with a foreword by Willa Cather. Richard Cary edited *The Uncollected Short Stories of Sarah Orne Jewett* (1971), as well as *Sarah Orne Jewett: Letters* (1967). The Library of America's edition of Jewett's *Novels and Stories* (1994), edited by Michael Davitt Bell, reprints three novels and thirty stories. Paula Blanchard's *Sarah Orne Jewett: Her World and Her Work* (2002) is an informative biography; a good introductory study is Josephine Donovan's *Sarah Orne Jewett* (1980). Perry D. Westbrook's *Acres of Flint: Sarah Orne Jewett and Her Contemporaries* (1981), Gwen L. Nagel's *Critical Essays on Sarah Orne Jewett* (1984), Louis A. Renza's *"A White Heron" and the Question of Minor Literature* (1985), and Sarah Way Sherman's *Sarah Orne Jewett: An American Persephone* (1989) are valuable. For more recent critical work, see June Howard's essay collection, *New*

Essays on The Country of the Pointed Firs (1993), Richard Brodhead's *Cultures of Letters: Scenes of Reading and Writing in Nineteenth-Century America* (1993), Joseph Church's *Transcendent Daughters in Jewett's Country of the Pointed Firs* (1995), Margaret Roman's *Sarah Orne Jewett: Reconstructing Gender* (1997), Karen L. Kilcup and Thomas S. Edwards's *Jewett and Her Contemporaries: Reshaping the Canon* (1999), Judith Fetterley and Marjorie Pryse's *Writing Out of Place: Regionalism, Women, and American Literary Culture* (2003), Paul R. Petrie's *Conscience and Purpose: Fiction and Social Consciousness in Howells, Jewett, Chesnutt, and Cather* (2005), and Mitchell Robert Breitwieser's *National Melancholy: Mourning and Opportunity in Classic American Literature* (2007).

Emma Lazarus

Mary Lazarus and Annie Lazarus, Emma Lazarus's sisters, edited the two-volume *The Poems of Emma Lazarus* (1888), which includes a biographical sketch. In 1939 Ralph L. Rusk edited *Letters to Emma Lazarus in the Columbia University Library*. Morris U. Schappes edited *The Letters of Emma Lazarus, 1868–1885* (1949) and *Emma Lazarus: Selections from Her Poetry and Prose* (1967). Newer editions include the Library of America's *Emma Lazarus: Selected Poems* (2005), edited by John Hollander; Bette Roth Young's *Emma Lazarus: In Her World* (1995), a collection of unpublished letters to friends and literary figures; and Gregory Eiselein's *Emma Lazarus: Selected Poems and Other Writings* (2002). Esther Schor's fine biography *Emma Lazarus* (2006) is now the standard account of her life and work. For discussions of Lazarus's writings, see also Ranen Omer-Sherman's *Diaspora and Zionism in Jewish American Literature* (2002), Meredith McGill's *The Traffic in Poems: Nineteenth-Century Poetry and Transatlantic Exchange* (2008), and Daniel Morris's *Lyric Encounters: Essays on American Poetry from Lazarus and Frost to Ortiz Cofer and Alexie* (2013).

Jack London

Important editions of London's writings include the three-volume *Letters of Jack London* (1988) and the three-volume *Complete Short Stories of Jack London* (1993), both edited by Earle Labor, Robert C. Leitz III, and I. Milo Shepard. Editions of material otherwise difficult to track down are *Jack London Reports* (1970; essays and newspaper articles), edited by King Hendricks and Irving Shepard; *No Mentor but Myself: Jack London on Writers and Writing* (1999), edited by Dale L. Walker and Jeanne Campbell Reesman; the Library of America *Jack London:*

Novels and Stories (1982), edited by Donald Pizer; and The Portable Jack London (1994), edited by Earle Labor. Jonah Raskin's The Radical Jack London: Writings on War and Revolution (2008) offers a selection of London's political writings. The Road (Subterranean Lives) (2006), edited by Todd Depastino, collects nine of London's essays from his days as a hobo, many first published in Cosmopolitan during 1907–8. Dan Wichlan edited Jack London: The Unpublished and Uncollected Articles and Essays and The Complete Poetry of Jack London, both published in 2008. Bibliographical work on London has languished since the publication of Joan Sherman's Jack London: A Reference Guide (1977) and Hensley C. Woodbridge, John London, and George H. Tweney's Jack London: A Bibliography (1966). The Jack London Online Collection is managed by Roy Tennant and Clarice Stasz at Sonoma State University: www .london.sonoma.edu.

Earle Labor's comprehensive biography Jack London: An American Life (2013) is an excellent guide to London's life, and Jay Williams has published the first volume of a more exhaustive, two-volume literary biography— Author Under Sail: The Imagination of Jack London, 1893–1902 (2014)—that is likely to become the standard account of London's writing life. In addition, Jean Campbell Reesman's critical biography of London emphasizes his racial ambivalences. Critical books and collections of essays include Jacqueline Tavernier-Courbin's Critical Essays on Jack London (1983), Charles N. Watson Jr.'s The Novels of Jack London: A Reappraisal (1983), Earle Labor and Jeanne Campbell Reesman's Jack London: Revised Edition (1994), Susan Nuernberg's The Critical Response to Jack London (1995), Leonard Cassuto and Reesman's edited collection Rereading Jack London (1996), Jonathan Auerbach's Male Call: Becoming Jack London (1996), Reesman's Jack London: A Study of the Short Fiction (1998), Sara S. Hodson and Reesman's edited collection Jack London: One Hundred Years a Writer (2002), Gina Rossetti's Imagining the Primitive in Naturalist and Modernist Literature (2006), Daniel Métraux's The Asian Writings of Jack London (2010), and Michael Lundblad's The Birth of a Jungle: Animality in Progressive-Era U.S. Literature and Culture (2013).

Mark Twain

As the center for authoritative editions of his writings, The Mark Twain Papers at the University of California at Berkeley has been producing annotated volumes since the 1960s. Their editions to date, including Adventures of Huckleberry Finn (2003), Mysterious Stranger Manuscripts (1969), A Connecticut Yankee in King Arthur's Court (1983), Roughing It (1996), and several volumes of Mark Twain's Letters and his Notebooks and Journals, are scholarly landmarks. For Twain books that have yet to receive this treatment, however, a good recourse is the series The Oxford Mark Twain (1997), edited by Shelley Fisher Fishkin. Essentially facsimiles of all first editions of Twain works published in his lifetime or soon after, the series is important because in the years when Clemens was head of his own publishing company, he could control everything that was produced with "Mark Twain" on the cover—including the numerous illustrations in his most famous books. These facsimiles show what American readers encountered when these books were fresh on the market, and help readers understand how Mark Twain included printed images in the creative process.

There are three encyclopedic recent guides to Twain's life and works: Gregg Camfield's The Oxford Companion to Mark Twain (2003), R. Kent Rasmussen's two-volume Critical Companion to Mark Twain: A Literary Reference to His Life and Work (2007), and Rasmussen's shorter and earlier Mark Twain: A to Z (1995). Also worth consulting are Forrest G. Robinson's The Cambridge Companion to Mark Twain (1995) and Peter Messent and Louis J. Budd's A Companion to Mark Twain (2005). Much briefer introductions to Twain's work and his literary legacy include Peter Messent's The Cambridge Introduction to Mark Twain (2007) and Stephen Railton's Mark Twain: A Short Introduction (2004).

Because the life of Samuel Clemens has become an American novel and legend in its own right, biographies abound; the 2010 centenary of his death brought a fresh wave, including Jerome Loving's Mark Twain: The Adventures of Samuel Clemens (2010) and Michael Shelden's Mark Twain: Man in White (2010). Also recent and well received is Ron Powers's Mark Twain: A Life (2005). These comprehensive narratives make use of journals and letters, and also a welter of previous retellings of the Twain story, including Justin Kaplan's still-reliable Mr. Clemens and Mark Twain (1966) and Albert Bigelow Paine's very early, extensive, but doubtfully authoritative Mark Twain: A Biography (1912). Other accounts of Clemens center on the Hannibal boyhood, the adventures in the West, the episodes of European and worldwide travel, and life on the lecture circuit; lately, much attention has concentrated on the final decade of his life. Recent revelations and opinions about this period include Laura Skandera Trombley's Mark Twain's Other Woman: The Hidden Story of His Final Years (2010) and Karen Lystra's Dangerous Intimacy: The Untold Story of Mark

Twain's Final Years (2006). Both of these build upon Hamlin Hill's *Mark Twain: God's Fool* (1973) and Van Wyck Brooks's *The Ordeal of Mark Twain* (1920), decisive works in transforming an author into an archetypal "wounded" American celebrity. Twain's anti-imperialism at the turn of the century has also recently engaged critics. *Following the Equator and Anti-Imperialist Essays*, edited by Fred Kaplan (1996), provides a good collection of Twain's works, and Hsuan L. Hsu's offers a critical analysis in *Sitting in Darkness: Mark Twain's Asia and Comparative Racialization* (2015).

Other biographical studies emphasize the imaginative experience, the business realities, and the cultural contexts of Mark Twain in his most productive years; notable among these are Victor Doyno's *Writing Huck Finn: Mark Twain's Creative Process* (1993), Bruce Michelson's *Printer's Devil: Mark Twain and the American Publishing Revolution* (2006), Roy Morris Jr.'s *Lighting Out for the Territory: How Samuel Clemens Headed West and Became Mark Twain* (2010), Morris's *American Vandal: Mark Twain Abroad* (2015), and Ben Tarnoff's *The Bohemians: Mark Twain and the San Francisco Writers Who Reinvented American Literature* (2014).

Louis J. Budd's *Our Mark Twain: The Making of His Public Personality* (1983) describes how Twain's reputation expanded, with embellishments, in the opening decades of the twentieth century. See also Shelley Fisher Fishkin's recent Library of America volume on the international response to Twain: *The Mark Twain Anthology: Great Writers on His Life and Works* (2010). The most influential studies of Twain's wit and humor include James M. Cox's *Mark Twain: The Fate of Humor* (1966), Bruce Michelson's *Mark Twain on the Loose: A Comic Writer and the American Self* (1995), Linda Morris's *Gender Play in Mark Twain: Cross-Dressing and Transgression* (2007), and Judith Yaross Lee's *Twain's Brand: Humor in Contemporary American Culture* (2012). For controversies about *Huckleberry Finn* as a "great" American novel, see Tom Quirk's *Coming to Grips with Huckleberry Finn* (1993), Shelley Fisher Fishkin's *Lighting Out for the Territory: Reflections on Mark Twain and American Culture* (1996), Jonathan Arac's *Huckleberry Finn as Idol and Target* (1997), and Andrew Levy's *Huck Finn's America: Mark Twain and the Era That Shaped His Masterpiece* (2015). *The Autobiography of Mark Twain* was published in three volumes from 2010 to 2015, becoming a national best seller.

Booker T. Washington
Louis R. Harlan edited *The Booker T. Washington Papers* in fourteen volumes (1972–89).

William L. Andrews edited a Norton Critical Edition of *Up from Slavery* (1996). Louis R. Harlan's two-volume biography, *Booker T. Washington: The Making of a Black Leader, 1865–1901* (1972) and *Booker T. Washington: The Wizard of Tuskegee, 1901–1915* (1983), is standard, but it should be supplemented by Michael Rudelph West's *The Education of Booker T. Washington: American Democracy and the Idea of Race Relations* (2006), Michael Bieze's *Booker T. Washington and the Art of Self-Representation* (2008), and Robert J. Norell's *Up from History: The Life of Booker T. Washington* (2009). Robert B. Stepto's chapter on Washington's *Up from Slavery*, in *Behind the Veil: A Study of Afro-American Narrative* (1979), is a classic analysis, as is James M. Cox's "Autobiography and Washington" in his *Recovering Lost Ground: Essays in American Autobiography* (1989). Also worth consulting are Kevern Verney's *The Art of the Possible: Booker T. Washington and Black Leadership in the United States, 1881–1925* (2001); Houston A. Baker Jr.'s *Turning South Again: Re-Thinking Modernism / Re-Reading Booker T.* (2001); Wilson Jeremiah Moses's *Creative Conflict in African American Thought: Frederick Douglass, Alexander Crummell, Booker T. Washington, W. E. B. Du Bois, and Marcus Garvey* (2005); Rebecca Carroll's edited collection *Uncle Tom or New Negro?: African Americans Reflect on Booker T. Washington and Up from Slavery 100 Years Later* (2006); and Michael Bieze and Marybeth Gasman's edited collection of essays, *Booker T. Washington Rediscovered* (2012).

Edith Wharton
R. W. B. Lewis edited *The Collected Short Stories of Edith Wharton* (1988) in two volumes. Frederick Wegener edited *Edith Wharton: The Uncollected Critical Writings* (1991), and Laura Rattray edited *The Unpublished Writings of Edith Wharton* (2009). The Library of America published several volumes of Wharton's works (1986, 1990, 2001), including novels, novellas, stories, and poems. *The Correspondence of Edith Wharton and Macmillan, 1901–1930* (2007), edited by Shafquat Towheed, helps to illuminate Wharton's relationship with her publisher. R. W. B. Lewis's groundbreaking *Edith Wharton: A Biography* appeared in 1975, and Cynthia Griffin Wolff's important critical biographical study, *A Feast of Words: The Triumph of Edith Wharton*, followed in 1977. However, Hermione Lee's deft and insightful *Edith Wharton* (2007) is likely to be the standard biography of Wharton for many years. George Ramsden's *Edith Wharton's Library: A Catalogue* (1999) inventories about half of her library—more than 2,200 books. Janet Beer and Elizabeth Nolan's *Edith Wharton*

(2006) is a reference work about contemporary views of the author. On reception, see also James W. Tuttleton, Kristin O. Lauer, and Margaret P. Murray's *Edith Wharton: The Contemporary Reviews* (1992) and Helen Killoran's *The Critical Reception of Edith Wharton* (2001).

Book-length critical studies include Elizabeth Ammons's *Edith Wharton's Argument with America* (1980), Susan Goodman's *Edith Wharton's Women* (1990), Goodman's *Edith Wharton's Inner Circle* (1994), Donna Campbell's *Resisting Regionalism: Gender and Naturalism in American Fiction, 1885–1915* (1997), Carol Singley's *Edith Wharton: Matters of Mind and Spirit* (1998), Hildegard Hoeller's *Edith Wharton's Dialogue with Realism and Sentimental Fiction* (2000), Jill M. Kress's *The Figure of Consciousness: William James, Henry James, and Edith Wharton* (2002), Julie Olin-Ammentorp, *Edith Wharton's Writings from the Great War* (2004), Emily J. Orlando's *Edith Wharton and the Visual Arts* (2007), Jennifer Haytock's *Edith Wharton and the Conversations of Literary Modernism* (2008), Jennie A. Kassanoff's *Edith Wharton and the Politics of Race* (2008), Judith P. Saunders's *Reading Edith Wharton through a Darwinian Lens: Evolutionary Biological Issues in Her Fiction* (2009), and Pamela Knight's *The Cambridge Introduction to Edith Wharton* (2009). A useful reference work is Sarah Bird Wright and Clare Colquitt's *Edith Wharton A to Z* (1998). For wide-ranging collections of essays, see Alfred Bendixen and Annette Zilversmit's *Edith Wharton: New Critical Essays* (1992), Millicent Bell's *The Cambridge Companion to Edith Wharton* (1995), Colquitt, Goodman, and Candace Waid's *A Forward Glance: New Essays on Edith Wharton* (1999), Singley's *Historical Guide to Edith Wharton* (2003), and Laura Rattray's *Edith Wharton in Context* (2012).

Walt Whitman
The study of Whitman has been revolutionized by the *Walt Whitman Hypertext Archive* www.whitmanarchive.org, directed by Kenneth M. Price and Ed Folsom. Before going to the printed sources listed below, students should explore this huge and superbly organized hypertext archive, which includes a lengthy and reliable biographical essay by Folsom and Price, all the known contemporary reviews, all the known photographs, the various editions of *Leaves of Grass* and other of Whitman's writings, and a current bibliography of scholarship and criticism.

The Collected Writings of Walt Whitman was under the general editorship of Gay Wilson Allen; part of this edition is *Walt Whitman: The Correspondence* (1961–69), a six-volume set with two supplements (1990–

91), edited by Edwin H. Miller. Essential, in three volumes, is *"Leaves of Grass": A Textual Variorum of the Printed Poems* (1980), edited by Sculley Bradley, Harold W. Blodgett, Arthur Golden, and William White. Michael Moon's Norton Critical Edition of *Leaves of Grass* (2002) includes discussion of textual variants and compositional development. Important documents can be found in *Notebooks and Unpublished Prose Manuscripts* (1984), edited by Edward F. Grier, and *Walt Whitman's Selected Journalism* (2014), edited by Douglas A. Noverr and Jason Stacy. For Whitman's temperance novel, *Franklin Evans; or, The Inebriate: A Tale of the Times* (1842), see Christopher Castiglia and Glenn Hendler's informative edition (2007); and Ed Folsom has edited a new facsimile edition (2010) of Whitman's 1870 *Democratic Vistas*. For useful documentary materials, see Joel Myerson's *Whitman in His Own Time* (1991, rev. 2000), and Gary Schmidgall's *Intimate with Walt: Selections from Whitman's Conversations with Horace Traubel, 1888–1892* (2001).

Important biographies include Gay Wilson Allen's *The Solitary Singer* (1967). It should be supplemented by Roger Asselineau's *The Evolution of Walt Whitman* (1960, 1962; reissued 1999), the first biography to deal openly with Whitman's sexuality; Justin Kaplan's *Walt Whitman: A Life* (1980); David S. Reynolds's *Walt Whitman's America: A Cultural Biography* (1995); Gary Schmidgall's *Walt Whitman: A Gay Life* (1998); Jerome Loving's *Walt Whitman: The Song of Himself* (1999); and Ed Folsom and Kenneth M. Price's *Re-scripting Walt Whitman: An Introduction to His Life and Work* (2005). For close attention to the Civil War period, see Roy Morris Jr.'s *The Better Angel: Walt Whitman in the Civil War* (2000), and Ted Genoways's *Walt Whitman and the Civil War* (2009); and for a good general introduction, see M. Jimmie Killingsworth's *The Cambridge Introduction to Walt Whitman* (2007). Useful resources are the 1998 *Walt Whitman: An Encyclopedia*, edited by J. R. LeMaster and Donald D. Kummings, and Charles M. Oliver's *Critical Companion to Walt Whitman* (2006).

On Whitman's critical reception, see Graham Clarke's four-volume *Walt Whitman: Critical Assessments* (1996) and Kenneth M. Price's *Walt Whitman: The Contemporary Reviews* (1996). Valuable collections of critical essays include Betsy Erkkila and Jay Grossman's *Breaking Bounds: Whitman and American Cultural Studies* (1996), David S. Reynolds's *A Historical Guide to Walt Whitman* (2000), Donald D. Kummings's *A Companion to Walt Whitman* (2006), Susan Belasco, Ed Folsom, and Kenneth M. Price's *Leaves of Grass: The Sesquicentennial Essays* (2007), and David

Haven Blake and Michael Robertson's *Walt Whitman: Where the Future Becomes Present* (2008); John Evan Seery's *A Political Companion to Walt Whitman* (2011); Joanna Levin and Edward Whitley's *Whitman among the Bohemians* (2014); and Ivy G. Wilson's *Whitman Noir: Black America and the Good Gray Poet* (2014). Important critical works include Betsy Erkkila's *Whitman the Political Poet* (1989), Kenneth M. Price's *Whitman and Tradition* (1990), Michael Moon's *Disseminating Whitman: Revision and Corporeality in "Leaves of Grass"* (1991), Ezra Greenspan's *Walt Whitman and the American Reader* (1991), Ed Folsom's *Walt Whitman's Native Representations* (1994), Martin Klammer's *Whitman, Slavery, and the Emergence of "Leaves of Grass"* (1995), Vivian R. Pollack's *The Erotic Whitman* (2000), Jay Grossman's *Reconstituting the American Renaissance: Emerson, Whitman, and the Poetics of Representation* (2003), M. Wynn Thomas's *Transatlantic Connections: Whitman U.S., Whitman U.K.* (2005), David Haven Blake's *Walt Whitman and the Culture of American Celebrity* (2006), Michael Robertson's *Worshipping Whitman: The Whitman Disciples* (2008), Edward Whitley's *American Bards: Walt Whitman and Other Unlikely Candidates for National Poet* (2010); Martin T. Buinicki's *Walt Whitman's Reconstruction: Poetry and Publishing Between Memory and History* (2011), and Gary Schmidgall's *Containing Mul-*

titudes: Walt Whitman and the British Literary Tradition (2014).

Zitkala-Ša (Gertrude Simmons Bonnin)

Dexter Fisher's 1986 edition of Zitkala-Ša's *American Indian Stories* (1921) includes an expert and insightful introduction to this collection of autobiography, fiction, and nonfiction prose. P. Jane Hafen helpfully edited a number of Zitkala-Ša's works in *Dreams and Thunder: Stories, Poems and "The Sun Dance Opera"* (2001), and Cathy Davidson and Ada Norris edited a one-volume collection for Penguin Books, *American Indian Stories, Legends, and Other Writings* (2003), which has a useful introduction and set of textual notes. Dexter Fisher's *Zitkala-Ša: The Evolution of a Writer* (1979) and Dorothea M. Susag's *Zitkala-Ša (Gertrude Simmons Bonnin): A Power(full) Literary Voice* (1993) are among the few critical and biographical studies that focus exclusively on Zitkala-Ša. For discussions of her writing in a variety of cultural contexts, see Michael Elliott's *The Culture Concept: Writing, Difference, and the Age of Realism* (2002), Molly Crumpton Winter's *American Narratives: Multiethnic Writing in the Age of Realism* (2007), and Mark Rifkin's *When Did Indians Become Straight? Kinship, the History of Sexuality, and Native Sovereignty* (2011).

AMERICAN LITERATURE 1914–1945

Reference Works and Histories

Chapters on the period may be consulted in the *Columbia Literary History of the United States* (1988), general editor Emory Elliott; the *Columbia History of the American Novel* (1991), general editor Emory Elliot; the *Columbia History of American Poetry* (1993), edited by Jay Parini; *The History of Southern Literature* (1985), edited by Louis D. Rubin et al.; A. LaVonne Brown Ruoff's *American Indian Literature* (1990); and *The Cambridge History of American Poetry* (2015), edited by Alfred Bendixen and Stephen Burt. Relevant volumes in the eight-volume *Cambridge History of American Literature* are volume 5, *Poetry and Criticism, 1900–1950* (2003), edited by Sacvan Bercovitch, and volume 6, *Prose Writing, 1910–1950* (2002), edited by Sacvan Bercovitch and Cyrus R. Patell. Reference works dedicated to the period and some of its important movements include *A Companion to Modernist Literature and Culture*, edited by David Bradshaw and Kevin J. H. Dettmar (2006); *The Cambridge Companion to American Modernism* (2005), edited by Walter Kalaidjian; *The Cambridge Companion to the Harlem Renaissance*, edited by George Hutchinson (2007); *A Companion to Twentieth-Century Poetry*, edited by Neil Roberts (2001); *A Companion to Twentieth-Century American Fiction*, edited by David

Seed (2010); *The Cambridge Companion to Modernist Poetry*, edited by Alex Davis and Lee M. Jenkins (2007); *A Companion to Twentieth-Century American Drama* (2005), edited by David Krasner; *A Companion to the Modern American Novel 1900–1950* (2009), edited by John T. Matthews; *The Oxford Critical and Culture History of Modernist Magazines*, Volume 2, *North America, 1894–1960* (2012), edited by Peter Brooker and Andrew Thacker; *The Cambridge Companion to the Literature of the American South* (2013), edited by Sharon Monteith; *A Companion to Modernist Poetry* (2014), edited by David E. Chinitz and Gail McDonald; *A Companion to the Harlem Renaissance* (2015), edited by Cherene Sherrard-Johnson; and *The Cambridge Companion to Modern American Poetry* (2015), edited by Kalaidjian.

For early histories of the period authored by critics who were active in the rise of modernism, see Malcolm Cowley's *Exile's Return* (1951), *After the Genteel Tradition: American Writers, 1910–1930* (1964), and *A Second Flowering: Works and Days of the Lost Generation* (1973); and Edmund Wilson's *The Shores of Light: A Literary Chronicle of the Twenties and Thirties* (1952). Other important early surveys include Alfred Kazin's *On Native Grounds: An Interpretation of Modern American Prose Literature* (1942); Frederick J. Hoffman's *The Twenties: American Writing in the Postwar Decade* (1955); Harold Clurman's *The Fervent Years: The Story of the Group Theatre and the Thirties* (1957); Walter Rideout's *The Radical Novel in the United States, 1900–1954* (1956); Joseph Wood Krutch's *The American Drama Since 1918* (1957); Daniel Aaron's *Writers on the Left* (1961); Louis D. Rubin's *Writers of the Modern South* (1963); Howard Taubman's *The Making of the American Theater* (1965); Warren French's *The Social Novel at the End of an Era* (1966); Brooks Atkinson's *Broadway: Nineteen Hundred to Nineteen Seventy* (1970); Nathan I. Huggins's *Harlem Renaissance* (1971); Hugh Kenner's *The Pound Era* (1971); and Kenner's *A Homemade World: The American Modernist Writers* (1975).

General books on literary and cultural history appearing since 1980 include David Levering Lewis's *When Harlem Was in Vogue* (1981); Daniel J. Singal's *The War Within: From Victorian to Modernist Thought in the South 1919–1945* (1982); Shari Benstock's *Women of the Left Bank: Paris 1900–1940* (1986); *Modernism and the Harlem Renaissance* (1987), edited by Houston Baker Jr.; Cecilia Tichi's *Shifting Gears: Technology, Literature, Culture in Modernist America* (1987); Joan Shelley Rubin's *The Making of Middlebrow Culture* (1992); Michael North's *The Dialect of Modernism: Race, Language and Twentieth-Century Literature* (1994); George Chauncey's *Gay New York: Gender, Urban Culture, and the Making of the Gay Male World, 1980–1940* (1994); George Hutchinson's *The Harlem Renaissance in Black and White* (1995); Cheryl Wall's *Women of the Harlem Renaissance* (1995); Walter Benn Michaels's *Our America* (1995); Ann Douglas's *Terrible Honesty: Mongrel Manhattan in the 1920s* (1995); Ross Posnock's *Color and Culture: Black Writers and the Making of the Modern Intellectual* (1998); William J. Maxwell's *New Negro, Old Left: African-American Writing and Communism between the Wars* (1999); Christine Stansell's *American Moderns: Bohemian New York and the Creation of a New Century* (1999); David G. Nicholls's *Conjuring the Folk: Forms of Modernity in African America* (2000); Michael Szalay's *New Deal Modernism: American Literature and the Invention of the Welfare State* (2000); Edward Pavlic's *Cross-*

roads *Modernism: Descent and Emergence in African-American Literary Culture* (2002); Catherine Turner's *Marketing Modernism between the Two World Wars* (2003); Tim Armstrong's *Modernism: A Cultural History* (2005); Daphne Lamothe's *Inventing the New Negro: Narrative, Culture, and Ethnography* (2008); Sarah Wilson's *Melting-Pot Modernism* (2010); Erick King Watts's *Hearing the Hurt: Rhetoric, Aesthetics, and Politics of the New Negro Movement* (2012); Jeffrey Hart's *The Living Moment: Modernism in a Broken World* (2012); Pearl James's *The New Death: American Modernism and World War I* (2013); Hazel Hutchison's *The War That Used Up Words: American Writers and the First World War* (2015); and Ichiro Takayoshi's *American Writers and the Approach of World War II, 1930–1941* (2015).

Literary Theory and Criticism

For an introduction to the ideas of literary criticism during the period, see Rene Wellek's *A History of Modern Criticism: American Criticism, 1900–1950*, volume 7 (1987); and Vincent B. Leitch's *American Literary Criticism from the 30s to the 80s* (1988). Gordon Hutner's *American Literature, American Culture* (1998) reprints a number of critical statements from the period. Gerald's Graff's *Professing Literature: An Institutional History* (1987); Lawrence H. Schwartz's *Creating Faulkner's Reputation: The Politics of Modern Literary Criticism* (1988); and Mark Jancovich's *The Cultural Politics of the New Criticism* (1994) analyze aspects of American literary criticism in the period and its aftermath.

Theoretical treatments of modernism (often in international perspectives) include Andreas Huyssen's *After the Great Divide: Modernism, Mass Culture, Postmodernism* (1986); Ashadur Eyssteinsson's *The Concept of Modernism* (1991); Joseph N. Riddel's *The Turning Word: American Literary Modernism and Continental Theory* (1996); Leonard Diepeveen's *The Difficulties of Modernism* (2003); Michael Trask's *Cruising Modernism: Class and Sexuality in American Literature and Social Thought* (2003); Susan McCabe's *Cinematic Modernism: Modernist Poetry and Film* (2005); Robert Scholes's *Paradoxy of Modernism* (2006); and John Carlos Rowe's *Afterlives of Modernism: Liberalism, Transnationalism, and Political Critique* (2011).

Criticism of poetry published since 1980 includes M. L. Rosenthal and Sally M. Gall's *The Modern Poetic Sequence: The Genius of Modern Poetry* (1984); William Drake's *The First Wave: Women Poets in America, 1914–1945* (1987); Albert Gelpi's *A Coherent Splendor: The American Poetic Renaissance, 1910–1950* (1987); Lisa M. Steinman's *Made in America: Science, Technology, and American Modernist Poets* (1987); *Shadowed Dreams: Women's Poetry of the Harlem Renaissance* (1989), edited by Maureen Honey; Cary Nelson's *Repression and Recovery: Modern American Poetry and the Politics of Cultural Memory, 1910–1945* (1989); Elisa New's *Fictions of Form in American Poetry* (1993); Frank Lentricchia's *Modernist Quartet* (1994); Elizabeth Gregory's *Quotation and Modern America Poetry: Imaginary Gardens with Real Toads* (1996); Rachel Blau DuPlessis's *Genders, Races, and Religious Cultures in Modern American Poetries, 1908–1934* (2001); Merrill Cole's *The Other Orpheus: A Poetics of Modern Homosexuality* (2003); Jennifer Ashton's *From*

Modernism to Postmodernism: American Poetry and Theory in the Twentieth Century (2005); Rachel Potter's *Modernism and Democracy: Literary Culture, 1900–1930* (2006); Charles Altieri's *The Art of Twentieth-Century American Poetry: Modernism and After* (2006); and Joel Nickels's *The Poetry of the Possible: Spontaneity, Modernism, and the Multitude* (2012).

Critical studies of fiction published since 1980 include Hazel V. Carby's *Reconstructing Womanhood: The Emergence of the Afro-American Woman Novelist* (1987); Linda Wagner-Martin's *The Modern American Novel, 1914–1945* (1990); J. Gerald Kennedy's *Imagining Paris* (1993); Barbara Foley's *Radical Representations: Politics and Form in U.S. Proletarian Fiction, 1929–41* (1993); David Minter's *A Cultural History of the American Novel* (1994); Laura Hapke's *Daughters of the Great Depression: Women, Work, and Fiction in the American 1930s* (1995); Gordon Hutner's *What America Read: Taste, Class, and the Novel, 1920–1960* (2009); Lawrence Buell's *The Dream of the Great American Novel* (2014); and David M. Ball's *False Starts: The Rhetoric of Failure and the Making of American Modernism* (2014).

Critical studies of drama published since 1980 include C. W. E. Bigsby's *A Critical Introduction to Twentieth-Century American Drama*, volume 1, *1900–1940* (1985); Ethan Mordden's *The American Theatre* (1981); Brenda Murphy's *American Realism and American Drama, 1880–1940* (1987); David Krasner's *A Beautiful Pageant: African American Theatre, Drama, and Performance in the Harlem Renaissance, 1910–1927* (2002); Julia A. Walker's *Expressionism and Modernism in the American Theatre: Bodies, Voices, Words* (2005); Soyica Diggs Colbert's *The African-American Theatrical Body: Reception, Performance, and the Stage* (2011); and Andrea Most's *Theatrical Liberalism: Jews and Popular Entertainment in America* (2013).

Sherwood Anderson

In addition to works mentioned in the author's headnote, Anderson published *The Modern Writer* (1925); *Sherwood Anderson's Notebook* (1925); *Alice and the Lost Novel* (1929); *Nearer the Grass Roots* (1929); *The American Country Fair* (1930); and *Home Town* (1940). The Library of America published his *Collected Stories* (2012), edited by Charles Baxter. The Norton Critical Edition of *Winesburg, Ohio* (1996), edited by Charles E. Modlin and Ray Lewis White, includes background materials and critical essays, as does the edition edited by John H. Ferres (1996). White edited a variorum edition of *Winesburg, Ohio* (1997) as well as *Sherwood Anderson's Memoirs: A Critical Edition* (1969). *The Letters of Sherwood Anderson* (1953) were edited by Howard Mumford Jones and Walter Rideout. See also *Sherwood Anderson: Selected Letters* (1984), edited by Charles E. Modlin, and *Letters to Bab: Sherwood Anderson to Marietta D. Finley, 1916–1933* (1985), edited by William A. Sutton. A two-volume biography by Walter Rideout is *Sherwood Anderson: A Writer in America* (2006–7). For critical commentary see *Sherwood Anderson: A Collection of Critical Essays* (1974), edited by Walter Rideout; *New Essays on Winesburg, Ohio* (1990), edited by John W. Crowley; Allen Papinchak's *Sherwood Anderson: A Study of the Short Fiction* (1992); Judy Jo Small's *A Reader's Guide to the Short Stories of Sherwood Anderson* (1994); Ray Lewis White's *Winesburg, Ohio: An Exploration* (1990); and Clarence Lindsay's *Such a Rare Thing: The Art of Sherwood Anderson's Winesburg, Ohio* (2009).

Willa Cather

Cather's volume of verse, *April Twilights* (1903; rev. 1923; reissued with an introduction by Bernice Slote, 1990), and her collection of essays, *Not under Forty* (1936), supplement the standard edition of her fiction, *The Novels and Stories of Willa Cather* (1937–41), and the scholarly editions (1992–2015) under the general editorship of Guy Reynolds. Her stories, novels, poems, and essays were published in three volumes by the Library of America with notes by Sharon O'Brien (1987, 1990, 1992). *The Selected Letters of Willa Cather* (2013) was edited by Andrew Jewell and Janis Stout. Other sources include *Willa Cather on Writing* (1949); *Writings from Willa Cather's Campus Years* (1950), edited by James Shively; and

The Kingdom of Art: Willa Cather's First Principles and Critical Statements (1967), edited by Bernice Slote. William M. Curtin collected articles and reviews in the two-volume *The World and the Parish* (1970). Personal memoirs include Edith Lewis's *Willa Cather Living* (1953, 2000), and Elizabeth Sergeant's *Willa Cather: A Memoir* (1953, 1992). Janis P. Stout's *A Calendar of the Letters of Willa Cather* (2002), and the biography *Willa Cather: The Writer and Her World* (2000) are worthwhile. Phyllis C. Robinson's *Willa: The Life of Willa Cather* (1982) is a full-length biography, as is James Woodress's *Willa Cather: A Literary Life* (1987). Sharon O'Brien's *Willa Cather: The Emerging Voice* (1987) concentrates on Cather's early years.

Critical studies of Cather are David Stouck's *Willa Cather's Imagination* (1975); Marilyn Arnold's *Willa Cather's Short Fiction* (1984) and *Willa Cather: A Reference Guide* (1986); Susan J. Rosowski's *The Voyage Perilous: Willa Cather's Romanticism* (1986); Sally P. Harvey's *Redefining the American Dream: The Novels of Willa Cather* (1995); Joseph R. Urgo's *Willa Cather and the Myth of American Migration* (1995); Guy Reynolds's *Willa Cather in Context* (1996); O'Brien's *New Essays on My Ántonia* (1999); Ann Romines's *Willa Cather's Southern Connection* (2000); Joan Acocella's *Willa Cather and the Politics of Criticism* (2000); and David Porter's *On the Divide: The Many Lives of Willa Cather* (2008) on her relationship to the literary marketplace. Janis P. Stout edited *Willa Cather and Material Culture: Real-World Writing and Writing the Real World* (2005). Also useful is *Violence, the Arts, and Willa Cather* (2007), edited by Joseph R. Urgo and Merrill Maguire Skaggs.

Hart Crane

Langdon Hammer edited *Hart Crane: Complete Poems and Selected Letters* (2006) for the Library of America. Crane's *Collected Poems*, edited by his friend Waldo Frank, appeared in 1933. Lawrence Kramer edited *The Bridge: An Annotated Edition* (2011). *Correspondence between Hart Crane and Waldo Frank* (1998) was edited by Steve H. Cook. Other sources of primary and bibliographical material are *My Land, My Friends: The Selected Letters of Hart Crane* (1997), edited by Langdon Hammer and Brom Weber; *Hart Crane: An Annotated Critical Bibliography* (1970), edited by Joseph Schwartz; and *Hart Crane: A Descriptive Bibliography* (1972), edited by Joseph Schwartz and Robert C. Schweik. Gary Lane compiled *A Concordance to the Poems of Hart Crane* (1972). Biographies of Crane are John Unterecker's *Voyager: A Life of Hart Crane* (1969); Paul Mariani's *The Broken Tower: A Life of Hart Crane* (2000); and Clive Fisher's *Hart Crane: A Life* (2002).

Useful earlier studies are R. W. B. Lewis's *The Poetry of Hart Crane* (1967); Monroe K. Spears's *Hart Crane* (1965); and Hunce Voelcker's *The Hart Crane Voyages* (1967). See also Richard P. Sugg's *Hart Crane's "The Bridge"* (1976); Helge Norman Nilsen's *Hart Crane's Divided Vision: An Analysis of "The Bridge"* (1980); Edward Brunner's *Hart Crane and the Making of "The Bridge"* (1984); Paul Giles's *Hart Crane: The Contexts of The Bridge* (1986); Thomas E. Yingling's *Hart Crane and the Homosexual Text* (1990); Brian M. Reed's *Hart Crane: After His Lights* (2006); Daniel Gabriel's *Hart Crane and the Modernist Epic: Canon and Genre Formation in Crane, Pound, Eliot and Williams* (2007); and John T. Irwin, *Hart Crane's Poetry: "Appollinaire Lived in Paris, I Live in Cleveland, Ohio"* (2011).

Countee Cullen

The Library of America issued Cullen's *Collected Poems* (2013), edited by Major Jackson. Cullen's groundbreaking anthology of 1927, *Caroling Dusk*, was reissued in 1993. His poetry volume, *Color*, originally published in 1925, was also reissued in 1993. *My Soul's High Song*, a collection of his writings edited by Gerald Early, appeared in 1991. *And Bid Him Sing: A Biography of Countée Cullen*, by Charles Molesworth, appeared in 2012. Earlier work of interest includes Helen J. Dinger's *A Study of Countee Cullen* (1953); Margaret Perry's *A Bio-Bibliography of Countee P. Cullen* (1969); Blanche E. Ferguson's *Countee Cullen and the Negro Renaissance* (1966); and Alan R. Shucard's *Countee Cullen* (1984).

E. E. Cummings

Complete Poems 1904–62, edited by George J. Firmage, was published in 1991. Firmage also edited *Three Plays and a Ballet* (1967). Cummings's prose fiction includes *The Enormous Room* (1922) and *EIMI* (1933). *E. E. Cummings: A Miscellany Revised* (1965), edited by Firmage, contains previously uncollected short prose pieces. *Six Nonlectures* (1953) consists of the talks that Cummings delivered at Harvard in the same year. A gathering of works is *Another E. E. Cummings* (1999), edited by Richard Kostceanetz. *Selected Letters of E. E. Cummings* (1969) was edited by F. W. Dupee and George Stade. Firmage edited *E. E. Cummings: A Bibliography* (1960). Barry Ahearn edited *The Correspondence of Ezra Pound and E. E. Cummings* (1996).

Several of Cummings's earlier works have been reedited by Firmage in the Cummings Typescript Editions. These include *Tulips & Chimneys* (1976); *No Thanks* (1978); *The Enormous Room*, with illustrations by Cummings (1978); *ViVa* (1979); *XAIPE* (1979); and *Etcetera*, the unpublished poems (1983).

Biographies are Richard S. Kennedy's *Dreams in the Mirror* (1979, 1994) and Susan Cheever's *E. E. Cummings: A Life* (2014). Early studies include Norman Friedman's *E. E. Cummings: The Growth of a Writer* (1964); Robert E. Wegner's *The Poetry and Prose of E. E. Cummings* (1965); and Rushworth Kidder's *E. E. Cummings, An Introduction to the Poetry* (1979). See also Cary Lane's *I Am: A Study of E. E. Cummings' Poems* (1976), and Richard S. Kennedy's *E. E. Cummings Revisited* (1994). Norman Friedman edited *E. E. Cummings: A Collection of Critical Essays* (1972) and authored *(Re)Valuing Cummings: Further Essays on the Poet* (1996). David G. Farley's *Modernist Travel Writing: Intellectuals Abroad* (2010) compares Cummings and Ezra Pound.

Hilda Doolittle (H.D.)

H.D.'s poetry through 1944 has been collected and edited by Louis L. Martz in *Collected Poems 1912–1944* (1983). *Collected Poems of H.D.* was published in 1925. Subsequent volumes of poetry include *Red Rose for Bronze* (1931); the trilogy of war poems *The Walls Do Not Fall* (1944), *Tribute to the Angels* (1945), and *The Flowering of the Rod* (1946); the dramatic monologue *Helen in Egypt* (1961); the major collection of her late poems, *Hermetic Definition* (1972); and the long poem *Vale Ave* (1992). H.D.'s other book-length verse dramas are *Hippolytus Temporizes* (1927) and the translation of *Euripides' Ion* (1937). *Palimpsest* (1926), *Hedylus* (1928), *Bid Me to Live* (1961), *HERmione* (1981), and *Asphodel* (1992), edited by Robert Spoo, compose her major prose fiction. *By Avon River* (1949) celebrates Shakespeare in prose and verse. *Tribute to Freud* (1956) is her account of her psychoanalysis by Freud. Also important are two autobiographical works: *End to Torment* (1979) and *The Gift* (1982, complete edition 1998). Michael Boughn compiled *H.D.: A Bibliography, 1905–1990* (1993). *Richard Aldington and H.D.: The Early Years in Letters* (1992), edited by Caroline Zilboorg, collects correspondence. Zilboorg also edited a scholarly edition of *Bid Me to Live* (2012).

Barbara Guest's *Herself Defined: The Poet H.D. and Her World* (1984) is a biography; Rachel Blau DuPlessis's *H.D.: The Career of That Struggle* (1986); Susan S. Friedman's *Psyche Reborn: The Emergence of H.D.* (1981); and Janice S. Robinson's *H.D.: The Life and Work of an American Poet* (1982) combine biography and literary analysis. Among critical books are Gary Burnett's *H. D.: Between Image and Epic, The Mysteries of Her Poetics* (1990); Friedman's *Penelope's Web: Gender, Modernity, and H.D.'s Fiction* (1990); Eileen Gregory's *H.D. and Hellenism* (1997); Diana

Collecott's *H.D and Sapphic Modernism* (1999); Georgia Taylor's *H.D. and the Public Sphere of Modernist Women Writers 1913–1946* (2001); Adalaide Morris's *How to Live/What to Do: H.D.'s Cultural Poetics* (2003); and Annette Debo's *The American H.D.* (2012). Nephie J. Christodoulides and Polina Mackay edited *The Cambridge Companion to H. D.* (2011).

T. S. Eliot

Eliot's poetic works have been collected in *Collected Poems, 1909–1962* (1963) and *The Complete Poems and Plays of T. S. Eliot* (1969). *Inventions of the March Hare: Poems 1909–1917* (1997), edited by Christopher Ricks, contains early, previously unpublished poetry. The indispensable manuscript to *The Waste Land* is in *The Waste Land: A Facsimile and Transcript of the Original Drafts Including the Annotations of Ezra Pound* (1971), edited by Valerie Eliot. Michael North edited a Norton Critical Edition of *The Waste Land* (2001), and Lawrence Rainey edited *The Annotated Waste Land with Eliot's Contemporary Prose* (2005). Important critical writings include *The Use of Poetry and the Use of Criticism* (1933), *Poetry and Drama* (1951), *The Three Voices of Poetry* (1953), *On Poetry and Poets* (1957), and *To Criticize the Critic and Other Writings* (1965). Three volumes of social commentary are *After Strange Gods* (1934), *The Idea of a Christian Society* (1939), and *Notes toward the Definition of Culture* (1948). Valerie Eliot's edition of *The Letters of T. S. Eliot* (1988–2015) has reached five volumes, up to 1933. J. L. Dawson edited *Concordance to the Complete Poems and Plays of T. S. Eliot* (1995). Good biographies are Peter Ackroyd's *T. S. Eliot: A Life* (1984); Lyndall Gordon's *T. S. Eliot: An Imperfect Life* (1998, 2000), an updating of her earlier biographies; James E. Miller Jr.'s *T. S. Eliot: The Making of an American Poet, 1888–1922* (2005); and Robert Crawford's *Young Eliot: A Biography* (2015).

Influential earlier studies of Eliot include F. O. Matthiessen's *The Achievement of T. S. Eliot* (rev. 1947); Helen Gardner's *The Art of T. S. Eliot* (1950); Hugh Kenner's *The Invisible Poet* (1959), Northrop Frye's *T. S. Eliot* (1963); and Stephen Spender's *T. S. Eliot* (1976). Among numerous critical studies are Helen Gardner's *The Composition of Four Quartets* (1978); Derek Traversi's *T. S. Eliot: The Longer Poems* (1976); Louis Menand's *Discovering Modernism: T. S. Eliot and His Context* (1987); Jewel Spears Brooker and Joseph Bentley's *Reading "The Waste Land": Modernism and the Limits of Interpretation* (1990); Brooker's *Mastery and Escape: T. S. Eliot and the Dialectic of Modernism* (1994); A. David Moody's *Thomas Stearns Eliot, Poet* (1994); Anthony Julius's *T. S. Eliot, Anti-Semitism, and Literary*

Form (1996); Ronald Schuchard's *Eliot's Dark Angel: Intersections of Life and Art* (2001); David Chintz's *T. S. Eliot and the Cultural Divide* (2003); and Craig Raine's *T. S. Eliot* (2006). Moody also edited the useful *Cambridge Companion to T. S. Eliot* (1994). For collections of critical essays about Eliot, see *T. S. Eliot: A Collection of Criticism* (1974), edited by Linda W. Wagner (1974); *T. S. Eliot: The Modernist in History* (1991), edited by Ronald Bush; and *Gender, Desire, and Sexuality in T. S. Eliot* (2004), edited by Cassandra Laity and Nancy K. Gish. Gareth Reeves's *T. S. Eliot's "The Waste Land"* (1994) is a comprehensive introduction to the poem.

Donald C. Gallup compiled the standard bibliography, *T. S. Eliot: A Bibliography* (rev. 1969).

William Faulkner

The Library of America issued Faulkner's novels in four volumes: 1930–1935 (1985), 1936–1940 (1990), 1942–1954 (1994), and 1957–1962 (1999). In addition to the volumes mentioned in the author's headnote are *Early Prose and Poetry* (1962), edited by Carvel Collins; *Dr. Martino and Other Stories* (1934); *Pylon* (1935); *The Unvanquished* (1938); *Intruder in the Dust* (1948); *Knight's Gambit* (1949); *Collected Stories of William Faulkner* (1950); *Requiem for a Nun* (1951); *Notes on a Horsethief* (1951); *Big Woods* (1955); and *Essays, Speeches, and Public Letters* (rev. 2004), edited by James B. Meriwether. Transcripts of discussions and interviews with Faulkner include *Faulkner at Nagano* (1956), edited by Robert A. Jelliffe; *Faulkner in the University* (1959), edited by Frederick L. Gwynn and Joseph L. Blotner; *Faulkner at West Point* (1964), edited by Joseph L. Fant and Robert Ashley (1964); and *The Lion in the Garden* (1968), edited by Meriwether and Michael Millgate. Letters are collected in *The Faulkner-Cowley File* (1961), edited by Malcolm Cowley (1961), and *Selected Letters of William Faulkner* (1977), edited by Joseph L. Blotner. Noel Polk has produced editions of several Faulkner novels based on a study of the manuscripts. Michael Gorra and Polk have published a Norton Critical Edition of *The Sound and the Fury* (2014), and Gorra has also published one of *As I Lay Dying* (2010).

Blotner's *Faulkner: A Biography*, 2 volumes (1974) is condensed and updated in *Faulkner* (1984). Two shorter biographies based on Blotner's work are David Minter's *William Faulkner: His Life and Work* (1980) and Judith Wittenberg's *Faulkner: The Transfiguration of Biography* (1979).

Comprehensive guides are Thomas E. Connolly's *Faulkner's World: A Directory of His People and Synopsis of Actions in His Published Works* (1988); and *A William Faulkner Encyclopedia* (1999), edited by Robert W. Hamblin and

Charles E. Peek. Teresa Towner's *Cambridge Introduction to William Faulkner* (2008) and John T. Matthews's edited *New Cambridge Companion to William Faulkner* (2015) are useful. Influential early studies include Cleanth Brooks's *William Faulkner: The Yoknapatawpha Country* (1963) and Hyatt H. Waggoner's *William Faulkner: From Jefferson to the World* (1959). Later studies include John T. Irwin's *Doubling and Incest, Repetition and Revenge: A Speculative Reading of Faulkner* (1975); Thadious M. Davis's *Faulkner's "Negro": Art and the Southern Context* (1983); Eric J. Sundquist's *Faulkner: The House Divided* (1983); Robert Dale Parker's *Faulkner and the Novelistic Imagination* (1985); Warwick Wadlington's *Reading Faulknerian Tragedy* (1987) and *As I Lay Dying: Stories out of Stories* (1992); Minrose C. Gwin's *The Feminine and Faulkner: Reading (beyond) Sexual Difference* (1990); André Bleikasten's *The Ink of Melancholy: Faulkner's Novels from "The Sound and the Fury" to "Light in August"* (1990); Richard Moreland's *Faulkner and Modernism: Rereading and Rewriting* (1990); Joel Williamson's *William Faulkner and Southern History* (1993); Diane Roberts's *Faulkner and Southern Womanhood* (1994); David Minter's *Faulkner's Questioning Narratives: Fiction of His Major Phase, 1929–42* (2001); Philip Weinstein's *Becoming Faulkner: The Art and Life of William Faulkner* (2010); and Candace Waid's *The Signifying Eye: Seeing Faulkner's Art* (2013).

Edited collections of critical essays include Louis J. Budd and Edwin Cady's *On Faulkner* (1989); Linda Wagner-Martin's *Faulkner: Six Decades of Criticism* (2002); Annette Trefzer's *Global Faulkner: Faulkner and Yoknapatawpha, 2006* (2009); and Peter Lurie and Ann J. Abadie's *Faulkner and Film* (2014).

F. Scott Fitzgerald

Fitzgerald's novels are *This Side of Paradise* (1920), *The Beautiful and Damned* (1922), *The Great Gatsby* (1925), *Tender Is the Night* (1934; rev. 1939; rpt. 1953), and the unfinished *The Last Tycoon* (1941). His collections of stories are *Flappers and Philosophers* (1921), *Tales of the Jazz Age* (1922), *All the Sad Young Men* (1926), and *Taps at Reveille* (1935). Two recent editions of his fiction are the Library of America's *Novels and Stories 1920–1922* (2000) and Matthew J. Bruccoli and Judith Baughman's *Before Gatsby: The First Twenty-Six Stories* (2001). The Cambridge Edition of Fitzgerald's works (1991–2014) includes his novels, story collections, and *My Lost City: Personal Essays, 1920–1940* (2005). A satirical play, *The Vegetable, or From Presidents to Postman*, was published in 1923. Among collections of Fitzgerald's writings are *F. Scott Fitzgerald in His Own Time: A*

Miscellany (1971), edited by Jackson R. Bryer and Bruccoli, and *Afternoon of an Author* (1957), edited by Arthur Mizener. *The Crack-Up* (1945), edited by Edmund Wilson, collects essays, notebook entries, and letters from the 1930s; youthful work is collected in *F. Scott Fitzgerald: The Princeton Years; Selected Writings, 1914–1920* (1966), edited by Chip Defaa.

The fullest collection of letters is *Correspondence of F. Scott Fitzgerald* (1980), edited by Bruccoli and Margaret M. Duggan. Other volumes of letters are *Dear Scott/Dear Max: The Fitzgerald-Perkins Correspondence* (1971), edited by John Kuehl and Jackson R. Bryer; *As Ever, Scott Fitz* (1972), edited by Bruccoli and Jennifer McCabe Atkinson (letters between Fitzgerald and his literary agent, Harold Ober); and *Dear Scott, Dearest Zelda: The Love Letters of F. Scott and Zelda Fitzgerald* (2002), edited by Jackson R. Bryer and Cathy W. Barks. Biographies include Bruccoli's *Some Sort of Epic Grandeur: The Life of F. Scott Fitzgerald* (1981), Scott Donaldson's *Fool for Love: F. Scott Fitzgerald, A Biographical Portrait* (1983), James Mellow's *Invented Lives* (1984), Jeffrey Myers's *Scott Fitzgerald* (2000), and Andrew Turnbull's *Scott Fitzgerald* (2001).

Among guides are Robert Gale's *An F. Scott Fitzgerald Encyclopedia* (1998); Linda Pelzer's *Student Companion to F. Scott Fitzgerald* (2001); and Kirk Curnutt's *Cambridge Introduction to F. Scott Fitzgerald* (2007). Critical studies include Milton R. Stern's *The Golden Moment: The Novels of F. Scott Fitzgerald* (1970); Brian Way's *F. Scott Fitzgerald and the Art of Social Fiction* (1980); John Kuehl's *F. Scott Fitzgerald, a Study of the Short Fiction* (1991); and Scott Donaldson's *Fitzgerald and Hemingway: Works and Days* (2009). Among collections of critical essays are *The Short Stories of F. Scott Fitzgerald: New Approaches in Criticism* (1983), edited by Jackson R. Bryer; *New Essays on "The Great Gatsby"* (1985), edited by Bruccoli; *The Cambridge Companion to F. Scott Fitzgerald* (2001), edited by Ruth Prigozy; *F. Scott Fitzgerald in the Twenty-First Century* (2003), edited by Jackson R. Bryer, Prigozy, and Milton B. Stern; and *F. Scott Fitzgerald in Context* (2013), edited by Bryant Mangum.

Robert Frost

The Poetry of Robert Frost (1969) incorporated *Complete Poems* (1949) and Frost's last volume, *In the Clearing* (1962). The Library of America issued Frost's *Collected Poems, Prose, and Plays* (1995). Mark Richardson edited *The Collected Prose of Robert Frost* (2007), and Robert Faggen edited *The Notebooks of Robert Frost* (2007). Richardson and Donald Sheehy edited *The Letters of Robert Frost*, volume 1 (2014). Important collections

of letters appear in *Selected Letters of Robert Frost* (1964), edited by Lawrence Thompson; *The Letters of Robert Frost to Louis Untermeyer* (1963); and Margaret Anderson's, *Robert Frost and John Bartlett: The Record of a Friendship* (1963). Conversations and interviews with Frost include Edward C. Lathem's *Interviews with Robert Frost* (1966); Reginald L. Cook's *The Dimensions of Robert Frost* (1964); Daniel Smythe's *Robert Frost Speaks* (1954); and Louis Mertin's *Robert Frost: Life and Talks—Walking* (1965).

Lawrance Thompson completed two volumes of the authorized biography: *Robert Frost: The Early Years, 1874–1915* (1966) and *Robert Frost: The Years of Triumph, 1915–1938* (1970). The third volume, *Robert Frost, the Later Years (1976)*, was completed by Richard Winnick, and Lathem produced a shorter version of the biography in *Robert Frost: A Biography* (1981). Other biographies are Jeffrey Meyers's *Robert Frost* (1996) and Jay Parini's *Robert Frost: A Life* (1999). William H. Pritchard in *Frost: A Literary Life Reconsidered* (1984) is interested in the poet's art, not his personal life. James L. Potter's *Robert Frost Handbook* (1980) is a useful guide; Lathem produced a concordance to Frost's poetry (1994).

A brief critical introduction is Mordecai Marcus's *The Poems of Robert Frost* (1991). Other critical studies are Richard Poirier's *Robert Frost, The Work of Knowing* (1977, reissued with new material in 1990); John C. Kemp's *Robert Frost and New England: The Poet as Regionalist* (1979); George Monteiro's *Robert Frost and the New England Renaissance* (1988); Mario D'Avanzo's *A Cloud of Other Poets: Robert Frost and the Romantics* (1990); Judith Oster's *Toward Robert Frost* (1991); George Bagby's *Frost and the Book of Nature* (1993); Mark Richardson's *Robert Frost: The Poet and His Poetics* (1997); and Tim Kendall's *The Art of Robert Frost* (2012). Collections of critical essays include *On Frost* (1991), edited by Edwin H. Cady and Louis J. Budd, and Robert Faggen's *Cambridge Companion to Robert Frost* (2001).

Susan Glaspell

Susan Glaspell: The Complete Plays, edited by Linda Ben-Zvi and J. Ellen Gainor, appeared in 2010. *Major Novels of Susan Glaspell*, edited by Martha C. Carpenter, was published in 1995. Patricia l. Bryan and Martha C. Carnpentier edited *Her America: "A Jury of Her Peers" and Other Stories* (2010). Two biographies are Arthur E. Waterman's *Susan Glaspell* (1966) and Barbara O. Rajkowska's *Susan Glaspell: A Critical Biography* (2000). Critical studies include Marcia Noe's *Susan Glaspell: Voice from the Heartland* (1983);

Veronica A. Makowsky's *Susan Glaspell's Century of American Women: A Critical Interpretation of Her Work* (1993); Gainor's *Susan Glaspell in Context: American Theater, Culture, and Politics, 1915–48* (2001); and Brenda Murphy's *The Provincetown Players and the Culture of Modernity* (2005). A collection of critical essays is *Susan Glaspell: Essays on Her Theater and Fiction* (1995), edited by Ben-Zvi.

Ernest Hemingway

There is no collected edition of Hemingway's writings. In addition to works mentioned in the author's headnote, his fiction includes *Today Is Friday* (1926) and *God Rest You Merry Gentlemen* (1933). His tribute to Spain, *The Spanish Earth*, and his play *The Fifth Column* appeared in 1938, the latter in a collection *The Fifth Column and the First Forty-Nine Stories*. His journalism has been collected in *The Wild Years* (1962), edited by Gene Z. Hanrahan, and *By-Line: Ernest Hemingway, Selected Articles and Dispatches of Four Decades* (1967), edited by William White. His *Complete Poems* (1992) has been edited by Nicholas Gerogiannis. *The Letters of Ernest Hemingway*, vols. 1 and 2 (2011, 2013), have appeared under the general editorship of Sandra Spanier. Audre Hanneman's *Ernest Hemingway: A Comprehensive Bibliography* (1967) is thorough. Scribners published *The Complete Short Stories of Ernest Hemingway* (1987).

The authorized biography is Carlos Baker's *Ernest Hemingway: A Life Story* (1969). Jeffrey Meyers's *Hemingway: A Biography* (1985) and Kenneth S. Lynn's *Hemingway* (1987) are important. Michael Reynolds's detailed volumes include *The Young Hemingway* (1986), *Hemingway: The Paris Years* (1989), *Hemingway: The 1930s* (1997), and *Hemingway: The Final Years* (1999). Bernice Kert's *The Hemingway Women* (1983) tells about Hemingway's mother, wives, and lovers; John Raeburn's *Fame Became of Him: Hemingway as Public Writer* (1984) compares the life with the public image.

Paul Smith's *A Reader's Guide to the Short Stories of Ernest Hemingway* (1989) is useful; Peter B. Messent's *Ernest Hemingway* (1992) is a good overview. For collections of critical essays on Hemingway, see *Ernest Hemingway: Eight Decades of Criticism* (2009), edited by Linda Wagner-Martin; *The Cambridge Companion to Hemingway* (1996), edited by Scott Donaldson; and *A Historical Guide to Ernest Hemingway* (2001), edited by Wagner-Martin. Specialized studies include Wirt Williams's *The Tragic Art of Ernest Hemingway* (1982); Mark Spilka's *Hemingway's Quarrel with Androgyny* (1990); Robert W. Trogdon's *The Lousy Racket: Hemingway, Scribners, and the Business of Literature* (2007); Amy L. Strong's

Race and Identity in Hemingway's Fiction (2008); Robert Paul Lamb's *Art Matters: Hemingway, Craft, and the Creation of the Modern Short Story* (2010); and Mark Cirino's *Ernest Hemingway: Thought in Action* (2012).

Langston Hughes

A sixteen-volume standard edition of Hughes's complete works appeared in 2001–3. Arnold Rampersad and David Roessel edited *The Collected Poems of Langston Hughes* (1994), including *The Weary Blues* (1926), *Fine Clothes to the Jew* (1927), *The Dream Keeper and Other Poems* (1932), *Scottsboro Limited: Four Poems and a Play in Verse* (1932), *Montage of a Dream Deferred* (1951), and *The Panther and the Lash: Poems of our Times* (1967). His short stories were edited by Akiba Sullivan Harper (1996). Faith Berry edited *Good Morning Revolution: Uncollected Social Protest Writings by Langston Hughes* (1973). *Mule Bone* (1991), which he coauthored with Zora Neale Hurston, has been edited with contextual materials by George Houston Pope and Henry Louis Gates, Jr. Hughes's autobiographical volumes include *The Big Sea* (1940) and *I Wonder as I Wander* (1956); both were reissued in 1993. Charles H. Nichols edited *Arna Bontemps–Langston Hughes: Letters 1925–1967* (1980), and Rampersad edited his *Selected Letters* (2015).

Early biographies of Hughes include Charlemae Rollins's *Black Troubador: Langston Hughes* (1970), and James S. Haskins's *Always Movin' On: The Life of Langston Hughes* (1976). Faith Berry's *Langston Hughes: Before and Beyond Harlem* (1983, 1995) contains much about Hughes's life to 1940. Arnold Rampersad's two-volume *Life of Langston Hughes*—volume 1, *1902–1941: I, Too, Sing America* (1986), and volume 2, *1941–1967: I Dream a World* (1988)—is definitive.

Thomas A. Mikolyzk compiled *Langston Hughes: A Bio-Bibliography* (1990). Contemporary reviews were collected by Letitia Dace (1997). Full-length critical studies are Onwuchekwa Jemie's *Langston Hughes: An Introduction to the Poetry* (1976); Richard K. Barksdale's *Langston Hughes: The Poet and His Critics* (1977); Steven C. Tracy's *Langston Hughes and the Blues* (1988); R. Baxter Miller's *The Art and Imagination of Langston Hughes* (1989); W. Jason Miller's *Langston Hughes and American Lynching Culture* (2011); Vera M. Kutzinski's *The Worlds of Langston Hughes: Modernism and Translation in the Americas* (2012); and David E. Chinitz's *Which Sin to Bear? Authenticity and Compromise in Langston Hughes* (2013). Essay collections include *Langston Hughes: Critical Perspectives Past and Present* (1993), edited by Henry Louis Gates, Jr., and K. A. Appiah; *Langston Hughes: The*

Man, His Art, and His Continuing Influence (1995), edited by C. James Trotman; and *A Historical Guide to Langston Hughes* (2003), edited by Steven C. Tracy. Peter Mandelik and Stanley Schatt's *A Concordance to the Poetry of Langston Hughes* (1975) is useful.

Zora Neale Hurston

Robert Hemenway's *Zora Neale Hurston, A Literary Biography* (1977) initiated the Hurston revival; her work is mostly available in paperback editions. The Library of America published Hurston's writing in two volumes: *Novels and Stories* (1995) and *Folklore, Memoirs, and Other Writings* (1995); Jean Lee Cole and Charles Mitchell edited *Collected Plays* (2008). Her letters were edited by Carla Kaplan (2002). Biographies include Valerie Boyd's *Wrapped in Rainbows: The Life of Zora Neale Hurston* (2003) and Virginia Lynn Moylan's *Zora Neale Hurston's Final Decade* (2011). Book-length studies include Karla C. F. Holloway's *The Character of the Word: The Texts of Zora Neale Hurston* (1987); John Lowe's *Jump at the Sun: Zora Neale Hurston's Cosmic Comedy* (1994); Deborah G. Plant's *Every Tub Must Sit on Its Own Bottom: The Philosophy and Politics of Zora Neale Hurston* (1995); Margaret Genevieve West's *Zora Neale Hurston and American Literary Culture* (2005); and Lovalerie King's *Cambridge Introduction to Zora Neale Hurston* (2008). Hurston is linked to other writers in Cheryl A. Wall's *Women of the Harlem Renaissance* (1995); Carla Kaplan's *The Erotics of Talk: Women's Writing and Feminist Paradigms* (1996); and Trudier Harris's *The Power of the Porch: The Storyteller's Craft in Zora Neale Hurston, Gloria Naylor, and Randall Kenan* (1996). Collections of essays are *New Essays on "Their Eyes Were Watching God"* (1990), edited by Michael Awkward; *Zora Neale Hurston: Critical Perspectives Past and Present* (1993), edited by Henry Louis Gates, Jr., and K. A. Appiah; and *Critical Essays on Zora Neale Hurston* (1998), edited by Gloria L. Cronin.

Amy Lowell

Lowell's complete poems were published in 1955. Honor Moore edited her *Selected Poems* (2004) for the Library of America. Ferris Greenslet, who was her editor at Houghton Mifflin, has written an excellent family chronicle from the first settler to Amy Lowell, *The Lowells and Their Seven Worlds* (1945). Additional biographical material may be found in S. Foster Damon's *Amy Lowell: A Chronicle, with Extracts from Her Correspondence* (1935), and *Florence Ayscough and Amy Lowell: Correspondence of a Friendship* (1945), edited by Harley Farnsworth MacNair. Critical estimates of Lowell include Jean

Gould's *Amy: The World of Amy Lowell and the Imagist Movement* (1975); Glenn Richard Ruihley's *The Thorn of a Rose: Amy Lowell Reconsidered* (1975); Richard Benvenuto's *Amy Lowell* (1985); and Melissa Bradshaw's *Amy Lowell, Diva Poet* (2011). Adrienne Munich and Bradshaw edited *Amy Lowell, American Modern* (2004).

Claude McKay

Volumes of McKay's poetry include *Songs of Jamaica* (1912), *Constab Ballads* (1912), *Spring in New Hampshire and Other Poems* (1920)—published in England—and *Harlem Shadows* (1922). William J. Maxwell edited the *Complete Poems* (2004), including many poems previously uncollected. Books of prose published in his lifetime include the novels *Home to Harlem* (1928), *Banjo* (1929), and *Banana Bottom* (1933); a short story collection, *Gingertown* (1932, 1991); an autobiography, *A Long Way from Home* (1937), and an essay collection, *Harlem: Negro Metropolis* (1940). Collections brought out after McKay's death include *Selected Poems* (1953), *The Dialect Poetry of Claude McKay* (1972), *The Passion of Claude McKay: Selected Poetry and Prose* (1973); two books of short stories, *Trial by Lynching* (1977) and *My Green Hills of Jamaica* (1979); and an essay collection, *The Negro in America* (1979).

Three good biographies are James R. Giles's *Claude McKay* (1976); Wayne F. Cooper's *Claude McKay: Rebel Sojourner in the Harlem Renaissance* (1987, 1996); and Tyrone Tillery's *Claude McKay: A Black Poet's Struggle for Identity* (1992). A collection of interpretive essays is *Claude McKay: Centennial Studies* (1992), edited by A. L. McLeod. General works with material on McKay include Harold Cruse's still valuable *The Crisis of the Negro Intellectual* (1967); Kenneth Ramchand's *The West Indian Novel and Its Background* (1970; rev. ed. 2004); Nathan I. Huggins's *Harlem Renaissance* (1971); Addison Gayle's *The Way of the New World: The Black Novel in America* (1975); David Levering Lewis's *When Harlem Was in Vogue* (1981); Bernard W. Bell's *The Afro-American Novel and Its Tradition* (1987); and George Hutchinson's *The Harlem Renaissance in Black and White* (1995). Contrasting treatments of McKay's poetry are in Winston James's *A Fierce Hatred of Injustice: Claude McKay's Jamaican Poetry of Rebellion* (2001) and Josh Gosciak's *The Shadowed Country: Claude McKay and the Romance of the Victorians* (2006).

Marianne Moore

Each collection of Moore's verse excluded some earlier poems while subjecting others to extensive revisions and changes in format.

Her separate volumes include *Poems* (1921), *Observations* (1924), *The Pangolin and Other Verse* (1936), *What Are Years?* (1941), *Nevertheless* (1944), *Like a Bulwark* (1956), *O to Be a Dragon* (1959), and *Tell Me, Tell Me* (1966). Collections include *Selected Poems* (1935), *Collected Poems* (1951), and *The Complete Poems of Marianne Moore* (1967, repr. 1981, 1987), which included selections from her translation of *The Fables of La Fontaine* (1954). Grace Shulman's *The Poems of Marianne Moore* (2003) is now the fullest edition. Patricia C. Willis has brought together Moore's published prose in *The Complete Prose of Marianne Moore* (1986). Moore's correspondence with Robert Lowell is published in David Kalstone's *Becoming a Poet* (1991); her relation to Wallace Stevens is considered by Robin G. Schulze in *The Web of Friendship* (1995). Biographies are Charles Molesworth's *Marianne Moore: A Literary Life* (1990) and Linda Leavell's *Holding On Upside Down: The Life and Work of Marianne Moore* (2013). Bonnie Costello edited *The Selected Letters of Marianne Moore* (1997). Book-length studies include Bernard F. Engel's *Marianne Moore* (1963, rev. 1989); Costello's *Marianne Moore: Imaginary Possessions* (1982); John M. Slatin's *The Savage's Romance: The Poetry of Marianne Moore* (1986); Grace Shulman's *Marianne Moore: The Poetry of Engagement* (1987); Margaret Holley's *The Poetry of Marianne Moore: A Study in Voice and Value* (1987); Cristanne Miller's *Questions of Authority* (1995); Leavell's *Marianne Moore and the Visual Arts* (1995); Elisabeth W. Joyce's *Cultural Critique and Abstraction: Marianne Moore and the Avant-Garde* (1998); and Victoria Bazin's *Marianne Moore and the Cultures of Modernity* (2010). Bethany Hickock's *Degrees of Freedom: American Women Poets and the Women's College, 1905–1955* (2008) connects Moore with Elizabeth Bishop and Sylvia Plath. Essay collections include *Marianne Moore, Woman and Poet* (1990), edited by Patricia Willis, and *Critics and Poets on Marianne Moore: "A Right Good Salvo of Barks"* (2005), edited by Leavell, Miller, and Schulze. Craig S. Abbott compiled *Marianne Moore: A Descriptive Bibliography* in 1977. Gary Lane's *A Concordance to the Poems of Marianne Moore* appeared in 1972.

Eugene O'Neill

The Library of America collected O'Neill's plays in three volumes, *Complete Plays, 1913–1920*; *Complete Plays, 1920–1931*; and *Complete Plays, 1932–1943* (1988). The standard biography of O'Neill is still that of Arthur and Barbara Gelb, *O'Neill* (1962, rev. 2000). Other biographical treatments are L. Schaeffer's *O'Neill, Son and Artist* (1973, 1990); Stephen A. Bloch's *Eugene O'Neill: Beyond*

Mourning and Tragedy (1999); and Robert M. Dowling's *Eugene O'Neill: A Life in Four Acts* (2014). *The Theatre We Worked For: The Letters of Eugene O'Neill to Kenneth Macgowan* (1982), edited by Jackson R. Bryer, documents O'Neill's attitudes to the theater of his day. Brenda Murphy's *O'Neill: Long Day's Journey into Night* (2001) provides a production history. Bryer and Travis Bogard edited *Selected Letters of Eugene O'Neill* (1994). *Conversations with Eugene O'Neill* (1990) is edited by Mark W. Estrin. Literary analysis of O'Neill's plays can be found in Bogard's *Contour in Time: The Plays of Eugene O'Neill* (1972, rev. 1987); Michael Manheim's *Eugene O'Neill's New Language of Kinship* (1982); Judith E. Barlow's *Final Acts: The Creation of Three Late O'Neill Plays* (1985); Kurt Eisen's *The Inner Strength of Opposites* (1994; on O'Neill's techniques); Joel Pfister's *Staging Depth: Eugene O'Neill and the Politics of Psychological Discourse* (1995); Donald Gallup's *Eugene O'Neill and His Eleven-Play Cycle* (1998); Doris Alexander's *Eugene O'Neill's Last Plays: Separating Art from Autobiography* (2005); and John Patrick Diggins's *Eugene O'Neill's America: Desire Under Democracy* (2007).

Essay collections include *Eugene O'Neill's Century* (1991), edited by Richard F. Moorton Jr.; *The Critical Response to Eugene O'Neill* (1993), edited by John H. Houchin; and *The Cambridge Companion to Eugene O'Neill* (1998), edited by Michael Manheim.

Katherine Anne Porter

Primary sources include *Ship of Fools* (1962); *The Collected Stories of Katherine Anne Porter* (1965); *The Collected Essays and Occasional Writings of Katherine Anne Porter* (1970); *The Never-Ending Wrong* (1977), about the Sacco and Vanzetti case; *Letters* (1990), edited by Isabel Bayley; *"This Strange, Old World" and Other Book Reviews by Katherine Anne Porter* (1991), edited by Darlene Harbour Unrue; *Uncollected Early Prose of Katherine Anne Porter* (1993), edited by Ruth M. Alvarez and Thomas F. Walsh; and *Katherine Anne Porter's Poetry* (1996), edited by Unrue. The Library of America's *Collected Stories and Other Writings* (2008), edited by Unrue, includes Porter's literary reviews and her journalism from Mexico. Unrue edited *Selected Letters of Katherine Anne Porter: Chronicles of a Modern Woman* (2012).

Biographies are Joan Givner's *Katherine Anne Porter, A Life* (1982, rev. 1991), and Unrue's *Katherine Anne Porter: The Life of an Artist* (2005). Givner also edited *Katherine Anne Porter: Conversations* (1987). A *Bibliography of the Works of Katherine Anne Porter*, edited by Louise Waldrip and Shirley Ann Bauer, appeared in 1969.

Critical studies include Jane Krause DeMouy's *Katherine Anne Porter's Women: The Eye of Her Fiction* (1983); Unrue's *Truth and Vision in Katherine Anne Porter's Fiction* (1985); Willene and George Hendrick's *Katherine Anne Porter* (rev. 1988); Thomas F. Walsh's *Katherine Anne Porter and Mexico: The Illusion of Eden* (1992); Robert H. Brinkmeyer's *Katherine Anne Porter's Artistic Development* (1993); Janis P. Stout's *Katherine Anne Porter, A Sense of the Times* (1995); Mary Titus's *The Ambivalent Art of Katherine Anne Porter* (2005); and Stout's *South by Southwest: Katherine Anne Porter and the Burden of Texas History* (2013). Unrue edited *Critical Essays on Katherine Anne Porter* (1997).

Ezra Pound
Pound's early poetry, from *A Lume Spento* (1908) through *Riposter* (1912), is in the authoritative *Collected Early Poems of Ezra Pound* (1976), edited by Michael King. The same volumes, along with later volumes *Hugh Selwyn Mauberley* and *Homage to Sextus Propertius*, are collected in *Personae: The Collected Shorter Poems* (rev. ed. 1949; 2nd rev. ed. 1990). The New Directions edition of *The Cantos* (1993) is definitive. The Library of America's *Poems and Translations* (2003), edited by Richard Sieburth, excludes *The Cantos*. The most important of Pound's critical writings are *The Spirit of Romance* (rev. 1952); *Gaudier-Brzeska: A Memoir* (1916); *Instigations* (1920); *Make It New* (1934); *The ABC of Reading* (1934); *Guide to Kulchur* (1938); and *Patria Mia* (1950). His criticism has been collected in *Literary Essays of Ezra Pound* (1954), edited by T. S. Eliot; *Selected Prose, 1909–1965* (1973), edited by William Cookson; and Ezra Pound's *Poetry and Prose Contributions to Periodicals* (1991), prefaced and arranged by Lea Baechler, A. Walton Litz, and James Longenback in eleven volumes. *Ezra Pound Speaking: Radio Speeches of World War II* (1978), edited by Leonard W. Doob, collects his wartime radio addresses. D. D. Paige edited *The Letters of Ezra Pound, 1907–1941* (1950). Other correspondence is collected in *Ezra Pound and Dorothy Shakespear: Their Letters, 1909–1914* (1984), edited by Omar Pound and A. Walton Litz; *Pound/Lewis: The Letters of Ezra Pound and Wyndham Lewis* (1985), edited by Timothy Materer; *Ezra Pound and James Loughlin* (1994), edited by David M. Gordon; and *Pound/Cummings: The Correspondence of Ezra Pound and E. E. Cummings*, edited by Barry Ahearn. Reviews of Pound are collected in Eric Homberger's *Ezra Pound: The Critical Heritage* (1973, 1997).

James J. Wilhelm's three-volume biography includes *The American Roots of Ezra Pound* (1985), *Ezra Pound in London and Paris,* *1908–1925* (1990), and *Ezra Pound: The Tragic Years, 1925–1972* (1994). David Moody also has a three-volume biography, *Ezra Pound: Poet* (2007, 2014, 2015). Also useful are Noel Stock's *The Life of Ezra Pound* (1970, 1982); C. David Haymann's *Ezra Pound, The Last Rower: A Political Profile* (1976); and Wendy Stallard Flory's *The American Ezra Pound* (1989). *The Roots of Treason: Ezra Pound and the Secrets of St. Elizabeth* (1984), by E. Fuller Torrey, focuses on Pound's trial and incarceration.

Hugh Kenner's *The Pound Era* (1972) has been influential. Good introductions are Christine Brooke-Rose's *A ZBC of Ezra Pound* (1971) and James Knapp's *Ezra Pound* (1972). For *The Cantos* see the *Annotated Index to the Cantos of Ezra Pound* (1957) (through "Canto LXXXIV"), edited by John H. Edwards and William W. Vasse; Noel Stock's *Reading the Cantos* (1967); Ronald Bush's *The Genesis of Pound's Cantos* (1976); Wilhelm's *The Later Cantos of Ezra Pound* (1977); Lawrence S. Rainey's *Ezra Pound and the Monument of Culture* (1991); Carrol F. Terrill's *A Companion to the Cantos of Ezra Pound* (1993); George Kearn's *Guide to Ezra Pound's Selected Cantos* (1980); Anthony Woodward's *Ezra Pound and "The Pisan Cantos"* (1980); and William Cookson's updated *Guide to the Cantos of Ezra Pound* (2001). Tim Redman's *Ezra Pound and Italian Fascism* (1991) addresses the poet's politics, as does Leon Surette's *Pound in Purgatory: From Economic Realism to Anti-Semitism* (1999). Cultural approaches to Pound include Michael Coyle's *Ezra Pound, Popular Genres, and the Discourse of Culture* (1995); Daniel Tiffany's *Radio Corpse* (1995); and Rebecca Beasley's *Ezra Pound and the Visual Culture of Modernism* (2007). Marjorie Perloff's *The Dance of the Intellect* (1996) studies poetry in the Pound tradition; Jacob Korg's *Winter Love: Ezra Pound and H. D.* (2003) is a comparative study. Andrew Gibson edited *Pound in Multiple Perspective: A Collection of Critical Essays* (1993), and Ira B. Nadel edited *The Cambridge Companion to Ezra Pound* (1999).

Edwin Arlington Robinson
Collected Poems of Edwin Arlington Robinson (1921) was enlarged periodically through 1937. In addition to shorter verse, Robinson wrote long narrative poems, including the Arthurian Trilogy of *Merlin* (1917), *Lancelot* (1920), and *Tristram* (1927). Other books include *Roman Bartholomew* (1923), *The Man Who Died Twice* (1924), *Cavender's House* (1929), *The Glory of the Nightingales* (1930), *Matthias at the Door* (1931), *Talifer* (1933), *Amaranth* (1934), and *King Jasper* (1935). Ridgely Torrence compiled *Selected*

Letters (1940). Denham Sutcliffe edited *Untriangulated Stars: Letters of Edwin Arlington Robinson to Harry de Forest Smith, 1890–1905* (1947). Richard Cary edited *Edwin Arlington Robinson's Letters to Edith Brower* (1968).

Scott Donaldson's *Edwin Arlington Robinson: A Poet's Life* (2007) is comprehensive. Richard Cary documented *The Early Reception of Edwin Arlington Robinson* (1974). Introductions to Robinson's work include Wallace L. Anderson's *Edwin Arlington Robinson: A Critical Introduction* (1967), Hoyt C. Franchere's *Edwin Arlington Robinson* (1968), and Louis O. Coxe's *Edwin Arlington Robinson: The Life of Poetry* (1969). Ellsworth Barnard edited *Edwin Arlington Robinson: Centenary Essays* (1969). Other collections are *Appreciation of Edwin Arlington Robinson: Twenty-eight Interpretive Essays* (1969), edited by Richard Cary; and *Edwin Arlington Robinson: A Collection of Critical Essays* (1970), edited by Francis Murphy. Richard Hoffpair's *The Contemplative Poetry of Edwin Arlington Robinson, Robert Frost, and Yvor Winters* (2002) links Robinson to other poets.

Carl Sandburg
The *Complete Poems of Carl Sandburg* (1950) was revised and expanded in 1970. *Breathing Tokens* (1978), edited by Margaret Sandburg, prints unpublished poems. *Billy Sunday and Other Poems* (1993), edited by George and Willene Hendrick, contains some of his unpublished, uncollected, and unexpurgated poems. Paul Berman edited his *Selected Poems* (2006) for the Library of America. In addition to eight full-length volumes of poetry, Sandburg wrote a Pulitzer Prize–winning study of Abraham Lincoln: *Abraham Lincoln: The Prairie Years*, 2 vols. (1926), and *Abraham Lincoln: The War Years*, 4 vols. (1939); two collections of journalism and social commentary; *Rootabaga Stories* for children; a novel; and a book of American folk songs. *Fables, Foibles and Foobles* (1988), edited by George Hendrick, is a selection of unpublished humorous pieces. *More Rootabagas* (1993), edited by Hendrick, contains stories for children. *Selected Poems* (1996) was edited by George and Willene Hendrick. *The Letters of Carl Sandburg* (1968, 1988) was edited by Herbert Mitgang. *The Poet and the Dream Girl: The Love Letters of Lilian Steichen and Carl Sandburg* (1987, 1999) was edited by Margaret Sandburg.

Always the Young Strangers (1953) and *Ever the Winds of Chance* (1983), edited by Margaret Sandburg and George Hendrick, are segments of Sandburg's autobiography. A full-scale biography is Penelope Niven's *Carl Sandburg: A Biography* (1991). Critical studies include Richard Crowder's *Carl Sandburg*

(1964) and Philip R. Yannella's *The Other Carl Sandburg* (1996). John Marsh's *Hog Butchers, Beggars, and Busboys: Poverty, Labor, and the Making of Modern American Poetry* (2011) includes a chapter on Sandburg.

Gertrude Stein
The Library of America published Stein's writings in two volumes: 1903–32 and 1932–46 (1998). The Yale Edition of the *Unpublished Writings of Gertrude Stein* (1951–58), edited by Carl Van Vechten, contains eight volumes of poetry, prose fiction, portraits, essays, and miscellany. The Norton Critical Edition of *Three Lives and Q.E.D.* (2005), edited by Marianne DeKoven, supplies critical and biographical contexts. Among publications in Stein's lifetime are *Tender Buttons* (1914) and prose fiction, including *Three Lives* (1909), *The Making of Americans* (1925), *Lucy Church Amiably* (1930), *Ida: A Novel* (1941), and *Brewsie and Willie* (1946). *Geography and Plays* (1922), *Operas and Plays* (1932), and *Last Operas and Plays* (1949, 1995), edited by Carl Van Vechten, contain dramatic pieces. Biographical material and portraits of Stein's contemporaries may be found in *The Autobiography of Alice B. Toklas* (1933), *Portraits and Prayers* (1934), *Everybody's Autobiography* (1937), and *Wars I Have Seen* (1945). Other works, including meditations, essays, sketches, and sociolinguistic treatises, are *Useful Knowledge* (1928), *How to Write* (1931), *Lectures in America* (1935), *Narration: Four Lectures by Gertrude Stein* (1935), *What Are Masterpieces?* (1940), and *Four in America* (1947). Donald C. Gallup edited *Fernhurst, Q.E.D. and Other Early Writings by Gertrude Stein* (1971) and also a collection of letters to Stein, *The Flowers of Friendship* (1953). Her correspondence with Mabel Dodge Luhan is edited by Patricia R. Everett (1996), with Thornton Wilder by Edward Burns and Ulla E. Dydo (1996), and with Virgil Thomson by Susan Holbrook and Thomas Dilworth (2010). *Baty Precious Always Shines* (2000), edited by Kay Tarner, has selected love letters written between Stein and her partner, Alice B. Toklas. *Gertrude Stein: An Annotated Bibliography* (1979) was compiled by Maureen R. Liston.

W. G. Rogers's *When This You See Remember Me: Gertrude Stein in Person* (1948) and Alice B. Toklas's *What Is Remembered* (1963) are reminiscences of Stein by friends. Biographies include Howard Greenfield's *Gertrude Stein: A Biography* (1973); James R. Mellow's *Charmed Circle: Gertrude Stein and Company* (1974); Janet Hobhouse's *Everybody Who Was Anybody* (1989); Linda Wagner-Martin's *Favored Strangers: Gertrude Stein and Her Family* (1995); Brenda Wineapple's *Sister Brother: Gertrude* and Leo Stein (1996); and Janet Malcolm's Two Lives: Gertrude and Alice (2007). Critical studies include Robert B. Haas's A Primer for the Gradual Understanding of Gertrude Stein (1971); Richard Bridgman's Gertrude Stein in Pieces (1970); Wendy Steiner's Exact Resemblance to Exact Resemblance: The Literary Portraiture of Gertrude Stein (1978); Marianne DeKoven's A Different Language: Gertrude Stein's Experimental Writing (1983); Randa Kay Dubnick's The Structure of Obscurity: Gertrude Stein, Language, and Cubism (1984); Lisa Ruddick's Reading Gertrude Stein: Body, Text, Gnosis (1990); Jane P. Bowers's Gertrude Stein (1993); Linda Watts's Gertrude Stein: A Study of the Short Fiction (1999); Barbara Will's Gertrude Stein, Modernism, and the Problem of "Genius" (2000); Steven Meyer's Irresistible Dictation: Gertrude Stein and the Correlations of Writing and Science (2001); Dana Cairns Watson's Gertrude Stein and the Essence of What Happens (2005); and Karen Leick's Gertrude Stein and the Making of an American Celebrity (2009). Bruce Kellner edited the useful Gertrude Stein Companion (1988). A collection of critical essays, edited by Richard Kostelanetz, is Gertrude Stein Advanced (1990).

John Steinbeck
The Library of America issued four volumes of Steinbeck's work, Novels and Stories 1932–1937 (1994), The Grapes of Wrath and Other Writings (1996), Novels 1942–1952 (2002), and Travels with Charley and Later Novels 1947–1962 (2007). Two biographies are Jack J. Benson's The True Adventures of John Steinbeck, Writer (1984) and Jay Parini's John Steinbeck (1995). Elaine Steinbeck and Robert Wallsten edited Steinbeck: A Life in Letters (1975). Critical studies of Steinbeck include R. S. Hughes's Beyond the Red Pony: A Reader's Guide to Steinbeck's Complete Short Stories (1987); John H. Timmerman's The Dramatic Landscape of Steinbeck's Short Stories (1990); and Warren French's John Steinbeck's Fiction Revisited (1994). R. David edited John Steinbeck: A Collection of Critical Essays (1972); other collections are Rediscovering Steinbeck (1989), edited by Cliff Lewis and Carroll Britch; Critical Essays on Steinbeck's Grapes of Wrath (1989), edited by John Ditsky; Short Novels of John Steinbeck (1990), edited by Jackson J. Benson; John Steinbeck: The Contemporary Reviews (1996), edited by Joseph R. McElrath Jr., Jesse S. Crisler, and Susan Shillinglaw; Steinbeck and the Environment: Interdisciplinary Approaches (1997), edited by Susan F. Beegel; and Beyond Boundaries: Rereading John Steinbeck (2002), edited by Shillinglaw and Kevin Hearle.

Wallace Stevens
The Collected Poems of Wallace Stevens was published in 1954. Milton J. Bates's Opus Posthumous (1957, rev. 1989) includes previously uncollected poems, plays, and essays. The Necessary Angel: Essays on Reality and the Imagination (1951) is Stevens's prose statement on poetry. The Library of America issued his Collected Poetry and Prose (1997). Other resources are Letters of Wallace Stevens (1966, 1996), edited by Holly Stevens; The Contemplated Spouse: The Letters of Wallace Stevens to Elsie (2006), edited by J. Donald Blount; Concordance to the Poetry of Wallace Stevens (1963), edited by Thomas Walsh; and Wallace Stevens: A Descriptive Bibliography (1973), compiled by J. M. Edelstein.

Joan Richardson's Wallace Stevens: The Early Years, 1879–1923 (1986) chronicles the poet's youth and her Wallace Stevens: The Later Years, 1923–1955 (1988) completes the story. Another biography is Tony Sharpe's Wallace Stevens: A Literary Life (2000). A. Walton Litz's Introspective Voyager: The Poetic Development of Wallace Stevens (1972) traces Stevens's thought and style through his early and middle years. Harold Bloom's Wallace Stevens: The Poems of Our Climate (1977) considers intellectual influences on Stevens; Joseph N. Riddle's The Clairvoyant Eye: The Poetry and Poetics of Wallace Stevens (1969, 1991) reads many individual poems. Other good full-length studies include Eleanor Cook's Poetry, Word-Play, and Word-War in Wallace Stevens (1988) and A Reader's Guide to Wallace Stevens (2007); James Longenbach's Wallace Stevens: The Plain Sense of Things (1991); Alan Filreis's Modernism from Left to Right (1994); Janet McCann's Wallace Stevens Revisited (1995); and Edward Ragg's Wallace Stevens and the Aesthetics of Abstraction (2010). Jacqueline Vaught Brogan's The Violence within/The Violence without: Wallace Stevens and the Emergence of a Revolutionary Poetics (2003) and Malcolm Woodland's Wallace Stevens and the Apocalyptic Mode (2005) consider the relation of Stevens's poetry to war. Albert Gelpi collects essays on the poet in Wallace Stevens: The Poetics of Modernism (1990); other collections are Critical Essays on Wallace Stevens (1988), edited by Steven Gould Axelrod and Helen Deese; Wallace Stevens and the Feminine (1993), edited by Melita Schaum; and Wallace Stevens Across the Atlantic (2008), edited by Bart Eeckhout and Ragg.

Jean Toomer
Toomer's published works include Cane (1923, repr. 1975, pub. also in a Norton Critical Edition, 2011), Essentials (1931), Portage Potential (1932), and an address, "The Flavor

of Man" (1949). His *Collected Poems*, edited by Robert B. Jones and Margery Toomer Latimer, was published in 1988. *A Jean Toomer Reader* (1993), containing previously unpublished writings, was edited by Frederik L. Rusch; Robert B. Jones edited *Selected Essays and Literary Criticism* (1996). Mark Whalan edited *The Letters of Jean Toomer, 1919–1924* (2005). Brian Joseph Benson and Mabel Mayle Dillard's *Jean Toomer* (1980); Nellie Y. McKay's *Jean Toomer, Artist: A Study of His Literary Life and Work, 1894–1936* (1984); and Cynthia Earl Kerman and Richard Eldridge's *The Lives of Jean Toomer: A Hunger for Wholeness* (1989) are biographies. Studies include Charles Scruggs and Lee Van De Marr's *Jean Toomer and the Terrors of American History* (1998); Karen Ford Jackson's *Split-Gut Song: Jean Toomer and the Poetics of Modernity* (2005); and Barbara Foley's *Jean Toomer: Race, Repression and Revolution* (2014). Whalan's *Race, Manhood, and Modernism in America: The Short Story Cycles of Sherwood Anderson and Jean Toomer* (2007) is a comparative study. Essay collections are *Jean Toomer: A Critical Evaluation* (1988), edited by Therman B. O'Daniel, and *Jean Toomer and the Harlem Renaissance*, edited by Geneviève Faber and Michel Faith (2000).

William Carlos Williams

Williams's poems were first collected in three volumes: *Collected Earlier Poems of William Carlos Williams* (1951), *Collected Later Poems of William Carlos Williams* (1950), and *Pictures from Brueghel* (1962). More recent are *The Collected Poems of William Carlos Williams, volume 1, 1909–1939* (1996), edited by A. Walton Litz and Christopher MacGowan, and volume 2, 1939–1962, edited by MacGowan (1988). *Paterson's* five books, published individually between 1946 and 1958, were issued in one volume in 1963 and reedited by MacGowan (1992). The Library of America issued *Selected Poems* (2004), edited by Robert Pinsky. *Kora in Hell*, Williams's volume of prose poetry, is in the collection *Imaginations* (1970), edited by Webster Schott, along with essays, fiction, and creative prose. Williams's short stories are collected in *Make Light of It* (1950) and again, with several additions, in *The Farmers' Daughters* (1961). His novels are *A Voyage to Pagany* (1928), *White Mule* (1937), *In the Money* (1940), and *The Build Up* (1946). His dramatic pieces were published together in *Many Loves and Other Plays* (1961). Important essays are contained in *In the American Grain* (1925, 1940), *Selected Essays of William Carlos Williams* (1954), and *Imaginations* (1970), edited by Webster Schott. Williams's prose also includes *The Autobiography of William Carlos Williams* (1951); a book of recollections dictated to Edith Heal, *I Wanted to Write a Poem* (1958); and *Yes, Mrs. Williams* (1959), a portrait of the poet's mother. J. C. Thirlwall edited *The Selected Letters of William Carlos Williams* (1957). Selections from the Pound–Williams correspondence, edited by Hugh Witemeyer, appeared in 1996. Letters between Williams and Denise Levertov, edited by MacGowan, appeared in 1998. Barry Ahearn edited *The Correspondence of William Carlos Williams and Louis Zukofsky* (2003). *The Humane Particulars: The Collected Letters of William Carlos Williams and Kenneth Burke* (2003) was edited by James H. East. Emily Mitchell Wallace compiled *A Bibliography of William Carlos Williams* (1968). Reed Whittemore's *William Carlos Williams: Poet from Jersey* (1975) is a critical biography, as are Paul Mariani's more detailed *William Carlos Williams: A New World Naked* (1981), and Herbert Leibowitz's *"Something Urgent I Have to Say to You": The Life and Works of William Carlos Williams* (2011).

James E. Breslin's *William Carlos Williams: An American Artist* (1970) is a still-useful overview. Other general introductions are Thomas R. Whitaker's *William Carlos Williams* (1989) and Kelli A. Larson's *Guide to the Poetry of William Carlos Williams* (1995). Among specialized studies are Mike Weaver's *William Carlos Williams: The American Background* (1971); Joseph N. Riddel's *The Inverted Bell: Modernism and the Counter-Poetics of William Carlos Williams* (1974); Henry M. Sayre's *The Visual Text of William Carlos Williams* (1983); Ann W. Fisher-Wirth's *William Carlos Williams and Autobiography: The Woods of His Own Nature* (1989); Ron Callan's *William Carlos Williams and Transcendentalism* (1992); T. Hugh Crawford's *Modernism, Medicine, and William Carlos Williams* (1993); Brian A. Bremen's *William Carlos Williams and the Diagnostics of Culture* (1993); Peter Halter's *The Revolution in the Visual Arts and the Poetry of William Carlos Williams* (1994); Donald W. Markos's *Ideas in Things* (1994); Barry Ahearn's *William Carlos Williams and Alterity* (1994); Julio Marzan's *The Spanish American Roots of William Carlos Williams* (1994); Stanley Koehler's *Countries of the Mind: The Poetry of William Carlos Williams* (1998); and John Beck's *Writing the Radical Center: William Carlos Williams, John Dewey, and American Cultural Politics* (2001).

Linda Wagner's *The Prose of William Carlos Williams* (1970) and Robert Coles's *William Carlos Williams: The Knack of Survival in America* (1975) discuss Williams's prose. For *Paterson*, see Joel Conarroe's *William Carlos Williams' Paterson: Language and Landscape* (1970); Benjamin Sankey's *A Companion to William Carlos Williams's Paterson* (1971); and

Ann Marie Mikkelson's *Pastoral, Pragmatism, and Twentieth-Century American Poetry* (2011). Paul Mariani's *William Carlos Williams: The Poet and His Critics* (1975) considers Williams's critical reception, as does *William Carlos Williams, The Critical Heritage* (1980, 1997), edited by Charles Doyle.

Richard Wright
Wright's fiction includes *Uncle Tom's Children* (1938), *Native Son* (1940), *The Outsider* (1953), and *Eight Men* (1961). *Black Boy* (1945) is his autobiography; *White Man, Listen!* (1957) is an important work of nonfiction. The Library of America has published his writings in two volumes, including an unexpurgated version of *Native Son* (1991). Earle V. Bryant edited *Byline, Richard Wright: Articles from the Daily Worker and the New Masses* (2015). For a complete bibliography of his writings, see *Richard Wright: A Primary Bibliography* (1982), compiled by Charles T. Davis and Michel Fabre. A good sample of reviews can be found in *Richard Wright: The Critical Reception* (1978), edited by John M. Reilly; a massive bibliography of Wright criticism around the world has been assembled by Keneth Kinnamon (1988). Kinnamon and Michel Fabre edited *Conversations with Richard Wright* (1993). The best critical biography is Fabre's *The Unfinished Quest of Richard Wright* (1993); see also Margaret Walker's *Richard Wright, Daemonic Genius* (1993) and Hazel Rowley's *Richard Wright: The Life and Times* (2001). Critical studies include Russell C. Brignano's *Richard Wright: An Introduction to the Man and His Works* (1970), Kinnamon's *The Emergence of Richard Wright* (1972), Fabre's *Richard Wright: Books and Writers* (1990) and his essays in *The World of Richard Wright* (2007), and Robert Butler's *Native Son: The Emergence of a New Black Hero* (1991). Abdul R. Jan Mohamed's *The Death-Bound-Subject: Richard Wright's Archaeology of Death* (2005) is an ambitious theoretical study. Collections of criticism are Yoshinobu Hakutani's *Critical Essays on Richard Wright* (1982); *Richard Wright: Critical Perspectives Past and Present* (1993), edited by Henry Louis Gates, Jr., and K. A. Appiah; *The Critical Response to Richard Wright* (1995), edited by Robert J. Butler; *Richard Wright: A Collection of Critical Essays* (1995), edited by Arnold Rampersad; Kinnamon's *Critical Essays on Richard Wright's Native Son* (1997); and *Richard Wright: New Readings in the 21st Century* (2011), edited by Alice Mikal Craven, William E. Dow, and Gary Taylor.

AMERICAN LITERATURE SINCE 1945

Reference Works and Histories

Jennifer Ashton's *Cambridge Companion to American Poetry since* 1945 (2013) and John Duvall's *Cambridge Companion to American Fiction after* 1945 (2011) collect general essays well suited to introducing students and teachers to the broad contours of the period. Excellent treatment of the period up to the end of the twentieth century can be found in vol. 7 ("Prose Writing, 1940–1990"; 1999) and 8 ("Poetry and Criticism, 1940–1995"; 1996) of *The Cambridge History of American Literature* (Sacvan Bercovitch, general editor). The vast *Dictionary of Literary Biography*, under the supervision of Matthew J. Bruccoli, the Scribners *American Writers* series, edited by Jay Parini, and vol. 2 of David Perkins's *History of Modern Poetry* (1976) offer wide coverage of specific authors. A more general history appears in Robert von Hallberg's *American Poetry and Culture 1945–1980* (1985). An indispensable reference guide for poetry is *Contemporary Poets*, 7th ed. (2000), edited by Thomas Riggs. Specific areas are treated by editors Darryl Dickson-Carr's *The Columbia Guide to Contemporary African American Fiction* (2005), editor Eric Cheyfitz's *The Columbia Guide to American Indian Literatures of the United States since 1945* (2006), and José F. Aranda Jr.'s *When We Arrive: A New Literary History of Mexican America* (2003).

Gershun Avilez's chapter on the Black Arts movement and other essays in *The Cambridge Companion to American Civil Rights Literature* (2015) are especially useful for contextualizing American writing in the 1950s and '60s; Steven Conner's *The Cambridge Companion to Postmodernism* (2004) provides a guide to other cultural and aesthetic contexts of the period. Lawrence Jackson's *The Indignant Generation* (2011) gives the best fine-grained literary and social history of black writing between 1940 and 1960. Histories of specific movements in poetry are explored in Michael Palmer's *The San Francisco Renaissance* (1991) and David Lehmann's *The Last Avant-Garde: The Making of the New York School of Poets* (1998). Useful introductory series are the Modern Language Association's *Approaches to Teaching* . . . series, the University of South Carolina Press's *Understanding* . . . volumes, the University Press of Mississippi's *Conversations with* . . . , the *Critical Essays* books from G. K. Hall Publishers, the Greenwood Press *Critical Response* series, the *Cambridge Companion* series, and the *Modern Critical Views* collections edited by Harold Bloom. The University of Michigan's Poets on Poetry series offers volumes in which poets comment on their own and others' work.

Criticism

Criticism on the fiction, poetry, and drama of the second half of the twentieth century has reached a critical mass such that few critics or particular works can be said to dominate the discussion. Rather, excellent criticism— both monographs and articles—can be found on a range of topics and writers, much of which is flagged in bibliographies for the individual authors below. That said, a few works stand out for their broad arguments taking in a crowd of writers and artists working the period, representing a strong reading of what American literary production in the second half of the twentieth century, and in the opening decade of the twenty-first century, has accomplished artistically and culturally.

The study of poetics has remained important throughout the last several decades, and can generate a broad perspective through which to read and teach the poetry in this volume. Influential studies of contemporary poetics by Marjorie Perloff include *The Poetics of Indeterminacy* (1981), *Radical Artifice: Writing in the Age of Media* (1991), and *21st-Century Modernism: The New Poetics* (2001). Jennifer Ashton's *From Modernism to Postmodernism: American Poetry and Theory in the Twentieth Century* (2006), and Charles Altieri's *The Art of Twentieth-Century American Poetry: Modernism and After* (2006) share Perloff's theoretically sophisticated understanding of the period's writing. Anthony Reed's highly theoretical *Freedom Time: The Poetics and Politics of Black Experimental Writing* (2014) discusses contemporary poetics and experiment in relation to the distinct position of black and Caribbean writers; while his focus is not on writers included in this volume, his way of reading black poetics is essential alongside arguments such as Perloff's and Altieri's. (His prose, like theirs, is suited to the theoretically intrepid reader.) Timothy Yu's edited volume, *Nests and Strangers: On Asian American Women Poets* (2015) and Yu's monograph, *Race and the Avant-Garde: Experimental and Asian American Poetry since 1965* (2009) effectively bring together theoretical and cultural-studies approaches. Gillian White's *Lyric Shame: The 'Lyric' Subject of Contemporary American Poetry* (2014) joins a more recent body of criticism about lyric as a genre, a turn best captured in Virginia Jackson's and Yopie Prins's edited volume, *The Lyric Theory Reader: A Critical Anthology* (2014). Jahan Ramazani's monographs on poetry's transnational context and on poetry's relationship to prayer, song, news, and other genres open up fruitful new ways of connecting poetry of the twentieth and twenty-first centuries with the large context of human expression, even though his work is not exclusively about contemporary or American poetry.

The tradition of the poet-critic lives on in American letters today, and several works in this vein are particularly worthy of mention. In *Close Calls with Nonsense: Reading New Poetry* (2009), Stephen Burt opens difficult contemporary poetry (including Ashbery, Ammons, Berryman, Bidart, Gunn, and others) to readers. The poet and critic Elizabeth Alexander writes about black poets of the late twentieth century in *Power and Possibility: Essays, Reviews, and Interviews* (2007); poet Kevin Young reflects on black poetics more generally in *The Grey Album: On the Blackness of Blackness* (2012). On lyric, the poet Allen Grossman and Mark Halliday's *The Sighted Singer: Two Works on Poetry for Readers and Writers* (1992) is more theoretical but generative and accessible nevertheless. The history of thinking about poetry may also be traced through statements on poetics by both poets and critics: *Poetics of the New American Poetry* (1973), edited by Donald Allen, was groundbreaking, and *Twentieth-Century American Poetry* (2004), edited by Dana Gioia, David Mason, and Meg Schoerke, gathers statements on poetics from throughout the period.

Among the vibrant criticism on American fiction, Mark McGurl's *The Program Era* (2009) has been widely influential, documenting the rise and significance of the writing program since the 1930s. The book examines a host of writers in its capacious arguments about craft, multiculturalism, the university, and middlebrow reading. Mark Greif's *The Age of the Crisis of Man: Thought and Fiction in America, 1933–1973* (2015) sets a wide array of midcentury American writers and critics in the philosophical and political context of a mid-century sense of cultural "crisis." Min Hyoung Song's *The Children of 1965: On Writing, and Not Writing, as an Asian American* sets discussions of fiction by many American writers of East Asian or South Asian decent in a broad context of Asian American writing in the late twentieth century. His appendix, "Contemporary Asian American Literature 101," is indispensible as a resource, listing over a hundred works of contemporary literature by Asian American authors across genres of fiction, poetry, life writing, comics, and creative nonfiction. Loren Glass's *Counterculture Colophon: Grove Press, the Evergreen Review, and the Incorporation of the Avant-Garde* (2013) gives a detailed history of the literary environment of experiment and resistance to censorship in the 1960s through the story of Grove Press, influential publisher of many of the avant-garde American and European writers of the day. Dean Rader, in *Engaged Resistance: American Indian Art, Literature, and Film from Alcatraz to the NMAI* (2011), reads literature, film and visual art that puts Native authors such as Harjo, Silko, Erdrich, and Alexie in a broader aesthetic context.

George Cotkin's *Feast of Excess: A Cultural History of the New Sensibility* (2016) documents the literary counterculture across genres in chronologically arranged chapters on an array of writers and artists from the early fifties through the early seventies, including short chapters on six authors in this volume. Broad overviews of drama in the period can be found in Sanford Sternlich's *A Reader's Guide to Modern American Drama* (2002), Thomas S. Hischak's *American Theatre: A Chronicle of Comedy and Drama, 1969–2000* (2001), Christopher Bigsby's *Contemporary American Playwrights* (1999), and Herbert Blau's *The Dubious Spectacle: Extremities of the Theater, 1976–2000* (2002).

American literary studies in the last decade has attempted to see American literature in a global and transnational context. This trend can be felt in many of the more recent critical works mentioned here, but a fine introduction to the central issues can be found in the collection *Globalizing American Studies* (2010), edited by Brian T. Edwards and Dilip Parameshwar Gaonkar. A more reflective treatment about the contemporary situation of American literature among global readers can be found in Caroline Levander's thought-provoking *Where Is American Literature?* (2013).

While teachers and students of literature naturally focus on the written word, the period covered by this volume inspires many to consider the broader media landscape of the late twentieth and early twenty-first centuries as they seek to understand the literature of the time. A quartet of books provides a fine overview of the issues addressed by media studies, including insights from the rejuvenated field of the history of the book. These critical works do not refer to specific writers in this volume, but they abound in big, interesting ideas that will enliven consideration of the anthology's texts for teachers and students so inclined. See Lisa Nakamura, *Digitizing Race: Visual Cultures of the Internet* (2008), Matthew Kirschenbaum, *Mechanisms: New Media and the Forensic Imagination* (2008), Robert Darnton, *The Case for Books: Past, Present and Future* (2010), and Alan Liu, *The Laws of Cool: Knowledge Work and the Culture of Information* (2004). Liu and Darnton, widely admired critics of Romantic poetry and eighteenth-century French literature, respectively, are particularly helpful in thinking about literature's relationship to new forms of media. David Shields's provocative book, *Reality Hunger* (2010), offers a version of a manifesto for a wide range of work by creative nonfiction writers.

Many studies of American literature since 1945 have been motivated by the social and identity movements of the period and seek to document these in and through the history of American writing. Two important studies from a feminist perspective are Nancy J. Peterson's *Against Amnesia: Contemporary Women Writers and the Crisis of Historical Memory* (2001) and Linda S. Kauffman's *Bad Girls and Sick Boys: Fantasies in Contemporary Art and Culture* (1998). A feminist approach to the study of poetry can be found in *Gendered Modernisms: American Women Poets and Their Readers* (1996), edited by Margaret Dickie and Thomas Travisano. Multiculturalism concerns Martha J. Cutter in *Lost and Found in Translation: Contemporary Ethnic American Writing and the Politics of Language Diversity* (2005), Paula M. L. Moya in *Learning from Experience: Minority Identities, Multicultural Struggles* (2002), Robert Jackson in *Seeking the Region in American Literature and Culture* (2005). Multiculturalism in poetry is the subject of Satya Mohanty's *Literary Theory and the Claims of History: Postmodernism, Objectivity, and Multicultural Politics* (1997). African American writing is the focus in Bernard W. Bell's *The Contemporary African American Novel: Its Folk Roots and Modern Literary Branches* (2004), Cheryl A. Wall's *Worrying the Line: Black Women Writers, Lineage, and Literary Tradition* (2005), Suzanne W. Jones's *Race Mixing: Southern Fiction since the Sixties* (2004). *African American Theater: A Cultural Companion* (2008) by Gloria Dickerson covers its subject in a narrative manner. African American poetry is examined in Joanne Gabbin's *The Furious Flowering of African American Poetry* (1999) and Alden Lynn Nielsen's *Black Chant: Languages of African-American Postmodernism* (1992). Chicano/a work is treated by Charles M. Tatum in *Chicano Popular Culture* (2001), Mary Pat Brady in *Extinct Lands, Temporal Geographies: Chicana Literature and the Urgency of Space* (2002), Elisabeth Mermann-Jozwiak in *Postmodern Vernaculars: Chicana Literature and Postmodern Rhetoric* (2005), Tey Diana Rebolledo in *The Chronicles of Panchita Villa and Other Guerrilleras* (2005), Ramon Saldívar in *Chicano Narrative* (1990), and Ellie D. Hernandez in *Postnationalism in Chicana/o Literature and Culture* (2009). Deborah L. Madsen's *Understanding Contemporary Chicana Literature* (2000) examines the work of women poets.

Transnational Asian American Literature: Sites and Transits (2006), edited by Shirley Geok-lin Lim et al., includes essays covering issues from immigration to feminism and globalism. Xiaojing Zhou studies Asian American poetry in *The Ethics and Poetics of Alterity in Asian American Poetry* (2006). Arnold Krupat's *Red Matters: Native American Studies* (2002) looks beyond nationalism, indigenism, and cosmopolitanism to gauge Native American literature's importance to the ethical and intellectual heritage of the West. Catherine Rainwater's *Dreams of Fiery Stars: The Transformation of Native American Fiction* (1999) offers strong artistic analysis. John Lloyd Purdy's *Writing Indian, Native Conversations* (2009) combines criticism and interviews. Kenneth Lincoln's *Sing with the Heart of a Bear: Fusions of Native and American Poetry, 1890–1999* (1999) stresses poetry's flexible and adaptable nature rather than its conformity to rigid ethnic and literary categories. Robin Riley First's *The Heart Is a Drum: Continuance and Resistance in American Indian Poetry* (2000) provides cultural and historical readings of a wide range of poems.

Especially useful for understanding how and why contemporary writers produce their work is the critical interview. Larry McCaffery, with various coeditors, has produced a series of extensive dialogues with important authors of the past four decades: *Anything Can Happen* (1983), *Alive and Writing* (1987), *Across the Wounded Galaxies* (1990), and *Some Other Frequency* (1996). Individual bibliographies below routinely mention interview sources one may consult.

An increasing amount of high-quality material can be found online, including websites that offer audio versions of writers reading from their work. The Academy of American Poets' poets.org; the Poetry Foundation's poetryfoundation.org; and Penn Sound's website (writing.upenn.edu/pennsound) are the best general sites for poetry and including poems, biography, and troves of recordings and other resources. Over the years the *Paris Review* has conducted a series of interviews under the rubrics "Writers at Work" and

"The Art of Fiction"; these include some of the most important writers of this period and are now available in full, and without cost, on the *Paris Review* website. The Internet Public Library offers "Native American Authors" at www.ipl.org/div/natam/. Post45.org offers a small stream of free access, curated critical essays, reviews, and occasional writer interviews on American literature and culture in the period.

Edward Abbey

A prolific writer, Abbey published numerous nonfiction works of environmental writing as well as eight novels. His most significant works remain *Desert Solitaire: A Season in the Wilderness* (1968; nonfiction) and his novel *The Monkey Wrench Gang* (1975), which has become, for some environmentalists, a sort of handbook for protest tactics. An anthology, *The Best of Edward Abbey*, appeared in 1988. His poetry is collected in *Earth Apples: The Poetry of Edward Abbey* (1994). Two volumes with selections from Abbey's journals are *A Voice Crying in the Wilderness: Notes from a Secret Journal* (1989) and *Confessions of a Barbarian: Selections from the Journals of Edward Abbey, 1951–1989* (1995). His selected letters can be found in *Postcards from Ed: Dispatches and Salvos from an American Iconoclast* (2006). *Edward Abbey: A Voice in the Wilderness* (1993), produced and directed by Eric Temple, is a documentary film about Abbey's life.

Among the critical discussions of Abbey's work are Anne Ronald's *The New West of Edward Abbey* (1982), John Cooley's edited collection, *Earthly Words: Essays on Contemporary American Nature and Environmental Writers* (1994), James I. McClintock's *Nature's Kindred Spirits: Aldo Leopold, Joseph Wood Krutch, Edward Abbey, Annie Dillard, and Gary Snyder* (1994), Peter Quigley's *Coyote in the Maze: Tracking Edward Abbey in a World of Words* (1998), and John M. Cahalan's important biography, *Edward Abbey: A Life* (2001).

Sherman Alexie

Alexie's novels are *Reservation Blues* (1995), *Indian Killer* (1996), *Flight: A Novel* (2007) and, for young adult readers, *The Absolutely True Diary of a Part-Time Indian* (2007; his best-known book) and *Radioactive Love Song* (2009). *Blasphemy: New and Selected Stories* (2013) offers a selection of his best stories from several previous collections alongside new ones. The stories in *The Lone Ranger and Tonto Fistfight in Heaven* (1993) were adapted as a film script for *Smoke Signals* in 1998. He both wrote and directed the movie *The Business of Fancydancing* (2000). He has published eleven poetry collections to date, beginning with *The Business of Fancydancing* (1992); his most recent is *Face* (2009).

Daniel Grassian provides critical analysis in *Understanding Sherman Alexie* (2005); an array of critical perspectives on his major works can be found in *Sherman Alexie: A Collection of Critical Essays* (2012), edited by Jeff Berglund and Jan Roush.

Gloria Anzaldúa

Borderlands/La Frontera (1987), excerpted in this volume, includes memoir, historical analysis, and narrative poetry. Anzaldúa wrote in multiple genres throughout her career, authoring several novels for adults and for young readers, essays both autobiographical and theoretical, and short fiction. An influential cultural critic and feminist thinker, she edited *Making Face, Making Soul / Haciendo Caras: Creative and Critical Perspectives by Feminists of Color* (1990), and (with Cherríe Moraga) coedited the landmark collection *This Bridge Called My Back: Writings by adical Women of Color* (1981). In 2002 she coedited, with AnaLouise Keating, *This Bridge We Call Home: Radical Visions for Transformation*. After Anzaldúa's death, AnaLouise Keating edited *The Gloria Anzaldúa Reader* (2009), which includes previously unpublished writing and offers a well-chosen selection of the author's work across the several genres in which she wrote.

Anzaldúa's ouvre is studied by Deborah L. Madsen in *Understanding Contemporary Chicana Literature* (2000), Sonia Sandivár-Hull in *Feminism on the Border: Chicana Politics and Literature* (2000), Paula M. L. Moya in *Learning from Experience: Minority Identities, Multicultural Struggles* (2002), Catrióna Rueda Esquibel in *With Her Machete in Her Hand: Reading Chicana Lesbians* (2006), and AnaLouise Keating in *Extremundos / Between Worlds* (2008).

John Ashbery

Ashbery's most discussed collections are *Some Trees* (1956; his first) and *Self-Portrait in a Convex Mirror* (1975). *Notes From the Air* (2007) is a selection of his later poems, and Ashbery is now represented in the Library of America series by *John Ashbery: Collected Poems 1956–87* (2008). Ashbery's Charles Eliot Norton Lectures on Poetry appear in *Other Traditions* (2000), and he also published *Selected Prose* (2004).

Among useful critical essays are David Kalstone's *Five Temperaments* (1977) and John Shoptaw's book-length study of Ashbery's poetry, *On the Outside Looking Out* (1994). David K. Kermani's *John Ashbery: A Comprehensive Bibliography* (1975) is indispensable and amusing. See also *Beyond Amazement: New Essays on John Ashbery* (1980), edited by David Lehman, Charles Altieri's *Postmodernisms Now* (1998), John Emil Vincent's *John Ashbery and You: His Later Books* (2007). Ben Hickman's *John Ashbery and English Poetry* (2012) revises the critical tendency to read Ashbery as exclusively an American or a postmodern poet, showing his work's connections to canonical English poets such as Donne, Marvell, Clare, Wordsworth, and Auden. Jesse Zuba's chapter on *Some Trees* in *The First Book: Twentieth-Century Poetic Careers in America* (2016) examines how Ashbery's poetry first found its audience. Michael Clune's brilliant essay on Ashbery, "'Whatever Charms Is Alien': John Ashbery's Everything" (*Criticism*, summer 2008) offers a way to think about the difficulty of reading Ashbery by relating his work to science fiction.

James Baldwin
Baldwin published novels, short stories, essays, and plays throughout his career, but is best known for the early novel *Go Tell It on the Mountain* (1953) and for his politically charged essays, especially *The Fire Next Time* (1963). His literary critical essay on Stowe's *Uncle Tom's Cabin*, "Everybody's Protest Novel" (1949) is widely taught. His prose has been gathered in three Library of America volumes: *Early Novels and Stories* (1998), *Later Novels* (2015), and *Collected Essays* (1998, edited by Toni Morrison). Baldwin's nonfiction has been also been gathered as *Collected Essays* (1998) and *The Cross of Redemption* (2010).

Critical and popular interest in Baldwin has blossomed since the turn of the century. The first biography, James Campbell's *Talking at the Gates: A Life of James Baldwin* (1991), is now supplemented by Magdalena J. Zaborowska's *James Baldwin's Turkish Decade: Erotics of Exile* (2009); by Herb Boyd's *Baldwin's Harlem: A Biography of James Baldwin* (2008), which tells the story of Baldwin's life through his relationships with other Harlem writers of his time, including Langston Hughes, Malcolm X, and Countee Cullen; by Hilton Als's exceptional essay about Baldwin for the *New Yorker*, "The Enemy Within: The Making and Unmaking of James Baldwin" (February 16, 1998); and by stand-alone biographical essays included in the many recent collections of critical essays on his work. Criticism has embraced various topics in Baldwin's work,

including his religious themes, gay life and queer sexuality, transnational contexts, and his interest in performance and drama. Selected criticism would inclue: Lynn Orilla Scott's *James Baldwin's Later Fiction: Witness to the Journey* (2002), Clarence E. Hardy III's *James Baldwin's God: Sex, Hope and Crisis in Black Holiness Culture* (2003). D. Quentin Miller's edited collection of essays, *Reviewing James Baldwin: Things Not Seen* (2000), D. Quentin Miller, *"A Criminal Power": James Baldwin and the Law* (2012); *James Baldwin: America and Beyond* (2012), edited by Cora Kaplan and Bill Schwarz (an exceptional collection of essays by major writers and critics), and *James Baldwin Now* (1999), edited by Dwight McBride. Several works on Baldwin by critic Douglas Field include *A Historical Guide to James Baldwin* (2010), edited by Field, which lays out the state of what might be called "Baldwin Studies"; Field's introduction to Baldwin, *James Baldwin* (2011); and his recent analytical and historical essays on Baldwin in *All Those Strangers: The Art and Lives of James Baldwin* (2015). Consuela Francis, *The Critical Reception of James Baldwin, 1963–2010* (2014) reveals the changing understanding of Baldwin's work over the course of his career and beyond. The most recent overview of the field, useful for teaching, is *The Cambridge Companion to James Baldwin* (2015).

Amiri Baraka (LeRoi Jones)
In addition to his poetry and plays, Baraka authored four books on music: *Blues People* (1963), *Black Music* (1968), and *The Music: Reflections on Jazz and Blues* (1987), and *Digging: The Afro-American Soul of American Classical Music* (2009). His essays are collected in *Home* (1966), *Raise Race Rays Raze* (1971), and *Selected Plays and Prose of Amiri Baraka / LeRoi Jones* (1979). Baraka edited three important anthologies: *The Moderns* (1963), *Black Fire* (1968, with Larry Neal), and *Confirmation: An Anthology of African American Women* (1983), with Amina Baraka. In 1984 he published *The Autobiography of LeRoi Jones / Amiri Baraka.*

Early but still useful studies are *Baraka: The Renegade and the Mask* (1976) by Kimberly W. Benston and *Amiri Baraka / LeRoi Jones: The Quest for a "Populist Modernism"* (1978) by Werner Sollors. William J. Harris has written *The Poetry and Poetics of Amiri Baraka: The Jazz Aesthetic* (1985) and edited *The LeRoi Jones / Amiri Baraka Reader* (1991), supplying introductory literary history and a bibliography. Ross Posnock's *Color and Culture* (1998) locates the author's thought in the context of other writers and thinkers of color. On the relationship between Baraka's art and politics, see Jerry Gafio Watt's *Amiri Baraka: The Politics and Art of a Black Intellectual* (2001), Komozi Woodard's *A Nation Within a Nation: Amiri Baraka (LeRoi Jones) and Black Power Politics*, and Harry J. Elam's *Taking It to the Streets: The Social Protest Theater of Luis Valdez and Amiri Baraka* (1997). *Amiri Baraka and Edward Dorn: The Collected Letters* (2013) documents the extraordinary interracial epistolary friendship between these two avant-garde poets from the end of the 1950s to the middle of the 1960s. In the wake of Baraka's death in January of 2014, the journal *Callaloo* (Summer, 2014) published a cluster of essays on Baraka's legacy, as did the journal *Transition* (no. 114, 2014). Biography can be gleaned from these sources and his autobiography, and may be complemented by the memoir from Baraka's first wife, Hettie Cohen, *How I Became Hettie Jones* (1990).

John Berryman

Berryman's *Collected Poems: 1937–1971* appeared in 1991; *John Berryman: Selected Poems*, in 2004. Berryman's critical biography, *Stephen Crane*, appeared in 1950, and a collection of his short fiction and literary essays was issued under the title *The Freedom of the Poet* (1976). Berryman's unfinished novel about his alcoholism, *Recovery*, appeared in 1973. *Berryman's Shakespeare: Essays, Letters, and Other Writings by John Berryman* (2001, edited by John Haffenden) presents a substantial selection of work from Berryman's unfinished critical and biographical project on Shakespeare.

Valuable critical introductions to Berryman's poetry can be found in Helen Vendler's *The Given and the Made* (1995) and Thomas Travisano's *Midcentury Quartet* (1999). Paul Mariani's *Dream Song: The Life of John Berryman* (1996) and Eileen Simpson's *Poets in Their Youth* (1982) are useful biographical studies. Tom Rogers's *God of Rescue: John Berryman and Christianity* (2010) documents Berryman's lifelong engagement with religion.

Elizabeth Bishop

Bishop's poems are available in *The Complete Poems 1927–1979* (1983). *The Collected Prose* (1984) includes memoirs and stories, especially the memory-based story "In the Village," invaluable for a reading of her poems. A remarkable selection of Bishop's correspondence, *One Art* (1994), was edited by her friend and publisher, Robert Giroux, and *Words in the Air: The Complete Correspondence between Elizabeth Bishop and Robert Lowell* (2008), edited by Thomas Travisano and Saskia Hamilton, documents one of the great literary friendships in twentieth-century

poetry. Her correspondence with editors at the *New Yorker*, offering a glimpse into the contemporary publishing world, is collected in *Elizabeth Bishop and* The New Yorker (2011). Reproductions of Bishop's watercolor paintings appear in *Exchanging Hats* (1996). Alice Quinn edited *Edgar Allan Poe & The Juke-Box: Uncollected Poems, Drafts, and Fragments* (2006). Bishop also translated from the Portuguese *The Diary of Helena Morley* (1957, 1977, 1991), an enchanting memoir of provincial life in Brazil.

Critical study of Bishop has been steady and robust in the last twenty years, showing no sign of abatement. Useful critical essays on Bishop appear in Seamus Heaney's *The Redress of Poetry* (1995), Lorrie Glodensohn's *Elizabeth Bishop: The Biography of a Poetry* (1992), and David Kalstone's *Becoming a Poet* (1989). *Elizabeth Bishop and Her Art*, edited by Lloyd Schwartz and Sybil P. Estess (1983), includes two interviews as well as essays. A provocative essay on Bishop appears in Adrienne Rich's *Blood, Bread, and Poetry* (1986). The novelist Colm Tóibín offers a personal view of Bishop's writing and its meaning for his own life and work in *On Elizabeth Bishop* (2015). Among the most valuable of the many critical studies are Brett C. Miller's important biography, *Elizabeth Bishop: Life and the Memory of It* (1993); *Elizabeth Bishop: The Geography of Gender* (1993), a collection of essays edited by Marilyn Lombardi; *Conversations with Elizabeth Bishop* (1996), edited by George Monteiro; and Thomas Travisano's *Midcentury Quartet* (1999). Candace Mac-Mahon's *Elizabeth Bishop: A Bibliography* (1980) is indispensable. A dual biography of Bishop and the Brazilian architect Lota de Macedo Soares, Bishop's romantic partner from 1951 to 1967, can be found in Carmen Oliviera's *Rare and Commonplace Flowers: The Story of Elizabeth Bishop and Lota de Macedo Soares* (2003); the book was a best seller in Brazil, where the couple met and made their home, and it offers invaluable Brazilian context for the poems Bishop wrote during these years. Peggy Samuels's *Deep Skin: Elizabeth Bishop and Visual Art* (2010) documents the relationship between Bishop's poetry and her involvement with the museum world of the 1930s and '40s. *The Cambridge Companion to Elizabeth Bishop* (2014), edited by Angus Cleghorn and Jonathan Ellis, gives a fine overview of critical issues and resources. *Elizabeth Bishop in the Twenty-First Century: Reading the New Editions* (2012), edited by Angus Cleghorn, Bethany Hicok, and Thomas Travisano, collects critical essays that take into account recent developments in archival studies of Bishop's work. These developments are reflected in the 2011 editions of her poetry and prose published by Farrar, Straus and Giroux, in celebration of the centenary of her birth.

Gwendolyn Brooks

Brooks wrote twelve stand-alone collections of poetry, starting with *A Street in Bronzeville* in 1945. Many of these poems are collected in *Selected Poems* (1999), *The Essential Gwendolyn Brooks* (2005), and the *Gwendolyn Brooks CD Poetry Collection* (2005). She also wrote two prose autobiographies, *Report from Part One* (1972) and *Report from Part Two* (1996).

Other useful biographical material appears in *A Life Distilled*, edited by M. K. Mootry and others, and George E. Kent's *A Life of Gwendolyn Brooks* (1990). Valuable discussions of Brooks's poetry appear in *Black Women Writers (1950–1980)*, edited by Mari Evans (1984). Stephen Wright's *On Gwendolyn Brooks: Reliant Contemplation* (1996), Harold Bloom's *Gwendolyn Brooks* (2000), and Martha E. Rhynes's *Gwendolyn Brooks: Poet from Chicago* (2003) are recent critical studies. An interview with Brooks appears in Janet Mullaney's *Truthtellers of the Times: Interviews with Contemporary Women Poets* (1998). Brooks and Gloria Jean Wade Gayles published *Conversations with Gwendolyn Brooks* (2002). Passages on Brooks in Lawrence Jackson's magisterial account of African American literary culture at midcentury, *The Indignant Generation: A Narrative History of African American Writers and Critics, 1934–1960*, place Brooks in the context of her times.

Raymond Carver

Principal collections of Carver's extensive short fiction are *Put Yourself in My Shoes* (1974), *Will You Please Be Quiet, Please?* (1976), *Furious Seasons* (1977), *What We Talk About When We Talk About Love* (1981), *The Pheasant* (1982), *Cathedral* (1983), and *Where I'm Calling From* (1988). *Fires* (1983) is a sampling of essays, poems, and narratives. Carver's uncollected work has been edited by William L. Stull as *No Heroics, Please* (1991), expanded as *Call If You Need Me* (2000). The Library of America's *Collected Stories* (2009), edited by William L. Stull and Maureen P. Carroll, includes drafts of stories before changes were introduced by his long-time editor, Gordon Lish. A fine introduction to the controversies surrounding Lish's extensive editing of Carver's fiction can be found in "Rough Crossings: The Cutting of Raymond Carver," the *New Yorker*, December 24, 2007, by Simon Armitage, available online through the *New Yorker*'s web archives. Throughout his career Carver published poetry as well, the bulk of which appears in several volumes from *Near Klamath* (1968) to *A New Path to the Waterfall* (1989); *All of Us* (1998) collects all his poems.

Arthur M. Saltzman's *Understanding Raymond Carver* (1988) looks beyond the author's apparent realism, as does Randolph Runyon's *Reading Raymond Carver* (1992). Carver's return to traditionalism is celebrated by Kirk Nesset in *The Stories of Raymond Carver* (1995). Editors Sandra Lee Kleppe and Robert Miltner present a wide variety of critical commentaries in *New Paths to Raymond Carver* (2008). Sam Halpert sifts through comments by Carver's associates in *Raymond Carver: An Oral Biography* (1995). The standard biography is *Raymond Carver: A Writer's Life* (2009) by Carol Sklenicka. Important interviews with Carver are collected in *Conversations with Raymond Carver* (1990), edited by Marshall Bruce Genry and William L. Stull.

John Cheever

Cheever's seven volumes of short stories, which appeared between 1943 and 1973, are assembled in *The Stories of John Cheever* (1978); *The Uncollected Stories of John Cheever* appeared posthumously in 1988. Two Library of America volumes of his work, both edited by Blake Bailey, collect the complete novels and "collected stories and other writings." *The Letters of John Cheever*, edited by his son, Benjamin Cheever, was published in 1988. *The Journals of John Cheever* (1991) was edited by Robert Gottlieb.

Biographies include Scott Donaldson's *John Cheever* (1988) and Blake Bailey's well-researched and engaging *Cheever: A Life* (2009). *Home before Dark* (1984), by his daughter, Susan Cheever, is a personal memoir. Francis J. Bosha has edited *The Critical Response to John Cheever* (1994). Samuel Chase Coale provides an overview in *John Cheever* (1977), while George W. Hunt explores religious dimensions in *John Cheever: The Hobgoblin Company of Love* (1983). The stories are given close study by James Eugene O'Hara in *John Cheever: A Study of the Short Fiction* (1989) and in *John Cheever* (2004), Harold Bloom's edited collection of criticism in the Chelsea House series "Bloom's Major Short Story Writers."

Sandra Cisneros

The House on Mango Street (1984) has been described as both interrelated short stories and a novel, whereas *Woman Hollering Creek* (1991) collects more evidently independent short stories. *Caramello* (2002) is an epic novel telling a multigenerational family story that entwines with major developments of twentieth-century American history. Cisneros has published two major collections of poetry, *My Wicked Wicked Ways* (1987) and *Loose Woman* (1994). Her *Hairs/Pelitos* (1994), written in English and accompanied by a Spanish text translated by Liliana Valenzuela, and *Have You Seen Marie?* (2012), illustrated by Ester Hernández, are narratives for children.

Recent studies on late-twentieth-century fiction show Cisneros's importance to creative writing programs and the later evolution of the Chicano literature movements; see sections on Cisneros in Mark McGurl, *The Program Era* (2009) and John Alba Cutler, *Ends of Assimilation: The Formation of Chicano Literature* (2015). Jean Wyatt's *Risking Difference* (2004) focuses on *Women Hollering Creek*, as do the essays edited by Cecilia Donahue in *Sandra Cisneros's Women Hollering Creek* (2010). Ramón Saldívar discusses Cisneros's fiction in *Chicano Narrative* (1990), as do Tey Diana Rebolledo in *Women Singing in the Snow* (1995) and Sonia Saldivár-Hull in *Feminism on the Border* (2000). *Class Definitions: On the Lives and Writings of Maxine Hong Kingston, Sandra Cisneros, and Dorothy Allison* (2008), by Michelle M. Tokarczyk, provides a comparative perspective. *Border Crossings and Beyond: The Life and Works of Sandra Cisneros* by Carmen Hydée Rivera (2009) combines critical and biographical approaches. An extensive dialogue with her appears in *Interviews with Writers of the Post-Colonial World* (1992), edited by Feroza Jussawalla and Reed Way Dasenbrock.

Lucille Clifton

Clifton's poetry is now gathered in *The Collected Poems of Lucille Clifton, 1965–2010* (2012), edited by Kevin Young and Michael S. Glaser. Her memoir, *Generations* (1976), provides a valuable context for her work. Clifton published over twenty books for children during the course of her career. Critical discussions of her work include Hilary Holiday's *Wild Blessings: The Poetry of Lucille Clifton* (2004). Mary Jane Lupton has published *Lucille Clifton: Her Life and Letters* (2006).

Billy Collins

Among the many collections of Collins's poetry it is useful to begin with his two volumes of selected poems: *Sailing Alone Around the World: New and Selected Poems* (2001), and *Aimless Love: New and Selected Poems* (2013). *The Best Cigarette* (1997), an audiobook, provides a chance to hear Collins reading thirty-three of his poems. He selected and introduced the anthologies *Poetry 180: A Turning Back to Poetry* (2003) and *180 More: Extraordinary Poems for Everyday Life* (2005).

One can find more occasional prose by Collins (anthology introductions, forewords, etc.) and interviews than criticism of his work, attesting to his popularity among a wide audience of readers and, perhaps, the relative simplicity of his poetry, which seems not to cry out for explication. Nevertheless, some critical discussion of Collins's work can be found in David Baker's *Heresy and the Ideal: On Contemporary Poetry* (2000).

Edwidge Danticat

Danticat has published both fiction and nonfiction. Her nonfiction works include *After the Dance: A Walk Through Carnival in Jacmel, Haiti* (2002) and *Brother, I'm Dying* (2007). She also edited *The Butterfly's Way: Voices from the Haitian Dyaspora in the United States* (2003). Her fiction includes *Krik? Krak!* (1996), *The Farming of Bones* (1998), and *The Dew Breaker* (1994), as well as the young adult novels *Breath, Eyes, Memory* (1994), *Behind the Mountains* (2002), and *Anacaona: Golden Flower, Haiti, 1490* (2005). A video, audio, and print transcript of her 2011 interview on Democracy Now, "The Immigrant Artist at Work," can be found on the program's website www.democracynow.org.

Critical discussion of Danticat's work can be found in Meredith M. Gadsby's *Sucking Salt: Caribbean Women Writers, Migration, and Survival* (2006). *Edwidge Danticat: A Reader's Guide* (2010), edited by Martin Munro, offers an appreciative collection of analytic, biographical, contextual, and reflective essays (these last by writers who know or have been influenced by Danticat), and includes interview materials.

Don DeLillo

In addition to his many novels, DeLillo has written several plays and occasional essays. Of particular interest among the latter is "In the Ruins of the Future, Reflections on Terror, Loss, and Time in the Shadow of September 11," published in *Harper's*, December 2001. DeLillo's interviews are gathered in *Conversations with Don DeLillo*, edited by Thomas DePietro (2005).

Overviews useful for teaching *White Noise* include *The Cambridge Companion to Don DeLillo* (2007; edited by John N. Duvall); the short reader's guide, *White Noise* (2003) by Leonard Orr; *Approaches to Teaching DeLillo's White Noise* (2007), edited by John Duvall and Tim Engles; *New Essays on White Noise* (1991), edited by Frank Lentricchia; and *White Noise: Text and Criticism* (1998), edited by Mark Osteen. Significant monograph studies on DeLillo include Mark Osteen's *American Magic and Dread: Don DeLillo's Dialogue with Culture* (2000); David Cowart's *DeLillo's*

Physics of Language (revised edition, 2003); and Peter Boxall's *Don DeLillo: The Possibility of Fiction* (2004). Religion has been a dominant topic of critical interest: see Jesse Kavadlo, *Don DeLillo: Balance at the Edge of Belief* (2004); John McClure's *Partial Faiths: Postsecular Fiction in the Age of Pynchon and Morrison* (2010); Amy Hungerford's *Postmodern Belief: American Literature and Religion since 1960* (2010), which discusses DeLillo's Catholicism; Mark C. Taylor, *Rewiring the Real: In Conversation with William Gaddis, Richard Powers, Mark Danielewski, and Don DeLillo* (2013). Two excellent and well-maintained free websites offer updated bibliographies and myriad other materials; see "DeLillo's America" and the website of the Don DeLillo Society.

Junot Díaz
Drown (1996) collects Díaz's short stories; his two novels to date are *The Brief Wondrous Life of Oscar Wao* (2007) and *This Is How You Lose Her* (2012).

Jacquelyn Loss studies Díaz's fiction in *Latino and Latina Writers* (2003), edited by Alan West-Durán, as do Raphael Dalleo and Elena Machado Sáez in *The Latino/a Canon and the Emergence of a Post-Sixties Literature* (2007). Díaz's cultural context is examined by Lucia Suarez in *The Tears of Hispaniola: Haitian and Dominican Diaspora Memory* (2006). Díaz is an exceptionally sharp critic himself, and has granted many interviews; these are essential reading alongside his fiction. Online searches will easily turn up material suitable for teaching. Of particular interest are his interviews with Edwidge Danticat, available online and also print in *BOMB: The Author Interviews* (2014), edited by Betsy Sussler, and with Taryne Jade Taylor in *Paradoxa 26* ("A Singular Dislocation: An Interview with Junot Díaz," "SF Now").

Joan Didion
Didion's long and varied career as a writer includes works of both fiction and nonfiction as well as multiple screenplays. Among her nonfiction volumes it is helpful to start with *We Tell Ourselves Stories in Order to Live: Collected Nonfiction* (2006) and and *Vintage Didion* (2004). Her creative nonfiction memoir, *The Year of Magical Thinking*, appeared in 2005. Two interviews with Didion have appeared in the *Paris Review*, one in 1978; a second, "The Art of Nonfiction" (2006), is available online at www.parisreview.org.

Critical discussion of Didion's work can be found in James N. Still's "The Minimal Self: Joan Didion's Journalism of Survival" in *Literary Selves: Autobiography and Contemporary American Nonfiction* (1993), Doug Underwood's *Journalism and the Novel: Truth and Fiction, 1700–2000* (2008), and Steven Belletto and Daniel Grausam's edited collection, *American Literature in an Age of Cold War: A Critical Reassessment* (2012). A general introduction to her work can be found in *Reading Joan Didion* (2009), by Lynn Marie Houston and William Lombardi. *The Last Love Song* (2015), by Tracy Daugherty, is the first full-length biography of Didion.

Rita Dove
Dove has published eight volumes of poetry; a collection of fiction, *Fifth Sunday* (1985); a novel, *Through the Ivory Gate* (1992); plays; and a valuable collection of essays, *The Poet's World* (1995). *Conversations with Rita Dove*, edited by Earl G. Ingersol, appeared in 2003.

Therese Steffen's critical study *Crossing Color: Transcultural Space and Place in Rita Dove's Poetry, Fiction, and Drama* appeared in 2001; Malin Pereira's *Rita Dove's Cosmopolitanism*, in 2003, places Dove in the context of the aftermath of the Black Arts movement; and Pat Righelato's *Understanding Rita Dove* (2006) offers an overview of her whole body of work.

Ralph Ellison
In his lifetime Ellison published three books: a novel, *Invisible Man* (1952), and two volumes of essays, *Shadow and Act* (1964) and *Going to the Territory* (1986). The latter materials are combined with other nonfiction in *The Collected Essays of Ralph Ellison* (1995), edited by John F. Callahan with a preface by Saul Bellow. Fragments of his novel in progress are noted in the bibliography to Mark Busby's *Ralph Ellison* (1991) in the Twayne United States Authors series; *Flying Home and Other Stories* (1997) gathers thirteen short stories written between 1937 and 1954, six of which were previously unpublished. In 1999 Callahan, as Ellison's literary executor, drew on manuscripts to assemble *Juneteenth* as a posthumous novel, a fuller version of which is presented by Callahan and editor Adam Bradley as *Three Days Before the Shooting . . .* (2010). Robert G. O'Meally edited *Living with Music: Ralph Ellison's Jazz Writings* (2001). *Trading Twelves: The Selected Letters of Ralph Ellison and Albert Murray*, edited by Murray and Callahan, appeared in 2000.

In the last decade several major critics have turned their attention to Ellison. Tracking their footnotes will provide readers with citations for earlier works of criticism. Ross Posnock's edited volume, *The Cambridge Companion to Ralph Ellison* (2006), provides an overview of the texts and the scholarship. Arnold Rampersand's *Ralph Ellison* (2007) is a comprehensive biography. The author's lifelong growth is measured by Adam Bradley in *Ralph Ellison in Progress* (2010). Timothy Parrish's *Ralph Ellison and the Genius of America* (2012) argues against the version of Ellison Rampersad presents, recasting Ellison as an intellectual whose thinking drove the civil rights movement and intersected with that of figures such as Philip Roth; the historian of slavery, C. Vann Woodward; Martin Luther King Jr.; and novelist and poet, Robert Penn Warren. Lawrence Jackson's *Ralph Ellison: The Emergence of Genius* (2002) is a biography that emphasizes Ellison's connection to the political Left in the 1930s and '40s; Kenneth Warren's *So Black and So Blue: Ralph Ellison and the Occasion of Criticism* (2003) reads Ellison as a writer of his times.

Political interests shape Barbara Foley's *Wrestling with the Left: The Making of Ralph Ellison's* Invisible Man (2010) and the critical essays collected by Lucas E. Morel in *Ralph Ellison and the Raft of Hope* (2004); music focuses Horace A. Porter's *Jazz Country: Ralph Ellison in America* (2001). *Ulysses in Black* (2008) by Patrice D. Rankin considers Ellison's debts to the classics. Lena Hill's *Visualizing Blackness and the Creation of the African American Literary Tradition* (2014), based on extensive archival and biographical research, argues for the centrality of Ellison's interest in and practice of the visual arts.

Louise Erdrich
Erdrich is best known for her novels but she has also published several poetry collections, short stories, children's books, and two memoirs, *The Blue Jay's Dance: A Birth Year* (1995), her account of becoming a mother, and *Birds and Islands in Ojibwe Country* (2003).

Approaches to Teaching the Works of Louise Erdrich (2004), edited by Greg Sarris, Connie A. Jacobs, and James R. Giles, provides a fine pedagogical overview. Erdrich's fiction is set more extensively in the Native American tradition by Louis Owens in *Other Destinies: Understanding the American Indian Novel* (1992), in the essays edited by Allan Chavkin in *The Chippewa Landscape of Louise Erdrich* (1999), and in *Studies in the Literary Achievement of Louise Erdrich, Native American Writer: Fifteen Critical Essays* (2008), edited by Brajesh Sawhney. Interview material can be found in *Conversations with Louise Erdrich and Michael Dorris* (1994), edited by Allan Chavkin and Nancy Feyl Chavkin. Peter G. Beidler and Gay Barton provide a general overview in *A Reader's Guide to the Novels of Louise Erdrich* (2006).

Allen Ginsberg
Ginsberg's poetry is gathered in *Collected Poems, 1947–1980* (1984), *White Shroud: Poems, 1980–1985* (1986), and *Death and Fame: Poems 1993–1997* (1999). His individual volumes, with the exception of *Empty Mirror* (1961), have been issued in the now unmistakable City Lights paperbacks. *Deliberate Prose: Selected Essays, 1952–1995* (2000) is a useful complement to the poetry, as are the many published selections from his journals and letters. Particularly helpful are his lively interviews: *Composed on the Tongue: Literary Conversations 1967–1977* (1980), edited by Donald Allen, and *Spontaneous Mind: Selected Interviews, 1958–1996* (2001), edited by David Carter. Notable among the published letters are *Jack Kerouac and Allen Ginsberg: The Letters* (2011), which includes both sides of this very early correspondence, brilliantly edited by Bill Morgan and David Stanford; and *The Selected Letters of Allen Ginsberg and Gary Snyder* (2008), edited by Bill Morgan. Ginsberg's photography can be found in *Photographs: Allen Ginsberg* (1991), among other collections.

Jane Kramer's *Allen Ginsberg in America* (1969) is a brilliant documentary piece on Ginsberg in the 1960s. Biographies include Michael Schumacher's *Dharma Lion: A Critical Biography of Allen Ginsberg* (1997); Graham Caveney's *Screaming with* Joy (2001); and Bill Morgan's *I Celebrate Myself: The Somewhat Private Life of Allen Ginsberg* (2007). Connections to religion are explored in Amy Hungerford's *Postmodern Belief* (2011), John Lardas's *The Bop Apocalypse* (2001) and in Tony Trigillio's *Allen Ginsberg's Buddhist Poetics* (2007). On Ginsberg and race, see the first chapter of Timothy Yu's *Race and the Avant-Garde: Experimental and Asian American Poetry Since 1965* (2009). On *Howl* and its aftermath, see *The Poem That Changed America: Howl Fifty Years Later* (2006), edited by Jason Shinder.

Joy Harjo
Harjo's selected poems, *How We Became Human: New and Selected Poems 1975–2001* (2002), is a good introduction to her large body of work. In *Secrets from the Center of the World* (1989), she wrote the text to accompany Steven Strom's photographs of the southwestern landscape. Her memoir is *Crazy Brave: A Memoir* (2013). She has also edited an anthology of Native American women's writing, *Reinventing the Enemy's Language: Contemporary Native Women's Writing of North America* (1997). Two collections of interviews are especially helpful: *Soul Talk, Song Language: Conversations with Joy Harjo* (2011), edited by Tanaya Winder; and Laura Coltelli's edited collection, *The Spiral of Memory* (1990). Commentary on the contexts of Harjo's work appears in Paula Gunn Allen's *The Sacred*

Hoop: Recovering the Feminine in American Indian Traditions (1986), Norma Wilson's *The Nature of Native American Poetry* (2001), and Dean Rader's *Engaged Resistance: American Indian Art, Literature, and Film from Alcatraz to the NMAI* (2011).

Robert Hayden

Hayden's *Collected Poems* appeared in 1985; his *Collected Prose* appeared the previous year. Both were edited by Frederick Glaysher. Fred M. Fetrow's *Robert Hayden* (1984) is a critical study of Hayden's work. Essays on Hayden's work appear in *Robert Hayden: Essays on the Poetry* (2003), edited by Robert Chrisman and Laurence Goldstein; and in Harold Bloom's edited volume *Robert Hayden* (2005).

Patricia Highsmith

Highsmith wrote twenty-two novels, and published nine collections of short stories. Readers may begin with *Patricia Highsmith: Selected Novels and Short Stories* (2010) *and Uncollected Short Stories* (2002). She discusses craft in *Plotting and Writing Suspense Fiction* (1966).

There are two Highsmith biographies: *Beautiful Shadow: A Life of Patricia Highsmith* (2004), by Andrew Wilson, and *The Talented Miss Highsmith: The Secret Life and Serious Art of Patricia Highsmith* (2009), by Joan Schenkar. A useful reader's guide is Russell Harrison, *Patricia Highsmith* (1997). Fiona Peters give a psychoanalytic reading in *Anxiety and Evil in the Work of Patricia Highsmith* (2011). Readers can find an open-access cluster of essays in the online journal *Post45*, "On Patricia Highsmith" (2012) edited by Tom Perrin and Mary Esteve, with contributions from Mark Seltzer, Mary Esteve, and Michael Trask. The following critics place Highsmith in a larger context: Michael Trask, in *Camp Sites* (2013); Leonard Cassuto, in *Hard-Boiled Sentimentality* (2009); Marco Abel, in *Violent Affect: Cinema, Literature, and Critique* (2007); and George Haggerty, in *Queer Gothic* (2006).

Randall Jarrell

Jarrell's *Complete Poems* was published in 1969, and a *Selected Poems* appeared in 1991. A selection of Jarrell's brilliant critical essays is available in *No Other Book* (1999), edited by Brad Leithauser. His novel satirizing American academic life, *Pictures from an Institution*, appeared in 1954. *Randall Jarrell's Book of Stories*, an anthology of Jarrell's favorite stories and narrative poems, was published in 1958 with a substantial introductory essay by Jarrell, and republished by the *New York Review of Books* in 2002. Steven Burt and Hannah

Brooks-Motl edited Jarrell's writings and lectures on the poet W. H. Auden in *Randall Jarrell on W. H. Auden* (2005), which includes worthwhile essays by the writer Adam Gopnick and by Burt that frame the history and significance of Jarrell's engagement with Auden.

Some of the most valuable commentary on Jarrell's life and work is to be found in a memorial volume of essays edited by Robert Lowell, Peter Taylor, and Robert Penn Warren, *Randall Jarrell, 1914–1965* (1967). William Pritchard's fine *Randall Jarrell: A Literary Life* (1990) illumines Jarrell's life and work, as does Mary Randall's *Remembering Randall* (1999). Critical discussion of Jarrell's work appears in Thomas Travisano's *Midcentury Quartet* (1999). Stephen Burt's *Randall Jarrell and His Age* (2002) examines the poet's entire oeuvre, including previously undiscovered essays and poems.

Jack Kerouac

Kerouac published numerous novels, poetry collections, and works of nonfiction; his most famous novel is *On the Road* (1957). Kerouac also recorded his poetry for a number of LPs many of which have been re-released in newer media and are widely available. In 2004, Douglas Brinkley edited *Windblown World: The Journals of Jack Kerouac, 1947–1954*, and in 2007, Howard Cunnell restored and edited an important first draft of *On the Road*, *On the Road: The Original Scroll* (2007).

John Tytell's *Naked Angels: The Lives and Literature of the Beat Generation* (1983) situates Kerouac in his historical and critical context, as do Raj Chandarlapaty's *The Beat Generation and Counterculture* (2009) and Ann Charters and Samuel Charters's *Brother-Souls* (2010). Stylistic analyses of Kerouac are undertaken in Regina Weinrich's *The Spontaneous Prose of Jack Kerouac* (1987), Michael Hrebeniak's *Action Writing: Jack Kerouac's Wild Form* (2006), and Tim Hunt's *The Textuality of Soulwork* (2014). Kerouac's friend Carolyn Cassady has written a memoir, *Off the Road* (1990), as has Edie Kerouac-Parker, *You'll Be Okay: My Life with Jack Kerouac* (2007). Among many biographies, the best include Barry Gifford and Lawrence Lee's excellent *Jack's Book: Jack Kerouac in the Lives and Words of His Friends* (1978), Tom Clark's *Jack Kerouac* (1984), Gerald Nicosia's *Memory Babe* (1983), Ann Charters's *Jack Kerouac* (1987), and Jorge García-Robles's *At the End of the Road: Jack Kerouac in Mexico* (2014). Kerouac's papers are housed in the Berg Collection of the New York Public Library.

Maxine Hong Kingston

Beginning with *The Woman Warrior* (1976) and as recently as *Fifth Book of Peace* (2003),

Maxine Hong Kingston has blended together elements of memoir and fiction. Her early works were first received as autobiography, though Kingston scholars now recognize important fictive elements. *Tripmaster Monkey: His Fake Book* (1989) is her most obvious novel. Essays Kingston wrote in 1978 appear as *Hawai'i One Summer* (1999). *I Love a Broad Margin to My Life* (2011) is an autobiography that uses poetry to address the author's concerns about aging. Shirley Geok-lin Lim edited *Approaches to Teaching Kingston's "The Woman Warrior"* (1991); also helpful is Sidonie Smith's *A Poetics of Women's Autobiography: Marginality and the Fictions of Self-Representation* (1987). More cognizant of fiction's role in Kingston's writing is *Articulate Silences: Hisaye Yamamoto, Maxine Hong Kingston, and Joy Kogawa* (1993) by King-Kok Cheung and *Writing Tricksters* (1997) by Jeanne Rosier Smith. Kingston is discussed in Christopher Lee's *The Semblance of Identity: Aesthetic Mediation in Asian-American Literature* (2012).

Jamaica Kincaid
Kincaid is the author of five novels, a collection of short stories, *At the Bottom of the River* (1983), and many works of autobiographical nonfiction and reportage, much of which was originally published in the *New Yorker*. Her essay, "On Seeing England for the First Time" (originally published in *Transition* magazine in 1991) was selected by Susan Sontag for *The Best American Essays* (1992).

Critical discussion of Kincaid's work includes Moira Ferguson's *Jamaica Kincaid: Where the Land Meets the Body* (1994), Lisa Paravisini-Gebert's *Jamaica Kincaid: A Critical Companion* (1999), Justin D. Edwards's *Understanding Jamaica Kincaid* (2007), and Mary Ellen Snodgrass's *Jamaica Kincaid: A Literary Companion* (2008). *My Brother* (1997), Kincaid's nonfictional account of her brother's AIDS diagnosis and death, plays a significant role in Katherine Stanton's *Cosmopolitan Fictions: Ethics, Politics, and Global Change in the Works of Kazuo Ishiguro, Michael Ondaatje, Jamaica Kincaid, and J. M. Coetzee*.

Yusef Komunyakaa
Komunyakaa's first poetry collection was *Dedications and Other Dark Horses* (1977); his most recent is *The Emperor of Water Clocks* (2015). With Martha Collins he has translated Nguyen Quang Thieu's *The Insomnia of Fire* (1992). With Sascha Feinstein he has edited two volumes of jazz poetry. In 2000 he published *Blue Notes: Essays, Interviews, and Commentaries*. He wrote a verse play of *Gilgamesh* (2006), which he produced as a stage adaptation with Chad Garcia.

Critical discussions of his work include Angela M. Salas's *Flashback Through the Heart: The Poetry of Yusef Komunyakaa* (2004). His work is set into a broader context by Wai Chee Dimock, "Gilgamesh's Planetary Turns" in *The Planetary Turn: Relationality and Geoaesthetics in the Twenty-First Century*, edited by Amy J. Elias and Christian Moraru (2015) and by Stephen Burt, "2001: 'Comrades, Be Not in Mourning': Twenty-First-Century Free Verse," in *New Literary History of America*, edited by Greil Marcus and Werner Sollors (2009).

Jhumpa Lahiri
Lahiri's collections of stories are *Interpreter of Maladies* (1999) and *Unaccustomed Earth* (2008); her novels are *The Namesake* (2003) and *The Lowland* (2013). In *Other Words*, a collection of her autobiographical essays, originally written in Italian and translated by Ann Goldstein, appeared in 2016.

Criticism of her fiction is found in *Transnational Asian American Literature: Sites and Transits* (2006), edited by Shirley Geok-lin Lim et al., and in *Literary Gestures: The Aesthetic in Asian American Writers* (2007), edited by Rocío G. Davis and Sue-Im Lee. In the context of theoretical arguments about neoliberalism and cosmopolitanism, Susan Koshy has published two articles about Lahiri: "Neoliberal Family Matters," *American Literary History* 25.2 (2013): 36, and "Minority Cosmopolitanism," *PMLA* 126.3 (2011): 592–609. Min Song sets Lahiri's work in the context of a generation of Asian American writers born after 1965 in *The Children of 1965: On Writing, and Not Writing, as an Asian American* (2013).

Li-Young Lee
Lee is the author of four books of poetry and a memoir, *The Winged Seed: A Remembrance* (1995). Gerald Stern's foreword to the collection *Rose* (1986) provides useful biographical material on Lee. *Breaking the Alabaster Jar: Conversations with Li-Young Lee* (2006) is a collection of interviews, edited by Earl G. Ingersoll. Other interviews with Lee appear in *Words Matter: Conversations with Asian American Writers* (2000), edited by King-Kok Cheung and *Poetry in Person: Twenty-Five Years of Conversation with America's Poets* (2010), edited by Alexander Neubauer.

Critical studies of Lee's verse can be found in Steven G. Yao's *Foreign Accents: Chinese American Verse from Exclusion to Postethnicity* (2010) and Dorothy J. Wang's *Thinking Its Presence: Form, Race, and Subjectivity in Contemporary Asian American Poetry* (2014).

Denise Levertov
Levertov was a prolific poet, with more than twenty volumes of poetry from *Double Image*

(1946) to *The Great Unknowing: Last Poems* (1999). *Making Peace* (2005) is a posthumous collection of Levertov's poems, edited by Peggy Rosenthal, and *The Collected Poems of Denise Levertov* was published in 2013. *The Poet in the World* (1973), *Light Up the Cave* (1981), and *Tesserae: Memories and Suppositions* (1995) include essays on Levertov's own work, autobiographical fragments, reviews of other poets, and some theoretical essays. Levertov's *New and Selected Essays* appeared in 1992. *The Letters of Denise Levertov and William Carlos Williams* (1998), *The Letters of Robert Duncan and Denise Levertov* (2004), and *Conversations with Denise Levertov*, a 1998 collection of interviews, mark important contributions to the study of Levertov's life and work.

The most authoritative biography of Levertov is Donna Krolik Hollenberg's *A Poet's Revolution: The Life of Denise Levertov* (2013), and critical studies include *Critical Essays on Denise Levertov* (1991), edited by Linda Wagner-Martin, Audrey T. Rogers' *Denise Levertov: The Poetry of Engagement* (1993), Linda Arbaugh's *Poetics of the Feminine* (1994) and *Denise Levertov: New Perspectives* (2000), edited by Anne Little and Susie Paul.

Barry Lopez

Lopez is a prolific writer and has published numerous works of fiction and nonfiction; as is the case with many creative nonfiction writers, his work often combines these genres. Teachers might well begin with Lopez's interviews, many of which can be found in William Tydeman's *Conversations with Barry Lopez: Walking the Path of Imagination* (2013), and Mike Newell's *No Bottom: In Conversation with Barry Lopez* (2008).

Critical discussions of Lopez can also be found in turn-of-the-twenty-first-century "ecocriticism"; he is discussed in the context of a whole body of environmental writing in many of the essays in *The Ecocriticism Reader: Landmarks in Literary Ecology*, edited by Cheryll Glotfelty and Harold Fromm (1996) and in Lawrence Buell's important book, *Writing for an Endangered World: Literature, Culture, and the Environment in the U. S. and Beyond* (2001). See also Scot Slovic's *Seeking Awareness in American Nature Writing: Henry Thoreau, Annie Dillard, Edward Abbey, Wendell Berry, and Barry Lopez* (1992) and Willliam H. Rueckert's essay, "Barry Lopez and the Search for a Dignified and Honorable Relationship with Nature," in *Earthly Words: Essays on Contemporary American Nature and Environmental Writers*, edited by John Cooley (1994).

Audre Lorde

The Collected Poems of Audre Lorde (2000) brings together Lorde's poetry, while a collection of Lorde's essays and speeches, *Sister Outsider* (1984), provides a powerful context for reading her work. Her autobiographical writing includes *The Cancer Journals* (1980) and *Zami: A New Spelling of My Name* (1982). A useful interview with Lorde appears in *Women Writers at Work* (1998), edited by George Plimpton.

Critical studies of Lorde's work appear in Mari Evans's edited *Black Women Writers* (1984) and Cassie Steele's *We Heal From Memory: Sexton, Lorde, Anzaldúa, and the Poetry of Witness* (2000). Cheryl Clark's "*After Mecca*": *Women Poets and the Black Arts Movement* (2005) and Kelly Lynch Reames's *Women and Race in Contemporary U.S. Writing: From Faulkner to Morrison* (2009) situate Lorde within American literary history, while Catherine A. John's *Clear Word and Third Sight* (2003) considers Lorde within the context of diasporic writing.

Robert Lowell

Lowell published numerous books of verse, and he adapted works by Aeschylus, Racine, Hawthorne, and Melville for the stage. His *Collected Prose* (1987) is an indispensable companion to the poetry and contains valuable essays on the work of other writers. An edition of Lowell's letters, edited by Saskia Hamilton, appeared in 2005, and *Words in the Air: The Complete Correspondence Between Elizabeth Bishop and Robert Lowell* (2008), edited by Saskia Hamilton and Thomas Travisano, documents one of the great literary friendships in twentieth-century poetry.

Useful early critical works on Lowell are Stephen Yenser's *Circle to Circle* (1975) and Steven Axelrod's *Robert Lowell: Life and Art* (1978). *Robert Lowell: A Collection of Critical Essays* (1968), edited by Thomas Parkinson, includes an important interview with the poet, and *The Critical Response to Robert Lowell* (1999), edited by Steven Axelrod, provides an overview of criticism on the work. Thomas Travisano's *Midcentury Quartet* (1999), Nick Halpern's *Everyday and Prophetic* (2003), and Helen Vendler's *Last Looks, Last Books* (2010) all contain chapters on Lowell that situate him in the midcentury American poetic tradition. Paula Hayes studies Lowell's style in *Robert Lowell and the Confessional Voice* (2013). Ian Hamilton's biography, *Robert Lowell*, appeared in 1982.

Arthur Miller

Miller's early plays are brought together in *Arthur Miller's Collected Plays* (1957), which also includes a lengthy and useful introduction by Miller. Later dramas are available in *Collected Plays, 1957–1981* (1981), *Collected Plays 1944–1961* (2006), and individual volumes. Miller also wrote many nonfiction pieces, as well as radio plays, screenplays, short stories, and the novel *Focus* (1945). *Echoes Down the Corridor: Collected Essays, 1944–2000* appeared in 2000. Miller published *Salesman in Beijing*, an account of the production of *Death of a Salesman* in China, in 1984, and an autobiography, *Timebends: A Life*, in 1987.

Martin Gottfried's *Arthur Miller: His Life and Work* (2003) is the major biography, while Enoch Brater's biography *Arthur Miller: A Playwright's Life and Works* (2004) provides useful performance histories for Miller's plays. The best recent analysis of Miller's work is found in Christopher Bigsby's *Arthur Miller, 1915–1962* (2010), supplemented by Bigsby's *Arthur Miller: A Critical Study* (2005) and his edited *The Cambridge Companion to Arthur Miller* (1997). Also helpful are the essays in Steven R. Centola's edited *The Achievement of Arthur Miller: New Essays* (1995). *Death of a Salesman* is analyzed in-depth in Brenda Murphy's *Miller: Death of a Salesman* (1995), Matthew C. Rodané's *Approaches to Teaching Miller's Death of a Salesman* (1995), Eric J. Sterling's edited *Arthur Miller's Death of a Salesman* (2008), and Peter L. Hays's *Arthur Miller's Death of a Salesman* (2008). Jeffrey D. Mason treats Miller in the context of American political history in *Stone Tower: The Political Theater of Arthur Miller* (2008).

Toni Morrison

Morrison published eleven novels, from *The Bluest Eye* (1970) to *God Help the Child* (2015), and three books for children. Her plays are *Dreaming Emmett* (1986), *Desdemona* (2011), and a libretto, *Margaret Garner* (2005). Morrison wrote and edited a number of critical works, including the seminal *Playing in the Dark: Whiteness and the Literary Imagination* (1992) and *Race-ing Justice, En-gendering Power: Essays on Anita Hill, Clarence Thomas, and the Construction of Social Reality* (editor, 1992). Her *Nobel Lecture in Literature* was published in 1994.

General book-length studies include Trudier Harris's *Fictions and Folklore: The Novels of Toni Morrison* (1991), John N. Duvall's *The Identifying Fictions of Toni Morrison* (2000), and Linda Wagner-Martin's *Toni Morrison: A Literary Life* (2015), which covers Morrison's first ten novels and emphasizes her role as a public intellectual. Henry Louis Gates Jr. and K. A. Appiah have edited the useful *Toni Morrison: Critical Perspectives Past and Present* (1993). Victoria Burrows's *Whiteness and Trauma* (2004) and Evelyn Jaffe Schreiber's *Race, Trauma, and Home in the Novels of Toni Morrison* (2010) address trauma and race in Morrison's work, while La Vinia

Delois Jenning's *Toni Morrison and the Idea of Africa* (2008) and K. Zauditu-Salassie's *African Spiritual Traditions in the Novels of Toni Morrison* (2009) examine the Africanist presence in Morrison's novels. Gender in Morrison's fiction is analyzed in Andrea Reilly's *Toni Morrison and Motherhood* (2004) and Susan Neal Mayberry's *Can't Love What I Criticize: The Masculine and Morrison* (2007), while religion in Morrison's fiction is treated in John A. McClure's *Partial Faiths: Postsecular Fiction in the Age of Pynchon and Morrison* (2007) and Amy Hungerford's *Postmodern Belief: American Literature and Religion since 1960* (2010).

Flannery O'Connor

O'Connor's novels and stories are collected in a volume in the Library of America series edited by Sally Fitzgerald (1988), while her letters are collected in *The Habit of Being: The Letters of Flannery O'Connor* (1979). *The Presence of Grace, and Other Book Reviews* (1983) collects some of her critical prose, as does *Mystery and Manners* (1969), edited by Sally Fitzgerald and Robert Fitzgerald. *A Prayer Journal* (2013), edited by W.A. Sessions, reproduces O'Connor's journal from 1946 to 1947.

Jean W. Cash provides a biography in *Flannery O'Connor: A Life* (2003), as does Brad Gooch in *Flannery* (2009). Critical overviews include Richard Giannone's *Flannery O'Connor, Hermit Novelist* (2000), Sarah Gordon's *Flannery O'Connor: The Obedient Imagination* (2000), and *Flannery O'Connor's Radical Reality* (2006), edited by Jan Nordby Grettund and Karl-Heinz Westarp. Studies of religion in O'Connor's fiction include Lorine M. Gertz's *Flannery O'Connor, Literary Theologian* (2000), Susan Srigley's *Flannery O'Connor's Sacramental Art* (2004), and Jordan Cofer's *The Gospel According to Flannery O'Connor* (2014). Donald E. Hardy explores embodiment in *The Body in Flannery O'Connor's Fiction* (2007), while Jon Lance Bacon situates O'Connor in American history in *Flannery O'Connor and Cold War Culture* (1993). *Flannery O'Connor: A Descriptive Bibliography* (1981) was compiled by David Farmer, and *Flannery O'Connor: The Contemporary Reviews* (2009), edited by R. Neil Scott, Irwin H. Streight, and M. Thomas Inge, collects contemporaneous reviews of O'Connor's fiction. A chapter in Mark McGurl's *The Program Era* (2009) reads some of her early stories and discusses the importance of her time at the Iowa Writer's Workshop.

Sylvia Plath

Plath's books of poetry have been gathered in *Plath's Collected Poems*, edited by Ted Hughes

(1983). Plath's novel, *The Bell Jar*, was first published in England in 1963; her short fiction and other prose writing was collected posthumously by Hughes in *Johnny Panic and the Bible of Dreams* (1977). Plath's mother, Aurelia Schober Plath, edited the useful *Letters Home: Correspondence 1950–63* (1975). Karen Kukil edited *The Unabridged Journals of Sylvia Plath, 1950–1962* (2000).

Among the biographical and critical studies of Plath's work are Judith Kroll's *Chapters in a Mythology* (1976), Anne Stevenson's *Bitter Fame: The Undiscovered Life of Sylvia Plath* (1988), Jacqueline Rose's *The Haunting of Sylvia Plath* (1993), and Heather Clark's *The Grief of Influence: Sylvia Plath and Ted Hughes* (2011). Amy Hungerford's *The Holocaust of Texts: Genocide, Literature, and Personification* (2003) discusses the meaning of and responses to Plath's Holocaust imagery. In *The Art of Cruelty: A Reckoning* (2011), Maggie Nelson situates Plath's poetry in a lineage of violent and transgressive art in the twentieth century, emphasizing the ethical core of her work. *The Cambridge Companion to Sylvia Plath*, edited by Jo Gill, appeared in 2006.

Thomas Pynchon
Pynchon has published nine novels, from *V.* (1963) to *Bleeding Edge* (2013). *Slow Learner* (1984) collects early stories.

Book-length studies of Pynchon's early novels are Thomas H. Schaub's *Pynchon, The Voice of Ambiguity* (1981), David Seed's *The Fictional Labyrinths of Thomas Pynchon* (1988), and Alan N. Brownlie's *Thomas Pynchon's Narratives: Subjectivity and the Problems of Knowing* (2000). Newer critical essays are collected by Niran Abbas in *Thomas Pynchon: Reading from The Margins* (2003) and Ian D. Copestake in *American Postmodernity: Essays on the Recent Fiction of Thomas Pynchon* (2003). David Cowart's *Thomas Pynchon and the Dark Passages of History* (2012) and Joanna Freer's *Thomas Pynchon and American Counterculture* (2014) situate Pynchon in postwar history. The fiction's relationship to contemporary religious thought is explored by John A. McClure in *Partial Faiths: Postmodern Fiction in the Age of Pynchon and Morrison* (2007); C. Namwali Serpell considers Pynchon's ambiguity in *Seven Modes of Uncertainty* (2014); and Mark Greif sets his work among mid-twentieth-century writers considering the "crisis of man" in *The Age of the Crisis of Man: Thought and Fiction in America, 1933–1973* (2015).

Adrienne Rich
The Fact of a Doorframe: Poems 1950–2001 (2002) collects five decades of Rich's poetry.

Her last volume of poetry was *Tonight No Poetry Will Serve: Poems 2007–2010* (2010). Several valuable collections gather Rich's essays, lectures, and speeches: *On Lies, Secrets, and Silence* (1979), *Blood, Bread, and Poetry* (1986), *What Is Found There?: Notebooks on Poetry and Politics* (1993), *Arts of the Possible* (2001), *Poetry and Commitment: An Essay* (2007), and *A Human Eye: Essays on Art in Society* (2009). Rich is also the author of an important study, *Of Woman Born: Motherhood as Experience and Institution* (1976).

Valuable critical essays and an interview appear in *Adrienne Rich's Poetry* (1975), edited by Barbara Charlesworth Gelpi and Albert Gelpi. Other studies are *Reading Adrienne Rich* (1984), edited by Jane Roberta Cooper; Paula Bennett's *My Life, a Loaded Gun: Female Creativity and Feminist Poetics* (1986); Margaret Dickie's *Stein, Bishop, & Rich: Lyrics of Love, War, & Place* (1997); Molly McQuade's *By Herself: Women Reclaim Poetry* (2000); *"Catch If You Can Your Country's Moment": Recovery and Regeneration in the Poetry of Adrienne Rich* (2007), edited by William S. Waddell; and Sylvia Henneberg's *The Creative Crone: Aging and the Poetry of May Sarton and Adrienne Rich* (2010).

Theodore Roethke
The Collected Poems of Theodore Roethke was published in 1966. *Dirty Dinkey and Other Creatures: Poems for Children*, edited by B. Roethke and Stephen Lushington, appeared in 1973. Useful comments on poetic tradition and his own poetic practice are to be found in several collections of Roethke's prose: *On the Poet and His Craft: Selected Prose of Theodore Roethke* (1965), edited by Ralph J. Mills Jr.; *Straw for the Fire: From the Notebooks of Theodore Roethke, 1948–63* (1972), edited by David Wagoner; and *The Selected Letters of Theodore Roethke* (1970), edited by Mills.

Among the useful studies of Roethke's work are *Theodore Roethke: Essays on the Poetry* (1965), edited by Arnold Stein, and Laurence Lieberman's *Beyond the Muse of Memory: Essays on Contemporary Poets* (1995). Allan Seager's *The Glass House* (1968) contains useful biographical material.

Philip Roth
Roth wrote twenty-seven novels and novellas, beginning with *Goodbye, Columbus* (1959) and concluding with *Nemesis* (2010). *The Facts: A Novelist's Autobiography* (1988) and *Patrimony* (1991) are Roth's memoirs. *Reading Myself and Others* (1975) and *Shop Talk* (2001) collect essays and interviews.

Philip Roth (1982) by Hermione Lee is an excellent introduction, as is *Understanding Philip Roth* (1990) by Murray Baumgarten and

Barbara Gottfried. *Philip Roth and the Jews* (1996) by Alan Cooper considers religious and cultural dimensions of the author's work. The broad sweep of Roth's career is covered by Mark Shechner in *Up Society's Ass, Copper: Reading Philip Roth* (2003), Deborah Shostak in *Philip Roth—Countertexts, Counterlives* (2004), and David Brauner in *Philip Roth* (2007). Elaine B. Safer's *Mocking the Age: The Later Novels of Philip Roth* (2006) discusses his experiments in narrative, while Ross Posnock handles controversy in *Philip Roth's Rude Truth* (2005). David Gooblar's *The Major Phases of Philip Roth* (2011) and Patrick Hayes's *Philip Roth: Fiction and Power* (2014) evaluate the full scope of Roth's career. Claudia Roth Pierpont's biography *A Writer and His Books* (2013) situates Roth's fiction in his personal history.

George Saunders

In addition to his several short-story collections, Saunders has published an illustrated fable, *The Brief and Frightening Reign of Phil* (2005), and a book for children, *The Very Persistent Gappers of Frip* (2006). His essays are an excellent accompaniment to the fiction; see the collection *The Braindead Megaphone* (2007). Readers may also be interested in his published commencement speech: *Congratulations, by the way: Some Thoughts on Kindness* (2014). He has collaborated on two stage adaptations of stories, "Jon" and "CommComm," with playwright Seth Bockley.

Very little criticism exists to date; two articles in mainstream academic journals are David Rando, "George Saunders and the Postmodern Working Class," in *Contemporary Literature* 53.3 (2012); and Sarah Pogell, "'The Verisimilitude Inspector': George Saunders as the New Baudrillard?" *Critique: Studies in Contemporary Fiction* 52.4 (2011).

Anne Sexton

Sexton authored eight volumes of poetry starting with *To Bedlam and Part Way Back* (1960) and ending with *The Awful Rowing toward God* (1975). *Complete Poems* appeared in 1981. Diane Wood Middlebrook's biography, *Anne Sexton* (1991), and Sexton's *A Self-Portrait in Letters* (1977) give useful biographical material. Important interviews and critical essays are to be found in J. D. McClatchy's *Anne Sexton: The Artist and Her Critics* (1978) and Diane Hume George's *Sexton: Selected Criticism* (1988). An interview with Sexton appears in *Women Writers at Work* (1998), edited by George Plimpton.

Leslie Marmon Silko

Silko has written three novels, six collections of stories and poetry, and a Kindle Single novella called *Oceanstory* (2011). *Yellow Woman and a Beauty of the Spirit* (1996) collects Silko's essays on contemporary Native American life. *The Turquoise Ledge* (2010) is Silko's memoir. *Lullaby*, coauthored with Frank Chin, was dramatically adapted and produced in San Francisco in 1976. *Delicacy and Strength of Lace*, a collection of letters between Silko and the poet James Wright, edited by Anne Wright, was published in 1985, while Ellen L. Arnold edited *Conversations with Leslie Marmon Silko* in 2000. Silko's work also appeared in *Yellow Woman* (1993), edited by Melody Graulich.

Introductions to Silko's work are Per Seyersted's *Leslie Marmon Silko* (1980), Melody Graulich's edited *'Yellow Woman': Leslie Marmon Silko* (1993), and Louise K. Barnett and James L. Thorson's edited *Leslie Marmon Silko* (1999). Catherine Rainwater's *Dreams of Fiery Stars* (1999), Sean Kicummah Teuton's *Red Land, Red Power: Grounding Knowledge in the American Indian Novel* (2008), and Mishuana Goeman's *Mark My Words: Native Women Mapping Our Nations* (2013) situate Silko within Native American literary culture. Rosemary A. King's *Border Influences from the Mexican War to the Present* (2001) and Claudia Sadowsky-Smith's *Border Fictions* (2008) locate Silko in the history of America's borderlands.

Art Spiegelman

Spiegelman's most important books include the two parts of *Maus, a Survivor's Tale*, published in 1986 and 1991, and *In the Shadow of No Towers* (2004). *Be a Nose* (2009) excerpts Spiegelman's sketchbooks, while *MetaMaus* (2011) contains background material about *Maus*. *Breakdowns* (2008) and *Co-Mix* (2013) anthologize Spiegelman's shorter works. *MetaMaus* (2011) provides source materials, interview, and background about the making of *Maus*.

Joseph Witek locates Spiegelman's importance in the evolution of underground comics and the graphic novel in *Comic Books as History: The Narrative Art of Jack Jackson, Art Spiegelman, and Harvey Pekar* (1989), as do Charles Hatfield in *Alternative Comics: An Emerging Literature* (2005) and Hillary Chute in *Disaster Drawn* (2016). Amy Hungerford's chapter on *Maus*, "Surviving Rego Park," in *The Holocaust of Texts: Genocide, Literature, and Personification* (2003) discusses the relationship between history and identity in Spiegelman's work. Alan Rosen analyzes *Maus* in *Sounds of Defiance: The Holocaust, Multilingualism, and the Problem of English* (2005), as do contributors to Jeet Heer and Kent Worcester's *A Comic Studies Reader* (2009). Kristiaan Versluys analyzes Spiegelman's response to 9/11 in *Out of the Blue: September 11 and the Novel* (2009), while Nicole Stamant considers Spiegelman as an American memoirist in *Serial Memoir: Archiving American Lives* (2014).

Natasha Trethewey

In addition to her several poetry collections, Trethewey has published a book of nonfiction, *Beyond Katrina: A Meditation on the Mississippi Gulf Coast* (2010). *Conversations with Natasha Trethewey* (2013), edited by Joan Wylie, gathers useful interviews. Two of Trethewey's essays, "On Whitman, Civil War Memory, and My South," in Ivy Wilson's edited collection *Whitman Noir: Black America and the Good Gray Poet* (2014), and "Why I Write," in *South Central Review* 31.1 (2014) may be of special interest to teachers. *The Southern Quarterly* 54.4 (2013), collects critical essays in a special issue on Trethewey's work in honor of her naming as U.S. poet laureate.

John Updike

Updike authored twenty-three novels including the popular *Rabbit* tetralogy: *Rabbit, Run* (1960), *Rabbit Redux* (1971), *Rabbit Is Rich* (1981), and *Rabbit at Rest* (1990). His two-volume *Collected Stories* was published in 2013. Updike's early poems are gathered in *Collected Poems 1953–1993* (1993), while *Americana: and Other Poems* (2001) and *Endpoint and Other Poems* (2009) are later works. Fourteen collections of criticism and four children's books round out his oeuvre.

Donald J. Greiner's thorough examination of the early canon appears in his *John Updike's Novels* (1984) and *The Other John Updike: Poems/Short Stories/Prose/Plays* (1981). Longer views are taken by James A. Schiff in *John Updike Revisited* (1998) and by William Pritchard in *Updike: America's Man of Letters* (2000). *Conversations with John Updike* (1993), edited by James Plath, collects thirty-two interviews with the writer between 1959 and 1993. Jack De Bellis has prepared *The John Updike Encyclopedia* (2007) and, with Michael Broomfield, *John Updike: A Bibliography* (2007). In 2006, Stacey Olster edited *The Cambridge Companion to John Updike*, and Adam Begley provides a compendious chronicle of the author's life in *Updike* (2014). Updike's papers have been deposited in the Houghton Library at Harvard University.

Alice Walker

Walker has published seven novels, including *The Color Purple* (1982), three short-story collections, and eight collections of poetry. Her *Collected Poems* appeared in 2005. Walker's literary essays are collected in *In Search of Our Mothers' Gardens* (1983), *Living by the Word* (1988), and *Anything We Love Can Be Saved* (2000). She has also written *Warrior Marks: Female Genital Mutilation and the Sexual Blinding of Women* (1987, with Pratibha Parmar), *We Are the Ones We Have Been Waiting For* (2006), and *Overcoming Speechlessness: A Poet Encounters the Horror in Rwanda, Eastern Congo, and Palestine/Israel* (2010). Her children's books include an illustrated *To Hell with Dying* (1988), *Finding the Green Stone* (1991), and a biography, *Langston Hughes, American Poet* (1974). Rudolph P. Byrd has edited a collection of interviews, *The World Has Changed: Conversations with Alice Walker* (2010).

Evelyn C. White's *Alice Walker: A Life* (2004) is a comprehensive biography. Good samplings of scholarship on Walker are offered by Henry Louis Gates Jr. and K. Anthony Appiah's edited *Alice Walker: Critical Perspectives Past and Present* (1993) and Lillie P. Howard's edited *Alice Walker and Zora Neale Hurston: The Common Bond* (1993). *Alice Walker* (2011) is Maria Lauret's book-length study, while Melanie L. Harris's *Gifts of Virtue, Alice Walker, and Womanist Ethics* (2010) analyzes Walker's politics of "womanism."

Eudora Welty

Welty was the author of five novels, including the Pulitzer Prize–winning *The Optimist's Daughter* (1972), and one novella, *The Robber Bridegroom* (1942). The *Collected Stories of Eudora Welty* (1980) was followed by two more collections of short stories and one collection of autobiographical essays, *One Writer's Beginnings* (1984). Among Welty's many volumes of nonfiction prose are *The Eye of the Story: Selected Essays and Reviews* (1978), and *A Writer's Eye: Collected Book Reviews* (1994).

Biographies of Welty include Ann Waldron's *Eudora: A Writer's Life* (1998) and Suzanne Marrs's *Eudora Welty: A Biography* (2005). Critical introductions to Welty's fiction are available in Marrs's *One Writer's Imagination: The Fiction of Eudora Welty* (2002), Gail Mortimer's *Daughter of the Swan: Love and Knowledge in Eudora Welty's Fiction* (1994), Jan Nordby Gretlund's *Eudora Welty's Aesthetics of Place* (1994), and Ruth D. Weston's *Gothic Traditions and Narrative Techniques in the Fiction of Eudora Welty* (1994). The collection of essays *Eudora Welty and Politics: Did the Writer Crusade?* (2001), edited by Suzanne Marrs and Harriet Pollack, seeks to revise the critical consensus that Welty avoided political and historical engagement in her writing and photography.

Tennessee Williams

Most of Williams's plays are collected in the seven-volume *The Theatre of Tennessee Wil-*

liams (1971–81). Some later dramas are available in separate editions; a few others are still to be published. Other writings include a novel, *The Roman Spring of Mrs.* Stone (1950); his short-story collections are brought together in *Collected Stories* (1986), edited by Gore Vidal; a volume of screenplays, *Stopped Rocking* (1984); and poems collected as *In the Winter of Cities* (1964) and *Androgyne, Mon Amour* (1977). *Where I Live: Selected Essays*, edited by Christine R. Day and Bob Woods, appeared in 1978. *The Selected Letters of Tennessee Williams, Volume I, 1920–1945* (2000) was edited by Albert J. Devlin and Nancy M. Tischler. Margaret Bradham Thornton has edited Williams's *Notebooks* (2007).

John Lahr's *Tennessee Williams: Mad Pilgrimage of the Flesh* (2014) is the best biographical account. Williams's own *Memoirs* (1975) is interestingly revelatory but is not a reliable biographical guide. Judith J. Thompson provides a Jungian analysis of the plays and identifies structural patterns in *Tennessee Williams' Plays: Memory, Myth, and Sym-* *bol* (1987, rev. 2002). Time relationships are explored by Patricia Schroeder in *The Presence of the Past in Modern American Drama* (1989). Williams's homosexuality functions in a complex way in his writing, as demonstrated by Michael Paller's *Gentlemen Callers: Tennessee Williams; Homosexuality, and Mid-Twentieth Century Drama* (2005) and Michael S. D. Hopper's *Sexual Politics in the Work of Tennessee Williams* (2012). The difficult aesthetics of Williams's late plays are examined by Annette Saddik in *Tennessee Williams's Theatre of Excess: The Strange, the Crazed, The Queer* (2015). Williams's female characters are analyzed by James Grissom in *Follies of God: Tennessee Williams and the Women of the Fog* (2015). Brenda Murphy edited *Tennessee Williams: Critical Insights* (2010); Philip G. Kolin edited *Tennessee Williams: A Guide to Research and Performance* (1998); Matthew C. Rodané prepared *The Cambridge Companion to Tennessee Williams*.

PERMISSIONS ACKNOWLEDGMENTS

IMAGE CREDITS

p. 1: Granger, NYC - All rights reserved; p. 4: National Archives; p. 5: Courtesy of the Ellis Island Immigration Museum; p. 10: Library of Congress/Getty Images; p. 15: Library of Congress; p. 22: Library of Congress; p. 89: Fascicle 11, *Wild nights-Wild nights!* The Manuscript of Books of Emily Dickinson edited by RW Franklin. Vol.1, 1981. The Houghton Library/New York Public Library; p. 293: Rare Books Division, The New York Public Library, Astor, Lenox and Tilden Foundations; p. 315: Picture History; p. 334: Harper's Weekly, October 21, 1863; p. 339: Hulton Archive/Getty Images; p. 343: From *Daisy Miller & An International Episode* by Henry James. Illustrated from Drawings by Harry W. McVickar; p. 470: Library of Congress; p. 496: Manuscripts, Archives and Rare Books Division, Schomburg Center for Research in Black Culture, The New York Public Library, Astor, Lenox and Tilden Foundations; p. 523: The New England Magazine, January 1892, Courtesy National Library of Medicine; p. 525: Library of Congress; p. 560: National Portrait Gallery, Smithsonian Institution/Art Resource, NY; p. 612: Barrett Library, University of Virginia; p. 649: General Research Division, The New York Public Library, Astor, Lenox and Tilden Foundation; p. 654 (top): Archives and Special Collections, Dickinson College, Carlisle, PA; p. 654 (bottom): Archives and Special Collections, Dickinson College, Carlisle, PA; p. 667: Edward Hopper (American 1882–1967), *Nighthawks*, 1942. Friends of American Art Collection 1942.51 The Art Institute of Chicago. Photography © The Art Institute of Chicago; p. 668: Bettmann/Getty Images; p. 669: Library of Congress/Getty Images; p. 672: Smithsonian American Art Museum, Washington, DC/Art Resource, NY; p. 675: Smithsonian American Art Museum, Washington, DC/Art Resource, NY; p. 676: Smithsonian American Art Museum, Washington, DC/Art Resource, NY; p. 680: Merrill C. Berman Collection; p. 684: Provincetown Players, 1916; p. 730: The Sandor Family Collection. Richard & Ellen Sandor; p. 829: Bettmann/Getty Images; p. 949: Library of Congress; p. 962: Harry Ransom Humanities Research Art Collection, UT Austin; p. 1007: Courtesy Everett Collection; p. 1008: Norton; p. 1068: Roy Lichtenstein, *Blam*. Yale University Art Gallery, Gift of Richard Brown Baker, BA. 1935, (1995.32.9) © Estate of Roy Lichtenstein; p. 1071: National Archives & Records Administration; p. 1072: Keystone-France/Gamma-Keystone/Getty Images; p. 1074: Courtesy of and copyright The Gordon Parks Foundation; p. 1075: Bernard Gotfryd/Getty Images; p. 1076 (left): Tony Linck/The LIFE Picture Collection/Getty Images; p. 1076 (right): Margaret Bourke-White/The LIFE Picture Collection/Getty Images; p. 1077: The Estate of David Gahr/Getty Images; p. 1080: Courtesy of the California History Room, California State Library, Sacramento, California; p. 1084 (left): Beinecke Rare Book and Manuscript Library, Yale University; p. 1084 (right): Beinecke Rare Book and Manuscript Library, Yale University; p. 1085: Grace Paley at Sarah Lawrence College. Photograph by Gary Gladstone. Courtesy of the Sarah Lawrence College Archives; p. 1118: AP Photo; p. 1200: Lisa Larsen/Time Life Pictures/Getty Images; p. 1222: W. Eugene Smith/Time Life Pictures/Getty Images; p. 1317: Henry W. and Albert A. Berg Collection of English and American Literature, The New York Public Library, Astor, Lenox and Tilde Foundations; p. 1393: Jack Manning/The New York Times/Redux; p. 1522: © Roy Harte Jazz Archives/CTSIMAGES; p. 1556: Photograph by Francis Wolff © Mosaic Images; p. 1654: © Robert Altman/The Image Works; p. 1679: Skeet McAuley; p. 1682: Kwaku Alston Photography, Inc.

COLOR INSERT CREDITS

C1: Philadelphia Museum of Art, Pennsylvania, PA, USA/Bridgeman Images; C2 (top): Granger, NYC - All rights reserved; C2 (bottom): Private Collection/Peter Newark American Pictures/Bridgeman Images; C3 (top): Permission of the University of Nebraska Press © 1967 by the University of Nebraska Press. © renewed 1995 by the University of Nebraska Press; C3 (bottom): Library of Congress/Getty Images; C4: Image copyright © The Metropolitan Museum of Art/Image source: Art Resource, NY; C5: Hampton University Museum Collection Hampton University, Hampton, VA; C6: Library of Congress; C7: George Bellows, *Both Members of This Club*, 1909; Chester Dale Collection. Image © 2006 Board of Trustees, National Gallery of Art Washington; C8: Childe Hassam, *Manhattan's Misty Sunset*, 1911; Collection of The Butler Institute of American Art, Youngstown, Ohio; C9: Duchamp, Marcel (1887–1968) © ARS, NY. *Nude Descending a Staircase (No. 2)*, 1912. Oil on canvas, 57 7/8 × 35 1/8 inches (147 × 89.2cm). The Louise and Walter Arensberg Collection, 1950. The Philadelphia Museum of Art. Art © 2016 Artists Rights Society (ARS), New York/ADAGP, Paris/Succession Marcel Duchamp. Photo credit: The Philadelphia Museum of Art/Art Resource, NY; C10: Marsden Hartley, *Portrait of a German Officer*, The Metropolitan Museum of Art, The Alfred Stieglitz Collection, 1949 (49.70.42). Image copyright © The Metropolitan Museum of Art/Art Resource, NY; C11: Thomas Hart Benton, American (1889–1975). *Hollywood*, 1937–38. Tempera with oil on canvas, mounted on panel, 56 × 84 inches (142.2 × 213.4 cm). The Nelson-Atkins Museum of Art, Kansas City, Missouri. Bequest of the artist, F75-21/12. Photo by Jamison Miller. Art © T.H. Benton and R.P. Benton Testamentary Trusts/UMB Bank Trustee/Licensed by VAGA, New York, NY; C12: Hampton University Museum, Hampton, VA; C13: Charles Sheeler (1883–1965), *River Rouge Plant* 1932; Oil on Canvas, 20 × 24 1/8 in. Whitney Museum of Art, NY; Purchase 32.43; C14: Georgia O'Keeffe, *From the Faraway, Nearby*, The Metropolitan Museum of Art, Alfred Stieglitz Collection, 1959 (59.204.2) Photograph © 1984 The Metropolitan Museum of Art; C15: Granger, NYC - All rights reserved; C16: Edward Hopper, (American 1882–1967) *Nighthawks*, 1942; Friends of American Art Collection 1942.51 The Art Institute of Chicago. Photography © The Art Institute of Chicago; C17 (top): Jackson Pollock, *Autumn Rhythm (Number 30)*; The Metropolitan Museum of Art, George A. Hearn Fund, 1957 (57.92) Photograph © 1998 The Metropolitan Museum of Art © 2016 The Pollock-Krasner Foundation for the Visual Arts, Inc./Artists Rights Society (ARS), New York; C17 (bottom): Carl Van Vechten used by permission of The Van Vechten Trust; C18: Roy Lichtenstein, *Blam*; Yale University Art Gallery, Gift of Richard Brown Baker, BA. 1935, (1995.32.9) © Estate of Roy Lichtenstein; C19 (top): Robert Rauschenberg, *Estate*, 1963 (oil & screenprinted inks on canvas), Rauschenberg, Robert (1925–2008)/Philadelphia Museum of Art, Pennsylvania, PA, USA/Gift of the Friends of the Philadelphia Museum of Art, 1967/Bridgeman Images/Licensed by VAGA, New York, NY; C19 (bottom): Andy Warhol, *Campbell's Soup I (Tomato)* 1968;

TEXT CREDITS

Holt and Company, copyright 1936, 1942, 1944, 1951, 1958, 1962 by Robert Frost. Copyright 1964, 1967, 1970, 1975 by Lesley Frost Ballantine. Reprinted by permission of the publisher Henry Holt and Company, LLC.

Allen Ginsberg: "A Supermarket in California," copyright © 1955 by Allen Ginsberg. "Howl," copyright © 1955 by Allen Ginsberg. "Footnote to Howl," copyright © 1955 by Allen Ginsberg. From COLLECTED POEMS 1947–1980 by Allen Ginsberg. Reprinted by permission of HarperCollins Publishers and The Wylie Agency (UK) Ltd. Published in Great Britain in COLLECTED POEMS 1947–1997. Copyright © 2006 by the Allen Ginsberg Trust.

Alan Gribben: From the Introduction to MARK TWAIN'S ADVENTURES OF TOM SAWYER AND HUCKLE-BERRY FINN: THE NEW SOUTH EDITION, ed. by Alan Gribben. Reprinted with the permission of New South Books.

Joy Harjo: "Call It Fear," and "White Bear" from SHE HAD SOME HORSES by Joy Harjo, copyright © 1983 by Joy Harjo. Used by permission of the author and W. W. Norton & Company, Inc.

Robert Hayden: "Middle Passage," copyright © 1962, 1966 by Robert Hayden, "Homage to the Empress of the Blues," copyright © 1962, 1966 by Robert Hayden, "Those Winter Sundays," copyright © 1966 by Robert Hayden. Used by permission of Liveright Publishing Corporation.

H. D. (Hilda Doolittle): "Oread" from COLLECTED POEMS 1912–1944 by H.D. (Hilda Doolittle) Copyright © 1914 by Hilda Doolittle." "Helen," "Leda," and "Mid-day," from COLLECTED POEMS 1912–1944. Copyright © 1982 by The Estate of Hilda Doolittle. Reprinted by permission of New Directions Publishing Corp. and Carcanet Press Ltd.

Ernest Hemingway: "Hills Like White Elephants" from THE SHORT STORIES OF ERNEST HEMINGWAY. Copyright 1927 by Charles Scribner's Sons; copyright renewed © 1955 by Ernest Hemingway. All rights reserved. Published in Great Britain in THE FIRST FORTY-NINE STORIES. Reprinted with permission of Atria/Scribner/Gallery, a division of Simon & Schuster, Inc. and The Random House Group Limited.

Patricia Highsmith: "The Quest for *Blank Claveringi*" from ELEVEN. Copyright © 1945, 1962, 1964, 1965, 1967, 1968, 1969, 1970 by Patricia Highsmith. Used by permission of Grove/Atlantic, Inc. Any third party use of this material outside of this publication is prohibited. Rights in the British Commonwealth, excluding Canada, by permission of the Little Brown Book Group.

Langston Hughes: "The Negro Speaks of Rivers," "Mother to Son," "The Weary Blues," "I, Too," "Song for a Dark Girl," "Theme for English B," "Note on Commercial Theatre," "Visitors to the Black Belt," "Mulatto," and "Democracy" from THE COLLECTED POEMS OF LANGSTON HUGHES, edited by Arnold Rampersad with David Roessel, Associate Editor. Copyright © 1994 by The Estate of Langston Hughes. Used by permission of Alfred A. Knopf, an imprint of the Knopf Doubleday Publishing Group, a division of Penguin Random House LLC. All rights reserved. Any third party use of this material, outside of this publication, is prohibited. Interested parties must apply directly to Penguin Random House LLC for permission. Rights in the British Commonwealth, excluding Canada, by permission of Harold Ober Associates Inc. "The Negro Artist and the Racial Mountain" abridged from *The Nation*, June 23, 1926. Copyright 1926 by Langston Hughes. Used by permission of Harold Ober Associates Inc.

Zora Neale Hurston: "How It Feels to Be Colored Me." Reprinted by permission of The Joy Harris Literary Agency, Inc. "Sweat" as taken from THE COMPLETE STORIES by Zora Neale Hurston. Introduction copyright © 1995 by Henry Louis Gates, Jr. and Sieglinde Lemke. Compilation copyright © 1995 by Vivian Bowden, Lois J. Hurston Gaston, Clifford Hurston, Lucy Ann Hurston, Winifred Hurston Clark, Zora Mack Goins, Edgar Hurston, Sr., and Barbara Hurston Lewis. Afterword and Bibliography copyright © 1995 by Henry Louis Gates. Reprinted by permission of HarperCollins Publishers.

Randall Jarrell: "The Death of the Ball Turret Gunner," "Second Air Force," and "Thinking of the Lost World" from THE COMPLETE POEMS by Randall Jarrell. Copyright © 1969; renewed 1997 by Mary von S. Jarrell. Reprinted by permission of Farrar, Straus and Giroux, LLC and Faber and Faber Ltd.

Michiko Kakutani: From "Light Out, Huck, They Still Want to Sivilize You" from *The New York Times*, Jan. 6, 2011. Copyright © 2011 by The New York Times. All rights reserved. Used by permission and protected by the Copyright Laws of the United States. The printing, copying, redistribution, or retransmission of this Content without express written permission is prohibited.

Jack Kerouac: "Part One, Chapter One," and "Part Five" from ON THE ROAD. Copyright © 1955, 1957 by Jack Kerouac. Copyright renewed © 1983 by Stella Kerouac; copyright renewed © 1985 by Stella Kerouac and Jan Kerouac. Used by permission of Viking Books, an imprint of Penguin Publishing Group, a division of Penguin Random House LLC.

Jamaica Kincaid: "Girl" from AT THE BOTTOM OF THE RIVER. Copyright © 1983 by Jamaica Kincaid. Reprinted by permission of Farrar, Straus and Giroux LLC and The Wylie Agency LLC. Copyright © 1978, 1979, 1981, 1982, 1983 by Jamaica Kincaid.

Maxine Hong Kingston: "No Name Woman" from THE WOMAN WARRIOR: MEMOIRS OF A GIRLHOOD AMONG GHOSTS by Maxine Hong Kingston, copyright © 1975, 1976 by Maxine Hong Kingston. Used by permission of Alfred A. Knopf, an imprint of the Knopf Doubleday Publishing Group, a division of Penguin Random House LLC. All rights reserved. Any third party use of this material, outside of this publication, is prohibited. Interested parties must apply directly to Penguin Random House LLC for permission. Rights in the British Commonwealth, excluding Canada, by permission of the author and the Sandra Dijkstra Literary Agency.

Yusef Komunyakaa: "When Dusk Weighs Daybreak" from TALKING DIRTY TO THE GODS. Copyright © 2000 by Yusef Komunyakaa. Reprinted by permission of Farrar, Straus and Giroux, LLC. "Slam, Dunk, & Hook," "Facing It," and "My Father's Love Letters" from PLEASURE DOME: NEW AND COLLECTED POEMS. Copyright © 2001 by Yusef Komunyakaa and reprinted by permission from Wesleyan University Press.

Jhumpa Lahiri: "Sexy" from INTERPRETER OF MALADIES by Jhumpa Lahiri. Copyright © 1999 by Jhumpa Lahiri. Reprinted by permission of Houghton Mifflin Harcourt Publishing Co. and HarperCollins Publishers Ltd. All rights reserved.

Li-Young Lee: "Persimmons," "Eating Alone," and "Eating Together" from ROSE. Copyright © 1986 by Li-Young Lee. "This Room and Everything in It" from THE CITY IN WHICH I LOVE YOU by Li-Young Lee. Copyright © 1990 by Li-Young Lee. Reprinted by permission of The Permissions Company, Inc. on behalf of BOA Editions Ltd. www.boaeditions.org

Index

A Bird, came down the Walk, 92
A brackish reach of shoal off Madaket—, 1291
A hush is over all the teeming lists, 638
A narrow Fellow in the Grass, 99
A novice was sitting on a cornice, 1405
Abbey, Edward, 1642
Abortions will not let you forget, 1301
According to Brueghel, 794
Adolescence—I, 1610
Adolescence—II, 1610
Adventures of Huckleberry Finn, 108
Africa, 937
After Apple-Picking, 742
after the murder, 1303
Agony. As Now., An, 1484
Alexie, Sherman, 1677
All day long I have been working, 727
All Greece hates, 822
Although it is a cold evening, 1109
Although it is night, I sit in the bathroom, waiting, 1610
Although she feeds me bread of bitterness, 938
Always, the dark body hewn asunder; always, 1689
America, 938
Amiri Baraka (Leroi Jones), 1483
Among twenty snowy mountains, 782
An old man bending I come among new faces, 74
And I start wondering how they came to be blind, 1555
and the gulf enters the sea and so forth, 1498
And then went down to the ship, 800
Anderson, Sherwood, 761
Anecdote of the Jar, 782
Ante-Bellum Sermon, An, 634
anyone lived in a pretty how town, 966
Anzaldúa, Gloria, 1557
Applauding youths laughed with young prostitutes, 936
April is the cruellest month, breeding, 834
Armadillo, The, 1111
Art of Fiction, The, 584
Ashbery, John, 1403
At Melville's Tomb, 1029

At Navajo Monument Valley Tribal School, 1678
At ten A.M. the young housewife, 788
At the 'Cadian Ball, 448
At the Fishhouses, 1109
August and the drive-in picture is packed, 1624

Babylon Revisited, 991
Back out of all this now too much for us, 749
Baldwin, James, 1330
Barely tolerated, living on the margin, 1406
Barn Burning, 1015
Beast in the Jungle, The, 399
Because I could not stop for Death, 94
Because there was a man somewhere in a candystripe silk shirt, 1197
Berryman, John, 1205
Bierce, Ambrose, 326
Birches, 744
Bishop, Elizabeth, 1106
Black Mother Woman, 1493
Blackberrying, 1449
Brooks, Gwendolyn, 1300
Brother, I'm Dying, 1662
Buffalo Bill's, 964
Burnt Norton, 850
By the road to the contagious hospital, 790

Cain lifts Crow, that heavy black bird, 1680
Call It Fear, 1606
Call the roller of big cigars, 778
Cane, 968
Cantos, The, 800
Captured Goddess, The, 726
Carver, Raymond, 1531
Cathedral, 1532
Cather, Willa, 691, 812
Chaplinesque, 1028
Cheever, John, 1182
Chesnutt, Charles W., 479
Chicago, 773
Chickamauga, 333
Child, 1450
Chopin, Kate, 441
Chrysanthemums, The, 1045
Cisneros, Sandra, 1613
CivilWarLand in Bad Decline, 1665

Clifton, Lucille, 1494
Coal, 1491
Collins, Billy, 1553
Complacencies of the peignoir, and late, 779
Consider the Lobster, 1657
Crane, Hart, 1028
Crane, Stephen, 611
Crossing Brooklyn Ferry, 69
Crow Testament, 1680
Cullen, Countee, 1053
Cummings, E. E., 961
Cuttings, 1092
Cuttings (later), 1092

Daddy, 1447
Daisy Miller: A Study, 342
Dance, The, 794
Danticat, Edwidge, 1661
Dear John Wayne, 1624
Death of a Salesman, 1223
Death of the Ball Turret Gunner, The, 1201
Death of the Hired Man, The, 738
Defender of the Faith, 1462
DeLillo, Don, 1499
Democracy, 1042
Democracy will not come, 1042
Desert Places, 747
Design, 748
Désirée's Baby, 442
Díaz, Junot, 1708
Dickinson, Emily, 82
Didion, Joan, 1653
Directive, 749
Disillusionment of Ten O'Clock, 778
Diving into the Wreck, 1421
Do not weep, maiden, for war is kind., 631
Dolor, 1093
Dove, Rita, 1608
Dream Songs, The, 1206
Dreiser, Theodore, 595
Droning a drowsy syncopated tune, 1039
Drown, 1709
Du Bois, W. E. B., 559
Dunbar, Paul Laurence, 633

Eating Alone, 1638
Eating Together, 1638
Editha, 316
Editor's Study, 580
Elegy for Jane, 1094
Eliot, T. S., 827
Ellison, Ralph, 1209
Emperor of Ice-Cream, The, 778
Entropy, 1520
Erdrich, Louise, 1622
Eros Turannos, 690
Every day the body works in the fields of the world, 1556
Everyday Use, 1568

Facing It, 1576
"Faith" is a fine invention, 87

Far off, above the plain the summer dries, 1201
Fast breaks. Lay ups. With Mercury's, 1578
Faulkner, William, 1005
Fear and Loathing in Las Vegas, 1652
Feminist Manifesto, 806
Fire and Ice, 746
First having read the book of myths, 1421
Fish, The, 1108
Fitzgerald, F. Scott, 973
Fleur, 1626
Flood-tide below me! I see you face to face!, 69
Flowering Judas, 940
Fog, 774
Footnote to Howl, 1402
For authorities whose hopes, 825
For the Union Dead, 1298
Forgetfulness, 1554
Four Quartets, 850
1492, 431
Frederick Douglass, 638
Freeman, Mary E. Wilkins, 459
From my mother's sleep I fell into the State, 1201
Frost, Robert, 735

Georgia Dusk, 968
Gilman, Charlotte Perkins, 509, 593
Ginsberg, Allen, 1392
Girl, 1650
Glaspell, Susan, 750
Going to Meet the Man, 1331
Good Country People, 1367
Good Man Is Hard to Find, A, 1381
Goophered Grapevine, The, 481
Grass, 774
Graveyard Blues, 1684
Green Snake, when I hung you round my neck, 1328
Gribben, Alan, 302
Grief, 1626

Hair—braided chestnut, 972
Harjo, Joy, 1605
Harlem Dancer, The, 936
Harlem Shadows, 936
Harriet Beecher Stowe, 637
Harte, Bret, 306
Havasu, 1643
Hayden, Robert, 1191
H.D. (Hilda Doolittle), 816
Helen, 822
Hemingway, Ernest, 1030
Her body is not so white as, 789
Here, where the noises of the busy town, 430
Heritage, 1054
High-Toned Old Christian Woman, A, 777
Highsmith, Patricia, 1304
Hills Like White Elephants, 1032
His Spirit in smoke ascended to high heaven, 937
Hog Butcher for the World, 773
Hollow Men, The, 847

Holy ! Holy ! Holy ! Holy ! Holy ! Holy ! Holy !
Holy ! Holy ! Holy ! Holy !, 1402
homage to my hips, 1496
Homage to the Empress of the Blues, 1197
Hopkins, Pauline Elizabeth, 497
How It Feels to Be Colored Me, 958
How she sat there, 1613
How to Tame a Wild Tongue, 1558
Howells, William Dean, 314, 579
Howl, 1394
Huck, Jim, and American Racial Discourse, 296
Huffy Henry hid the day, 1206
Hughes, Langston, 816, 1036
Hurston, Zora Neale, 948

I, Too, 1038
I, too, dislike it: there are things that are
    important beyond all this fiddle, 824
I, too, sing America, 1038
I / is the total black, being spoken, 1491
I am inside someone, 1484
I cannot live with You, 97
I cannot recall you gentle, 1493
I caught a tremendous fish, 1108
I celebrate myself, and sing myself, 25
*I Chop Some Parsley While Listening to Art
    Blakey's Version of "Three Blind Mice,"* 1555
I doubt not God is good, well-meaning, kind,
    1054
I felt a Funeral, in my Brain, 90
I found a dimpled spider, fat and white, 748
I have done it again, 1444
I have eaten, 793
I have known the inexorable sadness of
    pencils, 1093
I hear the halting footsteps of a lass, 936
I heard a Fly buzz - when I died, 96
I Knew a Woman, 1095
I know that He exists, 92
I know what the caged bird feels, alas!, 636
I like a look of Agony, 90
I make a pact with you, Walt Whitman—, 799
I placed a jar in Tennessee, 782
I remember the neckcurls, limp and damp as
    tendrils, 1094
I saw the best minds of my generation
    destroyed by madness, starving, 1394
I saw the spiders marching through the air,
    1295
i sing of Olaf glad and big, 965
I started Early - Took my Dog, 97
I taste a liquor never brewed, 87
I wake to sleep, and take my waking slow,
    1093
I walk into the bar, after being gone for a
    while, and it's empty. The, 1679
I want Catullus, 1579
I Was Sleeping Where the Black Oaks Move,
    1625
i wish them cramps, 1497
Idea of Order at Key West, The, 784
If "compression is the first grace of style," 825

If We Must Die, 937
Illustration, 1405
I'm ceded - I've stopped being Their's, 91
I'm going out to clean the pasture spring, 736
I'm Nobody! Who are you?, 88
Impressions of an Indian Childhood, 655
In a Station of the Metro, 799
In Brueghel's great picture, The Kermess, 794
in Just-, 962
In Mind, 1329
In sixth grade Mrs. Walker, 1636
In the Jewish Synagogue at Newport, 430
In the steamer is the trout, 1638
In the Waiting Room, 1113
In water-heavy nights behind grandmother's
    porch, 1610
In Worcester, Massachusetts, 1113
Incident, 1054
Introduction to Adventures of Huckleberry
    Finn, 300
Introduction to the NewSouth Edition, 302
Invisible Man, 1210
is an enchanted thing, 826
It rained the whole time we were laying her
    down, 1684
I've known rivers:, 1037
I've pulled the last of the year's young onions,
    1638

Jacob's Ladder, The, 1329
James, Henry, 338, 584
Jarrell, Randall, 1199
Jewett, Sara Orne, 432

Kakutani, Michiko, 304
Kerouac, Jack, 1316
Kincaid, Jamaica, 1649
Kingston, Maxine Hong, 1543
kitchenette building, 1301
Komunyakaa, Yusef, 1574

Lady Lazarus, 1444
Lahiri, Jhumpa, 1691
Landscape with the Fall of Icarus, 794
*Last Quatrain of the Ballad of Emmett Till,
    The*, 1303
Lazarus, Emma, 429
Leda, 821
Lee, Li-Young, 1635
Lester, Julius, 295
Let the snake wait under, 794
Let us go then, you and I, 830
Levertov, Denise, 1327
licked in the palm of my hand, 1497
Lie still now, 1639
*Light Out, Huck, They Still Want to Sivilize
    You*, 304
*Little Girl, My String Bean, My Lovely
    Woman*, 1412
London, Jack, 590, 639
Long Day's Journey into Night, 857
Lopez, Barry, 1647

Lorde, Audre, 1490
lost baby poem, the, 1496
Love set you going like a fat gold watch, 1444
Love Song of J. Alfred Prufrock, The, 830
Lowell, Amy, 724
Lowell, Robert, 1289
Loy, Mina, 806
Luck of Roaring Camp, The, 307
Lullaby, 1580
Lynching, The, 937

Madonna of the Evening Flowers, 727
Making of Americans, The, 731
Man Who Was Almost a Man, The, 1059
Manifesto of Futurism, 805
Marinetti, F. T., 804
Marx, Leo, 292
Mary sat musing on the lamp-flame at the table, 738
Masculine Literature, 593
Maus, 1588
McKay, Claude, 934
Mending Wall, 737
Mid-day, 820
Middle Passage, 1193
Miller, Arthur, 1221
Mind Is an Enchanting Thing, The, 826
Mine - by the right of the White Election!, 93
Miniver Cheevy, 689
Miracle of the Black Leg, 1689
miss rosie, 1495
mississippi river empties into the gulf, the, 1498
Money burns the pocket, pocket hurts, 972
Moore, Marianne, 822
Morality and Adventures of Huckleberry Finn, 295
Morning Song, 1444
Morrison, Toni, 300, 1426
Mother, 767
mother, the, 1301
Mother to Son, 1037
Mowing, 736
Mr. Edwards and the Spider, 1295
Mr. Eliot, Mr. Trilling, and Huckleberry Finn, 292
Mrs. Spring Fragrance, 550
Much Madness is divinest Sense, 96
Mulatto, 1039
My black face fades, 1576
My daughter, at eleven, 1412
My Father's Love Letters, 1577
My long two-pointed ladder's sticking through a tree, 742
My Papa's Waltz, 1093
My swirling wants. Your frozen lips, 1420
Myrtle, 1408

Native Guard, 1685
Nature's first green is gold, 747
Nautilus Island's hermit, 1296
Negro Artist and the Racial Mountain, The, 816

Negro Speaks of Rivers, The, 1037
Neighbour Rosicky, 694
Neither Out Far Nor In Deep, 748
New Colossus, The, 432
New England Nun, A, 460
"next to of course god america i, 964
Night House, The, 1556
Nobody in the lane, and nothing, nothing but blackberries, 1449
Norris, Frank, 586
Not like the brazen giant of Greek fame, 432
Note on Commercial Theatre, 1042
Nothing Gold Can Stay, 747
Notorious Jumping Frog of Calaveras County, The, 104
Novel Démeublé, The, 812

O sweet spontaneous, 963
Occurrence at Owl Creek Bridge, An, 327
O'Connor, Flannery, 1366
Of Modern Poetry, 785
Often beneath the wave, wide from this ledge, 1029
oh antic God, 1498
Oh Sylvia, Sylvia, 1410
On Fridays he'd open a can of Jax, 1577
On the Road, 1318
Once riding in old Baltimore, 1054
One Art, 1115
One must have a mind of winter, 777
O'Neill, Eugene, 854
Open Boat, The, 614
Oread, 820
Other Two, The, 526
"Out, Out—", 746
Out walking in the frozen swamp one gray day, 743
Over the housetops, 726

Pact, A, 799
Paper Nautilus, The, 825
Parsley, 1611
Pasture, The, 736
Pawn Shop, 1679
Persimmons, 1636
Petrified Man, 1097
Photograph: Ice Storm, 1971, 1685
Pile the bodies high at Austerlitz and Waterloo, 774
Plath, Sylvia, 1442
Plea for Romantic Fiction, A, 587
Poem for Willie Best, A, 1485
Poetry, 824
Poetry is the supreme fiction, madame, 777
Porter, Katherine Anne, 938
Portrait d'une Femme, 798
Portrait in Georgia, 972
Portrait of a Lady, 789
Pound, Ezra, 794, 809
Publication - is the Auction, 99
Pynchon, Thomas, 1519

Quaker Graveyard in Nantucket, The, 1291
Queen-Anne's-Lace, 789
Quest for Blank Claveringi, The, 1306

Raven, The, 1647
Real Thing, The, 382
Recitatif, 1429
Red Wheelbarrow, The, 793
Retrospect, A, 810
Rich, Adrienne, 1414
Richard Cory, 689
River-Merchant's Wife, The: A Letter, 799
Road Not Taken, The, 744
Robinson, Edwin Arlington, 688
Roethke, Theodore, 1091
Roman Fever, 540
Rosa, 1613
Rose for Emily, A, 1009
Roth, Philip, 1460

Sails flashing to the wind like weapons, 1193
Sandburg, Carl, 772
Saunders, George, 1664
Say It Ain't So, Huck: Second Thoughts on Mark Twain's "Masterpiece," 299
Sculptor's Funeral, The, 714
Second Air Force, 1201
Separating, 1452
September, 1918, 728
September rain falls on the house, 1112
Sestina, 1112
Seventh Street, 972
Sexton, Anne, 1408
Sexy, 1692
She begins to board the flight, 1607
She fears him, and will always ask, 690
She sang beyond the genius of the sea, 784
She told the story, and the whole world wept, 637
Silko, Leslie Marmon, 1579
Sister Carrie, 597
Skunk Hour, 1296
Slam, Dunk, & Hook, 1578
Slouching Towards Bethlehem, 1653
Smiley, Jane, 299
Smith, David L., 296
Snapshots of a Daughter-in-Law, 1416
Snow falling and night falling fast, oh, fast, 747
Snow Man, The, 777
so much depends, 793
Soft-Hearted Sioux, The, 660
Some keep the Sabbath going to Church, 87
Some say the world will end in fire, 746
Something there is that doesn't love a wall, 737
Sometimes you have to take your own hand, 1626
somewhere i have never travelled,gladly beyond, 966
Song for a Dark Girl, 1041
Song of Myself, 25

Sonny's Blues, 1343
Soonest Mended, 1406
Sorrow is my own yard, 790
Sort of a Song, A, 794
Souls of Black Folk, The, 561
Spiegelman, Art, 1587
Spring and All, 790, 814
Starry Night, The, 1409
Stein, Gertrude, 729
Steinbeck, John, 1044
Stevens, Wallace, 775
Sticks-in-a-drowse droop over sugary loam, 1092
Stopping by Woods on a Snowy Evening, 747
Storm, The, 455
Story of an Hour, The, 446
Street in Bronzeville, A, 1301
Streetcar Named Desire, A, 1119
Sui Sin Far (Edith Maud Eaton), 549
Sunday Morning, 779
Sundays too my father got up early, 1198
Supermarket in California, A, 1402
Sweat, 950
Swimmer, The, 1183
Sylvia's Death, 1410
Sympathy, 636

Talma Gordon, 498
Tell all the truth but tell it slant, 100
Tell me, / Was Venus more beautiful, 727
The apparition of these faces in the crowd, 799
The art of losing isn't hard to master, 1115
The Bible is an antique Volume, 100
The buzz saw snarled and rattled in the yard, 746
The face sings, alone, 1485
The fog comes, 774
the football field rises, 1678
The houses are haunted, 778
The hunters are back from beating the winter's face, 1492
The instructor said, 1043
The light beats upon me, 820
The name of the author is the first to go, 1554
The old South Boston Aquarium stands, 1298
The people along the sand, 748
The poem of the mind in the act of finding, 785
The pure products of America, 791
The sky, lazily disdaining to pursue, 968
The Soul selects her own Society, 93
The stairway is not, 1329
The sun sought thy dim bed and brought forth light, 937
the time i dropped your almost body down, 1496
The town does not exist, 1409
The whiskey on your breath, 1093
Theme for English B, 1043
There is a parrot imitating spring, 1611
There is this edge where shadows, 1606

There was never a sound beside the wood but one, 736
There's a certain Slant of light, 90
There's in my mind a woman, 1329
These are the days when Birds come back, 86
these hips are big hips, 1496
They had supposed their formula was fixed, 1302
They pose the portrait outside, 1683
Thinking of the Lost World, 1202
Thirteen Ways of Looking at a Blackbird, 782
This afternoon was the colour of water falling through sunlight, 728
This August evening I've been driving, 1423
This Is Just to Say, 793
This is my letter to the World, 96
This is the time of year, 1111
This Room and Everything in It, 1639
This spoonful of chocolate tapioca, 1202
This urge, wrestle, resurrection of dry sticks, 1092
This was a Poet, 94
Thomson, Hunter S., 1651
Those Winter Sundays, 1198
Thou two-faced year, Mother of Change and Fate, 431
Time present and time past, 850
To a Snail, 825
To Build a Fire, 641
To Elsie, 791
To the Diaspora, 1304
To the Snake, 1328
To Whistler, American, 797
Toomer, Jean, 967
Transcendental Etude, 1423
Trethewey, Natasha, 1681
Trifles, 751
Truth be told, I do not want to forget, 1685
Twain, Mark (Samuel L. Clemens), 101
Two roads diverged in a yellow wood, 744

Up from Slavery, 471
Updike, John, 1450

Valediction Forbidding Mourning, A, 1420
Venus Transiens, 727
Vignette, 1683
Visitors to the Black Belt, 1041

Waking, The, 1093
Walker, Alice, 1567
Wallace, David Foster, 1656
War Is Kind, 631
Washington, Booker T., 469
Waste Land, The, 834
Way Down South in Dixie, 1041
We are the hollow men, 847
We are things of dry hours and the involuntary plan, 1301
We is gathahed hyeah, my brothahs, 634
We make our meek adjustments, 1028
We Real Cool, 1303

We watched from the house, 1625
We Wear the Mask, 636
We wear the mask that grins and lies, 636
Weary Blues, The, 1039
Well, son, I'll tell you, 1037
Welty, Eudora, 1096
Wharton, Edith, 524
What is Africa to me, 1054
What Life Means to Me, 590
What thoughts I have of you tonight, Walt Whitman, for I walked down, 1402
When Dusk Weighs Daybreak, 1579
When I see birches bend to left and right, 744
When I was small, a Woman died, 95
when i watch you, 1495
When Lilacs Last in the Dooryard Bloom'd, 76
When you set out for Afrika, 1304
Whenever Richard Cory went down town, 689
Where the slow river, 821
While my hair was still cut straight across my forehead, 799
Whirl up, sea—, 820
White Bear, 1607
White Heron, A, 434
White Noise, 1501
white troops had their orders but the Negroes looked like men, the, 1302
Whitman, Walt, 21
Whose woods these are I think I know, 747
Why I Wrote "The Yellow Wallpaper"?, 523
Why the rough edge of beauty? Why, 1685
Widow's Lament in Springtime, The, 790
Wife of His Youth, The, 488
wild blessings, 1497
Wild nights - Wild nights!, 88
Williams, Tennessee, 1116
Williams, William Carlos, 786, 814
Winesburg, Ohio, 763
Winter Dreams, 975
wishes for sons, 1497
Woman Hollering Creek, 1614
Woman Thing, The, 1492
Woman Warrior, The, 1544
Wood-Pile, The, 743
Wound-Dresser, The, 74
Wright, Richard, 1058

Yellow Wall-paper, The, 511
Yet Do I Marvel, 1054
You, once a belle in Shreveport, 1416
You also, our first great, 797
You can talk about, 1041
You do not do, you do not do, 1447
Young Housewife, The, 788
Your clear eye is the one absolutely beautiful thing, 1450
Your mind and you are our Sargasso Sea, 798
Your thighs are appletrees, 789
You've taken my blues and gone—, 1042

Zitkala-Ša (Gertrude Simmons Bonnin), 652